THE NEW INTERPRETER'S BIBLE
COMMENTARY

In Ten Volumes

Editorial Board

The credentials listed here reflect the positions held at the time of the original publication.

THE NEW INTERPRETER'S™ BIBLE
COMMENTARY

VOLUME TWO

ABINGDON PRESS
Nashville

THE NEW INTERPRETER'S BIBLE COMMMENTARY
VOLUME II

Copyright © 2015 by Abingdon Press

This volume is a compilation of the following previously published material:
The New Interpreter's® Bible in Twelve Volumes, Volume II (Introduction to Narrative Literature, Joshua, Judges, Ruth, 1 & 2 Samuel), Copyright © 1998 by Abingdon Press.
The New Interpreter's® Bible in Twelve Volumes, Volume III (1 & 2 Kings, 1 & 2 Chronicles), Copyright © 1999 by Abingdon Press.

This book is printed on acid-free paper.

ISBN 978-1-4267-3579-0

19 20 21 22 23 24—10 9 8 7 6 5

MANUFACTURED IN THE UNITED STATES OF AMERICA

CONTRIBUTORS

PETER D. MISCALL
Adjunct Faculty
The Iliff School of Theology
Denver, Colorado
(The Episcopal Church)
Introduction to Narrative Literature

ROBERT B. COOTE
Professor of Old Testament
San Francisco Theological Seminary
San Anselmo, California
(Presbyterian Church [U.S.A.])
Joshua

DENNIS T. OLSON
Associate Professor of Old Testament
Princeton Theological Seminary
Princeton, New Jersey
(Evangelical Lutheran Church in America)
Judges

KATHLEEN A. ROBERTSON FARMER
Professor of Old Testament
United Theological Seminary
Dayton, Ohio
(The United Methodist Church)
Ruth

BRUCE C. BIRCH
Dean and Woodrow W. and Mildred B. Miller
    Professor of Biblical Theology
Wesley Theological Seminary
Washington, D.C.
(The United Methodist Church)
1 & 2 Samuel

CHOON-LEONG SEOW
Henry Snyder Gehman Professor of Old
    Testament Language and Literature
Princeton Theological Seminary
Princeton, New Jersey
(Presbyterian Church [U.S.A])
1 & 2 Kings

LESLIE C. ALLEN
Professor of Old Testament
Fuller Theological Seminary
Pasadena, California
(Baptist)
1 & 2 Chronicles

* The credentials listed here reflect the positions held at the time of the original publication.

CONTENTS

VOLUME II

INTRODUCTION TO NARRATIVE LITERATURE

PETER D. MISCALL

I n the late 1960s increasing numbers of scholars suggested that the methods of historical criticism, particularly source and form analysis, had reached an impasse and new approaches were needed. In subsequent years, literary criticism, in its many contemporary forms, has become the area most consistently explored for new ways of studying biblical literature, particularly narrative. Muilenburg's influential essay "Form Criticism and Beyond" built the foundation for rhetorical criticism, one of the first of the new ways to read biblical narratives as they appear in the canonical text.[1] Rhetorical criticism is defined as "the isolation of a discrete literary unity, the analysis of its structure and balance, and the attention to key words and motifs."[2] Its early results are enshrined in the 1974 Muilenburg festschrift, *Rhetorical Criticism.* This approach can contribute much to the close reading of a text, but because of its limited focus, it has not developed into a major approach to biblical narrative.

Rhetorical criticism competed with the influx of French structuralism and of other traditional brands of literary criticism that were influenced by the American New Criticism of the 1930s through the 1960s. A 1971 collection of French essays appeared in translation in 1974 as *Structural Analysis and Biblical Exegesis.*[3] *Semeia*, a journal devoted to new trends in biblical studies, issued its first volume in 1974, "A Structuralist Approach to the Parables." "Classical Hebrew Narrative," its third volume, appeared the following year. The issue included both structuralist and traditional literary approaches. *Semeia: An Experimental Journal for Biblical Criticism* continues to be a major sounding board for new approaches to biblical studies. In its issues, one can track most of the developments in biblical studies over the past two and a half decades, whether these developments flowered and lasted or withered on the vine.

Structuralism is noted for its attention to structure, both manifest and deep. Rhetorical criticism shares its concern for the obvious textual marks of structure, such as repeated terms and phrases, plot elements, and characters. Deep structure, however, is a theoretical category referring to the arrangement of a story—e.g., in terms of plot elements or

1. James Muilenburg, "Form Criticism and Beyond," *JBL* 88 (1969) 1-18.
2. Bernhard W. Anderson, "Introduction," *Rhetorical Criticism: Essays in Honor of James Muilenburg*, ed. Jared J. Jackson and Martin Kessler (Pittsburgh: Pickwick, 1974) xi.
3. R. Barthes, F. Bovon, et al., eds., *Structural Analysis and Biblical Exegesis* (Pittsburgh: Pickwick, 1974).

of the relationships of the characters—that is abstracted from the actual text through the application of modes of structural analysis. Structuralism is characterized by this abstract concern, by its fascination with specialist terminology—"synchronic," "diachronic," "actant" (instead of character)—and by its use of diagrams and quasi-mathematical formulas, such as the semiotic square and cube. Structuralism and rhetorical criticism remain valuable to biblical studies for the detailed textual focus they demand and for the original insights they produce.

Structuralism in particular, with its technical terminology and quasi-scientific claims, contrasts with "standard" literary approaches—those that employ the more familiar terminology of plot, setting, character, and theme and focus on these issues. They are no less probing or fruitful in their analyses. A collection of essays entitled *Literary Interpretations of Biblical Narratives* was published in 1974.[4] Intended for literature teachers in secondary schools and colleges, the collection had an impact on biblical studies and was one of the earliest of a long series of works devoted to the study of biblical narrative. The entire methodological shift that was occurring in the 1970s affected all areas of biblical studies—Old and New Testaments—including narrative, prophetic, wisdom, and epistolary literature. Our concern, however, lies with the Hebrew narrative in the OT; comments on other areas will be indirect.

The Sheffield periodical, *Journal for the Study of the Old Testament,* began appearing in 1976. It continues to be a major forum for diverse studies of biblical narrative. As with *Semeia,* one can track in its pages many of the changes and developments over the past twenty years of biblical studies.

Robert Alter's "A Literary Approach to the Bible" appeared in December 1975; it was devoted to Hebrew narrative and was followed in ensuing years by a series of articles on biblical narrative.[5] These articles, rewritten to various degrees, were gathered into Alter's influential *The Art of Biblical Narrative,* published in 1981.[6] Without arguing for a strict dividing line, I use this book and date to mark the beginning of a new stage in work on Hebrew narrative.

To simplify the work of a decade, we can say that in the 1970s those biblical scholars who were disenchanted, for a variety of reasons, with the methods and results of historical criticism were in search of new approaches to biblical study. This was a time of experimentation and often of heated debate between historical critics and the practitioners of various types of literary study of narrative. In particular, those debates addressed the central issue of whether one should focus on the biblical text in its canonical form or attempt to reconstruct earlier forms of the text. "The text-as-it-stands" and "the final form of the text" were two catchphrases of the period. The debate continues to the present day, although it is less heated and less prevalent.

The 1980s and 1990s witnessed the multiplication of methods and of in-depth interpretations of biblical narrative. Alongside the traditional historical-critical approaches were others: narratology, literary criticism, feminism, post-structuralism, and ideology critique. Scholars who employed the newer approaches could be as, if not more, acrimonious in their disputes among themselves as in those with historical critics. The recent *The Postmodern Bible* is an excellent overview of this diversity as it has developed over the last few decades and as it stands today.[7] I turn now from these controversies to a presentation of the literary study of biblical narrative as it has developed in the last generation. The presentation is general, but with pointers to some of the twists that individual critics give to both method and interpretation.

NARRATIVE AND NARRATOLOGY

A *narrative* is the telling, by a *narrator* to an audience, of a connected series or sequence of events. The series of events involve *characters* and their interrelationships, and the events occur in a place or places, the *setting.* The *plot* is the events selected and the

4. K. R. R. Gros Louis, J. S. Ackerman, and T. S. Warshaw, eds., *Literary Interpretations of Biblical Narratives* (Nashville: Abingdon, 1974).
5. Robert Alter, "A Literary Approach to the Bible," *Commentary* 60 (1975) 70-77.
6. Robert Alter, *The Art of Biblical Narrative* (New York: Basic, 1981).

7. The Bible and Culture Collective, *The Postmodern Bible* (New York: Yale University Press, 1995).

particular order in which they are presented. A *theme* is an idea, an abstract concept, that emerges from the narrative's presentation and treatment of its material.

"Narrative" can refer to a short piece, to an episode (e.g., Rebekah and Jacob's deception of Isaac in Gen 27), or to a larger work, such as Genesis itself or even the whole of Genesis through 2 Kings. Although others may make a distinction, I use "story" as a synonym for narrative—e.g., the story of Sarah and Hagar in Genesis 16 and Israel's primary story in Genesis–2 Kings.

Twentieth-century study of narrative, ancient and modern, from the epic to the novel, has developed into the specialized area of *narratology*, which endeavors to define narrative and its categories (e.g., narrator and character) on a theoretical and abstract level. Narratology is a subdivision of the larger field of *poetics* (not to be equated with the study of poetry only), which strives for a science of literature, a study of the basic elements and rules of any type of literature. Poetics is to literature what the study of grammar and syntax is to language. In such theoretical studies, actual narratives provide examples and illustrations. Narratology and poetics describe specific categories, with various subdivisions, that can be applied in the analysis of any narrative (or other type of literature); they offer tools to the literary critic, but do not engage in the in-depth reading and interpretation of texts for their own sake. These are the fields that have both refined and expanded our understanding of the mechanics and intricacies of, for example, characterization and point of view.

The works of Berlin,[8] Bar-Efrat,[9] and Gunn-Fewell[10] are fine examples of the genre that focuses on Hebrew narrative. They all employ extended examples of analysis, and Gunn-Fewell intersperse their theoretical presentations with extended readings of given narratives, including the fiery furnace episode in Daniel 3. Both Alter's *The Art of Biblical Narrative*[11] and Sternberg's *The Poetics of Biblical Narrative*[12] are inextricable mixes of theoretical comments and involved readings of chosen stories, mainly from Genesis–2 Kings.

One of the more important changes in this methodological shift is the explicit concern to describe and to appreciate biblical narrative in its own right as a literary category. Scholars engaged in this work describe the narratives as they appear in the Bible, rather than judging them according to norms and expectations developed from other Western literature, especially those of the modern realistic novel. In the works just listed, the authors take pains to explicate the narratological terms and concepts they employ and, at the same time, to show in detail how they apply to actual biblical narratives. Narrative study is a contemporary response to the original, critical insight and demand of Spinoza and others that the Bible be read like other literature. At relevant points, I will note the impact of this shift in focus for the specific categories I am presenting.

Narrative and History. Before proceeding to biblical narrative itself, I address one final methodological issue: the relation of narrative study to the study of the history of Israel, on the one hand, and the history of biblical writing, on the other hand. Although it can have significant impact on both, especially the latter, narrative study can proceed on its own by bracketing historical questions that are presently characterized by wide-ranging diversity of opinion and heated controversy. That is, we can discuss the narrative of Samuel, Saul, and David in 1 Samuel and beyond without having to answer, or even ask, the question of what "really happened" in those ancient times. This does not deny the relevance of issues of historicity. It neither affirms nor denies the historicity of specific characters and events, whether Joshua and the conquest, Samson and his exploits, David's relationship with Bathsheba, or the courtship of Ruth and Boaz. It asserts that these stories can be fruitfully read for what they tell us about people and how they relate to others, including God, and for what they tell us about the workings of biblical narrative, general and specific.

8. Adele Berlin, *Poetics and Interpretation of Biblical Narrative* (Sheffield: Almond, 1983).

9. Shimon Bar-Efrat, *Narrative Art in the Bible* (Sheffield: Almond, 1989; Hebrew ed., 1979).

10. David M. Gunn and Danna N. Fewell, *Narrative in the Hebrew Bible* (New York: Oxford, 1993).

11. Alter, *The Art of Biblical Narrative*.

12. Meir Sternberg, *The Poetics of Biblical Narrative: Ideological Literature and the Drama of Reading* (Bloomington: Indiana University Press, 1985).

Moreover, it allows us to bracket questions of the historical development of narrative style—not to deny the relevance of the issues, but to be able to proceed with narrative analysis without becoming embroiled in all the debates about the history of the writing and editing of the biblical text. Narrative and literary analyses have enough debates and diversity of opinion of their own!

The Narrative and the Author. This topic takes us immediately to a central distinction developed in twentieth-century criticism that is relevant to all narrative, ancient and modern. The author is the actual historical person (or persons) who wrote the work in question. (In reference to the Bible, I am not taking a stand on the issue of oral or written composition.) For example, Herman Melville wrote *Moby Dick* in the mid-nineteenth century. The narrator, on the other hand, is a literary and abstract personage. Within the text, he tells us the story that we are reading and must be distinguished from the actual author. *Moby Dick* is narrated by Ishmael ("Call me Ishmael"), not by Melville.

This distinction allows biblical readers to discuss the narratives in depth, and in the detail of their presentation, without having to identify an actual author by name or impersonal title, by place, and by date. There is, in addition, the category of the "implied author," the hypothetical person inferred as the author from the text's style and content. This person might or might not be similar to the actual author. However, this category is too abstract and debated to be explored in this article.

STYLE

Style refers to form, to how a narrative is told. Style can be used across the spectrum to describe a single story (e.g., Gen 27), a traditional section (e.g., the Pentateuch), or an entire corpus (e.g., Gen–2 Kgs). At this point I shall describe three primary, and often noted, characteristics of biblical narrative—indeed, of the whole OT. Then I shall discuss how these and other stylistic features affect the respective narrative categories. These three traits are the *episodic nature* of the material; the great *diversity* in terms of both form and content; and the prevalence of *repetition* of many different aspects of narrative.

The *episodic nature* is my phrase for the quality that allows us to read stories individually and separate from their context without feeling that we have lost the heart of the tale. This quality creates the impression that large segments of narrative are composed of stories strung together in a loose chronological frame, without further significant connection or relation. Examples are the Abraham cycle in Genesis 12–25, the wilderness wanderings episodes in Numbers 11–36, the judges stories in Judges 3–16, and the accounts of the last years of Israel and Judah in 2 Kings. These share a *paratactic style*—that is, scenes or stories are juxtaposed without connecting or transitional phrases.

The paratactic style is present at the level of individual sentences in the narrator's preference for "and" over subordinating conjunctions such as "so," "then," or "because." This characteristic is often obscured in modern translations, including the NIV and the NRSV, that use subordinating conjunctions in order to avoid too many repetitions of "and." The story of the war of the kings and of Abram's rescue of Lot in Genesis 14 closes with Abram's declaration that he will accept nothing from the king of Sodom. The following episode of promise and covenant is introduced by the indefinite phrase "after these things" (NRSV) or "after this" (NIV). The narrator gives us no hint of how much time, if any, has elapsed or whether we should think of a change of place. And he relates the story in chapter 15 with sentences connected by "and"; both the NIV and the NRSV use "but," "then," and "also" in place of some of the simple connectives. The story closes with the Lord's far-reaching promise to Abram and his descendants. Genesis 16, like chapter 15, opens abruptly with no indication of any time lapse or change in locale: "And Sarai, the wife of Abram, bore him no children." Both the NIV and the NRSV attempt to lessen the abruptness by using "now" as an introduction. Others, such as the NJB and the REB, mirror the terseness with a plain "Abram's wife Sarai . . ." (Note, however, the shift in the order of the characters such that Abram is named first; the NIV and the NRSV keep Sarai first.)

Another well-known and diversely interpreted juxtaposition of two stories occurs in the two creation stories in Gen 1:1–2:4*a* and 2:4*b*-25. To cite this example does not mean that we must accept the hypothesis that two different sources or authors are in evidence here, nor does it mean that we must attempt to harmonize the two stories and explain away all contrasts. Rather, we should accept the juxtaposition, even if it produces sharp contrasts or even contradictions, as part of the narrative style and then work at describing its effects upon readers and intepreters. Episodic and paratactic are descriptive, and not judgmental or evaluative, terms.

The narrator frequently proceeds by presenting contrasting or opposing views, stories, character portrayals, and such, whether placed side-by-side or at some remove. One example of the latter is the Moses who displays weaknesses in Exodus 17–18 and the Moses of Exod 33:7-11 and 34:29-35, who speaks with God face to face. Another is the near-silent Bathsheba of 2 Samuel 11–12 and the politically effective speaker of 1 Kings 1–2. This episodic style leaves room for readers to infer and to conjecture possible transitions and connections, but it never provides enough textual evidence to cinch any one interpretation. The myriad ways that have been proposed for relating or not relating the two creation stories is ample evidence for the process of unending inference triggered by this stylistic trait.

Diversity is a second catchword frequently used to describe biblical narrative. Not only do the two creation stories differ in their depictions of God, of creation, and of humanity, but also they differ in how the narrator presents the material. The first story is so highly and tightly structured that some question whether narrative or story adequately describes the text; perhaps a theological treatise or an ancient "scientific" document is a better descriptor. The second tale is a looser narrative with characters in potential conflict, and with the segment on the rivers in 2:10-14 in the center but without explicit relevance to the rest of the story. It is a fine example of the paratactic style.

This diversity in both content and form, along with the episodic aspect, confronts the reader constantly from the opening pages of Genesis through the close of 2 Kings and beyond. Genesis comprises narratives ranging from the terseness of the depiction of Lamech in 4:18-24 and of the tale of divine beings and human women in 6:1-4 to the lengthy and tightly woven story of Joseph and his brothers. The sagas of Abraham and his family, and of Jacob and his family or families, lie between these two poles, with the Abraham story the more episodic. Indeed, the latter has been referred to as the "Abraham Cycle," but never as a tightly woven tale. The strictly narrative portions of Genesis are broken at points by genealogies (e.g., chaps. 5 and 36) and a poem, Jacob's blessing (49:1-27).

Once readers move beyond Genesis to the rest of the Pentateuch, however, they are confronted with an even greater range of diversity. The strictly narrative portions are mixed with genealogies; a wide variety of ritual, legal, and technical descriptions and prescriptions; and the lengthy rehearsal of all of this in the sermons in Deuteronomy. "Strictly narrative portions" refers to separate stories such as the call of Moses in Exodus 3–4, the manna in Exodus 16, spying out the land in Numbers 13–14, and Moses' final moments in Deuteronomy 34, as opposed to other materials. But all of this material, including stories, "laws," the description of the tabernacle, poems, and sermons, is still part of the overall narrative of Genesis–2 Kings. The flow of the narrative, the forward movement in time and events, may slow or even stop for the presentation of these other materials, but the latter are still part of the narrative. Much of Exodus through Deuteronomy consists of lengthy speeches by characters, mainly God and Moses. We must keep all of this together in order to describe accurately the narrative corpus of Genesis–2 Kings. Awareness of diversity in form and content is also necessary for reading other narrative portions of the OT, such as Chronicles, Ezra–Nehemiah, and Ruth. Diversity may appear in different aspects and ways in these works than in Genesis–2 Kings, but it is present nonetheless.

Joshua–2 Kings continues the mixing. In these books, the narrator relates the history of Israel in the land from conquest to exile. He does so with the same variation in style—from the comparatively tightly woven story of Samuel, Saul, and then David in 1–2 Samuel to the much looser episodes of Judges and 2 Kings. (I use the traditional term "books" without regarding them—e.g., Gen and Josh—as separate works by separate authors; for Gen–2 Kgs, I take the "books" to be more like chapters in a contemporary work.) At points the material is punctuated with poems, such as those in Judges 5, 1 Samuel 2, and 2 Samuel 22, and by the speeches of characters, e.g., of Jotham in Judges 9, of Samuel in 1 Samuel 12, and of Ahijah in 1 Kings 11. The speeches, including overviews by the narrator, such as in 2 Kings 17, place the particular narratives in the larger setting of the story of Israel from its creation to the disaster of the exile.

Repetition is the third and final trait I shall discuss. It, like the other traits, appears in the opening pages of the OT. Genesis 1 is divided into six days by the formula "And there was evening and there was morning, the X day." Genesis 2 "repeats" the first chapter. There are two genealogies for Lamech (Gen 4:17-24; 5:1-31), and three stories of a patriarch (Abraham, Isaac) claiming that his wife (Sarah, Rebekah) is his sister (Gen 12:10-20; and 26:6-11). Ten plagues ravage Egypt, and God produces two copies of the stone tablets. In Exodus 25–31 the Lord, in great detail, commands Moses and the Israelites to build a tabernacle; in Exodus 35–40, with much the same detail, the narrator describes the actual construction of the tabernacle. This is the longest and most detailed repetition in the OT.

One of the most, if not the most, repeated stories is that of Israel from Genesis through 2 Kings and beyond, which is recited by the narrator, by God, or by another character at many different stages in the larger narrative. The story is anticipated in the Lord's declarations to Abraham in Gen 15:13-16 and to Moses in Exod 23:20-33 and Deut 31:16-21. Moses refers to it often in his speeches in Deuteronomy (e.g., Deut 26:1-11; 31:26-29; Joshua summarizes it in Josh 24:1-15, as does the narrator in 2 Kgs 17:7-20).

The story is repeated in a wide variety of ways from the brief declaration of the first commandment, "I am the LORD your God, who brought you out of the land of Egypt, out of the house of slavery" (Exod 20:2), to the lengthy versions in Deuteronomy 31 and Joshua 24. The repetition of Israel's story exemplifies both diversity and *diversity amid regularity,* since the same story is repeated. Diversity in biblical narrative is not endless or unlimited, but variation within set boundaries and a set number of narrative elements. A notable example is the Decalogue. It appears first as the Lord's direct speech in Exodus 20 and then is cited by Moses, in slightly different form, in Deuteronomy 5.

The versions of the story of God and Israel vary not only in terms of their length, but also in terms of their content. The sentence cited from Exod 20:2 refers only to the exodus from Egypt, while Joshua traces the story from the days of Abraham to the entrance into the land in his own day. In Deut 31:16-21, the Lord begins the tale with Moses and then looks off into Israel's future of sin and misery. Moses himself speaks of this distant future in Deut 4:25-31 with a more optimistic view of the outcome. An unnamed prophet tells of the exodus and entrance into the land with no mention of patriarchs or the wandering in the wilderness (Judg 6:8-10). Ezra's recital in Neh 9:6-37 is a full, detailed version that includes all the stages down to Ezra's own day, a time of suffering for past sins.

THE NARRATOR

In accepted literary terms, the biblical narrator is *omniscient* in the sense of possessing potential knowledge of all the characters and events presented, even the thoughts of God (see Gen 6:5-7; 18:17-21). The narrator is *reliable* to the extent that we can trust what we are told. Gunn and Fewell define this characteristic:

> A reliable narrator always gives us accurate information; or put another way, does not make mistakes, give false or unintentionally misleading information, or deliberately deceive us.[13]

They recognize, however, that the many factual contrasts and contradictions in

13. Gunn and Fewell, *Narrative in the Hebrew Bible,* 53.

presence of ironic statements require us to modify our understanding of what is reliable. Their general rule is the one followed in this article: "In practice, some such scale of reliability is a helpful rule of thumb in reading biblical narrative."[14] Finally, this is a *third-person* narrator who is not identified by name or title and who does not use "I."

In most ancient literature, narrators are voices, disembodied presences who narrate what we are reading and who seldom explicitly identify themselves or mark their presence. Genesis opens, "In the beginning God created the heavens and the earth," with no textual comment as to who is telling us this. The same narratorial style is employed throughout Genesis–2 Kings. For contrast, we can turn to Nehemiah ("In the month of Chislev, in the twentieth year, while I was in Susa" [1:1]) or to Ecclesiastes/Qoheleth ("I, the Teacher [Qoheleth], when king over Israel in Jerusalem, applied my mind" [1:12]). These are the exceptions and not the rule in biblical narrative.

The narrator's *point of view* is generally from outside or above the characters and the actions of the narrative, but material can be presented through the eyes of a character. For example, part of the formula that closes each day of creation is the repeated "and God saw that it was good"—a report of God's reaction and evaluation, not of the narrator's. Genesis 18 opens with the narrator's report, followed by what Abraham himself saw: "The LORD appeared to Abraham. . . . He looked up and saw three men standing near him" (NRSV). A similar contrast is drawn between the report and a character's perception in Exod 3:2: "There the angel of the LORD appeared to him in a flame of fire out of a bush: he looked, and the bush was blazing, yet it was not consumed" (NRSV).

In narratology, both within and beyond biblical studies, critics have proposed a wide range of distinctions and subdivisions to deal with all the complexities and nuances of the narrator and the point of view in narrative, ancient and modern. These can be valuable in the close reading and analysis of a narrative, but they are beyond the scope of this article.

I refer the reader to the works of Berlin,[15] Bar-Efrat,[16] and Bal[17] for both the complexities and the varieties. There is little critical consensus in this matter of further distinctions.

These characteristics are only the general framework within which the very capable and resourceful narrator works. This storyteller may be able to know all about the characters and events but is very selective and deliberate in exactly what is told us about them and how and when we are told. Such sparseness of narrative detail, whether in terms of characters, events, or setting, has long been noted in biblical narrative. What has changed in the contemporary scene is the judgment and evaluation of this stylistic trait; this change applies to many of the other stylistic traits discussed above, particularly the episodic and repetitive nature of the narrative. These traits have been variously observed in the past, but have almost always been judged as marks of the primitive and simplistic nature of biblical narrative. Critics took them as signs of a lack of literary ability and sophistication and not as essential keys to reading and analyzing the narrative. Contemporary literary critics speak, on the other hand, of the art of biblical narrative and of the artistic sophistication of the narrator, who can accomplish so much with apparently so little.

I turn now to discuss each of the other aspects of narrative: theme, setting, plot, and character. I deal with the initial three first because they can be presented more briefly. This is not to turn our backs completely on the narrator, since all that we know about these other four comes through the narration. We will have opportunity to comment further on the narrator's style—diversity, repetition, selectivity, etc.—and to relate it to the particulars of the narrative.

THEME, SETTING, AND PLOT

Theme is a rich, overarching category containing all of the ideas, concepts, and issues that a narrative treats, explicitly or implicitly, in what it says and how it says it. Thematic

14. Gunn and Fewell, *Narrative in the Hebrew Bible*, 54.

15. Berlin, *Poetics and Interpretation of Biblical Narrative*.
16. Bar-Efrat, *Narrative Art in the Bible*.
17. Mieke Bal, *Narratology: An Introduction to the Theory of Narrative* (Toronto: University of Toronto Press, 1985).

content can derive from both narrative form and content, and it is developed from the study of all other aspects of a narrative. Themes are generally spoken of in abstract terms: e.g., covenant, divine and human responsibilities, justice and injustice, mercy, prophetic (charismatic) and monarchic (dynastic) leadership, war, wisdom, law, love, the strengths and the failings of families, friendship, loyalty, and betrayal. This short list illustrates the wide range of issues that biblical narrative addresses. In addition, themes can be grouped into comprehensive classifications, such as political, theological, sociological, and historical, and then studied in relation to other topics within those classifications. The relation of one classification to another can be developed—e.g., what does the depiction of the monarchy in Samuel–Kings tell us about the narrator's (or author's) theology of state and of history?

Plot comprises the events that occur in the course of a narrative and can be looked at from two different perspectives. First, plot reflects a *pattern,* since the events, the actions, occur in a certain order and arrangement; they form a series. Second, one central binding element in the series is a *temporal framework.* The events form a sequence, a continuum that is bound in large part by chronology, by the flow of time. Genesis–2 Kings presents the story of humanity, especially Israel, from the creation of the world to the fall of Judah and Jerusalem c. 600–580 BCE. But there is great variety in the presentation of the plot— e.g., the amount of space and detail accorded a given event or period of time and the clarity, or lack thereof, in noting the passage of time.

Focus on plot raises the issues of causality and resolution. They, especially the former, are complicated by the episodic nature and brevity of biblical narrative, whether on the level of individual scenes and even sentences of one story, or on the level of the grouping of narratives into larger works, such as Exodus or all of Genesis–2 Kings. Specific events, stories, and even whole books frequently follow one upon another in time with little or no indication of any other connection between them. I included one example of this in the discussion of Genesis 15–16. The final statement in the clash between Michal and David (2 Sam 6) is another good example of paratactic style characterized by the use of "and."

The mutual anger and resentment between Michal and her husband are revealed in their heated exchange. The story closes: "And Michal the daughter of Saul had no child to the day of her death" (2 Sam 6:23 NRSV). The narrator thereby reports "the objective fact of Michal's barrenness . . . but carefully avoids any subordinate conjunction or syntactical signal that would indicate a clear causal connection between the fact stated and the dialogue that precedes it."[18] Is the childlessness divine punishment, one spouse refusing conjugal relations with the other, or "a bitter coincidence, the last painful twist of a wronged woman's fate"?[19]

The transition from Joshua to Judges provides another example of a reading difficulty caused by the juxtaposition of stories without an explicit statement of chronology and the flow of events. The book of Joshua closes with Israel in firm possession of much of the land and unified in its worship of the Lord; Josh 24:31 speaks of Israel in the singular: "Israel served the LORD." In the final verses, the narrator reports the passing of Joshua and his generation. The book of Judges opens with "after the death of Joshua" without, however, specifying the amount of elapsed time. Further, we immediately encounter "the children of Israel," who see themselves as a group of tribes without a leader, not as the united people, the singular "Israel" of Josh 24:31 led by Joshua and his comrades.

The division and isolation of the tribes narrated in Judges 1 is mirrored in the narrator's jagged style, which recounts each event, however brief, separately. Narrative form reflects content. A brief speech from a divine messenger (Judg 2:1-5) in part accounts for this sorry state of affairs. In Judg 2:6–3:6, the narrator provides a lengthy explanation both for what has happened and for what will continue to happen. The narrator's exposition breaks the chronology by backing up and telling us, after the reports in chap. 1, what happened after the death of Joshua and his generation, and then by looking ahead to the pattern of the future, the careers of the judges (Judg 3–16). The narrative of Judges 17–21 is not explicitly anticipated in this overview.

18. Alter, *Art of Biblical Narrative,* 125.
19. Alter, *Art of Biblical Narrative,* 125.

Both the stories of the judges and those about the characters and tribes in Judges 17–21 are presented in an episodic manner. They are apparently bound by chronology, with one judge and crisis following upon the other in time; they are also connected by themes of violence and war, both foreign and civil, and by themes of ignorance, confusion, and anonymity. As with chap. 1, the confusions and divisions narrated continue to be mirrored in the broken, paratactic form of the narration. The narrator forces readers to experience some of the bewilderment and bafflement of the characters of the narrative.

The chronological ties are only apparent. The narrator punctuates the text with explicit statements of elapsed time—e.g., "the Israelites served Cushan-rishathaim eight years" (Judg 3:8 NRSV); "the land had rest forty years" (Judg 3:11; 5:31 NRSV); and "he [Samson] had judged Israel twenty years" (Judg 16:31 NRSV). Depending on how one adds up or overlaps the figures, a two- to three-century period is covered in the stories of the judges. However, the narrator, in an aside, jolts us with the information that Israel has moved only one generation from the close of Joshua. The last verse of the book of Joshua reports the passing of Eleazar, son of Aaron; and Judg 20:27-28 notes that "Phinehas son of Eleazar, son of Aaron, ministered before [the ark] in those days." This genealogical notice forces us to rethink the previous material in Judges as simultaneous events or as events narrated after or before they have occurred, and not as events narrated in a straightforward plot line.

In historical-critical analyses, Judges has served as a prime target for different types of source and traditio-historical methods that divide the book into separate stories, groups of stories, or redactional levels. Critics employing these methods regard the narrative traits as pointing to the lack of a consistent narrative and conclude that the book cannot be read as a whole.[20] A contemporary literary critic, such as Josipovici, recognizes the literary problems and then, reflecting the shift in how such literary characteristics are evaluated, accepts them as part of the book: "The book of Judges is indeed oddly fragmented

and jagged, even by the standards of the Bible, but that is part of what it is about, not something to be condemned."[21]

Plot, finally, leads us to question whether a narrative leaves its reader with a sense of resolution, a feeling that all the loose ends have been tied up. This applies to a single episode such as the Tamar and Shechem story in Genesis 34, the entire Abraham cycle in Gen 11:10–25:18, the book of Genesis, or the whole of Genesis–2 Kings. The endings of both the Abraham story and the entire book of Genesis leave the reader with a sense of completion. Abraham "died in a good old age, an old man and full of years, and was gathered to his people" (Gen 25:8); he was blessed by the Lord in all things (Gen 24:1). He had seen to the proper marriage of his son Isaac; and the matter of his other wives and sons, including Ishmael, is summarized in the genealogies in Gen 25:1-6 and chaps. 12–18. Genesis ends with the proper burial of Jacob in the family plot at Machpelah, and with all his remaining family in Egypt having finally reached a high degree of trust and reconciliation. The story continues in Exodus but centuries later, and with an almost entirely new cast of characters, except for God and Jacob's "sons," who have now become the people Israel.

On the other hand, Genesis 34 ends with the city of Shechem plundered and Jacob terrified that the violent acts of his sons will result in his and his house's destruction by the Canaanites. The story ends with a question: "Should our sister be treated like a whore?" Thus the story is left open-ended, in regard both to Jacob's fears and to the query itself. All of Genesis–2 Kings ends, perhaps "stops" is a better term, with the description of King Jehoiachin residing in Babylon and being maintained in fine style by the king of Babylon. The ambiguity of the scene is evident, in the divided opinion of many commentators. Is it a positive sign that the Judean king yet lives on with ample support, or is it a negative sign of pathetic subjection and a fast-fading, last glimmer of hope? Is eating at another king's table a mark of honor or of humiliation? Note the similar ambiguity surrounding Mephibosheth's presence at David's table

20. See Robert G. Boling, *Judges*, AB 6A (Garden City, N.Y.: Doubleday, 1975).

21. Gabriel Josipovici, *The Book of God: A Response to the Bible* (New Haven: Yale University Press, 1988) 110.

(2 Sam 9). Is this only the fulfillment of a pledge to Jonathan, or is it an effective way of keeping an eye on a survivor of the house of Saul?[22]

Setting is the locale, the place where events happen, where characters reside. It refers to the cosmic, the heavens and earth of Genesis 1; to the large scale of countries and areas such as Canaan, Egypt, and the wilderness; to the smaller scale of cities, towns, and designated sites such as Shechem, Zoar, and the field of Machpelah, and to particular places within these sites. When the Lord appears to Abraham, it is "by the oaks of Mamre, as he sat at the entrance of his tent in the heat of the day" (Gen 18:1). Such details, including the notice of the time of day, add specificity to the narrative and, in this case, can lead us to wonder if Abraham first thinks he is seeing a heat mirage. The absence of any explicit indication of setting can serve to keep our attention on other aspects of the narrative. Genesis 15 and 17, both covenant stories, are appropriate examples.

In Genesis–2 Kings one broad concern is whether the setting is in Canaan/Israel, in a foreign country such as Egypt or Babylon, or in the intermediate zone of the wilderness. The setting may be actual or potential—i.e., promised or threatened—and is closely related to the actions of the people Israel, of God, and of the other nations and people involved in the ongoing narrative. This relation of setting with plot and character is a major part of the entire thematics and pattern of covenant and promise, possession or loss of the land, and both exodus and exile.

On a smaller scale, setting, especially as it fits or does not fit with the characters and actions placed there, can be significant in a story. Abram, in Egypt, expects the Egyptians to be amoral and to resort to murder to avoid adultery (Gen 12:10-20). Pharaoh and the Egyptians do nothing of the sort, and Pharaoh is shocked at Abram's behavior when he learns the truth. In the future, an Israelite king in the holy city of Jerusalem will act in just this way as he arranges for Uriah's death to cover his adultery with Bathsheba (2 Sam 11). Awareness of similarities and contrasts in plot and setting heightens our appreciation of the characterization of the main players, particularly Abram and David.

A contrasting example of the significance of Jerusalem occurs in Judges 19. Late in the day a servant suggests to his Levite master that they spend the night in "Jebus" (i.e., Jerusalem), but the Levite wants to press on to Gibeah of Benjamin, since Jebus is "a city of foreigners, who do not belong to the people of Israel" (Judg 19:10-12). It soon turns out that the men of Gibeah are more like the men of Sodom than like those whom the Levite and most readers would expect to encounter in an Israelite city.

Sisera, the commander of Jabin's army and a man of cities and broad battlefields, dies at the hand of a woman, Jael, in the confines of her tent (Judg 4). The male space of cities and the great outdoors contrasts with the female space of indoors and tents to the detriment of males. Sisera dies in a tent, and Barak discovers his enemy's corpse there and not on a battlefield. The same contrast is found between Michal's looking "out of the window" at David dancing in the street (2 Sam 6:16) and Jezebel's looking "out of the window" at Jehu (2 Kgs 9:30). The contrast of male and female space at the beginning of the David and Bathsheba episode in 2 Samuel 11 anticipates the dark portrayal of David—one already foreshadowed by the story of Pharaoh in Gen 12:10-20. David is in Jerusalem in the king's house, while Joab and the army are away at war with the Ammonites; from the roof of his house, he sees Bathsheba, and this sets the sordid tale in motion.

Genesis ends and Exodus begins in Egypt. The same setting allows us to focus on the passage of time and on the change in characters and situation. The narrator passes over the intervening centuries in silence, but the arrival of a new king "who did not know Joseph" (Exod 1:8) expresses, in as brief a manner as possible, the potentially threatening new conditions. The gap in time does not pose a problem for the plot, since the narrator's concern is with how Israel first came to Egypt and then with why and how they left. Judges ends, in accord with its episodic style, with the grotesque story of the rape of the young women of Shiloh at the annual festival. In terms of plot resolution the book ends or

22. Leo G. Perdue, "'Is There Anyone Left of the House of Saul . . . ?' Ambiguity and the Characterization of David in the Succession Narrative," *JSOT* 30 (1984) 67-84.

stops with the noncommittal statement about Israel's having no king and the people's doing whatever they want.

In the Hebrew Bible, but not in the Septuagint arrangement that underlies most English Bibles, 1 Samuel follows immediately with the story of Hannah, Elkanah, and Samuel. It is set in Shiloh and revolves about events at the annual festival in that city. But this common setting with the close of Judges is not accompanied by common elements of plot or character. We have no idea of elapsed time, if there is any; perhaps we are to read 1 Samuel 1 as saying that Hannah and her family were at Shiloh during the mass rape. Only after reading further into 1 Samuel do we realize that the narrative is finally moving on beyond the repetitive cycles of Judges. The narrator does not signal this shift at the start.

CHARACTER AND CHARACTERIZATION

I discuss this topic last because many, if not most, contemporary narrative studies focus on it and, directly or indirectly, relate the treatment of other narrative aspects to the development of characters. This includes works such as Moyers's *Genesis* television series and Miles's *God: A Biography*,[23] both of which are outside the mainstream of biblical studies. Many of my previous examples point to the significance of plot, setting, and style for our appreciation of characters. *Character* refers to the personages depicted in the narrative— e.g., Abraham and Rebekah—while *characterization* refers to all of the means that the narrator employs to portray them.

Characterization was not dealt with in any depth by either rhetorical criticism or structuralism because of their central concern with the text's structure, apparent or deep, and because of the latter's strong tendency to regard characters as actants. An actant is described in terms of relationships to others and by the use of adjectives attached to the actant. This technical terminology reflects structuralism's desire to align itself with science.

Before the advent of contemporary literary approaches, biblical studies regarded characterization in biblical narrative as minimal because of its lack of many of the devices for character development (e.g., detailed physical descriptions and in-depth psychological portraits) employed in other literature, especially the modern novel. The inability to describe the portrayal of characters in biblical narrative left mainline biblical studies unable to explain or engage the testimony of so many artists, teachers, and other expositors—Jewish and Christian—to the existence of such powerful individual characters as Abraham, Sarah, Moses, Ruth, and David.

The change in the evaluation of the biblical style of characterization is signaled in the title of one of Alter's chapters, "Characterization and the Art of Reticence."[24] He, and many others, now celebrate the Bible's sparseness and laconic style, seeking to describe how the biblical narrator can depict such powerful and memorable individuals without employing all of the familiar narrative modes.

Alter describes an ascending scale of reliability in the ways that the narrator presents a character. Although his is not the final word on the subject, it is a solid and accessible starting point. The lowest level of the scale includes a character's actions or appearance; these facts reveal little or nothing about motivations for actions or about the significance of the physical trait. Next is direct speech, by a character or by other characters concerning him or her. This moves us into the realm of claims and assertions about motives, feelings, intentions, etc., but here too we have to evaluate the assertions, weighing them against what others, including the narrator, tell us about the situation. The Amalekite's claim to have killed Saul (2 Sam 1) is a lie that contradicts the narrator's reliable report that Saul killed himself in battle (1 Sam 31).

Next comes inward speech, a character's interior monologue, which gives us some certainty regarding what she or he feels and thinks. In Gen 18:17-19, we learn precisely why the Lord's plans for Sodom and Gomorrah will be revealed to Abraham; in contrast, we know *what* Abraham argues for regarding the city, but we do not know *why.* Because the men with the Lord are going toward Sodom

23. See Bill Moyers, *Genesis: A Living Conversation* (New York: Doubleday, 1996); Jack Miles, *God: A Biography* (New York: Random House, 1995).

24. Alter, *The Art of Biblical Narrative,* 114-30.

(Gen 18:16, 22), we assume that Abraham means Sodom when he says "the city." Perhaps Lot and his family are at the front of his mind, and not just the righteous in general. Such assumptions and conjectures are typical of the process a reader goes through in evaluating and developing a portrait of a character.

Finally there is the reliable narrator's report of what the characters feel, think, and plan. Even here, however, the narrator may only state the feeling or intention without offering any explanation or motive for it. At the center of the story of Absalom's revolt, the narrator informs us that "the LORD had ordained to defeat the good counsel of Ahithophel, so that the LORD might bring ruin on Absalom" (2 Sam 17:14 NRSV). This announces the intention but not the motives of the Lord, especially whether this ruin of Absalom is meant for the benefit of David. In Genesis 37, Joseph's reports of his dreams result in his brothers' hatred and jealousy, "but his father kept the matter in mind" (37:11 NRSV).

Since brevity and selectivity play major roles in the depiction of character, reliability needs qualification in the sense that we cannot rely on the narrator to tell us all the facts, motives, intentions, etc., that we need. The modes that grant certainty are employed sparingly and usually report minimal amounts of information. This reticence can clothe characters in varying ways and degrees in ambiguity, mystery, and depth. Abner's death at Joab's hands is the convenient removal of a potential rival of David, and readers have wondered whether David had some role in this murder, as he will in the subsequent death of Uriah (2 Sam 11). The narrator could resolve this question for us, but instead only asserts the king's popularity with the people and their conviction of his innocence: "All the people and all Israel understood that day that the king had no part in the killing of Abner son of Ner" (2 Sam 3:37). We learn that Isaac and Rebekah favor Esau and Jacob respectively; a motive is provided for Isaac's love but not for Rebekah's: "Isaac loved Esau, because he was fond of game; but Rebekah loved Jacob" (Gen 25:28 NRSV).

The narrator employs repetition to great effect in the depiction of characters. Repetition extends from specific details to whole stories and is one of the most, if not the most,

employed devices in the narrator's literary tool kit. A character's own statement can be repeated at a different time or in a different place. We gain insight into God's frustration with and eventual toleration of human sin in that God first sends the flood and then promises never to send another because the human heart is always inclined to evil (Gen 6:5; 8:21). The narrator can tell us one thing and the character another. The character may be lying outright or simply tailoring the facts to fit an agenda. Both David and Solomon speak of the Lord's presence and establishment of Solomon's reign (1 Kgs 2:45 NRSV). Solomon proclaims to Shimei that "King Solomon shall be blessed, and the throne of David shall be established before the LORD forever" (1 Kgs 2:44-45). But the narrator makes no mention of the Lord in the closing report: "The kingdom was established in the hand of Solomon" (1 Kgs 2:46 NRSV; see 2:12).

Similar are the many instances when a character repeats what another character has said but alters it. Determining what the alterations are and how they reflect on the characters and the situation is a central process in our development and appreciation of biblical characterization. In Isaac's proposal to bless Esau, he emphasizes the hunt and food and does not mention the Lord. When Rebekah repeats this to Jacob, she shortens the description of the hunt and adds that the blessing is to be "before the LORD" (Gen 27:1-7). She tailors the repetition to impress Jacob more strongly. When Elisha first hears of Naaman's request for healing, he asks that Naaman be sent to Elisha "that he may learn that there is a prophet in Israel" (2 Kgs 5:8 NRSV). Once Naaman, an Aramean, is healed, he asserts, "Now I know that there is no God in all the earth except in Israel" (5:15). The contrast redounds to the honor of the foreigner and to the disgrace of the self-centered prophet.

Issues of change and complexity are central to appreciating biblical characterization. Characters can change for the better or for the worse. Judah develops from the self-centered brother and father-in-law of Genesis 37–38 into the responsible and knowledgeable son and brother of Genesis 43–44. In 1 Samuel, Saul gradually degenerates from the capable, although wary, king and soldier of his early career into the crazed and jealous ruler who spends his time and resources in the pursuit of David. David, at the same time, learns a lesson about the political and personal value of restraint in his chance encounter with Saul in the cave and through Abigail's argument that killing Nabal would haunt him in the future (1 Sam 24–25). David then applies this lesson in deliberate fashion by hunting down Saul and demonstrating that he will not kill him, even though he has the ability to do so whenever he wants (1 Sam 26).

On the other hand, lack of change or the persistence of personality, particularly in new situations, adds to characterization. Esau's impetuous nature leads him to sell his birthright in Gen 25:29-34, but results in his emotional welcome of Jacob in Genesis 33. In both instances Esau is a man of the moment who does not consider matters of the future or of the past. Samuel, even in death, remains the harsh prophet and Saul's implacable foe (1 Sam 13–15; 28). Jacob, unlike David, does not learn from his own experience that parental favoritism can tear a family apart; he plays favorites with Joseph, who, like Jacob, ends up spending twenty years in a foreign land before seeing his brothers again.

Complexity points to the multifaceted aspect of many character portrayals, including both the change and the persistence of personality traits. Seldom do characters fit into simple moral categories, and seldom can they be described using only one or two adjectives. They are portrayed with personal and moral strengths and weaknesses, and they demonstrate these in a variety of settings. Complexity combines with the capability of change to produce the rich and full individuals we meet in the pages of the OT. Even characters who appear once are seldom mere stereotypes, present only to advance the plot or to serve as a foil to other people, as evidenced by Abraham's servant (Gen 24), by Rahab (Josh 2), by Samson's parents (Judg 13), and by Abigail (1 Sam 25).

Characters. Discussion of the portraits of a few individuals furthers the presentation and underlines differences in how specific biblical people have been perceived. The 1970s produced a growing number of studies of major personalities such as Joseph, Moses, and David that developed some of the aspects of complexity and change. In the 1980s, the rate of growth accelerated, and the tenor of many of these studies shifted. Again, Alter's work is a helpful benchmark.

Besides complexity and change, Alter discussed the role of ambiguity in the depiction of a character such as David. I use David as a major illustration because a large number of works treat him directly or indirectly and because of the distinct shift in the evaluation of his character. Ambiguity of character arises when we are given some information that leads us to speculate about a particular trait, motive, or such, but we are not given enough information finally to resolve the question. In the example from Genesis 25, we know that Rebekah loves Jacob. Because we are given a motive for Isaac's love of Esau, we can wonder what Rebekah's reasons might be.

At various points in his discussion, Alter draws attention to this mainly in the portrayal of David. We are at times told how others view and react to David, whether in fear or in love. Saul, Jonathan, Michal, and all the people love David (1 Sam 16:21; 18:1-3, 16, 20), and Saul comes to fear him (1 Sam 18:12, 29). But we are never told what David feels toward any of these people. David is "very much afraid of King Achish" (1 Sam 21:12 NRSV), so it is not that the narrator never tells us what David feels or thinks. When Saul proposes that David marry one of his daughters, Merab and then Michal, the narrator uses inner monologue to reveal Saul's ulterior motive (that David would die in battle with the Philistines, 1 Sam 18:17, 21, 25). Of David, he tells us that he "was well pleased to be the king's son-in-law" (1 Sam 18:26 NRSV) but not why he was pleased or whether he has any inkling of Saul's intentions. David kills two hundred Philistines to collect double the required number of foreskins, but the narrator provides no light on David's reasons.

In evaluating David's—indeed, any character's—assertions and claims about self, about others, and about the general situation, we must take account of the setting for the statements. It is striking how many of David's pronouncements are made publicly so that, in evaluating them for their sincerity and truth, we have to ask whether David speaks honestly, only for public effect, or for a mix of the two. When David confronts Goliath in view of both the Israelite and the Philistine armies, he proclaims the Lord's power (1 Sam 18:45-47). Once Goliath is dead, however, no one—including David and the narrator—makes any mention of the Lord or of the assembled people coming to acknowledge his feat. At a crucial point in his flight from Saul, David speaks "in his heart" or "to himself" of the necessity of fleeing to the Philistines to escape Saul; in this very private moment David says nothing of the Lord.

Ambiguity means that we are presented a choice of ways of understanding David, or any character depicted in this mode. Is David only the pious shepherd and chosen king of Jewish and Christian tradition? Is he a violent, grasping man who will stop at almost nothing to achieve his goals? Or is he a complex mix of both of these, a true "political animal," to use a contemporary phrase? He ends his life displaying the same mixture of piety and power. He speaks to Solomon of fidelity to the Lord and then gives him a "hit list" of potential enemies (2 Kgs 2:1-9). The various studies and commentaries of the last twenty or so years have developed, in their own ways, each of these views with a variety of nuances and perspectives.

Character studies of David are prime examples of changes in the study of biblical narrative in both method and content. The brevity, selectivity, and repetitive nature of the narrator are now celebrated as integral parts of the depiction of characters. In addition, the characters themselves are regarded as complex, multifaceted, and capable of change, and not as cardboard stereotypes of righteousness or sin, faith or disobedience, success or failure. This includes a willingness to recognize that the biblical narrators are deliberately portraying both positive and negative sides of people and institutions. Biblical narrative is not a one-sided story of saints versus sinners, evil kings versus good prophets, and so forth.

Instead of dividing 1 Samuel into pro-monarchical and anti-monarchical sources, for example, we can read the book as a sophisticated and multifaceted evaluation of monarchy. The presentation includes kingship and the related systems of priests, judges, and prophets. This mode of reading works with both the abstract (prophecy) and the concrete (Samuel) without trying fully to separate them. That is, we cannot talk of the narrator's view(s) of monarchy separate from the personalities of Samuel, Saul, David, and the others associated with them. The many, and often contradictory, critical and historical stands that scholars have taken concerning 1 Samuel reflect, in part, the very complexity of the multiple viewpoints and beliefs expressed in the text.

Samuel is another example of rich characterization. He is a leader with aspects of priest, judge, and prophet; and he is a leader who is asked by the people and commanded by God to appoint his own successor. In 1 Samuel 8, Samuel threatens the people with the reality of kingship, but both the people and the Lord repeat their request and command. Samuel responds ambiguously, and not with immediate obedience: "Samuel then said to the people of Israel, 'Each of you return home'" (1 Sam 8:22 NRSV). Chapters 10–11, then, depict a prophet dragging his feet in carrying out his commission. Since Samuel is unwilling to appoint a king immediately, God sends him a candidate, Saul. Samuel has a love/hate relationship with Saul that carries both personal and political implications. Saul, for his part, is a capable military leader in his campaign against the Ammonites, but he can never envision himself totally separate from Samuel. Because of this latter trait, Samuel, perhaps, thinks of Saul as a leader whom he can influence or even control. Hence Samuel's angry reaction to the Lord's regret at ever making Saul king is a complex mix of emotions (1 Sam 15:10-11).

The Role of Women. Concern with characters has heightened our awareness of the roles women play in biblical narrative. This awareness has been accompanied by a focus on the issue of gender in both biblical narrative and commentary. Phyllis Trible, in her rhetorical and feminist readings, was one of the first to focus on questions of gender in the creation stories and other biblical narratives.[25] She challenges traditional views that assert God's strict maleness in Genesis 1 and that see a straightforward story of disobedience in Genesis 3. Starting with her work, critics have produced more readings of the opening chapters of Genesis that explore in

25. Phyllis Trible, *God and the Rhetoric of Sexuality* (Philadelphia: Fortress, 1978; and *Texts of Terror: Literary-Feminist Readings of Biblical Narratives* (Philadelphia: Fortress, 1984).

detail the ways the narrator develops the plot, setting, and characters of the story.[26] In these readings, the garden story becomes a fuller and richer narrative, not the simple story of sin committed by the one-dimensional figures Adam and Eve.

This leads into the large and growing number of feminist studies of biblical narrative. Many focus on the women in the narratives, whether they are major or minor characters, and portray them in depth and with independence. Sarah, Rebekah, Miriam, Deborah, Michal, Bathsheba—all take on a life of their own and no longer exist solely as the mothers, daughters, or wives of men. This holds even if the women are not given proper names of their own—e.g., the wife of Manoach, Samson's mother, and the daughter of Jephthah.

In addition, and just as significant, feminist studies draw our attention to the patriarchal and male society that forms a narrative's setting. These studies do not have to deal only or mainly with women in the text. Setting here refers to the entire range of social, religious, and political beliefs, perspectives, and assumptions that form the often unspoken background for the stories. Setting in this sense is usually evident only after close study of the text. The fact that most studies refer to the biblical narrator as "he" reflects the dominant male perspective of the narrative. Feminist studies, however, show us that it is a dominant, but not a totally commanding, perspective. Finally, reflecting the contemporary willingness to look at the darker parts and aspects of the Bible, feminist studies can confront us with troubling issues such as the role and treatment of women in the world of biblical narrative.[27]

The Character of God. The LORD (*YHWH*), *God* (*Elohim*), has seldom been treated as a character, mainly because of the powerful influence of Christianity and Judaism. However, as with the shift to full character portrayal with humans, God as a character with strengths and weaknesses is often a major part of the study of biblical narrative. God is not viewed as above or outside of the story, but as an integral part of it: "We can read the character of God in Hebrew narrative more elusively, positing of God the enigmatic ambiguities found in complex human characters."[28] A character portrayal of God takes into account all divine actions and statements, as well as whatever is said of or to God by another, including the narrator. This data is then evaluated as with any human character.

The divine presence varies from the implicit to the explicit. As an explicit presence, the Lord speaks and acts as in Genesis 1–11 and 12–25 (the primeval and the Abraham stories, respectively) while as an implicit presence, the Lord is referred to by others, as in the Joseph story, but seldom appears directly. (The book of Esther is an extreme example of the latter.) The Lord appears only once in the Joseph story, when, in a vision of God, Jacob is assured of divine presence and support during his upcoming stay in Egypt. True to the narrator's selective style, the Lord says, "Joseph's own hand will close your eyes," and neither confirms nor negates Joseph's claims that his rise to power in Egypt was part of a divine plan to preserve the family (Gen 45:4-9; 50:19-20). This relates to the variation between clarity and ambiguity of the portrait in terms of whether the Lord is actually determining and involved in events and of any possible motives for such activity. Previously I noted the limited extent of the narrator's ascription of Absalom's fall to the divine intention (2 Sam 17:14).

Narrative critics are willing to look at the dark side of human characters like Abraham and David, and of human society in general. The latter is evidenced in the mistreatment of women and in the prevalence of violence as the chief way to deal with problems. The focus on the human side is matched by a concern with understanding and evaluating God, who is not only involved with this human scene but is often also the initiator, the one who sets violent events in motion. The flood, the conquest, the seemingly unending wars of Samuel–Kings, and the destruction of Judah and Jerusalem are prime examples. Humans, whether individuals or the whole people, are flawed or far worse; and God is the One who chooses them to play a role in the divine plan. Critics have begun raising the question of how all of this reflects on God.

26. Gunn and Fewell, *Narrative in the Hebrew Bible*, 194-205.

27. For example, see Danna N. Fewell and David M. Gunn, *Gender, Power, and Promise: The Subject of the Bible's First Story* (Nashville: Abingdon, 1993); J. Cheryl Exum, *Fragmented Women: Feminist (Sub) Versions of Biblical Narratives* (Valley Forge, Pa.: Trinity, 1993).

28. Gunn and Fewell, *Narrative in the Hebrew Bible*, 85.

Biblical studies are presently enmeshed in assessing and debating the impact and relevance of all these changes, particularly the emphasis on the dark side, both human and divine, of the story. The task is to read the Bible as it is and to hold together its glory and its dread, and not to deny one to maintain only the other.

BIBLIOGRAPHY

Alter, Robert. *The Art of Biblical Narrative.* New York: Basic, 1981.

Bal, Mieke. *Narratology: An Introduction to the Theory of Narrative.* Toronto: University of Toronto Press, 1985. An excellent introduction to general narratology.

Bar-Efrat, Shimon. *Narrative Art in the Bible.* Sheffield: Almond, 1989 (Hebrew ed., 1979). A solid introduction that covers more topics than Berlin's work.

Berlin, Adele. *Poetics and Interpretation of Biblical Narrative.* Sheffield: Almond, 1983. A solid introduction that focuses on character and point of view.

The Bible and Culture Collective. *The Postmodern Bible.* New York: Yale University Press, 1995. By a group of scholars; an overview of the variety of contemporary ways of interpreting the Bible.

Gunn, David M., and Danna N. Fewell. *Narrative in the Hebrew Bible.* New York: Oxford, 1993. A solid introduction that combines theoretical discussion with in-depth readings of a variety of narratives.

Josipovici, Gabriel. *The Book of God: A Response to the Bible.* New Haven: Yale University Press, 1988. An insightful, general reading of both the OT and the NT by a comparative literature scholar.

Miles, Jack. *God: A Biography.* New York: Random House, 1995. The depiction or biography of God in the OT from Genesis through Chronicles; a fine and non-technical introduction to the issues involved in regarding God as a character in the Bible.

Moyers, Bill. *Genesis: A Living Gonversation.* New York: Doubleday, 1996. The companion to the PBS series, which is available in video and audio forms; a powerful expression of the tensions between traditional views of Genesis and contemporary readings that raise moral issues from the narrative.

Sternberg, Meir. *The Poetics of Biblical Narrative: Ideological Literature and the Drama of Reading.* Bloomington: Indiana University Press, 1985. An often-cited and debated work noted for its insights, its detail, and its controversial claims.

THE BOOK OF JOSHUA

INTRODUCTION, COMMENTARY, AND REFLECTIONS
BY
ROBERT B. COOTE

THE BOOK OF
JOSHUA

INTRODUCTION

The book of Joshua tells of Israel's conquest of Canaan, which appears to climax the long opening story of the Bible. In Genesis, God promises to give the land of Canaan to the descendants of Abraham, Isaac, and Israel. After delivering the descendants of Israel from Egypt and forcing them to remain in the desert long enough for an entire generation to die out and a new generation to take their place, God fulfills this promise. Near the end of the book of Numbers, with Moses still in command, the Israelites conquer the promised land east of the Jordan River and finally arrive at the Jordan. Deuteronomy consists of a long speech by Moses to Israel, including the last major installment of the law Moses passes on to Israel. At the end of Deuteronomy, Moses dies.

The book of Joshua continues the story from this point. First God commissions Joshua. Then, in an orgy of terror, violence, and mayhem, God takes the land of Canaan west of the Jordan away from its inhabitants and gives it to Israel under Joshua's command. Joshua, with the help of the priest Eleazar, distributes the conquered land to the tribes of Israel. Having aged, like Moses he bids his people farewell, dies, and is buried. Thus the book of Joshua explains how under Joshua's command Canaan was conquered, the Canaanites were slaughtered, and their lands were expropriated and redistributed to the tribes of Israel. It forms a triumphant finale to the Bible's foundational epic of liberation, the savage goal toward which God's creation of Israel and delivery of Israel from slavery in Egypt appears to point from the start.

COMPOSITION DURING THE MONARCHICAL PERIOD

It is possible, but unlikely, that this story was recorded as it happened in history. The story is composed of diverse ingredients. These include set speeches, folk narratives (some with auxiliary additions), echoes of rituals, excerpts from supposed ancient sources, lists, territorial descriptions of differing kinds, material repeated elsewhere in the Bible but in different form, and a double ending. The story purports to be about tribal warfare, but several features point to a monarchical as much as a tribal viewpoint. These include the precise delineation of territory covering a sweeping area, the notion of a unified conquest involving mass murder, and the portrayal of strict military loyalty and absolute obedience to a single commander. While Joshua plays a singular role in the story, however, he appears only sporadically, mostly in frameworks, large and small, as though he might not have belonged originally to all the parts—or to any of them. It is surprising that a hero from the tribe of Ephraim, whose territory lay at the heart of early Israel, should be the protagonist of a conquest narrative that focuses almost entirely on the territory of Benjamin, with scarcely anything at all to say about Ephraim. Similarly, Joshua rarely, if ever, acts on his own initiative, but moves only on Yahweh's orders. This contrasts, for example, with the account of David, who acts for himself, albeit in response to God's election; but it comports, as will become clear, with the scheme behind the later composition of the book of Joshua. This scheme held that for centuries Joshua, together with Israel under his command, was unique in his obedience to Yahweh. The first five books of the Bible are composed of at least five distinctive layers and strands, and the book of Joshua appears to be in line with at least two of these, long known as D and P, the first in a major way and the second in a minor way. Many towns are destroyed in Joshua, and these often do not agree with the archaeological evidence of the period before the Israelite monarchy, when the story is supposed to have taken place. In sum, these features of the book of Joshua indicate that it was not composed all at once as an accurate account of an episode in the history of pre-monarchic Israel. Instead, they point to a gradual composition, which took place mainly during the period of the monarchy, from two hundred to six hundred years after the supposed events occurred. Other features make clear that the monarchic perspective of Joshua derives specifically from the house of David.

The book of Joshua is not a simple account of historical events. It is a complex narrative shaped by writers belonging to several different contexts. Most of these contexts can be identified with at least some probability. The clearest is what most scholars regard as the basic context of the D strand, or Deuteronomistic History—namely, the reform of Josiah (c. 640–609 BCE) in the late seventh century. A significant part of Josiah's reform was the reconquest of what had been Israel, and Joshua's conquest of Canaan was taken as a precursor of Josiah's reconquest of Israel. Another earlier context was the reign of Hezekiah (c. 714–687 BCE). Hezekiah was the first Davidic king to begin his reign after the fall of Samaria in 722 BCE, when the non-Davidic kingdom of Israel came to an end. Analysis has shown that much of the books of Kings was composed under Hezekiah, and it is possible that much in the books of Joshua and Judges comes from his reign as well. He, too, wanted to reconquer Israel. The likelihood is that it was Hezekiah who adopted Joshua as a Davidic hero. Before Hezekiah, Joshua was an Israelite hero, probably introduced into wider popularity by Jeroboam I, the usurper of what had been Davidic Israel, whose home was not far from the tomb of Joshua. While it is not always possible to assign particular parts of Joshua to an exact source, these are the main events that helped to shape the book prior to the Babylonian exile of the house of David. During the exile, a few minor changes may have been made in line with the exilic revision of the entire Deuteronomistic History. After the exile, the parts of Joshua that seem related to the priestly strand in the Pentateuch were written, during the Persian period. The source and context of a few parts of Joshua remain a mystery.

That the book of Joshua was written mainly during the period of the Davidic monarchy no longer occasions surprise. In the last twenty years, much research has been devoted to the study of early Israel, particularly with regard to the tide of village settlements that arose in the hill country of Palestine during the Early Iron Age.[1] The Early Iron Age lasted during the twelfth and eleventh centuries BCE, after the supposed time of Joshua and before the time of David. While an exact identification between these new settlements and early Israel cannot be proved, historians and archaeologists believe that the inhabitants of most of these villages were related in some way to Israel as described in the Bible.

Settlement shifts are not uncommon in the history of Palestine. They have been going on for at least five thousand years, and many are comparable to the Early Iron Age shift. While the interpretation of these shifts will remain under investigation for the foreseeable future, so far one

---

1. The standard work is Israel Finkelstein, *The Archaeology of the Israelite Settlement* (Jerusalem: Israel Exploration Society, 1988).

thing is clear: Century-long settlement shifts in Palestine are not typically caused by blitzkriegs; therefore, it is improbable that the Early Iron Age settlement shift was prompted by an onslaught of tribal outsiders of the sort described by the book of Joshua. Most scholars now think that the people of Israel were indigenous to Palestine, and were not outsiders. There is nothing in the archaeological record to suggest that the Early Iron Age population of highland Palestine had a mainly pastoral-nomadic background, as suggested by the Bible, or that any sizable segment of the population of Palestine at that time originated outside of Palestine, again as suggested by the Bible, except the Aegean "Sea Peoples," represented by the Philistines. (Hittites are named in Joshua, where they are seen as indigenous; it is conceivable that they settled in Palestine during the Late Bronze Age, but more likely the term has its Neo-Assyrian meaning of the inhabitants of greater Syria.)

Several passages in Joshua itself, as well as in Judges, contradict the picture of a single triumphant assault. Moreover, the picture in Joshua leaves an important question unanswered: What was the nature of early Israel? One of the biggest mistakes readers of the Bible can make is to project modern notions of nationalism onto the ancient world or to assume, with the eighteenth-century thinker Johann Gottfried Herder and his Romantic and modern followers, that a given people whose existence as such is mistakenly taken for granted naturally expresses its singularity through a homogeneous folk spirit. In the commentary, "nation" is used to refer to what historians call the "political nation," rulers over a changing body of subjects. Early Israel represented not a nation, but a shifting confederation of tribes.

A tribe was a political network of families united by external threat and claiming a common putative ancestor. Tribal loyalty competed with other political and social loyalties and tended to be stronger among the stronger members of the alliance. Thus "tribe," like "nation," referred mainly to the political identity and function of an elite. Anthropological study of tribal societies, combined with historical evidence, shows that notions of defined patriarchal descent and kinship like those described in the Bible tend to be putative and fictional, reflecting not historical kinship but political relations, both among tribes and tribal alliances and between tribes and a central government. The biblical descriptions of the tribes of Israel, like those in J and P, reflect the interests of a state or governing elite with the ability or desire to centralize. The description of the "tribes" in Joshua is no different: It reflects, not the disorderly tribal relations that must have characterized early Israel, as illustrated in the early "Song of Deborah" in Judges 5, but the politics of radical reform and centralization. Thus in Joshua the tribes of Israel are presented in a rationalized manner, united in harmonious kinship.

The sources used by the writers of the book of Joshua may contain sparse material going back in some way to early Israel, but the book of Joshua in its present form was written long after the time of early Israel. The emergence of Israel and its settlement of the central highlands of Palestine are now understood mainly through archaeology and comparative history rather than the Bible.[2] To inquire about the historical contexts of the book of Joshua means to look at the house of David, and not early Israel. In this regard, Joshua resembles the Pentateuch, which precedes it. Virtually all of the Pentateuch, while purporting to describe early Israel, was written during the period of the Israelite and Davidic monarchies or later and reflects chiefly their circumstances and concerns.

CONTEXT OF DEUTERONOMISTIC HISTORY

To understand the book of Joshua, it is important to recognize that it is part, and how it is part, of a much larger work: the Deuteronomistic History. This is a conglomerate of monarchic historical sources, some of them probably tracing back to the court of David himself, that

---

2. For early Israel, see Robert B. Coote, *Early Israel: A New Horizon* (Minneapolis: Fortress, 1990); Coote, "Early Israel," *Scandinavian Journal of the Old Testament* 5 (1991) 35-46; Coote, "Conquest," in *Eerdmans Dictionary of the Bible*, ed. David Noel Freedman, Astrid B. Beck, and Allen C. Myers (Grand Rapids: Eerdmans, forthcoming); Michael G. Hasel, "Israel in the Merneptah Stela," *BASOR* 296 (1994) 45-61; Israel Finkelstein and Nadav Na'aman, eds., *From Nomadism to Monarchy: Archaeological and Historical Aspects of Early Israel* (Jerusalem: Israel Exploration Society, 1994); Israel Finkelstein, "The Great Transformation: The 'Conquest' of the Highlands Frontiers and the Rise of the Territorial States," in *The Archaeology of Society in the Holy Land*, ed. Thomas E. Levy (New York: Facts on File, 1995) 349-65.

have been edited according to a single overarching conception. That conception is the house of David's claim to the sovereignty of Israel. The Deuteronomistic History was composed out of these sources mainly during the reigns of Hezekiah and later Josiah to support their programs of centralization. Joshua cannot be understood apart from the Deuteronomistic History. But what about the story of the Tetrateuch, the first four books of the Bible, which precedes the Deuteronomistic History? Should Joshua also be read in the light of the Tetrateuch, especially the parts that pre-date the great priestly revision of it in the late sixth century BCE? Joshua presumes aspects of the Tetrateuch's story, but there is little of importance in Joshua that must be understood mainly in terms of the pre-priestly Tetrateuch. (Joshua also contains priestly passages. These are considered briefly at the end of this Introduction.) For example, Joshua assumes the Tetrateuch's representation of Davidic sovereignty, even though the Tetrateuch contains hardly a hint of a forthcoming conquest.

If we ask what gave God the right to dispossess the Canaanites of their land, the scriptural answer is to be found near the beginning of the Tetrateuch, in Noah's curse of Canaan in Gen 9:25-26: "Cursed be Canaan;/ lowest of slaves shall he be to his brothers. . . . Blessed by [Yahweh] my God be Shem [an ancestor of Israel];/ and let Canaan be his slave" (NRSV; cf. Josh 16:10; 17:13; Judg 1:28; 1 Kgs 9:20-21). The reason why Noah cursed Canaan was that Canaan's father, Ham, had seen Noah naked when Noah lay drunk in his tent (Gen 9:21-22). This curse laid the basis for God's promise to Abram made "between Bethel and Ai" (Gen 13:3): "All the land that you see I will give to you and to your offspring forever" (Gen 13:15 NRSV; Bethel and Ai lie about a mile and a half apart; cf. Josh 12:19).

The source of this myth was the court of the house of David, which early on produced the "history" of the world and of Israel that forms the basis of the Tetrateuch. The myth of God's promise of land to Israel, essential to the story of Joshua, together with the related myths of a unified nation descended from a single family arriving from outside, originated in its present form to help the house of David explain its sovereignty over greater Israel. However, the house of David exercised such sovereignty for only a short period in its five-hundred-year history, during the reigns of its founder David and his son Solomon in the tenth century BCE. Thereafter the house of David ruled little more than the highland territory of Judah, while the rest of Israel had its own kings and foreign rulers. For centuries the house of David looked back on the reigns of David and Solomon as the Golden Age and never gave up the hope of reconquering Israel and restoring Davidic rule to its original glory.

Such claims are not uncommon in dynastic histories. For instance, in the Mayflower Compact of 1621, the Pilgrims acknowledged the sovereignty of their king, James I (of the King James Bible), whom they called "king of Great Britain, *France,* and Ireland." The kings of England had not ruled in France for a long time, but they maintained the title in theory up through the eighteenth century. James I inherited this proprietary title from his great-grandmother on both sides, Margaret Tudor, daughter of Henry VII, and she from distant forebears. In the same way, the house of David maintained its title to Israel, inherited from David, in theory for hundreds of years. The ambition to reconquer Israel and make that title real again became pronounced in the late Assyrian period, after the fall of Samaria, Israel's capital, in 722 BCE, when there were no more opposing kings of Israel. Two Davidic kings in particular are known to have pursued policies leading to a projected reconquest of Israel: Hezekiah in the late eighth century BCE and Josiah in the late seventh century.

To the extent that the promise of the land plays an important role in the Tetrateuch, the book of Joshua appears to bring the Tetrateuch's story to its expected conclusion. However, originally the book of Joshua was *not* the ending of this story. When this story was first composed, the book of Joshua had not even been thought of. As already indicated, the Romantic idea that a single popular folk narrative lies behind the various strands of the biblical story from Genesis to Joshua has no basis. Even within the Pentateuch, Deuteronomy does not belong to the original story, but begins a new story, the Deuteronomistic History, which apparently was meant to be a sequel to the original pre-priestly Tetrateuch story.[3]

---

3. Deuteronomy became a part of a five-book Pentateuch, or Torah, late in the OT period, when the notion of an "Age of Moses" became a primary basis for partitioning Scripture. At that time the rest of the Deuteronomistic History, beginning with Joshua, became a part of the section of the Scriptures later called the Prophets.

Two strands of narrative made up the bulk of the pre-priestly Tetrateuch story. These were the early house of David's history of Israel, called J, and a slightly later northern Israelite supplement, called E. The J and E strands give little indication of how God's promise of land is to be fulfilled. They seem to take it for granted that David (in the case of J) and the kings of Israel (in the case of E) possess sovereignty over the land of Israel, as sanctioned by God, and devote most of their attention to other concerns. These strands cannot be traced into Deuteronomy and Joshua. They end, not with a conquest, as in Joshua, but with the culmination of their own distinctive themes, in Exodus (for E) and in Numbers (for J).[4]

Not only do the earliest strands of the Pentateuch conclude before Deuteronomy and Joshua, fail to appear in Deuteronomy and Joshua, and fail to refer to a conquest, but they also give no indication that the promise of the land is to be fulfilled in a blitzkrieg and attempted ethnic cleansing. Nor is there a hint of God's command to exterminate the Canaanites, to say nothing of the particular contours and emphases of the book of Joshua. The curse of slavery on Canaan is not the same as extermination, as recognized in the book of Joshua (Josh 16:10; 17:13). The figure of Joshua himself appears in the Tetrateuch, but he has little if anything to do with the main themes of J and E, and was probably introduced there by scribes in the court of Hezekiah or Josiah. In Exod 17:8-16, a text that belongs to neither J nor E, Joshua appears out of nowhere to help defeat the Amalekites. He appears again in Numbers 13–14, also in connection with the Amalekites. This is a J story about the Judahite town of Hebron, later David's first capital, and its eventual Judahite conqueror, Caleb. Here Joshua, an Ephraimite, is introduced rather artificially as a new character (Num 13:8, 16) to play a supplementary and presumably secondary role to Caleb, who is of primary interest in the J strand. It is even implied in Josh 14:12 that Joshua was not one of the spies.

The Amalekites play a major role in the Deuteronomistic History (Deut 25:17, 19; Judg 3:13; 5:14; 6:3, 33; 7:12; 10:12; 12:15; 1 Sam 14:48; 15:2-3, 5-7, 18, 20, 32; 28:18; 30:1, 13, 18; 2 Sam 1:1, 8, 13; 8:12; most of these passages have a connection with the founding of the house of David), but only a minor part in the Tetrateuch, except for these two passages involving Joshua (Gen 14:7; 36:12, 16; Num 24:20).[5] As for the notion of mass extermination, it figures in the Tetrateuch in only two stories, Joshua's attack on the Amalekites in Exodus 17 and Israel's attack on Hormah in Numbers 21, a duplicate of the attack on the Amalekites in Num 14:39-45.[6] It may be no coincidence that the Amalekites were later said to have been finally exterminated under Hezekiah (1 Chr 4:41-43).[7] It was probably in the court of Hezekiah, where the overall plot of the Deuteronomistic History was first conceived and Joshua was first given a significant role in the Davidic history of Israel, that the association of Joshua with the Amalekites was apparently introduced into the Tetrateuch.

NARRATIVE STRUCTURE

The story of Joshua has two parts. Israel's land east of the Jordan has already been conquered under Moses. The story of Joshua concerns mainly the west side of the Jordan.[8] First, Joshua leads the tribes of Israel in the conquest of the west side of the Jordan. What begins in Josh 1:1-6 concludes in 12:7-24. Second, Joshua oversees the distribution to the twelve tribes of all the land conquered (Joshua 13–31). The distribution includes the designation of refuges for

4. Hans Walter Wolff, "The Kerygma of the Yahwist," in *The Vitality of Old Testament Traditions*, eds. Walter Brueggemann and Hans Walter Wolff, 2nd ed. (Atlanta: John Knox, 1982) 41-66; Robert B. Coote and David Robert Ord, *The Bible's First History* (Philadelphia: Fortress, 1989); Robert B. Coote, *In Defense of Revolution: The Elohist History* (Minneapolis: Fortress, 1991).

5. The first and last of these passages probably belong to the J strand. The middle two belong to a separate text regarding the Edomites that may have been incorporated into the J strand.

6. The verb החרם (*heḥĕrîm*, "dedicate" in the sense of "exterminate") occurs in the Tetrateuch only in Num 21:2-3, as a folk explanation of the name "Hormah," "Extermination" (cf. Josh 12:14). The name probably derives from the notion of a sacred or prohibited precinct.

7. Outside of Exodus 17 and Numbers 13–14, Joshua appears parenthetically in Exod 24:13; 32:17 (texts that belong to neither J nor E); 33:11 (Joshua is introduced as an aside, with no close tie to the story); Num 11:28 (Joshua is a superfluous double to the "young man" in v. 27); and Num 27:18, 22; 32:12, 28; 34:17, all texts, basically priestly, that come after the end of J and E. See George W. Ramsey, "Joshua," *ABD*, 3:999.

8. In the long history of Palestine, the Jordan has rarely formed a prominent natural boundary as it does in the Deuteronomistic History. The tribe of Manasseh traditionally occupied both sides of the Jordan precisely because it was not a boundary. In the biblical period, the Jordan as boundary appears to be attested for the first time in the eighth and seventh centuries BCE, as an administrative expedient instituted by the Assyrians, who, not surprisingly, were outsiders.

manslayers and the assignment of towns and pasture to the Levites. After giving permission to the tribes from east of the Jordan to build an altar beside the Jordan to witness to their desire not to be separated from the west-bank tribes, and after giving a double farewell—a speech followed by a covenanting ceremony, ending with the erection of a stone as a witness that all Israel has committed to Joshua's Yahweh—Joshua dies and is buried (Joshua 22–24).

The plot of conquest and distribution represents only the bare bones of the narrative. By the time most of the account of the conquest is completed (Joshua 1–9), only two towns have been captured and destroyed, Jericho and Ai, and the inhabitants of another town, Gibeon, accommodated. The three towns that dominate the narrative of conquest lie in the small territory of Benjamin, nearly within sight of one another. They represent a tiny part of the land to be conquered. Why is this the case? The story uses conquest not only to foreshadow the house of David's reconquest, but also to confirm its sovereignty and elaborate on its policy of centralization.

Most of the narrative of conquest is taken up with three localities of great significance for the house of David's claim to sovereignty: Gilgal, Bethel, and Gibeon. (This assumes that the story of Ai bears on its neighbor Bethel.) At Gilgal, Samuel determined to depose Saul in favor of David, thereby establishing the house of David (see Commentary on 4:19–5:12). Bethel plays a critical role in the entire Deuteronomistic History. Its altar symbolized the "sin of Jeroboam." By usurping the sovereignty of the house of David in Israel, Jeroboam violated the first law of Moses, which stipulates that the service of Yahweh has to be performed at one shrine only. The sin of Jeroboam was then committed by all the subsequent kings of Israel, who thus stood in the way of the house of David's reconquest of Israel. Gibeon played a decisive role in the conflict between the house of Saul and the house of David, which led to David's usurping the throne and becoming king of Israel. It was at Gibeon that David's men defeated Abner's men and launched David's war of usurpation (2 Sam 2:12–3:1). David later consolidated his sovereignty by complying with the Gibeonites' demand for the execution of seven remaining sons and grandsons of Saul on the grounds that Saul had "put the Gibeonites to death." Although the incident referred to is not mentioned elsewhere, it makes direct reference to Josh 9:3-27 (2 Sam 21:1-14).

The story signals radical Davidic centralization by highlighting Joshua's fulfillment of Yahweh's command. Following the quasi-royal commissioning of Joshua, in which he begins his career as not only a second Moses but also the prototype of the ideal king in the Deuteronomistic History, the main narrative focuses on three examples (involving the three localities Gilgal, Ai, and Gibeon) of how the law of חרם (*ḥērem;* Deut 7:1; 20:16-18), which requires that all opponents be killed and no booty be taken, applies in order to sharpen the definition of how people are to relate to Yahweh's command, as enforced by Joshua, and to God's service, or cult, in its extraordinary deuteronomistic form. The first example involves Rahab and her family. They are Canaanites, but because Rahab shows loyalty to Yahweh by saving the Israelite spies and making possible the conquest of Jericho, at Joshua's direction she and her family are not slaughtered with the rest of the people of Jericho. In contrast, in the second example the Judahite Achan violates the law of *ḥērem* by withholding booty from Jericho. Achan and his family are Israelites, but this does not protect them from the consequences of their disloyalty. As a result of Achan's violation, at Joshua's direction, Achan and his family are stoned to death by "all Israel." The stoning of Achan makes possible the conquest of Ai.[9] The third example involves the Hivites of Gibeon. They trick Joshua into thinking they live far away, and in line with Deut 20:10-15 Joshua exempts them from *ḥērem* annihilation. When he finds that he has been deceived, he keeps his oath to them and does not destroy them, but makes them slaves of Yahweh's cult, laying the foundation for David's later annihilation of the house of Saul.

The concluding section concerning the conquest in Joshua relates two short campaigns of extermination. The first was prompted by Joshua's compact with the Gibeonites and instigated by the Amorite king of Jerusalem, the future city of David. In the second, Joshua overthrows a horde of Canaanite and alien kings led by the king of Hazor. The section ends with a list of

---

9. This episode also sets up a contrast with the Judahite Caleb, whose clan figures in the rise of David (Joshua 14). Because once Caleb, unlike Achan, alone obeyed Yahweh's command in battle, he later became the first member of the first tribe to receive a land grant on the west side of the Jordan.

thirty-one kings defeated and killed, largely in the order in which they were killed in the narrative, starting with the kings of Jericho, Ai, and Jerusalem.

The second half of Joshua's story concerns the distribution of the conquered land. Following an age-old pattern, victory in war ensues in the division of the spoils. The spoils other than land have mostly been "dedicated" to Yahweh through *ḥērem*, leaving only the land to distribute. The distribution of land places the greatest weight on Judah (Joshua 14–15) and Benjamin (Josh 18:11-28). As followers of David, Judahites ended up in Jerusalem (15:63), but the town itself was located within the territory of Benjamin (18:28). The distribution of land is by lot at Gilgal for Judah, Ephraim, and Manasseh, then at Shiloh for the remaining tribes. The land goes to tribes defined in terms of specified territories, an artificial conception that reflects the point of view of a central state concerned to regulate a population that threatens to regard itself as opposed to the state and, therefore, ready to make its own use of tribal designations and tribal rhetoric.

Centralizing monarchs strove to curtail not only tribal independence, but also acts of revenge that subverted the rule of the king through royally sanctioned law. Hence, once the tribal allotments are defined, Joshua assigns the cities of refuge from the avenger of blood, required in Deut 19:1-13 (cf. Num 35:9-34). According to deuteronomistic law, Levites are to control the document of the law laid down by Moses and thus oversee the house of David's jurisdiction. Members of the tribe of Levi do not receive a tribal territory, but are assigned towns and pasturage throughout the other territories (Joshua 21). Then a lengthy account in Joshua 22 details how Joshua helps to settle a dispute over an altar that threatens to duplicate the altar destined to be located at the Davidic Temple in Jerusalem. This ostensible exception to the deuteronomistic law of centralization must be meticulously justified.

Finally, Joshua pronounces two farewells. In the first he stresses absolute obedience to the command of Yahweh, the same emphasis with which the entire narrative began. In the second farewell, he performs a covenanting ceremony at Shechem, deep in the heartland of Israel, where little else has happened to this point. Here the gathered people in formation are encouraged to vow their loyalty to Joshua's, or the deuteronomist's, Yahweh. This ceremony has points of contact with Deuteronomy 27 and Josh 8:30-35, though it does not appear to belong to the monarchic Deuteronomistic History.

The narrative concludes with the death and burial of Joshua. Joshua's burial is important, because Joshua was likely to have been revered as a local hero, or saint, after his death, in a saint's cult centered at his tomb. Especially after death, such saints (Elijah and Elisha are probably examples) could become the focal point of political movements among villagers in the countryside, and it was important for central authorities to suppress them or to co-opt them. This is probably why few instances of such movements are found in the Bible before early Christianity. The tomb of Moses was potentially so important that the deuteronomistic historian asserts that its location is unknown, presumably in a bid to prevent anyone from starting a resistance movement around it. The figure of Joshua, an Ephraimite hero, has been thoroughly pre-empted in the house of David's history of the conquest so that he will be of little use to Israelites who might want to continue to resist the house of David.

MAIN FEATURES OF THE DEUTERONOMISTIC HISTORY

Since Joshua must be understood as part of the Deuteronomistic History, it is essential to recall the main features of that work. It is a lengthy and multifarious work, a corpus of manifold overlapping sources in successive editions that probably span almost four hundred years. However, its basic story is straightforward. Like most basic stories in the Bible, it treats of sovereignty expressed in terms of jurisdiction exercised through a religious shrine and cult. In the world of the Bible, government, politics, and religion are inseparable. Translations using "religious" language, like "worship" in place of "fear," which occurs several times in Joshua, often do not adequately express the political significance of shrines and cults in the Bible. The reason is that such translations do not have a juridical and jurisdictional connotation in modern English, as terms referring to the services in and of cults invariably have in the Bible.[10] The deuteronomistic story is the story of a set of laws that must be obeyed and eventually established through a particular shrine and its cult if the promised land is to be kept. If this story is thought to be mainly "religious," despite the essential role of this law, then it may be seriously misunderstood.

The deuteronomistic story begins when this law is delivered to the "nation" by Moses. Keeping the law, Joshua conquers Canaan. After Joshua dies, the nation fails to keep the law. Enemies afflict the nation, as one "judge" after another succeeds only in temporarily saving some of them. The first law of Moses delivered at the Jordan calls for centering the cult of Yahweh at one shrine only (Deut 12:1-14). David captures Jerusalem, and there his son Solomon builds the Temple, and this turns out to be the one shrine. Solomon, however, tolerates other shrines. Therefore, Yahweh takes the sovereignty of Israel away from the house of David and gives it to Jeroboam, who is no better. He immediately reactivates the cult of Bethel, violating Moses' cardinal law. As a result, the sovereignty of Israel must ultimately revert to the house of David. The story leaves no doubt how: At the precise moment Jeroboam is to inaugurate the secessionist cult of Bethel at its forbidden altar, a "man of God" from Judah, still held by the house of David, suddenly appears. He proclaims that a future scion of the house of David, whose name, here revealed three hundred years in advance, will be Josiah, is destined to destroy that very altar (1 Kgs 13:1-6). Two hundred years later, the story reaches a preliminary climax. The kingdom of Israel, whose kings have persisted in the "sin of Jeroboam," is obliterated, and the sovereignty of what had been Israel is taken over by the king of Assyria. The cult at Bethel, however, remains intact. Within three more generations, the long-awaited Josiah is born. During refurbishment of the Temple, ordered by Josiah, the law of Moses, which seems to have dropped out of sight, is rediscovered. Like Joshua, Josiah obeys it. He embarks on a triumphant rampage, destroying every shrine in sight other than the Temple—and most notably Bethel—throughout Judah and what had been Israel, which now may be reconstituted and brought once again under the sovereignty and direct jurisdiction of the house of David.

In sum, the Deuteronomistic History tells of how Israel under Joshua acquired its land in the first place, then how the house of David took it over, lost it, and under Josiah looked to recover it. It is a story of revanchism: The land once lost is to be reconquered. At the end of the story, the reconquest is not told in detail. In fact, it seems scarcely to be mentioned (cf. 2 Kgs 23:19-20). It is not clear whether the writer of this stage of the Deuteronomistic History meant to end his work by referring to the reconquest in this highly abbreviated form or simply to present the basis for a policy of reconquest. Whether Josiah's reconquest ever actually took place, the structure of the overall deuteronomistic story shows clearly how that reconquest was conceived. The story begins with the proclamation and recording of the law of Moses and the conquest of the land. It ends with the rediscovery of the law of Moses and the reconquest of the land. Thus the earlier conquest prefigures the later reconquest. Joshua, as will become evident, prefigures Josiah and may be said to be modeled on Josiah. In essence, the book of Joshua is a representation, incorporating sources of various kinds, of either the plan for or the course of the house of David's reconquest of Israel under Josiah.

The main deuteronomistic account ended with Josiah. The debacle of the Babylonian exile of the house of David necessitated updating the history. Minor additions appear in several places, and a coda brings the story to about 560 BCE. This updating had little effect on Joshua. Joshua 23:15-16 is the best candidate for an exilic addition.

Josiah's reform is the goal of the Deuteronomistic History and the event that more than any other provides the context for the book of Joshua. Josiah's reform is an example of a practice known throughout ancient history, including numerous times in the Bible, in which a ruler refurbished the state shrine or temple and, in the name of the state god(s), promulgated a roster of reform laws that headlined the easement of debts. Such appeals to commoners were a standard

---

10. The NRSV translates forms of חרם (ḥāram, "devote," "consecrate," "sanctify") with "destroy" or "annihilate," thereby misleadingly excluding the "religious" sense of the term, presumably because the practice was perceived by the translators as highly negative and hence not religious, and limiting its meaning to a "secular" sense; this is the reverse of the translators' approach to "fear," where they chose to exclude its secular sense, which takes in the entire sphere of jurisdiction, and limit its meaning to the religious sense of "worship," a term that, perhaps, was felt to make "fear," which here was unmistakably religious, sound more positive. The traditional translation of ḥērem is "ban," emphasizing the prohibition.

feature of the reigns of the protodemocratic rulers called "tyrants" (an impartial term) in Greece during the seventh century BCE. The famous reforms of Draco (624 BCE) and Solon (594 BCE) in Athens were nearly contemporary with Josiah's reform. The centerpiece of such reform laws was usually debt remission. Other forms of debt easement included the manumission of debt slaves (indentured servants trapped in interminable indebtedness), the prohibition or limiting of interest, and regulations governing the holding of securities for loans. All these are found in Josiah's deuteronomistic reform law (Deut 15:1-18; 23:19-20; 24:6, 10-13, 17-18).

The purposes of such ruler reforms are well known. They are summarized by Chaney, who studied the many ancient parallels to the abundant biblical texts related to such reforms.[11] In the ancient world, the lower classes were usually heavily in debt. Periodically their accumulated indebtedness threatened economic, social, and political order. One purpose of debt reform was to "ameliorate economic abuses severe enough to threaten the viability of the state." By the time of Josiah's reform in 622 BCE, economy and society under the house of David had been extensively commercialized in the context of the Assyrian "peace." Such commercialization typically had the effect of concentrating agricultural land in the hands of the wealthy through a combination of high rents and taxation and manipulation of the debt mechanism. It is not difficult to imagine that Josiah's reform answered to a clamor for debt relief.

A second purpose was to restore the reputation of the ruler, to allow him to "project a public image as a just statesman who took good care of his subjects, especially the weak and disadvantaged." Josiah's reform came after eighty years of Assyrian domination of the house of David. The dynasty's tradition of strength, longevity, and autonomy only served to point up its current weakness, since it had been suffered to govern for the last three generations only by the indulgence of and at the behest of its imperial master. It is almost certain that the house of David encouraged the commercialization that swelled indebtedness in its realm, and at the same time was poorly positioned to prevent disregard for and abuse of debt easement provisions sanctioned by age-old custom or spelled out in existing law rosters. Thus the house of David was in need of a policy that would counteract charges of callousness and injustice from the impoverished.

The third purpose of such reforms was to undermine opponents by implementing debt remission laws in a selective, partial manner, in order to "weaken elite factions that threatened the ruler's hold on power." The dominant political relations and political conflicts concerned the ruling class, who were also the creditor class. This class typically divided into contending factions. The reform of Josiah appears to have been partly the work of a faction only recently come to power. Josiah himself, who became king at the age of eight, would have reached his majority only a few years before the reform. Upon coming of age, he had either to break out of the clutches of his regents altogether or to gain control of them and join forces with them to enhance their combined power. It is likely that Josiah followed the second course. It seems that with the backing of the court newcomers who had held the regency, he promulgated a policy of debt remission designed to weaken eminent households long in power in the court and its Temple in Jerusalem, some perhaps going as far back as the early years of the house of David.

The modern reader may react very differently to two of the most important aspects of Josiah's reform: debt easement, on the one hand, and, on the other hand, a revanchist reconquest patterned after the destructive devotion of Canaan's indigenous populace—men, women, and children—which amounts to ethnic cleansing if not genocide. Group-based debt easement may be regarded by most people today as a laudable policy, even an acceptable foundation for an entire ethical program, though in practice usually only so long as, unlike the ideal in Deuteronomy, creditors can control the process. The same people today, however, would probably regard ethnic cleansing as wholly outside the bounds of ethics, categorically indefensible under any circumstances. Yet God, through Moses, commands both, and both as part of the *same* policy and program, within the space of five chapters in Deuteronomy. Clearly the world of Joshua is not the same as our world, and this ambiguity, like many other features of the book of Joshua, requires careful attention to the ancient context.

---

11. Marvin L. Chaney, "Debt Easement in Israelite History and Tradition," in *The Bible and the Politics of Exegesis*, ed. David Jobling, Peggy L. Day, and Gerald T. Sheppard (Cleveland: Pilgrim, 1991) 131. The quotations on this subject that follow are from this article.

The deuteronomistic account of Josiah's reform is based largely on typical elements of ancient royal reforms (2 Kgs 22:3–23:24). These include the repair of the dynastic Temple, the announcement of a reform law featuring debt remission, radical centralization of cult and jurisdiction, and territorial expansion. These elements are integral to one another and together enhance the reforming monarch's sovereignty and jurisdiction. Such acts were performed by Josiah with one end in view: the greater power of the house of David embodied in Josiah.

In the deuteronomist's account, the reform begins when Josiah orders his high priest Hilkiah to supervise the refurbishing of the Davidic Temple. In the ancient Near East, repairing a temple was tantamount to rebuilding it, or even building it in the first place. It represented the reassertion of strong rule through the reconfirmation of the dynasty. According to the deuteronomist, only one previous Davidic king had ordered the Temple repaired, and that was Jehoash (2 Kgs 11:1–12:16). Jehoash and Josiah had much in common. Jehoash's father, Ahaziah, had been assassinated, just as Josiah's father, Amon, was. Like Josiah, Jehoash needed to overcome the detriment of a lengthy minority, begun when he was seven years old, much like Josiah at eight. Jehoash's minority, like Josiah's, began with the aggressive restoration of the house of David by a forceful priest. The restoration of the dynasty was carried out in spite of alien overlords controlling Jerusalem, in Jehoash's case the Omrids, in Josiah's the Assyrians. In both cases the overlords promoted exceptional commercial development, producing the need for a temple-centered debt reform.

In the course of the repair ordered by Josiah, Hilkiah discovers the law of Moses, ostensibly long lost or long in desuetude. This is the law laid out in Deuteronomy 12–26, which was immediately written down and then heeded, or nearly so, under Joshua (Josh 1:7-8). As noted, although it is possible that this document, the "document of the law" within the Deuteronomistic History, contains archaic elements predating the monarchy, it is not likely, and the whole clearly reflects a radical monarchic reform. The writing of supposedly ancient, hidden books of vision, law, and wisdom for discovery is a commonplace of history.[12] The writer of Deuteronomy may well have consulted ancient sources, but by and large those parts of the law in Deuteronomy not already composed for Hezekiah's reform were probably composed under Josiah, in preparation for Josiah's centralizing reform, the aim of the history as a whole. Moses had introduced his law by insisting over and over that it was essential if the Israelites were to keep the land they were about to conquer. No law of Moses, no land of Israel. Having transgressed this law, the political nation of Israel lost its land with the fall of Samaria. The only hope for recovering the land of Israel, to say nothing of keeping the land of Judah, is to recover the law. And here it is, in the hands of Josiah's priest Hilkiah, ready to launch the house of David on its long-anticipated reconquest of Israel.

The two primary accents of this law have been mentioned: centralization, both cultic and judicial, and the periodic remission of debt. These policies are effected by radical rulings indeed, in all likelihood previously unheard of among Israelites in the form in which they occur in Deuteronomy. The Temple of the house of David, the shrine that Yahweh is to choose to place his name there, makes all other shrines, including other shrines dedicated to Yahweh, illegitimate (Deut 12:2-12; 12:29–13:18). Throughout the Deuteronomistic History, the presence of Yahweh is signified by the presence of Yahweh's name. In the deuteronomistic conception, the name of Yahweh encapsulates the political character of the central cult, which, like all cults, combines the religious and judicial aspects of the cult. The name of Yahweh is invoked not only in worship and supplication, but also, equally important and sometimes simultaneously, in judicial oaths that sanction true witness and just judgment in the adjudication of cases and disputes. To judge from the account in Deuteronomy of Moses' appointment of the judiciary (which may borrow from the E-strand account in the Tetrateuch, Exod 18:13-27). Josiah proposed to extend and rationalize central Davidic jurisdiction and to this end planned, for judicial purposes, to organize the entire subject people into surveillance cells of ten households each (Deut 1:9-18; cf. Deut 16:18-20).

---

12. See Jonathan Z. Smith, "The Temple and the Magician," in *Map Is Not Territory: Studies in the History of Religions* (Leiden: Brill, 1978) 176, esp. note 19.

Shrines and their jurisdictions outlawed by Moses' first law include those devoted to other Palestinian deities like Baal, Astarte, and Asherah, as well as the sun, the moon, and the host of heaven (stars, constellations). The status of the cults of the foreign peoples deported to Palestine by the Assyrians (identified in 2 Kgs 17:29-31) is ambiguous, since Josiah is not said to destroy them. The outlawed shrines include those devoted to departed heroes similar to Joshua and Moses. Josiah preempts the shrine of Joshua rather than outlawing it. Preempting the shrine or shrines of Moses, which must have existed, was apparently thought to be beyond even the militant, insurgent power of Josiah. Accordingly, it was officially declared not only that Moses died on the far side of the Jordan (probably an accepted tradition, although neither J nor E had addressed the matter), but also that "no one knows the burial place of Moses to this day" (Deut 34:6). It is not likely that this was a popular or widely accepted view. In the face of popular piety and practice to the contrary, it probably is one of the pronouncements and rulings put forward in their account of Moses that Josiah and his faction were unable to maintain.

The main rite of the central shrine, like nearly all ancient shrines, is sacrifice, which often entails the eating of meat; so the deuteronomistic historian goes into where and how meat may be eaten (Deut 12:13-27; 14:3-29). This subject resumes in Deut 15:19-23 and continues by implication through the rulings regarding keeping the three main feasts at the central shrine (Deut 16:1-17). In addition, this opening section of laws regarding centralization deals with the disposition of the Judahite levitical priests, who seemed to preside at now outlawed non-Jerusalemite shrines. They are made wards of the central shrine, but are expected to reside throughout the kingdom (Joshua 21).

In Deuteronomy 15, the historian reaches the second primary accent of the law: debt remission. This was a radical law: "At the end of seven years you shall remit all debts" held by fellow Israelites, that is, subjects of the house of David who have covenanted to keep the laws of Moses. Foreigners may be dunned indefinitely; as Frick points out, the Deuteronomistic History, like the Tetrateuch, presents "national" identity, not class, as the primary social category and takes little interest in the amelioration of poverty in the rest of the history outside Deuteronomy.[13] Like all land reform and debt-reform laws, this one was short-lived, even though similar laws occur, like ruler's reforms, throughout biblical history (cf. Exod 22:25-27; Lev 25:8-55; Neh 5:1-13; and numerous prophetic oracles that assume such laws, like Isa 3:13-15 and Amos 2:6-8; Jer 34:8-22 is reminiscent of Deut 15:1-18 but seems not to represent a full-scale royal reform). The lender is not permitted to deny the needy person's request for a loan, no matter how close the seventh year, the year of remission, may be. The condition described in Deut 15:11 is frequently misunderstood because of the use of this verse in the New Testament (Matt 26:11; Mark 14:7; John 12:8); the Hebrew text in Deuteronomy does not say that the poor will never cease, an outcome that would be quite unlikely given this law as formulated and given the abundant produce of the land (Deut 15:4). Instead, it says that when you enter the land, "since the poor shall not yet have ceased," open your hand to them. An exceptional feature of this legislation is the optimism and goodwill it expresses: The Israelite is not only to forgive debts owed, but to do so readily and joyously. This attitude is expressed particularly in regard to the release of the debt slave, another form of debt remission, which in the deuteronomistic conception recapitulates the deliverance from Egypt (see Commentary on 2:1–6:27).

Josiah's reform continues when he orders all the elders of Judah—those town and village heads who are referred to throughout the law—to gather in Jerusalem, together with all the nobles, priests, cult emissaries, courtiers, and plebs already there. "In the ears" of this great assembled gathering, the entire nation under the house of David, Josiah himself reads the complete law of Moses, discovered in the Temple. Josiah then makes a covenant to keep the law in all its parts, and the assembled nation joins him with one accord (2 Kgs 23:1-3).

This pristine accord, reminiscent of Joshua's fighting nation, ignites Josiah's campaign of cult purification, beginning with Judah. In obedience to the first law, Josiah purges and purifies the cult of the Temple and suppresses or purges all other cults as rivals to the one shrine and one

---

13. Frank S. Frick, "*Cui Bono?*—History in the Service of Political Nationalism: The Deuteronomistic History as Political Propaganda," *Semeia* 66 (1994) 79-92.

cult serving the one Yahweh (2 Kgs 23:4-14). He dislodges and demolishes or incinerates the apparatus and artifacts of the cults of Baal, Asherah, and the sun, the moon, and the stars, presumably with Astarte and Ashtar at their head. These are the Canaanite deities that helped to advance the house of David's long-standing trade relations and are associated particularly with Solomon and, for the Assyrian period, with Ahaz and Manasseh. Like most populist reforms, Josiah's reform touts its aversion to commerce, a root cause of the creation of debt slaves out of villagers forced to mortgage their labor and of the amassing of landholdings mortgaged by debt slaves into cash-crop estates. Altars and high places in and about Jerusalem he destroys, as well as all altars in Judah, "from Geba to Beer-sheba." These include the "high places" at the gate of the governor of the city, whose name happens to be Joshua; these high places at the gate probably sanction the jurisdiction assumed by this strong man, until Josiah puts an end to his insubordination (2 Kgs 23:8). The priests of all these abolished cults are left in their localities, but now they are dependent on the central cult, to which are owed all the contributions previously made to the demolished shrines (2 Kgs 23:9). This has been taken as a signal expression of the economic exploitation entailed in cult centralization, as the priests called Levites in Deuteronomy are forced to become wards of the Davidic Temple.[14] Many scholars theorize that these priests were installed by the house of David early in its history as partisans for Davidic rule in the hinterland. Apparently Josiah feels this settlement calls for reorganization (cf. Josh 21:1-42). Josiah puts a stop to child sacrifice in Jerusalem, thus confirming his right to supplant household patriarchs in determining the fate of their sons and daughters. The culmination of Josiah's purge of Judah comes with the wrecking of the shrines installed by Solomon (23:13-14). These were the shrines that, in the reformers' view, brought about the house of David's loss of Israel in the first place. With their destruction, the way is cleared for the reconquest of Israel.

Having thus purged Judah, Josiah turns to Israel. The revanchism of the house of David, dormant for more than three hundred years but festering for the preceding one hundred years, has come to a head. The ancient prophecy of the man from Judah at the altar of Jeroboam in Bethel—the altar by which generations of kings of Israel presumed to sanction the hated non-Davidic jurisdictions of Israel, jurisdictions condemned from the very start by Moses as recorded in the document found in the Davidic Temple—is to be fulfilled. Josiah begins with the altar at Bethel (23:15-18). He destroys the altar and its shrine. He removes the bones from saints' tombs nearby and incinerates them on the remains of the altar, as the man from Judah foretold. The remains of that same man lie in his own tomb; his bones Josiah leaves in peace, a relic of three centuries of impudence and its epochal requital.

Josiah continues on from Bethel, ravaging the remaining shrines of Israel founded under the kings of Israel, treating them all as he had the shrine at Bethel. Apparently, Josiah spares the priests of the outlawed shrines in Judah, but slaughters the priests in Israel. Finally he returns to Jerusalem (23:19-20). The brevity of this account has been noted. The historian may leave the details of the reconquest of Israel to be worked out, having previewed its salient highlights in the conquest of Canaan by Joshua. The key detail of Josiah's rampage through Israel is what is not said; as noted, Josiah does not attack the cults of the Assyrian populace planted by imperial force within the territory of what had been Israel (2 Kgs 17:34), but only "the shrines of the high places . . . which kings of Israel had made" (2 Kgs 23:19 NRSV).

Josiah's historian thus makes a clear distinction between indigenous cults and alien cults. The significance of this distinction goes beyond the possibility that the writer wished to avoid arousing Assyrian ire or resistance over the extent of Josiah's reconquest. Josiah accepts Assyrian settlement policy in this territory, just as he defines the territory in terms of Assyrian bounds, and he respects the separate jurisdictions sanctioned by these recently established cults. These were presumably limited jurisdictions for each imperial local group represented, like the Babylonians, Cuthites, and Hamathites. In the absence of any indication to the contrary, Josiah apparently lets these groups be, along with the judicial and property relations, including landholdings, under their aegis.

---

14. W. Eugene Claburn, "The Fiscal Basis of Josiah's Reforms," *JBL* 92 (1973) 11-22.

Josiah's concern lies not only with the pre-Assyrian populace and their leaders and cults, represented both by the so-called Canaanite people and by the contemporary inhabitants who correspond to the other distinct groups peopling the land Joshua fought to possess. These were the Canaanite "nations," called in varying order and combinations Canaanites, Hittites, Hivites, Perizzites, Girgashites, Amorites, and Jebusites (Josh 3:10; 9:1; 11:3; 12:8; 24:11; later they were idealistically regarded as seven in number). These Canaanite entities are also thought of in general as either Canaanites or Amorites. The latter distinction appears to represent the notion that the Amorites are native to the uplands of Palestine and the Canaanites to the lowlands (Num 13:29; Josh 11:3; 13:2-5). The cultures of the uplands and lowlands were distinct from each other during both the Late Bronze and Iron ages in Palestine.[15]

Most of the leaders of this native populace, especially of those who were subject to the kings of Israel, had been dispersed and deported a hundred years earlier than Josiah. The populace came under the new leaders planted by the Assyrians. These, the deuteronomistic historian explains, had been forced by Yahweh to acknowledge the cult of Bethel and hence its laws and jurisdiction, as part of their duty for taking over landholding rights and privileges in territory disposed of by Yahweh (2 Kgs 17:24-28).[16] The primary landholding relations of the newcomers, in other words, were those regulated from Bethel, and these were abolished when Josiah ransacked Bethel. Their private cults, which they had set up after the arrangement with Bethel and continued to practice following Josiah's reconquest, had little or no bearing on the loyalty of landholders, including themselves, to Jerusalem. As the historian explains at length in 2 Kgs 17:24-41, the descendants of these people do not now adhere to the law of Yahweh (Bethel having been destroyed) and, falling for the most part outside the scope of rural landholding in Israel, do not come under the jurisdiction of the house of David. From the Josianic deuteronomist's perspective, their overlord remains the king of Assyria.

Some may find it surprising that the presence of Assyria, rather than its absence, figures in the background of Josiah's reform. It used to be thought that the main event that made Josiah's reform possible was the collapse of Assyria at the end of the seventh century BCE, leaving a temporary power vacuum into which Josiah could step. The great Assurbanipal died in 627, Nineveh fell in 612, and by 609 virtually nothing was left of the once great empire. Assyria was fast being replaced by Babylon. Here was a window of opportunity, it seemed, that induced Josiah to reform.

However, in recent years views have changed. It is true that Josiah's reform advanced a nationalist and populist revival in which all things foreign were open to ridicule. This meant that any natives of Palestine who as the result of a hundred years of Assyrian cultural domination continued to imitate Assyrian style or custom or tout Assyrian ties were fair game for disparagement. But such disparagement leaves no trace in the deuteronomistic account of Josiah's reform, or anywhere in the Deuteronomistic History. It is now clear that the Assyrians did not require conquered peoples to worship Assyrian gods and that Josiah's purging of the Temple and the cults of Judah was not an anti-Assyrian act.[17] Apparently the deuteronomist makes a distinction between regional and indigenous people, on the one hand, and the newcomers planted by the Assyrians, the people of Babylon, Cuth, Hamath, and Sepharvaim, and the Assyrians themselves, who were still in place in 622 BCE, on the other hand. Josiah attacks the cults of the indigenous, but not of the Assyrian newcomers.[18]

Astonishingly, Josiah's historian says nothing about Assyria or Assyrians at either the beginning or the end of his history. Moses says nothing about them, nor, most remarkably, do they appear at all after Hezekiah's reign. The Assyrians are treated with an understandably negative slant in the account of Hezekiah's reign, since Hezekiah was known to have rebelled against Assyria. That account may incorporate a source from Hezekiah's time, as indicated by the ample role played by the prophet Isaiah. The deuteronomistic writers themselves do not give the named

15. Rivka Gonen, *Burial Patterns and Cultural Diversity in Late Bronze Age Canaan* (Winona Lake, Ind.: Eisenbrauns, 1992), esp. 38-39; Elizabeth M. Bloch-Smith, "The Cult of the Dead in Judah: Interpreting the Material Remains," *JBL* 111 (1992) 213-24, esp. 214-19.

16. The lions sent by God to ravage the Assyrian plantations for not acknowledging the judicial authority of Bethel (2 Kgs 17:26) are ironically akin to the lion sent by God to kill the man of God from Judah for dining with the anonymous old prophet in Bethel (1 Kgs 13:11-32).

17. Mordechai Cogan, "Judah Under Assyrian Hegemony: A Reexamination of *Imperialism and Religion*," *JBL* 112 (1993) 403-14.

18. This distinction may have been disregarded or found unacceptable by the later writer who added 2 Kgs 17:34b-40 to the history written under Josiah. See *The New Oxford Annotated Bible*, ed. Bruce M. Metzger and Roland E. Murphy (New York: Oxford University Press, 1991) 489.

prophets so much attention, except when distinct sources are incorporated in their history, as with Samuel, Elijah, and Elisha. Thus it is not surprising that the Assyrians appear in a somewhat unsympathetic light in relation to Hezekiah. The deuteronomistic view is better seen in the treatment of the fall of Samaria, which immediately precedes the account of Hezekiah's reign. Here the king of Assyria is presented as simply carrying out God's judgment (2 Kgs 17:1-34).

In his attack against rivals in Israel, Josiah seems to defer to long-standing Assyrian administrative boundaries. Josiah probably remained a nominal Assyrian vassal to the end of his reign and never had a reason to be anti-Assyrian. If the main impulse of Josiah's reform was anti-Assyrian, there is no sign of it in the Deuteronomistic History.

Thus for understanding Joshua as much as Josiah, the account of Josiah's campaign against the cults of the north is significant as much for what it does not say as for what it does say. By not having to attack the Assyrian newcomers, Josiah's historian makes it all the easier to develop the era of Joshua as the prototype for Josiah's reconquest, in which the long-resident peoples, "Amorite" and "Canaanite" agriculturists and commercialists, are the primary target.

When Josiah arrives back in Jerusalem, two final acts bring his reform to a close. The first is the keeping of the feast of Passover "as prescribed in this document of the covenant" (2 Kgs 23:21-23). The deuteronomistic law of Moses requires that the feast be kept at the central shrine. Like most of the reform legislation, this is a radical innovation. As described in the Tetrateuch, the Passover is an intrinsically local, household rite, centered on the extended family as the patriarch's household. By now it comes as no surprise that Josiah wishes to suppress such extended family rites, as is implied clearly in Deut 16:1-17. In the deuteronomistic conception, as seen above, the Passover celebrates the archetypal release from debt. The history of the nation as the Davidic "nation" in the land of Canaan, therefore, begins and ends with a Passover. The first Passover is represented by the national crossing of the Jordan, followed by the celebration of Passover (Josh 3:1–5:10). On apparently the second day of that first Passover in the land, the manna ceases and the nation eats for the first time of the produce of the land (Josh 5:11-12). The second Passover comes under Josiah, at the conclusion of his reform, and is the first in history to be in full compliance with the final law of Moses. For this alone, Josiah would have ranked supreme among the kings of Israel in deuteronomistic terms.

The second of Josiah's final acts is to remove from Judah "the mediums, wizards, teraphim, idols, and all the abominations . . . in Judah and Jerusalem" (2 Kgs 23:24 NRSV). To the extent that these are not redundant, they refer to local saints and their devices and representations, of the kind prohibited in Deut 18:9-14. The burden of this act is clear from the juxtaposition of the prohibition in Deuteronomy 18 with the text in which Moses says that "Yahweh will raise up a prophet like myself, whom you shall heed" (18:15). To obey Moses is to refuse to consult an oracle or saint who does not represent Moses. Elijah, and to a lesser extent Elisha, came close to looking something like Moses, but no one in the Deuteronomistic History actually both looks and sounds like Moses. The only way Moses does reappear is in the document containing his words, found in the Temple at Josiah's instigation. The authenticity of this document is confirmed by the prophet Huldah, so no further search for judgment, wisdom, or truth is required.

THE POLITICAL CONTEXT OF JOSIAH'S REFORM

The political context of Josiah's reform forms the primary backdrop for the story of Joshua. Josiah's support came not from the political middle, but instead from the two political extremes. One was the empires in control of Palestine: Egypt and its ally Assyria.[19] The other was a

19. In this regard, Josiah followed in the footsteps of his grandfather Manasseh. See Anson F. Rainey, "Manasseh, King of Judah, in the Whirlpool of the Seventh Century B.C.E.," in *Kinattūtu ša dārāti*: Raphael Kutscher Memorial Volume, ed. Anson F. Rainey (Tel Aviv: Institute of Archaeology, 1993) 147-64; J. P. J. Olivier, "Money Matters: Some Remarks on the Economic Situation in the Kingdom of Judah During the Seventh Century B.C.," *Biblische Notizen* 73 (1994) 90-100; Israel Finkelstein, "The Archaeology of the Days of Manasseh," in *Scripture and Other Artifacts: Essays on the Bible and Archaeology in Honor of Philip J. King*, ed. Michael D. Coogan, J. Cheryl Exum, and Lawrence E. Stager (Louisville: Westminster John Knox, 1994) 169-87; Richard Nelson, *"Realpolitik* in Judah (687–609 B.C.E.)," in *Scripture in Context II: More Essays on the Comparative Method*, ed. William W. Hallo, James C. Moyer, and Leo G. Perdue (Winona Lake, Ind.: Eisenbrauns, 1983) 177-89; J. Maxwell Miller and John H. Hayes, *A History of Ancient Israel and Judah* (Philadelphia: Westminster, 1986) 365-401; Duane L. Christensen, "Zephaniah 2:4-15: A Theological Basis for Josiah's Program of Political Expansion," *CBQ* 46 (1984) 669-82, esp. 678-81; Robert Althann, "Josiah," *ABD* 3:1015-18.

particular rural family and its allies and clients, a non-Jerusalemite family with deep Israelite roots, whose most famous member was Jeremiah, from Anathoth in Benjamin, just north of Jerusalem. This family traced its putative lineage back to Shiloh and was eager to promote a populist correction. From Shiloh's once venerable shrine came the prophet Samuel, who anointed David and sanctioned his usurpation of Saul, and the prophet Ahijah, who sanctioned Jeroboam's usurpation of the house of David (1 Kgs 11:29-39; 12:15) and then turned to a third dynast (14:1-18). Jeroboam bypassed Shiloh when he restored the cult of Israel at his borders, a common strategy, in Bethel and Dan. The importance of traditions from Benjamin in the book of Joshua and its failure to mention Egypt or Assyria are among the direct reflexes of this twofold source of support for Josiah. Not everyone, conceivably even the partisans' original backers, was enthusiastic about Josiah's pretensions. The Deuteronomistic History deals extensively with opponents of and foils to centralization. Indeed, its treatment of opponents, whether actual or metaphorical, comprises the great bulk of the history, and an understanding of these opponents as the deuteronomist presents them is of great importance for interpreting the book of Joshua. First there are the "Canaanites" of various kinds, who play an essential role in the preview of Josiah's reconquest and reassignment of land titles played out under Joshua. Then there are the local heroes of the type represented by the "saviors" and "judges" of the book of Judges, climaxing with Saul, in all of whose days the Israelites, in the absence of a rightful king, do "each what is right in his own eyes," contrary to the deuteronomistic law of centralization. Then come the opponents of David from among the house of Saul and its supporters and from David's own sons, possibly not unlike bypassed sons of Manasseh. Then follow the several dynasties of the kings of Israel (especially Jeroboam I and Ahab) who reject the pretensions of the house of David and its cult in Jerusalem, even when allied with it. All of these represent in Josiah's own day the kinds of opponents he must vanquish if his plan of conquest and political dominance is to succeed: men who, like Hiel of Bethel, fortify strategic sites like Jericho to their own advantage (Josh 6:26; 1 Kgs 16:34); indigenous landholders and traders in the Assyrian provinces who may identify themselves as Israelites following the norms of Bethol but not of Jerusalem; popular regional warlords, strongmen, and outlaws; prophets other than those who directly support the house of David; opposing claimants to the sovereignty of Israel from rival elite households or from the house of David itself. None can rival Josiah, the Deuteronomistic History proclaims, for the cogency and legitimacy of his claim of sovereignty.[20]

Josiah and his supporters promote a policy of "ethnic" cleansing based on the idea that "Canaanites"—that is, opponents in both Judah and the north headed by landowners and urban elite with commercial affiliations and their families, a large group under the Assyrian and Egyptian empires in Palestine—deserved to be murdered and all their property destroyed by the monarchy. As a "nationality," the category "Canaanite," like that of "Israelite," was a social construction, not an unchangeable historical reality. In the world of the Bible, there were no such nations as we understand the term.[21] Like virtually all distinctions of race, ethnic identity, and nationality, as well as the very definitions of such concepts, categories like "Canaan" and "Israel" were not natural but cultural.

The several kinds of opponents to Josiah treated throughout the Deuteronomistic History appear in the book of Joshua in the character of the seven "great and strong nations" named in Josh 3:10 (cf. Deut 7:1; Josh 11:3; Acts 13:19). In the deuteronomistic conception, these are the original inhabitants of the land of Canaan, of whom the "Canaanites" in particular are only one group. "Canaan" was a general term of uncertain origin for the southeastern Mediterranean coast and its hinterland, for which the terms "Palestine" and "the land of Israel" are often used in modern academic literature. Use of the term "Canaan" goes back to the Egyptian New Kingdom period, when Egypt held imperial sovereignty in Palestine, and even earlier. The term occurs in the phrases "the inhabitants [i.e., landholding elite] of Canaan" (Exod 15:15) and "the

---

20. Richard D. Nelson, *The Double Redaction of the Deuteronomistic History* (Sheffield: JSOT, 1981) 122.

21. Benedict Anderson, *Imagined Communities: Reflections on the Origin and Spread of Nationalism* (New York: Verso, 1983); Ernest Gellner, *Nations and Nationalism* (Ithaca: Cornell University Press, 1983); Eric J. Hobsbawm, *Nations and Nationalism Since 1780* (New York: Cambridge University Press, 1990); Mario Liverani, "Nationality and Political Identity," *ABD* 4:1031-37; John Hutchinson and Anthony D. Smith, eds., *Nationalism* (New York: Oxford University Press, 1994).

kings of Canaan" (Judg 5:19) already in early Israelite women's battle songs. It refers to the territory destined to come under David's sovereignty in the J strand, which adapts early Israelite tribal traditions so as implicitly to pit David against the king of Egypt in the post–New Kingdom struggle for Canaan. In J, the land of Canaan is mythically pictured as a "land oozing milk and honey"—that is, a largely uncultivated land (cf. Isa 7:18-25), peopled almost exclusively by city dwellers, the "Canaanite" elite descended from Ham (Gen 10:15-18). In a few texts in the Bible, "Canaanite" appears to mean "merchant," functionaries of the "kings of Canaan." The most interesting of these texts is Zeph 1:11, in which the "people of Canaan" are condemned. In this text, probably written in the time of Josiah, and perhaps in his court, "the people of Canaan" parallel "all who weigh out silver"—i.e., traders from "Canaan" resident in Jerusalem—precisely the people Josiah was most determined to suppress. The deuteronomistic historian, therefore, appears to have taken over the term "Canaan" from the house of David's history of early Israel and added to it the nuance of "trader," if that nuance was not already present.

Then, still using traditional sources and with no independent knowledge of his own (note, for example, that six of the "nations" are listed in Exod 3:8, probably an original J text), the deuteronomistic historian peoples the land of Canaan with a multifarious ancient elite of seven or so "nations" (Canaanites, Amorites, Hittites, Hivites, Girgashites, Perizzites, Jebusites; in the MT, the group numbers seven only in Deut 7:1; Josh 3:10; 24:11). Some of their names occur in the historical record outside the Bible. This is particularly the case with "Hittite" and "Amorite," a Semitic term (meaning "Westerner") used by the Egyptians like "Canaan" as a general geographic designation, this time for the Mediterranean coast and its hinterland north of Canaan. All may have existed at some time in ancient Canaan. It is important to realize that although modern historians can show that among these "nations" at least so-called Amorites, Hittites, and possibly Hivites lived long before the time of Josiah, mainly outside of Canaan, Josiah's historian, like scribes of the house of David probably going back to its beginning, believed that all these "nations" were, unlike "Israel," indigenous to Canaan. Thus they were all "Canaanites" in the sense of the original elites of the land of "Canaan," and all, in terms of J's genealogy of the "nations," sons of Ham as distinct from the sons of Shem, from whom Israel was descended.

In sum, for his understanding of "Canaan" and "Canaanite," which in his history figure almost exclusively prior to Saul and David, the deuteronomist had to look no further than the scrolls available to him in Josiah's scriptorium. He simply followed the written tradition of the house of David, to which he belonged. In line with this tradition, the ancient "land of Canaan" was the territory destined to be held by the united tribes of Israel ruled by the house of David. The original "inhabitants" or "kings" of Canaan would have to be dispossessed. The list of thirty-one kings (petty city lords) of Canaan in Josh 12:9-24, however fictional, fits exactly the Davidic concept of pre-Davidic Canaan as the land of the "kings of Canaan." Such a concept of Canaan apparently existed among tribal Israelites who formed their ostensible political identity partly over against the petty states of Canaan long before David. But this pre-existence makes little difference for understanding the book of Joshua, since it has little to do with early Israel. In the context of Davidic sovereignty in "Canaan," "Canaanite" meant "not Israelite," and as a fictive representation of contemporary political identity it meant "not submitting to the sovereignty of the house of David."

As an expression of Josiah's reform, the story of Joshua's conquest, patterned on Josiah's reconquest, "functions as an instrument of coercion" and intimidation, encouraging the submission of all subjects.[22] The historian wants to terrorize the populace, particularly its recalcitrant political leaders, into submission to Josiah by showing what happens to a class of people ("Canaanites") whose interests are opposed to the interests of Josiah's monarchy and of the peasantry under him. The writer also shows that obedience to Josiah can take precedence over supposed ethnic affiliation: Canaanites can submit and be saved (Rahab, the Gibeonites), and if a Judahite belonging to the Israelite in-group disobeys the commander-in-chief, he can be repudiated and killed (Achan). "The primary purpose of the conquest narrative is to send a message to internal

22. Lori L. Rowlett, "Inclusion, Exclusion and Marginality in the Book of Joshua," *JSOT* 55 (1992) 15-23; Rowlett, *Joshua and the Rhetoric of Violence: A "New Historicist" Analysis* (Sheffield: Sheffield Academic, 1996).

rivals, potential Achans, that they can make themselves into outsiders very easily."[23] Josiah's historian "uses the rhetoric of warfare and nationalism as an encouragement and a threat to its own population to submit voluntarily to the central authority of a government struggling to organize itself and to [re]create its own ideological framework of inclusion. In order to justify violent action [to that end], the dynamics of the literature of warfare usually consist of a division [often outrageously overstated] between self and other," us and them.[24]

VALUES IN THE BOOK OF JOSHUA

Much about the book of Joshua is repulsive, starting with ethnic cleansing, the savage dispossession and genocide of native peoples, and the massacre of women and children—all not simply condoned but ordered by God. These features are worse than abhorrent; they are far beyond the pale. Excoriable deeds and many others of at least questionable justifiability have been committed with the sanction of the book of Joshua, such as the decimation of the Native American peoples. People who regard themselves as peaceable Christians tend to shun the book of Joshua as not simply unedifying but irreconcilable with their faith, or to justify a tacit Marcionism by equating the worst parts of the book of Joshua with the entire OT. The book of Joshua scarcely appears in the ecumenical lectionary for preaching used in many denominations; not only are its most repugnant passages ignored, but most of the rest of the book is too. The current lectionary prescribes only three passages from Joshua, all innocuous: the crossing of the Jordan (3:7-17), the keeping of Passover at Gilgal (5:9-12), and the covenant at Shechem (24:1-3, 14-25). That the last pericope, with its lofty if paternalistic avowal "as for me and my household, we will serve the LORD," is assigned twice while most of the book is assigned not at all only corroborates the aversion and bowdlerizing selectivity with which people attuned to "family values" tend to hold Joshua at arm's length.

It is possible to abstract the narrative of Joshua so as to extract from it pure qualities or values that are positive and affirmable. The stories can be taken to illustrate reliance on the power of God, whose provision, both short-term and long-run, does not fail. They illustrate the importance of grace, allegiance, obedience to authority, community solidarity, the family, and deterring hasty revenge. This is one way to rescue the text of Joshua from peremptory dismissal. However, with such a sidestepping approach study is not necessary, and commentaries need play no role.

The purpose of a careful study of the book of Joshua is not in the first place to redeem it but to understand it better, and through it to understand ourselves better. In order to understand the book of Joshua better, along with other helps we need to use the imperfect knowledge of it that is available—with all its mere likelihoods and probabilities, its uncertainties, puzzles, gaps, and voids. When looked at in terms of its historical context, the values represented in the book of Joshua, whether ostensibly bad or good, are not pure, like offhand abstractions, but multifaceted, mixed, and ambiguous. Even within the limited and relatively well understood context of Josiah's reform, significant interpretive issues arise that are difficult to address. Josiah marshaled the harsh forces of centralization for the sake of his poor subjects, promulgating a program of debt remission, which, if carried out, would have eliminated poverty among his subjects within

23. Rowlett, "Inclusion, Exclusion and Marginality in the Book of Joshua," 23.

24. Rowlett, "Inclusion, Exclusion and Marginality in the Book of Joshua,", 23. See also Danna Nolan Fewell, "Joshua," in *The Women's Bible Commentary*, ed. Carol A. Newsom and Sharon H. Ringe (Louisville: Westminster/John Knox, 1992) 63-66; Peter Machinist, "Outsiders or Insiders: The Biblical View of Emergent Israel and Its Contexts," in *The Other in Jewish Thought and History: Constructions of Jewish Culture and Identity*, ed. L. J. Silverstein and R. I. Cohn (New York: New York University Press, 1994) 35-60; E. Theodore Mullen, *Narrative History and Ethnic Boundaries: The Deuteronomistic History and the Creation of Israelite National Identity* (Atlanta: Scholars Press, 1992), which holds that the Deuteronomistic History is mainly an exilic composition. For more on Josiah's reform and the Deuteronomistic History, see Steven L. McKenzie, "Deuteronomistic History," *ABD* 2:160-68; Jeffries M. Hamilton, *Social Justice and Deuteronomy: The Case of Deuteronomy 15* (Atlanta: Scholars Press, 1992); Shigeyuki Nakanose, *Josiah's Passover: Sociology and the Liberating Bible* (Maryknoll, N.Y.: Orbis, 1993); Gary N. Knoppers, *Two Nations Under God: The Deuteronomistic History of Solomon and the Dual Monarchies*, vol. 1: *The Reign of Solomon and the Rise of Jeroboam* (Atlanta: Scholars Press, 1993), vol. 2: *The Reign of Jeroboam, the Fall of Israel, and the Reign of Josiah* (Atlanta: Scholars Press, 1994); William G. Dever, "The Silence of the Text: An Archaeological Commentary on 2 Kings 23," in *Scripture and Other Artifacts: Essays on the Bible and Archaeology in Honor of Philip J. Kings*, ed. Michael D. Coogan, J. Cheryl Exum, and Lawrence E. Stager (Louisville: Westminster John Knox, 1994) 143-68; Erik Eynikel, *The Reform of King Josiah and the Composition of the Deuteronomistic History* (Leiden: E. J. Brill, 1995); Hieronymus Cruz, "Centralization of Cult by Josiah: A Biblical Perspective in Relation to Globalization," *Jeevadhara* 25 (1995) 65-71; William Schniedewind, "The Problem with Kings: Recent Study of the Deuteronomistic History," *Religious Studies Review* 22 (1996) 22-27.

his lifetime—an unheard-of boon. Or did he marshal the sympathies of the poor for the sake of his program of centralization? Where does the balance lie? Such ambiguities cannot finally be resolved but must be grappled with if the Word of God is to be discovered in the book of Joshua.

What does the book of Joshua show us about ourselves? If we attend to it carefully, it may suggest to us our own affinities with the atrocities, violence, coercion, and prejudicial categorizing as means to social betterment that are its main events. The point of such insight through God's Word is not to exaggerate our sins or grovel in them, but to encounter a greater reality in which we may not be as innocent as we suppose when averting our gaze from this book or disavowing it out of hand. The book of Joshua can help us to overcome consciousnesses mystified through the ignorance, fear, and conflict that to one degree or another affect all human beings.

PRIESTLY ADDITIONS TO JOSHUA

The main priestly strand (P) as a unified composition is confined to the Tetrateuch. But at least one passage of priestly character is found in Deut 32:48-52. Some historians have argued that the priestly strand predates and hence provides a source for at least the beginning parts of the Deuteronomistic History. Most, however, continue to believe that, while preserving earlier tradition from the time of their service as the priesthood of the house of David in Jerusalem, P was composed in its present form during or just after the Babylonian exile of the house of David. This sequence suggests what is probably the simplest explanation for the quasi-priestly additions to the Deuteronomistic History as well, which are most evident in the book of Joshua.

The Deuteronomistic History reflects a levitical control of tradition against the established priesthood. In contrast, in the post-exilic period the reestablished priesthood, who identified with the figure of Aaron, again found themselves in power and thus in a position to modify the Deuteronomistic History to make it conform more with the priestly Tetrateuch and express their special interests, and this they seem to have done in a modest way. For example, while the list of levitical cities in Joshua 21 may date originally from the late eighth or seventh century BCE, in its present form it is a priestly composition that was probably composed in the post-exilic period. Thus its assignment of Anathoth to the Aaronid priests (Josh 21:18) may represent, not long-standing tradition, but a form of Aaronid revenge against the deuteronomistic cabal of more than a century earlier. The similar bias can be seen in the account of Josiah's reform in 2 Chronicles 34–35, which, like the rest of Chronicles, reflects the influence of both the Aaronid rulers of the post-exilic period and the Levite underlings. Ignoring a foundational theme of the Deuteronomistic History, the account in Chronicles makes no mention at all of Josiah's attack against Bethel, the erstwhile Aaronid shrine.

A less likely explanation of the priestly additions to Joshua is to suppose that an exilic deuteronomist used priestly sources. Either way, the priestly tradition met in Joshua should be understood primarily in relation to the priestly strand in the Tetrateuch rather than in relation to the Deuteronomistic History, even though it is doubtful that a continuation of the P strand or any other unified priestly substratum underlies the present book of Joshua.

A notable instance of a priestly addition is the insertion of Eleazar in Josh 14:1; 17:4; and 21:1. Eleazar was the third son of Aaron and his designated heir. In later genealogies, he is the link between Aaron and the Zadokite Aaronids displaced by Josiah but restored to power following the Babylonian exile, at least putatively (1 Chr 6:3-15, 50-53; Ezra 7:1-5). In the deuteronomistic view, Joshua is the direct successor of Moses and is obedient to Moses' charge and commands, both without intermediary. In Josh 14:1; 17:4; 19:51; and 21:1, however, Eleazar appears to come between Moses and Joshua, as in Num 32:28 and 34:17. This contrasts with the deuteronomistic emphasis. (Eleazar is mentioned in Deut 10:6, but this is likely to be a priestly addition.) In the priestly strand, Eleazar joins Moses to hear Yahweh's order to enumerate the clans of the tribes of Israel in preparation for the apportionment of the conquered land (Numbers 26:1). This order is given before Joshua is commissioned (Num 27:12-23). Then, at Joshua's commissioning, Yahweh makes it explicit to Moses that Joshua is subordinate to Eleazar (Num 27:20-21).

In Joshua 13–21, the word מטה (*maṭṭeh*) rather than שבט (*šēbeṭ*) is used for "tribe," and scholars have sometimes taken this, together with other supposed differences, to indicate a comprehensive priestly source for the account of the allotment of territories to the tribes. This remains doubtful. Clearly Joshua 13–21 as currently phrased fulfills priestly directions given in the book of Numbers, tying together the themes of promise and fulfillment in the Tetrateuch and Joshua. This is true even when there are differences between the two books on the same subject. Thus priestly writers had a hand in composing the agreements between Numbers and Joshua, and it is not necessary to look further to explain the priestly characteristics found in these chapters.

Others have noted similarities between the book of Joshua and Chronicles. Such may be particularly significant in the account of the crossing of the Jordan (Joshua 3–4). The liturgical character of this account, which apparently originated in a ritual reenactment, is enhanced by the ceremonial role of the priests, much in the style of Chronicles. Because circumcision appears nowhere else in the Deuteronomistic History but plays a cardinal role in the priestly strand, the account of circumcision in Josh 5:2-8, which appears to interrupt the narrative, represents a priestly addition.

BIBLIOGRAPHY

Boling, Robert G., and G. Ernest Wright. *Joshua*. AB 6 Garden City, N.Y.: Doubleday, 1982. A thorough treatment of textual, literary, archaeological, historical, and interpretive issues; the introduction was written by G. Ernest Wright before his death in 1974.

Chaney, Marvin L. "Debt Easement in Israelite History and Tradition." In *The Bible and the Politics of Exegesis*. Edited by David Jobling, Peggy L. Day, and Gerald T. Sheppard. Cleveland: Pilgrim, 1991. 127-39.

———. "Joshua." In *The Books of the Bible*. Edited by Bernhard W. Anderson. New York: Charles Scribner's Sons, 1989. A concise but nuanced analysis of the book of Joshua as a deuteronomistic composition.

Coogan, Michael D. "Joshua." In *The New Jerome Biblical Commentary*. Edited by Raymond E. Brown, Joseph A. Fitzmyer, and Roland E. Murphy. Englewood Cliffs, N.J.: Prentice Hall, 1990. 110-31. Pays particular attention to literary and archaeological issues, acutely sensitive to the problems of placing the book of Joshua in its historical context.

Curtis, Andrian H. *Joshua*. Sheffield: Sheffield Academic, 1994. A succinct and balanced introduction to the basic issues of Joshua interpretation, with a partly annotated bibliography for each issue.

Doorly, William J. *Obsession with Justice: The Story of the Deuteronomists*. New York: Paulist, 1994. An introduction written for laypeople by a retired minister; usable with congregations.

Hamlin, E. John. *Inheriting the Land: A Commentary on the Book of Joshua*. Grand Rapids: Eerdmans, 1983. A fluent commentary attuned to historical, social, and interpretive issues; the author, who taught for many years in Singapore and Thailand, uses his experience in Asia to draw out the implications of Joshua from an international perspective.

Hess, Richard S. *Joshua: An Introduction and Commentary*. Downer's Grove, Ill.: Inter-Varsity, 1996. A knowledgeable interpretation of Joshua as reflecting Late Bronze Age conditions, particularly attentive to historical and archaeological data and interpretation.

McCarter, P. Kyle. *Joshua*. Hermeneia. Minneapolis: Fortress, forthcoming.

Na'aman, Nadav. "The 'Conquest of Canaan' in the Book of Joshua and in History." In *From Nomadism to Monarchy: Archaeological and Historical Aspects of Early Israel*. Edited by Israel Finkelstein and Nadav Na'aman. Jerusalem: Israel Exploration Society (1994) 218-81.

Nelson, Richard D. *Joshua*. OTL. Louisville: Westminster/John Knox, 1997. Particularly useful for preaching and teaching in the church, by one of the foremost scholarly interpreters of the Deuteronomistic History.

Niditch, Susan N. *War in the Hebrew Bible: A Study in the Ethics of Violence*. New York: Oxford University Press, 1993. A lively and insightful contemplation of the many facets of this contentious issue.

Soggin, J. Alberto. *Joshua: A Commentary*. Philadelphia: Westminster, 1972. An older work still valuable for its concise articulation of basic exegetical matters.

Woudstra, Marten H. *The Book of Joshua*. Grand Rapids: Eerdmans, 1981. An intelligent and informed discussion by a scholar who believes "the picture drawn by the book of Joshua to be true and reliable," with a particular interest in theological considerations.

OUTLINE OF JOSHUA

I. Joshua 1:1-18, Joshua Receives His Commission

II. Joshua 2:1–12:24, Joshua Conquers Canaan and Destroys Its People

    A. 2:1–6:27, The Destruction of Jericho at Passover
        2:1-24, Rahab's Help
        3:1–4:18, Crossing the Jordan
        4:19–5:12, Camped at Gilgal
        5:13–6:21, Destruction of Jericho
        6:22-27, Saving Rahab and Her Family
    B. 7:1–8:29, The Destruction of Achan and Ai
    C. 8:30-35, An Altar on Mt. Ebal
    D. 9:1–10:43, Destruction to the South
        9:1-27, Saving the Gibeonites
        10:1-43, Destruction of the Jerusalem Coalition
    E. 11:1-15, Destruction to the North
    F. 11:16–12:24, Summary of Destruction

III. Joshua 13:1–21:45, Joshua Redistributes the Land

    A. 13:1-7, "Redistribute This Land"
    B. 13:8-33, Land for the Tribes Beyond the Jordan
    C. 14:1-5, Inheritance by Lot
    D. 14:6–15:63, Land for Judah
        14:6-15, Hebron for Caleb
        15:1-63, Land for Judah
    E. 16:1–17:18, Land for the Sons of Joseph
        16:1-10, Land for Ephraim
        17:1-13, Land for Manasseh
        17:14-18, The Hill Country for the Sons of Joseph
    F. 18:1-10, Land Survey and Lots at Shiloh
    G. 18:11-28, Land for Benjamin
    H. 19:1-51, Land for the Remaining Six Tribes

JOSHUA RECEIVES HIS COMMISSION

COMMENTARY

The Josianic book of Joshua begins and ends with characteristically deuteronomistic speeches and narratives (Joshua 1; 22–23; 24:29-31). The deuteronomistic opening consists of three speeches. In the first speech, Yahweh recommissions Joshua (1:1-9); in the second Joshua gives his first order to his army officers (1:10-11); and in the third, the two and a half Transjordanian, or east-bank, tribes declare their willingness to obey Joshua's orders and to guarantee obedience from others on pain of death (1:12-18). The opening thus establishes Joshua's authority. The whole is framed by the formulaic phrases "I/he will be with you . . . be strong and courageous" (1:5-7, 17-18).

The narrative opens with the phrase "after the death of Moses." This is the deuteronomistic writer's way of demarcating the end of the period of Moses, when the law was laid down, and the commencement of the period of Joshua. The period of Joshua ends, and the period of the judges begins "after the death of Joshua" (Judg 1:1). The period of the judges ends, and the period of the kings proper, starting with the rule of David and his establishment of what his distant successors insisted was the single shrine laid down by Moses, begins "after the death of Saul" (2 Sam 1:1).

The period of Joshua features the conquest and distribution of the land under the law of Moses, so it is not surprising that these are the main themes of Yahweh's opening speech to Joshua. Here Yahweh recommissions Joshua to succeed Moses and command Israel in the conquest of the land west of the Jordan. The deuteronomistic character of the first speech is particularly evident, as it repeats several phrases from the account of Yahweh's commissioning of Joshua in Deut 31:7-23. It also pictures Joshua reading the document of the law day and night, as is decreed for the king in Deut 17:18-20.

The words that frame the entire opening section also frame the first speech, in chiastic order. Yahweh commands Joshua to cross the Jordan and conquer the land, since "as I was with Moses I will be with you . . . be strong and courageous. . . . Be strong and courageous, for [I] Yahweh your God am with you" (1:5-6, 9; cf. 1:7). From the first commissioning of Joshua in Deut 3:28, it is clear that these repeated words reiterate the operative clauses of the commission: "Be strong and courageous. . . . I will be with you." Moreover, Yahweh's encouragement of Joshua to "be strong and courageous" is reminiscent of the encouragement Moses offered to Joshua (Deut 3:23; 31:7). Unfortunately, this correspondence is not evident in the NRSV, since the same Hebrew words are translated differently each time. The words also echo what Moses said to the entire nation as they prepared for conquest (Deut 31:6), and they are repeated by Joshua to encourage his fighters to debase their Canaanite captives before he executes them (Josh 10:25).

In Deuteronomy, the commissioning of Joshua (Deut 31:14, 23) is nested within the larger account of the disposition of the law of Moses (Deut 31:9-29). Both accounts of Joshua's commissioning (Deuteronomy 31; Joshua 1) thus stress the importance of the law of Moses. It is this law that justifies the house of David's claim to the land and thus justifies the conquest as reconquest, and it is this law through which the house of David will exercise its jurisdiction over the conquered land. This is one of many indications that Joshua is cast in the role of the monarch, a role he plays throughout this story. As Nelson explains, these indications suggested to listeners in Josiah's court the identification of Joshua with Josiah.[25] Like a king, Joshua is to study the law of Moses every day. As in the installation of a king, Joshua is commissioned with a form used for office holders in general, but with the addition of obedience to the law, which makes the installation specifically royal (cf. 1 Kgs 2:2-4).

Similarly, the opening section emphasizes that Joshua is the successor to Moses. Just as Yahweh was with Moses, so also Yahweh is with Joshua; what Yahweh commanded Moses, Joshua is commanded to do also; as the tribes obeyed Moses, they will obey Joshua; only may Yahweh be with Joshua as with Moses. Joshua's immediate succession upon the death of Moses does not follow the consensual or charismatic pattern of tribal leadership, but the royal pattern of smooth dynastic succession, like Solomon's succession (cf. 1 Kgs 2:2). This succession is stressed throughout the book. As Joshua is about to lead Israel across the Jordan, just as Moses led Israel through the sea, Yahweh tells Joshua that he will be exalted, so that "they may know that I will be with you as I was with Moses" (3:7). When the crossing is finished, the writer notes that "all Israel feared him as they had feared Moses." Here "fear" (ירא yārē) connotes obedience to Joshua's command as to Moses' law. Joshua meets the commander of Yahweh's army in a scene reminiscent of Moses' meeting with the angel of Yahweh at the burning bush (Exod 3:2-6).

There are still other indications that Joshua is portrayed royally. Like a king, Joshua is assigned to lead a united family of "tribes," a family that, contrary to a genuinely early tradition like the Song of Deborah in Judges 5, suffers no internal conflict or dissension. As Chaney observes, in phrases like "all the Israelites," "all Israel," and "all the men of Israel," the notion of national unity "punctuates the book of Joshua like a drumbeat."[26] Like a king, Joshua is to exercise the royal power to partition land taken in conquest. As though upon a king who individually embodies his subjects, Yahweh concentrates the promise of victory and land upon the single individual Joshua (Josh 1:5). In contrast, the same promise in Deut 11:24-25 had been expressed to the entire nation. In the third of the opening speeches, the people pledge their absolute obedience to Joshua in place of Moses, as to a king; this motif is a commonplace in ancient Near Eastern vassal treaties, which demand that loyalty owed to a sovereign must be transferred to that sovereign's successor.

The commissioning of Joshua involves more than the pattern of royal appointment and succession. It also involves what Assyrian kings in Josiah's time and for centuries before referred to as the "trust-inspiring oracle" of the king's god. The first speech of the book of Joshua is just such a war oracle. In it, Yahweh encourages his lieutenant Joshua by declaring that since Yahweh will be fighting in the same battle and "will not fail you or forsake you" (1:5), Joshua should "be not frightened or dismayed" (1:9). This is a routine battle motif in the ancient Near East.[27] Assyrian kings, for example, went to battle "at the command of my lord Ashur." In the Ugaritic texts, the god El visits King Keret in a dream and commands him to make war against Pabil, king of Udum. Thus the diction of Yahweh's speech parallels that of Deut 20:1, 8 in the law for making war, which, next to the slaughter of the Canaanite peoples, deals primarily with the need for dedication and fearlessness in the troops. Moreover, the comparison of Josh 1:9 and 10:25 should remove the modern temptation to treat Yahweh's "trust-inspiring" words as anything other than a prelude to rout and mayhem.

The priestly account of Moses' commissioning of Joshua (Num 27:12-23) is distinct from, but probably dependent upon, the deuteronomistic treatment of the same theme.

The land is the land Yahweh has given to the nation of Israel. Note the repetition of "give," "gave," and "given" (נתן nātan) throughout this opening section. The nation in this narrative consists of the idealized subjects of the house of David, and the land is the land claimed by those who held the Davidic title in the period after the fall of Samaria in 722 BCE. The narrator refers almost exclusively to the "land" rather than to its present inhabitants. The inhabitants are referred

25. Richard D. Nelson, "Josiah in the Book of Joshua," *JBL* 100 (1981) 531-40.

26. Marvin L. Chaney, "Joshua," in *The Books of the Bible*, ed. Bernhard W. Anderson (New York: Charles Scribner's Sons, 1989) 1:108.

27. Jeffrey J. Niehaus, "Joshua and Ancient Near Eastern Warfare," *JETS* 31 (1988) 37-50.

to only in 1:5, where it is evident that the trust Yahweh must inspire is trust that the inhabitants who are to be attacked will not destroy their Israelite attackers. Without this reference to the land's present inhabitants, it might be easy to forget that the land is not just to be claimed but expropriated, and that even as myth the story is not about giving a land without a people to a people without a land.

The scope of the claimed territory is described in two ways. One way reflects the ideal that the territory of Israel should match what was conceived to be the greatest extent of Davidic suzerainty under David and Solomon. The description in 1:4 is similar to several such descriptions, which differ from one another, usually in minor ways (Deut 1:7; 11:24; Josh 9:1; 10:40; 11:16; 12:7-8).[28]

The other way concerns the boundary of the Jordan River. The Jordan is often thought of as a natural boundary, a concept greatly reinforced by the eastern boundary of the modern state of Israel. The modern boundary was determined at the Conference of Versailles following World War I as part of the British Mandate in Palestine. The conference mapmakers based their work on the deuteronomistic conception. This boundary was based on the system of Assyrian provinces in Palestine. It is not surprising that the two known instances of treating the Jordan as a political boundary should represent state-level determinations and have nothing to do with the people in the area themselves, who rarely if ever have treated the Jordan as a boundary. Typically, those who held or inhabited one side of the Jordan at any point held the other side as well. The fact that during most of a history of six hundred years or more, including the time of Josiah, "Israel" held land on both sides of the Jordan is quite in line with regional custom. That the tribe of Manasseh was conceived as having been divided by the

deuteronomistic boundary makes the point even clearer.

Just as the first speech in the opening of Joshua refers immediately to the crossing of the Jordan as the archetypal boundary crossing, the second speech refers directly to the crossing. Joshua gives orders through his "officers." The Hebrew term שטרים (*šōṭĕrîm*) means "scribes" and is a clear indication of the organized, if not bureaucratic, character of their office and the monarchic character of the narrative's context. The order is for the people to use the following three days to prepare provisions for crossing the Jordan and campaigning on the other side. The three days represent the time Israelite spies were concealed in Jericho, as part of the narrative framing and contextualizing of the crossing of the Jordan during Passover.

The third exchange, which equals the first in length, addresses head-on the closest thing to an internal division that the book of Joshua admits: the two and a half tribes who hold land to the east rather than to the west of the Jordan. The theme of this exchange is the obedience of the two and a half tribes. The ones whose loyalty might most be in question, since they already possess their lands and are separated by the Jordan, show themselves to be model followers of Joshua, to the point of avowing the death penalty for disobedience. There is an ironic element to their protestation, since it looks forward to the deuteronomistic close of the book of Joshua. There the same two and a half tribes appear to commit a dire transgression of the first law of Moses, prohibiting more than one altar by building an altar in the territory of Manasseh on the west bank of the Jordan, before the site of the single shrine prescribed by Moses had been settled upon. This apparent transgression leaves the two and a half tribes open to the charge of disloyalty, and the rest of the tribes prepare to make war against them, until the misunderstanding is cleared up. Thus the deuteronomistic composer of the book of Joshua frames the whole with a narrative defusing of the issue of potential "tribal" disloyalty.

---

28. The phrase "all the land of the Hittites" does not occur in the LXX and is probably an example of the kind of expansion that recurs often in the Hebrew text of Joshua. See P. Kyle McCarter, *Textual Criticism: Recovering the Text of the Hebrew Bible* (Philadelphia: Fortress, 1986), 27-29; Emanuel Tov, *Textual Criticism of the Hebrew Bible* (Minneapolis: Fortress, 1992), 283-84, 327-29. However, there is nothing surprising in this designation for the late Assyrian period.

REFLECTIONS

1. Most modern societies have a strong democratic and republican ethos, and the embodiment of a cause in a single individual can become complex and subtle. The constant turnover in officeholders and in leaders of political parties at all levels reflects this ethos. Moreover, the causes that are important to most Americans do not look like agrarian guerrilla causes. In our diverse and pluralistic society, causes are often deliberately designed more or less to overarch significant differences among people. The broad evangelical movement in American Protestantism provides an excellent example of a typical American pattern. For a hundred and fifty years or more, it has encompassed a great diversity of denominations and produced a multiplicity of leaders, at the same time standing for an identifiable alternative form of spirituality. Leaders recognized as embodiments of causes with national scope might include Susan B. Anthony, Mary Baker Eddy, Martin Luther King, Jr., Barry Goldwater, Gloria Steinem, Ralph Nader, and Billy Graham. Innumerable parallels exist for regional and local causes. Leaders have the ability to sharpen one set of distinctions in order to neutralize and incorporate all the other many distinctions that mark our lives. This realization invites us to reflect on the diversity of forces and interests represented by Joshua, even though his biblical portrait is inevitably one dimensional. It also bears on the role of the minister, who as leader frequently is challenged to embody both the congregation's diversity and its sense of common purpose.

2. In the Gospel of Mark, the story of Jesus begins, like the story of Joshua, with a commissioning. God commissions Jesus, like Joshua, to embody his "nation" as the monarch. This notion did not originate with Mark. It represents the subjects' usual sense of their monarch, not just in ancient Israel, but in agrarian societies in general. It also represents part of the meaning of such notions as being "in Christ" or "the body of Christ," which occur frequently, especially in the letters of Paul, the earliest-known Christian writings. Although the meaning of such notions is not exhausted by their sociopolitical origin, it is worth remembering that they do not begin with a vague or mystical experience, but parallel concrete experience, in this instance the experience of a collective or social identity "in" the monarch. This dimension of being "in" Christ suggests a collective experience that can be added to the necessary individualistic feeling or understanding of the phrase.

JOSHUA 2:1–12:24

JOSHUA CONQUERS CANAAN AND DESTROYS ITS PEOPLE

JOSHUA 2:1–6:27, THE DESTRUCTION OF JERICHO AT PASSOVER

OVERVIEW

Nearly the entire first half of the conquest narrative deals directly or indirectly with the fall of Jericho. The battle of Jericho is the most famous incident in the book of Joshua and one of the most famous incidents in the Bible. Often people who know little else about the Bible are aware that Joshua fought the battle of Jericho and the walls came tumbling down. The picture of the mighty walls of Jericho collapsing at the mere blast of seven horns and the shouts of the Israelite host encircling the town has captured the imagination for centuries. The attention given Jericho in the book of Joshua is a measure of its importance as a paradigm for God's leading the campaign to conquer Canaan. The great fighting force of Israelites need do no more than march around the outside of the town, blow seven horns, shout at the appointed moment—and above all obediently follow these unusual commands. God does the rest, until the Israelites rush in to ravage the now defenseless town and annihilate its inhabitants.

Of course, the battle of Jericho was not always so singularly prominent. It is scarcely mentioned outside of Joshua (2 Macc 12:15; Heb 11:30; and indirectly 1 Kgs 16:34, referring to the curse of Joshua in Josh 6:26). Apparently it held less fascination for the biblical writers than it does for us. Moreover, the battle of Jericho is only one among many interrelated themes in this section of Joshua; the others, while perhaps less famous, are just as important, if not more so. The account of the fall of Jericho is plaited out of numerous thematic strands and interconnected plots, which intertwine like the multiple plots of an effective television drama. They all relate to one another, and the battle itself takes its place within the assemblage. In interpreting any one theme or plot from this section, it is essential to keep in mind how it is related to the others.

If there is a master plot that draws all together, it is not the battle per se, but the recapitulation of the first Passover, from the saving of the Israelite firstborn to the crossing of the sea. This is represented especially by the crossing of the Jordan, which is the centerpiece of the account. Among other links to the Passover, two stand out. Rahab is to hang out a red cord and keep her family inside to avoid slaughter by the forces of Yahweh, just as the Israelites marked their homes with streaks of blood on the first Passover night. The seven days of the battle of Jericho apparently fall on the seven days of Passover. For the writers of the Deuteronomistic History, this is the last authentic Passover before the one decreed by Josiah in his eighteenth year, which practically brings the Josianic stage of the Deuteronomistic History to its grand climax (2 Kgs 23:21-23).

All the other themes and plots in this section relate to one another through the Passover, although, like the elements of many passages in the Bible, they are intensely multivalent. There are many such themes and plots. We can scan them here briefly. Joshua replays the role of Moses in the deliverance from slavery in Egypt. Yahweh is with Joshua as he was with Moses, as proved by Yahweh's miraculous support of Joshua in the crossing and the battle in tandem. The role of the levitical priests in the crossing stresses their deuteronomistic importance as trustees of the law of Moses in the ark (they are called "the priests, the Levites" in Josh 3:3, typically the deuteronomistic designation). Their feet play the same role in the crossing that the hand of Moses does in the original, by signaling the parting of the water for the passing of the law of Moses. The Jordan serves as the great boundary, where the desert trek (and with it manna) ends and the promised land (and with it the produce of the land) begins. The fall of Jericho and destruction of everyone in it serve as paradigms for the guerrilla tactics favored by Joshua's "weak" band in the face of local power and for the projected success of Joshua's rampage, especially as regards obedience to God's command. When Jericho is destroyed, Rahab and her father's household are saved. Rahab's family is the subject of the frame to this entire section. She and her family represent two significant themes. One theme is the inclusion of Canaanites on the side of Yahweh in contrast to the exclusion of the Israelite Achan and his family in the episode that follows. The other theme, assuming that Rahab's prostitution indicates her family's poverty, is the rescue of Rahab's family from indebtedness, just as in the Deuteronomistic History Passover validates Josiah's septennial debt remission by commemorating the saving of Israelite debt slaves from Egypt. This second theme concerning Rahab is the only reason her family is mentioned at all. Rahab and her family are saved from the ban. The ban exemplified in the destruction of Jericho epitomizes the unconditionality of Josiah's reform and reconquest, in theory at least, and it ties this account of Jericho and Rahab to the ensuing account of Achan and Ai, which illustrates the consequences of violating the law of the ban. The two cairns of twelve stones memorialize "tribal" Israel, which might resist royal encroachment but which Josiah aims to incorporate. The second cairn also stands specifically for Gilgal, here established as a sacred shrine like that at Horeb, where Moses was confronted by the fire of Yahweh in the bush. Except for allusions to the present scene, Gilgal plays a role elsewhere in the Deuteronomistic History only as the shrine where Samuel both

appointed and determined to depose Saul in favor of David, for violating the law of the ban. Although based on the "cairn" of stones, the name "Gilgal" is taken by the narrator to refer to the "rolling away" of the "shame of Egypt," which from the deuteronomistic perspective at least, signifies debt slavery. By highlighting Gilgal, and hence the later rejection of King Saul in favor of David, the narrative reinforces the point that the entire Jericho episode, but especially the crossing of the Jordan (2:9-10; 4:23-24), is meant, as was the first Passover, to inspire fear in "all the inhabitants of the land" and "all the people of the earth," who are specified as "the kings of the Amorites" and "the kings of the Canaanites" (5:1). Finally, having completed the desert trek, the new generation of Israelite men are straightaway circumcised, a condition for keeping the Passover (Exod 12:48).

It may be difficult for a reader or preacher to hold together all at once the many interrelated motifs, themes, and plots contained in this major section of the book of Joshua. We can review them once again, one by one: Joshua's authority; the Passover allusions and their significance; Rahab and debt remission; the priestly curators of the law of Moses; the Jordan as a boundary; obedience to God's command; the unconditionality of Josiah's reform, but the inclusion of indebted "Canaanites"; and the support represented in Gilgal for the house of David against opposing "tribes" and kings. The best way to relate one theme to another is to ask regarding any particular element or incident what theme or themes it contributes to, and then how it is related to Passover, recalling that Passover in the Deuteronomistic History signifies the saving of a nation of debt slaves, the populist base for Josiah's reform.

The deuteronomist follows an interpretation of debt slavery that is extremely important for the book of Joshua. When debt slaves are set free in the seventh year, Josiah's law prescribes, they are to be liberally provided with sheep, goats, grain, and wine (Deut 15:12-14). The reason is given: "You yourselves were once slaves in Egypt and Yahweh freed you from slavery and provided you with plenty—so now you are to do the same" (Deut 15:15). This reason contains something of a surprise. In the Tetrateuch's version of the exodus, what Israel suffered in Egypt was continuous corvée, or a state-imposed statute tax on labor in the form of slavery. The deuteronomistic conception, which the writers of Deuteronomy and Joshua were probably not alone in holding, is different. For them the exodus from Egypt represented liberation from debt slavery, not corvée slavery.

The deuteronomistic historian certainly knew the important difference between corvée slavery and debt slavery, but in principle the historian had little problem with corvée slavery. No deuteronomistic law deals with corvée. Samuel may refer to it in 1 Sam 8:17, a text incorporated by the historian, but there no deuteronomistic elaboration is given. David himself instituted corvée (2 Sam 20:24), and Solomon's Temple, Yahweh's exclusive shrine, was built by Israelite corvée slaves (1 Kgs 5:13, 12:4; seemingly contradicted by 1 Kgs 9:22).

Just as debt remission was a great theme of temple reform in the ancient Near East, so also debt slavery becomes an overriding concern of the deuteronomist. As a commemoration of the exodus, therefore, the feast of Passover in the Deuteronomistic History marks liberation from debt slavery. That is why Passover is the next major subject addressed in the laws after the remission of debt (15:19–16:8).[29] The deuteronomistic interpretation

of the slavery in Egypt as debt slavery is also clear from the frequent deuteronomistic use of the verb "redeem" (פדה *pādâ*) as though from debt (cf. e.g., Exod 21:8; Lev 19:20), to refer to Yahweh's deliverance of Israel from the "house of slavery" in Egypt (examples include Deut 7:8; 9:26; 13:6; 15:15; 24:18; 2 Sam 7:23; Mic 6:4 (part of a deuteronomistic passage).

The importance of this deuteronomistic understanding of the Passover becomes clear in the interpretation of the crossing of the Jordan (as Israel crossed the sea in the exodus), the keeping of Passover, and the conquest of Jericho in Joshua 2–6. All these episodes are framed by the story of the deliverance of Rahab and her family. Rahab is a prostitute. That is, she is a woman who is forced by poverty—and by her poor father or brothers—to seek income that would either help to keep her family from falling disastrously into debt or to pay off the debt they have already incurred. The story of the deliverance of Rahab and her family expresses more than the safeguarding of one Canaanite family from death by *ḥērem,* the ritual slaying of enemies "devoted" to Yahweh for the sake of central rule. It also epitomizes, in combination with the epitome of the reconquest that the crossing of the Jordan and the fall of Jericho represent, the selective deliverance from debt servitude that stands at the center of Josiah's reform in the form of the law of debt remission.

29. The deuteronomistic treatment of Passover begins appropriately with rules concerning the eating of the firstborn of herd and flock. This is the subject that also forms an envelope around the law of Passover in Exod 13:1-16.

Joshua 2:1-24, Rahab's Help

COMMENTARY

The story of Rahab is the story of her father's house, as she repeats (2:12, 18; cf. 6:25): father, mother, brothers, sisters, and all who belong to them (2:13, 18; 6:23)— indeed, her entire extended family (6:23; the NRSV translates the phrase "father's house" [בית אב *bêt 'āb*] as "family"). The mention of Rahab's mother next to her father reflects the subverting of patriarchal households in Josiah's reform. Rahab's family's fate is tied to her own, not because as the wealthiest member of the family she provides for the rest of

them, as some have suggested,[30] but for just the opposite reason: It has fallen to her as a mere daughter to help supply her family's dire need through the unwanted and demeaning necessity of prostitution, for it is the poverty of her extended household that has forced her into prostitution in the first place.

There are several reasons besides the deuteronomistic Passover basis of this narrative for assuming that Rahab is a prostitute

30. See, e.g., Athalya Brenner, *The Israelite Woman: Social Role and Literary Type in Biblical Narrative* (Sheffield: JSOT, 1985) 79-81.

because her family is in debt. Poverty was by far the most common cause of prostitution in the ancient world, as it is in our world as well. Most of the story works like many of the folkloristic narratives of the Bible, by dealing in stereotypical extremes. Rahab takes the side of the "outside agitators," on the extreme margins of society, against the king, at the extreme pinnacle of society. She advises the spies to escape to the hills, the traditional refuge of outlaws against royal authority. Her story is basically a folk narrative about poor people against kingly power, not about a well-off, if socially marginal, sexual escort. The narrative's characters represent stock figures rather than nuanced individuals: a typical prostitute and her family, a typical king, typical outlaw spies. Moreover, the only reason why the prostitute's family is brought into the story is that her story is their story—her prostitution reflects their poverty, and their poverty in all likelihood means their indebtedness. The story is adopted to appeal to debtor families who, far from condemning Rahab because of her prostitution or her act of deception, would sympathize with her and her family as fellow indigents and cheer her on as she dares to make fools out of the king and his men, to whom her family would have owed their debts.

There is no indication that Rahab owns the house she resides in, as is often assumed. It is probably her father's house, since the rest of her family are assumed to be living in Jericho. The house would have been kept in the family in part through Rahab's prostitution. The phrase "the house of a prostitute" in v. 1 does not require that the prostitute own the house; the phrase "your house" in v. 18 does not occur in the Hebrew text, which has only "inside the house" (אליך הביתה *ēlayik habbaytâ*). There is no reason to regard Rahab as a "madame," as some do, or an innkeeper, as later tradition sometimes attempted to suggest (see the note to 2:1 and 6:17 in the NIV). Rahab's prostitution is the narrator's way of addressing the issue of indebtedness, for in most instances in the ancient world prostitution alternated with debt slavery. Often, if a poor family did not submit to one alternative, it was forced to submit to the other, if not

to both. Rahab represents the indebted, as we might expect in a deuteronomistic text highlighting Passover, and her deliverance and the deliverance of her father's entire house in conjunction with the slaughter of their creditors are tantamount to the remission of their debts.

The basic story of the prostitute against the king has been co-opted by the deuteronomistic writers for its populist appeal.[31] Most of the narrative assumes that Rahab and her family are on the side of the spies and opposed to the king and his henchmen. In this aspect, the story pits the poor against the rich, the marginal against the dominant, and Rahab belongs on the side of the poor Israelites. The deuteronomist is opposed to all local warlords and minor rulers, like those featured throughout the narrative of conquest and enumerated in 12:9-24, a list headed by the king of Jericho. These represent the likes of Josiah's adversaries, the potent oppressors of Josiah's poor subjects and the target of his law of debt remission. In origin, the story tells about collusion between disaffected insurgents and a disaffected prostitute who have an interest in joining forces but who need to give guarantees that can be trusted. For this reason, the bulk of the narrative details the dialogue between spies (called messengers in 6:17, 25) and a prostitute as they negotiate the risky business of agreeing to terms and taking the requisite oaths (2:9a, 12-21).

In contrast to such a theme, however, in a few lines Rahab refers to herself as one with the king (2:9b-11). These lines have been added to the basic story by the deuteronomistic historian, in line with the conceptual polarization of Israelite and Canaanite. They interrupt the thread of Rahab's opening to her parley with the spies: "I know Yahweh has given you the land . . . so, since I have dealt kindly with you, swear. . . ." The first of the interjected phrases, "that dread of you has fallen on us" (v. 9b), and the rest of vv. 10-11 have numerous deuteronomistic

---

31. For the social analysis of the Rahab story presented here, see Marvin L. Chaney, "Ancient Palestinian Peasant Movements and the Formation of Premonarchic Israel," in *Palestine in Transition: The Emergence of Ancient Israel*, ed. David Noel Freedman and David F. Graf (Sheffield: Almond, 1983) 67-69. Cf. Norman K. Gottwald, *The Tribes of Yahweh: A Sociology of the Religion of Liberated Israel 1250–1050 B.C.E.* (Maryknoll, N.Y.: Orbis, 1979) 885-86.

parallels, especially in Deuteronomy and Joshua.[32] Yahweh, the God of heaven and earth, promotes the interests of the "nation" of the chosen grantees against the other nations of the earth. In this aspect, the story pits the supposed Israelite nation against the Canaanite nations, and Rahab belongs on the side of the Canaanites rather than the Israelites (her "us," "we," and "our" include the king and his men). The flax drying on the roof of Rahab's house is the first direct indication that events are occurring during the time of Passover. Flax was harvested and laid out to dry just before the barley harvest, and, as reckoned by the agricultural calendar, it was the barley harvest that marked the time of Passover.

Rahab refers to two causes of her people's fear: the drying up of the sea at Passover and the slaughter of the Amorite kings, Sihon and Og. It is partly ironic that in this speech she mentions the Passover—and mentions it first—since it is in the context of Passover and the debt remission it validates that the rest of her story puts her on the side of the Israelite poor. Looked at another way, however, it is appropriate. Having completed the new trek through the Jordan on dry land, Joshua constructs the cairn of stones at Gilgal to commemorate the crossing on dry land ("dry" [יבש *yābēš*] is repeated three times) so that all the peoples of the earth may know that Yahweh is mighty and so that they may learn, like the Israelites, to fear Yahweh (4:22-24). In the deuteronomistic view, for both Rahab and Joshua the purpose of crossing on dry land is to put fear in the hearts of the nations so that they will collapse in the face of Joshua—that is, so that they are forced to acknowledge the justice of Israel's liberation from Egypt. This is what Joshua comments on when the spies report to him (vv. 23-24), even though they have spent three days scouting out the hill country as well.

The phrase "inhabitants of the land" can be and was construed in two ways, only one of which applied in the folk narrative. The Hebrew translated "inhabitants" (יושבים *yôšěbîm*) means, literally, "the ones who sit." In many passages, it can refer either to rulers who sit on thrones (e.g., Amos 1:5: "I will cut off the enthroned one [NRSV, inhabitants] from Emeq-aven, and the one who holds the scepter from Beth-eden") or to the strong who "sit" on their estates as the wealthy landowning class (e.g., the "lords" of Philistia and Canaan in Exod 15:14-15; note the parallels, "chiefs" and "leaders"). This is the meaning of the phrase in the folk narrative, which stresses the gulf between the rich (not "inhabitants," but "landowners") and the poor. The second phrase in v. 9 *b,* "all the landowners of the country melt in fear before you," is likely original to the folk narrative, since it is not deuteronomistic but is identical to the popular poetic line in Exod 15:15 (NRSV, "all the inhabitants of Canaan melted away"). From the perspective of Rahab's deuteronomistic avowals, however, for which the distinction between Israelite and Canaanite is primary, the phrase probably was taken to mean "inhabitants," as though "Canaanite" were a national category embracing all people regardless of social class, including women and children. From this perspective, king and prostitute, the richest and the poorest in the town, belonged to the same category of people.

As in the rest of Joshua, the LXX often represents a different Hebrew original from the MT. In several places in Joshua 2, the LXX seems more in tune with the folk narrative, in which the spies come to the town to make contacts there, than the deuteronomistic use of it. In the LXX of v. 2, the king is told that some spies have come to search out the *town,* not the land. In v. 13, the LXX has "the house of my father," again the social unit responsible for covering family debts, instead of the MT's "my father" at the head of the list of individuals. In v. 18, the LXX has "if we come to the edge of the town" rather than "come to the land" (NIV, "enter the land"; NRSV, "invade the land"). The idea that in origin the story applied only to some town fits with 6:17, 25, where the spies are called "messengers," as though they had had business with someone in the town. Finally, the long phrase in v. 15 *b,* "for her house was

---

32. In addition to numerous deuteronomistic phrases, note that Rahab says the Israelites carried out the ban of extermination against Sihon and Og (2:10; NIV, "completely destroyed"; NRSV, "utterly destroyed"). Her statement agrees in this respect with the deuteronomistic account of the battles against Sihon and Og in Deut 2:31–3:7 ("ban" in Deut 2:34; 3:6). The account in the Tetrateuch, in contrast, mentions no such ban (Num 21:21-35). This part of Rahab's deuteronomistic speech thus points up in retrospect the rescue of her father's house, which sets up the marked contrast between Josh 6:17-21, where the ban involves "Canaanite" exceptions, and Deut 2:31–3:6, where there are no "Amorite" exceptions.

on the outer side of the town wall and she resided within the wall itself," does not occur in the LXX and seems to be a late explanatory addition that accords poorly with the fall of Jericho's walls and survival of Rahab's house (6:20, 22). It is sometimes suggested that Rahab's house stood miraculously while the rest of the wall fell down. This is unlikely, since it finds no association or resonance elsewhere in the text.

As already indicated, the red cord hung out by Rahab to protect her family from the impending slaughter is intentionally reminiscent of the blood of the pascal lamb, which protected the Israelite debt slaves at Passover

(Exod 12:7, 13). Even this quasi-liturgical motif could have played a role in the original folk narrative, if conceived in terms of the Passover feast as a family rite rather than the state rite it becomes in deuteronomistic legislation.

Thus the historian conceives a role for both Rahabs: the Rahab who represents the impoverished in social terms and the Rahab who represents the Canaanites in national terms. The one is meant to appeal to the poor debtors among Josiah's subjects, the other to "Canaanite" clients of Josiah's landed elite opponents who might be enticed to submit to Josiah's sovereign command.

REFLECTIONS

1. Probably most readers of Joshua who reside in the so-called developed world, or First World, when presented with the story of a prostitute are apt to appropriate it primarily in moral terms. Prostitution is bad, and a prostitute is a morally reprehensible individual; so Rahab must be a questionable character. Thus it is not surprising, such an interpretation might conclude, that she is a Canaanite, and in the end never really better than the rest of her fellow Canaanites. Such an interpretive approach must be abandoned, however, because it fails to take account of the pre-industrial contexts and meaning of prostitution.[33] Furthermore, it lacks any realistic analysis of modern prostitution and its causes, lumping poor and dominated prostitutes together with wealthy and independent prostitutes, even though the former far outnumber the latter, and assuming that prostitutes may simply exercise freedom of choice to engage in "immoral" behavior.

As in the book of Joshua, debt, slavery, and extermination played an important role in the development of American identity and racial and ethnic classifications. In the colonial period of United States history, indentured servitude, a form of debt slavery, played a significant role in helping thousands of needy people, almost entirely young men, emigrate from Britain and begin a new life in America. These debt contracts provided a socially accepted and constructive way for landowners and householders to capitalize on the labor pool available for work in the colonies and for the sons of the poor to find a new dignity in the independence they soon achieved. At the same time, in using the debt contract to bootstrap themselves to prosperity, they became part of the advancing tide of deception, mayhem, and dispossession that confronted the Native American populace.

In the highlands of Central and South America, European colonists put Native Americans to work in mines and on vast latifundia as serfs and slaves. Descendants of these groups exist today in large numbers, though often they are poor and discriminated against. In the tropical lowlands, the colonists exterminated or expelled the natives and imported chattel slaves from Africa, mainly for sugar and later cotton production. This labor development led directly to the definition of "whites" versus "blacks" that still prevails in the United States. In the temperate climes, colonists drove back the native population and brought in British and northern European indentured

33. See, e.g., Gideon Sjoberg, *The Preindustrial City: Past and Present* (New York: Free Press, 1960).

servants, whose story eventually contributed to the myth of North American resource-fulness and self-reliance.

Debt slavery and debt prostitution still exist around the world. Debt slavery was outlawed in Pakistan in 1992, but is still common there, for example, on sugar planta-tions. Recently the president of Brazil was forced to admit that slavery, outlawed in Brazil in 1888, is common on the orange, coffee, and other plantations of the Amazon region. Most Brazilian slaves indenture themselves to estate owners to pay for the long journey from the northeast of Brazil. Once on location, they are forced to buy all their needs from the estate owner and soon find it impossible to repay their debt, which only continues to grow. In a similar way, prostitutes are frequently enslaved in East Asia and other parts of the world.[34]

It may come as more of a surprise that slaves are still found in the United States. Recently state officials in Los Angeles raided a sweatshop housing seventy-four immi-grant Thai workers, mostly women, being paid slave wages for seventeen hours of work a day, supposedly toward paying off their fares to America. The state figured they were owed $3.5 million in back-pay, but instead laid plans to deport them, against the desire of many locals that all seventy-four be given green cards—in other words, be treated the way Rahab was treated by Joshua. As with many such attempts to enforce the law, this incident was regarded as a sign of the much wider practice of peonage and prostitution among poor Asian immigrants in southern California.

In comparable ways, such practices could be verified in many other parts of the country. The picture is complicated by a recent case in Chicago in which a woman was charged with selling her child to pay off a drug debt. With the reformist values repre-sented in Joshua 2, God would attack the creditor, pay the woman's debt, and redeem the child. In Chicago, the public faulted all three parties in the case—dealer, woman, and child—but focused most attention on the mother's wrongdoing, as though Rahab were most at fault because she is a prostitute.

When interpreting biblical texts, it is often worthwhile to identify the protagonists not with most of the people in the church, but with others whose lives are more like those in the text. The examples of forced indebtedness mentioned here represent a burden that has weighed on the poor for at least four millennia, and one that will, it seems, continue in more or less the same guise for the foreseeable future. Those who interpret Scripture in churches that are not poor need to recognize how this text (and many others) resonates with the experience of the poor.

By the same token, even within the church there are many, especially women, who, while not slaves, are oppressed by coercion of one kind or another. Thus in satisfying the needs of others they are unable to maintain their own importance and well-being.

2. Rahab is mentioned twice in the New Testament. In Heb 11:31, Rahab becomes one in the train of forebears who survived or prospered by faith, and in James she is a model of those who are "justified by works and not by faith alone" (Jas 2:24). The partial contrast between these two texts (Hebrews expounds on faith, while James advocates works) points up inevitable partiality of interpretation, even for New Testa-ment writers dealing with the Scriptures. Nevertheless, these texts also complement each other. Brief though they are, both attribute to Rahab the same faith marked by the same work: safeguarding the Israelite spies. Thus in concert they articulate the familiar biblical theme that "faith without works is dead" (Jas 2:17, 26). From this biblical perspective, the figure of Rahab reminds the interpreter that faith may be expounded in terms not only of doctrine, but also of lives lived. Moreover, the lives of the faithful

34. For prostitution in the contemporary world, see Rita Nakashima Brock and Susan Brooks Thistlethwaite, *Casting Stones: Prostitution and Liberation in Asia and the United States* (Minneapolis: Fortress, 1996).

include not only deeds performed, but also perseverence and patience maintained in the face of adversity. To be faithful is both to do and to endure, and the vector of a person's faith manifests itself through both.

Joshua 3:1–4:18, Crossing the Jordan

COMMENTARY

The battle of Jericho may not be much celebrated in the rest of the Bible, but the main event that precedes it, Israel's march through the Jordan River on dry land, is referred to or alluded to in several important passages in the OT and plays an extremely significant role in the NT Gospels. One of the most famous references occurs in Mic 6:4-5. There God explains briefly what God has done for Israel, redeeming them from slavery in Egypt by leading them out behind Moses, Aaron, and Miriam; protecting them from Balak and Balaam; and having them pass over (a commonly accepted emendation) "from Shittim to Gilgal." This is one of those places in the Bible where the failure to mention Joshua along with the other prominent characters in the story occasions surprise, particularly since Miriam is mentioned only here outside the Tetrateuch and since the entire passage, Mic 6:1-5, has a marked deuteronomistic tone.[35] As with other references to it, the event itself holds more significance than does the leadership of Joshua, who probably was joined to this event no earlier than the time of Hezekiah. Many commentators have noticed what they consider to be repetitions and inconsistencies in the narrative that suggest a composite text and a complicated history of composition; the text is multivalent, but genuine inconsistencies are probably only apparent.

Perhaps the lack of reference to Joshua in Mic 6:5 is even more surprising, given that one of the main themes in Joshua 3–4 is the magnification (NIV, NRSV, "exalted") of Joshua to the stature of Moses. The section

is partially framed by the commencement and fulfillment of this theme in 3:7 and 4:14, with the result that all Israel "feared [Joshua] as they had feared Moses." Joshua's command, however, goes little further than giving orders. For drama, the main role is played by the priests bearing the ark containing the law of Moses, which more than anything else represents the presence of the "living God." (The phrase "the ark of the covenant of Yahweh your God" occurs only here and in Deut 31:26, where Moses commands the Levites to put the new document of law on the ark.) It is the priests who, by stepping into the river, accomplish what Moses did by extending his hand toward the sea to part the waters and who, by stepping out again, cue the waters to return, as again Moses did with his hand. It is they who station themselves in the midst of the watercourse as the massed assembly of Israelites, including forty thousand men armed for war, trek safely across at a distance of no less than two thousand cubits, or about two-thirds of a mile. It is their position in the watercourse that is marked by a cairn of twelve stones, gathered and placed by Joshua. Moreover, Joshua's commemoration of the event stresses Yahweh's power in dividing and drying up the waters, not his own (4:6-7, 21-24). In a surprisingly democratic gesture, Joshua orders the Israelites to appoint twelve of their number, one from each tribe, to gather the stones that will form the cairn at Gilgal. Nevertheless, the significance of the ark's crossing for Joshua is clear: The living God, whose law of dispossession and centralization rests in the ark and who gives orders through Joshua, will drive out the seven Canaanite nations before the Israelite host (3:9-11). In a word, this crossing of the Jordan spells reconquest under Joshua. This is the emphasis that Josiah's historian wants the story to have.

It was not always so. The crossing of the Jordan played various roles in the thinking

35. James L. Mays, *Micah*, OTL (Philadelphia: Westminster, 1976) 127-36. For example, the last phrase in Mic 6:5, "in order to know the judgments of Yahweh," is similar to Josh 4:24, "in order for all the peoples of the earth to know the hand of Yahweh." The NRSV translation of Mic 6:5 assumes that the unspecified subject of the infinitive "to know" is "you," but it is at least as likely to be the rest of the world, and more likely to be both, as in Joshua. The phrase "in order to know" occurs three times in the Deuteronomistic History and once in Ezek 38:16.

and writing found in the Bible and engendered several different interpretations. The deuteronomistic portrayal of the crossing of the Jordan has a ritual character and may have been based on a rite that was periodically carried out more or less as described.[36] The ritual involved a re-enactment of the crossing of the sea at Passover. The re-enactment entailed a division of the water in the river into two walls or heaps on either side and the crossing of Israel on dry land, exactly the points Joshua takes to be the significance of the stones. Scholars have noted that neither of these familiar features of the event is mentioned in the earliest accounts of the exodus victory at the sea—namely, the ancient victory song in Exod 15:1-18 and the J and E accounts in Exodus 14. These features were apparently introduced into the Exodus account on the basis of the ritual at the Jordan. The earliest allusion to the splitting of the waters at the Jordan is in 2 Kings 2, which concerns the Jordan, and not the sea. This account dates to the latter part of the ninth century BCE, but its use of the tradition of crossing implies that the ritual re-enactment is already a well-established practice. It is not known exactly what form the re-enactment took or how the splitting of the waters was accomplished, as through damming or rechanneling at Adam, about fifteen miles north of the crossing at Jericho, or otherwise represented. The stopping of the waters of the Jordan at Passover, however, or even just the idea of stopping them, would have been particularly dramatic at that time of the year, which saw the Jordan in flood following the winter rainy season and with snow beginning to melt on Mt. Hermon at its source (3:15).

The most explicit equation of the sea and the Jordan appears in Psalm 114: The sea fled, the Jordan turned back as Israel left Egypt for Judah, God's sanctuary, and Israel, God's sovereign possession. The original passage through the sea not only consists of dry land but it also leads into the desert; the passage through the Jordan, which is modeled after it, does so as well. In fact, nearly the entire way from the Jordan to either Ai or Jerusalem goes through the Benjaminite or

Judean desert, including some of the most barren landscape in the world. This way may have served as the ritual way reflected, for example, in the grand elaboration that is the subject of most of Isaiah 40–55, written less than a hundred years after the Deuteronomistic History. An ancient wayfarer in the new exodus proclaimed by Isaiah would have journeyed not directly west across the Syrian desert, a route that never would have entered the poet's mind under any circumstances, but via the fertile crescent all the way from Babylon to the Jordan at Jericho without passing through any desert at all. Thus the way of the new exodus in Isaiah's conception passes through the desert only metaphorically until its last stage, from the Jordan to Jerusalem. This ritual way may be reflected already in Exod 15:13-18, which, like Psalm 114, truncates the journey from the sea to Yahweh's sanctuary and abode in Palestine, presumably Jerusalem. Little is lost by reading the entire song in Exod 15:1-18 as though it referred to the Jordan in place of the "sea" named in Exod 15:4.

The equation of the sea and the Jordan River was ultimately based on the same myth that the Exodus narrative itself makes use of: the divine warrior's defeat of the forces of chaos and infertility, personified by the cosmic sea. The role of the sea is played by Tiamat in the famous Babylonian creation narrative called *Enuma elish.* The same role in the Ugaritic myth of Baal, culturally closer to Israelite tradition, is played by a character called Sea, but given the twofold epithet of "Prince Sea" and "Judge River."[37] This mythic motif is adopted many times in the Bible to describe the establishment of Yahweh's cult as the source of fertility. Among the oldest of these is Hab 3:1-19, in which Yahweh does battle against both River and Sea (3:8-10, 15). Elsewhere, "Sea" and "River" appear in the Bible in their mythic form as dragons (e.g., Job 26:12-13; Pss 74:11-15; 77:16-20; Isa 27:1; 51:9-11).[38]

---

36. See Frank M. Cross, *Canaanite Myth and Hebrew Epic* (Cambridge, Mass.: Harvard University Press, 1973) 77-144; Bernard F. Batto, *Slaying the Dragon: Mythmaking in the Biblical Tradition* (Louisville: Westminster/John Knox, 1992) 128-52.

37. The Ugaritic terms translated "prince" and "judge" both signify "ruler" with little distinction between them.

38. The dragon is sometimes called Leviathan. In Job 9:13; 26:12; Ps 89:11; and Isa 51:9, it is called "Rahab." The dragon is sometimes said to be split, like the waters in Joshua 3–4 and Exodus 14. Although the two names "Rahab," one of the sea dragon (רהב *rahab*) and the other of the woman in Joshua 2 (רחב *raḥab*), look alike in English, they are spelled differently in Hebrew and are not related, despite the proximity of the motif of splitting or cutting off the river in Joshua 3–4.

What is perhaps most striking about all of these references to the tradition in its archetypal form is that not only do they make no mention of Joshua, but also they imply nothing about conquest or reconquest. Joshua and conquest are developments of the tradition of the crossing of the sea or the river that must be attributed to the deuteronomistic writers, whether under Hezekiah or Josiah.

Having left Shittim headed west, Israel camps next to the Jordan for three days. After this time of ritual preparation, Joshua's officers tell the people to watch for the ark carried by the levitical priests. When they see it moving, they are to follow it, "because you have not passed over on [this] way previously" (3:4). This caution looks very much like an alert to participants in the ritual who might think they were quite well acquainted with the way they were to follow, either because they lived nearby and were used to using the designated route or one close by or because they had participated in the ritual before. Thinking they knew the route, people massed for the day for the crossing might, if not otherwise cautioned, be inclined to follow their whim and cross whenever they pleased, perhaps at one of the fords mentioned in 2:7, rather than in order and at a place requiring or reflecting the stopping of the waters. Furthermore, they move quickly (4:10), as the Israelites did on the first Passover night (Deut 16:3; cf. Exod 12:11; Isa 52:12). This is probably an allusion to the first Passover, although the Hebrew expression is different. The NRSV leaves no doubt about the allusion by translating מהר (*māhar*) as "in haste," as though the Hebrew were the same as in Deut 16:3; the NIV more accurately translates "hurried."

No wonder that Micah said "from Shittim to Gilgal," since next to the command of Joshua, a deuteronomistic accent, and the role of the levitical priests, a deuteronomistic or priestly accent, the main point of the narrative is the gathering of the stones for the two memorial cairns that give Gilgal its name. The association of the crossing with Gilgal goes back well before the Deuteronomistic History. That is the subject of the next section.

REFLECTIONS

1. Israel crosses the Jordan to reach the land granted to it by Yahweh at the very beginning of its history, beginning with Israel's grandfather Abraham. This grant was alluded to even earlier in human history, through Noah's curse of Canaan. In the Old Testament world, land was the fundamental good, the irreducible basis of life, joy, and fulfillment, the entity whose disposition most other forms of social existence were shaped to serve. Modern interpreters may tend to think of land as a material good, without quite the status or value of spiritual goods. To be religious today is to emphasize spirituality over materiality. Such a distinction was foreign to the Old Testament world. There was then no clearer knowledge of God than that God was the one who gave to Israelites their land and that to keep their land they must heed the law laid down by God, including stipulations governing material goods. Land, law, people— these are the components of historical existence in ancient Canaan or Palestine that pointed to the one known as Yahweh, the Lord of all. Moreover, materiality depends on particularity, and both are ultimate, not penultimate, essentials of faith in ancient Israel.

This understanding of God and God's people as particular sits awkwardly with the Christian propensity to universalize God and the related Protestant propensity to individualize and spiritualize the life of faith. Thus Christians rightly marvel at God's creation in general and give thanks for individual blessings, especially those involving personal relationships. The focus on the land in Joshua might suggest, in addition, special attention to some particularity of the created order, such as the ecological soundness of the local environment or the ecological impact of economic policy. Or it might suggest special attention to particular material blessings, those received as well as those not received, as they appear to depend on group affiliations like family, nation, race, or class. Both the universal and the particular are essential. Working out how they are related to each other is like working out how a nation or a church or a congregation can be unified and diverse, one and many, at the same time, affirming what is distinctive about individuals and groups and what all people have in common. It is especially important to be aware of how wealth as such sometimes encourages the tendency to spiritualize and individualize. The classical liberal heritage essential to most denominations and to our national well-being now must be tempered with a clear recognition that particular identities—troublesome, upsetting, and morally ambiguous though they may appear, especially when they are somebody else's—are as significant as universal identities.

2. The crossing of the sea and the river to the land serves as a great symbol in the traditions of Israel and the house of David. It is repeated, recalled, and recast as the nucleus of what it means to become the redeemed people of God. Thus this part of Joshua can often be interpreted with integrity in the light of latter narratives of redemption.

Perhaps the best example of such recapitulation in the Old Testament is found in the elaborate vision of the return from Babylon to Jerusalem laid out in Second Isaiah (Isaiah 40–55; cf. Isaiah 35). This is probably the longest and most elaborate example of sustained metaphorical and rhetorical brilliance in the Old Testament. The poet polemicizes against the complacency of the second and third generations of the court in exile, who have little interest in leaving the place they experienced as the capital of their world and returning to the provincial backwater of Zion. To fire them up, the poet puts before them an image of Israel departing from Egypt in order to make known God's redeeming justice. The central component of this image is crossing through the water on dry land. Over and over this figure is elaborated, ramified, and developed.

The people of Israel, those addressed by Second Isaiah, are again Yahweh's servant, as they were of old. They are the servant of Yahweh in three distinct senses: (1) as a slave redeemed by Yahweh, as in the original exodus; (2) as a suppliant to Yahweh, drawn to worship Yahweh, also as in the first exodus (in Second Isaiah, the servant in this sense has to be encouraged to ask for help); and (3), the most important, as an officer in Yahweh's court. As such, Israel is called and appointed to serve in the court of the greatest lord of all, the Creator of the world and of Israel at the sea, and his anointed one, Cyrus, instead of the false gods of Babylon, whose service looks attractive to the Judahites. The servant (in all three senses) once was afflicted: The generation of the court of the house of David who came before suffered the punishment of exile. But now the servant is to be requited, by being raised high once again (one of several metaphors for return to Jerusalem), so that the nations can once again see and fear.

The resonant strain of intense transitions and new beginnings, the fresh confidence of initiations and the liberating encouragement derived from evidences of God's renewed attentions—these features of the story of Israel crossing the Jordan are replayed in the significant places where Scripture recalls this story. The interpreter and preacher may develop these positive themes at length to reflect their intensity in Joshua and Second Isaiah. At the same time, the question of who might suffer under the onslaught of such exuberant assurance and determination can never be overlooked.

3. The figure of the suffering and raised servant in Second Isaiah, who re-embodies Israel's crossing the Jordan, subsequently plays a momentous role in the early church's conception of Jesus. This is especially the case with the earliest of the canonical Gospels, Mark. The Isaian background to Mark's portrayal of Jesus is clearly indicated by, for example, the quote from Isaiah regarding the coming of the Lord's servant in Mark 1:2-3. Just as myth and rite are combined in the Old Testament text, so also they are combined in the New Testament, especially in the rite of baptism, which recapitulates the crossing of the sea. The baptism of Jesus at the Jordan, repeating the experience of

Elisha in 2 Kings 2, serves as paradigm. Since the names "Joshua" and "Jesus" are the same, it would have come as no surprise for early Christians to hear the story of their Lord, Jesus, begin, as it does in Mark, with a scene reminiscent of Joshua's leading Israel across the Jordan River (Mark 1:1-13), as though Jesus were repeating that great episode in the story of his namesake, itself recapitulating Israel's escape from slavery across the parted waters of the sea on dry land (Exod 14:5–15:21).

To the modern reader, the reminiscence may not be obvious at first. The passage may seem to be nothing more than a description of the baptism of Jesus. But to the hearer conversant with Scripture, numerous allusions would be unmistakable, of which a few can be considered here. The writer of Mark even declares that he is going to make the allusions by citing a scriptural amalgam from Exodus, Isaiah, and Malachi, which together refer to the return of Elijah as a voice of one crying in the desert, heralding the "great and terrible day of the Lord" (Mal 3:1; 4:5). This reference to Elijah immediately draws the hearer back to the moment when Elijah was last seen on earth. That moment is described in 2 Kgs 2:1-14, in a scene intentionally modeled on Joshua's crossing the Jordan in imitation of Israel crossing the sea during Passover, and that in turn provides one of the models for Mark's description of Jesus' baptism. Elijah leads Elisha through the parted waters of the Jordan from west to east. As Elijah is swept alive into the heavens in a swirl of war chariots, his prophetic spirit passes to Elisha, who takes up Elijah's mantle, strikes the Jordan, and, like Moses at the sea and Joshua at the Jordan, passes through the parted waters from east to west.

This, in adapted form, is what happens to Jesus. Mark, having alluded to all of this and more, opens his Gospel with the appearance of John, who looks like Elijah on the same day he summarily destroyed troops of the state's hostile armed men by summoning fire from heaven (2 Kgs 1:8-12; Mark 1:6). Indeed, it seems that John the Baptist is Elijah (Mark 9:11-13). Elijah has returned to announce the coming of the Lord and the preparation of the way to the Temple, leading to the restoration of God's kingdom on earth on a "great and terrible day." The anointing of Jesus with the Spirit as he re-enacts the climactic event of Passover, the crossing of the sea (here the Jordan), makes him all at once the new Moses, the new Joshua, as well as the new David, ready to draw together a new fighting host, storm Jerusalem, recapture and restore the Temple of the house of David, and re-establish God's rule on earth.[39] In the light of the deuteronomistic paralleling of Moses, Joshua, and Josiah, Jesus as the Davidic Messiah might almost be thought of at this point (Mark 1:11) as Josiah redivivus. As the Gospel of Mark develops, however, it becomes clear that Jesus is the antitype of such a messiah and that those who mistake him for another Josiah are deeply mistaken and disloyal.

Prior to the writing of Mark, there had developed a great debate in the early church regarding just how and to what extent Jesus embodied the material hopes of the house of David. It is sometimes easy to forget that the earliest Christians did not always see eye to eye on even the most basic issues.[40] Most, if not all, of the writings in the New Testament take similar positions on subjects about which early Christians vehemently disagreed; so it is often necessary to look behind the New Testament texts to see what subjects the early Christians were debating. One such subject was political: the substantive relationship between the "kingdom of God" and the historical kingdom of the house of David. Would Jesus, having risen from the grave and thus foiled those of the Temple and imperial states who had tried to stop him, return at the head of the heavenly host that once swept away Elijah and then brought him back as John? Would Jesus as the new Joshua/Josiah complete the recovery and repurification of the Temple, the reconquest of Israel, the reassertion of the law of God through Moses as the basis of Israel's righteousness, and the installation of the church's members, starting with its "pillars," as Jesus' vice-regents to rule the world? Many believed this was what Jesus

---

39. The Greek εἰς (*eis*) in Mark 1:9 appears to mean "into and through," as in Mark 7:31.
40. See Michael Goulder, *St. Peter versus St. Paul: A Tale of Two Missions* (Louisville: Westminster John Knox, 1995).

meant to do. Others tended to focus attention on the church less as the new political nation in the usual sense and more as a new commonality with its own distinctive destiny.

There were several reasons for this debate, but it became particularly acute as more and more Gentiles were baptized as Christians. Many, if not most, Gentiles regarded the specifically Davidic political aspirations of the early church as the new Israel as of little moment. That was not what Jesus meant to them. Paul, who at first was probably something of a maverick in the church, became the spokesperson for many such Gentiles. The Jewish monarchy, the Temple (newly restored by the non-Davidic Herodians), and the law of Moses have their own validity, which even Gentiles may affirm, but Jesus as Messiah has introduced a new basis for righteousness quite apart from these fundamental Davidic institutions, for Gentiles and Jews alike. The dispute often came down to the question of whether circumcision, the sign of the covenant of Abraham that laid the basis for the covenant of Moses, would be required of Gentile male converts, as it had been of an entire generation of uncircumcised Israelite adult male followers of Moses and Joshua as soon as they had crossed the Jordan (Josh 5:2-8) and before keeping Passover (Josh 5:10; cf. Exod 12:48). That is, was the church, in essence, a new form of the old Davidic nation, bound to the law of Moses, or was it something else?

Mark was written in the midst of this debate. Much was at stake. The early Christian sect was a Jewish sect and struggled with the same basic issues other Jews struggled with: What, in line with God's will, was the basis of the ethnic and judicial integrity of the Jews, and how were Jews to relate to the Gentiles, with whom they shared life in the cities of the Roman and Persian empires, where most Jews lived? The Jewish position, ultimately abandoned by the "orthodox" church on the basis of divergent interpretations, nevertheless involved affirmations we can still understand and value, such as ethnic integrity and the refusal to compromise with the will of God as revealed in Scripture.

By making the rite of baptism and the baptism of Jesus a primary basis of his version of the gospel, and by showing how baptism recapitulates the basic themes of the exodus and the crossing of the Jordan under Joshua, Mark lays a basis for understanding the inclusion of the Gentiles in terms of just those scriptural texts that most clearly formed the basis for distinguishing between Israel and the Gentiles. In this sense, the Gospel of Mark represents a radical reinterpretation of the old Joshua in terms of the new Joshua, or Jesus. The preacher may wish to reflect on the importance of not simply rejecting or repudiating what appears to be non-Christian in Joshua, but of interpreting the New Testament transformation of the themes of Joshua in their first-century context, where the integrity of the ethnic and judicial identity of the Jews and their relationships with Gentiles were at stake.

Joshua 4:19–5:12, Camped at Gilgal

COMMENTARY

This entire section concerns Gilgal: the setting up of the twelve-stone cairn for which Gilgal is named (the cairn has its independent significance), the giving of the meaning of the name "Gilgal" for this narrative, and the keeping of the feast of Passover as the blessed nation at Gilgal. Israel no longer is to eat manna, as they did in the desert, but the newly harvested produce of the land. The keeping of Passover looks ahead to Josiah's Passover, on the deuteronomistic assumption that the rite had not been kept the way it should have been for the entire time between Joshua and Josiah (2 Kgs 23:21-22). In the midst of this section, a later priestly writer has inserted an account of the circumcision of the new generation in the promised land.

The Benjaminite shrine at Gilgal plays a significant role as early as the prophetic sources for the history of David. Gilgal was where Samuel anointed Saul king of Israel (1 Sam 11:14-15) and then later determined to depose him, because Saul had violated a battle command of Yahweh (the same חרם [ḥērem][41] command violated by Achan at Gilgal [Josh 7:1–8:29]). Gilgal was where Samuel anointed David king in Saul's place (1 Sam 13:8-14). In the deuteronomistic conception, the beginning of Saul's reign leads directly to its fruitless end, both tied to Gilgal.

Samuel anoints Saul king and tells Saul to wait for him at Gilgal for seven days, until Samuel comes and offers sacrifices (1 Sam 10:1-8). Saul arrives at Gilgal and waits seven days, but Samuel does not come. To prevent his forces from further slipping away from inaction, Saul offers the sacrifices himself. Instantly Samuel appears, with no explanation for his delay, and denounces Saul for his disobedience. The price for Saul's error will be the loss of his kingdom to a rival. This first hint of the coming greatness of the house of David is announced at Gilgal.

The turning point between Saul and David occurs in 1 Samuel 15, again at Gilgal, in the midst of Saul's ongoing conflict with the Philistines. Here the issue is ḥērem, the primary issue in the stories of Rahab (Joshua 2; 6), Achan (Joshua 7–8), and the Gibeonites (Joshua 9) that make up most of the narrative of conquest in the book of Joshua. Moreover, here the issue of ḥērem all of a sudden has to do not with the Philistines, but with the Amalekites, just as in the stories that introduce Joshua in the Tetrateuch. Samuel has ordered Saul to slaughter the Amalekites, man, woman, and child, together with all their livestock. Saul destroys the Amalekites, but spares their king, Agag, along with choice cattle and sheep, in order to sacrifice them, as he later claims, in Gilgal. When the book of Joshua was composed, this violation of ḥērem apparently became the example for

Achan in Joshua 7, whose violation of ḥērem also occurs at Gilgal. At Gilgal, where once again Samuel meets up with Saul, Samuel is again unimpressed with Saul's sacrifice. Again he accuses Saul of disobedience: "Since you have rejected the word of Yahweh, Yahweh has rejected you from being king over Israel." Saul repents, but to no avail. Samuel himself "hews Agag in pieces" and departs from Gilgal, never to see Saul again until the day Saul is to die in battle, when, again disobeying the deuteronomistic law, Saul summons the ghost of Samuel from the dead to consult him one last, futile time. Leaving Saul in Gilgal, Samuel proceeds immediately to anoint David as Saul's eventual successor (1 Sam 16:1-13), thereby initiating all that the deuteronomist holds dear: the sovereignty of the house of David over all Israel, exercised through the deuteronomistic law of Moses and centered in the Temple in Jerusalem.

Apart from these two extremely significant episodes—Joshua's crossing the Jordan and setting up a base camp at Gilgal and Samuel's rejection of Saul in favor of David—and allusions to them, Gilgal plays practically no role in the Bible. It is, however, also associated with the crossing of the Jordan in 2 Kgs 2:1-18, and as a camp for Elisha and an impoverished following in 2 Kgs 4:38. These last two texts were probably written in the late ninth or early eighth century, some hundred years before Hezekiah and two hundred years before Josiah. Gilgal is mentioned several times as an Israelite shrine in the eighth- or seventh-century BCE texts of both Hosea and Amos (Hos 4:15; 9:15; 12:11; Amos 4:4; 5:5), in addition to the passage in Mic 6:5, already noted. In four of these prophetic passages, Gilgal is paired with Bethel, as in 2 Kgs 2:1-2. The geography suggested by this combination has led many scholars to posit two different Gilgals (in addition to at least two others), one near the Jordan and the other in the hill country, but the matter is uncertain.[42] In this commentary, they are taken to be the same.

Elijah and Elisha journey from Gilgal to Bethel to Jericho to the Jordan, and then across the Jordan, heading east. Apart from Bethel, this is the journey of the Israelites in Joshua in reverse, and nearly such if Bethel

---

41. When someone or something falls into the classification ḥērem, he, she, or it is a possession of Yahweh and, therefore, not for general use. When the spoils of war (whether people, animals, or property) were declared ḥērem, they were to be destroyed. See P. Stern, *The Biblical Ḥērem: A Window on Israel's Religious Experience* (Atlanta: Scholars Press, 1991); N. Lohfink, "ḥaram," *TDOT* 5:180-99.

42. Wade R. Kotter, "Gilgal," in *ABD*, 2:1022-24.

should substitute for Ai, from which the Israelites returned to Gilgal (Josh 8:23; 9:6; the detour to the vicinity of Shechem in Josh 8:30-35 is a secondary addition). Gilgal is clearly an important Israelite shrine, with an early association with the ritual recapitulation of the crossing of the sea. The exodus allusions in 2 Kings 2 include not just the many ways in which Elijah and Elisha imitate Moses, which are easy to recognize, but the following story in which Elisha, having recrossed the Jordan westward, like Joshua, and ended up at Jericho, purifies a spring of water at Jericho. This purification follows the river crossing immediately just as the purification of the waters of Marah follows the crossing of the sea in Exodus 14–15 (Exod 15:22-25; cf. Exod 15:27). This sequence matches the most common sequence of themes in the mythic accounts of the defeat or splitting of sea and river, which is frequently followed by a production of fresh water or allusion to such an event (e.g., Job 9:9; 38:22-38; Pss 46:4; 65:9-13; 74:15; 77:20; 89:11-12; 114:6). The tie between Gilgal and the myth of the sea splitting was ancient and distinct.

Passover allusions continue in the entire Jericho account, right up to its end. These include the seven days of the siege of Jericho, which represent the seven days of the Passover begun in 5:10. The possibility that the seven days may have been added after the main composition of the Deuteronomistic History will be considered in the next section. Given that the siege occurs during Passover, the crossing of the Jordan, while symbolically representing the Passover, is said to occur four days before Passover (4:19). Since the crossing does not coincide with Passover, Joshua's interpretation of the stones that will form the cairn of Gilgal makes the comparison of the crossing at the Jordan with the crossing at the sea explicit, which is done only here. For twelve stones representing the twelve tribes of Israel, see Exod 24:4 and 1 Kgs 18:31.

The Amorite kings hear about the drying up of the Jordan and are utterly dispirited. The phrasing of this line recalls Rahab's deuteronomistic speech (2:10-11; a similar transitional phrase is used also in 9:1; 10:1; 11:1). The Amorites are specified as being "to the west" because "beyond the Jordan" usually means the east bank. The sequel to this

disheartening follows directly in 5:9, since the mass circumcision is an insertion. The local kings have heard about Israel's miraculous crossing to the land, and the shame of slavery in Egypt is removed. The conjunction of these two themes goes all the way back to Exod 15:13-17, ostensibly one of the earliest texts in the Bible. It is repeated numerous times, not least in Numbers 22–24 in the story of Balaam's refusal to curse the passing escaped slaves. This is the meaning the narrator hears in the name "Gilgal," a name that in fact more likely derives from the cairns. All three meanings given to the cairns and to Gilgal—"Yahweh cut off the waters for the ark" (4:7), "Yahweh dried up the waters for crossing so the nations might hear about it" (4:22-24), and "Yahweh removed the shame of Egypt" (5:9)—are related, and the second flows directly into the preface to the third: "so that all the nations may know . . . the Amorite kings heard."

On the fourteenth day of the month, Passover begins. The manna that fed the Israelites for forty years in the desert ceases, and the invaders eat of the produce of the land of Canaan (there is a pun between "produce" [עבור *'ābûr*] in 5:11, 12 and "pass on" or "cross over" [עבר *'ābar*] in 3:4, 6 and 4:5).[43] How do they get the grain, having just arrived? As invaders, they take it, just as they take the land itself.

A priestly writer has inserted an account of the circumcision of the new generation of Israelites who replaced those who died out during the forty-year desert trek. Priestly tradition makes circumcision a prerequisite for participation in Passover (Exod 12:43-49). Thus the writer inserted his account here because he wanted to make sure everyone was circumcised before Passover began. Except as a metaphor (Deut 10:16; 30:6), circumcision plays no role in the Deuteronomistic History outside of this text. Except for the phrase "not having listened to the voice of Yahweh," this insertion has no significant resonances with the text in the Deuteronomistic History that serves as its basis, the foundational account of the rebellion against Yahweh's command to conquer the land in

---

43. The Hebrew word for "produce" in 5:11-12 is rare in the Bible, occurring only here for certain and possibly one or two other places. There are indications that it is a loanword from Assyrian.

Deut 1:19-40, which set the scene for Joshua's succession and conquest.

For the P strand, however, circumcision is an extremely important rite. There is little doubt that Israelites, like nearly all people in the ancient Near East, practiced circumcision during the entire biblical period as a surveillance ritual designed to test the loyalty that men with sons owed to their fraternal interest group.[44] But circumcision became a significant article of Israelite or Davidic covenantal understanding only for the Davidic priestly tradition represented in the P strand. There circumcision represents nothing less than the sign of the second of the three "eternal" covenants of P: the covenant of Abraham, required of all sons of Abraham. While circumcision later came to represent a supposed distinctive feature of Jews among the "nations," this was not its significance for the P strand. The rite was too common for that, and in any case P itself presents Abraham as the father of a "multitude of nations" (Gen 17:5). Davidic priests probably stressed the importance of circumcision because of their special concern for reproduction ("be fruitful and multiply," Gen 1:28 and repeated many times in P) and interest in male privilege in the sacrificial cult.[45]

The phrase "a second time" (5:2) is potentially confusing. It does not mean that these Israelites have already been circumcised once. The phrase may be secondary, having arisen due to an ambiguity created by a word in Yahweh's command that occurs in the Hebrew text but is not directly translated in either the NRSV or the NIV: "sit" ($\kappa\alpha\theta\acute{\iota}\zeta\omega$ *kathizō* LXX) or "do again" (שנית *šēnît* MT): "make flint knives and sit/again circumcise the Israelites." The LXX may represent the original meaning of this Hebrew word; if so, when it took on the MT meaning "do again," it may have been reinforced by "a second time." Perhaps more likely the MT meaning was original, in the sense of "resume" a practice that has been suspended. The practice would then have been started, if not resumed, a second time: "Start again to circumcise the Israelites. . . ."

The phrase "a land flowing [better: oozing] with milk and honey" was present already in the ancient Davidic history of the nation, the J strand. There it described the land of Canaan as untilled and largely uncultivated (cf. Isa 7:14-25), as though the Canaanites were nearly all just town-dwelling rulers or merchants. The deuteronomistic concept of the land of Canaan is the opposite (Deut 8:7-8), and hence this phrase acquires the connotation of extreme abundance in the Deuteronomistic History, as though milk and honey could provide a square meal that a hardworking peasant man or woman would choose instead of a satisfying batch of bread and olives. It is the deuteronomistic concept rather than the J concept that came to dominate the biblical and modern use of the phrase.

---

44. On circumcision in P, see Robert B. Coote and David Robert Ord, *In the Beginning: Creation and the Priestly History* (Minneapolis: Fortress, 1991) 67-75, a discussion based in part on Karen Ericksen Paige and Jeffrey M. Paige, *The Politics of Reproductive Ritual* (Berkeley: University of California Press, 1981) 122-66.

45. Nancy B. Jay, *Throughout Your Generations Forever: Sacrifice, Religion, and Paternity* (Chicago: University of Chicago Press, 1992).

REFLECTIONS

1. Gilgal is named for a memorial cairn, which is seen to signify the removal of the shame of poverty, indebtedness, and peonage ("the shame of Egypt"). It is thus a memorial both to the war that was, the war against slavery in Egypt (cf. Deut 6:21; 26:6; 28:68), which resulted in crossing the sea, and the war that will be, the war against the Canaanites, whose land must be forfeited to the former slaves, while the Canaanites themselves, in line with the curse of Canaan, become Israel's slaves. It may be useful to think of our own war memorials, especially to the two great wars that took place on our own soil, the War of Independence and the Civil War. Both wars were fought against slavery, and hence monuments from those wars could be regarded, like Gilgal, as monuments against slavery. The first war was fought against "slavery" to a government in which the colonists felt they had no representation. During the American Revolution, the word *slavery* was used often to describe England's treatment of the colonists. The second war was fought to assert the right of the United States over the right of constituent states to decide issues of slavery. This war resulted in the emancipation of slaves and the outlawing of slavery in the United States.

The analogy with Gilgal holds if slavery is defined very broadly. It is also important, however, to recognize how the analogy does not fit, because if slavery is only broadly defined, then the full meaning of Joshua will not become apparent. Obviously nothing in Joshua or the deuteronomistic reform suggests the value of representation in government. The reform is authoritarian and largely totalitarian. The law is said to come from Moses not Josiah, but that does not mean that it is based on representation. The slavery eliminated by the Civil War was chattel slavery. The Deuteronomistic History takes no stand on chattel slavery, which figures prominently in the house of David's JE history without censure, and the history condones the imposition of corvée, or statute enslavement, on the Canaanites. Later parts of the Old Testament may take sides against chattel slavery, but the New Testament as a body ends up indifferent to it, and in some cases supportive of it, despite important texts like Gal 3:28. Using Scripture to help invalidate and eradicate slavery is a relatively recent development in the church's history, as in our nation's history.

Is it possible that by focusing on political slavery and chattel slavery, the two forms abolished by our great wars against slavery, Americans have given themselves permission to divert their attention from the ongoing jeopardy of poverty, which continues to lead to different forms of impoverished labor and debt slavery, which the Bible always opposes or sharply limits? Looking more closely at the relationship between poverty and work, even in an age when the world of jobs is drastically changing, leads to the realization that missing from our land are public monuments to a war against coercive, extortionate labor in all its forms. The gap between rich and poor is now greater in the United States than in any other so-called developed country. America's twentieth-century "war on poverty" has failed for a variety of reasons, and it has been replaced by a new form of what some are calling a "war against the poor."[46] The United States is not alone. The monument at Gilgal provides the opportunity to reflect on the chronic war against the poor that all rich people and nations have been accused of waging.

2. Circumcision is in some ways the most important subject in the New Testament. The basis for including uncircumcised Gentiles was a point of contention from the start. When the view represented by Paul eventually came to prevail, baptism in effect became a substitute for circumcision. The issue is basic to Paul's Letter to the Romans, 1 Corinthians, and most explicitly Galatians, and thus underlies a substantial portion of the Pauline corpus. In Mark, the Gospel that leads the way in integrating the Pauline perspective with the church's gospel, the paradigmatic scene of Jesus's baptism makes clear allusion to the extensive symbolization of the circumcision of the firstborn in order, like Paul, to set aside the significance of the rite in favor of baptism, whose imagery in turn is pervasive and fundamental.[47] There were many different views of baptism in the early church, but these all tend to merge inconsistently from the perspective of the New Testament canon, which is dominated by the writings and views of Paul and in which the primary concern is to invalidate the necessity of circumcision rather than give a single coherent explanation of baptism.

3. The keeping of Passover by eating the produce of the land recalls Deut 8:3. There, in the desert, bread is contrasted to the command of Yahweh. Here, in the land, bread and Yahweh's command, found in the law of Moses, come together: The abundance of prosperity made possible by possession of the land depends on obedience to Moses, to Joshua, and to Josiah. It is not clear whether the Israelites stole the grain or

46. Herbert J. Gans, *The War Against the Poor: The Underclass and Antipoverty Policy* (New York: Basic, 1996).
47. See Jon D. Levenson, *The Death and Resurrection of the Beloved Son: The Transformation of Child Sacrifice in Judaism and Christianity* (New Haven: Yale University Press, 1993) 173-232.

bartered for it, a gap that confirms that it functions mainly as a symbol here. The availability of grain rather than the lack of it is now to remind the Israelites of their dependence on Yahweh and the law. The weight of exhortation to this effect in Deuteronomy and Joshua is perhaps an indication of how easy it is for the opposite to occur: God's blessing often leads us to forget its ultimate source instead of remembering it.

Joshua 5:13–6:21, Destruction of Jericho

COMMENTARY

The focus now shifts again to Jericho, destined for siege and destruction. Recall why Jericho plays the role it does as emblem for the entire conquest. With its spring-fed oasis, Jericho dominated the lower Jordan plain, as it had for six thousand years or more. During Josiah's reign, and not during the pre-Davidic period of Israel's history, Jericho, which lay about four miles west of the Jordan, was the prime urban settlement beside the Jordan where it flows closest to Jerusalem in the highland. Thus Jericho helps to mark the boundary of the land to be conquered under Joshua. Jericho also dominated the route south to the rest of the western side of the Dead Sea basin. Here was concentrated the increased production of incense in Palestine, in which the house of David under Manasseh and Josiah took great interest.

Moreover, Jericho may have been a center of resistance to Josiah's rule. In defiance of Joshua's curse (Josh 6:26) Jericho was rebuilt, according to the Deuteronomistic History, during the reign of Ahab, more than two centuries before Josiah, by a certain Hiel of Bethel (1 Kgs 16:34).[48] The deuteronomistic historian probably takes this Hiel to be an example of the kind of semi-independent warlord whom Josiah must suppress. Thus Coogan suggests that Hiel's rebuilding of Jericho, which to judge by the poetic character of the reference in 1 Kings had a historical basis, "was a kind of rebellious secession, disapproved of by the deuteronomistic historians."[49] Indeed, it is quite conceivable that Hiel had a self-governing successor in Jericho in Josiah's day who would then have been the real "king of Jericho" targeted by the story in Joshua. During the Late Bronze and Iron ages, which began in the sixteenth century BCE and lasted for nine hundred years, until the fall of Jerusalem, Jericho was most extensively settled during the seventh and early sixth centuries; before then, settlement was sparse at best, though the site was well known, since it was always strategically important due to its location and springs, regardless of whether it was settled.

In the prelude to the battle against Jericho, the commander of Yahweh's army appears before Joshua with drawn sword. There is no indefinite "once" as in the NRSV; this scene belongs with what follows, including Yahweh's battle instructions and Israel's first march around Jericho. The entire episode takes place without a break on the first day of Passover (5:13–6:11). Angels often appear as men, even when they speak as Yahweh, so Joshua at first does not recognize the commander for what he is. Joshua challenges him: Is he an Israelite or an enemy? The commander reveals his remarkable identity. That such appearances, concomitant with the routine war oracle, are typical in traditional battle accounts is indicated by a remarkable Homeric parallel in which Athena, goddess of war and Odysseus' protector, appears to Odysseus prior to his battle with the suitors to assure him of victory.[50] In this scene, even in Athena's presence Odysseus wonders out loud how he is going to succeed; he seems no more aware than Joshua of the might that is standing before him.

Confronted by Yahweh's commander, Joshua instantly collapses in obeisance and asks what word the angel has for him. This represents an extremely critical moment,

---

48. The LXX of 1 Kgs 16:34 shows the full form of Hiel's name, Ahiel.
49. Michael D. Coogan, "Archaeology and Biblical Studies: The Book of Joshua," in *The Hebrew Bible and Its Interpreters*, ed. William Propp, Baruch Halpern, and David Noel Freedman (Winona Lake, Ind.: Eisenbrauns, 1990) 22; "Joshua," in *The Jerome Biblical Commentary*, 116.

50. Homer *Odyssey* 20:30-55.

since Joshua now knows that, as when he was commissioned by Yahweh, he is to learn in advance the outcome of the battle through the equivalent of a divine war oracle delivered directly from the source rather than through an intervening messenger or prophet. Joshua is not looking for a command (contrary to the NRSV), but that is the first thing he receives. The commander's instruction recalls Moses standing before the burning bush at Horeb (Exod 3:1-12). His instruction makes Gilgal equivalent to Horeb, the site where Moses was told at length, despite numerous protestations, that God would be with him (Exod 3:12–4:17), and where, after delivering Israel from slavery in Egypt, God formed a covenant with Israel, conveyed the first ten laws, and anticipated the entire rest of the law (Deuteronomy 5). At Horeb, God also referred to the land oozing milk and honey and to the seven nations inhabiting the land, who are to be dispossessed (Exod 3:8)—starting here at Jericho. The commander's instruction confirms that the shrine at Gilgal is to be a sacred shrine like Horeb.

What, then, is to be the outcome of the battle? The comparison implies that Yahweh will fight on the side of Israel to fulfill the salvation of the former slaves. This scene thus resumes the insistence that Yahweh is with Joshua as with Moses (3:7; 4:14) and forms a framework with the concluding line of the Jericho episode to the same effect (6:27). Thus the entire first quarter of the book of Joshua may be said to be dedicated to verifying that Joshua and his royal successor Josiah represent the authority of Yahweh.

The chapter division should be ignored. After a narrator's comment on the state of Jericho (6:1), Yahweh delivers the expected war oracle, including an assigned battle plan (6:2). The fluid alternation of the figure of man, angel, and Yahweh should occasion no surprise; such alternation occurs several times in Genesis (e.g., Gen 18:1–19:28). Yahweh's battle plan, while surprising, is not so preposterous as it may at first seem. It can be interpreted in terms of guerrilla tactics, where feint, deception, display, discipline, and surprise can go a long way toward compensating for a weak position, like that of a tribal force facing a well-armed and sealed fortress town. In addition, the narrative has a clear

theological point: Israel cannot fight without Yahweh's help, though Yahweh is able to do a great deal without Israel's help. The narrative highlights how Yahweh's might almost effortlessly makes up for Israel's weakness (6:16: "Yahweh has given you the town").

The battle plan consists mostly of normal military procedures: blowing horns (see, e.g., 1 Sam 13:3; Amos 2:2; Hos 5:8; Zeph 1:16), marching in formation, rallying behind the palladium, shouting, charging. Comparison can be made with Joshua's battle against Ai (Joshua 8) and with Gideon's battle against the Midianites, which conveys much the same theological point (Judg 7:2-23). The number seven—seven priests, horns, and days—is known in military contexts. For example, in the Ugaritic texts, King Keret sets out with a mighty force to besiege King Pabil in his town, and the journey takes seven days.[51] The seven plagues that Yahweh inflicts on Pharaoh and his household in the original J account of the exodus (the E and P strands add three more plagues) probably stem from such a tradition (see Deut 7:18-20). At the same time, all the military elements except charging are characteristic of liturgical acts as well. The LXX does not include a reference to these groups of seven in the instructions to Joshua, possibly pointing to an earlier stage of the story, before its liturgical elaboration, if not by the deuteronomists then perhaps by priestly writers in the exilic or post-exilic period. In any case, the "Day of Yahweh," the day on which Yahweh arrives to vindicate a just judgment (typically in battle), the language of war, and the language of liturgy merge into a common diction, based on the common symbolism of God's fearsome advent as divine warrior and magistrate. Such a merging can be seen in such passages as Hos 5:8–6:6; Joel 2; and Zephaniah 1. This characteristic merging makes it possible for a narrator to describe the fall of Jericho as virtually a liturgical continuation of the crossing of the Jordan, whether or not there was a later liturgical recasting of the narrative.

At the climactic moment when Joshua gives the command to shout, all must hold their breath while he expands on the dedication of the goods, livestock, and people to

51. Michael D. Coogan, *Stories from Ancient Canaan* (Philadelphia: Westminster, 1978) 60-64.

Yahweh—that is, their disposal to the temple or their annihilation (6:15-19). This dedication is the pivotal motif underlying both the exemption of Rahab and her family, because Rahab in effect has loyally championed the dedication of Jericho, and, in the sequel, the execution of Achan and his family for Achan's violation of the same dedication. The phrase "bringing trouble upon it/bring disaster on it" (6:18) links this narrative directly to the crime and punishment of Achan (7:25). References to dedications of various kinds using the term חרם (ḥērem) occur throughout the OT. The deuteronomistic law for the dedication, or ban, of enemy spoil is laid down in Deut 20:10-18 (cf. Deut 7:1-3) as part of the procedure for warring against the natives of Canaan, and in Deut 13:12-18 as part of the procedure for punishing Israelite localities that practice idolatry. Every living thing is to be slaughtered as the means of dedicating them to Yahweh, and indestructible (chiefly metallic; note the anachronistic mention of iron) property of any worth is to be dedicated to the treasury of Yahweh (6:19). The NIV translation of 6:18a accurately renders the MT; the NRSV follows a widely accepted emendation based on the LXX. The LXX reading provides a further direct link with the story of Achan in 7:21. The ambiguity of choosing between such variants, however, which occur often in biblical study, is illustrated by the ties that both variants have to Deut 7:25-26, which make them not only valid but apropos. The Aramaic version of 6:19 refers to the "treasury *of the temple* of Yahweh," as does the MT, though not the LXX, in 6:24 (NRSV and NIV, "house"). There is nothing startling about this variant, since the term "treasury" by itself implies the existence of a substantial and commanding central shrine. The mention of a temple, whether by a deuteronomistic writer or later scribes, makes an anachronistic reference to the shrine of the house of David in Jerusalem and an allusion to Josiah's program of centralization.

This anachronism is telling in more ways than one. The narrator may have been aware that the complete and unconditional dedication of enemy spoil is not a tribal but a state institution, and that it would not make sense in the narrative in the absence of a state temple. To see why this is true, it is necessary

to look more closely at the institution of dedication.

The Hebrew root used to mean "dedication" (חרם *ḥrm*) occurs in all the Semitic languages as a synonym of the root קדש (*qdš*), which in Hebrew is the more common root, usually translated by the English idea of "holy." Both roots mean "to set apart," "treat as sacred," "dedicate," or "forfeit." Concepts like holy, holiness, sanctuary, and sanctified that in Hebrew are usually formed from the root *qdš* are frequently formed in other Semitic languages from the root *ḥrm*. In Arabic, for example, a sanctuary precinct is called *ḥaram* and the sanctuary *ḥarîm*. The latter word has come into English as "harem," the section of the patriarchal household "set apart" for women and, like "banned" items in Hebrew, "prohibited." The two roots occur together in Hebrew in Lev 27:28: "every dedicated thing [*ḥērem*] is most holy קדש-קדשים *qōdeš-qādāšîm* to Yahweh," so that every person so dedicated must be put to death. A less barbaric use of the two terms occurs in Lev 27:16-25, concerning a field dedicated (*qdš*) to Yahweh, which under specified conditions "shall be holy [*qdš*] to Yahweh as a dedicated [*ḥrm*] field" (Lev 27:21). It must be realized that there is some redundancy in such phrases: Something "set apart" is something "set apart." The prohibitive use of *qdš* in Hebrew is illustrated in Deut 22:9: If a person sows a vineyard with seed, "the whole yield will be forfeit [תקדש *tiqdaš*—that is, will be holy, or prohibited]."[52]

Not surprisingly, the ritual dedication of rivals and enemies, an excellent excuse for exterminating them, was practiced elsewhere in the ancient Near East, but how extensively is not known. The closest parallel comes from the so-called Mesha Stela, a Moabite inscription from the mid-ninth century BCE. In it the king of Moab, Mesha (probably the king referred to in 2 Kgs 1:1; 3:5), vaunts his reconquest of territory earlier lost to Omri and Ahab, kings of Israel (making Mesha a sort of non-Davidic precursor of Josiah). Mesha's state god was an avatar of Ashtar named Kemosh. In the midst of the

52. See Marvin H. Pope, "Devoted," in *Interpreter's Dictionary of the Bible*, ed. George A. Buttrick (Nashville: Abingdon, 1962) 1:838-39; Norbert Lohfink, "*ḥrm*," in *Theological Dictionary of the Old Testament*, ed. G. J. Botterweck and H. Ringgren (Grand Rapids: Eerdmans, 1982) vol. 3.

account of his reconquest, Mesha declares that "Kemosh said to me, 'Go, take Nebo from Israel!' So I went by night and fought against it from the break of dawn until noon, taking it and slaying all, seven thousand men, boys, women, girls, and maid-servants, for I had dedicated [*hrm*] them to Ashtar-Kemosh. From there I took the vessels(?) of Yahweh and hauled them before Kemosh."[53]

Another parallel often pointed out comes from the Mari letters, clay tablets from Mari, located on the middle Euphrates River near the present border between Syria and Iraq, which were written a thousand years before Josiah.[54] These letters concern many subjects, including the struggles of the kings of Mari to curb, pre-empt, or accommodate the tribes inhabiting territory under their sovereignty. In these struggles, the king of Mari claimed propriety over the spoils of warfare or intimidation on behalf of his god, much like Joshua. The king termed the violation of his prerogative "eating the *asakku* of the king or god." Eventually this expression became generalized to cover any breach of contract. The Akkadian word *asakku* originated as a loanword from Sumerian, where it referred to a particular demon that could be relied on to avenge a violation of propriety, and hence to something prohibited or taboo. The Akkadian term, therefore, was functionally, though not semantically, equivalent to Hebrew *hērem*.

In a recent response to the comparison of "eating the *asakku* of the king or god" with the violation of *hērem*, it has been suggested that the *asakku* taboo at Mari was an administrative device for regulating the distribution of booty, whereas the biblical concept of *hērem* was religious, entailing a self-denying vow of abstinence from the normal fruits of victory in order to arouse God's sympathy with Israel's cause.[55] The latter point helps to broaden the function of *hērem* in war. However, the perceived contrast between the two institutions depends on the unlikely distinction between the realms of religion and taboo and may not

take seriously enough that in war *hērem* was imposed by decree rather than voluntarily adopted.

The last point forms an important part of another major response to the original proposal.[56] Gottwald agrees with the comparison of "eating the *asakku*" with the violation of *hērem*, but rejects the assumption that the Mari institution was comparable with Israelite tribal practice in the pre-monarchic period. As Gottwald points out, it was not the tribes of Mari who imposed proprietary taboo, but the king, representing the central government and dominant cult. The same applies, according to Gottwald, to the great majority of other parallels that have been adduced.[57] By the same token, therefore, the description of *hērem* in Joshua must be regarded as a reflection of the reform of Josiah and possibly Hezekiah, and not a description of pre-Davidic tribal warfare.[58]

Ironically the fall and capture of Jericho and the dedication of every living thing in it, the sum of what most people know about Joshua, only two verses (6:20-21; see Overview to 9:1–10:43). Much has been made of Jericho not only because it is the first of the cities Joshua destroys, and not only because of the particularly dramatic fashion in which it is destroyed, but because its destruction appears to lend itself to archaeological confirmation. The archaeological evidence from Palestine, however, fails to agree with a Late Bronze Age destruction of Jericho and with few, if any, of the other episodes of destruction described in Joshua. Most archaeologists now believe that Jericho, Ai, and Gibeon had no significant occupation during the Late Bronze Age, when the incidents in Joshua would have occurred. Some of the cities supposedly destroyed in Joshua's campaign show evidence of destruction more or less in the requisite period, but their dates of destruction can vary significantly; Hazor was destroyed as early as a century before Lachish.

53. James B. Pritchard, *Ancient Near Eastern Texts* (Princeton: Princeton University Press, 1955) 320-21; Klass A. D. Smelik, *Writings from Ancient Israel: A Handbook of Historical and Religious Documents* (Louisville: Westminster/John Knox, 1991) 33-34.

54. Abraham Malamat, *Mari and the Early Israelite Experience* (New York: Oxford University Press, 1989) 70-79.

55. Moshe Greenberg, "Is There a Mari Parallel to the Israelite Enemy-*hērem*?" *Eretz-Israel* 24 (1993) 49-53, Hebrew with English summary p. 233*.

56. Norman K. Gottwald, *The Tribes of Yahweh* (Maryknoll, N.Y.: Orbis, 1979) 543-46.

57. See further Moshe Weinfeld, *The Promise of the Land: The Inheritance of the Land of Canaan by the Israelites* (Berkeley: University of California Press, 1993) 76-98; Stern, *The Biblical hērem*.

58. See Paul D. Hanson, "War and Peace in the Hebrew Bible," *Int.* 38 (1984) 241-61; T. Raymond Hobbs, *A Time for War: A Study of Warfare in the Old Testament* (Wilmington, Del.: Michael Glazier, 1989); Sa-Moon Kang, *Divine War in the Old Testament and the Ancient Near East* (Berlin: De Gruyter, 1989); Stern, *The Biblical Hērem*; Susan Niditch, *War in the Hebrew Bible: A Study in the Ethics of Violence* (New York: Oxford University Press, 1993); J. P. U, Lilley, "Understanding the *hērem*," *TynBul* 44 (1993) 169-77.

It does not do, however, to deal with the sites selectively in order to focus on the few apparent consistencies between archaeology and the book of Joshua. For the aggregate of evidence, William Dever, the dean of American biblical archaeologists, summarizes as follows:

First, of a total of sixteen sites clearly said by the Bible to have been destroyed, only three have produced archaeological evidence for a destruction ca. 1200 B.C.: Bethel, Lachish, and Hazor. This is virtually the same evidence adduced by Albright and Wright a generation ago; we can add only the newer data from Lachish for changing Albright's 1230 B.C. date to ca. 1175–50 B.C. Of the remaining thirteen sites, seven claimed by the Bible as Israelite destructions either were not even occupied in the period, or show no trace of a destruction. Finally, for six of these sixteen Biblical sites, archaeology is simply silent: they have not been positively located, or they have not yet been excavated sufficiently to yield evidence.

Second, if we look at the picture the other way around, of the twelve sites said by the Bible *not* to have been destroyed by the Israelites (mostly in Judges 1), five have been excavated and indeed show no destruction ca. 1200 B.C. The other six either have not been dug or have produced evidence that is inconclusive.

Finally, there are at least twelve other Late Bronze-Iron I sites of this horizon, either unidentified or not mentioned by name in the Bible. Of these, six were destroyed in all likelihood by the Philistines or "Sea Peoples," and one by the Egyptian Pharaoh Merneptah. The other six were destroyed by unknown agents—perhaps one or two of them by the Israelites, although there is no Biblical tradition to that effect and no way of ascertaining archaeologically the identity of the destroyers.

In conclusion, it may be stated confidently that the archaeological evidence today is overwhelmingly against the classic conquest model of Israelite origins, as envisioned in the book of Joshua and in much Biblical scholarship until recently.[59]

In a more recent summary of the discrepancies between archaeology and Joshua, Israeli archaeologist Nadav Na'aman confirms Dever's conclusion. Many sites, Na'aman points out, supposedly conquered or otherwise mentioned were not occupied in the Late Bronze Age. These include Heshbon, Arad, Ai, Jarmuth, Hebron, and Gibeon. The first four were not occupied for the entire second millennium BCE. The destruction of Late Bronze Age urban culture was gradual, not sudden, over a period of more than a hundred years. Joshua 10–11 makes it appear that Lachish and Hazor were destroyed at practically the same time. The evidence shows that Hazor was destroyed about mid-thirteenth century, and Lachish in the second half of the twelfth century. During the thirteenth and most of the twelfth centuries, Egyptian forces were in Canaan and left a marked Egyptian influence on the material culture of Palestine, especially in the eleventh century, but there is no mention of Egypt in the account of Joshua's conquest. Many cities were destroyed as Egypt pulled out of Palestine in the 1130s, including Bethshean, Megiddo, Ashdod, Tel Sera, and Tell el-Fer'ah. These sites, however, were destroyed much later than the supposed conquest, and they were all in the lowland, not the highland settled by the Israelites.[60] Moreover, John Peterson's archaeological analysis of levitical settlements in Joshua 21, showing that on the basis of the history of occupation at each site, the list could not have been compiled before the eighth century BCE, has been widely accepted.[61] As pointed out by many, the same is probably true of the most complete of the site lists, that of Judah in Joshua 15.

See also Dever, "Archaeology and the Israelite 'Conquest,' " in *ABD* 3:545-58; Coogan, "Archaeology and Biblical Studies," 19-32.

60. Nadav Na'aman, "The 'Conquest of Canaan' in the Book of Joshua and in History," in *From Nomadism to Monarchy: Archaeological and Historical Aspects of Early Israel*, ed. Israel Finkelstein and Nadav Na'aman (Jerusalem: Israel Exploration Society, 1994) 218-81, esp. 223.

61. John L. Peterson, "A Topographical Survey of the Levitical 'Cities' of Joshua 21 and 1 Chronicles 6: Studies on the Levites in Israelite Life and Religion" (Th.D. diss., Seabury-Western Theological Seminary, Evanston, 1977).

59. William G. Dever, "The Israelite Settlement in Canaan: New Archaeological Models," in *Recent Archaeological Discoveries and Biblical Research* (Seattle: University of Washington Press, 1990) 61; see also 37-84.

Reflections

1. There is probably nothing in the Bible more offensive to modern sensibilities than God's sanction of genocide against the Canaanites. In a discerning discussion of biblical theology in relation to natural theology, James Barr notes that proponents of a pure biblical theology have unfortunately been left either excusing this offense on false grounds—the Canaanites were wicked and deserved God's judgment; or the practice was common, and thus the Israelites were no worse than their neighbors; or the practice negated an ethic of plunder and exploitation—or ignoring it in the hope that most people would regard it as a minor matter or forget that it was in the Bible. It is probably not possible, concludes Barr, to accept the divine sanction of the practice and remain moral at the same time.[62]

An alternative apologetic looks at first more promising. This is to take a quasi-Marcionite approach. Genocide was commanded by the God of the Old Testament, whereas the God of the New Testament takes the opposite approach by incorporating the Gentiles, symbolized by the same seven "nations" of Canaanites anathematized in the Davidic scriptures, in the new covenant in Jesus Christ. This approach can emphasize changes in God or in history, analogous to progressive revelation, in which the old is replaced by the new. Or from a historical perspective, it can point out an apparent major difference between the Old Testament and the New Testament. The Old Testament presumes the integrity of a functioning nation or subset of humanity constituted under monarchic sovereignty by a distinctive law for life in a given territory, and thus of the wars that such integrity requires. In contrast, the New Testament repudiates that concept of Israel in favor of the notion of a community of faith, or trust, constituted not by a law but by mutual deference and love, ruled not by an earthly monarch schooled in the martial arts and existing to be served, but by an ecclesiastical collective representing the heavenly prince of peace, schooled in the arts of concord and goodwill and existing to serve.

Such an approach is no sooner stated than its flaws become apparent. While there is significant truth to the contrast, at the same time there is a great deal in the Old Testament that accords with what has just been said about the New Testament, as the New Testament writers themselves endlessly aver. By the same token, it would be a selective reading of the New Testament, indeed, to deny that one of its central concepts is the victory of the church through a great war sustained by God in fulfillment of the church's earliest Scriptures, the Old Testament. In that war, some are to die and others live, according to the inscrutable will of God. Moreover, the history of the church, for at least the last seventeen hundred years, shows that its concept of power and authority owes more to supposed Old Testament notions of privilege, sovereignty, and rule, than to the New Testament ideal of universal peace. Until quite recently all the major churches have been extremely powerful institutions, often with the force of states at their disposal, and in some cases they were states or virtual states in their own right. Even today, to state the obvious, much military havoc continues to be wrought in the name of the Prince of peace.

2. God's war against the Canaanites gives the interpreter more than the occasion for disavowing genocide. It prompts us to reflect on at least two major issues: the function of violence and the dynamics of genocide in our own world. Recognizing that social order takes on the character of the sacred, even within modern secular societies, René Girard observes in his broad comparative treatment of the subject that violence in the name of the sacred usually represents a reaction to a threat to social order, whether actual or perceived.[63] Since communities that define the sacred deal in symbolic realities, they typically project the threat onto collective scapegoats who, whether more or less justifiably, symbolize the threat. Scapegoat victims can be enemies, ritual victims, or surrogate victims from the community itself. All ultimately represent the threat and must be destroyed. In the end, the tendency is to see all disorder as external rather

---

62. James Barr, *Biblical Faith and Natural Theology* (Oxford: Clarendon, 1993) 207-21.
63. See René Girard, *Violence and the Sacred* (Baltimore: Johns Hopkins University Press, 1977). See also James G. Williams, *The Bible, Violence, and the Sacred: Liberation from the Myth of Sanctioned Violence* (San Francisco: HarperCollins, 1996).

than internal to the community. The common enemy must be sacrificed so the community can survive. The political opportunism made possible by sacred violence is evident. Without reference to the Bible, Girard lists four essentials to scapegoating: a crisis, the involvement of the divine in the selection of victims, a perceived difference between scapegoat and scapegoaters, and the sacrality of the king or other figurehead of sacred social order. All these apply to the narrative of Joshua, and they can be illustrated in our own world.

As for the dynamics of genocide, the role of the state or a comparable governing entity is essential. Ethnic cleansing is not a process that emerges in the "natural" interaction of people with one another. People are not angels, but left on their own they will not form grandiose concepts of false identity with which to divide the world into types whose moral characters form such opposites that one type must be destroyed by the other. This is a feat, to judge from known instances, to which people must be induced. The treatment of Jews pursued by the Nazi government in Central Europe is only the most notorious example of this rule; obviously many average people participated willingly in the persecution of Jews, but without the Nazi government there would have been no genocide. The same is true of the treatment of Tamils in Sri Lanka; of Serbs, Croats, and Bosnians in the former Yugoslavia; of Tutsis and in turn Hutus in Rwanda, and so on. These modern instances of ethnic cleansing represent not the inevitable struggle of one essential kind of humanity against another, as many of the participants themselves have been led to believe, but the result of government manipulation of popular insecurity, residual resentments, and latent or perceptible distinctions in the populace.

Without historical analysis, of course, this feature of the book of Joshua has been, and is, quite invisible. Even today it is possible for most readers of the Bible to believe that Canaanites and Israelites were actually completely different from each other.

3. The interpreter may prefer to bracket the political assumptions of the text and focus on the *esprit de corps* demonstrated by the guerrilla tactics of Israel's band of fighters. Their faith in the God who fought with them and for them, and their fear of what God might do if they were disobedient (see Joshua 7), led them to extraordinary commitment and feats of bravery. This is the spirit needed by any group set on facing daunting challenges and achieving difficult goals.

Joshua 6:22-27, Saving Rahab and Her Family

COMMENTARY

In a typical narrative frame, the end of the story of Jericho returns to its beginning. Joshua sends the same two men whom he sent in 2:1 into Jericho, to the house of Rahab. In what amounts to a compound conclusion (a small frame at the end of the large frame) the narrator refers in v. 25 yet again to the sending of the two men. The entire extended family is safely removed and given quarters outside the Israelite camp. This act brings the narrative as such to a close. The rest is summary and result, as is clear from the Hebrew syntax. In contrast to the rest of Jericho, which is put to the torch, Rahab and all her family with all their property are saved, to endure as aliens in the midst of Israel, a living testimony to the value of loyalty to Yahweh's and Israel's cause. Rahab and her family do not become Israelites, but still she contrasts with Achan as a model of loyalty in contrast to Achan's disloyalty. It may be assumed that in the narrative world of this text Rahab, whether a historical or legendary character, was able to discontinue her prostitution; even if not Israelite and not in line to receive a land grant, a household playing the role that hers does can expect relief from poverty and its degradations.

The NRSV translation "her family" in v. 25 is preferable to the NIV's "she"; Rahab's family rather than she alone may, in fact, be the subject of the verb "live," but in any case the sense pertains to Rahab's entire family, and not just to Rahab herself. However, the NRSV's "lived in Israel" is a seriously misleading anachronism. The NIV gets this right: Rahab's family "lives among the Israelites." This is the meaning of the Hebrew expression "in the midst of" (בקרב *bĕqereb*) here, which occurs also in 13:13 and 16:10 with reference to Canaanites. As shown by its translation of the latter two passages, the NRSV takes "Israel" to be a territory, equivalent to the expression "land of Israel"; neither that expression nor its sense occurs in Joshua. "Israel" here means the populace under tribal heads subjected to the house of David.

The entire narrative concerning Jericho concludes with the best clue to its significance in the first place. Joshua puts a curse on anyone who dares to rebuild Jericho (v. 26)—and someone does. Rebuilding Jericho does not mean just residing there, as some apparently do in the interim (18:21; Judg 3:13; 2 Sam 10:5), but refortifying it as a center of power. In the days of Ahab, long before Josiah, Hiel rebuilt Jericho, and in fulfillment of Joshua's curse it cost him two sons (1 Kgs 16:34; reported in the LXX of Josh 6:26). Whether the sons died as intentional sacrifices to the rebuilding or in some other way is disputed. The text is ambiguous in this regard. The main reason for believing that sacrifice was the cause of their deaths is the convention of guaranteeing such an undertaking by child sacrifice. The poetic character of Joshua's curse may suggest the use of a ritual formula. Whether or not a rite of child sacrifice was involved, the death of Hiel's two sons answers to the saving of Rahab and her family; more important, it provides a

final allusion to Passover in this section. The prescription for the Passover meal in Exod 13:1-16 is framed by references to the sacrifice of all firstborn males, with children to be redeemed (13:1-2, 11-16), and the Passover law in Deuteronomy 16 is immediately preceded by the deuteronomistic equivalent of the same law of sacrifice (Deut 15:19-23). The sacrifice of the firstborn, of course, duplicates the devastating slaughter of the firstborn of Pharaoh and the rest of the Egyptians on Passover night. It can be no accident that the deuteronomistic historian brings his grand account of the first Passover in the promised land to a conclusion by referring to the fitting death of the firstborn sons of the rebuilder of Jericho. Like all the onetime kings of Canaan, he is no better than Pharaoh and deserves the same fate (see Deut 7:17-24), as does anyone who might be tempted to follow his example by trying to establish an independent center of power.

The final line of this section summarizes the entire story, beginning with the commissioning of Joshua (1:5). Joshua's success in the miraculous crossing of the Jordan and capture of Jericho demonstrates that Yahweh stands behind him—or before him. Joshua's fame reaches the entire land. The Hebrew for "fame" (שמע *šōmaʿ*) means literally "what was heard" about him. The phrase recalls one of the main themes of the exodus: When Yahweh brought Israel out of Egypt with miraculous shows of power, kings trembled in fear and prepared to resist. The implications of Yahweh's power on Joshua's behalf are the same. Having heard about Joshua, the fearful kings combine forces to attempt to repulse the arrogant expropriator and his pretentious God (9:1). Of course, failure and weakness can produce a comparable fame and embolden opponents (see 7:8-9).

REFLECTIONS

Joshua's unconditional good fortune and victory suggest that Yahweh was "with him," as the narrator categorically states (6:27). This continues the emphasis of Josh 1:5, 9, "I will be with you . . . Yahweh is with you." Here the statement looks forward more than backward. However, without the benefit of lengthy hindsight, to equate blessing with righteousness and success with God's favor constitutes an arrogant audacity. A common prophetic theme in the Bible is how often the confidence of those who attribute their success to God's favor turns out to be premature. As history unfolds, sooner or later apparent blessing turns into wretched curse, as God turns the tables on the wealthy, the self-confident, and the self-assured, whose prosperity and accomplishments prove to be delusions. The deuteronomist, a notoriously unequivocal champion of God's justice, knows that this is true as long as God's justice prevails and is manifest.

From a prophetic perspective, the deuteronomistic writer realizes that despite Joshua's success there is no way to indicate with certainty without the passage of narrative time that God was, indeed, with Joshua. Thus the writer juxtaposed this claim with a curse, or forecast, by Joshua that later—much later—comes true. Together, curse and fulfillment supply the necessary proof, once the hearer of this part of the story hears what happens to Hiel in the time of Ahab. Of course, it is likely that the writer included this prophetic curse precisely because hearers were already familiar with the fate of Hiel. The writer was not content to allow the conquest of Jericho, betokening the conquest of Canaan, the very foundation of the house of David's later distinction, to satisfy the need for the prophetic perspective of time, because the later reconquest of the land is just what was at issue. Joshua captured the land, and David ruled it, but whether God really was with Joshua and David and, therefore, was to be with the writer's contemporary, Josiah, and give to him the rule of the land is not yet proven, because at the time the writer wrote, Josiah had not yet completed the reconquest.

Thus the brief notice that "the LORD was with Joshua" (6:27 NRSV), placed as it is immediately following Joshua's foretelling of the future, evidences the deuteronomist's awareness that making theological pronouncements based on ostensible success but without the benefit of the history God still has in store is not only a risk, but vain presumption. Of course, the deuteronomist himself nevertheless ends up being presumptuous: He crafts a narrative proof, but the narrative goes on and on. There is history yet to follow, not just the fulfillment of Joshua's curse, and not just the reign of Josiah himself. From the prophetic perspective, history was not over, and it is still not over. God continues to reign and to shape history to accomplish God's just will; hence theological presumption grounded in success and prosperity remains as perilous as ever.

JOSHUA 7:1–8:29, THE DESTRUCTION OF ACHAN AND AI

COMMENTARY

The story of the capture and destruction of Ai is immediately related to the preceding story of the capture and destruction of Jericho by means of a similar beginning, in which Joshua sends men to spy out the land (2:1; 7:2), and a similar ending, in which a primary site is given an etymology related to a heap of stones (Gilgal in 4:7, 20; 5:9; Jericho is not a heap of stones because it was rebuilt by Hiel). Jericho and Gilgal play a central role in each story: Achan hides spoil from Jericho in the camp in Gilgal. More important, the story of Ai mirrors the story of Jericho in that both highlight an individual, in one case, Rahab, in the other, Achan. The two individuals are contrasted. Rahab is loyal to the Israelite cause; Achan is disloyal to the same cause. Moreover, the two stories are linked through the ḥērem at Jericho, the dedication of every living thing and all material goods to Yahweh. Rahab is spared from the application of that dedication, and Achan is snared for violating it. In other words, the loyal Canaanite is included and the disloyal Israelite is excluded. This correspondence alone is the basis for the integration of over half the narrative of conquest in the book of Joshua (chaps. 2–8).

Indeed, the correspondence extends to the following major episode as well, in chaps. 9–10 (8:30-35 is to be bracketed as a later addition). The following episode must be brought into the discussion of the present section. Joshua's campaign to the south in chap. 9 begins with the attempt of the Canaanite kings to band together to defend themselves. The men of Gibeon decide not to join their coalition and instead, at the risk of getting themselves dedicated to Yahweh, trek to Gilgal and trick Joshua into making a compact with them. Having escaped dedication to Yahweh, the Gibeonites submit to Joshua as servants of the central altar of Yahweh, "in the place that he should choose" (9:27; cf. Deut 12:2-5). The story of the Gibeonites, like the stories of Rahab and Achan, lays the groundwork for the related battle account. Joshua comes to the rescue of the Gibeonites when they are attacked by five Amorite kings in the Canaanite alliance, led by the king of Jerusalem. Joshua kills the five kings and captures and dedicates most of their towns and others (except Jerusalem, left for David to capture).

The Gibeonites are Canaanites (Hivites). The inclusion of the Gibeonites parallels the inclusion of Rahab and her family, forming a frame around the story of the exclusion of Achan (note the tie between 6:27 and 9:1, immediately surrounding the story of Achan and Ai). Together these three stories comprise over three-quarters of the narrative of conquest (chaps. 2–10). As a set they make this one point: Those who submit may be saved and included, while those who rebel will be excluded and exterminated. It is now widely recognized that this point provides a counterpoint to the ostensible premise of the conquest according to the law of dedication, which posits that for the sake of all Israelites, all Canaanites are to be exterminated. Thus the conquest narrative makes two conflicting points at once. The first point is that as "nations" the Canaanites and the Israelites are implacable and irreconcilable opponents without exception, the Canaanites to be eradicated and the Israelites to be delivered. The second point, or counterpoint, is that exceptions are possible: Canaanites may find a placable reception, and Israelites can be eradicated.

Point and counterpoint may not seem consistent with each other, but both are consistent with Josiah's goal of reconquering and ruling Israel as efficiently as possible. The first point applies mainly to the "kings" of Canaan and their forces, claimants to autonomous sovereignty in their own spheres. The narrative allows for no exception to these and at the end drives home the point by listing by locality, or jurisdiction, all thirty-one kings eradicated (12:7-24). The counterpoint applies to the indebted and intimidated commoners among the Canaanites, the erstwhile subjects and clients of these kings. For these, loyalty and submission may sometimes forestall eradication, providing a basis for the corvée, or statute servitude (NRSV and NIV, "forced labor"), of Canaanites remaining in Israelite territory at the conclusion of Joshua's campaigns of conquest (see 16:10; 17:13; Deut 20:11; Judg 1:28, 30, 33, 35; 1 Kgs 9:20-21; cf. Deut 20:16). Thus the Deuteronomistic History, like the Prophets in general, makes use of two distinctions at once, without either taking precedence, a quasi-ethnic, or "national," distinction and a quasi-socioeconomic, or "class," distinction.

The intersection of the two distinctions may be best represented by the conflicting treatments of Canaanites in Joshua. Most Canaanites are slaughtered, the narrative implies. Many others are subjected to corvée slavery; the Israelites treat them as slaves in the same manner as the Israelites were treated as slaves in Egypt. The latter correspondence seems not to mean much to the deuteronomist, even though he must have known that the slavery described in Exod 1:11-14 was corvée servitude. As previously shown, the deuteronomist thought of Israel's slavery in Egypt as debt slavery rather than corvée (see Commentary on 2:1–6:27). Israel's enslavement of Canaanites represents mainly the fulfillment of Noah's curse of Canaan in the foundational Davidic history of Israel, the J strand. The Gibeonites have a privileged form of corvée duty imposed on them when they submit to becoming slaves of the central shrine of Yahweh. A few Canaanites may be delivered outright, and these are represented by Rahab, whose family has palpably been, or is liable to be, reduced to debt slavery. The narrative, therefore, focuses particular attention on those Canaanites who, in terms of fundamental deuteronomistic ideals, look like Israelites—slaves serving Yahweh—and are, therefore, treated as such and are saved. The message seems to be that "Canaanites" looking for mercy had better have a demonstrable grasp of Josiah's program of debt remission, promulgated from Yahweh's altar in Jerusalem. Thus the pattern in which the two main points of Joshua intersect suggests not contradiction, but rather no more tension than is inherent in the policies of Josiah they are meant to reflect.

It is now possible to see that the story of the fall of Ai represents more than a temporary setback followed by one more step forward in Joshua's unstoppable conquest, or the deserved punishment of a man who disobeyed the word of the Lord—or, in terms of classical American liberalism, the much less condonable punishment of his innocent family. While it is important to look at the story of Achan and Ai in further detail, it is equally important to realize that it does not, and as such never did, stand in isolation. Nevertheless, like the stories of Rahab, the crossing of the Jordan, and probably the fall of Jericho, the story of Ai seems to be based in part on a separate folk narrative, reflecting outlaw or guerrilla tactics of just the kind that Josiah must have had to neutralize or co-opt in order to prevent their being used against him.

The name "Ai" means "ruin" (תל *tēl*), and a ruin it was, whether in the Late Bronze Age of the exodus or the Late Iron Age of Josiah. Two thousand years before Josiah, in the Early Bronze Age, Ai had been a significant highland town. Between then and the time of Josiah, however, the site had been settled as an unwalled village for only about a century and a half, during the Early Iron Age. By the time of Saul and David, it had fallen into desuetude. Ai lies not far from Bethel, with which it is clearly associated in the mind of the narrator (7:2; 8:17). It is likely that Ai symbolically stood in part for Bethel and its cult, loathed by the deuteronomists.[64] The

present story explains how Ai came to be a ruin, as Bethel would in the time of Josiah. It is thus one of the many etiologies in Joshua— i.e., stories that explain some notable feature of the landscape.

In the case of Ai, there are two such features, described in 8:28-29. The first is the ruin of the supposed town, which Joshua reduces to a "perpetual devastated ruin" that exists "to this day" (8:28). Here the Hebrew word for "ruin" is *tēl*. Even today the word "tel" is used to describe mounds artificially built up through centuries of human settlement at a site. Such tells dot the landscape throughout the Near East. Indeed, the present-day Aramaic name for Ai is et-Tell, "the tell." The second etiology is the one that ties this story to the story of Jericho. This etiology actually occurs twice. The first time is when the Israelites raise over Achan's corpse "a great heap of stones to this day" (7:26). The second time is when the king of Ai is captured alive and executed and his corpse exposed until it is deposited at the entrance to what is left of Ai and covered with "a great heap of stones to this day" (8:29). The word for "heap" (גל *gal*) is the same as in "Gilgal," associated with its two heaps of stones. (The name "Gilgal" results from a regular transformation of the reduplicated form גלגל [*galgal*], "stone heap" or "heaps.") Achan's crime occurs in the camp in Gilgal. Thus the same etiology applies to Achan and the king of Ai; its significance cannot be missed. The two etiologies for Ai at the end of the story are themselves linked by a pun on the word *tēl*, since the word for "hanging" the king's corpse on a tree in order to expose it is תלא (*tālā*; see 10:26; Deut 21:22-23).

Like the story of Jericho, the story of Ai is a story within a story. The two attacks on Ai, the first a failure and the second a success, enclose the story of the discovery and execution of Achan, which turns failure into success. However, since Achan is fully identified at the outset (7:1), the failed attack is itself framed by the Achan story, which thereby is shown to be equal in significance to the fall of Ai, just as Rahab's story is as significant as the fall of Jericho.

There are two important parallels to the story of the fall of Ai. One is the battle between the Benjaminites and Israelites at Gibeah in

---

64. This suggestion has nothing to do with the very unlikely theory still proposed by some scholars that the destruction of Ai, described in Joshua 8 as Late Bronze Age history, actually applied to Bethel instead, which, unlike Ai, was destroyed at the end of the Bronze Age, according to excavators. In this view, the account of the fall of Bethel became secondarily attached to the ruin at Ai, as over time Bethel was rebuilt and Ai abandoned. For the problems surrounding the interpretation of the supposed Late Bronze destruction of Bethel, see William G. Dever, "Beitin, Tell," *ABD* 1:651-52.

Judges 20. There the Benjaminites play the role of the men of Ai. The Israelites attack the Benjaminites twice and are put to rout, as in the story of Ai. The Israelites appeal to Yahweh, and when Yahweh indicates support, they prepare the same ruse as at Ai. One division lies in ambush. The other draws the Benjaminites out of the town, allowing the first to put the town to the torch. Seeing the town on fire, the Benjaminites retreat and are cut down in flight by the recombined Israelite forces. The two stories have nearly identical plots. One may be based on the other, but it is more likely that they are two exemplars of a common folk narrative of tribal or brigand warfare.

The first parallel does not include an Achan. The men of Gibeah have committed a great wrong, but their story does not mesh with the story of the battle, as Achan's does. For the combined plots, it is necessary to look at a second parallel. This is the story in Deut 1:9-45, which summarizes events in Numbers 13–14. This is an important story, because it lays the basis for the conquest under Joshua rather than Moses (Deut 1:37-40). Moses orders the Israelites to take the land, starting with the Amorites in the highland. They hesitate and appeal for a reconnoitering. The spies bring a favorable report, but out of fear they still refuse to attack. Yahweh punishes their disobedience: They shall die in the desert without ever entering the land, and Joshua will lead the next generation in taking the land. When they hear this, they change their minds and are ready to attack. Yahweh orders them not to, but they disobey once again and attack anyway. They are routed "as far as Hormah," the very town named for the *ḥērem* the Israelites are supposed to inflict (Num 21:2-3).

This story parallels the first half of the Ai story. The great wrong committed by Achan is paralleled by the disobedience of all the Israelites. As a result, the attack, when finally made, is a failure. The attack will succeed only when the crime is punished: An entire generation must die in the desert, and only then will Joshua's attack succeed. With respect to this story at the beginning of the Deuteronomistic History, which is followed by the several examples of successful Yahweh-ordered dispossessions (Deut 2:1–3:17), the parallel to the second half of the Ai story is

nothing other than the whole of the conquest under Joshua. The story of Ai has immense resonances, indeed.

It is not surprising that Achan plays the same role as all the Israelites in the foundational story in Deuteronomy 1, for a striking aspect of the Ai story is the assumption of collective punishment. One person's sin arouses God's wrath against the entire nation (7:11, 20). Put in terms of Josiah's program, a single violation of the reform law is tantamount to their wholesale violation. The term used in 7:1 for Achan's transgression, translated "broke faith" (מעל *māʿal*), is used elsewhere in the book of Joshua only in chap. 22, where it refers to the alleged violation of the fundamental law of cult centralization (22:16, 20, 22, 31). The narrative thus reflects not only the collective perspective of social solidarity and community responsibility, but also the theoretical extremism of Joshua's program of centralization and reconquest, enforced through the terror of collective guilt investigated by means of a judicial lottery.

Joshua's reform calls for a highly regimented society, what we might term today a police state. Josiah's plan, probably based on earlier tradition, is to organize the state magistry down to supervised units of ten (Deut 1:9-18), in which one member could easily spy on another. Such small and rationally demarcated surveillance cells could not always correspond to households or clans, and probably were intentionally designed not to. Within households, family members were required to inform on each other (Deut 13:6-11), in a militant undermining of the patriarchal household consonant with other components of Josiah's law, which tended to isolate individuals from their lineal networks of aid and support in the process of undermining patriarchal households in order to strengthen the power of the monarchy.

It is important to grasp this feature of Josiah's reform, which is evident in the laws in Deuteronomy (Deuteronomy 12–26) and has received considerable scholarly attention. The most important households under Josiah's power would have functioned as the magistrates of the realm, judging cases coming before them as they deemed appropriate. The mere publication of a law like Josiah's served to curtail the power of this class of patriarchs, regardless of what was in that law. When the law prescribes that every tenth person is to be a magistrate (Deut 1:15), then clearly the power of any one of them is circumscribed. The basic political conflict in most pre-industrial societies pitted the central power against peripheral powers. Peripheral powers came in many forms. The most common included rival claimants to the throne: landed aristocrats or great nobles, paramilitary commanders, regional warlords or outlaws (anyone beyond the law of the realm), and local saints, alive or dead, who claimed a separate power and authority. Beyond such prominent potential opponents, in a more general way every head of household in the realm represented an alternative power and authority, and Josiah was not the first monarch bent on centralizing authority and power in such a way as to curb the authority and power of every male head of household subject to his jurisdiction.

❖   ❖   ❖   ❖

EXCURSUS: DEUTERONOMISTIC REPRESSION OF PATRIARCHAL AUTHORITY

Like the laws centralizing the cult and remitting debts after seven years, those designed to curb the authority and prerogatives of patriarchal heads represented a fundamental departure from customary practice if not customary ideals. These laws appear mostly in the latter part of the collection of Moses' laws, mostly in Deuteronomy 19–25, but in some instances the same thrust is evident in earlier laws. A good example of how radical such legislation can be appears as a corollary of the law of the sole cult: "If your brother, son, daughter, wife, or kin entices you in secret with the words, 'Let us go and serve others gods' . . . you shall not yield to him or listen to him, nor shall your eye pity him, nor shall you spare him, nor shall you conceal him; but you shall kill him" (Deut 13:6-9 author's trans.). The patriarchal head of household, in other words, has lost the right to protect his kin from the state's ruling.

In an analysis of family transgressions in Deuteronomy carrying the death penalty, Stulman has shown that deuteronomistic legislation tends to limit the power of fathers and husbands and consolidate those powers in local tribunals under state authority, all under the jurisdiction of the central shrine (Deut 17:8-13).[65] The state—that is, the Davidic Temple and court—restricts the power of the male head of household by obligating the state to act against family wrongs, by involving town elders in the legal process, and by requiring punishment to be executed in public at the town gate. The household patriarch is no longer the final authority in his own household. As with many parallel examples, this centralizing state attempts to regulate sexual matters, like virginity, adultery, and incest, in the interests of controlling the families and their heads. The laws may seem to confirm the prerogatives of town elders, but this is unlikely to be the case; at the very beginning of the history, the basis of a nationalized and regimented judiciary exercised through local authorities is laid down (Deut 1:9-18; 16:18-20), and in many cases described in Deuteronomy, the scope of the elders' rulings is significantly reduced.

These findings confirm a similar study by Steinberg, who concluded that the laws in Deuteronomy 19–25 posit increased centralized control over family matters.[66] By supporting the nuclear family at the expense of the extended family, these laws tend

---

65. Louis Stulman, "Sex and Familial Crimes in the D Code: A Witness to Mores in Transition," *JSOT* 53 (1992) 47-63.

66. Naomi Steinberg, "The Deuteronomic Law Code and the Politics of State Centralization," in *The Bible and the Politics of Exegesis,* ed. David Jobling, Peggy L. Day, and Gerald T. Sheppard (Cleveland: Pilgrim, 1991) 161-70.

to subvert the venerable kinship-based social system in favor of government oversight through councils of regulated town and village elders. It is often noticed that these laws help to preserve the nuclear family by limiting the power of men and creating rights for women. The deuteronomist, however, is not interested in the rights of women for their own sake, but for the sake of the nuclear family, which is more important than the individual. In order to safeguard these new rights, legal decisions affecting the nuclear family are taken out of the hands of the father or husband and given to the town elders, who are often beholden to set orders. This departure from custom can be seen by comparing Exod 22:16-17 with Deut 22:28-29. Both texts deal with the case of a man who has intercourse with a virgin who is not engaged. In Exodus, a bride-price is negotiated between the man and the woman's father, and her father decides whether she is to marry the man. In Deuteronomy, the bride-price is fixed at fifty shekels of silver, marriage is required, and no divorce is allowed; the woman's father is not even mentioned. Nowadays, such legislation might be called an invasion of privacy, and that is certainly the way it would have been experienced by householding men under Josiah's rule.

There are many such laws in Deuteronomy. Some involve routine attempts at state imposition, such as regulating blood revenge instead of allowing it to run rampant as an excuse for falling into factions and gathering private forces among families and clans (Deut 19:1-13) or preventing a man's preference for one wife over another from overriding the rights of primogeniture for both the firstborn son and his mother (Deut 21:15-17). Other laws are much less expected. An alien woman captured in battle and then married may not later be sold as a slave (Deut 21:10-14). A father and mother may discipline a defiant son, but neither may kill him, as was the accepted custom (Exod 21:15, 17). They must turn him over to the town elders, or magistrates, at the gate and together make public proclamation of their complaint; the elders then would arrange for the public execution of the son by the men of the town, presumably after satisfying themselves that the case is valid. A man who charges that his bride was not a virgin must present his case, together with evidence collected by the father and the mother of the bride, to the town elders rather than settling the matter in private. If the case goes against the accuser, he is to be fined a hundred shekels of silver and may never divorce the woman. If his case is sustained, she is to be stoned to death at the door of her father's house by the men of the town rather than by her father (Deut 22:13-21). If a man has intercourse with a married woman, both are stoned to death; neither the woman's husband nor her father or brothers may save her (Deut 22:22). The law of levirate marriage may seem to be an exception (Deut 25:5-10), but it, too, is designed primarily to shift the emphasis from the extended family to the nuclear family by keeping the property of the dead man within the immediate family and by ensuring that later offspring born to his wife and brother bear the dead man's name and provide support to the widow in her old age. If a brother refuses, the widow initiates legal action against him before the elders, who supervise a rite of spitting and humiliation, so that the brother's shame is sure to be public "throughout Israel" (see Commentary on Josh 17:1-13).[67]

67. Tikva Frymer-Kensky, "Deuteronomy," in *The Women's Bible Commentary*, ed. Carol A. Newsom and Sharon H. Ringe (Louisville: Westminster/John Knox, 1992) 52-62.

As with the law of debt remission, it is important to understand the deuteronomistic repression of patriarchal authority for the sake of the monarch, because it is a part of the portrayal of Joshua. This connection with Joshua goes well beyond the provision of cities of refuge, for example (Joshua 20; cf. Deut 19:1-13). Joshua represents the single ruler at the head of a united Israel. One individual leads the conquest. In the account of the conquest and distribution of land, all references to managing the competing and conflicting interests of particular "tribes" and their heads are dispensed with (cf. Judges 4–5). Assuming that references to Eleazar the priest are not deuteronomistic, all mention of other collaborating or competing chiefs, of dependable or jealous chiefs, or of lieutenants or aids is suppressed. All these, it might be expected, would be essential to an account of a campaign like Joshua's, but they are missing. Just as Rahab and her indebted family are integral to the first major narrative in Joshua, so also it is no accident that Achan and his family are integral to the second narrative, the conquest of Ai. Just as Rahab's story illustrates the deliverance of the debt slave, so also Achan's story illustrates the authority and power of the monarch over local patriarchs, even if the patriarch, like Achan, belongs to the same "tribe" as the monarch. As Joshua narrows his probe by lot through tribes, clans, households, and individuals in search of the man who violated the law of ḥērem, the detailing of Achan's social location points up his social isolation. No one steps forward to take Achan's side, to protect him or save him, or to help him hide or escape. The entire "nation" unanimously joins the monarch in the pitiless eradication of lawlessness in the person of this patriarch—and his nuclear family (strangely, his wife is not mentioned). This is more than an expression of corps solidarity. It is an epitome of the potency and command projected in Josiah's reform.

Besides the guilt of the isolated and vulnerable Achan, Israel's collective guilt is the narrative version of the categorical rhetoric of the laws themselves. As in the case of the two seemingly contradictory principles explained above, the assumption of an absolute law must be weighed against exceptions. This narrative immediately declares an exception: No sooner is Achan executed than Yahweh gives the Israelites permission to keep the spoil of Ai (8:2, 27), just as they spared Rahab.

Achan also plays a significant role in the emergence of the house of David. Achan's violation of ḥērem finds its later echo in Saul's violation of ḥērem, especially since both take place in Gilgal (1 Sam 15:10-33). Saul's kingship was revoked for his disobedience at Gilgal (1 Sam 13:7-14) for having made a sacrifice against orders from Samuel while the Philistines were camped "east of Beth-aven," thus not far from Ai (Josh 7:2; 1 Sam 13:5).[68] Saul was not executed right away for his crimes, but his death and the death of his son and heir Jonathan in battle against the Philistines are regarded as due punishment for failing to kill the king of the Amalekites as Joshua had killed the king of Ai (1 Sam 28:15-19).

A few further details require comment. The initial proposal that only a small force would be needed to take Ai is ironic (7:3). The proposal makes clear that the spies trust Yahweh and are ready to rely on Yahweh's strength. However, they are unaware that Yahweh is angry, as the narrator has openly stated. The attack on Ai is doomed from the start, trust or not. The term "thousand" in military contexts like this probably does not mean "a thousand," but a much smaller number. What number it does mean is uncertain and was presumably variable. One suggestion is that the "thousand" (אלף 'elep) is the fighting unit of the "clan" (משפחה mišpāḥâ), the putative social unit above the extended household. A likely parallel has been found in the Mari letters (see Commentary on 5:13–6:21), in which the word for "thousand" also is used for a clan unit.[69]

Joshua's lament (7:7-9) concludes with an argument popular in prayers of complaint, the most common form of prayer in the Bible (e.g., Pss 74:10, 18; 79:9; 83:4, 16, 18; 106:8; 109:21; 143:11). "When the Canaanites have cut off our name," he asks, "what are you going to do to restore your name?" Petitioners frequently remind God of the risk of God's being mocked as powerless if those ready to acknowledge God's help suffer great harm. Joshua tears his clothes as he does in Num 14:6, but there the appeal is to the people rather than to God. Here Joshua's appeal

---

68. For these and further parallels between Achan and Saul, see Michael D. Coogan, "Joshua," in *The New Jerome Biblical Commentary*, ed. Raymond E. Brown, Joseph A. Fitzmyer, and Roland E. Murphy (Englewood Cliffs, N.J.: Prentice Hall, 1990) 117.

69. Abraham Malamat, "A Recently Discovered Word for 'Clan' in Mari and Its Hebrew Cognate," in *Solving Riddles and Untying Knots: Biblical, Epigraphic, and Semitic Studies in Honor of Jonas C. Greenfield*, ed. Ziony Zevit et al. (Winona Lake, Ind.: Eisenbrauns, 1995) 177-79.

to God is closer to that of Moses, his precursor in Deut 9:25-29.

Yahweh responds vehemently. Achan's sin is everyone's sin. The repetitive counts of the charge are driven home in a series of clauses joined with "also" (גם *gam*), repeated five times like a bass drum beat. This pounding accent has been left out of both the NRSV and the NIV translations (7:11). The measure-for-measure character of God's justice is evident: Because Israel has violated the *ḥērem*, they have become a *ḥērem*, until they purge the *ḥērem*, both the perpetrator and the goods stolen (7:12; cf. 7:25).

Joshua goes through the hierarchy of social units, from tribe to clan to household to the men of the household (גברים *gĕbārîm*, "men," 7:14, 18; the NRSV's "one" is gratuitous), apparently by lot. The closest parallel is 1 Sam 10:20-21, in which Saul, having been chosen by Yahweh to be king, is publicly selected by lot. The narrative makes the result of the process of selecting Achan known in advance. Therefore, the point of tracing the process step-by-step twice (7:14, 16-18) is not the suspense of discovering who did it, or even the sharpened resemblance between Achan and David's unruly adversary Saul, but the intense judicial urgency to get to the culprit, to zero in on him and deal with him. There is no trial, even by ordeal. Yahweh knows who did it (cf. 22:20-22), and the process allows what Yahweh knows to be dramatically revealed, a practice common to sacred violence. There is a thin line between doing God's will and engaging in a witch hunt. As part of the history behind Josiah's reform, the narrative resolves this ambiguity by demonstrating that the process leads to the truth. This makes the Achan story a judicial exemplar of the same magnitude as David's

self-condemnation for adultery and murder (2 Sam 12:1-15) or Solomon's solution to the case of the prostitute's son by using the discerning mind given to him by Yahweh (1 Kgs 3:3-28). When the lot falls on Achan, he is forced to confess. The parallel between "give glory to God" in 7:19 and the same phrase in John 9:24 is indicative: The man is known to be a sinner; the issue is getting him to admit it. The public process excludes the possibility that Achan's family may have informed on him, so they are guilty by association and accordingly suffer the same punishment of stoning, a form of both communal judicial responsibility and controlled mob violence.

Achan's name is taken as a pun on the word "trouble," for which the valley where Achan is executed is named, "Achor" (עכור *ʿākôr*). His name occurs as "Achar" in 1 Chr 2:7. The valley takes on a positive valence in Hos 2:17 and Isa 65:10.

Joshua's use of his lance (8:18, 26; NRSV, "sword"; NIV, "javelin") to signal the defeat of the town (not to launch the ambush) recalls Moses' holding high of his staff while Joshua, at his first appearance, defeated the Amalekites (Exod 17:8-13). Again a parallel from the Mari letters suggests an age-old practice or convention.[70] In the different textual traditions of 8:11-13, there is confusion over details, but the general picture is clear. The mention of Bethel in 8:17 is surprising; since it does not appear in the LXX, most take it to be secondary. Despite the proximity of Bethel to Ai, there is no reason for its mention other than the importance of Bethel to the deuteronomists. Hence it is impossible to tell whether it was one of the original historians who mentioned it or a late copyist.

---

70. Moshe Anbar, "La critique biblique à la lumière des Archives royales de Mari: Jos 8," *Bib* 75 (1994) 70-74.

Reflections

1. This lengthy passage plays collective responsibility off against individual responsibility. The killing of Achan's family does not take away from this point: Their fate is tied to his individual act, discovery, and punishment. The point is easy to see. As Joshua proceeds to make a conspicuous example of Achan, the culprit's fellow Israelites can breathe a sigh of relief that with his death the basic problem has been taken care of and things will now go well. Life turns out to be orderly and manageable, so long as people realize that the authority of the central power is absolute and, as indicated by success at the lottery, infallible. This is the nature of collective discipline under fire. Under such circumstances, in the face of perceived pressure, threat, and danger, it is more difficult than usual to assess the nature of the central power's authority. Where does it come from? How does it work? What does it want? How does it expect to get it? Sometimes it may be necessary not to question authority. However, people in authority almost always would prefer that their authority not be questioned. When disorder under their command can be reduced to a single person's wrongdoing, so much the better. If it takes blaming a particular group or class of people, that can be done, too, as long as a problem can be identified in such a way as to be eliminated when the guilty party is eliminated. This is why there is such a narrow gap between analyzing social problems as a matter of policy, on the one hand, and scapegoating, on the other hand.

2. Joshua's "lament" follows the form of a prayer of complaint, of which there are many biblical examples. One important feature of such complaints is that they were typically performed in public, as here, even when they concern primarily an individual. Job's complaint is another familiar example: Job cries out to God in the presence of his friends. Recently, the purposes of such performances have been analyzed.[71] The enemies are not always simply the well-to-do and powerful who make the psalmist suffer. They can be friends, neighbors, and even family members as well. Often plaintiffs can expect that their loud public prayer will be heard by their enemies. The plaintiff may thereby expose the enemies and gain protection from further harassment or may voice indictments or threats against the enemies without having to confront them directly or may issue harsh commands or advice to the enemies, in the hope of deterring or converting them. Such a practice makes the collective nature of biblical prayer evident and contrasts strongly with the modern sense that prayer is mainly private, especially if it is a complaint.

Like any ancient plaintiff, Joshua can expect to arouse the sympathy of the elders and through them of the entire "nation," for whom he prays in any case, and draw the community together into a tighter unit than before. Joshua's prayer is immediately answered, a somewhat rare occurrence with complaints in the Bible. Indeed, the rhetoric of complaint, which is probably much more familiar to church people in their private lives than in their worship lives, is mostly self-contained. The plea to Yahweh for a response tends to be simple, whereas the elaboration of the difficulties, charges, and instructions is voiced mainly to the overhearing community, where the cry may gradually work its effect. Yahweh's response begins in typical fashion: When the complaint concerns the nation, the fault usually lies with a collective enemy, even when the guilty party has been the nation itself. Having accused the nation of wrongdoing, however, Yahweh then orders a procedure for conspicuous public discovery and punishment.

Nowadays if a person in prayer dares to complain to God at all, the complaint is routinely voiced in solitary devotions as a personal matter between the individual and God. The rarity of individual public complaint in church is a measure not only of the commendable dignity and discretion that characterize modern well-to-do congregations, but also of the extent to which congregations have difficulty dealing with conflict openly. Modern congregants can be grateful if their lives are relatively free of the powerlessness, oppression, deceit, rancor, and anguish that afflicted the ancient suppliant and found expression in the open court, as it were, of public complaint. At the same time, disagreements, tensions, and conflict are a fact of modern congregational life, and little good comes from pretending otherwise. Congregants may want to consider regaining some of the communal integrity and mutual care in loving expressions of anger and frustration that seem to have existed in some biblical communities, while striving to avoid the hostility, backbiting, and self-righteousness that frequently seemed

71. Gerald T. Sheppard, " 'Enemies' and the Politics of Prayer in the Book of Psalms," in *The Bible and the Politics of Exegesis*, ed. David Jobling, Peggy L. Day, and Gerald T. Sheppard (Cleveland: Pilgrim, 1991) 61-82.

also to be included. Such care might be nurtured if prayerful complaints could be heard and respected in church.

There is no simple solution to the spiritual dilemma that openness and dignity can be difficult to reconcile. It is important to remember that the ancient cultic setting of judicial prayer is significantly different from the modern worship service. It may be that, following a discussion of needs and expectations and the formulation of a common understanding, a weekly prayer meeting would best serve for introducing prayerful complaints. It must also be remembered that while dignity is important, at the cost of communion among the faithful it is not a significant biblical value. The tendency of the Bible is for corporate reliance on the grace of God to make possible the openness that builds trust and to obviate individuals' struggle for dignity as crucial to self-worth.

JOSHUA 8:30-35, AN ALTAR ON MT. EBAL

COMMENTARY

Joshua makes an unexpected jump to and from Mt. Ebal, which lies just north of Shechem in the center of the northern highland, a long day's march each way, of which there is no mention. There he publishes the law of Moses by writing it on stones and reading it aloud, in its entirety, to the whole nation of Israel—men, women, children, and resident aliens—assembled on Mt. Ebal and Mt. Gerizim astride one of the most strategic passes in highland Canaan (in what by Josiah's time was the heart of Israel). This unopposed theatrical production supposedly takes place before the conquest of Canaan has scarcely begun; the book of Joshua posits no military campaign here at all (there is no king of Shechem listed in 12:9-24, and the only nearby town in that list is the last, Tirzah). Joshua does not reappear at Shechem until chap. 24, the last chapter, after his deuteronomistic farewell in chap. 23. This section thus comes as a sudden surprise and does not fit well with the surrounding narrative. The end of the Ai story flows smoothly into the beginning of the story of the alliance of the Canaanite kings and the covenant with the Gibeonites (8:29; 9:1-2; 10:1). This section is evidently not part of the main deuteronomistic narrative.

This widely held perception is based on more than intuition. The present section does not have a fixed place in the textual record. In the LXX, it appears after 9:1-2. In the fragments of the oldest known text of Joshua, 4QJosh[a] from the Hasmonean period (approximately 150–50 BCE), it is followed by the report of circumcision now found in 5:2-8 and evidently preceded by the crossing of the Jordan in Joshua 3–4, which might help to explain the similarities between 5:1 and 9:1-2. Whichever of the three attested placements of this section is the original one—if, indeed, there was an original placement—such textual differences in sequence, of which there are many in the Bible, often arise with sections whose positions are not fixed because of their secondary nature.[72] Moreover, this section is directly related to Deuteronomy 27 (with Deut 11:29-30) and Joshua 24, both of which also concern Shechem and themselves appear to be secondary to their contexts.

The affinities of this movable section are thus clear. Its significance is less so, but must depend in part on the role of Shechem. Shechem occurs seldom in the Deuteronomistic History. Besides the passage just mentioned and two incidental references in the town list of Manasseh (17:2, 7), Shechem figures in just six other places in the history, of which all except two are brief. However, together these show that Shechem laid claim to being one of the most important localities in highland Israel. Shechem is named as one of the towns of the Levites (21:21) and, much more important, the only town of refuge in the Israelite heartland (20:7). Another brief

---

72. Emanuel Tov, *Textual Criticism of the Hebrew Bible* (Minneapolis: Fortress, 1992) 339. Similarly, another suggested explanation for the sequence in 4QJosh[a] is that Josh 5:2-8, which also is a secondary addition, may have been placed after 8:30-35 following the battle of Ai.

mention (Judg 21:19) describes the main road north from Jerusalem and Bethel as the road to Shechem. The fourth mention (Judg 8:31; 9:1-57) is the lengthiest. It concerns the story of Abimelech of Shechem, said to have killed seventy of his brothers, induced the lords of Shechem to make him king, and ruled as a tyrant for three years, when, after he has foiled an attempted coup, a woman crushes his skull with a millstone while he is attacking the town of Thebez. For the Deuteronomistic History, next to the kings of Israel themselves and even more than Hiel of Jericho (Josh 6:26; 1 Kgs 16:24), Abimelech of Shechem serves as the plainest example of the dangers of letting an Israelite other than a Davidic king set himself up as an independent power.

This political significance of Shechem is confirmed by the final two references. Both occur in 1 Kings 12 and figure directly in the house of David's loss of Israel to a rival king. First, Solomon's heir, Rehoboam, goes to Shechem in order to get "all Israel" to make him king; all except the tribe of Judah spurn him and make Jeroboam their king instead (12:1-24; this treatment of Shechem has obvious similarities with the story of how Abimelech is made king). Then Jeroboam, now king of Israel, immediately rebuilds Shechem (cf. Hiel of Jericho) and resides there, making it the first capital of anti-Davidic Israel (1 Kgs 12:25). For the deuteronomist, there is no question that Jeroboam's rebuilding of Shechem both prefigures Hiel and echoes Abimelech, who is nothing but a useless bramble, as Jotham vividly proclaims (Judg 9:7-15) from the same Mt. Gerizim upon which half the Israelites are standing to hear the law of Moses in Josh 8:33-35, commencing with the law of Davidic centralization.

Shechem thus stands for the archrival power in Israel to the house of David. Shechem was destroyed by the Assyrians in the eighth century BCE, probably around the time of the fall of Samaria. It was shoddily reconstructed during the seventh century. Assyrian pottery styles suggest the domination of outsiders at that time. The irony is that, though secondary, this section of Joshua may fit the circumstances of Josiah's reform at least as well as the main narrative of Joshua. For Josiah, however, Shechem's importance would have been not its concentration of power, but its symbolic role as a historic political center in Israel.

Moreover, it is no accident that the two main texts dealing with Shechem and kingship describe something akin to an election of the king (Judg 9:6, 16; 1 Kgs 12:1, 20) and that Deuteronomy 27 and Joshua 24 both involve elements of a public covenanting ceremony. According to Judg 9:4, the god of Shechem was Baal-berith, "Lord of the covenant," perhaps known as El-berith, "God of the covenant."[73] Shechem was regarded as a covenant-making center. While this tradition clearly pre-dates Josiah—indeed, may go back as early as the Late Bronze Age—there is no reason to believe that the two additions to Joshua involving Shechem reflect the early history of Israel as such, any more than the folkloric elements on which the accounts of Joshua's battles in the main deuteronomistic narrative are partly based reflect the history of early Israel. While covenant-making forms were already ancient by the time of Josiah, the emphasis on covenant associated with Shechem in the OT is found exclusively in deuteronomistic texts, and for covenantal forms in the Deuteronomistic History one need look no further than common practice in the Neo-Assyrian period and later.

Deuteronomy 27 prescribes a ceremonial ratification of some facet of the deuteronomistic covenant under Moses, at a strategic location glaringly symbolic of both rebellion against Davidic rule and covenantal accord with it. Joshua 8:30-35 sees that ratification carried out, with Joshua in the role of Moses. Joshua 24:1-28, of a slightly different character, reiterates the ratification with a stress on the reincorporation of the putative tribes of Israel. The establishment of the shrine for Joseph's bones in Josh 24:32 may belong to the same set of additions. Recent study suggests that the particular form to which the covenantal elements in Deuteronomy 27 and Joshua 8 contribute is the sacred enactment of a land grant, akin to the Babylonian *kudurru*.[74] The typical land-grant ceremony included the setting up of a boundary stone, here represented by the stones on which the

73. G. Ernest Wright, *Shechem: The Biography of a Biblical City* (New York: McGraw-Hill, 1965) 133-37.
74. Andrew E. Hill, "The Ebal Ceremony as Hebrew Land Grant?" *JETS* 31 (1988) 399-406.

law is written; a description of the plot of land and the circumstances of its transfer (Deut 27:1-10); the witnesses present; and curses on violators of the grant (cf. Josh 8:17). If this comparison is correct, these two texts were inserted in order to supply a missing piece in the account of God's granting to the Israelites the land of the Canaanites. That missing piece is the public formalization of the grant, tied to Yahweh's basic judicial covenant with Israel (the deuteronomistic covenant).

If the first two texts (with Deut 11:29-30) relate in any way to Josiah's reform, they may reflect either an alternative, less dictatorial approach to the highland heartland of Israel, an approach not articulated in the main narrative, or a later stage in the reform, when forces of resistance aroused by the reform and organized around Shechem had to be simultaneously mastered and accommodated. It is striking that 8:30 describes the building of an altar, presumably a temporary central shrine that later was to be replaced by the Temple in Jerusalem. This represents a different concept of the central shrine from that of the main deuteronomistic narrative, which displays a vehement reaction to the building of an altar in Joshua 22 and makes no reference to an existing altar at Shechem. It is also noteworthy that resident aliens are mentioned in Joshua only in 8:33, 35 (cf. Deut 27:19) and 20:9. These were apparently socially and politically isolated and vulnerable non-natives who were not required to keep all the laws of Moses (see Deut 14:21), but who were expected to become clients of the house of David and its cult of Yahweh for the protection of their interests rather than of one of the organized alien groups planted by the Assyrians and coming partly under the jurisdiction of Bethel after the fall of Samaria (see Deut 1:16). The phrase that contrasts with "alien" in 8:33, "indigenous" (אזרח *'ezrāḥ*; NRSV and NIV, "citizen"), is a predominantly priestly term that occurs only here in the Deuteronomistic History.

The altar that Joshua builds harks back to the Tetrateuch. It is built, ostensibly in obedience to Deut 27:5-6, of rough stones, not hewn with tools of iron. This anachronistic reference to iron follows the rule in Exod 20:25, reflecting traditional tribal rather than state practice. It represents a concern

of little interest to the main deuteronomistic narrative, which describes the abundant use of dressed stones for building the Temple (1 Kgs 5:17; 7:9-12; cf. 6:7, which implies that there is a rule not against the use of iron tools but against hearing them being used at the building site). Most altars known from excavations at Israelite sites are made of hewn stones. The publication of law on plastered stones erected in a public place (Deut 27:2-4, 8) is also an activity of state and not a tribal custom. Joshua appears here as much in the guise of a monarch as he does in any other passage. Moreover, in having a "copy" of the law written, he fulfills the duty laid on the king in Deut 17:18. Joshua's copy is for public display rather than his private use, one more indication that this set of texts related to Shechem is secondary to the main Deuteronomistic History. After the blessings and curses are pronounced from the two mountains (cf. Deut 27:12-13), Joshua reads all the written blessings and curses, a standard part of ancient Near Eastern covenants, presumably here the same as those in Deut 28:1-68 (the curses in Deut 27:15-26 are not matched by blessings). The final confirmation that Joshua here plays the role of the king comes with the phrase "before all the assembly of Israel," which in the Deuteronomistic History occurs only in 1 Kgs 8:22, when Solomon, having just blessed "all the assembly of Israel" (1 Kgs 8:14), makes his prayer of dedication for the Temple (cf. Deut 31:30).

Joshua's altar received a great deal of renewed attention when an Iron I site that apparently included an altar and was used for cultic purposes was discovered on the slopes of Mt. Ebal in 1980. The excavator identified the site as probably Joshua's altar.[75] To others, such an identification made little sense. "Since the division of the land in Joshua is an ideal picture . . . the mere presence of premonarchic remains within the ideal tribal boundaries does not require their construction or use by the members of that tribe."[76]

---

75. Adam Zertal, "Has Joshua's Altar Been Found on Mount Ebal?" *BAR* 11 (1985) 26-43; "An Early Iron Age Cultic Site on Mount Ebal," *Tel Aviv* 13-14 (1986–87) 105-65.
76. Michael D. Coogan, "Archaeology and Biblical Studies," 27. For further, see Adam Zertal, "Ebal, Mount," *ABD* 2:255-58.

JOSHUA 9:1–10:43, DESTRUCTION TO THE SOUTH

OVERVIEW

With the destruction of Ai, the way lies open for the Israelites' wider assault in Canaan. So far the Deuteronomistic History has presented the conquest, which to this point has covered only a tiny part of the land, in terms of two attacks, one against Jericho and the other against Ai, construed as offensive actions on Joshua's initiative (2:1; 7:2), under Yahweh's orders (6:2-5; 8:1-2).[77] The conquest of the rest of the land is presented in terms of two wider campaigns, against kings to the south and kings to the north. Although still the populace is slaughtered, the focus shifts even more than before to the kings, whose role is also cast into profile by the Gibeonites, who are said to have no king.

These two campaigns are parallel in several ways. In both, Yahweh delivers a war oracle to Joshua ordering him to attack and assuring victory (10:8; 11:6); Joshua attacks the hostile kings and their armies by surprise (10:9; 11:7); Yahweh does battle on Israel's side (10:10-14; 11:8); and the Israelite force routs its foes (10:10, 14; 11:8). Then Joshua kills the salient kings and destroys their towns (10:16-39; 11:10-15). In each case, the narration concludes with an acclamatory summary of death and destruction (10:40-43; 11:16-20). These two narratives are construed as struggles first against highland opponents ("Amorites") in the south and then lowland opponents in the north, who use chariots and are joined by allies from all over Canaan. The difference between highland and lowland warfare was a reality, and Josiah had to succeed at both if he was to reconquer Israel. But the many parallels between the two accounts, and between them and stereotypical ancient Near Eastern campaign accounts, show that they are literary compositions rather than historical reports.[78]

In addition, both of these campaigns are construed as defensive actions against offensive alliances. The initiative for battle comes not from Joshua, but from the kings. Nevertheless, the kings are the pawns of Yahweh. Yahweh makes the kings too stubborn ("hardens their hearts") to yield submissively to Israel's takeover, in order to make sure that they can be dedicated and exterminated without mercy (11:20). Yahweh's act of provocation shifts the onus for the conquest onto the dispossessed rather than the usurper, while the ultimate justification for usurpation remains with the sovereign Yahweh, who, having granted the land of the supposedly powerful Canaanites to the supposedly weak Israelites, guarantees that the land is taken.

Yahweh thus grants the land, provokes its holders into aggression, contributes the main force in response, and orders that the opposing populace be annihilated. The decisive role played by Yahweh is one reason why the narratives of the battles per se in Joshua are as brief as they are, as was also the case with the paradigmatic battle against Jericho. The book of Joshua tells nothing like the elaborate detail and embellishments that characterize heroic descriptions of intrepid fighting and dying in the Homeric epics and comparable traditions. Not even particulars such as are found in more succinct women's songs, like those of Miriam (Exod 15:1-18; cf. Exod 15:20-21) or of Deborah (Judg 5:1-31), seem to figure much in these accounts. Instead, the campaign accounts are marked by the spare formulaic prose of scribal war diaries, royal campaign annals, and monarchic Egyptian "day books," which frequently put forth grandiose claims of victories achieved by the kings of the ancient Near East with the help of their gods, accounts rich only in stereotyped hyperbole.[79] This part of Joshua is interrupted

---

77. The MT and the LXX of Josh 9:3 show a variation between "what Joshua had done" and "what Yahweh had done."

78. K. Lawson Younger, *Ancient Conquest Accounts: A Study in Ancient Near Eastern and Biblical History Writing* (Sheffield: JSOT, 1990).

79. James K. Hoffmeier, "The Structure of Joshua 1–11 and the Annals of Thutmose III," in *Faith, Tradition, and History: Old Testament Historiography in Its Near Eastern Context,* ed. A. R. Millard, James Hoffmeier, and David W. Baker (Winona Lake, Ind.: Eisenbrauns, 1994) 165-79.

by varied detail only infrequently, as in the brief excerpt from the "Yashar" document, apparently an ancient collection of poems of diverse types (10:12-13; cf. 2 Sam 1:17-27; 1 Kgs 8:12-13).

The numerous great and petty kings who appear in the book of Joshua have suggested to many a picture of Canaanite society splintered by conflict and feud into myriad tiny city-states, with no overarching political organization and identity. This is the way Late Bronze Age Canaan is usually thought of, giving the book of Joshua the appearance of historical reliability. This picture has seemed to find confirmation in the Amarna letters, written by numerous rival rulers and governors to the Egyptian court at Thebes and Akhetaten during the fourteenth century BCE.

What sense does such a picture make for the time of Josiah, when supposedly political fragmentation was a thing of the past and the house of David and the kings of Israel had brought swaths of territory under their sovereignty for centuries? Of course, the kings of Israel were no longer in the picture, and in any case the success of these rulers in controlling territory varied greatly over the centuries. The maps of OT times showing homogeneous sovereignty are frequently deceptive in this regard, especially when a single map covers centuries rather than decades. The picture of society in the book of Joshua offers a poor match for the Amarna era. It has already been pointed out that the locales named in Joshua differ markedly from what is known of settlement at that time and that references to iron are a serious anachronism. Within roughly the bounds covered by the book of Joshua, the Amarna letters suggest altogether only a handful of kings or warlords at any one time, some controlling quite extensive areas, and not the thirty-three, including Sihon and Og, listed in Joshua 12 (Judg 1:7 refers to no less than seventy).

Moreover, the term "king" can refer to many levels and degrees of sovereignty, from the imperial monarch to the lord of a large town. The picture in Joshua is one of a peculiar uniformity, where each town has its own king. Such a picture would be a figment of imagination for any age, whatever the extent of its political fragmentation. It resembles the Homeric picture of the age of "kings," which,

like the book of Joshua, is an eighth- or seventh-century projection back to the Bronze Age. In Homer, "kings" are local lords and heads of households up against powerful but feuding local aristocracies striving to keep kingly prerogatives to a minimum. These kings must maintain their status "by might," like Odysseus's having to fight against the suitors. The picture of "kings" in Joshua is a negative idealization corresponding to the positive idealization of the twelve tribes of Israel as a uniformity.

There is little reason to look further than Josiah's reform for the source of these opposed idealizations. The opposition of "tribe" and "state" was a widespread and popular notion that by itself says nothing about time, place, and circumstance. The book of Joshua, however, as part of the Deuteronomistic History, gives this opposition a specific setting. In the context of Josiah's reform, the two "nations" represent antitheses. The "Israelite" populace under Josiah's rule are granted their traditional "tribal" identities in theory, opposed to "state" impositions and exactions by the likes of Canaanite "kings" or local and regional strongmen; in fact, these tribal identities are severely curtailed by the royal court's typical rationalizing of tribal policy and by the severe curtailment of patriarchal prerogatives represented by the deuteronomistic law of Moses.

In contrast, Josiah's opposition is embodied in the "kings" of the "Canaanite" peoples. These kings are nowhere described with qualities or actions, other than their plain opposition, which would justify their destruction. None is even named until Josh 10:3, and thereafter only the kings of Gezer, Hazor, and Madon are named; all the rest are nameless. They are given no family or extended household ties; as beneficiaries of commerce in the deuteronomistic conception, they are assumed to place money ahead of family ties, unlike "tribes." The destruction of the kings of Canaan is justified in the narrative, not by who they are or what they do, but simply by the claim of the divine territorial grant together with the categorical distinction of "tribe" versus "king" that permeates the narrative. The one person in the narrative who acts in any detail like a king—namely, Joshua—is, of course, never called a king. The "kings" as a lot are clones of the king of Jericho as the successor of Hiel. Like Hiel, they are strong-men who set up rival sovereignties and carve out rival jurisdictions, presumably once con-doned by Assyria and Egypt, who must be suppressed and when possible eliminated if Josiah's reform and reconquest are to suc-ceed. It is no accident that, according to the story, the Gibeonites, the foil to the kings of the south, live in a great town (10:2) but have no king (cf. 9:11).

Nowhere was this more the case than in the region of the Shephelah, or Judahite foothills to the west and southwest of Joshua's camp, and of the northern great valley under control of "kings" of the north. These two areas were of great strategic and economic importance in the late seventh century. Bringing them under the aegis of the house of David would repre-sent a major step toward assuring the submis-sion of the highland enclosed by them. Such a strategy was similar to the one David used to consolidate his power to the extent that he did. This strategy is probably the main reason why the deuteronomist can reduce the ac-count of Joshua's extensive conquest to the two campaigns in chaps. 10 and 11.

Joshua 9:1-27, Saving the Gibeonites

COMMENTARY

The construing of the conquest as defen-sive is brought to the fore through the story of the Gibeonites, which begins with this episode, nested within the story of hostili-ties with the Canaanite kings. For the main deuteronomistic narrative, the reaction of the kings in 9:1-2 must be to the destruction of Ai and its king. As the text stands, however, they could just as well be reacting to the threat to their sovereignties represented by Joshua's exhibition of Moses' law in Shechem in 8:30-35. But that passage is secondary, as explained above, and it would seem untidy first to focus attention on the hill country around Shechem and then to describe reactions far to the south or to the north of Shechem without mention-ing reactions in or around Shechem itself. Joshua attacks the five Amorite kings when they attack Gibeon; both attacks stem from the treaty between the Gibeonites and the Israelites.

Gibeon, which lay seven miles southwest of Ai and six miles northwest of Jerusalem, was not inhabited in the Late Bronze Age but in the time of David. It plays the role it does in Joshua for three reasons. First, it figured in the events surrounding David's rise to power against the house of Saul (2 Sam 2:12–3:1). Second, the house of David patronized the Gibeonites, who apparently already served as slaves of the cult of Yahweh, which David co-opted. Thus this story, for the deuteronomists at least, serves as the etiology of the Gibeon-ites' cult duty (9:24, 27; cf. 6:19; "the place that he should choose" is the central shrine in Jerusalem). Third, David used an attack by the rival house of Saul against the Gibeon-ites as his excuse to put to death the heirs of the erstwhile Israelite king (2 Sam 21:1-14; see Introduction). Thus David's avenging the Gibeonites echoes Joshua's defense of the Gibeonites against the Amorite kings (cf. Josh 9:18 with 2 Sam 21:2). Some have supposed that the later story served as the basis of the present story.[80]

The Gibeonites' story emphasizes their submission. They know, somehow, the law of ḥērem, which continues as a primary theme in the narrative, and its distinction between near and distant towns (Deut 20:10-18), and they decide to try to avoid being wiped out through an acquiescent ruse rather than resis-tance. Their ruse recalls Yahweh's care of the Israelites during their lengthy trek in Deut 8:4 and 29:5. Their deuteronomistic lines in 9:9-10 make them like Rahab, intimidated by the exodus and the killing of Sihon and Og (2:10), and they are saved by an oath, as was Rahab. The role of the "leaders of the congregation" or "assembly" marks a priestly addition to the story, as evident from priestly vocabulary in 9:15b, 17-21, from the way 9:22 follows on 9:16, and from the apparent

---

80. The tradition was that Gibeonites served in the Temple until at least the time of Josiah, if not in the Persian period as well. In 1 Chr 9:35-44, a Gibeonite genealogy follows immediately after the catalog of Temple servants. See Joseph Blenkinsopp, *Ezra–Nehemiah*, OTL (Philadelphia: Westminster, 1988) 90.

duplication between 9:17-21 and 9:22-27. Exactly what comes from the priestly writer is not entirely certain, but the reason for the addition seems clear. As far as the deuteronomist is concerned, the Gibeonites' ruse works because they pull it off, and they submit; Joshua is tricked, and once the covenant is sealed and corvée duty (Deut 20:11; cf. 29:11) is imposed on the Gibeonites, the matter is closed. The priestly writer, however, seems troubled by Joshua's responsibility and the possibility that Joshua himself failed to obey the law of Moses. The wrongdoing involved, therefore, is shifted to the "leaders of the congregation," whose oath, rather than Joshua's covenant, prevents the Israelites from dedicating the Gibeonites to death after discovering the ruse. It is probably the priestly writer who blames the "men" for not consulting Yahweh to avoid being tricked (9:14).

The NRSV's "live among us" (9:7, 16, 22) makes for a possible anachronism, as though Israelites live all around Gibeon. Like many features of the book of Joshua, this would fit the context of Josiah, but this time the translation is faulty. The NIV's translation, "live near us," is to be preferred.

REFLECTIONS

The Gibeonites are representatives of one of the indigenous "nations" in Joshua. These are the Gentiles, as they are later called on the basis of the Latin word for "nation." The book of Joshua is based in part on the sharp contrast between Israelite and Canaanite. In the New Testament, a similar contrast between Jew and Gentile plays an extremely significant role. The letters of Paul and the four Gospels make much of incorporating the Gentiles into the people of God. Although the history of how this came about is complex, one of the most important themes of the New Testament is this inclusion of outsiders within the new covenant in Jesus. Considering the book of Joshua, this is a striking development. It is possible to point to many clues in the Old Testament that this was God's intent all along, and Paul and the Gospels are quick to adduce the relevant passages from Scripture. The book of Joshua largely contradicts this point of view. Nevertheless, it is brought into service of it by pointing out the faith of Rahab and of the Israelites, since faith instead of circumcision became the new basis of belonging to the people of God.

The Gentile "nations" were traditionally said to be seven in number; this number refers to the lists of Canaanite nations that occur frequently in Joshua, even though only a few of these lists contain exactly seven nations. One of the great ironies of the Bible is that the Gentiles are conceived of in this way as belonging originally to the land of Canaan before the Israelites ever arrived. God first takes away the land of the "Gentiles," and then later incorporates them into the new "Israel." This stunning reversal imbues the New Testament, providing the core conviction behind some of its keenest polemic and most serene assurance.

No sooner did the church of both Jew and Gentile form, however, than it began drawing lines of demarcation and boundaries of its own for purposes of exclusion. Taking for granted our inclusion as "Gentiles," we perhaps assume too quickly that the problem of inclusion was resolved during the first centuries and is no longer relevant.

The basis on which Joshua accepted the Gibeonites clearly does not have to do with a principle of inclusion. But in relation to the New Testament it does raise the issue of the inclusion of the Gentiles (Hivites included) and points us toward an aspect of the New Testament that is too easily neglected: The New Testament favors the inclusion of those who have been excluded, and it does so to the remarkable extent of dispensing with the core institutions and values—the Temple and the law of Moses—that were important not only to the book of Joshua, but in the time of the early church played the primary role in defining what it meant to be Jewish as well. In the beginning, this issue represented a radical and threatening innovation (see Reflections at 3:1–4:18).

How might the church today express a similar commitment to inclusion? Some possible challenges that some churches have already taken on are dissolving denominational boundaries, dissolving national church boundaries, publicizing and instituting a commitment to diversity in the congregation to counteract the tendency toward congregational homogeneity, and welcoming the homeless into the church. In these and other ways, Christians can be challenged to renew the church's commitment to inclusion.

Joshua 10:1-43, Destruction of the Jerusalem Coalition

COMMENTARY

The campaign to the south sparked by Joshua's defense of Gibeon occurs in three stages. The first stage involves the attack against the five allied kings. This attack continues to feature Gibeon; in separate incidents, at Gibeon the Israelites slaughter the allied army, from Gibeon to Azekah Yahweh pommels the retreating enemy with giant hailstones, and at Gibeon the sun stands still, helping Israel against its enemies. But the spotlight of the campaign as such is first on a group of kings led by the king of Jerusalem, and then on a group of towns whose territories blanket the Shephelah and Judahite highland. In the second stage, Joshua pursues and executes the five kings. In the third stage, the towns of most of these kings, along with other towns, are dedicated and destroyed. The narrative structure of this third stage highlights the destruction of Gezer (10:33), which dominates the primary gateway to the Aijalon Valley and the road between the Philistine coast and the Benjaminite and northern Judahite hills around Jerusalem.

The five Amorite kings are organized by the king of Jerusalem. The relationship between Adoni-zedek and another king, Adoni-bezek, probably also of Jerusalem, in Judg 1:4-7 is unclear. Their names are less similar than they look in English, but the LXX of Josh 10:1, 3 takes Adoni-zedek to be Adoni-bezek. This is one of a group of related puzzles and inconsistencies. There appears to be a duplication between Joshua and Judges of the accounts concerning several of these towns. The account in Joshua 15 concerning Jerusalem (which, according to 2 Sam 5:6-9, was not captured until David did so) and Hebron and Debir, all in the Judahite highland, seems to have an approximate duplicate in Judges 1.

According to Judg 1:4-13, the Judahites, who take the lead in Judges 1 unlike in the wars of Joshua, capture these three towns in the era after the death of Joshua. Judges 1:8 describes the capture and destruction of Jerusalem, contrary to Josh 15:63 (with which Judg 1:21 agrees, except that in Joshua it is the Judahites who live in Jerusalem and in Judges it is the Benjaminites). Judges 1:10 describes the capture of Hebron, but with no mention of Caleb, as in Josh 15:13-14. Judges 1:11-15 describes the capture of Debir in a nearly verbatim doublet of Josh 15:15-19. Joshua 11:21 raises fresh questions about the destruction of Hebron and Debir. The parallels between Judges 1 and Joshua 15 must be placed next to the account concerning the same towns in Joshua 10: here Jerusalem under Adoni-zedek or Adoni-bezek is not captured, but Hebron and Debir are (10:36-39). To top things off, Debir, the king of Eglon (10:3), is the only person supposedly with this name; all other Debirs are names of places, of which there are at least two. Is the writer confused about Debir?

There is no simple solution to these discrepancies, which are not the only matters on which Joshua and the beginning of Judges disagree. It is not likely that these differences arose in conflicting traditions about whether the conquest of Canaan was quick or gradual, an explanation that was popular not long ago. More likely, they arose beginning with the differing deuteronomistic concepts of the two eras, one of Joshua, the other of the judges and saviors. In Joshua the conquest was in theory complete, or virtually so; exceptions were just that, as the Israelites took effective control of the land. In the era of the judges and saviors, from the start Israel's control was much less than complete, and the accent is on the troubling presence everywhere of Israel's opponents.

Judges 1 is a deuteronomistic composition based on the contrast between Jerusalem, on the one hand (Judg 1:4-8, 21), and Bethel and Dan, where Jeroboam established his anti-Jerusalem shrines, on the other hand (Judg 1:22-26, 34). The references to Jerusalem enclose an account of Judah's successes in conquest, and the references to Bethel and Dan enclose an account of the failure in conquest of the rest of the northern Israelite tribes that, under Jeroboam, broke away from the house of David. The capture of Bethel (Judg 1:22-26) forms an unmistakable parallel to the capture of Jericho under Joshua, but without explicit sanction for sparing the Canaanite helper and his family from dedication. The account of the northern tribes forms an antithesis to the book of Joshua: Each tribe fails to drive out the Canaanites (Judg 1:27-34), though some are able to subject them to corvee slavery (forced labor). In the case of Manasseh and Ephraim, this is true in the book of Joshua as well (Josh 16:10; 17:12-13).

The structural contrast between Jerusalem and Bethel and Dan in Judges 1 is confirmed in the scene at Bochim ("Weepers"), which the LXX correctly takes to be Bethel, where in violation of the deuteronomistic law of centralization "they sacrificed to Yahweh" (Judg 2:1-5). Following a duplication of the death and burial of Joshua, which re-marks the boundary between Joshua's generation and the next (Judg 2:6-10), the deuteronomistic lesson of the era of the judges is laid out in full (Judg 2:11–3:6): Without a monarch devoted to the law of Moses and surrounded by leftover Canaanite peoples, generation after generation of Israelites prove unable to resist, oppose, or do battle against Canaanite power and Canaanite gods. This lesson is illustrated many times over in the main narrative of Judges, leading off with the stereotypical case of the Judahite deliverer Othniel (Judg 3:7-11).[81]

Given these two different concepts underlying the era of Joshua in contrast to the era of Judges—the rapid and successful conquest of Canaan in contrast to the cyclical failure to control the land conquered—it is not surprising that similar names and traditions are given different treatment in them and that, as typical in textual transmission, further confusion has arisen through subsequent attempts to reconcile or harmonize accounts. The supposed gradual conquest in Judges 1 probably reflects no more actual history, to say nothing of better history, than the book of Joshua's sudden conquest, and there is no reason to continue to contrast the two accounts as history at all. From a historical perspective, the two books are both best interpreted as reflecting monarchical politics in the late eighth and seventh centuries BCE.

As the Amorites flee from the Israelites toward the southwest, Yahweh attacks them with hail. Yahweh controls the heavens; this use of meteorological elements in battle is a commonplace in biblical war (see, e.g., Judg 5:20-21, where the stars represent windows opened to let in the cosmic flood [cf. Gen 7:11]; Hab 3:8-12; Job 38:22-23).

The same conception lies behind the episode encapsulated in the poetic excerpt in 10:12-13, which is too fragmentary to give a clear picture (the LXX's "God" for "the nation" is probably a later interpretation, consistent with v. 14b). The prose interpretation in v. 13b takes it to refer to an extension of daylight, presumably in order to allow Israel to complete its slaughter of the enemy. This oldest interpretation is found also in Sir 46:4. However, the prayer puts the sun over Gibeon and the moon over Aijalon (hence it cannot refer to a solar eclipse), and thus must have been pronounced at daybreak, not late in the day. Moreover, the day is not unique because the sun stopped, but because God "heeded a human voice." This cannot mean that God has never answered a prayer; it probably means that God has never taken orders from anyone in battle. Several recent interpretations make a comparison between Joshua's prayer and ancient Near Eastern omens. Certain sets of omens use "wait" and "stand" to refer to the sun and moon in their normal motions, not their miraculous deviation from their usual course or pace. This is probably the case with

81. A somewhat lengthy addition to the end of Joshua in the LXX describes the life and burial of the priest Phinehas, the apostasy of the Israelites, and Yahweh's delivering them "into the hands of Eglon king of Moab and he ruled over them eighteen years." The mention of Eglon's rule connects this variant of the end of the book of Joshua to Judg 3:12, suggesting to some that at least in one edition of Joshua and Judges the entire Jerusalem-dominated or deuteronomistic section in Judg 1:1–3:11 may have been missing, to be added secondarily. See Alexander Rofé, "The End of the Book of Joshua According to the Septuagint," *Henoch* 4 (1982) 17-36; Emanuel Tov, *Textual Criticism of the Hebrew Bible* (Minneapolis: Fortress, 1992) 330-32.

Joshua's prayer. According to some omens, if the sun and the moon appear together on the fourteenth day after new moon, there will be peace in the land; if the sun and the moon do not appear together until the fifteenth day, there will be catastrophic war. One interpretation along these lines supposes that Joshua seeks a favorable omen.[82] Another suggests that Joshua does not believe in omens himself but wants the Amorites to receive a discouraging omen.[83]

Neither v. 15 nor v. 43 appears in the LXX, but the narrative cusps that these verses mark are obvious nevertheless. In typical framework style, the second stage of the battle is enclosed by references to the cave where the kings hide (vv. 16, 27). The cave is sealed with stones until the rout and slaughter of the enemy are complete. Joshua has the Israelites bring the kings out of the cave and symbolically vanquish them; then he executes them, hangs each corpse on a tree until sunset, removes them, throws them back into the cave, and seals the entrance with the same stones.

The final stage of the battle of the south entails the fulfillment of *ḥerem* against three of the kings' towns and several others: Makkedah, Libnah, and Lachish, then Eglon, Hebron, and Debir. In each town, every person is put to death. In between these two sets of three towns, Joshua does battle against the kings of Gezer and his force ("people" in such a context usually refers to the group under arms). The structure of the narrative gives Gezer a particular prominence.[84] Gezer is not destroyed, nor are the inhabitants of the town itself slaughtered (16:10; Judg 1:19). Gezer's location gave it great strategic importance, and it continued to be occupied following its destruction during Sen-nacherib's campaign. Assyrian tablets have been found in this stratum of occupation, and the likelihood is that it was for some time an imperial administrative center, under Assyrian or Egyptian control, whose destruction Josiah had no reason to portray (though what were probably similar circumstances did not discourage him from having the destruction of Hazor portrayed—indeed, singling it out for burning, possibly because it was in fact beyond his reach; 11:10-11).

The summary of the southern campaign is given by region (v. 40), boundaries (v. 41), and length of time (v. 42).[85] From Gibeon south, not one human survivor remained and nothing was left alive. This obvious exaggeration was not even intended to be consistent with other parts of Joshua and Judges. Its purpose is to contribute to the deuteronomistic idealization of the era of Joshua. The "slopes" are probably the eastern escarpment of the Judahite and Benjaminite hills, dropping down to the Jordan and the Dead Sea basin. Goshen is distinct from the region of the same name in Egypt.

82. John R. Holladay, "The Day(s) the Moon Stood Still," *JBL* 87 (1968) 166-78.

83. John H. Walton, "Joshua 10:12-15 and Mesopotamian Celestial Omen Texts," in *Faith, Tradition, and History*, 181-90.

84. K. Lawson Younger, Jr., "The 'Conquest' of the South (Jos 10, 28-39)," *BZ* 39 (1995) 255-64.

85. Younger, "The 'Conquest' of the South (Jos 10, 28-39)," 258-59, 264.

REFLECTIONS

1. The contradiction between a complete destruction and an incomplete destruction in the south points up what Daniel Hawk calls the "contesting plots" in Joshua.[86] Tensions tend to arise in Joshua either because the narrator juxtaposes contrary events or because the narrator gives an interpretation that is inconsistent with the events being narrated. This happens in two main areas. One is the complete (Josh 10:28-42; 11:12-23; 12:7-24; 21:43-45; 23:9-10; 24:11-13) versus the incomplete (Josh 9:14-27; 11:19, 22; 15:63; 16:10; 17:11-12; 19:47) conquest. The other is the contrast between a quick and total obedience to Yahweh (Josh 1:16-18; 4:10; 8:30-35; 24:16-18, 21) and a slow reluctance or inability to obey (Josh 2:1-21; 7:1; 9:1-27; 18:1-10; 24:19-20).[87] Hawk looks at the narrative all at once and sees these not as irreconcilable

86. L. Daniel Hawk, *Every Promise Fulfilled: Contesting Plots in Joshua* (Louisville: Westminster/John Knox, 1991).

87. Hawk, *Every Promise Fulfilled*, 15-16.

differences resulting from a complex process of composition, but as narrative facets integral to a plot that seeks to "exemplify the tension between the structuring operations of dogma and the circumstances of experience."[88] The narrator's struggle with ambiguity mirrors the reader's perception that while structuring life according to a plan is essential, "reality resists and provokes our concords with dissonances and uncertainties. Israel laid claim to fulfillment, but continued to tell its story under the impulse of a promise yet to be realized."[89] The ambiguities and inconsistencies of Joshua reflect a narrator grappling with a reality less plastic than desired and throwing up challenges to his tenets and assertions. In this view, reading the book of Joshua becomes an exercise in adjusting hopes and expectations to the way things are without abandoning basic principles, a continually startling metaphor for adult learning. For readers of the Bible in the church, this can be a worthwhile lesson in looking or listening carefully to what the Bible is saying despite the expectations inevitably brought to it.

2. The forced repulsion, expulsion, or eradication of peoples is an age-old story of domination and despair, of which the decimation of Native Americans is, for present-day Americans, the most trenchant and consequential instance.[90] The story does not abate, and the twentieth century has produced some of the worst examples in history. For many, the Jewish Holocaust in Nazi Europe marks the nadir of the human capacity for the heinous atrocity of genocide.[91]

The tragic sequel to the suffering of the Jewish people in Europe is the suffering of the Palestinian people in what became the state of Israel and, in 1967, the occupied territories of the West Bank. The history of twentieth-century Palestine is a vexed and contentious subject, but one thing is indisputable: The outcome for hundreds of thousands of natives of Palestine has been an unending disaster. In 1948 the conquest of Joshua was replayed, with Palestinians in the role of the Canaanites. Assisted by Arab armies, the Palestinians were able to hold on to much of the highlands of Palestine until 1967, when Israeli forces captured the rest of biblical Canaan west of the Jordan. The history of this period is complex, but the result for most Palestinians was oppression, expulsion, and destruction, and in many cases death. The 1948 war produced 750,000 Palestinian refugees, families and communities whose children fifty years later often still live in the same camps to which their parents fled.[92]

The story of expulsion and ethnic cleansing has been repeated innumerable times and in many places since. Notable recent examples include East Timor (where since 1975 one-third of the population has been killed by its own government), Cambodia (one-fifth of the population), Sri Lanka, the former Yugoslavia, and Rwanda. The historian does no service to the memory of the victims of these horrendous events by making facile comparisons between them; however, one common feature important for comprehending the book of Joshua stands out: Ethnic cleansing does not occur today, and probably never did occur, except as devised, promoted, organized, and carried out under the direction of a state or dominant government seeking to centralize and expand. As one recent commentator put it regarding recent wars in Africa, "Ethnic differences do not in themselves cause wars. But when they are exploited by politicians, in countries where one man or one party has taken over the state, the results can be disastrous."[93] Such generalizations confirm that the cleansing portrayed in the book of

88. Hawk, *Every Promise Fulfilled*, 20.

89. Hawk, *Every Promise Fulfilled*, 145.

90. Robert Allen Warrior, "A Native American Perspective: Canaanites, Cowboys, and Indians," *Christianity and Crisis*, September 11, 1989, 261-65; reprinted in *Voices from the Margin: Interpreting the Bible in the Third World*, ed. R. S. Sugirtharajah (Maryknoll, N.Y.: Orbis, 1995) 277-85.

91. Douglas K. Huneke, *The Stones Will Cry Out: Pastoral Reflections on the Shoah* (Westport, Conn.: Greenwood, 1995).

92. Walid Khalidi, ed., *All That Remains: The Palestinian Villages Occupied and Depopulated by Israel in 1948* (Washington: Institute for Palestine Studies, 1992); Nur Masalha, *Expulsion of the Palestinians: The Concept of "Transfer" in Zionist Political Thought, 1882–1948* (Washington: Institute for Palestine Studies, 1992); Naim S. Ateek, "A Palestinian Perspective: Biblical Perspectives on the Land," in *Faith and the Intifada: Palestinian Christian Voices* (Maryknoll, N.Y.: Orbis, 1992): 108-16, reprinted in Sugirtharajah, *Voices from the Margin*, 267-76; W. Eugene March, *Israel and the Politics of Land: A Theological Case Study* (Louisville: Westminster/John Knox, 1994).

93. See *The Economist*, July 1, 1995, 17.

Joshua did not originate among the populace of ancient Palestine, including the highland tribal people identified as Israel. One key feature of modern ethnic cleansing is the use of the media to foster hatred. Although probably publicized little further than Josiah's wider court, the book of Joshua, together with the rest of the Deuteronomistic History, helped to serve this function in Josiah's reform.[94]

94. To understand ethnic cleansing in the book of Joshua, interpreters should familiarize themselves with at least one well-studied modern example. For Cambodia: Ben Kiernan, *The Pol Pot Regime: Race, Power, and Genocide in Cambodia Under the Khmer Rouge, 1957–79* (New Haven: Yale University Press, 1996). For Sri Lanka: Anthony Spaeth, "Inventing an Ethnic Rivalry," *Harper's* (November 1991) 67-78; David Little, *Sri Lanka: The Invention of Enmity* (Washington: United States Institute of Peace, 1994). For Yugoslavia: Misha Glenny, *The Fall of Yugoslavia: The Third Balkan War* (New York: Penguin, 1992); Laura Silber and Allan Little, *The Death of Yugoslavia* (New York: Penguin, 1995); Norman Cigar, *Genocide in Bosnia: The Policy of "Ethnic Cleansing"* (College Station: Texas A. & M. University Press, 1995). For Rwanda: Alex de Waal, "The Genocidal State: Hutu Extremism and the Origins of the 'Final Solution' in Rwanda," *The Times Literary Supplement,* July 1, 1994, 3-4; Robert Block, "The Tragedy of Rwanda," *The New York Review of Books,* October 20, 1994, 3-8; Gérard Prunier, *The Rwanda Crisis: History of a Genocide* (New York: Columbia University Press, 1995); *Genocide in Rwanda: The Planning and Execution of Mass Murder* (New York: Human Rights Watch, 1996). In general: *Slaughter Among Neighbors: The Political Origins of Ethnic, Racial, and Religious Violence* (New Haven: Yale University Press, 1995).

JOSHUA 11:1-15, DESTRUCTION TO THE NORTH

COMMENTARY

Consistent with the standard narrative transition in Joshua (see 5:1; 9:1; 10:1), the king of the greatest of the far northern towns, Hazor, hears about what has just happened in the south, and he tries to turn the tables on the Israelites. He organizes a northern alliance similar to the southern alliance just defeated. The southern alliance involved a few Amorite kings; this alliance includes all the Canaanite groups, who together produce a multitude under arms, with a multitude of chariots, the ancient equivalent of tanks pitted against Israel's infantry. Joshua's counterpart is Jabin, the king of Hazor, and it is hard to separate him from the Jabin who is the "king of Canaan" ruling in Hazor in the time of Deborah, several generations after Joshua (Judg 4:2, 7, 23-24). Many scholars rightly believe that the two accounts in Josh 11:1-15 and Judges 4–5 are variants of each other, or that one is based on the other. Both involve a battle against a Canaanite coalition in the Jezreel Valley. The "waters of Merom" (11:5) compare with the "waters of Megiddo" (Judg 5:19) and may be involved in a pun in the phrase "heights of the field" (5:18). The nature of the woman's song, probably ancient, in Judges 5 and some of its contents suggest that some pre-Davidic battle involving tribal "Israel" might lie far in the background of these accounts.

The Israelites burn the chariots and hamstring the horses, making them unusable in warfare (Gen 49:6; 2 Sam 8:4). Surprisingly the Israelites leave the towns they attack "on their tells" (cf. 8:28), excepting Hazor, and as with Ai dedicate to God only the inhabitants of the towns, taking the livestock and other spoil as booty. How the precedent of Ai justifies this exception to the law of ḥērem is unclear. Regardless, the conclusion that follows immediately explains that this was not a violation of the law, since Joshua has from the beginning and without exception obeyed all that Yahweh ordered Moses to tell the Israelites to do.

REFLECTIONS

Christians have always looked to God for support in their battles with superior forces, both material and spiritual. Virtually every church and denomination has a tradition of overcoming adversity against great odds with the help of the Lord. Expressions of God's help are readily found in church liturgies and hymns. In the comparatively peaceful world of middle-class America, where such adversity is more likely to be experienced in a spiritual rather than a material mode, it is easy to forget the struggles our forebears in the faith had to endure. It might be useful to go through the church's hymnal and discuss some of these struggles. An example is the great Reformed hymn based on Psalm 68, "Let God Arise and Show His Face." Its lines, in their sixteenth-century context of religious wars, were not sung metaphorically:

And all that hate him shall give place,
and all his foes shall scatter.
Just as the smoke away doth blow,
so shall his arm disperse the foe,
and all opponents banish.
But let the righteous all rejoice.[95]

This "Battle Hymn of the Huguenots" was used by, among others, the Pilgrims at Plymouth. The mortal foes referred to in this hymn are fellow Christians, although Protestants did not always regard Catholics as such for the first two hundred years or so of the Reformation. The nature of the struggle in the Reformation use of this hymn—in France, Britain, the Lowlands, or elsewhere—tended to be a civil war, not a war against "external" enemies. In this respect, it may not be so different from the struggle represented in the book of Joshua.

It is too facile simply to dismiss such hymns as barbaric and hence irrelevant. How do we take sides with a God who battles cancer, oppression, and death without raising the flag for the "God of our side"? To be faithful is to be partisan, and there is no more poignant expression of partisanship than the church's heritage of militaristic hymns, even if today we choose to reject or muffle their martial blare and spiked animosity. In any case, except in churches that are explicitly and unreservedly pacifist, the muting of the church's legacy of bellicosity tends to be selective. Christians may intend no longer to kill like Joshua, but happily they can "choose their fight" within the often shifting and ambiguous constraints of love and justice. Then the great battle hymns may have a great positive effect. Models may include the writer of Eph 6:10-17, who does not stint in rhetorically arming the Christian warrior to the hilt, and the Reformer Martin Luther, who, in "A Mighty Fortress Is Our God," composed, in part with martial metaphor, one of the enduring monuments to the calling of Christian faith.

95. This hymn was translated by Margaret House in 1949 for the World Student Christian Federation hymnal, published in 1951.

JOSHUA 11:16–12:24, SUMMARY OF DESTRUCTION

COMMENTARY

The summary of the northern campaign (11:16-20) serves as the beginning of the summary of the entire war of conquest (11:23–12:24). The emphasis on kings and the significance of Yahweh's provocation have been discussed already. The first summary concludes with a seemingly unrelated note that

Joshua defeated the Anakim from Hebron, Debir, and Anab (11:21), major towns in the heart of Judah, and from the rest of Judah and Israel (note the geographical anachronism). The Anakim were strong giants (Deut 9:2), and they are said to remain in the Philistine towns that in the late seventh century

BCE lay in Egyptian-controlled territory well beyond Josiah's control. The Anakim were Judah's own indigenous giants, analogous to the Rephaim, Emim, and Zamzummim who were dispossessed by Yahweh in the accounts of Deuteronomy 2. If Joshua 12–14, containing further summary and introduction, were bracketed, the reference to Joshua's giving Israel its inheritances, mentioned here for the first time in the book of Joshua, could flow cleanly into 15. It is thus not a coincidence that the story that immediately precedes 15 concerns Caleb's inheritance of Hebron, whose earlier name was the "town of Arba," the greatest of the Anakim. The repetition of the concluding formula in both 11:23 and 14:15, "the land had rest from war" (a deuteronomistic formula; see 14:15; Judg 3:11, 30; 5:31; 8:28), confirms that the account of the whole, in which the grant to Judah is both the first and the most extensive land grant on the west side of the Jordan, lays great stress on the conquest and disposition of the first of David's towns, Hebron. This is probably also why Joshua plays his most extensive role in the Tetrateuch as a secondary addition to the narrative of spying out Hebron with Caleb in Numbers 13–14 (note the Anakim in Num 13:22, 28, 33; see Introduction and discussion of 14:6-15).

The grand summary of the war of conquest begins with a cover statement (11:23), then gives two lists of kings, those defeated on the east side of the Jordan (12:1-6) and those on the west side (12:7-24). The first list includes just Sihon and Og, who have already been referred to several times. Og is said to be one of the last of the Rephaim, another race of giants who once inhabited the lands of Israel (Deut 3:11). Traditionally the Rephaim were the "hale" ones, mostly upper-class ancestors sufficiently robust and vital to survive death and live in the underworld (Job 26:5; Isa 14:9; 26:14). Living warriors borrowed the title to suggest that they would be able to survive death. The territory of the kingdoms of Sihon and Og is delineated, and it is made clear that the two and a half eastern tribes have their title to that land from Moses. This brief description previews the more detailed account in 13:8-33.

The second list is thought by many to be an independent source. Josiah may have drawn up a list of towns to be brought under his jurisdiction to the west of the Jordan, including some abandoned settlements; recall that a "king" represents the embodiment of a jurisdiction. The inclusion of lists and catalogs was popular with ancient narrators. The list contains thirty-one kings in the MT, twenty-nine in the LXX. The meaning of the word "one" (אחד *'eḥād*), which follows each place name, is an intriguing mystery; it is missing from the most important LXX MSS. The overall description of the territory that introduces the list moves from north to south, possibly because the immediately preceding section ended with the territory of Og in the northern Transjordan. This list of kings begins by following more or less the order of appearance in Joshua until it reaches Geder, Hormah, and Arad, which lie in the south but are not mentioned in Joshua 1–11. The narrative order resumes with Libnah and Makkedah, to which Adullam is added. The rest of the list shows little order, except that certain places are roughly adjacent to each other, like Adullam, near Libnah and Makkedah; Tappuah, near Bethel; Hepher, near Aphek and possibly Lasharon (if it is in fact a place name); Taanach, near Megiddo; and Jokneam, near Dor. The "king of Goiim in Galilee" is of dubious identity. The MT has "Gilgal" for the LXX's "Galilee" (cf. NRSV and NIV), and "Goiim" (גוים *gôyim*) means simply "nations" (cf. Isa 9:1).

The inclusion of Gezer, where Canaanites are said to remain (16:10; Judg 1:29), shows that the list is indeed a list of kings who embody sovereignties or jurisdictions, and not a list of localities. As such, it represents not destroyed towns or even simply eliminated kings, but one by one the separate jurisdictions that Josiah means to appropriate, establishing in place of their multiplicity a single sovereignty based on a single law sanctioned by a single cult under one single God (cf. Deut 6:4).

REFLECTIONS

The final summary of the conquest comes as a list of kings. Given the appalling incidence of mass slaughter in the narrative of conquest, this focus comes as a bit of a surprise. It invites us to engage in an exercise that is almost always instructive when we are confronted with a binary opposition of any kind. That exercise is to look for the "hidden third." What is missing, the interpreter may ask, in the choice between two alternatives? What in the case of Joshua might be missing in the distinction between Canaanite and Israelite as categories? If "Canaanite" means the kings of the Canaanites, as it does in this passage, then we may spot an opening that suggests that subjects, in contrast to kings, may fall into a different category from that of kings, despite the earlier narrative. If so, the king's subjects of the one category and those of the other might fall into a single class, one opposed to kings. In such a new binary opposition, the missing third might be discovered to be the debt enslaved, possessing the characteristic that earlier grouped Rahab with the escaped slaves of Israel (see Commentary on 2:1–6:27). In this case, the narrator has already invited us to inquire about the "hidden third."

In our church life as much as elsewhere, we are frequently confronted with seemingly all-encompassing alternatives, from trivial matters to the sublime. There are people who dress up for church and those who do not. There are those who claim to have a personal saving relationship with Jesus and those who do not. There is social justice and personal piety. There are those who baptize infants and those who do not. There are those who go to church and those who do not. There are the married and the unmarried, those with children and those without, those who own their own home and those who do not, those with a college degree and those without.

Whenever we realize that the world has been dichotomized, it is worth asking whether the assumptions behind the dichotomy are as true as they at first seem. While there is, given the "descent rule" in the history of American racism, an important social reality to the simple distinction between "black" and "white" in American culture, it is also a profoundly false distinction. One person confessed that when she was quite young and heard the words *black* and *white,* she was confused. She looked around at her classmates and saw people of Chinese, Filipino, Japanese, African, and Nordic descent, and she looked at the color of their skin: ivory, biscuit, buff, brick, sandalwood, clay, tobacco, hazelnut, and so forth. We may become irritated with the "rowdy, assertive babble about definitions and categories" that other people use, but how often do we examine our own cherished assumptions about how the world divides up?[96]

Looking for the hidden third also has the propensity to lead to compromise. For instance, a reviewer of essays by the Israeli writer Amos Oz points out his "political conviction . . . that the struggle between Israel and the Palestinians is a struggle of 'right against right,' that it is futile to insist on pure justice. Compromise, however inconsistent and unsatisfying, is the only solution. 'I was not born to blow rams' horns and liberate the land from the 'foreign yoke,' " Mr. Oz writes.[97]

96. The phrase is from Frank Kermode, in *The New York Times Book Review,* July 9, 1995, 7.
97. Tova Reich in *The New York Times Book Review,* June 25, 1995, 18.

JOSHUA 13:1–21:45

JOSHUA REDISTRIBUTES THE LAND

OVERVIEW

J oshua and his men have conquered the land by dispossessing its holders and barbarously putting them to death. Now, in the pattern of the war leader, Joshua undertakes to distribute the confiscated land to his men and their families. Until now the Israelites have obediently forborne the taking of booty, a routine means of compensation, but it is high time for them to receive grants of land. The distribution is told as a story in which each tribe is granted a portion of land defined by lists of towns or regions or descriptions of boundaries. Modern readers are liable to find this part of the book of Joshua of less interest than the earlier part. The pace of the story slows so as hardly to seem like a story at all. Precisely where a given tribe's territory lies can be of little interest to anyone other than those directly involved at the time. Twenty-six centuries later, the interpreter may know little about the presumptions, stresses, contentions, and surprises contained in the account of allocation that no doubt gripped the interest of its first hearers.

Indeed, unlike the modern reader, the ancient hearer would have found this part of the story of great interest, including many details that are now lost to us, since it dealt with the most important factor in the life of practically every person in the ancient world: access to land. In North America and many other parts of the world today, what most tends to attract attention is violence and sex. In Joshua's world, it was violence and land.

This story is a fictionalized account of an existing administrative arrangement. Such fictionalizations are not uncommon in premodern literature, and in talking about them historians will sometimes say that a scheme or organization has been "narrativized." This story, however, would have been of limited, and now unknown, administrative usefulness. There is reason to believe that the tribal lists existed at least in part before Hezekiah's or Josiah's historian made use of them. The descriptions of the tribal allotments are quite uneven, as though they might have been incorporated as available from haphazard sources: Some are detailed, some spare; some consist mainly of town lists or of regional descriptions, others of boundary descriptions, and no tribe is given a full description using both types of material. They appear to be at best only partly adjusted to fit Josiah's particular administrative purposes. Comparable ancient Near Eastern lists often appear in administrative texts, including those dealing with landholdings, which are usually already in the hands of their holders, as they are for the most part in Joshua 13–19.[98]

The possible dates of the supposed constituent lists are much debated. Whatever the dates of the incorporated lists, the story of the allotment comes from the deuteronomist, though it may be based on an earlier version from the court of Hezekiah. Given the variety of the descriptions of the different allotments and the schematized nature of the whole, the primary point of the allotment cannot be administrative, but must involve the story as such. Moreover, the story seems designed to illustrate not just the range of the assertive lord's reconquest, which is immediately said to fall significantly short of its goal, but more important the magnitude of his momentous capacity to make land grants at will in the territories he does control.

A later priestly hand has introduced Eleazar into the picture next to Joshua, but only in the frame of the allotments, and spuriously named ahead of Joshua (14:1; 18:1; 19:51; 21:1-2; in 13:7 and 14:6, Joshua functions on his own or with the tribal heads, the

98. Richard S. Hess, "Asking Historical Questions of Joshua 13–19: Recent Discussion Concerning the Date of the Boundary Lists," in *Faith, Tradition, and History*, 191-205.

deuteronomistic concept). The same hand may also be responsible for mentions of the tent of meeting and the use of the characteristic priestly word for "tribe" (מטה *maṭṭeh*) throughout the allotments. Overall there are many differences between the MT and the LXX in the text of this whole section, suggesting that what often happens in the transmission of MSS has happened here: Attempts to make clearer a somewhat irregular text, which furthermore was susceptible to scribal adjustment as soon as political and administrative circumstances began to change, have only made the text muddier.

The story emphasizes the role of Joshua as the supervisor of allocation. Three distinct notions of land redistribution are combined in the story, based on three different model contexts. Joshua plays the dominant role in each. The three contexts are the warlord's council or monarch's court, the village, and the tribe. In real life it was unusual for these three forms of redistribution to overlap. In the story of Joshua, they do overlap, so that none appears complete in itself, but only as part of a political metaphor with three discernible dimensions. Each dimension makes an essential contribution to what the deuteronomist wants to convey through the story of allotment.

The monarchic dimension emerges directly from the narrative plot of the book of Joshua, as one more of its numerous monarchic features. The military chief distributes captured land to his loyal retainers and supporters and their families. The monarch as conqueror represents a sovereign or arbitrary power. Joshua acts on his own sovereign's behalf, directing the lottery through which Yahweh makes the otherwise inscrutable allocation known. The imperiousness of Joshua's allocation becomes evident when it is remembered that from a tribal viewpoint tribal territories are not assigned by the state but are negotiated among the tribes. The monarch's arbitrariness emerges most conspicuously in 18:2-7. There Joshua first orders a survey for setting up the divisions of the land. Once the divisions are demarcated, the lottery takes place to determine which tribe gets which division. The premise of the narrative is that the tribes do not already inhabit a particular territory, as though Joshua were like the king of Assyria,

able to transfer whole populations, urban or tribal, from one location to another by divinely sanctioned fiat. There is little doubt that Josiah accommodated the "tribes" under his sovereignty in their usual territories, at least for the most part, but such is not the message of this story. This story's message is that the monarch, in obedience to God, claims the power to put people where he wants—if he wants. The modern reader might regard God's command to slaughter innocent people as the most outrageous atrocity in the book of Joshua. Ancient tribalists probably would not have agreed, but were likely to have regarded Joshua's arrogation of the right to assign tribal territories as the greatest offense, if they grasped the implication of this story.

This dimension is probably the main one behind the use of the term נחלה (*naḥălâ*), translated "inheritance," although the term has an important part to play in the other dimensions as well. The basic meaning of this term is "land grant" and of its verb "to receive or make a land grant."[99] Such a grant frequently becomes heritable, so it is not surprising that the term can take on the meaning of inheritance. But inheritance is not its primary meaning in Joshua, even though the tribal territories are taken as permanent. The story of Joshua does not emphasize the land as it is to be inherited by later generations, but rather land that is to be granted and received as a grant now, when both strong men and commoners are forced to respond to the pretensions of this belligerent upstart. The grant originates with Yahweh, the leading conqueror, who here carries out the sovereign decision to give to the "Israelites" the land that belongs to the "Canaanites."

In the Deuteronomistic History, the grant, a basis of the covenant, is made on condition; hence it is limited as to heritability from the start. Typically such conditions lie within the prerogative of the sovereign making the grant. Even when grants are made "in perpetuity," they can be reassigned with little or no difficulty, since even such grants remain in effect only at the pleasure of the grantor. Many examples of such reassignment are known from ancient texts. In this dimension,

---

99. P. Kyle McCarter and Robert B. Coote, "The Spatula Inscription from Byblos," *BASOR* 212 (December 1973) 20-21 (with correction, *BASOR* 214, 41).

the grants may be represented as heritable to the extent that Josiah wishes to be seen empowering the "Israelite" debtors against the depredations of "Canaanite" large landholders and creditors engaged in agricultural trade. This dimension, however, addresses more than the peasants of tribal Israel. It also addresses the powerful among Josiah's followers or among those he wants to coax into following him, to whom the portrayal of allocation promises a grant not so much of land, but of the rights to the produce of lands farmed by the peasants of the towns and villages named in the form of taxes, rents, or tribute.

The second dimension concerns the village. Villagers in ancient Palestine typically practiced a form of periodic repartitioning of arable land by lot. The participants in the lottery were those who headed households who did not hold parts of the land itself, but cultivation rights to the whole of the arable land. This practice, which was widespread in agrarian societies and can still be found in many parts of the world today, had a number of purposes. In Palestine it made it easier to leave fallow a large proportion of the arable land belonging to the farmers of a given village as a single block of land. The village animals could then graze in and manure this fallow block without wandering into the patchwork of adjacent cultivated plots that would exist if the fallow land were not so blocked. Thus each year a different section of the village's arable land was available for cultivation. As year by year cultivation rotated from section to section, the land to be cultivated was repartitioned by lot among the farming families. Redistribution spread the advantage of farming the better lands among the families at random. It also allowed the village to pay its taxes on arable land as a commonality, affording leverage against the tax collector.[100] The repartitional lottery forms the background to a number of biblical texts, including Pss 16:5-6; 125:3; and Mic 2:5.

In this dimension, the land of Canaan is like a village's total arable land, Joshua is the foremost elder in the village, and the tribal heads, where they figure, are the heads of households holding cultivation rights in the village. The Israelite tribes represent villagers who find their cultivation rights newly authorized, like peasants whose debts have been remitted, rather than relentlessly jeopardized or already lost through unpaid arrears. Periodic redistribution stood for values that villagers held dear, such as security, stability, cooperation, solidarity, productivity, and equal opportunity. It is necessary not to romanticize these values, but to recognize that when the deuteronomist "narrativizes" the tribal territories as he does, among other things he confirms an entire set of popular ideals consonant with Josiah's radical program of debt reform.

The third dimension is tribal. As already seen, tribes tended to define themselves from the top down according to putative genealogies, often through tribal heads in negotiation with state authorities. The dynamics of internal tribal politics, and of relations between tribes and rival powers, were extremely fluid and variable.[101] Tribal states like the one projected by the Deuteronomistic History are by no means rare in the history of the Middle East, but their notions of tribal constituencies were subject to erratic alteration. Nevertheless tribal ideals typically expressed egalitarianism, opposition to the state, a seamless solidarity to which all contributed voluntarily, pride of superiority over the mere peasant, and the honor of both self-reliance and mutual aid. These are the ideals that the deuteronomist can affirm through his story of the allocation of the land of Canaan among the tribes of Israel.

More often than not tribes are a bother to strong rulers, who prefer to keep them under control on the periphery of their realm. Why would a centralizing monarch like Josiah agree to have his nation portrayed as a great tribal family? Josiah might instead be expected to follow in the footsteps of Solomon and attempt to neutralize tribal loyalty and influence in his realm. This is what many scholars believe Solomon did, on the basis of the list of districts in 1 Kgs 4:7-19. One reason why Josiah went along with the ancient Davidic concept of tribal Israel is that, although it is impossible to know for certain, it is doubtful that Israelite tribal sentiments played a significant role in his time independent of

---

100. Robert B. Coote, *Early Israel: A New Horizon* (Minneapolis: Fortress, 1990) 20.

101. Philip S. Khoury and Joseph Kostiner, *Tribes and State Formation in the Middle East* (Berkeley: University of California Press, 1990) 38-44, 109-26, 252-75; Coote, *Early Israel,* 75-83.

central policy, except possibly in Judah and Benjamin. Josiah had little to lose and much to gain from this portrayal, since he meant to control both it and the politics it represented. In its treatment of the tribes of Israel, the Deuteronomistic History clearly announced that among putative Israelites no tribal politics would be licensed that did not fall within the definitions laid down by the court in Jerusalem. The recognition of the tribes of Israel had been an important facet of central reform under Hezekiah and probably Manasseh, and when Josiah inherited this strategy he saw no reason to repudiate it.

In the Deuteronomistic History, the tribes of Israel play an important role before David. After David, they play practically no role at all, being scarcely mentioned in the book of Kings. Presumably like Hezekiah's scribe before him, the deuteronomist got his concept of the tribes from JE, the Davidic history of early Israel, with its Israelite supplement as reappropriated by Hezekiah's court. The tribes are in J because in the Late Bronze and Early Iron ages early Israel was a powerful, but shifting and variable, tribal entity, and in the tenth century BCE, when J was written, the tribal concept of Israel remained a lively and potent force. The portrayal of the tribes in J, however, is already highly idealized and stylized from the order of their birth, to their numbering exactly twelve over a period of several hundred years, to their stories, which are mainly two: the tension between Judah and Joseph, resolved in the crisis over Benjamin and in tearful reconciliation among all the tribal brothers, and their nearly problem-free solidarity in the exodus and desert trek, during which individual names scarcely appear, the same as under Joshua.[102] The fixed number of twelve tribes represents David's tribal policy, which, unlike Josiah, he was probably forced to adopt, because the tribes were strong and the monarchy weak. There is some indication of traditional relations and territories in J, especially in the etymologies of the tribes in Genesis 29–30 and the archaic blessings in Genesis 49. The overriding tribal issue in J, however, is the relationship between Judah and Joseph, the two core highland areas south and north, with Benjamin between them

and the key to their reconciliation. This is practically a geographical constant in the history of Palestine, and thus it occurs also in Joshua 14–18 (see 18:11).

There is an evident element of reality in Joshua's portrayal of the tribes. As indicated, the lists of towns and borders probably come from existing documents of some kind. In several cases the territories represent natural regions, though the bearing of this point can be questioned; historically, tribes in Palestine claim not natural regions over an extended period of time, but changeable territories determined by a complex combination of geographical, demographic, economic, and especially political factors. Again it is essential to remember that while some tribal names may persist for some time in the history of Syria and Palestine, the usual pattern is for at least some names and relationships to change in little more than decades, making the persistence of twelve names in exactly the same genealogical relationship over several centuries of extreme social change implausible. Seven years after the fall of Samaria, in about 715 BCE, Sargon II resettled four named Arab tribes within the bounds of former Israel.[103] The deuteronomist makes no mention of these tribes, even though they must have quickly related with whatever may have been left of old Israelite tribal identities at the time. In any case, the tribal territories in Joshua are based on a maximalist, hardly practical notion, that has, for example, highland Judah incorporating Ashdod and Gaza (15:47) and coastal Asher incorporating Tyre (19:29), bounds that are politically quite improbable.

The tribal dimension does more than affirm a set of supposed tribal ideals. It also expresses specific political relationships, as the tribal metaphor always does. In Joshua's account, as in Judges 1, Judah comes first and is given the most complete treatment of all the tribes (Joshua 15). This reflects the Davidic origin of the book of Joshua, despite Joshua's Ephraimite origin. Next, the boundaries of Ephraim and the western half of Manasseh are given. Their town lists are missing. The

102. Robert B. Coote and David Robert Ord, *The Bible's First History* (Philadelphia: Fortress, 1989) 167-206, 257-97.

103. D. D. Luckenbill, *Ancient Records of Assyria and Babylonia*, vol. 2 (Chicago: University of Chicago Press, 1927) par. 17; available also in James B. Pritchard, ed., *The Ancient Near East: An Anthology of Texts and Pictures* (Princeton: Princeton University Press, 1958) 196, and Pritchard, *Ancient Near Eastern Texts Relating to the Old Testament*, 3rd ed. (Princeton: Princeton University Press, 1969) 286.

statement is made, however, that Manasseh includes major towns within the bounds of Issachar and Asher (17:11-13). Clearly the concept includes more than a given territory. Manasseh is the heartland of political Israel during nearly its entire history, from pre-monarchic times to Josiah. Its dominance is expressed in its inclusion of the likes of Megiddo, one of the great towns of Palestine in many ages, not least the age of Josiah. By now five tribes have received their allotments.

Once the two tribes of Joseph, Ephraim and Manasseh, have received their allotments, the scene shifts to Shiloh in Ephraim, where the seven remaining tribes are dealt with, starting with Benjamin (Joshua 18–19). Following a list of towns of refuge for manslayers (Joshua 20), a list of the towns and pasturage assigned to the Levites brings the distribution to a close.[104]

104. See Kurt Elliger, "Tribes, Territories of," in *IDB*, 4:701-10; Zecharia Kallai, "Tribes, Territories of," *IDBSup*, 920-23.

JOSHUA 13:1-7, "REDISTRIBUTE THIS LAND"

COMMENTARY

Joshua is now all of a sudden old (14:10 suggests that five to seven years have passed since the beginning of the conquest), though not so old that "many years" cannot pass before his final address to Israel (23:1). This represents the deuteronomistic conception in which Joshua's career has three stages: He conquers, distributes the land, and bids farewell. Joshua conquers what he can between his maturity and his old age. Much land within the ideal borders is left to conquer, but Joshua has come to the end of his fighting years and must go ahead and distribute what he has captured before he dies. When the distribution is complete, he dies, but before doing so he makes a final deuteronomistic speech, again in the pattern of Moses.

Much land remains to be possessed. This phrase at first seems to anticipate the frequent references to the incomplete conquest that follow (13:13; 14:12; 15:63; 16:10; 17:12-13, 15-18; Judg 1:21-35; 3:1-6). However, these later passages refer almost entirely to Canaanites remaining within or near the bounds of conquest described in Joshua 2–12. The notable exception is Judg 3:1-6, which refers for the most part to the same coastal territory described in the present passage but then defines its inhabitants according to the standard list of seven "nations," minus the Girgashites. The land described in the present passage falls into three sections, covering the entire Mediterranean coastland from south to

north, with most of interior Lebanon as the hinterland of the third section.

The first section of land covers the territory of the Philistines. This includes the Geshur in the south (cf. 1 Sam 27:8), different from the Geshur in the north, mentioned in 12.5. Of course, for the Late Bronze Age the confederated pentapolis under five Philistine rulers is an anachronism; the Philistines did not come to Palestine before the twelfth century BCE, and the pentapolis is unlikely to have formed long before its earliest historical attestation, which probably occurs in 1 Samuel 4–6 in the Davidic era, two hundred years later. The Avvim or Avvites are the pre-Philistine giants of the region of the kind that Yahweh regularly dispossesses in favor of new inhabitants (Deut 2:23; cf. the Rephaim in Josh 13:12) as paradigms for dispossession of the Canaanites. The second section of land covers the "Canaanite" coast between the first and third sections, Philistia and Phoenicia, which were culturally distinct. This section is probably designated "from Arah to Aphek," as in the NIV, even though Arah is said to be under the rule of the Sidonians, the contemporary term for "Phoenicians." The third section comprises the Phoenician towns and their hinterland as far as the Anti-Lebanon mountains. The dominant rulers are those of Byblos (Gebal) and Sidon.

In the long history of Palestine, the stretch of coastal lowland from next to the Sinai

Peninsula to what is now Lebanon has often been part of a different cultural or political matrix from that of the highland, or hill country. Nowhere in the Bible is this difference better illustrated than in the story of Samson, who as the rough-and-ready highlander smashes, bumps, jostles, pushes, and shoves his blunt way through adventures, but never slices or cuts, sharp actions that are left to the supposedly refined and civilized lowlanders.[105] Material cultural differences between lowland and highland similar to those that contributed to the ethnic distinction between "Israelite" and "Canaanite"—a distinction that was always at least as much political and social as cultural—are attested in other regions of the Near East possessing a comparable topography.[106] During the roughly five hundred years of Israelite monarchies, the kings of Israel and Judah rarely controlled the great towns along the coast. Towns in this region thrived on sea trade and great swaths of arable land, which enabled them to withstand highlander sieges and to field chariots in battle, which highlanders on their own could not do. Lowland towns tended to remain under the power of local rulers or oligarchies, who themselves were frequently overpowered by imperial forces and brought directly under the sway of Egypt or Mesopotamia. Highland monarchs and chieftains frequently allied with lowland powers, local or imperial. During the reign of Josiah, who was probably allied with the rulers of Assyria or Egypt who were in virtual full control of the Palestine coastal area, highland rule along the coast could be nothing more than an ambition, part of a scheme presented for political effect. Even Josiah's supposed Davidic model fails him on this score, since particularly along the northern coast David could do no more than make agreements with existing rulers.

The NRSV is probably correct to suppose that Yahweh's promise in v. 6 refers to all the sections and peoples named, not just the highland Sidonians, as in the NIV. With the conquest of this territory in the offing, Yahweh instructs Joshua to distribute what territory he has.

105. David E. Bynum, "Samson as a Biblical *phēr oreskōos* [Wild Man of the Mountains]," in *Text and Tradition: The Hebrew Bible and Folklore*, ed. Susan Niditch (Atlanta: Scholars Press, 1990) 57-73.

106. Gloria A. London, "A Comparison of Two Contemporaneous Lifestyles of the Late Second Millennium B.C.E.," *BASOR* 273 (1989) 37-55.

REFLECTIONS

Much of the literature available for Bible study tends to be somewhat more tranquil and aseptic than the Bible itself. This is particularly true when it comes to dealing with matters of land and property. Land was the most important material resource for the people of the Bible, and yet it is rarely discussed, either for what it meant in the biblical period or for how it might shed light on our attitudes to the nearest modern equivalent: capital. One of the benefits of the book of Joshua is that it brings us quickly and unavoidably into the turmoil, tribulation, anxiety, and violence of land relations in ancient Palestine, and the sharing of resources in our own world, where often the same turmoil prevails.

JOSHUA 13:8-33, LAND FOR THE TRIBES BEYOND THE JORDAN

COMMENTARY

Before narrating the distribution of the land conquered west of the Jordan (chaps. 14–19), the narrator defines the land conquered by Moses east of the Jordan (13:8 13), just as he had earlier reviewed its conquest (1:12-15; Deut 2:24–3:22). He then defines the division of that land among the tribes of Reuben and Gad and half the tribe of Manasseh (13:15-32). Also included are two references to the tribe of Levi, who receives no land grant (13:14, 33).

Moses' triumph over the kings Sihon and Og serves as the great exemplar for dispossession by Israel, and the deuteronomist misses no opportunity to refer to it. As in chaps. 1–12, the capture of the territory of Sihon and Og is assumed to be complete. Sweeping conquest is one thing, total ethnic cleansing and the imposition of coercive jurisdiction another. Now for the first time it appears that the dispossession is incomplete; Geshurites and Maacathites survive, under the control of Moses' law. The possible implication of shifting the focus to kings rather than to the entire populace begins to be borne out. This is the first of five references in Joshua to incomplete dispossession (see 14:12; 15:63; 16:10; 17:12-13, 15-18). The inescapable and terrible force of Moses' law is exemplified: The Israelites kill Balaam (cf. Num 31:8) for practicing "divination" (Numbers 22–24) in violation of deuteronomistic law (Deut 18:10; 2 Kgs 17:17). This law is not alone in the OT in condemning "divination," which can include consulting the dead (1 Sam 28:8); the prophets condemn it, too, but nearly always for what the "diviner" says, in contexts where divining seems simply to parallel other mantic forms (see Isa 3:2; Jer 27:9; 29:8; Ezek 13:9; Mic 3:6, 8). In Gen 30:27, Jacob divines with no apparent stigma attached at all. Balaam is a particularly unfortunate victim of Moses' pogrom, since (according to his story in J) he obeyed Yahweh at considerable personal risk and pronounced four blessings upon Israel, despite being hired by the king of Moab to curse them. But even Balaam admitted that Yahweh left him no choice in the matter, and the deuteronomist remembers him as a prophet whose vocation would have condemned him regardless and who would have cursed Israel for the king's pay if Yahweh had not stopped him (Deut 23:4-5; cf. Josh 24:9-10).

The names "Geshur" and "Maacah" can stand for the people of Geshur and Maacah, as often is the case with the term "Israel" (13:13). Thus the NIV translates "in the midst of Israel" in this verse as "among the Israelites." This seemingly minor point is actually quite important. The NRSV may be potentially misleading: "Israel" here does not mean a territory, whether state or tribal, a modern anachronism. In four of the five references to incomplete dispossession, a similar description occurs, but three different expressions are used. The same expression as in 13:13, "in the midst of" (בקרב *bĕqereb*) occurs in 16:10. That the text is referring to "the Ephraimites" (NIV) rather than to the territory of Ephraim is clear from 15:63. The third reference (in 17:12) is to a territory rather than to a people, and so it makes that distinction explicit: "in that land."

Long before Josiah, the Levites are seen to possess no arable land. In his ancient "blessing" of Levi, Jacob curses their notorious ire and promises to "apportion" them out— instead of giving them a portion—in Jacob and so disperse them in Israel (Gen 49:7). It is tempting to suppose that Jacob's curse gets it backward, since it is easier to imagine that the Levites' ire may result from their landlessness rather than the other way around. Instead of land, they are assigned towns to live in with pasturage for grazing livestock (chap. 21; Num 35:1-8). In the present section, the Levites are mentioned twice, first after the summary introduction (13:14) and then after the details of the allotments and the conclusion (13:33). Several of the Levites' towns with pasturage (chap. 21) lie east of the Jordan, so the narrator includes a reminder that while Levites are to be found east of the Jordan, they are not included in the apportionment of land there. Their "grant" is Yahweh, meaning the cult of Yahweh, supplied with the produce of the land by others (Deut 10:9; 14:22-29; 18:1-8).[107] The Levites do not provide their own staples, but are wards of the monarchy, whether in their towns or at the central shrine. The phrase "the offerings by fire to" is missing from the LXX of 13:14; the two variants are juxtaposed in Deut 18:1-2. The Levites are discussed further in the Commentary on 21:1-45.

---

107. This idiom is the source of the word "clergy," which derives ultimately from the notion of service for God as κλῆρος (*klēros*), Greek for "lot" or "inheritance."

REFLECTIONS

The monarchic role is projected onto Moses, as it has been on Joshua, and not for the first time in Scripture, since Moses played a role akin to that of David in the house of David's early history, represented by the J strand in the Tetrateuch. The interpreter is reminded that the continual process of interpretation and reinterpretation of people, events, and passages as the Bible is produced over many hundreds of years often includes viewing the old in terms of the new, the unfamiliar in terms of the familiar, and the ostensibly unuseful in terms of the useful. This process of interpretation continues without a break to the present. Updating—making the text present today—entails the hermeneutical dilemma, with the inevitable benefits and perils, of loosening the grip of historical rootedness that defines the subject merely on its own terms.

The killing of Balaam reminds us once again of the dispensability of human beings to those in power who feel the need to put principle ahead of lives. Again the reader is faced with the profound clash of values between Josiah's publicized intent to end poverty in Israel and his unyielding determination to eliminate all sources of authority other than his own. The one requires the other, the revolutionary argument runs, and the lives of individuals cannot stand in the way of the greater good. Even people who do not stand to lose their lives immediately might find room for skepticism. Equivalents of this dilemma, with less at stake, frequently confront us: When can we be sure that some greater good really does justify the suffering or wrong along the way?

In some instances the answer is easy. No recognizable good can justify the deaths of millions in famine and of thousands in military purges. In other cases, the answer appears easy, but can become more complicated depending on perspective. Today so-called terrorism is frequently perpetrated in the name of the supposed greater good of national liberation. The outrage against this notion is nearly universal, even among those presumed to be its beneficiaries. Yet it is possible at least to begin to grasp the frustration of terrorists, without justifying their acts. In the land of Joshua, present-day Israel and the occupied territories of Palestine, for example, those able to countenance terrorism can point to the vast imbalance of Palestinian suffering resulting from the Israelis' struggle to secure the good of a Jewish state in Palestine. The justification of war itself is a grand and recurrent instance of the same problem. The extremities of war present genuine dilemmas in their own right. Toward the end of what many have called the last "Good War," for instance, the United States killed over a hundred thousand civilians of Hiroshima and Nagasaki in a successful attempt to avert the deaths of as many or more Americans and Japanese in the planned Allied invasion of Japan.

Comparable uncertainty attends many instances closer to home of suffering or potential wrong caused for supposed short-term or long-term gains. Civil disobedience involving coercion or harm, doctor-assisted suicide, abortion on demand, and capital punishment all pose social dilemmas of great public import. Moreover, in the workplace as well as among friends and family, most people at some time wonder whether to qualify the imperatives of telling the truth and honoring private property in order to achieve what they regard as a greater good.

In this way, the killing of Balaam along with the rest of the onetime inhabitants of Reuben's territory, to say nothing of the general slaughter described by Joshua or its apparent foundation in Josiah's revanchist reform, raises an issue that, in one form or another, no one escapes.

JOSHUA 14:1-5, INHERITANCE BY LOT

COMMENTARY

The tribal allotments east of the Jordan having been defined, the story turns to the tribes west of the Jordan in the land of Canaan. Here the scene is set for the entire main allotment. In this scene, the remaining tribes are treated as though they were farming households in a great village. The village elders—here the patriarchal heads of the tribes—have gathered along with all the heads of cultivating households for the periodic redistributive lottery, as described above. The main item of business before the lottery itself is to decide exactly how many parties or households, here tribes, are participating. Thus v. 2 is the key to this section: The grants are to be apportioned by lot, and nine and a half parties will be participating. The number is explained. The whole group comprises the twelve sons of Israel. Two and a half have already received their grants, and Levi is not to receive a grant of land. The number is now down to eight and a half. However, Joseph is represented by his two sons, to make up for Levi's receiving only towns and pasturage. The result is nine and a half lottery participants.

The Levites are similarly mentioned in 18:7 in the midst of a new setting up for apportionment, this time at Shiloh. Again the crucial question is how many cultivating units the land is to be divided among, and the answer (seven) is again painstakingly explained (18:5-7).

Throughout agrarian history the world over, periodic reallocations of land within cultivating communities have nearly always been carried out by lot. The lottery ensures fairness and allows a community to express its solidarity. As in Palestine, periodic reallocation has been practiced not because people in close communities love to share wealth with one another, but in order to meet a particular need. Although such needs may take different forms, they typically arise from the advantage to the community as a whole of not fixing land as permanent properties. As explained above, in Palestine the community of dry farmers, who must put their land in fallow every second or third year to maintain its productivity, benefits from being able to enclose all of a given year's fallow land in a single block rather than in scattered fields, thereby greatly reducing the fencing, hedging, or surveillance required and making it easier to graze flocks and other livestock safely. The main disadvantage of reallocation is that it takes away the incentive for individuals or households to improve the land they work. Since over time the advantage accrues to and the disadvantage diminishes the community as a whole, it is important for the community not only to share the benefits and drawbacks as equally as possible, by preventing individuals or households from taking particular advantage of the system, but also to make a public display of this intent to sustain the level of cooperation required for such a system to work. This the lottery does.

Redistribution applied only to arable land, which was used for raising grain. Arable land was cultivated anew each year it was not in fallow, and so it did not necessitate long-term investment. Redistribution was not used with land planted in perennial crops, on the other hand, chiefly vineyards and olive orchards. These did require an investment by individuals or households, which they would be reluctant to hazard in a common land pool. During periods of the commercialization of agriculture, such as the eighth and seventh centuries BCE in Palestine, land tended to concentrate in the hands of big landholders, including the deuteronomistic "Canaanites," who could pressure growers into raising grain, grapes, or olives as cash crops rather than diversifying production for subsistence and risk management. Such commercialization is what Josiah's reform was professed to have been designed to counteract.

There were other popular non-village uses of the lottery in land distribution. One took place when groups of tribal or village farmers agreed to cultivate a big landholder's tract of land under a collective sharecropping agreement. Yet another use sometimes compared with Joshua was the lottery imposed by the powerful planters of Greek colonies for the distribution of land, as prescribed, for example, in highly rational detail by Plato in his *Laws*. [108] By this analogy, the conquest constitutes a colonization, and colonizations often were conquests. The Greek concepts of lottery and inherited land were closely related, in the same way that a grant in Hebrew tended to become an inheritance. Indeed, the evidence for the use of the lot in the distribution of land is more common in the Greek sources than in the OT, especially since over 150 Greek colonies were founded around the Mediterranean and the Black Sea within roughly a hundred years, and most within fifty years, of Josiah's reform and the main writing of the book of Joshua.

The idea of this common Greek practice, which like Joshua's distribution was part of a complex mix of political and religious procedures centered in conquest and with a popular—or populist—tinge, may have been based on communal repartitioning like that just described, which it must be assumed was practiced. But what is most noteworthy is that virtually all of the attested instances involve a powerful leader or ruler whose lottery stands for an intrusion of supremacy, and that most of the instances may have been more idealistic than practical. The earliest is the famous example of Nausithoos, legendary king of the Phaiakians. [109] Described as "godlike," Nausithoos led his people to a faraway land where, after building a walled town and temples to the gods, he distributed land to his people by lot. Another example comes from Herodotus's description of the legendary Egyptian king Sesostris. [110] He was the legendary greatest of all Egyptian conquerors and the builder of all of Egypt's myriad canals. Herodotus reports that "it was this king who divided the land among all the Egyptians, giving to each man as an allotment a square, equal in size. . . . If the river should carry off a portion of the allotment, the man would come to the king himself and signify what had happened, whereupon the king sent men to inspect and

remeasure by how much the allotment had grown less, so that for the future it should pay proportionally less of the assigned tax. I think it was from this that geometry was discovered."[111] Sesostris was no ordinary individual. Although in his *Laws* Plato describes a government less autocratic than his earlier utopias, its rationalized regimentation, provisions for surveillance, and communal conformity under a powerful "lawgiver" who imposes the death penalty on anyone encouraging deviance provide illuminating parallels to Josiah's deuteronomistic Israel.

In the ancient world, distribution of land by lot was ubiquitous. It is also likely, however, that it was farming collectives who practiced it in fact, while rulers practiced it mainly in theory. What the Greek parallels suggest is not that Joshua engages in a procedure with historical veracity, but that his is the role of the powerful despot whose image of fairness and equality shows his determination to be an autocrat for the people—autonomous, self-reliant, and unconstrained by the powerful men and households of his realm. It has been pointed out that land division was the most important part of colonization and equality of division the most important issue (cf. Num 26:52-56; Ezek 47:13–48:35); at the same time, it is probable that "the highly oligarchic societies of Greece cannot conceivably have founded colonies in which the citizens were equal."[112] While evidence points to an insistence on equality in theory in the classical period, from which all literary references come, "archaeological evidence and strong arguments from probability make it doubtful if such principles were observed in the colonization of at least the early Archaic period."[113]

There is no reason to believe that Josiah's domain was any less oligarchic than Greece was at the same time. Plato's lawgiver must deal with intractable strong men and anyone

---

108. Plato *Laws* 745 b-3. See Moshe Weinfeld, "The Pattern of the Israelite Settlement in Canaan," in *Congress Volume: Jerusalem 1986*, ed. J. A. Emerton, VTSup 40 (Leiden: Brill, 1988) 270-83, esp. 271, 279-80. In Plato's theory, after capturing land, the lawgiver founds and builds the city and its temples and divides the city, the land, and the people into twelve equal divisions ("tribes"), to whom the land is then allotted.

109. Homer *Odyssey* 6.6-10.

110. Herodotus *History* 2.102-110.

111. Herodotus *History*, 2.109. See *Herodotus: The History*, trans. David Greene (Chicago: University of Chicago Press, 1987) 175.

112. A. J. Graham, "The Colonial Expansion of Greece," in *The Cambridge Ancient History*, 2nd ed. (Cambridge: Cambridge University Press, 1982), 3:151. The tribal allotments in Ezekiel illustrate the extreme theoretical pitch possible when equal distribution is seen by the ruling class: Israel falls exclusively on the west side of the Jordan, and the envisioned allotments, adjoining one another along absolutely straight-line borders, are equal in their north-south dimension only, regardless of topography or east-west breadth.

113. Graham, "The Colonial Expansion of Greece," 152. The Archaic period covers the eighth, seventh, and sixth centuries BCE in Greece and the Aegean.

else who might be reluctant to submit to an autocrat in return for a parsimonious parcel of land:

All the arrangements now described will never be likely to meet with such favorable conditions that the whole program can be carried out according to plan. This requires that the citizens will raise no objection to such a mode of living together, and will tolerate being restricted for life to fixed and limited amounts of property and to families such as we have stated, and being deprived of gold and of the other things which the lawgiver is clearly obliged by our regulations to forbid, and will sub-mit also to the arrangements he has defined . . . almost as if he were telling nothing but dreams, or molding a city and citizen out of wax.[114]

The deuteronomistic historian uses the narrative device of the redistributive lottery metaphorically, not unlike the Greek exam-ples just given. Whether Josiah made grants of land to retainers and followers by lot, or planned to do so, does not much matter. The metaphor of the lottery allows the narrator of Joshua to make several points about Josiah at once. One point is the implied power of the monarchic distributor. In effect, the lottery makes Joshua's allocations arbitrary rather than either rational or, ironically, according to custom. This is the prerogative every central-izing monarch covets and the Greek exam-ples illustrate: the latitude to ignore logic or convention and to neutralize individuals and families of long-standing influence. The result is analogous as well to that achieved in Ath-ens by the introduction, possibly as early as Cleisthenes (late sixth century BCE) or even Solon (early sixth century BCE) of election of

magistrates by lottery, making it more difficult for the long-standing elite to gain powerful positions by virtue of family connections or wealth.[115] A second point palliates the first. It is not Joshua who decides who goes where and who gets what, but Yahweh, whose will the lottery reveals. Ostensibly Joshua's role in the protracted narrative of distribution is quite restricted. This is one of the items in the book of Joshua that scholars sometimes take as an indication that Joshua has been secondarily made the hero of existing stories. This time, however, Joshua's detachment is integral to the story: The village headman stands by to guarantee—as far as his credibil-ity extends—the fairness of the lottery not by producing particular results in his own inter-est, but by ensuring that chance is random, or up to God. A third point is made by pictur-ing Joshua as distributing all the conquered land in a manner that reminds hearers of the way villagers redistribute their arable land in contrast to their vineyards and orchards. This picture might suggest that the amount of village arable land is to increase and the land devoted to cash crops decrease, so that villagers are less likely to be forced into the market, especially during the winter, to purchase staple grain at inflated prices.[116] A fourth point is to affirm the villagers' values expressed through the lottery. As mentioned above, these include security, mutual aid, and equal opportunity, all confirming the funda-mental value of the debt remission that forms the heart of Josiah's reform legislation.

114. Plato Laws, 745e, LCL.

115. Josiah Ober, *Mass and Elite in Democratic Athens: Rhetoric, Ideology, and the Power of the People* (Princeton: Princeton University Press, 1989) 76-79.
116. See Marvin L. Chaney, "Bitter Bounty: The Dynamics of Political Economy Critiqued by the Eighth-Century Prophets," in *Reformed Faith and Economics,* ed. Robert L. Stivers (Lanham: University Press of America, 1989) 15-30.

REFLECTIONS

The lottery outwardly manifests the sovereignty of God, since people receive by lottery whatever God chooses to grant. The sovereignty of God is an essential biblical doctrine, but a doctrine always in potential tension with reason. Christian theologians have struggled with this dilemma since the beginning of the church. The tension is seen clearly in the grant of Canaan to God's chosen people. Neither the grant nor the choice of Israel has a reason. Of course, for both a reason is given: to justify the grant, Ham saw his father naked; to justify the choice of Israel, having been blessed, Abra-ham obediently threw himself on the grace of God. But even if by these acts Ham and

Abraham set themselves apart from all other human beings, the interpreter can still ask whether these acts reasonably lead to and warrant Israel's barbarous dispossession of the "Canaanites." To ask such a question is not to question God's sovereignty, but to pose the problem of theodicy, or God's responsibility for evil, in terms of the biblical text historically rather than abstractly understood—even though in the biblical writer's eyes the conquest of Canaan was a great good. Conversely, the fictional distribution by lot of holdings that fall more or less where they already have in the past verges on making the lottery have no reason: What is the point of a lottery when the outcome is known in advance, from the perspective of writer and hearer? As previously noted, at best it points up the sovereignty of God, which in this instance is at least fair (for the Israelite tribes), if arbitrary. But divine sovereignty in this sense is little more than an abstraction. In reality, the doctrine of God's sovereignty has always served both to thwart power and to support power. The interpreter, therefore, must take the unavoidable next step and ask how the abstraction of God's sovereignty is applied in reality, whether by powers reflected in the text, like Josiah, or by modern claimants to the power of the text.

The Christian doctrines of God's sovereignty and election are based in the Bible on the metaphor of the caprice of the autonomous, all-powerful ruler. Yahweh, the God of both the Old Testament and the New Testament, is a gracious despot. Theologically these doctrines are indispensable, but they have posed an intellectual challenge to the church in all ages; and they produce especially troubling implications in the modern context. In the pre-industrial, agrarian era of the Bible, authority was hierarchical. Arbitrary authority was thus expected and in the end usually accepted, and often glorified. This biblical notion of authority did not drop from the sky. It derived from and was sustained by a clear and definable social and political context. The modern context is different, and hence the modern concept of authority is different. In the modern context, authority is experienced as fundamentally democratic, and hence arbitrary authority is fundamentally unacceptable. The ancient concept of authority found in the Bible cannot trump the modern concept, because the ancient concept had a social and political basis no less than the modern concept. The great watershed occurred in North Atlantic culture during the seventeenth and eighteenth centuries. The distinction now prevails over most of the world. In theory, God is treated as an exception to this development: God's authority is categorically other than democratic authority. In this way, the biblical concept is saved. However, theory becomes fact when in the name of God power is exercised by some individual, group, church, or nation. God may be absolutely sovereign and arbitrary, but humans using power in the name of God are not. They must be reasonable.

The tendency is to ignore these implications rather than grapple with them. A recent survey found that most Americans no longer thought of God as king, lord, or father, but as friend. Without denying the truth of the popular conviction that God is our friend, insofar as it sidesteps most questions of power it leaves most of the Bible out of the picture—and potentially allows the religious justification of the abuse of power in through the back door. When some people exercise power over or against others in the name of God without having to give a reasonable answer to the question, "What gives God the right. . . ?" then injustice is likely to occur.

As the basis for the use of power in the name of God, the sovereignty of God is a two-edged sword. The classical liberal approach to God's sovereignty is rooted in the Age of Reason and is now accepted, explicitly or implicitly, by most Western or Westernized Christians. This approach follows in the natural law tradition. It holds that justice can be discerned by reason and that God must be reasonable. This seems in theory to limit God's freedom, but the alternative may be worse. If God is not limited by reason, then anything is possible; and if anything is possible, then injustice can be justified. By what right does Josiah reconquer the jurisdictions of Davidic Israel? By right of inheritance and the rationale of social justice. What would Josiah's opponents argue against him? To begin with, they might point out that David himself usurped those jurisdictions from Saul. But what about David's purported divine right to usurp, a major theme of the Bible?

There is no ending point to this progression or to the dilemmas evoked in the doctrine of God's sovereignty, essential though it is. Today some Christians would think it presumptuous and arrogant to reason about God's sovereignty, authority, and justice. God is just, so their assumption goes, but God answers to no one. This doctrine leads directly to the problem of Job. In the face of God's overwhelming sovereignty, Job surrenders the right to question God's justice. In the world of the Bible, where the vast majority had no claim to a share in power, and in theory, it may be tolerable to look no further than Job. In our world and in the real world of power, the responsible interpreter and trusting believer, even while affirming the categorical otherness of God, does look further, and like the psalmist refuses to abandon the right to question God.

JOSHUA 14:6–15:63, LAND FOR JUDAH

OVERVIEW

The tribes gather at Gilgal for the distribution of their allotments of land. If the redistributive lottery implies that all the tribes are equal, the descriptions of their territories quickly dispel this impression. Among the tribes, Judah, the tribe of the house of David, takes precedence, both by being first to receive its land grant in Canaan and by having its grant be the one most thoroughly delineated. Judah takes precedence among the tribes because it is the homeland of David, and for Josiah it is the one best known, most important, and largely already held.

The description of Judah's holding falls into four sections. The first and third are narrative; they focus on Caleb and the taking of Hebron and Debir, towns in central Judah (14:6-15; 15:13-19). The second and fourth are lists; they detail the allotment of Judah, first according to its boundaries, then according to its towns, which are grouped in twelve districts (15:1-12, 20-63).

As they appear, the two lists cannot predate the seventh century, and probably Josiah, since they include towns not settled before then. Earlier dates for the lists are often proposed, but there is little agreement about their pre-Josianic form. The interpretation of these and subsequent tribal lists is made difficult by numerous variations in the texts and versions, which indicate a complex history of revision and adjustment, probably both before and after Josiah, and by doubt or complete ignorance about the location of many of the places. Judah's boundaries are not always consistent with the boundaries described for adjacent tribes; the most obvious disagreement may involve Jerusalem, which is mentioned apropos of Judah in 15:63 but assigned to Benjamin in 18:28.

Joshua 14:6-15, Hebron for Caleb

COMMENTARY

This is the first of two stories that feature Caleb as a champion in the allotment of Judah—and a parade example of just the kind of individual who was likely to raise an objection to the lottery on the grounds that he constitutes an exception. Caleb wants his grant before the lottery gets started. Caleb has good grounds, and Joshua recognizes them. Caleb is a living legend, a hero of a different order, not one more foot soldier.

These stories should not be mistaken for chance footnotes to the main theme. Caleb is not an incidental figure for the book of Joshua. At some stage the figure of Joshua was joined to the story of Caleb, which told how Caleb was the only faithful Israelite in a reconnoitering of the land. Once he had turned into the only faithful Israelite in the generation of the exodus and the only Israelite of that generation—including Moses—deserving to inherit land in Canaan (Numbers 13–14; cf. Num 32:12), the question of who will lead Israel into the land arises. Will it be Moses himself, or will someone else be required? And if someone else, why not Caleb? Maybe the house of David before Hezekiah told stories about Caleb's leading a conquest of Israel.

Caleb's name means "dog" (כלב *keleb*). Dogs were usually thought of as fierce curs in the ancient world, and the name carried mostly negative connotations, not much better than "rat" or "skunk" today. By itself it is the tag of a mean man, not simply "Yahweh's best friend." But the name, which was actually quite common in the ancient world, could also be used affirmatively to mean a faithful and submissive servant. Caleb and Joshua are the deuteronomists' models of faithful servants. Joshua got into Caleb's story to help connect the earlier Davidic history of Israel, the JE parts of the Tetrateuch, to the history of the house of David's right to reconquer Israel. Caleb's story is repeated at length by Moses at the beginning of the Deuteronomistic History as an object lesson in obedience to the command to conquer the land without fear (Deut 1:19-45). It has already formed part of the groundwork of Joshua's succession to Moses, since, unlike Caleb, even Moses is indeed prevented from crossing the Jordan (cf. Deut 3:23-28). Then two further related stories about Caleb are told here in Joshua 14–15, and the second is repeated in Judg 1:11-15. Finally, Caleb's nephew Othniel, who figures in the latter story, becomes the Judahite "judge" (Judg 3:7-11), the first to fill that role, serving as a paradigm for all the judges who follow.

Caleb plays an important role in the allotment of Judah for the same reason he was singled out in J. As the eponymous ancestor of a—possibly the—major clan of Hebron, he represents the center of Judah and the town that David made his first capital. For the modern historian, the Calebites' role in the rise of David remains indistinct, but enough evidence is preserved to indicate that it must have been significant.[117] Caleb is said to have descended from the Kenizzites, one of the "pre-Israelite" peoples of Canaan (Gen 15:19; cf. Gen 36:11). Apparently the Calebites came to prominence among the Israelites (cf. the example of Uriah "the Hittite," 2 Sam 11:3–12:10; 23:39) and were worked into the genealogy of Judah, a process of which the genealogies in 1 Chronicles 2 and 4:15 are somewhat confusing vestiges. The first husband of David's wife Abigail was a Calebite nicknamed Nabal, "fool," whom David may have had killed in a move to supplant him (1 Samuel 25:1).[118] The narrator in Joshua 14–15 has a grasp of this and much more of Caleb's part in the Davidic heritage (and possibly more that is unknown to us), and by telling two stories about Caleb's land holdings he pays homage to it.

The two stories imply that Hebron and Debir have not yet been captured and so contradict the earlier conquest of Hebron and Debir (10:36-39; 12:10, 13). This inconsistency, intensified by 11:21-22, where Joshua is given all the credit for defeating the Anakim and Caleb none, cannot be resolved—though clearly Joshua, the likely newcomer to the house of David's story, had to prove himself equal to the Judahite hero, who is not modest about his abilities (14:11). Along with the story of Caleb's faithfulness, these two stories derive from a pre-deuteronomistic tradition of Caleb's exploits, of much the same character as the saga accounts found, for example, in Joshua 2 and 7–8. The final phrase of the first story, "the land had rest from war" (14:15), is surprising, since there is no battle account, and it seems to contradict the summary phrase in 11:23. It is apparently used to cap the allusion to dispossession in the mention of the Anakim (14:12, 15), just as the elliptical version of the phrase caps comparable episodes in Judges (Judg 3:11, 30; 5:31; 8:28). Nonetheless it would seem to go better at the end of 15:19, after Hebron

---

117. Mark J. Fretz and Raphael I. Panetz, "Caleb," *ABD* 1:808-10.
118. Jon D. Levenson, "1 Samuel 25:1 as Literature and as History," *CBQ* 40 (1978) 11-28; Jon D. Levenson and Baruch Halpern, "The Political Import of David's Marriages," *JBL* 99 (1980) 507-18.

and Debir are again fully captured. A sure sign of the independence of the tradition of Caleb's faithfulness is 14:12, which implies that Joshua was not one of the spies in Numbers 13–14 (even in Deut 1:36-38, Joshua is almost an afterthought).

REFLECTIONS

Caleb gets his personal grant of land at the beginning of a distribution that finds Joshua getting his personal grant of land at the end (19:49-50). These two individual grants bracket the grants to the west-bank tribes. The two great heroes of obedience—the old-timer and the newcomer—are given equivalent recognition. This is a stately variation on the projection of Josiah's exploits into Israel's venerable past, in which attention is diverted from the big man of the present, Josiah, to his illustrious predecessors, and in deference to the traditional Judahite hero, Caleb receives his grant first. The careful balance between Caleb and Joshua is maintained only up to a point. Joshua defeats the Anakim of Hebron before Caleb offers to do the same. Joshua grants Caleb his land, not the other way around. It is always an act of graciousness to defer to predecessors and others of the past, to honor those who have gone before, who have spent their lives and thus may manifest more clearly than ourselves what God can do through a given individual. Leaders especially would do well to remember that it does not cost the living to honor the dead, or the young to honor the old, or the incumbent to honor previous holders of their office. Such respect gives the chance to show gratefulness for the gifts of life, youth, or responsibility by sharing the advantages they confer.

Joshua 15:1-63, Land for Judah

COMMENTARY

The territory of Judah is described in two sections, by boundaries (15:1-12) and by towns (15:20-63); only the descriptions of Benjamin (18:11-28) and Naphtali (19:32-39), and fragmentarily Zebulun (19:10-16), Issachar (19:17-23), and Asher (19:24-31) match this pattern. These two Judahite lists are separated by the second story of Caleb (15:13-19; cf. Judg 1:11-15).

Four boundaries of Judah are described in the order of south, east, north, and west. Judah is bounded on three sides by natural features—sink, desert, and sea—and consists of the southern portion of ancient Canaan. The southern boundary runs from the border with Edom in the Arabah below the Dead Sea west to the Mediterranean at Wadi el-Arish, on the edge of the Sinai desert southwest of Gaza (15:1-4), although a few localities named later may fall below this line. The eastern boundary is the Dead Sea (15:5a). The northern boundary runs from the mouth of the Jordan at the northern end of the Dead Sea west to the Mediterranean at Jabneel, modern Yavne south of Tel Aviv (15:5b-11). This boundary, which in the highland Judah shares with Benjamin and in the foothills and lowland with Dan, separates Judah from the rest of Israel. Hence it is not surprising that it is described in more detail than any other and that it agrees almost entirely with Benjamin's southern boundary (18:15-19, described west to east). The brief description of Dan includes no boundary list (19:41-46). Judah's western boundary is the Mediterranean Sea (15:12a).

The town list (15:20-63) almost certainly represents an administrative division of Judah into twelve districts. Because the districts are partly ideals, if not utopian, the list would seem to come from either Hezekiah's or Josiah's reform program. In Sennacherib's account of the siege of Jerusalem, Hezekiah is said to be allied with several of the Philistine towns named. Several of the towns were settled only in the seventh century BCE. Hezekiah, therefore, is the less likely candidate. The list's relatively high degree of clarity suggests a recently composed document.

Scholars do not agree on how exactly the list represents the assumed twelve districts. The best solution would seem to be that represented by the NIV paragraphs, which differ from the NRSV only in combining vv. 45-47. This division produces eleven districts: one in the Negeb; four in the Shephelah (the western foothills or lowland); five in the highland; and one in the desert. The missing district, the tenth in sequence, is supplied by the LXX of the end of v. 59. It was lost by a classic case of homoioteleuton (an occurrence in writing of the same or similar endings near together), in which a scribe accidently skipped from "villages" at the end of v. 59 to "villages" at the end of the lost text and continued to copy from there. The lost text, representing a sixth highland district, reads "Tekoa, Ephrathah (that is, Bethlehem), Peor, Etam, Koloun, Tatam, Sores, Kerem, Gallim, Bether, Manahath—eleven towns and their villages." This correction is worth noting because it restores a large district in the northeast corner of Judah. This district centers on Bethlehem and borders Jerusalem and thus is of utmost importance to the house of David. It represents a surprising gap in the MT and an unfortunate omission from the marginal notes of both the NRSV and the NIV.

The town lists' sums do not always match the number of towns named; there are more than 29 towns in the first district (15:21-32), as apparently the list has grown without the sum's being recalculated. The new eleventh district, consisting of only two towns (15:60), seems too small. Many believe that the list for this district may have been transferred to the list for Benjamin (18:21-28), since Kiriath-jearim occurs in both lists (however, cf. 18:14) and Beth-arabah from the last district (15:61) is included as well (18:22). Three great Philistine towns make up an extremely broad and rich fifth district (15:45-47) whose towns and villages are neither listed nor tallied. This region, which no king of Judah, including probably even David, ever controlled, shows that the entire town list for Judah resembles a wish list as much as an administrative list (cf. 11:22; 13:2-3). The section concludes by noting that the Judahites cannot expel the Jebusites from Jerusalem, a failure later laid on the Benjaminites and contrasted to Caleb's success in capturing Hebron (Judg 1:20-21). The capture of Jerusalem, the deuteronomistic center, awaits the arrival of David (2 Sam 5:6).

Between the two Judahite lists, the Calebite capture of Hebron and Debir is narrated (15:13-19; cf. Judg 1:11-15, 20). The deuteronomist gets the names of the individual Anakim from Num 13:22. The main episode explains how the Calebite Othniel came to rule Debir, but its principal theme is more specific than that. The purpose of the story is to answer the question, How did the ruler of Debir acquire the rights to the two springs that bubble into the brown soil a mile and a half north of the town, its closest fresh water supply?[119] Unfortunately, the answer, and thus the point of the story, is something of a mystery. The point hinges on the connection between what Achsah does while sitting on her donkey—or "from" her donkey—and the gift she receives. No one knows for certain what either of these is. The meaning of the verb translated "dismount" (צנח *ṣānaḥ*, which occurs only here, in the parallel in Judg 1:14, and in Judg 4:21) and the noun translated "springs" (גלת *gullōt*) is uncertain. Neither the verb nor the noun represents the usual expression for its respective translation, and both translations are probably incorrect. An Akkadian cognate to the verb means "have diarrhea" (leading the great philologist G. R. Driver mistakenly to translate it "make a noise"—that is, break wind—in the NEB); and the noun גלה (*gullâ*), which can mean "bowl," comes from a Hebrew root also found in several words for excrement (גל *gel*, גלל *gālāl*, גלול *gillûl*). One plain meaning of Caleb's question to Achsah is, "What's the matter?" If the visual and verbal pun is not the obvious but lamentably scatological one, in which Achsah's diarrhea leaves pools beneath her donkey, evoking both the likeness of and a term for muddy spring basins (גלת מים *gullōt māyim*, "watery excrement," "watery basins"), then it remains beyond our ken.[120]

119. Robert G. Boling and G. Ernest Wright, *Joshua*, AB 6 (Garden City, N.Y.: Doubleday, 1982) 376.

120. For an alternative view, see the comments of Danna Nolan Fewell in "Textual Incites: Achsah and the (E)razed City of Writing," in *Judges and Method: New Approaches in Biblical Studies*, ed. Gale A. Yee (Minneapolis: Fortress, 1995) 129-41.

REFLECTIONS

Judah is home to the deuteronomist, so Judah's allocation gets the most careful and complete description. The small land is subdivided into twelve districts, and the settlements in each are detailed in turn. Organized administration looks good to us, and so it did to the government in Jerusalem that gave us this list. To the people in the towns, villages, and tents of the land, it looked different. People in Palestine tended not to care for administration, just as they did not like the census, which was useful mainly for taxation, conscription, or surveillance (cf. 2 Sam 24:1-17). There is always a tension between the governing and the governed that goes quite beyond the civil realm. What are the purposes of administration? How are its purposes to be achieved? The governing and the governed must find a common answer to these questions if rule is to succeed. In the ancient era, self-justifying government tended toward an autocratic tyranny. In the modern era, it tends toward a bureaucratic tyranny, though autocracy is always a danger as well. The idealistic scheme of the allocation to Judah raises the issue of the ends of government policy, or of any policy imposed by one on another. Whose interests are served? Does Josiah know best? The question arises even when it is acknowledged that it is God's plan and that God knows best, since even God's plan may serve one side's interests more than another's. The interpreter is again catapulted into the hermeneutical circle.

For the community of faith today, these questions arise whenever individual believers undertake to assess the roles and policies of governments and administrations in the light of their Christian beliefs. The biblical pattern for connecting administrative policy with strategic commitments becomes visible in this and most texts in Joshua when one recognizes its relationship to the centralizing and reforming laws of Deuteronomy. In this case, the ideal of relief for the majority poor, encapsulated in Deut 15:1-18, is affirmed in a "national" covenant with God. In the modern world, the establishment of tolerance and pluralism in the United States Constitution, which by the intention of its authors, but to the frustration of many, makes no mention of God, means that commitments based on faith are expressed through individuals and groups, including those holding public office, attempting to influence government rather than through government as such. The ideal is for as many as possible of those who are under a particular government, including Christian believers, to participate in the process of influencing that government, from voting to lobbying to acting responsibly in office. This is the case not only in the United States, but in most constitutional democracies.

A closer parallel to the biblical pattern of policy and faith can be expressed in the church itself. Although in the modern era neither nation nor theocracy, the church is the institution wherein the policies of administration and the interests and requirements of members can be brought together in a common undertaking in obedience to God. Most modern churches are representative to some degree. Representation usually helps to reduce the gap between the interests of administrators and those of members. Ambiguities continue to arise, however, concerning who is to be represented and how, and concerning the potential tension between the authority of the Bible and the authority of the majority. As overall conserving institutions, churches also struggle with whether the inertia of bureaucracies and entrenched leadership works for or against God. The preacher might want to reflect on the attitudes appropriate to those who hold church office, including the office of preacher. Given the ambiguities of church governance, the classical disciplines of Christian discipleship take on all the more importance: prayer, ongoing Bible study, unassuming consultation, an eagerness to be guided by the Holy Spirit, and a generous respect for and estimation of fellow members.

JOSHUA 16:1–17:18, LAND FOR THE SONS OF JOSEPH

COMMENTARY

The allotments for Ephraim and Manasseh follow immediately without a transition. The two tribes representing the sons of Joseph rank with Joseph's brothers their uncles; long after the event, the priestly strand in Genesis explained that Jacob simply declared it so (Gen 48:5-6). Historical geography tells us more. Since before David the highlands of Ephraim and Manasseh had formed much of the heartland of Israel, the mountains whose productivity the tribes of Israel significantly enhanced, in which they found refuge, and from which they launched their offensives against lowland rivals. As mentioned above, the reconciliation of Joseph and Judah formed the core of the story of the sons of Israel in J, the early Davidic history of Israel, and the three towns that became capitals of Israel once the Israelites had thrown off the yoke of the house of David—Shechem, Tirzah,

and Samaria—lay in Manasseh. The younger son, Ephraim, precedes Manasseh (cf. 17:1) because Jacob crossed his hands when he blessed them, declaring that Ephraim would become the greater (Gen 48:8-20). This tale is from J and was known to the deuteronomists. The stress on both brothers' greatness in Gen 48:19 is recalled by the tribes' complaint that they are numerous and Joshua's response at the end of this section (Josh 17:14-18), even though the Hebrew terms differ. The importance of Manasseh is nowhere clearer than in the naming of Hezekiah's son and heir, likely part of his bid for Israelite support.

This section has four parts. The southern boundary is drawn (16:1-3), followed by the allotments of the two sons (16:4-10; 17:1-13). The section concludes with the tribes' appeal for more land and Joshua's response confining them to the highland (17:14-18).

Joshua 16:1-10, Land for Ephraim

COMMENTARY

The narrator launches right in by delineating the boundary between the tribes of Joseph and Benjamin, from Jericho to Gezer by way of Bethel. Jericho and Bethel themselves lie in Benjamin (18:21-22). In the hills north of this line are found the holdings of the sons of Joseph.

The heading (v. 4) marks the descriptions of the two allotments as parallel (vv. 5-10; 17:1-13). Both contain boundary lists, but no proper town lists. Both pay heed to towns under one tribe's jurisdiction but lying within

the bounds of another tribe (v. 9; 17:8-9, 11), an indication that traditional jurisdictions had to be honored notwithstanding the partly artificial tribal bounds postulated by the central government. Both descriptions mention that Ephraim and Manasseh are unable to expel all the Canaanites from large towns under their control, but are able to impose corvée duty on them (v. 10; 17:12-13; cf. Judg 1:27-29), at last fulfilling the curse of Canaan, which justified the conquest in the first place (Gen 9:25).

REFLECTIONS

The fulfillment of the curse of Canaan expresses at best a backhanded compliment. The Davidic historian gives these two tribes of Joseph—always troublesome to Judah—the credit for fulfilling the curse, but as little credit as possible. Each of the likely rulers behind the composition of this section, Josiah and Hezekiah, knows that he must compromise with these powerful folk of the old Israelite hills, so the writer acknowledges their power ("put to forced labor"), but at the same time recalls their weaknesses ("did not drive them out").

Sometimes it is necessary to limit the esteem bestowed on worthy rivals with whom compromise is unavoidable. Prudence suggests that those given charge should pay the necessary compliments to those who could stand in their way, but without exaggerating to disguise reluctance. Acknowledge the opponent's strength, but with moderation. This the text subtly but tactfully does. The text is in keeping with scriptural advice to speak moderately and treat enemies with kindness. A good example of such advice is found in Prov 25:11-28, which Paul cites in Rom 12:14-21 and which the Gospel of Matthew follows in Matt 5:43-48.

All three of these texts (Prov 25:22; Matt 5:45; Rom 12:19) place the treatment of rivals in the context of God's judgment (cf. Matt 13:24-30). Undergirded by the judgment of God, the prescribed ideal for rulers in both the Old Testament and the New Testament is meekness. Probably Hezekiah and Josiah each saw himself, on the model of their ancestor David, as appropriately meek in the face of God's judgment. The ambiguity in the text arises from the fact that such prescriptions for meekness were almost always made from a position of actual strength; the Bible's proverbial wisdom tends to be court wisdom. Whether the advice that the strong be meek is appropriate for those who are already weak and poor, or the best way to bring the judgment of God to bear on the plight of the weak and poor is a question worth careful consideration by anyone who is not.

Joshua 17.1-13, Land for Manasseh

COMMENTARY

Manasseh, the firstborn of Joseph, has to give way to Ephraim, but his own firstborn he treats better. To Machir (NIV, "Makir") goes the first grant, east of the Jordan in the fertile Gilead and Bashan (vv. 1-2; cf. 13:29-31). West of the Jordan, Manasseh's grant goes to clans descended from six sons, including the five granddaughters from one of them, making a total of ten main divisions (vv. 5-6). Lesser claimants join Machir in the east (v. 6).

The six clan names represent regions or localities. The significance of Shechem is obvious. Three others—Helek, Asriel, and Shamida—occur in the Samaria ostraca from the eighth century BCE as notable sources of wine and oil. These all cluster within eight miles of Samaria. Hepher is Zelophehad's father. His name appears in the district list found in the account of Solomon's reign (1 Kgs 4:10). The area of Hepher is now known to have been in the Dothan Valley north of Samaria. As suggested by the name

"Tirzah," Jeroboam I's second capital, northeast of Shechem, the groups tracing themselves to Hepher's granddaughters may cluster farther east.

The story of the daughters of Zelophehad (vv. 3-6) is taken directly from Num 27:1-11 so that Joshua can be said to fulfill another of Moses' commands. Whatever the source of the passage in Numbers, it is introduced there as part of the priestly editing of the Tetrateuch, and it appears here in the book of Joshua as a priestly addition as well (cf. Eleazar, v. 4).

The issue raised by the daughters in Numbers 27 is the order of inheritance in case a married man has no sons. The deuteronomists have their own solution to that problem—namely, levirate (brother-in-law) marriage (Deut 25:5-10). Based on ancient and widespread custom, the levirate law requires that when a man who has had no sons dies, regardless of whether he has had daughters, his brother is to marry his widow, the vulnerable and marginalized daughter-in-law in the family, and bestow the inheritance of the deceased on the widow's firstborn in the name of the deceased and in his line. Thereafter the firstborn, beholden to his mother, may marry with his inheritance on his own account, since he is male, regardless of the wishes of his paternal uncles, including his biological father. Whether or not the widow had daughters, the uncles neither acquire the land nor dispose of it. The purpose of the levirate is to strengthen the wife-centered nuclear family at the expense of the patriarchal extended family (see the Commentary on 7:1–8:29). Although widely attested in pre-industrial societies, the levirate was frequently unpopular (cf. Gen 38:1-11). The continuance of the deceased brother's inheritance diminished the size of the inheritances of the surviving brothers, especially if the deceased was the firstborn. By trying to enforce the levirate, Josiah hoped to reduce the concentration of wealth in a given patriarchal household's hands.

The priestly rule laid down in response to the daughters of Zelophehad is different (Num 27:8-11). It allows the widow to be ignored by requiring that the property pass unencumbered to the daughters, if there are any. Even though they are then without father and brothers, they are beholden as usual, being female, to marry with their inheritance not on their own account, but according to the

wishes of their paternal uncles, returning the advantage to the patriarchal family (cf. Num 36:1-12). If there are no daughters, the land passes directly to the paternal uncles of either the first or the second generation back. It is little wonder that the priestly writer of vv. 3-6 does not spell out the point of Moses' ruling regarding the daughters of Zelophehad, given its incongruence with the law of levirate marriage.[121]

The description of Manasseh's allotment is confined to vv. 7-9, even shorter than Ephraim's sketchy account. The dearth of information on the territory of these two tribes fits with the failure of the narrative of conquest to devote any attention at all to the conquest of this territory. The contrast with the full description of Judah (chap. 15) is meant to be noticed. However, people of Manasseh held the great towns of the Jezreel Valley even though they did not lie within the tribal bounds, a demonstration of their power (v. 11). Perhaps Josiah had to depend on the heads of Ephraim and Manasseh to organize their own administration. These Jezreel towns are on Joshua's list of conquest (12:21, 23), but the men of Manasseh are not powerful enough to carry out completely the ethnic cleansing of their territory (v. 12; Judg 1:27), unlike Judah.

---

121. For an analysis of feminist readings of Num 27:1-11, see Katharine Doob Sakenfeld, "In the Wilderness, Awaiting the Land: The Daughters of Zelophehad and Feminist Interpretation," *The Princeton Seminary Bulletin* 9 (1988) 179-96; also Sakenfeld, "Feminist Biblical Interpretation," *Theology Today* 46 (1989) 154-68.

REFLECTIONS

The inheritance of the daughters of Zelophehad represents an empowerment. The deuteronomist clearly regarded empowerment as a zero-sum game: Power given to nuclear households was power taken away from extended households. Such a notion of power is often a valid one, particularly in contexts where power is distributed unequally and a justifiable struggle for power ensues. In the Bible, God's judgment often takes just this form, taking power away from one and giving it to another. This understanding inheres in the pervasive biblical metaphor of justification and its rhetorical expression, which over and over hold that to declare one party innocent is to declare another guilty and that the justification of one requires the condemnation of another. If the wrongful use of power is at stake, as it usually is in the Bible, then the judgment of God against it is understandably construed as a dialectic. Moreover, it is often pointed out that in agrarian societies experience usually dictates a zero-sum notion of the common good, so that by analogy the redistribution of any quantity must entail mutual gain and loss.

An alternative view holds that to empower one person is to empower others. The amount of compassion, affirmation, capability, self-respect, and self-fulfillment available is limitless, more than enough for all to have all they need. This view, in keeping with the focus on self-actualization in our individualistic culture, likewise has validity. It works well in contexts in which the wrongful use of power is not at issue, and thus tends to neglect much of what is in the Bible. It is a view in tune not only with the individualizing tendencies in our society, but also with the classical liberal tenets of universal likeness of individuals, individual worth and the opportunity of choice, and general social amelioration and progress. These liberal assumptions are inherent in our national political, economic, and social institutions and in our sense of competition among competitors sharing equal opportunity. Thus they tend to prevail over the contending assumption of dissension and strife between inimical opponents. It is possible that the individualizing view is favored by those who are better off and do not have to struggle to make ends meet.

Joshua 17:14-18, The Hill Country for the Sons of Joseph

COMMENTARY

In case those great sons of Joseph begin to think they have a right to take over in power in those strong lowland towns, the narrator tells a story in which Joshua orders them to be satisfied with the highland (vv. 14-18). The "portion" (vv. 5, 14) is the same in Hebrew as a "cord" (חֶבֶל *hebel*), since a cord was laid out when dividing up parcels of farming land by lot (cf. Amos 7:17; Mic 2:5); this is a direct reflex of the communal practice behind the metaphor of division by lot (see Commentary on 14:1-5; elsewhere in Joshua, "portion" translates various words). The references to forests and maquis do not imply a Bronze Age date, as sometimes suggested. The forests, which by NT times may have been nearly as sparse as

they were into the twentieth century CE, were still widespread in the monarchic period, and it would have involved no strain of the imagination to picture the hills covered with them. (A number of reasons for the denuding of the Palestine hills have been suggested; goats may have been the main culprits.) The mention of iron, on the other hand, is an obvious anachronism, since iron did not come into common use in Palestine until the tenth century BCE or later (cf. 6:19, 24; 22:8). The sons of Joseph should have little difficulty in expelling Canaanites from the highland, since chariots of iron (weaponry, fixtures, plating) would not have been of much use to them in the hills (cf. Num 13:29).

JOSHUA 18:1-10, LAND SURVEY AND LOTS AT SHILOH

COMMENTARY

The scene shifts from Gilgal to Shiloh, situated halfway between Ai and Shechem, for the allotment of land to the remaining seven tribes. Eleazar is a priestly addition, as is probably the mention of the tent of meeting, which occurs only here and in the corresponding summary in 19:51 (cf. 1 Sam 2:22 MT). While sudden, the shift to Shiloh belongs

to the deuteronomistic story. Together the Deuteronomistic History and the book of Jeremiah imply that the family of Hilkiah, the priest of Josiah's reform, traditionally came from Shiloh. Shiloh is the only location before Jerusalem to be described, in a deuteronomistic text, as "my place . . . where I made my name dwell at first" (Jer 7:12 NRSV; cf.

Deut 12:5; Judg 18:31; 1 Samuel 1:1–3; Ps 78:60). This gives Shiloh a unique status in deuteronomistic eyes. Moreover, the significance of Hilkiah's name (חלקיהו *ḥilqiyyāhû*), which means "Yahweh is my portion," is made clear by v. 7 (cf. 13:14, 33; 14:3-4). The Levites have no "portion" of land (also 14:4), since "the priesthood of Yahweh is their grant" (also 13:33; as noted above, this phrase lies behind the origin of the English word "clergy," which ultimately derives from Greek κλῆρος [*klēros*, "lot," "inheritance"]). Hence Hilkiah's name: "[the priesthood of] Yahweh is my portion," in lieu of a portion of land. And hence in Hilkiah's ancestral home the majority of Israelite tribes, seven of twelve, receive their portions—and the Levites do too (21:2). (The assignment of Anathoth to the Aaronids in 21:18, which may be reflected in the epigonic prose of Jer 11:21-23, is probably a Persian period maneuver.)

The faction that most directly supported Josiah's partisan program appears to have been a Levite group originally from Shiloh in Ephraim and then from Anathoth in Benjamin. The nature of this faction goes far toward explaining the book of Joshua's enthusiasm for its Ephraimite hero and the special attention it gives to Benjaminite traditions in Joshua 1–9 and to Gilgal in Benjamin and Shiloh in Ephraim as the sites where the distribution of the land takes place (14:6; 18:1). As outsiders this faction represented the interests of a particular segmentary power rather than of the segmentary powers in general or of the ancestral priesthood in Jerusalem. The established priesthood had been made unpopular by their trade and debt practices, and they suffered discredit at court because of their inconsistent loyalties. It is also probable that the established priesthood, whose ancestry according to later texts went all the way back to Aaron, had deep ties with the early priests of Bethel. The priests of Bethel were also putatively descended from Aaron, as indicated by the similarity of Jeroboam's golden calves with the golden calf fabricated by Aaron in Exodus 32. As pointed out by Friedman, when Josiah turns the "Asherah" of the Temple and the extraneous altars into "dust" (NRSV has also "rubble") and scatters the dust on graves and in the wadi, he performs an act described only one other time in the Deuteronomistic History, indeed,

in the entire Bible—namely, what Moses said he did to Aaron's golden calves (Deut 9:21; 2 Kgs 23:6, 12; cf. Exod 32:20).[122]

From Jeremiah and the Deuteronomistic History, it is possible to know something about Josiah's upstart priestly supporters, though not nearly as much as desired. The reform faction centered on the priestly family of Hilkiah, who discovered the document of Moses' Torah in the Temple, and the scribal families of Shaphan, who brought the document to Josiah and read it to him, together with Neriah, the father of the prophet Jeremiah's amanuensis Baruch.[123] The "faithful priest" referred to in 1 Sam 2:35 is almost always taken to be Zadok, the eponym (supplied with an Aaronid genealogy) of the dominant priestly family in Jerusalem from Solomon onward. But despite Zadok's supposed importance, he is of practically no interest to the Deuteronomistic History except to be implicated in the failure of Solomon's reign. The "faithful priest" who is to perform what Yahweh "thinks and wills" is more likely, at least in the conception of Josiah's deuteronomist, to be the non-Zadokite Hilkiah than Zadok, the priest on whose watch the house of David polluted the cult of Yahweh and lost its sovereignty over Israel (cf. 1 Chr 5:29-31; 9:10-11).

Jeremiah belonged to this faction. Friedman gives a concise summary: "When Jeremiah sent a letter to the exiles in Babylon, it was delivered for him by Gemariah, son of *Hilkiah,* and by Elasah, son of *Shaphan.* When Jeremiah wrote a scroll of prophecies against Josiah's son Jehoiakim, it was read at the chamber of Gemariah, son of *Shaphan.* Gemariah, son of Shaphan, stood by Jeremiah at critical moments in his life, as did Ahikam, son of Shaphan, who saved Jeremiah from being stoned. And Gedaliah, son of Ahikam, son of Shaphan, when he was appointed governor of Judah by Nebuchadnezzar, took Jeremiah under protection."[124] The book

122. Richard Elliott Friedman, *Who Wrote the Bible?* (New York: Summit, 1987) 113.

123. Friedman, *Who Wrote the Bible?* 120-26; J. Andrew Dearman, "My Servants the Scribes: Composition and Context in Jeremiah 36:1," *JBL* 109 (1990) 403-21; Patricia Dutcher-Walls, "The Social Location of the Deuteronomists: A Sociological Study of Factional Politics in Late Pre-Exilic Judah," *JSOT* 52 (1992) 77-94.

124. Friedman, *Who Wrote the Bible?* 125. Hundreds of personal names from around the time of Josiah are attested on ostraca, seals, and seal impressions, but only a few agree with figures mentioned in the Bible. Of those that do, most are mentioned in Jeremiah 36 and related texts, particularly Baruch, Seraiah, and Gemariah.

of Jeremiah is the only prophecy to refer to Shiloh, which is described with the deuteronomistic phrase "the place where Yahweh caused his name to dwell" (Jer 7:12). Jeremiah was the son of a priest from Anathoth, just north of Jerusalem (Jer 1:1; 11:21-23; 36:6-15), presumably descended from Abiathar, the priest of the house of Eli at Shiloh who served David and was banished by Solomon to Anathoth. Jeremiah's prophetic book was composed with language and ideas practically identical to those of the Deuteronomistic History, and his father's name was Hilkiah.[125] It is usually assumed that the priest of Josiah's reform and Jeremiah's father were two different men, but Friedman has pointed out that they could have been the same. In any case, like the deuteronomistic historian (who may have been Shaphan), Jeremiah identified as his prophetic forebears Samuel, the oracle behind the house of David, and Moses, the medium of the house of David's law (Jer 15:1).

How did such village-based families, minor segmentary powers in their own right but with little or no obvious strength in Jerusalem, come to power in the house of David, presumably during Josiah's youth? There is no way to know for certain (just as there is no way to know how Draco and Solon came to power in Greece), but it is worth speculating about from what is known about the house of David in the later Assyrian period and from what little is said, but is implied on a grand scale, in the Deuteronomistic History. In the history's account, members of the court of Amon, Manasseh's son and successor and Josiah's father, murdered Amon after a rule of only two years. (It is not known why Amon was murdered, but since he was not born until Manasseh was forty-five years old, he is likely to have had, like Solomon, older brothers with connections who thought the throne was rightfully theirs.) In the ensuing turmoil, segmentary powers (the meaning of עַם־הָאָרֶץ [ʿam-hāʾāreṣ; NRSV, "the people of the land"] in this context) of some ilk intervened to avenge the murder (2 Kgs 21:24). Momentarily in control, the avengers placed on the

throne the eight-year-old Josiah and provided, it must be presumed, for a regency—today we might call them Josiah's handlers—to manage his responsibilities during his minority and to look after their own advantage. It is quite likely that their chosen partisans, Hilkiah and Shaphan and their families, were the regency.

These partisans developed a liking for power and, partly to further their own interests in local conflicts (cf. Jer 32:6-15), encouraged their ward, as he grew older, in renewing the house of David's offensive against opposing segmentary powers, who among other things may still have been attempting to gain their own hold on the house of David. The cabal's means was a partisan populist reform, designed to garner support from an oppressed populace. Depending on whether Josiah in his teens and twenties continued to be dependent on his segmentary patrons, he either turned the tables on them or, with his plan to reconquer Israel and reallocate its lands, set out to help them fulfill their greatest dream of regaining land in erstwhile Israel. (Again, Hilkiah's name means "Yahweh is my portion of land.") The partisans' work was made easier by Egypt and Assyria, who gave them permission, albeit ambivalent, to press the reform.

Shiloh is one of the few Early Iron Age sites potentially associated with early Israel that have been excavated. Scant remains were found at the Late Bronze Age level, but a major settlement existed in the Early Iron period, whose pottery was "strongly in the overall Late Bronze tradition with respect to all individual types," not distinctively "Israelite."[126] The same description applies, in Dever's view, to the possible shrine identified by the excavator.[127] Shiloh was resettled as a village during the period of the monarchy, as evidenced by scattered remains in Stratum IV at the site. Its significance for the deuteronomist may be more symbolic than substantive.

125. Baruch Halpern, "Shiloh," *ABD* 5:1215.

126. William G. Dever, *BAR* 21/6 (November-December 1995) 10, review of Israel Finkelstein, *Shiloh: The Archaeology of a Biblical Site* (Tel Aviv: Institute of Archaeology, 1993).

127. Dever, review of Israel Finkelstein, *Shiloh: The Archaeology of a Biblical Site*, 8.

REFLECTIONS

1. The scene of redistribution shifts to Shiloh as soon as the territory of the tribes of Joseph, where Shiloh lies, is alloted. From the standpoint of Josiah's age, as opposed to the putative age of Joshua, this privileging of Shiloh (under Josiah no more than a small town that for hundreds of years had had little or no import) is extraordinary. It is tied, of course, to the traditional background of the deuteronomistic cabal, who regarded themselves as small and insignificant, the truly powerless amid the struggles of the powerful, dependent on Yahweh alone for whatever success they achieve. Their history recalls how they were reduced to a thin line of survival that ended up in one lone individual, Abiathar, who lost out in contention with Zadok, priest of the Davidic temple, and was banished to Anathoth. Josiah's cabal thought of themselves as this thin line of succession come back, looking to restore the prerogatives of David's support of the tribal cult under Abiathar, possibly involving the Levites as well. This tribal cult originally functioned alongside of, but separate from, David's private household cult under Zadok. Since the latter had enjoyed all the benefits since Solomon, it was time for the descendants of Abiathar to have their turn. The desire to have their own privileges restored lies behind the role of Shiloh in the book of Joshua. Their sense of lone vulnerability is abundantly personified in Jeremiah as portrayed in the book of Jeremiah.

The concept of ethnic cleansing in Joshua does not pit the strong against the weak, as was the case with genocide against Jews in Europe and Native Americans in the United States. The deuteronomist pictures a weak Israel fighting against a strong Canaanite, whom they may nevertheless, with Yahweh's help, annihilate. The Canaanites are "great and strong nations" (23:9; Deut 7:1). "Israel" is weak and must fight using guerrilla tactics. The deuteronomistic examples of God removing one people in favor of another involve the dispossession of giants, as the Canaanites/Amorites are described in Numbers 14–15, and Israel in Joshua fights against kings and towns—that is, centers of power. The powerful in the deuteronomist's conception are the opponents: the indigenous commercial populace, opposing claimants to sovereignty, especially the erstwhile wicked kings of the north. Josiah thought of himself as the head of "a people humble and lowly who shall seek refuge in the name of Yahweh—the remnant of Israel" (Zeph 3:12-13). It is possible that Hezekiah (from whom Zephaniah may have been descended) thought the same before him. The basis of this attitude by Josiah is his experience: growing up a youth in court, dependent on his regents, heading up a cabal that, even if possessing some power, was only one power among many in the realm. In a populist vein, he aggressively took up the cause of the poor, and in this way was no different from many other kings, not least his ancestor David, who regarded himself as beset by enemies on all sides—as he may in fact, like Josiah, have been.

Feeling weak does not excuse genocide. This is always the claim of the perpetrators of ethnic cleansing or genocide, including the European settlers and Americans against Native Americans and the Nazis against the Jews. But in assessing any political violence, the relations of power must be examined carefully—even when it is difficult to see how they could justify certain forms of violence. This is particularly true of political terrorists, who in desperation lash out against civilians in their struggle for their nations in the face of state power.

2. The rehabilitation of Shiloh and its priesthood is not unlike affirmative action in our own time. In reflecting on the actions of Josiah's reform faction, we are led to think as well about the right that some people have for special consideration due to past wrongs. Affirmative action is a corrective policy based on the recognition that institutions tend to re-create themselves, unless acted on from outside. The deuteronomistic cabal were such outsiders, interfering with the age-old pattern of priestly privilege and service in Jerusalem. From the deuteronomists' perspective, some corrective to institutional inertia seemed justified.What do we as present-day Christians do with affirmative action policies designed to correct institutional inertia that favors whites over people of color? The book of Joshua obviously does not speak directly to the complexity of our multiracial society. But it does suggest a biblical precedent for taking seriously the reality of institutional inertia and for seeking possible remedies for it. The Shiloh issue remains important for us: What can be done to counter the disadvantages and wrongs of the past that still bear on the present?

JOSHUA 18:11-28, LAND FOR BENJAMIN

COMMENTARY

Benjamin consists of a lozenge-shaped territory, its northern boundary with Ephraim extending from Jericho to Kiriath-jearim, and its southern boundary reaching east from Kiriath-jearim back to the Jordan at its entrance into the Dead Sea (vv. 11-20). Thus its eastern border consists of a few miles of the Jordan River. Most of this recapitulates what has previously been recorded (15:5-9; 16:1-3). The two lists of towns (vv. 21-28) add up to twenty-six. Several of these have already been assigned to Judah. Jerusalem is on the border between Benjamin and Judah, but appears to be regarded as lying, like all the significant localities in the opening three-quarters of the conquest narrative, within the bounds of Benjamin.

JOSHUA 19:1-51, LAND FOR THE REMAINING SIX TRIBES

COMMENTARY

The remaining six tribes are given cursory treatment, as much because there is little related narrative material as because the lists are short. The allotments are numbered according to their order at Shiloh, beginning with Benjamin (18:11; 19:1). Having finished with Benjamin, Judah's neighbor to the north, the narrator turns to Simeon, Judah's close neighbor to the south, then to the remaining five tribes farther north, beyond Manasseh. Simeon lies wholly within Judah, and several of the towns listed occur in Judah's lists. Simeon seems to consist of two districts; the one centered on Beersheba contains fourteen towns, not thirteen as stated in v. 6. The ideal of fairness is touted again in v. 9. Asher includes great Phoenician towns within its bounds, another case of utopian dreaming (vv. 24-31). The towns listed for Naphtali are described as being fortified (vv. 35-38); for Palestine in the Late Bronze Age, only a handful of walled settlements are known from archaeology; most settlements were unwalled.

Dan (vv. 40-48) represents a case of a tribe that migrates. They move from their territory northwest of Judah (cf. Judg 5:17, 13-16) to the far north, around the sources of the Jordan River at the base of Mt. Hermon (v. 47). The story of Dan's migration is told more fully in Judges 18:1 (cf. Judg 1:34-35). Leshem probably is a variant of Laish (Judg 18:7, 14, 27, 29). Traditions of Dan relate to both locations, and it is possible that the tribe was divided (cf. Judges 13–18). The town list for Dan (vv. 41-46) applies to the southern location, for which the writer has left room between the facing western boundaries of Judah (15:10-11) and Joseph (16:3). The list is apparently artificially constructed, mostly out of names for the Judah lists. The compiler begins with Zorah and Eshtaol, which are known from the story of Samson (Judg 13:2, 25) and are named in Judah's second district (15:33). He may then incorporate what was originally the fifth district before that became the Philistine region (15:45-47), heedless of the overlap with several towns mentioned in the Judahite boundary list (Beth-shemesh [Ir-shemesh], Timnah, Ekron).

When all the tribes have been assigned their grants, the Israelites obey God's command (presumably delivered via Joshua himself) to give Joshua the land grant of his choice (vv. 49-50). Joshua chooses Timnath-serah in Ephraim, with which thereafter he is traditionally associated and where his tomb and shrine rest. The name of his town appears as Timnath-heres in the LXX and Judg 2:9. The tomb, a saint's shrine in the time of Josiah that the resurgent monarch wishes to control rather than outlaw, is mentioned three times in the space of a few chapters (here; 24:29; and Judg 2:9; see the discussion at Josh 24:29). The conclusion at v. 51 brings to a close the process of allocation that began in 14:1.

JOSHUA 20:1-9, TOWNS FOR REFUGE

COMMENTARY

It may seem at first that chaps. 20–21, the related lists of towns for refuge and the levitical towns, form an addition to the deuteronomistic Joshua, since its conclusion (21:43-45) apparently duplicates the conclusion at 19:51. But 19:51 concludes the grants of land in Canaan, and 21:43-45 concludes the whole of the allocation that began in 13:1. Chapters 20–21 include settlements on both the east and the west sides of the Jordan; thus they mirror the description of the eastern tribal territories in chap. 13.

Moreover, both chap. 20 and chap. 21 have a deuteronomistic logic in that they fit the known purposes of Josiah's reform. The towns of refuge are designed to enhance the central power's control of cycles of violence. Clearly Josiah's reform was not meant to eliminate or even to reduce violence. But one of its purposes was to take as much as possible of the violence that did occur out of the hands of families and commonalities and put it in the hands of the state. In Athens, Draco's reform in 621 BCE, the year after Josiah's reform, had as its main purpose the melioration of the vendetta.

The levitical towns contribute to Josiah's control of and solicitude for the Levites. Conceivably the levitical towns are the vestige of a genuinely ancient institution, perhaps going back, as many have suggested, to the house of David's patronage of a scattered tribe of militant supporters (a hypothesis that is often overly romanticized). Barred from holding arable land (thus limited to pasture-land) and, therefore, from turning into a landholding elite, as dependents of the centralizing monarch they could serve in the role of dispersed and intimidating trustees of the central shrine's law, well known for their militancy and readiness to use violence. However, whether these two chapters are primarily deuteronomistic or priestly in their present form is another question.

The tension between clan justice, especially as expressed in the blood feud or vendetta, and the prerogatives of central justice, with its interest in the supposed dispassionate weighing of evidence and circumstance, is an age-old theme. In industrialized societies, where large middle and influential upper classes have the benefit of well-developed systems of law, courts, and police, it is sometimes easy to forget how fragile and tenuous the maintenance of social order can be. In theory, people who are relatively poor or racially stigmatized enjoy the same benefits, but their lives often come closer than do those of well-off whites to the disorder, lawlessness, and capriciousness that characterized most societies before the modern era.

Under such circumstances, the blood feud functions as a form of primitive justice. According to the basic principle, in the absence of police and courts households undertake to avenge the murder of one of their own. The responsibility for revenge falls on kin in the same proportion as for redemption from debt, so that in Hebrew the "redeemer" (גאל *gō'ēl*) is also the "avenger." Justice is a private matter. In practice, blood guilt serves more often as the basis for a negotiated settlement with compensation than as a justification for answering one killing with another. People usually—not always—prefer to work things out rather than pursue the potentially endless cycle of revenge and counterrevenge. This is important, because it relates directly to the purpose of the biblical towns of refuge, which represent a kind of compromise between private justice and monarchic justice, which in the deuteronomistic conception is overseen by a controlled magistracy.

While the institution of assigned urban asylums seems to make sense, it has the look of idealistic central planning often found in biblical law. The term used for "asylum" (מקלט *miqlāṭ*) occurs only in reference to these towns in priestly texts (Numbers 35; 1 Chronicles 6; and priestly parts of Joshua 20–21). There are no stories or historical accounts in the OT in which such towns appear. Elsewhere in the OT, asylum is provided by altars, as prescribed in the ancient law in Exod 21:13-14 (cf. 1 Kgs 1:50; 2:28) Outside of deuteronomistic or priestly legislation, such altars might be available practically anywhere. It is likely that the idea for asylum towns originated with the deuteronomists, forced on them as a repercussion of their radical law of centralization: The monarchy must support asylum; if altars outside Jerusalem are now illegal and, therefore, no longer available for asylum, something must take their place, and that something cannot depend on the availability of altars (cf. Deut 19:6, which recognizes distance to asylum as the problem).

Moses' order for asylum towns is given in two places, Deut 19:1-13 and Num 35:9-34. The deuteronomistic law calls for assigning three towns in the three main regions of highland Canaan, and another three towns if the east bank of the Jordan is conquered. The conquest of the east is described in Deut 2:26–3:17, so the three asylum towns there are designated already in Deut 4:41-43, one for each tribal territory. They are apparently major towns in the seventh century BCE, but none is mentioned in Joshua other than in chap. 21, where all the towns of refuge appear also in the list of levitical towns. The towns

to the west are assigned by region rather than by tribe; Hebron and Shechem are the traditional centers of their regions ("Ephraim" [20:7] is used broadly, since Shechem belongs to Manasseh [17:2]), and Kedesh in Galilee serves for the deuteronomist the same northern urban and strategic functions as Dan did for the kings of Israel.[128] Killers who flee to one of these towns turn their case over to the magistracies of both the asylum town and the town of the person killed.

There is nothing in the priestly law that indicates the existence of asylum towns before Josiah's reform, even though there is no doubt that earlier monarchs wanted to control the vendetta. The protection of Cain at the beginning of the J strand (Gen 4:1-16) is an early reflection of this concern. However, several significant elements appear in the priestly law that are not in the deuteronomistic law. One is that the killer's justification for initial asylum is strictly defined rather than being left mostly to the town's magistrates. Second, the case is quickly brought to trial before the "congregation," the priestly concept of the collective of all Israel. Third, killers judged innocent of murder by the congregation may return to their asylum and must remain there "until the death of the high priest," when they can return home.

Both versions of the law of asylum are evident in Joshua 20, but an important textual variation affects the interpretation of these two versions and their origin. In the LXX, 20:4-6 is almost entirely missing; there the text of 20:1-3, 6 states simply that the towns required by Moses are to be designated so that the killer "without intent" (NIV, "accidentally") may flee there until there is a trial before the congregation. The phrase "by mistake" (NIV, "unintentionally") is missing from the LXX. Now "without intent" occurs in Numbers 35 and "by mistake" in Deuteronomy 19. It has also been noticed that the LXX text looks like it is based entirely on the priestly version of the law and that the longer MT version shows apparent deuteronomistic additions that have no part in the priestly law, not only "by mistake" (there is no "or" in the Hebrew text), but also the negotiations between killer and town magistracy by which they must make a preliminary judgment in

---

128. John L. Peterson, "Kedesh, 3," *ABD* 4:11-12.

the case, before it goes before the "congregation" (20:4-5).

Some have regarded the magistrate's preliminary judgment as seriously inconsistent with the priestly law. Believing that the LXX version of Joshua 20 preserves a consistent understanding of the law, they reason that it represents, excepting one or two phrases, the earlier form of Joshua 20, and therefore that the earlier form follows the priestly rather than the deuteronomistic law.[129]

It is important to remember, however, that people have an interest in making an institution like the asylum towns work and in order to do so would have to be willing to give a killer the benefit of the doubt in a preliminary trial. With this in mind, the simpler explanation is that the MT of Joshua 20, the version familiar from the translations, represents the text's pre-LXX form (a deuteronomistic text with later priestly supplements) and that the shorter LXX text represents the alterations of a later scribe who had no particular need to see the system work. This scribe was disturbed by an apparent inconsistency between Deuteronomy 19 and Numbers 35 and, assuming that with the more determinate priestly law at the magistrates' disposal no preliminary trial would be needed, removed it, along with the vague "by mistake." In sum, the deuteronomistic version is more workable, the priestly version more defined, organized, and indeed centralized, but at the same time more theoretical; the MT represents the usual combination of the two on a deuteronomistic base, the LXX a revision in the direction of priestly strictness.[130]

129. Alexander Rofé, "Joshua 20—Historico-Literary Criticism Illustrated," in *Empirical Models for Biblical Criticism*, ed. Jeffrey H. Tigay (Philadelphia: University of Pennsylvania Press, 1985) 131-47.

130. See A. Graeme Auld, "Cities of Refuge in Israelite Tradition," *JSOT* 10 (1978) 26-40.

REFLECTIONS

People who live in the so-called developed world, especially those who are not poor, may tend to take for granted the degree of basic law and order, or social peace, that they enjoy as the result of belonging to a comparatively democratic, wealthy, and well-policed society. There is vast room for improvement in the policing of society in developed countries, but compared with early agrarian and present-day poorer societies, the majority of their inhabitants are fortunate. Because we do not have to worry daily about ongoing vendettas, we may underestimate the boon that any attempt to control them, as with the town of refuge, represented. Such refuge may have been indispensable in the absence of effective alternatives.

JOSHUA 21:1-45, TOWNS WITH PASTURE LANDS FOR THE LEVITES

COMMENTARY

The list of levitical towns, which includes all the towns of refuge in Joshua 20, fulfills the command of Moses described in the priestly text in Num 35:1-8, of which it is an elaboration. Like all the town lists in Joshua, this one has generated much discussion regarding date, and proposals have ranged from the earliest to the latest periods, from pre-monarchic to Persian times. After surveying the archaeological evidence for the sites listed, Peterson concluded that the list could not have been composed before the eighth century BCE, and his results have been widely accepted.[131] The list is dependent on both the list of allotments in Joshua 13–19 and the list of towns of refuge in Joshua 21, and is duplicated with variations in the Persian-period priestly

131. John L. Peterson, "A Topographical Surface Survey of the Levitical 'Cities' of Joshua 21 and 1 Chronicles 6." This work is cited often in the secondary literature; see esp. Boling and Wright, *Joshua*, 487-96.

version of the house of David's history, in 1 Chr 6:39-66. Nowhere else does the Deuteronomistic History show an interest in the levitical genealogy by which Joshua 21 is structured. Once more the distribution is headed by Eleazar before Joshua, a priestly earmark (21:1). The list displays a degree of formality not found in the deuteronomistic parts of Joshua. Four levitical groups (the usual three plus the Aaronids) receive four towns from each of the twelve tribes, except that Judah and Simeon together give up nine instead of eight and thus Naphtali gives up three. Since all the towns in a given tribe go to one of the Levite groups, the four groups receive respectively 13, 13, 12, and 11 towns, the least possible deviation from the ideal of 12 towns apiece.[132] The imbalance is created by the Aaronids' receiving an additional town in Judah and Simeon. By itself the imbalance does not indicate, as some have supposed, that the writer was forced to accommmodate a pre-existing list; there is nothing to stop a writer from changing a source to fit his scheme. The so-called imbalance makes its own point: the primacy of Aaron.

The present list's emphasis is on the family of Aaron, and the imbalance contributes to this emphasis. The Aaronids claim the levitical towns in Judah, including Hebron, which has already in Joshua been granted to Caleb (14:6-15; 15:13), and including Debir, which Caleb has granted to his nephew (15:15-19). Technically Caleb's rights are honored by means of a distinction, which is found only here in the book of Joshua, between the town and its pasturelands, on the one hand, and its villages and their arable land, on the other hand (21:11-12). It is as if each town, consistent with the glaringly unrealistic scheme of Num 35:5, possessed no adjacent arable land. The Aaronids here also lay claim to Anathoth, the traditional home of the rivals of the Aaronids, the Elide remnant behind the deuteronomistic reform (21:18). Indeed, the Aaronids receive more towns than do all the rest of their Kohathite branch, or than either of the other two levitical branches.[133] The Aaronids claim the levitical towns of Judah, Simeon, and Benjamin, the three territories closest to Jerusalem, presumably a reflection of their Persian-period dominance.

In Num 35:1-8, Moses prescribes a mythical rational allotment of levitical towns: The pasturage extends exactly two thousand cubits from the town wall (Num 35:5; all 48 towns are walled)—where usually the best garden and arable land would be expected—and more towns are to be taken from the larger tribes (Num 35:8). In Joshua 21, Eleazar and Joshua distribute the towns by lot (21:4-6, 8, 10). Many have supposed that the two passages contradict each other, but this is unlikely. The difference between mythical theory and fulfillment by lot characterizes most if not all of the connections between Numbers and Joshua.[134] That the Aaronids are first to come up by lot does not contradict their appointment as the main priestly family in the Tetrateuch. The mythic picture of towns surrounded with pastureland is apparently confirmed in 21:42. The allocation is said to be in direct fulfillment of Moses' command (21:2-3, 8).

In sum, in Joshua 22, the Aaronids are the focus of an artificial composition dependent on deuteronomistic parts of Joshua but devoid of deuteronomistic features, excepting perhaps the sparseness of levitical towns in Ephraim and Manasseh. The Aaronids dominate the Jerusalemite heartland, and the other Levites are pushed to the margins, from the perspective of Jerusalem. The Aaronid towns lie beyond the bounds of the Persian province of Yehud to the south, in the Edomite marches, and to the west, in the Philistine marches. This distribution may express the hope of the Persian-period Aaronids to expand their power. As Ben Zvi has concluded, this list "provides a glimpse into the world of claims, disappointments and hopes of the post-monarchic period" when the Aaronid priests ruled Jerusalem.[135]

The grand concluding statement in 21:43-45 is contradicted many times in the book of Joshua. This represents the era of Joshua, according to the deuteronomistic concept, at its most prominent, and the contradictions serve only to point up how strongly held the ideal was.

132. Ehud Ben Zvi, "The List of Levitical Cities," *JSOT* 54 (1992) 86-87.
133. Ben Zvi, "The List of Levitical Cities," 77-106.
134. Ben Zvi, "The List of Levitical Cities," 81n. 1.
135. Ben Zvi, "The List of Levitical Cities," 105. See also Nadav Na'aman, *Borders and Districts in Biblical Historiography: Seven Studies in Biblical Geographical Lists* (Jerusalem: Simor, 1986) 203-36; John R. Spencer, "Levitical Cities," *ABD* 4:310-11.

REFLECTIONS

The traditional dominant priestly families of the house of David returned, under the putative headship of Aaron, to harass the Levites, whose reform was long since dead and whose protestations are most pronounced in Isaiah 56–66. This is one of the many turns of events in the history of God's people that make it difficult or impossible to state categorically what God is up to. Eventually the priestly offices behind this chapter fell into oblivion following the fall of the Temple in 70 CE, which radically changed the face not only of Judaism but of Christianity as well. Whether the early church looked for a priestly messiah in addition to their royal messiah is unclear, but following the fall of the Temple such an idea, if it was ever held, lost all appeal. The restoration of comparable offices—an established and endowed cult leadership allied with the state—awaited the establishment of Christianity in the fourth and fifth centuries CE. Even then, the established priesthood rarely became hereditary, as it was in the Bible.

The failure of the church's priesthood to become hereditary was a measure not of the church's weakness but of its strength, the ability to prevent the prorogative of appointing priests, and with them their endowments, from falling out of the hands of the church's central authorities. This principle came under greatest threat at the time of emerging modern states in the fifteenth and sixteenth centuries. Clearly the Reformation also represented a diminishing of the church's central power. In Protestant churches, typically whatever of their support wealthier ministers were able to preserve passed to their heirs rather than back to the church. More important, in many instances appointments to endowments ended up in the hands mostly of laymen, as in Scotland for over two hundred years.

The endowment of the church today and the relationship of that endowment to the ministry of the church raise significant issues regarding the future of churches. As churches become wealthier in endowment, frequently the ministers and priests of the church become poorer. This is particularly the case in Protestant old-line churches, where, for example, the educational indebtedness of the pastorate has reached unprecedented levels. Because the ministry and priesthood have become so thoroughly professionalized, and because a profession that pays poorly may fail to attract the most able and qualified persons to its ranks, churches run the risk of enhancing their financial stability at the cost of an effective ministry. Add to this potential development the shrinking of membership in old-line churches, and the picture of churches resting on secure endowments but unsure ministries and uncertain memberships begins to take shape. The threat of identities and ministries driven mainly by endowment rather than vision, not a new situation in the history of the church, must be taken seriously. The purpose of such reflection is not to presume to prophesy about the future of the church, but to prompt the interpreter to consider the church's endowment and its current disposition in the light of God's will for the church.

JOSHUA 22:1-34

A SECOND ALTAR: LEGAL OR NOT?

COMMENTARY

At last, with conquest and land distribution concluded, Israel's fighting force has dispersed to new homelands, whose ethnic cleansing they have well begun if not ended. For the first time in over forty-five years of migration and fighting, the descendants of Jacob can look forward to a settled existence. Five generations after God had, within sight of the scene of the great battle of Ai (Joshua 7–8), promised the land to Jacob and his offspring (Gen 28:13-15; cf. Gen 13:3, 14-17), that promise now reaches its fulfillment as the households and clans of the children of Israel embark on the final stage of their long journey home—unaware that the troubled period of the "saviors" and "judges," when "there was no king in Israel," lies just ahead.

Not only have the loyal east Jordan tribes fought side by side with their kin in the west bank, but with their own land grants from Moses already in hand, they have also patiently attended the ceremony in which Joshua allots the remaining land and sends the happy recipients home. Now the men of the east Jordan tribes stand alone before Joshua at Shiloh, waiting to be dismissed. Joshua applauds their loyalty and, with a last admonition to love Yahweh and obey Moses, sends them on their way back to their families. Scarcely out of Joshua's sight, they come to the Jordan and, before crossing, build an altar, as though Moses' law of centralization had gone in one ear and out the other. Fearful that God would answer such an outrageous act of hostility with collective punishment, the west-bank tribes hurry back to Shiloh to make war against their own people (cf. Judges 20). They dispatch a delegation to reason with the rebels. Surely, the delegation complains, the rebels remember what happened when one man, Achan, broke the law—the whole nation was made to pay the price of defeat. At once the alleged culprits invoke Yahweh as the God of gods (22:22, 34), reaffirming Yahweh's oneness, and declare their innocence. They built the altar, they say, in Manasseh on the west side of the Jordan, not in order to break away from Israel's one cult and jurisdiction and establish their own on the east side—the sin of Jeroboam before its time—but to create a suitable monument to their right to belong to the jurisdiction of Israel and to hold their lands by that right. Separated from the heartland by the Jordan, they will not allow themselves to be disowned and thereby dispossessed by some future kin who, mistaking the Jordan for a national boundary, might shout across the river, "You have no portion [of land] in Yahweh"—that is, "Since we bar you from the central cult of Yahweh, your claim to land under its sovereignty is invalid" (note how this theme both begins and ends the expression of the tribes' concern in 22:25-27). The delegation from Shiloh is convinced by this protestation, since after all the east-bank tribes had shared the struggle to the end, and they return and mollify the rest of Israel.

As just told, these events continue the deuteronomistic story. This is the second time a second altar appears in the book of Joshua (see 8:30-35). Unlike the previous altar, this altar belongs to the original deuteronomistic narrative of Joshua and, ironically, plays a central role. Despite appearances, it is not the main subject. The main subject is the Jordan River, to whose significance the altar is a witness. The point of these events is that the Jordan may be a symbolic and administrative boundary, but it is not a national boundary. The Deuteronomists have to make this point clearly at the end of the entire story of Joshua, since at the beginning of the story they laid so much emphasis on the Jordan as a boundary (e.g., 1:2, 11, 14-15; 3:1–5:1; 7:7; 9:1; 12:1, 7; 15:5; 16:1; Deut 2:29; 3:17; 9:1; 11:31; 12:10; 30:18; 31:13).

Quite by plan, this episode forms part of a fourfold frame around the whole deuteronomistic narrative of conquest and allotment. At the beginning: (1) Joshua received his commission and mustered the Israelites; (2) Joshua called on the east-bank tribes to fight with their west-bank kin until the war was over, and they loyally consented; (3) Rahab was loyal; (4) all Israel crossed the Jordan from east to west in a heroic entrance into the promised land. The last deuteronomistic parts of the book of Joshua mirror the first, in reverse order: The east-bank tribes arrive at the Jordan prepared to cross from west to east (compare 4); they commit an act that looks like Achan's disloyalty (presaged when Joshua mentions spoil, 22:8), in contrast to Rahab's loyalty (3); they reaffirm their loyalty to their west-bank kin (2); and Joshua musters all the Israelites to bid them farewell (1). This narrative plan shows that the writer matched the story of Israel's crossing of the Jordan (chaps. 3–5) with the story of the building of the altar at the Jordan (chap. 22), confirming that the main issue is the status of the Jordan, an issue for which the attention-getting apparent act of disregard for the cardinal law of centralization provides a perfect vehicle.

In the light of this correspondence, it is no accident that the place where the east-bank tribes arrive at the Jordan and build their altar is called גלילות (*gĕlîlôt*, v. 10). Whether this is a descriptive term (NRSV, "region near the Jordan") or a place name (NIV, "Geliloth"), it plays on the name "Gilgal," the site of the first crossing and of Achan's crime. The word is uncommon and puzzled the LXX translators. They rendered the first occurrence "Gilgal" and the second "Gilead"; the first makes some symbolic sense, the second

some geographical sense, since Gilead lies nearby to the east. Wordplay was already a feature of the tradition on which this episode is based. Like the story in Gen 31:44-54, it explains the meaning of Gilead, "the cairn of witness" (in vv. 9, 13, 15, 32, the name refers not just to Gilead proper, but to the east bank in general).

The discussion so far has ignored much of Joshua 22, because this chapter is filled with priestly language and motifs that have been added to make the original deuteronomistic story considerably longer than it once was.[136] Although it is not always certain what was added, most of the priestly phrases appear in the section of the story dealing with the delegation, of which Phinehas the son of Eleazar is made the leader, presumably in place of Joshua. Identifiable traces of priestly additions include the phrase involving "possession" (vv. 9, 19); the "sons of Reuben or Gad" in place of simply Reuben or Gad; the priestly word for "tribe" (v. 14 and elsewhere); "treachery"; the "whole congregation"; the ten "chiefs"; the sin of Peor, where Phinehas played the saving role (Num 25:1-13; cf. the absence of Phinehas in Deut 4:3-4); the "defiled land"; the phrase "where Yahweh's tabernacle now stands" (v. 19); the elaboration of altar offerings; probably "copy" (v. 28); possibly the phrase "that stands before his tabernacle" (v. 29); all of v. 31; and "destroying" the land (v. 33). The priestly additions seem designed to highlight Phinehas's concern for purity and the priestly succession from Eleazar to Phinehas, anticipating Eleazar's death and burial (24:33).

136. John S. Kloppenborg, "Joshua 22: The Priestly Editing of an Ancient Tradition," *Bib* 62 (1981) 347-71.

REFLECTIONS

The east-bank tribes are portrayed as so anxious not to be excluded from the "nation" under Joshua that they risk the appearance of violating what is arguably the chief of all the laws Moses laid down as they themselves first stood near the banks of the Jordan: the law of the central altar (Deut 12:1-14). How were the other tribes to know that their altar was meant as a memorial rather than as a bid either to build and control the central altar or to build a second altar to rival the future central altar? The grave danger of misunderstanding gives a poignant edge to the narrative's characterization of the fear of exclusion. The east-bank tribes' fear of exclusion went as deep as it did because the social boundaries of the "nation" were defined so unconditionally and so violently.

There lies here an acutely disquieting irony: The more exactly and emphatically the edge of the sword (overt, as in the world of Joshua, or covert, as often in ours) marks the dividing line between those who belong and those who do not, between those who are in and those who are out, the more those who are in may be troubled with the possibility of ending up with those who are out. Such is the nature of division and factioning, as prevalent with supposedly constructive as well as destructive acts of distinguishing. There is a lesson in this text worth reflecting on: Is it not often the case that the more definite the criteria distinguishing those who belong from those who do not, the more the purpose of such criteria becomes questionable and the criteria themselves self-defeating? Given the nature of human beings, the more precise and systematic the division of one group from another becomes, the more untidy it becomes. The probable reason is that division arises from fear, and fear engenders more fear.

In addition, the present narrative raises an important issue regarding how people in a group work out an understanding of themselves and their values and identity. The story is that the east-bank tribes felt they had to test an important point of possible future legal contention: Could the Jordan be construed as a national boundary? Nothing had been said or done that necessitated such a conclusion, but neither had it clearly been ruled out, and the great emphasis on the Jordan, despite the continued solicitude for the east-bank tribes, left the matter in potential limbo.

Perhaps the closest parallel to this episode today, when laws provide one of the best delineations of values, is the testing of laws in a constitutional or quasi-constitutional system of jurisprudence. If there is a question of the meaning of a law, let it be violated, either substantively or technically. Through the ensuing process, the exact limits of the law will be discovered.

Sometimes in order to determine one point of law, an ancillary or corollary point must be raised. The west-bank tribes ruled on the irregular altar, but what they were really addressing was the issue of the river, and the resulting "national" constituency.

In general, a group's values and identity can often best be measured by concrete actions or decisions rather than by statements of principle. What beliefs and commitments define a group, including a church or a congregation? The answer lies in what they do when particular uncertainties or dilemmas arise. It is often observed, moreover, that there is no better indicator of the values of a group or organization than its budget, which defines the investment of resources, time, and money. To what is a church or congregation committed? Read its budget.

JOSHUA 23:1–24:28

JOSHUA BIDS FAREWELL

OVERVIEW

At the end of his life, Joshua gathers all the tribes together one last time to hear his farewell speech. In the original deuteronomistic narrative, this speech was followed directly by Joshua's death and burial and the deuteronomists' final characterization of the period of Joshua (24:29-31). Joshua 24:1-28 interrupts this sequence to describe a covenant at Shechem. Joshua 24 is not clearly deuteronomistic (see Commentary on 24:1-28). Its historical and literary affinities are uncertain. It summarizes the history from Abraham to Joshua from available scripture, uses stock motifs from covenant rites, and has possible connections with Josh 8:30-35.[137] In some ways it is redundant with chap. 23, from which it may borrow the list of heads gathered (23:2; 24:1; but cf. 8:33), so that Joshua ends up admonishing both the political nation and the popular nation twice.

137. For recent study of covenant, see Robert A. Oden, Jr., "The Place of Covenant in the Religion of Israel," in *Ancient Israelite Religion* (Philadelphia: Fortress, 1987) 429-47; Robert Davidson, "Covenant Ideology in Ancient Israel," in *The World of Ancient Israel: Sociological, Anthropological and Political Perspectives,* ed. Ronald E. Clements (Cambridge: Cambridge University Press, 1989) 323-47; George E. Mendenhall and Gary A. Herion, "Covenant," *ABD* 1:1179-1202.

JOSHUA 23:1-16, LOVE YAHWEH OR LOSE YOUR LAND

COMMENTARY

Joshua's farewell speech is replete with deuteronomistic phraseology. As a set piece of exhortation, it compares with Moses' lengthy prologue and epilogue to the law (Deuteronomy 6–11; 29–31). This is not surprising, since Moses' entire speech in Deuteronomy, including the law, is cast, like Joshua's speech here, as a farewell. Joshua's last speech also compares with David's in 1 Kgs 2:1-9; moreover, Joshua and David are the only persons in the Deuteronomistic History who at death's door say they are "about to go the way of all the earth" (23:14; 1 Kgs 2:2). Joshua's last speech corresponds structurally to Yahweh's first (1:2-9), in which Joshua is commissioned like a monarch; thus Joshua takes his leave from the story the same way he entered it: looking like the Davidic dynast for whom he stands.

Joshua emphasizes that what made Israel's victories possible was Yahweh's fighting on their side. If their success is not to be reversed, the Israelites must remain subjects of Yahweh, obedient to the law of Moses. This is Moses' theme put in the diction of conquest: Obey the law and take the land; continue to obey the law or lose the land. When encountering this rhetoric, the reader must not lose sight of exactly what this law entails, beginning with chillingly brutal ethnic conflict, ruthless centralization, and benevolent debt remission. Joshua emphasizes the exclusive character of Israel, different in kind from the other "nations," so that association and intermarriage are excluded (vv. 7, 12). This exclusion has more than a polemical social or "ethnic" thrust. Marriages sealed alliances, and in Josiah's world the main purpose of alliances was to create political and economic networks for siphoning the produce of Palestine into the channels of trade. As conceived here, intermarriage is a facet of the commercialization that Josiah, through his reform, is seen to set himself against.

The interdiction of intermarriage does not correspond to any of the deuteronomistic laws of Moses and plays an explicit role elsewhere in the Deuteronomistic History only in Deut 7:3 and perhaps Judges 21, which it is sometimes thought to anticipate. It is perfectly consistent, however, with the reform plan to eliminate rival cults, stem the commodification of agriculture, and interpose the state in the affairs of patriarchal households. Intermarriage becomes an even greater concern in the Persian period, when, with the resurgence of Aegean traders in the eastern Mediterranean, commercialization remained a threat to the populace, and opposing it remained a useful basis for popular appeal.

The interdiction of marriage is thus a possible indication that the end of Joshua 23 may include changes or additions from the hand of the exilic or later editor of the Deuteronomistic History (see Introduction). The "if" in v. 12 is not ambiguous; however, the clauses in v. 15-16 are ambiguous and can be read as factual or conditional. Thus v. 15 may be understood modally: "Yahweh may bring upon you all the bad worse [curse]." Verse 16 may begin with either a conditional "if" (both NRSV and NIV) or a factual "when." The Hebrew may favor "when," the exilic sense.

The "great and strong" nations in v. 9 recall the description of the tribes of Joseph in 17:17, even though the Hebrew terms are different. Power is always relative, and Yahweh helps to keep it that way.

REFLECTIONS

The prohibition of intermarriage in terms of ethnic affiliation brings up the issue of definitions of race and ethnicity in our own culture. Race and ethnicity are socially constructed categories. This does not mean that they are unreal, but that they have no inherent or essential reality apart from the political, social, and economic history that gives rise to them. Not only particular "races," but also the notion of race itself has a historical origin. The "white" race in North America represents an instructive example. The historical contingencies that led to the emergence of "whites" were complex, but its many facets have been well studied in recent years. These include the development of the so-called descent rule for eliminating intermediate identities (a single identifiable black ancestor made one black); the bureaucratic fondness for the classification "Caucasian," as though it represented a scientific category, even though it was invented by an eighteenth-century German naturalist who simply thought people from the Caucasus were the most beautiful; and the process by which in the United States during the nineteenth century the Irish, who in the British context played a role similar to that of Africans in the United States, came to be identified as "white."[138]

The prohibition of intermarriage in Joshua 23 targeted marriage alliances between major land owners under the supposed jurisdiction of the Temple, and hence "Judean," on the one hand, who were in a position to commercialize agriculture to the detriment of commoners and, on the other hand, traders with Mediterranean links. The prohibition is stated in "ethnic" terms, but its purpose, like marriage among the elite in the ancient world, was largely political and economic. In reflecting on parallels to the prohibition in modern times, the interpreter thus should focus on the undue or unjust advantage gained by the wealthy through questionable alliances.

138. See Ivan Hannaford, "The Idiocy of Race," *The Wilson* Quarterly 18:2 (Spring 1994) 8-44, and *Race: The History of an Idea in the* West (Baltimore: Johns Hopkins University Press, 1996); Marvin Harris, *Patterns of Race in the Americas* (New York: Norton, 1974); Stephen Jay Gould, "The Geometer of Race," *Discover* 15:11 (November 1994) 64-69; Noel Ignatiev, *How the Irish Became White* (New York: Routledge, 1995).

JOSHUA 24:1-28, COVENANT AT SHECHEM

COMMENTARY

Joshua re-calls the tribes to Shechem, last seen in 8:30-35, here introduced with a similar jump in location (for Shechem, see the Commentary on 8:30-35). The most distinctive aspect of this secondary passage is at the same time its closest link to 8:30-35: Joshua's publication of statutes and ordinances, which are recorded with the rest of the ceremony in the "document of the law of God" (24:25-26; cf. 8:32, 34-35). Joshua's new role as lawgiver puts him unusually at odds with the exclusive authority of the commandments and laws of Moses elsewhere in the book of Joshua. The law document here is referred to in the same way that the whole law of Moses—not just the law in Deuteronomy—is referred to in Neh 8:18 (cf. Neh 8:8; 10:29-30), confirming the impression that this passage was written later than most of the Deuteronomistic History. In 24:5, Aaron joins Moses, just as he does in the priestly additions to the Tetrateuch. Part of the distinctiveness of this passage is the way Joshua stands alone over against the Israelites rather than as first among them (cf. Josiah in 2 Kgs 23:1-3) to challenge them to faithfulness (24:15). (Joshua's challenge, if not his stance, has often appealed to preachers, helping to gain this idiosyncratic pericope its place in lieu of nearly all of the rest of Joshua in the church's common lectionary.) In the preceding chapter, Joshua had admonished the Israelites, but in the same congratulatory vein in which he had sent the east-bank tribes on their way (22:2-7). In contrast, now all of a sudden he challenges the Israelites' apostasy to Mesopotamian and other gods. Even if these gods are meant to be the same as those mentioned in 23:16, read as fact rather than condition (see the Commentary on 23:1-16), the responses from Yahweh and Joshua contrast sharply: in the first instance immediate expulsion; in the second, the opportunity to repent. Precisely this contrast is what most typically differentiates the Josianic deuteronomist from the exilic deuteronomist. Whether or not Joshua 24 was written by the latter, its author was evidently not the former.

The central concern of this passage is the apostacy and idolatry of the Israelites. They apparently assume naively that they can serve Yahweh and other gods at the same time; this seems to be the reason for Joshua's response to their assertion of loyalty to Yahweh (24:16-19). Joshua induces them to foreswear their allegiance to "foreign gods" who are either of the east, in Mesopotamia, where Abraham left to migrate to Canaan, stopping first at Shechem (Gen 12:6), or of the Amorites in the conquered land (24:14-15; cf. 24:2). The rehearsal of the ancestors' history and the concern for idolatry are both reminiscent of the exilic deuteronomist (cf. Deut 4:1-40, especially the concern for idolatry in Deut 4:15-20 and the importance of the "fathers" [NRSV, "ancestors"] in Deut 4:31, 37; 2 Kgs 21:10-15); the concern for Mesopotamian gods appears to imply exile or continued residence in Mesopotamia. But there are still too few identifiable deuteronomistic features of the narrative to say that it was written by the same hand that is behind the main exilic deuteronomistic passages, as well as otherwise surprising omissions. Why, for example, does the writer of Joshua 24 not emphasize Baal of Peor (as Deut 4:3-4 does) in the account of Israel's history in 24:2-10? Much like Joshua 22, the narrative ends with the setting up of a monumental stone as a witness to the people's commitment to testify against themselves should they forsake Yahweh for foreign gods.

Shechem is a medial locale in the original Israelite highlands, including the region assigned to the tribes of Joseph. Thus it might be expected to play a greater role in the main narrative of conquest than it does. (This discrepancy is addressed in the discussion of Josh 8:30-35.) The present passage does not make up for this lack of attention—or Davidic slight—to Shechem, nor to the whole of Manasseh and Ephraim, excepting Shiloh, even though Joshua comes from Ephraim. In reality, Shechem lay more or less beyond the sphere of the house of David in every period but its beginning.

Verse 13 brings out as well as any other text in Joshua the nature of the conquest as dispossession and ethnic cleansing. It refers not to the historical Iron I settlement of the hill country, which occurred largely on previously unoccupied terrain, but to the unmerciful displacement of the vanquished.

Yahweh's deliverance of the Israelites calls for a response, which Joshua puts to the people in vv. 14-15. The NRSV's "revere" in place of "fear" (ירא *yārēʾ*; cf. NIV) reflects the contemporary change in many liberal churches from patriarchal piety to the piety of familiarity and friendship with God; in the world of the Bible, the meaning was fear and its effects, especially fealty toward the lord and his commandments—obedience to Yahweh and the law. Both the NRSV ("in sincerity and in faithfulness") and the NIV ("with all faithfulness") may miss the meaning of the Hebrew phrase "with integrity and with faithfulness" (בתמים ובאמת *bĕtāmîm ûbeʾĕmet*). It is possible that the phrase expresses a single idea, as the NIV suggests: "with a true

faithfulness." It is equally possible, though, that the first term retains a separate meaning—namely, the congruence of professed and actual obedience. "Sincerity" may be understood in this way, but in contemporary English it may have too strong a subjective valence to capture a congruence that can be measured point by point against the standard of specific stipulations. The patriarchal character of Joshua's charge, quite contrary to the individualism that is important to nearly all modern churches, comes through clearly: As head of his household (the בית-אב [*bêt-ʾāb*], or "house of the father"), Joshua not only speaks for all the men, women, and children in his charge, but he has also decided for them what they will do. The "people" who respond are not the whole populace, each individual speaking for himself or herself, but the "elders, heads, judges, and officials" (v. 1, apparently adopted from 23:2)—the patriarchal heads, who agree on behalf of the households in their charge.

REFLECTIONS

Joshua's charge at Shechem highlights loyalty and professions of loyalty. The text suggests reflecting on the character of loyalty and the object of loyalty.

The nature of loyalty in this text is typical for the Bible. Loyalty tended to be objective, definable according to a known norm or expectation, explicitly affirmed, and in principle strictly judged, even if by no one but God. Loyalty also had a significant subjective component; however, loyalty, including to God, centered not on the warm experience of acceptance, trust, and support that characterizes interpersonal relationships at their best in our culture, but on the trepidation, deference, habitual caution, and hopeful dependence that characterized a person's relationship with social superiors, those who truly were lord and master. Thus the fear commanded by Joshua included, and at the same time had to answer to, an element of anxiety that a lord might act erratically or impulsively. Joshua spells out the saving acts of God not only to magnify the burden on the listening patriarchal heads—feared in turn by their own subordinates—to respond, but also to assure the heads, and through them their subordinates, of God's consistency, to allay their fear of capriciousness.

In patriarchal or authoritarian settings, which some have opted for in the church as elsewhere, such loyalty may seem unexceptional. But for many others in the church, those influenced by modern ideas of democracy, self-responsibility, self-worth, toleration of differences, overlooking the faults of others, and liberal love, such loyalty may seem peculiar and repugnant. There are probably benefits and liabilities to both kinds of loyalty, biblical and modern, which careful reflection will bring out. Not everyone will choose to reflect in this way, however, since to do so is to embrace the great dilemma of faithfulness to God in modern times, approaching God, whom the Bible reveals as the supreme patriarch, as modern classical liberal individuals.

This dilemma is all the more profound because it arises within and is reinforced by the prevailing political context of modern times, the constitutional society, with the United States as the example to the world. As modern believers, we do what biblical believers did; we express our faith in terms of our political culture. In the Bible, political culture—relations of power for achieving and maintaining social order—meant that orders were handed down from above in an altogether patriarchal mode. For us, political culture ideally means that we ourselves determine the laws we live by. This is now true in most parts of the world, which comes as a source of encouragement and joy to most Americans. Hence, culturally speaking, "the people" in Joshua 24 are vastly different from the people featured as "we the people" in the preamble to the Constitution of the United States. This difference is eclipsed by the apparent choice made by the people in Josh 24:16-24. But it must be remembered that "the people" in Joshua 24 are not choosing the system of government they would institute or which laws they would live by, but simply which lord and master they would subordinate themselves to. The object of their loyalty is both *God,* who has handed down the law, and the *law* that comes from God. The object of our comparable loyalty is the state, which, in theory, we, the people, have constituted.

Practically speaking, for modern believers the acute dilemma epitomized by this text is resolved in the modern notion of religion, which excludes the political by definition. Thus those who want to include a political dimension in their definition of religion have to say so explicitly. As modern people, we instinctively accept this truncated notion of religion, the very foundation of the modern multiconfessional nation. It is essential to realize, however, that this notion of religion does not apply to the Bible and that if we wish to reflect wisely on the meaning of loyalty in the Bible, we have no choice but to include the political dimension in our thinking.

JOSHUA 24:29-33

JOSHUA IS BURIED

COMMENTARY

J oshua was an Ephraimite hero, a saint venerated at his tomb. This may be as close as we can get to the historical Joshua, who almost certainly existed, but whose celebrated deeds just as certainly lie hidden in the mists of time. There are many kinds of deeds for which legendary heroes were venerated. Having been an Israelite tribal paramilitary leader is more than consistent with such veneration, as would having played a role like that of a Greek colonizer, a comparison broached in the discussion of 18:1-7. However, the all-Israel concept of the book of Joshua is extremely unlikely, both politically and geographically, to derive from traditions about such an Ephraimite local hero. Timnath-serah was located in the western part of Ephraim, midway between the town of Bethel, high in the hills, and the town of Aphek, in the coastal plain (cf. 19:49; Judg 2:6-9).[139] It is nowhere near any of the locations that play a significant role in the account of conquest. As explained in the Introduction, Joshua's name was probably introduced into the wider political arena by Jeroboam, who was born and raised close by Joshua's tomb, and into the house of David's history in the time of Hezekiah.

In contrast to our sparse knowledge of the historical Joshua, often there is a good deal of historical evidence for the colonizers. Most of these were roughly contemporary with Josiah, about whom considerably more is known than about Joshua. The colonizers' power was great, as we have seen, but what happened to these powers after the colonizers' death is usually unclear. What is clear is something that can probably also be assumed about Joshua: After he died he "became a hero, who was worshiped with ritual and

offerings in the belief that he was immortal and would, if propitiated, care for the welfare of his foundation."[140] While barring possible offerings to the saint, Josiah apparently acquiesed in the veneration of Joshua at his tomb, a concession to popular piety made possible by the co-opting of his prestige in the Deuteronomistic History. To judge from a parallel to Josiah's suppression of popular saints, this may have saved him at least some trouble. In the 1830s the governor of Palestine was Ibrahim Pasha, who ruled during a nine-year Egyptian occupation. Ibrahim expropriated many of the lands that held the shrines of saints in an attempt to reduce their power and influence. It is said that when his soldiers tried to capture a village containing the tomb of a saint, they were attacked and driven back by a swarm of bees, which the villagers said were the saint himself defending his shrine.[141]

The LXX of 24:30 contains a significant addition. It says that placed with Joshua in his tomb were the flint knives used to circumcise Israelites at Gilgal as Yahweh had commanded them to do, and that the knives are there "to this day." This may belong to the original Deuteronomistic History or it may, like 5:2-7, be a priestly touch. Either way, the notion that artifacts associated with the hero rest in his tomb with him is an authentic one, no different from the innumerable examples from the veneration of saints worldwide. In addition, in Palestine it was believed that objects left at a saint's shrine—such as plows, jewelry, or other valuables—came under the care of the saint and would be protected from theft.

139. According to various Jewish, Samaritan, Christian, and Muslim traditions, the tomb of Joshua is located in seven widely separated places in Palestine, Lebanon, and Syria.

140. Graham, "The Colonial Expansion of Greece," 3:152. The generic role of such heroes in the local and regional politics of Palestine is explored in Scott D. Hill, "The Local Hero in Palestine in Comparative Perspective," in *Elijah and Elisha in Socioliterary Perspective,* ed. Robert B. Coote (Atlanta: Scholars Press, 1992) 37-73.

141. Philip J. Baldensperger, "Order of Holy Men in Palestine," *PEFQ* 25 (1984) 35.

The deuteronomistic summary of the period of Joshua follows directly on Joshua's death and burial. In the LXX this summary is placed before Joshua's death and burial, probably a rationalizing correction. The final two notices regarding Joseph's bones and the death and burial of Eleazar are secondary, the latter related to priestly additions to Joshua, the former possibly related to the addition of 24:1-28. It is striking that all three of these final burial notices pertain to the territory of the tribes of Joseph (Manasseh in the case of Joseph's bones, Ephraim in the case of Joshua and Eleazar), and not to the territory of Judah.

REFLECTIONS

Given that his tomb became enshrined, Joshua continued as a living spirit in his own right, so that Josiah did not simply pose as Joshua returned. However, the line between being a particular saint and only looking like that saint was less rigid and probably less significant in the biblical period than we might expect. For example, as is well known, in the Gospel of Mark, John the Baptist first appears at exactly the place where Elijah had last appeared, on the east side of the Jordan, and wearing a leather belt that makes him look like Elijah (Mark 1:6; cf. 2 Kgs 1:8). Not surprisingly, in the story some believe that John was actually Elijah returned (Mark 6:15). Modern readers might assume that the writer of Mark meant to make fun of such an idea. This would be a hasty assumption, though, since Jesus himself identifies John as Elijah (Mark 9:9-13), and he does so even though Elijah has just reappeared with Moses in his presence in the transfiguration (the mountain is symbolic of Mt. Horeb, which both Moses and Elijah visited; see Mark 9:2-8). Later this identification plays an important role in Jesus' death (Mark 15:34-37). Was Elijah on the mountain actually John come back? For the last time? This important irony in Mark partakes of the inevitable ambiguity that arises when a living individual reminds many of a deceased individual: The living person embodies the spirit of the deceased, not just in appearance or manner but frequently in quite substantial terms.

This is the way Josiah is presented in the Deuteronomistic History—that is, as the embodiment of the first heroic Israelite conqueror of Canaan, Joshua. Joshua's own separate role as a living spirit was not necessarily thereby usurped, even if the active veneration of Joshua might have been discouraged under deuteronomistic law. Josiah was not Joshua, but he might as well have been, given the important similarities between the two men, as between Elijah and John. Furthermore, we may think of saints as peace-loving doers of good for all people; but throughout history saints, whether in the Middle East or worldwide, including Christian saints, could be militant and brutal, as was Elijah, who on at least one occasion single-handedly slaughtered 850 people in cold blood (1 Kgs 18:1-40). Controlling cults of saints was important not only to Josiah in the biblical period or to Ibrahim Pasha in the nineteenth century, but to many other rulers, including Christian rulers.[142]

The veneration of saints and of the dead has varied much in the history of Christianity. Regardless of diverse official views regarding the dead, however, there may be few believers—or non-believers, for that matter—who doubt that the dead live on in some sense, especially those who lived exemplary or heroic lives, or whose lives were simply bound particularly close to ours. We often find that their continued presence is particularly intense at, but by no means limited to, the place of their burial or the disposal of their ashes. It may be useful to reflect on the continuing presence of the spirit of the departed, which can always be affirmed pastorally even without an elaborate or developed view of how such spirits relate to the fate of the dead or to material reality.

---

142. Peter Brown, *The Cult of the Saints: Its Rise and Function in Latin Christianity* (Chicago: University of Chicago Press, 1981).

Christians belonging to traditions with a less developed sense of the effect of departed spirits or the influence of saints may want at least to bring to mind the importance of such figures in other traditions more in keeping with the perceptions and experiences of the biblical world. There are probably hundreds of such figures in the contemporary Christian world, in addition to the existing canonized saints of the Roman Catholic Church. Jesus Malverde is one of them. Malverde's shrine is found in Culiacan, in the Pacific Coast state of Sinaloa in Mexico. Around the turn of the century, Malverde is believed to have roamed the Culiacan hills, robbing the rich and feeding the poor, until the government caught up with him and executed him in 1909. All year a continuous stream of devotees, drawn largely from the poor and highland inhabitants of Sinaloa, come to Malverde's shrine to ask for favors—for health, safety, job success, protection from the government—and to give him thanks for his continuous deeds of kindness and assistance. The stories about Malverde are legion. They differ greatly, however, even over critical details like the manner of the saint's death. Historians have found no clear evidence that Malverde ever existed. But to his followers, he not only existed but is more powerful than ever, and they can make contact with him at his shrine, not far from the site of his death. "Thanks to God and Malverde," one follower was quoted as having said, "there's something for everyone. Not much, but something."[143]

143. *San Francisco Sunday Examiner,* March 2, 1997.

THE BOOK OF JUDGES

INTRODUCTION, COMMENTARY, AND REFLECTIONS
BY
DENNIS T. OLSON

THE BOOK OF

JUDGES

INTRODUCTION

T he book of Judges is one of the most exciting, colorful, and disturbing books of the Bible. It combines stories of political intrigue and assassination, lies and deception, rape and murder, courage and fear, great faith and idolatry, power and greed, sex and suicide, love and death, military victories and civil war. The book portrays a major transition in the biblical story of Israel. Before the book of Judges, Israel was under the leadership of Moses in the wilderness (Exodus–Deuteronomy) and then Joshua in the initial conquest of the land of Canaan (Joshua). After the book of Judges, Israel was ruled by kings, beginning with Saul, David, and Solomon and concluding with Judah's defeat and exile to Babylon (1–2 Samuel; 1–2 Kings; see 2 Kings 24–25). The turbulent transition between Moses and Joshua, on one hand, and the kings of Israel, on the other hand, is portrayed in the book of Judges. The book presents the varied tales of twelve warrior rulers, called judges, who led ancient Israel for brief periods in times of military emergency.

The book's title, "Judges," may bring to mind images of wise people who arbitrate legal cases in courts. Indeed, one of the so-called judges, Deborah, appears to function in this way as a mediator of disputes (4:4-5). However, the term "judge" (שׁפט *šōpēṭ*) in Hebrew can also mean "rule" or "ruler," and it is this meaning of the term that applies to the major characters in the book.[1] They are primarily warrior rulers who led Israel in fighting oppressive enemies. The judges were also involved in maintaining Israel's religious life and institutions with varying degrees of success (2:17; 5:1-31; 6:25-27; 8:22-28).

JUDGES AND HISTORY

Scholars have debated the value of the book of Judges in reconstructing the early history of ancient Israel after its settlement in the land of Canaan in the twelfth and eleventh centuries BCE. Some commentators assume that many of the events and people recounted in Judges do

---

1. Temba L. J. Mafico, "Judge, Judging," in *The Anchor Bible Dictionary,* 6 vols. (New York: Doubleday, 1992) 3:1104.

reflect actual historical situations in this early period, although the stories have been significantly reshaped and edited.[2] For example, scholars argue that the ongoing struggle of the Israelites with other nations in Canaan over a long period of time in Judges may provide a more accurate picture of the conquest of Canaan than does the quick and total conquest as depicted in some parts of Joshua (Josh 11:23). Scholars also point to the Song of Deborah and Barak in Judges 5 as one of the most ancient parts of the Bible, with its origin in the period of the judges or the early monarchy.

Yet, scholars are also cautious about using Judges to reconstruct early Israelite history.[3] For example, if one adds all of the years of enemy oppression and the length of the judges' rule throughout the book (e.g., 3:8, 11), the total comes to 480 years. But, that is far too long a period to fit the roughly 300 years between the exodus, dated sometime in the thirteenth century, and the rise of kingship in the tenth century BCE. Moreover, some of the judges' stories may have originally been tales of local heroes and chieftains of small clan or tribal groups. The tales were then later rewritten so that they became stories of leaders of larger Israelite coalitions as they were incorporated into the book of Judges. Still other scholars believe that we simply do not have adequate evidence from archaeological or other textual sources to evaluate the overall historicity of the events in Judges.

METHODS IN THE INTERPRETATION OF JUDGES

The lively characters, the moral difficulties, the turbulent social context, and the theological questions that animate the book of Judges have occasioned a wide spectrum of response in the history of biblical interpretation. The rabbinic debate over whether Jephthah's daughter was actually offered as a burnt sacrifice and the ancient Christian interpretation of the death of Samson as a typological prefigurement of the death of Jesus are only two of many intriguing examples of the ancient approportion of Judges. Modern historical-critical interpretation of Judges has paid the most attention to the history of the composition of the book in the light of proposals for the growth of the larger Deuteronomistic History (Deuteronomy and Joshua–2 Kings). Most scholars agree that Judges emerged through several stages of collecting, writing, and editing.[4] Originally separate stories of local clan or tribal heroes were assembled into a larger connected narrative. Editorial sections were added at key junctures in and around the stories. A definitive two-part introduction (1:1–2:5; 2:6–3:6) and a two-part conclusion (17:1–18:31; 19:1–21:25) were also added in two or more editorial stages. This process occurred over many generations, culminating in two or three definitive periods of editorial shaping, including the time of King Hezekiah (eighth century BCE), King Josiah (seventh century BCE), and sometime after the exile of Judah to Babylon (sixth–fifth century BCE). The audience for the final form of Judges probably included the people of Judah, who had experienced the exile to Babylon and the disintegration of their social, political, and religious life (2 Kings 24–25). Judges continued to be read and interpreted in new contexts and thus lived on as a biblical paradigm for future generations.

The book of Judges has been an exceptionally fertile ground for a wide variety of newer approaches to biblical interpretation.[5] Narrative analyses of plot, character, point of view, repetition, and theme have proved to be profitable avenues of study. Judges contains one of the Bible's largest concentrations of female characters, nineteen in all. The variety of women in Judges has offered a rich resource for feminist scholarship on the relationship of women, power, and violence. Social-scientific criticism has found grist for its mill in the questions of the formation of Israelite society in the judges period, the function of kinship association in a tribal society, and the role of the judges as chieftains in the rise of Israelite kingship. Structuralist, deconstructive, and ideological criticisms have also found Judges to be amenable to their various strategies and

2. Robert G. Boling, *Judges*, AB 6A (Garden City, N.Y.: Doubleday, 1975) 9-29.

3. J. Alberto Soggin, *Judges*, OTL (Philadelphia: Westminster, 1981) 6-12.

4. An insightful survey and proposal for the editorial shaping of Judges is offered by Lawson Stone, "From Tribal Confederation to Monarchic State: The Editorial Perspective of the Book of Judges" (Ph.D. diss., Yale University; Ann Arbor: University Microfilms, 1987). Much of my view of the overall structure and movement of Judges is indebted to Stone's work.

5. A survey of new methods as applied to Judges is Gale Yee, ed., *Judges and Method: New Approaches in Biblical Studies* (Minneapolis: Fortress, 1995).

methods of reading. The approach of this commentary on Judges is somewhat eclectic, using insights from various methods as they seem most helpful with a given text or issue. However, this commentary has a general tilt toward redactional and narrative analysis of the final form of the text, along with an overriding theological interest in the questions, issues, and struggles raised by the text for understanding the relationships of God, humans, and the world. This study of Judges is also informed by the Russian literary theorist Mikhail Bakhtin and his notion of competing dialogical voices and themes that are held together but not absorbed into one another.[6]

THE SHIFT FROM REPETITIVE CYCLES TO GRADUAL DECLINE

The book of Judges is often associated with a repetitive pattern or cycle outlined in 2:11-19 and repeated throughout the narratives of individual judges: Israel does evil, God sends an enemy; Israel cries in distress, God sends a judge or deliverer; Israel again does evil, and the cycle repeats. The cyclical pattern probably defined an earlier editorial layer of Judges. However, editors of the final form made important changes and additions that redefined the basic movement of the book's plot. These changes redefined the judges era from its characterization as a series of flat cycles in endless repetition to a downward slide and increasingly severe disintegration of Israel's social and religious life. These changes included altering the two-part introduction to Judges so that it described the gradual deterioration of the twelve tribes' conquest of Canaan (1:1–2:5) and the gradual decline of Israel's faithfulness to the covenant with God (2:6–3:6).

The stories of the individual judges (3:7–16:31) also have been edited to exhibit a similar gradual decline from initial success and faithfulness among the early judges (Othniel, Ehud, Deborah, and Barak) to eventual ineffectiveness and unfaithfulness among the later judges (Jephthah, Samson). In the final chapters of Judges, Israel is portrayed as having no king or ruler, and "all the people did what was right in their own eyes" (17:6; 21:25). Israel disintegrates into religious and social chaos in this final phase of the judges era (17.1–21.25). God allowed Israel to hit bottom as punishment for its increasing sinfulness and idolatry. Yet in the midst of Israel's unraveling and near-death experiences, glimpses of hope emerge. Samson's shaved hair began to grow back (16:22). A faithful house of God remained functioning in northern Israel at Shiloh in spite of the idolatrous cult at Dan (18:30). The tribe of Benjamin was pulled back from the brink of extinction and death (20:46–21:24). God remained present and active even in the midst of sinful and tragic circumstances (20:18, 21, 28, 35).

IMPORTANT THEMES IN DIALOGICAL TENSION

The book of Judges contains a wide array of dialogical perspectives on key themes. The book holds together seemingly opposed or disjunctive viewpoints on the same subject. Only a few examples are cited here; more detailed discussions of these dialogical tensions will occur throughout the commentary. This dialectical character of Judges was the basis for Martin Buber's proposal that Judges contains two "books," an anti-monarchical book that opposes dynastic kingship (chaps. 1–12) and a pro-monarchical book that supports dynastic kingship (chaps. 13–21).[7] The first anti-kingship section offers a critique of foreign kings, like Adoni-bezek (1:5-7), fat King Eglon (3:15-25), and King Jabin of Canaan (4:23-24). In this same section, Gideon rejects the offer to become a king over Israel (8:22-23), and Jotham ridicules Abimelech's disastrous attempt to become an Israelite king (9:7-15). In contrast, Buber argued that the second half of Judges, chapters 13–21, is pro-kingship in that it laments the chaos and disintegration of Israel in a time when "there was no king in Israel" and "all the people did what was right in their own eyes" (17:6; 18:1; 19:1; 21:25).

---

6. Among other works, see Mikhail Bakhtin, *Problems of Dostoevsky's Poetics,* ed. and trans. Caryl Emerson (Minneapolis: University of Minnesota Press, 1984), and *The Dialogic Imagination: Four Essays by M. M. Bakhtin,* ed. Michael Holquist (Austin: University of Texas Press, 1981). An example of a biblical scholar's application of Bakhtin's insights to some aspects of Judges is Robert Polzin, *Moses and the Deuteronomist: A Literary Study of the Deuteronomic History* (New York: Seabury, 1980).

7. Martin Buber, "The Books of Judges and the Book of Judges," in *The Kingship of God* (New York: Harper & Row, 1967) 66-84.

However, in my judgment the book's view of kingship is more consistent throughout the book than Buber suggests, but no less dialectical.[8] The book of Judges affirms the need for human kingship in Israel *at this particular time in Israel's history* at the end of the judges era. However, the editors and readers of the final form of Judges and the Deuteronomistic History also know that kingship, like the institution of judgeship, will be flawed, temporary, and eventually collapse. Kingship in Israel, like the judges, will in time be replaced by another form of human leadership, which will be necessary but also provisional and imperfect. The era of the judges thus becomes a paradigm of any human institution, mode of governance, or ideology—necessary but provisional, helpful for a time, but eventually replaced by another.

Examples of other themes held in dialogical tension throughout Judges include the interplay of religion and politics, the well-being of women and the health of society, the benefits and threats of relationships with people of other nations, human character as both noble and deeply flawed, the subtle interplay of divine and human agency and actions, and small signs of hope in the midst of horrendous chaos and social disintegration. One final and overriding tension throughout Judges is the interplay of God's justice or punishment and God's mercy or compassion. God repeatedly punishes Israel for its continual evil, and yet God cannot let Israel go. This increasingly intense dance between divine justice and mercy raises questions as the reader moves through the chapters of Judges: How far can God's patience and mercy be stretched until it reaches a breaking point? How far can Israel stray from the covenant before God gives up on Israel altogether? The angel's words in 2:1-5 pose the tension. On one hand, God affirms to Israel, "I will never break my covenant with you" (2:1). But on the other hand, God promises to punish Israel because "you have not obeyed my command" (2:2). In the end, God's mercy will sustain God's relationship with Israel, but Israel will go through a time of national chaos and death in order for a new generation to be born and a new way forward to emerge as Israel's experiment in kingship opens up into the narratives about the rise of kingship in 1–2 Samuel.

---

8. Stone, "From Tribal Confederation to Monarchic State," 77-84, 373-89. Stone reaches similar but not identical conclusions on Buber and Judges' view of kingship.

BIBLIOGRAPHY

Commentaries:

Boling, Robert G. *Judges,* AB 6A. Garden City, N.Y.: Doubleday, 1975. A fresh translation with a commentary focused on linguistic, historical, archaeological, and text-critical matters; assumes that Judges underwent several stages of editing, although many of its narratives reflect actual historical events and persons dating from the twelfth and eleventh centuries BCE.

Gray, John. *Joshua, Judges, Ruth.* NCBC. Grand Rapids: Eerdmans, 1986. A historical-critical commentary concerned with understanding the history of composition and redaction of Judges and the meaning of terms and phrases in their ancient Near Eastern context.

Hamlin, E. John. *Judges: At Risk in the Promised Land.* ITC. Grand Rapids: Eerdmans, 1990. A commentary of theological reflection on Judges in dialogue with other biblical texts, including the New Testament; having taught for many years in an Asian context, the author seeks to make connections between Judges and contemporary global issues related to gender, race, class, and ecology.

Soggin, J. Alberto. *Judges.* OTL. Philadelphia: Westminster, 1981. A historical-critical commentary that is more skeptical about judgments concerning the historicity of the events and persons in Judges; covers issues of text, form, archaeology, geography, and history of composition.

Other studies:

Bal, Mieke. *Death and Dissymmetry: The Politics of Coherence in the Book of Judges.* Chicago: University of Chicago Press, 1988. A provocative feminist and literary analysis of the relationship of gender and violence throughout Judges as a sign of cultural upheaval and transition; argues that the male violence against the three daughters in Judges (Jephthah's daughter, Samson's wife, and Levite's concubine) is answered by the violent retribution of three displaced mothers (Jael, the woman with the millstone, and Delilah).

Brenner, Athalya, ed. *A Feminist Companion to Judges.* Sheffield: JSOT, 1993. A stimulating collection of feminist and womanist studies of the book's many and varied female characters, including leaders, mothers, wives, and daughters.

Klein, Lillian R. *The Triumph of Irony in the Book of Judges.* Sheffield: Almond, 1989. Argues for the widespread use of irony as one of the major literary devices at work in the book of Judges; traces the differing perspectives and levels of knowledge among the narrator, the characters, God, and the reader and the effects of such differences on interpretation.

Marcus, David. *Jephthah and His Vow.* Lubbock, Tex.: Texas Tech Press, 1986. A fascinating study of the history of traditional Jewish, Christian, and modern critical interpretation of the story of Jephthah and his vow concerning the sacrifice of his daughter.

Polzin, Robert. *Moses and the Deuteronomist: A Literary Study of the Deuteronomic History.* New York: Seabury, 1980. An insightful literary study of Deuteronomy, Joshua, and Judges that traces the thematic tensions and dialogic interplay between various narrative voices; argues that the central conflict is the voice of dogmatic authoritarianism versus the voice of critical traditionalism.

Trible, Phyllis. *Texts of Terror: Literary-Feminist Readings of Biblical Narratives.* Philadelphia: Fortress, 1984. Contains chapters on Jephthah's daughter in Judges 11 and the Levite's concubine in Judges 19; a close reading of the biblical text that follows its rhetoric and traces the effects of male violence on the women who become its tragic victims.

Stone, Lawson. "From Tribal Confederation to Monarchic State: The Editorial Perspective of the Book of Judges." Ph.D. dissertation, Yale University. Ann Arbor: University Microfilms, 1987. A detailed and well-argued redaction-critical study that proposes that later editors constructed a coherent and artful structure for the whole book of Judges, culminating in a pattern of deterioration from faithfulness and triumph among the early judges to tragedy and internal conflict among the later judges and the end of the judges period.

Webb, Barry. *The Book of the Judges: An Integrated Reading.* Sheffield: JSOT, 1987. A thorough literary and narrative analysis of the whole book of Judges, highlighting its literary artfulness, its structural coherence, and the meaningful repetition of key motifs throughout the book.

Yee, Gale A., ed. *Judges and Method: New Approaches in Biblical Studies.* Minneapolis: Fortress, 1995. Helpful methodological essays that explain and apply a number of new literary and sociological methods in biblical interpretation using selected texts from the book of Judges; the various approaches include narrative, social-scientific, feminist, structuralist, deconstructive, and ideological criticisms.

OUTLINE OF JUDGES

JUDGES 1:1–3:6

INTRODUCTION: JUDGES AS AN
ERA OF DECLINE

OVERVIEW

The first major section of Judg 1:1–3:6 establishes the definitive pattern or paradigm for understanding the movement and structure of the entire book. The pattern defines the era of the Israelite judges as a series of generations who slide downward from initial successes and faithfulness to increasing failures and apostasy. The pattern is presented twice from two different perspectives within this introductory section. Judges 1:1–2:5 focuses on Israel's increasing failure in the military *conquest* of Canaan, and 2:6–3:6 focuses on Israel's growing unfaithfulness to the covenant with God. Israel's military inability or unwillingness to eradicate the Canaanites from the promised land becomes a symptom of a deeper problem—namely, Israel's failure to keep the covenant and worship the Lord alone.

Many scholars believe that this introduction in two parts reflects at least two stages in the writing and editing of the book of Judges.[9] The earliest part of the introduction is embedded within 2:6–3:6 and may have once functioned on its own as a prelude to an earlier version of the book. This earlier introduction defined the era of the judges as a cyclical and repetitive pattern of Israel's apostasy, God's punishment, and God's deliverance through a judge. The elements of this cyclical pattern are evident in 2:11-19: (1) Israel worshiped other gods (2:11-13); (2) the Lord became angry and handed Israel over to an enemy, who oppressed them (2:14-16); (3) Israel cried out, and the Lord responded in mercy by sending a judge to deliver Israel from its enemy (2:18); and (4) Israel would relapse

into disobedience and apostasy, and the cycle would begin again (2:19). This cyclical pattern was then attached to a series of stories of heroic individuals called judges. These judges were temporary leaders who formed loose alliances of Israelite tribes, won military victories against enemies, resolved intertribal conflicts, and restored peace for a time, until Israel sinned again and the next enemy threatened Israel once more.

The theology implied in such a cyclical and repetitive pattern is more mechanical than relational, more static than dynamic, more predictable than surprising and unexpected. But generations of Israelites who heard and passed on these stories about God and the judges came to believe that more needed to be said about the ways of God with Israel. Israel's experience with God was not as cyclical or predictable as this early introduction suggested. Israel was constantly surprised by God's unexpected ways both in judgment and in deliverance. For example, the prophet Jeremiah stunned the complacent leaders of his day with a surprising word of judgment from God for ignoring the deep wound of unfaithfulness among God's people: "They have treated the wound of my people carelessly, saying 'Peace, peace,' when there is no peace" (Jer 6:14 NRSV). On the other hand, the prophet of Isaiah 40–55 delivered unexpected words of God's promise of hope and a return home to a beleaguered and despondent audience of exiles in Babylon: "For you shall go out in joy, and be led back in peace" (Isa 55:12 NRSV). God's interactions with God's people were often surprising and contrary to guaranteed or predictable cycles from a human perspective.

9. For various perspectives on the history of the composition of this introductory section of Judges, see Boling, *Judges,* 29-38.

Thus a later editor and community made additions to the earlier introduction that changed its orientation from a flat-line cyclical pattern to a downward slide, a decline from faithfulness in early generations to a deepening sinfulness and apostasy in later generations. The book of Judges explores the surprising ways in which God acted and related to Israel through the judges in the midst of this deterioration of Israel's social and religious life. As we shall see, one key addition was the insertion of 2:17, which demoted the judges from entirely positive and heroic deliverers to leaders who gained temporary military success but ultimately failed as religious leaders. Another addition was 2:20–3:6, including God's climactic pronouncement of a change in strategy in 2:20-21. Later generations also added a second and entirely new introduction to the book in 1:1–2:5.[10] Much of this later introduction that now begins the book of Judges is reworked material drawn from the preceding book of Joshua. This later introduction presents the last stages of the conquest of Canaan after the death of the leader Joshua as a downward spiral that moves from moderate successes by the southern tribe of Judah (1:1-21) to increasingly negative failures by the northern tribes of "the house of Joseph" (1:22-36).

These later editorial changes and additions created an important shift in the book's theology from a cyclical and mechanistic view of God's ways with Israel. The expanded two-part introduction paints a much more relational, dynamic, and intense portrait of God's anger and mercy in response to the growing failure and faithlessness of Israel in the period of the judges. The book of Judges is no longer a predictable cycle of temporary military heroes in Israel's history. Under the careful shaping

of later editors, Judges introduces the record of Israel's slow and bumpy decline into apostasy and disintegration, a decline that even the judges sent by the Lord could not finally prevent or impede. The actual narratives of the judges in 3:7–16:31 have been shaped in the final form of the book to reflect this gradual decline in Israel's life and faith as a community of God's people. By the time we reach the final chapters of the book, the reader will be shocked by, but not wholly unprepared for, the horrific disintegration of Israel's religious and social fabric that Judges 17–21 narrates in tragic detail. A major theological question remains hanging over the end of the book of Judges: Now that the conquest of Canaan has been only partial, and now that the era of the judges has ended in failure and tragedy, what new strategy will God adopt in relating to and leading God's people? By the time we reach the end of Judges, Israel's life as a community will be so dramatically flawed that God will need to find a whole new way of leading and relating to God's people.

One other element to note in this opening section is the different time sequence within the two parts of the introduction. The time period associated with the first introductory section in 1–2:5 begins only "*after* the death of Joshua" (1:1). The brief narratives or notices about the conquest of Canaan that follow are all set in a time when Joshua is gone and off the stage. However, the time associated with the second introductory section in 2:6–3:6 takes the reader back in time and opens with a flashback scene when Joshua is still alive: "When Joshua dismissed the people . . ." (2:6). This section then moves through a series of generational phases: the lifetime of Joshua (2:6-7), a faithful generation of Israelites who outlived Joshua (2:7), and a new generation who did not know the Lord (2:10). This latter generation marks the beginning of a series of generations to whom God sends the judges to rescue Israel.

---

10. For details and arguments for this later redactional shaping of the introduction to Judges, see E. Theodore Mullen, "Judges 1:1–3:6: The Deuteronomistic Reintroduction of the Book of Judges," *HTR* 77 (1984) 33-54; and Stone, "From Tribal Confederation to Monarchic State," 190-259.

JUDGES 1:1–2:5, FROM SUCCESS TO FAILURE: THE CONQUEST OF CANAAN

OVERVIEW

This first of two parts of the introduction to Judges begins "after the death of Joshua" (1:1). A later editor or writer carefully constructed this introductory piece by borrowing some source material from the book of Joshua, restructuring it, and then adding other material to form a three-part section. Each section is marked at the beginning by the verb "to go up" (עלה, ʿālâ) with the meaning of "invade" or "attack": "Judah *shall go up*" (1:1-2); "The house of Joseph also *went up*" (1:22); and "Now the angel of the LORD *went up*" (2:1).[11] This tripartite series of military engagements moves from some moderate successes by the southern tribes led by Judah in 1:1-21 to a spiral of declining failures by the northern Israelite tribes of the "house of Joseph" (1:22, 35) in 1:22-36 to a final "going up" by the "angel of the LORD" in a climactic judgment speech against "all the Israelites" (2:4) in 2:1-5. This culminating divine speech marks a dramatic reversal of the conquest of Canaan; previously God had gone up and fought *for* Israel, but now God goes up and fights *against* Israel!

This portrait of a decline from Judah's initial triumphs to the failures of the northern "house of Joseph" to the divine indictment against all Israel has been constructed by an editor who borrowed and shaped material taken from the book of Joshua. Judges 1:1–2:5 quotes directly from several texts within the book of Joshua with some subtle, but important, changes:[12]

Josh 14:6, 13, 15; ⟶ Judg 1:10, 20
15:13-14 (Judah captures
(Caleb captures Hebron)
Hebron)

Josh 15:13-19 ⟶ Judg 1:11-15
(Othniel captures (Othniel captures
Kiriath-Sepher Kiriath-Sepher
during the lifetime after the death
of Joshua) of Joshua)

Josh 15:63 ⟶ Judg 1:21
(Judah could not (Benjaminites could
capture Jerusalem) not capture
Jerusalem)

Josh 17:11-13 ⟶ Judg 1:27-28
(Manasseh's failure (Manasseh's failure
is given less is given more
prominence) prominence)

Josh 16:10 ⟶ Judg 1:29
(Ephraim's failure is (Ephraim's failure
given less is given more
prominence) prominence)

In addition to these direct quotations, Judges also draws a number of more indirect allusions from the book of Joshua:

Joshua 10 ⟶ Judg 1:5-7
(Joshua's victory (Judah's victory over
over King King Adonibezek;
Adonizedek; Jerusalem
Jerusalem not captured)
captured)

Josh 17:16-18 ⟶ Judg 1:19
(Ephraim's failure (Judah's failure in
excused by north excused by
enemy's iron enemy's iron
chariots) chariots)

Joshua 13–19 ⟶ Judg 1:30-35
(tribal list moves (tribal list moves
from south to from south to
north) north; added
failure reports to
some northern
tribes)

---

11. A. G. Auld, "Judges 1 and History: A Reconsideration," *VT* 25 (1975) 276; G. F. Moore, *Judges*, ICC (New York: Scribners, 1901) 40. The same verb (עלה ʿālâ, "to go up") is used in the sense of entering into a battle in Judg 1:1-4, 16, 22; 2:1.

12. This list of quotations and allusions drawn from Joshua and their interpretation is adapted from Stone, "From Tribal Confederation to Monarchic State," 196-248; Mullen, "Judges 1:1–3:6," 33-54; and Marc Brettler, "The Book of Judges, Literature as Politics," *JBL* 108 (1989) 395-418.

Josh 5:13-15 ————————→ Judg 2:1-5
(angelic commander   (angel of the Lord
  of the Lord's army   indicts Israel;
  is neither friend   allows Canaanites
  nor enemy of   to remain in land
  Israel)   as enemies of
    Israel)

A writer composed Judg 1:1–2:5 by gathering and shaping these quotations and allusions, cementing them together with the writer's own additions. The specifics of the quotations and the allusions will be considered in the Commentary sections below. However, a general anachronism or problem in time sequences arises in these reappropriations of material from Joshua into Judg 1:1–2:5. The book of Joshua assumes that these events happened *during* the lifetime of Joshua. However, when the writer of Judg 1:1–2:5 incorporated them into the introduction to Judges, the writer altered the chronological frame to a time "*after* the death of Joshua" (Judg 1:1). But this anachronism was allowed to stand in service to the writer's larger goal of portraying a graduated decline from Judah's initial successes to the growing failure of the northern tribes to a general indictment of all Israel.

Judges 1:1-21, Judah First: Moderate Success

COMMENTARY

This opening section of Judges is an example of inner-biblical exegesis. The later editor who wrote this introductory material did so by selecting, rearranging, and reinterpreting selected earlier biblical accounts of the conquest of Canaan, drawn from Joshua 14–19. The interpretive rewriting has given the material a moderately pro-Judah slant. The southern tribe of Judah is highlighted as the first tribe chosen by God to lead the next phase of the conquest of Canaan "after the death of Joshua." Judah leads several other southern groups in military engagements, some Israelite and some non-Israelite. The Israelite tribe of Simeon (vv. 3-17) was associated with Judah, since the tradition held that its allotted land lay within Judah's territory (Josh 19:1). Caleb and Othniel (vv. 11-15, 20) were apparently Kenizzites and not originally Israelites. Joshua 14:6, 14 narrates the adoption of Caleb the Kenizzite and his clan into the tribal allotment of Judah and celebrates Caleb's faithfulness as one of the Israelite spies of Numbers 13–14. The Kenites, another non-Israelite group whose ancestor was the father-in-law of Moses, joined Judah as well for a time (Judg 1:16).

The section divides into four subsections: vv. 1-7, Judah's defeat of King Adoni-bezek; vv. 8-10, Judah's conquest of the cities of Jerusalem and Hebron; vv. 11-16, the conquests of foreigners who have been adopted into Judah's tribe: Othniel, his wife Achsah, and the Kenites; and vv. 17-21, further conquests by Judah and Simeon and some minor setbacks. The material borrowed from the book of Joshua to write much of this section has been given a moderately pro-Judah slant. But the seeds of some failure and signs of Judah's weakness remain and prepare for the angel's indictment against "all the Israelites" in 2:1-5.

1:1-7. These verses begin with a time designation, marking the beginning of an entirely new era: "After the death of Joshua." The preceding era, when Joshua led Israel in battle against the Canaanites, had been marked by a similar notice of the death of Moses in Josh 1:1. In the same way, a future new era under King David will commence in 2 Sam 1:1 and be marked by the same formula: "After the death of Saul." Thus v. 1 launches the reader into an important time of transition between the conquest of Canaan under Joshua and the unification of all Israel under King David. The book of Judges forms the first half of that time of transition, a time when God will experiment with judges as a way of leading Israel. In the second half of the transition to the Israelite kingship in 1 Samuel, God will experiment for the first time with human kingship under Saul. Both of these experiments, the judges and the kingship under Saul, will begin favorably but end in tragedy.

Ultimately, the Davidic kingship itself will run aground at the end of the present form of 2 Kings as even southern Judah under a Davidic king will end up with the Jerusalem Temple destroyed, the city sacked, and much of Judah's population forcibly taken into exile in Babylon (2 Kgs 25:1-26). But the hope of a return of a Davidic king to Jerusalem continued even at the end of the book of 2 Kings (2 Kgs 25:27-30; see 2 Samuel 7) and in the prophetic promises of a Davidic messiah who would return to lead Israel in some distant future day (e.g., Isaiah 11).

However, in this time of transition after the death of Joshua and before the rise of the Davidic kingship, the Israelite tribes gather to initiate a second phase of the conquest of Canaan. The generation of Israelites under Joshua had not completely routed all the Canaanites from the land, and thus a second phase of military engagements was required. The tribes inquire of the Lord through an oracle, using a question very much parallel to an oracular inquiry at the end of the book of Judges in 20:18:

"Who shall go up first for us against the Canaanites, to fight against them?" (1:1 NRSV)

"Which of us shall go up first to battle against the Benjaminites?" (20:18 NRSV)

In each case of the twin oracles, the answer will be "Judah shall go up first." However, in 1:1 the enemy is external, the Canaanites. In 20:18, Israel will have disintegrated into civil war among the tribes; the enemy will become internal, Israel fighting against itself. But for now, Judah is chosen to lead first. The preeminence of Judah has been affirmed previously in the biblical narrative as far back as the blessing of Jacob in Gen 49:8-10 and in Judah's leadership in the arrangement of the holy war camp in Num 10:14. Joshua 14 begins the allotment of lands among the tribes with the tribe of Judah. The southern tribe of Judah will eventually become the southern kingdom of Judah. Jerusalem will become its capital and the site of Solomon's Temple and the palace of the Davidic kings. Thus Judah's prominence among the twelve tribes of Israel is a recurring theme throughout the biblical narrative, and Judah's leadership in this phase of the conquest is in line with that theme.

Judah invites its fellow southern tribe of Simeon (see Josh 19:1) to join its forces (v. 3). The first of Judah's conquests involves the defeat of an army of ten thousand at Bezek. Scholars are unsure about the location of Bezek, although it may be identified with the one other occurrence of the name in the OT in 1 Sam 11:8, where it is a place name near Shechem. But the focus of the narrative is on the enemy king who is captured, King Adoni-bezek. The name invites comparison with the text of Joshua 10, where the great leader Joshua defeated a king with a similar name, Adoni-zedek of Jerusalem (Josh 10:1). Like the great leader Joshua, who defeated Adoni-zedek, Judah defeats a Canaanite king, Adoni-bezek. But Judah goes even a step further. Joshua defeated the king of Jerusalem but did not actually capture the city, as it remained in Jebusite hands (Josh 15:8). According to Judg 1:8, Judah was able to do what Joshua could not—namely, capture Jerusalem. In this way, the story elevates Judah's accomplishments to the same level as Joshua and pushes them even a notch higher. In capturing the city of Jerusalem, Judah does what Joshua could not.[13]

King Adoni-bezek is captured. His thumbs and big toes are cut off as a sign not just of disablement but also of humiliation and revenge, a practice known elsewhere among the cultures of the ancient Near East. What is striking is that this foreign king acknowledges God's victory and the moral judgment of God. The king is reaping what he has sown; he is receiving the same punishment he had arrogantly exacted against countless other rulers. The text affirms the ability of those outside the community of God's people to discern God's ways and moral order. King Abimelech had feared God and corrected his unintentional error of taking Sarah, the wife of Abraham, as a wife (Gen 20:1-18). Likewise, even the Egyptian pharaoh acknowledged to Moses in the midst of the ten plagues, "This time I have sinned; the LORD is in the right, and I and my people are in the wrong. Pray to the LORD!" (Exod 9:27-28 NRSV). The story reminds Israel that even foreign rulers can

---

13. Stone, "From Tribal Confederation to Monarchic State," 214-16.

discern their own transgression against God's moral order. Even these kings know they cannot do "whatever is right in their own eyes" (see Judg 17:6).

Judah's army brings King Adoni-bezek to Jerusalem, where he dies (v. 7). There at the city of Jerusalem, where Israel's own kings will one day come to power in David and Solomon and all the Davidic kings who follow, we are reminded that the arrogance of power will come to ruin. Kingship itself lives under and is responsible to the rule of a larger and divine moral order. No political order or ideology, whether of Joshua or Judah or judges or kings, can escape responsibility or judgment under God's ultimate rule.

1:8-10. The narrative continues with Judah's temporary capture of the city of Jerusalem. The capture is temporary, because the city will apparently be entrusted by Judah to the tribe of Benjamin, since the city lay within the boundaries of Benjamin's allotment of land (Josh 18:16, 28). So although Judah is able to make the initial assault on the city, Benjamin will be unable to hold on to the city and will not be able to drive out the Jebusite inhabitants of Jerusalem (v. 21). This scenario is somewhat at odds with the previous conquest reports in the book of Joshua, which states that it was Judah (not Benjamin) who was unable to drive out the Jebusites from Jerusalem (Josh 15:63). The writer of Judges 1 has clearly constructed a more favorable portrait of Judah's military success in line with the overall goal of portraying a movement of decline in Judges 1 from success to failure. But in the end, even Judah will be included in the indictment and failure of "all the Israelites" in 2:1-5.

After Jerusalem, Judah moves to the Negev and other areas of southern Canaan, including the city of Hebron (vv. 9-10). Again, the writer of chap. 1 revises the narrative of the book of Joshua in order to exalt Judah's accomplishment. In Josh 15:13-14, Caleb the Kenizzite is named as the one who captures Hebron, but in Judg 1:10 it is Judah. Caleb becomes subsumed under the tribe of Judah, although the wider biblical tradition knows the Kenizzites as being descended from Edom and not Israel (Gen 15:19; 36:11, 15, 42).

1:11-16. The next story in vv. 11-15 recounts Caleb's promise to give his daughter Achsah in marriage to whoever attacks and conquers the city of Debir, otherwise known as the city of Kiriath-sepher. The story is almost a repetition of the same story told in Josh 15:15-19. Othniel son of Kenaz accepts Caleb's challenge, conquers the city, and receives Achsah as his wife. It is grammatically ambiguous who the phrase "Caleb's younger brother" modifies in v. 13, either Othniel himself (making Othniel a brother or cousin to Caleb) or Othniel's father (making Othniel a nephew to Caleb). The latter is more likely in terms of the narrative, since Caleb was a contemporary of Joshua and at least one or two generations have come and gone since the death of Joshua (2:7-10; 3:7-11). However, the central character in this mini-narrative is not Othniel but Achsah, the wife of Othniel and daughter of Caleb. Achsah emerges as a shrewd and able negotiator with her father, Caleb. The Hebrew text of v. 14 makes her the primary subject of the action: "*She* urged him [her husband, Othniel] to ask" her father Caleb for a piece of land to go along with Achsah. The Greek and Latin versions of the verse reverse the order, "*he* [Othniel] urged her to ask," but the NRSV and the NIV have rightly followed the Hebrew text. Achsah is in charge. She gets Othniel to ask for a piece of land. She herself then slides off her donkey, approaches her father, and asks him for yet another favor. Since she and Othniel are getting land in the dry region of the Negev, she also asks for Gulloth-mayim (גלת מים *gullōt māyim*), meaning in Hebrew "Springs/Basins of Water." Her father, Caleb, responds by giving her not one but two sources of water, Upper Gulloth ("Upper Springs") and Lower Gulloth ("Lower Springs").

While one commentator has dismissed this mini-narrative as "a charming personal tale," vv. 11-15 in fact play an important role in introducing key themes and characters that will emerge later in the book of Judges. Barry Webb summarizes the connections with later material in Judges:

All three characters in this vignette will assume greater significance in the larger narrative which is yet to unfold. Othniel will reappear as the first judge (3.7-11). In the light of 2.7, Caleb will appear as a representative of 'the elders who outlived Joshua' and in whose days Israel still served

Yahweh. On the other hand, his promise to give Achsah to whoever would take Debir for him (12bc) will find a grotesque and tragic parallel in Jephthah's vow (11:30-31). Achsah's practical shrewdness and resourcefulness in seizing the initiative from both Othniel and Caleb—the two male heroes of the story—introduces a motif which will recur at crucial points in 3.6-16.31, particularly at 4.17-22 (Jael), 9.53-54 (the 'certain woman' of Thebez) and 16.14-21 (Delilah). Othniel's marriage to Achsah will also assume greater significance in the light of 3.6.[14]

The last sentence in Webb's summary alludes to the primary indictment against Israel in Judg 3:6. Later generations of Israelites have been marrying wives from the Canaanites and other non-Israelite people of the land and, as a result, have worshiped their gods and neglected the worship of Yahweh, the God of Israel. Othniel's marriage to Achsah is a model of remaining within the fold of Israel both in marriage and in faithfulness to God. Othniel will be portrayed as a model judge. But gradually even the judges, as well as the people, will deteriorate into intermarriage and unfaithfulness, culminating in Samson's liaisons with foreign women (chaps. 13–16). Judges repeatedly affirms the interconnectedness of the social and theological dimensions of Israel's life; the character of Israel's social and human relationships reflects Israel's relationship to God. The two cannot be separated.

As if to underscore that Israel is still to remain open to some foreign nations while avoiding entanglement with other evil nations (e.g., the native Canaanites), v. 16 speaks well of the Kenites, descendants of Moses' father-in-law and adopted members of the Israelite community. The NRSV supplies the name of the Kenite ancestor, Hobab; the NIV reflects the Hebrew Masoretic Text, which lists no name, only "the Kenite." The difference in the translation reflects some confusion in the larger biblical tradition about the name of Moses' father-in-law. He is called Hobab the Midianite in Num 10:29, Reuel the Midianite in Exod 2:16-22, and Jethro the Midianite in Exod 18:1-27. Later in Judg 4:11, a note will appear about a man named Heber the Kenite,

a descendant of "Hobab, the father-in-law of Moses." Thus one can infer that within the book of Judges, the father-in-law of Moses is assumed to be Hobab the Kenite. The word "Kenite" (קֵינִי *qênî*) is related to the Hebrew word for "iron smith" (קַיִן *qyn*) and may reflect the group's vocation as metal workers, tracing their ancestry back to Cain and those who "made all kinds of bronze and iron tools" (Gen 4:22). The Kenites went up with Judah from the "city of palms" (probably Jericho; Deut 34:3) to the Negeb. The NIV reflects the MT, which says that the Kenites settled with "the people," meaning presumably the Israelites. The NRSV, however, bases its change of the text from the Kenites settling among "the people" to the Kenites settling "with the Amalekites" on the narrative in 1 Sam 15:6. There King Saul instructs the Kenites to flee from the Amalekites because Saul is about to invade and kill off all the Amalekites. But because the Kenites have been kind to the Israelites throughout their history (see Num 10:29-32), Saul wishes to spare them and so urges them to separate themselves from the Amalekites. In any case, the Kenites are portrayed as foreigners who are welcomed and have a favorable relationship with Israel. The Kenites live as a liminal people, able to move among various nations and cross boundaries among cultures. This characteristic will play a role later in the story of Heber the Kenite and his wife, Jael, in the story of the death of the Canaanite general Sisera in chap. 4.

1:17-21. These verses continue with a number of other victories by the tribes of Judah and Simeon against various Canaanite cities. Judah captured Zephath and "devoted it to destruction" in a holy war ban in obedience to the special laws of holy war in Deut 20:10-18; thus the city's name was changed to "Hormah," meaning "Destruction" (v. 17). Verse 18 names three out of five principal Philistine strongholds that Judah conquered according to the Hebrew text: Gaza, Ashkelon, and Ekron. The Septuagint version of v. 18 reads that "Judah did *not* take" these cities, which may reflect the following verse about Judah's inability to drive out the inhabitants of the plain (v. 19). The Septuagint may also have in mind the reports of the continuing existence of the lords of the five Philistine cities in 3:3; the continuing threat of the Philistines, including Gaza

14. Barry Webb, *The Book of the Judges: An Integrated Reading* (Sheffield: JSOT, 1987) 87.

in the Samson cycle (16:1-3); and the note in Josh 13:3 that these three Philistine cities were not conquered by Israel (see also 1 Sam 5:6-12). On the other hand, the Hebrew text, which affirms Judah's capture of the three Philistine cities, corresponds to the note in Josh 15:45-47 that these cities were part of the inheritance of the tribe of Judah.

In any case, v. 19 affirms that "the LORD was with Judah" so that they could take the hill country; at the same time it concedes that Judah could not drive out the inhabitants of the plain. The reason given is the enemy's superior military technology: "they had chariots of iron." The writer of Judges 1 has taken over this apparently reasonable explanation or excuse from Josh 17:16-18; there it was used to explain *Ephraim's* failure, but now in v. 19 it excuses the failure of *Judah.* A possible theological conundrum enters here. If Judah is obedient and the Lord is with Judah, why is Judah unable to be successful against any enemy and any odds? "Is anything too hard for the LORD?" (Gen 18:14). The underlying lesson is that it may take time and other circumstances for God to accomplish God's will against certain powers and enemies. God will eventually lead Israel to victory against Sisera and his "iron chariots" in 4:13, 16. God will "begin" to conquer the Philistines with Samson the judge (13:5), but the Philistines and their iron chariots will remain a threat until the time of the kingships of Saul and David, when they will finally be overcome (1 Sam 13:19-22; 2 Sam 8:1). God may not always act immediately or in the way we would like, but God does remain true to God's ultimate promises. Such apparent delays or alternate routes in God's work to overcome evil and oppression are not necessarily caused by the sinfulness of the person or community involved. Judah is obedient and faithful, and God is with Judah; nevertheless, Judah encounters some enemies that cannot be overcome in the present moment. The Aramaic Targum tries to take the blame from God and put it on Judah. The Targum paraphrases the text of v. 19 by adding, "Because they [Judah] sinned they were not able to drive out the inhabitants." But the Targum's explanatory addition commits the same error as did Job's friends, who tried to convince the righteous Job that some secret or unknown sin must have caused his suffering. In the end, God condemns the

friends and exonerates Job, who maintained his innocence in his suffering throughout his ordeal. Some failures, oppressions, or suffering occur without some sin causing them.

Finally, vv. 20-21 conclude with one positive note and one negative note. Verse 20 affirms that Caleb received the city of Hebron as his inheritance (see 15:13-14). Earlier in the chapter (v. 10), Judah was named as the one who captured Hebron; once again we see that the editor has subsumed Caleb the Kenizzite under the tribe of Judah. Caleb successfully drove out the "sons of Anak," who were notorious fighters in Canaan. When the Israelite spies had first surveyed the land of Canaan in Numbers 13–14, their reports about the unusually tall and powerful "sons of Anak" had frightened the Israelite people into disobedience so that they refused to enter the promised land and, as a result, were condemned by God to wander in the wilderness forty more years. Caleb had been one of two faithful spies (the other being Joshua) who urged the Israelites to trust God and enter the land, but to no avail (Num 13:22, 28, 30-33). Now Caleb defeats the "sons of Anak" and proves his words of assurance and trust in God to be true.

The final negative note reports that "the Benjaminites" did not drive out the Jebusite people who lived in Jerusalem (v. 21). This is a virtual quotation from Josh 15:63 with one major change: The writer of Judges 1 has substituted Benjamin for Judah as the one responsible for the failure to drive out the Jebusites. As the narrative of Judges 1 now stands, Judah is seen as having successfully conquered Jerusalem (v. 8) and then entrusted the city to the tribe of Benjamin, since it was in their territory (Josh 18:28). But the Benjaminites were not able to hang on to Jerusalem or defeat its inhabitants (v. 21). This is all in line with the generally pro-Judah character of Judges 1, which we have noted at several points. The mention of Benjamin, a northern tribe, and its failure provides a transition into the next section of Judges 1, which relates the gradual deterioration and failure of the northern tribes to drive out the inhabitants of Canaan as God has commanded (Deut 20:16-18). The negative note about Benjamin here at the beginning of Judges is also a precursor to the grievous crime committed by the Benjaminites in Judges 19–21.

REFLECTIONS

1. This introductory section of Judges consists largely of rewritten material borrowed from the book of Joshua that has been given a decidedly pro-Judah and pro-David slant. The two cities, Jerusalem (1:7-8, 21) and Hebron (1:10, 20), form inclusios at the beginning and end of the unit. These two cities figure prominently in the narratives about King David as sites of his coronation and his capital city (2 Samuel 5). Although Benjamin was not able to drive out the Jebusites (Judg 1:21), King David did and claimed Jerusalem as "the city of David" (2 Sam 5:6-10). Just as God was with the tribe of Judah in its victories (Judg 1:19), so also God was "with David" in his victories (2 Sam 5:10). But these claims are not just political ideology or propaganda, although such motivations probably played some role in the formation of this material. The pro-Judah and pro-David perspectives affirm God's faithfulness in carrying out the blessing and promises of God over time, extending from Jacob's blessing of Judah in Gen 49:8-12 to the promise of an eternal dynasty to King David in 2 Sam 7:8-17.

This section was labeled Judah's "Moderate Success" for two reasons. First of all, Judah was not solely responsible for its victories. Judah received assistance from the tribe of Simeon, Caleb the Kenizzite and his clan, the Kenites, and most important God (Judg 1:19). Thus the narratives are not just about Judah's solo achievements. Ultimately, Judah owes whatever victories it achieves to God. Second, Judah is explicitly unsuccessful in ousting "the inhabitants of the plain," which acknowledges a partial failure on Judah's part (Judg 1:19). This concession as it stands is not found in the source material in the book of Joshua. The text is apparently a creation of the writer of Judges 1, conflating two traditions in Joshua: Judah's inability to drive out the Jebusites from Jerusalem (Josh 15:63) and Ephraim's inability to drive out the inhabitants of the plain because of their iron chariots (Josh 17:16-18). The writer has not obscured Judah's failure, and the enemy's iron chariots provide some reasonable excuse. Yet the text causes the reader to linger a moment over Judah's failure and wonder whether somehow all is not well even with this leading and favored tribe of Israel. Judah seems faithful and obedient, and yet Judah is not invincible and may be pulled into the greater failures of the northern tribes, who will occupy our attention in the next section of Judges 1.

2. The question of Israel's relationship to foreigners is raised in Judg 1:1-21 by juxtaposing Judah's true foreign enemies ("Canaanites and Perizzites, 1:5) and Judah's true foreign friends (Caleb and the Kenizzites and the Kenites, 1:11-16). This tension between foreigners who are helpful and welcome and foreigners who are oppressive and dangerous resonates with the theme of Israel's fluid relationship to foreigners throughout the book of Judges. Jael, a foreign woman and a Kenite, will be an agent of God's saving Israel (Judg 4:11, 17-24). On the other hand, foreign nations will constantly threaten and oppress Israel. Deep in the ethos of the community of God's people is a concern to welcome the stranger and the foreigner because Israel remembered its primal memory of what it was to be a stranger and a foreigner in the land of Egypt (Lev 19:33-34; Deut 24:17-18). Yet, Israel's memory was also littered with the temptations and oppressions of foreign nations and their gods, which often caused Israel to lose its way. Discernment and vigilance were constant requirements in Israel's interaction with foreigners, their values, their culture, and their gods. The same remains equally true of communities of God today. In the end, however, the book of Judges also reminds Israel that its own worst enemy could be itself; the threat to God's people is as much internal as external (Judges 17–21).

3. The two mini-narratives in this opening section grab the reader's interest and attention: the story of King Adoni-bezek with his thumbs and toes cut off (Judg 1:4-7) and the story of Achsah, who boldly asked for a spring of water from her father and received a double portion, two springs (Judg 1:11-15). The two narratives juxtapose at the beginning two ruling metaphors that will weave in and out of the book of Judges: the metaphor of law, retribution, and just punishment for sin and the metaphor of gracious and generous parental love. This dialectic of retributional law and generous love will interlace with a variety of relationships within Judges: the relationship of God and Israel and of Israel with other nations, intertribal relationships within Israel, relationships of parents and children, relationships of men and women. The necessary dialogical relationship between the two will sometimes be balanced and appropriate. At other times, the balance will be skewed and the subsequent relationships will become increasingly distorted, with disastrous results. Like the twins Jacob and Esau wrestling within their mother's womb (Gen 25:22-23), this delicate tug between lavish parental love and forgiveness and a more legal retribution wrestles within the deepest recesses of God's character:

> a God merciful and gracious,
> slow to anger,
> and abounding in steadfast love and faithfulness,
> keeping steadfast love for the thousandth generation,
> forgiving iniquity and transgression and sin,
> yet by no means clearing the guilty,
> but visiting the iniquity of the parents
> upon the children . . .
> to the third and fourth generation. (Exod 34:6-7 NRSV)

The book of Judges will illustrate this dance between law and love as God struggles with an increasingly unfaithful and disobedient Israel. In the end, God's love will prevail in that God will remain faithful to the promises made to Israel. But it will be a tough love that allows Israel in various generations to experience the tragic consequences of its own increasing disobedience.

4. The book of Judges contains a greater number of interesting women characters than does any other book of the Bible. We are introduced to the first woman in Judges 1: Achsah, daughter of Caleb and wife of Othniel. Achsah is both a passive object, the prize offered by her father for a military victory, and an active subject, a bold petitioner who seeks to ensure her own well-being and the well-being of her family. Danna Nolan Fewell makes this observation about Achsah's role in Judges:

> Her status as a daughter sets the stage for all the other daughters of Judges whose fates will be decided by their fathers and husbands. Hence her story introduces the theme of female vulnerability, which will reach painful crescendos with the fates of Jephthah's daughter, Samson's bride, the Levite's wife, the women of Benjamin, Jabesh-Gilead, and Shiloh. And yet, Achsah's situation suggests that even in patriarchy women can sometimes have power, especially when they are treated with esteem by men in their family. Unfortunately, Achsah's endogamous marriage and her demand for a home on cultivable soil also serve to accentuate all the daughters who are sold to foreigners (Judg 3:6), who are, in fact, dispossessed from the landholdings of Israel. Consequently, as the story of a woman, Achsah's brief debut raises all sorts of unresolved issues about power, control, possession, personhood, and the social health of the Israelite nation.[15]

The picture of Achsah dismounting from her donkey in boldness and self-assurance to ask her father for springs of water (Judg 1:14) at the beginning of Judges contrasts

---

15. Danna Nolan Fewell, "Deconstructive Criticism: Achsah and the (E)razed City of Writing," in Yee, *Judges and Method,* 140.

with another picture at the end of Judges. There the limp body of another woman, the Levite's concubine, who has been gang raped and abused and finally murdered, is placed lifeless on a donkey (Judg 19:25-28). Somewhere between this beginning and this end of Judges, things have gone terribly wrong. The next text, Judg 1:22-36, will begin to explore Israel's descent into failure, unfaithfulness, and disintegration.

Judges 1:22-36, The "House of Joseph": Failed Conquests

COMMENTARY

The first introductory section of Judges now turns its attention from Judah's "going up" to fight the Canaanites in 1:1-2 to the "house of Joseph," who "went up" to fight against the city of Bethel in 1:22. The "house of Joseph" in the Joshua source material typically refers only to the two tribes of Manasseh and Ephraim, who traced their ancestry back to Joseph (Gen 48:1; Josh 16:4). But in chap. 1, the "house of Joseph" has a broader function and becomes the umbrella designation for all the northern tribes. The "house of Joseph" forms an inclusio from the beginning of the section in v. 22 to the end of the section in v. 35 with a number of specific northern tribes being named between the two occurrences. Just as Judah had represented the southern tribes, so also the house of Joseph represents the northern tribes of Israel.

Two narrative trajectories dominate vv. 22-36, one geographical and the other military. The geographical trajectory moves from south to north, from Bethel and the tribal territories of Ephraim and Manasseh (v. 22-29) northward through the territories of Zebulun, Asher, Naphtali (vv. 30-33), and on to the northernmost tribe of Dan (v. 34). The accompanying military trajectory involves a movement from initial victory (vv. 22-26) to growing military failures by the northern tribes, culminating in Dan's expulsion from its territory (v. 34). The correlation of these two trajectories suggests that the deeper one moves into northern territory in Israel, the more one moves into failure and deficiency. These two trajectories form part of the strategy of the pro-southern Judah and anti-northern perspective of the writer of Judges 1.[16]

1:22-26. The account of the military experiences begins with the northern tribes' successful campaign against Bethel, formerly known as Luz. Verse 22 affirms that "the LORD was with them," just as the Lord had been with Judah (v. 19). The small narrative of Bethel's capture involves an account of Israelite spies convincing a native of the city to show them the way into the city. God's presence and clever human ingenuity combine to bring a victory. But the price for the man's advice is that he and his family will be spared and let go when Israel invades the city. This story of Bethel echoes the story of Rahab, the Canaanite harlot, and Israel's defeat of the city of Jericho in Joshua 2 and 6. Like the man at Bethel, Rahab had helped the Israelite spies in Jericho in exchange for Israel's sparing of her and her family. In both cases, Israel had seemed to be obedient and victorious. But the careful reader will notice that something is missing in the attack against Bethel that was present in the account of Judah's victory against Zephath (v. 17). Judah devoted the whole city to destruction, every living being, in accord with the holy wars of Deut 20:16-18. Bethel's capture by the house of Joseph disobeyed the holy war laws, since the man and his family were allowed to live, disobeying the holy war provisions that everyone in the Canaanite city be killed and devoted to God. Indeed, the story of Israel's capture of Jericho when Rahab and her family were allowed to live may be read as an unintentional, but nevertheless real, violation of this same holy war law in Deuteronomy.[17] The same ambiguity and tension concerning Israel's disobedience of the holy war laws,

---

16. Stone, "From Tribal Confederation to Monarchic State," 237-39; Mullen, "Judges 1:1–3:6," 50-52.

17. L. Daniel Hawk, *Every Promise Fulfilled: Contesting Plots in Joshua* (Louisville: Westminster/John Knox, 199) 59-71, 92-93.

which prescribe total destruction, by allowing Rahab to live (Joshua 2; 6) is also evident in the story of Bethel and the resident of Bethel who was spared (Judg 1:22-26). God does lead Israel to victory in both cases, but the reader senses that the seeds of disobedience and disintegration may already have been sown.

1:27-36. The sequence of events involving the northern tribes and their military engagements now proceeds into a gradual decline in stages from this initial victory at Bethel. The first stage involves the northern tribes of Manasseh, Ephraim, and Zebulun. They "did not drive out" all the Canaanite inhabitants of several of the cities within their territory. They allowed the Canaanites to continue to live in their land (vv. 27, 29-30). In two of the three cases, they also put the Canaanites to "forced labor" so that the Israelite tribes remained the most numerous and dominant population in their territory (vv. 28, 30). The second stage of decline involves the next two tribes of Asher and Naphtali. Neither of these tribes drive out all the Canaanites. Moreover, in the case of Manasseh, Ephraim, and Zebulun, the Canaanites live among the Israelites. The Canaanites remain a minority among the more numerous Israelite population. But in the case of Asher and Naphtali, we have a reversal. The Canaanites do not live among the people of Asher and Naphtali; instead, Asher and Naphtali "lived among the Canaanites" (vv. 32, 33). Asher and Naphtali are portrayed as the less numerous minority within a predominantly Canaanite population. They have lost even more ground than the preceding tribes. But in the case of Naphtali, even as a minority Israel did manage to subject the Canaanites to forced labor (v. 33).

Finally, the whole tribe of Dan is unable to continue to live in its own designated territory, for the Amorites (an alternate name for the Canaanites) have driven them completely out of the plain "back into the hill country" (v. 34). Dan becomes a refugee tribe in search of a home territory. Dan's tragic story will resume at the end of the book of Judges with the story of Dan's forcible theft of the idolatrous shrine of Micah and Dan's migration with the shrine to the far north of Israel (chaps. 17–18).

As in the section concerning Judah in vv. 1-21, the writer of vv. 22-36 has selected, revised, and added to source material from Joshua 14–19 in order to construct this account. The failure of Manasseh and Ephraim to drive out the Canaanites completely is reported in Josh 17:11-13 along with a number of other items about these tribes. However, the writer of Judg 1:27-29 has highlighted only the account of the failures of Ephraim and Manasseh. Moreover, Josh 17:12 says that these northern tribes *could not* drive out the Canaanites. However, the writer of Judg 1:27, 29 deleted the "could not" and changed it simply to "did not" drive them out. The change is subtle but telling. The Joshua account makes the failure to drive out the Canaanites a matter of power and ability; they wanted to but were not able. The failure is somewhat excusable. The Judges 1 account, however, suggests less excusable reasons for the failure: The failure of Manasseh and Ephraim to drive out the Canaanites may have involved less a lack of ability and more a lack of desire. Perhaps they *could* have driven the Canaanites out, but they did not *want* to do so. If Manasseh was able to subject the Canaanites to forced labor, they also should have been able to drive them out (v. 28). The northern tribes apparently desired to enter into covenants with the Canaanites and their gods rather than obey the covenant with the Lord and worship the Lord alone. This theological issue will indeed be the underlying motivation for Israel's future, which will be revealed in the angel's speech in 2:1-5.

Another change made by the writer of Judges 1 was the addition of failure reports for the three tribes of Zebulun, Asher, and Naphtali. Failure reports for these three tribes do not exist in the Joshua source material, and so the editor of Judges 1 has composed and added them, using the Ephraim and Manasseh material as a model. The writer of Judges 1 clearly wishes to underscore the thoroughgoing failure of the northern tribes. Finally, concerning the tribe of Dan, the writer has again selected only the failure report (v. 34) out of a larger section detailing both Dan's successes and failures in Josh 19:40-48.

The section ends with a general summary of the overall experience of the "house of Joseph" (vv. 35-36). The Amorites or Canaanites continue to live in various cities, but the northern tribes continue to hold the balance of power and thus subject the Amorites to forced labor (vv. 30, 32-33). However, this affirmation that the Canaanites were allowed to live and were subjected to forced labor only reminds the reader of the northern tribes' transgression of the holy war law in Deuteronomy, which mandates the total annihilation of all Canaanites from the land. The holy war provision that allows the enemy to live and be subject to forced labor applies only to "towns that are very far from you" that lie outside the borders of Canaan (Deut 20:11, 15-18 NRSV). Once again we are reminded of the growing failure of the northern tribes to carry out the commands of God. Verse 36 concludes with a southern boundary established for the Amorites, as if to suggest that the Amorites and the Canaanites will now remain a permanent fixture in the land of Canaan with their own established borders. The Canaanites are here to stay!

REFLECTIONS

1. We see again the perspective of the writer of Judges 1 generally to be more charitable to southern Judah and less charitable to the northern "house of Joseph" in this summation of the continuing conquest of Canaan after the death of Joshua. But at least two factors mitigate against any kind of absolute distinction of good or bad in assessing the two groups. First of all, the text affirms that the Lord was with both Judah (1:19) and the house of Joseph (1:22). God plays no favorites and remembers the covenant promises to all Israel. Second, the descriptions of both Judah and the house of Joseph include successes and failures; neither group is all perfect or all evil. Judah could not drive out the inhabitants of the plain (1:19), although its portrait emerges as largely positive. The house of Joseph successfully captured Bethel (1:22-26), although its overall portrait emerges as largely negative. The narrative avoids the creation of an absolute villain in the northern tribes or an absolute hero in southern Judah. The character of these communities remains human, realistic, and as morally complex as any human community or individual. Rarely can blame be assessed simply on one party or another in any dispute, conflict, or tragedy. And rarely are motives absolutely pure and complex actions totally unambiguous. Although a relative distinction is possible between the more successful Judah and the less successful northern tribes of Joseph, their fate and destiny remain bound together as brother tribes. The apostle Paul spoke of the body of Christ and the need for one group or member to refrain from claiming absolute superiority over another member in order that "there may be no dissension within the body, but the members may have the same care for one another. If one member suffers, all suffer together with it; if one member is honored, all rejoice together with it" (1 Cor 12:25-26 NRSV). Relative distinctions remain from a human perspective. But as the divine angel's speech will reveal in 2:1-5, those distinctions dissolve as God views people and events through divine eyes. The angel will speak to "all the Israelites" as a community or body without distinction of its parts (Judg 2:4).

2. The geographical trajectory from southern Judah to the various northern tribes of Israel roughly reflects the same south-to-north sequence of geographical affiliations of the individual major judges that will appear in the narratives of Judges 13–16. The first major judge is Othniel, from southern Judah (3:7-11), and the last judge is Samson, from what will become the far northern tribe of Dan (13:2). The geographical progression of the individual judges runs in the following sequence: Judah (Othniel), Benjamin (Ehud), Issachar/Naphtali (Deborah/Barak), Manasseh (Gideon), Gad (Jephthah), and Dan (Samson). Thus Judges 1 provides a kind of geographical guide to the main body of judge stories that will follow in Judges 3–16.

This geographical trajectory will also be matched by a similar theological trajectory from initial success to a downward slide of failure and unfaithfulness among the individual judges. The stories will move from the initial victorious judges in Judges 3–5 to the ambiguous figure of Gideon, who moves from victory to unfaithfulness in Judges 6–8. The era of the major judges will end with the tragic figures of Jephthah and Samson (Judges 10–16). The final chapters (Judges 17–21) will conclude the internal religious social disintegration of Israel as a community. Thus Judges 1 functions as a road map, both geographical and theological, for the rest of the book.

3. The failures of the Israelite conquest and the disobedience of the holy war laws of Deuteronomy in allowing some of the Canaanites to live (contrary to the law in Deut 20:16-18) do not represent rash or overt rebellions against the Lord. Judah is not able to defeat its enemies because of their iron chariots. The northern Joseph tribes defeat some of the Canaanites, but not all of them. Those Canaanites who remain are subjected to forced labor. The Canaanites are at least subdued, albeit by a means the law reserves for nations far away from Canaan (Deut 20:10-15). At least on the surface, the Israelites seem to be making some good-faith effort to continue the conquest.

Yet Judges 1 gives the sense of a growing deterioration in strength and resolve of the Israelite tribes. Israel does not seem to intend to be unfaithful, but gradually the seeds of disobedience that were sown begin to grow. Step by step, the web of transgression and failure begins to be spun. Like the serpent's gradual temptation of Adam and Eve with a few seemingly innocent questions (Gen 3:1-7) or King David's gradual entanglement with adultery and then murder in the case of Bathsheba and Uriah (2 Samuel 11), Israel is gradually drawn into deeper disobedience and entanglements with the Canaanites and their gods. Such is often the nature of temptation and the downward spiral into disobedience. Originally good people and communities and institutions can become corrupted from the inside, even if on the surface all seems, at least for the moment, to be well. That will happen to the people of Israel, both north and south, to the institutions of the judges, and to the institution of Israelite kingship, which will follow the era of the judges.

Judges 2:1-5, Judgment on All the Israelites

COMMENTARY

The climactic conclusion to this first introductory section of Judges features the sudden appearance and judgment speech of "the angel of the LORD." Who is this angel or messenger of God who makes a dramatic intrusion into the narrative? The last appearance of the angel was back in Josh 5:13-15 near the cities of Jericho and Gilgal (Josh 5:10). There Joshua was about to lead the Israelite army in an attack against Jericho, when the angel suddenly appeared as a man with a drawn sword and confronted Joshua. Joshua asked this divine warrior, "Are you one of us, or one of our adversaries?" The angel replied, "Neither; but as commander of the army of the LORD I have now come" (Josh 5:13-14 NRSV). Joshua's response was to bow to the ground and worship, for he realized he was in the Lord's presence.

The Lord had promised Israel in the covenant at Mt. Sinai that the angelic divine warrior would lead Israel into the promised land (Exod 23:20-33; 33:2; Num 20:16). But on the eve of the conquest of the first Canaanite city of Jericho, the angel had reminded Joshua that God remains free to fight either for or against Israel. God is neither "one of us" nor "one of our adversaries." God ultimately transcends all humanly engineered divisions and remains sovereign to judge or deliver whomever God wills. The special name of God, Yahweh, from the Hebrew verb "to be" (היה hāyâ) conveys this divine freedom: "I AM WHO I AM" (Exod 3:13-14 NRSV) and "I will be gracious to whom I will be gracious, and will show mercy on whom I will show mercy" (Exod 33:19 NRSV). It is this same angelic agent of God's power and transcendent freedom who "went up from Gilgal [the site of the angel's last appearance] to Bochim" to encounter a new generation of Israelites "after the death of Joshua."

The verb "to go up" (עלה 'ālâ) had been used to mark the beginning of the military engagements of southern Judah (1:1-2) and then the engagements of the northern house of Joseph (1:22) against the Canaanites. In 2:1, the same verb signals a third "going up" in battle, but this time it is the divine angel's "going up" in a holy war attack, not against the Canaanites, but against the Israelites! The reader recalls the angel's reminder to Joshua (Josh 5:13-14) that God is absolutely free to be for us or against us. Israel cannot smugly assume that God will always fight on its side. The form of this holy war attack on Israel is not military weaponry but a verbal indictment: The angel speaks words of judgment like a prosecuting attorney presenting an airtight case of evidence against the accused defendant Israel.

The angelic prosecutor begins the case, reminding Israel that God has met all the divine obligations under the covenant made at Mt. Sinai in Exodus 19–24 and reaffirmed in the book of Deuteronomy. God brought Israel up from Egypt and has now brought them into the promised land of Canaan. The angel reports God's absolute and irrevocable commitment: "I said, 'I will never break my covenant with you' " (v. 1). Israel was obligated for its part of the covenant to maintain an exclusive relationship with the Lord. Israel was not allowed to make any covenants with "the inhabitants of the land," and Israel was required to tear down the altars of the Canaanite gods (v. 2).

The angel then levels the charge that while God has kept God's side of the covenant, Israel has not. The covenant at Mt. Sinai clearly stated Israel's covenant obligations to drive out the inhabitants of the land of Canaan and not make covenants with them or their gods. The Canaanites "shall not live in your land, or they will make you sin against me; for if you worship their gods, it will surely be a snare to you" (Exod 23:31-33 NRSV; see also Deut 7:1-6). Israel has disobeyed God's command of exclusive loyalty by allowing many of the Canaanites and their gods and worship sites to remain in the land.

The angel then points to the failures to oust the Canaanites from the land, which have just been narrated in Judges 1, and says, "See what you have done!" The evidence is plain enough: Israel has failed to carry out the conquest of Canaan as commanded.

The angelic prosecutor suddenly shifts roles and becomes a divine judge. The angel reports God's verdict, which involves a dramatic change in strategy in God's plans concerning Israel and the promised land. God's original plan and hope was that Israel would eliminate all the Canaanites from the promised land, leaving a secure paradise free from all temptations of other cultures and gods. The vision is not unlike the garden of Eden in Genesis 1–2, a perfect place of human habitation without enticements to disobey or follow other gods. But just as the plan for the humans in the garden of Eden collapsed and required a new strategy by God, so also the plan for Israel in Canaan has fallen apart. God resolves not to drive out the Canaanites but instead allows them to remain among the Israelites in Canaan. The Canaanites shall become ongoing "adversaries" (NRSV) or "thorns in your sides" (NIV); the difference in translation reflects a text-critical problem with the Hebrew text that requires some emending to make sense. But the issue is not just a social or political issue with the Canaanites. It is also theological. God resolves to allow the Canaanite gods to remain in the land as a continuing "snare" to test the faith and loyalty of Israel (v. 3).

The speech of the angel is concluded, but we as readers may wonder at whom this verbal onslaught is aimed. Judah seems to have been moderately successful in its conquest, and even the northern house of Joseph has made a determined attempt to oust or subdue at least some of the Canaanites. But the narrator quickly informs us that the angel's indictment targets "all the Israelites" (v. 4). No tribe is exempt from this blanket condemnation. All have sinned and fallen short. There is no room for one tribe to gloat over the misfortunes or denunciation of another.

In response to the angel's judgment speech and verdict, the people lift up their voices and "weep" with a loud and public wailing of lament and grief. They recognize that their relationship to God and the land in which they and their children will live has been dramatically altered. Canaan will not be a pure paradise of milk and honey without temptations or worries. Canaan will be for Israel a land like any other, with other nations, other cultures, other values, and other gods constantly gnawing at Israel's heart and allegiance. Like the garden of Eden, the perfect land of promise has been forever lost. Because this was a place where the Israelites wept at the loss of their great promise, they name the place "Bochim," which in Hebrew means "Weepers" (בכים *bōkîm*). This place of wailing and weeping becomes a memorial to dashed hopes and forfeited futures because of the sinfulness of Israel. The Israelites acknowledge the place as a holy site of divine revelation by making sacrifices to the Lord on the spot (vv. 4-5).

This dramatic and tearful climax to this introductory section of Judges finds an important counterpart at the end of the book. Only two places in the entire book of Judges explicitly mention "all the Israelites": 2:4, at the beginning, and 20:26, at the end of the book. Moreover, these two contexts also share the portrait of all Israel weeping and lamenting before God. In v. 4, the Israelites weep once, but by the end of the book the weeping and the wailing have intensified into a triple chorus of Israel's crying and lamenting to God on three closely related occasions at Bethel (20:23, 26; 21:2). This series of weeping and lament brackets the book, and the intensification of the cry at the end provides further indication that we are headed for a downhill slide in terms of Israel's fortunes and faithfulness as we move through the book of Judges. These bookends of weeping in Judges enclose numerous other cries and laments throughout the book. Israel repeatedly cried out to God because of the oppression of its enemies (3:9, 15; 4:3; 6:7; 10:10). Like Israel, Jephthah's daughter wept over the loss of what her life could have been had it not been for her father's foolish vow, which cut short her life (11:37-38). Israelite women continued to weep in an annual ritual in remembrance of her loss and pain (11:40). Judges is a book that takes seriously the reality of human suffering and anguish, whether brought on by our own sinfulness or by external forces and enemies who oppress us.

REFLECTIONS

1. The severe indictment of the angel of the Lord breaks into the narrative somewhat abruptly. The last things we have heard about the Lord's activity are the positive notes that the Lord was with Judah and with the house of Joseph in their victories (1:19, 22). Suddenly God breaks in as an angelic messenger and summarily condemns all the Israelites for the failure of their conquest of Canaan. In fact, a reader who has worked through both the book of Joshua and the first chapter of Judges may have reason to wonder what God thinks about Israel's moderate, but partial, success in defeating and eradicating the Canaanites. Even within the book of Joshua, which portrays a fairly successful conquest, one may see two "contesting plots" throughout the book, one affirming the success and obedience of the Israelite conquest and the other hinting at the conquest's failures and Israel's disobedience.[18] But now in Judg 2:1-5, we have the definitive divine assessment over all of Joshua and Judges 1: Israel has failed in the conquest and disobeyed God's command. The period of the conquest is over, and Canaanites will remain scattered over the land as a constant threat, temptation, and thorn in Israel's side.

2. For modern readers, the notion of holy war, the act of killing—especially the killing of women and children—and the near annihilation of a native population of Canaanites will seem alien and reprehensible in the extreme. From a larger biblical and moral view, the notion of a holy war seems hard to justify. Other texts in the Old Testament promulgate a very different vision for God's people, a vision of peace rather

18. Hawk, *Every Promise Fulfilled*, 56-116.

than war among nations (e.g., Isa 2:2-4). But Judg 2:1-5 reminds us that the holy war concept is only a temporary measure, confined to this limited period in Israel's story. No later biblical texts ever counsel Israel to take up a holy war again. The holy war as an act of human violence against other humans does not function in the Bible as a continuing paradigm for the actions of God's people. The goal of the holy war against Canaan was not achieved. The goal had been to define a clear boundary that would protect Israel from contact with the "other" in its social, political, and religious life. Israel was forced throughout its history to struggle to discern when to welcome and when to resist the culture, values, and philosophies of other nations and peoples. The struggle between separateness and absorption, strict isolation and negotiated assimilation, remains a challenge for every community of God's people who strive to live in the world but not be of it.

Although the paradigm of holy war as human violence against other humans was seen as a dead end, that does not mean that the notion of holy war and God as divine warrior ceased. In fact, the image of the divine warrior remains a lively theological motif throughout the Old Testament and on into the New Testament.[19] Israel continued to wage battles against the enemies of God's will, but the battles became more and more for Israel a battle of words, persuasion, obedience, and education through devotion and study of God's Word of Scripture (Josh 1:7-9).[20]

3. The two mini-narratives in Judges 1—the story of King Adoni-bezek, who received his just legal punishment, and the story of Caleb's daughter Achsah, who graciously received more than she asked for from her father—illustrate the dialogical dance between law and lavish love, between a *quid pro quo* legalism and a more familial model of forgiveness and unconditional love. This interplay between a legal-political model and a more domestic-familial model gets at the inherent tension in God's covenant with Israel. God pledges undying commitment to Israel in words similar to a parental vow to a child: "I will never break my covenant with you" (2:1). At the same time, God brings Israel to court in a forensic indictment more akin to a courtroom. The scene ends with one resolution (the Canaanites will remain in the land), but the next step God will take in responding to Israel's weeping is not resolved. Has the covenant relationship between God and Israel ended because of Israel's unfaithfulness? Or will God continue to work with Israel in spite of its ongoing disobedience? And if so, how will God proceed with Israel into the future? The answers to these questions remain open, but the second half of the two-part introduction to Judges in 2:6–3:6 will begin to address the root causes and the next steps God will take to address these issues.

19. Richard Nysse, "Yahweh Is a Warrior," *Word & World* (Spring 1987) 192-201.
20. Dennis T. Olson, *Deuteronomy and the Death of Moses: A Theological Reading* (Minneapolis: Fortress, 1994) 162-64.

JUDGES 2:6–3:6, FROM FAITHFULNESS TO SIN: THE COVENANT WITH GOD

OVERVIEW

Judges 2:6–3:6 presents the second half of the two-part introduction to the book of Judges. This two-part introduction provides the lens through which the reader will interpret the varied stories of individual judges that will follow in chaps. 3–16. The first half of this introductory interpretive lens, 1:1–2:5, focused largely on external events, reporting the successes and failures of Israel's military campaign in Canaan. Very little was said of God's reactions and feelings about the events until 2:1-5. Suddenly the angel appeared with a stinging rebuke of Israel's failure to oust the Canaanites totally from the land. The root causes of God's displeasure were only briefly touched on in the rebuke: "their gods shall be a snare to you" (2:3). This theological or religious dimension of Israel's failure will become the major theme to be explored in much more depth in the second half of the introduction, 2:6–3:6. The second introductory half will also reveal much more of God's inner emotions and feelings in relationship to Israel's constant rebellion and worship of other gods. Descriptions of the Lord's anger, sorrow, and compassion will swirl around the downward spiral of Israel's growing unfaithfulness like eddies in a wildly turbulent river. The river will have its moments of calm, but they will soon give way again to increasingly rocky rapids, heading inexorably toward the final waterfall that will dash Israel into a splintered social and religious heap (chaps. 17–21).

The reader will also notice a striking shift from specificity to generalization as we move from the first to the second half of the introduction to Judges. The first half, 1:1–2:5, was saturated with specific names of Israelite tribes, people, and places. Certain tribes were singled out in contrast to others. The second half, 2:6–3:6, speaks less of individual tribes or persons and much more about all the Israelites together. This pan-Israelite perspective ties in with the angel's speech, directed to "all the Israelites" at the end of the first introductory section (2:4). Only one person, Joshua, is highlighted as a faithful leader of a past generation. The distinctions in this section focus less on individual tribes or people than on differences among generations of Israelites; the faithfulness of the generations of Joshua and the next generation of elders (2:7-10a) contrasts sharply with the growing unfaithfulness of the generations after them, for they "did not know the LORD or the work that he had done for Israel" (2:10).

One major interpretive challenge is the need to account for the disjunction in time as we move from events in the first unit of 1:1–2:5 to the second unit in 2:6–3:6. All the events in the first unit are set in a time "after the death of Joshua" (1:1). Suddenly,

as we encounter the second unit beginning in 2:6, the clock winds back in time to a moment when Joshua is still alive: "when Joshua dismissed the people . . ." (2:6). Why do we have this abrupt flashback in time? We will see that it allows the writer to draw the necessary contrast between the faithful generation of Joshua and his contemporaries and the downward slide of subsequent generations of Israelites who worship other gods and rebel against the Lord. Just as the first half of the introduction had begun with a fairly positive portrait of Judah, to which the northern tribes' experience could be contrasted, so also the second half begins with a fairly positive portrait of Joshua and his generation, to which later generations can be contrasted. Thus the two introductions form a parallel portrait of Israel on a downward slope from initial victory and faithfulness to increasing defeat and apostasy. The parallels move along two axes, one tribal or geographical (south to north) and the other temporal or generational (from Joshua's generation to post–Joshua generations). Together, the two introductions invite the reader to understand the narratives that comprise the main body of the book in chaps. 3–16 as more than merely a revolving or cyclical circle of events that always returns to the same point. Rather, the stories of the judges trace a rough trajectory or line that moves toward deterioration, culminating in the tragedy of Samson and the religious crisis of chaps. 17–18 and the social and political crisis of chaps. 19–21.[21]

What can be known about the history of how this second part of the introduction to Judges was composed? Many scholars agree that 2:6–3:6 contains within it the remnants of an earlier preface to the stories of the judges. This earlier preface presented the era of the judges of Israel as a time of cyclical repetition in which God sent temporary deliverers, called judges, to save Israel from its enemies. This earlier preface accentuated the heroism and faithfulness of the judges as leaders of Israel; the judges were always able to bring Israel back to God and back to a

---

21. Similar conclusions about the larger function of the dual introductions in the light of the whole book of Judges have been argued independently from both a redaction-critical perspective (Stone, "From Tribal Confederation to Monarchic State," 248-59, 460-77) and a formalistic literary perspective (Webb, *The Book of the Judges,* 81-122). Both Stone and Webb build on a number of important earlier works on Judges, both literary and redaction-critical in scope.

sense of political and social security. The core of this early form of the preface is likely 2:10-16, 18-19 and 3:1-4. However, a later editor added a number of crucial verses to this core: 2:6-9, 17, 20-23 and 3:5-6.[22] These editorial additions changed the orientation of the preface from a repetitive cycle celebrating heroic judges to a linear story of Israel's gradual deterioration, a deterioration in which even the judges participated. These editorial changes brought this earlier preface in line with other parts of the book of Judges as they came to be edited later: the later preface in 1:1–2:5, the judges stories themselves as later edited and shaped to show a decline (chaps. 3–16), and the concluding chapters portraying Israel at its moment of greatest failure and disintegration at the end of the judges era (chaps. 17–21).

22. Rudolph Smend, "Das Gesertz und die Völker: ein Beitrag zu deuteronomistichen Redaktionsgeschichte," *Probleme biblische Theologie: Gerhard von Rad zum 70 Geburtstag,* ed. H. W. Wolff (Munich: Chr. Kaiser Verlag, 1971) 494-509.

Judges 2:6-10, A New Generation Is Born

COMMENTARY

2:6. The setting for the military campaigns in 1:1–2:5 was a time "*after* the death of Joshua." Judges 2:6-9 marks a brief flashback to a time *before* the death of Joshua and is essentially a rearrangement of material drawn from the scene in Josh 24:28-31 just before Joshua's death. Joshua had assembled all Israel in a great assembly at Shechem (Josh 24:1). He reminded the people of God's faithfulness, which the Lord had shown to Israel through the first phase of the conquest, and he called on the people of Israel to renew their commitment to the covenant with the Lord. Then Joshua dismissed the Israelites (Josh 24:28), and that is where Judg 2:6 picks up the action. All the Israelites who have been fighting together as one army in Canaan during Joshua's lifetime have disbanded into individual tribes, each responsible for completing the conquest within its individual tribal allotments of territory.

2:7. This verse underscores the faithful worship of the Lord by the people during the period of the leadership of Joshua and then the elders who outlived him. They had known and trusted in the Lord because they were eyewitnesses to "all the great work that the LORD had done for Israel." God's great works during the leadership of Joshua and the elders included protection and guidance of the new generation at the end of the wilderness period in Numbers 26–36 and the first stage of the conquest of Canaan in the book of Joshua. Thus Joshua and the elders who ruled the generation after him effectively taught and led the people in the ways of the Lord. They had been direct witnesses and participants in the drama of God's great acts of power and deliverance in the wilderness and in Canaan.

2:8-9. Joshua died and was buried in his home territory of Ephraim (Num 13:8, 16) at the age of 110 years. He received the honored title of "the servant of the LORD" (v. 8), first used for Moses (Josh 1:1) and to be used again for certain faithful kings (David, Hezekiah, Zerubbabel) and prophets, culminating in the Suffering Servant figure in Isaiah 40–55 (see Isa 52:13–53:12). But no leader comparable to Moses or Joshua with the title of "servant of the LORD" arose in the generation immediately after the death of Joshua and the next generation of elders. Moses and Joshua represent unique and unrepeatable leaders in a special time of Israel's history.

2:10. This verse sets the stage for a definitive shift from the era of Moses, Joshua, and the elders to a new era defined by a generation "who did not know the LORD or the work that he had done for Israel." The phrase is reminiscent of the dramatic change in relationships that occurred at the beginning of the book of Exodus. Israel had enjoyed good fortune when Joseph had been favored by an earlier pharaoh. But then "a new king arose over Egypt, who did not know Joseph" (Exod 1:8). This lack of knowing caused a sudden shift in the nature of Israel's relationship to pharaoh and the Egyptians. They became slaves instead of a favored people. In 2:10, it is Israel who no longer knows the Lord, and as a result the nature of the relationship between God and Israel will dramatically change. The verb "to know" (ידע *yāda*ʿ) signifies here an intimate and personal knowledge and relationship with another. The verb can describe the intimacy of sexual intercourse between a man and a woman (Gen 4:1). Moses described the special bond between God and himself with the words, "I know you by name" (Exod 33:12). Knowing God involves loyalty in a covenant relationship, a sense of mutual trust, obedience to God's commands, and an acknowledgment of God's power and sovereignty (Exod 29:45-46). The generations of Joshua and the elders had such a knowledge of the Lord because of their direct and personal experience of God's mighty acts of deliverance. But a new generation arises without such a foundation and knowledge and relationship with God.

The narrative movement from one generation to another has formed an important structural framework for much of the OT narrative up to this point. Genealogical formulas that mark the end of one generation and the beginning of another form the major narrative backbone for the book of Genesis (e.g., Gen 2:4; 5:1; 10:1; 25:19). The beginning of the book of Exodus marks the rise of a new generation of Israelites along with the rise of a new king who did not know Joseph (Exod 1:1-8). Two census lists of the twelve tribes of Israel in Numbers 1 and 26 define the structure of Numbers as the story of two very different generations. The first generation counted in the census list in Numbers 1 was increasingly rebellious against God and Moses in the wilderness. Because of their rebellion, climaxed by the refusal to enter the promised land in the spy story of Numbers 13–14, God condemned this generation to die in the desert without entering the land of Canaan. The Lord would allow only the new generation of their "little ones" born in the wilderness to come into Canaan, along with the two faithful spies out of the old generation, Joshua and Caleb (Num 14:20-35). The rise of this new generation of hope and promise was marked by the second census list in Numbers 26. The census included no members of the old rebellious wilderness generation of Israelites except Joshua and Caleb (Num 26:63-65).[23]

The theme of a generational transition from an old rebellious generation to a new generation of hope and promise in the book of Numbers was taken up again in Moses' speech in the book of Deuteronomy (Deut 1:26-40). This shift from an earlier unfaithful generation to a later faithful generation (led by Joshua) provides the necessary background to Judg 2:6-9, which is a mirror image of what happens in Numbers. In Judg 2:6-9, an earlier faithful generation (led by Joshua and then the elders who outlived Joshua) dies and a later unfaithful generation, who "did not know the Lord," rises up. Thus, while the book of Numbers had ended on a hopeful note about the rise of a new faithful generation of promise, the book of Judges begins on a pessimistic note about the rise of a new unfaithful generation of rebellion.

23. Dennis T. Olson, *Numbers,* Interpretation (Louisville: John Knox, 1996) 3-6, 75-89.

Reflections

1. The text raises the issue of the nature of faith and knowing God and the role of eyewitness testimony from those who have seen the works of God directly and firsthand. Being a firsthand witness to God's powerful acts of mercy and deliverance does not automatically create or guarantee faith. The old wilderness generation in the book of Numbers had been eyewitnesses to the dramatic Red Sea deliverance out of Egypt and God's thunderous revelation on the top of Mt. Sinai in the book of Exodus. But those direct experiences of God's awesome presence and power did not prevent the old generation from constantly rebelling against God. Faith in God is a fragile gift that must be continually nurtured and nourished through a community of faith, prayer, study, and practice. No faithful person can rely on any one dramatic event or conversion or miracle to sustain faith over the long haul. Many in Jesus' time saw firsthand the powerful signs of healing and forgiveness and teaching of Jesus' ministry, but even then many did not believe in him or understand his ministry (Mark 6:6). Even some of Jesus' own disciples had difficulty understanding the shape and purpose of his life and work (Mark 8:31-33; 9:32). His own disciple Judas betrayed him (Matt 26:14-16; 47-50). Even Peter "the rock" denied Jesus three times (Matt 26:69-75). When the apostle Paul preached at Athens about what he had seen and heard about Jesus, some listeners scoffed, some were mildly interested, and still others actually joined Paul and became believers (Acts 17:32-34).

2. If seeing God's work directly does not always lead to believing, then it is also true that believing and knowing God can happen without seeing in some direct, firsthand way. The fact that the new generation in Judg 2:10 did not see the great works of God firsthand, as had the previous generation of Joshua and the elders, did not excuse the new generation from the expectation that they too would come to know, love, and obey the Lord. Jesus' words in response to doubting Thomas's demand for tangible proof remind us that believing without seeing not only is possible but also promises a particular blessing: "Have you believed because you have seen me? Blessed are those who have not seen and yet have come to believe" (John 20:29 NRSV). A deep faith and knowledge of God can come through hearing, learning, and doing as well as through seeing.

3. This text raises the urgent question of how faith is or is not passed from one generation to the next. The text reminds us that the heritage of faith is not something automatically inherited by passive osmosis from one generation to the next. A faithful generation can have unfaithful children. Faith and the knowledge of God are always only one generation away from extinction. The question, Will our children have faith? remains a pressing and urgent issue in the community of God's people. The traditions of faith require constant attention, teaching, discussion, and living out day by day if they are to have a chance to be passed on to the next generation (Deut 6:1-9). Even when parents are diligent in teaching the faith to their children, it may be that faith will not sprout or will die down for some period in a child's life. Faith is not something even parents can program into their children; it is finally a matter between God and the individual or community in question. We may contribute to the process, but we have no ultimate control over whether someone has faith in God.

Judges 2:11-23, The Pattern: Apostasy, Punishment, and Mercy

COMMENTARY

With the announced death of Joshua in 2:8 and the rise of a new generation after him, we have arrived back again at the same time frame with which the book of Judges began, "after the death of Joshua" (1:1). What follows in 2:11-23 will describe God's unique angle of interpretation and reaction to the military campaigns reported earlier in 1:1-36. In a sense, God's judgment on the new generations and their unfaithfulness in 2:11-23 functions as an expanded commentary on the angel's brief indictment speech, which has already appeared in 2:1-5. This

expansion of God's reaction will zero in on the underlying problem for which the partial military failures in Judges 1 are only symptoms. The root problem is not military strategy or ideological differences among tribes or the relative failure of one tribe or group in comparison to another. The core problem is *all* Israel's abandonment of the Lord and *all* Israel's increasing propensity to worship other gods. The real issue is a religious and theological problem that applies to "all the Israelites."

2:11-15. These verses provide the details of what Israel has done and God's reaction to it. The Israelites did "evil" and "worshiped the Baals." The plural "Baals" likely refers to numerous local cults in Canaan all directed in worship to the principal Canaanite god, Baal. This god is mentioned with some frequency in the OT, but the Bible provides few details of the Canaanite fertility cult with which Baal is associated. However, archaeologists have uncovered and deciphered cuneiform tablets from Ugarit that provide some of the background myths for the Baal cult. Baal is portrayed in the Ugaritic myths as a weather god, manifested in thunderstorms ("Rider of the Clouds"), who struggles with the sea god, named Yam, and the god of death, named Mot. The chaos of the sea and the threat of death threatened the annual cycles of rain and fertility, but Baal in the end overcomes the forces of death and ensures the annual springtime rains and seasons of agricultural planting and harvests. The worship of Baal probably involved annual rituals that dramatized and encouraged Baal's victory over death and infertility. The cult was no doubt popular in an agrarian setting like Canaan, and this new generation of Israelites has been drawn into Baal worship instead of observing their covenant obligation to worship and love the Lord alone (Deut 5:6-7; 6:4-15). Verse 13 mentions Baal again, along with a Canaanite fertility goddess named Astarte, who was a consort of Baal and part of the broader Canaanite pantheon.

The flip side of worshiping other gods is abandoning the Lord. Israel's abandonment is particularly egregious for two reasons: The Lord is "the God of their ancestors," and the Lord is the one "who had brought them out of the land of Egypt" (v. 12). The Lord has been Israel's faithful God reaching far back into Israel's history to the time of Abraham, Isaac, and Jacob. Moreover, the Lord is the one who gave Israel its future by rescuing it from slavery and bringing it to the land of Canaan. Now Israel has taken the gift of the land and rejected the gift-giver by worshiping other gods. These reminders of God's past faithfulness prepare the reader for God's heated response of anger, which appears in triplicate in this section (v. 12, 14, 20).

God's righteous anger gives way to action in judgment on Israel, described as "giving them over" to plunderers and "selling them into the power" of their enemies (v. 14). God drops all divine defenses from around the Israelites so that they become vulnerable to those who attack them. But God also takes a more active role as well. Whenever Israel's army marched into battle, the Lord's hand "was against them to bring misfortune" (v. 15). Here the motif of God as enemy mirrors the angel of the Lord, who "went up" in a reversal of the holy war to fight against Israel with a verbal indictment in vv. 1-5. God's reaction should have been no surprise, since God had clearly stated time and again that the worship of other gods would lead to God's anger and destructive fury. Deuteronomy 7:4 is an example where Moses speaks on behalf of God about the consequences of Israel's worshiping other gods: "Then the anger of the LORD would be kindled against you, and he would destroy you quickly." According to the covenant, God has the legal right to impose the death penalty on Israel as a people; such is the severity of the transgression of bowing down to other deities.

2:16. What seemed to be a screaming locomotive heading for Israel's destruction is suddenly derailed. God raised up "judges, who delivered them out of the power of those who plundered them." God is both enemy and friend, both wounder and healer. The judges provide temporary relief from the enemy's oppression. The earlier nucleus of this section probably presented this sequence of events in a revolving or cyclical pattern:

(a) Israel worshiped other gods.

(b) God became angry and allowed enemies to attack Israel.

(c) God raised up a judge who delivered Israel and returned Israel to worshiping the Lord.

(d) Israel reverted to its old ways of worshiping other gods after the judge died, and then the cycle started all over again (a-d).

2:17. This cyclical pattern appears if the reader moves from v. 16 immediately to vv. 18-19, skipping v. 17. Verse 17 is probably a later editorial addition to the old nucleus of this section. Once added, v. 17 transforms the earlier positive characterization of the judges as military leaders and religious reformers into something else. According to v. 17, the judges do, indeed, remain effective military deliverers who rescue Israel from enemies. But they fail in the more important theological task of teaching the people about their sole loyalty to the Lord: The Israelites "did not listen even to their judges; for they lusted after other gods and bowed down to them."

2:18-19. These verses add two more pieces of important information, one about God and one about Israel. Concerning God, we are told the reason why God repeatedly sent judges generation after generation to deliver Israel from the very enemies God had allowed to plunder Israel. The Lord was "moved to pity by their groaning." The verb נחם (*niham*, niphal), translated "move to pity" (NRSV) or "had compassion" (NIV), signifies sorrow at the hurt or pain of another and a desire to come to the victim's aid. The word "groaning" (נאקה *nĕʾāqâ*) refers not to any repentant attitude on the part of the Israelites, but to cries of lament due to pain and oppression. God responds to deliver them not because Israel has promised to reform or is sorry for sin. God responds simply because God has compassion on this oppressed but still rebellious people. The same Hebrew word is used in Exod 2:23-24 for the groaning of the Israelite slaves in Egypt, which caused God to hear and to act to deliver them from oppression. The cries of oppressed people have a special avenue to God's heart and a unique claim on God's compassion, irrespective of whether the oppressed are themselves wholly virtuous.

Concerning Israel, v. 19 informs us that the Israelites during the era of the judges are on a downhill slide into apostasy and idolatry. Whenever the judges died, the Israelites who were not faithful even during the tenure of the judges (v. 17) behaved even worse than the previous generation of ancestors. God's hope was that the judges would not only save Israel from its enemies but also strengthen Israel's resolve to drive the Canaanites and their gods totally out of the promised land. But Israel under the judges refused to drop any of their sinful ways. They increasingly strayed from the Lord and continued more and more to worship other gods. In their final edited form, vv. 6-19 have portrayed a steady decline from the faithfulness of the early generations under Joshua and the elders to the increasing apostasy and rebellion of Israel throughout the era of the judges. We see, then, a parallel movement in the characterization of Israel from good to bad to worse in the two parts of the introduction to the book of Judges: 1:1-36, increasing military failure to oust the Canaanites, and 2:6-19, increasing theological failure to worship the Lord alone.

2:20-23. The first part of the introduction to Judges ended with a climactic speech by the angel of the Lord. The speech indicted Israel and reported God's change in plans. God would allow the Canaanites to stay in the land, and their gods would remain as a constant "snare" to Israel (vv. 1-5). This second half of the introduction also ends with a climactic speech by God, indicting Israel and reporting God's change in plans concerning the Canaanites (vv. 20-23). The third appearance of God's anger in this section occurs in v. 20. The previous two occurrences of the divine anger had been part of the repeated cycle of God's anger in the more global response of God's looking back over the whole sweep of the many generations of the judges era and their failures and disappointments. Thus God, in a culminating but understandable and righteous rage, gives up on the holy war plan to wipe out the Canaanites. Instead, the Canaanites will remain in the land "in order to test Israel, whether or not they would take care to walk in the way of the LORD" (v. 22). Israel will never be free from temptations and forces that will seek to lure its faith and allegiance away from the Lord. Israel's faith will be under constant scrutiny and testing. God's dream of bringing Israel into the promised land of milk and honey with no cares or temptations where Israel would have no choice but to worship the Lord alone has been forfeited and lost forever. Verses 6-23 have revealed God's inner struggle and process to arrive at that painful conclusion. The divine dream has been shattered. Yet God's compassion moves God to pick up the pieces and move on with a new reality and strategy for continuing in relationship with the inescapably unruly people of Israel.

REFLECTIONS

1. The book of Judges does not go into great detail in describing the particulars of the other religions and gods that Israel worshiped. The narrative mentions the names of Baal and Astarte, but little other information is provided. The lack of specificity and the repeated general charge of "worshiping other gods" invites later generations to fill in this story with the particular temptations and gods of their own age and setting. What gods in our own time and place lure us away from loyalty and devotion to the Lord? What temptations in our surrounding culture cause us to ignore the call to "love the LORD your God with all your heart, and with all your soul, and with all your might" (Deut 6:5 NRSV)? Such temptations are not limited to other organized religions or cults. All the many pressures, values, and enticements of our culture that demand our time, energy, resources, and loyalty can become false gods insofar as our devotion to them supersedes our devotion to the Lord. For example, Deuteronomy 7–11 explores the ways in which devotion to arrogant militarism, self-sufficient materialism, or self-righteous moralism can become substitutes for true worship of God (Deut 7:7, 17; 8:17; 9:4). The nature of the false gods we worship may be as varied as the human imagination that manufactures them.

2. We encounter again the theme of the dialogical struggle between God's anger and God's compassion, the battle between the requirements of the law and the compassion of gracious love. As was noted earlier, there is a juxtaposition of these two competing paradigms in the legalism of the judgment of King Adoni-bezek (Judg 1:4-7) and the compassion and generosity of parental love shown by Caleb to his daughter Achsah (Judg 1:11-15). The angel's speech in 2:1-5 displayed a similar tension between God's unconditional covenant faithfulness (2:1) and Israel's covenant disobedience and God's just punishment (2:2-3). This dialectical dance between God's heartfelt compassion and God's angry judgment becomes the dominating theme of 2:6-23. As Israel accelerates its downward slide into rebellion and apostasy, God allows enemies to plunder Israel in punishment for its sin. But at the same time, God interrupts the judgment for a time by sending judges who deliver Israel from their enemies. Israel experiences God as both enemy and friend. Just as the angelic divine warrior who confronted Joshua (Josh 5:13-15) was not solely an adversary or solely an ally, so also God both judges and delivers God's people. In the Song of Moses in Deuteronomy 32, God proclaims:

> See now that I, even I, am he;
> there is no god beside me.
> I kill and I make alive;
> I wound and I heal;
> and no one can deliver from my hand. (Deut 32:39 NRSV)

Like Jacob in the wrestling match with God in Genesis 32, God wrestles and injures, but also blesses and cares for, God's people. This is the painful lesson the rebellious people of God must constantly learn: There is no other god or savior to heal our woes other than the same God who alone has the power both to judge and to deliver.

3. The power of the cry of the oppressed Israelites to move God, even though they remained mired in their idolatrous sin, reminds us of the hold that the poor and the oppressed have on God's heart. It was the cry of the Israelite slaves that caught God's attention and initiated the course of events that toppled an arrogant pharaoh from power (Exod 2:23-24). As a result, God later commanded the Israelites to treat those who were poor or oppressed in their own communities with generosity and compassion. Otherwise, "your neighbor might cry to the LORD against you, and you would incur guilt" (Deut 15:9 NRSV). The cry of the oppressed peoples of the earth has power to provoke God's action to judge the arrogant and the powerful and to raise up the poor and the downtrodden (1 Sam 2:1-10; Luke 1:46-55).

Judges 3:1-6, Nations Remain to Test Israel

COMMENTARY

The two-part introduction to Judges (1:1–2:5 and 2:6–3:6) concludes with a brief summary of the nations that God allowed to remain in the promised land. God had resolved in 2:21 not to drive out "any of the nations that Joshua left," and 3:1-6 tells the reader precisely who those nations are. The list of nations in v. 3—Philistines, Canaanites, Sidonians, and Hivites—was probably derived from Josh 13:2-6 and includes nations that were neighbors to the central part of Canaan on its northern and western boundaries. The king of Hazor in the far north of Canaan will be featured in the story of Deborah, Barak, and Jael (chaps. 4–5), and the Philistines will be the prime oppressors in the Samson story (chaps. 13–16). The additional list of nations in v. 5 is the more conventional summary of the inhabitants of Canaan that one finds scattered throughout the book of Joshua (Josh 3:10; 9:1; 11:3; 12:8; 24:11).

Why did the Lord allow these nations to remain in Canaan? Two seemingly contradictory reasons are given. Verses 1-2 argue that the other nations were left in Canaan to help succeeding generations of Israelites learn how to fight in a war and gain military experience. The text says this was the "only" reason. Verse 4 offers a second, different reason. God allowed the other nations to remain in Canaan to test Israel "to know whether Israel would obey the commandments of the LORD." This second reason has been the primary way in which the preceding verses explained why God allowed the Canaanites

to stay in the land (2:3, 22-23). Many scholars simply dismiss the first reason about pedagogy for military battle an insertion by a later naïve or inept editor. That may be the case, but the two reasons can be read as more complementary than contradictory. God's commandments do include rules on how to conduct holy war (cf. Deut 20:10-18, which has the same list of nations as in Judg 3:5). Thus a good part of knowing whether Israel would obey God's commandments (reason 2) includes testing how Israel will fight its battles against other peoples and other gods (reason 1). Also, following God's commandments inevitably draws the faithful person or community into some sort of conflict with other forces, powers, and communities who may resist God's will and God's way. The challenge to obey God in the face of countervailing forces entails learning how to do battle against such forces. Such battles need not be fought with weapons of violence, but with weapons of words, Scripture, study, persuasion, prayer, worship, community support, and acts of love, reconciliation, and forgiveness. Future visions of nations and their vocation in the world moved away from military violence to visions of peace, servanthood, and education in the ways of the Lord (Isa 2:1-4):

They shall beat their swords into plowshares,
and their spears into pruning hooks;
nation shall not lift up sword against nation,
neither shall they learn war any more.
(Isa 2:4 NRSV)

REFLECTIONS

1. Some people may be troubled by the notion that God deliberately places tests and temptations before us to try our souls. After all, we pray in the Lord's prayer,

"Lead us not into temptation" (Matt 6:13 NIV). However, the motif of God's testing the faith of God's people is a significant theme in the Old Testament. God tested Abraham when God ordered him to sacrifice Isaac (Gen 22:1). The psalmist invites such testing: "Prove me, O LORD, and try me; test my heart and mind" (Ps 26:2 NRSV; cf. Ps 66:10). The prophets likewise speak of God's testing of Israel (Jer 9:7; Zech 13:9). The entire book of Job involves God's test of Job's faith and devotion to God (Job 1:1). While some New Testament traditions likewise affirm God's testing of the faithful (Heb 11:17), other traditions deny that God tempts anyone (Jas 1:13). Satan, or the devil, is often portrayed as the chief source of temptation and testing (Matt 4:1-11; Luke 22:3; Rev 2:10).

How are we to understand these disparate traditions about God's testing and tempting of God's people? It seems clear that God does at times test people and their faith. But God tests them not to tempt them into sin but to refine and strengthen their commitment to God. Using the analogy of the purification of precious metals, God will at times put the people of God "into the fire, refine them as one refines silver, and test them as gold is tested" (Zech 13:9 NRSV). But, of course, there are times when suffering or evil comes upon us from forces or powers other than God or ourselves. Then we join with God in battle against a common enemy. But each challenge and difficulty in life is an opportunity to ask the question, Is God testing me and my community? But even when we discern that God may be testing our faith, the apostle Paul reminds us that God is both the one who tests and the one who provides:

> No testing has overtaken you that is not common to everyone. God is faithful, and he will not let you be tested beyond your strength, but with the testing he will also provide the way out so that you may be able to endure it. (1 Cor 10:13 NRSV)

Again we see the portrait of God as both enemy and friend, judge and deliverer, tempter and rescuer. In the book of Judges, God resolves to leave the Canaanites in the land to tempt Israel as a test of faith (3:1, 4). But in the course of the generations of testing, God will provide judges who will deliver Israel for a time. God will not abandon Israel entirely to its own devices. God will ensure that somehow the story of God and of God's people will go on in spite of the testing, the failures, and the unfaithfulness of God's people.

2. The concluding verse in this unit, 3:6, provides a narrative transition that sets the stage for the series of individual judge stories that will typically begin with Israel doing evil in the sight of the Lord. Verse 6 describes the nature of Israel's evil as the intermarriage of Israelite men and women with the sons and daughters of the other nations. The consequence of such intermarriage was that the Israelites "worshiped their gods." This association of intermarriage and apostasy takes seriously the risks and challenges of close and intimate relationships with those who do not share our core values, beliefs, and faith. Marriages, close friendships, peer groups, gangs, and other tightly knit communities (such as cults) have enormous power to shape our loyalties and thinking. As was noted in the Commentary on 1:1-21, Israel often had to wrestle with the nature of its relationships to other peoples and nations. Sometimes Israel fought against and isolated itself from other nations (Judg 1:4; cf. Ezra and Nehemiah), and sometimes Israel embraced people of foreign nations (Judg 1:16; cf. Ruth and Jonah).

A curious double message exists in the biblical material concerning intermarriage. On the one hand, prominent ancestors and leaders of Israel intermarried in good faith with women of other nations and peoples (Joseph and his Egyptian wife, Gen 41:45; Moses and his Midianite wife, Exod 2:21; Moses and his Cushite wife, Num 12:1; Boaz and his Moabite wife, Ruth, Ruth 4:13). On the other hand, some biblical laws and narratives offer strict warnings against intermarriage because it may lead to abandoning the Lord and worshiping other gods (Exod 34:11-16; Num 25:1-18; Deut 7:1-6; 1 Kgs 11:1-13).

Two things need to be said. First of all, many of the warnings against intermarriage occurred only in regard to certain transitional times in Israel's history and in regard to certain evil nations, like the Canaanites, at the time of the settlement in the land. The settlement in Canaan was the moment of Israel's birth as a nation. Such times of transition in Israel's history were precarious. Israel's identity as the people of God was fragile, vulnerable, and easily swayed. Israel needed a time of separation to gain a sense of its boundaries and identity as a people among the other nations. The time of Ezra and Nehemiah and the rebuilding of a fragile community of returned exiles in Judah in the post-exilic period was also a time of delicate transition and community formation. In that context, the leaders decreed an end to intermarriage with foreign spouses, echoing the concerns of these earlier texts from Exodus, Deuteronomy, and Judges (Ezra 9–10).

Second, other traditions in the Old Testament are much more open to the notion of intermarriage and regular interaction with people of other nations. Books like Ruth and Jonah come to mind, along with the stories in Genesis in which the foreigners sometimes appear more noble and virtuous than do the Israelites (Gen 12:10-20; 20:1-18; 34:1-31). Some of these stories may have come from a time when Israel was more secure in its identity and thus better able to be open and inclusive of other peoples and nations. In any case, as we come to the end of this two-part introduction to the book of Judges, we know that we are about to embark upon a path that will lead from Israel's initial success and faithfulness downward into the growing disintegration and unfaithfulness of the fragile Israelite community.

JUDGES 3:7–16:31

THE INDIVIDUAL JUDGES: A DOWNWARD SPIRAL

OVERVIEW

The two-part introduction to the book of Judges in 1:1–3:6 provided the defining pattern for understanding the movement and structure of the book of Judges. This generalized pattern portrayed the time of Israel's judges as a series of Israelite generations who experienced a downward political and religious spiral in their leadership, in their faith in God, and in their social unity. The individual judge stories in the main body of 3:7–16:31 have been edited and shaped to conform to this same introductory paradigm of military, political, and religious decline. The tales of individual judges begin with the model judge Othniel (3:7-11), who stands apart from the rest and provides the standard of proper judgeship by which all the other judges may be evaluated. The individual judge narratives include a total of twelve judges, six "major judges," with extended narratives (Othniel, Ehud, Deborah, Gideon with his son Abimelech, Jephthah, and Samson), and six "minor judges," with brief notices interspersed among the major judge stories (Shamgar, Tola, Jair, Ibzan, Elon, and Abdon).

The Six Major Judges: From Victory to Tragedy. We may discern a downward progression in three phases or stages among the six major judge stories.[24] The first phase (3:7–5:31) includes judges who are largely victorious and faithful: Othniel, the model judge; Ehud, the left-handed Benjaminite ("son of the right hand"); and the story of Deborah, Barak, and Jael. This first phase culminates in the poetic Song of Deborah, which sings the praises of God and humans. The second

phase (6:1–10:5) is transitional in character and begins the downward slide of the judges. Gideon is himself a transitional figure, moving from victory and faithfulness (albeit in a somewhat cowardly and tentative manner) to idolatry and hints of political power grabbing in the midst of a rhetoric of pious humility. The subtle negative shift in Gideon's character emerges full blown in his son Abimelech, whose arrogance and power grabbing are anything but subtle. Abimelech declares himself king and kills his own brothers in a familial and civil war. He dies in shame fighting a war started over a challenge to his personal honor. Gideon and Abimelech mark a turning point from positive to negative in the succession of individual judges. More and more the judges will fight for themselves and against Israel's interests rather than for God and for the interests of a united people of Israel.

The third group of judges after Gideon and Abimelech descend further into military failure, religious unfaithfulness, and personal tragedy (10:6–16:31). Jephthah the judge is victorious in battle but feels forced to kill his one and only child, a daughter, because of a foolish vow to God. Jephthah also fights and kills 42,000 members of a fellow Israelite tribe, an act as abhorrent as killing one's own family member. The other tragic figure in this third and last group of Israelite judges is Samson. Although great expectations are attached to his birth as a specially chosen Nazirite, Samson is a judge who leads no one but himself. He is a playboy who parties with foreigners, a hot-headed rogue who regularly violates his nazirite vows to God, and a love-struck fool who is humiliated by Israel's enemies. In the end, Samson kills himself along

---

24. My understanding of the overall shape of the book of Judges, 3:7–6:31 in particular, is informed by the redaction-critical study of, among others, Stone, "From Tribal Confederation to Monarchic State," 260-391, and the literary work of Webb, *The Book of the Judges,* 123-79.

with a large number of Philistine leaders in one last desperate act of personal revenge.

This three-stage descent from victory and faithfulness to tragedy and religious distortion among the individual judges is the result of an intentional process of careful literary editing in two or more stages. Many of the judge stories probably originated as entertaining heroic tales about the military victories or exploits of a local tribal ancestor. These independent tales were retold and gradually came to be collected and edited into a coherent series of deliverers or judges. The resulting series of judge stories may have been formed on the model of a common genre of ancient Near Eastern literature called the royal annals or chronicles, in which a succession of rulers and their stories were brought together into a coherent whole.[25] The role of these originally local judges was expanded to a national level; they were portrayed as leading not only a local tribe or small coalition but "all Israel" for a given period of years. Much of the local color and detail of each of the stories remained. However, later editors also reworked the stories in crucial ways so that the reader was given a sense of a gradual and progressive deterioration in the quality of the judges and their rule.

Six important elements of the first judge story, that of Othniel (3:7-11), functioned as a definitive norm or standard of a faithful judge against which all the other judge stories could be implicitly assessed. These six elements include (1) the nature of the evil done by the Israelite people, (2) the description of the enemy's oppression, (3) the divine reaction to the Israelites' cry, (4) the judges' success in uniting and delivering Israel, (5) a focus on God's victory against the enemies of Israel versus a focus on the details of the judge's own personal life and desire for vengeance, and (6) the proportion of the number of years the judge ruled in peace versus the number of years the enemy oppressed Israel. As we move from the earlier to the later judges in chaps. 3–16, we will note the progressive deterioration in actualizing these six criteria of the model judge. As the discussion below will show, these six criteria have been used by the writers and editors of Judges to portray

a dramatic religious and political decline during the era of the judges:

(1) The nature of Israel's evil moves from an unspecified evil in the early judge stories (3:12; 4:1a) to a more and more explicit charge of idolatry and worshiping foreign gods in the later judge stories (6:10; 8:24-27, 33-35; 10:6).

(2) The descriptions of the enemy's oppression in the early judge narratives are relatively short and generic (3:13; 4:2), but the descriptions of the oppression in the last two stages of the judge narratives become longer and more severe (6:1-6; 10:6-16).

(3) God's reaction to the Israelites' cry of distress is immediate and positive in the early judge tales (3:15; 4:3-7). In contrast, Israel's cry of distress in the later stories evokes a mediated rebuke from God (6:7-10) and then a direct divine rejection (10:10-14) because of Israel's increasing sinfulness and the judges' increasing failure to lead. This decline culminates in the final judge story of Samson, which contains no Israelite cry of distress at all; the traditional power of the oppressed human's cry to God has been lost (13:1).

(4) The judges' success in uniting and saving Israel from its oppressing enemy begins on a high note. The early judges are victorious (3:29-30; 4:23-24). They united Israel, including the northern Ephraimites, to their cause (3:27; 5:14). The degree to which the Israelite tribe of Ephraim is included or excluded becomes an indicator of Israel's health throughout these narratives. The later judges have some success against external enemies (8:28). However, Gideon becomes entangled in a brief internal conflict with his fellow Israelite tribe of Ephraim (8:1-3). Gideon's conflict with Ephraim is quickly resolved without bloodshed, but this intra-Israel conflict escalates with the later judges who slay fellow Israelites. Abimelech murders seventy of his own brothers (9:5), Jephthah kills his own daughter and fights and kills 42,000 people of the tribe of Ephraim (12:1-6). The last judge, Samson, is a one-man army who does not unite or lead any tribes of Israel in concerted action against their enemy. His success is limited, as he will only "begin to deliver Israel from the hand of the Philistines" (13:5).

25. Barnabas Lindbars, *Judges 1–5: A New Translation and Commentary* (Edinburgh: T. & T. Clark, 1995) 125.

(5) The focus of the early judge narratives is less on the human judge in terms of biographical detail and more on God and the praise of God (3:15, 28; 4:23; 5:1-11, 31). We know very little about the origins, divine call, or personal lives of the early judges, Othniel, Ehud, and Deborah. The spotlight in their stories is on the military victory itself and on God's role in achieving it. However, the later judge stories gradually lessen the attention on God and increase the amount of biographical detail dedicated to the individual judges, beginning with Gideon. By the time we reach Jephthah and Samson, their personal stories and self-serving desire for personal vengeance simply crowd out the actual account of any military victory or of God's role in it. Like the later judges, Israel has become more and more concerned with looking at itself and less and less concerned with looking to God for guidance and help.

(6) The decreasing proportion of the number of years Israel had rest or peace under each judge to the number of years of enemy oppression is yet another marker of the decline of the judges period. The ideal standard is set in the Othniel account with a long forty years of peace (a round number for a generation), in contrast to only an eight-year period of oppression (3:8, 11). The early judges all meet or exceed this standard.

Judge	Years of Peace	Years of Oppression
Ehud (3:14, 30)	80	18
Deborah (4:3; 5:31)	40	20
Gideon (6:1; 8:28)	40	7
Jephthah (10:8; 12:7)	61	8
Samson (13:1; 16:31)	20	40

Gideon is a transitional figure in the decline of the judges. He meets the standard set by Othniel in chap. 3 of at least forty years of peace (8:28), but this notice is marred by an accompanying indictment that "all Israel prostituted themselves" to an idolatrous ephod made by Gideon (8:27). Gideon's son Abimelech solidifies the decline in that he kills members of his own Israelite family and then himself is killed in battle, so no years of peace are recorded for him; Abimelech falls entirely outside the paradigm. The notices for the last two judges, Jephthah and Samson, reveal that the decline has continued. The formula that the "land had rest" for a specified number of years is absent in the later stories of Jephthah and Samson, replaced simply with the number of years they were judges. In the case of the later judgeships, the years of oppression far exceed the number of years the judge actually ruled. The progression in these chronological notices associated with major judges throughout 3:7–16:31 clearly reveals a gradual decline in the fortunes of Israel and the judges' effectiveness as leaders.

The Six Minor Judges: From Victory to Trivial Pursuit. The same sense of gradual decline appears in the sequence of the six so-called minor judges. The brief notices of these judges intrude at three junctures among the major judge narratives: Shamgar in 3:31, Tola and Jair in 10:1-5, and Ibzan, Elon, and Abdon in 12:8-15. These three junctures correspond to the three phases or stages in the decline of the judges as a whole. The first minor judge, Shamgar, successfully kills six hundred of the dreaded enemy, the Philistines, and is said to have "delivered Israel" (3:31). The focus only on Shamgar's military success fits his present literary location among the early judges who were faithful and successful. The next two minor judges, Tola and Jair, who rule twenty-three and twenty-two years respectively, appear in the second transitional stage after Gideon and the disastrous rule of his son Abimelech. The narrator reports that Tola "rose to deliver Israel," but the narrator provides no indication that the second minor judge, Jair, accomplished anything for the well-being of Israel. All that is reported is the rather bizarre personal note that Jair had thirty sons who rode on thirty donkeys and had thirty towns. This mixed report of deliverance of Israel and no deliverance of Israel mirrors the transitional nature of this section of Judges, moving from success to failure in Gideon and Abimelech.

Finally, the third interpolation of minor judges (Ibzan, Elon, and Abdon) in 12:8-15 appears between the narratives of Jephthah and Samson. In line with the relative decline and failure of the last of the major judges, no mention of delivering Israel or any other beneficial effect is reported for these three minor judges. Moreover, the length of their successive judgeships is relatively short: seven years

(Ibzan), ten years (Elon), and eight years (Abdon). The relative shortness of their tenures corresponds to the relative brevity of the judgeships of Jephthah and Samson, indicating again a sense of decreasing effectiveness as leaders. The focus of the brief reports concerning these later minor judges, like the later major judges, is on their personal lives and individual concerns rather than the national welfare (finding spouses for their sons and daughters, the number of their children and grandchildren riding on donkeys). The concern for Israel's national welfare among the early judges has been gradually diluted into personal agendas, individual familial concerns, and trivial pursuits among the last judges.

Geographical Sequence and the Decline of the Judges. It was noted in the discussion of the introductory section of Judges 1 that a trend from positive success to gradually increasing failure characterized the geographical movement from southern to northern Israel in the first chapter of the book of Judges. A similar geographical movement from southern Judah through middle and northern Israelite tribes and clans is evident in the sequence of individual judge stories in 3:6–16:31. The sequence begins with the positive model of Othniel, who is related to Caleb from the tribe of Judah. The sequence then continues from south to north through Israel's landscape as we move through the tribal designations provided for many, but not all, of the judges: Judah (Othniel, 1:10-15; 3:9), Benjamin (Ehud, 3:15), Ephraim (Deborah, 4:4), Issachar (Tola, 10:1), Zebulun (Elon, 12:12), and Dan (Samson, 13:2). These geographical progressions from southern Judah to the far northern Dan are accompanied by a deteriorating progression in the effectiveness and faithfulness of the judges and the Israelites. Both of these progressions—geographical and religious-political—mirror the structure and progression evident in the introduction to the book in chap. 1. Many of the other judges, particularly those in the latter stages of the judges era, are not listed by their affiliation with one of the twelve tribes of Israel. They are listed only by their minor clan or village designations: Abiezrite (Gideon, 6:11), Gilead (Jephthah, 11:1), Bethlehem (Ibzan, 12:8), and Pirathon (Abdon, 12:13). These increasingly minor clan affiliations, as opposed to full tribal attachments, contribute further to the sense of increasing disunity and disintegration within the nation of Israel toward the end of the period of the judges.

Thus the editing of the six major judge narratives, the three minor judge interpolations, and the overall geographical progression from the southern to the northern tribes all conspire to shape the reading of these judge stories. The once independent judge narratives have been brought together and formed into a sequence of gradual decline and disintegration. The judges' political leadership and Israel's religious faithfulness begin on a high note with the earliest judges, but end in tragedy and disunity with the last judges, Jephthah and Samson. Although the political and religious institution of the judges and their temporary mode of leadership was satisfactory for a time, it soon proved to be inadequate for the long haul. Israel and God would together need to find a new way to unify and lead Israel as its national life continued in the land of Canaan.

JUDGES 3:7-11, OTHNIEL, THE MODEL JUDGE

COMMENTARY

The numerous episodes of individual judges or deliverers in 3:7–16:31 begin with a judge who is a relative of the honored ancestor Caleb and a member of the prestigious southern tribe of Judah. His name is Othniel. We have encountered Othniel already in the first chapter of Judges. Caleb, of the tribe of Judah, offered his daughter Achsah in marriage to the one warrior who would attack and defeat the Canaanite city of Kiriath-sepher. Caleb's nephew Othniel accepted the challenge, defeated the Canaanites, and married Achsah (1:11-15; see Josh 15:13-19). None of these details are carried forward into this brief narrative in 3:7-11. Instead, what we have is a collation of all the stock formulas and stereotypical phrases that occurred in the summary framework in 2:11-19 and will recur with important and meaningful variations over the course of the more expansive individual judge narratives that will follow in chaps. 3–16. Scholars have long recognized the stereotypical form of the Othniel episode as being composed of these formulaic phrases and motifs: Israel's doing evil, the Lord's anger, oppression from the enemy, the Lord's raising up of a judge, and so forth. Some scholars have concluded from its brevity and artificiality that the Othniel episode is of little value for interpreting Judges, perhaps functioning only to make up a judge for the tribe of Judah, since Judah did not have a representative among the other judge stories.

However, the Othniel episode in the present form of Judges has a central role as the standard against which all the other judge stories may be compared and evaluated.[26] As was discussed in the Overview to 3:7–16:31, the variations in key motifs and phrases in the judge stories portray a sequence of gradual degradation in the political, military, and religious effectiveness of the Israelite judges. Othniel's story gathers together all the significant stereotypical phrases that are scattered among the other judge stories as if to say to the reader, "Now these are the phrases and elements to which you should pay attention as you evaluate the following stories of judges." The Overview to 3:7–16:31 also noted how six elements or criteria embedded within the Othniel story play a crucial role in the appraisal of the judges who will follow Othniel: (1) the nature of Israel's evil, (2) the description of the enemy's oppression, (3) God's reaction to the Israelites' cry of distress, (4) the judge's success in uniting and delivering Israel, (5) a focus on God's victory or the judge's personal life and desire for vengeance, and (6) the proportion of the number of years the judge ruled in peace ("the land had rest X years") and the number of years

the enemy oppressed Israel. The Othniel episode contains largely positive dimensions of these six elements, while later judge stories will gradually exhibit more negative dimensions relative to the criteria implied in the model story of Othniel.

Othniel's story is the first specific example of the generalized pattern of what will occur in the era of the judges, laid out earlier in 2:11-19. The story begins with the Israelites doing evil, which is expressed as both "forgetting the LORD" and "worshiping the Baals and Asherahs." The time period presumably returns the reader to the time of 2:11, when Joshua and his generation have died. The new generation has forgotten all that Israel's God has done for them and instead has sought security and salvation in the gods of Canaan, the local cults of the male god Baal and the female consort Asherah. This apostasy provokes God's anger so that God gives the Israelites over to an enemy king named Cushan-rishathaim from Aram-naharaim. The king's name in Hebrew means "Cusan of Double Wickedness," an obviously villainous and perhaps satirical royal name for which we have no historical record. The place name Aram-naharaim means "Aram of the Two Rivers" and refers to the area of northwest Mesopotamia where two rivers flow.

God and the Cry of the Oppressed. The enemy oppression of Israel lasted only eight years, one of the shortest periods of oppression among the judge stories (3:8). In the midst of their oppression, the Israelites "cried out to the LORD," and God responded by sending the judge-deliverer named Othniel to save them. Some interpreters have understood this cry to God as Israel's cry of repentance and remorseful acknowledgment of the sin of worshiping other gods. However, the Hebrew verb זעק ($z\bar{a}^{c}aq$, "to cry out"), as it is used elsewhere in the OT, does not carry the connotation of repentance but simply someone in distress who is calling desperately to God for help. That the cry of the oppressed has a special power and leverage with the gods is a common ancient Near Eastern motif that the OT shares.[27] However, the story of Othniel adds an additional

---

26. Stone, "From Tribal Confederation to Monarchic State," 260-89.

27. Richard Boyce, *The Cry to God in the Old Testament* (Atlanta: Scholars Press, 1988); Stone, "From Tribal Confederation to Monarchic State," 311-26.

religious and moral dimension. In spite of Israel's worship of other gods, Israel's God graciously responds to their cry and saves them in spite of their sin (3:9). However, the time will come in the judges era when Israel's idolatrous transgression will increase to such an extent that God will respond with a rebuke when the Israelites cry out about oppression (6:7-10). Later, God will respond even more negatively to Israel's cry with a word of outright rejection, even though Israel adds words of confession and repentance to the cry for help (10:10-16). The growing depth of Israel's sin will eventually make even the powerful cry of the oppressed ineffectual in moving God to saving action. For now in the Othniel story, Israel's cry for aid receives an immediate and positive response: God quickly sends Othniel to save Israel.

The Spirit of the Lord and the Judges. God raises up Othniel as "the spirit of the LORD" comes upon him. The effect of the divine Spirit on the judge is another important criterion by which to evaluate the judges. With Othniel, the effect is positive as he is empowered and immediately victorious (3:10). However, the divine Spirit in the book of Judges can have either positive or negative effects. For Othniel, God's Spirit is a positive gift that changes him and leads him into powerful, decisive, and faithful action. The result is similar to the effect of God's Spirit coming upon Saul in 1 Sam 10:6-7. For the other early judges, like Ehud and Deborah, the text does not say that they were given a divine Spirit at all but rather a divine word (3:20; 4:6). When God's Spirit does return to play a role in the judges narrative, it comes upon Gideon—but with little effect or change. Before the Spirit of the Lord comes upon him, Gideon is cowardly, hesitant, and secretive (6:11-33). After the Spirit of the Lord has come upon him (6:34), Gideon does not change. The cowardly Gideon continues to need repeated reassurance from God through signs and dreams (6:36–7:15). The effect of the divine Spirit's coming on Jephthah is even more negative. Before receiving the Spirit, Jephthah had been an able and cool-headed negotiator of conflicts (11:1-28). After "the spirit of the LORD" comes upon him (11:29), Jephthah begins to act in rash, careless, and impulsive ways by making a foolish vow that

causes his daughter's death (11:30-40). The Spirit-filled Jephthah also erupts in a hot-headed killing spree, slaying 42,000 fellow Israelites over a petty disagreement (12:1-6).

The misuse of the divine Spirit's power comes to a climax in Samson, upon whom the divine Spirit comes several times (13:25; 14:6, 19; 15:14). Again, however, the Spirit of the Lord simply impels Samson to act powerfully but with unthinking impulse, violence, and faithlessness. The Spirit's untamed power leads Samson to slay a lion and later eat honey from its carcass. The spirit-driven Samson kills thirty and then a thousand Philistine warriors at close range with the jawbone of an ass. The problem is that Samson is a Nazirite from birth (Judges 13) and is prohibited from touching anything unclean, especially a dead body or corpse. His close contact with countless corpses, both animal and human, repeatedly breaks his nazirite vow to God. Therefore, Othniel embodies the ancient ideal of a faithful judge empowered in a special way by the Spirit of the Lord. But when the divine Spirit gradually reappears in later judges, the Spirit is no longer a positive force. In the hands of unfaithful leaders like Gideon, Jephthah, and Samson, the divine Spirit becomes ineffectual and ultimately dangerous and destructive in the extreme.[28]

The Lord's Rest. The brief episode of Othniel ends with the affirmation that it is "the LORD" who gave the enemy king into the hands of the judge Othniel (3:10). The ultimate agent of Israel's deliverance is not Othniel's personal skills or prowess but God's faithfulness and compassion. Even though Israel forgets the Lord and worships other gods, God remains true to the covenant relationship and promises made to Israel's ancestors over many generations. Thus "the land had rest forty years," roughly the equivalent of one generation. The land at rest signifies peace, security, and the absence of conflict with enemies. The land at rest is the ultimate goal of the judge's leadership and deliverance according to the ideal set by Othniel, but it will be a goal that later judges (Jephthah and Samson) will not be able to achieve (12:7; 16:31).

---

28. Stone, "From Tribal Confederation to Monarchic State," 332-38.

REFLECTIONS

1. Othniel is the first ideal and faithful leader within a system of Israelite governance and polity depicted as the era of the judges. This system of temporary leaders who arose at certain crisis periods in Israel's early nationhood will eventually deteriorate and collapse by the end of the book of Judges. The judges were eventually replaced by kings who ruled as an ongoing dynasty in ancient Israel (1–2 Samuel; 1–2 Kings). But even within the flawed system and structure of the judges, Othniel emerges as an ideal ruler for this time and context. Good leaders can work faithfully and successfully within any number of secular political systems or religious polities. We are sometimes prone to label some governmental or economic systems as inherently "anti-Christian" or "evil," especially when they are different from our own. But God's success with Othniel as part of the ultimately flawed system of judges suggests that we need to be open to the possibility of God's faithful working in and through a wide variety of human political systems, social organizations, and economic structures. God is not permanently tied to any one human institution or structure or ideology.

2. The role of "the spirit of the LORD" with Othniel and the other judges suggests the need to accompany reliance on God's Spirit with leaders who have been shaped by faithful guidance from the tradition and memory of what God has done and proclaimed in the past. God's Spirit does, indeed, give special power to leaders, but that power may be abused by unfaithful or misguided leaders. Thus leadership that claims legitimacy through God's Spirit needs to be evaluated and checked by appeals to Scripture, by conformity to the church's tradition, and by other voices both within and outside the community.

3. The victory against the enemy king and the resulting rest or peace Israel enjoyed during Othniel's tenure as their temporary leader was ultimately the work of God. It was "the LORD" who gave the king into Othniel's hand. Human beings are the vehicles through which God works, but God is the one who in the end accomplishes God's purposes. In similar ways, the apostle Paul spoke of his work and the work of his colleague Apollos in proclaiming the gospel in the Christian community of Corinth. Growth in faith had been the result, but Paul knew it was ultimately not his doing: "What then is Apollos? What is Paul? Servants through whom you came to believe, as the Lord assigned to each. I planted, Apollos watered, but God gave the growth." Othniel may have planted and watered, but it was God who won the victory. Thus the first judge we meet recedes into the background with little detail about his personal life. As God is remembered as the One who finally is responsible for the victory, the final words of the story usher the first judge off the stage with the words, "Othniel the son of Kenaz died."

JUDGES 3:12-31, EHUD AND SHAMGAR

COMMENTARY

The first judge who appears after the model judge, Othniel, is a crafty and deceptive assassin named Ehud. The narrative of Ehud contains entertaining elements of satire, suspense, and humor that probably reflect a previous history of oral storytelling as the tale was passed from one generation to the next. The present literary form of the story retains these elements and adds to them a theological concern in line with the larger framework of the cycle of judge stories. Two of the central theological issues that emerge in this story are the interaction of human and divine agency or causality and the hidden and unexpected ways in which God acts to save God's people.

3:12-14. The story of the judge Ehud begins with the Israelites again doing "what was evil in the sight of the LORD." This refrain echoes the opening formula at the beginning of the recurring pattern, noted in the Introduction (2:11-19) and in the paradigm established by the judge Othniel (3:7-11). The nature of Israel's evil is not spelled out in any detail. In the later judges, such as Gideon and Jephthah, the evil will increasingly be described as the serious offense of worshiping other foreign gods (6:8-10; 10:6); here the evil is unspecified. The evil is sufficient to move God to punish the Israelites by "strengthening" King Eglon of Moab against Israel. The other judge stories portray God as either "selling" or "giving over" Israel to its enemy, suggesting a more active and direct divine role in handing Israel over to its oppressors (4:2; 6:1; 10:7; 13:1). In the Ehud story, God simply strengthens the Moabite king in his own already established plans to conquer and oppress Israel. Moreover, the Moabite King Eglon engineers some strengthening of his own by forming a military alliance with the neighboring "Ammonites and Amalekites" (3:13). Thus the Moabite Eglon and his Ammonite and Amalekite allies unknowingly carry out God's purposes to defeat and punish Israel for a period of eighteen years. They capture in particular "the city of palms," usually identified as the town of Jericho, near the Jordan River and the border between Israel and Moab and Ammon.

3:15-30. After eighteen years under the tyranny of the Moabite King Eglon, Israel cries out to God, and God responds by raising up a "deliverer" named Ehud. Ehud is from the tribe of Benjamin, a tribe whose territory is just north of Judah and thus in line with the general south-to-north trajectory of the tribal affiliations of the individual judge stories, beginning with Othniel of southern Judah (vv. 7-11). The other significance of Ehud's being from the tribe of Benjamin is that the name "Benjamin" in Hebrew (בנימין binyāmîn) means "son of the right hand." The text notes that Ehud is "a left-handed man" (v. 15). In other words, Ehud is a "left-handed son of the right hand"! As a reader, we may expect something extraordinary,

unusual, and unexpected from this character Ehud, and we will not be disappointed. His left-handedness will play an important role in a crafty assassination plot against the king of Moab. But what exactly does it mean that Ehud is left-handed? The phrase in Hebrew literally means "bound or restricted in his right hand." Some interpreters have suggested that Ehud was handicapped with a deformed or withered right hand. Others suggest he was simply left-handed. Still others link Ehud with an elite group of Benjaminite warriors who were specially trained to be left-handed or ambidextrous, which gave them an advantage in battle (20:15-16). For the purposes of the Ehud story, all that is required to make the story work is that he is left-handed, and thus we assume its straightforward meaning.

The Israelites choose Ehud to be their envoy to carry tribute to the Moabite King Eglon. The tribute is a burdensome tax of money or produce exacted as a reminder that the Israelites are under the rule of the Moabite king, who is free to take from them whatever he wishes for his royal coffers. In choosing Ehud as tribute bearer, the Israelites are apparently unaware that Ehud himself has a secret plan in mind to bring down the Moabite king. Ehud manufactures a "sword with two edges," which symbolizes the double-edged nature not only of the sword but also of the words Ehud will use with King Eglon at the opportune moment. Ehud fastens the sword on his right thigh so that he can cross over with his left hand and draw the sword. The plan seems to be that since most people are right-handed, the bodyguards to the king will assume that Ehud is right-handed and thus check only Ehud's left thigh for a weapon. If so, they will fail to notice the concealed weapon on his right side.

After these preparations, Ehud leads an entourage of Israelites to offer the tribute of produce and money to King Eglon (vv. 17-18). The vocabulary of "presenting the tribute" is related to religious rituals of offering sacrifices to the gods as an acknowledgment of their power and the people's allegiance. Such a ceremony may have been involved in Ehud's presenting the tribute. The ritual and sacrificial charater of the scene is further suggested by the narrator's interjection, "Now Eglon was a very fat man." Eglon's name in Hebrew (עגלון

'eglôn) is related to the noun "young bull" or "fatted calf" (עגל 'ēgel), which is an animal that may be killed or sacrificed on an altar in an offering to God (Lev 9:2-3, 8). What we have, then, is a very fat "young bull" king who himself is about to be killed and offered as a tribute and a sacrifice. Ehud leaves with his Israelite companions to go back home after presenting the tribute. However, Ehud turns back at the "sculptured stones" (NRSV) or "idols" (NIV) near Gilgal (v. 19). When he does his deed against the king and returns back home on his escape, he will again pass by the same "sculptured stones/idols" (v. 26). The reference to these carved stones or idols and Ehud's passing by or passing over them forms a meaningful inclusio to the scene about to be narrated: Ehud's killing of the fat Moabite king is his way of leading Israel to bypass and leave behind the Moabite powers and gods that have oppressed them for eighteen years. Politics and religion are here intimately tied together.

As Ehud returns to the king's palace, he is allowed to speak with the king since he has just presided over giving a lavish tribute or offering to Eglon. Ehud says to King Eglon, "I have a secret message for you, O king." The Hebrew word for "message" (דבר dābār) can mean a "word" or a "thing." Like his sword, Ehud's words are double-edged. The king expects to hear "a secret word," but Ehud really has "a secret thing," a sword. The Moabite king immediately orders "Silence!" All the king's attendants take the order as an invitation to exit the throne room, leaving the king and Ehud alone in the "roof chamber" of the palace. In double-edged irony, Ehud speaks a second time to the king and reveals the divine origin of this "message": "I have a message [word/thing] from God for you." The king anxiously rises from his throne to receive the secret and divine message, unseating himself from the seat of power. Ehud promptly reaches "with his left hand," takes the dagger "from his right thigh," and thrusts it into Eglon's very fat belly (v. 21).

The text pauses here with some grotesque detail: The king's mountain of fat swallows up the sword, handle and all, so that Ehud does not draw the weapon back out. The final phrase in v. 22 contains an unusual Hebrew word whose meaning is uncertain. Some

translate it as does the NRSV: "the dirt came out," meaning the contents of the king's colon. This translation, derived from the Aramaic Targum and the Vulgate versions, would give some added reason why the king's attendants would later assume he was taking his time on the toilet. Another translation is represented by the NIV: "[the sword] which came out his back." Still others suggest the phrase refers to Ehud's escape route: "and he [Ehud] went out the hole [of the toilet?]." Ehud next goes out into the vestibule or porch and locks the outer doors to give himself time to escape (v. 23).[29]

The scene shifts to the king's servants who had exited and now come back to check on the king. They note that the doors of the roof chamber are locked from the inside. The locked doors and perhaps the smell of defecation cause them to assume the fat king must be "relieving himself" on his royal toilet. They wait until they are embarrassed and become concerned. Finally, they take a key and unlock the doors. As they fling open the doors, their eyes witness a horrifying sight: "there was their lord lying dead on the floor" (v. 25).

While the Moabite servants are left frozen and staring in horror, the scene shifts once again to Ehud as he escapes. He again passes by "the sculptured stones/idols," a sign of leaving behind the Moabite lords and their gods (v. 26). Ehud's crafty assassination of King Eglon earns him the loyalty of the Israelites as they make him their military leader. Ehud reveals the real force behind his success as he exhorts the Israelites, "Follow me, for the LORD has given your enemies into your hand" (v. 28). The Moabite "lord" was already dead, and Israel's Lord had already sealed the victory of Israel against its oppressors. The military victory against the Moabites that follows again involves craft and deception. The Israelite warriors lie in wait at the fords of the Jordan River, which separates Moab from Canaan. They ambush about ten thousand Moabites who try to cross the river "and so Moab was subdued that day under the hand of Israel" (v. 30). The result was eighty years of rest in the land.

29. For a detailed historical reconstruction of Eglon's assassination, see Baruch Halpern, *The First Historians: The Hebrew Bible and History* (New York: Harper & Row, 1988) 39-75.

3:31. After the conclusion of the Ehud narrative, we encounter the first of the six so-called minor judges who appear at three junctures among the other major judge stories (3:31; 10:1-5; 12:8-15). The first minor judge is "Shamgar son of Anath." Most of the other judges have tribal or clan designations that indicate they are clearly of Israelite origin, but Shamgar does not. He is listed as the "son of Anath." "Shamgar" is not a typical Israelite name, and "Anath" is the name of a Canaanite goddess and consort to the god Baal. Thus some have argued that Shamgar may have been a foreign mercenary who joined and led Israel's federation of tribes for a time. All we are told of Shamgar is that he killed six hundred Philistines "with an oxgoad" (v. 31). Just as Ehud's exploits centered on the uniqueness of his method and the weapon used,

so also the brief note about Shamgar focuses on his single-handed and heroic method and weapon, the oxgoad. Shamgar is not as subtle or secretive as Ehud; Shamgar uses brute strength and a blunt oxgoad to defeat the enemy, the Philistines. For all of his suspect lineage and his brutal tactics, however, Shamgar is affirmed as part of the line of judges. Shamgar comes "after him [Ehud]," and the narrator affirms that Shamgar "too delivered Israel" just as Ehud had done (vv. 15, 31). The Song of Deborah will later recall and celebrate "the days of Shamgar son of Anath" (5:6), and Israel will be reminded that God had previously defeated the Philistines (10:11). Using Shamgar, God saves Israel for a time but does so again through quite unexpected and unpredictable means and people.

REFLECTIONS

1. The story is first and foremost about the "left-handed" ways of God both to judge and to deliver Israel. God's ways are not our ways. The unexpected and often hidden means by which God works should make us cautious about being overly confident that we know exactly where, when, and how God will act in a given situation or context. God begins by choosing an unlikely fat Moabite king and his Ammonite and Amalekite allies who unknowingly carry out God's punishment upon a sinful Israel. In response to Israel's cry of distress, God reverses course and compassionately chooses another unlikely agent, a deliverer named Ehud whose odd left-handedness, hidden weapon, and deceptive words lead to the death of the Moabite oppressor and temporary rest for Israel. The hand of God works through the "left hand" of Ehud to subdue the Moabites "under the hand" of Israel and to give Moab "into the hand" of Israel (3:15, 21, 28, 30).

2. A related theme that emerges from this story is the intricate way in which God's agency is woven in and through the words, actions, and plans of human groups and individuals. God "strengthens" the Moabites in their already existent plan to conquer Israel. At the same time, the Moabites strengthen themselves by joining an alliance with Ammon and the Amalekites. Ehud devises on his own initiative an intricate plan to kill the Moabite king, but he (unlike the Moabites) acknowledges that it was "the LORD" working through him. Ehud's plan of assassination was in many ways ingenious. Yet the high number of fortuitous coincidences that were required to make Ehud's plan effective suggests a divine hand working behind the scenes to ensure success. Ehud just happened to be the one chosen to carry Israel's tribute to King Eglon. Ehud just happened to be allowed to have a second audience with the king. Ehud happened to be left-handed, and the bodyguards of the king just happened not to check Ehud's right side for a sword. The servants just happen to exit the throne room and leave Ehud alone with the king when the king had simply told the servants to be quiet and not necessarily to leave. Ehud somehow fortuitously found the time and the means to escape undetected. The large number of seeming coincidences suggests a divine hand behind it all.

As we look back over our own lives, Ehud's story may lead us to consider whether those seemingly chance encounters, fortuitous opportunities, and timely coincidences we have experienced may not have had a divine hand at work in them. It may be difficult to know at the time of the events themselves, but time and hindsight sometimes allow us to look back and trace a divine plan at work, sometimes faintly and sometimes quite clearly.

3. This story about the very fat King Eglon of Moab and his stupid Moabite servants may be seen as an example of antagonistic and even vicious ethnic humor. One can well imagine Israelites laughing heartily at the "toilet joke" about the obese king of Moab. Is this just an ethnic slur against Moabites that has inadvertently found its way into the Bible? Or does the satire of the Ehud story play a larger role within the increasing deterioration of Israel within the book of Judges? In terms of bawdy humor and bumbling characters who are constantly outwitted, the story of Ehud and Eglon at the beginning of the judge stories finds its closest counterpart at the end of the judge stories in the story of Samson (Judges 13–16). Like the story of Ehud and the Moabites, the tale of Samson and the Philistines is full of humor, riddles, bumbling mistakes, and deceptions. But the biting satire in the tale of Samson turns the tables on Israel: Samson, the hero and symbol of Israel, becomes the bumbling fool, the deceived playboy, and finally the one who brings death on himself. The laughter over Ehud's victory over the Moabites will become the weeping over Samson's tragic life and suicidal death. By the end of Judges, Israel will be no different from any other nation or group.[30] In fact, Israel will become its own worst enemy. God's people cannot claim greater numerical strength, material advantage, or moral superiority to the Moabites, the Philistines, or even the Canaanites (Deut 7:7; 8:17; 9:4-7). In the end, the only thing that makes Israel distinct from every other nation is that God's presence and activity stir among this chosen people of God, both to judge and to save (Exod 33:16). The same is true of God's people today. Writing to the Christians at Rome, the apostle Paul reminded them that they had no right to boast about their superiority over any other people: "Therefore you have no excuse, whoever you are, when you judge others; for in passing judgment on another you condemn yourself, because you, the judge, are doing the very same things" (Rom 2:1 NRSV).

30. Lowell Handy, "Uneasy Laughter: Ehud and Eglon as Ethnic Humor," *Scandinavian Journal of the Old Testament* 6 (1992) 233-46.

JUDGES 4:1–5:31, DEBORAH, BARAK, AND JAEL

OVERVIEW

Judges 4–5 concludes the first of three phases in the story of the gradual decline of Israel and the decline in the effectiveness of the individual judges as leaders of Israel. The three phases move from (1) victorious and faithful judges (3:7–5:31) to (2) a transitional stage that begins a decline into idolatry and social disunity within Israel (6:1–10:5) to (3) an increasingly serious deterioration of Israel as a social and religious community led by increasingly tragic and misguided judges (10:6–16:31). Chapters 4–5 contain some seeds of Israel's future deterioration, but these chapters largely celebrate a positive victory over Israel's Canaanite enemies.

Judges 4–5 follow the general pattern of judge stories established in the paradigm in 2:11-19 and in the story of the model judge Othniel (3:7-11). The Israelites do evil, the Lord sells them into the hand of the enemy, Israel cries out to the Lord, and the Lord raises up a judge who delivers them for a period of time. One of the unique wrinkles in Judges 4–5 is that it is not altogether clear who the actual judge is in this account. Indeed, the task of the judge as exemplified in the previous judge stories (Othniel, Ehud, Shamgar) is shared among three major characters in the story: Deborah, who is a woman prophet and acts as a judge in the sense of arbitrating disputes rather than leading military attacks; Barak, who is Israel's military general but is never called a judge; and Jael, who is a non-Israelite woman who kills the enemy Canaanite general named Sisera when he comes to her tent for refuge. This ambivalence about the real judge or hero of this story will play an important role in the narrative's plot as well as in the theological interpretation of the account.

Another major distinguishing element of Judges 4–5 is that the same account of Deborah, Barak, and Jael is conveyed to the reader in two different versions: a prose narrative account (chap. 4) and a poetic song that combines elements of a hymn of victory and a ballad that retells a story in poetic form (chap. 5). The closest biblical analogy to this juxtaposition of narrative and song to recount the same event is the account of Moses leading the Israelites in the crossing of the Red Sea in Exodus 14 (prose) and Exodus 15 (song). The two versions, the narrative in Judges 4 and the song in Judges 5, display a number of similarities as well as key differences. The story and the song both contain the same list of main characters: the Lord, Deborah, Barak, Jael, and Sisera the Canaanite general. They both recount the battle and victory against the Canaanite Sisera and the roles played by Deborah and Barak as leaders of Israel. In both the song and the narrative, Jael the Kenite woman offers hospitality to Sisera and then kills him.

Significant differences also characterize the prose and poetic versions of the Deborah-Barak-Jael account. Although playing no direct role in the story itself, the name of the Canaanite King Jabin appears in the outer framework of the prose story at the beginning (4:2) and at the end (4:23-24). In contrast, Jabin is not mentioned at all in the song of Judges 5, although there is a reference to unnamed "kings of Canaan" (5:19). A number of themes are present in the poetic song that are absent from the prose narrative: a more extensive description of the conditions of Israel's oppression (5:6-8), the description of cosmic disturbances and effects with the appearance of the Lord as the divine warrior (5:4-5, 19-22), the contrast between some Israelite tribes who participated in the battle and those who refused to participate (5:13-18), and the final scene of Sisera's mother and her advisers waiting for the return of her son, who will never come back home (5:28-30).

Two other broader differences between the narrative and poetic versions of Judges 4–5 have been proposed and debated among interpreters of these texts. One debate revolves around the question of whether the narrative and the poem differ in their primary focus on human activity or divine activity. A second debate argues about whether either the poem or the narrative reflects a woman's perspective versus a man's perspective.

On the contrast between a focus on divine agency versus human agency, some interpreters have argued that the story in Judges 4 subsumes all human action under the providential and divine plan of God with the oracle that Sisera would be defeated by "the hand of a woman" (4:9). God is the focus of the narrative version. On the other hand, these same interpreters argue that the poem in Judges 5 places human motives, emotions, and actions in the foreground (the oppressed Israelites, 5:6-8; the enthusiasm and the hesitation of some Israelite tribes, 5:13-18; the emotional scene of Sisera's mother waiting for her son to return, 5:28-30). Other scholars argue just the opposite: The prose narrative in chap. 4 highlights the interactions among the humans, while the poem of chap. 5 places the spotlight on God and plays down the role of the humans (the song's opening praise of God, 5:1-5; the refrain "bless the LORD," 5:2, 9; the battle as "the triumphs of the LORD," 5:11; the concluding prayer concerning the enemies and the friends of the Lord, 5:31). Still others claim that both the narrative and the poem place God as the center, subsuming all human action to the divine purpose and plan.[31] In fact, the widely divergent views of

31. See Julius Wellhausen, *Prolegomena to the History of Israel* (Gloucester, Mass.: P. Smith, 1973 [1878]) 240-42; Webb, *The Book of the Judges,* 141-44; Mieke Bal, *Murder and Difference: Gender, Genre and Scholarship on Sisera's Death* (Bloomington: Indiana University Press, 1988) 38, 44-50; Yairah Amit, "Judges 4: Its Content and Form," *JSOT* 39 (1987) 89-111; James W. Watts, *Psalm and Story: Inset Hymns in Hebrew Narrative* (Sheffield: JSOT, 1992) 86-87.

human and divine agencies suggest a complex intertwining and subtle dialectic between the divine plan and human freedom that cannot be easily distinguished or separated in either the prose or the poetic account.

Another broad category of proposed differences between the narrative of Judges 4 and the poetry of Judges 5 involves whether one or the other version reflects a feminine versus a masculine perspective. Mieke Bal argues that cultural studies of oral cultures suggest that certain genres tend to be tied to women and other genres to men. Feminine genres tend more toward lyric poetry, contain few details, and highlight activities around the village and family. Bal finds these feminine characteristics more evident in the poem of Judges 5. The poem's images of Deborah as "a mother in Israel" (5:7), Jael as "most blessed of women" (5:24), and the pathos of the scene with Sisera's mother and her female advisers suggest a feminine orientation to the song of Judges 5. In contrast, masculine genres tend to favor epic narrative, the inclusion of many details, and adventures centered outside the village or family. Bal finds these elements more clearly in the narrative prose of Judges 4 and argues that the main plot line in the narrative of chap. 4 wrestles with the distinctly masculine issue of honor and shame in relation to a woman: The two males in the story, Barak and Sisera, lose honor and status because of a woman, Jael, who either kills or steals glory from the men.[32] Other interpreters have argued the opposite. The narrative in Judges 4, they suggest, displays more of a woman's perspective, celebrating the prowess of a woman and upsetting the expected conventions of a typical male heroic tale. On the other hand, they maintain that the poem in Judges 5 has a more masculine character, since the focus is on the battle with Sisera's army and God's fighting on behalf of the Israelites.

As with the false dichotomy of divine versus human agency, both the prose and the poetic accounts defy any simple attempts to separate them into discrete masculine and feminine perspectives. The prose account in Judges 4 does feature powerful women in Deborah and Jael. Some of Barak's glory as a

male warrior does fall upon Jael when Barak discovers that she is the one who has killed the Canaanite general Sisera (4:9, 22). However, Barak remains the victorious leader of Israel's militia who defeated all of Sisera's army. That Barak received help from God (4:6-7, 15) and from Deborah (4:8-9, 14) as well as from Jael is not a matter of great shame. Rahab, the Canaanite harlot, helped the faithful Joshua and his army in conquering the city of Jericho with no shame or dishonor upon Joshua for having received aid from a woman (Josh 2:1-24; 6:22-25). The death of Sisera at the hands of Jael is a different matter. A great warrior's being killed at the hands of a woman was an ignoble death (Judg 9:52-57). However, the Canaanite Sisera had already been dishonored by his retreat and abandonment of his army; Jael's killing of him simply caused him further dishonor.

In the present form of the text, with the song of chap. 5 following the prose account, the reader sees both Barak and Deborah together singing a song (5:1). Barak does not appear woefully shamed or dishonored but praised along with others. The song does not praise only men or only women but all those who participated in saving Israel: God (5:2-5, 20-21, 31), Deborah (5:7, 12), Jael (5:24-27), some of the Israelite tribes (5:13-18), and Barak (5:9, 12). The praise of God begins and ends the song as an affirmation that God integrates and works across the many boundaries of gender, tribe, nation, and creation within the poem (male/female, Israelite/non-Israelite, some tribes/not other tribes, human/non-human forces of nature). The only boundary that remains is the one between Israel and their Canaanite foes. But even that boundary may be crossed by God in the light of 5:31, which speaks of judgment upon the Lord's enemies and blessing upon the Lord's friends. The next verse tells us that "the Israelites did what was evil in the sight of the LORD" (6:1), suggesting that Israel will soon become again God's enemies, virtually indistinguishable from the Canaanite enemies of God (2:1-5). God will fight against Israel until it again cries in distress.

The existence of two versions of the same event, the narrative in Judges 4 and the poetic song in Judges 5, raises issues of relative dating and dependence of each text on the

32. Bal, *Murder and Difference*, 111-34; A Globe, "The Literary Structure and Unity of the Song of Deborah," *JBL* 93 (1974) 495.

other. Which of the two accounts is earlier? Was one account written on the basis of the other? Or were the narrative and the poetic versions written independently from a common source and later combined? Most scholars agree that the poetic song in Judges 5 is the earlier of the two accounts because of its archaic Hebrew language and style. The prose narrative reflects standard classical Hebrew from a time later in Israel's history. The most plausible reconstruction of the composition of the two accounts may be that the poetic Song of Deborah and Barak was written first. The narrative of Judges 4 was composed on the basis of the earlier poem in Judges 5 and perhaps also in the light of the Ehud story in 3:12-30. Notable echoes exist between the Deborah-Barak-Jael story and the preceding Ehud narrative. The prose version retold the story with important thematic differences and thus may have functioned independently for a time. But eventually an editor brought the prose (Judges 4) and poetic (Judges 5) versions together and placed them within the larger framework and collection of individual judge stories to make up the present book of Judges.

Two principal motifs intimated in Judges 4–5 will play an increasing role in portraying the gradual deterioration of Israel under the judges in chapters that follow. The first motif is the leader's desire for reassurance or a sign when called to fight against the enemy. In 4:6-10, the Israelite general Barak places a condition on accepting God's call to go and fight the Canaanite oppressors. Barak refuses to go into battle unless Deborah, the prophet

of the Lord, goes along with him. As we move into the later stories in Judges, this motif of a leader's need for divine assurance or a sign will become more prominent in the stories of Gideon (6:36-40) and Jephthah (11:29-33). Increasingly, the leaders of Israel will be less trusting and require more divine guarantees to bolster their confidence. The second motif, which will become ever more significant in the deterioration of Israel's social and political fabric, is the disunity within the tribal confederation of Israel. The Song of Deborah and Barak in Judges 5 chastises several of Israel's tribes for their failure to join the other Israelite tribes in the battle against the Canaanites (Judg 5:13-18, 23). This theme of tribal disunity will recur in mild form in the Gideon episode (8:1-3), but it will begin to grow more grave in Abimelech's killing of his own brothers (9:5), in Jephthah's killing of 42,000 of his Ephraimite countrymen (12:1-6), in Samson's inability to lead any Israelite tribal coalitions at all and Judah's betrayal of Samson (15:9-17), and ultimately in the civil war among the Israelite tribes against the tribe of Benjamin in the concluding section of Judges (20:12-48). Thus Judges 4–5 begins to plant the seed for the gradual decline in Israel's fortunes and sense of unity as we move through the book of Judges. However, the story of Deborah, Barak, and Jael remains for the most part a positive portrait of a time in Israel when judges ruled effectively and faithfully as the Canaanites are defeated, the Lord is praised, and "the land had rest forty years" (5:31).

Judges 4:1-24, The Story of Sisera's Death

COMMENTARY

Judges 4 is a narrative account of a coalition of three judge-like figures who save Israel only through the combination of unique contributions that each person makes. Deborah is a prophet and a judge in the sense of arbitrator. She brings God's word to fight the Canaanites and accompanies the Israelite warriors into battle with words of encouragement and guidance. Barak is the general of Israel's army who leads the victory against

the Canaanites but fails to kill his Canaanite counterpart, the general Sisera. Jael is not an Israelite but a Kenite who invites Sisera, the Canaanite general, into her tent and then proceeds to kill him. All three contribute to saving Israel, but none of them can lay sole claim to the title of "judge" in this period. This shifting and inconclusive identity of the major judge in this story will contribute to a sense of suspense within the narrative plot as well as the theological significance of the story.

4:1-3. The cycle of events in this chapter begins in the same way the earlier judge paradigm had established (2:11-19) and the previous model of Othniel had confirmed (3:7-11). "After Ehud died," Israel "again" begins to do evil in God's sight (v. 1). The death of the previous judge Ehud leaves a vacuum into which Israel slips in disobedience to God. The next step is also expected: God sells Israel into the hand of an enemy, King Jabin of Canaan. The Canaanites are the fourth set of enemies Israel has faced in this first phase of the judges period. With the judge Othniel, the enemy had come from some distance in the far north and east in Mesopotamia. With Ehud, the enemy had been a closer neighbor to the east, Moab. Shamgar fought against the Philistines, Israel's close neighbor to the west. Now for the first time Israel faces a more internal enemy, King Jabin of Canaan, who is said to reign in the far north of Canaan at Hazor (v. 2). Many interpreters believe this King Jabin may be related in some way to the "King Jabin of Hazor" who led a coalition of Canaanite kings against Joshua and Israel as reported in Joshua 11. Joshua successfully conquered the coalition, and Josh 11:10 notes that Joshua "took Hazor, and struck its king down with the sword." Is this the same Jabin, or is "Jabin" a common royal name among Canaanite rulers? Some scholars suggest that Judges 4–5 is a retelling of the same event as recorded in Joshua 11 with some changes. Others suggest that the name of Jabin has been imported into the present text of Judges 4, since Jabin plays no active role in the story itself and is never mentioned in the song in Judges 5. The mention of "the kings of Canaan" in 5:19 may have occasioned the link with the account in Joshua 11. In any case, King Jabin remains a shadowy figure in the background to Judges 4; general Sisera is the one Canaanite who grabs the spotlight and generates any narrative interest in the story.

As we would expect, the next step in the cycle of events is Israel's cry to God for help (v. 3). However, a note is added that the Canaanite commander "had nine hundred chariots of iron." The mention of iron provides a glimpse into the major cultural shift in technology occurring in the ancient Near East at this time from the earlier Bronze Age to the early phase of the Iron Age (1200–1000 BCE). The Canaanites were the more established, powerful, and richer culture in comparison to the Israelites. Thus the Canaanites had access to the most recent military technology, which they used to maintain their power and "cruelly" oppress the Israelites. The Canaanite oppression lasted a total of twenty years, slightly longer than the eighteen years before Ehud and the eight years before Othniel (3:8, 14).

4:4-11. In the previous judge stories, Israel's cry of distress had immediately caused God to raise up a judge to save Israel (3:9, 15). Thus we expect the next person named to be the judge who will lead Israel's army against the enemy. That person is Deborah, a woman described as a prophet, the wife of Lappidoth (or alternatively "woman of torches"), and who was "judging" Israel. The Hebrew word "judge" (שֹׁפֵט *šōpēṭ*) can have the sense either of ruler and military commander (as in the preceding judge stories) or arbitrator of disputes (as in the story of Moses in Exod 18:13-16). Deborah fulfills the latter sense of judging as she sits "under the palm of Deborah" in the hill country of Ephraim and the Israelites come to her for judgment in disputes (v. 5).

As the reader wonders whether Deborah is, indeed, the expected judge or deliverer sent to lead Israel into battle against the Canaanites, the narrative introduces a second possible candidate. His name is Barak. Deborah delivers an oracle from the Lord to Barak, commanding him to take ten thousand warriors from the tribes of Naphtali and Zebulun to fight the Canaanites. God promises to "draw out" the Canaanite commander Sisera with his chariots and troops, "and I will give him into your hand" (v. 7). The vocabulary of God's giving the enemy "into your hand" echoes similar words used for the preceding judges (3:10, 28). We now expect Barak to step immediately into the shoes of previous judges, bravely leading Israel against Sisera and his troops. But Barak interrupts with unexpected words of caution and hesitation. Barak seeks the reassurance of Deborah's presence with him as he goes out into battle. If Deborah is willing to go with him, Barak will go. But if Deborah will not go with him, Barak will not go, in spite of God's direct command to him (v. 8).

Barak's request for Deborah's presence has been variously interpreted. Some see Barak here as cowardly, afraid, and distrusting of God. A real judge would not need the assistance of anyone, much less a woman, to lead Israel into battle. In this understanding, the request for Deborah's presence would be unusual and unnecessary. Other interpreters see Barak's request as a gracious and insistent invitation to Deborah as God's prophet to join him so that she might bless the military expedition and share in the glory of the Lord's victory over the Canaanites. In this understanding, it would not be unusual for the woman prophet Deborah to accompany a military expedition and offer divine oracles of encouragement and strategy. The narrator does not provide an explicit evaluation of Barak's statement, and so we are left to wonder about Barak's inner motivation.

Deborah's response to Barak is no less ambiguous. Her reply is emphatic: "I will *surely* go with you." But what is the tone of her speech? "Of course I will go with you, Barak; that's what I would expect to do, since I am a prophet of God and this is God's battle." Or is the tone more like this: "Well, all right, if you insist, I will surely go with you, but it really shows a lack of trust in God on your part"? The same ambiguity pertains to the second half of her response, and here the NRSV and the NIV translations differ significantly in the nuances they give to the Hebrew. In the NRSV, Deborah says she will surely go with Barak, but Barak should know that the road on which he is going will not lead to his glory, since the Lord will give his counterpart, the Canaanite commander Sisera, "into the hand of a woman" (v. 9). Although susceptible to either a negative or a positive reading, the NRSV translation could suggest that Deborah's words are merely a statement of fact that does *not* reflect negatively on Barak's request for her presence with him. Losing some glory to a woman may well be a trade-off Barak is quite willing to make in exchange for Deborah's prophetic presence with his army. The NIV gives a more one-sided and negative interpretation to Deborah's response. She agrees to

go with Barak, but she adds, "because of the way you are going about this, the honor will not be yours, for the LORD will hand Sisera over to a woman" (v. 9). Here the lack of honor for Barak is interpreted as a negative punishment for the unfaithful request to have Deborah accompany him. The way Barak is going about this is all wrong and a punishable offense against God.

In my judgment, the NIV interprets Deborah's statement too narrowly. As the NRSV rightly translates, Deborah's response is ambiguous and should be translated in a way that maintains the uncertainty. The narrative is intentionally drawing the reader in to ponder the ambiguous possibilities in the statements of these two characters. The ambiguity is part of a larger narrative strategy that builds suspense and leads the reader on to determine who the real judge might be. In the flow of the narrative, the reader initially would think that Deborah was the judge (v. 4), but then Barak takes over as a more likely candidate (vv. 6-7). However, Barak's ambiguous statement makes us think twice about his suitability (v. 8). Now Deborah's declaration that Sisera (the individual or Sisera and his whole army?) will be delivered into the hand of a woman causes us to wonder whether Deborah will after all emerge as the true judge and heroine in place of Barak (v. 9). But we are not sure at this point, and so we read on. Deborah does go up with Barak to the place of battle at Kedesh, and Barak does summon his ten thousand warriors, so the stage is now set for the battle to begin (v. 10).

One peculiar note suddenly drops into the story without any preparation. It is a piece of information provided by the narrator to the reader that will become important later in the story. A man named Heber from the non-Israelite nation of the Kenites had separated himself from the other Kenites and encamped "near Kedesh," the place where the battle is about to begin. The Kenites had a special relationship with Israel in that Moses' father-in-law, Hobab, had been a Kenite (v. 11; see 1:16). One interesting possibility concerning Heber the Kenite is the Kenites' traditional association with iron smithing and iron work (see Gen 4:22). Although Heber had a familial association with Israel, had Heber separated from the other Kenites in order to ply his trade as an iron smith with the 900 iron chariots of the Canaanites? Is Heber an ally of Israel or of Canaan? Later in this story, we will learn that "there was peace between King Jabin of Hazor and the clan of Heber the Kenite" (v. 17). That fact will play a role in the ongoing suspense and drama of the story. For now, the note about Heber the Kenite (v. 11) is simply inserted between Israel's preparing for battle (vv. 6-10) and Canaan's preparing for battle (vv. 12-13). Heber's placement between Israel and Canaan signifies his ambiguous position on the narrative boundary between them. With all the other ambiguities of this story, the reader wonders what the role of this liminal character and his clan will be.

4:12-16. The Canaanite commander Sisera hears of Israel's preparations for war and assembles "all his chariots, nine hundred chariots of iron, and all the troops" (vv. 12-13). As for Israel, Deborah speaks an oracle of divine encouragement to Barak: "Up! For this is the day on which the LORD has given Sisera into your hand" (v. 14). What does this oracle mean? Has the earlier oracle that Sisera would be given into the hand of a woman (v. 9) been rescinded? Or is this merely a way of saying that Barak and his forces will win a general victory against the Canaanites, even though Sisera himself will fall under the hand of a woman? Again, we as readers do not know. We do know that God is with the Israelites and fights for them as the divine warrior. Thus the Lord throws Sisera's army and chariots into confusion and panic, just as the Lord had done against Pharaoh and his chariots in the exodus from Egypt (Exod 14:24). Barak defeats the entire army of Sisera with the Lord's help, except for Sisera, who runs away on foot (vv. 15-16).

4:17-22. As in v. 11, the narrator interrupts the flow of the story with another note informing the reader that the fleeing Sisera has escaped to the tent of Jael, who is the wife of Heber the Kenite. Sisera had fled there, "for there was peace" between Heber's Kenite clan and the Canaanite king Jabin, whose army Sisera commanded (v. 17). Now we surmise that Heber had separated from the other Kenites (v. 11) in order to ally himself and his family with the Canaanites.

The narrative resumes with Jael welcoming Sisera warmly into her tent, addressing him as "my lord" and insisting that he need have no fear. He enters Jael's tent, and she covers him with a rug. He asks for "a little water to drink," and Jael gives him sleep-inducing milk instead (vv. 18-19). Jael here acts as a mother. The mighty warrior Sisera is turned into a little child, tucked into bed for the night and hiding from any monsters who might threaten him. Sisera instructs Jael to stand watch at the entrance to the tent. If anyone comes by and asks "Is anyone here?" Sisera tells Jael to say no (v. 20). The question in Hebrew (היש־פה איש *hăyēš-pōh 'îš*) can mean literally, "Is a *man* here?" Ironically, Sisera's own words reveal that his masculinity has been reduced to that of an infant. On the surface, Sisera seems safe and secure in the womb-like tent of mother Jael, falling asleep from the weariness of battle and the heaviness of milk.

The story suddenly takes a dramatic and wholly unexpected turn. Jael takes a sharp tent peg and a hammer "in her hand" and drives the peg forcefully into the soft temple of Sisera's sleeping head so that he dies (v. 21). Commentators have long observed the sudden shift from maternal to sexual imagery here in a scene of reverse rape, the woman Jael forcibly thrusting and violently penetrating Sisera's body. The sexual imagery will become more explicit in the poetic version in 5:26-27.[33] The Israelite general Barak pursues Sisera but arrives after Jael has killed Sisera in his sleep. Jael welcomes Barak into her tent and shows him the body of Sisera, "lying dead, with the tent peg in his temple" (v. 22). Is Barak happy to share the glory with Jael? Is he despondent that he did not have the singular glory of killing his Canaanite counterpart? The narrative does not tell us.

Now the perplexity over whether Deborah or Barak is the true judge or hero is in some ways made even more complicated. Jael, a non-Israelite woman, is added to the list of those who helped save Israel from its Canaanite enemy. She replaces Deborah as

33. See Robert Alter, *The Art of Biblical Poetry* (New York: Basic, 1985) 43-50; Meir Sternberg, *The Poetics of Biblical Narrative: Ideological Literature and the Drama of Reading* (Bloomington: Indiana University Press, 1981) 270-83; Bal, *Murder and Difference*, 111-34; and Danna Nolan Fewell and David Gunn, "Women, Men, and the Authority of Violence in Judges 4:1 and 5," *JAAR* 58 (1990) 389-411.

the one who fulfills Deborah's oracle that Sisera would be given "into the hand of a woman" (vv. 9, 21). Neither Deborah, Barak, nor Jael emerges as the singular hero or judge in this story. Moreover, the puzzle continues with new questions. What motivated Jael to kill Sisera? Why did she defy the peace agreement between her husband and the Canaanites? Did she act out of a deep loyalty to Israel and Israel's God? Or did she realize the Israelites had won the battle and so defect to the Israelite cause for pragmatic reasons to save her own life? Her motives remain a mystery. All we know is that God used Jael for the purpose of defeating Israel's enemy, no matter what her motives were.

4:23-24. The artful indirection, suspense, and sharing of glory among Deborah, Barak, and Jael point ultimately to the overarching and integrating agency of God. In the final analysis, "*God* subdued King Jabin of Canaan" (v. 23). God and Jabin were the shadowy but ultimate power brokers in the battle between Israel and Canaan. In that ultimate struggle, it was God who prevailed. But God's purposes were achieved through a coalition of human actors, none of whom could take ultimate credit for the victory.[34] The final verse in the narrative suggests that Israel continued to wage war against other Canaanite forces of King Jabin for a time, bearing harder and

34. Yairah Amit, "Judges 4: Its Content and Form," *JSOT* 39 (1987) 89-111.

harder upon him until he was destroyed (v. 24).

The climactic point in chap. 4 is not the battle but the scene in Jael's tent and the assassination of Sisera. Several similarities between this central scene in chap. 4 and the stories of the preceding two judges, Ehud and Shamgar (3:12-31), stand out. Like Ehud, Jael kills the enemy alone in a private room through an act of deception. Like Ehud, who had brought tribute to King Eglon to seek his favor, Jael offers milk, refuge, and rest to Sisera. The same Hebrew verb (תקע *tāqaʿ*, "to drive," "to thrust") is used for Ehud's assassination of Eglon (3:21) and for Jael's assassination of Sisera (4:21). Just as Ehud's deed was unexpectedly done by his left hand, so also Jael's deed was unexpectedly done through a foreign woman's hand (4:9). Like Shamgar, who fashioned an unconventional weapon out of an oxgoad (3:31), Jael used a tent peg as her unusual weapon. Thus the three judge stories—Ehud, Shamgar, and Deborah-Barak-Jael—are tied together as examples of temporary victories that God leads on behalf of an oppressed Israel through the agency of unexpected human agents. This first phase of the judge stories in 3:7–5:31 portrays faithfulness and effectiveness on the part of Israel's leaders and judges. When the judge or judges are alive, Israel prospers. But when the judge dies, Israel reverts to its old evil ways.

REFLECTIONS

1. The most dramatic feature of this story is the image of two strong, independent, and courageous women: Deborah, the prophet and arbitrator of disputes, and Jael, the non-Israelite assassin. These are not the first strong women in Judges. Achsah, daughter of Caleb and Othniel's wife, had been a strong and independent negotiator with her father (1:11-15). Indeed, the book of Judges contains the largest number of women characters of any book of the Bible, nineteen in all. But the portraits and fate of the women of Judges follow a trajectory similar to that of the judges period as a whole. The judge stories and the portraits of women begin as healthy, strong, and faithful. The first women we encounter all have names (Achsah, Deborah, Jael). But increasingly, as Israel and the judges begin their decline, the fate of women will decline as well. The many women characters become nameless (except for Delilah in the Samson story). Women gradually lose their independent power and become objects and victims, first inadvertently and willingly (Jephthah's daughter and his foolish vow in chap. 11), but then more intentionally and unwillingly (Samson's women in chaps. 14–16, the Levite's concubine in chap. 19, the 400 young virgins of Jabesh-Gilead and the women dancers at Shiloh in chap. 21). The book of Judges offers a wide spectrum of the possible experiences of women, both positive and negative. In the ancient world as well as our own, the health and well-being of women provide an important barometer to measure the core health and values of a society or community.

2. Judges 4 depicts God's working in and through a nexus of human activities involving shared leadership, mutual responsibility, and glory that is distributed among several of the main characters (Deborah, Jael, and Barak). Although many interpreters argue that Judges promotes a strictly centralized and royal mode of leadership (see the refrain in 17:6 and 21:25), Judges 4 also appears to recognize the ability of God to work effectively through more complex systems where power may be decentralized, duties may be distributed, and no one leader need take all the credit or responsibility. As we reflect on various models or polities within our families, congregations, denominations, or other political entities, we may be assured that God is able to work through any variety of structures or systems. The question may be what is most appropriate and helpful in a given context, time, and tradition.

3. The Bible honors the common ancient Near Eastern custom of hospitality to strangers and sojourners. Abraham and Sarah welcomed three strangers who turned out to be the Lord present among them (Genesis 18). Hebrews 13:2 uses their story to commend its readers to show hospitality to strangers, "for by doing that some have entertained angels without knowing it" (NRSV). Many of Israel's laws urged hospitality to strangers and sojourners, since Israel had been a sojourner in Egypt (Exod 22:21; Lev 19:33-34; Deut 10:19). Jael breaks this hospitality code rather egregiously in first welcoming and then killing Sisera, the Canaanite general. Not only does she break the hospitality code, but she also breaks the peace pact between the Canaanites and her own Kenite clan. Yet the narrative never explicitly condemns or raises concerns about her act; indeed, her slaying of Sisera is praised in the next chapter in the song (Judg 5:24-27). But Jael's act inevitably raises difficult moral questions, and the narrative does not let the reader off the hook by providing much insight into Jael's motives or thoughts. On this issue, the story in Judges 4 draws the reader into moral reflection without providing an explicit evaluation. The situation is similar to the scene of Moses killing the Egyptian foreman in Exod 2:11-15; no overt moral assessment is made in the text of Moses' act of using violence for the sake of social justice. However, the story raises the questions and issues in a way that forces the reader to wrestle with them.

4. Two narrative strategies seem to be working at cross-purposes in Judges 4. On one hand, the cyclical framework (4:1-3, 23) commonly found in the other judge stories suggests a foreordained sequence of events with God clearly in control. The predictability of the sequence of events affirms the ultimate sovereignty of God. On the other hand, the intensity of misdirection and suspense throughout Judges 4 (will the real judge please stand up?) suggests unpredictability and the need for God to adjust the divine plan to make room for human freedom and decisions. God's oracle through Deborah promises Barak that the Lord will deliver Sisera into his hand (4:7). However, his request that Deborah accompany him seems to cause a change in God's oracle and plan: "the LORD will sell Sisera into the hand of a woman" (4:9). But later, Deborah reiterates that God has given Sisera into Barak's hand (4:14). In the end, God accomplishes the salvation promised, but we as human readers ponder the often untraceable combination of human and divine "hands" at work in a given situation. In the end, God's will for the world will prevail, but God also makes adjustment to human freedom and actions along the way. As the people of God, we can be confident that God is at work in and through our lives and communities to accomplish God's will, even when we may be unaware. Indeed, God may work through outsiders or those on the margin of our community in ways we would never expect. At the same time, we can be hopeful that the prayers, words, and actions of faithful individuals, leaders, and communities will be taken seriously and incorporated into the larger plans of God to bring about change and redemption in line with the purposes of God.

Judges 5:1-31, The Song of Deborah and Barak

COMMENTARY

The Song of Deborah and Barak in this chapter is considered by most scholars to be one of the oldest pieces of literature in the Old Testament, perhaps dating to the twelfth century BCE. Its archaic Hebrew vocabulary and syntax have caused significant debates and disagreements about how best to translate certain lines of the poem. A comparison of the NRSV and the NIV translations reveals significant differences in 5:2*a,* 7*a,* 14*a,* and 16*a,* and these represent only the tip of the scholarly iceberg of studies devoted to this ancient poem.[35] The poetic song in Judges 5 provides an alternative version of the story of God's victory and the Canaanites' defeat, narrated in prose form in Judges 4. The song fills in some additional details, adds whole new scenes, lacks the narrative version's important theme of Barak's loss of glory, and adds other themes not present in Judges 4. The song seems to assume that the reader is familiar with the events as narrated in the story. For example, Sisera appears without prior explanation or introduction in the poem itself in 5:20. The poem combines elements of a hymn of praise and a ballad that recounts a story in poetic form.

5:1-11. The overriding theme of this section of the poem is the overwhelming power of God contrasted with the weakness of Israel in the face of the Canaanites' oppression. The song is sung by both Deborah and Barak "on that day," presumably immediately after the victory narrated in chap. 4, which concludes with the same phrase in 4:23, "on that day." This first section is framed by a related pair of themes at the beginning and the end: a note of joy and thanksgiving for those Israelites who volunteered to fight, followed by the refrain, "Bless the LORD!" (vv. 2, 9), and an imperative call for foreign kings to hear the song that Deborah and Barak are singing to the Lord (v. 3), matched by an imperative call to foreign travelers to listen to musicians as "they repeat the triumphs of the LORD" and "of his peasantry in Israel" (vv. 10-11).

Between these two framing sections, the poem draws a striking contrast between the powerful appearance of God as a divine warrior and the oppression and weakness of Israel in the face of the Canaanite tyranny (vv. 4-8). The scene in vv. 4-5 depicts the awesome cosmic disturbances that accompany the appearance of the Lord, who is ready for battle against the enemies of God. As God the divine warrior marches from the east in Edom to Israel, nature erupts with explosive force: Mountains quake; the earth trembles; the skies unleash a powerful and pounding rainstorm.

In contrast, Israel in the days of Shamgar and Jael was weak and powerless. Travelers and caravans avoided the roads for fear of the Canaanites. Normal life and commerce were interrupted (vv. 6-7). The NIV may be closer than the NRSV to the meaning of v. 7*a*: The normal life of Israel's peasantry ceased. This negative situation continued "until" (NIV) Deborah arose "as a mother in Israel." The phrase is probably more than just an endearing title. "Mother in Israel" (אם בישראל *ʾēm bĕyiśrāʾēl*) may represent the place and office of a wise woman prophet who delivers divine oracles to resolve disputes (see 4:5; 2 Sam 20:16-19).[36] Verse 8*a* is difficult to understand, having to do either with Israel's apostasy in choosing new gods (NIV and NRSV) or, more probably, with Deborah's choosing

35. A few representative studies include Michael D. Coogan, "A Structural and Literary Analysis of the Song of Deborah," *CBQ* 40 (1978) 143-66; Frank M. Cross and David Noel Freedman, *Studies in Ancient Yahwistic Poetry* (Missoula, Mont.: Scholars Press, 1975); and A. Globe, "The Literary Structure and Unity of the Song of Deborah," *JBL* 93 (1974) 493-512. On the importance of contrasts in the structure of the poem, see G. Gerleman, "The Song of Deborah in Light of Stylistics," *VT* (1951) 168-79; and Frank Yamada, "The Rhetorical Use of Contrast in the Song of Deborah (Judges 5:1)," a paper presented at the Society of Biblical Literature Annual Meeting, San Francisco, November 22, 1997.

36. Watts, *Psalm and Story,* 90.

new recruits for Israel's army. Unfortunately, these new recruits had no weapons: "not a shield or spear was seen" (v. 8). Thus a weak and weaponless Israel will face the mighty Canaanites in battle. But the determining factor will not be the relative weakness or strength of these human forces. In this holy war conflict, the one truly relevant factor will be that God, the powerful divine warrior, will be fighting for Israel and against Canaan. Thus the rag tag army of Israel marches down from its humble highland settlements to the lowland walled and gated cities of Canaan: "Then down to the gates marched the people of the LORD" (v. 11*b*).

5:12-18. The important contrast in this section is between those Israelite tribes that valiantly joined the battle and those other tribes who were reluctant or refused to do so. The section begins with a call to Deborah to "utter a song" as a call to battle and a call to Israel's military leader, Barak, to lead away his captives. A "remnant" (שריד *śārîd*) of all the Israelite tribes responds to their leaders' call to battle as they march down "against the mighty" Canaanites (v. 13). This faithful remnant includes the tribes of Ephraim, Benjamin, Zebulun, Issachar, Naphtali, and the half-tribe of Manasseh, known as Machir (vv. 14-15*a*, 18). However, other Israelite tribes were hesitant and stayed at home rather than help their fellow Israelites. The "clans of Reuben" experienced "great searchings of heart" in deciding whether to leave their flocks of sheep to go to war (vv. 15*b*-16). The east Jordan tribe of Gilead refused to cross the Jordan River and come to the aid of Israel's other tribes. The tribes of Dan and Asher preferred the relative security of their ships and the seacoast to the dangers of war (v. 17). The tribes' reluctance reveals a lack of trust in God and a lack of commitment to the unity of Israel as the people of God. Nevertheless, the war against Canaan begins with an already weak Israel at half strength but, more important, with God fighting on Israel's side.

5:19-22. This section of the poem narrates the battle scene between Israel's God and the Canaanite kings. The section begins with the confident Canaanite kings who come and fight beside the waters of Megiddo (v. 19). The section ends with the loud beating of Canaanite horses' hooves galloping in retreat (v. 22). On the surface, it seemed that Canaan's army was fighting only a weak and weaponless Israelite militia. But Israel's God was also fighting. God used the forces of nature, the stars and the rainstorm, to defeat the Canaanite general Sisera and his army of chariots (vv. 20-21; see 4:2). The torrential rains and flooding torrents of the wadi Kishon rendered Sisera's chariots useless in the lowland mud. God unleashed forces far beyond the control or power of Israel's small human army to win the victory over Israel's Canaanite oppressor.

5:23-30. The next poetic unit juxtaposes a vehement curse and a lavish blessing. The curse is aimed at a presumably Israelite clan, Meroz, for its unwillingness to "come to the help of the LORD . . . against the mighty" (v. 23). The blessing is pronounced upon Jael, the non-Israelite wife of Heber the Kenite, who is remembered as "the most blessed of women" (v. 24). The rest of the unit retells in gory detail the way in which Jael assassinated the Canaanite general Sisera. The unit concludes with a poignant scene depicting Sisera's mother waiting in vain for her son to return home from battle.

Sisera had come to this "tent-dwelling woman" and asked her for water. But Jael gave him milky "curds in a lordly bowl," a mild sedative to set him up for her deadly deed (v. 25). The action slows down to a slow-motion crawl in the next two verses as Jael takes a tent peg in one hand and a mallet in the other. She then strikes Sisera with a crushing blow to the head, shattering and piercing his temple. Unlike the narrative version of this scene, where Sisera is lying asleep in the tent (4:18-21), here he appears to be standing or perhaps sitting in a chair. When Jael penetrated his body with the tent peg, "he sank, he fell, he lay still . . . he sank, he fell . . . he fell dead" (v. 27). Sisera falls dead literally in Hebrew "between her feet" or "between her legs" (בין רגליה *bên ragleyhā*, v. 27), a sexual euphemism found elsewhere in the Bible (Deut 28:57; Ezek 16:25). The sexual overtones of this death scene have been frequently noted, reaching as far back as the ancient Jewish rabbinical interpreters. This woman nurturer-turned-warrior symbolizes the close interplay of sexuality and death, of rape and war.[37] But the tables have been turned. Used to killing men and raping woman, general Sisera is himself killed and "raped" by a woman. The non-Israelite Jael here becomes a cipher for Israel and Sisera a cipher for Canaan's military might. The supposedly weaker Israel had been repeatedly oppressed and pillaged by the arrogant Canaanites in the past. But now with the help of Israel's divine warrior, mighty Canaan has fallen into defeat and death.

For the closing scene of this unit, the narrator turns our attention to a scene in a Canaanite city where the mother of general Sisera waits at her window for her son to return from battle. Sisera's mother wonders aloud and discusses with her women advisers why her son is taking such a long time to return (vv. 28-29). Their arrogant confidence that Sisera has surely been victorious is matched only by their greedy anticipation of fine clothes and other spoil that Sisera will steal from those whom he has defeated (v. 30). But one line in this chatter of smug Canaanite women leaps out in the light of what has happened earlier in the poem. One of the reasons they imagine for the delay in his return is the time it takes to rape the women of those who have been defeated. The NRSV and the NIV translations read "a girl or two

37. Susan Niditch, "Eroticism and Death in the Tale of Jael," in *Gender and Difference in Ancient Israel*, ed. Peggy Day (Minneapolis: Fortress, 1989) 43-57.

for every man" (v. 30). The Hebrew is even more crude: "A womb [רחם *raham*] or two for every man." But these Canaanite women (and their men) have not reckoned with the "one or two women" who are the heroes of this poem, Deborah and Jael. Nor have they reckoned with the God of Israel, against whom no human army can withstand. Thus Deborah, Barak, Jael, and God upended the prideful plans of Sisera and his Canaanite soldiers: the Canaanites "got no spoils of war" (v. 19), and Sisera "fell . . . between her feet . . . there he fell dead" (v. 27).

5:31. The poem comes to a close with a final prayer that contrasts the enemies and the friends of the Lord: "So perish all your enemies, O LORD!" The defeat and death of the Canaanites represent the fate of all God's enemies, those powers and principalities that resist the will of God for Israel and the world. But the poem requests of God a very different fate for those who are faithful and love God: "But may your friends be like the sun as it rises in its might." After the turbulent rainstorm and the clouds of battle and the stars fighting from heaven have concluded their work (vv. 4, 20-21), they now can step aside and allow a faithful Israel to assume its place of honor like the sun shining in full strength in the sky. Judges 5, so filled with the noise and tumult of war and earthquakes and thunderstorms, now ends quietly with the words, "And the land had rest forty years."

REFLECTIONS

1. The dominant feature of the Song of Deborah and Barak is its series of strong and dramatic contrasts: the powerful divine warrior and a weak Israel, the willing bravery of some Israelite tribes and the passive reluctance of others, the defeated human army of the Canaanites and God's victorious forces of nature and the stars of heaven, Jael as a woman killing and "raping" Sisera, and Sisera's mother under the illusion that her son would be the one killing and raping. Poetry is elevated speech that heightens contrasts, interprets reality, discerns truth, stretches imagination, and leads us deeper into mysteries in more playful, poignant, and powerful ways than ordinary prosaic discourse. Judges 4 provides us with the prose narrative version of the story, but the poetry of Judges 5 leads us to see more deeply the meanings and mysteries of God, who fights against God's enemies and for God's friends. One of the ministerial tasks of preaching, teaching, and counseling in a community of faith is to help people take up the prosaic and mundane realities of their lives and the events of our world and explore the deeper and divine realities, truths, and mysteries that lie embedded within them. The poetry of Judges 5 provides one of many models for thinking about ministry as poetic reflection on the seemingly mundane and ordinary parts of our lives. Just as poetry interprets prose, so also the pastor interprets the everyday life of his or her parishioners.

2. If the poem of Judges 5 is a series of contrasts, the primary contrast is between God's power and effective use of forces from outside Israel versus the weakness and the timidity of Israel's contribution to the major battle with the Canaanites. Israel was relatively poor, militarily weak, virtually weaponless, and not unified in its resolve. The source of Israel's salvation would have to come from outside itself—from God, from the forces of nature that God used against Canaan (the thunderstorm), and from Jael the Kenite. Similarly, as Christians we confess that our salvation against the enemy forces of sin and death is rooted, not in our own efforts or capacities to save ourselves, but in the work of God and the agents through whom God works to bring to us the words and deeds of God's sustaining love. Just as Israel was saved through God's complex integration of forces of nature, Jael the Kenite, and the bravery of some of the Israelite tribes, so, too, God works to ensure that we are nurtured in our faith and life through a complex integration of people, communities, family, friends, gifts of nature, and the like. Life in its fullness is a true gift from God.

3. Although God and forces outside of Israel itself were largely responsible for the victory against the Canaanites, the poem also makes clear that it matters whether God's own people remain unified and work together toward the purposes of God. God has chosen in some way to be contingent on active human participation in the ongoing drama of God's saving ways with God's people and the world. God's people ought not to take lightly the obligation to help one another, particularly in times of crisis, threat, or danger. The body of Christ requires all its members to be united together under the one head, who is Christ: "If one member suffers, all suffer together with it; if one member is honored, all rejoice together with it" (1 Cor 12:26 NRSV). The poem in Judges 5 is an important model in this regard. The prose story of Judges 4 tells of how Barak lost glory when Jael killed the Canaanite commander Sisera before Barak had the opportunity (4:9, 22). But the poem of Judges 5 shows Barak immediately afterward joining Deborah in singing not only the praises of God but also the praises of Jael, the "most blessed of women" (5:24). Some commentators argue that the song in Judges 5 was originally only the Song of Deborah (5:7) and that Barak's name was added only later to the introduction in 5:1. If that is true, the present form of the text still affirms Barak's willingness to overcome his loss of glory and rejoice together with other members of the community.

4. Some features of this poem may be troubling to those people of God who cherish the hopes for peace (Isa 2:1-11), the resistance to violence (Matt 5:38-48), and the refusal to take vengeance (Rom 12:9) that are themes we find elsewhere in the Bible. What do we do with Judges 5 and its image of God as divine warrior; the ruthless violence of Jael against Sisera, which seems to be applauded; and the desire for vengeance against one's enemies (5:31)? These are not issues that can be easily resolved, because they require ongoing reflection over all of Scripture and its diverse witnesses. But we can offer a few brief guidelines.

First of all, the image of God as divine warrior is pervasive throughout many different traditions in the Old Testament and even into the New Testament. But typically, as in Judges 5, God as divine warrior fights on behalf of the weak and the powerless against arrogant forces of oppression, death, and rebellion against God. When Jesus sent out seventy of his followers to preach and to heal and they returned to him, Jesus proclaimed that underlying the apparently mundane character of their ministry was an ongoing cosmic battle against the power of evil: "I watched Satan fall from heaven like a flash of lightning" (Luke 10:18 NRSV).

Second, the violence of Jael against Sisera was done by a non-Israelite acting as an advocate for the sake of others, and not to save herself. The poem portrays the act as

God's just punishment upon the arrogance and greed of an oppressor as exemplified in the scene with Sisera's mother (5:28-30). The narrator of the poem does not present the story of Jael as a model to be emulated by God's people when they are attacked so much as it is a portrait of the judgment God will bring upon those who live by violence and oppression. The Bible is fully aware of the ambiguity and danger in any use of violence even for reasons we may convince ourselves are just, but there are times when oppressors will bring God's judgment of violence on themselves. Sisera is one such example.

Finally, the prayer to God that all the Lord's enemies might perish (5:31) relinquishes this natural human desire for vengeance to God. The petitioner can let go of these negative feelings toward an enemy and entrust any just vengeance to God. The book of Psalms contains many so-called imprecatory psalms asking God for vengeance, and they serve this positive purpose, letting go of our sinful human inclinations to do vengeance and entrusting God to perform whatever justice needs to be done (see Psalms 7; 54; 143).

JUDGES 6:1–10:5, THE DOWNHILL SLIDE BEGINS: GIDEON AND ABIMELECH; TOLA AND JAIR

OVERVIEW

The accounts of the individual judges or deliverers in 3:7–16:31 divide into three major phases of gradual decline in military effectiveness and religious faithfulness. The first phase included Othniel, the model judge (3:7-11), and the two faithful and victorious judges, Ehud (3:12-30) and Deborah (4:1–5:31). As we move into the second phase of the judges period, two major characters stand out: Gideon (6:1–8:35) and his renegade son Abimelech (9:1-57). This second phase of the judges period is marked by a transition from victory and faithfulness to idolatry and the reckless and selfish use of military might and violence. Gideon's initial military victories against the Midianite enemies are impressive, but Gideon is also cowardly, hesitant, and often doubtful of God's ability to accomplish what God has promised. Moreover, Gideon himself shifts from being an idol breaker to an idol maker. Although Gideon secretly destroys an altar of the pagan god Baal early in his career, he later fashions a golden ephod, used in obtaining oracles from God. The ephod itself becomes an object of worship and thus an idol in place of the Lord.

The transition into decline in this second phase of the judges period becomes even more pronounced with Gideon's son Abimelech (9:1-57). Abimelech's mother, a Canaanite, was a concubine or a woman servant whom Gideon had taken as a wife. Abimelech declares himself king over Israel after Gideon's death. He kills Gideon's seventy other Israelite sons to solidify his power. He enlists the support of his mother's people, the residents of Shechem. However, Abimelech eventually falls out of favor even with the Shechemites and ends up destroying their town and killing all the inhabitants of Shechem. Finally, Abimelech himself is killed in an ignoble manner as God's repayment for the disgraceful way in which he ruled over Israel (9:56-57). Previous and effective judges like Ehud and Deborah had united Israel, defeated the enemy, and praised God for their victories. Abimelech does the opposite: He causes divisions within Israel, kills his own people, and fights for his own honor and glory. Abimelech is a sign that the strategy of leading Israel through the temporary leaders called judges is in serious danger of unraveling.

The two minor judges who conclude this second phase, Tola and Jair (10:1-5), provide a parallel to the pair of major judges in this section. The major judge Gideon had been somewhat successful. In a similar way, Tola, the first minor judge, likewise "rose to deliver Israel." But just as the second major judge, Abimelech, had been a failure and gained nothing for Israel, so, too, there is no notice that the second minor judge, Jair, accomplished any deliverance or victory for Israel. The period of the judges has clearly moved into a transition into decline in this second phase. The third phase of the individual judge accounts will slide even further into internal dissension, fragmentation, civil war, and tragedy with the stories of Jephthah (10:6–11:15) and Samson (13:1–16:31). But that downward slide has already begun in this second phase with Gideon, Abimelech, Jair, and Tola.

One recurring image that binds together the stories of Gideon and Abimelech is that of the rock or stone. The first rock is the one on which Gideon sets his offering or present to the angel of God. The angel miraculously causes fire to burn on the rock, consuming Gideon's offering (6:17-21). In this case, the rock is part of a sign of reassurance to Gideon that God is indeed powerfully present with him as he fights the enemy. The second rock or stone image is the "one stone" on which Abimelech kills the seventy sons of Gideon in order to protect his arrogant claim to power (9:5, 18). The third stone is the "millstone" that "one woman" throws from atop the city wall of Shechem onto Abimelech's head, crushing his skull. Lying half-dead next to the millstone, Abimelech orders his servant to kill him with a sword so that people will not say of Abimelech, "A woman killed him" (9:53-54). In these stories, the motif of the stone moves from a sign of divine assurance for Gideon to the stone as an executioner's block for the murder of seventy of Abimelech's half-brothers to a skull-crushing millstone that brings poetic justice onto Abimelech's own head. The stone image further illustrates the transition from faithfulness to disaster in the stories of Gideon and Abimelech.

Judges 6:1–8:35, Gideon: From Idol Breaker to Idol Maker

OVERVIEW

Two features of the story of Gideon the judge merit special attention by the reader. The first feature involves the important alterations or additions to the normal judge cycles of events, first given in 2:11-19. The elements of that recurring cycle include (1) Israel's doing evil, (2) the Lord's becoming angry and sending enemies against Israel, (3) Israel's crying in distress, and (4) the Lord's sending judges to save them. But when the judge died, Israel again did evil, and the cycle would repeat. The Gideon story modifies and expands some of these cyclical elements. First of all, the nature of Israel's evil is left unspecified in the early judge stories (3:12; 4:1). The Gideon account, however, charges the Israelites with the specific and serious evil of worshiping idols and other gods (6:10; 8:24-27, 33-35). Second, the severity of the oppression of the enemy (the Midianites, the Amalekites, and people of the east) is spelled out in much more detail than in the earliest judges accounts (6:2-6). Third, God had previously responded to Israel's cry of distress by immediately sending a judge to save them. In the Gideon story, however, God first rebukes the Israelites for their worship of other gods through the judgment speech of a prophet (6:7-10). Fourth, the Gideon story greatly expands the process of raising up or calling a judge. Gideon is hesitant and resistant to God's call (6:11-24). When Gideon does finally accept God's call to be a judge, he acts like a secretive and cowardly trickster in need of constant reassurance. He is not the bold, confident, and courageous military leader we have seen before in Ehud and Deborah (6:25-40; 7:9-15). Finally, Gideon's function as judge is to be not only a military leader but also a religious leader who unifies the people in the praise and worship of the Lord. The Song of Deborah and Barak in Judges 5, which precedes the Gideon story, illustrates this religious function of the judge. Gideon does well in this regard early on when he breaks down an idol and pulls down an altar to the pagan god Baal (6:25-32). However, by the end of his career, Gideon himself constructs an object that becomes an idol that the Israelites worship as a god (8:25-28). Unlike the Deborah story, which ends in the praise of the Lord, Gideon's story ends in the worship of the Canaanite god Baal-berith (8:33). All of these changes to the typical judges cycle suggest that we have entered into a new and more negative phase in the judges era.

A second feature of the Gideon story is the number of allusions to other important biblical figures and events that echo throughout the episodes. The exodus out of Egypt (Exodus 14–15), the call of Moses (Exodus 3), the idolatry of the golden calf at Mt. Sinai (Exodus 32), the golden calves of King Jeroboam (1 Kings 12), Micah's idolatrous ephod of silver (Judges 17–18), the angels' visit to Abraham and Sarah (Genesis 18), Jacob's combative encounter with God and his name change to "Israel" at Penuel (Genesis 32), Elijah's encounter with the Baal prophets and the burned sacrifice on the altar on Mt. Carmel (1 Kgs 18:20-40), and Joshua's victory at Jericho with the trumpets and the falling city walls all find echoes in this Gideon story. These reverberations suggest that an earlier version of the Gideon story has been significantly reshaped and edited in dialogue with a wide range of other biblical traditions.[38] The task in the commentary below will be to determine the function of these many echoes in the interpretation of the stories. In general, these parallels will reflect negatively on Gideon's career. Gideon is somewhat successful in his military victories, but in the end he loses the most important battle, which is trusting the Lord and keeping Israel faithful.

38. A. Graeme Auld, "Gideon: Hacking at the Heart of the Old Testament," *VT* 39 (1989) 257-67.

Judges 6:1-32, A Timid Gideon Pulls Down Baal's Altar

COMMENTARY

The story of Gideon is a tale of a leader who changes from a timid but faithful leader who relies on God to a bold but ultimately unfaithful leader who takes matters into his own hands. Militarily, Gideon ends up relying on his own skill and direction rather than God. Religiously, Gideon ends up crafting an idol with his own hands that leads Israel away from God. As we begin the Gideon story, however, we encounter a faithful Gideon who works in the mold of Moses when he was called to lead Israel out of the slavery of Egypt (Exodus 3).

6:1-10. The familiar refrain of v. 1 marks the start of another major episode in the judges stories: Israel again does evil in the sight of the Lord (see 2:11; 3:7, 12; 4:1). The quick return to evil on Israel's part is disappointing in the light of the exuberant song that praised God's faithfulness so strongly in Judges 5. In response to Israel's ingratitude, God predictably hands Israel over to an enemy. The previous enemy in chaps. 4–5 had been the native Canaanites. The defeat of the Canaanite army left a power vacuum in Canaan, which allowed marauding desert tribes from the east to invade the land. Thus the enemy God sends against Israel is the desert peoples of the "Midianites," "Amalekites," and "the people of the east" (v. 3). These roving desert nations were traditional enemies of Israel dating back to the period of Moses and the wilderness (Exod 17:8-16; Num 31:1; Deut 25:17-19). The effects of their attacks against Israel are described in great detail. Their military incursions force Israel to hide and live in mountain caves like cowering animals (v. 2). The desert marauders destroy Israel's crops and steal all their livestock (vv. 3-4). The vast number of Midianites is like a locust plague swarming over the land, causing images of the plagues of Egypt to sweep across the mind's eye (Exodus 7–13). This time, however, it is Israel who suffers God's torments.

Israel's economic devastation is immense (v. 6). Predictably, Israel "cried out to the LORD for help."

On the heels of this cry, the reader has come to expect God's swift appointment of a judge or deliverer (3:9, 15). In 4:3-4, God had worked through a woman prophet named Deborah to guide Israel's general Barak to victory. Now in 6:7-8, God again raises up a prophet. But this prophet has a mission different from that of Deborah, who immediately called up Israel's army to fight. This unnamed prophet rebukes Israel, reminding the people that their cry of distress is not to be taken as an automatic guarantee of God's gracious response. The prophet rehearses God's past faithfulness in liberating Israel from Egypt and bringing them to the land of Canaan (vv. 8-9). The single most important obligation Israel had in its relationship with this faithful God was exclusive loyalty to the Lord and the worship of no other gods (v. 10). But God concludes in the words of the anonymous prophet, "You have not given heed to my voice." There is something of a narrative pause here, and we wonder as readers whether God has reached the limits of divine patience. Will God decide at this point not to send a judge to deliver Israel as God had done in the past?

6:11-24. The answer to the question of whether God will respond to Israel's cry comes in the form of an "angel of the LORD." God's deliverance in chaps. 4–5 had begun with Deborah the judge, who "used to sit under the palm of Deborah" (4:5). Similarly, God's deliverance in chap. 6 begins with the "angel" who "sat under the oak at Ophrah" (v. 11). The oak tree belongs to an Israelite named Joash from the Abiezrite clan, which is part of the tribe of Manasseh (Josh 17:2). Joash has a son, Gideon, who has been secretly threshing grain in the unlikely locale of a winepress in order to avoid detection by the Midianites (v. 11). For the first time in Judges, an angel of the Lord speaks directly to one who will become a judge—that is, to Gideon. We have heard this angel speak before to all Israel in 2:1-5. In that speech, the angel had reaffirmed God's unconditional commitment to the covenant with Israel. Yet at the same time, the angel condemned Israel for not tearing down the altars of the

Canaanite gods in their midst. This tension between God's faithfulness and Israel's continual failure to maintain exclusive loyalty to the Lord alone returns as a major theme here in the Gideon story.

The angel addresses young Gideon, hiding in the winepress, with words of affirmation: "The LORD is with you, you mighty warrior." The dissonance between this timid young man hiding in fear from the enemy and the angel's description of him as a "mighty warrior" introduces an ongoing theme in the early part of Gideon's career as a judge. But Gideon is interested in discussing another dissonance with the angel. If the angel's assurance that "the LORD is with us" is true, and if the prophet's earlier words about God saving Israel from Egypt are true, then why "has the LORD cast us off and given us into the hand of Midian" (v. 13)? The angel, to whom the question is addressed, suddenly becomes "the LORD." The Lord turns and points at Gideon and says, in effect, "You are the answer to your own question." God orders Gideon to use "this might of yours" to go and save Israel from the hand of Midian. The Lord concludes by answering Gideon's question with another question: "Am I not sending you?"

However, Gideon intends this encounter with God to remain in the realm of the theoretical and abstract. Gideon does not anticipate becoming an active part of the solution to the problem he posed to the angel. Thus Gideon strenuously objects to God's commission to save Israel from the Midianites. Gideon asks, "How can I deliver Israel?" He is the weakest member of the smallest clan of the tribe of Manasseh. Gideon does not have the qualifications or the resources for the job. But in the ways of the Lord, Gideon's weakness is a virtue. Gideon's inadequacy allows room for what is most important and determinative in this mission: God's presence and God's strength. What really matters in the end, says God, is that "I will be with you" (v. 16). Gideon is still not satisfied. He trades on God's favoring of him and asks for an additional "sign" to prove that "it is you who speak with me" (v. 17).

The angel promptly responds to Gideon's request and miraculously lights a fire on a rock with the tip of a staff. The fire burns Gideon's sacrifice of meat and unleavened bread. Then the angel disappears as soon as the sign or proof of the angel's divine identity is given (vv. 19-21). When Gideon sees this sign, he knows he has seen "the angel of the LORD face to face." A recurring tradition in the OT states that no human can see the dangerous holiness of God face to face and live (13:22; Gen 16:13; 32:30; Exod 20:19; 33:23). Although God's visible angelic form has disappeared, the Lord's invisible presence remains and soothes the terrified Gideon with the words, "Peace be to you. . . . You shall not die." Gideon gratefully responds to this promise by doing the same thing Jacob had done when the angel appeared to him with similar assurance that "I will be with you" (Gen 28:10-22). Like Jacob, Gideon builds an altar near the rock where the sacrifice had been burned. In the light of God's promise of peace, Gideon calls the place "The LORD is peace." At his hometown of Ophrah, Gideon sets up an altar to the Lord (v. 24).

This opening portrait of Gideon connects with three other biblical figures: Moses, Elijah, and Jacob. God's call to Gideon to save an oppressed Israel mirrors God's call to Moses to deliver an enslaved Israel from Egypt in Exodus 3. Like Gideon, Moses objected to God's call, but God promised Moses, "I will be with you" and then gave a "sign" of reassurance (Exod 3:11-12). God also infused Moses' staff with miraculous power to convince the people of God's presence with him (Exod 4:1-5), just as the angel used a staff to light a fire as proof for Gideon. The miraculous fire on the altar is also reminiscent of the prophet Elijah and his contest with the prophets of Baal on Mt. Carmel when the Lord caused a water-soaked altar built by Elijah to burst into flames (1 Kgs 18:20-40). And like Gideon, the ancestor Jacob built an altar at a special stone or rock where God appeared and gave the place a name (Gen 28:10-22). Like Gideon, Jacob also saw God face to face and lived when he wrestled with God at Penuel (Gen 32:30). This cluster of associations with some of the most important figures of the OT raises enormous expectations about Gideon's tenure as judge and deliverer of Israel. Will Gideon be the one to end Israel's oppression, like Moses, to defeat the Baal cults of Canaan, like Elijah, or even to wrestle a blessing from God, like Jacob?

6:25-32. God begins Gideon's career as judge by instructing him to use a bull to pull down his father's altar. This family altar was dedicated to the worship, not of the Lord, but of the Canaanite god Baal, and the accompanying sacred pole was for the worship of Asherah, a Canaanite goddess and consort to Baal. The bull was also a frequent image for the god Baal. Thus Gideon uses a bull to pull down the altar of Baal the bull. Then Gideon kills the bull and sacrifices it on the new altar dedicated to the worship of the Lord. The initial temptation to cheer enthusiastically for Gideon's brave act of religious reform is tempered by a note concerning his timidity; he does the deed at night and in secret for fear of his family (v. 27). Gideon has not yet fully lived up to the angel's description of him as a bold and "mighty warrior" (v. 12).

The townspeople are outraged when they discover the desecrated Baal altar the next morning. When they determine Gideon is responsible and seek to kill him, Gideon's father intervenes and urges the people to let the god Baal fight his own fight. "Will you contend for Baal?" he asks. "If he is a god, let him contend for himself" (v. 31). The Lord had earlier told Gideon that victory would come not because of Gideon's human strength or weakness but because of the Lord's presence and power. Gideon's father applies the same test to the god Baal. If Baal is truly a god, then Baal by his own power will exact revenge on Gideon for destroying his altar. The incident becomes the occasion for a second name given to Gideon: "Jerubbaal." The name is taken to mean "Let Baal contend [ריב *rîb*] against him" (v. 32). Some scholars believe "Jerubbaal" may have referred to an earlier individual with whom the later and separate tradition of Gideon became secondarily identified. The story of Abimelech, son of Jerubbaal, in Judges 9 consistently uses only the name "Jerubbaal." Moreover, other OT references to the judges mention only Jerubbaal and not Gideon (1 Sam 12:11; 2 Sam 11:21). However, the present form of the text clearly attaches the two names to one person: "Jerubbaal (that is, Gideon)" (7:1; 8:35). Gideon's oscillation between two names will reflect his double-sided character. Early on, Gideon is a faithful but weak servant of the Lord, a destroyer of idols and entirely dependent on God's leading. Later, Gideon will become a bold military leader who relies not on God but on his own human skill. He will end up making God into his own humanly crafted idol (8:24-27). Such a complex character may well deserve at least two different names.

REFLECTIONS

1. Like Moses and Jeremiah and countless others whom God has called to service, Gideon felt inadequate to do the task God had given him. The Bible continually reminds us, however, that success in the vocations to which God summons people depends primarily on God's presence and God's power working in and through them. God will work in spite of and sometimes through their weaknesses. When the apostle Paul repeatedly complained to God about the "thorn in his flesh" that made him weak, the Lord replied, "My grace is sufficient for you, for power is made perfect in weakness" (2 Cor 12:9 NRSV). Elsewhere Paul describes the gospel of a crucified and broken Messiah as foolishness for unbelievers. But that portrait of suffering love on the cross is the power and wisdom of God, which exceeds all human wisdom and power. Paul reminds his hearers that they are in the same cruciform mold as their Lord: "Consider your own call, brothers and sisters: not many of you were wise by human standards, not many were powerful, not many were of noble birth." But God chose what was weak and despised in the world so that "no one might boast in the presence of God" (1 Cor 1:26-29 NRSV). The God of Gideon is the God of Jesus Christ, choosing the weakest of the weak to accomplish God's mission in the world.

2. In the course of being called by God, Gideon raises a recurring issue in the life of faith. God has been faithful in the past and has promised God's blessing into the present and the future. In the midst of his people's blessing, however, Gideon asks the hard question: "If the LORD is with us, why then has all this happened to us?" The Bible provides many different responses to that question of theodicy posed elsewhere in the psalms of lament, the confession of Jeremiah, or the complaints of the righteous sufferer Job. The answers to the "Why?" of suffering varies, depending on the circumstances. Sometimes the sin of the people has brought it upon them. Sometimes God uses evil to accomplish a greater good (Gen 50:20). Sometimes the reason for suffering remains a profound mystery without any rational resolution, as in the book of Job. In the case of Gideon's question and circumstance, the narrative gives two responses. One response is implied already in the beginning of the story: "The Israelites did what was evil in the sight of the LORD" (6:1). Their own sin brought their enemy upon them. But God's second and more direct response to Gideon's query about their suffering is this: "Go . . . and deliver Israel" (6:14). Get involved. Do something about it. But at the same time, remember that success depends on the faithfulness and promise of God: "I will be with you" (6:16).

3. Gideon is the first judge whose inner character and feelings are explored in depth. What emerges is a complex character who will develop and change over his lifetime. His two names, Gideon and Jerubbaal, suggest a split personality, two inner masters fighting to control the one person. Gideon begins in this early part of his story as faithful and dependent on God's guidance. At the same time, he is timid, weak, and afraid. Later, Gideon will become much bolder and stronger as a leader. But he will also rely less on God and more on his own power and wisdom. In the end, he will lead Israel into idolatry, even as he tries to be faithful to God and refuses the kingship offered to him by the Israelites.

The tug of war within Gideon reflects the tensions and divided loyalties within many of God's people who seek to be faithful to God and yet who feel constantly pulled to other commitments and loyalties. We struggle to pull down altars to other gods and allegiances in our lives and erect a true altar of worship and service to the Lord. But we remain divided and wrestle with God all through our lives. As a desperate father pleaded with Jesus to help his afflicted child, he knew his own divided self, "I believe; help my unbelief!" (Mark 9:24 NRSV). The apostle Paul also knew of this civil war within his own body: "For I do not do the good I want, but the evil I do not want is what I do" (Rom 7:19 NRSV). Gideon's own divided character testifies to these inner civil wars of allegiance that rage within many who struggle to be faithful servants of God.

Judges 6:33–8:3, Gideon's Victory

COMMENTARY

After God's call to Gideon and his secretive destruction of the Baal altar, Gideon faces his next challenge. He must lead a military battle against the Midianite and Amalekite invaders. He is successful in his military endeavors only because of God's involvement. But Gideon remains fearful and in need of reassurance from God until the end of this section, when he begins to assert more of himself and his own diplomatic skill as a leader.

6:33-40. "The spirit of the LORD" comes upon Gideon in preparation for the battle against the Midianites, the Amalekites, and other desert peoples of the east (v. 34). God's Spirit had once earlier come upon a judge, the model deliverer named Othniel (3:10). Then the Spirit had given Othniel the power and courage to unite Israel and defeat the enemy. In the case of Gideon, however, the Spirit of the Lord seems to have little effect in changing Gideon in any significant way. *Before* receiving the divine Spirit, Gideon had been timid, fearful, and in need of signs of reassurance (vv. 15, 17, 27). Now *after* receiving the Spirit, Gideon still remains tentative, doubtful, and in need of signs of reassurance (vv. 36-40; 7:9-15). When the Spirit of the Lord returns and comes upon later judges, like Jephthah and Samson, the unbridled power of the Spirit will create more negative and even disastrous consequences. Already with Gideon, the era of the judges inspired by a temporary divine Spirit has taken a negative turn, a decline that will become more pronounced as the period of the judges continues.

As Gideon musters his armies from some of the middle and northern tribes of Israel (Manasseh, Asher, Zebulun, and Naphtali),

he asks God for a sign that "you will deliver Israel by my hand" (v. 36). He lays out fleece or wool shorn from sheep on the threshing floor overnight. If there is moist dew on the fleece alone and the ground remains dry, then Gideon will take that as a sign that God will deliver Israel. However, that dew would condense on wool and evaporate from the warmer stone floor of a threshing floor in the coolness of night is a completely natural and expected result in everyday experience. This may be a sign of a natural sort, but it is no miracle. So using the words of old Abraham when he once bargained with God over the fate of Sodom and Gomorrah, Gideon says to God, "Do not let your anger burn against me, let me speak one more time" (v. 39; cf. Gen 18:32). Gideon requests that the opposite be done with respect to the dew and the fleece: This time the dew should appear on the ground but *not* on the fleece. Remarkably and patiently, God complies with this second request for a sign that will be more extraordinary than the first (vv. 39-40). Only then is Gideon ready to go off to battle.

7:1-23. God had chosen a weak and unlikely leader in Gideon (6:15). Similarly, God also desires a small and weak army to fight the Midianites. A small number of warriors in Israel's army would compel Israel to acknowledge that it was God alone who had won the victory, and not human strength. Israel could not boast, "My own hand has delivered me" (v. 2). Gideon begins with thirty-two thousand soldiers, which would have been an emormous army in this ancient period. The Hebrew word for "thousand" (אֶלֶף *'elep*) can also mean tribal "unit." Thus an earlier version of the story may have been about 32 "units" (not "thousands") of soldiers with perhaps ten soldiers in each unit, for a total of 320 soldiers. Even 320 would be a large army in this time period.

Whatever the earlier version, the text's present form presumes the huge army of 32,000 men. (We will later learn that the Midianite army numbers 120,000 soldiers!) God seeks to reduce the number of Gideon's army through two tests. The first test is drawn from the laws of the books of Deuteronomy. The law specifies that if any warrior is "afraid or disheartened," he should return home from battle lest he discourage the other troops (Deut 20:8). When Gideon instructs the fearful to return home, 22,000 men leave, and only 10,000 remain. Given Gideon's past fearfulness, we may wonder whether he was tempted to join those who went back home. Gideon does stay, perhaps a signal that he himself is beginning to change. Still not satisfied, God devises a second test to reduce the number of soldiers even more. All the fighters who kneel down at a watering hole and drink by putting their hands to their mouths are excluded. The tiny minority of 300 who lapped the water with their tongues like dogs are chosen as Gideon's little army (vv. 4-7). This small band of doglike soldiers will take on the hordes of Midianites, who are as "thick as locusts" so that they cannot be counted (v. 12; cf. 6:5).

God commands Gideon to attack, "for I have given it into your hand" (v. 9). Such divine assurance ought to have been sufficient grounds for Gideon's ready obedience. But God knows this fearful Gideon and offers him another sign of reassurance. Gideon and his servant sneak down to the enemy camp and overhear words spoken by the Midianites about their fear of Gideon and his army. Gideon is encouraged, worships God, and calls his soldiers to attack (vv. 9-15). Their unorthodox military strategy involves a nighttime raid as Gideon's men surround the enemy camp. Each of the 300 soldiers will blow a trumphet and then smash a clay jar that conceals a torch inside. The Midianites' still dark night will be pierced by the simultaneous sound of 300 trumpets coming from every direction and the explosion of light as 300 torches suddenly light up the night sky.

The enemy soldiers will be so terrified and confused they will fight and kill one another. As Gideon's army performs this strategy to instill terror in the enemy, Gideon tells them to shout, "For the LORD and for Gideon!" (vv. 18, 20). The praise of Gideon along with the Lord may suggest a subtle shift in Gideon's perception of himself. Gideon had earlier felt that he was nothing (6:15) and the Lord was everything (7:15). But now in this shout Gideon claims a piece of the spotlight along with God.

This subtle shift is also apparent when we compare Gideon's attack in Judges 7 with Joshua's attack on the city of Jericho in Joshua 2. The tactics of Israel's army surrounding the enemy, blowing trumpets, and shouting all find a parallel in Joshua's conquest of Jericho. However, Joshua's command to shout did not give glory to Joshua himself but only to the Lord: "For the LORD has given you the city" (Josh 2:16). In contrast, Gideon desires to claim credit along with God in his shout: "For the LORD *and* for Gideon." Gideon is taking over some of God's prerogatives.

7:24–8:3. Gideon initially gathered his army from some of the middle and northern tribes of Israel in Canaan (Manasseh, Asher, Zebulun, and Naphtali; 6:35; 7:23). Gideon had not at first invited the important northern tribe of Ephraim to join in the battle. However, he does call them to help in the very last phase of the battle against the Midianites. They succeed in capturing the two "captains" of the Midianite army, Oreb ("Raven") and Zeeb ("Wolf"). The psalmist lists these two names as enemy leaders of Midian whom Israel had conquered during the time of the judges (Ps 83:11).

The warriors from the tribe of Ephraim bring the heads of Oreb and Zeeb to Gideon, but they also bring a complaint to him. They are angry that Gideon did not call them at the beginning of the conflict with Midian, and "they upbraided him violently" (8:1). The possibility of internal conflict or even civil war within Israel arises for the first time in the book of Judges. As the judges era continues, this internal conflict or social disintegration will emerge as a major theme as the judges become less and less effective as unifiers of the Israelite people. The book of Judges will end with an all-out civil war as Israelite tribes attack and nearly exterminate their brother tribe of Benjamin (Judges 20–21). This time the conflict between Gideon and the tribe of Ephraim does not end with civil war but with negotiated resolution. Gideon demonstrates diplomatic skill as he flatters the Ephraimites for achieving what Gideon could not do in capturing the two Midianite generals: "What have I been able to do in comparison to you?" Gideon has learned well from God's skill in responding to Gideon's own objections and laments. Gideon follows God's example and patiently offers a gracious response to the Ephraimites' complaint. Gideon soothes their anger and averts a crisis (8:2-3).

REFLECTIONS

1. Before going into battle, Gideon sets up a test for God involving the fleece of sheep's wool and the morning dew. Other biblical figures used conditions and tests to determine whether God was present and active in a given situation. Sometimes the conditions involved natural or ordinary needs. For example, Jacob agreed to accept the Lord as his God if the Lord would "give me bread to eat and clothing to wear" and return him "to my father's house in peace" (Gen 28:18-22 NRSV). At other times, miraculous or extraordinary signs of God's power were requested. Moses requested a sign that he could bring to the Israelites to convince them that God was the power behind his leadership. God gave him two miraculous signs: the healing of his leprous hand and the staff that turned into a serpent (Exod 4:1-9). Jesus also used both ordinary and miraculous signs of God's power in his ministry. In the story of the paralyzed man who was lowered through a hole in the roof, Jesus first spoke ordinary words, "Friend, your sins are forgiven you" (Luke 5:20 NRSV). But some onlookers grumbled that Jesus' words were blasphemy, since forgiving sins was something only God could do. Thus Jesus gave an extraordinary sign of God's power by healing the paralyzed man "so that you may know that the Son of Man has authority on earth to forgive sins" (Luke 5:24 NRSV).

Like Gideon, we yearn for signs, both ordinary and extraordinary, that God is alive and at work in our lives. The disciple Thomas wanted such tangible signs of Jesus' presence after the resurrection. Thomas was not satisfied with ordinary words and reports; he demanded to see the miracle of Jesus risen from the dead for himself. Jesus granted him that direct evidence of his presence. But Jesus also reminded him, "Blessed are those who have not seen and yet have come to believe" (John 20:29 NRSV). The story of Gideon reminds us of God's graciousness in giving us those occasional signs and glimpses of God's presence and power at work in our lives. Sometimes those signs are natural and ordinary glimpses of God's quiet blessings that are always there but often go unnoticed or unappreciated. At other times and more rarely, God may give us a more dramatic or extraordinary sign. Others may brush off such experiences as coincidence or blind chance, but the eyes of faith may perceive them as the hand of God. At still other times, God's people may yearn for a sign from God that never comes. At such times, we join the psalmist's lament and cry, "How long, O LORD? Will you forget me forever?/ How long will you hide your face from me?" (Ps 13:1 NRSV)?"

2. One of the major thematic tensions in this section involves the balance between divine agency and human participation in accomplishing God's work in the world. On one hand, God reduces Gideon's huge army from 32,000 to 300 in order to demonstrate that the victory will rely primarily on God's power alone, and not on human strength. God is concerned that Israel will wrongly "take credit away from me, saying, 'My own hand has delivered me' " (7:2). On the other hand, Gideon inserts his own name in the shout of praise and glory associated with the victory to come: "For the LORD and for Gideon" (7:18-20).

This tension reflects a larger, ongoing dialogue within Scripture about the balance between divine agency and human responsibility. On the one hand, Moses emphasizes the primacy of God's action and the passivity of humans in the conflict with Pharaoh and Israel's exodus out of Egypt. Moses advises the Israelites, "The LORD will fight for you, and you have only to keep still" (Exod 14:14 NRSV). The apostle Paul speaks of the death of his human self and its replacement with Christ: "I have been crucified with Christ; and it is no longer I who live but it is Christ who lives in me" (Gal 2:19-20 NRSV). On the other hand, the Bible contains many laws and proverbs that presume that humans have the ability, freedom, and responsibility to work with God to do God's will. Scripture also includes stories of human action that caused God to adjust or alter divine plans. Moses' prayer changed God's mind when Israel worshiped the golden calf (Exod 32:11-14). The pleas of the Syrophoenecian woman caused Jesus to reverse his decision and heal her daughter (Mark 7:24-30). God clearly takes into account human actions, words, and freedom as God works in the world. Indeed, even within the book of Judges itself God used the freedom and actions of many human actors to achieve God's purposes. Ehud's devious trick with his hidden sword (3:12-30) or Jael's feigned hospitality to the Canaanite general Sisera (4:17-24) were human actions that God did not seem to plan but that did contribute to God's defeat of Israel's enemies. The Song of Deborah and Barak in Judges 5 praises God for the defeat of the Canaanites (5:2-5, 31), but it also praises humans like Deborah, "the mother of Israel" (5:7), the commanders "who offered themselves willingly" (5:9), and Jael as "the most blessed of women" (5:24). As few in number as they were, even the 300 soldiers of Gideon played some role in God's defeat of the Midianites.

Thus we may affirm Gideon's insistence that recognition be given to him along with the Lord in defeating Midian. We generally applaud those with feelings of worthlessness, like Gideon, who discover over time a sense of self-worth and value. But God's concern about Israel's taking all the credit for itself instead of attributing it to God flashes a warning light at the same time. Surely humans contribute to the divine cause, but God knows that humans have a tendency to cross the line, forget God, and take all the credit for themselves. Maintaining a balance between primary reliance on God and an affirmation of human talents and creativity in achieving God's will in the world is difficult, but necessary. In the case of Gideon, we will see that he will begin to cross the line and lose that balance when he crosses the Jordan River in the next section, beginning with Judg 8:4. Gideon's worthwhile self-affirmation will eventually begin to evolve into self-absorption.

Judges 8:4-35, A Complex Gideon: Kingship and Idolatry

COMMENTARY

The typical model of the judges cycle would conclude the story of Gideon at this point with a statement about the victory over the enemy Midian and the number of years of rest that followed. But the Gideon narrative does not end here. Rather, the story begins a new scene in 8:4 as Gideon crosses the Jordan River out of Canaan in hot pursuit of two Midianite kings named Zebah and Zalmunna. The psalmist mentions their names as Midianite princes who coveted Israel's land (Ps 83:11). Gideon's 300 soldiers are "exhausted and famished" from all their fighting (v. 4). The Lord plays no role in the action of these last episodes. One gets the sense that it is Gideon alone, not his soldiers or the Lord, who is pushing the action and calling the shots.

8:4-21. Gideon and his army come to the towns of Succoth and then Penuel, east of the Jordan. They ask for some bread, but the residents of these cities refuse to offer them hospitality. The story does not explicitly say who the residents of Succoth and Penuel are. Are they Canaanites? Are they fellow Israelites from the east Jordanian tribe of Gad? The town of Succoth was settled by the tribe of Gad, according to Josh 13:24-28. Penuel is a town associated with the ancestor Jacob and his wrestling match with God (Gen 32:30-32). These associations suggest that the townspeople are Israelites refusing to help fellow Israelites. In response to their inhospitality, Gideon promises revenge upon them after he returns from capturing the two Midianite kings (vv. 7, 9). Later Gideon will do what he threatened. He will trample the inhabitants of Succoth with wilderness thorns and briars, and he will topple the tower of Penuel and kill its people (vv. 16-17).

The violence and severity of the revenge Gideon takes on his fellow Israelites for their admittedly inhospitable attitude seems out of proportion. The taunting of Gideon by Succoth and Penuel (vv. 6, 15) was hardly just cause to kill everyone in the towns. Gideon has seemingly lost his diplomatic skill and graciousness, displayed in the dispute with the Ephraimites (vv. 1-3). He has crossed a line as well as the Jordan River (v. 4). He displays the overweening arrogance of the primeval and brutish Lamech, who boasted to his wives, "I have killed a man for wounding me, a young man for striking me. If Cain is avenged sevenfold, truly Lamech seventy-sevenfold" (Gen 4:23-24 NRSV). These themes of Israel's own inhospitality toward other Israelites and the severe revenge and civil war that ensue will grow larger as we move through Judges. The final episode of chaps. 19–21 describes a full-blown version of these themes, which will mark the total collapse of Israel's unity and the end of the judges era.

Personal revenge or retribution plays a role not only with Succoth and Penuel but also with Gideon's motivation in pursuing the two kings of Midian, Zebah and Zalmunna. When Gideon finally captures them, he asks them about the Israelites they killed at Tabor. The kings' answer to Gideon is interesting: "As you are, so were they, every one of them; they resembled the sons of a king" (v. 18). The implication is clear: Gideon has the appearance of a "son of a king." Moreover, Gideon is about to kill two kings. Does that mean

that Gideon will himself step into their role of king in their stead? In this context, Gideon issues his own law of vengeance much as a king might do. He justifies his execution of the kings as revenge for their having killed his brothers. He thus instructs his oldest son to kill the kings. However, his son refuses out of fear and timidity (v. 20). Gideon's son is a reflection of the earlier and more timid Gideon who had refused God's command to kill the enemy early in his career (6:15). But Gideon has changed. He has become bolder, more self-assured, and more willing to take matters into his own hands without the help of the Lord. Thus Gideon kills the kings himself. He also takes the royal emblems, the crescents hanging from the necks of the kings' camels, as booty and keeps them for himself (v. 21). Has Gideon begun to step over the line from a temporary judge to a king? And if so, is that a good thing or a bad thing? The next episodes will explore those questions.

8:22-28. The Israelites are impressed with Gideon's newly discovered boldness, independence, and assertiveness as a leader. They say to Gideon, "Rule [מְשֹׁל *māšal*] over us, you and your son and your grandson also." They do not use the word "king" (מֶלֶךְ *melek*), but they do suggest a dynasty of Gideon's line to rule into the future. The reason the people offer to Gideon is that "you have delivered us out of the hand of Midian." The Lord had earlier been concerned that Israel might take credit away from the Lord and say, "My own hand has delivered me" (7:2). These words to Gideon that *he* was the one who delivered Israel with no mention of the Lord suggest that what God feared has come to pass. Israel has forgotten all that God had done, just as the prophet had warned earlier in the Gideon story (6:7-10).

Gideon seems to turn down the people's request that he and his son and grandson become rulers over Israel. Sounding quite pious, Gideon replies, "I will not rule over you, and my son will not rule over you; the LORD will rule over you" (8:23). Gideon appears to wash his hands of any role in guiding Israel into the future and instead leaves it up to God alone. Gideon's statement is taken by some scholars as a positive reflection of the view of the writers of this story. The intended meaning of the story, they argue, is a critique of all human kingship or dynastic rule in favor of a theocratic ideal in which God alone is King and Ruler over Israel. This implies an affirmation of total human equality that plays down the need for human hierarchy or leadership. However, the message of the Gideon story in this regard seems more nuanced than a simple rejection of all human kingship or leadership. The narrator of the story has placed Gideon's claim—that God alone rules Israel with no room for human leadership—in a literary context that suggests something is wrong with this statement. First of all, Gideon has been acting more and more like an independent and improper king. He had no need of the Lord when he took the law into his own hands and went on his spree of personal revenge in this chapter. Moreover, he accumulates gold (vv. 24-26), a sign of a bad king, according to the law of the king in Deut 17:17. Second, Gideon crafts a cult object, called an ephod, which becomes an idol: "All Israel prostituted themselves to it, and it became a snare to Gideon and to his family" (v. 27). This, too, is a sign of a bad king, according to the law in Deut 17:20.[39]

How does this religious ephod relate to the issue of human politics and kingship? An ephod is associated with ceremonial garments of priests (Exodus 28; 39). It was probably used as a device for receiving oracles and guidance from a deity. Since Gideon had renounced any overt claim to rule for himself, he makes an ephod as an instrument of divination to provide a way to maintain contact between God and Israel. However, his manufacture and sole control of the ephod and the connection to God suggest that Gideon may in fact be hiding his power and rule behind the cloak of religious trappings and pious claims that "the LORD will rule over you." In this sense, the ephod becomes an idol, a graven image of God that Gideon controls. Israel worships a humanly constructed image instead of the true God, who is beyond human control and who judges all human beings and their institutions of power. The God of Israel surely can work in and through human beings and their structures of community and national life. But this God of Israel cannot be captured or uncritically identified with any one human form, image, or institution.

We can also read this connection of Gideon's refusal to rule Israel and the making of an ephod in a more straightforward way. Gideon may simply want no part in trying to rule Israel, with all its difficulties and conflicts. He constructs the ephod as a mechanical device for divine oracles so that he will not need to take responsibility for guiding the affairs of the nation. The ephod becomes a substitute for human leadership of the community. However, the ephod can never take the place of the dynamic and complex interactions of God, human leaders, and the people of Israel. In this reading, Gideon has acted wrongly, but not because he veils his human power behind an idolatrous image of God. Rather, Gideon abandons his responsibility to lead Israel as a servant and partner with God. His refusal leaves a power vacuum that is only inadequately filled by a mechanical and idolatrous oracular device. The narrative may be intentionally ambiguous and suggestive of both readings. Either reading of Gideon's actions—that he is a covert king or that he has abandoned all responsibility for leadership—indicates that something has gone terribly wrong with the system of the judges.

The full extent of Gideon's offense in making the idol emerges when one considers the episode in Israel's history that it most resembles. In effect, Gideon replays the sin of Aaron and the Israelites when they made and worshiped the golden calf at Mt. Sinai (Exodus 32). When God conquered Pharaoh and his army, Israel received booty of gold and silver jewelry from the Egyptians (Exod 3:21-22; 12:35-36). Later at Mt. Sinai, Aaron the priest collected all the gold earrings the Israelites had received from the Egyptians and melted them down to make a golden calf. They worshiped the golden calf, proclaiming it to be the god "who brought you out of the land of Egypt" (Exod 32:8 NRSV). Gideon does what Aaron did. He asks the Israelites to give up their golden earrings plundered from the enemy, makes an ephod from the gold, and sets the ephod up at his home in Ophrah, and Israel worships it as an idol. Just as their ancestors had claimed that the golden calf had delivered them out of Egypt, so also the Israelites now claim that Gideon

39. David Jobling, "Deuteronomic Political Theory in Judges and 1 Samuel 1–12," in *The Sense of Biblical Narrative: Structural Analyses in the Hebrew Bible*, JSOTSup 39 (Sheffield: JSOT, 1988) 1:66-67.

and not the Lord was the one "who delivered us out of the hand of Midian" (8:22). More than any other OT story, the golden calf story represents the defining paradigm of Israel's rebellion against the Lord. The association of Gideon's ephod with that story suggests that the road of the judges era has taken a decidedly negative turn.

The ominous character of Gideon's idolatry is further signaled by the fact that Gideon's ephod is a literary echo of a later story in the book of Judges. The story of Micah and his idolatrous "ephod" marks the culminating endpoint of Israel's downward spiral into religious disintegration (17:5; 18:14-20). The Gideon story begins the transition into that downward slide. At the start of his career, Gideon had broken down pagan altars and idols in his hometown of Ophrah (6:24-27). At the end of his life, Gideon constructs an idol, which leads Israel astray in his hometown of Ophrah (8:27). The final portrait of Gideon is mixed. He failed as a religious leader, but he remained successful as a military leader. He subdued Midian, and Israel had rest for forty years (8:28; see 3:11; 5:31).

8:29-35. These verses conclude the Gideon cycle and show again the complexity and ambiguity of Gideon's character. Both names for Gideon reappear together: Jerubbabel (v. 29) and Gideon (v. 30). On one hand, Jerubbaal, or Gideon, seems to retire from any role in leading the people of Israel; he "went to live in his own house" (v. 29). On the other hand, Gideon has "many wives" and seventy sons (v. 30). Both details provide a hint that Gideon has become more than just a simple wheat farmer from Ophrah (6:11). Larger numbers of wives and offspring often accompany kingship. The law of the king in Deuteronomy explicitly prohibits Israel's king from acquiring "many wives for himself, or else his heart will turn away" (Deut 17:17); King Solomon violated the prohibition of having many wives (1 Kgs 11:3). The mention of Gideon's seventy sons reflects the large number of offspring kings typically have. In

particular, the wicked King Ahab of Samaria had "seventy sons" (2 Kgs 10:1). Moreover, Gideon takes a female slave from the city of Shechem as a wife or concubine. Sexual entanglements with Shechem had led to disastrous results before in Israel's history (Genesis 34). This time the relationship between Israel and the concubine in Shechem leads to the birth of a son, whom Gideon names "Abimelech," meaning "My Father Is King" (v. 31). Through his son's name, Gideon may be covertly proclaiming himself king. He was a successful ruler in terms of military victories (v. 28), but Gideon was a poor leader in religious affairs involving the idolatrous ephod (vv. 24-27). Gideon is an ambiguous figure, refusing to accept the office of ruler or kingship (vv. 22-23), and yet he is acting in some ways as a covert king. In the next generation, Gideon's son Abimelech will openly declare himself king in spite of Gideon's claim that "my sons will not rule over you" (v. 23). Abimelech's attempt at monarchy will be short and violent, and it will end in tragedy (chap. 9).

For now, however, Gideon's life ends peacefully "at a good old age." Gideon achieved much that was good in his life, but his reign as judge also showed the cracks of a deteriorating system of leadership. While Gideon was alive, Israel worshiped his ephod as an idol, a graven image of the Lord. When Gideon dies, Israel goes even further in violating the first of the Ten Commandments: Israel "relapsed and prostituted themselves with the Baals." Their religious situation returns to what it was at the beginning of the Gideon story, before Gideon pulled down his father's Baal altar (6:25-27). They forgot the Lord, but they also committed another major sin: "they did not exhibit loyalty to the house of Jerubbaal (that is, Gideon) in return for all the good that he had done in Israel" (v. 35). The details of this offense against Gideon's house, or family, will be the subject of the next chapter in the judges era, Abimelech's disastrous attempt to become king in Israel.

REFLECTIONS

1. Gideon is a character who changes radically over the course of his reign as a judge. He begins as an overly passive and fearful leader, constantly in need of reassurance. At the midpoint of his career, he finds a balance of both self-affirmation and the affirmation of God's role as deliverer: "For the LORD and for Gideon" (8:18, 20). By the end of his battles with Midian, Gideon begins asserting himself to the exclusion of God in unwarranted acts of personal revenge, even against his fellow Israelites. The final blow comes when Gideon makes the ephod, which replaces the Lord as an object of worship.

Remarkably, God works through Gideon all through his life. When Gideon was hesitant and fainthearted, God patiently gave him the signs he needed to bolster his courage. When Gideon later became focused on his own glory more than the praise of God, God still gave forty years of peace to Israel by defeating the Midianites. As one surveys the Scriptures, it becomes clear that God repeatedly works through flawed and imperfect people. Abraham sometimes doubted and endangered God's promises to him, but God continued to use him and his descendants as a blessing to "all the families of the earth" (Gen 12:3 NRSV). Jacob was hardly an exemplary person, deceiving his father and stealing his brother's birthright. Yet God chose him as the carrier of the promise. King David committed adultery and murdered his loyal soldier Uriah to cover up his affair. Yet God chose him and his dynasty forever. The disciple Peter denied Jesus three times, and the other disciples all deserted Jesus during his trial, which led to Jesus' execution on the cross. Yet God used Peter and the other disciples as the first preachers of the gospel (Acts 2). Whether we feel wholly inadequate for what God calls us to do or whether we sometimes think too highly of ourselves and forget God, the lesson of Gideon teaches us that God can still accomplish God's will through us and sometimes in spite of us.

2. The story of Gideon raises the issue of the relationship of religion and politics. In the end, did Gideon hide his drive for power and self-glorification with the word and power of God? Or did he run away from his responsibility and the responsibility of his family to lead Israel on a more permanent and stable basis, since the system of temporary leadership by judges was starting to unravel? Either option seems to be rejected by the writer or narrator of the Gideon story. The book of Judges does not promote a theocratic ideal in which God alone is King and no human leader exists. When Gideon expressed such an ideal, his words were set in a negative context that implicitly condemned his claim. In the end, Judges affirms the need for a king, a human ruler, who guides Israel to faith and allegiance to the Lord. This pro-king perspective of Judges is demonstrated by the important refrain that encloses the last section of the book, describing Israel's basic problem as Israel spins out of control into political and religious chaos: "In those days there was no king in Israel; all the people did what was right in their own eyes" (17:6; 21:25). Israel comes to need a more stable form of human leadership.

On the other hand, the Gideon story makes clear that this king must be of a special type, conforming to certain criteria. The king must take seriously the responsibility to rule. Those in authority must be open and accountable in the exercise of power. They stand under divine scrutiny and judgment. The mediation of the Lord's will should not be too closely identified with the ruler's will as it was with Gideon's ephod. God's word must remain free, independent, and able to critique the governing power. A prophet like the one who appeared earlier in the Gideon story (6:7-10) typically fulfilled this role in Israel's monarchy. Examples include the prophets Samuel (1 Samuel 15), Nathan (2 Samuel 12), and Elijah (1 Kings 18). Each spoke God's critical words of judgment to Israel's kings. Governments and leaders in communities of all kinds continue to need independent voices who are willing to speak the truth boldly and to criticize constructively. The quality of Gideon's rule fell short in a number of these criteria of good leadership and good kings. The kingship of Gideon's son Abimelech will move even further away from the ideal kingship to which Judges looks forward.

Judges 9:1-57, Abimelech: A Troubled Foray into Kingship

COMMENTARY

Two observations begin the exploration of Judges 9: Abimelech is the first person in the Bible overtly to assert for himself the title of "king," and Abimelech's violent and vengeful brand of kingship is the antithesis of the kind of ruler the book of Judges advocates. This judgment appears most clearly in Jotham's fable, which Martin Buber has called "the strongest anti-monarchical poem of world literature."[40] Abimelech's experiment in kingship ultimately comes to an ignoble and abrupt end. After Abimelech, Israel's mode of governance will revert to the system of temporary judges in Jephthah and Samson (chaps. 10–16). Ultimately, however, the experiment in judgeship itself will suffer the same fate as Abimelech's violent brand of kingship and come to a similar disastrous end (chaps. 17–21).

9:1-21. Abimelech's father was a son of Gideon. His mother was a concubine or woman slave from the city of Shechem. As the son of a slave woman, Abimelech had less status than the seventy other sons of Gideon, whose mothers were not concubines. Abimelech desires to overcome his low status by first establishing a power base with the inhabitants of Shechem, his mother's hometown. He argues that his single leadership would be less taxing and preferable to being ruled by all the seventy sons of Gideon. He also appeals to his kinship with the Shechemites: "I am your bone and your flesh." The leaders of Shechem agree to support him because "he is our brother" (v. 3). They give him money to hire an army of "worthless and reckless fellows" (v. 4). His first act is to go and kill "his brothers," the seventy sons of Gideon, "on one stone." Two ironies flow from this brutal mass murder. The first irony is that Abimelech's macho savagery against his seventy Israelite brothers "on one stone" will be answered at the end of his life by a woman's "millstone" thrown upon his head

(vv. 5, 53, 56).[41] The second irony is that the Shechemites, who felt secure in their support of Abimelech because "he is our brother," should have learned from this massacre how Abimelech treats his "brothers." Indeed, Abimelech will eventually attack and kill all his Shechemite "brothers" just as he had killed his brothers who were the sons of Gideon (vv. 3, 34-49, 57).

After Abimelech kills Gideon's seventy sons, the leaders of Shechem and Beth-millo make him "king" in a covenant ceremony at "the oak of the pillar at Shechem." The mention of the oak and the pillar is likely a reference to a Canaanite worship site (see Gen 35:4). Shechem as a city had both positive and negative memories for Israel. Israel remembered a brutal confrontation with the Canaanites of Shechem headed by a man named Hamor (Genesis 34). After Joshua's conquest of Canaan, Shechem became a famous Israelite site for covenant ceremonies of blessing and curse (Joshua 24). The bones of the revered ancestor Jacob were also buried at Shechem (Josh 24:32). Later in Israel's history, Shechem gained more negative associations after King Solomon's death when the united kingdom of Israel was split into two kingdoms, northern Israel and southern Judah. Solomon's son Rehoboam, who ruled the southern kingdom of Judah, was initially crowned king at Shechem (1 Kgs 12:1). Rehoboam's rival, King Jeroboam of the northern kingdom of Israel, then built his own royal palace at Shechem as a rival of the southern capital of Jerusalem (1 Kgs 12:25). Thus Shechem conjured up associations with covenants of curse and blessing as well as troubled and divisive kingships in Israel's memory.

Once Abimelech is declared king at Shechem, Jotham steps onto the stage. Jotham is the one remaining son of Gideon

---

40. Buber, "Books of Judges and Book of Judges," 75.

41. T. A. Boogart, "Stone for Stone: Retribution in the Story of Abimelech and Shechem," *JSOT* 32 (1985) 45-56; J. Gerald Janzen, "A Certain Woman in the Rhetoric of Judges 9:1," *JSOT* 38 (1987) 33-37.

who had escaped the slaughter of Gideon's family. He stands on top of Mt. Gerizim, a place tradition had associated with covenants and proclaiming a blessing (Deut 27:12; Josh 8:33). However, Jotham proclaims not a blessing but a curse on Abimelech and the residents of Shechem in the form of a fable about trees and a bramble bush (vv. 8-15). In the fable, the trees symbolize the people of Shechem who are looking for someone to anoint as king over them. They ask various fruit trees and vines, who all say no to kingship (vv. 8-13). Finally, they ask a worthless bramble bush, who invites them to "come and take refuge in my shade" (v. 15). "Shade" (צל *ṣēl*) as protection was a frequent image associated with kings in the ancient Near East. However, the scrawny bramble bush offers little actual shade; its only real value is as kindling for fire. The bramble bush represents Abimelech, who becomes the king of the "trees" of Shechem. They join forces in a covenant with a meager blessing—the thin shade of a bramble bush—and a much more dangerous curse—a forest fire started with the kindling of the bramble (v. 15).

In the fable itself, curse and blessing are dependent on whether the "trees" of Shechem act "in good faith" in anointing Abimelech as king (v. 15). Jotham's explanation of the fable expands this key condition for curse or blessing. The central question is this: Did the people of Shechem act "in good faith and honor *with Jerubbaal and with his house*" when they crowned Abimelech king (vv. 16, 19-20)? Gideon, or Jerubbaal, had risked his life to save Shechem from the Midian invaders. Is Shechem showing proper gratitude and honor toward Gideon by crowning the murderer of his sons as king? If the answer is yes, then Shechem will rejoice. On the other hand, if crowning Abimelech, who massacred the seventy sons of Gideon (or Jerubbaal), dishonored the house of Gideon, then "let fire come from Abimelech" to destroy the towns of Shechem and Beth-millo, and let fire from Shechem and Beth-millo also destroy Abimelech (v. 20). Of course, Jotham's conditions already contain their answer. Abimelech, and by association the Shechemites, has grievously dishonored Gideon's house, and thus the curse will indeed come into effect. The rest of the story of Abimelech recounts the working out of this curse.

9:22-57. Abimelech rules for only three years (v. 22). Other rulers of Israel in the judges period typically ruled for forty years or longer. The brevity of Abimelech's reign is the eventual result of God's sending "an evil spirit between Abimelech and the lords of Shechem" (v. 23). God's Spirit had inspired the model judge Othniel to victory (3:10). God's Spirit had also come upon Gideon with somewhat less dramatic effect, but he was at least successful in uniting some of the Israelite tribes (see the Commentary on 6:34). In Abimelech's case, the divine Spirit actually causes division and conflict between people rather than uniting them. God sends the evil and divisive spirit as just retribution for the murder of Gideon's seventy sons. The conflict starts as the Shechemites begin to ambush and rob travelers "out of hostility" to Abimelech (v. 25). The conflict intensifies when a Canaanite named "Gaal" (related to the Hebrew verb געל [*gā'al,* "to loathe," "to abhor"]) moves into Shechem and wins the loyalty of the lords of Shechem away from Abimelech. Just as Abimelech had appealed to his mother's kinship with the Shechemites, so also Gaal appeals to the Shechemites' kinship bond to their earlier Canaanite ancestor "Hamor father of Shechem" (v. 28; see Genesis 34:1).

Zebul is Abimelech's one remaining supporter in Shechem. He gets wind of Gaal's plot to win the allegiance of Shechem away from Abimelech and promptly informs him. Abimelech then launches a surprise attack on the city of Shechem that moves in three phases. First, Abimelech's army defeats Gaal and his forces (vv. 34-41). It would have been reasonable for Abimelech to have ended his attack at that point, satisfied with eliminating Gaal and his supporters. However, he takes revenge to an extreme in a manner similar to his father, Gideon. Gideon had earlier destroyed the towns of Succoth and Penuel, including the tower of Penuel, in retaliation for their taunts against him (8:4-17). Abimelech likewise takes vengeance to an extreme. In the second phase of his attack on the next day, he kills all the common people of Shechem who came out in the morning to work in the fields outside the city. Abimelech's disagreement was with Gaal and the lords of Shechem, not with these commoners of Shechem. Yet he kills them all. Then Abimelech enters the city itself, burns it to the ground, and sows it with salt so that nothing will ever grow there again (vv. 42-45). The third phase of Abimelech's attack is aimed at the inner circle of Shechem's leaders, the "lords of the Tower of Shechem." These lords shut themselves up in the tower, which functioned as a temple of the Canaanite god El-berith (meaning "god of the covenant"). The god's name recalls the covenant that Abimelech made with Shechem, which Jotham interpreted in his fable as a covenant of curse. The fable's curse about Abimelech as the fiery bramble bush (v. 20) literally comes true as Abimelech and his army frantically gather bundles of brush and set fire to them at the base of the tower to burn it, killing about a thousand men and women in the process (vv. 46-49).

Abimelech's frenzied attacks of unwarranted and extreme revenge show a portrait of a madman out of control. The final episode in this violent despot's life is his seemingly random attack on the town of Thebez, which was not involved in the Shechem affair. One senses that Abimelech is randomly slaughtering people for no apparent reason. Attacks on towers characterize the vengeful rampages of both Gideon and Abimelech. Gideon had attacked the tower at Penuel (8:17); Abimelech had earlier attacked the tower of

Shechem (9:46-49). Abimelech assaults still another tower, the tower of Thebez (9:50-52). It is at this tower that Abimelech meets his end when "a certain woman" at the top of the tower throws a "millstone," which hits Abimelech and crushes his skull (v. 53). Before he dies, Abimelech commands his armorbearer to drive his sword into him lest people say of Abimelech, "A woman killed him." For this macho, violent madman, that would be the ultimate shame. The irony is, of course, that this story has been remembered throughout the ages. Abimelech is repaid with death and shame for his savagery against Gideon's sons every time the story is retold. Abimelech joins the ranks of the Canaanite general Sisera, who also died at the hand of a woman. The major difference is that Sisera had been an enemy, a Canaanite. Abimelech was the son of one of Israel's judges who killed and fought against his own people. The enemy is no longer only foreign generals. The enemy has become one of Israel's own rulers. The social fabric of Israel has experienced a major tear. The question will be whether Abimelech's tenure was a momentary lapse from which Israel will shortly recover. Or has Israel begun an irreversible downhill slide into social and religious chaos? The stories of the next major judges, Jephthah and Samson, will lead us further into answers to those questions.

REFLECTIONS

1. It may trouble us to read that God may at times send an evil spirit within communities or groups to stir up conflict, divisiveness, and disunity. God usually seems on the side of harmony, unity, and reconciliation within communities. The apostle Paul urges the Christian community to live harmoniously together as the body of Christ, whose members "though many, are one body" and who live "in the one Spirit" (1 Cor 12:12-13 NRSV). Psalm 133 declares, "How very good and pleasant it is when kindred live together in unity. . . . For there the LORD ordained his blessing, life forevermore" (Ps 133:1, 3 NRSV). Yet there are circumstances when God does disrupt unified communities when they have become too powerful and their actions stand too strongly in opposition to the will and purpose of God. The classic example is the story of the tower of Babel (Gen 11:1-9), another tower story in the Bible, which echoes the attack on the tower of Shechem. Humanity had unified itself for the purpose of building a tower to reach to the heavens in order to "make a name for ourselves" (Gen 11:4 NRSV). God discerned that this world-unifying project had self-centeredness and rebellion written all over it. Thus God confused the tower builders' language and scattered them across the earth. The humans' rebellious power was thereby dispersed and limited. The violent alliance of Abimelech and the Shechemites was similarly self-centered and rebellious in its intentions. Thus God's spirit stirred up divisions among them so that their power would be diffused and their treachery finally ended.

The rise and fall of modern-day empires, hate groups, dictators, and oppressive systems invite consideration of how God may be working today in our own world and time in analogous ways. Even communities of God's people who are severely conflicted with hateful feelings of vengeance must ask themselves hard questions. Is the community's extreme ill will in part God's judgment on the community for past purposes and actions that have run counter to the purposes God may have envisioned for that community? Of course, some conflict and disagreement within a community are normal and even desirable for a vital and creative group. However, a given community can reach a point when conflict becomes so hurtful and deep that it paralyzes rather than energizes the community or groups within the community. Then it is time for soul searching and serious evaluation of the community's mission and its relationships to God and to other communities with whom it relates.

2. The story of Abimelech is sometimes interpreted as a general indictment of any form of kingship or centralized form of government within Israel. However, Judges 9 and its fable indict a specific form of kingship characterized by gaining power through brute force and violence. The major issue with Abimelech and Shechem is that they did not "exhibit loyalty to the house of" Jerubbabel/Gideon when they participated in the massacre of Gideon's seventy sons (8:35; 9:16-20, 56-57). Gideon had risked his life for them, and they returned evil for good. In the final analysis, the book of Judges will support certain forms of kingship and centralized authority. The positive attributes of such a model of kingship for the book of Judges would include the following elements: (1) a dynasty or family line of rulers whom God would choose; (2) a king who would unite all Israel, not by force or violence, but by persuasion and an earned loyalty; and (3) a king who would be faithful and subject to God's guidance and who would lead the people in devotion to the one true God of Israel. Abimelech fell short in every category. The politics of Abimelech—ruthless violence, hunger for power, back-stabbing vengeance, irrational assault, the worship of other gods—are roundly condemned in the strongest terms in Judges 9. Such violence in political life repeated itself often in Israel's history of kingship (1 Kgs 15:29; 2 Kgs 9:1–10:17), and violence has continued to mar the political struggles of human communities across the globe and throughout history up to the present day. Judges 9 provides a realistic portrait of the potential evil of human politics, power, and violence.

3. The disloyalty and ingratitude that Abimelech and the Shechemites displayed to their deliverer Gideon is a mirror of the disloyalty and lack of gratitude that Israel as a people showed toward the Lord. Religion and politics are intertwined in the stories. Israel's disloyalty to God begins and ends the Gideon cycle (6:7-10; 8:33-35). That religious disloyalty seeps into the political life of Israel. Israelites forgot how to show gratefulness and fidelity both to their God, who saved them from Egypt, and to their human leader Gideon, who delivered them from Midian. The quality of our theology shapes and influences the quality of both our political and our personal relationships. Good theology ought to have practical effects on how humans relate to each other.

Judges 10:1-5, Tola and Jair: Two Minor Judges

COMMENTARY

A second interlude of the so-called minor judges appears at the end of this middle phase of the judges period (6:1–10:5). Three separate notices of minor judges appear in the book of Judges, one for each of the three phases of the judges era: (1) Shamgar, at the middle of the first victorious and faithful phase in 3:31; (2) Tola and Jair at the end of the transitional phase in 10:1-5; and (3) Ibzan, Elon, and Abdon at the middle of the third tragic phase of the judges in 12:8-15. The first minor judge, Shamgar, mirrored the positive success of the major judges of the first phase (Ehud, Deborah/Barak) as he was victorious over Israel's enemy and "delivered Israel" (3:31). The two minor judges in 10:1-5, Tola and Jair, reflect the ambiguous and transitional character of the two judges or rulers in this middle phase of the judges, Gideon and Abimelech. On one hand, Gideon successfully defeated the Midianites and gave Israel rest from its enemies for forty years (8:28). On the other hand, Gideon led Israel into idolatry (8:27),

Abimelech violently seized power as king (9:5-6), and both of them used excessive violence in acts of personal revenge (8:4-17; 9:22-57).

Similarly, the first minor judge in this period, Tola, successfully "rose to deliver Israel" and ruled for twenty-three years. Tola's success mirrors the success of Gideon. However, the second minor judge, Jair, never is said to have delivered Israel or defeated an enemy. Jair's judgeship of twenty-two years seems selfishly preoccupied with internal consolidation of the family's power and wealth: thirty sons who ride on thirty donkeys and possess thirty towns. Jair seems less oriented to helping Israel or serving God and more oriented to helping himself and his own family. Thus the transition from Tola's successful deliverance of Israel to Jair's preoccupation with himself and his family's welfare is a microcosm of the turn from Gideon's deliverance to Abimelech's self-absorbed grab for power.

REFLECTIONS

1. The interludes of the minor judges have the literary effect of providing pauses of relative calm and stability within the increasingly chaotic and unstable era of the judges. God's work through these minor judges suggests not so much God's dramatic intervention as God's quiet and often hidden sustaining work within the ordinary life of families, communities, and nations. Such momentary respites of order and stability in the lives of individuals and communities allow time for renewal before we face the next round of challenges and difficulties. The minor judge episodes function as "narrative sabbaths," brief moments of relative quiet and refreshment. The minor judge interlude allows some brief narrative time for readers to ponder their reactions and their role in the events that have transpired before we are thrown again into the dilemmas, struggles, and tragedies of major judges like Jephthah and Samson.

2. The two minor judges, Tola and Jair, represent a transition in the era of the judges, as do the major judges Gideon and Abimelech. As implied readers of Judges who have read only this far in the book, however, we may not be able to discern whether these judges in the middle section of Judges represent a major turning point downward in Israel's national life or only a momentary relapse from which it will recover with the subsequent judgeships of Jephthah and Samson. Of course, when we survey the whole book with the chaos and the tragedy of the final chapters, Judges 17–21, we then can know the answer. The events of 6:1–10:5 do indeed mark a major turning point and a defining moment of decline and transition.

This experience of readers who may have some unclarity about the significance of events when we are still in the midst of them and cannot see the long view or the final outcome is analogous to our experience in the life of faith. When in the midst of a time of despair or other difficulty, we may not be able to know what our future holds. Are we at the beginning of a downward slide into a long and arduous experience of suffering with no foreseeable end? Or is this only a momentary setback, a brief time of struggle from which we will soon recover? In such times, we remember God's faithfulness to God's people over the long haul in the past. Remembrances of God's past loyalty and love provide a long view, reaching backward, that may help to put moments of difficult transition in perspective. We also have God's promises for the future of divine presence, strength, and ultimate victory over all things—even death—to sustain us with a long perspective that reaches forward (Rom 8:37-39). Even as Israel turns toward social and religious disintegration at this point in the book, Israel can be sustained by God's past love and future promises that somehow God will continue to preserve and shape Israel toward a hopeful future. Out of Israel's struggle and transition into decline will eventually come Israel's new life, new promises, and new hope. However, it may be difficult to see any of that clearly now. Israel, as God's people in every time and place, must live by faith and not by sight.

JUDGES 10:6–12:15, JEPHTHAH, IBZAN, ELON, AND ABDON

OVERVIEW

The narrative of Jephthah begins the third and final phase of the individual judge stories. The first phase (3:7–5:31) had featured consistently faithful and victorious judges (Othniel, Ehud, Deborah/Barak). The second transitional phase (6:1–10:5) included the judge Gideon and his son Abimelech, who represented the beginning of the downfall of the judges. Gideon was successful in defeating Israel's enemies and giving Israel rest for forty years. However, the leadership of Gideon and Abimelech began to degenerate into religious idolatry and selfish acts of violence aimed not only at external enemies but also at other Israelites. The third phase of the judge stories (10:6–16:31) portrays two major judges, Jephthah and Samson. These judges continue the descent into a widening distance from God and a growing inability to unite and defend Israel against its enemies for a sustained period of time. Both Jephthah and Samson experience a deeply tragic turnabout in their lives. A foolish vow compels Jephthah to sacrifice the life of his only daughter, and a reckless revelation to Delilah leads Samson into disgrace and death. Their individual stories of tragedy become precursors of Israel's collective tragedy and disintegration in the final section of the book, chaps. 17–21.

A key theme in the Jephthah narrative is the entrapment of human language that leads to death. Jephthah's vow forces him to kill or sacrifice his one child, his daughter, who represents his only link to future life. The name "Jephthah" means in Hebrew "he opens" (יפתח *yiptāḥ*), and the climax of his story is when Jephthah opens his mouth to speak the terrible vow he cannot take back: "For I have opened my mouth to the LORD, and I cannot take back my vow" (11:35-36). In the final scene, fellow Israelites from the tribe of Ephraim are forced to say a single word with a different dialect ("sibboleth" instead of "shibboleth"). Because they pronounce this one word differently, 42,000 of the Ephraimites die at the hands of Jephthah and his army. Human words and dialogue are important throughout Jephthah's story; five scenes form the structural backbone, and a dialogue stands at the center of each scene.

The scenes include (1) Israel and the Lord (10:6-16), (2) the elders of Gilead and Jephthah (10:17–11:11), (3) Jephthah and the Ammonite king (11:12-28), (4) Jephthah and his daughter (11:29-38), and (5) Jephthah and the Ephraimites (12:1-7).[42]

These five scenes and their central dialogues reveal Israel's deepening failure to remain faithful to God and united to one another. This growing failure emerges when we compare the Jephthah narrative with the preceding judge stories and the plot that is repeated in each story. The early judge stories spoke of Israel's sin in brief and general terms, but the Jephthah story concentrates more extensively on Israel's sin as the worship of other gods (10:6; cf. 3:12; 4:1). The enemy's oppression is briefly noted in the earlier stories but occupies much more space in the Jephthah cycle (10:6-16; cf. 3:13; 4:2). Israel's cry of distress led to immediate divine deliverance in the earlier stories (3:15; 4:3-7). But Israel's cry and repentance in the Jephthah tale lead to God's harsh rebuke of Israel's sin and God's initial refusal to deliver Israel (10:10-14). Previous judges had united several Israelite tribes (including Ephraim) in the battle against their enemies (3:27; 5:14). Jephthah is unable to unite even one entire tribe but only the district or clan of Gilead, located east of the Jordan. Moreover, he ends up killing 42,000 Ephraimites who were part of the Israelite people. Disunity rather than unity in Israel characterizes Jephthah's tenure as judge. Gideon had also had a dispute with the Ephraimites, but he had resolved the quarrel peacefully (8:1-3). In contrast, Jephthah's dispute with Ephraim ends with a slaughter (12:1-6). The early judge stories kept the spotlight on God and the military deliverance, but Jephthah's story focuses much more on the human judge and less attention on God. The early judges gain forty or more years of "rest" from Israel's enemies (3:30; 5:31; 8:28). However, Jephthah reigns for only six years and does not gain "rest" from Israel's enemies (12:7). At every point of comparison, Jephthah indicates a degradation from previous judge stories.[43]

43. Stone, "From Tribal Confederation to Monarchic State," 260-391, provides an extended argument for the redactional shaping of the individual judge stories into three phases of gradual decline.

42. Webb, *The Book of the Judges*, 41-78.

Judges 10:6–11:11, Israel, the Lord, and Jephthah

COMMENTARY

The two scenes that begin the Jephthah narrative function as mirror images. In the first scene (10:6-16), *the Lord* rebuffs Israel for asking for help after the Israelites had earlier rejected the Lord: "You have abandoned me and worshiped other gods" (10:13). In the second scene (10:17–11:11), *Jephthah* rebukes the elders of Gilead for asking for his help after the elders had earlier rejected him. His words closely resemble the words used by the Lord: "Are you not the very ones who rejected me?" In spite of the initial rebuke, however, both scenes end with the Lord and Jephthah responding favorably to the pleas for help. Although similar, these paired scenes also illustrate a crucial distinction. The Lord responds graciously to Israel's cry of distress with no appreciable benefit to the Lord. In fact, Israel increasingly rejects the Lord in favor of other gods in spite of the Lord's favor.

On the other hand, Jephthah's response to the cries of distress leads to his elevation from the status of a rejected son of a prostitute to "the head and commander" of the people of Gilead. God acts out of unrequited love, while Jephthah acts out of self-interest.

10:6-16. The Jephthah cycle opens with the usual introductory description of Israel again doing "what was evil in the sight of the Lord." However, the nature of the evil involving the worship of other gods has worsened. In the previous era of Gideon, Israel had worshiped only Canaanite or Amorite gods (6:10, 25; 8:33). In the era of Jephthah, the Israelites extend their religious devotion to a virtual supermarket of foreign gods from Canaan, Aram, Sidon, Moab, Ammon, and Philistia (v. 6). As punishment for their increasing disloyalty, the Lord allows the foreign nations of Philistia and Ammon to oppress Israel for

eighteen years. As in the other judge episodes, the Israelites "cried to the LORD" for
help (v. 10; see 3:9, 15; 4:3; 6:7).

But this time the Israelites add something
to their typical cry for aid. They speak words
of repentance and remorse for their sinful
ways: "We have sinned against you" (v. 10).
Israel has never confessed its sin in this way
before in the judges stories. Unfortunately,
the condition of the people has deteriorated
to such a state that the Lord receives these
words of repentance as a shallow ploy to
manipulate God. The words do not convince
the Lord in the light of the repeated backsliding of Israel in the past. God had saved the
Israelites from seven different oppressors in
the past. Yet, each time the Israelites had
rejected the Lord and returned to worshiping
the gods of those same oppressing nations (cf.
v. 6 and vv. 11-12). Thus the Lord comes to a
startling and terrifying conclusion: "therefore
I will deliver you no more" (v. 13). The divine
pronouncement is Israel's death sentence.
Without God's presence and deliverance,
Israel is doomed. The Lord urges Israel to "go
and cry" for help from these other foreign
gods that Israel had repeatedly worshiped.
"Let them deliver you" (v. 14).

The Israelites are persistent, however, and
beg God with a second word of repentance
(v. 15). Moreover, the Israelites bolster their
words with action: They "put away" their
alien gods and worship the Lord. The next
line is crucial, but its meaning is debated. The
Lord "could no longer bear to see Israel suffer" (v. 16). Many commentators assume that
Israel's actions and words have convinced the
Lord of Israel's genuine and deep remorse.
This profound repentance, they argue, is
what causes the Lord to alter the earlier pronouncement of never again delivering Israel.
Another biblical example of this divine change
of heart in response to human repentance to
which these commentators point is that of
the city of Nineveh in the book of Jonah. The
inhabitants of Nineveh repented after hearing
Jonah's words of doom, and their repentance
caused God to spare the city from destruction
(Jonah 3:10; see Jer 18:7-8). Many commentators conclude that the same dynamic is at
work here.[44]

However, the Lord's reaction in v. 16 is
more ambiguous and indeterminate than
such an interpretation allows. The verb
translated "to bear" (קצר *qāṣar*) often carries
connotations of frustration, loss of patience,
anger, and exasperation (Num 21:4-5; Zech
11:8-9). It is the verb used when Samson
becomes so exasperated with Delilah's constant nagging that he reveals the secret of his
strength (16:16). Thus one might well read
the Lord's response in v. 16 not as God's joyful agreement to deliver Israel because of its
genuine and sustained repentance. Rather,
the Lord knows that this repentance will
again be temporary and shallow, but the Lord
in total exasperation and anger "cannot bear
to see Israel suffer." It is Israel's *suffering,* not
Israel's deep repentance, that motivates any
potential change in the Lord's plans.[45] We
assume that God will somehow reluctantly
intervene. However, the text does not say that
the Lord immediately raises up a deliverer as
in the earlier judge stories. The reader is left
to wonder how God is involved in the next
series of events and whether those events will
lead to Israel's deliverance from its enemies.
As we shall see, this ambiguity about God's
role in the judgeship of Jephthah is the first
of a number of indeterminate moments in the
story of Jephthah the judge.

10:17–11:11. The next scene opens with
the Ammonite army getting ready to fight
Israel. Meanwhile, the Israelites in the Transjordan region of Gilead are frantically scrambling to find a military leader who is willing
to fight the Ammonites. They offer a reward
to the one who will step forward: "He shall
be head over all the inhabitants of Gilead"
(10:18). The narrator interrupts the flow of
the story to introduce a "mighty warrior"
named Jephthah. Jephthah is an Israelite from
Gilead, but he has some deficits according to
Israel's social code: He is "the son of a prostitute," an outcast from his family, and a leader
of outlaws who raid villages in the foreign
"land of Tob" for a living (10:1-3). Jephthah's
character reminds us of the ill-fated Abimelech, who was the despised son of a concubine (8:31), in conflict with his other brothers (9:5), and the leader of outlaws (9:4).
These associations with the negative figure

---

44. See Boling, *Judges,* 193; Soggin, *Judges,* 203.

45. Polzin, *Moses and the Deuteronomist,* 177; Webb, *The Book of
the Judges,* 45-48.

of Abimelech do not bode well for Jephthah's future, but in the end (unlike Abimelech) he will be called one who "judged Israel six years" (12:7).

In 11:4, the narrator returns to the story about the Ammonites' making war on the Israelite people of Gilead. Although the Gileadites had earlier rejected Jephthah as one of their own, the elders of Gilead beg Jephthah in their distress to return home and save his people from the Ammonite oppressors. Just as Israel had earlier rejected God and then returned to call on God for help, so also the people of Gilead return to call on Jephthah for help. Jephthah asks a legitimate question: "Are you not the very ones who rejected me?" But the Gileadites insist and offer Jephthah the position of leader "over all the inhabitants of Gilead" if he conquers the Ammonites. Jephthah then accepts the offer to fight the Ammonites with a condition that links his mission with the Lord's plan: if "the LORD gives them over to me" (11:9). This is Jephthah's first vow involving the Lord; his second vow will be more problematic (11:29-40). The elders of Gilead then pledge, "The LORD will be witness between us," and the deal is struck "before the LORD at Mizpah" (11:9-11). This sudden cluster of references to "the LORD" suggests to the reader that Jephthah may indeed be the Lord's chosen agent to deliver Israel in spite of his questionable character. Our interest is piqued and focused on this ambiguous character, who is both "mighty warrior" and "son of a prostitute," both pious adherent to the Lord and shrewd negotiator for his own interests.

REFLECTIONS

1. Israel's words of repentance and God's refusal to accept the repentance as sufficient or genuine invite reflection on the role of human repentance in motivating God's forgiveness and acts of compassion. God often does accept repentance and a change of heart as sufficient grounds to grant a person or group mercy and compassion. The psalmist reminds us that "the sacrifice acceptable to God is a broken spirit;/ a broken and contrite heart,/ O God, you will not despise" (Ps 51:17 NRSV). God speaks through the prophet Jeremiah in a similar vein: "At one moment I may declare concerning a nation or a kingdom, that I will pluck up and break down and destroy it, but if that nation, concerning which I have spoken, turns from its evil, I will change my mind about the disaster that I intended to bring on it" (Jer 18:7-8 NRSV).

Yet even in cases of true repentance and God's change of mind concerning judgment, the repentant people sometimes must still suffer negative consequences from their misdeeds. For example, God forgave the Israelites for their worship of the golden calf at Mt. Sinai (Exod 32:10, 14). However, some of the Israelites still suffered death and a plague for their sin (Exod 35:25-28, 34-35). Later in the wilderness, Moses' appeal to God's merciful nature caused God to forgive Israel's sin of refusing to enter the promised land of Canaan (Num 14:10-20). But again severe consequences accompanied the forgiveness: The old generation of Israelites would have to die in the wilderness, and God would allow only a new generation of Israelites born in the wilderness to enter the land of Canaan (Num 14:21-35).

At other times in the Bible, words and even actions that display human repentance have no effect on God. At times, the people have become so corrupt and disloyal at their core that no hope for true and sustained repentance seems possible. An important example is God's indictment of Israel's shallow repentance in Hos 5:8–6:6. Israel utters words of repentance, but God knows these words are manipulative, hollow, and not heartfelt. God seems genuinely at a loss on how to turn Israel around:

What shall I do with you, O Ephraim?
What shall I do with you, O Judah?

Your love is like a morning cloud,
　like the dew that goes away early. (Hos 6:4 NRSV)

A classic example of Israel's shallow repentance is recorded in Jeremiah 34. The prophet Jeremiah proclaimed doom on the city of Jerusalem and its king, Zedekiah. As a result, the king issued a decree setting all Israelite slaves free in accordance with a widely ignored biblical law that commanded the periodic release of all Israelite slaves. The king hoped the freeing of Israelite slaves would demonstrate to God that Zedekiah and his people were truly repentant. This in turn would motivate God to deliver Israel from the Babylonian army, which had surrounded the city. However, when the Babylonian army got up and left for a time to attend to another crisis elsewhere, the Israelites immediately rescinded the decree and took back all their slaves once again. God angrily denounced Israel's shallow repentance and promised that the Babylonian army would return to destroy Jerusalem (Jer 34:12-32). Israel had become so rebellious at its very core that it was no longer capable of sincere and sustained repentance. That is the situation in which we find Israel in Judg 10:10-16. At this point, Israel has rejected the Lord so many times after the Lord's repeated interventions to save Israel that Israel can no longer be trusted.

The Bible is well acquainted with the full range of human responses to God's compassionate and loving nature. Sometimes God's love causes a person to see the error of his or her ways and to begin a whole new life of faithfulness and obedience (Luke 19:1-10). More often, God's promise and love may begin a process of slow growth and change, with ups and downs that offer glimpses of genuine repentance that may not be fully realized on this side of the grave. Major biblical figures like Abraham, Jacob, and King David, for whom we have more biographical detail, offer realistic examples of lives of faith that sometimes falter. At other times, an individual or community may reach a point of such degradation or entrapment in misguided rebellion or sinfulness that they may be incapable of true and lasting repentance. Like an addict who will say anything to get another fix or an abuser who will deny everything to avoid exposing an awful secret, people can become almost hopelessly entangled in their self-delusions and manipulative ploys. The only resort to genuine transformation in such cases is to "hit bottom" so that the lie is exposed, the truth is set free, and the old pattern reaches an end. In such extreme cases, only then does new life have a chance to emerge as a genuine possibility. This is where the book of Judges is heading. Israel will hit bottom in chapters 17–21 as the social fabric of Israel will disintegrate and its sense of faith and morality will descend into chaos. People of faith need much wisdom and much humility when they try to discern at what point they and those with whom they minister stand on the continuum of human repentance. Is it genuine, partial, or a shallow manipulative ploy? In some cases, we may need to leave judgments concerning the genuineness of human repentance to God's wisdom when our own insights in such matters reach their limits.

2. One of the most remarkable features of the Lord's response to Israel's shallow repentance is that the Lord does not simply abandon Israel entirely. Instead, the story reports that God "could no longer bear to see Israel suffer" (10:16). This is a word of grace in the midst of human failure. Even though Israel deserves to be oppressed by the very nations and foreign gods whom they had worshiped, the Lord is moved to save them from the punishment the Lord had imposed. The manner of God's salvation in this particular case is not immediately apparent. Such bewilderment and unclarity are often what we experience when we stand in the midst of a time of trial and suffering. Where is God in this? How will God act to save? In the midst of our wonderment, we can be supported by the knowledge that God cannot bear too long to see God's people suffer, no matter how deserved the suffering may be. We can hope and expect that God will not allow us to undergo more difficulty or trial than we can endure with God's help (1 Cor 10:13).

3. God has used many unlikely people to accomplish God's purposes throughout the book of Judges. God's agents have included a left-handed assassin named Ehud, a woman judge and prophet named Deborah, a non-Israelite woman named Jael, and a timid Gideon, who was the weakest of the weak. Yet Jephthah appears to be the most unlikely person of God among them all. He is the son of a prostitute, an outcast from his own family, and the leader of a band of outlaws. He is also a sly negotiator as he gains for himself the position of leader of all Gilead in return for his willingness to fight Ammon. At the same time, he acknowledges the Lord's role in giving him victory over Ammon (11:9) and brings his political covenant with the elders of Gilead into the realm of religious faith (11:11). We are left wondering at this point whether Jephthah, at his core, is a genuinely good and faithful person who has simply made the best of the unfortunate circumstances of his life, which were beyond his control. Or is Jephthah a cynical politician who is looking out only for his own interests, using religion to mask his quest for political power and position? Even by the end of the story of Jephthah, we will not be able to answer these questions definitively. Jephthah will remain an ambiguous character. Yet God will use him to judge Israel for six years (12:7), and Jephthah will be listed in the New Testament Letter to the Hebrews as one of Israel's heroes of faith (Heb 11:32). God does not use plastic saints but flesh-and-blood sinners to work God's will in the world. That may be a comforting word of reassurance for those who yearn to be useful to the purposes of God and yet who know all too well their own failures and inadequacies.

Judges 11:12-40, Jephthah, His Daughter, and the Ammonites

COMMENTARY

The dramatic point of tension and resolution in previous judge stories involved the defeat of the enemy and its leader. Othniel defeated the king of Aram (3:10). Ehud assassinated the fat King Eglon (3:21-23). Deborah foretold and Jael actually committed the assassination of the Canaanite general Sisera (4:9, 21). Gideon annihilated the Midianites in a surprise attack at night (7:19-23). We would expect that the climax of the Jephthah story would be his military defeat of the Ammonites, who were oppressing Israel. Jephthah does defeat them, but the battle is narrated in only two short verses (vv. 32-33). What replaces the military victory as the center of the story's tension and climax is the vow Jephthah makes to the Lord before the battle (vv. 30-31) and its fulfillment after the battle (vv. 34-40). Jephthah vows to offer to the Lord as a burnt offering whoever or whatever comes out of the door of his house when he comes home from battle (v. 31). The one

to be sacrificed ends up being Jephthah's only child, his daughter. As we shall see, a number of uncertainties and ambiguities surround this climactic episode. The history of interpretation of this text runs the gamut from extolling the virtue of Jephthah and his daughter in their willing sacrifice to vilifying Jephthah as an evil father and perpetrator of patriarchal violence. However, before we examine the ambiguities of Jephthah's vow, the scene opens with an extended set of negotiations between Jephthah and the king of the Ammonites in vv. 12-28.

11:12-28. Jephthah has been elevated by the elders of Gilead from a rogue leader of bandits to the more honored role of a military commander of Gilead's army. Before leading the army into battle, however, Jephthah steps into another role as statesman and diplomat in an attempt to broker a peaceful resolution to the conflict with Ammon. Jephthah demonstrates his verbal abilities in presenting persuasive arguments about conflicting claims to the land of Gilead. Unfortunately, the Ammonite king in the end remains unpersuaded, and military conflict becomes the only option.

Jephthah begins the negotiations by sending a messenger to the Ammonites to ask why Ammon is attacking the Israelite region of Gilead. The Ammonite king sends a messenger in reply who argues that Israel wrongly stole this land of the Ammorites in the Transjordan area when Israel first came from Egypt on its way to the promised land (v. 13). In a lengthy rejoinder, Jephthah rehearses the story of Numbers 21, which recounts Israel's experience in this region. As the Israelites tried to reach Canaan, which was the land the Lord had given them, the Israelites had to cross one of three nations that lay on the eastern boundary of Canaan. Those nations included Moab, Edom, and the land of the Amorites. Israel did not seek to take away "the land of Moab or the land of the Ammonites" or any other land besides Canaan (v. 15). However, Edom and Moab refused to allow Israel to cross their territories to get to Canaan (vv. 16-18). The only option left to Israel was to go through the land of the Amorites, whose leader was King Sihon. The Amorites also refused to honor Israel's reasonable request to pass through the land. In addition to refusing Israel's request, the Amorites also viciously attacked Israel in an act of aggression. But "the LORD" saved Israel and defeated the aggressive Amorites. As a result, the Lord gave the Amorites' land to Israel as their rightful possession in the area east of the Jordan River (v. 21-23).

Jephthah then asks the Ammonites two key questions in his argument: "Should you not possess what your god Chemosh gives you to possess? And should we not be the ones to possess everything that the LORD our God has conquered for our benefit?" (v. 24). The questions imply that each nation has its legitimate god with a certain territory alloted to it, no more and no less. This view is in line with that of Deut 32:8-9:

When the Most High apportioned the nations,
    when he divided humankind,
he fixed the boundaries of the peoples
    according to the number of the gods;

the LORD's own portion was his people,
    Jacob his alloted share. (NRSV)

One difficulty in the Judges text is that the god Chemosh is usually portrayed as the chief god of the nation of Moab and not of Ammon. Ammon's chief god is Milcom, or Molech (Num 21:29; 2 Kgs 23:13). However, Jephthah apparently assumes an almost interchangeable identification of the nations of Ammon and Moab. This close association of Moab and Ammon appears elsewhere in Judges (3:13) and in the OT (Gen 19:36-38; Deut 2:17-19). The association with Moab and the god Chemosh may also recall the remarkable narrative of the Moabite king who offered up his only son as a burnt offering in a conflict with Israel, causing Moab to be spared (2 Kgs 3:26-27). The upcoming scene with Jephthah's sacrifice of his only child as part of a vow before a military battle may be an echo of this Moabite act, an act that was at once effective and also abominable.

Jephthah continues his argument as he moves from history and theology to practicality. If the east Jordan region of the Amorites belonged to Ammon, why did Ammon allow the Israelites to dwell in the region for three hundred years (v. 26)? It makes little sense for Ammon suddenly to raise objections when Ammon has been silent for such a long time. In the end, however, Jephthah correctly senses that none of these arguments will likely sway the Ammonite king. Thus Jephthah throws down the gauntlet by inviting the Lord to be the judge of this dispute and "decide today for the Israelites or the Ammonites" (v. 27). Jephthah takes on the role of a prosecuting attorney in a lawsuit with Ammon with the Lord sitting as judge in the divine court. The statement is in effect a declaration of war as the Lord's decision will be determined by whomever wins the military battle between the two opponents. Jephthah's extended arguments indeed have no effect in persuading the Ammonites to back down, and so the stage is set for the conflict to begin (v. 28).

The literary effects of this extended negotiation are several. First, the negotiations retard the building tension and push back the climax to a point further into the story. Second, Jephthah's diplomacy establishes him as an able (if not always successful) negotiator. Knowing of his ability to negotiate will later cause the reader to wonder why the skillful Jephthah does not negotiate with God when his foolish vow forces him to sacrifice his daughter. Third, the references to Moab and the god Chemosh suggest a negative association of Jephthah with the Moabite king who offered his child as a burnt offering as a means of inducing his god to give him a victory (2 Kgs 3:26-27). Fourth, Jephthah's arguments also suggest positive aspects of his character. He seems to know the faith traditions of Israel's past, and he presents himself as a rational statesman who desires peace rather than war. He is not an aggressor, and yet he is also not a coward. He refuses to back down in fear before the Ammonite threat. He ultimately entrusts his future and his fate into the hands of the Lord. Jephthah emerges as a complex character with both negative and positive dimensions that will continue throughout the next climactic scenes involving his vow and his daughter.

11:29-40. When the negotiations with the Ammonite king conclude, "the spirit of the LORD came upon Jephthah" (v. 29). This is the first explicit indication in the story that the Lord has indeed chosen Jephthah to deliver Israel from the Ammonites. Everything up to this point has involved human initiative: the elders of Gilead negotiating with Jephthah to be their leader, and Jephthah negotiating on his own initiative with the Ammonite king. The Lord's name has been invoked along the way at several points, but no overt statement has indicated the Lord's actual involvement with Jephthah. But now the Spirit of the Lord has come upon Jephthah just as the Spirit had come upon previous judges. The divine Spirit was a positive element in Othniel's defeat of the enemy king of Aram (3:10). The Spirit of the Lord had relatively little positive effect on Gideon, however, who remained timid and fearful even after receiving the Spirit (6:34). In the case of Abimelech, God sent an evil spirit that did not cause unity and strength but conflict and discord among the Israelites. Thus, when we read that Jephthah received the Spirit of the Lord, we are poised to wonder whether this will have a positive or a negative effect. Part of the effect of the Spirit is an ability to unite and call forth volunteers from among the tribes of Israel. Jephthah accomplishes

this rallying of troops with some success as he passes "through Gilead and Manasseh." This is not a large call of many Israelite tribes but involves only a small localized area in the territory outside of Canaan and east of the Jordan River. The judges seem less and less able to muster substantial coalitions of tribes as we move through the individual judge stories from Othniel to Ehud to Deborah/Barak and Gideon. Indeed, the next and final judge after Jephthah, Samson, will lead no Israelites in battle. Samson will fight all his battles against the Philistines alone. This increasing inability to unify Israel's tribes is part of the social disintegration of the nation as the era of the judges waned.

Once we have been assured that the Spirit of the Lord has come upon Jephthah, we are prepared by the previous judge stories to assume that battle and victory for Israel will follow immediately. However, that assumption is disrupted by a startling and somewhat ambiguous pledge or vow made by Jephthah to the Lord. If the Lord gives Jephthah victory over the Ammonites, then Jephthah promises to offer as a burnt offering either "whoever" (NRSV) or "whatever" (NIV) first "comes out of the doors of my house to meet me" when he returns home from the battle. The Hebrew text (אשר 'ăšer) is ambiguous as to whether Jephthah intended his vow to involve the offering of a human being ("whoever") or an animal ("whatever"). Some scholars argue that Jephthah's words must intend a human sacrifice. G. F. Moore offers his own strong opinion, "That a human victim is intended is, in fact, as plain as words can make it; the language is inapplicable to an animal, and a vow to offer the first sheep or goat that he comes across—not to mention the possibility of an unclean animal—is trivial to absurdity."[46]

Other scholars argue just as adamantly that Jephthah's vow would assume an animal sacrifice in the light of the structure of Iron Age houses unearthed in this area. Domesticated animals apparently lived along with humans inside the typical house of this period.[47] In my judgment, Jephthah's language is left intentionally ambivalent by the narrator so that the reader cannot know for sure what Jephthah's real intention was.

46. Moore, *Judges,* 299.
47. Boling, *Judges,* 208.

Another issue arises in trying to understand the significance of Jephthah's vow. What is the relationship of Jephthah's vow and the coming of the Spirit of the Lord upon him? Phyllis Trible argues that Jephthah's vow is an act of unfaithfulness. She assumes Jephthah is aware that he has just received the Lord's Spirit. Knowing this, the Spirit-filled Jephthah should trust that God's Spirit is all he needs to guarantee victory over the Ammonites. However, his additional vow after receiving the Spirit means that he does not yet trust God sufficiently. His vow is a calculated ploy to manipulate God as a way to ensure victory.[48] In contrast to Trible, who separates the good spirit from Jephthah's bad vow, Cheryl Exum maintains that the vow is not made in opposition to the divine Spirit. Rather, the vow is made under the influence of the Lord's Spirit. The problem is not the vow as such, argues Exum. Faithful Israelites frequently made vows to God. The revered ancestor Jacob vowed to worship the Lord if the Lord would take care of his needs (Gen 28:20-22). The pious Hannah vowed to dedicate her son to the Lord's service if the Lord would grant her the ability to have children (1 Sam 1:9-11). The problem with Jephthah's vow was not making the vow itself but its careless wording and content. Jephthah recklessly vowed to offer "whoever" or "whatever" came out of his house as a burnt offering. If he had promised to erect an altar or worship the Lord when he returned in victory, the vow would have been much less problematic.[49]

I would argue that the act of taking the vow in itself *in this specific context* is indeed problematic, but not for the reason Trible cites. We are not told whether Jephthah is aware of having received the divine Spirit. Therefore, we cannot join Trible in condemning him for failing to trust in a divine Spirit that he may not have been aware he had been given. Yet there is another basis on which we can condemn Jephthah. While vows may be properly offered to God in some contexts, Jephthah wrongly uses the vow *in this particular context* as a bribe or leverage

to influence the divine judge in the context of a court case. Jephthah has himself set up the conflict with the Ammonites as a court battle with the Lord as judge (11:27). According to Deuteronomy's laws, any bribes or gifts to judges are strictly prohibited lest they unduly influence the judges' decisions (Deut 16:19). This prohibition is grounded in Israel's understanding of God, who "is not partial and takes no bribe" (Deut 10:17 NRSV).[50] Thus Jephthah's vow in itself violates a deeply held Israelite norm in regard to the prohibition of gifts or bribes to judges. Exum is surely correct that the wording and content of the vow are also reckless and problematic in that it opens the door to all kinds of inappropriate sacrifices, including unclean animals or humans. But any vow, no matter its content, in this particular setting of a court case with God as judge is illicit and inappropriate.

Jephthah has received "the spirit of the LORD" as a gift of strength, and he has made the vow as a bribe to influence God's decision as judge in order to guarantee himself the victory. What will God's response be? We learn immediately that the Lord gave the Ammonites into Jephthah's hand, and Jephthah "inflicted a massive defeat on them" (vv. 32-33). Ordinarily such a victory would be the climax of an individual judge story, but in this case the attention of the narrator rests elsewhere. Jephthah returns home from his victory. Remembering his open-ended vow, the reader wonders who or what will first come out of his house. The narrator reports the tragic scene: "there was his daughter coming out to meet him with timbrels and dancing." Jephthah's daughter was doing what Israelite women often did: welcoming victorious soldiers home with music and dance. Women led by Miriam celebrated Israel's victory over Egypt at the Red Sea (Exod 15:19-21), and women later celebrated King David's military victories in a similar manner (1 Sam 8:6-7).

But this moment of great triumph for Jephthah turns into bitter tragedy and pain. His thoughtless vow meant that he would have to sacrifice his daughter as a burnt offering to the Lord. The sacrifice is all the more poignant because she is his only link to future

48. Phyllis Trible, "The Daughter of Jephthah: An Inhuman Sacrifice," in *Texts of Terror: Literary-Feminist Readings of Biblical Narratives* (Philadelphia: Fortress, 1984) 93-116.

49. J. Cheryl Exum, "The Tragic Vision and Biblical Narrative: The Case of Jephthah," in *Signs and Wonders: Biblical Texts in Literary Focus,* ed. J. Cheryl Exum (n.p.: SBL, 1989) 66-67.

50. Michael Goldberg, "The Story of the Moral: Gifts or Bribes in Deuteronomy?" *Int.* 38 (1984) 15-25.

generations: "she was his only child; he had no son or daughter except her" (v. 34). Jephthah's first words are somewhat troubling, for they paint him as the victim and offer no consolation to his daughter. Jephthah accuses his daughter of bringing trouble on him, as if she is somehow responsible for his reckless vow (v. 35). He appears capable of seeing the world only through his own eyes. His self-centered character is heightened by the contrast with his daughter. She dutifully accepts her fate for the sake of her father and Israel's security: "do to me according to what has gone out of your mouth" (v. 36). She makes only one request: that she and her companions be allowed to "wander on the mountains" and "bewail my virginity" for a period of two months (v. 37). She does so, and then she returns to her father, "who did with her according to the vow he had made." No description of the actual killing of the daughter is given beyond this. An additional note emphasizes her virginity: "she had never slept with a man" (v. 39). The scene concludes with an ongoing custom in which the daughters of Israel would go out for four days each year either "to lament" (NRSV) the death of Jephthah's daughter or to "commemorate" (NIV) her willing sacrifice (v. 40).

In a thorough and helpful study of this text, David Marcus summarizes the fascinating history of interpretation of this tragic and troubling text, which divides into two major groups.[51] On one hand, Jewish and Christian interpreters up to the Middle Ages consistently assumed that Jephthah did indeed kill his daughter and offer her up as a burnt offering to God. For example, the Aramaic Targum acknowledged that while Jephthah did sacrifice his daughter, the practice was henceforth prohibited in Israel. The Church Father Origen believed the sacrifice of Jephthah's daughter to prefigure the willing sacrifice and death of the Christian martyrs. Jewish exegetes like Rashi and Nachmanides appealed to the "plain sense" of the text's meaning that Jephthah did indeed kill his daughter as a sacrificial offering.

On the other hand, a second major group of interpreters have argued that Jephthah did *not* actually kill his daughter, but rather

dedicated her to a life of virginity or celibacy. The earliest example of this line of interpretation is the medieval Jewish commentator David Kimchi, who wrote:

It is quite clear that he did not kill her because the text [in verse 37] does not say "I will mourn for my life," [but only "will mourn for my virginity"]. This indicates that he did not kill her but rather that she did not know a man [remained a virgin], because the text says [verse 39] "she did not know a man."[52]

Many subsequent Jewish and Christian interpreters adopted this line of interpretation, assuming that Jephthah's daughter remained alive but celibate. Indeed, Christian scholars associated the medieval practice of nuns vowing their lives to celibate service to God with the model of Jephthah's daughter. In support of their position, these interpreters point to v. 39, which does not actually state that Jephthah killed his daughter but simply that he "did with her according to the vow he had made." This line of interpretation found its way into George Frederic Handel's oratorio entitled *Jephtha* first performed in 1752. In Handel's retelling of the biblical story, an angel intervenes just when Jephthah is about to kill his daughter and sings these words:

Rise, Jephtha. And ye reverend priests, withhold the slaughterous hand. No vow can disannul the law of God, nor such was its intent, when rightly scanned, yet still shall be fulfilled. Thy daughter, Jephtha, thou must dedicate to God, in pure and virgin state for ever.

This angelic interruption of the sacrifice mirrors a similar motif in Abraham's near sacrifice of his son in Genesis 22.

Despite these alternative renderings, the dominant interpretation remains that Jephthah did indeed kill his daughter and offer her as a burnt offering. Martin Luther's comment on the text is typical: "Some affirm he did not sacrifice her, but the text is clear enough."[53] However, I find more convincing the conclusion of the careful study by David Marcus that the Jephthah story contains

---

51. David Marcus, *Jephthah and His Vow* (Lubbock, Tex.: Texas Tech Press, 1986) 8-9.

52. Quoted in Marcus, *Jephthah and His Vow*, 8.
53. Martin Luther, *Die Deutsche Bibel* (Weimar: Hermann Böhlaus Nachfolger, 1939) 131.

"ambiguities consciously devised by the narrator" to be "open to a number of interpretations" so that "the text, as it stands now, admits the possibility of either conclusion."[54] The effect of the ambivalence is to heighten suspense, to draw the reader into wrestling with the moral dilemmas and ambiguities of the story, and to increase the sense of horror at a possibility so repulsive that it is not described but left only as an imagined potentiality. This central ambiguity of the entire story—whether Jephthah killed his daughter or not—reflects the overall ambiguity of Jephthah's character. In the end, whether Jephthah's daughter was sacrificed or lived a life of celibacy, Jephthah's vow remains foolish, wrong, and unnecessary. Yet at the same time, Jephthah received "the spirit of the LORD" and successfully delivered Israel from the Ammonite oppression. The scale of evaluation, however, will be tipped more toward the negative and against Jephthah in the concluding episode as he deals treacherously with his fellow Israelites from the tribe of Ephraim (12:1-6).

54. Marcus, *Jephthah and His Vow,* 52.

REFLECTIONS

1. Part of the ambiguity of this story is that it touches upon the opposition of two strong convictions or values promoted in biblical literature. On one hand, the offering up of children as burnt offerings to the gods was viewed as an abhorrent pagan abomination that profaned the name of the Lord (Lev 18:21; 20:2-5; 2 Kgs 23:10; Jer 32:35). Indeed, this repugnant practice was most closely associated with the god Molech, the god of the Ammonites, the very people against whom Jephthah was fighting. On the other hand, the Old Testament expresses the conviction that every firstborn child belonged to the Lord and was theoretically to be offered up as a sacrifice to the Lord (Exod 13:2; 22:29). This conviction lay in the background of the account of the Lord's killing of the firstborn of the Egyptians in the tenth plague of the exodus story (Exod 4:22-23). God commanded certain provisions by which the firstborn children of the Israelites could be "redeemed" and thus spared from death. Parents could substitute certain animals as burnt offerings (Exod 13:13; 34:20). They could also substitute for their children individual members of the special tribe of Levites who were dedicated to lifelong service in the Lord's sanctuary (Num 3:12-13; 8:15-18). The Lord's legitimate claim on all firstborn children likely underlies in part the story of God's command to Abraham to offer his son Isaac as a burnt offering to the Lord in Genesis 22. The same theme of the sacrifice of the firstborn child lies behind Paul's understanding of the death of Jesus as God's offering up his only Son as a sacrifice: "He who did not withhold his own Son, but gave him up for all of us, will he not with him also give us everything else?" (Rom 8:32 NRSV). Jon Levenson has argued that this theme of the death and sacrifice of the firstborn or beloved child is deeply rooted and common in both Jewish and Christian theological traditions.[55] The willingness to give up what is most precious in service to God remains an enduring biblical value. At the same time, the protection of children against violence and abuse, even if religiously motivated, is demonstrated by the many ways in which the firstborn children could be "redeemed." Abraham's willingness to sacrifice Isaac is never held up as a model to be emulated; it was a one-time and unique demonstration of faith from which all subsequent sacrifices in ancient Israel of animals, grain, or acts of justice and contrition drew merit. In the same way, God's willingness to allow Jesus to die on the cross was a one-time, unrepeatable sacrifice and not a literal example for human parents to follow in regard to their children.

55. Jon Levenson, *The Death and Resurrection of the Beloved Son: The Transformation of Child Sacrifice in Judaism and Christianity* (New Haven: Yale University Press, 1993).

As for Jephthah's willingness to sacrifice his daughter, we must remember its place within the larger structure of thematic development within the book of Judges. Jephthah's judgeship represents the third and most negative phase of the individual judges. We have moved from good and faithful judges in 3:7–5:31 to a transitional phase of somewhat effective but religiously unfaithful judges in 6:1–10:5 to the third phase of tragic and ultimately failed judges in 10:6–16:31. Jephthah falls within the last and most negative period of the era. His willingness to kill or sacrifice his daughter in an unnecessary and illicit vow must be evaluated as a symptom of a deteriorating system of leadership under the judges.

2. Feminist scholars have rightly condemned Jephthah's callous and unjust treatment of his daughter. Her meek and submissive acquiescence to her father's foolish vow cannot excuse Jephthah, nor can it be taken as an enduring model for women or daughters in their relationship to men or fathers. As is often the case in many communities and societies, the woman here is anonymous, powerless, and the victim of deathly forces over which she has little control or involvement. Her negative experience differs markedly from the first woman and daughter we encountered at the beginning of Judges. There the daughter had a name, Achsah. She took bold initiatives for the sake of her own well-being as she asked her father for life-giving springs of water as part of her inheritance (1:11-15). In contrast, Jephthah's daughter can ask her father only for two months reprieve from her death sentence or (in some interpretations) two months of mourning for her life of celibacy.

What emerges as one surveys all the women in the book of Judges is that the welfare and status of women become signs of the religious and political health of the society. In the initial stages of the judges era, when Israel was united and faithful to God, the women in the stories held positions of some power and exercised independent initiative. The women who appear early in the judges period—Achsah (1:11-15), Deborah, and Jael (chaps. 4–5)—are among some of the strongest women characters in the Bible. By the time we have reached the third phase of the era in the judgeship of Jephthah, the fate of women has deteriorated along with Israel's social and religious life, as the fate of Jephthah's daughter illustrates. That deterioration in the role of the women will continue with the fate of several women in the Samson story (chaps. 13–16). This social and religious regression will reach a horrifying low point with the rape and murder of the Levite's concubine in chapter 19 and the forcible kidnapping of hundreds of young women by the men of the tribe of Benjamin in chapter 21. The book of Judges suggests that the well-being and treatment of women and children (especially daughters) in a community or nation can serve as a measuring stick for the overall health and faithfulness of the community's religious and political life. In a similar way, the Old Testament prophets saw the mistreatment of widows and orphans and other marginalized groups as a symptom of a deeper social and religious deterioration at the core of the nation (Isa 10:2). This measuring stick remains an enduring and relevant index for the health of contemporary communities and societies as well.[56]

3. Certain tensions emerge in attempting to understand the nature of God's involvement in the events of Jephthah's story. The Lord vows never again to deliver Israel because of its repeated disloyalty, and yet the Lord cannot bear to see Israel suffer (10:13, 16). Jephthah negotiates his own rise to the position of judge over Israel. In every other case, God has been the prime mover in calling the judges to their role. The Lord does give the victory to Jephthah (11:32), but it is not entirely clear whether the victory comes solely as a result of the Lord's giving Jephthah the divine Spirit (11:29). Did Jephthah's vow to the Lord help in any way to convince God to secure the victory

---

56. For a survey of women characters in the book of Judges, see Michael O'Connor, "The Women in the Book of Judges," *HAR* 10 (1986) 227-93; and J. Cheryl Exum, "Feminist Criticism: Whose Interests Are Being Served?" in Yee, *Judges and Method,* 65-90.

over the Ammonites (11:30-31)? The story does not give a clear answer. One senses that God is somehow more distant and not as directly in control of events as in the previous judge stories. Although God remains involved, God seems at the same time to be growing increasingly frustrated with Israel and more willing to allow Israel to go on its misguided course and suffer the consequences. The elders of Gilead choose the son of a prostitute as their judge, and the Lord allows it. Jephthah vows to sacrifice what first comes out of his house. When it is his daughter, God does not intervene to nullify the tragic consequences as God had done in Genesis 22 with Abraham and Isaac. There may be times in our lives when God remains present, but may also allow us to suffer the tragic consequences of our own rebellious actions and sin. God does not save us from every mistake. God often allows us the freedom to fail. Such failures and acts of rebellion may become opportunities to reconsider our priorities, to mature in our decision making, and to grow in faith. At other times, such failures may drive us to despair. Whether we take advantage of those opportunities for growth in the midst of failure remains an open question and an ongoing challenge that we are likely to encounter more than once in our lifetime.

Judges 12:1-7, Jephthah and the Ephraimites

COMMENTARY

The final episode in the Jephthah cycle involves his conflict, not with an external enemy but with a fellow Israelite tribe, the tribe of Ephraim. Ephraim is a northern tribe located on the western side of the Jordan River in the hill country of Canaan. Ephraim was a dominant and important northern tribe throughout much of ancient Israel's history. The book of Judges uses this tribe as a barometer of Israel's cohesion and social unity as a people. In the earliest and most positive phase of the judges era, the individual judges called on the tribe of Ephraim to join in the conflict against the enemy, and they immediately responded (3:27; 4:5; 5:14). In the second transitional phase under the judge Gideon, the tribe of Ephraim is called into the conflict against Midian at a late stage. The Ephraimites complain bitterly to Gideon about not being invited earlier to join in the battle. Gideon soothes their hurt feelings and peacefully resolves the internal dispute with Ephraim (7:24-25; 8:1-3). In this third and most negative phase of the judges era, beginning with Jephthah, the Ephraimites are bitterly disappointed that they were not invited to join Jephthah's fight against the Ammonites. Although a skillful negotiator in the past, Jephthah does not deal with their complaint diplomatically. Instead, he fights

against the Ephraimites and kills 42,000 of them. This civil war with Ephraim uncovers a growing rift within Israel itself. This intra-Israelite conflict is a sign of the dissolution of the nation of Israel, which will only worsen when a full-scale civil war erupts in Judges 19–21 with devastating results.

12:1-3. Verse 1 opens the scene with the Ephraimites preparing for battle and confronting Jephthah with a question. Why did he not call on the Ephraimites to join in his fight against the Ammonites? The question is a close parallel to the Ephraimites' question to Gideon in 8:1. However, their hostility is much more intense now than at the time of Gideon. The Ephraimites vow to burn Jephthah's "house" down over him. The threat is somewhat hollow in that the death or lifelong virginity of Jephthah's only daughter guarantees that he has no "house" in the sense of future progeny. Jephthah responds that he had, indeed, called on the Ephraimites to help in fighting the Ammonites, but they "did not deliver me from their hand" (v. 2). Jephthah's claim to have invited Ephraim to join the fight is not attested anywhere in the preceding story (see 11:29). The reader is led to conclude that this is a bald-faced lie. We begin to wonder whether any of Jephthah's many words, including his confessions of faith in God, were genuine and true. The Ephraimites are not satisfied with his answer to their complaint, and so the battle between Jephthah and his fellow Israelites from Ephraim begins.

12:4. One of the other causes of the fight is the Ephraimites' taunt or accusation that the Transjordanian people of Gilead are only פליטים (pĕlîṭîm), "fugitives" (NRSV) or perhaps better "renegades" (NIV), from Ephraim who have abandoned their true home tribe (v. 4). Such taunts and desires for personal vengeance had earlier led Gideon to attack his fellow Israelites (8:4-9, 13-17). Once again, matters involving the judge's personal pride and tribal jealousies override the need for unity and cohesion as the people of God. Jephthah's leadership fails to offer any substantive or positive vision for uniting Israel once the Ammonite enemy has been defeated. Instead, Jephthah engages in ruthless power politics to defeat and kill what he perceives to be the internal enemy of Ephraim.

12:5-6. One of the methods Jephthah employs to identify and isolate his internal enemies is the boundary of language and of dialect. Jephthah knows well the power of words to entrap and bring death. Jephthah's army of Gileadites secures the fords, or crossing points, on the Jordan River, the geographical boundary between his parochial region of Gilead east of the Jordan and the rest of Israel in the land of Canaan, which lies to the west of the Jordan River. Jephthah's defeat of the invading Ephraimite army causes the Ephraimite soldiers who escaped from the battle to become the "fugitives of Ephraim," the same derisive label the Ephraimites had used for the men of Gilead (v. 5; see v. 4). When these Ephraimite fugitives try to cross

the Jordan to leave Gilead and return home to Ephraim on the western side, the Gilead soldiers first make them say the word "Shibboleth" (שבלת šibbōlet), which means either "ear of corn" or "stream." People of Gilead east of the Jordan pronounced this word with an initial "sh" sound in their dialect. People of Ephraim from west of the Jordan pronounced the same word with an initial "s," and not "sh," sound. Thus Jephthah's soldiers are able to detect the Ephraimites by their dialect, and they kill them as they try to cross the river. The narrator reports that an enormous number, 42,000 Ephraimites, were killed at that time (v. 6). This scene at the fords of the Jordan River recalls an earlier judge, Ehud, who also seized the fords of the Jordan River and killed thousands there. However, Ehud fought against Israel's enemies, the Moabites, and not against fellow Israelites (3:28-29). In contrast, Jephthah has slaughtered his countrymen, the Ephraimites, at the fords of the Jordan. Jephthah's massacre of his own people suggests a disintegration of Israel's unity from the inside, a growing threat more ominous than any outside enemy.

12:7. This gradual decline in Israel's well-being as a nation is also suggested by the fact that Jephthah's reign as a judge is the shortest of any of the judges thus far. Previous judges had won periods of forty to eighty years of peace and "rest" for Israel (3:30; 5:31; 8:28). Jephthah judged Israel for only six years. In contrast to the previous judges, the narrator does not report that Israel obtained any period of "rest" or peace in his time. Jephthah dies a parochial "Gileadite" more than a unifying and heroic judge who left a lasting legacy for all Israel (v. 12).

REFLECTIONS

Up to this point, Jephthah's character has appeared to be quite ambivalent. At times he seems a faithful follower of the Lord and an able leader of the army who defeats the Ammonites. At other times, Jephthah appears manipulative, unwilling to trust the Lord, and tragically entrapped by his own words. In this last scene of his life, the scales of judgment tip decidedly against him in comparison to previous judges and their treatment of the tribe of Ephraim. Earlier judges had successfully rallied the Ephraimites to their side. But Jephthah succeeds only in antagonizing the Ephraimites and then slaughtering them. Just as Jephthah had killed his own daughter and family member, so also now he kills his own Israelite brothers and members of the broader Israelite family.

When a common external enemy is defeated or disappears, a power vacuum often occurs within a group or community. This is true of large groups and nations, and it is true of small groups, religious communities, and families. The sudden disappearance of a common enemy or purpose often allows old tribal jealousies and conflicts over power within the group to erupt. What is required is something Jephthah did not offer. Such groups or communities need strong leadership to help them discover and unite behind a positive and compelling vision for their identity and mission. Good leaders help individuals and groups within their community to form and rally around positive goals and purposes. Such goals transcend parochial interests and center the community's attention on the larger good of the group and its mission within the larger context in which it lives and works.

Judges 12:8-15, Ibzan, Elon, and Abdon: Three Minor Judges

COMMENTARY

The three so-called minor judges in 12:8-15 appear in the midst of the major judgeships of Jephthah (chaps. 10–12) and Samson (chaps. 13–16). These three judges—Ibzan, Elon, and Abdon—reflect the same progressive decline in effectiveness that has been noted among the major judges Jephthah and Samson, who comprise this third and most negative phase of the judges era. This third cluster of minor judges emerges as ineffectual leaders in comparison to the two previous groups of minor judges, associated with phase one and phase two of the judges period. The first minor judge in the positive phase was Shamgar (3:31), who defeated the Philistines and "delivered Israel." The second group of minor judges included Tola and Jair (10:1-5) during the second transitional phase of the judges era. Tola successfully "delivered Israel" and reigned for twenty-three years. The description of Jair's tenure as judge is less positive in that he did not "deliver Israel." His reign focused less on Israel as a whole and more on the welfare of his own family and their possession of donkeys and towns. His reign, however, lasted for a fairly long period of twenty-two years.

The third group of minor judges here does not compare favorably with the previous minor judges. No minor judge in this third group is said to "deliver" Israel. Their rule brings benefit only to themselves and not to the nation of Israel as a whole. The details about these judges involve only their own families and their deaths and burials. The lengths of their reigns (seven years, ten years, eight years) are relatively short in comparison to the previous minor judges (10:1-5, 23 years, 22 years). These minor judges (Ibzan, Elon, Abdon) combine with Jephthah and Samson to embody the disintegration of Israel in the third and most negative phase of the individual judge stories.

This uneventful interlude of three minor judges has a literary effect similar to treading water and going nowhere. It is almost as if God needs this time to consider the options of what to do next with this people Israel who seem repeatedly inclined toward rebellion and self-destruction. God had earlier said there would be no more deliverance for Israel (10:13). Would God return to that position after the misguided judgeship of Jephthah? Or would God dramatically intervene in some new way when the next cycle began with Israel's evil and the resulting oppression by an enemy? The brief respite of the minor judges provides some time for God and the reader to interrupt the cycle of major judgeships, to contemplate the implications of the disturbing events of the past, and to consider the range of options for Israel's future.

REFLECTIONS

The temporary intermission provided by the minor judges at this unsettled point in the era of the judges may provoke some reflections on those times in our own lives when we need such moments of respite. Significant or traumatic events and transitions in our lives often require that we interrupt our normal routine and pattern to make some space for contemplation and assessment. We need to carve out space and time for thoughtful reflection, prayer, decision making, discussion, and rest. Such moments are especially important in times of chaos, transition, uncertainty, or conflict. Israel was going through such unsettled times, and the minor judges provide a moment of calm in the midst of a turbulent and uncertain future.

JUDGES 13:1–16:31, SAMSON, THE LAST JUDGE

OVERVIEW

The seventeenth-century poet John Milton retold the biblical story of Samson in an epic poem entitled *Samson Agonistes.* Milton himself had tragically become blind, and he put this searching question into Samson's mouth:

Why was my breeding ordered and prescribed
As of a person separate to God,
Designed for great exploits; if I must die
Betrayed, captive, and both my eyes put out . . . ?
(Line 30)

Milton's question captures the essential riddle of great expectations and tragic humiliation that is the story of Samson. More than any previous judge, Samson is wondrously chosen by God from birth. He is a special judge, a Nazarite called to deliver Israel from the oppressive Philistines. Tragically, all our expectations about what a judge should be fall apart in Samson. He leads no Israelites into battle. He marries a Philistine woman. He attends drinking parties with the enemy. He spends the night with a foreign prostitute. He engages only in personal vendettas with little sense of working in service to God or for the well-being of all Israel. He succumbs to Delilah's pleas to know the secret of his strength, which leads to imprisonment, torture, and blindness. In the end, Samson prays to God to let him die and destroy the Philistines and

the temple of the god Dagon in the process. Samson is no ordinary judge. He plays an important and even climactic role as the last of the judges of Israel in the book of Judges.

The importance of the Samson cycle for the book of Judges is demonstrated by the extensive number of motifs the writers or editors have borrowed from earlier judge narratives and incorporated into the Samson saga. The following is a list of sixteen important allusions to other parts of Judges, both allusive parallels and contrasts.[57]

(1) In the first chapter of Judges, the role of the tribe of Judah was positive, bold, and courageous in leading the fight against Israel's enemy (1:1-15). In the Samson story, the people of Judah simply acquiesce to the Philistines' oppressive rule over them. They show no courage or ability to resist the enemy (15:9-11). Instead, they betray their own judge Samson, bind him with ropes, and hand him over to the Philistines (15:12-13).

(2) Judges 3:6 condemned the Israelites for intermarrying with other nations, since marriage with foreigners led to worshiping foreign gods. Samson loved and married a foreign woman (14:1-4). His marriage violated God's prohibition to the Israelites in 2:2: "For

---

57. The list of allusions to other sections of Judges and their significance has been drawn primarily from the discussion of Edward Greenstein, "The Riddle of Samson," *Prooftexts* 1 (1981) 237-60; and Webb, *The Book of the Judges,* 162-74; in addition to my own independent work.

your part, do not make a covenant with the inhabitants of this land" (2:2). Moreover, Samson also slept with a foreign prostitute (זנה zōnâ, 16:1-3). The same Hebrew root (זנה znh) is used to describe Israel's "prostituting" and "lusting" after foreign gods elsewhere in Judges (2:17; 8:33).

(3) The last rogue judge, Samson, is the reverse image of the first model judge, Othniel (1:11-15; 3:7-11). Othniel's exemplary marriage to the Israelite Achsah contrasts with Samson's troubled marriage and relationships with foreign women. Othniel leads Israelite soldiers in a successful holy war. Samson is a loner who has no desire to lead Israel in any way. Othniel "delivered" Israel from its enemy and gave Israel "rest," or peace, for forty years (3:9, 11). Samson will only "begin to deliver Israel" from the Philistines, and no period of rest will result from his judgeship (13:5; 16:31).

(4) In all the previous judge stories, it is always *Israel* who cries in distress and causes God to intervene (3:15; 4:3; 6:7; 10:10). In the Samson story, *Samson* replaces Israel as the one who cries out to God, once when he is dying of thirst (15:18-19) and once at the end of his life, when he desires revenge on the Philistines (16:28-30). In both cases, God responds to Samson's cry just as God had responded to the Israelites' cry of distress in the previous stories.

(5) The early judge Ehud approached the fat king Eglon with a sword hidden at his side, and he said, "I have a secret message for you, O king" (3:19). Similarly, secrets figure prominently throughout the Samson story: the angel's secret identity (13:17-18), the secret that Samson's marriage to a Philistine woman is from the Lord (14:4), the riddle and its secret solution (12:18), the secret of Samson's strength in his uncut hair (16:4-17), the secret that the Lord had left Samson when his head was shaved (16:20), and the secret of Samson's hair growing back, which allowed him one last opportunity to bring revenge on the Philistines (16:22-30).

(6) One of the early minor judges, Shamgar, killed six hundred Philistines with an oxgoad (3:31). Samson killed one thousand Philistines with the jawbone of an ass (15:14-17).

(7) Jael the Kenite killed the Canaanite general Sisera by putting him to sleep in her tent and then secretly "driving" a tent peg into his head (4:21). Similarly, Delilah tries to capture Samson by putting him to sleep and "driving" (תקע tāqa'; the same verbs as in 4:21) a tent peg or pin into the long braid of hair on his head (16:14). In the end, Jael succeeds in killing Israel's enemy, Sisera, and Delilah succeeds in the plot to kill Israel's judge, Samson (16:18-31).

(8) The judge Gideon began his career by pulling down the altar of the Canaanite god Baal (6:25-27). Samson ends his career by pushing down the pillars of the temple of the Philistine god Dagon (16:23-31).

(9) Gideon's main mission to fight the Midianites was momentarily diverted by a personal vendetta against the inhabitants of the towns of Succoth and Penuel who had taunted him (8:4-9, 13-17). Similarly, Jephthah's primary fight with the Ammonites was interrupted when as an act of personal revenge he killed thousands of Ephraimites who had taunted him (12:1-6). Samson's career as a judge was devoted entirely to personal vendettas and individual acts of revenge against the Philistines (14:19; 15:7, 14-17; 16:28-30). What was occasional with Gideon and Jephthah became Samson's whole mission: a self-centered desire for personal revenge with no awareness of serving God or leading all Israel.

(10) Several elements in God's call of Gideon to be a judge in 6:11-24 reappear in the story of Samson's birth and call to be a deliverer of Israel in 13:1-25. Shared motifs include the dramatic appearance of an angel of the Lord (6:11-12; 13:3); the request for confirmation and repetition of signs (6:17-18; 13:8); the fear of death due to seeing the Lord (6:22; 13:22); the reassurance that the people involved will not die (6:23; 13:23); the offering of a kid and a grain offering to the Lord on a rock (6:19-20; 13:19); a divine fire that springs up from the altar, accompanied by the disappearance of the angel (6:21; 13:20-21); and the divine commissioning of Gideon and Samson to deliver Israel (6:14; 13:5).

(11) Gideon employed three hundred men with torches in the attack against the Midianites (7:16, 20-23). Samson employed three hundred foxes with torches tied between their tails in the attack against the Philistines (15:1-8).

(12) It is only with Samson that the Philistine threat, first mentioned in the Jephthah story, is addressed (13:5; 16:30).

(13) A centerpiece of the Jephthah story is that he keeps his vow to sacrifice his daughter, despite the tragic consequences (11:29-40). One of the central elements of the Samson story is that he does *not* keep his vows. He breaks all three nazirite vows by eating unclean food, drinking alcohol, and cutting his hair (13:4-5; see Num 6:1-8). He ate unclean food in the form of honey from a lion's corpse (14:8-9). He drank alcohol or wine at a seven-day drinking festival in honor of his wedding to the Philistine woman (14:10-12). He allowed his hair to be cut after Delilah's incessant pleas (16:17-20).

(14) Jephthah's victory against the Ammonites led unintentionally to the death and burning of the daughter whom he loved (11:30-31, 34-40). Samson's victory against the Philistines led unintentionally to the death and burning of the wife whom he loved (15:1-6).

(15) In 14:3 and 7, Samson desired the woman from Timnah as a wife because "she pleased Samson." The phrase in Hebrew literally reads, "she was right in the eyes of Samson." The phrase is unusual when applied to humans as an object, but it appears to be an intentional echo of a key phrase that frames the last section of Judges (chaps. 17–21). The same phrase is used for all Israelites in 17:6 and 21:25: "All the people did what was right in their own eyes." Samson's roving eyes, illicit sexual liaisons, and vengeful murder of Philistines resemble the Israelites' doing whatever was right in their own eyes in Judges 17–21. They worshiped idols (17:1-6). They committed sexual immorality and murder (19:22-30). And Israelites killed each other, nearly exterminating the tribe of Benjamin (20:35-48).

(16) Samson's shaved head portends his imminent capture and death at the hands of the Philistines (16:17-21; see 13:3-5). However, a note of hope emerges when "the hair of his head began to grow again" (16:22). Similarly, the Israelites' attack and near extinction of their own fellow tribe of Benjamin portends the end of Israel's twelve-tribe union (19:22–20:46). However, a note of hope emerges when six hundred Benjaminite

soldiers manage to escape the battle and live on to repopulate the tribe (20:47).

How are we to interpret these many allusions to other parts of the book of Judges in the Samson story? These literary echoes suggest that the present form of the story was shaped and edited at a late stage of the book's composition, when much of the other material in Judges had already been written and set in place. Also, Samson is an embodiment of all that was wrong with the judges who preceded him. On one hand, Samson is the opposite of what the good judges were in the early part of the judges era. He is the reverse image of the first model judge, Othniel. Samson also embodies the worst of the negative characteristics that began to appear in the last two phases of the judges era with Gideon and Jephthah: personal vendettas, selfish rage, reluctance to lead, inability to rally the tribes of Israel into a united community, covenants with foreigners, and breaking of covenant vows. In short, Samson represents the implosion of the whole judge system. The judges have gradually deteriorated in effectiveness as religious and military leaders over the course of three distinct phases in the book of Judges. Samson is the end of the line in that deterioration. He is the judge who no longer leads Israel or obeys God. Moreover, he only begins to deliver Israel from the Philistines (13:5), and he does not gain any years of rest for his people.

Samson is the embodiment not only of the judges but also of the whole nation of Israel.[58] He breaks all of his covenant vows as a Nazirite in the same way that Israel repeatedly broke its covenant obligations in worshiping idols. Samson's entanglements with foreign women are a metaphor for Israel's "lusting" after foreign gods. Samson spurned all the obligations of the nazirite covenant to which his parents had been faithful (13:1-24). In the same manner, the new generation of Israelites after the death of Joshua spurned the covenant of their faithful parents (2:6-23). Just as God responded repeatedly to Israel's cry of distress in spite of its disobedience, so also God responded each time to Samson's cry of distress (15:18-19; 16:28-30).

Just as Samson embodies the judges and Israel, so also he embodies one other important

58. Greenstein, "The Riddle of Samson," 247-55.

feature of the book of Judges: the kind of divine love that simply cannot let go. Samson loves even when the loved one repeatedly betrays that love and loyalty. Samson's wife betrayed the answer to his riddle (14:17), and yet he continued to love her (15:1). One scholar has argued that the answer to the riddle in 14:18 ("What is sweeter than honey? What is stronger than a lion?") implies an additional and unspoken answer—namely, love.[59] Delilah betrayed Samson four different times, and yet he continued to return to her and love her (16:1-21). Samson was betrayed not only by the women he loved but even by his fellow Israelites. The tribe of Judah betrayed their own judge, Samson, to the Philistines, and yet he did not take revenge on Judah (15:9-17). The special intensity of Samson's connection with God—the special birth

involving the angelic visitor and the frequent infusion of the divine Spirit (13:25; 14:6, 19; 15:14)—suggests that Samson's character may reveal something deeper and more direct about God's character than did previous judges. Samson's tenacious and often irrational love provides a metaphor for God's unfailing love in spite of Israel's repeated betrayals. Samson was a pushover whenever his beloved cried, begged, and pleaded with him. If we shake our heads in puzzlement over Samson's relentless love for those who betrayed him, then we must do the same for God's amazingly patient and relentless love for Israel throughout the book of Judges. Ironically, the most disobedient and ineffective of all Israel's judges becomes the best window into the heart and character of Israel's God. With Samson, we come to the core of the meaning of the book of Judges for our understanding of the judges, of Israel, and of God.

59. Philip Nel, "The Riddle of Samson (Judge 14, 14.18)," *Biblica* 66 (1985) 534-45.

Judges 13:1-25, The Birth of Samson

COMMENTARY

The Samson narrative opens with the usual introductory formula, announcing that Israel again has done evil and the Lord has allowed the Philistines to oppress them for forty years. If this were the typical judges cycle, we would expect the Israelites to cry in distress, prompting God to send a deliverer. In this case, the Israelites do not know enough even to cry out. Instead, God must take the initiative in sending an angel to announce the birth of a son "who shall begin to deliver Israel from the hand of the Philistines" (v. 5). The deliverance will be partial, suggesting that the judge paradigm is increasingly losing effectiveness. The Philistines will return as Israel's oppressors later in 1 Samuel under the kingships of Saul and David (see 1 Sam 4:1-11).

The birth of this deliverer is announced to the barren, or childless, wife of a man named Manoah from the tribe of Dan. The angel instructs the mother-to-be not to drink wine or alcohol and not to eat unclean food. These same prohibitions presumably apply to the son about to be born, along with one

additional prohibition: "no razor is to come on his head" (vv. 4-5). The reason for the prohibitions is that this son will be a "Nazirite" to God from birth. The word "nazirite" (נזיר *nāzîr*) means "separated one" or "consecrated one," signifying someone specially dedicated for service to God. The law for the Nazirite is found in Num 6:1-21 and specifies three obligations: no wine, no cutting of hair, and no touching of a corpse. The laws in Numbers 6 assume that the nazirite vow is taken on voluntarily by an adult for a limited period rather than given at birth for a lifetime. However, the special dedication of a Nazirite from the womb suggests an extraordinary act of consecration by God. The special character of this son who is about to be born is underscored by the fact that the mother is barren. The motif of the barren wife to whom God gives a child is associated with several famous female ancestors of Israel's history: Sarah and her son, Isaac (Gen 11:30; 21:1-7); Rebekah and her sons, Jacob and Esau (Gen 25:21-26); Rachel and her sons, Joseph and Benjamin (Gen 29:31;

30:22-24; 35:16-20); and Hannah and her son Samuel (1 Sam 1:1-28). The nazirite vow and the barren woman who gives birth raise enormous expectations in the reader to look for something extraordinary from this son who is about to be born.

The wife of Manoah reports the encounter to her husband. She tells him that "a man of God" whose appearance was like that of "an angel of God" came to her with the news of the imminent birth of a son. She simply accepts his words as true, not pressing to know from where he came or what his name is (vv. 6-7). Manoah's wife explains that the boy will be a Nazirite to God from birth, as the man of God had said. Then she adds her own ominous words: His nazirite mission will extend from birth "to the day of his death" (v. 7). Her words allude in a tragic way to the final scene of the Samson story (16:23-31).

The husband, Manoah, is not satisfied with this secondhand report from his wife. He prays to God to send the man of God again to confirm the news and to teach them what they are to do with the boy who will be born. God grants Manoah's request. The man of God comes to Manoah's wife in the field, and she runs and brings her husband to meet him. After the man of God, who is indeed an angel of God, repeats the Nazirite instructions, Manoah invites him to stay and eat. Manoah wants to prepare a kid or young goat as a meal. The hospitality is reminiscent of Abraham's invitation to the three men of God in Gen 18:1-15. The angel of God demurs, saying he will not eat the food, but Manoah can offer the kid as a burnt offering to the Lord. Still unaware that this is an angel,

Manoah asks, "What is your name?" The angel replies, "Why do you ask my name? It is too wonderful" (vv. 17-18). This exchange is a direct allusion to the famous wrestling match between the ancestor Jacob and the angel of God (Gen 32:29).

After Manoah offers up a burnt offering, the angel ascends in the flame up to heaven. Now Manoah knows this was an angel of the Lord. He is fearful that he and his wife will die because "we have seen God" (v. 22). This concern reflects a common OT notion that any human who sees God face to face will die (Exod 33:20). But Manoah's wife assures him that they will not die. God has come, not to destroy them, but to give them life in the form of a son soon to be born (v. 23). In due time, Manoah's wife gives birth to a son, whom she names Samson. The Lord blesses the boy as he grows, and "the spirit of the LORD began to stir him" (v. 24).

This opening episode of the Samson story is saturated with allusions to the wider biblical tradition. The famous barren mothers, the nazirite vow, the angels' visit to Abraham and Sarah, the wrestling match with Jacob, and seeing God face to face all point to the birth of this son as an extraordinarily momentous event. These allusions all suggest that God has pulled out all the stops and is investing enormous divine power and hope in this one son about to be born. After the debacle of the Jephthah story and the brief respite of the minor judges in 12:8-15, God is now intervening in a dramatic and unprecedented way to save Israel. Even so, God realizes that even this child will only "begin to deliver Israel from the hand of the Philistines" (v. 5).

REFLECTIONS

1. When it comes to believing and trusting in what God promises, the Bible affirms that a variety of responses is available and legitimate. The first scene of the story presents us with two quite different approaches in the wife of Manoah and Manoah himself. The wife of Manoah simply trusts what the man of God tells her. She does not require or ask for his source of authority or his name (13:6). In spite of the obstacle of her barrenness, she is willing to trust that God will somehow find a way to make the promise come true. Her strong faith finds a New Testament counterpart in the angel's promise to Mary that she would be the mother of Jesus. Mary accepted the angel's words, saying, "Let it be with me according to your word" (Luke 1:38 NRSV). Likewise, the women at Jesus' tomb on Easter morning believed without question the angels' words that Jesus had risen from the dead (Luke 24:1-9).

However, not all of God's people find it easy to trust God's promises without some sort of sign or confirmation. In Judges 13, the husband, Manoah, needs some assurance that his wife's report is truly a word from God. His request echoes the experience of Abraham and his struggle to believe God's promise of a son and of a land in Genesis 15. On one hand, Abraham trusted God's promise of a son (Gen 15:6). On the other hand, a part of Abraham needed an additional sign and confirmation of God's promise of the land (Gen 15:8-19). In the New Testament retelling of the first Easter story, the women came from Jesus' tomb and relayed to the disciples what the angel had said about Jesus' resurrection. But the text reports that "these words seemed to them an idle tale" (Luke 24:11 NRSV). The confirmation came in Jesus' resurrection appearances to the disciples. Examples include the scene on the road to Emmaus (Luke 24:13-35) and the confrontation of the risen Jesus with doubting Thomas, the disciple who wanted proof that Jesus was alive (John 20:19-29). In each of these cases, God took seriously and accepted those who expressed their doubts and struggles to believe. To those who doubt, God often offers signs and assurances that are visible to the eyes of faith.

2. The parents of Samson emerge as faithful and obedient models of faith who desire that God "teach us what we are to do concerning the boy" (13:8). We have seen this motif of a faithful generation of parents once before in the book of Judges. In chapter 2, the previous generation of Israelites under the leadership of Joshua had "worshiped the LORD all the days of Joshua" (2:7). However, after the death of that generation, "another generation grew up after them, who did not know the LORD" (2:10). The parents of Samson display a strong faith similar to that of the generation of Joshua. As readers at this early point in the Samson story, we wonder whether the son Samson and the generation of Israelites he represents will continue to be faithful. Or will Samson and his generation fail to maintain their covenant loyalty to the Lord? By the end of the Samson saga, we will see that the paradigm of an old faithful generation of parents, followed by a disobedient and rebellious generation will, indeed, be repeated in the story of Manoah and his wife and their son, Samson. The paradigm raises the ever-present challenges of an older generation's passing on its faith tradition to a new generation.

3. The many allusions to important biblical traditions of consecration and special service in Judges 13 demonstrate that the divine investment in this son named Samson as a deliverer of Israel is enormous. At the same time, the continuing decline in the effectiveness of the whole judges system of leadership and the degradation of Israel's social and religious life pose massive obstacles to God's will to deliver Israel yet again. This combination of intense divine energy and a resistant people and system of leadership will result only in Israel's partial deliverance: Samson "shall begin to deliver Israel from the hand of the Philistines" (v. 5). This observation may lead us to reflect on the role of humans and human systems and institutions both to advance and to thwart the efficiency and effectiveness of God's will's being done in a given situation. Ultimately, God's final will and loving purpose for the people of God and for the whole creation will be done. As the apostle Paul affirms, nothing "in all creation will be able to separate us from the love of God in Christ Jesus our Lord" (Rom 8:39 NRSV). However, God's specific will in particular circumstances may be helped or hindered by what humans and other forces in the world may do.

Judges 14:1-20, Samson the Riddler

COMMENTARY

Judges 13 had prepared the reader to have great expectations for Samson as a deliverer of Israel. However, his first recorded action as an adult seems quickly to dash those expectations. He falls in love with a Philistine woman and orders his mother and father, "Get her for me as my wife" (v. 2). Samson's parents know that their covenant with God condemns intermarriage with foreigners (3:6) and making covenants with non-Israelites (2:2). Thus they try to dissuade Samson from marrying the Philistine woman, but he will not take no for an answer. He insists that "she pleases me" (בעיני ישרה היא *hî' yāšĕrâ bĕ'ênāy*, lit., "she is right in my eyes"). The phrase is an echo of the important refrain that characterizes all Israel in the final and most tragic section of Judges: "all the people did what was right in their own eyes" (17:6; 21:25).

14:4. Just when we are ready to condemn Samson for his roving eye, however, the narrator interrupts with a word to the reader. Samson's parents did not know that "this was from the LORD"! The Lord wanted Samson to marry the Philistine woman in order to create "a pretext to act against the Philistines." Remarkably, God steers Samson to disobey God's own covenant prohibitions against intermarriage in order to help Israel and act against the Philistine oppressors. This is one of many ironies and inverted expectations that we will encounter in the chaotic and unsettled situation in which Samson lives and through which God works at the end of the judges era. The parents' lack of knowledge about the unexpected ways in which God was working in Samson will also be a recurring theme in the narrative.

14:5-9. Samson convinces his parents to join him in "going down" to the town of Timnah to marry the Philistine woman. Their journey into Philistine territory will lead to Samson's breaking two of his three nazirite vows: drinking wine or anything produced from the grapevine (13:4; Num 6:4) and eating anything that is unclean, especially anything associated with the corpse of an animal or a human (13:4; Num 6:6-8). They come to the "vineyards of Timnah." The mention of a vineyard immediately raises warning flags, since the Nazirite is to avoid anything produced from grapes. Suddenly a young lion roars at Samson, the Spirit of the Lord rushes upon him, and he tears apart the lion barehanded. The nazirite instructions in chap. 13 had said nothing about a prohibition against Samson's touching a corpse; that prohibition is mentioned only in the general nazirite law in Numbers 6. Thus the reader may wonder whether Samson's touching the corpse of a lion (itself an unclean animal, Lev 11:27) may technically not be a violation of his nazirite covenant. Samson's parents again do not know about the incident with the lion. In any case, Samson and his parents visit the Philistine woman and then return home. Sometime later, Samson is on his way to the wedding and travels the same road as before. He sees the carcass of the lion he had killed with a swarm of bees and their honey in the carcass. He eats the honey, which is ritually contaminated by the unclean corpse of an unclean animal. The reader now knows that Samson has broken his first nazirite vow, but again his parents are unaware (vv. 8-9).

14:10-11. Samson's father goes down to arrange for the marriage, and Samson "made a feast" as was the custom for weddings (v. 10). The word for "feast" here (משתה *mišteh*) suggests a drinking feast, and so Samson seems to have broken now the second of his nazirite vows: "be careful not to drink wine or strong drink" (13:4; Num 6:3-4). However, the reader may wonder still whether these are serious infractions, since the angel had applied these two prohibitions to the parents but not explicitly (perhaps implicitly?) to Samson. At least Samson's hair remains uncut, and it will be that third and last vow of his nazirite covenant that will remain fulfilled until the last episode with Delilah.

14:12-18a. As part of the seven-day feast, Samson proposes a riddle to his wedding guests and places a wager of sixty garments that the guests cannot solve it. The riddle is this: "Out of the eater came something to eat. Out of the strong came something sweet." The answer to the riddle, on the surface, is Samson's dead lion with its sweet honey, about which the guests know nothing. After three days of guessing, the guests demand that Samson's new wife beg him for the answer to the riddle "or we will burn you and your father's house with fire" (v. 15). She begs Samson for the answer until the seventh day of the feast. He finally relents and tells her the answer to the riddle, and then she passes it on to the Philistine guests: "What is sweeter than honey? What is stronger than a lion?" (v. 18). There may be more than this surface-level meaning to the riddle, however, in the context of the larger Samson story. The solution is given in the form of two questions. The interrogatives invite further searching on the reader's part to consider another level of meaning as to what might be stronger than a lion and sweeter than honey. One scholar has argued that a more subtle answer to the

two questions and an implied solution to the larger riddle of the Samson story itself is the answer "love." Love is both incredibly strong and incredibly sweet for both Samson and his women, but more significantly for God and the people of Israel. God's powerful and sweet love cannot let Israel go, no matter how disobedient they are.

14:18b-20. Samson gives a sexually crude and angry response to the wedding guests: "If you had not plowed with my heifer, you would not have found out my riddle" (v. 18). The Spirit of God rushes on Samson yet again. He then angrily goes to the neighboring Philistine city of Ashkelon, kills thirty men, steals their garments, and gives the stolen clothing to the wedding guests in payment for the wager they had made and Samson had lost. Hot-headed Samson heads back home, leaving his wife with the Philistines. In Samson's absence, his wife is married off again to the best man at Samson's wedding (vv. 19-20).

REFLECTIONS

In the topsy-turvy world of a disintegrating Israelite society, the Lord works in mysterious and seemingly contradictory ways. The Lord is behind Samson's desire for a Philistine wife, a desire that contradicts earlier covenant prohibitions for inter-marriage in Judg 2:2 and 3:6. The Spirit of the Lord rushed on Samson two times in this episode, and each time Samson disobeyed clear prohibitions of the covenant. The divine Spirit gave Samson the strength to kill the young lion (14:6). Yet that eventually led to his breaking the nazirite prohibition of touching a corpse or eating anything unclean. The Spirit of the Lord also rushed upon Samson when he murdered the thirty men of Ashkelon, stole their clothing, and then used his ill-gotten gains to pay off his wager. Samson kills and steals out of personal revenge and hot-headed anger, violations of the commandments against killing and stealing without community sanction (Deut 5:17, 19).

God seems constrained to work through such devious and sinful means in the disordered context of a splintered and rebellious Israelite nation. God is free to contravene the very laws God has given to Israel for the sake of God's mercy and love for the people and for the sake of the punishment of the oppressive Philistines. Although laws and ordered structures are important and helpful, the priority remains on God's will and God's compassion, which may at times override institutional policy, governmental regulation, and even divine law.

Judges 15:1-20, Samson the Avenger

COMMENTARY

15:1-8. Samson's hot-headed exploits of personal revenge against the Philistines continue. Samson discovers that his Philistine wife has been given to another man and vows to "do mischief to the Philistines" in retaliation. He implies that his earlier killing and stealing (14:19) had been reckless and sinful when he says that this time his revenge "will be without blame" (v. 4). Samson's "mischief" involves attaching torches to the tails of three hundred foxes and letting them loose to burn up the grain fields, vineyards, and olive groves of the Philistines. When the Philistines learn that Samson was behind the "mischief," they up the ante in a spiral of retaliatory violence by burning Samson's Philistine wife and her father (v. 6; see 14:15). Samson then vows revenge, and "he struck them down hip and thigh with great slaughter" (v. 8).

15:9-13. The spiral of revenge keeps growing as the Philistines in turn attack the tribe of Judah in the hope of capturing Samson. The tribe of Judah had been an exemplary leader among the Israelites in chap. 1. They had been the first and most successful tribe to lead an attack against the Canaanites (1:1-15). However, in this period of the disintegration of Israel under the judges, even the tribe of Judah cannot or will not resist Israel's oppressors. Instead, they betray God's designated deliverer, Samson, by binding him and surrendering him to the Philistines (vv. 12-13).

15:14-17. The Spirit of the Lord once again rushes upon Samson, and he breaks the ropes that bind him. He finds a jawbone of a donkey. As with the lion carcass (14:5-9), Samson again touches a part of an animal corpse, which defiles him and breaks his nazirite vow (Num 6:6). Samson uses the jawbone to kill a thousand Philistines and then utters a proud boast about the "heaps upon heaps" he has killed (v. 16). The boast is reminiscent of the primeval figure Lamech, who boasted of the revenge he took upon those who hurt him (Gen 4:23-24). Samson's exploits also find a parallel in the earlier minor judge Shamgar, who killed six hundred Philistines with an oxgoad (3:31). The hill on which Samson threw away the donkey's jawbone is remembered by its name, "Ramathlehi," "The Hill of the Jawbone" (v. 17).

15:18-20. The next scene introduces the first of two times when Samson calls upon God for help. Although God's Spirit has repeatedly rushed upon Samson, it is not clear whether Samson is aware that God has been working through him. Samson seems, in his own mind, to be driven by the desire for personal revenge and nothing else. However, now he acknowledges that it is the Lord who has "granted this great victory by the hand of your servant" (v. 18). In spite of Samson's disobedience and breach of his nazirite covenant, Samson stays connected to God. He prays to God, asking, "Am I now to die of thirst?" In previous judge stories, it was always Israel who cried out in distress, and not the judges. Samson, who is both judge and a metaphor for Israel itself, cries out to the Lord. And as in previous judge stories, the Lord responds to Samson's cry. God splits open a rock, and water flows from it. The place was named "En-hakkore," "The Spring of the One Who Called" (vv. 18-19). This scene of thirst and the provision of water recalls Israel's experience in the wilderness as the people traveled from Egypt to the promised land and God miraculously provided water from a rock (Exod 17:1-7). The parallel with Israel's experience further cements the identification of Samson not only as a judge but also as a metaphor for all Israel.

REFLECTIONS

The central theme of this section of the Samson story is best summarized by Samson himself, "As they did to me, so I have done to them" (15:11). Samson's relationship to the Philistines dances between two poles, either legalistic vengeance as expressed in Samson's statement or a passionate and reckless love as expressed for his Philistine wife (14:3) and later for Delilah (16:4). Samson loves his women, even though he is repeatedly betrayed by them. This dance between vengeful legalism and unrelenting and generous love first appeared in the book of Judges in the juxtaposition of the story of the Canaanite king Adoni-bezek (1:5-7) and the story of Achsah, daughter of the Israelite Othniel (1:11-15). After his capture and punishment, the Canaanite king conceded, "As I have done, so God has paid me back" (1:7). He sees the world through the lens of legalistic retribution. On the other hand, Achsah received from her father an inheritance of land as a gift. Then she boldly asked for an additional area that contains springs of water, and her father graciously and generously gave her two such areas with springs of life-giving water (1:14-15). Achsah saw the world through the lens of a parent's unconditional and generous love. Both of these themes have been weaving in and out of the stories of the judges throughout the book. Israel has done evil, and God has sent an enemy in punishment. Israel has cried out in distress, and God has sent a deliverer to save them. As Israel's sin and disloyalty have increased over the course of the judges era, however, God's love and generosity have been strained to a near breaking point. God's work in and through Samson is one more attempt by God to embody in a leader both responsible accountability and retribution and an unconditional divine love that cannot let Israel go.

God strains to reconcile these two poles in the relationship with Israel throughout Judges. On one hand, God proclaims to Israel, "I will never break my covenant with you" (2:1). On the other hand, God threatens to end the relationship and let Israel receive its just punishment: "You have abandoned me and worshiped other gods; therefore I will deliver you no more" (10:13). Samson embodies these two poles—vengeful retribution and unrelenting love—in his life and relationships. Ultimately, like the two pillars of Dagon's temple (16:30-31), these two opposing poles of vengeance and love will crush Samson and lead to his death. The reader may wonder how God is faring under the strain of holding this rebellious Israel accountable for its actions even as God loves Israel with an unfailing love.

Judges 16:1-3, Samson and the Prostitute

COMMENTARY

Samson's love life continues with a brief nocturnal liaison with a Philistine prostitute in Gaza (v. 1). If Samson can point, however imperfectly, to the vastness of God's love, Samson can also symbolize the fickle love and loyalty of Israel. His night with the "prostitute" (זנה *zōnâ*) recalls God's charge against the Israelites for "prostituting" (זנה *zānâ*) themselves with all manner of foreign gods (2:17; 8:33).

The Philistines in Gaza discover that Samson is in town. Seeking further revenge, they decide to wait until dawn to capture Samson as he leaves the prostitute and departs through the city gate. But Samson leaves at midnight and eludes capture. With his enormous strength, Samson also picks up the city gate and its two posts and carries them for miles to the Israelite town of Hebron, where he sets them up on a hill as an act of humiliation and defiance aimed at Israel's Philistine oppressors (vv. 2-3).

REFLECTIONS

Samson's illicit sexual relationship with the Philistine prostitute reminds the reader in some ways of the two Israelite spies who visited Rahab, the Canaanite prostitute, in the city of Jericho (Josh 2:1-24). One key difference between the two stories is that Samson is there for his own personal gratification. The two Israelite spies were in Jericho not for their own pleasure but on a spy mission on behalf of all Israel. Samson's liaison with the prostitute signifies Israel's lusting after other gods for the sake of personal gratification and self-centered desires. The Jericho spies were doing the opposite. They risked their lives and well-being for the sake of the larger community.

However, there are also significant similarities between the two stories. Both stories proclaim the ultimate power and authority of Israel's God over all other gods and powers. Jericho's walls came tumbling down. Samson's theft of Gaza's city gates makes a similar statement about God's authority even over the Philistines. The city gate is the place of political decision making and the rendering of justice. Samson's feat of pulling up the city gate and planting it on a hill in Israel portends the eventual political and military defeat of the Philistines by the Israelites. It also prefigures Samson's final act of defiance when he will push down another entrance and two pillars in the Philistine temple of Dagon. That final act in the Samson saga will entail not only Israel's partial triumph over the Philistine oppressors but also the Lord's ultimate victory over the Philistine god Dagon (16:23-31).

Samson's act of political defiance stands in a long series of biblical people of God who have defied the powers of human authority and government when they have acted oppressively and contrary to God's will. Moses defied Pharaoh and the Egyptian empire, saying, "Let my people go" (Exodus 5–15). Amos boldly condemned King Jeroboam for the nation's ill treatment of the poor (Amos 7:10-17). Daniel remained faithful in the face of persecution for his faith because he knew God's authority supersedes all worldly authorities (Daniel 1–12). When the authorities tried to prevent Peter and the other apostles from proclaiming the gospel of Jesus Christ, they replied, "We must obey God rather than any human authority" (Acts 5:29 NRSV). Samson's placing the Gaza gates on the hill outside Hebron is one more affirmation that "thine is the kingdom and the power and the glory forever and ever. Amen."

Judges 16:4-31, Delilah and the Death of Samson

COMMENTARY

16:4-5. After the one-night liaison in Gaza, Samson "falls in love" with a woman named Delilah (v. 4). She is from the valley of Sorek, which lies within the Israelite land of Canaan, not far from Jerusalem. Scholars disagree about whether Delilah is an Israelite, a Canaanite, or a Philistine. The text remains intentionally ambivalent about her ethnicity so that the reader may wonder whether Samson has at last "come home" to Israel in obedience to his parents' wishes to find a woman to love from among "our people" (14:3). The name "Delilah" (דלילה *dĕlîlâ*) means "flirtatious," which fits her role in the story. The

Philistines had earlier coaxed Samson's wife to betray him in the matter of the riddle (14:15-20). Similarly, the Philistines coax Delilah to find out the secret to the riddle of Samson's superhuman strength. Whereas earlier the Philistines had threatened Samson's wife with death (14:15), this time they offer Delilah an enormous bribe of "eleven hundred pieces of silver" (v. 5).

16:6-14. Delilah then tries to coax the secret of Samson's strength from him. On three different occasions he lies to Delilah about the secret of his power. First, Samson tells her that his strength will vanish if he is bound by seven fresh bowstrings. Then he suggests that he will lose his power if he is bound by new ropes. Finally, he tells Delilah that he will become a normal man if his hair is plaited into seven braids, which are then woven into a web and made tight with a pin. All of these are lies. It is this third false reason that begins to build suspense. Samson's admission that his strength has something to do with his hair is getting dangerously close to the truth about the one nazirite vow he has not yet broken (13:5). Moreover, the scene with Samson sleeping and Delilah weaving the hair of his head and "making it tight with the pin" (lit., "she thrust the pin/tent peg") reminds the reader of an earlier story in Judges 4. Jael, the Kenite woman, like Delilah, was not clearly allied with either Israel or Israel's enemy Sisera. As he slept, she "thrust" (תקע *tāqa'*; the same verb as in 16:14) a tent peg into his temple and killed him (4:17-21). The parallel is a foreboding sign that Samson is moving closer to his own downfall and death.

16:15-22. Delilah pleads one more time with Samson to reveal his secret, appealing to his love for her. After days of nagging, Samson is "tired to death" (v. 16), a figurative image that will soon become a literal fact. Samson gives in and tells her the secret of his nazirite vow and that his hair cannot be cut: "If my head were shaved . . . I would become weak, and be like anyone else" (v. 17). Delilah senses that this time Samson is telling the truth. She again lets him fall asleep in her lap and then has a man cut Samson's hair. Samson's strength begins to leave him, but he appears unaware of his loss: "he did not know that the LORD had left him" (v. 20). Samson's figurative blindness to his real condition of weakness and divine abandonment is made literal and physical as the Philistines capture him and "gouged out his eyes" (v. 21).

Samson is bound and forced to do what is traditionally the work of women and slaves: "he ground at the mill in the prison" (v. 21; see Exod 11:5; Job 31:10). Samson has been totally transformed and humiliated. He was once a paragon of male bravado, a man of extraordinary physical strength and the knower of deep secrets unknown to others. Now Samson takes the role of a blind female servant, a captive of war, an exile in a foreign land. Indeed, his fate is a mirror image of the later experience of Israel in exile. Lamentations 5:13 laments that in exile "young men are compelled to grind." Samson's shaved head is not only a violation of his nazirite vow but also the mark of a person who is taken into exile. Isaiah 7:20 predicts the exile of the northern kingdom of Israel by the Assyrians with this image: "On that day the Lord will shave with a razor hired beyond the River—with the king of Assyria—the head and the hair of the feet, and it will take off the beard as well." Deuteronomy 21:12 speaks of the treatment of female captives of war: "suppose you see among the captives a beautiful woman whom you desire and want to marry . . . she shall shave her head." Samson is a feminized captive and exile, a paradigm of Israel in exile, seemingly abandoned by God.

However, the scene does not end in total despair but with what James Crenshaw has described as "one of those pregnant sentences that is the mark of genius."[60] Verse 22 concludes, "But the hair of his head began to grow again after it had been shaved." The new growth of Samson's hair may yet provide hope for some kind of vindication and purpose in the midst of Samson's captivity and exile among the Philistines.

16:23-27. The setting for the final scene of the Samson story is the grand temple of the Philistine god Dagon, which is filled with "the lords of the Philistines." The Philistines are celebrating a grand festival of sacrifice and thanksgiving to their god, who "has given Samson our enemy into our hand" (v. 23). Samson had entertained the Philistines once before at the wedding feast of his Philistine wife. Then he had offered a secret riddle to which they found a solution. The Philistines again command Samson to entertain them; he performs to a full house with standing room only for an additional 3,000 Philistines who are on the roof of the temple (v. 27).

16:28-30. Once before Samson had called upon God in prayer when he was weakened by thirst (15:18). One more time he calls on God in prayer. "Strengthen me," he prays, "so that with this one act of revenge I may pay back the Philistines for my eyes" (v. 28). Samson continues to define his actions in terms of

60. James Crenshaw, "The Samson Saga: Filial Devotion or Erotic Attachment?" *ZAW* 86 (1974) 501.

personal vendetta and revenge. He remains blind, however, to the larger significance of his mission as an agent of God's deliverance for the sake of the future of the whole people of Israel. Nevertheless, God will use Samson for one last defeat of the Philistines.

In a story filled with secrets and riddles, Samson accomplishes his final act of defeating the Philistines through one final secret. Samson pretends that he is so weak that he must lean on the "pillars on which the house rests" (v. 26). Then, calling on the Lord, Samson leans his full weight aganst the middle pillars of the temple. Dramatically, he prays, "Let me die with the Philistines" (v. 30). Samson strains "with all his might," which has returned along with his growing hair. The pillars buckle, the roof collapses, and the victory party for Dagon becomes a Philistine disaster of death and destruction. Samson dies along with thousands of Philistines. Ironically, Samson has killed more Philistines in his death than all those he killed during his life (v. 30). In the midst of this final triumph, Samson remains a tragic figure, forever blind

to the larger purposes for which God had used him. Samson saw only personal revenge in this event; the Lord sees deliverance for God's people and the Lord's victory in the cosmic battle against Dagon, the god of the Philistines.

16:31. Samson's family takes his body and buries him in the tomb of his father, a sign of a life that has ended and come full circle. In the end, Samson "judged Israel twenty years," as compared to the much longer forty years of Philistine oppression (13:1). God had invested enormous divine energy in this last of the judges. Even so, Samson was only able to "begin to deliver Israel" from the Philistines (13:5). The Philistines would return as a major threat to Israel, beginning with the events in 1 Samuel 4. In Samson, the line of Israel's military deliverers called judges comes to an end within the book of Judges. The system of leadership under the judges has finally self-destructed and collapsed under its own weight along with the Philistine temple of Dagon.

REFLECTIONS

1. Samson's many relationships with women invite critical reflection on the role and portraits of women in the Samson saga. His mother is a positive model of faithfulness and trust. However, the other women in his life are not so positively portrayed. They are objects of desire, nagging and tempting Samson into economic ruin, sexual immorality, and ultimately death. Moreover, each of these women is in some way caught in the web of the pressures, economics, and powers of a male-dominated society. Samson's wife is threatened and forced to betray him. She is ultimately killed and burned along with her father (14:14; 15:16). Samson uses the prostitute at Gaza for a night of self-gratification (16:1-3). Delilah is pressured by an enormous bribe from the Philistines to betray her lover. Both the prostitute and Delilah are used by men in exchange for money.[61]

It was noted in the reflections on Jephthah's daughter in Judges 11 that the decline in the well-being of women as we move through the book of Judges parallels the gradual disintegration and decline of Israel as a society and a religious community. The women in the Samson story continue to reflect this downward trend in social and religious degradation. Their portraits will find parallels in our own time and communities.

2. One of the most dramatic points in Judges 16 is Samson's request for God to let him "die with the Philistines" (v. 30). This expression to God of a death wish is not unique to Samson. Other great figures of the Bible reached such points of despair that they also asked God to let them die. Moses was overcome with the burdens of leading the rebellious Israelites through the wilderness and requested that God put him

---

61. See J. Cheryl Exum, "Samson's Women," in Fragmented Women: Feminist (Sub)versions of Biblical Narratives (Valley Forge, Pa.: Trinity, 1993) 61-93.

to death (Num 11:10-15). The prophet Elijah sat under a tree in despair because he alone had been faithful to God and yet had been no more effective than his predecessors in leading Israel to faith in God. So he asked God, "take away my life" (1 Kgs 19:4). Jeremiah was so severely persecuted for prophesying God's word that he wished he had been killed in his mother's womb (Jer 20:17). The prophet Jonah sulked under a bush because God had shown mercy to the Assyrian city of Nineveh. Jonah was so upset by God's generosity to this pagan city that he asked God to "please take my life from me" (Jonah 4:3). In each of these cases, however, God always refused the request to put the person to death and instead sent the person on to continue his mission. Samson's request for God to let him die is the only time such a request is granted in the Old Testament.

Samson's uniqueness in this regard may stem from two reasons. One reason is that Samson represents the end of the line of the judges. He is more than just another judge. He embodies the office of the judge, which comes to an end with him. Thus, God's allowing Samson to die is God's allowing the office or system of judge as a means of leading and saving Israel to die. Another reason for Samson's uniqueness is that he embodies Israel as a nation. The shaved head, the forced grinding at the mill, and the binding and captivity of Samson are all images of exile and captivity. They prefigure the exile Israel will later experience under kingship. The northern kingdom of Israel will be conquered by the Assyrians and be sent into exile (2 Kings 17). Later, the southern kingdom of Judah will succumb to the power of the Babylonian empires, and its population will be exiled (2 Kings 24–25). The exile will be a kind of death for Israel. The Temple in Jerusalem will be destroyed as was the Philistine temple of Dagon. The system of kingship will end, just as the era of the judges also came to an end. Israel and Judah will lose their strength as Samson had done. The prophets will castigate Israel for its blindness to its sin before the exile (Isa 6:9-13) and its blindness to the deliverance God is working out for the sake of the exiles (Isa 43:19). The prophet Ezekiel spoke of Israel's exile as the death of a nation in his image of Israel as a valley filled with dry bones (Ezek 37:1-14). Thus Samson's request to die and God's acquiescence to that request reflect Samson's larger role as a symbol of the system of judges as an institution and a metaphor for Israel as a nation and its eventual fate of exile.

3. The Samson story holds on to a thread (or hair) of hope as it notes that Samson's hair begins to grow back after it has been shaved (16:22). If his shaved head represents exile and captivity, then the new growth of hair represents hope in the midst of exile. The Deuteronomistic History of Joshua–2 Kings ends with Israel in exile. But it also ends with a brief note of hope that parallels Samson's growing hair. In 2 Kgs 25:27-30, the king of Judah, who is in exile, is released from prison and allowed to dine with the king of Babylon. This hint of hope and opening to some kind of possible future functions in a way similar to the growing hair of Samson. As we emerge from the tragedies and downfalls that beset us, we may yet discover such glimpses of hope, such openings to the future, such hints that God is working in hidden ways to redeem and save and heal, of which we may not be fully aware.

4. One of the overriding themes of the Samson story is Israel's learning that its future depends entirely on God's guidance and strength, not its own. Samson represents the prideful and boastful Israel who goes it alone, thinking for the most part that he does not need anyone else to help him. Yet there are glimpses of Samson's recognition of his limits, once when he was dying of thirst and a final time when he was dying at the hand of the Philistines. It is only when Samson reaches the end of his rope and slams up against his dependence on God that he comes to some realization of his need for God.[62] This was God's experience with Israel as well. That experience is definitively summarized in the Song of Moses in Deuteronomy 32:

62. J. Cheryl Exum, "The Theological Dimension of the Samson Saga," *VT* 33 (1983), 30-45.

Indeed the LORD will vindicate his people,
    have compassion on his servants,
when he sees that their power is gone. (Deut 32:36 NRSV)

Israel will then begin to come to the realization that its future and hope lie not in a particular institution of leadership (whether judges or kings) or in its own strength or virtue. The future of God's people lies in trusting and worshiping the one God who is worthy of such trust:

See now that I, even I, am he:
    there is no god besides me.
I kill and I make alive:
    I wound and I heal;
    and no one can deliver from my hand. (Deut 32:39 NRSV)

5. In the history of Christian biblical interpretation, one of the dominant ways in which Samson has been interpreted is as a prefigurement, or type, of Christ. In spite of his dubious moral character, Samson has functioned over the centuries in sermons, art, and interpretation as a precursor to Jesus' life and death. The parallels are many. Samson's special birth and the angel's announcement to his mother in Judges 13 functioned as a model for the writer of Jesus' birth story and announcement in Luke 1–2. The title of "Nazorean" is applied to Jesus, a possible allusion to the special status of a "Nazirite," similar to Samson, in Matt 2:23. The Spirit of the Lord came upon Samson just as it came upon Jesus as he did battle with Satan in the wilderness (Luke 3:21-22; 4:1-13). However, the most important parallels involve Samson's suffering and death as a type of Jesus' suffering and death on the cross. Samson was betrayed by his own people, by Judah and by the women he loved. He was beaten and tortured. Samson's outstretched arms on the two pillars of the Philistine temple were read by Christian interpreters as a prefigurement of Jesus' outstretched arms on the cross. In his death, Samson destroyed the enemy and its god. Similarly, interpreters saw Jesus' death as destroying sin and death and defeating the powers and principalities of this world who resisted God's will for creation.

Perhaps at a deeper level, the Samson story affirms God's willingness to enter into the full sinfulness and rebellion of humankind in order to accomplish the purposes of God in the world. At some level, the figure of Samson embodies not only the institution of judgeship or the nation of Israel, but also God's amazing and relentless love. God keeps coming back to God's sinful people, responding to their cries of distress and promising to stay with them in and through their failures, their captivities, their exiles, and even their deaths. Whether it is the human nation of Israel or the individual person of Jesus, God is present and at work in an incarnational way in the blood and mess and chaos of human life. In that promise is a word of hope even when we come to the end and death of the era of the judges in the man Samson.

JUDGES 17:1–21:25

CONCLUSION: ISRAEL'S DISINTEGRATION

OVERVIEW

The stories of chaps. 17–21 conclude the book of Judges with a portrait of Israel in religious and social chaos. The gradual decline in the individual judge stories from the ideal of Othniel in chap. 3 to the tragic judgeships of Jephthah and Samson in chaps. 10–16 ends in chaps. 17–21 with Israel's near disintegration as a covenant community of God. In these chapters, the era of the judges has ended. Idols are worshiped. Priests are hired for personal gain. Defenseless foreigners are mercilessly attacked. Strangers are mistreated. An Israelite woman is brutally raped and murdered by Israelites. The entire Israelite tribe of Benjamin is nearly exterminated by fellow Israelites. Additional Israelite men, women, and children are killed. Other women are kidnapped and forced to become wives of Benjaminite men. Israel seems oblivious to the extent of its disobedience and disloyalty to the covenant with God. Yet God remains to work in and through the perverse actions of Israel in order to preserve its life and prepare for a whole new way of leading and guiding Israel through the institution of the king (1–2 Samuel).

The narratives in chaps. 17–21 no longer follow the cyclical pattern of the individual judge stories of chaps. 3–16, in which Israel does evil, God sends an enemy, Israel cries to God, God sends a judge to deliver Israel, and Israel again does evil (see 2:11-19). Instead, Judges 17–21 is a collection of originally disparate stories that contain no foreign aggressor or enemy and no judge or deliverer to lead Israel. These varied and originally separate stories have been brought together and artfully shaped to form a dramatic conclusion to the book. The stories divide into two major sections: Chapters 17–18 focus on the religious dimensions of Israel's decline (idols, priests, abuse of holy war), and chaps. 19–21 deal more with the social dimensions of Israel's disintegration (inhospitality, rape, murder, deception, civil war, the near extinction of an Israelite tribe). This two-part conclusion corresponds with the book's two-part introduction, which likewise focuses on the social fragmentation (1:1–2:5) and religious deterioration (2:6–3:6) of Israel in the land of Canaan.

Although different in focus, the two sections of chaps. 17–18 (religious chaos) and chaps. 19–21 (social upheaval) contain several overlapping details and themes. Both sections feature an individual "Levite," a member of the special priestly tribe of Israel (cf. Josh 18:7; 21:1-42). In the first section, a Levite man travels from the southern town of Bethlehem in Judah to the hill country of Ephraim (17:7-8). In the second section, another Levite man travels from the hill country of Ephraim to Bethlehem of Judah and then back to northern Ephraim (19:1, 18). One Levite is originally from southern Judah, and the other Levite is originally from northern Ephraim. The actions of the two Levite men, representing the major tribes of northern and southern Israel, are implicitly condemned. Both sections begin with an event involving the individual Levite and personal or family matters (chaps. 17; 19), which then spirals into a larger tribal conflict involving either foreigners (chap. 18) or fellow Israelites (chap. 20). The conclusion of each section involves the preservation of an Israelite tribe through abhorrent but seemingly necessary means. After having lost its original land allotment in Canaan, the tribe of Dan migrates to the foreign town of Laish.

Dan destroys the small and defenseless village on the northern margins of Canaan and takes it over as its own city and territory, so that the tribe can have a place to live (18:27-31). Likewise, after having been nearly exterminated as a tribe in a civil war with the rest of Israel, the six hundred surviving men of the tribe of Benjamin secure their tenuous future by kidnapping young girls who will become their wives (21:8-24). In each case, innocent victims suffer with no mechanism for accountability or redress because of the absence of political leadership.[63]

An important refrain brackets the concluding section of chaps. 17–21, at both its beginning (17:6) and its end (21:25): "In those days there was no king in Israel; all the people did what was right in their own eyes." Part of the refrain, "In those days there was no king in Israel," also appears in 18:1 and 19:1. Scholars generally agree that this refrain provides a key insight into the perspective of the later writers and editors who shaped the book of Judges. However, scholars disagree about the meaning of the refrain. Some argue that it was added at a late date in Israel's history, sometime after the exile of Israel by the Assyrians (2 Kings 17) and the exile of Judah by the Babylonians (2 Kings 24–25). They point to the key reference to the period of Israel's exile in the phrase "the time the land went into captivity," in 18:30. These scholars view the meaning of the refrain in a positive light, arguing that it is a declaration of moral freedom and spiritual renewal for the Israelites in exile under either the Assyrians (722 BCE) or the Babylonians (586 BCE). According to this perspective, the refrain signals an opportunity to start over in hope and promotes creative experiments for community life after the demise of kingship in Israel.[64] Other scholars view the refrain as an entirely negative evaluation of Israel in the period of the judges. They tend to date the final form of the book and its refrain to the time either before the Assyrian exile or before the Babylonian exile, when the Israelite monarchy was still in place. The refrain, they argue, points to the need for a king as the only viable solution to protect Israel from its own self-induced social and religious dissolution. Some scholars argue that the concluding chapters of Judges and the refrain were intended negatively, either as a polemic against the northern kingdom's worship centers in Dan and Bethel (see 2 Kgs 12:25-33), as an attack against the erratic leadership of Saul in comparison to the stable kingship of David, or as a general apology for dynastic kingship, as opposed to the occasional and flawed leadership of the judges.[65]

As the analysis of the individual chapters will show, the refrain and the concluding section of Judges as a whole should be understood as both a negative portrayal of Israel in this period at the end of the judges era and as an affirmation of the hope of God's continuing presence with the community in spite of its unfaithfulness. The flip side of the refrain about the absence of a king and everybody's doing what is right in his or her own eyes is the phrase repeated frequently throughout Judges: "the Israelites did what was evil in the eyes of the LORD" (2:11; 3:7, 12; 4:1; 6:1; 10:6; 13:1). In the present form of Judges, the Israelites' doing "evil in the eyes of the LORD" is functionally equivalent to doing "what is right in their own eyes." This negative interpretation of the refrain in 17:6 and 21:25 is further supported by the use of the same phrase for Samson's errant and misguided yearning for a Philistine wife: "she is right in my eyes" (NRSV, "she pleases me"; 14:3, 7). Elsewhere in the OT, humans' "doing what is right in their own eyes" typically connotes presumption, arrogance, and failure to act according to the will of God. In Deut 12:8, Moses commands Israel, "You shall not act as we are acting here today, everyone doing what is right in their own eyes" (literal translation of the Hebrew; NRSV, "all of us according to our own desires"; NIV, "everyone as he sees fit").

63. F. Crüsemann, *Der Widerstand gegen das Königtum* (Neukirchen-Vluyn: Neukirchener Verlag, 1978) 157-58.

64. Examples of positive readings of the refrain include Robert Boling, "In Those Days There Was No King in Israel," in *A Light Unto My Path: Old Testament Studies in Honor of Jacob M. Myers*, ed. H. Bream et al. (Philadelphia: Temple, 1974) 33-48; and William Dumbrell, " 'In Those Days There Was No King in Israel; Every Man Did What Was Right in His Own Eyes': The Purpose of the Book of Judges Reconsidered," *JSOT* 25 (1983) 23-33.

65. Martin Noth, "The Background of Judges 17–18," in *Israel's Prophetic Heritage*, ed. B. W. Anderson and W. Harrelson (London: SCM, 1962) 68-85; Yairah Amit, "Literature in the Service of Political Studies in Judges 19:1–21," in *Politics and Theopolitics in the Bible and Postbiblical Literature*, ed. H. G. Reventlow et al. (Sheffield, JSOT, 1994) 28-40; and Stone, "From Tribal Confederation to Monarchic State," 458, 471-77.

Moreover, the narratives in Judges 17–21 portray the systematic breaking of nearly all of the Ten Commandments (see Exod 20:1-17; Deut 5:6–21). Israelites worship other gods and idols (17:3-5), take the Lord's name in vain (17:13), dishonor parents (17:1-2), brutally kill innocent victims (18:27; 19:26-29; 21:10), commit adultery and rape (19:22-25), steal other's property (17:2; 18:21-27), bear false witness (20:1-7), and covet what belongs to their neighbor (18:27-31; 21:8-24). This failure to obey the central commandments outlined in Deuteronomy 5 suggests that "doing what was right in their own eyes" was something less than a positive experience of spiritual renewal (see 2:17; 3:4).

Was the absence of a monarch ("there was no king") the basic cause of this moral and religious failure in Israel? And would the rise of kingship in Israel rectify the chaos at the end of the judges period by creating a permanent state of obedience and faithfulness in Israel? As noted above, this concluding section of Judges and the entire book itself had a long history of composition and editing. Early stories of individual judges were collected and edited over many generations, probably extending from a time early in the Israelite monarchy to the exilic or post-exilic period. At an earlier stage, the book of Judges likely functioned as an apologetic piece to support kingship in Israel, particularly the southern Judean dynasty of King David and his successors. The geographical progression of both the introduction in 1:1–2:5 and the individual judge stories in 3:7–16:31 suggest a preference for the southern tribe of Judah as success and faithfulness among the southern tribes gradually decline into failure and disobedience as one moves further north among the tribes of Israel. The introduction concludes with the expulsion of what will be the northernmost tribe, Dan, from its land (1:34-36), and the individual judge stories conclude with the tragic death of the judge Samson, who is also from the northern tribe of Dan (13:2; 16:23-31). This pro-Judean and pro-kingship perspective may well have been the product of the editors who worked on the books of the Deuteronomistic History (Deuteronomy–2 Kings) during the reigns of Hezekiah (2 Kings 18–20) and Josiah

(2 Kings 22–23) or at other times during the monarchy.

However, the narratives of the exile of the northern kingdom (2 Kings 17), and especially the exile of the southern kingdom of Judah (2 Kings 24–25), suggest that the final form of Judges came to be read within the broader perspective of the whole Deuteronomistic History, which extends from Deuteronomy to 2 Kings. That history encompasses Israel's narrated experience through a number of different political contexts: the unique office of Moses as covenant mediator, Joshua's leadership of the conquest and the temporary judges who followed him, Israel's kings in both northern Israel and southern Judah, and the time of the exile and the end of kingship. Looking back from the perspective of the exile, Israel came to know that each of these human political contexts and institutions was initially moderately successful but in the end ultimately flawed. Each period of leadership (Moses, Joshua–Judges, Kings) evidenced a similar pattern of initial success followed by deterioration and the ultimate dissolution of the old system. Moses successfully led Israel out of Egypt, but Israel in its trek through the wilderness grew increasingly rebellious against God (Deut 31:27-29). The old wilderness generation of Israelites, including Moses himself, was condemned to die in the desert without entering the promised land. An entirely new generation would inherit the land of Canaan (Deut 1:22-45; see Numbers 13–14). During the period of Joshua and the judges, Israel experienced initial success in its conquest. However, the book of Judges traces the gradual decline of the judges era from moderate success into gradual decline, culminating in social and religious chaos and disintegration (Judges 17–21). During the period of the kings in Israel, the initial success of David and Solomon in the united monarchy gradually deteriorated into the divided kingdoms of north and south (1 Kings 11–12), the exile of the northern kingdom (2 Kings 17), and finally the exile of the southern kingdom of Judah and the apparent end of the Davidic kingship in its traditional form (2 Kings 24–25).

Thus Judges, within the final form of the Deuteronomistic History, functions as a sober and realistic example of what eventually happens to any form of human governance or polity among the people of God. Every form of human leadership or power, whether a Mosaic covenant mediator or a judge or a king, may be moderately appropriate and helpful for a given time and context. But no human institution or structure is immune from the larger and deeper problem that infects humanity itself: namely, human sinfulness, rebellion against God, and self-absorbed quests for power, vengeance, and resources through strategies of violence, delusion, and theft. The book of Judges is not simply an apology for kingship, as if the presence of kings would be the one, ideal guarantee of Israel's long-term adherence to the covenant with God. Rather, the institution of Israelite judges was a paradigm of the way in which God must work in an imperfect world through necessary but inevitably flawed human structures, ideologies, and institutions. Such human structures and arrangements of power and resources may work for a time in given contexts and periods, but they will eventually deteriorate. God allows such institutions and structures to run their course and die in order

that new arrangements and structures may be born. God allowed the structure of leadership through temporary judges to "hit bottom" in the social and religious chaos of Judges 17–21. Israel would struggle to find a new way of governance through the new institution of kingship (1–2 Samuel, 1–2 Kings). Like the judges, the institution of kingship would function effectively for a time, but eventually disintegrate in the exile. Israel would then need again to struggle to find an appropriate polity and structure to reconstitute itself as the people of God, whether it remained in diaspora or returned to the land. Aspects of kingship remained alive in Judaism in the form of a hope for the Messiah, but leadership in the community took other forms in the meantime. Thus the book of Judges is a sober and mature portrait of the necessity for human structures of leadership and power, the inevitability of their corruption and eventual decline, and the gracious willingness of God to work in and through such flawed human structures and communities in order to accomplish God's purposes in the world.

JUDGES 17:1–18:31, IDOLS, HIRED PRIESTS, AND UNHOLY CONQUESTS

COMMENTARY

17:1-13. The narrative of Israel's degeneration into religious chaos begins with a man named Micah (v. 1). In Hebrew (מיכה *mîkâ*), this name means "*Who is like the Lord?*" The name implies that no god, idol, or other representation can ever compare with or substitute for the Lord. The Lord resists being tamed or captured by any humanly created image, structure, or institution. Ironically, this man named Micah will in the end seek to do what his name denies is possible: He will try to capture God in an idol and manipulate God for his own personal gain (vv. 4-5, 12-13). The reader senses immediately the topsy-turvy nature of this family's religious life. The son, Micah, stole from his own mother eleven hundred pieces of silver, an enormous sum equal to what Delilah received for betraying her lover Samson (16:4). He had

knowingly taken the money, even though he had heard his mother utter a curse against anyone who would steal it. Micah's actions as an individual reflect the actions of the nation of Israel. Israel was repeatedly warned about the consequences and curses for violating God's covenant (2:1-5, 20-23; 6:7-10; 10:10-16), and yet the nation repeatedly and openly disobeyed God. The son, Micah, returns the silver to his mother. She does not offer any word of reproof at all but asks for the Lord's blessing on him. One senses the total absence of accountability and responsibility in this family. The mother then consecrates the silver to the Lord "to make an idol of cast metal" (v. 3). She offers only two hundred of the eleven hundred pieces of silver to a silversmith to make the idol for her son (v. 4). Religion is here twisted and distorted. Curses become blessings. Consecration to the Lord becomes idolatry. Vows of offerings are only partially fulfilled. The scene ends with a tidy personal shrine for the son, Micah, with the silver idol, devices for getting oracles from God ("an ephod and teraphim"), and Micah's own son as a priest. The refrain about no king and everybody's doing "what was right in their own eyes" (v. 6) reflects the religious chaos exemplified in this opening scene of chap. 17 and functions as an overarching commentary on the entire period described in chaps. 17–21. The same refrain is repeated at 21:25 and thus brackets this entire concluding section of Judges.

The scene shifts from Micah and his personal shrine to another young man, a Levite from the town of Bethlehem in Judah. The Levites in Judah were descendants of the priestly line of Aaron (Josh 21:4). The Levite leaves his home in Judah "to live wherever he could find a place" (v. 8). The sense of the Levite's aimless wandering without any guide again reflects Israel's loss of leadership in this period when "there was no king" (v. 6). Eventually, the Levite comes to Micah's house in Ephraim, and he hires the Levite as his own priest for ten pieces of silver (vv. 8-12). The levitical priest simply sells his clerical services to anyone with sufficient money. Micah's theology of divine manipulation becomes clear in his comment that he now knows God will prosper him "because the Levite has become my priest" (v. 13). Micah believes that just as God can be captured in a humanly crafted idol, so also God's favor can be guaranteed by buying the right priest. Religion has been reduced to a privatized manipulation of God for personal gain.

18:1-31. The narrative action shifts from the private shrine of Micah to "the tribe of the Danites," who are in search of a new territorial home. The narrator reminds the reader once again of Israel's lack of leadership: "in those days there was no king in Israel" (v. 1; see 17:6; 19:1; 21:25). Like the aimless and wandering Levite in 17:8, the Danites are wandering aimlessly in search of land. The tribe of Dan had originally settled in their inheritance of land in the western border of Canaan, but they had been driven out by the native Amorites (1:34-36; Josh 19:40-47). Dan was among several Israelite tribes

in Judges 1 that allowed foreigners and their gods to remain in Canaan in violation of the holy war laws, but the tribe of Dan was the only Israelite tribe that was so weak that it was actually chased off its inherited land.

Having lost their initial land inheritance, the Danites engage in a new conquest for land. An earlier story in Josh 19:47 recounts Dan's conquest of a city called Leshem. Judges 18 provides an alternate version of the same conquest, but the name of the city is changed from "Leshem" to "Laish." The actions of the tribe of Dan follow roughly the narrative pattern of previous Israelite conquests, especially the spy story in Numbers 13–14 and the conquest of the city of Jericho in Judges 2 and 6. Elements of this holy war pattern in Judges 18 include sending spies (v. 2), receiving a divine command to conquer the land (vv. 3-6), gaining inside information about the inhabitants (v. 7), the spies' report and the people's reaction (vv. 8-10), and the march and the actual conquest of the city or land (vv. 11-13, 27-28).[66] The story of the Danite conquest of the city of Laish, however, distorts three crucial elements of the conquest pattern. One element is the oracle from God. Previous conquest stories included a clear oracle and command from the Lord to conquer the land or city, mediated through a reliable messenger, either Moses or Joshua. In the case of Dan's conquest, the hired levitical priest in Micah's idolatrous shrine is unreliable as a messenger for the Lord. The Levite seems more than willing to sell his soul as well as his oracles to the highest bidder (vv. 18-20). Moreover, the Levite provides an ambiguous oracle that in Hebrew (לכו לשלום נכח יהוה דרככם *lĕkû lĕšālôm nōkaḥ YHWH darkĕkem*) literally reads: "Go in peace. Your way is *in front of the Lord*" (v. 6). The NIV translates the second sentence of the oracle as indicating "the LORD's approval" of the Danites' plan to conquer Laish. The NRSV provides an equally plausible translation, indicating that the Danites' plan is subject to God's critical judgment: "The mission you are on is under the eye of the LORD." The ambiguity of the oracle invites readers to question the legitimacy of the Danites' plan to conquer Laish.

66. Abraham Malamat, "The Danite Migration and the Pan-Israelite Exodus-Conquest: A Biblical Narrative Pattern," *Bib* 22 (1992) 1-17.

A second element of the holy war conquest pattern that is distorted in comparison to previous conquest accounts is the strength and aggression of the enemy relative to Israel. The model of holy war conquest emphasizes Israel's weakness, the enemy's strength and aggressiveness, and the Lord's ability to overcome the odds and give Israel the victory (Num 13:27-33; Josh 6:1, 16, 20; 10:1-11; 11:1-5). The Danites' conquest of Laish turns this model of holy war on its head. The Danites are the military aggressors. The inhabitants of Laish are "living securely" without the need for military defenses, walls, or strong allies nearby. They are "quiet and unsuspecting" (vv. 7, 27-28). The Danites' attack on the weak and peaceful people of Laish seems less like a legitimate holy war conquest and more like Amalek's wicked aggression against the "faint and weary" Israelites in the wilderness (Deut 25:17-19). The Lord remains largely uninvolved in carrying out the actual conquest, another sign of the illegitimacy of the Danites' attack on Laish.

A third element of the holy war pattern is a prohibition on anyone's ever living again in the city once it has been destroyed (Josh 6:26) and the devotion of all the city's wealth to the Lord (Josh 6:17-19; 7:1-26). In violation of the holy war laws, the Danites "rebuild the city and lived in it" (v. 28), changing the name of the city from "Laish" to "Dan." Moreover, the Danites covet the wealth of Laish (vv. 7, 10), and there is no report that they dedicate any of the wealth to the Lord. Instead, they steal the Levite and the idols from the personal shrine of Micah and forcibly transfer them to their rebuilt city of Dan (vv. 14-26, 30-31). The Danites worship at this illegitimate site of idolatry even though the true "house of God was at Shiloh," where the ark of God was maintained (v. 31; see 1 Samuel 1–3). The Danite sanctuary remained, along with a levitical priest in the line of Moses, "until the time the land went into captivity" (v. 30), a reference to the exile of the northern kingdom of Israel in 721 BCE (2 Kings 17). The sanctuary at Dan eventually became associated with the idolatrous golden calves set up by the Israelite king Jeroboam in Dan and Bethel (1 Kgs 12:25-31). Therefore, although the Danite conquest of Laish seems to have the general outline of a holy war conquest, the distortions of three crucial elements condemn the Danites in their aggressive military takeover of Laish. The ambiguous divine oracle is given through a suspect mediator (a hired Levite and idolator). Dan is the powerful aggressor against the weak and defenseless city of Laish. Finally, Dan fails to devote the city and its wealth to the Lord, taking it over for themselves and setting up an idolatrous worship site. The portrait of the tribe of Dan that emerges from this chapter is that of a greedy bully who picks on the weak and serves idols of wealth and power rather than God.

REFLECTIONS

On the surface of these stories, a tone of religious devotion swirls in the air. There is talk of God, dedication to worship, the hiring of priests, the seeking of divine oracles, the building of worship sites, and many of the elements of a holy war conquest. However, scratch a little deeper, and these surface features of religiosity and piety reveal a profound ailment that reaches to the core of Israel's heart. Israel has lost touch with God and God's covenant traditions and commandments. Israel is devoted to other gods, idols, wealth, and power as substitutes for knowing and loving the Lord alone (Deut 6:4-5). Manipulation of God for private gain replaces sacrifices and service to the purpose and mission of God in the world. Individuals try to shrink God to a private household shrine rather than bow down in worshipful humility before the God who is the maker and judge of all creation. Micah and the Danites are examples of Israel's attempt to make God small and manageable. But attempts to confine or domesticate God will lead to judgment and disaster. Israel will suffer a near-death experience in the final chapters that follow. What will be even more amazing is that the Lord will not give up on Israel. God will find a way to remain faithful to the promises God made to this recalcitrant people, preserving them and bringing creative new forms of community life out of the chaos of religious and social degradation.

The stories of Judges 17–18 invite us to reflect critically on the practices of individual congregations, institutions, denominations, and religions. To what extent do our surface rhetoric and actions reflect and promote a true and deep knowledge and love of the God of Jesus Christ? Do our lives and practices embody a lively and devoted commitment to God and familiarity with Scripture? Or are our religious words and actions simply a smoke screen to veil real devotion to the interests of self, the power politics of the world, the worship of greed, and the resistance to responsibility and accountability for the well-being of others? Scripture reminds us that not everything that is "spiritual," "religious," and "godly" is necessarily true, good, or of the Lord. The devil delights to dress in religious garb. Thus 1 John 4:1 counsels the faithful to "test the spirits to see whether they are from God; for many false prophets have gone out into the world" (NRSV). Jesus reminds his followers, "Not everyone who says to me, 'Lord, Lord,' will enter the kingdom of heaven" (Matt 7:21 NRSV). Jesus asked, "Why do you call me 'Lord, Lord,' and do not do what I tell you?" He followed this question with a parable about a man who dug deeply and built his house on a solid rock foundation that resisted the devastating floods that inevitably come. Another person built a house on shallow ground without any foundation, and "great was the ruin of that house" (Luke 6:46-49). Judges 17–18 reflects the ruin of Israel as it built its house on the shallow ground of idolatry, greed, and power. The catastrophic flood of social disintegration will soon follow in chapters 19–21, the horrific consequence of everybody's doing "what was right in their own eyes."

JUDGES 19:1–21:25, THE LEVITE'S CONCUBINE AND WAR WITHIN ISRAEL

OVERVIEW

It has been noted throughout the book of Judges that the changing power relationships, independence, and treatment of the many women characters in the book function as benchmarks for the health and faithfulness of God's people. Early on in the judges era, women like Achsah (1:11-15), Deborah (4:4-10), and Jael (4:17-22) displayed glimpses of boldness, leadership, and power as subjects of their destinies in the midst of a largely patriarchal context. Israel seemed to function more effectively as a religious and social community. As the period of the judges began its long decline, women became objects of men's foolish vows (Jephthah's daughter, 11:29-40), the objects of men's desire (14:1-3; 16:1), and the purchased instruments for schemes of male vengeance (16:5). This general decline from woman as the subject of independent action to woman as the object of men's actions and desires in the book of Judges coincides with the gradual decline in the health of Israel's social and religious life during the judges era. That decline culminates with the atrocity of rape and murder committed against the Levite's concubine in Judges 19, certainly one of the most brutal and violent scenes in all of Scripture.

The interplay of an individual Israelite (Samson, Micah) or a particular tribe (Dan) functioning as a symbol or metaphor for all Israel is a narrative device that continues into Judges 19–21. Certainly the horror of the rape and murder of the Levite's concubine must be taken seriously in its own right as a matter of patriarchal violence against women. However, its juxtaposition with the fractious civil war in chaps. 20–21 invites the reader to consider the fate of this woman, who has been raped, murdered, and cut into twelve pieces, as a gruesome metaphor for the social body of the twelve-tribe union of Israel. Increasingly in the book of Judges, Israel has been dishonored, attacked, killed, and split into pieces by other Israelites. Hints of these internal tribal divisions and conflicts began already in the Song of Deborah and Barak in 5:15-17 and in Gideon's conflict with the Ephraimites and the people of Penuel and Succoth (8:1-9, 13-17).

The internal violence and social dissolution within Israel gradually escalated with Abimelech's murder of his seventy half-brothers (9:5), Jephthah's killing of 42,000 Ephraimites (12:1-6), Judah's betrayal of Samson to the Philistines (15:9-13), and Samson's unwillingness to lead any Israelite tribes in a coalition against the Philistines. The fabric of Israel's tribal union gradually unraveled into a disheveled heap of threads.

Judges 19:1-30, The Atrocity at Gibeah

COMMENTARY

19:1-3. Judges 19 begins by describing again the absence of leadership and accountability in this period of Israel's life: "In those days, when there was no king in Israel . . ." (v. 1; see 17:6; 18:1; 21:25). The refrain builds an expectation that chaos, disorder, and disobedience will characterize the stories that follow. The earlier narrative in chap. 17 had featured a Levite from Bethlehem in southern Judah who traveled north to Ephraim. This narrative in chap. 19 features a Levite from northern Ephraim who travels south to Bethlehem in Judah. His "concubine" or wife of secondary rank had left the Levite, her husband, four months earlier and returned home to live with her father. The reason for her leaving is open to two different interpretations. The NRSV translates the Hebrew verb זנה (zānâ; lit., "to commit adultery," "prostitute oneself") in v. 2 as "she became angry with him," implying that the Levite had done something wrong to cause her to leave. Since a woman could not initiate a divorce in ancient Israel, the very act of a woman's leaving her husband would be construed as committing adultery. But leaving her husband in such a way suggests the husband probably had been abusive or done something else wrong, causing her to be angry and to leave. The NIV translates the same verb as "she was unfaithful to him," indicating that the concubine was the one responsible for causing the separation through her adulterous action with another man. However, the subsequent actions of the Levite, who goes to the father's house "to speak tenderly to her and bring her back," seem to imply that he had been in the wrong. The similar phrase, "to speak tenderly to her" (לדבר על־לבה lĕdabbēr ʿal-libbāh), was used to describe the man Shechem as he sought to persuade the Israelite woman Dinah to marry him after he had already raped her (Gen 34:3). This association with Shechem plants a seed of suspicion in the reader's mind about the dubious character of this Levite. While the concubine's father appears delighted to see his daughter's husband come for her (v. 3), the reader does not know the feelings of the concubine herself. She remains an object passed from father to husband with no apparent opportunity for her to approve or disapprove of their decision concerning her fate.

The concubine's father practices an exaggerated hospitality, repeatedly insisting that the Levite remain to eat and drink and enjoy himself in a feast of male bonding over the course of five days. The Levite appears weak and unable to say no to his father-in-law until finally, late into the fifth day, the Levite and his concubine take off to return to northern Ephraim (vv. 9-10). The Levite's unwise decision to leave so late in the day forces him and his party (the concubine, a servant, and two donkeys) to seek shelter overnight in a stranger's house. The Levite avoids seeking shelter in the city of Jerusalem because non-Israelites, Jebusites, lived there: "we will not turn aside into a city of foreigners" (vv. 10-12). The Levite wrongly assumes he will receive more hospitality in the Israelite town of Gibeah, which is located in the tribal territory of Benjamin. As things turn out, the Levite and his party would probably have fared better with foreigners than with their fellow Israelites.

19:14-15. The Levite enters the Israelite town of Gibeah and sits waiting in the open square for an invitation from some hospitable resident to spend the night at his or her house. Extending hospitality to strangers was an important and deeply held custom in the ancient Near East, and particularly so in Israel. The covenant code in Exodus (Exod 22:21; 23:9), the priestly laws of Leviticus (Lev 19:33-34), and the deuteronomic law code (Deut 16:14; 26:12) all command Israel to extend generous hospitality to the stranger or sojourner. God "loves the stranger," and God instructs Israel, "You shall also love the stranger, for you were strangers in the land of Egypt" (Deut 10:18-19). The deuteronomic law also instructs Israelites to be generous in hospitality to Levites, since they have no land of their own and their lives are to be dedicated in service to the Lord (Deut 16:14; 26:12). Therefore, if the Israelites in the town of Gibeah had known their religious traditions and values well, they would have fallen all over each other to offer hospitality to this man who is both a sojourner and a Levite. "But no one," says the text, "took them to spend the night" (v. 15). This is a time when there is no king, no teacher of the law, and no knowledge or fear of the Lord in the land. Ironically, it is the Levites as a tribe who were charged by Moses to teach the Israelites "to observe diligently all the words of this law" (Deut 31:12). If Gibeah is any sign of what is typical in Israel, the Levites have failed miserably as teachers of the law in regard to hospitality.[67]

19:16-26. Finally, late into the evening an old man who was originally from Ephraim but is living as a resident alien in the Benjaminite town of Gibeah offers them a place to sleep in his house (vv. 16-21). It is questionable whether such a resident alien even had the legal right to extend hospitality to strangers. At any rate, his generosity puts the native residents of Gibeah in an extremely bad light. The Levite assures the old man that they have plenty of provisions; all they need is a roof over their heads. While they eat and drink and enjoy the old man's generous hospitality, "the men of the city, a perverse lot" surround the house and pound on the door. They demand that the strange man, the Levite, be brought out "so that we might have intercourse with him" (v. 22; lit., "so that we might know him"). In an act of twisted male hospitality, the old Ephraimite man refuses to cave in to this threat of homosexual rape against the Levite, offering instead his virgin daughter and the Levite's concubine. The Levite suddenly intervenes, "seized his concubine, and put her out to them" (v. 25). In the Levite's hands, his concubine becomes a dispensable victim and a substitute sacrifice who undergoes the horror and abuse that he would have experienced. "They wantonly raped her, and abused her all through the night until the morning" (v. 25). The concubine manages to crawl to the door of the old man's house and then collapses, either unconscious or dead (v. 26).[68]

The scene is a clear echo of the Genesis story of Sodom and Gomorrah, in which the two angels of the Lord were traveling and received hospitality from Lot (Gen 19:1-29). The wicked men of Sodom similarly surrounded the house and pounded at Lot's door. They demanded that the two strangers come out "so that we may know them" (Gen 19:5). Lot offered his two daughters in their stead. However, before this could be done, the two angels of the Lord struck blind the residents of Sodom. On the next day, God destroyed the two wicked cities of Sodom and Gomorrah in a hail of fire and brimstone. The two cities became legendary in Israel's tradition for their wickedness, their inhospitality to strangers, and God's total annihilation of them (Deut 29:23; Jer 49:18; Amos 4:11). The atrocity at Gibeah in Judges 19 offers no divine intervention to protect the woman. Thus Gibeah's evil men go over the edge and transgress in ways even worse than the residents of Sodom.[69]

67. Victor Matthews, "Hospitality and Hostility in Genesis 19 and Judges 19," *BTB* 22 (1992) 3-11.

68. Insightful analyses of this story are offered from a feminist-literary perspective by Trible, "An Unnamed Woman, The Extravagance of Violence," in *Texts of Terror,* 65-91; and from a womanist perspective by Koala Jones-Warsaw, "Toward a Womanist Hermeneutic: A Reading of Judges 19:1–21," in *A Feminist Companion to Judges,* ed. Athalya Brenner (Sheffield: JSOT, 1993) 172-86.

69. For various perspectives on the literary, historical, and thematic relationship between Genesis 19 and Judges 19–21, see Stuart Lasine, "Guest and Host in Judges 19: Lot's Hospitality in an Inverted World," *JSOT* 29 (1984) 37-59; Susan Niditch, "The 'Sodomite' Theme in Judges 19–20: Family, Community, and Social Disintegration," *CBQ* 44 (1982) 365-78; and Matthews, "Hospitality and Hostility in Genesis 19 and Judges 19," 3-11.

19:27-28. Although subtly construed, the most sinister character in the narrative may be the Levite himself. He had earlier "spoken tenderly" to his concubine in an effort to persuade her to return with him from her father's house (v. 3). But the reader even then may have wondered what the Levite had done to cause her to leave him in the first place. The events following the concubine's rape may provide some reasons. After having handed over his concubine to the mob outside the house, the Levite might be expected to be tortured all night by guilt, shame, and remorse for his action. Instead, he apparently goes to bed and sleeps (v. 27). He does not rush out of the house in the morning in search of his concubine. Instead, he makes preparations to leave and opens the door only when he is ready to continue his journey. The Levite is totally self-absorbed, unremorseful, and unfeeling.

When the Levite finally opens the door, "there was his concubine lying at the door of the house, with her hands on the threshold" (v. 27). The image of this tortured and raped woman on the doorstep should have brought to tears any human with an ounce of compassion. Now would be a moment for him to "speak tenderly" to her, gently lifting her battered body and carrying her to a bed in the house where she could be nursed and allowed time to begin to heal her broken body and spirit—if she was not already dead. What we get instead are the callous and gruff words of the Levite to the concubine, "Get up, we are going." She does not answer. Her inability to respond suggests either unconsciousness or death, and the reader is left wondering. The Levite picks up her limp body, puts it on the donkey, and "sets out for his home" (v. 28). The scene is a reversal of the first woman we encounter in the book of Judges, Achsah, daughter of Caleb. In 1:11-15, a bold and buoyant Achsah had dismounted from her donkey to ask her loving father for the gift of life-giving springs of water. Her father, Caleb, generously gave his daughter not one but two springs of water. The love, generosity, and promotion of life and well-being that characterized the relationship between women and men at the beginning of Judges are tragically absent here at the end of Judges.

19:29-30. When the Levite arrives at his home, he takes a knife and grasps his concubine (v. 29). The verb "to grasp" (חזק *ḥāzaq*) is the same Hebrew verb used in v. 25 when the Levite "seized" his concubine to put her out and expose her to the mob of wicked men. The verb suggests a rough and abusive handling of her body. The Levite then "cut her into twelve pieces, limb by limb" and sends each piece of her dismembered body to one of the twelve tribes of Israel as a grisly call to arms. His act is a morbid and twisted adaptation of a customary means of calling up an emergency military force in the ancient Near East. King Saul, for example, summoned the twelve tribes of Israel to join in a battle by cutting up and sending out twelve parts of an ox (1 Sam 11:7). But when did the Levite's concubine actually die? When she lay at the doorstep after the night of abuse? During the journey home on the donkey? Or at the hands of the Levite as he cut her into pieces? The reader is never actually told. Mieke Bal suggests that "as her death began at her exposure and ends with her dismemberment, we cannot know when exactly she dies, and we must not know it. . . . She dies several times, or rather, she never stops dying."[70] In any case, the Levite is as culpable in her death as anyone in the story from his first "seizing" of her in v. 25 to the last "grasping" of her in v. 29. As the Levite sends her body parts out to Israel, he accompanies them with a message, "Has such a thing ever happened since the day that the Israelites came up from the land of Egypt until this day?" (v. 30). But what exactly is the outrageous "thing"? Is it the brutal rape of this woman? The inhospitality shown toward the Levite? Or, at least in the reader's mind, is it the truly outrageous and brutal dismemberment, desecration, and perhaps even murder of the woman by the cold and calculating Levite? Has the concubine become simply an instrument for the Levite to use to drum up support for his desire for personal revenge for the inhospitality shown to him? We will learn more in the next scene.

70. Mieke Bal, "A Body of Writing: Judges 19," in *A Feminist Companion to Judges*, ed. Athalya Brenner (Sheffield: JSOT, 1993) 222. See also Bal, *Death and Dissymmetry: The Politics of Coherence in the Book of Judges* (Chicago: University of Chicago Press, 1988) 83-93.

REFLECTIONS

1. The dismembered body of a woman who has been raped constitutes an outrageous horror in the midst of Israel. The portrait of this woman is a tragedy that has been repeated time and again throughout history from the ancient period until today. Violence, sexual abuse, neglect, and suffering have been the experience of far too many women in countries and cultures across the globe. The unnamed concubine in Judges 19:1 is a metaphor for all the nameless women who endure public or private abuse and suffering in our societies. This story of the Levite's concubine calls the reader to "consider it, take counsel, and speak out" (19:30).

2. The pattern of exaggerated hospitality followed by violent inhospitality occurred in an earlier narrative in Judges when the Kenite woman Jael invited the Canaanite general Sisera into her tent for protection, food, drink, and rest. She then proceeded to pound a tent peg into the temple of his sleeping head (4:17-22). This breach of the ancient hospitality code had occurred among foreigners, but Jael's act contributed to the victory Israel won against the Canaanites. It was part of the strange means by which "God subdued King Jabin of Canaan before the Israelites" (4:23). The story of Judges 19 likewise portrays an exaggerated hospitality followed by violent inhospitality. Unlike Judges 4, this act of inhospitality occurs "in the family" of Israel. The attack against the Levite's concubine involves Israel's attack, not against a foreign enemy, but against its own body politic. To paraphrase Pogo, Israel has met the enemy, "and the enemy is us!"

Israel's worst internal enemy emerges as the Levite, the holy man who is supposed to be dedicated to the service of the Lord. The shocking implications for the critique of religious leaders parallel the effect of Jesus' story of the good Samaritan (Luke 10:25-37). The two holy men, the priest and the Levite, passed by the man who had been robbed and beaten, much as the Levite gruffly stepped over the body of his concubine with the words, "Get up, we are going." It was only the outsider or foreigner, the Samaritan, who stopped and offered help, hospitality, and generosity to the man. We wonder how much better it would have been for the Levite and his concubine had they agreed to stay overnight with the non-Israelites in Jerusalem, the Jebusites (vv. 10-12). Even the great ancestor Abraham looked less than virtuous next to the fear of God displayed by the Canaanite king Abimelech in Gen 20:1-18. These stories suggest that outsiders and foreigners often display values and virtues closer to the biblical tradition than do God's own people, who claim to follow the will of God."

3. Israel's actions in Judges 19 contradict the instructions concerning the treatment of strangers and outsiders found elsewhere in Scripture. According to the larger biblical tradition, extending hospitality to strangers may be an opportunity to encounter God in the form of a human being in need. Abraham and Sarah offered hospitality to three men who visited them with a promise, and the strangers turned out to be the Lord visiting them (Genesis 18). The New Testament Letter to the Hebrews alludes to Abraham and Sarah's experience: "Let mutual love continue. Do not neglect to show hospitality to strangers, for by doing that some have entertained angels without knowing it" (Heb 13:1-2). In the last judgment scene in Matthew 25, when the good sheep are separated from the wicked goats, the good sheep are those who have fed the hungry, clothed the naked, visited the prisoners, and welcomed the stranger. Without realizing it, those who practice such hospitality to others do it to Jesus as well: "Truly, I tell you, just as you did it to one of the least of these who are members of my family, you did it to me" (Matt 25:40). Offering hospitality to strangers is an opportunity to encounter God. The abuse or neglect of strangers is an affront to God.

Judges 20:1–21:25, An Unholy Civil War

COMMENTARY

20:1-48. The Israelites respond en masse to the Levite's urgent call to arms precipitated by the rape of his concubine and the distribution of her body parts to all twelve tribes. In ironic contrast to the concubine's dismembered body, "all the Israelites" assemble "in one body" at Mizpah (v. 1). The mention of Mizpah recalls the story of Jephthah and his daughter. Jephthah was selected as a judge at Mizpah, and it was there that he made his tragic and reckless vow, which led to the death and sacrifice of his daughter (11:29-40). The association with Jephthah does not bode well for what is about to take place. Previous attempts to unite Israel's twelve tribes against foreign enemies gradually deteriorated over the course of the judges era, culminating in the later judges who attacked fellow Israelites (Gideon, Jephthah) and in the individualistic Samson, who did not lead or unite any Israelites but carried out his personal acts of revenge by himself. However, in this period of chaos and distintegration, the Israelites come together for the purpose of taking revenge on one of their own tribes, the tribe of Benjamin. They gather to consider taking revenge on Benjamin because its territory includes the town of Gibeah, the site of the atrocity against the Levite's concubine (19:12-15).

The Israelites ask the Levite to explain what happened at Gibeah in Benjamin. The Levite responds with a distorted and edited version of events. His report of the outrage at Gibeah differs markedly at certain crucial points from the actual narrated events in 19:22-30. The Levite's distortions begin with his claim that it was "the lords of Gibeah" who rose up against him (v. 5) rather than the less significant group of "perverse men of the city" (19:22). The Levite claims that the men "intended to kill me" (v. 5), while the actual intent was to "have intercourse with him" (19:22). The Levite fails to mention that he was the one who "seized his concubine" and threw her out to the mob. Moreover, he claims that "they raped my concubine until she died" (v. 5). The actual narrative never makes it clear that the men of Gibeah killed

her; the reader knows that the Levite himself probably had a role in killing her either through neglect, forcing her to ride the long journey on the donkey, or cutting her body into pieces. The Levite's version of the story is designed to exaggerate the guilt of the people of Gibeah and to avoid any guilt or responsibility on his own part for having exposed his concubine to rape and murder. The Levite engages in the age-old game of creating an enemy in order to avoid his own responsibility or role in perpetuating an evil situation or action.

The Israelites respond to the Levite's accusation against the city of Gibeah by sending troops to attack the city and "repay Gibeah of Benjamin for all the disgrace that they have done in Israel" (v. 10). The text emphasizes again that "all the men of Israel" are "united as one" in their attack against Gibeah (v. 11). A matter of personal revenge involving a Levite has now expanded to become a national and tribal affair. A total of 26,000 troops from the tribe of Benjamin (including some specially skilled left-handed warriors) come out to support the city of Gibeah against the attack of the huge army of 400,000 warriors from the other Israelite tribes (vv. 14-17).

Like the tribe of Dan, who had misused a holy war model in its conquest of the city of Laish (18:27-31), the Israelites use aspects of the holy war in this ill-conceived civil war against one of their own tribes. They go up to the holy site of Bethel and inquire of God, "Which of us shall go up first to battle against the Benjaminites?" The Lord answers, "Judah shall go up first" (v. 18). The question and the oracle's response echo the opening scene in the book of Judges, when the Israelites had asked the Lord who should be first to go up to fight against "the Canaanites." God had also answered then, "Judah shall go up" (1:1-2). The oracle in Judges 1 had shown the favored status of Judah, and God gave Judah victory in its battle with Canaan (1:4-10). But in Judges 20, the choice of Judah to lead the assault against Benjamin implicates Judah along with the other tribes in their ill-conceived attempt to destroy a part of Israel. Insofar as "all Israelites" are involved in this civil war, all Israelites are implicitly condemned by these actions, including Judah.

The judgment against all Israel, including Judah, is further demonstrated by the results of the three separate battles against the Benjaminites in Judges 20. In the first battle, the Benjaminites are victorious and kill 22,000 Israelites. Israel weeps before the Lord, crying out for help as they had done when the Lord sent enemy oppressors to attack them for their disobedience (vv. 19-23; see 2:1-5; 3:9, 15; 4:3; 6:6; 10:10). As earlier in the book of Judges, Israel's weeping and crying are reactions to the oppression of enemies that God used to punish Israel for its evil ways. In previous episodes of the judges, God used foreign nations, such as the Canaanites or the Ammonites or the Philistines, as instruments of judgment. In chap. 20, God uses one of Israel's own tribes, the tribe of Benjamin, as an instrument of judgment against the rest of Israel.

The Israelites again seek an oracle from the Lord, asking, "Shall we again draw near to battle against our kinsfolk the Benjaminites?" God says yes, but the oracle again does not promise victory (v. 23; note the transposition of vv. 22 and 23 in the NRSV). The Israelites dutifully attack Benjamin a second time, but they suffer another defeat and the deaths of an additional 18,000 men (vv. 24-25). The Israelites weep again and seek a third oracle from God, and this time God promises Israel's victory and Benjamin's defeat (vv. 26-28). In their third battle with Benjamin, the Israelites employ a military strategy of ambush and deception similar to the strategy used in the successful holy war campaign against the city of Ai (Josh 8:29-42). The successful strategy is a sign that this battle is God's just punishment on the tribe of Benjamin for its disobedience, just as the two previous battles had been God's judgment on the other tribes of Israel.

The battle scene concludes with a body count of Benjaminites killed in battle. The Benjaminites had started out with about 26,000 warriors (v. 15). In various phases of the third and last battle, the Israelites killed a group of 18,000 Benjaminite soldiers (v. 24), then a group of 5,000 Benjaminites (v. 45), and finally a group of 2,000 Benjaminite

warriors (v. 45). Only 600 Benjaminite men remain of the whole tribe; these 600 had escaped the battle and "fled toward the wilderness" (v. 47). The Israelites then proceed to kill all the remaining Benjaminite population of elders, women, children, and animals. The tribe of Benjamin was nearly exterminated from the face of the earth, except for the slender thread of 600 escaped survivors. Would a part of Israel be forever destroyed by fellow Israelites? That is the question that hangs over the narrative as we move into the next scene.

21:1-25. The question of the survival of the tribe of Benjamin is heightened by a foolish vow the Israelites had made in the course of their deliberations at Mizpah. They had promised that none of them would give their daughters in marriage to any Benjaminite man (v. 1). Mizpah was the same location where Jephthah had made his reckless vow to offer as a burnt offering whatever or whoever first came out of his house when he returned victorious from battle. What came first out of his house happened to be his one and only child, his daughter. Jephthah was thus forced to sacrifice her, effectively wiping out his family line (11:29-40). The Israelites' vow at Mizpah threatens to create a similar result for the tribe of Benjamin, effectively wiping out any hope for the tribe's future life. The remnant of the tribe of Benjamin consists of only 600 men and no women to bear children for a new generation (20:46-48). The Israelites cry for a third time to God, but their cry reveals their ignorance about their own responsibility and guilt in nearly exterminating the tribe of Benjamin. They ask God, "Why has it come to pass that today there should be one tribe lacking in Israel" (v. 3)? They need only look in the mirror for the answer. The sinfulness of all Israel, including Benjamin, is responsible for this crisis (20:11). Israel seems unable to acknowledge its own guilt in the matter, much as the Levite in the rape and murder of his concubine.

The Israelites suddenly wake up and realize that they cannot allow Benjamin as a tribe to be annihilated in spite of their foolish vow. They remember a second vow they had made at Mizpah: that any group who did not come to Mizpah and join the coalition against Benjamin would "be put to death" (v. 5). They also recall that one group of Israelites from Jabesh-gilead had not been present at Mizpah (vv. 8-9). Thus, in a bizarre move, they decide to attack the residents of Jabesh-gilead out of "compassion for Benjamin their kin" (v. 6). Where is their compassion for their kin of Jabesh-gilead? The Israelites kill everyone in Jabesh-gilead except "four hundred young virgins who had never slept with a man" (v. 12). They offer the 400 virgin women of Jabesh-gilead to the 600 Benjaminite men who had escaped the battle and proclaim peace to them (v. 13-14).

However, 200 of the 600 Benjaminite men still have no wives. Thus the Israelites come up with another bizarre scheme. They instruct the Benjaminites to lie in wait at the yearly festival at Shiloh and kidnap the young virgins as they dance during the festival. In this way, the Benjaminites will get wives for themselves. But since these women were not given voluntarily by the fathers or brothers at Shiloh, the Israelites will not technically have violated the Mizpah vow, which involved willingly giving daughters to the Benjaminite men (vv. 15-22). The Israelites seem unaware that kidnapping and rape violate basic covenant obligations more severely than any single vow. The Israelites are simply multiplying the crime that was first committed against the Levite's concubine. The Benjaminites do indeed kidnap the virgin women at Shiloh and return to their tribal territory to raise families and build up their tribal population once again (vv. 23-24).

The book of Judges comes to a close with the refrain that began this section in 17:6: "In those days there was no king in Israel; all the people did what was right in their own eyes" (v. 25), reminding the reader again of the chaos and disintegration that have occurred between the two refrains. Religious idolatry, unholy wars of conquest against a peaceful and defenseless people, abuse of strangers, rape, murder, personal revenge, deception, civil war, and more rape, murder, and kidnapping of young women all combine to portray an Israel in turmoil and near death. What is most remarkable is that God has been at work in and through this chaos, even as God's Spirit moved over the primeval chaos of creation to form the heavens and the earth (Gen 1:1-5). God has been true to the divine promise to preserve Israel's survival in the land in spite of its constant and escalating rebellion and disobedience. And just as surely as God created the cosmos out of chaos, so too God will create a new Israel out of the chaos at the end of the judges period. The stories that follow in 1–2 Samuel and 1–2 Kings chronicle a bold new experiment with kingship in Israel, a new venture with its own set of glorious heights, culminating in King David, and tragic lows, ending in the exile of the nation to a foreign land.

REFLECTIONS

1. The Levite dodged his role and responsibility for the concubine's rape and death by misrepresenting the complex moral texture of the events leading up to the crimes that were committed. He simplified the calculus of guilt by laying all the blame on the residents of Gibeah. Similarly, the tribes of Israel seem totally unaware of the ways in which their evil actions have led to the near extinction of one of their own tribes, the tribe of Benjamin. "O LORD," they ask, "why has it come to pass that today there should be one tribe lacking in Israel?" The desire to pass the buck and not acknowledge our own sin and failure goes back as far as the story of Adam and Eve in the garden of Eden (Gen 3:8-13) or to the story of Aaron and the golden calf at the foot of Mt. Sinai (Exod 32:3-4, 22-24). Humans regularly resist taking responsibility for their own misdeeds. We seek to place blame on anyone but ourselves. Some find it difficult to offer a true and heartfelt confession of failure to God and to people whom they have hurt. But such confession and acknowledgment of wrongdoing are a necessary first step in restoring broken relationships with God and with other human beings. Confession is good for our souls, but it is often hard for our lips to speak the words with integrity and truthfulness.

2. Scholars have often understood the final section of Judges (chaps. 17–21) as propaganda by one group aimed against other groups within Israel. Some argue that these stories condemn the northern kingdom of Israel and favor the southern kingdom of Judah. Others suggest that the stories imply a condemnation of the kingship of Saul (who was from Gibeah of the tribe of Benjamin, 1 Sam 10:26) and support for the kingship of David, based in Jerusalem. Still others see an implied critique of one levitical group of priests versus another group of Levites. Some of these intra-Israelite rivalries may have played a role in earlier stages in the writing and shaping of these stories. But in their present form, these narratives intentionally include all tribes and groups as taking part in and being responsible for the social and religious collapse of Israel at the end of the judges period. One idolatrous Levite or priest is from the south and the tribe of Judah, and the other callous and self-absorbed Levite is from the north and the tribe of Ephraim. "All Israel" is involved in the misguided civil war and the killing and kidnapping of women that follow. All the tribes of Israel experience defeat in the battle, a sign of God's judgment against them. Benjamin (the tribe of King Saul) is defeated and judged, but so is the tribe of Judah (the tribe of King David). This blanket condemnation of all Israel echoes the angel's words of judgment against all the Israelites at the beginning of the book (Judg 2:4). All have sinned and fallen short of the glory of God (Rom 3:23).

3. The Israelite tribes acted in bizarre and reprehensible ways to avoid the technicalities of violating the reckless vow that prohibited them from offering their daughters to the remnant of Benjaminite men. On one hand, their actions display a rigid legalism in trying to keep the vow at any cost. On the other hand, their actions show a total disregard for the basic covenantal obligations of love and preserving the life and well-being of their neighbor. When the Israelite tribes totally annihilated Jabesh-gilead and sanctioned the kidnapping of the women of Shiloh in order to protect themselves from breaking their vow, they give evidence of having lost their moral and covenantal bearings. Preoccupation with legalistic and technical obedience to certain rules or laws without an accompanying sense of the principles of faithfulness and love that undergird such laws and temper their rigid application is a recipe for disaster.

4. The singular tragedy of the rape and murder of the Levite's concubine is compounded and multiplied many times over by the events that follow the Levite's manipulation of the facts. His distorted report leads to a spiraling cycle of violence and revenge, which only multiplies the crime. Thousands more people are killed. Hundreds more women are forcibly taken. Such is the demonic power of group evil, mob violence, and the human desire for ever more vengeance and retribution. The Bible recommends a good and more perfect way in which vengeance belongs to God alone, evil is answered with good, and enemies are loved rather than hated (Lev 19:18; Matt 5:38-48; Rom 12:14-21). Such ideals are often difficult to translate into reality, but even the so-called *lex talionis*—"an eye for an eye, a tooth for a tooth, a life for a life"—at least puts a limit on retribution and revenge. We may, perhaps, begin there and then work, however imperfectly, toward the more difficult but preferred ideal.

5. Lingering theological questions remain at the end of the book of Judges about the place and role of God in the midst of this unholy mess of human violence, idolatry, blind disobedience, war, and atrocities. God remains involved in these tragic events to judge and punish the Israelites through their own ill-conceived plans and strategies (20:18, 23, 27-28, 35). God remains ominously silent in response to the Israelites' question of "why has it come to pass. . . ?" (21:3). But the reader knows well that the Israelites have brought this crisis upon themselves through their own disobedience.

There is no king in Israel, no leader, no teacher, no guide who can unite Israel in renewed commitment to God and to the covenant God made with Israel. For the moment, everyone is doing what is right in his or her own eyes. As we come to the end of Judges, God has allowed Israel to experience the violent harvest of its long history of disobedience.

But God is not finished with Israel yet. Just as Samson's hair began to grow and offered a glimpse of hope, so also the tribe of Benjamin is pulled back just in time from the brink of extinction. Israel's twelve tribes are preserved. God remains committed to this people, because God has promised to do so: "I will never break my covenant with you" (2:1). God's patient love has been stretched nearly to the breaking point during the era of Gideon, Jephthah, Samson, and the Levite's concubine. But the Spirit of God is stirring again in new ways in Israel in the chaos at the end of Judges. God will raise up a new order of kings and prophets in Israel who will lead God's people effectively for a time. But the time of kings and prophets, like the era of the judges, will also come to an end. The kings of Israel, like the judges of old, will give way to new means of leadership, new structures of community, and new avenues for the Spirit of God to work in the world.

The book of Judges invites us to assess our own times and communities and modes of leadership. Are they effective and faithful instruments for promoting the will and purposes of God in the world? Are we sufficiently open to the new futures and possibilities God is creating out of the chaos and churning of our own time? In the words of God speaking through a prophet in a time of exile and chaos, "I am about to do a new thing;/ now it springs forth; do you not perceive it?" (Isa 43:19 NRSV).

THE BOOK OF RUTH

INTRODUCTION, COMMENTARY, AND REFLECTIONS
BY
KATHLEEN A. ROBERTSON FARMER

THE BOOK OF
RUTH

INTRODUCTION

T he book of Ruth contains an artistically constructed, kaleidoscopic narrative that is more like an extended parable than a historical report. The story is told with extreme narrative economy (a style that includes deliberate gaps or silences that leave many details unexplained) and with a characteristic disregard for historical or political details. The narrator uses symbolic names (such as the names of Naomi's sons, signifying in advance that they are not long for this world), word play (such as puns and double entendres), and the purposeful repetition of words and phrases to highlight themes and underline ambiguities. The "sophisticated literary artistry of the author" is marked by "the conscious intentional employment of multiple levels of meaning in the narrative."[1]

THE INTERPRETIVE CHALLENGE

In form and function, the book of Ruth closely resembles both the book of Jonah and the story Nathan tells to David in 2 Sam 12:1-7, without Nathan's accusatory line ("You are the man!") at the end. Like Nathan's story, and like Jonah, Ruth has the power of revealing us to ourselves *as we are* rather than as we think we ought to be. But unlike Nathan's story, Ruth and Jonah are *not* presented to us by a prophet who is willing and able to tell us who we are within the dynamics of the story.

Thus the interpretive challenge in both stories lies in the area of identification. We can rather easily argue that Jonah was a personification of the Jewish audience to whom the book itself was addressed. "Israel itself is symbolized in Jonah's person, a stubborn and self-isolating Israel that is always occupied with itself, evading the actual will of God, and unaware that God loves other peoples just as much as Israel itself."[2] But which of the characters in the book of Ruth can be said to mirror the people of God?

---

1. Moshe J. Bernstein, "Two Multivalent Readings in the Ruth Narrative," *JSOT* 50 (1991) 15-16.
2. Gerhard Lohfink, *The Bible: Now I Get It! A Form-Criticism Handbook,* trans. Daniel Coogan (Garden City, N.Y.: Doubleday, 1979) 83.

Generations of interpreters have held up the character of Ruth as a model of morality. Like the "good Samaritan" in Luke 10:30-37, Ruth is an admirable character from an ethnic group that was despised and rejected by those who considered themselves to be the "people of God." Ruth's admirability tempts interpreters to tell themselves and their audiences, "We *ought* to be or act like this." But an interpreter's advice to "go and do likewise" (as wise as it may be) never comes to an audience with the force of revelation. Nathan's exclamation in 2 Sam 12:7 has revelatory power because it uses the mirror of the story to reveal David to himself. But seeing themselves mirrored in the character for whom the book of Ruth is named will not lead an audience either to repentance or to hope for their own redemption.

REDEMPTION AND IDENTIFICATION

The purposeful repetition of key terms in the book of Ruth encourages us to consider Naomi as the character who most closely mirrors the attitudes and experiences of the people of God, including both Israel and the church. Repetition indicates that "redemption" is a key concern in the story of Ruth. The book is only eighty-five verses long, but the word "redeem" (גאל *gā'al*) and its derivatives ("redeemer," "redemption") are used some twenty-three times. Asking who or what is redeemed leads to the discovery that Naomi is the ultimate recipient of redemption in the story.

On a superficial level, we might say that the story of Ruth is about redemption defined in a secular manner, as the restoration of property to its original owners or as the healing of a break in a branch of a family tree. The final scene in the story (4:13-17), however, hints at a deeper level of meaning. In 4:14 the audience discovers that Naomi is to be "redeemed" through the child whose conception was said to have been given by the LORD (4:13). The women of Bethlehem, who know how bitter Naomi has been about the emptiness of her life, tell us that this "redeemer" will "restore" or "reverse" Naomi's "life" (using the word נפש [*nepeš*], which is often translated "soul").

Reversal is the essence of redemption. Within the story world Naomi is the primary object of redemption. It is Naomi whose life is turned around, whose feelings of bitterness, emptiness, and hopelessness are reversed. Ruth's faithfulness is only the *instrument* God uses to accomplish Naomi's redemption.

If the story told in the book of Ruth is to be redemptive for the people of God, then the people of God must identify themselves with the one who *is* redeemed. The story of Ruth becomes a story of redemption for Israel only if Israel can be persuaded to believe that the redemptive efforts made by God on Naomi's behalf will be made by God on Israel's behalf as well.

Ruth, the outsider, the representative of a group that Deut 23:3 refuses to admit to "the assembly of the LORD," is the agent or tool God uses to bring about the redemption of Israel/ Naomi. The parable-like form of the narrative encourages us to see not just that we *ought* to be like Ruth but that we *are* like Naomi. And when we see ourselves reflected in the story as we really are (rather than as we think we ought to be), the good news comes to us as revelation rather than application.

Thus a redemptive reading of Ruth will assume that the story is primarily concerned with the faithfulness of God rather than with the faithfulness of the people of God. In Ruth, redemption is based on grace, not merit. Redemption is not a reward given to Naomi because of her exemplary behavior. God chooses to redeem those who seem to have done little to deserve redemption. And God chooses to use those who seem unqualified according to human standards of judgment to accomplish God's purposes in the world. The admirability of the "other" in the story (be they Samaritan or Moabite) should serve primarily to convict us of our own repeated failures to recognize the despised "other" as an agent of God's redemptive activity in the world.

CANONICAL LOCATIONS AND THEIR IMPLICATIONS

Different Bibles place the book of Ruth in different locations. In Christian Bibles (following the Septuagint), Ruth is found in the "Former Prophets," the traditional name for the narrative sequence from Joshua to 2 Kings. But the Hebrew Bible puts Ruth among the Writings, the division of the canon that includes wisdom literature and Psalms. In the Hebrew text, Ruth is one of the *Megilloth* ("The Five Scrolls") set apart for liturgical use in the major religious festivals of Judaism. Ruth is read aloud in the synagogue as a part of the two-day celebration of *Shavuot*, the Feast of Weeks (which is also called Pentecost because it falls fifty days—seven weeks plus one day—after the beginning of Passover). The Feast of Weeks celebrates both the end of the grain harvest season and the giving of the Torah, marking the covenant between Yahweh and the people of Israel.[3] The connection between the festival and the book is both seasonal (the action in Ruth takes place during the grain harvest) and symbolic (God's love for Israel culminates in a marriage/covenant oriented toward redemption).

The canonizers responsible for the order of the books in Christian Bibles may not have intended to convey any particular theological meaning by their placement of Ruth between Judges and 1 Samuel. They may have intended merely to put as many books as possible in chronological order. However, once it was done (for whatever reason) it must be acknowledged that "the narrative that includes [Ruth] differs from the narrative that excludes it."[4] When Ruth is read in between Judges and Samuel, it functions both as a spacer and as a bridge between the end of the period when "there was no king in Israel" (Judg 21:25) and the beginning of the united monarchy. On the one hand, the opening of Ruth ("In the days when the Judges ruled") implies that the period of the judges is an era now gone by, making the book of Judges seem quite distant and separate from the action in 1 Samuel. On the other hand, the way Ruth begins with a reference to the judges and ends with a reference to David informs the reader in advance that the episodes in Samuel dealing with Saul are little more than a detour on the road to the dynasty that really matters, the Davidic line of kings.[5]

Taken together, Judges 19–21 and Ruth seem to condemn the origins of Saul and commend the origins of David for ethical rather than ethnic reasons.[6] God's rejection of Saul can be anticipated by the reader who notes that Saul comes from Gibeah (the source of the appalling behavior described in Judges 19–21). Saul has an ethnically "pure" family tree, but he seems to have inherited his ancestors' tendency to disregard God's sovereignty. In contrast, David's family tree is rooted in the remarkably loyal behavior of a foreigner who has voluntarily chosen to join herself and her future to the Lord. Thus if Ruth is read in between Judges and 1 Samuel, it seems to function as a "witness to the moral legitimacy of the Davidic monarchy."[7] When Judges, Ruth, and Samuel are read together as a single story, it seems that David, with his "outsider" blood, is more of an insider with God than is Saul, whose bloodlines are not tainted by intermarriage but whose ancestors *acted* in a tainted way.

In the Hebrew Bible, Ruth is surrounded by post-exilic, poetic and wisdom-oriented texts. The reader who encounters Ruth among the Writings is more inclined to see the story as a parable than as an apology, or as an example story rather than royal propaganda. Many of the psalms are assigned to David, and a large section of 1 Chronicles (chaps. 10–29) is devoted to the kingship of David. In this literary context, the book of Ruth seems to assume the greatness rather than defend the legitimacy of the Davidic line of kings. Thus readers of Ruth in the Hebrew Bible are more likely to conclude that it teaches a lesson that could function equally well in any historical setting. An early rabbinic interpreter says Ruth was written "to teach how great is the reward of those who do deeds of kindness,"[8] and a modern literary critic says that the moral of the story is, "Common people achieve uncommon ends when they act unselfishly toward each other."[9]

3. See Abraham P. Bloch, *The Biblical and Historical Background of the Jewish Holy Days* (New York: KTAV, 1978) 179-89.

4. David Jobling, "Ruth Finds a Home: Canon, Politics, Method," in *The New Literary Criticism and the Hebrew Bible*, ed. J. Cheryl Exum and David J. A. Clines (Valley Forge: Trinity Press International, 1993) 126.

5. Jobling, "Ruth Finds a Home," 130-31.

6. See Warren Austin Gage, "Ruth Upon the Threshing Floor and the Sin of Gibeah: A Biblical-Theological Study," *Westminster Theological Journal* 51 (1989) 369-75.

7. See Gage, "Ruth Upon the Threshing Floor and the Sin of Gibeah," 370.

8. *Ruth Rabbah* II.14, L. Rabinowitz, trans. (London: Socino Press, 1939).

9. Jack M. Sasson, "Ruth," in *The Literary Guide to the Bible*, ed. Robert Alter and Frank Kermode (Cambridge, Mass.: Harvard University Press, 1987) 321.

Since many of the Writings are obviously post-exilic in origin, Ruth's placement in the Hebrew Bible tends to support those who think the story of Ruth was developed in the fifth century BCE as a way of casting doubt on the wisdom of Ezra and Nehemiah's attempt to cast all foreign wives out of the restoration community of Israel.[10]

THE AMBIGUITY OF DATING

We cannot date the composition of the book of Ruth with any degree of certainty. The linguistic evidence is so ambiguous that equally valid arguments can be formulated to support either an early or a late date.[11]

Some readers jump from the observation of Ruth's function in its literary context in Christian Bibles to the conclusion that Ruth was *written* in David's time as an attempt to establish David's right to the throne. However, an apology for the righteous origins of the Davidic dynasty might have served the purposes of later writers as well. The exilic editors of the Deuteronomic History (the narrative sequence from Joshua to Kings) were interested in reflecting on faithful and unfaithful forms of leadership in Israel and Judah, and the post-exilic work of the chronicler was dedicated to exalting the successful kingship of David over against the failures of Saul.

In his own lifetime, David would have been known as a successful and powerful king who had overcome the military opponents of Israel and expanded the borders of the kingdom, while creating a sense of national identity among various tribal and ethnic groups. But David's greatest fame in Israel came in retrospect, as people in later times looked back on the beginnings of the Davidic dynasty, which had become remarkable for its stability and longevity. Long after David's own time, as the gap between the theological ideals projected onto human kingship and the historical realities perpetrated by human kings continued to widen, the faithful in Israel began to look for a future king descended from David (a "messiah" [משיח *māšîaḥ*], meaning "an anointed one") whose reign would bring about true security, justice, and well-being. Thus David's significance did not diminish with time but grew even greater in the years just before and just after the Babylonian Exile (587–539 BCE).

READING RUTH IN VARIOUS LIFE SETTINGS

Reading history through the lens of Ruth is more like looking through a kaleidoscope than a microscope. While the dominant themes of redemption and insider/outsider dynamics remain constant within the story, every rotation of the proposed background against which the story is read causes these themes to fall into a different pattern. Every attempt to fill in the silences in the story produces a new shade of meaning.

If we imagine an audience of people in David's own time concerned with the purity of David's bloodline, we can see how reading Ruth might have persuaded them that the Moabite "taint" in David's ancestry was "redeemed" when the Moabite in question was shown to be an admirable convert to Judaism.[12] If we imagine an audience at a later date concerned with what it was that qualified one line of kings to rule "forever," we can see how reading Ruth may have convinced them that lovingkindness (not ethnic purity) gave birth to the messianic line of kings. If Ruth is read by people who are gravely concerned over the fragmentation of Israel, it may seem that "in the reunion of Ruth and Naomi, whom even death will not separate, the old sad break between the families of Lot and Abraham is repaired, and from that reforging of patriarchal bonds, there will be a new birth of salvation."[13] And if the book is read and studied by people who are being forced to choose between those who want to cast all foreign influences out of their community of faith (Neh 13:1-3) and those who insist that the "house of the LORD"

---

10. Although this idea has circulated since the early 1800s, it has been given its best modern presentation by André LaCocque, "Ruth," in *The Feminine Unconventional: Four Subversive Figures in Israel's Tradition* (Minneapolis: Fortress, 1990) 84-116.

11. Edward L. Greenstein, *Essays on Biblical Method and Translation,* BJS 92 (Atlanta, 1989) 14-15.

12. Murray D. Gow, *The Book of Ruth: Its Structure, Theme, and Purpose* (Leicester: Apollos, 1992) 182.

13. Harold Fisch, "Ruth and the Structure of Covenant History," *VT* 32 (1982) 435.

should be a "house of prayer for all peoples" (Isa 56:1-8), such an audience must have heard the story of Ruth as supporting the fruitfulness of the inclusive position.

In fact, the parabolic nature of the narrative makes tenuous every attempt to pin its origins down to one particular setting in the life of Israel. The enduring appeal of Ruth depends precisely upon this non-specificity, which allows the story to function effectively as revelation in our own as well as in Israel's eyes. When the kaleidoscope of history spins into our own time, we must consider how people in a country that is in the process of tightening its immigration laws in order to protect its cultural identity will see or hear themselves reflected in the dynamics of the text. Every new reader is challenged afresh to recognize his or her own present reality mirrored in a narrative that both convicts us of our lack of merit and assures us of God's redemptive inclinations.

BIBLIOGRAPHY

Verse-by-verse analyses plus theological reflections that will be helpful in preaching, teaching, and personal study can be found in:

Bush, Frederic. *Ruth/Esther.* WBC 9. Dallas: Word, 1996. Extensive bibliographies and detailed analyses of the Hebrew text make this volume an outstanding resource for further study.

Campbell, Edward F., Jr. *Ruth.* AB 7. Garden City, N.Y.: Doubleday, 1975. Although slightly dated, this is still the most accessible, well-balanced, and theologically sound commentary available in English.

Hubbard, Robert L., Jr. *The Book of Ruth.* NICOT. Grand Rapids: Eerdmans, 1988. Contains very helpful surveys of the range of opinions and the arguments used to support scholarly theories of the origins, purposes, themes, and theological perspectives of Ruth.

The following give readers helpful or provocative insights into the different ways Ruth can be understood, depending on the assumptions one brings to the reading of the text:

Bos, Johanna W. H. *Ruth, Esther, Jonah.* Knox Preaching Guides. Edited by John H. Hayes. Atlanta: John Knox, 1986.

Fewell, Danna Nolan, and David Miller Gunn. *Compromising Redemption: Relating Characters in the Book of Ruth.* Literary Currents in Biblical Interpretation. Louisville: Westminster/John Knox, 1990. Uses both interpretive storytelling and formal literary analyses to question traditional assumptions about the exemplary nature of the characters in Ruth.

Kates, Judith A., and Gail Twersky Reimer, eds. *Reading Ruth: Contemporary Women Reclaim a Sacred Story.* New York: Ballantine, 1994. Allows women's experiences in the modern world to illuminate and be illuminated by the book of Ruth.

LaCocque, André. "Ruth." In *The Feminine Unconventional: Four Subversive Figures in Israel's Tradition.* OBT. Minneapolis: Fortress, 1990. Pictures Ruth as a post-exilic parable that subverts the xenophobic policies of Ezra and Nehemiah.

Sasson, Jack M. *Ruth: A New Translation with a Philological Commentary and a Formalist-Folklorist Interpretation.* Baltimore: John Hopkins University Press, 1979. Casts a great deal of light on the way traditional literary forms affect our readings of the biblical text.

Trible, Phyllis. "A Human Comedy." In *God and the Rhetoric of Sexuality.* OBT. Philadelphia: Fortress, 1978. Presents Ruth and Naomi as admirable examples of how brave and bold women can survive in a man's world and become both the recipients and the agents of God's blessings.

OUTLINE OF RUTH

RUTH 1:1-22

TURN TURN, TURN

OVERVIEW

The action in the opening chapter of the book of Ruth revolves around Naomi. She provides the thread of narrative continuity in the chapter. We follow her from Bethlehem to Moab and back. She turns away from the promised land in a time of need and turns back in a time of plenty. Naomi is the object of Ruth's pledge of loyalty. And, when Naomi and Ruth arrive in Bethlehem, Naomi is the center of the whole town's attention (1:19).[14]

The word שוב (šûb), variously translated as "turn," "return," "go back," "turn back," and "brought back," occurs fifteen times in the book of Ruth, twelve times in the first chapter (1·6, 7, 8, 10, 11, 12, 15a, 15b, 16, 21, 22a, 22b). In the HB, šûb ("turn"/"return") is frequently used in a figurative sense to describe mental, emotional, or spiritual reversals. The word can refer to apostasy (turning away from God, as in Judg 2:19) as well as to repentance (turning back to God, as in 1 Kgs 8:33). Thus even when "turn"/"return" or "turn back" is used in a seemingly neutral (geographical) sense, it retains some of these moral overtones. Ruth and Naomi can both be said to be "returnees" ("who came back from the country of Moab," 1:22, 2:6; 4:3) in more than one sense of the word.

The frequent repetition of "turn" may also be used to alert the audience to the role that reversals play in this part of the story (as well as in the book as a whole). The chapter begins in the midst of a famine and ends in the midst of a barley harvest. The ones who look for more abundant life in Moab find death there instead. Naomi's life turns from "full" in the midst of famine to "empty" in the midst of plenty, and Naomi herself turns from "sweet" to "bitter" (1:20-21). In chapter 4, the word

šûb will be used again to describe the final reversal in the story: The child born to Ruth and Boaz will be "a restorer of life" (משיב mēšîb; lit., "will cause life to turn around") for Naomi.

The fact that this story is said to take place "in the days when the judges 'judged' " may carry more meaning than merely a historical identification. Several indicators suggest that the narrator wants us to connect the beginning of Ruth with the end of Judges. The twofold repetition of "Bethlehem in Judah" in Ruth 1:1-2 prods us to make a mental connection between this unidentified man and the escalating spiral of sin and violence portrayed in the final chapters of Judges (which in the LXX and in the Christian canon immediately precede Ruth).

The story in Judges 17–18, about the opportunistic levite who tended the idolatrous shrine that was eventually appropriated by the Danites, begins with nearly identical language: "Now there was a young man of Bethlehem in Judah" (Judg 17:7). Similarly, the story of gang rape, murder, dismemberment, civil war, and genocide told in Judges 19–21 begins with "a certain Levite" who took for himself a "concubine from Bethlehem in Judah" (Judg 19:1).

Furthermore, when the character called "a certain man" in Ruth 1:1 is given a name in 1:2, it is a name that is guaranteed to remind the reader of the recurring theme of Judges 17–21. The name "Elimelech" can be taken as an affirmation meaning "My God is King." But the final chapters in Judges illustrate in a stark and graphic manner that in those days no one (not even God) was king in Israel (Judg 17:6; 18:1; 19:1; 21:25). Thus the story of Ruth begins in a way that reminds us of the evil that can happen when the LORD does *not* reign supreme in Israel. The book of Judges illustrates the ways in which lack of

---

14. Vincent L. Tollers, "Narrative Control in the Book of Ruth," in *Mappings of the Biblical Terrain: The Bible as Text,* ed. Vincent L. Tollers and John Maier (Lewisburg: Bucknell University Press, 1989) 255.

loyalty and kindness among the children of Israel leads to division and death. In contrast, Ruth demonstrates what can happen when even a foreigner whose origins are despised in Israel chooses loyalty and kindness as a way of life.

RUTH 1:1-5, TURNING AWAY

COMMENTARY

1:1. Biblical authors sometimes speak of famines as a consequence of or punishment for the sins of the people of God (see Amos 4:6; Hos 4:1-3). But the phrase "there was a famine in the land" may also be used as the conventional beginning of an example story (as in Gen 12:10; 26:1).

1:2. The sojourners are said to be "Ephrathites," which in this context seems to be the name of a clan or sub-tribal grouping. The source of 1 Chr 2:19-20, 50 suggests that Bethlehem was founded by the descendants of a woman named Ephrath, the wife of Caleb. It is particularly appropriate for a story that centers around a woman to identify her family by the name of the clan's matriarch. The narrator in Gen 35:19 considers "Ephrathah" simply another name for Bethlehem, which would also be congruent with the usage of "Ephrathah" in Ruth 4:11. The only other time the whole term "Ephrathite from Bethlehem in Judah" is used in the OT is in 1 Sam 17:12, when David is identified as the son of "an Ephrathite of Bethlehem in Judah." However, the speaker in Judg 12:5 uses "Ephrathites" to refer to people from Ephraim. This latter usage suggests still another connection between the beginning of Ruth and the end of Judges, since both of the stories in Judges 17–21 begin "in the hill country of Ephraim." The word "Ephrathites" may also have ironic overtones as it is used here, since it apparently comes from a root (פרה *pārâ*) meaning "fruitful," "fertile," or "productive." These travelers, who come from either a clan or an area known for its "fruitfulness," find only barrenness and death in Moab.

The term translated "country of Moab" is spelled in two slightly different ways in Ruth. "Country" is spelled שׂדי (*śĕdê*, construct form) in 1:1-2 and in one of the two occurrences in 1:6 (as well as in 1:22; 2:6) but שׂדה (*śĕdēh*, construct form) in the second occurrence in 1:6 (and also in Ruth 4:3). The latter spelling is the more common in texts other than Ruth (see Gen 36:35; Num 21:20; 1 Chr 1:46; 8:8). This variation in spelling may be more significant than it seems at first glance. In the unpointed (unvocalized) Hebrew text, "country" (*śĕdê*) is identical to Shaddai (שׁדי *šadday*), the name Naomi uses for God in 1:20-21. Thus the place where Naomi's troubles begin and the name of the God she blames for bringing these troubles upon her would have looked as well as sounded alike in the earliest forms of the text. (See Commentary on 1:20-21.)

In modern English usage, the word "country" is an ambiguous term that can refer either to a political state or to a rural (as opposed to an urban) area. There is some question as to how the terms *śĕdê* and *śĕdēh* should be translated here. Since the singular form of the same word (שׂדה *śādeh*) is used later in Ruth to refer to the "field" in which Ruth gleans (2:2-3, 8, 22) and to the parcel of land that Naomi is selling (4:3), we might reasonably infer that the narrator uses *śĕdê mô'āb/śĕdēh mô'āb* to refer in a nonspecific way to rural areas under cultivation, where there is some hope of escaping the famine that prevails in Bethlehem.

In any case, the symbolic force that the name "Moab" would have had in the minds of Israelite audiences matters here more than does the travelers' geographical destination. In the ears of an Israelite audience, almost any reference to Moab would have carried negative moral and emotional connotations. Genesis 19 reflects Israelite feelings of contempt for Moabites, claiming that Moab (and Ammon) had incestuous beginnings. When the Israelites were traveling in the wilderness after their escape from bondage in Egypt, their encounters with Moabites were either hostile (Numbers 22) or shameful (Numbers

25). After the Israelite tribes began to settle in Canaan, their enmity with Moab continued (Judges 3); and hostilities flourished through the periods of the united and divided monarchies (2 Samuel 8; Isaiah 15–16; Jer 48:38; Ezek 25:8-11; Amos 2:1-3; Zeph 2:9). Deuteronomy 23:3 bans Moabites and their descendants down to the tenth generation from entering "the assembly of the LORD."

1:3-5. The narrative begins (as an ancient audience would have expected a story to begin) by naming the man, the head of the family, first. In the first two verses, Naomi is merely a member of Elimelech's family. She is "*his* wife," and Mahlon and Chilion are "*his* two sons." But in v. 3 the storyteller shifts the focus of attention to Naomi: Elimelech becomes "the husband of Naomi," and Naomi is left with "*her* two sons." When the sons also die, we are told that "the woman was left without *her* two sons and *her* husband"

(1:5). Naomi will be the center of narrative attention throughout the rest of the chapter.

The names given to Naomi's sons are symbolic of the short-lived role they will play in the story. "Mahlon" sounds like the disease that hit the Egyptians before the exodus (Exod 15:26), and "Chilion" seems to come from the root כלה (*kālâ*), meaning "to perish." The narrator tells us that Mahlon and Chilion "married" Moabite women (NIV) or "took" (NRSV) Moabite wives, using the root נשא (*ns'*) instead of the more usual word for "take" (לקח *lqh*). The term used in Ruth 1:4 (נשא *ns'*) is used only nine times in the OT to refer to marriage: in Judg 21:23 (reminding us once again of the links between the beginning of Ruth and the end of Judges); in Ezra 9:2, 12; 10:44 and Neh 13:25 (where the taking of foreign wives is condemned); and in 2 Chr 11:21; 13:21; 24:3 (in reference to the taking of multiple wives).

REFLECTIONS

The book of Ruth begins with a series of small ironies. Famine covers the area known as the "House of Bread" (Bethlehem). Members of a clan named "Fruitfulness" move to Moab in order to live, but end up dying one after another, leaving no "fruit" (children) behind them. Even audiences who were not already predisposed to seeing Moab as a symbol of evil would be able to infer that Moab in this story is a place of death and destruction, swallowing up those who turn to it for sustenance.

The parabolic nature of the introduction to Ruth encourages us to see ourselves and our own lives reflected in the circumstances of the story. But the revelatory power of a parable depends on its audience's understanding of the *implications* of the facts of the story. When Jesus told the parable of the good Samaritan to his Judean audience, he knew the implications involved in making the hero of the story a Samaritan. The parable would not have made its point if most of the people in the audience had not considered themselves morally superior to Samaritans. In order to hear the same point in our own time, modern audiences need to recognize (but not share or condone) the ancient audience's cultural prejudices. Before we can decide what corresponds to Moab in our lives today, we have to ask, "What are the things we think we despise until we are forced to turn to them in times of crisis?" Or "What do we seek out in desperate times that ends up killing us or making our lives unfruitful?"

A deuteronomistic historian may have seen the use of נשא *nāśā'* in 1:4 (they "took" wives) as a way of highlighting the relationship between the end of Judges and the beginning of Ruth. But an audience in the post-exilic period must have heard in the use of this term for "marriage" an echo of the language Ezra and Nehemiah were using as they tried to persuade the Jews to abandon the foreign wives they had "taken." It has been suggested that Ruth is a subversive parable that was written specifically to undermine the authority of the priests who were trying to "purify" Israel by ostracizing foreign women.[15] Like parables in general, Ruth begins in a way that encourages

15. LaCocque, "Ruth," 84-116.

people to identify themselves with the characters and their attitudes. An audience that had begun to be persuaded by Ezra and Nehemiah's language might have felt that the use of *nāśā´* gave an appropriately negative connotation to the joining of Israelite men with Moabite women. But, again like parables in general, the story of Ruth will eventually subvert, or cause the audience to question their initial assumptions. Whether the story of Ruth was originally written for this purpose, it certainly must have functioned this way in Second Temple Judaism (i.e., after 520–515 BCE).

When conflicts of opinion arise in our own communities of faith concerning who is acceptable and who is not, we can encourage people to notice that more than one opinion is expressed by the faith communities reflected in the biblical text. Part of the good news to be preached on the basis of the book of Ruth is that the attitudes toward outsiders expressed in Ezra 9–10 and Neh 13:23-27 were not shared by all biblical authorities. The xenophobia reflected in Ezra–Nehemiah is contradicted explicitly in Isaiah 56 and implicitly in the book of Ruth.

RUTH 1:6-22, TURNING BACK

Ruth 1:6-14, "Return to Your Mother's House"

COMMENTARY

1:6-7. Clearly Naomi is the focus of the narrator's attention. *She* started to return with *her* daughters-in-law, because *"she* had heard. . . . " (v. 6), and *"she* set out from the place where *she* had been living" (v. 7). The phrase "back to the land of Judah" in v. 7 must also refer to Naomi alone, since Ruth and Orpah had not come from there originally.

In v. 6, the word translated "food" is לחם (*leḥem*), which can mean either "bread" or "food." The narrator uses an implied pun to make a point: Naomi decided to return home after the deaths of her husband and sons, because she had heard that "bread" (*leḥem*) had returned to "The House of Bread" (בית־לחם *bêt-leḥem*).

The word that is translated "daughter-in-law" (כלה *kallâ*) in 1:6-8, and 22 is used in most other passages to mean "bride" (as in Isa 49:18; 61:10; 62:5). Ruth and Orpah are Naomi's sons' "brides." The narrator may use this particular term to add a further touch of pathos to the story and to make the two women seem younger and more eligible for second marriages. Naomi herself is said to address the younger women as "my daughters" in 1:11-13.

1:8-9. Naomi wants her sons' brides to remarry. Commentators have sometimes been puzzled by the use of the phrase "mother's house" in v. 8. Elsewhere in the HB widowed women are expected or advised to return to their fathers' houses (Gen 38:11; Lev 22:13). The term "mother's house" (בית אמה *bêt ´immāh*) occurs only four times in Scripture: once here in Ruth 1:8, once in Gen 24:8 (the Rebekah story), and twice in the Song of Songs (3:4; 8:2). In each case this phrase appears in a story about or by a woman, and in each case the context is related to marriage arrangements. Naomi's statement in v. 9 makes it clear that urging each of them to go back to her "mother's house" is equivalent to encouraging them to look for new husbands. Going back to the mother's house is a first step in the process that will allow them to find "rest" or "security" (מנוחה *měnûḥâ*) in another husband's house.

In the written form of the Hebrew text, v. 9 is a declarative sentence: "The LORD *will* deal kindly with you." The early scribes amended it to read as a wish. Read as a declarative statement, Naomi's words might seem like an affirmation of faith. However, if we take what Naomi says as an affirmation, rather than a wish, then Naomi would seem to be implying that her own miserable situation has come about because she has not dealt kindly with the dead! (See further discussion at Commentary on 1:21.)

The terms "kindly" (NRSV) and "kindness" (NIV) in v. 8 are feeble attempts to translate the Hebrew word חסד (*ḥesed*). In the HB, *ḥesed* has far more theological significance than "kindness" has in common English usage. *Ḥesed* is considered an essential part of the nature of God and is frequently used to describe God's acts of unmerited grace and mercy. But (as v. 8 implies), human beings are also able to do or to show *ḥesed* to one another. To do or to show *ḥesed* means to demonstrate lovingkindness and loyalty that extends far beyond what the law requires, beyond anything the recipient expects or deserves to receive.[16]

Naomi's wish in v. 8 implies that both of her sons' brides have been kind and loyal to their husbands and to her beyond the call of duty. Naomi hopes that the LORD will follow *their* example! Furthermore, Naomi clearly thinks that the LORD's *ḥesed* toward Orpah and Ruth should provide them with "security" or "rest" (*měnûḥâ*) in the form of new husbands.

1:10-13. When the younger women say they would rather return with Naomi to her home than return to their own homes (v. 10), Naomi comes up with a series of arguments meant to persuade them that they will be better off going back to their own mothers' houses. Naomi's logic seems to be based on a customary practice known in modern times as the "levirate marriage" (after the Latin word *levir,* meaning "brother-in-law"). If an Israelite man died before he produced any offspring, his brother was expected to marry the widow and to allow the firstborn son of their union to carry on the dead man's "name" (Deut 25:5-10). Similar practices were customary in Hittite, Assyrian, and Ugaritic societies, and texts from these neighboring cultures indicate that such marriages allowed the deceased man's family to keep his property

under their control.[17] It is unclear whether this was the rationale behind Deut 25:5-10. In any case, Naomi seems to assume that if she had other living sons, they might have married their brothers' widows and thus provided them with the "security" they needed.

Naomi's statements that she "has no more sons in her" and is too old now to have another husband are followed by two rhetorical questions in v. 13 that assume the answer no. Naomi knows she is not able to provide Orpah and Ruth with the husbands she thinks they need in order to have "security" or "rest." The word used twice in v. 15 to mean "sister-in-law" reminds the listener of the levirate code in Deuteronomy. The only biblical uses of the root יבם (*ybm*) are found here in Ruth (in the feminine, translated "sister-in-law") and in the "law of the levirate" in Deut 25:5-10 (in the masculine, translated "brother-in-law").

The questions Naomi asks in v. 13 are also meant to remind us of the story of Tamar and Judah (Genesis 38), which illustrates how levirate marriage customs functioned (or failed to function) on at least one occasion in Israel's memory. After Tamar's first two husbands (both sons of Judah) had died, Judah said to his daughter-in-law, "Remain a widow in your father's house until my son Shelah grows up," all the while intending to ignore any further claims she might make upon his family (Gen 38:11). Naomi's argument implies that Ruth's and Orpah's situation is even more hopeless than Tamar's was. Naomi thinks there is not even the remotest possibility that levirate customs could provide a satisfactory solution to their mutual dilemma. Later in the story, Naomi's next of kin will be called a "redeemer," but never a "brother-in-law."

Naomi's final argument has to do with her own apparently hopeless situation. The future may seem uncertain for Orpah and Ruth, but Naomi thinks her own situation is even more bitter than theirs. They might still remarry and have children, but the older woman seems to have "no hope" (v. 12). In v. 9, Naomi expressed the wish that the LORD would deal even more kindly with Orpah and Ruth than they deserved. But v. 13 indicates that Naomi does not think the LORD has dealt

16. Katherine Doob Sakenfeld, *Faithfulness in Action: Loyalty in Biblical Perspective,* OBT (Philadelphia: Fortress, 1985); H. J. Zobel, *Theological Dictionary of the Old Testament,* vol. 5 (Grand Rapids: Eerdmans, 1986) 44-64; Edward F. Campbell, "Naomi, Boaz, and Ruth: *Hesed* and Change," in *God's Steadfast Love: Essays in Honor of Prescott Harrison Williams, Jr.,* Austin Seminary Bulletin (1990) 64-74.

17. Raymond Westbrook, *Property and Family in Biblical Law,* JSOTSup 113 (Sheffield: Sheffield Academic, 1991) 69-89.

kindly with her at all. Unlike the land of the Ephrathites, which is able to recover from famine, Naomi expects never to become fruitful again.

Naomi is "bitter" (מר *mar*, v. 13), as she will say again in vv. 19-20, and she blames the LORD for bringing about the situation in which she finds herself: "the hand of the LORD has turned against me." She argues that it does not make logical sense for Orpah and Ruth to align themselves with someone who seems to have the hand of the LORD turned against her.

The narrator uses the same root word for "turn"/"return" (שוב *šûb*) in all of the turning points in this scene: When Naomi decides to *return* home, she tells her daughters-in-law to *return* to their homes because the LORD's hand has *turned* against her. "Turn"/"return" occurs both in the narration and in the dialogue, serving to integrate both components of the text,[18] and it "carries the whole movement and tension of the episode."[19]

1:14. In vv. 6-13 the daughters-in-law are addressed as a unit and respond as a unit: "they wept" (v. 9), and "they said" (v. 10).

18. Basil Rebera, "Lexical Cohesion in Ruth: A Sample," in *Perspectives on Language and Text*, ed. Edgar W. Conrad and Edward G. Newing (Winona Lake, In.: Eisenbrauns, 1987) 131-38.
19. Edward F. Campbell, Jr., *Ruth*, AB 7 (New York: Doubleday, 1975) 79.

Here they again weep in unison, and then they become individuals, acting separately for the first time in the story. Orpah's leave-taking is recorded in the briefest possible manner. Having been persuaded by Naomi's arguments in vv. 11-13, Orpah kisses Naomi good-bye and then simply vanishes from the narrator's point of view. Orpah functions as a foil for Ruth, who acts in an exactly opposite way. Unlike Orpah, Ruth is not persuaded. She "clings" to her mother-in-law (note the verb דבק [*dābaq*], which can also be used to refer to a marriage relationship, as in Gen 2:24; 1 Kgs 11:2, or to Israel's ideal relationship with God, as in Josh 22:5). And unlike Orpah, who is never given a speaking voice in the story, Ruth makes a lengthy, forceful, and impassioned speech that dismisses all of Naomi's arguments as irrelevant.

The word for "mother-in-law" (חמות *hāmôt*) occurs here for the first time. The narrator uses this term, meaning "husband's mother" here and in 2:11, 18, 19, 23; 3:1, 6, 16. But Ruth herself never uses this word to address Naomi. Ruth uses the term only when she tells Naomi that *Boaz* has said, "Do not return to your mother-in-law empty-handed." Outside the book of Ruth, "mother-in-law" is found only in Mic 7:6.

REFLECTIONS

The formal, written record of a society seldom reflects a true picture of day-to-day life within that society. Historians, reporters, journalists, filmmakers, and storytellers may neglect the mundane details of everyday relationships, but these are the "facts" of life that affect the majority of people in the most significant ways. Naomi's reference to the "mother's house" gives us an oblique glimpse into one of the (most unreported) roles played by Israelite women in daily affairs.[20] The narrator who reports that Ishmael's mother "got a wife for him" does not seem to think this was exceptional behavior on Hagar's part (Gen 21:21), and Naomi does not see marriage from "the mother's house" as a foreign institution. Although the official, formal records speak only of a father's power over his daughter's choices, "Israelite women apparently had a role equal to if not greater than their husbands in arranging the marriages of their children."[21]

Orpah (whose name seems to mean "back of the neck") does everything society, custom, and the authority figures in her life expect her to do. She obeys her mother-in-law's instructions and returns to her own mother's house, weeping as she goes. While rabbinic legends say that the four giant warriors mentioned in 2 Sam 21:22 were Orpah's sons, the official biblical records ignore her. Orpah seems to have been a

20. Carol Meyers, "Returning Home: Ruth 1:8 and the Gendering of the Book of Ruth," in *A Feminist Companion to Ruth*, ed. Athalya Brenner (Sheffield: Sheffield Academic, 1993) 113.
21. Meyers, "Returning Home," 112.

model of obedient womanhood, and the LORD may have eventually dealt kindly with her, as she had dealt with Naomi and her family (1:8); but no one elected to tell her story. In a similar way, many modern women who have chosen traditional life-styles, living lives of obedience to the expectations of society or of the authority figures in their lives, may feel that no one is interested in telling their stories. "Orpah's journey home helps us to reconsider the silent and silenced among us, the women who stand both on the threshold of the women's movement and on the threshold of traditional beliefs and practices."[22]

We should stress that the biblical narrator does not condemn Orpah. Nor should we. The Orpahs as well as the Ruths among us deserve to be remembered and celebrated. But considering Orpah's choice to return to her mother's house encourages us to ask, "What in one's past does one reclaim? To what does one return? How does one return to the 'mother's house' without losing the redefinition of self and society discovered in the wilderness?"[23]

It is very important for the interpreter of Ruth to note that the relationship between Ruth and Naomi is *described* by the narrator, not *prescribed* as a rule for anyone else's behavior. If Ruth's actions are taken to be prescriptive (if the interpreter moves from the observation that this is the way Ruth acted to the conclusion that this is the way *all* daughters-in-law should act), then the book of Ruth becomes an oppressive instrument. Katherine Doob Sakenfeld describes a gathering of Japanese women who "expressed strong distaste for the story [of Ruth], explaining that it was much used by male church leaders as biblical warrant for completely self-sacrificing devotion of daughter-in-law to mother-in-law, a cultural tradition they sought to challenge."[24] While the relationship between mother-in-law and daughter-in-law translates differently in different cultural settings and among different persons, there is nothing in the biblical text of Ruth to justify our using it to impose or to reinforce standards of behavior in our own times.

22. Bonnie Miller-McLemore, "Returning to the 'Mother's House': A Feminist Look at Orpah," *The Christian Century* (April 17, 1991) 430.

23. Miller-McLemore, "Returning to the 'Mother's House'," 430.

24. Katherine Doob Sakenfeld, " 'Feminist' Theology and Biblical Interpretation," in *Biblical Theology: Problems and Perspectives,* ed. Steven J. Kraftchick, Charles D. Meyers, Jr., and Ben C. Ollenburger (Nashville: Abingdon, 1995) 257.

Ruth 1:15-18, "Don't Tell Me to Turn My Back on You!"

COMMENTARY

1:15. Both the NRSV and the NIV refer to Orpah's "gods" with a lowercase letter *g*, which seems to indicate to the English reader that Orpah and her fellow Moabites worshiped a variety of gods. But when the same Hebrew word אלהים (*'ĕlōhîm*) occurs again in v. 16, both translations use an uppercase *G* to indicate that Ruth intends to worship Naomi's one and only God. However, an impartial observer must note that the words used in vv. 15-16 are identical in Hebrew. The difference occurs in English only because the translators have come to their readings of the text with some previous assumptions concerning Moabite worship practices. It might be argued that OT references to Moabite religion seem to know of only one Moabite deity: Chemosh (see Num 21:29; Judg 11:24; 1 Kgs 11:7, 33; 2 Kgs 23:13; Jer 48:7, 13, 46; except for Baal-peor in Num 25:1-3, which seems to mean "The Lord of Peor" and also probably refers to Chemosh). So when *'ĕlōhîm* is used in the context of Orpah's return to her mother's house, it may be that "the most natural assumption is that Chemosh is intended."[25]

1:16. When Ruth finally speaks up, her words have overtones of indignation that the usual English translations fail to capture.

25. Alastair Hunter, "How Many Gods Had Ruth?" *Scottish Journal of Theology* 34 (1981) 433.

The word עזב (ʿāzab), translated "leave" in this verse, frequently connotes "changing primary allegiance" (as in Gen 2:24, which uses both דבק [dābaq, to "cling to"] and עזב [ʿāzab, to "leave"]).[26] ʿĀzab is the word used when Israel is said to "abandon" or "forsake" the LORD (as in Judg 10:10) or the LORD's commandments (as in Deut 29:24). Ruth is indignant because Naomi is urging her to abandon her present loyalties and to turn her back on her previous commitments.

Ruth uses verbs that state her intentions for the future: "I will go"; "I will lodge"; "I will die"; and "I will be buried." But the clauses translated here as "your God *will be* my God" and "your people *will be* my people" actually contain no verbs at all. In Hebrew, this simple juxtapositioning of nouns ("your God, my God; your people, my people") most frequently represents a statement of present rather than future reality. It is possible that Ruth means for these clauses to stand as an explanation for the rest of her declaration. Ruth has *already* committed herself to the LORD by whom she swears in v. 17. She has already committed herself to the

family into which she married.[27] These firm and present loyalties explain Ruth's determination to "cling" to Naomi and her indignation at being asked to return to her family of origin. In effect, Ruth says: "Your God *is* my God, and your people *are* my people; *therefore,* where you go I will go, and where you lodge I will lodge. And it makes me angry when you urge me to abandon these commitments!"

1:17. The oath formula used here is found elsewhere in the OT (e.g., 1 Kgs 19:2), but only in 1 Sam 20:13 and in this verse from Ruth does it use Yahweh (יהוה *YHWH,* "LORD") rather than Elohim (אלהים *ʾĕlōhîm,* "God"). The oath assumes that the LORD is one who reads the intentions of the heart and punishes lies. If Ruth's husband had been alive, or if she had been living in her father's house, such an oath might not have been considered binding. But according to Num 30:9, "every vow of a widow or of a divorced woman, by which she has bound herself, shall be binding upon her."

1:18. The Hebrew can be understood in at least two ways. Either Naomi stopped urging Ruth to go back (as the NIV assumes), or Naomi stopped speaking to Ruth altogether. The NRSV translation ("she said no more to her") leaves room for either understanding.

---

26. Ilona Rashkow, "Ruth: The Discourse of Power and the Power of Discourse," in *A Feminist Companion to Ruth,* ed. Athalya Brenner (Sheffield: Sheffield Academic, 1993) 31.

27. Rashkow, "Ruth," 32.

REFLECTIONS

Ruth was neither legally required nor customarily expected to remain with her mother-in-law. Thus her speech in vv. 16-17 must be understood as an act of *ḥesed,* showing love and loyalty over and beyond what is considered normal or expected. Ruth's actions seem to reflect her name, an apparent pun recalling the sounds of the words for "woman friend" (רעות *rěʿût,* as in Exod 11:2) and "satiation" or "full-to-overflowing" (רויה *rěwāyâ,* as in Ps 23:5). Naomi takes a commonsense approach to the future as she tries to reason with Ruth. She sees no way that Ruth could benefit personally from continued association with her. Reason alone could not justify Ruth's decision to "cling" to her mother-in-law. Her words and actions are governed by loyalty and love, rather than by logic.

In Jewish tradition, the interchange between Naomi and Ruth is used as a pattern for testing the sincerity of converts to Judaism. Noting that Naomi says "go back" (שבנה *šōbnâ*) three times (v. 8, 11, 12) to both Orpah and Ruth, the rabbis concluded that "a would-be proselyte should be repulsed three times." And, as Naomi tried to convince Ruth that accompanying her would have its disadvantages, the rabbis concluded that the would-be convert must be told about the possible hardships involved in becoming a Jew.[28] Naomi says "go back" once more to Ruth alone (v. 15), but after Ruth's firm response, "she stopped urging her," leading the rabbis to think that "a proselyte is not to be overburdened or cross-examined too closely."[29]

How do we read Naomi's character? The narrative does not assign an emotion or an attitude to the statement in v. 18 that says, literally, "When she realized she was determined to go with her she ceased speaking to her." The narrator does not tell us how to interpret Naomi's silence. Is Naomi overwhelmed with gratitude and thus silenced, or does she refuse to speak as a sign of anger?

Some readers suggest that Naomi may have preferred to go back home without the burden of a Moabite daughter-in-law. After all, Naomi's people had despised the Moabites for generations before and after the time in which this story is set. If we assume that she shared the "conventional prejudices" of her society against Moabites, then "Naomi's silence at Ruth's unshakable commitment to accompany her emerges as resentment, irritation, frustration, unease."[30] This reading of Naomi's reaction to Ruth's clinging is supported by the way she appears to ignore Ruth in the next scene, when they arrive back in Bethlehem (vv. 19-21). At the very least we might say that Naomi did not want to go home to Bethlehem accompanied by a Moabite reminder of all she had lost.

However, those who prefer to interpret Naomi's silence as appreciation or gratitude argue that "Naomi is the only one who could have told the Bethlehemites about Ruth's kindness, later mentioned by Boaz (2:11)."[31] Or they claim that "it could only have been because of Naomi's conduct that both her daughters-in-law cleaved to her, were prepared to surrender their past" on her behalf.[32]

28. *Ruth Rab.* II 16; *Yebam,* 47a; *Rashi* i 16. See D. R. G. Beattie, *Jewish Exegesis of the Book of Ruth,* ISOTSup 2 (1977) 101, 005 6.

29. *Rashi* i 16, Beattie, *Jewish Exegesis of the Book of Ruth,* 104.

30. Danna Nolan Fewell and David M. Gunn, " 'A Son Is Born to Naomi!': Literary Allusions and Interpretation in the Book of Ruth," *JSOT* 40 (1988) 104.

31. Tollers, "Narrative Control in the Book of Ruth," 254.

32. Frieda Clark Hyman, "Ruth—A Pure Dove of Israel," *Judaism* 38 (1989) 61.

Ruth 1:19-22, Turning Bitter

COMMENTARY

1:19. The "whole town" was stirred, but only the women speak to Naomi. Their communal question may simply express surprise at her sudden appearance, after an absence of more than ten years, or it may imply that Naomi's appearance has changed considerably during her absence.

1:20-21. Naomi's circumstances have certainly turned for the worse, as she makes clear with a bitter pun based on the root meanings of two Hebrew names. Naomi says that her given name, which sounds like the Hebrew words for "pleasant" (נעם *nōʿam*) or "sweet" (נעים *nāʿîm*), does not fit her current circumstances. It would be more accurate now for her friends to call her Mara (which

sounds like מרה [*mārâ*], the feminine form of the Hebrew word for "bitter").

Two sets of opposites are rhymed (in antithetical parallelism) in order to explain Naomi's bittersweet pun. In meaning, bitter is as far from sweet as empty is from full. "Sweet" may have been an appropriate name for Naomi when she was "full." But "bitter" better fits her "empty" state. The polarity between *full* and *empty* will come up again in 3:17, when Ruth brings an apron full of grain back from the threshing floor and tells Naomi that Boaz had told her not to go back to Naomi "empty."

Once again (in v. 20 as in v. 13) Naomi's bitterness is connected with her assumption that the LORD's hand has been turned against her. Early rabbis saw three possible ways of reading the consonants of the word מרה (*mrh*), translated "dealt harshly with me" (NRSV) or "has afflicted me" (NIV). The word might mean "to testify," "to afflict," or "to be concerned with." Early Greek and Latin translations opted for the meaning "afflict." The Masoretic Hebrew text chose the form meaning "testify against."[33] If Naomi is using the legal term "testified against me" (as in 1 Sam 12:3; 2 Sam 1:16), then her statement would seem to imply that she feels she has done something wrong and is being punished by God. The reader's sense that Naomi feels guilty is strengthened if a declarative sense of the verb is kept in v. 9 (the LORD will deal kindly with you, as you have dealt kindly with the dead and with me).

Naomi uses two different names for God in vv. 20-21. The poetic parallelism equates *Shaddai* (translated "Almighty" in most English versions) with *Yahweh* (traditionally translated LORD). This is not a particularly new idea: Exodus 6:2 also implies that the LORD (Yahweh) was known to the patriarchs as El Shaddai (traditionally translated "God Almighty" or "Almighty God"). But Naomi's use of "Shaddai" in this context of fertility (fullness) reversed to barrenness (emptiness) is particularly striking.

As mentioned in the Commentary on 1:2, the word "Shaddai" (שׁדי *šadday*) is similar in sound and identical in spelling (in the consonantal text) to the word שׁדי (*šĕdê*), which is used in Ruth for the "country of" or the "fields of" Moab. At the very least, a Hebrew-speaking audience must have noticed the echoing of sounds between the use of *"Shaddai"* in vv. 20-21 and *šĕdê* in v. 22. The narrator has already demonstrated a penchant for wordplay. Thus we should seriously consider the possibility that this phonological echo was a deliberate attempt to call attention to the ironic possibilities inherent in the similar sounds of Hebrew words.

The original meaning or actual derivation of the divine name "Shaddai" is open to debate. Based on similarities between *shaddai* and other words in Hebrew, as well as in related Semitic languages, suggestions have been made ranging from "mountain" to "fields," from "breasts" to "demons" or

"destroyers." Greek and Latin translators decided that "Shaddai" must refer to "the omnipotent one," and English versions followed suit with the traditional rendering "Almighty."[34]

Whatever the origins of the name may be, there is no doubt that Shaddai sounds very much like the Hebrew words שׂדה (*śādeh*, "field"/"fertile country"), שׁדי (*šĕdê*, "breasts of"), and שׁד (*šōd*, "destruction"). Hebrew storytellers have never been known to limit their puns to linguistically derived etymologies. The narrator in Ruth may have been aware of nothing more than the polar possibilities of meaning inherent in the sound of the traditional name "Shaddai." But such an awareness on the part of the speaker and the audience would give an ironic twist to Naomi's complaint. Both her former fullness and her present emptiness originate with the God whose name reminds people of both fertility and destruction. The narrator may also have expected listeners to connect Naomi's God language with her experiences in the "fields" (fertile country) of Moab. A few texts suggest that the name "Shaddai" may once have had Moabite connections.[35] In the third and fourth oracles of Balaam (the prophet who was called by the king of Moab to curse the Israelites as they camped in Moabite territory), Balaam describes himself as one who "sees the vision of Shaddai" (Num 24:4, 16).

1:22. The final verse of the first chapter looks both backward and forward. It summarizes the essential happenings of the first chapter and sets the stage for the action in the second chapter, which takes place in the period between "the beginning of the barley harvest" and "the end of the barley and the wheat harvests" (2:23).

The thematic term "turn"/"return" is used twice in the final verse of the first chapter. The first usage in v. 22 (ותשׁב *wattaāšob*) is identical in form to the very first usage in the book (1:6). This repetition creates an envelope structure around the first part of Naomi's story. The second usage in this verse takes the form השׁבה (*haššābâ*, "the returnee"), which will appear again in 4:3.

34. For an excellent overview of scholarly suggestions and arguments, see David Biale, "The God with Breasts: El Shaddai in the Bible," *History of Religions* 21 (1982) 240-56.

35. Jo Ann Hackett, *The Balaam Text from Deir 'Alla*, HSM 31 (Chico, Calif.: Scholars Press, 1984) 85-89.

33. Campbell, *Ruth*, 77.

In the homecoming scene (vv. 19-21), Naomi seemed to be so involved in her own bitterness that she ignored the presence of Ruth. But now the narrator reminds us that Ruth is still very much in the picture. She is called by name and described according to both her family of origin (Moabitess) and her family of choice (daughter-in-law). This is the first time in the story that Ruth is called "the Moabite/Moabitess." This designation may be used by the narrator to reflect the way the people of Bethlehem think of Ruth—as an outsider. In the coming chapters there will be a repeated emphasis on Ruth's ethnic background, even when it does not seem natural or needed in the narrative (note 2:2, 6, 21; 4:5, 10). The fact that the story belabors this aspect of Ruth's identity may indicate something of the author's intentions.[36]

36. LaCocque, "Ruth," 85.

REFLECTIONS

No matter how central her role in the story may be, Naomi comes across in this first chapter as a rather unattractive character. She knows that her name means "sweet" or "sweetness," but she does not feel sweet. Life has not been sweet for Naomi. Furthermore, Naomi does not act in the way we expect the faithful to act. She blames the LORD for the emptiness she now feels. She neither asks nor expects the LORD to come to her aid as God had come "to the aid of his people by providing food for them."[37] In modern times we might say that Naomi is in one of the stages of the grieving process. Like many of us who have suffered losses that leave us feeling empty, Naomi fears that her loss of husband and sons is the result of divine judgment. She may even feel that she is somehow to blame for their deaths.

Also like others who are caught up in the throes of their own grief, Naomi seems to lack gratitude for the support she has received from Ruth. When the two travelers arrive in Bethlehem, Naomi complains that she went away full—with a husband, two sons, and a promising future—and that she is coming back empty, because of the LORD. She speaks to the women of the town as if Ruth were neither present nor important to her. In this stage of her grief, Naomi's emptiness has not been affected by Ruth's pledge of undying loyalty.

From the beginning of the story it has been clear that Naomi is the character who is most in need of redemption. Her situation cries out for a reversal or a recovery. If members of a modern audience feel no need to be redeemed, they may be reluctant to identify themselves and their own situations with Naomi's situation. Thus, if you are inclined to preach or to teach Ruth as a parable of God's grace, you will need to lead your listeners to recognize that they, like Naomi, have pockets of emptiness in their lives that cannot be filled through their own efforts.

The narrative we call the story of Ruth will eventually tell us how Naomi is persuaded to let go of her bitterness, how her emptiness is filled with new life, how her redemption becomes the first step in the redemption of the people of God. Nevertheless, the memory of Naomi is a bittersweet one. We know more about the bitter side of Naomi than of the sweet. Might we not say the same about most of the people of God? Are not most of us really more like Naomi than we are like Ruth? At best most of us might say we have lived bittersweet lives of faith. Most of us can probably say that (like Naomi) we have more often been the recipients than the givers of loving kindness/ faithfulness. Yet it can be said:

that this bitter, grieving Naomi has succeeded in achieving what many missionaries hope for: someone has chosen to follow her God, and she (Naomi) has become an instrument for this choice not by putting on a "happy face" but by being her true self. For Ruth,

37. D. F. Rauber, "Literary Values in the Bible: The Book of Ruth," *JBL* 89 (1970) 27-37.

Naomi's truthful expression of her grief and bitterness does not obscure what Ruth has seen as a member of her family for the last ten years nor what she knows about Naomi's faith.[38]

Thus it seems that Naomi's story would serve as an appropriate basis for a sermon on All Saints Day. Just as Memorial Day is a secular holiday meant to honor those who have died in the country's service and to remember those we continue to love, even though they are no longer a physical part of our lives, so also All Saints Day is a time set aside in the church year for the remembrance of those who have died in the faith. This "memorial day" of the church is celebrated either on the first day of November (the day after Halloween) or on the first Sunday in November.

In older English versions of the Bible, we find references to the "saints" in the Old Testament as well as in the New Testament. One of the words that gets translated as "saints" in the Old Testament is a form of the Hebrew word for lovingkindness or faithfulness above and beyond the ordinary. According to that definition, we might easily say that Ruth should be included among the "saints" whom we remember on All Saints Day. It is easy to see how Ruth's actions toward Naomi might be described as faithfulness above and beyond the call of duty. Ruth probably comes as close to conforming to our traditional expectations of what a saint is like as any Old Testament character ever does. However, in the Christian tradition the people who are called saints have not all demonstrated an extraordinary degree of faithfulness, patience, or piety. In fact, the apostle Paul uses the term "saints" to refer to all who are a part of the body of Christ. Under this definition, all Christians, past, present, and future, can be considered a part of the communion of saints. And in Matt 27:52 the saints are even said to include the pre-Christian faithful.

It is easy to see how we might include Ruth among the communion of saints. Ruth plays an important, even an essential role in the carrying out of God's will in the world. Ruth is the change-agent whose loving faithfulness reflects God's faithfulness to Naomi. But in the last analysis, we need to acknowledge that this festival of All Saints is not about the faithfulness of the saints at all. It is, rather, a celebration of the faithfulness of God.[39] Because Naomi does not come across as a model of sainthood or faithfulness as we usually understand it, because Naomi does not act as we expect the faithful to act, it is easier for us to see that her story is about the faithfulness of God, and not about the faithfulness of humankind. Thus there is a message of good news for those who can see themselves mirrored in the character of Naomi: God can use us, as weak and as faulty as we may be, just as God used Naomi, even in the midst of her bitterness and grief, to accomplish some small part in the work of God in the world. Like Naomi, we can be called "saints," not because we have been extraordinarily faithful to God but because God has been extraordinarily faithful to us.

38. Nancy V. Lee, "Choices in the Book of Ruth," *The Japan Christian Quarterly* 54 (1988) 236.
39. Marion Soards, Thomas Dozeman, and Kendall McCabe, *Preaching the Common Lectionary Year B: After Pentecost 2* (Nashville: Abingdon, 1993) 132-33.

RUTH 2:1-23

KNOWN AND UNKNOWN

OVERVIEW

The center section of Ruth is organized around the polarities of knowing and not knowing, leaving and cleaving. Various forms of ידע (*yāda'*, "to know") are used in chaps. 2–3, along with other words having similar meanings (such as "recognize," "eyes"/"sight," etc.). Boaz is "known" as a member of Elimelech's clan. Ruth is a foreigner (one who is unknown) who comes to a people that she "did not know before" (2:11 NRSV). Boaz, who is "known" to Naomi, "notices" the one who is unknown (2:10) and acknowledges her right to his protection. In keeping with the narrator's interest in knowing and not knowing, we find a pattern of repetition of the word for "eyes" (עינים *'ênayim*) in this section of the book. Ruth uses the phrase "to find favor in the eyes of" in 2:2 (to Naomi, about her intentions), in 2:10 (to Boaz), and again in 2:13, at the end of her conversation with Boaz. Boaz also tells Ruth to keep her "eyes" on the field that is being reaped (2:9).

Chapter 3 will exploit the sexual as well as the cognitive connotations of "knowing," but chap. 2 merely hints at potential relationships that might develop between members of the clan and the stranger in their midst by exploring the thematic contrast between the polarities of leaving and cleaving (forsaking and clinging), which were first introduced in the preceding chapter. In chap. 1 Ruth was said to "cling"/"cleave"/"stay close" (דבק *dābaq*) to her mother-in-law, whom she stubbornly refused to "leave"/"forsake"/"abandon" (עזב *'āzab*). In this chapter, Boaz tells Ruth to "cling"/"cleave"/"stay close" (*dābaq*) to his workers (v. 8) and praises her for having "abandoned" or "left" (*'āzab*) her father, her mother, and her native land in order to accompany Naomi back to Bethlehem (2:11). Boaz uses the word *'āzab* again when he orders his workers to "leave" some extra stalks of grain for Ruth to glean (2:16); Naomi uses *'āzab* in 2:20, as she praises the one "whose kindness has not *forsaken* the living or the dead;" and both Ruth and Naomi use *dābaq* ("stay close") again in 2:21, 23.

Chapter 2 should raise questions in the audience's mind with regard to insider/outsider dynamics in Israel as well as in our own communities. Who is "family," and who is not? Who is "foreign," and who is not? How does an outsider become an insider? What are the rights, the privileges, and the obligations shared by those who belong to the "insider" group?

Once again, an interpretive ambiguity arises with regard to the discernment of Boaz's character. How do we explain his motives? Why does Boaz do and say what he does? Does his piety go any deeper than the words he speaks in 2:4, 12? Does this portrayal of Boaz picture him as a totally admirable man or not? Is he magnanimous in his treatment of Ruth, or does Ruth have to nudge him into a sense of his responsibilities?

RUTH 2:1-16, PORTRAIT OF A "WORTHY" MAN

Ruth 2:1-7, "Happening" to Find the Right Field

COMMENTARY

2:1. The narrator's introduction of Boaz begins (v. 1) and ends (v. 3) with a reference to the family/clan of Elimelech. He and Boaz are said to be members of the same sub-tribal grouping, but the specific relationship between them is left vague. The narrator says that Boaz is Elimelech's מידע (*mĕyuddāʿ*), spelled in a way that usually means "acquaintance," "close friend" or "companion" (as in Ps 55:14). Scribal notations in the Masoretic text suggest that it should be read as מדע (*mōdāʿ*), which seems to mean "kinsman" or "relative" in its only other biblical occurrence (in Prov 7:4). Both *mĕyuddāʿ* and *mōdāʿ* are derivatives of the root meaning "to know."

Since Boaz is from the same clan as Elimelech, the two men clearly must be related in some way. However, given the ways in which the narrator plays with the various permutations of the root "to know" in this center section of the book, it seems more than likely that the original spelling (connoting an acquaintance rather than a close relative) represented the narrator's deliberate intentions. Boaz may be a relative, but the narrator does not want to raise our hopes prematurely concerning his degree of closeness to Elimelech. Rather, the storyteller allows the tension in the story to build. It is not at all clear at first just how Boaz's relationship to Elimelech is going to be of help to Naomi. Only after Ruth reports on her successful encounter with Boaz does Naomi tell us he is a "near one" (קרוב *qārôb*) and a גאל (*gōʾēl*), a relationship that involves certain obligations. (See the discussion of *gōʾēl* in the Commentary on 2:20.)

Whether we read the word as *mĕyuddāʿ* or as *mōdāʿ*, it is very likely that the relational term used in v. 1 is neutral with regard to Boaz's family obligations. The narrator introduces Boaz without implying that he

has any legal or moral obligation to support Naomi.[40] In contrast, the terms that will be used in v. 20 suggest that Boaz either can or should do something to alleviate the widow's "emptiness."

In v. 1, this man Boaz (who is related in some way to Naomi's husband) is also called a גבור חיל (*gibbôr ḥayil*). Both *gibbôr* and *ḥayil* have root meanings associated with the concepts of strength and power. The phrase is used as a statement of approbation in a variety of situations and seems to have different connotations, depending on the context in which it is used. In Josh 1:14; 6:2; 8:3; and Judg 11:1, *gibbôr ḥayil* clearly refers to "warriors," to "soldiers" (NRSV), and to "fighting men" (NIV). But translators have decided that in 1 Sam 9:1 its usage best describes Kish as "a man of wealth" (NRSV) or "a man of standing" (NIV); that David was "a man of valor" (NRSV) or "a brave man" (NIV) in 1 Sam 16:18; that Jeroboam was "very able" (NRSV) or "a man of standing" (NIV) in 1 Kgs 11:28; and that Naaman was "a valiant soldier" (NIV) or "a mighty warrior" (NRSV) in 2 Kgs 5:1. In a few contexts, *ḥayil* seems to mean "procreative power" or "the ability to produce offspring" (as in Job 21:7; Joel 2:22); thus it might be translated as "virility."[41]

Most interpreters think the context in Ruth implies that Boaz is "a man of substance"[42] or "a property holder."[43] The most creatively appropriate suggestion comes from Danna Nolan Fewell and David M. Gunn, who think *gibbôr ḥayil* should be translated "a pillar of society."[44] Fewell and Gunn explain that this

---

40. Cf. Campbell, *Ruth*, 88-90, who notes the use of the verb ידע *ydʿ* in treaty-covenant terminology and translates מידע (*mĕyuddāʿ*) as "covenant-brother."

41. C. J. Labuschagne, "The Crux in Ruth 4:11," *ZAW* 79 (1967) 365.

42. Campbell, *Ruth*, 90.

43. Jack M. Sasson, *Ruth: A New Translation with a Philological Commentary and a Formalist-Folklorist Interpretation* (Baltimore: Johns Hopkins University Press, 1979) 39.

44. Danna Nolan Fewell and David M. Gunn, "Boaz, Pillar of Society: Measures of Worth in the Book of Ruth," *JSOT* 45 (1989) 45-59.

English idiom . . . plays well on both the notion of strength (*hayil*) and the fact that "Boaz" is also the name of one of the pillars of the temple (1 Kgs 7:1.15-22, 41-42). Furthermore, we understand the phrase to suggest that Boaz is an important man in the community, a man of reputation, a man of worth, a man of social and economic standing.[45]

The NIV combines both words into a single meaning that emphasizes Boaz's reputation in the community ("a man of standing"), while the NRSV says that Boaz is both "prominent" (*gibbôr*) and "rich" (*hayil*). However, when Boaz uses *hayil* to describe Ruth (3:11), the NRSV translates the word as "worthy." Consistency as well as context would be better served by using "worthy" to describe both Boaz and Ruth (in 2:1 and 3:11). In both contexts, *hayil* refers to the way Boaz and Ruth are perceived in the community. The use of *hayil* in both verses seems to suggest that they are a well-matched pair.

2:2. The narrator once again calls Ruth "the Moabite/Moabitess," even though the designation seems superfluous and redundant in the context. The narrator clearly wants us to keep Ruth's ethnic identity in mind. However, referring to Moab here also creates a phonological echo between this verse and 1:22. Ruth uses שדה (*śādeh*) to mean "field." Thus the same two words (*śādeh* and Moab) are used in this verse as were used in 1:22 (where they meant the "country of Moab"). Ruth says she wants to "glean," which the NIV accurately translates as "pick up the leftover grain." The laws in Lev 19:9-10 and 23:22 forbade Israelite landowners to strip their fields completely clean as they harvested their crops. Harvesters were supposed to leave both the standing grain at the edges of every field and the grains that were accidentally missed during the regular harvesting process for the use of the "poor" and the "resident alien," who had no land of their own to cultivate. Deuteronomy 24:19 states a slightly different version of the law: "When you reap your harvest in your field and forget a sheaf in the field, you shall not go back to get it; it shall be left for the alien, the orphan, and the widow" (NRSV).

2:3. "As it happened" (NRSV) or "as it turned out" (NIV) is literally "her happening happened." This phrase appears to mean "as luck would have it" or "by chance she happened onto." When the word is used elsewhere in the Hebrew Bible (e.g., Gen 24:12; 27:20), it is God who is said to cause something to happen. But here the narrator carefully avoids any specific reference to God's agency.

2:4. The first interchange between Boaz and his workers may reflect a standardized greeting formula. We have heard Boaz described in the third person as a "pillar" of the community. Now we are allowed to hear for ourselves the manner in which such a "pillar" speaks. Both Boaz and Naomi seem to use a slightly archaic form of Hebrew, indicating (perhaps) that they belong to an older generation.

2:5-7. Boaz addresses "the servant who was in charge of the reapers" (NRSV), called "the foreman of the reapers" in the NIV. In the NRSV, the masculine form of the word נער (*na'ar*) is translated "servant" in vv. 5-6, but the feminine form of the same word (נערה *na'ărâ*) is translated "young woman" in v. 5. The basic sense of both terms has to do with youth rather than with servanthood. But both words are used in a secondary sense to connote a person with subservient status. Thus when Boaz asks the *na'ar* who is in charge of the reapers, "To whom does this *na'ărâ* belong?" he might mean "To whom does this 'servant woman' belong?" (in the sense of ownership) or "To which clan or family does this 'young woman' belong?"

In v. 6 the young man/servant in charge of the harvesters clarifies Ruth's status by describing her first of all as "the Moabite woman" and then as the one "who came back with Naomi from the country of Moab." In v. 7 he tells Boaz that Ruth asked both to "glean" and to "gather" (אסף *āsap*) "among the sheaves."

The meaning of the last part of the foreman's speech is unclear in Hebrew. All translations emend the text in some way in an attempt to make sense of what the foreman says about Ruth. With emendations, the text can be taken to mean either that Ruth has been working in the field since morning or that she has been standing there waiting

45. Fewell and Gunn, "Boaz, Pillar of Society," 54.

for Boaz to arrive.[46] Many critics think that Ruth (either out of ignorance or out of boldness) has asked the foreman for permission to do something out of the ordinary.[47] The word "gather" (used in addition to "glean") may imply a departure from the usual way in which gleaning was done, or Ruth's request to glean "among the sheaves" may go beyond the usual practice.[48] It is not even clear whether the custom of the land guaranteed Ruth the right to glean. The laws in Lev 19:9-10; 23:22; and Deut 24:19 give gleaning

rights to the "sojourner" or to the resident alien (using the Hebrew word רֵג *gēr*). But in v. 10 Ruth calls herself a נכריה (*nokriyyâ*, a female foreigner), which may mean that she is not entitled to glean and needs to get permission first.[49]

The NIV follows those emendations that picture Ruth as already working in the field before the arrival of Boaz. The NRSV preserves some of the ambiguity of the Hebrew text by using the phrase "on her feet," which could imply either that she was standing and waiting or that she was working. (See Reflections at 2:8-16 and 2:17-23.)

46. Campbell, *Ruth,* 94-96; Sasson, *Ruth,* 47; Robert L. Hubbard, *The Book of Ruth,* NICOT (Grand Rapids: Eerdmans, 1988) 149, 152.
47. See Frederic Bush, *Ruth/Esther,* WBC 9 (Dallas: Word, 1996) 114.
48. Hubbard, *The Book of Ruth,* 148, 176.

49. Deut 15:3 and 23:20 seem to indicate that Israel's laws did not protect the "foreigner" (m. s. נכרי *nokrî*) as they protected the "sojourner" (רֵג *gēr*) from exploitation.

Ruth 2:8-16, Boaz "Notices" Ruth

COMMENTARY

2:8-11. The way in which one emends v. 7 makes a difference in how one understands Boaz and his actions. If Ruth is standing at the edge of the field when Boaz arrives, it is easy to see why Boaz notices her immediately. If she is already working in the field with a number of others, his noticing her seems more remarkable. If Ruth has been waiting for the landowner's permission to begin working, then vv. 8-9 can be seen to mean little more than the granting of that permission. But if Ruth is thought to have been working in the field already, then what Boaz does in vv. 8-9 appears to be an unsolicited act of kindness, above and beyond the expectations of custom or duty. This latter reading is the traditional interpretation, bolstered by the observation that Ruth's response to Boaz's first speech seems to indicate that his actions go beyond the strict performance of the laws on gleaning (v. 10).

In v. 8 Boaz addresses Ruth as "my daughter," which could be understood as either a traditional form of address from an older person to a woman who is considerably younger (cf. 1:11-13) or as a form of address that emphasizes the superior status of the speaker. When Boaz tells Ruth to stick close to his "young women" (NRSV) or "servant girls"

(NIV), he uses דבק (*dābaq*), the same word for "cling" or "keep close," which the narrator used in 1:14 to describe the way Ruth "clung" to Naomi.

Ruth's question in v. 10 involves a pun based on two different forms of the same word.[50] The word translated "foreigner" (נכריה *nokriyyâ*) comes from the same root (נכר *nkr*) as the word translated "take notice." In effect, Ruth says, "Why do you 'recognize' me [notice me], when I am 'one who is not recognized' [a foreigner]?" Boaz's answer in v. 11 picks up the two central themes in the chapter. He knows (has been told) that Ruth had to forsake the people and places she knew so well in order to come to live with a people she did not know.

2:12-13. Like Naomi in 1:8-9, Boaz makes a pious wish for Ruth's future, based on her commendable behavior in the past. The word כנף (*kānāp*) is translated in its usual sense of "wing" in v. 12, but in 3:9 the same word will be translated "cloak" (NRSV) or the "corner of a garment" (NIV). Boaz's metaphor implies that the God of Israel is like a mother hen (or some other type of bird) that protects its young by sheltering them under its wing (as in Deut 32:11; Ps 91:4). Since the "wings"

50. Campbell, *Ruth,* 98.

represent a place of refuge, the metaphor refers essentially to the LORD's protection.

Boaz apparently assumes that Ruth's future is in the hands of the LORD. Ruth's reply in the first part of v. 13 subtly suggests that the LORD may be waiting for Boaz to act! In modern colloquial terms, we might say that Ruth challenges Boaz to "put his money where his mouth is."

In the last half of v. 13, Ruth says that Boaz has treated her as kindly as he would treat one of his own "servants" (using the word שׁפחה [šiphâ, which is traditionally translated "maid" or "maidservant"), even though she is not in fact one of his servants.

We know very little about the functioning of social hierarchies in Israel. Translators have assumed that the meaning of šiphâ varies according to the context in which it is used. In Exod 11:5, the "maidservant" is associated with menial labor and seems to be at the opposite end of the social spectrum from the ruling classes. In some OT texts, the šiphâ seems to be a maid who is eligible to bear the children of her mistress' husband (such as Hagar, Dilhah, or Zilpah). In some texts, šiphâ is translated "female slave" (as in Gen 12:16; 24:35). However, šiphâ is also closely related to the Hebrew word for "clan" or "extended family" (משפחה mišpāhâ). These overtones of kinship connected with servitude might be better communicated in English by translating šiphâ as "family servant." It is possible that a family servant was considered a member of his or her owner's clan, and thus could expect better treatment from family members than could the נכריה (nokriyyâ), "foreign woman," Ruth knows herself to be. (See the laws in Lev 25:35-46 regarding the treatment of fellow Israelites who have been forced by poverty into positions of servitude.)

When Ruth uses the phrase "speak to the heart of" in v. 13, she is using language that could be construed in one of two ways. The phrase can mean simply to speak kindly (as in

Gen 50:21) or to "encourage" someone (as in 2 Sam 19:7). But in several other texts the idiom is used in the context of courtship or persuasion in a sexual sense (as in Gen 34:3; Judg 19:3; Hos 2:14).[51] Ruth (or the narrator) may be hinting that Boaz's speech sounds like "sweettalking."

2:14-16. In the ancient world, traveling away from home, leaving the protection of one's friends and relatives behind, was a risky business. Travelers had to depend on hospitality customs, which changed a stranger into a temporary member of the host's family, in order to survive. When hospitality was offered and accepted, it was generally understood that the protection of the host's clan was extended to the guest. Hospitality codes were a matter of custom rather than law, but several Old Testament narratives give us a glimpse of these customs at work in biblical times. When unknown travelers are invited into people's homes in Genesis 18–19; 24 and Judges 19, the sharing of food is always mentioned. Thus it seems that the sharing of food is a hospitality ritual associated with the offering of protection to the unprotected. When Boaz gives Ruth food and drink, he may be offering her (or acknowledging that she has) a kind of honorary membership in his clan.[52]

In v. 7 the young man in charge of the reapers said that Ruth had asked to glean "among the sheaves." This is what Boaz now tells his men to let her do (v. 15), suggesting that this was not the usual way gleaning was done. Furthermore, Boaz tells them deliberately to "abandon" (עזב 'āzab) an extra amount of the standing grain for Ruth's benefit.

In v. 9 Boaz said he had told his men not to "touch" Ruth. Now he orders them neither to "humiliate" her (v. 15) nor to "restrain" her from gathering as much as she can (v. 16).

51. Campbell, *Ruth*, 100-101.
52. Sasson, "Ruth," 324-25.

REFLECTIONS

The story of Ruth lives within the sociocultural assumptions of its narrator. The modern interpreter of Ruth needs to recognize (but need not approve of) the world pictured by the narrator. However, if Ruth is to function as a revelatory text in the modern world, modern audiences will need to see how the situations of the characters in the story correspond to modern situations. The preacher or teacher needs to ask, What types of people in our society face the same kinds of problems as Naomi and Ruth faced in the world they inhabited? The narrator assumes that Ruth and Naomi live in a rural, agrarian society in which women have to depend on men in order to survive. This is a world in which women are valued primarily for their ability to produce sons to carry on the patrilineal system;[53] a world in which women without fathers, husbands, or sons are denied access to the legal and financial structures of the community. The narrator (and the original audience) assumes that women like Naomi and Ruth have no socially acceptable means of supporting themselves except begging and gleaning.

Thus, in order to decide who corresponds to Ruth and Naomi in our own society, we have to ask, Who is forced by circumstances beyond their control to glean what they can from the bounty of others? Who in our world has no choice but to live on what is left over after those in control of the basic resources for life have taken everything they want or need? The modern interpreter thus concludes that a "widow" is not merely a woman who has lost her husband but anyone in our society (male or female) who has to rely on the charitable whims of others for food and shelter.

Furthermore, Naomi comes from and Ruth immigrates to a community in which foreigners (particularly foreign women) traditionally were viewed with suspicion, as a potential source of temptation to sin (as in, e.g., 1 Kgs 11:1-8; Prov 5:1-20). Many biblical references indicate that Ruth's ancestry and culture were held in contempt by the people of her new homeland. If Israel had an official "immigration policy" in the time of the judges, undoubtedly Moabites would have been listed as "undesirable elements." Moabites were banned from the assembly of the LORD because of their ancestors' sins. In order to decide who corresponds to a "Moabite" in our society, we need to consider not just those who are strangers in our midst, but those whom we have banned from the fellowship of worshiping Christians.

In modern times, ongoing debates over immigration laws indicate that many people feel burdened by the presence of foreigners in their midst—even if these outsiders profess undying allegiance to us and to our God, as Ruth did to Naomi. The people in our congregations may find it hard to believe that refugees, immigrants, or people requesting political asylum might someday become the instruments of our redemption. But there is no doubt that the biblical narrator pictures Ruth as an immigrant, entering the "promised land" from the same direction and for many of the same reasons as Naomi's ancestors had done in previous generations. Thus interpreters of Ruth will need to lead their audiences to consider some of the characteristics Ruth has in common with "outsiders" who are seeking entrance into our own country or into our communities today. For instance, it might be argued that Ruth came into Israel seeking (and finding) greater economic security than she had in her native land. (Elimelech and his family had gone to Moab for the same reason.) Impoverished Israelites may have complained that Ruth took work or resources away from the native poor of Bethlehem.

Some readers might be tempted to see Ruth as a model immigrant, one who is acceptable because she is perfectly assimilated into the society and religion she has adopted as her own. But this "melting pot" perspective has a shadow side. Some groups of immigrants have discovered that promises of assimilation into the dominant culture raise false hopes. United Methodist Bishop Roy Sano has said, "If there is any biblical account that describes the story behind Asian Americans' dreams in America, it appears in the book of Ruth. . . . The greater part of our people came with a determination to live the same story in its secular or religious versions. However, an analysis of our actual situation suggests that another story would be more honest and humanizing."[54]

---

53. See Esther Fuchs, "The Literary Characterization of Mothers and Sexual Politics in the Hebrew Bible," in *Feminist Perspectives on Biblical Scholarship,* ed. Adela Yarbro Collins (Chico, Calif.: Scholars Press, 1985) 117-36, who argues that the narrator makes Ruth behave in ways that reflect and promote male desires and prerogatives.

54. Roy Sano, "Ethnic Liberation Theology: Neo-Orthodoxy Reshaped or Replaced?" *Christianity and Crisis* 11:10 (1975) 258-59.

In fact, many immigrants' experiences have not matched the "dream" that an assimilated Ruth represents. We might ask which is flawed—the dream or the reality? Perhaps the "parable" of Ruth should be addressed only to the dominant majority in each community of faith. The dominant (insider) group needs constantly to be reminded that they can neither survive nor accomplish the mission to which they are called without the active assistance of "foreigners" in their midst.

RUTH 2:17-23, "KINDNESS" HAS NOT FORSAKEN THE LIVING OR THE DEAD

COMMENTARY

2:17-20. Thanks to Boaz's largess, Ruth is able to bring a large amount of barley (about half a bushel) home to Naomi, plus whatever she has left over from the "parched grain" Boaz had given her to eat (v. 14). When Naomi finds out that it is Boaz who has taken such "notice" of Ruth (using the same word used in v. 10), she calls down a blessing upon him. The antecedent of the expression "whose kindness has not forsaken the living or the dead" (v. 20) is unclear. Naomi's words may mean that Boaz's recognition of Ruth proves that *Boaz* has not "forsaken" either them or their deceased husbands. Or the words may mean that Boaz's actions indicate that the Lord has not "forsaken" them. The NIV takes the decision away from the reader by inserting the word "Lord" as the subject and making the relative clause into a declarative sentence. The NIV clearly wants the reader to conclude that Naomi sees the Lord's hand at work in Boaz's actions.

Now, for the first time, Naomi tells Ruth that Boaz is a "close relative" (קרוב *qārôb*, from the root meaning "near"). In fact, Naomi says, he is a גאל (*gō'ēl*), "one of our nearest kin" (NRSV) or "one of our kinsman-redeemers" (NIV). The word *gō'ēl* comes from the root גאל (*gā'al*, "to redeem" or "to recover"). In Israelite law codes, a *gō'ēl* is a designated male family member (brother, uncle, or cousin) who is expected to recover (rescue, ransom, buy back, redeem) that which has been (or is in danger of being) removed from family control by poverty, war, death, etc. The literature of ancient Israel refers to customs and duties related to the recovery (or redemption) of people (Lev 25:47-55), of

property (Lev 25:25-34; Jer 32:6-15), and of prestige (through the taking of revenge, Num 35:19-27; 2 Sam 14:4-11). But the circumstances in Ruth (at least as far as they have been explained by the narrator) do not seem to conform to any of the legal codes preserved in Scripture. At this point in the story, it is not at all clear to the modern reader what Boaz might be expected to "redeem."

In 1:12-13 it seemed that Naomi had given up hope that traditional levirate marriage practices would ever be of benefit to her. Now, however, Naomi seems to think that "the living and the dead" will be able to benefit in some way from the attraction between her *gō'ēl* and her daughter-in-law. It would seem that the dead could benefit only if their names were kept alive in Israel, as levirate marriages were meant to do. But the legal codes contained in the Bible do not speak of a connection between levirate marriage practices and the redemption or recovery of property. The story of Ruth seems to excerpt elements associated with both customs and to combine them in a unique way. It would be reasonable for us to assume that ancient audiences were familiar with a much larger body of customary law than the codes preserved in Scripture. Naomi's excitement in v. 20 seems to indicate that she sees possibilities that we do not. It also seems that Naomi's attitude toward Ruth is changing. Naomi includes Ruth in the kinship circle when she says that Boaz is "one of *our* closest relatives."

2:21-23. In v. 21, Ruth quotes Boaz as having said "cling to my young men," whereas, in fact, he said (in v. 8) "cling to my young women." Like Boaz, Naomi tells

Ruth to stick close to the *women* workers (v. 22). Naomi is afraid that Ruth might be importuned (פגע *pāga*ʾ), using the same word that was translated "urge" (NIV) or "press" (NRSV) in 1:16, if she tries to better herself by going to some other landowner's field.

Taken at face value, Naomi's advice to Ruth sounds very motherly: Stick close to the *women* workers in Boaz's fields. However, it is also possible that Naomi's concern is prompted by self-interest. Now that it appears that Boaz has taken more than a passing interest in Ruth, Naomi may be beginning to see how a marriage between her *gōʾēl* and her daughter-in-law could result in a solution to her own problems.

As in the previous chapter, the final verse both summarizes the essential points made in this chapter and sets the stage for the action in the following chapter. Verse 23 tells us that about seven weeks have passed since Ruth and Naomi had arrived in Bethlehem (the usual period of time between the beginning of the barley harvest in 1:22 and the end of the wheat harvest in 2:23). However, Ruth and Naomi are still widows, still living on the leftovers of the harvest in Bethlehem. Naomi's expectations that "the living and the dead" would benefit from Boaz's attraction to Ruth have not been met. Thus we are persuaded that their situation is dire enough to justify the drastic measures that will be taken in the following chapter.

REFLECTIONS

Providence, like beauty, is in the eye of the beholder. While the narrator does not specifically say that Ruth's "happening" to find Boaz's field was a part of God's plan, members of the audience may conclude that such happenings only seem accidental to human eyes. "For Ruth and Boaz it was an accident, but not for God."[55] Naomi's exclamation in 2:20 can also be taken as the perception of God's providence at work, as the NIV translation dictates.

This chapter in Ruth raises the question of the relationship between divine plans and human agency. To what extent does the working out of God's plans depend on the willingness of humans to be God's "hands" (or in this case "wings") in the world? After Boaz piously wishes that the LORD will repay Ruth for her loyalty to Naomi, Ruth reminds Boaz that he can (and should) act as God's agent in ameliorating her present circumstances. Ruth's reply, "May I continue to find favor in *your* sight" (2:13 NRSV, italics added), reminds Boaz that she and her mother-in-law also need earthly, physical help, which he is in a position to supply. Ruth even has to hint to Boaz that he might help make his pious wish come true by accepting her as a member of his extended family.[56]

In an oral performance, a narrator can use intonations and gestures to communicate attitudes such as sarcasm and irony, boldness, and feigned or genuine deference on the part of the speakers. But the written text lacks intonation patterns, and the narrator gives us very few clues with which to judge the motives or the emotions of the characters in the story. The narrator in Ruth (in line with the practice of most biblical storytellers) usually reports only *what* the characters say and do, not why or how. These gaps or silences in the text lure members of the audience into drawing their own conclusions about the sincerity (or the sarcasm) of any statement.

When Boaz was first described as a "worthy" man in the story, the original storyteller may have used an intonation pattern that turned the phrase "a worthy man" into a tongue-in-cheek evaluation of Boaz's character. The sound of the original speaker's voice may have made the listener wonder whether Boaz's "worthiness" was only skin deep. Is Boaz a man who speaks in a pious manner but has to be nudged into giving his close relatives' widows a helping hand? It is equally possible that the original

---

55. Ronald M. Hals, *The Theology of the Book of Ruth* (Philadelphia: Fortress, 1969) 12.
56. Sasson, *Ruth*, 49-52.

speaker's tone of voice assured the audience that Boaz truly was an admirable man. It is up to the reader of the text to decide whether Ruth's speeches in 2:10, 13 are genuinely humble, submissive, and grateful or whether she speaks with a tinge of impatience or irony in her voice. How would you feel if you were Ruth, waiting for this pillar of the community to give you permission to glean enough for you and your mother-in-law to live on, and all he said was "may the LORD reward you"? Would you feel more sarcastic than humble as you reminded this "worthy" man that he himself has a part to play in God's plans for you (2:13)?

When the narrator has Ruth use the term *nokriyyâ* to describe herself in 2:10, a post-exilic audience must have heard echoes of the contempt Ezra and Nehemiah had for the נכריות (*nokriyyôt*, "foreign women") who had married Israelite men. Although the early rabbis thought that a convert like Ruth should be accepted as an equal in Israel,[57] a close examination of Ruth's first attempts to act like a normal member of the Bethlehem community raises a few doubts concerning the community's initial willingness to accept her as one of their own. Why, for instance, was it necessary for Boaz to tell his men (on three separate occasions) not to bother this stranger in their midst? Although the translations sound neutral with regard to where Ruth sat when Boaz invited her to share the harvesters' lunch, the Hebrew hints that she sat to the side of the other workers, not among them. The narrator continues to call Ruth "the Moabite/Moabitess" from the beginning of the chapter (2:2, 6) to the end (2:22).

Boaz may have been worried that the other community members would think less of him if he gave special favors to a Moabite. What would the people of Bethlehem say if he, a pillar of the community, allowed an outsider—someone from a despised ethnic group, someone who has never before worked or paid taxes in their community—access to the fields they have cultivated all year? What would happen to the work ethic if she were given more grain than the law strictly allowed? Would other poor people flock to his fields expecting the same? Would his current field hands demand special privileges as well?

This chapter in Ruth also raises the question of how the faithful should deal with the "widows" (the dispossessed and the powerless) in their communities. Israelite laws regarding the care of the poor assumed that most people lived in rural, agriculturally based communities (see Exod 22:21-24; 23:6-11; Lev 19:9-10; Deut 10:17-19; 14:28-29; 15:7-11; 24:17-22; 26:12-13). The change to a largely urban, industrialized society in our time makes it difficult to decide how we should translate into modern practices these ancient instructions for the care of the people. Interpreters of the biblical text need to consider whether (and how) the laws of gleaning and tithing and protecting the powerless apply for us today.

Again, it may be necessary for the interpreter of Ruth to examine the role of the reader's identification within the dynamics of the story. Unlike an accusatory prophetic text, which prompts people to react defensively, a parable like Ruth allows people to make discoveries about themselves that have the force of revelation. But the content of that revelation will vary according to the location of the reader's identification. As teachers and preachers of the parable of Ruth, our task is to retell the story in such a way that our listeners recognize their own present realities mirrored in the dynamics of the narrative. Who shall we say seems to play a Boaz-like part in the modern world? Do we resemble Boaz and the reapers in the field in our dealings with the dispossessed and the powerless in our society? Do we give them pious words in response to their pleas instead of material relief for their needs? Do we allow those without resources of their own to "glean" only after we have taken everything we want from our "fields"? Do we give them the leftovers that we, the pillars of the community, do not want or do not want to bother with? Are we reluctant to set aside perfectly good resources for their use, telling ourselves that they have not helped to "grow" or to "tend" them? Are food pantries the modern equivalent of gleaning? What would be the modern equivalent of offering hospitality to an unknown traveler?

---

57. *Ruth Rab.* III.5.

RUTH 3:1-18

UNCOVERING AND RECOVERING

OVERVIEW

The third chapter of Ruth consists of three distinct scenes. The word גלה (*gālâ*, "uncover") dominates the first scene (vv. 1-7), and the similar-sounding גאל (*gā'al*, "recover," "redeem," "act as next-of-kin") prevails in the second (vv. 8-13). The deliberate use of word play, ambiguity, and *double entendre* in these first two scenes creates a dramatic tension that the final scene (vv. 14-18) serves to prolong rather than resolve. The words שכב (*šākab*, "lie down") and ידע (*yāda'*, "know") occur in all three scenes and weave a thread of continuity between them.

In this chapter, the narrator's penchant for puns develops into a mischievous use of words and phrases that may be understood to have either innocent or sexually suggestive meanings. In other Old Testament texts, "to know" and "to lie down" are each used as euphemisms for sexual intercourse. When Ruth asks Boaz to take her "under his wing" in v. 9, she uses the same phrase that is used in Ezek 16:8 as a metaphor for marriage. The word מרגלות (*margĕlôt*, "feet") comes from a root commonly used in euphemisms for the genitals (see Isa 7:20); "uncover" is frequently found in texts prohibiting sexual relationships between close relatives (Lev 18:6-19); and "threshing floors" were traditionally associated with sex for hire (Hos 9:1).

The clustering together of so many terms that have both innocent denotations (face-value meanings) and sexually suggestive connotations must be considered a deliberate narrative ploy.[58] Misplaced prudery may tempt modern readers to cover up the sexually suggestive nature of the text, but doing so robs the story of an essential element of its meaning.

The suggestive language used here encourages us to compare this situation with other, similar situations recorded in Scripture. Naomi's plan is not without biblical precedent. Both Ruth and Naomi could trace their ancestry back to women who had decided to take similarly drastic actions in order to accomplish similar ends (Genesis 19 and 38).[59]

Again in this chapter narrative gaps or silences force each reader to evaluate and to come to some conclusions about what motivates the words and actions of the characters. The reader must decide whether Ruth appears to be "a willing marionette in the hands of a crafty, strong-willed mother-in-law"[60] or whether she demonstrates initiative, pluck, and *chutzpah* as she manipulates Boaz into giving her what she wants and needs.[61]

Does Ruth merely encourage a shy or hesitant Boaz to follow his own inclinations, as traditional piety often assumes? Or does the plan formulated by Naomi and carried out by Ruth constitute entrapment, as some other readers suggest?[62] In order to evaluate Boaz's character, we must first decide whether Boaz had a moral or legal obligation to do something about Naomi and Ruth's precarious economic situation. If we decide that he did, then we must ask, Why had he not done so before? Did Boaz have to be shamed into doing his duty, or had he truly not seen a way to help until Ruth pointed it out to him? Did Ruth have to prick his conscience, or did she simply help him to see a way in which he could do חסד (*ḥesed*), "kindness" beyond the call of obligation or duty?

---

58. Barbara Green, "The Plot of the Biblical Story of Ruth," *JSOT* 23 (1982) 61; Campbell, *Ruth,* 131; Calum Carmichael, "Treading in the Book of Ruth," *ZAW* 92 (1980) 248-66.

59. The notable similarities between these stories have been highlighted and analyzed persuasively by H. Fisch, "Ruth and the Structure of Covenant History," *VT* (1982) 425-37; and Anthony Phillips, "The Book of Ruth—Deception and Shame," *Journal of Jewish Studies* 37 (1986) 1-17.

60. Tollers, "Narrative Control in the Book of Ruth," 254.

61. Sasson, *Ruth,* 230.

62. See Athalya Brenner, *The Israelite Woman: Social Role and Literary Type in Biblical Narrative* (Sheffield: JSOT, 1985) 107; Phillips, "The Book of Ruth—Deception and Shame," 14-16.

Some interpreters suggest that Boaz finds it difficult to justify his attraction to a Moabite woman and needs some way to make his inclinations seem like a virtuous concern for the interests of the living and the dead.[63]

Others think that Boaz had to be shamed into doing what he ought to have done all along.[64] As you read chapter 3, keep an open mind to the multiple interpretive possibilities inherent in the text.

63. Fewell and Gunn, "Boaz, Pillar of Society," 49.

64. E.g., Phillips, "The Book of Ruth—Deception and Shame."

RUTH 3:1-7, THE PLAN: UNCOVERING

COMMENTARY

3:1-2. In the first chapter, Naomi urged Ruth to return to her mother's house, praying that the LORD would grant her מנוחה (měnûḥâ), "security" (NRSV) or "rest" (NIV), by giving her a second husband (1:9). In 3:1 the term מנוח (mānôaḥ, which the NRSV translates as "security" and the NIV as "home") is spelled slightly differently and seems to refer to a "resting place," or a place to settle down (see Gen 8:9) rather than to rest itself. As a widow and a foreigner, without property or protector, Ruth has no home of her own. As the last few words in the preceding chapter remind us, "she lived with her mother-in-law." Gleaning would have provided Ruth and Naomi with little more than hand-to-mouth subsistence. So Naomi sees the need to plan for her daughter-in-law's (and her own?) future. Naomi's hopes had been raised by the attention Boaz paid to Ruth at their first encounter. But as the harvest season draws to an end without any further action from Boaz, Naomi sees that she and Ruth will need to "work out their own destinies."[65]

It was clear that Naomi had marriage in mind when she used the term "rest" in 1:9, and the same seems to be true here. Naomi mentions Ruth's need for security in one breath (v. 1) and Boaz in the next (v. 2).

The word Naomi uses in v. 2 to describe Boaz as their "kinsman" differs from the relational terms she used in 2:20. In 2:20, Naomi called Boaz a גאל (gōʾēl, a "kinsman-redeemer"). But in 3:2, as in 2:1, she uses a kinship designation derived from the root meaning "to know" (ידע yḏʿ). Other forms of

knowing appear in vv. 3, 11, and 18, providing a framework for the rest of the narrator's "carefully contrived ambiguity."[66]

3:3. Washing, anointing (or perfuming oneself), and donning one's best clothes may symbolize either the end of a period of mourning (cf. 2 Sam 12:20) or the preparation of a bride for a wedding (cf. Ezek 16:9).[67] Audience members who were fully aware of the euphemistic uses of "know" (see, e.g., Gen 4:1, 17, 25) must have been amused at the double meaning inherent in Naomi's advice, "Do not make yourself *known* to the man until he has finished eating and drinking."

3:4-7. The storyteller uses "uncover," "feet," and "lie down" both in Naomi's instructions and in the description of Ruth's actions (vv. 4, 7). In Hebrew, each of these words carries suggestive associations that are not obvious in English translations. Before the reader tries to decide what Naomi wants to happen on the threshing floor, some attention must be given to the secondary freight these words must have carried in the minds of a Hebrew-speaking audience.

Like the English word "sleep," the word שכב (šākab, "lie down") can be used in an innocent manner. But the word is also frequently used to imply sexual intercourse (e.g., Gen 19:33-35; 30:15-16; 38:26). Similarly, the word translated "uncover" (גלה gālâ) assumes sexual overtones when it is used in combination with words such as "nakedness" (ערוה ʿerwâ), as in laws governing sexual relationships (Lev 18:6-19). "Nakedness" in such contexts seems to be a euphemism for genitalia (see Isa 47:3). However, in

65. Phyllis Trible, "A Human Comedy," in *God and the Rhetoric of Sexuality,* OBT (Philadelphia: Fortress, 1978) 195.

66. Campbell, *Ruth,* 131.

67. Green, "The Plot of the Biblical Story of Ruth," 61.

other combinations, the same root meaning of "uncover" is carried over into the realm of religious experience, where it becomes a technical term for "revelation" (as in Deut 29:29; Isa 40:5; 53:1).

In Deut 27:20, *gālâ* means "removed" (the man who "lies down" [*šākab*] with his father's wife is cursed, because he has "removed" [*gālâ*] his father's "wing" or garment [כנף *kānāp*]). But in other contexts, *gālâ* becomes a political or historical term when it refers to a person who is "removed" from the land (taken into captivity or exile), as in 2 Kgs 25:21 and Jer 52:27. And in the account of Ezra's post-exilic campaign to eliminate all marriages between Israelite men and foreign women, this same root is used a collective noun (גולה *gôlâ*), designating those who had returned from exile (see Ezra 9:4).

By juxtaposing the similar-sounding words *gālâ* ("uncover," "reveal," "remove") and גאל (*gāʾal*, "recover," "redeem," "restore"), the narrator encourages the audience to consider

ways in which "uncovering" (with all its possible innuendoes) can lead to "recovering"— to the redemption of what was lost.

Naomi tells Ruth to uncover Boaz's "feet" (or the place where his feet are), rather than his "nakedness," but the word translated "feet" is also commonly used as a euphemism meaning "private parts." It would be more accurate, then, to translate the word as "lower body" than "feet." Modern translations sometimes substitute modern euphemisms, so that the reader of an English version is seldom aware of the way the word "feet" functions in the Hebrew text. Thus, for instance, both the NIV and the NRSV use "relieving himself," where the Hebrew idiom says, literally, "uncovering his feet" (see, e.g., Judg 3:24; 1 Sam 24:3), the NRSV of Ezek 16:25 says, "offering *yourself* [lit.. your feet] to every passerby," and Deut 28:25 says "the afterbirth that comes out from between her *thighs* [lit., her feet]."

RUTH 3:8-13, RECOVERING: MIDNIGHT ON THE THRESHING FLOOR

COMMENTARY

The stories preserved in Genesis 19 and 38 (both of which involve tricks played by women without husbands or children on men who are related to them in some way) must lurk in the background of our minds as we listen to Naomi's plan and watch Ruth carry the scheme out with a variation or two of her own. "No one could have heard the story of 'Ruth the Moabitess' without thinking of Lot's daughter (Ruth's ancestress) and the incestuous beginning of the Moabite nation."[68] A reader who remembers how Lot's daughters managed to impregnate themselves without their father's knowledge might suspect that Naomi's plan "depends on Boaz being merry with wine and consequently having no clear memory of what happened."[69] It is quite possible that when he is startled awake and finds himself lying half naked next to

a Moabite woman, "Boaz imagines that Ruth has done what her ancestress, Lot's daughter, did before her."[70]

The root word גאל (*gʾl*) is used six times in vv. 9-13 (once in v. 9, twice in v. 12, three times in v. 13) and thus comes to dominate this midnight scenario. As a verb, *gāʾal* is translated "redeem" in the NIV and "act as next-of-kin" in the NRSV. The noun form, *gōʾēl*, is translated "next-of-kin" in the NRSV and "kinsman-redeemer" in the NIV. The term is difficult to translate because the same root is used to describe (1) the action of recovering that which was lost (or about to be lost) to a given family and (2) the family member who was expected to perform that action.

3:8-9. Verse 8 begins with ויהי (*wayĕhî*), sometimes translated "and it came to pass." usually indicates the start of a new scene. In the previous scene, Naomi had said "he

---

68. Gage, "Ruth Upon the Threshing Floor and the Sin of Gibeah," 370.
69. Phillips, "The Book of Ruth—Deception and Shame," 14.
70. Phillips, "The Book of Ruth—Deception and Shame," 14.

will tell you what to do" (v. 4), and Ruth had promised to do everything Naomi told her to do. But Ruth does not wait until Boaz tells her what to do. Rather, *she* tells *him* what he should do, using words that were not supplied by Naomi.[71]

In her earlier conversational exchanges with Boaz, Ruth had referred to herself as a נכריה (*nokriyyâ*), a foreigner (2:10), who had been treated more like a שפחה (*šipḥâ*), a family servant (2:13). Now in v. 9 she tells Boaz that she is his אמה (*'āmâ*), again translated "servant" in both the NRSV and the NIV. Although in most biblical contexts the words *šipḥâ* and *'āmâ* seem to be interchangeable, many scholars think that an *'āmâ* has higher social status than a *šipḥâ*.[72] Sasson[73] and Campbell[74] think that there is some reason to believe that an *'āmâ* was eligible for marriage with her master, and Ilona Rashkow suggests that Ruth has used "three progressively more familiar terms . . . to describe herself to Boaz."[75]

First Ruth identifies herself as his *'āmâ*, then she asks Boaz to "spread" his כנף (*kānāp*; NRSV, "cloak"; NIV, "corner of garment") over his *'āmâ*. The NIV takes this second use of *'āmâ* as "over me." Boaz had used the plural of the word *kānāp* ("wing") in 2:12 to refer to the protection of the LORD. Now Ruth repeats Boaz's words back to him in a context that gives a new shade of meaning to his original utterance. In Ruth's request (v. 9), the word *kānāp* ("wing"/"cloak") retains the connotation of protection it had in 2:12. But when a woman asks a man to take her "under his wing," the metaphor assumes sexual overtones (as in Deut 27:20; Ezek 16:8). Again in 3:9, as in 2:13, Ruth challenges Boaz to take action to make his pious wishes come true.

Interpreters are divided over two issues related to Ruth's speech in v. 9: (1) Should the words "spread your wing" ("spread the corner of your garment/your cloak over

your servant") be understood as a marriage proposal or merely a request for sexual relations? (2) Is Ruth making one request or two? Should we understand her words to mean that she equates the function of redemption with marriage (or sexual relations) with Boaz? Is she saying, "Since you are a *gō'ēl* [next-of-kin/kinsman-redeemer], you should marry me?" Or should Ruth's mention of "redemption" be considered a separate issue from marriage?

While many readers assume that Ruth is asking Boaz to fulfill the levirate marriage customs, in fact the biblical laws concerning "redemption" say nothing about marriage, let alone levirate marriage. However, it is quite possible that the laws preserved in Scripture represent only a fraction of the customary laws that existed in any given period or locality. The narrator may assume a body of customary law in which marriage and redemption are equated or closely linked. If so, these laws have not been preserved for our edification.

There is no doubt that the institutions of redemption and levirate marriage (as they are described in the biblical texts) had similar purposes. While the levirate laws state that they are concerned with keeping a "name" alive, a large body of evidence indicates that one's name is more closely connected to inheritance than to bloodline or memory. The complaint that the daughters of Zelophehad brought to Moses (Num 27:1-11) "presupposes that the 'name' of a man . . . could be preserved only in association with the inheritance of land by his descendants."[76] A levirate marriage was meant "to provide the deceased with an heir to his estate,"[77] so that his family would not lose title to his land. Redemption was similarly concerned with keeping family property under family control.

3:10-13. It can be argued that Boaz's words in these verses provide adequate clues for deciding between the interpretative possibilities presented to us in vv. 9-10.[78] Since Boaz says, "I will do for you all that you ask" (v. 11), and then proceeds to arrange his marriage with Ruth, we should be able to

71. Johanna W. H. Bos, "Out of the Shadows: Genesis 38; Judges 4:17-22; Ruth 3," *Semeia* 42 (1988) 62.

72. E. M. MacDonald, *The Position of Women as Reflected in Semitic Codes of Law* (Toronto: University of Toronto Press, 1931) 62; Paul Joüon, *Ruth: Commentaire philologique et exégique,* Subsidia Biblica 9 (Rome: Pontifical Biblical Institute, 1986) 57; Adele Berlin, *Poetics and Interpretation of Biblical Narrative,* Bible and Literature 9 (Sheffield: Almond, 1983) 88-89.

73. Sasson, *Ruth,* 53.

74. Campbell, *Ruth,* 101.

75. Rashkow, "Ruth," 39.

76. Martin Noth, *Numbers,* OTL (Philadelphia: Westminster, 1968) 211.

77. Westbrook, *Property and Family in Biblical Law,* 74.

78. Barbara Green, "The Plot of the Biblical Story of Ruth," *JSOT* 23 (1982) 63.

assume that he understood Ruth's request as a proposal of marriage, rather than a request for sexual relations per se. This assumption is further supported by the observation that in Ezek 16:8 the image of "spreading a wing over" is closely connected with "pledging" oneself and entering into a covenant with the one over whom the wing or cloak is spread.

The fact that the storyteller has Boaz give two different answers in vv. 11-12 (each beginning with ועתה [wĕʿattâ], indicating that they are separate conclusions to separate requests)[79] suggests that Ruth's request for the protection of marriage is separable from (not automatically tied to) her request for "redemption." In v. 11 Boaz responds to Ruth's request for marriage, and in v. 12 he responds to her reminder that he is a גאל (gōʾēl). "The first he can promise to do; the second depends on one factor outside his control."[80]

Boaz says that someone has a prior claim, or a closer kinship, to Naomi (or to Naomi's husband) than he does. Leviticus 25:48-49 lists brothers, uncles, or uncles' sons (first cousins) as responsible for the redemption of family members who are forced to sell themselves into bondage. However, the story never tells us precisely how Boaz was related to Elimelech (see Commentary on 4:3).

Assuming that Ruth's request for marriage is not automatically tied to Boaz's status as a potential "redeemer" allows us to address another debated point in the interpretation of this text. In v. 10 Boaz says that this current act of "loyalty" or "kindness" (חסד ḥesed) on Ruth's part is greater than her former ḥesed. But the narrator leaves it up to the listener (or reader) to decide what Boaz means either by Ruth's former act of ḥesed or by *this* act of ḥesed.

The word ḥesed has been used two times before in this story, both times by Naomi. In 1:8, Naomi prayed that the LORD would show ḥesed to her daughters-in-law as they had shown it to her and to "the dead." In 2:20, Naomi takes Boaz's tokens of favor to Ruth as a sign that the LORD had not stopped showing ḥesed "to the living and the dead." It seems reasonable to assume that, in Boaz's mind,

Ruth's former ḥesed was directed to her now-deceased husband, brother-in-law, and father-in-law and to her still-living mother-in-law.

It is somewhat more difficult to determine what Boaz means by this latter act of ḥesed on Ruth's part, which he takes to be even greater than the first one (3:10). Does Boaz think that he is the beneficiary in this latter act of ḥesed? Does he think that Ruth has done *him* a kindness by choosing him (an old man, with no heir of his own) as a marriage partner in preference to a younger man? Or does Boaz see that both the living (Naomi) and the dead (Elimelech, Mahlon, and Chilion) will benefit from Ruth's action here, just as they benefited from Ruth's ḥesed in the past?

Separating Ruth's request for marriage from her request for redemption allows us to distinguish between the beneficiaries of these separate requests. Boaz's remarks in v. 10 indicate that Ruth could have remedied her own situation by getting any one of the younger men to marry her (which may explain her initial interest in the men who worked in Boaz's fields). But only marriage to one of Elimelech's closest relatives (a kinsman-redeemer) could address both the needs of Ruth's family of choice (living and dead) and Ruth's needs for the security of a home of her own. If we assume that Ruth makes two separate suggestions, one for her own benefit ("Take me under your wing") and one for the benefit of the living and the dead ("Act as the redeemer you are qualified to be"), then it seems that the action Boaz calls "this last instance of your loyalty" refers to Ruth's concern for Naomi and her "emptiness" (i.e., her dead family).

In v. 11 Boaz agrees to marry Ruth, assuring her that the townspeople think she is "a worthy woman," and in v. 13 he swears that one way or another he will see to the recovery (redemption) of what was lost after the deaths of Elimelech, Mahlon, and Chilion. Up to this point in the story, we have not been told precisely what Boaz is being asked to redeem or recover. We can only deduce, from what has been said so far, that "Boaz as a redeemer will provide Naomi, as well as Ruth, with [economic] security."[81]

79. Sasson, *Ruth*, 86.
80. Green, "The Plot of the Biblical Story of Ruth," 63.

81. Bos, "Out of the Shadows," 63.

The term אשת חיל ('ēšet ḥayil; NRSV, "a worthy woman"; NIV, "a woman of noble character") is the feminine equivalent of what Boaz was called in 2:1 (גבור חיל gibbôr ḥayil). Boaz might be saying that Ruth's first marriage (to Mahlon) "had conferred upon her credentials proper enough for her to (re)marry a gibbôr ḥayil."[82] But it seems

82. Bos, "Out of the Shadows," 63.

just as likely that Boaz uses this term because Ruth has already earned a reputation for good works (as 2:11 indicates). Since this chapter is so heavily packed with double entendre, we ought also to remember that ḥayil can have overtones meaning "procreative power," the ability to have a large family (see the Commentary on 2:1 and 4:11). (See Reflections at 3:14-18.)

RUTH 3:14-18, THE BEGINNING OF AN END TO EMPTINESS

COMMENTARY

3:14. The final scene takes place at first light. Given the common association between threshing floors and prostitution, we might interpret Boaz's wish for Ruth to leave the threshing floor "before anyone could be recognized" as an attempt to protect either her reputation as a "worthy woman" or his own reputation in order not to jeopardize the plan he will carry out in the next chapter.

3:15. Various attempts have been made to explain the significance of the barley Boaz gives to Ruth. The text says that Boaz gave her six "barleys," usually interpreted as six "measures" of one size or another. This amount of grain might represent a bride-price or a marriage settlement.[83] It might be the price for the option to buy the parcel of land that we learn about in the next chapter. It could be interpreted as a token of apology to Naomi, because her scheme did not work out precisely as she had hoped,[84] or it might be understood as Ruth's payment for services rendered during the night.[85] Some think the phrase "six barleys" should be understood as six grains, symbolizing the restoration of "seed" to Elimelech's line.[86] Early Jewish interpreters thought the six grains (seeds) represented six male descendants, each of whom

would be blessed with six blessings.[87] Phillips concludes that having been tricked into thinking he has been compromised, "Boaz seeks to save his own reputation and keep Naomi quiet at the same time by signaling by the gift of grain that he will now do what he ought all along to have put in motion."[88]

3:16. Naomi's question is literally, "Who are you, my daughter?" Boaz used the same words in v. 9. But Naomi is not really asking for identification. The phrase may simply be an idiom suggesting that Ruth has arrived home before it is light enough for Naomi to see for sure who it is (in which case, it should be translated, "It is you, my daughter?"). But the words might also be understood as Naomi's way of asking whether Ruth's status has changed overnight. Both the NIV and the NRSV translations imply that Naomi is asking Ruth whether her plan has succeeded. This interpretation is justified by the observation that Ruth replies to Naomi's question by telling her "all that the man had done for her."[89]

3:17-18. Back in v. 15, the narrator did not tell us whether Boaz said anything at all when he gave the grain to Ruth, so it is unclear whether we should take Ruth's words in v. 17 as a factual report of events. However, it is clear that the word ריקם (rêqām; NIV and NRSV, "empty-handed") is identical to the term used by Naomi to describe her "emptiness" in 1:21. Whether Boaz in fact said, "Do

83. Sasson, Ruth, 98. See also Étan Levine, The Aramaic Version of Ruth, AnBib 58 (Rome: Pontifical Biblical Institute, 1973) 95-96.
84. See Pierre Crapon de Caprona, Ruth la Moabite (Geneva: Labor et Fides, 1982) 88-89.
85. G. May, "Ruth's Visit to the High Place at Bethlehem," Journal of the Royal Asiatic Society of Great Britain and Ireland (1939) 77.
86. Bos, "Out of the Shadows," 56.

87. Ruth Rab. VII.2; Levine, The Aramaic Version of Ruth, 96.
88. Phillips, "The Book of Ruth—Deception and Shame," 14.
89. Gow, The Book of Ruth, 72.

not go back to your mother-in-law empty," it seems likely that the barley given to Ruth was meant to send a message of some kind to Naomi. Naomi's words in v. 18 indicate that she understands the barley as a sign from Boaz that "he will settle the matter today."

Ruth has asked for marriage and redemption. Boaz has pledged to see both done. If Naomi is the intended recipient of the redemption (as 4:14 seems to indicate), then the suspense generated in this chapter has to do with how Boaz will accomplish this task. The levirate marriage laws, at least in the form in which we know them, do not expect Boaz to offer marriage to Ruth. If Boaz had been one of Elimelech's brothers, he might have felt obliged to marry *Naomi*. But such a marriage would not have solved Ruth's problems. Nor would a marriage between Naomi and Boaz keep the "name" of the dead alive in Israel, since Naomi was past the age of childbearing (1:11). Thus the narrator cleverly builds suspense by leading the audience to wonder how both women's problems can be solved by a marriage between Boaz and Ruth.

REFLECTIONS

1. Again, the eyes of faith may see God working behind the scenes in chap. 3, but the narrator carefully avoids saying anything about divine agency. The evidence could just as easily lead one to conclude that "God only helps those who help themselves,"[90] or that "God's plan is unconsciously carried out by the Naomis of this world who think they are only working out their own destiny."[91]

In this chapter as in the preceding one, the narrator uses echoing phrases to raise the question of correspondences between human actions and divine actions. On the threshing floor at midnight, Ruth repeats Boaz's words back to him, as she did in the gleaning scene. This time she hints to Boaz that shelter under the LORD's "wings" (1:12) might very well take the shape of shelter under Boaz's "wing" (3:9). In other words, Ruth "challenges Boaz to be the occasion of divine blessing in her life."[92] Preachers and teachers may conclude that, like Boaz, we need more than one reminder that we have a role to play in making our pious wishes for others come true. And, like Boaz, those of us who are the "pillars" of our own religious communities may need to be taught how to do *ḥesed* by the "foreigners" in our midst.

2. The most heated debates concerning the interpretation of the book of Ruth revolve around the action on the threshing floor. What really happened there? Are we supposed to know? Should we be shocked by Naomi's plan and Ruth's behavior? Or should we admire the way these women have taken steps to guarantee both their own futures and the continuity of their family tree?

The similarity between chapter 3 of Ruth and the story of Tamar in Genesis 38 reminds us that Tamar's father-in-law, Judah, acknowledged that Tamar's behavior (which might have been condemned as incestuous by normal standards) was more justifiable than his. He had avoided doing what was right: providing Tamar with a child to carry on the "name" of the dead. Judah's failure to do what was right forced Tamar to take drastic measures to see justice done. In a similar way, Boaz acknowledges that Ruth's behavior is actually an act of *ḥesed*. This does not mean that Ruth's behavior (if known to the people of Bethlehem) would have been condoned. Even if nothing more happened between Ruth and Boaz than the conversation reported in 3:8-13, Ruth's actions (coming to the threshing floor, lying next to a sleeping man who was not her husband) would undoubtedly have been judged scandalous according to the standards

90. Phillips, "The Book of Ruth—Deception and Shame," 16.
91. Tollers, "Narrative Control in the Book of Ruth," 252.
92. Trible, "A Human Comedy," 184.

of the society in which she lived. The question is whether the end result in this case justifies the means.

The reluctance of modern readers to see any scandalous overtones in this scene may stem from a need to reinforce deep-seated beliefs that the virtuous are rewarded. Since Ruth's actions seem to have had positive results, what she did must have been something good. This wishful thinking is aided and abetted by translators who fail (or refuse) to communicate the undertones as well as the overtones of the original language to the non-Hebrew-speaking audience. If we acknowledge that what Ruth did is both scandalous (in the eyes of the world) and an act of loving-kindness, then we can prompt modern audiences to consider which canons of socially acceptable behavior they might be willing to defy in order to "do" *ḥesed*—loving-kindness above and beyond the call of duty.

3. The debate that rages over the admirability (or lack thereof) of the actions portrayed in Ruth 3:1-13 is not trivial. There are serious theological implications. If Ruth is read with a "merit theology," then the happy ending that comes in the final chapter will seem to be the result of the courage, initiative, loyalty, and altruism of the human characters involved in the scene at the threshing floor. There are ample warrants for reading the story in this way. While the biblical texts frequently remind us that it is not our faithfulness that causes God to love us, it is clear that human faithfulness is highly valued by God. The book of Ruth can be said to suggest that the effective communication of God's love in the world depends on faithful human behavior, that God uses faithful human behavior to communicate God's love.

A number of appealing sermon topics can be derived from a merit-based reading of Ruth. We can truthfully say that the story of Ruth demonstrates that loving-kindness (*ḥesed*) can transform emptiness into occasions for hope, that *ḥesed* alone (and not the purity of one's ancestral line) qualifies us to become servants of the LORD. We might conclude that the book of Ruth and Gal 3:26-29 agree that it is not our physical ancestry but our faithfulness to God that identifies us as descendants of Abraham and heirs to the promise. Ruth might be pictured as the model foreigner Isaiah of Babylon had in mind when he said that the LORD will give a monument and a name better than sons and daughters to foreigners who choose to join themselves to the LORD (Isa 56:3-7). We could say that Ruth's willingness to commit herself and her future to the LORD allows God to work through her to transform Naomi's emptiness into fullness. Ruth acts as an agent of God's *ḥesed* when she herself shows *ḥesed* to Naomi.

Reading Ruth with a theology of grace (unmerited love) allows us to consider that none of the human characters acted in totally admirable or altruistic ways. The deliberate ambiguity of the narrator allows us to choose. Is redemption (which plays such a large part in the story) given as a *reward* for the behavior portrayed in this chapter or in spite of it?

RUTH 4:1-22

THE ROOTS OF ISRAEL'S REDEMPTION

OVERVIEW

In the preceding chapter, Ruth *uncovered* Boaz and asked him to *recover* ("redeem") that which was lost. In this chapter, Boaz *uncovers* the ear of the "nearer redeemer" and challenges him to *recover* (redeem) the land that had belonged to Elimelech. Used in a technical sense in legal texts, "redemption" seems to refer to the process by which people, property, and prestige are restored to a family who has lost them through poverty, violence, or some other cause. But the word "redeem" is also used figuratively to mean to "rescue," "save," or "liberate" people from danger, distress, or oppression.[93] When Ruth tells Boaz, "You are a redeemer" (see 3:9), it is not completely clear what she is asking Boaz to do. In 4:3 we hear for the first time in the story that there is property that needs to be redeemed.

The difficulty in trying to understand what is going on in chap. 4 stems from two facts: (1) The customs or laws assumed by the story world are no longer known to us; they have been lost in the mists of time. (2) In the process of transmitting the text, some changes have been made, so that none of the solutions suggested by interpreters can make complete sense of the text as it now stands.

It becomes apparent in 4:14-17 that the loss that mattered most to Naomi is one that can be redeemed by the birth of a child. This may be related to the "parcel of land" mentioned in 4:3 by assuming that a male child is needed to carry on the title to the property that had belonged to Elimelech. In order for the property to remain in Elimelech's family,

there needs to be a male heir to inherit it. But we can only speculate as to whether the purchase (or redemption) of the field triggers the levirate obligation to raise up an heir for the dead,[94] or whether the redemption of property and the raising up an heir for that property are considered separate and unconnected actions until Boaz makes the connection voluntarily, as a surprise move.

In v. 4, the word "redeem" (גאל *gāʾal*) is equated with "acquire," "make one's own" (קנה *qānâ*). The encounter between Boaz and the nearer redeemer is structured around the word *qnh* (translated "buy" or "acquire"), which occurs six times in vv. 4-10 (once in vv. 4, 8, 9, 10, and twice in v. 5).

The word שׁם (*šēm*, "name") occurs seven times in this chapter (once in vv. 5, 11, 14; twice in vv. 10 and 17), but only the final use of the term seems to be part of an actual naming formula. In vv. 5 and 10, "name" takes on the connotation of "title to the land," while in vv. 11 and 14 it seems to refer to reputation or fame.

The genealogy with which the book of Ruth ends looks forward to the birth of David and backward to Perez, the child of a Canaanite widow who tricked the father of her deceased husband into having intercourse with her. Thus we are told that neither of Obed's parents has an impeccable line of descent. Ruth's ancestry can be traced to an incestuous union between Lot and one of his daughters (Genesis 19), and Boaz is descended from an illicit union between Judah and his daughter-in-law (Genesis 38)!

---

93. See Ringgren, *TDOT* 2:353-54.

94. Westbrook, *Property and Family in Biblical Law*, 67.

RUTH 4:1-11a, BOAZ SETTLES THE MATTER

Ruth 4:1-4, The Trap Is Baited and Set

COMMENTARY

4:1-2. Archaeological digs have revealed that the gate area of most Israelite towns included a courtyard lined with benches. Biblical texts indicate that many business transactions, including the settling of disputes, were conducted in this area, with townspeople acting as witnesses or as the jury. When Boaz gets the next-of-kin and ten elders to sit down with him in the gate, he is in effect convening a court of law.

As soon as the stage is set, the closer kinsman arrives on the scene. Both the NRSV and the NIV have Boaz call the next of kin "friend," but in fact Boaz uses פלני אלמני (*pĕlōnî 'almōnî*), a Hebrew idiom that suggests that the man's name is not important to the story. When the same phrase is used to describe a place rather than a person in 2 Kgs 6:8, both the NIV and the NRSV have "such and such a place." Thus it seems that the English idiom "so and so" might better communicate the storyteller's intentions. The medieval Rabbi Rashi seems to have been the first to suggest that *pĕlōnî 'almōnî* should be translated "So-and-So," explaining that "his name is not written because he was not willing to redeem."[95]

4:3. There are a number of interpretive ambiguities in this verse. For the first time in the story a piece of land or a field belonging to Elimelech has been explicitly mentioned. Is this simply a literary device to preserve the surprise of the story? Or should we have known from Naomi's and Ruth's references to a redeemer that a parcel of land was implied? Is Boaz saying that Naomi *is about to sell* or that she *has already sold* this piece of property? Should the phrase "our brother Elimelech" be understood literally or figuratively?

The verb that Boaz uses (מכר *mākar*, "sold") is in the perfect tense, which ordinarily indicates a completed action. Thus we could understand Boaz to mean that Naomi

(or Elimelech) had already sold the field in question, perhaps during the famine that motivated the family's move to Moab. So what is needed is a redeemer to buy the property back, and thus restore it to the control of the clan or extended family. But if this were the case, Boaz's words in vv. 5 and 9 would not make sense. Thus both the NIV and the NRSV opt for a present-tense translation: Naomi "*is* selling."

Women could own, buy, sell, and inherit property in Israel (see Num 27:1-8; 36:1-12; Job 42:15; Prov 31:16). Most of the cultures of the ancient Near East allowed men to make their wives or daughters their heirs.[96] Texts from the Jewish community on the island of Elephantine in the sixth century BCE indicate that a childless widow in that community could inherit property from her husband, and the apocryphal book of Judith is about a widow who both inherited from her husband (Jdt 8:7) and had the right to bequeath her property as she wished (Jdt 16:21-24). The biblical laws "specify those who have a right to the property insofar as there are no contrary provisions made. They do not say the wife cannot inherit if the husband, before he dies, chooses to make her his heir."[97] Thus Naomi may have inherited from her deceased husband the parcel of land to which Boaz refers. One way of reading v. 5 even suggests that both Naomi and Ruth could claim ownership of the land in question. Since the story says that Naomi and Ruth have been living on gleanings from the grain harvest, however, we can assume that mere ownership of the field was not enough to support the two women.

It is highly unlikely that a piece of arable land would have been left unclaimed and unused during the ten or more years that

---

95. Beattie, *Jewish Exegesis of the Book of Ruth*, 109.

96. Eryl W. Davie, "Inheritance Rights and the Hebrew Levirate Marriage: Part I," *VT* 31, 2 (1981) 138.
97. Thomas Thompson and Dorothy Thompson, "Some Legal Problems in the Book of Ruth," *VT* (1968) 98.

Elimelech and his family stayed in Moab. So it is conceivable that the task of buying or redeeming the land would include regaining control of it from someone who had held it in Naomi's absence. This seems to have been the problem faced by the woman whose son was revived by Elisha. When she returned home after having lived elsewhere during seven years of famine in her own land, she had to "appeal to the king for her house and her land" (2 Kgs 8:1-6). It may even have been So-and-So who had claimed and used the land in the intervening years, since he knew that he was the next-of-kin. If that is the case, then Boaz would be suggesting in v. 4 that So-and-So should pay Naomi for the land he has been using since Naomi and her family left for Moab.

In speaking to So-and-So, Boaz calls Elimelech "our brother" (אחינו *ʾaḥînû*). Interpreters who are inclined to take this term literally conclude that Boaz, So-and-So, and Elimelech shared at least one parent. Other interpreters note that the common Hebrew usage of "brother" is seldom precise. The word "brother" can also be used to describe relationships between cousins (brothers' sons) and between uncles and nephews.

4:4. When Boaz reminds So-and-So that it is his duty to buy (or to pay for) the field that legally belongs to Elimelech's heirs, he uses an idiom that in Hebrew means "I thought I would *uncover* your ear." The insipid English translations (NRSV, "I thought I would tell you of it"; NIV, "I thought I would bring it to your attention") obscure the way in which the narrator links the uncovering done by Ruth on the threshing floor with the uncovering done by Boaz at the city gate. In chap. 4, as in chap. 3, uncovering is closely related to recovering. The NIV inserts the word "right" ("to redeem") into Boaz's sentence. But it is really not clear whether redemption in this case involves a right of first refusal or an obligation to buy.

Boaz has chosen to call So-and-So to account for his actions in a very public forum. Having been openly challenged in the presence of ten elders (and assorted other townspeople), So-and-So states his willingness to make amends. He says, "I will buy." (See Reflections at 4:13-17.)

Ruth 4:5-6, The Trap Is Sprung

COMMENTARY

Interpretations of the interchange between Boaz and So-and-So can vary widely, because a word that was written one way in the consonantal text was vocalized by the Masoretes to read another way.[98] The original consonants in the text of v. 5 (קניתי *qnyty*) imply that Boaz says, "The day you acquire the land . . . *I* acquire the dead man's widow." But both the NIV and the NRSV accept the scribal emendation that changes the written form of the verb ("I acquire") to קניתה *qānîtâ*), "you acquire" or "you are acquiring."

The amended form ("you acquire") implies (1) that a levirate-type of obligation is connected to the ownership of the land and (2) that So-and-So either does not know, has forgotten, or wants to ignore this connection. Beattie thinks this emendation originated

because of a misunderstanding: "Since, when he buys the land, Boaz also takes Ruth as his wife (vv. 9, 10), it was assumed that the two things belonged together and that the redeemer of the land should take Ruth in marriage as a condition of his redemption, and so קניתי *qānîtî* was taken to be second person."[99] If we assume that the levirate customarily applied to more than brothers-in-law, and if we read the text as it was pointed by the Masoretes ("The day you acquire the field . . . *you* acquire the widow, to maintain the dead man's name on his inheritance"), then it seems that Boaz is saying that "if the nearest relative is willing to perform one legal custom which was to his advantage, he should in logic be willing to perform the other which was not. . . . He could not decently choose one and reject the other."[100] This

98. See D. R. G. Beattie, "Kethibh and Qere in Ruth 4:5," *VT* 21 (1971) 490-94.

99. Beattie, "Kethibh and Qere in Ruth 4:5," 494.
100. Phillips, "The Book of Ruth—Deception and Shame," 9.

reading assumes that Boaz has shamed the nearer redeemer by publicly exposing his willingness to perform only the profitable parts of his redemptive duties. However, if we keep the original consonantal spelling, so that Boaz says, "*I* have acquired" or "*I* am acquiring," then it seems that marrying Ruth in order to produce a child who will keep Elimelech's line alive is not necessarily connected with the redemption of the land.

The words used in v. 5 (NIV, "to maintain the name of the dead with his property"; NRSV, "to maintain the dead man's name on his inheritance") echo the levirate language used in Deut 25:6-7. But neither Boaz nor So-and-So fits the category of persons to whom the law in Deuteronomy 25 is addressed (i.e., they are not "brothers living together" with Elimelech). Commentators have proposed a number of theories to explain the differences between what the Ruth account seems to assume and what the law in Deuteronomy commands. It has been suggested that the "rules" assumed in Ruth (1) represent a local, geographical variant; (2) that they testify to customs that preceded the codification of the law; or (3) that they reflect later stages of development in the application of the spirit of the laws to concrete situations.[101]

So-and-So's reaction to Boaz's announcement indicates that more is at stake here than literally keeping the name of the dead alive. Since neither Ruth nor Tamar (whose story in Genesis 38:1 more closely fits the levirate laws) actually called her children by the name of the deceased husband, we may deduce that "name" (שׁם *šēm*) was not meant to be taken literally in this context. Furthermore, Boaz says he intends to "maintain the dead man's name *on his inheritance*." Thus it seems that this use of "name" might have the sense of "title" or "claim of ownership" of the land. In other words, Boaz firmly intends to let his and Ruth's first child be known as Elimelech's heir. In effect, Boaz says, "I feel it

is only fair to tell you, before you redeem [or acquire] this piece of property, that I plan to marry Ruth in order to raise up a future claimant to the title of that land."

The laws concerning the redemption of land say that land that was sold to a redeemer "shall remain with the purchaser until the year of jubilee; in the jubilee it shall be released, and the property shall be returned" (Lev 25:28). However, the command to return the property assumes that someone with a legitimate claim to its title would still be alive to accept its return. In this case, it must have seemed quite likely that Elimelech's line would die out. So-and-So was willing to buy or redeem the land as long as it seemed that he would never have to give the land back. Once So-and-So had paid for the land in question, it would remain a part of his own inheritance. But if Boaz provided Elimelech and Mahlon with an heir, So-and-So (and his heirs) would eventually lose both the purchase price and the land itself.

It seems best to assume that neither Boaz nor So-and-So was legally obliged to "maintain the dead man's name on his inheritance." It makes better logical and narrative sense to assume that Boaz's announcement comes as a surprise to both So-and-So and the audience.[102] If we keep the original form of the text (*I* am acquiring), then it seems that the surprise Boaz springs on So-and-So is the announcement that Boaz *voluntarily* is going to take on the duties of a levirate marriage. So-and-So had not foreseen the possibility that Boaz would marry Ruth or that Boaz would pledge "to raise up the name of the deceased over his inheritance." The suspense engendered by events in the preceding chapter is thus resolved in a satisfying manner. The audience is supposed to think, "Aha! What a clever (and unexpected) solution to both widows' problems!" (See Reflections at 4:13-17.)

---

101. Westbrook, *Property and Family in Biblical Law*, 63.

102. Green, "The Plot of the Biblical Story of Ruth," 59.

Ruth 4:7-11a, Legal Formalities

COMMENTARY

4:7-8. A shoe, or a sandal, functions as a symbol for the right to buy or redeem the land that had belonged to Elimelech.[103] Giving up the sandal signals So-and-So's willingness to give up his right to claim or redeem the property Elimelech had left behind when he went to Moab. The narrator's statement that "this was the custom in former days" indicates that the story is being told to people who live in a much later time than the time in which Boaz and So-and-So lived. The narrator's audience no longer exchanged sandals in order to confirm or legalize a transaction, so this detail in the story needed to be explained to them.

Deuteronomy 25:7-10 says that a widow whose husband's brother refuses to perform the levirate duties has the right to pull the sandal off his foot and spit in his face in the presence of elders. Ruth 4:7 indicates that taking off a sandal in front of witnesses represents a legal transaction. However, the verbs "to pull off" (שׁלף *šālap*) and "to take off" (חלץ *ḥālaṣ*) come from completely different Hebrew roots. Apparently the law of the levirate allowed the widow to perform an action that publicly declared that the brother-in-law had given up all claims to the land that had belonged to his deceased brother. If he was not willing to marry the widow and raise

up sons for the deceased man, then he had to forfeit his right to claim or to redeem the land. Some critics think that Boaz (in 4:5) was making the same point to the nearer redeemer.[104] However, So-and-So is never called "brother-in-law."

4:9-11a. Once the sandal is in his possession, Boaz turns to the elders and to all the townspeople who happen to be in the area at that time, publicly declaring that he has acquired both the land and Ruth (vv. 9-10). The legal nature of his declaration is underscored by the fact that his speech begins and ends with the formula "today you are witnesses" (vv. 9-10). Since Boaz uses the same word to describe what he has done both to the land and to Ruth, some readers have wondered whether Ruth is being bought and sold like a piece of property. However, the word קנה (*qānâ*), translated here as "acquire" or "buy," has a spectrum of meanings ranging from "purchase" to "create" to "possess." In Ps 74:2 and Exod 15:13-16, *qānâ* is used as a synonym for "redemption." Thus we should probably understand *qānâ* here to mean "make one's own."[105] In front of witnesses, as if in a court of law, Boaz declares that he has made both the land and Ruth his own. The people reply, "We are witnesses," and the legalities are concluded. (See Reflections at 4:13-17.)

103. Robert Gordis, "Love, Marriage, and Business in the Book of Ruth," in *A Light Unto My Path: Old Testament Studies in Honor of Jacob M. Myers*, ed. H. N. bream et al. (Philadelphia: Temple University Press, 1977) 247.

104. Phillips, "The Book of Ruth—Deception and Shame," 9.
105. Campbell, *Ruth*, 159.

RUTH 4:11b-17, NAMING THE MOTHERS OF THE MESSIAH

Ruth 4:11b-12, Blessing the Union

COMMENTARY

After they have performed their legal function as witnesses, the same collective voice of the elders and the people assembled at the gate pronounces a blessing on the upcoming marriage. The blessing contains three wishes: The first concerns Boaz's bride; the second concerns Boaz himself; and the third concerns his "house." The first and third parts of the blessing refer to the "house" of Israel and the "house" of Perez. Jacob-Israel was the father of Judah through Leah, and Judah was the father of Perez through Tamar. Boaz is a descendant of both houses.

"House" (בית *bêt*) is clearly a figure of speech meaning "lineage" or "descendants." In the first part of the blessing, it is clear that the wish is for Ruth to produce as many offspring as did Rachel and Leah (the wives of Jacob-Israel). The last part of the blessing is a wish that the descendants of Ruth and Boaz will rival those of Judah and Tamar. But the middle part of the blessing is more difficult to understand. Literally, the Hebrew says, "May you make/do חיל [*hayil*]" in Ephrathah and "call a name" in Bethlehem. As we saw earlier, the word *hayil* can mean "strength" or "worth" derived from physical, moral, or financial power. But *hayil* also occurs in the

special sense of "potency" or "the ability to produce offspring." Thus it seems that all three parts of the blessing are concerned with the fruitfulness of the marriage. The NRSV understands *hayil* in this way when it translates the middle wish, "May you produce children in Ephrathah and bestow a name in Bethlehem." While Ephrathah is the name of the clan to which Boaz belongs, mentioning it again at this point makes particularly good sense because of the name's association with fertility.[106]

While the blessing is addressed to a man, each of its parts reminds us of the women who have had essential roles in maintaining the continuity of the family in the past: Leah, the mother of Judah; Ephrat, the mother of the clan named after her; and Tamar, the mother of Perez. (See Reflections at 4:13-17.)

---

106. C. J. Labuschagne, "The Crux in Ruth 4:11," *ZAW* 79 (1967) 365-66.

Ruth 4:13-17, Redemption Incarnate

COMMENTARY

4:13. In 1:4 we were told that Mahlon and Chilion "took" Moabite wives (using the verb נשא *nāśāʾ*). In 4:10, Boaz declared that he had "acquired" Ruth (using the verb קנה *qānâ*). But when the narrator reports on the actual marriage between Ruth and Boaz, two more traditional terms are used: לקח (*lāqaḥ*, also meaning "took") and ותהי–לו לאשה (*watĕhî-lô lĕʾiššâ*, "she became his wife"). Then the narrator tells us (with a euphemism) that "Boaz went into her" (NRSV, "they came together"; the NIV leaves out this bit of information). The consummation of the marriage is clearly a human activity. However, in the narrator's eyes, the conception of a child is a gift from God ("the Lord made her conceive"). Like Rachel and Leah—indeed, like all the mothers of the promised line— Ruth conceives only by the grace of God (Gen 21:1-2; 25:21; 29:31-32; 30:22-23).

4:14-17. When the women say that the child is Naomi's "redeemer" (גאל *gōʾēl*) in v. 14, the legally minded may see this as a reference to the property that had once belonged to Elimelech. If Naomi had had another son

of her own, presumably that son would have inherited everything from his dead father and brothers. As Naomi's "son," Obed is the heir who will "maintain the name of the dead with his property." But the women of the town define the child's role in a different way. In their opinion, the child's significance is formulated completely in terms of his meaning for Naomi.[107]

The phrase קרא שם (*qārāʾ šēm*, "to call a name") occurs twice in vv. 17, creating the impression that the women of Bethlehem give the baby more than one name. The NIV changes the first use of *qārāʾ šēm* to "say," but the NRSV represents the Hebrew accurately. Naming speeches usually consist of a pun linking the baby's name with an explanation of its meaning. If the way Rachel and Leah named their children is used as a pattern (see Gen 29:32-35; 30:6, 8, 11, 13, 18-19, 24), then we would expect the first part of v. 17

---

107. Fokkelien Van Dijk-Hemmes, "Traces of Women's Texts in the Hebrew Bible," in *On Gendering Texts: Female and Male Voices in the Hebrew Bible,* ed. Athalya Brenner and Fokkelien Van Dijk-Hemmes (Leiden: E. J. Brill, 1993) 106.

to say that the child's name resembled sounds in the phrase "a son is born to Naomi." But there seems to be no relationship between this phrase and the name "Obed." Since the phrase "to call a name" is also used in vv. 11 and 14 in the sense of becoming famous, its first use in v. 17 might be taken to mean "significance" or "importance." If so, then the verse should be translated as "A son has been born to Naomi."[108]

Ruth's son is Naomi's "redeemer," but redemption for Naomi takes the form of a reversal of the emptiness that has embittered her. It is poetically fitting for the narrator to use the same women who absorbed Naomi's bitterness in 1:20-21 to assure her that the LORD has not abandoned her; the child whose conception was given by the LORD will turn Naomi's life around. This fifteenth use of

108. Hubbard, *The Book of Ruth*, 15.

the word שוב (*šûb*; NRSV, "restore"; NIV, "renew") marks the final reversal in Naomi's story. The word נפש (*nepeš*; NIV and NRSV, "life") refers to the whole person or to the innermost self. When Ps 23:3 uses the same two words, most translations render them as "restore" and "soul." Naomi's "life" has gone from fullness to emptiness and back to fullness again. Because Ruth the Moabite loves her, Naomi will be "sustained" (NIV) or "nourished" (NRSV) rather than empty in her "old age." Clearly the women think there is more to redemption than the retention of property within the family.

Obed, the ancestor of the Davidic kings, personifies Naomi's redemption. After political kingship disappears altogether from Israel and Judah, the faithful will still look for a descendant of Obed (a "messiah") to become redemption incarnate for the people of God.

REFLECTIONS

1. In the story world, the townspeople's blessing is presented as a traditional wish, something they might have said to any bride and groom. Presumably, the people sitting at the gate were unaware of Ruth's clandestine visit to the threshing floor. But for the narrator's audience, the blessing must seem ironically appropriate. For the audience who knows both the traditions of Israel and the story of Ruth, the blessing is more than a generic wish for fruitfulness in a marriage. The audience is aware that the three women who are named in the blessing have well-known stories attached to them in Israel's tradition. Not only did these women play a part in building up the house of Israel, but they did so in particularly deceptive ways. Tamar, Rachel, and Leah are all remembered as tricksters whose deceptions had reproductive consequences (Gen 29:21–30:19; 38:1-30). A further touch of irony results from the recollection that Rachel and Leah once complained to Israel that their own father (Laban) treated them like *nokriyyōt*, foreign women (Gen 31:15)!

Although Rachel, the younger of Jacob's wives, is listed first in the blessing, Leah is the mother of Judah. The people of Bethlehem traced their ancestry to Judah through Perez, one of the twins born after Tamar tricked Judah into having intercourse with her. But this reference to Tamar and Judah must remind the audience of more than just the Bethlehemites' ancestry. An audience familiar with Tamar's story must have seen resemblances between her situation and Ruth's situation, between Tamar's actions and Ruth's actions. Both women are childless widows. Both widows have male relatives who might be expected to ameliorate their situations, but who choose not to do so. Each woman takes her reproductive future into her own hands. Each "uncovers" a man who can give her a child qualified to keep the "name" of the dead alive in Israel. The genealogy in Ruth 4:18-22 will trace the family tree through the fathers, but the blessing in 4:11-12 reminds us that it is the mothers of the messianic line who made sure that the continuity of the family line remained unbroken. To modern eyes, these women may seem to have sold out to "the patriarchal institution of the levirate, which ensures the patrilineage of a deceased husband."[109] But it might also be argued that they have undermined the male Israelites' belief that God favors submissive, non-aggressive behavior on the part of women.

2. The references to Rachel and Tamar might also have had political significance. Rachel was the mother of Joseph and thus was the ancestress of the northern kingdom's dominant tribes (Ephraim and Manasseh). Leah was the mother of Judah, the dominant tribe of the southern kingdom. Tamar appears to have been a Canaanite woman. Ezra 4:1-3 tells us how the returned exiles (the remnants of Judah/Leah's descendants) spurned the remnants of Rachel's descendants, and Ezra 10 tells us how they rejected the foreign wives of men descended from Judah. But the first part of the blessing in Ruth 4:11*b* names Rachel (the northern ancestress) first and emphatically declares that both Rachel and Leah together built up the house of Israel. And in the final part of the blessing, "Boaz is blessed by the prayer that his house may be like that 'of Perez whom Tamar [a Canaanite!] bore' to the patriarch Judah as the result of an irregular connection (so the Judeans were in no position to throw stones at their northern neighbors)."[110]

3. Boaz and his well-wishers in 4:11-12 think of Ruth's value in terms of her ability to "build up" her husband's "house." In the world of the story, women seem to acquire value in men's eyes primarily by giving birth to sons who will carry their fathers' "names" (both gene pools and property claims) into the future. But the women of Bethlehem refuse to be limited by this patriarchal evaluation. They tell Naomi that "the son is to be valued because of his *mother!* This child will be a blessing, they say, 'for your daughter-in-law, who loves you, has borne him, and she means more than seven sons!' "[111]

The story thus ends, as it began, with Naomi. After all is said and done, Naomi is the recipient of redemption. Ruth is neither seen nor heard to speak in the conclusion of the book bearing her name. Nevertheless, Ruth (not Naomi) will be remembered as one of the mothers of the Messiah.

4. Whether or not the book of Ruth was *written* in post-exilic times, when it was *heard* in that era it must have made a difference in people's attitudes toward the foreigners in their midst. Clearly Naomi is the character who best reflects the experiences of the *gôlâ,* the remnant who returned home after the exile: "Naomi is a figure for the Jewish people in a phase from which God has hidden his face."[112] Naomi herself was a remnant; she was the one who was "left" (1:3, 5). If the people of Israel in the post-exilic period could identify with Naomi's bitterness, if they felt as empty as Naomi felt returning to Judah after a long sojourn away from home, then they might also have understood from the story of Ruth that redemption (recovery from the emptiness and the bitter losses of the exile) could come from the very foreigners Ezra and Nehemiah wanted to cast out of the covenant community. If, on the other hand, the listeners identified with the "worthy" Boaz, they might have noticed that this pillar of Israelite society had to be called to responsibility by a foreign woman.[113] Identification within the dynamics of the Ruth story might very well have helped to persuade people in the time of Nehemiah-Ezra that "foreigners who joined themselves to the Lord" (Isa 56:6) were an essential part of the Lord's plan for Israel's redemption.

---

109. Fuchs, "The Literary Characterization of Mothers and Sexual Politics in the Hebrew Bible," 130.
110. See M. Smith, *Palestinian Parties and Politics That Shaped the Old Testament* (New York: Columbia University Press, 1971) 161-62.
111. Nancy V. Lee, "Choices in the Book of Ruth," *The Japan Christian Quarterly* 54 (1988) 242.
112. Haim Chertok, "The Book of Ruth—Complexities Within Simplicity," *Judaism* 35 (1986) 295.
113. Trible, "A Human Comedy," 184.

RUTH 4:18-22, DAVID'S FAMILY TREE

COMMENTARY

When the Anchor Bible commentary on Ruth was published in 1975, it could accurately be said that "there is all but universal agreement that verses 18-22 form a genealogical appendix to the Ruth story and are not an original part of it."[114] But more recent scholarship is inclined to argue that the genealogy functions "as an integral part of the text as it has been received."[115] Since there is no genealogy of David in the books of Samuel, this list of ancestors in Ruth serves an essential purpose: "to situate the characters of this story among the body of known personalities in the tradition."[116] Thus it seems that the attachment of the genealogy to the story of Ruth must be at least as old as the inclusion of the book in the narrative sequence from Genesis to Kings.

The genealogy begins with Perez, which makes Boaz the seventh "son" named in the list of David's ancestors. David himself was said to be a seventh son in 1 Chr 2:15, although 1 Sam 17:12-15 calls him the youngest of Jesse's eight sons.

Since the narrative puts so much emphasis on maintaining the name of the dead on

his inheritance, the failure to mention either Elimelech or Mahlon in the genealogy is striking. Boaz is counted as the father of Obed, and Obed "builds up the house" of Boaz, not the house of Mahlon. Whatever legal fiction was maintained in order to make Obed the heir to Elimelech's property, the narrator clearly thinks that the line leading to the birth of David runs through Boaz.

In most Hebrew manuscripts, the name of Boaz's father is spelled "Salma" (here and in 1 Chr 2:11). Some manuscripts of the Septuagint spell the name "Salmon," as does Matt 1:5. Matthew's list of ancestors from Abraham to Jesus names Rahab as the wife of Salmon and the mother of Boaz (a detail that is not found in the Hebrew Bible). Most commentators assume that Matthew is referring to the Rahab whose story is told in Josh 2:1-21; 6:22-23. Like Ruth, Rahab was a non-Israelite woman who chose to align herself with Israel and with Israel's God. If Rahab, the Canaanite prostitute from Jericho, was the mother of Boaz, then Obed, the "root" of David's family tree, had both a Moabite mother and a Canaanite grandmother. On one side, the line leading to Obed runs from the unnamed mother of Moab to Ruth. On the other side, the line leads from Leah, the mother of Judah, to Tamar, the mother of Perez, and to Rahab, the mother of Boaz.

114. Campbell, *Ruth,* 172.
115. Ernst R. Wendland, "Structural Symmetry and Its Significance in the Book of Ruth," in *Issues in Bible Translation,* ed. Philip C. Stine, UBS Monograph Series 3 (New York: United Bible Societies, 1988) 36. See also Adele Berlin, *Poetics and Interpretation of Biblical Narrative* (Winona Lake, Ind.: Eisenbrauns, 1994) 109-10; Johannes C. de Moor, "The Poetry of the Book of Ruth, Part II," *Orientalia,* N.S. 55 (1986) 42-43.
116. Berlin, *Poetics and Interpretation of Biblical Narrative,* 110.

REFLECTIONS

In 4:13 the narrator tells us that the LORD made Ruth conceive. This assertion stands out as the only place in the book in which the narrator makes a statement about God's actions. All of the other references to God in the story are found in the mouths of the characters, who express a variety of beliefs about the nature and purposes of God.

Naomi's picture of God reflects (or perhaps is distorted by) her grief. When Naomi speaks to Orpah and Ruth in 1:13 and to the women of Bethlehem in 1:20-21, she blames the LORD for her bereavement. It is not clear whether she thinks she has done something wrong (perhaps fleeing to Moab in the midst of a famine) for which she is being punished, or whether she thinks the LORD's hand has been arbitrarily raised against her.

As her grief begins to heal, Naomi invokes the LORD's blessing on Boaz when Ruth brings back a load of grain from gleaning in Boaz's field (2:20). While it is not clear whether the phrase "whose kindness has not forsaken the living or the dead" refers to Boaz or to the LORD, it is clear that Naomi is now thinking of the LORD as a potential source of blessing.

In a similar way, we can see that what Boaz says and thinks about God is shaped (or perhaps distorted) by the fact that Boaz is wealthy and secure in his position in the community. Feeling blessed by God, he repeatedly calls upon the LORD to bless or to reward those with whom Boaz is pleased (2:12; 3:10).

Ruth, the non-Israelite convert to the mother-in-law's faith, has the least to say about the LORD. After she tells Naomi that "your God will be my God," she swears an oath by the God of Israel, which means something like, "May the LORD strike me dead if I don't keep my pledge" (1:17). Ruth is confident that she has put her future into the hands of a God who has power over life and death.

The women of Bethlehem also see the LORD as a source of life. They praise God with a collective voice in 4:14, because it is clear to them that God has provided Naomi with a "redeemer." However, it might also be said that human beings personify and communicate the loving-kindness of God to each other in this story. Everything the LORD gives, including the conception of the child, comes through human interaction. We might conclude that God's love embodied in humankind gives birth to the messianic line.

Interpretations of the book of Ruth in the life of the church can be divided into essentially two groups, depending on how the following questions are answered: Is the line of the redeemer "chosen" *because* of the faithfulness of its human components or *in spite of* their all-too human behavior? Are Tamar, Rahab, and Ruth included in Matthew's genealogy because of or in spite of who they were? Do we credit their *ḥesed* or God's *ḥesed* for the birth of the messianic line?

On the one hand, it is quite possible to argue that "the genealogy . . . underscores the great reward granted Ruth for her loyalty; she is the honored ancestress of a great Israelite leader."[117] Ruth's faithfulness seems to be an essential element in the carrying out of God's plans for the world through the lineage of David. "It is the faith of Rahab and Ruth, not their pedigree, that commends them to be the mothers of kings."[118]

On the other hand, it is equally possible to argue that the story of Ruth is more about the faithfulness of God than about the faithfulness of humankind. If we consider the role the book of Ruth plays as a part of the Deuteronomistic History, we might conclude either that the ancestry of the Davidic line of kings is better than the line of Saul, or that *both* lines leading to human kingship in Israel are flawed. The marriage between Ruth (the descendant of Moab) and Boaz (the descendant of Tamar) can be seen either as a redemption of their ancestors' stories or as one more echo in Israel's sustained confession of sin as recorded in Joshua through 2 Kings.

Within the context of the whole canon, the book of Ruth can be considered a parable of the nature of God's love. The parable says that Ruth persisted in offering Naomi love and support, even in the face of Naomi's rejection, just as God persists in loving us, even in the face of our rejection. But the specific stories associated with the line of the Messiah read more like a confession of sin than a catalog of virtues. The stories told about the ancestors of Ruth and Boaz make it clear that the messianic king comes from a well-established line of tricksters who have mixed and not always admirable motives for what they do. Whatever determined David's eligibility to father the messianic line of kings, we can be sure that it was neither the ethnic nor the moral purity of his ancestral line! The collective point these stories make is *not* that the mothers and fathers of the Messiah were exceptionally worthy people, but that God can use even the least

117. Hubbard, *The Book of Ruth*, 22.
118. Gage, "Ruth Upon the Threshing Floor and the Sin of Gibeah," 375.

likely agents to bring about redemption. When the Gospel of Matthew adds Rahab to the list of David's ancestors and Jesus to the list of those whose ancestry is nothing to brag about, the theological point remains the same: It is God's grace and not our own merit that brings forth the redeemer of the world.

We who consider ourselves the people of God are frequently tempted to think that redemption comes as a reward to those who are faithful. We need to be reminded on a regular basis that God's faithfulness, not our own, brings about redemption. All of the characters in the story of Ruth have mixed motives. They have both self-serving and altruistic agendas. "They are all human, yet out of the tangle of human interactions God's redemption occurs."[119]

Because Ruth is the human catalyst for the redemptive transformations in Naomi's life, and because Ruth's acts of loving-kindness communicate the persistence of God's love to Naomi, we are tempted to hold Ruth up as a model for our own morality. But, in fact, most of us should see ourselves mirrored in the character of Naomi. Naomi reflects the reality of who we are: We are the recipients of unmerited love, and our redemption is due to someone else's *hesed,* not our own.

At the same time, however, it must be said that readers who recognize that there are ways in which they *are* like Ruth may also hear a redemptive message in the story. Renita Weems notes that an African American woman might at various times see her life experiences reflected in "Ruth the woman, Ruth the foreigner, Ruth the unelected woman, Ruth the displaced widow, or, perhaps, Ruth the ancestress of the king of Israel, King David, to name a few."[120] Seeing one's own reality mirrored in the character of Ruth may assure those who feel like Moabites in their own modern contexts that God does not choose agents of redemption according to human standards or according to the expectations of society, that God can and may be working through them and through their relationships with others to transform emptiness into fullness. But for someone else (teachers, preachers, or writers of commentaries) to insist that a reader *ought* to be like Ruth must be considered repressive rather than redemptive.

We who think we have been chosen by God are often tempted to exclude those we perceive to be "the other." Thus we need to be reminded on a regular basis that God often chooses "the other" to help carry out God's purposes in the world. Rather than encouraging people to be like Ruth, we need to challenge them to *see* Ruth reflected in the "other," however the "other" is currently defined. In preaching or teaching from the book of Ruth, we need to ask, Who is the "Moabite" in the eyes of *our* community of faith? Who do we despise on the basis of their origins (Gen 19:30-37) or blame for the decline in our own morals (Num 25:1-2)? To whom do we deny admittance into "the assembly of the LORD" (Deut 23:3-6)? Might God use such a one to bring about *our* redemption?

119. Alice Ogden Bellis, *Helpmates, Harlots, Heroes: Women's Stories in the Hebrew Bible* (Louisville: Westminster/John Knox, 1994) 211.
120. Renita J. Weems, "African American Women and the Bible," in *Stony the Road We Trod,* ed. Cain Hope Felder (Minneapolis: Fortress, 1991) 67-68.

THE FIRST AND SECOND BOOKS OF SAMUEL

INTRODUCTION, COMMENTARY, AND REFLECTIONS
BY
BRUCE C. BIRCH

THE FIRST AND SECOND BOOKS OF

SAMUEL

INTRODUCTION

T he books of 1 and 2 Samuel witness to one of the most crucial periods of transition and change in the story of ancient Israel. At the opening of 1 Samuel, Israel is a loose federation of tribes, experiencing both external threat from the militarily superior Philistines and internal crisis because of the corruption of the priestly house of Eli at Shiloh, where the ark was maintained and covenant traditions were preserved (see Overview for chaps. 1–7). At the conclusion of 2 Samuel, an emerging monarchy is firmly in place under David. He has weathered various threats to the integrity of the kingdom, and is preparing to establish a hereditary dynasty in Israel. The momentous changes necessitated by this transition to kingship provide some of the most dramatic stories in the Old Testament. These stories not only narrate dramatic events but also introduce us to some of the most striking characters in the biblical story. Samuel, Saul, and David, whose stories overlap, dominate the pages of the books of Samuel. Moreover, even the supporting cast is remarkable for the variety of sharply drawn characters that flesh out the pages of these stories—Hannah, Eli, Jonathan, Michal, Joab, Abigail, Abishai, Abner, Bathsheba, Nathan, Amnon, Tamar, Absalom, Mephibosheth, to name only a few. Yet, beyond these personalities and events, the books of Samuel make clear that the Lord is at work in these turbulent times. On the surface, these stories may seem preoccupied with political power, but we will discover that these narratives testify to the true power of the Lord, acting in and through personalities and events to bring Israel to a new future in keeping with God's purposes.

TITLE AND DIVISION OF THE BOOKS OF SAMUEL

The books of 1 and 2 Samuel were originally one book. The oldest Hebrew manuscript from Qumran (4QSamª) includes both 1 and 2 Samuel on a single scroll. Moreover, the Talmud references allude to a single book of Samuel. The division into two books was probably introduced by the Greek translators (the Septuagint), perhaps to create scrolls of a more manageable size. In Septuagint manuscripts, the books of Samuel and Kings are divided into four books called

1–4 Kingdoms. This division and its designations were adopted by Jerome in his Latin translation (the Vulgate) and became the common designation in Roman Catholic Bibles until the mid-twentieth century. The manuscripts of the Masoretic text (Hebrew) assume a one-book arrangement. The division into 1 and 2 Samuel did not appear until the fifteenth century and became common with the first printed editions of the Hebrew Bible in the sixteenth century.[1]

The decision about the place at which to divide the books was undoubtedly influenced by the custom of concluding books with the death of a major figure (e.g., Joseph/Genesis; Moses/Deuteronomy; Joshua/Joshua). Thus the division of the books of Samuel was placed after the death of Saul. It is curious, however, that the two versions of Saul's death are separated by this division (1 Samuel 31; 2 Samuel 1). The retention of the name "Samuel" for the divided arrangement also creates the anomaly of a 2 Samuel named for the prophet Samuel, who does not appear at all in the book.

TEXT OF THE BOOKS OF SAMUEL

The Hebrew text of 1 and 2 Samuel (the Masoretic text) on which English translations have been routinely based is in extremely poor condition.[2] Its text for these books is much shorter than the text of the ancient Greek translation of the Hebrew Bible, the Septuagint (LXX), and other ancient versions of the text of 1 and 2 Samuel. Until recently, many scholars assumed that the Greek translators had simply added traditions known to them and thus expanded the text. However, other scholars offered a different explanation—namely, that the Hebrew text had suffered numerous omissions and copying errors. This latter assumption was confirmed by the discovery, beginning in 1952, of three fragmentary Samuel manuscripts in the library of the ancient community of Qumran, beside the shores of the Dead Sea.[3] The most important of these, 4QSam[a], was written in the first century BCE and contains large portions of 1 and 2 Samuel in a well-preserved condition. The second, 4QSam[b], dates from the mid-third century but contains only poorly preserved fragments of a small portion of 1 Samuel. And the third, 4QSam[c], also from the first century, contains only fragments of 1 Samuel 25 and 2 Samuel 14–15.

The failure to publish many of the Qumran texts promptly has delayed the impact of this material on English translations of the books of Samuel. However, the work of Ulrich and McCarter (both cited above) has given wide circulation to the longer LXX/Qumran readings for 1 and 2 Samuel. Frank Cross used the Qumran material in translating the books of Samuel for the NAB (1970). More recent translations (including the NRSV and the NIV, used in this commentary) have been able to use this textual material, and as a consequence have often adopted many of the longer readings reflected in the LXX and Qumran texts.

LITERARY COMPOSITION OF THE BOOKS OF SAMUEL

It is generally agreed that analysis of the process by which the books of Samuel were composed comprises one of the most complex subjects in twentieth-century biblical study. Current views on the literary composition of 1 and 2 Samuel offer no clear-cut consensus. I can only summarize briefly some of the major positions and approaches concerning the formation of the books of Samuel. Later, some of the critical assumptions that serve as the basis for this commentary will be made clear.

Earlier Approaches. Repetitions, doublets, contradictions, and contrasting viewpoints in the stories and traditions of 1 and 2 Samuel led scholars in the late nineteenth and early twentieth centuries to look for multiple literary strands or sources that could be traced throughout the books of Samuel.[4] Some identified literary sources in the books of Samuel that they thought

1. See P. Kyle McCarter, *I Samuel*, AB 8 (Garden City, N.Y.: Doubleday, 1984) 3-4.
2. McCarter (*I Samuel*, 5-11) has the fullest description of the textual witnesses for the books of Samuel, and the textual sections of his chapter-by-chapter commentary represent the most detailed treatment of textual problems in these books.
3. See E. C. Ulrich, Jr., *The Qumran Text of Samuel and Josephus*, HSM 19 (Missoula, Mont.: Scholars Press, 1978).
4. For a detailed discussion of representative scholars and viewpoints in early and recent research on the books of Samuel, see James W. Flanagan, "Samuel, Book of 1-2: Text, Composition and Content," in *The Anchor Bible Dictionary*, 6 vols., ed. David Noel Freedman (New York: Doubleday, 1992) 5:958-61.

were continuations of those present in the Pentateuch, but this view was largely abandoned in the early twentieth century. A more prominent theory involved the view that the books of Samuel were made up of an early and a late source. Although details differed, many scholars until the mid-twentieth century defended some variation on this hypothesis. The early source was thought to offer a more positive assessment of the development of monarchy in Israel and also to be more historically reliable. The late source was responsible for additions to the text that created inconsistencies and redundancies. This late source was negative toward kingship and considered to provide a less reliable historical source for the period. This theory of an early and a late source has been largely abandoned. Both supportive and antagonistic attitudes toward kingship in Israel are likely to have arisen from Saul's time onward and not simply to be the product of late experience with kings. Furthermore, the negative views associated with the kingship of Saul disappear in positive approval of David when he enters the story. In sum, theories of composition for the books of Samuel have become more complex. Moreover, few scholars think that the traditions now included in the books of Samuel offer a neutral historical reconstruction of that period.

In 1926, Leonhard Rost published his influential study of 2 Samuel 9–20 and 1 Kings 1–2,[5] which he identified as an independent narrative written by a single author who lived close to the time of the events themselves. Rost believed that the focus for this narrative was in answering the question, Who will succeed David on the throne? Building on Rost's hypothesis, Gerhard von Rad argued that the succession narrative was an early example of history writing, albeit a history that assumes divine providence acted through persons and events in the narrative.[6] Rost's work has been the starting point for an unusual degree of interest in these chapters of 2 Samuel, and many of Rost's conclusions have been modified, including the contention that succession is the central interest of these chapters (see Overview for 2 Samuel 9:1–20:26). Nevertheless, his view of a coherent pre-existing narrative used as a source by the author of 1 and 2 Samuel is still widely accepted.

This claim for the existence of a succession narrative as a source document for the compiler of 1 and 2 Samuel has influenced a flurry of claims for other independent pre-existing sources that were incorporated into the books of Samuel—not as intertwined sources but as stories in a sequence. Other proposed sources included an ark narrative (1 Samuel 4–6; 2 Samuel 6), a history of David's rise (1 Samuel 16–2 Samuel 5:10), and a birth story of Samuel (1 Samuel 1–3).

In 1943, Martin Noth proposed that the whole of the Former Prophets (Joshua–2 Kings, excluding Ruth in the English Bible) constituted a single great history work influenced by deuteronomic theological perspectives and written during the time of the Babylonian exile.[7] His basic argument for a deuteronomistic historian (Dtr) is still widely accepted, although some now argue persuasively that this Deuteronomistic History was written before the destruction of Jerusalem and was then supplemented to take account of those events. Noth did identify the deuteronomic historian with most of the material and viewpoint attributed to the so-called Late Source of earlier scholarship—that is, negative to kingship and historically unreliable. This broad identification is no longer accepted. Most now regard the final shape of 1 and 2 Samuel to be the work of the deuteronomistic historian, but the extent of that role is debated, with some claiming that the deuteronomist did little more than mechanical redaction with occasional theological comment and others claiming single, unified authorship of the whole of 1 and 2 Samuel by the deuteronomist.[8]

5. Leonhard Rost, *Die Überlieferung von der Thronnachfolge Davids*, BWANT 3/6 (Stuttgart: Kohlhammer, 1926); English trans.: *The Succession to the Throne of David*, trans. Michael D. Rutter and David M. Gunn (Sheffield: Almond, 1982).

6. Gerhard von Rad, "Der Anfang der Geschichtsschreibung im alten Israel," *Archiv für Kulturgeschichte* 32 (1944) 1-42; English translation: "The Beginning of History Writing in Ancient Israel," in *The Problem of the Hexateuch and Other Essays*, trans. E. W. Trueman Dicken (New York: McGraw-Hill, 1966) 166-204.

7. Martin Noth, *Überlieferungsgeschichtliche Studien. Die sammeln and bearbeitenden Geschichtswerke im Alten Testament* (Tubingen: Niemeyer, 1943); English translation: *The Deuteronomistic History*, trans. J. Doull, JSOTSup 15 (Sheffield: JSOT, 1981).

8. The most careful and nuanced treatment of the deuteronomistic influences and traditions in the books of Samuel is that of T. Veijola, *Das Konigtum in der Beurteilung der deuteronomistischen Historiographie. Eine redaktionsgeschichtliche Untersuchung*, Annales Academiae Scientiarum Fennicae B, 193 (Helsinki: Suomalainen Tiedeakatemia, 1977). Robert Polzin has recently argued in a series of volumes that the text from Joshua through 2 Kings is the work of a single deuteronomistic author. His volumes on the books of Samuel are *Samuel and the Deuteronomist: A Literary Study of the Deuteronomic History*, Part Two: *1 Samuel* (San Francisco: Harper & Row, 1989) and *David and the Deuteronomist: A Literary Study of the Deuteronomic History*, Part Three: *2 Samuel* (Bloomington: Indiana University Press, 1993).

Recent Emphases. Scholarship on the books of Samuel since 1960 has been prolific and varied, but one may highlight several prominent areas in the discussion. Many scholars continued to work with the traditional tools and approaches of historical-critical scholarship but with much greater attention to the complexity of the Samuel material. In addition, they have tended to examine longer segments of the Samuel narratives and with greater attention to the final form of the text in these segments as well as in the books of Samuel as a whole. Significant studies, based on historical-critical methods, have focused on the ark narrative, the rise of kingship in Israel, the history of David's rise, David's consolidation of his kingdom, the court history of David (the succession narrative), and the so-called appendixes to the books of Samuel. (See the Overview sections on each of these narrative segments for more detailed discussion and bibliography.)

Recent Emphases. Scholarship on the books of Samuel since 1960 has been prolific and varied, but one may highlight several prominent areas in the discussion. Many scholars continued to work with the traditional tools and approaches of historical-critical scholarship but with much greater attention to the complexity of the Samuel material. In addition, they have tended to examine longer segments of the Samuel narratives and with greater attention to the final form of the text in these segments as well as in the books of Samuel as a whole. Significant studies, based on historical-critical methods, have focused on the ark narrative, the rise of kingship in Israel, the history of David's rise, David's consolidation of his kingdom, the court history of David (the succession narrative), and the so-called appendixes to the books of Samuel. (See the Overview sections on each of these narrative segments for more detailed discussion and bibliography.)

Some scholars still discern evidence of pre-deuteronomistic editions of Samuel traditions incorporating, and in some cases helping to form, the larger narrative segments just mentioned above. Perhaps the most thoroughgoing example of such a viewpoint appears in McCarter's Anchor Bible commentary. Building on the work of Weiser and Birch, McCarter argues that

the First Book of Samuel derives its basic shape from a prophetic history of the origin of the monarchy that was intended to present the advent of kingship in Israel as a concession to a wanton demand of the people . . . the history was written to set forth according to a prophetic perspective the essential elements of the new system by which Israel would be governed. The prophet, whom the example of Samuel showed to be capable of ruling alone, would continue to be the people's intercessor with Yahweh. The king . . . would be subject not only to the instruction and admonition of the prophet acting in his capacity as Yahweh's spokesman but even to prophetic election and rejection.[9]

This prophetic history, dating to the late eighth century, is especially evident in segments of narrative on the birth of Samuel (1 Samuel 1–3), the role of Samuel as judge and deliverer (1 Samuel 7), the rise of kingship and the role of the prophet in those events (1 Samuel 8–12), the rejection of Saul (1 Samuel 13 and 15), the anointing of David (1 Samuel 16), Saul's consultation with the ghost of Samuel (1 Samuel 28), elements of the dynastic oracle (2 Samuel 7), the sin of David and his confrontation by Nathan (2 Samuel 11–12), and David's census and God's judgment (2 Samuel 24).

Recent decades have seen the impact of social-scientific methods and comparative social-world models on study of the books of Samuel and the transition period these traditions represent in the history of Israel. The publication of Gottwald's groundbreaking study on tribal Israel in the period of Joshua and Judges[10] had a catalytic effect on Samuel studies. Interest focused on describing the centralization process that moved Israel from its tribal existence to a monarchic nation-state. Most social-world critics think a complex pattern of social and economic pressures led toward centralization, but also produced resistance to that centralization. Many believe the political reality of the Philistines' pressure and the economic reality of limited resources led not

9. McCarter, *I Samuel*, 21. McCarter builds on work by Artur Weiser, *The Old Testament: Its Formation and Development,* trans. B. M. Barton (New York: Association Press, 1961; German original 1948); and Bruce C. Birch, *The Rise of the Israelite Monarchy: The Growth and Development of 1 Samuel 7–15,* SBLDS 27 (Missoula, Mont.: Scholars Press, 1976).

10. Norman K. Gottwald, *The Tribes of Yahweh: A Sociology of the Religion of Liberated Israel, 1250–1050 B.C.* (Maryknoll, N.Y.: Orbis, 1979).

to a full-fledged kingship under Saul and David, but to something more like a paramount tribal chieftaincy, which was not free politically or economically to embrace fully the model of a royal state.[11] That remains for Solomon to accomplish. The narratives of Samuel represent not history per se but a telling of Israel's story that seeks to unify diverse perspectives in the service of a social unity centered in Jerusalem and based on Yahwistic religion.

Differences and contradictions in the stories have ecological, political, social, economic, and religious bases. By their existence, the texts signal continuing hope for social unity grounded in belief. The unifying force of Yahwist religion is central to the stories. Tensions among factions and perspectives that can be felt, for the most part, follow from contemporary differences rather than successive revisions of the texts. Hence, 1–2 Samuel, although formed from separate traditions, cycles, and stories, is a unified account that captures the urgency of the compilers' time.[12]

Recent scholarship has also seen the application of literary-critical methodologies to 1 and 2 Samuel. These studies have focused on the final form of the text with little interest in traditional questions of sources or processes of composition. Literary critics assume that the narrative as it stands possesses artistic integrity and must be analyzed as such. These approaches have been largely uninterested in historical questions and are largely skeptical that genuine correlations are possible between these stories and the actual course of Israel's history. The study by David Gunn, devoted to the succession narrative, represented a break with many of the assumptions of traditional historical criticism and treated the succession narrative as a part of a larger integrated whole in the books of Samuel.[13] More recently, works by Polzin and Fokkelman involve a close literary reading of the texts of 1 and 2 Samuel that has moved in an entirely different direction from traditional historical-critical scholarship on the books of Samuel.[14] Their treatments postulate and seek to demonstrate a literary integrity in the books of Samuel that neither admits to previous sources or editions in these narratives nor shows any interest or confidence in these texts as sources for Israel's history in the time of Saul and David. The narrative is understood to be largely the product of the literary efforts and theological concerns of a later single author (for Polzin, it is the deuteronomist).

Finally, there has been a resurgence of interest in the theological interpretation of the books of Samuel. In the search for sources and in the effort to identify various historical elements in the text, the theological importance of the books of Samuel as a whole had been neglected. However, this situation has changed dramatically since 1970. There is increasing recognition that the books of Samuel represent Israel's theological struggle to adapt its faith to radically changed social realities and that many of the issues concerning the relationship of God's providence to human power are of continuing concern to the Jewish and Christian communities. The work of Walter Brueggemann has been of critical importance in the renewal of theological interest in the books of Samuel. In countless articles, monographs, and books he has pioneered the reshaping of traditional assumptions that these books are only of "historical" interest. His commentary on the books of Samuel represents the culminating statement of his work on this literature.[15]

Recent Samuel scholarship has been rich and eclectic. There is no clear consensus on many of the critical issues in interpreting the book, but a general agreement seems to be emerging that scholarship on the books of Samuel in the future is likely to draw on a variety of approaches and methodologies (historical-critical, social-world, literary, theological). Perhaps such multifaceted approaches are the best hope of doing justice to the complexity and richness of these books.

---

11. See James W. Flanagan, "Chiefs in Israel," *JSOT* 20 (1981) 47-73; Frank S. Frick, *The Formation of the State in Ancient Israel: A Survey of Methods and Theories*, SWBA 4 (Sheffield: JSOT, 1985).

12. Flanagan, "Samuel, Books of 1–2," *ABD* 5:961.

13. David M. Gunn, *The Story of King David: Genre and Interpretation*, JSOTSup 6 (Sheffield: JSOT, 1978).

14. See Polzin, *Samuel and the Deuteronomist* and *David and the Deuteronomist;* J. P. Fokkelman, *Narrative Art and Poetry in the Books of Samuel*, 2 vols. (Assen: Van Gorcum, 1981; 1986).

15. Walter Brueggemann, *First and Second Samuel*, Interpretation (Louisville: John Knox, 1990). His many other articles and books related to the books of Samuel are too numerous to mention here, but they are cited throughout this commentary.

CRITICAL ASSUMPTIONS

The Commentary and Reflections on the books of Samuel make a number of critical assumptions that need to be made explicit.

1. The emphasis of this work will be on the *final form* of 1 and 2 Samuel as a literary witness whose integrity and meaning do not depend on analysis and recovery of the earlier sources and editions that have brought the narrative to its present final form. This final form is probably the product of the deuteronomistic historian, who allowed earlier sources and editions to remain visible. These earlier elements may contribute distinctive emphases to the narrative. The concern, however, will not be to separate and recover these earlier sources and editions from the final form of the text, but to examine how they contribute to the books of Samuel in their present form. The long process by which these traditions have been shaped is not recoverable. My analysis will begin with the whole rather than the parts. Where earlier sources and editions have been left visible, I will comment on the emphases of these elements as they contribute to an enriched understanding of the books of Samuel in their present final form.

For the purpose of this commentary, the most important of the earlier sources and editions are listed here:

Independent literary units that existed prior to the work of the narrator and are responsible for the final shape of the books of Samuel. These include an ark narrative (1 Samuel 4–6); a history of the rise of David (1 Sam 16:1–2 Sam 5:10); and a court history (so-called succession narrative; 2 Samuel 9–20). Other narrative segments of 1 and 2 Samuel seem intentionally shaped as literary units, but it is less clear that they predate the work of the artistic hand responsible for the whole of these books.

A prophetic edition of these narratives may have joined and interpreted early traditions and sources prior to the work of the deuteronomist. The conclusions of McCarter, mentioned earlier, seem to have merit, though I am not as confident as McCarter that the work of this prophetic editor can be as precisely identified as he believes. It is not possible to isolate a prophetic edition in the present form of the books of Samuel. Rather, one may identify a prophetic theology of kingship and an emphasis on the peculiar role of the prophets in relation to kings within certain narratives. These prophetic interests and emphases will be noted as they appear in the final form of the text. This emphasis is apparent especially in 1 Samuel 1–3; 7–15; 16; 28; and 2 Samuel 7; 11–12; 24 (see Commentary on these sections and chapters).

Even if the deuteronomistic historian is responsible for the whole of 1 and 2 Samuel, there are certain *narrative segments that reflect deuteronomistic language and theological interests.* Compared to other portions of the Deuteronomistic History, there are fewer of these distinctively deuteronomistic passages, which suggests that a large part of the narrative of 1 and 2 Samuel already existed in a form that the deuteronomistic historian found congenial. Many of the distinctly deuteronomistic passages incorporate the Samuel narratives into the form and structure adopted elsewhere for the Deuteronomistic History—e.g., elements of the farewell speech of Samuel (1 Samuel 12) or the archival notices on Saul's kingship (1 Sam 13:1-2; 14:47-51). In general, I will not try to identify every verse that might be argued as distinctively deuteronomistic;[16] instead, I will simply note those places where a deuteronomistic perspective or use of language influences the analysis of the larger narrative. I do not regard the deuteronomist as simply an annotator. By what has been included, excluded, and added to earlier sources, the deuteronomist has worked as the literary artist and theological commentator responsible for the books of Samuel as we now have them.

2. There is an identifiable and significant *socio-historical context* to which the narratives of 1 and 2 Samuel give witness, even if that witness is now interpretively shaped by the perspectives and contexts of later Israelite generations. These stories are rooted in a time of considerable social and political transformation in the life of Israel, and these realities challenged the theological categories by which Israel understood its life in relation to God. This transformative period

---

16. A helpful and thoughtful delineation of the deuteronomistic portions of 1 and 2 Samuel may be found in McCarter, *I Samuel*, 14-17, and *II Samuel*, 4-8, although McCarter is generally more confident than I in arguing the presence of a deuteronomistic hand in very small additions to some chapters.

was so crucial to Israel's understanding of itself that its events and personalities were still being assessed politically and theologically at the time of the exile, when the work of the deuteronomistic historian fixed these narratives in their present form.

The books of Samuel open with a loose federation of tribal groups gripped by a crisis, both external and internal, that threatens the very existence of Israel, and they end on the eve of an emergent hereditary monarchy that will preside over an established nation-state. This transformation represents a considerable achievement. The narratives in 1 and 2 Samuel are not historical in the sense of our modern positivistic understandings of history. Rather, they blend historical realism with artistic and theological imagination. Attention to the imaginative elements of these narratives has led some to miss the historically realistic style by which these narratives depict the nature of this historical crisis and social transformation. Likewise, the historically realistic style has led others mistakenly to treat the books of Samuel as history writing and to overlook the artistic and imaginative freedom with which many elements of the story have been shaped.

The socio-historical context at the beginning of 1 Samuel includes the external threat of incorporation into a Philistine empire that sought to expand into Israelite territory c. 1000 BCE (1 Samuel 4). The internal crisis in this same period is reflected in the loose tribal association that proves incapable of meeting such a crisis (1 Samuel 4) and the corruption of the institutions of Yahwism, which gave tribal Israel whatever unity it possessed (1 Samuel 2–3). The end of the book of Judges describes a state of political chaos and moral decadence that results in idolatry and barbarous behavior (Judges 17–21), a time when "there was no king in Israel; every man did what was right in his own eyes" (Judg 17:6; 18:1; 19:1; 21:25). There is little reason to think that Israel could survive these internal and external crises.

Yet, by the end of 2 Samuel, Israel has been transformed socially and politically. Although details may be debated, it is clear that this transformation included political centralization and the emergence of governantal structures (first to chieftaincy then to monarchy) capable of uniting tribal Israel and coping with the crises it faced. This transformation included movement economically from marginal tribal, agrarian existence to a period of prosperity that included extended trade and the emergence of wealth. This development also required new structures of social management and practice. Many of the narratives of 1 and 2 Samuel are concerned to make legitimate, politically and theologically, these newly emerging political and economic structures. Saul, David, Jerusalem, the Temple—all in turn are the subject of narrative apologists in the books of Samuel (e.g., Saul, 1 Sam 9:1–10:16; David, 1 Sam 16:1–2 Sam 5:10; Jerusalem, 2 Sam 5:6-10; 6:1-19; Temple, 2 Sam 24:18-25). But the narratives also reflect the resistance to new centralized political and economic structures: Kingship is opposed (1 Samuel 8); David cannot build the Temple (2 Samuel 7); David's census brings judgment (2 Sam 24:1-17). These narratives reflect the challenge, tensions, and promise of a transformative moment in Israel's life. Elements of historical realism in the narratives allow us a view of the socio-historical context for this moment in Israel's story, but the narratives exercise artistic imagination in presenting the personalities, the events, and the divine will that mediated Israel's transformation.

3. *The role of personality* in Israel's story of this period is central. Samuel, Saul, and David loom over the story in overlapping domination of the narrative landscape (Samuel, 1 Samuel 1–28; Saul, 1 Samuel 9–2 Samuel 1; David, 1 Samuel 16–2 Samuel 24). First, Samuel, then Saul, and finally David are presented as crucial to Israel's future, but where any two are present in the story, tension and conflict arise, as if there is room for only one of these dominant personalities in the spotlight. In the end, it is David, "the man after God's own heart," who fascinates Israel's storytellers.

Yet, for all the intense interest in David, these narratives do not neglect the role of others in the story. No segment of the Old Testament is filled with a richer cast of characters, and their portraits are vividly drawn. Even characters that occupy a single episode (e.g., Abigail, 1 Samuel 25) are often drawn as full and intriguing figures who play crucial roles in the drama that will find its climax in David. More than in earlier narratives in the canon (the Pentateuch, Joshua, Judges) the personalities of 1 and 2 Samuel are described in terms of inner motives and struggles as well as actions.

The telling of these stories depicts the personalities in artistic as well as historical terms. A historically realistic style is blended with artistic imagination. The narrator is not concerned with just the "truth" of fact but with the "truth" of meaning for Israel, especially where David is concerned. It does not matter who really killed Goliath (David, 1 Samuel 17, or Elhanan, 2 Sam 21:19). The combination of piety and courage in the dramatic, but fanciful, story of a youthful David's triumph captures the imagination of Israel and allows one to be confident that Israel's new future is assured. The story of Israel's transformation from tribe to kingdom is grounded in a historical experience, but the story of this time is peopled by characters that are, at times, portrayed in painstakingly realistic terms and, at other times, seem to stride off the page larger than life. Both the imaginative and the realistic elements are important in conveying Israel's memory of this crucial time.

4. To paint David and other crucial characters solely in human historical terms might suggest that Israel's transformation in that period was simply the product of human activity. But the authors of 1 and 2 Samuel understand that Israel's new future results from the working of *the providence of God.* It is the Lord (Yahweh) who shapes the events and personalities of this time. Sociopolitical realities and leadership are bent to the divine purpose.

In a world of human politics preoccupied with the issues of power, the issue for the narratives of Samuel is, Where does true power lie? These narrators understand that, in the juxtaposition of human power and divine will, God possesses the final authority. The poetry of Hannah's song (1 Sam 2:1-10) and of David's song (2 Sam 22:2-51) frames the entirety of 1 and 2 Samuel by announcing a divine purpose at work in the world that overturns and reverses the usual patterns of power. Consistent with this literary frame, a barren woman can give birth to the prophet of God's future for Israel (1 Samuel 1), a devastating Philistine victory can be turned into Philistine defeat without human help (1 Samuel 4–6), the king demanded by the people can nevertheless become God's anointed one (1 Samuel 8–10), even anointed kings can be rejected for unfaithfulness (1 Samuel 13; 15), an eighth son of an obscure family can become the future of Israel and the man after God's own heart (1 Samuel 16), a fugitive with a renegade band of followers sought by the king can receive the divine promise of eternal dynasty (2 Samuel 7), and even Israel's greatest and most beloved king can be judged by God (2 Samuel 12) and bring tragedy upon his own family (2 Samuel 13–18). In human terms, many of these events seem unlikely, but the narratives of Samuel understand all of these (and more) as a part of God's providence at work to bring Israel's future into being.

In 1 and 2 Samuel, the divine shaping of events is assumed, and even stated by the main characters in the narrative. This working of divine power does not usually occur by direct intervention in events, although the ark narratives (1 Samuel 4–6) suggest that God's purposes might not require human agency. Nevertheless, God's will is usually brought to pass through human events and personalities. The narratives make clear that divine power lies behind the human drama. For example, the lengthy narration of David's rise (1 Samuel 16–2 Sam 5:10) has as its central theological motif the conviction that "God was with him" (1 Sam 16:18; 18:14, 28), and it concludes after David is fully enthroned over Israel and Judah, "David became greater and greater, for the LORD, the God of hosts, was with him" (2 Sam 5:10 NRSV).

NARRATIVE UNITS AND EMPHASES IN THE BOOKS OF SAMUEL

Completely apart from judgments about earlier independent sources still visible in 1 and 2 Samuel, there is a developing scholarly consensus about the major segments into which the narrative falls. A brief description of these units gives a sense of the flow of the narrative and its major emphases. For a fuller description of these units and their themes, as well as references to the relevant scholarly literature, see the Overview sections for each of the segments.

1 Sam 1:1–4:1a. As the books of Samuel open, Israel is faced with a grave crisis, both internal and external, but we are not introduced to that crisis directly. Instead, we hear the story of Hannah, a barren woman who prays to the Lord and makes a vow (1:11). She asks the Lord to remember her, which the story tells us the Lord does (1:19). The story of Hannah's barrenness opens to the story of Israel's barren future. She bears a son, Samuel, the prophet who leads Israel through its time of crisis and through whom God will establish a kingship in Israel. Hannah's song (2:1-10) speaks of a God who brings the future in dramatic reversals and foreshadows the remarkable emergence of David as the climax of this story, an eighth son who becomes king. Childs has identified this song as "an interpretive key for this history which is, above all, to be understood from a theocentric perspective."[17] He has also shown that it has a counterpart at the end of 2 Samuel (chap. 22), a song that celebrates the Lord as the power behind David's successes. Thus a story that will be rich in human characters and events is framed as the work of the Lord.

This opening segment of 1 Samuel goes on to depict the tragic corruption of the priestly house of Eli at Shiloh (2:11-36). But against this background of covenant disobedience at the heart of Israel, chaps. 1–3 provide a story of the birth, growth, legitimization, and establishment of Samuel as the prophetic leader who will bring Israel through crisis to a new day. By the end of chap. 3, Samuel is established as God's prophetic voice, and judgment has been pronounced on the house of Eli.

1 Sam 4:1b–7:1. This section of narrative identifies the external crisis of Israel. It tells a dramatic story of Philistine threat, defeat of Israel, and capture of the ark (chap. 4). Nevertheless, the Philistines do not turn out to have the upper hand. The ark of the covenant itself mediates the powerful presence of the Lord, defeating the Philistine god Dagon and bringing plagues upon the Philistine people. In humiliation, the Philistines finally send the ark on a cart back into Israelite territory (chaps. 5–6). I agree with those who have argued that this so-called ark history did not originally continue in 2 Samuel 6 (see the Overview on this section for a detailed discussion). That story does, of course, include the ark, but it focuses on David in a way quite unlike the style in 1 Samuel 4–6, where human characters play a small role.

These stories about the ark are remarkable, because Samuel, who was so carefully introduced in the preceding chapters, is absent. The only connection to chaps. 1–3 is the report of the death of Eli's sons when the ark is captured and of Eli's death when he hears the tragic news (4:12-22). Human leadership plays no role in these events; the divine power mediated by the ark is equal to the challenge of the Philistine crisis. As a result, the ensuing human demand for a king seems unnecessary. The Lord is sovereign and governs Israel's history, even in the face of threat from Philistine armies and gods. Whatever is to unfold in Israel's story in 1 and 2 Samuel will be because God allows or wills it.

1 Sam 7:2-17. Suddenly Samuel reappears in the story. In this unusual narrative, Samuel faces a Philistine threat and leads Israel to victory, but not through his own military leadership. Through prayer and mediation of divine power against the enemy, Samuel meets the threat (7:2-14). This victory is followed by the notice of a circuit that Samuel travels, "administering justice" in Israel (7:15-17). The portrait in this chapter is of Samuel single-handedly carrying on the covenant tradition and giving the leadership necessary for Israel's welfare. Once again, the narrative's effect is to render the coming request for a king unnecessary. Israel has the power of God and the leadership of Samuel. What more is needed? If kingship is nevertheless to come, then it is because God wills it, not because the situation of Israel demanded it.

1 Sam 8:1–15:35. These chapters focus on the establishment of kingship in Israel and the installation of Saul as the first holder of this office. There can be little doubt that these narratives have gone through a complex literary process that cannot be entirely recovered (see earlier discussion in this Introduction and also the Overview for these chapters). There is also an emerging consensus that the socio-historical realities behind these narratives were more complex than response to the Philistine crisis. Economic developments leading to accumulation of wealth and to the centralized forms of government needed to safeguard that wealth undoubtedly played a role in the development of Israelite monarchy, but these processes lie in the background of the narrative.

As the narratives now stand, the internal and external crises of Israel have driven some to demand a king. These chapters preserve a divided opinion on this matter. Some narratives clearly view kingship as sinful, allowed by an indulgent God (chaps. 8 and 12), while other narratives

---

17. Brevard S. Childs, *Introduction to the Old Testament as Scripture* (Philadelphia: Fortress, 1979) 273.

see the choice of Saul and his kingship as an act of God's providential grace (9:1–10:16; 11:1-15). This divided opinion is now widely understood as being rooted in genuine division within Israel at an early time. These traditions undoubtedly reflect Israel's struggle over the appropriate relationship of human power to divine power as expressed in the institutions of governance in Israel. Economic and political pressures were demanding new patterns of institutional leadership, but how was covenant obedience and divine authority preserved when human power grew more centralized and prominent in Israel?

The prophet plays a crucial role in representing the initiative of God (anointing, 10:1), in voicing the covenant demands of God on king and people (Samuel's farewell address, chap. 12), and in holding kings accountable to God (Saul's rejection, 13:8-15; 15:1-35). This prophetic role also occurs in David's story. The roles of the prophet in these narratives have led some scholars to suggest a prophetic editing of significant portions of the narratives in 1 and 2 Samuel, including the diverse material on the establishment of kingship (see the fuller discussion in the Overview on this section).

The political and theological interests reflected in 1 Samuel 8–15 are played out around the person of Saul. Many interpreters have noted the tragic character of his story (see the Overview on this section). The narratives reflect an awareness that David is the true climax of the story and of God's purposes in the story. Saul, in spite of his gifts, beyond what seems deserved by his faults, appears destined for failure and tragedy. Saul's story is not his own; it is a preparation for David. Saul's shortcomings are exposed in these stories (esp. chaps. 13–15). He does not appear to have the gifts required to usher in Israel's new future. Yet, the narrator is aware that Saul pays the personal price for Israel's future as one destined to fail so that another might succeed. It is fitting that much later in the narrative, after David has become the focus of attention, there is a pause for compassion and tribute to Saul and his son Jonathan on the occasion of their tragic deaths (2 Samuel 1).

1 Sam 16:1–2 Sam 5:10. The focus shifts to David. Story after story celebrates the courage, leadership, resourcefulness, piety, and political skill of David. Saul appears as a foil to David—driven, impulsive, cruel, fickle, and ineffective. Many scholars believe these narratives existed as an earlier collection, often called the "History of David's Rise" (see the Overview on this section).

With the appearance of David, the divisions and struggles evident in 1 Samuel 8–15 begin to recede into the background. The theme of Hannah's song reappears forcefully in these stories; God is at work in great historical reversals—to bring low and to exalt. In 1 Samuel 16, we are introduced to an eighth son of an obscure family who tends sheep. By 2 Sam 5:3, he has become the king of Judah and Israel. The activity of God through these events is made explicit at the conclusion of the whole narrative segment, "David became greater and greater, for the LORD, the God of hosts, was with him" (2 Sam 5:10 NRSV). God's presence with David is a central theme of this narrative section (see 1 Sam 16:18; 17:37; 18:12, 14, 28; 20:13). David is portrayed as a man of piety and prayer alongside his prowess as warrior and leader (e.g., 1 Sam 17:45-47; 23:1-5).

The narrator is concerned to legitimize the kingship of David and to overcome objections that might be raised against his claim on the throne. Thus various episodes in this section seek to counter charges that might be made against David. McCarter has listed the following charges that these narratives seek to refute and explain:[18]

1. David sought to advance himself at Saul's expense.
2. David was a deserter.
3. David was an outlaw.
4. David was a Philistine mercenary.
5. David was implicated in Saul's death.
6. David was implicated in Abner's death.
7. David was implicated in Ishbaal's death.

18. P. Kyle McCarter, "The Apology of David," *JBL* 99 (1980) 499-502.

Alongside these apologetic efforts is a growing procession of witnesses who acknowledge David's right and destiny to Israel's throne: Jonathan, Michal, the servants of Achish, Ahimelech, Abigail, and finally Saul himself (1 Sam 24:20). After Saul's death (1 Samuel 31; 2 Samuel 1), David first becomes king over Judah (2 Sam 2:1-4), and after a series of complicated events, which includes the deaths of Abner and Ishbaal, David becomes king over Israel as well (2 Sam 5:3). In the final event of this drama of David's rise, David takes Jerusalem as his capital city (2 Sam 5:6-9). In David and Jerusalem, God has established a new future for Israel.

2 Sam 5:11–8:18. David remains the focus of the narrative, but in this segment the tone is not as celebrative as it was for David's rise. Enthusiasm gives way to official records and affairs of state. David sits on the throne; bureaucracy and ideology seem to close around him. Flanagan has observed a symmetry of arrangement that suggests a shift from tribal, covenant realities to state, royal ideology.[19] Family genealogy (2 Sam 5:13-16) gives way to officers of the court (2 Sam 8:15-18). War to bring deliverance from the Philistine threat (2 Sam 5:17-25) gives way to wars of national expansion and empire building (2 Sam 8:1-14). The central symbol of tribal covenant relationship to God, the ark, is brought to Jerusalem (2 Sam 6:1-20) and made secondary by God's announcement through the prophet Nathan of an eternal covenant with David (2 Sam 7:1-29). The center of Israel's life has shifted. God's covenant promises for Israel's future are now identified with the future of the Davidic dynasty. Conflict in Israel over kingship has now disappeared or been overridden by the claim that David is the destiny for Israel toward which God has been moving.

2 Sam 9:1–20:26. This is the segment of 2 Samuel usually designated as the succession narrative or the court history of David. Most scholars agree that this narrative segment existed independently prior to the time it was incorporated into the larger narrative of the books of Samuel. However, recent arguments have been advanced against considering 1 Kings 1–2 to be the continuation or conclusion of this narrative (see the Overview on 2 Sam 9:1–20:26 for a detailed discussion of critical issues).

There is a general consensus that, with these chapters, the narrative makes a sudden and dramatic shift in its portrayal of David. The key to this shift is 2 Samuel 11–12, which recount David's adultery with Bathsheba, his murder of Uriah, his marriage to Bathsheba, and his confrontation by the prophet Nathan. David's repentance spares his own life, but Nathan announces God's judgment of violence unleashed in David's own family. The remaining narratives provide detailed accounts of the tragic consequences of David's own sin: Amnon's rape of Tamar (13:1-22), Absalom's killing of Amnon and his banishment (13:23-39), Absalom's rebellion and David's humiliating retreat from Jerusalem (chaps. 14–17), the defeat and death of Absalom; David's overwhelming grief (chaps. 18–19), and continued rebellion in the kingdom (chap. 20).

As many have noted, literary style and emphasis change markedly in this segment of David's story. Gone is the assurance of state ideology that marked the previous narrative on David as king and the exuberance of the narrative on David's rise. These are stories in which the humanity, pathos, and vulnerability of David come to the fore. We are allowed to see David in decline and suffering. The literary style is unusually subtle and sensitive (see the Overview on this section for further details on style and perspective in this narrative). It focuses on human agency in these stories of tragedy in David's family; yet, it makes clear, in understated ways, that God's providence nevertheless encompasses even these painful human moments (cf. 2 Sam 11:27*b;* 17:14*b*). The result of this intensely human portrait of David is that readers approach the end of the books of Samuel in a chastened mood. The achievement of human political power is not without its dangers. The temptation to think of human power as autonomous is considerable. To wield that power in the service of self-interest and in disregard of God's ultimate authority and rule is to incur judgment. Even David takes such a course of action at considerable cost.

2 Sam 21:1–24:25. These chapters, commonly called appendixes to the books of Samuel, have been most often treated as a miscellaneous collection of David traditions inserted by a rough hand prior to David's deathbed scene in 1 Kings 1–2. However, there is a symmetrical arrangement to these materials that suggests a significant intention. There are two narratives,

19. James W. Flanagan, "Social Transformation and Ritual in 2 Samuel 6," in *The Word of the Lord Shall Go Forth,* ed. Carol L. Meyers and M. O'Connor (Winona Lake, Ind.: Eisenbrauns, 1983) 361-72.

one focused on expiation of Saul's guilt (2 Sam 21:1-14) and the other on expiation of David's guilt (2 Sam 24:1-25). There are two lists of heroes and their deeds (2 Sam 21:15-22; 23:8-39). Finally, at the heart of this section are two songs: a thanksgiving by David for the Lord's deliverance (2 Sam 22:1-51, parallel to Psalm 18) and a song that celebrates God's promise to David (2 Sam 23:1-7). This pattern reminds us of the pattern in 2 Sam 5:11–8:18 and has led some to suggest that the earlier movement from tribal to royal realities is being reversed in these appendixes—to reassert tribal, covenantal perspectives at the end of David's story (see the Overview on 2 Sam 21:1–24:25 for fuller discussion of scholarly proposals on these chapters).

In many ways the ideology of royal absolutism has been deconstructed by the judgment on David's sin with Bathsheba and Uriah, and the tragic events in David's family that ensued. Yet, at the end of chap. 20, David's power is reestablished, and he asserts that power to quell a rebellion. Without the so-called appendixes, the story would continue in 1 Kings 1–2 with deathbed vendettas by David and bloodbaths by Solomon. This material (chaps. 21–24) stays or moderates the reconstruction of royal absolutist power. The narratives in these chapters provide a reminder that, even when David feels most powerful, he is accountable to forces and authority beyond his own (the execution of Saul's son, chap. 21; the census, chap. 24). The lists of heroes make clear that it was never David alone through whom God was working to bring Israel's future. David was the leader of a heroic community. The two great songs at the heart of this section place into the mouth of David acknowledgment and celebration of the power of God working through him. In spite of earlier sin and judgment, these final appendixes return to the David anticipated by the song of Hannah at the start of the books of Samuel. It is the Lord who "brings low and exalts" and who "exalts the power of his anointed" (1 Sam 2:7*b*, 10*b*). Just as the Lord had heeded the prayer of Hannah (1 Sam 1:19) to open the story of kingship in Israel, so also that story concludes with the Lord heeding the prayer of David (2 Sam 24:25).

BIBLIOGRAPHY

Commentaries:

Anderson, A. A. *2 Samuel.* WBC 11. Waco: Word, 1989. A comprehensive critical commentary with valuable surveys of previous scholarly work.

Brueggemann, Walter. *First and Second Samuel.* Interpretation. Louisville: John Knox, 1990. An expository commentary with valuable theological insights.

Gordon, R. P. *1 and 2 Samuel.* Old Testament Guides. Sheffield: JSOT, 1984. A brief but reliable guide to the main interpretive issues.

Hertzberg, Hans Wilhelm. *I and II Samuel.* OTL. Philadelphia: Westminster, 1964. A classic historical-critical treatment of the books of Samuel.

Klein, Ralph W. *1 Samuel.* WBC 10. Waco: Word, 1983. A comprehensive critical commentary with valuable surveys of previous scholarly work.

McCarter, P. Kyle. *I Samuel.* AB 8. Garden City, N.Y.: Doubleday, 1980.

————. *II Samuel.* AB 9. Garden City, N.Y.: Doubleday, 1984. The best available treatment of text-critical issues in the books of Samuel, valuable for its careful critical analysis of literary and traditio-historical issues.

Other Helpful Studies:

Alter, Robert. *The Art of Biblical Narrative.* New York: Basic Books, 1981. A foundational study of the features of Hebrew narrative texts.

Birch, Bruce C. *The Rise of the Israelite Monarchy: The Growth and Development of I Samuel 7–15.* SBLDS 27. Missoula, Mont.: Scholars Press, 1976. A dissertation that advanced the thesis of prophetic interests evident in a pre-Dtr editing of materials in the books of Samuel.

Brueggemann, Walter. *David's Truth in Israel's Imagination and Memory.* Philadelphia: Fortress, 1985. Theological essays on focal themes for different segments of the narratives that give Israel's testimony concerning David.

————. *Power, Providence, and Personality: Biblical Insight into Life and Ministry.* Louisville: Westminster/John Knox, 1990. Insightful studies of selected texts and theological themes in the books of Samuel.

Carlson, R. A. *David, the Chosen King: A Traditio-Historical Approach to the Second Book of Samuel.* Stockholm: Almqvist och Wiksell, 1964. A helpful discussion of 2 Samuel organized around the themes of David under blessing and under curse.

Childs, Brevard S. *Introduction to the Old Testament as Scripture.* Philadelphia: Fortress, 1979. Discussion of the canonical shape and context for the books of Samuel.

Fokkelmann, J. P. *Narrative Art and Poetry in the Books of Samuel.* 2 vols. Assen: Van Gorcum, 1981 and 1986. Detailed analysis of the literary structures and functions of the texts in the books of Samuel.

Gunn, David M. *The Fate of King Saul.* JSOTSup 14. Sheffield: JSOT, 1980.

————. *The Story of King David.* JSOTSup 6. Sheffield: JSOT, 1978. Analysis of the literary features of these key narratives and the central characters around which they are constructed.

Miller, Patrick D., Jr., and J. J. M. Roberts. *The Hand of the Lord: A Reassessment of the "Ark Narrative" of 1 Samuel.* Johns Hopkins Near Eastern Studies. Baltimore: Johns Hopkins University Press, 1977. The most thorough treatment of the "ark narrative" in 1 Samuel 4–6 and of the scholarly theses related to these narratives; distinguished by its use of comparative Near Eastern materials and its cogent argument against inclusion of 2 Samuel 6 as a part of the "ark narrative."

Polzin, Robert. *David and the Deuteronomist: A Literary Study of the Deuteronomic History.* Part Three: *2 Samuel.* Bloomington: Indiana University Press, 1993.

————. *Samuel and the Deuteronomist: A Literary Study of the Deuteronomic History.* Part Two: *1 Samuel.* San Francisco: Harper & Row, 1989. Detailed literary analysis of the books of Samuel that argues the case for a single author of the Deuteronomistic History of which these books are a part.

Rad, Gerhard von. "Der Anfang der Geschichtsschreibung im alten Israel." *Archiv für Kulturgeschichte* 32 (1944) 1-42. English translation: "The Beginning of History Writing in Ancient Israel." In *The Problem of the Hexateuch and Other Essays.* Translated by E. W. Trueman Dicken. New York: McGraw-Hill, 1966. A classic essay that still marks the starting point for all modern discussion of the theological perspective of the "succession narrative" in 2 Samuel.

Rost, Leonhard. *Die Überlieferung von der Thronnachfolge Davids.* BWANT 3/6. Stuttgart: Kohlhammer, 1926. English translation: *The Succession to the Throne of David.* Translated by Michael D. Rutter and David M. Gunn. Sheffield: Almond, 1982. The classic study that popularized the hypothesis that 2 Samuel 9–20 and 1 Kings 1–2 are a connected literary product of a single author focused on the theme of succession to the throne of David.

Other important studies on particular narrative sections of the books of Samuel are cited in the notes to the Overview sections spread throughout the commentary.

OUTLINE OF FIRST AND SECOND SAMUEL

1 SAMUEL 1:1–31:13

1 SAMUEL 1:1–7:17, SAMUEL AND THE CRISIS OF ISRAEL

OVERVIEW

These chapters introduce the books of 1 and 2 Samuel as the story of a reshaping moment in Israel's history. As 1 Samuel opens, a transformation is about to take place in Israel's life. By the end of 2 Samuel, that transformation, for good or for ill, has been completed. The time of the judges has ended, and the reign of Israelite kings has begun. The threatened conquest of tribal Israel by external enemies, such as the Philistines (the threat at the end of Judges and at the opening of 1 Samuel), is over and the kingdom of David is established with secure borders. The violence and lack of moral direction signaled by the closing chapters of Judges (Judges 17–21)[20] is replaced by the mediators of God's Word: the prophets and God's anointed ones, the kings. No longer will it be said, "In those days there was no king in Israel; all the people did what was right in their own eyes" (Judg 21:25).

First Samuel 1–7 sets the stage for these transformations in Israel. The reader is drawn into an Israelite world in crisis. On the one hand, the crisis is internal. The sons of Eli, the priest at Shiloh where the ark of the covenant is kept, have corrupted the religious practices of Israel for their own gain (2:11-17). Eli seems powerless to change or control their behavior (2:22-25). Since God will not tolerate such faithlessness (2:25*b*, 27-36), there is no future for the house of Eli (4:12-22). On the other hand, the crisis of Israel is external. The Philistines wage a war of conquest on Israel and even capture the ark of the covenant as the spoils of victory (4:1*b*-11), but God will not tolerate the victory of Israel's enemies or the humiliation of the ark

(5:1–7:1). There is no future for Philistine conquest of Israel (7:3-14).

Chapters 1–7 introduce not only Israel's crisis, but also the key figure through whom God will work to resolve the crisis, Samuel. We are told of his birth as the gracious act of God (1:1-28), his childhood and vocational shaping at Shiloh (2:11, 18, 26; 3:1-18), his establishment as the prophet of God's Word (3:19–4:1a), and his leadership in the face of the Philistine threat (7:3-17). Samuel plays the central role in these chapters as the instrument of God's will in the midst of Israel. Samuel is the first of three great men whose overlapping stories dominate this time of transition in Israel and who take up the whole of the books of Samuel: Samuel, Saul, and David. One may see Samuel as the representative of older, tribal Israel and its traditions. Yet, Samuel will also be the instrument through whom God will act to bring about a new, royal Israel with its perils and possibilities.

It has long been recognized that 1 Samuel 1–7 contains at least three distinct literary segments: (1) Chapters 1–3 tell of Samuel's birth and childhood and the corruption of the house of Eli; (2) chaps. 4–6 narrate the Philistine threat and the capture of the ark; and (3) chap. 7 establishes the leadership of Samuel. The sudden and total absence of Samuel in chaps. 4–6 especially suggests that the deuteronomistic historian (see Introduction) has used separate sources in compiling the books of Samuel. These segments may have originated separately, but in their present place in the Deuteronomistic History they are closely interconnected. Scholars such as Willis and Polzin[21] have made a strong case for a reading

---

20. In the Deuteronomistic History, which stretches from Joshua to 2 Kings, the book of 1 Samuel follows immediately after Judges. Early English Bibles changed the order of books in the canon and placed the book of Ruth between Judges and 1 Samuel.

21. See John T. Willis, "An Anti-Elide Narrative Tradition from a Prophetic Circle at the Ramah Sanctuary," *JBL* 90 (1971) 288-308; "Samuel Versus Eli: I Sám. 1-7," *TZ* 35 (1979) 201-12; Polzin, *Samuel and the Deuteronomist*, 18-79.

that focuses on the literary continuity of these segments in the story of Israel as it is now told by the deuteronomistic historian. Although this commentary will break the text into segments at logical points for convenience of discussion, the chief focus nevertheless will be on the final form in which these chapters (and, indeed, the whole of 1 Samuel) tell and interpret the story of Israel in this time of transformation.

1 Samuel 1:1–4:1a, Samuel and the Word of the Lord

OVERVIEW

These chapters provide a crucial introduction to the books of Samuel. In the story of a single family and an elderly priest at Shiloh, we are made aware of important events that will transform Israel's future and of a past way of life in Israel that will be no more. These chapters look back to the book of Judges and to the historical and moral limitations that have brought Israel to a moment of crisis. At the same time, they look forward to a future that God's transforming initiatives will make possible for Israel in the midst of crisis.

There are several distinct segments in these chapters. We hear the story of Samuel's birth (1:1-28), an account of the corruption of the priestly house of Eli at Shiloh (2:11-36), and a narrative that establishes the authority of Samuel in Israel as an alternative to the house of Eli (3:1–4:1a). But the song of Hannah (2:1-10) stands at the center of this section. It not only celebrates the grace-given birth of a child, but also it looks beyond that moment to celebrate the birth of a new Israel with a king as a grace-given possibility for Israel's future. The song of Hannah tells us that we are hearing more than the local stories of Elkanah's family and Eli's family. The events that link the fate of these two families will determine the future of Israel.

Of course, these chapters introduce us to Samuel as the key figure who will give leadership for the beginning of this period of crisis and transformation. This section begins with his birth as a gift of grace in response to Hannah's plea and vow (1:1-28), and it ends with Samuel fully established in Israel as a prophet of God's Word (3:19–4:1a). Yet, as important as Samuel is, these chapters even more importantly establish God as the One who will determine Israel's future. Samuel is an agent of God's sovereignty and initiative. Every segment of this opening section to the books of Samuel stresses God's role as the One whose will and word will shape Israel's new life. Samuel will play a key role, but it will be as the instrument of what God is doing in Israel.

The initial chapters of the books of Samuel focus on God's raising up of new leadership in Israel to meet the moral crisis created by the corruption of Eli's sons (2:11-36). It is significant that moral crisis takes priority over political crisis in the opening of the books of Samuel. We do not hear of the Philistines and the grave threat they represent to Israel's political future until chapter 4. Instead, the concern is initially for the lack of faithful and decisive leadership in Israel. The reader of the Deuteronomistic History cannot help connecting this lack of leadership to the violence and moral lack of direction that characterized Israel at the end of the book of Judges (e.g., the rape and murder of the Levite's concubine, Judges 19; the near genocidal war that follows, Judges 20–21; and the summary comment, Judg 21:25). God must raise up faithful leadership, first Samuel and ultimately David, before the political crisis of Israel can be resolved.

God begins Israel's transformation in this time of crisis not with great men and events, but with the distress of a barren woman. Such a beginning reminds us of the unlikely paths God's grace often takes, and it signals to us that the coming kingdom itself is to be understood as the gift of divine grace.

1 Samuel 1:1-28, The Birth of Samuel

COMMENTARY

The book of 1 Samuel opens with a localized story of dynamics in a single family, but this story is more than it seems on first glance. The story ends with the birth of Samuel and his dedication at Shiloh. Samuel is to play a central role in the transformation from a tribal Israel to an Israelite kingdom. Further, this family story introduces not only a main character in the story ahead but also many of the themes and issues that will mark the telling of that story.

On one level, 1 Sam 1:1-28 is a family drama. We meet the family of Elkanah and his two wives, Hannah and Peninnah. The tension in this family comes from the barrenness of Hannah. Although Elkanah loves Hannah and treats her with kindness, Peninnah taunts and provokes Hannah for her childlessness. With this situation as background, the focus shifts to Hannah. On a visit to the sanctuary at Shiloh, she prays fervently to the Lord for the gift of a child and vows to dedicate any such child to the Lord. The priest of Shiloh, Eli, observes her at prayer and, after initially mistaking her behavior as drunkenness, blesses the vow she has made. Subsequently, Hannah does bear a son to Elkanah and names him Samuel. After the child is weaned, she brings Samuel to Shiloh and leaves him there in service dedicated to the Lord. Throughout this family drama, God is the determining power. It is God who has "closed her womb" (vv. 5-6); it is God to whom Hannah prays and makes her vow (vv. 10-11); it is God whom Eli invokes to grant Hannah's petition (v. 17); it is God who "remembers" Hannah and grants her request (v. 19); and it is God to whom the child, Samuel, is given in service (vv. 27-28). God works providentially in the events of this story.

On another level, this story does more than simply get Samuel onstage. There are many ties between the telling of this family story and the wider story of Israel's journey to kingship and kingdom, which is the central focus of 1 and 2 Samuel. Robert Polzin has suggested that the situation in Elkanah's family is intended as a parable of Israel's situation at this moment in its history.[22] Hannah's anxiety over having no children, even though Elkanah loves her, parallels Israel's anxiety over having no king in spite of the care and love of God. The taunting of Peninnah, described as a rival (see Commentary on 1:6), suggests the taunts of Israel's neighboring "rival" nations, who have kings. The granting of a son to Hannah and the future granting of a king to Israel do not occur without conditions. The son (the king?) is to be dedicated to the Lord. Elkanah, who loved Hannah even without a child, voices the central condition that comes with all gifts of God's grace, whether child or king: "May the LORD establish his word" (v. 23). When Israel's first king, Saul, is later rejected from kingship, God tells Samuel it is because Saul has not "established my word" (1 Sam 15:11; NRSV, "carried out my commands"; NIV, "carried out my instructions").

The narrative of 1:1-28 contains several distinct elements. Verses 1-2 introduce us to Elkanah, Hannah, and Peninnah and state the central issue of Hannah's childlessness. Verses 3-8 serve as exposition, giving the reader information on the rivalry with Peninnah, the love of Elkanah, and the bitterness of Hannah that are necessary background to the story of Hannah's vow at Shiloh and her encounter with the priest Eli, which follows in vv. 9-18. This vow and the narration of its fulfillment (vv. 19-20) constitute the central focus of the chapter. What precedes is background exposition, and what follows in the final section—with the weaning, presentation, and dedication of Samuel (vv. 21-28)—suggests future implications for Israel flowing from Hannah's vow and its fulfillment.

1:1-2. Elkanah is introduced as an Ephraimite from Ramathaim. A later tradition in 1 Chr 6:27, 34 (MT 6:12, 19) makes Elkanah a Levite, but this may be a late attempt to give Samuel a proper priestly ancestry. Ramathaim is mentioned only here; Elkanah's hometown appears in v. 19 and in 2:11 simply as Ramah. In subsequent

22. Polzin, *Samuel and the Deuteronomist*, 18-30.

chapters, Samuel is associated with a town named Ramah in the tribal territory of Benjamin. These two places are probably not the same, but it is impossible to sort out the confusion with certainty. Elkanah's ancestor Zuph seems to give his name to both a clan (Elkanah is a Zuphite, v. 1*a*) and a geographic region (Saul's search for lost asses takes him to a land called Zuph, where he encounters Samuel, 9:5).

Elkanah has two wives. Monogamy was not yet established as the only acceptable practice, and many biblical figures had multiple wives (e.g., Abraham, Jacob, David). Hannah was the first wife, and Peninnah was the second (MT, "second"; NRSV and NIV, "other"). The main issue creating the drama in this story is stated simply and clearly at the end of v. 2: "Peninnah had children, but Hannah had no children." This note may imply that the reason why Elkanah took a second wife was to give him children and heirs, since Hannah remained childless. The names of the wives may connote something of their role in the story: "Hannah" (חנה *ḥannâ*) means "charming," "attractive," indicating her role as the wife Elkanah loves (v. 5); "Peninnah" (פננה *pĕninnâ*) means "fertile" or "prolific," indicating her identity as childbearer.

1:3-8. This section gives us background on the tensions among Hannah, Peninnah, and Elkanah that arose year after year on the occasion of a special pilgrimage to the sanctuary at Shiloh. It appears to have been an act of special devotion on the part of Elkanah, and not a pilgrimage as a part of a stipulated observance (1:3, 21). It was a time for family worship and sacrifice.

Shiloh, at this time, was a major sanctuary of the Israelite tribes and was the resting place for the "ark of God" (3:3). As such it is a place especially associated with the presence of the God of Israel, whom Elkanah worships here as the "LORD of hosts" or "Yahweh of the armies" (v. 3). This is a longer form of the proper name for Israel's God, which some have suggested may mean "one who creates [heavenly] armies."[23] This name may especially be connected with God as the warrior who fights for Israel against its enemies, as in the hero/heroine stories of the book of Judges or in the victory of Samuel through God's aid (1 Samuel 7).

The passing reference to Eli and his two sons, Hophni and Phinehas (v. 3*b*), foreshadows the significant role they play in the story a short time later (cf. 1 Sam 2:12-17).

This annual visit to Shiloh was a time when Hannah's childlessness became a particular burden. The distribution of meat from the sacrifice underlined her solitary state. While Peninnah and her sons and daughters would receive a large portion of the sacrifice, Hannah would be entitled only to her one portion. Elkanah would give Hannah a double portion out of his love for her (v. 5), but this surely only emphasized her isolation in a society where wives were valued when they bore children.

This situation was made worse by the taunting of Peninnah, whose provocation and irritation of Hannah, year after year, reduced her to tears and refusal to eat (vv. 6-7). Peninnah is described as a "rival" (צרה *ṣārâ*), a term seldom used in describing family relationships and often translated as "enemy" or "adversary" in describing relationships between peoples or nations. The choice of language here suggests that the relationship of Israel without a king taunted by its neighboring kingdoms may be reflected in the family tension between Hannah and Peninnah. The themes of barrenness and the rivalry between wives is known from the earlier biblical stories of Sarah and Hagar (Genesis 16), and Rachel and Leah (Gen 29:31–30:24), where these mothers and their sons also represent the relationships between tribes and peoples.

Elkanah appears in the midst of this conflict as a kind and well-intentioned man. He loves Hannah and tries to treat her with care (v. 5), but he cannot quite understand the depth of her despair. In v. 8, he pleads with her to eat and not be sad. He rather plaintively asks if his love is not worth more to her than ten sons. As we shall see, Hannah's answer to this question is no. She still desires a son, much as Israel will still desire a king in spite of God's love and care (1 Samuel 8). Elkanah may mean well, but he places himself, and not the plight of Hannah, in the central focus. He significantly does not tell Hannah that *she* is worth more to *him* than ten sons.[24]

23. See McCarter, *I Samuel*, 59.

24. See Yairah Amit, "'Am I Not More Devoted to You Than Ten Sons?' (1 Samuel 1.8): Male and Female Interpretations," in *A Feminist Companion to Samuel and Kings*, ed. A. Brenner (Sheffield: Sheffield Academic, 1994) 68-76.

Twice in this section the reader is told that "the LORD had closed her [Hannah's] womb" (vv. 5-6). On the one hand, this statement reminds us of God's ultimate power to determine all futures, whether Hannah's or Israel's. But, on the other hand, both of these statements describe Hannah's state by someone else. Others may see Hannah's barrenness as a sign of God's rejection. Elkanah loves her, though God has closed her womb; Peninnah taunts her, because God has closed her womb. Both lover and provoker treat Hannah as God-forsaken. It is eventually God's response to Hannah that will prove this to be a premature judgment.

1:9-18. Here we come to the heart of the story. The narrative moves from what happened year after year to the events of a particular year when Hannah left the sacrificial meal and "presented herself before the LORD" (v. 9). Such action probably occurred near the entrance to the sanctuary where the ark was housed, because Eli, the head of the priestly family that served the sanctuary at Shiloh, was seated there. In her distress and bitterness, Hannah has nevertheless taken the initiative to bring her case to God. She prays and makes a vow (vv. 10-11).

Hannah's vow (v. 11) appeals to the same "LORD of hosts" to whom Elkanah brings his annual sacrifice. She asks that God "remember" her, and her appeal is brought as one in misery, with only the lowly state of a servant before God. She assumes that the God of Israel might care for those hurting and without status, an assumption beautifully elaborated in Hannah's song in 2:1-10. The "God of armies" might also remember a distressed, childless woman like Hannah.

Her request is straightforward: She asks for a male child. But if she were to receive this gift of God's grace, she vows to give back to God the gift she receives. She promises to dedicate her son as a Nazirite. Nazirites marked their commitment by abstaining from wine or other strong drink and by never cutting their hair (v. 11*b*). Such vows of dedication did not usually last for a lifetime, as the regulations in Num 6:1-21 suggest. They did set aside individuals for unusual service to God, sometimes in military service. Samson is the chief biblical example of a Nazirite. Perhaps Hannah knew his story because Samson's unnamed mother,

too, was childless when God promised her a son and laid down the conditions of his dedication as a Nazirite (Judg 13:1-24). Samson's dedication was also to be lifelong, although as we know it did not turn out that way.

At this point, we discover that Hannah has been praying silently while moving her lips, and that Eli, who observed her, mistook this for drunken behavior and rebuked her (vv. 12-14), which initiated dialogue between them. Hannah responds with a passionate defense of her actions. It is not wine or strong drink, but her soul that she has been "pouring out" before God (v. 15). She admits to being a "deeply troubled" woman, a phrase (קשת־רוח *qĕšat-rûaḥ*) that Ahlstrom has proposed is better translated as "hard, obstinate or stubborn of spirit."[25] Hannah persists in her request for a child from God, an act that effectively foreshadows the persistence of Israel in its request for a king. Hannah further admits to "great anxiety and vexation" but begs of Eli that she not be counted as a "worthless woman" (v. 16). The word "worthless" (בליעל *bĕliyyaʿal*) appears later in 1 Sam 2:12 to describe the sons of Eli and in 10:27 to describe troublesome opponents of the kingship of Saul. It also describes the violent wrongdoers of Gibeah in Judg 19:22 and the power of chaos in Ps 18:5. What Hannah has requested out of her great anxiety will indeed have great effect on the future of Israel. Hannah's petition and vow have been laid in the hands of God.

Eli responds without ever learning the content of Hannah's vow. Perhaps he responds to the passion of her trust in God's grace. He simply announces a blessing on her request and sends her forth in peace (v. 17). His comment is as much an expression of confidence that God *will* respond to such a fervent and trusting petition as it is a hope that God will do so. Little does he realize what the child who results from this vow will mean to his own priestly family. Eli's language in this speech introduces the first two of seven uses of the verb "to ask" (שאל *šāʾal*) in this chapter. Instead of "the petition you have made," this expression might be rendered "the asking you have asked." This verb appears in the name of Samuel and his connection to Saul. It will be commented on further in relation to vv. 20 and 28.

25. G. W. Ahlstrom, "1 Samuel 1:15," *Biblica* 60 (1979) 254.

1:19-20. Hannah responds with a modest request to be viewed favorably by this priest who has mistaken her for a drunken woman, and then she returns to her husband. No longer sad, she has rested her future in God's hands. That trust is well placed. When Hannah returns home and has sexual relations with Elkanah, "the LORD remembered her" (v. 19). It is the precise fulfillment of the request Hannah had made in v. 11. She gives birth to a son and names him Samuel (v. 20). She explains this name by linking it to the verb "to ask" (*šaʾal*), which we have already noted in Eli's speech (v. 17). But Samuel's name (שמואל *šĕmûʾēl*) does not seem derived from this verb. It is Saul (שאול *šāʾûl*) whose name is drawn from the verb "to ask." This has led many previous commentators to suggest that this was originally a birth story for Saul and that at a later time Samuel displaced him in the story.[26] Such a view does not seem likely. There is little in this story that fits Saul's story in any way (i.e., different parents and home, no evidence of Saul's being dedicated to service at Shiloh). Perhaps the play on words here is instead intended to link the future of Samuel to that of Saul (see Commentary on 1:28).

1:21-28. Elkanah and his family returned to Shiloh for their yearly sacrifice, but Samuel is not immediately dedicated to God's service, as Hannah had vowed. Hannah does not go to Shiloh but asks that she might wait until the boy, Samuel, is weaned and reaffirms her intention to dedicate the boy as a Nazirite at that time (vv. 21-22).

Elkanah readily agrees but makes a statement that sounds an important theme for the opening of 1 Samuel: "Only—may the LORD establish his word" (v. 23). Elkanah alludes to the larger purpose for which the boy Samuel is to be dedicated. The issue of Nazirite vows is no longer in view. Samuel is to become a prophet, a mediator of God's Word to all of Israel (3:19–4:1a). In this role, Samuel is later to reject Saul as one who did not establish God's word (15:11). We become aware in Elkanah's statement that we are not simply beginning the story of Samuel, but the story of God's Word working through Samuel in Israel. The actual dedication of Samuel may occur after his weaning, but God's Word will not ultimately be stayed.

In due course, Hannah takes Samuel to Shiloh along with appropriate offerings and sacrifices (v. 24) and presents the boy to Eli. She identifies herself as the distraught woman with whom Eli had spoken (v. 25). She then uses the very words Eli had used in v. 17: "The LORD has granted me the petition that I made to him" (v. 27). The child Samuel is "the asking that I asked," once again returning to the verb *šāʾal*, "to ask." Further, she continues (v. 28) to link Samuel even more directly to this verb. The verb *šāʾal* can also have the meaning "to lend" in the sense of "requested" or "designated for a purpose." Hannah says, "I have *lent* him to the LORD," and further, "as long as he lives, he *is given* to the LORD." The form of this final verb is identical to the name of Saul (שאול *šāʾûl*). For as long as Samuel lives, "he is Saul to the LORD." This statement comes as a climactic conclusion to the chapter. Samuel is both requested from and loaned back to the Lord. But his future, as one dedicated to God, is inextricably linked with Saul, as we shall later see. It is not Samuel who has invaded a birth story of Saul; it is Saul whom the narrative has caused to invade Samuel's story, linking their futures together in God's purposes for Israel. Samuel, "as long as he lives," has no future that does not include Saul. Hannah has spoken her son's future, and with that, she leaves him in Shiloh "for the LORD" (v. 28b).

26. See, e.g., McCarter, *1 Samuel*, 62-63. For a discussion of the problems with this view and alternatives along the lines I have taken here, see John T. Willis, "Cultic Elements in the Story of Samuel's Birth and Dedication," *ST* 26 (1972) 54; and Polzin, *Samuel and the Deuteronomist*, 24-25.

REFLECTIONS

The books of Samuel begin with a salvation story. New life comes out of barrenness. Hope rises from hopelessness. Despair is transformed into thanksgiving and praise.

In 1 Samuel 1, the focus is on Hannah, a woman distraught over the limits faced by childless women in her world and taunted by a rival who has no compassion. By trusting her plight to God, Hannah claimed the new future God can make possible to those in barren, hopeless circumstances. Her story has roots in Israel's past. God had remembered Rachel, and she had been given a child (Gen 30:22). God had remembered the Hebrews in bondage in Egypt (Exod 2:24) and delivered them into new life as a people. Hannah opens her misery and need to God and asks for God to remember her.

Hannah's story also points to Israel's future. It is significant that a story that is to climax in the royal greatness of David begins in the bereft circumstances of Hannah. The future of Israel is to be a gift of God's grace as surely as Israel's past had been. Over and over again in the books of Samuel, God will find possibilities for new life and hopeful futures in persons and circumstances that seem impossible by human standards. Threatened by external enemies and internal corruption, Israel's future at the time of Hannah's story is bleak, but the birth of Samuel to a barren woman who boldly asks for God's grace gives hope that God can transform Israel's future even as Hannah's future is transformed—and Hannah's son, Samuel, is to play a central role in God's plan. God remembered Hannah; God will once again remember Israel.

If this is a story of God's grace for Hannah and for Israel, it can also be the story of God's grace for us. As persons of faith and as the church, we can learn from Hannah something of the dynamics of grace that might transform our futures and address the forms of hopelessness and pain that we face.

1. We can learn from Hannah the importance of expressing our need before God. Sometimes we are more intent on presenting a portrait of the vigor of our faith than in confessing our struggles, our anxieties, and our pains. This is true of individuals, congregations, and denominations. In our religious life, we admire positive thinking, goal setting, problem solving, and program planning. We often seem to believe that the right spiritual discipline, the proper church-growth program, or the most thoroughgoing strategic planning process will meet our needs. Hannah simply and straightforwardly expressed her need to God. In doing so, she recognized that wholeness in her life lay beyond those things she could control and rested in God as the larger reality of her life. Sometimes facing our needs as persons and as churches can open new possibilities, not of our making but of God's.

2. We can learn from Hannah the trustful persistence required to claim God's grace. Hannah boldly asked that God remember her. She prayed passionately, as a woman of "stubborn spirit" (see Commentary on 1:15), and she trusted that God's grace was available to her. There is an audacity to this persistent trustfulness that does not always fit well with the gentility of Sunday morning religion in the modern church. Some years ago, a well-known government official stopped attending a Washington, D.C., church that included a time for sharing of concerns before intercessory prayers. He claimed he did not come to church to hear people "let their guts hang out." There is a certain audacity to the insistence that God's grace is ours. Those who passionately express their hopeful claim on that grace may be judged unacceptable in their behavior, even as Hannah was judged by Eli to be drunk. The bold and passionate claim that God's justice is a promise for all people regardless of race issued in behavior by early civil rights advocates that many judged inappropriate and thus condemned.

God responded to the stubborn insistence of Hannah. Elkanah's love was not enough. She asked of God yet further expressions of grace, and God gave it. We will learn soon in 1 Samuel that the grace of God in the leaders of Israel's past was not enough. Israel insisted on a king, and God complied. In reading these stories, some might judge Hannah and Israel as audaciously ungrateful. Yet, Jesus spoke in praise of the persistent widow in Luke 18:1-8, and he urged his followers to persist in making their needs known to God in prayer. God has constantly created new possibilities of grace out of our stubborn insistence that God remember us yet again.

---

3. We can learn from Hannah that the proper response to the gift of God's grace is to give it back. If we attempt to keep it as a possession, we will lose it. Hannah knew this from the beginning and vowed to give back of the grace God might grant. When the time comes, Hannah's response teaches us something of proper response to the gifts of God. When the infant Samuel is weaned, Hannah returns to the sanctuary with offerings and sacrifices, and she dedicates the child to God.

When grace brings new life, we, too, must give back of the grace we have received. This will include worship, which is the giving back of grace as praise. It will further include dedicating the grace we have received to the service of God. In every generation there has been a need for some in the church to move beyond receiving grace to returning grace. The curious possibilities in the word שאל (šā'al) model the needed response. *What was asked* must become what is *lent back.* People and communities of faith must become less concerned over who and how many have received God's grace and more concerned with the ways in which God's grace is given back into God's service.

1 Samuel 2:1-10, The Song of Hannah

COMMENTARY

1 Samuel 2 begins by telling us that Hannah prayed, but what follows is not just a prayer but a hymn. Hannah sings! Her song is offered to us as the only appropriate response to her experience of God's wondrous grace. Hannah's song (2:1-10) is only loosely connected to the narratives that precede and follow it; nevertheless, on several different levels it serves an important role in these opening chapters of 1 Samuel.

First, these verses are a song of praise and thanksgiving by a barren woman whose womb has been opened. There is much in this hymn appropriate as a response by Hannah to the miracle that has issued in the birth of Samuel (chap. 1). The language of v. 1 is the language of personal praise to God, and Hannah gives praise for "my victory" (NRSV, reading with Qumran MSS; the NIV reads "your" with the MT). The "enemies" of v. 1b and the references to arrogant and proud speech in v. 3 can be read as references to Peninnah and her taunting of Hannah. Verse 5b speaks of God's reversal of fortunes to give the barren one seven children while one with many children is left forlorn. Although Hannah is later recorded as bearing only five more children (v. 21), her hope for seven (a common number representing completion and fulfillment) is appropriate at this point in the story. She has certainly experienced the reversal wrought by God's power, of which this verse speaks.

It has long been recognized, however, that the reference of this hymn is broader than the story of Hannah's barrenness and the birth of Samuel. Many have noted the similarities of language and style to Psalm 113 and other hymns of praise in the psalter. It may well be that Hannah's praise has been drawn from a pool of hymnic praise known to Israel in its worship traditions. This possibility has led many to treat Hannah's song as a late and secondary intrusion into the text. Even though Hannah's song may draw on wider doxological traditions in Israel, however, it functions here as a key text to introduce the whole of the books of Samuel by relating Hannah's new future to a new future opening up for Israel.

Thus a second level of meaning for the song of Hannah becomes available when we recognize that she sings not just as the mother of Samuel but as a mother of Israel. It is a song that moves from lifting high the horn of Hannah (v. 1a, NIV; NRSV, "strength is exalted") to lifting high the horn of God's anointed (the king, 10b, NIV; NRSV, "power of his anointed"). The song suggests hope for the movement of struggling, perishing Israel to established nation, which is the story of the books of Samuel. Hannah's singing further reinforces what we have seen foreshadowed in chap. 1: Samuel's birth is tied to the birth of kingship in Israel. Israel's fortunes, like Hannah's, can be reversed. Thus the song of Hannah is intended to broaden our horizons beyond that of Hannah's personal story. Her song speaks of a whole catalog of reversals that are possible through the power of God: weakness made strength, the lowly made exalted, the hungry filled, the poor made rich, the barren given children (vv. 4-8a). At the end of Hannah's song, God's anointed one, the king, is to be understood as the gift of God as surely as was the child whose birth is celebrated at the opening of the song.

Although many have commented on similarities between Hannah's song and Psalm 113, only a few have noted the remarkable similarity of language and theme with 2 Samuel 22 (which appears in almost identical form in Psalm 18).[27] The superscription to Psalm 18 says that David addressed this song of thanksgiving to God "on the day when the LORD delivered him from the hand of all his enemies and from the hand of Saul" (Ps 18). The whole saga of the books of Samuel is bracketed by the singing of Hannah and David. Hannah's victory, given by God, points forward to God's anointed one. David, God's anointed king, celebrates God's victory on his behalf, reflecting on the many obstacles he has overcome. Both songs stress the power of God to reverse apparently fixed human fortunes. Both Hannah's son, Samuel, and David must face conflict with Saul as God's failed king and their enemy. Again Hannah's song anticipates God's power to overcome such conflict, while David's song recalls such conflict already overcome. Seen in tandem with 2 Samuel 22, Hannah's song in 1 Sam 2:1-10 cannot be regarded as a mere intrusion into the flow of the narrative. Rather, it states doxologically the theological motifs that will dominate the whole of the story about to unfold in the books of Samuel. We shall expect to find these motifs echoed at various points throughout the story.

27. See R. A. Carlson, *David, the Chosen King* (Stockholm: Almqvist & Wiksell, 1964) 45-46; Childs, *Introduction to the Old Testament as Scripture*, 274; Walter Brueggemann, "I Samuel 1: A Sense of a Beginning," *ZAW* 102 (1990) 33-48; and Polzin, *Samuel and the Deuteronomist*, 31-34. Polzin includes a detailed chart of linguistic and thematic similarities. Randall C. Bailey, "The Redemption of YWH: A Literary Critical Function of the Songs of Hannah and David," *Biblical Interpretation* 3 (1995) 213-31, sees these bracketing hymns focused for exiles on a more hopeful aspect of God's character than the character of God displayed in the rest of the books of Samuel.

Finally, the song of Hannah should be understood as a witness to the central role of God's providence. Her song is a clear and unequivocal offering of praise to God, who is the power behind all of the events about to unfold, as surely as God was the power that opened the womb of Hannah. In the story of Hannah in chap. 1, and in all the episodes that will unfold in the chapters ahead, we will encounter the influence of remarkable men and women on the fate of Israel in the midst of extraordinary historical circumstances. Yet, central to the witness of 1 and 2 Samuel is the conviction that it is the presence of God with these characters and in the midst of this history that makes the crucial difference for Israel's future. Hannah's song celebrates and gives witness to this power of divine providence to create possibilities for the future that seem impossible through human and historical resources alone. Who would have thought there was a new future for Hannah? Who would think that Israel, as its plight unfolds in 2:11–7:2, has any future? It is the Lord (Yahweh) who is incomparable (v. 2), who knows and weighs (v. 3b), who reverses the fortunes of the strong and the weak (vv. 4-8a), who is the creator of the earth itself (v. 8b), who guards the faithful (v. 9a), who judges the earth (v. 10c), and who upholds the king (v. 10de). Behind the human drama and the historical circumstances of these stories in the books of Samuel lies the certainty of God's providential working. Hannah's song passionately affirms God's providential presence in human history.

2:1-3. The song begins in an intensely personal style more characteristic of songs of thanksgiving than the more generalized praise of hymns. This is appropriate to the setting as Hannah's passionate offering of praise for God's deliverance. She sings in v. 1 of "my heart," "my strength," "my God," and "my enemies," and speaks of the victory in which she rejoices.[28] Such praise is immediately followed by three statements about the incomparability of God (v. 2). There is no one like the Lord, the Holy One, the Rock. Hannah's personal joy depends on divine power, a power manifested in holiness and strength, a power worthy of worship but offering safety

28. The NRSV also includes "my victory" by adopting the reading from Qumran MSS. The NIV stays with the MT and reads "your victory," thus creating a contrast. It is Hannah's celebration, but it is God's victory.

in times of trouble. Hannah's singing gives praise to God as the source of her deliverance.

In the second phrase of the song, she uses a Hebrew idiom רמה קרני (*rāmâ qarnî*), literally, "my horn is raised" (v. 1a). This is a common metaphor in Hebrew poetry, used to evoke the image of a horned beast. The horn itself is a sign of strength; to "raise a horn" is to affirm power and dignity; hence, the NRSV abandons the metaphor and simply translates the image as "strength." The image of the horn appears in Hebrew literature as a sign of victory or success (e.g., Pss 89:17; 92:10), and it is sometimes used with specific reference to God's giving of children (see esp. 1 Chr 25:5, "All these were the children of Heman . . . in accordance with God's promise to raise up his horn," author's trans.). Such usage makes the image of the horn particularly appropriate for expressing Hannah's joy. The special significance of this image in Hannah's song is that what begins in v. 1 as the raising of Hannah's horn concludes in v. 10 with the raising of the king's horn. The power of God, which can make the barren woman rejoice in a child, can also transform threatened tribal Israel into a kingdom.

Verse 3 provides a warning. If Hannah rejoices, those who are inclined to pride or arrogance must beware. God both knows (presumably of such prideful and arrogant attitudes) and weighs actions (if such prideful arrogance is acted upon). In the light of Hannah's story, Peninnah's taunting and ridicule of Hannah come immediately to mind (1:6). But this hymn does not identify Peninnah, leaving the text open for us to consider all who might arrogantly oppose God's will or pridefully think they can control their own destiny apart from God.

2:4-8. In these verses, Hannah's song becomes a catalog of surprising reversals that are wrought by God's power. The recital is divided into two groups with dramatic effect. Verses 4-5 speak in passive voice of groups whose fortunes are reversed, but God is not named as the agent of these transformations. The text focuses on the strong who are made weak (the mighty, v. 4; the full, v. 5a) and the weak who are made strong (the feeble, v. 4; the hungry, v. 5a). Verse 5b reverses the order, beginning with the weak. This time the subject is the barren woman who is

given seven children, while the woman with many children is forlorn. The poem confirms Hannah's experience, given emphasis in this recital of God's power to transform the customary human realities. The number seven is probably an ideal number here and does not need to be reconciled with the five additional children Hannah later bears (v. 21). We might also observe that this first group of reversals begins with the "mighty" whose bows are broken (v. 4a). Perhaps this allusion foreshadows the reversal of fortunes that will bring David to the throne when Saul and Jonathan are killed in battle against the Philistines, with David mourning, "How the mighty have fallen" (2 Sam 1:19, 25, 27).

In vv. 6-8d, Hannah's song names the Lord as the power behind these reversals. The focus shifts from the hope of those in need of God's transforming power to a doxology in praise of the transforming One. An astonishing series of active verbs emphasizes God's power behind both negative and positive human experience. It is the Lord who "kills," who "brings down to Sheol," who "makes poor," who "brings low." The Lord also "brings to life," "raises up," "makes rich," "exalts," "raises up," "lifts," and "makes them sit and inherit." The positive list is longer, naming the "poor" and the "needy" as recipients (v. 8). Further v. 8cd describes the fate of these poor and needy people as sitting with princes and inheriting a throne. The poet points the reader ahead both to lowly Israel's taking a place among the kingdoms and to David as a shepherd and eighth son who nevertheless will be king.[29]

The identity of this God who can accomplish such reversals is revealed in v. 8ef. God is the Creator. The hope of Hannah and the hope of Israel are rooted in the same power that holds the cosmos aloft over the seas of chaos. God has placed the world on its foundations, and God is the Rock (v. 2b) on which those in need and without power can rely. Hannah has experienced the power of the Creator in her time of need, and she sings about it as the reality to which all in need may turn.

2:9-10. Moral implications flow from this recital. The God of these reversals is a God who distinguishes between the faithful

---

29. At this point, the LXX adds "He grants the vow of the one who vows," which would seem to give a more explicit reference to Hannah's story; but the LXX also omits much of the preceding verse. The NRSV takes note of this alternative in a footnote.

and the wicked (v. 9ab). Indeed, "the LORD will judge the ends of the earth" (v. 10c). The faithful are those who trust God's power to transform their lives and the social realities in which they live. The wicked are those who trust in their own might, power, and wealth. The list of groups whose fortunes are reversed in vv. 4-8d is here equated with the faithful and the wicked in the eyes of God. God will care for the faithful, but the wicked, God will "cut off in darkness" (v. 9b).

The last phrase of v. 9 serves not just as a conclusion to the verse, but also as a key to all of Hannah's song. It states a crucial principle for the story of Israel that unfolds in the books of Samuel: "For not by might does one prevail" (v. 9c). Human efforts to secure one's own destiny will not prevail apart from trust in what God is doing. In Hannah's song, all of the ways of human power can be reversed through the power of God: military might, wealth, family. It is God's power that endures.

At this point (v. 10a), the song bursts forth in an ecstatic cry of God's name—the Lord (Yahweh)![30] A series of phrases (v. 10a-c)

celebrates the power of God, who shatters adversaries, thunders on high, and judges the earth. Who can doubt that it is the power of such a God that prevails and not human might?

Finally, and rather surprisingly, the power of God so passionately celebrated is linked to the king. Hannah's song concludes in v. 10de by announcing that God will give strength to the king and raise the "horn" (NRSV, "exalt the power") of the anointed (מָשִׁיחַ *māšîaḥ*). God's investment in this king is underlined by the use of the possessive. It is God's king and God's anointed one. The song, which began by celebrating God's gift of a child to Hannah, anticipates the gift of God's king to Israel; and it is Hannah's son, the prophet Samuel, who will anoint Israel's kings, Saul (10:1) and David (16:13). As we shall see, the advent of kingship in Israel was controversial. But Hannah's song at the beginning of this story makes clear that God is at work in these events; there will be no king but that he is God's king.

---

30. The NRSV is to be preferred over the NIV, which has omitted the conjunction "for" or "because" that links the final phrase of v. 9 causally to the first two phrases. In v. 10a, it is unlikely that "LORD" can be read as an object the way the NIV has it. There are longer additions to v. 10 in the LXX and in 4QSam. The LXX addition is similar to Jer 9:23-24, and the Qumran addition is different but fragmentary. See McCarter, *I Samuel*, 69-70, for a full discussion of these textual problems.

REFLECTIONS

1. The song of Hannah is one of the Bible's most eloquent voices, testifying to God as the true source of transforming power. Its key line, "For not by might does one prevail" (1 Sam 2:9c NRSV), is a needed word in every generation, for it speaks to one of the most perennial of human temptations: the temptation to believe that we can control our own destiny and, perhaps, the course of history as well.

We live in a world that constantly evidences a belief in human might. Militarism, in its modern technological guise, has made the twentieth century the bloodiest century of human history; yet it is easier to raise budgets for weapons than for diplomacy. Consumer-driven market realities control our cultural preferences and appetites, and elections are influenced more by financial resources than by political ideas. Even at the personal level we live within a culture that worships self-fulfillment and the many programs to achieve it. Even in the church, energy seems too often directed to issues of membership growth, institutional maintenance, and popularity of programs than to discernment of what God is doing in the world.

The experience out of which Hannah sings offers hope to Israel and to us that a different reality is at work in the world from what we customarily acknowledge. Hannah's hope becomes hope for Israel and for us that power is not irrevocably tilted in favor of those the world defines as powerful—definitions that leave many powerless and without hope. Hannah sings of a God whose transforming power can reverse those patterns. She sings of a God who does not accept the world's power arrangements. She sings of a God whose might is not wielded in a disinterested fashion. God is heavily invested in the welfare of the weak, the powerless, the poor, the hungry, the dispossessed, the barren.

It is not accidental that Israel's hope for a king is voiced through the experience and the song of a barren woman whose petition has been heard. If God's transforming power for Israel takes the shape of a king, then Israel's king cannot be disinterested. Israel's king must be God's king, God's anointed one (1 Sam 2:10). The leadership of such a king must reflect the priorities of a God invested in those without power and might by the world's standards—those the world believes cannot possibly prevail. God's anointed one must serve the reversals of power about which Hannah sings (see Ps 72:1-4, 12-14).

This connection of anointed king to barren woman suggests that leadership in God's community in every generation cannot be either disinterested or self-serving. Leadership of God's people must reflect God's investment in the transformation of social realities that are biased against the weak, the poor, and the powerless. The church must identify with those who wait for God's reversals of grace. It is the surprising shape of God's power to which Paul points in 1 Cor 1:27-29:

> God chose what is foolish in the world to shame the wise; God chose what is weak in the world to shame the strong; God chose what is low and despised in the world, things that are not, to reduce to nothing things that are, so that no one might boast in the presence of God. (NRSV)

The raised horn of those who have been anointed to leadership in the church must be rooted in the raised horn of those who once were barren but are given new life in God's grace and power.

2. For Christians, the melody of Hannah's song is echoed in the song of Mary, known as the Magnificat (Luke 1:46-55). The strong similarities of language and theme have led many scholars to suggest that the song of Hannah was known to the Gospel writer. Both songs celebrate a wondrous birth, enabled by God's grace. Both songs preface and look to the coming of an anointed one (Messiah), although only Hannah's song uses this actual word. Both songs see the power of God as transforming power in behalf of the powerless.

Thus Mary, the mother of Jesus, is part of a long tradition. The mother of the Messiah (the "anointed one") for the church has an ancestry that includes the mothers of Israel, like Hannah. Many of these mothers, like Hannah and Mary, were singers. Miriam sang of God's deliverance in Exodus 15. Deborah sang of God's victory in Judges 5. These mothers were singers of new possibilities. They were singers of new communities and new power arrangements. The songs of mothers remind us that our story as the church is a part of what God has been doing since creation itself (1 Sam 2:8*b*), since the first giving of God's promise to raise up a people (Luke 1:55). The history of God's salvation does not originate with Jesus or with the church. The church is a part of the larger activity of God from creation onward. To be the community of Jesus as the Messiah is to be related to a God whose story is always larger than the church's story. It is to be related to a God whose transforming power on behalf of the powerless does not originate in Jesus Christ but was already known to Hannah and simply finds new expression in the song Mary sings for the church.

1 Samuel 2:11-36, Corruption of the House of Eli

COMMENTARY

After Hannah's song, the narrative resumes to begin the story of disaster facing the priestly house of Eli. The author identifies the corruption of Eli's sons and the abuse of the priestly office as the precipitating cause for the coming judgment of God against the house of Eli. The counterpoint to this story of impending disaster is a constant thread of attention to the rise of Samuel. In this story of corruption and doom, there is, nevertheless, a developing sense of anticipation for the new things in store for Israel, which God will do through Samuel.

The literary structure of this section seems very carefully crafted so as to contrast the wickedness of Eli's sons, Hophni and Phinehas, with the goodness of Hannah's son, Samuel.[31] The most fully developed portions of the story focus on the corruption of Eli's sons and the consequences that flow from their behavior. Verses 12-17 identify the past patterns of consistent and habitual abuse of the priestly office by Eli's sons. Verses 22-25 tell of an ineffectual attempt by Eli to curb their behavior. The sons ignore him, a response that characterizes the present lamentable state of affairs in the story. Finally, vv. 27-36 shift to the future disastrous consequences of this behavior for the house of Eli by means of an oracle of judgment brought to Eli by a "man of God."

A brief episode in the middle of the sorry story of Eli's sons concludes the prior story of Hannah (vv. 19-21). It brings closure to Hannah's story in ironic fashion, since Eli pronounces a blessing for her faithfulness even as his household is falling under a curse for its lack of faithfulness.

Threaded throughout this largely negative story are six short notices on Samuel's rise and growth in favor with God and people. They provide an understated counterpoint to the story of Eli's sons in this last portion of chap. 2 (vv. 11, 18, 21 *b*, 26), but they extend

into chap. 3, where they bracket a more fully developed story of Samuel as the vehicle of God's word (3:1, 19). Each of these notices of Samuel's positive development is immediately prefaced or followed by a comment about the sin and corruption of Eli's sons. The contrast is especially heightened by use of the Hebrew verb גדל (*gādal*), meaning to "become great" or "grow." Verse 17 notes that it was the sins of Eli's sons that "became great," while three of the five following references to Samuel note that he "grew up in the presence of the LORD" (v. 21 *b*), "in stature and in favor with the LORD and with the people" (v. 26), and as a man for whom God "let none of his words fall to the ground" (3:19 NRSV).

2:11-17. The narrative resumes with the notice that Elkanah returns home (Hannah is not mentioned), while Samuel, identified only as "the boy" (נער *na'ar*), stayed to serve the Lord under the tutelage of Eli (v. 11). The section ends by referring to Eli's sons also as "boys" (נערים *nĕ'ārîm*), but they are contemptuous of the Lord and have become great sinners in the Lord's eyes (v. 17). The term *na'ar* is here used as an indicator of subordinate status and not simply chronological age. Samuel must have been quite young, just beginning his service in Shiloh, whereas Eli's sons clearly were old enough to be given some priestly responsibilities. This section describes their failure in those responsibilities.

The account gives a harsh and unequivocating judgment. Eli's sons are not named (except to announce their death, v. 34), but their sinful behavior is carefully noted. They are identified as "scoundrels" (בליעל *bĕliyya'al*, v. 12; NIV, "wicked men"), a title Hannah disavows when she pleads with Eli not to think her a "worthless woman" (1:16). Eli's sons have achieved this dubious status by showing disregard for the Lord (v. 12*b*) and for the duties of priests (v. 13*a*).

Verses 13*b*-14 describe the customary practice of providing the priests' portion at Shiloh, while vv. 15-16 detail the abuse of this practice (this is made clearer in the NIV translation). Ordinarily, while the meat was

31. This view is opposed to those that see the Samuel material in this chapter as separate and redactional. See John T. Willis, "Samuel Versus Eli: I Sam. 1-7," *TZ* 35 (1979) 201-12, for a detailed defense of the unity of this chapter and, indeed, the whole of 1 Samuel 1–7.

boiling, a fork would be thrust in and whatever it brought out would go to the priests. Eli's sons, however, would send a servant to insist on a choice cut from all of the meat, including the fatty portions, which were specially reserved for dedication to the Lord. Further, they insisted that their choice be made before it was boiled so that the priests could roast the choicest portions for themselves. If Israelites objected to this arrogant behavior, hoping at least to burn the fatty portions before the Lord, they were threatened with violence (v. 16). The narrative affirms that such practices are contemptuous and constitute great sin in the eyes of God (v. 17).

2:18-21. The failure of Eli's sons in their priestly duties is followed by a notice concerning Samuel's education as a priest. The "linen ephod" he wore is not to be confused with a more elaborate outer garment also called an ephod and worn by priests (see v. 28). The white linen fabric here is elsewhere associated with priests and angels. David wears a "linen ephod" when he dances before the ark (2 Sam 6:14).

This notice about Samuel's clothing bridges to a brief account of the small robe Hannah would make and bring to Samuel each year. Verses 19-21 bring closure to Hannah's story. Eli blesses her; she then has five additional children. Soon the story will announce the death of Eli's children (v. 34). The verb שָׁאַל (šā'al) is used again to describe Samuel as the "gift" or "asking" that Hannah has now "lent" to the Lord, a play on words that, we have seen, ties the fate of Hannah's son Samuel to Saul, Israel's first king (see Commentary on 1:20, 27-28). A final notice of Samuel's growth in the presence of God (v. 21b) signals a return to the story of Eli's sons and their growth in sin.

2:22-26. A poignant encounter unfolds. Eli has heard of his sons' despicable behavior. Indeed, he has additionally heard that they are having sexual relations with women serving in the sanctuary (v. 22). He attempts to confront them. Using strong words, he calls their actions "evil dealings/wicked deeds" (v. 23), informing them that their actions are widely known (v. 24) and making clear that such acts constitute sin against God (v. 25). But he speaks to no avail. They will not listen (v. 25b). Eli, who is very old (v. 22a; 4:15

reports him to be ninety-eight), cannot exercise authority over these wanton sons. Perhaps this confrontation between father and sons has come too late.

The final phrase of v. 25 is difficult to understand: "for it was the will of the LORD to kill them." The text assumes that the coming deaths of Hophni and Phinehas are encompassed in the will of God for Israel at this time in its life. As surely as God is bringing something to birth for Israel through Hannah and Samuel, God is the power that will bring Eli's sons to the death their sin has made necessary. The description of the sins of Eli's sons makes clear that they have chosen this particular path. The path of corruption represented by Eli's sons must end so that something new can begin for the life of Israel.

Verse 26 makes it clear where that new life is emerging. Even as we learn from Eli's words to his sons that their evil reputation has spread among the people (v. 24), we hear that Samuel is growing in favor not only with God but also with the people. This notice of Hannah's son is particularly reminiscent of a later comment—about Mary's son in Luke 2:52.

2:27-36. A "man of God" appears before Eli and pronounces a prophetic oracle of God's judgment on the house of Eli. Many have suggested that this speech came from the hand of the deuteronomistic historian (Dtr). Particularly toward the end of this speech, the perspective shifts from the immediate events that will involve Samuel and Eli's household to concerns for the priestly office in Solomon's Temple. Such a perspective would be consistent with Dtr's wider view in telling the whole story of Israel. Dtr elsewhere uses programmatic speeches at crucial points to clarify the direction and perspective of his theological view of history (see esp. the speech by a "man of God" to Jeroboam in 1 Kgs 13:1-3). Certain phrases are characteristic of deuteronomistic vocabulary—e.g., "do according to what is in my heart and in my mind" (v. 35).

This speech may indeed reflect the broader interests of Dtr, but it also plays an important and carefully crafted role in the flow of the surrounding narrative. The deaths of Hophni and Phinehas are announced. The beginning of the end is at hand for the priestly house of Eli and for Shiloh. Samuel will be the immediate successor to Eli's authority in Israel, even if Dtr gives us a glimpse over a longer term.

This speech is a classic example of a prophetic judgment speech. It opens with the use of the messenger formula ("Thus says the LORD . . ."), making clear that the "man of God" is speaking for God. The first half of the speech provides an accusation in which the sin of Eli's house is made clear (vv. 27-29). Signaled by "therefore," the oracle moves to an announcement of judgment against Eli's house (vv. 30-36). There is no narrative conclusion to the chapter. It ends abruptly with the conclusion of the speech.

As is customary in prophetic speech, God speaks in the first person through the "man of God" to Eli. God reminds Eli that his priestly service may be traced back to the time of bondage in Egypt, when Eli's ancestor was chosen to be priest (vv. 27-28). Three priestly duties given to that ancestor and his descendants are named: "to go up to my altar, to offer incense, to wear an ephod," and in return certain offerings were given to the priests (v. 28). Many think the ancestor intended here is Moses and that Eli is a part of a Mushite line of priestly authority that could trace its genealogy to the time of the Israelite bondage in Egypt; "Hophni" and "Phinehas" are Egyptian names.[32] Eli is simply reminded that he holds office and authority by God's designation, handed down through generations of Eli's ancestors. Moreover, that designation assumes the faithful discharge of the lineage's priestly duties.

In the context of these expectations as God's priest, Eli is charged with abuse of his priestly office in relation to sacrifices and offerings and with honoring his sons more than God (v. 29). Perhaps Eli's sons were the prime offenders, but God's judgment charges Eli with complicity in their apostasy. Did Eli also eat the choice parts pirated from worshipers? Could he have done more to stop such behavior? However, it is now too late; the speech moves to the pronouncement of judgment for the contempt shown to God.

God acknowledges the making of a promise to Eli's ancestor that his line should serve God as priests forever (v. 30a). However, God also declares that only those who honor God can be honored by God. Those who despise God can only be treated with contempt (v. 30b). God's promise does not offer an unconditional guarantee of privilege. God promises to return honor for honor and contempt for contempt. The consequences are dire. No one in the entire priestly family of Eli will live to old age (vv. 31-32). This priestly house is to end.

There is one exception, and here is where the horizon of Dtr broadens beyond the immediate story of Eli and Samuel and the coming kingship. One will be spared, but even he shall eventually die weeping and grieving (v. 33). The other members of Eli's house will die violent deaths. It is widely agreed that this verse alludes to Abiathar and his survival from Saul's massacre of the priests at Nob (22:6-23). Abiathar becomes high priest, along with Zadok, under David; but in the purge after Solomon takes the throne, Abiathar is deposed and banished (1 Kgs 2:27). The sign to Eli that these events shall come to pass will be the deaths of his sons, Hophni and Phinehas, on the same day (v. 34). This brings us back to Eli's family, and the fulfillment of this sign is recorded in 4:11.

Again, in vv. 35-36, the longer view of Dtr asserts itself. God promises to raise up a "faithful priest" to do what is in God's heart and mind and to serve "before my anointed one forever." God promises to build a "sure house" for this priest (a phrase reminiscent of the sure house God promises to establish for David in 2 Sam 7:16). Most scholars believe this statement is a reference to Zadok and Solomon's designation of Zadok and his house as the permanent priesthood of the Temple in Jerusalem. Priestly house and royal house become closely linked. The Zadokite priesthood is generally thought to trace its ancestry to Aaron rather than to Moses. Dtr may be commenting on later post-exilic priestly conflicts. Verse 36 is puzzling, but it may indicate later descendants of Eli's house (through Abiathar?) who were forced to beg for bread from the Temple. Scholars have suggested that this may reflect the later menial and subservient status of Levites at the Temple (see Deut 18:6-8; 2 Kgs 23:9).

32. The history of priestly office in Israel is a complex subject, and some of these genealogical claims may be attempts to justify authority among later priestly groups. See the discussion in Richard D. Nelson, *Raising Up a Faithful Priest: Community and Priesthood in Biblical Theology* (Louisville: Westminster/John Knox, 1993) 1-16. The view of a Mushite connection to Eli still rests largely on the work of Frank M. Cross, "The Priestly Houses of Early Israel," in *Canaanite Myth and Hebrew Epic* (Cambridge, Mass.: Harvard University Press, 1973) 195-215.

REFLECTIONS

Any preaching or teaching from 1 Sam 2:11-36 will bring the reader face to face with the issue of God's judgment. This is a story of sin and its consequences. Many North American Christians are not very comfortable with these themes. Optimism, positive thinking, joyful possibility—these sound so much more promising for an attractive, upbeat faith. Stories like this one come as a shock.

How do we make sense of the notion that God's promises can be abrogated or rejected? God made a promise forever to Eli's ancestor (2:30), but God cancels the promise because Israel has treated God with contempt. There are consequences to the contempt of God, and in this story the consequence is death. We in the church like to think of ourselves as recipients of God's promise. Could our sin lead to the cancellation of that promise?

We are shocked by the statement at the end of 2:25, "It was the will of the LORD to kill them" (NRSV). This does not mean that God desired their deaths. But God must exact the consequences of sin. In general, the Bible does not deal with this difficult theme in a rigid or mechanistic way. God does not determine the actions of Eli's sons. God does not choose the moral course that leads to death, but the death Hophni and Phinehas bring upon themselves is from God because God will not rescue them from the consequences of their own sin. Nor can we expect guarantees for life if we make death-dealing moral choices. The promise inherent in life itself can be broken if we render it meaningless. An old spiritual sings, "God gave Noah the rainbow sign; no more water, the fire next time." God's promises are not given with immunity from God's judgment. We can refuse the grace inherent in God's promise, and the consequence may be death.

The God angrily confronting Eli is no warm, fuzzy God. We cannot speak of the grace of God, seen growing in Samuel, without acknowledging the wrath and judgment of God, exacting consequences for the sins of Eli's sons. To preach this text is to acknowledge that moral choices as leaders in God's community do have something to do with life and death. Relationship to God is demanding and dangerous. Those who would serve God place themselves under both God's grace and God's judgment—not just under God's grace. This would certainly alter concepts of ordained ministry in an age where too many see the role of pastor or priest as only a job or a profession. Perhaps this episode concerning Eli's sons can help us to reflect on the risky business of leadership in God's community. To treat leadership roles in self-serving ways is to treat God with contempt, and there might be more at stake than a job.

1 Samuel 3:1–4:1a, The Call of Samuel

COMMENTARY

This chapter, traditionally labeled "The Call of Samuel," does more than that title suggests. It authorizes and legitimizes Samuel as the only source of God's Word during the oncoming period of radical dislocation and transformation in Israel. Simultaneously it provides the final word of judgment on and removal from authority of the priestly house of Eli (although we have had previous word of this in 2:27-36). The chapter begins with Samuel as a boy, learning from Eli, and it ends with Samuel as God's prophet (3:20), replacing Eli as the authority at Shiloh (3:21).

3:1. This verse reintroduces us to the cast of characters, Samuel and Eli, and suggests that the main focus of the reader's concern should be on the rarity of God's word. No longer a child, Samuel has become a young man in the service of the Lord under Eli at Shiloh. The text has carefully noted the progress of Samuel's growth and service (1 Sam 2:11, 18, 21, 26). He has learned from Eli, gained favor with the people, and, most important, matured in the presence and favor of the Lord. All this prepares him for his transformation to a new role of leadership.

Eli has just received an extended pronouncement of judgment on his priestly house from an unknown prophet (1 Sam 2:27-36). We must read chap. 3 under the shadow of this judgment, waiting to see how the Lord will provide for leadership in Israel when the priestly leadership at Shiloh has failed so utterly. Nevertheless, as the chapter opens Samuel is still serving "under Eli."

The central issue of this chapter is introduced in v. 1*b:* The "word of the LORD" is rare, and "visions" have become uncommon in Israel. Consequently, what is about to happen to Samuel is unusual and prepares us for his unique role. Verse 7 explains that, during the night, Samuel was experiencing the "word of the LORD," but he did not know it. In v. 11, Samuel does receive the Lord's word, and in v. 15 the experience is described as a "vision." In the person of Samuel, the situation of v. 1*b* is about to be reversed. The chapter closes with an extended notice of Samuel's new role as the channel of the Lord's word in Israel (3:19–4:1*a*). This special concern for the word of the Lord and the authorization of Samuel as its medium is consistent with the theological concerns of the prophetic editor whom many scholars believe had a crucial role in the shaping of 1 Samuel (see the Introduction).

3:2-18. This narrative gives an account of Samuel's revelatory experience at Shiloh. Although these verses are usually described as the call of Samuel, they do not show the typical pattern of a prophetic call narrative. There is neither a formal commissioning of Samuel to be a prophet nor the typical expression of a prophet's unworthiness for the call (cf., e.g., Isa 6:1-13). This passage is better understood as a theophany, a report about God's appearance in the human world. This account would seem to have much in common with Egyptian and Mesopotamian theophanic narratives of religious functionaries who sleep in a shrine in order to receive a

dream or visionary message from the deity.[33] First Samuel 3 serves less to call Samuel as a prophet than to inaugurate him as a prophet, mediating the word of the Lord.

The story of Samuel's theophanic experience falls into three distinct parts: vv. 2-9 describe the initial setting and experience in which Samuel does not recognize the approach of the Lord; vv. 10-14 report the Lord's message to Samuel; vv. 15-18 tell of Samuel's reluctant reporting of the message to Eli. Although Samuel is the central figure in the story, Eli plays an important role in each segment as well.

The story takes place during the night in the temple (tent sanctuary) at Shiloh. Samuel is sleeping near the ark of the Lord (v. 3), while Eli is lying down in his usual place, presumably somewhere outside the inner temple precincts (v. 2).

We are told that the "lamp of God had not yet gone out" (v. 3). At its most literal level, this expression may indicate the time prior to dawn. Priestly protocol called for the burning of lamps in the sanctuary from evening to morning (Exod 27:20-21). But this phrase may convey multiple levels of meaning. As Polzin has noted, this story opens with the vocabulary of sight and insight.[34] *Visions* are infrequent. Eli's *eyesight* is growing dim; he cannot *see.* The *lamp* has not yet gone out. This visual vocabulary prepares us for an ironic contrast. The boy Samuel sleeps near the ark, which is a source of divine presence and illumination, but he cannot perceive what is really happening, whereas the priest Eli, nearly blind and sleeping apart from the divine presence of the ark, finally perceives that the Lord is speaking to Samuel. In this context, the expression "the lamp of God had not yet gone out" may refer both to the near extinguishing of divine vision in Israel (v. 1*b*) and to the waning of Eli's literal vision as well as his role as a priestly source of spiritual vision (v. 2).

33. Some continue to defend this chapter as a modified call narrative, following the position of Murray Newman, "The Prophetic Call of Samuel," in *Israel's Prophetic Heritage*, ed. B. W. Anderson and W. Harrelson (New York: Harper & Row, 1962) 86-97. More convincing seem the treatments of those who see the chapter as a theophanic narrative: e.g., Ralph W. Klein, *1 Samuel,* WBC 10 (Waco: Word, 1983) 31; Michael Fishbane, "I Samuel 3: Historical Narrative and Narrative Poetics," in *Literary Interpretations of Biblical Narratives*, vol. 2, ed. K. R. Gros Louis and J. S. Ackerman (Nashville: Abingdon, 1982) 192.

34. Polzin, *Samuel and the Deuteronomist,* 49-54.

Three times God calls Samuel, and each time he runs to Eli, presuming the old priest has summoned him (vv. 4-8). We need not think, as some commentators have suggested, that Samuel is unusually naive or dense. He is still a youth and living in a time when the word and vision of the Lord are rare. In fact, the text goes to unusual lengths to suggest that Samuel has no basis on which to recognize the Lord's summons. Verse 7 tells us that Samuel did not yet *know* the Lord, nor had the word of the Lord been *revealed* to him. Since Samuel has been ministering under the instruction of Eli at the Lord's sanctuary in Shiloh, we may presume that Samuel knew something about the Lord, but that he had not yet had revelatory experience of the Lord. Therefore, it is not reasonable to expect Samuel to recognize what is taking place.

When Samuel comes to Eli a third time, the old priest *perceives* "that the Lord was calling the boy" (v. 8*b*). The blind priest *sees* what is taking place, whereupon Eli gives Samuel a proper response to make (v. 9).

Verses 10-14 record the full content of the divine revelation to Samuel. The climactic moment follows the three futile calls. Together they form an emphatic number sequence (cf. Num 22:22-33; Amos 1:3, 6, 9, 11, 13). Samuel makes the response suggested to him by Eli, but he omits the explicit use of the divine name (v. 10), perhaps reinforcing the notice of v. 7 that Samuel does not yet *know* the Lord.

At this point, the Lord "came and stood" before Samuel, indicating a visionary as well as an auditory experience. The message of the Lord begins with the announcement that the Lord is "about to do something in Israel that will make the ears of everyone who hears of it tingle" (v. 11; see the same expression in 2 Kgs 21:12; Jer 19:3). The divine word to be pronounced bears immediate significance for the house of Eli. Simultaneously, it announces a divine action that will be recognized by all who hear of it as a turning point in God's relationship with Israel.

God pronounces a word of judgment on the priestly house of Eli. The wording of v. 12 recognizes that judgment has already been pronounced on Eli's family in 2:27-36. This new word confirms and makes irrevocable that judgment. Once again it is clear that Eli

himself is not corrupt or unfaithful. His sons have engaged in despicable and corrupt activities, and Eli has not been able to "restrain" (כהה *kāhâ*) them (v. 13). Standard Hebrew lexicons give the meaning of this word as "rebuke," and some translations (e.g., NEB) have followed this meaning. However, this meaning surely cannot be correct, since Eli did "rebuke" his sons (2:22-25). The NRSV and the NIV both follow the suggestion that this word is related to a root meaning "to be weak," thus in this text meaning "to restrain" or "to weaken." Eli rebuked his sons, but he could not control them. The judgment is harsh: Eli and his entire priestly lineage, once promised authority forever (2:30), are now to be "punished" (NRSV; NIV, "judged") forever (v. 13). This judgment cannot be ritually averted either by sacrifice or by offering (v. 14).

Unlike the previous announcement of God's judgment against the house of Eli, there is no mention of survivors (2:33) or successor priestly houses (2:35). The emphasis here is less on this divine word of judgment as news to Eli than on the inauguration of Samuel as the prophetic recipient and proclaimer of the divine word.

In the final section of this story (vv. 15-18), Samuel must communicate the Lord's harsh word of judgment to Eli. He delays until morning, afraid to face Eli with this difficult judgment (v. 15). The statement that Samuel "opened the doors of the house of the Lord," which may have been his usual duty, takes on new meaning, since Samuel is opening a new means of access to God's word in Israel.

Eli takes the initiative by calling to Samuel, and he softens a difficult moment for Samuel by gently addressing him as "my son." Ironically, Samuel makes the same response ("Here I am") that he made in the night when he mistakenly thought Eli was calling him (v. 16). Eli instructs Samuel to report his experience, leaving out nothing. When Samuel does so, Eli wins our admiration by the integrity of his forthright response (v. 18). The aging priest again identifies the source of this revelatory word: "It is the Lord." He then gracefully accepts the divine verdict. Although he knows that the consequences of his sons' sins have fallen upon him personally and on his whole house, he can nevertheless respond in terms of acceptance rather than self-interest. God knows what is good even though this means relinquishment and loss for Eli and his family. It is remarkable that, in spite of Eli's inability to control his sons, he is never described in these chapters as personally culpable or lacking in integrity and faithful intent. God's way into the future for Israel will not include Eli, but Eli acknowledges the priority of divine will over his own. The roles of Eli and Samuel have now been reversed. It is Eli who looks to Samuel for instruction in the word of the Lord. Eli's authority has ended, but Samuel's has just begun.

3:19–4:1a. The real climax of this passage comes in the final notice that identifies Samuel as the Lord's fully authorized prophet. The first half of 4:1 functions as the concluding word to this unit rather than as the opening word to the ark narrative that follows. (The LXX has a much longer reading for this verse, which includes mention of the continued wickedness of Eli's sons.) The situation described in 3:1 has changed. The word of the Lord is no longer rare, but reliably present in the midst of Israel through Samuel.

Verse 19 implies that Samuel has grown to adulthood, but in sharp contrast to 3:7, the Lord is now present with him and lets "none of his words fall to the ground." Samuel's words prove reliable and trustworthy. Indeed, we are told that this reputation stretched the length of the land, "from Dan to Beer-sheba" (3:20). But this reputation is now identified with a definite role. All of Israel knows Samuel to be "attested as a prophet of the Lord" (3:20; the NRSV inexplicably changes the verb into an adjective, "was a trustworthy prophet . . ."). Samuel is a נביא (*nābî'*), the Hebrew term for "prophet." The narrator in 2:27 was reluctant to use this formal term for the "man of God" who gave the oracle of judgment to Eli. In 1 Samuel, this term is reserved for Samuel, the Lord's prophet.

With great irony, 3:21 reports that the Lord continued to appear at *Shiloh*. Although the place remains the same, the reader is aware that a great change has been made. What had been the ritual center under the leadership of Eli has now become the center for the prophetic word under the leadership of Samuel.

An interesting pattern appears in the concluding lines of this account. The Lord continues to give Samuel revelatory experience "by the word of the Lord" (3:21*b*; the NIV reduces the divine name to a pronoun, "through his word."). The following clause states that "the word of *Samuel* came to all Israel" (4:1*a*). This progression is a telling comment on the way in which a prophet mediates the divine word. The prophet may be the channel through whom God speaks, but one should not confuse the divine word with the prophet's words. God's word comes to the prophet, but the prophet must pass that word on in his own words. The prophet speaks *for* God, not *as* God.

REFLECTIONS

1. In the church's use of this text the focus has almost always been on 3:2-10 as a simple story of God's call and the way in which we often fail to recognize it. In such traditional use, the passage becomes a generalized story of God's calling and the need for discernment so that we do not mistake God's voice for the human voices of authority that surround us.

Although this reading depends on a legitimate element of the story, it ignores the fact that God's call did not come to Samuel—nor does it come to us—in general circumstances. This is not a narrative of Samuel's general religious awakening. It is not simply another experience on the road to religious maturity. Samuel is called by God in a time of spiritual desolation, religious corruption, political danger, and social upheaval. The word of the Lord is rare; the sons of Eli are corrupt; the Philistines are about to threaten Israel's survival; the pressures to move toward kingship will soon grow to overwhelming.

If the context for Samuel's experience is harsh, so too is the message he is told to bring. We sometimes celebrate so-called mountaintop religious experiences as ends in themselves, without considering what the God we encounter in religious experience demands of us. Samuel is called to deliver a harsh message of judgment that is necessary if there is to be a hopeful new beginning for Israel in this trying time. There is no time to dwell on childlike faith experiences. The call is to a prophetic task. The text will not allow us to dwell on the theophanic experience as an end in itself. This text reminds us of the spiritual challenges and social transformations that God's call brings. We are urged not only to discern God's voice but to listen to what it asks of us as well. We are called to become the channel for God's prophetic word to our own time.

2. First Samuel 3:1–4:1 *a* reminds us of God's constant presence in the endings and the beginnings of human history. This is a story of endings. The people despair at the corruption of Eli's sons and the failure of leadership in a crucial time. But the message of this story is that corrupt institutions and oppressive practices need not endure. God opposes them. In the harsh word of judgment given to Samuel for Eli is the hopeful proclamation that God will not acquiesce to evil. This has already been anticipated in doxological terms by Hannah's song in 2:1-10. It now finds concrete historical reality in God's announced end to the house of Eli.

Eli's calm and faithful acceptance of this harsh word is itself a model of faith in difficult circumstances. He is not the central cause of corruption in the order God will sweep away, but he is invested in that order. He, too, will pay a price in God's judgment on his sons. Historically the church, too, has found itself invested in corrupt orders it did not entirely create. Accepting God's judgment in times of social transformation and spiritual challenge involves us in the pain of Eli's complicity and calls us to reflect his trustful willingness to let God "do what is good."

But this is also a story of new beginnings. To dwell on the judgment of Eli's house is to fail to rejoice in God's initiative to raise up new prophetic leadership. We cannot mourn so deeply what seems to be passing that we miss the signs of what God is bringing to birth: "There is a chance for newness, and that chance is rooted in Hannah's piety, in Israel's daring doxology, in Eli's yielding, in Samuel's availability, in God's resolve to do a new thing."[35]

God's new beginning is not just the stirring of a boy's religious sensitivities. The chapter opens with the absence of God's word and ends with the proclamation of God's word through Samuel. The story opens with corrupt and discredited religious leadership in place and closes with new and vigorous leadership, recognized by all Israel. We are being prepared to recognize that, in the difficult days of social upheaval ahead for Israel, there is already a new beginning: God's initiative for new possibilities in spite of the failure and the passing away of old patterns. The movement of Samuel is from messenger of God's word of judgment for Eli to ongoing prophet of God's word for all Israel. Those who read this text need to see the link between the proclamation of endings and the provision for ongoing leadership that enables God's new beginnings. It will not be enough to proclaim judgment without taking responsibility for what lies beyond judgment.

3. This story reminds us that the divine word is often mediated through human words. In our efforts to discern God's will, we recognize in this story the need for community. First Samuel, then Eli, and finally all Israel requires the mediation of others to hear and understand God's word for their lives.

With humility, we realize that, like Samuel, we may not ourselves recognize the call of God. It may be others, like Eli, who discern the divine presence first and name the divine name so that we may be enabled to respond. This text calls for openness to seeking the advice and wisdom of others who might aid us in discerning God's call.

35. Brueggemann, *First and Second Samuel,* 27.

In fear and trembling, we understand with Eli that the harsh words others may speak in criticism of our practices may be the word of God's judgment. The person through whom such words of judgment are mediated may be as unlikely as an apprentice sleeping in the sanctuary, but the word delivered is nonetheless the word of God. The response demanded of us may be as difficult as Eli's relinquishment of vested interest to trust in God's will. We are challenged by this text to recognize that God's word for us sometimes comes harshly, and asks of us difficult choices.

In gratitude, we recognize with all Israel the continuing presence of God's word in our midst, and we give thanks for God's prophets who bring us hope as well as judgment. God's word requires prophets, but this text reminds us that the two cannot be confused. God's word comes to Samuel, but Samuel's words come to all Israel. This is a foundation stone in understanding the preaching task in the life of the church. Our words rest on faithful discernment of God's word, but they will never be identical to God's word. Humility is an appropriate posture as we respond to the call to mediate God's word. Further on in the story, we may have occasion to wonder whether Samuel has remembered this. Nevertheless, we are reminded in this text of the necessary mediation to the community by those who audaciously receive the gift of God's word and attempt to communicate it in their own words.

1 Samuel 4:1*b*–7:1, The Philistine Crisis and the Capture of the Ark

OVERVIEW

First Samuel 4:1 *b*–7:1 provides an abrupt change of scene and focus. Chapter 4 tells the story of a Philistine military campaign against Israel. Not only is Israel defeated initially, but when the ark of the covenant, a sacred symbol of the presence of Yahweh, is brought onto the field to ensure victory, it is captured, and Israel suffers an even greater defeat. The sons of Eli are killed, and Eli himself dies in shock at the news of the ark's capture. In chap. 5 we have an account of what happens while the ark is with the Philistines, and chap. 6 tells how the Philistines finally sent the ark back to Israelite territory. The entire story stresses the ultimate sovereignty of the Lord (Yahweh) over the Philistines and their gods despite appearances to the contrary in the initial defeat of Israel.

Since the work of Leonhard Rost, most scholars have viewed 1 Samuel 4–6 as a separate story, usually referred to as the "Ark Narrative."[36] In this view, the main character of

chaps. 4–6 is the ark of the covenant itself. This ark narrative concludes in 2 Samuel 6 with the story of David's finding and installing the ark in Jerusalem. This narrative was written in the late Davidic or early Solomonic period to legitimize the Davidic dynasty by associating it with the ark, which was a sacred symbol of God's presence during the time of the tribal league. Then the ark narrative was incorporated into the later Deuteronomistic History. Most scholars think its presence there is somewhat intrusive.

Recent studies have raised some serious alternatives to this view. Patrick D. Miller and J. J. M. Roberts[37] have argued forcefully that an original ark narrative included the portions of 1 Samuel 2 that deal with the corruption of the house of Eli. They argue that this original narrative did not include 2 Samuel 6 and that it dates prior to David's defeat of the Philistines. The account stresses the hand of Yahweh as an expression of divine power and encourages trust in God's control of events even

36. Rost, *The Succession to the Throne of David.* Anthony h Campbell, *The Ark Narrative (1 Sam 4–6; 2 Sam 6): A Form-Critical and Traditio-Historical Study,* SBLDS 16 (Missoula, Mont.: Scholars Press, 1975), represents a development of Rost's classic view and contains an excellent history of research on these chapters.

37. Patrick D. Miller and J. J. M. Roberts, *The Hand of the Lord: A Reassessment of the "Ark Narrative" of 1 Samuel* (Baltimore: Johns Hopkins, 1977).

in a time of apparent defeat. Robert Polzin[38] is representative of recent literary studies of the books of Samuel that are little concerned with the early history of the text. He stresses the interconnections between chaps. 4–6 and the surrounding material in 1 Samuel 1–7 and discusses the role these chapters might play in the larger Deuteronomistic History addressed to exiles in Babylon. He finds these interconnections so numerous and so skillfully made that he sees little value in speculating on the prior existence of an independent ark narrative.

It seems likely that these chapters did have a separate history. Even the casual reader has the sense of an abrupt change with chap. 4. Samuel, whose birth and future leadership have dominated chaps. 1–3, drops entirely out of the story. With no introduction, the Philistines are threatening the future of Israel. Events rather than characters occupy the attention of the story. Although the deaths of Hophni and Phinehas serve in the present arrangement of 1 Samuel to fulfill the words of the man of God to Eli in 2:34, chap. 4 itself makes nothing of this. In fact, chap. 4 does not reflect any anti-Elide sentiment or suggest that the death of Eli's sons (or of Eli himself) had anything to do with their sin. Chapter 2, with its careful counterpoint between Samuel and the sons of Eli, seems too much a literary unity to support the suggestion that the ark narrative originally included the anti-Elide portions of the chapter (contra Miller and Roberts).

Although 1 Samuel 4–6 may have had a separate literary pre-history, these chapters have been artfully incorporated into the context of 1 Samuel 1–7 and into the larger purposes of the Deuteronomistic History. To perceive these interconnections as skillfully created does not necessitate the suggestion of a single author (contra Polzin), but can be seen as a tribute to the skill of a historian who utilized a variety of materials to produce a telling of Israel's story for the sake of a generation in exile. The story of Israel's early loss of the ark would have been of obvious interest to exiles who had lost the ark in the destruction of Jerusalem (with Polzin). Although we may see evidence of earlier source materials

used by the historian and make observations about them, our primary emphasis must be on the story of Israel in this transformative period as it is now told in the full text before us.

We can now make some observations about the nature of the narrative material in 1 Samuel 4–6 and about the way in which this narrative segment now functions in its present position in the books of Samuel. Miller and Roberts have made an especially important contribution to the study of these chapters by their investigation of numerous texts from the ancient Near East that chronicle the capture of a nation's gods in battle and their subsequent return.[39] Taking images of gods as spoils of war was common, as was displaying them in the victorious nation's temple. Frequently these images were returned. Miller and Roberts cite texts that interpret such events not only from the point of view of the victor but also those that speak from the perspective of the defeated. For the victor, such events demonstrated the superiority of their gods. Told from the perspective of the defeated, it was important to reaffirm the sovereignty of their god and to assert that even the defeat was an act of their god's will, perhaps out of anger with the people. The eventual return of the image was understood as having been compelled by the god's desire to return and not by the magnanimity of the enemy.

Miller and Roberts make a convincing case for understanding the ark narrative in 1 Samuel 4–6 as an account of a disastrous defeat and the capture of the ark from the point of view of an Israel trying to understand how this could have happened. The account seeks to interpret events theologically by seeing the "hand of Yahweh" in the entire course of events. God has allowed the defeat and the ark's capture (chap. 4); in captivity, the ark serves as the vehicle for Yahweh to humiliate the Philistines and their god Dagon (chap. 5); and God's power ultimately brings the ark home to Israel (chap. 6). Although events appear to suggest otherwise, the ark narrative makes clear that the Lord (Yahweh) was always the determinative power behind the course of events. Within 1 Samuel 4–6 it is not made clear what motivated Israel's God to allow such a defeat. However, the placement of the ark narrative in 1 Samuel

---

38. Polzin, *Samuel and the Deuteronomist*, 2-8, 55-79. See also John T. Willis, "Samuel Versus Eli: I Sam. 1-7," *TZ* 35 (1979).

39. Miller and Roberts, *The Hand of the Lord*.

1–7 suggests an answer to this question: It was the corruption of the priestly leadership of Israel in the house of Eli at Shiloh.[40] The deuteronomistic historian has artfully used the ark narrative to play an important function not only in the immediate context of 1 Samuel and the story of the rise of kingship in Israel but also in the larger context of the Deuteronomistic History as a narration of Israel's story addressed to exiles.

In 1 Samuel 1–7 everything points toward the emergence of kingship in Israel. First Samuel 1–3 introduced the reader to the internal factors that contributed to the need for kingship. The priestly house of Eli at Shiloh had become corrupt. Yet, God was at work. Samuel was born as the gift of God to Hannah, and he was raised to be given authority as God's prophet, replacing Eli at Shiloh as the trustworthy representative of God in Israel (3:19–4:1*a*). Chapters 4–6 now introduce the reader to the external factors leading to kingship in Israel. The Philistines have defeated Israel and have captured the ark. There is a danger that political autonomy and identity for Israel may be swallowed up permanently by this enemy. But the message of the ark narrative is that here, too, God is at work. God is still in control of these events, allowing the capture of the ark (chap. 4), humiliating the Philistines and their god Dagon (chap. 5), and motivating the return of the ark to Israelite territory (chap. 6). In their present arrangement, these two segments are tied together by the deaths of Eli and his sons in 4:12-18. These deaths now function as the fulfillment of God's judgment on the corruption of the house of Eli, announced by both the unnamed man of God (2:27-36) and Samuel (3:11-18). As we shall see, chap. 7 brings together these internal and external forces that move Israel toward kingship.

Samuel meets the Philistines, and the Philistines are defeated. Once again, God is at work, using the prophet Samuel, who replaced Eli, to meet the external threat of the enemy. The perspective of this story seems to be that kingship was coming, but that it was not really needed. God was at work dealing with the internal and the external crises.

In the larger framework of the Deuteronomistic History the ark narrative may have a special significance for the community of exiles to whom that history was addressed. The exiles had also suffered defeat and lost the ark. They could not fail to identify with the plight of Israel when the ark was captured by the Philistines. This connection to the experience of exile seems explicit in the naming of Phinehas' son by his dying wife in 4:21-22, "The glory has *gone into exile* from Israel" (author's trans. גלה [*gālâ*]; the NRSV and the NIV use the less descriptive "departed"). The "glory" (כבוד *kābôd*) refers to God's own being and is strikingly similar to the image in Ezek 10:18 for the departure of God's glory from the Temple in the exile experience. Chapters 5–6 of the ark narrative, which emphasize the continued sovereignty of God, the humiliation of the enemy, and return to the land, would be especially hopeful for exiles who read this history, trusting that God was also continuing to be active on their behalf. For exiles who read 1 Samuel 4–6, the message is that God continues to be at work even in apparent defeat. For exiles, kingship has ended, but God's sovereignty has not. In this larger deuteronomistic context, kingship has come and gone. First Samuel 4–6 may suggest that kingship had not really been needed. God's sovereignty is sufficiently reliable.

In the commentary below we will look more closely at each of the distinct episodes in the drama of the Philistines and the ark.

---

40. It is not necessary to include portions of chap. 2 in an original ark narrative (as do Miller and Roberts) in order to observe this connection in the present arrangement of 1 Samuel 1–7. An original ark narrative may have included some other motivation for Yahweh's action or none at all. See Willis, "Samuel Versus Eli," 204-7.

1 Samuel 4:1b-22, The Philistines, the Ark, and the House of Eli

COMMENTARY

This chapter is divided into two distinct segments. The first segment (vv. 1*b*-11) tells the story of a Philistine attack on Israel. After an initial defeat, the elders of Israel decide to bring the ark of the covenant onto the field of battle. Although fearful, the Philistines do battle again. The defeat of Israel is catastrophic, and the ark itself is captured. The remainder of the chapter (vv. 12-22) offers a detailed response to the disastrous news of the defeat and capture of the ark. The priest of Shiloh, Eli, dies in shock upon hearing that his sons are dead and the ark has been taken, and his daughter-in-law dies in childbirth.

4:1b-11. Abruptly the Philistines enter the story. Nothing in chaps. 1–3 has prepared us for this external threat to Israel. The Philistines gather for war at Aphek, a site east of modern-day Tel-Aviv, while the Israelites gather to meet them at Ebenezer (probably a different site from the Ebenezer of 7:12). No motivation is given for the battle. This account is not interested in political history. We know of animosity between Israelites and Philistines from the stories of Samson in Judges 13–16. Moreover, throughout the books of Samuel the Philistines are among the chief adversaries of Israel until David's decisive victories over them (2 Sam 5:17-25). In the ark narrative, the Philistines are treated as a general threat to Israel's security and well-being.

The Philistines were a people who established themselves on the coastal plain to the southwest of Israelite territory as a part of an invasion of sea peoples in the late thirteenth century BCE. They became the ruling class of the Canaanite population, already settled in the coastal plain, and were largely associated with the five great cities mentioned in 6:17. Some of the accounts of conflict with Israel found in 1 and 2 Samuel suggest that the Philistines had ambitions to expand their territory at the expense of the Israelite tribes (e.g., the suggestion in 1 Samuel 13–14 of Philistine garrisons in Israelite territory).

The first section of chap. 4 has a symmetrical (chiastic) structure.

vv.1*b*-2	first defeat by the Philistines
vv.3	speech of the elders of Israel
vv. 4-5	bringing of the ark to battle
vv.6-9	speech of the Philistines
v.10	second defeat by the Philistines; capture of the ark

The ark stands at the center of this account, and its fate will be the main concern of chaps. 5–6. The speeches on either side of the appearance of the ark concern Israelite and Philistine perceptions of what the ark symbolizes about Israel's God.

In the initial skirmish, Israel is defeated with a loss of four "thousands" of men. It is widely agreed that the Hebrew term for "thousand" (אלף *'elep*) designates a tribal or a military unit of an indeterminate size.[41] The loss is probably fewer than fifty men. This first defeat is a humiliation but not yet a disaster for Israel.

When the elders of Israel hear the report of this battle they immediately have a diagnosis of the situation (v. 3): The Lord has caused their defeat. The situation can be remedied by bringing the "ark of the covenant of the LORD" from Shiloh. Then, God will "come among us and save us from the power of our enemies." The problem for the elders is no more than the need to have God present at the scene of battle. The reader, however, has information not apparent to the elders. When we hear in v. 4 that Hophni and Phinehas are to carry the ark into battle, we suspect that the defeat might have more to do with God's judgment than with God's absence, and this judgment is not yet complete.

In v. 4, the people send to Shiloh and bring "the ark of the covenant of the LORD of hosts, who is enthroned on the cherubim." This lengthy epithet for the ark implies that

41. See McCarter, *I Samuel,* 107, for a fuller discussion.

it functioned in several ways in Israelite tradition. The ark was a box or chest that served as a repository for the tablets of the law given to Moses on Mt. Sinai (Exod 25:21; Deut 10:3-5); thus it was called the "ark of the covenant" (e.g., Josh 3:6) or the "ark of the testimony" (e.g., Exod 25:22). Further, the ark was the sign of the enthroned presence of Yahweh. It was regarded as a throne pedestal above which Yahweh was invisibly enthroned. Thus the ark could be referred to as God's footstool (1 Chr 28:2; Pss 99:5; 132:7; Lam 2:1). God's invisible throne was flanked by winged cherubim, part animal and part human figures known to us from Canaanite iconography, in which the god El is depicted on a throne supported by cherubim. Usually kept in the sanctuary (during this period at Shiloh), the ark symbolized the royal presence of Yahweh in the midst of Israel. But the ark was also fitted with rings and poles to make it movable (Exod 25:12-13), and it played a special role in Israel's holy wars. It was carried into battle to ensure that Yahweh would be present and fight on behalf of Israel (see Joshua 6:1 and the ark's crucial role at Jericho). In v. 3, the elders clearly understand the presence of the ark as the key to deliverance from their enemies, the Philistines. The title "Lord of hosts" (יהוה צבאות *YHWH ṣĕbā'ôt*, v. 4) is a reference to this military role of the ark and might be rendered "Lord of the armies."

When the ark arrives in the Israelite battle camp, the army raises the prolonged ritual shout associated with holy war (תרועה *tĕrû'â*), whereupon, the earth itself trembles (v. 5). This noise has the desired effect: When the Philistines hear the roar, they respond anxiously over this turn of events.

The Philistine speech initially demonstrates the dread that falls upon them. They are startled by the ritual outcry coming from the camp of Israel (whom they refer to as "Hebrews," probably a somewhat pejorative designation, v. 6). Informed of the arrival of the ark, they interpret this as the arrival of "gods" in Israel's camp. "Woe to us! For nothing like this has happened before," they cry (v. 7). They despair at their chances before the "power of these mighty gods" (v. 8). The Philistines may be intentionally portrayed as ignorant of Israelite belief, since the use

of the plural "gods" suggests that Israelites were polytheists. This statement makes their next utterance even more remarkable. It is the Philistines who draw a parallel with the great moment of Israelite deliverance in the exodus. It is the Philistines who confess exodus faith (v. 8*b*). They know of the plagues with which Yahweh struck Egypt, although they suggest that this happened in the wilderness and, again, was done by "gods." They are informed but not entirely accurate in their information. Nevertheless, it is the Philistines who alert the reader to exodus parallels and possibilities (a theme to which the Philistines return in 6:6).

The tide seems to be turning toward Israel. The ark is present; the shouting is invoking terror in the enemy; the God of exodus is at work. But the Philistines do not respond as expected. They do not retreat in panic. They admonish themselves with calls to have courage, to "be men and fight" (v. 9). They will not be slaves to Israel, suggesting that this was what Israel had been to them. This may indicate an oppressive history between Philistines and Israelites behind the story, but it is not of central concern in the telling of this story.

The outcome of a second battle is reported with devastating economy (v. 10). The verbs dominate: "fought," "defeated," "fled," "fell," "captured," "died." Both armies fight, but Israel is defeated. It is Israel's army that flees, not just retreating but dispersing and going home. Thirty "thousands" of Israelites have fallen (see Commentary on 4:2). The ark is captured; Hophni and Phinehas die. This last notice prepares us for the shift of scene to Shiloh in v. 12.

The account simply reports the outcome of the battle, but the dilemma left in the wake of battle is theological, and not just political. The ark had been present. The elders assumed that God would be present as well. Yet, the outcome was again defeat. This could mean that Israel's God was powerless, but subsequent events (chap. 5) will demonstrate that this is not the case. The theological crisis of these events arises out of the recognition that defeat must have been the will of God.

4:12-22. The scene shifts to Shiloh, opening with a messenger's arrival from the battlefield. We are immediately made aware of Eli, the priest at Shiloh, as the focus of this account. He sits anxiously beside the gate, waiting for news, and his anxiety is not for his sons but for the ark (v. 13). The messenger has torn his clothes and placed dirt upon his head, traditional signs of grief; but Eli is ninety-eight years old and blind, so he cannot see these visible signs of bad news (v. 15). When he first enters the city, the messenger gives the news, and the city cries out (v. 13). Eli hears this outcry and asks about its meaning.

The messenger's report to Eli is remarkably similar to the report given to David of Saul's death in 2 Sam 1:1-4, also by a messenger who arrives with torn clothes and dirt on his head (cf. esp. 1 Sam 4:16-17 with 2 Sam 1:3-4). In each case, the messenger refers to his recent escape from the battle, is asked about the situation, reports a defeat and scattering of the army, and brings news of the death of two persons in the battle. Verse 17 also reports the capture of the ark. In chap. 4 the defeat of Israel foreshadows a later time when the future of Israel will be in jeopardy. The enemy is the same, but the consequences quite different. The one signals the end of the house of Eli, but the other marks the rise of the house of David. Israel may be defeated, but God's purposes for judgment or grace will go forward.

To our surprise, Eli does not respond to the news of his sons' deaths. It is at the news of the capture of the ark that he falls from his seat, breaks his neck, and dies (v. 18). The ark narrative itself makes no connection to the statement by the man of God to Eli that the deaths of Hophni and Phinehas would be the sign of God's eventual judgment against the whole of the house of Eli (2:34). We as readers are left to make that connection. We are positioned to understand the events of chap. 4 as a part of God's judgment, although chap. 4 itself displays no interest or awareness of this theme.

The final phrase of v. 18 reports that Eli "judged Israel forty years." We would not have thought to number Eli among the judges of Israel. He appears in 1 Samuel 1–4 solely as a priest at Shiloh. This note is probably an effort of the deuteronomistic historian to incorporate Eli into the chronological scheme of his history. To Dtr, all of the leaders in Israel before the start of kingship were understood as judges and their years were reported, usually in round numbers of forty or twenty (see the book of Judges).

The final episode of this chapter (vv. 19-22) gives us a brief and poignant human vignette, used to make a theological comment on the meaning of these events. An unnamed woman, identified only as Eli's daughter-in-law and the wife of Phinehas, is pregnant. The tragic news of the capture of the ark and the deaths of Eli and Phinehas brings on labor (v. 19). It does not go well, and she is near to death, but she gives birth to a son (v. 20). We presume that she dies, but not before naming her son "Ichabod." Although the precise derivation of the name is uncertain, the mother interprets the name to mean "the glory has departed from Israel" (v. 21), which refers specifically to the capture of the ark (v. 22). The verb used here means "to go into exile" (גלה *gālâ*), and "glory" (כבוד *kābôd*) refers not to the ark itself but to the presence of God enthroned over the ark. God has gone into exile. It is an image reminiscent of Ezekiel's vision of God's glory departing from the Temple over the mountains (Ezek 10:18). It seems like the end of the story for Israel. The Philistines had invoked exodus imagery, but this seems like a reverse exodus: God departs, leaving Israel in bondage. It is well to remember that this material, although speaking of events near the end of the twelfth century BCE, is part of a larger history work addressed to Babylonian exiles. We can imagine a particularly sharp identification of exiles with this moment in the story, which would also make subsequent developments in chaps. 5–6 of special interest to those readers.

REFLECTIONS

The end of chapter 4 focuses the central question raised here for Israel and for every generation: How do we maintain faith when "the glory has departed"? What becomes of our trust in God when God appears to be absent or impotent? It is a perennial question of human experience. For Christians, it is the question of Good Friday, the moment when human hope seems lost forever in the suffering of the cross, and Jesus himself cries out with the words of Ps 22:1, "My God, my God, why have you forsaken me?"

The story of 1 Samuel 4 suggests for our initial reflection on this unfolding drama (we must remember that this is only the first episode in a longer ark narrative) both a false and a hopeful response to this question of the absence of God. Clues to these responses are found in the contrasting speeches of the elders of Israel (4:3-4) and of the Philistines (4:6-9).

1. In the response of the elders of Israel to the news of the first defeat by the Philistines we see the danger of equating the presence of God with the material trappings of religion. It is easy to mistake our symbols for the God to whom they point. The elders of Israel assumed that the presence of the ark would ensure God's presence, and that that presence would take the form of a victory. Perhaps exiles reading this tale through the work of the deuteronomistic historian would have thought of a similar attitude toward the Temple as a guarantee of God's presence and Israel's security (see the temple sermon in Jeremiah 7). Modern readers of this story would do well to ponder the ways in which we tend to equate the presence of God with impressive buildings or furnishings, with burgeoning memberships, or with popular programs. In response to perceived "enemies" of the church, we are likely to wheel out these evidences of success as testimony to God with us.

The witness of this opening episode in the ark narrative is that trust in symbols alone is misplaced trust. It is a form of idolatry. A pastor recently confided to me that a catastrophic fire that had destroyed a large and imposing church building may have been the best thing to happen to that congregation in some time. "We discovered that the building may have been distracting us from some of the things God had in mind for us."

The tragedy for Israel, and perhaps for us, is that idols must sometimes fail for us to see what we have done. The failure of the ark was a national tragedy with painful consequences. Likewise, confrontation with our misplaced trust is often painful. Cherished programs and beloved buildings must sometimes be lost in order for us to see that the presence of God is not defined by such things.

2. It is, perhaps, an intentional irony that it is the Philistines who give us the clue to a more faithful and hopeful response in times of the apparent absence of God. In their somewhat panicked, not quite accurate way, they nevertheless point us to the exodus tradition. While the elders of Israel trust in the ark, the Philistines remind us to remember how the presence of God has been made known in the past. In the face of defeat, it is the enemy who voices the memory of exodus and God's deliverance from bondage in Egypt. The Philistines voice what they do not fully understand, but they remind us of the importance of reclaiming our own exodus memory.

It is from exodus memory that Israel and the church have discerned a pattern of exodus faith, claimed and reclaimed by countless generations. In situations of distress we, like Israel at the sea, despair of hope for any way into the future. Death seems about to have the final word; we can see no possibilities for life. It is the faith growing out of the experience of those who walked through the midst of the sea to new life, that through God unexpected deliverance is made available. In God there is always a way into the future and a further word of life to be spoken over against the apparent finality of death.[42]

In 1 Samuel 4, death seems to have spoken a final word—the four "thousands," the thirty "thousands," Hophni and Phinehas, Eli, the unnamed wife of Phinehas,

42. Bruce C. Birch, *Let Justice Roll Down: The Old Testament, Ethics, and Christian Life* (Louisville: Westminster/John Knox, 1991) 131-32.

the hopes of Israel—all dead! Exodus faith believes this is not the final word, and the Philistines remind us to remember. Perhaps it is significant that the chapter ends with a birth. It is a shadowed birth in ominous circumstances, but it is new life in the midst of death nevertheless. Exodus faith urges us to trust that in God death is never the final word, but life has a further word to speak. In 1 Samuel 4, it is not yet clear what that word of new life might be for Israel, so the chapter ends with the necessity of trustful waiting—trust that God is not finished yet with Israel. It is a word to us as well. In times when God seems absent, we are called to trustful waiting because we know of the exodus God. With the prophet of the exile we can affirm that "those who wait for the Lord shall renew their strength, they shall mount up with wings like eagles, they shall run and not be weary, they shall walk and not faint" (Isa 40:31).

1 Samuel 5:1-12, The Ark with the Philistines

COMMENTARY

Although Israel has been defeated by the Philistines, the message of this chapter is that the Lord (Yahweh) has not. The theme of chap. 5 is the power of the Lord. This theme is emphasized by the repeated use of the phrase "the hand of the Lord/God" (vv. 6, 7, 9, 11). In all four instances, the "hand of the Lord/God" is exercised against the Philistines as a demonstration of the power of Israel's God, Yahweh. Use of "hand" (יד *yād*) in this way indicates strength, might, or power. By contrast, the Philistine god Dagon loses his hands in this episode (v. 4). Further, three times the author states that the "hand of the Lord" is "heavy" (vv. 6, 7, 11). The word "heavy" in vv. 6 and 11 is from the same root as the word "glory" (כבד *kbd* ; v. 7 uses another root [קשה *qšh*], also meaning "to be heavy"). In 4:21-22, the "glory" had departed from Israel, but now this same *kābôd* ("glory," "heavy") is evident in the Lord's power against the Philistines. The account of chap. 5 makes clear that God has not been vanquished or lost power. Rather, the course of events serves God's purposes.

This episode of God's power unfolds in two stages. First, there is a drama in which the Lord (Yahweh) defeats the Philistine god Dagon (vv. 1-5). Then there is an account of the affliction of the Philistines with a plague of tumors, which progresses from one Philistine city to another and leaves the Philistines urging that the ark be relinquished (vv. 6-12).

5:1-5. The Philistines carry the ark of the covenant triumphantly to Ashdod (v. 1), one of the five principal cities of Philistia, located roughly in the center of Philistine territory, close to the sea. They install the ark in a temple for the god Dagon and place it next to Dagon's image (v. 2). This portion of the ark story seems to regard Dagon as the primary god of the Philistines (see also Judg 16:23; 1 Chr 10:10), but his background is Semitic. The Philistines probably adopted his worship along with other practices of the essentially Canaanite population they ruled. Dagon was present in the pantheon of a number of ancient cities (e.g., Ebla, Mari, Ugarit), and in the Ugaritic texts he appears as the father of Baal. The name "Dagon" is related to Semitic words for "rain clouds" and "grain," fitting connections for a fertility god. The temple of Dagon in Ashdod was later destroyed by the Hasmonean ruler Jonathan in 147 BCE (1 Macc 10:83-84; 11:4).

It was a common practice in the ancient world to carry off the image of the god of a vanquished enemy.[43] Although the ark was not an image of Yahweh, the Philistines' reaction in 4:5-9 shows their awareness that the ark symbolized the presence of the Israelite deity. To place the ark next to the image of Dagon in his temple would certainly indicate the submission and perhaps defeat of Yahweh by Dagon; it may also have reflected the incorporation of Yahweh's power as a subordinate deity into Dagon's sovereignty. The superiority of Dagon over Yahweh was made visible in the ritual sphere, even as

---

43. See Miller and Roberts, *The Hand of the Lord*, for discussions of ancient Near Eastern parallels to the practices reflected in this chapter.

Philistia had defeated Israel in the political sphere. These Philistine expectations were not, however, to be fulfilled.

On the first morning after the installation of the ark in the Philistine temple, the people of Ashdod found the image of Dagon lying face down before the ark (v. 3). It must have been a shock to find the great Dagon in a posture of obeisance and submission before the "ark of the covenant of the Lord of hosts" (4:4 NRSV). They put Dagon back in his place. When they rise early on the next morning and come to Dagon's temple, they again find his image face down before the ark, but this time his head and his hands are broken off and are lying on the threshold of the temple (v. 4). Dagon is "reduced to a stump, without a head for thinking or hands for acting."[44] The text provides a dramatic portrait of a vanquished Dagon. He is rendered helpless before Yahweh. Perhaps Dagon's hands on the threshold even suggest that he made a futile attempt to escape, or perhaps that the demons and spirits sometimes said to guard thresholds (in this instance to a sacred place) could not help him. Almost as an aside, the story includes an etiological note (v. 5), citing this event as the reason why priests and others do not step on the threshold of the temple of Dagon in Ashdod. In any event, a great reversal has taken place. The one apparently without power has proved powerful; the one thought to have been defeated has emerged victorious. The reader is reminded of Hannah's song in 2:1-10 and its celebration of God's power to make such reversals. Lest there be any doubt, the story moves from Dagon rendered powerless without hands to an account of the heavy hand of the Lord against the Philistines.

5:6-12. The biblical author mentions the hand of the Lord four times in this section (vv. 6, 7, 9, 11). This image of the power of God is now directed against the Philistines, who had dared to challenge that power. Dagon, their god, has been exposed as helpless and ineffectual. The consequences fall upon the Philistines, who now are without protection.

A plague of tumors breaks out among the people of Ashdod (v. 6). The Septuagint and the Vulgate include a longer version of v. 6, which most recent commentators and a number of recent translations have adopted as the preferred reading (the NIV includes it in a footnote). The addition to v. 6 might be translated: "Mice [or rats] swarmed up from their ships, and the mice [or rats] went into their land. Then there was a deathly panic in the city."[45] This reference to mice or rats in the longer text makes sense of the symbolic golden offerings of tumors and mice sent back with the ark in 6:4-5, 11. They are offerings intended to ward off a plague in the cities associated with mice (or rats) swarming out of Philistine ports into the cities.

The Hebrew word translated here as "tumors" (עפלים 'ŏpālîm) means "hill," "mound," or "swelling." Since Martin Luther, most commentators have associated these tumors with the bubonic plague. This dreaded disease takes its name from its most visible symptom, the growth of inflamed tumerous boils called "buboes." It is also well known that bubonic plague was associated with the fleas that infested rodents as carriers of the disease and often spread through rodents on ships in port cities.[46]

For the ark story, however, the ultimate cause of this plague is the hand of the Lord. Plague is one of the ways in which God's power and judgment on enemies are expressed in the Hebrew tradition (see 2 Samuel 24:1; Hab 3:5). The Philistine references to the exodus tradition in 4:8 and 6:6 would certainly prompt the reader to remember the role of plague in the exodus drama as well (see esp. Exod 9:15-16). In the ancient world, widespread disease was usually considered to be of divine origin. With Dagon defeated and a plague upon them, it is not surprising that the Philistines quickly turned to appease Israel's God by returning the ark to Israel.

An assembly of the lords of the Philistines is hastily convened (v. 8). Each of the five Philistine cities was ruled by a lord, and in times of crisis they acted in concert. The people of Ashdod say that the ark cannot remain

---

44. Klein, *1 Samuel,* 50. Miller and Roberts, *The Hand of the Lord,* 46, also note a reference in the Ugaritic texts to the goddess Anat wearing a girdle of hands from vanquished enemies and with their heads hanging down her back.

45. See McCarter, *1 Samuel,* 119-20, for a full discussion of the textual problems here.

46. Apparently the term used in the Septuagint can indicate not only the swelling of a hill or a tumerous growth but also the buttocks. This led the Jewish historian Josephus (*Antiquities of the Jews* 6.3) to associate the plague here with dysentery. The MT repoints the Hebrew word to give a meaning associated with dysentery.

among them, because they blame its presence for the fate of Dagon and the plague (v. 7). Almost arrogantly the people of Gath say they will take it (v. 8*b*); but when the ark arrives in Gath the hand of the Lord turns against them, and the plague breaks out in Gath (v. 9). Without consultation or request, the ark is sent on to Ekron, where it is received with despair (v. 10). The hand of the Lord and the plague also take a toll of the Ekronites (vv. 11*b*-12). The lords of the Philistines are again called, and the people demand that the ark be returned to its place in Israel (v. 11*a*). The ark and the accompanying hand of the Lord have been on a procession of death through the Philistine cities. In each of these cities, the language of plague is accompanied by the language of holy war. We are told in vv. 6 (LXX), 9, and 11 that a "panic" (מהומה *měhûmâ*) swept the cities, a word used to describe the holy panic that sweeps the enemy when God fights for Israel (14:15, 20, 22; Deut 7:23).

This is what Israel had hoped for when they brought the ark to the field of battle against the Philistines. The holy panic had been withheld on that occasion, but now it breaks forth against all three of the Philistine cities that hold the ark captive. God had allowed the defeat of Israel for other purposes, but God is not powerless before Philistine enemies. Panic and plague sweep their cities. Verse 12 ends this segment of the ark story with the outcry of a Philistine city to match the outcry of Shiloh (4:13).

The power of the Lord associated with the ark has now been experienced by Israelite and Philistine alike. Israel experienced that power in the withholding of God's hand; the Philistines experienced it in the striking of God's hand. In terms of the larger story, it is now clear that the Philistines are a threat to Israel, but not to the Lord (Yahweh). The Philistines need not be feared by those who trust and honor the Lord.

REFLECTIONS

"God has no hands but our hands," states an aphorism popular in many contemporary church circles. This episode of the ark story (chap. 5) is a dramatic rebuttal of that notion. The aphorism suggests that God has no power to act in the world apart from human agency. Yet, in this episode the "hand of the LORD" is constantly at work without the mediation of any human agent, and the enemies of God are rendered handless (Dagon) and helpless (the Philistines). It is remarkable for the books of Samuel to include this story in which human characters play no role at all in the course of events, for most of the stories in Samuel are dominated by powerful and often charismatic personalities. The absence of human characters in the drama of the ark story may serve as a reminder of the ultimate reality of divine power when royal power gets under way.

It can serve as a reminder to us as well. Not everything is of our making in matters of faith and ultimate purpose in history. We live in a society frequently tempted to worship human power. Human capacities have been extended. We can affect our own future from the manipulation of the psyche to the destruction of the planet. These are heady powers. Yet, in this century of the greatest human power we have witnessed the results of those powers used only for human self-interest: holocaust, ethnic cleansing, racism, apartheid, terrorism, war, environmental destruction.

This attitude carries over to the church as well. We often imagine that God's grace is dependent on our efforts. We are sometimes so busy doing things for God that we fail to notice what God is doing. We need the reminder of this ark story that the hand of God is constantly at work exposing the idols in our midst as impotent and directing us to real power in the divine purposes at work in the world. When our programs and missions become efforts to manage and control God's grace for the sake of institutional success, we run the risk of finding our efforts reduced to powerless torsos without hands. Our idolatrous efforts cannot really make a difference, and we run the risk of finding ourselves numbered among God's enemies.

Walter Brueggemann calls our attention to important Gospel parallels here:

> The phrase "They rose early on the next morning" (v. 4) calls to mind the Easter formula of the Gospels (Matt. 28:1; Mark 16:2; Luke 24:1). Like those women in the Gospel narrative, the Philistines came to the temple "early the next morning" expecting to find a triumphant Dagon and a defeated Yahweh. In the Gospel they came expecting to find the power of death regnant and the defeat of Jesus. In neither case did the morning visitors find what they expected. The expectation of both the Philistines and the women in the Gospel failed to recognize that the power for life belongs to Yahweh.[47]

For resurrection people, the word is the same as this word to Israel in the ark story: The hand that makes the difference between life and death in the world belongs to God. What our hands do must be decided in the light of that truth.

47. Brueggeman, *First and Second Samuel*, 36.

1 Samuel 6:1–7:1, The Return of the Ark

COMMENTARY

This section constitutes the final act in the drama of the ark of the Lord. The Philistines, hoping for an end to the afflictions that have plagued them, devise a plan for returning the ark (6:1-9). The plan is carried out, and the ark is welcomed with rejoicing and sacrifice by the people of Beth-shemesh (6:10-16). Following a short summary of the reparation offerings sent with the ark (6:17-18), there is a final episode concerning an outbreak of divine power against the people of Beth-shemesh and their subsequent decision to lodge the ark at Kiriath-jearim (6:19–7:1).

As in chap. 5, the story does not emphasize the ark itself, but the power of the Lord, who acts in freedom and sovereignty. This power is acknowledged by the Philistines in their references to God's "hand" against them (vv. 3, 5, 9), and this episode ends with God's power mysteriously breaking out against the Israelites of Beth-shemesh after the ark arrives there (v. 19). The power of God is not controlled by any party, but shows itself in ways that emphasize the sovereign freedom of God.

In the larger framework of 1 Samuel, the ark story of chaps. 4–6 is now complete. The Philistines, who constituted the external threat to Israel's future, have proved ineffectual before the superior power of the Lord (Yahweh). Their apparent victory was but a passing moment, and the hand of the Lord exposed the Philistines and their god Dagon as weak and powerless. The Philistine threat is not yet removed, however. That development will occur in chap. 7. In the course of dealing with the external Philistine threat, God has also brought to an end the corrupt house of Eli at Shiloh (4:12-18). This development ties the ark story to the previous story of Hannah, Eli, and Samuel in chaps. 1–3 and prepares the reader for the return of Samuel to the story in chap. 7. This passage concludes with the designation of a priest, Eleazar (7:1), to care for the ark. Yet, the question of political leadership for Israel's future remains unresolved.

6:1-9. The ark remained in Philistine territory for seven months (v. 1); we may presume these were months of continued afflictions of tumors and mice (see Commentary on 5:6). In the light of the prominent exodus language and imagery in this chapter, we are reminded of the seven days of the first plague against Egypt in Exod 7:25. The Philistines summon priests and diviners (not lords as in 5:8, 11) and ask them both what to do with the ark and what they should send with the ark when returning it to its place (v. 2). The tone seems exasperated, and the questions seem to assume that the ark must be returned; but the question is over the proper method for doing so.

What unfolds in vv. 3-9 is an elaborate plan focused on two elements: the sending of a reparation offering with the ark (vv. 3-5) and a plan for the physical return of the ark that allows for a final testing of the power of Israel's God (vv. 7-9). In v. 6, the Philistines, as they did at the beginning of the ark story (4:8), make a remarkably direct reference to the exodus experience. It is Israel's enemies, the Philistines, who give us the key: The ark story is an exodus story. We have already seen exodus language and themes in chaps. 4–5. Chapter 6 is heavily influenced by exodus images and parallels as well.[48]

The priests and diviners urge that the ark not be sent from Philistine territory empty. This calls to mind God's promise to Moses that Israel would not go from Egypt "empty-handed" (Exod 3:21). In Exod 11:2 and 12:35-36, this promise is fulfilled with objects of gold and silver (כלי [kĕlî], "objects," is used in 1 Sam 6:8, 15 and Exod 12:35). Deuteronomy 15:13 also urges that slaves not be freed and sent out "empty-handed," because Israelites were once slaves in Egypt. In 1 Samuel, the priests and diviners counsel the payment of a "guilt-offering" (vv. 3-4, 8, 17). The Hebrew word used here (אשם 'āšām) is most often a substitutionary offering to remove impurity, but in this instance it is to be understood as the payment of reparations to appease Israel's God and to obtain relief from the afflictions the people have suffered. The priests and diviners hope that such an offering would provide for healing and ransom and that it would turn aside the "hand" of Israel's God (v. 3b). In effect, the Philistines now acknowledge the power of the Lord (Yahweh). In chap. 5, the narrator spoke of events as the "hand of the LORD"; in chap. 6 the Philistines speak of events as the "hand of the God of Israel" (vv. 3, 5, 9).

The "guilt offering" is to take the form of "five gold tumors and five gold mice" (v. 4; NIV, "rats"). These were to be placed in a container and transported with the ark out of Philistine territory. The number, shape, and material of these objects all give meaning to this symbolic act. The number five corresponds to the five lords of the Philistine cities (v. 4). All are said to have been afflicted,

even though chap. 5 mentioned only three of the five. In v. 17, the five cities are named in connection with the five gold tumors, but v. 18 suggests that there were many more gold mice. The number of mice is said to represent every Philistine habitation, "both fortified cities and unwalled villages." These objects are made of gold, making them very valuable and, therefore, suitable for the payment of reparations to appease the anger of Israel's God. The shape of these objects clearly represents the afflictions that have come upon the Philistines. By sending away these representations of the tumors and the rodents that have plagued their people and cities, the Philistines hope to rid themselves of God's judgmental hand (v. 5). The extent to which this "hand" has been felt is reflected in the hope that God's hand will be lightened from upon "you, your gods and your land" (v. 5b).

Verses 5b-6 justify the Philistine plan by means of a remarkable appeal to the exodus tradition. The strategy is described as intended to "give glory to the God of Israel." This development is a reversal of the departure of "glory" from Israel after the capture of the ark in 4:21 22. We are also reminded of Exod 14:4, 17, where God describes the exodus deliverance as "gaining glory" over Pharaoh and Egypt. In both instances, God's glory is contrasted to the "hardening" of the pharaoh's heart. This tradition is known to the Philistines in the ark story, and in v. 6 the priests and diviners argue against a "hardening" of Philistine hearts lest they meet the same fate as Pharaoh and Egypt. God had "made fools" (התעלל hit'allēl, hithpael) of the Egyptians (the same word is used in Exod 10:2), and they still had to let the Israelites go. The argument seems to be that delay in letting the ark go could only result in further harm and humiliation. The return of the ark may be understood as a new exodus event—a release from bondage and a return to the land of Israel. Perhaps in the light of the exile language in 4:21, exiles were also meant to take hope in this story told to them through the Deuteronomistic History. Release and return are possible through the power of the Lord.

The Hebrew root כבד (kbd) continues to play a key role here, as it did in chaps. 4–5. This root is behind both the words for "glory" and for "heavy." In v. 6, it is also the root translated "harden," which we might read as

48. See David Daube, *The Exodus Pattern in the Bible* (London: Faber & Faber, 1963).

"to make heavy." The root "lighten" (קָלַל *qll*) is the semantic opposite of this root. Thus vv. 5b-6 urge the Philistines to "give glory" (*kbd*) to God; maybe God will "lighten his hand"; but do not "make heavy/harden" (*kbd*) your heart.

In vv. 7-9, the focus shifts to plans for the physical return of the ark to Israelite territory. The use of a new cart and cows that have not yet known a yoke (v. 7) is consistent with other biblical and ancient references to the care for the purity of objects and animals used in rituals or associated with holy objects like the ark. The cows are eventually sacrificed by the people of Beth-shemesh (v. 14), which may have been the Philistines' intent as well. The selection of milk cows and their separation from their calves seems to be a peculiar Philistine wrinkle designed to make a final test of Yahweh's power. The cows, unused to the yoke and separated from their calves, are to be set loose to pull the cart with the ark and the golden offerings. If they go toward Beth-shemesh into Israelite territory, then it was indeed God's hand that had afflicted them; but if they should instead return to their calves or wander aimlessly, then the affliction might be mere chance (v. 9). The Philistines hold out one final hope that they might discredit Israel's God and salvage some relief from their humiliation. It proves to be a false hope.

6:10-16. The test begins. The cows do not waver. They go straight toward Beth-shemesh, "turning neither to the right nor to the left" (v. 12). Trailing in their wake are the lords of the Philistines, who watch as the ark arrives in the fields of Beth-shemesh. Fourteen miles west of Jerusalem, not far from the Philistine city of Ekron, Beth-shemesh may have been territory disputed by Israel and Philistia (see 2 Chr 28:18).

The people of Beth-shemesh greet the ark with great rejoicing (v. 13). The outcries of Shiloh when the ark was captured (4:13) are now replaced by the cries of celebration in Beth-shemesh at its return. The cart provides the wood and the cows become the sacrifice as the people of Beth-shemesh use a large stone in the field of Joshua as an altar upon which to offer ritual thanks to God for what must have seemed a miraculous turn

of events. The Philistine lords watch this celebration and return to Ekron (v. 16).

Verse 15 is often considered a secondary addition to the story. Levites are rarely mentioned in the books of Samuel (only in 2 Sam 15:24), and their removal of the ark and offering of sacrifices repeats what has already taken place in v. 14. It may be that later editors thought the ark should only properly be handled by priests.

6:17-18. These verses summarize the guilt offerings and their significance. The five gold tumors symbolize the five central cities of the Philistines, which are named here. Verse 18 suggests that the golden mice (or rats) represent all Philistine towns and villages and must number many more than five. This notice may indicate that all Philistia participated in the payment of reparations. Verse 18 adds an etiological note that the stone in Joshua's field remains as a witness "to this day."

6:19–7:1. Just when the story seems to be over, we encounter a disturbing episode. The ark story began with the Israelites' presumption that the ark gave them some control over the use of God's power. They were mistaken, as the capture of the ark and their defeat made clear (chap. 4). As the ark story comes to a close and the ark returns to the Israelites, this episode seems like a warning that the presence of God is still a dangerous matter and cannot be presumed upon. Israel, in the time of David, learns this lesson again when Uzzah is struck down for touching the ark as it is transferred to Jerusalem (2 Sam 6:6-7).

The Masoretic Text and the Septuagint differ on what took place. Some Israelites, the sons of Jeconiah, either looked into the ark (MT) or refused to join in the celebration (LXX; the NRSV follows the LXX; the NIV follows the MT). Because of this violation of the ark's holiness, or because of a refusal to honor the ark, God strikes down seventy men (v. 19).[49] The mood of welcome disappears. The people of Beth-shemesh mourn and ask whether anyone can stand before this holy God. They want to get rid of the ark (v. 20). They send to the town of Kireath-jearim, a Gibeonite city, which may have included

---

49. The Hebrew text adds 50,000 men, but the additional number is inserted in ungrammatical fashion, is absent in the LXX, and is rejected by most translators and commentators. See McCarter, *I Samuel*, 131, for a full discussion of the textual problems in 6:19.

a ritual center. The references to the "house of Abinadab" and the "consecration" of his son Eleazar to care for the ark may refer to a priestly household, which would seem to be an appropriate place for a holy object like the ark. Josephus, the Jewish historian, suggests that the reason for God's smiting of men at Beth-shemesh was that none of them were priests (his text does not appear to contain the reference to Levites in v. 15).[50] If this was the issue, then the move to Kireath-jearim placed the ark in the proper priestly care it deserved. Eleazar is not an Israelite, and he plays no wider role in Israel's story. The ark now has a proper custodian, but Israel still has no real political or ritual leadership to replace the house of Eli. God's power is not defeated or diminished, but it is not yet clear what God has in store for Israel's future.

50. Josephus *Antiquities of the Jews* 6:16.

REFLECTIONS

Chapter 6 completes the story traditionally called "the ark narrative." The ark of the covenant does, indeed, play a central role in the story, but is the ark really the focus? Both Israelites and Philistines thought so, but each learned, with some difficulty, that the ark symbolized the presence and power of the Lord (Yahweh), but that the ark did not guarantee control of that power. Israel expected victory by the ark's presence on the battlefield (4:1-11). They were defeated. The Philistines expected triumph when they installed the ark as a trophy in the temple of Dagon (5:1-12). They were humiliated and afflicted. The Israelites of Beth-shemesh expected restored well-being to accompany the return of the ark (6:19–7:1). They were assaulted. In each episode, Israelite or Philistine failed to see that true power lies not in the ark but in the holy God to whom the ark pointed, and that God will not be managed or controlled.

This is not the portrait of a warm, fuzzy, friendly deity. The God of the ark story in 1 Samuel 4–6 is mysterious, dangerous, and, above all, possessed of sovereign freedom. This is not the portrait of God favored by positive-thinking, make-God-appealing, church-growth strategies. "God is so good" a well-known praise song croons repeatedly. Well, yes! God is good. But God is also holy, mysterious, and powerful. This story reminds us that there is a side of the reality of God that cannot be reduced to a tool for providing positive life experiences. Relationship to God can be demanding and even risky. Manipulation and management of holy symbols for our own ends can be downright dangerous.

We live in a time when politicians almost routinely invoke religious language and symbolism in their political campaigns and public image making. How different is this from bringing out the ark in the hope that our enemies will flee in panic? Is there a true sense of God's holy power as the reality behind the symbols and images? A recent American president was well known for his use of religious language to gain support for policy initiatives, but it was equally well known that he was a member of no church and did not participate in public worship except for official occasions. Such seemingly cynical use of religious symbols reflects a disregard for the divine reality to which those symbols point. The disturbing message of the incident at Beth-shemesh is that the judging hand of God can be felt by those who claim to be divine allies but fail to honor God, as easily as it is felt by those who openly declare opposition to God's purposes in the world.

It is, perhaps, in the nature of institutionalized religion to want to control or manage divine power and to limit divine freedom. But the God of the ark story is similar to the God who spoke through Moses on Mt. Sinai, saying, "I will be gracious to whom I will be gracious, and will show mercy to whom I will show mercy" (Exod 33:19; see Paul's quote of this text in Rom 9:15). To modern sensibilities, this may seem like divine arbitrariness, but it is instead divine freedom. In every generation there are those in the church who imagine that they can make lists of those who are deserving of God's mercy (or, as in the ark story, deserving of God's judging hand). In Jesus' time, some of his opponents among the scribes and Pharisees objected to his association with those they had defined as being outside of God's mercy. In our own time, voices claiming to speak for God have put forward lists of those deserving of God's judgment and unworthy of God's mercy. Such lists have included persons with AIDS, feminists, immigrants who do not speak English, gays or lesbians, non-middle-class African Americans, those who would allow abortions, and the poor in general. Even in localized and personal relationships there is a distressing tendency to treat those with whom we disagree as apostates and ourselves as being backed by divine power. The ark story suggests that the freedom of God will not allow God's power to be wielded on behalf of self-serving interests or in disregard of the need to honor God's purposes above our own. No cause, regardless of how righteous it seems, can claim God's grace as a possession or God's judgment as a weapon. Both God's grace and God's judgment come as a divine gift, and that gift is given out of sovereign freedom.

The Israelites of Shiloh and Beth-shemesh were clear about who deserved the judging hand of God against them: the Philistines. When the Philistines won the battle, they were clear about who had been deserted by the hand of God: the Israelites. Both were wrong. God's purposes went forward according to God's plan. Those who fail to discern what God is doing and insist on trying to control God's power for their own plan court disaster. Lives of faith lived in respect for God's freedom are lives of discernment. We seek to discern what God is doing in the world and align our efforts to God's. The tendency of the church is to think it is incumbent on God to follow our carefully laid plans. We must scan the horizon, seeking to discern God at work in people, movements, events, and programs that make for wholeness, justice, and love. To our surprise we may sometimes find testimony to God at work in the mouths of those we thought were Philistines.

Perhaps, in the end, the Philistines ironically modeled the proper response. They sought to understand God's activity in their own time by remembering what God had done before. It was the Philistines who called to mind the exodus-shaped activity of God. They gave God gifts that suggested honor and respect for God's holiness and power. They acknowledged the freedom of God by allowing the ark to make its own way toward its own future—and they followed. Maybe their only real mistake at this point was that they eventually turned back.

1 Samuel 7:2-17, Samuel as Judge of Israel

COMMENTARY

With chapter 7 we come to an important crossroad in the story of 1 Samuel. In chaps. 1–3, we were introduced to the internal crisis in Israel. Eli's sons had become corrupt, and the entire priestly house of Eli at Shiloh was judged and condemned. In chaps. 4–6, the external crisis in Israel was introduced. The Philistines defeated Israel in battle and captured the ark of the covenant. In each of these crises, God was at work creating unexpected, new possibilities. To meet the internal need for faithful and authentic leadership, God raised up Samuel to be God's prophet. To meet the external need to demonstrate where true power lies, God humiliated the Philistine god Dagon and afflicted the Philistine cities with tumors and mice, forcing the return of the ark. At the end of chaps. 1–3, *God's word,* mediated through the prophet Samuel, has replaced the authority of Eli and his corrupt sons (3:19–4:1). At the end of chaps. 4–6, *God's hand* has been felt by Philistine and Israelite, making clear that God's sovereign freedom and power are unrivaled in the world.

Now these two strands of Israel's story come together in chap. 7. Samuel, absent from chaps. 4–6, appears again in a central role, exercising authentic and legitimate leadership over Israel. The Philistines appear again as a military threat, and this time, through the mediation of Samuel, a great victory is won and Israel enjoys a time of release from Philistine threat.

In bare outline, chap. 7 includes a ceremony in which Samuel leads Israel in putting aside foreign gods (vv. 3-4); an assembly at Mizpah, interrupted by a Philistine attack and a subsequent victory over the Philistines through the intercession of Samuel (vv. 5-12); a summary of the extent of Philistine subjugation during the time of Samuel (vv. 13-14); and a notice of the circuit Samuel regularly made as judge of Israel (vv. 15-17).

The role of Samuel is central in each segment of chap. 7. Indeed, it is Samuel's role in chap. 7 that brings together and resolves for the moment the issues of crisis for Israel raised in chaps. 1–6. We have already seen Samuel as a "trustworthy prophet of the LORD" (4:20). We may also presume that by being reared and mentored by Eli at Shiloh, Samuel had some training in priestly duties. In chap. 7, we see both a continuation and an expansion of these prophetic and priestly roles for Samuel as well as the addition of a judicial role.

Samuel appears in the role of intercessor for the people before God (v. 5). The verb used here (פלל *pālal*; NIV, "intercede"; the NRSV unsatisfactorily translates as "pray") is the same verb used in Eli's question to his corrupt sons in 2:25: "If someone sins against the Lord, who can make intercession?" Samuel himself now seems to be the answer to that question. In 12:19, the people implore Samuel to continue in the role of intercessor (*pālal*), and Samuel responds in 12:23, "Far be it from me that I should sin against the Lord by ceasing to intercede [*pālal*] for you" (NIV; the NRSV again simply translates "pray"). In 7:5, Samuel intercedes for the people in a ceremony of repentance, but the role of intercessor is also consistent with the people's appeal for him to call on God for aid

against the Philistine threat in 7:8. Representing the people's needs before God is a role frequently taken up by later prophets (e.g., Amos, Jeremiah, Joel), and it reminds us of the role of Moses as intercessor. Indeed, Samuel is twice mentioned alongside Moses in the role of intercessor for the people (Ps 99:6; Jer 15:1).

Samuel appears in vv. 7-12 as the prophetic performer of holy war rites prior to the victory of the Lord.[51] Samuel is not himself a charismatic deliverer but a prophetic agent helping to mediate God's deliverance. The connection of prophets to such holy warfare is seen in 1 Kgs 20:13-14; 22:5-12; and 2 Kgs 3:11-19. We are also reminded of Deborah, who was called a prophetess and was not herself a military deliverer (Judges 4). The roles of both intercessor and mediator of the holy war elaborate Samuel's leadership as a prophet and are primarily connected with the account of victory over the Philistines in vv. 5-12. This heightening of Samuel's role as a prophet would be consistent with the existence of a prophetic version of Israel's story for this period (see Introduction).

Another role for Samuel, not necessarily related to his identity as a prophet, is reflected in the four references to him as "judging" Israel (vv. 6, 15, 16, 17). The root שפט (*špt*, "to judge") implies the administration of justice and probably involves the interpreting of covenant law and tradition related to the Mosaic covenant. Samuel's role as judge is connected in vv. 15-17 with a small circuit in central Israelite territory (mainly Benjaminite land), in which Samuel apparently traveled to interpret and administer covenant justice. He is often viewed here as keeping older covenant traditions alive in a time when the ark is lost, Shiloh may be destroyed, the leadership of the house of Eli is ended, and, in spite of the optimistic notice of v. 13, the Philistine threat is not yet ended. The reference in v. 6 seems to be an effort to identify the judge of vv. 15-17 with the prophet of vv. 5-12; they are both Samuel. This title of "judge" also makes Samuel the clear successor to Eli (who was said to have judged Israel

51. The nature of holy war traditions will be further discussed in connection with a closer look at 7:5-12. For additional detail on the prophet's role in holy war, see Birch, *The Rise of the Israelite Monarchy*, 17-19; Patrick D. Miller, "The Divine Council and the Prophetic Call to War," *VT* 18 (1968) 100-107.

for 40 years [4:18]) and to earlier "judges" of Israel in the book of Judges. These earlier "judges" included military deliverers and those who played some judicial function as covenant interpreters. Samuel's activity in vv. 15-17 seems more like the latter. The final statement in v. 17 tells us that Samuel built an altar at Ramah. In this chapter, he also conducts a water ritual related to penance (v. 6) and offers a burnt offering (v. 9). These suggest priestly activities, even if Samuel does not appear fully in the role of priest.

These testimonies to the breadth and efficacy of Samuel's leadership suggest that God has raised up the leadership necessary to meet Israel's crises and that a king is not really necessary (the people's request comes in the next chapter). Prophetic leadership would have been enough. McCarter thinks that Samuel's role and accomplishments reflect David's later success and are intended to diminish the unique role of David.[52]

First Samuel 7 shows some evidence of the process through which the traditions developed. The episode of victory over the Philistines and the heightened role of Samuel in that episode (vv. 5-12) are consistent with an earlier prophetic version of Israel's story for this period (see the Introduction). The special language and interests of the deuteronomistic historian (Dtr) are reflected in vv. 3-4, the last phrase of v. 6, and vv. 13-15 (some of the evidence for this judgment will be commented upon in the detailed examination of this chapter). Whatever the earlier history of these materials, however, they have now all been assembled into the present form of the text by the creative work of the deuteronomistic historian, and it is this final telling of Israel's story that should occupy primary attention. After a closer look at the various segments of this chapter, we will return to comments on the role of chap. 7 as a whole in its wider contexts.

7:2-4. Verse 2 forms a transition from the ark story in chaps. 4–6 to the narrative of chap. 7. It assumes that we know something of the story that led to the ark's lodging at Kireath-jearim and speaks of the passage of twenty years. The expression that Israel "lamented [NRSV; NIV, "mourned"] after the LORD" suggests that this was an unsettled and difficult time for Israel. The attack of the Philistines in v. 10 indicates that the threat from these perennial enemies had continued in spite of the experience with the ark.

In vv. 3-4, Samuel challenges all of Israel to give up idolatrous practices as a condition for deliverance from the Philistines. These verses have been widely recognized as deuteronomistic in both language and theme.[53] The concern for purity of worship and the theme of return to the Lord are central to the theology of Deuteronomy and Dtr.[54] Verses 3-4 seem very similar to Josh 24:23-24 and Judg 10:6-16, both thought to show Dtr influence. Each of these texts calls for Israel to put away foreign gods and identifies those gods with the Baals and Astartes of Canaanite worship. They further call on Israel to "direct your heart to the LORD" and "serve" the Lord. Baal was the Canaanite storm god and chief god related to the fertility of the land; Astarte was a Canaanite goddess of fertility and war and closely associated with Baal. Their names almost became clichéd expressions for any idolatrous deities (see 12:10; Judg 2:13; 3:7; 10:6, 10).

Verses 2-4 seem to be a deuteronomistic passage creating a transition from the ark story of chaps. 4–6 to the story of Samuel and the Philistine victory in 7:5-12. This transition has two important effects. First, these verses now imply that the disaster when the ark was captured was due to Israel's idolatry and not to the corruption of the house of Eli. The crisis with the Philistines did not end with the return of the ark. The people now need to repent of their apostasy if they are to be delivered out of the hand of the Philistines. Second, these verses now tie this episode into the pattern of sin (usually idolatry), distress as punishment, appeal to God, repentance, deliverance, and a period of peace that organizes the stories of the book of Judges; this pattern is described in Judg 2:11–3:6. Israel's story in 1 Samuel 1–7 is to be read as a continuation

---

52. McCarter, *I Samuel,* 150. See also Polzin, *Samuel and the Deuteronomist,* 76-77.

53. See Birch, *Rise of the Israelite Monarchy,* 16-17; Klein, *I Samuel,* 64-66; McCarter, *I Samuel,* 142-43. The expression "with all your heart" is common in Deut and Dtr (Deut 4:29; 6:5; 10:12; 11:13; 13:4; 26:16; 30:2, 6, 10; Josh 22:5; 23:14; 1 Sam 12:20, 24; 1 Kgs 8:23; 14:8; 2 Kgs 10:31). The fuller phrase "to return to the LORD with all the heart" is found in Deut 30:10; 1 Kgs 8:48; 2 Kgs 23:25.

54. See Hans Walter Wolff, "The Kerygma of the Deuteronomic Historical Work," in *The Vitality of Old Testament Traditions* (Atlanta: John Knox, 1975) 83-100.

of the story of tribal Israel. Israel has sinned, and that sin is now interpreted as idolatry. They have suffered oppression and distress at the hands of the Philistines (twenty- or forty-year periods are typical in Judges). They have appealed to the Lord (v. 2, "lamented after the LORD"). They respond to Samuel's appeal and put away the foreign gods. The stage is now set for deliverance, for Samuel portrayed as judge, and for the ensuing period of peace (see Commentary on 7:13-14 and 7:15).

7:5-12. Samuel calls an assembly of the people at Mizpah for the purpose of interceding for the people's sin (v. 5). This seems to repeat the assembly Samuel addressed in vv. 3-4, and the people's fasting and confession in v. 6 seem unnecessary in light of their action of putting away the Baals and Astartes in v. 4. The water pouring ritual in v. 6 is unknown elsewhere, but is clearly a part of a ritual of penitence here.

Mizpah is an important cultic center in the tribal territory of Benjamin, north of Jerusalem. It plays an important role in 1 Samuel as part of Samuel's judicial circuit (7:16) and the site where Saul was selected as king by lot (10:17). The notice that Samuel "judged" the people there (v. 6) is unexpected, since no judicial activity is involved. In this verse, Dtr is probably reminding us to read the coming story of deliverance from the Philistines in the light of the pattern of the book of Judges. The notice here identifies the intercessor/holy war agent/prophet Samuel with the Samuel who judges Israel in vv. 15-17.

The Philistines hear of this assembly, and the lords of the Philistines bring a force up against Israel (v. 7) and attack them (v. 10). Perhaps the Philistines considered the assembly a prelude to rebellion or simply an opportune moment to gain advantage; their motives are not made clear.

The Israelites turn in fear to Samuel and insist that the prophet who interceded for their sins also act as intercessor to seek God's salvation from the Philistines. They asked Samuel to *cry out* and *pray* so that God might *save* (v. 8). Samuel offers a lamb as a whole burnt offering; then he *cries out,* and God *answers* (v. 9). The verbs in these verses expose an important dynamic in Israel's faith. It is the cry of human distress that mobilizes God's response and salvation (see, e.g., 12:8,

10; Exod 2:23; 3:7). The people do not cry directly to God, but Samuel is asked to cry out on their behalf. This action emphasizes his role as prophetic mediator. Prayer now stands as the middle term between the outcry on behalf of the people's need and the advent of God's salvation. The burnt offering, a sacrifice devoted entirely to God, represents utter reliance on God's deliverance; and when Samuel takes up the people's petition and cries out, God's answer follows (v. 9b).

The events of v. 10b (v. 10a simply notes the Philistine attack) make clear that trust in God is all that was necessary.

The tradition of miraculous delivery from the Philistines . . . seems clearly to be a holy war tradition. The encounter is prefaced by sacrifice (vs. 9); it is Yahweh himself who fights, calling into service the forces of nature (vs. 10) and throwing the enemy into confusion (vs. 10). These are among the primary motifs of holy war. The language itself is the language of holy war. The verb המם [*hmm* "to throw into confusion or panic"] appears five times and always in a holy war context [Josh 10:10; Judg 4:15; 1 Sam 7:10; 2 Sam 22:15//Ps 18:14]. In all but Judg 4:1 Yahweh's victory is accompanied by meteorological phenomena such as thunder, lightning or hail.[55]

The victory belongs entirely to the Lord, and the enemy is routed before Israel (v. 10b), with Israelites engaging in the pursuit after the outcome is decided (v. 11). This victory reverses the rout of the Israelites by the Philistines attested in 4:3.

Samuel erects a stone and names it Ebenezer, "stone of help," to commemorate the Lord's help against the Philistines (v. 12). This act recalls the place where Israel assembled to do battle with the Philistines on the disastrous occasion when the ark was captured (4:1). It seems unlikely that this Ebenezer near Mizpah and the earlier Ebenezer near Aphek could be the same place, but geography is not the crucial matter here. What matters is that, by God's power and through the mediation of God's prophet, the defeat of Israel at Ebenezer (chap. 4) has been reversed

---

55. Birch, *Rise of the Israelite Monarchy,* 17-18. On features of holy war, see R. de Vaux, *Ancient Israel: Its Life and Institutions* (London: Darton, Longman and Todd, 1961) 258-60, and F. M. Cross, "The Divine Warrior in Israel's Early Cult," in *Biblical Motifs,* ed. A. Altmann (Cambridge, Mass.: Harvard University Press, 1966) 11-39.

by a victory of Ebenezer (chap. 7). The Philistines have been routed and defeated. Most significantly, God has not been defeated, as the capture of the ark might have implied. When Israel was in need, God helped, and that help sufficed.

7:13-14. These verses show Dtr completing the framework begun in vv. 2-4. Such a framework is common in the book of Judges. Now that God has brought deliverance, the land enjoys a time of peace for the lifetime of the judge ("all the days of Samuel"). In form and vocabulary, these verses are similar to the notes that conclude the deliverance accounts in the book of Judges.[56]

The far-reaching effects claimed by vv. 13-14 for the victory over the Philistines cannot be regarded as accurate. The claim here is that the Philistines were not only subdued but also did not even enter the land of Israel during Samuel's lifetime (v. 13), that the territory was returned to Israel, and that there was peace with the Amorites (v. 14). Many episodes in the subsequent story of 1 Samuel show the Philistines occupying Israelite territory and engaging in military actions against the Israelites (e.g., chaps. 13–14; 17–18) during the life of Samuel. Eventually, Saul loses his life in a great battle against the Philistines (1 Samuel 31; 2 Samuel 1); it is David who finally removes the Philistine threat (2 Sam 5:17-25).

The importance of these verses is not historical but theological. The "hand of the LORD" has proved victorious against the Philistines (v. 13). Israel, under the leadership of Samuel, has nothing to fear from the "hand of the Philistines" (vv. 3, 8, 14). This theme of the power of God's hand also ties the victory of chap. 7 to the humiliation and affliction of the Philistines, brought by the "hand of the LORD" in the ark story (chaps. 5–6). The claim here is that Israel can trust this demonstrated power of the Lord and the leadership of Samuel. There is no need for the king whom the people will request in chap. 8. That the idealized picture of vv. 13-14 does not become historical reality may be understood as the

product of the people's failure to trust in the Lord's power and the Lord's prophet by insisting on a king.

7:15-17. In the present form of this chapter, the notice of Samuel as judge of Israel for his lifetime (v. 15) makes Samuel the successor to Eli, who was said to have judged Israel in 4:18, and places Samuel in the long succession of judges over Israel recorded in the book of Judges. Verses 16-17 give us a glimpse of the activity of Samuel that might lie as reality behind such a title. Samuel traveled a small circuit of towns to administer justice. In a time when the Shiloh priesthood is scattered and discredited and Shiloh itself may be destroyed or left non-functional by the Philistines, Samuel appears here as one laboring to keep the tradition of the covenant law alive. Since we are told he built an altar at Ramah, perhaps we can imagine him performing ritual as well as judicial functions. Ramah was the hometown of Samuel, and the other places were towns with important cultic backgrounds (Bethel, Gilgal, and Mizpah). All are close together, so we should imagine that Samuel is maintaining a foothold for the endangered covenant tradition, not making grand rounds throughout Israel.

Having looked more closely at the segments of the chapter, it is now possible to comment on the role of 1 Samuel 7 in its wider contexts. This chapter seems to play a pivotal role both in the opening section of 1 Samuel (chaps. 1–7) and in the wider Deuteronomistic History.

Chapter 7 concludes the epoch of Israel's history that began with the book of Judges. Samuel becomes the last of the judges. He is made the successor both of those judges who were connected with Israel's deliverance from an enemy[57] and of those judges who are connected with the administration of justice and the oversight of covenant traditions (the so-called minor judges). The picture of 1 Samuel 7 is intended to convince us that this pattern of leadership and of trust in the Lord was adequate to Israel's needs. Chapter 8 will begin the story of kingship, and the era of judges will be gone forever.

56. The verb (כנע *kāna'*, "subdue") appears in the niphal primarily in the Dtr framework of Judges (Judg 3:30; 8:28; 11:33; in hiphil Judg 4:23). The expression "the hand of the LORD was against . . ." appears in Deut 2:15; Judg 2:15; 1 Sam 12:15, which are deuteronomistic, and also in 1 Sam 5:9, which connects this episode back to the ark narrative. The term "Amorite" (v. 14) is also the term used by Deuteronomy (and the Elohist) for the non-Israelite peoples of the area.

57. Samuel is not himself a military deliverer but is the agent through which God's deliverance is mediated. His role is most analogous to that of Deborah, one of the earlier judges.

Chapter 7 serves as the resolution of Israel's internal and external crises that have been described in 1 Samuel 1–6. The infant Samuel, a gift of God's grace to Hannah, has grown to adulthood as a prophet, a gift of God's grace to Israel. As God's prophet, Samuel is the successor to the corrupt house of Eli, which has been discredited and removed from influence. As God's prophet, Samuel is the mediator of the power of the Lord's hand, which can give deliverance from enemies. The power that humiliated the Philistines through the ark is now mediated through God's prophet. This could be the happy ending to the story, but the people in chap. 8 will insist on a king instead.

Chapter 7 plays an important role as a reference point in the ongoing story of Israel as told by the deuteronomist. Most immediately it is the counterpoint against which we must read the story of the people's request for a king in 1 Samuel 8. Samuel led the people to put away foreign gods and serve the Lord *only* (7:3-4). In 8:7-8, God interprets the request for a king as equivalent to Israel's rebellions in idolatry. Serving a king is equated to serving other gods. The result of such folly is also made clear in relation to chap. 7. Whereas Samuel cried to the Lord and the Lord answered (7:9), the people, with the king they have chosen, will cry to the Lord, and the Lord will not answer (8:18). In the broader perspective of the deuteronomist, this chapter (and its negative counterpoint in chap. 8) may present a word to the generation of exiles to which this history is addressed. They have trusted kings, and the result was exile. Chapter 7 suggests to such exilic readers that they can still cry out, and God will answer if their trust is truly in the Lord (and the Lord's prophets?), and not in their own institutions.

REFLECTIONS

The second verse of the well-known hymn "Come, Thou Fount of Every Blessing" begins:

Here I raise mine Ebenezer;
Hither by thy help I'm come;
And I hope, by thy good pleasure,
Safely to arrive at home.

Countless Christians have sung these lines, affirming their need for help and safe arrival home without having any idea what it means to "raise mine Ebenezer." It is 1 Sam 7:12 from which we learn that an Ebenezer ("a stone of help") is a reminder of the only sure source of help and safety. God helps! This chapter is a witness to the dangers of false security and the source of true security.

1. False security is ultimately a matter of idolatry. It is not just a deuteronomistic conceit that this chapter begins with a call to put aside foreign gods (7:3-4). Loyalty and trust in the Lord are the basic issue here. The appeal of the Baals and the Astartes must be understood in broad terms as the failure to "direct your heart to the LORD" (7:3 NRSV). They represent the many other things that can claim the loyalty of Israel and of us. In 1 Samuel 7, we read this call to "put away foreign gods" and "serve the LORD only" in the light of the ark, on one side (chaps. 4–6), and the king, on the other (chap. 8). Neither is worthy of ultimate trust. The ark is an object, and the king is a man; neither can save of its own accord. The attempt to manipulate the ark for the sake of security led to disaster. To trust in a king ultimately leads to exile. Both ark and king have value only as representatives of the true power that lies with the hand of the Lord.

It is the Philistines who represent the fears of Israel over their own security. The Philistines are, in 1 Samuel, the representatives of worldly, political, and technical power. They are organized, efficient, technologically superior in military might. Israel had been defeated by them twice, and they had captured the ark. Israel feared that the Philistines were the wave of the future, and they were afraid (7:7). But Philistine power had already been exposed as idolatrous. Their god Dagon had no true power. Philistine might, however, could not protect their cities and people from the hand of the Lord. The Philistines proved as fearful and vulnerable as the Israelites. They may have taken the ark, but they could not hold it. In 1 Samuel 7 the Philistines are defeated, not by superior technical and political power, but by the thunder of God.

We live in a world that cannot imagine this turn of events. We admire, even worship, political power and technical expertise. We consider this realistic and not idolatrous. We sometimes see the dangers in such loyalties, but then we want symbols (arks) or leadership (kings) that yoke our trust in God to political and technical power. It is seldom that we dare serve God *only.* Even our frequent preoccupation with efficient, successful, technically up-to-date congregations and denominational structures seems more like an emulation of the Philistines than a trust in God's power to bring new possibilities in unexpected ways.

We are so allied with public power and technical expertise in our culture that it is hard for us to grant reality to this story of God's victory. Brueggemann notes, "Insofar as this text concerns war and national public power, it is, in our day, the marginal peoples who rely on strategies of thunder in the face of superior technology."[58] It is the oppressed and the dispossessed who know they stand no chance if their hope rests in power defined by the world's terms. It is also in personal experiences of powerlessness, grief, and loss that we know reality is not defined ultimately by worldly, technical, and political power. The history of the faith communities who have gone before us gives frequent testimony to the unlikely reversals, societal and personal, that have been made possible by God's hand, much to the bewilderment of the world's power arrangements. Even in our recent history, we have seen the dismantlement of the Soviet Union, the destruction of the Berlin wall, the fall of dictatorship in the Philippines, the end of apartheid in South Africa, and an agreement between Palestinians and Israelis. These are the reversals of which Hannah sang and seemed unlikely judged solely by human capabilities and stratagems. They are the reversals hoped for by those who can only trust that the thunder of God can rout the Philistines.

2. The verbs of 7:8-9 tell us something of Israel's covenantal alternative to idolatrous loyalties. In the face of Philistine threat, the people ask Samuel to *cry out* and *pray* on their behalf, so that the Lord might *save* them. In response to their request, Samuel does *cry out,* and the Lord does *answer.* Further, this chapter is bracketed by *fasting* and *confession* in 7:6 and the *administration of justice* in 7:15-17. All of these verbs speak of a reliance on covenantal relationship to God's power, and not of reliance on human power and capability. Such a pattern of trust in the Lord contrasts with the apparent superiority of Philistine power, which strikes fear in Israelite hearts. We know from chaps. 4–6 that Philistine power rests on idolatrous loyalties that cannot save.

God's salvation is mobilized by the outcry of human need and distress, but it is focused by prayer, repentance, and the administration of justice. The outcry alone brings divine response (7:9). From Exodus onward (e.g., Exod 2:23; 3:7), Israel's God has been known as a God who responds to the cry of human distress. God's salvation is seen in the new possibilities for life and hope that arise in the midst of and in spite of that distress. In reading again in this story of God's willingness to answer the outcry, we can take renewed hope that God is at work even in the most oppressive and hopeless circumstances. This is true completely apart from any human activity. But prayer, repentance, and the administration of justice are ways in which the covenantal faith community aligns with and joins in the saving activity of God.

---

58. Brueggemann, *First and Second Samuel,* 53.

The people ask Samuel to cry out and to pray for them. The outcry is the voicing of pain, but prayer is the conscious sharing of our experience with God and openness to God's experience shared with us. Does the victory of 1 Samuel 7 suggest that prayer can save? No, it is God who saves. But is God responsive to prayer? Yes, but in God's own time and way. We dare to pray for our needs, even to pray for the defeat of enemies, but we must then trust that the future and its possibilities will be opened in God's own way. God is not manipulated by our prayers.

Likewise, repentance and the administration of justice are the ways in which the covenant community seeks to renew its own life and the life of its society through alignment with the purposes of God. In repentance, we examine our own lives and institutions for patterns that serve our self-interests rather than God's. We recognize in repentance that we, too, can align ourselves with the enemies of God. In the administration of justice, the covenant community seeks to create structures that make for the wholeness (*shalom*) that is the goal of covenant life to which God has called us. Like Samuel, we are often called upon to preserve a witness to such wholeness in the midst of and in spite of considerable brokenness. We dare to say in a broken world that there is another reality, and justice points to that reality by seeking to value and bring to wholeness every human life and the whole of creation.

These activities also do not themselves "save" us, although the frenetic activities of some congregations suggest a belief that salvation can be programmed. God's salvation always comes as freely and unexpectedly as the thunder of the Lord. Repentance and justice are part of covenant community lived in trust that the God who thunders is the locus of true security, and the loyalties that we seek to manage through human means are idolatrous. They are not worthy of ultimate trust. The ark story, followed by this story of Samuel and the victory of God, teaches us that God's ways of saving will sometimes surprise our expectations. If God responds to our outcries, it will not be in mechanical or managed ways. We will be surprised by grace, but we can trust its reality. The world will still urge us to loyalties and trust that are idolatrous, but covenant faith insists that only the hand of the Lord can save us.

1 SAMUEL 8:1–15:35, THE KINGSHIP OF SAUL

OVERVIEW

With these chapters we come to the main subject of the books of Samuel: the beginnings of kingship in Israel. Chapters 1–7 provide a prologue to this main story. The establishment of kingship represented a major transformation for Israel. It was not only a change in institutional structures but also a major shift in categories for understanding the nature of Israel's life as a community and its relationship to God. Such transformations could not take place without stresses and conflicts. The books of Samuel in general, and chaps. 8–15 in particular, reflect the tensions and ambiguities of these transitional times. These tensions are evident in distinct but interrelated dimensions of the story that unfold in 1 Samuel 8–15.

Israel's transformation was *theological.* The old traditions of covenant community resisted and came into conflict with the emerging ideology of royal community. Covenant community had been rooted in an understanding of the sovereignty of God. Israel was the people of a divine king. When Gideon was asked by some of the people to become king following his victory over Midian he refused, saying, "I will not rule over you, and my son will not rule over you; the Lord will rule over you" (Judg 8:23). Earthly kingship was seen by some as a rejection of divine kingship.

Covenant community was understood as a tradition of special relationship to God, who had been made known to Israel through the exodus experience and the covenant making at Mt. Sinai. Israel's understanding of this covenant God and the community that lived in relationship to this God set them apart from other communities in the world. The desire to have a king arises in 1 Samuel 8 as the impulse to be "like other nations" (vv. 5, 20). For Israel, the available models for kingship were to be found in the small kingdoms that were Israel's neighbors. How could the uniqueness of Israel's faith and relationship to God be maintained if Israel's life became patterned more like the surrounding nations? How could Israel have an earthly king without undermining the sovereignty of God?

Israel's transformation was *sociopolitical.* The emergence of kingship in Israel did not result from an abstract theological debate. Real crises, both internal and external, exposed the weaknesses of Israel's tribal life and created the pressure to adopt kingship as an alternative. When Samuel became old, his sons proved to be corrupt and unworthy successors to judge Israel (8:1-3). The house of Eli before Samuel had fallen under God's judgment for its corruption. It is in this context that the elders of Israel come to request a king (8:4-5). Even after a king is chosen, tensions over spheres of authority remain and can be seen in the conflicts between Samuel and Saul (13:1-15; 15:1-35).

External sociopolitical pressures came in the form of the Philistine military threat. The deuteronomistic historian does not want to present the Philistines as a legitimate reason for kingship. Samuel is presented as ending the Philistine threat in 7:13-14, and the Philistine crisis does not figure at all in the elders' request for a king in chap. 8 (although it may be hinted at in v. 20). Nevertheless, other texts in this section make clear that the threat of permanent Philistine conquest was a factor in the establishment of kingship. Saul is anointed in 10:1 with the explicit charge to deliver Israel from the Philistines. Chapters 13–14 show Saul addressing all of his initial efforts at relief from the Philistine threat. Kingship implies centralized leadership, standing armies, and unified authority. These are needed to defeat an enemy like the Philistines, but these are all new patterns for the life of Israel and stand in tension with older patterns. The conflicts with Samuel in chaps. 13–15 are not only theological in character, but also represent conflicts over authority and conduct in military matters. Samuel represents older holy war traditions, and Saul represents emerging patterns common to the ways in which kings conduct military campaigns.

Recent work on the sociological background to this period of transformation to monarchy has made clear that emerging population pressure and economic surplus were a part of the pressure to move from localized tribal patterns to centralized royal systems of social organization.[59] New patterns of land consolidation and political power necessitated a strong centralized system to protect these emerging vested interests. Kingship was the logical development to meet these needs. A military crisis, like the Philistine threat, may have provided the opportunity for transition to kingship, but vested economic and political power interests stood to gain more than simply relief from Philistine pressure. It must be stressed that these social and demographic factors are never explicitly stated in the text of the books of Samuel as a justification for kingship. They are the factors we can discern behind and through the story.

These social factors also create theological tensions. Covenant faith arose in response to oppression and marginalization and was never at home with vested-interest power arrangements. The theological unease of the covenant tradition with some of the emerging sociopolitical power arrangements that accompany kingship will be a source of tension visible at various points in the books of Samuel (e.g., "the ways of the king," 1 Sam 8:11-18).

Israel's transformation was *character driven.* The testimony of the books of Samuel is that this crucial transition period in Israel's life was dominated by the leadership and personalities of Samuel, Saul, and David. The character and activity of Israel's God,

---

59. See, e.g., L. Marvin Chaney, "Ancient Palestinian Peasant Movements and the Formation of Premonarchic Israel," in *Palestine in Transition,* ed. D. N. Freedman and D. F. Graf (Sheffield: Almond, 1983) 39-90; James W. Flanagan, "Chiefs in Israel," *JSOT* 20 (1981) 47-73; Frank S. Frick, *The Formation of the State in Ancient Israel* (Sheffield: JSOT, 1988); Norman K. Gottwald, "Early Israel and the Canaanite Socioeconomic System," in Freedman and Graf, *Palestine in Transition,* 25-37.

Yahweh, also play a pivotal role in the story of this period and in the lives of these three leaders. In 1 Samuel 8–15, David has not yet entered the story, although his crucial place in the story is sometimes foreshadowed (e.g., 13:14; 15:28). In these chapters, the characters of Samuel, Saul, and the Lord (Yahweh) all reflect the tensions and ambiguities of this transition time.

Samuel appears as God's prophet. As such he is commanded by God to give the people a king (8:7, 9, 22), and he is God's agent in designating and anointing Saul (9:27–10:8, 17-27). But Samuel also represents the older tribal traditions, and he sometimes appears as intransigent and subversive of kingship in general and of Saul in particular (8:6, 10-17; 10:17-19; 13:1-15; 15:1-35).

Saul, as Israel's first king, is portrayed as an attractive, effective leader (esp. chap. 11), and the reader sympathizes with him when he seems undermined by Samuel (13:1-15; 15:1-35). Yet, he also at times seems vacillating and indecisive, prone to impulsive decisions, and unable to see the consequences of his actions (e.g., 14:36-46; Saul's character problems come out more strongly in chaps. 16–31). He represents, at times, Israel's bright future, but at other times, Israel's miscalculation. He does not appear effective at bridging from the old order to the new.

God clearly authorizes the establishment of kingship in Israel (8:7, 9, 22) and designates Saul as the first king (9:15-18). Yet, God clearly regards this development as sinful and as a rejection of God's own rule (8:7-9). It is God's prophet who claims that God has rejected Saul (15:26), but then it is God who chooses David as the "man after God's own heart" (13:14). God clearly directs the course of events, but God's motives and goals are not always clear. Some of this ambiguity may reside in traditions that differ on whether kingship can be reconciled with the covenant tradition.

These tensions of a transition time in Israel's life are reflected in the complexity of the literature in 1 Samuel 8–15. These chapters have proved notoriously difficult for both the scholar and the church reader. Kingship seems condemned at one point and welcomed at another. Saul seems to become king three times. He is rejected by Samuel twice. Later in 1 Samuel, David is introduced to Saul twice, David spares Saul's life twice, and Saul commits suicide twice. The times were complex. So, too, the literature of 1 Samuel (esp. chaps. 8–15) probably went through a complex history of development. Here are some observations that may help in reading this section of 1 Samuel.

(1) In these chapters, we are not dealing with history writing as such but with literary and theological interpretations of history. The storytellers make no effort to be objective. They have perspectives on the stories they want to share, and those perspectives often reflect the situations of later Israel, to whom they are telling the story (e.g., exiles in Babylon).

(2) The episodes that form the present shape of 1 Samuel probably went through a complex process of development. Older views of 1 Samuel divided the book into an early source that was positive to kingship and a late source that was negative to kingship. This approach has largely proved unsuccessful and has been abandoned, although many Bible reference books still reflect this theory. Most scholars now recognize that support and opposition to kingship were a part of the experience of Israel at the time of the transition to kingship.

There is wide agreement that a deuteronomistic historian is responsible for the final shape of these chapters as a part of his larger work from Joshua through 2 Kings. He was more than just an editor, but a creative storyteller in his own right, telling the story of Israel's life for the sake of a generation in exile in Babylon. At times he contributed material of his own (e.g., chap. 12), while at other times he shaped an already extant story through additions and transitions (e.g., chap. 8). We will see his special interests showing through more clearly at some points than at others.

There was also an earlier prophetic edition of these stories (see the Introduction for fuller details), and his interest in the role of prophets and in a prophetic view of kingship can be seen clearly at various points. It is not possible or even desirable to divide the traditions of 1 Samuel into "sources" or to become preoccupied with the pre-canonical development of the text. It is helpful to see the way the tradition picks up the witness of previous generations and incorporates that witness into a new telling of the story. Although the text of the canon is now relatively fixed, this process continues as church and synagogue read and tell the story of Israel in ways that speak to a new generation.

(3) It is the final shape of the story as it now appears in the canonical text of 1 and 2 Samuel that we must seek to understand and appropriate. In the commentary that follows on chaps. 8–15, we will reflect on the story as a theological and literary witness in its present form. This form is not the product of haphazard editing but is a final creative telling of the story. Although occasionally evidences of the process through which the traditions passed will be observed, the overriding concern will always be to understand and to find meaning in the story of Israel's establishment of kingship as it is now presented to us in the book of 1 Samuel and in the larger frame of the story of Israel from Joshua to 2 Kings.

In general terms, 1 Samuel 8–15 divides into two large segments. Chapters 8–12 tell us how Saul became king; chaps. 13–15 tell us how Saul lost kingship. Each of these segments begins and ends in an encounter with the prophet Samuel, who is obviously a key figure for this segment of 1 Samuel.

1 Samuel 8:1-22, Demand and Warning

COMMENTARY

In this chapter, the elders of Israel come to Samuel and demand a king. The kingship, which was hinted at in various ways in chaps. 1–7, now becomes the explicit focus of the story. This is the issue we have been prepared for in the opening chapters of 1 Samuel. We have seen kingship coming, but in 1 Samuel 7 we are told, in effect, that it is not needed. The leadership of God's prophet Samuel was enough. His faithful judging of Israel had replaced the corruption of the house of Eli, and his mediation of God's power had resulted in the defeat of the Philistines. We are prepared and meant to be unsympathetic to the elders' request in 8:4-5.

After a brief report on the corruption of Samuel's sons, the main episode unfolds as a series of conversations between three participants: the elders of Israel, Samuel, and God. The long recitation by Samuel on the "ways of the king" in vv. 10-18 forms the centerpiece for the chapter.

Most scholars have found evidence of the special themes and vocabulary of the deuteronomistic historian in this chapter. This will be particularly noted in the discussion of vv. 8 and 18 and in the theme of apostasy raised in God's speech in vv. 7-9. The mediating role of Samuel between God and people makes this material consistent with the emphasis on his role as a prophet in an earlier prophetic edition of this tradition.[60] The emphasis in this commentary will be on chap. 8 as it now functions in its present form.

8:1-3. Samuel has grown old (vv. 1, 5). We presume he has judged Israel faithfully and well. When he addresses Israel a final time and proclaims his innocence, none can raise complaint against him (12:3-5). But all is not well.

Ironically, it is Samuel's sons who have grown corrupt. Samuel himself had replaced Eli, not because of the sin of the old priest himself, but because of the perverse practices of Eli's sons, Hophni and Phinehas (2:12-17). This notice of the sin of Samuel's sons prepares us for the elders of Israel to request a new arrangement in vv. 4-5.

Samuel had appointed his two sons, Joel and Abijah, to be judges in Beersheba. It is surprising to have two individuals exercising this function in the same location, and to imagine that Samuel's influence stretched as far south as Beersheba. The Jewish historian Josephus knew a tradition that assigned one of the sons to Bethel.[61] These sons, however, were no Samuels. In a series of blunt phrases, the problem is stated in v. 3. They have not followed in their father's ways; they seek profit for themselves; they accept bribes; they "perverted justice." These include explicit violations of covenant law on profits (Exod 18:21), bribes (Exod 23:8), and the administration of justice (Exod 23:2, 6, 8). They

---

60. See Birch, *The Rise of the Israelite Monarchy*, 22-29; and McCarter, *I Samuel*, 156-59.

61. Josephus *Antiquities of the Jews* 6.32.

were practices later harshly condemned by the prophets (see Isa 1:23; 5:23; Amos 5:7, 12). These actions struck at the heart of the covenant relationship that judges in Israel were intended to protect and uphold.

Justice is the fundamental issue at stake in this episode of the story. The Hebrew verb שפט (*šāpaṭ*, "to judge") and the noun משפט (*mišpāṭ*, "justice") play an important role here. Chapter 7 concluded with a notice that Samuel "judged" Israel and "administered justice" (7:15-17). Chapter 8 opens with a notice that his sons "judged" Israel and "perverted justice" (vv. 1-3). The request of the elders (vv. 5, 20) is for a king "to judge us" (*šāpaṭ*; NRSV, "to govern"; NIV, "to lead"). When God later tells Samuel to warn the people, it is to tell them the "*mišpāṭ* of the king" (NRSV, "ways of the king"; NIV, "what the king . . . will do").[62] A central question posed by this chapter is, Where is justice to come from with Samuel growing old? It does not appear that his sons are the answer. Samuel is displeased (v. 6) by the request for a "king to judge us," and his speech later (vv. 10-17) does not hold out the hope that justice can come from a king. Perhaps only God's prophet, like Samuel, can be trusted to guard justice in Israel. When Israel does have kings, it is the prophets Samuel (1 Samuel 13; 15) and Nathan (2 Samuel 12) who will have the authority to confront Saul and David with violations of justice and covenant obedience.

8:4-9. The elders of Israel approach Samuel in his hometown of Ramah (v. 4). It is not clear what segment of Israel this represents. Verse 10 refers to them as "the people who were asking him for a king," which seems to imply that this is not a representative, all-Israel delegation. The fact that they are not worried by Samuel's suggestion of the burdens of kingship in vv. 10-17 has led some to speculate that this gathering represents the more influential and wealthy in Israel, who were most likely to gain from the move to kingship.

The complaint of the elders (v. 5*a*) repeats the language of the notice in vv. 1-3: Samuel is old, and his sons do not follow in his ways.

There is no suggestion in the text that this was an illegitimate concern. But the remedy proposed by the elders takes a bold turn (v. 5*b*). They ask for a king! They want this king to govern them. Since the verb here is *šāpaṭ*, "to judge," it seems clear that they envision this king as a successor to Samuel, who had been "judging" them (7:15-17). They want Samuel to "appoint" this king, but most surprising in their request (demand?) is that they want to be "like other nations." This phrase is repeated in the people's insistence on a king in v. 20. The law of the king in Deut 17:14 uses a similar phrase to describe the people's desire for a king, and then surrounds this desire with laws that guard and restrict the role of the king. To become "like other nations" represented a significant shift for Israel—a shift away from distinctive community to conformity with the patterns of other peoples. What was at stake was Israel's identity and particularity.

Samuel does not pick up on this issue. He is displeased, but his displeasure seems personally focused on his replacement as judge by a king (v. 6). When Samuel prays to God, we have the sense that the people are being reported to a higher authority by someone who has been personally affronted. God certainly saw Samuel's response as one of personal rejection and thus soothed him (v. 7).

God's response is surprising. God commands Samuel to "listen to the voice of the people" (v. 7). God repeats this command twice (vv. 9, 22), each time in slightly stronger terms. The imperative of שמע (*šāma'*, "to listen" or "to hear") often carries the implication of "obey." God immediately acquiesces to the demand of the people and proceeds to soothe Samuel. Only then does God voice the divine concerns raised by the people's request. To seek an earthly king was a rejection of God's rule as divine king. It was a challenge to divine sovereignty, and at root it was idolatrous. God equated the desire for a king with Israel's forsaking of the Lord in favor of serving other gods. Israel had been doing this since God brought them out of Egypt (an adroit reminder of exodus as the origin of Israel in God's deliverance, v. 8). The elders' request is a rejection of God, not of Samuel. The issue is idolatry (like other nations) and apostasy (only God is king), not personal

---

62. The "*mišpāṭ* of the king" will be discussed further below. It can be noted here, however, that the NIV translation is woefully inadequate. It obscures the connection of this term to "justice" and the fact that the text may be referring to a formal document or code of royal responsibilities (see 10:25; Deut 17:18-19).

affront. What Samuel is now experiencing is the same idolatrous behavior God had seen before ("so also they are doing to you," v. 8*b*), not something uniquely directed at Samuel.

The Hebrew term מאס (*māʾas*, "to reject") is a key term. The people's action is described here and later in Samuel's speech at Mizpah (10:19) as a "rejection" of God as king. The term next appears as a description of God's action toward Saul, "Because you have rejected the word of the LORD, he has also rejected you from being king" (15:23; cf. 15:26; 16:1). As Gunn has observed, "The use of the motif of rejection . . . formally links Saul's fate with Yahweh's understanding of his own treatment at the hands of the people."[63] This rejection of God casts a shadow over Saul's kingship from the beginning.

Nevertheless, God instructs Samuel again to "listen to their voice" (v. 9*a*). God does not approve, but God permits. The tone is indulgent and tolerant, almost resigned. But Samuel is also told to "solemnly warn them" (v. 9*b*, the verb is given emphasis by the addition of an infinitive). The verb עוד (*ʿûd*) means to "give witness" and in this emphatic form can mean to "give warning." In effect, Samuel as God's prophet becomes witness to the dangers of the path the people have chosen. The content of Samuel's witness is to be the משפט המלך (*mišpaṭ hammelek*, vv. 9, 11). The phrase seems to indicate some formal standard for the behavior of kings. Both 1 Sam 10:25 (using a similar phrase) and Deut 17:18-19 imply a written document to which kings were accountable. Both of these passages, however, imply that the document was some sort of restraint on the abuse of kingship, whereas Samuel's speech in vv. 10-18 provides a catalog of abuse. Some have seen the phrase as connoting the rights of the king, while others have seen it merely as descriptive of the conduct of the king. Clearly there is an ironic contrast between the concern of the elders for "justice" and the use of the term "justice" (*mišpaṭ*) for this recitation of oppressive royal behavior. Veijola, noting the common use of the term "witness" or "warn" in connection with treaties or agreements, suggests that Samuel is instructed by God to lay out before the people, with proper

warnings, the terms of an ironic royal treaty.[64] In effect, God tells Samuel to let them know what they're in for. "They wanted justice? Tell them the kind of justice they can expect from a king." Still, God granted the people's request. Samuel was to warn them, but he was also to do what they asked.

8:10-18. Samuel's speech is a catalog of the royal abuse of power. Many have observed that it seems to reflect Israel's later experience with its own kings, especially Solomon. Thus the deuteronomistic historian may be suggesting that the request for a king was the beginning of the path to exile. Mendelsohn, however, has shown that this picture could also fit Canaanite royal practices as early as the thirteenth century BCE (Ugarit and Alalakh).[65] If so, Samuel's speech may describe the excesses of pagan kingship rather than being a description of Israel's own royal experience. The practices reflected in vv. 11-17 fit well with the foreign practices forbidden to Israel's kings in the law of the king (Deut 17:14-20). Perhaps these views are not mutually exclusive. An old document detailing the abusive practices of foreign kings may well have suited the deuteronomistic historian's needs in critiquing Israel's royal abuses.

Whatever the origin of this portrait of kingship, it is clear that Samuel is using it in an attempt to dissuade the Israelite elders from their request for a king. Although v. 10 says that Samuel reported the words of the Lord, there is no suggestion that he revealed to the elders the Lord's instruction to grant their request. In fact, after God instructs Samuel a third time to "listen to their voice," Samuel still does not tell the people of God's acquiescence in their request and sends them home (v. 22). For Polzin, this is evidence that Samuel is dragging his feet in spite of God's willingness to grant a king. He believes the *mišpaṭ hammelek* must have included duties of the king toward the people as well as the privileges Samuel details; thus Samuel is intentionally giving only half the picture.[66]

63. David M. Gunn, *The Fate of King Saul: An Introduction of a Biblical Story* (Sheffield: JSOT, 1980) 60.

64. T. Veijola, *Das Königtum in der Beurteilung der Deuteronomistischen Historiographie*, Annales Academiae Scientiarum Fennicae Series B 198 (Helsinki: Suomalainen Tiedeaktemia, 1977) 60.

65. Isaac Mendelsohn, "Samuel's Denunciation of Kingship in the Light of Akkadian Documents from Ugarit," *BASOR* 143 (1956) 17-22.

66. Polzin, *Samuel and the Deuteronomist*, 85-88. Polzin also holds the opinion that the practices Samuel details are typical and expected of kings and do not constitute abuse of power. Samuel merely gives these normal royal practices a negative spin.

Whatever Samuel's motives, he clearly paints a negative portrait of kingship, and it is clearly intended to convince the people to withdraw their request. The royal practices Samuel highlighted were those of conscripting young men for military service, farming royal holdings, and manufacture of implements (vv. 11-12) and young women for perfumers, cooks, and bakers (v. 13). The king would also take the best of the productive land and redistribute it to his own retainers (v. 14). He would require a tenth of all forms of wealth—grain, vineyards, flocks, cattle, donkeys, and slaves (vv. 15-17). All these are practices attested for Israelite and non-Israelite kings.[67]

Samuel's speech portrays royal privilege as grasping and debilitating. Four times he uses the verb "to take" (לקח *lāqaḥ*) and twice the verb "to confiscate one tenth" (עשׂר *'āśar*) as the main action of his description (vv. 11, 13, 14, 15, 16, 17). What is the "justice" of a king? A king will take, take, take, take, take, take! Even more dramatically, Samuel describes the end result of this grasping: "you shall be his slaves" (v. 17b). To serve a king is to return to bondage, to reverse what God had done in the exodus deliverance (v. 8). The fate Samuel described would undercut the very identity of Israel as God's delivered people. For the security of a king, the people would surrender their freedom. "The monarchy substitutes human power for the availability of Yahweh."[68]

Samuel concludes by saying the day will come when the people will "cry out because of your king . . . but the LORD will not answer" (v. 18). The cry and answer that brought deliverance under Samuel (7:9) are reversed. The pattern of outcry and divine answer, which had been Israel's hope and security from the exodus onward, is now broken (Exod 2:23-25; 3:7-8). This sequence had particularly marked the period of the judges, but under a king the time of divine answer is ended. The phrase "in that day" may indicate the historian's word to his audience that in exile "that day" had already come, and "in that day" God could not save them from the fate they had chosen. Significantly, v. 18 describes this choice as the king "you have chosen for

yourselves." Even in the law of the king in Deut 17:15, which allows a king in Israel, it is to be one "whom the Lord your God will choose." The people's request is seen in v. 18 as an attempt at self-willed choice by the people. God will allow a king, but the ongoing story in 1 Samuel suggests that God will choose him. Chapter 9 is a story of Saul's designation by God, not by the people.

8:19-22. In counterpoint to God's instruction that Samuel "listen to the voice of the people" (vv. 7, 9, 22), the people "refused to listen to the voice of Samuel" (v. 19). Samuel's warning has no effect. The response is a resounding "No!" Some have suggested that the people's disregard of Samuel's speech shows that these were the Israelites who would benefit from a royal system. The story seems to suggest their stubbornness in the face of Samuel's warning more than their sense that it would not apply to them. In any case, Samuel offered no real alternative, so it is not surprising that the people insisted on having a king.

The reasons for having a king are expanded. The people still desire to be "like other nations" and to have a king "to govern" them, but in addition they want the king to "go out before us and fight our battles" (v. 20). This is the first hint of a military justification for kingship. Perhaps the Philistine threat is behind this vague remark.

When Samuel reports the people's determination to the Lord, he is instructed a third time to "listen" and to "set a king over them." Instead of immediately doing so, Samuel sends the people home (v. 22). This could be read as intentional recalcitrance on Samuel's part, but it may simply be an ending of this episode in order to move the story on to the various traditions on how Saul became the first king (chaps. 9–11).

When we look back at the entire episode in 1 Samuel 8, it is clear that the people have a legitimate complaint. The system is breaking down, and Samuel seems unwilling or unable to offer a remedy. It would seem that both Samuel and the elders, with their request, appear in the story as false options. Samuel is defensive and foot-dragging. He sees the request as a personal affront and is not immediately responsive to the people's needs or God's command. The elders, on

---

67. See Klein, *1 Samuel*, 77-78, for particulars on these practices.
68. Brueggemann, *First and Second Samuel*, 65.

the other hand, seem to want more than the corrective to a legitimate problem. They are motivated by the desire to emulate their neighbors and to give up the difficult vocation of covenant community, which makes them different. Self-interest and status seem to occupy them, and they make a more emotional than thoughtful response to the issues raised by Samuel's warning.

It is God who seems willing to risk a new choice, even against the divine self-interest. God's acquiescence does seem more indulgent than gracious, but there is a sense that God knows more and is willing to risk more than Samuel or the elders. Or perhaps God is willing to let his covenant partners take their own risks, even when God believes their choice to be unwise. God knows that kingship in these terms is idolatrous and sinful. Still, kingship is authorized and perhaps not unredeemable (as Samuel later suggests in 12:14), but the risk is great. Saul will fall victim to that risk. Perhaps God is already looking ahead to David and his special role in the story of Israel's kings. It may take the failure of Saul to allow the possibilities of David.

REFLECTIONS

1. It was not easy for Israel to live as covenant community in partnership with God. It was clear from Exodus onward that the covenant model was an alternative to the models of community that prevailed in the world of Israel's neighbors.[69] That alternative model included a recognition of God's sovereignty, which did not require hierarchical forms of leadership in the human community. But the lure of conformity is seductive, and the pressures toward cultural accommodation are great. "Appoint for us a king . . . like other nations" (8:5). The people said to Samuel, in effect, "We don't want to be different anymore. We want to be like everyone else. The pressures of alternative living are too great." One of the issues raised by this episode for the community of faith in every generation is the lure and the danger of cultural accommodation.

Like Israel, the church is called to be in the world, but not of the world. The pattern of the church's life is defined by relationship with God in continuity with the covenant model of Israel and with the community of new covenant in Jesus Christ, shaped by the early church. The qualities of such faith communities include love, justice, peace, compassion, and worship. This is not an easy calling. The pressures toward cultural conformity are great, and we live in a culture that often elevates a different set of qualities from those of the covenant model. They include self-interest and self-fulfillment, political and military power, acquisition and consumption. It is understandably tempting to want to be like everyone else, both as persons and as institutions.

The special warning for us in 1 Samuel 8 is the way in which authentic crisis may support the desire to be "like other nations." The crisis of leadership created by Samuel's age and the corruption of his sons was real, but in the response to this crisis Israel's authentic identity as a covenant people was compromised. Likewise, the church's greatest temptations to accommodation often come in struggles to deal with authentic challenges or to respond to genuine crises in the church or the society.

A man whose father was a pastor in California at the start of World War II confided that his father had been guilt stricken for his entire life because he had failed to say a word of protest when a close personal friend and neighbor of Japanese descent was taken to an internment camp and had his home and business seized. As a pastor in the community, he thought he might have made a difference, but he remained silent. The crisis of the war with Japan was real, but he compromised his deepest faith commitments because of the pressure of public sentiment and the fear of seeming different. It is a pressure to be "like other nations" that we all have known. At its simplest, it is

---

69. For fuller discussions of covenant community as an alternative model, see Walter Brueggemann, *Prophetic Imagination* (Philadelphia: Fortress, 1978) chap. 2, and Bruce C. Birch, *Let Justice Roll Down*, 172-84.

a personal unwillingness to be identified as a person of faith in our communities and workplaces. At its most demonic, it is a church that accommodates itself to evil in the name of patriotism and produces a Nazi Germany or an ethnic cleansing.

The church as an institution is vulnerable to this danger of responding to crisis by becoming "like other nations." Many denominations and congregations have become concerned over membership decline. Outreach and evangelism are always legitimate concerns for the church, but not at the cost of the church's basic faith identity. In contemporary America the emphasis on individual independence and self-reliance is enormous, and the notion of relating to others in community is not always popular. In our eagerness to reach the world, the temptation is to compromise the basic identity of God's covenant people. But it is simply not possible to be a person of covenant faith without being a part of the covenant community. The church could become "like other nations," but it would cease to be the church. In its desire to be relevant, the church must also guard against sacrificing its authentic calling and identity for the sake of the latest fad, success scheme, or ideology that comes along. The desire to be "like other nations" is never a legitimate motivation for change or unwillingness to change.

2. Reflection on 1 Samuel 8 raises questions on the difficult relationship of faith community to political institutions. Israel did not have the sharp separation of sacred and secular institutions that American society assumes, but the basic issues remain the same. When does trust in human power become a rejection of divine power? How does our recognition of divine authority relate to our recognition of human authority? How do citizenship and discipleship interact? Chapter 8 does not so much offer answers to these questions as it puts them on our agenda. These questions provide a lens and a focus for reading the stories of Saul and David, which lie ahead. These questions also provide a framework for reflection on the uneasy relationship between divine power and human power in our own settings and institutions as citizens of a modern nation and members of contemporary churches. This chapter reminds us that communities of faith are not isolated from the arenas of public power. Our decisions about relationship to God affect the way we live in the sociopolitical world.

In this story, the elders and Samuel both suggest dangers that still face us in the modern church. The elders have a legitimate concern for justice, but are willing to erode the authority of God for the sake of stronger centers of human power. Samuel is protective of the integrity of God, but represents a vested interest in the way things have always been done. Chapter 8 offers no simple right-and-wrong way to adjudicate the claims of citizenship and faith. It merely demands an awareness of the interrelated character of these claims.

The elders' initial approach asks us to consider where the church's support of traditional ways of doing things has allowed or perpetuated injustice. Have we raised up leaders who close their eyes to patterns of abuse in the name of protecting the status quo? The elders' request for a king raises questions about our willingness to grasp for security when the need is for justice. To what degree does the church support public policies that provide instant gratification at the expense of long-term problem solving? We want forceful, even authoritarian, leaders to deal with issues of crime, drug trafficking, deteriorating cities, welfare abuse, and the collapse of family structures. But there is often little support for long-term systemic efforts to address the underlying issues of poverty, consumerism, racism, and societal values that create the dysfunctions in our communities and families. Samuel's catalog of oppressive royal practices ought to give us pause as citizens and as people of faith. Like other nations before us, we may be too willing to sacrifice freedom and justice for the sake of security.

The ultimate issue raised by 1 Samuel 8 is, To what degree have we let our trust in human authority overshadow our trust in God? This is the issue placed before us for the reading of the remainder of 1 and 2 Samuel. It is also placed before us as people of faith who must grapple with issues of public power and authority. Where does faith draw its boundaries? At what point do our loyalties to human institutions have to give way to the higher loyalty we owe to God? There is no set answer, but there are many examples of those who were forced to make such a decision. Martin Luther opposed the ecclesiastical power of a pope. Martin Luther King, Jr., opposed the civil power of a state. In 1 Samuel 8, God gives Israel the freedom to choose a king, but God does not give up the claim of divine sovereignty. We, too, have the freedom to participate boldly in making the decisions of public life, but if we read this chapter carefully we should do so with some degree of humility (and repentance?) in recognition that human power is only subordinate to divine power.

1 Samuel 9:1–11:15, Saul Becomes King

OVERVIEW

The spotlight shifts from the question of whether to have a king to the question of who will be king. These chapters contain three separate stories relating how Saul was designated as the first king of Israel. In 9:1–10:16, Saul is anointed and commissioned by the prophet Samuel. In 10:17-27, Saul is chosen by lot and found hiding among the baggage before being acclaimed by the people. In 11:1-15, Saul delivers Jabesh-gilead from the Ammonites in a style reminiscent of the judges, and the people make Saul king.

Yet kingship arrives uneasily in Israel. Samuel's speech in 10:18-19 reminds the people that their desire for a king is a rejection of God's rule. Even after Saul is chosen by lot and legitimated by the people, there are those who complain and withhold their allegiance (10:27). After Saul's deliverance of Jabesh-gilead, some desire to put such complainers to death (11:12-13). Samuel's farewell speech in chap. 12 renews and extends Samuel's objections to kingship and his warnings about its dangers. In 13:1-15 and 15:1-35, Saul has no sooner become king than he is rejected from kingship by Samuel. In chaps. 9–11, Saul has his brief moment in the story, but it is clear that the older Israelite tradition represented by Samuel is still ambiguous about kingship. Saul is not able to win over the Israelite tradition. It remains for David to do that.

These chapters may have gone through a complex literary history. Traditionally these stories were each assigned to an early pro-monarchical source and a late anti-monarchical source. This approach has been largely abandoned. Nevertheless, each episode does seem to have a different perspective on kingship in general and Saul in particular. It is likely that these episodes had separate literary origins, but they are now connected and interrelated by a creative hand that presented these traditions as part of a single witness to this important period of transformation in Israel. It is my belief that this artful, interconnected story was first the product of prophetically influenced circles with a distinctive theology of kingship in mind. I will note places where this prophetic theology comes into view. This prophetically influenced telling of the story was incorporated into the Deuteronomistic History work, and the Dtr historian made his own creative literary contributions. Nevertheless, the emphasis will not be on the literary prehistory of these chapters, but on their witness in the present final form of the text. The full text as we now have it is the telling of the story of kingship that Israel itself finally fixed and passed on as its accepted version of these important events. Listening to the voice of this full witness is our chief task.

1 Samuel 9:1–10:16, The Anointing of Saul

COMMENTARY

With the opening of chap. 9 there is a sudden shift in scene and subject matter. Chapter 8 ended in ambiguity. There would be a king in Israel. God had ordered Samuel to listen to the people's request. But the matter of kingship is still problematic. God would grant the request, but understood it as a rejection of God's own rule; and Samuel had warned of the oppressive policies of such a king. In chap. 9, these ambiguities are left behind for the moment. The attention of the narrative shifts to the questions of who and how. In three separate episodes, of which this is the first, the answer to who is always Saul. The answer to how is a bit more complex.

In this story, Saul is anointed for his role by the prophet Samuel. Saul is designated by God and brought to Samuel through the circumstances of a search for lost donkeys. In the anointing by God's prophet, Saul is legitimized for his role as ruler (נגיד *nāgîd*, "ruler," leader," not מלך *melek*, "king"; see Commentary below) to deliver Israel from the Philistines (9:16; 10:1), and he receives God's Spirit (10:10). Saul's commissioning is declared by Samuel to be the "word of God" (9:27*b*).

There is no hint of ambiguity about kingship or Saul in this account. There is no reluctance evidenced by Samuel or by God to this authorization of Saul to his role. The motive for this designation of Saul is God's salvation. God has chosen Saul to bring deliverance from the Philistines (a motive absent in chap. 8). There is no indication in this account that God is acting in response to the people's desires. Saul and kingship have their moment in the story without qualification.

The anointing of Saul by the prophet Samuel is bracketed by the story of a young man's search for his father's lost donkeys. After a brief introduction of Saul's background in vv. 1-2, a tale unfolds of lost donkeys, young men, journeys, and a seer who might help them (vv. 3-13). This story seems totally unrelated to any of the matters that have occupied the attention of 1 Samuel 1–8. Since the work of Gressman, most scholars have agreed

that this material is marked by folkloristic elements: indefinite time, an unnamed city, the motif of journeying and searching, and an ideal youth as hero.[70] Saul and his young servant companion search for the lost animals. Their search is futile, and they resolve to consult a man of God at a nearby city. They have run out of bread and discuss how they will pay for his advice. They meet maidens coming to draw water who tell them in some detail of the arrival of a man of God to offer a sacrifice. These verses (vv. 3-13) are rich in detail, leisurely in pace, and seemingly unrelated to matters of significance in the wider story of 1 Samuel.

At v. 14 there is a dramatic shift. The unknown man of God/seer is revealed to be Samuel. The reader knows him, although Saul does not. The pace and mood of the story shift. In a flashback we are told that God had told Samuel of Saul's coming (vv. 15-17). We learn that Saul is God's choice for king, and, in a series of events, Saul is anointed, receives the Spirit of God, and prophesies with a band of prophets. This segment of the story (9:14–10:13) has been shaped by the pattern typical of prophetic call narratives (see Excursus, "The Call Narrative Form in 1 Samuel 9:1–10:16"). Samuel disposes of the matter of the lost donkeys (v. 20). This is no longer the focus. God's purposes, Israel's deliverance, rulers, prophets, God's Spirit—these are the central focus of the story, and they are related to the larger themes of 1 Samuel 1–7. In 10:14-16, Saul returns home, and the focus again becomes the lost donkeys. Saul keeps the "matter of the kingship" a secret (v. 16*b*).

It is possible that the story of the lost donkeys and the story of the anointing by Samuel originated separately, but if so, they have now been artfully combined and interrelated. The episode as it now stands may well have originated from prophetic circles that emphasized the importance of the prophetic role in

---

70. For a fuller discussion, see Bruce C. Birch, "The Development of the Tradition of the Anointing of Saul, 1 Sam 9:1–10:16," *JBL* 90 (1971) 57-58.

authorizing Israel's kings. To be legitimate, kings must be anointed by God's prophet and receive God's Spirit. This prophetic perspective on kingship may be behind the arrangement of the ongoing story. In 10:17-27, Saul, God's anointed one, is given public recognition; and in 11:1-15, Saul demonstrates the power of God's Spirit by delivering the people of Jabesh-gilead. We will see a similar pattern in the beginning of David's story in 1 Samuel 16–17.

In 1 Sam 9:1–10:16, each segment of the story is constructed around dialogues with two brief narrative intervals and a stylized introduction.

9:1-4	Introduction of Saul and the search for the donkeys
9:5-10	Saul and his servant companion
9:11-14	Young men and the maidens
9:15-17	God and Samuel
9:18-21	Samuel and Saul—first day
9:22-25	(Narrative of the banquet)
9:26–10:8	Samuel and Saul—second day
10:9-13	(Narrative of Saul's prophesying)
10:14-16	Saul and his uncle

These first two conversations and the final one focus on the lost donkeys. The three conversations in the central portion of the story give us the theological center and the narrative climax of the story. In 9:15-17, we learn that it is God's initiative that is theologically central to these events. In 9:26–10:8, God's initiative is fulfilled and the story reaches its climax in the anointing of Saul as ruler to deliver Israel. Samuel the prophet is the connecting link between God and Saul.

9:1-2. Saul is introduced into the story for the first time by the use of an introductory formula, giving us his genealogy and some basic information about him. The pattern is a bit unusual, since it begins not with Saul but with his father, Kish (see 17:12; Judg 3:15; 1 Kgs 11:26). Saul is from an influential family in the tribe of Benjamin. The phrase "man of wealth" (חיל גבור *gibbôr ḥayil*) can also mean "mighty warrior," and we might take it to mean that Saul's father is a powerful and influential man. Further, we are told that Saul

is both more handsome and physically taller than most men. This notice is reminiscent of other specially destined characters in the biblical story (Joseph, Gen 39:6; David, 1 Sam 16:12, 18; 17:42; Absalom, 2 Sam 14:25). This is not a story of humble beginnings or of the ugly duckling. Saul is introduced to us as a young man with good prospects.

9:3-10. Saul is sent by his father to find some strayed donkeys, and he takes a young man (probably a servant) with him. The pace of the story is unhurried, and it lingers over many details, such as the route of the search through territories of uncertain identity (v. 4). After a futile search, Saul wants to turn back out of concern that his father might become more worried about him than about the donkeys (v. 5); but his companion has heard of a man of God in a nearby town and suggests that they ask him about the donkeys (v. 6). Saul worries about what to give for payment, since they are out of bread (v. 7). But the young man finds a quarter shekel of silver (v. 8), and so they go to find the man of God (v. 10). Elements of their conversation will come back to mind later in the story when Samuel tells Saul of signs that he will receive. The first sign would be a man bringing news that the donkeys have been found and that Saul's father is worried about him (10:2), and the second would be a man who will give them bread (10:3-4).

In our first encounter with Saul, he seems young and inexperienced. The servant-companion seems more resourceful than Saul. There is little to make us think that Saul is a man of destiny. Perhaps this is in itself significant. Saul does nothing to appear ambitious or in any way seeking kingship. We are introduced to Saul completely apart from the usual political maneuverings that lead to leadership or high office. At this point, Saul is a passive participant in the story of his own destiny. He is to be chosen, not to choose.

There is a brief parenthetical comment in v. 9. The author of this story felt the need to explain to readers that a man who used to be called a "seer" was the same as what was now known to the readers of the story as a "prophet." Both terms designated one to whom inquiries could be made about matters of concern seeking insight into the future or advice on a course of action. This is a bit confusing, since the term "seer" is not used until v. 11. There the "man of God" is referred to as a "seer." It would seem that all three terms are being used somewhat interchangeably in this chapter. The nameless "man of God" will suddenly be revealed as Samuel in v. 14. The author apparently thought readers would be confused when the prophet Samuel is addressed as "seer" instead of as "prophet."

9:11-14. As Saul and his companion approach the city, they meet young girls coming down from the hill to draw water. They ask the maidens, "Is the seer here?" (v. 11). They receive an effusive answer, detailing the arrival of the seer, his custom to offer sacrifice at the shrine there, and his practice of hosting a banquet for invited guests after the sacrifice (vv. 12-13). After they leave the girls and enter the city, the two young men meet the seer on his way to the shrine, and it is none other than Samuel (v. 14). Saul clearly does not know Samuel (cf. vv. 18-19), but the reader now suspects that something more significant than lost donkeys is afoot.

9:15-17. A flashback informs the reader that behind Saul's seemingly innocent search is a divine initiative. What is taking place is a part of God's plan. A day earlier God had spoken to the prophet Samuel that on the next day God would send to him a man from the tribe of Benjamin. There is no rationale for God's choice. Saul, as we know from our glimpse of him earlier in the chapter, has not sought leadership of the kingdom. God has not picked him out because he has already distinguished himself in leadership in any way. The choice of Saul is to be an act of sovereign freedom on the part of God. It surely is not what the elders had in mind in their request for a king. Perhaps Samuel thought he would have a voice in the choosing. When Saul comes into view the next day, God speaks again to Samuel, saying, "This is the man" (v. 17). God alone has chosen, bypassing Samuel and the elders and offering no explanation for the choice.

God's intended course of action, however, is made very clear. There is a role for Samuel and for Saul in what God is doing. The verbs and their subjects are straight to the point: "I will send . . . you shall anoint . . . he shall save" (v. 15). God's own motive for this plan of action is also clear, "I have seen." What

God had seen was the suffering of Israel at the hand of the Philistines. The outcry of the people had come to the Lord. Three times in the brief speech to Samuel (v. 16) God speaks of Israel as "my people." The language of God's concern is the language of the exodus God, who sees suffering, hears the outcry, and acts to deliver (Exod 2:23-25; 3:7-8). Ironically, in 1 Samuel 1–8 it has been primarily the Philistines who have reminded us of the exodus God (4:8; 6:6; but see also God's reminder in 8:8). Once again this exodus God acts to bring salvation to Israel.

Samuel is to "anoint" Saul to be "ruler" (v. 16 NRSV; NIV, "leader") over Israel. It is significant that the term "king" (מלך *melek*) is not used. Instead, both here and in 10:1, we find the term נגיד (*nāgîd*). The precise meaning of this term has been widely debated. Some have argued that Saul was not initially authorized as king but as some sort of military commander in the face of the Philistine threat. His role only developed toward full kingship as he continued in office, acquired court officers, and hoped to begin a dynastic succession with his son Jonathan. However, both David (25:30; 2 Sam 5:2; 6:21; 7:8) and Solomon (1 Kgs 1:20, 35) are referred to as *nāgîd* in contexts that are related to kingship. Even though the term "king" is not used in the story of Saul's anointing, the final line declares that Saul kept the "matter of the kingship" to himself (10:16). Clearly, the story as it now stands understands Saul's role as royal and not just military. Mettinger has made a convincing case for understanding *nāgîd* as a term for king-designate.[71] This meaning would fit well here, since Saul has been designated as king but has not yet taken office in Israel. The intention in God's command is to start Saul on a path to a royal destiny.

Whatever *nāgîd* came to designate as an office in Israel, we should not overlook an important significance to the title within the literary framework of the story itself. The noun *nāgîd* seems to be derived from the verb נגד (*nāgad*, "to make known"), which appears mainly in its hiphil form

---

71. T. N. D. Mettinger, *King and Messiah: The Civil and Sacral Legitimation of the Israelite Kings,* CB Old Testament Series 8 (Lund: C. W. K. Gleerup, 1976). Mettinger builds on an earlier suggestion by A. Alt, "The Formation of the Israelite State in Palestine," in *Essays on Old Testament History and Religion* (Oxford: Basil Blackwell, 1966) 195.

הגיד (*higgîd*). This verb appears six times in the story (9:6, 8, 18, 19; 10:15, 16). Literally, *nāgîd* means "the made known one" or "the designated one." The use of the noun and the verb stresses that Saul does not on his own become king. He is "designated" by God. This role for Saul is "made known" by God to Samuel and through Samuel to Saul.

The act of anointing legitimates Saul in this office.[72] There are many references to the anointing of kings in Israel; some are by the people (2 Sam 2:4; 5:3; 2 Kgs 11:12; 23:30) and others by God's prophet (9:16; 10:1; 15:1, 17; 16:12-13; 2 Sam 12:7; 2 Kgs 9:3, 6, 12; 2 Chr 22:7). Both types may well reflect God as the ultimate source of authorization, with people or prophet acting as God's signifying agent in the ritual of anointing. Certainly prophetic circles would stress the necessity of God's prophet in this role for the legitimization of kings. The account of Saul's anointing seems to be from such circles, since it highlights the role of Samuel. As we will see in the discussion of 10:1, an important consequence of anointing in this prophetic tradition may be the receiving of God's Spirit. In any case, kings in Israel came to be known as Yahweh's "anointed one" (משיח *māšîaḥ*). When the hope for God's "anointed one" was projected into the future as an eschatological hope, it became the expectation of God's coming Messiah. In a sense, Saul is Israel's first "messiah"; thus important themes in Israel's story find a beginning.

In v. 17 (see also 10:1), Samuel is told that Saul will "rule" over Israel. This term (עצר *ʿāṣar*) means literally "to keep in bounds." It may be taken in the sense of "govern" or "administer" and is an activity not limited to kings. It indicates more than a military role for Saul.[73]

It is important to note that for 9:1–10:16, the motivating factor for the establishment of kingship in Israel is the Philistine crisis. There is no hint of a request from the elders or of the situation with Samuel's sons. Kingship

and Saul as the king-designate appear in this story as a part of God's saving response to Israel's cry of distress. None of the ambiguity that was noted in connection with kingship in chap. 8 is present in this account.

9:18-21. Saul obviously does not know or recognize Samuel, and he inquires about the seer. After a curt acknowledgment that he is the seer, Samuel gives a more elaborate response that must have amazed Saul (v. 19). In quick order, Saul is ordered up to the shrine, invited to dinner with Samuel, and told he is staying the night. Samuel further says that he will tell Saul everything on his "mind" (לב *lēb*, "heart," often translated "mind," since ancient Israelites understood the heart to be the seat of thought and understanding). Saul undoubtedly thought that the lost donkeys were uppermost in his "mind." Samuel dismisses this concern by informing Saul that the donkeys have been found. Saul is to give no further "thought" (*lēb*) to them (v. 20*a*). Something new and more significant is about to be placed on the "mind/heart" of Saul. In the end, he will be transformed; God will give him "another heart" (*lēb*, 10:9).

Samuel ends his speech to Saul with an enigmatic question (v. 20*b*): "On whom is Israel's desire fixed, if not on you and on all your ancestral house?" In this NRSV translation (and the similar one in the NIV), the emphasis seems to be on Saul and his family as the fulfillment of Israel's desires—namely, a leader, a king. It may also be translated, "To whom belong all desirable things in Israel . . . ?" This rendering highlights the wealth and benefits that might flow to Saul and his family when he rules Israel. In either case, lost donkeys are of little consequence when Saul has these prospects ahead of him.

In v. 21, Saul finally senses that something extraordinary is taking place. He may not fully understand what Samuel is alluding to, but he objects that he is not the right person. He claims that he is from an insignificant tribe and a humble family. In a somewhat bewildered tone he asks why Samuel has spoken to him in this way. Saul's objections sound much like those raised by earlier figures in the biblical story, particularly Moses and Gideon. Such objections are a standard feature of call stories, in which God calls and commissions persons to a task in the divine plan. The

---

72. On anointing and its significance, see E. Kutsch, *Salbung als Rechtsakt im Alten Testament und in alten Orient*, BZAW 88 (Berlin: Alfred Topelmann, 1963). For the importance of anointing to the prophetic ideology of kingship, see Rolf Knierim, "The Messianic Concept in the First Book of Samuel," in *Jesus and the Historian*, ed. T. Trotter (Philadelphia: Westminster, 1968) 31.

73. Polzin, *Samuel and the Deuteronomist*, 94, takes this verb to mean "constrain," "hinder," "imprison" and sees it as a divine prediction of the dire consequences of kingship. Given the positive outlook on Saul throughout this account, such negative meanings seem unlikely.

standardized pattern of such call narratives has influenced the shape of this story about Saul. Since this pattern stretches over several sections of this episode it is appropriate to briefly consider the call narrative pattern as a whole and its influence on this story.

❖   ❖   ❖   ❖

EXCURSUS: THE CALL NARRATIVE FORM IN 1 SAMUEL 9:1–10:16

Norman Habel has provided the most definitive description of a basic literary structure in prophetic call narratives.[74] He based his work on examination of the calls of Moses, Gideon, and the classical prophets for whom we have a call story. All of the elements Habel discerned in such call narratives are present in the Saul story (1 Sam 9:1–10:16). They occur in a somewhat altered order, modified to account for the presence of the prophet Samuel as a third-party mediator of God's call to Saul. This role of Samuel is one of the special interests and emphases of this story and is consistent with the view that the story was shaped in prophetic circles.

The elements of this formal structure in the Samuel/Saul account are: (1) divine confrontation, (2) introductory word, (3) objection, (4) commission, (5) sign, and (6) reassurance.

THE DIVINE CONFRONTATION, 9:15

It is God who takes the initiative. In most call stories, God confronts directly the one to be commissioned, but here God contacts Samuel, God's prophet. The situation is similar to that of the prophet Elijah (1 Kgs 19:15-16), when the prophet is commanded to anoint Elisha as his successor (interestingly, also to anoint Jehu as king of Israel). The direct nature of the divine encounter is emphasized by the Hebrew idiom for direct revelation, "the LORD had uncovered Samuel's ear" (9:15 NRSV; NIV, "revealed").

THE INTRODUCTORY WORD, 9:16-17

This element in the structure spells out the basis for the commission to come later. God is still speaking to Samuel, and the purpose of the call is simple and clear: It is to raise up a deliverer for Israel against the Philistines. The urgency is underlined by the statement that God has seen the affliction and heard the outcry of "my people." The language is reminiscent of the call of Moses (Exod 3:7-9), and the need for a deliverer against an enemy is like the situation in Gideon's call (Judg 6:11-24).

This revelatory word to Samuel anticipates the actual commissioning of Saul, which comes later. The language of 9:16-17 is substantially repeated in 10:1. In God's eyes, Saul has already been commissioned, even though Samuel has yet to communicate this fact to Saul. The Hebrew word שׁלח (šālaḥ, "send") is a key word in most prophetic call narratives, but in this Samuel/Saul story it appears in the word to Samuel (9:16) and not in the actual commissioning (10:1). In a sense, Saul is already "sent" by God before he ever encounters Samuel and is told of this "sending."

---

74. Norman Habel, "The Form and Significance of the Call Narratives," *ZAW* 77 (1965) 297-323. Wolfgang Richter, *Die sogenannten vorprophetischen Berufungsberichte. Eine literaturwissenschaftliche Studie zu 1 Sam 9:1-10, 16; Ex 3f.; und Ri 6:11b-17*, FRLANT 101 (Göttingen: Vandenhoeck und Ruprecht, 1970), sees the calls of Moses, Gideon, and Saul following a different format from that described by Habel. In my opinion, what Richter describes are variants of Habel's pattern adapted to different stories and settings, and not a separate formal type. See my fuller, more technical discussion of the call pattern for Saul in Birch, "The Development of the Tradition of the Anointing of Saul," 60-68.

THE OBJECTION, 9:21

The recipient of God's call now objects that he is unworthy or inadequate of such a calling. Ordinarily this element would come after the commissioning. Here Saul receives only a foreshadowing of the commission in Samuel's statement that he and his family have been singled out for a distinctive role in Israel (v. 20*b*). Of course, the reader knows the full commission, since it was revealed to Samuel the day before. The content of Saul's objection is much like Gideon's. However, since it comes before the full statement of the task before him, Saul's objection, unlike Gideon's, is not that he is unequal to the task (Judg 6:15), but that he is unworthy of the choice itself.

THE COMMISSION, 10:1

The commissioning itself is prefaced by Samuel's statement that this is the "word of God" (9:27; cf. NIV, weakly, "message from God"), emphasizing the role of the prophet as a mediator of God's call in this story. The commission is virtually identical to God's words given to Samuel on the day before, except that the Philistines are not specifically named. Saul is to be a deliverer for Israel from all its "enemies." The commission is similar to that of Gideon (Judg 6:14), beginning with a rhetorical question (see NIV; the NRSV makes it a statement) that emphasizes divine initiative and ends in a commission to be a deliverer from military threat. Unlike Gideon, Saul's commission is accompanied by an act—Samuel's anointing of Saul. This is a new element, not typically present in call narratives, because this story deals with a king. Saul is to be God's anointed one, as נגיד (*nāgîd*), "leader," or as מלך (*melek*), "king." The Lord is the one who anoints Saul, a claim made twice in this verse (reading the longer version of the Greek).

THE SIGN, 10:1*b*, 5-7*a*, 9-10

In most call narratives, the sign comes after the reassurance. It confirms the presence of God with the one called. Here Samuel promises a "sign" already at the end of Samuel's commissioning and anointing (10:1*b*) and speaks of "signs" just prior to the words of reassurance given to Saul in v. 7. Although Samuel predicts these "signs" before the reassurance, they are fulfilled in vv. 9-10.

There has been considerable debate over the nature of this sign. Verse 1*b* speaks of a "sign" in the singular, but vv. 7 and 9 refer to "signs." Samuel's speech to Saul in vv. 2-6 speaks of three events that will befall Saul, but vv. 10-11 narrate the fulfillment of only one of these events. These discrepancies cannot be resolved easily. As it now stands, the story seems to regard the episode of Saul's encounter with a band of prophets and his receiving of God's Spirit with them as the most important confirming event—the sign of God's presence with Saul. The other two events predicted by Samuel have to do with the lost donkeys portion of the story, and this element of the story has given way to the more important call of Saul to be God's deliverer. Their fulfillment is not the focus of the story's interest.

THE REASSURANCE, 10:7*b*

The reassurance formula "for God will be with you" is an important part of call stories. Usually it occurs in the first person as God speaks directly to the one called, but here it is in the third person as God's call is mediated to Saul through the prophet Samuel.

All of the elements of Habel's description of the typical call narrative are here, although somewhat altered by the mediating presence of Samuel as God's prophet. The call narrative and the role of Samuel emphasize the importance of the prophets as God's agents in authorizing and legitimizing kings in Israel.

9:22-25. Saul and his servant companion are brought to a banquet hall, where a sumptuous meal has been prepared, and Saul is treated as the honored guest. There are thirty guests, and Saul is given a special portion of the meat. Some have wished to see symbolic significance in these particulars. Others have seen the banquet itself as foreshadowing a coronation feast. However, such suggestions are speculative. We can say with certainty only that Saul, as an inexperienced young man just arrived in the city, dined as an honored guest with the great prophet Samuel on that day (v. 24b). Saul is then taken to spend the night, presumably at Samuel's house, to end a remarkable day. But even more remarkable events are to come on the next day.

9:26-10:13. The next morning Samuel takes Saul to the edge of the town and sends his servant on ahead. Then Samuel, announcing this moment as an occasion to "make known" the "word of God" (9:27b), anoints Saul and commissions him as *nāgîd* to deliver Israel from its enemies (10:1; most of this verse is missing in the Hebrew text, but the longer version is present in the Septuagint and the Vulgate; the NRSV and most recent translations have adopted this longer reading. The NIV includes it in a footnote). The nature of anointing and the role of *nāgîd* have already been discussed in connection with 9:15-17. The anointing and the commissioning of Saul (10:1) repeat the language of God's instructions to Samuel earlier, except that specific mention of the Philistines is replaced by a more general reference to "enemies" of Israel. This is the climactic moment of the story. Saul, a young man in search of lost donkeys, has instead been designated to rule a kingdom. The reader is left to marvel at the boldness of God's initiative. This is not likely the candidate the elders would have chosen. Even Samuel is bluntly told, "Here is the man!" (9:17). Whatever happens in subsequent episodes to win approval for Saul's kingship among the people, we are clear that in the beginning Saul was God's man.

Samuel promises a sign (10:1b), and then speaks of three events that will take place after Saul leaves him. First, two men will meet him to say that the donkeys have been found and that his father is worried about him. Saul had earlier suggested that his father would be worried (9:5), and Samuel had told him the donkeys were found (9:20). This report to Saul would seem only to confirm what he already knows and resolve the lost donkeys theme in the story. Second, Saul will encounter three men who will give him bread. This seems to resolve the lament of Saul in 9:7 that they were out of bread.

The third event is most important in the story. Saul will meet a band of prophets coming down from a shrine, playing instruments. They will be caught up in a prophetic ecstasy, and Saul will be seized by the "spirit of the Lord" and join them in their charismatic prophesying. This is the only one of the three predicted events for which the fulfillment is narrated. According to 10:10, Saul does meet this band of prophets, becomes possessed of God's Spirit, and prophesies with them.

There is an important connection between anointing and the receiving of God's Spirit in 1 Samuel.[75] David also receives God's Spirit after being anointed by the prophet Samuel (16:13). Later, when the Spirit of God empowers Saul to deliver the people of Jabesh-gilead, it is a public demonstration of the power of the Spirit Saul has already received in his anointing. God's anointed kings are the recipients of God's Spirit, and for Saul both the anointing and the Spirit are mediated to him by the prophets.

Through the events of anointing and possession of God's Spirit, Saul is transformed. Twice in this segment of the story there are indications of the radical nature of this transformation. In v. 6b, Samuel says that when the Spirit comes upon him Saul will "be turned into a different person," and in v. 9a the text tells us that as Saul left Samuel "God gave him another heart." There is a tension of timing here. Was Saul a changed man before or after meeting the prophets and receiving the Spirit? It matters little. Through these events Saul is changed from the naive young man we saw at the beginning of the story. Then his "heart/mind" (לב *lēb*) was only on donkeys (see Commentary on 9:19-20), but now Saul has a new "heart" (*lēb*, 10:9). Saul's story begins with another witness to a common biblical theme: the power of God to

75. See Rolf Knierim, "The Messianic Concept in the First Book of Samuel," in *Jesus and the Historian,* ed. T. Trotter (Philadelphia: Westminster, 1968).

choose and use persons who seem unlikely agents of God's purposes when measured in human terms (Jacob, Moses, Gideon, Ruth, David, Amos, a peasant woman from Nazareth named Mary). God sees with a different eye. Through God's Spirit, Saul becomes a "different man."

Just how "different" Saul is may be in part measured by the response of witnesses to Saul's prophesying (10:11-13). People who know him as the son of Kish are amazed, and this amazement gives rise to a popular saying, "Is Saul also among the prophets?" Another story of how this saying arose appears in 19:18-24. Gunn has pointed out that the saying appears to have an affirming context in 1 Samuel 10 but a disapproving context in chap. 19. In the first passage, Saul is recognized to have the status of a prophet, while in the second it seems to confirm him as a raving madman.[76] Of course, one comes before Saul's rejection and the other after. In the context of 1 Samuel 10, the people's amazement becomes a confirmation that Saul is indeed a different person. He is Spirit-filled, therefore, God empowered. In the wake of chap. 8, we have to wonder if this is what the elders had in mind. This is not a king who will come to the throne through the usual processes of politics and power. If there is to be a king in Israel, this story seems to suggest that he will be chosen on God's terms. The reign of such a king, then, will also be judged on God's terms. This idea has ramifications for the fate of Saul as the story continues.

In 10:7 Saul is authorized to "do whatever you see fit to do." This would seem to be the permission to get about the business for which he has been commissioned: to bring deliverance. Many would see this actualized in chap. 11 when Saul, through the power of God's Spirit, delivers the people of Jabesh-gilead.

76. Gunn, *The Fate of King Saul,* 63.

But immediately in 10:8 Samuel commands Saul to go to Gilgal and wait for him to come and offer sacrifices. The wait is to last seven days, and Samuel will "show you what you shall do." It is as if Saul is authorized in 10:7, and in 10:8 Samuel asserts that he is still in charge. This verse clearly is the background to the first conflict between Samuel and Saul (13:1-15), which leads to Saul's rejection by Samuel. It reminds us that however positive the picture of Saul and kingship is in 9:1–10:16, there is a deep ambiguity in the wider tradition about kingship in general and Saul in particular. Israel was not of one mind as it faced these transforming changes from old order to new.

10:14-16. At the end of 10:13 we are told simply that Saul went home. Suddenly we are back in the lost donkey story. Saul's uncle questions him and learns that the two men went to Samuel for help in finding the donkeys (v. 14). Perhaps finding this encounter with the eminent Samuel surprising, the uncle asks what Samuel said (v. 15). All Saul reports is that Samuel told him that the donkeys had been found. The episode concludes with the notice that Saul intentionally kept the "matter of the kingship" a secret (v. 16). This gives the reader a way of understanding why subsequent episodes on Saul's accession to the kingship do not seem to know of this anointing by Samuel. But this final notice makes clear that, as the text now stands, Saul's anointing was a "matter of the kingship," and *nāgîd* as used here (9:16; 10:1) is not understood in some narrow meaning of military leadership alone. This story is intended as the first step by Saul to the throne. The kingdom remains a secret for the moment, but the reader knows that God has acted. In spite of ambiguous beginnings (chap. 8), if there will be a king in Israel, it will be God's king.

REFLECTIONS

1. The most obvious point to be drawn from 1 Sam 9:1–10:16 is that God uses unexpected persons and works through surprising circumstances. This is, of course, a common biblical theme (Joseph, Moses, Gideon, Ruth, Esther, Mary, Paul); and it is seen again in 1 Samuel when David is chosen as the man after God's own heart, even though he is the eighth son and but a boy (1 Sam 16:1-13). That this theme is so common in the Bible should not lead us to the conclusion that it is trite, but that it is centrally important. Over and again the biblical story tells us that men and women who become crucial to God's purposes would have been overlooked if measured only by the usual human standards. God looked beyond these standards and saw new possibilities. God saw in Saul the "different person" (10:6) and the "other heart" (10:9) that lay within this inexperienced young man. It would seem that Saul's story (and the many other stories of unlikely persons called by God) might urge the church to reconsider the standards of discernment that usually prevail in identifying and nurturing leadership in the church. It is often easier to tick off lists of qualifications than to discern the capacity to be transformed by God's Spirit and to become one of those who manifest the heart received from God.

Saul is not just a surprising choice, but the circumstances of his anointing are unlikely as well. It is commonplace to refer to this story as one in which Saul went looking for lost donkeys but found a kingdom. There is a word here both for those who experience God's call (like Saul) and for those who might be God's agents in mediating God's call (like Samuel). The person God needs and the occasion for claiming that person to God's purposes may present themselves in the most ordinary and unexpected circumstances. The church is prone to develop "leadership training events" or "Christian vocation conferences" and the like in its formal efforts to develop and nurture leaders for the faith community. These have their place, but Saul's story suggests that a part of our energies must be devoted to listening for God's voice to say, "Here is the one." This will not always come through our formal programs.

We must be careful not to romanticize this theme. Saul was not a person of no real gifts miraculously transformed into a king. We cannot expect a sense of God's calling and authorization to give us gifts and talents we never had before. We can, however, expect that through the power of God's Spirit we can become persons that we never were before, and the gifts we possess can be put to new purpose and given new focus by God's giving of "another heart" (10:9): " 'Another heart' (10:9) suggests a total revisioning of the world in a way that shatters old perceptions, invites new commitments, and requires new actions."[77] Saul has been given new possibilities for his life, and the text suggests such new possibilities for Israel as well. To read this text in the church is to expect transformation and change if we are open to God's calling. We cannot settle for business as usual. We cannot settle for more efficient leadership. We cannot settle for success defined as safety and stability. What those who saw Saul seized by the Spirit observed was unsettling and disturbing to them. "There is a new creation: everything old has passed away; see, everything has become new!" (2 Cor 5:17 NRSV).

2. The real point of this story of Saul's calling (and of our own) focuses on the one who calls. This is a story of *God's initiative* and *God's Spirit* as the source of newness. The newness of God for Saul and for Israel does not come from calculating reason or careful political maneuvering. This was surely what the elders wanted and expected (chap. 8). They wanted a general, an administrator, and a royal symbol of stability and safety. Instead they got Saul, seized by the power of the Spirit in ways that amazed, perhaps embarrassed, those who knew him (10:11-12). He did not look like a leader who could be managed in the people's interests. The Spirit often appears unmanageable in the world's terms. When the Spirit powerfully filled those present at Pentecost, onlookers sneered that they were drunk (Acts 2:13), even as Hannah had been accused of drunkenness by Eli when she was merely occupied with God (1:14).

For the people of God, whether Israel or the church, genuine newness comes first from *God's initiative.* The people may demand, as did the elders of Israel (chap. 8), but God will choose, as made evident in Saul ("Here is the man," 9:17). In the church, most denominations or traditions have elaborate structures and mechanisms

---

77. Brueggemann, *First and Second Samuel,* 77.

for making choices of leadership or program. It is important that we constantly and prayerfully examine these to ensure that they are accountable to the choosing of God. The church's processes should always be, in part, a discernment of what God has chosen as the path to newness in the church's life and mission.

For the people of God, genuine newness is not only initiated by God but also empowered and made possible by *God's Spirit*. In God's Spirit, Saul was made new, and it took surprising, amazing form as he prophesied with the prophets. Openness to God's Spirit in the community of faith will lead us down unexpected paths. In its institutional forms, the church is like other human institutions. It tends to prefer patterns that can be managed and controlled. If kept oriented to faithful purposes, this can even be good stewardship. But the power of God's Spirit, constantly working to transform the church and the world, means that a central element of our life will be unmanageable and uncontrollable. God's Spirit seizes, surprises, upsets, transforms, and reorients. Without openness to this empowerment of the Spirit, the church cannot be made new.

The pattern of God's choosing and the Spirit of God empowering is one with considerable resonance in the biblical tradition. In 1 Sam 9:1–10:16, Saul is chosen by God, is anointed by the prophet Samuel on God's command, and receives God's Spirit. The result is to give Israel its first king. In 1 Sam 16:1-13, David is singled out as God's choice, is anointed by Samuel, and receives God's Spirit. The result is not only a king for Israel, but also a dynasty (the house of David) descended from the man "after God's own heart." In Luke 3:21-22//Matt 3:13-17//Mark 1:9-11, Jesus is baptized (anointed) by John, the Spirit descends upon Jesus, and God's voice claims him as "beloved Son" (the language of God's affirmation is taken from Ps 2:7, a royal psalm, and Isa 42:1). The result is the beginning of the career of Jesus as Messiah, the anointed one. In Acts 2:1 the apostles and those assembled with them are anointed by tongues of flame, and the Spirit descends upon them. The result is the Pentecost birth of the church. This places us as the church today in the line of the pattern that began with Saul. Are we still the God-chosen, Spirit-filled church? Saul is eventually rejected and loses the Spirit. Could the church suffer the same fate? Do we continue to live out the promise of newness that the Spirit brings, or have we like Saul gotten diverted by our own self-interest? We may continue on in Saul's story with more than a little interest in his fate.

1 Samuel 10:17-27a, Saul Among the Baggage

COMMENTARY

The scene shifts to an assembly of Israel, called by Samuel, at Mizpah. The transition is not smooth. No passage of time is noted, but the Saul who is chosen by lot and acclaimed king is not the boy we just left in the previous episode. Samuel, who had anointed Saul in 10:1, does not seem to know him now. This may well have been an independent story of how Saul became king. In its present position, following the story of Saul's anointing by Samuel, this episode now functions as the public acclamation of Saul's designation as king, which was kept secret until this moment

(v. 16*b*). Here the people become involved in acknowledging God's choice for king (v. 24).

Samuel's speech at the beginning of the Mizpah assembly (vv. 18-19) recalls the negative evaluation given of kingship in chap. 8. Some have claimed this speech to be the work of the deuteronomistic historian, but the text includes no special Dtr vocabulary; it is more appropriately understood as a prophetic judgment speech (see Commentary on 10:18-19). The later portion of this episode at Mizpah involves God in directly selecting Saul and proclaims Saul as God's chosen one. Thus the

Mizpah story seems to reflect the deep ambiguity in Israel over kingship. In fact, the story ends with references to supporters and detractors of Saul (vv. 26-27a). The public beginnings of kingship in Israel were unsettled and disturbing. How can the people's rejection of God still result in Saul as God's chosen one?

10:17-19. We have already encountered Mizpah as the scene of the penitential ceremony Samuel was conducting when the Philistines attacked (7:7-11). On that occasion, through the mediation of Samuel, a great victory was won. Chapter 7 seemed to show that kingship was unnecessary to deal with the Philistine threat. To assemble Israel at Mizpah for kingmaking may have been intended to recall that victory and to suggest that this activity was unneeded.

Certainly Samuel's opening speech to this assembly set a negative tone for the proceedings. The pattern of this speech is typical of prophetic judgment speeches against the nation,[78] and it underlines Samuel's prophetic role. His speech opens with a long form of the prophetic *messenger formula* ("Thus says the LORD, the God of Israel," v. 18a). The words that follow are in the first person, as if God were speaking directly through Samuel as God's prophetic messenger. God's speech to Israel begins with a *recitation of saving acts.* God recalls the exodus deliverance out of bondage in Egypt and also mentions deliverance from "all the kingdoms that were oppressing you" (v. 18b). This phrase may refer to those who opposed Israel's settlement in the land or to threats from enemies during the time of the judges. What is significant is that these enemies are described as "kingdoms." It was Israel's enemies who had kings, and they were overcome by God's power acting through and for Israel without benefit of a king! This opening to God's speech through Samuel reminds Israel that they have been the recipients of God's salvation.

By contrast, the *accusation* in v. 19a charges that Israel had "rejected your God who saves you from all your calamities and your distresses." Israel had done this by asking for a king. This charge is emphasized by characterizing Israel's response to the Lord as an emphatic "No!" This accusation

recalls the assembly at Ramah in chap. 8 and the people's demand to Samuel for a king. Israel's sin is its rejection of God. The verb "reject" (מאס *mā'as*) is common in prophetic judgment speeches. This is the same charge against Israel as in 8:7, but there God added the accusation that Israel worshiped foreign gods (8:8). This motif is more typical of the deuteronomistic historian but is missing in 10:18-19.[79]

The *announcement of judgment,* often introduced by the words "Now, therefore . . ." (as in v. 19b), usually follows the accusation in a prophetic judgment speech. What we expect is God's judgment as a response to the people's rejection of the God who saved them. What we find instead is a bland summons for the people to present themselves by tribes and clans. That this is "before the LORD" indicates some cultic ceremony. What follows in vv. 20-24 is the account of God's choosing of Saul as king. As we will see, God is active in this process, and Samuel proclaims Saul as "the one whom the LORD has chosen" (v. 24). The divine will asserts itself, not in judgment, but in claiming Israel's king as the Lord's king. The story suggests that time will tell whether Saul in particular or kingship in general is a judgment. But it will not be because God has withdrawn from Israel in this kingmaking moment.

10:20-24. The actual drama of Saul's selection is played out in two acts. First, there is a lot-casting ceremony (vv. 20-21). Then there is the search for Saul among the baggage and his acclamation by Samuel and the people (vv. 22-24).

Assembled before the Lord, Israel is "brought near" by tribe, and the tribe of Benjamin is "taken." The families of Benjamin are "brought near," and the family of Matri is "taken." The men of Matri are "brought near" man by man, and Saul, the son of Kish, is "taken." The process is very similar to the lot-casting described in Josh 7:14-18, where lots were cast to identify Achan as the violator of the holy ban. Lots were also cast to indicate Jonathan as the vow breaker in 14:40-42, although the process there probably involved the Urim and Thummim and the choice between two options until a final

---

78. Claus Westermann, *Basic Forms of Prophetic Speech* (Philadelphia: Westminster, 1967) 98-101, 182-83.

79. Those who argue that 10:17-27a is deuteronomistic often compare 10:18-19 to Judg 6:7-10 and 1 Sam 8:7-8, but the Dtr influence in those passages is clearest in the theme of the worship of foreign gods, which is absent in 10:17-27a. For fuller discussion see Birch, *The Rise of the Israelite Monarchy,* 47-50; and McCarter, *I Samuel,* 195.

decision is made. Both of these parallels are stories for the designation of an offender against God and Israel, which may suggest that the use of lots was an intentional continuation of the negative tone toward kingship in v. 19; still, positive statements on Saul as God's chosen one in v. 24 make this claim doubtful.

The final phrase of v. 21 says that when Saul was sought, he could not be found. This is problematic, since the method described for casting lots requires the physical presence of tribes, families, and individuals. They are "brought near," and one is then "taken" (i.e., designated). In v. 21, the people inquire of God (the Hebrew word is שׁאל [*šā'al*], from which the name "Saul" is derived; thus they "sauled" for Saul). According to the Hebrew text, the people question God: "Is there a man yet to come here?" (v. 22). This query seems to imply that the lot-casting was unsuccessful and that the people turn to the Lord for further help. Both the NRSV and the NIV adopt a Septuagint reading that merely indicates that Saul cannot be found. This leaves the mystery of how he could have been designated while hidden. Some scholars believe that two accounts, one of lot casting and one of Saul's being pointed out directly by God among the baggage, have been combined. As it stands, we have to imagine Saul designated by lot and then somehow running to hide before he is really noticed.

In any case, God becomes very active in designating Saul from v. 22 onward. The people "inquire" of the Lord; the Lord points Saul out, hiding in the baggage (v. 22); and Saul is proclaimed by Samuel as the one "chosen by the LORD" (v. 24*a*). There is a sense of excitement and affirmation regarding Saul in this portion of the story. When Saul stood, he was "head and shoulders taller than any of them" (v. 23; cf. 9:2), a physical sign that Saul was, indeed, the divine choice. Samuel, normally dour, seems to be enthusiastic when he says, "There is no one like him among all the people." The people shout, "Long live the king!" (v. 24*b;* a cry associated elsewhere with accession to the throne, 2 Sam 16:16; 1 Kgs 1:25; 2 Kgs 11:12).

Apart from Samuel's opening speech in vv. 18-19, this account is very positive, even joyous, over the selection of Saul. Saul is God's chosen and is now acclaimed by Samuel and the people. The people had rejected God (v. 19), but God has chosen Saul (v. 24). The people may have sinned, but God refuses to withdraw from their future.

10:25-27. Samuel next recites to the people the משפט המלכה (*mišpaṭ hammĕlukâ*), some set of regulations to govern the rule of the king (NRSV, "rights and duties of the kingship"; NIV, "regulations of the kingship"). Samuel records them in a book and deposits it before the Lord—i.e., in a sanctuary (v. 25). This immediately brings to mind the law of the king in Deut 17:14-20, which defines the obligations of the king and requires him to make a copy of "this law" (perhaps meaning all of Deuteronomy). In any case, v. 25 seems to indicate some written, legal document to hold the king accountable before God.

Is this *mišpaṭ hammĕlukâ* to be identified with the המלך משפט (*mišpaṭ hammelek*), which Samuel makes known to the people in 8:9? Translated as "ways of the king" (NRSV), 8:9 introduces Samuel's negative speech about the oppressive practices of kings as a warning to the people. The two references (8:9; 10:25) are most often taken as unrelated. Yet, the similarity in terminology is striking. In Samuel's speech (chap. 8), he could well have drawn from a document on the practices of kings but for his purposes highlighted only the negative burdens that royal privilege would impose on the people. The NRSV rendering of 10:25 as "rights and duties of the kingship" emphasizes the usual expectation that the Hebrew word משפט (*mišpāṭ*, "justice") would include responsibilities as well as privileges attached to kingship.

According to the final phrase of v. 25, Samuel sends everyone home, including Saul, who goes back to Gibeah (v. 26*a*). This seems odd. It would seem that Saul should now begin the business of being king. It may be that his return home is necessary to prepare for chap. 11, where Saul is summoned from his fields to rescue Jabesh-gilead and is again proclaimed king. The historian is combining and harmonizing several stories detailing Saul's accession to kingship.

Verses 26*b*-27 include an especially interesting note indicating Israel's divided mind over kingship. Even after the acclamation at Mizpah, there were both supporters and opponents of Saul's kingship. Saul was accompanied to his home by supporters described as "warriors" (NRSV) or "valiant men" (NIV). The word so translated is חיל (*ḥayil*), which can indicate strength or prowess in battle, but can also signify wealth and influence. Since economic wealth and political influence were often accompanied and protected by military power in Israel's world, it is easy to see how this word includes all these nuances. We may have here an indication that the support for kingship in general and Saul in particular came from those with influence and wealth in Israel. The elders who approached Samuel asking for a king in chap. 8 would also seem to possess power and privilege. According to v. 26, God had touched the hearts of these men. Saul's support from the influential and powerful was surely essential if he was to have a chance at success, and God's hand is involved even in this garnering of support.

Yet kingship comes to Saul and to Israel as an ambiguous thing. There are detractors, described in v. 27*a* as בליעל (*bĕliyya'al*; NRSV, "worthless fellows"; NIV, "troublemakers"). These renegades and malcontents sneer, "How can this man save us?" They despise Saul and give him no gifts (which may have symbolized fealty to the new king). But Saul holds his peace. This notice is surely related to 11:12-13. Following Saul's victory at Jabesh-gilead, his supporters want to put his detractors to death. Saul had been the source of "saving" in Israel, and he refuses to allow such bloodshed. (This incident will be discussed further in the Commentary on chap. 11.)

The word *bĕliyya'al* was used in 2:12 to describe the unscrupulous sons of Eli. It is clear that this word usually indicated the most undesirable people in Israel. Yet we should remember that Eli mistook Hannah for *bĕliyya'al* in 1:14-16. Later, when David gathers men around him in the wilderness, his support comes from the discontented and outcasts of Israel (22:1-3). In the story of 1 Samuel, true power comes from God, and its form in the life of Israel does not always follow the usual patterns of human power and privilege. The elders may demand a king, but God will choose an inexperienced boy. The men of power may collect around the newly acclaimed Saul, but the "worthless ones" may have the final word as they later gather around a fugitive David.

Indeed, the worthless ones may voice the crucial question at this point in the story: Can Saul save? In the unfolding drama of 1 Samuel, there are both immediate and long-term answers to this question. In the very next episode of the story (chap. 11), Saul does save the city and the people of Jabesh-gilead. But in the longer term, God rejects Saul, who commits terrifying and unbalanced deeds. Can Saul save? Perhaps God working through Saul could save. The deliverance of Jabesh-gilead was made possible by the possession of God's mighty Spirit (11:6). His rejection will come when he ignores the command of God through God's prophet (chaps. 13 and 15), and his demented behavior will come after God's Spirit leaves him (16:14). The story of 1 Samuel may be a story of the source of true saving. Saul alone cannot save. The worthless ones raised a more important question than they knew.

REFLECTIONS

First Samuel 10:17-27*a* has been a neglected episode among the stories of the rise of kingship in Israel. At best it is considered curious that the chosen king should be hiding among the baggage. Yet, themes are touched on in this brief episode that are among the most central aspects of the biblical message.

1. This passage begins with God's word through Samuel that in spite of God's past deliverance Israel has rejected "your God who saves you" by desiring a king (10:18-19). Yet, a short time later it is God who reveals Saul hiding among the baggage (10:22), and Samuel declares him "the one whom the LORD has chosen" (10:24). This has struck many commentators as inconsistent or at least odd. How could a passage that begins with God's rejection of the people because of their desire for a king end in the designation of Saul as God's chosen king? Many have resorted to theories of divergent accounts unskillfully wed in 10:17-27*a,* one negative to kingship, another positive.

It would seem that those who find this pattern strange have forgotten how frequently in the biblical story God responds to human sin with grace. Sin is judged and called to account, but it is not God's final word. In this passage, Samuel's speech is a prophetic judgment of the people in direct and unvarnished terms. But God's final action is to redeem even the kingship through the grace of divine election. The king will be *God's* chosen one, not the people's. One is reminded of God's speech in Hosea's well-known oracle:

> When Israel was a child, I loved him,
>   and out of Egypt I call my son.
> The more I called them,
>   the more they went from me . . .
>   My heart recoils within me;
>   my compassion grows warm and tender.
> I will not execute my fierce anger . . .
> I will return them to their homes, says the LORD.
> (Hos 11:1-2*a,* 8*b*-9*a,* 11*b* NRSV)

Time and again in the biblical story, God's saving occurs in spite of human sin. God turns potential disasters as a result of human sin into opportunities for divine grace. Joseph says to his reconciled brothers, "Even though you intended to do harm to me, God intended it for good" (Gen 50:20 NRSV). From the flood story to Jonah's message of doom to the Ninevites, God's grace has a way of having the last word. It is the very same dynamic that stands at the heart of the Christian gospel, "But God proves his love for us in that while we still were sinners Christ died for us" (Rom 5:8 NRSV). In the story of Israel's kingship, the people may have turned away from God in desiring a king; but it is clear that God will not turn away from them, even in the matter of a king. Saul will have his chance as God's chosen one.

2. A second important theme in this episode focuses on the unlikely moments of Saul's hiding in the baggage (10:22-23) and on the complaining of "worthless fellows" that Saul cannot save them (10:27*a*). This question recurs in many forms throughout 1 and 2 Samuel: "Who can save?" The question has individual and social dimensions.

On an individual level, Saul is apparently reluctant to be chosen. Like Moses and Gideon before him, he does not think he is the one to save Israel. God must seek him out and insist that he is the chosen one. It is not up to Saul alone to save. It is God with Saul (10:7) who can save. Over and over again those called in the biblical story must be reassured that it is God with them who saves: "I have chosen you and not cast you off; do not fear, for I am with you, do not be afraid, for I am your God; I will strengthen you, I will help you, I will uphold you with my victorious right hand" (Isa 41:9*b*-10 NRSV).

Most of us today are inclined to hide in the baggage. We are reluctant to think that we might be the very one through whom God's salvation might work. Our fear frequently arises because we only gauge our own human resources and fail to trust in what God might work through us and our limited gifts. The life of the church is full of baggage-searching efforts, insisting that with God's grace this one or that one might really give the leadership needed. The trick is to be certain that we are prayerfully attuned to God's choices and not our own. God's choosing may lead, as with Saul, to some less obvious nominees through whom God's saving grace might work.

The question of who can save is also a social question. All Israel is divided by this question. It is the worthless ones who dare to voice it (10:26-27*a*). The question is directed to our corporate institutions and those who hold office in them. For Israel, it was kingship in general and Saul in particular. For us it may be denominational structures and leaders (bishops, elders, presbytery executives, moderators, officers, and staff members) or it may be secular institutions of governance and the officeholders or civil servants who work in them. Israel's story once again suggests that the structures and the persons alone cannot save. The worthless ones are properly skeptical if Saul's supporters think that kingship or Saul of their own accord can save Israel. The story of 1 Samuel has already made this point. The piety and integrity of Eli could not save his sons or his household; the ark could not save Israel. It is God's power that saves, and that power can work through persons and institutions. Through Samuel, God saves Israel from the Philistines in chap. 7. In the power of God's Spirit, Saul will save Jabesh-gilead in chap. 11. But when Saul tries to save on his own terms and in disregard for God as the source of saving power, he is rejected as God's chosen one and his story takes a tragic turn (chap. 15).

It has always been tempting for the church and its leaders to trust institutional structures and officeholders as the source of salvation rather than the God who might work through those institutions and leaders. As with the kingship, God can redeem even our sometimes sinful churches—but only if we recognize the choices God is making in our midst, rather than insisting on our own customs or preferences.

The same observation can be made about secular societal institutions and leaders. They, too, can become idols, and there are many who believe, in the name of patriotism, that some pattern of government or legislation or leadership can save us. Alone these things cannot save us. Only when self-interest and vested interest are given up to God's interests can salvation be fully present in our societal structures.

It is significant that the skeptical question of who can save is raised by those whom Israel labeled "worthless ones." Often, from biblical times to the present, it is through those whom society labels worthless that the patterns of God's grace in our midst are revealed. In the end the skepticism toward Saul is, unfortunately, well founded. Jesus associated with outcasts and sinners. The early church broke down barriers between Jew and Greek, male and female, slave and free (Gal 3:28). Saint Francis reclaimed the gospel as good news for the poor. John Wesley left comfortable pews to preach to miners in open fields. African Americans and black South Africans declared that racist institutions could save no one and acted accordingly. It would do well for Christians and citizens today to listen to the voices of those dismissed as worthless ones. Perhaps their voices can be a reminder that even the most cherished customs, economic systems, political platforms, or religious systems cannot save. It is only through constant discernment of what God is doing in our midst, and attention to the surprising patterns of God's grace, that any institution or leader can become a part of God's saving work in the world.

1 Samuel 10:27b–11:15, Saul Delivers Jabesh-gilead

COMMENTARY

If we had not already been introduced to Saul as Israel's first king in previous chapters, this episode would look like a story from the book of Judges. Saul seems like one of the charismatic deliverers of Israel, empowered by God's Spirit in times of crisis. The crisis here is caused by the cruelty and oppression of Nahash, the king of Ammon, who has laid siege to Jabesh-gilead (vv. 1-4). When the inhabitants of Jabesh send a desperate appeal for help, it is Saul who hears the news while plowing his field, whereupon he is filled with the Spirit of God. He summons the tribal militia and mounts a campaign that successfully delivers the people of Jabesh-gilead (vv. 5-11). Following this victory, some want to put to death those who opposed Saul, but Saul intervenes (vv. 12-13), and he is then made king in Gilgal (vv. 14-15). Until the kingmaking at the end of the chapter, this story shows no knowledge of Saul in connection with kingship. There is no indication of any previous anointing (10:1) or public acclamation (10:24) of Saul as king over Israel. The account is very positive toward Saul, picturing him as a hero and deliverer of Israel. It would appear that this story is an independent tradition indicating that Saul became king as a spontaneous acclamation following his demonstrated leadership in delivering Jabesh-gilead. As we will see later, some attempt has been made to harmonize this account with other stories on Saul's rise to kingship by having Samuel suggest in v. 14 that the people are going to Gilgal to "renew" the kingship. Verse 15, however, says straightforwardly that the people "made Saul king before the LORD in Gilgal."

Chapter 11 may have originated as an independent tradition on Saul's rise to kingship, but in its present context it confirms a kingship already revealed to Saul and to Israel. Saul had already received the Spirit of God as a result of his anointing by Samuel (10:5-6, 10), and he had been presented and acclaimed before the people at Mizpah (10:17-24). Still, Saul had not begun active rule over Israel. Samuel had sent him and the people home from Mizpah (10:25*b*). The coming of God's Spirit on Saul in this episode (11:6) empowers him not to prophesy but to lead Israel to deliverance from an enemy, the Ammonites. Saul publicly demonstrates the power of God's Spirit in leadership of Israel. The "renewal" of the kingship in Gilgal (11:14) now marks the beginning of Saul's active rule of Israel as a proven leader possessed of God's Spirit.

Chapter 11 is also tied to its wider context by the key concept of salvation. Chapter 10 had ended with the crucial question of the "worthless ones": "How can this man *save* us?" (10:27*a*). The Hebrew root ישע (*yš'*) plays a key role in this chapter. As a verb, it is translated "save" or "deliver," and as a noun, "salvation" or "deliverance." Brueggemann has seen that this theme is central to each part of the dramatic story of chap. 11.[80]

The problem: If there is no one to *save* us (v. 3)

The intervention: You shall have *deliverance* (v. 9)

The resolution: The LORD has wrought *deliverance* in Israel (v. 13)

Saul can save, but only as an agent of God's deliverance, which he himself confesses in v. 13. Those whom the supporters of Saul want to put to death in v. 12 are likely the "worthless ones/troublemakers," who cast doubt on Saul's ability to save in 10:27*a*. Saul refuses to allow their death, and in doing so begins to function as an authority for sacral justice in Israel (see discussion below). This ironically casts a shadow forward, since it will be Saul's later violations in matters of sacral justice that lead Samuel to reject Saul as king (chaps. 13 and 15).

10:27b–11:4. The story opens with a description of the cruel siege of Jabesh-gilead by Nahash the Ammonite. The NRSV includes a long addition to the text that now appears at the end of chap. 10 (the addition is actually unnumbered but will be treated here as 10:27*b*). This material is from a manuscript found at Qumran (Dead Sea Scroll 4QSam[a]) and was also known by the Jewish historian Josephus.[81] The NIV has chosen not to include it. The addition provides helpful background on the siege. Nahash, the ruler of Ammon, is described as a cruel oppressor. The name "Nahash" is related to the Hebrew for "snake" (נחש *nāḥāš*). Nahash had systematically gouged out the right eyes of the men of Gad and Reuben, and seven thousand men from these tribes had taken refuge in Jabesh-gilead. Gad and Reuben were Israelite tribes located to the east of the Jordan in territory perennially under dispute with the Ammonites, one of several Transjordanian kingdoms. Jabesh-gilead is usually located in the Transjordanian portion of the tribe of Manasseh and has always seemed too far north to have been an object of Ammonite conquest. The longer text from Qumran makes clear that Nahash is pursuing refugees from his oppressive campaign against Gad and Reuben. His intent in gouging out eyes was to deprive the Israelites of a *deliverer* (a theme that returns in 11:3). Presumably, one-eyed men are not

---

80. Brueggemann, *First and Second Samuel*, 83.

81. Josephus *Antiquities of the Jews* 6.68-71. See McCarter, *I Samuel*, 199, for a discussion and reconstruction of the Qumran text.

very effective warriors. This cruel policy of Nahash, outlined in the Qumran addition, provides the background to Nahash's terms of surrender to the besieged inhabitants of Jabesh-gilead in 11:2. They had offered to surrender and make a treaty of service to Nahash (11:1), but Nahash had accepted only on condition that their right eyes be gouged out, thus disgracing Israel.

The elders of Jabesh-gilead asked for seven days to send out word through Israel. Their intent was to find someone to *save* them. If no one was found, they would surrender (v. 3). Surprisingly, Nahash does not respond. Perhaps he was simply confident that nothing could save Jabesh-gilead in so short a time.

In v. 4, messengers from Jabesh-gilead reach Gibeah (identified here with Saul), and the inhabitants weep at the news of the desperate situation. The book of Judges reports a special relationship between these two cities that grew out of an earlier crisis. The tribes of Israel went to war against the tribe of Benjamin for atrocities committed by the men of Gibeah against the concubine of a Levite from Ephraim (Judges 19–21). Jabesh-gilead had refused to send men to participate in the punishment of Gibeah, and for this they were attacked and four hundred virgin daughters of Jabesh-gilead were given to the survivors of Benjamin to rebuild the population of the tribe (Judg 21:1-14). Thus many families of Gibeah included ties of kinship to Jabesh-gilead. It is now in Gibeah that a deliverer for Jabesh is found in the person of Saul. Later in the books of Samuel, the men of Jabesh-gilead repay the deliverance of Saul by retrieving his body at great risk from the Philistines to give it a proper burial (1 Sam 31:11-13; 2 Sam 2:4*b*-7).

11:5-11. This section of the story focuses entirely on Saul and his response to the plight of Jabesh-gilead. It is his response that makes a difference and brings deliverance. When the news of the siege comes, Saul is simply working in the fields with oxen like any ordinary citizen (v. 5). This account knows nothing of royal designation for Saul. When Saul asks why people are weeping and is told the news, the response is immediate. Simultaneously the Spirit of God comes upon him with power, and he becomes very angry (v. 6). The language is strikingly similar to that

used of Samson in Judg 14:6, 19; 15:14, and many of the heroes of Judges were said to have received God's Spirit as the source of their power (Othniel, Gideon, Jephthah). For Saul, human anger at oppression and divine empowerment to effect a change through God's Spirit come together. It is out of this combination of righteous anger and divine power that the action of salvation comes in this story. Although Saul is clearly the hero of this story, there is a clear stress on God as the ultimate source of deliverance. It is the Spirit of God that empowers Saul; it is the dread of the Lord (v. 8) that fell upon Israel and brought response to Saul's summons; and it is the Lord to whom Saul finally gives credit for deliverance (v. 13).

Saul summons the tribal levy. This is the only example of this calling out of tribal military resources outside of the book of Judges. He does this by cutting his oxen into pieces and sending them throughout Israel with the threat that whoever does not respond to the call might face a similar fate (v. 7). This is reminiscent of the Levite's sending pieces of his concubine's body to summon Israel to punish those responsible for her death (Judg 19:29-30). The reference to Samuel in this verse is widely regarded as a secondary addition. Samuel plays no role in this story until the kingmaking at the end of the chapter.

The "dread of the LORD" falls upon Israel, and the people respond (v. 7*b*). This phrase and the motif of God's Spirit suggest that we are dealing with the influence of holy war traditions. It is God who fights for Israel in such righteous causes. When the people are mustered by Saul at Bezek, they number three hundred thousand. The word for "thousand" in Hebrew (אֶלֶף *'elep*) may also be translated as "contingent," which may be a more realistic rendering.

Word is sent to Jabesh-gilead that before midday on the next day they would have *deliverance* (v. 9), and the people of Jabesh-gilead rejoice. The inhabitants then give Nahash an ambiguous message. The Hebrew word יָצָא (*yāṣā'*) means literally "come out." It can be used in the sense of "surrender" or "give ourselves up" as in v. 3, but it can also mean "come out to do battle." The people of Jabesh-gilead give a cleverly ambiguous reply to Nahash: "Tomorrow, we will come out to you, and you may do to us whatever seems good to you" (v. 10). Nahash is lulled into believing capitulation is at hand, when the people of Jabesh-gilead plan to join in Saul's attack on the Ammonites. Both the NIV and the NRSV obscure this play on words.

The actual battle and Saul's victory are recorded briefly in v. 11. Saul divides his company into three forces. They attack the Ammonites in the morning and complete the victory during the heat of the day. Presumably the Ammonites are taken off guard, thinking that surrender is near. The victory is complete, and no further interest is shown in Nahash or the Ammonites. Interest focuses on Saul.

11:12-15. In the aftermath of victory, people approach Samuel demanding that those who questioned the reign of Saul be put to death (v. 12). This group may be the "worthless men/troublemakers" of 10:27*a* who wondered aloud whether Saul could save them. Now Saul has saved Israel, and those who doubted are in jeopardy. This incident is widely interpreted as a desire for petty vengeance and Saul's response as evidence of his magnanimity. However, Knierim has emphasized that the matter is one of sacral justice and not simple vengeance and mercy.

The request of the people for the punishment of Saul's slanderers is not at all an act of "petty vengeance." It is a necessity of sacral justice. . . . After Saul's victory, it was proven by divine judgment that the despisers had not merely slandered Saul but also Yahweh's messiah, and with that Yahweh himself. . . . The desire of the people . . . is a legitimate and necessary demand to execute judgment against the convicted slanderers of Yahweh.[82]

In 10:27*a* these opponents of Saul are already called בני בליעל (*běnê běliyya'al,* "worthless ones"). In the Old Testament, a "worthless man" is one who slanders God or breaks sacral law (1:16; 2:12; Deut 13:14; Judg 19:22; 20:13; Nah 1:11), destroys justice (1 Kgs 21:10; Prov 19:28), destroys life (Prov 16:27), or rebels against the king (2 Sam 16:7; 20:1; 23:7; Job 34:18)—and all of these acts call for the judgment of death. The

text itself is quite clear that Saul did not pardon these opponents because he was feeling generous. He states in apodictic form:

No man shall be put to death on this day . . . because God has delivered Israel. A legal pronouncement is made on the basis of God's act of salvation and not because of Saul's magnanimity. What is significant about this is the apparent transfer to Saul of the right to make judgments in the sacral/legal realm. . . . In v. 12 the people approach Samuel with the matter, but in v. 13 it is Saul who deals with the question. It is natural that Samuel as the judge of Israel and authority in such matters should be approached, but it is clear that the outcome shows Saul in the position to act authoritatively [instead of Samuel].[83]

Saul's exercise of authority properly recognizes God as the ultimate authority both for this judg-ment and for the victory that preceded it. Ironically it will be a disregard for sacral law and God's authority that Samuel will use as the basis for Saul's later rejection."

In v. 14, Samuel summons the people to Gilgal with the curious purpose of "renewing" the kingship, but in v. 15 it is the people who make Saul king before the Lord. This text may reflect a tradition of the people involved in kingmaking without the involvement of God's prophet. Verse 14 would then represent the prophetic tradition introducing Samuel into this story and harmonizing it with the earlier kingmaking role of Samuel by speaking of the Gilgal ceremony as a "renewal" of kingship. The effect of the text as it now stands is to make Saul's victory and the ceremony at Gilgal a confirmation of Saul's earlier designation as Israel's king.

This narrative provides an overwhelmingly positive portrait of Saul and the basis for his kingship. It is appropriate that the story ends with the rejoicing of Saul and all Israel at Gilgal (v. 15*b*). However, the biblical tradition associated with Gilgal does not remain entirely positive. In the time of Hosea, when Israel had suffered from the abuses of royal power, the prophet proclaimed, "They made kings, but not through me. . . . Every evil of theirs began at Gilgal; there I came to hate them" (Hos 8:4*a;* 9:15*a* NRSV).

82. Rolf Knierim, "The Messianic Concept in the First Book of Samuel," in *Jesus and the Historian,* ed. T. Trotter (Philadelphia: Westminster, 1968) 33.

83. Birch, *The Rise of the Israelite Monarchy,* 61-62.

REFLECTIONS

There can be no doubt that Saul is the narrative center of this story. It is his heroic moment, and the tone of the story is one of unstinting approval for Saul. But if Saul is the narrative center, the theological center of this story is focused on the theme of salvation. This is a story of salvation, both in the immediate sense of the crisis in Jabesh-gilead and in a larger sense within the book of 1 Samuel.

The immediate context for this focus on salvation begins in 10:19. Including that verse, there are five uses (10:19, 27; 11:3, 9, 13) of the root ישׁע (*yš'*) as either a verb ("to save," "to deliver") or a noun ("salvation," "deliverance"). Samuel claims that Israel has rejected their God, who *saves* them (10:19). Some have doubts that Saul can *save* them (10:27). The people of Jabesh-gilead fear that no one can *save* them (11:3). Word is sent that Saul will *save* them (11:9). Saul affirms that it was God who *saved* them. At the center stands the perennial fear in times of crisis that no salvation is possible. On one side stand the rejection of God and the doubts about leadership. Can they possibly save us (see the Reflections in previous chapter)? On the other side stands the affirmation that our leaders can bring salvation, but only if it is understood that the salvation they bring originates in God. This salvation drama in the story of Israel and Saul can teach us much about our own continuing quest for salvation.

1. Salvation is ultimately from God. It is God who truly saves. Samuel feared that in demanding a king the people were rejecting the God who saves (10:19). At least at this moment in the story Saul's response in 11:13 suggests that even a king can recognize God as the true source of all deliverance. For us, who live in a time that values individual self-sufficiency and puts increasing trust in technological solutions to problems, it is sometimes difficult to recognize our need for the salvation that comes from God. Israel was in a time of transition when it must have been tempted to leave God behind as part of the old order. But even in a story of new leadership and heroism there must be recognition that God is the source of all genuine salvation in every age, old and new.

2. God's salvation does not operate in isolation from human agency. The biblical story is filled with examples of the men and women God has involved in the work of salvation in the world. In this story, the agent of God's salvation is Saul. God's Spirit is at work to bring deliverance, but it is Saul who is seized by God's Spirit and empowered by it (11:6). What is kindled in Saul is anger, and that anger is directed at the cruel oppression that Nahash has inflicted on the people of Jabesh-gilead. The order here is significant. Saul does not become angry and then become Spirit-filled; it is the reverse. The anger is, of course, Saul's, but the implication is that it also grows out of the Spirit of God, which has grasped him. The suggestion is that the anger is also God's. Perhaps this story is teaching us what can happen when divine Spirit and human anger are focused together on oppression. The story of Saul as an instrument of God's deliverance here will help us to recognize that through God's Spirit, power beyond our rational and pragmatic expectations is available to us. But it will also require human involvement in the pain and struggle of those whose plight should rouse us to anger and action.

3. Salvation is sociopolitical as well as spiritual. Stories such as this one are important reminders that God's salvation has to do with the divine desire for human wholeness in all aspects of broken human existence. There are many voices in our time that use the concept of salvation only in reference to religious or spiritual matters. They imagine that God desires only to "save" us by establishing or restoring faith relationship in communion with God. The biblical concept of God's salvation is much broader than this; God's salvation includes not only a concern to establish faith but also to foster justice and to seek peace. In our time, the liberation theologies have seen the sociopolitical dimensions of God's salvation most clearly. Indeed, the Hebrew words for "save" and "salvation" can also be translated as "liberate" and "liberation." God's salvation is at work not only in the holy moment of covenant making on Mt. Sinai but also in the liberating spirit that rouses Saul to righteous anger on behalf of justice for Jabesh-gilead. In our own time, perhaps, God's salvation is best seen in those whose lives have exemplified deep biblical and spiritual roots combined with the active work of compassion and justice—the love of God joined with and reflected in the love of neighbor—Dietrich Bonhoeffer, Dorothy Day, Martin Luther King, Jr., Thomas Merton, Mother Teresa.

4. Salvation cannot remain passive in the face of suffering. It must act. God's Spirit is roused to action by human suffering, and those who would live in relation to the divine Spirit will likewise be stirred. Jesus inaugurated his ministry by reading from Isa 61:1-2:

> The Spirit of the Lord is upon me,
>   because he has anointed me to bring good news to the poor.
> He has sent me to proclaim release to the captives
>   and recovery of sight to the blind,
>   to let the oppressed go free,
> to proclaim the year of the Lord's favor. (Luke 4:18-19 NRSV)

In the power of God's Spirit upon him, Saul is "proclaiming release to the captives" in 1 Samuel 11. The Spirit empowers us to action in the face of oppression and suffering, but it is not without cost. Some are troubled that "saving action" in this story involves war as an instrument of divine and human justice. The salvation wrought by the Spirit does not operate as a *deus ex machina,* magically righting wrong with no human cost. It is not war that is affirmed in stories such as this. What is affirmed is the value of those who live and suffer on the underside of history. What is affirmed is that God has not forgotten them. What is affirmed is that violence is already being done in situations of oppression, and not to respond would be violence itself. God cannot will that nothing be done in the face of such brutality—whether in Jabesh-gilead or in countless modern experiences of oppression and suffering. The fall of oppressors is often costly and violent because of the violence that oppression introduces into human experience, not because violence is what God desires. In biblical times or our own, to do nothing in the face of brutality and injustice is sometimes the greater violence.

1 Samuel 12:1-25, Samuel's Address to Israel

COMMENTARY

Chapter 12 consists entirely of a speech by Samuel to Israel, with occasional responses by the people. There is a curious lack of narrative framework for this address. No time or place is given. The voice of the narrator merely tells us when Samuel or the people begin to speak and narrates the fulfillment of a sign in v. 18.

This chapter is frequently called the "farewell address" of Samuel because of the prophet's reference to his advanced age in v. 2 and the clear implication that some transitions of leadership are taking place with the advent of kingship. But it is not really accurate to treat this as Samuel's retirement. Toward the end of this chapter, Samuel emphasizes that he will continue to pray for Israel and to "instruct you in the good and the right way" (v. 23). He is still active in the course of events hereafter, as his two rejections of Saul in chaps. 13 and 15 make clear. Further, it will be Samuel who anoints David as Saul's successor (16:1-13) and who gives David refuge when he flees from Saul (19:18-24). In this last episode, Samuel remains active as the leader of a community of prophets. It is well to take Samuel's speech as a marker of transition in his role, but not as his farewell.

Since the work of Martin Noth[84] most scholars have recognized 1 Samuel 12 as one of the key passages, often in the form of speeches by main characters, that stand at turning points in the Deuteronomistic History (Dtr) and serve to integrate its various sections (e.g., Josh 1:11-15; 23–24; 2 Samuel 7:1; 1 Kgs 8:14-61). There is much evidence of deuteronomistic language and themes, but these occur primarily in vv. 6-15 and 20-25, leading some scholars to suggest that vv. 1-5, 16-19 may reflect an earlier tradition that the deuteronomistic historian has used as the context for his programmatic speech by Samuel.[85] The earlier verses focus on a vindication and demonstration of authority for Samuel as God's prophet. The Dtr additions in vv. 6-15 and 20-25 focus on the vindication of God and the faithlessness of the people as a basis for renewed covenant possibilities even in the age of kings. The vindication of God's prophet in vv. 1-5 gives added authority to Samuel's affirmation of God and judgment of the people in the remainder of the chapter.

The chapter falls into distinct segments: vv. 1-5, the exoneration of Samuel; vv. 6-15, covenant-influenced address contrasting faithfulness of God and sin of the people; vv. 16-18, the giving of a sign; v. 19, the people's confession of sin and request for intercession; vv. 20-25, closing homiletical admonitions.

12:1-5. Since the place is not named, we must assume that the scene is still Gilgal, where chap. 11 ended. Samuel's speech to the people uses both legal ("testify," "witness") and cultic ("before the LORD and before his anointed") language, so the matter of Samuel's innocence seems to be set in terms of sacral justice. The fact that testimony

takes place "before God's anointed" and that "God's anointed" is affirmed as a witness (vv. 3a, 5a) suggests that the king played a role in sacral justice. We have seen this role developing (perhaps at the expense of Samuel) in 11:12-13.

The thematic focus of this first speech is on Samuel's vindication of himself before the people. There are several important particulars. First, he declares that he has fulfilled his role as kingmaker (v. 1). He has set a king over Israel in response to what the people requested. This action obviously calls to mind the demand of the elders in chap. 8, but there is no hint in 12:1-5 that this was a sinful request (as it was in chap. 8). Indeed, the king is twice called "God's anointed" (משיח *māšîaḥ*) in these verses (3a, 5a), a designation that relates to the very positive tradition of the anointing of Saul in 9:1–10:16. The idea of the request for a king as something sinful is introduced only in the second part (vv. 6-15, the Dtr portion) of Samuel's speech in chap. 12, and then in connection with the defeat of Nahash, the Ammonite. Clearly, the relationship of chap. 12 to the preceding chapters is a complex one. It may well be that vv. 1-5 stem from an earlier prophetic edition of this literature (see the Introduction) that stresses Samuel's prophetic role but treats kings positively as the Lord's anointed. In any case, Samuel here cites his role in kingmaking as a proper carrying out of his responsibilities.

Samuel acknowledges the presence of the new king and draws a contrast to his own advanced age (v. 2). He also refers to his sons as part of the people. There is no hint of the problematic behavior of these sons that led to the demand for a king (8:1-4). Samuel calls attention to the long years of leadership he has given, reminding the people that he began as a youth and has led them until he is now old and gray. Clearly Samuel is alluding to a change of leadership even if he is not signaling his complete retirement. If one may judge from subsequent developments in 1 Samuel, the king will now give leadership in governance and military matters. Samuel, as prophet, intends to retain some authority and leadership in covenantal matters. This notion fits well with his intention, declared later in this chapter, to pray and provide moral teaching (v. 23) to the people. That these matters

84. Martin Noth, *Überlieferungsgeschichtliche Studien,* 2nd ed. (Tübingen: Max Niemeyer, 1957) 5; Eng. trans.: *The Deuteronomistic History* (Sheffield: University of Sheffield Press, 1981).

85. See McCarter, *I Samuel,* 212-21, which includes an excellent listing of the deuteronomistic influences in the chapter. See also Birch, *The Rise of the Israelite Monarchy,* 64-68.

have not been so neatly separated in Israel will lead to trouble between Saul and Samuel.

Finally, Samuel declares that he is innocent of any charge that he has used his leadership role for personal gain. Samuel asks five questions in which he declares his innocence of corrupt practices: taking an ox, taking a donkey, defrauding, oppressing, and taking a bribe (v. 3). He calls for testimony by anyone who might challenge him and say that he has done these things. The assumption is that if no one comes forward, Samuel's protestation of innocence stands (cf. Num 16:15; Deut 26:13-14; Job 31:1). Significantly, three of the five potential violations of office use the term "take" (לקח *lāqaḥ*). This is the same verb used frequently in Samuel's warning speech about the practices of a king (8:11-18). Kings "take," but Samuel has not "taken." It is not just the person of Samuel that is vindicated here, but the type of leadership represented by the authority of prophets rather than the authority of kings. It is the community of covenant contrasted with the unknown shape that monarchy may take in Israel.[86]

The people respond to Samuel's demand for exoneration with a ringing endorsement of his innocence (v. 4). They declare that Samuel has not used his office for gain. Samuel then formalizes this as a matter of sacral justice by declaring the Lord and the Lord's anointed as solemn witnesses to his innocence, with the people acknowledging this witness (v. 5).

12:6-15. There is almost universal agreement that this portion of chap. 12 is from the hand of Dtr and stands as one of the programmatic speeches that the historian uses to mark the transition from one period of Israel's story to the next. This speech marks the transition from the era of the judges to the era of the kings in Israel's life. There is also broad agreement that the speech reflects the influence of the covenant form also attested in Joshua 24 and the book of Deuteronomy. The role of Samuel here is that of covenant mediator, as was also the case with Moses and Joshua. Formal elements of a covenant pattern influenced by the patterns of ancient treaties have frequently been pointed out in this speech.[87] This pattern includes an introduction or summons to hear, historical prologue, stipulations or requirements, blessings and curses, and divine witnesses. The pattern, perhaps influenced by ancient treaty forms (often involving investiture of kings in office), has been adapted to the particular viewpoint of Dtr that the request for a king was a sin of the people. The emphasis throughout is on the fidelity of the people rather than on the king.

Verse 6 opens with an invocation of the Lord as witness (NRSV, which reads with LXX). McCarthy has noted that in ancient treaty forms divine witnesses were often listed at the opening of the treaties.[88] The God called upon to witness this solemn recitation is identified as the God of the exodus tradition, and in particular the God who appoints leaders like Moses and Aaron. With God as witness, Israel is called upon to "take your stand . . . before the LORD" (cf. Josh 24:1). The express purpose here is Samuel's intention to "enter into judgment with you" (v. 7*a*). The ceremony is not for covenant making but is occasioned by covenant breaking, and perhaps intended for covenant renewing.

Samuel announces a recitation of the Lord's saving deeds toward Israel (v. 7*b;* cf. Josh 24:2-13). The emphasis of this recitation is on God's faithfulness to Israel in times of crisis, with particular attention given to the way in which God has provided leadership for these crises. By contrast, Samuel emphasizes the people's recurring sin, usually in the form of forgetting the Lord (v. 9) and worshiping idols (v. 10). The pattern in this historical recital is the pattern present in the book of Judges: the people sin, a crisis (usually an enemy) arises, the people cry to the Lord, and the Lord sends a deliverer. Samuel begins with the exodus story (v. 8), which opens not with Israel's sin, but with Jacob's simple entry into Egypt, where the Egyptians oppressed them (Israel), and then God's sending of Moses and Aaron, who delivered Israel out of Egypt.

86. So Brueggemann, *First and Second Samuel,* 90; McCarter, *I Samuel,* 218-19. McCarter argues that the original account had a three-fold shape reflecting prophetic interests and editing. Verses 1-5 contrast the prophet favorably to the king; vv. 16-19 demonstrate the power of the prophet; v. 23 foretells the future shape of the office of prophet. The Dtr historian has added to this account the admonitions and evaluations of kingship found in vv. 6-15 and portions of vv. 20-25.

87. This discussion of covenant form in 1 Samuel 12 is especially indebted to Dennis J. McCarthy, *Treaty and Covenant: A Study in Form in the Ancient Oriental Documents and in the Old Testament* (Rome: Pontifical Biblical Institute, 1963) 141-44, and James Muilenburg, "The Form and Structure of the Covenantal Formulations," *VT* 9 (1959) 347-65.

88. McCarthy, *Treaty and Covenant,* 141.

Samuel then moves to the period of the judges (vv. 9-11). Here the cycle begins with the people's sin and proceeds through the pattern typical of the book of Judges (crisis, cry, deliverer). Samuel names three enemies who brought crisis to Israel (v. 9): Sisera/King Jabin, the Philistines, and the king of Moab. These cases do not reflect the order of events in the book of Judges. Sisera was defeated by Deborah and her general Barak (Judges 4–5). The Philistines appear as a threat in connection with the deliverance of Shamgar (Judg 3:31), the exploits of Samson (Judges 13–16), and the holy war of Samuel (1 Samuel 7). We do not know to which of these moments Samuel was referring. King Eglon of Moab oppressed Israel and was killed by Ehud (Judg 3:12-30). In v. 10, Samuel recalls the outcry of the people in these crises, confessing their sin and renewed loyalty to the Lord. The language of this verse is strongly deuteronomistic in tone—e.g., the reference to serving the "Baals and Astartes" (cf. 7:3-4). In v. 11, Samuel moves on to name deliverers raised up by God in response to the people's cry of need and repentance: Jerubbaal (another name for Gideon), Bedan, Jephthah, and Samuel. Except for Samuel, those named do not correspond to any of the enemies listed in v. 9. Bedan is not known to us except for an obscure reference in 1 Chr 7:17; the LXX reads "Barak" instead of "Bedan," a reading adopted by both the NRSV and the NIV. The LXX also reads "Samson" instead of "Samuel" (adopted by the NRSV, but mentioned in a footnote in the NIV). Despite these ambiguities, Samuel's point is clear: God provided the leadership necessary to meet crises and give Israel security and peace (v. 11*b*).

Samuel moves on to the most recent crisis with Nahash of Ammon (v. 12). The prophet charges that Israel has changed the pattern out of a failure to trust in God's deliverance. When this crisis arose, Israel did not cry out to God and confidently await God's response. Instead, they demanded a king, and in doing so rejected the kingship of God. This is a different version of events from what we have seen in 1 Samuel 11, where Saul was pictured as a deliverer empowered by God's Spirit in the mold of the judges. The elevation to kingship in that story came after the victory, and in earlier chapters the people's demand for a

king came long before the crisis with Ammon (1 Samuel 8). Again, although the ambiguities cannot be resolved, we understand Samuel's claim. Israel in the present moment is accused of a failure to trust in God's deliverance. Instead of crying to God for help, Israel has demanded a king.

Verse 13 shifts from recitation of the past to presentation in the present. Samuel presents the king; he acknowledges kingship as an accomplished fact. Surprisingly, the king is presented both as chosen by the people and as established in authority over Israel by God. The people have demanded, but the king they receive is still from God.

Then vv. 14-15 present the conditions under which people and king can still live within the framework of covenant relationship to God. Even though the kingship originated out of sinful request, there is a future for king and people in relation to God—though with conditions. The listings in vv. 14-15 correspond to the listing of stipulations or requirements in other covenant texts and in ancient treaties (Deuteronomy 12–26; Josh 24:14). The consequences, good and bad, that flow from obedience or disobedience to these requirements reflect the blessings and curses associated with this covenant/treaty form (Deuteronomy 28; Josh 24:20). There are five conditions from which blessing flows, and all reflect the loyalty to the Lord required of Israel and its king. These are followed by two conditions, which will result in judgment:

Obedience to the Lord (v. 14)		Disobedience to the Lord (v. 15)	
If you will:	fear	If you will not:	
	serve		
	heed his voice	heed his voice	
	not rebel	If you do:	rebel
	follow		
Then:	it will be well	Then: the hand of the LORD will be against you and your king	

The judgment stated in v. 15 is especially interesting, since the hand of the Lord was prominent in judgment against both

Philistines and Israelites in the ark story of 1 Samuel 4–6. It is also worth commenting that Samuel includes people and king together in presenting covenant possibilities and covenant dangers. Israel may have a king, and the king may be established by God as a concession to Israel, but the king must obey the covenant.

12:16-19. Samuel has ended his covenant speech. Now he demonstrates his prophetic power: his ability to call and have the Lord answer. It was the time of the wheat harvest when rain was rare, but Samuel called upon the Lord to send a thunderstorm as a sign of the people's sin in asking for a king, and the Lord sent a thunderstorm. This act is reminiscent of events in Samuel's victory over the Philistines in 7:8-10 (see also Elijah's calling forth a drought from the Lord, 1 Kgs 17:1). Thunderstorms are also connected with the appearance of God (theophany). The fear of the people that they may die (v. 19) suggests that they feared the holy presence of God in this storm. They ask for Samuel to intercede for them, and they confess that their demand for a king was evil. The effect of this development is not only to reassert divine authority but to establish Samuel's prophetic authority as God's representative as well. "All the people greatly feared the LORD and Samuel" (v. 18 b; cf. Exod 14:31 b for a similar statement on the Lord and Moses). Samuel had vindicated himself (vv. 1-5) and God (vv. 6-15) before the people, and the authority of God and the prophet are now demonstrated to powerful effect. This is hardly a retirement ceremony for Samuel. Kingship may be an accomplished reality in Israel, but God's prophet still claims considerable authority. He has not asked for the undoing of kingship. Indeed, Samuel has helped to establish the king, but the future of king and people still lies within the framework of covenant obedience, and Samuel remains the covenant mediator.

12:20-25. This section is less formal and more homiletical in tone. It even has a pastoral quality as Samuel responds to the people's fearful confession with the classic formula of reassurance, "Do not be afraid" (v. 20 a). This section again shows marks of the deuteronomic historian—e.g., the phrase "serve the LORD with all your heart" (v. 20). When we remember that Dtr probably wrote and compiled his history in the context of Babylonian exile, we might wonder whether this last section is particularly directed at reassuring and admonishing the exiles. The "fear not" formula is perhaps best known from the great prophet of the exile we know as Second Isaiah (e.g., Isa 41:10, 14; 43:1, 5). There are reassurances that the people can turn back to the Lord and serve the Lord in spite of sin (v. 20 b), and reaffirmations of God's election of Israel and the tie of God's name to Israel as a people (v. 22). The people are admonished not to turn aside after "useless things." The Hebrew word תהו (*tōhû*) is used in Gen 1:2 to indicate chaos and by Second Isaiah in reference to idols (Isa 41:29; 44:9). Samuel ends his homily with a more concise statement of conditions for blessing and curse (vv. 24-25; cf. vv. 14-15). Israel is called to fear and serve the Lord, but if they do wickedness then Israel and its king will be "swept away." Again, in the context of exile, the possibility of being permanently "swept away," both king and people, is a very real fear. Samuel offers some hope, but the consequences of failure are harsh. For exiles reading this historian's story of early Israel—Samuel, Saul, and eventually David—the story is often a parable of their own struggles.

In the midst of Samuel's final speech (v. 23), the prophet speaks about his own future role (perhaps reflecting the role of prophets in Israel's later history, including the exile experience). For all of his judgment pronounced on Israel's sin, Samuel vows never to sin against the Lord by ceasing to pray for the people and to instruct them in the "good and right way." The people can count on the prophet's continual intercession and moral instruction. It is an interesting and instructive view of the prophet's role beyond the announcement of God's word.

REFLECTIONS

First Samuel 12 is the ideal preaching and teaching text. Its form is already a teaching sermon. Of course, Samuel's words to Israel may need some translation to the situation of the modern church, but not as much as we might think. The issues with which Samuel and Israel were struggling are perennial issues in the life of the church in every generation, including our own.

1. On one level, Samuel's concern and the focus of this chapter are on the way in which old and cherished values can relate to new realities. Situations of change for the faith community and the social contexts in which faith is lived can bring both threat and possibility. Samuel spoke to Israel at a time when many saw the king as a hopeful new reality in their midst. The patterns of covenant community and Samuel's lifelong investment in the leadership of Israel seemed threatened and were probably regarded by many as outmoded. Samuel saw this as an issue of trust in God. The danger was that the God of covenant might seem as outmoded as the older patterns of community and leadership.

Samuel's speech is a word against moral compromise in the name of realistic politics. Changing situations may demand new institutions and new social structures, but Samuel asserts that fundamental moral reality has not changed. That moral reality is rooted in the God who covenants with the community and is faithful to that covenant. Samuel's recital of God's faithfulness in times of crisis can be continued down to the present. New kings or new elected officials or new political parties or new patterns of regulations and governance may become necessary, but these things do not ultimately endure and cannot be the locus of our trust. When we lose sight of God's reign, we risk idolatry in the worship of structures we have made for ourselves. We place ourselves in danger of being "swept away" because these things do not endure.

> Chapter 12 asserts without reservation that there is another governance that merits and must have more of our attention. There is a leadership that does not "take," that does not seek its own. There is a community that could "serve faithfully." This chapter intends to renew in ancient Israel a moral vision of the historical process when that moral vision was skewed by fear, calculation, and vested interest. The renewed moral vision of the historical process is as urgent now as then—lest we all be "swept away."[89]

There is also in this text another insight into times of transition. The speech of Samuel also asserts that the affirmation of old values (covenant) can embrace new forms and realities (kingship). Samuel judges the request for kingship sinful, but this new reality can be encompassed within the covenant framework. Samuel does not ask the people to depose the king, but challenges king and people to renewed covenant obedience. Moral steadfastness need not be reactionary and backward looking. Faithful response need not go back to the future, but can go on to the future—even in changed circumstances we might not have chosen—in confidence that all futures are God's future. In the book of 1 Samuel, there is much that looks back to what God has done and seeks to preserve the covenant relationship forged in that history. But at the same time, much in 1 Samuel looks ahead, beyond the struggles within and without, to David, the man after God's own heart. And in the larger perspective of the canon, it looks beyond David to the Messiah, God with us. Those in our own time who are troubled by changes that threaten valued faith perspectives are right to call for care, lest we reject the reign of God for the sake of our own constructions of reality. But equal care must be exercised that we do not fail to discern what God is doing new in our midst and mindlessly hold to the old and familiar. Times of change, even crisis, bring not only

89. Brueggemann, *First and Second Samuel,* 96-97.

threat but also new possibility. Samuel's speech in the context of a history for exiles may have been intended both to renew covenant loyalties and to affirm that God is still at work in the radically changed realities of their lives: "I am about to do a new thing; now it springs forth, do you not perceive it?" (Isa 43:19*a* NRSV). Samuel's speech is a word to the increasingly polarized political climate of our times. God both preserves and makes new. The challenge is to discernment, not to the choosing of sides.

2. This chapter is also an important text for reflection on the meaning of leadership in the faith community or in the society. Both Samuel and the new king (unnamed here) are assumed in this text to be accountable to the same covenant demands for obedience that are laid upon the people. Samuel opens his conduct as a leader to the people's judgment and witness (12:1-5). In Samuel's challenge to covenant obedience and warning of dangers to disobedience (12:14-15, 24-25), no distinction is drawn between king and people. This text is a fundamental rejection of the notion that leadership brings privileged position. Not even prophets or kings could claim this. This has been a perennial issue in political and religious institutions. Recent decades have seen a constant stream of revelations exposing violations of trust by those who hold offices of leadership in society or church. Often these corrupt practices grow less out of pure malevolence than out of the misguided notion that offices of leadership confer privileged position on their holders—that to hold such offices is to escape the standards expected of the people. The flagrant cases make news headlines. The list includes presidents and Wall Street managers, Republicans and Democrats, men and women. In the church, leadership has suffered the same abuses and illusions of privileged position. The list here includes bishops, denominational treasurers, pastors of local churches, and lay officeholders. These are the offenders, but Samuel's speech suggests that their offenses may grow out of a flawed notion of office and leadership. Can we affirm with Samuel that office should confer no privilege or personal gain? Can we agree that the future of a leader is intimately tied to the future of the people? Do we accept or even promote patterns of deference and privilege between office holder and citizen, or between clergy and laity, that create the climate for abuse?

Along with his warning about kingship in chap. 8, the text of Samuel's speech in chap. 12 has a rich history in the English tradition. English politicians and writers have cited Samuel as support for making the monarchy accountable to the people in the signing of the Magna Carta and for constitutional monarchy in the seventeenth century. Early American patriots, such as Thomas Paine, used Samuel to support democratic forms of leadership that are fully accountable to the people.

Samuel has sometimes been pictured as defensive and crotchety. This may reflect our unhappiness with him in his treatment of Saul later in the story (chaps. 13; 15). It is possible, however, to view him in chap. 12 as a model of admirable traits of leadership. He is unswerving in his determination not to use his office for personal gain. He recognizes that God, and not he, is the true shaping force of history. Although with warnings, he makes a place for the new reality of kingship in Israel. And perhaps his new role, outlined in 12:23, is an especially important word about leadership. When the time of Samuel's formal leadership at the head of the people came to an end, he did not simply abandon his tie to the people but promised to be unceasing in prayer and instruction in the good and right way. One wonders whether the activities of prayer and instruction might sometimes be more enduring than the activities of office and power. Recent American presidents have often left office simply to lead lives of personal pleasure and relaxation. Jimmy Carter, however, a man of prayer and religious conviction, has devoted himself since his presidency to mediation of international conflicts, Habitat for Humanity, and his center in Atlanta dedicated to issues of peace and justice in the world. One wonders whether this is not more in the spirit of Samuel, who did not leave office to go home to his own interests, but continued in prayer for and instruction of the people he had once led in power.

1 Samuel 13:1–15:35, The Exploits and Rejection of Saul

OVERVIEW

Now that Saul is firmly established as king, and Samuel's speech in chap. 12 has given us a pause for theological reflection on covenant, king, and people, the narrative resumes with the career of Saul. It is to be brief and unhappy. The two central episodes are rejection stories (13:8-15; 15:1-35). Again, Samuel plays a central role as God's prophet. He confronts Saul with violations of covenant obedience and sacral law, and then announces God's judgment. The section ends with the mournful note that "the Lord was sorry that he had made Saul king over Israel." Saul will remain in the story for the rest of 1 Samuel, but the focus will shift to David beginning with chap. 16.

Surrounding these two rejection stories are traditions that narrate Saul's efforts against the Philistines. These sections provide a good deal of data about the historical circumstances of the time. Israel exists in a desperate position. Saul's efforts seem admirable and sometimes effective, but even here Saul seems overshadowed by his own son Jonathan. The episode in chap. 14 that almost leads to the death of Jonathan already begins to cast a shadow over Saul's leadership and judgment. In this entire section we have the feeling that we are not really hearing about Saul's reign but are being prepared for the appearance of David.

1 Samuel 13:1-23, Saul Rejected from Dynasty

COMMENTARY

The use of a special formula (although incomplete) announces the formal beginning of Saul's reign in v. 1. Saul is now king, but the story of his rise to the throne almost immediately becomes the story of his fall from kingship. In Saul's story there is no honeymoon for the new monarch. Chapter 13 is a narrative of Saul's external conflict with the Philistines and internal conflict with Samuel. Saul does not succeed in overcoming either of these conflicts, and they eventually bring him to a tragic end.

The immediate challenge for Saul's reign is the war against Philistine domination. Verses 2-7a begin a detailed account of military encounters with the Philistines and the particular exploits of Saul and his son Jonathan (introduced here for the first time). The story of these military campaigns and their eventual limited success in parts of the tribal territory of Benjamin continues in vv. 15b-23 and on into chap. 14.

In the midst of this account of military tactics and maneuvers we find an episode of conflict between Saul and the prophet Samuel (vv. 7b-15a). Saul, faced with a deteriorating

military situation, had offered the sacrifices necessary to begin battle. Samuel had told him to wait for his arrival. One presumes that the prophet would have offered these sacrifices. When Samuel arrives to find that Saul had proceeded without him, he angrily denounces Saul and announces that God will seek another "man after his own heart" to whom the kingdom will be given.

There are numerous problems in this chapter: (1) Samuel's instruction of Saul to wait at Gilgal for seven days (v. 8) seems related to the command of Samuel in 10:8, but in chap. 10 Saul was a boy and not yet king. In chap. 13, Saul is a warrior king with a grown warrior son. (2) The narrative seems to speak of the military exploits of Saul and Jonathan in a confused and overlapping way (cf. v. 3 with v. 4). This situation has led some scholars to suggest that an account of a successful campaign by Saul has been interwoven with an account of Jonathan's deeds.[90] (3) Almost all

---

90. See Klein, *1 Samuel*, 123-28, for a more detailed discussion of various proposals.

commentators have recognized a confusion in biblical references to Gibeah (גבעה *gib'â*) and Geba (גבע *geba'*). Although these two places have traditionally been seen as separate locations only three miles apart in Benjaminite territory, the two often appear interchangeably in different manuscript traditions and within narrative episodes (e.g., cf. v. 15 with v. 16). Miller has made a plausible case that references to Geba, to Geba of Benjamin, to Gibeah, to Gibeath, to Gibeah of Benjamin, to Gibeah of Saul, and to Gibeath-elohim all refer to the same general geographic location.[91] Some of these matters are commented on further below, but in general the difficulties of this chapter cannot be fully resolved. Chapter 13 does not seem an entirely smooth literary piece, but the significance for Saul's story of conflicts with the Philistines and with Samuel seems clear, and that will be our focus.

13:1. This is the formula typically used to introduce the reign of a king in the books of Kings (e.g., 1 Kgs 14:21; 22:42). It is also used later for Ishbaal (2 Sam 2:10) and David (2 Sam 5:4). The formula usually states the age of the king at accession and the number of years of his reign, but in Saul's case the formula appears to be incomplete. The MT literally reads that Saul was one year old when he began his reign. A number may have dropped out, as the NRSV rendering suggests by leaving a blank space. Three LXX manuscripts read the number 30, which the NIV has adopted, but most LXX texts omit the entire verse. The age of thirty seems young for Saul to have a warrior son like Jonathan a verse later, however.

The last part of the formula is also incomplete. The Hebrew text reads two years for Saul's reign, but in an unusual form of the number 2 that would seem to require another number before it. Many have felt two years too short to account for the events of Saul's reign, in any case. The NIV reads forty-two by appealing to the use of the round number 40 for Saul's reign in Acts 13:21. Josephus also reads forty,[92] but forty is a round number often used for a generation when more precise numbers are unknown. We must content ourselves by saying that these numbers

were either unknown to the historian or lost somewhere in the process of transmission. Most agree that the deuteronomistic historian is responsible for these chronological markers in the books of Samuel and Kings. Some argue that two years fits the Dtr chronological scheme, and was used for that reason whether it was historically accurate or not. In any case, the formula signals the beginning of Saul's kingship. What follows, for good or for ill, is the tradition's record of his reign.

13:2-7a, 15b-23. This material reflects the hostilities between Israel and the Philistines. The accounts include details concerning troop movements, strategic locations and deployment of forces, and numbers of men. There is no dialogue and little character development. The literary style is straightforward and almost bare of stylistic devices (vv. 5-6 show a brief descriptive flourish). The impression is of annalistic material or official records of these military encounters.

This military material in chap. 13 sets the stage for the more developed narrative of events in chap. 14. Saul is presented as a capable military leader who has assembled a significant force (v. 2). He is encamped at Michmash and Jonathan at Gibeah/Geba. Jonathan takes bold action (foreshadowing his role in chap. 14?) and wins a victory over the garrison of Philistines at Gibeah/Geba (v. 3). This act gains the attention of the Philistines and causes Saul to blow the trumpet and summon the Israelite levy (v. 4). A major Philistine army encamps at Michmash to put down this rebellion (v. 5).

In Saul's summons (v. 3*b*), he says, "Let the Hebrews hear!" This expression is problematic, because Israelites never referred to themselves as Hebrews. Elsewhere the term is pejorative and is applied to them by others. Later, in v. 7, the scattering of Israelite troops includes a further reference to "some Hebrews." Many scholars have emended the text to remove these references. Norman Gottwald has proposed that in addition to calling out the Israelite tribal levy Saul is appealing to Israelites who have become *apiru*/Hebrew mercenaries fighting for the Philistines, as David and his men later do in 1 Samuel 27:1. The term "Hebrew" is often said to have its origin in reference to

91. J. M. Miller, "Geba/Gibeah of Benjamin," *VT* 25 (1975) 145-66.
92. Josephus *Antiquities of the Jews* 6.14.9.

an outlaw class called *apiru* who sometimes served as mercenary military retainers.[93]

With the arrival of a Philistine army, Saul's situation deteriorates. Only a brief time earlier in Saul's story, the empowerment of God's Spirit had enabled a victory over the Ammonites against even greater odds (chap. 11). The contrast could hardly be greater in chap. 13. The people are trembling with distress and take cowardly flight, hiding themselves in panic wherever they can find a refuge (vv. 6-7). Saul seems helpless to rally them, and in v. 15b he can only count 600 who remain with him. This is not the Spirit-filled leader of chap. 11. It is the moment of Saul's helplessness in the face of the desertion of his army that becomes the setting for the story of conflict and rejection in the encounter with Samuel (vv. 7b-15a). Saul's loss of God's Spirit is not noted until 16:14, but the power of God's Spirit seems already dormant in Saul.

The last portion of the chapter gives further reports on military movements and deployments. The Philistines are encamped at Michmash and send out smaller forces in three directions (vv. 17-18). Saul and Jonathan remain at Gibeah/Geba with their depleted force (vv. 15b-16), but the chapter ends by calling attention to the Philistine force deployed to the pass at Michmash. The stage is set for the bold raid of Jonathan, which begins chap. 14.

As an aside from the main story, vv. 19-22 report that the Philistines had a monopoly on ironworking in the region. The Israelites (called Hebrews by the Philistines, v. 19) were not allowed to have smiths. Even farm implements had to be obtained from the Philistine smiths, and at considerable cost as well (vv. 20-21). Thus Israelite armies under Saul did not have iron fighting weapons. Only Saul and Jonathan possessed sword or spear of iron (v. 22). The impact of this note is to heighten the readers' sense of the overwhelming odds faced by Saul, Jonathan, and the Israelite warriors.

13:7b-15a. This is the first of two episodes telling of Saul's rejection by Samuel (cf. also chap. 15). In the present form of the text, this story is tied to the instruction of Samuel to the young Saul in 10:8. The prophet commands Saul to go to Gilgal and wait seven days for Samuel's arrival to offer sacrifices. Verse 8 sets the stage for following events by reporting that Saul waits the seven days appointed by Samuel, but the prophet does not come to Gilgal. We have already briefly noted the problems with this chronology. The events of 10:17–12:25 could hardly have taken place in seven days. Further, the young Saul of 10:8 is now a man with a grown son in 13:8. Nevertheless, there is no other possible reference for the command to wait at Gilgal. The historian has apparently chosen to ignore the chronological problems in favor of focusing on Saul's obedience to the command of the prophet Samuel. The story even seems artificially to move Saul to Gilgal (v. 7b) and back again to Gibeah/Geba (v. 15) to make this possible.

Saul is occupied with the strategic military situation. His troops are scattering in panic after having seen the superior strength of the Philistines. A battle seems imminent, but in the holy war traditions of Israel sacrifices must be offered before a battle in order to seek the Lord's favor. It is not only a matter of required ritual but also for Saul a matter of his troops' morale. How can he hold his men if they do not have confidence that the Lord will aid their cause against the oppressor Philistines?

Saul fails to see that this is a theological as well as a strategic situation. Samuel had commanded him to wait, and the prophet had specified that he would arrive to make the sacrifices. The burnt offering and the offering of well-being (peace or fellowship offering, NIV) are the very sacrifices Samuel mentioned in 10:8 and reserved to himself. We have already seen Samuel offering sacrifices before battle (7:9-10) in a victorious encounter with the Philistines. Hence, the ritual may be a prophetic prerogative, and thus not to be usurped by kings. Kings, after all, were new to Israel and had no claim on traditional rituals.

No sooner does Saul proceed with the sacrifices than Samuel appears. It is hard to avoid some suspicion at the timing of his entrance. Samuel's encounter with Saul occurs in the form of a prophetic accusation and announcement of judgment. Samuel responds to Saul's greeting with an accusing question, "What have you done?" (v. 11a). "The prophetic

93. Gottwald, *The Tribes of Yahweh*, 423-24.

accusation to an individual person was often a matter of the prophet's establishing the facts of the case through questions exactly as it occurs in the regular judicial process. . . . [It is] similar to a hearing in which the prophet is one who hears and the king is the one heard."[94] Saul's response is defensive, shifting responsibility to Samuel, "The people were slipping away from me, and . . . *you* [the pronoun here is emphatic] did not come" (v. 11*b*). Saul goes on to state his desire to have the favor of the Lord in battle and claims that he "forced himself" to make the sacrifices (v. 12). He offered them reluctantly, he claims.

Saul seems sympathetic here. To most readers his rationale sounds reasonable and his actions understandable. We are unprepared for the harshness of Samuel's response. He brands Saul's actions foolish and charges Saul with failing to keep the commandment of the Lord (v. 13*a*). Prophetic accusation is then followed by announcement of punishment, and again Samuel's response seems exceptionally harsh. Samuel announces that the Lord would have established Saul's kingdom forever (v. 13*b*). This is a new motif in 1 Samuel, and it foreshadows the dynastic promise later given to David by the prophet Nathan (2 Samuel 7:1). Samuel continues by saying that now Saul's kingdom will not continue (v. 14*a*). Saul is denied the hope of dynasty for his house. The reader has just been introduced to Jonathan; both here and in the following chapter he appears as an attractive and capable leader. However, Samuel makes clear that Jonathan will not succeed his father as king. Further, Samuel declares that the Lord has already selected Saul's successor, "a man after his own heart," and has appointed him נגיד (*nāgîd*, "ruler," "prince," "designate to the throne," v. 14*b*). This is clearly a reference ahead to David, who will be anointed by Samuel in 16:13 as Saul's successor. David's shadow is cast over Saul from the very beginning of his reign. The phrase "a man after his own heart" is often taken as a reference to David's character, as if it refers to some special quality that singled David out. McCarter has shown clearly, however, that this phrase refers not to David's character but to God's freedom.[95] The kingdom is given to

"a man of God's own choosing" (cf. the use of this phrase in 14:7; 2 Sam 7:21; Ps 20:4; Jer 3:15). This phrase looks ahead to David because this is the direction God wills. This emphasis on God's free choice of the anointed one as designated through prophets is consistent with the prophetic theology of kingship, visible in 9:1–10:16, the episode to which this story is tied through the command of Samuel the prophet.

Again Samuel asserts with finality that Saul has not kept the Lord's commandment (v. 14*b*). What was this commandment? What does Samuel see as the offense? Is the failure to follow Samuel's instructions the equivalent of violating the commandment of the Lord? Is the punishment announced by Samuel out of proportion to the offense? The text does not answer all of our questions. We are inclined to respond to the personalities at play here. Saul seems well meaning and concerned for his people. Samuel seems angry, temperamental, and reactionary. The modern reader is inclined to feel that he is overreacting. We should probably not underestimate the depth of the issues involved in the transitions taking place with the establishment of kingship for the first time in Israel. How much power are kings to have? Should their authority extend to religious matters? Should the office of king usurp the office of the prophet/covenant mediator? Should kingship in Israel include the concept of dynasty? Samuel is not an attractive personality in these stories, but the issues are more than a clash of personalities. They are issues that will prove to be life-and-death matters in Israel, and from the perspective of the historians who later shaped this narrative (perhaps both prophetic and deuteronomistic) the deathly possibilities inherent in royal power seem more obvious than they may be to the contemporary reader. Perhaps these historians knew of later times in Israel's story when hundreds of prophets were co-opted by royal power in the time of Ahab (1 Kgs 22:6).

Saul is not to be Israel's future, and in chap. 15 he is even rejected as the legitimate king of Israel's present in the story of 1 Samuel. Perhaps the tradition does not itself fully know why Saul deserved this fate, but it does know that David was God's choice for Israel's future and that Saul's brief reign was not finally characterized by the presence of God's Spirit.

94. Westermann, *Basic Forms of Prophetic Speech*, 144.
95. McCarter, *I Samuel*, 229.

REFLECTIONS

This first story of Saul's rejection before he even has a chance to establish his reign is a tale with sober lessons to teach. These reflections grow out of the beginning of a tragedy that will not, perhaps cannot, be averted.

1. This tale of conflict between Samuel and Saul is set in a context that calls for the exercise of power on several different levels. Military power must be exercised in the face of the Philistine threat. The power of leadership is called for to maintain readiness and morale among Saul's own fighting men. The power of religious authority is crucial in Israel, where all wars are to be fought as holy wars in obedience to God's purpose and will. In each of these interrelated arenas there were decisions to be made and actions to be taken, and these were a matter of life and death.

But these issues of power could not be decided in the abstract. They came entangled in the personalities of Samuel and Saul. Samuel is a reluctant participant in the enterprise of kingship. He is fearful that kingship will erode the covenant tradition he has upheld faithfully. He will be supplanted to some degree by any shape of developing royal leadership. In his prophetic role, he designated Saul, and he feels bound to hold Saul accountable to the Lord whom Samuel serves as prophet. Saul is a young man in a role with no precedent in Israel. His inexperience as king is matched by Israel's inexperience at having kings. He is faced with an overwhelming military challenge and a deteriorating capability for meeting that challenge. He seems naive in his understanding of relationship to the religious authority of Samuel.

What begins in the conflict here, continues in the total rejection of chap. 15, and finally ends when Saul takes his own life in 1 Samuel 31 is a tragedy borne of the peculiar mix of personality and power issues that mark the lives of Samuel and Saul. What we must understand is that this mixing of personality and power is always the case. We wish it were not so. We long for purity in moral decision making, hoping for some rational, objective method of knowing the will of God and determining the ethical course of action. Or we long for ideal personalities with no human flaws to make these decisions for us. If only we had the ideal president or the ideal pastor. But this difficult story of Samuel and Saul reminds us that moral decisions are made in the context of complex, often ambiguous, power dilemmas, and they are made by real people, with their personal flaws and vested interests.

In the ongoing story of 1 Samuel it is clear that alongside the messy issues of personality and power, God is at work opening new possibilities for Israel. Beyond the arenas of human power is a working of divine power. The ark stories in chaps. 4–6 make the reality of this power visible. The hand of Yahweh is at work in these events. This episode already looks ahead to God's choosing of David (v. 14). This seems a quick and harsh verdict on Saul, but the stakes for Israel are high. It is not too early to suggest that the constant prayer and inquiry after God's will that mark so many David stories are in distinct contrast to the well-meaning, but self-possessed blundering forward of Saul. Saul always seems to act on his own authority rather than in communication with God. It is a warning to our own well-intentioned efforts that are, nevertheless, centered only in our own power and authority.

2. The conflict between Samuel and Saul is a matter not only of personalities but also of role or office. Samuel is a prophet, but in the circumstances of his time he also serves in judicial and priestly roles that maintain the older covenant traditions of Israel. Saul is Israel's new king, an office not known before in Israel and considered by some antagonistic to the covenant tradition. The conflict here is a reflection of the need to determine the relationship that should exist between the authority of kings and the authority of prophets.

While modern readers often sympathize with Saul in this and subsequent episodes (Samuel comes off as a considerably unlikable grouch!), it would be well for American readers in particular to remember their own history. The founders of the United States thought there were good reasons to separate religious and governance roles. They did not wish kings to control religious rituals and practices, and they had in some cases come to the American colonies to escape the abuse of such royal authority used to restrict religious practice. Eventually in Israel kings began to co-opt many of the prophets or persecute those whom they could not co-opt. We may sympathize with Saul as a person, but we should not be so quick to dismiss his actions as trivial. It is often by seemingly innocent and trivial acts that authority is undermined or liberties eroded, in our own time as surely as in ancient Israel. Samuel may be a harsh character in this story, but we would do well to consider him a warning to our complacency when religious symbols are appropriated for civil or political purposes or for partisan ideological commitments in our own time. This is surely one of the issues to be considered in the heated debate over prayer in public schools. Even if the intention is noble, do we want to set the precedent of allowing civil authority to authorize or, as some would have it, administer religious observance? Those who answer this question in the negative may seem as harsh and unreasoning as would Samuel to some.

1 Samuel 14:1-52, Jonathan and Saul Against the Philistines

COMMENTARY

This is Jonathan's story. He boldly initiates action against the Philistines and leads the Israelites in a decisive victory against their enemy. Saul also plays a major role in the story, but in contrast to his son Jonathan, Saul appears cautious, given to pious ritual, and ultimately foolish in his decisions. Saul's actions prevent the victory from being as great as it might have been and jeopardize Jonathan's life.

Chapter 14 presupposes the background on the Philistine war that was reported in 13:1-7a, 15b-23, but stylistically this episode is very different. Unlike the sparse, annalistic quality of chap. 13, the account in chap. 14 is a masterpiece of narrative storytelling. It uses dialogue extensively, includes plot and subplot, and develops two characters (Jonathan and Saul). Numerous studies have demonstrated that this chapter is one of the finest examples of narrative prose in the Hebrew Bible.[96]

There is also a constant influence in this chapter from the holy war theology and its understanding that it is Yahweh who fights for Israel and can alone give victory. This influence pervades the entire chapter.[97]

v. 6	In the very making of his proposal to attack the Philistine garrison, Jonathan affirms that it is the Lord who must in reality win the victory. God's power bears no relationship to numbers of men.
vv. 10, 12	Entry into the fray depends on a sign that the Lord has "given them into our hand." This phrase is one of the most typical formulae in holy war texts (Josh 6:2, 12; 8:1, 7; 10:8, 12, 19; Judg 11:30, 32; 12:3). It is used (vv. 36-37) in an oracular inquiry directed to the Lord.
v. 15	The enemy is stricken with God's panic (Gen 35:5; Exod 23:27; Isa 2:10, 19), and there is an earthquake (1 Sam 4:5; Amos 8:8; Joel 2:10).
v. 20	The enemy is thrown into confusion (Judg 7:22, and in verbal form 1 Sam 7:10; Exod 14:24; Josh 10:10; 2 Sam 22:15).

96. For detailed discussion of the literary features of 1 Samuel 14, see J. Blenkinsopp, "Jonathan's Sacrilege, 1 Sam 14:1-46: A Study in Literary History," *CBQ* 26 (1964) 423-49; David Jobling, "Saul's Fall and Jonathan's Rise: Tradition and Redaction in 1 Sam 14:1-46," *JBL* 95 (1976) 367-76.

97. The following list is an adaptation from Birch, *The Rise of the Israelite Monarchy,* 89-90.

v. 23	Victory is ascribed to the Lord by a salvation formula ("The LORD saved Israel on that day," 1 Sam 4:3; 7:8).
v. 31	The totality of victory is expressed in a common formula used in holy war texts ("The LORD struck down the Philistines that day from Michmash to Aijalon," 1 Sam 15:5-7; Num 21:30; Judg 11:33; Josh 10:10).
v. 45	Even in the attempt to ransom Jonathan's life, the people ascribe the victory to divine aid.

The victory is Yahweh's victory. It is Jonathan who trusts in and defers to God's providence even as he takes bold action. As he proposes the attack to his weaponbearer, Jonathan says, "*Perhaps* [NIV; NRSV, "It may be"] the LORD will act in our behalf. Nothing can hinder the LORD from saving, whether by many or by few" (v. 6). Jonathan does not presume on God's freedom, but he is certain that if victory is possible it will come from the Lord. He then acts in confidence that God will save when God wills it.

Saul, in contrast, relies excessively on ritual. He tends to remain passive and unresponsive until he can ensure the Lord's favor by oracular means or by the taking of oaths (vv. 2-3, 18-19, 24, 36-37, 46). Perhaps this puts his rejection in chap. 13 in a new light as a part of Saul's need to hide behind ritual assurance even at the expense of infringing on Samuel's prerogatives. He might have fared better to go boldly into battle without the sacrifices. We will return to these issues at a later point.

In any case, chap. 14 introduces us to Jonathan as a hero, but exposes Saul as a man whose cautious piety and foolish actions nearly lead to the tragic cost of Jonathan's life. The people must redeem Jonathan from Saul's own folly. Perhaps the larger tragedy of Saul's story in 1 Samuel is that no one can eventually redeem Saul from the tragic cost of his own folly. In the end, Saul's piety is revealed as self-serving, not God-fearing. It is Jonathan who truly trusts in divine freedom and divine saving. Ultimately, Saul stands in contrast not only to Jonathan but also to David.

14:1-5. This story begins dramatically with Jonathan's proposal to attack the Philistine garrison accompanied only by his armorbearer (v. 1). Only then does the storyteller set the scene. The Philistines are at Michmash, while Saul and only six hundred men are at Gibeah (vv. 2, 16; Geba in v. 5). Saul is sitting under a tree, accompanied by Ahijah, a priest in the line of Eli, who carries an ephod (vv. 2-3). The text opens with Jonathan as a man of action and Saul passively waiting for something to develop. The priest and the ephod are significant in the light of the role that ritual plays for Saul in this story. Here the ephod seems to be a ceremonial garment that contains in a pocket or pouch the sacred oracles, Urim and Thummim, which are used later in the story.

No one in Saul's camp knows that Jonathan and his armorbearer have gone. They must climb down through a rocky gorge that separates Philistines and Israelites and come back up the other side (vv. 5-6).

14:6-23. With the scene set, action resumes with Jonathan again stating his intention (v. 6), but he adds a derogatory reference to the Philistines as the uncircumcised. More important, he sets his action in the context of God's providence: "Perhaps the LORD will act for us." He does not infringe on divine freedom or presume somehow to control God's action. He expresses a hope in what he trusts is possible through the Lord, "for nothing can hinder the LORD from saving by many or by few" (v. 6).

The armorbearer, in his only speech, expresses solidarity with Jonathan (v. 7). Such men were more than servants; they were also close martial companions to leaders like Jonathan. David later becomes Saul's armorbearer and distinguishes himself in battle. In this story, Jonathan's armorbearer is a full participant in the crucial battle that Jonathan precipitates with the Philistines.

Jonathan proposes a method for determining whether his proposed attack is the will of the Lord (vv. 8-10). The sign will be that the Philistines who first see them urge them to come up (taunting them to come up and fight?). Jonathan and his companion show themselves, and the Philistines taunt them, calling them "Hebrews" (a derogatory term) who have come up out of their holes from hiding (v. 11). The Philistines dare them to come up, whereupon they will show them a thing or two (v. 12). A battle ensues in which Jonathan and his companion wreak havoc on the Philistine ranks (vv. 13-14). It is clear that the Lord is, indeed, with them, as is evident in the onset of panic and an earthquake, which characterize the Lord's fighting for Israel (v. 15).

Saul's camp at Gibeah notices the fighting in the Philistine camp (v. 16). Instead of joining the fray immediately, Saul takes the roll of his troops and discovers that Jonathan and his armorbearer are missing (v. 17). He calls for the priest Ahijah, presumably to consult after God's will in this situation. The Masoretic Text (Hebrew) reads that Ahijah brought the ark out to Saul (v. 18). This does not seem likely, given the fate of the ark in 1 Samuel 6 and the need for David to find it later in 2 Samuel 6. The LXX (Greek) text reads "ephod" here. This seems a more appropriate reading, particularly in the light of v. 3, where the ephod is mentioned. This reference also makes sense of v. 19, where the tumult grows so great among the Philistines that Saul finally decides he can wait no longer. He commands Ahijah to "withdraw your hand." Presumably Ahijah was interrupted in the process of consulting the Urim and Thummim (mentioned later in v. 41). They may have been carried in a pouch on the ephod (see Exod 28:30; Lev 8:8), from which they would be withdrawn to give their judgment on Saul's military prospects. Eight times in 1 Samuel the ephod is mentioned as a priestly garment from which a divine oracle is often sought (2:28; 14:3, 18; 21:9; 22:18; 23:6, 9; 30:7).

Saul and his men join the conflict (v. 20), whereupon they are joined by Hebrew mercenaries who had been fighting for the Philistines (v. 21) and Israelites who had hidden in panic earlier (v. 22; see 13:6-7). The text makes clear that it is the Lord who gives Israel victory on that day (v. 23*a*). The battle extends far beyond the area around Gibeah and Michmash into the hill country of Ephraim, with Saul's army swelling to ten thousand men (v. 23*b*).

14:24-30. Against the backdrop of this improbable victory another deadly drama begins to unfold as a result of an oath Saul lays upon his troops (v. 24). The narrator labels this action from the beginning as "very rash" (the NRSV and most commentators read with the LXX here; the Greek text specifies an act regarded as a blunder). Saul's oath lays a curse on any of his troops who eat food before nightfall and the completion of Saul's vengeance on his enemies. The purpose of such an oath is to help ensure victory by making a sacrificial commitment. However, this was a foolish move, for two reasons. First, Saul's army eventually becomes faint for lack of food (vv. 28, 31), and they cannot physically pursue the victory to its fullest extent. More important for this story, not everyone— including Saul's son, Jonathan (v. 27)—is present to hear of this oath.

In the course of battle, Jonathan, seeing a honeycomb, dips his staff into the honey and eats from it (v. 27). The food energizes him ("his eyes brightened"). Then others tell him of his father's oath. Remarkably, Jonathan immediately criticizes his father openly: "My father has troubled the land. . . . How much better if today the troops had eaten freely . . . for now the slaughter among the Philistines has not been great" (vv. 29-30). Father and son are now set ominously against each other. It will not be the last time, for Jonathan eventually becomes the friend of David and his supporter for the throne (1 Samuel 20). For now, Jonathan's innocent act of nourishment places him inadvertently under the curse of Saul's oath.

14:31-35. For a brief moment the story's attention shifts from Jonathan to the wider consequences of Saul's foolish oath. Famished after long fighting without food, Saul's troops begin to slaughter sheep and cattle and eat the meat without the ritual draining of the blood required by Israelite law (vv. 31-32). Saul's oath has led to massive sacral sin by his army. Saul orders that a large stone be placed in front of him, which becomes an altar for ritual slaughter and draining of the blood (vv. 33-34). It is said to be the first altar Saul built to the Lord, implying that others had been made as well (v. 35).

14:36-46. In the flush of victory by day, Saul proposes to pursue the Philistines through the night, but Saul, heeding the urging of his priest, pauses to consult the Lord (v. 36). Presumably this meant the seeking of some oracular assurance through the priest

(Urim and Thummim?) before taking action. However, on this occasion there is no answer (v. 37). Saul does not then make his own decision. He presumes that he cannot get assurance because of someone's sin (v. 38), and he, again rashly, proclaims that even if this sin is in his own son Jonathan, he will surely die (v. 39). There follows an elaborate process of lot-casting with the Urim and the Thummim. The names of these two objects, cast or withdrawn in the process, seem to mean "cursed" and "counted whole," hence each inquiry could give a positive or a negative verdict. This process could be used by posing questions (as in v. 37) or by choosing between groups of potentially guilty persons (as in vv. 40-42). Saul's first question forces a choice between the people on one side and Jonathan/Saul on the other. When father and son are taken, Saul poses a choice between himself and Jonathan. (The LXX includes additional material claiming that the people tried to dissuade Saul from continuing at this point.) Jonathan is taken; he confesses to having eaten honey and expresses a willingness to die (v. 43). The irony at this point in the story is significant. Jonathan ate food in utter ignorance of his father's oath. If there was sin here, it was in the making of such a misguided oath (one recalls the oath of Jephthah and the willing death of his innocent daughter, Judges 11) or the widespread, knowing violation by the people in eating meat with the blood still in it, which violates sacral law. But it is Jonathan, the undisputed hero of the day, who is taken by lot and who offers himself to die. Distressingly, Saul states his willingness to carry out this death penalty (v. 44), but the people will not hear of it. Claiming that Jonathan worked with God in bringing them victory, they counter Saul's oath with one of their own, "As the LORD lives, not one hair of his head shall fall to the ground" (v. 45). Sadly the story ends with a report that the moment for a wider Israelite victory had

passed. The pursuit ends, and the Philistines return to their own strongholds (v. 46).

14:47-52. The final section of this chapter includes three small notices. The first (vv. 47-48) is a summary of Saul's military campaigns. It assesses positively Saul's leadership in matters of warfare. Some have thought the list too extensive and suggest that a later list of David's victories has been placed here. However, such an explanation is not really necessary. Independent traditions confirm Saul's campaigns against Ammonites, Philistines, and Amalekites. It is not unreasonable that he had conflicts with others among Israel's traditional enemies. What remains important is that a portion of the tradition remembers Saul as successful and valiant. In answer to the earlier question of the skeptics, "Can Saul save?" (10:27), this notice says, "Yes, Saul did save Israel for a time." It is significant that this positive notice is placed before the final story of Saul's rejection from kingship in chap. 15.

A second notice tells us of Saul's family (vv. 49-51). His son Ishvi is mentioned only here, unless this is a variant name for Ishbaal (2 Samuel 2–4). Jonathan, Malchishua, and Abinadab (not named here) are reported to have died with Saul at Mt. Gilboa in 31:2 (see 1 Chr 9:49). Saul's two daughters, Merab and Michal, play a later role in connection with marriage to David (18:17-27), with Michal becoming David's wife. This is the only time Saul's wife, Ahinoam, is named. Abner, the commander of Saul's army, plays a key role in the later story, and he appears here as Saul's uncle, although confusion over the relationship of Kish and Ner may mean that Saul and Abner were cousins (see 9:1; 1 Chr 8:33; 9:36, 39).

In the final notice (v. 52), we see Saul's method for gathering fighting men to his service. It reflects the beginning of a standing army in Israel and constitutes the very manner by which David later enters Saul's service (16:18) and becomes Saul's armorbearer (16:21).

REFLECTIONS

On the surface, this story is about warfare, heroic deeds, and strange rituals. At a deeper level, this story concerns the relationship between piety and moral responsibility, particularly the moral responsibility that comes with leadership.

The commentary has pointed to the great contrast between Jonathan and Saul. It is ironic that Jonathan seems the more kingly of the two, but we know from chap. 13 that he will not be king after his father. On initial glance, Jonathan seems pragmatic, a man of action and bold initiative. Yet, it is Jonathan who trusts in God's purposes to work through "many or by few," who gives God credit for victory, and who knows that human desires and divine purpose may not always coincide. "Perhaps," he says, "the LORD will act for us." Saul seems the more pious, surrounding himself with priest and ephod, resorting to ritual assurance before taking action, pledging solemn oaths as a sign of commitment. Yet, it is Saul who seems unable to act in trust that God's purposes will go forward one way or another. He wants assurance of outcomes before he begins. He wants his piety to be recognized and perhaps obligate God to his purposes. From the drama played out between this father and son, we learn important things about the nature and limitations of true piety when faced with the moral decisions of public policy (in this instance, warfare against oppressors).

1. Piety is not a substitute for human wisdom and responsible action. Jonathan acted boldly to take an initiative he thought promising. In his "Perhaps . . ." of v. 6, he holds open the possibility that the course of events could show that his action was not the direction of God's purposes, and he would then have broken off his attack or changed strategies. By contrast, Saul let his acts of piety (rituals and oaths) substitute for his own wisdom and his own action. His nervous consultations at strategic moments and his foolish oath did not impress or obligate God. They sapped the war effort, almost took the life of his own son, and left the end result short of what it might have been.

It is endlessly tempting, from Saul's generation to our own, to let piety become an end in itself, as if acting religious were the chief thing required of those who would serve the God who can save. We refrain from our own saving activity in favor of energy spent on rituals and institutional patterns that divert our attention from moral challenges rather than focusing us on them. Such self-serving religious ritual and practice are ultimately a failure of trust in God and a failure to understand that the world is the arena of God's activity. We, like Jonathan, are called to discern what actions might best serve God's salvation and to move forward. Such discernment and action may have to be modified in the light of further understandings of God's will, but inaction coupled with fearful hiding behind religious rituals and practices will never serve God's saving purposes.

2. Piety, especially ritual observance, cannot protect us from moral risk taking. Even the most faithful among us are given no path to certitude that guarantees the outcome of our actions. Saul wanted to resolve the "perhaps" of Jonathan's initiative before he took action. In an apt phrase, Robert Polzin accuses Saul of engaging in "ritual conceal-ment."[98] Saul is so obsessed with rituals and oaths that might determine or even influence the course of divine action that he borders on sorcery and divination. He wants a formula for success before he risks his resources. Needless to say, this is not an attitude limited to the time of Saul. Too many leaders in church and society are reluctant to take positions until it is clear which way the wind is blowing. In politics, this is expediency; but in the church it is a lack of faith.

3. Piety must ultimately honor the freedom of God. We cannot by our pious practices and observances coerce or obligate divine grace. Nothing can hinder the salvation of the Lord, and we will never cease to be surprised by grace. The "Perhaps . . ." of Jonathan was a more authentic expression of faith than the fearful ritual seeking of certitude by Saul, because it grew out of trust in God's saving purposes and a willingness to live and act within the mysteries of God's saving grace. Some of the opponents

98. Polzin, *Samuel and the Deuteronomist,* 138.

of Jesus in the Gospels thought they knew the paths of observance that would guarantee divine favor and grace. There is no lack of such attitudes in some quarters in the church today.

The freedom of God does not depend on popular support or large numbers. Jonathan knew that God can save through the many or the few. Saul thought he could do nothing with his six hundred, and Jonathan acted with two. Trustful action in the hope that "perhaps the Lord will act for us" happens too seldom in the modern church. We wait for full funding, additional staffing, rising memberships, fully resourced programs, and denominational authorization. We could find ourselves under the tree with Saul, consulting priest and ephod, or taking oaths in the form of resolutions when God chooses to act for justice and salvation. God's action may be served by the few who can choose to move boldly in trust that the path of God's grace will be revealed as we move forward.

1 Samuel 15:1-35, Saul Rejected from Kingship

COMMENTARY

In this chapter Saul is rejected as legitimate king over Israel. As in chap. 13, he has violated the instructions of Samuel, the prophet of the Lord. Twice we are told that the Lord "regretted" having made Saul king over Israel (vv. 11, 35) because "he has turned back from following me, and has not carried out my commands" (v. 11). In the confrontation with Saul, Samuel claims that God has already "torn" the kingdom from Saul and "given it to a neighbor of yours, who is better than you" (v. 28). The text is already looking ahead to David, who waits just offstage (chap. 16) and will occupy the central attention of the tradition for the remainder of the books of Samuel. Saul's career as God's anointed king over Israel ends almost as soon as it starts.

The setting for this episode is a war with the Amalekites, an ancient enemy of Israel. Samuel, speaking as the Lord's prophet, commands Saul to exterminate the Amalekites in order to avenge wrongs committed against Israel when they came out of Egypt (vv. 1-3). The Amalekite background and the holy war practice of חרם (*ḥērem*) will be discussed further below. It is important to note here that both Amalekites and *ḥērem* are secondary interests in this episode. Instead, the primary issue is obedience to the direct command of the Lord. No question is raised by the text (though it is by some commentators) about the appropriateness of a campaign against the Amalekites or the morality of the utter extermination of enemies (*ḥērem*). These

questions often arise out of sympathy for the hapless Saul and in reaction to the harshness of Samuel. For this story, the issue is Saul's obedience to God's commands; no suggestion is made that these commands were illegitimate. If we raise those issues, we must recognize that they are our concerns and not those of 1 Samuel.

As we will see, this chapter includes prophetic patterns and concerns. Samuel is a prophet of the Lord. He announces the word of the Lord with the use of the full messenger formula (v. 2), receives the word of the Lord expressing divine regret, and pronounces an oracle of judgment against Saul for his failure to obey the word of the Lord (see esp. vv. 22-23). As many have observed, the key word around which the entire episode hinges is שמע (*šāmaʿ*, "to hear"), which, particularly in conjunction with the term "voice" or "command of the LORD," often means "to obey." This verb appears in vv. 1, 14, 19, 20, 22 (2x), and 24. Saul's failure to "hear/obey" is the reason for his rejection as king. This theme would have been theologically important to the prophetic circles that shaped the Saul story, and it was also an important concern to the deuteronomistic historian (cf. 12:14-15), who incorporated this material into his larger history work (see Introduction).

Chapter 15 has important thematic ties to its larger context. There is a reference in v. 1 to the anointing of Saul in 10:1 (another episode with strong prophetic emphases).

The theme of obedience to God's voice and commandment is the condition laid down by Samuel for the well-being of king and people in 12:14-15. Chapter 15 must also be read with chaps. 13 and 14 as the final episode in a section on Saul's career as king that seems primarily concerned with explaining the reasons for Saul's failure. There are similarities to 13:7b-15a, which have led some to see chap. 15 as a variant account of that earlier rejection story. But both seem to have been shaped by prophetic circles so as to present a growing pattern of crisis, leading first to the loss of dynasty and then to the loss of Saul's own kingship. Chapter 16 begins with the grief of Samuel, mentioned at the end of this episode (v. 35), and Saul's encounter with Samuel's ghost in chap. 28 clearly knows and uses the rejection story in chap. 15.

Just as Saul's obedience is at issue, so also is the people's obedience. Saul's references to the people's role in the violation of the ḥērem (vv. 15, 21, 24) are often treated simply as efforts by Saul to avoid full blame. But it is the narrator, and not Saul, who reports (v. 9) that "Saul *and the people* spared. . . ." Saul was the people's king. God acquiesced, but commanded Samuel in 8:22, "Make for *them* a king." In Samuel's speech to Israel (chap. 12), Saul is "the king whom *you* have chosen, for whom *you* have asked" (v. 13), and the people confess that they have sinned by "demanding a king for *ourselves*" (v. 19). Both king and people are held accountable: "If both you and the king . . . will follow the LORD your God, it will be well. . . . But if you do wickedly, you shall be swept away, both you and your king" (vv. 14, 25). In the present story, chap. 15 involves the people in the charge of disobedience along with Saul. His rejection is the rejection of the people's king. Chapter 16 then opens significantly with God's announcement that "I have provided for *myself* a king among his [Jesse's] sons" (v. 1b).

Since this chapter signals an end to Saul's legitimized rule, it is a natural point at which to raise questions of meaning concerning this abortive experience with kingship. One may also assess the character of Saul and his confronter, Samuel, as well as the role of God in this failed enterprise. Was Saul guilty? Was his offense so great? Was God fair? Had God

doomed Saul from the start? Was Samuel too harsh? Was he representing God or his own reactionary interests? Earlier responses to these questions paint a harsh portrait of Saul as surely deserving of what he received. "What wonder was it then, that the Lord rejected him, whose best service was an act of vile dissimulation? . . . He continued, to the last, proud, and cruel, and profane."[99] Scholars have more recently tended to see Saul as a tragic figure and, hence, treat both Samuel and God rather harshly in assessment of this episode. "Samuel's passion for covenant requirements reaches ideological proportions, because he is unwilling (or unable) to relate his demands to the political realities with which Saul must struggle. . . . Samuel's absolutist claims here are subtle and multidimensioned. Most broadly, Samuel's one issue is uncompromising loyalty to Yahweh. At another level, his claim is uncompromising loyalty to Samuel, who is the only valid voice of Yahweh."[100] Opinion on this chapter and on the assessment of Saul, Samuel, and God at this point is more varied than for any other issues in the books of Samuel. We will return to discuss these matters further after a closer look at the text of chapter 15.

15:1-3. The episode opens with Samuel's report to Saul of a divine command. He begins by reminding Saul about the source of his authority. It was Samuel whom God sent to anoint Saul in the first place (v. 1a). It is the prophet who speaks and who now voices what is to be the crucial issue of this chapter, "Now therefore listen to the words of the LORD" (v. 1b). The Hebrew verb שְׁמַע (šāmaʿ) means "listen" or "hear," but in covenantal contexts (especially deuteronomistic) it often means "obey." To obey is not only to hear but also to do. Saul is called to hear and to do "the words of the LORD." Saul may be king, but he is still subject to the word of the Lord as mediated by the prophet Samuel.

Samuel begins his speech with the full messenger formula, which underlines his

99. Thomas Robinson, "The Character of Saul," in *Scripture Characters or a Practical Improvement of the Principal Histories from the Time of the Judges to the End of the Old Testament* (London, 1790) 49, quoted in Gunn, *The Fate of King Saul*, 42-43.

100. Brueggemann, *First and Second Samuel*, 109-10. See also Gunn, *The Fate of King Saul*; W. Lee Humphreys, "The Tragedy of King Saul: A Study of the Structure of 1 Sam 9:1-31," *JSOT* 6 (1978) 18-27; and J. Cheryl Exum and William J. Whedbee, "Isaac, Samson, and Saul: Reflections on the Comic and Tragic Visions," *Semeia* 32 (1984) 5-40.

claim to speak God's word, "Thus says the Lord of hosts" (v. 2a). The term "hosts" (צבאת *ṣĕbā'ôt*) means "armies" and emphasizes the God who fights as a warrior for Israel—an appropriate way of referring to God on this occasion. Samuel orders a campaign against the Amalekites as punishment for the opposition of the Amalekites against Israel at the time of the exodus from Egypt (v. 2). Saul is to attack and "utterly destroy" the Amalekites—every person and every animal (v. 3).

The Amalekites were a nomadic people living primarily in the Negeb and the Sinai, south of Israelite territory. On the journey through the wilderness from Egypt, Israel had been attacked by the Amalekites and won a victory over them at Rephidim (Exod 17:8-16), after which God promised to "blot out the remembrance of Amalek from under heaven" (17:14). Samuel's announcement that the time of Amalek's punishment had come is similar to the command in Deut 25:17-19 that Amalek should be destroyed for its past crimes. Brueggemann has suggested that Samuel's command is a "dangerous political irrelevancy" because there is no evidence that the Amalekites posed any real threat to Israel's life, but instead is an ideological test.[101] We should remember, however, that David was later forced into military encounter with the Amalekites on three occasions (27:8; 30:1-31; 2 Sam 8:12). In the positive summary of Saul's military achievements in 14:48, the victory of the Amalekites is listed as a rescue from the hands of those who plundered Israel. Conflict with Amalekites seemed to be a frequent factor in the life of Judah especially, and one could see Saul undertaking a campaign against them as a way of extending his influence into this important southern tribe (exactly what David did later). Hence, it does not seem necessary to see the Amalekite campaign as an occasion manufactured by Samuel for a test of Saul's obedience.

Saul is to "utterly/totally destroy" every man, woman, child, and beast belonging to the Amalekites. The Hebrew verb חרם (*ḥāram*, also translated "to exterminate," "to place under the ban") is used in connection with warfare for the practice of dedicating to God all of a conquered enemy and their possessions by killing and burning. The practice is associated with holy war, in which the battle has sacral purpose and God is often said to fight as a warrior for Israel (Josh 6:17; 10–11). Deuteronomic law (Deut 13:12-18; 20:1-20) provides prescripts for such practices. Even though the practice is primarily attested for the period before kingship in Israel, the *ḥērem* seems to be an ideal kept alive among the prophets. Ahab is confronted by the prophets for not carrying out the ban (1 Kgs 20:42), and later oracles of judgment may reflect the concept applied to those who become the enemies of God's purposes in the world (e.g., Joel 2). Although associated with the concept of holy war, the practice seems infrequently applied, and recent scholarship has stressed that the notion and institutions of holy war itself do not seem standardized or uniformly applied at different times and places in Israel's story.[102] What seems to be at stake in 1 Samuel 15 is not Saul's violation of a norm for holy war. It is, instead, his failure to carry out the explicit command of the Lord as mediated by the prophet Samuel on this occasion. The text does not reflect at all upon whether the command of *ḥērem* is legitimate or morally worthy of obedience (an area often explored by those seeking to justify Saul's actions). The text treats the content of the command matter-of-factly and focuses entirely on the issue of obedience or disobedience to God's words/commands.

15:4-9. These verses describe Saul's campaign against the Amalekites. The numbers for Saul's men seem inflated; the word אלף (*'elep*) may not mean "thousand" but instead "group," "battalion," or "unit" (v. 4). Significantly, a force for Judah is listed separately, which suggests that Saul may be undertaking this campaign as a way of building alliances with this large southern tribe. A "city of the Amalekites" (v. 5) has not been identified with any certainty and stands in tension with the nomadic life usually associated with the Amalekites. The Kenites, another southern desert people who lived among the Amalekites, are offered amnesty before the battle begins out of respect for past cooperative relations between Kenites and Israelites (v. 6;

---

101. Brueggemann, *First and Second Samuel,* 110.

102. See the excellent survey in Norman K. Gottwald, "War, Holy," in *IDBSup* (Nashville: Abingdon, 1976) 942-44; and the comprehensive study by Susan Niditch, *War in the Hebrew Bible: A Study in the Ethics of Violence* (New York: Oxford University Press, 1993).

cf. Exodus 18:1; Judg 4:11-22, and David's similar treatment of the Kenites in 1 Sam 27:10; 30:29). Amalek is defeated over a wide territory (v. 7).

The report on the carrying out of the command to "utterly destroy" (ḥāram) is crucial for this episode. Verse 8 states that Agag, king of Amalek, was spared but that the rest of the Amalekites were destroyed. The reference must be to a particular group of Amalekites, since Amalekites continue to give trouble later to David (chap. 30). The next verse (v. 9) significantly states that "Saul and the people" not only kept Agag alive, but they also kept the best of the sheep, cattle, fatlings, and lambs. What was valuable was saved, and only what was "despised and worthless" was destroyed. Offering God only what is despised and worthless would seem a thoughtless act at best and contemptuous at worst. In any case, commanded by God to "utterly destroy," Saul and the people have "spared."

15:10-23. The word of the Lord comes again to Samuel (v. 10), and its content is surprising. God "regrets" having made Saul king (v. 11). The confrontation with Saul is bracketed with divine regret, for the chapter ends by saying again that the Lord was "sorry" to have made Saul king (v. 35b; the Hebrew word here is the same [נחם nāḥam]; this verb also appears as the expression of divine regret over the creation of humankind prior to the flood in Gen 6:6-7). The experiment with Saul is over. God has already rendered a judgment, and it remains for Samuel to confront Saul and deliver that judgment. The basis of God's judgment is clear: "He has turned back from following me, and has not carried out my commands" (v. 11a).

The report of Samuel's anger and night-long crying out to the Lord has been variously interpreted. Some see it simply as an expression of Samuel's outrage at Saul expressed in a venting of that anger in communion with God. Others have seen the verse as an expression of prophetic intercession to God, perhaps hoping to avert such a final judgment against Saul. The text does not resolve this ambiguity.

Samuel then journeys to meet Saul, ironically finding him at Gilgal (v. 12), the place of Saul's confirmation in kingship (11:14-15) and his first confrontation with Samuel (13:7b-15a). Samuel had heard that Saul was erecting a monument for himself at Carmel (v. 12), probable evidence of self-aggrandizement on Saul's part.

The meeting of Samuel with Saul is shaped by the influence of prophetic speeches of indictment (accusation) and judgment (as also in 13:7b-15), with the accusation becoming clear through a series of questions posed by Samuel to Saul in a process resembling a judicial hearing (vv. 13-21). When the indictment against Saul is clear, Samuel announces judgment in the form of a poetic oracle that is remarkably similar to passages in the classical prophets (vv. 22-23; cf. Hos 6:6).[103]

Saul greets Samuel warmly and explicitly claims that he has fulfilled the Lord's command (v. 13). But countering Saul's implicit claim to have "listened," Samuel listens and hears the sound of sheep and cattle (v. 14). Saul admits this livestock is from the Amalekite raid, but he claims "the *people* spared the best" of the livestock for sacrifice. The rest, he claims, "*we* have utterly destroyed" (v. 15). Saul excludes himself from the sparing, but includes himself in utterly destroying. It is a pattern to which Saul returns in vv. 20b-21a, where he claims, "*I* have utterly destroyed the Amalekites. But from the spoil the *people* took sheep and cattle" for sacrifice.

In the ensuing exchange between Samuel and Saul, the issue of listening/obedience is central. Samuel interrupts Saul's justification for sparing the livestock to announce God's word (v. 16). Although v. 17 is difficult to interpret, Samuel seems to claim that Saul, as king of Israel, is responsible for the people's actions. He cannot separate their actions from his own. After reminding Saul of the task to which he has been commanded (v. 18), Samuel challenges, "Why did you not obey [שמע šāma] the word of the LORD?" The taking of spoil is labeled as "evil in the sight of the LORD" (v. 19). Yet, Saul insists that he has "obeyed the voice of the LORD," but in the same breath comes the revelation that he has brought the Amalekite king Agag as a captive (v. 20). We are given no clue in the chapter to the purpose of this hostage taking. Could it have been for the prestige of parading the captive king? Could it have been to

103. See Birch, *The Rise of the Israelite Monarchy*, 98-103, for a fuller treatment of these prophetic speech forms.

force some agreement or cessation of hostilities with other Amalekite groups? We do not know, but Agag as a captive violates the commanded ban.

Samuel then announces judgment on Saul. Samuel rejects the notion that bringing sheep and cattle for sacrifice provides an acceptable substitute for obedience to the command of the Lord. The Lord does not delight in such rituals when they become a substitute for obedience (v. 22; the verb שָׁמַע [šāmaʿ] is used twice in this verse, and a synonym, הִקְשִׁב [hiqšîb, hiphil, "to heed"], is used as well). This elevation of obedience over sacrifice is a central theme in the prophets (Isa 1:10-13; Amos 5:21-24; Hos 6:6; Mic 6:6-8). Saul's disobedience is called "rebellion" and "stubbornness" and is equated with the sins of divination, iniquity, and idolatry (v. 23a). It is a harsh judgment, one that often seems disproportionate to Saul's deeds, but this is because most modern readers do not accept the command of ḥērem as legitimate. It is clear from Samuel's judgment speech that the issue was not the specific "sparing" of livestock and king but the matter of obedience to the word of the Lord. Verse 23b contains the devastating consequence: Because Saul "rejected" the Lord's word, the Lord has "rejected" him as king. The verb here is the same as that used in 8:7 for God's statement that the people had "rejected" (מָאַס māʾas) the Lord as king over them. The rejection of Saul is also a rejection of the people's king. Rejection has come full circle. King and people stand convicted in this account.

How guilty was Saul? Did he really believe he had carried out the command of God? Did he really bring all of those sheep and cattle (the best) for sacrifice? David Gunn is representative of a number of scholars who want to defend Saul as a tragic victim here.

If Samuel's bitter contrast between obedience and sacrifice only makes sense when it is assumed that he saw a significant incompatibility between "devotion" (ḥrm) and "sacrifice" (zbḥ) of the booty, so Saul's (and the people's) actions and subsequent protestations that the command had been fulfilled only make sense when it is assumed that they, for their part, saw no significant incompatibility. . . . Saul's crime is either that he was ignorant of some technical implications of two sacral concepts (ḥrm

and zbḥ) or, if he were aware of them, that he wrongly evaluated them as unimportant.[104]

Gunn and others with similar viewpoints are correct in their assumption that the story intends to generate some sympathy for Saul and that the harshness of the penalty for Saul seems disproportionate. The account is too rich and nuanced for simplistic readings that simply make Saul a villain (likewise Samuel or God). We must remember that the account is trying to make sense of historical events that resulted in Saul's tragic demise and David's eventual triumph. History often does not seem fair, but historians and storytellers seek to understand these events (in this case theologically as well as historically). In this account, Saul is treated sympathetically; but his attempt to pass responsibility to the people, his later confession that he "listened" to the people and not to God (v. 24), and his sparing of King Agag, for which no purpose is given, are enough for the tradition to judge him guilty of disobedience, even if his intention to sacrifice the livestock at Gilgal were an honorable delay of "utterly destroying" rather than a hasty justification of taking plunder. Disobedience ("not listening") is unacceptable in God's anointed king. Saul is not just any man, and he is not rejected as a man, but as the holder of the office of anointed one (v. 17 recalls this status).

15:24-31. Saul responds to Samuel's announcement of judgment with a confession. Again the issue is expressed, not in terms of the specifics of ḥērem but as violation (sin, transgression) of the commandment of the Lord and the words of the Lord's prophet. Saul explains that he "feared the *people* and *listened* to their voice" (v. 24). He pleads for forgiveness and asks that Samuel return with him to worship the Lord (v. 25); but Samuel will not do that, and he repeats the devastating judgment (v. 26; cf. v. 23b).

The author has painted a desperate picture. Samuel turns to go; Saul grasps for him in pleading. Samuel's robe is caught and torn (v. 27). The moment gives Samuel one last opportunity, and he seems harsh indeed. He uses the ripped garment as a symbolic action to reinforce God's word, in a manner characteristic of later prophets. One thinks

---

104. Gunn, *The Fate of King Saul,* 50, 53-54.

especially of the prophet Ahijah of Shiloh, who meets Jeroboam on the road and tears a cloak and symbolically gives him the pieces, which represent the tribes torn from the rule of Solomon's son Rehoboam (1 Kgs 11:29-32). Samuel declares that God has torn the kingdom from Saul "this day." But he adds one very significant piece of information: God has already given the kingdom to "a neighbor of yours, who is better than you" (v. 28), referring, of course, to David. Saul's kingship has effectively ended, although he continues in the trappings of royalty for some time. David waits in the wings to make his entrance in the next chapter.

Verse 29 has long been recognized as problematic. Samuel claims that the "Glory of Israel" (i.e., God) does not "lie" (the NRSV's "recant" is an odd choice for the word here) or "change his mind; for he is not a mortal that he should change his mind." The word translated here as "change his mind" is נחם (niham, niphal), the same word used in vv. 1 and 35 to say that God "regretted" (i.e., "changed his mind," also sometimes translated "repented") the choice of Saul. Most interpreters have read v. 29 as a general statement of divine character reinforcing the irrevocability of Saul's rejection. Still, this verse seems a puzzling contradiction of the "regret" of God seen in vv. 1 and 35. Fretheim has argued convincingly that v. 29 refers not to Saul's rejection but to God's commitment made to David (without David's name) in v. 28b.[105] God may have "regretted/repented" of the choice of Saul, but v. 29 now announces an unshakable commitment to David. The text foreshadows the divine covenant with David. The intention is not to say that God never repents of anything but that this particular commitment is unshakable. The two places where niham is used to speak of God as "not repenting" both refer to God's commitment to David. Verse 29 is a near duplicate of a passage in Balaam's speeches in Num 23:19, where the concern is also a foreshadowing of divine commitment to David. The same verb used to speak of God's not repenting appears in a Davidic covenant setting in Ps 110:4. Although the

verb is different, the theme is equivalent in Ps 132:11: "The Lord swore to David a sure oath, from which he will *not turn back*" (NRSV). The theme of God's character being revealed in regretting/repenting and not regretting/repenting will be discussed at a later point.

Saul again confesses his sin, but he asks Samuel at least to honor him before the people by returning with him to worship the Lord (v. 30). Samuel agrees, an act that shows some compassion in allowing Saul to save face before Israel (v. 31).

15:32-35. Samuel is not finished. He commands that Agag, the Amalekite king, be brought before him. Agag seems to foresee his doom (v. 32). After a brief oracle of judgment (v. 33a), Samuel himself completes the *ḥērem* against the Amalekites by cutting Agag to pieces (v. 33b), presumably with a sword, even as Agag had killed many people with the sword.

Samuel leaves for Ramah and Saul for Gibeah (v. 34), but it is the prophet's permanent exit from Saul's story. We are told that Samuel does not see Saul again until the day of Samuel's death (v. 35). This notice foreshadows Saul's later encounter with Samuel's ghost (chap. 28) before the battle that ends with his own death. The brief encounter in 19:18-24 stands in tension with this statement.

Samuel grieves over Saul (v. 35), a motif that continues into the beginning of David's story (16:1). The author does not hint that this grief is false or only over the failure of Samuel's plans. The narrative portrays Samuel as a complex character of harsh words and actions, but also with his own indications of humanity.

The chapter ends with the statement again that the Lord "regretted" the choice of Saul (v. 35b). God's purposes are central to 1 Samuel, and God has determined that a new course must be set. The kingship of Saul can no longer serve God's intentions for Israel.

What do we make of this story and its role in 1 Samuel? The answer to this question revolves around both the actions and the character of the three central figures: Saul, Samuel, and God.

Did Saul sin? Yes. The charge of "not listening" to the command/word of the Lord

105. Terence E. Fretheim, "Divine Foreknowledge, Divine Constancy, and the Rejection of Saul's Kingship," *CBQ* 47 (1985) 595-602. This provocative and insightful article has informed my discussion of many of the issues in this chapter.

is a serious one in many OT texts. Did he sin knowingly, and was his punishment proportionate to his misdeeds? These questions are not so easy to answer. The witnesses to Saul's story clearly have some sympathy with him. He is treated not as a villain, but as a tragic man who meant well for Israel. To this degree, the treatments of Gunn, Humphreys, Exum/Whedbee, and others have provided important correctives to excessive vilification of Saul in many earlier studies. But in 1 Samuel, God focuses on Israel's future, not Saul's. Saul is not devoid of admirable human traits, but he has weaknesses as well. Chapters 13–15 are designed to show that the course of his kingship is not going well. Israel's future is at stake, and the theme of God's regret in 15:1, 35 expresses the divine decision that Saul is not the direction. God will chart a new course with David, and Saul will not be Israel's future.

Gunn and others have suggested that chap. 15 (and its wider context in 1 Samuel) reveals the "dark side" of God. Saul is fated to fail, and God is ruthlessly manipulative and less than honorable [106] There are certainly questions of fairness to be raised concerning the actions of God, if our perspective were only from the personal fate of Saul. There is a "dark side" to the portrait of God here because God's larger purposes for Israel and for kingship are judged incapable of fulfillment through Saul and through kingship as defined in the story of Saul. Saul was not fated to fail. God had intended that Saul would deliver Israel (9:16; 10:1) and empowered him with the divine Spirit for such tasks (chap. 11). Saul's failures were his own, and were not forced on him by God. It is clear by chap. 15 that the tradition, although sympathetic to Saul, sees in David God's new enterprise for the sake of Israel. Saul could not have gotten them there. In fact, kingship as defined by Saul was not working to benefit Israel. Kingship itself had to be put on a new basis.

Saul was the people's king (8:22), whereas David will be the king God makes for "myself" (16:1). Saul and the people were a conditional experiment that depended on obedience (12:14-15, 25), but Davidic kingship would rest on God's unconditional commitment. God's choice of David would ultimately lead to a new basis for the role of the anointed one. That role rested not on the people and the king's obedience, but on God's faithfulness. Does this mean the divine relationship to the king changed from Saul to David? Perhaps so. The tradition recognizes a difference.

I will establish the throne of his kingdom forever ... when he commits iniquity I will punish him ... but I will not take my steadfast love from him, as I took it from Saul, whom I put away from before you. (2 Sam 7:13-15 NRSV)

Fretheim addresses these issues in a similar fashion:

While the kingship of Saul was explicitly conditioned by the obedience of both king and people (12:14-15, 25), the kingship of David was not. God placed the kingship on an entirely new footing compared to that of Saul. Why? Because God learned something from the experience (and experiment) with Saul. ... Given what has happened to the conditionally established kingship of Saul, God determines that only a new tack will have a chance of succeeding, viz., an unconditional commitment to the Davidic king. ... It is of great importance to recognize that God's primary concern in all of this is for the future of *Israel* (cf. 9:16; 10:1; 12:22). Saul's disobedience and other unkingly behavior may not seem to our minds to be sufficient justification for the divine rejection. But chaps. 13–15 (cf. 1 Sam 28:18) would seem to be concerned to chart a trend or direction in the nature of Saul's kingship. ... It is possible that the whole people would be swept away (12:14-15, 25) if this pattern in the kingship were allowed to continue.[107]

Measured in individual terms, this seems unfair to Saul, but the portrait of the books of Samuel is of a God responding to human history, not unrolling a predetermined script. The theme of divine regret/repentance especially suggests a God who responds and alters course in the pursuit of divine purposes. I mentioned earlier that the theme of divine regret (נחם *niḥam*, niphal) also appears in the story of the flood in Gen 6:6; the analogy

---

106. See Gunn, *The Fate of King Saul*, 123-24, and also the others cited in n. 78.

107. Fretheim, "Divine Foreknowledge, Divine Constancy, and the Rejection of Saul's Kingship," 599-601.

with 1 Samuel 15 is an apt one. God's regret results both in judgment and in a new beginning based on God's covenant commitment, even in spite of human sin (see Gen 8:21-22). According to the story of 1 Samuel, kingship will find a new basis in David, which is guaranteed by God's commitment in spite of the conduct of people and the king. The tradition recognizes that it was different for Saul (2 Sam 7:13-15), and in that sense he was a tragic figure. David, too, will sin, and he will suffer consequences for his sin (see 2 Sam 11:1-20); but God's faithfulness will allow the lineage of God's anointed one to endure as the source of hope in Israel even when earthly kingdoms seem to have perished through disobedience and when only the eschatological hope of a coming anointed one ("messiah") remains.

What of Samuel? Is he unduly harsh? Is he a single issue ideologue?[108] Prophets would not win personality awards. Samuel, indeed, is representative of an older, threatened political and religious order, and we know he was resistant to the idea of kingship (chap. 8). But the tradition portrays him in chap. 15 as one whose central focus is the word of the Lord. The text matter-of-factly reports Samuel's command to Saul as coming from the Lord. When Samuel's vested interests got in the

way of God's purposes, the tradition forthrightly showed God dealing with Samuel as an obstruction (chaps. 8; 16). There is no suggestion of that in chap. 15. Samuel does represent the old order, which is passing away in Israel, and we may fairly judge that he does not possess the full vision of God's future. In chap. 16, as we will see, he is still looking for the wrong things and must be directed by God (16:7). But Samuel not only rejects Saul—he anoints David, an even more radical departure from the old order. Samuel has limits and shortcomings, and he is harsh and often unlikable, but the tradition seems to believe that in chap. 15 he was doing the will of God in rejecting Saul so that the project with David could begin. If he is unbending in chap. 15, it is because the tradition reflected in that chapter regards listening/obedience as non-negotiable. The ongoing Jewish tradition remembered Samuel as faithful prophet, not as an ideological obstructionist (Sir 46:13-20).

In the end it is fitting, perhaps, that Samuel's grief marks the end of Saul's time as king (v. 35). There is no reason to regard this as self-serving or inauthentic sorrow. Samuel began his career announcing rejection to a man he probably cared for deeply (Eli, chap. 3). There is a certain symmetry in his career (even beyond the grave, chap. 28) that it ended in the same fashion.

108. See Brueggemann, *First and Second Samuel*, 110, for a vigorous argument on behalf of this view.

REFLECTIONS

Chapter 15 is an important turning point in the story of 1 Samuel, but it has also proved a difficult episode for modern readers in response to the story. It is important to separate several issues that necessarily arise for the reader.

1. In reading and appropriating this story, we must forthrightly acknowledge that holy war, as its practice is reflected in this story, cannot be a morally defensible practice for us. In devoting both plunder and people of a vanquished enemy to the Lord, the practice of holy war treats people as mere property and shows no regard for the sanctity of life. Once defined as an enemy, Amalekite lives were given no worth. Such practices are not, of course, limited to ancient times. Holocaust and Hiroshima stand as symbols of modern policies of extermination in dealing with enemies. But such policies, even in war, no longer have broad moral support, and readers of 1 Samuel 15 are often shocked that God and Samuel would order such an action.

It is important to note that the text of 1 Samuel 15 treats the command of holy war against the Amalekites as a legitimate command of the Lord. We may disagree that such a policy could ever be God's will, but this is not questioned by Saul or by the storyteller. Thus Saul's action in sparing King Agag cannot be seized upon as the act of a moral reformer demonstrating compassion over against the hard-heartedness of Samuel. The motive for bringing back a captive king is glory, not compassion. In preaching this text, we can (perhaps must) reject the content of ancient standards of morality in the matter of holy war while at the same time taking seriously the confrontation over obedience to the divine word in this story.

2. The episode in chap. 15 provides occasion to reflect on how often we know what the word of the Lord demands, but alter it to suit our own needs. If we set aside the difficult issue of holy war for a moment, the issue for us in this text is, as it was for Saul, obedience. What happens when we know the will of God but fail to do it—worse, when we only do it in part—the parts that are convenient? Paul lamented, "For I do not do the good I want, but the evil I do not want is what I do" (Rom 7:19). We can fill in our own issues and experience, but almost all of us, if we are honest, know how easy it is to make our own adjustments to what we know God is demanding of us. We want to honor God in our own way, not in God's way. We want to make our own adjustments ("Just a small difference really!"). When the rich young ruler came to Jesus, he was certain he was ready for full obedience. But when Jesus told him to sell all he had, it was not the shape of obedience he had in mind (Matt 19:16-30; Mark 10:17-31; Luke 18:18-30). I'm certain the price of discipleship seemed harsh to the young ruler. When we read of the rejection of Saul for his failure to do what he knew was demanded of him as God's command, we can sympathize with him and the high price he paid for a few alterations in carrying out the command. But if we choose to follow his path and make our own alterations in what we know God is asking of us in obedience, then we had better look over our shoulders occasionally for the approach of a Samuel.

3. Much of the focus of modern readers' discomfort and assessment of Saul as a tragic figure centers on the issue of proportionality. Was the judgment of God announced by Samuel against Saul harsher than his infraction deserved? He had hardly begun his reign before he was rejected as king. Saul may have used poor judgment, but he does not seem a man of ill will.

We live in a society that gives fairness a high value. We make bestsellers out of books such as *When Bad Things Happen to Good People.*[109] Although Saul, unlike Job, is not a completely innocent man, many still feel that 1 Samuel 15 raises a theodicy issue. Did Saul's actions completely justify rejection by God? As modern readers, all too aware of our own flaws, we identify with Saul and doubt that we could meet such rigorous divine standards.

Yet, the story of Saul and of our lives does not operate solely in a retributive-justice framework. Saul is not rejected because he passed some dividing line of behavior that is marked "deserving" on one side and "undeserving" on the other. It has simply become clear in the story that Saul cannot be God's future for Israel. Disobedience to God's Word, Saul's need for the assurance of ritual and oath, his indecision and inability to assess situations clearly (all demonstrated in the episodes of chaps. 13–15) have made this evident. Israel's future is at stake, and God acts to move toward a new future in David.

In our society, both secular and religious institutions struggle over the standards that should apply and the judgments that should be made concerning leadership. Too often matters of seniority, goodwill, old-boy networks, or simple avoidance of conflict stand in the way of judgments over what will move us forward in obedience to God's will and in concern for the welfare of our communities and churches. We allow general qualities of goodness to substitute for the gifts of leadership. A "Peanuts" cartoon shows Charlie Brown saying to Linus that when he grows up he would like to be a prophet. Linus replies that this is an admirable goal, but "most turn out to be false

109. Harold S. Kushner, *When Bad Things Happen to Good People* (New York: Schocken, 1981).

prophets." Charlie Brown responds, "Well, at least I'll be a sincere false prophet." There are those who at times must make decisions that remove persons from leadership or deny them access to leadership roles (e.g., judicatory bodies that assess candidates for ministry). These persons will often be worthy and admirable in other ways. If our unwillingness to make difficult decisions causes us to allow persons to continue in leadership when they do not have the gifts for that role, then we will have failed the future of the institutions we serve. Those who make such difficult decisions will often seem as harsh as does Samuel in this account.

4. Samuel has sometimes been accused of rejecting Saul out of vested interests in maintaining the ideology of an old order. This is always a danger for those who must make judgments concerning leadership. But this story suggests that Samuel acted out of obedience to God's command and that he was personally filled with grief for Saul. We, like Samuel, cannot come to decisions concerning leadership without vested interests. But we can submit our decisions to prayerful discernment of God's will for the future rather than our own, and we cannot make such decisions in isolation from the personal pathos all such decisions involve. We do well to remember that if Samuel rejected Saul with any thought of returning to the safety of an old, familiar order of things, God did not let this happen. God summoned Samuel out of his grief and sent him to anoint David (16:1), an even more radical departure from the old patterns and ideologies of the tribal league. If we are tempted to reject leaders in the name of God, hoping for the comfort of the "way we've always done things," we can be certain that God will find yet more challenging ways of raising up leaders to move us toward the future of God's kingdom.

1 SAMUEL 16:1–31:13, THE RISE OF DAVID AND THE DECLINE OF SAUL

OVERVIEW

David comes onstage at this point in the story and does not relinquish center stage for the remainder of the books of Samuel. Other major characters recede into the background or play only supporting roles. Samuel, the prophet whose forceful presence has dominated the early chapters of 1 Samuel, anoints David as king and then disappears from the story. Saul, Israel's first king, still occupies the throne, but Israel has no future with Saul; he seems, in the remaining chapters of 1 Samuel, to be primarily a foil for the rising star of David. His death, at the end of 1 Samuel, provides a tragic counterpoint to the final accession of David to the throne. David is the climactic point to which the story of 1 Samuel has been building, and we now hear his story in astonishing detail. The tradition clearly understands that God's intentions for Israel's future are bound up in this man David.

Since the work of Leonhard Rost, most scholars have accepted the identification of a unified literary composition, commonly called the history of David's rise, that tells the story of David until his accession to the kingship of Judah and Israel.[110] The precise beginning and ending of this history Rise remain in dispute.[111] I agree with those who see the beginning of this composition in 16:14-23 with the introduction of David to Saul's

110. The original work of Leonhard Rost was published in 1926, but is now available in English translation as *The Succession to the Throne of David.* Rost's brief suggestion of a history of the rise of David has received considerable attention in recent years. See the treatment of this scholarship in P. Kyle McCarter, "The Apology of David," 489-504. For a minority view that understands all of 1 Samuel as a unified literary composition rather than a product of several sources or editions, see Polzin, *Samuel and the Deuteronomist.*

111. Some would see the beginning of the history of David's rise at 16:1, and others would even include chap. 15. A few would see the conclusion extending beyond 5:10 in 2 Samuel. See the discussion of these critical issues in P. Kyle McCarter, "The Apology of David," 499-502, as well as his summary of the role of the history of the Rise of David in the larger composition of 1 Samuel in McCarter, *I Samuel,* 27-30.

court as a musician and armorbearer. The conclusion may be found in the formula that declares God's presence with David in 2 Sam 5:10. The story of David's anointing (6:1-13) is an important introduction to the history of David's rise, added by a prophetic historian who incorporated the history into his larger work, covering most of 1 Samuel (see the Introduction). This prophetic historian used the story of David's anointing to create a bridge between the rejection of Saul (chap. 15) and the beginning of David's story (16:14-23) and is also responsible for the episode with the ghost of Samuel in chap. 28.

This history of the rise of David does not focus on David as an established royal figure. Rather, it conveys a David who begins as an eighth son and a shepherd, yet becomes king of all Israel through an unlikely series of trials and successes. David is the outsider who makes good, the underdog who triumphs, the outcast who returns in power. Brueggemann reminds us that such stories are told and celebrated by the marginal, who find hope in the early David stories for their own rise from marginalization.[112] David is a marginal figure himself, a nobody whose successes are resented by the established power (Saul) and who is forced to become something of an outlaw.[113] These stories celebrate David as the raw yet charismatic hero of those denied the gentility of established power. The David we will encounter in these stories is not idealized. He is both pious and pragmatic, idealistic and self-serving, fearless and calculating.

A compelling argument has been made that a central purpose for the writing of the history of the rise of David was to legitimate his claim to the throne and to provide an apology to counter claims that might have been made against David's right to the kingship.

McCarter offers the following list of potential charges against David that this narrative seeks to counter:

1. David sought to advance himself at court at Saul's expense.
2. David was a deserter.
3. David was an outlaw.
4. David was a Philistine mercenary.
5. David was implicated in Saul's death.
6. David was implicated in Abner's death.
7. David was implicated in Ishbaal's death.[114]

In each of these instances the storyteller takes pains to show that David was guiltless and that his rise to power was lawful and legitimate. Each of these charges is argued as untrue or understandable in the circumstances. We will see this more clearly in discussing individual chapters.

If David occupies the stage in these stories, God is nevertheless the director of the drama. The clear and constant theological theme of these chapters is that the Lord was with David. This claim occurs first in the mouth of a servant speaking to Saul of David (16:18), and it recurs explicitly in 17:37; 18:12, 14, 28; 20:13; and 2 Sam 5:10. This final reference provides a theological summary of the history of David's rise: "And David became greater and greater, for the LORD, the God of hosts, was with him." Throughout these stories, even where the formula of divine presence does not explicitly appear, it is clear that David represents what God is doing to secure Israel's future and well-being. As we will see in 16:1-13, God initiated the David story in Israel by choosing David "for myself" (16:1). What follows in the remaining chapters of 1 Samuel is a unique combination of theological confidence in God's presence with David and honesty about the raw events of this political process and the men and women who lived through it.

112. Walter Brueggemann, *David's Truth in Israel's Imagination and Memory* (Philadelphia: Fortress, 1985) 19-23.

113. Both Niels Peter Lemche, "David's Rise," *JSOT* 10 (1978) 23, and George Mendenhall, *The Tenth Generation: The Origins of the Biblical Tradition* (Baltimore: Johns Hopkins University Press, 1973) 135-36, treat David as a Habiru (a kind of outlaw class of the socially marginal in the ancient world). John L. McKenzie, *The Old Testament Without Illusion* (Chicago: Thomas More, 1979) 236, calls David a "bloodthirsty, oversexed bandit."

114. McCarter, "The Apology of David," 499-502. McCarter is building on the earlier work of Artur Weiser, "Die Legitimation des Königs David: zur Eigenart and Entstehung der sogen. Geschichte von Davids Aufstieg," *VT* 16 (1966) 325-54.

1 Samuel 16:1-13, The Anointing of David

COMMENTARY

Chapter 16 contains two episodes that introduce David. The first (vv. 1-13) designates David as God's choice; the second (vv. 14-23) identifies David as Saul's choice. The narrator wanted to emphasize the priority of God's initiative. The human actions that occur in the coming chapters constitute the acting out of a divine plan for Israel's future. The stories about David are the stories of God's anointed one. God's designation of David takes place in secret, and the reader thus possesses knowledge that only Samuel and David's family possess in the story. The episode of David's introduction to Saul's court (vv. 14-23) is thus a public presentation of David, and the reader knows more of the significance of this debut than does Saul. In v. 1, God chooses David "for myself" as a king, while in vv. 14-23 Saul thinks he is only choosing a musician and armorbearer.

The account of David's anointing by the prophet Samuel was probably placed as an introduction to the history of David's rise, which begins with v. 14. No mention is made of Samuel's anointing of David outside of 16:1-13. The theme of the Spirit that comes upon David (v. 13) and leaves Saul (v. 14) links the two episodes that introduce us to David. Likewise, the theme of Samuel's grief in v. 1 links this episode backward to the story of Saul's rejection, where Samuel's grief is mentioned (15:35).

The key word in vv. 1-13 is ראה (rā'â, "to see," vv. 1, 6, 7, 12). It is also used in vv. 17-18, where it provides a thematic link between the episodes of the chapter. Chapter 15 described the rejection of Saul as a function of not "listening." The election of David is now presented as an exercise in right "seeing." Twice in this chapter the verb rā'â is used with the specialized meaning of "provide"—seeing in the sense of discerning or choosing. In v. 1, God says, "I have provided [seen] for myself a king," and in v. 17, Saul says, "Provide [see] for me someone who can play." God sees more than Saul can see in David. In the anointing episode, God sees more than Samuel. In vv. 6-7, Samuel (the

seer! 9:19) sees only outward appearance, but God sees the heart. The story has now gone full circle. At the beginning of Samuel's story it was Eli who could not see, visions were rare, and the lamp of God was dim (3:1-2). Now it is Samuel who does not see clearly, and God must directly indicate the proper choice. At the center of this episode is a drama of right seeing. In it, the author underlines the theme of appearance and reality, which is central to this text. The reality of God's future for Israel does not always appear clear to human eyes, even to those of a prophet.

The anointing of David also follows a pattern we have seen before in the story of Saul. The career of God's anointed one (משיח māšîaḥ) involves anointing by a prophet, after which both Saul and David experience the possession of God's Spirit (10:1, 9-10; 11:6 for Saul; 16:13 for David). David's reception of the Spirit seems more immediate and is said to be effective "from that day forward" (v. 13). Both men then make a public debut (10:17-27; 16:14-23) and subsequently perform a mighty deed of valor that validates them as individuals possessed of God's Spirit (chaps. 11 and 17). But Saul's actions led to rejection, whereas David's story will culminate in confirmation and covenant.

Central to this theology of God's anointed one is the role of the prophet, who is God's agent to anoint, reject, or confirm (Nathan, 2 Samuel 7). In chap. 16, the prophetic interests are still clear, but the portrait of Samuel as an individual performing the prophetic role is less than flattering. He must be roused out of immobilizing grief (v. 1), he is fearful of the task laid out for him (v. 2), and he is rebuked for rushing to judgment (vv. 6-7). He seems old and passive, unable to see as God wishes him to see. Throughout the chapter, there is a constant dialogue between God and Samuel, as if he must be instructed at each step. Nevertheless, he is the prophet through whom God chooses to work. One has the impression that the prophetic role is being honored by the tradition even when the individual is not totally effective.

16:1-5. The story of David begins with divine initiative. God's speech in v. 1 begins with a note of reproof to Samuel. The season of grief is over (cf. 15:35). God has rejected Saul, and Samuel is dwelling on what might have been. God is already looking to the future. Indeed, the choice has already been made: "I have provided [seen] for *myself* a king." This new chosen one is among the sons of Jesse in Bethlehem. Samuel is told to fill his horn with oil (for an obvious anointing) and go there. Samuel had been commissioned to "make for *them* [the people] a king" (8:22). This act will provide a new dimension of God's initiative for Israel's future, with its twin crises of leadership and Philistine threat. David will be God's own king.

Samuel responds in fear: "If Saul hears of it, he will kill me" (v. 2*a*). To anoint a new king while Saul still physically occupies the throne would be treason. God tells Samuel to take a heifer along so that he can claim to be journeying to Bethlehem for a sacrifice (v. 2*b*), but once there the purpose is clear. Samuel is to invite Jesse and his sons to the sacrifice and anoint the one God names. God almost seems indulgent with Samuel in saying, "I will tell you what to do." The suggestion·that God has participated in a lie (the God who claimed not to lie in 15:29) is a false issue. As in 9:19-24, the anointing would almost certainly have been accompanied by sacrifice and ritual eating together. God appears to be simply instructing Samuel on practicalities that he seems unable to decide for himself in his fearful state. In effect, he is told by God, "You don't have to confess treason, Samuel. Tell them something acceptable." If in chap. 8 God was willing to step back a little to let the people chart the course they demanded, that time has now ended. God is firmly in authority over the course of events this time. Kingship will have a new basis in God's initiative, not that of the people.

The elders of Bethlehem are afraid and ask Samuel if he comes peaceably (v. 4). It seems less that they fear danger from Samuel directly than the controversy with Saul that he might bring into their midst. They do not know that he has come to anoint a successor to Saul, but they know that he is in conflict with Saul. Samuel soothes them by declaring peaceable intent. He merely announces a sacrifice and invites Jesse and his sons to join him (v. 5).

16:6-11. In this drama, Jesse and his sons seem to be the only persons present with Samuel. The sons of Jesse are brought before Samuel one at a time. When Eliab (the eldest, 17:13) comes forward, Samuel is ready to choose him. But the issue is proper "seeing." The text says that Samuel "looked on [ראה *rā'â*] Eliab" and thought that Eliab surely must be the Lord's anointed. God immediately replies with a rebuke. Samuel, God warns, must not "look" at appearance or stature. The verb here is נבט (*nābaṭ*) rather than *rā'â*, "to see." The implication may be that Samuel was "looking" but not really "seeing." Saul had been handsome and tall (9:2; 10:23). Such matters of appearance did not justify a decision. God pronounces Eliab to be "rejected" (מאס *mā'as*), the same term used of Saul in 15:23, 26 when he was "rejected" as king. It is also the same word used in 8:7 to describe the people's "rejection" of God as king. Eliab cannot move Israel beyond the stalemates of "rejection." Mettinger has suggested that "Eliab is something of a 'new Saul,' so that in his rejection Saul is denounced in effigy." He further suggests that the process here is something like the choosing of Saul by lots. As each son is brought forward, Samuel in some manner determines a divine judgment of yes or no. As with Saul, Samuel almost took Eliab's stature as the sign of his chosenness. But when God finally makes a choice, the chosen one is absent and must be brought onstage.[115]

God declares further that the Lord "sees" differently from mortals, who settle for outward appearance. The Lord "sees" the heart (v. 7), the inner person, and not the outward appearance. "Heart" has to do with the will and character of a person. David is the man after God's own heart (13:14), the man whom God has chosen. Human appearance will not determine reality for Israel this time.

The other sons of Jesse are paraded forward (vv. 8-10). Two are named, Abinadab and Shammah, but the other four are lumped together and left nameless. All are designated as "not chosen." Samuel asks Jesse if all his sons are present, and Jesse reports that there is one other who is tending the sheep (v. 11).

---

115. Mettinger, *King and Messiah,* 175-79.

Samuel sends for him. Virtually all scholars agree that David's identity as a shepherd (a theme mentioned in each of the three introductory stories for David, 16:19; 17:15, 34-36) foreshadows his role as king. "Shepherd" was a common title for kings both in Israel and in the ancient Near East. It is also significant that David is the eighth son. This means that he is far down in the line of succession. God, as with Jacob and Joseph, once again reaches out to take a younger son, an unlikely prospect for success, and finds in him the hope of Israel's future. From this moment and throughout the stories of the rise of David there is an element of cheering on the underdog and the outsider.[116] God "sees" possibilities even when others do not: "God chose what is low and despised in the world, things that are not, to reduce to nothing things that are" (1 Cor 1:28).

16:12-13. At last David makes his appearance. He is passive, the object of our regard. It is not yet time for him to take action. Remarkably, when he enters, the text tells us, he is "ruddy, had beautiful eyes, and was handsome" (v. 12a). Appearance may not be what counts for God's choice, but the text almost seems to delight in saying that

116. This is a theme particularly stressed by Brueggemann's treatment of the stories of the rise of David, Brueggemann, *David's Truth in Israel's Imagination and Memory*, 19-40.

he could be handsome anyway. "This is the one!" God declares (v. 12b). This handsome one must also be the one with the heart to be God's anointed. So Samuel is commanded to anoint him, and he does so before all the sons of Jesse (v. 13a). Then "the spirit of the LORD came mightily upon David from that day forward" (v. 13b). God's anointed one is marked, as was Saul, by the receiving of the Spirit. But unlike Saul, the Spirit comes upon David as soon as he is anointed and stays with him from that day forward. Saul's experience with the prophets (10:9-13) and in delivering Ammon (11:6) suggests a different understanding of the way in which the Spirit might be present for Saul, although the departure of the Spirit from Saul (v. 14) might indicate the Spirit was with him until that moment. In any case, David is now fully God's anointed king, with oil and with Spirit.

It should be noted that although David's name has been used throughout this discussion he is not named in the text until this final verse of the anointing story. The naming of this anointed one as David comes as a dramatic and climactic introduction to one whose story will become the very center of Israel's life and who will grasp Israel's imagination for generations to come. Samuel, by contrast, quietly leaves the stage and returns to Ramah (v. 13b). His time is over.

REFLECTIONS

1. Once again we have a story that reminds us of the unlikely vessels of God's grace. God's choice is David, a shepherd, an eighth son, from the village of Bethlehem, from a family that has no obvious pedigree. The theme of David as an unlikely instrument for Israel's hope continues throughout the story of his early years. We are always in wonder that this man David is the one for whom God has prepared us, of whom Hannah sang in hope. Can this boy defeat the Philistine champion? Can this upstart warrior escape the wrath of Saul? Can this fugitive and outlaw become a king? Can a man who hires himself out to the Philistines win Israel's heart?

One of the most basic themes of the entire biblical message is that God finds possibilities for grace in the most unexpected places and through the most unlikely persons. To choose the youngest son, who labors as a shepherd, to be Israel's future king is to ignore the usual arrangements for power and influence in the ancient world. Unlike Saul's father, Kish, David's father, Jesse, is not described as "a man of wealth" (9:1, the word can also mean "power"). The family tree of David is not distinguished. Jesse's grandmother was Ruth, an immigrant Moabite woman (Ruth 4:17). His grandfather was Boaz, whose ancestors included a Canaanite woman who was almost executed for adultery (Tamar, Genesis 38) and a Canaanite prostitute from Jericho (Rahab, Joshua 2). In the world's usual power arrangements, this would not be the stuff of royal lineage, but in God's plans sometimes "the last shall be first" (Matt 19:30; 20:16; Mark 10:31; Luke 13:30), even an absent eighth son tending the sheep. Of course, the unlikely journey of God's grace through the line of David leads to Jesus, born in a stable, a Galilean, a carpenter's son, and finally a crucified criminal. But Jesus is the true anointed One (Messiah) in whom God meets us for the most unlikely of all moments of grace. And the genealogy of Jesus in Matthew 1 includes younger sons like Jacob, David, and Solomon as well as naming those unlikely mothers Tamar, Rahab, and Ruth.

This story of the choosing of David can serve as a reminder that we still live in communities for which the patterns of power seek to become permanently entrenched. Too often we fail to look for possibilities of grace and hope beyond the traditional channels of power, influence, and success. We ignore the possibilities in those who are customarily absent from the gatherings of power (the inner cities, the elderly, immigrants who speak languages other than English, those of a different race from ours). We do not believe that God can find hope for a new future among the marginalized and the dispossessed. In our own personal moments of estrangement and self-doubt, we do not believe that God can find possibilities for grace in us.

2. Related to this theme of God's unexpected choices is our tendency, like Samuel, to confuse appearance for reality. It is almost trite to note that we live in a culture oriented to image and appearance. Products are sold by the appearance of youth and sexuality, which have nothing to do with the product itself. Tobacco brings cancerous death, but sells by appeal to chic and macho appearances. Children are ostracized at school for not wearing the proper brand names, and sometimes robbed of coveted items when they do wear them. Political campaigners seek to polish a successful media image rather than to convince voters by their positions on issues.

God's word to Samuel (16:7) is hopeful in such a time. When so many are fooled by appearances, it is comforting and encouraging to hear that God looks on the heart, that God can see past the preoccupation with image and appearance that characterizes our time. If the church is both to discern and to mediate God's grace in the world, then it, too, must seek to look on the heart—to see as God sees. It must look beyond appearances in order to grapple with the concerns and address the needs of the human heart. Nothing less will be acceptable for the life of God's people, no matter how successful our institutional appearance might be. If we succumb to the temptation to choose for appearance alone, then God's rebuke to Samuel will be our own.

The irony of this text is that when David appears, he, too, is handsome. This text does not argue against our efforts to make ourselves, our communities, our programs attractive. It is a question of priorities. Appearance alone is no substitute for matters of the heart, but if we tend faithfully to matters of the heart, the grace of God within will often show an attractive face to the world.

1 Samuel 16:14-23, David Is Introduced to Saul's Court

COMMENTARY

This is the second of three episodes that introduce David into the story. No one of the three shows knowledge of the others, but together they introduce David from complementary perspectives. What was a secret, subversive choosing of David by God (vv. 1-13) becomes a public, visible choosing of David by Saul (vv. 14-23). On the surface, Saul seems to be the subject of this episode, with his needs for relief from an "evil spirit" occupying central attention. A young musician named David is brought in to aid him. But the reader, because of the anointing story in vv. 1-13, knows that David is more than just a musician in this story. Saul has brought the future king into his own court.

Fokkelman has highlighted the irony of this moment, "While Saul and his court think they are welcoming a musician, we realize that the Saulide monarchy is dragging in a Trojan Horse."[117]

The key word that sets the theme for this episode is רוח (*rûaḥ*), "spirit." It provides a link back to the anointing story, where "the spirit of the LORD came mightily upon David from that day forward" (v. 13). Now v. 14 reports that "the spirit of the LORD departed from Saul" (v. 14*a*) and "an evil spirit from the LORD tormented him" (v. 14*b*). Both Saul and David may have been anointed, but it seems that only one of them may possess the Lord's Spirit at a time and thus be the legitimate anointed one in the eyes of God and on the throne of Israel. The evil spirit that plagues Saul seems to be some sort of affliction that comes and goes, since David's playing can make it depart (v. 23). The various references to "spirit" will be commented on further in the discussion of the verses below. The notion of an evil spirit "from the LORD" is disturbing to us. Does this simply make Saul a victim of God's anger? We must remember that seldom does the biblical story recognize secondary causation. All things ultimately come from God. This does not absolve Saul from responsibility for his own behavior. We must also avoid rationalizing this text too quickly. The evil spirit here is more than just some ancient code for what we might call sickness or mental illness. Saul is a troubled man, and as the people's king he reflects a troubled Israel (as we have seen in previous chaps., esp. 8 and 15). Both Saul and Israel are alienated from God. David is God's solution for both. This episode in 16:14-23 brings David immediately into the household of Saul, and with healing results. In the longer term, the episode introduces David into the household of Israel with hope for its future well-being. Although the immediate context is Saul's malady, God's ultimate plan for Israel in David is recognized and given voice through Saul's servant, "the LORD is with him" (v. 18).

16:14-19. We have noted that the Lord's Spirit departs from Saul and that an evil spirit arrives to plague him (v. 1). Although God's Spirit came more than once to Saul (10:10; 11:6), its departure here seems permanent. Possession of God's Spirit was a sign of Saul's status as God's anointed one, and it is now David who possesses God's Spirit (16:13). By contrast, the evil spirit can come and go repeatedly as the troubled mind and spirit of Saul are given healing attention, in the case of this account, by David's music (v. 23). This is apparently some affliction that is not without precedent, for Saul's servants suggest that a musician skilled with the lyre can soothe and bring relief to him (vv. 15-16). There is a possible known remedy for such troubling of the spirit. It is not fruitful to attempt some precise medical or psychological diagnosis of Saul as some have done. We know that Saul, at later points in the story, evidences brooding and melancholy states, fits of anger and rage that issue in violence, and irrational actions that divert him from the needs of his kingdom and finally lead to his own suicide. That this evil spirit is attributed to God indicates that, for the author, Saul's condition has a spiritual dimension. He is alienated from God and from the power of God's Spirit for well-being. All things come from God, but the preceding chapters help us to understand that Saul's actions have cut him off from the well-being that would be available to him in relationship to God.

Music is often associated, in both ancient and modern literature, with healing powers. Saul's servants are certain that music will help to soothe his troubled state, and they suggest a search for a musician skilled on the lyre. Saul accepts the suggestion and commands that his servants "provide for me someone who can play well" (v. 17). The verb here is the same focused use of *ra'ah*, "to see," "to search out," that was used by God in 16:1, "I have provided for myself. . . ." David was first provided by God, and now provided to Saul. A young servant immediately responds to Saul's command with "I have seen [*ra'â*] a son of Jesse the Bethlehemite" and reports that this son of Jesse is "skillful in playing." Here is the first testimony in the biblical tradition to David as a musician. David's skills as a musician, singer, and composer of songs become a standard part of the tradition about him. He is called the "beloved singer of Israel" in

117. J. P. Fokkelman, *Narrative Art and Poetry in the Books of Samuel,* vol. 2: *The Crossing Fates (I Sam 13–31 and II Sam 1)* (Assen: Van Gorcum, 1986) 135.

2 Sam 23:1 (NIV; the NRSV abandons this reading; see Commentary on 2 Sam 23:1-7). He is cited as a composer of psalms and patron of music in 2 Sam 6:5; 1 Chr 6:31; and 16:7-42 and in the superscriptions of more than eighty psalms. Klein cites a reference in the Qumran materials that David wrote 3,600 psalms and 450 songs.[118]

The testimony of the servant continues on to cite a number of other qualities of this son of Jesse. He is a "man of valor, a warrior, prudent in speech, and a man of good presence" (v. 18). This recital goes beyond the needs of this episode, where only a musician is sought. These qualities anticipate the actions and qualities of the David we will see in the chapters immediately ahead (chaps. 17–20). Most important, the servant testifies that "the LORD is with him" (v. 18b), a major theological theme in the stories of David's rise, culminating in the great summation of 2 Sam 5:10 (see also 1 Sam 17:37; 18:12, 14, 28; 20:13). We are placed on notice that what begins here is part of a larger divine plan and not just a strategy to relieve Saul's illness.

The man described here is not the untried boy of vv. 11-13. He is also not the boy, untested in battle, who fells Goliath in chap. 17, a tension we will deal with in later discussion. Apparently this able man is still doing some sheeptending, as Saul's request of Jesse in v. 19 suggests. Saul's request (command?) names David publicly for the first time. It is ironic that the first utterance of David's name in the Bible is on the lips of Saul, the man he will replace as Israel's king.

16:20-23. David makes his appearance and enters Saul's service. His role is still

largely passive. He is the subject of only two verbs here, "David took the lyre and played it" (v. 23). We await chap. 17 for the introduction of David as a man of bold action, although the qualities cited by the servant in v. 18 anticipate such bold leadership.

Jesse sends gifts to Saul (v. 20), whereupon Saul receives David into his service (v. 21). We are reminded of Saul's recruiting of able warriors into his service (14:52b). It does not appear that Saul received David only for his abilities as a musician. In fact, v. 21 says that David became Saul's personal armorbearer, which, as we have seen in the story of Jonathan's exploits (chap. 14), signifies someone like a companion at arms. Most significant, v. 21 notes that "Saul loved him greatly." Alongside the public story of emerging kingship in Israel there begins here a personal story of relationships between David and the household of Saul. The tragedy of Saul's insane jealousy toward David at a later point in the story is compounded by this simple statement of Saul's great love for David. It is not only Saul's kingdom that is torn (chap. 15) but his heart as well.

Saul requests of Jesse that David remain permanently in his service (v. 22), which highlights Saul's special regard for David. Verse 23 returns to the theme of Saul's illness/evil spirit. When it plagues him, then it is indeed David who can lift this oppressive spirit. David is the source of well-being, the possessor of the Lord's Spirit who can drive back evil spirits. The word translated as "relieved" (רוח *rāwaḥ*) is a verbal form from the same root as "spirit." David not only removes the troubling spirit but also is the source of life and well-being through the Spirit. David provides momentary relief to Saul; he is the long-term hope for Israel.

118. Klein, *1 Samuel,* 165. See also James L. Mays, "The David of the Psalms," *Int.* 40 (1986) 143-55.

REFLECTIONS

There is a famous painting of Saul and David by the Dutch master Rembrandt van Rijn. Saul is in the foreground dressed in the turban and finery of an oriental potentate. His expression is sad and melancholy. We know that this is a man in despair. He grips a spear, and something about his grasp on that weapon and the set of his jaw tells us that there is not only sadness here, but danger as well. There is a potential for evil in this troubled man. In the background, almost hidden in the shadows, is David, with harp in hand. We know the story. We know that his task is to soothe this troubled man. There is something hopeful about his presence. We know there is another reality than this powerful, troubled, and potentially evil man in the foreground. David is present as the future, but we know it is an endangered future. We hope he will be good at dodging spears.

Our tendency is often to define power as dangerous and potentially evil. As we move into the twenty-first century, distrust of those in authority is very high. We have seen the madness come forward and brandish the spear—in holocausts, gulags, ethnic cleansings, tribal wars of genocide. Our text does not absolve God of these evil spirits, and we, too, wonder why God's world should allow for such possibilities. Even short of horrors and atrocities, we often view those who have the power of governance or leadership as troubled and self-serving. The episode of David's introduction to Saul's court and Rembrandt's painting remind us that troubled and corrupt power is not the only possibility.

God has allowed for such evil in the world, but both spear and harp can represent power used faithfully for God's purposes. If our world is plagued, like Saul, by evil spirits that are also ultimately from God, then God has not left us defenseless against such evil.

In this episode it is the harp we find first in David's hand. David will, in future episodes, also be a warrior, and the spear can be wielded for good (David) or ill (Saul). But against the evil spirits that trouble the holders of power, David comes first as a singer of hope. It may well be that the church, like David, will be called to sing in the face of power edging into madness—to sing of hope, alternative possibilities, new futures. Such singing is not a substitute for faithful action in the arenas of power and influence, but perhaps faithful singing must precede faithful action as acknowledgment that the Spirit that drives out evil comes from God with us and not from our power alone.

In the painting Saul holds the spear. He has not used it yet, but he will later use it in an attempt to kill David, the singer (chap. 18). But the spear or the sword (used in these stories as symbols of military power) will be used in David's hand to kill Goliath and eventually drive oppressors from the land. There may be a part of us that wishes God's purposes worked only through the harp or that the providence of God included only benevolent spirits and not evil spirits. But God has become active in human history with all of its complexities and ambiguities. In order to move toward David, God must move away from Saul, and this leaves Saul plagued and troubled. This, too, is God's doing. The hope of harp and song simply reminds us that God has not left us defenseless in the face of troubled power and that the spear will not always be in Saul's hand.

1 Samuel 17:1-58, David Defeats Goliath

COMMENTARY

This is certainly the best known of all the stories of David. People who have no religious background or biblical knowledge recognize and know the broad outlines of the story of David and Goliath. Moreover, within 1 Samuel this story seems to occupy a special position. It is the most detailed in the telling of all the stories of David. Robert Alter says that this chapter represents as close as one can come in the Hebrew Bible to an epic style of storytelling—rich and explicit detail,

extensive use of vivid dialogue, strong characterization and interaction of characters.[119] At the center of this epic drama, David emerges as the central actor whose bold action and unwavering faith capture our imagination. He is unquestionably the man for Israel's future, and the popularity of the story suggests that he becomes here a man for future generations as well.

119. Robert Alter, *The Art of Biblical Narrative* (New York: Basic Books, 1981) 150-51.

Many scholars think that David did not kill Goliath. In 2 Sam 21:19 (cf. also 23:24), a biblical author reports that Elhanan of Bethlehem killed Goliath the Gittite. In 1 Samuel 17, Goliath is named only twice (vv. 4, 23), and David's opponent is usually referred to simply as "the Philistine." The Goliath killed by Elhanan was said to possess a spear with a shaft "like a weaver's beam," a detail also used in describing the armor of David's opponent in 17:7. The name "Goliath" may have been transferred from Elhanan's deed to the account of David's victory over a Philistine champion. The chronicler attempts to harmonize these stories by having Elhanan kill Lahmi, a cousin of Goliath (1 Chr 20:5). Whatever the historical truth, the name "Goliath" became firmly fixed in the tradition as the giant warrior vanquished by the courageous boy David. In fact, it became one of the defining stories of the tradition about David in early Judaism and on through generations in church and synagogue. The writer of Sirach, singing the praises of famous men in Israel's past, wrote of David:

In his youth did he not kill a giant,
    and take away the people's disgrace,
when he whirled the stone in the sling
    and struck down the boasting Goliath?
For he called on the Lord, the Most High,
    and he gave strength to his right arm
to strike down a mighty warrior,
    and to exalt the power of his people.
(Sir 47:4-5 NRSV)

In its present form, this chapter serves as the reader's third introduction to David. As we shall see, this introduction shows no awareness of the previous episodes of David's anointing or introduction to Saul's court as a musician (chap. 16). This creates certain tensions in the flow of the larger story that cannot be resolved or harmonized. The dramatic story of 1 Samuel 17:1 does provide an important complement to the episodes of chap. 16. There David was first "provided" by God in the story of his anointing (16:1-13) and then "provided" to Saul to banish his evil spirits (16:14-23), but in both of these stories David is essentially passive. He never speaks; his only action is to play the lyre (16:23). Now, in chap. 17, David reveals a talent for speech and action. He is not just the object of others' descriptions. His two rhetorically powerful speeches to Saul (vv. 34-37) and to Goliath (vv. 45-47) form the theological heart of this story. His actions are reported throughout the chapter, but especially in the climactic moment of the battle with the Philistine champion, David becomes a man of bold and effective action. In vv. 48-51, David is the subject of fifteen verbs, placing him at the center of a bold action drama. He ran—put his hand—took out—slung—struck—prevailed—striking down—killing—ran—stood over—grasped—drew—killed—cut off. David is now introduced to us not only as God's man and Saul's man, but also as his own man. Speaking of the contrast and complementarity of chaps. 16 and 17, Alter wrote:

The joining of the two accounts leaves us swaying in the dynamic interplay between two theologies, two conceptions of kingship and history, two views of David the man. In one, the king is imagined as God's instrument, elected through God's own initiative, manifesting his authority by commanding the realm of spirits good and evil, a figure who brings healing and inspires love. In the other account, the king's election is, one might say, ratified rather than initiated by God; instead of the spirit descending, we have a young man ascending through his own resourcefulness, cool courage, and quick reflexes, and also through his rhetorical skill. . . . Without both these versions of David's beginnings and his claim to legitimacy as monarch, the Hebrew writer would have conveyed less than what he conceived to be the full truth about his subject.[120]

Unfortunately, 1 Samuel 17:1 poses difficult textual problems.[121] The Old Greek text (LXX and other related MSS) is considerably shorter than the Hebrew text (MT) on which our translations of chap. 17 are based. Missing from LXX are vv. 12-31, 41, 48b, 50, and 55-58 (also 18:1-5). These verses are present in other manuscript families of the LXX, but the majority of scholars at present argue that the shorter text is the more original and that the MT and other LXX manuscripts represent

---

120. Alter, *The Art of Biblical Narrative*, 152-53.
121. See McCarter, *I Samuel*, 286-309; and Klein, *I Samuel*, 168-75, for detailed discussions of the textual issues.

an expansion of the story. A few would even see this expansion as the combination of two completely independent accounts, but the verses missing from LXX do not really make a very complete or coherent account on their own. In short, the textual history of this chapter is complex. In this commentary, I will interpret the text in its present form as it now stands in the Hebrew text of 1 Samuel, though occasionally noting problems posed by variant readings.

17:1-11. Verses 1-3 set the scene. The Philistines are back. This relentless enemy still poses a serious threat to Israel's future. Saul was anointed and commissioned to face this threat (9:16; 10:1), and in this tale he is attempting to do so—although, as we shall see, his efforts seem to have bogged down. The Philistine and Israelite armies are encamped on opposite ridges with a valley in between. This confrontation occurred in the southwest of Judah near the Philistine border and the cities of Ekron and Gath.

Into the valley, a man named Goliath of Gath comes to challenge Israel (v. 4). The name is thought by many to be an authentic Philistine name similar to names from other regions settled by the sea peoples. He is called a "champion" (אש–הבנים *'îš-habbēnayim;* lit., "a man between the two"). Roland de Vaux has collected a number of references, from the Bible and from the ancient Near East, that indicate that a tradition of single, representative combat was not unusual in the ancient world (see, e.g., 2 Sam 21:15-22; 23:20; Paris/Menelaus and Hector/Achilles in the *Iliad*).[122] Goliath has come forth to challenge an Israelite representative to such combat (v. 8). The fight will be to the death. Moreover, the Philistine asserts that the army of the losing combatant would become the servants of the opposing army (v. 9). In fact, as de Vaux's study shows, such combats seldom resolved the issue so completely, and battles usually ensued, as at the end of this story; but the winning of such a combat could give great psychological advantage to the victorious side.

The text does not rush quickly to describe the combat. Instead, it lingers in detail on the

intimidating appearance of the challenger. The MT gives his height as six cubits and a span (all LXX texts read four cubits and a span). The greater of these would make Goliath 9 feet 9 inches tall, while the lesser would make him 6 feet 9 inches. By ancient standards, even this lower figure would be an impressive height. The larger figure would be taller than any known human remains. In any case, this imposing stature is the source of the notion popular from ancient times to the present that David's victory was over a giant.

The text is more impressed with Goliath's armor than with his height. Three verses (vv. 5-7) are devoted to detailed descriptions of his armaments. The portrait is of an invulnerable warrior. His entire body is covered with state-of-the-art armor. We are intended to envision him as impregnable—an impression David will prove wrong! Not only is he armored, but also he is armed. He has a javelin slung on his back (some think this is a scimitar); he carries a huge spear with a massive iron head; and we know from the end of the story (v. 51) that he has a sword.

This intimidating champion of the Philistines issues his challenge and then taunts Israel, "Today I defy the ranks of Israel! Give me a man, that we may fight together" (v. 10). Challenge becomes humiliating taunt. The Philistine's demand for a "man" foreshadows his later judgment (and Saul's) that Israel instead sends a "boy" (vv. 33, 42). David will prove this judgment wrong, but for the time being the intimidating tactics of the Philistine are effective. Saul and all Israel are "dismayed and greatly afraid." The king who was to be Israel's deliverer and all his army are immobilized by fear.

17:12-30. This entire section is missing in the shorter LXX[B] text, which goes immediately to v. 31 and David's appearance before Saul as a potential champion for Israel. In the present shape of the story, this lengthy section introduces David in a way that sharpens the contrast with the bombastic bully Goliath.

At an almost leisurely pace, David is introduced as the eighth son of Jesse from Bethlehem in Judah (v. 12). As in chap. 16, David is a shepherd (v. 15), but, significantly, his three oldest brothers have joined the service of Saul and are with Saul's army (v. 13). In the larger narrative of the rise of David, this

122. Roland de Vaux, "Single Combat in the Old Testament," in *The Bible and the Ancient Near East,* trans. D. McHugh (Garden City, N.Y.: Doubleday, 1971) 122-35.

is an important portrait of Jesse's family as loyal servants to Saul. David has the menial task of shuttling back and forth from flock to father's house to battlefront, carrying supplies and messages while still having responsibilities for tending sheep (vv. 15, 17-18). After the Philistine's challenge has gone unanswered for forty days (v. 16), David is serendipitously sent to the battlecamp with grain and bread for his brothers, along with cheese as a gift for their commander (vv. 17-18). He is to return with news and tokens from his brothers for Jesse. The introduction of David in this story is as ordinary and unremarkable as the introduction of Goliath is dramatic and intimidating.

As chance would have it, David arrives at Saul's camp just as the armies are taking their positions on opposite sides of the valley, with war cries splitting the air (v. 20). He seems typical of what we would expect of a young man come to the scene of the action. He quickly dumps his baggage with the quartermaster to find his brothers and see what is happening on the front lines (v. 22; Would Saul have been hiding in the baggage? 10:22). He finds his brothers just as Goliath (named here for the second time, v. 23) steps forth to issue his challenge. The response around him is fear and retreat (v. 24). The men of Saul's army speak of him in awe ("Get a load of that guy!") and have no doubt that Goliath's arrogant challenge is meant to defy Israel (v. 25a); but they can report the rewards offered by the king to face him only in wistful tones. There is no hint that, even in return for such rewards, anyone will go out against the Philistine. The king has offered wealth, marriage into the royal family, and "to make his family free in Israel" for the man who kills Goliath (v. 25b). It is not clear what this final phrase means. Most believe it represents some remission of obligations (taxation, military service) to the family of a victorious volunteer. As if he has not heard correctly, David asks the man to repeat this recital of rewards, but in doing so he adds comments of his own that are revealing (v. 26). He characterizes one who would win such rewards as "taking away the reproach from Israel." David understands the lack of Israelite response as shameful. Israel lies discredited as long as none dare take up the challenge. Further, the reproach is not

merely to Israel or to Saul. It is to Israel's God, for David understands that these are "the armies of the living God" that Goliath has defied. David becomes the first to describe this confrontation in theological terms. It is not Saul, the king anointed to bring God's deliverance, who invokes the power of God. It is this newly arrived shepherd boy. He sees clearly what Saul and the rest of Israel apparently do not: that to respond only in terms of the Philistine trust in force of arms leaves them in the clutches of fear and death, but to understand the Philistine offense as being against a living God is to open up powerful and unexpected resources for life. It is David, and not Saul, who will embody this.

In what almost seems a distraction from the main story, Eliab, the oldest son of Jesse, overhears his young brother quizzing soldiers about the royal rewards, and his reaction seems typical of older brothers to kid brothers (v. 28). He is angry; he overreacts; he accuses David of abandoning his responsibilities with the sheep; he labels David as presumptuous and evil-hearted; he accuses David of boyish voyeurism, just showing up to gawk at the battle. David does what all little brothers do. He says, in effect, "Who asked you?" (v. 29), and goes right on with what he was doing (v. 30). This encounter only serves to heighten the coming drama. The reader knows that David has not abandoned his sheep (v. 20), that he is there at his father's bidding, and that, far from being "evil-hearted," David is the man after God's own heart (13:14) and the one whom God has chosen by looking on the heart (16:7). We suspect what Eliab does not, that in this seemingly ordinary, curious boy there is a surprising possibility for God's response to the "reproach of Israel." In the camp of the faint-hearted, this boy accused of an evil heart will prove to have the most courageous heart.

17:31-40. Saul hears about David's inquiries and sends for him (v. 31). There is no indication that Saul is already acquainted with David or knows anything about him. Just as the reader was introduced to David again in v. 12, so also Saul must now be introduced to him.

David is certainly not in awe of the king's presence. He speaks first and does so to console the king by urging him not to lose heart because of the arrogant Philistine (v. 32*a*). Referring to himself as Saul's servant, David then volunteers to go out against the Philistine (v. 32*b*). Saul is dismayed and responds that David is only a boy in contrast to the seasoned Philistine warrior (v. 33). The contrast between boy and man is made throughout the account until David proves he is more than man enough in the end. Saul's judgment is next echoed by Goliath himself (v. 42).

David makes the first of two great speeches in this chapter, which reveal both his rhetorical skill and the foundation of faith on which his actions rest. Saul has assumed that the power necessary for deliverance must lie in the realm of military might. Of armies and arms, David has no experience. David's speech is designed to demonstrate to Saul that power and courage can have other sources than military experience, and these sources for David are both practical and spiritual.

David speaks first of his life as a shepherd, an ordinary occupation but one with its own dangers and challenges (vv. 34-35). David already has experience with deliverance. When lions and bears would seize a lamb, David would not hesitate to confront these beasts, even if they turned on him. He would pursue, rescue, seize, strike down, and kill these animals. The verbs are similar to those used in the action climax of David's battle with the Philistine champion. Indeed, after speaking of his experience with marauding beasts, David vows to do the same to one who had "defied the armies of the living God" (v. 36). We might note that those armies stand paralyzed while a boy proposes to defend the honor of the living God. The armies do not act as if they believe in such a God.

David has spoken boldly of his own courage and strength, but in v. 37 he gives the credit for this to God. It was "the LORD" who "saved" from lion and bear; it is "the LORD" who "will save" from the hand of the Philistine. David is the first in this account to offer the name of Israel's God, Yahweh (trans. "LORD"). It is Yahweh who saves and who is the true source of any power David may have—to save from beasts of animal or human variety. Saul, the would-be deliverer from the hand of the Philistines, is reduced to echoing the faith of this boy. He is convinced

and bids him go and then pronounces the name Yahweh himself, not as the source of his strength but as the One who goes with David (v. 37). First, Saul's servant had pronounced this theme to the stories of the rise of David (16:18); now Saul himself recognizes this truth, "The LORD is/will be with him."

Saul may have uttered the divine name, but he cannot give up his own reliance on human military power. He attempts to clothe David in his own armor (vv. 38-39).

Saul does not understand anything. He has uttered Yahweh's name. But he wants to outdo Goliath on Goliath's terms. . . . So he offers armor, helmet, coat of mail, sword—David "tried in vain to go" with such encumbrance. David's contrast is with both Saul and Goliath. Unlike them, he goes unencumbered ("I am not used to them"). Both of them—the one a braggart, the other a coward—trust in arms.[123]

David is the model of another way, of those without the benefit of superior arms and armies who nevertheless trust that God can make deliverance possible against the odds, that there is hope even when faced with apparently hopeless situations. David refuses the armor, and he takes only his staff, his sling, and five smooth stones—the equipment of a shepherd (v. 40)—to meet the Philistine.

17:41-47. The Philistine champion can hardly believe his eyes. As he approaches, shieldbearer in front of him, he sees David is only a boy, "ruddy and handsome" (vv. 41-42), and he responds with contempt, "Am I a dog that you come to me with sticks?" (v. 43*a*). The reader, of course, remembers that this Philistine has been ominously compared with animals (v. 36). Goliath curses David by his gods, but they are left nameless and by implication are judged insignificant and ineffectual (v. 43*b*). He taunts David, threatening to leave his flesh to the birds and the beasts (v. 44). The portrait is of a warrior who is arrogant, boastful, self-assured.

By contrast, David seems calmly confident. To Goliath he directs a second remarkable speech. As he did to Saul earlier, David gives voice to the source of his confidence in

123. Brueggemann, *David's Truth in Israel's Imagination and Memory*, 33.

the Lord's power to deliver. He begins with the contrast that is obvious to all who view them on the field of battle. Goliath comes with the confidence of armed might (sword, spear, and javelin), but David comes only in the name of the Lord—here given full title "the LORD of hosts, the God of the armies of Israel" (v. 45). It is that Lord who delivers, David declares, and will give the Philistine into his hand. David will strike him down, cut off his head, and leave the bodies of the entire Philistine army as carrion for the birds and beasts (v. 46). David can give it back to the Philistine in the rhetorical battle as well as the coming physical one.

Verses 46b-47 attest to the true purpose of this contest. It must happen so that "all the earth may know there is a God in Israel, and that all this assembly may know that the Lord does not save by sword and spear; for the battle is the Lord's and he will give you into our hand." Deliverance does not come through trust in human might. God delivers in spite of "spear and sword" for the sake of the world's knowledge of the source of true power and the special relationship of that power to Israel. This theme was also central in the exodus story of God's deliverance (see, e.g., Exod 7:5; 14:4, 18), and it was central to the exiles when the power of their God among the nations was in doubt (see, e.g., Ezek 6:7, 10, 13-14; 7:4, 9, 27). In this story, those who need to "know" include both the Philistines and the Israelites of Saul's army. Both parties must know that the Lord saves! The array of swords and spears on either hillside represents power that cannot ultimately save. David "calls Israel away from its imitation of the nations and calls the nations away from their foolish defiance of Yahweh."[124] David comes with courage and hope, not because of superior weapons or training, but because his trust is in the surprising possibilities of God's deliverance.

17:48-51. When the combat comes, the narrative moves swiftly. Action verbs tumble over one another. After all the buildup, the climax is almost over as quickly as it starts (vv. 48-49). David runs, puts his hand in the bag, takes a stone, slings it, and strikes the Philistine. The stone finds a vulnerable,

unarmored spot on the forehead. The stone sinks; the Philistine falls.

Verse 50 almost seems like an aside, observing what we have already seen, but perhaps emphasizing the odds against it by noting that David did not even carry a sword. David finishes the matter by drawing the Philistine's own sword, killing him, and cutting off his head (v. 51). David has carried out his intentions declared to the Philistine challenger (v. 46). The reaction of the Philistine army is immediate: They flee. They had no intention of passively becoming the servants of Israel, as Goliath's challenge had proposed.

17:52-58. There remains only the aftermath of this sudden and surprising victory. Israel's army pursues the Philistines back into their own cities and territories (v. 52) and returns to plunder their camp (v. 53). In a problematic note, v. 54 says that David takes the head of the Philistine to Jerusalem and puts Goliath's armor in his own tent. Jerusalem is not an Israelite city until David himself captures it in 2 Sam 5:6-9. As for the armor, David later retrieves the sword of Goliath from the sanctuary at Nob (21:8-9). It may be that Goliath's head ended up at Jerusalem later as a relic of David's victory. No widely accepted resolution of these tensions has been suggested.

The episode of David's victory ends with a strange incident. After Saul has watched this improbable victory, he asks his commander, "Abner, whose son is this young man?" Abner does not know (v. 55). Saul instructs Abner to make inquiries and find out whose son he is (v. 56). Finally, Abner simply brings David before Saul (dragging the severed head! v. 57), and Saul asks David, "Whose son are you?" to which David replies, "I am the son of your servant Jesse the Bethlehemite" (v. 58). David noticeably does not give his name. What is going on here? How could Saul not know the boy he tried to outfit with his armor and talked with before the battle? Certainly this story shows no knowledge of David as a member of Saul's inner court circle (16:14-23).

Polzin has ingeniously proposed that Saul's question of David was really a demand to acquire David's allegiance as a "son" of Saul—i.e., one committed in loyalty to Saul. "Saul thereby asks David formally to renounce

124. Brueggemann, First and Second Samuel, 132.

Jesse's paternity in favor of his own."[125] David shrewdly avoids this commitment by citing only his biological sonship and noting Jesse as the king's servant, but refusing to pledge such loyalty in his own name. Polzin thus affirms that Saul knew David as his armorbearer all along and was now seeking to secure David's pledge of loyalty. The withheld pledge marks the beginning of tensions between the two. Polzin's thesis of continuous, single authorship for virtually the whole of 1 Samuel (including chaps. 16–17) forces him to play down the problems with this view of v. 58. It makes less sense to see Saul's question of Abner (v. 55) and his command to inquire about David (v. 56) as matters of David's allegiance to Saul. It also remains problematic to

see David as Saul's musician and armorbearer, who entered permanent service with Saul in 16:21-22, as the same David who is commuting from the sheepfold to bring food to his brothers at Saul's camp. Further, would Saul's armorbearer be so unfamiliar with arms and armor as in 17:38-39, or would Saul show no signs of recognition or familiarity? It is far more likely that the episodes of 16:1-13, 14-23 and 17:1-58 are three separate introductions to David with differing conceptions of how David became known to Saul. They have come together in a collection of David traditions without any extensive effort to resolve the tensions between them. I believe Polzin is correct, however, to see David's reply in v. 58 b as a wary one, not even revealing his name. The exchange seems tense and foreshadows further tension to come.

125. Polzin, *Samuel and the Deuteronomist,* 175, see the full discussion, 171-76.

REFLECTIONS

The story of David and Goliath has become one of the best known of all biblical stories and something of a cultural icon. Its imagery and influence can be seen in an amazing variety of ways from biblical times to the present. Painters, sculptors, musicians, and poets have made the story their subject. For example, David was the patron saint of Florence during the Renaissance, and that city's remarkable cadre of painters and sculptors almost all used David as a subject, the favorite view being of David with the head of Goliath. In a single month recently, I heard a recording of a song on David and Goliath by the jazz group Take 6, had a student share with me delight at discovering Joseph Heller's comic rendering of this story in his novel *God Knows,*[126] rediscovered Emily Dickinson's David/Goliath poem "I Took My Power in My Hand," and viewed the magnificent Flemish tapestries of the David and Goliath story hanging in the Washington National Cathedral.

The use of the David/Goliath story as a metaphor for the hopes of the underdog has become a cultural cliché. In the 1996 United States presidential elections, Bob Dole compared his election hopes against Bill Clinton to David versus Goliath. Cereal ads used the imagery of this story to suggest that cereal can make Davids out of young boys. The victory of the U.S. Women's Gymnastics team at the 1996 Atlanta Olympics was praised as a David over Goliath victory, even though the gender of the participants was different.

Some of these uses of the story are, of course, superficial. Some simply illustrate the natural appeal of stories in all cultures that feature resourceful children winning over evil forces against the odds. But even these witness to a deeper level of meaning that has made the David and Goliath story such a perennial favorite. The story is not simply a matter of rooting for the underdog. It embodies the hopes of all persons when they are faced with overwhelming and evil power that there is a way to overcome that power and win the future. This story has been told and retold especially by the weak, the oppressed, the marginal, and the powerless—those who do not simply hope for a David but see themselves as David, faced with the giants of oppression, and who know

126. Joseph Heller, *God Knows* (New York: Knopf, 1984).

that their only hope lies with a living God. Their own courage and resourcefulness will not be enough, and the human power even of their friends will lie paralyzed and ineffectual like the armies of Saul. It is the oppressed and the marginalized who know better than most of us that the Philistines of the world cannot be bested on their own terms. Whole systems of power, technology, and violence cannot be beaten by creating countersystems of power, technology, and violence. Arms races may create stalemates between opponents bristling with arms, but cannot bring peace. This is the reason why the violence of crime is not overcome by counterviolence in brutal prisons and capital punishment. The David and Goliath story is the story of those who know the truth of David's words, "The Lord does not save by sword or spear."

David is not just the courageous underdog. He is the one who knows that there are resources beyond the technology of kingdoms. His is an alternative to the way of swords and empires. To be sure, his way in this story is not a pacifist option. The enemy is struck down, and David must stand bravely in opposition to oppressive power. But his way, if not pacifist in the face of oppressive power, is subversive of that power. Ultimately his trust is not in the technology of force but in the subversive power of truth. And the truth in this story is that God is ultimately in opposition to arrogant and self-serving power and its violence. Trust in God nurtures hope that there is a way into the future where there seems no way, that there may be a chink in the impregnable armor, that a well-placed stone of opposition can bring down seemingly impregnable systems of oppression that loom as armored giants. We must relearn this lesson of God-trusting opposition to oppression in every generation. I confess that I did not believe that I would see in my lifetime the collapse of the Berlin Wall (and all that it symbolized) or the end of the system of apartheid in South Africa. I had forgotten this story of God-trusting persistence in the face of the giants.

This story also reminds us that speech is as important as action. David's two speeches to Saul and to Goliath give meaning to the action he takes. The affirmation of a "living God" enables one to go forth against the technologies of death. The affirmation that our purpose is that "all may know there is a God" saves our opposition to evil from becoming self-serving and arrogant. The acknowledgment that "the Lord does not save by sword or spear" makes us imaginative and resourceful in seeking alternatives to the intimidation of the powerful.

The contrast in this story is not just between David's God and the nameless (and ultimately powerless) gods of the Philistines. It is also between David's faith and the lack of faith of Saul and Israel. They can think of nothing more to do than to imitate poorly the very forces of oppressive power they oppose. Well-meaning movements and efforts for justice in the church and society sometimes clank around in the armor of Saul, attempting to imitate and best oppression on its own terms. When the church imagines that its mission can go forward only with massive numbers, large budgets, corporate styles of planning, and hierarchical structures of authority, then maybe we should read this story again. It is God who saves, not Goliath. God saves, not without human agents, but in ways that astonish us in our usual ways of measuring influence and power.

The David and Goliath story is the truth needed by those who are "the least of these" and face the overwhelming power of violent and death-dealing systems. This story teaches and hopefully engenders trust that the resources of a living God can still best the "principalities and powers" of this world. This is not a passive, inactive posture. It requires faithful and truthful speech, courageous confrontation, and the trust that by God's grace a well-placed stone might prove superior to the armor of a Goliath or a Saul.

1 Samuel 18:1–20:42, David and the Household of Saul

OVERVIEW

Now that David has been introduced—as shepherd anointed by Samuel, as musician brought into the service of Saul, and as unlikely hero against Goliath—there follows a series of chapters that trace David's relationships—with Saul, with Saul's family, and with the wider public in Israel. These chapters establish key themes for the remainder of the stories about Saul and David. These themes will make clear why the end must come in the triumph of David and the tragedy of Saul. In chap. 18, David is both the object of love—from Jonathan, Michal, and all Israel—and the object of growing hostility from Saul. The danger from Saul's jealous anger appears in chap. 18 but escalates in chap. 19 into a direct threat that forces David to become a fugitive from the royal household. Chapter 20 is a moving story of the love and friendship between David and Jonathan, which nevertheless cannot bring David back into favor. Their pledges foreshadow the transfer of the kingdom from Saul to David and not to Jonathan. From this point forward, David is a fugitive, on the run from Saul's anger.

A number of scholars understand 18:1-5 as the conclusion of the David and Goliath story in chap. 17.[127] I disagree and take these verses as the first episode of a chapter focusing on David's relationships in the royal household and the implications of this situation for the future of king and kingdom in Israel. It may well be that the first phrase of 18:1 is intended to create a bridge to chap. 17 ("After David had finished talking to Saul . . ."), but Jonathan, the focus of 18:1-5, does not appear and plays no role in the Goliath story. However, his love for David (stated twice, vv. 1, 3) provides one of the major themes of chap. 18: the growing love for David both in the royal household and in all Israel (vv. 16, 20, 22, 28). This love for David, especially in Saul's own family, is the counterpoint for Saul's anger and growing hostility toward David. Saul is losing the throne to David. These issues were not yet on the table in chap. 17, but 18:1-5 introduces them in a way tied crucially to the remainder of chap. 18 and the two chapters that follow (19–20).

127. See Klein, *1 Samuel*, 168-83; McCarter, *1 Samuel*, 299-309; H. W. Hertzberg, *I and II Samuel: Introduction and Commentary*, OTL (Philadelphia: Westminster, 1964) 142-55.

1 Samuel 18:1-30, Saul's Jealousy at David's Success

COMMENTARY

This chapter consists of four distinct narrative episodes and a concluding comment. The narratives each feature a member of the royal household in some kind of relationship to David: vv. 1-5, Jonathan's love for David; vv. 6-16, Saul's growing hostility toward David; vv. 17-19, the proposed marriage of David to Merab; vv. 20-29, Michal's love for David and their marriage; v. 30, concluding comment.

Saul's relationship to David is the focus of vv. 6-16, but Saul and his actions are a part of the three episodes involving his children as well. The context for the events narrated in this chapter is twofold. Much of the action

occurs within the royal household of Saul, to which David clearly has access in the beginning of the chapter and to which David gains membership as the king's son-in-law by the end of the chapter. At the same time there is regular attention throughout the chapter to David's growing public following. His larger reputation and the deeds that build public acclaim are a constant element in the development of events and the actions of characters in this chapter.

The episodes of this chapter are linked by interwoven themes of David's rise, on the one hand, and Saul's decline, on the other hand. There are three linking elements to the positive portrait of David's inexorable movement toward the kingship.

(1) David is surrounded and gifted with *love*. Six times in this chapter we are told that David is loved. Two of Saul's children loved David, and that love is mentioned twice for each: Jonathan in vv. 1, 3, and Michal in vv. 22, 28. All of Israel and Judah loved David (v. 16). Even Saul's servants loved David, a fact Saul cynically uses in setting up what he hopes will be David's death (v. 22; see also v. 5). In this chapter David does little to promote or reciprocate this love (but see chap. 20). Love seems to come to him as gift and destiny.[128] We catch only distant glimpses of his public leadership in military campaigns as any offered explanation of what inspired such love. Ironically, Saul was first said to love David (16:21), but as his family, household, and all Israel come to love David, Saul cannot. This may be an important clue to the character of Saul.

(2) The love David receives is coupled with the *success* he achieves. Four times in the chapter we are told that David is successful: as a warrior (v. 5), in all his undertakings (v. 14), in the eyes of Saul (v. 15), and especially against the Philistines, which leads to his fame (v. 30). David's success comes primarily in accomplishing what Saul was anointed and commissioned to do: to bring deliverance from the Philistines. To observe that Saul saw this success (v. 15) is to note his bitter recognition of David's effectiveness and, by implication, his own failure. At least this seems to be how Saul takes it, for he seems unable to enjoy David's successes as a part of the leadership he has raised up and encouraged. For Saul, David's success is not reason for celebration but for his removal. Part of the building drama of the chapter is that the obstacles Saul throws up to David's success become the foundations for David's greater successes—his dispatch to the battlefront (v. 13); his offer of Michal in exchange for Philistine foreskins as the bridal price (vv. 24-27).

(3) The picture of the love and success that come to David is built up through the events and personalities reported in narratives of public and court life. However, this narrative detail leads to a theological conclusion. Not only is David loved and successful, but also *the Lord is with him.* Twice the narrator gives us this theological comment as an explanation for the unfolding events (vv. 12, 14). It is the sounding again of a key theme already introduced in 16:18, and that will continue as a theme throughout the narratives of the rise of David (see the concluding affirmation in 2 Sam 5:10). The theme appears a third time in this chapter, significantly to record Saul's own realization that "the LORD was with David" (v. 28). Saul, along with the reader, is forced to recognize that within the human events narrated here a divine intention is at work. David is God's future for Israel, and he will not be denied.

Over against this celebration of David unfolds a dark counterdrama for Saul. When the love and success surrounding David find expression in the song of the women, praising David more extravagantly than they praise Saul (v. 7), Saul's response is *anger* (v. 8) and an "eyeing" of David (v. 9), which must be interpreted as "suspicion" and/or "jealousy." Most of Saul's actions throughout the chapter can be understood as expressions of this anger and jealousy. Saul once loved David (16:21), but at the end of this chapter the final verdict is that "Saul was David's enemy from that day forward" (v. 29).

Coupled with the acting out of Saul's anger is Saul's growing *fear.* Anger and fear, as modern psychology knows, often go hand in hand. Saul has been rejected by Samuel as king; now his actual grip on the kingdom is slipping. Saul becomes the first to voice that the future of the kingdom is David (v. 8), although the reader has known this since Samuel's anointing of David (16:1-13). So beneath Saul's angry and hostile response to David is an escalation of fear and anxiety. "Saul was *afraid* of David" (v. 12). Then Saul "stood in *awe* of him" (ירא *yārē*', a term that indicates anxiety, apprehension, v. 15). Finally, after David has turned every obstacle from Saul into success, and Saul has acknowledged that "the LORD was with David," we read that "Saul was *still more afraid* of David" (v. 29).

In the midst of this human drama, the narrator discerns a divine intention. For Saul,

128. See D. M. Gunn, "David and the Gift of the Kingdom," *Semeia* 3 (1975) 14-45.

this finds expression in "an evil spirit from God" that seizes him and sends him into a rage against David (v. 10). Saul's own anger and fear exemplify a deeper alienation from God and God's purposes for Israel. Saul cannot be Israel's future. His own actions demonstrate why this must be so, but the giving and withholding of God's Spirit for good or for evil will make certain that it is so.

Is Saul fated to fail and David destined to succeed? Some recent treatments of this narrative have seen Saul as only, or primarily, a victim and have understood his story as one of tragic fate.[129] David, of course, in such a view is destined to greatness. Both men are little more than pawns in the plot of a story predetermined by the storyteller's conception of divine intention. Such a view does not, however, do justice to the complexity of these stories. Chapter 18 offers a good example of this complexity. Before the "evil spirit from God" comes upon Saul (v. 10), he has already responded to the success of his own commander with anger and jealousy, seeing only danger to his throne and not benefits to his kingdom (vv. 8-9). The evil spirit that comes upon Saul intermittently does not appear responsible for Saul's actions, fating him to failure, but in this instance its presence almost seems brought on by Saul's turn to self-serving and eventually evil responses to David's success.[130] Paul Ricoeur has suggested that in this narrative we should understand Saul as both victim and perpetrator.[131] Saul is not compelled to evil action by the "evil spirit from God." Indeed, chap. 18 goes to unusual lengths to expose the inner thoughts and motives of a man, Saul, bent on sinful protection of his own interests (see esp. vv. 17, 21, 25). The narrator tells us of both the actions or motives of the human characters and of the divine purposes that can be discerned acting through and in spite of these human agents. God's purpose in these narratives is fated to have its way, but Saul and David may, nevertheless, choose their courses

of action within those divine purposes. It is part of the artistic complexity and brilliance of these stories that both human action and divine intent are made credible.[132] Such excellence helps to account for the appeal of these stories to those confessing communities who today affirm both human freedom and divine providence.

As in chap. 17, the text of LXX[B] is considerably shorter than the Hebrew text reflected in most translations. Most scholars believe the shorter Greek text may have been original and that the Hebrew text represents later expansion. These additions are scattered throughout chap. 18 and seem to emphasize the hostility of Saul for David, making clear that David was innocent of any provocation for this hostility. For example, the entire Merab incident is missing in LXX[B]. The addition shows David as humbly professing himself unworthy and Saul as underhanded and double-dealing. I will make occasional observations on important textual variants, but, in general, will interpret the Hebrew text on which most translations are based.[133]

18:1-5. Abruptly Jonathan enters the story. The opening phrase of v. 1 tries to bridge back to the close of chap. 17, but the themes of vv. 1-5 all point forward to the remainder of chap. 18 and beyond. Jonathan experiences an immediate bonding with David—his soul was bound to David's soul (v. 1). No motivation is given for this bonding, but it is obviously deeply personal. The word translated here as "soul" is נפשׁ (nepeš), a word that indicates the essential life of a person or animal. It encompasses the whole being of a person (hence, the NIV translation using the word "spirit" is misleading and potentially confusing, since the Hebrew word for "spirit" [רוח rûaḥ] does play a role in this chapter at a later point [v. 10]). Further, Jonathan "loved" David; such love transcended Jonathan's own self-interest. His love for David was indistinguishable from that of his own life. Saul's action in not allowing David to return home (v. 2) almost constitutes an adoption of David into the royal household, a

129. See Gunn, *The Fate of King Saul*; W. Lee Humphreys, *The Tragic Vision and the Hebrew Tradition*, OBT (Philadelphia: Fortress, 1985) esp. 38-41.

130. Polzin, *Samuel and the Deuteronomist*, 180, discusses the evil spirit that plagues Saul as potentially both cause and effect of Saul's deranged and evil actions.

131. Paul Ricoeur, *The Symbolism of Evil* (Boston: Beacon, 1969) 232-60. This work came to my attention through the use of Ricoeur's categories by Walter Brueggemann, "Narrative Coherence and Theological Intentionality in 1 Samuel 18," *CBQ* 55 (1993) 229, 241-42.

132. For a helpful discussion of 1 Samuel 18 as an "imaginative construal" of human and political events as divine providence see Walter Brueggemann, *Power, Providence, and Personality* (Louisville: Westminster/John Knox, 1990) 24-48, esp. 40.

133. For a fuller discussion of textual matters see McCarter, *I Samuel*, 301-21; Klein, *I Samuel*, 185-87.

status further authorized by David's marriage to Saul's daughter Michal at the end of this chapter (v. 27).

Recent studies of the term "love" (אהב '*āhab*) have emphasized that in addition to the implications of personal and emotional commitment the term often carries dimensions of social and political loyalty.[134] In v. 3, Jonathan's love is stated again, using the same language as in v. 1, but this time it is connected with the making of a covenant with David. One is tempted to see these two expressions of Jonathan's love as indications of personal (v. 1) and political commitment (v. 3) to David. Jonathan has, for good or for ill, cast his future with David. He has bound himself to David not only in terms of personal loyalty (see the expansion of this to the concept of חסד *ḥesed* in chap. 20), but also, more formally, in a covenant.

We are not explicitly told the content of the covenant between David and Jonathan, but Jonathan's actions in v. 4 may give an indication. Jonathan strips off his robe, his armor, his sword, and his belt and gives them all to David. This, though undoubtedly a generous personal gesture, is surely more than that. The robe, in particular, symbolizes the kingdom. Hence, Jonathan's action authorizes David for the throne.[135] The tearing of a robe represented the tearing of the kingdom from Saul in 15:28, where Samuel also promised that it would be given into the hand of "a neighbor of yours, who is better than you." Jonathan is the potential heir to Saul's throne, but now he gives his robe and other royal accoutrements to David at the start of a chapter clearly designed to show David as better than Saul—prospering in success as Saul descends into fearful and jealous actions. The implication seems to be that Jonathan already sees David as Israel's future. The covenant between them might well be a formal recognition of loyalty to that end. (This reading gains support as the continuing relationship of David and Jonathan unfolds in chaps. 19–20.)

We hear nothing of David's response to Jonathan's remarkable expressions of love for him. At this point we receive only a first report of David's success (v. 5). The verb the NRSV translates here as "went out" (יצא *yāṣā*; the NIV has a remarkably free translation of this verse) often indicates a military mission against an enemy, and David's success leads to Saul's appointment of him as commander of the army. David's initial success is as a warrior in Saul's service. In this role he receives the approval of "all the people" and significantly of "the servants of Saul." Almost before we know it is an issue, the affections of Saul's family, household, and subjects have been captured by David.

18:6-16. This long central section narrates the transformation of Saul. By the end of v. 16, it is clear that Saul has become unworthy of the throne. He has given in to petty and self-serving hostility toward David.

The turning point is the song of the women who are welcoming Saul and David home from "killing the Philistine" (v. 6). It is unlikely that we are intended to see this as the return from the victory over Goliath. Verse 5 makes clear that David has been given a command and was sent out in the service of Saul, and the women's welcome home implies some passage of time for David to establish his reputation in battle. To the accompaniment of instruments, the women from the towns of Israel come dancing and singing, "Saul has killed his thousands, and David his ten thousands" (v. 7). This couplet of Hebrew poetry is in a familiar pattern of intensifying parallelism, in which the second element expands and intensifies the meaning of the first element.[136] In fact, the word in the second element does not have the precise meaning "ten thousand" but can be translated "many" or "multitude"; nevertheless, the pattern requires it to mean more than the thousand attributed to Saul. Usually the subject in such parallelisms does not change, but here the subject of the first is Saul and of the second David. The implication seems to be that the women did not simply unintentionally offend Saul, but really elevated David's deeds over those of the king.

134. See J. A. Thompson, "The Significance of the Verb *Love* in the David-Jonathan Narratives in 1 Samuel," *VT* 24 (1974) 334-38.

135. See David Jobling, *The Sense of Biblical Narrative: Structural Analyses in the Hebrew Bible I*, JSOTSup 7 (Sheffield: JSOT, 1986) 19-20. Gunn, *The Fate of King Saul*, 80, points out that David will receive equipment from Jonathan that he would not accept from Saul in 17:38-39, but Brueggemann rightly notes that Saul is trying to equip David for battle (which he does not need), but Jonathan is legitimating him for the throne (which he does need), Brueggemann, "Narrative Coherence and Theological Intentionality in 1 Samuel 18," 233.

136. See Robert Alter, *The Art of Biblical Poetry* (New York, Basic Books, 1985); Adele Berlin, "Parallelism," in *Anchor Bible Dictionary* (New York: Doubleday, 1992) 5:155-62.

Saul clearly understands the song as belittling to him, and his response is to be angry and displeased (v. 8), which is the seed from which violence and madness will grow. Ironically Saul first gives voice to the ultimate issue at stake. He correctly perceives that the issue is legitimate claim to the kingdom, and he correctly senses that his own grip on that legitimate claim is slipping: "What more can he have but the kingdom?" (v. 8*b*). The note that he "eyed" David thereafter alludes to suspicion and jealousy (v. 9). Saul is unable to see David's success and growing reputation as anything but threatening.

It is significant that Saul's hostile and self-protective response is followed by a notice of his possession by "an evil spirit from God" (v. 10). Saul seems to suffer intermittent seizures by this "evil spirit," which does not seem the cause of his other problematic behaviors so much as additional evidence of his unbalanced state. We are told that Saul "raved"; the word here is the verb often translated as "prophesy" (נבא *nābā*). In 10:10 Saul was seized by God's Spirit and he "prophesied" as a positive sign of his anointing. Now his seizure by "an evil spirit from God" results in the ravings of a madman.

These "ravings" come upon Saul while David is playing music to soothe him (cf. 16:23). Saul is holding a spear, and as David plays, Saul throws the spear at him, forcing David to elude him twice (vv. 10*b*-11). For the first of several times in this chapter, the narrator gives us access to Saul's thoughts and, thus, his motives. In this case, outward action and inner thought coincide, for Saul thought to pin David to the wall and then threw his spear to do so. Later, Saul seems to become more duplicitous, saying one thing outwardly while the narrator lets us hear entirely different motives inwardly. Saul is now caught in a vicious cycle with David. David's music soothes him at the onset of his seizures by this "evil spirit," but the presence of David kindles Saul's anger and jealousy toward the growing popularity of his servant. Saul is a troubled and torn man.

Verses 10-11 are a near duplicate of 19:9-10. They are missing from LXX[B], and many scholars think they have become displaced and inserted here from chap. 19. In any case, the incident shows well the increasing instability and hostility of Saul at this point in the story.

Although David's life was in danger (v. 11), Saul was the one "afraid" (v. 12). The narrator is clear about the reason for such fear. Saul is afraid because God was with David but had parted from Saul. These human events are a part of what God is doing in and through these events. For Saul, fear leads to increasingly self-serving actions. He sends David out to battle (v. 13). This commission has the effect of removing him from court and placing him in a position of threat. Some see a demotion in David's placement as commander of a thousand (a military unit), when v. 5 reported that Saul set him over the army. Whatever Saul's intent, David is neither killed nor relegated to obscurity. He is "successful" in everything he does (v. 14), and the whole land comes to "love" him (v. 16). As before, the narrator makes sure we know that such success happens because "the LORD was with him" (v. 14). Saul's fear escalates to "awe" of David (the NIV translates "afraid of" for both of the different words in vv. 12 and 14, but the word in v. 14 indicates something more like "anxiety" or "trembling").

18:17-19. Saul's fear and awe lead to murderous plots against David. Saul offers his daughter Merab to David, saying he desires only David's bravery and skill as a warrior in return (v. 17*a*). But immediately after Saul's speech the narrator opens Saul's inner dialogue to us. Saul intends that when David attempts to prove himself worthy of this status, he will be killed by the Philistines (v. 17*b*). Saul's offer of marriage may be related to the reward promised to the one who killed Goliath (17:25), but the biblical author does not make this connection explicit. Saul seems to be growing increasingly duplicitous. When the time comes for Merab to marry, he gives her to another (v. 19). Royal daughters are given and royal wives are acquired throughout the books of Samuel largely as an outgrowth of political purposes on the part of the kings themselves and those seeking to influence them.

David simply responds with a statement of humility concerning his unworthiness for the position of son-in-law to the king (v. 18). In this segment and the next, we are given information about the thoughts and feelings of both Saul and Michal, but we gain no access to David's inner thoughts and motives. We do not know whether he saw through Saul's plots, how he felt about this betrayal, whether he reciprocated Michal's love (v. 20), or whether he saw the plots as opportunities to further ambition. While we gain remarkable insight into the character of Saul and Michal, the character of David remains opaque.[137]

18:20-30. This section opens with a remarkable and revealing statement that "Michal loved David" (v. 20).[138] It is the only time in Hebrew Scripture where a woman is said to love a man, and where a woman's feelings precipitate a marriage. In this case, the fact of Michal's love pleases Saul because of his own devious purposes. His interior thoughts are again revealed by the narrator as being focused on a plot to have David killed by the Philistines (v. 21). But it is bold for Michal to both love and to make that love known (reported twice, vv. 20, 28) in a time of politically arranged marriages. We are told nothing of what motivated this love, and we are never told that David reciprocated it. In fact, when the offer of marriage to Michal is made known to David, his response is distinctly pragmatic and impersonal, "David was well pleased to be the king's son-in-law" (v. 26). It was the position, and not the woman, that attracted David.

Most of this section is taken up with the plotting of Saul, a portrait of distinctly inappropriate royal behavior. The offer to become the king's son-in-law is made a second time (v. 21 b), but through the mediation of Saul's servants. They are commanded to flatter David with a strange mixture of truth and falsehood (v. 22): the king delights in you (lie); his servants "love" you (probably true, cf. v. 5). They are further instructed on what to say when David makes another self-effacing statement about his unworthiness (as with Merab). Are these statements genuine? Does David see through the plot? Is he playing along because he sees an opportunity? These matters are left unclear. The servants are to say that Saul expects no bride-price except one hundred Philistine foreskins (v. 25). Just so the reader will not fail to get the point, the narrator interrupts to say explicitly that Saul was sending David out to be killed (v. 25 b). Ironically, David adopts a similar strategy of removing a man by sending him into battle when he sends Uriah to his death in 2 Samuel 11.

David goes immediately to gain the bridal price, and he returns with *two hundred* Philistine foreskins. The Greek text (LXX) and 2 Sam 3:14 both have "one hundred"; the NRSV adopts this reading, but the NIV stays with the MT's "two hundred." Perhaps David is so enthusiastic to become the son-in-law Saul does not want that he actually doubles the number of foreskins. The marriage is made; the brevity of the report about it may suggest Saul's reluctant compliance.

The text makes explicit Saul's recognition of the realities facing him (v. 28). The Lord is with David, and Michal loves him. Saul has been betrayed by his God and his family. Little wonder that v. 29 a reports Saul as "still more afraid of David." Since Saul seems unable to join in the celebration of David, whom he also once loved (16:21), he now sadly becomes "David's enemy from that time forward" (v. 29 b). Saul has cast his lot with enmity against David, and tragically this act places him in opposition to what God is doing in behalf of Israel's future.

In a final verse (v. 30) we hear a report of David's "success" against the Philistines and his growing fame. David is fulfilling the task originally given to Saul.

137. Alter, *The Art of Biblical Narrative,* 114-20, uses chaps. 18-19 as the primary focus for his discussion of "Characterization and the Art of Reticence" in Hebrew narrative. His detailed discussion of the various techniques for revealing character, as well as keeping character hidden, is extremely helpful. All of these techniques are used in Samuel 18: inference from actions, outward speech, interior dialogue, and the narrator's explicit statements.

138. For this and all subsequent discussions of texts involving Michal, I am indebted to a remarkable collection of scholarly and artistic treatments of Michal's story, *Telling Queen Michal's Story: An Experiment in Comparative Interpretation,* ed. David J. A. Clines and Tamara C. Eskenazi, JSOTSup 119 (Sheffield: JSOT, 1991). Included in this collection is a previously published article that has especially influenced my own views of these texts: J. Cheryl Exum, "Murder They Wrote: Ideology and the Manipulation of Female Presence in Biblical Narrative," in *The Pleasure of Her Text: Feminist Readings of Biblical and Historical Texts,* ed. A. Bach (Philadelphia: Trinity Press International, 1990) 45-68.

REFLECTIONS

1. Walter Brueggemann has made an imaginative use of 1 Samuel 18 in reflecting on pastoral care in the practice of ministry.[139] He suggests that because our own lives have the quality of narrated story, our attentiveness to narratives such as this chapter can have transforming effect. The key lies in imaginatively attending to our stories alongside the biblical story. Pastoral care in the context of biblical faith is an act of imaginative attending to texts such as this one and to the narratives of our lives. The imaginative juxtaposition of biblical story with personal story creates new possibilities both for understanding the claims of faith and for living transformed lives in the light of those claims.

In 1 Samuel 18 the text models for us ways in which the data of "love" and "success" can be described. The biblical story shows a complexity of human interactions and motives, yet reveals within those human stories an insistent divine story ("Yahweh was with him"). Pastoral care attends to the human stories of our lives while challenging us to imaginatively perceive the insistence of another story that changes us beyond the ability of psychology or sociology to describe. Stories like those in 1 Samuel 18 provide opportunity for transforming pastoral care, because in the retelling these texts are experienced as both our story and not our story. Such texts provide a ground for redescribing and reconstructing our own lives.

> It takes no great imagination, while considering Saul or David, to find our life peopled with Jonathan and Merab and Michal and singing women and ruthless spears and applauding crowds. We draw very close to the narrative and we participate. When we do draw close, criticism is overcome and the text narrates for us another world, a world in which love is possible and hatred goes crazy, in which success is rampant and the king fails, in which Yahweh is present in transformative ways. David's world is rich with people. In our *retelling* of David's story and David's world, "our story" is *repeopled.* . . . When these stories are absent from our experience, everything is likely to be "explained." But then noticing is not possible: thrones are never risked, songs are never sung, swords are never thrown, foreskins are never acquired, names are never precious. When everything is "explained" life is denied and no new life is imaginable.[140]

2. By the end of chap. 18, Saul is engaged in a devious plot to end David's life, and his own life is gripped by fear and enmity. But the chapter did not begin that way. All of this grew from the seed of anger, envy, and jealousy at the success of another. The escalation from this small beginning to Saul's eventual tragic collapse was not necessary. All of us experience occasions of unwarranted and self-serving anger, jealousy that the successes of another were not our own. What the episodes of this chapter make clear is that evil and tragedy grow first from the small seeds of ordinary acts born of our own worst impulses. We cannot blame God for these acts, nor could Saul, but God's judgment will not be absent when we act to injure others out of our own anger and envy. We may not plot murder, but there are many ways to do hostile injury, from malicious gossip to political campaigns of character assassination. Saul is a sad reminder that jealous anger is a common human experience, but it makes all the difference whether we resolve it in repentance and reconciliation or take the escalating road to evil and madness.

By the same token "love" and "success" are not guaranteed by God's grace apart from the acts of responsibility and commitment taken in the dailiness of our lives.

---

139. Brueggemann, *Power, Providence, and Personality,* 41-48.
140. Brueggemann, *Power, Providence, and Personality,* 47-48.

Jonathan and Michal heard the same praise given for David that Saul heard. Jonathan in particular could have acted as Saul did in jealous protection of his own interests. What makes for the love and success of David's story here, in contrast to the fear and evil that overshadow Saul's story, are the simple acts of David's attention to the tasks given him, the courage of Jonathan and Michal to love without regard to self-interest, and the willingness of the women to sing in honest celebration of things that deserve celebrating. This narrative insists that God is at work in our lives, but not apart from ordinary acts of human courage and faithfulness or human sin and madness. If God is with us, or if we have become alienated from God, it is not simply preordained. It is the daily conduct of our own lives that will allow others to make those judgments about us.

1 Samuel 19:1-24, Saul's Threat to David's Life

COMMENTARY

This chapter tells the tale of four escapes (vv. 1-7; 8-10; 11-17; 18-24). Although it is David whose life is in danger, the chapter focuses on Saul. His descent into degenerate violence and madness becomes complete.

The entire narrative presents an escalation of Saul's murderous intent toward David. Saul no longer disguises his efforts to have his rival killed. In each of the four episodes, Saul takes direct action against David in full public view.

In this chapter, the extent of opposition to Saul is exposed, as is the breadth of David's support. Saul's efforts to kill David are thwarted by his own children, Jonathan (vv. 1-7) and Michal (vv. 11-17), by David's own agility (vv. 8-10), and by the prophet Samuel with the aid of God's Spirit (vv. 18-24).

By the end of the final episode we have witnessed the final and total delegitimation of Saul as he lies prostrate before Samuel, naked and raving (v. 24). He has moved from anger, fear, and devious plotting in chap. 18 to obsessive murderous action and madness in chap. 19. There may be some episodes yet to be played out, but there is no doubt that Saul is no longer God's anointed king. In fact, God may have rejected Saul as king (chap. 15), but Saul's own actions have made himself a despicable and pitiable human being.

19:1-7. Saul's murderous intentions are now in the open. He speaks to his son Jonathan and his servants about killing David (v. 1). His plots to get the Philistines to do his dirty work had failed (chap. 18), so Saul intends to take matters directly into his own hands. The irony is that he makes this known to those whom we know love David (18:1, 3, 22). Saul does not seem in touch with reality. In v. 1 b we are told that Jonathan "took great delight" in David. The verb here (חפץ ḥāpēṣ) is the same as the one Saul used in lying to David that the "king is delighted with you," while in reality Saul was plotting his death (18:22). Jonathan's delight in David is the truth, and he warns David of Saul's intention to kill him (v. 2), helps him devise a hiding place, and offers to be David's advocate with Saul (v. 3). David seems to hide in the very field where Jonathan speaks with his father, suggesting to some scholars that David was intended to overhear the conversation (v. 3).

Jonathan's speech is both passionate and eloquent. He seems to have a flair for rhetoric, which reminds us of the eloquent speeches of David to Saul and Goliath in chap. 17. Perhaps this was a common trait that drew these friends together. Jonathan's attempt to sway his father begins by contrasting the sin Saul intends against David with David's innocence of any sin against Saul (v. 4). Further, David has rendered "good service" to Saul (v. 4). Most would see in this phrase affirmation of David's loyalty to a formal commitment of service required of those who serve the king. In v. 5 a, Jonathan argues that David has even gone beyond the simple doing of his duty and courageously risked his life in vanquishing the Philistine (Goliath). This led to a great victory for Israel, and Jonathan reminds Saul that the king had seen and rejoiced in this mighty deed and that the Lord had been behind this victory. Jonathan then concludes by returning to the theme of David's innocence (v. 5b). By emphasizing that Saul would be killing David without cause, Jonathan may be raising the threat of bloodguilt on the house of Saul for the taking of innocent life (cf. Abigail's effort to keep David from bloodguilt in 25:31).

Saul is persuaded; he even swears an oath in the name of the Lord (Yahweh) that David shall not be put to death (v. 6). Jonathan completes his mediation on David's behalf by personally bringing him the news and escorting him back to the court to resume his duties (v. 7). It is to be a brief restoration.

19:8-10. In v. 8, further conflict with the Philistines is reported. David goes out to meet them in battle (we hear no report of Saul's involvement), and, as before, he is successful. The Philistines flee before his attack. As in chap. 18, David does nothing more throughout these episodes of Saul's growing hostility than carry out his duties as a warrior (and musician) in the service of Saul.

The battle notice is immediately followed by a repeat of the incident reported in 18:10-11 (many scholars think 19:9-10 is the original location and that the incident has been duplicated by addition to chap. 18). The evil spirit from God once again comes over Saul (v. 9), and he is caught up in a moment of madness. As with 18:10-11, the notion of an evil spirit may be a way of describing a psychological or emotional disorder. Such illness was for Israel from God and encompassed in God's purposes. Especially in these stories of the rejected Saul, his illness or madness was evidence of his alienation from God.

As David is playing music, to soothe Saul in such times, Saul attempts to kill David with a spear, but David is too agile. The spear is embedded harmlessly in the wall (v. 10). Now Saul has directly attempted to kill David, and David is forced to escape. We are forced to some disturbing conclusions about Saul. The juxtaposition of the battle notice and the attempt on David's life forces us to see a relationship between the two. In the light of chap. 18 (esp. v. 8), we must assume that Saul is motivated by jealousy at David's success in the very task Saul himself was commissioned to perform—deliverance from the Philistines. Saul's deadly actions against David have nothing to do with an offense by David, but grow from Saul's sense of his own inadequacy.

Saul has also now become an oath breaker. The oath he swore in the Lord's name (v. 6) has been quickly and very personally broken. It apparently meant nothing. Brueggemann notes how lightly Saul has broken this oath to preserve a life when he tenaciously held on to an oath for death that almost took Jonathan's life in 14:24, 44.[141]

19:11-17. First it was Jonathan who intervened to save David from Saul, now it is Michal who saves him, for like Jonathan she "loved" David (18:20, 28). Saul has placed men at David's house, intending to kill him the next morning (v. 11a). Michal apparently has some knowledge of her father's intent, and she warns David that he must escape that night (v. 11b). This initiative on her part is like that taken by Jonathan in v. 2.

Michal's efforts on behalf of David are, however, quite different from Jonathan's. Jonathan became David's rhetorical advocate with Saul, but Michal takes direct action in David's behalf. Perhaps Saul was beyond rhetoric. Michal lowers David out of a window to enable his escape (v. 12). She then creates a cover story to buy him time. She takes a teraphim (some kind of household idol; cf. Gen. 31:19-35; Judg 17:5; 18:14, 17-18, 20) and places it as a dummy in David's bed, using goat hair for the head, and covers it with clothes (v. 13). When Saul's men come to take David and kill him, she tells her first lie by reporting that he is sick (v. 14). Saul sends his men back, telling them to bring David in his sick bed and that he will kill him anyway (v. 15). Saul has even lost any sense of honor in his obsession with ridding himself of David. Michal's deception is then discovered (v. 16), and Saul confronts his daughter, demanding to know why she has aided his enemy (v. 17a). Michal then tells a second lie on David's behalf, but also to mollify her father and, perhaps, to protect herself. She says that David threatened her (v. 17b). In reality, she has been the initiator at every point. Adele Berlin has pointed out that in terms of usual biblical expectations, Jonathan has acted the more feminine role and Michal the more masculine.[142] It is Jonathan

141. Brueggemann, *First and Second Samuel,* 142.

142. Adele Berlin, "Characterization in Biblical Narrative: David's Wives," *JSOT* 23 (1982) 70-72. Berlin also points out that this same reversal can be seen in David's response to Jonathan and Michal: "The feelings of love and tenderness that David might have been expected to have for Michal are all reserved for Jonathan." See 1 Sam 20:41; 2 Sam 1:26.

who uses words and Michal who takes aggressive and physical action. She boldly made her love for David known in the beginning (not the usual woman's prerogative in those times), and she took greater risks in protecting David by actively deceiving and lying to Saul.

As for Saul, he is now exposed as both murderous and obsessed. He has been abandoned and betrayed by his own family. He is isolated without support in his efforts and bereft even of his own honor.

19:18-24. The chapter concludes with a strange episode. David escapes from Saul's capital in Gibeah and goes north to Ramah, the hometown of the prophet Samuel (v. 18). It seems unlikely that he would have gone north, since his own tribal territory is Judah, and all of his subsequent adventures as a fugitive occur in this southern territory. This episode, which will later include an encounter between Samuel and Saul, also stands in tension with the notice (15:35) that Samuel did not see Saul again until the day of his death. It may be that these tensions are less important to the storyteller than the need to use a story that affirms public support for David from the prophet Samuel and that underscores Saul's isolation and madness.

David reports to Samuel all that has transpired (v. 18*b*). We cannot imagine him being too surprised. They settle at Naioth in Ramah. Naioth is probably not a place name, as the NRSV and the NIV suggest. It may best be translated as "camps" or "huts" and seems to be a location at Ramah, perhaps the kind of settlement that housed communities of prophets.[143] Saul hears of David's presence there and sends men to capture him (vv. 19-20*a*).

When Saul's men arrive, they see Samuel standing at the head of the assembly of prophets who are caught up in the ecstatic state of prophesying. Then the "spirit of God" falls upon these messengers of Saul, and they, too, fall into a prophetic frenzy (v. 20). We saw this ecstatic behavior associated with the prophets and the possession of God's Spirit

in 10:9-10 when Saul was seized by God's Spirit as a sign of his special status as God's anointed one. At that time, Saul was given another heart, indicating some transformation to enable him in his commission as the anointed one (10:9). Here Saul's messengers seem immobilized by the Spirit's frenzy and unable to carry out their mission. When Saul hears of this situation, he sends a second group of men who have the same experience. Saul sends a third group, with like results (v. 21).

Finally, Saul must go himself (v. 22); no one can do his dirty work for him. Before he even reaches the place where David and Samuel are, he is also seized by the Spirit of God (v. 23). He falls into the same ecstatic frenzy as the others while apparently continuing to Naioth in Ramah. When there, he strips off his clothes and falls on the ground before Samuel and lies naked for an entire day and night. It is a scene of Saul's final and total humiliation and his complete loss of authority as God's anointed king. Before God's prophet, the Spirit of God, which once authorized him (10:9-10), now leaves Saul naked, prostrate, humiliated, and powerless. David then makes good his escape (20:1*a*).

The final phrase of v. 24 relates this experience once more to the saying "Is Saul also among the prophets?" In 10:11-12, this proverb seems to imply an answer of yes and to confirm Saul as God's anointed one. He is given "another heart" to pursue his commission to deliver Israel. Saul is once again "among the prophets," but this time it is only as an object of humiliation and pity. The Spirit of God can both authorize and judge. Saul is no longer worthy. Instead of receiving another heart, Saul is immobilized, and David, the man after God's own heart, escapes. It is even possible, as Wilson suggests, that the implied answer to the saying "Is Saul also among the prophets?" has now become "No, Saul is no prophet; he is insane!"[144]

---

143. See the discussion in McCarter, *I Samuel*, 328.

144. Robert R. Wilson, *Prophecy and Society in Ancient Israel* (Philadelphia: Fortress, 1980) 183.

REFLECTIONS

The theme of this chapter is sad but obvious. It is a chronicle of the total undoing of Saul. David himself and even Yahweh recede for a moment into the background. This is the final unfolding of the cautionary moral tale of Saul that began in chap. 18 with anger and jealousy at the success of another. It is often our failure to address the roots of evil in the ordinary that allows evil to flourish and corrode our lives. Saul was not an inherently evil man who rose to high places only to have his sinful nature finally catch up with him. He had his flaws and failures, but until 18:8 he seemed basically a good man who intended well. Those who do terrible and violent deeds do not usually begin by intending such actions. To ignore or justify our own petty thoughts and deeds is to risk the path of Saul. Saul was rejected by God as king; he could not bring Israel into the future God intended. But he was the sponsor and mentor of that future for Israel in David. He was not rejected as a man, and he, like his son Jonathan, could have allowed the throne to pass to David, a man he once loved (16:21).

Again we encounter a notice of the "evil spirit from the LORD" that came upon Saul and led to his attempt on David's life with the spear, which seems so constantly present with Saul. This theme reminds us of Saul's alienation from God and God's rejection of Saul as a part of the divine plan for Israel. God has, indeed, caused the anguish that grips Saul and sends him periodically into a rage, but the text takes care to comment on Saul's own human motives of anger, jealousy, and self-interest. These are not the Lord's doing. The "evil spirit from the LORD" may indicate intermittent losses of control and judgment, but Saul's descent into murderous obsession and madness is largely accomplished in chaps. 18–19 in those moments of complete self-possession rather than spirit possession. He became ruled by anger, jealousy, rage, obsession, and fear. He allowed these emotions to overwhelm his beginning with David, when he loved David (16:21). Saul's end as a king may have been rooted in his rejection by God through Samuel, but his end as a good and faithful man began in ordinary moments where jealous anger was allowed to obscure love.

But if David is in the background here, Jonathan and Michal are not. Their courageous speech and deeds form a counterpart to Saul's descent into madness and murder. Their disregard for self-interest is a total contrast to Saul's obsession with his own standing. These profiles of faithfulness and courage motivated by love are worth noting for their modeling of alternative paths to the self-destructive path taken by Saul.

1 Samuel 20:1-42, The Friendship of Jonathan and David

COMMENTARY

David's time in the court of Saul is over. He dare not return, because Saul will kill him. He will be a fugitive for the immediate future. But there is a final scene yet to play. The deep and committed friendship of Jonathan with David is the focus of this chapter. Although the external issue revolves around determining whether David must permanently absent himself from Saul's court, the real issue is focused on the ability of the friendship of Jonathan and David to survive this crisis and on the meaning of that commitment for Israel's future and the future of their descendants. Jonathan must struggle with conflicting loyalties to family responsibility and covenanted commitment to his friend. David must balance his instinct for survival with his loyalty to Jonathan and his need to honor Jonathan's obligation to Saul, even though Saul is now David's enemy. The exchanges between them are moving, honest, and, in the end, heartbreaking, for these friends will be forced to part. There are no portraits in the Bible of love and loyalty between friends to match this one. It is a friendship, with personal and political dimensions, that shapes Israel's future as surely as it shapes the futures of Jonathan and David themselves.

The first half of the chapter is taken up by an extended conversation between David and Jonathan. Initially, David petitions Jonathan for help in determining his status in Saul's court and the seriousness of Saul's threats on his life (vv. 1-11). They devise a plan involving David's absence from an important banquet. In a second segment of the conversation (vv. 12-17), the roles are reversed, and Jonathan petitions David to remember him and his descendants when he comes into the power of his kingdom. Many scholars believe this section is a secondary addition to the text because it anticipates the kind treatment David gives to Jonathan's son, Mephibosheth, in 2 Samuel 9.[145] They note that David's question in v. 10 is answered in vv. 18-23 and suggest that the addition of vv. 12-17 was a later attempt to bridge between the history of David's rise and the succession narrative. In any case, the present form of the text makes the friendship and loyalty between David and Jonathan the context for commenting on David's relationship to the house of Saul on two horizons. On the near horizon, David's innocence of wrongdoing against Saul is acknowledged and affirmed by Saul's own son. David did not come to power through any injustice against the house of Saul. Innocence is a major concern of the history of David's rise. On the distant horizon, David's loyalty to the house of Saul through Jonathan, even after he becomes king, is promised and anticipated. This loyalty is a concern for the succession narrative in 2 Samuel. The extended conversation between David and Jonathan ends with a plan for communicating what Jonathan has discovered (vv. 18-23).

The second half of the chapter carries out the two friends' plan. David is absent from the banquet, and Jonathan offers an explanation (vv. 24-29). Saul lashes out angrily at Jonathan, and his murderous intentions toward David become clear (vv. 30-34). Jonathan gets news to David, and the chapter ends with a tearful and moving parting of the friends (vv. 35-42).

A key theological term in this episode is חסד (hesed), which is difficult to translate adequately. It appears often in connection with Israel's covenant with God where it is frequently used to describe God's covenant love and loyalty. It has often been translated as "steadfast love," "lovingkindness," or "mercy." In this passage, both David and Jonathan appeal to this concept (vv. 8, 14-15). The NRSV translates as "deal kindly" (v. 8) and "faithful love" (vv. 14-15); the NIV uses "kindness" for all three occurrences. Sakenfeld, in the most thorough and useful study of hesed, suggests that the term really indicates both the attitude and the action of loyalty in relationships. Her analysis is particularly helpful in reflecting on the role of loyalty in this relationship between David and Jonathan.[146]

This is a story of conflicting claims of loyalty. The conflict is between the familial and the covenantal. Jonathan has responsibility as a son to his father; for that matter, David has obligations as a son-in-law to Saul. But Saul's intention to kill David places family loyalty in conflict with a covenant made between Jonathan and David (vv. 8, 16; 18:3). In 1 Samuel 20, hesed is used only in reference to this covenant commitment between the two friends. The conflict of loyalties also occurs between the personal and the political. The "love" (v. 17; 18:1, 3) and "loyalty" (vv. 8, 14-15) between David and Jonathan are not limited to the personal and intimate relationship between them. Both terms also reflect sociopolitical loyalties and commitments. Jonathan and David both understand that it is not just their personal future at stake but the political future of Israel. Saul angrily insists that Jonathan's political interests as heir to the throne require that he set aside the shameful choice of personal commitment to David (vv. 30-31). Jonathan knows that loyalty to David is not simply to a friend but to one who will be king instead of him, and he asks of David loyalty as a king and not just as a friend (vv. 13-16).

Some have seen Jonathan in this chapter choosing exclusively for David and against Saul.[147] This is true, in a sense. Jonathan not only supports and protects David against the wrath of his father, but he also seems to see

---

145. See McCarter, *I Samuel*, 342-45; Klein, *I Samuel*, 205.

146. Katharine Doob Sakenfeld, *Faithfulness in Action: Loyalty in Biblical Perspective*, OBT (Philadelphia: Fortress, 1985) 1-15.

147. Brueggemann, *First and Second Samuel*, 153.

the most clearly of anyone in the story that David represents God's future for Israel. Jonathan alone gives voice to a sense of the Lord's working through David in these events (vv. 12, 14, 16, 22, 23, 42). In a way, Jonathan chooses for the Lord and not just for David. But this choice is not allowed to be absolute and unambiguous. Jonathan must, for the sake of loyalty to David, oppose his father and risk his father's violence (v. 33); but he refuses to abandon his father or the demands of familial loyalty. He knows his father, Saul, is doomed; he knows David is Israel's future. He can protect that future, but he cannot go with it. In this chapter, the term "father" (אב *'āb*) is used fourteen times, emphasizing the painful relationship that Jonathan cannot escape. Saul is his father. He loves David, but he does not go with him. He stays with Saul at some personal risk and with the knowledge that he is on a sinking ship. In the end, he dies fighting with his father in a battle that cannot be won (31:2). It is little wonder that David, who better than anyone knows of Jonathan's loyalty, can sing on hearing of the death of father and son, "Saul and Jonathan, beloved and lovely! In life and in death they were not divided" (2 Sam 1:23*a*).

20:1-11. David is on the run. After leaving Ramah, he meets with Jonathan to plead his innocence (v. 1). Jonathan refuses to believe that his father wishes to kill David and appeals to his close relationship with Saul to argue that Saul would have told him (v. 2). This does not fit well with the notice of 19:1 that Saul spoke with Jonathan in particular about killing David. Either separate accounts of events have been combined without regard to such tensions or episodes are not necessarily in chronological order. David hypothesizes that Saul wouldn't tell Jonathan because he knew such a plot would grieve his son (v. 3). This statement foreshadows reality; when Jonathan learns beyond doubt that his father intends to kill David, he does indeed grieve (v. 34). The depth of relationship between Jonathan and David is shown by Jonathan's ready willingness to do what David asks without knowing yet what it is (v. 4).

Although the events of chap. 19 would seem to leave no doubt about Saul's intent, David enlists Jonathan's help in determining his standing with Saul and the extent of his

danger. David plans to absent himself from an important feast he would have been expected to attend. When his absence is noted by Saul, Jonathan is to say that David has gone to Bethlehem for a yearly sacrifice with his family (vv. 5-6). If the king accepts the excuse, all is well; but if the king is angry, then it will indicate that Saul means to do evil toward David (v. 7).

David concludes his petition by asking that Jonathan show *ḥesed* "loyalty" toward him because of the "covenant" between them (v. 8*a;* see 18:3). Further, David declares that if he is guilty he would just as soon Jonathan would kill him (v. 8*b*). In this verse, the depth of loyalty and commitment that supports this friendship is exposed. The relationship is not just a casual attraction between youthful comrades in arms. Their friendship is a covenanted relationship originating in love (v. 17; 18:1, 3) and maintained in a loyalty prepared to accept the personal and the political implications of the commitment between them. In the larger framework of 1 Samuel, this account once again affirms David's innocence of offense against the house of Saul and shows Saul's son supporting David in this claim.

David asks how Jonathan will bring news to him if the news is bad (v. 10). The presumption is that if Saul does wish to kill David, it will be risky to be seen with him. The two friends walk out into a field (v. 11). The narrative appears to continue in v. 18, where the plan devised involves David's hiding in the field. In the present form of the text, however, Jonathan opens a new conversation in which roles are reversed. Jonathan now petitions David.

20:12-17. This section begins with Jonathan's vow not only to tell David if his father means him harm, but also to help him escape to safety. He swears in the name of "the LORD, the God of Israel" and invokes the name of the Lord repeatedly throughout this speech (vv. 12-16). He even places himself at risk if he fails to honor this vow (v. 13*a*). Jonathan sees that they are players in more than a human drama. It is God's future for Israel that is at stake, and not simply his personal friend David.

Jonathan's focus shifts to that future in blessing and petition. In blessing, Jonathan invokes the Lord's presence with David "as he has been with my father" (v. 13*b*). The theme of "God is with him [David]," a major motif of the history of David's rise, is now invoked by Saul's own son. But Jonathan also seems to be recognizing a transfer of divine presence from his father to David. Implicit in his language is acknowledgment that the Lord is no longer with Saul, but Jonathan willingly invokes the Lord's presence for David as Israel's future. Saul already belongs to Israel's past.

Blessing for the future gives way to petition for the future in vv. 14-15. The roles of Jonathan and David are reversed. David, who was in danger at the present, had asked Jonathan for help. Jonathan now foresees a danger to his descendants and requests David for help in the future. Both of these friends appeal to *ḥesed* "loyalty/faithful love/kindness" and the covenant between them as the basis for aid. Jonathan first appeals to *ḥesed* for himself if he is still alive (v. 14), and then to *ḥesed* for his descendants (v. 15). Jonathan sees a future when David will become king and the Lord will destroy his enemies and the enemies of Israel (v. 15); indeed, he covenants with David that it may be so (v. 16). In effect, Jonathan acknowledges the coming kingship of David, but he also knows that the house of Saul has become the enemy of this future king. He knows that the enemies of the Lord's anointed will be "cut off" (כרת *kārat*, a verb used twice in v. 15) and appeals to David that he and his house not be numbered among those enemies. (The LXX of v. 16 reads, "may the name of Jonathan not be 'cut off' from the house of David.") Jonathan separates himself from the opposition of the house of Saul to David and asks David to make a place for his name and his household in the coming future kingdom. He makes David swear an oath out of love (v. 17). The text notes "for he loved him as he loved his own life"; it is unclear whether the subject is Jonathan or David. It would seem that David is swearing on the basis of his love for Jonathan (v. 17*a*). This would make the swearing of David's love a complement to Jonathan's love of David "as his own soul" in 18:1, 3.

What Jonathan fears and the help he requests both come to pass at a later point in the story. In 2 Samuel 9, when David's enemies have been vanquished, including most of the house of Saul, David seeks out the surviving son of Jonathan, Mephibosheth, to show him *ḥesed* (2 Sam 9:1, 3, 7) for the sake of Jonathan. David restores land to him and gives him a place at the royal table.

20:18-23. The two friends devise a plan that will enable Jonathan to communicate to David what he finds out about Saul's intent. Jonathan will shoot arrows in the field near where David is hiding. Then, when Jonathan instructs his servant where to find the arrows, he will, by his instructions, reveal to David what he knows about Saul's plan (vv. 19-22). Jonathan's sense of the Lord's providence is evident. If David must flee for his own safety, Jonathan is confident that the "LORD has sent you away" (v. 22*b*). As the friends part, Jonathan invokes the Lord as witness to what has passed between them (v. 23). It is no light thing; it is "forever."

20:24-34. The scene shifts to the feast of the new moon at Saul's court, where David's chair is empty (vv. 24-25). His absence elicits no response for the first night of the feast because Saul assumes that David has become unclean for some reason and cannot attend (v. 26). There were a variety of ways this could occur (e.g., contact with a dead body, an emission of bodily fluids, etc.). But when David is absent a second night, Saul asks for an explanation from Jonathan. Jonathan uses the prepared excuse that David has been summoned to be with his family in Bethlehem (vv. 27-29). Interestingly, Jonathan reports that David came to him, and he gave permission for his absence, which seems a bit presumptuous on Jonathan's part.

The mood suddenly and violently shifts. Saul, perhaps with the clarity of his own paranoid obsession with David, has seen straight through Jonathan, and he turns his anger on his own son (v. 30). He launches into a merciless tirade, slandering even Jonathan's mother in the process. But in his anger he sees clearly: Jonathan has "chosen" David, and Saul believes it is to Jonathan's shame. The reference to the shame of Jonathan's mother's nakedness or genitals is perhaps a suggestion that Jonathan was a shame from the moment of his birth. Saul cannot even bring himself to pronounce the name of David (also v. 27). Throughout this tirade, he calls David only the "son of Jesse," as if this were an epithet.

Perhaps it is a derogatory comment aimed at David's humble family.

Saul, in his anger, knows the future. He simply does not accept it. He angrily declares to Jonathan what Jonathan already knows: As long as the "son of Jesse" lives, there will be no kingdom for Jonathan (v. 31a). Lest Jonathan have any doubt, Saul demands that he bring the "son of Jesse" to him, for he is a "son of death" (v. 31b; the NRSV and the NIV lose the graphic imagery here by rendering "he will surely die/he must die"). Jonathan makes one last desperate attempt to plead David's innocence (v. 32). It is more than Saul can take. Rejected by God, he now seems rejected by his own son. The violence directed heretofore at David explodes toward Jonathan, and Saul hurls his spear at his son (v. 33a). Jonathan knows that David was right; only violence and death can await David in Saul's court (v. 33b). He leaves the table and the court in anger and grieves (as David had known he would, v. 3), over his friend's fate and his own disgrace (v. 34).

20:35-42. The scene shifts to the field where Jonathan and David had arranged their rendezvous. The narrative lingers over the details of Jonathan's shooting of arrows and his instructions to the boy with him (vv. 35-40). It is almost as if the narrative is reluctant to end, for at its end these two friends will part forever. The signal is given in the coded responses to the servant boy: David is not safe in the court of Saul. Jonathan's speech offers a double meaning when he urges his servant, "Hurry, be quick, do not linger!" (v. 38). It is an instruction David, too, must heed.

Jonathan dismisses his servant, and the friends meet for a final time face to face. It is a scene of considerable pathos, and for once David, often the passive objective of passions around him, becomes the proactive partner. He prostrates himself before Jonathan three times; the two men kiss and weep, but the text says, "David wept the more" (v. 41). There is no embarrassment at the deep affection that passes between these two warriors and friends. The author of this political drama of the kingdom pauses to note the passion and the grief of this moment.

Jonathan has the last word, and, as previously, it is Jonathan who sees with the eyes of faith and trusts that the Lord is at work even in these painful events. He sends David forth in peace (a contrast to the violence manifested by Saul), and he recalls the mutual oaths sworn in the name of the Lord. His words invoke the presence of that same Lord as the guarantor of the ties between Jonathan and David and between Jonathan's house and David's house "forever" (v. 42). They physically part from each other, but they are forever bound in covenant loyalty.

REFLECTIONS

This chapter is centrally important to any biblical reflection on a theology of friendship. The Bible is filled with many stories that illustrate the importance of relationships, but on closer examination most of these have to do with relationships of family (husbands, wives, parents, children, extended family) or of roles in society (governance, economics, religious leadership, military crises). There are not many texts that deal with relationship of friends, adults who need not have established relationships of commitment to each other, but have done so nevertheless. Jonathan and David could have related to each other at greater personal distance through the positions and roles each held: crown prince to military commander; son of Saul to son-in-law of Saul. But from the beginning the relationship of these two went beyond that of family and social role. Jonathan loved David "as his own soul" (18:1, 3), and David loved Jonathan "as his own life" (20:17). Modeled here is friendship that chooses for a depth of intimacy and commitment that was not a given responsibility of family or social position. It was grounded in covenant between the two and was practiced through the loyalty each gave to and claimed from the other.

The danger here, of course, is that we may give in to a romantic sentimentality about friendship and wax eloquent about all of the positive virtues of love, commitment, and loyalty as if they operated in detachment from the historical, social, and even theological contexts where friendship must be lived. It is perhaps significant and thought-provoking that our most eloquent story of human friendship in the Bible does not end happily ever after. Perhaps this helps us to guard against rendering the important truths of this story of friendship in the pastels of a Madison Avenue commercial.

As Sakenfeld has reminded us, "loyalty" (*hesed*) is the key to understanding the human commitments modeled here in the friendship of Jonathan and David.[148] But it is good to remind ourselves of the breadth and depth of this key theme.

1. This story tells us of the ambiguity and pain of loyalty. The commitment between friends modeled here is not without cost. The choices made are not always simple and clear-cut. The friendship of these two men requires risk and self-sacrifice. Commitments of loyalty are not made in a vacuum.

Jonathan is not free to choose for David in isolation from responsibilities to his father, Saul. He must make painful choices that honor his commitments as loyal friend while not giving up responsibilities as a son. While Jonathan helps David to safety, he also chooses to remain with his father, even to death. In D. H. Lawrence's play *David,* much of the drama is centered on the tension between Jonathan's ties to his friend as future king and his father as rejected king. Jonathan realizes that his soul belongs to David, but that his life belongs to Saul. When the friends finally part, Jonathan says to David, "I would not see thy new day, David. For thy wisdom is the wisdom of the subtle and behind thy passion lies prudence. Thy virtue is in thy wit and thy shrewdness. But in Saul have I known the magnanimity of a man."[149]

The story of friendship between David and Jonathan suggests that love and loyalty are always experienced in the midst of ambiguous claims and responsibilities. The experience of friendship can lead to painful as well as fulfilling decisions. We live in a societal context prone to cheap relationships. Many live under the illusion that their own self-fulfillment and self-gratification are the primary goals of relationship. But pursuit of such shallow relationships can never result in the experience of loyal friendship given and received. Loyalty requires honoring of commitments, concern for the other as fully as for self, parting as well as being with, giving rather than grasping, pain along with joy.

2. This is also a story of the politics of loyalty. In the commentary it is noted that key terms such as "love" and "loyalty" are not limited in their meaning to the personal and intimate dimensions of human relationship. The love and loyalty in the friendship of Jonathan and David surely had such personal dimensions, as the moving scene of their parting demonstrates. But at every point in the story it is clear that these two friends knew that their commitment had implications for the kingdom. Jonathan's choice for David was a matter of shifted political loyalty as well as personal loyalty.

Friendships always have social contexts and social consequences. This is clear, for example, in our society in the matter of interracial friendships and relationships. To bind oneself in loyal friendship to a person of another race is to move against the grain of a society still blighted by significant elements of racism and to model an alternative to that racism, often at considerable risk and pain. Jonathan saw a different future for Israel in David and chose that future as well as that person in his friendship for David. In our friendships, we make not only personal choices but also choices for the future of the communities of which we are a part. To choose friendships with those most like ourselves will limit the future open to our communities. Jonathan chose against what tradition dictated as his self-interest. The challenge to find loyalty in relationships today across traditional lines of race, class, sexual orientation, and national self-interest

148. Sakenfeld, *Faithfulness in Action.*
149. D. H. Lawrence, *David,* reprinted in *Religious Drama I: Five Plays,* ed. M. Halverson (New York: Meridian, 1957) 265-66.

will determine the future. The church in such a time would do well to read Jonathan's story carefully.

3. Finally, this story points to God as guarantor of loyalty. Over and again, largely in the voice and witness of Jonathan, we are reminded that loyalty in human relationships finds its full meaning as commitment made in the name of the Lord. It is trust that the future is God's future that makes pain and ambiguity endurable. It is the hope that God's future will come that allows us to risk challenging the vested interests and human cowardice that, in the name of stability and convention, undermine loyalty and love. Jonathan could choose against his own self-interest and his father's restricted vision of the future because his horizon was God's future. His vision encompassed more than the present realities of homicidal father, fugitive friend, risky intercession, and tearful parting. Beyond these events, Jonathan could see God's future for Israel, and David could respond in loyal commitment even to Jonathan's descendants in trust that God's future would come. In the complexities of our own relationships, our horizons are often too limited to the human possibilities that seem available in the present moment. One of the functions of this text and of the church that reads it is to offer the horizon of God's future as hopeful possibility to those who struggle to see past the pain and ambiguity of present circumstance to suggest that there is a larger vision that our relationships can serve. Those who would offer loyal friendship in the midst of life's struggles give up self-interest and risk painful struggle not only for the sake of the friend but also for the future of God's kingdom that such loyalty makes possible.

1 Samuel 21:1–26:25, David as Fugitive

OVERVIEW

These chapters contain stories from the period of time when David was a fugitive trying to stay one step ahead of Saul. The character of David becomes more active in these stories in contrast to his largely passive role in the stories of his time in Saul's court. During this period, David gathers a personal military force around himself (22:1-5) and lives the life of an outlaw. These episodes, as a part of the history of David's rise, explain David's actions in ways that avoid public disapproval and maintain his innocence of wrongdoing.[150] David has been forced into fugitive life by the unjust pursuit of Saul. Although Saul commits violent atrocities (22:6-23), David spares Saul's life and seeks reconciliation with him (24:1-22; 26:1-25). David receives the support of important figures, and their support shows his innocence of wrongdoing and the growing recognition of his coming kingship. Ahimelech willingly shares holy bread with him (21:1-9). The king of Moab gives him refuge (22:3-4). The prophet Gad supports him (22:5). Abiathar seeks refuge with David as a survivor of Saul's massacre at Nob, and David is in no way responsible for that act of madness (22:6-23). Abigail's resourcefulness keeps David from bloodguilt in the death of Nabal (25:1-44). Although David is a fugitive, he is not a lawless man who acts in ways inappropriate for one who would be king. Eventually, in a rare lucid moment, even Saul recognizes David's innocence and blesses him (26:21-25).

150. P. Kyle McCarter, "The Apology of David," 500.

1 Samuel 21:1-9, David and Ahimelech at Nob

COMMENTARY

When David is on the run, his first encounter is with the priest Ahimelech at Nob. This is only the first portion of a dramatic story that has its tragic resolution in 22:6-23, when Saul has the entire priestly community at Nob massacred for helping David. Here we read the story of Ahimelech's assistance to David, which leads to that tragedy. In this first story of David as fugitive, we see two elements emerge that are characteristic of this entire section on David's adventures as a fugitive from Saul. First, David becomes much more proactive than he has appeared in chaps. 18–20. He is not content to react to the actions of others, but he asserts himself, often in unconventional ways. Second, Ahimelech is the first of what will be a growing list of those who recognize David as future king. This recognition is not always explicit, but David's influence is seen as broadening and his support growing. The king's own son and daughter had already helped David escape from Saul. This episode adds the aid of Ahimelech, the head of the surviving Elide priesthood that once served the ark in Shiloh.

21:1-6. David's flight brings him to Nob, where remnants of the priestly line of Eli settled after the destruction of Shiloh and the loss of the ark. Ahimelech, the leader of this priestly community, was the son of Ahitub, Eli's grandson (22:9), and a brother of Ahijah, who carried the ephod for Saul in his earlier campaign against the Philistines (14:3, 18).

Ahimelech comes trembling with fear to meet David (v. 1). He asks David why he has come alone. It would presumably be unusual for a commander of Saul's army to be about by himself (also unarmed, as it turns out); so it is understandable that Ahimelech would fear that something was amiss. David boldly lies, claiming that Saul has sent him on a secret mission (v. 2). Ahimelech does not seem to question this statement. Word of David's fugitive status may not have been widely known at this point.

David further reveals that he has a force of men somewhere nearby. He needs food for himself and his men. He asks for

five loaves but also expresses willingness to accept anything that is at hand (v. 3). Ahimelech answers that he has no "ordinary" bread, but only "holy" bread (v. 4). The two terms here make an important contrast that David will also use in his reply (v. 5). The word חל (*ḥōl*) means "ordinary," "profane," "secular" and is the opposite of קדש (*qōdeš*) "holy," "sacred." Ahimelech was referring to the holy bread of the presence (see v. 6), twelve loaves baked from pure wheat flour and placed before Yahweh on each sabbath. According to Exod 25:30; 35:13; and Lev 24:5-9, such bread was to be eaten by Aaron and his sons—i.e., the priests. Ahimelech is willing to give this bread to David, but only if he has met the conditions of ritual holiness. In this case, Ahimelech inquires after only one such condition. David and his men must not have engaged recently in sexual intercourse (v. 4b). The laws of purity required that those in contact with holy things must observe sexual abstinence. David replies that he and his men always observe sexual abstinence when on a military mission (v. 5a). He is probably referring to practices associated with holy war, when those fighting a righteous cause were expected to observe certain rules of purity (see Deut 23:9-14; Josh 3:5). (Ironically, it is later Uriah's dedication in keeping himself pure for battle that prevents him from sleeping with his wife, Bathsheba, to David's annoyance and his own doom [2 Sam 11:11-12].) David tells Ahimelech that even though the mission might be "secular" (*ḥōl*) his men keep their "vessels" (bodies, sexual members?) "holy" (*qōdeš*). He implies that this is especially the case on this occasion (v. 5b). Ahimelech is apparently convinced by David's word on this matter. As a result, he gives David the bread of the presence as food for his men.

The text has provided an interesting play on the words for the "holy," "sacred" and the "profane," "ordinary." Ahimelech has only "holy" bread, but gives it up to those in need of "ordinary" bread. David is on an "ordinary," "common" mission, but claims to observe the rules of "holiness" and receives "holy" bread for provision. The ordinary boundaries between the sacred and the profane have been collapsed in the face of David's need and God's kingdom, which is coming in David.

Did David tell the truth? We do not really know. Jesus refers to this incident as a violation of ritual law (Matt 12:3-4; Mark 2:25-26; Luke 6:3-4), but this may not indicate that David was impure, only that by Jesus' time ritual law reserved such holy bread only for priests, and it would not have mattered whether David and his men were ritually holy. The importance of this story does not lie so much in the truth of David's statements but in the availability of holy things for what God is doing through David. David obtains the help of the most influential priestly authority in the land. He certainly exercises a bold freedom in ritual matters, in marked contrast to Saul's behavior (see esp. chap. 14). Were Samuel to rebuke him for this incident, one cannot imagine David agonized and undone by it.

21:7-9. The episode closes with two brief notes. This exchange between David and Ahimelech is observed by Doeg, an Edomite and a servant of Saul (v. 7). Nothing is made of this now, but in 22:6-23 it is Doeg who becomes the informer to Saul of this exchange, and Doeg eventually is ordered to do Saul's dirty work of slaughtering the priests. Edomites are traditional enemies of Israel throughout the Bible, so Doeg's identity as an Edomite is probably intended to mark him for the reader as a potential villain.

David had apparently fled Saul's court in such haste that he took no weapons, and he asks Ahimelech if any can be supplied to him (v. 8). In response to this second request, Ahimelech reports that what is available is the sword of Goliath, which has been carefully kept, wrapped in fine cloth and stored behind the ephod. He offers it, and David gladly takes it (v. 9). We do not know how it came to be at Nob. This does not accord with the note in 17:54, although the LXX there reads that it was placed in the "temple of the LORD," which might indicate a sanctuary like Nob. Of greatest importance here is the way in which possession of the sword makes visible and explicit the memory of David's greatest public triumph. Power, prestige, and recognition are flowing David's way throughout these stories in spite of the sense of danger and urgency in his flight.

REFLECTIONS

In this story of David and the holy bread it is clear that David represents the future God is bringing for the sake of Israel. The laws of holiness are intended to show honor and respect for the holiness of God, but never as an end in themselves. When such rituals and traditions themselves stand in the way of God's larger purposes, they must give way to the needs of God's kingdom. One has a sense in reading this story that Ahimelech is properly discharging his duty as keeper of holy things, but he does not question David too closely or draw the lines of ritual purity too closely (e.g., limiting the eating of the bread to priests only). He asks of David a respect for those holy traditions, but willingly gives holy things for God's purposes in a world that is itself profane and ordinary. What good are holy things if they cannot make a difference in a world where some seek to kill others and prevent the advent of God's kingdom?

For his part, David has boldly asserted that he has honored the requirements of holiness but insists on the importance of his needs in the struggles for God's kingdom taking place in the profane world. In a well-known article, Walter Brueggemann has suggested that David is put forward in the tradition as God's trusted creature. This story is one of the texts to which he points to show David modeling the freedom God has given to humankind—a freedom to seize boldly the possibilities of every moment. In David we see a man who understands that God has trusted him with his moment in history and can risk new understandings and new possibilities. In this story, David breaks the notion of "holy" away from the shrine and moves it out into the normal affairs of men. . . . David is not bound by the normal notion of what is *qōdeš*. He subordinates that conventional notion to the problem at hand, namely his safe get-away. . . . If *qōdeš* still functions as a meaningful term, it now means the well-being of his party on the way to royal power. Against the narrower notions of holy which had been held he risks a new understanding . . . . Both David and Jesus overturn conventional notions of what is sacred.[151]

Notions of the holy are still often held within the sanctuary and the traditions of institutional religious practice. David's story asserts that holiness received in the sanctuary can make holy the struggles of the ordinary, and it is in that wider, profane world that God is bringing the kingdom. But make no mistake—it is risky business to discern and choose for what God is doing in the world and to offer the sanctuary's holy resources for the sake of God's work in the world. We will see this in its starkest terms when the story of Nob continues to its tragic end in chap. 22. Then we must return to reflect on the cost of leaving the enclave of the sanctuary to become involved in the coming of the kingdom.

In the Gospels, Jesus uses this story of David in one of his earliest confrontations with the Pharisees (Mark 2:23-28; Luke 6:1-5; Matthew puts it later in Jesus' ministry, Matt 12:1-8). He was confronted by the religious leaders for plucking grain on the sabbath. Jesus appealed to the example of David, who, in need of food, ate the bread of the presence, "which it was not lawful for any but the priests to eat," and gave it to his companions. In the Gospel of Mark, Jesus then states that "the sabbath was made for humankind, not humankind for the sabbath" (Mark 2:27). For Jesus in Mark's Gospel, human need takes priority over ritual observance, and he implies, in approval of David, that laws of ritual holiness are subordinate not only to human need but also to the larger purposes and priorities demanded by God's kingdom. In all three of the Gospel accounts, Jesus proclaims that "the Son of Man is Lord of the sabbath." David's bold redefinition of holiness stands as a precedent for a christological claim that Jesus, the son of David, has likewise redefined holiness in keeping with the needs of God's kingdom rather than the requirements for ritual holiness or sacred institution. To oppose the powers that defend such ritual holiness is, however, serious business. For Jesus, this leads to the cross; for David, this act leads to a later massacre of all of the priests at Nob (22:6-23).

151. Walter Brueggemann, "The Trusted Creature," *CBQ* 31 (1969) 488-89.

1 Samuel 21:10-15, David Plays the Madman

COMMENTARY

This brief and strange episode adds Achish, the Philistine king of Gath, to the growing list of those who recognize David as king. The use of the term "king" (מלך *melek*) for David by the servants of Achish (v. 11) is sometimes taken as a textual mistake (an editorial slip, a redactional inconsistency). More likely it is but one more addition to the growing list of those who clearly see David as Israel's future and know Saul is king in name only.

Why did David go to Gath? We are not told. Perhaps he sought anonymity and safety from Saul by hiring himself out as mercenary to Achish, the king of Gath. He does this at a later point, but with full knowledge of his identity by Achish. Achish accepted his service and placed David in charge of Ziklag (27:1–28:2). In this story, one of the points seems to be the growing reputation and recognition of David. He cannot hide—even in a non-Israelite setting. The servants of Achish (Philistines no less) not only recognize him, but pronounce him the king of the land (as opposed to Saul, who thinks he is). They even know the songs sung in celebration of David's killing of their fellow Philistines (v. 11)!

David makes a quick assessment of this situation and decides he has miscalculated in thinking Gath was a place he could hide. He is afraid, as well he should have been (v. 12). Thinking quickly (our more active David in this section), he bangs/marks/spits on the gateposts (translators read this difficult text differently) and lets spit dribble down his beard. In short, he acts insane. He acts like a fool while they try to restrain him (v. 13). The strategy works. Achish, thinking David mad, announces that he has enough madmen without bringing one more into the house. Apparently they release him, since 22:1 has him escaping from there to another place. No doubt this story was told with the intent to ridicule the Philistines as well—"Don't we all know those Philistines have more than their share of madmen?"

This brief story serves to introduce Achish, who plays a larger role later in the story. It shows David as resourceful when in danger. That the story, though brief, was enjoyed by Israel is reflected by two references to it in the superscriptions of Psalms 34 and 56. But the greatest significance of this odd encounter lies in the growing accumulation of witnesses to David's coming kingship. David is God's anointed one. Samuel knows it. Jonathan and Michal know it. Many in Israel seem to sense it, even if they do not fully recognize it. Ahimelech seems to know it. Now even the nations begin to acknowledge God's anointed one. What the Philistines see in David is not a fugitive but the king of the land (v. 11), and a moment later "a madman." This strategy bespeaks cleverness on David's part, but in the larger biblical drama the nations often see the ways of God's anointed and the coming of God's kingdom as madness.

REFLECTIONS

This strange episode comes immediately after David's bold redefinition of holiness in the taking of the bread of presence for food (see Reflections at 21:1-9). David's masquerade as a madman reminds us of the odd form holiness can sometimes take. The Philistines discern the truth of David as Israel's future king, but they dismiss its significance because his madness does not fit their definition of a threat to their interests. Likewise, we may often see God's holy purpose at work in the world, but ignore its significance because it does not fit our expectations for the activities of grace. Many great figures in the history of the church have been considered "mad" for their actions, only to have history judge them to have been instruments of God's holy purposes. This is an odd tale, but it is the first recognition of David's kingship by the nations. To the nations, God's anointed one seems a harmless madman. To proclaim a crucified criminal as God's anointed one (Messiah) must have seemed equally mad to the nations in Jesus' time.

1 Samuel 22:1-5, The Entourage of David

COMMENTARY

This brief portion of the story consists of two short notes. The first tells of the growing entourage that begins to form around David (vv. 1-2). The second reports on David's brief trip to Moab, apparently to take his parents out of harm's way (vv. 3-5). These notes continue the accumulation of witnesses and support that David is gathering.

22:1-2. David takes refuge in the cave of Adullam. Although the precise location is uncertain, it was definitely in the tribal territory of Judah, probably somewhere between Hebron and Gath. From this location David could get word to his family. Hence, we are not surprised to learn that he is joined by his brothers and all of his father's household (v. 1). They could well have been in danger from Saul's anger at David. This seems confirmed when David moves his own parents to Moab for a while (v. 3). David seems to have had the unqualified support of his family throughout his career. Even the quarrel with Eliab in 17:28-30 is not a serious division, but only the natural squabbling of older and younger brothers.

Of greater interest is the notice (v. 2) that David is joined in his fugitive enclave by the distressed, the indebted, and the discontent. David becomes their leader, and their number grows to four hundred (later to six hundred, 23:13; 25:13; 27:2; 30:9-10). In short, David's personal force is made up of those who are marginal or outcast in society. This group is the beginning of a personal military force that David maintained as loyal to him and that stood apart from the kingdom's own military even after he became king. The origins of this group suggest that there may have been a socioeconomic basis to the conflict between David and Saul in addition to personal jealousy and animosity. David, as an eighth son of a rather undistinguished family, may be seen as the hero and champion of socially and economically marginal groups over against wealthier landholders. Certainly Saul continues to avoid David's name and call him a "son of Jesse," as if this were derogatory (see 22:7), which may indicate a contempt for David's humble birth and lack of social position. The rise of David may threaten social realignment in Israel. Mendenhall has taken this text and others as evidence that David is a "Hebrew," a term used in a derogatory way

about groups that live as outlaws without social status or power.[152] There may also be a northern Israel/southern Judah split reflected here as David begins building a southern, Judean, power base for himself; Saul was from the northern tribe of Benjamin.

22:3-5. David apparently enjoys friendly relations with Moab. He makes a trip to Mizpeh, where he asks the king of Moab to keep his father and mother safe until he is clear about his future (v. 1). Of course, the book of Ruth preserves a tradition that David's own great-grandmother was a Moabite woman (Ruth 4:18-22). It is noteworthy that in asking for this favor David again casually expresses confidence that his future is in God's hands: "until I know what God will do for me" (v. 1b). He does not view the kingdom as something he seizes by his own efforts, but constantly sees the possibilities of his future as expressions of God's will. David does leave his parents in Moab for a time, although it is uncertain what is meant by the phrase "all the time that David was in the stronghold" (v. 4). Now the king of Moab has been added to the list of those who seem to support David as the future of Israel. David's influence and political base are broadening.

Suddenly a prophet named Gad appears and orders David back to Judah (v. 5). We know nothing about Gad; later he functions as a court prophet during the reign of David (2 Sam 24:11-19). This small note is significant in two ways. First, it indicates prophetic support for David, along with his anointing by Samuel and the incident at Ramah (19:18-24). Second, it moves David back into Judah, where the remaining drama of David's rise to kingship will be played out and where David will build his own base of support.

152. Mendenhall, "The 'Vengeance' of Yahweh," in *The Tenth Generation,* 135-38.

REFLECTIONS

We cannot read this notice in 1 Sam 22:2 about David's attracting to himself the outcasts of the land without remembering that Jesus, the son of David, also attracted the outcasts of his time. There is a word about the nature of God's kingdom as opposed to human kingdoms here. God's kingdom does not find its membership in the usual patterns of power and influence. It is often "the least of these" who become significant, and the "last will become first." David is clear in the midst of the mundane concerns of these verses that his kingdom will be a result of what "God will do for me." It will not be of his own making.

This is an important reminder about the nature of God's people and God's kingdom for a time like ours, when strategies of church growth urge homogeneity and upward mobility as growth principles. I am certain that those gathering to David did not look in his time like a formula designed for success. Certainly, the representatives of institutional religion in Jesus' time did not think he was making wise choices about those who became associated with him. But if David and Jesus drew the troubled and the outcast to themselves because they offered hope and new life to all, can the church in our time do less and still serve the kingdom of God? "Come to me, all you that are weary and are carrying heavy burdens, and I will give you rest" (Matt 11:28 NRSV).

1 Samuel 22:6-23, Saul Massacres the Priests at Nob

COMMENTARY

This episode resumes the story line begun in 21:1-9. Doeg the Edomite, who saw David with Ahimelech (21:7), reports this meeting to Saul. The consequences are tragic. In this story, Saul hits bottom in his madness. He is possessed by his violent obsession with David and is out of control. We suspected something ominous might come from the note about Doeg in 21:7, but as readers we are shocked at the massacre that results. In the larger context, David has been gaining support from key figures and broadening his base among the people. Here we see Saul alienating and turning against his own support.

22:6-10. Saul is at Gibeah, his hometown and capital. As is frequently the case, Saul holds a spear (18:10; 19:9, 10; 26:7-8, 11-12, 16; 2 Sam 1:6). He has already hurled it at David and Jonathan on separate occasions. He is sitting beneath a tamarisk tree, and his servants are around him (v. 6). Saul addresses them as "Benjaminites," suggesting that this group is made up only of those closest to Saul, his own tribesmen and kinfolk (v. 7). Saul seems to be brooding. The immediate tone of his address to these close servants is accusatory. He asks a rhetorical question (Will David reward you?), followed by an amazing accusation: "Is that why all of you have conspired against me?" (v. 8a). He apparently believes that all of these kinsmen in his service would conspire against him for gain. The suggestion must have been a shock. It was customary to reward service with land and promotion to military command. Surely Saul had already

done so for some of these. Perhaps he is calling to their attention that David, a fugitive, can hardly offer such reward.

Saul's bill of particulars for the charge of conspiracy includes the accusation that none of them have disclosed the covenant (NRSV, "league") made between his son Jonathan and David (whom Saul only refers to disparagingly as "son of Jesse"), or that Jonathan has stirred David up "to lie in wait" (v. 8). This means that Saul believes his own son is plotting with his enemy for his death, an accusation we, as readers, know is untrue. This reference may be preparing us for the two stories in which David does, indeed, have the life of Saul in his hand, but refuses to take the life of God's anointed one (chaps. 24 and 26). There is a pathetic quality to Saul's speech. At one point (v. 8b) he pleads, "None of you is sorry for me." Saul seems to know about the commitment of Jonathan in loyalty to David. They had already confronted each other over this matter (20:30-34). Saul's madness seems to have taken a paranoid turn. He imagines that Jonathan's commitment to David is a plot to ambush him, and he accuses his own men of knowing about this. This must have seemed outrageous and unwarranted to Saul's men. In the text, they remain speechless.

It is Doeg, a non-Israelite, an Edomite, who finds his tongue. In v. 9 he reports having seen David with Ahimelech at Nob, and he levels three charges. He claims that Ahimelech "inquired of the LORD" for David, gave him provisions, and gave him the sword of Goliath (v. 10). We know the last two of these to be true based on the account in 21:1-9. It is the first we have heard of the first charge, although Ahimelech later seems to admit that it is true (v. 15). "To inquire of the LORD" means to seek an oracle of guidance, in this case for David. This is a function associated with priests or prophets, and persons presumably would seek them out to make such inquiries. As we have seen before in 1 Samuel, there is an ironic play on words here, since the verb שָׁאַל (šā'al, "to ask," "to inquire") is the root of Saul's own name. While Saul was seeking David, David was seeking a šā'al from Ahimelech.

22:11-19. Saul demands the appearance not only of Ahimelech but also of the entire company of priests who live at Nob (v. 11). These priests are the remnants of the house of Eli. According to 14:3, Ahimelech's brother Ahijah has accompanied Saul on his Philistine campaigns and used the ephod to help give him guidance. There is little to suggest that this entire Elide priesthood had been anything other than completely loyal to Saul. Yet, when Saul greets Ahimelech, it is with a contemptuous command to "Listen!" and a refusal to use his name. Ahimelech respectfully makes himself available and refers to Saul as "my lord" (v. 12), but Saul without preamble accuses him of conspiracy and repeats the three charges made by Doeg. Saul adds to this his own paranoid notion that this enables David to "lie in wait" to ambush Saul.

Ahimelech's response and defense are extraordinary and masterful. He defends himself by defending David's innocence (v. 14). Why should he not receive and aid David? David is known as the most faithful of Saul's servants; he is the king's son-in-law; he is the commander of Saul's bodyguard (NIV, reading with the LXX; the NRSV adopts a strange translation here that has no textual support). He is honored in the royal household. Ahimelech could well imagine that he would be in trouble should he not aid one such as this. It should be noted that throughout his speech, Ahimelech, in contrast to Saul, always uses David's name.

Ahimelech continues his defense by appealing to precedent (v. 15a). He admits inquiring of the Lord for David, but argues that he has done it many times before. Further, he claims that he and his whole priestly house knew

nothing of the enmity between Saul and David (v. 15b). He had no reason to think things had changed from his previous dealings with David. Throughout this last plea, Ahimelech refers to himself as Saul's "servant."

Saul does not hesitate for a moment. There is no discussion, no debate. The sentence is death, presumably for treason against the king, and it is death not just for Ahimelech but for the entire company of priests (v. 16). The hesitation comes not from Saul, but from the king's own royal bodyguard. Saul orders them to carry out the death sentence, and they refuse (v. 17). It is a telling moment in Saul's story. He is now isolated in his madness from his own men. They will not attack priests of the Lord. Their respect for God's priests is greater than Saul's. Saul is alone in his obsession. Almost pathetically Saul turns in his isolation to Doeg the Edomite (v. 18). He has no stake in priests of the Lord, so he does Saul's bidding and slaughters eighty-five priests that day (v. 19). Tradition amplifies the horror of this moment; the LXX reads 305 priests, and Josephus reads 385 priests. The massacre is carried to the city of Nob itself, which Saul puts to the sword, killing men, women, children, and livestock (v. 20). Saul, who disobeyed the command to put the Amalekites to the ban (חרם ḥērem; see chap. 15), now totally exterminates the remaining members of the priestly family, who served before the ark of the covenant, as if they were the enemies of the Lord. Saul's mad act brings to sad fulfillment the judgment pronounced on the house of Eli in 2:31-32.

22:20-23. The judgment against the house of Eli speaks of one who would escape to weep and grieve (1 Sam 2:33). This prediction is fulfilled when Abiathar, the son of Ahimelech, escapes the massacre and flees to David (v. 20) and reports the news of this tragedy to David (v. 21). In contrast to Saul's irresponsible actions, David immediately takes the responsibility (v. 22). He remembers seeing Doeg, and he says flatly, "I am responsible for the lives of all your father's house." It is Saul who has acted like a criminal, and it is David who acts like a king. David receives Abiathar into his entourage with reassurance, along with the warning that Abiathar is now marked by Saul even as David is marked (v. 23).

REFLECTIONS

What can be said about the violent madness seen in a story such as this? We want to cry out in protest. Truthfully we want God to do something about it—to intervene. After all, we have seen constant evidences of God's hand moving David toward Israel's future. We have seen God rejecting Saul, and an evil spirit from God coming to plague him. Is not God in control here? But in the books of Samuel, God is at work largely through and in spite of human agency. God does not remove either David or Saul from responsibility for his own actions. Even the evil spirit that plagues Saul is an indication of his alienation from divine power and the guidance of God's Spirit, but it is not in evidence as a coercive power making Saul's decisions for him.

The hard truth of this terrible story is that Saul has become an evil man. He was not inherently so or destined to be so. He is not devoid of qualities even now that arouse our sympathy. But he has become evil in the obsessive desire to maintain his hold on power. At its worst, evil cannot distinguish between friend and foe, and now Saul has turned on his allies and imagines conspiracy from his friends. The outcome is terrible to behold.

The hard truth of human freedom is that God does not stay the hand of one bent on evil. God does not intervene to save the priests of Nob, whose lives are devoted to the service of the Lord. In our own century, we wish that God had stayed the hand of evil—in the holocaust deaths of millions in the death camps, in the genocidal wars and ethnic cleansings of resurgent tribalism and nationalism, in Vietnamese villages destroyed in misbegotten efforts to save them—but God has not intervened. In our time, as in Saul's, human freedom may be used for evil. The desire to gain or maintain power over others still leads to acts of mindless violence.

God does not intervene to prevent the possibilities of evil in the service of power. In 1 Samuel, God is at work making clear that Israel's future of promise lies with David and that Saul cannot be that future. But God, in these stories, works through human agency. If God is with David, it is not to supernaturally predetermine his successes. They are the product of David's gifts used in the service of God. Unfortunately, this story is centered on a man alienated from God, and God does not limit what Saul can do in the grip of evil and madness. The trust that God gives in human freedom, which is apparent in the books of Samuel, means that such freedom can be used for good or for evil. We know this is also true in our own time, for acts of terrible violence are a part of our daily news. If God is present at such times, it is not to make decisions or to determine actions for us. It is to support and enable the response of good in the face of evil. It is to provide alternatives for our future that move away from evil.

In this story, David models what is required in the face of evil. David takes responsibility for what has come to pass and moves on toward God's future. The violence was Saul's, but it is David who says, "I am responsible." The priests of Nob are tragically gone, but Abiathar can be sheltered, and a different kingdom from Saul's can be brought into being. The realities of evil are evident in every generation. The names Auschwitz, My Lai, Soweto, Hiroshima, Belfast, Sarajevo, Rwanda, Mogadishu, and Selma are a partial roll call of evil in our own time. Those who would participate in the bringing of God's future cannot be those who say, "We had nothing to do with those things." God's future lies with those who, like David, say, "We are responsible." It is a choosing of responsibility when the perpetrators of evil have chosen irresponsibility. As David then offered to Abiathar, we must also then offer the vision of a future free from fear, allied with life, and safe for all (1 Sam 22:23).

1 Samuel 23:1-29, Narrow Escapes from Saul

COMMENTARY

On first glance this chapter has nothing new to tell us. Saul—still obsessive and dangerous—is pursuing David. David stays just out of Saul's reach by virtue of his own wits and astute judgment. At first this seems to be just another chase and escape episode. But on second reading, some important additions to the portrayal of David's character appear. In his rescue of the inhabitants of Keilah (vv. 1-5), David risks his own best interests for the sake of others in need. There seems to be little to gain politically, and Keilah does not prove grateful or reliable (v. 12). David, however, shows himself capable of more than pragmatic, political self-interest. In addition, the entire episode with Keilah shows David engaged in an ongoing exchange with God that seems both natural and comfortable. He inquires of God as a matter of course in important matters. We have seen David gaining support throughout the preceding chapters. Although he is a fugitive, it is clear that David is Israel's future and Saul is in decline. Now v. 14*b* makes clear why Saul cannot succeed in his efforts to destroy David, "Saul sought him every day but the LORD did not give him into his hand." What we witness here is not constant divine, supernatural intervention. It is the simple truth that David, as a man who inquires naturally and regularly of God, has the strength of faith at his disposal. Along with his own courage and resourcefulness David has the resources of his own trustful relationship with God, and for the narrator of these chapters that makes all the difference between David and Saul. God is committed to David as Israel's future and is present in these events to bring that future to pass, but David must trust and act in accord with that divine commitment. It is not enough to trust in his own considerable gifts. Saul, however, has given in entirely to his own self-interested need for power and to violence in support of maintaining that power.

23:1-5. A report reaches David that the Judean city Keilah is under attack by the Philistines, who were apparently taking grain from the threshing floors (v. 1). Keilah was in the region of Judah, close to Philistine territory and vulnerable to attack. Faced with a situation calling for action, David prays. He asks God if he should go to Keilah's aid. God's answer is, "Yes! Go! Save them!" (v. 2). We are not told the means of inquiry. It may have been by use of the ephod in the possession of Abiathar and mentioned in v. 6 (see chap. 14 on use of the ephod to inquire of God). It is significant that David is immediately responsive to Keilah's predicament. No special tie to this town is mentioned; there is no obvious political advantage to David. Rather, the risk is great to David, not only from the Philistines, but also, as events develop, from exposing himself to the pursuit of Saul. Apart from building general goodwill in Judah, David's primary motivation seems to be compassion for Keilah's plight.

David's men are afraid (v. 3). It is understandable that fighting the Philistines almost on the borders of Philistia might be a daunting prospect. To allay their fears, David prays again (v. 4). This time the Lord's response is even more specific, "I will give them into your hand." So David fights for Keilah and is victorious (v. 5). He captures the Philistine livestock and delivers the city. The narrative focuses on David, both as a man of prayer and as a man of action. It is a combination seldom seen for Saul. Even in chap. 14, where he consults God through his priest, Saul seems unwilling to act in trust of the guidance he has sought.

23:6-14. Verse 6 notes the presence of Abiathar and the ephod he carries as a part of David's retinue. The resources of the religious establishment of Israel (what is left of it) are now with David.

The scene then shifts to Saul and his obsession with David. Saul believes David has made a mistake by entering a closed city where he can be trapped (v. 7), hence Saul gathers his army for a siege of Keilah (v. 8). The situation is reminiscent of those who thought they had Samson trapped inside a city (Judg 16:1-3). It is interesting that Saul here voices the belief that God has given David into his hand—an unbelievable delusion on the part of Saul, who has just slaughtered all of God's priests. Either he is deluded and unaware of his true situation, or he refuses to acknowledge it. The truth is made clear to the reader at the end of this episode: "The LORD did not give him into his hand" (v. 14b).

We are not told how, but word of Saul's mobilization reaches David, whereupon he summons Abiathar (v. 9). Now David explicitly uses the ephod to inquire of the Lord. He asks if Saul really will come against Keilah, and God responds that Saul will (vv. 10-11). Twice in this inquiry David refers to himself as God's servant. He is also clear that Keilah is endangered because of him. David inquires further. Will the men of Keilah surrender David to save themselves? The Lord answers that they will (v. 12). David cannot stay. With his six hundred men, he leaves Keilah before Saul can arrive (v. 13). Having no destination, they "wandered wherever they could go." Saul gives up the siege of Keilah, but not the pursuit. Verse 14 says that he seeks David every day. David stays in the hill country, finally moving to the wilderness of Ziph, an area closer to Hebron.

23:15-18. Verse 15 actually begins in the MT with "David saw," but the unpointed consonants of the verb are identical to the verb "to be afraid." It does not make sense that David is just now "learning/saw" that Saul had come out to kill him (as the NRSV and the NIV have it). In the light of Jonathan's reassurance in v. 17, it would seem that this episode begins in v. 15 by noting David's fear, his vulnerability: "David was afraid, for Saul had come out to seek his life; David was in the wilderness of Ziph, at Horesh."

It is in the time of David's fear that his friend Jonathan comes to him (v. 16). We hear nothing of the communication or the logistics that made this possible. In the moment of need, Jonathan is there to strengthen him, but he does so "through the LORD." This is a friendship shared in the context of faith. Jonathan seems to understand that they participate in the larger purposes of God's future for Israel. Jonathan's initial words are words of reassurance that we associate with divine messengers, "Fear not!" Jonathan speaks further in the confident tones of pronouncement. David need not fear, because Saul will not find him—because David will be king—because Jonathan gives up his first position in inheritance of the throne to become second to David—because even Saul knows that this is true (v. 17). This is a remarkable series of assertions. Perhaps the confident tone is because Jonathan spoke "through the LORD." The mood is almost one of prophetic pronouncement. Most amazing is Jonathan's final assertion that Saul also knows David will be king. We do not question that what Jonathan says is true. We have suspected that Saul's compulsive pursuit of David is rooted in what Saul dares not admit to himself. Now his son has said aloud what Saul cannot himself yet voice. That final confession of David as Israel's future king is yet to come from Saul himself (24:20). All know the truth of David's coming kingship. Saul will be the last to know, or at least to acknowledge publicly that he knows. Again the friends covenant together (as in 18:3; 20:16-17), and they go their separate ways. It is their last face-to-face meeting.

23:19-29. This chapter contains yet one more tale of escape. Perhaps the author intends that we not forget that David still has enemies and the danger is real. We have seen support coming to him so often in the previous stories that we may forget how perilous David's situation really is.

While David is hiding in the region of Ziph, some men of that region go to Saul at Gibeah. They reveal David's hiding place and offer to hand him over to the king (vv. 19-20). Saul's response is ironic. He invokes God's blessing on these Ziphites for showing him "compassion" (חמל hāmal, v. 21). It is the very word used when Saul spared King Agag's life in 15:3, 9, 15. Now he would connect compassion with the taking of David's life. He sends the men of Ziph back for a precise reconnaissance and promises to join them for the final hunt when David is located (vv. 22-23). Saul recognizes that David is "very cunning" (v. 22) and knows that capture of David is no sure thing until it is accomplished.

The time for speeches is over. Verses 24-29 are all action—a kind of cat and mouse game. Saul is now on the chase, and David is on the run (v. 25). In the wilderness of Maon, Saul gets close to his objective. David is on one side of a mountain and Saul on the other, but

Saul seems to be circling in on his prey (v. 26). Just then messengers come with word of a Philistine attack (v. 27). We are not told precisely where or in what strength, but it is a situation serious enough to cause Saul to break off the effort to capture David and to turn his attention to the Philistines (v. 28). Even Saul cannot ignore the threat Philistines posed to Israel's survival. How ironic that the Philistines whom David attacked at the beginning of the chapter should save him now. They name the place "Rock of Division or Parting" or "Rock of Escape" to commemorate this incident. David makes good his escape and moves to En-gedi, beside the Dead Sea (v. 29).

REFLECTIONS

Once again this chapter invites us to ponder the interrelationship between divine will and human circumstances. In these escape stories, God does not dramatically intervene to save David. Everything is explainable in human terms. David takes courageous action; he makes wise decisions; he reacts swiftly to circumstances. Yet the narrative is confident that divine providence is at work. The workings of divine grace are not radically separated in character from the workings of David's considerable human skills.

Especially significant is David's confidence that divine providence plays a role even as he marshals and uses his own skills effectively. He not only acts, but he also prays. He has resources of faith as well as a capable mind, a fleet foot, and a strong arm. His prayers do not seem perfunctory or merely habitual. David prays and acts in crisis situations as if both efforts make a difference. This suggests that for the narrator of these stories divine providence is understood to require both the trust and the agency of David. God is at work, but God also counts on David to be at work. It is together that God and David will bring Israel's future.

For people of faith in the modern church the temptation is often to separate the workings of divine providence from our own human agency. Even further, many choose to emphasize only one or the other. Some imagine they can pray for God's will and do nothing. Others seem to think they can build the kingdom of God by their own efforts alone. Prayer groups and social action committees in congregations frequently have no overlapping membership. David models a different response. His constant combination of prayer and action suggests that we, too, must stand in the tension between trust in what God is doing and response as we ourselves do what we can do. It is, perhaps, trustful prayer that enables wise discernment of what we must do. In discussion of David's story, I have heard some remark that they wish God were with them as God was with David. Perhaps it takes bold prayer, like David's, to claim the truth that God *is* with us in our own faithful actions to move toward God's future.

1 Samuel 24:1-22, David Spares Saul's Life

COMMENTARY

One of the dangers of power is its seduction to violence.[153] The temptation is to resort to violence as a way of gaining, maintaining, or holding on to power. Saul has fallen victim to this temptation. Although he did not gain his throne by violence, but by the gift of God, he has resorted to increasing violence as he felt power shifting from himself toward David. Thus far, the balance of power has

153. Brueggemann, *Power, Providence, and Personality*, 49-89, has used the stories of David's rise to kingship as the focus for reflection on the interrelationship of power and violence. He has given special attention to 1 Samuel 24–26 as crucial for understanding David's relationship to these issues. My own discussion is indebted at many points to the stimulus of his treatment of these chapters.

been on Saul's side. He is the king; he has the power. As the popularity of David grew, Saul first became violent toward David himself. David was forced to become a fugitive from Saul's murderous intentions. But violence tends to breed violence. Saul's paranoid grasping after his own power led to violent turns toward those who supported David, and eventually toward those he only imagined to support David. His violence lashed out at his own son Jonathan, his own servants, and in deadliest fashion to the whole community of the priests of Nob.

In chaps. 18–23, as Saul's bent to violence increased, his hold on power ironically decreased. We have seen in these chapters a shifting of power away from Saul and toward David, as one after another the witnesses to David's future kingship step forward. At the beginning of these chapters, Saul was powerful and David was vulnerable; but in 1 Samuel 24 the situation is reversed. In this episode, it will be Saul who is vulnerable and David who holds power over his life. In the final speech of this chapter, Saul himself will finally confess this knowledge that David will be king (24:20). The shift of power to David is finally complete; even Saul must acknowledge it. It is a great reversal like those Hannah's song foresees (1 Sam 2:1-10). The eighth son from a family of little influence or wealth, forced to live as an outlaw and fugitive, nevertheless will be Israel's future king because he is the man after God's own heart (13:14).

In this great reversal of power, David now faces the temptation to violence that power brings. This is the first of three chapters (chaps. 24–26) that focus on whether David will use violence in order to gain or hold power. Like Saul, power has come to him as a gift. Will he, like Saul, resort to the violence that power makes so readily available?

Chapter 24 relates an incident in which Saul's life is unexpectedly placed in David's hands, but out of respect for God's anointed one David cannot kill him, as his men urge him to do. Instead he cuts off a piece of Saul's robe and uses it to confront Saul. David speaks of his own innocence and compassion, and he presents the evidence of his sparing of Saul. Saul, shocked out of his madness into lucidity, confesses his own repayment of David's goodness by evil and acknowledges that the

future of Israel's kingship lies with David. The chapter is organized with a succinct narrative account of the incident (vv. 1-7), followed by the two lengthy and eloquent speeches, the first by David (vv. 8-15) and the second by Saul (vv. 16-21).

This episode is closely paralleled by the story in 1 Samuel 26. Most scholars believe that these stories are variant witnesses to the same incident. Although some details differ, there are extensive similarities of language, detail, and theme in the two accounts.[154] There is no agreement on which account is earlier or more authentic. In the present arrangement, the two similar episodes are used to build a sequence (with the story of David/Nabal/Abigail in 1 Samuel 25 between them) on David's facing of issues of power, violence, bloodguilt, and innocence.

The viewpoint of the narrator and editor of these stories as they now stand is that David refused to gain or hold power by violence. David spares Saul's life (v. 24); he is persuaded by Abigail to spare Nabal (v. 25); he spares Saul again (v. 26).[155] In this first episode of the sequence in chaps. 24–26, David has the opportunity to kill Saul, who has become his enemy and seeks his life, but David refuses. The claim of the story is that David is free of bloodguilt toward the house of Saul. He did not gain power by raising his own hand against God's anointed one. He has received the kingdom as the gift of God's grace and not by the grasp of his own hand.[156] The story suggests that David models an alternative to the usual power arrangements and breaks the connection of power with violence, although he must live close to its temptations. Subsequent chapters continue to raise these issues. Can such an alternative to the interconnections of power and violence be maintained?

---

154. Klein, *1 Samuel*, 236-37, gives a detailed chart of the extensive parallels between 1 Samuel 24 and 26.

155. Traditional historical-critical treatments of these chapters have been preoccupied with similarities between chaps. 24 and 26 and have focused on questions concerning historicity and the history of composition. More recent commentators have observed that the sequence of chaps. 24–26 as it now stands serves to shift from David as one whose life is endangered to David as one who spares life. Each of these chapters is connected to important earlier themes in the narrative of David's rise. Polzin, *Samuel and the Deuteronomist*, 203-15, provides an excellent and representative discussion of these matters.

156. Gunn, "David and the Gift of the Kingdom," 14-45, has helpfully developed the categories of gift and grasp for understanding the successes and failures of David. When David receives the kingdom as a gift of God and acts accordingly, all is well; but when David attempts to grasp the power of the kingdom for his own purposes, all goes awry.

24:1-7. Surely this story was told with amazement and humor. Saul again receives a report on David's whereabouts (v. 1). He sets out with three thousand men into the wilderness around En-gedi (v. 2). Saul comes to a convenient cave and, feeling the urge of nature, he goes inside to defecate (v. 3*a*). The expression "to cover his feet" is a euphemism for this bodily function. Saul's circumstances are surely intended to emphasize both the fact that he had reason to enter the cave alone and that he was in an extremely vulnerable position. Remarkably, David and his men are hiding in the back of this very cave (v. 3*b*). It is an astonishing turn of events. The hunter has now become the potential prey.

David's men are immediately certain that this opportunity has been given to them by the Lord, and they urge David to take advantage of it. They quote a promise of the Lord, unknown to us elsewhere, that predicts a day when the Lord will give the enemy into David's hand and he should "do to him as it seems good to you" (v. 4*a*). They clearly have in mind the ending of Saul's pursuit by the ending of Saul's life. Perhaps David is tempted by this; the text does not say. But clearly he will lose face or leadership if he does nothing with such an opportunity. The possibility of violence could easily be justified in such circumstances. Saul has amply made clear his violent intent toward David. With Saul gone, would not David's way be clear to the throne? We imagine many such possibilities churning within David, but what he does amazes us (and surely his men as well). He creeps forward and cuts off a piece of Saul's robe (v. 4*b*).

How could this happen? The text is short on details. Perhaps it was very dark, and they were very close. Perhaps Saul had laid his robe aside while relieving himself. Perhaps he fell asleep afterward. The focus is not on the details, but the act itself is full of meaning. We know that the royal robe itself is a powerful symbol of authority. Jonathan symbolizes his willingness to pass royal authority on to David by clothing him in his own robe in 18:4. The torn robe of Samuel in 15:28 was used by the prophet to symbolize the tearing of the kingdom from Saul and giving it to his neighbor, "who is better than you." Now David holds in his hand the torn piece of Saul's robe, and

Saul's very life is effectively in David's power. The verb "cut off" (כרת *kārat*) is used four times in this chapter (vv. 4, 5, 12, 22). Jonathan uses this verb to plead with David that his family not be "cut off" when David comes to the throne (20:14-16), and at the end of this encounter Saul will similarly ask David to swear that he will not "cut off" Saul's family or name in Israel (v. 21). David Gunn makes a plausible case that the literal phrase here, "to cut off the skirt," is a euphemism for cutting off the penis, thus leaving Saul without manhood or future. David does not actually do this, but the phrase suggests to the audience of this story the possibility of this drastic act and the extent of Saul's vulnerability.[157] This act of cutting off potentially represents David's power over Saul's life, over his royal authority, over his manhood, over his descendants, and over his future.

David has acted magnanimously and spared Saul's life, but he is still immediately filled with remorse. He is "stricken to the heart" (v. 5) at what he has done, but one has the impression that he is most devastated by what he might have done. He refers to Saul twice in v. 6 as "the Lord's anointed" and calls him "my lord." David's fear is that he might have "raised my hand against him." David has acted with compassion, but he has stared into the abyss of violence. He knows how close he was to raising his hand against the Lord's anointed one. Power has been shifting from Saul to David, and now Saul is completely in David's power. David knows the ease by which vulnerability can be violently exploited and how thin is the line between knowing this and acting on it. He is overwhelmed by what he has discovered within himself. On this occasion he holds back the violence and resists it successfully. At a later point in David's story, at the height of his royal power, he gives in. He takes Bathsheba, and he kills Uriah (2 Samuel 11). Even now, in a cave in the Judean wilderness, David knows and recoils from this capacity within himself.

David's stress on Saul as "the Lord's anointed" (twice in v. 5) also shows a knowledge on David's part that to strike Saul is to strike the office itself. He comes back to his respect for the office of "the Lord's anointed"

157. Gunn, *The Fate of King Saul,* 92-95.

when he speaks to Saul (v. 10). After all, David is himself "the LORD's anointed." The respect for one designated by the Lord may be genuine, but it cannot be without some degree of self-interest. David surely does not want to set a precedent that violence can be legitimately authorized against one God has chosen.[158] David restrains his men, perhaps with some difficulty, since he is forced to "scold them severely," and allows Saul to exit the cave (v. 7).

24:8-15. David follows Saul from the cave and places himself in the vulnerable position. He addresses Saul respectfully by his office as "My lord, the king" and bows to the ground in homage (v. 8). We do not immediately have Saul's reaction, for David begins a lengthy speech.

David first declares himself innocent of the charge that he ever desired to harm Saul (v. 9). We must remember that while David is speaking to Saul within the story, the larger narrative is defending David of such a charge. David offers as dramatic evidence of his innocence the piece of Saul's robe and rehearses the circumstances of Saul's vulnerability in the cave (vv. 10-11). David is explicit about what might have happened, "I could have killed you; others urged me to do it." David even uses the language of divine providence, "The LORD gave you into my hand" (v. 10). This is the language used most often in holy war for the disposal of God's enemies. David implies that Saul has become God's enemy, and David could have been the instrument of God's judgment on Saul. But David "spared" him.

At the moment David shows Saul the piece of robe, the evidence of his compassion, he shifts to more intimate language and calls Saul "my father" (v. 11a). David contrasts his action with Saul's, "I have not sinned . . . you are hunting me" (v. 11b).

Finally, David shifts to juridical language in his appeal to Saul (v. 12). David is willing to let the Lord judge between them. David has not taken vengeance but will leave such vengeance to God: "My hand shall not be against you." He reinforces this affirmation with a saying, "Out of the wicked comes forth wickedness" (v. 13). David is not among the wicked, so his hand will not do violence to Saul. By contrast, Saul, the king of Israel, seeks to do violence—and against whom? David self-deprecatingly describes himself as "a dead dog" or "a flea" (v. 14) compared to Saul's royal power. David's refusal to raise a hand against Saul seems more than a refusal for the moment; it seems almost to be a vow. David will not seize the throne by violence against the person of Saul. It is for the Lord to judge such things, not David, and David is certain that in the Lord's judgment he will be vindicated (v. 15).

David's speech is a remarkable and impassioned refusal of the usual patterns of power and violence. He chooses not to take vengeance and seize power over Saul, who has become his enemy. Although the word is not used, David in effect forgives Saul and offers to end the enmity between them. By a bold act of compassion, David breaks the cycle of violence that Saul has initiated.

24:16-22. Saul now speaks. We have been in suspense, wondering what his response might be. It is not what we would expect: "Is this your voice, my son David?" (v. 16). Saul returns the intimate address of David, who spoke to him as a father (v. 11). We remember that once Saul loved David (16:21). Brueggemann has pointed out that Saul's plaintive question echoes the question of the aged Isaac, uncertain of the identity of his son (Gen 27:18, 32).[159] The effect is to stress Saul's vulnerability and fearfulness. Like the blessing stolen from Isaac by Jacob, the kingdom is about to be transferred from a once, but no longer, powerful Saul to the bold youth of David.

Before speaking further, Saul weeps (v. 16b). It is a moment filled with pathos. One imagines all the failed possibilities for Saul's life caught up in this weeping. David has made Saul face what he has become. Perhaps he weeps for what he might have been or what he once was.

The Saul who speaks after the weeping seems a different man from the one we have seen in recent chapters of the story. He can lucidly face and speak the truth of his life, although it is a harsh truth. He begins with the juridical language that concluded David's speech, and he pronounces a verdict

---

158. This element of David's self-interest is discussed very helpfully in Keith Whitelam, "The Defense of David," *JSOT* 29 (1984) 73.

159. Brueggemann, *First and Second Samuel*, 171.

(v. 17): David is the righteous one in this conflict. Saul has repaid good with evil. Saul equates his actions with evil. Out of Saul's own mouth, David is acquitted and declared righteous. The telling of this story will vindicate David from charges of conspiring against Saul. It is an unexpected reversal: The fugitive is righteous and good; the king is evil. One is reminded of the same verdict ("she is more righteous than I") by Judah concerning Tamar when she was about to be executed (Gen 38:26).

Saul continues in a remarkable series of candid acknowledgments. It is as if he is suddenly empowered to recognize and speak the truth, even though it convicts him of evil.

He acknowledges David's magnanimity in sparing his life (v. 18a).

He acknowledges that it was the Lord who gave him into David's hand (v. 18b).

He acknowledges that he cannot be David's enemy, for who would send an enemy away safely (v. 19a)?

He acknowledges that David deserves good as a reward for what he has done (v. 19b).

Finally, in one of the climactic moments of the history of David's rise, Saul utters the words "I know." His confession is what others in the story and the reader have known for some time: "I know that you shall surely be king, and that the kingdom of Israel is in your hand" (v. 20). The verb מלך (*mālak*) is formulated in a particularly emphatic way, "you shall surely be king." Saul is the last to know. Jonathan told David that Saul knew (23:17), but we must hear it from the mouth of Saul himself. Now the transition is complete. Saul has conceded the kingdom and acknowledged David as the future—a future Saul had failed to forestall.

Saul has one final plea. He asks David to swear an oath that he will not "cut off" his descendants after him or wipe out his name (v. 21). The verb "cut off" is the same as the word used for the action of "cutting off" Saul's robe; thus David holds Saul's future in his hands. But David had already made a covenant with Jonathan not to "cut off" his descendants (20:14-17). Even in this matter, David has acted ahead of Saul in "steadfast love" (*hesed*) toward Jonathan. David swears this also to Saul, but with no comment (v. 22).

The two depart, but Saul to Gibeah and David to his wilderness stronghold. Saul may have acknowledged David's coming kingship, but David will not put himself into Saul's hand again. The transfer of power is complete, but the final days of Saul must still be completed; David must wait.

REFLECTIONS

Even Saul has now confessed David as Israel's future. It is an important moment in the plot of this story, but the context in which this confession comes is equally important because this moment has not been reached by the usual power arrangements. Power has been transferring to David throughout these stories, but David has not used it to seize the kingdom. In this dramatic episode, Saul, who has become David's enemy, is in David's power. David could have killed him, but he did not. He spared Saul. David was even remorseful over his temptation to do violence against Saul. He refused to exploit Saul's vulnerability and returned good for evil. He refused to act in vengeance. These are not the usual ways in which power is exercised in David's world—or, for that matter, in our own. It reminds us of Hannah's song, which already signaled that the coming of God's kingdom would be marked by reversals from the usual patterns of power: "The LORD makes poor and makes rich; he brings low, he also exalts" (2:7).

In David's action in this story, we see one whose final moment in receiving power is enabled by forgiveness and compassion. He breaks the cycle of violence and vengeance, and new possibilities are opened. Even Saul is freed for a lucid moment of knowing and speaking the truth—about David, about himself, about the future of Israel. All who come to hold power must face the issues of violence. There is no alternative in the human world. Power always lives close to the possibilities of violence by some means. In this story, it is David who must face that reality. He must look squarely at the possibility of violence within himself. He quails at what he sees, for violence is closer to the surface than most are forced to recognize or admit. But he does not give in to the violence within him.

To hold power does not mean that we will surrender to our violent impulses. David models an alternative to such surrender. Compassion, remorse, forgiveness, and responsibility can allow power to turn from violence. Such qualities of grace can break the tenacious connection between power and violence and allow new options.

To forgive and to act with compassion does not mean to ignore the realities of violence and evil that confront us. David's appeal to Saul asked for an end to pursuit and a declaration of innocence. But to follow David's alternative way is to refuse to return violence with violence. Recent studies in the patterns of abuse within families document the sad truth that many victims become victimizers themselves. They are caught in a vicious and continuous cycle of abuse and violence. The cycle is broken not by acceptance of the evil done, but by forgiveness that frees the victim from the need for vengeance and enables a new future. David and Saul do not go home together as if nothing had ever happened between them, but David's bold refusal of violence and his compassion on his own enemy broke the cycle and enabled them to go their separate ways into a new future.

It would seem that this alternative of forgiveness and compassion holds the hope for breaking some of the societal patterns of violence in which we are enmeshed as well. One wonders if widespread and strident support for capital punishment and the right to carry concealed weapons is not the desire for vengeance that returns violence for the violent assaults of crime, drug trafficking, and loss of respect for authority that afflict our communities. The desire to return violence for violence is a part of longstanding conflicts such as the Israeli/Palestinian hostilities. When Soviet-sponsored oppression was lifted from the Balkan states, freedom did not lead to peace but to vengeful ethnic cleansings, inflicting violence on supposed enemies in return for years of violence suffered under oppression. Such cycles of violence can go on endlessly unless someone courageously breaks the cycle.

What might happen if persons in power chose to practice a politics of compassion and forgiveness in place of the politics of coercion, manipulation, and violence? What would happen if the alternative practiced by David replaced the usual patterns of power? The kingdom gained by compassion and not by violence was the dream of prophets who hoped for a time when swords would be beaten into plowshares (Isa 2:4; Mic 4:3). For Christians, such an alternative is modeled in Jesus of Nazareth, who announced a kingdom that did not conform to the usual power arrangements—that called for the forgiveness of enemies (Matt 5:24; Luke 6:27, 35), the love of the neighbor (Matt 22:39; Mark 12:31; Luke 10:25-37), the giving of one's life for the sake of the kingdom (Matt 10:39; Mark 8:35; Luke 17:33). In 1 Samuel 24 and David's refusal to gain the kingdom by violence, we can, perhaps, see why the early church also proclaimed Jesus of Nazareth to be the son of David.

1 Samuel 25:1-44, Abigail Saves David from Bloodguilt

COMMENTARY

This is the second account in a sequence of three chapters dealing with the temptation to violence that comes with power. In each account, David's innocence of such violence is demonstrated, and his coming kingship is cleared from suspicion of bloodguilt. In chap. 24 and in the similar episode yet to come (chap. 26), David restrains his impulse to do violence against Saul and refuses to take the king's life. In chap. 25, David must be restrained by the intervention of Abigail to keep from incurring bloodguilt by taking revenge on her husband, Nabal.

Numerous scholars have commented on a sense of stereotyped character and formal, unrealistic plot to chap. 25. Berlin writes, "The plot, as well as the characters, is unrealistic. It could be reduced to: 'fair maiden' Abigail is freed from the 'wicked ogre' and marries 'prince charming.' This suggests that this is not just another episode in the biography of David, but an exemplum."[160] These observations in no way diminish the important role of chap. 25, particularly the role it plays in the sequence on David's refusal to use violence in chaps. 24–26. All three of these chapters, with long rhetorical speeches placed in the mouths of the key characters, seem somewhat artificial. This itself, however, may give us a clue that the author is using this sequence of chapters to make some major points of his own.[161]

Chapter 25 is constructed in such a way that character and plot point beyond the narrative boundaries of the chapter. We can sketch the broad outline of some of these interconnections and will discuss details in the verse-by-verse commentary.

The character of Nabal in this story seems to represent Saul in many details.[162] In the immediate context of chaps. 24–26, Nabal, like Saul, is spared from the vengeful hand of David, although chap. 25 requires the intervention of Abigail. Nabal is also one who returns evil for good, a characteristic Saul admits about himself (24:17). Nabal's name and actions are the marks of a fool (25:25) and reflect the confession Saul makes in 26:21, "I have been a fool." Nabal's response to David's request is to treat him as a servant breaking away from a master (25:10), which reflects David's treatment by Saul since chap. 19. Most important, Nabal's death, not by the hand of David but by the hand of the Lord, prefigures Saul's death. Abigail's speeches twice look ahead to Saul's death while also speaking of her husband. In 25:26, Abigail swears by the Lord, "Let your enemies and

those who seek to do evil to my lord be like Nabal." The only one "seeking" to do evil to David outside this story is Saul. When Abigail later says, "If anyone should rise up to pursue you and to seek your life" (v. 29a), it is impossible not to think of Saul's pursuit, which has dominated the story in recent chapters. She continues, "The lives of your enemies he [God] shall sling out as from the hollow of a sling" (v. 29b). Immediately we think of Goliath, vanquished by a stone from David's sling. But when Nabal is later struck dead by the Lord, the act is accompanied by the notice that "he became like a stone" (v. 37). David's enemies, whether Goliath, Nabal, or Saul, are slung out like a stone to their own death. Both Nabal and Saul die because they opposed David, and in doing so opposed God's future for Israel.

David is saved from incurring bloodguilt by Abigail, but in the process we are exposed to a darker side of David's character than we have seen thus far. Although he is restrained by Abigail's timely intervention, David is willing to kill, and to do so on a major scale in wiping out all the males in Nabal's household (v. 22). Some have characterized David's activity in this episode as a protection racketeer. This assessment will require discussion, but could add to the darker Davidic portrait drawn in this chapter. This side of David's character foreshadows a later time when his willingness to kill is not restrained, and he sends Uriah to his death in order to take Bathsheba for himself (2 Samuel 11). The consequences of this surrender to his own violent side are monumental for David and his family (2 Samuel 12–20). In both incidents, David seeks to kill a man and then marries his wife. Due to Abigail, who acts as an instrument of the Lord, David does not kill Nabal, and the later marriage is not tainted by bloodguilt. With Uriah and Bathsheba, David does kill, and the marriage is shadowed by blood.

Abigail is the central character in this episode, even though David's coming kingship remains the larger context. She appears as the agent through whose gifts the Lord is at work to restrain David from violence.[163] In contrast to Nabal and his foolishness, Abigail recognizes in David the future king of Israel and understands the danger that bloodguilt would

---

160. Berlin, "Characterization in Biblical Narrative," 77.
161. See Polzin, *Samuel and the Deuteronomist*, 268n. 10, for a response to critics who use the artifice of chaps. 24–26 as an excuse to dismiss their significance in the larger history.
162. Numerous scholars have noticed the Saul-Nabal connection. Polzin (*Samuel and the Deuteronomist*, 211-12) gives one of the more detailed discussions of the issue.

163. See Brueggemann, *Power, Providence, and Personality*, 62.

constitute to that kingship. It is through her remarkable human gifts that the word and will of God are made clear to David and he is able to step back from the danger. Her gifts include intelligence, beauty, excellence in speech, resourcefulness, and a willingness to take action. Levenson sees her as the model of the wise woman (contrasted to the fool) and relates her to the "ideal woman" of Prov 31:10-31.[164] Bach objects that she can hardly be the "ideal woman," since she "refers to her husband as a fool (v. 25), sides with his enemy, and does not even mourn his death." Bach sees her as a figure with prophetic connections, speaking God's word to David and pronouncing the first prophecy of a "sure house" for David (v. 28).[165] This phrase certainly looks ahead to Nathan's dynastic oracle in 2 Samuel 7. It may be significant that Abigail's story comes after the death of Samuel (v. 1) and before Nathan has entered the story. Abigail is the bridge between these prophets for God's Word, whether she holds an overt office as prophet or not. An additional element of Abigail's character has been recognized by Berlin, who sees her as a mirror image of Bathsheba.[166] Uriah is a good man, but Bathsheba can do nothing to save him. Nabal is a worthless man, but Abigail goes to great lengths to save him. David is drawn to Bathsheba in an encounter of illicit sex, but Abigail, though she marries David, is not involved sexually with him at all, and the marriage is completely legitimate. For Bathsheba, David kills; for Abigail, David refrains from killing.

Through the characters and the roles they play in this story, chap. 25 serves as the central piece in the defense of David (chaps. 24–26) against the charge of using violence to gain the throne. At the same time, this chapter brings to fruition the themes of divine destiny in David's rise and foreshadows the themes of dynasty and downfall in David's future.

25:1. With the briefest of notices, we learn that Samuel has died. It is the end of an important time of transition in Israel. For good or for ill, Israel now stands fully in the era of kings. Samuel had anointed Saul and presided over his rejection. He had anointed David and saw the beginnings of his rise to kingship. Perhaps the narrator has waited until this moment to report Samuel's death so that we can first hear the confession of David's kingship from the mouth of Saul himself (24:20). David's kingship and Israel's future are secure. The notice that David went down to the wilderness of Paran is changed by almost all commentators to read with the LXX, "the wilderness of Maon."

25:2-8. The story opens with the introduction of two characters we have not previously met. The first is Nabal, but we are introduced to his property and wealth before we ever learn his name (v. 2).[167] We are told that he is a "very great man" (NRSV; NIV, "rich"; the phrase probably indicates influence as well as wealth). He has "three thousand sheep and a thousand goats," and we are told that it is shearing time, a time of celebration and profit-making from the flocks. Finally (v. 3) we are told his name. This must have raised the eyebrows of Hebrew readers, for his name means "fool" or "churl." The word נבל (*nābāl*) appears frequently in wisdom contexts as the opposite of the wise man, one who is a glutton (Prov 30:22), a miser (Jer 17:11), who does not believe in God (Pss 14:1; 53:1), and is a general embarrassment (Prov 17:21). A *nābāl* is stupid, but in a vicious and mean-spirited manner, not in the harmless way of the simpleton. In v. 3*b*, Nabal is characterized as "surly and mean." Especially interesting is the long description of a *nābāl* in Isa 32:5-8, which includes the refusal of the *nābāl* to give food and drink to those in need of them (Isa 32:6), the precise violation of hospitality that Nabal commits against David in this story. Verse 3*b* also tells us that Nabal was a Calebite, one of the most influential clans of Judah, with its chief city in Hebron.

In the midst of v. 3 we are also briefly introduced to Abigail, who provides a contrast to Nabal. We are given her name first and then told that she is "clever/intelligent" (NRSV/ NIV) and "beautiful." The word used here is שׂכל (*śekel*, "understanding," "intellect"), and Abigail is said to have "good understanding." She is a striking contrast to her husband,

164. Jon D. Levenson, "1 Samuel 25 as Literature and History," *CBQ* 40 (1978) 11-28. This excellent article has influenced much of my understanding of this chapter.

165. Bach, "The Pleasure of Her Text," 29, 34.

166. Berlin, "Characterization in Biblical Narrative," 76.

167. Levenson, "1 Samuel 25 as Literature and History," 13-17, includes this observation in a detailed and helpful characterization of Nabal.

who is "surly and mean," but we cannot help thinking that she matches better with David, who is described as "handsome" in 16:12, using the same term as used here for Abigail's beauty. Both have inner qualities of "heart" (David) and "understanding/intelligence" (Abigail) that distinguish them beyond their good looks.

The action of the story begins with a delegation of ten men sent from David, who had heard it was shearing time (vv. 4-5). This time was one of revelry and feasting, and David believes this is the opportune moment to make a request of Nabal in Carmel. The emissaries are given careful instructions in courtesy and respect. They are to greet Nabal with a threefold greeting of "Peace" (שלום *šālôm*), a wish for well-being and wholeness to Nabal, to his house, and to all he has (v. 6). David's request is then to be conveyed to Nabal. His men have been with Nabal's shepherds, and David avows that no harm has come to them and nothing has been missing during that time (v. 7). On the basis of this protection, he asks for consideration at this feast time and is willing to take whatever Nabal might have at hand to give them by way of provisions (v. 8). David closes his message by referring to himself and his men as Nabal's servants, and to himself as "your son David," an intimate term of address used by Saul in chaps. 24 and 26 to address David.

Is this request legitimate or is it a veiled threat? Some commentators have seen David's greeting of peace and his statement affirming that the shepherds have not been harmed as veiled language for the lack of peace and the harm that will come to the shepherds if his request is not granted. In this view, David is a racketeer engaged in a protection scam.[168] This view seems more influenced by old gangster movies than by the biblical narrative. The shepherds themselves elaborate enthusiastically about David to Abigail and describe David's men as "a wall to us both night and day" (v. 16). In the protection rackets of gangster imagery, no real protection is ever given from any danger except from the collectors themselves. In the wilderness areas of Judah, the dangers to flocks from predators and thieves were quite real, but with David's men there, no sheep

had been lost (even to David's men). Nabal's shepherds seem to believe that the presence and protection of David's men is an asset. David himself seems to believe that a genuine service had been rendered (v. 21). Certainly David's request seems respectful rather than demanding, although one would think that the simple rules of hospitality and common sense would warn Nabal against offending a man with an armed band of six hundred men. It would seem well for us to avoid seeing David's request as racketeering without further information on the customs of the time in such matters.

25:9-13. After Nabal has heard the request from David's men (v. 9), his response is as contemptuous as their tone had been respectful. He asks mockingly, "Who is David? Who is the son of Jesse?" (v. 10a). The implication is that David is a nobody. Even worse, Nabal suggests that David is no more than a runaway servant or slave, escaping from a master (v. 10b). The reference may be intended for us to think of Saul's pursuit of his "servant" David. There is considerable irony here, since a few verses later Nabal's own servants turn against him, describing him as "so ill-natured that no one can speak to him" (v. 17). Nabal ends his contemptuous response by claiming that his food and drink are for his own shearers and not for men without standing, like David and his entourage (v. 11). Not only has Nabal refused the request, but also he has demeaned those who brought it.

David's response is swift and harsh. Upon hearing the report (v. 12), David orders his men to strap on their swords and arms himself as well. He leaves two hundred men to guard the baggage and sets out with four hundred armed men (v. 13). David clearly intends to revenge the insult to his men and their request with violence, and unlike his opportunities to strike Saul (chaps. 24 and 26), he does not hesitate to choose this violent course of action.

25:14-17. Remarkably one of Nabal's servants comes to Abigail in distress about the situation (v. 14). He appears to be one of the shepherds in the field, for he seems to know of David and his men and to represent those who enjoyed their protection while in the field. He speaks of this experience with David in the first-person plural, and, as we

168. See, e.g., Brueggemann, *First and Second Samuel,* 176, 179.

have noted, he speaks to Abigail very positively about David and the servants' relationship to him (vv. 15-16). Somehow he has learned of Nabal's insults to David's messengers and reports to Abigail of her husband's behavior (v. 14b). He also seems to know that this response will bring disaster ("evil") upon Nabal's whole household (v. 17). Whether he has a report of David's armed approach or simply knows from experience how David will respond we do not know. It is clear that he expects Abigail to be able to do something about the situation. He calls Nabal a בן-בליעל (ben-bĕliyya'al), "a worthless man, a good-for-nothing" (NRSV, "ill-natured"; NIV, "wicked man"). This is the same term used of those who were contemptuous of Saul in 10:26-27; Nabal has, like them, spurned the future king. The same term was also used of Eli's worthless sons (2:12) and of Eli's mistaken judgment about Hannah (1:16). Nabal is now labeled by his own servant as a worthless fool. But the servant clearly hopes for more from Abigail.

25:18-31. Abigail takes over the story at this point. If David was quick to take action for violence, Abigail matches his decisiveness in the effort to avoid violence. She takes action by gathering elaborate provisions for David's men. The narrative lingers over the precise details of the food and drink as they are loaded on donkeys, perhaps marveling at Abigail's ability to assemble so much on such short notice (v. 18). She sends the provisions on ahead with servants, promising that she herself will follow (v. 19). One is reminded of the gifts sent ahead by Jacob to soothe a potentially murderous Esau (Genesis 32). The narrative makes a point of noting that she does not tell her husband, Nabal (v. 19b).

Abigail follows after the provisions on her donkey, whereupon she meets David and his men on the way (v. 20). It is noteworthy that she is not willing to sit home and hope the provisions will appease David. Her own personal involvement carries considerable risk, given the hostile intentions of David. The meeting of Abigail with David gives the narrator the opportunity to reemphasize that hostile intent. We are given access to David's vow of vengeance (vv. 21-22). David recalls his protection of Nabal's men and flocks and characterizes what Nabal has done as having

"returned me evil for good." This clearly links Nabal with Saul in 24:17 and suggests that the narrator does not see David as being engaged in some morally questionable scam. But David is on the brink of violence for the sake of vengeance, having vowed to kill all the males of Nabal's household (v. 22). The Hebrew text here translates literally "all who piss upon the wall," a euphemism for male gender by reference to their means of urination (cf. v. 34).

The account returns to Abigail, who dismounts and falls on the ground in obeisance before David (v. 23). At this point the focus shifts from the actions of Abigail to the speech of Abigail. She is as eloquent as she is decisive, but she is also strategic. Constantly throughout her speeches she addresses David as "my lord" and speaks of herself as "your servant," literally "your maidservant." Her initial words are disarming in the light of David's vow. She boldly claims all the guilt as hers alone (v. 24). What is David to do? He has vowed the death of all males in Nabal's household, and a woman is now taking all the blame. At the very least it blunts David's resolve and allows her a hearing. Although she has accepted blame, she does not hesitate to indicate where actual blame belongs, nor is she reluctant to describe her husband with candor (v. 25a). She pleads that David not take seriously an איש הבליעל (*'iš habbĕliyya'al*), a "worthless man." She boldly claims that his name, "Nabal," describes him. "Fool [*nābāl*] is his name, and folly [נבלה *nĕbālâ*] is with him." (Isa 32:5 also makes this connection, "For the fool utters foolishness [*nĕbālâ*].") She subtly contrasts herself to her husband. If David had dealt with her, none of this would have happened, but she did not see the young men David sent (v. 25b).

Abigail counters David's vow with a vow of her own, taken in the name of the Lord and of David's own life (v. 26a). Abigail's language in this section of her speech makes constant reference to the Lord (Yahweh) and to what the Lord is doing in these events. Abigail gives voice to the word and will of God here in a manner very reminiscent of the prophets. She claims that the Lord has restrained David from bloodguilt and the taking of vengeance with his own hand (v. 26b). Since the intervention has been entirely through the agency of Abigail, we must conclude that her actions of intervention were God's actions. God, through Abigail, has kept David from actions that would argue against his worthiness for kingship. In chaps. 24 and 26, David makes clear that God's anointed one is not to be killed; in this chapter, he must learn that neither is God's anointed one to engage in unnecessary killing. To take violent vengeance on Nabal would constitute serious moral and practical impediments to David's future kingship. One could hardly imagine the later crowning of David at Hebron (2 Sam 2:1-4) if he had wiped out the entire household of a prominent Calebite.

Abigail goes on to express the hope that David's "enemies and those who seek to do evil to my lord be like Nabal" (v. 26*b*). According to Abigail's speech, Nabal is as good as dead, but not by David's hand. It is Saul who "seeks" David for evil. Saul's death, not by David's hand, is foreshadowed here as well (as chaps. 24 and 26 make clear).

The provisions are offered as a blessing (NRSV, "present"; NIV, "gift") for David's men (v. 27), and Abigail, having already accepted guilt, asks for forgiveness (v. 28*a*). What Abigail offers in return is a word about David's future. Her words are prophetic in tone and explicitly anticipate the dynastic oracle of the prophet Nathan (2 Samuel 7). Abigail proclaims that the Lord will make for David a "sure house" in Israel (v. 28*b*). It is the first direct reference to the Davidic dynasty and is the same phrase used for dynastic promise in 2 Sam 7:11, 17, 26-27; 1 Kgs 2:24; 11:38. This affirmation of David for Israel's future goes beyond even Saul's confession in 24:20. Abigail implies that such a promise is deserved because David is fighting the battles of the Lord. It is less clear what she means by claiming that evil will not be found in David for his entire lifetime, since this is not the case as his story unfolds. Some believe she is speaking primarily of his innocence at this point in the story.

Abigail again turns to speak of those who pursue David as enemies who seek his life (v. 29). Saul is the only one who comes to mind. In a colorful metaphor, she announces God's protection for David. He will be "bound in the bundle of the living under the care of the LORD your God." Enemies like Saul receive

their own metaphor, apparently drawn from David's victory over Goliath. They will be "slung out as from the hollow of a sling." Nabal, as David's enemy in this story, is eventually struck by the Lord and becomes "like a stone" (v. 37).

Abigail understands that David will be instrumental for Israel's future, and she knows this from the Lord. She boldly sums up what she has done for David and proclaims his future at the same time. When the Lord has done all the good spoken about David (Abigail seems privy to this divine information) and has appointed him "prince over Israel" (נגיד *nāgîd*, the term used in 9:16 for king-designate, referring to Saul), then David will be free of guilt over spilling innocent blood. His kingship can be claimed without taint. The implication is that David has been saved from this fate. Abigail subtly takes credit by asking that when the Lord has dealt well with David, he "remember" her (v. 31). This request eventually results in David's marriage to Abigail.

25:32-35. David's response is simple and direct, and in most ways it defers to Abigail as the chief actor in this drama. He speaks in doxology by pronouncing a threefold blessing. In these blessings are both praise and recognition. He recognizes that it is the Lord who has met him in Abigail (v. 32). He recognizes Abigail's "good sense/good judgment" (v. 33*a*), a quality that again marks her as a wise woman (see Prov 11:22). He recognizes that her action has kept him from bloodguilt and vengeance by his own hand (v. 33*b*). It is this last recognition that gives David pause for further reflection. Without Abigail, David's impulse to do violence against the men of Nabal's house would have been unrestrained (v. 34), and David's claim to the kingdom would have been clouded by bloodguilt against a prominent Calebite family in Judah. David has stared into the abyss of his own violence yet again. As he reflects on what might have been, we learn that Abigail herself had been in danger, for David credits the Lord God of Israel with restraining him from hurting Abigail (v. 34*a*). David is sober and chastened after having faced this woman of courage, resourcefulness, and persuasive speech. David receives the provisions she has brought and sends her home with the blessing of peace that he had tried to give to her husband, Nabal (v. 35). David acknowledges her persuasive voice and grants her petition (lit., "I have lifted up your face," v. 35 b).

25:36-38. When Abigail returns home, Nabal is feasting and drunk, a state consistent with the gluttonous behavior associated elsewhere with a "fool." She tells him nothing until the next morning (v. 36). His feast is described as "like a king," but ironically he has left an actual king outside the feast and without provision except for the intervention of Abigail. The next morning, when the wine has drained out of Nabal (perhaps a wordplay, since *nābāl* can also mean "wineskin"), Abigail tells him what she has done (v. 37 a). His reaction is immediate and harsh: "His heart died within him; he became like a stone" (v. 37 b). Nabal's "merry heart" (v. 36 b) is now stilled and hardened. Ten days later, the Lord strikes Nabal so that he dies (26:10 suggests this could also become the fate of Saul). It is the Lord who takes vengeance, and not David. "The fool has said in his heart there is no God" (Pss 14:1; 53:1), but here God has struck the heart of the fool. Nabal has offended God in treating God's anointed one with contempt. In chaps. 24 and 26 David refrains from acting against God's anointed one, knowing that one cannot injure God's anointed with impunity. Nabal, the fool, demonstrates the wisdom of David in this matter. Abigail has saved David from interfering with this divine justice.

25:39-44. David responds to the news of Nabal's death with another doxology (cf. vv. 32-33). His offer of praise to the Lord clearly acknowledges the right of God to judge him and the evil that he had almost committed (v. 39). In praising the Lord for keeping him from such evildoing, he tacitly equates the action of Abigail with the action of God. In these events, Abigail was the embodiment of God's activity on behalf of David.

David woos Abigail; he sends a delegation to "take you to him as his wife" (v. 40). This "taking" does not seem like the royal actions in the warning of Samuel (8:11-18) or the illicit seizure of Uriah's wife, Bathsheba (2 Sam 11:4). Abigail is a free woman and responds willingly (although some feel her response in v. 41 is excessively subservient). As she had done before, she rides out to meet David. The accompanying five maids signify her wealth and importance. She becomes David's wife (v. 42).

Verses 43-44 are not a part of the story itself. They offer further notices about David's marriages, undoubtedly placed here because of his marriage to Abigail. We are told that David also married Ahinoam of Jezreel (v. 43). Most believe this is the Jezreel mentioned as a city in Judah, near Maon and Carmel (Josh 15:56), and not the northern and better-known Jezreel. Levenson and Halpern have made clear the probable importance of these marriages in solidifying Judahite support for David and explaining the quick action to crown David king in Hebron after the death of Saul (2 Sam 2:1-4).[169] In Abigail's case, David became the head of a wealthy Calebite household, and the marriage to Ahinoam at least made him part of another important clan of Judah. Levenson's suggestion that Ahinoam was the same one who was the only named wife of Saul (14:50) has little support.[170] It seems unlikely that such an audacious act, with its claim on the throne of Saul, would stand without comment in the biblical narrative. Ahinoam later gives birth to David's first son, Amnon, whose rape of Tamar sets off a series of violent episodes in David's family (2 Samuel 13:1). Abigail also bears a son, named either Chileab (2 Sam 3:3) or Daniel (1 Chr 3:1).

While David is concluding influential marriages in Judah, Saul acts to deprive him of his own daughter Michal by giving her to another man, Palti (v. 44). This act would appear to be an effort to deprive David of any legitimate claim on the Saulide line.

169. Jon D. Levenson and Baruch Halpern, "The Political Import of David's Marriages," *JBL* 99 (1980) 507-18.
170. Levenson, "1 Samuel 25 as Literature and History," 27.

REFLECTIONS

1. "Beloved, never avenge yourselves, but leave room for the wrath of God; for it is written, 'Vengeance is mine, I will repay, says the Lord' " (Rom 12:19 NRSV; cf.

Heb 10:30). The story of Abigail's saving David from bloodguilt could almost use this line from the apostle Paul as an Aesop-like moral at the end of the story. First Samuel 25 could serve as a parable on the truth and importance of this statement by Paul. Yet, Paul himself is actually quoting the Torah in Deut 32:35, and the principle of vengeance reserved to God and not to be taken into one's own hands is an important Hebrew moral principle (see also Prov 20:22; 24:29).

This notion that vengeance belongs to God is widely misunderstood. Many modern Christians would read Paul's statement as a remnant of some harsh, judgmental Old Testament God. But Mendenhall has shown that God's vengeance is not an arbitrary or capricious divine wrath, but an expression of divine governance related to justice and righteousness as operative and maintained by God in the world.[171] Even more important, the reservation of vengeance to God removes justification for human vengeance. If "vengeance is mine, says the Lord," then it cannot be yours or mine. Both Abigail and David state the most important outcome of Abigail's intervention—namely, that David did not take vengeance into his own hands (vv. 26, 33).

The forestalling of vengeance by one's own hand opens the possibilities for creative moral action and discernment of God's providence. Paul's reflection on vengeance as the Lord's is followed by this statement: "No, 'if your enemies are hungry, feed them; if they are thirsty, give them something to drink' " (Rom 12:20 NRSV). Paul is quoting Jesus' teachings (Matt 5:44; 25:35; Luke 6:27), but it is Abigail who has already acted this out. In her actions to forestall vengeance, new possibilities are made available. Lives are saved, of course, but the future kingdom God is making for Israel through David is saved as well. God does act against Nabal, but David is not tainted with Nabal's blood. In their marriage, both David and Abigail claim a future that could not have been possible in the aftermath of a vengeful raid. In the surrounding chapters 24 and 26, David's restraint from violence leads to Saul's concession of the kingdom, a legitimization David could never have had by killing Saul.

2. "Blessed are the peacemakers, for they will be called the children of God" (Matt 5:9 NRSV). Peacemaking and acting as a partner in God's family are allied in this saying of Jesus. Abigail models it. David is reminded of it by Abigail on the verge of violating the peace, and he sees God's action in Abigail (1 Sam 25:32, 39). To do good rather than evil is to align our actions with what God is doing. To be peacemakers is to seek the unity of human moral agency with divine agency; Abigail models this. Her husband Nabal models its opposite. Evil appears as foolishness and removal from God.

Peace in the Hebrew sense of *šālôm* means wholeness and well-being. David announces such a hope for peace through his men (v. 6), but the actions of Nabal prevent it. To act the fool is to create brokenness. Evil appears here as moral disregard and self-preoccupation. This also characterizes Saul, who has become evil in the sense of playing the fool (which he admits in 26:21). He was not inherently evil and did not begin his kingship by intending the evil use of power. He became one who returned evil for good (24:17) through his own foolishness. In our own time, it is often easier to confront great forces of obvious evil (Hitlers and Stalins, KKK and Bull Connors, apartheid and ethnic cleansing) than to confront our own mean-spirited foolishness and the evil that results. It is easy to desire peacemaking and turning from vengeance as the work of diplomats and Nobel prize winners. It is more difficult to rush, like Abigail, into the breaches of daily life where foolishness provokes violence and standing between the two is risky business.

3. This is an unusual story in the Hebrew Bible because a woman, Abigail, appears as the chief protagonist. Hebrew biblical narrative in general is the product of a highly patriarchal culture, and women usually appear as secondary characters in men's

---

171. Mendenhall, "The 'Vengeance' of Yahweh," 69-104.

stories, with some notable exceptions.[172] Even in Abigail's case, the story is in the context of the larger story of David's rise to kingship. But this distinct episode belongs to Abigail. She is the only character in contact with all the other characters in the story. After the initial description of the crisis, she is the clear decision maker and action taker. Except for his initial resolve to violence, which is seen as a rash and unconsidered action, even David primarily responds to her initiatives. Abigail is pictured with bold qualities of character: intelligence, direct and persuasive speech, decisiveness, good sense, and vision. Most unusual is that Abigail is seen as the surrogate for Yahweh (the LORD). Her actions are the agency for God's actions and are recognized as such by David (and, therefore, by the narrator of this history). Abigail both acts for God and speaks for God, and this acting and speaking are the salvation of the future king. She saves him from bloodguilt and the terrible burden this would place on his kingship.

Some have reacted negatively to Abigail because of her deferential speech and her initiation and acceptance of marriage to David. We should not be too harsh on her for acting within the framework of her own time. It was a patriarchal culture, and there was little place in it for unmarried women. Unusual to her time was her bold initiative to secure a marriage of her own choosing. That she secures a safe place for her own future we should not begrudge her.

Abigail is an important biblical model of moral courage and peacemaking. She dealt with both the evil of Nabal and the danger of David in a forthright and resourceful way, and at considerable risk to herself. She could well have experienced violence from Nabal or from David. It is significant that, as a woman of wealth and privilege, she was approached in trustful confidence by the servants of the household seeking help. She models peacemaking in her ability to see issues at stake beyond the immediate situation and in enabling others (here most notably David) to see the long-term consequences of immediate acts of passion and self-gratification.

In her own initiatives, Abigail never loses sight of the larger movement of divine initiative, but she boldly claims a part in that providential movement. She persuasively relates present moral action to the larger vision of God's future and dares to place herself in a position to mediate the present in the light of that vision.

We live in a world constantly needing restraint from violence, and we could always do with more Abigails. She stands as a model in her own context for actions that avoid vengeance and make for peace. Our context is radically different from that of Abigail, but the tasks are no less urgent. Abigail acted boldly within the framework available to her, and in doing so she shaped the future of God's kingdom. Men and women may find in her example the encouragement to act for God's kingdom in opposition to the violence of our own time.

172. See Alice Ogden Bellis, *Helpmates, Harlots, Heroes: Women's Stories in the Hebrew Bible* (Louisville: Westminster/John Knox, 1994), for a helpful survey of women's stories and the considerable scholarly literature now available on them.

1 Samuel 26:1-25, David Spares Saul's Life Again

COMMENTARY

This episode is a close parallel to chap. 24. Both have the same basic plot, though with differing details and some new emphases appearing in chap. 26. This is also the final chapter in a sequence of three episodes dealing with the temptation to violence that comes with power and David's avoidance of such violence. In chaps. 24 and 26, David has the opportunity to kill Saul, but he chooses against violence. In chap. 25, he is saved from violence against the house of Nabal by the intervention of Abigail. In all three chapters, the narrator understands violence to have been avoided because God was working providentially to bring David's kingdom to fruition. Violence would have created an impediment to his kingship over all Israel.

These three chapters also represent Saul's last hurrah. What remains after these stories are only the details surrounding his death (chaps. 28 and 31). In chaps. 24–26, we see Saul's relinquishment of the kingdom. Saul himself acknowledges David's coming kingdom in chap. 24. In chap. 25, Saul's death is foreshadowed in the fate of Nabal, and in chap. 26, Saul's death is even more explicitly foretold.

Many of the basic elements in the story of chap. 26 have already been treated in the discussion of chap. 24. The commentary on chap. 26 will stress those elements that differ from chap. 24. Some of these new and distinctive elements are:

- ❖ the role of Abishai as David's companion in the venture;
- ❖ the heightened sense of divine providence;
- ❖ the foreshadowing of Saul's death;
- ❖ the taking of Saul's spear and water jar;
- ❖ the taunting of Abner;
- ❖ David's suggestion of motivation for Saul's pursuit;
- ❖ Saul's final benediction to David.

26:1-5. Ziphites again report to Saul about David's whereabouts (v. 1; cf. 23:19). As before, Saul gathers a sizable force (3,000 men) to pursue his obsession (v. 2). Saul makes a base camp, and David, hearing that Saul has come into the area, sends out spies to locate him (vv. 3-4). With this information, David himself goes to find Saul asleep for the night, with Abner his commander at his side, and the army encircling him (v. 5). Unlike chap. 24, Saul has not come serendipitously into David's power. David has sought him out, and he will next take the initiative to go into Saul's camp. It is a more active David, seeking advantage over Saul, than we saw in chap. 24.

26:6-12. David speaks to Ahimelech the Hittite and to Abishai, Joab's brother, to see if they are daring enough go with him into Saul's camp. Abishai takes up the challenge eagerly (v. 6). We presume that Ahimelech declined. Abishai is one of the sons of Zeruiah, David's sister (1 Chr 2:16). Abishai and his two brothers, Joab and Asahel, are prominent members of David's warrior band. Joab becomes David's chief military commander, and Asahel is killed in an incident that starts a blood feud with difficult consequences for David (2 Samuel 2). Abishai was a member of David's elite "Thirty" and had been involved in numerous exploits that required a ready sword (2 Sam 2:18-24; 3:30; 10:9-14; 16:5-11; 18:2-14; 20:6-10; 21:16-17). David complains at one point, "These men, the sons of Zeruiah, are too violent for me" (2 Sam 3:39). Given this reputation, it is not surprising that Abishai volunteered for David's daring mission.

They find Saul sleeping with his spear stuck in the ground beside him, while Abner and the army surrounding him also sleep (v. 7). Abishai is ready to kill Saul. He claims that "God has given your enemy into your hand," but then wishes to be the extension of David's hand and pin Saul to the ground with one thrust of Saul's own spear (v. 8). David restrains him by claiming that no one can strike God's anointed and remain guiltless (v. 9). David's restraint no doubt reflects a mixture of compassion and respect for the office of king as God's anointed one. After all, David is himself God's anointed (see discussion of 24:1-22).

Abishai must have been difficult to hold back. David argues that the life of Saul must be in God's hands, not theirs. He details three ways in which Saul might meet his fate (v. 10): He will be struck down by God (as was Nabal, 25:38); he will die of natural causes ("his day will come to die"); or he will die in battle. It is this last possibility that is to be Saul's fate, although the fatal blow is not to be from the enemy's hand (chap. 31). David's urgent argument to Abishai is that Saul's death is coming, and it should not come at their hands.

David proposes that they take the spear and a water jug nearby and leave (v. 11). These will prove that they had the opportunity to harm Saul. They take these things and make their way out of the camp with no one knowing of their presence (v. 12a). But the note in v. 12b suggests that this act of human daring was assisted by divine providence: "Because a deep sleep from the LORD had fallen upon them." More than in chap. 24, the narrator has emphasized the activity of God through and beside the actions of the human participants in the story. The events leading to Israel's future in David are subject to divine governance. David seems to sense this. His refusal to burden his coming kingship with the blood of Saul grows out of trust that God's way with Saul will take its own course. Five times in his speech to Abishai (vv. 9-11) David mentions the name of the Lord. The narrator, by telling us of the deep sleep from the Lord (v. 12), lets us know that God is also enabling the course of David's future.

26:13-16. Standing on a hill at a distance, David calls to the sleeping army and singles out Abner in particular (vv. 13-14). Abner, the commander of Saul's army (14:50-51), plays a crucial role in future events. He does not seem initially to recognize David (v. 14*b*). David addresses him with contempt, as a soldier who has failed in his duty. He taunts Abner for having a reputation as a warrior but failing to keep adequate watch over "your lord, the king" (v. 15). David boldly claims that Abner deserves to die for having failed to protect the Lord's anointed, and he calls attention to the missing spear and water jug—proof that the king's life had been in jeopardy even while Saul slept in the midst of his army (v. 16). It may be that David's death sentence against Abner is intended to foreshadow and justify Joab's later killing of Abner, even though the immediate cause at the time was a matter of family vengeance for Joab (2 Sam 3:27). The protection of the life of God's anointed one is no small matter in these stories. David succeeds in ridiculing Abner for disregard of Saul, while David places himself in the position of honoring Saul by sparing his life when the king was in his power. It is the fugitive and outlaw who has best guarded the king's life.

26:17-25. Instead of two formal monologues by David and Saul, as in chap. 24, there is here an exchange of speeches between the two. It is Saul who recognizes David, and his initial response is unexpectedly intimate, "Is this your voice, my son David?" (v. 17). In all three of Saul's speeches he addresses David as

"my son" (vv. 17, 21, 25). Even more remarkable, in each of these places he also uses David's name. We have become accustomed in previous chapters to Saul's contemptuous and dismissive reference to David as "the son of Jesse." Unlike 24:11, however, David does not address Saul as "my father." He addresses Saul formally but respectfully as "my lord, O king" and refers to himself deferentially as Saul's "servant" (vv. 17*b*-18).

As in chap. 24, David declares his innocence of wrongdoing toward the king (v. 18), but his speech in v. 19 probes further the motivation of Saul's pursuit of David. He raises the possibility that the Lord has roused Saul to pursue him; but it does not appear that David believes this, and he suggests that an offering would be enough to put the relationship right. David then ventures that other men have stirred Saul against him. Here he seems more passionate, suggesting this is where he believes blame belongs. "May they be cursed before the LORD," David exclaims. Such opponents, he claims, are driving him out of the land of Israel, the heritage of the Lord. David surprisingly suggests that they are driving him to the service of other gods (v. 19*b*). David's claim here may be a preparation for his move in chap. 27 into the service of Achish, the Philistine king of Gath. This must have been a controversial element in David's career, and his speech (v. 19) suggests that others have driven him to seek refuge outside the land of Israel. It would not have been David's choice. In fact, David pleads with Saul to relent from his pursuit so that David might not die away from the land of the Lord (v. 20*a*). Saul has mounted a big-game hunt for a mere flea (v. 20*b*).

Saul responds in a confession (v. 21). It is briefer than Saul's speech in 24:16-21, but it is more striking because Saul admits to wrongdoing. Bluntly Saul states, "I have done wrong." He calls himself a fool (recalling Nabal in chap. 25) and admits he has made a mistake. In the midst of this self-critique, Saul also invites David to return, although it is not clear whether this means to the service of Saul or back to the royal household. He vows no harm will come to David and recognizes that David has already had opportunity to harm him but has not done so. As it turns out, this is the last story in which Saul pursues David, but 27:4 suggests that this is only because David left Israelite territory.

David dramatically shows the spear (perhaps the same one previously thrown at him) and offers to return it (v. 22). Although he continues to speak to Saul, David's focus shifts to his own vindication before the Lord. He seeks nothing from Saul. Perhaps he realizes that he already has the kingdom from Saul and can ask for nothing more. Instead, David gives voice to his hope and trust that the Lord rewards righteousness and faithfulness, that David's own life will be precious in the sight of the Lord, and that the Lord will deliver him from all trouble (vv. 23*a,* 24). He recognizes that the Lord was present in the events that gave Saul into his hand (v. 23*b*). David gave back Saul's life, but it is to the Lord that David looks for his life (v. 24*a*). In the parallel accounts of chaps. 24 and 26, the trustful faith of David is more evident in chap.

26. David has refrained from the temptation to violence as a means to power, but it was trust in the Lord's ability to bring David's future in God's own way that enabled David to refuse violence as a means to his own future. This is David's last speech to Saul, and in it he has moved away from concern with Saul. David now focuses on the Lord as the source of Israel's future and his own.

Saul's final response is a less explicit concession than his conceding of the kingdom to David in 24:20, but it is more sweeping. He pronounces a blessing on David and acknowledges that David's success is assured. Saul's final sentence uses two intensive grammatical constructions (infinitives absolute) to express the strength of his final knowledge of David's future: "You will *indeed* do many things and will *surely* succeed in them" (v. 25). David and Saul part for the last time.

REFLECTIONS

Saul and David are finished with each other. Kingship has been conceded to David. David has refused violence as a means to achieve power. Chapters 24–26 have had moments of intense human drama with life and death hanging in the balance (see Reflections on chaps. 24 and 25). Yet, through it all it is clear that the Lord is at work in these human events. For the most part, there is no effort in the telling of the story to demarcate human and divine action. God's actions are often seen in and through the action of human events (the exception is the deep sleep of 26:12). It is together that divine providence and human agency have modeled a way to power that is not based on violence. The restraint of David and the intervention of Abigail are significant as human moral acts in the face of violent potential. But their actions are not without resources rooted in trust that the Lord is at work, and both Abigail and David give credit for God's presence in their own actions.

In our own modern experience, the tendency is to separate human and divine agency in dealing with the issues of violence and power. There are those, on the one hand, who expect God to make moral decisions for them or to take the crucial moral actions. They pray for righteousness, peace, and justice but do nothing to enable it. They treat the Bible as a prescriptive rule book through which they hope God will direct them. On the other hand, there are those who imagine that human resources alone are adequate to build the future. They trust only those possibilities that emerge out of empirical data or rational analysis. They do not trust that God is also at work. They miss opportunities that come as surprises of graceful possibility and are overlooked by inventories of human resources alone. Particularly in the arenas of power politics there often seems to be little room for qualities of compassion, restraint, patience, and mediation. Such qualities are often considered soft—not realistic politics in the world's terms.

Chapter 26 suggests that there are alternatives in dealing with the issues of power and violence. David models a willingness to receive the kingdom on God's terms by refusing violence as a means to power and trusting that God will open other options for dealing with Saul. The alternative to David in this story is Abishai, who knows no way but violence on his own terms. The boundary between the two is small. David knows how close he is to Abishai's way, and the story of Abigail's intervention in chap. 25 tells us that David is capable of choosing that way. But Abishai's way would have polarized David's kingdom. To seize by force the objects or goals we desire is often to destroy the very thing we hoped to gain. Whether we look at hardened lines of conflict in international disputes or in family dynamics, one often suspects that Abishai's way has prevailed. We try to force the future we desire through various degrees of physical, political, and emotional violence. Like David, we all live too close for comfort to the temptation to force our will, to retaliate, and to justify our attempts to control.

In this story, David does restrain Abishai, even as he was himself restrained by Abigail. It suggests that there is a moral alternative to the violent practices of power that are evident in our marriages and families, our power politics and military might, and our economic and racial divisions. But this alternative requires imaginative discernment of God at work in the midst of our own actions. Qualities of compassion, righteousness, faithfulness, and trust are evident in these stories. But reading these stories teaches us that such qualities will appear only when we give up our own attempts to force the future and instead choose partnership with God, who constantly gives us our future as a gift and bids us receive it rather than grasp it.[173]

173. See Gunn, "David and the Gift of the Kingdom," 14-45.

1 Samuel 27:1–28:2, David in the Service of the Philistines

COMMENTARY

In spite of chaps. 24 and 26, the enmity between David and Saul has not ended, or at least David is not willing to trust that it has ended. David believes that he can only find safety by leaving the area of Saul's authority. He feels compelled to take refuge in Philistine territory and to support his company by doing service to Achish, the king of Gath. In the history of David's rise, this episode justifies the Philistine interlude in David's career by claiming that it was forced by Saul. The story goes on to claim further that David was not really disloyal. Rather, he turned the occasion of his service to the advantage of Judah and duped the Philistines in the process.

This chapter, and its continuation in chap. 29, includes no explicit theological interests. God remains hidden in this portion of the story. As for David, we have seen much to admire in him thus far. Much of what we have seen bears out the judgment of the servant who first brought him to Saul's attention in 16:18: He is "skillful in playing, a man of valor, a warrior, prudent in speech, and a man of good presence; and the LORD is with him." In this chapter, we are reminded that David can also be tough, opportunistic, and cunning. He is capable of ruthless behavior. We have seen some of this side of David as well from time to time (most notably in the rage from which Abigail restrains him, chap. 25). David is presented here as a warrior, looking out for himself and his entourage as best he can. He could be ruthlessly effective in pursuit of his own needs for security and political gain.

27:1-4. David does not think he is safe from Saul's murderous intentions. David has six hundred men with him, along with their entire households, including women and children; he himself now has two wives (vv. 2-3). With such a large party, he cannot indefinitely elude Saul. He can think of no better alternative than to leave Saul's territory, and that means moving into Philistine territory as the one place Saul certainly will not pursue him (v. 1). It is a calculated risk. For one who aspired to the throne of Israel, such consort with Israel's enemy would be hard to explain. Perhaps only David would have dared it. He seems to have considered this strategy earlier (21:11-16), but he was recognized and forced to abandon the attempt. Perhaps this was too close in time to some of his own exploits against the Philistines. It may be that David is now perceived as the enemy of the king of Israel, Saul. In any case, David and his company, including Abigail and Ahinoam, are received into residence in Gath. When Saul hears that David is in Gath, he does abandon his pursuit (v. 4). It is the permanent end of the threat from Saul, for he is soon caught up in the events that end his life.

27:5-7. David approaches Achish, the king of Gath, with a proposal. He asks that he be assigned a town where he can be of service to Achish rather than living in Gath itself (v. 5). We presume that David would have to render service to the Philistine king in some way in order to be allowed to live in Gath or any other place in his kingdom. David's move is a shrewd one, since it places the execution of his service to Achish at a remove from close scrutiny by the king. Achish accepts the proposal and assigns David the town of Ziklag as the location for David's service (v. 6a), perhaps as a kind of feudal territory. The text notes that Ziklag continued to be regarded as a personal holding of the Davidic kings in Judah down to the time of the writing of the account (v. 6b). Verse 7 inserts a chronological note that David was in Philistine service for one year and four months.

27:8-12. Presumably David's assignment was to pacify the enemies of Philistine Gath in the region of Ziklag, which lay on the boundary between the territory of Gath and a region that included the settlements of the Israelite tribe of Judah as well as a number of other settled and semi-nomadic peoples of the southern region known as the Negeb. David's actions while at Ziklag were calculated to build his own power base in Judah while fooling Achish into believing that he was giving exemplary service.

Using Ziklag as a base, David made raids on the Geshurites, the Girzites, and the Amalekites (v. 8). These were traditional enemies of the Israelites, particularly the tribe of Judah. These peoples lived in the wilderness areas south of Judah into the Sinai peninsula, but often raided Judahite villages. David's own people are victimized at Ziklag by an Amalekite raid (chap. 30), although this act may be in retaliation for what David had done. David's forays against these traditional enemies surely enhanced his reputation in Judah, and in the process extended David's political base in Judah. In these raids, David leaves no one alive—man, woman, or child—but takes considerable spoils in the form of livestock or garments, which he brings back to Achish (v. 9). This activity seems ironic, since Saul was rejected for taking such spoil after a war with the Amalekites (chap. 15). But David is under no prophetically mediated divine command of *ḥērem* here. Indeed, his killing of all the people in these raids turns out to have a ruthless but practical purpose for David and does not involve holy war strictures. Warfare against enemies is also outside the framework of concern for bloodguilt, which occupied our attention in chaps. 24–26.

Achish, who is no doubt pleased with the additions to his wealth and the subduing of troublesome enemies, asks David for a report on his raids. David shrewdly but falsely reports that he has been raiding "the Negeb of Judah," "the Negeb of the Jerahmeelites," or "the Negeb of the Kenites" (v. 10). The Jerahmeelites and the Kenites are both southern peoples allied with Judah and perhaps considered their kindred. David casually lies to Achish that his raids have been in the general southern region (Negeb) against Israelite villages of the tribe of Judah and their allies. It is to cover this lie that David must leave no witnesses alive to tell the truth of his raids (v. 11). The subterfuge seems to work, for Achish believes that David must have made himself utterly odious to his own people (after all, David is himself from the tribe of Judah), and as a result Achish considers David to have proved himself an entirely trustworthy servant (v. 12).

28:1-2. David's strategy may have worked too well. The worst possible situation develops: war against Israel by the gathered forces of the Philistines (v. 1a). Achish is so confident of the loyalty of David and his men that he calls them out as part of the military force from Gath to take part in the campaign against Israel (v. 1b). David is in an extremely difficult political dilemma. If he is forced to fight against Israel, he will be unable to justify any claim on the Israelite throne; but if he refuses loyal service to Achish, his own life and those of his company will be in immediate danger. David chooses to bluff for the moment. He almost casually responds to Achish that he is ready to serve him (v. 2*a*). Matters go from bad to worse when Achish, perhaps pleased with David's ready response, makes David and his men the personal bodyguard of the Philistine king (v. 2*b*). Now David cannot even hope to seek refuge on the obscure outskirts of the battle. A king's bodyguard must surround the king and fight for his protection. Such a position in battle is visible and prominent. Achish considers this an honor to David, but David is in a terrible position.

Suddenly, the account breaks off. We are left suspended. The outcome of David's dilemma will not be told until this story resumes in 29:1. Instead, the scene shifts to give us a last pathos-filled glimpse of Saul on the eve of this coming battle with the Philistines (28:3-25).

REFLECTIONS

This is a report that revels in David's shrewd manipulation of enemies and justifies what might otherwise be a questionable time of service with the Philistines. There is no need to import artificial theological comment into the chapter. David is God's future for Israel, but he is no saint. The narrative does not flinch from this reality. We know God's hand is with David, but in this moment it is hidden. We are left with a story that reflects the brutal realities of the time, and a David who seeks to survive within the framework of those realities. In this story, David cannot wait for more favorable options but must choose boldly for his own survival and the lives of his company. We are asked simply to attend to the story of these events in confidence that the reality of God's purposes behind the story has not changed.

In similar fashion, people of faith in every generation are asked to attend to the story of their own lives in trust that God is the reality that moves history—even when the hand of God seems hidden and the brutal realities that are a part of human experience seem remote from God's purposes. It is in facing harsh circumstances that are so often a part of human experience that we avoid a naive, romantic view of God's purposes in the world, and how we effectively serve those purposes. We, like David, may also be asked to act boldly in circumstances that do not give us ideal options or absolute moral clarity.

1 Samuel 28:3-25, Saul and the Ghost of Samuel

COMMENTARY

This episode records the final desperate hours of Saul before his death. On the eve of battle with the Philistines, Saul violates his own proscription of necromancy in Israel by seeking out a medium to bring up the ghost of the prophet Samuel. Instead of the reassurance or release he seeks, Saul is reminded by a hostile Samuel of his rejection and is told of his impending death in battle along with his sons. Even from the grave, Samuel remains Saul's nemesis.

Saul has reached absolute bottom. He is fearful and anxious and seeks to inquire of the Lord, but no mode of inquiry brings results (v. 6). He comes to the full realization that God is not with him. We have known it, and perhaps Saul has suspected it, since he was forced to acknowledge David as future king (24:20). But on the eve of battle with the Philistines, the full realization of his isolation from God drives Saul to despair. He understands rightly that Samuel had been the key to God's presence with him earlier. Indeed, the fates of Samuel and Saul have been intertwined from the beginning. Even Samuel's birth story (chap. 1) was filled with allusions to Saul's name. It seems only fitting that the two should appear together at the end.

In a sense this is the end of Samuel's era as well as of Saul's. Saul has failed as the people's king, but God's alternative to Saul is not a return to the rigid orthodoxy and old traditionalism of Samuel. Samuel began in a time when there was no word of the Lord in the land (3:1). Now chap. 28 returns to a situation where there is no word of the Lord (v. 6), and even the ghost of Samuel can only speak harshly of endings, not of beginnings. Another avenue for the presence of God in Israel has become available with David. Samuel anointed him, but he has operated quite independently of the old ways represented by Samuel. A central theme of the stories of David's rise has been, "God was with him" (e.g., 16:18; 2 Sam 5:10). Unlike Saul, David has no problem inquiring of God and receiving a response (22:10, 13, 15; 23:2, 4; 30:8; 2 Sam 2:1; 5:19, 23). Through David, God has opened a new path for God's future with Israel. Saul and Samuel are both about to be left behind. A new boldness and directness in relating to God have appeared in David that reject both the anxious ritualism of Saul and the inflexible orthodoxy of Samuel. Saul and Samuel together in this story point only to deathly realities for Israel. By contrast, David bears God's possibilities of life for Israel.

An introductory word must be said about the woman in this story. She is a necromancer, whose practices were consistently forbidden in Israel as inconsistent with the worship of Yahweh. Translators have often labeled her a "witch" (see discussion of the Hebrew terms below). It is a term that carries dark and sinister connotations, and is not at all specific to the actual meanings of the terms used in the story. Older commentary on this text often vilified her and even suggested that she was somehow responsible for leading Saul astray in his final hours. Yet, in the context of a careful reading of the story, this unnamed woman is a person of courage and compassion. Her vocation may not be compatible with the worship of Yahweh, but she is intended in her strength and caring to be a

contrast to the weak, pathetic, and unfaithful Saul. The story intentionally compares this so-called king to this forbidden woman and finds Saul the loser in the comparison.

Scholars have frequently pointed out difficulties in the placement and composition of this chapter.[174] According to v. 4, the Philistines are already encamped at Shunem, near the site of the final battle, but in 29:1 they are still gathering much farther south at Aphek. The chapter would fit better chronologically after chap. 30. Such a reorganization would, of course, remove the chapter from its disruptive position in the story of David's dilemma in the service of the Philistines. Still, we should also reckon with the possibility that it was just such a pause in David's story that was intended by those who placed chap. 28 here. Saul's tragic fate is then contrasted with David's near miraculous good fortune in chap. 29. The close ties of this chapter to chap. 15 (cf. 28:16-18 and 15:16-28) and the heightened role of Samuel suggest that this chapter received some reworking as part of a prophetic edition of these stories (see Introduction).

28:3-7. The episode opens bluntly. It quickly gives us three pieces of information:

(1) Samuel is dead (v. 3*a*). This restates the notice of 25:1 and serves to reintroduce Samuel into the story.

(2) Saul had expelled "mediums" and "wizards" (NRSV)/"spiritists" (NIV) from the land. This is consistent with what seems to be a constant opposition of Yahwism to such practices (see Lev 19:31; 20:6, 27; Deut 18:11). This notice introduces unauthorized means of seeking guidance alongside notice of Samuel, who was a prophet, an authorized means of seeking guidance. Saul will soon be in the awkward position of seeking to consult a prophet (authorized) through a medium (unauthorized), which he had forbidden in Israel.

(3) The Philistines are gathering for a major military campaign against Israel. Forces are already arrayed opposite one another in the valley of Jezreel (v. 4), the Philistines at Shunem on the north and the Israelites at Gilboa on the south.

With this background, the scene shifts to Saul, who remains the central focus throughout. Saul is terrified at the sight of the army

174. See McCarter, *I Samuel*, 422-23; Klein, *I Samuel*, 268-74.

the Philistines have assembled (v. 5). His impulse is not to devise a plan of action (even a strategic retreat), but to find some instruction about what to do. He tries to inquire of the Lord. There is a play on words here, for the verb "to ask," "to inquire" is שאל (šā'al), the word from which Saul's own name is derived. Saul "sauled" the Lord. He uses three traditional means of inquiry: dreams, the casting of sacred lots (here only Urim mentioned; usually Urim and Thummim), and prophets. The scene is reminiscent of chap. 14, where Jonathan took bold action, voicing trust in the Lord, while Saul sought ritual reassurance before doing anything until it was almost too late. On the eve of his battle with the Philistines, Saul is seeking ritual certainty rather than drawing up battle plans. He is ruled by fear and not by trust. The Lord does not answer. It is ironic that another means of seeking guidance from the Lord—namely, through priest and ephod—has been lost to Saul by his own deadly violence against the priestly community at Nob (22:6-23). Abiathar and the ephod are now with David, and in 30:7-8 David will use them confidently and successfully to receive a word from the Lord.

In his anxiety and fear, Saul goes beyond the bounds of faithful covenant practices to seek out a medium, violating his own prohibition. He sends servants to find a medium so he can "saul" (inquire of) her. They find one at Endor (v. 7), which is behind the Philistine lines.

The word translated "medium" in vv. 3, 7, 9 and as "spirit" in v. 8 is אוב ('ôb), a word referring to ancestral spirits or images representing them. Lust, who has written the most detailed analysis on wizardry and necromancy in ancient Israel, connects the word with the Hebrew for "father" (אב 'āb), referring to the spirits of "fathers" who have died.[175] It often appears in the plural, as in vv. 3 and 9, and connotes those who summon such spirits or ancestors, a "medium." Verse 7 is more explicit and speaks twice of "a woman of [i.e., dealing with] ancestral spirits." Verse 8 speaks in the singular of the "spirit" Saul wishes the woman to conjure up. Other texts suggest that such necromancers

may either summon and "inquire of" spirits (Deut 18:11) or be possessed by spirits and speak for them (Lev 20:27). The term translated "wizard" or "spiritist" (vv. 3, 9) is ידעני (yiddĕ'ōnî), a word related to the verb "to know" (ידע yāda'), which Lust understands as ghosts knowledgeable of the future. Saul's prohibition in vv. 3 and 9 implies a banning of those who traffic in such ghosts, hence a "wizard."

28:8-14. Saul goes to the woman at Endor, in disguise and at night, accompanied by two of his men (v. 8a). He must furtively sneak behind enemy lines to seek this forbidden reassurance. It is not a picture to inspire confidence in Saul's leadership. He requests the woman to call up a specific ancestral spirit ('ôb), whom he will name (v. 8b). She is cautious. She cites Saul's prohibition of mediums and wizards and wonders aloud if they are trying to entrap her (v. 9). To violate royal decree is to risk death. She does not seem to be in the business of regularly flaunting this royal prohibition. Ironically, to reassure her that she will come to no harm, Saul swears by the Lord (Yahweh), even as he violates the commandments of covenant with the Lord (v. 10).

The woman still seems cautious as she asks, "Who do you want brought up?" Saul answers, "Samuel" (v. 11). The narrative shows no interest in rituals or details of the conjuring process. Suddenly, Samuel is there. Some commentators have suggested that he appeared before the woman could do anything to summon him. When she sees Samuel, the woman suddenly also recognizes Saul. She cries out at the deception and names what Saul has sought to hide, "You are Saul!" (v. 12). Saul reassures her but rushes on to the matter he came for, "What do you see?" (v. 13a). At first she reports that she sees "a divine being" or "a god" (v. 13b; the NIV reads "spirit," but the word is אלהים ['ĕlōhîm], "god" or "gods") coming up from the ground. Saul anxiously asks for her to describe its appearance, and she reports seeing an old man wrapped in a robe (v. 14a). It is enough; Saul knows him, and he bows to the ground before Samuel (v. 14b). The word for "robe" (מעיל mĕ'îl) is associated both with Samuel and with royalty. It is the word for the robe that Samuel tore at the time of

---

175. J. Lust, "On Wizards and Prophets," in *Studies in Prophecy,* VTSup 26 (Leiden: E. J. Brill, 1974) 133-42. See Klein, *1 Samuel,* 270, for other etymological suggestions.

Saul's rejection in 15:27. It is the word for the robe Hannah brought to the boy Samuel each year at Shiloh (2:19). It is the word for the robe passed to David by Jonathan (18:4) and the robe that David cut a piece from when Saul was in his power (24:5). The ghost of Samuel comes cloaked in the robe associated with prophecy and kingship, and Saul cannot help knowing him. But it is the cloak of authority that Saul cannot possess or keep. It appears now on the dead Samuel like a shroud, and when Samuel is finished it represents the shroud of Saul as well. Saul greets the ghost of Samuel on the ground, which is where Samuel last saw him in humiliating circumstances (19:24).

28:15-19. Death has not mellowed Samuel. He is as harsh and unyielding as we remember him. He is angry at being disturbed from the sleep of death (v. 15a). We wonder what Saul could possibly have had in mind to summon this crotchety nemesis in his time of need. Yet, Saul pours out his troubles in a rush of words: the Philistines—war—God—turned away—no answer (v. 15b). Finally, Saul truthfully speaks the heart of his problem: "I have summoned you to tell me what I should do." We cannot imagine this line from David. David constantly inquires of God, but he is never at a loss for what to do in crisis. At the risk of using a cliché, there is something of the old piece of folk wisdom that "God helps those who help themselves" in the contrast between Saul and David. David may inquire of God over a course of action (as in 30:7-8), but Saul seems to want God or God's prophet to tell him what to do.

Samuel replies scornfully, "Why then do you ask [שָׁאַל *šāʾal*] me?" He voices what Saul now knows: God has abandoned him and is his enemy (v. 16). The ghost of Samuel has seized the floor, and his harsh rhetoric pours over the hapless Saul. Saul is reminded that what has happened is just what Samuel said would happen: The kingdom has been torn

from him and given to his neighbor (v. 17). The language is identical to 15:28, except that Samuel now names the neighbor: David! Saul is reminded of his sin in not exterminating the Amalekites; the emphasis is not on the deed itself, however, but on Saul's failure to "obey the voice of the LORD" (v. 18). David will take spoils from Amalek without criticism (chap. 30). But the day of Samuel and holy war commandments of tribal covenant practice is over.

The final word of Samuel's ghost addresses neither the past nor its fulfillment in Saul's present crisis. It concerns the future and Saul's final fate. Samuel reveals that the Lord will give Israel into the hand of the Philistines, and Saul, along with his sons, will die in the battle on the next day (v. 19). As if to signal the abruptness and the finality of Saul's end, the séance with Samuel is ended. There is no word of departure, no appeal, no discussion, no further conversation. It is over—the séance, the coming battle, the experiment with the people's king, the life of Saul!

28:20-25. Saul once again is on the ground, a powerless man, at the departure of Samuel (v. 20; cf. 19:24). These last verses are anticlimactic. Saul is devastated emotionally and weak physically. He has eaten nothing all day and night, perhaps fasting in preparation for battle (v. 20b). The woman takes charge in caring response to Saul's terror-stricken state (v. 21a). She demands that Saul listen to her because she has listened to him and risked her life (vv. 21b-22a). She offers Saul food to strengthen him, and he refuses; but his servants join the woman in urging him until he finally rises from the ground to sit on the bed (vv. 22b-23). Quickly and generously, the woman slaughters a calf, bakes cakes, and prepares them for Saul (v. 24). In the house of this forbidden woman, behind enemy lines, and in the dead of night, Saul eats a final royal meal and departs (v. 25).

REFLECTIONS

Saul is faced here with a genuine crisis and deserves our sympathy. But the portrait of Saul in this episode is not one of courage in the face of crisis. The Saul of this story is sad and pathetic—a despairing, beaten man. His energy is not spent facing crisis and giving leadership in what must have been a terrifying moment for all of Israel.

Instead of facing his destiny, he is still seeking ways to know and control his destiny. In desperation, he turns to idolatrous practices. In fear of the future, he returns to a past that cannot save him.

The episode of chapter 28 is strange. This story of mediums and ghosts is easy to dismiss as odd or interesting, but in no way our story. Yet, in many ways we live in a very Saul-like era. We are deeply anxious and fearful of the future. The hostile forces that face us are different from Saul's Philistines, but no less deadly. We are assaulted by media-driven consumer values that erode our sense of self-worth, reduce our sexuality to a marketing commodity, and create a deadly acceptance of violent behavior in streets, schools, and homes, as well as between nations.

People of faith should be able to respond with resources of life in the face of such death-dealing crises. But too often we, like Saul, have lost touch with the future as God's future. The trustful living and bold facing of the future modeled by David in these stories is replaced by anxious Saul-like efforts to know and control our destiny, efforts that seem cut off from trustful confidence that God is with us.

1. The failure of a trustful faith leads us to embrace idolatrous practices in the effort to know and control our destiny. We live in an age of the popularity of the soothsayer and the quick fix on the future. Horoscopes may be mere entertainment for some people, but are taken very seriously by others as daily guides for living. Bestseller lists regularly carry titles that promise to make ancient secret knowledge available to modern readers. Psychic hotlines peddle their wares regularly on late-night television. Radio and TV evangelists urge us to purchase their explanations of biblical prophecies that will supposedly make clear the course of future events. Even something as benign as the Meyers-Briggs test indicators is sometimes misconstrued as dictating what is possible and what is not, what will happen and what will not. There seems to be an unending stream of new corporate management systems, and the church is often tempted to adopt the latest as the means to congregational growth and success.

Some of these examples may be empty hoaxes, while others misapply useful tools. All risk becoming idolatrous substitutes for openness to the future God is bringing. These and many other modern systems and devices tempt us to seek knowledge and control of our future as a substitute for trustful receiving and responding to the future. Like Saul, we often want certainty in advance.

2. The failure of trustful faith also leads us to refuse God's future by desperately calling up the past. In politics this often leads to a kind of nostalgia for the past as a time free of the crises that beset us. But the past is to be remembered and not reborn; the past is to be learned from and built upon, not resurrected. Restoration of our past, like the ghost of Samuel, often turns out crankier than we remembered. A recent presidential candidate remembered and extolled the community spirit he knew and valued in the late 1940s and early 1950s. He claimed that we could recover it, but African Americans from the South and women who lived in that time do not share his nostalgia.

In religious life we also call up the past as a way of refusing the future. "We've always done it that way" is an old familiar cry in the church. We invoke tradition, hoping, like Saul, that it will tell us what to do. But the ghosts of our past, if we dare to listen to them, may tell a word about the death of one way into the future so that another can be born. Like the tragic, coming death of Saul and his sons, such deaths of failed faithfulness are genuinely painful. The prophetic spirit of our own past as people of faith will always point us forward to God, who will not be confined to the past. We must sometimes face our own death so that God's future can be born. Sometimes "those who would gain their life must lose it" (Matt 10:39; Mark 8:35; Luke 17:33; John 12:25).

1 Samuel 29:1-11, David Dismissed from the Battle with Saul

COMMENTARY

This chapter is a continuation of 27:1–28:2. David had offered himself and his men in service to Achish the king of Gath and had been given Ziklag as an outpost for keeping the enemies of Gath pacified and enriching the coffers of Achish. Although David had launched campaigns against the traditional enemies of Judah, he had fooled Achish into thinking he was raiding his own people. In 28:1-2, David was placed in an awkward position by being called out to join Philistine forces in a campaign against Israel. We were left in suspense while the scene shifted to Saul's meeting with Samuel's ghost in 28:3-25. This episode tells us how David was saved from the politically disastrous position of doing battle against Israel. Saul's total desolation (28:3-25) stands in contrast to this story of David's astonishing resilience and good fortune.

29:1-5. The Philistines have gathered at Aphek, the same site where the disastrous capture of the ark had occurred earlier (4:1). The Israelites are already in Jezreel below Mt. Gilboa, where the final battle with Saul will take place (v. 1). The troops mustered by the lords of the five Philistine cities are passing in review before the commanders (presumably those designated for command of the combined military forces) when David and his men ride past near the rear of the column as a part of Achish's troops (v. 2). The commanders seem astonished, "What are these Hebrews doing here?" (v. 3*a*). They use the derogatory term "Hebrew" (עברי *'ibrî*), signifying a marginal, socially outcast class of people. It is a term found elsewhere on Philistine lips concerning Israelites (4:6, 9; 13:3, 19; 14:11, 21). Again the account reminds us of David's ties to the marginal and oppressed groups within Israel.

Achish makes the first of three vigorous defenses of David's acceptability in this chapter (v. 3*b*). He identifies David by name and by calling him the servant of King Saul of Israel. This does not seem to help,

whereupon Achish goes on quickly to say that David has been in his service for some time. He identifies David as a deserter, which perhaps explains his initial linking of David with Saul. He avows to have found no fault in David. As readers, of course, we know differently. David has been duping Achish while ingratiating himself to the people of Judah (27:8-12).

The commanders are not easily persuaded. They are angry with Achish and demand that he send David back to Ziklag. They regard him as a liability in battle, one who could turn on the Philistines during the heat of battle (v. 4). They raise the possibility that David would buy his way back into favor with his lord (Saul) by offering the heads of Philistine soldiers. Further, now that Achish has named him, the commanders know his reputation. He is the same David celebrated in song and dance, along with Saul, for having killed Philistines (v. 5): "Saul has killed his thousands, and David his ten thousands." It is easy to understand the commander's unease about David's presence. It may be fortunate that they let David leave unimpeded.

29:6-11. Achish must break the news to David. Oddly, he does so by swearing an oath in the name of the Lord (Yahweh). Perhaps this was an honor to David's God, or perhaps it is just an anachronism. For the second time Achish vigorously defends David (v. 6). Ironically, he begins by citing David's honesty; we know David does not deserve this accolade. Achish argues that David should be included in the campaign; he has found nothing wrong with David. Now Achish says the lords of the Philistines do not approve, presumably backing up their commanders' objections. Achish sends David home in peace, but warns him to do nothing to offend the Philistine lords (v. 7). Perhaps this indicates that David's safety is somewhat in question; he had better not call any more attention to himself.

In what must surely be a tongue-in-cheek response, David protests his loyalty and expresses disappointment at not being included in the Philistine military effort (v. 8). He must surely have been inwardly relieved. Many have suggested that David's final phrases have an intended double meaning. When he expresses the desire to "fight against the enemies of my lord the king," he does not name the king. Achish assumes it is a reference to himself, but David may have been referring to Saul. Perhaps in battle David thought he would seize the opportunity to turn the tide for Israel.

A third time Achish declares David innocent of wrongdoing. Here he seems to get carried away rhetorically: "You are as blameless in my sight as an angel of God" (v. 9). Surely there was some humor in the telling of a story in which a Philistine king sees David as an angel of God! Still David must return home; he cannot do battle. He will have to be content with the good regard of Achish and not take the commanders' disapproval ("evil report") to heart (v. 10; the longer NRSV text in this verse reflects a reading with the LXX, which the NIV does not adopt). David leaves for Ziklag as the Philistines move north to meet the Israelites at Jezreel (v. 11).

REFLECTIONS

There are no explicit theological statements in this chapter, but in the larger history of David's rise we have heard many times that "God was with him." Even without an explicit statement, that seems obvious once again in this chapter.

Everything seems to come up roses for David. The future of Israel in David simply will not be denied or shadowed. What looks compromising of that future always seems to take a turn for the best. This story, as with most of the stories of David's rise, seems to be told from the perspective of the marginal who revel in the adventures and triumphs of one of their own. Even Philistine kings (Achish) declare David guiltless, but they do not know the half of it. He is really guiltless from Israel's perspective, because he has used his service to Achish to dupe the hated Philistines and to serve Judah. For marginal and embattled Israelites of future generations, this becomes literature of hope in times when there is little to hope for and even less to celebrate.

Yet in David, and the telling of his stories, it can be affirmed that God's future is coming. Those in power are not quite as in control as they think. This is why David's remarkable stories have been read and reread with wonder and hope, generation after generation. Even today, those who read these stories in the church of the marginal and the oppressed will recognize their hope in David and be heartened and astonished by his narrow escapes, bold actions, and faithful trust. Those who read these stories in the church of the powerful must suspect that they may not know the full story of what God is doing (like Achish) unless they can strive to read outside their own privileged context. They must seek to read stories such as this one in solidarity with those who know that grace usually comes as subversive power—like David.

1 Samuel 30:1-31, David and the Amalekite Raid on Ziklag

COMMENTARY

David returns to Ziklag to find it burned and looted by Amalekite raiders. All the women and children, including David's two wives, have been taken captive. David immediately pursues the Amalekites, defeats them, and recovers the captives, along with considerable spoils. This victory for David, of course, provides a simple and immediate contrast to the defeat Saul and the Israelite army suffer in chap. 31. Yet, the real interest of the story does not seem to be in David's victory over the Amalekites itself, but in David's character—the way he conducts himself—throughout the episode. Here, too, David stands in contrast to Saul, but it is the inept and despairing Saul of chap. 28 in view rather than the Saul dying in battle of chap. 31. Key elements in this contrast include:

(1) Both Saul and David are described as being in "great distress" (28:15; 30:6). Both men are in leadership crises. Saul is on the eve of a great battle with the Philistines and does not know what to do. His response to "great distress" is to consult in desperation a medium, forbidden to worshipers of the covenant Lord, and to ask the ghost of Samuel what he is to do. David is in "great distress" because he has returned to the destruction of Ziklag and the capture of its women and children, and his men are so angry that they threaten to stone him (v. 6). The NRSV translates this verb (צרר *ṣārar*) as to be in "great danger," but this is inadequate. The reference is not to external threat but to David's inner turmoil. The key phrase comes at the end of v. 6, "But David strengthened himself in the LORD his God." David knows where his greatest strength lies. His confident faith here is the very antithesis to the desperate and fearful Saul creeping by night to the medium at Endor.

(2) When Saul inquired of the Lord (28:6) he received no answer from any of the acceptable forms of inquiry. In contrast, David calls on Abiathar to bring out the ephod, and he inquires of the Lord whether he should pursue the Amalekites (30:7-8). David receives strong reassurance from the Lord, "Pursue, for you shall surely overtake and shall surely rescue" (two emphatic infinitive constructions). We could interpret this contrast simply as the difference between divine disfavor and divine favor. The story is deeply biased in favor of David as God's future for Israel. But it would be a mistake to see this contrast simply as a victimization of Saul and to understand his distance from God as solely of divine making. Saul was rejected as the king God desired for Israel, but apart from a desire for ritual certainty before crucial battles (see chaps. 13; 14; 28) Saul is never portrayed as a man who "strengthened himself in the LORD." He does not pray to the Lord. He does not express

trust in the Lord. The ephod is with David because Saul massacred the priestly community where it resided. Saul has been driven by his own jealousy, anger, and violence without reference to what he perceived the Lord to be doing. If the Lord does not answer Saul (28:6), he should hardly be surprised, since he has lived in separation from the Lord. By contrast, David has prayed to, consulted with, and given credit to the Lord throughout the course of these stories. There is a trustful confidence that marks David's interaction with the Lord. David is in communication with the Lord because he has never broken off the lines of communication.

(3) In the sad episode at Endor, Saul is a king who can hardly be recognized as such. His behavior is the antithesis of royal behavior. He violates his own royal decrees. He seeks ghosts who might tell him what to do. He is fearful and without authority. In the end, even the medium must command him to act in his own best interest (28:21-22). In chap. 30, David, who is not yet king, gives royal leadership that prefigures his coming kingdom. After consulting with God, he takes command with a bold plan of action. But he seems even more the king after the victory is won when he makes the decision to share the spoils with those who stayed to guard the baggage (vv. 21-25). It is a judicial decision that reorders the social hierarchy that has previously prevailed. The decision treats all who participate, in whatever role, with equity and moves against the creation of haves and have-nots. It no doubt reflects David's own experience of being an eighth son, a fugitive, and one whose own entourage was gathered from the dispossessed (22:2). But it also reflects the authority to make such decisions that goes with kingship. In equally generous spirit, but with calculated political gain, David also distributes spoils to the chief cities of Judah, building and broadening his political base (vv. 26-31). Again such generous, diplomatic, and pragmatic action bespeaks royal authority. Saul is the king who acts as no king; David is the not-yet king who acts with royal authority.

30:1-6. The Amalekites seem to be constantly entangled in Israel's story. When David and his men return to find Ziklag in ashes and their women and children taken captive (vv. 1-3), it seems natural to assume that this was

Amalekite retaliation for the raids David had conducted against them while in the service of Achish (27:8). David's absence had provided them with an opportunity. The Amalekites had taken captive everyone left in Ziklag (v. 2), whereas David had systematically left no survivors in his Amalekite raids (27:9). This contrast does not arise out of some more compassionate inclination on the part of the Amalekites but on the difference in strategic situation. David could not allow word to reach Achish of the true character of his raids. The Amalekites' taking of prisoners was probably more common, since women and children could be considered plunder and were profitable. Their capture alive was a matter of economics, and not mercy.

The immediate response to this catastrophe is grief (v. 4). The people weep, and David weeps with them for his wives, Ahinoam and Abigail, who were both taken (v. 5). But weeping is followed by bitterness and anger, and it focuses on David (v. 6). After all, he was their leader. Perhaps he should have foreseen the vulnerability of Ziklag when all the fighting men were taken to join the Philistine force. Their anger is so great that the people speak of stoning David. This causes David "great distress," but "David strengthened himself in the Lord his God." It is a marvelous view of a man in crisis who knows he possesses faith resources as well as his own human resources. There is a quiet, confident trust that characterizes David's faith here. Piety alone will not suffice. David goes on in this story to take action, utilizing his own considerable skills as leader and warrior. But David models the man of faith who knows that something beyond his own human skills is available to those who trust in the God of whom Hannah sang (2:1-10)—the God who reverses the fortunes of the powerful on behalf of the powerless.

30:7-10. David calls for Abiathar to bring the ephod (v. 7). Abiathar had brought the ephod with him as the lone survivor of Saul's massacre of the priests of Nob (23:6). David inquires of God through priest and ephod, "Shall I pursue? Shall I overtake?" God's answer comes without elaboration, "Pursue! You shall surely overtake. You shall surely deliver" (v. 8). The answer is immediate and emphatic. We have already noted the stark contrast to the silence of God and the isolation of Saul (28:6). It is still up to David to give leadership in a concrete plan of pursuit and deliverance. He takes six hundred men who have already traveled three days from Aphek and pursues the Amalekites to the Wadi Besor, presumably south into the Negeb. Here David leaves two hundred men who are too exhausted to go farther (vv. 9-10). It seems clear that these two hundred also served to guard the supply baggage so that the pursuit could make all necessary speed (v. 24). We hear no more of anger toward David. Leadership has channeled grief and frustration into action.

30:11-15. David and his men get a helpful break when they encounter an Egyptian abandoned in the desert for three days without food or water. David immediately gives him hospitality, and the food and water revive him (vv. 11-12). He had been a slave of the Amalekites and had been abandoned in the desert when he became ill (v. 13). He confirms that this was the very band of Amalekites who had burned Ziklag (v. 14), and David recruits his help to take them to these Amalekites. The young Egyptian agrees, on the condition that his life be spared and that he not be returned to his master (v. 15). This Egyptian is the first of several parties in this account to receive the generosity of David. In each instance, David seems compassionate and responsive to those without power, but in each he also acts in ways that enhance his reputation and claim for kingship. In short, David is acting as a wise king might act.

30:16-20. With the help of the Egyptian, the Amalekites are overtaken. They are eating, drinking, and dancing in celebration of their victory and enjoyment of their plunder (v. 16). The picture is of raiders who think they are beyond the reach of any possible pursuit. David attacks, and the battle extends through the following day. Only four hundred Amalekites on camels escape, too swift for David to overtake (v. 17). The success is complete. David's wives and all the other captives are recovered (vv. 18-19). All of the plunder of the Amalekites is taken, along with extensive herds of livestock. All of the material goods are given over to David's authority as if he were a triumphant king, "This is David's spoil" (v. 20).

One cannot help remembering that Saul was condemned for having taken Amalekite spoil (chap. 15). Now, David is celebrated for the taking of Amalekite spoil. Clearly things have changed in Israel. It should be remembered that although the occasion is the taking of Amalekite spoil and the preserving of King Agag's life, the explicit sin of Saul was in failing to obey the explicit command of the Lord through the prophet Samuel. Samuel had declared the Amalekite campaign a holy war and commanded the total destruction of all people and goods. What has changed in Israel is not simply that David can do what Saul could not, although the story is certainly biased toward David. What has changed is that Samuel and the old traditions of the tribal league, such as holy war, have passed from the scene. David's military campaign stands under no divine command. There is no Samuel to disobey. The taking of Amalekite spoil is set in a new and different context. Indeed, David himself sought authorization for his Amalekite campaign; he did not need a prophet to order it or a holy war tradition to structure it. The issue was never Amalekite spoil but a new freedom exercised by David in relationship to the Lord that was not possible for Saul. The strictures of tribal Yahwism no longer hold, and there is no longer a Samuel to maintain them.

30:21-25. When David and his men return to where the two hundred had been left with the baggage, an issue arises. Those who had done battle do not wish to share the spoil with those who remained behind (vv. 21-22). Some among David's men, labeled "corrupt and worthless men," wish to allow those with the baggage only the recovery of their wives and children. This surely was the traditional economic arrangement; those who fought got the plunder. David intervenes and demonstrates both generosity and a willingness to make a

decision about the distribution of these goods that is kingly in character. David determines that all should share equally in the economic goods gained in the Amalekite victory whether they fought in the battle or guarded the supplies (v. 24). David declares a theological basis for his policy: It is the Lord who gives the victory, so any gain comes as a gift of grace, even to those who did battle; thus all are to share in these gifts (v. 23). Further, David makes this "a statute and an ordinance," and it will hold until the time of the narrator who tells this tale (v. 25). The declaration of new laws for the basis of distributing economic goods is an action we would expect of a king. David boldly decides the issue and claims an authority that anticipates his kingship. This authority is exercised on behalf of generosity and equity by one who himself has been deprived in the context of traditional economic arrangements— an eighth son, one left to run errands for his brothers who did battle, a fugitive, a leader of marginal men in Israel.

30:26-31. David's generosity is not ended. He distributes the goods captured from the Amalekites even beyond the circle of his own men. He sends spoil to his "friends, the elders of Judah" (v. 26*a*). His message to them is an invitation to share in the "spoil of the enemies of the LORD" (v. 26*b*). The implication is interesting. One is either a "friend of David" or an "enemy of the LORD." David is established as the mediator of relationship to the Lord. To be for David is to join in God's purposes for Israel. David's largess to the elders of Judah is not without important political implications. David is building the base in Judah from which his kingship will first be declared. The names of the cities of Judah are listed like the roll call of a political convention (vv. 27-31); the list ends with Hebron, where David will first be declared and crowned king (2 Sam 2:1-4).

REFLECTIONS

The kingdom of Saul is finished. He is not yet crowned, but in this chapter it is David who acts like a king. David is already demonstrating qualities of the kingdom God is bringing to Israel.

1. It is a kingdom that finds its pragmatic power in giving, and not taking. With the abandoned Egyptian, the two hundred men left exhausted with the baggage, and in the distribution of spoil to the cities of Judah, David acts out of generosity, and not possession. Samuel had warned of a king who would take and take and take (8:11-18), but David is not to be that king. One of the important dimensions observed here about David's generosity is that it is not separated from his exercise of pragmatic power and authority. We so often treat acts of generosity as acts apart from normal reality. We step back to do an altruistic deed or to give a generous gift, assuming that we will then resume the patterns of realistic economics and politics. David's generosity is genuine, but it also serves him well in his own political goals. From the Egyptian, he receives the intelligence he needs to overtake the Amalekites. Among his own men, he establishes a cohesive solidarity that was not possible in the usual arrangements of haves and have-nots. With the cities of Judah, he builds a broad base for future rule based on a confidence that David will seek the welfare of all and not simply the enrichment of the royal house. Simply put, this chapter suggests that the politics of giving not only makes good theological and ethical sense, but it also makes better political sense than the politics of taking.

This is difficult for many to understand or accept in our consumer society, based on profitability. The study of American values entitled *Habits of the Heart* suggests that as a society we are abandoning communitarian values in favor of individualistic values, and one of the casualties is a traditional spirit of generosity in American life.[176] In one of the lowest taxed of all developed nations, there is a growing resentment at having to give up any of our economic resources to the common good of the community. In churches we are now told that the baby boomer generations do not appreciate the concept of stewardship. They resent the notion of giving and are more comfortable with patterns of funding that move to a payment-for-services mode. One recent stewardship expert suggested posted fees in churches for weddings, funerals, Sunday school registration for children, and the like. David's story suggests that community based on taking, holding, and possessing cannot be the community of God's kingdom.

2. It is a kingdom that is willing to rearrange the customary patterns of economic distribution. David boldly declared a new equity in economic resources between those who fought the battles and those who maintained the supplies and guarded the base camp. After all, if some had stayed to guard Ziklag, the Amalekites could not have raided them, but all the fighting men probably wanted in on the glory and profit of the Philistine campaign. Although the matter immediately at hand dealt with the sharing of goods from a military campaign, David showed a willingness to examine and change traditional arrangements of economic power for the sake of equity and justice.

Walter Brueggemann reminds us of the similarity between David's decision and Jesus' parable of the workers in Matt 20:1-16. Those who began work early in the day were paid the same wages as those who came late. When some complain, the householder says, "I choose to give to this last as I give to you. . . . Do you begrudge my generosity? So the last will be first, and the first last" (Matt 20:15-16). Brueggemann remarks, "This Matthean text is a parable of the kingdom. Our narrator has some sense that with David a new kingdom is at hand. Israel is at the threshold of the last becoming first. The new king orders a new social possibility."[177]

3. It is a kingdom that knows its resources for crisis are spiritual as well as sociopolitical, economic, or psychological. Nowhere is the character of the kingdom God is bringing in David made clearer than in v. 6. In the midst of grief over his own loss and a leadership crisis that could become life-threatening, "David strengthened himself in the Lord his God." David was possessed of considerable resources of his own: courage, leadership, prowess as a warrior, resourcefulness. Yet, David always seemed to be aware that these alone were not sufficient apart from a faith that placed his human

---

176. Robert Bellah et al., *Habits of the Heart: Individualism and Commitment in American Life* (Berkeley: University of California Press, 1985).

177. Brueggemann, *First and Second Samuel,* 205.

skills in partnership with what God was doing in Israel and in his own life. For David, faith was not a separate reality to be honored apart from the other arenas of his life. It was in and through his faith in the Lord that David approached all else and utilized his considerable human gifts.

We live in a society prone to isolate and compartmentalize religious experience. After honoring the spiritual dimensions of our life on Sunday, we return to work and personal relationships, where we often try to operate entirely by rational and empirical modes of knowing and doing that are in our own control. Without a nurturing of spiritual resources, we suffer a loss of identity and our doing becomes indistinguishable from all of the other interests that seek to influence public policy and societal conduct. David, without strengthening himself in the Lord, would have been just one more minor ancient Near Eastern potentate. Instead, he was the man after God's own heart.

1 Samuel 31:1-13, The Battle of Gilboa and the Death of Saul

COMMENTARY

It is ended. The kingdom of Saul is no more. There will be no deliverance. Saul and his sons lie dead on Mt. Gilboa at the hand of the Philistines. It is for David to have the final word about Saul and Jonathan in 2 Sam 1:19-27. In 1 Samuel 31, the account of Saul's death is told in simple, straightforward terms. The narrator gives us no additional comment. Except for David's eulogy, all has been spoken of Saul.

There is a second, variant account of Saul's death in 2 Sam 1:1-16, where an Amalekite comes to David claiming to have ended Saul's life at the king's own request. This account will be evaluated in discussion of that chapter. It is unclear whether it should be taken as a differing account or simply as a boastful claim by an Amalekite.

31:1-7. With the briefest of reports, it is clear that the battle with the Philistines has gone disastrously for Israel. The Israelite troops have been slaughtered in their flight on the slopes of Mt. Gilboa (v. 1). The reader has an uncanny feeling of returning to the beginning of this story of 1 Samuel. Nothing seems to have changed from the time of the Israelite defeat and the capture of the ark in 1 Samuel 4. Saul had made no real difference in the Philistine crisis. Kingship, as Saul had exercised it, was no more effective than the tribal levy that was defeated in that earlier disaster.

Saul has lost his army, and in short order he loses his sons in battle as well—three of them: Jonathan, Abinadab, and Malchishua (v. 2). A fourth son survives to play a role in later events (2 Sam 2:8-11). Saul had been left alone by God and Samuel, and he is now alone on the battlefield. The archers are turning attention to his position, and Saul has been wounded (v. 3).

Saul had been unable to make decisions on the eve of this battle (chap. 28), but in his final moment he is decisive. He asks his armorbearer to draw his sword and kill him, lest the Philistines capture and humiliate him (v. 4a). He retains enough fight to scornfully call them the "uncircumcised." He will not give his enemies the pleasure of taking him alive and shaming Israel. The armorbearer is afraid and will not do it. Perhaps he is too devoted to Saul, or he is afraid to strike down God's anointed one. Without hesitation or word, Saul falls upon his own sword in a final heroic gesture (v. 4b). Seeing this, the armorbearer falls upon his sword and dies with his king (v. 5). King, sons, servants, and army all lie dead upon Mt. Gilboa (v. 6). The Israelites of the region, even beyond the Jordan, hear of this massive defeat and flee from their cities. The Philistines occupy the entire territory (v. 7). It is the end of Saul; the defeat is of such proportions that we wonder whether it is the end of Israel.

31:8-13. The Philistines find the bodies of Saul and his sons (v. 8). They do not seem to be looking for him or to know that Saul is dead. It was the ordinary practice to strip the battlefield dead for items of value. No doubt Saul and his sons would be recognizable by their armor and weapons. Saul's bold act has robbed them of the possibility of humiliating his person. All they can do is mutilate his body. They cut off his head, strip his armor, and send news of the extent of their victory to their people (v. 9; the text also notes their idols, probably a scornful comment). Beheading was probably intended as an act of triumphant scorn. We remember David's beheading of Goliath after his victory (17:51). The Philistines place Saul's armor in the temple of Astarte, a goddess associated with Canaanite religion. Such a display is no doubt intended to show the superiority of Philistine deities over the God of Israel. We remember the display of the ark in the temple of Dagon (5:2) and the deposit of Goliath's sword in a holy place (17:54; 21:9-10). Saul's body (we do not know if this included his head) is hung on the walls of Beth-shan, a northern city under Philistine control (v. 10). This was probably intended as an act of public humiliation, although Saul's self-inflicted death robbed the Philistines of a more effective public ridicule. The Philistines did not capture him; they did not even kill him.

The final word of this chapter is not, however, of death and humiliation but of honor. When word of Saul's fate reaches the people of Jabesh-gilead (v. 11), they do not hesitate. All of the fighting men of the city march through the night to retrieve the bodies of Saul and his sons from where the Philistines have hung them. They return with the bodies and burn them (v. 12). They then bury the bones under a tamarisk tree in Jabesh-gilead and fast in Saul's honor (v. 13). The people of Jabesh-gilead could not forget or ignore the debt they owe Saul for his swift and valiant rescue when they were at the mercy of Nahash, the king of Ammon (chap. 11). Saul had begun his time as king with courageous and effective leadership as befits a king. For the people of Jabesh-gilead, this moment remains worthy of honor, and they act to ensure that this honor be bestowed even in death. Saul is not to have a place in Israel's future, but the people of Jabesh-gilead ensure that Saul's royal moments in Israel's past will be remembered.

REFLECTIONS

This is not the moment to celebrate or evaluate Saul. He could not be the king Israel needed or God desired, but he deserves the dignity of recognizing his own courageous death and the notice of the honor given him by the people of Jabesh-gilead as royal moments. Preachers should resist coming to this text for moral reflection on suicide, for the tradition makes no moral comment about the means of Saul's death. He did not have the choice of life or death, only the choice of further humiliation for Israel through his capture and execution or a kingly act that brought an end to this moment of Israelite defeat. This is a moment to acknowledge the need for communal silence and grieving and to resist explanatory words for a brief time. Such restraint is often needed in the midst of our own moments of personal and corporate grief. It remains for David to celebrate Saul and Jonathan (2 Sam 1:17-27). It is fitting that David should have the last word on Saul, because beyond Saul, David is God's next word for Israel. (See 2 Sam 1:1-10 and 1:11-27 for further Reflections on the death of Saul.)

2 SAMUEL 1:1–24:25

OVERVIEW

The division between the books of Samuel is artificial. In the Hebrew manuscripts they were one continuous book, but the division was introduced in the Greek and Latin versions. It must have seemed convenient to divide this lengthy book into two, and the death of Saul seemed a natural point of division. After all, several other biblical books end with the death of important figures (Moses, Joshua). This, however, creates the impression that 1 Samuel is Saul's story and 2 Samuel is David's. Any careful reader of 1 Samuel to this point will know that this is not the case. David has been the primary focus since he was introduced in 1 Samuel 16. He is even anticipated in several passages before that (e.g., 1 Sam 13:14; 15:28).

2 SAMUEL 1:1–5:10, DAVID BECOMES KING

OVERVIEW

Second Samuel 1:1–5:10 is the conclusion of the history of the rise of David, which began with 1 Sam 16:1. Most scholars believe this was an independent narrative, now incorporated into the larger Deuteronomistic History (see Introduction and the Overview on 1 Sam 16:1–31:13). This narrative of David's rise to the throne concludes with the formula in 2 Sam 5:10, "And David became greater and greater, for the LORD, the God of hosts was with him." The purpose of this narrative on David's rise was not simply to report events, but to make clear in the telling that David achieved the throne by legitimate means. He was both worthy of the throne and intended by God for Israel's throne.

The narrative task of bringing David to the throne and legitimizing him on it is not finished with the death of Saul (1 Samuel 31). It was clearly not self-evident to all in that time that David should become king. He becomes king immediately only over Judah (2 Sam 2:1-4). The rest of Israel, although in disarray following the Philistine defeat, follows Saul's son Ishbosheth/Ishbaal, who was supported on the throne by Abner, Saul's commander (2 Sam 2:8). Complex events that eventually bring David to the throne of Israel as well as Judah include the assassinations of Abner and Ishbosheth/Ishbaal (3:6-39; 4:1-12). The narrative of these events clearly has as a central purpose the exoneration of David from any blame in these deaths. It is not enough that David become king but that he is legitimated in doing so. He is not tainted by bloodguilt, nor has he conspired against the house of Saul. These chapters have as their central purpose the legitimization of David's claim on the throne. What better way to begin than by reporting David's genuine anger and grief over the deaths of Saul and Jonathan?

2 Samuel 1:1-16, A Report of Saul's Death

COMMENTARY

The book of 2 Samuel opens with another report of Saul's death. The narrator has given us a report of Saul's final moments on Mt. Gilboa in 1 Samuel 31, but, in the context of the story, David does not yet know of Saul's fate. This episode reports Saul's death as it comes to David.

Such a reporting to David would simply reinforce what we already know, except that when the report is given it provides a somewhat different accounting of Saul's death. The messenger is an Amalekite. Saul seems to be fatally entangled with Amalekites (see 1 Samuel 15). This Amalekite brings word that he chanced upon the wounded Saul, who asked him to take his life. The Amalekite did so and has brought David the insignia of royal office—crown and armlet. He no doubt expected reward and favor for this. This accounting is quite different from that of 1 Samuel 31, where Saul takes his own life rather than be captured and humiliated by the Philistines. The existence of these two accounts has raised questions. Which is the story of what really happened? Have two sources with different versions been combined here? The two accounts, however, need not raise such questions. The Amalekite could be a mere opportunist who chanced upon Saul's body and enhanced his tale in order to seek David's favor. Since the narrator has given us another story of Saul's death already (1 Samuel 31), we may regard the Amalekite report with suspicion. We will probably never know what really happened. What is important in this version (2 Samuel 1) is that David has no other information than this Amalekite's report, and David's response is based on that information.

To focus on questions of historicity or sources would be to miss the genuinely new element in this account—namely, David's response to the news of Saul's death. It is spontaneous grief, not joy and celebration. It is not what the Amalekite expected. David himself speaks of it later, "When the one who told me, 'See, Saul is dead,' thought he was bringing good news, I seized him and killed him" (4:10). David's grief and execution of the Amalekite constitute the most important focus of this episode. David is cleared of complicity in Saul's death. (How did he get those royal insignia?) He is innocent even of unseemly celebration. (Look how spontaneous was his grief!) He has given honor and protection to the Lord's anointed one. (He is himself the Lord's anointed.)

1:1-10. The phrase "after the death of Saul" signals the basis on which 1 and 2 Samuel are divided. The era of Saul has ended. Although David's story had already begun, he is now left alone at center stage.

David has been back at Ziklag for two days (v. 1), following the Amalekite campaign (1 Samuel 30). This notice subtly reminds the reader that David was occupied with the Amalekites far to the south at the time of the battle on Mt. Gilboa, thereby suggesting that he could not have been involved in Saul's death. On the third day, a messenger arrives from Saul's camp. It is clear that the news is not good, for his clothes are torn and he has dirt on his head, in keeping with traditional signs of mourning (v. 2). After he falls in homage before David, there follows a battle report in the form of an interrogation. David asks three questions and receives answers that convey what has happened (vv. 3-10). The reader of the books of Samuel has a strange sense of having seen this scene before. The messenger, the signs of mourning, the questions and answers resemble closely the account of the messenger who brought news to Eli of the defeat of Israel, the death of his sons, and the capture of the ark (1 Sam 4:12-18). Once again the news is of catastrophic defeat, the end of a family's leadership in Israel, and the emergence of an overriding question of what has happened to God's presence in Israel's midst. This time the answer to the question of God's presence will be David!

Still, it is not yet time for David. This episode involves a report of endings, not new beginnings. In answer to David's rapid-fire questioning, the messenger reveals that he has come from Israel's camp (v. 3) and brings news that the Israelite army has fled. Many have fallen in battle, including Saul and Jonathan (v. 4). One can almost sense David's suspicions that all is not simple and straightforward when he asks the messenger how he knows of the deaths of Saul and Jonathan (v. 5).

The answer requires a tale. The messenger reports that he was on Mt. Gilboa. It is not at all clear what his role was. He does not seem to have been a part of the army of Saul or of the Philistines. It would seem that he is a scavenger of the battlefield, a pilferer among the fallen. He reports that he encountered Saul, leaning upon his spear, with Philistine chariots and horsemen closing in on his position (v. 6). How appropriate—even ironic—that Saul should lean in his final moments on the spear that seemed always with him—to throw at David or at Jonathan or to be stolen from his side at night by David. The messenger relates that Saul called to him and asked his identity (v. 7). The messenger answered him, "I am an Amalekite" (v. 8). An Amalekite! As we listen in on this report, we are astonished. Is Saul fated to encounter Amalekites at all his moments of loss—of kingdom (1 Samuel 15) and of life? The Amalekite reports that Saul beseeched him to kill him (v. 9a). Saul seems to be already badly wounded in this accounting. He tells the Amalekite that he is seized by "convulsions" (NRSV; NIV, "throes of death"), yet his life lingers (v. 9b). So the Amalekite reports that he killed Saul; he believed Saul could not have lived anyway (v. 10a). The tone is matter-of-fact, almost casual. The Amalekite presents David with Saul's crown and armlet, emphasizing that he has brought them to "my lord" (v. 10b). Such royal insignia were signs of office and authority. It is now clear that the Amalekite knew of David's potential claim on Israel's throne. We will learn that one of Saul's sons, and Saul's general Abner, survived the battle and sought to continue the house of Saul; but the Amalekite did not seek to return Saul's royal insignia to his own house. He brought them to David, seeking to win favor. He no doubt believed that David would celebrate the death of Saul as his enemy, and that he, having brought not only the good news but also the symbols of kingship and its authority, would be celebrated too. He must have expected a reward.

It shows, however, how little this outsider, this Amalekite, really understood of Israel's kings as God's anointed ones or of David's complex relationship to Saul.

1:11-16. David's response was immediate and must have been surprising to the Amalekite messenger. David responds in unreserved grief—tearing his clothes, weeping, fasting until the evening—and he is joined by all the men with him (vv. 11-12). There is no suggestion of pretense or artificiality in David's grief. The Amalekite had come with news he no doubt judged worthy of celebration. He did not understand the importance of Saul or of the office of king as God's anointed to Israel. He did not understand the depth of loss when Saul, Jonathan, and the army of Israel had all been swept away.

At evening David returns to question the young man who had come as messenger. He asks, "Where do you come from?" And he hears in answer, "I am the son of a resident alien, an Amalekite" (v. 13). An Amalekite, living as a sojourner in Israel—it is as if the identity of the messenger had not registered with David earlier. No doubt David's recent loss to the Amalekite raid and his subsequent pursuit and victory were fresh in his mind (1 Samuel 30). Now, he has suffered loss at the hands of an Amalekite again. One can feel the growing menace in David's voice as he asks a question that is in effect an accusation, "Were you not afraid to lift your hand to destroy the LORD's anointed?" (v. 14). David had been afraid to do so. On two occasions, Saul had been in his power, and David had refused to strike him out of respect for Saul as the Lord's anointed one (1 Samuel 24 and 26). Now Saul has been struck down by an Amalekite—a people with a long history of animosity toward Israel and a nemesis to both Saul and David. David cannot allow the inviolability of God's anointed to be broken. He cannot allow the precedent of letting violence to God's anointed go unpunished. He cannot allow his own loyalty to Saul as God's anointed one to be questioned. The Amalekite has unknowingly violated sacred territory, expecting a reward. His ignorance cannot save him; he receives a death sentence instead. David quickly and summarily orders the Amalekite struck down (v. 15). His own confession has condemned him, and David announces the bloodguilt that lies upon the Amalekite for his deed (v. 16). By implication, David declares his own innocence of bloodguilt in Saul's death. He has avenged Saul's death, not taken advantage of it. The opportunism of the Amalekite led to death, and not favor. As an outsider, he never fully understood what was at stake.

REFLECTIONS

Much of the attention to this text has focused on issues of historicity in relation to the account of Saul's death in 1 Samuel 31. What really happened? Which account is accurate? This is not, however, an important issue to the narrator of the history of David's rise or to the larger Deuteronomistic History of which it is a part—and it should not be the focus of our reading. It does not matter whether the Amalekite was lying or telling the truth. Either way, David acted on the basis of what he knew of how Saul died, and the focus is on his loyalty and grief overriding his ambition and self-interest. This theme is further heightened by the song of lament for Saul and Jonathan that follows in 1:17-27. David responded as much for the community as for himself. Whatever Saul had done to David, the striking of God's anointed one (whether an Amalekite deed or an Amalekite lie) struck at the heart of Israel, and such an act could not be allowed to stand unavenged.

Readers often find this account oddly troubling. If Saul were really mortally wounded, they feel that the Amalekite really did nothing very wrong. Even if he just happened along and took the crown and armlet to David with a tale, hoping for reward, they do not feel that he deserved to die. In this country, we are raised to admire opportunism. We often have little loyalty to anything beyond the opportunistic advance of our own interests. The lovable con man is a staple of our novels and movies. The important study of American values *Habits of the Heart*[178] documents the diminishment of communitarian values in favor of a purely individualistic value structure. In American religious life, there has always been a strong segment of believers who elevate personal salvation above considerations of commitment to church or human community. Such perspectives often seem little more than pious opportunism.

The character of David certainly has an opportunistic streak. He knows how to protect and advance his own self-interests, and even in this episode it is in his political interest not to seem in any way complicit in Saul's death. But David also has genuine loyalties that transcend and restrict his opportunism. He has loyalty to Israel and is genuinely grieved at the Philistine defeat of Israel's armies. He has loyalty to the commitments he makes. He had joined in covenant to Jonathan and will honor that commitment, even to Jonathan's descendants (chap. 9). He has loyalty to the Lord. Saul was God's anointed one, and even though Saul treated him as an enemy David refused to harm Saul (1 Samuel 24 and 26). At many points in David's story his relationship to God affects the course of his own personal actions. Even following the grieving of Saul's death, David inquires of God before taking political action (2:1-4). The Amalekite, who believed that he was bringing good news that cleared the throne for an opportunistic David, found that his news was not immediately good news. He did not reckon with loyalties that transcended personal ambitions. Our own reading of this story often fails to credit David with motives or loyalties that transcend his own self-interest. Perhaps this is a reflection of our own predilections rather than a careful reading of David's own story.

A story such as this one calls us to examine our own loyalties and behavior. In a society that often admires and rewards self-interested behavior, we are summoned in this story to witness David's righteous anger on behalf of the community's loss and in

---

178. Bellah et al., *Habits of the Heart.*

loyalty to God's anointed one—even when this loss might bring him personal advantage. Do we still have the capacity to become as righteously angry over violations of community as over violations of our personal ambitions? Are we prepared to grieve over the loss of the community's authority and integrity as well as over our own? Our answers to such questions will determine where we find our place in this story—with the Amalekite or with David.

2 Samuel 1:17-27, David's Lament for Saul and Jonathan

COMMENTARY

David's grief finds moving expression in a lament for Saul and Jonathan. The poetry is passionate, unreserved, and genuine in its communication of loss. This song of lament is widely regarded as the composition of David himself. It is a fitting memorial to Saul and Jonathan and their accomplishments on behalf of Israel, and it is especially appropriate that this memorial should be from David. His song reminds us of the depth of loss that the death of Saul and Jonathan meant for Israel. The focus of 1 Samuel 16–31 on the rise of David and the conflict between David and Saul causes us to lose sight of the full meaning of Saul's kingship for Israel. We have seen Saul's obsession and jealousy, and we have watched his descent into desperation and fear. Nevertheless, in a time of Philistine conquest and domination, Saul led Israel back to some sense of identity and renewed freedom. His small kingdom and his successes against the Philistines kept alive the hope that Israel's story had not ended. The courage and leadership of his son Jonathan was well-known and widely admired. Now Saul is gone; the crown prince Jonathan is gone; Israel has been defeated and dispersed by yet another Philistine army. As readers we have hope that in David Israel's kingdom and its story may yet find a new future. But David and the remnants of Israel have no assurance of this. The depth of loss and defeat is so great that it must be acknowledged and mourned before one may dare to hope for any future. David's personal story is set aside for public grief. His time may come, but in this moment of loss it is the time of Saul and Jonathan that must be honored. Without Saul and Jonathan, David's story would not be possible.

David's song is in the form of a dirge or lament for the dead, known in Hebrew as a קינה (*qînâ*). It is a type of song in honor of the dead that looks backward on the accomplishments of those being remembered and honored. It often addresses the dead in the second person. There is a frequent contrasting of "then" and "now" or "past" and "present" in such dirges. The song honors the dead, and, hence, no ill is spoken of them. There is no mention or address to God in a *qînâ*. As in David's lament here, even theological concerns are set aside in the experience of a deeply human moment. There is a distinctive poetic rhythm to the *qînâ*, although variations in it are possible, as is the case in this text. This type of funerary lament is distinguished from the lament of distress found in the psalms. Such distress laments are cries for help addressed to God, which realistically express the distress of the moment but look forward in anticipation of deliverance. There is no *qînâ* in the psalter.[179]

The poetic lament occurs in vv. 19-27. Verses 17-18 form an introduction to the song. The refrain "How the mighty have fallen" is used three times (vv. 19, 25, 27). It appears at the beginning and end of the piece, and its presence in v. 25 seems to divide the lament into two unequal segments. The first part focuses on the exploits of Saul and Jonathan and the mourning of their deaths (vv. 19-24), whereas the second focuses more on David's personal grief over the loss of Jonathan (vv. 25-26).

1:17-18. These verses introduce the poetic piece, which starts in v. 19. David's song is announced in v. 17 as a *qînâ* in honor of Saul and Jonathan. Even the verb in this

---

179. Claus Westermann, "Struktur und Geschichte der Klage im Alten Testament," *ZAW* 66 (1954) 46, gives a detailed sketch of the differences between these two types of lament.

verse is derived from the same root as the noun *qînâ*.

Verse 18 has been subject to a variety of translations and interpretations.[180] There are three distinct elements to the verse. The first is the phrase "to teach the sons of Judah." The second is the single Hebrew word for "bow" (קשת *qešet*), the same weapon of war used by Jonathan in v. 22. The third element is the expression "[Behold], it is written in the Book of Jashar." There is general agreement that this final expression indicates a collection of poems or songs from which this lament of David was taken by the editor, who placed it appropriately after the narrative accounts of Saul's death. The Book of Jashar is also mentioned in Josh 10:12-13 as the source of the poem celebrating the standing still of the sun at Gibeon. This may have been an anthology of poems (now lost to us) celebrating the heroic deeds of various Israelites. The word "Jashar" is sometimes translated as "the Upright" or "the Just" (הישר *hayyāšār*).

The first two elements of the verse may be understood in two different ways. These may constitute a superscription to David's song in the fashion of the superscriptions that preface many of the psalms. According to this model, the first phrase would be an admonition that the song should be taught to the sons of Judah. It is to be preserved as an important memory in Israel. The word "bow" would then be the title of the poem. Such a title could be taken as a key word from the mention of Jonathan's favorite weapon in v. 22, or it could be an epithet for Jonathan and/or Saul themselves, much as "the chariots of Israel and its horsemen" is used to designate Elijah and Elisha (2 Kgs 2:12; 13:14). Another view would combine these first two elements and read them as a single phrase, "to teach the sons of Judah the bow." In this view, the phrase would announce the intention to use this lament to encourage the sons of Judah to learn military skills following the example of Saul and Jonathan. There are difficulties of grammatical construction that make the second option less likely, and the phrases are likely a superscription and a title to the poem.

1:19-20. In grand and poetic language David addresses Israel to mourn its "glory," which has been slain (v. 19*a*). This is not the common Hebrew word for "glory." The word here is צבי (*ṣĕbî*), which means "beauty," "honor," or "splendor." It can also mean "gazelle." In either usage the term is commonly regarded as an epithet for Saul (or for both Saul and Jonathan). Kings are frequently described in idealistic and heroic terms as handsome and magnificent. Animal images are often used for heroes in ancient literature as well. Either as the "Splendor of Israel" or as the "Gazelle of Israel," this invitation to grief would seem to have Saul, the king, as its object.

The phrase "slain upon your high places" uses a term (במה *bāmâ*) that is later associated with the wooded heights of idolatrous worship and sacrifice. Accordingly some have wanted to see here a comment on Saul's death as idolatrous sacrifice—perhaps a deuteronomistic comment on Saul's kingship and eventually all kingship as idolatrous.[181] If, however, as most suppose, this is early poetry authored by David himself, the term *bāmâ* need not indicate a place of idolatrous worship. Indeed, the basic meaning of the word seems to indicate any rounded swelling of landscape or even of body parts—e.g., buttocks. Given Saul's well-attested death on Mt. Gilboa and the reference to this location in v. 21, we should take the term here to mean only a "height."

The first use of the refrain is in v. 19*b*. The term "mighty" (i.e., mighty men, warriors) does not mean Israelite warriors in general but Saul and Jonathan in particular. Israel's heroes have perished. The refrain becomes a punctuation of grief for this song of loss.

The opening exclamation of grief is followed in v. 20 by a fervent wish that is nevertheless contrary to reality. David's wish, and surely that of all Israel, is that news of this loss could be kept from the Philistine home cities, for there the news will be greeted with rejoicing and exultation. In reality the Philistines sent news of victory to their home cities immediately, perhaps with Saul's armor as a trophy (1 Sam 31:9). Ashkelon and Gath are two of the five Philistine city states, and, of course, Gath is where David served the

180. For a full discussion of the various proposals, see A. A. Anderson, *2 Samuel,* WBC 11 (Dallas: Word, 1989) 15; P. Kyle McCarter, *II Samuel,* AB 9 (Garden City, N.Y.: Doubleday, 1984) 67-68.

181. See Polzin, *David and the Deuteronomist,* 15-16.

Philistine king Achish for a time. He knows the Philistines well. It is particularly galling to think of Philistine joy at the expense of Israelite loss. A measure of David's contempt for this Philistine foe can be seen in the use of the term "uncircumcised" as a derogatory description (see also 1 Sam 17:26, where David uses the term in contempt of Goliath). The description of the daughters of the Philistines in arrogant rejoicing is balanced later in the poem by a summons to the daughters of Israel that they may weep over Saul, a more fitting response to such a great loss (v. 24).

1:21. David turns to the mountains of Gilboa, where Saul was killed, and calls for them to be without dew or rain and to have no fields of bounteous harvest (v. 21*a*).[182] In effect, David has uttered a curse upon Gilboa. Such desolation on its slopes is the only fitting memorial to such a loss. Cut off from its life-giving water both above and below, Gilboa would only be a place of death because there the shield of the "mighty" was defiled (v. 21*b*). The poetic parallel makes clear that Saul is the warrior meant here. It is his shield that will no longer be oiled in preparation for battle. The use of the phrase "anointed with oil" also reminds us that Saul himself was God's anointed one, but that he, too, no longer exists.

1:22-24. We have already mentioned the contrast between "then" and "now" as a characteristic of the *qînâ*, or funerary lament. In this segment, the present reality of loss and defeat is contrasted with the memory of Saul and Jonathan as magnificent and valiant warriors for Israel. The tone of this section is more intimate and personal, more passionate.

In v. 22 we are suddenly in the heat of battle, but it is not the final battle of defeat. The imagery attests to the prowess of Saul and Jonathan as warriors. Jonathan with bow and Saul with sword did not hesitate to draw the blood or pierce the flesh (fat) of the enemy. Blood and fat are often associated with sacrifice, and this language may suggest that the victories of Saul and Jonathan were like sacrifices offered up to the Lord. The weapons of

Saul and Jonathan found their mark and were victorious even over the "mighty" (גבורים *gibbôrîm*; the same word used of Saul and Jonathan in vv. 19, 21, 25, 27) who fought for the enemy.

David's song looks beyond the exploits of battle to remember Saul and Jonathan as beloved in Israel and as gracious or charming (v. 23*a*). The NRSV's use of "lovely" suggests appearance, but the word here (נעים *nā'îm*, "gracious," "charming"; it can also mean "pleasant," which may be how it is used in v. 26*b*) is more indicative of manner or character. Further, David sings that in life and in death this father and son were not parted. The NRSV translation is to be preferred. Life and death form a poetic merism, with two opposites indicating a totality—i.e., Saul and Jonathan were never divided. In the final images of the verse (v. 23*b*), these two mighty men of Israel are compared in swiftness to eagles and in strength to lions. In this verse, we may be dealing with the natural hyperbole that is characteristic of eulogies. Because so much of our encounter with Saul has involved his obsessive and violent pursuit of David, we do not think of him as gracious and beloved, although our portrait of Jonathan might fit these terms. We certainly do not think of the relationship between Saul and Jonathan as one of constant unity. They quarreled violently, and because of David (1 Sam 20:30-34; 22:8). No doubt the portrait here is due in part to the graciousness of David, placing Israel's departed king in the best light. Nevertheless, we should also remember that Israel's experience with Saul was not seen primarily through the lens of the struggle with David. David's memory of a loved and gracious Saul may be his own memories of a time before their conflict, when Saul loved David (1 Sam 16:21); but it may also speak for Israel, who saw in Saul and his son Jonathan those who gave them hope in the face of Philistine threat and pride in identity as Israelites. If Jonathan and Saul had conflicts, we should remember that Jonathan loyally stayed by his father's side rather than go with David. Jonathan chose against his love for David to honor and support Saul in spite of their differences. They were not divided, even by their dispute over David, and they died together on the field of battle. David sings of a truth in Israel's

---

182. The words translated "bounteous fields" (NRSV) and "fields that yield offerings of grain" (NIV; שדי תרומת *śĕdê tĕrûmōt*) are notoriously difficult to translate, and numerous emendations of the text have been suggested, none of which have received a wide following. See Anderson, *2 Samuel*, 21; and McCarter, *II Samuel*, 69-71, 75-76, for fuller discussion of the proposals.

experience of Saul and Jonathan that transcends the flaws and struggles of their lives to celebrate their gifts and mourn their loss.

In contrast to the arrogant rejoicing of the daughters of the Philistines (v. 20), David summons the daughters of Israel to weep for Saul (v. 24). It is tears that are appropriate, not laughter. They are to mourn for his loss, remembering the honor and glory with which he had clothed them. The imagery of crimson garments and gold ornaments represents the well-being that Saul returned to Israel. Crimson and gold are the trappings of royalty. In a time of Philistine defeat and occupation, Saul brought a royal presence into the midst of Israel and dared in such a time to dream of kingdom. If he failed to establish an enduring kingdom, he nevertheless gave birth to that possibility for Israel. Again the language is poetic hyperbole. It should not be taken to mean that David is addressing only the daughters of the wealthy.[183]

1:25-27. The use of the refrain in v. 25*a* marks the transition to a new section of the lament. It is the most personal segment in its use of language, almost as if we have moved from leadership in public grief to David's own private sorrow. It is the only segment of the lament cast in the first person. The focus of this section is on Jonathan and the deep personal loss his death meant for David. The king is put aside for the moment in this intimate mourning of the loss of a friend. It is no longer the "splendor" or "glory" of Israel that lies slain upon the high places. It is simply and tragically Jonathan who lies slain there (v. 25*b*).

The poetry of grief in v. 26 reflects the deep and personal relationship of David and Jonathan and the covenant bonds between them, portrayed in 1 Sam 18:1-4; 20:1-42; 23:15-18. David speaks of his own deep distress and speaks of Jonathan as "brother" (v. 26*a*). This term of familial relationship and closeness may refer both to David's relationship to Jonathan as the husband of his sister Michal and to their commitment in a covenant based on *ḥesed* ("faithfulness," "steadfast love"). Covenant partners are often referred to as "brothers."

David speaks of the depth of personal relationship between them. The two verbs used are the same two used in v. 23*a* to speak of Saul and Jonathan, but the application is more personal. The NRSV confusingly translates נעם (*nā'ēm*) as "beloved," which makes it seem as if the verb "to love" (אהב *'āhab*) appears three times in v. 26*b* and points to the wrong corresponding verb in v. 23*a*. David speaks here of the great pleasure and graciousness he found in Jonathan. The NIV translates it more felicitously, "you were very dear to me." David calls to memory Jonathan's love (18:1, 3; 20:17). It was wonderful, and it surpassed the love of women (v. 26*b*). David unreservedly gives public expression to the love on which his friendship with Jonathan was based. As observed in the Commentary on 18:1-4, such love was not only personal but political in character as well. Jonathan's love for David found expression in the surrender of his claim to the throne (18:4), and the verb "to love" appears often in connection with covenant partners to indicate commitment. It was, indeed, wondrous that Jonathan could give up so much for the love of his friend.

Some have felt that the statement of this love, which for David surpassed the love of women, is indicative of a homosexual relationship between David and Jonathan.[184] There is nothing in the language of this verse that explicitly suggests this or rules it out. Of course, David's many liaisons with women are well known and in some cases notorious (2 Samuel 11). We should be alert to the possibility that this phrase says less about David's sexual orientation than it says about the status of women in ancient Israel. In an era of arranged marriages, love was not considered the basis of most relationships between men and women. Liaisons with women existed either in the context of marriage, where the purpose was child-bearing, or in illicit contexts, where the purpose was to satisfy lust. Love of women in such limited contexts might indeed pale in comparison to the deep and personal commitment represented by the love of David and Jonathan for each other.

The final use of the refrain in v. 27 signals the end of David's song of lament. The "weapons of war" that have perished here are Saul and Jonathan themselves. David

---

183. Contra Brueggemann, *First and Second Samuel*, 216.

184. See Tom Horner, *Jonathan Loved David: Homosexuality in Biblical Times* (Philadelphia: Westminster, 1978).

has been the instrument of the unreserved and public expression of grief. He has dared to speak both personally of his own loss and corporately of Israel's loss. Set aside for this moment are both political prospects and divine intentions for Israel's future. It is a deeply human moment that belongs to Saul and Jonathan.

REFLECTIONS

David's singing of Israel's grief and his own invites us to consider our own capacity for public grief and the healing that can flow from such expression.

In 1963 I was a seminary student in Dallas, Texas, when President John F. Kennedy was assassinated. I remember vividly the days of public and national grief. My mind still fills with the images of the caisson and the riderless horse and the endless lines of mourners who filed past the bier while millions filed with them via the television screen. There were poetic words of tribute and loss to accompany the rituals. And there was a strange unity and community in grief, as if in acknowledging our loss we were bound together in a human experience that transcended partisan politics and vested interests. As it was for David, the customary politics of the kingdom were set aside for the moment. The humanness at the heart of the political process was exposed and cared for. In this spirit, bipartisan efforts passed the Civil Rights Act of 1963 in the days following the death of JFK. It was by no means politics as usual.

Only a few short years later, the assassination of Martin Luther King, Jr., in 1968 also brought the country to a standstill. Grief this time was also expressed as rage, and many cities experienced violent outbursts of anger and loss. The hope and promise of a man who symbolized unity beyond the deep racial divisions in our country had been cut down by an assassin's bullet. In the wrenching aftermath of this tragedy, it was again an occasion for public grief that captured a nation's attention, refocused the dream for which King had died, and turned a nation's loss toward new resolve in the struggles against racism. King's nationally televised funeral service brought the nation to a standstill and focused the public attention on King's legacy, which lives beyond the loss felt so deeply by so many.

Unfortunately these signal events in American life may be exceptions and not the rule. Only a short distance from the Lincoln Memorial in Washington, D.C., is the Vietnam War Memorial. It does not announce its presence in monumental fashion. It is a silent, dark granite gash in the green earth inscribed with the mute names of every American military person lost in the Vietnam war. Endless lines pass by its surfaces and stop to find and read names that represent their losses in the midst of a nation's loss. It is the most visited monument in the nation's capital and obviously speaks eloquently to the need of many to acknowledge public grief. But this monument speaks in silent testimony to those who make their way to its site while the nation as a whole has yet to speak much publicly about this chapter of defeat and loss. Vietnam veterans returned to a nation that did not want to hear about their war. They are often called a lost generation of veterans whose sacrifices have been largely unacknowledged because to do so would be to face our moment of national loss and pain in that war. Triumphal politics silence the Davidic voices who would grieve the slain and mourn the defeats. In similar fashion, we are only now learning that voices of triumph obscured the cost and loss suffered in the Persian Gulf War.

David has introduced into this ongoing story of politics and kingdoms the truth taught by all of Israel's laments. It is as important to sing publicly of our hurts as it is to sing of our triumphs. It is only by acknowledging the depths of loss that we can open to God's new thing in our midst. David sings Israel to an acknowledgment of loss that will allow them to surrender Saul as a future that can no longer be. Such singing enables the turning to God's new future. We must remember that David's story not only has roots in the experience of his own time but is being retold by the deuterono-mistic historian, who is telling the story to exiles in Babylon who have also lost a king and a kingdom. Imagine the meaning of David's song of lament heard anew beside the rivers of Babylon by those who despaired of singing the Lord's song (Ps 137:4). David summons those non-singers to sing their loss, and his singers invite us to join in the singing. It is the singing of our hurts that truly orders our priorities. Even the kingdom can wait. Politics and consuming as usual can wait when we allow our grief and pain to teach us what is genuinely valued and needed in our lives. We know the truth of this in moments like the JFK and the King funerals, when much that seemed important was put on hold for a while.

David's singing may model a role for the church. The church should be the place where death can be faced for the painful reality that it is and where our human loss and grief can be voiced. It should be a place where we dare to speak of kingdoms we hoped for that have suffered defeat and have left us despairing of justice or peace or hope. This is the point of the cross as a central symbol of the Christian faith. The brokenness of our lives and our world must be acknowledged and voiced. David teaches us that we cannot move to joy, renewal, and praise too soon. We must make a place for our pain. Our wounds cannot heal if they are not exposed. It is only after encounter with the cross and the loss it represents that resurrection can speak a meaningful word of life. The poetry of pain and grief allows the lost kingdom of Saul to give way to the renewed kingdom of David. The church can sing with David and become a place where pain and loss are acknowledged publicly and their power over us is broken. This can enable a turning toward God's new future for ourselves, for our nation, for our world.

2 Samuel 2:1-11, David Becomes King at Hebron

COMMENTARY

Abruptly the time of mourning is ended. Political realities will not wait. Saul is dead, and the Israelites have scattered. The Philistines occupy the country. If David is to be a part of Israel's future, he must act. The first part of this chapter consists of three brief reports, each suggesting elements in the complex politics of the kingdom. Saul's death has left a vacuum of leadership, and various forces rush to fill the space he has left: vv. 1-4a, after inquiring of God, David moves to Hebron, where he is anointed king by the men of Judah; vv. 4b-7, David responds to the loyalty of Jabesh-gilead in rescuing the body of Saul. His first act as king in Judah is to offer favor to a key group of Israelites; vv. 8-11, Abner makes Ishbosheth king over Israel in Mahanaim.

There is no simple way forward after Saul's death. This portion of the story marks the beginning of a period of conflicting loyalties and ambitions. It is a story of politics and violence, but at the same time a story of

God's future for Israel that finally comes to fruition in David.

2:1-4a. David is still at Ziklag. Saul is dead. Israel's future is at stake. David does not hesitate to act and move toward power, but characteristically his first act is to inquire of the Lord. He has a specific course of action in mind, and the posing of the question in this form suggests that he is using the sacred lots (see 1 Sam 23:9; 30:7). But the narrative has no interest in ritual processes. Only the question and its answer are important: "Should I go up to one of the cities of Judah?" "Yes!" says the Lord. "To which one?" David asks. "Hebron!" (v. 1). David's natural impulse is to consult with the Lord before taking action. This may be an intentional contrast to the way in which Abner makes Ishbosheth king in Mahanaim (vv. 8-9). David's strength ultimately rests in divine power, not in human power.

Hebron was one of the towns to which David distributed the spoil of his Amalekite victory (1 Sam 30:31). It has a long history of connection with Israel's ancestors (Gen 13:18; 23:19; 35:27; 37:14), but in the tribal period of Israel it was a Calebite town (Josh 15:13-14; Judg 1:20) and may not have been considered a city of Judah until after David unified the territory. It is significant that David's two wives are named in the notice that he went up to Hebron. Abigail had been the wife of Nabal, a prominent Calebite land-holder, and Ahinoam was from Jezreel, which was a town near Carmel, the city of Nabal. The account emphasizes that David is already related by marriage to two important clans in the area of Hebron and may already have claims on important landholdings by virtue of those marriages.

In v. 3, David, all of his men (presum-ably six hundred; cf. 1 Sam 27:2), and their households settled in the "towns of Hebron." This would imply at least 2,000 people, and even if the "towns of Hebron" implies the surrounding region rather than just the city of Hebron, this is a sizable population trans-fer. Many scholars have suggested that this sounds more like a takeover of Hebron than a simple move, although it may have been an acceptable takeover to the inhabitants of Hebron. The verb עלה ('ālâ, "to go up") is used elsewhere with a military connotation (e.g., 5:17, 19), and David does "go up" with a seasoned fighting force of six hundred men. Hebron would hardly be in a position to refuse David hospitality. Some have suggested that David may have done this with Philistine approval.[185] There is not yet any notice in the story that he has left Philistine service or positioned himself as a Philistine enemy. His break with the Philistines does not seem to come until he is made king of Israel (5:17).

Only after David has, in effect, occupied Hebron do the "men of Judah" come to Hebron and "anoint" David king over the house of Judah (v. 4a). These may be the same individuals as the "elders of Judah" who received David's gifts in 1 Sam 30:26. What-ever the earlier relationship between Judah and Hebron, they are now joined in David's kingship over a "house of Judah," with its capital in Hebron.

It is significant that the people "anoint" David. He had already been secretly anointed by the prophet Samuel (1 Sam 16:13). This earlier anointing led to David's receiving God's Spirit and being designated as the "anointed of the LORD." Here we seem to be dealing with an anointing ritual that does not confer sacral status but represents the people's authorization of the ruler. In 19:10, the people anoint Absalom as a sign of their authorization, but it does not make him the Lord's anointed. The significance here is that David is legitimated by both God and people. His rule is established with the broadest pos-sible basis. The immediate contrast to this will be the imposition of a king on the throne of Israel by Abner in vv. 8-9.

Judah has for the moment separated from Israel. Judah has chosen one of its own as king. The fate of Israel, scattered and defeated, is not immediately clear, whereas the people of Judah have acted to secure their own future. Such Judahite action may be seen as a rebellion against Israel as a Saulide kingdom. This would help to explain the hos-tilities that break out into war between Israel and Judah in 2:12-32.

2:4b-7. David is given a report on the people of Jabesh-gilead (v. 4b), who rescued Saul's body from the walls of Beth-shan and gave it a proper burial (1 Sam 31:11-13). Their kindness to Saul was in gratitude for his rescue of Jabesh-gilead from the siege of Nahash, the king of Ammon (1 Samuel 11).

David's first act after becoming king of Judah is to send a gracious message to a northern Israelite group (vv. 5-7). Jabesh-gilead was an important town in the Transjor-dan and was not far from Mahanaim, where a Saulide capital would be established under the reign of Saul's son Ishbosheth (vv. 8-9). David offers commendation and friendship to an Israelite community in the heart of the remaining Saulide kingdom.

David begins by blessing them in the name of the Lord because of the loyalty they had shown to Saul in his burial (v. 5). The term for "loyalty" here is חסד (ḥesed), a word associated with covenants and commitments (also translated as "kindness," "faithfulness," or "steadfast love"). It was a term favored by David and Jonathan in describing the depth of their friendship and commitment to each other (1 Sam 20:8, 14-15). It is a principle respected and employed by David in honor-ing his personal and royal commitments (9:1,

185. Anderson, *2 Samuel*, 22-23.

with Jonathan's son, Mephibosheth; 10:2, in a treaty with the Ammonites).

In return, David invokes the "steadfast love/kindness" (ḥesed) and "faithfulness" of the Lord on behalf of the Jabesh-gileadites (v. 6a). Further, David himself promises "favor" toward them. The term used here is טובה (ṭôbâ; lit., "goodness"). The NRSV's translation "reward" suggests material benefits, but David is simply offering friendship and goodwill. He offers relationship and not "reward." It is significant that David invokes God's beneficence before offering his own goodwill. It conveys a sense that David understands his own authority as being derived from that of the Lord. It also serves to make his own goodwill an extension of God's favor, a connection that he no doubt hopes the people of Jabesh-gilead will find attractive. His final word is not quite so subtle. Although he encourages them to be brave and strong, he bluntly reminds them that Saul is dead, but Judah has just anointed David king (v. 7). The message to Jabesh-gilead is that they can hang on to those things that are gone, or they can look to new beginnings with David. At this point, David cannot realistically expect an explicit political alliance with Jabesh-gilead. They are too far north, and both Philistines and the remnants of a Saulide kingdom lie between. He is, however, building influence and goodwill in the north, and this effort seems to bear fruit in the future (5:1-3).

2:8-11. The first two verses of this section narrate the establishment of a continuing Saulide kingdom (vv. 8-9). The narrative does not dwell on this continuation of Israel, but strikes a contrast with the beginnings of David's kingdom, described earlier in the chapter.

David's kingship in Judah begins with his inquiring of the Lord (v. 1). David seeks divine authorization. By contrast, vv. 8-9 report that Abner *took* Ishbosheth, and *brought* him to Mahanaim, and *made* him king. The harsh verbs of these verses portray an Israelite kingship authorized by the political and military power of Abner.

Abner was the commander of Saul's army (1 Sam 17:55; 20:25; 26:5) and a cousin (or uncle) of Saul (1 Sam 14:50). It seems clear that, after the death of Saul, Abner was the effective power in Israel, but he does not have

a clear claim to the throne and must install the remaining son of Saul on the throne as a figurehead. This assessment of Abner's power seems confirmed by later events when his defection to David and subsequent death leave Ishbosheth vulnerable to assassination (3:6–4:12).

Ishbosheth appears to be the remaining son of Saul. His name, as it appears in 2 Samuel, has always been considered a scribal comment. His name is reported in 1 Chr 8:33; 9:39 as "Eshbaal," which means "Baal exists." Some would, with a slight emendation, read "Ishbaal," "Man of Baal." Most scholars consider the name reported in 1 Chronicles as historically original,[186] and many translations have adopted this name in place of Ishbosheth in 2 Samuel (including the NRSV). However, the actual text for 2 Samuel reads the name as "Ishbosheth," which means "Man of shame." The widely accepted hypothesis is that later editors or scribes (perhaps the deuteronomistic historian), reflecting the struggle with Baalism in later periods, replaced the offending Baal element of the name with the Hebrew word for "shame" (בשת bōšet). Such a linguistic substitution as a theological comment is known elsewhere in the biblical tradition (e.g., Jer 11:13). In Saul's time, the term בעל (baʿal), which means "lord," was not yet connected with Canaanite idolatry as a threat to the worship of Yahweh. The noun may even have been used as a term of honor and respect for God. Jonathan also had a son with a name that included the element baʿal, and the text of 2 Samuel also shows his name altered by the use of the term bōšet (see Commentary on 2 Sam 9:1-13). We do not know much about Ishbosheth/Ishbaal. He was not with Saul and his other sons at Mt. Gilboa, and most assume that this means he was too young to join the fighting men.

Mahanaim is an important town in the Transjordan. It seems clear that any continuation of Israelite rule would have been forced to locate its center outside of Philistine-dominated territory. There is no evidence that Philistine hegemony extended beyond the Jordan River, so Mahanaim was a safe place for Abner to attempt a rebuilding of the Israelite

---

186. See McCarter, *II Samuel*, 85-87, for a detailed discussion of the linguistic and textual proposals related to this name.

kingdom. The list of geographic territories for Ishbosheth's rule in v. 9 is a claim to most, if not all, of Saul's previous kingdom, but it is a hope rather than a reality.

The chronological notes of vv. 10-11 are characteristic of the deuteronomistic historian and are probably from his hand. The actual figures used present some problems. It is highly unlikely that Ishbosheth was forty years old at the start of his reign. This would make him older than Jonathan and heir to the throne ahead of Jonathan. David was only thirty years old when his reign began (5:4), and he was of similar age to Jonathan. There are many indications that Ishbosheth was a boy. He did not fight at Gilboa. He was dominated and controlled by Abner as if Abner were regent to the throne. In the later dispute over Rizpah, Saul's concubine, it is Abner who has sexual relations with her, and not Ishbosheth. The taking of the king's harem was a frequent sign of accession to the throne in ancient times (see Absalom later, 16:21-22). Ishbosheth may have been too young to have exercised this sign of authority himself (see Commentary on 3:6-11).

The note of two years for Ishbosheth's reign may well be accurate (v. 10), but it is difficult to explain why David's reign at Hebron is listed as having been so much longer (seven and a half years, v. 11). The usual assumption has been that when Ishbosheth was killed and the elders of Israel made David king as well, he soon thereafter moved his capital to Jerusalem. This note, if accurate, would suggest that David reigned from Hebron for five and a half years after becoming king over Judah *and* Israel.

REFLECTIONS

It would be understandable if readers took a cynical view of these notices in 2:1-11. Saul has received his moment of honor and respect. Now it is politics as usual. Yet, even the honored past must give way to the future, and the realities of power must be acknowledged.

The short notices of this passage do, however, offer a contrast in dealing with the realities of power. Abner *takes, brings,* and *makes* a king. He imposes authority and forces a political ideology on the land. David inquires of God, acts decisively himself, and submits to the anointing of the people. He is not without his own authority or the influence of his own considerable will. But he is willing to submit his own authority to a partnership with God, on the one hand, and with the community, on the other hand.

What an instructive metaphor this is for any calling to leadership in the secular world or in the church. Whether in our churches or in our governments, we want leaders with authority who can take decisive action. But too often our leadership is exposed as exercising such authority with no loyalty beyond their own self-interest. Hardly a month goes by without the news of some major scandal of failed public or ecclesiastical trust—presidential advisers, bishops, senators, denominational treasurers. It is significant that in the notice that stands between the models of David and Abner for kingship, David commends the men of Jabesh-gilead for their loyalty to the interests of a king who cannot repay their deed. It is an act of integrity utterly without self-interest. Leadership appropriate to God's kingdom is always shared leadership, accountable to God and community. Whether we speak of pastors or of presidents, David's model has much to commend it.

2 Samuel 2:12-32, A Battle and a Blood Feud

COMMENTARY

The background to this episode is war between the house of Saul and the house of David (cf. 3:1, 6). This is probably not the story of the outbreak of that war, although it would seem to be the account of a major confrontation at an early point in this period of hostility. When the forces of Abner and the forces of Joab confront each other across the pool at Gibeon, the assumption is that there will be a battle of some sort (vv. 12-14). The narrative of 2 Samuel is not interested in telling us why the house of Saul and the house of David are at war. Does Israel regard David's kingship over Judah as a rebellion and a seizing of territory belonging to Israel? Has David made overt claims on the throne of Israel? We do not know of any such claims. It may well be that David, even as king in Hebron, is still working as a vassal of the Philistines. We do not have any record of a break with the Philistines at this point. Only after he becomes king of Israel (5:1-3) does David seem to become an enemy of the Philistines. If Abner and his men are at Gibeon trying to reassert Israelite control of the central hill country, Saul's home area in Benjamin, then an encounter with Joab could well be an encounter with forces in service to the Philistines.

The narrator of this episode is less concerned with the larger geopolitics of the region than with this encounter as the setting for the killing of Asahel by Abner (v. 23). This act sets in motion a complex series of events that do constitute a threat to David's kingship over all of Israel. These events will continue to unfold beyond this episode through chaps. 3–4. God's kingdom under David does not come in a vacuum but in the midst of difficult political realities and personal tragedies.

2:12-17. Abner, who was commander of the army under Saul and is now the power behind the rule of Ishbosheth, leads a military party back into the central hill country from which Israel had been driven by the Philistines (v. 12). The verb יצא (yāṣā', "to go out") used in this context has military connotations. They have come from Mahanaim, the Transjordanian town from which Ishbosheth

now perpetuates the rule of the house of Saul, to Gibeon, a non-Israelite city aligned with Israel since the days of Joshua (Joshua 9). Gibeon is in the middle of Benjaminite tribal territory and close to Saul's capital at Gibeah. Several times in this account the Israelites with Abner are referred to as Benjaminites (vv. 15, 25, 31). This may well be a mission sent to test the extent of Philistine control over Benjaminite home territory.

At the same time, Joab, commanding some of the men of David, went out (yāṣā') to meet them at the pool of Gibeon (v. 13). Joab is David's nephew, the son of his sister Zeruiah (1 Chr 2:16). This is our first meeting with him, but he will figure prominently in the story of David from this point onward. Joab and his men seem already to be in Gibeon, and they meet with Abner's force at a place called the pool of Gibeon. The two groups face each other across the pool (v. 13b). We have already mentioned the possibility that David's men are still serving as vassals of the Philistines. They may be patrolling this territory for the Philistines.

Perhaps in an attempt to avoid full-scale conflict Abner proposes a representative combat between twelve of his men (called Benjaminites) and twelve of Joab's men; Joab agrees to this (vv. 14-15). Older commentary on this text describes this encounter as a game or a contest that got out of hand and turned deadly. More recent scholarship has made clear the widespread use of representative combat in the ancient Near East and has advanced evidence that the verb שחק (śāḥaq), often translated as "to play," can also mean "to contest in hand to hand combat."[187]

The fight is quickly over (v. 16). This verse may represent only the final stage of the combat. It would appear that each pair of opponents became locked in struggle with daggers so that all twenty-four opponents fell wounded if not dead. The narrator reports that this event gave rise to the naming of the place as "Field of Daggers or Hostilities"

187. Vaux, "Single Combat in the Old Testament," 122-35.

(v. 16b). Suddenly, without explanation, a wider battle is reported, and it is one that Abner and the Israelite men lose (v. 17). Did some not honor the terms of the representative combat? Of course, such a battle broke out after David killed Goliath as well (1 Samuel 17:1). This battle following the combat of the young men seems to be the context in which the events of vv. 18-32 are narrated. It was those events, and not the wider battle, that was of interest to the narrator.

2:18-32. The three sons of David's sister Zeruiah are the macho men of the books of Samuel. They are fierce and formidable warriors, but also are rash and intemperate. We already met Abishai, who, as the companion of David, had to be restrained from killing Saul in his sleep (1 Sam 26:6-12). Joab eventually becomes the commander of David's armies, but he will also be involved in numerous events that require a quick sword and a willingness to use it. In this story, the focus is on the third brother, Asahel, who is said to be as fast of foot as a gazelle (v. 18).

In the heat of battle, perhaps as the Israelites are trying to retreat, Asahel pursues Abner with dogged persistence (v. 19). The impression is that Abner is not as fast as Asahel, but he is a more seasoned warrior. Abner clearly knows Asahel and makes certain of his identity (v. 20). Twice he tries to persuade Asahel to break off the pursuit. He urges him to seize one of the other men and take spoil for himself (v. 21). When Asahel persists in pursuit, Abner pleads that he does not wish to hurt him. He worries about facing Joab if he should strike down Asahel (v. 22). As it turns out, this worry was warranted (see chap. 3). Asahel refuses to break off the pursuit. The end comes quickly with the practiced efficiency of the experienced warrior. When Abner sees that there is no alternative but to kill or be killed, he strikes Asahel with the butt of his spear so that the end passes through his body (v. 23a). It may have been an unexpected stroke with the back of the spear. The account seems to be at great pains to show that Abner was forced into combat against his will in killing Asahel. Others come to the place where Asahel lies and stand silent and still, perhaps in shock at the loss of one of these seemingly invincible brothers (v. 23b).

The remaining brothers, Joab and Abishai, take up the pursuit of Abner, but they do not seem as fleet of foot (v. 24). At nightfall Abner and his remaining Israelites/Benjaminites take a stand on a hilltop with Joab, Abishai, and their men apparently at a distance, perhaps on an opposite hill (v. 25). Abner calls out a proposal to end the fighting. He speaks of his men and the men of David as kinsmen and suggests that their battle can only become more bitter (v. 26). Joab takes the opening. Perhaps it allows him to disengage with honor. He, too, refers to the two opposing forces as kinsmen and admits that without Abner's initiative the battle would have continued until morning (v. 27). Joab sounds the trumpet, and the battle ends (v. 28). There is irony in Abner's proposal to cease hostilities. He asks the question, "Is the sword to keep devouring forever?" (v. 26a). The imagery of the "sword devouring" appears only one additional time in 2 Samuel. Instead of a plea for peace, it is a casual justification for the murder of Uriah, which David orders Joab to carry out, saying, "The sword devours one and then the other" (11:25).

There remains of this account only the sad aftermath of war: the return home of those who survived (vv. 29, 32b); the listing of the body count for those who cannot return home (nineteen of David's men, but three hundred and sixty of Abner's men, vv. 30-31); and the burial of Asahel in his father's tomb in Bethlehem (v. 32a). It has been a great loss for the men of Israel, but the death of Asahel clearly leaves Joab without any feeling of victory. The full repercussions of this event have yet to play themselves out.

REFLECTIONS

It is in the Advent season that churches sing of the angelic proclamation of "Peace on earth! Goodwill to all people!" It is a most satisfying way to think of the advent of God's kingdom and the coming of God's anointed one. But this text is far from that imagery. David is God's anointed one, and the kingdom God will establish through him is being born. Yet, the events of this narrative are of war, not of peace—of violence, and not of goodwill.

It is natural for readers to ask why David's lament over the cost of war in the lives of Saul and Jonathan (1:19-27) and David's praise for the "loyalty/steadfast love" of Jabesh-gilead (2:4b-7) must be followed by a story of such senseless violence and death. We want God's kingdom to be announced and fully present. We want to think about God's kingdom as abstracted from the realities of war and blood feuds, politics and ideologies. This text reminds us that God's kingdom cannot take shape in human history without recognition of these realities. David cannot establish God's kingdom for Israel, and God's purposes cannot go forward apart from facing and dealing with such realities. David will have to deal with the Abners and the Joabs, the civil wars and the Philistine wars, his own faithfulness and the seductions of his own power.

In our own time, we may sing with the angelic choirs at Christmastide, but the gospel story and the church calendar will eventually take us to Herod's court, to Pilate's judgment, and to Golgotha. It is good to sing of our hope for "peace on earth," but the church in our time will have to listen to the stories of atrocities in Rwanda, renewed ethnic killing in Bosnia, and widespread abuse and rape of women in our own society that fill our newspapers. It is these stories, like the war story of 2 Sam 2:12-32, that remind us why God's kingdom is needed in our midst. We need God's kingdom to come precisely because the world is often violent, unjust, and cruel. Blood is shed, and death is real in our world just as in David's.

The story of this war episode offers no glib answers or moral aphorisms. It tells us what the world, where David must establish his kingdom, is like. His first act as king of Judah was to praise the *hesed* of Jabesh-gilead. He must now deal with the political realities that drive the violence of Abner and Joab and their men. In the chapters just ahead (chaps. 3–4), events actually get more complex politically, and more people die. David must face these realities and nevertheless find a way to establish the kingdom. If we in our turn are to be agents for the bringing of God's kingdom, it will not be enough to sing of peace and settle for a fuzzy hope that it will come. We, like David, will have to find realistic strategies that deal with the ambiguous political realities standing as barriers to the coming of the kingdom. To do that, we will have to face the realities of wars and rumors of wars. We will have to hear and tell the stories of violence that make clear the tragic cycle of injury and revenge that threatens God's kingdom in our time as surely as it threatened God's kingdom through David. Only by recognizing such patterns of violence and naming the blind self-interest that motivates such patterns can we hope to break the hold of violent patterns and move toward the fullness of God's kingdom.

2 Samuel 3:1-5, David's Sons

COMMENTARY

This short section includes a summarizing note (v. 1) and a list of the sons born to David at Hebron (vv. 2-5). It seems intrusive here, since v. 6 resumes the story of the enmity between Abner and Joab, which began with the death of Asahel in 2:18-32.

Verse 1 is an important programmatic statement reminding us that David's kingship over a unified Israel did not come immediately or without cost. There was a "long war." Interestingly, this war is characterized not by geography (north and south) but by the two houses claiming the throne. It was a war between the house of Saul and the house of David. The ghost of past conflict between David and Saul is not easily exorcised. Yet, the path to the future is clear. David grew constantly stronger while the house of Saul grew progressively weaker. Perhaps the conflict went on so long precisely because David would not seize a unified kingdom by frontal assault. As we shall see, he is careful not to be seen as having plotted the deaths of Israel's leaders. It is important that Israel come to him with the gift of kingdom. We should imagine the war, then, as one of border hostilities and skirmishing rather than as a campaign by David to impose his rule on Israel.

The list of David's sons is information that is not directly pertinent at this point in the story, but it is the first hint of the issue of succession, which will loom so large at a later point in the story. We know almost nothing about three of these sons beyond their names in this list (cf. 1 Chr 3:1-9, where it is combined with the list in 5:13-16): Chileab (whose mother, Abigail, is known to us from 1 Samuel 25), Shephatiah, and Ithream. The remaining three will become well known to us in later struggles over succession to the throne. Amnon, Absalom, and Adonijah all play significant roles in the difficult and tragic events of David's later life (see 2 Samuel 13–20; 1 Kings 1–2).

2 Samuel 3:6-39, The Death of Abner

COMMENTARY

This episode constitutes an unfolding drama with Abner at its center, but the innocence of David as its objective. This drama falls into several distinct acts within the narrative of the chapter: vv. 6-11 tell of Abner's conflict with Ishbosheth; vv. 12-21 detail Abner's negotiations with David and the planned covenant with Israel; vv. 22-27 narrate the circumstances of Abner's death at the hands of Joab; vv. 28-39 describe David's cursing of Joab and his elaborate lamentation and honoring of Abner. The purpose of the episode within the larger history of the rise of David is made clear by v. 37: "So all the people and all Israel understood that day that the king had no part in the killing of Abner, son of Ner." David is innocent of the violence that took the life of Abner, commander of the northern armies. The bloodguilt falls on Joab (v. 29), and not on David. It is conceivable that David benefited from Abner's death, if Abner is seen as a potential rival of David, but a similar case could be made that this untimely death was problematic for David's relationship to northern Israel and robbed him of an important strategic ally in terms of other goals (e.g., ridding Israel of Philistine domination).

The account of Abner's death possesses a viewpoint of its own for this complex series of events. No doubt the telling of this story would be different from other viewpoints. The present account is *biased positively toward Abner.* Abner appears as a strong and forceful leader of Israel. By contrast, Ishbosheth is weak and vacillating. After Abner's death even David voices the opinion that "a prince and a great man has fallen this day in Israel" (v. 38). Abner is not viewed as a threat to David. In fact, it is Abner who gives voice on two occasions to the conviction that David is the man the Lord has chosen to lead all Israel and to bring deliverance from the Philistines (vv. 9, 18). The present account is equally clear about the *guilt of Joab.* Joab's cause against Abner is not presented as a just cause, but as a petty personal feud that has placed the interests of David and Israel in jeopardy. David curses Joab and lays the bloodguilt for Abner's death upon Joab and his family (vv. 28-29). Joab's act of killing is a murder (v. 30), and this bloodguilt may eventually be what allows Solomon to take Joab's life at a later point when it suits Solomon's interests (1 Kgs 2:31-34). The present account, by contrast, is concerned to demonstrate *David's innocence.* David is not involved in plotting Abner's death and does not incur bloodguilt (v. 37). He curses Joab and gives Abner the honor of a state funeral with elaborate lamentation. Of course, it is also notable that Joab, unlike the Amalekite who took Saul's life (1:1-16) or the two who will bring Ishbosheth's head to David in the next episode (4:1-12), is not killed. David curses him, but seems still to need him. Perhaps David could not move to take Joab's life because he was related to David by family or was simply too influential and powerful. What seems to begin here is a dark and complex relationship between Joab and David. David will often rely on Joab for both honorable and sinister purposes (cf. 10:7-19 and 11:14-25). He seems to need Joab, but seems also to recognize in him a violence that is dangerous and compromises the kingdom (v. 39).

These events might have been told from other perspectives and have taken quite a different shape. The story would have a different spin were it told from the perspective of Joab's clan or the perspective of those in Israel still suspicious of David's motives or the perspective of the surviving members of the house of Saul (e.g., Ishbosheth and Michal). The invective of Shimei (16:7-8) when David is retreating from Jerusalem suggests that some thought David had incurred bloodguilt in the events that led to his kingship and the collapse of the house of Saul.

The present narrative is biased in favor of David's innocence, but it is the only telling of these events that we have. One can only speculate about the relation of this telling to the historical course of events or David's so-called true motives behind his public actions. Some, desiring to paint a more cynical portrait of David, have ventured so far as to suggest that David desired and plotted the death of Abner. His public shock and lamentation, then, were a sham.[188] In the absence of other tellings of this story, such alternative reconstructions are mere speculation and should be treated with caution.

3:6-11. Verse 6 seems to be a further comment on v. 1 and resumes the main story line after the insertion of the notice on David's sons in vv. 2-5. War continues between the houses of Saul and David, but the focus now shifts to Abner, who has made his position stronger within the house of Saul (v. 6*b*). Since Abner was already acknowledged as the power behind the throne of Ishbosheth (2:8-9), this development is not a surprise.

A tale of conflict between Abner and Ishbosheth unfolds in vv. 7-11. (The NRSV, following 1 Chr 8:33; 9:39, reads "Ishbaal"

instead of "Ishbosheth" for the name of Saul's son. See Commentary on 2 Sam 2:8-11 for a discussion of this matter.) Ishbosheth confronts Abner over having had sexual relations with Rizpah, a concubine of his father, Saul. In this story, Rizpah does not emerge as a character in her own right, but is a symbolic pawn in power struggles related to the throne. In a later story (21:8-14), she appears in a tragic episode involving the death of her sons. Her courage and perseverance eventually command the attention and response of David himself. Here, however, she is simply named as the concubine of Saul.

The status of such concubines is a matter of some debate. Some regard Rizpah as a slave attached to the household of Saul who attained significance by bearing him two sons.[189] Others believe that such concubines were legitimate wives of a second rank, perhaps drawn from lower economic classes.[190] The naming of her father would tend to confirm that she was not a slave. In any case, it is clear that her two sons fathered by Saul were considered a legitimate part of the house of Saul and certainly gave Rizpah additional status in the royal household.

It has long been noted that sexual relations with a king's wives or concubines is an act used by claimants to the throne to establish their right to succession. Such action can establish legitimacy to a claim on the throne or serve to usurp the claim of the present occupant of the throne. In this instance, Ishbosheth may have taken Abner's relations with Rizpah to be an implicit threat to his own kingship and a potential claim on the throne by Abner himself. Similar events occur in two other instances with David's sons. Absalom asserts his claim on David's throne by sleeping with David's ten concubines (2 Samuel 20–22). Later, Adonijah asks for Abishag, the concubine of David's old age, as a wife. This is treated as an act of sedition by Solomon and is used as a pretext to kill his half brother and rival for the throne (1 Kgs 2:17-25). Such symbolic sexual acts with royal wives and concubines by claimants to the throne are known elsewhere in the ancient world as well, and many believe the action of Abner

---

188. See, e.g., J. C. VanderKam, "Davidic Complicity in the Deaths of Abner and Eshbaal: A Historical and Redactional Study," *JBL* 99 (1980) 521-39.

189. See McCarter, *II Samuel*, 112-13, for this view.
190. See Anderson, *2 Samuel*, 55-56, and the more technical studies he cites for this view.

must be seen as a challenge to Ishbosheth's royal authority.[191] Why did Ishbosheth not take Rizpah as a wife himself? Then Abner could have sexual relations with her only by committing the crime of adultery. It may be that Ishbosheth was too young and was still only a boy (see Commentary on 2:10-11).

Abner's angry response leaves unclear whether Ishbosheth's charge was just or not. Abner is indignant, but his indignation could be construed as anger over Ishbosheth's accusation as false or over the accusation as dealing with a trivial matter compared to the loyalty Abner had shown to the house of Saul. He begins his angry response by claiming that Ishbosheth's accusation has insulted him as a "dog's head of Judah," presumably an epithet of worthlessness (v. 8a). Abner feels publicly demeaned. He contrasts this with his loyalty (*hesed*) shown to the house of Saul and specifically states that he has not given Ishbosheth over to David (v. 8b). Perhaps this remark is intended as a veiled threat. To Abner, the matter of Rizpah is of small consequence compared to his service, and Ishbosheth has demeaned that service.

Abruptly, Abner seems to resolve to do the very thing he had threatened. In vv. 8-9, he vows by his own well-being before God to shift his support to David and establish his kingdom from Dan to Beersheba. Surprisingly he cites the promise of the Lord to David for such a kingdom and places his own support in the service of that promise. Abner vows to become the agent of God's promise to David. We do not have any record of so specific a divine promise made to David, although his anointing by Samuel and the many references to David as God's choice for king would carry the implicit promise of such an established kingdom. Certainly there is no story of a divine oath sworn to David, but this may simply indicate the widespread recognition of divine favor attached to David and his future reign. We should note that Abner refers to David's reign over Israel and Judah, indicating the dual nature of David's kingship from the beginning.

Our final picture of Ishbosheth is of a pitiful, fearful man. He is powerless to do anything to stop the defection of Abner. The real power clearly rests with Abner, not Ishbosheth, and Ishbosheth is afraid (v. 11).

3:12-21. In v. 12, Abner makes good his threat and enters into negotiations with David. He sends messengers to propose a covenant with David. It is clear that Abner approaches David not as a refugee but as a chieftain with considerable power and influence. He offers as his part of a covenant with David to deliver not only his own support but also the allegiance of the northern tribes of Israel. We have no reason to doubt that he can deliver on the promise. However, the rhetorical question that begins Abner's negotiations with David is not entirely clear. It may be that the question, "To whom does the land belong?" is a reference to Abner's acknowledgment of the Lord's oath to give all of the land into David's rule (vv. 9-10). The answer to the rhetorical question is, then, "To David, of course!"

David readily agrees to a covenant with Abner, but not without his own condition. If Abner is to meet with David to negotiate an alliance, then he is to bring Saul's daughter Michal with him (v. 13). The language is forceful. Abner may not even appear before David without bringing Michal. Saul had been forced to marry his daughter Michal to David when he produced the brideprice of Philistine foreskins (1 Sam 18:20-27). David now alludes to this brideprice (v. 14) as his legal claim that the marriage to Michal is still in effect. When David had been forced to flee from Saul's court, with the aid of Michal and Jonathan, Saul had married her to a man named Palti (1 Sam 25:44). Saul hoped to remove any claim by David on kinship to the house of Saul that might strengthen Davidic claims on the throne. Now that second marriage is declared void by the reassertion of David's claim, and Michal is forcibly taken from Paltiel (v. 15, a longer form of the name), who follows her, weeping, until Abner threateningly tells him to return home (v. 16). Although Michal's arrival at David's capital is not recounted, we may assume that she was delivered to him, since she makes a later appearance as part of David's household (6:16, 20-23). By reclaiming his marriage to Michal, David solidifies both a legal and a popular tie to the house of Saul. This no doubt increases his acceptability to a broad

191. See M. Tsevat, "Marriage and Monarchical Legitimacy in Ugarit and Israel," *JSS* 3 (1958) 237-43.

segment of the northern Israelite populace. In all of this Michal has no say. She once loved David (1 Sam 18:20), but she has now become a pawn in a larger complex of political maneuvering.

It is odd that David's formal request for the return of Michal goes to Ishbosheth, who then has her taken from Paltiel (vv. 14-15). In v. 16, however, it is clearly Abner who is delivering her to David. It is likely that Ishbosheth was not aware of Abner's actual negotiations with David or of David's condition. David's legal claim on Michal is asserted through the official channel of the Saulide king Ishbosheth, because the negotiations with Abner are still secret. Abner is still the true power behind Ishbosheth, so it is not surprising that Ishbosheth complies, although he must certainly have known it would strengthen Davidic claims.

After negotiations with David, Abner turns to deal with the elders of Israel (v. 17a). This should not be understood as a formal body, but simply a meeting of representative leaders from the northern tribes. Abner's speech to them implies that there has already been considerable support in the north for David as king (v. 17b). Abner announces to them that the time has come to make it happen, and he supports that claim by making an appeal to David as the one promised by the Lord to bring deliverance from the Philistines (v. 18). This must have been a powerful incentive to those who had only recently suffered a brutal defeat at the hands of the Philistines, and Abner's appeal is also a reminder of the failure of the house of Saul to bring relief from Philistine oppression. Abner makes a special effort to speak directly to the Benjaminites, the tribesmen of Saul's house (v. 19a). It is not clear if this was in a separate meeting, but it does imply that negotiations with Saul's own tribe required additional attention and delicacy. Nevertheless, the word brought to David at Hebron by Abner is pointed in its statement that Israel and the "whole house of Benjamin" are ready to act in David's favor (v. 19b).

With a company of only twenty men, Abner meets with David at Hebron, where he is welcomed with a feast (v. 20). Final negotiations are completed for a covenant-making ceremony with Israel that will establish David's rule over "all that your heart desires" (v. 21). Abner addresses David as "my lord, the king," and the mood is festive. When Abner departs to rally Israel for the covenant ceremony, the text tells us for the first of three times that Abner departed in "peace" (שלום *šālôm*, vv. 21b, 22b, 23b). The narrator wants to be clear that all was well between David and Abner. Perhaps of equal importance, the narrative is clear that alliance with Israel was not made through coercion but through negotiations and covenant.

3:22-30. Joab enters the story, and events take a dark turn. He had just returned from leading one of David's raiding parties, presumably of the sort that David conducted in the name of the Philistines from Ziklag (v. 22a). In the light of subsequent events, one wonders if Joab's absence from Hebron at the time of Abner's visit was intentional on David's part. Joab comes with the spoils of war, and the text reminds us again that Abner had departed in peace (v. 22b). Immediately Joab receives a report that Abner has been in Hebron and again that Abner left David in peace (v. 23). Joab's response is immediate and bitter. He confronts David and suggests that David has allowed an enemy to escape (v. 24). He argues that Abner could only have deception and spying as his purposes in coming to David (v. 25). No response of David is recorded, but Joab clearly received no encouragement, since he subsequently took matters into his own hands. Joab must be seen as a figure with two interests that work against the acceptability of an alliance with Abner. The first is his hatred and distrust of Abner, stemming from Abner's killing of Joab's brother Asahel in the battle described in 2:12-32. Joab sees himself as the legitimate bearer of a claim for vengeance against Abner, although ordinarily bloodguilt would not be recognized for a death suffered in war—i.e., it was not considered murder. The second of Joab's interests in this matter has to do with influence on David. Joab eventually becomes commander of David's armies (8:16), but it is reasonable to think that Abner might have assumed this role if he had lived. In any case, Abner would have been a powerful and influential military adviser and leader within David's kingdom, and this would make him Joab's natural rival for David's favor.

Joab does not hesitate to take ruthless action in his own interests. He sends messengers to intercept Abner and seek his return to Hebron (v. 26). Again, the cautious narrative makes clear that David knew nothing of this (v. 26*b*). When Abner returns, Joab pulls him into a chamber of the gate as if to confer with him, but instead Joab stabs him in the stomach, and Abner dies (v. 27). Twice the narrative attributes this death to vengeance for Asahel's death (vv. 27*b*, 30; Joab's brother Abishai is included in v. 30, although he seems to have played no direct role). However, the verdict of the narrative on this deed is clear. The death of Abner is called a murder, while the death of Asahel in battle is named a killing (v. 30).

It is murder that carries bloodguilt, and this is David's immediate concern in response to news of Abner's death. David declares himself and his kingdom innocent of this wrongfully shed blood (v. 28), and he lays the guilt upon Joab and the house of Joab's father (v. 29*a*). David goes farther and pronounces a curse upon the house of Joab (v. 29*b*) that includes disease, violence, and hunger. The reference to one "who holds a spindle" may imply men who are not fit for battle and must do women's work. The curse is vigorous and unflinching in its terms, but why did David not act more directly against Joab as he did in avenging the bloodguilt incurred by the Amalekite in killing Saul (1:1-16), or as he will later do in avenging the death of Ishbosheth (4:1-12)? In effect, David leaves this particular matter to the Lord (explicit in v. 39*b*), while David himself continues to make extensive use of the services of Joab (e.g., 8:16; 20:23). It may be that Joab and his family are too influential and centrally important in David's military forces to act against him or dispense with him. Certainly, v. 39 indicates some frustration on David's part for his lack of political options in dealing with the violence of the sons of Zeruiah. It is clear that even kings have political limitations on their choices—at least if they are to continue as king. Eventually Joab's bloodguilt for the death of Abner is cited by David from his deathbed as reason for Solomon to kill him (1 Kgs 2:5-6). It may be that the story here is shaped to help justify the death of Joab as part of an initial Solomonic court purge.

3:31-39. David may be innocent, as the narrative claims, but it is also possible that no one will believe him. The need to establish public credibility for David's claim to non-involvement is clearly a factor in the elaborate public mourning and state funeral given for Abner. David is sending a message to the northern tribes that this killing was not his desired outcome. Indeed, Abner's death seems more a problem to David than an asset.

David orders the people, including Joab (a public humiliation?), into mourning for Abner with the tearing of clothes and the wearing of sackcloth (v. 31). David himself follows the bier and leads in weeping at Abner's burial in Hebron (v. 32). He sings a lament for Abner (vv. 33-34), recalling his similar but much more elaborate lament for Saul and Jonathan (1:17-27). The first line is addressed to Israel as a rhetorical question, suggesting that Abner did not deserve such an ignoble death (that of a fool or an outlaw, v. 33*b*). The remaining lines are addressed in the second person to the deceased, a feature common to funerary laments (although this one is not composed in the קינה *qînâ* pattern as in 1:17-27). Although Abner was not bound and fettered like a criminal, he died like one (v. 34*a*). David labels those who killed Abner as the wicked before whom Abner fell by treachery (v. 34*b*). David fasts the entire day, in spite of the people's urging him to eat (v. 35). David is the chief of the mourners for Abner, and although his sentiments may be genuine, it is clear that his mourning bears political significance.

From the perspective of this narrative, David's efforts are efficacious. The people noticed and were pleased by David's response, although the narrator admits that the people seemed to be pleased with almost everything David did (v. 36). We have already noted the declaration of David's innocence and the people's recognition of his innocence in v. 37 as the key verse to this chapter. David is not complicit in the death of Abner. The people know it; the narrative wants the reader to know it. Indeed, David's final words in this matter are a magnanimous tribute to Abner as "a prince and a great man" (v. 38) and a final statement of impotence in the face of the violence of Joab's family (v. 39). David's vow in v. 39b entrusts vengeance in this matter to the Lord.

Was David innocent of the death of Abner? Those who take a more cynical view of David believe not and argue that David plotted Abner's death.[192] It is hard, however, to maintain the case that Abner's death was an advantage to David rather than a setback. David was on the verge of achieving kingship over all Israel when Joab impulsively acted. What is important to observe is that this narrative is not in doubt about David's innocence. Historical possibilities beyond this telling of the story are possible, but completely speculative, and this way of telling the story is what Israelite tradition has preserved as its belief. Others, ancient and modern, will no doubt continue to believe David somehow guilty in these matters. Conspiracy theories were probably as popular in ancient Israel as in modern America. Shimei's outburst against David is probably a good example (16:7-8). There remains one more death to be narrated (Ishbosheth, 4:1-12) before we can reflect fully on these complex interrelationships of power and violence, innocence and guilt.

Although the larger concern is David's innocence, this episode is unusual because David is not its center. It is Abner who dominates this story—even in his death. David's words of honor and respect in v. 38 do not ring hollow. David, as a "prince and a great man" himself, can recognize and pay tribute to another, even though David had once taunted Abner over his failure to protect the king (1 Sam 26:14-16).

Abner does not have the aura of divine destiny about him as does David. No narrator claims that "God was with him." Perhaps he is a secular counterpart to David—warrior, leader, diplomat—but he is not God's anointed. Abner does recognize the Lord at work in the events bringing David to the throne, and he is able to align himself willingly with those divine purposes (3:9, 18).

No doubt Abner acted with all the self-interest that we might expect a warrior and a man of influence to possess. In 2:8-9, he acts with decisive power to establish Ishbosheth on the throne and himself as the power behind the throne. Yet, it was a time of crisis when Israel was scattered and defeated. Without Abner, it is clear that no Israelite kingdom would have continued in the north. In spite of self-interest there is a kind of integrity to Abner. He did not seize the throne himself. Even the incident with Rizpah does not seem like a move toward the throne for himself, since the result was a move toward David. His claim of loyalty to the house of Saul is believable (3:8). Even in moving his allegiance to David there is no hint that he would do violence to Ishbosheth, although Ishbosheth's accusation wounded and angered him (3:7-8). His address to the elders of Israel suggests that the move to David was motivated by the best interests of Israel against their most deadly enemy, the Philistines (3:17-18).

Abner must have possessed a great deal of power, but in this episode and the preceding story of Asahel's death he does not act with raw power. He tried twice to dissuade Asahel from pursuit before he was forced to kill him (2:18-23). He negotiated terms with David. He negotiated terms with the elders of Israel. He moved to base Israel's future on covenant agreements and not simply on his personal influence (3:12, 21).

Abner is no saint, but he seems very different as a warrior and as a man from Joab. Ironically, it is Joab and not David who gains the most from Abner's death. Although cursed in the moment he rises to ever greater power and influence under David, Joab is at his most visible in the stories of David's decline and his troubled family. What would the mature years of David's reign have been like with Abner as a right-hand man rather than Joab? Joab is such an ambiguous figure that David from his deathbed feels compelled to advise Solomon to kill him in final payment for the bloodguilt incurred with the death of Abner (1 Kgs 2:5-6, 28-34). Of course, Joab had opposed Solomon for the throne and would have been dangerous to leave alive.

192. See VanderKam, "Davidic Complicity in the Deaths of Abner and Eshbaal," 533, who writes, "David both desired and planned the death of Abner." See also N. P. Lemche, "David's Rise," JSOT 10 (1978) 17-18.

REFLECTIONS

1. We live in an age enamored of superstars. We want to focus on the Davids who rise to the top. We often fail to look beyond to those who make a difference in the second, third, or fourth ranks of leadership. It may make a difference whether those places are filled by Abners or Joabs. It may be worth caring whether people of integrity are neutralized by violence, although the weapon for our time is as likely to be the violence of ideology as that of the knife. We tend to expend great energy on processes to elect presidents, to choose bishops, to select school superintendents, or to hire chiefs of police. But we need to devote far more energy to opposing those persons and processes that drive good people from the lesser offices of public or church service, from day-to-day ministry, from classroom teaching, or from routine police work. Those who might serve the Davids of our time with integrity are too often victims of the self-interested, calculated violence of the Joabs among us. The weapons of violence include more than physical assault. Persons of integrity are often driven from leadership in church and community by character assassination, intolerable pay and working conditions, polarized ideological rhetoric, and lack of support. We can hope for leaders of integrity in our highest levels of political or church leadership, but they will fail if we do not find ways to support them with scores of Abners rather than Joabs.

2. The issues of violence are never far from the arenas of public or ecclesiastical power. We cannot naively hope for unblemished Davids who will save us. In this story, David may be innocent; but thanks to Joab, David's kingdom can never be innocent again, and Abner is dead. We must read the story of yet another death, Ishbosheth (4:1-12), and then we can reflect more fully on the complex interrelationship between power and violence and the future of God's kingdom in the midst of these realities. (See Reflections at 4:1-12.)

2 Samuel 4:1-12, The Death of Ishbosheth

COMMENTARY

This episode recounts the third death to which David must respond during his ascent to the throne of Judah and Israel. The death of Ishbosheth now leaves the throne of Israel unoccupied. The story of Ishbosheth's death and David's response is remarkably similar to that of the death of Saul at the hand of the Amalekite (1:1-16). In each story someone kills a king and brings the news to David, expecting to find favor with him. Instead, they pay with their own lives for the bloodguilt they have incurred. The narrative of Abner's death is longer and more complex but raises the same issue of bloodguilt in relation to David's kingdom (3:6-39).

The issue of bloodguilt has been a central concern in the history of the rise of David. The episode on the death of Ishbosheth is the end of a long sequence of narrative episodes seeking to establish David's innocence of bloodguilt. In 1 Samuel 24–26, David avoided bloodguilt. Twice he resisted the opportunity to take the life of Saul and incur bloodguilt for the killing of the Lord's anointed (1 Samuel 24 and 26). In 1 Samuel 25, the intervention of Abigail saved David from angrily killing Nabal and incurring bloodguilt. Now, David cannot avoid association with killings that incur bloodguilt, but the narratives seek to demonstrate that the bloodguilt does not belong to David. He is innocent of involvement and instead acts to avenge the slain and exact the consequences of bloodguilt. He orders the deaths of the Amalekite who took the life of Saul (1:1-16) and the sons of Rimmon, who bring to David the head of Ishbosheth (4:1-12). Following the death of Abner, David cursed his own military commander, Joab, and elaborately mourned the fallen Abner (3:6-39). Violence and death have come close to the kingdom, but David has not taken innocent blood to advance his kingdom, argues the narrative.

Undoubtedly there were those in Israel who did not regard David as innocent of bloodguilt in these deaths. When David retreats from Jerusalem at the time of Absalom's rebellion, a man named Shimei comes out to curse the seemingly defeated David:

Out! Out! Murderer! Scoundrel! The LORD has avenged on all of you the blood of the house of Saul, in whose place you have reigned; and the LORD has given the kingdom into the hand of your son Absalom. See, disaster has overtaken you; for you are a man of blood. (16:7-8)

Recently a number of interpreters have argued in favor of David's complicity in these deaths. They view the present story as political propaganda used to whitewash a politically calculating and opportunistic David. For example, in the death of Ishbosheth, Lemche writes of the two murderers, "No sooner had they murdered their master than they hastened to Hebron to receive their reward, and of course David perforce had to execute his hired assassins if he was to maintain his innocence."[193] Such a reading reflects a more cynical view of David and political power in general, but there is little explicit support in the text for this view of David's role. To be sure, we must recognize the apologetic character of the entire history of David's rise. Moreover, David may well have benefited from deaths that he did not himself arrange. Still, there is no clear evidence for his complicity in these deaths.

The accounts of Davidic innocence in these matters are not naive political idealizations, at least not as they are now incorporated into the larger framework of the books of Samuel and the Deuteronomistic History. David may be innocent, but these narratives clearly imply that violence is, nevertheless, a reality in the kingdom. David's faithful rule must be established in the face of brutal and violent realities, and David must deal with these realities in spite of his innocence in eating them. We begin to understand that

power in the kingdom can never be totally innocent so long as the kingdom itself is brutal and violent. In the longer view of David's story, we are being prepared for the day when David gives in to the temptations of power and commits violent acts for reasons of pure self-interest (adultery with Bathsheba and the murder of Uriah, 2 Samuel 11). Using the helpful vocabulary of David Gunn, we must first hear the story of how the kingdom came to David as a *gift* before we can fully comprehend the dangers of seeking to gain or maintain the kingdom by *grasp*.[194] The narrator understands that David has received the kingdom as the Lord's gift, not as the result of his grasping manipulation of events and propaganda. The story does not idealize David, but makes even clearer the dangers of believing that the kingdom can be grasped through one's own power. The story of David's grasping of power and its consequences lies yet ahead of us.

4:1-3. The scene shifts to the north for reaction to the death of Abner. Ishbosheth's (in accordance with the chronicler, the NRSV reads "Ishbaal" rather than "Ishbosheth"; see the Com-mentary on 2:8-9 for a discussion of the alternatives for the name of Saul's son) courage fails, and all Israel is distressed (v. 1). Of course, Ishbosheth was afraid of the threat Abner posed when he was alive (3:11); now that Abner is dead, Ishbosheth is still afraid. It is hard to know what Ishbosheth or Israel knew about Abner's negotiations with David. Since Abner had conferred with the elders of Israel, their dismay must reflect not simply the loss of Abner but the loss of the alliance he was negotiating with David. It is clear that without Abner the prospects of the north and their bargaining power with David are diminished. As for Ishbosheth, he was properly fearful. With or without Abner, he seems to have no future.

Verse 2 introduces Baanah and Rechab, who were captains of raiding bands in Ishbosheth's army. The account is at some pains to establish that they were Benjaminites, even though they were from Beeroth, which was a traditional Gibeonite city. This makes Ishbosheth's assassins his own kinsmen. Although details are not supplied, it is clear that Beeroth was annexed by the tribe of Benjamin, forcing the Gibeonite inhabitants to

193. Lemche, "David's Rise," 17.

194. Gunn, "David and the Gift of the Kingdom," 14-45.

relocate in Gittaim (v. 3). These events may lie behind the blood feud that led the Gibeonites to exact vengeance upon the house of Saul in 2 Sam 21:1-9.

4:4. This verse is a parenthesis, which does not advance the story of this episode, but prepares us for a later story in chap. 9. It tells us that Saul's son Jonathan had a son named Mephibosheth. He had been injured and permanently crippled by a fall suffered in the hasty escape from Jezreel at the time of Israel's defeat on Mt. Gilboa and the deaths of Saul and Jonathan. The name "Mephibosheth" is reported in 1 Chr 8:34; 9:40 as "Meribbaal." Most scholars believe that this is another instance where later editors were offended by the element "baal" as part of a royal family name. They substituted בשת (*bōšet*), the Hebrew word for "shame," in place of the supposed idolatrous element of the name (see the discussion of Ishbosheth in the Commentary on 2:8-9).

The insertion of this note is odd. It may be that the narrator wishes us to know that with the death of Ishbosheth the line of Saul will not end. Further, it anticipates the loyalty (חסד *ḥesed*) that David will yet show to the house of Saul in keeping with the covenant he made with Jonathan (1 Samuel 20). In the midst of a story of violence and treachery against the house of Saul, loyalty and commitment are also anticipated.

4:5-8. The account of the murderous deed itself starts at an oddly leisurely pace as Baanah and Rechab come to Ishbosheth's house during his noontime rest (v. 5). The literary style implies careful deliberation, not impulsive action. The next two verses almost seem like variant versions of the killing of Ishbosheth. Each could stand alone. In v. 6, the men come inside on the pretext of obtaining wheat (a communal storehouse?), strike

Ishbosheth in the stomach, and escape. In v. 7, they enter the house and find Ishbosheth lying on his couch. The fatal action is narrated in a brutal series of verbs: "They attacked him, killed him, and beheaded him." Then they take his head and travel through the night to Hebron. It may be that v. 7 simply added detail to the spare account in v. 6.

Arriving at Hebron, they present Ishbosheth's head to David, clearly expecting praise and honor for their deed (v. 8). They present their grisly trophy as vengeance for David on Saul, an enemy who had sought David's life. They clearly do not understand David or the situation they have created. Reward or favor will not be their lot.

4:9-12. David answers Baanah and Rechab with an oath taken in the name of the Lord, whom David recognizes as the source of his deliverance from adversity (v. 9). He ominously recalls for them the fate of the Amalekite who had brought news that he had killed Saul, thinking it good news. His fate was death (v. 10). Saul had been wounded and asked for his own death to avoid being captured by the Philistines. Now, David reminds his would-be benefactors, a righteous man has been murdered in his own bed. Ishbosheth is not, like his father, God's anointed king, but he is righteous (i.e., innocent). That makes Baanah and Rechab evildoers, and their blood is required to recompense the bloodguilt they have incurred (v. 11). In verbs as harsh and quick as the reporting of their own deed, David commands the fate of these two assassins: "They killed them; they cut off their hands and feet, and hung their bodies beside the pool at Hebron." While his assassins are humiliated in their death, Ishbosheth is honored in his death. It is ironic, however, that his burial is in the same tomb as Abner.

REFLECTIONS

As has been noted, this episode on the death of Ishbosheth is the last in a sequence of stories dealing with the juxtaposition of power and violence, guilt and innocence, in the history of David's rise.[195] In our reading of these stories and in reflection on their intersection with our own experience, two dangerously distorted interpretive readings must be avoided.

---

195. Walter Brueggemann also reads these stories in terms of the issues of violence and power in *Power, Providence, and Personality,* 49-85. Our readings are congenial, but with different emphases.

The first is a reading that makes the mistake of thinking that the claims for David's innocence mean that the kingdom is innocent or that the seductive temptation to violence for the sake of power can be ignored. David's innocence cannot be read as an end in itself. This is the danger of *pious naïveté*. David's claim to innocence was not bought at the price of non-involvement in the brutal realities of a violent world. He was forced to recognize the temptation to violence in himself (1 Samuel 24–26) and to respond justly and faithfully to the violence of others (2 Samuel 1–4). In our own world, the temptation to think that innocent faith can provide an escape from the realities of a broken world is a delusion and an abdication of responsibility. As in David's story, God's kingdom is come in the midst of the world and its sinful realities, not apart from them. People of faith cannot use their own supposed innocence to hide from or ignore a world enamored of violence. To do so is to work against the coming of God's kingdom.

The second reading that must be avoided is one that believes that no innocence can be preserved in the midst of violence and cannot see the possibilities of God's kingdom in the midst of a brutal world. This is the danger of *secularized cynicism*. In our cynical age, there are many who believe that faithfulness and integrity are not possible in the precincts of power. They believe that religious faith is either irrelevant to political power or a mere tool of political power. Reading David's story from this perspective sees only propaganda for Davidic power and is certain that David was manipulating events behind the scenes. Such readings see manipulation, self-interest, survival, and compromise with violence as the only possibilities for dealing with power in our own world.

Over against these dangerous and distorted readings, the church must read David's story in these episodes with the conviction that there is an alternative to our naïveté and our cynicism. The church's attentive reading of these stories of David's encounters with violence on the way to power in God's new kingdom can teach us about the realities of violence, power, and God's kingdom in our own time.

1. These stories teach us that there is no completely innocent power. Power is never far from violence or the temptation to violence. As an individual, David may be innocent of bloodguilt in these stories. But as a king he must rule in a kingdom saturated with violence. To have power is to have responsibility for recognizing and responding to violence, in David's world or in our own. The Christian faith radicalizes this understanding in its central salvation story. Jesus—the Messiah, the anointed One, the son of David—must face the violence of the world in his own crucifixion in order to bring God's kingdom. The innocent one, nevertheless, takes on the bloodguilt of a violent world.

2. These stories also teach us that there can be faithful leadership in the face of violence. Brutality, violence, manipulation, and self-interest do not have the final word in these stories. One can responsibly exercise power without giving in to the violence that is always near at hand. David's innocence in these stories is not merely political propaganda but is serious moral witness on the part of the community that preserved and told these stories. (The portion of David's story that unfolds from the adultery with Bathsheba and the killing of Uriah in 2 Samuel 11 deals with the consequences that result when power does give in to the temptations of violence.)

Faithful leadership for the sake of God's kingdom requires action in opposition to violence. Like David, we must oppose and hold accountable those who promote and condone violence in the expectation of profit, fame, or pleasure. A recent news article told of the recasting of two films with additional scenes of sex and violence to avoid a PG rating and gain a more profitable R rating. "On any given day in America, 480 women and children will be forcibly raped, 5,670 women will be assaulted by a male intimate partner and four women and three children will be murdered by a family member."[196] Every season of political campaigning is now marred by "attack ads" and character assassination in the hopes of gaining electoral favor. The church must be in

196. Mary Pipher, *Reviving Ophelia: Saving the Selves of Adolescent Girls* (New York: Ballantine, 1994) 219.

the forefront of those willing to join decisive action against these predilections to violence in our midst.

Faithful leadership for the sake of God's kingdom requires grief at the losses we have suffered. David could not bring a new kingdom apart from his ability to lead his people in grief over their losses of Saul, Jonathan, Abner, and Ishbosheth. The church, too, will not be credible in its leadership for alternatives to dangerous streets, troubled homes, and desensitized public appetites for violence if it is not seen as grieving over the losses we have experienced. A church perceived as merely tending to its own institutional health will have no credibility in leadership for alternatives to violence in our time. It was the prophet Amos who indicted those who, even though not guilty of direct violence, "lie on beds of ivory . . . sing idle songs to the sound of the harp . . . but are not grieved over the ruin of Joseph" (Amos 6:4-6 NRSV). It is our grief that sharpens our awareness of the price we have paid for violence and enables us to look beyond to the new possibilities of God's kingdom. Resurrection does not immediately follow crucifixion in the gospel story. The grief of the disciples while Jesus lay three days in the tomb is a necessary prelude to the new hope of resurrection.

3. These stories, finally, teach us that it is ultimately God who redeems the kingdom. Throughout the stories of the rise of David there have been constant reminders that as David moved toward his own power, he recognized that the ultimate power for newness in Israel comes from the Lord. God makes faithful leadership possible in the midst of and in spite of violence. It is God's kingdom that stands as the alternative to human kingdoms ruled by violence and self-interest. To give faithful leadership in God's kingdom does not require perfection (David is far from that), but it implies an integrity rooted in an alternative vision of the source of true power. David is cunning, resourceful, formidable in battle, and shrewd in his political dealings. He can compete on the fields of human power. But what sets him apart in these stories is his constant possession of a vision that transcends human power and is rooted in the power of God as the hope for newness in Israel. He refuses to accept the kingdom from those who would give it on violent terms. In the Christian gospel story, human kingdoms flex muscles in crucifixion, but resurrection has the final word of newness in spite of such violence. For David and for us, it is God's kingdom that brings newness and will not be denied. Between the blindness of naïveté and the paralysis of cynicism, enabled by our own action and grief, lies the possibility of God's faithful kingdom in a world of violence.

2 Samuel 5:1-5, David Made King by Israel

COMMENTARY

This brief report brings us to the climactic moment of the history of David's rise. He had earlier been anointed king over Judah (2:4a). Now the northern tribes of Israel, the remnants of the kingdom of Saul, come to anoint David as their king. David becomes king of all Israel.

As the elders of Israel affirm David, they recall a promise of the Lord that David would be "shepherd of my people Israel" (v. 2). Hearing this phrase, we realize with a start that we have completed an incredible journey, starting with David as shepherd of his father's flocks to David as "shepherd of my people Israel." He has moved from boy to king—from eighth son to the throne. The narrative recounting this climactic moment is surprisingly brief and matter-of-fact. The narrative has confidently foreseen this moment all along. It now simply states in the voice of the people that the Lord's promises have been fulfilled in David.

5:1-3. The tribes of Israel come to David at Hebron (v. 1a). The text no doubt implies that tribal representatives were sent; v. 3, in fact, refers to this delegation as the "elders of Israel." They appeal to David to become their king. They have nowhere else to go. Ishbosheth is dead, and there is no likely successor. They have no bargaining power. Their military leader, Abner, is dead, and his position of strength for negotiations with David is now lost. They come now to David almost as petitioners, beseeching him to accept them and rule over them.

This very compact narrative of only three verses articulates a basis for this completion of David's rise to kingship over all Israel in the words and actions of the elders of Israel. They appeal to kinship (v. 1 a), to their previous experience with David (v. 2 a), and to the promise of the Lord (v. 2 b). Then they enter into covenant with David (v. 3 a) and anoint him as king (v. 3 b).

The elders open their petition to David by claiming, "We are your bone and flesh." This expression usually denotes blood kinship (cf. Gen 29:14; Judg 9:2). At a later point in the story, David uses a similar phrase to note his kinship to Judah in contrast to all of Israel (19:13), but this would not rule out Israel's use of the phrase to appeal to kinship as the basis for agreement with David. David has now reclaimed Saul's daughter Michal as his legal wife (3:13-16). Although tribal ties represent the closest kinship (e.g., David with Judah and Saul with Benjamin) the notion of a broader kinship among the tribal groups of Israel emerged fairly early. By the time of the Deuteronomistic History, the notion of the kinship of all Israel was a fixed dogma. For that reason, some have suggested a deuteronomistic influence in these verses.[197] It does not seem likely that this phrase is being used as a covenantal formula rather than a plea based on kinship.[198]

In v. 2 a, the Israelites appeal to their past experience with David. They do so in a way that explicitly renounces their loyalty to Saul. They recall that even in the days of Saul "it was you who led out Israel and brought it in." This phrase specifically refers to David's military leadership in command of Israelite troops (1 Sam 18:13, 16). Perhaps these were some

of the people who cheered that "Saul has slain his thousands, but David his ten thousands." It was not Saul who gave them hope, they now claim—it was *you*! As readers, we have known from 1 Samuel 16 on that the future of Israel belongs to David and not to Saul. This scene is the final moment of recognition.

The elders of Israel are also clear that the Lord has been at work in bringing them to this moment (v. 2 b). They know of a promise by the Lord that David should be "shepherd over my people Israel" and "ruler over Israel." We do not know of such a promise verbalized in the narrative by the Lord in these terms. But we have known David as the man to whom God promised kingship over Israel, and the roles of shepherd and ruler are consistent with the destiny toward which God has constantly moved David's journey. The term "shepherd" (רעה *rō'eh*) is a common designation for kings and political leaders, both in Israel and in the wider ancient Near East.[199] The title is a reminder of responsibility to care for and protect the people as a shepherd would do for the flock. One suspects, however, that in this context we are intended to recall David's own beginnings as a shepherd boy (1 Sam 16:11; 17:15). Now he has become a shepherd king. Israel also uses the term נגיד (*nāgîd*), "prince," "king-designate" (see the discussion of this term in Commentary on 9:16; 10:1). Some have suggested that Israel was cautiously avoiding the term "king." However, David does not become king until the covenant making and anointing in v. 3, where the term "king" is used twice. The use of *nāgîd* in v. 2 may simply be as "king-designate."

Of special significance is the use of "shepherd" and *nāgîd* together in reference to David in Nathan's oracle of dynastic promise: "I took you from the pasture, from following the sheep to be prince over my people Israel" (7:8). The promise of the Lord here articulated by the elders of Israel seems to anticipate and prepare us for Nathan's oracle. This connection may be further support for those who see deuteronomistic influence in 5:1-2, since such influence is generally recognized in the final shaping of 2 Samuel 7.

In v. 3, the elders of Israel come to Hebron (did they come twice?) for covenant making.

---

197. See McCarter, *II Samuel*, 131-32.

198. Contra Walter Brueggemann, "Of the Same Flesh and Bone (Gen 2,23a)," *CBQ* 32 (1970) 535.

199. See Anderson, *2 Samuel*, 76.

It is King David (note the full title) who is the subject of the verb here. The basis of Davidic rule over Israel will not be raw power, but willingness on his part to enter covenant. His kingship is established on the basis of a covenant involving mutual recognition of needs and responsibilities. The people then anoint him as king over Israel. This anointing is the counterpart of the anointing by Judah in 2:4*a*. But both of these anointings by the people only serve to ratify the anointing of David by the Lord through the prophet Samuel (1 Sam 16:13). David's journey to the throne as the Lord's anointed one is now complete.

5:4-5. These are chronological notes, probably from the deuteronomistic historian. David is surprisingly young by our standards—only thirty—when he begins to reign. He rules surprisingly long by ancient standards—forty years, making him a ripe age of seventy when he dies. The number forty may be a rounded number, as it often is in the Old Testament, but it fits rather closely into other chronological data on David. Verse 5 seems more specific, giving us years and months at Hebron along with years and months at Jerusalem. This, of course, is premature on the part of the historian, since Jerusalem is not yet in David's hands.

REFLECTIONS

God keeps promises. David is now king in Israel, and the kingdom is established with God's king and not the people's. Already this kingdom promises newness. The shape of power in this kingdom will be governed by shepherding and covenant making. The imagery is of care and mutuality. Israel's future hope has for the moment become its present hope.

Although the shape of human governance, political and religious, has seldom maintained the ideal of shepherding and covenant making, these have remained significant images in the vision of Israel and the church through generations to the present. From the Twenty-third Psalm to Jesus' declaration of his own death, "I am the good shepherd who lays down his life for the sheep" (see John 10:11), the image of the shepherd has been a central expression of the church's vision of leadership in the service of God's kingdom. Covenant has likewise been central to the understanding of Israel and the church that leadership never functions apart from a mutual community of recognized needs and responsibilities. This brief passage only lifts these images briefly into view, but it is a beginning in David that points us to rich new understandings of God's kingdom for Israel's future and for our own.

2 Samuel 5:6-10, David Captures Jerusalem

COMMENTARY

David is now king over all Israel, north and south, but oddly the final episode in the history of David's rise does not focus on the royal office but on the royal capital. The final note involves the politics of geography, not the politics of leadership. In a brief, almost cryptic, passage we are told that David captured the Jebusite city of Jerusalem and made it the "city of David" (vv. 7, 9). It is a text fraught with many problems of translation and interpretation, as the verse-to-verse

commentary will make clear. Verse 10 pronounces a theological verdict on the entire history of David's rise: "David became greater and greater, for the LORD, the God of hosts, was with him." God's presence with David throughout the trials of his rise to the throne of Israel has been a major theological theme since it was first sounded in 1 Sam 16:18 (see the Overview for 1 Sam 16:1–31:13). It now stands almost as a benediction on all that has transpired in the story of David to this point.

Beyond this point, we encounter traditions on the manner in which David consolidated and conducted his rule of Israel.

As for Jerusalem, it is fitting that this city make its appearance alongside David as he takes up the kingship of all Israel. This brief episode is only a beginning, but as a royal theology develops from the reign of David onward, it will rest on two great pillars of belief and trust. The first is that God has chosen David and his dynasty forever. David is clearly chosen for the throne of Israel by God, and in the dynastic oracle from the prophet Nathan in 2 Samuel 7, this election extends to the Davidic dynasty forever. The second conviction of royal theology is that God has chosen Mt. Zion in Jerusalem as the holy habitation of God. This belief obviously received its great boost from Solomon's building of the Temple on Mt. Zion. Jerusalem becomes not just David's city, but a holy city. Nevertheless, this Jerusalem element of royal theology begins in this brief story of David's capture of Jerusalem to be his capital. It will be further developed by the story of David's transfer of the ark of the covenant to Jerusalem in the next chapter. Psalm 132, which commemorates David's search for the ark, ends in praise for each of these elements of Davidic royal theology: the promise to David and the choice of Mt. Zion in Jerusalem. This understated story of David's capture of Jerusalem provides the beginning of that city's important role in Israel's faith and its continued existence today as a city considered holy by three great religions: Judaism, Christianity, and Islam.

This story of David's capture of Jerusalem gives no rationale for the undertaking. Why did David want or need Jerusalem? It has long been commonplace in analyzing David's action to suppose that he was looking for a way to locate his capital on neutral ground, unrelated to either Judah or Israel. Jerusalem is almost on the boundary between the tribal territories of Judah and the northern tribes who finally came to David in 5:1-3. Since Jerusalem was a Jebusite city, neither Judah nor Israel could claim David's capital city as its own. David captured it with "his men" (v. 6), and it became the "city of David" (vv. 7, 9). Jerusalem was also a well-known city from ancient times. It is mentioned in the Ebla archives (c. 2500 BCE), Egyptian execration texts (19th cent. BCE), and the Amarna letters (14th cent. BCE). It is usually identified with the city of Salem, where Abraham encountered the priest-king Melchizedek (Gen 14:17-20). Jerusalem is described as one of the Canaanite centers that Israel could not capture or assimilate (Josh 15:63; Judg 1:21); a successful raid or skirmish with the Jebusites of Jerusalem may be indicated in Judg 1:8. A deity named Shalem is mentioned in the Ugaritic texts, and thus the name of Jerusalem may mean "establishment of (the god) Shalem." In later Israelite times the name is associated with the Hebrew word שלום (šālôm), meaning "peace/wholeness." To possess Jerusalem as his capital undoubtedly added a measure of credibility and prestige to David's infant kingdom.

5:6-9. Without any explanation or hint of motivation, David and his men march against the Jebusite city of Jerusalem (v. 6a). There can be little doubt that the phrase "his men" refers to the mercenary force loyal to David that has been with him through much of his time in the wilderness and his service to the Philistines. David's capture of Jerusalem will owe nothing to the militias of Judah or Israel. This means that there is a literal sense to David's naming of the city as "the city of David" (v. 9a; see also v. 7). It could be regarded as a personal, royal possession.

We know little about the Jebusites. Opinion is divided among scholars on whether they are a Canaanite clan or a small, autonomous ethnic group apart from the Canaanites. Either is possible. In spite of the exchange of some hostile words and taunts in this brief episode, it seems clear that David took the city without great loss of life and, as Gottwald argues persuasively, "retained the Jebusites in their former home, even though this put them in the administrative heart of his new Israelite kingdom."[200] Mendenhall believes this gave David the administrators, managers, scribes, and merchants who enabled him to successfully launch a nation-state. The tribal cultures of Israel and Judah would not have required or possessed many of these skills.[201]

In v. 6b, the Jebusites appear to taunt David, believing their city to be impregnable.

200. Gottwald, *The Tribes of Yahweh*, 571.
201. George E. Mendenhall, "The Monarchy," *Int.* 29 (1975) 160.

Their taunt is the first of three puzzling references in this passage to the "blind and the lame" (see also v. 8). Most believe that this first reference expresses the Jebusite belief that Jerusalem is so strong and secure that even "the blind and the lame" could defend it. The narrator even shares the Jebusites' thoughts that David could be disregarded as a threat: "David cannot come in here." One presumes that David, with his force of men, is outside the wall, threatening siege.

The narrative is so eager that it gives outcome before any details. Verse 7 simply announces, as if in response to the Jebusite taunt, that David did capture the "stronghold of Zion" and that further he audaciously renamed it after himself, "the city of David." This is the first reference to Zion, and this is usually taken as a designation of the hill on the southeast of the city that may have been a citadel at this time. It becomes better known, of course, as the designation of the hill on which Solomon builds the Temple, Mt. Zion.

An extremely brief account suggests the manner of David's capture of Jerusalem in v. 8. The text is so cryptic in its details that it has been often suggested that the text has become corrupted or shortened. It seems clear that David took the city by stealth rather than by force. David issues a challenge to those who would join him in attacking the Jebusites. Both the NRSV and the NIV follow the majority opinion and depict David and his men using a water shaft to enter the city, perhaps taking it by surprise. The difficult word here is צנור (ṣinnôr), a rare word appearing elsewhere only in Ps 42:7, where it is generally taken to mean "waterfall." Various other proposals have been made for this word, including "grappling hooks," "weapon," and even the "male sexual organ" in an oath-taking ceremony. McCarter believes the term means "windpipe" and that David is instructing his men to strike a lethal blow, thereby not leaving any lame or blind.[202] The classic suggestion that David used the city's access to its own water supply as a vulnerable point from which to take the city seems most likely. The verb may imply the cutting off of the water supply rather than scrambling up a shaft. The shaft discovered in 1867 connecting the spring of Gihon with the old stronghold of Jerusalem is probably not the Jebusite ṣinnôr.[203]

In 1 Chr 11:4-9, the account of the capture of Jerusalem is elaborated by an offer from David that the first to attack the Jebusites would be made commander in chief of his army. In this account, Joab meets this challenge and is the first to attack. Accordingly, he is put in a position of command by David. This may be an authentic detail that has been omitted by the writer of 2 Samuel, since this book often demeans Joab.

The references to the "lame and blind" in v. 6 are puzzling. The first reference may simply be a turning back of the Jebusite taunt. David refers to the defenders of Jerusalem as the "lame and blind" and declares his hatred of them. This may be simply the rhetoric of battle taunts. The final sentence of v. 8 takes this matter of the blind and the lame as the etiology of a custom or prohibition denying the lame and the blind access to the Temple ("house"). We do not know of such a regulation, although disabled persons could not become priests (Lev 21:18). Since the Temple did not even exist in David's time, the verse seems artificial and contrived. It does not help to consider "house" to mean "palace," as some have suggested, since we know of no such regulation for the palace either. No proposal has gained a consensus.

The final outcome of this encounter is stated clearly in v. 9a. David not only captured Jerusalem but also occupied it and renamed it as his own city, "the city of David." In v. 9b, we are told that David did some building. The meaning of "Millo" is uncertain. The NRSV leaves the term untranslated to indicate a region of the city. Recent archaeological work suggests that the term may refer to a system of terraces supported by retaining walls, and the NIV translation reflects this understanding. Solomon is also said to have done construction work on the Millo (1 Kgs 9:15, 24; 11:27), which suggests that he extended or improved terracing already begun by David.

5:10. We have already noted this verse as a final theological comment for the history of the rise of David. The longer, formal name of God is used: "the LORD, the God of hosts."

---

202. See the discussion in Anderson, *2 Samuel*, 84, and the alternative proposed by McCarter, *II Samuel*, 139-40.

203. See J. Shiloh, "The City of David: Archaeological Project: Third Season—1980," *Biblical Archaeologist* 44 (1981) 170.

At the beginning of the books of Samuel, this name was associated with the ark of the covenant and the hope of Israel, expressed in the prayer of Hannah (1 Sam 1:11; 4:4). Now the ark is lost, but God has raised up David. Just as the ark represented God's presence in Israel, so also God is with David. Significantly, in the next chapter David brings back the ark to Jerusalem, but it will no longer be the chief sign of God's presence. God's presence in Israel is now seen in David, who grows stronger and stronger. There is an implicit contrast here. The house of Saul has grown weaker and weaker and has all but disappeared. The threat of the Philistines will be immediately addressed in the remainder of chapter 5. David's strength has now grown until he can meet this deadly enemy of Israel, and they will then grow weaker and weaker. We have followed David's story as the hope for Israel's future. That future has now arrived.

REFLECTIONS

We have come to the concluding moment in a remarkable tale of God's newness for Israel. That newness has taken the shape of David, but it now also introduces Jerusalem. God's future for Israel is tied up not only with a man but also with a place. Jerusalem (Zion) becomes a holy place. This has not yet fully taken place. Here Jerusalem becomes David's city. With the later building of the Temple by Solomon, it will become God's holy habitation. Here we stand only at the introduction of this city that is to figure so remarkably in Israel's story. Just as Moses is forever connected to Sinai, so also David will be forever connected to Zion. Gese has spoken of this as a reshaping of Israel's memory from Sinai-Torah to Zion-Torah.[204] That reshaping process has begun in this moment when Jerusalem becomes David's city.

This beginning of the Jerusalem tradition seems unpromising. It speaks of conquest and of exclusion of the disabled. Jerusalem was a Jebusite city, perhaps named after a Jebusite god. One can hardly see here the beginning of an expansive and hopeful vision for Jerusalem as God's holy habitation. Yet, we should remember that David began as the unpromising eighth son who tended sheep for his undistinguished family. It is God who makes something of the boy and of the place.

From this unpromising beginning unfolds an expansive vision of God's city to complement God's king. Jerusalem becomes the focus of a new vision of God's presence in our midst. This finds expression, of course, in the building of Solomon's Temple (1 Kings 6). God's dwelling on Mt. Zion becomes the sign of God's involvement in the midst of God's people and human history: "For the LORD has chosen Zion; he has desired it for his habitation: 'This is my resting place forever; here I will reside, for I have desired it' " (Ps 132:13-14 NRSV). When Jerusalem and the Temple are destroyed, this expansive vision survives as hope for more than an earthly city. The vision of God's new Jerusalem becomes ultimate hope for the triumph of God's rule and measure for all earthly cities where human rulers hold power. From Ezekiel's elaborate vision of the new Jerusalem (Ezekiel 40–48) to the apocalyptic vision of God's new Jerusalem descending from the heavens (Rev 21:1-4), the vision that arises from Jerusalem both encompasses and transcends the possibilities for earthly cities and those who govern there. If David's city begins with exclusion of the lame and the blind, this is not where it ends. The vision of Jerusalem expands to become inclusive of all human hopes and possibilities: "I saw the holy city, the New Jerusalem, coming down out of heaven from God. . . . 'See, the home of God is among mortals. He will dwell with them as their God; they will be his peoples, and God himself will be with them; he will wipe every tear from their eyes. Death will be no more; mourning and crying and pain will be no more, for the first things have passed away' " (Rev. 21:2-4).

204. Hartmut Gese, "The Davidic Covenant and the Zion Tradition," in *Essays on Biblical Theology* (Minneapolis: Augsburg, 1981) 60-92.

The text of 2 Sam 5:6-10 should be preached as the humble beginnings from which this expansive vision grows. Jerusalem occupies a special and passionate place in the Israelite tradition that survives even into the present day, when Jerusalem is a unique and holy place to three of the world's great religions: "If I forget you, O Jerusalem, let my right hand wither! Let my tongue cling to the roof of my mouth, if I do not remember you, if I do not set Jerusalem above my highest joy" (Ps 137:5-6 NRSV). If these passions give rise to tensions, they also give rise to a hopeful vision that transcends the tensions: "Pray for the peace of Jerusalem: May they prosper who love you. Peace be within your walls, and security within your towers. . . . For the sake of the house of the Lord our God, I will seek your good" (Ps 122:6-7, 9 NRSV).

This text encourages us to reflect on the importance of holy place in religious experience. In our mobile society, we lose sight of the possibilities for place as a bearer of tradition and a repository for the sense of God's presence. In reading the story of David, we are not only reading of kings and kingdoms, but of the dwelling of God in their midst. Jerusalem becomes a reminder of this, lest the course of human events become an end in itself. It is good in our own time to consider the way in which our sanctuaries and the historic places of our various denominations can be for us holy places that serve as repositories of memory and tradition—that remind us of God's story in the midst of our own. It is also good to rekindle in our preaching, our teaching, our hymnody, and our liturgies the expansive vision of God's new Jerusalem. This vision, grown from the modest beginnings of David's city, reminds us of the larger vision that our modest places must always serve and be judged by. When the places of our religious life begin to become "our" places rather than God's place—when we only exclude and have failed to open to God's more inclusive vision—then we need to hear again the story of Jerusalem with its beginnings in conquest and its completion as the crown of God's coming kingdom. Like Jerusalem, our places can be transformed by the vision of God's presence.

2 SAMUEL 5:11–8:18, DAVID CONSOLIDATES HIS KINGDOM

OVERVIEW

It is almost anticlimactic for the story to continue. We began with a hope and an expectation of newness in Israel with the birth of Hannah's child Samuel, and the singing of Hannah's song of God's reversals of customary power in 1 Sam 1:1–2:10. The focus of 1 Samuel 1–7 was on Israel's crises and the hopeful expectation, symbolized by the prophet Samuel, that God would bring newness into the midst of crisis. That expectation for God's new future has been identified with the hope for a king in Israel since 1 Samuel 8. Expectation for God's new future has focused on David since 1 Samuel 16. It became clear that David was God's future for Israel and God's king for a new Israelite kingdom. We

have been moving with growing anticipation toward David's ascent to Israel's throne, and now it has come to pass.

Nevertheless, Israel's story and David's story continue. This section (2 Sam 5:11–8:18) is concerned with the consolidation and legitimization of David's kingdom. It is one thing to become king and another thing to establish a secure and enduring kingdom. David the tribal hero and chieftain must become David the ruler of a nation.

From a literary standpoint, this section does not possess the thematic coherence and unity that have long been noted for the great artistic literary pieces that stand on either side. The history of David's rise (1 Sam

16:1–2 Sam 5:10) provides the passion and excitement of David as hero of the tribes, opposed by Saul but destined for greatness by the enduring presence of God. The succession narrative, which follows (2 Samuel 9–20; 1 Kings 1–2), chronicles the decline of David and his family into excesses of power and intrigue, with God's judgment articulated by Nathan's oracle (2 Sam 12:1-15) as the background. This section on David's consolidation of the kingdom presents neither the passion nor the pathos of these other narrative segments of David's story. The narrative segments within the chapters seem to be a collection of independent narratives ranging from battle report to prophetic oracle of promise and reflect no common author or narrative style.

The collection of these independent traditions is not, however, haphazard. James Flanagan has persuasively argued that this section has six segments that have been artistically arranged to suggest a movement in David's story from settlement with the old order to the emergence of genuinely new patterns for Israel's life.[205] The units are arranged chiastically:

A 5:13-16, list of David's family
  B 5:17-25, defeat of the Philistines; kingdom secured
    C 6:1-23, the ark brought to Jerusalem
    C´ 7:1-29, Nathan's oracle of dynastic promise
  B´ 8:1-14, defeat of Israel's neighbors; kingdom expanded
A´ 8:15-18, list of David's officials

The first three units represent the foundation of David's kingship in concerns appropriate to the earlier tribal existence of Israel as God's covenant people. David's marriages and his children (5:13-16) witness to the importance of kinship networks in earlier tribal life. His victory over the Philistines (5:17-25) ends the threat of a perennial enemy of tribal Israel. The bringing of the ark to Jerusalem (6:1-23) makes the royal capital also the

205. Flanagan, "Social Transformation and Ritual in 2 Samuel 6," 361-72.

covenant shrine, as was Shiloh, and the ancient symbol of God's presence and power is honored in the new kingdom. In these notices and actions, David is presented as one who makes alliances with the old order of covenantal Israel in order to secure the kingdom and to settle or make peace with old issues that brought Saul to grief.

In the last three units of the section, David's story moves to new horizons. New bases of security are established for Israel's future. Kinship gives way to royal bureaucracy as the basis of power (5:13-16; 8:15-18). Security from a threatening enemy gives way to royal conquest and expansion of borders and the security of territorial domination (5:17-25; 8:1-14). At the center of the section, the theology of God's presence symbolized by the ark gives way to a theology of God's promise that makes Davidic dynasty itself a theological symbol of God's care for Israel (6:1-23; 7:1-29). Kingdom is theologically wedded to God's continuing guidance of Israel's future.

The reader is gripped by a tension between two responses that seem naturally invoked by these stories and reports. On the one hand, we acknowledge the passing of the old order even as David makes his peace with that older reality in Israel. On the other hand, we celebrate the arrival of full nationhood and the emergence of new and unexpected patterns of God's grace in David and his dynasty. Both are authentic responses to God's truth revealed in passing order and emerging order. The emergence of Israel as a nation is not without cost. As we shall see, the new bases of royal power bring new threats of royal ideology and abuse of power. But to remain in the tribal patterns of covenantal Israel had already proved costly, as seen in the crises that opened the books of Samuel (see Overview for 1 Sam 1:1–7:17). The key to this section is the great oracle of God's promise to David in 2 Samuel 7. If the kingdom is to be more than ideology or power, it will be because God redeems it and works through it.

2 Samuel 5:11-25, Economic and Political Security

COMMENTARY

The remainder of chap. 5 contains several short notices that deal primarily with the economic and political security of David's new kingdom. There is a brief mention of trade and diplomatic relations established with Hiram king of Tyre (vv. 11-12); a listing of the children born to David in Jerusalem (vv. 13-16); and two accounts of decisive victories over the Philistines (vv. 17-21, 22-25). The cumulative effect of these notices shows David as being effective in making his fledgling kingdom secure and viable. David ends the ongoing threat from the Philistines, which Saul had failed to meet. The building of a palace with cedar obtained from Hiram of Tyre reflects the beginning of new economic patterns with Jerusalem as the new center of the emerging Davidic kingdom.

5:11-12. Suddenly the scope of David's story expands. We no longer read of local realities, which were the focus of the narratives of David's rise to the throne. The scope has become international, and David receives ambassadors from a neighboring king, Hiram of Tyre (v. 11a). Further, along with the ambassadors come cedar and the skilled carpenters and masons who will build a palace for David. This, no doubt, suggests the establishment of trade relations between David's fledgling kingdom and the Phoenician trading center of Tyre. Hiram would have not supplied such goods and services without getting something in return. We do not have the details, but it is clear that new economic arrangements have been made. Kingdoms require economic bases to survive and grow beyond the simpler needs of tribal life. It is significant that this notice of economic arrangements with Tyre is the first action reported for David as king of all Israel.

We have moved from tribal reality to royal reality. Cedar is the symbol of wealth, but its opulence is also the source of the temptation to imagine that wealth makes a king self-sufficient and aloof from covenant demands for justice. Jeremiah speaks of kings who build houses of cedar and imagine themselves great while ignoring the concerns of justice and righteousness that demonstrate knowledge of the Lord (Jer 22:13-18). New possibilities for kingdom bring new dangers, but for the moment David is certain that these new realities are further evidence of the favor of God on his kingdom (v. 12). The costs and dangers of such kingdoms are to be faced in the future.

5:13-16. These verses list the children born to David while in Jerusalem. It corresponds to the list of his children born at Hebron in 3:2-5. Unlike that list, only the names of the sons are mentioned here. Their mothers remain anonymous, except for the mother of Solomon, whom we know from 2 Sam 12:24 was Bathsheba. This is the first reference to Solomon and points us toward a significant development in the story of David and the kingship.

The other, nameless mothers of David's Jerusalem children are lumped together in the notice that David "took" more concubines and wives (v. 13a). The verb "took" (לקח lāqaḥ) recalls the warning of Samuel in 1 Sam 8:11-18 about the "ways of the king" and anticipates David's "taking" of Bathsheba in 2 Sam 11:4 (the NRSV and NIV translate it weakly as "get"). This is also the first mention of concubines (v. 13a). The acquisition of a harem of wives and concubines was a symbol of power and influence among ancient kings (see Solomon's later practice in 1 Kings 11:1). David is indeed beginning to give Israel a king "like the other nations" (1 Sam 8:5, 20). Verse 13b also mentions the birth of daughters, but like the mothers they are left nameless. Women do not figure in the usual patriarchal patterns of royal reality. Except for Solomon, none of the sons mentioned here will play any further role in Israel's story.

5:17-25. In two brief accounts, David seems to end the Philistine threat that had clouded Israel's future for over a generation. David succeeds in the task for which Saul was anointed as Israel's first king, but that ended for Saul in failure and death. It is likely that David's ending of the Philistine menace involved more than two battles (2 Sam 8:1

may reflect this). These may have been decisive victories and may have been intended to balance the two great defeats suffered by Israel in the earlier stories of the books of Samuel (1 Samuel 4 and 31). These accounts symbolize David's success at giving Israel military security; they do not seem to occur in the chronological order of David's actions in the early days of his kingship. For example, many commentators have suggested that at least one of these victories must have come before the capture of Jerusalem. Certainly the chapter should not be regarded as giving a reliable historical sequence of events.[206]

As it now stands, the encounters with the Philistines are initiated by the news of David's acceptance of kingship over Israel (i.e., the northern, previously Saulide, tribes who had been the constant enemies of Philistia). We must consider the possibility that, until this point, the Philistines had still regarded David as a vassal of the king of Gath. The narrator has not reported that David had broken this relationship. Hence, his kingship over Judah may have been considered a development in David's control over a southern territory that he was supposed to be managing for the king of Gath. In any case, the break with the Philistines is made inevitable by his kingship over all Israel, which would have made clear his intention to throw off Philistine domination. David is now clearly the enemy, and the Philistines must act against his perceived rebellion (vv. 1-2).

Initially David is forced to seek refuge in his stronghold (perhaps Adullam, 1 Sam 22:1, 4; 24:22). In v. 19 we still see the David known to us before he became king. He inquires of the Lord whether he should engage the Philistines. The means of inquiry is not clear but could have been by ephod or lots. The Lord answers that David should engage them, for the Lord will give the Philistines into David's hand. The theme of God's presence with David and David's recognition of his reliance on God's guidance has carried over from the narratives of David's rise. He has not yet become the self-sufficient monarch. When David defeats the Philistines (v. 20a), he gives the credit to the Lord, using

the metaphor of a flood bursting upon the enemy; from that image is derived the name for remembrance of the place, Baal-perazim (v. 20b).[207] In the abandonment, capture, and removal of Philistine idols (v. 21), the reader cannot help recalling the Philistine capture of the ark and its subsequent sojourn in Philistine territory (1 Samuel 4–6). Through David, God has reversed Israel's fortunes.

The second battle occurs in the same general region (v. 22). It is not clear what the relationship of the two encounters might have been. Perhaps this is a force sent out in response to the first defeat, but it could also be a separate incident at another time, suggesting a period of hostilities between David and the Philistines. Once again David inquires of the Lord, and the Lord's response this time involves a particular strategy (vv. 23-24). David is not to engage them directly, but he must flank the Philistine force and come against them from the rear through a stand of balsam trees. When David hears "the sound of marching in the tops of the balsam trees" he is to strike, for he will know that the Lord has already gone ahead to strike the Philistines. This imagery is probably intended to refer to a rush of wind in the treetops. Wind is often an image of divine power in battle accounts that reflect the holy war imagery where God fights for Israel (see the storm imagery in 1 Sam 7:10; 12:18). David follows the Lord's instruction and wins a great victory, driving the Philistines back into their home territory (v. 25). Except for a brief reference in 8:1, this is the last we hear of the Philistines as a threat to Israel. David accomplishes what Saul could not and ends the time of Philistine domination.

At the end of this chapter, David has brought his new kingdom fully into the arena of nations. His united kingdom of Israel and Judah has a capital in Jerusalem, the beginning of international trade, and military security against its most feared enemy. David is now fully a king and has established a

---

206. See the discussion of these matters in Anderson, *2 Samuel,* 92-94, and in N. L. Tidwell, "The Philistine Incursions into the Valley of Rephaim," VTSup 30 (1979) 190-212.

207. C. L. Seow, *Myth, Drama, and the Politics of David's Dance,* HSM 44 (Atlanta: Scholars Press, 1989) 80-90, argues that Yahweh should be seen here as the divine warrior of holy war tradition "bursting forth" against the waters as in primordial battle. This "bursting forth" is paralleled in the Lord's "bursting forth" against Uzzah in 2 Sam 6:8. Certainly Seow is correct that both of the battle accounts in 5:17-25 reflect the holy war tradition associated with the ark. McCarter, *II Samuel,* 183, in a similar vein argues that these battle accounts, with their holy war language, are intended as a necessary introduction to the procession of the ark, symbolizing the God of holy war tradition, which follows in chap. 6.

kingdom in more than name only. It is the Lord who is still recognized by David and by the narrator as the power at work through David, but the ominous seduction of cedar, with its implications of wealth and power, is now also a part of the story.

REFLECTIONS

No one would deny the importance of achieving economic and political security for a nation. In these stories, David does so and appears to maintain his sense of the kingdom as ultimately relying for true security on the Lord. This unit, with its brief episodes, is significant for its record of David's achievements and for its hint of the dangers that come with the power to make such achievements. A palace of cedar is little to ask as a reward (v. 11), and even in its building David is quick to acknowledge the Lord as the source of all he has achieved. But cedar and victory are dangerous commodities and require careful handling. These dangers remain for later episodes in David's story to explore.

Economic wealth and political victory are still seductive and dangerous commodities, and recent decades have given us a procession of political and ecclesiastical leaders who have fallen victim to these seductive dangers. Our text suggests no remedy but constant recognition of our true security in the Lord and our awareness of the dangers that come with the necessary exercise of power.

2 Samuel 6:1-23, David Brings the Ark to Jerusalem

COMMENTARY

Scholars generally agree that David's installation of the ark of God in Jerusalem was of pivotal significance to the establishment and legitimization of his kingdom. Yet, interpretation of 2 Samuel 6 has been extremely varied.

Leonhard Rost first proposed that this chapter was part of an independent ark narrative that began with 1 Samuel 4–6 and concluded with the bringing of the ark to Jerusalem in 2 Samuel 6.[208] Following Rost, the ark narrative was understood until recently as one of the sources incorporated into a larger history work by the deuteronomistic historian. More recent scholarship has raised questions about the inclusion of 2 Samuel 6 in such an ark narrative.[209] This chapter seems to be part of David's story, and, unlike 1 Samuel 4–6, the ark itself does not seem to be the major character of the story. The transition between 1 Samuel 4–6 and 2 Samuel 6 is not a smooth one and has led many to propose that something must have dropped out if these chapters existed as an independent document. Nevertheless, it seems clear that the author responsible for writing and placing 2 Samuel 6 knew of the ark narratives in 1 Samuel 4–6 and intentionally built on that earlier episode concerning the ark of God. Certain patterns seem to be an intentional relating of the two ark-related narratives. In 1 Samuel 4, there are two Philistine victories that lead to the loss of the ark, whereas two victories of Israel over the Philistines (2 Sam 5:17-25) and the loss of the Philistine idols (5:21) preface the recovery of the ark in 2 Samuel 6. The loss of the ark signaled the end of the house of Eli (1 Sam 4:12-18); now the recovery of the ark occasions a confrontation with Michal that signals with finality the end of the house of Saul (2 Sam 6:20-23). The religious and political futures of Israel now focus on David. Even the ark seems to need his patronage as it is restored to a central place in Israelite life. The ark (and the Lord it represented) seemed to take care of itself in 1 Samuel 5–6.

208. Rost, *The Succession to the Throne of David*.
209. Miller and Roberts, *The Hand of the Lord*, make a convincing argument that 2 Samuel 6 was not a part of an independent ark narrative. For an opposing view, see Anthony F. Campbell, *The Ark Narrative (1 Sam 4–6; 2 Sam 6): A Form-Critical and Traditio-Historical Study*, SBLDS 16 (Missoula, Mont.: Scholars Press, 1975).

Psalm 132 has long been recognized as a liturgical remembrance of David's transfer of the ark. It opens by describing a search for and a procession of the ark (Ps 132:1-9) and concludes with affirmations of God's promises concerning David and Zion (Ps 132:10-18). This is similar to the progression in 2 Samuel—from procession of the ark (chap. 6) to the oracle of dynastic promise to David (chap. 7). Psalm 132 may well be an older remembrance of the ark procession and the Davidic promise than the present narrative forms of 2 Samuel 6–7. Influential Scandinavian scholars have stressed the ritual and mythological background of the ark procession, arguing that 2 Samuel 6 was a story composed to justify later liturgical practices of processing the ark and was without historical basis in the reign of David.[210] More recent scholarship has reasserted the importance of 2 Samuel 6 as the record of a pivotal historical moment in David's kingship, although the telling of the story has been shaped to help legitimate Davidic rule.[211] Liturgy, as reflected in Psalm 132, celebrates this event but does not create it.

The procession of the ark to Jerusalem, initiated by David, was significant on many levels. Flanagan has suggested that this complexity of meanings marks the ark procession as a rite of passage that allows and encourages transformations from old order to new order that would not have been possible in a less liminal moment.[212] Although they are interrelated, different levels of meaning can be discerned in the ark procession story.

(1) The transfer of the ark served to legitimate Davidic rule. The ark of God was the most sacred symbol of tribal, covenantal Israel. It represented the holy war traditions of Yahweh as the divine warrior who fought for Israel, and the traditions of Yahweh as divine king whose enthroned presence was

represented by the ark (see Commentary on 1 Sam 4:4). David's transfer of the ark to Jerusalem links the kingship of God to Davidic rule. Likewise, God's protection of Israel was now channeled through the protection of God's anointed king.

(2) The removal of the ark from the house of Abinadab and the death of Uzzah, Abinadab's son, sever previous arrangements for custody of the ark. Custody is transferred to the house of David. In effect, David becomes the patron of the ark—a priestly role—and the older covenantal religious traditions it represents. By honoring the ark and restoring it to a position of respect, David avoids the conflict that brought grief to Saul. He positions himself as the preserver rather than the threat to the older religious traditions.

(3) The procession of the ark serves as a public ritual to inaugurate Jerusalem, not only as royal capital but also as the religious center of Israel's life.[213] This makes Jerusalem the successor to Shiloh and ties religious center and political center together in David's city and David's rule. The kingdom of David and the city of Jerusalem possess both theological and political implications, leading to the emergence of a David-Zion theology.

(4) The narrative of the ark procession reveals David's personal character, especially his unique ability to blend piety and politics. On the one hand, the honoring of the ark is a pious act, acknowledging the centrality of the Lord's rule in David's kingdom. On the other hand, the procession of the ark is a shrewd and calculated move by David to appease forces that might otherwise oppose him. It is a part of David's uniqueness in Israel's story that both of these aspects seem authentic to David. Brueggemann captures the ambiguity of Davidic character in such moments:

Insofar as the narrative looks back, the advent of the ark bespeaks genuine religious seriousness on David's part. Insofar as the event looks forward, there is a hint of political calculation and manipulation in David's act. Both factors are present. The wonder is that David is able to hold them together in a kind of personal authenticity that resists choosing one factor or the other.[214]

210. Norwegian Sigmund Mowinckel first advanced his arguments for an ark procession as part of an annual Israelite New Year's festival in the 1920s. His most definitive work was translated into English as *The Psalms in Israel's Worship*, 2 vols., trans. D. R. Ap-Thomas (Nashville: Abingdon, 1962). A. Bentzen had earlier argued that 2 Samuel 6 reflects ancient combat myths and is a narrativizing of liturgical motifs. See "The Cultic Use of the Story of the Ark in Samuel," *JBL* 67 (1948) 37-53.

211. See Terence E. Fretheim, "The Cultic Use of the Ark of the Covenant in the Monarchical Period" (Th.D. diss., Princeton Theological Seminary, 1967); and P. Kyle McCarter, "The Ritual Dedication of the City of David in 2 Samuel 6:1," in Meyers and O'Connor, *The Word of the Lord Shall Go Forth*, 273-78.

212. Flanagan, "Social Transformation and Ritual in 2 Samuel 6," 361-72.

213. McCarter, "The Ritual Dedication of the City of David in 2 Samuel 6:1," 273-78, particularly stresses this narrative as involving the inauguration of Jerusalem for its important role in Israel's life.

214. Brueggemann, *First and Second Samuel*, 249.

(5) The procession of the ark helps to establish a ritual, liturgical base for the development of a theology of kingship in Israel. Certainly the evidence from Psalm 132, as well as other references in the psalms, makes clear that the transfer of the ark to Jerusalem was the subject of ongoing liturgical celebration in Israel's worship life. C. L. Seow, in an important study of this chapter, suggests persuasively that David may have shaped this procession as a ritual drama drawn from an ancient mythic pattern chronicling the victory of the divine warrior and his subsequent victorious procession to ascend the royal throne.[215] Such a pattern seems to shape the narrative of 2 Samuel 6. The ritual pattern associated with the divine warrior in the ancient Near East is now claimed for Israel's God, Yahweh. The various elements of this ritual drama include:

❖ victory over enemies (5:17-25) as the necessary prelude to the victory procession of chap. 6;

❖ a ceremonial procession of the victorious divine warrior in joyous celebration;

❖ demonstrations of divine power, such as the smiting of Uzzah (Seow suggests that this might have been a ritual battle at the threshing floor [v. 6] to reenact the death of the Lord's enemies, but this must be regarded as somewhat speculative);

❖ the role of dancing as reflective of the dance of all creation in celebration of the divine warrior's victory;

❖ the ascent and installation of the ark (vv. 17-18) as an enthronement of the divine warrior in kingship;

❖ a ritual banquet and distribution of food, displaying the divine king's graciousness (v. 19).

In effect, this ritual drama enacts the procession of the victorious divine warrior to his rightful place as divine king. In the narrative of 2 Samuel 6, this ritual drama is appropriated in a manner that makes David and his kingship the representative of the Lord as divine warrior king.

In vv. 16 and 20-23, an intense drama is played out within the larger narrative between David and Saul's daughter Michal. This episode seems intrusive within the story of the transfer of the ark, and opinion is divided on whether the encounter with Michal is an original part of the narrative. Much has been written recently on the character of Michal.[216] She has been depicted both as a vindictive nag and as a rightfully incensed victim of political manipulation by David. The episode will be examined more carefully below, but the encounter in its present form has less to do with the personalities of Michal and David than with the delegitimizing of Saulide claims. The episode serves to announce the end of any possibility of an heir to the throne through Michal.

6:1-5. We have just read about two great victories over the Philistines (5:17-25). When v. 1 tells us that David "again" musters "thirty thousand men," we expect a further account of military engagements. Instead David and his entire entourage go to Baalah of Judah (NIV; NRSV, "Baale-judah") to bring the ark of God to Jerusalem. Instead of a new military engagement, this is to be the triumphal procession of the God responsible for those victories against the Philistines (5:20b, 24b).

Unlike the apparent implication of Ps 132:6, no search for the ark is necessary. The ark of God is not lost, but it has been neglected. According to 1 Sam 6:21–7:1, the ark had rested in the house of Abinadab in Kireath-jearim, a Gibeonite town in the territory of Judah. According to 2 Sam 6:3-4, the ark is removed from the house of Abinadab, placed on a new cart, and sent on its way accompanied by the two sons of Abinadab, Uzzah and Ahio. The discrepancy in place names for the ark's resting place may be explained by alternative names for the same location. Kiriath-jearim is identified with Kiriath-baal in Josh 15:60; 18:14, and with Baalah in Josh 15:9. Baalah of Judah could be a variant of these alternative names for Kiriath-jearim.

The full formal designation for the ark is used in v. 2: "the ark of God which is called by the name of the LORD of hosts who is enthroned on the cherubim." This same full name of the ark is also used in 1 Sam 4:4 at the beginning of the ark narrative (see Commentary on 1 Sam 4:1b-11). The use of this full designation connects David to the range of traditions connected to the ark. For tribal

---

215. Seow, *Myth, Drama, and the Politics of David's Dance.*

216. An outstanding collection of writings on Michal is found in David J. A. Clines and Tamara C. Eskenazi, eds., *Telling Queen Michal's Story,* JSOTSup 119 (Sheffield: JSOT, 1991). Particularly helpful is Exum, "Murder They Wrote," 45-68.

Israel, the ark of God was the chief symbol of the Lord's presence in the midst of Israel. It was a gilded box made of acacia wood (Exod 25:10-22; 37:1-9) surmounted by winged cherubim, which served as a pedestal for the invisibly enthroned Yahweh (the LORD). The title for Israel's God as "LORD of hosts" is rooted in the holy war tradition of Israel's God as a divine warrior who fights for them and is the true leader of the armies ("hosts"). By the use of the ark's full title, the reader is reminded that when David brings the ark to Jerusalem he is associating his own kingdom with the presence, the military power, and the kingship of Israel's covenant God, Yahweh. David is, in effect, proclaiming a powerful divine alliance for himself in this public ritual.

The procession moves toward Jerusalem. The use of the cart and oxen is reminiscent of the Philistines' ridding themselves of the ark in 1 Samuel 6. Once again the ark moves to a new resting place, but this time it is not accompanied at a distance by watchful and anxious Philistines (1 Sam 6:12). David himself and the whole house of Israel dance and play instruments "before the LORD with all their might" (v. 5). The mood is one of joy and celebration appropriate to the triumphal procession of the Lord, who had been victorious over the Philistines.

6:6-11. The procession of the ark to Jerusalem is interrupted. As the ark approaches the threshing floor of Nacon, the oxen stumble and the ark teeters. Uzzah reaches out his hand to steady the ark (v. 6). The anger of the Lord flares, and God strikes Uzzah dead (v. 7). We are shocked. What has Uzzah done to deserve this? The Hebrew text uses an obscure word of uncertain meaning. The NIV has translated the phrase as "because of his irreverent act." The NRSV follows the reading in 1 Chr 13:10, which is supported by a fragmentary Qumran manuscript, "because he reached out his hand to the ark." What is clear is that the ark possesses great holiness and power. It may not be treated casually. The death of Uzzah is reminiscent of the fate that befell the inhabitants of Beth-shemesh when they looked inside the ark (1 Sam 6:19). Uzzah may have desired to help, but his casual touching of the holy ark carries a terrible price. David clearly does not find this price acceptable. With unusual candor, v. 8 records David's anger toward God. The note about David's anger uses the same verb, translated as "burst forth" (פרץ *pāraṣ*), that was used for the "bursting forth" of God's power against the Philistines in the holy war account of 5:20.[217] Uzzah has been treated like the enemy of God and of Israel, and David does not find this acceptable. He fears bringing such a dangerous holy object into his own city (vv. 9-10a). Accordingly, the procession is halted, and the ark is lodged in the house of Obed-edom, a Gittite who presumably lives nearby (v. 10b). There the ark remains for three months, which v. 11 tells us were months of blessing for Obed-edom and his household. Ironically, just as David had sojourned among the Gittites before receiving his kingdom and claiming Jerusalem as his capital, so, too, the ark of God rests with a Gittite before proceeding to Jerusalem and the triumphant installation of Israel's divine warrior-king, Yahweh.

6:12-19. The death of Uzzah ends any authority that the house of Abinadab might have had over the ark of God. In v. 12, David receives word that the house of Obed-edom has been blessed, so he resumes the procession of the ark into Jerusalem. There is no further word of Abinadab or his sons as custodians of the ark. David seems more directly involved than before. It is David who "brought up" the ark (v. 12); it is David who "sacrificed" an ox and a fatling after processing only six paces (v. 13); it is David who "danced before the LORD with all his might" clad only in a linen ephod (v. 14). It is David's house that now serves as custodian of the ark.

With great ceremony, the ark is installed in Jerusalem. The ark, and the God whose presence it represents, is given an honored place and is housed in a special tent sanctuary where burnt offerings and offerings of well-being are made (v. 17). Blessings are pronounced on the people in the name of the Lord of hosts (v. 18). The divine warrior has now become a source of blessing in the midst of the people. Food is distributed among the

217. Because of the similarity of the verbs, Seow, *Myth, Drama, and the Politics of David's Dance,* 97-104, speculates that the procession of the divine warrior represented by the ark may have included a mock battle, reenacting the victory over the Philistines. But he admits that the present text treats Uzzah's death entirely as a historical occurrence and not as a mock death of Philistine enemies.

people—bread, meat, and raisins—as a ceremonial meal befitting the conclusion of the triumphant processional of Israel's victorious God (v. 19). Banquets and public distribution of food were common in ancient Near Eastern coronation rights, which would support the notion that Israel's God is being installed as a divine king. God's enthroned presence, represented by the ark, now resides in the midst of David's city.

In the midst of this public ritual and celebration, v. 16 pulls us aside as observers of one who has not participated in the joy of the day. Michal, identified every time she is mentioned in this chapter as the "daughter of Saul," is inside looking on from a window. This position alone marks her as a non-participant. She focuses on David's dancing, described here as exuberant in his leaping before the Lord. We are told only that as she sees David dancing, she "despised him in her heart." For now we know nothing of the motivations for such despising. The notice anticipates the later confrontation between David and Michal after the celebrations are over (vv. 20-23).

6:20-23. The account of the ark's transfer to Jerusalem does not end on a high note of celebration and joy. The final verses of the chapter are taken up in a bitter family dispute between David and Michal.[218] She is always identified in this chapter as the daughter of Saul, underlining her role as the representative of the Saulide line. Saul had reluctantly given her as wife to David after his payment of a brideprice of two hundred Philistine foreskins (1 Sam 18:20-29), but she was given to Palti as wife when David became a fugitive from Saul (1 Sam 25:44). David required Abner to restore Michal to him as a condition for accepting Abner's support, and Michal was forcibly taken from a weeping Palti and brought to David (2 Sam 3:15-16). At one time, the story reported that "Michal loved David" (1 Sam 18:20), but nothing of that love remains.

David seems to know nothing of the impending confrontation and returns to bless his own household following the public ceremonies with the ark (v. 20a). He is met by Michal, who immediately confronts David with criticism of his public behavior (v. 20). She begins with sarcasm, "How the king of Israel honored himself today." It is clear from what follows that she believes he has dishonored himself.

Much has been written about Michal's displeasure.[219] There are three elements in her angry tirade (v. 20b). The first is that David has uncovered himself. In his dancing, presumably he exposed his genitals. This may well have been unusual behavior for a king. A second motive for her anger is that this took place before "the slave girls of his servants" (NIV; NRSV, "his servants' maids")—in other words, before women of the lowest socioeconomic class. It seems to matter to Michal that David has behaved this way before lower-class women, but we are not told why. Finally, Michal calls David a "vulgar fellow" who has "shamelessly" uncovered himself. She seems to feel that his behavior was inappropriate for a king. He has lowered himself to the basest of men. Perhaps as a royal herself she has her own conception of protocol, and this son of a shepherd does not meet the standard. Michal's feelings have been made clear, but we are left to speculate on all that lies behind them.

David's response to Michal clearly makes the issue one of legitimacy for his kingship and as a corollary the end of Saulide hopes for a royal future (vv. 21-22). David immediately contrasts his status as God's chosen king with God's rejection of Saul ("your father") and all of his household (v. 21a). David reminds her that he is "prince over Israel" by the Lord's choice, and it was for the Lord that he danced (v. 21b). David seems to agree that his behavior was shameless, undignified, and humiliating even in his own eyes (v. 22a), but it was for the Lord. As for the servants' maids, David accepts their honor even when Michal believes he has only earned dishonor (v. 22b). Michal is put in her place as the daughter of a dishonored and rejected king. David is the chosen of God and is honored by even the lowest classes of his people. The political implications are clear: The house of Saul

---

218. Two articles by David J. A. Clines have been particularly helpful on this segment of Michal's story: "Michal Observed: An Introduction to Reading Her Story," and "The Story of Michal, Wife of David, in Its Sequential Unfolding," both in Clines and Eskenazi, *Telling Queen Michal's Story*, 24-63, 129-40.

219. See Clines's survey of the many suggestions and positions taken relative to Michal in this story, "Michal Observed: An Introduction to Reading Her Story," in *Telling Queen Michal's Story*, 52-61.

has no say in matters of the kingdom. David draws his authority and legitimation from the Lord and from the people.

The final verse of the chapter (v. 23) ends all Saulide hopes. Michal will remain childless to her death. There will be no son to unite the Davidic and Saulide houses. Again the text leaves details unclear. Many have speculated that David put her aside as a wife; others have suggested that Michal would have nothing to do with David. Some have interpreted this verse as implying God's judgment on Michal. None of these things are said. All are left as possibilities for our speculation.

In this brief episode, we are told about the substance of the confrontation, but most of the motives behind it are left unstated. Robert Alter suggests that this invitation to "multiple interpretations" may be precisely the point:

With a fine sense of the tactics of exposition, the narrator tells us exactly what Michal is feeling but not why. . . . The scorn for David welling up in Michal's heart is thus plausibly attributable in some degree to all of the following: the undignified public spectacle which David just now is making of himself; Michal's jealousy over the moment of glory David is enjoying while she sits alone, a neglected co-wife, back at the provisional palace; Michal's resentment over David's indifference to her all these years, over the other wives he has taken, over being torn away from the devoted Palti; David's dynastic ambitions—now clearly revealed in his establishing the Ark in the "City of David"—which will irrevocably displace the house of Saul. The distance between the spouses is nicely indicated here by the epithets chosen for each: she is the "daughter of Saul," and she sees him as the king. Michal's subsequent words to David seize on the immediate occasion, the leaping and cavorting, as the particular reason for her anger, but the biblical writer knows as well as any psychologically minded modern that one's emotional reaction to an immediate stimulus can have a complicated prehistory; and by suppressing any causal explanation in his initial statement of Michal's scorn, he beautifully suggests the "overdetermined" nature of her contemptuous ire, how it bears the weight of everything that has not been said but obliquely intimated about the relation between Michal and David.[220]

220. Alter, *The Art of Biblical Narrative*, 123.

REFLECTIONS

1. There have been many occasions when 2 Samuel 6 has been used as a justification for dance and bodily movement as a part of Christian worship. It is no doubt true that dance was a more natural part of Israelite worship than our own, but such a use of this text misses its main point. Dance is not here simply a neutral method for the praise of God. David's dancing before the ark as it is transferred to Jerusalem, the city of David, points to a pivotal transfer of political power and a transforming possibility for new theological understandings of God's power in relation to public power. David's intense personal involvement is either a genuine recognition and honoring of true power in the Lord (represented by the ark) or a manipulation of religious symbols for the sake of his own enhanced power. This account invites us to reflect on how thin the line is between these two possibilities.

I am writing these words on the very day of the inauguration of a president of the United States. The ceremony will be filled with religious symbols and personalities. These religious trappings embody both possibilities and dangers. They symbolize ties to older traditions in honor and respect for the values of religious customs that we wish to preserve and draw upon in public life. They represent the danger of cynically manipulating religious symbols for the advancement of ideologies or personal power. There is no easy mediation between these two alternatives, and unless religious values are to be totally absent from the public arena we must run the risk of these dangers for the sake of the possibilities. To separate religious symbolism and public power is to risk giving up the notion of moral accountability in public life altogether.

Worship, in our experience, is seldom this risky. Unlike David, we mostly observe rather than participate. Unlike those who saw Uzzah fall, we seldom recognize the power of God's holy presence. Unlike Michal, we fail to voice the political threat that arises from the juncture of religious symbol and political power.

This text and these reflections can offer no glib antidotes to the safe and comfortable rituals of our sanctuaries or the taken-for-granted use of religious symbols in public ceremonies. It would seem that 2 Samuel 6 simply reminds us that divine power and human political power must be intentionally brought together as David is trying to do. It is a risky business, as Uzzah's death reminds us and Nathan the prophet will later point out to David (2 Samuel 12). The alternative is to live with the illusion that our own structures of political power are the ultimate reality, to live with the illusion that religious symbols can be hoarded away from public responsibility or cynically manipulated for the sake of human power arrangements. It is out of such illusions that kingdoms have fallen and nations have perished.

2. While it is clear that the confrontation between Michal and David is intended to address matters of Davidic and Saulide claims on the kingdom, the story is also revealing of gender politics in ancient Israel. Michal had boldly dared to love David and to make that love known (1 Sam 18:20). Yet, David is never said to have loved her, although marriage to her was politically advantageous to him. Three times Michal is given to a man as wife for political reasons (David, 1 Sam 18:27; Paltiel, to spite David, 1 Sam 25:44; David again, as the price for alliance with Abner, 2 Sam 3:14-16). In all of this we lose sight of her love, for love was not allowed a role in such political matters. By 2 Sam 6:20-23, this love appears long dead. When her resentment pours out upon David, the text treats the issue as one of the legitimation of claims on the kingdom. Michal is always called the daughter of Saul, for she is used here as the representative of Saulide claims.

But that is just the point: Michal is always getting used for claims other than her own. Her claim of love was given no power in her world. Her sad and bitter story may be used by the writer to further the men's story of kingdom and power, but it reminds us that the books of Samuel know another reality that David ignores at his peril. The books of Samuel began in the Lord's regard for another childless woman, Hannah. Hannah's song testified to the Lord's commitment to reverse the fortunes of the oppressed and the exploited. David has known this reversal of grace himself in his rise as God's chosen one, from shepherd to king. As his kingdom interests bring Michal's story to a bitter end, David is in the dangerous position of claiming to honor the Lord while completing the final humiliation of one who had once offered him love. Michal's story anticipates the day when David will learn that even God's chosen king must face God's judgment for having been preoccupied with his own power and self-interest (the Bathsheba story, 2 Samuel 11–12). In reading Michal's story, we do well to examine our own refusals of love for the sake of power, our own disregard of women's interests as irrelevant to the public interest, our own efforts to honor the Lord while not fully honoring the priorities to which the Lord has called us.

3. It is the death of Uzzah that most often disturbs readers of this chapter. Why should he be struck dead for what seems a helpful act? It is unlikely that any response we may give will make us comfortable with this God who brings death rather than life. But the point of this strange and disturbing episode may well be that encounter with God is a risky business—not to be taken causually or lightly, as is frequently our custom.

We know nothing about Uzzah. We do know that the ark was, by law, to be carried on poles by Levites, but it has instead been loaded on an oxcart (reminiscent of the Philistines in 1 Samuel 6). Was Uzzah responsible for this? Is his haste to prevent the toppling of the ark but his own attempt to avoid the consequences of poor judgment in transporting the holy presence? As a priest, did he not know that touching the ark is forbidden? Such questions cannot be answered, but the death of Uzzah can stand as a reminder of the danger of trying to manage God's holiness. What should be reverence and awe before God gives way to the notion that we can put our hands on God. That way lies death—perhaps not as dramatic as Uzzah's but just as fatal. Jesus called those who thought they could control God's holiness by their own efforts "whitewashed tombs . . . full of dead men's bones" (Matt 23:27 NRSV).

2 Samuel 7:1-17, Nathan's Dynastic Oracle

COMMENTARY

This chapter is the most important theological text in the books of Samuel and perhaps in the entire Deuteronomistic History. With the kingdom secure and his own house (palace) built, David expresses the desire to build a house (temple) for the Lord. Initially, the prophet Nathan approves of this task (vv. 1-3). God's word comes to Nathan in the night with an oracle in response to David's desire (vv. 4-16): The Lord does not need or desire a house (vv. 4-7). The Lord has chosen and cared for David (vv. 8-11*a*), and, instead, the Lord will establish a house (dynasty) for David (v. 11*b*). A son will come after David and be established on the throne; he will build a house (temple) for the Lord (vv. 12-13). This throne will be established forever; the Lord will relate to these descendants of David as father to son; they may be chastised for their sin, but, unlike with Saul, God's steadfast love will be with them forever (vv. 14-16). Nathan conveys this oracle to David (v. 17).

It is readily apparent that this chapter relies on a word play, involving the variant meanings of a single word, to convey its central theme. The common Hebrew noun בית (*bayit*) can, depending on context, mean "house," "dwelling," "palace," "temple," or "dynasty." All of these meanings may play a role in 2 Sam 7:1-17, but the crucial theological focus is on the relationship between temple and dynasty.

This passage is foundational for the appearance and development of a Davidic theology in Israel alongside the covenant theology of tribal Israel. The text of this chapter did not appear full blown in David's time. Most scholars agree that the text of 2 Sam 7:1-17 has undergone a complex history, and, as it

now stands, it reflects the development and appropriation of many generations in Israel. There is no scholarly consensus, however, on the details of the literary history of this text.[221] Almost all would see the final form of 2 Sam 7:1-17 as having been shaped by the deuteronomistic historian (in the verse-by-verse commentary, evidence of deuteronomistic language and themes will be noted). McCarthy proposed that 2 Samuel 7 should be regarded as one of the programmatic speeches that appear at crucial junctures in the Deuteronomistic History (e.g., Joshua 23; 1 Samuel 12; 1 Kgs 8:14-66).[222] These speeches look back on the past and ahead to the future and offer theological evaluations of Israel's history and prospects. His proposal has proved widely persuasive. A substantial majority of scholars would also see some elements of 2 Sam 7:1-17 as having originated with David, but proposals for the development of the chapter between the time of David and the Deuteronomistic History vary significantly. McCarter has offered a proposal for the development of 2 Sam 7:1-17 in three stages, each reflecting differing interests and emphases, which seems helpful and persuasive: "The earliest form of Nathan's oracle was a promise of dynasty to David made in connection with his declared intention to build a temple for Yahweh. This ancient document was expanded by a writer with a

221. See the extremely helpful survey and evaluation of the vast literature interpreting 2 Samuel 7 in McCarter, *II Samuel*, 209-31. His treatment is an invaluable guide to the many proposals made concerning the development of this key chapter. A few recent voices argue for the literary unity of 2 Samuel 7 and deny any history of development reflected in the text. John Van Seters, *In Search of History: Historiography in the Ancient World and the Origins of Biblical History* (New Haven: Yale University Press, 1983) 273, argues "from the point of view of form criticism there is no reason why the whole chapter cannot be considered the work of one author."
222. Dennis J. McCarthy, "II Samuel 7 and the Structure of the Deuteronomic History," *JBL* 84 (1965) 131-38.

less favorable view towards the temple and towards David himself. The final form of the passage was the work of a Deuteronomistic editor who further amended it to express his own point of view."[223] McCarter identifies the second stage in this process with circles reflecting a "prophetic theology of kingship coming to terms with the historical reality of the Davidic dynasty."[224] He characterizes the progression of theological perspectives through these stages as follows:

(1) "You have promised to build a house for me. Therefore I shall build a house for you."[225] Dynastic promise was initially understood as divine response to David's intention to build God a temple. This earliest level is found in vv. 1a, 2-3, 11b-12, 13b-15a.

(2) "You will not build me a house. I shall build you a house."[226] A prophetic editing of the text, found in vv. 4-9a, 15b, argues that a temple was not needed and that the gift of dynastic promise was not a response to David's plan to build a temple but a free act of divine grace.

(3) "You will not build me a house. Your son will build me a house."[227] The final version of the deuteronomistic historian, present in vv. 1b, 9b-11a, 13a, 16, softens the negative attitude of the prophetic version toward the Temple. It makes God's refusal to David only temporary and allows for a positive attitude toward Solomon's building of the Temple.

One could argue with the attribution of particular verses or phrases, but in general the process of development McCarter suggests makes sense against the backdrop of Israel's changing history and the place of temple and dynasty in that history. Psalms 89:19-37; 132:11-18; and 1 Chr 17:1-15 represent other important texts in which the themes of dynastic promise to David and God's dwelling on Mt. Zion (Temple) are seen as pillars of the royal theology that develops in Israel from David onward.

In its present form, 2 Sam 7:1-17 serves multiple purposes in the ongoing story of 1–2 Samuel as well as in the larger biblical story. It serves to explain why David did not build a Temple but why his son Solomon later is able to do so. It seeks to legitimize the principle of dynastic succession, which was new to Israel, by making it the will and promise of the Lord. It made clear that God's graceful presence was not dependent on a temple, even though Solomon would later be allowed to build one. It makes clear that God's promise to David would endure, even though times of chastising judgment would arise. (This emphasis might have been especially important to the exilic audience of the Deuteronomistic History.) Finally, it became an important text to articulate Jewish messianic expectations in a time when there was no Davidic monarch on the throne. This development, of course, led to the appropriation of this text by the early Christian church, who understood Jesus as the continuation of this promise to the line of David.

The oracle of Nathan in 2 Sam 7:4-16 locates God's grace toward Israel in an unconditional and everlasting promise to the line of David. This was a new theological understanding in Israel and stood in tension with the conditional "if" of the Mosaic covenant at Mt. Sinai.[228] Yet, the Davidic promise did not displace the Sinai covenant. God's promise to David was understood to stand in continuity with God's previous acts of salvation on behalf of Israel. The conditional "if" of covenant is now encompassed by the "nevertheless" of unconditional promise. Obedience to covenant requirements is still demanded. Judgment, even of Davidic kings, is still the consequence of covenant disobedience (7:14b), but the commitment of God to steadfast love toward David's line and the Davidic kingdom is everlasting and cannot be broken (7:15-16). As will be discussed further below, this notion advances a theme of unconditional divine grace that makes this text centrally important to later Protestant understandings of justification by grace rather than works.

223. McCarter, *II Samuel*, 223.
224. McCarter, *II Samuel*, 229.
225. McCarter, *II Samuel*, 224.
226. McCarter, *II Samuel*, 225.
227. McCarter, *II Samuel*, 230.

228. Ps 132:12 contains a conditional form of the dynastic promise: "If your sons keep my covenant and my decrees that I shall teach them, their sons also, forevermore, shall sit on your throne" (NRSV). The covenantal "if" is preserved here, and this may be an earlier form of the dynastic promise than 2 Sam 7:4-16. The unconditional character of the promise develops as the line of David does, in fact, consolidate its power and establish its continuity. A theology to justify this in spite of the inevitable better and worse occupants of the throne has developed that understands God's promise as unconditional, although allowing for chastisement, and this is now reflected in 2 Sam 7:4-16.

The theology of 2 Sam 7:1-17 is not politically disinterested, and this text has not always been seen or used in accordance with high-minded purposes. Especially in its present position in David's story, this text legitimizes dynastic power and the interests of the Davidic state in maintaining power. As Flanagan's understanding of the structure of these chapters reminds us (see the Overview to 2 Sam 5:11–8:18), 2 Samuel 7 represents the turning point from continuity with older tribal realities and traditions (symbolized by the ark, chap. 6) to new understandings of God's presence in the Davidic kingdom.[229] The struggle for survival against the Philistines is over (5:17-25), and the expansion to empire is about to begin (8:1-14). Brueggemann calls the perspective of this chapter "the sure truth of the state" to emphasize the ideological orientation and interests of this text.

In the move from tribe to state, we are moving into ideology, into a justification of present forms of power and social organization and into propaganda, in which truth is what is advantageous. Note, I do not argue that this is dishonest or lightly perverted. I argue rather that the shift of perception caused by a monopoly of wealth and power invites such distortion, which then becomes systematic distortion. . . . I do not believe there is a predistorted text of these things. That is, there never was a "Nathan oracle" which was not ideologically intentional. Moreover, I shall say that this "sure truth," distorted as it is, is foundationally the vehicle for important faith resources.[230]

Israel's theology is now invested in the Davidic kingdom and its particular shape of political power. Chapter 7 is a recital by those who see new possibilities given by God in commitment to David. Nathan's oracle becomes the source of trust in the certainty of God's promise. But 2 Samuel 7 is also a recital by those likely to benefit from the power arrangements of kingdom. The oracle, then, becomes the source of temptation to manipulate the language of God's promise for the sake of vested interests. This text is at one and the same time a locus for both hope and danger.

7:1-3. David is now settled in his newly built "house of cedar" (see 5:11), and the kingdom is at peace (v. 1). The concept of "rest from enemies" given by the Lord (see also v. 11a) is a frequent theme in deuteronomistic texts (Deut 12:9-10; 25:19; Josh 21:44; 22:4; 23:1; 1 Kgs 5:4; 8:56). David is disturbed by the contrast between the luxury of his own house and the "tent" that houses the ark of God (v. 2). The clear implication is that David would like to build a temple for the Lord. Temple building was an activity often undertaken by ancient Near Eastern kings to legitimize their rule and to ensure favor from their gods.[231] A temple in Jerusalem would relate the Lord's presence, symbolized by the ark, to a permanent structure in David's city.

David expresses his concern to Nathan, the prophet (v. 2a). This is the first mention of Nathan, and we receive no information about him except that he is a "prophet" (נביא nābî). He appears to have been an influential member of David's court in Jerusalem, with access to the king. He later confronts David over his sin with Bathsheba (2 Samuel 12) and plays a role in the accession of Solomon (1 Kings 1). Nathan's initial response to David's desire to build a temple for the Lord is one of approval. Nathan tells David to carry out his intentions and blesses him with the formula "the LORD is with you" (v. 3). We have seen this formula as a central theme in the history of David's rise (see Commentary on 5:10). David came to power through bold action in confidence that the Lord was with him. In v. 3, it appears that this pattern will continue with a bold Davidic plan to build the Lord a temple.

7:4-7. Nathan spoke too quickly. The Lord has a word to communicate on this matter, and it comes to Nathan in the night (v. 4). The word that Nathan is to take to David (vv. 5-16) is introduced with the messenger formula characteristic of prophetic oracles: "Thus says the LORD. . . ."

The initial element of God's word to David focuses on divine rejection of David's proposal to build a temple for the Lord (vv. 5-7). The tone is not angry but firm. David is God's servant and is addressed as such (vv. 5, 8), but David is not the one to build such

---

229. Flanagan, "Social Transformation and Ritual in 2 Samuel 6."
230. Brueggemann, *David's Truth in Israel's Imagination and Memory,* 72.

231. G. W. Ahlstrom, *Royal Administration and National Religion in Ancient Palestine* (Leiden: E. J. Brill, 1982) 3-8.

a house for the Lord (v. 5*b*). God has not desired or needed a house (i.e., a permanent, fixed dwelling). God recalls that the divine dwelling has been a tent since the days of the deliverance out of Egypt (v. 6) and that at no time has a divine request been made of Israel's leaders to build a "house of cedar" for the Lord (v. 7). The issue here is one of divine freedom, represented by the movable tent-sanctuary, which is threatened by the notion of a permanent, localized temple and the implication that divine presence can be confined or captured. God, who is accustomed to "moving about among all the people of Israel," treats the desire to build a temple as an attempt to domesticate and control the presence of God. It is an abridgment of sovereign freedom. This clearly stated attitude against the building of a temple makes v. 13 problematic, since it seems to approve the later building of a temple by David's son Solomon.

7:8-11a. The use of the words "Now, therefore . . ." and a repeated messenger formula signal a new focus in God's word to David through the prophet. What follows is a review of God's favorable history with David and an extension of that favor through David to Israel's future. God's refusal to permit David to build a temple is not to be seen as a sign of divine disfavor. God has been with David, and through David God will bless Israel's future. This section is powered by verbs of decisive divine action. The first three point to God's gracious history with David:

I took you from the pasture (v. 8*b*)
I have been with you (v. 9*a*)
I have cut off all your enemies (v. 9*a*)

The second three point to a future of God's graciousness with David and Israel:

I will make you a great name (v. 9*b*)
I will appoint a place for my people Israel (v. 10*a*)
I will give you rest from all your enemies (v. 11)

Many have suggested that the three phrases that point to the future show deuteronomistic influence and the desire to reassure a generation in exile that God's promise still holds. The theme of rest from enemies is a common deuteronomistic theme (see Commentary

on 7:1-3), and v. 10, in particular, appears to address a generation that has lost a kingdom, rather than David, who has just gained one."

7:11b-17. Verse 11*b* begins a new section of God's promise, as indicated by the connecting word *moreover.* But it also signals the theological and literary center of this oracle. The expression "The Lord declares to you that the Lord himself will establish a house for you" (v. 11*b*) alone is cast in third-person rather than first-person address. This shift calls attention to the climactic character of the verse and has led some to argue that it was originally the continuation of v. 3 and represents the oldest literary layer of the text (see the discussion of McCarter's proposal above).

Startlingly, God reverses David's proposal. David cannot build a house for the Lord; the Lord will build a house for David. Using the potential for multiple meanings in the word ביח (*bayit,* "house"), God rejects "temple" but promises "dynasty." The grace shown to David in the past will now extend into the future. This promise is not simply for David, but for the line of David that will come after him.

The immediate consequence of this promise is to be a son who will succeed David on the throne (v. 12). This, of course, will be Solomon (1 Kings 1). It is this son who will be allowed to build "a house for my name" (v. 13*a*). This verse is thought by many to be from the deuteronomist. It seems to be a later legitimization of the Solomonic Temple in spite of God's rejection of such temples in vv. 5-7. The effect is to make God's refusal of a temple only temporary, but the remaining tension between vv. 5-7 and v. 13*a* is still evident. Verse 13*a* uses the typical deuteronomistic idea that it is God's name and not God's own self that dwells in the Temple (see Deut 12:11; 14:23; 16:2; 26:2).

The promise of a "house" for David extends beyond Solomon. The throne of the kingdom is to be established and made secure "forever" (repeated three times in vv. 13, 16). Abigail had already foretold a "sure house" for David (1 Sam 25:28), and God has now promised everlasting dynasty extending from David to secure a future of promise for Israel.

This promise will establish intimate relationship. The relationship between God and the king will be as that of a father to a son (v. 14; cf. the language of Pss 2:7; 89:26-27). It was not uncommon in the ancient world to conceptualize the king as the adopted son of the national god. Further, this promise is unconditional. God may chastise the king for disobeying God's covenant demands ("iniquity"), and there will be appropriate consequences (v. 14*b*). But even this will not cause God to cease in "steadfast love" toward David's line, as had happened to Saul (v. 15). The tragedy of Saul cannot be repeated. God is permanently and unconditionally committed to David and what flows from David for Israel's future. God's commitment takes the form of "steadfast love" (חסד *hesed*), a term connected with the loyalty required of covenant relationships. Verse 17 reports that Nathan conveyed to David all that the Lord had spoken.

REFLECTIONS

1. Nathan's oracle speaks to us of the necessary risk of deep faith held close to political ideology. It speaks to us out of the recognition that God has taken the risk of historical concreteness. Chapter 7 is the witness of those who have discerned God's unconditional grace in relation to David and to David's kingdom. It is a bold and audacious claim, and such a claim is not without its dangers. There are clear ideological interests in this text. It runs dangerously close to political propaganda. Indeed, later kings of Judah seem to use Davidic royal theology to simply undergird their own privileged position of power without regard to the God whose promise they exploit (e.g., see the indictment of a king by Jeremiah, Jer 2:3-19).

In spite of the danger, this text is a summons to stand boldly in the tension created by faith commitment and political engagement—to stand between God's interests and the world's interests. The pressure is to resolve the tension. Indeed, readings of 2 Sam 7:1-17 tend to read the oracle either as a bold statement of grace or as cress political propaganda.[232] Likewise, the church resists reading this text as a challenge to stand in the tension of faith and ideology. We are prone either to withdraw from the world's interests into unengaged piety or to ignore God's interests and slip into ideologically co-opted or culturally accommodated religiosity.

God has taken the risk of engaging with the political interests of kingdom. This text summons the church to risk such engagement as well. To respond to this summons will be to get ecclesiastical hands dirty: debating public policy on important issues; upholding value commitments and integrity in public institutions; standing in opposition to power structures when God's justice demands it; supporting power structures when mutually affirmed goals allow it. We may, like David, have occasions to repent when the interests of power tempt us over the line and we act in our own interests (personal or institutional) rather than in God's interests. Second Samuel 7 reminds us that the alternative to this risky tension of faith and political ideology cannot be disinterested, unengaged religion. That is not what God has modeled for us. In David, God risks the dangers of ideological manipulation of faith for the sake of bringing the grace of divine promise into close engagement with public and political realities. The church can do no less.

2. Nathan's oracle introduces a new theological language of unconditional grace into Israel's story. "This ideological utterance is the root of evangelical faith in the Bible: that is, faith that relies on the free promise of the gospel. Heretofore, God's commitments to Israel are regularly and characteristically conditional."[233] The promise to

---

232. McCarter, *II Samuel,* 210, cites the views of R. H. Pfeiffer, *Introduction to the Old Testament,* rev. ed. (New York: Harper and Bros., 1948), who regarded 2 Samuel 7 as "a mire of unintelligible verbiage" (p. 372), characterized by confusion and illiteracy and a "complete misunderstanding of the religion in the period of . . . David" (p. 373). The author, whose style is "consistently wretched," is at once "prolix" and "banal" (p. 372); he "repeats himself *ad nauseam*" (p. 373).

233. Brueggemann, *First and Second Samuel,* 257.

David does not remove the "if" of moral demand that we associate with God's covenant given to Israel at Sinai. Even kings may be chastised and made to suffer the consequences of their sin. This promise, however, does encompass the "if" in a divine commitment that endures in spite of sin. God's grace provides a bedrock of hope even in the midst of sin's consequences.

This unconditional promise may be one of the very reasons why Israel's tradition endures. Exile to Babylon came as a particular challenge to Israel's faith. Seemingly, nation, king, Temple, and national identity had been swept away. The retelling of David's story by the deuteronomistic historian in exilic times offered the chance to reclaim this promise and reaffirm that God is never finished with this commitment to David and to David's line. The promise holds and offers a constant basis of hope to God's people. This theme of unconditional grace in the promise to David is consistent with the articulation of "justification by grace" in the letters of Paul (cf. Rom 3:28; Gal 2:16-21). For that reason, 2 Samuel 7 has been an important text in Protestant traditions in which it is frequently cited and preached upon in connection with the theme of God's grace.

3. The promise of an enduring line for David is one of the foundations for the rise of messianic hopes in Judaism. When the prospects of the present kingdom seemed bleak, the prophets turned to this statement of enduring promise through David for the hope that God is always bringing a new David in every circumstance. God has promised an anointed one who will again bear God's Spirit and establish God's intended kingdom.

> A shoot shall come out from the stump of Jesse,
>   and a branch shall grow out of his roots.
> The spirit of the LORD shall rest on him,
>   the spirit of wisdom and understanding,
> the spirit of counsel and might,
>   the spirit of knowledge and the fear of the LORD.
> (Isa 11:1-2 NRSV)

In the circumstances surrounding exile and its aftermath, Judaism relied on the promise of God to David for the hope that God had not abandoned the historical enterprise. Even when there was no political kingdom, there was a David coming and a hope that God's anointed one would set things right. Exile contributed to an understanding that God's kingdom might not be tied to any one political kingdom, but the promise is nevertheless trustworthy within the historical process. The people of Israel could remain hopeful even under successive dominations by the empires.

The early Christian church saw Jesus in the light of this promise. The claim that Jesus was born in the line of David and thus inherits God's promise to David is not casually made. Jesus was seen as the Messiah, God's anointed one, announcing a kingdom of God with transforming power in this world. In the church today, 2 Sam 7:1-11, 16 appears in the *Revised Common Lectionary* as the lection for the fourth Sunday in Advent, Cycle B, the season when we anticipate Jesus' coming as the promised one. It is coupled with the Gospel reading of the annunciation to Mary (Luke 1:26-38) to indicate the church's recognition of continuity between Mary, the mother of Messiah, and David, the father of the messianic line. The angel Gabriel's announcement is, in part, a reaffirmation of the everlasting promise to David:

> And now, you will conceive in your womb and bear a son, and you will name him Jesus. He will be great, and will be called the Son of the Most High [cf. 2 Sam 7:14], and the Lord God will give to him the throne of his ancestor David. He will reign over the house of Jacob forever, and of his kingdom there will be no end. (Luke 1:31-33 NRSV)

Incarnation is connected to Davidic promise. Each brings divine presence close to human political realities. Each suggests that we cannot know God's promises apart from engagement with the risks and possibilities of the human historical process. In the lections of Advent we wait again each year for the coming of the son of David and the Son of God, confident that God's promise still holds in the historical moment of every generation.

Mary's response to the news of her son was to sing the beautiful song that we call the Magnificat (Luke 1:46-55; it appears as an alternative reading for the psalm in the lections for the fourth Sunday of Advent, Cycle B). Mary's song is a celebration of the transforming reversals of hope that the Messiah (her son, God's Son) will bring in the political and economic orders of human history. As we listen to her song in anticipation of Jesus, we remember that it is based on Hannah's song (1 Sam 2:1-10). Hannah's song also anticipated such reversals of hope in the coming of God's anointed king and the transforming grace he would bring. God's anticipated king in Hannah's song was David.

To read God's enduring promise to David in this text today is to be reminded of the roots and the challenge of our own messianic hope. To trust in God's promise to David and to claim Jesus as having been born into the line of that promise is to understand God's work as being endlessly engaged with the issues of justice and power that must be faced to establish God's kingdom in every age. In the light of this biblical promise, the church must understand its own faith as being endlessly engaged with these same realities.

2 Samuel 7:18-29, The Prayer of David

COMMENTARY

David responds to the oracle of dynastic promise with a prayer. It is a remarkable prayer and quite unlike the spontaneous, almost conversational, communication with God that has marked David's story to this point. In style, this prayer is formal, and in mood it seems calculating. It manages to be both deferential and audacious, qualities revealed in key repetitions in the prayer. David refers to himself ten times as "your servant." He addresses God with the exceedingly formal title "Lord GOD" (אדני יהוה *ădōnāy YHWH*; cf. NIV, "Sovereign Lord") seven times and as "LORD of hosts" twice. The divine appellation "Lord GOD" is used nowhere else in the books of Samuel. These repeated designations suggest an acknowledgment of divine power by a deferential David. Such deference is matched, however, by an audacious David who forcefully reminds God of the dynastic promise, perhaps even demanding fidelity to this promise. The use of the word "house" to mean "dynasty" appears seven times (see Commentary on 7:1-17),

and the term "forever" (עולם *ôlām*) is used five times. These repetitions are largely in the last six verses of the passage.

In structure, the prayer begins with David's expressions of deference (vv. 18-21), moves to praise of God's incomparability and benevolence toward Israel (vv. 22-24), and concludes with David's insistent restatement of the dynastic promise (vv. 25-29). Brueggemann felicitously refers to this threefold structure of David's prayer as "deference, doxology, and demand."[234] The final section of this prayer actually contains two petitions, both bold claims on God's fidelity to the promise of the dynastic oracle. David asks that God "do as you promised" (v. 25) and that God "bless the house of your servant" (v. 29).[235]

There has been considerable debate about the literary history of this text. Most scholars

234. Brueggemann, *First and Second Samuel*, 259. See also the discussion in Brueggemann, *David's Truth in Israel's Imagination and Memory*, 77-81.

235. See the analysis of this prayer in Patrick D. Miller, *They Cried to the Lord: The Form and Theology of Biblical Prayer* (Minneapolis: Fortress, 1994) 345-46.

agree that there is evidence of the deuteronomistic historian in the passage, especially in vv. 22-26.[236] There may have been a version of David's prayer that accompanied earlier versions of Nathan's oracle. It is hard to separate out such an earlier version with any certainty. The urgency with which David appeals for the fulfillment of God's promise to the line of David suggests that the present text reflects a time when historic circumstances have called that promise into question. This would, of course, fit well with the deuteronomistic historian's setting in exile. The urgent need of exiles to hear this promise anew and to hear David insisting on its fulfillment may be the shaping influence of David's prayer as we now read it. A supporting piece of evidence might be found in the unusual use of the divine designation "Lord GOD," which is never used elsewhere in the books of Samuel but is characteristically used by the exilic prophet Ezekiel (217 times).

7:18-21. David begins with a formula typically used for polite deference to a superior, "Who am I . . . ?" and continues in this deferential tone (v. 10). He refers to himself as ser vant (vv. 19-21) and addresses God four times as "Lord GOD" (vv. 18-20). David speaks of himself and the matter of his house (dynasty) as being "small" in God's eyes (v. 19; cf. also this usage in Solomon's prayer, 1 Kgs 3:7). All that has happened to bring David this far (v. 18) and to bestow whatever "greatness" (v. 21) David possesses is credited to the "word" and to the "will" of God (NIV; the NRSV uses "promise" and "heart" of God).

In its language, the opening to David's prayer bespeaks humility before God. Yet, the formal tone is quite different from the previous occasions when David "inquired" of the Lord. Gone is the sense of intimate piety, and it seems replaced by more florid, court language. Has this public prayer been shaped by reasons of state rather than by habits of faith? It is hard to say, but the prayer of David the king seems different from the prayer of David the shepherd/warrior/fugitive.

7:22-24. This section is given over entirely to praise of God. The stress is on the incomparability of God (v. 22), as evidenced

in graciousness toward Israel (v. 23). This makes Israel unique among the nations (v. 23a). The entire salvation history of Israel is suggested in the phrases of v. 23. It is here that most scholars find language that evidences the deuteronomistic style (e.g., the stress on the Lord's "name," v. 23).

Verse 24 links God to Israel in a version of the well-known covenant formula, "I will be their God and they will be my people" (Exod 6:7; Lev 26:12; Ezek 11:20; 37:27; Hos 2:23). Interestingly, the status of God's people will last "forever" (v. 24b). The conditional covenant of Sinai relating God and people is now altered by the unconditional language of the Davidic dynastic promise (v. 16). Praise of God has been inescapably linked to the future of the Davidic regime as implied in the commitment to the people "forever." This tie to Davidic promise is made explicit in the final section of the prayer.

7:25-29. The climactic section of David's prayer is signaled by the use of the Hebrew word ועתה (wĕ'attâ), "and now." This adverb is used, especially in covenantal formulations, to move from past remembrance to present action and is usually used by a stronger party to demand an action from a lesser party.[237] David uses this adverb three times in this section (vv. 25, 28, 29), giving his prayer an exceptionally audacious tone. David is now demanding fidelity from God.

Verse 25 moves directly to audacious petition. After reminding God of the word already spoken (i.e., Nathan's oracle), David petitions God to "confirm it forever; do as you have promised." The term "forever" (עולם 'ôlām), applied to the people in covenant with God (v. 24), is now applied to dynastic promise to David. David's prayer then immediately links this to the glorification of God's name, which will be "forever" (v. 26a), but not in its own right. The magnification of God's name is tied to Israel and the house of David (v. 26b). David demands God's fidelity to an everlasting link of God's name, Israel, and the house of David. Brueggemann writes:

David has gone very far in . . . taking the initiative for the relation with God. That is exactly what we expect from state truth, with reference to God.

---

236. A few scholars have seen the entire prayer as a deuteronomistic composition, e.g., Cross, *Canaanite Myth and Hebrew Epic*, 254. Most have seen the Dtr influence only in 7:22-26, e.g., Mettinger, *King and Messiah*, 51.

237. See Muilenburg, "The Form and Structure of the Covenantal Formulations," 347-65, for a discussion of this adverb in covenantal texts.

Its program is to make God a responsive patron. In 7:26 we have a shrewd piece of dynastic self-service. It is promised that Yahweh's name will be magnified . . . but he has now linked it to the dynastic claim. He has fixed it so that Yahweh cannot be magnified unless David is magnified as well. Thus David is linked to Yahweh. And along the way, Israel is identified with David.[238]

In v. 27, David recalls and restates the central promise of the dynastic oracle, "I will build you a house [dynasty]" (cf. v. 11b, where the verb is "make"). He claims that it is the remembrance of that promise that has given him the courage to pray so boldly. With two additional phrases introduced by *wĕ'attâ*, David continues in this bold vein. In v. 28, David acknowledges that "God is God" and that God's words are true, but he then links God's divine truth to the promise of this "good thing" to David. David audaciously suggests that the veracity of God's word is at stake. In v. 29, David further

238. Brueggemann, *David's Truth in Israel's Imagination and Memory,* 80.

petitions for a blessing. One would think that the promise of dynasty was enough, but the point here seems to be the continuity of the promise. The word "forever" is used twice, and the blessing asked for—demanded—is but a further way of stating the "good thing" that has been done for David in the promise of dynasty. This verse is a not-too-subtle reminder to God that this promise was to be everlasting. Significantly, the prayer ends on the word "forever." The prayer that began in deference ends with unmitigated demand.

Throughout his story, David has prayed. Perhaps it is to be expected that his prayers as shepherd and as warrior would be different from his prayers as king. He must now lead a nation's prayers and represent a people's interests. The language is now formal, public language. The interests are in a dynastic future and not a personal future. But the object to which prayer is directed is still an acknowledged sovereign God. David boldly claims the promise; he will later also experience the accountability that comes with that promise (cf. 7:14; 12:1-14).

REFLECTIONS

It is doubtful that David's prayer would ever be used as an Old Testament reading alongside the Lord's prayer. It is not the model we desire in answer to the disciples' request, "Lord, teach us to pray" (Luke 11:1). Although David's prayer acknowledges divine sovereignty, it also boldly makes claims on the sovereign God. Its tone is not that of disinterested praise or acknowledgment of need before God. The interests of state ideology are not far beneath the surface.

Yet, there is a quality to David's prayer, and to Hebrew prayer in general, that has much to teach us. Our tendency in prayer is to seek both language and tone that we imagine acceptable before God. By contrast, Hebrew prayer brings before God the entire gamut of human experience and the moods appropriate to them. The laments of the psalter are often cited in this regard. Anger, resentment, desire for vengeance, frustration with God's seeming inattention—a whole range of human feeling and experience seldom expressed in our prayer (esp. public prayer) finds expression in Hebrew prayer. God does not require a sanitized version of our most passionate struggles.

The boldness of David's prayer is in keeping with this quality of Hebrew prayer. David unabashedly expresses his claim on God's fidelity to the promise given to his dynasty. If this is tainted by ideological state interests, God must also know that these political interests are of concern to David. They are often of concern to us, but they seldom are offered to God in prayer. David, while boldly making his claims, constantly acknowledges divine sovereignty and freedom. To lay our claims before God is not to imagine that we actually control God.

To pray on behalf of our political self-interest is, of course, dangerous prayer. We run the risk of thinking we can domesticate God in our own interests. We may forget to lay such prayer alongside acknowledgment of divine sovereignty and thereby render prayer a mere instrument of public propaganda. This sometimes happens in the cynical uses of religious language and symbols that political candidates imagine will win votes.

But to pray on behalf of our political self-interest, while dangerous, is also necessary lest we submit only a portion of our humanity to the sovereignty of God's will in the conscious act of prayer. There is a need to pray about our political arrangements lest we think final authority lies in such arrangements. The act of prayer itself is a recognition of God's interests, which extend beyond our own self-interest. God is capable of judging the heart by which such prayers are offered and of responding to the humility or cynicism found there. It may ultimately be more dangerous to pray only the "safe" prayers on what we imagine are the "acceptable" topics in the "appropriate" moods. Such prayers are ultimately a failure of trust in the comprehensive freedom and sovereignty of God.

2 Samuel 8:1-14, David's Victories

COMMENTARY

This section records the military triumphs of David and the territorial expansion of his kingdom. The style is annalistic rather than that of storytelling. The chapter seems to be a collection of archival notices. Each segment records a people conquered or brought into the sphere of Davidic influence. This chapter records the movement from small kingdom to small empire.

The order of reporting in the chapter should not be taken as a chronological history. The record presents victories and annexations of territory stretching over many years during David's reign. This section parallels the section on David's victories over the Philistines in 2 Sam 5:17-25. The purpose of David's military exploits has shifted from defense to empire building. This is in keeping with the symmetrical structure Flanagan has detected for 5:11–8:18 as David's story moves from older, tribal connections to emerging patterns of kingdom and empire[239] (see the Overview to 5:11–8:18). Because David's victories over the Philistines occupy an earlier position in this structure, there is only a very brief mention of Philistine victory here (v. 1).

The key theological theme in this chapter is sounded in vv. 6b and 14b, where it is noted that "the LORD gave victory to David wherever he went." There is little doubt that the intention of the historian[240] is to picture the growth of a small Israelite empire by the subjugation of neighboring territories as evidence of divine favor toward David. By itself this would be a theme in continuity with the "God was with him" theme of the history of David's rise. However, the theological statement of vv. 6b and 14b stands in some tension with the tendency of empires to trust in human power. Verse 13a begins by stating that "David won a name for *himself*," and almost every segment of the chapter records David's prowess, and often his cruelty, as a conqueror. The reader arrives at the end of the chapter with an overall impression of reliance on human power in empire building in spite of the attributions of David's victories to the Lord in vv. 6b, 14b. This tension between divine power and human power arrangements will frequently occupy our attention in the episodes that lie ahead in David's story.

8:1-2. The chapter begins with brief notices of victories over the Philistines and the Moabites. David's victory over the Philistines has already been recorded in 5:17-25, and for that reason probably receives little attention here. This may be an additional victory not specifically mentioned earlier. We have little idea of the proper chronology for the several Philistine battles mentioned here and in chap. 5. This particular battle may be mentioned because it involves annexation of territory. The NRSV and the NIV treat "Metheg-ammah" as a place name, but such a place is unknown to us otherwise. The parallel text in 1 Chr 18:1 reads, "Gath and its surrounding villages."

Verse 2 records a victory over Moab, although no reason is given for hostilities with this neighboring kingdom. Indeed, the

---

239. Flanagan, "Social Transformation and Ritual in 2 Samuel 6."
240. McCarter, *II Samuel,* 251, believes the deuteronomistic historian is responsible for compiling this section from available archival material. There is little by way of language that indicates deuteronomistic composition, so this conclusion is possible but unlikely.

king of Moab had given refuge to David's family while he was a fugitive from Saul (1 Sam 22:3-4), and later tradition claims that David's great-grandmother was the Moabite woman Ruth (Ruth 4:21-22). This makes David's harsh treatment of Moabite captives even more surprising. The method of measuring with a cord to determine those to be singled out for mass execution is particularly gruesome and is not attested elsewhere. The writer of 1 Chr 18:2 omits the matter altogether, and the Greek text changes the ratio to half and half for survivors and those executed. The crucial matter for the interests of this chapter is that Moab becomes a vassal state in a growing Davidic empire.

8:3-8. These verses give a more detailed report of a campaign against Aramean contingents in Syria. David's primary adversary is King Hadadezer of Rehob of Zobah (v. 3). Zobah is an Aramean territory east of the Anti-Lebanon mountain range and north of Damascus. We know of a Beth-rehob near the southern slopes of Mt. Hermon, and this may have been Hadadezer's home. David seems to have attacked Hadadezer's territory when he was away to the north near the Euphrates River (v. 3b). The battle probably widened into a general Aramean conflict, since the Arameans of Damascus come to the aid of Hadadezer (v. 5) and since David's final victory is over this entire Aramean territory (v. 6). Damascus, a vassal or ally state of Zobah at this point, will rise to become the dominant Aramean capital by late in Solomon's reign (1 Kgs 11:23-25).

It is uncertain what the relationship is between this report and the account of campaigns against the Arameans in 10:6-19. Since these accounts also involve Hadadezer and end in Aramean defeat and subjugation, most interpreters would regard the two passages as reports drawn from the same Davidic campaign against the Arameans. Whether these reflect different battles and events in such a campaign or are variant accounts of the same battles is not clear (see Commentary on 10:1-19).

David's victory is decisive, and significant attention is given to the plunder. We are told of large numbers of horses and men captured by David (v. 4). He keeps only 100 chariots and hamstrings the remaining 1,600 horses. He apparently could not incorporate more into his own forces and refused to leave them usable by his enemy. Verse 5b records that 22,000 Aramean fighting men have been killed by David's forces. Gold shields belonging to Hadadezer are carried triumphally to Jerusalem (v. 7), and great quantities of bronze are taken (v. 8), perhaps as part of the tribute exacted in v. 6. The chronicler claims that this bronze was used by Solomon to fashion ritual objects for the Temple on Mt. Zion (1 Chr 18:8).

The tone of this account is harsh. Again no explicit motive for war with the Arameans is mentioned. The motivation seems to be territorial expansion of David's realm (v. 6). The note attributing David's victories to the Lord's hand (v. 6b) seems incongruous when it appears in the midst of this account of territorial conquest and plunder.

8:9-12. Hamath was a neo-Hittite city-state to the north of Zobah, and King Toi of this city was delighted with David's victory over Hadadezer, with whom he had often been at war (vv. 9-10). King Toi sends his son Joram with congratulations and tribute of gold, silver, and bronze to David (v. 10). David dedicates this tribute to the Lord, along with the booty he took in his other campaigns (v. 11). Verse 12 goes on to list David's conquests from which the dedicated plunder has come. In addition to the campaigns mentioned in this chapter, this summary mentions Edom, the Ammonites, and Amalek. The verb used for David's action toward these people is "subdue" (כבש *kābaš*), indicating conquest and subjugation. None of the campaigns reported in this chapter seem to have been a response to provocation.

8:13-14. These verses contain two concluding formulae that stand in tension with each other and a brief note on the subjugation of Edom. The latter appears as an added note, almost an afterthought to the previous notices. It records a great slaughter of Edomites (18,000, v. 13) and the incorporation of Edom into David's growing empire as a vassal state (v. 14).

The two formulae attribute David's success on the one hand to the Lord (v. 14b, a repeat of v. 6b), and on the other hand to David's own considerable powers (v. 13a, "David won a name for *himself*"). Empire as a testimony to human power stands in tension with kingdom as the gift of God.

REFLECTIONS

The theological issue of this chapter lies in the very tension with which it ends. Is David's success as an empire builder a testimony to his own achievement or to the grace of God? For the moment, these attributions stand side by side, but it is clear that the successes of power raise the temptation to imagine such power to be autonomous. The David who inquired of the Lord at almost every turn in the stories of his rise to kingship does not ask for divine guidance in these conquests. He simply "defeats," "takes," "kills," "strikes down," and "subdues." These are the verbs of autonomous power. When it is reported that the Lord gave him victory, it almost seems to be a divine indulgence of David's imagined autonomy. A dangerous tension has been established nonetheless. That tension is resolved in divine judgment on David in 2 Samuel 12, when the illusion of autonomous power leads to injustice and violence.

We should be disturbed by the unjustified exercise of power for ideological political purposes here. There are no suggested motives for David's campaigns beyond expansion of his own political power and influence. And the means for achieving this expansion of power are violent. The word for "victory" in 8:6*b*, 14*b* is more frequently translated as "salvation," "deliverance," or "liberation." It is a sobering reminder that it is all too easy to justify our own ideological interests as divinely sanctioned. God's salvation becomes our victory. The text here walks a thin line. God may, indeed, be at work in these matters of the kingdom, but the tendency of human power to act as if it were autonomous stands side by side with the claim of divine activity.

In our own successes, we are much more prone to take credit for ourselves, our congregation, or our nation than to recognize the enabling activity of God. When we fail to give this recognition, the methods by which we pursue success are even more likely to do violence in some way to others as the price of our accomplishments. Power brings with it the dangerous illusion of autonomy. The temptation is then to invoke the name of God only after the fact as a blessing on what we have done for our own purposes. Nevertheless, persons and communities of faith cannot avoid the exercise of power in the public arena, for to do so would be a failure of trust that God is at work in those arenas. The alternative is the constant prayerful discernment of the divine will in the very processes of making decisions in the exercise of power. Early in his career, David modeled such a constancy of prayer and seeking of the divine will. Here, David at the height of his career is in danger of forgetting this process. To preach this chapter is to be warned of the danger that results when God is acknowledged only as an afterthought. The next step is to forget God altogether and risk the violent consequences of our own unchecked temptations to autonomous power.

2 Samuel 8:15-18, The Officers of David's Court

COMMENTARY

This small section is generally regarded as a conclusion to the material on the consolidation of David's kingdom before the start of the succession narrative in chap. 9 (see Introduction). It offers a summarizing statement of David's rule (v. 15) and a listing of his most important officials (vv. 16-18). The section on David as king began with a listing of David's family (5:13-16), in keeping with tribal concern for kinship. But with the kingdom secure, a dynastic promise given, and an empire begun, the stress shifts from family to officers of the court. Loyalties to family and tribe must give way to loyalties to king and kingdom.

8:15. As David's reign over all Israel is affirmed (v. 15*a*) there is a significant acknowledgment of "justice and equity" at the heart of David's rule, and this is for the sake of "all his people." Things have changed in Israel. Many tribal patterns have been replaced by the emerging power arrangements of the kingdom. Yet, this text suggests that centrally important covenant commitments have not been left behind, but have been transferred to new royal structures. David, as king, takes up the mantle of administrator of covenant justice. David has now reached the pinnacle of his power, and yet he is presented as remaining aware of covenant obligation and the welfare of all Israel. This perspective is in keeping with portraits elsewhere of the ideal king (Ps 89:14; Isa 9:7; Jer 22:3; 23:5). It will remain to be seen whether David will keep these commitments in view as he settles into a position of power and influence heretofore unknown in Israel.

8:16-18. Here we get a closer look at the organization of the royal bureaucracy. Under David, Israel is taking on the shape of kingdoms known elsewhere in the region. David is consolidating and organizing royal power in ways that will run the risk of the very dangers against which Samuel warned (1 Sam 8:11-18). He places pairs of officials in control of military, economic, and religious life. A similar list appears in 2 Sam 20:23-26 with the addition of Ira, the Jairite, a priest, and Adoniram as supervisor of the labor details.

Joab is to command the army, and Benaiah is in charge of mercenary forces (Cherethites and Pelethites, v. 18b). Both of these commands represent something new in Israel: a standing professional army and the use of mercenary forces. Reliance on tribal levies for defense is a thing of the past, and military power now centers its loyalty on the king, and not on the tribe. The identity of the two mercenary groups cannot be determined with certainty. The Cherethites have often been identified as Cretans and the Pelethites as a sub-group of the Philistines. They may

be groups who, like the Philistines, came to the area as part of the Sea People's invasion, and they seem to have been recruited into the force David assembled around himself while at Ziklag (see the reference to "the Negeb of the Cherethites" in 1 Sam 30:14).[241]

Jehoshaphat, who is listed as "recorder," should be considered the chief civil servant in charge of state records and documents (v. 16b). Among the functions of such records would be provision of the basis for taxation and conscription. Seraiah (v. 17b), listed as "secretary," was more than just a scribe but should probably be seen as a "secretary of state" (the rendering used in the NEB) and an adviser to David.[242]

In the listing of priests under David, the names of Ahimelech and Abiathar have probably become reversed (v. 17a). The parallel list in 20:25 lists Abiathar (not Ahimelech) as David's priest, and 1 Sam 22:20; 23:6; 30:7 identify Abiathar's father as Ahimelech.[243] Zadok and Abiathar share the office of high priest under David until Abiathar is banished by Solomon after David's death (1 Kgs 2:35). Abiathar was the only survivor of Saul's massacre of the priests of Nob and joined David's entourage at that time (1 Sam 22:6-23). The final reference to David's sons as priests is curious (v. 18b). This may mean that the priesthood was not yet hereditary or was limited to those of Levite descent. The chronicler, concerned with levitical matters, seems to have changed the designation to make David's sons only "high officials" (1 Chr 18:17). David's sons do not seem to be designated as priests in the larger public role given to Zadok and Abiathar. They may have functioned as priests in the royal household—i.e., chaplains within the royal family.

---

241. See the fuller discussion of these groupings in McCarter, *II Samuel*, 256.

242. See T. N. D. Mettinger, *Solomonic State Officials*, ConBOT 5 (Lund: CWK Gleerup, 1971) 52-62, for a full discussion of officials during the time of David.

243. See McCarter's discussion of the textual problems and their solution, *II Samuel*, 253-55.

REFLECTIONS

The ideals of covenant loyalty stand side by side with the organization of state bureaucracy. Therein lies both the challenge and the danger for David and for all who would seek to relate faith to public power. David may actualize the dangers against which Samuel warned (1 Sam 8:11-18); the mechanisms for royal "taking" are all in place. Or David may remain committed to the covenant God, who has been "with him" to this point. These are the perennial choices of people who would not compartmentalize religious faith away from the public arena. One of the lessons to be learned from the books of Samuel is that God is not removed from the arenas of public political power. God cannot be served in a privatized fashion. But the juxtaposition of covenant values and bureaucratic power arrangements implies a genuine risk. David will fall victim to the temptations of autonomous power in his taking of Bathsheba and his murder of Uriah (2 Samuel 11). So, too, has our own history known such abuses of power, from the taking of Native American land to the violent defense of racial segregation to the arrogance of Watergate. But while the nearness of covenant to power may tempt David and us to the sins of power, the nearness of power to covenant allows for the judgment and redemption of power. Such judgment and redemption will also be a part of David's story, because commitment to covenant loyalty allows access to the voice of the prophet Nathan (2 Samuel 12). Such judgment and redemption will be possible for us only to the degree that our bureaucratic arrangements allow access to covenantal voices within the arrangements of power.

2 SAMUEL 9:1–20:26, DAVID'S FAMILY AND DAVID'S THRONE

OVERVIEW

Since the work of Leonhard Rost, most scholars have assumed that 2 Sam 9:1–20:26 and 1 Kgs 1:1–2:46 are a unified narrative incorporated into the Deuteronomistic History.[244] Rost, and most scholars since him, called this piece the "succession narrative," because, he claimed, the central concern of these texts was to answer the question of 1 Kgs 1:20, 27: "Who should sit on the throne of my lord the king after him?" This question of succession to the throne of David is resolved by the accession of Solomon and the purging of his opponents (1 Kings 1–2). Earlier portions of the story remove Amnon (2 Samuel 13) and Absalom (2 Samuel 14–19) as potential heirs to the throne and make clear that there will be no descendants of Saul to claim the throne (2 Samuel 9). The calamitous family events that surround this drama of succession are given theological justification by the story of David's sin and judgment in the matter of Bathsheba and Uriah (2 Samuel 11–12).

Following Rost, great stress has been placed on the unusual artistic quality of the succession narrative. Its rich use of narrative detail and its full development of character, especially the intimate portraits of personal emotions and motivations, have been widely praised. Von Rad has persuasively argued that the succession narrative represents the advent of a new form of history writing in ancient Israel that elevates and celebrates human reality by demonstrating "an emancipated spirituality, modernized and freed from cultus."[245]

Although there has been general agreement on the conclusion of the succession narrative with 1 Kgs 2:46b, "So the kingdom was established in the hand of Solomon," there has been less agreement about its beginning."[246] Rost suggested that it commenced in 2 Samuel 9, but he recognized earlier elements that might be a part of the succession theme (e.g., 2 Sam 6:23). Other suggestions

---

244. The English translation of Leonhard Rost's 1926 work is available as *The Succession to the Throne of David.* See Anderson, *2 Samuel,* xxvi-xxviii, for a discussion of earlier work on which Rost's influential hypothesis was based.

245. Gerhard von Rad, "The Beginnings of Historical Writing in Ancient Israel," in *The Problem of the Hexateuch and Other Essays,* trans. E. W. Trueman Dicken (New York: McGraw-Hill, 1966; orig. German edition, 1944) 204.

246. See Anderson, *2 Samuel,* xxv-xxxvi, for a survey of critical views on the character and limits of the succession narrative.

have been made, but without an emerging consensus. The proposed beginning in 2 Samuel 9 does seem abrupt. The story of Gibeonite revenge on the house of Saul, which now appears as an appendix in 2 Samuel 21, may belong with the story of David's hospitality to the remaining Saulide survivor (2 Samuel 9). Still, although the beginning is difficult to determine, most scholars continue to view the so-called succession narrative as one of three already existing compositions incorporated by the deuteronomist into his larger history work: ark narrative (1 Samuel 4–6 [some include 2 Samuel 6]); history of David's rise (1 Sam 16:1–2 Sam 5:10); succession narrative (2 Samuel 9–20; 1 Kings 1–2).

Although Rost's hypothesis has proven very influential, recent challenges have been raised to fundamental aspects of his view. First, the question has been raised as to whether succession to the throne is really the central theme of this entire block of narrative. Gunn suggests that the focus of this narrative is not on legitimizing Solomon for the throne. Rather, the focus is on "David's fortunes through accession, rebellion and succession."[247] McCarter would agree with Gunn that succession is a central concern only for the final portion of the narrative (1 Kings 1–2).[248] He argues that the so-called succession narrative is really a series of independent thematic pieces (e.g., David's treatment of the surviving sons of Saul; David's sin with Bathsheba; Amnon's rape of Tamar; Absalom's rebellion) that are organized as a more personal history of David's family and fortunes in the later years of his reign and are related to succession only by the addition of 1 Kings 1–2. Gunn and McCarter are only representative of numerous recent challenges to Rost's hypothesis.

Questions have also been raised about the narrative in 2 Samuel 9–20 and 1 Kings 1–2 as the product of a superior artistic hand separate from the rest of 1 and 2 Samuel. Robert Alter has asserted that "the evidence for a unified imaginative conception of the whole David story seems to me to be persuasive."[249] Robert Polzin has subjected the entire David story to close analysis as part of his argument that David's story, as well as the whole of the Deuteronomistic History, stems from a single author.[250] Both represent a growing number of voices arguing that changes in style or emphasis in this portion of David's story constitute an intentional artistic strategy rather than evidence of a separate narrative source. Most scholars, however, continue to discern some stylistic differences between the history of David's rise and the succession narrative and find the episodes devoted to David's actions as king (2 Sam 5:11–8:18) even more distinct. They would see the present shape of 2 Samuel as the product of a gifted editor using multiple sources rather than the product of a single authorial hand.[251]

A number of recent interpretations of David's story have focused on the character of David rather than on the literary history of the text. Seen from this perspective, there seems to be a sharp division in David's story, with the dividing point coming in the Bathsheba/Uriah episode (2 Samuel 11–12). R. A. Carlson has argued that stories prior to this account of David's sin show David as the recipient of blessing. From that point onward, however, we read the story of David under a curse. The David we see under blessing is confident, bold, decisive, and energetic. David under curse appears tentative, anxious, inactive, and anguished.[252] Alter and Brueggemann have observed a similar shift in the narrative portrait of David, but they have characterized this as a shift from focus on David's public life to his private life. The former is a story of unparalleled success, but the latter is filled with considerable ambiguity and anguish.

One of the most striking aspects of the entire David story is that until his career reaches its crucial breaking point with his murder-by-proxy of Uriah after his adultery with Bathsheba, almost all his speeches are in public situations and can be read as politically motivated. It is only after the death of the child born of his union with Bathsheba that the personal voice of a shaken David begins to emerge.[253]

247. Gunn, *The Story of King David*, 14.

248. McCarter, *II Samuel*, 9-16. See also Peter Ackroyd, "The Succession Narrative (So-called)," *Int*. 35 (1981) 383-96.

249. Alter, *The Art of Biblical Narrative*, 119.

250. Polzin, *David and the Deuteronomist*, esp. 221n. 1.

251. See McCarter, *II Samuel*, 4-16, for a discussion of major hypotheses on the literary structure and history of this material.

252. Carlson, *David, the Chosen King*.

253. Alter, *The Art of Biblical Narrative*, 119.

[In] the "Rise of David," the narrative focuses exclusively and with severe discipline only upon the *public* David, screening out any probe of David's person, attitude, or motive. . . . The incredible miscalculation (sin?) with Uriah and Bathsheba opens David, according to the narrator, to the awareness of ambiguity of a moral kind. . . . And from that shattering moment, the narrator, the community around the story, and perhaps David, are permitted to enter a new world of personal interiority with all its problematic of anguish, ambiguity, ambition, and ambivalence. The public David continues to function, but the public David is no longer able or permitted to override, censor, and ignore the personal David. Now the two are placed in a deep and unresolvable tension.[254]

In 2 Samuel 9–20 and 1 Kings 1–2, the focus is on David the man, not on David the king. As readers of this segment of David's story, we will be forced to ponder the meaning of our humanity in the face of power. These narratives are not devoid of ideological interests, but reflection on political power must stand side by side with reflection on human vulnerability. Such stories of humanness in the midst of power have implications for our understandings of kingdom and of our own humanity.[255]

If a shift in the presentation of David takes place in 2 Samuel 9–20 and 1 Kings 1–2, this is also true for the depiction of God's role in this story. Gerhard von Rad, in a classic treatment of this narrative, has argued that God is more hidden in these stories than in previous narratives.[256] This feature allows a greater role for and emphasis on human freedom,[257] but this less overtly visible God has not surrendered the historical process to human autonomy. Although David models freedom in all its possibilities and temptations, the narrative makes clear that God has not let go of David and is still acting to shape the course of Israel's future through David. Von Rad has noted three crucial texts in which God's continued engagement with David's story becomes visible: 2 Sam 11:27; 12:24-25; and 17:14. These texts will receive special attention in the subsequent commentary.[258] In addition to these references to explicit divine involvement, Brueggemann has called attention to two texts in which David expresses faith and trust in God's continued engagement with his life and Israel's future: 2 Sam 15:24-29 and 16:12.[259] These, likewise, will receive special attention.

Beginning with chapter 9 and ending with chapter 20, each episode is part of a continuous narrative. The logical conclusion of this narrative comes in 1 Kings 1–2 with the death of David and the accession of Solomon, but these chapters obviously lie beyond the scope of our commentary on the books of Samuel. Chapters 21–24 are a diverse collection of materials that do not stand in narrative sequence with chaps. 9–20. They are usually referred to as appendixes to the books of Samuel. Questions pertaining to the arrangement, placement, and purpose of these chapters will be taken up in the Overview to 2 Sam 21:1–24:25.

254. Brueggemann, *David's Truth in Israel's Imagination and Memory*, 42-43.

255. Indeed, Brueggemann has suggested that these stories of David's human vulnerability provide the clues for understanding the generalized reflections on created humanity found in the Yahwist narratives of Genesis 2–11. See Walter Brueggemann, "David and His Theologian," *CBQ* 30 (1968) 156-81.

256. Von Rad, "The Beginnings of Historical Writing in Ancient Israel."

257. See Walter Brueggemann, "The Trusted Creature," *CBQ* 31 (1969) 484-98, and "On Trust and Freedom: A Study of Faith in the Succession Narrative," *Int.* 26 (1972) 3-19.

258. Von Rad, "The Beginnings of Historical Writing in Ancient Israel," 198.

259. Brueggemann, *David's Truth in Israel's Imagination and Memory*, 53. Brueggemann also adds 1 Kings 2:2-4 to the three texts identified by von Rad as texts witnessing to God's continued involvement.

2 Samuel 9:1-13, David's Hospitality to Mephibosheth

COMMENTARY

With his kingdom secure, David abruptly becomes concerned about his covenant with Jonathan, which required David to show loyalty to Jonathan's descendants (cf. 1 Sam 20:14-17, 42; 23:18; 24:21-22). David's fulfillment of this covenant obligation provides the theme for this chapter. Together with 2 Samuel 10, this passage portrays David as a man of loyalty and good faith in his personal and royal dealings. The term חסד (ḥesed) appears as David's intention in 9:1, 3, 7 and in 10:2.

David's dealings with Jonathan's surviving son, Mephibosheth, is foreshadowed by the brief account of the accident that left Mephibosheth lame (2 Sam 4:4). This episode is also related to later material—when Mephibosheth and the servant Ziba play important roles in the encounters that mark David's retreat from Jerusalem at the time of Absalom's rebellion (cf. 16:1-4; 19:24-31).

Many scholars believe that 2 Samuel 21 originally preceded 2 Samuel 9.[260] In the necessary chronological sequence of events the execution of the sons of Saul to revenge Saul's wrongdoing against the Gibeonites, which is the subject of chap. 21, must come prior to David's searching out of Mephibosheth as the sole survivor of the house of Saul. Although it is possible that chap. 21 has been displaced from its original literary context prior to chap. 9, there is no clear evidence for this point as its original placement. As we shall see, chap. 21 plays an important role in the structure of the appendixes to 2 Samuel 21–24.

Chapter 9 opens with David's question and then proceeds by means of three dialogues: David/Ziba (vv. 2-4); David/Mephibosheth (vv. 5-8); David/Ziba again (vv. 9-11a). Concluding comments in vv. 11b-13 make clear that David's intentions to provide hospitality to Jonathan's son were carried out.

9:1-4. David's question (v. 1) introduces the theme of the chapter: David's covenant with Jonathan. With his kingdom secure, David turns his attention to the fulfillment of the covenant he swore to Jonathan (1 Sam 20:14-17, 42). He intends to show ḥesed (the loyalty often associated with covenants; see the Commentary on 1 Samuel 20) to any who are still left from the house of Saul. The use of the word "still" implies that events have preceded this account that leave in doubt the question of survivors in the line of Saul. This doubt has led to the suggestion, mentioned above, that the account of the killing of seven sons of Saul to satisfy Gibeonite demands for vengeance (2 Sam 21:1-14) originally preceded 2 Samuel 9. Indeed, the sparing of Mephibosheth from these acts of revenge is

mentioned explicitly there (21:7). But, even without the grim tale of 2 Samuel 21, there would be some doubt about the survival of Saul's line. Following Saul's own death (1 Samuel 31; 2 Samuel 1) David's kingship is established through events that include the killing of Saul's general, Abner, and the assassination of Saul's son Ishbosheth (2 Samuel 2–4).[261] These events, which mark the fall of any vestige of Saulide rule, no doubt signaled the confiscation of Saulide land holdings and the dispersal of the remaining family of Saul. When David announces his desire to show "loyalty" or "kindness" (חסד ḥesed) to the house of Saul in keeping with his commitment to Jonathan, one has reason to wonder about the sincerity of such a declaration.

Ziba is introduced as a servant of the house of Saul who is summoned by David and then offers David his service (v. 2). David has clearly sought Ziba out in his quest for surviving descendants of Saul, and he asks Ziba the same question he voiced earlier (v. 3). Ziba knows of a son of Jonathan and identifies him as being "crippled in his feet" (see 2 Sam 4:4); he is living in the household of Machir in Lo-debar, which is in the Transjordan (v. 4). This site is close to Mahanaim, where Ishbosheth located his capital, and to Jabesh-gilead, a city with special ties to the house of Saul (see 1 Sam 11:1-13; 31:11-13; 2 Sam 2:4b-7).

9:5-8. David sends for this son of Jonathan (v. 5), and only when he appears before David is he finally named, both by the narrator and by David (v. 6). The chronicler records his name as Meribaal (1 Chr 8:34; 9:40), probably another instance where the deuteronomistic historian has replaced the element בעל (ba'al, "lord" or "master") in the name with the word בשת (bōšet, "shame") because of the association of the title ba'al with the name of the Canaanite deity Baal.[262]

---

260. See McCarter, *II Samuel*, 263.

261. Gunn, *The Story of King David*, 68, makes a strong case for the relationship of 2 Samuel 9 to the events narrated in 2 Samuel 2–4. This raises doubts about chap. 9 as the beginning of a new narrative and suggests a closer connection between the history of the rise of David and the succession narrative than usually argued.

262. See McCarter, *II Samuel*, 124-25, 128, for a detailed discussion of the textual evidence and the various proposals made in relation to the name "Mephibosheth." A similar emendation was also made for the name "Ishbaal," which appears in 2 Samuel as "Ishbosheth." See the Commentary on 2 Sam 4:1 and the discussion of "Mephibosheth" in the Commentary on 2 Sam 4:4. It should also be noted that Rizpah, the concubine of Saul, also had a son named Mephibosheth (21:8). Most scholars agree that these are two individuals with the same or similar names.

There is a strong emphasis in this account on the difference in power between David and Mephibosheth (also with Ziba earlier). Mephibosheth falls on his face, does obeisance (the Hebrew word here is often translated as "worship" [שחה šāḥâ]), and refers to himself as David's servant (v. 6). Following David's gracious act toward him, Mephibosheth again does obeisance ("worships") and refers to himself not only as servant but self-deprecatingly as a "dead dog" as well (v. 8). The implication is that he is worthless compared to David. The result of this subservience by Mephibosheth is to highlight David's power and privilege and to make David's act of kindness toward Mephibosheth seem remarkably gracious. David addresses Mephibosheth with the classic formula of reassurance associated with salvation oracles, "Fear not!" (v. 7a). He then cites his covenant obligation to Jonathan, Mephibosheth's father, and restores the land of Saul to this grandson of Israel's first king. David further vows that Mephibosheth will henceforth eat at the king's table (v. 7). To sit at table with the king is a privilege that accords Mephibosheth status akin to the sons of the king (v. 11). Some have said that there is a political purpose to David's invitation to the royal table—namely, that he is placing the remaining heir of Saul where an eye can be kept on him.[263] This may be true, but such a motive is not made explicit in the text, and the narrator of the story clearly considers this an honor, and not house arrest (v. 11). The restoration of Saulide land to Mephibosheth implies that it had been confiscated, perhaps after the death of Ishbaal, and was in David's possession as royal property until this time.

9:9-11a. Abruptly David again summons Ziba (v. 9a). Mephibosheth's departure is not mentioned. David reports his action in returning land to Mephibosheth (v. 9b) and commissions Ziba, his sons, and his servants to work and manage the land on behalf of this new master (v. 10a). Ziba's household is substantial: fifteen sons and twenty servants (v. 10b). It seems possible that Ziba, a former servant of Saul, was already managing this land as royal property for David and that he is here simply informed that he and the land have a new master in Mephibosheth. Ziba's management of the land is to provide Mephibosheth

263. See, e.g., Hertzberg, *I and II Samuel*, 299.

with food, even though the narrator reports again that he will eat at the king's table (v. 10b). Perhaps Mephibosheth, now as a royal landowner, must provide his share for the provisioning of the royal court. Ziba, deferentially referring to himself again as David's servant, accepts this commission and vows to carry it out (v. 11a).

9:11b-13. These verses conclude the account by reporting on the outcome of the matters revealed in the dialogues between David, Ziba, and Mephibosheth. The text refers twice again to Mephibosheth's eating at the king's table (vv. 11b, 13a). One of these references (v. 11b) adds the note equating this role to the status of one of the king's own sons. Mephibosheth has a son named Mica (v. 12a), who is included in the list of four sons born to Mephibosheth according to the chronicler's account (1 Chr 8:34-35; 9:40-41). Thus the line of Saul, through Jonathan, continues. The covenant vow made by David to Jonathan is kept, and David appears as a man of loyalty (*ḥesed*) to his commitments.

The final verse of the chapter mentions again that Mephibosheth was "lame in both his feet" (v. 13b; see v. 3; 4:4). This description reminds readers that this malady makes him an unlikely candidate for the throne; hence, he is not a threat to David.

Four times it is stressed in this chapter that Mephibosheth was to eat at the king's table the rest of his days (vv. 7b, 10b, 11b, 13a). As mentioned above, some have seen this as a form of house arrest—David shrewdly keeping an eye on a potential rival for the throne. In such a reading, this becomes a story of ideological politics masquerading as compassion. We are led to question whether power can act with genuine compassion rather than solely in its own self-interest.

But this reading does not seem supported by the text itself. The stress on covenant relationship with Jonathan, the reference to making Mephibosheth like one of the king's sons, and the restoration of land to Mephibosheth are all elements that seem genuinely in the interests of Mephibosheth's welfare. It is true that the acts of a king were never neutral and without political significance, but in this case David's interests seem well served by his appearing magnanimous rather than coercive toward the remnant of the house of Saul.

The question remains as to why unusual stress is given to Mephibosheth's eating at the king's table. Robert Polzin has made the intriguing suggestion that this theme in 2 Samuel 9 must be read in connection with the reference in 2 Kgs 25:29 that Jehoiachin, the Davidic king carried into exile from Jerusalem to Babylon, "every day of his life dined regularly in the king's presence."[264] Although English translations vary slightly, the Hebrew phrase, appearing only in 2 Sam 9:7, 10, 13 and 2 Kgs 25:29, is אכל תמיד ('ākal tāmîd), "to eat continually." Mephibosheth, the remnant of Saul's house, "eating continually" at the king's table foreshadows Jehoiachin, the remnant of David's house in exile, "eating continually" at the king's table. Through this connection within the Deuteronomistic History, 2 Samuel 9:1 suggests that the last word for the house of Saul, for the house of David, and for Israel's future is that of *ḥesed*, "covenant loyalty."

The foundational character of that *ḥesed* may appear in v. 3 of this chapter, when David refers to the *ḥesed* he intends to demonstrate as the "*ḥesed* of God" ("the kindness of God"). David acts not just out of friendship to Jonathan but out of covenant commitment between the two that finds its grounding in God's covenant commitment. "Show me the faithful love [*ḥesed*] of the Lord," Jonathan implores David (1 Sam 20:14). If David's treatment of Mephibosheth foreshadows Israel's story in exile and the fate of his own royal line, then this account suggests to the exilic readers of the Deuteronomistic History that they, too, can count on God's *ḥesed*, and the land that belonged to them might also be restored.

264. Polzin, *David and the Deuteronomist,* 103-4. Polzin also connects this theme in 2 Samuel 9 with the reference in 1 Sam 2:36 to the survivor of Eli's priestly house requesting "one of the priest's places that I may eat a morsel of bread." The parallel suggested does not contain the phrase "eat continually," refers to priestly remnants rather than to royal remnants, and does not draw on the image of being invited to the royal table. In short, the connection seems less compelling here than that suggested with 2 Kgs 25:29.

REFLECTIONS

1. Seen in the light of the hopeful meaning this episode may have held for exiles, a seemingly odd episode of David's loyalty and kindness becomes a testimony to divine loyalty and kindness. We read as those who constantly find ourselves cut off from our full future—existing as remnants with little hope for fullness of life except for the *ḥesed* of God, a divine sovereign who restores us to wholeness and invites us to sit at table.

Medieval and Renaissance Christian artists sometimes pictured David and Mephibosheth in the paintings, stained-glass windows, and sculptures they produced. Often when they did, the food they depicted on the king's table was the bread and the cup of the eucharistic meal. David's kindness was understood as God's kindness (v. 3), and the king's table to which we are all invited is ultimately God's table.

2. This episode, however, can also be read within its own framework in David's story as a witness to the capacity for compassion to co-exist with political expediency. David's actions need not be read as simply one or the other. In our own experience, we often react cynically to expressions of compassion or altruism by public officeholders. We suspect their motivation is solely for public image and political advantage.

We are correct to examine such expressions for evidence of genuine regard and, perhaps more important, to remember and hold officials accountable for actions that are consistent with their statements of compassionate concern. Nevertheless, people of faith should welcome the notion that commitments born of compassion and regard for the well-being of others should be considered politically advantageous. If such values were consistently rewarded, it would encourage more persons committed to those values to seek public office. Unfortunately, we too often say we want our leaders to demonstrate qualities such as compassionate regard for others, but we reward political actions that are advantageous only to the special interests from which we profit.

David had no interest in encouraging the house of Saul to make claims on the throne, but he honored the covenant of friendship that he had made with Jonathan and acted with *hesed*. We need not apologize for pursuing or supporting others in appropriate political goals. But the measure of our actions in pursuit of political ends must be in terms of values such as those honored by David in this story: loyalty, respect, steadfast love, and the well-being of others.

2 Samuel 10:1-19, War with the Ammonites and the Arameans

COMMENTARY

This chapter contains the first two of three reports on conflicts in a war between David's Israelite kingdom and a coalition of Ammonite and Aramean kingdoms. The first report tells of the Ammonite insult to David's envoys, the assembling of an Ammonite-Aramean coalition to oppose David's army under Joab, and an initial victory for Israel (vv. 1-14). David seems to follow this victory with separate campaigns against the Arameans and the Ammonites. A second report tells of David's victory over a widened coalition of Aramean kingdoms (10:15-19). A final report will narrate the siege and eventual capture of Rabbah, the capital of Ammon (11:1; 12:26-31).

These military accounts allude to the theme of David's חסד (*hesed*, "loyalty") in chapter 9. There David showed *hesed* toward Mephibosheth in loyalty to the covenant of friendship between David and Mephibosheth's father, Jonathan. In chap. 10, David seeks to show *hesed* in his public political dealings by sending envoys to reaffirm his loyalty to Ammon on the occasion of the death of their king, Nahash (v. 2). The portrait of chaps. 9 and 10 is of David as a man who honors commitments and acts with integrity to uphold those commitments in his personal and public dealings.

The military campaign against Ammonites and Arameans also defines the context for the story of David's adultery with Bathsheba and the arranged killing of her husband, Uriah, during the siege of Rabbah (11:2-25). There is a sad and ironic contrast between David's willingness to go to war to defend an insult to his *hesed* (chap. 10) and his subsequent willingness to abandon *hesed* to his subjects by committing adultery and murder.

10:1-5. Nahash, the king of the Ammonites, has died and has been succeeded by his son Hanun (v. 1). David sends envoys to express his condolences to Hanun, an action that David understands as an expression of loyalty (*hesed*) to Hanun in return for loyal treatment (*hesed*) David had received from Hanun's father, Nahash (v. 2). This language toward Ammonite kings may surprise the reader. Nahash had been a brutal enemy of Israel during the days of Saul and had been defeated by Saul when Nahash laid siege to the city of Jabesh-gilead (see 1 Samuel 11). However, the language in the opening verses of this chapter reflects the relationship of allies. Some have speculated that friendly relations developed between David and Ammon when David was fleeing from Saul. Nahash and David became allies against a common enemy in Saul.[265] Others speculate that the alliance was not between equals and that Ammon had been forced by Saul's victory into a relationship of subservience to Israel, which now carries over to David's kingdom.[266] This background would help to explain the hostile treatment of David's envoys by Hanun, but it assumes a vassal relationship of Ammon to Israel that seems unlikely during the tenuous kingship of Saul.

Whatever the earlier relationship, David is now king of a secure and increasingly powerful Israelite kingdom. Hanun's advisers among the Ammonite princes see David's

265. So Anderson, *2 Samuel*, 146; and McCarter, *II Samuel*, 270. McCarter, however, thinks the act of loyalty from Nahash to David was when David was received at Mahanaim by a son of Nahash, named Shobi, while retreating from Absalom (2 Sam 17:27). He believes the account of the war in chap. 10 has been misplaced chronologically in the present arrangement.

266. So Brueggemann, *First and Second Samuel*, 269-70.

envoys as potential spies for an eventual Israelite overthrow of Ammon (v. 3b). They discount any honorable intention in the sending of envoys with condolences (v. 3a), and they humiliate David's representatives by shaving half of their beards and cutting off the lower portion of their garments, exposing their manhood (v. 4). Such acts explicitly reject the loyalty (ḥesed) that David had sought to demonstrate.

When the envoys return to Israelite territory, David, hearing of their treatment and their shame, goes compassionately to meet them at Jericho. He urges them to remain there until their beards grow back, erasing the external signs of their shameful treatment. David's personal attention to their plight is characteristic of his regard for his subjects, especially those in his service. Small acts of compassion like this make David's treatment of Uriah in the following chapter even more shocking.

10:6-14. The intentional humiliation of David's official envoys functions as an act of war. The Ammonite king has insulted David himself. David's honor and the integrity of his ḥesed toward Hanun's father have been called into question. The Ammonites clearly understood that war would result, and they proceeded immediately to recruit allies among the Aramean kingdoms of the region. The Arameans of Beth-rehob and Zobah may be the same coalition of kingdoms located south and east of Mt. Hermon that were mentioned in David's campaigns in 8:3-8, particularly since the Arameans are led by a king named Hadadezer, who is also mentioned later in this account (10:16). Most scholars believe that 8:3-8 represents the final victory in the war described in chap. 10.[267] Chapter 8 is a summary of David's conquests and was not intended to imply that all these victories took place at that early point in David's kingship. Maacah and Tob are also small Aramean kingdoms located in the region east of the Sea of Galilee and probably under the influence of Hadadezer and the larger Aramean kingdom of Zobah (10:16). The numbers of men may not be as large as most translations suggest, since the Hebrew word usually translated "thousand" (אלף 'elep) can also mean a "military unit" of variable

size. The account in 1 Chr 19:6-7 suggests that the Ammonites hired the Arameans as mercenaries.

David does not himself go to battle. He sends his general Joab (v. 7), a trusted commander who had been with David from the days of his conflict with Saul. Joab brings his army up to face the Ammonites outside the gate of their city (presumably their capital, Rabbah), and finds himself with two battle-fronts, since the Aramean forces draw up in the open country behind him (v. 8). It is not clear whether Joab was surprised by this tactic or anticipated it, but he responds quickly by taking a picked force under his own command to face the Arameans while leaving the rest of his army under the command of his brother Abishai to face the Ammonites (vv. 9-10). If possible, they are to assist one another should either front prove too difficult (v. 11). Joab's final admonition before battle is notable. He urges courage, both for the sake of "our people and for the cities of our God" (v. 12a). This may refer to the cities of David's kingdom in general or to the Israelite cities of the Transjordan, which would be in more immediate danger if the battle were lost. Finally, Joab offers a statement of reliance on the will of the Lord: "May the LORD do what seems good to him" (v. 12b). We are accustomed to hearing this kind of trustful expression of faith from the mouth of David, but not from Joab, who usually displays a more pragmatic inclination.

Joab's two-front attack is successful. The Arameans are routed, and the Ammonites retreat back into their walled city (vv. 13-14). Apparently, Joab and his army are not prepared either to lay siege to the city or to pursue the Arameans back into their own territory. The Israelites return to Jerusalem (v. 14b), but the war is far from over. This was only the opening skirmish.

10:15-19. The Arameans correctly understand that David is not through with them, and they decide to take the initiative against him. Under the leadership of Hadadezer (cf. 2 Sam 8:3-8), the Aramean city-states from beyond the Euphrates River (NIV, "the River") gather to oppose David. Hadadezer places the army under the command of his own general, Shobach (vv. 15-16). This time, David himself leads an Israelite force to meet

267. See Anderson, *2 Samuel,* 146.

the Arameans, a measure of the seriousness with which he takes this threat (v. 17). By contrast, in the following chapter David will remain at home for the siege of Rabbah. Such a siege may have required a longer campaign, and the king's protracted absence was not desirable; nevertheless, there seems to be an intended contrast between the active David of chap. 10 and the idle David of chap. 11.

The place or region where these armies engage one another is Helam, probably located in the northern Transjordan (v. 17). The outcome never seems in doubt: David and his army rout the Arameans, with a great loss of Aramean lives and the death of Shobach, their general (v. 18). The coalition of Aramean kings under Hadadezer recognize their defeat and sue for peace, but peace in this instance is clearly acceptance of subjection to Israel and the end of Aramean assistance to the Ammonites (v. 19). The borders of David's kingdom are expanded, and the enemy who started this war is now isolated. The campaign against the Ammonites will follow in short order (11:1).

REFLECTIONS

This chapter reminds us that David, as God's anointed king, is forced to deal with the same matters of state that all political leaders must face. We are reminded that David is a man of war as well as a man of faith. Israel, even as a kingdom ruled by God's chosen king, must live among the nations and deal with the conflicts that arise between nations. Covenant faith and covenant community cannot function in a vacuum apart from the world. Indeed, in the books of Samuel, piety is always held close to politics, and chap. 10 reminds us that God's people are not protected from the messiness of the world. This chapter does not reflect deeply on these matters, but there do seem to be two small clues worthy of notice.

1. It is clearly important to the narrator of this text that David sought to act with the integrity of *hesed* in dealing with the politics of nations and did not limit such "loyalty" to personal relationships (as in chap. 9). The same commitment to loyalty that marks the covenant relationship between Israel and God is to mark our personal and public dealings with one another. We are not to hold separate sets of values and commitments in our personal and public lives. Both are to be governed by the *hesed* that God, in covenant relationship, demonstrates toward us.

2. Joab voices a willingness to place trust ultimately in God while doing his human best to cope with a situation of grave conflict (v. 12). In the stories of David, Joab often represents the pragmatic warrior. He is certainly not a figure of piety and faith. Yet, in David's kingdom power is to be wielded in the presence and promise of God. David most often models this trust, but it is here also a hallmark of those who serve him. Even in the messy conflicts of power that erupt in war there is the need to recognize the power of God that holds any exercise of power accountable. In the recognition of God's power to do what "seems good to him" is the safeguard against the service of our own self-interests. When power is used in the service of self-interest and in the illusion of human autonomy, divine presence can be experienced as judgment. David is about to learn this.

2 Samuel 11:1-27, David's Adultery with Bathsheba

COMMENTARY

In this chapter, the reader senses a major shift in David's story. The shift may be described in a variety of ways: from the public to the personal, from power to vulnerability, from blessing to curse,[268] from gift to grasp.[269] In the course of this subtly crafted narrative, David's world is transformed. Things will no longer be the same. David uses royal power abusively to satisfy his own personal desires. Moreover, the violence he had earlier avoided (1 Samuel 24–26) spirals out of control in his own personal life. Adultery and deceit lead to murder, and the violence that stains David's hands will spread to his own family (chaps. 12–19).

The story may be seen as a tale of royal power told in four episodes, each with a complication that further enmeshes David in sin: (1) v. 1, an introductory verse that places David at home while his army lays siege to Rabbah; (2) vv. 2-5, the adultery. David sees a beautiful woman (Bathsheba) bathing and exercises royal privilege to "take" her. Complication: Bathsheba becomes pregnant; (3) vv. 6-13, the cover-up; David brings Uriah, Bathsheba's husband, home from the front to sleep with his wife and remove suspicion over the child's paternity—complication: Uriah is too dedicated as a soldier and will not "go down" to his house while comrades are still in the field; and (4) vv. 14-25, the murder. David arranges with Joab for Uriah to die in battle. Complication: Other innocent lives are lost in an ill-advised military tactic; and (5) vv. 26-27, the aftermath. David and Bathsheba marry to preserve public honor, and they have a son. Complication: What David had done was "evil in the eyes of the LORD."

The final sentence of chap. 11 points beyond the boundaries of the story. In the books of Samuel, the story is not just about the rise of royal power in Israel. It is also story of God's power as the true force shaping Israel's future. For chap. 11 as a story of David, a king, the marriage and birth would have been the end of the matter. But as a story

of David, God's anointed king, the matter is not ended. The story continues in chap. 12 when Nathan the prophet confronts David by announcing divine judgment for what he had done in taking Bathsheba and killing Uriah.

The narrative of David and Bathsheba is also set more widely in the context of public events. The war with Ammon and the siege of Rabbah provide the framework and the backdrop for the story. The siege begins in 11:1 and concludes in 12:26-31. In 1 Sam 8:20, the elders of Israel had demanded a king who would "go out before us and fight our battles." The prophet Samuel had warned them of the dangers from kings who "take" from the people for their own interests (1 Sam 8:11-18). Now David no longer leads his troops into battle. He remains idle in Jerusalem while his men are fighting at Rabbah (v. 1), and he "takes" what he sees and desires for himself (v. 4).

The repercussions go beyond the framework of the war with Ammon. David's use of power for personal desire is like a virus unleashed in his own family (see Nathan's oracle of judgment on David, 12:10-12). Episodes of rape, murder, and rebellion mark the unfolding tragedy of David's family history (chaps. 13–19).[270] David in chap. 11 charts a tragic path of abused power for his own sons to follow.

11:1-5. The background for the story is the siege of Rabbah. This campaign against the capital city of Ammon is the final chapter of the wars narrated in chap. 10. David sends Joab to lay siege to Rabbah, while David remains in Jerusalem. The taking of Rabbah is not narrated until 12:26-31. We see the events of this story against the backdrop of the public realities of a nation at war with a neighbor. The embedding of this story of sexual violence within a story of the violence of

---

268. Carlson, *David, The Chosen King.*
269. Gunn, *The Story of King David.*

270. McCarter, *II Samuel,* 290-91, sees 2 Samuel 11–12 as a preface added by a prophetic author to a story on the events surrounding Absalom's rebellion (2 Samuel 13–19), although the prophetic author's direct contribution may be limited to 11:27b-12:15a. This may well be the case, since chaps. 13–19 do not refer explicitly to the events of chaps. 11–12. These chapters seem more like a lens through which to view David's sin and judgment in subsequent chapters.

war may be intentional. David, left behind in Jerusalem, "takes" the woman he desires (v. 4) and eventually is summoned to Rabbah to personally "take" the city (12:28-29).[271]

The reason why David remains in Jerusalem is not explained. It seems to be a part of the narrative art of the author to leave ambiguities that allow us to imagine differing possibilities.[272] Has David lost interest in military leadership? Is he now too valuable as king to go on such campaigns (see 21:17)? Is the siege a tedious matter, and can David give time only to the final "taking" of the city? In any case, the picture is that of an idle king, pacing about on the roof of his palace when he spies a beautiful woman at her bath (v. 2). Further, a contrast is established between the stay-at-home David and the wronged husband, Uriah, who is away fighting the king's battles.

The story unfolds with a remarkable economy of narration. The author emphasizes the action with little mention of motivations, emotions, or feelings. About the woman we are told only that she was bathing and beautiful. From this slender evidence some have been certain that Bathsheba had conspired to be seen by the king. Hertzberg accuses Bathsheba of "feminine flirtation": "We must, however, ask whether Bathsheba did not count on this possibility [of being seen]."[273] Nicol suggests that "even if it was not deliberate, Bathsheba's bathing in a place so clearly open to the king's palace can hardly indicate less than a contributory negligence on her part."[274] Others are equally clear that Bathsheba is simply the victim, both of David and of the narrator by objectifying her in the story.[275] The matter of Bathsheba's complicity is left unaddressed and, therefore, ambiguous. It must be observed, however, that the account shows no interest in Bathsheba's guilt in this matter and does not suggest that Bathsheba's bathing was an act of seduction. The

narrator lays the moral responsibility entirely on David. It is what "David had done" that "was evil in the eyes of the LORD" (v. 27b), and it is against David that Nathan announces God's judgment (12:7).

David inquires after the identity of the woman he has seen (v. 3). He asks, "Is this not Bathsheba, daughter of Eliam, the wife of Uriah the Hittite?"[276] David receives no confirmation of this identification. The purpose of the question is to identify her for the reader. She is identified primarily by her ties to father and husband. In fact, she is not again called by her own name, Bathsheba, until after the death of the child she conceives with David (12:24). She is called only "the wife of Uriah" or "the woman." Even in the genealogy of Jesus in Matt 1:6 she is called the "wife of Uriah." The emphasis here is on the adultery of David and his guilt, but it is a point made at the expense of robbing Bathsheba of any developed character or identity in the story. Adele Berlin observes that Bathsheba is "a complete non-person. She is not even a minor character, but simply part of the plot. This is why she is not considered guilty of adultery. She is not an equal party to the adultery, but only the means whereby it was achieved."[277]

The actual act of adultery is narrated with surprising economy in v. 4. The narrative is powered by verbs in short phrases. David "sent," "took," and "lay." Bathsheba "came," "returned," and "conceived." Is this the record of a rape? According to Exum, "the text seems ambivalent on the matter. 'Sent' and 'took' indicate aggression on David's part; on the other hand, the two verbs of which Bathsheba is the subject, 'came' and 'returned,' are not what one would expect if resistance were involved. The king sends for a subject and she obeys. His position of power gives him an advantage: he 'takes.'"[278] This is coercive, self-indulgent use of power to satisfy sexual lust on David's part. He intentionally violates a marriage and breaks the law of the Lord. If Bathsheba "came" to

271. For discussion of the significant combination of war, sex, and violence in this chapter, see Mieke Bal, *Lethal Love: Feminist Literary Readings of Biblical Love Stories* (Bloomington: Indiana University Press, 1987) 10-36; J. P. Fokkelman, *Narrative Art and Poetry in the Books of Samuel*, vol. 1: *King David* (Assen: van Gorcum, 1981) 41-70.

272. The crucial role of ambiguity in the narrative art of this chapter has been convincingly discussed in Gale A. Yee, " 'Fraught with Background': Literary Ambiguity in II Samuel 11," *Int.* 42 (1988) 240-53.

273. Hertzberg, *I and II Samuel,* 309.

274. George G. Nicol, "Bathsheba, a Clever Woman?" *Expository Times* 99 (1988) 360.

275. J. Cheryl Exum, *Fragmented Women: Feminist (Sub)versions of Biblical Narratives* (Valley Forge: Trinity Press International, 1993) 170-201.

276. The verbs in this sentence give no other subject than David. Both the NRSV and the NIV imply a third party reporting back to David, but the question is David's seeking of confirmation. See Randall C. Bailey, *David in Love and War: The Pursuit of Power in 2 Samuel 10–12,* JSOTSup 75 (Sheffield: JSOT, 1990) 85. David's inquiry after the woman's identity need not imply others voyeuristically gazing with David at the bathing Bathsheba, contra Exum, *Fragmented Women,* 174-75.

277. Berlin, "Characterization in Biblical Narrative," 73.

278. Exum, *Fragmented Women,* 172.

him, it implies passivity more than consent. It is a verb that follows the statement that the king "sent messengers and he took her." Both the NRSV and the NIV soften the text here and inaccurately imply consent by translating "David sent messengers to get her." In these translations, there is no "taking," as Samuel warned that kings would do (1 Sam 8:11-18), and the messengers, rather than David, are made the implied subject of the verb. "Taking" is reduced to "fetching," and Bathsheba's "coming" is made the response to a summons rather than acquiescence in a seizure.[279] In the ongoing story of David's family, this scene of coercive sex foreshadows Amnon's rape of Tamar (chap. 13) and Absalom's rape of the ten wives of David (on the very same palace roof, 16:21-22). In this narrative, David is clearly treated as the offender and Bathsheba as a used woman. David did not take her with a desire for ongoing relationship or marriage. It is only the pregnancy that keeps the episode from being a one-night stand, and even then David hopes to deceive Uriah into thinking the child is his rather than David's. It is only the lack of attention to Bathsheba's point of view altogether that allows issues of seduction, honor, or consent on her part to be raised at all.[280]

The parenthetical statement (v. 4) that Bathsheba was "purifying herself after her period" is not an explanation of the bathing in v. 1. It is a note that makes clear the paternity of the child conceived by Bathsheba. Since she had just had a period and since her husband is on the battlefront, the child must be David's.

A tawdry but straightforward story of royal lust is suddenly complicated. Bathsheba, who has not spoken at all, now makes a transforming speech. She conceives and reports to the king, "I am pregnant" (v. 5). David is now threatened with exposure of his lustful

taking of Bathsheba, his violation of another man's marriage, and his breaking of the law of the Lord (see Deut 22:22). David thought his power gave him control, but he could not control Bathsheba's body and the conception that took place within her. Her words now propel the story into a new and tragic dimension.

11:6-13. In response to Bathsheba's words, David launches a cover-up. He sends a message to Joab, summoning Uriah home from the battlefront (v. 6). Joab always seems somewhere nearby when questionable actions are afoot. David intends to get Uriah to sleep with his wife so that he might appear to be the child's father.[281]

Uriah was a member of David's elite thirty (23:39). He is consistently identified as "the Hittite." This may mean that he was a mercenary serving as an officer in David's military, but some think the Jerusalem nobility may have had Hittite associations and were incorporated into Israel with David's capture of Jerusalem.[282] "Uriah" is a Yahwistic name meaning "Yahweh is my light," which would indicate identification with Israel's God.

As with Bathsheba, David "sends" and Uriah "comes," but there is no "taking." This time David must persuade and manipulate. When Uriah appears, David inquires after the progress of the siege, as if this report were the purpose of the summons (v. 7). He asks after the welfare (שלום šālôm, "peace," "well-being") of Joab, the army, and the war (the NRSV and the NIV obscure this threefold asking about šālôm). These queries are ironic, since David's actions will later cause death—the absence of šālôm—to dominate the story (vv. 15, 17, 21, 24-26).

David urges Uriah to "go down to your house and wash your feet" and sends a present with him (v. 8). The phrase "wash your feet" is a euphemism for having sexual intercourse, which v. 11 shows Uriah clearly understood. But Uriah does not "go down." He sleeps with the king's servants at the gate (v. 9). David is told that Uriah did not "go

279. Hertzberg, *I and II Samuel,* 310, writes that "her consciousness of the danger into which adultery was leading her . . . must have been outweighed by her realization of the honour of having attracted the king." It is troubling that coercive use of power for the sake of royal lust is so easily transmuted into an honor.

280. Exum refers to this objectivization of Bathsheba by the narrator as being "raped by the pen." This is the title of her chapter on Bathsheba in *Fragmented Women,* 170-201. I would stop short of accusing scholars who note the ambiguities left by the narrator as complicit in the crime of "narrative rape." Those who resolve those ambiguities by scapegoating Bathsheba and softening David's guilt may deserve the accolade. For a response to the issues Exum raises, see George G. Nicol, "The Alleged Rape of Bathsheba: Some Observations on Ambiguity in Biblical Narrative," *JSOT* 73 (1997) 43-54.

281. It is David's persistent attempts to pass paternity of the child onto Uriah that undercut Randall Bailey's thesis (*David in Love and War,* 88) that this story is concerned with "political marriage" rather than "sexual lust." David is clearly trying to avoid marriage. The notion that David required the wife of another man to produce a legitimate heir when he had so many other wives and sons stretches credulity and forces Bailey to locate this episode unconvincingly after the death of Absalom.

282. See Anderson, *2 Samuel,* 153.

down," and he summons Uriah to ask why he did not (v. 10). The constant concern to get Uriah to "go down" to his house gives an urgent, almost frantic tone to the story. David is desperate that the cover-up succeed.

In contrast to David's desperation, Uriah seems calm and principled. He tells David that he cannot enjoy his house—eating, drinking, and taking sexual pleasure with his wife—while the ark, Joab, and the armies of Israel and Judah remain encamped in the field, enduring the hardships of the siege at Rabbah (v. 11). The reference to booths (Sukkot) here may refer to temporary camp structures or be taken as a place name for the encampment, Succoth. This statement seems a genuine expression of loyalty and commitment on the part of one of David's elite military men. There is no suggestion in the text that Uriah knew of his wife's pregnancy and suspected David's true purposes.[283]

The mention of the ark reminds us that David was once ill at ease until there should be a house for the ark (2 Sam 7:2; Ps 132:1-5). Now he is at ease in Jerusalem while the ark is still in the field with the army.

David makes one more attempt to get Uriah to his house. He gets Uriah drunk, but when evening comes Uriah still sleeps with the king's servants and does not "go down" to his house (v. 13). Unwittingly, Uriah has sealed his own doom, but the picture left with the reader is one of contrast between the principled obedience of Uriah and the increasingly desperate actions of David. David has once again encountered the limits of royal power. He cannot control Uriah's principles.

11:14-25. It is chilling how easily cover-up plan shifts to murder plot. As before, it begins with a message from David to Joab, but this time Uriah must carry the cruel order for his own death (v. 14). The letter orders Joab to place Uriah in the midst of heavy fighting and withdraw support (v. 15). Thus Uriah is to be given a hero's death in battle. He is to be honored in death for the sake of preserving David's honor in life. This section of the story is dominated by forms of the verb "to die" (מות *mût*, vv. 15, 17, 21, 24, 26). God's anointed king has become an agent of

death. Self-interested use of power has led David into a deadly chain of events from seizure to deception to death.

Joab quickly carries out David's order, and Uriah is killed (vv. 16-17), but not without further cost. The effort to expose Uriah leads to the death of others from among "the servants of David" (v. 17). This leads to an elaborate reporting of events to David. Joab sends a messenger to David (v. 18) but anticipates that David will become angry at the loss of troops that resulted from a foray so close to the city walls (vv. 19-20) and that he will recall the death of Abimelech when a woman threw a millstone on him from the wall (v. 21; cf. Judg 9:50-55).[284] If David responds in this angry manner, the messenger is to add the news, "Your servant Uriah the Hittite is dead too" (v. 21*b*).

In v. 22, the messenger makes his report to David, and the Hebrew text does not report an angry response on his part. Nevertheless, vv. 23-24 report a speech by the messenger justifying the tactic that took them close to the wall and cost lives among the servants of David. He ends with the news that Uriah was also dead. The Greek text of these verses does include the angry response of David in virtually identical language to the anticipation of his anger by Joab. This fuller text makes more sense out of the messenger's defensive response and the mollifying news of Uriah's death.

David sends a callous and cynical response back to Joab (v. 25): "Do not let this thing be evil in your eyes, for the sword devours now one, now another." The NRSV and the NIV soften the opening phrase and in the process lose a precise parallel with the closing comment of the chapter (v. 27*b*). David presumes to say that what has happened is not an evil thing. It is just the unfortunate cost of war. Get on with the siege. David engages in a moral cover-up to match the cover-up of his actual deeds. Perhaps he is trying to convince himself as much as Joab that this was an act of war and not an act of murder. He is not so calmly accepting of the costs of war when the reported death is that of his own son Absalom

283. Contra Hertzberg, *I and II Samuel,* 310; Meir Sternberg, *The Poetics of Biblical Narrative* (Bloomington: University of Indiana Press, 1985) 201-13.

284. The reference to Abimelech seems awkward and ill placed. Some have suggested that it is a reference intended to function metaphorically as a comment on aspects of the wider story in chap. 11. See Bal, *Lethal Love,* 10-36, for extensive discussion of the options here and the connection of this text with the emergence of a biblical theme of the "lethal woman."

(18:33). David speaks as if the matter is finished. He imagines his sinful deeds can be masked by the inevitable loss of life that takes place in war.

11:26-27. These verses report the developments David had hoped for in arranging the death of Uriah and one further development beyond his control. In quick succession, Uriah's death is reported to Bathsheba; she observes the proper rituals of mourning for her husband; David "sends" and "brings" her to the palace; David and Bathsheba marry; and a son is born. This is the course of events for which David had hoped and plotted. The king's honor has been publicly preserved. David surely imagines that all is well and the matter is finished.

At this point, the moral perspective of the Lord enters the picture. David had urged Joab not to let this matter be "evil in your eyes" (v. 25a), setting aside any human moral qualms. But the text now tells us that "the thing that David has done was evil in the eyes of the LORD" (v. 27b, author's trans.). Again both the NRSV and the NIV soften the moral judgment made in the text and obscure the parallel with v. 25a. From God's perspective this matter is not finished. David's power cannot control the judgment of God. David believes the story has ended, but this final notice of God's viewpoint alerts the reader that there is a further act to this drama, and chap. 12 will make this clear to David as well when he is confronted with his sin by the prophet Nathan.

REFLECTIONS

1. This is a classic story of the arrogant misuse of power for personal whim. It is remarkable that a story so negative to David was preserved and passed on in the tradition. Indeed, the idealized Davidic portrait by the chronicler omits this episode. We should be grateful that the tradition had the courage to present Israel's greatest king with a portrait that includes his weaknesses and vulnerability as well as his accomplishments and power. This sordid and disillusioning episode in David's story serves as a cautionary tale on the nearness of violence to those who live with power. It reminds us that even those most admired and most accomplished are not immune to the temptation of power.

Those possessed of power and surrounded by admirers and supporters often succumb to the illusion that they are in control of their own destiny and can define the terms of the morality that governs their actions. David experienced the limits of his power and control. He could not control Bathsheba's pregnancy, Uriah's principles, or God's moral judgment. One can hardly consider this a word limited in application to an ancient king when our own news has been filled in recent years with stories of politicians, clergy, military officers, and teachers guilty of sexual misconduct and manipulation of others for the sake of self-interest. In many of these instances, abuses were committed under the illusion that the authority of their office, rank, or influence would protect them. The tragedy of lives undone and accomplishments overshadowed by acts committed under such an illusion of power is an almost weekly story in our communities and nation.

The story of David's adultery and murder reminds us of the deadly spiral of violence that can escalate from a single sinful act. For David, an initial act born of lust led to an elaborate and deceitful attempt at cover-up and finally to murder. Perhaps the dramas of our lives are not always on this grand scale, but we should not imagine that because we have stopped short of murder that this is not our story. We all know that we have at times acted to exploit others for our own self-interest, and we know too well how easily a lie to cover our tracks can involve us in complex deceits and additional acts that compound and deepen our original complicity.

2. Evidence that this story strikes close to home can be seen in the many efforts to soften the impact of the story. This is apparent in the endless fascination with the tale of David and Bathsheba through the generations and the many efforts to find some justification or mitigating circumstances that avoid the simple conclusion that David, the hero of our story, has become an adulterer and a murderer. These efforts are seen not only in scholarly treatments, from the ancient rabbis to modern academics, but also in numerous treatments of the David and Bathsheba story in art, poetry, literature, and film.[285]

As modern readers, teachers, and preachers, we must face the harsh realities of the story and avoid the temptation to soften them. To do so will mean countering many distorted readings of this story already present in past interpretation and popular cultural. These distorted readings take several forms:

Scapegoating. Perhaps the most common distortion of this story through the ages is the effort to portray Bathsheba as a seductress or co-conspirator, thereby transforming David to some degree from perpetrator to victim. The story gives us nothing explicit to substantiate such views and, in fact, shows little interest in Bathsheba as a subject at all. Yet, the following excerpt from a turn-of-the-century treatment of this story has been typical of many treatments of the episode down to the present: "No one of good moral character could have acted as she did in her seduction and conquest of David. She doubtless exposed herself that the king might be tempted; she willingly came to the palace when she was sent for; and conspired with David for the murder of her husband."[286] This scapegoating of Bathsheba as the temptress who led David astray was present in some ancient rabbinic efforts to soften David's guilt, and it is still present in some church education curriculum treatments. Recent movie and television treatments of the story uniformly show Bathsheba engaging in seductive behavior and usually portray her as the initiator of the relationship by means of such behavior.[287] Joseph Heller's novel on David has Bathsheba say, "I made up my mind to meet you. A king and all that too—who could resist? So I began bathing on my roof every evening to attract you."[288] These efforts to make Bathsheba the initiator are unfortunately consistent with a common defense in cases of the rape and abuse of women: "She asked for it." Even the NRSV's and the NIV's softening of the verb "take" to make David's messengers merely "getting" Bathsheba (v. 4*a*) shows our unwillingness to face the coercion in David's action. This would suggest that it might be difficult to face similarly coercive behaviors between the sexes in our own experience.

Rationalizing. Another common effort to soften the harsh realities of this story is the search for mitigating circumstances that help to explain, if not justify, David's actions. In a 1985 film, *King David,*[289] Bathsheba reveals to a shocked David that Uriah is an abusive husband, thus giving David a noble motive for the act of murder and the rescue of an abused woman. The ancient rabbis sought to lessen David's guilt in a variety of ways. Some claimed the chain of events was due to the marriage of a Hittite man to an Israelite wife and that the marriage to David rectified that unacceptable state. Others claimed that Satan appeared as a bird and when David shot an arrow at it, the screen shielding Bathsheba at her bath was toppled, and the chain of events was begun.[290] Another form of rationalizing David's great sin has been to claim that his repentance was correspondingly great, as evidenced by Psalm 51. Such a traditional argument usually seems to mean that we can ignore the sordid story of 2 Samuel 11.

Romanticizing. Some readers prefer to describe Bathsheba as the beautiful woman with whom "David fell in love when he saw her bathing." What better way to soften the harshness of this story than to make it a love story? Indeed, David and Bathsheba

---

285. See J. Cheryl Exum, "Bathsheba Plotted, Shot, and Painted," in *Plotted, Shot, and Painted: Cultural Representations of Biblical Women,* JSOTSup 215 (Sheffield: Sheffield Academic, 1996) 19-53.

286. Morton Bryan Wharton, *Famous Men of the Old Testament* (New York: E. B. Treat, 1903) 213.

287. See Exum, "Bathsheba Plotted, Shot, and Painted," 19-53.

288. Joseph Heller, *God Knows* (New York: Dell, 1984) 312.

289. *King David,* Paramount Pictures, directed by Bruce Beresford, produced by Martin Elfand, starring Richard Gere.

290. Reported in Michael E. Williams, ed. *The Storyteller's Companion to the Bible,* vol. 3: *Judges–Kings* (Nashville: Abingdon, 1992) 122-23.

often make the list of the world's great lovers, alongside Romeo and Juliet, Anthony and Cleopatra, and others. Hollywood could not resist this temptation, and many people's view of this story is colored by the sweeping romance of Gregory Peck and Susan Hayward in Darryl F. Zanuck's 1951 film *David and Bathsheba.*[291] This film presents Uriah as a soldier with no interest in his wife, David as lonely in his royal office, and Bathsheba as a neglected wife who finds her true love in David. But the biblical text does not give us a romance. David has no interest in an ongoing relationship or marriage until Bathsheba becomes pregnant, and even then he prefers the solution of making Uriah the father. Romances do not begin with "taking" and end with murder, and we romanticize this tale at our own peril. There is too much in present popular culture that romanticizes violence and the abuse of women.

When we preach and teach this story, we must be clear: It is a story of a fallen hero. One cannot help recalling David's own lament over Saul and Jonathan, "How the mighty have fallen" (2 Sam 1:19). This time it is David who has fallen, and the fall is not in battle but in moral character. The difficulty we have in facing the harsh reality of this story is a testimony to the ease with which we excuse our own sin. But if we can face David's sin for what it is, we may better face our own. This theme will continue in the confrontation with Nathan in chap. 12.

To preach this story will require an honest facing of our own complicity with David. To face the sin of our greatest biblical heroes can allow us to face our own impulses to use others for the fulfillment of our own desires and to face the tragic ease with which we can become entangled in growing webs of sinful acts as we try to cover up and avoid accountability for our own manipulation of others. This story is especially directed to those whose positions of power, leadership, and influence provide constant opportunity for manipulating or exploiting those in more vulnerable positions. Our newspapers today are filled with stories of those—from presidents to pastors—who have abused the power of their offices for the fulfillment of their own self-interested desires or gains. Perhaps we need to preach this bleak side of David's story more often, not simply to point fingers at the sins of the mighty but to acknowledge how often we excuse and emulate them.

291. *David and Bathsheba,* Twentieth Century Fox, directed by Henry King, produced by Darryl F. Zanuck.

2 Samuel 12:1-15a, Nathan's Confrontation of David

COMMENTARY

In the previous chapter David "sent" in order to "take" (11:4). Now it is the Lord who "sends," and it is in order to speak. God sends Nathan, a prophet, to David. Nathan is to confront David and speak of God's judgment of him, because the "thing that David had done was evil in the eyes of the LORD" (11:27*b*, author's trans.).

It has often been noted that Nathan's confrontation with David in 12:1-15*a* stands out as different in style and content from the storytelling style of the succession narrative (2 Samuel 9–20; 1 Kings 1–2).[292] For most of

292. See the discussion of the interpretive history of this chapter in George W. Coats, "Parable, Fable, and Anecdote: Storytelling in the Succession Narrative," *Int.* 35 (1981) 368-82.

the succession narrative, God's perspective and God's shaping of events are conveyed in minimal comments that remind the reader of a larger reality at work. The verse quoted above (11:27*b*) is such a comment, and the story would flow smoothly from that notice of God's displeasure to the consequence stated in 12:15*b,* "The LORD struck the child that Uriah's wife bore to David, and it became very ill." So it is unusual to have a prophet arrive and offer a detailed spelling out of God's judgment on David's sin. McCarter has argued compellingly that chaps. 10–12 have been affixed by a prophetic editor "as a kind of theological preface" to the subsequent story of Absalom's rebellion and the havoc in

David's family that preceded and followed that rebellion[293] McCarter admits, however, that only 12:1-15*a* may actually stem from the hand of this prophetic editor.[294] In my opinion, the story of David's sin and the tragic events that culminated in Absalom's rebellion were already joined in the succession narrative. The knowledge of David's adultery and the death of Uriah could not be ignored by that historian. The prophetic addition of the confrontation and judgment from the Lord through Nathan additionally makes the case that David has already been judged, has repented, and has suffered the consequences of his sin in the tragedies that afflict his family, so the dynasty (Solomon in particular) could continue free of taint from these events.

The account of this prophetic encounter has three parts: vv. 1-7*a*, the parable and David's response to it; vv. 7*b*-12, a prophetic oracle announcing judgment; vv. 13-15*a*, David's repentance.

12:1-7a. David had thought the matter of Bathsheba and Uriah to be finished, but the Lord has not finished with it. The Lord sends Nathan to him. The introduction of the prophet into the story is abrupt and unexpected. We met Nathan previously in chap. 7, where he announced the oracle of God's promise to David. He is present now for a quite different purpose. Readers often assume that Nathan had access to David and could speak to him openly. Nevertheless, even a prophet must frame his speech carefully in the presence of power; so Nathan does not approach the matter of concern directly. Instead, he tells David a story involving a case of injustice.

Nathan's story is usually understood as a parable.[295] Parables operate out of a tension between the expected and the actual events. Actual events usually reverse the expectations of the hearer and in doing so make the point intended by the recital of the parable. Some have called this text a "juridical parable," which intentionally disguises a real-life situation in order to draw a guilty party into passing judgment on himself.[296] Other

examples of juridical parables are 2 Sam 14:1-20; 1 Kgs 20:35-43; and Isa 5:1-7.

Nathan's parable presents David with a tale of contrasts. There is a rich man and a poor man. There are the large flocks and herds of the rich man, and the single ewe lamb that is the prized possession of the poor man (vv. 2-3). Nathan's story expands at this point to describe the closeness of the poor man to his lamb. It was like his child; it ate, drank, and slept with him (v. 3*b*). When a guest came to the rich man's house, he was reluctant to take a lamb from his own flocks to feed his guest. It is at this point that the parable takes its unexpected turn. Without explanation, the rich man simply takes the poor man's beloved lamb and feeds it to his guest (v. 4). We are shocked at such a heartless act, particularly since it is disguised to the rich man's guest as hospitality—crass injustice masquerading as graciousness.

Before speaking of David's reaction, we should note that this scene does not seem like a customary session of royal judicial practice. Kings did have a role in administering justice, but this instance is not presented as a real-life case for David to decide. No names, places, witnesses, or other petitioners are in evidence. Instead, we find an encounter between prophet and king in which Nathan has chosen the rhetorical device of a parable of injustice for his purpose in confronting David.

David's reaction is like our own. He is shocked and angry by the arbitrary action of the rich man (v. 5*a*). Yet, he does not yet recognize his own "taking" (11:4) in the "taking" of the rich man (v. 4). David does not yet realize that he has become the king against whose "taking" Samuel warned the people (1 Sam 8:11-19). David swears by the life of the Lord that any man who would do such a thing is a בֶן־מָוֶת (*ben-māwet*), literally, a "son of death" (v. 5*b*). This is usually interpreted to mean "one who deserves to die" (cf. 1 Sam 20:31-32, where Saul refers to David as a *ben-māwet* and Jonathan responds, "Why should he be put to death?"). This comment, however, expresses David's feeling toward such a man and does not constitute a formal sentence of death. In v. 6, David's sense of legal remedy for such a situation is expressed in terms of fourfold restitution (see

293. McCarter, *II Samuel*, 276.

294. McCarter, *II Samuel*, 304-9.

295. See W. M. W. Roth, "You Are the Man! Structural Interaction in 2 Samuel 10:1-12," *Semeia* 8 (1977) 1-13. See also Coats, "Parable, Fable, and Anecdote," although Coats unconvincingly wants to argue that Nathan's story is more like a fable than a parable.

296. Uriel Simon, "The Poor Man's Ewe-Lamb: An Example of a Juridical Parable," *Biblica* 48 (1967) 207-42.

Exod 22:1). His sense of the offense is made clear in v. 6*b*, "because he had no pity." The Hebrew word for "pity" (חמל *hāmāl*) here may be thought of in terms of "compassion," especially the "compassion" that saves from death.[297] Lacking compassion, the rich man sent the poor man's lamb to slaughter; likewise, David sent Uriah to his death.

The dramatic climax of Nathan's strategy and the moment of recognition for David come in v. 7*a*: *"You are the man!"* David is the one who had much and took the possession of one who had little; David is the exploiter, the perpetrator of injustice. Some have argued that Nathan's parable does not correspond exactly to David's crimes. The lamb seems to represent Bathsheba, the one wife of Uriah, whereas David had many wives. Yet, it is the lamb that is killed, not its owner, who loved it. But the parable is not intended as an allegory in which each detail corresponds to the exact crimes of David. David's use of his position of power and wealth to "take" what belonged to another is like the deed of the rich man. The exact detailing of David's crimes remains for the direct and explicit speech of the judgment oracle that follows (vv. 7*b*-12). The parable creates the moment of recognition after David has himself rendered a judgment on the injustice of such privileged "taking."

12:7b-12. Nathan leaves the indirection of parable and risks the directness of confrontational speech that takes the form of a prophetic announcement of God's judgment. It opens with the messenger formula, "Thus says the LORD . . ." (repeated again at the start of v. 11), which emphasizes the prophet's role in speaking God's word and signals that the prophet will speak in the first person, as if the Lord were speaking directly. God recites to David the benevolent deeds done on his behalf (vv. 7*b*-8). This is followed by the accusation detailing David's offenses (v. 9). The formulaic element "Now, therefore . . ." signals the announcement of punishment that will come as judgment for David's sin (vv. 10-12).

God reviews the history of divine graciousness toward David; it is a history dominated

by "giving," in contrast to David's "taking" (vv. 7-8). The anointing probably refers to David's anointing by the prophet Samuel (1 Sam 16:13). God saved David from Saul and gave all that was Saul's to David, eventually including the kingdoms of Israel and Judah. It is uncertain what is meant by the reference to "your master's wives," since there is no tradition that David ever took the wives of Saul for himself. Surprisingly, God states a willingness to have given David even more (v. 8*b*), but David has now moved from gift to grasp.[298]

What was veiled and implied in Nathan's parable becomes bold and explicit in the indictment of v. 9. What David has done is given theological meaning in the opening of this indictment. He has "despised the word of the LORD" and done "what is evil in his sight" (v. 9*a*). This is dangerous language, for Saul was rejected as king because he had "rejected the word of the LORD" (1 Sam 15:26). Again David's deeds are named as "evil" in God's eyes, echoing the language of 11:27*b* and contradicting David's false reassurance to Joab that their murderous deeds were not "evil" but the mere by-product of war (see Commentary on 11:25). David's deeds are not just offenses against Bathsheba and Uriah; they are offenses against God's Word. Even in the later announcement of punishment, God makes clear that in taking Bathsheba for his own wife, "you have despised me" (v. 10*b*).

Again the indictment names David's sin as "taking" Uriah's wife for his own and brackets that accusation of adultery with a twofold statement of David's murder of Uriah (v. 9*b*). David was not present when Uriah was killed in battle ("struck down by the sword"; "killed him with the sword of the Ammonites"), but God's indictment is explicit: *"You . . . struck down . . . killed."*

"Now, therefore . . ." signals God's pronouncement of punishment for David's sin. The "sword will never depart from your house" (v. 10*a*). "I will raise up trouble against you from within your own house" (v. 11*a*). The violence David has done against Uriah and Bathsheba will be visited on David's own family. The story of David, as it unfolds from this point forward, is indeed violent and tragic. It includes the death of a child, an incestuous rape, a murder of revenge, a

297. George Coats, "II Samuel 12:1-7a," *Int.* 40 (1986) 171-72, finds this same Hebrew root used for the "compassion" that Pharaoh's daughter showed in saving the infant Moses from death and that later Moses showed in intervening to save Israel from death at the hands of God's judgment for the golden calf at Sinai.

298. See Gunn, "David and the Gift of the Kingdom," 14-45.

son's armed rebellion, and that son's subsequent death. God's statement of having given David's wives to a "neighbor" who will lie with them in public, doing before all Israel what David did in secret (vv. 11*b*-12), foreshadows Absalom's public taking of David's wives and concubines in a tent on the palace roof (16:21-22). It was an act of defiance, a taking of David's royal prerogatives to symbolize Absalom's seizure of David's throne. That shameful moment is here given a theological interpretation as being retribution for David's own adultery.

12:13-15a. The shock of Nathan's dramatic accusation "You are the man!" is almost equaled by David's immediate response to God's judgment, "I have sinned against the LORD" (v. 13*a*). David has not lost the capacity to choose for the Lord, and the only avenue back to relationship is the one he has taken, confession and repentance. Power defers to piety. David did not turn on Nathan or reject Nathan's harsh words. He did not assert his authority or attempt to justify or deny. His confession is as simple and direct as was the moment of recognition that followed the parable. David is the man; David is the sinner. David has dealt violence and death, and violence and death are to return as his judgment. But in his confession, life continues to assert itself. Nathan announces that David's sin has been put aside, and he will not die (v. 13*b*). God's forgiveness can be as simple and direct as David's repentance. But the continuing claim of life made possible by David's response does not remove all consequence of sin. What David has done cannot be undone. Life can be reclaimed and continue in the midst of the consequences of sin, but the tragic reverberations from David's sin will continue to be felt in his family. David has "utterly scorned the LORD," and he may live, but the child conceived by Bathsheba from her union with David will die (v. 14). Nathan has spoken God's word, and he departs the scene as quickly as he appeared (v. 15*a*).

REFLECTIONS

1. This story concerns the speaking of judgment to power. Power is always tempted to live in the illusion that it is autonomous and self-sufficient. Powerful people in powerful positions often imagine that they can define reality in their own terms. David had succumbed to the illusion of royal reality as ultimate authority. Nathan has come to speak to him the truth of the matter, that there is a divine reality before which royal reality is judged. In our own time, the prophetic task is still to speak the truth of divine reality in a world that is obsessed with the self-defining realities of political and economic power. If the church would speak prophetically as a part of its ministry, then it must be willing to speak the truth in the presence of power. There is a divine governance of history that transcends human institutions. There is a divine power at work in history that judges human uses of power. In the eyes of God, the powerless are as valued as the powerful, and the exploitation of these powerless ones is evil. The achievements of power will mean nothing if they are bought at the price of exploiting the weak and the vulnerable. This is the reality of the world the prophet (and the prophetic community) speaks as truth in the presence of power.

But such speech is dangerous. Those who would be prophetic must risk speaking directly to those who hold power. It is not enough to speak about the misuse of power at a distance from power. If the church would make a difference with its prophetic speaking, it must find ways to be heard by those who hold power. This may necessitate finding ways of commanding attention, as Nathan did in his use of parable. "One cannot address royal power directly, especially royal power so deeply in guilt. It is permissible to talk about speaking truth to power, but if truth is to have a chance with power, it must be done with some subtlety."[299] But even for Nathan, there came a moment

---

299. Brueggemann, *David's Truth in Israel's Imagination and Memory*, 63.

when royal power was attentive and the unvarnished truth of evil in the service of power had to be named and faced. The risk of this moment is real, and the church cannot imagine that the speaking of truth to power will not be costly at times. It will not always be a David who stands before us. At other times in the biblical story, the response to prophetic confrontation of the king was not repentance. Ahab and Jezebel sought Elijah's life; Manasseh slaughtered the prophets; Jehoiakim held Jeremiah's words in contempt.

2. An important and overlooked aspect of this story is that both Nathan and David stand within and represent the community of faith. As the church, we cannot afford to read this story as a call simply to become Nathans, pointing fingers at and naming the sins of others. Both Nathan and David are part of God's covenant community, and each plays a role in God's plan for Israel.

> This story is not concerned with the opposition of the wholly righteous to the unredeemably wicked. Its lesson is that righteousness and sin exist side by side even within the covenant community. Thus, the church is never in the position of selecting only one of these roles. It is called to *proclaim God's judgment* on all that opposes God's desire for justice and fullness of life, but it is also required to *receive and acknowledge judgment* for its own participation in the conditions that create brokenness.[300]

3. This story focuses primarily on the speaking of judgment, but it also speaks of the possibilities of confession and repentance in the face of judgment. David's immediate and direct confession of sin (v. 13*a*) is almost as surprising as Nathan's climactic, "You are the man!" (v. 7*a*). David has committed crimes, and from this brokenness will come consequences. They will unfold in the death of the child and the tragedies that will infect David's family. David has unleashed death, but in his confession he reclaims the possibilities of life in the midst of death. He moves from his own self-pronounced verdict that he is a "son of death" (12:5*b*) to Nathan's quiet word, "You will not die" (12:13*b*).

If, as the church, we attend only to Nathan's judgment and fail to note David's repentance, then we run the risk of settling for guilt as the goal of our prophetic speech. Dramatic confrontation and naming of sin in sermons, resolutions, and public forums can often be quite successful in stirring guilt for complicity in the brokenness that is present in our world. But guilt is ultimately static and backward-looking in regret for things done that cannot be undone. David's confession models a first step toward repentance. In the Hebrew concept, repentance is related to the word meaning "to turn." To repent is to turn and go in a new direction. Repentance is dynamic and forward-looking in hope for a new direction away from patterns of brokenness. The good news of this text is that we are not left in guilt but are called to repentance. This does not mean that we are free from the consequences of sin. David has enacted self-centered abuses of power that will return to haunt him through his own children. It does, however, mean that judgment is not the final word; repentance makes a further word of life possible in the face of judgment. If the church speaks the truth to power, it should never be with a self-satisfied assumption that judgment is the final word. We should always speak judgment in the hope that confession and repentance might make life possible in spite of the deathly powers unleashed by sin.

In many medieval synagogue manuscripts of 2 Samuel 12, a gap was left by the copyist in the text following David's confession of sin in v. 13*a*. This was to give the opportunity for the reading of Psalm 51, the great penitential psalm that carries this superscription: "A Psalm of David, when the prophet Nathan came to him, after he had gone in to Bathsheba." This psalm expresses the attitude of repentance, rather than guilt, which the church seeks when it speaks in judgment:

---

300. Bruce C. Birch and Larry L. Rasmussen, *The Predicament of the Prosperous* (Philadelphia: Westminster, 1978) 128.

Have mercy on me, O God,
  according to your steadfast love;
according to your abundant mercy
  blot out my transgressions.
Wash me thoroughly from my iniquity,
  and cleanse me from my sin

.   .   .   .   .   .

Create in me a clean heart, O God,
  and put a new and right spirit within me.
Do not cast me away from your presence,
  and do not take your holy spirit from me.
(Ps 51:1-2, 10-11 NRSV)

2 Samuel 12:15*b*-25, The Death of the Child of David and Bathsheba

COMMENTARY

This segment of the text leaves the didactic style of Nathan's prophetic oracle and returns to a storytelling mode. This section may be the original continuation of 11:27*b,* before the prophetic addition of Nathan's confrontation with David. The death of David and Bathsheba's child becomes only the first of a series of tragic experiences of death and/or violence in David's family. Moreover, we now understand these experiences in the light of Nathan's pronouncement of God's judgment on David. David's confession reclaims his own life, but such reclaiming is costly. David's own life continues in the midst of the deadly realities he has himself introduced into his own personal story. The first costly experience of this deathly presence in the royal household comes in the death of the son conceived in David's adulterous liaison with Bathsheba. Nathan had already said that the child would die (v. 14). Verses 15*b*-23 narrate the events surrounding the child's death. Verses 24-25 anticipate a new future and new life with the birth of Solomon, whom the Lord loves and who will become the first king in an ongoing dynasty from David.

12:15b-23. The opening of this bitter story leaves no room for doubt: "The LORD struck the child that Uriah's wife bore to David, and it became very ill" (v. 15*b*). The death that David brought to another family now enters his own. In the view of this narrator, there was a cost to be paid, and the Lord is the agent exacting the moral cost of David's deathly crimes. Since the price is the life of a child, we may find this view of God difficult to understand and accept, but the text does not address this issue.

The narrative focuses on David. By now we should not be surprised at this. David is clearly attached to the child and pleads with God for the child's life (v. 16*a*). The conception of this child altered the life of king and kingdom. To have lost so much and then lose the child as well seems unbearable. David refuses food, keeping vigil through the night, and his servants become distressed, urging him to eat (vv. 16*b*-17). After seven days, the child dies, and the servants are afraid to tell David. They fear that his grief will deepen and that he may even do himself harm (v. 18). David perceives the reality of the moment without being told. He asks his whispering servants if the child is dead, and they confirm that it is so (v. 19).

It is at this point in the story that David's actions confound his servants (and readers). Custom dictates that mourning should begin, with its attendant lamentation and ceremonies of grief. Instead of these expected practices, David begins a series of purposeful activities not usually associated with a time of mourning (v. 20). The verbs dominate the story: David rose, washed, anointed himself, changed clothes, entered the house of the Lord, worshiped, went to his own house, requested food, and ate. In short, David resumed his life and the practices of his customary routines.

His servants, who were disturbed over David's unrestrained distress during the child's illness, are equally dismayed at his behavior after the child's death. David has reversed the usual custom. His servants cannot restrain themselves. "What are you doing?" they ask (v. 21). David's response shows a remarkable ability to face the realities of life and death and his own complicity in those things that make for life and death. He fasted and wept while the child was ill in petition for the graciousness of God and in hope that God's mercy would grant the child life (v. 22). But when this was not to be, David accepted the reality of death and rejected fasting and weeping in favor of relinquishment and resumption of life (v. 23). He refuses to bow to the power of death and accepts his inability to restore his son. "I shall go to him, but he will not return to me" (v. 23*b*).

Walter Brueggemann has seen in this story one evidence of a new portrait of humanity that emerges in the story of David. David is the model of God's "trusted creature" who acts with boldness and freedom to claim the gifts of life with which humanity is trusted.

David's reaction to the death of his child and thus to the reality of all death is not to be viewed as stoic resignation. . . . David has a fresh view of the meaning of life and death, where his proper hopes and proper fears are to be located. This is more than a violation of common practice. It is an act of profound faith in the face of the most precious tabus of his people. David had discerned, for whatever reasons, that the issues of his life are not to be found in cringing fear before the powers of death, but rather in his ability to embrace and abandon, to love and to leave, to take life as it comes not with indifference but with freedom, not with callousness but with buoyancy. . . . For him there is none of the conventional paralysis in death. He knew death belonged legitimately to history, and

he had no illusions about entering some kind of faith which did not know death.[301]

12:24-25. David's affirmation of life in the face of death is followed by a report of new life. In rapid succession, David comforts Bathsheba, goes to her, lies with her, and she then bears a second son (v. 24*a*). This is the first time since Bathsheba was introduced (11:3) that she is named in her own right and not referred to as "the wife of Uriah." In the birth of this second child, she becomes more than the occasion for David's sin. In fact, Bathsheba is later to play a very active role in helping this son succeed to the throne of David (1 Kgs 1:11-31).

This son is named Solomon (v. 24*b*), a name usually associated with the word שָׁלוֹם (*šālôm*, "peace," "wholeness"). This is an ironic name in the light of the events that preceded his birth, but perhaps it should be seen as the "peace/wholeness" hoped for in the new beginning of his birth. That this is a genuine new beginning with hope of a new future is affirmed by the notice that "the LORD loved him" (v. 24*b*). Further, God sends the prophet Nathan, this time as a bearer of hope rather than judgment. Nathan names the child "Jedidiah," a name that means "beloved of the LORD [Yahweh]" (v. 25). This name is not used elsewhere about Solomon and may be considered a private name, while "Solomon" was to be the child's throne name as Israel's third king.

The consequences of death and violence unleashed by David's sin are not yet played out. Tragic events lie ahead, but this notice already foreshadows that the promise of dynasty to David will remain firm and that Solomon need not carry into his own reign the judgment given to his father. Indeed, this may be part of the purpose of this entire narrative: to show that the sins of David have been judged and paid for. Solomon and the Davidic dynasty are free from guilt.

301. Walter Brueggemann, "The Trusted Creature," *CBQ* 31 (1969) 490.

Reflections

1. This is a difficult story for modern readers in the church. We do not wish to think that the lives of innocent children are exacted by God as punishment for a parent's sin. But this text assumes that all things ultimately come from God, including the illness of this child. From this point of view, all deaths are a part of the mystery of God's providence. God can and does use the circumstances of our lives to further the purposes of divine grace and judgment. This story does not, however, make a generalized claim about the deaths of all children.

The emphasis in this story is on David, who thought he could be the controller of life and death for his own ends, but must now discover that he is not autonomous and cannot control life and death, even though he is the king. Life and death exist in human history as a part of the mystery of God's providence, and not as a matter to be taken into human hands.

What also offends modern readers is the total focus on David. It is David who is the subject of this narrative—his loss, his grief, and finally his response in the face of the tragic cost. The child and Bathsheba are only elements of the plot in this episode of David's story, and they are not even named. This storytelling is simply endlessly fascinated with David and his meaning for Israel. This is less an intentional belittling of other characters in the story than a mark of the enormous importance David came to hold for Israel. That attention still focuses on David even in these episodes of sin, judgment, loss, and pain is a remarkable testimony to the ability of Israel's storytellers to face the realities of David's weakness and vulnerability while yet affirming his vitality and importance in Israel's story. This suggests that the tradition about David has something to teach us in observing his vulnerable moments and not simply in celebrating his triumphs.

2. This story reminds us that in the community of faith, life always has a further word to speak. There is something about the death of a child that heightens the offense of death. Life is unexpectedly cut short. Such a death seems unnatural, unfair. It is surely this same sense of offense that leads David to his severe pain and grief when faced with the potential loss of his son. David's grief and our own when faced with the reality of such untimely death is an appropriate acknowledgment of the reality and power of death in our human existence. It is an expression of our vulnerability and a recognition that we are not autonomous and in control. Even a life of piety and faith does not give us safe conduct around the necessity of facing death's power. The death of a child brings us more unexpectedly and harshly into the presence of that power. In our own grief, in our care of others in their grief, we must allow for the acknowledgment and voicing of the pain that comes with death's power. We must refuse to deny the reality of death's power.

But David's response to the death of the child is an important word to us about the power of life, which does not take away the offense of death. It simply refuses to let death have the final word. Death invades and inflicts its pain, but life goes on. In grieving the death of a child, it is all too easy to let that child's death become the most important thing about him or her. But even in a foreshortened life, the gift of that child's life among us is more important than his or her death. If, like David, we dwell not on death but on life, then we align ourselves with the importance that the gift of a life be remembered and affirmed. That life need not be eclipsed by letting death have the final word. To go on with life is not heartless or stoic and does not require us to deny the pain of loss. It is to affirm that the power of life is stronger than the power of death, and if we live that as true for our own lives we can affirm it as true for our children who die before us.[302]

302. See Bruce C. Birch, "Biblical Faith and the Loss of Children," *The Christian Century* 100 (1983) 965-67.

For Christians, this understanding is at the heart of resurrection faith. Christ's resurrection does not remove or nullify the offense of the cross. Resurrection is simply God's refusal to let death have the final word. There is a further word of life that God speaks in the face of death and against the power of death (see Romans 6). David claimed the power of life at the very moment that death seemed to prevail. To read his story is to understand that we can do the same.

2 Samuel 12:26-31, The Capture of Rabbah

COMMENTARY

The story moves from private matters back to the public arena and resumes the account of the Ammonite campaign, left off at 11:1. This military confrontation with a neighboring kingdom had begun in the humiliation of David's ambassadors in 10:1-5 and now concludes with the capture and pillage of the Ammonite capital city, Rabbah.

Developments in this final stage of the siege of Rabbah take an ironic turn. David had remained in Jerusalem while Joab conducted the siege (11:1). This simple fact provides the context for the account of David's adultery with Bathsheba and subsequent murder of her husband Uriah. Further, Nathan had confronted David with his crimes and pronounced God's judgment on him. Now, with all the personal damage done, Joab summons David to participate in the final defeat of Rabbah (v. 27). Joab has brought the city to submission by attacking its water supply (v. 27*b*). But out of loyalty to David, he sends word that he believes it more appropriate that David's name be associated with the fall of the city rather than his own (v. 28). It is a worthy and perhaps prudent gesture on the part of a loyal commander.

David responds to this summons and goes to Rabbah. The account is dominated by the verb "to take" (לכד *lākad*, vv. 28 [2x], 29). How much more appropriate it is for David to be engaged in "taking" the city of Israel's enemies than for him to be idle in Jerusalem "taking" the wife of his loyal commander Uriah (11:4). David "takes" not only the city but also spoils from the city (v. 30*b*), including a massive gold and jewel-encrusted crown taken from the idol of Ammon's god, Milcom, which is placed on David's head (v. 30*a*). He subjects the people of Ammon to forced labor to dismantle the defenses of their own cities (v. 31). Ammon was almost certainly incorporated territorially into the Davidic empire. The tradition allows David to capture, take plunder, use slave labor, and return to Jerusalem without moral comment. There is no memory of the story of Saul, who had been judged for such actions. There is no prophet Samuel to declare such campaigns as governed by the laws of holy war and חרם (*ḥērem*; see the Commentary on 1 Sam 15:1-35). The prophet Nathan is silent about such older tribal institutions. We have left tribal reality behind, and the Israelite tradition now stands fully in the reality of kingship. Royal concerns for territory, enemies made subject people, and economic gain now govern the story. In this military report, these concerns are assumed as appropriate to the reality of kings without further comment. (These few verses simply complete the narrative of David's Ammonite-Aramaean wars, begun in chap. 10. See Reflections at 10:1-19.)

2 Samuel 13:1-22, Amnon Rapes Tamar

COMMENTARY

This shocking episode narrates a brutal and incestuous rape. Tamar is the object of lustful desire by her half brother Amnon. The story reports in graphic detail Amnon's plot to get Tamar alone, his violent rape of her, and his callous discarding of her afterward. Her brother, Absalom, urges her silence and broods on his own plans for vengeance and ambitions. Their father, David, is angry but takes no action against Amnon. The story is truly what Phyllis Trible has labeled "a text of terror."[303]

Unlike Bathsheba (chap. 11), Tamar has voice and action in this story, and she speaks and acts with wisdom and courage. Nevertheless, in significant ways this remains a story of men set in the man's world of power and politics. Tamar is introduced not in her own right but as the sister of Absalom and the object of Amnon's desire (v. 1). Absalom and Amnon are sons of David and rivals to succeed him on the throne. For the narrator of this story, the rape of Tamar is not of interest as a personal tragedy for Tamar but as an offense to the family of Absalom, which leads to Absalom's vengeful killing of Amnon and his subsequent banishment by David. Tamar's rape sets in motion a course of events that eventually eliminates the two leading contenders for the Davidic throne. Tamar is an event rather than a person in this story. When the event is over, she disappears, while Absalom and Amnon play out the effects of the event that are of greatest interest to the narrator.

In the larger context, this story is a part of an unfolding chronicle of the violence David has unleashed in his own family.[304] He has himself modeled the wanton behavior that "takes" by power whatever is desired (Bathsheba, chap. 11) and is willing to kill for his own self-interest (Uriah, chap. 11). Now his sons follow in his footsteps, to the grief of Tamar. In this larger context, these violent events are also a part of the "trouble against you from within your own house" (12:11a), which Nathan the prophet announced as God's judgment for David's sin. Tamar is a victim not only of Amnon's lust but also of David's sin and God's judgment.

We have little choice but to attend to the drama of tragedy in David's house and power politics in David's kingdom, for David is the fascination and focus of the books of Samuel. Nevertheless, we can also choose to see the tragedy and pain of Tamar the person in spite of the narrator's emphasis on her rape as the excuse for Absalom's revenge. We need not victimize Tamar again by failing to note her courage and resourcefulness in the face of danger or by refusing to acknowledge the full reality of the suffering and humiliation inflicted upon her, not only by Amnon, who raped her, but also by David and Absalom, who see her tragedy primarily as a complication in kingdom politics.[305]

13:1-7. The story begins with the naming of David's son Absalom, for it is in his fate that the narrator is interested. Tamar is named only after her identity as Absalom's beautiful sister is stated (v. 1a). Indeed, she is bracketed by two princes, for Amnon, the half brother of Absalom, is said to love her (v. 1b). Amnon is David's oldest son (3:2-5) and, therefore, David's likely successor. Absalom was probably next in line for the throne, since Chileab (3:3) does not appear in any stories and is believed to have died. This story is not told for its own sake but for its effect on the succession to the throne.[306]

It becomes increasingly apparent that Amnon's so-called love is really lust. He is described as being obsessed with Tamar to the point of illness (v. 2a). Tamar is not available to him. She is his sister, a fact reinforced by constant use of brother/sister language in this chapter. She is a virgin, undoubtedly sequestered and protected in women's quarters with other marriageable women of the court. The narrative is straightforward; Amnon's so-called love is frustration that he cannot do with Tamar what he pleases (v. 2b).

Jonadab is introduced as a friend of Amnon, the nephew of David, and a "crafty" man (v. 3). Amnon reveals the problem of his

303. Phyllis Trible, "Tamar: The Royal Rape of Wisdom," in *Texts of Terror: Literary-Feminist Readings of Biblical Narratives* (Philadelphia: Fortress, 1984) 37-64.

304. Burke O. Long, "Wounded Beginnings: David and Two Sons," in *Images of Man and God: Old Testament Short Stories in Literary Focus*, ed. by Burke O. Long (Sheffield: Almond, 1981) 26-34, treats this episode as a short story in its own right that is incorporated into the plot of the larger compositions of the succession narrative and the Deuteronomistic History.

305. A notable example of telling and interpreting this story from Tamar's point of view can be found in Pamela Cooper-White, *The Cry of Tamar: Violence Against Women and the Church's Response* (Minneapolis: Fortress, 1995) 1-14. My discussion has also been informed by an unpublished seminar paper on this chapter by Mary Petrina Boyd.

306. Anderson, *2 Samuel*, 172, suggests that "Amnon's love for Tamar was, largely, part of his plan to put Absalom and his family in their place! . . . Although Amnon was attracted by Tamar's beauty he hoped, even more so, both to gratify his sexual desires and to humiliate Absalom through Tamar, at the same time." Although this is possible, there is little explicit evidence of this in the text.

"love" for Tamar (again identified as Absalom's sister, v. 4). The tone of the text is misleading. Amnon's intentions are later exposed as the violence of incest and rape, but the text treats his plotting with Jonadab as if the issue were merely the plight of a lovesick young man. We are well warned by this story of the innocent guises that can mask violence. Jonadab devises a plan, with the sole intent of isolating Amnon alone with Tamar. Amnon is to feign illness, and when he is visited by his father, David, he is to ask that Tamar be sent to make cakes and feed him in his illness (v. 5). Amnon follows this plan to the letter (v. 6). David once again becomes complicit (this time probably unwittingly) in sending someone to a violent fate—first Uriah, now Tamar (v. 7).

13:8-14. Tamar comes innocently to Amnon's house, and what the reader knows to be a charade is played out. Her actions are efficient and caring. She performs all the necessary operations for the baking of cakes (v. 8), but Amnon refuses to eat and instead sends everyone from the room (v. 9). Amnon implores her to come into his chamber and feed him (presumably a separate bedchamber where he is lying in bed feigning illness, v. 10). It is at this point that all pretense vanishes on Amnon's part (v. 11). There is no illness; there is no love. There is "grasping/seizing" (חזק ḥāzaq, a verb that emphasizes strength) and desire, "Come, lie with me, my sister." It is uncertain whether laws against incest were in force at this time (Lev 18:9, 11; 20:17; Deut 27:22) or whether they applied to the royal family. Tamar later suggests that marriage would have been possible (v. 13b). It may be that the frequent use of "brother/sister" language points to disregard of filial loyalties rather than to a charge of incest.

The intent to rape, however, is clear. Amnon has not made an invitation; he has voiced a demand and will not be denied. Tamar names the intent, "No, my brother, do not force me" (v. 12a). The meaning of the verb ענה ('ānâ, "force") is connected with concepts of humiliation and oppression. Tamar sees clearly that rape is Amnon's intention (the same verb is used in v. 14, when Amnon carries out that intention).

Unlike Bathsheba in 11:4, Tamar resists the lustful grasp of royal power—in speech and in action. Trible has emphasized Tamar's courageous voicing of wise counsel in the face of dire threat.[307] She quickly marshals arguments against Amnon's intended violence, in his own interests as well as hers. She first argues that such a thing is simply not done in Israel, and she names this act with the term נבלה (nĕbālâ, v. 12b). A widely used traditional translation of this term is "folly" or "foolishness" (KJV, RSV), but recent scholarship and translators have recognized the inadequacy of this rendering. Phillips notes that this term is "a general expression for serious disorderly and unruly action resulting in the breakup of an existing relationship. . . . It indicates the end of an existing order consequent upon breach of rules which maintained that order."[308] The renderings in the NRSV ("vile [thing]") and the NIV ("wicked thing") are more appropriate. Tamar argues that Amnon's deed would violate deeply held principles that guard the Israelite social order.

Taking a second, more practical tack, Tamar laments that she would have to live in shame, but more pointedly Amnon's reputation would be ruined. He would be regarded as "one of the [נבלים nĕbālîm] in Israel"—i.e., "a fool," "a scoundrel" (v. 13a). We are reminded of Nabal, in 1 Samuel 25, whose name and actions were from this same root word.

Finally, Tamar begs Amnon to speak with David and arrange a marriage. She believes David would not refuse the relationship (v. 13b). It is not clear whether such marriages of half siblings in the royal family were acceptable, but Tamar is probably right that David would agree to it rather than face the scandal that is about to erupt. After all, David has defied convention for the sake of lust himself. This plea on Tamar's part is a sad testimony to her recognition of the powerless role that women occupied in ancient Israel. She knows that if Amnon is determined, he can have her, but she urges him to do this in a way that accords her some honor and respect.

Tamar's speech is remarkable for its wise counsel under such desperate circumstances. Her arguments are compelling, and she is able to appeal to Amnon's interests as well as her own. Yet, Amnon refuses to listen to her. He

---

307. Trible, *Texts of Terror,* 36-64.
308. A. Phillips, "NEBALAH—a Term for Serious Disorderly and Unruly Conduct," *VT* 25 (1975) 241.

rejects wise speech in favor of physical power and violence. The rape is reported in direct and brutal terms (v. 14). Amnon was stronger than Tamar, so he forced her (the verb is *ʿānâ* again; cf. v. 12). The final verb שׁכב (*šākab*, "to lay") appears in the Hebrew text without its customary preposition "with," used to indicate consensual sexual intercourse. The result is a construction that accords with the brutal crudity of our modern expression, making the final phrase of this verse, "and he laid her." The NIV combines the effect of the verbs "force" and "lay" to tersely translate, "he raped her." The notice that Amnon was stronger than Tamar implies physical resistance on her part. To wise speech, Tamar adds courageous action, but she is overpowered.

13:15-19. Just as this account began with Amnon's feelings, so also now that rape has been committed, Amnon's feelings continue to occupy the narrative. He is filled with intense hatred (v. 15; NRSV, "loathing"). His so-called love (v. 1) is exposed as lust and the power to do violence. The reversal from desire to repulsion is immediate and revealing. He had no regard for Tamar beyond the gratification of his own desires. Now he cannot face what he has done. He orders Tamar, "Get up and get out!" (v. 15*b*). Amnon has used Tamar, and he is now through with her.

Again Tamar boldly protests. Although bruised, bleeding, and humiliated, Tamar understands the repercussions of what is happening. She is not paralyzed by Amnon's violence and hatred, but sees her interests clearly. She argues that to send her away now would be an even greater wrong than he has already committed (v. 16). According to Israelite law, Amnon is now guilty of the rape of an unbetrothed virgin, and the law demanded that he make the bridal payment and marry her (Exod 22:16-17; see also Deut 22:28-29). Although she has been brutalized, to be sent away would subject Tamar to the cultural horror of a life of permanent shame, unmarriageability, and childlessness. She would be deprived even of the limited opportunities available to women for life as a full part of the community. The marriage required by law in such a situation would at least give her some rights and some sense of public honor.

For the second time, Amnon will not listen to Tamar (v. 16*b;* cf. v. 14*a*). He calls his servant and has Tamar forcibly removed from his presence and the door bolted (vv. 17, 18*b*). It is the last recorded contact he has with her; he is through with her. No shred of regard for her fate is revealed.

Perhaps Amnon thought that was the end of the matter and that Tamar would slink away in silence and shame. But Tamar will not participate in a conspiracy of silence. She boldly makes public what Amnon has done and forces the world of power and kingdom to face the reality of this violence and her humiliation. Apparently princesses wore a special garment that signified their virginity and marriageability (v. 18*a*). Tamar now tears this garment and goes forth in grief and public lamentation, with ashes on her head, with her hand raised upon her head, and with loud weeping (v. 19). Tamar's public outcry ensures that the chain of consequences will now flow unbroken from Amnon's act (and originally from David's acts of adultery and murder). Violence will beget violence.

13:20-22. Tamar's speaking and acting are finished in the story. The narrator's interest shifts to the repercussions of these events in the world of royal power. It is Absalom who will now be the central figure. He meets his sister in her grief and humiliation and seems to know that it is Amnon who has done this thing (v. 20*a*). Absalom urges Tamar to "be quiet for now, my sister; he is your brother; do not take this to heart" (v. 20*b*). Absalom's response minimizes Tamar's pain and humiliation and suggests to Tamar that not much can be done, since it is a family matter. She is urged to silence and the stifling of feelings. Some suggest that in the light of Absalom's later revenge against Amnon, he is not minimizing Tamar's experience but merely biding his time.[309] Absalom was certainly deeply offended by Amnon's assault on his sister. Nevertheless, he does not share with Tamar his anger toward Amnon or even his sympathy with her plight.[310] Absalom's revenge

---

309. C. C. Conroy, *Absalom, Absalom! Narrative and Language in 2 Sam 13–20,* AnBib 81 (Rome: Pontifical Biblical Institute, 1978) 35, finds in Absalom's spare response a "tone of tenderness." Trible, *Texts of Terror,* 51, suggests that Absalom is not minimizing but using euphemisms that underscore the unspeakable horror of the rape. See Cooper-White's response to Trible and discussion of this issue in *The Cry of Tamar,* 8-9, 265.

310. Brueggemann, *First and Second Samuel,* 288-89, writes that "Absalom assures his sister he will carry her wrong in his heart." Although subsequent events may show that he did so, the text does not depict Absalom as assuring Tamar that her burden is shared. In fact, though he may take the matter to heart, he tells Tamar not to do so (v. 20).

seems to be more a matter of restoring family honor and securing his own place in the succession than a matter of solidarity with Tamar. He does take her into his house, where she remains a "desolate" woman, a term that indicates her status as a woman without hope of marriage or family who must live with permanent public humiliation (v. 20b).

On hearing of this atrocity, King David responds by becoming "very angry" (v. 21a). But his anger is of little consequence. We are told that he will not punish Amnon because he loves him as his firstborn (v. 21b).[311] David does nothing. We have known David

as a man of decisive action, but in this and subsequent episodes narrating the drama of his own family, David is curiously passive and indecisive. Perhaps David is himself so morally compromised by his own flagrant crimes (chap. 11) that he cannot confront the excesses of his sons. David may be angry, but he joins the conspiracy of silence around the rape of Tamar, and in doing so he unwittingly allows Absalom's murderous revenge to run its course. It is to this further violence that v. 22 points. Absalom speaks neither "good nor bad" to Amnon, which may mean he avoided him altogether. Instead Absalom nurtures hatred for his brother because Amnon had raped (the word is ʿānâ again) his sister, Tamar.

311. The Septuagint, with some support from the Qumran texts, is the basis for the fuller text of the NRSV. Most commentators have adopted this reading, but the NIV follows the briefer Hebrew text.

REFLECTIONS

1. Although this is a story of princes and princesses in an ancient kingdom, the violence it narrates is shockingly timeless. Pamela Cooper-White has found in the text of this ancient story a witness to issues of violence against women that are still with us.

Tamar's story, sadly, is still modern:
❖ Tamar was sexually assaulted, not by a stranger, but by someone she knew.
❖ The violation took place not in a dark alley or in a desolate park, but by a member of her own family in his home.
❖ Tamar was exploited through one of her most vulnerable traits—her kindness and her upbringing to take care of the other.
❖ Tamar said no; her no was not respected.
❖ When Tamar sought help, she was told to keep quiet.
❖ The process for achieving justice and restitution was taken out of her hands entirely and carried forward by her brother—it became men's business.
❖ In the end, it was her perpetrator for whom her father mourned, not for her.
❖ The end of Tamar's story happens without her.[312]

The pattern of Tamar's story is repeated in the story of many modern women who are the victims of rape or incest, yet whose experience has been denied or hidden.

This text is not read publicly in the church, and it is seldom preached. Persons experienced at Bible study in the church are often shocked to have this story called to their attention. They had no idea such a story was a part of the biblical tradition. It is as if the silence counseled by Absalom (v. 20) has extended through the centuries to the present. It is easy to understand why the story has been ignored. We do not like to be faced with the brutal realities of which this story speaks. Even less do we like to think such stories are a part of our Scripture. What does it mean that David's line, from which the Messiah is to come, has been determined by the course of such violent events?

While it is easy to understand why many would prefer not to read this story, there are important reasons why it should be read. In reading this story, we are forced to recognize our own experience in this ancient tale. There is an empowerment that

312. Pamela Cooper-White, *The Cry of Tamar: Violence Against Women and the Church's Response* (Minneapolis: Fortress, 1995) 4-5.

comes from recognizing that this story names present realities as well as those long past. If such stories are read as part of our biblical tradition, similar stories can be faced in our own lives, in the lives of our family and friends, and in the life of our communities. To read of the courage and wisdom of Tamar may encourage those who have been victimized in our own time to give voice to their own experience, so that conspiracies of silence do not allow continued violence to be denied or ignored. To read of Tamar's pain can enable others to voice their own pain so that it is not borne alone. If the church can be the place of such reading and such voicing, then there is hope that the church might provide a community prepared to take action against continued patterns of violence against women in our culture and to stand in caring support of those who have already been victimized.

2. This story is also a reminder of the way in which resorting to violence and exploitation gives rise to continuing chains of tragedy and suffering. Acts of violence are seldom isolated events. David's own actions in the "taking" of Bathsheba and the murder of Uriah provided the model for Amnon's violent use of power to fulfill his own desires. Amnon's brutal rape of Tamar kindles a hatred in Absalom that will lead to further violence (13:23-36). Absalom's violent revenge will result in alienation, which leads to rebellion, war, and further death (chaps. 15–19). It is no different in our own time. Those who brutalize others have often been witnesses to or victims of such violence themselves.

In this story, it is David who might have broken the chain of violence he himself had begun. But, though angered, he does nothing, and his refusal to act continues the chain. In reading this story, we are encouraged to recognize the ways in which we grow angry at the violence of our society, but choose not to act. We live in a society in which gun ownership continues to rise and schools have been forced to develop policies to deal with weapons brought to school. Drive-by shootings are a reality in every urban area of the country. Bombings of the federal building in Oklahoma City and at the Atlanta Olympics in 1996 raise the specter of domestic terrorism. Dozens of African American churches have been burned in senseless acts of destruction. We live in a violent world in which genocidal war masquerades as "ethnic cleansing" in Bosnia, where tourists are slaughtered in Luxor for the sake of a political statement, and where the potential for peace in the Middle East is undermined by violent Arab and Israeli extremists. These are dramatic evidences of violence, but they are fueled by a tolerance of violence in smaller ways, such as an unwillingness to face the acceptance of violence as commonplace in our entertainment media (where women are often the victims of graphic and sexually charged acts of violence), and a growing lack of civility in personal and political relationships. David's example should teach us that anger is not enough. Tolerance and inaction in the face of violence fosters further violence. Because David did nothing, this story ends with a hatred that will continue the chain of violence. Our tolerance and inaction in the face of violence will likewise ensure the continuity of violence in our midst.

2 Samuel 13:23-39, Absalom Kills Amnon

COMMENTARY

The unfolding story of tragic events in David's family continues. After biding his time for two years, Absalom takes revenge for the rape of Tamar by killing his half-brother Amnon. Although this act has the immediate effect of forcing Absalom into exile from

Jerusalem, nevertheless, it places him next in the line of succession to David's throne. In this ongoing story, family events are never far separated from the machinations of power in the affairs of the kingdom, and it is the eventual outcome of these power struggles that most interests the narrator. Although this episode records Amnon's death, Absalom is the main focus of the narrative. These events are part of the prelude to Absalom's rebellion (chaps. 15–19).

13:23-29. Absalom invites the royal household to a sheepshearing at his properties some miles to the north of Jerusalem (v. 1). This was undoubtedly not an invitation to the special work of shearing but to the celebration and feasting that follow the work (see 1 Sam 25:2-8). Although the initial invitation is to the "king's sons," presumably accompanied by their usual entourages, Absalom makes a special invitation to David, the king, himself (v. 2). This may have been an expected custom and courtesy. David graciously declines the invitation, on grounds that the king's presence with all of the necessary attending servants would be a burden on Absalom's hospitality. Although Absalom presses, the king maintains his refusal, but gives a royal blessing on the occasion (v. 3).

There is no way to know whether Absalom had already planned this event as the setting for his revenge or if the absence of David gave him an opportune moment, which he seized. Perhaps David was suspicious when Absalom singled out Amnon as one whose presence he especially desired. David questions the need of Amnon's attendance (v. 4), but when Absalom insists, David finally allows Amnon and all the other princes to travel to Absalom's feast (v. 5). Whether planned or serendipitous, Absalom finally has what his vengeance requires: the presence of Amnon away from the watchful eye of David and a location away from Jerusalem that will allow for his own escape.

Absalom orders his servants to murder Amnon. He instructs them to wait until Amnon is drunk with wine and to kill him at Absalom's command (v. 28a). Lest his servants waver in their loyalty, Absalom assures them that he will take full responsibility for the command and urges their courage and valor (v. 28b). Like his father, Absalom does not kill

directly but orders murder through the hands of loyal servants (cf. David's order to Joab, 11:14-15). Absalom's trust in his servants' loyalty is well placed. With the command, "Strike Amnon!" the deed is done; no details of the actual murder are recorded. We hear only that the servants did as commanded and that the rest of the king's sons flee on mules. They undoubtedly feared a wholesale massacre of royal heirs. Absalom's purpose at the moment seems limited to revenge. He does not yet plan a rebellion and seizing of power. If so, he might have waited until an occasion when David was present and struck him as well.

13:30-39. The narrative lingers dramatically over a false report that came to David claiming that Absalom had killed all of the king's sons (v. 30). David tears his garments and lies prostrate in grief over the prospect of such a terrible loss (v. 31). His grief proves misplaced, but it foreshadows a later moment of terrible grief when it is Absalom who lies dead (18:33[19:1]). Strangely, Jonadab, the friend who had plotted with Amnon in his rape of Tamar, advises the king that it is surely only Amnon who is dead (vv. 32-33). He has no explicit report to this effect, but he cites the rape of Tamar as the source of Absalom's animosity. Jonadab expected something like this, perhaps because he himself feared retaliation for his part in the matter.

Jonadab's confident assertion is borne out a short time later when the watchman sees many people coming on the road to Jerusalem (v. 34). They are the king's sons, who arrive weeping bitterly over the assassination of their brother, and no doubt out of fear for their own lives (v. 36). Jonadab takes credit for his accurate prediction (v. 35).

In the midst of this narration of David's anxious waiting, we are told for the first of three times that "Absalom fled" (vv. 34a, 37, 38). Absalom takes refuge with his maternal grandfather, Talmai, the king of Geshur (v. 37; cf. 3:3). He remains there for three years (v. 38). We are told that David mourned daily for his son (v. 37b), but the text is ambiguous at first about which son he mourned— Amnon, who was dead, or Absalom, who was a fugitive in exile from his own land. Verse 39 resolves this ambiguity. It is Absalom for whom David's heart longs. The text tells us that he is consoled over Amnon's death; now he misses the son who yet lives. David's ability to face death and go on with life reminds us of the story of the death of his first son with Bathsheba (12:15b-23). We wonder why David did not simply bring Absalom home. Yet, there are limits to what even a king can do. Absalom is guilty of the murder of the crown prince. Even David might find it difficult to excuse such a crime publicly, in spite of his personal longings. It takes a complicated negotiation, engineered by Joab, to bring him home (chap. 14).

REFLECTIONS

This tragic story of revenge and murder is yet another link in the chain of violence that began with David's adultery with Bathsheba and murder of Uriah. Now David's two oldest sons have repeated his actions: One has taken for himself the object of his sexual desire, and the other has killed for the sake of his own personal and political interests. Tragically, the result of following their father's path is that one son is dead and the other in exile. The overriding message of this text is once again that violence leads to yet more violence (see Reflections at 13:1-22).

The difference here is that Absalom believed his violence against Amnon was just recompense for Amnon's rape of Tamar (although we cannot rule out Absalom's political interests in the succession as a factor). But this does not end the matter. Absalom has continued the chain of violence, and the chain has not yet played out its consequences. It is in reading this story in our time that we must learn that righteous violence continues the chain of violence, as surely as violence done out of baser motives. Absalom's solution of taking justice violently into his own hands is as unacceptable as David's refusal to take action at all (v. 21). Neither denial nor violent retaliation ends the chain of violence.

Recently, the FBI made arrests of a group planning to bomb the homes of anti-abortion leaders. The actions of this group were intended to be righteous retaliation for the bombing of several abortion clinics in which one person had been killed. What a strange turn of events. In the name of preserving life and protecting freedom of choice, opposing groups are willing to take life and permanently end choice. The cycle of violence will continue unless someone steps forward willing to break that cycle.

One wonders whether the rising tide of public opinion in support of capital punishment is not motivated more by a righteous desire for revenge than by any real desire to break the patterns that lead to violent crimes. Such a willingness simply to justify the return of violence for violence will not break patterns of violent crime in our communities. The way of Absalom runs the risk of deepening the alienation in our own communities rather than resolving it. As with Absalom, so with us, the consequences could be great.

2 Samuel 14:1-33, The Restoration of Absalom

COMMENTARY

This chapter continues the narration of events in the aftermath of Amnon's rape of Tamar (13:1-22) and Absalom's vengeance killing of Amnon (13:23-39). Absalom has passed three years in exile from Jerusalem, fearing retribution (13:38). This chapter tells first of Absalom's return to Jerusalem, through the timely intervention of David's right-hand man, Joab, and a wise woman from Tekoa, whom Joab recruits for his scheme (vv. 1-24). David is involved in rendering a hypothetical judgment that is used in a manner similar to Nathan's parable (12:1-7) to enable David to see his own action and allow Absalom's return to Jerusalem, but not into the king's presence. Verses 25-27 give the reader a fuller description of Absalom's attractiveness. Finally, the story tells of Absalom's use of Joab again, after two years, to bring about a personal restoration of relationship to his father, David (vv. 28-33). The relationship may be genuine, but it is fragile. Five years of bitter separation between father and son cannot be easily bridged or forgotten. The kiss of reconciliation comes too late (v. 33), and almost immediately Absalom begins his plans for rebellion (chap. 15).

Many scholars believe vv. 15-17 have become displaced and that they properly follow v. 7.[313] These verses return to the hypothetical case of the woman's surviving son after David has already rendered judgment in this matter and the woman has given up her role as the aggrieved widow (vv. 8-11). The argument in favor of this reordering is persuasive, and the discussion will follow that reordered pattern.

14:1-7, 15-17. Joab takes the initiative to restore Absalom because of his regard for David (v. 1). As subsequent events reveal, Joab has no personal concern for Absalom (cf. 14:29-33; 18:14). Perhaps Joab believes that he can take David's mind off of Absalom and restore his mind to matters of the kingdom (cf. 19:1-8).

Without preamble, Joab launches a stratagem by bringing a wise woman from Tekoa, approximately ten miles south of Jerusalem. He instructs her to take on the role of a widow woman in mourning and to go before the king (v. 2). Joab gives her the words to say. There has been some debate about the character and role of the woman from Tekoa.[314] The use of the adjective "wise" (חכמה ḥǎkāmâ, v. 2a) probably does not indicate a formal office (e.g., sage or teacher). It may indicate that she was "clever" or "shrewd." Joab may have given her the "words" that define the

hypothetical case she brings to David, but her interaction with David and the skill with which she manipulates his response draw the reader's admiration. She flatters David, saying that he has "wisdom like the wisdom of the angel of God" (v. 20). Since she clearly enables David to see things he cannot see for himself, we are left with the judgment that she is certainly as wise as the king and, therefore, deserving of the adjective that describes her in v. 2.[315]

In vv. 4-7, the woman comes before David as a petitioner seeking the king's aid. She plays the hypothetical role of a widow whose two sons have fought, and tragically one has killed the other. Now, her family demands that the surviving son be given up and executed as a murderer, thus leaving her with no sons and with no one to carry on her dead husband's name and lineage. Verses 15-17 seem to continue this telling of the woman's story and express the motivation that caused her to bring her case before the king. She seeks deliverance by the king from the strict demands that justice would impose upon her, cutting her and her son off from the "heritage of God" (v. 16). She ends with the appropriate flattery of the king's ability to discern "good and evil" and invokes the name of the Lord (v. 17).

Like Nathan's parable (12:1-4), the woman's story seems to be a juridical parable designed to elicit a judgment from David on his own situation and then point out to him the parallels in his own life.[316] Unlike Nathan, the woman's case is directed toward eliciting an action of reconciliation on David's part rather than evoking a judgment against the king. The outcome is not as sharp and dramatic as in the case of Nathan's parable,[317] but it succeeds in forcing David out of the strict

313. See McCarter, *II Samuel,* 345-46; Anderson, *2 Samuel,* 185-86.

314. The poles of opinion are defined by Claudia V. Camp, "The Wise Women of 2 Samuel: A Role Model for Women in Early Israel," *CBQ* 43 (1981) 14-29, who argues that this woman must have had considerable standing and authority in her own community, and by Bellis, *Helpmates, Harlots, and Heroes,* 154, who writes, "The woman is merely playing a role that has been scripted for her by a man. Although she is called wise, there is a problem. Either her own work is attributed to a man, a real enough possibility, or she is not really wise." The first of the positions probably argues for more than can be said on the basis of this text, and the second underestimates the skill and latitude the woman exercises in the role assigned her by Joab.

315. Brueggemann, *First and Second Samuel,* 292, writes, "Perhaps 'wise' means one who is able to discern, articulate, and practice life outside the categories of bureaucratic perception, the capacity to see connections and hidden forces that are not visible in conventional modes of administrative thought."

316. On juridical parables, see Simon, "The Poor Man's Ewe-Lamb," 207-42.

317. Willey makes the interesting argument that the woman's story is a "clever parody" of the Nathan parable: "By setting up a tale similar to the Nathan tale, the narrator raises our expectations for a similarly luminous outcome, but then fails splendidly to deliver. This importunate woman reads not as a second Nathan, come again to set things straight, but as a parody of his methods, fit for a king doomed to moral confusion." See Patricia K. Willey, "The Importunate Woman of Tekoa and How She Got Her Way," in *Reading Between Texts: Intertextuality and the Hebrew Bible,* ed. Danna Nolan Fewell, Literary Currents in Biblical Interpretation (Louisville: Westminster/John Knox, 1992) 115-31, esp. 128.

dictates of the law, which he must uphold as king, and into the thinking of unthinkable alternatives. He is forced to consider the possibilities of mercy, new future, and an end to violence and vengeance.

14:8-11. The king is moved to mercy and promises to issue orders on the woman's behalf (v. 8). The woman constantly interrupts the king in the process of his ruling. She declares that she will bear the guilt (v. 9a), presumably the guilt that might be incurred from going against the letter of the law. She further declares that the king and his throne will be guiltless (v. 9b). Even if David does not yet see his own situation in the woman's story, the reader certainly catches the irony of such a declaration. David and his throne are not guiltless. The reader is forced to remember the chain of violence that stretches from David to Amnon and to Absalom. David's throne and the pretenders to it are awash in guilt. David reassures the woman that his own authority will reach out against any who speak against her (v. 10).

The woman persists and wants explicit reassurance in the name of the Lord that the "avenger of blood" will not take her son's life (v. 11a). Some regard this "avenger of blood" as an officer in the community for seeing that justice is done in cases such as the murder the woman reports. Others see this role as one assumed by a member of the family with the responsibility to seek blood vengeance in such cases. Indeed, the woman does refer to her family as having "risen against" her (v. 7).[318] In any case, David gives her the reassurance she desires and pronounces an oath: "As the LORD lives, not one hair of your son shall fall to the ground" (v. 11b). It is the same guarantee of safety that the people used to protect Jonathan against Saul's unwise execution of the letter of the law (1 Sam 14:45). It also binds David by an oath, after which the woman abandons her role and reveals the true matter that David has pronounced upon. Whether such an oath is binding when the hypothetical case is unmasked may be debatable, but the real force here is moral, and not legal suasion.

14:12-14, 18-20. David has been led by the woman's skillfully played role to compromise the law of blood vengeance. As Brueggemann has aptly stated it, "When the 'killer' is acknowledged to be a beloved son, vengeance can be overcome."[319] The woman can now drop her ruse and reveal the true nature of the concern for which Joab sent her. It is a moment of risk and courage. One does not meddle lightly in the king's family matters. Her tone becomes deferential as she asks and receives permission to speak a word to the king (v. 12).

The intent of the woman's speech is clear, although some elements are problematic and uncertain. She tells David straightforwardly that in rendering judgment on her hypothetical case he has convicted himself, inasmuch as he has allowed himself to lose a beloved son by banishment (v. 13b). In effect, David has played the role of the blood avenger toward Absalom. She suggests that this is an offense against the people of God, perhaps indicating Absalom's popularity with the people (v. 13a). Verse 14a seems to be speaking of Amnon's death as something that cannot be undone, much as water spilled on the ground cannot be retrieved. She argues that God would find a way to restore an outcast (v. 14b). This section of the woman's speech is awkward and oblique in its application to David. Perhaps the indirection is a mark of deference before the king. Nevertheless, the intent of the speech is clear: If David can restore the son to the woman in her hypothetical case, then he can find a way to restore Absalom to his own family and kingdom.

David not only sees the woman's point, but he sees behind it. He insists on her candor (v. 18) and asks if the hand of Joab is in this charade (v. 19a). The woman admits that it was Joab's doing, but not without considerable flattery of the king and his wise ability to see and know all things (vv. 19b-20). With the stratagem uncovered, the woman no doubt fears how the king will react. So she praises David extravagantly as having "wisdom like the wisdom of the angel of God."

14:21-24. Now that he sees, David acts. He sees that the case brought to him is really a petition about Absalom, and he grants the petition and orders that Absalom be brought home (v. 21). He deals directly with Joab, who seems to be present, and the woman is suddenly gone from the story. Joab knows he

---

318. See the discussion in Anderson, *2 Samuel*, 188.

319. Brueggemann, *First and Second Samuel*, 293.

has pushed the boundaries of his friendship and loyalty to David, and he acknowledges David's decision with deference, flattery, and blessing. But he also clearly takes credit for the idea (v. 22).

But the matter is not settled. David has been pressed to act as a father, but he cannot give up the role of king. Joab brings Absalom to Jerusalem (v. 23), but David will not allow Absalom into his presence (v. 24). The father has brought him home, but the king will not receive him. This situation will continue for two full years (v. 28). A reconciling moment has come near, but it has passed without actualization.

14:25-27. The narrative pauses for a personal note about Absalom. We are told of his handsome appearance (v. 25), and we remember the striking appearance of Saul (1 Sam 9:2) and his tragic fate. We also recall the Lord's reminder to the prophet Samuel that God looks not on appearance but on the heart (1 Sam 16:7); nevertheless the story-teller cannot resist noting the handsome appearance of David when he enters the story (1 Sam 16:12). Absalom is admired for his physical perfection and a magnificent head of hair (vv. 25b-26). This particular description foreshadows Absalom's fate, when he will be caught fast by his hair in a tree while attempting to escape the defeat of his military force. This is usually interpreted as the entanglement of his hair; his vanity becomes his undoing. A final and poignant personal note is added when the narrator reports that Absalom has three sons and one daughter, but only the daughter is named (v. 27). Her name is Tamar, a testimony to the feelings Absalom carried for his violated sister. Even if he took Amnon's life in part for his own political purposes, there is little reason to doubt that Absalom was deeply troubled by the defiling of his sister, Tamar.

14:28-33. Two years have passed without Absalom's return to the court. It is almost as if he is under house arrest (v. 28). Absalom takes the initiative to change this situation, and, like his father, he knows that Joab is the man to make things happen. Absalom sends for Joab, but twice Joab ignores the prince's summons (v. 29). Joab is loyal to the father, not the son. Absalom resorts to extreme measures. He orders his servants to set Joab's field on fire (v. 30), and this brings Joab to ask what in the world Absalom is doing (v. 31). Absalom then makes clear his desire to be brought before the king and suggests he would rather be in exile or even executed if he is still considered guilty (v. 32). It is a risky and bold move. David must make good his full rehabilitation at court or complete the demands of blood guilt, now delayed five years.

Again Joab is the go-between, and when David hears the message he does send for Absalom. With appropriate deference, Absalom prostrates himself before the king, and "the king kissed Absalom" (v. 33). This is often treated as a reconciliation between father and son. The NRSV subtitles this section "David Forgives Absalom." Perhaps David's kiss could have signaled a restored relationship, but we have the impression that the kiss came at least two years too late. At no point does David take the initiative to restore Absalom to relationship. When the kiss finally comes, it is because Absalom forces the moment. David has not seen Absalom for five years. Even when official forgiveness allows Absalom's return to Jerusalem, David makes clear that personal forgiveness is not offered. David's mind was on Absalom (14:1), but he seems unable to allow the father in him to take precedence over the king. The text is clear: It is the king who kisses Absalom, not the father. David's kiss seems grudging and formal, and we are given no indication that David's heart, which may long for Absalom (14:1), is allowed to take precedence over royal policy. We are not surprised when chap. 15 begins the story of Absalom's overt rebellion and attempt to seize David's throne.

REFLECTIONS

This episode in the drama of David's family and kingdom speaks to us of the opportunity for new beginnings and of how easily those opportunities can be missed.

1. The first part of the story is a hopeful testimony that it is possible to move beyond vengeance to a new beginning. The cycle of violence and the dislocations it creates can be broken. This is genuine good news for those of us who read this story in a time when violence has reached such deadly and far-reaching proportions in our society. That the cycle of violence can be broken is also good news for those who know the deadly patterns of violence and vengeance in their own families. Patterns of abuse, exploitation, and alienation have divided our own families as surely as the family of David, and the results are often a paralysis that imagines no new beginnings are possible and the continuation of patterns of abuse from one generation to the next.

In this narrative on the possibility of a new beginning, Joab, of all people, first envisions an alternative future—a future not dictated by custom, traditional patterns, or juridical realities. Why was it not possible for Absalom to come home and make a new beginning? But the real power for new beginnings comes through courageous and imaginative speech that allows David to perceive an alternative future. A wise and resourceful woman tells a story that imagines vengeance could be foregone in favor of compassion. In that story, David sees new possibilities for his own story and breaks the demands of custom and law to allow the return of an outcast and the dropping of demands for further blood.

In our society, our churches, and our own lives we are often so busy analyzing the reality of our situations that we fail to imagine more hopeful scenarios and tell stories that make them possible. Pastoral care in our churches has borrowed the insights of the psychotherapy movement and understood how helpful it can be to retell the story of our past and claim the past without being controlled by it. This story suggests that we should also be telling stories of our future in ways that open new possibilities and release us from the tyranny of our own present. We have identified the form of the woman's story as "parable," a type of story that speaks of the familiar but surprises the listener with new realities about his or her own life. Christians, of course, think of Jesus' parables and the way in which they opened new possibilities for the listener. For this story, we cannot help recalling the parable of the prodigal son (Luke 15:11-32), a story of a son whose choices alienated and exiled him from the love of a father. Like the woman's story to David, Jesus' parable suggests that separation need not be the accepted reality. There can be return, forgiveness, and new beginnings.

The church is also in the business of telling stories through which persons can come to see themselves and their possibilities in new ways. The biblical story itself can serve in this way. In our preaching and teaching, in our study and devotion, we should seek ways to allow the biblical story to intersect our own stories and encourage openness to the new possibilities that come out of those intersections. Likewise, the sharing of our own faith stories and the witness of ways in which we have experienced the overcoming of fear and alienation can allow others to envision those same possibilities in their lives. The woman's story was one in which she refused to let the law have the last word about her son. The community of faith, like the woman, should constantly tell stories that affirm the ultimate worth of all persons regardless of the circumstances that make them outcasts and separate them from one another. This enables the church, like David, to act in ways that redeem the outcast and move beyond alienation.

2. Tragically, this episode in David's story is not just about new beginnings made possible, but also about opportunities lost. Because of the woman's courageous and imaginative speech, David saw an alternative future in relationship to his son, but when Absalom returned to Jerusalem, David failed to actualize that new future. He does not see his son or receive him. Two years of silent proximity pass, and Absalom forces an encounter. David kisses Absalom, but the kiss comes too late.

In the parable of the prodigal son, the father also kisses the son (Luke 15:20), but there the kiss marks the graceful seizing of the moment when a new future can be realized. The father's kiss comes immediately, spontaneously, unconditionally. David could not act in grace and forgiveness when the moment for it came, and the moment passed. The kiss comes too late, and a resentful Absalom begins to plot rebellion (15:1-12).

The courageous and imaginative telling of our biblical and faith stories can create possibilities for new beginnings. But the moment for those new beginnings must be acted upon. Whether it is the moment of hopeful new alternatives for our lives, for our churches, or for our communities, it requires a giving up of past realities defined by habit, custom, tradition, or fear for the risk of grace. We cannot embrace the future and nurse the wounds of the past. David wanted his son nearby, but he could not embrace him. David wanted a new beginning as a father, but he could not abandon the juridical judgment of the king.

In Israel's story, God has the experience of a parent with an exiled child in the time of Israel's Babylonian exile. God's response, through the prophet of the exile, is to say: "I, I am He who blots out your transgressions for my own sake, and I will not remember your sins" (Isa 43:25 NRSV). God risks the speaking of forgiveness and understands such forgiving as being for God's "own sake." For his own sake, David needed to forgive and claim the new future opened by the wise woman's imaginative speech. For our own sake, as persons of faith and as the church, we need to model God's forgiveness in the world. We must speak imaginatively of new beginnings in lives and communities, leave alienated pasts behind in forgiveness, and embrace the new futures made possible in God's grace.

2 Samuel 15:1–20:22, Absalom's Rebellion

OVERVIEW

The story of Absalom's rebellion stands as the centerpiece of the so-called succession narrative. The stories of Amnon's rape of Absalom's sister, Tamar, and Absalom's subsequent murder of Amnon (chaps. 13–14) are primarily narrated to explain how it came to be that David's son Absalom was so alienated from David that he tried to seize the throne. This entire course of events is the grim fulfillment of the judgment pronounced by the prophet Nathan on David for his sin in the adultery with Bathsheba and the murder of Uriah (chap. 12).

The narration of Absalom's rebellion unfolds primarily in a series of conversations between characters in the story. There is a noticeable lack of interest in historical detail while the focus remains on the unfolding personal drama between David and his rebellious son. Other characters enter the story as they support or oppose David in this time of revolt. While Absalom's rebellion is an event dealing with the future course of political power in Israel, it is in the end a personal tragedy that ends in David's grief over yet another son (18:33).

2 Samuel 15:1-12, The Seeds of Revolt

COMMENTARY

This episode divides into two scenes. The first (vv. 1-6) describes the activity of Absalom as he ingratiates himself to the people of Israel and gathers popular support at the expense of David's reputation. The second scene (vv. 7-12) tells of Absalom's overt declaration of

rebellion against David from the ancient capital city of Judah in Hebron.

15:1-6. Apparently only a short time after Absalom's reunion with David (14:33), Absalom surrounds himself with the trappings of a royal prince and heir apparent. The chariot, horses, and fifty men (presumably soldiers) that accompany him on his movements in and around Jerusalem (v. 1) must have given Absalom considerable public visibility. We do not know whether he was officially considered the heir to the throne; at a later point when David's son Adonijah declares his claim to the throne, he, too, surrounds himself with chariots, horses, and fifty men (1 Kgs 1:5). This may well be an entourage that indicates potential royal status.

Absalom embarks on a strategy of ingratiating himself with those who are discontent with David's system of administering justice. Absalom would position himself in the gate to encounter those who brought a suit before the king (v. 2). He would express sympathy with their case as well as decry the lack of anyone available to hear the case (v. 3). Absalom then avowed that if he were judge in the land all who had a cause could come before him and receive justice (v. 4). Clearly Absalom is exploiting a weakness in David's system of justice in order to build public support, but it is difficult to tell just what the nature of the discontent was toward David's justice. The king in Israel had a judicial function and was required to render judgments on difficult cases that could not be clearly ruled upon in other judicial arenas (cf. Ps 72:1-4, 12-14; Isa 11:3-5). Twice we have seen this role of the king exploited to bring personal matters before David (by Nathan, 12:1-15; by the wise woman of Tekoa, 14:1-24). It may have been that in this time it had become too difficult to gain access to David in order to bring a case before him. Or perhaps there was a feeling that David should appoint an official to hear cases on his behalf. Some believe that Absalom's offer to act in this role is an effort to appear as an innovator proposing solutions on the people's behalf.[320] David may have been unwilling to delegate royal authority in this manner, a reluctance Absalom now exploits.

Whatever the particulars, discontent with David's justice must have been widespread, as evidenced by Absalom's success at garnering support for his rebellion. Absalom, whom we know was handsome (14:25-26), clearly also possesses personal charm. He embraces

and kisses those who bow before him (vv. 5-6a) and in this way "stole the hearts of the people of Israel" (v. 6b). The people are made to feel that they have a friend in the royal court. No doubt, Absalom's appeal to those who felt they were denied adequate attention from the king's justice were supplemented by those who had other reasons to want David's rule overturned. When David retreats from Jerusalem, for instance, he encounters those who still hold a grudge against him for having displaced the house of Saul (cf. 16:3, 5-8).

15:7-12. Absalom has built his popular base of support, and now the moment for overt rebellion has come. Most take the reference to four years in v. 7 as the time since his reunion with David (14:33). Only then would Absalom have had the freedom to engage in the activities of vv. 1-6. That Absalom felt the need to seize the throne while David was yet alive may be the best evidence that he was not clearly designated as the successor to the throne. His rehabilitation may not have included restoration of his succession rights.

Once again Absalom asks permission of David to make a journey with an entourage from the court (cf. 13:23-29). One would think David might think twice about this request. This time Absalom claims the need to go to Hebron to offer sacrifices in fulfillment of a vow he made while exiled in Geshur (vv. 7-8). The king gives permission and ironically wishes him peace (v. 9).

Absalom's true intent becomes clear in v. 10. He sends secret messengers throughout Israel. With the blowing of the ram's horn (a traditional part of enthronement rituals; see 1 Kgs 1:34; 2), Absalom is to be pronounced king at Hebron. Hebron was a symbolically appropriate place for this announced coup. It was an ancient Yahwistic shrine and the capital of the tribe of Judah. Absalom himself was born there (3:2-3), but more important David was anointed king in Hebron over both Judah (2:4) and Israel (5:1). It may well be that the people of Hebron were disgruntled over the movement of David's capital from Hebron to Jerusalem and welcomed Absalom's attention to its status. In any case, Absalom's launch of revolt from the capital of Judah makes clear that his rebellion had the support of both the northern and southern tribes of Israel. He

320. See K. W. Whitelam, *The Just King: Monarchical Judicial Authority in Ancient Israel*, JSOTSup 12 (Sheffield: University of Sheffield Press, 1979) 140-41.

was not simply exploiting discontent from die-hard Saulides.

Absalom had shrewdly brought two hundred men as his guests from Jerusalem. The text tells us they were innocent and did not know what was about to happen (v. 11). This was a clever move on Absalom's part. No doubt the two hundred were primarily those whom Absalom considered friends and supporters. By being with him in Hebron, they are already implicated in his declared usurpation of the throne. They are hardly in a position to disavow loyalty to Absalom, as some might have done in the greater safety of Jerusalem. From David's side, it appears that many influential men have cast their lot with Absalom. The story particularly calls our attention to the defection of one of David's "counselors" (advisers) to give assistance to Absalom (v. 12). His name is Ahithophel,

and the effort to thwart his shrewd advice becomes a chief interest later in the story (16:15–17:29).

Absalom's attack on Jerusalem must have come quickly but not immediately. Verse 12b suggests that some time was spent in Hebron to allow for support to gather strength. Interestingly, the narrator calls Absalom's rebellion a "conspiracy" (קשר qāšar), the same word used much earlier by Saul in accusing his own supporters of having collaborated with David against him (1 Sam 22:8, 13). The decisive moment has passed. Israel faces a civil war, and shockingly Absalom has seized the initiative and appears to have growing strength and numbers (v. 12b). We thought David's fugitive days were over, but he must flee for his life once again. (See Reflections at 15:13–16:14.)

2 Samuel 15:13–16:14, The Retreat from Jerusalem

COMMENTARY

The central portion of the narrative of Absalom's rebellion has a symmetrical structure.[321]

A   15:13–16:14, David's retreat from Jerusalem

B   16:15–17:23, the conflict of advisers

B′   17:24–19:8, the conflict of armies

A′   19:9-43, David's return to Jerusalem

This account of David's retreat from Jerusalem in the face of Absalom's advance on the capital city provides the opportunity for narration of five encounters that reveal to us something of David's support and opposition as well as evidence of his still considerable strength of character in the face of adversity. Information on the panicked beginning and the progress of David's retreat is found in 15:13-18, 23, 30-31; 16:5, 14. The encounters along the way include those with Ittai the Gittite (16:19-22), Abiathar and Zadok

(16:24-29), Hushai the Archite (15:32-36), Ziba (16:1-4), and Shimei (16:5-13). This account conveys an atmosphere of near panic, and decisions are made quickly in the heat of the moment with no opportunity for careful planning or strategy on David's part. The advantage seems to rest with Absalom, although he is himself offstage, and we hear only of his arrival to Jerusalem in v. 37.

15:13-18. A messenger brings David the ominous news that the "hearts of the Israelites have gone after Absalom" (v. 13). By contrast, David's constituency seems to be the bureaucracy of Jerusalem, whom he now summons to escape (v. 14). These verses speak of David's household, his officials, his servants, and the mercenary troops that are in his personal service. The implication is clear: The people are with Absalom. The odds do not look good for David.

The message brought to David must have indicated that Absalom was on the move toward Jerusalem. David's pleas are urgent, yet David takes command, and the order of the day is haste. He clearly does not regard Jerusalem as the ground on which he wishes to meet Absalom. Perhaps he

321. For a more detailed analysis of literary structures in these chapters, see Conroy, *Absalom, Absalom!* 89. See also Anderson, *2 Samuel*, 202.

fears encirclement or harm to the city. What David orders is a strategic retreat so that he may choose a more suitable time and place to meet Absalom's threat. All who are loyal to David in Jerusalem are evacuated except for ten concubines left to care for the royal household (v. 16). This reference clearly prepares for Absalom's action reported in 16:22.

David stops at the outskirts of the city to take stock of his entourage (v. 17). Those who pass in review (v. 18) are intended to give us some idea of David's remaining military resources. These consist primarily of non-Israelite mercenaries whose loyalty is to David and not to Israel as a nation. The manuscript evidence for this verse is very uncertain,[322] and many commentators believe the reference to the "six hundred" is an indication of David's personal army, retained from the days of his wilderness skirmishes with Saul and his service of the Philistines at Ziklag (cf. 1 Sam 23:13; 27:2; 30:9). Cherethites, Pelethites, and Gittites are mercenary groups of non-Israelites in David's service.

15:19-23. The first of five encounters for David during his retreat from Jerusalem is with Ittai, the commander of the Gittite troops in David's service. This may well be a contingent of fighting men from Gath whose loyalty David had won while serving as the Philistine commander of Ziklag under the king of Gath. David suggests in his comments to Ittai that he joined David only "yesterday" (v. 20a), which may indicate that the Gittite troops were not a part of David's longstanding personal army, but had joined him more recently.

David's speech to Ittai is gracious and generous. He speaks of Ittai's foreign status and suggests that this need not be Ittai's battle. He releases Ittai and his men from obligation, along with their families and households, and blesses them with steadfast love (חסד *ḥesed*) and faithfulness from the Lord (v. 20). Ittai's response is equally gracious and generous. He pledges loyalty to David in the name of David's God, Yahweh (the Lord), and by David's own life. Ittai declares that his lot is with David in life or in death (v. 21). David accepts this pledge, and Ittai, his men, and their families all march into exile with David

(v. 22). Sakenfeld has called attention to the parallel of this encounter with Naomi's effort to bid farewell to Ruth and her subsequent pledge of loyalty in Ruth 1:8, 16-17.[323] Like Ruth, Ittai is a foreigner who chooses loyalty to an Israelite and to Israel's God over alternatives that might have led to greater safety and less risk. In this context, we may be intended to see a contrast between Absalom, the disloyal son, and Ittai, the foreigner who is more loyal than the son. In the final battle against Absalom, Ittai is made one of the three top commanders (18:2, 5).

The route of David's retreat is through the Kidron Valley, which lies between Jerusalem and the Mount of Olives. The procession is one of weeping and sorrow. The wilderness, into which the procession heads, seems symbolic (v. 23).

15:24-30. David next encounters the priests Abiathar and Zadok, who come bearing the ark of the covenant (v. 24). It would seem logical to bring the ark with David's entourage as a sign of God's presence in their midst, but David rejects this alternative in a characteristic mixture of piety and pragmatism. He sends the ark and the priests back into Jerusalem. He realizes that possession even of this sacred object offers no guarantee of God's favor (cf. Israel's experience in 1 Samuel 4). It is not for David to command the presence of God. If David finds favor in God's eyes, then God will bring him back into the presence of the ark and Jerusalem, where it resides (v. 25). But if David finds no favor in God's eyes, the ark will not save him. God will do what seems right in the divine will (v. 26). David places his trust in the providence of God, not in the ark as a sacred object he can possess. This speech by David is reminiscent of the pious trust he relied on in the period when he was a fugitive from Saul in the wilderness. It is appropriate as he heads into the wilderness again as a fugitive that his faith should once again become the basis of his trust. His future is entrusted to the hand of God.

Yet, David's trustful faith does not rule out his own pragmatic action. This mixture of piety and pragmatism has often marked David's bold actions in the past. If Zadok and

322. McCarter, *II Samuel*, 363-64, discusses the textual issues in detail.

323. Katherine D. Sakenfeld, *The Meaning of Hesed in the Hebrew Bible: A New Inquiry*, HSM 17 (Missoula, Mont.: Scholars Press, 1978) 1-8.

Abiathar must return to Jerusalem with their two sons (v. 27), they can at least be David's eyes and ears in Absalom's city. David lays the foundation for an intelligence network and informs the priests where he will be waiting so that word can be brought to him (v. 28). The two priests return with the ark to Jerusalem to carry out this mandate.

David and his people proceed on their way over the Mount of Olives (v. 30). David weeps; his head is covered; he walks on bare feet. This is not the portrait of a political or military retreat. It is a penitential procession. David has cast his fate in the hands of God, and he moves forward in penance and in supplication for God's mercy. His people join him in these acts of ritual penance.

15:31-37. Even on his penitential journey David is active, receiving intelligence, meeting friends and foes, and making decisions. He receives word that one of his trusted advisers, Ahithophel, has joined Absalom's rebellion against him (cf. v. 12). His first response is to place this matter in God's hands—he prays. He asks God to turn the counsel of Ahithophel to foolishness (v. 31). We are reminded of David's frequent resort to prayer in time of trial before he became king. As he arrives at the summit of the Mount of Olives, where there was a place of worship, Hushai appears to meet him (v. 32), almost as if he were the answer to David's prayer. Indeed, Hushai will become the means for defeating the counsel of Ahithophel.

Hushai arrives in torn garments and with dirt on his head, clearly prepared to join the grieving procession into exile (v. 32). But David has other plans for this loyal friend. We are seeing David at his best. He has no master strategy, but seizes opportunities as they are presented and makes them work in his favor. David reminds us in the encounters during his retreat of the opportunistic, yet piously trustful David we saw in his early career. Ittai, the military man, is most useful in the wilderness with David. But his priests and now his friend will be of greater use in Jerusalem. David sends Hushai, like Abiathar and Zadok, back to the city to infiltrate Absalom's followers. Hushai is to pretend to defect to Absalom. David hopes that Hushai might find ways to counter the defection of Ahithophel (v. 34). It would seem that David thinks of

Hushai primarily as a spy, working with Abiathar and Zadok to send information to David by means of their two sons (vv. 35-36). What David cannot foresee is that Hushai will actually be called upon to advise Absalom, thus directly countering Ahithophel's advice (cf. 16:15–17:14). Hushai, referred to as David's friend, does return to the city just as Absalom is entering it (v. 37).

16:1-4. David's next encounter, as he passes beyond the Mount of Olives, is with a figure we have met before. Ziba, a servant of Saul who had been assigned by David to care for properties of Jonathan's remaining son, Mephibosheth (chap. 9), meets David bearing gifts (16:1). Ziba's appearance is something of a surprise. As an old Saulide loyalist, he might have welcomed the overthrow of David and thus support Absalom. But Ziba is shrewd; he may know enough not to count the father out in this struggle. He may see this moment as his opportunity to become more than a servant to those with land and authority. He brings substantial provisions to David and his company, surely a welcome gift for this hasty departure, and the king is pleasantly surprised at such largess (16:1-2). Such a gift makes clear that Ziba sides with David. But David shrewdly asks where Mephibosheth stands (v. 3a), and Ziba replies that Mephibosheth has remained in Jerusalem hoping that Absalom's rebellion will see the return to him of Saul's kingdom (v. 3b). We do not know the truth of this matter, and Mephibosheth will later dispute this report (19:24-30). It does not seem reasonable that Absalom's seizure of the throne should raise hopes for the return of the throne to the house of Saul. Is Ziba simply opportunistic at Mephibosheth's expense? For the moment we are left to wonder, but David acts on what he hears and declares that all of Mephibosheth's holdings are now Ziba's property (v. 4a), a decision for which Ziba is appropriately grateful and deferential toward David (v. 4b).

16:5-10a. David has received the loyalty of an old Saulide supporter, but his next encounter is with the unleashed anger and venom of a Saulide supporter who has not reconciled himself to the reign of David in Saul's place. When David reaches Bahurim, moving toward the Jordan River, a man named Shimei, whose family belongs to the house of

Saul, comes to meet David—not with gifts, but with cursing (v. 5). He throws stones at David and his party and hurls accusations as well (vv. 6-8). His voice must represent many yet remaining in Israel who hold David responsible for the deaths of Saul, Ishbosheth, and Abner. Shimei calls David a murderer and a man of blood. It may well be that the handing over of Saul's sons to Gibeonite vengeance (recorded in 21:1-9) had also taken place prior to this time in David's story. Shimei calls for blood vengeance against David for the blood of the house of Saul, and he sees Absalom's revolt as the instrument of the Lord's judgment against David. Saulide hopes and animosities are alive and well in Israel. Shimei thinks the moment for Saulide vengeance has come, and he boldly announces as much to David, even in the presence of David's loyal fighting men.

Naturally, it is Abishai, brother of Joab and one of the hotheaded sons of Zeruiah, who wants to respond by calling Shimei a "dead dog" and cutting off his head (v. 9). David has had to deal with the hot-tempered and violent responses of Abishai and his brother Joab before (1 Sam 26:8-9; 2 Sam 3:30, 39), and he quickly heads off Abishai's retaliatory response (v. 10a). David's response reveals his trustful faith in the face of grave challenge.

16:10b-12. David cannot afford petty retaliation at this moment, but his response is more than pragmatism. David takes this moment of cursing to reflect on his position before God and his trust that it is God's grace and not Abishai's sword that can counter Shimei's cursing. David reflects that Shimei's cursing may be a part of what God has done in this moment (v. 10b), and he chooses to endure the curses as a part of what God's providence has brought to him. After all, David muses, his own son Absalom is in open revolt against him (v. 11). What are curses and stones compared to the threat from which they are in retreat? David recognizes that it is not the goodwill of Shimei that he needs, but the grace and mercy of God in his time of distress (v. 12a). He expresses a hope, almost a prayer, that Shimei's curses may be countered and replaced by God's goodness (v. 12b). In this moment we again see David as we have seen him before at his best. He trusts God and recognizes his reliance on God's providence, while moving forward himself with the most effective action he can take on his own behalf. It is a juxtaposition of political realism and trusting faith that is part of what so fascinates us about David and has made him such an influential figure in Jewish and Christian tradition.

16:13-14. So the procession continues on down to the Jordan, with Shimei unmolested in his cursing and stone throwing. One senses that David is out of immediate danger once he reaches the Jordan River. The scene now shifts to Absalom's court and the strategic counsel he receives.

REFLECTIONS

This segment of the narrative gives us a portrait of David marked by considerable pathos. He is a man under judgment whose own son has turned against him. He has experienced tragedy and death; now he faces the shame of flight from his own capital city. We can hardly help recalling the words of David's own lament over Saul and Jonathan, "How the mighty have fallen" (1:19b).

Yet there emerges in this account of retreat a remarkable testimony to the resilience of David's faith and the strength of his character. The David we see is not without the flaws that have brought tragedy to him, but he is, nevertheless, a David who models for us the power of faith to overcome the power of sin and death. In the midst of what is almost a Davidic passion narrative, we begin to see the power of God to bring new life.

1. David begins this journey as a sinner who has paid a high price as the consequence of his sin. But he is not undone by this realization of his own guilt. David teaches us that in the face of sin and its death-dealing consequences, we must ultimately rely on the power of God's grace. David will return if he "finds favor in the eyes of the LORD" (15:25) and if the "LORD will look on my distress" and "repay me with good" (16:12). This is not the "good" he deserves but the "good" that comes only as God's grace. He trusts that in spite of sin there is a future to be received in God's providence. In contrast, many who come to the realization of their own sin and are faced with its consequences in their lives find themselves mired in guilt, unable to move on from a past that has crumbled and move toward the possibilities of God's new future. Sometimes when our own sinful choices have resulted in broken relationships and ruined lives, we seem to believe that broken reality is all we deserve. David models the bold faith that believes the good news—new life is available to us through the "goodness" of God, even when we do not deserve it. In the midst of the apparent loss of his kingdom, a consequence of his own sin, David trusts that in God there is a future for him. Although he does not know that this future will mean his kingdom regained, he trusts boldly in God's providence to give him a future: "Let him do to me what seems good to him" (15:26).

David also teaches us in this story that piety is not passive in its waiting for God's goodness to bring new life and new future. On this journey in retreat from Jerusalem, David is meeting and dealing with friends and enemies in a way that reflects his considerable skill at shaping his own future while trusting that its shape ultimately rests with God. He plans, deploys, gathers information, and makes careful decisions. Piety does not ask for the abandonment of political realism or shrewd decision making in our own interests. Some persons of faith seem to assume that piety necessitates a kind of political naïveté and passivity in the face of life's personal and societal challenges. God may provide openings to new life, but we surely must be willing to open doors and find ways to move forward through them. Faith does not ask us to resign ourselves to the future God has in store, but to boldly claim that future and participate with God in its emergence.

2. A special notice must be given to David's unwillingness to use the ark to his advantage. He refused to manipulate the authentic religious symbol of covenant faith for his own self-interest. In a day that sees frequent appeal to religious symbols for the promotion of narrow ideological claims, it is refreshing to read of David's refusal. We, also, should be wary of too easily claiming the symbols of our faith to lend authority to causes that cannot stand on their own merits. This is not an appeal for the absence of religious language in public life. It is an appeal that we not use such language or symbols as a cynical Madison Avenue technique to lend respectability to our causes. David refused to use the ark, but he did not hesitate to speak the language of faith in his dealings with those he met and in the strategic decisions he made on his journey. It is the substance of our faith and its values that must be present in the public arena, not simply its symbols for the sake of appearances and public image.

2 Samuel 16:15–17:29, The Strategies of Ahithophel and Hushai

COMMENTARY

It is Absalom's time onstage. The scene shifts from the pathos of David's retreat from Jerusalem to the self-confident air of Absalom's triumphant procession into Jerusalem. The narrator emphasizes the strategic moves by which Absalom will consolidate his grip on David's kingdom. The developments within Absalom's camp unfold in several scenes: 16:15-19 Hushai, David's friend, insinuates himself into the counsel of Absalom;

16:20-23, on Ahithophel's advice Absalom publicly takes possession of David's concubines; 17:1-4, Ahithophel gives his advice on the strategy Absalom should follow in defeating David; 17:5-14, Hushai offers competing advice; 17:15-22, David is warned and makes good his escape; 17:23, Ahithophel commits suicide; 17:24-29, David and Absalom maneuver their forces and prepare for battle.

Some questions have been raised about the literary unity of this section.[324] Absalom's taking of David's concubines (16:20-23) seems a strange diversion when he appears otherwise to be in hot pursuit of David. Further, Hushai's advice is declared the better (17:14), and Ahithophel appar ently commits suicide in disgrace (17:23); but in the end, it is Ahithophel's advice that is taken (17:24), and Hushai warns David in time to escape (17:15-16). However, the narrator is less interested in these idiosyncrasies than in the theological issues that shape the account. For example, Ahithophel's advice is confounded by the misleading advice of Hushai in answer to David's prayer in 15:31, "O Lord, I pray you, turn the counsel of Ahithophel into foolishness." Further, David may have been warned in a timely way by Hushai and may have taken appropriate action (17:15-16, 22), but the crucial power at work behind these events and on David's behalf is the Lord: "For the LORD had ordained to defeat the good counsel of Ahithophel, so that the Lord might bring ruin on Absalom" (17:14b). The incident involving the concubines reminds us of Nathan's prophecy against David that "I will take your wives before your eyes, and give them to your neighbor, and he shall lie with your wives in the sight of this very sun. For you did it secretly; but I will do this thing before all Israel and before the sun" (12:11-12). The narrative emphasizes that David has been judged. This violence from the hand of his own son is a part of that judgment. But the Lord has not taken the kingdom from David. He has been chastised, but the promise to David's dynasty is a firm promise, stated in 7:14-16 in Nathan's oracle.

16:15-19. When Absalom enters Jerusalem, Ahithophel is with him, and their first encounter is with David's friend Hushai (v. 15). Hushai's task, following David's instruction (15:32-37), is to make believable his own defection to Absalom's camp and to attempt to counter Ahithophel's advice. His words to Absalom display a marvelous facility with rhetorical duplicity. He greets Absalom with "Long live the king!" carefully avoiding mention of the name of the king whose long life he desires (v. 16). When Absalom questions the "loyalty" (חסד ḥesed) of one who would desert a friend (v. 17), Hushai coyly claims loyalty only to the one chosen by God and the people (v. 18). The reader, of course, knows that Hushai believes this to be David, while Absalom's ego, no doubt, allows him to believe it is he. Finally, however, even clever phrases must give way to the bold lie that allows Hushai access to the inner councils of Absalom: "I will serve you," he lies (v. 19).

16:20–17:14. Absalom turns first to Ahithophel for counsel (16:20). Ahithophel's advice is so highly regarded that it is treated as if it were an oracle from God (v. 23). Ahithophel's reputation is a force to be reckoned with, and the danger to David from his advice is serious. His advice comes in two parts.

First, Ahithophel advises Absalom to humiliate David publicly by openly engaging in sexual intercourse with the ten concubines David had left at the palace (v. 21; cf. 15:16). Ahithophel suggests that this action will make Absalom "odious" to David in the hearing of all Israel and will strengthen Absalom's supporters (16:21b). Absalom pitches a tent on the roof and publicly takes his father's concubines (16:22). Such action fulfills Nathan's judgment against David (12:11-12) that his wives will be taken publicly, whereas he had taken Uriah's wife in secret. Perhaps Absalom's tent is pitched on the palace roof from which David first viewed Bathsheba. It does not seem likely, as some have suggested, that Absalom's action established any legal claim on the throne.[325] His action seems symbolic; it is an act of defiance and a seizing of David's prerogatives as king. Such defiant public gestures often do win public support from those who gravitate to the apparent winning side in political conflicts. Ironically, Absalom's

---

324. See Anderson, *2 Samuel*, 212-13, for a discussion of various proposals.

325. See the discussion of these matters in Anderson, *2 Samuel*, 214. See also the Commentary on 2 Sam 3:7-10, where Abner's taking of Saul's concubine raises similar issues.

dramatic act is for the reader a fulfillment of Yahweh's judgment and thus serves notice that Absalom, even in this moment of apparent humiliation of his father, is not really in control of events.

Ahithophel's second piece of advice is strategic. He offers Absalom a plan to end his campaign swiftly and surgically (17:1-3). Ahithophel himself proposes to lead a force of twelve thousand (the word for "thousand" [אלף *elep*] can also mean a "contingent" or "battalion") in a quick strike on David that very night while he is "weary and discouraged." In the ensuing panic and flight, Ahithophel will strike down David alone, minimizing the loss of life among the others with David. Ahithophel assumes that with David gone, the others can be pacified and returned to their homes without need of a protracted war. He uses the imagery of a bride returning to her husband to describe this strategy. It is a bold and brilliant plan, one that pleases Absalom and the elders of Israel (17:4). This plan might have worked, except for the intervention of Hushai. David's hasty retreat from the fords of the Jordan after hearing of this plan suggests that he knew he would be in danger from such a strategy (17:22).

Absalom decides to consult Hushai for advice as well, and reports to him what Ahithophel has already counseled (17:5-6). Wasting no time, Hushai declares that Ahithophel's plan is not good (17:7). Whereas Ahithophel's advice was offered directly and succinctly, Hushai's speech is eloquent and complex. He marshals all of his considerable rhetorical resources to sway opinion away from Ahithophel's plan (17:8-10). Hushai does not move directly to an alternative plan. He recalls David's considerable reputation as a warrior and notes the field experience of the seasoned warriors who are with him. Such a cunning warrior would not allow himself to be found dispirited and unprepared in the midst of his troops; he would be hidden (17:8b-9a). David and his troops are enraged like a bear robbed of cubs (17:8a); therefore, they are more dangerous at present. Hushai suggests that when Absalom's less experienced troops meet David's seasoned warriors, it is Absalom's troops who are likely to panic at the first losses to David and his warriors (17:9b-10). While pretending to give Absalom advice, Hushai actually pays tribute to David and builds up the image of David's invincibility among Absalom's supporters.

Hushai offers an alternative plan that involves the raising of an army from all Israel (17:11a, Dan to Beersheba suggests that Absalom's support is not regionalized). He may be appealing to Absalom's ego by suggesting that he should lead this mighty army personally (17:11b). In Hushai's plan, this mighty army would sweep over David's force wherever they encountered him, and if he took refuge in a city they would drag it into the valley to capture him (vv. 12-13). Hushai is in wonderful form as a rhetorical orator at this point. The reader knows that Hushai's plan is intended to buy time for David to organize his resistance, but its grandiose design and the lure of a heroic battle and its accompanying victory win the day with Absalom and his advisers. They declare Hushai's plan better than Ahithophel's (17:14a). However, the narrator lets the reader in on the reality truly at work here: "The LORD had ordained to defeat the good counsel of Ahithophel" (17:14b). David had prayed while Absalom marched, and David's prayer (15:31) has been answered. Kings and pretenders struggle for the throne, but the Lord controls the ultimate course of Israel's history and David's dynasty.

17:15-23. Hushai seems to have prevailed, but the events that follow presume that Ahithophel's strategy is followed. Hushai sends a warning to David, carried by the sons of Zadok and Abiathar, David's priests who have stayed in Jerusalem to spy on Absalom's activity. Although Hushai reports on the counsel given by Ahithophel and himself, he urges David to move quickly so that Ahithophel's plan would not have a chance of success (vv. 15-16). The narrator includes a dramatic episode concerning the narrow escape of the messengers, Jonathan and Ahimaaz, who are hidden in a well by supporters (vv. 17-20). When they report to David, they emphasize the danger imposed by Ahithophel's strategy (v. 21). David quickly crosses the Jordan and moves out of reach of Ahithophel's proposed quick-strike force. The account exhibits no trust that Hushai's apparent triumph as an adviser will hold. Indeed, the military movements that follow in the story show little relation to either strategy. The narrative about dueling advisers may be intended primarily to emphasize the conviction that God will ultimately determine the outcome of events.

Ahithophel responds to the defeat of his plan (perhaps also to intelligence that David's quick action had rendered it unfeasible) by setting his house in order and hanging himself (v. 23). Many have noted the similarity to the report of Judas's death in the Gospels (cf. Matt 27:5). Both men betrayed God's anointed one.

17:24-29. The final verses of this chapter report troop movements and preparations in advance of the final military encounter, in which the success or failure of Absalom's rebellion will be determined.

David moves to Mahanaim in the Transjordan, while Absalom crosses the Jordan, too late to catch David at the fords there (v. 24), and Absalom goes on to camp in Gilead (v. 26). Absalom appoints Joab's nephew Amasa to lead his troops (v. 25). Perhaps by this move he hopes to claim for himself some of the charisma of Joab's warrior family.

Verses 27-29 report that David is given extensive provisions at Mahanaim by three prominent families of supporters, one Ammonite and two Israelite. The reader learns that not all have deserted him for Absalom. David still has support and resources to draw upon. Hushai's rhetoric and warning have bought him time, and he is now rested and provisioned. The stage is set for the final confrontation of father and son.

REFLECTIONS

Sixteenth- and seventeenth-century English writers were fascinated with this confrontation between Ahithophel and Hushai.[326] From Chaucer to Shakespeare to Dryden, Ahithophel has been seen as synonymous with treachery, disloyalty, and political machination for one's own gain. Ahithophel has been compared with Judas, and their suicides are considered appropriate for their disloyalty. A verb was even coined in seventeenth-century England for the act of disloyal treachery: "to Ahithophel." Hushai, quite the opposite, has been widely admired for his loyalty and willingness to risk his own welfare for the sake of that loyalty. John Dryden, in *Absalom and Achitophel,* may have seen his own satire as the wisdom of Hushai. In that work, he sought to confound the treachery of Absalom-like politicians and the deception of Ahithophel-like advisers, which he saw leading England astray in his time.

The story and the metaphors it affords are no longer so familiar, but the moral types represented by Ahithophel and Hushai are as prominent in the modern imagination as ever. The clever but treacherous turncoat and the undercover loyalist are staples of modern fiction and caricatures that often appear in analysis of public affairs. Loyalty and betrayal remain topics of modern fascination.

We are not as prone as our seventeenth-century counterparts to read biblical stories as straightforward allegories of our own times, events, and personalities. Yet, the story of these two advisers raises probing questions for us in a time when loyalties are perhaps too easily shifted and we are often reluctant to take risks even for the loyalties we have chosen. How often are our loyalties shifted in order to be on a "winning side," as with Ahithophel? Are we, like Hushai, willing to risk rejection, ridicule, even danger for the sake of the commitments we have made? The retreating, humiliated, and betrayed David of these stories does not look like a good investment for the loyalty of Hushai. The tendency of modern predilections is to be with the majority, the popular, the apparent locus of power. But God's future often does not accord with expectations measured in terms of human power and success. David was the eighth son of a little-known family, but he was the man after God's own heart. For Christians, commitment

326. For specific references on the wealth of 16th- and 17th-century references to Ahithophel and Hushai, see Larry Carver, "Ahithophel," in *A Dictionary of Biblical Tradition in English Literature,* ed. David Lyle Jeffrey (Grand Rapids: Eerdmans, 1992) 27-28.

to a "crucified One" seems a poor investment of loyalty if measured by the standards of modern realpolitik.

Ultimately, the proper reading of this story requires that we acknowledge the working of God's will as the measure of all loyalties. God is at work preserving a future for David and confounding the rebellion of Absalom. Trust in this providential working of God in the course of human history is not a reason for resigned and passive waiting. Like Hushai, we work on behalf of those loyalties that seem most worthy and in line with what we understand God may be doing. In these efforts, we make ourselves available as the channels through which God's providence may operate. Like Hushai, we may become the means whereby God confounds treachery, self-serving ambitions, and murderous intent in the cynical politics of our own Ahithophels.

2 Samuel 18:1-18, The Defeat and Death of Absalom

COMMENTARY

The story of Absalom's rebellion now moves quickly to its tragic climax. The description of the final battle and David's victory is reported briefly and matter-of-factly (vv. 6-8). What clearly concerns the narrator more is making clear that David was in no way involved in the death of Absalom. This may have been a necessary apologetic for reestablishing David's rule in an Israel where Absalom had received widespread support. In this telling of the story of Absalom's defeat and death, the narrator is at great pains to explain that David was not even allowed to participate personally in the battle (vv. 2b-4) and that David went to great lengths in attempting to ensure the personal safety of Absalom (vv. 5, 12). Joab is given total responsibility for Absalom's death. His role in David's story seems to be that of the heavy who does the dirty work while David remains apart with reputation intact (cf. the deaths of Abner, 3:27; Uriah, 11:16-17).

18:1-5. David organizes his troops for the battle with Absalom using the traditional military units of "thousands" and "hundreds" (v. 1; these terms do not indicate precise numbers). He divides his force into three contingents (v. 2), two commanded by his long-time companions, the warrior brothers Joab and Abishai, and the third by the mercenary Ittai the Gittite, whose loyalty was noted in the report of David's retreat from Jerusalem (15:19-22).

The account lingers over the details of two claims that are clearly of great importance

in this story. The first is that David does not actually participate in the battle that leads to the defeat and death of Absalom. He wished to accompany his troops (v. 2b), but they would not allow it. The king is considered too valuable ("worth ten thousand of us," v. 3), and he is urged to remain in the city (Mahanaim?), providing support. David acquiesces to their judgment (v. 4).

Second, David gives explicit instructions to Joab, Abishai, and Ittai, which "all the people heard," that Absalom is not to be personally harmed (v. 5). It is David, the concerned father, who dominates the moments before the final battle, not David the aggrieved king. "Deal gently," David pleads and urges this for his own sake, not for the sake of Absalom. The author pictures David as being personally invested in the welfare of his son, a portrait that may have been designed by the narrator to assuage Absalom's followers after his death and to aid in reestablishing David's rule.

18:6-8. The battle is joined; its description is terse and pointed. The fighting takes place in the "forest of Ephraim," probably a forested area in the Transjordan (v. 6). The "men of Israel" are massively defeated by "the servants of David" (v. 7). These phrases may suggest that Absalom's largely conscripted army was no match for the seasoned professional warriors of David. Hushai's advice and warning bought David the time to organize and choose the field of battle, and in these conditions Absalom's people's army was no match for the experienced warriors of David.

The loss of twenty thousand may be intended to indicate losses of twenty units designated as "thousands" rather than indicating actual numbers.[327] As the battle widens, the report indicates that the forest claims more than the sword (v. 8), a tribute to David's wise choice of terrain for what may have been a battle more like guerrilla warfare than the open meeting of armies in the field.

18:9-18. The scene shifts to Absalom. It is not clear whether he is leading troops in battle or attempting to flee the battlefield. What happens, however, is not the result of a military encounter. Absalom's mule takes him beneath an oak tree, and his head becomes caught in its branches, leaving him suspended "between heaven and earth" (v. 9). Since the time of Josephus,[328] interpreters have related this event to the notice of Absalom's magnificent head of hair (14:26) and assumed that his hair became entangled in the overhanging boughs of the tree. Brueggemann suggests that Absalom's suspension reflects the tensions in which the narrative itself now stands suspended. "Absalom is suspended between life and death, between the sentence of a rebel and the value of a son, between the severity of the king and the yearning of the father."[329] Over against the harshness of the battle and its terrible losses stand the last words of David, "Deal gently."

The desire of the father does not dominate events in this moment. Rather, the harsh pragmatism of Joab assumes control of events, perhaps intended by the author to shift any blame that might attach to David for Absalom's death. A soldier reports Absalom's predicament to Joab (v. 10), and Joab admonishes him for not having killed Absalom on the spot. The exchange between Joab and the soldier emphasizes for the reader the clarity of David's desire and command concerning the safety of Absalom. The soldier would not risk raising his hand against the king's son for any amount of reward, because he had clearly heard the king's command (v. 12). Furthermore, he does not believe Joab would have backed him up if he had killed Absalom (v. 13). Absalom's death cannot be blamed on overzealous troops. Joab must personally take matters into his own hands. He takes three spears and thrusts them into Absalom; only then do his personal armor-bearers also join in ensuring the death of the rebellious son (vv. 14-15). Absalom's blood is on Joab's hands alone. Only with Absalom's death are the battle and the pursuit ended (v. 16).

Absalom is buried in the forest, his grave marked by a heap of stones (v. 17). This is an honorable burial; he is not left dishonored as carrion for the animals (cf. the fate of Saul's sons in 21:1-14). Nevertheless, Absalom is not buried with the royal family. He is left on the field of battle where his rebellion ended in failure. The note in v. 18 seems to be an added parenthesis by an editor who wanted to take note of a pillar that Absalom himself had erected in the Valley of the Kings (perhaps the Kidron Valley in Jerusalem), which still stood in his own time and was known by Absalom's name. The notice that Absalom had no sons may mean that the three sons mentioned as having been born to Absalom in 14:27 had not survived into adulthood. The monument mentioned here no doubt led to the naming of a later Roman period tomb in the Kidron Valley as the "Tomb of Absalom," a popular designation that this Hellenistic tomb retains today. (See Reflections at 18:19–19:8a.)

327. McCarter, *II Samuel*, 405, suggests the losses may have been as few as between 100 and 280, but most would estimate the numerical strength of a "thousand" as more than five to fourteen soldiers. This may be more the strength of a "hundred" (cf. v. 1). In any case, we should think of the loss to Absalom's army in this battle as twenty "units." See G. E. Mendenhall, "The Census Lists of Numbers 1 and 26," *JBL* 77 (1958) 52-66, for a comprehensive discussion of the term אלף (*'elep*), "thousand."

328. Josephus *Antiquities of the Jews* 7.239.

329. Brueggemann, *First and Second Samuel*, 319.

2 Samuel 18:19–19:8a, David's Grief Over Absalom's Death

COMMENTARY

The narrative continues with a report of the aftermath of Absalom's death. The tragic news of the son's death is brought to the waiting father, and his all-consuming grief threatens to overwhelm the effect of the victory. The pathos of David's grief is portrayed in a graphic manner that has touched the hearts of generations who have read this story and made it a virtual icon of parental anguish.

The story builds dramatically to the moment when David receives the tragic news of Absalom's death. Fourteen verses (18:19-32) stretch the tension as rival runners bring word to an anxious father who pleads for news of the welfare of his son. David receives word of the victory, but almost dismisses it, seeking news of Absalom. When David learns of Absalom's death, the victory is entirely hidden from view by the magnitude of his grief (18:33). David's role as father, protecting even a rebellious son, is allowed to prevail over any portrait of him as ruthless king putting down a rebellion against his rule. It remains for Joab to see the demoralizing effect of David's grief on his supporters and the belittling of their service on behalf of David and his throne. Joab, in his usual direct way, confronts David and coaxes him to resume the role of king in spite of the pain of the father (19:1-8).

18:19-32. This detailed narration of the messengers sent to bring word to David heightens the drama of the waiting father and the terrible news that he must hear. Ahimaaz, the son of Zadok, wishes to bring the report to David. He is bubbling with youthful excitement about the great victory, which he understands as the Lord's deliverance of David (v. 19). Joab knows that since Absalom is dead, David will not receive this as good news. He tells Ahimaaz that he cannot go "because the king's son is dead" (v. 20). It would not do to send the son of a high royal official, the priest Zadok, with such news. David has killed the bearer of bad tidings before (cf. 1:15-16). Joab knows that the news of this death will not be welcomed as was the news of Uriah's death

(11:21). David will not dismiss this death as the unfortunate consequence of war (11:25). Better to send a Cushite, a foreigner, an outsider, with such news (v. 21). But even after the Cushite departs, Ahimaaz pleads to run to David as well. He seems aware of the risk, but asks to be allowed to run "come what may!" (vv. 22-23). Joab reminds him that this news will carry no reward (v. 22), but he gives in, and Ahimaaz, taking an alternative route, outruns the Cushite (v. 23).

The focus of the narrative shifts to David's perspective, waiting at the gates of the city with a sentinel, straining for first sight of the messengers who might bring news of the battle (v. 24). First one runner is sighted, then another. The first is recognized as Ahimaaz, and David leaps to grasp a straw of hope. Ahimaaz is a good man; he must bring good news (vv. 25-27). Perhaps David assumes that Joab would not risk the life of the son of Zadok with bad news and David's anger.

Ahimaaz blurts out an "All is well" as he falls prostrate before David. His formal report is in the form of a thanksgiving to the Lord,[330] and he speaks only of the victory (v. 28). This is not what interests David; he presses for information on "the young man" Absalom (v. 29a). Ahimaaz suffers a failure of nerve. Joab told him that Absalom was dead, but he cannot bring himself to tell David (compassion for David? fear for his own safety?). He reports only a commotion but no knowledge of its meaning (v. 29b). He does not have news of what David most wants to know. The victory is of little interest to the anxious father. He tells Ahimaaz to stand aside (v. 30).

It remains for the Cushite unwittingly to bring the tragic news to David. He, too, reports the news of victory as the welcome deliverance of the Lord (v. 31), and when David asks of Absalom, the Cushite reports his death as the welcome death of one who rose up to harm the king (v. 32). There is no sense that this would not come as good news

---

330. See Conroy, *Absalom, Absalom!* 72, esp. n. 116.

to a threatened king. But it is not the king who receives the news; it is the father.

18:33. There is no more poignant portrayal of human grief and desolation in all of Scripture than in this single verse. David, who had received the news of his infant son's death with stoic resignation (12:19-23) is undone by news of Absalom's death. The battle, the rebellion, the throne—all of this is irrelevant in this moment. David is wracked with unrestrained grief and cries out in anguish. No longer is Absalom the "young man" (18:5, 29, 32). He is "my son" (five times in this verse), and Absalom (three times in this verse). David has grieved with poetic eloquence over Saul and Jonathan (1:17-27), and with stoic resignation over his infant son (12:19-23). But this time there is no capacity for eloquence, and the king is not resigned to this ending of a father's hopes. This is the most elemental and deeply human moment in all of David's story. David has now borne the full cost of his own descent into violence, and the judgment pronounced by Nathan has now played itself out in the violent consequences to his own family. It may be David's knowledge of his own role in bringing this moment of lost hopes and shattered relationship that makes his grief so inconsolable.

19:1-8a. As usual, Joab notices that there is a kingdom to run here. It is to Joab that the grief of the king and the effect of his mourning on the people are reported (vv. 1-2). Reports of the king's reaction cause troops that should have returned in celebration of victory to creep back into the city as if they had done something wrong and should be ashamed (v. 3). David does not even notice this behavior. The cries of "my son, Absalom," which seemed moving and understandable in 18:33, begin to seem self-indulgent in 19:4.

Joab boldly enters the royal residence and confronts the king. Perhaps only Joab could have spoken as directly and candidly as he now speaks to David. He tells David that he has shamed those who supported him, fought for him, and saved his life and the lives of his family (v. 5). Joab accuses David of having twisted values, loving those who hate him and hating those who love him (v. 6*a*). Joab shares his impression that David would gladly have heard news of the death of every member of his company if Absalom, a rebel and a murderer, were yet alive (v. 6*b*). It is a remarkable speech for anyone to make to a king, but Joab is not finished. He ends with a threat: David must appear in public to speak a word of kindness to his supporters or, Joab swears by the Lord, not a single man will stay the night with him, and David will be finished (v. 7). This almost sounds like a threat by Joab to lead a rebellion or desertion of David himself.

To his credit, David gathers himself and takes a seat in the gate, presumably as a sign of support and welcome to his returning and victorious warriors (v. 8). Word of this royal presence passes among the troops, and they gather around the king for whom they have fought. We cannot imagine that the grief we have glimpsed is assuaged, but in the necessities of the moment, the king takes the place of the father.

REFLECTIONS

The heart-rending scene of David's grief over Absalom's death is a scene of such universal human pathos that it has attracted unusual attention, from ancient times to our own era. The tragic moment addresses the reader on multiple levels.

1. First and foremost, David depicts the depths of a father's grief at the loss of a son. Whatever the circumstances, whatever the strains on the relationship, every parent can identify with the pain of having one's own child die first. Many know and recognize the cry of David's loss without understanding any of the complexities of the relationship between David and Absalom. David's poignant statement that he would willingly have died in Absalom's place has become particularly emblematic of parental willingness to sacrifice one's own welfare to preserve the life of one's child. Those who know something of Absalom's rebellion find this story particularly relevant to parents of children who take self-destructive paths from which parental love, though willing to sacrifice, cannot save them. The power of this portrait of parental grief gives this moment in David's story a familiarity and emotional identification that function apart from the complexities of the story in 2 Samuel.

2. The preaching of this text, however, should point beyond emotional identification with parental loss to some of the deeper issues encompassed in this climactic moment of David's grief. David is caught in a tension between his roles as father and as king. Absalom is a rebel and a traitor against the king, but he is nevertheless loved by the father. Earlier David, alienated from Absalom, had called him only "the young man Absalom" (18:5), but now Absalom is "my son," and David utters this phrase repeatedly (five times) in anguish and grief.

David is caught in a tragic conflict between public and private roles. As king, he must regard Absalom as a criminal whose fate is deserved, but as father he cannot accept such an end for his son. As king, he has vast power to influence events, but as a grief-stricken father he has no power to bring his son back to life. Frederick Buechner reminds us that when David wished he had died instead of Absalom, "he meant it, of course. If he could have done the boy's dying for him, he would have done it. If he could have paid the price for the boy's betrayal of him, he would have paid it. If he could have given his own life to make the boy alive again, he would have given it. But even a king can't do things like that. As later history was to prove, it takes a God."[331]

This poignant moment in David's story is a reminder to us of the difficulty of balancing public responsibility and familial loyalty. Like David, we often learn to love when it is too late. When David's love would have made a difference, he was only the king—allowing Absalom's return, but not allowing access to the father's love. In our own society, the lesson of David's grief is not simply a matter of personal relationships but of societal ones as well. We grieve the violence that breaks out all too often in the rebellion of sons and daughters, but we have not reached out in ways that would have forestalled violence and rebellion. Issues of poverty, education, familial dysfunction, substance abuse, and consumerist values distort the future of many of our sons and daughters who then attempt to seize their birthright in violent ways—increased gun violence, the growth of paramilitary cults, increased intolerance in public discourse, and growing lack of respect for all forms of authority. We may mourn, like David, when inattention to such alienation produces an Oklahoma City federal building bombing or a Unabomber, but the time for addressing alienation with compassion, forgiveness, and attention to genuine needs comes, as with David, before the point of tragic consequences. David's weeping must move us in response to those of our sons and daughters who are alienated and in rebellion before we, too, must weep the tragic consequences. The challenge is to break the cycle before we come to these tragic moments of grief, personal or societal. David's human emotions became visible when it was too late. In his story, one wonders what might have been avoided if David's heart had overflowed with love and forgiveness at an earlier moment rather than with grief in this tragic demonstration after Absalom is gone (see Reflections at 14:1-33).

3. But David's weeping may in part be for himself as well as for Absalom. David's suffering and loss are not innocent. It is David's own modeling of grasping, arrogant power that Absalom has emulated. It is judgment on David's sin that is playing itself out in the tragedies of his family. This drama of sin and judgment, passing tragically from fathers to sons, is a theme that has attracted the attention of Christian writers from Augustine to the present. They have found in this final scene of the drama of Absalom's rebellion a tragic and sobering outcome to the conflict between the exercise of self-interested human free will and the irresistible workings of divine providence.

---

331. Frederick Buechner, *Peculiar Treasures: A Biblical Who's Who* (San Francisco: Harper & Row, 1979) 6.

This they believed was a perennial tension in human existence lived within the framework of divine will. Absalom's loss was not just a human tragedy but a result of divine justice. Augustine writes in *On Christian Doctrine :* "He mourned over his son's death, not because of his own loss, but because he knew to what punishment so impious an adulterer and parricide had been hurried."[332] It may well be that this scene continues to have a tragic attraction for modern readers for this same reason. David's grief speaks to us not simply of parental loss but of his recognition that his own sins, Absalom's sins, and God's justice have all helped to bring this tragic moment to pass. We recognize in David's grief our own grief over many losses we have experienced not simply as victims but as perpetrators. How much greater the grief when we know that we have helped to bring its cause. It is the despair of our soul coupled with the grief of our heart.

With the advent of the novel in the eighteenth century, writers were drawn to the universal elements of this story of a divided father and son ending in the father's grief. Thomas Hardy called this chapter the "finest example of [prose narrative] that I know, showing beyond its power and pathos the highest artistic cunning."[333] The two most celebrated uses of this story of a son's rebellion and a father's grief are in William Faulkner's *Absalom, Absalom!* and Alan Paton's *Cry, the Beloved Country.* Both find in the racially divided societies of the early twentieth-century American South and mid-century South African apartheid parallels to the story of Absalom and David. In both novels and the modern settings they chronicle, sons are brought to grief by the injustices their fathers first put in place and the sons inevitably imitate. Too late the fathers must recognize the price their sons have paid for their father's sins as well as their own, and the emptiness of the grief with which the fathers are left.

Absalom went to war against his father in an effort to seize for himself a place he had lost by imitating the violence his own father had used to get what he desired. This vicious cycle is not unknown to the parents and children of every generation. We know that we have modeled behavior and values that subsequent generations will imitate—to our sorrow. If we identify with the grief of David over his son, it is because we too often experience it as our own, or that of others close to us.

This scene of David's desolation will forever touch the human heart with its portrait of a father's pain. One can hope that it will also remind us that time can run out. There are stories in which the prodigal son does not come home and the waiting father's embrace is empty.

332. Augustine, *On Christian Doctrine*, 3.21.30, cited in De Bruyn, "Absalom," in *A Dictionary of Biblical Tradition in English Literature,* ed. David Lyle Jeffrey (Grand Rapids: Eerdmans, 1992) 12.

333. Cited in Augustine, *On Christian Doctrine*, 3.21.30, cited in De Bruyn, "Absalom," 14.

2 Samuel 19:8b-43, David Returns to Jerusalem

COMMENTARY

Absalom's rebellion and the civil war it brought are over, but the aftermath of these events leaves a troubled political reality in the kingdom as David retakes his throne. The grieving father must give way to the judicious king if David's reign is to be effectively reestablished. Not even David's return to Jerusalem is without troublesome political details, and the first portion of this section details the negotiations that make David's return possible (vv. 8*b*-18*a*). As David crosses the Jordan to begin the final leg of his return journey, he encounters three persons. They remind us of the encounters that marked his retreat from Jerusalem (15:13–16:14). In fact, two of these are direct counterparts of those earlier encounters: with Shimei (vv. 18*b*-23) and with Mephibosheth (vv. 24-30). The third is with a powerful supporter of David, Barzillai, with whom David negotiates a continuing alliance (vv. 31-40; cf. 17:27-29). The chapter closes with a confrontation between the northern tribes of Israel and Judah over David's crossing of the Jordan and his escort back to Jerusalem (vv. 41-43). This dispute apparently sets the stage for a further rebellion against David, led by a man named Sheba (chap. 20).

David's retreat from Jerusalem in the face of Absalom's advance was discussed earlier as being narrated in the manner of a procession of penance. Now that Absalom is dead and David's forces have been victorious, we might expect a triumphant and celebratory return to Jerusalem. Yet, the tone of this narrative is not triumphal. The wise, if world-weary, David we saw in the retreat from Jerusalem (15:13–16:14) is the David we still see in this report of return. He makes judicious and compassionate decisions. He takes decisive action when needed. There is no overt expression of theological themes in this account, but one wonders if this telling is not still governed by David's expression in his retreat from Jerusalem: "If I find favor in the eyes of the LORD, he will bring me back and let me see both it and the place where [the ark] stays" (15:25). David is returning, not in triumph, but in humility. He is a sinner, but he still finds favor in the eyes of the Lord.

19:8b-18a. Although the victory over Absalom is won, these verses make clear that it is no simple matter for David to resume the throne. There are political complexities to be addressed and political loyalties to be won. The reference to the anointing of Absalom (v. 10), about which we had not heard before, suggests that David may have been officially deposed by the people. He may have won the victory, but the people must invite him to resume the throne, perhaps even by being anointed again. This is what some scholars believe took place at Gilgal, an ancient site connected with kingship from Saul's time (1 Sam 11:15), where David meets the representatives of Israel and Judah (vv. 15, 40).[334]

The notice that the Israelites had fled to their homes (v. 8*b*) indicates the dispersal of the army raised by Absalom, but the political division among the people is not ended. Some remember the deliverance from enemies that David had won for them in the past and urge

that he be brought back now that Absalom is defeated (v. 9). Not all agree, as the use of dispute to describe the advancing of this argument suggests. David takes political action in the face of this uncertainty. He uses his loyal priests, Zadok and Abiathar, to make a political overture to the elders of Judah. David urges Judah to take the initiative in restoring him to the throne, and he bases his appeal on his kinship with Judah (vv. 11-12). He was a Judean himself, and Judah had been the first to make him king (2:4). Ironically the appeal to "my bone and my flesh" echoes the claim of kinship that northern Israel made in asking David to be king (5:1). Now David is playing Judah off against northern Israel.

David is willing to make concessions to win back Judah's political loyalty. In an astonishing bid for the loyalty of those in Judah who supported Absalom, David offers to make Amasa commander of his army, replacing Joab (v. 13). Amasa was a distant kinsman of David and Joab, and he was chosen by Absalom to lead the rebel army (17:25). This move would be as if President Lincoln had invited Robert E. Lee to replace Ulysses S. Grant at the conclusion of the American Civil War. Such a dramatic concession must speak to the uncertainty of David's political situation that he should feel such a gesture was needed. Further, he is directly displacing Joab, a reality that Joab could not accept. David may harbor animosity toward Joab for having killed Absalom, although we are never explicitly told that David knew this. The young man refusing Joab's urging to kill Absalom may have been right when he said, "There is nothing hidden from the king" (18:13).

David's political strategy seems to work, since Amasa sways Judah and they send an invitation for David to return (v. 14). Representatives of Judah meet at Gilgal to welcome David as he crosses the Jordan on his return to Jerusalem (v. 15). This apparently effective political overture to Judah will, however, create new problems in David's relationship to the northern tribes of Israel (vv. 41-43).

Among those who hurry to Gilgal to meet David are Shimei, the pro-Saulide Benjaminite who had cursed David on his retreat (v. 16; cf. 16:5-8), and Ziba, the servant of Saul to whom David had given the land allotted to

334. See Mettinger, *King and Messiah*, 118-23.

Mephibosheth, also on the retreat from Jerusalem (v. 17; cf. 16:1-4). Now on his return journey David must deal again with these men and issues.

19:18b-23. Although it was primarily Judah who came to escort David back to Jerusalem, Shimei had arrived with a thousand Benjaminites (v. 17*a*). Shimei had good reason to be worried. When David seemed near to defeat and was barely escaping Jerusalem ahead of Absalom, Shimei had cursed David and attributed David's fate to the blood of Saul's house on his hands. David had restrained Abishai from killing Shimei (16:5-13). Now Absalom is defeated, and David has the upper hand. Shimei takes the initiative by falling before David, confessing the wrong he has done to him, and asking for mercy (v. 19). He claims that he is the first from the "house of Joseph" to meet David (v. 20), which means the first from the northern tribes to support David.

Again it is Abishai who wants to kill him, but we should not take this simply as a violent impulse. Abishai cites Shimei's offense as cursing the Lord's anointed, which is indeed a serious crime (v. 21). But as before, David intervenes on behalf of Shimei. David mildly rebukes Abishai (and his brother Joab), suggesting that he is distancing himself from the violence of these "sons of Zeruiah" and does not wish them as adversaries (v. 22*a*).[335] David had voiced reservations before about the "sons of Zeruiah" at the time of Abner's death (3:39).

David relates the mercy he shows on "this day" as appropriate to the day he is "king over Israel." We are reminded of the time Saul's supporters wanted to put some of his opponents to death, and Saul declared that "no one shall be put to death this day" (1 Sam 11:13). Immediately after this Saul was anointed at Gilgal (1 Sam 11:14-15). Such a sequence has led some to believe that David is being anointed again at Gilgal and that amnesty for opponents such as Shimei has become a part of the tradition surrounding the anointing and accession of Israel's kings.[336] Of course, David has ample political motives for showing such

mercy to Shimei, since his support among the northern tribes is not yet assured. Conciliation toward Shimei seems wise on David's part as an effort to renegotiate his own kingship and its necessary base of support.[337]

David pronounces his verdict, "You shall not die," and gives it force by taking an oath (v. 23). But political memories are long. Shimei's curse against the Lord's anointed one has still not been avenged. On his deathbed, David will charge Solomon to deal with Shimei in accordance with his offense (1 Kgs 2:8-9). David's oath and his need for northern support prevented him from doing so, but Solomon is not restrained by this oath. On a pretext, Solomon will have Shimei put to death (1 Kgs 2:36-46).

19:24-30. David is next met by Mephibosheth, the son of Jonathan and the grandson of Saul (see chap. 9). He is unkempt and dirty, since he has not washed or otherwise taken care of himself since the day David left Jerusalem (v. 24). The implication is that Mephibosheth's actions were acts of mourning and solidarity with David in his plight. David meets him with a challenge, "Why did you not go with me, Mephibosheth?" (v. 25). Mephibosheth was not one of those whom David met on his desperate retreat from Jerusalem. It was Ziba, the servant of Saul who had been charged with the care of the Saulide lands David had given to Mephibosheth, who met David on the road. Ziba had brought provisions for David and charges against Mephibosheth that he had remained in Jerusalem in hopes of regaining the kingdom of Saul (16:1-4). David had rewarded Ziba by declaring that all that had belonged to Mephibosheth henceforth belonged to Ziba.

Even now, as David crosses the Jordan, Ziba has come with fifteen sons and twenty servants to help transport David's household and be at his service (v. 17*b*). But Mephibosheth is now here to speak for himself, and he tells quite a different story. In answer to David's challenge, Mephibosheth claims that Ziba had deceived David. Mephibosheth had charged Ziba to saddle a donkey so he could join David. Being lame, he must ride to do so. But Ziba, he claims, had taken the donkey for

---

335. The noun שׂטן (*śāṭān*) may not mean "adversary" in the sense of an opponent of David, but "accuser" in the sense of the legal accuser of Shimei (cf. Zech 3:1). David would be rejecting Abishai's attempt to play that accusatory role.

336. Mettinger, *King and Messiah,* 119.

337. Whitelam, *The Just King,* 145, gives a detailed accounting of the negotiating process that may have been necessary for David's return to the throne.

himself, left Mephibosheth helpless behind, and slandered his good name before David (vv. 26-27*a*). Mephibosheth throws himself on David's mercy and whatever David might decide (v. 27*b*). He claims that he has already received David's generosity and has no right to ask more (v. 28). He is eloquent and convincing in his claim that he would not violate David's goodwill. Who is telling the truth? David is faced with utterly contradictory stories, and the narrator offers no hints about where the truth might lie.

David does not hesitate; he makes a royal decision. The land, and presumably the household that accompanies the land, is to be divided between Ziba and Mephibosheth (v. 29). There is no time to adjudicate this dispute. David chooses to believe that Mephibosheth could be speaking the truth, and he acts to ensure his continued generosity to the house of Saul. Mephibosheth might well have protested that all of the land should be his and that Ziba should be punished, but he does not. He responds in loyalty and gratitude and with the surprising statement that Ziba could take all the land, since David had returned in safety (v. 30). This statement alone seems to confirm that Mephibosheth speaks out of loyalty and not expedience.

19:31-40. Barzillai is a Gileadite who had helped to provision David's army in the Transjordan when he was preparing for the battle with Absalom (v. 32; cf. 17:27-29). He, too, now meets David at the crossing of the Jordan (v. 31). He appears in the role of David's host, bidding farewell to his royal guest, and David attempts to repay the kindness by urging Barzillai to come and live at David's court (v. 33). No doubt David is anxious to continue the alliance with this powerful and influential supporter, but one need not see his offer as an effort to co-opt or control Barzillai. Indeed, Barzillai is probably more valuable to David in the Transjordan, which is where

Barzillai desires to remain. Barzillai cites his age of eighty years, and with an appealing sense of mild self-mockery claims that he is well beyond the ability to enjoy courtly pleasures (v. 35). He will only accompany David a short way and then return to live out his years in his own family home (vv. 36-37*a*).

Barzillai does ask that Chimham, who must be his son, be taken into David's court to serve at David's pleasure (v. 37*b*). David gladly accepts this offer (v. 38); indeed, on his deathbed he urges Solomon to offer continued generosity toward the sons of Barzillai (1 Kgs 2:7). When David and those accompanying him have crossed the Jordan, he kisses Barzillai, who then departs for his home (v. 39). The procession continues on to Gilgal, but, significantly, those accompanying David now include "half the people of Israel" as well as the people of Judah (v. 40).

19:41-43. It is the people of Israel, the representatives of the northern tribes, who now speak up in resentment of the initiative taken by Judah to bring David back to Jerusalem (v. 41). Tribal and regional animosities boil to the surface in an angry exchange of claims about who has priority in David's kingdom. Judah claims kinship to David and innocence of any intention to gain from their initiative (v. 42). But Israel claims to have a larger stake in the kingdom by virtue of having ten tribes, and they were the first to speak of bringing David back (v. 43). These jealous claims are not resolved. The text states that Judah's words were fiercer than Israel's, giving the impression that Judah simply outshouted or even threatened their northern counterparts. Absalom may be defeated, but the tribal divisions that he exploited are still present in the kingdom. As old animosities resurface, one final episode of rebellion against David's kingship occurs: the rebellion of Sheba (chap. 20). (See Reflections at 20:1-22.)

2 Samuel 20:1-22, Sheba's Rebellion

COMMENTARY

The intertribal rivalries and political tensions that threatened David's kingship during Absalom's rebellion have one more

convulsive episode to be played out. A man named Sheba, from the Saulide tribe of Benjamin, declares a secession from Davidic rule and apparently receives significant northern Israelite support. This separatist movement seems to have been provoked by the dispute between representatives of Judah and Israel at the end of chap. 19 over priority in support of the restoration of David's rule. It is doubtful, especially in the light of the outcome, that Sheba's revolt enjoyed the support of most northern Israelites. His separatist movement more likely reflects the political rivalries and fragmentation that Absalom exploited. David's victory over Absalom did not immediately end those tensions. To reestablish his reign, David must deal with rebellious leaders like Sheba if he is to reunify his kingdom. Even though Sheba is finally betrayed and his threat ended, the episode makes clear that the final years of David's reign were not years of halcyon contentment. The divisions that finally permanently rupture the kingdom after Solomon's death are already present in David's kingdom. In fact, the rallying cry for secessionist northern dissenters is the same later in Jeroboam's time (1 Kgs 12:16) as in Sheba's (v. 1).

Sheba's revolt also functions as the backdrop for narrating a further dark episode in Joab's story. This time he is responsible for the murder of Amasa (vv. 4-13), whom David had appointed to command the army in his place (19:13). As with his killing of Abner (3:27), Uriah (11:16-17), and Absalom (18:14), Joab does not hesitate to kill when he judges it to be in his own interest or his own assessment of the king's interests. The narrative simply reports the murder of Amasa without comment, but on his deathbed David charges Solomon to hold Joab accountable for the blood of Abner and Amasa (1 Kgs 2:5-6). Political memories can be long in Israel.

The completion of chap. 20 seems to represent a break in the narrative of David's later years. Most have judged chaps. 21–24 to be appendixes to the book. These chapters do not continue the chronological narration of events toward the end of David's kingship. Some have believed that 1 Kings 1–2 are the continuation of the main narrative and conclude the so-called succession narrative with the account of Solomon's accession to the throne (see the Overview for chaps. 9–20). In their present form, those chapters certainly conclude David's story by narrating

his death and the events immediately surrounding it, but they were probably not originally connected to 2 Samuel 20. With chap. 20 we come to the conclusion, not of David's life, but of an apologetic account of the events that led to and resolved Absalom's rebellion against his own father. The slant is pro-David, narrating tragic events but making clear that they were not of David's making (including the murder of Amasa). David may have suffered struggles and setbacks, but he is still worthy of God's promise, and so is his dynasty.[338]

20:1-3. Sheba, identified as a scoundrel or troublemaker, was one of the Israelites present at the angry confrontation between Israelites and Judahites in 19:41-43. His response to the apparently successful claims of Judah for priority with David is to declare that Israel has nothing to do with David (v. 1). His outcry is a call to secession and separatism for the northern tribes of Israel, and it may have been a traditional separatist slogan. In any case, it is used again in a remarkably similar situation of failed negotiations between north and south when Jeroboam leads the north into the breakaway that permanently divides the Israelite kingdom (1 Kgs 12:16). Sheba is a Benjaminite, perhaps even a distant relative of Saul, if Bichri is related to Becorath (9:1). Perhaps Sheba is part of the one thousand Benjaminites who accompanied Shimei to meet David (19:16).

Sheba's cry receives support, but it is unclear what is meant by the expression "all the people of Israel followed Sheba" (v. 2). It surely does not mean that the whole of the northern tribes joined Sheba's rebellion, for no battles with northern forces seem to ensue. The phrase could indicate that the Israelites present at the crossing of the Jordan left with Sheba in an act of defiance. The second half of the verse narrows the reference to those who met David at the Jordan to accompany him back to Jerusalem. Since those present on that occasion were primarily Benjaminites, like Sheba himself, it may have been that Sheba's tangible support came primarily from his own tribe. That he does not gain widespread support in Israel seems clear by his ignoble end (vv. 14-22).

338. See McCarter, *II Samuel,* 9-16, for a detailed discussion of this view and its alternatives.

David's first act in Jerusalem is to set aside the ten concubines he had left in Jerusalem (15:16). These are the women of his household whom Absalom had violated sexually in a public display of contempt for David and assertion of his own author- ity as king (16:20-23). Although David provides for their care, they are condemned to a future without husbands or children, as if they were widows (v. 3). David's act here does not have any clearly discernible connection to Sheba's revolt. It seems unlikely that this is an act to appease northern sensibilities, and even less likely that David is giving up the keeping of concubines (his son Solomon takes the practice to new heights).[339] More likely, David acts to preserve his own honor by refusing to restore to his household the women Absalom has defiled. The narrator is concerned not only with Sheba's rebellion but also with other matters that took place in this same period.

20:4-13. The murder of Amasa by Joab is another drama that plays itself out against the backdrop of Sheba's rebellion. Amasa was the Judahite commander of Absalom's army whom David appointed over his own army in a conciliatory gesture to win back support of the tribe of Judah and others who had followed Absalom (19:13). This appointment displaced Joab, who was out of favor with David for killing Absalom. Joab had, earlier in David's career, reacted to the defection of Abner, Saul's general and a potential rival, by killing him (3:27).

In the wake of Sheba's defiance, David summons Amasa with his first assignment as commander of David's army. He is to gather the militia of Judah and come ready before David in three days. He does not do so in the time allotted (v. 4). Scholars offer various interpretations of this failure.[340] Was it an act of deliberate refusal to obey on Amasa's part? Was the time simply too short to accomplish the task? Was the short time limit a deliberate trap to ensure Amasa's failure? We do not have enough information to determine which of these was the case.

David turns to one of his old warrior companions, Abishai (one of the sons of Zeruiah and the brother of Joab), to take the mercenary forces, which were under separate command from the tribal militia, and pursue Sheba quickly (vv. 6-7). David is presented as being genuinely worried about the threat from Sheba—one potentially greater than that posed by Absalom. Absalom fomented a rebellion against David, but Sheba represents a potential threat to the unity of the kingdom itself. David will, in this successful campaign against Sheba, keep this unity intact by force; but Sheba's separatist movement foreshadows the eventual division of the kingdom under Jeroboam (1 Kings 12).

Belatedly, Amasa comes to meet Joab and the army at Gibeon (v. 8a). The troops of Judah may have been with him. Joab goes out to meet him and, in an apparent ruse, intentionally drops his sword, only to retrieve it and plunge it into Amasa's belly as he grasps Amasa's beard to kiss him in greeting (vv. 8b-10). It is a scene narrated with grisly details: Amasa's entrails fall onto the ground; Joab strikes only one blow and leaves Amasa to die wallowing in his own blood on the road (v. 12). An ultimatum is issued: Whoever favors Joab and David should follow Joab (v. 11). The order of loyalties expressed here is significant. The ultimatum does not work immediately. With Amasa's agonized body in the road, people (presumably Amasa's troops) simply stop in the road (v. 12). Finally, Joab's man drags Amasa's body aside and covers it; only then do all the troops join in the pursuit of Sheba (v. 13).

This episode is probably narrated in such detail to make clear that Amasa's murder was not David's doing. Amasa was, no doubt, an influential man in Judah, and his murder presented a serious political complication for David. This account is apologetic in character. "This was the work of Joab, acting on his own initiative and motivated by his usual sense of ruthless expediency, probably augmented in this case by envy and injured pride."[341]

20:14-22. Sheba does not seem able to generate an effective army. He is described primarily as being on the run with David's force in pursuit. David's haste in ordering this pursuit was probably an effort to keep Sheba from having time to gather a force and organize a campaign. Ironically, David's strategy is consistent with the advice of Ahithophel to

---

339. Contra Brueggemann, *First and Second Samuel*, 330.
340. Cf. Contra Brueggemann, *First and Second Samuel*, 330-31; Anderson, *2 Samuel*, 432.

341. McCarter, *II Samuel*, 432.

Absalom and might well have been effective against David if Hushai had not intervened (16:15–17:14).

David's initial fear that Sheba would hole up in a fortified city (v. 6) comes to pass. Sheba takes refuge in Abel of Beth-maacah, a city in the north of Israel near Dan (v. 14); it may be associated with the Aramaean kingdom of Maacah (10:6). He seems to have only a force from his own clan, the Bichrites, with him. Joab lays siege to the city, a matter in which he has some expertise (11:1; 12:26-31). The siege proceeds methodically and would no doubt have been effective (v. 15), but Joab is halted by the words of a "wise woman" from the walls of the city (v. 16).

The woman describes herself as a representative of peace and faithfulness in Israel and speaks of the "heritage of the LORD." She presents alternatives to the destruction of her city, known for its wisdom and as a "mother in Israel" (vv. 18-19). The contrast with Joab could hardly be greater. He represents ruthless power and the will to violence in settling issues. He considers his actions in the light of pragmatic self-interest, not out of concern for the "heritage of the LORD." He would not hesitate to destroy even the most important city if it stood in his way. The wise woman of Abel reminds us of other women in the books of Samuel who offered peaceful and conciliatory alternatives to violence and confrontation: Abigail (1 Samuel 25) and the wise woman of Tekoa (2 Sam 14:1-24).

But Joab is willing to deal if he can get what he is after. He is nothing if not pragmatic. Joab declares that his real objective is not to destroy the city, but to capture and deal with Sheba, a rebel against David's rule. If he alone were given up, the city and all in it would be left alone; Joab would withdraw (v. 21a). The wise woman promises the head of Sheba (v. 21b). It is a peaceful alternative for the city, but not for Sheba. After proper consultation with the people, Sheba's head is thrown over the wall, and the siege is lifted (v. 22). The unity of the kingdom is restored—but by force, not by persuasion.

REFLECTIONS

1. The events that follow Absalom's death show David and his kingdom enmeshed in a complex series of political and military dealings. God is not explicitly visible in these chapters, and the kingdom reflects abiding tensions that foreshadow a troubled future. In his retreat from Jerusalem, David had trusted his troubled future to the goodness of God and the faithfulness of God's promises (16:12). As the narrative of David's story through this troubled period comes to an end, we are forced to understand that if God's promise is trustworthy it will be in the midst of the troubled realities of power and politics, not as a way around those realities.

Many in our own day turn to faith in the hope that the promises of God can give them a means to bypass the harsh realities of the world. That hope is an illusion. Like David, we will be forced to trust in those promises through days that are filled with conflict, difficult decisions, shifting human loyalties, and the seeming lack of God's presence. In the midst of harsh realities in politics and relationships, we will also encounter loyal relationships (like Barzillai) and wise words (like the woman of Abel), and we must receive and be guided by them. But beyond these human moments of hope must be a trust that God's promises are sure even in a troubled world and in the troubles of our lives.

Trust is a quality that is often in short supply in our materialistic world. Trust requires an ability to look beyond the immediacy of our struggles and brokenness. Trust requires remembering and living out of God's promises even in days when God seems distant or absent. God is not overtly visible in the account of troubling political events in this chapter, and David has been through tragic events that were a consequence of his own sin. But God's promise has not been revoked, and in the midst of his troubles, David chose to trust in that promise (16:12). It may be that trust, rooted in the memory of God's promise, gives us eyes to see God's goodness in the midst of trouble—in the loyalty of a friend, in wise words from an unexpected source, in the faithful support of a community, or in the opening of unforeseen possibilities.

2. Chapters 19–20 are not resurrection moments in David's story. They are testimony to the realities of brokenness and violence that surround the exercise of human political power. But the promise has been voiced and is still certain. David is God's anointed king. He has been to the depths of personal despair in the death of Absalom and to the desperation of political failure in the loss of his kingdom, and he has trusted in the goodness of God's promise (16:12). We, like David, can trust God's promise; but we, like him, must do so in continued engagement with the complexities of our personal and political lives. We could do far worse than to face those complexities with compassion for those who have wronged us (Shimei), acceptance of ambiguities we cannot resolve (Ziba and Mephibosheth), appreciation for the loyalties of friends and family (Barzillai), decisiveness when difficult action must be taken to avoid further division (Sheba), and willingness to entertain wise alternatives (the wise woman of Abel).

These stories of the struggles and brokenness of David's later years do not contain dramatic religious experiences to reassure David of God's presence. In our own troubled world and the troubled moments of our own lives, we, too, seldom receive dramatic religious experiences to reassure us. Like David, we are required to remember God's promises as they have been made known to us and to trust that God is in the midst of our decisions and relationships, enabling our most faithful responses to the events of our lives.

2 Samuel 20:23-26, David's Officers

COMMENTARY

The final segment before the "appendixes" to the books of Samuel (chaps. 21–24) is a list of David's officers. It is a parallel to the list in 8:15-18. Most scholars believe the list in chap. 8 reflects an earlier period of David's reign and that the list here reflects David's later kingdom.[342] The presence of this bureaucratic list as the conclusion to this section (chaps. 9–20) suggests that, for the moment, stability has been restored and the administrative apparatus of the kingdom is in place.

Most of the officers of the court are listed in pairs: two military, two administrative, two priestly offices. This arrangement may reflect an interest in preventing too great a concentration of power in any one of the persons in these areas.

There are some additions to and variations on the list of 8:15-18. Sheva is now secretary rather than Seraiah. There is a new office:

342. Mettinger, *Solomonic State Officials* 7.

"Adoram was in charge of the forced labor" (v. 24*a*). The practice of using forced labor, a policy continued and expanded by Solomon (1 Kgs 5:13; 9:15-22), came to be much hated. This practice may have begun as a use of slaves or non-Israelite laborers, but eventually Israelites were also conscripted for the building of Solomon's royal buildings and the Temple. Such conscription of labor sounds like the dangers of which the prophet Samuel warned (1 Sam 8:10-18), and such an office in this list seems to move farther from the ideals of covenant community into royal bureaucracy. We know nothing about Ira the Jairite or what it means to say that he was David's priest (v. 26). His position in the list displaces the listing of David's sons as priests in 8:18. Ira does not seem to have the cultic status of Zadok and Abiathar, who are elsewhere connected with the ark and the corporate cultus of Jerusalem. Perhaps Ira was a royal chaplain to David.

2 SAMUEL 21:1–24:25, A FINALE OF DAVID TRADITIONS

OVERVIEW

These final chapters represent an interruption in the chronological narration of David's story. Those who have defended the hypothesis of a succession narrative see the account of Solomon's accession to the throne (1 Kings 1–2) as the natural continuation of 2 Samuel 20. The narratives of 21:1-14 and 24:1-25 are not set in the later years of David's life and have nothing to do with royal succession. The poems of 22:1-51 and 23:1-7 possess no narrative setting, and the lists of 21:15-22 and 23:8-39 are drawn from the period of David's exploits against the Philistines. Most scholars have treated these chapters as intrusive appendixes, a miscellany of David-related material that was appended to the story in a complex and fragmented redactional process at a point prior to his deathbed scene.[343] Interpreters have also recognized the symmetrical or ring-like arrangement of these chapters:[344]

A 21:1-14, a narrative on the expiation of Saul's guilt
 B 21:15-22, a list of heroes and their deeds
  C 22:1-51, a song of thanksgiving for the Lord's deliverance
  C´ 23:1-7, a song in celebration of God's promise to David
 B´ 23:8-39, a list of heroes and their deeds
A´ 24:1-25, a narrative on the expiation of David's guilt

Despite this literary structure, these chapters have been treated primarily as a miscellany without intentional or substantive connection to the preceding books of Samuel. Only recently have voices begun to suggest that these chapters conclude the book of 2 Samuel with a distinctive ideological and theological voice. Scholars have suggested that these chapters taken together make a concluding comment on the story of kingship in Israel and the story of David in particular as that has been narrated in the books of Samuel.[345]

My own position on these chapters is similar to that taken by Walter Brueggemann in his recent studies of these chapters.[346] He notes the symmetrical arrangement of narratives in 2 Samuel 5–8, chapters that move David's story from tribal ideology to royal ideology (see the Overview for 2 Samuel 5–8), and suggests that these final chapters of 2 Samuel move in the other direction, from a high royal theology back to tribal, covenantal understandings of David's story. He notes that "the story ends with a king beset by self-serving political arrogance and autonomy" and argues that "chapters 21–24 are a gathering of materials to form a counterpart to the aggrandizement of absolute David, and perhaps intend to reverse the *rite of passage* in chapters 5–8 in order to provide David 'passage' back into the pre-absolute world of tribal fidelity . . . [these chapters are] a dismantling or deconstruction of an extravagantly royal David who has become unacceptable to the old tribal theory."[347]

I would suggest a slightly different relationship of these chapters to their preceding context. Chapter 20 does not leave us with a reality of royal absolutism that needs deconstruction. Royal absolutism in David's story was at its height in 2 Samuel 10 (conquest of nations) and 2 Samuel 11 (the personal behavior of "taking"). David's acting out of royal absolutism is reflected in the behavior of his sons Amnon (in the rape of Tamar, chap. 13) and Absalom (in his seizing of the throne, chaps. 15–18). But such absolutism as acceptable royal behavior for God's king has

343. See Anderson, *2 Samuel,* 247-48; McCarter, *II Samuel,* 18-19.
344. This symmetrical arrangement was first given detailed description by Karl Budde, *Die Bucher Samuel erklart,* KHCAT 8 (Tubingen: Mohr, 1902) 304, and his description has been adopted by many since.

345. Most notably, Childs, *Introduction to the Old Testament as Scripture,* 273-75; Walter Brueggemann, "2 Samuel 21–24: An Appendix of Deconstruction?" *CBQ* 50 (1988) 383-97; Polzin, *David and the Deuteronomist,* 202-14.
346. See Brueggemann's recent treatments of these chapters in *First and Second Samuel,* 336-57, and Brueggemann, *Power, Providence, and Personality,* 86-115.
347. Brueggemann, *Power, Providence, and Personality,* 88, 90.

already been deconstructed in the narrative by the judgment of the Lord pronounced by Nathan (chap. 12), and in the tragic events that unfold in David's own family, bringing him to grief as a king and as a man (chaps. 13–20). In these tragic episodes, we see a newly vulnerable and fallible David, but we also glimpse some of the qualities that made David God's king earlier in his story. These qualities are especially evident in his expression of trust to God's mercy and will in 15:25-26 and in David's wise and compassionate dealings with enemies and friends both as he retreated from Jerusalem (15:13–16:14) and as he returned (19:8b-40). The ideology of royal absolutism has been exposed and found wanting; glimpses of David as the Lord's anointed, covenantal king are visible in spite of David's vulnerability.

At the end of chap. 20, however, David has been reestablished as king. Moreover, Joab's actions suggest the possibility of a return to rule by absolute royal power. Without the intervening testimony of chaps. 21–24, David's story would proceed to the cynical

politics of deathbed vendettas by David and political bloodbaths by Solomon (1 Kings 1–2). What intervenes in chaps. 21–24 is not a deconstruction of royal absolutism but the effort to stay or to moderate its reconstruction. David is still vulnerable and capable of self-serving political acts (e.g., the execution of Saul's sons, chap. 21; the census, chap. 24), but he is capable of recognizing an authority beyond his own, that of the Lord. The lists show David not as the sole hero of a royal public relations effort, but as the leader of a heroic community. The two great songs celebrate David only in relation to the Lord, who chose him and acts through him, and in spite of David's sin and God's judgment. When the story moves on to Solomon and the ideology of empire, it does so only after including the testimony of these so-called appendixes. But these chapters bracket David's story by ending on the same note that was struck by Hannah's song in the beginning of the story of Israel's kingship. It is the Lord who "brings low and exalts," and it is the Lord who "exalts the power of his anointed" (1 Sam 2:7b, 10b).

2 Samuel 21:1-14, Gibeonite Vengeance

COMMENTARY

This narrative describes how a claim of bloodguilt on the house of Saul, for a wrong committed against the Gibeonites, led to the execution of seven of Saul's remaining sons. The cursing of Shimei as David retreats from Jerusalem accuses David of having the blood of Saul's house on his hands (16:8). This accusation may have as its background the events narrated in 21:1-14. The events narrated here do not follow chronologically on the rebellion of Sheba in chap. 20. This story comes from an earlier time in David's reign, although we find no mention of these events elsewhere in the books of Samuel or Chronicles. The narrator knows of David's kindness to Mephibosheth because of his oath to Jonathan (v. 7). Moreover, 2 Samuel 9, which tells the story of David and Mephibosheth, seems to presuppose that he is the only one left of the house of Saul (9:1). This reference has caused some to propose that chap. 21 has been displaced from an original position prior

to chap. 9, but there is no evidence to support this hypothesis.

Although the story is grim and tragic, the narrative may be intended to absolve David of any direct responsibility for the elimination of Saul's heirs. Taken in this straightforward fashion, an unspecified offense of Saul against the Gibeonites has caused a famine because that offense has not been expiated. David is only the one to whom God reveals the cause of the famine (v. 1). Further, David has no direct responsibility for the death of the remaining sons of the house of Saul; it is the Gibeonites who carry out vengeance on Saul's heirs (vv. 4-6). David even spares one of Saul's sons (v. 7) and later gives these seven, along with the bones of Saul and Jonathan, honored burial (vv. 12-14).

But the account is capable of a more cynical reading. We have no knowledge of the offense against the Gibeonites that issued in this charge of bloodguilt against the house of Saul. This is unusual in a pro-David narrative that lost no opportunity to discredit Saul. In this story, the bloodguilt of Saul is made known only to David, although the Gibeonites seem to feel the accusation is warranted. It is David, however, who initiates negotiations with the Gibeonites over this matter. Brueggemann has suggested that the charge against Saul could simply be a piece of "Davidic fabrication" that serves as a pretext for David to eliminate any future Saulide claim on his throne, and does so in the name of religious expiation of guilt.[348] But even if the offense against the Gibeonites is not fabricated, we can judge David to be capable of political opportunism in using an old charge of bloodguilt to eliminate potential rivals. At the point in David's story where a vulnerable and chastened David has regained power and used it to consolidate his reign (chap. 20), this narrative begins a series of appendixes that step outside the chronology of David's story and remind the reader that royal reality is not identical with the royal ideal of efficient, bureaucratized, religiously sanctioned power. Instead of high royal ideology, we see either a local chieftain who must expiate bloodguilt and bow to powers beyond his control or a ruthless politician who takes advantage of a suspicious charge against an old enemy to eliminate his heirs as potential rivals. In either case, this narrative works against any idealized high theology of kingship focused on David.

21:1-6. A three-year famine grips the land. In this crisis, David inquires of the Lord, only to be told that the land suffers under bloodguilt incurred by Saul for an offense against the Gibeonites. But there are gaps in this information. Why does the land now suffer punishment during the time of David for an offense committed by Saul, who has already been rejected and met a tragic death for his failures before God? What did Saul do to the Gibeonites? By what means did David inquire of God? How is it that he alone comes to know of Saul's bloodguilt? These questions are never answered and leave the account ambiguous. Is this an innocent story of the expiation of guilt or a convenient pretext for political opportunism by David?

We have no record elsewhere of an action by Saul against the Gibeonites. Verse 2 says that Saul tried to exterminate them and attributes this to excessive nationalistic sentiment for Israel and Judah, which caused him to violate the special covenant made between Israel and the Gibeonites in Joshua's time (Josh 9:3-27). Although the Gibeonites were a non-Israelite people (here called Amorites), they had enjoyed a special relationship to Israel. However, their city and territory were very near Saul's capital and home at Gibeah. Saul may have tried to annex or somehow control this territory and met resistance that led to Gibeonite deaths.

The Gibeonites are pictured as reticent in this entire matter. They do not call for vengeance, but are approached by David (v. 2a), who alone seems to have received divine word that the famine is connected with Saul's bloodguilt. David seeks a renewed blessing from the Gibeonites and asks them to name the means of expiation (v. 3). The Gibeonites cautiously advise the king that it is not within their authority to exact monetary reparations or to exact the death penalty (v. 4a). Again David takes the initiative by assuming the authority for any penalty exacted in expiation of Saul's bloodguilt (v. 4b). It is by royal authority that things will be put right.

When the Gibeonites finally speak their mind, it is to seek the penalty against Saul's house that he supposedly sought against the Gibeonites—extermination. Saul's offense is described as genocidal in character (v. 5), though details are still vague and unspecified. The proposed penalty for Saul's act is the execution of seven of Saul's sons at the hands of the Gibeonites (v. 6). The meaning of the verb יקע (yāqaʿ) is uncertain here, and translators have argued on behalf of an astonishing range of options ("impaling," "dismemberment," "crucifixion in the sun," "hanging," "hurling down").[349] Since this is to be done "before the Lord," it should be envisioned as a ritual execution. David agrees to hand over these seven sons. The act may be intended as more symbolic than actually effective in ending the house of Saul. Perhaps the number seven represents completion. As we shall see, David spares Jonathan's son, Mephibosheth

---

348. Brueggemann, *First and Second Samuel,* 336-38.

349. See R. Polzin, "HWQY' and Covenantal Institutions in Early Israel," *HTR* 62 (1969) 236.

(v. 7; chap. 9), and the seven sons of Saul who were executed surely included some old enough to have sons of their own to carry on the Saulide line. For David's political purposes, it does eliminate all possible immediate Saulide rivals to the throne.

21:7-9. The executions are carried out, with the notable exception of David's protection of Mephibosheth (v. 7), Jonathan's son, because of the covenant sworn between David and Jonathan (1 Sam 18:3; 20:17, 42; 23:18). Chapter 9 tells the story of David and Mephibosheth in some detail, and the opening of that chapter seems to imply that Mephibosheth is the only remaining direct descendant of Saul. For this reason, some have suggested that chap. 21 once preceded chap. 9.

The seven executed sons are named in v. 8. They include two sons of Saul by Rizpah, who was Saul's concubine and, after Saul's death, was the object of tension between Abner and Ishbosheth (3:7-11). One of Rizpah's sons is also named Mephibosheth, but he is in no way to be identified with Jonathan's son. The remaining five were grandsons of Saul, born to his daughter Merab,[350] who was married to a son of Barzillai. If this is the same Barzillai associated with the support of David during Absalom's revolt (17:27-29; 19:31-40), it is surprising that his grandsons would be killed with David's tacit approval. Some have argued that these two men are not the same person.[351]

David hands these Saulide sons into the hand of the Gibeonites, who carry out the executions at the beginning of the barley harvest (v. 9). This timing may have been significant—as an expectation that expiation of Saul's bloodguilt would bring an end to the famine.

21:10-14. Suddenly and surprisingly the narrative focus shifts away from David to Rizpah, the concubine of Saul and mother of two sons executed by the Gibeonites. Dressed for mourning, she keeps vigil by the bodies of her sons and the others who have been executed (v. 10). The bodies have apparently been left exposed to birds and wild animals as a further act of humiliation and dishonor, but Rizpah refuses to accept this fate for her sons and fends off the scavengers day and night.

When Rizpah's lonely vigil is reported to David (v. 11), he is apparently moved to action. We are not told of David's inner motivation, but he acts to honor the dead. He begins by retrieving the bones of Saul and Jonathan from the people of Jabesh-gilead, who had stolen the bodies of their heroes from their humiliating display on the walls of the Philistine city of Beth-shan (v. 12; cf. 1 Sam 31:11-13). He gives their bones and the bodies of those now executed an honorable burial (vv. 13-14*a*). Saul and Jonathan are laid to rest in the tomb of Saul's father, Kish (v. 14*a*). Only after their burial does God heed prayers on behalf of the famine-parched land (v. 14*b*). Some scholars think this story stands in conflict with 1 Sam 31:12, where it is reported that the bodies of Saul and Jonathan had been burned, but v. 13 clearly states that after the burning their bones were buried under a tamarisk tree in Jabesh-gilead. The burning of the bodies was not so intense or protracted as to destroy the bones.

350. The Hebrew text reads "Michal," but Michal was never married to a son of Barzillai and is explicitly said to have borne no children (6:23). The Greek text reads "Merab," and most translations have followed this reading.

351. See Hertzberg, *I and II Samuel*, 384.

REFLECTIONS

1. This story is told in a manner that does not allow certainty on whether to read it as an innocent but somewhat primitive story of the expiation of guilt or as a cynical exercise in royal political opportunism (see Commentary). This ambiguity may well point to a reality worth noting for our time as well as for David's: the ease with which political expediency can masquerade as religious duty. It is often as difficult to distinguish innocent religiosity from self-serving hypocrisy in our modern public forums as it is in this story. Since the stakes, as in this tale, are often serious life-and-death issues, it behooves us to examine carefully religious calls to action. The clothing of religious duty cannot provide a safe conduct around careful public scrutiny of proposed policies or programs. This is not a call to "keep religion out of politics," but to recognize that religious values and claims in the political arena must be subject to the same critical scrutiny as secular claims. If religious motivations prove sincere and recommended policies prove sound, the outcome will be stronger for undergoing careful scrutiny. But if closer examination reveals hypocrisy and cynical self-serving uses of religious language, then all will be well served by the exposure of such tactics. Determination of David's motives lies beyond our further examination, but the ambiguous telling of this story serves to make us more vigilant in writing our own story.

2. The brief moment in the spotlight occupied by Rizpah in this story is worthy of our notice. David, the king, holds all the power, but Rizpah, with quiet moral persistence, forces the king to act on the side of honor and humanity. Too often we give in to the claims of human political power to be all-powerful, but Rizpah reminds us that this is not the full truth about reality. There is a moral power that can affect even kings, if we choose to wield it. In our own time, women in Argentina and El Salvador have stood up publicly and persistently as the "mothers of the disappeared," insisting that disregard for the common humanity of countless sons and husbands could not go unremarked. Like Rizpah, they kept a vigil that brought the notice of powers that could eventually make changes. Oppressive regimes were forced to change and give way in the face of a witness devoid of apparent political power, but possessed of moral power that proved capable of making a political difference. Rizpah's moment in this story is small, but her moral persistence makes her witness great.

2 Samuel 21:15-22, David's Warriors

COMMENTARY

The second element in the appendixes is a list of the exploits of David's warriors during the war with the Philistines. The list is composed of four items, each with some narrative detail, describing the triumph of one of David's men over a giant warrior of the Philistines. Each item begins with a report about a battle with the Philistines (vv. 15, 18-20), and v. 22 summarizes the entire list, "These four were descended from the giants in Gath; they fell by the hands of David and his servants."

Although David is valued as the "lamp of Israel" (v. 17), such a judgment occurs in a context of his weariness and removal from battle. David may be the king whose very being is important to Israel, but he no longer leads heroically in battle. In all four segments of the list, David's men do the heroic deeds. David's elevation to the high role of "lamp of Israel" seems hollow when placed alongside the diminishment of his actual deeds in leading Israel. The attribution of his triumph over Goliath to another hero (v. 19) may be a part of this intentional diminishment of David.

The author may be suggesting that the claims of importance for the "lamp of Israel" may be exaggerated and that Israel does not really need David.

21:15-17. David plays a role only in the first part of the list (vv. 15-17), a portrait with some tension in its portrayal of David. He grows weary in battle and is about to be overcome by one of the giants who fought for the Philistines (vv. 15-16). This Philistine warrior and the subsequent three are all described as "descendants of הרפה" (*hārāpâ*, vv. 16, 18, 20, 22), which is taken by some as a reference to the "Rephaim," who were legendary giants in Canaan before the coming of the Israelites (Gen 15:20; Deut 2:11; 3:11; Josh 17:15), hence, to be translated here as "giants" (NRSV). But others have taken this term for a family name and have translated it as "descendants of Rapha" (NIV).

David is rescued by Abishai from the threat occasioned by his weariness (v. 17*a*). Again he is forced to rely on the sons of Zeruiah (Abishai's brother is Joab). Following this narrow escape, David's men swore that he should no longer go into battle. As king, he is too valuable to risk in battle (cf. 18:3). They fear that his death would "quench the lamp of Israel" (v. 17*b*). This phrase represents a high theology of kingship that values the king as light and life in the midst of Israel, but ironically it works against the exercise of genuine leadership or the direct action on the part of David. Brueggemann has suggested that the juxtaposition of David's weariness and his removal from the arena of mighty deeds in these verses makes the affirmation that David is the "lamp of Israel" ironic and ambiguous.[352] The high theology of kingship is called into question. Is such a symbolically valued king needed if he no longer leads? In the following list of mighty deeds against the Philistines, David is conspicuous by his absence.

21:18-22. David no longer appears in this list of heroic exploits. The heroic victories of three of his men are celebrated. It is the second of these three that has provoked greatest comment. In v. 19, Elhanan, a Bethlehemite,

is given credit for having killed Goliath. In the far better known story of 1 Samuel 17, it is, of course, David who is the Bethlehemite who kills Goliath, whose spear, in both stories, is described as being like a "weaver's beam" (1 Sam 17:7). Scholars have offered numerous suggestions to explain this discrepancy.[353] They range from suggesting that Elhanan is another name for David himself to the view that this is an intentional debunking of the David mystique by attributing his greatest victory to another warrior. The chronicler reports (1 Chr 20:5) that Elhanan killed Lahmi, a brother of Goliath, which is widely taken as an attempt by the historian to harmonize these two traditions. We cannot resolve this discrepancy with certainty, but the effect of the notice here is to diminish David's role in the Philistine wars. The final notice of v. 22 makes the mention of David alongside his men seem irrelevant. David does nothing in this listing of mighty deeds except to retire in weariness from the field of battle.

---

352. Brueggemann, *Power, Providence, and Personality,* 92-93.

353. See the discussion of various proposals in Anderson, *2 Samuel,* 255.

2 Samuel 22:1-51, A Psalm of Thanksgiving from David

COMMENTARY

This is the first of two songs that stand at the heart of the appendixes to the books of Samuel. It is a royal psalm of thanksgiving, attributed to David "when the LORD delivered him from the hand of all his enemies, and from the hand of Saul" (v. 1), and is a duplicate of Psalm 18. McCann has made a strong case that this psalm of thanksgiving had an eschatological orientation in Israel and in the psalter. It functioned to proclaim "the reign of God amid circumstances that suggest God does *not* reign."[354] Even in its setting in 2 Samuel, this psalm refers less to a celebration of the end of troubles for David himself and more to a confidence that God will bring deliverance for the house of David into the future (v. 51*c*).

This song, probably shaped in Israel's liturgical history, is now placed at the end of the

books of Samuel as David's reflection on his entire career and as a theological comment on the books of Samuel. It complements the song of Hannah (1 Sam 2:1-10), celebrating in retrospect the same ultimate reality of the Lord's sovereignty that Hannah's song anticipated.[355] As we shall see, many themes appear in both these poetic pieces, which bracket the narratives of 1 and 2 Samuel.

The song falls into three distinct pieces. The separate emphases of these segments are crucial to understanding the role this song now plays when it is placed in the mouth of David at the conclusion of his career (i.e., when the kingdom is secure from enemies).

The first section (vv. 1-20) is a thanksgiving for deliverance. It emphasizes the celebration of God's power to deliver from the threat of chaos. The king appears only as a

---

354. J. Clinton McCann, Jr., *Psalms,* in *The New Interpreter's Bible Commentary,* vol. 3 (Nashville: Abingdon, 2015) 349.

355. See Childs, *Introduction to the Old Testament as Scripture,* 273-74; Brueggemann, *First and Second Samuel,* 339.

supplicant. Verse 7 is the thematic key of this section, "I called . . . he heard. . . ." The poet focuses exclusively on the grace-filled activity of God's salvation.

The second section (vv. 21-28) extols human moral virtue and the power of righteousness to gain the Lord's favor. Both wisdom and deuteronomic influence have been attributed to this section, because it seems to accept a doctrine of strict retribution that is characteristic of these two traditions. The thematic key to this section comes in v. 24, "I was blameless before him." Here the emphasis is on human ability to claim God's grace by virtue of one's own righteousness.

The final section (vv. 29-51) offers yet another perspective. In the king's voice, God's ultimate power is acknowledged as central (e.g., v. 29, "Indeed, you are my lamp, O LORD"), but side by side with this acknowledgment is an affirmation of the king's own abilities and deeds (e.g., v. 30, "By you I can crush a troop"). This section is filled with the affirmation of heroic acts and mighty gifts, all celebrated in action verbs whose subject is "I." But constantly alongside the deeds of the royal "I," the poet acknowledges the divine, empowering "Thou." The king achieves great things through admirable abilities, but all that he does is enabled by the grace-filled activity of God, who deserves to be praised (v. 50). But God's salvation and steadfast love are given through God's king and God's anointed one: "David and his descendants forever" (v. 51). As a theological comment on David's story—indeed, the whole story of God's movement in Israel toward and through David—the final section of this psalm serves as a corrective to the first two segments.

God's salvation (emphasized in vv. 1-20) is crucial to Israel's future, but the stories of the books of Samuel stress the unique combination of divine providence with human personality, through which God has chosen to work. These stories do not fit the dictum of the exodus experience, "The LORD will fight for you, and you have only to keep still" (Exod 14:14). God's grace in deliverance is worthy of celebration, but if 1 and 2 Samuel celebrate divine power they also celebrate the man after God's own heart: David. Even when David grew weary (21:15), there were mighty men and mighty deeds through which God's deliverance was made visible.

In section two of this psalm (vv. 22-28), the emphasis on the king's righteousness and obedience as the source of God's blessing also does not ring completely true. At this point, near the end of David's story, we know that he did not remain blameless and without guilt. The king's moral virtue alone, even when the king is David, cannot assure God's salvation. A developing ideology of kingship may wish to assert royal control over the destiny of Israel, but the story of David makes clear that such an ideology stands on shaky ground. We can only read the assertions of vv. 21-28 ironically in the light of David's career, marred by his own guilt in "the matter of Uriah the Hittite" (1 Kgs 15:4).

It is only in section three of this song (vv. 29-51) that we come to the combination of royal gifts with the ultimate empowering (and forgiving) grace of God, which makes the future possible for God's people. "The outcome of such a three part juxtaposition is that the king who might wish to claim virtue and achievement for himself is like every other Israelite. He is only an empty-handed supplicant before Yahweh, totally dependent on Yahweh's willingness to listen and to answer and intervene."[356] The king is nothing without the grace of God; nevertheless, God has chosen to work through David and the subsequent kings of his line. God has chosen to work messianically—that is, through God's anointed one. It is this combination of divine providence and human action that uniquely summarizes the books of Samuel and the story of David in particular.

22:1-20. Verse 1 serves as a superscription to this psalm, identifying the first-person royal voice in the psalm as David and identifying the occasion as the day when David was delivered from all his enemies and from Saul. The psalm itself does not derive from a specific time of deliverance, but instead to God's deliverance of God's king in all times of distress.

356. Brueggemann, *Power, Providence, and Personality,* 97. Unlike Brueggemann I do not see the third section as a return to single-minded emphasis on God's grace alone, as in section one. God's willingness to act as "Thou" to the king's "I" is unique. The psalm ultimately affirms God's intention to act in and through God's "anointed" one in spite of human sin and guilt, which makes it so appropriate as a theological summation to the books of Samuel, and for Christians a prelude to God's "messianic" future.

These initial verses are a thanksgiving for deliverance from distress. They open with a doxology in praise of the Lord that utilizes a rush of terms and titles signifying God's role as rescuer and protector (vv. 2-4). All of these terms are personalized by "the royal narrator" with the use of the possessive pronoun "my": rock, fortress, deliverer, refuge, shield, horn of salvation, stronghold, savior.

Doxology gives way to descriptions of distress in vv. 5-6. Such language is associated elsewhere with descriptions of chaos and Sheol (cf. Ps 116:3; Jonah 2:5-6a), and the stress is on the powerlessness of the royal suppliant before such chaotic forces: waves of death, torrents of perdition, cords of Sheol, and snares of death.

Verse 7 is the dramatic turning point in this part of the psalm. The king cries out, and God hears. It is classic exodus language, reflecting the covenantal traditions of Israel (Exod 2:23). What follows in vv. 8-20 is a richly embroidered poetic portrait of God's salvation—eminently capable of meeting the challenge of the chaotic powers described in vv. 5-6 and resulting in the salvation of the royal suppliant. The king's only role in this first segment of chap. 22 is that of one in need who cries out to God. God is the deliverer, described in theophanic terms arriving in power to work deliverance in a time of distress. Elements of earthquake, smoke, and fire accompany God's appearance (vv. 8-9). God commands the clouds, rides on cherubs and the wind, thunders with his voice, hurls the lightning, and lays bare the sea and the earth's foundations with a blast from the divine nostrils (vv. 10-16). God's theophany delivers the suppliant. Matching the torrent of doxology in vv. 2-4 is a rush of verbs signifying deliverance in vv. 17-20: God "reached . . . took . . . drew me out . . . delivered . . . was my stay . . . brought me out . . . delighted in me." We reach the end of this first segment of the psalm surfeited in the language of divine salvation and grace. The poem focuses exclusively on God as the bringer of salvation.

22:21-28. Some have found the shift in language so startling with these verses that they discern a different author. In my view, this dramatic shift is an intentional literary device that serves well the purpose of this psalm. These verses shift the emphasis from divine saving initiatives to human righteousness and obedience and human moral ability to deserve God's blessing.

In tones reminiscent of Deuteronomy or Proverbs, this portion of the psalm asserts the importance of righteousness and obedience to God's covenant as moral qualities that God takes seriously. The psalmist parades terms indicative of the moral life for our attention: "righteousness," "cleanness of hands," "his ordinances before me," "his statutes I did not turn aside," "blameless," "kept from guilt," "loyal," "pure," "humble." We are torn between two sentiments as we read this section. We are properly impressed with the demands of the moral life lived in covenant obedience. Surely the Lord does regard such qualities, and we are reassured that such values matter in the eyes of God. But we also remember that these words are placed in the mouth of David, and when this Davidic voice claims, "I was blameless before him, and I kept myself from guilt" (v. 24a), we know that this has not always been the case. The words of such lofty ideals placed in the mouth of the man who took Bathsheba and killed Uriah become ironic and self-indicting. The words of this section are no less true as statements of what God desires, but David does not stand guiltless. This segment of the psalm stands as a testimony to the moral demands placed upon one who would be God's person, but in the light of David's story, we are grateful that we have already heard testimony in vv. 2-20 to God's grace given without merit. Taken alone, these verses might well become the basis of a high royal theology that imagines the king can control his own fate or is blameless because he stands above blame. But because we know David's story, we know that this can never be true. Even David stands guilty before God. Fortunately, this segment of the psalm does not stand alone and must be read in the context of the full psalm.

22:29-51. The final segment of this psalm is a song of victory. It celebrates both the success of human action and the enabling power of God that makes such actions effective. In the first two verses of this section, we hear praise for God as "my lamp" who "lightens my darkness" (v. 29), followed by the affirmations that "I can crush a troop" or "leap over a wall" (v. 30). Even these human feats of prowess, however, are accomplished only "by you" and "by my God." It is significant that David here celebrates God as "lamp" when in 21:17b David's men feared to risk his life lest it quench the "lamp of Israel." David's light depends on God's light.

Throughout the remainder of this psalm, the royal voice celebrates the feats he has accomplished against enemies. Such language is sometimes placed in an exultant first-person voice: "I pursued . . . destroyed . . . did not turn back . . . consumed . . . struck down . . . they fell" (vv. 38-39). But the affirmations of the royal "I" are constantly balanced by acknowledgment of a divine "Thou" who enables victory against enemies and prowess as warrior. The voice speaking here admits that "your help has made me great" (v. 36b).

Celebration of victory is punctuated with praise for the Lord who gives the victory (vv. 32, 47, 50).

It is with the final verse (v. 51) that the full contrast of this final section with the first two sections of the song becomes clear. God is the true source of deliverance (vv. 2-20), and human righteousness does count (vv. 21-28). But in David and his descendants, God has chosen to work salvation through the Davidic king and to show steadfast love by means of the anointed one. The king alone cannot secure the future in righteousness—even David is a sinner—and God has chosen not to act alone but through David, God's anointed king. In the end, this psalm celebrates this partnership for the sake of Israel's salvation.

REFLECTIONS

Many important elements of this psalm are given reflection in the section on Psalm 18 in volume III of *The New Interpreter's Bible Commentary.* I limit reflections here to aspects that seem especially significant to the setting of this psalm at the conclusion of David's story.

1. Some of the imagery of this psalm will seem strange to our modern ears, especially the dramatic theophanic images of 22:8-20. Yet, the threat of chaos is a reality with which most can identify. Brueggemann writes, "Indeed, chaos (and not guilt) is the besetting issue in our common experience. The threat of chaos is known most intimately in broken interpersonal relationships. The same threat is known most massively and publicly in relation to the looming danger of nuclear holocaust."[357]

2. In some ways we have retained a sense of the invading reality of chaos and its threat to our attempts at ordered meaning to our lives, but we have lost the corresponding language of deliverance that speaks in the same elemental way against the threat of chaos. We live in a time enamored of our own human capacities. When these capacities fail to deliver us from the crises (the times of chaos) in our life, we often discover that we have lost touch with a sense of divine power capable of driving back the darkness and restoring order in the midst of chaos.

Recovery of a sense of a power beyond our own human capacities requires a boldness of speech about God's power beyond our power, as this psalm models. Such speech does not allow denial of our need for deliverance, as if we could save ourselves. Such speech does not sink into despair that chaos cannot be overcome, for it boldly speaks of a power capable of overcoming chaos.

In terms of this psalm, our generation (and especially the church) has been drawn to the ordered, moral universe suggested by the second section of this psalm (22:21-28). The cool, rational, didactic approach of obeying commandments and seeking righteousness tempts us into thinking that our own efforts can control chaos. In the face of difficult and divisive moral issues (such as sexual orientation, abortion, the changing shape of the family, economic materialism, and nuclear war), the church is more

357. Brueggemann, *First and Second Samuel,* 342.

prone to establish study commissions, to pass carefully worded resolutions, or sometimes to seek settlement of the issue by legislation that defines righteousness. One of the teachings of this psalm may be that such didactic approaches to vexing moral questions only have their place in the context of a more elemental confidence and celebration of God's power to overcome chaos and to establish the kingdom. Such a confidence in God's ultimate reign over creation and history may let us regard our own efforts as less ultimate. Such a confidence may allow acceptance of differences in the confidence that God will ultimately vanquish the genuine enemies of God's kingdom. Such a confidence will require a boldness of speech about God's salvation that recognizes that our own moral efforts remain important, but cannot alone save us.

3. In the end this psalm teaches us something about God's willingness to act with, through, and even in spite of our humanness—both in David's story and our own. This psalm declares that God has chosen to make Israel's salvation (and ours) a divine-human enterprise. In this psalm, it is the confession of the human "I" that what enables wholeness and success in our own efforts is the power of the divine "Thou." In the Christian faith, the word for this confessional reality is *incarnation.* We know God's steadfast love through God's "anointed" (v. 51), through "messiah" (the Hebrew term for "anointed one"). For Christians, the claim that Jesus Christ was born in the line of David is precisely made in order to claim as a part of the meaning of Christ the story of God acting in, through, and in spite of David. In incarnation, Christians claim the tradition summarized by this psalm and its ultimate celebration of a divine-human partnership through which salvation comes. Hannah's song (1 Sam 2:1-10) began the story of God's salvation through David, and Mary's song (Luke 1:46-55) echoed it to begin the story of God's salvation through Jesus. Now this psalm of deliverance, obedience, and partnership between God and God's anointed one ends David's story and is echoed in the New Testament claim that Jesus, divine and human, is the son of David.

2 Samuel 23:1-7, David's Last Words

COMMENTARY

This is the second of the two songs that stand together at the heart of the so-called appendixes (2 Samuel 21–24). Although it is considerably shorter, this poetic piece, like 22:1-51, is a statement of idealized royal theology. Together these two songs at the end of David's career serve as a counterpart to the song of Hannah in 1 Sam 2:1-10. Hannah sang in anticipation of God's anointed one and the power of God through this royal agent to reverse the injustices of the world. The songs set in the mouth of David in 22:1-51 and 23:1-7 make clear that God has not abandoned the divine resolve to work through God's anointed king. These "last words of David" in 23:1-7 emphasize that God's covenant promise is everlasting (v. 5). Moreover, the well-being of God's people requires that the king rule "justly" and in the "fear of God" (vv. 3-4). After the stories of David's abuse of

power and the tragic re-enactment of those abuses by his sons and others in his kingdom (2 Samuel 11–20), these last words of David come as a reminder of the royal ideal to which God will hold the anointed one in spite of the temptations presented by royal power. This poem articulates the continuing hope that God's king can be an agent of God's Word and Spirit (v. 2), in spite of the shortcomings of David. It speaks of the hope for just rule through kingship understood as divine gift, not simply as the result of human power. It is against such hope, centered in what God is doing in Israel's midst, that not only David but all future kings in the line of David can be held accountable, and God's commitment to "everlasting covenant" can be understood. The politics of royal power must be measured against the demands of divine justice and the certainty of divine commitment.

Interestingly, these "last words of David" are presented as an "oracle" of David (v. 1*a*). The word נאם (*ně'um*), here translated "oracle," usually refers to a "prophetic utterance." Since David speaks of God's word on his tongue and the Spirit of the Lord speaking through him (v. 2), we conclude that David is portrayed here as a prophetic figure, receiving and proclaiming the word of the Lord as well as functioning as God's anointed king (v. 1*b*). Perhaps this picture of David as prophet originated with some of the other prophetic influences that we have noticed earlier in the books of Samuel (see Introduction).

In keeping with a common pattern for such oracles (see Balaam's oracle, Num 24:3, 15), there is an introduction of the oracle giver and an acknowledgment of God as the source of this word in vv. 1-2, followed by the direct reporting of God's word in vv. 3-4. David interrupts this word from the Lord (v. 5), affirming that his rule has embodied this word and that, as a consequence, he has received God's covenant and blessing (v. 5). Verses 6-7 resume and conclude God's word. It has often been noticed that the word of the Lord in vv. 4, 6-7 bears similarities to wisdom literature in its contrast of the righteous and the wicked, its use of metaphors drawn from nature, and its appeal to the fear of God.

23:1-2. Following a superscription that labels this song as the "last words of David" (v. 1*a*), David announces that he speaks an "oracle," which comes through him as God's "word" enabled by the "Spirit of the LORD" (vv. 1-2). The vocabulary is that of prophetic utterance, and the opening formula is virtually identical to that used by Balaam in beginning his oracle in Num 24:3. As readers of 2 Samuel, we have seen the temptation to understand royal power through taking and grasping (as the prophet Samuel had warned, 1 Sam 8:10-18), but now in the poetic oracle of a prophetic David, we hear him acknowledge that it is God who exalts a man to kingship (v. 1*b*);[358] it is not a human accomplishment. The king is the anointed of God (v. 1*b*) and not of the people. It is from the "Strong One of Israel" that favor comes (v. 1*b*),[359] and not from the wielding of political power. The testimony of this song does not come as a summing up of David's wisdom and experience. It comes through the "Spirit of the LORD" as God's "word" on David's tongue (v. 2). At the end of David's story, we are reminded in this song that God has been the initiator and shaper of a new future for Israel.

23:3-4. David announces and speaks the word of God; the text of this word begins in v. 3*b* (the NIV indicates this with quotation marks). The king is to rule justly and in the fear of God (v. 3*b*). When justice and piety are joined in the rule of the kingdom, then the result will be like the benefits of light from the sun and rain on the land in a well-ordered creation (v. 4). The imagery from nature and the admonition to the fear of God are reminiscent of wisdom literature. But wise rule here clearly arises from attending to matters of justice that temper the exercise of self-interested power. And wise rule requires that the king recognize God as the source from which royal power is derived, if it is to give life as sun and rain give life to the earth.

David's story has not always reflected this commitment to justice. As a result, death rather than life became actualized in his family and kingdom. But the ideal of kingship as God's anointed requires justice at the heart of any exercise of power, lest it be used to exploit, manipulate, or oppress. Those responsible for these final chapters of 2 Samuel have not allowed the tragic stories of grasping, self-interested power that marked the later years of David and his family to have the final word. Israel's poets can imagine a vision of the just and faithful king that outlives the realities of David's failures. This song leaves as David's legacy a royal ideal that is more enduring than royal reality, which always falls short of God's intentions (see Psalm 72 for a fuller poetic articulation of this ideal). The king can be a source of life and renewal to God's people, but only by attending to the justice and faithfulness that are the conditions of life-giving rule.

---

358. We read אל (*'ēl*, "God"; see NRSV) with the Dead Sea Scroll fragment 4QSamᵃ in place of על (*'āl*, "on high" or "Most High"; see NIV) in the MT. See McCarter, *II Samuel*, 477, for a detailed discussion of alternatives.

359. The traditional rendering of this phrase as "the sweet singer [or psalmist] of Israel" (NIV, "Israel's singer of songs") is possible, but most recent commentators and translations have read the terms זמרות ישראל (*zĕmirôt yiśrā'ēl*) as an epithet for God parallel to the phrase "God of Jacob" in the preceding line. It is variously translated as "protector of Israel," "Strong One of Israel" (NRSV), or "Stronghold of Israel." See McCarter, *II Samuel*, 480.

23:5. This verse seems like a comment by David instead of God's word. Read in this way, there is an exuberant quality to David's break into the moment with his own word: "Is not my house like this with God?" Our first reaction might be incredulous. David's house has been far from justice and faithfulness in previous episodes, and yet the humility of David in retreat from Jerusalem and the grief of David as bereft father have shown us a David defined by more than self-serving power.

The key to David's outburst may be found in his answer to his own question (v. 5b). The capacity for David's house to be just and faithful lies not in what David or those who come after him can achieve, but in God's commitment in "everlasting covenant" with David and his line (reflecting 2 Sam 7:14-16). If justice and faithfulness were left to human capacities alone, all would be doomed to fail. David can sin, but he can reclaim the vision of just and faithful rule because God's commitment never wavers. God is the true source of order, security, prosperity, and help (v. 5b). These do not exist as human achievements but as God-given possibilities, given again and again in everlasting covenant. David's house cannot be "like this" alone, but only "with God" (v. 5a). God's fidelity makes justice and faithfulness possible in spite of our sinful grasping after power.

23:6-7. These verses resume the divine oracle David is declaring. They provide an antithesis to vv. 3b-4. If the just and faithful king brings the renewal of life, then the "godless" (NRSV) or "evil" (NIV) bring death. The poet uses imagery, not of renewed and productive nature, but of thorns that choke life and cause pain (v. 6). Their fate is to perish (v. 7). The Hebrew word here is בליעל (*běliyyaʿal*), a word often translated as "worthless ones" but is also associated with injustice and impiety—i.e., the opposite of God's king as envisioned in v. 3b. It is interesting to note that, following Hannah's song (1 Sam 2:1-10), with its anticipation of God's justice through God's anointed one, we immediately see the contrast to God's anointed in the injustices committed by Eli's sons, who are also called *běliyyaʿal* (1 Sam 2:12).

REFLECTIONS

Those responsible for the appendixes in chaps. 21–24 knew the realistic story of David's misuse of power and its consequences. As readers of 2 Samuel, we, too, have seen David misuse his power to take and kill, and we have seen the consequences in his own family. We know the unfortunate reality alongside the hoped-for ideal of God's anointed king. But the segments of the appendixes, and this poetic song in particular, seek to reimagine the future from the perspective of what God is doing in David (and in kingship), and not through what David has done. This is the key. Israel's future and our own future are not dependent on what human power has realistically done or can do. For those who dare to imagine it, and give poetic voice to it, the future is God's future and, therefore, is always open to the possibilities of justice, faithfulness, and life no matter how realistic might be our assessment of the powers of oppression, sin, and death. Surrounded by a troubled and broken world and the crises of our own lives, we lose sight of God's power at work beyond and in spite of our own human limitations and sin. In the name of realism, we define ourselves, our goals, our communities by our failures and not by our visions. We settle for problems to solve rather than ideals to embody.

We live in a world where even the best of our leaders, in church and nation, seem to acquiesce in the so-called realities of violence, marketplace, self-sufficiency, and arrogant certitude. Even in facing these realities as problematic we allow them to define the terms of our life. There is a dearth of those who would reimagine the future in different terms. In particular, the church should give leadership in such reimagining because we know the reality of God beyond the realities of the world. We should dare to dream dreams and see visions, because we trust that God is at work to bring possibilities for life, hope, love, and justice that go beyond the sum total of our human capacities. To read David's final song should not lead us to sneer at its unrealistic idealism. We should instead hear in its images the call to declare anew for our time that God's justice and faithfulness define the vision that leads to life. This is the truth of the world's reality, no matter how often we fall short of fully actualizing that vision. David's song calls us to reimagine our future as God's future. If we are so busy in the church realistically analyzing our institutional and societal issues that we fail to dream dreams or see visions, then we will perish like the "worthless ones" of 23:6-7. If, however, we claim with David the everlasting covenant of God's promise (23:5), then the hope of our future will be based in a reality that transcends the powers of this world. Our hope can never settle for the realistic assessment of human possibilities. Just and faithful human rule is always rooted in the trustworthiness of God's promises.

2 Samuel 23:8-39, Exploits of David's Warriors

COMMENTARY

In the symmetrical arrangement of the appendixes to 2 Samuel, this list of David's warriors and their exploits corresponds to the list in 21:15-21. This section, however, is actually composed of two lists separated by a brief narrative about David and his men: vv. 8-12, a list of the Three and their exploits; this list identifies David's most prominent warriors and documents their prowess in single-handed combat against the Philistines; vv. 13-17, a narrative account of an incident involving David and three unnamed warriors (the editor may have assumed they were the Three); the account stresses the solidarity between David and his men.; vv. 18-39, a list of the Thirty, apparently a military unit made up of David's most effective fighting men; the list details exploits of two who rose to military command positions and simply names others; the list concludes with Uriah the Hittite (see 2 Samuel 11).

This section is in keeping with the tendency of the appendixes to offer alternatives to the bureaucracy and ideology of kingship that characterize the narratives of David at the height of his power. The lists here are remarkable for the absence of any reference to David. Israel had other heroes than David. The kingdom and its successes, particularly against the Philistines, were not totally dependent on David. However, the mention of victory as the gift of the Lord (vv. 10, 12) makes clear that the kingdom's future has been in God's hands. Brueggemann sees theonomous and democratic tendencies working together here in an alternative reading of the David tradition:

It is likely that the *theonomous* inclination of the narrative, which credits Yahweh, and the *democratic* tendency, which names other heroes, are related to each other. State absolutism will attempt to silence theonomy and to nullify democracy. The list thus makes an important statement about social power. The list specifies and celebrates theonomous, democratic power as the proper way of David's rule; and it warns against absolutism which would credit neither Yahweh nor other human heroes.[360]

When David does appear in this section, it is in a narrative (vv. 13-17) that stresses his solidarity with his men, the common humanity he shares with them, and his wise refusal to elevate himself above them. It cannot be accidental that the list of the Thirty ends this section with the naming of Uriah the Hittite (v. 39). The mention of his name speaks eloquently without explicit moralizing. He is among those heroes on whose exploits the kingdom and David's successes depended. He was among those with whom David once acknowledged a deep solidarity. Our knowledge of the reason for his untimely departure from the ranks of the Thirty (2 Samuel 11) speaks volumes about the dangers of a royal ideology and practice that loses touch with its

360. Brueggemann, *First and Second Samuel*, 348.

foundations in the work of the Lord and the support of the community.

23:8-12. Three great warriors are named and praised for their effectiveness in single-handed combat against the Philistines, often in situations where the Israelite army had fled in panic. Their names are Josheb-basshebeth,[361] Eleazar, and Shammah. We know nothing of their deeds outside of these notices. They do not appear as companions of David elsewhere in the stories of David, although the editor who arranged the material of this chapter may have assumed they were the unnamed three of vv. 13-17. Josheb-basshebeth was the chief or commander of the Three. The "Three" seems to be a designation for a formal elite unit or rank in Israel's militia under David, at least in the early period of the Philistine wars (note vv. 8, 19, 23).

Twice in recounting the exploits of the Three, the narrator gives credit for their victory to the Lord (vv. 10, 12). This recognition of the power of God working through human exploits characterizes the traditions about the early David and his successes (see the concluding summary of the rise of David, 2 Sam 5:10), but is notably absent in the accounts of David's wars as king (2 Samuel 8 and 10). The narrator responsible for arranging these appendixes may have intended to reaffirm this theonomous principle as a corrective to the tendency of royal ideology to self-sufficiency.

23:13-17. This brief narrative tells of a time when a Philistine garrison occupied David's home in Bethlehem (v. 14). David, who is at his stronghold in the cave of Adullam (v. 13), tells three of his warriors that he wants a drink from the well in Bethlehem (v. 15). In this very human and intimate portrait, David is unfettered by royal pretensions and office. He shares his basic, human desires with his men.

But this story is also about the loyalty of David's men to him. At considerable risk, they break through the Philistine defenses at Bethlehem, draw water from the well there, and bring it back to David (v. 16a). It is an act

of foolishly touching bravery and solidarity with their leader.

David's response is truly remarkable for its instinctive grasp of what is at stake here. David perceives that water brought at such risk and such commitment cannot be treated as the ordinary drink that might be brought by a subordinate to one in authority. In the mere bringing of such a costly gift there was a solidarity between David and his men that could not be broken by the exercise of his own satisfaction. David pours the water on the ground, but he does so as an act of offering to the Lord (v. 16b). The water is treated, not as worthless, but as so valuable that it can be offered only to God. David stands in solidarity with his men, refusing to be the one worthy of such a gift. He treats the water as a sacrament, saying that it represents the very blood of the men who risked their lives for it (v. 17).

This is not the David of kingly office and royal authority who is "worth ten thousand of us" (18:3). David's leadership is recognized here as rooted in solidarity with his men, not his elevation above them. It is a fitting reminder near the end of David's story of the qualities that brought him to leadership and eventually to the throne, lest the temptations of royal power isolate him from the possibilities of solidarity with his people.

23:18-39. The chapter closes with a list of the Thirty. This group, like the Three, seems to be an elite corps of warriors on whom David relied, particularly early in his career. The author gives two of them special treatment by reporting some of their heroic exploits. One of these is Abishai, the brother of Joab, and a frequent, if hotheaded, companion of David in his early exploits (see, e.g., 1 Sam 26:6-8; 2 Sam 16:9-12). Abishai is credited here with becoming commander of the Thirty (vv. 18-19). Benaiah is also accorded this extended treatment (vv. 20-23), and his mighty deeds are recounted. He, too, rises to a position of command. He was placed in charge of David's bodyguard (v. 23), which probably meant the mercenaries who formed David's own personal militia. Benaiah later plays a role in the palace intrigues around the succession to the throne when David is on his deathbed (1 Kings 1–2).

---

361. Some Greek MSS read this name as "Eshbaal" or "Ishbaal," which may have been deliberately altered to remove the element "baal" from the name (see Commentary on 2:8). 1 Chr 11:11 has the name as "Jashobeam." The chronicler also has variant names for many in the list of the Thirty as well as some additional names. See McCarter, *II Samuel,* 489-99, for a detailed discussion of the many textual variants in the names listed here and in 1 Chronicles.

The remainder of the Thirty are simply listed by name, with some reference to family or place (vv. 24-39). The concluding formula states that there were thirty-seven men in all (v. 39), but it is impossible to find this many names even with the inclusion of Abishai, Benaiah, and the Three. The most striking feature of the list is the absence of one name, Joab. Joab is David's most frequent military companion, and, aside from David, the most prominent military leader in Israel. He is listed twice as the commander of David's army (8:16; 20:23). He was the brother of Abishai, commander of the Thirty, and of Asahel, also listed in the Thirty (v. 24), who was killed by Abner in an incident while David was king of Judah (2:18-23). Perhaps, as commander of the army Joab was considered to be above and outside the Three and the Thirty. Ending this list of heroes with the name of Uriah the Hittite makes a final comment on a less than heroic side of David's tradition.

REFLECTIONS

1. Effective and charismatic leaders always face the danger of creating a cult of personality among their followers, thus losing touch with the very people who admire them and helped to make for their success. History is replete with examples. The two lists (23:8-12, 18-39) and the intervening narrative (23:13-17) of this section seem intended to warn of this danger with respect to David. David was not the only man helping to forge Israel's future by brave and sacrificial deeds, and what made him most effective as a leader was his solidarity with his men, not his authority over them.

This intended corrective to the David tradition can serve as a warning to us as well. It is all too easy for those in positions of leadership to become isolated and to forget the many contributions made by persons who contribute without getting as much recognition—elected officials forget voters, clergy ignore laity, teachers patronize students, parents demean or overprotect children. The configurations of power that seem most admired in our society and in our churches tend to be hierarchical, self-sufficient, and self-promoting. This section suggests that this is a false perception. Real leadership and true power arise out of recognition of solidarity with community and with God. Such solidarity is offered here as a corrective to the ideology of royal power that led David into tragedy and loss. We may read this section as a corrective to our own tendencies to follow David's example (2 Samuel 11–20) into false ideologies of autonomous and isolated power.

2. There is a helpful insight for the church in the story of David's thirst and the water his men procured at great risk, only to have David pour it out before the Lord. The story suggests that the church might think more carefully about the role of liturgical acts in acknowledging and calling us to solidarity with one another. Liturgical acts, when properly focused on God and engaged in as the work of the community, have the power to subvert the imagination in favor of possibilities that undermine accepted notions of power and authority in the world. When we come together as a community before God, liturgical acts call us away from autonomy into solidarity, away from grasping into giving, and away from self-congratulation to acknowledgment of interdependence and mutual need. If the church is to participate in the emergence of new power arrangements for a new community, then it will first have to risk acts of liturgical imagination that, like David's pouring out of the water, create a sense of solidarity with one another before God. We refuse to allow personal satisfaction or fulfillment (drinking the water) as an appropriate goal for our liturgical life together. Worship is directed to God rather than to our own needs. Worship is the work that makes community, not our own self-fulfillment.

2 Samuel 24:1-25, David's Census and the Threshing Floor of Araunah

COMMENTARY

This unusual narrative forms the counterpart to the narrative that opened the appendixes to the books of Samuel (21:1-14). The word "again," which begins v. 1, suggests a formal link between the two stories as episodes that begin with the Lord's anger. Some have suggested that these two stories originally belonged together and were located earlier in the collection of David's stories. Yet others have found several different and independent traditions brought together in chap. 24. These efforts to reconstruct an earlier, complex literary history for this chapter have neither been convincing nor generated a consensus.[362] It seems more likely that, whatever the earlier literary history of this narrative, it was placed here in its present form as a part of the symmetrically arranged appendixes to the books of Samuel (see Overview for 21:1–24:25) to play a role in the conclusion of the David tradition.

The story is organized into three distinct but related episodes: vv. 1-9, the census—incited by God, ordered by David, carried out by Joab; vv. 10-17, the judgment—David's repentance, Gad's announcement, the plague, God's mercy, David's confession; vv. 18-25, the altar—Gad's announcement, the purchase of the threshing floor, the building of an altar, the end of the threat. The story leaves many questions unaddressed. Why was God angry with Israel? Why is a census such a threat to the people? How does David come to realize that he has sinned? Why does God show mercy in the judgment by pestilence? The narrator does not seem interested in reporting motives behind events but instead to allow the character of David to be revealed in the course of events. Such an interest makes chap. 24 an appropriate final comment on David for the books of Samuel.

24:1-9. The story opens with the unexplained anger of God toward Israel. Further, God "incited David" to commit an act that later in the story is clearly regarded as sinful (v. 1). We are uncomfortable with questions these assertions raise about the justice of God, but the narrator gives no attention to this concern and passes quickly on to the course of events with the focus on David. The portrait of God as the instigator of sinful actions must have made subsequent generations uncomfortable, since the retelling of this story by the chronicler attributes the instigation to the "adversary" (שׂטן śāṭān) instead of to the Lord (1 Chr 21:1). The issues raised are similar to those raised by the prologue to the book of Job, in which both the Lord and the "adversary" (śāṭăn) play a role in trying to instigate Job to sin.

David is to "count the people"—i.e., take a census (v. 1b). It is never clear that David realizes that this administrative impulse has been instigated by the Lord. David, as so often before, entrusts this task to his chief of staff, Joab, and presents it as his own royal command. David says nothing about divine initiative, nor does he say anything about royal purpose in wanting to know "how many there are" (v. 2).

We begin to sense that there is more to this issue than meets the eye when Joab, with great deference but unmistakable firmness, questions David's wisdom in undertaking this census (v. 3). Joab's opposition is even more persistent in the parallel account in 1 Chr 21:2-6, where he even refuses to carry out the order fully. We notice that this task is to be carried out by Joab with the commanders of the army (i.e., it may require military force) and that they disapprove as well, which is made clear when David must override the objections of Joab and the commanders by royal fiat (v. 4a). In the face of full royal authority, Joab and the commanders obey the king (v. 4b). Verses 5-8 report the carrying out of the census. The locations mentioned refer to the extremities of the Davidic kingdom, implying that all who fell within these boundaries were counted. The phrase "from Dan to

---

362. See Anderson, *2 Samuel*, 282-84, for a discussion of the many proposals made for the literary formation of this chapter.

·Beersheba" commonly designates the whole of Israel (v. 2). The process took nine months and twenty days (v. 8).

What was so threatening about a census, and why did it require the participation of the army? We begin to sense an answer to this question with Joab's report back to David (v. 9). The census enumerated the number of fighting men in the kingdom—800,000 in Israel and 500,000 in Judah. Only the able-bodied men have been counted. Such a census is the prelude to a military draft. Later, under Solomon, it is clear that such a census also provides the basis for conscripting forced labor and for taxation (1 Kgs 4:7-19, 27-28; 5:13-14). No wonder such a census might be resisted by the people and require the army to carry it out. David has taken a major step away from tribal military behavior and toward centralized royal control of such matters. His census constitutes a step toward the fulfillment of the prophet Samuel's dire warning against kings who "take" from the people (1 Sam 8:10-18). Such a royal census is not a neutral act, but a testimony to state power and intent to use that power. David (even though "incited" by God) has given in to the temptation to order his kingdom in the manner of state politics in the other kingdoms of the ancient world. David's Israel is becoming "like the other nations" (1 Sam 8:4, 20).

24:10-17. This section is bracketed by David's realization and confession of the sin he has committed (vv. 10, 17). We are not told how David came to this realization, but what is significant (perhaps the more so for seeming so spontaneous) is that David is not wholly captured by the ideology of state power and its bureaucratic practices. He retains a capacity for governance that considers the perspective of the people and a willingness to acknowledge and respond to his own weaknesses. Even in his two confessions of sin in this section, he progresses from petitioning God for his own forgiveness (v. 10) to petitioning God to spare the people of Israel and to let judgment fall entirely on David and his house (v. 17).

A new character enters David's story at this point, but it is not a new role. A prophet brings the word of God's judgment and its consequences, but the prophet is not Nathan (chaps. 7 and 12); it is a prophet named Gad (v. 11). The word Gad brings is odd. David may choose the consequences of the sin he has committed—but what a choice it is! Gad offers the terrible triad of famine, war, and pestilence, known in later prophetic preaching on God's judgment (Jer 14:12; 15:2; 21:7, 9; 24:10; 27:8; Ezek 5:12; 6:12). The time sequences occur in descending order: three years of famine (reading with the Greek text and 1 Chr 21:12; the Hebrew text reads "seven"), three months of military pursuit by enemies, or three days of pestilence (v. 13).

David's response to this terrible dilemma of choice is in keeping with the portrait of his faithful side presented in these final chapters. He places his trust in the God who is now judging him, and, in the face of the judgment, he expresses hope in God's mercy (v. 14). In the hands of God, one might hope for mercy—not so from human hands. This choice eliminates one of the possible consequences—namely, pursuit by an enemy—but it leaves famine and pestilence as possibilities. David chooses no further, and it is the Lord who apparently makes the final choice and sends a pestilence (v. 15).

It is unclear how long the pestilence runs unchecked, but "until the appointed time" is not the full three days threatened because God's mercy does intervene. David's trust is justified. The damage is still great; seventy thousand die from disease (v. 15b). Without explanation, an angel of the Lord appears in the story as the agent of God's judgment by pestilence. As the angel approaches Jerusalem, God stays its destroying hand with the declaration: "It is enough" (v. 16).[363] The spot where the pestilence stops is the threshing floor of a Jebusite named Arauna, which is significant for the final episode of this chapter. Verse 17 records David's second confession of sin prior to God's relenting mercy, since it treats his words as a response to the destruction wrought by the angel of pestilence. Just as God responds in mercy, so also David responds by offering himself in place of the people. But God's mercy is not the result of David's confession; it is the unexplained grace of God in which David trusted (v. 14).

363. The angel has a more extended and dramatic role in the chronicler's account, where he stands with sword drawn over Jerusalem while David's repentance and the episode with the altar and sacrifice at the threshing floor of Arauna (Chronicles, Ornan) are played out. Only after the sacrifice is the sword sheathed (1 Chr 21:15-27).

If God can judge, God can also show mercy (cf. Hos 11:8-9). The Lord repents of anger, and David repents of sin. In this divine and human responsiveness lie the hope of Israel's future and the possibility of renewed relationship between God and God's king.

24:18-25. The prophet Gad instructs David to build an altar at the threshing floor where the plague had stopped (v. 17). David's response is one of obedience, and the subsequent course of events completes David's faithful response to God's judgment and mercy in an act of ritual piety. Verses 18-24 narrate the negotiations for the purchase of the threshing floor by David from Arauna. Arauna is initially awed by the king's presence and the gravity of the occasion, so he offers to give the threshing floor as well as oxen and wood for sacrifice (in 1 Chr 21:20-23, this generosity is also motivated by the presence of the angel with a drawn sword). David refuses this offer by saying that he cannot offer to the Lord what cost him nothing, and he insists on paying full price (v. 24).

Only when the altar is built and the sacrifice has been made does the account end by saying that the Lord answered David's supplications and ended the plague (v. 25; in 1 Chr 21:27, the angel sheaths his sword). The impression is that God initiated mercy, but that David's response in acknowledging God and confessing his own sin with appropriate acts of ritual piety were necessary to end the threat of judgment completely. The confession is enacted in worship wherein the gift of God's mercy is acknowledged and received. Anything less than authentic worship would not restore relationship broken by sin.

This final episode may have been preserved because of a tradition that linked this altar on Arauna's threshing floor with the eventual site of the Jerusalem Temple. In 1 Chr 22:1, David declares this Jebusite threshing floor to be the site of a future temple and actually begins making preparations for its construction by stockpiling building materials (1 Chr 22:2-16).

With chap. 24 we come to the end of the books of Samuel and to the end of David's story. (1 Kings 1–2 focus on the accession of Solomon; David is dying.) It is significant that the books of Samuel end with the prayerful petition of David in a time of need and with God's merciful response to that need. The books of Samuel began in a similar way, with the prayerful petition of Hannah and God's merciful response (1 Samuel 1). At beginning and end, this story turns on trust in the mercy of God. Early in 1 Samuel we are told that Israel's old system of leadership was corrupt (Eli's sons), and in the end David himself has been corrupted. However, God's mercy endures. Moreover, the true source from which Israel's future always comes is acknowledged in acts of worship (Hannah's and David's) that frame the books of Samuel. Brueggemann speaks of these framing stories in this way:

The Samuel corpus is thus framed at beginning and end with powerful affirmations about God's fidelity and Israel's (Hannah's and David's) capacity to trust, submit, and pray. The decisive affirmation at beginning and end of the narrative concerns the overriding sovereignty of God.[364]

Chapter 24 (and the appendixes of chaps. 21–24) redirects our attention from the flawed David, seduced by the availability of royal power and co-opted by the patterns of state ideology. The David we finally see in the appendixes is the David who, in spite of his human vulnerability, has a capacity for faith, for prayer, for worship that points beyond himself to the Lord as David's true source of power, as Israel's genuine hope for a future, as every generation's sure promise of mercy.

364. Brueggemann, *First and Second Samuel*, 256.

REFLECTIONS

1. At first glance, many readers feel that the events that develop in this chapter seem out of proportion to the taking of a census, which precipitates the crisis. But much depends on where we locate ourselves as readers. To those who have power, or feel they have access to those in power, bureaucratic processes most often seem benign, necessary, or neutral. But to those who live their lives outside the circles of power and on the margins of the social order, such processes are threatening and dangerous—even a census. For the 1990 United States Census, the percentage of those who remained uncounted in the inner cities of the largest metropolitan areas has been estimated as high as 25 percent. Among the poor and the immigrant residents of our cities, many felt that to be found and counted was to be put at risk. The bureaucracies of state power were not to be trusted; better to be anonymous and uncounted. To give information to such bureaucracies was to be uncertain of how that information would be used. Would such information be shared with taxation authorities, with immigration officials, with police departments?

To read this final story of David is to realize how casually those who hold authority and power exercise it without considering how the bureaucracies of power are experienced by those at the margins of society. Even programs designed to help those in need are sometimes burdened with such bureaucratic complexity that many conclude that the help offered is intended to be unobtainable. Too often the practices of institutional power structures have as their primary interest their own self-perpetuation. It is too easy for political or ecclesiastical institutions to lose sight of the communities they are to serve. This odd story of a census stands as a reminder that we must look at our programs and policies through the eyes of those at the margins if we are to be certain that our efforts contribute to the wholeness of all whom our actions touch.

2. What makes this story remarkable, however, is that David, in the midst of his own exercise of self-serving bureaucratic power, recognized his actions for what they were—sinful—and he confessed. What opened from that confession were new possibilities for facing the consequences of his action, for rekindling his care for the community, and for restoring relationship to God.

The dangers of self-interested power do not go wholly unrecognized in our own time, but the response is often reform rather than repentance, renewed practice rather than renewed prayer. David's example here might encourage us, in the face of the dangers brought by uncaring power, not to rush so quickly into new blueprints for more responsive institutions or better-flowing organizational charts. Confession and prayer, whether in secular or religious settings, offer possibilities for the future that grow out of restored relationships, rather than new solutions offered out of the same old institutional assumptions. Confession and prayer offer foundations for facing unpleasant consequences that spring from our self-interested exercise of power, rather than attempting to cover those consequences (or postpone them) with a flurry of new activity.

In our own time, we have watched the remarkable proceedings of South Africa's Truth and Reconciliation Commission, chaired by Bishop Desmond Tutu, as it has engaged in the public practice of confession in an effort to heal a deeply divided nation. It is not insignificant that this commission is led by a bishop of the Anglican Church, for if the church reads its own Scripture, including stories like this one, then it knows something of the power of confession to create new possibilities.

The practice of confession and prayer is the foundation for recognizing where God's mercy is at work in the midst of the brokenness our human actions inevitably bring. Prayer does not so much mobilize God's mercy as articulate our own trust in God's mercy. God's mercy is already at work, but our own trustful prayer makes the possibilities that grow from divine mercy more visible. Prayer changes the horizon of our vision to include discernment of what God is doing alongside our analysis of the human possibilities. Prayer that encompasses our own self-examination and confession—that reaches in hope for restored and renewed possibilities—is the first act on the path to actualizing God's new future in our lives and in our communities.

3. It is appropriate that the books of Samuel end with worship and the responsiveness of God in mercy (v. 25). In a story filled with remarkable personalities and complex political events, we might be tempted to think that the stories of Samuel, Saul, and David are stories of human power. But from the story of Hannah to this final story of census, plague, and altar, we have been reminded that God's providence is at work in the characters and the events of this decisive period in Israel. Worship as the final act of this story is the appropriate recognition of divine reality working in and through human history. To read this story is to know that this is true for our history as well as for Israel's. In the consequences that flow from our own acts of bureaucratic disregard and institutional power, we experience God's judgment and contribute to our own brokenness. If in confession and prayer we recognize our failings and trust in God's mercy, new possibilities for restored relationship are opened to us. Community and communion, with others and with God, can be imagined in ways that transform our future and provide new paths of response. Like David at the end of these books of Samuel, our only appropriate response to this gift of new future in God's mercy is worship—the acknowledgment of God as the true source of all futures and our only hope for a foretaste of God's kingdom in the midst of our human kingdoms.

THE FIRST AND SECOND BOOKS OF KINGS

INTRODUCTION, COMMENTARY, AND REFLECTIONS
BY
CHOON-LEONG SEOW

THE FIRST AND
SECOND BOOKS OF
KINGS

INTRODUCTION

The books of 1 and 2 Kings cover more than four hundred years of Israelite history, from the death of David and the accession of Solomon in the tenth century, to the release of Judah's exiled king Jehoiachin in the sixth century BCE. The story begins with the court intrigues that propelled Solomon to power, dwells on his many worldly accomplishments and his widespread reputation, and focuses on the terrible precedent for syncretism that he set for other kings after him. From the start, one discerns the inevitable interplay of divine will and human will in history. That interplay of wills continues to be evident in the rest of the story of the monarchy, from the division of the kingdom into Judah and Samaria, through the reigns of various kings of Israel and Judah, to the fall of Samaria and, eventually, to the fall of Jerusalem. In the chaotic arena of history and amid the court intrigues, internecine warfare, and international conflicts, the story relentlessly conveys the confidence that God's will is being worked out. The story as a whole testifies to divine purposefulness in the messiness of history. Despite the impression that the affairs of the world are determined by political maneuverings and military strivings of rogues and scoundrels, it is God who will have the final say when all is said and done. History moves inexorably according to the will of the sovereign God.

THE UNITY OF 1 AND 2 KINGS

The two biblical books now known as 1 and 2 Kings originally constituted a single work. The artificial division into two books was first made in the Greek version, where the materials now known as 1–2 Samuel and 1–2 Kings are broken up into four manageable portions called the "books of Reigns/Kingdoms" (chapter and verse divisions were not introduced into biblical manuscripts until the medieval period). Thus the point of division between the books appears to be purely arbitrary; the end of 1 Kings (1 Kgs 22:51-53) and the beginning of 2 Kings (2 Kgs 1:1-18) together constitute a single literary unit, a report on the reign of King Ahaziah of Israel. The Hebrew tradition, in fact, assumed a single literary work, and it was only in the late Middle

Ages when, under the influence of the Greek and Latin versions, the division began appearing in Hebrew manuscripts as well. Hence, from a literary viewpoint at least, it is more accurate to speak of a "book of Kings" rather than the "books of Kings."

In the Jewish tradition, the book of Kings belongs—together with the books of Joshua, Judges, and Samuel—to the Former Prophets, a collection of works that provide a prophetic interpretation of Israel's history from the conquest of Canaan to the end of the monarchy. Modern scholars call this biblical corpus "the deuteronomistic history" because the narratives therein share a common vocabulary, literary style, and theological perspective that is heavily influenced by the book of Deuteronomy, which many scholars now regard as the introduction to the corpus. Although it appears likely that there were earlier editions of the deuteronomistic history—in the reigns of Hezekiah (c. 715–686 BCE) and Josiah (c. 640–609 BCE)—it seems clear that the work was given its final form sometime during the exilic period (c. 586–539 BCE). The precise identification of the various stages of redaction, however, is too complicated a task to be pursued in a commentary like this one. Thus, although it may be more accurate to speak of several deuteronomists, I will presume that the final form of the text is broadly coherent and will refer to the final editor as "the (deuteronomistic) narrator." While acknowledging the likelihood of a complex compositional and redactional history behind the present form of the text, the primary focus in this commentary will be on the interpretation of the text as we have it now.

STRUCTURE

The book may be divided into three parts. The first part (1 Kings 1–11) is focused on the kingdom under Solomon. The narrator explains how Solomon succeeded David, even though Solomon was not the heir apparent to the throne (1 Kings 1–2). This succession, to the narrator, was according to the will of God, for God's promise to David was being fulfilled in Solomon's accession to the throne. From the start, therefore, the reader gets the message that God's purpose was being worked out behind all the scandals and human schemes. God's will was fulfilled despite, and even through, human devices and plots. Then the reader is introduced to Solomon the king, and the picture of him is mixed (1 Kgs 3:1-15). Solomon loved God, but he had other loves as well, and his priorities were not always right (1 Kgs 3:1-3). Still, God responded to Solomon's imperfect love and graciously granted him a gift—a gift on which Solomon's reputation would be built. The rest of the account of Solomon's reign depicts him as a king who was successful in all the worldly ways: He was famous, rich, and powerful. Among his many accomplishments was his building of the Temple in Jerusalem. Clearly the dedication of the Temple (1 Kings 8) was a highpoint within the structure of the story, for the Temple was the very symbol of God's presence in the midst of the people, and God's presence was assured, as long as God's people were faithful. Yet, to the narrator, Solomon was no ideal king. Indeed, in many ways, Solomon violated the expectations of faithful kingship laid out in Deuteronomy (Deut 17:14-20). Above all, Solomon's many loves opened the doors to all kinds of compromises to faith in the Lord. Hence, God promised to divide the kingdom into two.

Narratives about the divided kingdom constitute the bulk of the second part of the book of Kings (1 Kings 12–2 Kings 17). It begins with the secession of the ten northern tribes under Jeroboam, who established two heterodox sanctuaries at Bethel and Dan to rival the Temple of the Lord in Jerusalem (1 Kgs 12:25-33). To the narrator, this was blatant apostasy, and Jeroboam had provided a horrible precedent for all his successors to follow. Henceforth, all the kings of Israel (the northern kingdom) would be judged according to their failure to depart from "the way of Jeroboam," and all of them would fail miserably (1 Kgs 15:30, 34; 16:2, 7, 19, 26, 31; 21:22; 22:52; 2 Kgs 3:3; 9:9; 10:29, 31; 13:2, 6, 11; 14:24; 15:9, 18, 24, 28; 17:21-22). Jeroboam had set an indelible pattern of apostasy in the north; it remained possible for each of his successors to turn back to the Lord, but none would do so. Hence, the destruction of the north was inevitable. Throughout the account of the kings of the north, the imperative of obedience to God's demands is emphasized, and the narrator makes the point that destruction is the consequence of Israel's will to disobey.

Meanwhile in Judah, God's promise of an enduring dynasty for David was being preserved by the sheer grace of God. Unlike Israel, there was continuity on the throne of David in Judah, as God had promised. Yet, there was the expectation of faithfulness to the Lord. Just as the kings of the north were judged according to failure to depart from the apostate ways of Jeroboam, so also the kings of the south were judged according to the standard of piety set by David (1 Kgs 14:8; 15:3-5, 11; 2 Kgs 14:3; 16:2). Unlike the northern kingdom, however, there were a few good kings in the south, reformists like Asa (1 Kgs 15:9-15), Jehoshaphat (1 Kgs 22:41-50), and Joash (2 Kgs 12:1-21). Yet, even these reformist kings failed to do all that was necessary to ensure the centralization of worship in Jerusalem. Hence, even though Judah would last a little longer than Israel, it was also set on a path of destruction.

The third major portion of the book focuses on the kingdom of Judah (2 Kings 18:1-25), the northern kingdom's having been destroyed because of its persistent will to disobey God (2 Kings 17). There is hope when one reads about the reign of reformist King Hezekiah. Indeed, when the Assyrians besieged Jerusalem, they were unable to take the city and had to turn back (2 Kings 18–19). The destiny of Judah appeared to be embodied in the person of Hezekiah, who was on the brink of death, but because of his piety was miraculously granted a reprieve and recovered to live for a while longer (2 Kgs 20:1-11). Yet, all was not well, because Hezekiah, who has been portrayed as one who trusted the Lord, instead trusted the Babylonians and finally cared most about preserving his own well-being (2 Kgs 20:12-21). Even worse for Judah, Hezekiah was succeeded by Manasseh, who thoroughly undid what good Hezekiah had done (2 Kgs 21:1-18). Indeed, Manasseh's heretical counterreformation was so horrifying to the narrator that he portrayed this king as Judah's equivalent of Jeroboam of Israel: Just as Jeroboam had caused Israel to sin, so also Manasseh caused Judah to sin. On account of his offenses, the fate of Judah was sealed. The pious reforms of Hezekiah were rendered as nothing. Even the all-encompassing reformation of Josiah could not save Judah (2 Kgs 22:1–23:30). So Judah was finally destroyed; Jerusalem was devastated; the Temple, the symbol of God's presence, was razed to the ground; and the people of Judah were exiled.

THE BOOK OF KINGS AS THEOLOGICAL NARRATIVE

Arguably the most challenging task for the interpreter of Kings is to make sense of it in one's own day and age. To be sure, there are the memorable stories that warm our hearts, like the story of Solomon's receipt of the gift of wisdom from God (1 Kgs 3:4-15) or his swift and simple administration of justice in a complex case (1 Kgs 3:16-28). There are also stories that obviously testify to the power of God and God's prophets, like Elijah's victory on Mt. Carmel (1 Kgs 18:1-46) or Elisha's healing of the leprous Aramean general through a cleansing at the Jordan River (2 Kgs 5:1-19). These are the passages that one finds repeatedly in lectionaries. Yet, there is much in the narratives that is difficult to appropriate as Scripture. The book is filled with all kinds of peculiar details, not only the unfamiliar names of many kings and the dates of their reigns, but also administrative lists (e.g., 1 Kgs 4:1-34) and pedantic descriptions of the Temple and its appurtenances (e.g., 1 Kgs 6:1–7:51). Many of the stories seem tedious and repetitive (cf. 1 Kgs 15:1–16:28), horribly violent (e.g., 2 Kgs 9:1–10:36), ethically challenging (e.g., 1 Kgs 1:1–2:46; 13:1-33), or just plain odd (e.g., 2 Kgs 6:1-7; 13:14-21). Our challenge in reading these texts—indeed, all of Kings—is to make theological sense of them. That will be the primary focus of the commentary.

At one level, the book of Kings reads like a historical document. By presenting the events in a chronological sequence, by its frequent chronological notices and synchronisms (coordination of the reigns of the kings of Israel with the reigns of the kings of Judah), and by its use of and references to historical sources ("the Book of the Acts of Solomon"; "the Book of the Annals of the Kings of Israel"; "the Book of the Annals of the Kings of Judah"), the book of Kings seems to present itself as a work of history. Much of what we know of the history of Israel in this period is, indeed, derived from this source; some of its information has been corroborated by extra-biblical inscriptions and other archaeological sources.

Yet, the purpose of the book is not to present a comprehensive history of the period, as if it were written for general information about the period in question. Rather, by its frequent references to fuller accounts elsewhere (e.g., 1 Kgs 14:19, 29), the text implicitly admits to the selectivity of its data. Rather, the history is a decisively theological one. It has to do with the working out of God's will. Other historical data are of secondary interest to the narrator or, indeed, of no interest at all. So, for instance, Omri, who is known from extra-biblical sources to have been a powerful monarch, warrants only passing notice, for to the narrator he was merely an unfaithful king who was a failure in the eyes of God. Likewise, Ahab is known to have accomplished much politically and militarily, but the narrator presents him as a bungling and rather weak king. By the same token, there are many tantalizing historical allusions that cannot be verified from other records, historical details that cannot be easily reconciled with what we know from other sources, synchronisms that contradict one another, and places that cannot be identified and the significance of which cannot be discerned. Although the pursuit of such historical questions may yield satisfying results, the reader must keep in mind that the purpose of the book of Kings is to impart a theological message. That is what this commentary will strive to highlight.

BIBLIOGRAPHY

Brueggemann, Walter. *1 Kings*. KPG. Atlanta: John Knox, 1983. A preaching guide, full of homiletical ideas.

————. *2 Kings*. KPG. Atlanta: John Knox, 1982. A helpful preaching guide.

Cogan, Mordechai, and Hayim Tadmor. *2 Kings*. AB 11. Garden City, N.Y.: Doubleday, 1988. A detailed commentary, especially helpful on philological and historical issues.

De Vries, Simon J. *1 Kings*. WBC 12. Waco, Tex.: Word, 1985. Detailed attention to the compositional history of the text and to text-critical matters.

Gray, John. *1 & 2 Kings, A Commentary*. OTL. Philadelphia: Westminster, 1970. Especially good on ancient Near Eastern background.

Hobbs, T. R. *2 Kings*. WBC 13. Waco, Tex.: Word, 1985. An insightful commentary, especially on literary and historical issues.

Jones, Gwilym. H. *1 and 2 Kings*. NCB. 2 vols. Grand Rapids: Eerdmans, 1984. A commentary that pays careful attention to historical-critical issues.

Long, Burke O. *1 Kings, with an Introduction to Historical Literature*. FOTL 9. Grand Rapids: Eerdmans, 1984. An insightful work that focuses on literary forms. Especially good on literary matters.

————. *2 Kings*. FOTL 10. Grand Rapids: Eerdmans, 1991. See preceding annotation.

Montgomery, James A., and Henry Snyder Gehman. *A Critical and Exegetical Commentary on the Book of Kings*. ICC. Edinburgh: T. & T. Clark, 1986. Originally published in 1951. A technical commentary designed for specialists.

Nelson, Richard D. *First and Second Kings*. Interpretation. Atlanta: John Knox, 1987. An excellent commentary written with pastors in mind. It is rich with theological insights.

Rice, G. *1 Kings: Nations Under God*. ITC. Grand Rapids: Eerdmans, 1990. A good commentary written with the laity in mind.

Walsh, Jerome T. *1 Kings*. Berit Olam. Collegeville, Minn.: Liturgical Press, 1996. Emphasis on a literary reading of the text.

OUTLINE OF FIRST AND SECOND KINGS

1 KINGS 1:1–11:43

THE REIGN OF SOLOMON

1 KINGS 1:1-53, HOW SOLOMON BECAME HEIR TO DAVID'S THRONE

OVERVIEW

The narrative in the book of Kings begins with the demise of King David, the focal character in 2 Samuel. For much of the twentieth century, there has been something of a consensus among scholars that this account of the power struggle and transfer of authority at the end of David's reign is properly part of the conclusion of an originally unified "succession narrative," a Davidic court history comprised of 2 Samuel 9–20 and 1 Kings 1–2, with 2 Samuel 21–24 as a secondary addition. There are, to be sure, tantalizing literary and thematic links between the opening two chapters of 1 Kings and much of 2 Samuel. Some scholars have maintained, however, that these chapters in 1 Kings were never part of an original succession narrative. Rather, 1 Kings 1–2 may be better viewed as part of a Solomonic *apologia*, composed not as the conclusion of some Davidic court document but as a part of a separate work that, nevertheless, drew on Davidic court history.[1]

Indeed, the very reference to the old age of David in v. 1 ("King David was old and advanced in years") presupposes knowledge of some tradition about David's reign. The

introductory words sound very much like the continuation of a story that the reader is supposed to know already. Similar words are found in Gen 18:11; 24:1; Josh 13:1; 23:1; and 1 Sam 17:12, and in all those cases the words appear in continuation of a story. One may contrast, for instance, the opening of the books of Samuel ("There was a certain man . . . " [1 Sam 1:1]), or the book of Ruth ("In the days when the judges ruled . . . " [Ruth 1:1]), or the book of Job ("There was a man in the land of Uz . . . " [Job 1:1]), none of which assumes an antecedent account. Be that as it may, the report of David's demise in this opening chapter functions now—in its present literary and canonical contexts—as an appropriate introduction to a *new* story: The passing of an old era is the beginning of a new one. The copulative ו (*wĕ*) at the very beginning of the first verse (RSV, "Now") suggests that this introduction should be read with the preceding story in mind, although it also signals a turning point. The RSV's rendering ("Now King David was old . . ."), correctly understanding the copulative *wĕ* to be disjunctive rather than conjunctive, conveys well the sense that one is at a narrative juncture.

1. So P. K. McCarter, "Plots, True or False," *Int* 35 (1981) 355-67.

1 Kings 1:1-4, The Demise of King David

COMMENTARY

King David is now old (about seventy years old, according to 2 Sam 5:4-5; 1 Kgs 2:11) and infirm. Like one suffering from arteriosclerosis, he is unable to keep warm despite the

best efforts of his courtiers. At their behest, a young virgin is brought to attend to him. She would be his סכנת (*sōkenet*, "governess"), a term that has been variously interpreted to mean "nurse," "companion," "concubine," or "queen" (NRSV, "his attendant"; NIV, "take care of him").[2] This maiden is supposed to "lie in [his] bosom" (v. 2), an expression that recalls Nathan's parable in reference to the ewe lamb, a metaphor for Bathsheba, the wife of Uriah: "She used to lie in his bosom" (2 Sam 12:3). The translation in the NIV ("lie beside him") misses the subtle allusion. It is important to keep that allusion in mind, for one will soon encounter Bathsheba again.

The woman in view now is not Bathsheba, however, but Abishag "the Shunammite"—that is, one from the town of Shunem, where the prophet Elisha would later revive a dead child by lying on him and warming the dead body (2 Kgs 4:32-37). But there is no miraculous healing in the case of David. Even when the most beautiful young virgin in all the territory of Israel is brought, the old man simply cannot be warmed. Despite David's oft-noticed penchant for beautiful women (e.g., 1 Sam 25:3; 2 Sam 11:2), the aged king apparently did not have sexual relations with her; literally, "he did not know her" (v. 4).

2. The masculine form of the term is found in Hebrew and other Semitic languages for people in positions of power and responsibility.

The implicit inability of David to respond to the beautiful virgin in his bosom suggests his impotence in more ways than one. At the beginning of his career, in contrast to his predecessor Saul, he had grown "stronger and stronger," and his increasing strength in those days was reflected in the increase in the number of his wives (see 2 Sam 3:1-5). Even though he had been given Saul's house and Saul's women to be in his bosom (בחיקך *běḥêqekā*, "in your bosom," 2 Sam 12:8), David still desired someone who was in the bosom of another man, Uriah (2 Sam 12:3). Yet, the aged David is unable to respond now. He is also no longer in control of his house. Rather, he appears to be at the mercy of his courtiers and requires a "governess" to take care of him. The stage is set, then, for the transfer of power and authority from David to a successor. The reader, who is assumed to be familiar with the story of King David, is implicitly presented with a predicament at this critical juncture in history: Who will be heir to the throne of David, which God had promised would be established forever (see 2 Sam 7:1-17)? (See Reflections at 1:5-40.)

1 Kings 1:5-40, Succession Is in Question

COMMENTARY

1:5-6. Immediately after the account of David's pathetic conditions (vv. 1-4), we learn that Adonijah the son of Haggith is elevating himself. Neither the NRSV nor the NIV adequately captures the emphasis in the Hebrew, for Adonijah says, literally, "I, I will be king." This story of an ambitious prince attempting to seize power is reminiscent of the Canaanite *Legend of King Keret*, where we read of an effort by a prince—the heir-presumptive by the custom of primogeniture—to depose his old and infirm father on the grounds of the old man's ineffectiveness and impotence.[3] The prince tells the old king to abdicate (Ugaritic *yrd*, "to come down," semantically opposite to Hebrew נשא [*nāśā*], "to elevate"])

3. *The Legend of King Keret*, in *Ancient Near Eastern Texts*, ed. J. B. Pritchard (Princeton: Princeton University Press, 1969) 142-49.

so that he himself might become king: "Come down from kingship [and] I will be king, from your rule [and] I will sit enthroned, even I" (author's trans.). The prince is trying to elevate himself at the expense of his impotent father.

The narrative about Adonijah's attempted *coup d'état* also recalls a previous abortive putsch by another son of David, Absalom (2 Samuel 15–18). Indeed, the narrator probably intends the linkage between these two sons. Like Absalom (2 Sam 14:25-26), Adonijah is said to be very handsome; like Absalom (2 Sam 15:1), Adonjah gathers to himself chariots, horses (not "horsemen" as the NRSV has it),[4]

4. We should probably repoint the text to read פרשים (*pĕrāšîm*, "horses"), rather than פרשים (*pārāšîm*, "horsemen"). Cf. Jer 46:4; Ezek 27:14; Joel 2:4, where פרש (*pāraš*) is used as a parallel term for סוס (*sûs*), the common word for "horse." The word refers to horses used for pulling chariots (e.g., Gen 50:9; Josh 24:6; 1 Sam 8:11). The cavalry, with horsemen riding horses, was not known in Palestine until the ninth century BCE.

and royal escorts (cf. 1 Sam 8:11); like Absalom (2 Sam 15:12), Adonijah invites others to a sacrificial feast. The narrator notes that Adonijah was born "next after Absalom," meaning probably that Adonijah is the heir-presumptive by primogeniture (see 2:15, 22).

Adonijah is the fourth of David's sons who were born to him in the Judean town of Hebron (2 Sam 3:2-5).[5] David's firstborn, Amnon, had raped his half sister Tamar and was killed by Absalom, Tamar's full brother (2 Samuel 13). Absalom, the third son, was banished for the murder and killed when trying to usurp the throne (2 Samuel 18). We know virtually nothing of Chileab, the second son (2 Sam 3:3; 1 Chr 3:1); one can only conjecture that he had died in childhood. In any case, Adonijah is the oldest surviving son of David and, now, the presumed heir. He is seen as someone who has not been disciplined by his father (v. 6).[6] One recalls, again, the prophecy of Nathan, in which it is predicted that because of David's adultery with Bathsheba (the "ewe lamb" that used to lie in the bosom of her master), trouble would plague David from within his own house, initiated by those very people closest to him (2 Sam 12:11).

1:7-8. In his usurpation of power, Adonijah turns to people who had been with David before he became king in Jerusalem. Joab was a commander of the Judean militia when David ruled in Hebron (2 Samuel 2). Abiathar the priest had served David in his early struggle against Saul (1 Sam 22:20-23; 23:6). These are the conservative elements, the "old guard" in David's regime based in Hebron. Opposing them are Zadok the priest;[7] Benaiah, the captain of the royal bodyguards, comprised of mercenaries; and Nathan the prophet, all of whom came to prominence only after David began ruling in Jerusalem (2 Sam 7:2; 8:17-18), along with Shimei (perhaps "Shimei the son of Ela," 4:18) and Rei (of whom nothing else is known), and David's own special corps of elite warriors.

David's choice of Jerusalem as capital had been a calculated one, for the city had belonged neither to the tribes of Judah nor to the tribes of Israel. It was in Jerusalem that David united the various tribal confederacies, north and south. There he had ruled with a coalition of old guards from Judah and new personnel in Jerusalem drawn from a variety of backgrounds. Hence, he had two high priests (Abiathar and Zadok) and two military commanders (Joab and Benaiah), one apparently in charge of the militia and the other commanding the professional troops. Yet now, in David's last days, the fragile coalition appears to be disintegrating.

1:9-14. The usurper Adonijah hosts a sacrificial feast, an act fraught with political symbolism (see vv. 18-19, 24-25; cf. 2 Sam 15:7-12), and he invites other sons of the king and the court officials who are Judeans. The event is held at a landmark known as "the Stone of Zohelet" near En-Rogel in the Kidron Valley, on the boundary between Benjaminite and Judean territories, just beyond the capital city. Solomon and his supporters are not invited to Adonijah's exclusive gathering (v. 10). Although Adonijah is the heir apparent, he obviously does not trust Solomon, who was not born, as he was, in the Judean town of Hebron but in the new capital city of Jerusalem and who has the support of the more cosmopolitan officials in that city. Nathan the prophet, always a supporter of Solomon (see 2 Sam 7:1-17; 12:25), brings the matter to the attention of Bathsheba, the mother of Solomon, identifying Adonijah as "the son of Haggith"—that is, the son of a rival wife to Bathsheba—and charging that "Adonijah has become king" (v. 11; cf. 2 Sam 15:10, "Absalom has become king"). Nathan presents the attempted takeover as something that has already happened (מלך *mālak*, "has become king," v. 11), and he warns that Solomon and Bathsheba will be in mortal danger if Adonijah remains unchallenged (v. 12). He lays out their strategy for dealing with the problem: First, Bathsheba will approach David and "remind" him of an oath that he had made to name Solomon as his successor, and then Nathan would appear to "confirm" (מלא *millē*'), in the piel; lit., "fill out") her words (vv. 13-14).

1:15-19. Bathsheba appears before David, not in the court of the palace, but in his private bedroom (v. 15). The narrator reiterates at this point that David is very old, thus

---

5. See Josephus *Antiquities of the Jews* 7.14.4.

6. David is elsewhere seen as an indulgent father. See 2 Sam 13:21 (an addition in the Greek) and 2 Sam 19:1-8.

7. There is much confusion surrounding the background of Zadok (see 2 Sam 8:17, a problematic text; 15:24-29), but he is almost certainly not Judean.

bringing us back to the introductory words about the king's old age and infirmity (vv. 1-4). Bathsheba, who had been desired by David even though she was in the bosom of another man, now speaks to the old king in front of the young and beautiful Abishag, who was brought to lie in his bosom. Bathsheba tells David that Adonijah has become king without his knowledge (v. 18); David is not "in the know," as it were. Even as he does not *know* Abishag (v. 4), he does not *know* that Adonijah is plotting to take over the throne (vv. 11, 18). This lack of knowledge on his part is telling, for the king was once assumed to have had great wisdom and the ability "to know all things that are on earth" (2 Sam 14:20). Here, however, David is clearly in his waning years, and he does not seem to know very much at all.

Nathan and Bathsheba seem to be taking advantage of the old man's senility. The prophet suggests that Bathsheba ask David if the king himself had not sworn to her that Solomon would be his successor. In Bathsheba's own rendering, however, the leading question posed by Nathan turns into an indicative statement, an outright reminder of the king's supposed commitment to her: "My lord, you yourself swore to me" (v. 17). It is in Nathan's prompting of Bathsheba (v. 13) that the reader first learns of this putative commitment on David's part; nothing is said of such an oath in earlier narratives or, indeed, anywhere else in the Bible, which would be completely surprising, given the importance of such a tradition to the Davidic monarchy. If such a decisive oath had actually been made, or if it had been made in private between David and Bathsheba (perhaps as "pillow talk"), it would be very strange that she should have to be reminded of it by Nathan. Moreover, when Nathan appears to "confirm" (*mille*) Bathsheba's words (v. 14), he makes no mention at all of such a promise (vv. 22-27). He asks only if David has, in fact, designated Adonijah to be the successor, implicitly conceding that to be a legitimate option (cf. 1 Kgs 2:15).

Bathsheba and Nathan both draw attention to the political implication of Adonijah's sacrificial feast. They also indirectly implicate all those who joined Adonijah (vv. 19, 25). At the same time, both Bathsheba and Nathan

subtly turn Adonijah's snub into a political virtue for Solomon. She points out that Solomon is not among those invited by Adonijah, thus exonerating her own son from complicity in the treasonous plot. The Hebrew word order is emphatic in its exclusion of Solomon from the reported conspiracy, and Bathsheba deliberately calls attention to Solomon's allegiance to David by referring to her son as David's "servant" and not just his "son": "But as for Solomon, your servant, [Adonijah] did not invite" (v. 19). In other words, Abiathar and Joab are complicitous in the plot, but Solomon is the king's servant.

1:20-27. No doubt to rouse David to action, Bathsheba tells him that "the eyes of all Israel" are on him to see who he will designate as his heir (v. 20). What is at stake here in Bathsheba's plea is not merely David's prestige and credibility, as many commentators have observed, but the unity of the country. The reference to the opinion of "all Israel" is poignant in the light of the fact that all of Adonijah's supporters were Judean and the emphasis in the narrative that Adonijah had specifically invited "all the men of *Judah* who are royal officials" (v. 9). The eyes of the whole nation ("all Israel"), she warns, are watching to see how David will respond to the crisis.

Bathsheba speaks as a mother whose primary interest is to protect her son; if Adonijah's actions are not negated, she points out to David, she and Solomon will be in trouble. Filling out her account, the prophet Nathan adds that Adonijah has already been acclaimed king by the rebels (v. 25) and that Nathan himself ("your servant"), Zadok the priest, and Benaiah the son of Jehoiada have not been party to Adonijah's plot (v. 26). Thereby he identifies for David the non-conspirators who could be trusted to counter Adonijah's gang.

The climax of Nathan's speech before David is an indignant question: Has David indeed chosen Adonijah as his successor without ever informing his loyal servants? Nathan's real purpose here is not so much to indict David for his ignorance and the violation of "due process," as some have suggested. Rather, he means to point out that those who are *not* with Adonijah are still loyal to David—they are truly *his servants*.

1:28-31. This time David speaks and acts decisively. Perhaps not trusting his own memory, he is simply accepting the case made by Bathsheba. Or perhaps he is genuinely moved by the plea of Bathsheba and the arguments of Nathan, and so decides to act. Whereas the reader has only heard questionable references to a previous commitment that David made to Bathsheba regarding the succession to his throne, one now hears the oath in David's own words that Solomon is indeed the heir-designate (v. 30). If one does not know whether there had really been an oath before this occasion, one certainly hears the oath sworn now in David's own words, an oath made in the name of "the LORD, the God of Israel." Bathsheba responds with gratitude, saying, "May my lord King David live forever!" (v. 31). This is surely not an expression of hope for David's physical immortality, but a wish that David would live on through his lineage upon the throne, as promised by the deity in Nathan's oracle (2 Sam 7:12-16).

With David's oath explicitly designating Solomon (vv. 28-30) and Bathsheba's benediction (v. 31), the story takes a decisive turn. Medieval Hebrew scholars noticed the shift and placed the strongest marker of a paragraph division after the words of Bathsheba (v. 31)—the only such marker in the chapter. Leading to this pivotal moment, the narrative speaks of Adonijah's elevation of himself, followed by the intervention of Nathan and Bathsheba on Solomon's behalf. Beyond this point we read of the acclamation of Solomon as king and the fall of Adonijah, ending in his humiliation before Solomon.

1:32-40. David instructs Zadok the priest, Nathan the prophet, and Benaiah the commander of the royal guards—three persons who are not implicated in the conspiracy—to install Solomon as king (מלך *melek*) and as designated ruler (נגיד *nāgîd*). In stark contrast to the divisive and provincial assembly of Adonijah, which was attended by Judeans only, Solomon is said to have been installed amid pomp and circumstance, all marking the legitimacy of his accession over the whole country ("over Israel," v. 34; "over Israel and over Judah," v. 35).

Solomon is thus presented as a duly designated and legitimate heir in the dynasty and as a ruler accepted by all the people. He is placed upon David's own mule, the mule having become a status symbol in those days (cf. 2 Sam 13:29; 18:9). He is publicly anointed with "the oil from the tent," no doubt referring here to the movable "tent of meeting" or "tent of YHWH" that had been the symbol of divine presence in the midst of Israel (2:28; 2 Sam 7:2, 7). In this way, then, he is anointed just as Saul (1 Sam 10:1) and David (1 Sam 16:1, 13) had been.

The ceremony takes place near the spring of Gihon, beneath the City of David, whereas Adonijah's feast is held at another spring outside the city. Moreover, throughout the account, the narrator presents Adonijah's actions as having arisen from ambition and personal will. Adonijah exalted himself, openly declared his wish to be king, prepared for himself the trappings of kingship, and approached his co-conspirators himself. By contrast, Solomon's accession is not his own doing. He is presented as a passive figure throughout the process: Others plot and plead his case, others cause him to ride the mule, others bring him to Gihon and anoint him. They blow the *shophar*—the ram's horn—and proclaim him king amid joyous public fanfare, rather than in an exclusive ceremony, as was the case with Adonijah. Accordingly, then, "all the people" (v. 40)—not just a select group of Judeans—follow Solomon and celebrate his accession publicly.

1 Kings 1:41-53, Solomon's Succession Is Ensured

COMMENTARY

Adonijah and his guests hear the loud noise in town (v. 41), for En-Rogel, although outside the city limits, is less than half a mile away. The significance of the sound is reported by an intelligence scout, Jonathan, the son of Abiathar the priest (see 2 Sam 15:27, 36; 17:17-20). Adonijah apparently expects the noise to indicate the success of his *coup d'état*, for he assumes that Jonathan is a harbinger of "good news." He expects a positive word from Jonathan because the messenger is "a man of substance" (v. 42; NRSV and NIV, "worthy man"), here meaning that he is a loyal subject (cf. v. 52; 1 Sam 18:17; 2 Sam 2:7; 13:28). Furthermore, the Hebrew root used here for the bringing of good news (בשׂר *bśr*, in the piel) is related to the one used in Canaanite mythology for the announcement of Baal-Hadad's successful bid for kingship (Ugaritic, *bšr*). Upon Baal-Hadad's victory over Mot (deified Death), his brother and rival for cosmic kingship, the consort of the former brought "good news" (*tbšr . . . bšrt*) that a palace befitting Baal's kingship would be constructed for him.[8]

In Adonijah's case, however, there is no good news. In fact, the messenger reports that David has already designated Solomon as heir, that Solomon has already been installed upon the throne, that the subordinates of the king have accepted the succession as legitimate, and that David himself has affirmed that Solomon's accession is in accordance with divine will (see 2 Sam 7:12). The hopelessness of the situation for Adonijah is conveyed in the messenger's speech through the threefold repetition of the particle גם (*gam*, "also," "moreover"), a particle that is not consistently represented in the English translations. The text says, literally: "*Moreover* Solomon has sat enthroned" (v. 46), "*moreover* the king's servants came to bless our lord"

8. *ANET*, 133.

(v. 47), "*moreover* thus said the king . . . " (v. 48). Adonijah's failure is indicated in other ways, as well, for not only does Jonathan relate the cold facts of Solomon's success, but also his language betrays his shifting loyalty: Twice he refers to David as "our lord" (vv. 43, 47). Adonijah's guests, too, are quick to abandon him; they "rose in alarm and dispersed" (v. 49).

Fearing for his life, then, Adonijah seeks temporary asylum in the sanctuary: He "went and grasped the horns of the altar" (v. 50). The "horns of the altar" refers to the four horn-like protuberances at the four corners of the altar, on which sacrificial blood is smeared and atonement is symbolically effected (Exod 27:2; 29:12; 30:10; Lev 4:7; Ezek 43:20). Hence, the grasping of these horns came to signal an appeal for asylum. The prophet Amos would later threaten Israel that the horns of the altar at Bethel—one of two national sanctuaries of the northern kingdom—would be cut off (Amos 3:14), meaning that the Israelites would have no place to go when their pursuers sought their lives. The mere grasping of the horns of the altar does not, however, guarantee one safety forever (Exod 21:14). Adonijah has to secure Solomon's agreement, sealed by an oath, that Solomon would spare him. He refers to himself as Solomon's servant (v. 51) and pays homage to Solomon. But he is simply dismissed with the words, "Go to your house" (v. 53). Thus the story of Adonijah's *coup d'état* comes full circle, as Solomon agrees to spare him, but only if Adonijah behaves like a loyal citizen.

REFLECTIONS

The story in 1 Kings 1 may be read in different ways. It may be read as an ancient historical document. Insofar as it presents the characters "warts and all," it may be viewed as an attempt—despite the inevitability of its particular biases—to present a factual record of the past, an account so detailed that some have surmised that the author must have been an eyewitness in the Davidic court. Hence, the narrator has been characterized as an early historian writing "history for history's sake," a sort of Israelite forerunner of classical writers of history like Thucydides and Herodotus. The narrative may, at the same time, be read most readily as a political document, a (re)telling of the events primarily for propagandistic reasons—most commentators say to legitimize the reign of Solomon, to justify his elevation from among his brothers, and to praise the superiority of his reign over against that of David. Others argue that the narrative is part of a larger novella told and written primarily for entertainment. The text contains all the elements that make a good story: contrast of characters, dialogue, conflict, suspense, humor, irony, colorful details, and pathos. It is a fascinating account that sounds remarkably contemporary, with factional strifes among groups with different political views (conservative and liberal), from different branches of the armed forces, belonging to different religious factions, and having different agendas.

There is validity to each of the approaches to the chapter, and they are not mutually exclusive. The text is a historical narrative, written from a particular sociopolitical viewpoint probably for political purposes at first, and it is constructed aesthetically. These perspectives all seem rather obvious when one reads the chapter. What is not so immediately evident in the story itself, however, is its theological message. There is little suggestion of direct divine intervention in the text. There is no divine manifestation, no direct word from on high, not even communication from God delivered by a messenger. Indeed, God is not mentioned very frequently in the text, only in connection with oaths, whether putative or real (1:17, 29-30), and in a couple of blessing and prayer formulas (1:36-37, 47-48). The narrative seems more concerned with human plots, schemes, and machinations.

It is difficult to find moral lessons here. The pro-Solomonic narrator discredits Adonijah as overly ambitious, impatient, and divisive. With that assessment, one might readily agree. Adonijah cannot wait until the king has passed away or given his official word about the succession, but tries to seize power by turning to certain factions in the country. Yet, his opponents do not seem morally much more compelling. Bathsheba and Nathan conspire to deny Adonijah the throne and to win it for Solomon. One may even charge that they were taking advantage of David's senility and pride, apparently fabricating an oath that David was supposed to have made and casting aspersions on Adonijah. Through their manipulation of the aged king, Solomon is designated and publicly anointed as the successor to the throne. This outcome the narrator dares to put in theological terms: God's promise to David is being fulfilled (1:36-37, 47-48). The story is utterly scandalous.

Yet there is a subtle, even subliminal, message throughout the story.[9] Quietly conveyed in this very entertaining story is a conviction that the will of God is somehow being worked out behind all the scandals and human schemes. In the first place, the elevation of Solomon may be contrary to what people might expect. Adonijah was handsome, confident, and influential. He is just the kind of person whom we would choose to rule over us. He had become first in line to the throne. Had he waited a little while longer, one wonders, might he not have been properly enthroned? Adonijah, however, was self-willed and undisciplined. He tried to impose his will and achieve kingship in his own way. He tried to seize the throne for himself. History would not be dictated by human will, however. God's promise to David would not be fulfilled by the priority of birth or by personal ambition. God's promise would be fulfilled in God's own way, through one whom God had chosen for reasons that may not be revealed to humanity. This is what one learns, too, from other stories in the Bible. God's promise to Abraham, for example, would be fulfilled, not by Ishmael, who was born to Abraham by Hagar, nor by Eliezer, the Damascan slave whom Abraham had adopted. Rather, the promise would come only through Isaac, whom God had chosen (Genesis 12–22). Divine election is a mysterious thing.

In contrast to Adonijah, Solomon is elevated despite all human odds. He was not the obvious choice, according to the custom of primogeniture. Indeed, there is no reason given for the choice of Solomon, save the sense that it was the will of God. Through him the promise of God is somehow fulfilled. To be sure, others did plot and scheme on his behalf, but the narrative puts Solomon above the fray for the time being. Throughout the intrigues, Solomon remains a passive figure. Whereas Adonijah exalted himself, Solomon was exalted by others—and by God. That is the simple

---

9. On the subliminal nature of the theological message, see S. E. McEvenue, "The Basis of Empire, A Study of the Succession Narrative," Ex Auditu 2 (1986) 34-45, esp. 41-45.

conclusion of the story: One who tries to elevate himself is brought down, but one who does nothing to promote himself is exalted. It is God's will that will be done, not the will of an ambitious prince.

The case the narrator makes for Solomon as David's heir is not a logically compelling one. There is still much that is ambiguous, even questionable. Still, the reader is implicitly given the choice: whether or not to concur with the judgment of those who confessed that God's will is somehow being worked out in human reality *despite*, and sometimes even *through, human plots.*

In the end, one must recognize that this is not a tale with a moral lesson. One is not asked to emulate any of the characters in the story—not a king like David, not a prophet like Nathan, not a queen like Bathsheba, not priests like Abiathar and Zadok, not even the blessed Solomon. It is, rather, a simple but memorable story, one that the modern reader may appreciate for no other gain but enjoyment. For one who comes to the text as Scripture, however, this captivating story is more than entertainment. It poses a peculiar dilemma of faith: Whether to believe that there is divine purpose behind, and despite, such scandalous events in history. The Bible is full of such accounts of God's surprises: the exaltation of Jacob over his elder brother, Esau—indeed, through human duplicity and deceit; the election of an enslaved people over a powerful nation; the triumph of a small shepherd boy over a giant; the choice of David over his elder brothers; the birth of Solomon through David's marriage with Bathsheba following their adultery and his murder of her husband. One may even perceive this to be at the heart of the Bible: God's purpose is constantly worked out as history moves along and human beings scheme. But human plots cannot derail God's plan. Ambitious politicians cannot stand in the way: Their purposes, if contrary to God's, will only be thwarted; their actions, if consonant with the fulfillment of God's promises, will be allowed to take place, whether they know the full consequences or not (Acts 4:27-28). God's will is worked out even though human conspirators may have personal and political agendas in mind. For the narrator of 1 Kings, Solomon's succession is just part of the mysterious working out of God's eternal promise made to David (2 Sam 7:1-17).

For the Christian believer, the scandals that attend Solomon's succession to the throne of David is part of the gospel story—the good news that God comes to us through the very arena of human history, through ordinary human beings—sinners all (see Matt 1:1-17). The scandalous story of Solomon's succession is only part of a larger story of God's plan being worked out. The climax of this biblical (hi)story comes in the scandal of the gospel—the coming of Jesus, who is called "the son of David," despite the adverse circumstances attending his birth. It is this one, this son of David, whom God has ultimately exalted as king, and now he sits enthroned "at the right hand of the Majesty on high" (Heb 1:3). The subliminal message in 1 Kings 1 is that God is at work—despite the plots of Adonijah and his supporters and even through the wicked plots of Solomon's supporters. One who so believes may be prompted to respond with the narrator, in the words spoken by Benaiah: "Amen! May the LORD, the God of my lord the king, so ordain!" (v. 36). May God's will be done.

1 KINGS 2:1-46, SOLOMON CONSOLIDATES POWER

OVERVIEW

The preceding chapter ends with the elevation of Solomon to the throne of David and the simultaneous debasement of Adonijah. Some loose ends are still untied, however.

Although Solomon has already been designated, anointed, and acclaimed "king," it is clear that David is still alive, suggesting that there was some sort of co-regency during the transition from one reign to the next. Moreover, Solomon had spared Adonijah, his brother and rival, only if Adonijah would show himself to be a "person of substance" (1:52; NRSV, NIV, "worthy man"). Despite the turn of events narrated in chap. 1, there is still some uncertainty about the future of the kingdom. Now, in this new literary unit, the reader will be told how that kingdom came to be consolidated under Solomon's rule.

1 Kings 2:1-12, Solomon's Kingship Is Firmly Established

COMMENTARY

2:1-4. On his deathbed, David delivers his final testament in the form of instructions to his son and successor. The introduction of David's valedictory oration ("when the time drew near for David to die . . .") is reminiscent of the opening of the account of the patriarch Jacob/Israel's final testament in Gen 47:29–50:14: "when the time drew near for Israel to die . . ." (Gen 47:29). The antiquity of the latter tradition is suggested by the archaic language in Gen 49:1b-27, a poem that is widely regarded by Hebraists as being among the oldest in the Bible. It is possible, too, that the original core of David's final valediction may have been quite ancient, possibly going back to the Solomonic era. Certainly the genre of the final testament of the king is already well attested in the ancient Near East by the third millennium BCE, as is evident in the Egyptian *Instruction for King Merikare* (c. 2100 BCE) and the *Instruction of King Amenemhet I* (c. 1970 BCE).[10] Both are presented as pragmatic advice of a dying king to his successor on political survival.[11] Each was intended to legitimate the new king and justify the elimination of any opposition that may yet remain. In the light of the sapiential character of the Egyptian royal testaments, it is not amiss to note that Solomon is expected to show "wisdom" in his dealings with those who may be a threat to his rule (see vv. 6, 9).

Despite the formal and thematic analogies with the Egyptian royal testaments, however, one should not assume that the text in 1 Kings 2, as we have it, is from the united

monarchy. Indeed, the hand of the deuteronomist is most readily evident in vv. 2-4, for the text is replete with deuteronomistic idioms and themes (see Introduction). First of all, valedictory orations are one of the hallmarks of deuteronomistic style. Thus, just as Moses (Deuteronomy 33), Joshua (Joshua 23), and Samuel (1 Samuel 12) all made farewell speeches exhorting faithfulness to the way of the Lord, so, too, David utters a final oration for posterity. In the *Instruction for King Merikare*, the new king is exhorted to be observant of the teachings of the ancestors, as they have been written and passed down. Similarly, Solomon is charged to be faithful to the legacy of Moses, here expressed in deuteronomistic terms (v. 3): "statutes" (חקות *ḥuqqôt*; NIV, "decrees"), "commandments" (מצות *miṣwōt*), "rules" (משפטים *mišpāṭîm*; NRSV, "ordinances"; NIV, "laws"), and "stipulations" (עדות *ʿēdôt*; NRSV, "testimonies"; NIV, "requirements"). All these are said to be "as written in the תורה (*tôrâ*) of Moses," referring here essentially to the materials in the book of Deuteronomy, the constitutive document for Israel's existence as a political entity.[12]

Moshe Weinfeld makes the astute observation that the editor has superimposed a deuteronomistic theology on the original royal testament, thereby subsuming the original (largely political) intention of the account to its own *theological* agenda.[13] This is part of

---

10. See M. Lichtheim, *Ancient Egyptian Literature*, 3 vols. (Berkeley: University of California Press, 1975) 1:97-109, 134-39.

11. See L. G. Perdue, "The Testament of David and Egyptian Royal Inscriptions," in W. W. Hallo et al., eds., *Scripture in Context II: More Essays on the Comparative Method* (Winona Lake, Ind.: Eisenbrauns, 1983) 79-96.

12. Both the NIV and the NRSV translate תורה (*tôrâ*) as "law," which, given the dominance of the later Pauline notion of "law," is unsatisfactory. The Hebrew word may be taken variously to mean "teaching," "instruction," "direction," or even, as S. D. McBride has suggested, "polity" or "constitution." See McBride, "The Polity of the Covenant People: The Book of Deuteronomy," *Int* 41 (1987) 229-44.

13. Moshe Weinfeld, *Deuteronomy and the Deuteronomic School* (Oxford: Clarendon, 1972) 11. This does not mean that the old document was pro-Solomonic, whereas the deuteronomistic perspective was anti-Solomonic. Rather, it means that the deuteronomistic editor has theologically reappropriated the original account.

the theological framework within which one is now meant to understand the account as a whole. The theologian affirms that God will keep the promise made to David (v. 4), no doubt referring to the promise of an ongoing dynasty in Nathan's oracle (2 Sam 7:12-16), with the proviso that the successors of David are unwaveringly faithful. Implicitly, then, Solomon's place in history will be judged by his faithfulness, or the lack thereof, to the Mosaic standards hereby reiterated through the authority of the founder of the dynasty.

2:5-9. As the narrative has it, it was David who ordered the pre-emptive moves against any threat to his successor's absolute hegemony. Solomon's violent expurgation of his rivals is thus justified as filial and proper obedience to the will of his father. This is the same perspective that one sees in the Egyptian royal testaments, essentially apologies for the successor to the throne; the radical changes of the new king are legitimated in the name of his predecessor.

First, David orders the extermination of Joab, the commander of Adonijah's military forces. The basis for this sentence is Joab's previous actions against two military officers Abner and Amasa, both of whom Joab had killed. The incidents in question are reported in 2 Sam 3:6-39 and 20:4-10. Abner was a commander in Saul's army when David battled the house of Saul. But Abner later negotiated with David to defect, promising to rally support for him. David granted Abner safe passage, and Joab was specifically informed (2 Sam 3:21-23). Still, Joab murdered Abner to avenge his brother, whom Abner had actually killed in self-defense (2 Sam 2:18-23; 3:37). In consequence, Joab is said to have brought blood guilt upon David's house (see 1 Kgs 2:31). Hence, David supposedly took personal offense, claiming that Joab "did it to me" (1 Kgs 2:5). One wonders, however, why David himself had not punished Joab all those years since that incident. Or was the pro-Solomonic apologist attributing to David the decision to eliminate Joab, who posed a threat to Solomon?[14] Whatever the original intention, the point in the text as we have it now seems to be that David is weak, but Solomon is strong and courageous—even as David

in his last testament had urged him to be. In the account of Abner's murder in 2 Samuel 3, one learns of David's weakness and, in particular, his inability to deal decisively with "the sons of Zeruiah" (2 Sam 3:39). In contrast to David, Solomon will have the character to do the things that need to be done to secure the kingdom. He will deal appropriately with Joab, "the son of Zeruiah."

Amasa was a kinsman both of Joab (2 Sam 17:25) and of David (2 Sam 19:13). He was appointed by Absalom in place of Joab as commander of the army during Absalom's rebellion against David. Although retained by David as an officer in the Judean army after the rebellion had been quelled, Amasa was later treacherously and brutally murdered by his rival, Joab (2 Sam 20:4-10). The precise point that is being made about the murder of Amasa in David's last testament, however, is unclear. The Hebrew text itself is uncertain. All one knows is that Joab's murder of Amasa is in view and, since Amasa was retained as an officer by David, Joab's offense supposedly injured David. One wonders, again, if the pro-Solomonic apologist was attempting to exonerate Solomon from the execution of Joab or if the point is that Solomon is truly bolder and stronger than David was.

On account of his "wisdom," Solomon is expected to dispose of Joab properly (v. 6). The Hebrew word חכמה (ḥokmâ), translated as "wisdom" (true also of the related Hebrew adjective for "wise" and the verb "to be wise") is used much more broadly than the English implies. It may be used of any skill one may have, including skill in magic, divination, interpretation of dreams, handicrafts, social etiquette, sailing, military maneuvers, diplomacy, political craft, survival instincts, or even duplicity (2 Sam 13:3) and wickedness in general (Jer 4:22). In Solomon's case, "wisdom" should enable him to handle the delicate political crisis at hand. In the Egyptian royal testaments, too, the king is expected to be a "wise" person who knows how to handle those surrounding him, neutralizing his adversaries and rewarding his allies.

In contrast to the retaliatory measure that Solomon is to take against Joab, the descendants of Barzillai the Gileadite are to be "among those who eat at [the king's] table," meaning that they are to be pensioned

---

14. Cf. the insistence in 2 Sam 3:28 that David and his kingdom are *not* guilty for the blood of Abner, shed by Joab.

by the government. This is a dubious honor, for those who "eat at the king's table" are often so privileged in order that they may be kept under surveillance (2 Sam 9:7, 13; 1 Kgs 18:19; 2 Kgs 25:29 = Jer 52:33). The expressed basis for this decision is the help that David received from Barzillai when he was fleeing from Absalom. In return for the hospitality and assistance that he received (2 Sam 17:27-29), David later offered Barzillai permanent residence in Jerusalem. The latter declined, citing his old age, and sent his son to take his place (2 Sam 19:31-40). Now Solomon is to continue keeping the family in Jerusalem through the government's largess.

The wealthy Barzillai (2 Sam 19:32), whose name is derived from the word for "iron" (ברזל barzel), probably made his fortune in the iron business. The region of ancient Gilead was rich in iron ores, and archaeologists have uncovered evidence of an extensive and technologically advanced iron industry at the end of the second millennium BCE at various sites in that region, in present-day Jordan. Mahanaim, the Gileadite administrative center where David had met Barzillai, has, in fact, been convincingly identified with iron-rich Telul edh-Dhahab. One may speculate, therefore, that the king's interest in securing the presence of the Barzillai family in Jerusalem may have arisen not simply out of gratitude for the earlier hospitality of the Gileadite. There may have been pecuniary and strategic motivations as well. Iron was the metal of choice in the production of military materiel in that period, and success in warfare depended on knowledge of iron technology, as the Israelites had learned in their earlier wars with the Philistines (1 Sam 13:19-22).

As David was on his way to Mahanaim, he was confronted by a Benjaminite kinsman of Saul, Shimei the son of Gera, who cursed David grievously (v. 8; see 2 Sam 16:5-13). On his way back to Jerusalem, however, the victorious David was met again by Shimei, now apologetic and thoroughly obsequious, although not insignificantly backed by a force of a thousand. Thereupon, perhaps to gain the loyalty of Shimei's Benjaminite kinfolks at a time when his own power had not yet been consolidated, David swore that Shimei's life would be spared (2 Sam 19:16-23). It is peculiar, therefore, that David should now include vengeance on Shimei in his last testament, contrary to his reported earlier belief that Shimei had cursed him because God had asked him to do so (2 Sam 16:11), as well as his own oath to spare him.[15] At least, the pro-Solomonic apologist would have the reader believe that it was David who told Solomon to punish Shimei. Solomon is supposed to handle the situation with the shrewdness ("wisdom") that is expected of him as king (v. 9).

2:10-12. A concluding regnal summary marks the transition between the reign of David and the reign of Solomon. Similar formulae are found throughout the book of Kings (so, e.g., 1 Kgs 11:41-43; 14:19-20, 29-31; 15:23-24, 31-32). This is an editorial device used by the Deuteronomist in his periodization of monarchical history. Here, the editor notes that David "rested with his ancestors," a formula certifying the peaceful passing of the king. Also noted in the regnal summary is the length of David's reign, rounded to forty years—seven years in Hebron and thirty-three in Jerusalem (cf. 2 Sam 5:4-5).

The establishment of Solomon as the successor to David is verified through David's charge to him (so 2:1-12). There may be a slight nuance in the Hebrew of v. 12b as opposed to v. 46b, an indication of progression in the story that is lost in the translation of NRSV: Solomon's *kingship* (מלכות *malkût*) is firmly established (v. 12), and then the kingdom (ממלכה *mamlākâ*) was established in his power. (See Reflections at 2:13-16.)

---

15. If the record in 2 Sam 19:23[24] is accurate, David made a general promise to spare Shimei's life: "You shall not die!" In David's last testament, however, the promise is stated much more narrowly: "*I* [David] will not put you to death *by the sword*" (italics added). So Shimei's death by some other person or by some other means would still be a fulfillment of the "original" promise.

1 Kings 2:13-46, The Kingdom Is Consolidated Under Solomon

COMMENTARY

Despite David's final testament and the accession of Solomon to the throne, the latter's kingship having been "firmly established" (v. 12*b*), the narrator now calls attention to various threats that remain within the kingdom.

2:13-25. Adonijah, the deposed heir apparent and the chief contender for the throne, is still around. Highlighting the blood rivalry between the two brothers, the narrator refers to the former as "the son of Haggith," whereas Solomon is identified with his mother, Bathsheba. Adonijah comes to Bathsheba with a proposition that is apparently so delicate and audacious that he dares not broach it with Solomon directly. Bathsheba seems, once again, to be a conduit for the dangerous petitions of men—first of Nathan before David (1:11-27), and now of Adonijah before Solomon (vv. 13-18).

Adonijah and Bathsheba encounter each other ever so cautiously. Despite the successful enthronement of her son, she continues to be suspicious of Adonijah, the son of Haggith. In their conversation, Adonijah manages to slip in his own view that the kingdom was his to begin with and that all Israel had fully expected him to be king (v. 15), a gross exaggeration at best. He concedes, though, that there has been a turnaround in the matter and that this happened because the kingdom was meant by the Lord for his younger brother. Only in his final turn of the conversation does Adonijah state his "one request": that Abishag the Shunammite be given to him for a wife. She is, of course, the beautiful young virgin who was brought to David to lie in his bosom.

Bathsheba promises to speak to the king, although what she says may be double-edged. She does not say that she will relay the petition itself to the king, but that she will speak to Solomon "about you" (עליך *'āleykā*). Accordingly, she comes to the royal court and speaks to Solomon "about" Adonijah. In her mouth, Adonijah's "one request"

(v. 16) becomes "one small request" (v. 20). One cannot tell if the characterization of the request as a small one is intended to suggest that Bathsheba actually sees no harm in granting it or if she means it ironically. One also cannot be sure if her reference to Adonijah as "your brother" (v. 21) is intended as an argument in favor of the petition or if it is meant to signal the danger of it. Solomon certainly does not take the matter lightly; it is not just "one small request" to him. He recognizes, too, that Adonijah is not just a brother but, indeed, his *elder* brother (v. 22). Despite the propriety of Solomon's etiquette before the queen mother, and his initial assurance to her that he will not reject her request, he is thoroughly indignant. "Ask for him the kingdom also," he retorts, betraying a sense of insecurity over his domain.

Behind Solomon's paranoia is, perhaps, the notion that a king's harem may become a trophy for his challenger or successor. So David, having succeeded Saul, is said to have been given "your master's house and your master's wives into your bosom" (2 Sam 12:8). By the same token, because of David's own illicit affair with Bathsheba, Nathan predicted that God would bring about a tragedy in David's house and give his wives to someone else (2 Sam 12:11). One thinks, too, of Ishbaal's accusation that Abner was trying to take one of Saul's concubines, a charge tantamount to treason, to which Abner responded in rage (2 Sam 3:6-11). Most poignantly, when Absalom was rebelling against David, he was counseled by Ahitophel, his shrewd adviser: "Have intercourse with your father's concubines, whom he has left to keep the house, and all Israel will hear that you have become odious to your father, and all your supporters will be encouraged" (2 Sam 16:20-21).[16]

Moreover, Adonijah has the support of two influential Judean officials, Abiathar the priest

---

16. On the political implications of the marriage of royal consorts in these texts, see M. Tsevat, "Marriage and Monarchical Legitimacy in Ugarit and Israel," *JSS* 3 (1958) 237-43.

and Joab the military commander.[17] Both of them are supported by the free elements in the kingdom, whereas Zadok and Benaiah are feudal retainers appointed by the authoritarian power of the king.

Solomon swears in the name of the Lord and invokes the Lord's promise to David (yet another allusion to Nathan's oracle, 2 Samuel 7), promising that Adonijah will be put to death for his conduct. The reader is supposed to remember at this point that Adonijah was earlier spared his life only on condition of his loyalty (1:52). But now the deal is off, his present quest being evidence to Solomon that Adonijah is not "a person of substance," after all. So Solomon sends Benaiah, his hatchet man, to kill Adonijah, thus putting an end to whatever claims his brother may have had to the throne. Whereas David had been weak and indulgent to Adonijah (1:5), Solomon is strong and acts boldly.

The narrator leaves many questions unanswered in this story. Is Adonijah a hopeless "romantic," who naively believes that Abishag is legitimately available to him because her relationship with David was never consummated? Or has he really been exposed as a desperate and deceitful manipulator, trying to use two women (Abishag and Bathsheba) to achieve his political ambition? Is Adonijah's concession of defeat (v. 15b) merely a sinister ploy verbalized only to get what he really wants? Or does his action reflect a genuine, if bitter, recognition that the kingdom is truly beyond him now and only a consolation prize is possible? Is Bathsheba merely a nice old woman who is easily manipulated? Or is she coldly calculating and shrewder than she seems at first blush? Does she, in fact, know her son so well that she could anticipate his reaction and the dire consequences for Adonijah and, possibly, also for young and lovely Abishag? What about Abishag's role? Is she merely a pawn, the silent object of other people's schemes? Is Solomon so astute that he sees through the true (political) agenda of Adonijah? Or is he merely paranoid or, even

worse, wicked in using Adonijah's innocent, if unwise, request as a pretext to eliminate his brother? Whatever the truth, the outcome is a death sentence for Adonijah, and Solomon justifies it as the fulfillment of God's promise that he himself will be the heir to David's throne.

2:26-46. Having already mentioned the threat posed by Abiathar and Joab (v. 22), the narrator proceeds to explain how they are also neutralized. The priest is exiled to his estate in the Benjaminite town of Anathoth, three and a half miles northeast of Jerusalem. Unlike all the others who are punished, no charge is explicitly leveled against Abiathar; the only reason why he is sentenced, one gathers, is his complicity in the anti-Solomon conspiracy; this is implied in v. 22. Abiathar deserves death, but extenuating circumstances are cited for the supposed leniency of his sentence: He had carried the ark before David and had shared in David's afflictions (v. 26). During the rebellion of Absalom, Abiathar was with Zadok and the Levites in carrying the ark back into Jerusalem (2 Sam 15:24-29), the ark having presumably been brought out of the city when David fled. This is probably the incident that the narrator has in mind when he links the carrying of the ark with David's hardships (cf. Ps 132:1).

The narrator notes that the rustification of Abiathar fulfills an oracle against the priestly family of Eli in Shiloh (v. 27; see 1 Sam 2:27-36).[18] Abiathar is thus identified with the old guard associated with the shrine at Shiloh, the central sanctuary of the tribal confederacy before the construction of the Temple in Jerusalem. The way is now clear for the elevation of Zadok as the sole high priest in Jerusalem (v. 35), and his descendants will control the Jerusalem Temple continuously until the end of the monarchy. These two priests are representatives of two traditions of divine dwelling: Abiathar stood for the tent-shrine in Shiloh, and Zadok, in time, the Jerusalem Temple. Now the latter is promoted at the expense of the former. In the light of this background, it is interesting to note that the prophet Jeremiah, who was born of a priestly family in Anathoth, would appear centuries

---

17. The Hebrew has, literally, "and for him and for Abiathar the priest and for Joab the son of Zeruiah," a reading adopted by the NRSV and the NIV. That is possibly corrupt, however. One should read with other ancient versions, with only a slight emendation of the Hebrew: "and for him is Abiathar the priest and for him is Joab the son of Zeruiah." The point is that they are on his side. For the idiom, see Exod 32:26; Josh 5:13; 2 Kgs 10:6.

18. Abiathar's father was Ahimelech (1 Sam 30:7), one of the priests of Nob and a son Ahitub (1 Sam 22:9), the brother of Ichabod, the grandson of Eli (1 Sam 14:3).

later, delivering scathing critiques of the Temple and its establishment (Jer 3:16-17; 7:1-15; 26:1-6).

The next target in Solomon's purge is Joab, the chief military commander who had supported Adonijah (v. 28). The news of Solomon's intention comes to the general, "because Joab had supported Adonijah and had not supported Absalom" (v. 28). Taken at face value, the Hebrew suggests that Joab receives the news *because* he has supported Adonijah (the heir apparent to the throne of David), but he has not supported Absalom, who had rebelled against David. That is, Joab is a Davidide loyalist through and through and, as such, is a beneficiary of the pro-Adonijah underground network.[19] Thus forewarned, he flees. Like his patron, Adonijah, he seeks asylum by coming to the tent of the Lord and grasping the horns of the altar (see Commentary on 1:50).

Given Adonijah's experience, Joab must surely expect no more than temporary reprieve. Even so, he refuses to leave the sanctuary and apparently gets away with it for a while. Benaiah, who is sent after him, dares not pursue him into the sanctuary but reports the standoff to Solomon. In effect, Joab dares Solomon and his hatchet man, Benaiah, to violate the law of sanctuary: If anyone wants to kill him, it will have to be there, right by the altar in the sanctuary! The fact that Benaiah has to try to get Joab to leave the sanctuary first suggests that Joab probably has a case. Nonetheless, Solomon orders the execution, citing not so much Joab's disloyalty or his political affiliation (v. 22), for which asylum in the sanctuary is provided for by law, but his murder of Abner and Amasa, the intentional and treacherous nature of which annuls any right of refuge (Exod 21:12-14). On this pretext, which is already set forth in the last testament of David, Joab is killed. Solomon goes to great lengths to place the guilt squarely on the head of Joab, emphasizing that, while Joab had killed Abner and Amasa treacherously, David had not known of it and is, therefore, not complicitous. Hence, David and his successors are free from guilt for putting Joab to death, even death in the sanctuary. Accordingly, even as Zadok becomes

the sole high priest, taking over the position of Abiathar, Benaiah is appointed the commander in chief, taking over the position of his rival. Adonijah and his most important allies (1:7) have all been eliminated.

Besides the two principal supporters of Adonijah, the narrator accounts for the elimination of Shimei, who embodies the threat of Saulide loyalists, notably the Benjaminites.[20] Shimei is put under house arrest in Jerusalem and, on pain of death, forbidden to leave the Kidron Valley, east of Jerusalem. He accepts the conditions and does in fact live in Jerusalem for some time. The restriction given to Shimei, a Benjaminite from Bahurim, was no doubt to undermine his influence at home,[21] the actual weakening of which is evident in the escape of two of his slaves to Gath, one of the five principal Philistine cities. Gath is the Philistine city closest to the territory of Davidic Judah (1 Sam 17:52). The narrator notes that the slaves had escaped to "Achish, the son of Maacah, king of Gath," thus emphasizing that they are in Philistine domain. Solomon apparently does not even know of Shimei's trip until after he returns to Jerusalem. One can only speculate as to what must have been in Shimei's mind— whether he had flagrantly violated the letter of the law but not the spirit of it, as one might say. The elaborative restriction of the house arrest stipulates the Kidron Valley as the limit. That stipulation, however, might have been interpreted by Shimei to mean that Gath, which lies west of Jerusalem, was actually permissible to visit. What is clear is that he was already beyond Solomon's orbit, having reached Philistine Gath. He returns in any case. But Solomon interprets the restriction narrowly and claims to have made Shimei take a sacred oath and that the penalty for going anywhere at all from Jerusalem is death. Such details, curiously enough, are not found in the account of their agreement earlier in the passage; no oath is mentioned, and the death penalty is stipulated only for crossing the Kidron Valley, not for leaving Jerusalem per se. In fact, Shimei did not cross the Kidron, for the valley is to the

20. The possibility of a Benjaminite secession from the kingdom is evidenced earlier in the revolt of Sheba (2 Samuel 20).

21. This is evident in the specific prohibition for leaving the Kidron Valley, which provides access to Bahurim, where Shimei has his ancestral home.

19. So Jerome T. Walsh, *1 Kings*, Berit Olam (Collegeville, Minn.: Liturgical Press, 1996) 57.

east of Jerusalem, whereas Philistine Gath is to the west. It is, perhaps, in recognition of the disputable nature of the accusation that Solomon adds the charge of Shimei's offense against David long ago, a wrong that Shimei is supposed to know "in his own heart" (v. 44). Shimei must have denied the charge—that is with his lips—because Solomon accuses him of lying. The excuse for the execution of Shimei is flimsy at best, but the whole setup is precisely what one might expect, for David had expressed confidence that Solomon would know just what to do with that tricky situation, since he is a "wise" man. So Shimei is put to death, Solomon is blessed, and the kingdom is, finally, consolidated in his hand.

REFLECTIONS

This passage of Scripture has come to us through a long process of transmission, the details of which are still elusive, perhaps irrecoverably so. From a moral viewpoint, the passage is difficult to appropriate. Herein one finds attitudes and actions that are utterly deplorable. We see examples of human cunning, vindictiveness, pettiness, insecurity, and sheer dishonesty. David and Solomon, God's anointed ones, are just as guilty of questionable ethics as are the others—if not more so. They are no role models for righteous conduct, except in negative ways. One might attempt a defense of their conduct in the light of ancient Near Eastern cultures, arguing that their actions sprang from culturally specific and antiquated attitudes about the power of curses, the abiding consequences of blood guilt, and the like. Still, the text remains morally problematic in the light of the totality of Scripture's teachings about right relationships among human beings.

The text "will not preach," if its primary message is ethics. When one discerns its deeper theological message, however, this passage of Scripture offers rich lessons. One may begin with the precedent set by the deuteronomistic editor-narrator, who wrestles theologically with history. David's charge to Solomon is couched in deuteronomistic idioms: Courageous and uncompromising obedience to the way of the Lord is the king's obligation (2:2-3). No doubt, for the deuteronomist, the actions of Solomon are to be judged according to this requirement of obedience to the will of God, as written in the Torah of Moses.

One might argue that the narrator is glossing over the ruthless pragmatism of ancient politicians by recourse to the language of Torah piety. That is to say, the narrator considers Solomon's unscrupulous elimination of his adversaries to be in accordance with the manifestation of courageous and uncompromising obedience. Indeed, just as Moses had charged Israel and Joshua to "be strong and courageous" in following the way of the Lord (Deut 31:1-6; Josh 1:1-9), a charge that mandated the extermination of all those who opposed Israel's possession of the promised land, so also David charges Solomon to be "strong and courageous" (2:2), a charge that is taken to mean the elimination of every threat to the fulfillment of God's promise. In an earlier period, the nations that opposed Israel's taking of God's gift of the land were defeated, and only those who did not stand in their way were spared. Now, similarly, the individuals who opposed Solomon are neutralized, while benefactors of the government are treated well. Just as God's promise of the land brooks no compromise, so, too, God's promise of succession in the Davidic kingdom brooks no compromise. Solomon did whatever it took to bring about God's promise.

That is surely not what we are to get out of the text, however. Indeed, in the light of the rest of Scripture, Solomon's actions—even if politically and legally justifiable—are morally reprehensible. It is significant that the narrator quotes Nathan's oracle, where the promise of God to David is, ironically, *unconditional* (2 Sam 7:12-16); the enduring character of the Davidic dynasty is ensured by unilateral divine decision. We see profound theology at work here. The unconditionality of promise, as we know it in

Nathan's oracle, is now *conditioned* by a demand for faithfulness, introduced by the conditional particle "if": "*If* your descendants take heed to their way, to walk before me in faithfulness with all their heart and with all their being, [then] there shall not fail you a person for the throne of Israel" (2:4).

The narrator-editor insists on obedience to the Torah, and that is what we must proclaim. At the same time, however, the modern reader must ask what it means to be faithful in our time. In other words, one may accept the theological mandate of the text without necessarily agreeing with the culturally conditioned application of it. The text highlights the importance of obedience. At the same time, however, it indicates how people might use the letter of the Torah to realize their personal ambition and to justify their fundamentally unscrupulous actions. The Christian believer has to honor the "letter of the law" in ways that are always true to the "spirit of the law," as it were (see 2 Cor 3:4-18).

There is, indeed, tension and ambiguity throughout the narrative. On the one hand, one detects a certain inevitability in the accession of Solomon, for the Lord has willed the succession to be just so (see 2:15, 24). All this happens in fulfillment of God's promise. On the other hand, Solomon has to be uncompromisingly faithful to the way of the Lord in order that the promise might be fulfilled. As the narrative has it, he tries to be true to the charge by guarding the house of David against the blood guilt, curses, and disloyalties that threaten it. The tension is never resolved.

Here one encounters two seemingly irreconcilable truths about the relationship between God and people. On the one hand, there is faith in the sovereignty of God to bring about the divine will apart from human decisions and despite human failures. On the other hand, there is the insistence upon unwavering faithfulness to God's way. It is a dialectic of the absolute control of God in history as one pole, and the freedom of the human will to respond or not to respond to God as the other. That is a dialectic that persists even today in various theologies within the communities of faith, with some traditions emphasizing the absolute sovereignty of God to bring about the divine will despite human responses or lack thereof and others stressing the divinely granted freedom of humanity to respond or refuse to respond to God. But both theological realities—of God's sovereignty and human freedom—must be preserved, as they are in this passage of Scripture.

Even as the promise is relativized and made provisional by the condition of obedience, the limitations of human ability to be truly faithful are also relativized by the failures and mortality of humanity. God brings about the promise despite the questionable and presumptuous conduct of human beings.

It is, in fact, the deity who ensures that the succession is worked out as promised. This is the significance of the concluding regnal summary in 2:10-12. David dies, but history moves on inexorably to the inevitable end that God has determined. The kingdom of God is, indeed, guaranteed by God, and Solomon's enthronement is indisputably a result of divine intention. By God's will and, somehow, through the coincidence of human manipulation, the kingdom is established in the hand of Solomon. The promise of God transcends the historical presence and activities of David and Solomon. There is no letup on the demand of obedience, but the fulfillment of God's promise is not dependent on human will but on the will of God. Hence, even if mortals fail and behave as mortals only can, the will of God is nevertheless brought about.

In a similar manner, the death and burial of David are interpreted theologically in the New Testament. David's mortality only points to the transcendence of divine will, as manifested in the person of Jesus Christ (Acts 2:29; 13:36). The promise of God did not die with David. Nor would it die with Solomon. Rather, the promise of God lives on by the will of God.

1 KINGS 3:1-15, SOLOMON'S PRIORITIES AND HIS GIFTS FROM GOD

1 Kings 3:1-3, Solomon's Alliance with Egypt

COMMENTARY

This episode comes on the heels of Solomon's takeover from the now-deceased David. The new literary unit begins immediately with Solomon's marriage alliance with an unnamed king of Egypt, probably Pharaoh Siamun (c. 978–959 BCE). It was a diplomatic deal sealed by Egypt's cession of the newly conquered city of Gezer to Solomon as a dowry, according to the historical notation of 9:16. Politically, the marriage signaled Solomon's rise to prominence in the international arena. He was leading his tiny new nation into the realm of world-class diplomacy, and the ruler of the powerful Egyptian Empire had to come to terms with him, even giving the Egyptian princess to him. That was a remarkable achievement since, according to one of the Amarna letters, the Egyptians did not like to make such concessions on their part: "From time immemorial no daughter of the king of Egy[pt] is given to anyone."[22]

In terms of the overall agenda of the narrator, however, this alliance surely foreshadows problems in which Solomon and his kingdom would soon become embroiled. The narrator hints at this by mentioning the Temple of the Lord that is still to be built and the fact that the people were sacrificing at the "high places" (local cultic installations) because the Temple had not yet been built.[23] The narrative presents Solomon's marriage alliance with Egypt as the first of his acts after the kingdom was firmly established in his hand.

The Egyptian princess is brought into the City of David. Solomon apparently could not wait to bring her in, for he had not yet built his own palace and certainly not the Temple, which would have made possible the centralization of worship in Jerusalem according to the stipulations in Deuteronomy (Deut 12:13-14). The defense of the city, too, had been put off. The implication is that the consequent syncretism had compromised the security of the nation, so much so that no walls could ever shield it from destruction in the end.

The narrator no doubt intends the reader to come to the story with the Torah of Moses in mind. Thus the episode may be viewed against the backdrop of the deuteronomistic prohibition against marriages with foreigners, for such alliances would cause the people to turn away from following the Lord and, consequently, lead to destruction (Deut 7:3-4; Josh 23:11-13; 2 Kgs 8:18). It is probable, too, that one is to think of the warning in Deut 17:16, put in the mouth of Moses, that a king must not "cause the people to return to Egypt." Indeed, Israel's return to Egypt is an inevitable outcome of Solomon's action, and the division of the kingdom would be a prelude to its complete disintegration (see 11:26-40).

The Temple of the Lord in Jerusalem is said to be a temple (בית *bayit*; lit., "a house") built for "the name of the LORD" (v. 2). For the deuteronomist, the "name of the LORD" is a virtually independent entity that stands in place of the actual presence of the deity in the sanctuary (so NIV: "Name" rather than "name"). By recourse to the notion of the "Name" that represents God's presence, the theologian is able to associate the deity's presence with the sanctuary without ever implying that the deity is confined to that physical structure (see 8:27-30). The Temple is a place where God's name may be invoked, and so that presence may be brought about as and

22. Amarna letter no. 4, line 4, in W. L. Moran, trans., *The Amarna Letters* (Baltimore: Johns Hopkins University Press, 1997) 8. Although there are exceptions under certain conditions, the pharaoh's boast does reflect official Egyptian double standards in the practice of diplomatic marriage. The Egyptians typically demanded the hand of foreign princesses, but they themselves would not give up their princesses in such arrangements. The concession to Solomon indicates the weakness of Egypt and the strength of Israel in the 10th century BCE.

23. The NIV partially exonerates Solomon by introducing the word "still" (not in the Hebrew) before "sacrificing," thus placing the blame before Solomon's time; the people had already been worshiping at the high places and only continued to do so because of Solomon's negligence. The Hebrew may, in fact, be taken to mean that the people were sacrificing at the local high places precisely because of Solomon's delay in building the Temple.

when God wills, but the Temple is not the house of God per se.

Solomon "loved the LORD," the editor tells us in characteristic deuteronomic language (Deut 6:5; 10:12; 30:16, 20), inasmuch as he was "walking in the statutes of David his father" (v. 3). Yet, that positive judgment seems to be tempered by the observation that he also offered sacrifices and burnt incense at the high places (v. 3b). Again, to the narrator, Solomon is setting a dangerous precedent. Indeed, by the end of the account of Solomon's reign, what is emphasized in the narrative is not his love of the Lord but his love of foreign women, the result of which was the syncretism that ultimately led to the destruction of the kingdom (see 11:1). (See Reflections at 3:4-15.)

1 Kings 3:4-15, God's Self-revelation and Gifts to Solomon

COMMENTARY

Solomon goes to sacrifice at Gibeon, a Benjaminite city, identified with the modern village of el-Jib, on a hill about seven miles northwest of Jerusalem. Gibeon is chosen because "that was the great high place" (NRSV, "that was the principal high place"; NIV, "that was the most important high place"), its reputation as a sacred location is corroborated by the chronicler, who portrays it as a place where "the tabernacle of the LORD" or "the tent of meeting of God" was (1 Chr 16:39; 21:29; 2 Chr 1:3, 6, 13). Yet, it is peculiar that Solomon should seek to worship at the high places or the particular one in Gibeon, for the ark, the very symbol of the Lord's presence, was in Jerusalem, as v. 15 confirms. He went to Gibeon to worship, even though the ark was already in Jerusalem! Solomon cannot be easily exonerated for having gone to that great high place.

The account of Solomon's encounter of God at Gibeon has been compared with other dream accounts in the ancient Near East, especially that of Tuth-mose IV of Egypt (c. 1421–1413 BCE), a dream in which the crown prince receives a divine promise of kingship.[24] As in the report of Tuth-Mose IV and a number of other royal dream accounts, this episode in the book of 1 Kings provides divine legitimation for the ruler in question. Not only does the very appearance of the deity confirm Solomon's favored position in this case, but it is also implied in the narrative that he is king of all Israel, both because he is the scion of David, as southern (Judean) dynastic ideology dictates, and because he is divinely endowed with charisma, as northern (Israelite) notions of leadership would have it.

Solomon's request is sometimes viewed as part of an ancient Near Eastern royal coronation ritual, where the king is given the privilege of a special petition to the deity (see the royal psalms, Pss 2:8; 20:4-6; 21:2). This is suggested by the litany-like reply of God (v. 11):

"Because you asked for yourself this thing,
  but you did not ask for yourself longevity,
  you did not ask for yourself wealth,
  you did not ask for yourself the life of your
    enemies,
but you ask for yourself discernment to hear
    what is just."

Moreover, the king's reference to his youth should be seen not as a chronological datum, a historically reliable indication of Solomon's actual age at the time of his accession. Rather, it is to be understood as a formulaic assertion of divine election, suggesting that Solomon is chosen despite overwhelming odds; although he is only a youth (cf. Jer 1:6) and incapable of leading his people (see Num 27:17; Deut 31:2; Josh 14:11; 1 Sam 18:13; 29:6; 2 Kgs 11:8). References to one's youth are quite common in ancient Near Eastern propaganda, where kings, especially those who come to the throne as usurpers, frequently call attention to divine election in and despite of their youth. So the original dream account

24. *ANET*, 449.

may have been a part of a larger propagandistic work composed to legitimate the kingship of Solomon.

Accepting this pro-Solomonic perspective, modern interpreters have observed that the king's request for wisdom to govern (שׁפט *šāpaṭ*, lit., "to judge") his people (v. 9), rather than for the more selfish and worldly desires of longevity, riches, honor, and victory over enemies, indicates the depth of his character. Here is, as it were, a model of faith that seeks first the good of God's kingdom, the just and proper rule of God's chosen multitudes, rather than one's private interests, and because of that righteous attitude, Solomon is richly blessed (vv. 13-14; cf. Matt. 6:33; Rom 8:28-30). Yet, the elevation of wisdom over against other values is hardly unique in the Hebrew Bible. Indeed, in the wisdom tradition, longevity, honor, and material possessions are all seen as benefits that derive from wisdom (Prov 3:13-18). These things are given to anyone who acquires wisdom. So it only makes practical sense that one should seek wisdom first; all the other benefits will follow.

The account of Solomon's experience at Gibeon makes clear, however, that his wisdom was not something that he acquired through his own efforts. Nor was it an innate quality he was born with. Rather, wisdom was given by God upon Solomon's proper response to God's invitation. All the other benefits, too, were not merely the derivatives of wisdom. They were, rather, also graciously given by God without Solomon's asking, the only condition being, according to the narrator, obedience to God's way (v. 14).

Then Solomon awoke from the dream and returned to Jerusalem. Whereas he had been worshiping at the high places and had gone to Gibeon to worship, he returned in the end to Jerusalem, where the ark was (v. 15). And there, in addition to the burnt offerings that he offered at Gibeon and other high places, he offered שלמים (*šĕlāmîm*; NRSV, "offerings of well-being"; NIV, "fellowship offerings"), probably referring to communal sacrifices accompanied by public feasting.

REFLECTIONS

Solomon's fame is legendary. Most modern readers know, as the ancient reader also did, that his reign was long and exceedingly prosperous and that he was well known for his wisdom. This account seems to confirm all that. Indeed, the original account may historically have served as political propaganda—an account to aggrandize Solomon.

Whatever the original intention of the episode, however, the editor-narrator now sets forth his own explanation. Neither Solomon's legendary wisdom, which made him an effective ruler in the eyes of all the world, nor his other attainments of longevity, wealth, honor, and victory over his enemies, is due to his own righteousness. It is true that he loved the Lord, and it is true that he came before God with the proper attitude of humility. That is neither the beginning nor the end of the story, however. In fact, it was God who came to Solomon first, despite the fact that the king had endangered the integrity of the kingdom by bringing it into alliance with Egypt. Solomon, too, was slow to build the Temple and the defenses of the city, because he was more interested in his own marriage to the Egyptian princess and in building his own palace. He worshiped at the high places, which faithful reformers like Josiah later on had to eliminate. Yet, God came to him with an open invitation. God took the initiative, while Solomon was yet in sin and darkness, as it were.

The passage as a whole seems to convey mixed messages about Solomon. It appears to vacillate between commendation and condemnation of him. On the one hand, Solomon seems to be favorably portrayed, as the builder of the Temple of the Lord in Jerusalem, as one who loves the Lord, who walks in "the statutes of David his father," who has his priorities right inasmuch as he asks for wisdom rather than worldly attainments for himself. And this attitude is explicitly affirmed by God (3:10-14). On the other hand, the salutary character and actions of Solomon are colored by the unsavory effects of his decisions. He built the Temple to be sure, but not before he had brought a foreign wife into the City of David, in contravention of deuteronomic law. He planned to construct the Lord's house only after he had built his own, and, in the meantime, his people burned incense and offered sacrifices at the local cultic installations—something that the establishment of the Jerusalem Temple would have obviated. He loved the Lord, yet Solomon offered sacrifices and incense at the high places, again in violation of deuteronomic law. The pious Solomon, who is given wisdom by God to be a wise ruler, stands in stark contrast to the unscrupulous Solomon of the earlier chapters, who is supposed to be already "wise" enough to know how to deal with all who might threaten his place (see esp. 2:6, 9).

Many commentators are inclined to see Solomon's approach to the Lord as something of a paradigm for faithful prayer. In his petition before God, he first acknowledges God's grace to him (3:6), recognizes that he is undeserving of God's special favor (3:7), and then asks for God's gift of wisdom so that he can carry out his duty as ruler of God's people, the chosen people (3:8-9). His thoughts are, it seems, noble; his primary desire is to seek the good of the kingdom. Accordingly, because of his appropriate attitude, God grants his wish for that gift, along with other benefits that he does not explicitly request. In other words, because he seeks first the kingdom of God, all these things are added unto him (see Matt 6:33).

Solomon's attitude of humility before God is admirable, and there is, indeed, a practical lesson about faith and prayer that one may learn from this story. Yet, the most salient point of the passage is surely *not* that one should emulate Solomon. If it were so, the passage would be theologically banal. Those who view the story as exemplary are, in fact, forced to concede that the picture of Solomon here, contradictory as it is to other characterizations in other passages, represents only "the ideal Solomon . . . as he ought to have been, not necessarily as he was in historical reality."[25] Moreover, that interpretation would make sense only if one were to isolate the episode of Solomon's encounter at Gibeon from the opening subunit about the more selfish and thoughtless first acts of his reign (3:1-3). Whereas the words of his prayer may indicate that his priorities were right in that he put God and duty before self, there is hardly any way to exonerate him in his marriage with the Egyptian princess and in his putting the building of his own house ahead of the construction of the centralized Temple in Jerusalem and the defenses of the city. Finally, such a reading makes no sense in the light of the larger context of chapters 1–11, for the devastating effects of Solomon's selfishness for the kingdom as a whole are plainly laid out at the end.

The lectionaries typically include only 3:5-15 (omitting even v. 4, which should properly be included on literary grounds), but not the preceding verses. Thus truncated, the text calls attention only to the self-revelation of God, the divine invitation, Solomon's admirable response, and the fact of God's gifts. Such a truncation, however, misses the theological tensions that the juxtaposition of these accounts poses: It is the very human, selfish, negligent Solomon who benefits from God's self-revelation and gifts. Solomon loved God only in a qualified way. Still, the deity appeared to him. Such is the nature of God in Scripture: God responds to the *imperfect love* (3:4), the sincere if inadequate response of mortals, with undeserved blessings, only to summon one yet again to love and to obey (3:14).

25. Simon J. De Vries, *1 Kings*, WBC (Waco, Tex.: Word, 1985) 55. De Vries notes, however, that "the two [portrayals] were not irreconcilably divorced, for elements of the real and the ideal are present in every person."

1 KINGS 3:16-28, SOLOMON'S WISDOM IN JUDGMENT

COMMENTARY

Immediately following the account of Solomon's encounter with the deity at Gibeon is an anecdote of his sagacious judgment in an extremely difficult case involving two prostitutes (3:16-28). This episode is a sequel to the Gibeon encounter (3:3-15). It is a sequel that does not appear in the parallel account in Chronicles, and one can only speculate as to reasons why it is in one history but not the other.

The temporal adverb אָז (*'āz*, "then"; NRSV, "later"; NIV, "now") marks the transition from one passage to the next. It indicates that we have a new turn in the narrative, an event taking place in a specific temporal context, in this case, the reign of Solomon. To some commentators, the story originally had nothing to do with Solomon. Accordingly, it is argued, Solomon is not mentioned by name anywhere in the story; indeed, none of the characters is named. Thus "the king" mentioned throughout the story (vv. 16, 22-28) is a typical figure, but that type has been secondarily applied to Solomon within this literary context. In support of this view, it is often pointed out that there are folkloristic elements in the narrative and parallels found in other cultures, both in the Levant and as far away as India and eastern Asia.

In the light of such parallels, many view the story of the king's judgment of the two prostitutes as an Israelite version of a cross-cultural folktale, one that was originally told for pedagogical reasons (perhaps as an example-story of wisdom) or for pure entertainment, but that folktale was later incorporated as a part of Solomonic propaganda. Debates about the origins of such texts and the related issues of their historicity are, of course, impossible to resolve. Whatever its provenance, the story must now be read in the aftermath of Solomon's receipt of the gift of wisdom and its ancillary benefits. In its context, the story serves as an illustration of either the efficacy of Solomon's wisdom or its limitations or, as I would contend, *both*.

The Hebrew has it that two "women, prostitutes" (נשים זנות *nāšîm zōnôt*) came and stood before the king. Earlier on in the book, we read of Bathsheba, who appeared first before David (1:11-21) and then before Solomon (2:13-22) to persuade the king to do her bidding. Here, however, are two women who are related to the king neither by marriage (as Bathsheba was to David) nor by birth (as Bathsheba was to Solomon). Rather, they are commoners. Not only that—they are prostitutes. This detail is important, for the sociocultural assumptions about prostitutes are such that their credibility is immediately in question. They are women of "ill-repute" or women who "turn tricks," so to speak—deceitful women who simply cannot be trusted. That is a large part of the king's problem; the credibility of both the complainant and the respondent is in question from the beginning. The fact that they are prostitutes probably also means that no man is likely to come forward to claim their children. Only the words of these women of disrepute—the charge of the one and the denial of the other—are to be considered in the judgment.

The circumstances are laid out largely through the petition of the complainant, "the one woman," as she is called in v. 17. The two were apparently living in the same house when they each gave birth to a son at about the same time—three days apart, according to the Hebrew text and most ancient witnesses. The fact that they were at home is stressed repeatedly in the Hebrew text (four times in vv. 17-18, a fact reflected in the NRSV but not in the NIV), suggesting that there were no eyewitnesses who could have been passing by. Indeed, there were apparently no witnesses at all, for there was no one (lit., "no stranger") in the house.[26] Since the two prostitutes were "together" (so NRSV), they were

---

26. We expect אִין-אִישׁ (*'ēn-'îš*), the normal idiom for "no one." That אִין-זָר (*'ēn-zār*, lit., "no stranger") is used may well mean that no clients of the prostitutes were present, as some scholars believe. It may simply mean, however, that there was no objective witness, no one who is not kin or friend of either of the two prostitutes.

the only ones responsible for the happenings therein; no one else could be blamed for any mishap (so NIV, "we were alone"). Without witnesses, there was also no one to verify or to challenge their words. Ironically, the fact that they were together alone meant that they must now be separated: One of them had suffered an injustice, and the other had to be culpable.

According to the complainant, they were both asleep when the respondent smothered her own baby by sleeping on it. So in the middle of the night, the mother of the deceased baby exchanged the dead child for the living one. The crime in darkness came to light only with the break of day, according to the complainant, when she arose to nurse her child and, upon closer examination, discovered that the dead child on her bosom was not hers.

The account is flatly denied by the respondent, without any elaboration (v. 22). A simple denial is all that it takes to bring about the legal impasse. Since no evidence whatsoever is here offered by the complainant, it is the word of one woman against another, indeed, one prostitute against another.

The Hebrew text is vivid, even tedious, in its portrayal of the impasse (vv. 22-23). As indicated below, the words of the respondent (A) reverse those of the complainant (B), and Solomon adds to the repetitiveness by summarizing the arguments of the one (C) and then the other (D):

A: "*My son is the living one*, and **your son is the dead one**."

B: "**Your son is the dead one**, and *my son is the living one*."

C: "*My son is the living one*, and **your son is the dead one**."

D: "**Your son is the dead one**, and *my son is the living one*."

The argument appears to be going around in circles, with no end in sight.

Then the king calls for a sword and orders that the living infant be cut in two and each half be given to one of the women. Thereupon, the mother of the living child yields, because her tender emotions are stirred up for her son (NRSV, "because compassion for her son burned within her"; NIV, she was "filled with compassion for her son").

Although it is obvious in the context that it is "mother love" that is meant, some interpreters go too far to make the case on etymological grounds, noting that the term for the mother's emotions (רחמיה *raḥămeyhā*, "her compassion") is the plural form of רחם (*reḥem*, "womb"). Yet the word, either in the singular or the plural, was never meant to be anatomically specific; it may refer to the uterus or the womb (e.g., Gen 29:31; 30:22; Job 38:8; Jer 1:5; 20:18; Job 38:8), but it is certainly not limited to that. It is, rather, a generic term for one's "gut." Accordingly, the Hebrew word may be used of male and female emotions alike, and cognates in other Semitic languages have the same wide range. Indeed, the very Hebrew idiom "emotions stirred up" (נכמרו רחמים *nikměrû raḥămîm*) is used of Joseph's emotional breakdown as he is being reconciled with his brothers: "his emotions stirred" (נכמרו רחמיו *nikměrû raḥămāyw*, Gen 43:30). It is the context that suggests that motherly love is at issue, not the etymology of the Hebrew term.

It is usually presumed that the woman whose compassion is so stirred is the complainant, perhaps because she seems utterly hysterical, as it were, whereas the respondent, with only one line of her response recorded, seems cool and detached. The text in v. 26, however, is ambiguous. It states merely that the mother of the child was so stirred by the impending threat to her son's life that she conceded the case. This "woman whose son is the living one" may, indeed, be the complainant, but she may also be the respondent.

The real mother's "gut reaction" is to give up her claim to the living child: "Give her the boy who is alive and by no means kill him!" The text is still ambiguous when it refers to the true mother's rival, who is not called "the second woman" or even "the other woman," but simply "this one" (זאת *zō't*), a term the king uses to refer to each of the women (v. 23). "This one" (NRSV, NIV: "the other") replies in a startlingly matter-of-fact way: "It shall be neither mine nor yours! Divide [him]!" It seems sensible that the one who so coldly responds to the threat of the boy's life is not the true mother—"the woman whose son is the living one"—but it is not absolutely clear whether she is the complainant or the respondent. At best, given one's assumptions about the normal psychology of mothers, one may conclude that the mother is *probably* the complainant. The one who is selflessly concerned about the infant's well-being is the "real" mother, one presumes. Mothers are not supposed to be willing to kill their own children. Yet, we know that there are exceptions to the rule, as many well-publicized cases of the murder of infants and young children by their own mothers have shown. Complicating one's evaluation, too, is the obvious caricature of the monstrosity of the woman who is willing to let the baby be killed and divided. This is not a case that the readers, if they were the jury, could decide beyond a reasonable doubt.

Unfortunately, the judgment of the just king is questionable. He never interrogates the two women. He accepts at face value the complainant's claim that there were no other witnesses. He does not point to the obvious gaps in her version of events and the purely circumstantial nature of her charge. He does not notice that she claimed to have been so soundly asleep that she did not know that her infant had been taken from her and another placed in her bosom, and yet she is able to report on all that was happening that night. He does not point to the inconsistency of her statement, inasmuch as she herself admits that she did not know the child was already dead until the morning. Neither does the king question the respondent, choosing merely to accept her denial as adequate. Neither woman is required to take an oath or undergo some kind of test, as the law stipulates for disputes involving no witnesses (see Exod 22:10-11; Deut 19:15-18; Num 5:11-15). He does not visit the site of the crime, nor does he send investigators to look for possible clues that may have been overlooked. Instead, he threatens the life of an innocent child, expecting the horrendous threat to provoke the responses he expects from his own stereotypes of the good mother and the deceptive woman. He does not consider the possibility that one or both women might be calling his bluff. So he pronounces one of them to be the mother of the child, curiously echoing the very words of the unspecified "woman whose son is the living one": "Give her the boy who is alive and by no means kill him!" (vv. 26-27). Most translators are uncomfortable with the ambiguity of

the king's words, and so they substitute "the first woman" (i.e., the complainant) for the confusing pronoun "her" (so NRSV and NIV). The Greek translators tried to clarify the text even further: "Give her, the one who says 'Give her the living child' "—leading a few commentators to assume that some words were omitted accidentally and to emend the text. All Hebrew witnesses assume the more ambiguous reading, however. What is more, the immediate antecedent of the pronoun "her" is not the complainant, but the one who calls for the splitting of the baby. Is this intentional on the narrator's part, or is it just sloppy narrative style?

Perhaps the king was pointing to the "real" mother when he ordered that the boy who is alive be given to *her*, because "she is his mother!" The reader is not given any clarity of vision, however, only the words of the verdict that are, in fact, couched in the very words of the mother's concession. Are we to take it that the king is ironically using the words of the mother to grant her the living child—that is, she asks that the boy be given to "her" (the liar), but the king is ordering that he be given to "her" (the truth teller)? Is he, as it were, granting the unspoken desires of the mother's heart but not the words of her petition? Or is he doing what she has suggested, sparing the baby and giving him to the other woman? Moreover, if the judge is proclaiming the complainant to be the mother here, as the NRSV and the NIV have it ("to the first woman"), is he perhaps being too hasty? Should he not have considered the possibility that the one who seems to be telling the truth is merely more astute than the other in catching on to his judicial hoax and, hence, is giving him precisely the response that Solomon is expecting of a true mother? Is she merely countering his hoax with her own? And what if the other woman had not been so naive as the narrator caricatures her to be? What if she, too, sensing that the king is trying to trick them, is cool enough to play along?[27] What if she is merely trying to call

27. In recognition of this possibility, some early interpreters suggested that Solomon finally knew who the real mother was only because a "heavenly voice" (קול בת *bat qôl*) revealed it to him: "How did Solomon know? Perhaps the woman had spoken craftily, so that Solomon would award the child to her. But it was a heavenly voice that came forth and said: *She is the mother thereof.*" See *Midr. Teh.* 72:2; cf. 17A.17. Translation in W. G. Braude, *The Midrash on Psalms*, Yale Judaica Series (New Haven: Yale University Press, 1959) 1:226, 560.

Solomon's bluff, daring him to take responsibility for his threat of violence? What would the king have done if both mothers had said the "motherly thing" that he expects? Has the king's shock tactic, in fact, proved irrefutably who the real mother is?

Most interpreters seem to come down on the side of the complainant, assuming that she is the real mother and that justice has been done. That assessment is not based on the specifics of the report, however. Not only is the account lacking in details, but also one is left to interpret the words according to one's perception of the truth. Much is left to the reader's imagination and personal inclination.

The passage concludes by taking the reader outside the court of the royal arbiter to the outside world, as it were. All Israel, we are told, heard of the king's judgment and, the Hebrew text says, literally, "they feared the king, for they saw that divine wisdom was in him to do justice" (see v. 28). The most obvious interpretation of the narrator's concluding observation about the effect of the king's judgment is that it was unquestionably the correct one; divine wisdom was "in him" (NRSV, correctly, rather than NIV, "he had"), and so the entire nation stood in awe of him. This is the interpretation reflected in the translations of both the NRSV ("they stood in awe of the king") and the NIV ("they held the king in awe"). Yet, if one is cynical, if doubt lingers still in the reader's mind about the limitations of human wisdom, one might hear the text differently—that is, when all Israel heard of the judgment, *they were afraid of the king*, because they saw that this judgment was the outcome of his "divine wisdom," which was internal to him alone—"in him," as the Hebrew text ambiguously has it.

Even if one grants the first interpretation, however, history has not been as sanguine about the wisdom of the king's judgment as all Israel is supposed to have been. Josephus, who felt the case was so complicated that he had to report it in detail, says that there were those present in Solomon's time who were not convinced that he had acted wisely. On the contrary, "all the people secretly made fun of the king as of a boy."[28] That tradition is partially corroborated in a midrashic passage that tells of how witnesses to the

event initially pitied the country because its ruler was just a boy: "Woe to you, O Land, whose king is a boy!"[29] The same negative assessment of Solomon's judgment is said to have been made by Rabbi Judah, the son of Rabbi Ilai, who thought that Solomon's decision was contemptible: "If I had been there, I would put a rope around Solomon's neck, for one dead child was apparently not enough for him—no, he had to command that the second be divided in two."[30] More recent interpreters have been similarly critical of Solomon's failure to interrogate the women involved, to look for possible unnoticed witnesses, to consider possible clinical clues, such as the differences between the navels and the stools of babies born three days apart, and so forth.[31] Others, too, have faulted Solomon for allowing his ends to justify his means—that is, for threatening the life of a child in order to make what he thought would be a correct decision. Finally, Brueggemann points out that the story shows no indication of the king's compassion at all and, if anything, should serve to warn one "about the gift and the danger of public power, about cold objectivity as a stern form of compassion, about the practice of justice being very close to cold cynicism."[32]

As with other passages in the book of 1 Kings, it seems possible for one to view Solomon here either in a positive or a negative light. Neither perspective can be easily dismissed. On the one hand, the story may have been intended at one time as a positive example of Solomon's wisdom. This is just the sort of account that could have been circulating as part of the legend of the great Solomon. It may be, therefore, that the narrator is merely conceding the reality of Solomon's fame and material successes. On the other hand, it is conceivable that the narrator is exploiting the gaps and ambiguities in the story to subvert the legend. The wisdom of Solomon, its divine origin and its much-vaunted fame notwithstanding, is finally limited. Wisdom, even if divinely imbued, can take one only so far. Solomon's gifts and successes are limited after all.

28. Josephus *Antiquities of the Jews* VIII.2.32.

29. *M. Teh.* 72.2, quoting Eccl 10:16. Translation in Braude, *The Midrash on Psalms I*, 559.

30. Braude, *The Midrash on Psalms I*, 559.

31. See S. Lasine, "The Riddle of Solomon's Judgment and the Riddle of Human Nature in the Hebrew Bible," *JSOT* 45 (1989) 65-86; S. Levin, "The Judgment of Solomon: Legal and Medical," *Judaism* 32 (1982) 463-65.

32. Walter Brueggemann, *1 Kings*, KPG (Atlanta: John Knox, 1983) 14.

REFLECTIONS

This section of 1 Kings contains the quintessential example-story of Solomon's wisdom. This legendary judicial decision of King Solomon has been celebrated throughout history: It is retold in medieval manuscript illustrations, oratorios, plays, paintings, sculptures, and literature.[33] In the Middle Ages, the scene was frequently depicted in law courts, and Solomon's decision was held out as a model of true justice.

At one level, the memorable story tells of the possibility of justice for people who are not in positions of power, even for people whom society has marginalized and whose credibility is not generally accepted. A modern-day attorney, whether prosecuting or defending, would probably have a field day cross-examining these prostitutes as witnesses. Perhaps these women would not even be called upon to speak for themselves, for aspects of their private and professional lives not directly relevant to the litigation at hand might surface that would cause them more harm than good. Essentially, the case revolves around the words of one "whore" against another. One of these "whores" is telling the truth, however, and she is a compassionate mother who is more concerned about the infant's welfare than with her rights. She would be called a "slut" in contemporary moralistic parlance, but she also happens to be a loving mother. And the latter character seems to be the one that matters most.

Romantic idealists are probably inclined to side with the "real" mother, despite any moral reservations about her profession. Perhaps some would even identify emotionally with her. Yet, the other woman may actually have the law on her side. Her demand that the infant be divided equally between herself and her adversary may have some basis in Israelite property law. In the event of an unprovable dispute over property, the parties are supposed to divide the property equally (Exod 21:35; 2 Sam 19:29). In the absence of evidence, she demands that each person be given the "same pain and same gain." Many jurists today would argue the same way in disputes over custody of children and family property: When there is no clear evidence in favor of one or the other party, the fairest, safest settlement may be to divide everything down the middle and "split the baby"—a cliché still popularly used in legal circles in the United States.

In such a reading of the story, the narrator ventures a judgment in the name of Solomon. The king shocks the women into two kinds of responses: a response of love that favors life for the child over against a response that insists on one's legal rights. The true mother in this interpretation is the one who chooses life over death, love over right. Biological relationship is perhaps assumed, but it does not appear to be at issue here. Love is at issue.

The real mother is willing to surrender her right to be with her son in order that he might live. If that is true, the story makes an ironic point: Because the mother is willing to give up her son, she receives him back. Her emotionally wrenching words of surrender turn out to be the king's words of justice: "Give *her* the baby!"

This story may be compared to another famous Old Testament story involving the life of another beloved son: Abraham's sacrifice of Isaac in Genesis 22. In that story, the father is also willing to give up his son—in this case, in obedience to God. Like the unnamed living son of the unnamed mother, the life of Abraham's son Isaac, too, hangs in the balance as Abraham prepares to sacrifice him in order to be faithful to God's command. Yet, because Abraham is willing to give up the son whom he loves, he receives the boy back *as a gift*. In obedience, he is willing to surrender his beloved son.

In contrast to the story of Abraham's sacrifice of Isaac, the mother of the boy who is alive in this story is not prepared to have her son killed. That is not her sacrifice. Yet, she is prepared to sacrifice her son in the sense of losing him for herself. She would surrender him for the sake of his life. In love, she is willing to surrender her beloved son.

33. For a convenient overview, see the article on Solomon in *Encyclopedia Judaica* XV, cols. 108-11.

Supreme love sometimes prompts a parent to give up his or her child in order that life—perhaps even an abundant life—might be possible for that child.

The king in our story seems to present a commonsense solution, one that especially appeals to modern readers frustrated by the slow turns of the wheels of justice. In view of legal cases that take months, if not years, of judicial hairsplitting, millions of dollars spent on teams of high-priced jurists, flamboyant prosecutors, expert testimonies, jury-selection consultations, reams of legal depositions, and extensive media coverage, only to reach decisions that are dubious and divisive, "Solomonic justice" may seem very appealing to us. A number of sensational cases in the United States in the late 1990s may come to mind. In each of these judgments, some observers came away believing that justice had been served by the tedious and expensive legal process, but others were equally convinced that there had been a gross miscarriage of justice. And often one's opinion about the verdict is colored by one's ethnic background and socio-economic context. The tedium of due process in the American judicial system yields no certain results, it seems. It is understandable, then, to find an American interpreter of this passage suggesting that the story means "that the community of faith has a stake in letting justice in the public domain be nine parts simplicity and one part common sense."[34]

Yet, such "Solomonic justice" may be more of an ideal than a reality that can be achieved in our world of sin and darkness. In our most cautious moments, most of us would not be willing to sacrifice the rule of law and due process for such a brand of justice. How many of us living in a free and open society would trust a single individual to have that kind of power, no matter how "wise" that person may appear to be? That is why, in democratic societies, we have built into our systems of government a series of checks and balances. Perhaps the often frustrating system could be eliminated, we think, if only our rulers would have divine wisdom and rule just as Solomon did. Or would we? The wisdom of Solomon's judgment turns out to be a debatable matter upon a closer consideration of the account. At best, we may view him as a benign dictator, like many rulers throughout the world today, who simply demand that their citizens trust them alone to do what is right for everyone. Some of these rulers, too, use propaganda and appeal to special divine privileges, just as Solomon did. Some are truly intellectually gifted and have brought genuine benefits to their people—possibly better administration of justice, better management of the economy, more respectable international standing, perhaps even better opportunities for religion, just as Solomon gave to Israel (so we read in 1 Kings 3–10). These rulers dismiss the ability of the general populace to decide matters for themselves. They spurn the legal processes as unnecessarily complicated, and they hold themselves to be the sole trustworthy custodians of right. They think themselves wiser than others. For such leaders as these, the story of Solomon may provide scriptural sanction for dictatorship and oppression.

So, too, Solomon may have been viewed, and may continue to be perceived, as a gifted ruler. Perhaps his citizens were truly awed by him, as most English translations (including the NRSV and the NIV) would have it. Yet, the ambiguities in the text, perhaps deliberately left there by the narrator, subtly subvert any purely positive image one might have of the king. Thereby, it warns us that his dictatorship may not have been so benign after all, and it foreshadows the dire consequences of his reign for his kingdom. Even under the best of circumstances, human beings must contend with the limitations of wisdom—even wisdom given by God.

34. Brueggemann, *1 Kings*, 14.

1 KINGS 4:1-34, SOLOMON'S RECORD

OVERVIEW

This passage is at once tantalizing and frustrating. It is especially intriguing to historians, for the two registers of officials (vv. 2-6, 7-19) and the commissary inventory (vv. 22-28) resemble records from a royal archive. References to two of Solomon's otherwise unknown sons-in-law (vv. 11, 15) also lend an air of authenticity to the report. Here, then, is a possible window—a broken window though it is—into the administration of the early Israelite monarchy, its various offices, perhaps even the specific names of the officials, and its administrative districts.

The task of historical reconstruction is, however, severely hampered by a number of obstacles. Most problematic are the text-critical problems: The readings in the Hebrew text are often called into question by other ancient versions, and it is almost impossible to reconstruct what the original account might have been. Moreover, while some of the place-names are readily identifiable (like Beth-shemesh, Naphath-dor, Taanach, Megiddo, and Bethshean), others are uncertain (like Elon Beth-Hanan) or even obscure (like Makaz, Arubboth, and Bealoth).

In terms of form, parallels may be drawn with numerous ancient Near Eastern royal inscriptions that boast of the successes of specific kings and their superiority over other rulers. Some Egyptian records contain precisely the sorts of administrative details that we find here. Indeed, so suggestive are some of these parallels that scholars have argued that Solomon's government may have been modeled after its Egyptian counterpart.[35] This is likely, given the alliance Solomon made with Egypt, an alliance the narrator has noted at the outset (3:1).

Other commentators have noticed continuities between this passage and various Assyrian royal inscriptions, including the itemizing of the daily provisions of the palace. Some annals boast of the king's literacy and wisdom, which surpass those of his rivals. Parallels may also be drawn with the Phoenician inscription of Azitawadda, which calls attention to the ruler's accomplishments, including the subjugation of neighboring countries, his reputation for wisdom, and peace and plenty in the land.[36] The inscription specifically observes that because of Azitawadda's benevolent rule, his people "ate and drank."

The resemblance of the account to other royal inscriptions cannot be gainsaid. Ostensibly, Solomon is being compared to other rulers in his efficiency, power, wealth, and wisdom. Despite the rhetoric of superiority that is typical of royal propaganda, however, the reader comes away with the feeling that Solomon's kingship was becoming just like that of his neighbors. In this account, we find a despotic and imperial Solomon—just as imposing and glorious as the others, to be sure, but also no less repressive, self-serving, and ostentatious.

35. See T. N. D. Mettinger, *Solomonic State Officials*, ConBOT 5 (Lund: Gleerup, 1971).
36. *ANET*, 653-54.

1 Kings 4:1-6, Solomon's Cabinet

COMMENTARY

As the Hebrew text has it, there were eleven officers in Solomon's administrative inner circle. They included a number of holdovers from the reign of David, such as Benaiah (v. 4a), the officer of the mercenary guards under David (2 Sam 8:18; 20:23; 1 Chr 18:17) who was promoted by Solomon to be the supreme commander of the army (2:35), and the old priests Zadok and Abiathar (v. 4b). Indeed, Abiathar, who had earlier been exiled by Solomon (2:26-27), seems to have been brought back. Jehoshaphat, the son of Ahilud (v. 3), "the recorder," appears to have been a minister in David's cabinet (2 Sam 8:16; 20:24; 1 Chr 18:15), and Adoniram (v. 6), chief of the corvée laborers, may be the same as "Adoram, the chief of the corvée" under David (2 Sam 20:24). In addition, there are a few cabinet members who may have been related to former officials of the Davidic court—namely, Azariah, the son of Zadok (v. 2), who had apparently taken over his father's function as high priest, and the two sons of Nathan (v. 5)—possibly Nathan, the court prophet who helped Solomon seize power, or Nathan, a son of David (2 Sam 5:14). The two "secretaries" are identified in the Hebrew as sons of Shisha (v. 3), a name that looks suspiciously like that of variant names of the secretary in David's cabinet (2 Sam 8:17; 20:25). With the exception of Ahishar (v. 6), then, the entire cabinet seems to be composed of people with long-standing connections to the center of power in Judah.

The responsibilities of some of the officials seem clear enough, including a commander of the army, an official supervising the corvée workers, and an overseer of the royal palace. Benaiah the commander is already known to the reader, and there is no explanation needed for his title. As for the chief of the corvée ("in charge of forced labor," NRSV and NIV) and the chief steward of the palace, both are attested elsewhere in the Bible and in Hebrew inscriptions. We gather from references elsewhere that the chief of the palace was a powerful position in the monarchical period, perhaps something comparable to the Chief of Staff in the executive branch of United States government.

The duties of the two "secretaries" are more ambiguous. Since they are included in a list of "officials" (v. 2), and since they are juxtaposed with other powerful functionaries,

one might consider it likely that they were secretaries of state rather than mere scribes assigned to transcribe diplomatic correspondence or royal records. In this connection, one notes that "the royal secretary" is mentioned along with other high court officials—the high priest (2 Kgs 12:10 = 2 Chr 24:11) or the royal steward in charge of the palace (2 Kgs 18:18; 19:2; Isa 36:3, 22; 37:2). Moreover, in 2 Kgs 25:19, we find a reference to "the secretary, the official of the army."

The NRSV and the NIV take the office of Jehoshaphat, son of Ahilud, to be "recorder" (v. 3), but other scholars have argued that the term מזכיר (*mazkîr*) designates a "herald"—that is, one who makes proclamations on behalf of the king or makes known the name of the king.[37] It is also possible that the word refers to one who mentions legal matters to the king, hence, a chief attorney or the like. This meaning is perhaps corroborated by the forensic use of the same Hebrew root in Isa 43:26.

Finally, the role of the "king's friend" (v. 5) is also unclear. The designation recalls Hushai's role as a "friend" of David (2 Sam 15:37; 16:16; 1 Chr 27:33). Hushai was clearly an ally and personal adviser of David, although he does not appear in any list of David's court officials. Scholars have called attention to analogies for the designation "king's friend" in Mesopotamia, Egypt, and Canaan. Still, since the title does not occur again after the reign of Solomon, one cannot be sure what the functions of such an official might have been in the Israelite-Judean context.

There remains much that is uncertain in the text. What seems clear, however, is that Solomon has surrounded himself with old-timers and insiders, no doubt to secure his own kingship. (See Reflections at 4:29-34.)

37. Mettinger, *Solomonic State Officials*, 29-30.

1 Kings 4:7-19, Solomon's Other Appointees

COMMENTARY

In this section, there is a list of twelve individuals who are said to be "over all Israel" (v. 7). Since Solomon is also said to be king "over all Israel" (v. 1), we understand these twelve to be representatives of the king throughout the country. These individuals are called "officials" in the NRSV and "district governors" in the NIV. The Hebrew term נצבים (*niṣṣābîm*) literally means something like "one set in place," hence "appointee."

There are still a number of problems. First of all, a number of these appointees are known only by their fathers' names (thus, lit., "Son of So-and-So"): Ben-Hur, Ben-Deker, Ben-Hesed, Ben-Abinadab, and Ben-Geber. The emphasis on the patronyms may indicate that the appointments were made primarily on the basis of family ties.

The fact that two of the appointees in Solomon's list are identified as his sons-in-law (vv. 11, 15) indicates the extent of nepotism and favoritism in his administration. Baana, the son of Ahilud, is possibly the brother of the entrenched court "recorder," Jehoshaphat, the son of Ahilud (v. 2; cf. 2 Sam 8:16; 20:24). Ahimaaz may be the son of Zadok (2 Sam 15:27; 18:27). Baana, the son of Hushai, may be the son of David's friend (2 Sam 15:32-37). Abinadab, the son of Iddo, may be the son of the same Iddo who ruled Gileadite Manasseh during David's reign (1 Chr 27:21). All these men are apparently connected to the Judean court. Yet, they are all appointed to rule over non-Judean districts.

This observation is all the more poignant when one takes the Hebrew text in v. 19 as it is, without emendation. If this is correct, Judah is not mentioned at all in the register (so NIV), suggesting that it was exempt from the tax system. Indeed, if one adds "Judah" with the Greek, as the NRSV does, one ends up with a list of thirteen officials—twelve for "all Israel" (v. 7) and an unnamed appointee for Judah. One would have to argue that "all Israel" in v. 7 means only the north, thus different from "all Israel" in v. 1, which refers to Israel and Judah.

The NIV takes the appointee in v. 19 to be Geber, son of Uri: "He was the only governor over the district." But that is a free reading of the Hebrew, and it is somewhat misleading, since the appointees in vv. 5 and 7 are called "*district* governors," where the word "district" is supplied by the translators. The Hebrew may better be rendered: "and one prefect who was in all the land."[38] We may take this cryptic notation as the narrator's

summary assessment on the administration of "all Israel" (v. 7); although there are twelve appointees over various regions, there is only one prefect, a stand-in for the king, as it were, in the whole country. If that is the case, then the reference here is to Azariah, the son of Nathan, who is in charge of all the regional appointees (v. 5). Power ultimately resides in Solomon's court.

Traditionally, it has been assumed that the twelve districts correspond roughly to the territories of the twelve tribes of Israel. Yet, the only tribal names that appear are Ephraim, Benjamin, Naphtali, Issachar, and Asher. Moreover, the first district is not called simply "Ephraim" but "the hill country of Ephraim" (v. 8), a designation that elsewhere includes portions of Manasseh (see Josh 17:14-18). In addition, a number of the other districts seem to have been administered in cities that had been beyond Israelite tribal control: Naphathdor, a stronghold of the Sea Peoples, was outside the tribal allotment (Josh 17:11-12; Judg 1:27); Taanach, Megiddo, and Bethshean were Canaanite strongholds. One can only speculate on the reasons for the choice of these centers. Solomon may have simply incorporated the more recently acquired domains and capitalized on the superior facilities that the old urban centers now afforded. Still, the choice of these traditionally non-Israelite centers may have been politically motivated as well.

It has been proposed that Solomon's restructuring was done largely for fiscal reasons. Instead of the conservative tribal system, he radically reorganized his kingdom into twelve districts of roughly comparable economic capacities.[39] The Samaria Ostraca from the eighth century BCE may provide a glimpse at the workings of the system as it continued in the north after the division of the kingdom. These inscriptions are apparently receipts recording the delivery of produce to the northern capital of Samaria from various administrative regions, including not a few sites from the district of Hepher (see "land of Hepher" in v. 10). Other archaeological discoveries also confirm that there were government fiscal centers throughout the

---

38. The word נצבים (*niṣṣābîm*), translated as "prefects" here, is a variant of the word for "appointees." For its usage, see 1 Sam 10:5; 13:3-4; 2 Sam 8:6, 14.

39. See G. E. Wright, "The Provinces of Solomon (1 Kings 4:7-19)," *EI* 8 (1967) 58*-68*.

monarchical period, centers to which taxes-in-kind were delivered. This is not to say that Solomon's motivation in the restructuring is purely economic. Indeed, economics and politics are inextricably intertwined; the economic restructuring no doubt undermined the political claims of the individual tribes.

The political implication of the restructuring is evident in the emphasis on the appointees rather than on the districts themselves, and in the fact that a number of these appointees are Judeans with old connections to the Davidic dynasty. If analogies with other administrative texts from the Levant are any indication, Solomon probably granted control over land to his family, friends, and other favorites in return for periodic taxes, the contribution of labor for the military and the corvée laborers, and, of course, loyalty. This connectedness may explain the emphasis on the appointees and the fact that their family ties seem more important than their personal names.

The irony in the passage should not be overlooked: Solomon is king over "all Israel" (v. 1); yet, his officials in the cabinet and his appointees over the districts are not representative of all Israel. Solomon may have the gift of administrative wisdom, a genius for organization, but his record shows that he has a penchant for taking care of himself and his favorites first. (See Reflections at 4:29-34.)

1 Kings 4:20-28, Solomon's Domains and His Provisions

COMMENTARY

In these verses we have something of a commentary on the economic and political consequences of Solomon's reign. The text seems at first blush to exalt Solomon unequivocally. Yet there are startling contradictions within it that give one pause. Solomon's administrative reorganization includes plans for forced labor and taxes that were explicitly to support the king's household and cronies. The king's appointees abundantly provided for the government, ensuring that nothing was left out (v. 27). Yet, the citizens are characterized in typically propagandistic terms: "They ate and drank and were happy" (v. 20). Solomon's reign is portrayed in idealistic and exaggerated terms; his domain is said to have included all the kingdoms from the Euphrates to the border of Egypt. Yet, we know that Solomon did not, in fact, have such control. The Phoenicians of Tyre, at least, were independent, as we know from Solomon's dealings with Hiram in the next chapter. Further, the populace is said to have dwelt securely (v. 25). Yet, that seems an unlikely environment, given the fact that this passage has to do with tax burdens for each district. These burdens are all the more onerous given the preposterous daily provisions expected for the court and the military. (In v. 26, the Hebrew records that Solomon has "forty thousand" stalls for horses [so NRSV], but that figure is played down to four thousand in the Greek [so NIV], perhaps because the figure seems too exaggerated. Yet, the extraordinarily high figure may have been intentional.)

Despite the overall impression of benevolent rule, there are subtle indications that not all is well. It is apparent that the economy is healthy, the military is strong, the country is efficiently run, and the ruler's authority is widely recognized. Still, there are implicit questions about who is served and exalted in all of this. Clearly, it is Solomon whose interests are protected, whose coffers are full. It is he who receives "offering" (NRSV, NIV, "tribute") and he who is "served" (v. 21). The text refers ambiguously to the charge to bring goods to "the place," but what the officials bring are not offerings for God but supplies for the military (v. 28).

One might argue that the similarities of Solomon's record to royal inscriptions from elsewhere in the ancient Near East point to the influence of other cultures upon Israel or to the mutuality of cultural influences. That may or may not be the case. What seems clear is that the account here is stereotypical. It is evident that Solomon was becoming a king just like the other kings of the region. This is precisely what some had warned would be the consequence of establishing a monarchy in Israel: The king might become just like the other rulers of the region, demanding forced labor, taxes for imperial expansions and the maintenance of the royal court, and the glorification of the king at the expense of the populace (Deut 17:14-20; 1 Sam 8:10-18). Indeed, the resemblance of Solomon's administration to other self-serving and repressive regimes may be the very point of the passage. The fate of the kingdom—the fate of God's people—is not secured despite Solomon's

efficiency, wealth, and power. With the machinery for imposition of the king's will as regards the resources of the country, one wonders whether the narrator is being a little ironic to concede that the people were happy or that they could, indeed, live securely. One is impelled to ask questions about the benefits of Solomon's successes in the light of larger issues about what God may intend for God's people. (See Reflections at 4:29-34.)

1 Kings 4:29-34, Solomon's Reputation for Wisdom

COMMENTARY

The narrative returns explicitly to the subject of God's gift of wisdom to Solomon (see 3:1-28). The king's wisdom surpassed that of all others, and he became internationally famous for it. Like the ideal sage of the ancient Near East, he had a reputation for his aesthetic interests. He was a patron of the arts—indeed, a prolific composer himself. He also delved into nature, discussing various botanical and zoological matters. From the narrator's point of view, Solomon's successes are well known and beyond dispute. Yet, nowhere does the narrator equate giftedness with character or faithfulness. There is possibly a hint in the text as to an unsavory side

to his enormous gift, for he is said to have had a phenomenal "broadness of heart/mind" (v. 29; NRSV, NIV: "breadth of understanding"). In the choice of words here is perhaps a warning, a foreshadowing of the troubles in which Solomon will be caught. The Hebrew idiom for "broadness of heart/mind" (רחב לב *rōḥab lēb*) may, if the context requires, also be interpreted as intellectual arrogance. So in Prov 21:4 and Ps 101:5, the expression "broad of heart/mind" is used for the arrogance of the wicked. Similarly, the expression "largeness of heart/mind" is used for arrogance (Isa 9:9; 10:12). Solomon's gift of wisdom may have a dangerous side as well.

REFLECTIONS

Solomon is in an enviable position. We were told earlier that he was blessed by God with the gift of wisdom and all the trappings of a good life (3:3-15). Now we get a sense of his power, wealth, intellectual capacity, and fame. One would like to think that Solomon has received all these because he came before God with unimpeachable character, the right attitude, or sincere prayer. Yet, that does not appear to be a point that the passage makes; nothing about Solomon here suggests that he deserves to have it so good.

One may well envy Solomon, but this is not someone whom most of us would like. Apparently insecure in his power, he surrounds himself with people he trusts, promoting his cronies, ensuring his own comfort. He seems to undermine traditional sociopolitical structures in order to ensure his influence throughout his domain, now reorganized into fiscal regions to support the prodigious expenses of his palace and his military machinery.

Inasmuch as the passage concerns government, one might be tempted to find scriptural warrant here for one's own political agenda. Arguably, we have a paradigm for a proactive central government; through Solomon's capital initiatives the people prosper, live securely, and have peace on every side. Political appointees provide the central government with every provision, making sure that nothing is lacking.

Other readers may not be so sanguine about the governmental interventions, however, particularly if the story is read within its larger literary context. The presence of a secretary of labor only foreshadows problems that the people will encounter later. That "tax-and-spend government" would, after all, lead the nation to destruction. To be sure, the economy may have been doing well under Solomon's administration so that other questions pertaining to his character do not seem to matter. Yet all that will change as the story progresses. Character matters, after all, and the fate of the country does depend, at least in part, on the faithful responses of its leaders.

The Bible is dangerous that way. It is easy to justify our political and personal agendas therein. That is not the purpose of Scripture, however. The story has power, not because of any political or social paradigm it may provide, but because of its affirmation that God does act in the arena of history with all its limitations, through real human beings with all their gifts and despite their failings. One is at once puzzled and amazed.

There is no question that Solomon is capable. He is efficient, savvy, and cosmopolitan. Still, this man who has been anointed by God is no perfect soul. We have the distinct impression that he is insecure, self-indulgent, and vain. It does not help that the passage ends with affirmation of his extraordinary giftedness. It paints a picture of Solomon as a person incomparable in the scope of his intellectual and creative ability. He is something of a genius, a veritable Leonardo da Vinci or Mozart of his time, with an abiding international reputation. But one wonders why it is *this* ruthless, self-centered, and vain man whom God has blessed with such extraordinary gifts. Why is it not someone else more deserving, less rapacious, more faithful, less pompous?

The difficult truth for us in this story is that it has no easy answers to our questions about the seeming arbitrariness of God's election. It is a mystery that God's purpose in history should be fulfilled through people who have their own biases, political agendas, and limited visions. It is a mystery, too, that God should bless some who are so unworthy or even unfaithful, more than those who seem to us more deserving. That same mystery of God's surprising grace, however, is the good news in the story. The instruments of God are at best imperfect. So are we.

1 KINGS 5:1-18, SHADY DEALS AND OPPRESSIVE POLICIES

COMMENTARY

The chapter begins with Solomon's ties to the Phoenicians, represented here by Hiram (a variant form of Phoenician "Ahiram"), king of Tyre. The alliance is not a new one, for it had been established already since the reign of David (2 Sam 5:11-12). This reference to David provides the narrator with an opportunity to place Solomon's intention to build the Temple within the larger history of the Davidic dynasty. Alluding to Nathan's oracle (2 Sam 7:1-17), the narrator asserts that David had not been able to carry out his desire to construct a temple because he had

been beset by wars. Solomon is not similarly troubled by political problems, and so he could carry out the project as the anointed successor to David.

A deal is cut between Solomon and Hiram, on terms that are more favorable to the Phoenicians than to the Israelites. In chap. 4, we learned that Solomon had taxed his people in order to support the royal palace. Foreign nations, too, supposedly supplied provisions for him. Yet, he is now agreeing to provide for the household of the Tyrian king and gives him 20,000 cors (approx. 125,000 bushels) of wheat and, according to the Hebrew text, 2,000 cors (almost 700,000 gallons) of refined oil "year after year" (v. 11),[40] and he will do so for a couple of decades (9:10-11).

Hiram agrees to supply the materials and the professional expertise. Solomon conscripts people from Israel—not just outsiders, as with the permanent corvée that was engaged in the fortification projects (9:20-21)—for a term of three months each. In addition, there are 150,000 burden bearers and hewers of stone, supervised by a force of 3,300, all under the charge of Adoniram, a cabinet minister, chief of the levy (4:6).

40. So the Hebrew text. The Greek, followed by the NIV, has "20,000 baths" instead of "2,000 cors."

Despite the allusion to Solomon's wisdom (vv. 7, 12), the alliance foreshadows the problems the kingdom will soon face. Solomon notes that God has given him peace and that he has neither adversaries nor misfortunes. Yet, because of his alliances with outsiders, his kingdom will soon be threatened by one adversary after another (11:14, 23). Solomon has turned to foreigners for his most public religious project, paying an exorbitant price and even promising that his servants will be with the Phoenicians: "My servants/slaves will be with your servants/slaves" (v. 6). He has also conscripted forced labor out of Israel, probably referring to those from the north. That forced conscription of Israelites (as opposed to Judeans) will later be the cause of the kingdom's division.

REFLECTIONS

Solomon had an ambition, one that his father, David, had but was unable to fulfill. David proposed to build a permanent house for the Lord in Jerusalem, for he himself already had a cedar palace there (2 Sam 7:2). So, too, Solomon wants to build a temple in the capital city as a symbol of God's abiding presence there.

The peace and prosperity of his time made it feasible for him to carry out this plan, and he prepared for it by making a pact with a Phoenician wheeler-dealer who was insistent that his own wishes be carried out. Solomon seemed willing to compromise with anyone in order to achieve his own goals, which is admittedly stated in traditional religious terms (5:3-5). He was also willing to impose his will on his citizens. Although the project may have legitimated his place as the designated successor to the Davidic throne, he had to sell out his people in order to achieve it. The plan is articulated in theological terms, but its consequences for God's people were dire: They had to bear the burdens and suffer injustices for the sake of Solomon's Temple.

In this story one is prompted to consider the price that others have to pay for *our* pet projects that may be motivated by a mixture of true religious conviction and personal vision and ambition. Even in a worthwhile project done in the name of God, one must consider the possibility that one's personal agenda may get in the mix, and that the questionable deals that one has to make and the oppressive costs one has to pay may compromise the integrity of the project. How often has a church building, the symbol of divine presence, involved such costs!

1 KINGS 6:1-38, THE TEMPLE IS BUILT

COMMENTARY

Solomon's temple project is dated, according to the Hebrew text, to the 480th year of the exodus, meaning probably twelve generations of forty years each. (The Greek version, however, corrects the date to read "four hundred and fortieth year.") The project is said to have begun in the fourth year of Solomon's reign, in the month of Ziv (according

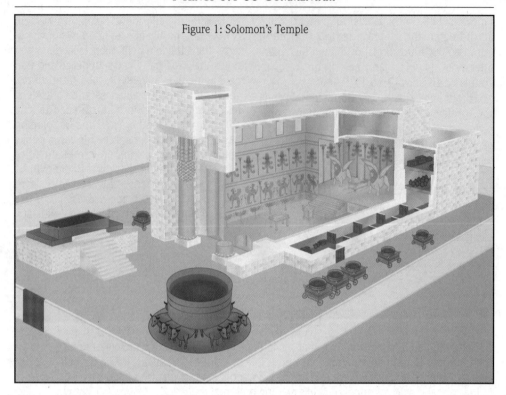

Figure 1: Solomon's Temple

to the obsolete Canaanite calendar), which is explained as the second month (according to the more current Babylonian calendar, which begins its reckoning in the spring). The narrative thus recalls the time when Israel was enslaved under foreign oppressors. Long after Israel had been liberated, when the nation is supposed to be at the peak of its power, its own king is placing an enormous burden upon it through his alliance with another foreigner. Solomon endangers the freedom of his people and puts them under servitude with the slaves of Hiram; ironically, he does so in an effort to bring about and to ensure divine presence.

The Temple is described in all its ornate architectural detail, with all its dimensions. It is 60 cubits (90 feet) long, 20 cubits (30 feet) wide, and thirty cubits (45 feet) high; if one includes the portico, it is even larger, for a total area of about 100 feet long and 50 feet wide.[41] This would make the Jerusalem Temple larger than any temple known in

Palestine. The tripartite structure—with the porch (NIV, "portico"; NRSV, "vestibule"), the main hall (NRSV, "nave"), and the inner sanctuary—corresponds, however, to other exemplars from the region. Indeed, the Temple that Solomon built may well have been constructed after Canaanite and, especially, Phoenician models.

In the midst of the structural details comes an important theological condition, which is perhaps deliberately intrusive. It is a "word of the LORD" for Solomon regarding the building of the Temple (vv. 11-13). As if disregarding all the structural and decorative specifications, the divine word emphasizes obedience to God and the freedom of God's presence. The validity of the project is qualified by an explicit condition: *If* God's commandments are obeyed, *then* the promise to David will be made good; God will "dwell" in the midst of the people and not abandon them. The presence of the Temple will not ensure the dynasty's stability, nor will it bring about God's presence in Israel's midst. Only obedience will. Moreover, the verb used for God's dwelling is not the typical one used

41. A cubit is the distance from the elbow to the tip of the index finger on the hand of an average-size man. It is about 17.5 inches in length.

for the inhabitation of a house, ישב (yāšăb, "sit," "live"), as is the case when the narrator speaks later of Solomon's residency in his palace (7:8). Rather, the verb is שכן (šākan, "tabernacle," "stay over"). For all its splendor, the Temple will not house the presence of God per se, but, provided that the people keep faith, God will somehow be present with them and not forsake them. One has to keep this condition in mind as one reads the rest of the details about the Temple and its furnishings.

The Temple is said to have been completed according to its elaborate specifications after seven years, in the month of Bul (according to the old Canaanite calendar), which is explained as the eighth month of the year (according to the Babylonian calendar), around the end of August and early September.

REFLECTIONS

Richard Nelson makes an apt analogy between the description of the Temple's architectural and decorative details and the commentary that one might get from a tour guide when visiting a famous building.[42] In this case, the reader is "guided" through the historic complex, the Temple, which is visible only in the imagination of the reader, for the physical structure no longer exists. The meticulous description accounts for the various measurements, structural peculiarities, architectural techniques, blend of materials, and so forth.

For some, such a tour may be utterly fascinating, if not awe-inspiring. At one level, that may have been the original intent of this commentary; the core of it may have been an official source that promoted the glories of the Temple. For many modern readers, however, the pedantic details may be overwhelming, particularly since the edifice exists no longer. The Temple is a relic that seems to be of interest primarily to history buffs.

There are many texts like that in the Bible. They seem to have a museum-like quality about them, and one wonders what all this has to do with the life of contemporary believers. Sometimes the length and pedantic character of the text drive one to ask in frustration: "So what?" The believer might and, perhaps, should ask: "What is the word of God in all of this?" This is what preachers struggle to answer with every text in Holy Scripture.

In this case, however, the text provides the answer. Intruding into the imagined visit to the historical edifice comes the divine word: "As for this temple . . . if you walk . . . then I will . . ." (6:12-13). The intrusive word of God seems to be a non sequitur in the midst of the architectural and decorative details. The received Hebrew text presents this word of the Lord despite its apparent discord. It is the imposing voice of another guide that points one beyond the glories of the edifice to another interrelation of parts, the excellence of which is measured neither in cubits nor in aesthetics. Rather, the significance of the Temple is tied to faithfulness: *If* people are faithful to the commandments, *then* God will be faithful to God's promises. The validity of the structure is dependent on the validity of the interrelationship between God and people. This is the word of the Lord about the sanctuary wherein we are to worship God.

42. Richard D. Nelson, *First and Second Kings*, Interpretation (Atlanta: John Knox, 1987) 43-46.

1 KINGS 7:1-51, A DIGRESSION ON SOLOMON'S HANDIWORK

COMMENTARY

7:1-12. In contrast to the Temple, which had taken seven years to build (6:38), we are told that Solomon's own house took nearly twice as long—thirteen years. The contrast is all the more striking when we keep in mind the fact that the original text had no chapter divisions, which were introduced only in medieval times. Disregarding the chapter division, then, one discerns possibly a criticism of Solomon, a criticism that is subtle and more evident in the Hebrew than in the English translations: literally, "He built it [the Temple] seven years, but as for his own house, he built [it] thirteen years and completed all of it." Moreover, the royal complex, which comprised several buildings, appears to be considerably larger than the Temple. The "House of the Forest of Lebanon," apparently the palace treasury and armory (10:17, 21; Isa 22:8), is alone larger than the Temple. It is 100 cubits (150 feet) long, fifty cubits (75 feet) wide, and 30 cubits (45 feet) high (cf. 6:2). The narrator also makes special mention of Solomon's construction of a house for Pharaoh's daughter whom he had married (lit., "received," v. 8).

7:13-51. Solomon not only "received" (לקח *lāqaḥ*) the daughter of Pharaoh (7:8),

something he did early in his reign (3:1-3), but he also "received" (*lāqaḥ*) Hiram, a professional bronze-smith from Tyre, who is said to have done all of Solomon's work (v. 14). The smith's mother was a widow from the Israelite tribe of Naphtali, and perhaps this tie was once used to emphasize his legitimacy as the builder of the Lord's Temple in Jerusalem. Yet, the narrator seems to take pains to point out that Hiram was "received" from Tyre, that his father was a Tyrian, and that he had acquired his skills from his father. It is noteworthy, too, that he has the same name as the king of Tyre, with whom Solomon is dealing in order to attain materials to build the Temple.

The passage makes it clear throughout that it was the Phoenician who had done all the work: He cast, he made, he set, and "he finished all the work" (v. 40). The emphasis on his handiwork is tedious. Solomon, too, is responsible: He did all the work of the Temple and finished it (v. 51). The Temple here is clearly the product of human hands. Perhaps the narrator means for us to keep this in mind as we read about the dedication of the Temple.

REFLECTIONS

This chapter stands out mainly as an intrusion. The preceding chapter ends with the completion of the Temple. The next chapter will give an account of its dedication. In between the two stands this odd chapter highlighting Solomon's construction of his own palace and the emphasis that the building is the work of Hiram, the Tyrian artisan, and Solomon. It was they who made it; it was they who completed it.

The digression is, perhaps, not accidental. In any case, whether or not it has been deliberately put in this context, this intrusion is theologically important. It serves at once as a postscript to the account of the completion of the Temple and a preface to the account of the Temple's dedication.

If only in an implicit way, the text raises some questions about Solomon's worldly ambition (7:1-12). It was not for purely altruistic and pious reasons that the Temple was built so gloriously. It is a reflection of the vanity of Solomon and the dangerously compromising character of his reign.

Most important, the passage also stresses the Temple and its furnishings as human handiwork, just as the palace complex is. This is the perspective of the martyr Stephen: "It was Solomon who built a house for [God]. Yet the Most High does not dwell in houses made with human hands" (Acts 7:47-48 NRSV). Jesus, too, notes that while human beings may be enamored of the physical beauty of a temple, it is, in fact, a destructible edifice (Luke 21:5-6). By contrast, the metaphorical "temple" that God brought about on earth, culminating in the resurrection of Jesus from the dead, is not a temple made with human hands (Mark 14:58; John 2:19-22).

1 KINGS 8:1-66, THE DEDICATION OF THE TEMPLE

OVERVIEW

This literary unit, the end product of generations of theological struggles, is structured around the prayer of Solomon at the ceremonial dedication of the Temple (see also 2 Chronicles 5–7). The passage begins with the assembling of the people (v. 1), and it concludes with their departure (v. 66). The tensions between the various traditions about divine presence are still discernible; the seams are still evident. The present unit is carefully quilted, broadly patterned to focus on the dedicatory prayer:

A Commencement of the ceremony, vv. 1-13

  B Solomon's preliminary remarks, vv. 14-21

    C Solomon's prayer, vv. 22-53

  D´ Solomon's closing remarks, vv. 54-61

A´ Conclusion of the festival, vv. 62-66

1 Kings 8:1-13, Commencement of the Ceremony

COMMENTARY

8:1-2. Solomon's temple building project culminates in the dedication of the edifice in the month of Ethanim (v. 2), the seventh month—that is, late September and early October. Since the Temple was already completed according to all its specifications in the month of Bul, the eighth month (6:38), this means that the official dedication was held off for nearly a year, possibly to coincide with the festival known as the Feast of Tabernacles (Lev 23:34, 39; Num 29:12-34), in the seventh month, when a large crowd of people would have come into the city. The Feast of Tabernacles was recognized as the time for the ceremonial renewal of the covenant (Deut 31:9-13), and this may be significant as well. Some scholars also believe that the festival was associated with the autumn new year and the celebration of divine enthronement.

8:3-5. The leaders of the nation gather in Jerusalem, together with the multitudes for that occasion. The ark of the covenant, at once a symbol of divine presence in the midst of God's people and a tangible reminder of Israel's covenant relationship with the Lord, is brought in procession from its location in the City of David, called by its ideologically loaded name "Zion" (2 Sam 5:7; Pss 2:6; 9:11; 14:7; 48:2; 50:2; 74:2; 78:68; 99:2). Clearly, it was believed that God was somehow present in the procession, for the ark of the covenant was brought with the "tent of meeting" (v. 4), and generous sacrifices were made "before the ark" (v. 5).

8:6-11. In some ways, the ritual is reminiscent of the dedication of cultic images elsewhere in ancient Canaan and Mesopotamia, even though the ark is not a divine image.

At the climax of the ceremony, it is placed under the cherubim (v. 6), a pair of sphinx-like creatures with their wings spread across the inner sanctuary. Some scholars who have reconstructed the scene argue that the cherubim with outstretched wings represented a gigantic throne, smaller versions of which have been found in ancient Near Eastern iconography. Accordingly, the cherubim symbolized the royal seat on which the deity was thought to have been invisibly enthroned, and the ark was viewed as the footstool. An ivory plaque excavated at Megiddo and a sarcophagus of the Phoenician king Ahiram (a form to which the name "Hiram" is related) both depict a cherubim-throne with a seated king, whose feet rest upon a box-like footstool.[43] Elsewhere in the ancient Near East, treaty documents were sometimes placed in boxes that doubled as footstools for the kings. So it is interesting to note that the ark is said to have contained the two tablets placed in it by Moses when the covenant was made on Mt. Horeb.

The narrative emphasizes, too, that the ark comes with carrying poles, although that fact may not be obvious to everyone, since the poles could not be seen outside the inner sanctuary. The poles indicate the mobility of the ark and, hence, also the freedom of the deity from the sanctuary; this was no footstool of a deity permanently enthroned in the building. In Israel's persistent sanctions against the use of cultic images, the ark was merely a reminder of God's suzerainty and the covenant that bound Israel to the deity. Here, as elsewhere in the deuteronomistic tradition, the ark is called "the ark of the covenant of the LORD" (vv. 1, 6) and, lest there be any doubt, it is observed that there is nothing else in the box except the tablets that have represented God's covenant with Israel since the time of Moses (v. 9; cf. Deut 10:1-5). In these ways, the ark is demythologized, and the mention of the poles for carrying it (vv. 7-8) is part of a theological effort to move away from any misunderstanding of God as a king permanently enthroned in the Temple.

8:12-13. Still, the notion of the deity as a king lies in the background. In an archaic poetic fragment retained in these verses,[44] Solomon declares that he has built the Lord "an exalted house" (or, perhaps, "a princely house"). Both the NRSV and the NIV have "dwell." There are, in fact, two different verbs in these two verses. Whereas the verb in v. 12 (שכן *šākan*) refers to the settling of the "thick darkness" that accompanies the Lord's theophany (see Deut 4:11; 5:22; Ps 18:10-11; 97:2), the verb in v. 13 (ישב *yāšab*) may also mean "sit" and, more specifically, "sit [enthroned]." So here, again, the imagery of divine kingship is in the background.

One should pay attention to the fact that two different words are used here to describe God's presence in relation to the Temple. Subtle theological nuances may, in fact, have been intended. We should translate the Hebrew of the poetic fragment as follows:

The LORD has said he would tabernacle in thick darkness.
I [Solomon] have, indeed, built you a royal house, an establishment of your enthroning.
(author's trans.)

The notion of God's tabernacling presence is prominent in some theological traditions in Israel. It is a way of conveying the free presence of the deity, an avoidance of the language of an enthroned and entrenched deity. So Ezekiel and the Priestly tradition of the Torah speak not of God enthroned in the Temple, but of God's *glory*, represented by a cloud that "tabernacles" at the sanctuary, coming and going as God wills (Exod 25:8; 29:45; Ezek 10:19, 22; 43:1-12). The use of imagery of the Temple's being filled with the cloud of the Lord's "glory" (vv. 10-11) and the tabernacling of the Lord through thick darkness is a way of expressing the mysterious and free presence of the deity.

As for the Temple, the "princely house" itself, it is an establishment of God's "enthroning." Inasmuch as the verb for "enthroning" (לשבתך *lĕšibtĕkā*) is used for all kinds of sitting and residing, it is easy to see how that view might have led to an understanding of the Temple as God's actual dwelling place. This is a notion, a theological

---

43. See J. B. Pritchard, *The Ancient Near East in Pictures*, 2nd ed. (Princeton: Princeton University Press, 1969) 111, 157-58.

44. According to the Greek text, these words are from "The Book of the Song," probably an allusion to the lost "Book of Yashar," mentioned in Josh 10:13; 2 Sam 1:18.

misinterpretation, that the present narrative about the dedication tries to dispel. In combination with the language of the tabernacling presence of God through the mysterious "thick darkness," one ought to understand the Temple not as the earthly dwelling place for God, but as a tangible establishment of (the fact of) divine enthroning. One might say that the Temple is a concrete representation of the reality of the sovereignty of God. The Temple is God's "princely house" only in this sense. (See Reflections at 8:62-66.)

1 Kings 8:14-21, Solomon's Preliminary Remarks

COMMENTARY

In the early monarchical period, such a dedicatory ceremony would have been fraught with political symbolism. The public ritual signified at once the election of the Davidic dynasty (in this case the choice of Solomon) and also the election of Zion (see v. 1). This dual election, especially important in Judah, is affirmed. Despite echoes of the notion of God's kingship, the Temple is not the place in which God is enthroned. Indeed, the Temple is not the Lord's palace, but is very deliberately identified as a house for the Name of the Lord. The theology of divine presence as regards the Temple is carefully nuanced. In this context, the biblical writer-theologian is able to affirm simultaneously the transcendence (remoteness) and immanence (nearness) of God. The deity is not enthroned in the Temple per se, yet divine presence is somehow represented by the Name of God in the Temple. The authority of God is there, whether or not God is personally present. Additionally, despite Solomon's words in vv. 12-13, the Temple is specifically identified as a place for the chest that contains the tangible symbols of the covenant, namely, the covenant documents (the tablets). Here the theologian moves beyond the promise to David that undergirds much of Judean theology to point to the exodus from Egypt and the covenant that God made with Israel. It is the salvific presence of God, culminating in the covenant with Israel, that the Temple affirms. The Temple is not so much the *locus* of God's presence as it is a reminder of God's free presence that is made good in the covenant. (See Reflections at 8:62-66.)

1 Kings 8:22-53, Solomon's Dedicatory Prayer

COMMENTARY

8:22-30. Solomon's prayer is at the heart of the entire account of the dedication ceremony. The theological disposition of the narrative is nowhere more evident than in this long prayer. We are told that Solomon comes "before the altar" and "before the assembled people" and that he "spread his hands out to heaven" (v. 22; in v. 22 Solomon is standing, but in v. 54 he is kneeling). The wording is particularly poignant when one compares this account with Isaiah's description of Hezekiah in prayer at the Temple (Isa 37:14-16). The southern prophet, who stands in the Judean tradition that emphasizes God's presence as King in the Jerusalem Temple (see Pss 46:4-5; 76:2), speaks of Hezekiah's coming to the house of the Lord, spreading his petition "before the Lord," and praying to the God enthroned upon the cherubim (Isa 37:14-16). Hezekiah's posture is that of a lone petitioner appearing before an enthroned, though invisible, King. This is not what we have here in 1 Kings. Rather, the narrator is careful to say that Solomon stood "before *the altar* of the Lord," rather than "before the Lord." This account also emphasizes the covenant, entirely appropriate if the festival does, indeed, coincide with the Feast of Tabernacles. God is confessed as an incomparable One both in heaven and on earth, thus unlike the other deities of Israel's neighbors. The Lord, Israel's God, is the suzerain who keeps covenant promises. Perhaps the narrator also means that the deity is not locally enthroned, as the images of the other deities would be depicted. There is no denial of God's kingship, to be sure, but the focus is on the keeping of God's promise and on the obligation of the vassals to conduct themselves properly before their suzerain.

The movement away from the notion of God's enthroned presence in the Temple is especially clear in the rhetorical question posed in v. 27: "Will God indeed sit [enthroned] on the earth?" The verb here is the one used in v. 13, and, again, the NRSV and the NIV both translate it as "dwell." That is the same verb used in the old divine epithet associated with the ark at Shiloh: "The ark of the LORD of Hosts, who sits [enthroned] upon the cherubim" (1 Sam 4:4; 2 Sam 6:2). That is the epithet used by Hezekiah when he comes to pray to the Lord as King (Isa 37:16). The perspective in 1 Kings, however, offers a corrective to any such misunderstandings of divine presence. If there was any doubt as to the nature of God's "enthroning" presence before (v. 13), it is clarified here. Even the heaven and the highest heaven cannot contain God; how much less, then, can the Temple that a mere mortal has built? One cannot help reading this rhetorical question with v. 13 in mind. The Temple is a reminder of God's kingship; it is an establishment of God's eternal "enthroning." That enthroning is not limited by any place; it is certainly not limited to the Temple, for Solomon pleads that God's attention be turned toward it.

A curious convergence on the Temple is created by the repetition of the preposition "toward" in v. 29: Solomon asks God to respond "toward this house," while prayer is simultaneously directed "toward this place" (see also vv. 35, 38, 42), even though the petitioner may also actually be praying "in" the Temple (cf. vv. 31, 33). The Temple is neither God's residence nor the place where the petitioner personally encounters the deity. Rather, it is a place at which the needs of the petitioner coincide with the willingness of the deity to respond. The Temple is not the place where the very person of God is; rather, it is merely the place where God's presence

may be known, where the authority of God is proclaimed.

Prayer is directed toward the Temple, while God's realm is associated with "heaven." One might argue that the reference to God's "enthroning" in heaven is a polemic against the notion of God's "enthroning" in the Temple. This is anti-Temple theology, as it were: God is enthroned, not in the earthly Temple, but in heaven. Yet, the biblical writer confesses that not even the heaven and the highest heaven can contain the deity. Locality is not at issue in all this talk of God's realm. God's transcendence and sovereignty are.

The translations in the NRSV and the NIV locate God's residence in heaven: "in heaven your dwelling place" (NRSV); "from heaven, your dwelling place" (NIV). The Hebrew is admittedly strained, as perhaps any reference to God's realm must be, and one should perhaps retain the ambiguity of the text: "Hear, unto your dwelling/enthroning, unto heaven" (v. 30).

8:31-53. There follows a series of circumstances in which God's "enthroned" presence is desired, including individual sins and corporate sins, prayers offered within the Temple and without the Temple, prayers from near and far, prayers for deliverance from natural disasters and from war, prayers by the people of Israel and prayers by outsiders. The disasters mentioned in the litany are reminiscent of the covenant curses that we read in Deuteronomy 28:1 and in various vassal treaties from elsewhere in the ancient Near East. They are tragedies that would befall covenant violators.

The details of these circumstances are probably less significant than the fact that there seven situations are identified, seven being the number of completeness in the ancient Near East. One notes, too, the comprehensive coverage: "whatever plague, whatever sickness" (v. 37); "whatever prayer, whatever plea" (v. 38); "whenever the foreigner comes and prays toward this house" (v. 42); "whenever they call" (v. 52). The seventh situation, the longest and most detailed one, is the climax of the series, and there is reason to believe that the text intends to convey the idea of completeness. Humanity will always be in need of divine presence, for "there is no one who does not sin" (v. 46).

In vv. 46-50, there is a tantalizing word-play involving the Semitic roots suggesting captivity (שבי *šěbî*) and repentance or turning around (שוב *šûb*) and, perhaps, also the Hebrew word for God's "enthroning" presence (שבת *šebet*). The English translations do not adequately convey this wordplay. The litany suggests the way by which one may avert disasters that inevitably come with the violation of the covenant, calamities expressed by the metaphor of captivity (*šěbî*). The hope lies in a change of heart, or repentance (*šûb*). Only with such a turnaround may the captive offender appeal for the forgiveness that is possible because God's presence is both heavenly (transcendent) and "enthroning" (sovereign). The litany appeals to God's compassion in the face of captivity (v. 50), and the basis for that appeal is God's sovereign grace manifested in salvation from bondage, God's election of a particular people, and God's promise made long ago. (See Reflections at 8:62-66.)

1 Kings 8:54-61, Solomon's Closing Remarks

COMMENTARY

Together with vv. 14-21, these remarks of Solomon bracket his prayer. The two subsections are approximately the same length—seven verses each, according to all modern editions of the Bible. The preliminary remarks (vv. 14-21) are preceded by an account of the commencement of the festival (vv. 1-13); the final remarks (vv. 54-61) are followed by an account of the end of the celebration (vv. 62-66). In the king's opening remarks, reference is made to the promise of God made through David, a promise that is sustained by God alone and marked by the dual election of David and Zion. This dual election is stressed in Judean theology. Now, in this post-prayer public commentary, Solomon calls attention to God's blessing of the people of Israel through Moses (Deut 12:10), a tradition that predominated in the north. Moreover, just as the opening emphasis on the Judean covenant theology is balanced with allusions to the exodus and the Mosaic covenant, so also the closing remarks stress obedience to the covenant, even while assuring the people of God's presence in language that echoes Judean theology, with its emphasis on the abiding presence of God: "The LORD our God is with us" (cf. Isa 7:14). (See Reflections at 8:62-66.)

1 Kings 8:62-66, Conclusion of the Ceremony

COMMENTARY

Like the Feast of Tabernacles elsewhere (Lev 23:39; Num 29:35), the temple-dedication celebration ends on the eighth day. Solomon, who had convened the assembly at the beginning (vv. 1-2), now dismisses the people. They all "went to their tents," happy and united. Reflecting a convergence of northern and southern covenant traditions, the narrator says that the people were glad for the goodness that God had shown both to the Davidic dynasty and to the people of Israel. At a later time, however, a call for the people to return to their tents will signal the division of the kingdom into two—Judah and Israel (12:16).

REFLECTIONS

Theologically, this is one of the richest passages in the book of Kings, and there are a number of issues one might highlight in the context of a faith community.

1. God tabernacles in "thick darkness," the text says (8:12). One might think of this as a metaphor for the mystery of God's presence. The text is strained at a number of points, at times even sounding contradictory as it tries to characterize the divine presence. One may wish for more clarity, more specificity, more certainty about that reality, but there is none. What we have, rather, is something of a collage of various articulations, various imageries of that mysterious but undeniable presence: Temple, ark, cloud, glory, name, deep darkness. Faith speaks with only a limited vocabulary. It paints impressionistic pictures. Together these idioms convey a sense of divine nearness that is only God's to give.

2. The Temple is an establishment of God's "enthroning" (8:13). This is biblical language for what we might call God's sovereignty. The sanctuary is but a human establishment that represents that sovereignty of God. God's rule is not tied to any one locale on earth or even in heaven or the highest heaven. God is transcendent and free of human manipulation.

Like the Temple that Solomon built, the existence of any sanctuary is a concrete representation of the possibility of God's presence amid a community in worship, but God's freedom transcends any building made by human hands—or any structure, any institution, for that matter (see Mark 11:15-19). In the New Testament, the presence of God is made manifest most decisively through Jesus. More than any building, it is in Jesus that the presence of God is "fleshed out," as it were. He "dwelled [lit., "tabernacled," "stayed over"] among us" and the "glory" of God is manifest in him (John 1:14; cf. 1 Kgs 8:10-12). The New Testament even uses the analogy of the Temple to speak of the death and resurrection of Jesus, relativizing the existence of any other temple (Mark 14:58; John 2:19-22). The point is that the living presence of God is known in the salvific acts of God, not in any structure or in any institution. With this in mind, we dare not take lightly the apostle Paul's reference to the church as God's temple (1 Cor 3:16-17; 2 Cor 6:16).

3. God, though wholly transcendent, will nevertheless hear the prayers of human beings and will respond accordingly. Solomon's prayer portrays human desperation in terms of their personal, political, social, and natural circumstances. People will always be in desperate need of divine attention because of their sins, both small and large, against other people and against God (8:31, 33-36, 46-48). No one escapes the captivity of sin, since "there is no one who does not sin" (8:46). Yet, with faithful response, including obedience and repentance, there is hope of relief. There is hope because of God's enthroning presence—that is, divine sovereignty and freedom to intervene. Because of that "enthroning," people may come to God in the face of "whatever plague, whatever sickness" with "whatever prayer, whatever plea" (8:38). Because of that "enthroning," even the foreigners—those who are not from Israel—may come to God in prayer. The existence of the "temple" of God in every sense of the term is a testimony to the hope that the sovereign God will freely forgive, freely save.

1 KINGS 9:1-9, A SECOND REVELATION

COMMENTARY

The narrative beginning of Solomon's reign is marked by a divine revelation to him at the greatest high place of that time, Gibeon (3:4-15). Following that encounter, the king proceeds to use the gift of wisdom that God has given him to judge his people (3:16-28), to administer his domain (4:1-34), to deal with his allies (5:1-18), and, above all, to build the Temple and his palace (6:1–7:51). Now, after the completion of the construction projects that culminated in the dedication of the Temple (8:1-66), Solomon has another revelatory encounter, this time presumably in Jerusalem. The account of the second revelation in 9:1-9 thus forms a literary bracket, together with the first revelation (3:4-15).

In direct response to Solomon's prayer at the dedication of the Temple (8:22-53), God acknowledges the special place of the Temple Solomon had built: It has been "consecrated"—set apart as a holy place—and God promises that God's name and attention will be there "forever" (v. 3). That "forever" is immediately qualified, however, by two "if . . . then" conditions (vv. 4-5, 6-7). In the Hebrew, the addressee shifts from the singular in vv. 4-5, referring to Solomon ("as for you," v. 4), to the plural in vv. 6-7, referring to all the Davidic kings ("you and your children," v. 6), although the people of Israel as a whole are also implicated (v. 9). Interestingly, the first condition is stated in terms of the validity of the promise of God to David (v. 5; cf. 2 Sam 7:13; 1 Kgs 8:25-26); that promise is good, provided that Solomon is faithful. The second condition is expressed as a threat that extends far beyond the dynasty: Israel will be exiled (vv. 7-9). The preservation of the Davidic dynasty "over Israel," the continuation of Israel in the land that God has given them, and the survival of the Temple are all at stake. Disobedience and disloyalty to the covenant will bring destruction. Even the Temple, set apart as a holy place, will be cast from God's sight (v. 7), thus negating Solomon's plea and God's promise to focus God's attention on it forever (v. 3; cf. 8:29-30). Israel, God's elect, will become the object of scorn and ridicule among the nations. This is one of the curses for disobedience (Deut 28:37). The destruction of the Temple (the NRSV emends the text at 9:8 ["shall be a heap of ruins"], following some ancient witnesses; the NIV is closer to the Hebrew text here; see also 2 Chr 7:21), too, will lead onlookers to conclude that it is the Lord who has brought destruction and exile on Israel, but they will rightly conclude that the Lord is entirely justified (cf. Deut 29:22-28).

Conditionality of the covenant is nothing new in the story. It is present already in the account of God's first revelation to Solomon (3:14). Still, whereas the emphasis in the first revelation is on divine initiative and grace shown to Solomon, indicated especially by God's gift of wisdom and its corollary benefits to Solomon while he loved God only in a compromising way (see Commentary on 3:1-15), the emphasis in this second revelation seems to be on the conditions for him and his successors. The two accounts are, in fact, meant to be read as complementary to each other: The first is clarified and balanced by the second. God has freely given, but the validity of the covenant relationship with God is indicated not so much by the gifts of God already received but by loyalty to God's demands.

REFLECTIONS

The second revelation to Solomon makes a theological counterpoint to the message of God's abundant grace manifest in the first revelation (3:1-15). God first came to Solomon while Solomon was "yet in sin and darkness," as it were. Although he loved God only in a limited way, God freely blessed Solomon. The narrator makes plain that God's blessing is the reason for Solomon's fame and success. Yet the magnitude of God's grace does not mean that there are no conditions for Solomon.

The passage makes a connection between human suffering in exile and destruction with the people's unfaithfulness. Israel's suffering in exile comes because of the people's disobedience to God, because of their disloyalty to the covenant. The same attitude toward suffering is evident also in Solomon's prayer, where natural calamities like drought and famine, along with defeat in war and exile (8:33-53), are also associated with sin. That cause-and-effect explanation is applied by the deuteronomistic theologian to Israel's experience in 587 BCE. Such explanations cannot be generalized for all human suffering, however, and other parts of the Bible (such as the book of Job) resist this blanket association. The abiding theological message in the text, however, is not that God is justified for human suffering. Read together with its counterpart in the literary bracket, this revelation can be understood as expounding on the *implications* of God's grace. The recipient of God's promise and consequent blessings is not to "sin the more that grace may abound" (cf. Rom 6:1). By no means! Rather, we need to remember that God's grace makes possible a divine-human relationship and, as in any relationship, there are demands and responsibilities. Those who are blessed are called to be faithful to God in worship and in conduct. If that relationship with God is not maintained and nurtured, no tangible symbol of divine presence, not even the sanctuary, has any abiding value.

1 KINGS 9:10–10:29, SOLOMON IN ALL HIS GLORY

OVERVIEW

After the balancing of perspectives provided in the account of God's second revelation to Solomon (9:1-9; cf. 3:1-15), the narrator proceeds to give an awe-inspiring review of Solomon's reign in all its glitter and glory. Our separation of this scriptural portion from the preceding unit is largely for practical reasons. We should, in fact, read the passage in the light of 9:1-9, keeping in mind the conditions stipulated in that passage as we assess this overview of Solomon's reign.

There is no apparent order of presentation; indeed, the order varies in different ancient versions. Logical order seems secondary to the overall impression that the collage makes. The report of Solomon's deal with Hiram (9:10-14), which revolves around Solomon's ambitious building projects, probably prompted thoughts about the use of forced labor and the supervision of the work-force (9:15-23; cf. 5:13-18). The mention of the fortification at Gezer (9:15) necessitated a parenthetical explanation regarding the acquisition of the city from the Egyptians as a dowry for Solomon's marriage to the pharaoh's daughter (9:16), which then led to an aside about Solomon's devotion to her (9:24). There is a digression about Solomon's public religious performance (9:25) before the narrator returns to Solomon's alliance with Hiram, this time to their joint maritime ventures to Ophir, a rich and exotic land probably somewhere in East Africa (9:26-28). That reference to a distant land then leads to an account of the historic visit of the queen of Sheba, an enchanting ruler from another faraway place (10:1-10). The author then returns briefly to the joint Israelite-Phoenician expedition to Ophir (10:11-12), then back again to the queen of Sheba (10:13), before going on to Solomon's other transactions with the nations at the far reaches of the then-known world: Arabia, Egypt, Kue (Cilicia) in Asia Minor, the Hittite kingdom and Aram/Syria (10:14-29). Aspects of the account are no doubt historically accurate; claims of fortifications at Hazor, Megiddo, and Gezer may be confirmed by archaeological excavations, and trade with Ophir is corroborated by an eighth-century BCE inscription from Tell Qasile, a port on the estuary of the Yarkon River (just north of modern Tel Aviv) since the twelfth century BCE. Other aspects, however, sound like the stuff of which legends are made: unprecedented amounts of spices (10:2, 10, 25), silver's being as common as stones in Jerusalem (10:27), and cedar as plentiful as the sycamore/fig trees of the Judean hill country (10:27). There are staggering amounts of treasures (gold, silver, precious gems, ivory), rare wood (cedar, cypress, "almugwood"), and quaint creatures (apes and תכיים [*tukkiyyîm*], an unknown Hebrew word interpreted as "baboons" in the NIV and "peacocks" in the NRSV). And Solomon's brilliance was without match.

1 Kings 9:10-28, Solomon's Commercial Forays

COMMENTARY

Solomon has ruled for twenty years (v. 10), during which period he completed the Temple (7 years, according to 6:38) and the palace complex (13 years, according to 7:1). This is the midpoint, perhaps the peak, of his forty-year career (11:42). Now, in addition to all the positive and negative reports about his reign in the narrative thus far, we get a summary assessment of his reign. The overall impression one receives is that Solomon was an extraordinarily gifted ruler, just as one might expect from the account of the first revelation (3:4-15): Solomon's God-given wisdom has brought him untold riches, power, and honor.

The king was able to deal shrewdly with the cunning Hiram, king of Tyre (9:10-14). Although Solomon had to make territorial concessions (which were not entirely to the Tyrian ruler's satisfaction), he managed to gain some material benefits from that transaction.[45] The narrator cites an unknown and evidently derogatory explanation for the ceded territory, which is called "the land of Cabul" (v. 13), meaning somehow that Solomon had taken advantage of his ally.[46] This advantage Solomon gained over the Phoenician king stands in contrast to an earlier report about the hard bargain driven by the Tyrian Hiram (5:1-18). Here we find Hiram

paying Solomon 120 talents of gold in addition to whatever other exchanges they may have made to seal their treaty.[47] Solomon gained some and lost some, as it were, all within the bounds of international law. What he gained was prestige and wealth for himself, symbolized above all by the completion of the Temple and his palace. What he gave up was territory that God had granted to Israel (see v. 7). The reference to the surrender of northern (Israelite) territories also foreshadows the division of the kingdom into north and south in the near future.

Solomon undertook significant public constructions, including the Temple, the palace complex, the "Millo" (probably some kind of terraced structure), storage cities, fortifications at various locations, and other military installations. Indeed, he reportedly "built whatever he desired in Jerusalem, Lebanon, and all his domain" (v. 19). He was able to carry out these projects through a combination of power and administrative know-how; his labor force came from a permanent levy of foreign slaves in his domain, Israelite laborers who were drafted for three months each (cf. 5:13-18), and, presumably, paid warriors, all under a trusted corps of his officers. He engaged in all sorts of diplomatic deals, international trade, and other foreign ventures. He attended to his public religious duties, offering sacrifices at the central sanctuary three times a year, thus fulfilling the law (Deut 16:16-17). (See Reflections at 10:1-29.)

45. The parallel account in 2 Chr 8:2 says that it was Huram (Hiram) who conceded territories to Solomon. Since the chronicler's account does not specify the "twenty cities of Galilee," we may think of both accounts as different perspectives on a historic territorial exchange.

46. The reading and the etymology of the name are disputed in the ancient versions and by commentators. Notes in the NRSV and the NIV suggest the meaning "as nothing," but that assumes a Hebrew word that is not attested elsewhere. In any case, the reference is probably to the towns of Asher in the northern coastal plain. See Josh 19:27.

47. According to the Babylonian standard currency throughout the ancient Near East in the sixth century BCE, a talent was the equivalent of 3,600 shekels.

1 Kings 10:1-29, Solomon's Other Successes

COMMENTARY

Indicative of the worldwide prestige Solomon had gained is the historic visit of the mysterious queen of Sheba, a place identified in the NT as a land in the southern reaches

of the world (Matt 12:42; Luke 11:31).[48] Scholars suspect that it was for political and

48. Josephus, *Antiquities of the Jews* 8.6.5-6, calls her "the Queen of Egypt and Ethiopia," and later traditions also identify her as Ethiopian.

economic reasons that the queen of Sheba journeyed to Jerusalem—it was a historic trade mission. She had come to Jerusalem to resolve difficult diplomatic issues surrounding the expanding world economy—perhaps the "hard questions" mentioned in v. 1. Whatever the reason for her visit, the narrator makes plain that it was a personal triumph for Solomon. The queen had heard of this king's reputation (v. 1), and she came to Jerusalem to verify these reports personally. She came bearing splendrous tributes and tested the king's intellect. She was so impressed by his brilliance, wealth, and the luxury of his palace that she was left breathless (v. 5; NRSV, NIV, "she was overwhelmed").

Through the persona of the queen of Sheba, we are presented with the deuteronomistic narrator's perspective on Solomon. According to this version of the story, she came to Jerusalem to confirm for herself "the reputation of Solomon as regards the name of the Lord," or, more literally, "the hearing of Solomon as regards the name of the Lord" (v. 1). The reference to the name of the Lord is an additional deuteronomistic twist that one does not find in the parallel account in 2 Chr 9:1, which has the queen visiting only to authenticate the rumors. Regardless of the evidence of Solomon's personal successes, reported in the review, the narrator points to what is theologically crucial in all of this: It is Solomon's conduct as regards the name of the Lord that is in question.

Moreover, through the congratulatory words of the queen of Sheba (vv. 6-9), the narrator reiterates that it is God's will (חפץ *ḥāpēṣ*) that Solomon sit on the throne and that it is for the love of the people of Israel that God has so willed (v. 9). Solomon is to execute justice and righteousness. The mention of God's will (*ḥēpeṣ*) is especially poignant in the light of the allusions elsewhere in the report to the desire of Solomon (*ḥēpeṣ*, 9:11) or the desire of the queen of Sheba (10:13).

The communiqué of the queen of Sheba may be just the sort of rhetorical nicety one might expect in a diplomatic mission. No one who has followed the account of Solomon's reign so far will take her words as anything but empty flattery that does not quite fit the Solomon we know. To be sure, Solomon is recognized as a brilliant and glamorous ruler. There is no question about his fame or the splendor of his reign. He has also carried out his public religious duties in accordance with the law (9:25; Deut 16:16-17). Still, the reader is prompted by the diplomatic words of the foreign queen to wonder about his support for "justice and righteousness," which are supposed to accompany divine election (see Deut 16:18-20). The choice of Solomon is supposed to have been by the will of God and for the sake of the people—in order that justice and righteousness might be brought about. The reader may even remember that Solomon had asked for wisdom so that he could govern his people properly (see 3:9, 11). Yet, what we read about in this review is the expression of Solomon's will, the will of the queen of Sheba, the enrichment of the king and his allies, and the pomp that surrounds him. We read about the alliance with Hiram, which resulted in the concession of land to the foreign leader that God had given to the people of Israel. We read about Solomon's prejudicial exploitation of forced labor to build all the projects that "he desired" (9:11, 21). We read about the non-Israelite people who remained in the land, who should have been eliminated by the law of the ban (Deut 7:1-5; 20:16-18). Even though Solomon was then in control, he did not eliminate them in accordance with the law. Instead, he compromised by distinguishing them from the Israelites, while he exploited them for his own purposes. We read about the increased contacts Solomon established with foreigners from the farthest corners of the world and, especially, his marriage alliance with the Egyptian pharaoh, whose daughter Solomon married and brought into his capital. We read of his appointment of officials to run his workforce, just like the kings of the other nations (1 Sam 8:12). We read about all the gold that went into the making of Solomon's throne, and we wonder about a particular detail that is pointed out in the report. According to the Greek text, a calf's head (the NRSV, following the Hebrew tradition, has "rounded top") was on the back of Solomon's throne. We read about his accumulation of wealth for himself and his acquisition of horses. Indeed, Solomon had become a king *just like those of the other nations*, thus contrary to the deuteronomic ideal of the faithful king (Deut 17:14-20; 1 Sam 8:1-18).

Reflections

It is difficult not to be overawed by King Solomon "in all his glory." He seems to have it all: personal abilities, enormous wealth, international prestige, and power. From the beginning of the book of 1 Kings, the reader has been told that Solomon was chosen by God to be the successor to the throne of David and that the king was blessed with wisdom, riches, honor, and victory over his adversaries. There is no doubt regarding the initiative and concern of God: It was God who invited Solomon to request whatever he wanted, God who granted his request and even more. The characterization of Solomon throughout the narrative is, however, ambiguous. At times he is portrayed positively as one who loves God, is humble in acknowledging the grace of God, is desirous of wisdom to fulfill his responsibilities to his people, and is capable of composing a dedicatory prayer so beautiful and profound that it still provides the church with material for liturgy and for theological reflection on divine presence. At the same time, however, Solomon is depicted as ruthless, scheming, self-absorbed, oppressive, greedy, and vain. This unusually gifted king is, after all, like all of other mortals: imperfect and sinful. The mystery in the story is that God should choose such a one and bless him so richly. That mystery is also the good news, however: God's grace overcomes human limitations, and the transcendent God is free to forgive when sinners repent.

The tension between the grace of God and the demand of faith, distinctly framed between two divine revelations (3:1-15; 9:1-9), is evident throughout the narrative. The grace of God is never intended to be without demands on the part of humanity: God's promise is good, *provided* that the king and his people are faithful to God's demands. This is stated as the word of God in Solomon's first revelation (3:14); it is acknowledged by Solomon himself in his prayer at the dedication of the Temple (8:25); and it is reiterated in the second revelation to him (9:4-7). Indeed, the deuteronomist tells us that even the queen of Sheba, a foreign woman from a distant land, knew that what mattered in terms of Solomon's reputation was his conduct regarding the name of the Lord (10:1). Even this foreign woman understood that it was God's will that mattered, not Solomon's or that of any other ruler; that Solomon was chosen because of God's love for Israel; and that the king was to do justice and righteousness. In the end, the question one must ask about Solomon in his glory is this: Has he been faithful to the will of God? Has he been obedient to God's demands?

The author of Ecclesiastes, writing in the guise of the king who had it all, raises questions about the abiding value of human desire to take control of one's future and worldly accomplishments (Eccl 1:12–2:26). The author says that he, as king, surpassed all others (Eccl 1:16, 2:9; cf. 1 Kgs 10:23). He built all that he desired and accumulated enormous wealth. He indulged in pleasure, and he was gifted in wisdom. Still, he comes to realize that all these things are ephemeral—they are as futile as trying to chase the wind. For the writer of Ecclesiastes, all wisdom, wealth, success, pleasure, and fame are finally unreliable. All is "vanity" in this sense.

The words of Ecclesiastes are echoed in the New Testament parable of the rich fool who accumulates wealth and is concerned only with his material successes (Luke 12:13-21). Jesus, however, cautions against covetousness, for "one's life does not consist in the abundance of possessions" (Luke 12:15 NRSV), and there are those "who store up treasures for themselves but are not rich toward God" (Luke 12:21 NRSV). Whereas people strive to assure their own successes, Jesus points out that the lilies of the field do not so strive and yet, "even Solomon in all his glory was not clothed like one of these" (Luke 12:27 NRSV). Jesus observes that some people are too much like the unbelievers, "like the nations of the world," who are concerned with material things. Instead of living such a life-style, he urges his disciples to seek first the kingdom of God and God's righteousness (cf. 1 Kgs 10:9), promising that God's blessings will then be granted to them (Matt 6:33).

1 KINGS 11:1-43, THE DEMISE OF SOLOMON

OVERVIEW

The preceding passage (9:10–10:29) depicts Solomon as a ruler just like those of other nations, even surpassing them all in his accumulation of wealth and horses, especially horses acquired from Egypt. He had clearly violated deuteronomistic law (Deut 17:14-17; 1 Sam 8:1-21). Now the narrator goes on to point out how Solomon had been unfaithful to the Lord.

1 Kings 11:1-13, Solomon's Unfaithfulness

COMMENTARY

Contrary to the law (Deut 17:14-17), Solomon loved many foreign women (v. 1). The daughter of the pharaoh of Egypt is singled out, but the narrator mentions also Moabites, Ammonites, Edomites, Sidonians (Phoenicians), and Hittites—women from the nations surrounding Israel. Indeed, Solomon had seven hundred royal wives and three hundred concubines (v. 3). For the narrator, the problem was not with the multiplicity of women per se, but that these foreign women had led Solomon's heart astray (vv. 2-4, 9). David also had many wives and concubines (2 Sam 3:2-5; 5:13-16; 11:27; 1 Chr 3:1-9), but, unlike Solomon, David's heart remained true to his God (vv. 4, 6). The danger of intermarriage with the foreign women lies in one's deviation from the worship of the Lord alone. The narrator says, literally, if somewhat ambiguously, "Solomon held fast [דבק *dābaq*] to loving" (v. 2). The context suggests that the objects of Solomon's love were these foreign women and their foreign gods; he held fast to them. The language is theologically loaded, for elsewhere in the deuteronomistic tradition, the love of the Lord requires one to "hold fast" (*dābaq*) to God (Deut 11:22; 30:20; Josh 22:5) and to God alone (Deut 4:4; 10:20; 13:4). It must be noted, too, that in deuteronomistic literature, "love" is more than a term to express an emotion. As the concept is used elsewhere in ancient Near Eastern treaties, "love" is an idiom for committed relationship. So Israel is exhorted to love the Lord without wavering: "Love the LORD your God with all your heart, and with all your soul, and with all your might" (Deut 6:5 NRSV).

At the beginning of Solomon's reign, we are told, he "loved the LORD" (3:3) and was blessed with wisdom (3:4-14). Even at that time, however, his actions presaged his later troubles. His first act after ascending to the throne was to enter into a marriage alliance with Egypt, taking the daughter of the pharaoh as bride (3:1). That marriage seems particularly irksome to the narrator, who mentions it repeatedly, sometimes even digressing from his story to do so (7:8; 9:16, 24). The theological problem for the narrator is that Solomon's love of the foreign women compromised his allegiance to the Lord; these foreign women caused his heart to turn from devotion to God, so that he did not follow his Suzerain wholeheartedly (vv. 4, 6).

Before the construction and completion of the Temple, Solomon had worshiped at the local high places: "Solomon loved the LORD, walking in the statutes of his father David, except that he sacrificed and offered incense at the high places" (3:3). Now, despite the presence of the Temple, Solomon built high places for the gods of his foreign wives. Some of these high places were even blatantly raised on the hill facing (על-פני *'al-pĕnê*, "to the face of") Jerusalem—that is, on the Mount of Olives.

Solomon's unfaithfulness is especially disconcerting because God had appeared to him twice (v. 9), once graciously giving him gifts (3:1-15) and another time firmly reiterating the demand for faithfulness (9:1-19). On account of Solomon's flagrant violation of the covenant, God promises to tear the kingdom from him and to give it to one of his servants (v. 11). In this way, the narrator anticipates the rise of Jeroboam, son of Nebat (vv. 26-40). Still, the deity was apparently reluctant to undo the promise to David by giving the kingdom entirely to an outsider, a servant. Referring to the dual election of David and Jerusalem, the narrator speaks of God's assurance to let hope for the Davidic promise stay alive by giving one tribe to Solomon's successor. (See Reflections at 11:14-43.)

1 Kings 11:14-43, God Ends Solomon's Kingship

COMMENTARY

The epitome of Solomon's achievements was his construction of the Temple of the Lord in Jerusalem. Whereas his father, David, had been preoccupied with warfare and was unable to carry out the project, Solomon boasted to Hiram, the Tyrian king, that he himself was able to do so because he had neither disasters nor adversaries (5:3-5). His good fortunes would be reversed, however, for God would raise up against him two adversaries from without (11:14-25) and one from within his kingdom (11:26-40).

11:14-22. In the time of David, the Israelites had defeated the Edomites in war, virtually annihilating the population (2 Sam 8:13-14). The young Edomite crown prince, Hadad, managed to escape and was brought to Egypt. The story of the Edomite's sojourn in Egypt provides some details that initially seem tangential to the point that he would be an adversary of Solomon: The refugees fled with the young crown prince to Egypt by way of Midian and Paran, desert locations important in the history of the Israelite nation. In Egypt, the Edomite married into the house of the pharaoh and produced a son who was taken in by the Egyptian queen and raised among the Egyptian royal children. Elements of the story—the reference to Midian, the birth of a child in Egypt, the raising of the child by an Egyptian queen in the Egyptian palace—find echo in the story of Moses, the mediator through whom God had freed the Israelites. The allusion to the exodus is unmistakable in the plea of the Edomite prince for freedom from Egypt: "Let me go (שלחני *šallĕḥēnî*), that I may return to my country" (v. 21; cf. v. 22). These are words that recall God's own words, uttered through Moses, in demand of Israel's release by the pharaoh of Egypt: "Let my son/people go" (see Exod 4:23; 5:1; 7:16; 8:1; 9:1; 10:3). The deuteronomistic narrator is not so sanguine about the Edomites as to suggest that the worship of the Lord would be the consequence of their release, as was the argument made before Pharaoh for Israel's freedom. Still, the text leaves no doubt that it was the Lord who raised up Hadad, despite the initial adversity of Hadad's circumstances. By a tissue of verbal allusions to the exodus experience, the narrator touches the core of Israelite belief in the particularity of their election. The text does not go so far as to state that the Edomites were liberated by the Lord and chosen by the Lord, as Israel had been. The universalism of God's salvation is not a point that the deuteronomistic narrator makes. The Lord had raised Hadad not so much to be the savior of the Edomites as to be an adversary to Solomon, who had sealed his alliance with Egypt through marrying the pharaoh's daughter. In any case, the text is clear that the will of God was being worked out even through foreigners.

11:23-25. Besides Hadad the Edomite, God also raised up Rezon. This was a man who had rebelled against his master, Hadadezer king of Zobah (an Aramaic state; see v. 23). Although the defeat of Hadadezer of Zobah is recounted elsewhere in the Bible (2 Sam 8:3-8; 10:1-19 // 1 Chr 18:3-8; 19:1-19), there is no hint anywhere else in the OT of Rezon's role. In the 1 Kings account, however, Rezon is given prominence. He is seen as the leader of a marauding band in rebellion against their overlord, just as David had led a band of men against King Saul. Rezon went on to capture Damascus, which he made the capital of a new Aramean dynasty, even as David captured Jerusalem and made it the capital of the Israelite kingdom. To the reader who knows the tradition of David's rise and the taking of Jerusalem as evidence of God's dual election of the king and the capital, the allusions cannot be missed. Again, the narrator does not make any claim that Rezon or Damascus were chosen in the same way that David and Zion had been. Still, the deliberate analogies are astounding. The narrator touches the very core of Israel's covenant theology. He points ironically to God's use of foreigners to undermine the Israelites' special relationship with God—the relationship established in the election of Israel (evident in the exodus experience) and the dual election of David and Zion.[49] There is no claim of God's universal salvation in the story here, but it is clear that history is being worked out completely under the will of the Lord—even if foreigners were used against God's chosen one!

11:26-43. Like Rezon the Aramean and David, Jeroboam rebelled against his king. Jeroboam is identified as the son of Nebat, who is called an אפרתי (*'eprātî*), a word that may be taken to mean either "Ephraimite" (as opposed to "Judean") or "Ephrathite" (someone from Ephrathah). The NIV and the NRSV both take the designation to mean that Jeroboam's father was an "Ephraimite," and that is probably correct. Still, the gentilic form *'eprātî* recalls David as the "son of an *'eprātî*" (1 Sam 17:12). The narrator acknowledges that Jeroboam the son of Nebat was no biological scion of the Davidic dynasty; yet, there are hints of other connections with David. Jeroboam is called by his patronym, perhaps to allow the cryptic note about his connection with the *'eprātî*: "son of Nebat, the *'eprātî*" (v. 26). He is also identified as a son of the widow Zeruah (meaning "leprous"?), perhaps in derogation, and he is called Solomon's "servant" (the NIV, less satisfactorily, has "one of Solomon's officials"). It may be significant that up to this point in the narrative of 1 Kings, every contender to the Davidic throne is associated with his mother: Adonijah, whose mother was Haggith (1:5, 11; 2:13), and Solomon, whose mother was Bathsheba (1:11; 2:13). Moreover, Jeroboam

was a "servant" of Solomon (v. 26), just as David was a "servant" of Saul (1 Sam 17:32).

The connections with David pile up as the story continues. Jeroboam's rebellion against Solomon was set in motion by a "word" (רבד *dābār*, v. 27), possibly a reference to the divine word (NIV, "account"; NRSV, "reason"), just as the rejection of King Saul and the rise of David were set in motion by a (divine) "word" (1 Sam 15:10). Indeed, Jeroboam was encouraged in his rebellion by the word of God through Ahijah, a Shilonite prophet, even as David was encouraged to rise against Saul by God's word through Samuel, a prophet from the central sanctuary at Shiloh. Jeroboam was a youngster when he was called to service by Solomon, just as David was chosen by Saul when David was a youngster (1 Sam 17:33, 42). Despite his youth, Jeroboam is said to have been "a substantial hero" (גבור חיל *gibbôr ḥayil*, v. 28; NIV, "man of standing"; NRSV, "very able"), just as David was recommended to Saul as "a substantial hero" (*gibbôr ḥayil*) while he was still a youth (1 Sam 16:18; cf. 17:33). Jeroboam initially impressed Solomon (v. 28), just as David initially impressed Saul (1 Sam 16:21-22). The tragic fate of Saul was sealed by the tearing of a garment that symbolized the tearing of the kingdom from him, a kingdom that would be given to David (1 Sam 15:27-28). The rejection of Solomon, too, was marked by the symbolic act of the rending of a garment, in this case a *new* garment, ten fragments of which were given to Jeroboam (vv. 12, 30-31). The prophet Samuel interpreted the torn garment as God's rejection of Saul for his disobedience to the Lord. So, too, the prophet Ahijah interpreted the new torn garment as symbolic of the deity's rejection of Solomon. The rejected and jealous Saul tried to kill David (1 Sam 18:1–19:17), whom he initially favored. So, too, Solomon tried to kill Jeroboam, who had impressed him earlier (v. 40). David escaped to seek the protection of the Philistines (1 Sam 27:1-12), and he remained a fugitive until Saul's death. Likewise, Jeroboam escaped and received the protection of the Egyptians, and he remained there until Solomon died (v. 40). Most important, God promised to build Jeroboam an enduring dynasty, just as God had done for

---

49. The exodus experience was central in the northern traditions ("Israel," as opposed to "Judah"), while the dual election of David and Zion was basic in Judean ideology. So the narrator of Kings is thorough in responding to the traditions of the north and the south.

David—provided that Jeroboam keep the covenant (v. 38).

Despite the unmistakable allusions to the fall of Saul and the consequent rise of David, there are important differences between that story and the story of Solomon's fall and Jeroboam's rise. In Saul's case, the kingdom of Israel was torn from him and given to another, who was said to be better than he (1 Sam 15:28). In Jeroboam's case, the text is explicit that the kingdom would not be taken in its entirety out of Solomon's hand (vv. 13, 34). Nor is Jeroboam praised as a better person than Solomon. Only ten of the twelve fragments, symbolizing the ten tribes that belonged to the north, were given to Jeroboam. God's dual election of David and Jerusalem would not be violated, for one tribe will be retained for the "son of David" in order that there will always be "a lamp" in Jerusalem (v. 36; cf. 2 Sam 21:17). The narrator performs a remarkable balancing act here, at once preserving hope in God's promise that the Davidic dynasty would endure forever and maintaining the threat of severe punishment for any violation of the covenant stipulations. David had received assurance through Nathan's oracle that God's "covenant loyalty" (חסד ḥesed) would never be removed from his dynasty, as God had removed it from Saul (2 Sam 7:16). Now, through the rebellion of Jeroboam, it appears that God is removing the "kingdom of Israel" from the Davidides. By the allusions to God's action with regard to the fall of Saul, the narrator impels the reader to think of that incident, thus making the difference between the two cases stark: "But I will not take all the kingdom from his hand" (v. 34); "Only I will not tear away all the kingdom" (vv. 11-13). The promise to David is still good, inasmuch as Solomon will remain king until his death, and hope will remain in Jerusalem, for there will remain one tribe over which a scion of David will rule.

The careful reader will no doubt notice that the math does not add up in this passage. Ahijah had torn twelve fragments of the new garment to represent the twelve tribes. If ten tribes were given to Jeroboam and one to the Davidides, only eleven are accounted for. Ancient interpreters noticed the discrepancy as well, and, indeed, the Greek translation reflects a tradition that says two tribes were given to the Davidides—probably an attempt to harmonize the math. Commentators sometimes argue that the author did not care much about the precise figures. Yet, the narrator states in 12:20 that, while Jeroboam was given control over "all Israel" (the ten tribes of the north), only the tribe of Judah remained faithful to the house of David. Even though the Benjaminites did ally themselves with Judah under Rehoboam, Solomon's son (see 12:21-24), the unity of the south remains an open question.

REFLECTIONS

These passages raise a number of interesting theological issues that confront the faith community.

1. The negative role foreign women seem to play in Solomon's demise is troubling to the reader. Although Solomon was the one who was ultimately punished for his unfaithfulness, the story puts the blame on the foreign women. It was they who caused his heart to turn astray, as if he would not have strayed on his own or on account of other foreign alliances, such as his economic and political compromises with Phoenicia and Egypt. No, he had strayed because the women had led him to do so. To be sure, that is how the Torah sees it: The Israelites must not marry foreigners because their hearts would be turned away from loving the Lord (Deut 7:3-5; cf. Exod 34:15-16; Josh 23:12). That law was taken at face value in the post-exilic period, when, in the face of the community's losses through intermarriage, the leaders of the Jewish community called for reforms that would enforce the old prohibition against foreign marriages, the divorce of foreign wives, and the abandonment of the children of such marriages (Ezra 9–10). To modern readers, that approach to outsiders smacks of xenophobia, and its enforcement, with its demand for keeping "the race" pure (Ezra 9:2), sounds dangerously similar to what is now euphemistically called "ethnic cleansing." It is also troubling that only marriages of Israelite men to foreign women were at issue in the reforms of Ezra. No explicit sanction is made against Israelite women marrying foreign men.

Whatever the cultural, social, political, and economic circumstances that generated such laws in the Bible, it is important to understand that the biblical theologians were ultimately interested in the issue of faithfulness to the Lord alone. That is finally what is at stake in these laws. The critical theological issue in the condemnation of Solomon is his unfaithfulness to God, manifested in his love for other gods. The fundamental problem here is not the multiplicity of women or their foreignness or even their particular religions. For modern readers, Ashtoreth, Milcom, Chemosh, or other gods of Israel's neighbors are probably not serious threats. These cults have roundly been condemned for their promotion of fertility rites, their use of idols, and so on. Reading the stories in their historical contexts alone, we may be smug that we are no longer subservient to those sorts of "primitive" beliefs. The key theological issue that this text raises, however, is absolute devotion to our God. The fate of Solomon warns us against allegiance to other gods—and their names are still legion. The love of God in the biblical sense is an exclusivistic one. It brooks no compromise; it allows allegiance to no other "gods," whatever their names, whatever their forms.

2. In the light of the particularistic view in 11:11-13, with its polemic against Solomon's devotion to his foreign wives with their gods, 11:14-25 sounds almost universalistic. The particularity of Israel's claims—of God's election of the people as attested by their experience of liberation from Egypt and of the dual election of David and Zion—is astoundingly relativized. The story implies that even the Edomites had experiences of liberation analogous to those of Israel in Egypt. The narrator does not explicitly state that the liberation of the Edomites from Egypt was also the Lord's doing, but it does say that the Lord is the one who raised up Hadad, presumably the Edomite liberator, as an adversary to Solomon. The foreigner was used by God—negatively, in this case—to fulfill the divine plan as regards Israel.

By the same token, the Arameans also had a story to tell about the rise of their king that has parallels to David's rise and the taking of Jerusalem. The narrator of 1 Kings does not make the positive case that the rise of the enduring dynasty that Rezon brought and the choice of Damascus as the center of Aramean influence are evidence of God's election of the Arameans. Yet, the narrator does not doubt that it is the Lord who has raised up this Aramean—if only to be an adversary to Solomon, God's chosen king.

The narrator speaks of God's use of the foreigners only as foils for Israel. The implicitly universalistic assertion is that God is in control of all human history, not only of Israel's particular history. The passage does not make an explicit case for God's involvement in the positive experiences of the foreigners that are analogous to those of Israel, but biblical theologians do. In the face of Israel's flagrant violation of the covenant, the prophet Amos points to the liberation experiences of other nations that are, like Israel's exodus from Egypt, evidence of God's handiwork (Amos 9:7). The book of Jonah makes the case for God's love extending well beyond the boundaries of Israel to include foreigners in distant lands. Above all, the persistent message of the New Testament is that God breaks down the boundaries of ethnicity, gender, class, and nationality to proclaim the power of the love of God for all human beings, Jew and Gentile alike. The passage in 1 Kings recognizes the inclusivity of God's will alongside the claims of exclusivity that the covenant makes. So, too, the church must be exclusively devoted to the Lord and, at the same time, be open to the possibility that God might act much more inclusively than we may imagine.

3. The punishment of Solomon is a testimony to the integrity of God's demands as Suzerain. Violations of the covenant will have their consequences. This is a standard expectation in ancient Near Eastern treaties. The good news that is proclaimed throughout the Bible and that goes beyond standard covenant ideologies—the *good news* that is reiterated in this passage—is God's faithfulness to God's promises. The threat of God's punishment for sin is real, and so is the promise, even if the signs of God's judgment and God's faithfulness do not quite add up. Mathematicians cannot resolve the mystery of that tension.

The validity of God's promise will be made manifest in the endurance of the Davidic line through the tribe of Judah. That persistence of hope through the scion of David will be the "lamp" ever before God. For many believers, that lamp shining in the midst of the darkness is most decisively manifested in the ministry of Jesus (see John 1:4-9). He is the "son of David" and a descendant from the tribe of Judah (Matt 1:1-17). That light will, by the divine promise and freedom, always be before God. In that promise, we dare to believe that God will be faithful forever.

1 KINGS 12:1–2 KINGS 17:41

THE DIVIDED KINGDOM

1 KINGS 12:1-33, FRAGMENTATION OF THE KINGDOM

OVERVIEW

In the preceding chapter, Ahijah the Shilonite had prophesied the fragmentation of the kingdom, with ten tribes given to Jeroboam, son of Nebat, an Ephraimite (11:26-40). Now in chap. 12, we see how that prophecy is fulfilled (12:1-24) and what Jeroboam's priorities were when he became king (12:25-33). Although Rehoboam has a prominent role to play in the first part of the chapter, his reign is not at issue here—that will come later (14:21-31). The point the narrator makes, rather, is that Rehoboam's oppressive and arrogant ways were instrumental in the fulfillment of the will of God, announced through Ahijah's prophecy (v.

15). By the same token, Rehoboam's surprising obedience to the word of God spoken through Shemaiah, the man of God, was decisive in the fulfillment of the will of God (v. 24). Jeroboam is ironically silent in this story of his rise to power; throughout the account in vv. 1-24, he does not speak or act, except as part of the assembly that petitioned Rehoboam (vv. 3, 12). In this way, the narrative effectively conveys the message that Jeroboam's rise to power is in accordance with the will of God; it has nothing to do with Jeroboam's ability or character. When Jeroboam does finally act and speak (vv. 25-29), it is in his own selfish interest, and his initiatives are unsavory.

1 Kings 12:1-24, Ahijah's Prophecy Is Fulfilled

COMMENTARY

12:1-19. Upon the death of Solomon, his son Rehoboam went to Shechem to be crowned king (922–915 BCE). Political considerations seem to have been at play in previous choices of coronation sites—David at Hebron (2 Sam 5:1-5), Adonijah at En Rogel (1 Kgs 1:9-10), Solomon at Gihon (1 Kgs 1:32-37). Shechem was perhaps a politically sensible choice for the kingdom that threatens to disintegrate. It has pride of place as the first locale Abram visited when he migrated from Haran (Gen 12:6). It was also the site of a covenant ceremony involving the whole Israelite confederacy (Joshua 24). Set in "the hill country of Ephraim" (v. 25), it was an important city for the northern tribes. So its

selection may be viewed as a conciliatory overture to the northern tribes by the Judean successor to the throne. Rehoboam, however, is not portrayed by the narrator as a tactful and compromising man. It is more likely that his coronation at Shechem was a deliberate assertion of his authority over the northern tribes.

Whatever the case may have been historically, the mention of a coronation at Shechem recalls a similar event that occurred before the establishment of the Davidic monarchy. In the days of the judges, a certain Abimelech, son of Jerubbaal, tried to make himself king there. He viciously murdered all his rivals and ruled over Israel for three years, contrary to the antimonarchical tradition of the northern tribal confederacy (Judg 9:1-57). That early experiment in monarchical rule failed, however, and the Lord again raised up judges to deliver Israel (Judg 10:1-2). Rehoboam apparently had not learned a lesson from history, for history would soon repeat itself: His assumption of kingship at Shechem would be immediately challenged.

Figure 2: Chronology of the Kings of the Divided Monarchy*

Judah	Israel
Rehoboam (922–915 BCE)	Jeroboam I (922–901 BCE)
	Abijam (915–913)
Asa (915–873)	Nadab (901–900)
	Baasha (900–877)
	Elah (877–876)
	Zimri (876)
Jehoshaphat (873–849)	Omri (876–869)
	Ahab (869–850)
	Ahaziah (850–849)
Jehoram (849–843)	Jehoram (849–843/2)
Ahaziah (843/2)	
Athaliah (843–837)	
Jehoash (837–800)	Jehu (843/2–815)
	Jehoahaz (815–802)
	Joash (802–786)
Azariah/Uzziah (783–742)	Jeroboam II (786–746)
	Zechariah (746–745)
	Shallum (745)
Jotham (742–735)	Menahem (745–737)
	Pekahiah (737–736)
	Pekah (736–732)
Ahaz (735–715)	Hoshea (732–724)
	Fall of Samaria (722/1 BCE)
Hezekiah (715–687/6)	
Manasseh (687/6–642)	
Amon (642–609)	
Jehoahaz (609)	
Jehoiakim (609–598)	
Jehoiachin (598/7)	
Babylonian conquest of Jerusalem and first deportation (597 BCE)	
Zedekiah (597–587/6)	
Destruction of Jerusalem and second deportation (587/6 BCE)	

*Dates following the kings' names are approximate years of their rule

---

Ahijah the Shilonite had dramatized in a sign-act that Jeroboam, son of Nebat, would be instrumental in the dismantling of the kingdom (11:26-46). Solomon had temporarily removed that threat by driving Jeroboam into exile in Egypt. According to the Hebrew text, Jeroboam was still in Egypt at this time.[50] He

50. The NRSV and the NIV both emend the Hebrew text to read "and he returned from Egypt," following the parallel text in 2 Chr 10:2, the Greek, and the Vulgate.

was immediately summoned back, no doubt by the northerners because of his previous experience as leader of the corvée (11:28). The northern leaders appeared before the newly crowned king to ask that the workload be lightened, for they had borne the brunt of Solomon's demands for corvée workers for his various projects (see 4:1-17). Apparently there is still a chance that Ahijah's prophesied fragmentation might be averted; the decision lay in the hands of Rehoboam to follow the path of oppression set by his father or to take a different course.

Rehoboam managed to buy some time in order to seek advice. The veterans who had served Solomon counseled a conciliatory approach. Despite their links with Solomon, they advocated a reversal of policy. Their sage advice was to take a long view of the matter: If the king would accommodate the request of the Israelites now, then they would be beholden to him forever. Rehoboam, however, rejected the advice and turned instead to his peers "who had grown up with him." His bias is evident in the fact that he identifies himself with them: "What do you advise that *we* answer this people . . . ?" (v. 9; cf., "How do you advise *me* . . . ?" in v. 6). His companions—derogatorily called "the boys" (הילדים *haylādîm*), even though they must have been about forty years old (see 21:14; hence, the NRSV and the NIV have "the young men")—advocated an uncompromising approach, even urging Rehoboam to use what is probably a vulgar idiom: "My little [thing] is thicker than my father's loins!" (Most translators supply the word "finger" to clarify the substantive קטן [*qĕṭōn*, "little one," "little thing"], but that only obscures the idiom.) They encouraged Rehoboam to increase the burden and the scourge—to use "scorpions" (perhaps a reference to spiked lashes) instead of ordinary whips.

Like Pharaoh, whose heart was hardened when he was asked to grant the Israelite slaves some reprieve from their oppressive burdens, Rehoboam was recalcitrant. Just as Pharaoh did with the Israelites, so also Rehoboam promised even more hardship and more painful afflictions (Exod 5:1-23). Here, again, Rehoboam has apparently not learned from history; he "did not listen to the people" (v. 15). The narrator portrays this turn of events as something brought about in accordance with God's will in order that the prophecy of Ahijah might be fulfilled.

The northern tribes sounded the cry of rebellion with words that echo the revolt of Sheba the Benjaminite in the time of Saul (2 Sam 20:1). Again, history repeats itself, and Rehoboam is still not learning from it.

The consequence is the division of the kingdom. "All Israel" (presumably ten tribes, as Ahijah had predicted) were led by Jeroboam. Rehoboam remained in control over only the Israelites living in the Judean towns. Still, he did not appear to have learned his lesson. Of all people, he sent Adoram, the minister of forced labor, to the Israelites, possibly the same Adoram or a descendant of the Adoram who was in charge of the forced labor in the days when Sheba revolted (see 2 Sam 20:24)! The taskmaster was stoned to death, and Rehoboam had to flee to Jerusalem. The division of the kingdom had become a fact "to this day" (v. 19)—that is, in the generation of the editor.

12:20-24. While Jeroboam, son of Nebat, was made king over the ten tribes of Israel (922–901 BCE), only the tribe of Judah remained loyal to the house of David, just as Ahijah had prophesied. The tribe of Benjamin apparently did not join the northern group, but neither did they pledge allegiance to the Davidides. Despite the fact that he was in the minority, Rehoboam was willing to take up arms to restore the kingdom. Obviously, he had the seasoned military units under his command. He was on the verge of bringing the Benjaminites over to his side when he was stopped by Shemaiah, "the man of God," who declared that the division of the kingdom was in accordance with the will of the Lord. The word of the Lord somehow prevailed, and Rehoboam gave up his fight. Instead of trying "to restore" (להשיב *lĕhāšîb*, in the hiphil) the kingdom by force, the people "returned" (שוב *šûb*) to their homes. The foolish young king who began by insisting on his way finally obeyed the word of God. The will of God, as conveyed in the prophecy of Ahijah, was thus fulfilled. (See Reflections at 12:25-33.)

1 Kings 12:25-33, Jeroboam's Priorities

Commentary

Jeroboam is largely a passive figure in the preceding verses, even though his rise to power is at issue. Except for his presence with the rest of his people before Rehoboam, he is silent. Twice he had to be summoned to the scene of action (vv. 2, 20). Yet, he has come into power because it is the will of God. It is only after the division of the kingdom has become a fact that we see Jeroboam in an active role.

Shechem, an ancient city that once was the site of a covenant renewal ceremony for all Israel (Joshua 24), was rebuilt and established as Jeroboam's capital. Penuel, a sacred site in the Jacob tradition (Gen 32:24-31) and, hence, also among the northern tribes, was also rebuilt. Now the narrator lets the reader in on the private thoughts of Jeroboam so that his true intentions may be known. Fearing that the dedication to the Jerusalem cultus would lead to disloyalty to him, he established royal sanctuaries at Bethel, a sacred site long associated with Jacob, and at Dan, near the northern border of Israel. The reader gathers from Jeroboam's soliloquy that his interests were purely political and selfish; they had nothing to do with faith in the Lord, even though he cast the issue in religious terms before his people (v. 28). He made two golden calves at these sanctuaries and called for worship there.

Like the rebuilding of Shechem and Penuel, Jeroboam's initiative at Bethel and Dan was a political one: He wanted to retain the loyalty of the populace and, no doubt, also the wealth that their offerings would bring into the state coffers. It was probably not his purpose to have the calves set up as idols to be worshiped; politically, it would have been exceedingly foolhardy for him to try to found a new religion when the country was in such turmoil. Rather, the calves were probably symbols of God, who was known from antiquity as "the Bull of Jacob" (see Gen 49:24; Ps 132:2, 5). In one tradition at least, the calf imagery was probably associated with the god of the exodus: "These are your gods, O Israel, who brought you up out of the land of Egypt" (Exod 32:4, 8 NRSV; see TNK and NAB). Thus, just as the ark and the cherubim in the Jerusalem Temple were thought to have been the symbols of an invisibly enthroned deity, so also the calf was probably intended as the pedestal for an invisible God. Accordingly, the TNK renders the Hebrew of v. 28 thus: "This is your god, O Israel, who brought you up from the land of Egypt." The allusion to the exodus experience is not accidental, for the experience of the northern tribes under the rule of the southerners was analogous to the bondage of Israel in Egypt.

Whatever the original intention of Jeroboam, from the perspective of the deuteronomistic editor, who is vehement that the Jerusalem Temple is the only acceptable one, the initiative of Jeroboam was nothing but sin, and the fact that there were two calves allows the editor to imply the polytheistic nature of Jeroboam's innovations. He feared that his people would continue to go to "the house of the LORD" (v. 27), so he built an alternative "house of high places" (v. 31; NRSV, "houses on high places"; NIV, "shrines on high places") and he appointed non-Levites to serve as priests, both actions in contravention of deuteronomistic law (Deut 12:5-7; 18:1-8). Jeroboam is also accused of changing the festal calendar; he ordered the celebration of a festival just like *the* festival in Judah—that is, the Feast of Booths (Sukkot) on the fifteenth day of the eighth month, rather than the fifteenth day of the seventh month, as stipulated in the law (Lev 23:33-36). The charge of heresy is perhaps unfair in the light of Jeroboam's original intention. Yet, it is true that his initiatives at Bethel and Dan did lead to idolatry; the calves did become objects of worship (Hos 10:5; 13:2), and the northern shrines did become centers of heterodoxy (Amos 5:4-5), in which the priests were more interested in protecting the political establishment than in following the demands of the Lord (Amos 7:10-17). By letting the reader in on the thoughts of Jeroboam, the narrator makes it clear that Jeroboam's actions were for his own political goals.

REFLECTIONS

The narrator paints a caricature of a despicable dictator in Rehoboam: He is foolish, tactless, crass, recalcitrant, and oppressive. We can name many modern dictators who would fit this description perfectly. Inevitably our sympathy lies with the oppressed people they rule. We rejoice at the people's liberation, and we are not at all surprised to learn that it is the will of God that their revolution should succeed.

The story in 1 Kings 12, however, warns us not to romanticize revolution. Jeroboam, the acknowledged leader of the liberated people, is no ideal figure himself. He has his own political agenda and is perfectly willing to manipulate religious symbols to fit it. He speaks the language of liberation theology ("who brought you out of the land of Egypt"), but his allegiance is to himself.

On the one hand, the passage teaches us that it is the will of God to liberate the oppressed. On the other hand, we learn not to idealize every liberation movement.[51] In the end, it is the will of God that really matters (12:15), and it is not too late for even the worst of sinners to obey the will of God (12:24).

51. See Nelson, *First and Second Kings*, 82.

1 KINGS 13:1-34, WHEN ONE DOES NOT OBEY THE WORD OF THE LORD

OVERVIEW

This chapter is a continuation of the preceding account of Jeroboam's heterodox innovations. The account of Jeroboam's encounter with an unnamed man of God from Judah (vv. 1-10) seems logical enough in the context. It is followed, however, by a peculiar report of the fate of this man of God that seems to be entirely intrusive in the narrative (vv. 11-32). Yet, the unity of the chapter is not in doubt. The phrase "the word of the LORD" is repeated throughout the chapter (vv. 1-2, 5, 9, 17-18, 20-21, 26 [twice], 32). Various forms of the Hebrew root שׁוּב (*šûb*, with its range of meanings) appear sixteen times (vv. 4, 6 [twice], 9, 10, 16, 17, 18, 19, 20, 22, 23,

26, 29, 33 [twice]), and the word for "way" or "road" also appears repeatedly (vv. 9, 10 [twice], 17, 24 [twice], 26, 33). The story of the man of God is, in fact, not an insignificant diversion. Rather, it is an illustration of what might happen when one does not obey the word of the Lord. Even a man of God, who is scrupulously obedient most of the time and who falls short on just one seemingly understandable situation, is punished. Yet, the recalcitrant Jeroboam did not seem to learn that lesson (vv. 33-34). Thus the chapter as a whole is about Jeroboam's disobedience of the word of the Lord and the predicted consequences of that disobedience.

1 Kings 13:1-10, Consequences of Jeroboam's Disobedience

COMMENTARY

The story actually begins at 12:32. Among the heretical religious innovations of Jeroboam was the celebration of a feast, probably the Feast of Booths (Sukkot), on the fifteenth day of the eighth month. This was in contrast to the rule in Judah, where the feast was celebrated in the seventh month.

Jeroboam had apparently come to Bethel to inaugurate the festival by offering sacrifices at the altar—sacrifices offered to the golden calves he had set up, according to the narrator (12:32). He was standing by the altar to offer incense when an unnamed man of God came from Judah "by the word of the LORD" (v. 1). It is clear that the Lord was not at Bethel. Rather, the word of the Lord was brought by someone from Judah.

As the present text has it, the man of God predicted the coming of Josiah, a descendent of David, almost three centuries later. Reflecting the events related in 2 Kgs 23:15-20, the man of God predicted Josiah's desecration of the altar by slaughtering the priests of the high places and burning their bones upon the Bethel altar. To confirm the prophecy, the man of God proclaimed an accompanying sign—namely, the splitting apart of the altar. Jeroboam stretched out his hand to order the arrest of the man, but his hand withered and his arm became paralyzed and the altar was split apart accordingly (v. 5). Jeroboam had earlier successfully "raised his hand" against Solomon (11:26, 27), but his hand is now stretched out in an attempt to prevent a sign from the Lord. His hand is dramatically stopped.

Jeroboam pleaded for the man of God to intercede for him. When the man did so, Jeroboam's hand was restored. Clearly, it was the Lord who granted the restoration. The king appeared not to get that point either, however. He invited the man of God to dine with him, promising him a gift. The holy man declined the invitation, stating that he had been commanded "by the word of the LORD" not to eat or drink or to return by the way he had come. No reason is given for this injunction. Whatever the rationale for that commandment, there is no question that the man of God knew that he was so charged. (See Reflections at 13:33-34.)

1 Kings 13:11-32, No Excuse Is Acceptable for Disobedience

COMMENTARY

The encounter was reported to an unnamed old prophet who lived in Bethel. His response is immediate. He hastens to find the man of God from Judah to invite him to dine with him. We are not told the reason for this eager invitation, but one recognizes the similarity to Jeroboam's bidding in v. 7. In any case, it is plain now that Jeroboam was not motivated by gratitude for the healing of his withered hand. When the man of God declined the invitation of the old prophet, as he did that of Jeroboam, the old man blatantly lied, saying that he had been visited by an angel who told him to issue the invitation. So, despite his own certainty of what the Lord had commanded him earlier (vv. 9, 17), the Judean man of God was lured home by the unnamed prophet from Bethel.

It is clear by now that the old man from Bethel was a false prophet. Yet it is he who received and pronounced the word of the Lord against the man of God from Judah. For his disobedience, the latter would be deprived of burial in his ancestral tomb. Then, on his way home after the forbidden communion, the man of God was met by a lion and killed. Contrary to expectations, the lion merely stood beside the corpse instead of mauling it, a fact that is reiterated by the narrator (vv. 24-25, 28). It also did not attack the man's donkey (vv. 24, 28), as would be natural. The narrator thus makes the point that the killing was divinely ordained.

The old prophet declared that it was the Lord who had slain the man of God because of the man's disobedience. He buried the man in the grave that he had apparently reserved for himself, and he mourned for the man of God, calling him "my brother" (v. 30). Then, he instructed his sons that he, too, should be buried in that grave with the man of God.

Apparently, the false prophet wanted to be associated with the man whose prophecy he knew would certainly come to pass and, according to the Greek, because he knew that the tomb of the man of God would not be desecrated. (See Reflections at 13:33-34.)

1 Kings 13:33-34, Jeroboam Continues His Disobedience

COMMENTARY

The deuteronomistic editor concludes that Jeroboam did not repent despite the preceding story. The introductory words are ambiguous in Hebrew: אחר הדבר הזה (*'aḥar haddābār hazzeh*), "after this word/matter/event." We cannot be sure if the preceding incident itself or the account of it or the word of the Lord is meant. To the deuteronomistic editor, the fate of the man of God should have been an object lesson to Jeroboam; the story was the word of the Lord. The man of God who had prophesied the truth, who had tried so assiduously to obey the Lord but was finally tricked into disobedience, was slain for his disobedience. How much more certainly would a blatant sinner like Jeroboam be punished? Yet, Jeroboam remained unrepentant.

Rather, he continued to appoint priests at the local sanctuaries—indeed, appointing anyone who wished to be a priest, without regard for lineage. Through the prophecy of Ahijah the Shilonite, the Lord had promised Jeroboam that he would reign over Israel (the ten tribes of the north) and that he would have an enduring house like that of David, provided that he remain obedient to the Lord's commandments (11:37-38). Jeroboam, however, sealed his own fate through his disobedience, and he set Israel on the course for destruction. By contrast, Rehoboam and the house of Judah, "obeyed the word of the LORD" (12:24), and so there would remain "a lamp" before the Lord in Jerusalem (11:36).

REFLECTIONS

1. This passage raises a number of awkward theological and ethical questions. It offends our moral sensibilities to think that God might actually have allowed a deceitful prophet to lure a sincere, but naive, man of God to sin. Not only that, but as if to rub salt in the wound, God then uses that false prophet to proclaim a word of judgment against the man of God. Nothing is said of the punishment of the false prophet, and, indeed, he was able to make arrangements regarding the proper interment of his own remains. The poor man of God from Judah seems to suffer more than the other characters in the story, all because of one naive error in judgment. Even Jeroboam lived to see another day.

Despite such an offending issue, the main point of the narrative seems clear enough: God demands obedience without compromise. From beginning to end, Jeroboam seemed oblivious to this truth. Even the frightening account of the fate of the man of God did not seem to have fazed him, and so he did not turn from his evil ways. The consequences of his disobedience are dire, however—not for him alone but for an entire nation. Disobedience to God can have devastating consequences that affect more than the disobedient person. This is the primary issue that the narrative raises.

2. Still, there is a lesson for us in the fate of the man of God. Whatever the author's intention might have been, we cannot help being drawn to that peculiar story. It is, after all, with that man of God that most of us readily identify. Most of us probably do not see ourselves as flagrant sinners like Jeroboam. Nor are we deliberately deceptive like the old prophet from Bethel. Rather, like the man of God, most of us probably are sincere in our desire to obey God and do try our best to do so. For us, the lesson is, perhaps, that we should not be too quick to cast the proverbial stones. Even as we proclaim the word of the Lord to the likes of Jeroboam in our time, we must recognize that we, too, are susceptible to the same tendency to be disobedient (see 1 Cor 10:12). The danger may, indeed, lie in the fact that our sins are usually not quite so blatant as Jeroboam's or that they seem so much more excusable. Most of us do not have the kind of clout to commit sins that so affect the nation as a king in Israel might have had, or as an American president might have. Our offenses are not "high crimes and misdemeanors." Lacking an exalted post, most of us are faithful, decent people. In the fate of the man of God, however, we find a warning not to be too complacent and not to be too sure that we are on the side of God. Jeroboam did not heed this word (13:33), but we must.

3. Finally, we have to admit that the moral problems we have with the text cannot be explained away and that we may have no answers to them. We recognize that the word of God comes to us through this culturally conditioned and imperfect story. That is the amazing thing about the way God works. The word of God may be heard despite the story's limitations. So, too, the word of God was proclaimed through the man of God who was imperfect—as we all are.

1 KINGS 14:1-20, JUDGMENT ON THE HOUSE OF JEROBOAM

COMMENTARY

Chapter 13 ends by noting the recalcitrance of Jeroboam, despite the word of the Lord. Therefore, it is stated as a matter of fact that the house of Jeroboam will be "cut off" and destroyed from the face of the earth (13:33-34). Immediately, then, we are told of the illness of Jeroboam's son (probably his firstborn) "at that time" (14:1; Abijah's position as the heir apparent is, perhaps, indicated by the fact that all Israel mourned for him when he died [v. 18]). The reader knows that this is the beginning of the end of the house of Jeroboam. The king, too, must have had an inkling of what his son's illness portended, for he sent his wife to the prophet Ahijah at Shiloh.

It was Ahijah, of course, who had prophesied Jeroboam's coming to power. This fact is noted by Jeroboam himself in his instruction to his wife. What he does not mention, but the reader already knows (11:33-34), is that the prophecy included the promise of an enduring dynasty for him, provided that Jeroboam was obedient to the Lord (11:38). It is probably his recognition of this fact that prevents him from going to see the prophet himself; it is probably this fact that necessitates his wife's disguise and bringing of offerings of gifts that commoners might bring—only ten loaves, some cakes, and a jar of honey. Apparently Jeroboam did not want to remind the prophet of what had been prophesied in regard to him, but he wanted to know what would happen to his son and no doubt hoped to receive a different word from the prophet.

The ploy fails. Ahijah is now old and cannot see, so the disguise of Jeroboam's queen is for nought. Indeed, the Lord tells the prophet what to expect and what to say. The narrator thus makes the point that it is not so much the predictive ability of Ahijah that is at issue but the will of the Lord. The disguised queen does not get a chance to go through with her charade. As soon as Ahijah hears her footsteps, he identifies her and tells her that he has bad news for her. Even though he is blind, he hears and he sees through the disguise. He sends an oracle to Jeroboam through her, reiterating the word of the Lord that was first delivered to Jeroboam (vv. 7-8; see 12:27-38). Jeroboam's sins are enumerated (v. 9), sins that have provoked the anger of God. And that terrible anger is evident as the punishment for the house of Jeroboam is spelled out in harsh, even vulgar, terms (vv. 10-11).[52] Not only will the men of the dynasty be killed, but they will be left unburied as well, abandoned to the dogs in the city and to the birds of prey in the countryside. The immediate consequence of this oracle is that Abijah will die as soon as the queen returns to the capital. This is the direct answer to the question that Jeroboam never had a chance to ask.

The oracle points beyond familial questions, however. It points to the destiny of the entire kingdom, from the disastrous succession to Jeroboam's throne (v. 14), through the instability of the kingdom (they will be shaken like a reed in the water), to their destruction and exile by the Assyrians ("beyond the Euphrates," v. 15). Clearly, the sins of Jeroboam affect not only his family and his generation, but also the future of his people. Accordingly, Abijah dies as soon as the queen returns. Jeroboam himself dies and is succeeded by Nadab (901–900 BCE), although the reader already knows that the fate of the kingdom has been sealed.

The story of Jeroboam's reign has been told in a fast-paced manner in 1 Kings 11–14. Events occur one after another: Israel breaks free of the oppression of Rehoboam, Jeroboam comes to power, he strengthens his position in the north and establishes rival sanctuaries there, his actions are condemned, and judgment is proclaimed upon his house. The editorial note in vv. 19-20 jolts the reader into the realization that these events, in fact, took place over a twenty-two-year period. There are other details regarding Jeroboam— "how he warred and how he reigned"—that were supposedly in the "Book of the Annals of the Kings of Israel," readily available for the original readers to consult. Modern readers interested in various historical details may, likewise, turn to other sources for such details and reconstruct other explanations for the demise of Jeroboam's dynasty. The narrative in 1 Kings provides only the theological rationale for the fall of Jeroboam and the eventual destruction of his kingdom. The focus of the narrative, therefore, is judgment on the house of Jeroboam for the sins that he committed.

Yet, there are elements that cannot be easily harmonized with the harsh and decisive judgment. Despite the certainty of Abijah's death as the first installment in the fulfillment of the prophecy of doom, he would apparently not be denied a burial, as the word of judgment had proclaimed for all males in the house of Jeroboam. Not only would he be accorded proper burial, but also he would even be mourned by all Israel. Amid the reality of divine anger there was ever so slight an indication of God's favor: "There is found in him [Abijah] something pleasing to the LORD" (v. 13). Jeroboam himself does not suffer the fate prophesied for all the males in his family, and the dynasty does not end immediately; Nadab, another son of Jeroboam, comes to power as one "raised up" by the Lord (v. 14). As for Jeroboam's people, their punishment would come not strictly because of Jeroboam's sins but because their own idolatrous acts (v. 15): Jeroboam caused them to sin, but they would do so themselves. Hence, despite their destined destruction, a question comes that almost invites a response—a question that makes no logical sense in its context and, accordingly, baffles all translators: "This is the day! What, then, even now?" (14:14). The question—perhaps a later gloss—leaves open the possibility that the Israelite reader might alter the inevitable destiny with death after all.[53]

---

52. Most modern translations use euphemisms, but the Hebrew for "male" (משתין בקיר *mašṭîn běqîr*) is literally "one who pisses against the wall" (see KJV). The idiom ועזוב עצור (*āṣur wĕ 'āzub*) is obscure (NRSV, "bond or free"; NIV, "slave or"). The idiom may refer to those who are still under parental control (lit., "restrained") and those who have been left to their own devices, hence "minors [or] adult" or the like.

53. On the hermeneutical function of this "gloss," see Nelson, *First and Second Kings*, 96-97.

REFLECTIONS

The most obvious lesson of this chapter, of course, is the importance of faithfulness and obedience: God's punishment is inevitable in the face of the persistence of sin. The passage makes plain, too, that one's sin may have deadly consequences for others as well. Jeroboam sinned, but others died because of it or were drawn also to sin and, thus, to bring destruction upon themselves. Still, there are other important insights that the text raises for the reader.

1. God is in charge, even though people may be inclined to think that they can resolve their problems at the human level. Jeroboam sees his problem in purely human terms and tries to resolve it by manipulating others to give him the answers he seeks. God, however, intervenes with a word of judgment. The passage makes the point that our true intentions are known to God, even if we try to hide them. God sees through our pretenses, our charades, our attempts to cover up our sins.

2. Human sins bring the inevitable judgment of God; yet, God may still provide signs of grace and glimmers of hope amid the darkness of sin and death. Despite the certainty of doom that sin brings, God persistently holds out the possibility of an appropriate response from those whom God so loves.

1 KINGS 14:21–15:24, REHOBOAM, ABIJAH, AND ASA OF JUDAH

OVERVIEW

The preceding unit ends with the death of Jeroboam and the accession of his son Nadab to the throne in Israel (14:19-20). As if to reinforce the point about the end of the house of Jeroboam, the narrative focus shifts immediately to the house of David in the south, where the Davidic dynasty continues in relative peace and apparently without regard for the characters of the kings in Jerusalem: Rehoboam, the son of Solomon, is succeeded by his son Abijah, who is succeeded by his own son Asa. Whereas the fate of Israel is sealed by the disobedience of Jeroboam, hope remains in Judah because of the dual election of Jerusalem and David.

1 Kings 14:21-31, The Reign of Rehoboam

COMMENTARY

The reader has already been introduced to Solomon's son Rehoboam in 12:1-24. There, however, Rehoboam is not the main interest of the narrator. Rather, he is a foil for Jeroboam; Rehoboam's arrogant and oppressive ways provided the immediate cause for the rebellion of the ten tribes of Israel. Now in this section of the text, the report is focused on Rehoboam's own reign in Judah (922–915 BCE).

Rehoboam is said to be king not only "in Judah" but also, specifically, *in Jerusalem*. His successors are also typically said to reign over Judah in Jerusalem (15:2, 10). This detail is significant, for Jerusalem is identified as a city that the Lord "had chosen out of all the tribes of Israel" (v. 21). The divine election of Jerusalem stands over against the absence of an acceptable shrine for the Lord in the northern kingdom. It is partly for this reason that Judah appears to be judged less harshly than Israel.

At the beginning and the end of the unit (vv. 21, 31), Rehoboam is identified as the son of Naamah, an Ammonite woman. Solomon had married many foreign women who had led him away from complete devotion to the Lord (11:1-8). Accordingly, he had "followed" various foreign gods, including "Milcom the abomination of the Ammonites," and he also built high places for these gods, including one for Milcom of the Ammonites in the mountain opposite Jerusalem—namely, the Mount of Olives. The stage had been set for Judah to sin, and this is what they did. In Rehoboam's reign, Judah even sinned "more than all their ancestors" (v. 22). Along with the high places that they built for themselves, they erected מצבות (*maṣṣēbôt*; NRSV, "pillars"; NIV, "sacred stones") and אשרים (*ăšērîm*; NRSV, "sacred poles"; NIV, "Asherah poles"), various Canaanite cultic objects that the people of God were supposed to smash and cut down (Deut 7:5; 12:2-5). They committed "all the abominations of the nations" that the Lord had driven out of the land for Israel's sake. The implication, of course, is that they themselves deserved to be driven out of the land.

Pharaoh Shishak's invasion and the consequent plunder of the Temple in Jerusalem are inevitably seen as the results of the sins of Judah. They foreshadow future plunder and the eventual destruction of the Temple in the chosen city. The glory of Solomon's Temple is tarnished in the hands of his son. Rehoboam replaced Solomon's shields of gold with shields made of bronze. Even so, the Temple survived Shishak's raid because it was the place that the Lord had chosen.

Despite the sins of Judah in the reign of Rehoboam, there is no oracle of doom corresponding to the lengthy one that Jeroboam received (vv. 7-16). For his sins, the house of Jeroboam will be cut off; his dynasty will be brought to an end. By contrast, the house of Rehoboam survives, despite the chastisement that God brought by way of Shishak's invasion and plunder. Thus, whereas Abijah the son of Jeroboam dies prematurely, Abijah the son of Rehoboam lives to succeed him (v. 31).[54] (See Reflections at 15:9-24.)

54. The NRSV, following most Hebrew MSS, has the name as "Abijam" (a unique and improbable name in Hebrew), whereas the NIV follows some Hebrew MSS and the parallel account in 2 Chr 12:16 in reading the name as "Abijah," a name reflected also in the Greek translation and in Josephus *Antiquities of the Jews* 8.9.1.

1 Kings 15:1-8, The Reign of Abijah

COMMENTARY

According to a parallel text (2 Chr 11:20-22), Abijah was the son of Rehoboam and his favorite wife, Maacah, and resigned around 915–913 BCE.[55] This Abijah sinned as his father had done. Yet, he did not suffer the fate of the other Abijah, Jeroboam's son, who died prematurely. Clearly, the continuation of the house of David was not due to the righteousness of David's successors in Jerusalem, but simply because of the will of the sovereign God. Despite the sins of David's successors, there will always be a lamp in Jerusalem for David's sake (v. 4; see 11:36). This everlasting promise was given because David did what was right in the eyes of the Lord. Yet, it is acknowledged that David's righteousness, which is regarded by the narrator as paradigmatic for the Judean kings, was not without blemish: David did not turn aside from what the Lord had commanded him, "except in the matter of Uriah the Hittite"—i.e., the murder of Uriah to cover up David's scandalous affair with Bathsheba, Uriah's wife. God's acceptance of David and his house was from beginning to end an act of sheer grace. (See Reflections at 15:9-24.)

55. This, however, contradicts 2 Chr 13:2, which gives Abijah's mother's name as "Micaiah the daughter of Uriel of Gibeah." For a discussion of this crux, see S. Japhet, *1 & 2 Chronicles*, OTL (Louisville: Westminster/ John Knox, 1993) 670-72.

1 Kings 15:9-24, The Reign of Asa

COMMENTARY

Abijah is succeed by his son Asa (913–873 BCE), who came to the throne in Jerusalem while Jeroboam was still in power in Israel and reigned forty-one years. Accordingly, his reign overlapped with seven of his counterparts in the north: Jeroboam, Nadab, Baasha, Elah, Zimri, Omri, and Ahab (see 16:29). He was, by all accounts (see 2 Chr 14:1-8), a reformist king who (1) expelled the cult prostitutes,[56] (2) removed all the idols that his predecessors had set up, (3) deposed the idolatrous queen mother,[57] and (4) destroyed the queen mother's cult image of Asherah. Although the high places of the land were not eliminated, Asa's heart was true to the Lord until the day of his death. He returned the votive gifts of his father to the Temple and he himself brought votive gifts.

56. The masculine plural in Hebrew (קדשים *qĕdēšîm*) is probably intended to be inclusive of male and female cult prostitutes (see NIV; NRSV).
57. Assuming the correctness of 15:2, we should probably follow the NIV in taking the word אם (*'em*) in 15:10 to mean "grandmother," instead of " mother" (so NRSV).

In contrast to his father, Abijah, Asa is depicted in relatively positive terms. Indeed, his attitudes and actions anticipate those of reformist kings Hezekiah (2 Kgs 18:3-6) and Josiah (2 Kgs 23:1-26). Yet, all was not well in Judah. Conflict with Israel prompted Asa to take drastic action. He removed the temple and palace treasures to bribe the Arameans to break off their alliance with Israel. Ironically, he did to the Temple and the palace what Pharaoh Shishak had done during the reign of Rehoboam (14:26). While Asa brought in votive gifts for the Temple, he also removed treasures from it.

REFLECTIONS

The accounts in this unit are poignant in their contrast to the preceding story of Jeroboam's demise (12:25–14:20). Whereas the emphasis in the latter is on the essentiality of obedience to the Lord, the underlying emphasis in the accounts of the reigns of David's successors in Jerusalem is the election of Jerusalem and the eternal promise of God to David. The sovereign God who demands obedience uncompromisingly also mysteriously saves without regard for one's character.

1 KINGS 15:25–16:34, ISRAEL'S KINGS FROM NADAB TO AHAB

OVERVIEW

Following the account of the long reign of the Judean king Asa (15:9-24), we find a series of reports on six of his contemporaries in the northern kingdom: (1) Nadab (15:25-32); (2) Baasha (15:33–16:7); (3) Elah (16:8-14); (4) Zimri (16:16-20); (5) Omri (16:21-28); and (6) Ahab (16:29-34). On the one hand, the reports read like a historical work: The duration of each reign is specified and synchronized with the reign of the Judean counterpart. At the end of each report, the reader is referred to the further materials in the archives, as it were. On the other hand, the accounts are rather formulaic: The overriding criterion for evaluation of the kings is their wickedness, notably how

they have followed the way of Jeroboam. Consequently, the reports are all more or less of the same length: Baasha's twenty-two-year reign receives about the same amount of space as the two-year span of Nadab and Elah, or even the seven-day rule of Zimri. Likewise, Omri, who reigned twelve years and began a powerful dynasty, gets the same brief and negative evaluation. Despite the chronological notices, cross-referencing, historical details, and the mention of archival materials, these reports are not intended to be read as a disinterested history of these kings. Their purpose is, rather, primarily theological: to show the consequences of unfaithfulness to the Lord.

1 Kings 15:25-32, The Reign of Nadab, Son of Jeroboam

Commentary

The predicted end of the house of Jeroboam did not come immediately with Jeroboam's demise. Ahijah the Shilonite had prophesied the annihilation of all males in the family, and accordingly Abijah, presumably the firstborn of Jeroboam, died prematurely. Upon Jeroboam's death, however, his son Nadab succeeded him on the throne. The accession and reign of Jeroboam's son might have raised the possibility of hope in Israel. Nadab, however, did nothing to warrant the

reversal of the doom prophesied against the house of Jeroboam; he acted wickedly and followed the way of his father. Accordingly, he was assassinated by Baasha of the house of Issachar; Nadab and all his family were killed, thus fulfilling the prophecy of Ahijah (14:10-11). Despite the harsh judgment against Jeroboam's house, the narrator makes it clear that Nadab paid for his own sins, and not for the sins of his father. (See Reflections at 16:29-34.)

1 Kings 15:33–16:7, The Reign of Baasha of the House of Issachar

Commentary

Despite being in power for nearly a quarter of a century (900–877 BCE), Baasha receives a report of about the same length as that of Nadab, who had reigned only two years. The main point that the deuteronomistic historian wants to make is that Baasha also did what was evil in the sight of the Lord and that he perpetuated the sin of Jeroboam. Just as the end of the house of Jeroboam had been

proclaimed by the prophet Ahijah, so also the fate of Baasha was proclaimed by the prophet Jehu, in language reminiscent of Ahijah's words (16:2-4; see 14:9-12). Baasha was killed because he, like Jeroboam, sinned (15:34; 16:2-3, 7) and because he had murdered the family of Jeroboam (15:29; 16:7). (See Reflections at 16:29-34.)

1 Kings 16:8-14, The Reign of Elah, Son of Baasha

Commentary

As with the house of Jeroboam, Baasha was succeeded by his son. Here, again, there is ever so slight a sign of hope that the prophetic prediction of the end of the house of Baasha might be stayed. Elah, the son and successor of Baasha (877–876 BCE), did

nothing to warrant that hope, however. He acted faithlessly. Hence, he was assassinated by a usurper after having reigned only two years. Elah paid for his own sins, and not for the sins of his father. (See Reflections at 16:29-34.)

1 Kings 16:15-20, The Reign of Zimri, Commander of the Chariotry

COMMENTARY

The usurper Zimri reigned only seven days, committing suicide in the palace when he knew that he had been defeated. He, too, is judged to have done evil in the sight of the Lord, perpetuating the sin of Jeroboam. (See Reflections at 16:29-34.)

1 Kings 16:21-28, The Beginning of the House of Omri

COMMENTARY

From the standpoint of secular history, Omri's reign (876–869 BCE) was a significant one. We know from the Moabite Stone that in his reign Israel extended its influence over its neighboring states.[58] Indeed, with Omri we have a dynasty that lasted through the reigns of his son Ahab and his grandsons Ahaziah and Joram. His influence was so great that even after his dynasty had come to an end, the Assyrians continued to refer to the Israelites as "the house of Omri." Yet, Omri's secular successes were of little interest to the deuteronomistic historian, who simply refers the reader to the archival materials for Omri's acts, not mentioned in this account. Of his achievements, only the establishment of Samaria as the capital of the northern kingdom is noted. Otherwise, Omri is dismissed with the other kings who sinned against the Lord and continued in the idolatrous ways of Jeroboam. (See Reflections at 16:29-34.)

58. See *ANET*, 320.

1 Kings 16:29-34, Ahab the Son of Omri

COMMENTARY

These verses introduce the reader to Ahab (869–850 BCE), whose reign becomes the focus through the end of 1 Kings. Like his father, Omri, Ahab is recognized in extra-biblical sources as a powerful king. He is mentioned in the "Monolith Inscription" of the Assyrian king Shalmanezer III as having contributed a substantial force to the anti-Assyrian coalition at the Battle of Qarqar in 853 BCE.[59] His secular success, however, is of little interest to the deuteronomistic historian. Rather, the deuteronomist is primarily concerned with the religious implications of Ahab's activities. Accordingly, the first notice of his reign concerns his marriage to Jezebel, a Sidonian princess and devotee of the Canaanite god Baal. Ahab reportedly erected an altar for Baal in the temple of Baal that he had built in Samaria. He also built an אשרה (*'ăšērâ*; NRSV, "a sacred pole"; NIV, "Asherah pole") in the city, in contravention of deuteronomic law. Thus he is judged to have done more to provoke the anger of God than had all his predecessors (vv. 30, 33).

59. See *ANET*, 279.

REFLECTIONS

It is a commonplace in modern scholarship to point to the incompleteness of the historical records in the book of Kings. Particularly in the accounts of the reigns of Omri and Ahab, there are extra-biblical records that show that the kings who are summarily dismissed as unfaithful leaders of Israel may, in fact, turn out to have been powerful and influential rulers according to secular criteria. Yet, the lesson in this version of history is that God judges leaders not by popular measures of success but by their faithfulness to divine will. These stories prompt us to consider history beyond the interplay of social, economic, and political factors to the issues of faith and obedience. Beyond this general lesson, the accounts also convey two theological truths that are not easily reconciled: the will of God, on the one hand, and human responsibility, on the other hand.

1. God's will is being worked out in history. Even though human beings seem to be the principal actors in the historical arena, it is God who works behind the scenes to bring about events. Leaders owe their positions to God, for it is God who exalts them and grants them their place in history (16:2). It is the same God, however, who brings them down. The reader already knows that the tumultuous events were brought about in Israel because it was God's will to punish Jeroboam for his apostasy.

2. Despite the will of God, human beings are responsible for their actions. Nadab was punished, not because of the sins of his father, Jeroboam, but because of his own sins. Elah was not punished because of the sins of his father, Baasha, but because of his own sins. Even though it was the will of God to destroy the house of Jeroboam, Baasha was held responsible for their destruction (16:7).

1 KINGS 17:1-24, THE LIVING GOD WHO SUSTAINS AND REVIVES

OVERVIEW

In this chapter, the reader encounters the prophet Elijah for the very first time. This prophet will be the focus of the narrator's interest in 1 Kings 17–19, 21 and 2 Kings 1–2. The chapter itself may be divided into three subunits: (1) vv. 1-7, God's provision for Elijah through the ravens; (2) vv. 8-16, God's provision for Elijah through a Sidonian widow; and (3) vv. 17-24, God's resuscitation of the widow's dead child. Unifying the literary unit are two themes: *Life* is made possible by the Lord alone, and the importance of the *word*, meaning the word of the Lord as spoken through the prophet. Accordingly, various forms of the Hebrew verb חיה (*ḥāyâ*, "to live") recur (vv. 1, 12, 22-23), alongside repeated occurrences of the Hebrew term דבר (*dābār*, "word," vv. 1-2, 5, 8, 13, 15, 24). Over against Baal, the Canaanite god of life, it is affirmed that Israel's God is the true Lord of life, with power over the forces of nature and even over death itself.

1 Kings 17:1-7, Elijah Is Fed by Ravens

COMMENTARY

Elijah appears on the scene abruptly. Apart from his name, he is identified only as "the Tishbite," an obscure designation that the ancient versions understood to be a reference to his place of origin, an unknown site somewhere in Gilead called "Tishbe" (so NIV, NRSV).[60] His first utterance is an oath in the name of the Lord: "As the LORD the God of Israel lives . . ." (v. 2). Although this oath formula is quite common in the Hebrew Bible, its usage in this context is particularly suggestive, for the issue at hand is the Lord as the source of life. The formula is especially poignant inasmuch as it is addressed to Ahab, who, we learned in 16:31-33, has married Jezebel, a devotee of the Canaanite god Baal, and has built an altar and a temple for Baal in Samaria, thus provoking the anger of "the LORD, the God of Israel." In Canaanite religion, Baal the storm god is the one who brings rain and, thus, the possibility of life on earth. When there is drought, it is presumed that death (which is deified in Canaanite mythology) has been victorious and that Baal is dead. Conversely, when there is rain, it is presumed that Baal is alive and that death has been defeated:

Let the heavens rain oil,
The wadis run with honey
Then I will know that Mightiest B[aal] lives,
The Prince, Lord of the earth is alive.[61]

Elijah's oath, however, affirms that it is the Lord who lives, and the rest of the narrative will make plain that it is the Lord who makes life possible (see, esp., v. 23). Elijah, as the servant of the Lord ("before whom I stand,"

v. 1), also dares to declare that there will be "neither dew nor rain," except by his word. The servant of the Lord thus challenges the power of Baal directly, for drought is a sign of the powerlessness of Baal, according to Canaanite lore:

Seven years Baal is absent,
Eight, the Rider of Clouds:
No dew, no downpour,
No swirling of the deeps,
No welcome voice of Baal.[62]

The narrator does not tell us the reaction of King Ahab, but it is obvious that Elijah's life is in danger, for he is instructed by the Lord to flee to the Wadi Cherith, presumably one of the many deep and wide ravines east of the Jordan. Elijah is called to leave the promised land, as it were, and to go east of the Jordan, whence Israel came. There he is to drink from the wadi, and the Lord ordains ravens to feed him. The latter element is ironic in two important ways: Ravens are regarded in the Torah as unclean birds (Lev 11:15; Deut 14:14), and they are birds of prey (Job 38:41; Prov 30:17; Isa 34:11). These unclean birds of prey miraculously feed Elijah, and he is, indeed, fed well—with bread and meat twice a day. The narrator is clear that this feeding is done at the command of the Lord. The water in the wadi, however, dries up because there is no rain. In other words, the provision that might possibly be construed as having come from Baal, who is understood in Canaanite religion to be the lord of the rain, ends. In contrast, the provision that is explicitly a consequence of the Lord's command is abundant. The Lord provides miraculously and in ways that people might not expect—even through creatures that are deemed unclean. (See Reflections at 17:17-24.)

---

60. Whereas the Greek translations read "the Tishbite from Tishbe," the Hebrew has Elijah as one "among the sojourners of Gilead," and "Tishbe" does not appear as a place-name anywhere.

61. Translated by Mark S. Smith in *Ugaritic Narrative Poetry*, ed. Simon B. Parker, SBL Writings from the Ancient World Series, vol. 9 (Atlanta: Scholars, 1997) 157, col. III, ll. 6-9. In this text, Baal is known as the prince (Ugaritic *zbl*, an element in the name "Jezebel").

62. Translation by Simon B. Parker in Parker, *Ugaritic Narrative Poetry*, 69, col. I, ll. 42-46.

1 Kings 17:8-16, Elijah Is Fed by a Sidonian Widow

COMMENTARY

Elijah is ordered by the Lord to go to the city of Zarephath ("Sarepta" in the Greek), a Phoenician commercial capital known for its exporting of various goods, including wine, grain, and oil. Yet, this city in Baal's territory is ironically in dire straits because of a drought. Just as the Lord ordained the ravens to feed Elijah, so also the Lord now ordains a widow to feed him. Although she apparently does not know it, this Sidonian woman is to be used by the Lord for salvific purposes. In this she stands in contrast to the other Sidonian woman, Jezebel, the Sidonian princess whom Ahab married (16:31) and who would be a champion for Baal in Israel. Again, it is ironic that the Lord would have a Phoenician, presumably a worshiper of Baal, to feed Elijah. Not only that, but she is a widow, which in ancient Near Eastern cultures means that she is probably destitute. In the OT, widows are typically associated with the neediest elements of society, the orphans and the poor

(Job 24:3-4; 31:16-17; Isa 10:2; Zech 7:10). Yet, it is this widow in a land devastated by drought who is to feed Elijah, and it is to her that he turns for sustenance. She who has such scarce means is instrumental in God's plan to provide for others (cf. Mark 12:41-44).

The widow swears that she has little to spare, using the very oath formula that is put in the mouth of Elijah at the beginning of the passage: "As the LORD your God lives . . ." (v. 12; see also v. 1). According to Elijah, the Lord gives assurance that the provisions at hand will not be diminished: "The jar of meal will not be emptied and the jug of oil will not fail until the LORD sends rain on the earth." If it had not been clear before in the narrative, it is certainly clear now that it is the Lord who gives rain, not Baal. This is, indeed, the word of the Lord proclaimed to a worshiper of Baal in the territory of Baal, the homeland of Jezebel. (See Reflections at 17:17-24.)

1 Kings 17:17-24, The Resurrection of a Dead Boy

COMMENTARY

The final crisis in the chapter involves the fate of the Sidonian woman's son, who had become so severely ill that "there was no more breath left in him" (v. 17). The stakes are raised higher in this instance than in the other two vignettes in the chapter. Whereas the Lord has been able to avert death by providing first for Elijah through the ravens (vv. 1-7) and then through the widow (vv. 8-16), the challenge is now posed in the form of a boy who has already died. Elijah, who has

apparently been received as a guest in the house of the woman, intercedes on the boy's behalf. The Lord hears his intercession, and the boy is miraculously revived. Thus the story claims that Elijah's deity, the God of Israel, is truly the Lord of life, for even one who has already died could be brought to life again by that deity's power. Important, too, is the claim that the miracle was accomplished as a result of the prophetic word (v. 24).

REFLECTIONS

1. Along with other stories pertaining to Elijah, the miracles in this chapter have been commemorated in music and in art. In these re-creations of the story, attention is invariably drawn to the supramundane origin of Elijah's experiences. That is, indeed, the main point of the passage: It is the Lord, the God of Israel, who brings about these wonders. So, too, we dare to believe that things that seem impossible to human beings can be brought about by the Lord: Birds of prey may provide nourishment; the poor may have their victuals wondrously replenished; and even the dead may be resurrected. It is the Lord and no other god who performs such miracles. So we are called to believe as well.

2. The wonder of these stories resides not merely in their supernatural character, however. One is amazed, too, at the wondrous freedom and sovereignty of God. The deity uses even creatures that are regarded as ritually unclean to fulfill the divine purpose. So, too, the sovereign God is free to act beyond the borders of Israel, even through Gentile worshipers of foreign gods. This point is picked up by Jesus in his inaugural sermon in his hometown synagogue (Luke 4:25-26). Jesus observes that there were many widows in Israel in Elijah's time; yet, the man of God went to a foreign land and sought out the foreign woman. The Sidonian woman is apparently not a worshiper of Elijah's God, for she refers to Elijah's deity as "your God" (17:12). Yet, she is the recipient of God's miraculous provision. In receiving divine favor, the Phoenician woman becomes a prototype for other Gentile women who receive God's grace through their encounters with Jesus (see Matt 15:21-28; Mark 7:24-30). God's universal love reaches beyond the boundaries of nationality, ethnicity, and even religious affiliation.

3. Elijah is seen in the New Testament as a forerunner of Jesus. Explicitly and implicitly, Elijah's ministry is seen as a model for the ministry of Jesus. Appropriately, therefore, most lectionaries that list 1 Kgs 17:17-24 juxtapose the passage with the account of Jesus' raising of the son of the widow of Nain (Luke 7:11-17). There are, indeed, suggestive parallels between the two accounts: the city gate, the plight of a widow, a son who has died, the miraculous resuscitation, the return of the son to his mother. The miraculous resuscitation of life in each case leads to the recognition that God has acted through an earthly intermediary.

In the New Testament, however, Jesus surpasses Elijah. Whereas Elijah is the beneficiary of God's miraculous provision of nourishment and he proclaims that God will sustain the hungry despite the meagerness of what is available, Jesus himself would miraculously feed a multitude with a seemingly meager amount of food (Matt 14:13-21; 15:32-39). Whereas Elijah appeals to God to revive the widow's son, Jesus himself commands the dead to rise again. Indeed, the culmination of the story of Jesus in the New Testament is that he represents the power of God to grant and sustain life, his own resurrection from the dead being the ultimate testimony to the triumph of God over death (1 Cor 15:20-26).

1 KINGS 18:1-46, EQUIVOCAL FAITH

OVERVIEW

This chapter concerns the reemergence of Elijah from hiding and his face-to-face confrontation with Ahab, which results in a contest on Mt. Carmel to demonstrate the power of the Lord and the powerlessness of Baal. The dramatic contest on Mt. Carmel was prompted by the people's religious equivocation as a result of Ahab's troubling patronage of Baal religion within Israel.

1 Kings 18:1-2a, Introduction

COMMENTARY

The introductory words of chapter 18 indicate continuity with the preceding literary unit. A long time has passed since the drought had come by the word of the Lord given through Elijah (see 17:1). Now the word of the Lord comes again to Elijah "in the third year," presumably the third year of the drought (the NRSV supplies "of the drought" in v. 1). This notice of the drought's duration is important, for it establishes the fact that at least one full cycle of the seasons has come and gone, with no sign of the timely return of rejuvenating rain, which in Canaanite mythology would have been a testimony to Baal's resurrection.[63] To the narrator, the deadly dry

spell would end neither by the power of Baal nor by the ritual manipulation of his worshipers, but by the word of the Lord through the prophet. There will be no rain except by the Lord's word (see 17:1). So that is why Elijah has to emerge from hiding: He is to effect the return of life-giving rain by the word of the Lord. Of the various English translations, the NAB best captures the purposeful nature of the Lord's command: " 'Go, present yourself to Ahab,' [the Lord] said, '*that* I may send rain upon the earth' " (italics added). Accordingly, Elijah obeys, and so the reader should now expect the rain to come.

63. The "third year" may imply three actual years or just one full year with a part of the preceding and part of the succeeding year.

1 Kings 18:2b-16, Obadiah's Equivocation

COMMENTARY

18:2b-6. The narrator does not immediately report on the expected encounter between Elijah and Ahab, however. Instead, the reader is introduced to Obadiah, who is said to be the chief steward in Ahab's palace, the ancient Israelite equivalent of the chief of staff in the U.S. White House. Like its modern American counterpart, the position of chief steward of the palace in ancient Israel and Judah was a powerful and prestigious one. Obadiah would have had to earn Ahab's complete trust, and the extent of that trust is evident in the fact that it is to Obadiah alone that Ahab turns to deal with the national crisis at hand. Yet, Obadiah, whose name means "servant/worshiper of the LORD" in Hebrew, also "feared the LORD greatly" (so we should read with the KJV, rather than the NRSV's "revered the LORD greatly" and the NIV's "was a devout believer"). Hence, when Jezebel tried to have all the prophets of the Lord killed off, Obadiah hid a hundred of them and sustained them with food and water. On the one hand, his furtive action is reminiscent of

the Hebrew midwives in Egypt, who "feared God" (so the NRSV and the NIV correctly have it) and helped to save the infant boys whom Pharaoh had ordered to be killed (Exod 1:15-29). On the other hand, his feeding of the prophets who were in hiding (v. 4) recalls the feeding of Elijah by the ravens (17:4) and by the widow in Zarephath (17:9); the Hebrew verb (כול *kûl*) is the same in all these instances. Obadiah is seen as an instrument of the Lord, even though he is also a trusted official in Ahab's government.

The severity of the famine in the capital forces Ahab to act. His first priority, it seems, is the care of his "horses and mules"—that is, animals used for the convenience of military personnel, nobles, and members of the royal family.[64] Famine and drought are in the land, but the king is concerned, not about his people, but about the stables. The prophets of the Lord are being killed off (v. 4), but the king is more worried about his animals being

64. Commoners who could afford beasts of transport ordinarily used donkeys or camels.

killed off (v. 5). So he sends Obadiah to assist him in looking for fodder and water, the two of them dividing the country between them.

18:7-16. On his way, Obadiah meets Elijah, whom he recognizes (although he is surprised to see him) and before whom he, despite his office, does obeisance. It is interesting to note the number of times the word "lord" appears in the conversation between Elijah and Obadiah. Even though Obadiah is a high-ranking official in Ahab's government, he refers to Elijah as "my lord" (vv. 7, 13) and calls himself Elijah's "servant" (vv. 9, 12). At the same time, however, Elijah refers to Ahab as Obadiah's "lord" (vv. 8, 11, 14), and Obadiah himself acknowledges Ahab as "my lord" (v. 10). Thus the narrator paints a picture of Obadiah as one who pays allegiance to two lords at the same time.

There is more at stake here, however, than loyalty to king or to prophet. Obadiah is said to be a fearer of the Lord, Elijah's God (vv. 3-4, 12-13), secretly saving and sustaining the Lord's prophets from Jezebel's pogrom. Yet, his conversation with Elijah makes it clear that he also fears Ahab immensely. He is unwilling to announce Elijah's emergence without some assurance from the latter that it would be safe for him to do so. Elijah's charge to Obadiah is repeated three times

in the passage (vv. 8, 11, 14), which is an interesting detail in the light of the Hebrew; the announcement "Elijah is here" (הנה אליהו *hinnēh 'eliyyāhû*) may also be heard in Hebrew to mean "Lo, the LORD is my God!"[65] Obadiah's reluctance to make the announcement is, therefore, tantamount to a denial of his allegiance to the Lord. Indeed, in an oath formula (v. 10), Obadiah goes so far as to refer to the Lord as Elijah's God ("your God"), thus echoing the oath formula as used by the Sidonian woman from Zarephath (17:12). He, like the Sidonian woman, fears that Elijah's presence might bring death (see 17:18). Ironically, the foreign woman, no doubt a worshiper of Baal, helped Elijah in public—at the city gate (see 17:10)—and even brought him home as a guest in her house. Meanwhile, Obadiah, who is supposed to be a fearer of the Lord and whose name in Hebrew means "servant/worshiper of the LORD," would only help the Lord's prophets secretly, and he is obsequious to Elijah when they encounter each other away from the public eye. The account of Obadiah's equivocation anticipates Elijah's accusation that the people of Israel are trying to keep all their options open (v. 21). (See Reflections at 18:41-46.)

65. See Walsh, *1 Kings*, 241.

1 Kings 18:17-40, The Summit Challenge

COMMENTARY

18:17-19. Elijah finally confronts Ahab, who immediately accuses him of being "the troubler of Israel." The Hebrew word for "troubler" (עכר *'ōkēr*) suggests someone whose action or presence is destructive to others. Jacob's sons Simeon and Levi "brought trouble" to their father by an act of vengeance that resulted in Jacob's becoming *persona non grata* to his neighbors (Gen 34:30). Achan "brought trouble" to the rest of Israel by his violation of the ban (Josh 6:18; 7:25). So Ahab's charge is that Elijah is an unsavory influence in Israel. Ahab does not spell out the charge, however. Perhaps he means that Elijah's uncompromising polemics against Baal have caused the god to be angry and, hence, have brought the drought. Perhaps

he means that Elijah has disturbed the interreligious harmony that Ahab has been trying to promote. In any case, Elijah replies that it is Ahab himself who has troubled Israel by following his father's idolatrous ways, specifically, by following "the Baals"—a reference to various local manifestations of the Canaanite deity. The decisions of Ahab as king adversely affect his people's fate. The reader already knows what "trouble" Ahab has been even to a fearer of the Lord like Obadiah. Elijah will soon demonstrate the infection of Ahab's ways upon his people's faith. He issues a challenge, asking Ahab to assemble all Israel on Mt. Carmel, along with 450 prophets of Baal and 400 prophets of Asherah.

18:20-24. Elijah asks the people how long they will continue to equivocate (v. 21). The NRSV has them "limping *with* two opinions," while the NIV says that they "waver *between* two opinions" (italics added in both cases). Other modern English translations similarly interpret the idiom to mean "hopping between two opinions" (TNK), "limping between the two sides" (ASV), "straddle the issue" (NAB), "sit on the fence" (NEB), or the like. The Hebrew idiom פסחים על שתי הסעפים (*pōsĕḥîm ʿal-štê hassĕʿippîm*) means, literally, "hobbling upon two branches."[66] The imagery is probably that of a bird hopping from branch to branch or of a person hobbling on two crutches made of branches. Whatever the literal meaning of the metaphor, however, there is no doubt about Elijah's point, for he challenges the people to choose between the Lord and Baal. To this challenge, they do not respond.

Elijah proposes a test to see whether the Lord or Baal is the true God, and he gives Baal every opportunity to succeed, every advantage. On the one side of the contest would be the 450 prophets of Baal. On the other side would be the lone figure of Elijah, representing the Lord. Each side would offer a bull on an altar, and each side would invoke the name of its deity. The one who responded by fire would be the true God.

18:25-29. With the consent of the audience, the contest gets under way. Baal's representatives go first. They call on their god from morning until noon, but they get no response. They perform some kind of a ritual dance, hobbling around the altar, but, again, there is no response. Their failure prompts Elijah to taunt them by suggesting that perhaps their god, not being omnipotent and omnipresent, is preoccupied with other matters, mundane things. The prophets of Baal

fall into a frenzy, lacerating themselves and desperately calling upon Baal to respond. There is, however, "no voice, no one who answers, no notice" (v. 29).

18:30-40. For his part, Elijah begins by repairing the Lord's altar, which had been destroyed. The impropriety of setting up an altar for the Lord outside of Jerusalem is momentarily forgotten as Elijah restores the altar to vindicate his God in this contest. Twelve stones are used to represent the twelve tribes of Israel, thereby recalling the unity of the tribes before the monarchy (Josh 4:3, 8-9, 20)—indeed, the time of Moses (Exod 28:21; 39:14). That act symbolically represents Elijah's claim of authority over against Ahab. Around the altar, the prophet digs a trench that has the capacity for two *seah*-measures of seed.[67] Wood is piled upon the altar, and the sacrificial bull is laid upon it. Then Elijah gives instructions to have the entire setup thoroughly drenched with water—twelve pitchers in all.

Thus ensuring that any fire that comes upon the altar would not be accidental, Elijah calls upon the Lord as the God of Israel's ancestors. Accordingly, the Lord's fire consumes not only the burnt offering, but also the water-drenched wood, the stones, the dust, and even the water that is in the trench. The people are duly awed, for they fall down in worship and acknowledge that it is the Lord who is God, echoing Elijah's name ("The LORD is my God," v. 39). Elijah orders that the prophets of Baal be killed in the Kishon Valley, where Israel's judge Deborah had battled and slain the Canaanites long ago (Judg 4:7, 13; 5:21; Ps 83:9). (See Reflections at 18:41-46.)

---

66. On the meaning of the noun for "branches," see Isa 10:33; 17:6; 27:10; Ezek 31:6, 8.

67. The NRSV and the NIV both take the text to mean that the trench is capable of holding two *seah*-measures of seed (approximately seven gallons), which would be too small for an altar large enough to hold a sacrificial bull. If, however, one takes the capacity to refer to the area of land required for sowing that amount of seed (see Lev 27:16; Isa 5:10), then the area around the altar would need to be about 1,800 square yards, which seems too large for twelve pitchers of water to fill.

1 Kings 18:41-46, Conclusion of the Contest

COMMENTARY

The passage concludes with the coming of rain, as the Lord had promised through

Elijah at the beginning (v. 1): "the sound of the rumbling of rain" (v. 41), "rain" (v.

44), "heavy rain" (v. 45). Throughout these concluding verses, Elijah is in charge, while Ahab merely takes his cues from him. Elijah hears the sound of approaching rain and orders Ahab to ascend the mountain and to eat and drink. The summit meal no doubt signals the end of drought and famine. More important, however, it recalls the covenant meal that Moses and Aaron and the seventy elders of Israel partook at the mountain of God long ago (see Exod 24:9-14). For all his offenses, Ahab is apparently still included as a member of the covenant community, but he is clearly under prophetic authority. Elijah, then, goes off to the very peak of Mt. Carmel, just as Moses had left the rest of the party to wait for him while he retreated high up the mountain of God to commune with the deity. Elijah crouches on the ground, placing his face between his knees in what must have been a posture of intense prayer. He has an assistant with him, just as Moses had an assistant with him when he left the rest of the group waiting at the mountain of God. The unnamed servant is to look toward the sea, and he does so without result until the symbolically signficant seventh time. Then the servant sees a little cloud "no bigger than a person's hand" arising from the horizon. The approaching cloud, though appearing small in the distance, is reminiscent of the cloud of glory that represented the Lord's presence at the mountain of God in the time of Moses.

Through his servant, Elijah then instructs Ahab to leave in his chariot before the rain comes and he will be unable to do so. The long-awaited rain that would end the drought, the rain that is supposed to be a blessing, would be an obstacle for Ahab. Just as surely as Elijah had said, the sky turns dark and heavy rain falls, while the king flees on his chariot to Jezreel, Ahab and Jezebel's winter palace some seventeen miles away. Empowered by the Lord, however, Elijah outpaces him on foot.

REFLECTIONS

This is an enormously entertaining chapter. Here we find a story of a high government official furtively subverting a quasi-state-sponsored pogrom and paying homage to the most wanted dissident in the country. We have an account, too, of a confrontation between a king and a prophet, with each accusing the other of culpability in the suffering of others—a veritable power struggle between "church" and "state." Above all, we have the high drama of a mountaintop contest between the representatives of two different religions, each trying to prove the superiority of its deity.

These stories are recounted not just for entertainment, however; they are narrated for theological reasons. Herein one finds important theological lessons that continue to be instructive for the community of faith.

1. The passage obviously asserts the power of Israel's God, who is omnipotent and sovereign over the world. Just as important, although conveyed more subtly, however, are God's persistent grace and mercy. Despite the blatant unfaithfulness of human beings, God nevertheless responds to human needs even when people do not ask. In the case the text discusses, it is God who initiates the end of the drought and the return of rain. God may act wondrously and publicly—whether in the liberation of slaves from oppression, in sending fire from heaven, in the resurrection, or in some other salvific event in order to bring people to faith.

2. At the heart of biblical faith is the demand for allegiance to only one God. For most people who are already in the community of faith, however, the challenge is not theism per se, for few would deny God outright. Rather, the greatest challenge lies in faithfulness to one God and no other; it lies in the willingness to trust that one God, even in times when other alternatives seem more practical, more immediately relevant, or more popular. Human needs and wants are so great that there is always the temptation to keep one's theological options open to hedge against the possibility that our God may not adequately provide for our needs. Polytheism allows one to so hedge, but that is not the case with the religion of Moses (see Exod 20:3; Deut 5:7), after whose ministry Elijah's own is modeled. For Elijah, then, there can be no theological compromise; we have to choose to be on one side or the other. In this perspective, *not* to choose is already to choose an alternative other than the way of the Lord. It is not only in genuine polytheism that such a threat exists, however, for even people who do not believe in the actual existence of other gods might have other equally pernicious delusions of alternative powers. Jesus called attention to one such alternative in his generation, pointing out that the command to love God allows no other allegiance: "No one can serve two masters; for a slave will either hate the one and love the other, or be devoted to one and despise the other. You cannot serve God and wealth" (Matt 6:24 NRSV).

3. The chapter illustrates the demand of Mosaic religion quite well—not only in Elijah's call to the people to choose either the Lord or Baal, but also in the realistic example of Obadiah. In Obadiah we have someone with whom most people in the community of faith might identify much more readily than with Ahab or even the people of Israel assembled on Mt. Carmel. Obadiah is a believer, a fearer of God. His loyalty to the Lord is attested by his name ("servant/worshiper of the LORD"). He is even instrumental in saving the lives of others, secretly undermining the will of the queen. Obadiah, however, has other allegiances and fears, as well: He has his boss to serve, his career to protect, his own life to preserve. He is one with whom we readily sympathize, and we wonder whether the narrator had been a tad too harsh in comparing him implicitly with the Sidonian widow, a woman outside the community of faith. The text warns us, however, of the dangers of the insidious or the seemingly excusable compromises, as well as the blatant ones. Herein lies the threat to faith for most of us.

1 KINGS 19:1-21, THE PROPHET'S PLIGHT

OVERVIEW

The chapter is anticlimactic. On the heels of the great victory on Mt. Carmel, the reader may be surprised to find the protagonist of that contest now on the run for his life. In chaps. 17–18, Elijah is a bona fide hero of faith. He is larger than life—faithful, confident, and authoritative. He is able to bring about miracles through prayer, even raising the dead and calling fire down from heaven. He is able to confront a powerful king and accuse him of sin, and he dares to challenge a large crowd of Baalists. He is able to outrun Ahab's chariot in a seventeen-mile race. So we certainly would not expect to find an easily intimidated, suicidal, self-doubting yet self-righteous Elijah in chap. 19. Indeed, the tone of this chapter is so different from the previous ones that most critics assume that the link to the preceding units of thought suggested by vv. 1-3 is artificial; the rest of the chapter, it is sometimes argued, does not return to Jezebel or to her death threat. There are, moreover, a number of elements in the chapter that suggest a complex compositional history.

All that may be true. Yet, there are signs that the text as we have it is intended to be read as a whole and, indeed, to be read as a sequel to the Mt. Carmel episode.

1 Kings 19:1-3a, Why Elijah Is on the Run

COMMENTARY

As the preceding chapter ended, Ahab was rushing off to Jezreel (18:45), presumably to the winter palace that he and his queen have there (see 21:1). As the new chapter begins, we find him reporting to his wife, Jezebel, a princess from Sidon (16:31) and a fanatical devotee of Baal (see 18:4, 13), all the details of what Elijah had done. Specifically, Ahab reports on Elijah's killing of "all the prophets," meaning the 450 prophets of Baal (18:40) and perhaps the 400 prophets of Asherah who have been supported by the queen (18:19).

Jezebel immediately reacts by sending a message to Elijah, vowing to kill him. Yet, if that is what she really wants to do, it seems strange that she does not simply send an assassin to finish him off or a bailiff to arrest him. Instead, she tips him off, giving him time to escape. One must not press the details too hard, however, for this is not so much a historical report as it is literature. This introductory account simply sets up the rest of the story. It explains why it is that Elijah is fleeing despite his triumph on Mt. Carmel: He is persecuted for doing the Lord's work; his life threatened. Duly warned, he is frightened and flees for his life (v. 3a). (See Reflections at 19:19-21.)

1 Kings 19:3b-8a, Two Epiphanies in the Desert

COMMENTARY

Elijah goes to Beersheba, the southernmost town in the land of the Lord's people, as we know from the cliché "from Dan to Beersheba" (Judg 20:1; 1 Sam 3:20; 2 Sam 17:11; 24:2, 15). The narrator reminds the reader that Beersheba was at that time under Judah's control. So Elijah is legally well beyond the reach of Jezebel. Still, he does not remain there. Whereas on Mt. Carmel he had counted on his servant to help him look out for sign of impending rain (18:43-44), now he leaves the lad in Beersheba, while he himself ventures into the wilderness beyond Judah. He takes shelter under a solitary desert bush ("broom tree," NRSV and NIV) and cries out, presumably to the Lord. "Too much [רב *rab*; NIV, "I have had enough, Lord"; NRSV, "It is enough"]!" he says summarily, and asks to die because he is no better than his forebears (אבות *ʾābôt*; NRSV, NIV, "ancestors"). His requesting that the Lord let him die ("for I am no better than my forebears") is usually understood to mean that he thinks his life is no better than those of his dead ancestors. It is also possible, however, that the "forebears" refers, not to his ancestors per se, but to his predecessors in the prophetic ministry. That is, despite his stupendous success on Mt. Carmel, he is no better than his vocational predecessors after all. Perhaps he has in mind Moses, who also complained to the Lord in the wilderness that his burden was too heavy to bear alone, and so he asked the Lord to let him die (Num 11:14-15). So, too, Elijah goes into the wilderness to complain that he is bearing too much and asks to die. He would later insist that he is by himself ("I alone am left," vv. 10, 14). Elijah, in other words, is in no better situation than were his forebears inasmuch as he, like them, is left with too much to bear on his own.

Elijah is then touched by an angel and provided with a cake baked on hot coals and a jug of water, hardly things one should expect to find in the desert. The Hebrew word used for "hot coals" (רצפים *rĕṣāpîm*) is a rare one. It is found elsewhere only in Isa 6:6 for a hot coal that a seraph takes from the altar of the Lord's Temple and with which he touches the lips of Isaiah in response to the prophet's expression of unworthiness to accept the Lord's commission. The word used for "jar"

(צפחת *ṣappaḥat*) is also uncommon. It is found in two other passages, 1 Sam 26:10-16 and 1 Kgs 17:8-16, the latter having to do with the Lord's provision for Elijah's needs through the widow of Zarephath when Elijah was hiding from Ahab.

Through the device of a second epiphany, the narrator is able to identify the angel specifically as an angel of the Lord and to give a reason for the provision and the command to eat. In the account of the first epiphany, we read only of "an angel," which is noteworthy because the word for "angel" (מלאך *mal'āk*) is the same one used for Jezebel's "messenger" in v. 2. Rhetorically, this ambiguity heightens the tension, for the reader is momentarily uncertain whether the mysterious intermediary will bring death, which

Jezebel had promised and which Elijah had self-piteously requested, or whether the intermediary will somehow deliver Elijah from his persecutor and from himself.

The account of the second epiphany clarifies that the intermediary is, in fact, from the Lord. It explains, too, that Elijah is to eat because "the way is too much for you" (רב ממך הדרך *rab mimměkā haddārek*, v. 7). NRSV understands the text to be referring to the journey ahead of Elijah ("the journey will be too much for you"), but the text is ambivalent. Moreover, the reference to the excessive difficulty of "the way" harks back to Elijah's own complaint in v. 4: "too much!" (br rab). Elijah has to accept the nourishment that the Lord provides in the wilderness because "the way" is "too much" for him. So he complies. (See Reflections at 19:19-21.)

1 Kings 19:8*b*-18, Encounter with God on Mount Horeb

COMMENTARY

19:8b-10. Elijah goes on a journey of forty days and forty nights to "Horeb the mount of God," an alternate name for Mt. Sinai (see Exod 3:1). The period of forty days and forty nights, significantly, also echoes the time Moses spent on the same mountain, where he encountered God (see Exod 24:18; 34:28; Deut 9:9, 11, 18, 25; 10:10). On that mountain, Elijah comes to a cave (so NIV, NRSV); the Hebrew has the definite article, "the cave" (המערה *hammě'ārâ*, v. 9), which is perhaps a reference to the "cleft of the rock" where Moses stood as the Lord "passed by" (Exod 33:22).

In response to the Lord's question as to his purpose on Horeb, Elijah replies that he has been "very zealous for the LORD" because the people of Israel have forsaken the covenant, torn down the altars of the Lord, and killed the Lord's prophets. The term used for Elijah's zeal here (קנא קנאתי *qannō' qinnē'tî*), however, is used most frequently for God's "jealousy" as regards Israel's loyalty (Exod 20:5; 34:14; Deut 4:24; 5:9; 6:15; 32:16, 19, 21; Josh 24:19). Elijah, in other words, is jealous on behalf of the Lord, and he is angry because he has been left by himself to do God's work and because he is persecuted for it. So he has come to this mountain where Moses long ago

had encountered God, indeed, spoken to God "face to face" (Deut 5:4).

Elijah appears to be overly zealous, however. He does not seem to recall the affirmative response of the people of Israel on Mt. Carmel (18:39). He charges them with having torn down the altars of the Lord, perhaps thinking of the altar that he had to repair to offer the sacrificial bull in the contest with Baal's prophets (18:30). Yet, the destruction of altars outside Jerusalem would be in accordance with the deuteronomic program of centralization. The reference to the killing of the Lord's prophets is also puzzling, because the only record of such killing is that ordered by Jezebel (18:4, 13), and not by the people of Israel. Elijah also does not seem to remember that Obadiah had rescued a hundred prophets of the Lord, so he is not technically left by himself.

19:11-14. The Lord tells him to go out and stand on the mountain, for the Lord is "about to pass by" (so the NIV correctly has it in v. 11). The words are probably meant to evoke the tradition of Moses standing at the "cleft of the rock"—perhaps this very cave— where he encountered the Lord's passing by (Exod 33:19-23). Signs that typically accompany theophanies appear in succession: the accompaniments of a rainstorm, an earthquake, fire (e.g., Exod 19:16-19; Judg 5:4-5; Pss 18:13; 68:9; Nah 1:3-5; Hab 3:4-6). In particular, in the preceding chapter rainstorm and fire are associated with the power of God. Yet, in each case now, Elijah discovers that the Lord is not present despite the familiar signs.

Finally, after the fire, there is an eerie calm, literally "a sound of fine silence" (קול דממה דקה *qôl děmāmâ daqqâ*). The traditional translation of the phrase as "a still small voice" (so KJV) has been popularized in hymns, but it does not convey the oxymoron. The NRSV takes it to be "a sound of sheer silence," which is what the words mean, and yet, Elijah is able to hear something (v. 13). The Hebrew words for "sound" and "silence," in fact, occur together in Job 4:16, where that combination is generally taken as an expression for a barely audible sound (NIV, "a gentle whisper"). That is probably what is meant by the "sound of fine silence"—that is, a hushed sound. The Hebrew word for "silence" (דממה *děmāmâ*) is attested in Ps 107:29 as well, where it refers to the end of a storm. What Elijah hears, apparently, is the calm that comes after the storm. Perhaps the narrator means to contrast this hushed sound with the sound of the rumbling before the storm, קול המון הגשם (*qôl hămôn haggāšēm*; see 18:41). In any case, the structure of the text implies that it is in this stillness that Elijah somehow encounters the Lord: The Lord was not in the storm, not in the earthquake, not in the fire, but after the fire there is this "sound." Thereupon, Elijah covers his face with his mantle, a gesture that suggests that he is, indeed, encountering the numinous in that stillness (cf. Exod 3:6; 33:22).

Elijah then hears a sound (v. 13)—perhaps another sound, perhaps the same sound. In any case, this time the sound is clearly a personal voice, and the reader knows from the query the voice poses that it is the voice of the Lord. To that question, Elijah gives the same answer as before. The manifestation of divine presence described in the preceding verses apparently has made no difference in Elijah's understanding; he apparently does not get the point of the "sound of fine silence."

19:15-18. The Lord speaks to him a symbolically significant third time, telling him, literally, "Go, return to your way [לך שוב לדרכך *lēk šûb lĕdarkĕkā*]" (v. 15). The last reference in the passage to a "way" (דרך *derek*) is in v. 7, in reference to the way that would be "too much" for Elijah without divine sustenance in the wilderness. This time, however, the wilderness is not in the south, but in the north: the wilderness of Damascus. Elijah is to anoint Hazael as king of Aram (the Syrians), Jehu as king of Israel, and Elisha as his successor. The reference to Hazael and Jehu anticipates events recorded in 2 Kgs 8:7–10:31, only there it is not Elijah who is the principal prophetic figure but Elisha. It is Elisha who announces to Hazael that he will be king (2 Kgs 8:7-15), and it is Elisha who indirectly anoints Jehu as king (2 Kgs 9:1-15). Critics discern here a complex redactional process, perhaps a secondary insertion at this point of a reworked fragment from the Elisha cycle. Whatever the reality, the charge to Elijah in vv. 11-21 in its present literary context stands as an explication of the "sound of fine silence" that Elijah heard on Mt. Horeb. It also provides a conclusion to the story of Elijah's flight. The answer to the threat posed by Jezebel will not come in the spectacular and immediate manner, as on Mt. Carmel. It does not come by way of a fire from on high. It does not come by way of a rainstorm. Rather, it is to come in a quiet fashion, through the rather unspectacular fact of prophetic succession. The answer will come through the working out of divine will in the historical process. The anointing of Elisha will lead, if only indirectly, to the anointing of Hazael and Jehu. The seemingly mundane event of the ordination of Elijah's successor will turn out to be the resolution to the problem of Jezebel. Eventually, in the reign of Jehu years later, Jezebel will be killed (2 Kgs 9:30-37), as will her fellow devotees of Baal (2 Kgs 10:18-28). Moreover, contrary to the view of Elijah that he alone is left, the Lord will leave "seven thousand" (a symbolic figure) who will not bend their knees to Baal or give him their allegiance. In contrast to the events on Mt. Carmel, these events are unspectacular. They are even difficult to perceive, for they occur indirectly and over a period of time in history. Yet, that is how the Lord may appear—in "a sound of fine silence" that comes after the fire (see chap. 18). (See Reflections at 19:19-21.)

1 Kings 19:19-21, The Call of Elisha

COMMENTARY

Elijah does not respond by going to the wilderness of Damascus to anoint Hazael, as one might expect from a surface reading of his commission in vv. 11-18. Rather, he responds to the essence of the divine charge, quietly beginning the process of fulfilling the Lord's word by passing on the mantle of prophetic authority to Elisha. Elijah leaves Horeb, the Mount of God, and finds Elisha, presumably in the latter's hometown of Abel-meholah (v. 16), in the western Jordan valley. Elisha is plowing the field with twelve teams of oxen, suggesting an extremely large operation and, hence, considerable wealth. Strangely, as Elijah passes him by, he throws his mantle upon Elisha and keeps on going. The cultural significance of this admittedly bizarre action is unknown. Some scholars discern a literary allusion to the Lord's "passing by" before Elijah in front of the cave in Mt. Horeb—that is, Elijah passes by Elisha, just as the Lord had passed by Elijah.[68] The mantle is presumably the one that Elijah used to cover his face from the theophany at Horeb (v. 13). With this mantle, Elijah would later strike the water of a river and cause it to miraculously part (2 Kgs 2:8), and Elisha would follow suit

68. See Robert B. Coote, "Yahweh Recalls Elijah," in *Traditions in Transformation: Turning Points in Biblical Faith*, ed. Baruch Halpern and Jon D. Levenson (Winona Lake, Ind.: Eisenbrauns, 1981) 115-20.

(2 Kgs 2:13-14). So the mantle is to Elijah what the staff was to Moses (Exod 7:17-18; 14:16). Elisha must have had a sense of the symbolic significance of that gesture, whatever that might have been, for he leaves his oxen to follow Elijah, asking only to return home first to bid his parents farewell. Elijah tells him to do so, using words that echo the Lord's commission to him in v. 15, "Go, return [שוב לך *lēk šûb*]." The remark that immediately follows this call to return is, however, enigmatic: "What have I done to you?" It is often understood to be a rhetorical question: "What have I done to prevent you?" (NEB) or "Have I done anything to you?" (NAB). Elijah, however, may be alluding to the symbolic meaning of the gesture—that is, what the tossing of the mantle to Elisha implies. He means, perhaps, that Elisha's acceptance of the call would entail a radical break from his familial and social moorings. Elisha clearly understands that his farewell will be more than a ritual kiss. He sacrifices the capital and tools of his trade, slaughtering the oxen and using the equipment that comes with them for fuel. Duly severed from his past, then, he sets out to follow Elijah "and attended to him" (וישרתהו *wayšārĕtēhû*), the Hebrew recalling the role that Joshua, Moses' successor, played before Moses passed on (Num 11:28; Josh 1:1). Elisha plays Joshua to Elijah's Moses.

REFLECTIONS

It is for good reason that chapter 19 is one of the most frequently preached sections in the book of Kings. There are a number of New Testament allusions to it, and all subsections in the unit appear in various lectionaries. There is no question that this is a theologically rich passage.

1. Arguably the most memorable words in the entire chapter are the oxymoronic expression "sound of fine silence," famous in the traditional rendering, "a still small voice." The passage is perhaps theologically most important as a counterpoint to the high drama of chapter 18. There the Lord is known in spectacular manifestations of fire from heaven and sudden rainstorm after a drought. Here, however, the point is made quite deliberately that God is not locked into any one mode of appearing. Sometimes God is not made known to us through flashy theophanies. Sometimes God is known in unspectacular ways, through the quiet working out of history. For Elijah, who had known the presence of God through God's providence and through miraculous acts that clearly demonstrated God's power, divine will was also manifested in his role in the ordination of his successor. Unbeknownst to him at that time, that one act in the countryside would lead to other events in the fulfillment of God's will in history. Elsewhere in Scripture, we learn that God's "voice" is sometimes present in unspectacular events and ordinary people. Indeed, God's "voice" may be present even amid God's silence, as in the birth of a child to an unwed mother amid scandalous circumstances or in the death of an innocent man on the cross.

2. A second lesson is related to the first. We learn that the ministry may take many forms. We may recognize Elijah's tasks in chapter 18 as traditional forms of ministry: He confronts a powerful leader with his sins; he calls on people to be faithful to God's demands; he acts to convert others by the powerful word of God. Here in chapter 19, however, we learn that ministry may include the passing on of the mantle of leadership. Faithfulness to God's calling may entail the preparation of others for their own ministries.

3. The chapter is blatantly honest about the humanity of God's servants. Even the prophet who has experienced God's providence and power has his moments of darkness. Elijah has been blessed with much success, but at the slightest sign of a reversal of fortune, he is ready to quit. In this story we find all the signs of ministerial burnout. Those who are psychologically inclined might point out that Elijah manifests all the signs of depression. He appears to be totally worn out, fatigued. This prophet who used to refer to himself as one standing before the Lord (17:1; 18:15) seems to be sleeping a lot in this passage. He complains. He is suicidal. He needs to be told to eat. His view of reality is distorted. He is quick to blame others for the situation in which he has found himself. He feels all alone. Given his attitude, one should expect a divine rebuke. There is not one, however. Instead, there is a series of epiphanies. Elijah is touched by a divine intermediary and, when he fails to get the point, the Lord speaks to him a third time. Elijah's perspective is strongly challenged, and a lesson is offered to him; but he is never rebuked for showing weakness. Rather, Elijah is accepted as he is and is merely called back to his ministry: "Go, return to your way!" God does not let him go simply because he is burned out and depressed.

4. God's persistence with Elijah does not at all imply that God's will can be carried only through him. Indeed, Elijah is assured that there are many others—unnamed heroes of faith—who have "not bent their knees to Baal." In the New Testament, this "remnant" that God has left untainted is evidence of the enormousness of divine grace (see Rom 11:3-5).

5. The account of Elisha's calling says something about the kind of commitment that it would take to accept the call to ministry. Elisha returns to bid farewell to his family and sacrifices the essential equipment of his trade. This view of faithfulness logically follows upon the call in the preceding chapter for unequivocal commitment to the way of the Lord. In the New Testament, the demand for absolute commitment in following Jesus is stated even more radically: "No one who puts a hand to the plow and looks back is fit for the kingdom of God" (Luke 9:57-62 NRSV, esp. v. 62; see also Matt 8:18-22; 19:23-30; Mark 10:23-31). Discipleship can be costly!

1 KINGS 20:1-43, AHAB'S HANDLING OF A FOREIGN-POLICY CRISIS

OVERVIEW

This chapter purports to be about a foreign-policy crisis Ahab had to face—namely, the war that Israel was forced to fight with Aram (Syria) under a certain King Ben-Hadad. Critics point out, however, that there are a number of discrepancies in the historical details, and they argue compellingly that it is more likely that the story originally concerned events that occurred later, in the reign of Jehoahaz (see 2 Kgs 13:1-9).[69] The account here is not to be read as a historical record, however, but as theological literature. Whatever its origin and compositional history, the story in its present context needs to be read as a theological assessment of Ahab's faithfulness—or lack thereof.

The story's literary context poses a problem as well. Whereas Elijah is the conduit of the Lord's word in the preceding three chapters and will make a comeback in the next chapter, he is completely absent from chap. 20. To some scholars, that fact again indicates that we have intrusive material here. Yet, we may read the text in the light of the preceding materials. Here the deity does not work in the foreground—through supernatural acts and theophanies, as in chaps. 17–19—but only in the background, through the unfolding

of history. This is, in fact, the point of the "sound of fine silence" in 19:12. Moreover, the fact that Elijah is silent while several other prophetic figures convey the will of God (see vv. 13-14, 22, 28, 35-43) is testimony to the truth of the claim in 19:18 that there are numerous other people in Israel who are still loyal to the Lord (the "seven thousand in Israel who have not bent their knees to Baal"), despite Elijah's claim to be the only one left. Moreover, countering Ahab's charge that Elijah was Israel's "troubler," Elijah replied that it was Ahab who was the real "troubler," the word implying that his presence and actions would bring trouble upon others (18:17). Now the narrator will show how Ahab did, indeed, bring trouble to his people (see v. 42).

Finally, in terms of the overall flow of the passage, vv. 1-34 seem to be a self-contained unit: War turns to peace; the king of Israel is victorious over the king of Aram. Thus the final section (vv. 35-43) seems to have been tacked on. The coherence of vv. 1-34, however, is a literary setup by the narrator. One might read the end of this section with some satisfaction, only to be surprised by the two prophetic episodes in vv. 35-43. These concluding verses are, in fact, crucial for the passage, for they provide a theological lens through which to view Ahab's overall performance in his handling of the crisis.

69. See, e.g., the careful study of Wayne T. Pitard, *Ancient Damascus* (Winona Lake, Ind.: Eisenbrauns, 1987) 114-25.

1 Kings 20:1-12, How the War Begins

COMMENTARY

The story begins with the naked aggression of Ben-hadad of Aram, who led a coalition of foreign rulers against Samaria. At first, he seems to demand a declaration of submission from Ahab. At least that is how Ahab chooses to interpret the demand, and he concedes to it. Ben-hadad, however, is not satisfied with that. Although it is unclear in the

initial command (v. 3), Ben-hadad insists that he had asked Ahab to deliver the personal tribute (v. 5). Indeed, he expands his demand now to include freedom for his representatives to enter the capital to plunder it at will.

Ahab consults with the elders of the land and receives popular support. With that, he reiterates his willingness to give a personal tribute but asserts that he cannot comply with the amended demand. Already looking for any pretext to invade Israel, Ben-hadad swears that he will so devastate Samaria that when he is finished there will not even be enough dust in the city for his troops to bring home a handful each (v. 10). Ahab retorts (v. 11), citing a proverb that says essentially that one who is only getting dressed for combat (lit., "one who girds") should not boast like one who is removing the battle gear.[70] In other words, one must not presume to know the results of the battle. Or, as we might say in contemporary parlance, "It ain't over until it's over!" Thereupon, Ben-hadad orders the Aramean troops to prepare for battle. (See Reflections at 20:35-43.)

70. For the idioms used here, see 1 Sam 17:39; Isa 45:1.

1 Kings 20:13-34, How Quickly the Tide Turns

COMMENTARY

20:13-21. An unnamed prophet—apparently one of the "seven thousand" who remain loyal to the Lord (see 19:18)—comes to Ahab with an oracle. The Lord will deliver the vast Aramean army into the hand of Ahab as a self-revelatory act, says the prophet. Indeed, the promise "that you may know that I am the LORD" echoes similar promises given by God in connection with the exodus (Exod 6:6-7; 7:17; 10:2; 16:12). Ahab does not dispute the theological basis of the promise of deliverance, but he seems most interested in the pragmatic questions of strategy: Who will be the key players, and who will direct the battle? Ahab asks, literally, "Who will bind the battle?" The meaning of the idiom is, unfortunately, not clarified by its only other occurrence, in 2 Chr 20:3. The NRSV and the NIV both take it to mean "to begin the battle," but the idiom may simply refer to the control of battle strategy.

Although the Israelites attack in broad daylight ("at noon"), they still catch the enemy in a drunken stupor. Moreover, despite advance warning, Ben-hadad apparently does not have any strategy and merely gives a vague order to take the attackers alive (v. 18). The result is a rout of the Arameans, and Ben-hadad himself has to flee.

20:22-25. The prophet urges Ahab to strengthen his position and to strategize carefully because the Arameans will attack again. Meanwhile, Ben-hadad also gets advice from his counselors. They suggest to him that the coalition army lost the battle because Israel's "gods are gods of the hills" (v. 23). So they propose that the next battle be fought in the plain where the Arameans would presumably be more at home. They also urge that the conglomeration of kings in the coalition be replaced by commissioned officers (lit., "governors"), thus revealing the coalition to be the sham that it is. Ben-hadad should, of course, rebuild his army before going into battle again.

Military strategists will no doubt agree that the recommendations make perfect sense. The point about the advantage of fighting the Israelites in the plain instead of in the hill country is sound and probably well known in regional military history (see Josh 17:16-18; Judg 1:19). The problem, as the narrator sees it, is that the issue is framed in ignorant theological terms. The Aramean advisers comically presume that Israel is supported by gods whose power is geographically defined. For the narrator, this is no mere battle for the kings. It is the Lord's holy war.

20:26-30a. As the prophet predicted (v. 22), the Arameans attack again. This time, the battle takes place at Aphek. There are a number of places known as Aphek in the Hebrew Bible. Most notable is a site on the plain of Philistia, where the Philistines defeated the Israelites and carried away the ark of the covenant as a trophy, an emblem of their god's victory over the God of Israel (1 Sam 4:1-11). This time, however, there will be no victory for Israel's enemy, even though the Israelites are significantly outnumbered (v. 27). A man of God—another one of those who have not bent their knees to Baal—delivers another oracle of the Lord that repeats the divine promise in the beginning and its theological rationale: the self-disclosure of the Lord. Accordingly, the Arameans are roundly defeated; their troops are slaughtered, and those who escape into the city are killed by a collapsing wall. The implication is that the wall falls by divine will and so 27,000 are killed thereby. The collapsing of the wall in connection with a battle that is fought after a seven-day waiting period (v. 29) reminds one of the wall of Jericho, which miraculously fell because the Lord was fighting for Israel (Josh 6:15-27). This is an important clue that the narrator sees this as a holy war, a battle in which the Lord fights.

20:30b-34. Once again, Ben-hadad is able to escape. His advisers suggest that they go to Ahab with symbols of surrender: sackcloth around their waists, a sign of sorrow, and a rope around their heads, perhaps to symbolize captivity. The story faintly echoes the ploy of the Gibeonites in the time of the conquest, who tricked the Israelites into sparing them from slaughter and entering into a treaty with them instead (Josh 9:1-27). In any case, when Ahab learns that Ben-hadad is alive, he is exceedingly magnanimous. Whereas Ben-hadad refers to himself as "your servant," Ahab is quick to come to terms with him as a peer ("my brother"; cf. 9:13). The Israelite king brings Ben-hadad up on a chariot (lit., "caused him to go up on a chariot") and

makes a treaty with him. In political and economic terms, Ahab's deal is sagacious: He gets his towns restored and gains trading privileges for Israel in Damascus, one of the most important trading centers in the ancient Near East.

Despite the negative portrayal of Ahab in chaps. 16–18, we here find a picture of Ahab as a shrewd politician. In practical terms, he has managed the entire foreign-policy crisis remarkably well. Faced with a demand for personal tribute from his enemy, he was willing to concede. Yet, when the demands escalated unreasonably, he did not yield. Rather, he consulted with the elders and gained popular backing for resistance. Still, he tried to keep the diplomatic solution alive. He sent word that he was willing to give what he could, but steadfastly refused to give an unconditional surrender. Indeed, in contrast to the pompous and impulsive Ben-hadad, Ahab is the model of a judicious king. He is, moreover, a pragmatic strategist. He listened to the advice of others, but he quickly cut to the chase to establish his plan of action. Then, when he is finally victorious, he looks ahead. Instead of annihilating his enemy, he makes a deal that brings material advantages for his country. The portrayal of Ahab in the chapter thus far is positive. (See Reflections at 20:35-43.)

1 Kings 20:35-43, Assessment of Ahab's Performance

COMMENTARY

Following the apparently glowing account of Ahab's leadership are a couple of related prophetic episodes that put Ahab in perspective. The first of these (vv. 35-36) is enigmatic, and its meaning is unclear until one gets to the end of the second episode (vv. 37-43).

Yet another unknown prophetic figure, a member of a guild of prophets (lit., "sons of prophets"), approaches a colleague at the command of the Lord with a strange request to be attacked. When that colleague declines to do so, the first prophet pronounces a death sentence upon him for disobeying the Lord's command, promising him a fate reminiscent of the unnamed man of God who was killed for what seems like very reasonable

and faithful conduct (13:11-32): A lion will attack him. Accordingly, the prophecy comes to pass.

The man who had received the command of the Lord then approaches a second colleague, who does as he is told: He strikes and wounds the prophet. The prophet then disguises himself as a wounded soldier. He waits at the roadside until he sees Ahab and then approaches him with a petition, something every citizen has the right to do (see 3:16-28; 2 Sam 14:1-20; 2 Kgs 6:26-31; 8:3-6). No doubt Ahab thinks that this is one of the soldiers who fought with him in his victory over the Arameans. The "soldier" claims that he was in the thick of battle when he was approached by a colleague to guard a prisoner, likely one seized as personal booty of the captor. It was stipulated that if the prisoner were missing, the "soldier" would be killed or pay an exorbitant cash penalty.[71] While the "soldier" was "busy here and there," the prisoner disappears. The "soldier" implies that the loss was excusable, since he was in the midst of a battle and busy with other things.

The case seems straightforward to Ahab, who thinks that the "soldier" already knows the answer: The "soldier" deserves whatever punishment has been stipulated because he understood full well what he was supposed to do. Thereupon, the prophet removes his disguise and the king recognizes him for who he is, suggesting that there must have been some identifying marks of prophetic authority on the prophet's person. Like the prophet Nathan, who told the parable of the unfairly appropriated ewe (meaning Bathsheba) to condemn David (2 Sam 12:1-15), and like the wise woman of Tekoa, who tricked David into sparing Absalom's life (2 Sam 14:4-20), the prophet now informs the king that the parable was about him. The prophet proclaims

71. A talent of silver would be about a hundred times the average price of a slave. Such a penalty on a poor soldier, then, would be tantamount to a death sentence, for he would surely be enslaved for life.

the Lord's judgment on Ahab for his release of Ben-hadad, contrary to the custom of the ban, whereby all persons and property seized in a holy war were to be utterly destroyed (see Deut 7:2; 20:16-18; 1 Sam 15:1-35). Ahab is condemned by his own words, for he did not realize that the "soldier" was a cipher for himself. Only Ben-hadad did not escape on his own; Ahab had released him, even though it was not within his authority to do so. The battle was the Lord's, and Ben-hadad was reserved for the Lord. Ahab and, along with him, his people are condemned. Elijah was correct to say that it was Ahab who brought trouble to Israel. Like Achan, a troubler from an earlier time (Joshua 7:1), Ahab violated the ban and, in doing so, has brought condemnation upon not only himself but his people as well.

The meaning of the strange episode of vv. 35-36 is now clarified. Like the story of the man of God who was tricked into disobeying the Lord (13:11-32), the current story makes the point that there is no excuse for disobeying the Lord's command. Like the wounded "soldier," Ahab is not excused because of his preoccupation with the matters of war or of the state. Death is his punishment for disobedience to the Lord.

REFLECTIONS

Modern readers will no doubt read the story in this chapter with much sympathy for Ahab. By most criteria of leadership, he would be judged an able king. He may even be admired for the way he stood up to a vain foreign dictator and aggressor. Ahab was diplomatic and courageous under duress, and he is magnanimous in victory. What is more, his deal with his erstwhile enemy allowed him to open trade with that country, thus ensuring new opportunities of economic prosperity for his nation. Were a modern leader to have the kind of foreign policy successes Ahab achieved, one might be inclined to overlook his or her minor offenses. If the country is strong and the economy is sound, we are content to overlook the personal flaws and excusable infractions of our leaders. Yet, Ahab is condemned for what seems to us like a very humane and farsighted deed: the sparing of his enemy.

The notion of the ban that is associated with the assumptions of holy war is difficult for us to understand today. It is one of those regulations in the Bible to which we must say no. Yet, this passage of Scripture warns against our tendency to place pragmatic considerations ahead of a right relationship with God. It also warns us against making excuses for shunning our responsibility to the Lord—against claiming that we are too "busy here and there," too preoccupied with matters that seem more pressing than do matters of faith.

1 KINGS 21:1-29, AHAB'S DOMESTIC POLICY

OVERVIEW

The preceding chapter concerns Ahab's handling of a particular foreign-policy crisis. The present chapter concerns an incident that illustrates his performance in the domestic arena. Taken together, both chapters show him to be an unacceptable king according to the standards of deuteronomic law. Accordingly, then, this chapter anticipates Ahab's death (vv. 19, 21-24; see also 20:41-42).

Most scholars agree that the story of the judicial murder of Naboth (vv. 1b-14) must have originally circulated independently. Its artificial placement in its present context is evident from the presence of the obvious redactional link to the preceding material ("after these events") in addition to the circumstantial introduction ("Naboth the Jezreelite had a vineyard in Jezreel"). Some would also argue that the story as a whole fits better in a later period, while others speculate that there may have been different versions of the story that are conflated in the present account. These and other historical-critical issues, however, need not detain us in the necessary task of interpreting the passage in its present form and in its larger literary context.

The literary unit may be divided into two halves. The first half (vv. 1-16) outlines the story in considerable detail; the second half (vv. 17-29) provides the prophetic perspective on the offense.

1 Kings 21:1-16, Ahab Takes Possession of Naboth's Vineyard

COMMENTARY

21:1-2. The Hebrew of v. 1 is awkward. It reads literally: "It came to pass after these events, Naboth the Jezreelite had a vineyard in Jezreel." This may suggest that the story originally circulated independently, introduced by the words "Naboth the Jezreelite had a vineyard in Jezreel" (cf. the introduction of the Song of the Vineyard in Isa 5:1b, "My beloved had a vineyard on a very fertile hill"). That story has been appropriated by the narrator in this particular context and placed temporally after the events just presented.[72]

At the end of chap. 20, Ahab is said to have returned home to Samaria, "resentful and sullen" (20:43). Here, too, he is called "King of Samaria" (v. 1) and later is said to return home "resentful and sullen" (v. 4). Whatever the provenance, the narrator apparently wants the reader to think of the preceding events when reading this story.

Although Ahab has returned home to Samaria (20:43), he is thinking about a piece of real estate adjacent to his winter palace in Jezreel. Its considerably lower elevation makes Jezreel a warmer location than Samaria and, hence, a suitable site for a winter palace. The narrator refers to him as "King of Samaria," an unusual designation (found elsewhere only in 2 Kgs 1:3), perhaps to emphasize that his primary residence is in that city or to allude to the fact that Samaria was acquired as crown property only a generation earlier and has no Israelite tradition associated with it (see 16:23-24). In contrast, the desired property in Jezreel is owned by a local, "Naboth the Jezreelite."

Ahab wants to acquire the property in order to plant a vegetable garden because it is adjacent to his seasonal residence. He already has a palace in Samaria and one in Jezreel, but now he covets additional property (see Isa 5:8; Mic 2:1-2). Yet, the narrator may not merely have Ahab's covetousness in mind. He

---

72. That is, assuming the Hebrew tradition. The Greek text places the story after chapter 19 and before the account of the war with Aram.

tells us that Ahab intends to convert the vineyard into a "vegetable garden" (גן ירק *gan yārāq*), using an expression that occurs only one other time in the Hebrew Bible, in Deut 11:10. That passage contrasts the land that God has promised Israel's ancestors with the land of Egypt, where people have to depend on irrigation in order to grow a vegetable garden, whereas the promised land would be watered by rain from the sky. Moreover, elsewhere in Deuteronomy the promised land is described as a place where vineyards thrive naturally (Deut 6:10-12; 8:8-10). It is not surprising, therefore, that vineyards are often viewed in the Bible as a sign of God's blessings (Hos 2:15) and that Israel is sometimes depicted through the metaphor of a vineyard or a vine (Isa 3:13-15; 5:1-7; Jer 2:21; 12:10; Ezek 19:10-14; Hos 10:1). The proposed conversion of the vineyard into a vegetable garden, then, is ominous. It signals that there may be more at stake than a private real estate transaction. Indeed, this story is especially poignant when one recalls that the promised land is regarded as an inheritance given by the Lord (see, e.g., Exod 15:17; 32:13; Lev 20:2), and that portions of that land are but portions of this divinely given inheritance (Num 34:1-29; 35:8). Moreover, the term for Ahab's seizure of the land, ירש (*yāraš*, "take possession," vv. 15-16, 18), is the term used for Israel's possessing of the inheritance given by the Lord (Lev 20:24; Num 33:53; 35:2, 8; Deut 1:39).

21:3-4. Ahab's offer seems fair enough. He gives Naboth a choice of a better vineyard or a fair market price for the property. Naboth declines the offer: "the LORD forbid!" What he utters here is not a belligerent or indignant exclamation, however. The Hebrew expression means something like, "It is profanation for me because of the LORD!" The vineyard, Naboth says, is an ancestral inheritance. Israelite laws stipulate that ancestral estates should remain within the family or the clan; these rights are generally inalienable (Num 27:8-11; 36:1-12). Such laws were intended to preserve the territorial integrity of the original tribal assignments; that is the reason why, for example, intermarriages were not allowed in Israel, for such compromises would inevitably result in the loss of Israelite property to foreigners. The laws guard against the loss of

Israelite territory for economic or other reasons. Thus it is not merely for sentimental reasons that Naboth wants to hold on to his inheritance; it is a religious obligation for him to do so, and it would literally be profanation for him simply to trade it away. As one text puts it, in the mouth of the Lord, "The land shall not be sold in perpetuity, for the land is mine; with me you are but aliens and tenants" (Lev 25:23). One wonders, too, if the mixed marriage of Ahab and Jezebel does not makes the transaction so much more unacceptable. In any case, the land (which ultimately belongs to the Lord) is not for Ahab to take, just as the booty of holy war is not for him to spare. Hence, just as he returned home "resentful and sullen" because of the Lord's condemnation of his release of Benhadad (19:43), so also he now returns home "resentful and sullen" (v. 4), having had his offer to purchase Naboth's ancestral estate rejected. Naboth's invocation of the Lord's name makes further negotiations impossible. Ahab sulks and acts rather peevish, but he does not force the issue at this point, probably because he knows that he, even as king, is subject to the law. Not so Jezebel.

21:5-7. It is, perhaps, not a surprise that it is Jezebel, Ahab's Phoenician wife, who comes to the fore in the matter of the vineyard. She was the one who caused him to turn to patronize the Baal cult. It was she who tried to massacre the prophets of the Lord. It was to her that Ahab fled to report on Elijah's annihilation of Baal's prophets, and it was she who threatened Elijah's life. Now she mocks Ahab for not exercising his royal power, which suggests that she has no knowledge of or regard for the sort of constraints that Israelite law places on the king (Deut 17:14-20). So she arrogantly promises that she herself will give him the vineyard, as if it is within her rights to do so.

21:8-14. Jezebel literally takes over Ahab's royal authority. She writes letters in his name and seals them with his seal, sending them to elders and nobles who live with Naboth in his city—that is, the local leadership, charging them to proclaim a fast. In ancient Israel, a public fast may be called when there is a special need, particularly when a community faces a great distress or calamity (see, e.g., Judg 20:26; 1 Sam 14:24; 2 Chr 20:3) or when there is a grave sin that threatens the well-being of the entire community (1 Sam 7:6). The reason for the fast is not given here, but it will soon be clear that the pretext is the fabricated offenses of Naboth, which will be "exposed" at the gathering. So she instructs the elders and nobles, the latter perhaps people beholden to the crown for their wealth, to place Naboth in front of the assembly, a prominent place that Naboth probably would think is a mark of honor or indicative of his having a role in the proceedings. Opposite him would sit two "scoundrels" (בני-בליעל *běnê-běliyya'al*), meaning probably people without scruples, for they would commit perjury as witnesses to the trumped-up charges against Naboth. Jezebel is apparently sufficiently acquainted with Israelite law, for she knows that it would require two or three witnesses to corroborate the charges in a trial for a capital offense (Deut 17:6; 19:15). Naboth is to be charged with blasphemy and treason, both of which are subject to the death penalty (see 2:8-9; Lev 24:15-16; 2 Sam 16:9). So he is to be taken outside and stoned to death.

21:15-16. Jezebel's wishes are carried out to the last detail. Naboth is killed, and, the reader learns later, his corpse is left ignominiously unburied (v. 19). Thereupon, she tells Ahab to go and take possession of the vineyard, which he is now able to do, no doubt because there is no one left in Naboth's family to claim the inheritance; according to 2 Kgs 9:26, all the sons of Naboth were killed as well. Ahab, who released a foreign king whom he had defeated in a holy war, has allowed his queen to massacre a family of innocent Israelite citizens. Ben-hadad was not his to spare, but he spared him. Now there is no mercy for the innocent, and Ahab takes possession of a vineyard that is not his to take.

Naboth is only the human victim, the most immediate and obvious victim, of Ahab and Jezebel's malice. In one fell swoop, the very principles of Israelite society have been challenged as well. The office of the king has been usurped by a foreigner and corrupted with the king's acquiescence, if not consent. Neighbor has turned against neighbor. Those who are entrusted with the responsibility of upholding justice have perverted it. A solemn religious ritual becomes a pretext for a sham trial and, indeed, an occasion for perjury and murder. The law is manipulated to perpetrate gross injustice. The avarice of Ahab has led to the deaths of Naboth and his family, but that is by no means the only consequence of it. As one interpreter puts it, "The religious uniqueness of Israel, rooted in covenant and enshrined in law and tradition, is equally assaulted."[73] (See Reflections at 21:17-29.)

---

73. Walsh, *1 Kings*, 327.

1 Kings 21:17-29, Elijah Brings the Word of the Lord

COMMENTARY

Elijah, as usual, appears abruptly. It is unclear where he is when he is commanded to "go down" to meet Ahab, but that imperative suggests that Ahab is in Jezreel, which is only some 370 feet above sea level (see v. 18, where Ahab goes down to Jezreel). Accordingly, even though the Hebrew text refers to Ahab as "king of Israel, who is in Samaria," the NRSV and the NIV take it to mean that he is a king "who rules in Samaria." Like the reference to Ahab as "king of Samaria" (v. 1), however, the mention of Samaria may be an allusion to the capital mount as an Omride acquisition with no Israelite tradition. Indeed, the text tells us immediately that the king is in Naboth's vineyard, where he has gone (lit., "gone down") to take possession. Regardless of the indirect way by which Ahab has gone about acquiring the property, he is charged with murdering Naboth and taking possession of another person's property (see Exod 20:13, 17; Deut 5:17, 21). Hence, Elijah proclaims an oracle of doom against Ahab, promising him that he will receive the ignominious fate of Naboth upon his death, an oracle that is fulfilled later (see 22:38).

Even though Jezebel is the main schemer in the story, it is clear that Ahab is complicitous. Hence, when he hears Elijah's words of doom for him, he calls the prophet his enemy who has found him out (v. 20). Except for his initial offer to Naboth and the actual taking of the property, Ahab has been above the fray, allowing—perhaps even subtly manipulating—Jezebel to carry out his will. He is not innocent, however, for he has sold himself.

The reference to the death of Ahab leads the narrator to the stylized proclamation of the end of the dynasty in accordance with curses for the violation of the covenant (vv. 20-24; see also 13:33-34; 14:10-11; 16:1-4). The narrator manages, however, to work in a special word of doom for Jezebel (v. 23). There is no denial of Ahab's personal culpability, but the narrator notes that Jezebel has incited Ahab (cf. Deut 13:7). This assessment of Ahab is similar to the view of Solomon, whose marriage to foreign women caused him to stray from the way of the Lord (11:1-13). For the narrator, the issue boils down to idolatry or, to put the matter in terms of the covenant, disloyalty to the divine sovereign. Ahab has shown that he loves to possess Naboth's property more than he loves the Lord. Ahab's marriage to Jezebel, a devotee of Baal, has led to all this trouble.

At this point, one expects the story to conclude with an account of Ahab's death and how his dynasty comes to an abrupt end. That is not the case, however. Despite his use of the formulaic proclamation of the end of the dynasty, the narrator no doubt knows that Ahab's dynasty did not end with him, but would continue through the reigns of his sons Ahaziah and Jehoram. This delay of the end of Ahab's dynasty, according to the narrator, is a sign of the deity's grace. Surprisingly, Ahab acts penitently (v. 27; see also 2 Kgs 22:11, 19; Jonah 3:6), and that is enough for the Lord to turn back divine judgment, if only for a while.

REFLECTIONS

This passage paints a vivid picture of the abuse of power and social injustice. It tells of how a failed real estate transaction between a powerful king and an ordinary citizen leads to the frame-up of that citizen, a death sentence for him, and the confiscation of his property. Although the story is set in ancient Israel in the time of Ahab, it could be told with equal power and relevance in any period of human history. For those who take the passage as Scripture, this story, as well as the prophetic perspective on it, provides much material for theological reflection.

1. The issue at hand is an attempted business transaction between unequal partners, one who has all kinds of political and economic resources over against one who relies only on tradition and whatever protection society may provide through its legal and religious institutions. This is the kind of struggle that continues to take place today, not just between kings (or their modern equivalents) and their citizens, but also between large corporations and small businesses, powerful nations and nations that have only limited resources. The powerful in every generation will always have advisers who are clever enough to devise technically legal or quasi-legal means to achieve their clients' objectives. This passage lifts up a prophetic word against the manipulation of the legal and religious institutions to achieve such goals. It affirms that these activities do not take place without the notice of God. Ahab is found out, even though he has been mostly passive, allowing others to do the dirty work for him.

2. Chapter 21 is, in a sense, a profound exposition of the tenth commandment, the injunction against coveting something that belongs to another (Exod 20:17; Deut 5:21). We learn here that the problem lies not so much in our private desire to have something that another person has. The danger lies in the intensity of the greed that prompts someone to commit acts of violence against others in order to achieve his or her goals. Social order may be indirectly endangered by covetousness; on account of one individual's avarice, others may be quickly drawn into a web of betrayal and deceit. Moreover, this example shows how easily sin escalates. Covetousness leads quickly to perjury and murder; disregard for the tenth commandment leads to violation of the ninth and the sixth. It is no accident either that the narrator of this passage views Ahab's sin as idolatry—that is, violation of the first and second commandments (v. 26). Covetousness, in other words, is a form of idolatry: It is placing other priorities and desires before God; it is the elevation of material things to the status of gods. We hear the same warning in the New Testament: "Be sure of this, that no fornicator or impure person, or one who is greedy [that is, an idolater], has any inheritance in the kingdom of Christ and of God" (Eph 5:5 NRSV; see also Col 3:5).

3. The conclusion of the chapter (21:27-29) is jarring, but it is theologically profound. Ahab, having already been found out and judged harshly, goes through a ritual that suggests penitence. Given his track record, one might fairly question his motives. Is it a genuine expression of remorse, or is it an attempt to gain some reduction of sentence? Is he expressing sorrow for what he has done, or is he only sorry that he has been found out? God, however, does not second-guess Ahab's motives. Rather, despite the gravity of Ahab's offenses, God is quick to extend grace to the sinner. Ahab does not get off scot-free to be sure, but he is given the benefit of the doubt. This is the way God is: always ready to accept us, no matter how grave our sins may be, when we manifest the slightest will to repent.

1 KINGS 22:1-40, THE END OF AHAB'S REIGN

OVERVIEW

This literary unit, with the concluding regnal summary in vv. 37-40, brings the account of Ahab's reign (begun in 16:29-34) to a close. The present form of the narrative works well as a coherent unit, whatever its sources may have been. The bulk of the story has an almost verbatim parallel account in 2 Chr 18:3-34, which is somewhat surprising because the chronicler generally shows little interest in the affairs of northern kings. The 1 Kings account, however, has the additional chronological notice in vv. 1-2, the reference to Ahab's death as the fulfillment of Elijah's prophecy (vv. 37-38; see also 21:19-20), and the concluding regnal summary (vv. 37-40). The chapter is meant to be read as a part of the larger narrative, extending at least from 16:29.

1 Kings 22:1-5, Ahab Decides to Go to War

COMMENTARY

The narrator begins by noting that there was peace between Israel and Aram (Syria) for three years, meaning probably that the peace treaty signed by Ahab and his Aramean counterpart had been effective (20:34). The reader has already been apprised, however, of the fact that the treaty was not sanctioned by God, who, in fact, condemned Ahab for having spared the Aramean king's life and sentenced Ahab to death for that offense (20:42).

It is not a surprise to the reader, therefore, to learn that the peace would not last long— only long enough, it seems, to see Ahab further seal his fate through other offenses committed in his own kingdom (21:20-24). Ironically, Ahab is the one who now breaks that peace treaty and initiates hostile action that would lead to the fulfillment of the prophecies of the unnamed prophet in 20:42 and Elijah (21:19-20) regarding his death.

After years at war with Judah (14:30; 15:6-7, 16-22), there is now peace between the two sister nations as well. It was probably Jehoshaphat of Judah who had sued for peace (v. 44), forging a new, though unequal, alliance between Israel and Judah that was sealed by the marriage of Ahab's daughter to Jehoshaphat's son (2 Kgs 8:18, 26; 2 Chr 18:1). The relatively strong position of Ahab over his Judean counterpart is indicated by the subservient role Jehoshaphat plays throughout this narrative. Here we see him appearing before Ahab (v. 2), perhaps having been summoned to hear Ahab's proposal.[74]

74. In accordance with the mythopoeic assumption of Jerusalem as being set on the highest mountain, the narrator speaks of Jehoshaphat's going down to Ahab, who is presumably in Samaria.

Ahab wants to recover from the Arameans the city of Ramoth-gilead in a region of the Transjordan that was probably assigned to Israel when the kingdom was divided in the late tenth century BCE. The city had fallen into Aramean hands at some point, possibly during the reign of Ben-hadad, son of Tabrimmon (15:20); but it had not been returned to Israel as Ahab's peace treaty with Ben-hadad stipulated (20:34). This is clearly Ahab's war to fight (see vv. 4, 6, 11-12, 15), but Jehoshaphat pledges his support, no doubt because he does not have much of a choice in the matter, only urging Ahab to get an oracle from the Lord first, which is standard practice in ancient Israel (see Judg 20:27-28; 1 Sam 14:36-37; 23:1-5; 30:7-8; 2 Sam 5:19). (See Reflections at 22:29-40.)

1 Kings 22:6-12, Ahab Finds Prophetic Consensus

COMMENTARY

Ahab gathers "about four hundred" prophets together (the parallel account has simply "four hundred"; see 2 Chr 18:5). The narrator does not say that they are prophets of the Lord and may, indeed, be implying that they are not. The number 400 is reminiscent of the four hundred prophets of Asherah whom Ahab gathered on Mt. Carmel (18:19-20).[75] Elijah is said to have killed the 450 prophets of Baal (18:22, 40), but nothing is said about the fate of the other four hundred. After Ahab's prophetic advisers encourage him to proceed with the attack,[76] Jehoshaphat asks if there is no prophet of the Lord left who might be consulted, saying, literally, "Is there not here a prophet of the Lord anymore of whom we may inquire?" (v. 7).[77]

Ahab admits that there is still one person left whom he can consult. Taken literally, that claim would be untrue, of course, for we know that Elijah, Elisha, the hundred prophets saved by Obadiah, and other prophets are still around. The reader is probably supposed to think of the previous confrontation between a large contingent of illegitimate prophets and a single prophet of the Lord (see chap. 18). The lone prophet this time is a hitherto unknown Micaiah son of Imlah, and Ahab dislikes him, just as he disliked the other lone prophet who confronted the majority whom Ahab had earlier mustered. Still, with the encouragement of Jehoshaphat, Ahab quickly summons Micaiah.

Meanwhile, the two kings hold court at a "threshing floor" outside the city gates of Samaria, apparently an open area where a public event might be witnessed by a large audience. There, the four hundred prophets prophesy, and a certain prophet named Zedekiah, the son of Chenaanah, performs a prophetic sign-act (cf. Deut 33:17), a dramatization that is supposed to set the fulfillment of a prophecy in motion (see, e.g., 11:29-31; 2 Kgs 13:14-19; Isa 20:1-6; Jer 13:1-7; Ezek 4:1-5:4). The prophecy in this case is victory for Ahab at Ramoth-gilead![78] This message has the concurrence of all the prophets present. (See Reflections at 22:29-40.)

75. Apart from this passage and its parallel (see 2 Chr 18:5), the precise Hebrew idiom for gathering the prophets occurs only in 18:20, in connection with Ahab's assembling of the prophets of Baal and Asherah.

76. The NRSV assumes that the prophets are promising victory from "the LORD" (i.e., יהוה *Yahweh*), but the best Hebrew MSS read אדני (*ʾădōnāy*). The parallel account has "God" (2 Chr 18:5).

77. The NRSV's translation ("Is there no other prophet of the LORD here?") suggests that the 400 are prophets of the Lord, but the text is ambiguous—perhaps deliberately so.

78. This time there is no question that the divine name is meant. One interpreter thinks that Ahab's prophets are now acceding to Jehoshaphat's request for an oracle from the Lord. See Walsh, *1 Kings*, 347.

1 Kings 22:13-28, The Lone Voice of Micaiah, Son of Imlah

COMMENTARY

22:13-18. Pressure is put on Micaiah to go along with the consensus of Ahab's prophets and "speak favorably," but Micaiah promises only to speak what the Lord tells him. When Micaiah is first queried by Ahab, he simply repeats the answer of the majority. The king knows, however, that this is not the truth. He knows this, perhaps, because of the tone and manner of Micaiah's delivery. Or it may be that the king knows all too well that Micaiah would not say anything favorable to him (see v. 8). In any case, Ahab adjures the prophet to speak the truth "in the name of the LORD," something that Micaiah did not do in his initial response. Yet, when Micaiah prophesies disaster in the Lord's name (v. 17), Ahab says it only confirms his impression of Micaiah: that the prophet is always going to be a naysayer as far as Ahab is concerned.

Micaiah is clearly prophesying the demise of Ahab; "mountains" is probably an allusion to Ramoth-gilead (the name in Hebrew means "the Heights of Gilead"), and "shepherd" is a commonly used metaphor throughout the ancient Near East for kings (see 2 Sam 5:2; Isa 44:28; Jer 23:4; 25:34, 36; Ezek 34:23; 37:24; Zech 13:7). Ahab, however, is not interested in a genuine oracle from the Lord. He accepts only the oracles that are favorable—namely, those that corroborate his intention and support the action that he plans to take. Perhaps he is going through the farce of getting an oracle only for political reasons—to placate his ally, Jehoshaphat, and to convince the populace to follow him, which is probably the reason for the public drama at the threshing floor outside the gates of the capital city.

22:19-25. Micaiah then describes a vision of the Lord sitting enthroned in the celestial court, surrounded by members of the divine council (the "heavenly host"). This vision, which bears some resemblance to the inaugural vision of Isaiah (Isa 6:1-8), authenticates Micaiah's role as a prophet of the Lord. It points to him as a true prophet, for a true prophet is given the opportunity to witness the proceedings in the divine council (Jer 23:18-22). The issue at stake here, as in Jeremiah 23:1, is the question of true prophecy versus false prophecy.

In Micaiah's vision, the Lord asks for a volunteer from the divine council to go and trick Ahab into going into battle, only to be struck down. One of the members of the council comes forward, proposing to be a "lying spirit" in the mouth of Ahab's prophets in order that they might entice him into going to war (see Jer 20:7; Ezek 14:9; see also 2 Thess 2:11). The volunteer is duly charged with the task by the Lord and is promised success. Micaiah then interprets the vision for Ahab, telling him that the false prophets who give him what he wants to hear are speaking for the lying spirit. When Zedekiah points out through a sarcastic question that it is difficult to prove the validity of one claim over the other (v. 24), Micaiah replies that it will become clear when Zedekiah will have to hide, the imagery being reminiscent of Ben-hadad's hiding to avoid being killed (see 20:30).

22:26-28. Ahab orders Micaiah's arrest and imprisonment, no doubt because his negative utterances undermine Ahab's war efforts. Yet, Ahab apparently wants the prophet alive, perhaps as insurance, in case his plan fails after all. Still, the king expects to return safely. The prophet retorts, however, that Ahab's safe return would prove that Micaiah is a false prophet, which means probably that Micaiah would be killed (see Deut 18:20-22).

1 Kings 22:29-40, Ahab Dies

COMMENTARY

For all his bravado, Ahab seems to know the seriousness of Micaiah's oracle, which supports the predictions of Ahab's death by both the unnamed prophet (20:42) and Elijah (21:20-24). Ahab is determined to carry out his plan, but, as a precautionary measure, he disguises himself and asks Jehoshaphat to put on the royal garb of the Israelite king. Thereby Ahab intends not only to deceive the enemy, but also to thwart the will of the Lord. The narrator tells us that the Arameans focus all their attention on getting Ahab; he is their sole target.

Ahab's deception works initially. The Arameans go after Jehoshaphat, thinking that he is Ahab, but they turn back when they realize that they have been tricked. The Lord, however, is not duped. Someone shoots an arrow, unintentionally striking Ahab, and manages to wound him at one of the few vulnerable spots in his armor. The text does not tell us whether the arrow is shot by an enemy soldier or if it is "friendly fire," only that Ahab is hit by someone. Ahab may be able to deceive his enemies, but he is not able to outwit the Lord after all. One suspects that what seems accidental is in reality an act of God.

Ahab asks to be taken out of the battle, presumably to be treated. The fighting is too intense, however. His soldiers merely prop him up on the chariot facing the enemy to disguise the fact that he has been wounded, and he remains in the chariot that way, bleeding until his death at the end of the day. The incapacitated king does not, of course, provide any leadership, thus fulfilling the oracle of Micaiah in v. 17. The troops are able to return home safely, despite the absence of Ahab's leadership, again fulfilling the prophecy of Micaiah: "These have no masters, let them go home in safety" (v. 17). The Hebrew word בשלום (*bĕšālôm*) may mean "in safety" (so TNK) or "in peace" (so NRSV, NIV). The point is not that they will have peace but that they will return home without hindrance.

The fact that Ahab bled in the chariot for a long time also explains why the chariot is thoroughly soaked with blood, so that dogs could lick it, thus at least partially fulfilling the prophecy of Elijah (21:19; Elijah prophesied that Ahab's blood would be licked by dogs "in the place" where dogs licked up Naboth's blood. If that place refers to Jezreel, then the prophecy is only partially fulfilled). The reference to prostitutes bathing in the blood, perhaps meaning the blood that stains the pool in Samaria, is enigmatic. It seems to refer to an oracle for which there is now no record. The account of Ahab's reign, then, ends in the stereotypical manner, with references to further documentation of Ahab's performance as king and a note about his successor (v. 39).

REFLECTIONS

Chapter 22 is not a passage for anyone who comes to Scripture in search of easy moralistic lessons, for there are none. At the heart of the story is an account of God's initiative in the perpetration of a lie, the divine commissioning of a spirit that intentionally deceives people into self-destructive action. That perspective will not sit easily with the church. Yet, the story must be told and its lessons taught.

1. The first lesson is a negative one. In this story we see just how recalcitrant human beings can be. Here is Ahab, a man who has personally witnessed the manifestation of God's power, who has heard the word of the Lord through several prophets, and, despite his sins, has experienced the grace of God when he expressed penitence. Still, he does not seem to understand what it is that God demands. He has little understanding of the nature of God. He has a personal agenda that he is determined to carry out.

So he musters all his resources. He gets his subordinates and allies to do his bidding and does not hesitate to manipulate the religious establishment to support his questionable goals. He ignores what he knows to be the truth and suppresses any voice of dissent. He even tries to thwart God's will by deceit in order to achieve his goal. Ahab is a model of what we can become when we are not attentive to the will of God.

2. The passage, however, acknowledges with remarkable honesty that it is not an easy thing to discern the will of God. Sometimes we are confronted with conflicting truth claims, the veracity of which can be authenticated only in retrospect, when it is too late. Even a "true prophet" (like Micaiah) sometimes speaks untruth. The passage does not provide a direct answer to the implicit question of how one may in practice discern what truth is, but it does warn against equating majority opinion, or even consensus, with truth. There are too many positive-thinking people who give us feel-good messages, proclaiming, "Peace! Peace!" when there is no peace (Jer 6:14). Or there may be some who are all too ready to pander to the powerful. Those who wish to know the will of God cannot simply find the messengers who will confirm their outlook and support their agenda but who will tell it like it is, even if the message is contrary to what we might expect or desire. Indeed, the word of God may not come through the popular majority but through those whom we may regard as troublers or enemies or naysayers. Perhaps we should listen especially carefully when the word makes us uncomfortable.

3. The most profound, if also confounding, theological message in this passage is that God may not fit our preconceived image of unimpeachable goodness. The passage jolts us into the realization that such a notion of deity, ironically, is too limiting for God. Such a god would be an idol, a god of our own creation. Rather, the passage forces us to deal with a God who is sovereign, a God who is absolutely free to use any means— even those contrary to human reason or standards of morality—in order to bring divine purpose to fulfillment. The God of the Bible is a sovereign deity who oversees all that goes on in the world, darkness as well as light, woe as well as weal (Isa 45:7). The biblical God may harden people's hearts so that they do not respond to God aright (Exod 4:21; 9:12; 10:1, 20, 27; 11:10; 14:8; Deut 2:30; Isa 6:10; Rom 9:18), incite people to do wrong and then condemn them (2 Sam 24:1), deceive people (Jer 4:10), or send lying spirits (2 Thess 2:11). Yet, God's thoughts are not our thoughts, neither are God's ways our ways (Isa 55:8). The sovereign God will use whatever means necessary to bring about divine will—whether in judgment or in salvation.

1 KINGS 22:41-53, JEHOSHAPHAT OF JUDAH AND AHAZIAH OF ISRAEL

OVERVIEW

The remaining verses of 1 Kings concern the reigns of two rulers: Jehoshaphat of Judah (vv. 41-50) and Ahaziah of Israel (vv. 51-53). The account of Jehoshaphat is much shorter than what one finds in the chronicler's version (2 Chronicles 17–21), for the narrator of 1 Kings is not interested in much of the details of royal history, only with the performance of the kings according to the standards set forth in Deuteronomy. The brief account is, in any case, self-contained: It begins and ends with the typical regnal summaries for Judean kings. By contrast, the account of Ahaziah's reign is incomplete. It is, in fact, only the introduction of a longer account that continues through 2 Kgs 1:18.

1 Kings 22:41-50, The Reign of Jehoshaphat of Judah

COMMENTARY

Jehoshaphat (873–849 BCE) has already been mentioned as the successor to Asa (15:24) and in connection with his alliance with Ahab. Now comes the formal report of his reign, and it is a relatively positive one. He is said to have "walked in all the way of his father Asa," not turning aside from it and doing what was right in the sight of the Lord (v. 43). Yet, the high places (local sanctuaries) were not removed, and people continued to sacrifice and offer incense there. He continued his father's policy of removing the cult prostitutes from the country (15:12).[79] He is also credited with making peace with Israel (v. 44), with the domination of Edom (v. 47), and with engaging in maritime activities (v. 48).

While the report echoes the assessment of Asa (15:9-24), both positively and negatively, it also calls to mind Solomon's reign in many ways. The observation that the king followed the ways of his father faithfully, except for the problem of the local sanctuaries, recalls a similar evaluation of Solomon (3:2-3). The mention of peace with Israel brings to mind the peace that Solomon wrought (4:24; 5:12) and recalls the unity of Israel and Judah under him. Like Solomon, too, Jehoshaphat was able to control Edom and, hence, gain access to the Red Sea port of Ezion-geber (see 9:26-27). Apparently, he also attempted to repeat the maritime successes of Solomon by sending expeditions to find gold in Ophir (9:28; 10:11). Yet, Jehoshaphat was unable to repeat Solomon's successes: His expeditions were aborted because the ships were wrecked at the port of Ezion-geber, and, despite the peace with Israel, he was unwilling to let the Israelites go on his ships. Jehoshaphat, in fact, was not like Solomon in giftedness or achievements. He was like Solomon, however, in that he was an heir to the Davidic throne. He ruled in Jerusalem, the Lord's chosen city, and was buried, like all his Judean predecessors, in the city of "his father David" (v. 50). (See Reflections at 22:51-53.)

79. As in 15:12, we should take the word קדשים (qĕdēšîm) as an inclusive term for all cult prostitutes and not just the male ones, as the NRSV and the NIV have it.

1 Kings 22:51-53, The Reign of Ahaziah of Israel

COMMENTARY

Just as Jehoshaphat walked in the ways of his father, Asa (v. 43), so also Ahaziah (850–849 BCE) walked in the ways of his father, Ahab, and his mother, Jezebel (v. 52). Moreover, just as Jehoshaphat's reign is associated with those of Solomon and David, so also Ahaziah's reign is linked with Jeroboam's. Jehoshaphat did what was right in the sight of the Lord (v. 43), but Ahaziah did what was evil in the sight of the Lord (v. 52). Finally, Jehoshaphat was buried in the city of David "his father" (v. 50), but Ahaziah provoked the anger of the Lord "just as his father had done" (v. 53).

REFLECTIONS

Most readers of the concluding verses of 1 Kings will no doubt notice the different tones in the brief reports of the two reigns: One is generally positive, the other utterly negative. Jehoshaphat tried to be faithful, while Ahaziah was faithless. One may, of course, point to the importance of faithfulness to the Lord, surely a legitimate lesson to be drawn from the text. Yet, the larger and more important issue is that both kings came short of the Lord's demands. The real difference between the two is that one of them, by God's will alone, was heir to the throne of David. Whatever place Jehoshaphat may have in salvation history, it will not be because of his righteousness, but because of the sovereign will of God.

2 KINGS 1:1-18, AHAZIAH'S APOSTASY

OVERVIEW

The end of 1 Kings (22:51-53) begins the formal account of Ahaziah's reign. That report is continued and completed in this passage, with the stylized regnal summary at the end (vv. 17-18). The story echoes Elijah's encounter with Ahaziah's father, Ahab, on Mt. Carmel (1 Kings 18:1). Elijah comes into the picture, as before, on account of a summons from on high. As in the previous encounter of prophet and king as well, the initial contact between the two is through intermediaries. Above all, the presence of Elijah on top of a mount echoes the contest on Mt. Carmel, as does the descent of fire from heaven.

2 Kings 1:1, The Rebellion of Moab

COMMENTARY

The reference to Moab's rebellion is awkward, for it seems to have nothing to do with the rest of the chapter. Moab, in fact, does not become a factor in the narrative until 3:4-27. It is possible, therefore, that this verse has been misplaced (note the similar notice of Moab's rebellion in 3:5). Yet, it is not impossible to read the reference in its context. The narrator may intend to point to the loss of hegemony over Moab as a consequence of the Israelite king's unfaithfulness (see 1 Kgs 22:51-53). Moab had been subjugated since the time of David (2 Sam 8:12), but now Israel is beginning to lose control of it and will completely do so by the time of Jehoram, who is similarly unfaithful to the Lord (2 Kgs 3:4-27). By contrast, Judah gained influence over Edom in the reign of Jehoshaphat, Ahaziah's contemporary (1 Kgs 22:47).

2 Kings 1:2-4, Ahaziah Turns to Baal-Zebub

COMMENTARY

The introduction of the account of Ahaziah's reign (1 Kgs 22:51-53) casts him as a servant and worshiper of Baal, just like his father Ahab (1 Kgs 16:31). Now we see the extent and effect of Ahaziah's apostasy. When he injures himself as a result of a fall, he sends messengers to Ekron to seek an oracle from the local manifestation of Baal, called Baal-Zebub ("Baal the Fly" or, as one might say, "Baal the Pest"),[80] a deliberate distortion by the narrator of the name "Baal-Zebul" ("Baal the Prince"; cf. "Beelzebul" in the NT: Matt 10:25; 12:24, 27; Mark 3:22; Luke 11:15, 18-19).[81] Ekron is a Philistine town some twenty-two miles west of Jerusalem, so it appears that Ahaziah is going out of his way to seek this god rather than the Lord in Jerusalem.

Like his father, Ahab, Ahaziah is also challenged by Elijah, who, as usual, appears

---

80. The Greek translators understood the name to mean "Baal the Fly." In the HB, flies are considered a nuisance (Eccl 10:1; Isa 7:18).

81. This designation of Baal, attested in Ugaritic mythology, is also suggested by the name "Jezebel" (איזבל ʾîzebel).

on the scene abruptly. "An angel" (מלאך *mal' āk*) of the Lord tells Elijah to intercept Ahaziah's "messengers" (מלאכים *mal'ākîm*) and deliver a word of judgment for the king through them. (See Reflections at 1:9-18.)

2 Kings 1:5-8, The Messengers Report Their Encounter

COMMENTARY

Ahaziah's emissaries apparently do not complete their task for him, for they have been turned back by Elijah. They tell the king about their encounter with the prophet, without naming him. Whereas Elijah had asked them why they were going to ask for the oracle in Ekron, they interpret the problem to be Ahaziah's initiative in sending them. That is, of course, a logical conclusion on their part, since doom is pronounced not on them but on the king, an oracle that they duly repeat.

They tell Ahaziah that the man who confronted them was, literally, "a man, a possessor of hair" (איש בעל שער *' îš ba'al śē'ār*) who wore a leather belt. The first description probably alludes to a hairy mantle that may have been a mark of prophetic authority (see Zech 13:4). In any case, Ahaziah immediately recognizes the description as fitting Elijah. (See Reflections at 1:9-18.)

2 Kings 1:9-18, Ahaziah Challenges Elijah

COMMENTARY

The king sends "a captain of fifty with his fifty men" to Elijah. Whereas Elijah previously had to "go up" to intercept the king's messengers, Ahaziah's men now have to go up to meet Elijah, who is on top of the "mount" (הר *har*, the same Hebrew word used for *Mount* Carmel, so we should not translate it as "a hill" as in the NIV and the NRSV). The captain addresses Elijah as "man of God" and gives the king's command to "come down." Elijah's reply plays on the similarity of the term for "man" (איש *' îš*) to the word for "fire" (אש *' ēš*). Ahaziah wishes to bring the man of God down, but he succeeds only in bringing down a fire from heaven that consumes all his men—just like the consuming fire on Mt. Carmel. The king apparently has not learned the lesson from recent history. He has learned nothing from his father's mistakes. Worse still, he does not seem to learn from his own mistakes, for he sends a second squad of fifty to bring the man of God down, with the same consequences as before, and then a third squad. The captain of the third group, however, does not obey the king. Rather, he pleads with the prophet to spare his life and the lives of his men.

The angel of the Lord then reappears to order Elijah to go down with the captain to face the king and to reiterate in person the Lord's word of doom for his having turned to Baal-zebub. The command to "go down" is reminiscent of God's command to Moses to "go down" from the mount of God because the people of Israel had turned away from God and become idolatrous (see Exod 32:7; Deut 9:12).

The story ends with the death of Ahaziah as the fulfillment of prophecy and the typical regnal summary, with its references to further information on the reign.

REFLECTIONS

The fundamental issue that this passage treats is the violation of the first commandment, God's initial charge to the covenant people: "You shall have no other gods before me" (Exod 20:3 NRSV; Deut 5:7). Ahaziah's problem is that he believes that Baal-zebub, rather than Israel's God, is the lord of life. The passage makes plain, however, that life is the Lord's to give and to take away and that life is mediated through the proclamation of the word of the Lord. This is a lesson that two disciples of Jesus, James and John, had to learn (Luke 9:54-55). Angry that the Samaritans (descendants of the northern kingdom) seemed to have rejected Jesus, James and John offered to bring down fire from heaven to consume the unbelievers. In other words, they wanted to do what Elijah had done to the northerners. Jesus, however, rebuked them, and they simply went on. It is the Lord who takes away life and the Lord who spares life.

2 KINGS 2:1-25, PROPHETIC SUCCESSION

OVERVIEW

This chapter is sandwiched between the regnal summary of Ahaziah's reign (1:17-18) and the introductory résumé of Jehoram's (3:1-2). The historical accounting of the performance of the kings of Israel and Judah is interrupted by the momentous event of prophetic succession.

The chapter marks both the end of Elijah's ministry and the beginning of Elisha's. The latter has already been introduced in 1 Kgs 19:19-21, where we find an account of his calling by Elijah. Yet, Elisha is not mentioned again until now. Henceforth, however, he will be the key prophetic figure—through the reigns of the next four kings of Israel (Jehoram, Jehu, Jehoahaz, Jehoash)—that is,

during the second half of the eighth century BCE (2 Kings 3–13).

The chapter may be divided into two parts: the first concerns the ascension of Elijah to heaven and Elisha's taking of the mantle of prophetic leadership (vv. 1-18); the second reports two incidents that show the power and authority of Elisha as Elijah's successor (vv. 19-25). The second portion is deliberately joined with the first and is meant to be read with it. Note, for instance, that "the city" and "this city" in v. 19 must refer to Jericho (see vv. 15-17), and the mention of "Bethel" (v. 23) takes the reader back to the beginning of the story (vv. 2-3).

2 Kings 2:1-18, Elisha Succeeds Elijah

COMMENTARY

2:1-8. The narrator tips the reader off right away that Elijah will soon be taken up to heaven in a whirlwind, an event that is recounted in vv. 11-12, the climax of the passage. Elijah has, of course, been the key prophetic voice throughout the reigns of Ahab and Ahaziah. Although there have been others speaking for the Lord during that period, he looms larger than all others and

is portrayed by the narrator as a prophet like Moses (see Commentary on 1 Kgs 18:30-46; 19:4-18; 2 Kgs 1:1-15). Now that Elijah is departing the scene, the narrator takes great pains to show that there is a worthy successor to him: Elisha, who has already been chosen (1 Kgs 19:19-21).

The rite of passage begins with a journey taken by both Elijah and Elisha (vv. 1-8). They travel from Gilgal down to Bethel,[82] then from Bethel to Jericho, and finally from Jericho to the Jordan River. At each stop, Elijah tells his disciple to remain behind while he continues on the journey, but Elisha refuses to leave him (vv. 2, 4, 6). The point is probably Elisha's profound commitment to his master and his determination to follow him to the end (cf. Ruth 1:16-17). One should perhaps also compare the initial call of Elisha and how Elijah merely tossed the mantle at him and passed on, while Elisha had to chase after him (1 Kgs 19:19-21). Elisha had sacrificed the capital and tools of his trade to follow Elijah and attend to him. Now Elisha persists in staying with his master. He has, indeed, understood the significance of Elijah's symbolic gesture of throwing the mantle of the prophet upon him (see Commentary on 19:20).

Elisha clearly knows what he is doing, as we note from his reply to the prophetic colleagues who ask him, literally, "Do you know that today the Lord is taking your master from over your head?" (vv. 3, 5).[83] They probably mean that Elijah would no longer be in charge of Elisha ("over your head"), but the reader, duly tipped off by the narrator in v. 1, knows that Elijah would be taken literally above the head of Elisha—that is, up to heaven. Elisha is not being led unwittingly into his new role, it seems. He is fully cognizant of the implication of the rite of passage, although he tells his inquirers to be silent (cf. Mark 9:9, 30).

At last, the two prophets come to the Jordan (v. 6-8). At their other stops, these prophetic witnesses spoke with Elisha, but now they remain in the distance as Elijah and Elisha come to the bank of the Jordan. There Elijah rolls up his mantle, probably into some semblance of a rod, and strikes the water of the river. Thereupon, the waters part and the two prophets cross over on dry ground. Elijah's mantle, the symbol of his authority and power, is apparently the equivalent of Moses' rod (Exod 14:16). Specifically, the event recalls Moses' parting of the water of the Sea of Reeds (Exod 14:21-22). The implication of the act is that Elijah is a prophet like Moses.

That kind of prophetic leadership is now at stake.

2:9-12. Having crossed the Jordan, they are now in the region where Moses had died. There, Elisha asks to inherit a "double portion" of Elijah's spirit, an allusion to the legal right of the firstborn (Deut 21:15-17). Elisha, in other words, is asking to be treated as Elijah's principal heir. The "double portion" refers to two-thirds of the inheritance (the term שנים [šěnayim] is used in this sense in Zech 13:8), not twice the measure of the prophetic spirit that Elijah possesses. Here the "spirit" refers to the divinely endowed charisma that may be apportioned and transferred to others (see Num 11:16-17, 24-26). Elijah says that the request is difficult, meaning that it is difficult for a human being to meet. He states, in essence, that the privilege is not his to give (cf. Mark 10:38); if Elisha witnesses Elijah's departure, then his wish will be granted.

Accordingly, as the two are busy walking and talking, "fiery chariots and fiery horses" (NEB) suddenly separate them from each other, and Elijah ascends to the heavens in a tempest.[84] Since fire is often associated with the numinous in the Bible (e.g., Exod 3:2; 19:18; 24:17; Deut 4:12; 9:3), the reader is meant to understand these chariots and horses to be vehicles of the celestial hosts. Amid the pandemonium, Elijah ascends into the sky in a tempest (cf. Job 27:20; Nah 1:3).

Witnessing the whole scene, Elisha cries out: "My father, my father! The chariots of Israel and its horsemen!" The significance of Elisha's outcry is disputed. The same expression occurs in 13:14 in reference to Elisha, almost as a title, probably an indication of the prophet's role in the holy war against Aram (see 6:8-23; 13:14-19). In any case, it is difficult to separate "the chariots of Israel and its horsemen" in v. 12 from the fiery chariots and horses in v. 11. In Israel's ideology of holy war, the Lord's celestial hosts fight along with and on behalf of the terrestrial hosts, the armies of Israel; the latter is but a microcosm of the former (see Num 10:35-36; Deut 33:2).[85] The vision, like Joshua's vision

---

82. There are a number of locations in the Bible known as Gilgal ("Circle"). Since the prophets *go down* from there to Bethel, it is unlikely that the Gilgal beside the Jordan (Joshua 3–4) is meant. Rather, many scholars have identified the Gilgal in 2 Kings 2 with a site seven miles north of Bethel and on a higher elevation.

83. The NIV and the NRSV both interpret the expression to mean simply that Elijah will be taken from Elisha.

84. The word רכב (*rekeb*) here probably refers not only to a single chariot (NRSV, NIV), but also, as in the next verse and frequently in the HB (see also 13:14; Exod 14:23; Dan 11:40), to a group of chariots. Elijah is taken up in the whirlwind, not in a chariot.

85. See Patrick D. Miller, *The Divine Warrior in Early Israel*, HSM 5 (Cambridge, Mass.: Harvard University Press, 1975) 134-35.

of the captain of the celestial host (Josh 5:13-15), is an empowering one. It foreshadows the kind of ministry that Elisha will have—he will have a role to play in Israel's wars—and hints at the source of his power. Elisha then rends his garment in two, a sign of mourning (see Gen 37:34; Josh 7:6; Judg 11:35; 2 Sam 13:31).

2:13-18. The story has reached its climax. Elisha has, indeed, seen Elijah "taken" from him. Now Elisha picks up the mantle of Elijah, first thrown on him by the master (1 Kgs 19:19), and begins the second half of his rite of passage, returning whence he came: first to the Jordan (vv. 13-14), then to Jericho (vv. 15-22), on to Bethel (vv. 23-24), and finally to Mt. Carmel and Samaria (v. 25).[86] Elisha returns to the bank of the Jordan. Once again, he plays Joshua to Elijah's Moses (see Commentary on 1 Kgs 19:21). Just as Elijah parted the water with his mantle, so also Elisha parts the water with the same mantle. Elisha's reenactment, in fact, recalls Joshua's marvelous crossing of the Jordan to enter the promised land after the death of Moses (Josh 3:7-17).

The members of the prophetic guild who had witnessed Elijah and Elisha crossing

the Jordan from a distance (v. 7-8) now see Elisha, again from a distance (v. 15). They know, no doubt from Elisha's repetition of Elijah's miraculous act, that the spirit of Elijah now rests upon Elisha. Joshua, the servant and eventual successor of Moses, had also received the spirit when Moses laid his hands upon him (Num 27:18-23; Deut 34:9). So, too, Elisha is endowed with the spirit of Elijah. The company of prophets bow down to Elisha, just as Obadiah had bowed down to Elijah (1 Kgs 18:7), and offer to search for Elijah. They were apparently not privy to the vision that Elisha saw across the Jordan, although they know that something marvelous has happened (cf. Dan 10:7; Acts 9:7). Elisha, knowing what has happened, tries to discourage them from looking for Elijah, but is unable to dissuade them. They look for three days without success. The narrative purpose of the episode is to show that Elijah has, indeed, disappeared from the face of the earth without a trace. In some ways, then, he was like Moses, who left the earth without leaving a burial site that could be known to anyone (Deut 34:5-6). Elisha is aware, and the reader is likewise privileged to know, however, that Elijah had ascended to the heavens.

---

86. Cf. Elisha's trip with Elijah from Gilgal to Bethel (vv. 2-3), Jericho (vv. 4-5), and the Jordan (vv. 6-8).

---

2 Kings 2:19-25, Elisha's Power Illustrated

COMMENTARY

2:19-22. Immediately following the account of his assumption of the mantle of Elijah, the narrator illustrates the power and authority of Elisha through two episodes. The first tells of a miraculous act at Jericho (cf. the miracles wrought by Elijah at the beginning of his ministry, 1 Kgs 17:8-24). Elisha learns that the water at Jericho is not potable ("bad"), apparently causing the land to be unproductive (lit., "bringing bereavement"). Rationalistic explanations have been proffered for that situation. One theory, citing hydrological studies, suggests that geological disturbances caused a high amount of radioactive pollutants to be released into the springs of the region, yielding water that has been shown

by laboratory tests to cause sterility.[87] Another hypothesis traces the problem to certain species of freshwater snails that have been found in excavations at Jericho; these snails are known to be carriers of a disease responsible for high infant mortality.[88] Whatever the explanation, Elisha miraculously purifies the water by throwing salt into it, a formula that has also tantalized rationalists. The chemical formula necessary to purify the contaminated water is, of course, of no interest to the narrator, who notes only that it is the Lord who

---

87. See I. M. Blake, "Jericho (Ain es-Sultan): Joshua's Curse and Elisha's Miracle, One Possible Explanation," *PEQ* 99 (1967) 86-97.

88. E. V. Hulse, "Joshua's Curse and the Abandonment of Ancient Jericho: Schistosomiasis as a Possible Medical Explanation," *Medical History* 15 (1971) 376-86.

has made the water drinkable. Despite the difference in method, the incident is reminiscent of Moses' sweetening of the bitter water at Marah by throwing wood into it (Exod 15:23-25). Elisha has even surpassed Moses. The latter had only sweetened water that was bitter, but the former has "healed" deadly water: "there will no longer be death or bereavement from there" (v. 21).[89]

2:23-25. The next incident, however, is not so savory. Elisha is on his way from Jericho to Bethel when he comes across a group of young lads who deride him: "Go up, baldy! Go up, baldy!" (v. 23). Elisha curses them in the name of the Lord, whereupon two female bears appear from the woods to maul forty-two of the youngsters. Elisha's harsh reaction to the seemingly innocuous taunt seems horribly out of proportion. Interpreters through the centuries have tried to exonerate the prophet by explaining the taunt as something more than a ridiculing of the prophet's physical appearance—an attack on his prophetic office (indicated by his "tonsure"), an insult directed at the prophet that is tantamount to an attack on God, an attempt to prevent him from going to the Bethel sanctuary, a taunt that he should go to the heretical Bethel sanctuary, and the like. No explanation is convincing, however. If the taunt meant more than what it seems now, that original meaning is lost to the modern reader, who cannot even be certain if the imperative in Hebrew means "Go away!" (NRSV), "Go on up!" (NIV), or simply "Go up!" (KJV). What is evident, when all is said and done, is that the narrator has juxtaposed this episode illustrating the prophet's power to inflict deadly punishment (cf. 1:9-16) alongside the story of his power to turn away death (vv. 19-22). Perhaps the point is that Elisha's ministry, like that of Moses, offers the possibility of blessings or curses, life or death.

The story concludes with Elisha going to Mt. Carmel, the mountain best known for the manifestation of the Lord's power over Baal and his prophets, and then to Samaria, where the kings of Israel reign. These destinations signal to the reader that the prophet has truly taken up the mantle of his predecessor.

89. For the parallelism of "death" and "bereavement," see Lam 1:20 and cf. Theodore J. Lewis, *Ugaritic Narrative Poetry*, ed. Simon B. Parker, SBLWAW (Atlanta: Scholars Press, 1997) 208, ll. 8-9.

REFLECTIONS

Of all the wonders associated with Elijah, there are none that have been more important in shaping his reputation than the account of his ascension to heaven. No other story of the prophet has had a more vigorous hermeneutical "afterlife" than this one; no other account has fired the imagination of interpreters more. By contrast, no other passage in the Elisha cycle has offended the moral sensibilities of readers more than the episode of the prophet's deadly curse of the youngsters for what seems like mischievous behavior. Both portions deserve further reflection.

1. Although Enoch is said to have been "taken by God" upon his death (Gen 5:24), no other Old Testament personality has been said explicitly to have ascended to heaven. Elijah's dramatic departure has given rise to expectations of his return as the harbinger of the "day of the LORD" (Mal 4:5) and to speculations of his association with the messianic age (see Sir 48:1-11; Matt 11:10-14; 16:13-14; 17:10-13; 27:47, 49; Mark 6:14-15; 8:27-28; 9:11-13; 15:35-36; Luke 1:17; 9:7-8, 18-19). It is important, however, to note that the text is about the glorious ascension of the master as much as it is about prophetic succession. The disciple follows the master resolutely, until he has been given the gift of the spirit for his task. The main point of the passage is, in fact, the continued availability of people who would proclaim the word of the Lord. The people of God are not left forlorn, it seems. As one prophet passes on, another is immediately raised. The ministry in God's name will go on.

Elisha is given the privilege of witnessing the glorious assumption of his master. What is most significant about that experience, however, is not so much the manner of the master's departure but Elisha's vision of celestial power in the midst of human struggles, conveyed by the mirroring of the celestial and terrestrial hosts. Elisha is empowered by that knowledge. The same point is made in the New Testament accounts of the transfiguration (Matt 17:1-9; Mark 9:2-8; Luke 9:28-36). Witnessing the event, Peter is quick to focus on its glorious aspect and makes an enthusiastic proposal out of ignorance. In Luke's account, the disciples overhear the conversation about Jesus' departure (lit., "his exodus"; cf. the reenactment of the exodus by Elijah in 2 Kgs 2:8), but that departure/exodus is not one of glory but of suffering. Likewise, when Luke speaks later of Jesus' being "taken up" (Luke 9:51), the focus is on Jesus' fulfillment of his mission. We are, perhaps, inclined to focus on the glory of the ascension of Elijah and of Jesus, but what is equally important is the fulfillment of God's will.

One may note, too, that in the account of Jesus' ascension in Acts, the immediate concern of Scripture is with the continuation of the ministry, the empowering of the disciples of Jesus with the presence of the Holy Spirit (Acts 1:2, 11, 22).

2. The episode of Elisha's cursing of the youngsters is challenging for anyone who comes to the Bible as Scripture. Elisha's response seems vindictive, petty, and morally unjustifiable. The passage provides no paradigm of righteous conduct, however. Ethics is not at issue. The point, rather, is a theological one. Read in tandem with the preceding episode concerning a salvific act wrought in the name of God, it points to a dialectical understanding of the character of God. The sovereign deity is free to save and to punish, to bless and to curse, to give life and to take it away. It was probably on account of such an understanding of the sovereignty of God that Jesus rebuked his disciples who wanted, like Elijah, to call down fire from heaven to punish those who rejected their master. It is entirely up to God to bless or to curse.

2 KINGS 3:1-27, JEHORAM'S CAMPAIGN AGAINST MOAB

OVERVIEW

Elisha's vision of the celestial hosts—the fiery chariots and fiery horses (2:11)—and his connection of that vision with Israel's chariots and horsemen (2:12) signaled the fact that his ministry will involve him in Israel's wars. This chapter, which reports on his campaign against Moab, is but the first of several stories of Elisha's role in Israel's military conflicts (see also 6:24–7:20; 13:14-19).

Modern scholars have generally assumed that the regnal summary in vv. 1-3 is editorial and was not originally a part of the report on the Moabite war. That may be so. Nevertheless, the text as it stands places the Moabite campaign in the specific context of Jehoram's reign and, indeed, suggests that one should read the account of the war in the light of the ambivalent assessment of Jehoram in vv. 1-3.

2 Kings 3:1-3, Regnal Résumé of Jehoram

COMMENTARY

Ahaziah, the son of Ahab, died as a result of his fall from the window (1:2, 17). Apparently having left no son, he is succeeded by his brother Jehoram (849–843 BCE; his name also appears in its variant form, Joram; e.g., 8:16-29; 9:14-26). The summary assessment of Jehoram's reign in this section is fairly typical for northern kings. Despite the admission that he was not as bad as his parents (Ahab and Jezebel) because he did carry out some reforms, Jehoram gets a negative evaluation overall. The problem of heterodoxy created by Jeroboam had not been eradicated.

In its present context, the regnal résumé provides a chronological setting for the narrative about the war with Moab. In its canonical context, the story of Israel's war with Moab (vv. 4-27) is to be read in the light of the assessment of Jehoram's reign in vv. 1-3. Hence, the deviation of this regnal résumé from the stereotypical form for northern kings is noteworthy. There is some ambiguity as

regards Jehoram's performance, an ambiguity that is conveyed twice by the Hebrew adverb רק (*raq*, "only") and twice by the verb סור (*sûr*, "to turn aside"): "only not like his father and mother, for he turned aside the pillar of Baal that his father had made, only he clung to the sin of Jeroboam son of Nebat, which he caused Israel to commit; he did not turn aside from it" (vv. 2-3). This ambiguity is reflected in the story that follows: in Elisha's initial reluctance ("Go to your father's prophets and your mother's") becomes consent to give the word of the Lord to Jehoram. It is also reflected in the results of the war: Israel scores a victory over Moab but has to withdraw and return to their land. (See Reflections at 3:20-27.)

2 Kings 3:4-8, Jehoram Forms an Alliance Against Moab

COMMENTARY

Much has been made of the fact that Jehoram's Moabite counterpart, Mesha, is known from a Moabite inscription, wherein Mesha acknowledged that Moab had been subjugated by Israel since the time of Omri, but claimed to have liberated his country sometime after that.[90] Despite difficulties in the interpretation of details, it seems clear that Moab did assert its independence during the reign of Mesha, and it is possible that Moab gained control of Israelite territory, as Mesha claimed. Still, there is nothing mentioned in the inscription of this particular campaign or

any of its details. Our understanding of this passage as Scripture will come primarily from our reading of it as a literary and theological text, and not as a historical record.

As in the case of Ahab's war against the Arameans to win back Ramoth-gilead, it is the king of Israel who initiates the war (see 1 Kgs 22:3). As in that war, Jehoram wants to involve the Judeans, and so he asks Jehoshaphat, who had been allied with his father in the Aramean war, a question similar to the one Ahab had posed (v. 7, cf. 1 Kgs 22:4). Jehoshaphat, who is apparently still a weaker partner in the alliance, gives the same answer that he gave Ahab (v. 8, cf. 1 Kgs 22:4). (See Reflections at 3:20-27.)

90. See *ANET*, 320.

2 Kings 3:9-19, Attack, Setback, and Prophetic Prediction

COMMENTARY

Jehoram decides to attack Moab from the south, marching through Judean and Edomite territories in so doing. Israel and Judah were allies at this time, and Edom was a vassal of Judah (see 1 Kgs 22:47). The reason for this roundabout strategy is unclear. One can only speculate that the Moabites would have

strengthened the defenses where they might have expected the attack to come, and so the long march from the south may have been a way of circumventing that defense.

The allied forces are on their way when they run into logistical problems: a shortage of water. Jehoshaphat suggests, as he did with

Ahab (1 Kgs 22:5), that they seek an oracle from the Lord. One of Jehoram's ministers proposes that Elisha be called, adding that he "used to pour water on the hands of Elijah" (v. 11). The idiom here no doubt refers to Elisha as Elijah's assistant, but it also points to Elisha as the one who would be able to solve the water-shortage problem. More important, Jehoshaphat confirms that the word of the Lord is with Elisha.

The narrator's ambivalence about Jehoram is evident throughout the passage. Elisha is said to have been initially reluctant to acknowledge Jehoram, sending him instead to his father's and mother's prophets (cf. 1 Kgs 18:19). Yet, Elisha relents, reportedly because of Jehoram's ally, Jehoshaphat. Elisha needs music to be induced into a trance (cf. 1 Sam 10:5). Nevertheless, the "hand of the LORD" (v. 15; NRSV, "power of the LORD") does come upon him, whereupon he delivers to the king a promise of a divine miracle: The

wadi will be filled with water, even though there will be neither wind nor rain. Ordinarily, the wadi would contain water only during the rainy season, but Elisha predicts that it will be full without wind or rain, elements that the Canaanites associated with the power of Baal. This miracle, which is but a small matter to the deity, will turn out to be salvific for the allies; it will be the means by which God will deliver Moab into the "hand" of the allies (v. 18).

According to Elisha's prediction, the allies will not only conquer all the cities, but will also totally devastate the land, destroying the good trees and ruining every arable plot, in contravention of deuteronomic law (Deut 20:19-20). This is probably to be read, not as a promise of what the Lord will give to the allies, but as a prediction of what they will do. God will give them victory (so vv. 17-18), but they will carry out unacceptable atrocities. (See Reflections at 3:20-27.)

2 Kings 3:20-27, Fulfillment of Prophecies

COMMENTARY

The predictions of Elisha come to pass the next day, specifically, "when the tribute is offered up" (v. 20). One wonders whether it is only a coincidence that the decisive moment corresponds to the time of the day when Elijah called down the fire of heaven in the contest with the prophets of Baal (1 Kgs 18:36), a contest that led to the annihilation of all those prophets.

Water flows from the direction of Edom until the country is filled with water. Through Elisha, "who used to pour water upon the hand of Elijah" (v. 11), comes this miracle of abundant water that more than resolves the problem of water shortage that the allies face.

The Moabites, arrayed for battle, see the water opposite them "as red as blood," leading them to think that the allies are killing one another. Thus misled, they proceed to take the spoil and, consequently, suffer defeat. Rationalistic explanations have been proffered for the bloodred water: redness caused by the laterite soil of the region, reflection of the sun, or the like. Water becoming blood, of course, recalls the first of the plagues that

led to the exodus from Egypt (Exod 7:14-25, esp. v. 21). There is, in any case, a wordplay on the name "Edom" (אדום 'ĕdôm) in the phrase "red as blood" (אדמים כדם 'adummîm kaddām, v. 22). Whatever the explanation, the water that is a blessing for some turns out to be a curse for others.

The Israelites, as Elisha predicted, carry their victory to its extreme conclusion, destroying good trees and arable land, in contravention of deuteronomic law. In desperate straits, the king of Moab sacrifices his first-born son, the crown prince to the Moabite throne. One expects this to be the denouement of the story, an indication of decisive victory for Israel. Instead, we find a surprising conclusion: a great wrath comes upon Israel, and so they withdraw and return home. The text is ambiguous about the source of the "great wrath." We might take the sudden withdrawal of Israel as indicative of the efficacy of the human sacrifice and, hence, take the "great wrath" as coming from Chemosh, Moab's patron deity. Some interpreters, however, have proposed that the "wrath" (קצף

qesep) refers to human passion: the outrage of the Moabites that prompted them to muster all their resources to beat back the coalition, the anger of the attackers because of the protracted battle, and so on. It should be noted that the Hebrew expression for "good wrath" (קצף גדול qesep gādôl) is used in the Bible only for the wrath of the Lord (Deut 29:27; Jer 21:5; 32:37; Zech 1:15; 7:12).

Moreover, the expression היה קצף על (hāyâ qesep 'al, "there was a wrath against") is always used in reference to divine wrath. It seems most probable, therefore, that the text is referring to the wrath of the Lord for the violation of the deuteronomic prohibition of the scorched—earth policy in war. For the narrator, the Lord gave victory to Jehoram-but not a complete victory.

REFLECTIONS

This chapter reflects the conviction that God responds to people who come to the deity in time of need, even when they have been undeserving of God's help. Here we have a story of a king who is judged a sinner, a man who has embarked upon a course with nary a thought of the will of God. Yet, in his moment of need, God comes through with a promise of salvation for him. The freedom of God to save does not mean, however, that one has received a "blank check." The passage does not provide a prooftext for a triumphalistic theology—that God will fight for us, come what may. The very last words (v. 27), in fact, offer the most profound theological truth, a warning that God's salvation may instantly turn to wrath in the face of human excesses and mercilessness.

2 KINGS 4:1-44, ELISHA'S MINISTRY OF LIFE

OVERVIEW

Following the chapter on Elisha's role in Israel's war with Moab, we have a chapter on the prophet's ministry of life. It is likely, as most critics believe, that the legends contained herein originally circulated independently or as parts of various collections. Still, the various pieces in this literary collage seem to fit together rather well. They all revolve around the issue of life and death, Elisha in each case acting to bring, sustain, or restore life and avert death. The following sub-units may be discerned:

I. The miracle of abundant oil (vv. 1-7)
II. Elisha ministers to a wealthy woman (vv. 8-37)
    A. The gift of a son (vv. 8-17)
    B. Death and resurrection (vv. 18-37)
III. Elisha feeds the hungry (vv. 38-44)
    A. Death in the pot (vv. 38-41)
    B. Feeding many with little (vv. 42-44)

2 Kings 4:1-7, The Miracle of Abundant Oil

COMMENTARY

The first story in this chapter concerns Elisha's miraculous rescue of the family of a member of the prophetic guild, probably one of his followers (see v. 1: "You yourself know that your servant feared the LORD"). The man

had died, leaving his widow and two children liable for debts that he had incurred. According to the law, if a man's debt is unpaid at his death, the creditor may seize the debtor's property and children (see Exod 21:7; Isa

50:1; Amos 2:6; 8:6; Mic 2:9; Neh 5:3-5). Like the widow of Zarephath, whom Elijah had encountered (1 Kgs 17:8-16), this widow is in desperate straits. Elisha cannot legally prevent the creditor from seizing the children, so if he is to help the widow, it will have to be through some other means.

The widow has nothing in her house save one cruse of oil. So Elisha instructs her to borrow containers from her neighbors. Just as Elijah had provided the widow of Zarephath with an unending supply of oil, so also Elisha miraculously provides this widow with an abundant amount of oil, instructing her to sell it to pay off her debt. She and her children may live on what is left over, he says. The episode thus moves from the problem that death has caused (v. 1) to the renewed possibility of life through the miracle wrought by Elisha (v. 7). (See Reflections at 4:42-44.)

2 Kings 4:8-37, Elisha Ministers to a Wealthy Woman

2 Kings 4:8-17, The Gift of a Son

COMMENTARY

The second episode concerns the promise and birth of a son to a Shunammite woman who has shown hospitality to the prophet. Unlike the widow of the first episode, this woman is said to be a woman of status (lit., "a great woman"; cf. 5:2; 10:6, 11; 1 Sam 25:2; 2 Sam 19:33). In contrast to the first woman, too, she does not come to Elisha with a request for help. Indeed, she has the resources to invite the prophet to dine with her family whenever he passes though her town, and she and her husband even build and furnish a guest room for him.

On his own accord, Elisha offers to peddle influence on her behalf, but the woman says she has no need of that. She seems to have everything she needs. It is pointed out to Elisha, however, that the couple have no son and that there is no prospect of their having one, since the husband is old. Elisha, therefore, tells her that she will have a son "in due time"—that is, within the year. Accordingly, the woman conceives and gives birth to a son. The prophet is able to bring the blessing of new life, even when that possibility is dimmed by biological realities. (See Reflections at 4:42-44.)

2 Kings 4:18-37, Death and Resurrection

COMMENTARY

This episode is related to the preceding one, although some time has now passed. In the preceding scene, Elisha is in the house of the woman in Shunem (v. 11), but he is now at Mt. Carmel (v. 25), about fifteen miles from Shunem. The boy is now old enough to look for his father among the reapers and to complain of a headache. The father orders the boy to be carried to his mother, perhaps because he is too old to carry him there himself. The child, however, dies on his mother's lap. The woman puts the boy on Elisha's bed (in the room that the family had built for him, v. 10) and rushes off to see the "man of God" who had promised her the son without her having asked. Oddly, her husband does not seem to share her sense of urgency; indeed, he asks her why she is visiting the prophet when it is not a holiday. She presses on, however, with only one word to him: "It is all right!" (שלום šālôm).

Elisha's servant, Gehazi, is sent to greet her first, but she is eager to see the prophet face-to-face. She brushes aside his questions of her family's well-being with the same word she spoke to her husband as she left home:

šālôm ("It is all right!"). There is no time for explanations to her husband and no time for a perfunctory exchange of greetings with the prophet, it seems. All is, in fact, not well, but she is pressing on to seek that *šālôm* from the one who can give it to her.

Elisha recognizes that she is greatly distressed, but admits that he has not been apprised of the situation by the Lord. When he learns what the problem is, he immediately dispatches Gehazi to go to the boy to place his staff on him. The mother's instincts and love for the child are great, for she will not settle for anything less than the personal attention of Elisha. Sure enough, Gehazi is not successful in reviving the boy. Indeed, several times in the text, it is asserted that the boy is dead (vv. 20, 31-32). Still, Elisha comes and prays to the Lord, just as Elijah had done when he revived the son of the widow of Zarephath (1 Kgs 17:20). After applying a technique similar to that Elijah used, Elisha gets off the boy and paces around the house once. Then, he hears the boy sneezing seven times and, returning to the room, notices him opening his eyes. He gives the boy back to his mother, who bows down to the man of God, presumably in gratitude. (See Reflections at 4:42-44.)

2 Kings 4:38-44, Elisha Feeds the Hungry

2 Kings 4:38-41, Death in the Pot

COMMENTARY

The next story is reminiscent of the episode of Elisha's "healing" of the contaminated water at Jericho (2:19-22). When Elisha returns to Gilgal (see 2:1), he discovers that there is a famine. Still, he is able to provide for "the company of prophets." However, the servant assigned to prepare a stew inadvertently includes some poisonous ingredients. Those who taste it realize immediately that "there is death in the pot." Elisha then orders that flour be thrown into the pot, thereby detoxifying the stew. (See Reflections at 4:42-44.)

2 Kings 4:42-44, Feeding Many with Little

COMMENTARY

The final scene in the chapter concerns Elisha's miraculous feeding of one hundred people with a relatively small amount of food. The servant is initially skeptical, but Elisha repeats the order to feed the group, declaring that the Lord will provide more than enough food for everyone.

REFLECTIONS

What we have in this chapter is a collage of Elisha's extraordinary deeds: miraculously filling empty vessels with oil, granting a childless couple a son, raising a person from the dead, neutralizing poisonous food, and feeding a multitude with food for but a few. In his role as a wonder-worker, Elisha foreshadows the miracle worker of whom the New Testament speaks, the one whose marvelous deeds would surpass Elisha's (see Matt 9:18-26; 14:13-21; Mark 5:21-43; 6:34-44; Luke 7:11-17; 8:40-56; John 2:1-11). Although these acts all serve to demonstrate that the one who performs them does so by the power of God, they are not performed merely for their awe-inspiring effects. Rather, in each case, the marvelous deed is for the sake of others, specifically to bring, to sustain, or to restore life and avert death. The power of the "man of God" to carry out these miraculous deeds testifies to the power of God over life and death.

For all its emphasis on the miraculous nature of these acts of Elisha, however, this passage is noteworthy that the needs to which he ministered are remarkably mundane: freedom and life for the destitute, hope for the childless, restoration of a dead child to a desperate mother, food for the hungry. The man of God acts on more than just a grand political scale, bringing the word of God to kings about God's will as regards the nations (as in chap. 3). The man of God also acts to address the mundane, personal needs of people living life day to day. That is at the heart of the ministry. To be sure, one may not have the power of Elisha to fill empty vessels with oil. Yet, in the face of the desperate plight of the destitute, one may take a cue from Elisha about the economic enablement of the poor. Elisha provides a means by which the destitute widow is able to resolve her economic problem and save her children from enslavement. Indeed, the miracle of economic enablement may take many forms—it only takes the eyes of faith to discern those forms in our day and age. By the same token, one may not be able to resurrect a dead child, as Elisha did. Yet, the story makes a poignant point that there are critical moments in the ministry that may demand our immediate, personal, direct, and prayerful involvement in the problem at hand. The grieving mother in desperate need of the senior minister's attention will not be comforted by "passing the buck" to an associate with a mere emblem of the senior pastor's authority. We may not have the technical know-how to detoxify poisonous food or to cause limited quantities of food to multiply. Yet, it is imperative that we feed the hungry with whatever resources we may find. Proclamation of the word of the Lord involves much more than words; it involves reactive and proactive action to bring life and to give hope to others. As one New Testament writer puts it: "If a brother or sister is naked and lacks daily food, and one of you says to them, 'Go in peace; keep warm and eat your fill,' and yet you do not supply their bodily needs, what is the good of that?" (Jas 2:15-16 NRSV).

2 KINGS 5:1-27, NAAMAN AND GEHAZI

OVERVIEW

The issue of the unity of the passage primarily revolves around the place of the episode about Gehazi's greed (vv. 19b-27). For many interpreters, this account is entirely secondary, constituting an appendix of sorts to the story of the healing of Naaman (vv. 1-19a). Yet, there are strong indications of the coherence of the chapter or, at least, indications that the narrator intends the Gehazi episode to be read with the preceding material. Most poignantly, the present form of the text begins with the skin affliction of Naaman (v. 1) and ends with the skin affliction of Gehazi (v. 27): The "outsider" is healed, while the "insider" is afflicted. Moreover, the faithfulness of Naaman's slave girl at the beginning of the story stands in stark contrast to the treachery of Elisha's servant at the end of the chapter.

2 Kings 5:1-7, Naaman Seeks Help in Israel

Commentary

The story begins with Naaman, the chief military commander of the Aramean army. He is a "great man" (איש גדול *ʾîš gādôl*, v. 1; cf. אשה גדולה *ʾiššâ gĕdôlâ* in 4:8) who is favored by the king of Aram (ancient Syria) because of his victory over Israel, here perhaps an allusion to the Aramean victory in the conflict over Ramoth-gilead (1 Kgs 22:19-23).[91] That victory by the Aramean army is said to have been granted by the Lord, a standard way in Israelite writings of explaining the defeat of Israel as God's people (see, e.g., Judg 6:1; 13:1; 2 Chr 28:5; Dan 1:2), for in Israelite theology no foreign army can be victorious over Israel unless it is by the will of the Lord. Indeed, as we read the story in 2 Kings 5, we gather that Israel's defeat must have been in accordance with the will of the Lord, for that defeat would result in the conversion of a powerful Gentile and the glorification of the Lord. This is no doubt the sort of story that the Israelites, particularly those in exile, liked to tell. Despite the tragedy of defeat and captivity, it seems, greater good may be achieved.

In spite of all his accomplishments and greatness, Naaman has a problem: He suffers from a terrible skin disease,[92] one that carries with it a social stigma and is associated with death (see Num 12:10-12). Ironically, salvation for this "great man" would come by way of "a young girl" from Israel, captured by the Arameans on one of their raids. This Israelite captive would bring hope for her Aramean captor. She suggests that Naaman might be healed of his disease were he to seek help from "the prophet who is in Samaria" (v. 3)— that is, Elisha, who has apparently already gained a reputation for performing miracles, doubtless because of the kinds of legends that we read in chap. 4. The young girl's proposal makes it all the way to the king of Aram, who sends a letter to his counterpart in Israel, presumably Jehoram (see 3:1). No doubt, a visit to Samaria by the Aramean general who was responsible for the defeat of Israel in their previous military engagement could not proceed in peacetime without at least some diplomatic arrangements.

Armed with extravagant gifts and a letter from his king, the general comes to the king of Israel. The letter dictates that the king of Israel is to cure Naaman of his disease. The king is in despair, for he takes the content of the letter literally as a demand for him to perform the miracle himself. He realizes that curing such a terrible affliction is not something that any human being can accomplish. It is only God who gives death or life (see Deut 32:39; 1 Sam 2:6; Hos 6:2). The faithless king sees the challenge as a political problem, a pretext on the part of the Arameans for war. That may, indeed, be the real motive for the Aramean king's letter, which, curiously, does not mention the prophet. Whatever the Aramean king's intentions, however, the narrative will show that things would work out according to God's will. Ironically, the king of Israel does not seem to know what the captive slave girl in Damascus knows: that there is a prophet in Samaria who could perform the miracle. He sees only the impossibility of the case; she sees its possibility. (See Reflections at 5:19*b*-27.)

91. There is even a tradition that Naaman was the one who shot the arrow that "accidentally" killed Ahab in that battle. See Josephus *Antiquities of the Jews* 15.5. See also the Targum on 2 Chronicles 18.

92. Most translations retain the traditional rendering of the disease as "leprosy," more as a convenient term rather than a medically accurate one. Most scholars now agree that the Hebrew word does not refer to leprosy as we know it (i.e., Hansen's disease), but to skin afflictions of various sorts, here probably psoriasis or vitiligo. See David P. Wright and Richard N. Jones, "Leprosy," in *ABD*, 4:277-82.

2 Kings 5:8-14, Naaman Is Healed

Commentary

Elisha hears of the king's despair and comes forward to help, in order that Naaman "may learn that there is a prophet in Israel" (v. 8). So Naaman comes to the entrance of the prophet's house with his impressive entourage. Although his visit brought grave anxiety to the king, the prophet does not even deign to come out to meet the "great man." A more subtle point, perhaps, is the power of the prophet. Without ever seeing Naaman, he is able to bring about Naaman's healing. Elisha merely sends instructions through a messenger, telling Naaman to wash himself seven times in the Jordan River and promising that his flesh will be restored as a result and that he will be clean (for the significance of "seven times," see Lev 14:7, 16, 27, 51; cf. 2 Kgs 4:35).

Naaman is indignant at his treatment by Elisha, for the general had already imagined how it would all work, perhaps because he had seen healing rituals being performed before. He probably expects Elisha to come out, call on the name of the Lord, wave his hand over the problem area, and heal it. Although it is not readily evident in the English translations, the Hebrew word order suggests a wounded ego: "I thought, 'Unto me he would surely come out and stand. . . .'"

Naaman's national pride is also insulted, it seems. If he has to wash himself in a river, he does not see why he has to come all the way from his own country, for he deems the local rivers of Damascus, the Abana (properly, the Amanah) and the Pharpar, better than all the waters of Israel. So he turns away in rage. His servants point out that he would no doubt go to great lengths to do what Elisha says, if it had been something difficult, so he should give the simple formula a chance to succeed. For all his greatness and pride, Naaman is able to listen to the advice of his servants. The words of the Israelite servant girl caused him to come to Israel in the first place, and now, his own servants are prompting him to heed the Israelite prophet. Accordingly, Naaman follows the instructions of Elisha and is healed, just as Elisha had promised. The flesh of the "great man" is restored (שוב *šûb*) like that of a "young boy" (v. 14). Naaman is now in some sense like the "young girl" from Israel whom he had enslaved. (See Reflections at 5:19*b*-27.)

2 Kings 5:15-19*a*, Naaman's Conversion

COMMENTARY

Naaman returns to Elisha and stands before the prophet (v. 15). Unlike the previous occasion, when Elisha merely instructed him through a messenger, the prophet now speaks to him directly. Whereas Naaman had previously expected the prophet to come to him and "stand" (עמד *ʿāmad*, v. 11), it is now Naaman who stands (*ʿāmad*, v. 15) before Elisha. Moreover, whereas Naaman previously referred to the Lord as Elisha's God (v. 11), now he himself confesses the uniqueness of the Lord. Elisha had come forward to heal Naaman in order that Naaman might "know that there is a prophet in Israel"; now we hear Naaman's confession that "there is no other god in all the earth except in Israel."

Naaman offers Elisha a gift (ברכה *běrākâ*; lit., "a blessing"), but Elisha steadfastly refuses it, even when pressed upon to do so (cf. Num 22:18; Dan 5:17; Amos 7:12; Mic 3:5, 11). Naaman then asks that he might

be allowed to take home soil from Israel. Like any new convert, Naaman's theology is apparently unsophisticated. He properly confesses that "there is no God in all the earth except in Israel," perhaps because that is what he has been taught. He takes the confession literally, however, assuming that the Lord is to be worshiped only on Israelite soil. Hence his proposal to take some of that soil home, because he does not want to offer burnt offerings or sacrifices to other gods. At the same time, however, he realizes that his position will entail certain expectations; as the king's right-hand man (see 7:2, 17), as it were, he would have to accompany the king to worship Rimmon, the storm deity Hadad-Rimmon ("Hadad the Thunderer"), the patron god of the Arameans (Zech 12:11). For that anticipated compromise of his allegiance to the Lord, he asks for forgiveness in advance (cf. 1 Kgs 8:41-43). He is clearly aware that such an act would be contrary to expectations of him in his newfound faith; thus the awkward repetition about his anticipated obeisance in the temple of Rimmon in v. 18 may indicate some embarrassment on his part about the request. Elisha replies with neither condemnation nor permission, but he tells Naaman to "go in peace" (cf. Exod 4:18; 1 Sam 1:17; 20:42; see also Mark 5:34; Luke 7:50; 8:48; Acts 16:36). (See Reflections at 5:19*b-27.*)

2 Kings 5:19*b*-27, Gehazi's Treachery

COMMENTARY

Elisha has been firm that he will not receive any remuneration from Naaman. His servant Gehazi, however, thinks that Elisha has been too easy on Naaman, whom he obviously regards as still an outsider (נעמן הארמי הזה [*na ʿămān hāʾărammî hazzeh,* "Naaman, that Aramean"], v. 20). Elisha had sworn ("as the LORD lives") that he would accept nothing from Naaman (v. 16). Gehazi, however, swears ("as the LORD lives") that he will get something out of Naaman (v. 20). He lies that Elisha has changed his mind about the gift because two prophets have suddenly shown up. The lie is credible because the request is relatively modest, only a small fraction of what Naaman had brought (see v. 5). Gehazi's deviousness stands in contrast to the graciousness of Naaman, who urges him (v. 16; cf. v. 23) to take twice the amount of cash requested, packages it nicely, and has his servants carry the packages for Gehazi. As soon as Gehazi returns to the capital, he sends away the helpers and conceals the loot. One deception leads to another, for Gehazi then lies to Elisha, saying that he has not gone anywhere. The prophet, however, has extraordinary powers of knowledge and knows that Gehazi has been "on the take" (the verb לקה [*lāqaḥ,* "to take"] appears twice in v. 26). So he condemns Gehazi and his descendants with Naaman's disease. Thus Gehazi, who contrives to take the "blessing" that Naaman had meant for Elisha, is cursed.

REFLECTIONS

The story of the healing of Naaman is surely one of the most fascinating in the book of Kings. It is a remarkably entertaining drama with a rich cast of characters, a well-developed plot, many ironic twists and turns, comic relief (like the image of the panicky king), keen insights into human flaws (a war hero's ego and ethnocentrism; a servant's avarice and deceitfulness), and a satisfying conclusion. Here are the essential materials for a compelling church play—one that offers many theological vignettes.

1. The most important message is, of course, the inclusivity of God's saving activity. The reader is told from the beginning that it is God who gives victory (the Hebrew word also means "deliverance" or "salvation") to Naaman. It is God's will from the start, it seems, to bring "salvation" to Naaman, even though Naaman was not among God's chosen people. This message is all the more poignant when one considers the ironic reversal that the chapter as a whole conveys: The Gentile Naaman is restored, while the Israelite Gehazi is cursed. It is appropriate, therefore, that Jesus should later point to this story to justify the inclusivity of his ministry (Luke 4:27). Just as Elijah ministered to the Phoenician widow of Zarephath, and just as Elisha ministered to Naaman the Aramean, so, too, Jesus proclaimed good news to the outcasts of Jewish society as well as to some Gentiles.

2. Naaman's path to restoration was by no means a straightforward one. He was amenable to heeding the suggestion of a captive slave and desperate enough to travel all the way from Damascus to find the prophet at his home in Samaria. Naaman had, however, his own idea of how the restoration of health would be carried out. Elisha's instructions sounded ridiculous to Naaman, and his pride was wounded. Yet, he was restored only when he submitted himself to the seemingly silly ritual of taking a bath. He expected something dramatic, but salvation came to him through the words of a prophet, conveyed to him by a messenger—and it entailed a baptism. This is the way God cleanses people of their afflictions, it seems—not through the dramatic performance of a human healer, but through a simple act of obedience. Salvation comes mysteriously when we submit to God's script and not our own.

3. Naaman's experience of restoration leads to his confession of faith in the Lord. One might have expected the reverse (confession before restoration), but that is not the case. God initiated the entire process of salvation for Naaman—while the Aramean was yet afflicted with the deadly disease—by giving him victory (also meaning "deliverance" or "salvation"). God restored Naaman and cleansed him when he obeyed, without understanding anything of the mystery of that experience (see Titus 3:4-5). Even when Naaman finally confessed the Lord, his theology was simplistic, his notion of God's presence inadequate, his allegiance to God not without distractions. The reader may be inclined to be impatient with Naaman for his bad theology and his unwillingness to risk all that he has for the Lord. Elisha did not, however, condemn him. Rather, Elisha sent him away with a benediction: "Go in peace!" There was much room for grace in Elisha's theology.

4. Unlike Elisha, Gehazi was not so gracious. There is something disdainful, too—perhaps even exclusivistic—in the way he spoke of Naaman ("Naaman, this Aramean," 5:20). He thought that Naaman was getting off easy when he should have had to pay a price, and so he tried to squeeze something out of Naaman. Gehazi tried to make a profit from Naaman's experience of healing, and for that he was condemned (see also Acts 8:18-24). There are people in every era who are so terribly afflicted with diseases and other ailments, who are desperate to find any word of hope from spiritual leaders. And there are always opportunists like Gehazi who are ready to make a quick profit in the name of the Lord. This text sternly warns against such opportunism.

5. In stark contrast to Gehazi is the unnamed Israelite slave at the beginning of the chapter. Despite her lowly status and her captivity in a foreign land, she is faithful. Although far from her homeland, her eyes of faith perceive hope for her Aramean master. The king of Israel, on the other hand, could only despair, even though salvation was at hand in Samaria.

2 KINGS 6:1-23, MORE MIRACLES OF ELISHA

OVERVIEW

There are two stories concerning Elijah's ministry in 2 Kgs 6:1-23. The first, taking place in a somewhat private and domestic setting, tells of the prophet's raising of a sunken ax head (6:1-7). As with the preceding story concerning the healing of Naaman, the event in this account is set at the Jordan River, and that setting perhaps explains its place in this literary context. The miracle of healing at the river is followed by the miracle of the floating iron ax head. The second story concerns an international incident in which Elisha effectively neutralizes certain acts of aggression by the Arameans against Israel (6:8-23). The account may have been placed here because of the reference to a large Aramean army in Israel (see 5:9) and the allusion to Elisha's gift of "second sight" (vv. 8-10; cf. 5:26).

2 Kings 6:1-7, Elisha Raises a Sunken Ax Head

COMMENTARY

A group of Elisha's prophetic disciples realize that they have outgrown their meeting place (NIV, "the place where we meet with you") or quarters (NRSV, "the place where we live under your charge"). The Hebrew may be taken to mean, literally, "the place where they were sitting before him" (cf. 4:38)—that is, as his disciples. So they decide to go to the Jordan to cut down trees to build a new one, and they invite Elisha to come along. As one of them is working, his iron ax head slips off the handle and falls into the river, causing him great consternation because the ax had been borrowed. Elisha, however, saves the day. When he finds the spot where the ax head fell into the river, he cuts a piece of wood and throws it into the water, causing the iron ax head to float and thus be easily retrieved.

Commentators have been tempted to see this feat as an illustration of "sympathetic magic" or to offer rationalistic explanations of what might have happened. The text is silent about the details, however. It merely reports it as a wondrous deed that was brought about on account of Elisha's presence and intervention on behalf of the man in distress. Whereas axes were relatively inexpensive in modern times, they were not so in ancient Israel, where iron was scarce and, in time of war, largely reserved for military use. The members of "the company of prophets" seem to have been quite poor (see 4:38-41; 5:22), and this story is set in a context of famine and war, so the loss of a borrowed ax was no trivial matter. Elisha's intervention probably saved the poor man from incurring a debt that he could not afford to pay. This miracle thus ranks with others that Elisha performed on behalf of individuals in dire need (see 2:19-22; 4:1-7, 38-41). Sandwiched between accounts of the prophet's role in the international arena, the story of his attention to the plight of an individual disciple is testimony to the range of Elisha's prophetic ministry. He does not save only mighty generals like Naaman (5:1-19a). He is concerned not only with the affairs of kings and nations (6:8–7:20). Elisha's salvific activity touches the daily and mundane needs of individual persons as well. (See Reflections at 6:8-23.)

2 Kings 6:8-23, Elisha Overcomes the Troops of Aram

COMMENTARY

Unlike the preceding story regarding Elisha's ministry among his own disciples, this account concerns his role in the arena of international politics. It is set in a time of war between Israel and Aram; the peace assumed by the story of the healing of Naaman (5:1-27) no longer held.

The unnamed Aramean king repeatedly devised secret plans to attack Israel, but each time Elisha learned of the plans through his extraordinary powers (cf. 5:26) and passed on the secret to the Israelites, who used the information to thwart the Arameans.[93] This was not a coincidence, the narrator implies, for the same thing recurred (v. 10). The king of Aram suspects treason (v. 11), but he was told that it was Elisha who had been responsible for the security leaks (cf. Eccl 10:20). Thereupon, he orders the prophet's capture (v. 13).

93. Josephus identified the Aramean king as Ben-hadad and the Israelite king as Joram, but that is entirely speculative. See Josephus *Antiquities of the Jews* IX.51-78.

The single prophet apparently caused such concern to the Aramean king that the latter dispatches a huge force—"horses and chariots and a great army" (v. 14)—to capture him in Dothan (10 miles north of Samaria), where Elisha is reported to be (v. 13). Moreover, despite the fact that Elisha had previously known of the king's secret plans through his extrasensory powers, the Arameans think it would make a difference for them to approach under the cover of darkness (v. 13). At dawn, Elisha's attendant expresses consternation upon seeing the Aramean troops, his cry echoing the distressful cry of the disciple whose ax head had fallen into the river Jordan: "Alas! My master!" (v. 15; cf. v. 5). The prophet assures him cryptically that "there are more with us than there are with them" (v. 16). The meaning of this assurance is made plain when, upon the prayer of Elisha, the servant is given to see something of what Elisha himself had seen at his inauguration as Elijah's successor (2:11). The servant apparently sees a celestial host ("the mountains full of horses and chariots of fire") surrounding Elisha. This will be the secret of Elisha's success. The Arameans, who obviously are not privy to this vision, attack. Elisha prays for them to be struck by "a blinding light" (TNK). The NRSV and the NIV take the word סנורים (sanwērîm) to mean "blindness." Yet,

the troops were not completely blinded, for they were able to follow Elisha to Samaria. The Hebrew word, which occurs elsewhere in the Bible only in Gen 19:11, is probably a loan word from Akkadian *šunwurum* ("having dazzling brightness"). The humor of the narrator surfaces again as one reads of Elisha's encounter with the Aramean troops. The very prophet whom they were sent to capture tells them that they are going in the wrong direction. When he volunteers to lead them to the man they seek to capture, they blindly follow him. Accordingly, Elisha brings them to Samaria, where the Israelites presumably had military superiority. Then he prays for their ability to see (v. 20), even as he had prayed for his servant to see (v. 17); and they realize where they are.

The Israelite king reacts as an excited child might. "Father, shall I kill them? Shall I kill them?" he asks the prophet. Elisha demurs, noting that these troops were not brought into Samaria by Israel's military might but by the will of God alone. Instead of doing violence to them, then, Elisha tells the king to extend hospitality to the enemy troops and then to release them. There is perhaps nothing more humiliating than for the great invading army to be fed and then sent on its way. In consequence, according to the narrator, the Arameans no longer harassed Israel (v. 23).

REFLECTIONS

The juxtaposition of the two stories highlights dramatically the range of Elisha's ministry. In one instance, he is involved in the daily activities of his disciples, their concern to have a suitable place for their group, the panic of a person who has lost something expensive. In the next instance, the prophet is involved in international politics, as it were, working to thwart the naked aggression of the Arameans, on the one hand, and preventing violence on the part of the Israelites, on the other hand. The ministry in God's name can be like that.

1. Richard Nelson has observed that the miracle of the floating ax head is "something of an embarrassment for modern readers" and that "it seems trivial and pointless."[94] That is especially the case when one reads it after the account of the dramatic healing of Naaman in 5:1-28 and before the story of Elisha's dazzling of the massive Aramean army in 6:8-23. Yet its very domestic and mundane character may itself be instructive. The presence of stories like this one is a powerful reminder to us that ministry involves attending to the seemingly ordinary needs and anxieties of people coping with life's routines.

94. Nelson, *First and Second Kings*, 184.

2. Elisha's ministry calls attention to the fact that the battles of the world are not fought by the great armies of the earth alone. In the face of overwhelming odds, the prophet prays for his servant to see that there are celestial forces fighting on the side of God's people against those who threaten them, "for there are more with us than with them" (v. 16).

3. Against those who may be eager to annihilate their enemy, the narrator elevates a response of hospitality and kindness instead of violence. This passage offers a perspective that is different from the harsh demands of holy war ideology (cf. 1 Kgs 20:31-42).

2 KINGS 6:24–7:20, THE SIEGE OF SAMARIA

OVERVIEW

This literary unit contains an account of another of Israel's encounters with the Arameans. The story is loosely linked to the preceding one by the temporal expression אחרי-כן ('aḥărê-kēn, "afterward"; NRSV, NIV, "sometime later"). The unit is, however, quite different from the preceding one. Whereas the preceding passage ends with the cessation of Aramean hostilities, the new unit concerns a direct attack on Samaria (v. 24). Whereas the king of Aram is not named in the preceding unit, he is now identified as Ben-hadad, the name of several Aramean kings in the ninth century BCE. Given the relative weakness of Israel and the might of Aram, it is likely that Ben-hadad, son of Hazael, is meant. He ruled in Damascus at the end of the ninth century BCE and the beginning of the eighth. Cf. 2 Kgs 8:15; 13:3-7; 22–25.

Whereas 6:1-23 contains stories of miracles performed by Elisha, 6:24–7:20 highlights a prophetic oracle and its fulfillment. Despite the chapter division in most modern Bibles, it seems clear that the original unit included not only the description of the siege and its consequences (6:24-33), but also Elisha's prediction of the end of the siege and the fulfillment of the prophecy (7:1-20). Moreover, whatever its origin might have been, 7:18-20 now appears as a final reiteration of the fulfillment of the oracle in 7:1-2, for 8:1 clearly begins a brand-new story.

2 Kings 6:24-31, The Siege and Its Effects

COMMENTARY

According to the conclusion of the preceding unit, the Arameans "no longer came raiding into the land of Israel" (v. 23). In the new story, set in a different time, however, Ben-hadad of Aram succeeds in laying siege to Samaria (v. 24). The Aramean siege causes such a severe famine in the city that even an unappetizing item like a donkey's head and a very small amount ("one-fourth of a kab" is about a quarter of a quart) of "dove dung" fetch exorbitant prices (v. 25). The NIV interprets the "dove dung" (חרי יונים ḥărê yônîm) to be a popular term for some kind of "seed pods" (NJV, "carob pods"; NEB and REB,

"locust-beans"); there is some evidence for this interpretation in an Akkadian lexical text, in which "dove dung" is defined as "seed of the false carob."[95] Even such inedible husks (cf. Luke 15:16) were scarce during the siege.

Jehoram, the king of Samaria, apparently is surveying the devastation, when a distressed woman approaches him for deliverance (v. 26). The king recognizes that it is beyond his ability to alleviate the situation, for he is unable to supply any grain from the threshing

---

95. See Mordecai Cogan and Hayim Tadmor, *2 Kings*, AB 11 (New York: Doubleday, 1988) 79. Josephus, too, long ago suggested that "dove dung" might have been some sort of food, specifically something used as a salt substitute. See Josephus *Antiquities of the Jews IX.62.*

floor or wine from the vats (6:27; cf. Num 18:27, 30; Deut 15:14; 16:13). Unwittingly, he points to the true source of their salvation: the Lord (v. 27; see 7:6). Nevertheless, he listens to the woman's complaint; through that complaint, the reader learns of the extreme horrors the famine has produced (vv. 28-29). Cases of cannibalism in times of siege are known from the Bible (Deut 28:56-57; Lam 2:20; 4:10; Ezek 5:10) and are corroborated by extra-biblical sources.[96]

In some ways, the case that this woman presents before the king, in which she and another woman agreed to cannibalize each other's son, but one reneges, echoes the case of the two harlots who came before Solomon in 1 Kgs 3:16-28.[97] Yet, there are stark differences. Whereas the "real" mother in the case before Solomon was overwhelmed by sorrow and moved by compassion for her dead child, the mother who presents her case to Jehoram does not express her sense of loss

96. See *ANET*, 298.
97. See Stuart Lasine, "Jehoram and the Cannibal Mothers (2 Kings 6:24-33): Solomon's Judgment in an Inverted World," *JSOT* 50 (1991) 27-53.

or her guilt at having killed her son. Instead, she complains that the other woman has reneged on their agreement so that she, the plaintiff, is being deprived of her right to have the child of the other woman as food. The famine has brought about savage desperation and callousness.

The king goes into public mourning (v. 30), another indication of the severity of the national crisis (cf. 19:1-2; 1 Kgs 20:32; 21:27). He blames Elisha for the situation (v. 31). One might speculate that the king thought the problem would not exist if he had been allowed to kill the Aramean army that had been trapped in Samaria (vv. 22-23). Perhaps he reckoned that Elisha could have performed a miracle to provide food for the people (cf. 4:42-44). The king does not give any reason, however, for placing the blame on Elisha, and that is perhaps the point that we are meant to get. The king takes no responsibility whatsoever for the situation, preferring to find a scapegoat and to divert attention from the problem by killing someone, as if the famine had not already caused death enough. (See Reflections at 7:3-20.)

2 Kings 6:32–7:2, Confrontation Between the King and Elisha

COMMENTARY

The confusing sequence of events in 6:32-33 is difficult to sort out. The king sends a man to Elisha (v. 32*a*), but the mission of that man is not spelled out in the narrative. One expects him to be an assassin or a bailiff, but, as in another instance involving a threat to the life of a prophet, he may be a messenger who is sent to issue the death threat (1 Kgs 19:2-3). The narrator here identifies the man as a messenger (v. 32*b*).

Elisha is at home with the elders of the city who had come to visit him. Through his extraordinary power of perception (cf. 5:26; 6:8-10), the prophet knows that the man is coming and that his life is in danger. Still, Elisha refers to the man as a messenger and expects the king to come behind him. The scene is thoroughly comical. Elisha calls on a bunch of old men to hold the door shut

as the message from the king is delivered, either by the messenger (so the Hebrew text, followed by the NIV) or by the king in person (so NRSV, with a slight emendation of the text). In any case, the king is apparently present when the message was delivered (7:2). Just as he had held Elisha responsible in some way for the tragedy (v. 31), so also the king blames the Lord and expresses a loss of faith in the Lord (v. 33). As the Targum would have it, he was so disheartened that he even refused to pray.

Elisha responds with a surprisingly positive oracle issued in classical prophetic style (7:1). He predicts that the dire circumstances will end the very next day; the prices of food will be back to the usual levels one might expect at the marketplace ("at the gate of

Samaria").[98] Nothing is said of the king's reaction. Jehoram's right-hand man, however, is skeptical that there could be such an instant turnaround. Even if the Lord were to open the floodgates of heaven (cf. Gen 7:11; Mal 3:10), the officer suggests, there could

not be an immediate reversal such as Elisha predicted (v. 2). No doubt, he meant that it would take some time for the new growth to bear fruit. The officer cannot conceive of another way for deliverance to come, except by the natural process. For that lack of faith, the prophet declares, the officer will witness the miracle but not be able to partake of its benefits. (See Reflections at 7:3-20.)

98. The "measure" (סאה *sĕ'â*) was six times larger than the קב (*qab*, "dove dung"). Yet a *sĕ'â* of choice meal would sell for only a fifth of the price of a *qab* during the siege, and the same amount of money would buy two סאים (*sĕ'îm*) of barley.

2 Kings 7:3-20, How the Siege Was Lifted

COMMENTARY

The miracle is fulfilled through unexpected agents. Four starving "lepers" (see Commentary on 5:1) outside the city are pondering their options. They could go into the city, where there was a famine and where they were not permitted to go (see Lev 13:11, 46; Num 12:14-16), or they could face death outside the city (vv. 3-4). With nothing to lose, they decide to defect to the Aramean camp, where there is food aplenty. When they come to the Aramean camp, however, they find it deserted, with all the supplies left intact.

The narrator pauses at this point to explain how that situation came about. The Lord had caused the Arameans to hear a huge commotion like the sound of an enormous host, perhaps the sound of the celestial host (2:11-12; 6:17). Assuming that the Israelites must have forged an alliance with the mighty Hittites and Egyptians, the Arameans fled for their lives, ironically leaving the very vehicles of transport—the horses and donkeys—that would have aided their hasty flight. The lepers enter the camp and help themselves to its abundance, but they quickly decide, both out of guilt and out of fear of punishment, that they are not acting appropriately "on the day

of good news" (v. 9). So they decide to report to the Israelite king that the Arameans have deserted their camp.

The practical, but faithless, king suspects a trap, which is not an unreasonable conclusion. After all, such tactics had been used before (cf. Joshua 8; Judges 9). One of his advisers, however, proposes that they risk sending scouts on five of the remaining horses that will probably starve anyway. Accordingly, the scouts discover that the Arameans really have fled in haste, for their clothing and equipment litter their escape route. Accordingly, the good news is brought to the Israelite king.

The Israelites plunder the Aramean camp, which was so well stocked with food that the instant increase in supply causes the prices of food to drop immediately, just as Elisha had predicted. The king's right-hand man, who earlier expressed skepticism about the possibility of an instant economic recovery, is assigned to have charge at the gate, the marketplace, and is trampled to death by the mob. Thus the prophecy of Elisha is fulfilled, and, in case the reader should somehow miss the point, the narrator clarifies it (vv. 18-20).

REFLECTIONS

The story related in this section of 2 Kings tells of the power of God to bring hope in the face of overwhelming odds, even though human authorities cannot deliver salvation.

1. For the king of Israel, expression of confidence in the ability of God to save had become a cliché a convenient way of abdicating his responsibility (6:27). He might have led his people in seeking God's deliverance. He might have turned to the prophet for a word from the Lord. He might have prayed. He might have done any number of things that a faithful leader should have done. But he did not. Instead, he was quick to blame others and to blame God. Even worse, he was prepared to give up hope in God's ability to save.

2. Given the king's murderous intent, his bitter words, and his lack of faith, it is rather remarkable that Elisha did not react adversely to the king's message. Instead of proclaiming a word of judgment upon the king, the prophet offered a surprising, unsolicited word of hope from God. That is the marvelous testimony to the grace of God. To one who could wait no longer, the word of God was the promise of an almost immediate reversal of the adverse circumstances.

3. Curiously, the text does not report the reaction of the king to Elisha's proclamation of hope. That is apparently left to the reader's imagination. The story is horribly graphic in its description of the famine. Encountering such a portrayal of human tragedy, the reader may furtively share the perspective of the angry king, who asked the question that we may not dare to ask: "Why should I hope in the LORD?" Taken in that light, the silence regarding the king's reaction (surely he had one!) is an invitation to readers to fill in the blanks with their own responses.

4. Whereas there is no response from the king, the narrator does report one reaction—namely, the skepticism of the king's right-hand man. The officer was a realist. He thought only in pragmatic terms, considering the possibility of a reversal of Israel's economic condition to come only through the natural processes. To him, the power of God could be manifested only within the scope of his limited vision. He could not see the power of God beyond what he thought was possible. However, the story here, like other stories in the Elisha cycle, makes the point that God's ways are not necessarily the ways of human beings (cf. Isa 55:8-9). Just as God may act through forces ordinarily invisible to human eyes (see 6:16), so also God may act in ways that do not conform to human experience and expectations.

5. Certainly one of the surprises in the story is the key role that the lepers play. These outcasts of society appear out of nowhere, starving and desperate. Yet, they were given the privilege of discovering the good news that the Arameans have deserted their camp. They were concerned first and foremost with their own needs, but they decided to pass the news on to the authorities out of a twinge of guilt and a large amount of fear. Still, it is through them that the good news was conveyed, while those in power doubted the possibility of divine deliverance. By the same token, while the faithless king was slow to accept the good news for what it was, a nameless servant provided a viable solution that led eventually to the fulfillment of prophecy. This is the way of the God of the Bible, who may bring about great miracles—indeed, salvation for people—through the outcasts and the lowly ones of society.

2 KINGS 8:1-29, A FEW LOOSE ENDS

OVERVIEW

The reigns of the kings of Israel's powerful Omride dynasty have been in focus since the accession of its founder, Omri (1 Kgs 16:21-28). During the reign of Ahab, the son of Omri, Elijah had prophesied the end of the dynasty (1 Kgs 21:21-24). Now, the narrator is about to tell the story of the end of the house of Omri (chaps. 9–10). Before he gets to that, however, there are a few loose ends to be tied up.

Chapter 8 consists of three passages that appear to be unrelated to one another. The first unit (vv. 1-6) returns to the woman from Shunem, to whom Elisha had previously ministered in wondrous ways (4:8-37). An unspecified amount of time seems to have lapsed since the earlier story, for the woman now appears to be the head of her household, and the hitherto wealthy woman is now vulnerable to the threat of an impending famine. Perhaps the story of the terrible famine in the preceding chapter prompted the placing of this account here. Famine is not the principal problem in this case, however. We know already from previous accounts that threat of famine can be miraculously averted (see 4:38-44) or overturned (6:24–7:20). The narrative purpose of the famine in the present account is to explain how the woman had lost her property and is now in need of powerful intervention on her behalf. That situation provides occasion for the demonstration of the power of the traditions about the prophet's mighty deeds; the traditions affect life and cause justice to be brought about, even when the prophet is physically absent. The story begins with the threat of famine, which turned out to have been rather easily avoided (the woman only had to take refuge in the land of the Philistines, not far away), but it ends with the demonstration of prophetic authority, even when the prophet is not present.

The second passage (vv. 7-15) does not appear to be related to the first. It takes place in a completely different setting, concerns a different subject matter, and, save for Elisha, involves different characters. It begins with the illness of the Aramean king and his attempt to discover whether he would recover. The king's illness and his inquiry turn out, however, to be a pretext for the narrator to tell of Elisha's role in the rise of the usurper Hazael. If only in an indirect fashion, Elisha now fulfills the word of the Lord given to Elijah in 1 Kgs 19:15-18. To be sure, Elijah is no longer present to anoint Hazael, but Elijah's role in the calling of Elisha as his successor has brought about this expected possibility of Hazael's accession through the word of an Israelite prophet. So the story begins with the illness of the king and his inquiry, but it ends with a demonstration of prophetic authority, even when the prophet Elijah is no longer present.

The third passage consists of the reports of the reigns of two Judean kings, Jehoram (vv. 16-24) and Ahaziah (vv. 25-29). These accounts may be seen as necessary "asides," inserted here for the sake of completeness in the overall history of both kingdoms. Still, both kings are presented as having such intimate ties with Israel that the two kingdoms are practically merged as one. Ahaziah is said to have reigned only one year, but during that brief reign, he managed to join Israel in its war with Hazael and even joined his Israelite counterpart in Jezreel, where Jehu would seize power and put an end to the Omride dynasty, thus fulfilling the prophecy of 1 Kgs 19:15-18.

2 Kings 8:1-6, Reprise of the Woman from Shunem

COMMENTARY

The narrator makes it clear that the woman who is the focus of this account is the one "whose son [Elisha] had restored to life" (4:8-37). In the earlier story, one gathers that she was a wealthy woman who, together with her husband, provided a guest room for Elisha's use whenever his itinerary brought him to their town. The prophet now warns her of an impending seven-year famine called forth by the Lord and urges her to leave the country with her household. The language suggests that she is head of her family, with her husband now presumably dead. The coming famine, then, is not the same one that is mentioned in 4:38, immediately following the account of Elisha's miraculous resurrection of the boy (4:18-37). It is also apparently not the famine that occurred during the siege of Samaria, mentioned in the preceding chapter (6:24–7:20). In any case, this famine does not appear to be widespread, for she goes only as far as the land of the Philistines, in the coastal region southwest of Judah.

When the woman returns home at the end of the seven-year period, she has to petition the king that her property be restored to her. The reader is not told why she had lost her property. Perhaps some unscrupulous neighbor had seized it during her absence. Perhaps it had been taken over and held in trust by the crown. Whatever the case, she is now in need of royal attention. In the earlier story, Elisha had offered to peddle influence on her behalf, but she declined his offer because she was dwelling among her own people (4:13). Now, having lost her home, she comes to the king on her own accord. Elisha has not sent her, and he is absent in this sequence. Fortunately for her, however, the king has become a fan of Elisha (cf. 6:31) and is eager to hear Elisha's attendant Gehazi tell stories about the wondrous deeds of the master. Indeed, Gehazi is telling the story of the resurrection of the woman's son when she arrives with her petition before the king. Perhaps because of her connection to the prophet, she easily wins the king's favor. He appoints an officer to settle her case, returning her property to her, together with whatever revenue it may have accrued during her absence.

The story illustrates the abiding effect of Elisha's mighty deeds. In this instance, Elisha himself is absent, but the mere retelling of his wonders, particularly the story of the resurrection of the dead child, is enough to affect the king, causing him to bring about justice. (See Reflections at 8:16-29.)

2 Kings 8:7-15, Elisha Plays Kingmaker

COMMENTARY

The scene shifts from Israel to Damascus, where Ben-hadad, the king of Aram, is sick.[99] Upon learning of Elisha's presence in the city, the king sends an officer named Hazael to inquire whether the king will recover from his illness. The Aramean king's action stands in marked contrast to that of Ahaziah, an Israelite king who in his illness preferred to seek an oracle from Baal-Zebub of Ekron (1:2-8). Moreover, whereas Elisha had previously been considered such a threat that an enormous Aramean army had to be dispatched to capture him in Israel (6:8-14), he is now portrayed as a welcome presence in the capital of Aram. Like Naaman, the Aramean general who had been healed of his affliction by Elisha (5:1-19a), Hazael brings generous presents from the king to the prophet and refers to the king as the prophet's "son," a term suggesting filial devotion (cf. "father" in 5:13; 6:21; 13:14). The portrayal of the king is entirely positive, and so the reader is set up to expect a positive word from the man of God.

Elisha's response in v. 10 is confusing, to say the least. The NRSV and the NIV both follow a scribal tradition that has Elisha telling Hazael to say that the king will certainly recover, while Hazael is informed that the king actually will die. The consonantal Hebrew text, however, suggests that Hazael is to say that the king will certainly *not* live. Instead of לו (*lô*, "to him"), this tradition reads לא (*lō'*, "not"), thus: "Say, you shall certainly not live!" This reading, however, probably represents resistance to the idea that the prophet might have urged Hazael to lie. Josephus, likewise, tried to exonerate the man of God by having him forbid Hazael to tell the king that he would not recover.[100] These and other moves cannot,[101] however, eliminate the problem, which goes beyond the question of truthfulness and deceit. Elisha is, in fact, deliberately setting Hazael up for his role as the usurper of the throne. A long and awkward period of silence ensues

99. Despite the narrator's obvious belief that this Ben-hadad was the predecessor of Hazael, whose reign is known from extra-biblical sources, his identity and historicity are matters of scholarly dispute. For a possible reconstruction, see Pitard, *Ancient Damascus*, 132-38.

100. Josephus *Antiquities of the Jews* IX.92.
101. For other views, see John Gray, *1 & 2 Kings*, OTL (Philadelphia: Westminster, 1964) 530-31; C. J. Labuschagne, "Did Elisha Deliberately Lie? Notes on 2 Kings 8:10," *ZAW 77 (1965) 327-28.*

between the two men "until he was embarrassed [עד-בש 'ad-bōš]." Then Elisha breaks down. He weeps, he explains, because he knows the atrocities that Hazael will do to Israel. This is further clarified by the explanation that Hazael will become king.

Taking the cue that the prophet may (or may not) have intended to give, Hazael· returns to Damascus and gives Ben-hadad the prophet's assurance that the king will live. The next morning, Hazael takes some kind of woven material (the Hebrew word מכבר [makbēr] is of uncertain meaning), dips it in water, and apparently suffocates the king in his sleep. Thus Hazael usurps the throne.[102] In a rather indirect fashion, the accession of Hazael is the fulfillment of 1 Kgs 19:15. To be sure, Elijah in his lifetime did not anoint Hazael. Yet, Elijah had been instrumental in the calling of Elisha to the ministry, and Elisha has been instrumental in the accession of Hazael. (See Reflections at 8:16-29.)

102. In the Akkadian inscriptions, too, Hazael is known as a usurper, "a son of a nobody."

2 Kings 8:16-29, The Reigns of Jehoram and Ahaziah of Judah

COMMENTARY

8:16-24. Jehoram (Joram), the son of Jehoshaphat, has already been mentioned incidentally in 1 Kgs 22:50 and 2 Kgs 1:17. Now comes the brief report of his reign (849–843 BCE). In contrast to the reigns of his two predecessors, Asa (1 Kgs 15:9-24) and Jehoshapat (22:41-50), both of whom are portrayed in generally positive terms, Jehoram's reign receives a strongly negative evaluation. He "walked in the ways of the kings of Israel" because he married the daughter of Ahab (v. 18), a marriage made, no doubt, for political convenience (cf. 1 Kgs 22:2). Just as Solomon was corrupted by his marriages to foreign women who led him down an idolatrous path (1 Kgs 11:1-8) and just as Ahab's marriage to Jezebel, the Sidonian princess, led him to patronize the cult of Baal (1 Kgs 16:31-34), so also Jehoram's marriage to Ahab's daughter has corrupted him. Still, the pro-Judean narrator tells us, the Lord's promise to David is still binding: The dynasty will continue, and Judah will not be destroyed (see 1 Kgs 11:36; 15:4). That does not mean, however, that there are no consequences for Jehoram's sins (cf. 2 Sam 7:14-16). Edom, which had been a vassal of Judah (3:8; 1 Kgs 22:47) would become independent of Judean control, and even Libnah, a town near the border with the Philistines, would revolt (v. 22).

8:25-29. On the one hand, the promise of an enduring dynasty in Judah (8:19; 1 Kgs 11:36; 15:4) seems to hold good, for Jehoram, despite his sins, is succeeded by Ahaziah, his son (v. 25). On the other hand, it is ominous that Ahaziah reigned only one year (843/2 BCE), at the young age of twenty-two, and nothing is said about an heir to him (v. 26). The promise of an enduring Davidic dynasty now seems threatened. The threat is all the worse because of Judah's dalliance with the north. All the notices about Ahaziah's brief reign have to do with his associations with Israel. His mother was Athaliah, the granddaughter of Omri and daughter of Ahab. Ahaziah also walked in the ways of Ahab, just as his father, Ahab's son-in-law, had done. Ahaziah joined Joram, his northern counterpart, in a war against the Arameans. He visited the wounded Joram in Jezreel after the Aramean campaign.

REFLECTIONS

This chapter is fragmented and difficult to appropriate in the community of faith. Nevertheless, it does offer important theological and practical insights.

1. As we so often find in the Elisha cycle, the prophet is involved in the lives of individuals in domestic settings immediately before and after dramatic successes in the international arena. Immediately after playing a major role in Israel's war with the Moabites (3:4-27), we find him attending to the economic and other mundane needs of various people (4:1-44). Immediately after his wondrous healing of Naaman, the Aramean general (5:1-27), we find him helping a disciple retrieve a lost ax head (6:1-7), before returning to international politics (6:8-23). Now, again, the man of God moves from playing a key role in a national crisis that is both economic and military (6:24–7:20) to turn his attention to an individual (8:1-3), before returning to play a role in international politics again. Such is the nature of the prophetic ministry: It attends to the needs of individuals as well as of nations.

2. The first story in the chapter illustrates how the wondrous acts of the past may continue to have their effects in the present through the retelling of the story. In this case, the retelling of the story of the resurrection of the son touched a king so much that he immediately moved to help a woman in need. The miracle happened not only in the resurrection itself, but also in the power that the story has to affect lives long after the event, even without the presence of the original performer of the miracle.

3. The story of Elisha's role in the demise of Ben-hadad and the accession of Hazael is troubling to many modern readers. The man of God apparently tells Hazael to lie and, whether he had intended it or not, is complicit in the assassination of the king. Within the narrator's larger view of history, however, this event fulfills the word of the Lord that promises an end to the horrible reigns of the apostate kings of the north. God's larger purpose will be worked out, it seems, even through human deceit (cf. 1 Kings 22:1) and unjustified death. The story defies our moral logic, but the Bible as a whole tells the story of a God whose will is accomplished in ways that sometimes defy human logic and moral categories.

2 KINGS 9:1–10:36, THE REIGN OF JEHU

OVERVIEW

In 1 Kgs 19:15-16, Elijah is told to anoint Elisha as his successor, Hazael as king of Aram, and Jehu as king of Israel. Although Elisha was not, strictly speaking, anointed, Elijah did pass the prophetic mantle on to him (1 Kgs 19:19-21). Hazael, too, was not anointed, but Elisha, duly commissioned by Elijah, was instrumental in his accession (8:7-15). There remains now only the anointing of Jehu, which will be carried out by one of the disciples of Elisha at the behest and with the authority of the master (9:1-13). Elijah had predicted the manner of death of Ahab and Jezebel and the obliteration of their descendants because of the murder of Naboth the Jezreelite (1 Kgs 21:17-24). The prophecy concerning Ahab's death has already been fulfilled (cf. 1 Kgs 22:37-38). Jezebel is still alive,

however, and Ahab has been succeeded by one son and then another. Now the narrator will show how the wrong done to Naboth the Jezreelite will finally be righted. The Hebrew root שלם (*šlm*, "to be complete/whole/in order") reverberates throughout the story with different nuances of the meaning of the root (9:17-19, 22, 31), most notably in the question, "Is all well?" (השלום *hăšālôm*; 9:11). The root occurs, too, in the word of the Lord to Ahab regarding the murder of Naboth: "And I will repay [ושלמתי *wěšillamtî*] you" (9:26); there can be no שלום (*šālôm*), no closure, as it were, until Naboth's murder has been fully avenged. Jehu states that there can be no *šālôm* until all the "whoredoms and sorceries" of Jezebel are eliminated (9:22). And that justifies the massacre of the worshipers of Baal (10:18-22). Finally, the root appears in the admission of Ahaziah's kin, who tell Jehu that they have come to Israel "to salute" (לשלום *lišlôm*, 10:13; NRSV, "to visit"; NIV, "to greet") him. They would be put to death, no doubt because they are related to Ahaziah, who is related to Ahab through his mother,

Athaliah. Only with the death of the last descendant of Ahab will the wrong committed against Naboth the Jezreelite be righted. Only with the complete destruction of the cult of Baal can there be *šālôm*. So complete is the judgment of God against the sins of the house of Ahab.

2 Kings 9:1-13, Jehu Is Anointed King

COMMENTARY

Joram, king of Israel, is wounded in the course of battle at Ramoth-gilead, and so he withdraws to Jezreel to recuperate (8:28-29), leaving some of his troops behind. Elisha sees an opportunity to anoint Jehu as king, according to the word of the Lord spoken to Elijah (1 Kgs 19:16). He does not, however, personally anoint the king. Rather, he tells one of his disciples to go immediately to Ramoth-gilead (v. 1), where Ahab had been killed earlier (1 Kgs 22:1-40), and to anoint Jehu as king in place of Joram. The idiom "gird up your loins" (NRSV) or "tuck your coat into your belt" (NIV) probably suggests urgency (see 1 Kgs 18:46; 2 Kgs 4:29). Elisha apparently wants to seize the moment and anoint Jehu before Joram recovers and returns to take control. Whereas 1 Kgs 19:16 has it that Elijah was to anoint Jehu, that is accomplished only indirectly, through Elijah's commissioning of Elisha (1 Kgs 19:19-21), who now charges one of his disciples to do the anointing. The gradual and indirect fulfillment of the word of the Lord in history is part of what Elijah was intended to understand by the almost imperceptible silence he heard on Mt. Horeb (1 Kgs 19:12). The task the young disciple of Elisha has is, in any case, a dangerous one, for he is told by Elisha to do the job and then to flee immediately (v. 3), but the precise nature of that danger is not spelled out.

Jehu, who is elsewhere called "the son of Nimshi" (v. 20; 1 Kgs 19:16; 2 Chr 22:7), is here called "son of Jehoshaphat the son of Nimshi" (vv. 2, 14). The inclusion of the grandfather's name in the patronym is rather unusual. Hence, some scholars surmise that Nimshi might have been Jehu's clan name or that Jehu's grandfather must have been better

known than his father.[103] It is possible, however, that the grandfather's name is provided to make it clear that Jehu is not the son of Jehoshaphat, the son of Asa, king of Judah. The point is that Jehu is not of royal descent. He is, in fact, though a high-ranking military officer in the Israelite army stationed at Ramoth-gilead, a commoner.

When the young prophet arrives at the camp, the officers are sitting in council (v. 5). Perhaps they are already plotting a coup. If that is the case, then Jehu's official anointing by the authority of the prophet (cf. 1 Sam 9:16; 10:1; 15:1; 16:1-13) would no doubt have given the rebellion prophetic legitimation. As the narrator would have it (v. 7), Jehu is to destroy the house of Ahab as a retribution against Jezebel (Ahab is already dead!) for her role in the killing of the prophets and other servants of the Lord (1 Kgs 18:4; 19:10, 14). The elimination of the descendants of Ahab would also fulfill the prophecy of Elijah regarding the matter of Naboth the Jezreelite (vv. 9-10; 1 Kgs 21:21-24). Despite the secretive ceremony (see vv. 2, 6) and the private conversation between the young prophet and Jehu, the other officers at Ramoth-gilead are quick to pledge their allegiance to the new king-designate (vv. 11-13; unlike the elevation of Omri [1 Kgs 16:16], this acclamation of Jehu to king appears not to have had universal support of the military). Although they disparage the prophet, referring to him as a madman (v. 11; cf. Jer 29:26; Hos 9:7), they do not hesitate to use his prophetic authority to support their cause. So Jehu is proclaimed king (cf. 11:9-12; 1 Kgs 1:38-40; Matt 21:8-11).

---

103. See, e.g., Gray, *1 & 2 Kings*, 540.

2 Kings 9:14-29, Joram and Ahaziah Are Killed

COMMENTARY

9:14-20. Jehu leaves instructions for his fellow officers to keep their proceedings a secret in Ramoth-gilead (v. 15), while he rushes off to Jezreel with some troops, no doubt intending to get there before word gets to the king of the conspiracy. A sentinel in Jezreel, seeing the troops approaching from afar, reports to Joram. The king sends two scouts out in succession, apparently to discover the intentions of the encroaching party. In each case, the scout is instructed to inquire of Jehu, and each in turn asks: "Is all well?" (השלום *hăšālôm*, vv. 17-19; cf. NJV, NAB). The question is the same one that Gehazi asked the Shunammite woman who was going to see Elisha because her child had died (4:26), the question only highlighting the fact that all was not well. It is the same question Naaman asked Gehazi when the latter ran after him to extract a gift from him; in that episode as well the question highlighted the fact that all was not well for Gehazi (5:21). It is also the same question that Jehu's comrades asked him when he emerged from his meeting with Elisha's emissary (v. 11). The NRSV and the NIV apparently understand the king and his scouts to be asking whether Jehu is coming in peace. While that is certainly a meaning of the question, the narrator may intend more—indeed, implying that in reality all is not well.[104] This is suggested by Jehu's question to the scouts and his invitation for them to join him on the side of שלום (*šālôm*): "What do you have to do with *šālôm*? Get around behind me!" (vv. 18-19). Each of the scouts does get behind Jehu, and the sentinel duly reports the fact to Joram. The reckless pace of the encroaching party suggests to the sentinel that it must be Jehu, "for he drives like a madman" (v. 20), a designation that prompts the reader to associate Jehu with Elisha, who is earlier also called a madman (v. 11). The reader is given a signal that Jehu is on the side of Elisha.

9:21-22. At last, Joram sets forth, accompanied by Ahaziah of Judah in a separate chariot, to meet Jehu. Poignantly, the parties meet at the property of Naboth the Jezreelite. This is probably the very plot of land where Elijah had earlier proclaimed judgment on the house of Ahab for his murder of Naboth (1 Kings 21:1). Joram now asks Jehu directly if all is well (*hăšālôm*), perhaps meaning the military situation at the battlefront in Ramoth-gilead. To that question Jehu replies that there can be no שלום (*šālôm*) so long as the "whoredoms and sorceries" of Jezebel continue (v. 22). The "whoredoms" here should not be taken literally; the language of promiscuity is often used in the Bible for association with other gods (cf. Exod 34:16; Lev 17:7; Deut 31:16; Judg 2:17; 8:33; Jer 2:1-13; Hosea 1:1–3). Likewise, "sorceries" should be taken as a metaphor for general wickedness (cf. Isa 47:9, 12; Nah 3:4).

9:23-26. Joram now recognizes the rebellion for what it is and shouts a warning to Ahaziah: "Treason!" (מרמה *mirmâ*) (v. 23)[105] and then tries to flee. Ahab had already paid for his crime when, in the heat of the battle at Ramoth-gilead, an archer shot an arrow that struck and killed him while he was in his chariot (1 Kgs 22:34). Now Jehu shoots an arrow that kills Joram in his chariot (v. 24). Joram is then thrown onto Naboth's plot, thus fulfilling the prophecy of Elijah against Ahab (1 Kgs 21:19) and against his descendants (1 Kgs 21:21-22). Specifically, the death of Joram is seen as the Lord's righting of the wrong that Ahab and Jezebel had done to Naboth the Jezreelite: "And I will repay [ושלמתי *wĕšillamtî*] you on this very plot of ground." To the narrator, then, this is the reason for Jehu's mission, hinted at by the repetition of the question, "Is it well?" (vv. 11, 17-19, 22). All is, in fact, not well. There can be no *šālôm* as long as Jezebel lives, and there can be no *šālôm* until wrong is righted (שלם *šillēm*, in the piel).

---

104. On the polyvalence of the root שלום (*šlwm*) and its use in this passage, see Saul Olyan, "*Hăšālôm*: Some Literary Considerations of 2 Kings 9," *CBQ 46 (1984) 652-68.*

105. Olyan, "*Hăšālôm*," 667, has pointed out that מרמה (*mirmâ*) is the opposite of (*šālôm*). See also Burke O. Long, *2 Kings*, FOTL (Grand Rapids: Eerdmans, 1991) 121-22.

9:27-29. Ahaziah of Judah, who has already cast his lot with Joram, flees south in the direction of Beth-haggan (ancient Jenin), apparently trying to return to Judah. He, too, is shot by an arrow and dies in Megiddo (v. 27), but his corpse is brought back to Jerusalem to be buried with his ancestors (v. 28;

2 Chr 22:9, however, suggests that Ahaziah was hiding in Samaria). It is unclear why Jehu wants to have Ahaziah killed. We may surmise that it is because of Ahaziah's various ties with Ahab and that Jehu wants to eliminate all threats to his own power in Israel and Judah.

2 Kings 9:30-37, Jezebel Is Killed

COMMENTARY

With Joram now dead, Jehu turns next to Jezebel. She is, however, defiant. She puts on her makeup, adorns her head, and comes to the window, probably in order to be viewed as queen. When Jehu appears, she also asks him the question that pervades the narrative: "Is it well?" (v. 31). Here she is surely not wondering whether Jehu is coming in peace, as the translations of the NIV and the NRSV would have it, for she has already heard of what he has done (cf. v. 30). Her question is a bitingly sarcastic one, implying that all is not well for Jehu, despite his triumphs thus far.[106] Her sarcastic intention is corroborated by her insult of Jehu, for she calls him "Zimri," referring to the usurper of the Israelite throne who managed to rule for only seven days

(1 Kgs 16:9-16). Zimri, too, was an officer in the army and had murdered his master, but he was not accepted by the troops. In fact, it was Omri, the father of Ahab, who had replaced that usurper!

At the behest of Jehu, two palace officials throw Jezebel down from the window, perhaps onto the very plot of ground once owned by Naboth the Jezreelite (vv. 36-37; cf. 1 Kgs 21:1). Her blood spatters on the wall, and her corpse is trampled by horses. Jehu celebrates his victory and only as an afterthought orders her burial (because she is a princess), but his henchmen find that there is not much left of her body to be interred. This event is recognized as a fulfillment of the prophecy of Elijah (cf. v. 10), although Jehu's quote expands on the original oracle as we know it in 1 Kgs 21:23.

106. Olyan, "Some Literary Considerations," 668.

2 Kings 10:1-17, Ahab's Descendants Are Killed

COMMENTARY

Jehu sets out next to deal with Ahab's "seventy sons" (v. 1), a figurative expression referring to all possible claimants to the throne (Judg 8:30; 9:5; 12:14). Just as Jezebel had written a letter to the elders of Jezreel in order to frame Naboth (1 Kgs 21:8), so also Jehu writes a letter to the local authorities—the commanders, the elders, and the guardians of Ahab's family—inviting them to select one of the descendants of Ahab as heir to the throne. The leaders, of course, perceive the dare implied in the invitation. They quickly pledge their allegiance to Jehu. He is not satisfied with words of allegiance, however, and demands that they present, literally, "the

heads of the men of your master's sons" and to come to him in Jezreel the next day (v. 6). The word "heads" (ראשים *rā'šîm*) is ambiguous, for it could refer literally to anatomical heads or figuratively to leaders. The officials assume the literal meaning and decapitate the remaining descendants of Ahab. Instead of going to Jezreel, however, as they have been ordered, they send the heads in a basket to Jehu, who has the heads put in heaps at the city gate until the next morning.[107]

107. The Assyrian kings did similar things as a warning to the general populace of the kings' willingness to resort to violence to achieve their goals. See *ANET*, 276-77.

The precise intent of Jehu's public statement is unclear (vv. 9-10). It is evident that he accepts responsibility for the death of the king, and he implies that he had not ordered the killing of the rest of the Omrides. There is great ambiguity, however, in his initial words, when he calls the people "righteous" (צדקים *ṣaddîqîm*). Does he mean to exonerate them from guilt in the king's murder, as the translation in the NRSV and the NIV suggests ("you are innocent")? Does he mean that they are impartial witnesses who would surely recognize that he is not responsible for this atrocity (REB, "you are fair-minded judges")? Does he imply that they are, in fact, implicated in the offense (NJV, "Are you blameless?").[108] Whatever the case, the narrator sees the slaughter of the descendants of Ahab as the fulfillment

of the prophecy of Elijah (1 Kgs 21:21-22, 24). With this theological legitimation, then, Jehu proceeds to kill all those who may still be associated with the house of Ahab in any way, until there are no survivors left (v. 11).

With his rivals thus eliminated, Jehu proceeds to the capital city, Samaria, no doubt to claim the throne formally (v. 12). On his way, he comes to Beth-eked of the Shepherds (an unknown location), where he meets associates of Ahaziah of Judah, who apparently do not seem to have been aware of what has happened to their king. Ironically, they inform Jehu that they are on their way "to salute" (לשלום *lišlôm*) the royal princes and the sons of the queen mother, Jezebel. Jehu has them arrested and killed—forty-two men in all (cf. 2:24). Thus he has eliminated all supporters of the house of Ahab, including those from Judah. (See Reflections at 10:28-36.)

---

108. See Long, *2 Kings*, 136; Gray, *1 & 2 Kings*, 555.

---

2 Kings 10:18-27, Jehu's Zeal

COMMENTARY

Jehu next meets an enigmatic figure, Jehonadab "son of Rechab." Apart from this passage, the latter is mentioned in Jeremiah 35:1, where he is remembered as the ancestor or founder of the house of the Rechabites. According to Jer 35:6-7, Jehonadab "son of Rechab" forbade the drinking of wine, viticulture, or, indeed, sedentary life in general. This is commonly seen as a rejection of all aspects of life in Canaan, and so Jehonadab is viewed by many scholars as a conservative worshiper of the Lord who advocated a return to the faith in its pristine purity, as in the wilderness days. Other interpreters, however, noting that the "house of Rechab" is associated with the Kenites or "smiths" in 1 Chr 2:55, argue that the Rechabites were really a guild of metallurgists, specifically chariot makers.[109] If the latter is the case, then בן־רכב (*ben-rēkāb*) would not be a patronym ("son of Rechab") but an indication of Jehonadab's association with the Rechabite guild ("a chariotmaker,"

or the like).[110] Whatever the reasons, Jehu and Jehonadab form an immediate bond (v. 15), and Jehu treats Jehonadab as a close ally (see 1 Kgs 20:33).

With his newfound ally, Jehu sets about eliminating Baal worship in Israel. The story is told with great irony. Jehu announces that Ahab had served Baal a little and that Jehu would serve Baal much. There is an apparent wordplay here, for the Hebrew verb for "to serve" (עבד *'ābad*) sounds like the verb "to destroy" (א אבד *'ābad*; cf. v. 19). So Jehu summons the worshipers of Baal to one place, just as Ahab had done on Mt. Carmel (1 Kgs 18:20), where they were eventually slaughtered by Elijah (1 Kgs 18:40). The occasion, according to Jehu, would be a great "sacrifice" (זבח *zebaḥ*) for Baal; the root for "sacrifice" is used of the slaughter of idolaters (cf. 1 Kgs 13:2). Lest the reader miss the point, however, the narrator states that Jehu is acting with cunning (v. 19).

When the Baal worshipers are assembled at the temple, no doubt the temple of Baal

---

109. See Frank S. Frick, "The Rechabites Reconsidered," *JBL* 90 (1970) 279-87. In this view, the injunction against wine (Jer 35:6-7) is not an indication of asceticism but a rule of the guild designed to prevent accidental divulgence of metallurgic secrets.

110. See T. R. Hobbs, *2 Kings*, WBC 13 (Waco, Tex.: Word, 1985) 128-29.

---

that Ahab had built (1 Kgs 16:32), they pack the building "from end to end" (v. 21; lit., "mouth to mouth"). The number of Baal worshipers in Israel at that time must have been considerably greater than those assembled, but the narrator heightens the drama by having the worshipers of Baal destroyed in Baal's very own temple. Ironically, too, Jehu orders the baalists to be properly attired for the occasion (v. 22) and takes steps to ensure the exclusion of "the servants of the LORD" from this special occasion (v. 23). Then he orders his officers to slaughter all of the people, and they desecrate and destroy the temple, indeed, turning it into a latrine, thus ensuring that it could never again be used as a sanctuary (vv. 24-27). (See Reflections at 10:28-36.)

2 Kings 10:28-36, Summary Assessment of Jehu's Reign

COMMENTARY

Jehu's purge of baalism wins him praise from the deuteronomistic narrator (v. 28). Jehu is considered to have done so well that God rewards him with four generations on the throne; in fact, his dynasty will be the longest lived that the northern kingdom will ever know (v. 30). For all this, however, the evaluation of Jehu is negative. He is said to have failed to keep the Torah of the Lord with all his heart, and he did not turn away from the sin of Jeroboam, for the golden calves at Dan and Bethel were not destroyed (v. 31). The closing summary of Jehu's reign includes observations about the losses of Israelite territory east of the Jordan (vv. 32-36).

REFLECTIONS

This passage is surely one of the most violent portions of the Bible. The greatest difficulty for those who come to 2 Kgs 9:1–10:36 as Scripture, however, is not the reality of extensive violence per se, but the contention of the narrator that Jehu was anointed by the will of God and the implication that his massacres were a fulfillment of the will of God (see 9:7-10, 22, 26, 36-37; 10:10, 30). Jehu is unscrupulous, cunning, ruthless, and brutal. He reminds us of the most extreme kind of religious fanatic, who resorts to deceit and brutality to exterminate those who do not share his or her religious views. Yet, Jehu is affirmed as the one who has brought שלום (šālôm). He is praised for his elimination of the house of Ahab (v. 30) and for eradicating Baal worship (v. 28). The text is not unequivocal in its commendation of Jehu, however. He is judged negatively for not turning away from the sins of Jeroboam (v. 29) and for his failure to keep the Lord's instructions with all his heart (v. 31). Jeroboam was also the acknowledged leader of a revolution, but he served his own ambitions and was perfectly willing to manipulate religion to suit his own purposes; his idolatry was not so much the worship of statues (the golden calves) but his own agenda (see Commentary and Reflections on 1 Kgs 12:1-33). Jehu was cut from the same cloth.

1. On the one hand, then, the text affirms the judgment of God: Injustice will not be overlooked, disloyalty to God will be punished, and idolatry will have its deadly consequences. The judgment may not be carried out immediately, but it will be carried out in due time, perhaps through the complicated plots of human history and even through self-serving and wicked opportunists who are, nevertheless, unwitting agents of God's will. On the other hand, the text makes it plain that the responsibility of human beings is to obey God with all their hearts. God looks beyond the results of one's actions into the inner motivation.

2. The story in 2 Kings 9–10 is ironic in its suggestion that *šālôm* is achieved through violence. The narrator's point of view, conveyed by Jehu, is that there can be no *šālôm* as long as human atrocities are not requited. Yet, all is not well, even with the death of Ahab and Jezebel and their descendants. Jezebel's question to Jehu remains as yet unanswered: "Is all well?" (9:31). The reader has a sense that the terrible violence cannot really bring *šālôm*. Soon, in some remote site off the beaten track, the paranoid Jehu has to kill the unnamed associates of the Judean king who were seeking *šālôm* (10:13). As for Jehu himself, all was not well: His territory was trimmed, and he died with the condemnation of the Lord for his unfaithfulness. A century later, the prophet Hosea would proclaim the judgment of God against the house of Jehu for the violence committed at Jezreel (Hos 1:4-5). Still, the narrator's point that there can be no *šālôm* in the face of unrequited sin vexes, and the point that *šālôm* may paradoxically come out of violence haunts the reader. That unsettling perspective is consonant with the rest of the Bible, however, culminating in the view, central to the New Testament, that in God's mysterious dispensation, *šālôm* for sinful humanity does come about in the aftermath of violence. That is how the will of God is worked out sometimes. Indeed, that is the paradox of the cross.

2 KINGS 11:1–12:21, THE ACCESSION AND REIGN OF JOASH

OVERVIEW

The narrator turns from the revolution in the north to a crisis in the south. The idolatrous ways of the house of Ahab had insidiously but surely infected the house of David. Jehoshaphat was forced to fight alongside Ahab and his son Jehoram, although in each case he had tried to coax the Israelite kings to turn to the Lord (1 Kgs 22:1-40; 2 Kgs 3:1-27), and he tried to do what was right in the eyes of the Lord (1 Kgs 22:41-44). His son and successor, Jehoram, however, was married to Athaliah, the daughter of Ahab, and behaved in the manner of the idolatrous northern kings (8:16-18). Still, despite his recalcitrant ways, the Lord would not destroy Judah and would continue to uphold the promise to David that one of his descendants would always sit on his throne (8:19). Jehoram's son and successor, Ahaziah, had continued in the ways of his father—indeed, associating so closely with the house of Ahab that he, in effect, tied Judah's fate with that of Israel (8:27-29). Poignantly, in the report of his reign, there is no reiteration of the Lord's promise that the Davidic line will endure. The revolution that took the life of the Israelite king also killed the king of Judah (9:27-29) and, along with him, some of his relatives (10:12-14). The foolhardy exploits of Ahaziah left him dead after having reigned only one year. The promise of God to David is now threatened as never before. The queen mother, Athaliah, an Omride princess (8:18, 26; 2 Chr 21:6; 22:2), seizes power and attempts to kill all the sons in the royal family (11:1). Although Athaliah rules for seven years, the typical regnal summaries are omitted in the report, for the narrator does not consider her to have been a legitimate ruler.

2 Kings 11:1-3, Athaliah's Usurpation of the Davidic Throne

COMMENTARY

Athaliah is to Judah what Jezebel was to Israel. Jezebel, the Phoenician princess and devotee of Baal, held an unsavory influence over the house of Ahab, leading eventually to Jehu's revolution. Athaliah is a daughter of Ahab and, one presumes, of Jezebel. Like the ruthless Jezebel, Athaliah is willing to commit murder in order to have her way. She orders a purge of all possible claimants to the throne (v. 1), thus endangering the promise of God to David that there will always by a "lamp" in Jerusalem (1 Kgs 11:36). Indeed, the Omrides had been eradicated by Jehu in Jezreel and Samaria, but Athaliah threatens to continue the ways of that dynasty in Jerusalem. The purge of Ahaziah's heirs is foiled, however, by Ahaziah's sister Jehosheba, who hides the infant Joash, together with his nurse (v. 2).[111] Safe from Athaliah, the baby Joash (the form of the name alternates with its variant; "Jehoash") spends six years in the "house of the LORD" (v. 3). Indeed, the parallel account in 2 Chr 22:10-12 provides the additional information that Jehosheba is the wife of Jehoiada, the priest who will have a dominant role to play in the restoration of "the king's son" (see v. 4) to the throne.

111. Jehosheba is said to be the daughter of Joram and Ahaziah's sister, but the text does not specify whether she is also Athaliah's daughter. Not surprisingly, Josephus (*Antiquities of the Jews* IX.7) and others have speculated that Jehosheba is the daughter of Joram through another marriage and, hence, is a half sister of Joash, thus explaining her loyalty to him.

2 Kings 11:4-21, The Davidic Monarchy Is Restored

COMMENTARY

In the seventh year of Athaliah's illegitimate reign, Jehoiada, the chief priest of the Temple of the Lord (see 2 Chr 24:6), orchestrates a return of the legitimate heir to the throne. He secures the support of the Carites, mercenaries of uncertain origin, who are charged with guarding the Temple and the palace, swearing them to secrecy and loyalty.[112] The instructions given to them are rather confusing (cf. the NIV and the NRSV of vv. 5-8), partly because of our ignorance of military organization of that time and the layout of the city and partly because the Hebrew is ambiguous.[113] It appears that the guards are divided into three detachments, one of which is further divided into three details and is assigned to three strategic stations, while the other two are to protect the boy, Joash. The troops are provided with weapons from the Temple that had belonged to King David (v. 10; cf. 2 Sam 8:7). This is a subtle but important detail inasmuch as the countercoup is seen by the narrator as an effort to restore the promise made by the Lord to David. Then these guards bring out Joash, put the crown upon his head, and give him some kind of emblem of kingship (v. 12). The Hebrew word for that emblem (עדות *'ēdût*) is used elsewhere in the Bible for covenant documents (e.g., Exod 25:16, 21; 31:18; 32:15; 34:29; 40:20) and occurs in conjunction with David's kingship in Ps 132:12. Hence the NIV interprets it as "a copy of the covenant" (NRSV, "the covenant"; REB, "the testimony"), although the word has been taken by some interpreters to refer to some sort of royal insignia.[114] In any case, Joash is proclaimed king (v. 12).

112. The Hebrew consonantal text in 2 Sam 20:23 also speaks of the "Carites," but later scribes preferred reading "Cherethites," who may or may not be related to the Carites.

113. The "house" (בית *bayit*) at the end of v. 6, for instance, is interpreted as "palace" in the NRSV but "temple" in the NIV. Indeed, it has even been interpreted as the "house" of Baal mentioned in v. 18. See Iain W. Provan, *1 and 2 Kings,* NIBC (Peabody, Mass.: Hendrickson, 1995) 221-22.

114. See Cogan and Tadmor, *2 Kings,* 128.

Athaliah is caught off guard; her protestations of treachery are of no avail, as Jehoiada orders her arrest and the guards kill her, but only after they have taken her away from the sacred precincts (vv. 13-16). Jehoiada then initiates a covenant renewal between the Lord and the king and his people (v. 17), a renewal necessitated by the rupture in the relationship between the Lord and the nation, caused by Ahaziah's allegiance to the house of Ahab, which seemed to have intertwined Judah's fate with Israel, and by the subsequent illegitimate rule of Athaliah. The people move to destroy the hitherto unmentioned temple of Baal (presumably built by Athaliah), its cultic appurtenances, and Mattan, its priest (v. 18). In contrast to the carnage that attended the revolution in the north, there is no massacre; only Mattan, the priest of Baal, and Athaliah are killed. Instead of the terror and uncertainty that Jehu's revolution brought, the narrator reports that all the people rejoice and that the city is quiet (v. 20).

2 Kings 12:1-16, The Reign of Joash

COMMENTARY

The reign of Joash (837–800 BCE) is focused almost entirely on the renovation of the Temple, symbolic of the rededication of Judah to the Lord. The mother of Joash is identified as Zibiah of Beersheba, a site at the southern border of Judah—that is, as far south from the border with Israel as possible. The narrator seems to imply that it is this parentage, together with the fact of Jehoiada's tutelage, that accounts for the relatively faithful reign of Joash, although he, too, is criticized for failing to remove the high places.

Joash orders the priests to collect the money from the census taxes (see Exod 30:11-16) and from the voluntary offerings that are given in repayment of vows (Lev 27:1-8) and instructs them to oversee the renovation of the Temple (vv. 4-5). The fundraising mandate seems to be a general one;

it is not clear whether the funds are specifically designated for the project. Hence, more than two decades later, the repairs are still not done (v. 6). Joash dismisses the priests from the project because of the obvious conflicts of interest. Henceforth the priests are no longer to receive the contributions, and they are also released from the obligation of overseeing the temple repairs (vv. 7-8). A chest is set up to receive additional contributions, and whenever it is full, representatives of the state and the Temple together disburse the money for payment of the workers. The funds were not to be used for the maintenance of the temple appurtenances, but only for the workers commissioned to do the repairs. The priests, though, are still paid out of the funds accumulated from the guilt offerings and sin offerings (see Lev 4:1–6:7; Num 15:22-31).

2 Kings 12:17-21, Hazael Threatens and Joash Dies

COMMENTARY

All the efforts of Joash to do right seem to be negated, however, when Hazael of Aram threatens Jerusalem. To buy Hazael off, Joash takes from the temple treasury the votive gifts deposited there by his predecessors, Jehoshaphat, Joram, and Ahaziah. History seems to repeat itself, for the reformist king Asa had long ago taken from the same treasury in order to buy off the Arameans (1 Kgs 15:18).

The temple treasury, which was depleted by Asa and slowly replenished by his successors, is again being raided by a reformist king in the face of an Aramean threat. Even reformist kings like Asa and Joash do not perform adequately in the interest of the Lord's house.

The regnal summary of Joash includes a note about his assassination by his own courtiers. No reason is given by the narrator for this murder, but the chronicler adds the information that Joash is killed for having murdered the son of his former patron, Jehoiada the priest (2 Chr 24:23-27).

REFLECTIONS

In this chapter, we see how God's promise of an enduring Davidic dynasty is threatened by a ruthless usurper determined to eliminate all the royal family. A single baby is saved, however, by a hitherto unknown and never again mentioned woman who takes it upon herself to hide him from his would-be killers. This is not the first time, of course, that a baby is saved from a royal pogrom. Pharaoh tried to have all the male infants of his Hebrew slaves killed, but Moses was secretly hidden and saved from harm, and he grew up to be an agent of God's liberation (Exod 2:1-10). Nor is the deliverance of baby Joash the last time that such a deliverance of an infant would occur. Indeed, the deliverance of Joash from death in some ways foreshadows the deliverance of another baby, another "son of David," from the efforts of King Herod to have all male infants killed (Matt 2:1-23). To be sure, God is silent in this story of the deliverance of the infant Joash. In the light of the repeated emphasis in the book of Kings on the working out of God's will in history, however, there can be little doubt that the reader is to understand that God is working behind the scenes, too, in this deliverance of an infant. God does not have to act or speak in order for God's will to be accomplished. In history there will always be agents, witting or unwitting, who will bring about the divine will.

The story also points to the potential and limitations of human beings who strive to serve God. Jehoiada, who so valiantly and efficiently orchestrated the restoration of the heir to the throne of David, does not seem to have the ability to manage the finances of the Temple efficiently enough to carry out the needed repairs. By the same token, King Joash had initiated the fund-raising campaign to repair the Temple, but he seemed so out of touch with the project that it took him more than two decades to realize that the repairs had not been done. He who had taken steps to raise funds for the Temple's renovation is the same king who robbed the temple treasury in order to pay off an outsider. He who had been rescued as an infant was struck down forty years later by his own servants, perhaps because he had betrayed the very person who had instructed him in his youth (2 Chr 24:23-27).

2 KINGS 13:1–14:29, THE DYNASTY OF JEHU THRIVES

OVERVIEW

Having addressed the crisis in Judah (chap. 12), the narrator now returns to the situation in Israel. The crisis in Judah was not merely a political one; it was also a theological crisis. The conduct of Joram of Judah and his son Ahaziah had so tied Judah to Israel that the two nations had practically become one. It was no accident, therefore, that Ahaziah was murdered along with his northern counterpart in Israel. The foolhardy actions of Ahaziah brought consequences not only to himself, but to the Davidic dynasty as well. Athaliah, a princess from the house of Ahab, seized power and moved to eradicate all legitimate claimants to the throne in Jerusalem. It looked as if the house of Ahab, annihilated in Jezreel and Samaria, would simply continue in Judah through Athaliah. Moreover, God's promise of an enduring Davidic dynasty hung in the balance for a while, thwarted only by the deliverance of a lone baby, the future King Joash, from death. At last, the crisis had blown over, as the legitimate scion of David was placed on the throne; the covenant was renewed among God, king, and people; and the Temple was refurbished. Things were as God had intended them to be for Judah. But what about Israel?

Unlike Ahaziah, who had pandered to the house of Ahab, Jehu had been effective in destroying it and eliminating Baal worship from Israel. For his accomplishments in those areas, Jehu was commended and rewarded with the promise of a relatively enduring dynasty—one that would last four generations. Now in the new unit (13:1–14:29) we find a report of how Israel fared through three generations of the descendants of Jehu. In that period, Israel seemed to have been treated in a manner more typical for Judah: The ruling dynasty endured, and Israel experienced the persistence of God's grace despite the sins of the kings.

These two chapters look like a collection of loosely connected and haphazardly placed units. The reports of the reigns of Jehoahaz (13:1-9) and Jehoash (13:10-13) appear to be already closed out, when we find Jehoash active again and performing sign-actions at the behest of Elisha (13:14-19). An account of an odd incident occurring after the death of Elisha appears in 13:20-21; it concerns the resurrection of an unknown man and seems at first blush to have nothing to do with the national and international events in the rest of these chapters. Then, the focus turns again to the international arena, with a reference in the narrative to the Aramean oppression of Israel during the reign of Jehoahaz (13:24), together with allusions to victory for Israel under Jehoash (13:25). There follows a report on the reign of Amaziah of Judah (14:1-14), with a closing summary of that reign (14:17-22). Intruding into that report, however, is a regnal summary of the reign of Jehoash that most commentators regard as anomalous (14:15-16) and some believe to be a secondary duplication of a similar summary in 13:12-13. Finally, there is a report of the reign of Jeroboam II (14:23-29). Not surprisingly, some scholars posit that a series of originally independent pieces has been brought together over a period of time and through a series of redactions.[115] That may be the case, but it is still possible to read the entire unit as one literary piece, as some scholars have attempted to do.[116] As it stands, the narrative is about the fulfillment of God's promise to Jehu that his dynasty will last four generations (10:30). Regardless of the sins of Jehu's descendants, therefore, God has continued to grant Israel salvation and victory.

115. See, e.g., the survey in Long, *2 Kings*, 163-65.
116. Long, *2 Kings*, 162-70.

2 Kings 13:1-13, Jehoahaz and Jehoash Reign in Israel

COMMENTARY

Jehoahaz (variant of "Joahaz") has already been mentioned in 10:35 as the son and successor of Jehu. Now comes the formal report of his reign (vv. 1-9). He is evaluated in the manner typical for the northern kings. Accordingly, Jehoahaz followed the ways of Jeroboam, son of Nebat, causing Israel to sin, and he did not depart from them (v. 2; cf. 1 Kgs 12:26-32; 16:26; 22:52; 2 Kgs 3:3; 10:29; 13:11; 14:24; 15:9, 18, 24, 28). The account in vv. 3-6 echoes the typical cycle of events that one finds in early Israel's history: Israel sins, God sends an oppressive enemy as retribution, the people cry to God for mercy, God sends a deliverer, things return to normal for Israel, but soon the people sin again (see Judg 2:11-23; 3:7-15, 30; 4:1-3, 23; 10:6-10). Whereas the "savior" is typically named in the analogous depictions from Israel's early history (it was typically the next ruler), however, he is not explicitly identified here (v. 5). Scholars have variously suggested that the allusion is to a third-party aggressor whose pressure on the Arameans brought a reprieve for Israel (such as the Assyrian king Adad-nirari III or even Zakkur of Hamath), another Israelite king like Joash or Jeroboam (II), or Elisha.[117] Despite the

117. See Cogan and Tadmor, *2 Kings*, 143.

fact that it is the reign of Jehoahaz that is in view, it seems clear that the narrator has in mind the problem of Aramean aggression over a considerable period of time; God repeatedly gave Israel into the hands of the Arameans during the reigns of Hazael and then of his son, Ben-hadad (v. 3), certainly a period extending well beyond the rule of Jehoahaz. The "savior" (מושיע *môšîaʿ*), then, would not be one specific individual, but anyone who was instrumental in the deliverance of Israel from its plight. Indeed, in the course of the narrative, the Hebrew root ישע (*yšʿ*, "save") is used in conjunction with Elisha (13:14-21), Joash (13:17), and Jeroboam (14:27), each of whom will in some way bring salvation/victory (the Hebrew word is the same) to Israel in its times of distress.

It is important to observe that God responds to the cry for deliverance from oppression, even when the entreaty comes from the recalcitrant Jehoahaz. Nothing is said in the text about repentance, yet God heeds the prayer of the king. Still, the people persist in following the ways of Jeroboam, and unacceptable sacred objects, like the "sacred pole," were not purged from Samaria (v. 6). Jehoahaz is left with a remnant of an army as insignificant as the dust on a threshing floor, vulnerable to every wind that blows across it (v. 7). This remnant is, paradoxically, a testimony to both God's judgment and God's grace: The army's diminution is certainly a sign of divine judgment, but the fact that a remnant survives is a sign of grace. For now, Israel is like Judah inasmuch as it is punished for its offenses against God, but there is continuity on the throne in Samaria as in Jerusalem. So when Jehoahaz dies (v. 9), he is succeeded by his son Jehoash (variant of "Joash"). The new king, too, does not depart from the ways of Jeroboam (vv. 10-11). Yet, he triumphs mightily over Judah (v. 12), and he is succeeded by his son Jeroboam (v. 3). (See Reflections at 14:23-29.)

2 Kings 13:14-21, Elisha Dies, But His Ministry Lives On

COMMENTARY

Given the importance of the "savior" (מושיע *môšîaʿ*) in the survival of Israel, the impending death of Elisha (אלישע *ʾĕlîšaʿ*; lit., "My God Saves") is certainly ominous, and Jehoash knows it. The king's weeping before the prophet suggests a recognition of the role that the celestial hosts have played in Israel's victories on account of Elisha's presence (see 2:11-12; 6:16-17). Elisha had cried as Elijah ascended into heaven, "My father, my father! The chariotry of Israel and its horses!" (2:12). So now Jehoash cries as Elisha lies on his deathbed, "My father, my father! The chariotry of Israel and its horses!" (v. 14). Is it conceivable, one might wonder, that Jehoash could somehow be in the position that Elisha had been in when he succeeded the great Elijah?

Elisha tells Joash to shoot an arrow eastward, out of the window (vv. 15-17). This is a prophetic sign-act, akin to Ahijah's tearing of the garments into twelve pieces to symbolize the fragmentation of the kingdom (1 Kgs 11:29-32). Such prophetic sign-acts, intended as the initial realization of the prophecy, are typically performed by prophets (e.g., Isa 7:3; 8:1-4; 20:1-6; Jer 13:1-11; 18:1-12; 27:2-11; 32:1-15; Ezek 4:1-11; 5:1-12; 12:1-20; 24:15-27). Here it is Jehoash who acts out the prophetic event under the instruction of Elisha. Then, when Jehoash shoots the arrow out the window, Elisha announces that it is the Lord's "arrow of victory, the arrow of victory over Aram," the Hebrew word for "victory" (תשועה *tĕšûʿâ*) being the same as the word for "salvation," a word consisting of the same root as the word for "savior" (*môšîaʿ*) in v. 5 and found in the name "Elisha." Poignantly, Elisha places his hand upon the hand of Jehoash after the king has shot the arrow, as if the prophet is passing on to the king his prophetic power or authority. It is as if the agency of salvation or victory made possible through the person of Elisha is now somehow passed on to the king of Israel. Even after the death of the prophet, there will be a "savior"; there will be salvation/victory through a king, even one as sinful as Jehoash. Elisha stipulates, however, that Jehoash is to fight Aram at Aphek "unto completion" (עד-כלה 'ad-kallēh). The mention of Aphek recalls Ahab's victory over the Arameans at that same site, although Ahab did not completely destroy the Arameans, as he was supposed to do in a holy war (1 Kgs 20:26-43). The fact that the arrow shot out of the window is called "the LORD's arrow" suggests that the battle belongs to the Lord (cf. other references to arrows of the divine warrior in Deut 32:23; Pss 77:18; 91:5; Hab 3:11; Zech 9:14). As in the case of the war Ahab had earlier fought against the king of Aram at Aphek, this war belongs to the Lord, and victory in it belongs to the Lord.

The prophet further instructs the king to strike the ground with the arrows (v. 18). The Hebrew word for "strike" (הכה hikkâ, in the hiphil) is also the word used in the defeat of enemies, and the word for "earth" (ארצה 'arṣâ) is the same one used for "country." Given the context, therefore, one may understand the command to be a call to defeat the country of Aram. When Jehoash strikes the ground with the arrow only three times and stops, he is chided for having carried out the command inadequately (v. 19). Elisha interprets this to mean that the king should have struck "unto completion" (v. 19; cf. v. 17). Jehoash's failure is sometimes explained as evidence of his "tendency to think small,"[118] of his "vacillating character,"[119] or the like. The anger of Elisha, too, seems unreasonable to some scholars, who note that the prophet did not tell the king precisely how many times to strike the arrows on the ground.[120] In view of Elisha's call (v. 18) to "strike" (hikkâ) Aram "unto completion" ('ad-kallēh), and in the light of the account of the earlier battle of Israel with Aram at Aphek, however, it seems clear that the issue here is not the insufficiency of Jehoash's enthusiasm, but his

flagrant disregard for the will of God in holy war (see the Commentary on 1 Kgs 20:35-43). The incident anticipates the report on Israel's limited success against Aram in v. 25.

In all, the account provides an explanation for the success of Israel against Aram during the years under the house of Jehu. It explains why the dynasty endured four generations, despite the flaws of the descendants of Jehu. God somehow provides a "savior" whenever there is a need for one, whether that "savior" is a prophet or a king, a man of God or a sinner. At the same time, however, the passage provides a rationale for the impending end of that period of grace: The kings of the house of Jehu, like Jehoash, are just like the willfully disobedient Ahab after all.

As if to ensure that the point is not missed that the abiding effects of Elisha's ministry will continue even after his death, the narrator then tells a somewhat comical, but nevertheless powerful, story of an event that happened after Elisha had died and was buried. A funeral of another man is taking place when a marauding band of Moabites come to a region in Israel. In their hurry to avoid the Moabites, the people burying the man simply throw the corpse into a grave, which just happens to be Elisha's. When the corpse comes into contact with Elisha's skeleton, the dead man is revived. The possibility that this resurrection was a result of the contact of the dead man's body with that of Elisha is reminiscent of the resurrection of the dead child of the Shunammite woman in 4:32-35. The present story is even more poignant, however, for Elisha has long been dead and buried, his body having decayed until only the skeleton is left. Yet, even in death, Elisha's power lives and enlivens, even as the mere retelling of his power empowers and enlivens, despite his absence (8:1-6). As in life, so even in death, his power not only affects kings in the international arena (vv. 14-19), but it also brings life to ordinary folk, even an unnamed dead man! (See Reflections at 14:23-29.)

118. Hobbs, *2 Kings*, 170.

119. Norman Snaith, "2 Kings," in *The Interpreter's Bible* (Nashville: Abingdon, 1954) 3:257.

120. See, e.g., Paul J. Kissling, *Reliable Characters in the Primary History: Profiles of Moses, Joshua, Elijah, and Elisha*, JSOTSup 224 (Sheffield: Sheffield Academic, 1996) 179-80.

2 Kings 13:22-25, Victories over Aram

COMMENTARY

The narrator summarizes the situation during the reigns of Jehoahaz and Jehoash. The Lord had been gracious and merciful to Israel on account of the covenant with the ancestors (see Gen 15:1-21; 26:23-25; 28:10-22). Without parallel anywhere in the book of Kings, this claim explains the survival of Israel despite the sins of its kings. In effect, this appeal to the covenant with the ancestors functions as the equivalent of the appeal to the Davidic covenant (2 Sam 7:1-17) for the kings of Judah. It explains why salvation came to Israel, despite the lack of any appropriate response by Israel's kings (vv. 1-9). Hence, Israel is able to have victories over Aram, just as Elisha had predicted in the symbolic actions of Jehoash (vv. 14-19). There are hints in the text, however, that the respite God has granted Israel will not last forever, the narrator's historical viewpoint being evident in the words "until now" (v. 23). Jehoash does "strike" (הכה *hikkâ*; NRSV, NIV, "defeated") Aram three times and recovers the towns of Israel (v. 25). The reader has been apprised, however, that the victories of Jehoash will not last (v. 19). (See Reflections at 14:23-29.)

2 Kings 14:1-22, The Reign of Amaziah of Judah

COMMENTARY

14:1-6. The attention of the narrator shifts from north to south, as we now find a report on the reign of Amaziah (800–873 BCE), a contemporary of Jehoash of Israel. The report is a typical one for Judean kings. It is a generally positive evaluation: Amaziah, like David, did what was right in the sight of God (cf. 1 Kgs 3:3; 15:11; 22:43). Yet, he was not quite like David, for Amaziah failed to destroy the local sanctuaries (vv. 1-4). To the narrator, the overall faithfulness of Amaziah is evident in the fact that he avenged the murder of his father, Joash (cf. 12:19-21)—but he did so within the limits of the law (vv. 5-6; cf. Deut 24:16).

14:7. Amaziah is relatively successful against the Edomites, killing ten thousand of them in the Valley of Salt (cf. 2 Sam 8:13) and capturing Sela (v. 7).[121] So far in the narratives of Kings, Judah's relation with Edom has been something of a gauge of the status of the Davidic king in the eyes of God. When the king has been generally faithful, Edom has been a vassal of Judah (so in the reign of Jehoshaphat, 1 Kgs 22:47; 2 Kgs 3:8). When the king has been unfaithful, however, Judah has lost control of its neighbor (so in the reign of Joram, 8:20). The implication of Amaziah's successes over Edom, therefore, is a sign of divine favor. Still, as the account that follows suggests, Israel under the descendant of Jehu is even stronger than Judah.

14:8-14. Perhaps emboldened by his triumphs over Edom, Amaziah sends emissaries to his northern counterpart, apparently in an attempt to shake off Judah's vassal status (2 Chr 25:6-16 provides a plausible explanation for Amaziah's desire to work things out with his northern counterpart before things got out of hand). His proposal for a face-to-face conference assumes parity of the two states. Jehoash, however, is disdainful of the proposal. He cites a fable, comparing Judah to an insignificant thornbush that tries to behave as an equal or even a superior to a cedar tree (v. 9), and he urges Amaziah to stay home and behave himself (v. 10).[122] When Amaziah refuses, Jehoash indeed meets him face-to-face, not in a diplomatic conference but in combat at Beth-shemesh, not far from Jerusalem (v. 11). To distinguish

---

121. Sela has traditionally been identified with Petra, although there are no remains there dated earlier than the seventh century. The site is more likely near es-Sela', where traces of a fortified city dating from the ninth to the seventh centuries have been discovered. The name "Jokthe-el" is otherwise used of a town in the Judean foothills around Lachish (Josh 15:38).

122. For other examples of plant fables, see Judg 9:7-15 and Ezek 17:1-10.

the town from others with the same name (cf. Josh 19:22, 38), the narrator specifies that this town is Beth-shemesh of Judah. That is, despite the challenge issued in Samaria, the battle was fought just outside the Judean capital. In consequence, Judah is defeated, Amaziah is captured, a large portion of the wall of Jerusalem is torn down,[123] the treasuries of the palace and the Temple are raided, and hostages are seized (vv. 12-14).

14:15-16. The regnal summary of Jehoash in these verses seems out of place and, since it duplicates the regnal summary in 13:12-13, is usually regarded as an intrusive anomaly.[124] Yet, the presence of this regnal notice makes good narrative sense, for the account of Amaziah's reign is really subordinated to the larger story of Israel's period of favor under the kings of the Jehu dynasty. Not even Amaziah, with all of his attempts to do right and his triumphs over the Edomites, can stand in the way of Israel's success. Israel's victory over Judah is merely part of the larger story of the accomplishments wrought in Israel through Jehoash. The theological importance of this point necessitates the insertion of this regnal notice here, even if it duplicates the similar summary in 13:12-13.[125]

---

123. Although the major battle took place in Beth-Shemesh, southwest of Jerusalem, it is the northern wall that is breached. The breach was 400 cubits, approximately 600 feet, long.
124. See, e.g, Hobbs, *2 Kings*, 177; Gray, *1 & 2 Kings*, 612.
125. Some scholars have plausibly suggested that the earlier text (13:12-13) is, in fact, the secondary text. See Cogan and Tadmor, *2 Kings*, 145.

14:17-22. With that theological point now scored, the narrator returns to complete his report on Amaziah. Although still called "king," Amaziah is said to have lived for fifteen years after the death of Jehoash. Whether he was, in fact, still ruling in Jerusalem, the narrator does not say. Despite the claim that he reigned twenty-nine years in Jerusalem (vv. 1-2), there are hints that he might have been deposed (see 14:23; 15:8). Indeed, in contrast to the regnal summary for Jehoash, which speaks of the "might" of that king of Israel (v. 15), we read only of the "deeds" of Amaziah (v. 18). Even worse, the summary notes a conspiracy against him in Jerusalem, of his flight to Lachish, and of his murder (v. 19). Like that of his ancestor Ahaziah (9:28), his body had to be brought back to Jerusalem for burial (14:20). Jehoash, the descendant of Jehu, dies peacefully, while Amaziah, the descendant of David, is murdered while in enemy captivity. Despite the promise to David of an everlasting dynasty, Amaziah dies a humiliated man, succeeded by his sixteen-year-old son Azariah, during whose reign the Edomite city of Elath, on the northern coast of the Gulf of Aqaba, will be restored—only after Jehoash has passed away (v. 22; cf. v. 17). (See Reflections at 14:23-29.)

2 Kings 14:23-29, The Reign of Jeroboam II of Israel

COMMENTARY

The narrator has already noted that Jehoash was succeeded by his son, Jeroboam II (786–746 BCE; 13:13; 14:16). Now he gives a brief report of Jeroboam's reign. As the reader has come to expect of northern kings, the evaluation of him is basically negative: Jeroboam did evil in the sight of God and did not turn from the ways of Jeroboam, son of Nebat (v. 24). Even so, the narrator notes Jeroboam's expansion of Israel's border "from Lebo-hamath as far as the Sea of Arabah" (v. 25)—that is, to the extent of Israel's territory in the days of Solomon (1 Kgs 4:21; 8:65).

This achievement was "according to the word of the LORD, the God of Israel, which he spoke by his servant Jonah son of Amittai" (v. 25). The territorial expansion is apparently understood as a fulfillment of an oracle by the prophet Jonah, son of Amittai. No such oracle has been preserved, however, and nothing else is known about Jonah, except what we may extrapolate from the biblical book that bears his name. Still, it is significant that we have an allusion to a positive prophetic word to Israel, despite the sins of its kings. Noteworthy, too, is that the Lord is called "the God of

Israel" (v. 25). This "God of Israel" responded to Israel's distress (see 13:5) and, seeing that there was no one else who could help Israel, saved it through Jeroboam. The assertion that "the LORD had not said that he would blot out the name of Israel under heaven" is remarkable, for it implies that Israel is the chosen people of God (cf. Deut 9:14; 1 Sam 12:22). The summary of Jeroboam, like that of his father and predecessor (vv. 15-16), notes the main accomplishments of Jeroboam. It notes, too, that he is succeeded by Zechariah, thus bringing up the name of the last king of the Jehu dynasty (v. 29).

REFLECTIONS

These chapters of the book of Kings are remarkable for the ways they contradict and nuance the pattern that we have come to expect. One who reads through the reports of the reigns of the various kings of Israel and Judah from 1 Kings 12 to 2 Kings 14 will notice the rhythmic quality in the accounts. The kings of Israel are uniformly regarded with disdain, and reports of their reigns typically include harsh words of judgment for Israel. The kings of Judah, however, are judged much more sympathetically. Even when they are evaluated negatively, the narrator typically calls attention to the validity of God's promise to David: For the sake of David, who did what was right in the eyes of the Lord, God had promised that there would always be a scion of David on the throne in Jerusalem (see, e.g., 1 Kgs 14:21 16:34). In 2 Kings 13–14, however, Israel is the undeserving recipient of God's favor. Despite the fact that all the kings of Israel named in this context are as sinful as their predecessors, the narrator speaks of Israel in idioms that recall other texts that describe God's chosen people (see especially 13:4-5, 23; 14:26-27). At the same time, the reader gets a hint that Judah, the recipient of God's grace through the promise to David, cannot count on divine favor forever. God's dealings with humanity cannot be reduced to any easy formula, for the deity saves whomever the deity wills.

The God who delivers people from oppression does so through unexpected agents. In the first place, we are astounded to learn that God answers the prayers of people even when they show no signs of repentance. For the sake of the oppressed, God heeded the prayers of a person as sinful as Jehoahaz. Not only that, God even calls sinners to be saviors! That is a remarkable claim that this text makes. It violates our expectations, for we tend to think of saviors as heroes, and we idealize heroes as people of irreproachable character. God's salvation, however, breaks our preconceived molds. Salvation may come from prophets like Elisha, but succeeding Elisha in the role of the one who brings salvation is the sinful king Jehoash. It is through Jehoash that God brings Israel salvation from the Arameans. Then it is the sinful king Jeroboam who brought salvation to his people. What a remarkable lesson that is for those of us who tend to see good coming only from people who are perfect or, at least, generally of good character. God, however, works for good through whomever God chooses—through faithful ministers of the word (like Elisha), and even through evil people (like Jehoahaz, Jehoash, and Jeroboam)!

2 KINGS 15:1–16:20, KINGS OF ISRAEL AND JUDAH

2 Kings 15:1-7, Azariah/Uzziah of Judah

COMMENTARY

Azariah (783–742 BCE), the son of Amaziah, of Judah is also known as Uzziah (see vv. 13, 30, 32, 34). The former is probably his personal name, whereas the latter is his throne name (so it is used in references to his reign in Isa 1:1; 6:1; 7:1; Hos 1:1; Amos 1:1; Zech 14:5). He became king at the age of sixteen (v. 2), when his father was deposed after a humiliating defeat by Jehoash of Israel (14:1-22). According to the narrator, Azariah reigned a remarkable fifty-two years (v. 2), probably including a period of co-regency with his father. The evaluation of his reign is typical of the positive analyses of Judean kings. Like Amaziah (14:3), he did what was right in the eyes of the Lord (v. 3), except that he failed to centralize worship in Jerusalem (v. 4). The text speaks of a skin affliction ("leprosy") that he suffered—later in life, according to the parallel account in 2 Chr 26:16-21. The disease is said to have been an affliction from the Lord (v. 5). No reason is given here for that affliction, but according to the 2 Chronicles version, the king grew arrogant in his autumn years and flagrantly violated

ritual regulations (2 Chr 26:16-21).[126] He was not banned from the city, as might be expected (Lev 13:11, 46; Num 12:14-16; cf. 2 Kgs 7:3), but he did live in בית החפשית (*bêt haḥopšît*), literally, "the house of freedom."[127] Since he was unable to perform his royal duties because of his condition, the king probably went into early retirement, while his son Jotham served as regent. That is perhaps the reason for the occasional reversion to his personal name. In any case, despite his disease, his long reign brought considerable stability to Judah. According to the chronicler, Azariah/Uzziah repaired the defenses of the capital, reformed the army, gained control of the trade routes to the south, and extended the borders of Judah at the expense of its Philistine and Edomite neighbors 2 Chr 26:6-15. (See Reflections at 16:1-20.)

---

126. See also Josephus *Antiquities of the Jews* IX.222-25.

127. The NIV and the NRSV both have "a separate house," presuming that the king was quarantined, an interpretation supported by the Targum, which has Azariah living outside the city. Another interpretation, already found in the medieval commentator Qim'i, takes "house of freedom" to mean release from all duties. See Gray, *1 & 2 Kings*, 619-20.

2 Kings 15:8-31, A Succession of Kings of Israel

COMMENTARY

Following the report of Azariah's reign comes a series of brief accounts of the reigns of a rapid succession of Israel's kings, each of whom (except for Shallum, who reigned only one month) is said to have done evil in the sight of the Lord and followed the ways of Jeroboam, son of Nebat (vv. 9, 18, 24, 28). Zechariah (746–745 BCE), the son of Jeroboam II, was the last king of the house of Jehu. He reigned only six months before being assassinated in public by a man named Shallum, "son of Jabesh" (a reference probably to his

clan, Jabesh of Gilead, rather than to his parentage), who then ruled as king for only one month, before being himself assassinated (see Amos 7:9, 11; Hos 7:6-7, 16). Shallum's killer was Menahem, who reigned 747–737 BCE, during which time he sacked Tiphsah and committed atrocities there.[128] During his reign, the Assyrian king Pul (an alternate

---

128. Tiphsah was a city in northern Syria, on the west bank of the Euphrates. It was a border town in the days of Solomon (1 Kgs 4:24). The reading of the name, however, is uncertain. Some Greek witnesses assume the name "Tappuah," a town on the border of Ephraim and Manasseh.

Hebrew name for Tiglath-pileser III) became a dominant force in the region. Menahem had to buy him off with increased taxes (v. 20). Menahem was succeeded by his son Pekaiah, who reigned two years (737–736 BCE) before being assassinated by Pekah, son of Remaliah (vv. 23-25). Pekah held the throne from 736 to 732 BCE, during which time Tiglath-pileser III raided the country several times, taking many cities and carrying off captives to Assyria. Pekah was killed by Hoshea, who reigned 732–724 BCE. Thus the narrator races through history, naming six kings of Israel, five of whom were assassinated. The narrator seems to be hastening toward the end of Israel's existence as an independent nation. (See Reflections at 16:1-20.)

2 Kings 15:32-38, Jotham of Judah

COMMENTARY

Uzziah's son Jotham reigned sixteen years (742–735 BCE). He gets an evaluation typical of a good Judean king: Jotham did what was right in the eyes of the Lord but failed to remove the high places (vv. 34-35). In addition, he is said to have built "the upper gate of the temple of the LORD," the location of which is unknown. (See Reflections at 16:1-20.)

2 Kings 16:1-20, Ahaz of Judah

COMMENTARY

16:1-9. Following the disastrous reigns of Jehoram (8:16-24) and Ahaziah (8:25-29) and the debacle of Athaliah's coup (11:1-3), the Judean monarchy seems to be back on track. Kings Joash, Amaziah, Azariah/Uzziah, and Jotham are all said to have done what is right in the eyes of God, even though they did not remove the local sanctuaries (12:2-3; 14:3-4; 15:3-4, 34-35). Ahaz, however, receives an overwhelmingly negative evaluation. He did not do what was right in the eyes of God, as his ancestor David had done, but instead, "walked in the ways of the kings of Israel" (v. 3; cf. 8:18, 27). The narrator accuses him of practicing child sacrifice like the nations that were driven out of the land at God's command when Israel entered it (v. 3). The narrator, no doubt, is referring here to certain religious practices of the cult of Molech (cf. 1 Kgs 11:7) that are banned by deuteronomic law (Deut 18:9-14; see also Lev 18:21; 20:2-5; Jer 7:31; 19:5; 32:35).[129] Such a horrible offense is given as one of the reasons for Israel's eventual destruction (17:17-18). The only other king of Judah who committed such a sin was Manasseh, the archrogue of the Davidic dynasty (21:6). Ahaz, of course, is also accused of personally worshiping at the "high places" (local cultic sites condemned by the deuteronomists), the first Judean king to be so accused after the completion of the Temple in Jerusalem (v. 4; cf. 1 Kgs 14:23-24).

It was during the reign of Ahaz that the so-called Syro-Ephraimitic War was waged by a coalition of Aramean (Syrian) forces and Israel against Judah. The alliance was attempting to depose Ahaz and coerce Judah into joining in its rebellion against Assyria (cf. Isa 7:1-8, 10). During that period, the Edomites retook Elath, on the northern coast of the Gulf of Aqaba (v. 6; cf. 2 Chr 28:17), which had been seized by Judah during the reign of Azariah/Uzziah (cf. 14:22). Against Aram and Israel, Ahaz pledged vassalage to Tiglath-pileser III of Assyria (v. 7). In consequence, Judah had to pay tribute to the Assyrians, which then prompted Ahaz to draw on the temple treasury, as other kings before him had done (v. 8). Hence, the Assyrians marched against

129. See John Day, *Molech: A God of Human Sacrifice in the Old Testament*, University of Cambridge Oriental Publications (Cambridge: Cambridge University Press, 1989) 31-33.

Damascus, captured it, carried its people into exile to Kir (said to be the original home of the Arameans in Amos 9:7), and killed Rezin, the Aramean king.

16:10-20. In Damascus to meet with his Assyrian suzerain, Ahaz saw an altar in that city that particularly impressed him. So he sent a model of it to Jerusalem and commissioned one just like it to be built in Jerusalem. The old bronze altar in the Temple (cf. 1 Kgs 8:64) was moved (v. 14), now for the king to seek oracles (v. 15). Some of the furnishings were removed and apparently were used as part of the bribe.

REFLECTIONS

These chapters appear to contain straight historical records that have no explicit theological messages. Indeed, when we compare various portions of this text with parallel accounts found elsewhere in the Bible, we find a strange silence in chapters 15–16 where theological implications of the stories are fleshed out in the parallel passages. Regarding Azariah/Uzziah, for instance, the chronicler tells of the king's initial faithfulness and his successes because of it. When the king became arrogant and disregarded the ritual regulations, however, he was afflicted with a skin disease. By contrast, the narrator of the passage in 2 Kgs 15:1-7 is remarkably terse in his report about Azariah/Uzziah, mentioning his skin disease as a divine affliction but not giving the cause of it. Similarly, whereas the chronicler presents Jotham as a righteous king who held firm to the ways of the Lord (2 Chr 27:1-9), the narrator in 2 Kgs 15:32-38 only makes formulaic judgments about this king, noting without comment Jotham's construction of the upper gate of the Temple. Although Isaiah observes Ahaz's dependence upon military prowess instead of trusting the Lord (Isa 7:1–8:10), the narrator in 2 Kgs 16:1-20 does not make such an explicit theological claim, even though he acknowledges Ahaz's apostasy. Ahaz's innovations at the Temple are passed over without any theological judgments. Instead of such overt theological moves, the narrator conveys a subtle, even subliminal, message: God's sovereign will is being worked out in separate tracks. On the one hand, the kingdom is moving inexorably toward destruction because its leaders will not turn the nation away from the sinful course on which it has been set. On the other hand, another nation is being preserved because of God's promise, despite the inadequacies of its rulers.

2 KINGS 17:1-41, THE FALL OF SAMARIA

OVERVIEW

This long chapter, containing an account of the fall of Samaria (722/721 BCE) and its aftermath, is widely believed to be the product of a long and complex compositional-redactional history. There is little agreement among critics, however, about the details of that history, except for the fact that the final form of it is a showcase of the deuteronomistic theology of history.[130] The fall of Samaria is, in any case, a key moment in the history of the monarchy. It is the moment anticipated since the very beginning of the divided monarchy, when Jeroboam established the sanctuaries in Dan and Bethel together with the golden calves therein (1 Kgs 12:25–14:18). Henceforth there will be only the state of Judah, the focus of the rest of 2 Kings. In any case, the present text is coherent in broad outline. The chapter may be divided into three parts: (1) an account of the fall of Samaria, vv. 1-6; (2) a lengthy theological rationale for the event, vv. 7-23; and (3) the aftermath of the destruction, vv. 24-41.

130. See Hobbs, *2 Kings*, 224-25; Long, *2 Kings*, 180-82.

2 Kings 17:1-6, How Samaria Fell

COMMENTARY

Hoshea, son of Elah (c. 732–724 BCE), was the last king of the northern kingdom, the king in whose reign the fall of Samaria would actually begin (v. 1). The history of Israel has been leading up to this point ever since the days of Jeroboam. On account of Jeroboam's sins, which all the succeeding kings of Israel followed, God is expected to bring the nation to an end, uprooting the people from the land given to their ancestors and sending them into exile beyond the Euphrates (1 Kgs 14:15). Hence, the reader anticipates the harshest judgment on the king's conduct as the story of the end is told. One expects the narrator to observe that things really came to a head with Hoshea, the last king, who was more sinful than all his predecessors. That is not what the text says, however. Rather, the narrator acknowledges the sinfulness of the king, but quickly adds that Hoshea was not as bad as the kings who preceded him (v. 2). This toning down of judgment is unprecedented in the history of the northern kings. Moreover, the standard negative assessment of the kings of Israel—that the king followed the ways of Jeroboam, son of Nebat—is absent here (cf. 1 Kgs 16:2, 19, 26, 31; 22:52; 2 Kgs 3:3; 9:9; 10:29; 13:2, 11; 14:24). Indeed, this evaluation of Hoshea stands in stark contrast to that of Ahaz of Judah, who is said to have "walked in the ways of the kings of Israel" (16:3). In this way, the narrator indirectly makes the

point that the destruction of Samaria is not due to the conduct of its present king alone. Rather, the pattern of behavior that has led to the destruction had been set long ago. Israel's history of unfaithfulness to the Lord has led to this point, and destruction cannot now be averted.

The Assyrian king Shalmaneser—in this case Shalmaneser V (c. 727–722 BCE), the son and successor of Tiglath-pileser III—threatened Israel (v. 3). Hoshea duly paid him tribute and submitted to him as a vassal, but soon flirted with the possibility of making an alliance with Egypt (v. 4).[131] Assyrian retribution was swift. Shalmaneser besieged Samaria (vv. 5-6),[132] but one gathers from Assyrian records that he apparently died while the three-year-long siege was going on in Israel, and the city was actually taken by his successor, Sargon II (722–705 BCE).[133] The citizens of Israel were exiled to various parts of the Assyrian Empire (v. 6)—to Hallah (a region northeast of Nineveh) and to the area around the Habor (a tributary of the Euphrates), which is said to be "the river of Gozan" (Gozan being the capital of an Assyrian province and in the cities of the Medes). (See Reflections at 17:24-41.)

131. The identity of "So" has sparked vigorous debate, for no such king is known from the Egyptian records. See Cogan and Hayim, *2 Kings*, AB 11 (New York: Doubleday, 1988) 196.
132. For some of the historical details behind this account, see John H. Hayes and Jeffery K. Kuan, "The Final Years of Samaria (730–720 B.C.)," *Bib* 72 (1991) 153-81.
133. See *ANET*, 284-85.

2 Kings 17:7-23, Why Samaria Fell

COMMENTARY

The explanation for the fall of Samaria is couched in terms of violation of the covenant: The people sinned against the God of the exodus (v. 7); conducted themselves like the nations that had been driven out of the land (vv. 8, 15); constructed unacceptable sanctuaries (v. 9); set up idolatrous symbols (vv. 10, 16); worshiped idols, astral deities, and other gods (vv. 11-12, 15-16); practiced

child sacrifice (v. 17); turned to divinations and auguries (v. 17); and generally violated the covenant and various stipulations laid down by God (vv. 14-16; see especially Deut 6:4-15; 7:1-6; 12:2-4; 18:9-14). God had sent them warning "by every prophet and every seer," but they did not turn back from their wicked ways (vv. 13-14). Poignantly, the narrator notes that the people had gone after things ephemeral (ההבל *hahebel*) and, hence, themselves became ephemeral (see v. 15). The Hebrew word הבל (*hebel*; NJV, "delusion"; NRSV, "false idols"; NIV, "worthless idols") literally means "wind" or "puff." It refers to things that are insubstantial, ephemeral, or unreliable. They will not last because they have chosen relationships that do not last. Against the Lord they "secretly" did things that were not right (v. 9).

Remarkably, woven into the present text is a subliminal message for Judah. Although the issue at hand is the fall of Samaria, the narrator notes that God's warning through the prophets and seers had been for Israel *and* Judah (v. 13). Israel fell because the Lord was angry, says the narrator, so that Judah alone remained (v. 18). Implicit here is a warning to the Judeans not to take the lesson of Israel's fall lightly; even though they may still be standing, the fate that befell Israel may yet await them. Indeed, as the present text has it, Judah also did not keep the commandments of God and had, in fact, followed the customs that Israel had introduced (v. 19). The theological explanation, then, seems to be directed not at Israel but at Judah. It is not only a justification of God's action against Israel, but also a theological lesson directed at the people of Judah, calling for them to turn back to God before it is too late. As one scholar sees it, the narrator "looks back on what has been to set forth what will be for the future."[134]

The narrator summarizes the issue in vv. 21-23, where we find the history of the divided kingdom in a nutshell. It all began with Jeroboam, son of Nebat, who drove the people of Israel from God and provoked them to sin (v. 21). Yet, the responsibility for proper conduct rests squarely on the shoulders of the people themselves. They continued in all the ways of Jeroboam, and they did not turn back from those ways (v. 23) until the Lord finally removed them from God's presence, thus fulfilling the proclamations of the prophets. (See Reflections at 17:24-41.)

134. Pauline A. Viviano, "2 Kings 17: A Rhetorical and Form-Critical Analysis," *CBQ* 49 (1987) 559.

2 Kings 17:24-41, The Resettlement of Samaria and Its Consequences

COMMENTARY

While the Assyrians deported Israelites from the land to distant places, they also brought in outsiders from various parts of the empire (v. 24).[135] To the narrator, however, the land still belonged to the Lord, who sent lions to attack the foreign settlers who did not worship God (v. 25). When this was reported to the Assyrian king, he sent an exiled Israelite priest, a man from Bethel, to return to his country to teach the settlers the true religion (vv. 26-28).

The damage had been done, however, for the settlers continued to worship their foreign gods with their strange-sounding names (vv. 29-31).[136] Syncretism became the order of the day, as the settlers worshiped the Lord along with their own gods (v. 32). They even appointed all sorts of people as priests in the local sanctuaries, ironically replicating what Jeroboam had done when he founded the heterodox sanctuary at Dan and Bethel (1 Kgs 12:31). That is perhaps not surprising, since the one person whom the Assyrians found to save the situation turned out to be a priest from the heterodox sanctuary at Bethel that Jeroboam had built (v. 28). Evidently, the consequences of Jeroboam's sins were felt long after his death, for now the deuteronomic laws that were supposed to be constitutive in the land became irreparably compromised (vv. 34-41).

135. The Assyrian practice of repopulating conquered territories is well attested in extra-biblical texts. See, e.g., the record of Sargon II in *ANET*, 284-85.

136. Of the names of the gods mentioned, only Nergal may be identified with certainty.

REFLECTIONS

Most scholars recognize that 2 Kings 17 is a key passage illustrating the deuteronomistic editor's message to the exiles in the sixth century BCE. The narrator's temporal viewpoint is evident throughout the narrative, most notably in the phrase "to this day" (17:23, 34, 41). Here the theologian justifies God's destruction for disobedience and warns against syncretism in the face of the temptation to do so as the exiles dwell among foreigners in faraway places. There are theological lessons in this text, however, that are as pertinent for people in the modern community of faith as they were for those living in the sixth century BCE.

1. The text is ultimately more than a justification of the doom that God brought upon a nation long ago. It is a homily to those of us for whom there is still an opportunity to do what is right. It is a homily about what happens when we violate the first commandment and betray God, from whom no secrets can be kept (see 17:9).

2. The narrator makes the point that God's judgment in the present does not come because of what someone else did in the past. Accordingly, the destruction of Israel occurred not because of what Jeroboam, son of Nebat, had done generations before or, for that matter, because of what Hoshea did when the Assyrians came. Rather, God's judgment is against what the people themselves have been doing. Jeroboam did sin, but the people of Israel continued in his ways and did not depart from them. Moreover, the judgment is not so much against specific offenses at any one time as it is against people's refusal to turn back despite God's persistent pleas through human messengers. The problem is with the assumption that grace entails no responsibility. We cannot expect God's patience in the face of the persistence of our rejection of God's call.

3. Paradoxically, the narrator also believes that sin has consequences beyond the experiences of individuals in the present. The sins of Jeroboam, son of Nebat, did have consequences far greater and longer lasting than he could ever have imagined. Largely for pragmatic and political reasons, he had established heterodox sanctuaries in Dan and Bethel. The tradition that he began had become so entrenched that when the Assyrians decided to send someone back to Israel to teach the ways of the Lord to the settlers there, the only person who could be found to do so was a priest from Bethel; the narrator seems to imply, however, that this priest only managed to teach them unacceptable practices. The heterodoxy of "Samaria" and the "Samaritans" is an indirect result of what both Jeroboam and the people of Israel had done.

2 KINGS 18:1–25:30

THE LAST DAYS OF JUDAH

2 KINGS 18:1–20:21, HEZEKIAH, THE TRUSTING KING

OVERVIEW

This literary unit, which focuses on the reign of Hezekiah, son of Ahaz, is neatly framed by the regnal summaries at the beginning (18:1-8) and the end (20:20-21). The accounts here find extensive parallels elsewhere in the Old Testament (2 Chronicles 29:1–32; Isaiah 36:1–39), not to mention accounts in the Assyrian annals.[137] Scholars posit that the text as it stands is a compilation of a number of originally independent units, including two variant accounts of the confrontation between the representatives of the Assyrian king and Hezekiah. Whatever the reality, the entire unit as we have it reads reasonably well as a continuous report. The chronological notices scattered throughout the chapters suggest a sequential framework. The story begins with the beginning of Hezekiah's reign (18:1-8), followed by accounts of events in the fourth, sixth, and fourteenth years of his reign (18:9–19:7; 19:8-34); Hezekiah's illness and the extension of his life by fifteen years (20:1-19); and, finally, a reference to his death (20:20-21).

137. See *ANET*, 287-88.

2 Kings 18:1-8, Introduction to Hezekiah the Reformer

COMMENTARY

The regnal notice in v. 1 notes that Hezekiah began his reign in the third year of King Hoshea of Israel (i.e., 729/728 BCE), but that date does not square with the information in vv. 9-10 and 13. There have been many attempts to explain or harmonize the discrepancies,[138] but such moves are perhaps unnecessary, for the text is finally to be viewed, not as a historical document, but as theological literature. Most scholars now agree that Hezekiah reigned from around 715 to 687/686 BCE (the parallel text in 2 Chr 29:1-2 omits the synchronism).

Hezekiah receives an unequivocal endorsement from the narrator (v. 3), the first of its kind so far in the book of Kings. Like many of his predecessors, Hezekiah is said to have done what is right in the sight of God. However, in contrast to the others, whose failure to centralize the cult in Jerusalem in accordance with deuteronomic law is invariably noted (1 Kgs 22:43; 2 Kgs 12:3; 14:4), Hezekiah is commended for removing the "high places" (local sanctuaries) and the cultic symbols that accompanied such heterodox religious sites (see 1 Kgs 14:15, 23; 15:14; 22:43; 2 Kgs 12:3; 14:4; 15:4, 35; 17:10). He is portrayed as being faithful to the deuteronomic law (cf. Deut 7:5; 12:3), a monotheistic reformer like Gideon (Judg 6:25-32), and, perhaps, even like Moses (Exod 34:11-17; Deut 9:21). Indeed, whereas Moses had set up a bronze serpent, a cultic object for treating snakebites

138. See, e.g., Gray, *I & 2 Kings*, 669-70; E. Thiele, *The Mysterious Numbers of the Hebrew Kings*, 2nd ed. (Grand Rapids: Eerdmans, 1965) 132-33.

(Num 21:8-9), Hezekiah surpasses him by removing that object (נחשתן [nĕḥuštān] is a play on the words for "bronze" and "serpent"), because it had come to be venerated (v. 4).

The narrator reports that Hezekiah "trusted" the Lord as no other king before him had done (v. 5)—indeed, apart from Hezekiah (the Hebrew root occurs eight other times in this story, in vv. 19 [twice], 20, 21 [twice], 22, 24; 19:10), the verb is not used of any other ruler in the book of Kings. Unlike Solomon, who "held fast" (דבק dābaq) to his foreign wives (1 Kgs 11:2), Hezekiah "held fast" (dābaq) to the Lord and did not depart from the law of Moses (v. 6). As a result, the Lord was with Hezekiah as God was with David (v. 7; cf. 1 Sam 16:18; 18:12, 14; 2 Sam 5:10), and Hezekiah became successful, just as David had been (1 Sam 18:5, 14-15). Like David, too, he was given victory over the Philistines (v. 8; 1 Sam 18:27; 19:8). Finally, in contrast to Ahaz, who turned readily to the king of Assyria for security (16:7), Hezekiah rebelled against the Assyrians (v. 7). Hezekiah was, by all accounts, a faithful king. (See Reflections at 20:12-21.)

2 Kings 18:9-12, Perspective on the Fall of Samaria

COMMENTARY

The fate of the northern kingdom at the hands of the Assyrians is retold here in virtually the same detail as in 17:1-6, except for the attempt to synchronize the events with the reign of Hezekiah (vv. 9-10). It appears that Hezekiah had rebelled against the king of Assyria (v. 7) but was able to survive foreign invasion because he had been obedient and faithful, whereas Samaria was destroyed because the people of Israel were disobedient (v. 12). The narrator implies that Hezekiah's trust (v. 5) had put Judah on the side of the Lord. Thus expectation is raised on the part of the reader that Judah will survive the Assyrian threat.[139] (See Reflections at 20:12-21.)

139. Long, *2 Kings*, 198. Cogan and Tadmor, *2 Kings*, 221.

2 Kings 18:13–19:7, Sennacherib's First Challenge

COMMENTARY

Given the auspicious start in the narrative in vv. 1-8 and the implication in vv. 9-12 that, because of Hezekiah's faithfulness, the fate of the southern kingdom would be radically different from that of the northern kingdom, the account of the fall of Judean cities at the hands of the Assyrians is utterly astounding. Suddenly we are in the fourteenth year of Hezekiah's reign (cf. Isa 36:1)—that is, 701 BCE—and the Assyrian king now is Sennacherib (705–681 BCE). Indeed, two decades have passed since the destruction of Samaria in 722/721 BCE (see vv. 9-12). Now the Assyrians are at the doorsteps of Jerusalem, Sennacherib having captured "all the fortified cities" (v. 13).

18:13-16. In its present literary context, Sennacherib's attack might be understood as Assyrian retribution for Hezekiah's rebellion (vv. 7, 20), and historians might point out that Hezekiah probably joined other anti-Assyrian states in the region in the widespread insurrection that followed the death of Sargon II in 705 BCE.[140] Hezekiah had, indeed, strengthened the defenses of Jerusalem and taken steps to ensure an adequate water supply for the city (20:20).[141] Such historical details, however, are of little interest to the narrator, for whom Sennacherib was simply an arrogant king who would not be appeased. Sennacherib was bent on humiliating Hezekiah and challenging the God of Judah.

140. Cogan and Tadmor, *2 Kings*, 221.
141. See Amihai Mazar, *Archaeology of the Land of the Bible*, ABRL (New York: Doubleday, 1990) 405, 420-22.

In the face of Sennacherib's aggression, Hezekiah is as accommodating as one might expect: He admits to his wrongdoing (perhaps referring to his role in the insurrection of the vassal states in Palestine), pleads for the Assyrians to withdraw, and agrees to pay indemnity (v. 14). Although Sennacherib's price is enormous,[142] Hezekiah complies fully (v. 15), giving Sennacherib "all the silver" in the temple and palace treasuries, even stripping the temple doors and doorposts of their gold inlays in order to do so (v. 16).

18:17-18. Yet, Sennacherib would not leave Jerusalem alone. The Assyrian king sends a triumvirate to Jerusalem, including the "Tartan"(Assyrian *turtanû*, the highest official after the king, hence, "the Viceroy"), the "Rabsaris" (Assyrian *rab ša rēši*, "the chief courtier"), and the Rabshakeh (lit., "chief cup-bearer," a reference to the adjutant). They come to Jerusalem with a sizable force and stand just outside the city walls.[143] Meeting the Assyrian delegation of three are three Judean emissaries: Eliakim, "the one over the house" (the chief of staff in the palace); Shebna, "the secretary" (keeper of royal records?); and Joah, "the recorder" (perhaps "the herald").

18:19-25. Through the speech of the Rabshakeh (vv. 19-23), the narrator calls attention to what was at stake for Hezekiah: "What is this security [הבטחון *habbiṭṭāḥôn*] on which you trust [בטחת *bāṭāḥtā*]?" (v. 19). The poignancy of the speech is more evident in Hebrew than in English, for the root בטח (*bṭḥ*, "trust") has already been used to depict Hezekiah's faith in v. 5 and is repeated several times (vv. 19-22, 24). The Assyrians accuse Hezekiah of trusting in Egypt, which was an untrustworthy alliance since Egypt was but a crushed reed that would, in fact, pierce the hand of anyone who tried to lean on it (vv. 20-21). The Rabshakeh takes the view, proffered also by the prophet Isaiah, that Judah should not turn to Egypt for help (cf. Isa 30:1-5; 31:1-3).[144] To the charge that Judah had relied on Egypt, however, the Judean delegation (the first "you" in v. 22 is plural in Hebrew) apparently assert that their trust

is really in the Lord ("We trust the LORD our God"), rather than in Egypt (v. 22). Yet, the Rabshakeh, who clearly believes that the local high places are legitimate Yahwistic sanctuaries, points out that Hezekiah had removed them and so could not have been on the side of the Lord (v. 22). This was no doubt a view shared by many in Judah as well. The Assyrian officer implies that Hezekiah's decision to centralize worship in Jerusalem is so unpopular that, even if Hezekiah were given two thousand horses, he would not be able to find riders for them to fight the Assyrians (v. 23).[145] Egypt was finally what Hezekiah was really counting on, says the Rabshakeh, who suggests that Assyria might, indeed, have been sent by the Lord to punish Hezekiah (vv. 24-25).

18:26-35. The Rabshakeh made a compelling case. Certainly there would have been Judeans who would have agreed with some or all of his arguments, which were made to them in their own language. Hence, Hezekiah's negotiators request that the Assyrians speak in Aramaic (v. 26), the language of diplomacy in the Near East in those days, a language that was not accessible to the populace. The Assyrians insist, however, that the message is not just for the king and his emissaries, but is also for the people who would have to suffer the horrible consequences of a siege (v. 27; cf. 6:25-29).

Directly addressing the people in their own language, the Rabshakeh urges them not to let Hezekiah mislead them into thinking that he can deliver them or believing that the Lord can save them (vv. 28-30). The issue is now viewed in terms of the ability of the Lord to deliver the Judeans from the power of the Assyrians. Through the Rabshakeh, Sennacherib presents himself as a benevolent suzerain, inviting the Judeans literally to "make a blessing" (ברכה *běrākâ*) with him and to depart with him (v. 31). The Assyrian king offers himself as a suzerain in place of the Lord, urging the Judeans to choose him over their God. Whereas the Lord promised blessing to those who would obey the Lord and are brought into the promised land (cf. Deut 30:15-16; 28:8), the Assyrian king invites them out of that land, promising them

142. See *ANET*, 288, where the amount is 30 talents of gold and 800 talents of silver.

143. The precise location of the conference (v. 17) is uncertain. For a survey of various options, see Hobbs, *2 Kings*, 260-62.

144. For the imagery of the fractured reed, cf. Isa 42:3; Ezek 29:6.

145. Indeed, Sennacherib claimed massive desertion on the part of the Judean soldiers. See *ANET*, 288.

abundant food to eat and water to drink (cf. the conditions of siege, 6:25). His offer to take them out of their land to a new promised land, as it were, is an indirect challenge to the Lord, implying that it is in the promised land of Sennacherib where they will find an abundant supply of food and wine and where they will live and not die (v. 32; cf. Deut 8:7-9). Hezekiah's talk of deliverance by the Lord is surely a delusion, Sennacherib maintains, for the gods of the nations that had previously been attacked by him have not been able to deliver their people from him. The gods of the other nations, too, had not been able to deliver the citizens of Samaria from Sennacherib's power, and now neither would the Lord be able to save Judah.

18:36–19:7. Hezekiah has no answer to the taunts of Sennacherib's spokesman and instructs his people not to give one. The emissaries return in mourning to the king (v. 37). Hezekiah, too, goes into mourning (19:1). Then he sends a special delegation to consult with the prophet Isaiah (v. 2), calling the moment "a day of distress, of rebuke, and of disgrace" (v. 3). The king cites a proverb in v. 3*b*, suggesting that the crucial moment for deliverance has arisen but that the participants in it have not been able to bring it about. The Lord has heard the insults and challenges from the Assyrian delegation and responds through the words of Isaiah, noting Sennacherib's challenge as such and promising that a spirit will be sent into the Assyrian king that will cause him to hear a rumor and to return to his homeland, there to be killed (vv. 6-7). (See Reflections at 20:12-21.)

2 Kings 19:8-37, Sennacherib's Second Challenge

COMMENTARY

19:8-13. Despite the word of the Lord spoken through Isaiah (vv. 6-7), the Rabshakeh returns to his headquarters to find that Sennacherib has already left Lachish, the principal fortress west of Jerusalem, and is now fighting against Libnah (v. 8), a smaller site probably to be located to the east of Lachish. Instead of turning back, Sennacherib appears to be pressing on toward Jerusalem. He hears word, however, that the Tirhakah of Cush (NRSV, "Ethiopia") is fighting against his armies (v. 9).[146] The Assyrian king, no doubt fearing that this development might encourage Hezekiah, threatens the Judean again. This time, Sennacherib intensifies his rhetoric. Whereas he had previously told the people not to let Hezekiah deceive them into trusting the Lord (18:30), Sennacherib now tells Hezekiah himself not to let the Lord deceive him into trusting the Lord (19:10). He asserts, once again, that the Lord will not be able to deliver Jerusalem any more than the gods of the other nations were able to deliver their cities (vv. 10-13; cf. 18:19-35).

19:14-19. One gathers from v. 14 that the message this time is delivered in written form. Whereas Hezekiah had previously sent representatives to the Temple to ask the prophet Isaiah to pray (v. 2), the king himself now prays to God (v. 15). In the Temple, probably facing the symbols of divine presence in the holy of holies (cf. 1 Kgs 8:6-13), the king spreads the document "before the LORD" (v. 15). He appeals to God, using an epithet that affirms the deity as king ("enthroned above the cherubim") and acknowledges that the Lord alone is God over all the kingdoms of the earth—not just over Judah, but over Assyria as well. He appeals to God as the sovereign Creator of heaven and earth and prays that God might take note of Sennacherib's blasphemous challenge, despite the fact that the Assyrian gods are but wood and stone (vv. 16-18). Then he asks God to save the Judeans from Sennacherib's hands, in order that the whole world might know that the Lord alone is God (v. 19). Nothing less than the sovereignty of God is at stake in this theological crisis.

146. Tirhakah, in fact, became pharaoh of Egypt, but not until 690 BCE. In 701 BCE, however, he was probably a military commander of the Egyptian army, which, according to Sennacherib's Assyrian annals, fought against the Assyrians in the Plain of Eltekeh. See Kenneth A. Kitchen, *The Third Intermediate Period in Egypt (1100–65)* (Warminster: Aris & Phillips, 1973) 157-61.

19:20-28. Isaiah delivers an oracle of the Lord concerning Sennacherib (vv. 20-34; cf. Isa 10:12-19; 14:24-27). The word of the Lord is set over against the words of Sennacherib (vv. 20-21). Although the oracle begins by depicting personified Jerusalem as a woman scorned and mocked by personified Assyria, it quickly becomes clear that the issue is not between two women, two cities, or even two nations. Rather, it is a dispute between an arrogant king and the Lord, whom Hezekiah trusts. Sennacherib is addressed directly, for the challenge has become an intensely personal one for the Lord: It is Sennacherib against the Holy One of Israel (v. 22). The deity quotes the Assyrian king's boast—precisely the sort of boast that one finds in the Assyrian annals about how the king has ventured into the remote recesses of the world, felling the tallest trees and drying up rivers in doing so (vv. 23-24). God points out, however, that Sennacherib's victories have, in fact, been part of God's plan from long ago, meaning that Assyria is merely being used as an agent of God's plan (vv. 25-26; cf. Isa 10:5-11). The power of the Assyrian king is but a manifestation of divine will and power. God knows Sennacherib's every move, and the Assyrian will be harnessed like an animal (vv. 27-28).

19:29-37. Then Hezekiah is addressed directly and is promised a sign (vv. 29-31). The ravaged land will not recover immediately, and the people will have to eat what grows naturally. But by the third year, the agricultural routines will return fully. This cycle is a sign that the land will be repopulated from the remnant of people now left in Jerusalem. As for Sennacherib, he will not be successful in his attack of Jerusalem but will be turned back, for the Lord will personally defend the city and save it, for the Lord's own sake and for the sake of David (vv. 32-34).

That very night, the angel of the Lord attacks the Assyrian army, decimating it (v. 35). Suddenly, Sennacherib has to return to Nineveh, where he is assassinated by his own sons while he is worshiping in the temple of his god, an otherwise unknown deity named Nisroch (vv. 35-37). (See Reflections at 20:12-21.)

2 Kings 20:1-11, Hezekiah's Illness and Recovery

COMMENTARY

The temporal introduction ("in those days") vaguely links this passage with the preceding unit (chaps. 18–19)—namely, the time of Hezekiah and Sennacherib (v. 1). The narrator becomes more precise in v. 6, however, in placing the story at the time of Sennacherib's siege of Jerusalem—that is, in the fourteenth year of Hezekiah's reign, 701 BCE (v. 6; cf. 18:13).

When Hezekiah becomes critically ill, the prophet Isaiah comes to him with the word of the Lord, telling Hezekiah to give his last injunction (cf. 1 Kgs 2:1),[147] for he will not recover (v. 2). Hezekiah does not accept that fate, however. He prays fervently for God to remember (cf. Ps 132:1) his wholehearted devotion and faithful conduct before the Lord (v. 3). Thereupon, Isaiah, who has scarcely left Hezekiah's presence (v. 4), is told to return to the king with the promise that God has heard his prayers and seen his tears, and thus will bring healing to the sick king so that he can go again to the Temple (v. 5). Hezekiah is given an extension of his life span: He will live fifteen more years (v. 6a). It is important to note here that reprieve and recovery for the king are linked to the same good fortune for Judah (v. 6b). The fate of the king and the fate of the city are bound together.[148] God will deliver both the king and Judah from the hands of the Assyrian king for God's own sake, as well as for the sake of David. Read in its larger literary-theological context, the deliverance of Jerusalem can be understood as being partly God's specific response to Sennacherib's blasphemous challenge and partly the manifestation of God's grace extended to David. Thus Hezekiah's personal recovery is the working

---

147. See Gray, *1 & 2 Kings*, 397.

148. See Long, *2 Kings*, 238.

out of God's will in microcosm. Isaiah then makes a poultice of figs and applies it to Hezekiah's boils to heal them (v. 7).

Hezekiah requests a sign as a confirmation of the promise of his recovery (v. 8). Unlike his father, Ahaz, who had refused to ask for a sign even when invited to do so by Isaiah (Isa 7:11-13), Hezekiah wants a sign from the Lord. Isaiah's response to the request comes not as a straight-forward announcement of the sign, but initially in the form of a question: "The shadow has advanced ten steps, will it return ten steps?" (vv. 8-9; cf. Num 20:10; Ezek 37:3). The "steps" here refer to the "steps of Ahaz" in v. 11, which the NRSV, following most interpreters, takes to be a sundial ("dial of Ahaz"), presumably a series of steps on which the movement of a shadow cast by the sun marked the hours of the day. Hezekiah replies that it is natural for the shadow to lengthen ten steps, but not for it to retreat ten steps (v. 10). When a shadow has been cast, it ordinarily will not recede. Isaiah then prays to God, and the shadow on the dial miraculously retreats after it has advanced (cf. the miracle of the sun's standing still in Josh 10:12-13). The miracle is dramatized in the recovery of Hezekiah. Isaiah had already proclaimed that Hezekiah is about to die (v. 1). Yet, when Hezekiah prayed to the Lord (v. 3), Isaiah was commanded to *turn back* (v. 5) and tell Hezekiah that fifteen years had been added to his life (v. 6). So, too, even though the shadow has already advanced ten degrees on the "steps of Ahaz" (i.e., time has passed), Isaiah prays to the Lord, and the Lord turns back the shadow (v. 11). Even if the word of death or destruction has been proclaimed, it is possible, through prayer, to turn back that word of judgment. (See Reflections at 20:12-21.)

2 Kings 20:12-21, From Assyria to Babylon

COMMENTARY

This story is loosely connected to the present context by the temporal phrase "at that time" (v. 1). The Mesopotamian ruler with whom Hezekiah deals in this case is not the king of Assyria, as in chapters 17–18, however, but the king of Babylon, the power that within a century would defeat the Assyrians and invade Judah, capture Jerusalem, and send the Judeans into exile. According to the narrator, Babylonian emissaries had made overtures to Judah when Hezekiah was ill (v. 12), although nothing is said of the purpose for their having come to Jerusalem. The chronicler has them coming to learn about the sign that had been given to Hezekiah (2 Chr 32:31). Whatever the case, they are willingly received in Jerusalem and are shown all its resources (vv. 13, 15). When Isaiah learns what has transpired, he predicts that the day will come when the Babylonians will return to take all the wealth of the city and the king's descendants will be taken as captives to Babylon (vv. 16-18).

The king's response is somewhat enigmatic.[149] Taking the Hebrew text at face value, it appears that Hezekiah has two responses. The first is the public one that he states to Isaiah: "The word of the LORD that you have spoken is good" (v. 19a). That response is consonant with Hezekiah's image of a compliant, pious king who is ready to accept God's judgment. The other response, however, made known to the reader by the narrator, is Hezekiah's private response: "Why not, if there will be peace and security in my days?" (v. 19b). Apparently Hezekiah is willing to take the judgment, since it does not affect him directly. During his own reign, he seems to think, there will be peace and security. The publicly pious king is willing to accept the judgment of God, knowing full well that it does not affect him personally.

With that shocking assessment of the private side of Hezekiah, the narrator simply moves on to give the standard closing summary of the king's reign, calling attention to his famous public project—namely, the provision of a water supply through the cutting of the Siloam tunnel.

149. For various interpretations of Hezekiah's response, see Peter R. Ackroyd, "An Interpretation of the Babylonian Exile: A Study of 2 Kings 20, Isaiah 38-39," *SJT* 27 (1974) 335-38.

REFLECTIONS

1. In both obvious and subtle ways, this lengthy report addresses the issue of trust, a term that appears numerous times in the text. It begins with a portrayal of a king who trusted God as no other king had done before him (18:1-8). That trust entailed bold and decisive compliance with the will of God, and it brought divine favor. In contrast, those who did not trust God did not survive (18:9-12).

2. Despite the introductory verses of the story, the narrator seems to know that such talk of trust in God and its payoffs is difficult to work out in the "real world." In the real world, even those who trust in God are confronted with political realities. For all his trust in God, Hezekiah had to suffer humiliation at the hands of a foreign invader, and he even had to strip the Temple of its wealth, removing gold from the doors and doorposts of the Lord's house in order to pay off the bully (18:13-16). Trust in God will not necessarily stave off actual political threats. Trust in God may not have immediate or manifest results.

3. The text implicitly concedes that the rhetoric of trust in an invisible God is difficult to authenticate in the nitty-gritty of worldly affairs. People may speak of trust in God while they work on political solutions, their trust being in military alliances and the like (18:19-25). By the same token, talk of God's blessings is often difficult to corroborate. In the face of war's atrocities and the deprivations that people suffer, it is tempting to respond to the invitation of the most powerful ruler in the world to "make a blessing" with him and to go on an exodus with him from one's God-given place (18:30-32). It is tempting to believe his claim that it is he who would provide us with the necessities and luxuries of life. In view of the verifiable evidence of military might, and in view of the absence of any divine resistance to such demonstrations of power, it is tempting to believe that God cannot rescue us from such political and military power (18:33-35). In such circumstances, the people of God may, indeed, have no answer and ought not to try to give one (18:36). There is no answer in human disputation. In such circumstances, the only answer, if one is forthcoming, is a word from God—difficult though that word may be to verify (19:1-7). Thus this story asserts that prayer can make a difference.

4. The silence of God may prompt arrogant individuals to believe that they are in a place to challenge God directly, to believe that they are in control of the destiny of the world. Such people miss the point, however, that even they may actually be instruments of God. Their power and their every plan may, indeed, be known to God and may be utilized in the working out of God's will in the world (9:8-34). When all is said and done, it is God who will have the last word. The text, therefore, invites the reader to believe that even in the face of the atrocious manifestation of military power—indeed, even evil, destructive power—nevertheless, the sovereign Creator of the world is in control.

5. The story of Hezekiah's recovery from a deadly illness is something of a parable about the possibility of life even when death is all too certain. The Hebrew word translated as "recover" in the NRSV (20:1, 7) is also the word for "live." Hezekiah was about to die, but his faith made the impossible possible (20:3-6). For the individual, as well as for the people of God as a larger community, there is hope in trusting God, even if no hope seems possible (20:6). Even if the shadow has been cast and it has lengthened ten times, God can reverse it (20:8-11). This is the kind of trust that the text challenges the reader to have. The grace of God through faith makes it possible for death to be overcome (Rom 3:21-31; 4:2-4; Gal 2:1-10). This is at the heart of the gospel story in the New Testament.

6. Readers may prefer that the story of Hezekiah ended with his miraculous recovery by grace through faith, for that would make a wonderful theological denouement. That is not the final word, however. Hezekiah's trust in God does not seem so firm after all. He, who has been portrayed as a model of faith and piety, turns to the Babylonians, for reasons that the narrator does not bother to explain. When confronted with a prophetic word of judgment (a prediction of the eventual destruction of Jerusalem and the consequent exile), Hezekiah responds with appropriate humility in public, declaring the word of the Lord to be "good" (v. 19*a*). Publicly he is still the humble and obedient king. He accepted the word of the Lord. The narrator tells us, however, that his private thoughts may not have been entirely commendable. Hezekiah was more concerned, it seems, with his lame-duck reign than with the long-term consequences of his misplaced trust in the Babylonians. Interpreters from time immemorial have been uncomfortable with this negative portrayal of Hezekiah at the end of the mostly positive assessment of his reign. One must not try to exonerate Hezekiah for the sake of literary coherence, however. If anything, the presence of this story after the crescendo in 20:1-11 is a powerful reminder to the reader not to hold any human being, however attractive, however faithful, as a model. The Bible is not finally a story about faithful people but a story about a faithful God. The story of the lapse of pious Hezekiah is a lesson to us about post-recovery life: Despite one's experience of God's wondrous, life-renewing grace, there remains the possibility—indeed, the likelihood—that one may not fully trust God. As the apostle Paul warns us: "If you think you are standing, watch out that you do not fall" (1 Cor 10:12 NRSV).

2 KINGS 21:1-26, IRREPARABLE DAMAGE TO JUDAH

OVERVIEW

The preceding chapter already hinted at the impending destruction of Judah. Even faithful and pious King Hezekiah somehow lost perspective at the end of his reign, completely exposing Jerusalem and its resources to the unsavory gaze of the Babylonians (20:12-15). For that, the prophet Isaiah predicted that in time the Babylonians would invade Jerusalem and take captives to Babylon (20:16-18). For all his dedication, Hezekiah's reaction to that word of judgment was less than faithful; while he publicly accepted the word of God as "good," he privately thought only of the peace and security that his reign would enjoy (20:19). The future of God's people mattered less to him than did his own reign.

In chapter 21 the reader witnesses Judah's rapid downward spiral toward destruction and exile. Any good that was accomplished through Hezekiah's reforms is undone by the two wicked kings, his son (21:1-18) and grandson (21:19-26). Manasseh reigned for more than half a century, around 687/686 BCE–642 BCE. To the deuteronomistic narrator, this was the worst of times. Manasseh did such harm to Judah that no reform, however well intentioned, could ever save it from destruction. Manasseh was the most evil of all the kings of Judah, doing to that kingdom what Jeroboam and Ahab did to Israel. Partly because of him, Judah did everything Israel did that led to the fall of Samaria (17:7-20). Manasseh was succeeded by his son Amon, who reigned for only two years (642–640 BCE) before being assassinated in his own palace. Amon followed in his father's faithless footsteps. Thus Judah was led down the inevitable path of doom.

2 Kings 21:1-18, The Reign of Manasseh

COMMENTARY

Unlike the slightly lengthier parallel account in 2 Chr 33:1-20, which portrays Manasseh in a more favorable light (including a report of his repentance and restoration), the depiction of him in 2 Kgs 21:1-18 is entirely negative. Indeed, no other king in Judah received such an unrelentingly negative evaluation. Unlike his father, Hezekiah, who did what was right in the sight of the Lord (18:3), Manasseh did what was evil (v. 2). In violation of deuteronomic law (Deut 12:29-31), he "followed the abominable practices of the nations that the Lord had driven out" from before the people of Israel (cf. 16:3; 17:7). He rebuilt the local sanctuaries ("high places") that Hezekiah had torn down (v. 3; cf. 18:4), sanctuaries that were roundly condemned in Kings as heterodox sites, contrary to the ideal of worship centralized in Jerusalem (1 Kgs 11:7; 12:31-32; 13:32-33; 14:23; etc.; cf. Deut 12:2-7). He erected altars for Baal and other heterodox cultic symbols (v. 3), just as Ahab had done in Israel (16:11). Even worse, Manasseh introduced various foreign cultic objects into the Temple of the Lord in Jerusalem, constructing altars for astral deities and crafting an image of Asherah (consort of the high god in the Canaanite pantheon) in it (vv. 3-5). He followed Ahaz in the practice of child sacrifice (v. 6; 16:3) and sanctioned divination (v. 6; cf. Deut 18:9-14; 2 Kgs 17:17). Not only did he out-sin his predecessors and the worst kings of Israel, he even outdid the former inhabitants of the land in his atrocities (see Deut 9:5).

Despite the warning of the Lord proclaimed by unspecified prophets, Manasseh continued in his wicked ways (vv. 10-11). Hence judgment will come upon Israel as it has upon Samaria (vv. 12-13). Indeed, the deity will clean out Jerusalem as one might clean out a dish, turning it upside down to ensure that everything in it is removed (v. 13b).

Although Manasseh has done irreparable damage, the narrator does not mean that the destruction would come because of his sins alone. Rather, the people of Israel as a whole are culpable, for they have been provoking the Lord to anger since the time of the exodus (see v. 15). Manasseh sinned horribly and he caused Judah to sin (v. 16), even as Jeroboam son of Nebat had caused Israel to sin; but Judah is culpable because of its collective response (cf. 17:7-20). (See Reflections at 21:19-26.)

2 Kings 21:19-26, The Reign of Amon

COMMENTARY

Manasseh is succeeded by his son Amon, who is said to have followed in his father's footsteps, doing evil in the sight of God, serving idols, and generally turning away from the God of Israel's ancestors. He is assassinated by his servants in the palace, and his son Josiah is placed on the throne.

REFLECTIONS

There is no question that the picture in this chapter is a gloomy one. Humanity seems utterly incapable of sustaining anything good. Any hope of a proper response of faith that Hezekiah might have raised is dashed against the rocks of Manasseh's and Amon's faithlessness. Doom is inevitable because human beings are bent on their destructive course, turning away from the way of God. Yet the text does not merely proclaim the inevitability of judgment. The point is not simply that people deserve punishment because they sin. Rather, woven into the account that justifies God's judgment is a subliminal message of God's grace. Even as one hears the word of judgment, one hears a message of God's persistent grace: God brought the people out of bondage (v. 15b), made it possible for Israel to possess the promised land (vv. 2b, 9b), gave the people rest (v. 8), promised to be present in the midst of the people (vv. 4, 7), and preserved a remnant as God's heritage (v. 14). When one considers the subliminal message of grace, one understands that judgment comes not so much because of isolated acts of disobedience, but because of a people's history of willful rejection of grace.

2 KINGS 22:1–23:30, THE JOSIANIC REFORMATION

OVERVIEW

Up to this point in Kings, the history that the narrator presents is a history of failure. From Solomon on down, the kings have failed to live up to the high standards of faithfulness that the Torah demands. Solomon began reasonably well and he received God's gift of gracious wisdom (1 Kgs 3:1-15), but he soon showed that he was not up to the standards. He turned out to be a self-serving, oppressive, and syncretistic despot (1 Kings 3–11). As a result of his unfaithfulness, the kingdom was divided into two: Israel and Judah.

Things still did not improve, however. Indeed, the kings of the northern kingdom all turned out to be complete failures. They invariably followed the idolatrous ways of Jeroboam the son of Nebat, and that history of willful disobedience led eventually to the destruction of Samaria and the dispersion of the people. Judah's kings fared somewhat better, for there were a few kings who generally did right by God, kings like Asa (1 Kgs 15:9-24), Jehoshaphat (1 Kgs 22:41-50), Jehoash (2 Kgs 12:1-16), and, above all, Hezekiah (2 Kgs 18:1–20:21). Still, the southern kingdom did not survive because of the righteousness of its kings, for none of them lived up to the standards of the Torah. Even Hezekiah, who is acknowledged as one who trusted the Lord, endangered the well-being of his people by unduly trusting the Babylonians (2 Kgs 20:12-15). Moreover, when he heard the word of judgment delivered by the prophet Isaiah, he was more concerned about his own reign than he was with the destiny of

God's people (2 Kgs 20:16-19). In any case, any hopes of recovery that Judah might have had were utterly shattered by the blatantly syncretistic counter-reformation of Manasseh and by his equally impious son and successor, Amon (2 Kgs 21:1-26).

Then comes Josiah, the ideal king according to the standards of deuteronomic law, the paragon of kingly righteousness (2 Kgs 22:1–23:30). There has never been and never will be a king like him, the narrator says (23:25). Josiah earned the narrator's praise primarily because of his reform efforts based on a rediscovered "book of the תורה (tôrâ)," a document that, to judge by the nature of the reform, with its emphasis on the elimination of syncretism and on the centralization of worship in Jerusalem, is probably some form of the book of Deuteronomy. The parallel account of Josiah's reign traces his reform efforts to an earlier period in his career (2 Chr 34:3-7), but the narrator of Kings has no interest in all that. What he considers most important is that Josiah's reforms were based on the rediscovery of the Torah and, in that regard, Josiah was completely faithful. The narrator has nothing but positive things to say about Josiah and his reforms.

Yet, the shocking conclusion of the story is that the reforms came too late. As thorough as Josiah was, his reforms could not overcome the horrible effects of Manasseh's counter-reformation. So Judah was doomed despite the righteousness of Josiah (23:26-27).

2 Kings 22:1-2, Introduction to Josiah's Reign

COMMENTARY

The narrator's evaluation of Josiah (c. 640–609 BCE) is entirely positive. Like a few other reformist kings of Judah, he is judged to have done right in the sight of the Lord and to have walked in the way of his ancestor David (cf. 1 Kgs 15:11; 22:43; 2 Kgs 12:2; 18:3). Of all these kings, only Hezekiah and Josiah are praised without qualification; the rest are commended for generally doing well before God, but each is noted for failure to remove the heterodox "high places" and centralize worship in Jerusalem. Josiah alone, however, is said to have walked in *all* the ways of David, and of no one else is it said that "he did not turn aside to the right or to the left" (v. 2), an allusion to Moses' charge (Deut 5:32; 17:11, 20; 28:14) that is reiterated to and by Joshua (Josh 1:7; 23:6). In Josiah, then, we have an image of the ideal king according to deuteronomic law (Deut 17:14-20). In his utter devotion he is reminiscent of Moses, Joshua, David, and Hezekiah.

2 Kings 22:3-11, Rediscovery of the Book of the Law

COMMENTARY

Josiah is, first and foremost, a reformer. Just as Jehoash had refurbished the Temple after the six-year usurpation of the throne by Athaliah daughter of Ahab (12:4-16), so also Josiah, who comes to power after the disastrously syncretistic reigns of Manasseh and Amon, orders the Temple to be repaired (vv. 3-7). According to 2 Chr 34:3-7, Josiah began to seek God in the eighth year of his reign, and his reforms began in the twelfth year of his reign, information that interests many scholars because that date more or less coincides with the death of Assyria's highly effective king, Asshurbanipal. Many scholars believe that the chronicler's account may, in fact, reflect historical realities. The narrator of Kings, however, has little interest in the events prior to Josiah's eighteenth year (622 BCE), the year when the so-called book of the law was rediscovered. The reformation effort that grew out of that pivotal event is the narrator's primary focus.

During the renovation of the Temple, the high priest Hilkiah discovers a copy of the "book of the law," which, some scholars speculate, had been hidden away during the anti-deuteronomic counter-reformation of Manasseh (21:2-9). This archaeological "discovery" is reported to Shaphan the secretary, who has come to the Temple to disburse funds for the project. Shaphan reads the book (v. 8) and then informs the king of the find and reads it aloud to him (v. 10). On hearing the content of the document, Josiah is greatly distressed (v. 11; cf. Josh 7:6; Job 1:20; 2 Kgs 5:7; 6:30). His reaction suggests that he recognizes the content not merely as information about the past, but as a prophetic word for the present--not as instruction only, but as prophecy (cf. 17:13).[150]

150. See Long, *2 Kings*, 262.

2 Kings 22:12-20, A Prophetic Oracle

COMMENTARY

The king dispatches a delegation to seek an oracle for himself and for his people, noting that their ancestors had not obeyed the document's dictates and hence had brought the document's covenant curses upon themselves (v. 13). Like his great-grandfather before him (cf. 19:2), Josiah is portrayed as one who is willing to seek the counsel of the prophets.

Prophetic word comes from a hitherto unnamed prophetess, Huldah (v. 14). She confirms Josiah's fears, pronouncing judgment upon Jerusalem and its inhabitants because they have been disloyal to God and have served idols (vv. 15-17). The anger of the Lord will be kindled against Jerusalem ("this place") and its inhabitants (meaning the citizens of Judah), says Huldah, and it will not be quenched (v. 17). As for the king, because he has heard God (vv. 18, 19), God has also heard him (v. 19). Huldah prophesies that Josiah will "be gathered to [the] grave" with his ancestors and will be buried "in peace" (v. 20). The idioms used imply that Josiah will die a non-violent death (cf. Gen 15:15; 25:8), yet the meaning of that prophecy is clarified immediately: "Your eyes shall not see all the disaster that I will bring upon this place." In comparison to the disaster that will befall Jerusalem, Josiah's death (23:29-30) will be a peaceful one.

2 Kings 23:1-25, Josiah's Reforms

COMMENTARY

Despite Huldah's prophecy of doom for Judah, Josiah gathers all the people for a public reading of the "book of the law," and he leads them in a covenant renewal ceremony (vv. 1-3; cf. Deut 5:1-5; 29:2-28; 31:9-13), just as his ancestor Jehoiada had done (11:12-18). He immediately institutes sweeping reforms in accordance with the stipulations of the law. He removes all the heterodox cultic paraphernalia and structures in Jerusalem and its vicinity (vv. 4, 6-7, 10-12), deposes the idolatrous priests (vv. 5, 8-9) and diviners of various sorts (v. 24), and destroys the local sanctuaries and all things associated with them (vv. 8, 13-15). He extends his reforms beyond Judah into the northern kingdom (vv. 4, 15-20). Indeed, Josiah removes all the heterodox elements that had been introduced by preceding kings of Judah and Israel, undoing the unacceptable innovations of recent kings, like Manasseh and Ahaz (v. 12), and of kings from long ago, like Solomon (v. 13) and Jeroboam son of Nebat (v. 15). The narrator makes it clear that Josiah takes no chances and leaves no stone unturned. He removes from the Temple "all the vessels made for Baal" (v. 4), removes "all the priests" from the Judean towns "from Geba to Beersheba" (v. 8). Indeed, he does not merely remove offensive objects, he burns them, pulverizes them, and thoroughly defiles them so that they could never again be used (vv. 4, 6, 14, 20). He does not merely depose the priests from the local sanctuaries, he even goes beyond deuteronomic laws in banning these priests from sacrificing in Jerusalem (v. 9; cf. Deut 18:6-8). He does not stop his reforms in Judah but extends them into Samaria. Then he commands the celebration of the Passover (v. 21), the festival that is rooted in Israel's experience as a chosen people (Exod 12:1-28), following the prescription in "the book of the covenant" (cf. Deut 16:1-8). The festival had been neglected since the emergence of Israel as a nation (cf. Josh 5:10-12), but Josiah restores it (v. 22). To the narrator, Josiah is the quintessential good king: There has been none like him who has turned to the Lord with heart and soul and might (cf. Deut 6:5) "according to all the law of Moses," and none will arise after him who will be as faithful (v. 25).

2 Kings 23:26-30, The Failure of Josiah to Stem the Tide of Destruction

COMMENTARY

Following the detailed report of Josiah's thorough reform, and especially the summary assessment of v. 25, the conclusion of the story is anticlimactic. Josiah's salutary efforts could not undo the destructive effects of Manasseh's sins. Despite what Josiah has done, Judah will fall like Israel; even Jerusalem, the place God has chosen as the site for God's Temple, will be destroyed (vv. 26-27). Repentance and reformation could not stem the tide of destruction that sin has set in motion.

Josiah's regnal summary (vv. 28-30) notes his death at the hands of Pharaoh Neco of Egypt. Historians point out that the Egyptian army was on its way to Carchemish to join forces with the Assyrians in a last-ditch effort to deny victory to the emerging power of Babylon. Josiah tried to intercept them at the strategic pass of Esdraelon, where Megiddo was the principal fortress, and there, in 609 BCE, he was killed. The details are, however, of little interest to the narrator, who notes the death only to get to the peaceful burial of the king in Jerusalem. The prophecy of Huldah is fulfilled inasmuch as Josiah is buried with his ancestors in Jerusalem and does not witness the final destruction of the city (22:20).

REFLECTIONS

The reader of Kings may be forgiven for feeling a little betrayed by the narrator. From the very beginning of this long story, the narrator has stressed the need for obedience and repentance. The history told so far has been a history of the failure of the kings to obey God fully and to repent of wrongs committed against God. Over and over again, the narrator emphasizes the need for repentance and reform. Now, near the end of the story, comes, at last, the ideal king according to the standards of deuteronomic law. This is the king who is obedient in every way. He leads his people in a renewal of the covenant. He initiates all-encompassing reforms in accordance with the stipulations of the Torah, and the narrator goes through the long catalog of the reforms. Yet the conclusion of all this is that the efforts of Josiah have come too late. The sins of Manasseh trump the righteousness of Josiah and have consequences for all his people, including those who come after him, but the righteousness of Josiah does not have salvific effects for the people. What an infuriating conclusion that is! Is there a redeeming, liberating word of God in this story? What theological lessons might one draw from this admittedly depressing conclusion?

1. The story points out that the faithful response of one good leader does not gain salvation for others. Josiah is spared because he is pious, penitent, and humble, but Judah is not spared on account of Josiah's faith. Josiah in this story evokes memories of Moses, Joshua, David, and Hezekiah. Yet his personal faithfulness cannot bring deliverance to others. The text thus invites readers to consider their own responses to God, for it implies that deliverance cannot be received without one's own response of faith.

2. It is significant that Josiah carried out his reforms despite the word of doom for Judah. He leads his people in covenant renewal, repentance, and reform. Significantly, however, there is no prayer for deliverance, no call for God to turn back the word of judgment, as one might expect. To be sure, the acts of repentance may be intended to turn back God's wrath. Yet that is not how the narrator has presented his account. Josiah's initial desire to turn back God's wrath (22:13) is met by the prophetic word stating the inevitability of destruction for Judah (22:16-17). Still, Josiah proceeds with the reforms. One gathers, then, that we obey God neither for the sake of rewards nor for the aversion of judgment. Rather, obedience to God is simply what faith brings about. Even in the face of God's judgment and without promise of relief, one is to obey and worship God, for that is what faith calls one to do.

3. The most important lesson of all that the passage offers is a negative one. It teaches that human acts of righteousness, even those as thorough and as sincere as Josiah's, are no guarantee of salvation. The story is a warning against all who dare to believe that salvation can be earned through perfect works of righteousness (cf. Romans 1–3). Here is the story of an admirable reformation, one carried out in strict accordance with "the book," and yet it ends in destruction. Josiah initiated an ancient equivalent of a "back to the Bible" movement, as it were, but the rediscovery of the law does not save. Despite his zealous adherence to "the book," there is no salvation for Judah. Salvation, if it comes at all, will be by the grace of God alone, through faith (Eph 2:8).

2 KINGS 23:31–25:30, THE END

OVERVIEW

With the death of Josiah, the thoroughly faithful reformer, all hopes of recovery appear to be dashed. The narrator now recounts the story of Judah's inevitable demise, culminating in the report of Jerusalem's destruction in 586 BCE. Four kings reigned during this period (609–586 BCE): Jehoahaz (3 months), Jehoiakim (11 years), Jehoiachin (3 months), and Zedekiah (11 years). All are judged by the narrator to have done evil in the sight of the Lord (23:32, 37; 24:9, 19). Jehoahaz is the first Judean king to be deposed by a foreign power and exiled, a foretaste of what is to come. God appears to have abandoned the Davidic dynasty, whose fate now seems to be determined by the winds of international politics. Indeed, all these kings apparently reigned at the will of foreign powers. Jehoiakim was installed as an Egyptian puppet, although he vacillated between Egypt and Babylon; he died as the Babylonians moved to punish him for rebellion. Jehoiachin, who succeeded Jehoiakim, was removed from power by the Babylonians and exiled. Zedekiah was first placed on the throne by the Babylonians, but he was eventually deposed, humiliated, and taken captive by them. The narrator tells the story in a matter-of-fact manner, focusing on the two invasions of Jerusalem in 598/597 BCE and 587/586 BCE. He does not conclude with destruction and exile, however. Rather, a surprising epilogue appears at the very end (25:27-30), with the release of Jehoiachin from prison. While still in Babylon, he is nevertheless set free and treated well, a living testimony to the fact that the house of David has not been extinguished forever.

2 Kings 23:31-35, The Reign of Jehoahaz

COMMENTARY

On the death of Josiah in 609 BCE, his son Jehoahaz was placed on the throne by a pro-Babylonian faction in the country, the so-called "people of the land" (v. 30), even though he was not the eldest son of Josiah (compare vv. 31 and 36). He did evil in the sight of God, the narrator reports (v. 32), and reigned only three months before Pharaoh Neco deposed him and deported him first to Riblah in Syria and then to Egypt (vv. 33-34). In his place the Egyptians installed a pro-Egyptian puppet, an elder son of Josiah by the name of Eliakim ("my God will raise up"), who assumed a Yahwistic throne-name, Jehoiakim ("the LORD will raise"). That token of loyalty to the Lord would, however, make little difference in stemming the tide of destruction.

2 Kings 23:36–24:7, The Reign of Jehoiakim

COMMENTARY

Jehoiakim, who reigned eleven years (609–598 BCE), is also judged to have done evil in the sight of God (vv. 36-37). Completely at the mercy of foreign powers, he allied himself now with Egypt and now with Babylon in order to survive. Thus when the Babylonians under Nebuchadnezzar won the Battle of Carchemish (605 BCE), Jehoiakim, who had been placed on the throne by the Egyptians, threw his lot in with the Babylonians, and Judah became a vassal of Babylon for three years (604–602 BCE). When the Babylonians were later (c. 602/601 BCE) defeated, however, Jehoiakim changed sides again.

Unfortunately for Jehoiakim and for Judah, Nebuchadnezzar's setback proved to be temporary. The Babylonians quickly recovered, and Nebuchadnezzar sent a coalition army from his vassal states to punish Judah for its disloyalty. To the narrator, however, God was working behind the scenes, as it were (24:2-4). The invading army was, in fact, sent by the Lord to fulfill the promised punishment of Judah for the sins of Manasseh (see 21:1-16; 23:26). Jehoiakim apparently died during the Babylonian invasion, although the details of his death are unclear (v. 5).

2 Kings 24:8-17, The Reign of Jehoiachin

COMMENTARY

Jehoiakim was succeeded by his son Jehoiachin (v. 6), who is also judged to have done evil in the sight of God (v. 9). The new king reigned only three months (598/597 BCE). When Nebuchadnezzar reached Jerusalem and laid siege to it, Jehoiachin surrendered himself along with his family and palace staff (vv. 10-12). Nebuchadnezzar raided the temple and palace treasuries and stripped the Temple of its gold inlay (v. 13). The elite of society were deported to Babylon, along with the king and the royal household (vv. 12, 14-16). In place of the deposed king, Nebuchadnezzar installed Mattaniah, who was an uncle of Jehoiachin (v. 17) and a younger brother of Jehoahaz (v. 18; cf. 23:31). Once again, it was an outsider who determined the one who would reign over Judah, and the pro-Babylonian puppet was not a legitimate heir to the throne. It is perhaps telling, therefore, that Mattaniah took the throne name Zedekiah ("my Legitimacy is the LORD!").

2 Kings 24:18–25:21, The Reign of Zedekiah

COMMENTARY

Zedekiah was on the throne for eleven years (596–587/586 BCE). Like all other kings after Josiah, he is judged to have done evil in the sight of God, thus provoking the wrath of God and leading God to exile the Judeans (24:19-20). It is on the final devastation of Jerusalem and the consequent exile of its citizens that the narrator is focused.

The story of the final days of Judah is told elsewhere in the Bible (2 Chr 36:11-21; Jer 39:1-14; 52:1-34). Zedekiah is portrayed as a tragic figure in Jeremiah's accounts: The king desperately wanted to do what was right, turning to Jeremiah again and again for a word from the Lord (Jer 37:1-10, 16-21; 38:14-28), and yet he was unable to stand up to the officials and other leaders who opposed the prophet. The narrator of Kings, however, does not focus on Zedekiah's personal struggles, only on the tragedy of the fall of Jerusalem. Zedekiah rebelled against Babylon, the narrator reports, probably meaning that Judah was once again counting on the protection of a resurgent Egypt under Pharaoh

Psammeticus II, who came to power in 592 BCE. Nebuchadnezzar's response was swift. The Babylonian siege of Jerusalem began in the ninth year of Zedekiah's reign (January 587 BCE) and lasted eighteen months (until July 586 BCE), during which time there was a famine (25:1-3). The king fled when the city walls were breached, but he was captured and brought before Nebuchadnezzar in Riblah (vv. 4-6; see 23:33). Then, his captors murdered his sons in his sight, put out his eyes and brought him in chains to Babylon (v. 7). The Temple in Jerusalem was subsequently burned, its sacred vessels were carried off to Babylon, and the elite citizens of the city were exiled (vv. 8-17).

2 Kings 25:22-26, Gedaliah Becomes Governor

COMMENTARY

To bring about stability in the region, the Babylonians appointed a prominent citizen named Gedaliah as governor of Judah (v. 22; cf. also Jer 40:7–41:8). Gedaliah's grandfather, Shaphan, had been a secretary during the reign of Josiah (22:3) and his father, Ahikam, had been a part of the delegation sent to consult with the prophetess Huldah (22:12) and was a friend to Jeremiah (Jer 26:24). The officers of the remnant army came to Gedaliah at the administrative center in Mizpah (vv. 23-24), probably a site about eight miles north of Jerusalem, only to hear Gedaliah counsel cooperation with the Babylonians (a stance shared by the prophet

Jeremiah [Jer 27:1-22; 40:1-6]). One of the officers, a certain Ishmael (a member of the extended royal family), led a rebellious group to assassinate the governor, along with the Judeans and Babylonians who were with him (v. 25). The assassins then fled to Egypt, apparently with other Judean citizens (v. 26). Their intended refuge is ironic, for God had once freed the people from bondage in Egypt. Indeed, only recently Jehoiakim had been captured and taken there by force (23:34). Yet it was to Egypt that "all the people" of Judah fled. The people thus willfully reversed the exodus.

2 Kings 25:27-30, Jehoiachin Is Released from Prison

COMMENTARY

In this brief epilogue, the narrator turns to the exiled king, Jehoiachin, in Babylon (cf. Jer 52:31-34). The Davidide ruler is now in the thirty-seventh year of his exile (that is, 561 BCE) and Evil-Merodach has succeeded

Nebuchadnezzar as king in Babylon. Jehoiachin is released from prison and treated well by the Babylonians. He is even exalted among the other captive kings, eats regularly at the king's table, and receives an allowance.

REFLECTIONS

The story of Judah's end is, of course, a story of God's unrelenting judgment against disobedience. For the narrator, the events were not accidental, for God was behind it all. Even Nebuchadnezzar's invading force of coalition troops was sent against Judah by none other than the Lord, in fulfillment of the prophetic word of destruction proclaimed because of the sins of Manasseh (24:2-3). The people's persistent and willful rejection of the Lord could not go unpunished, and so God had abandoned them, leaving Jerusalem and the Temple of the Lord to be destroyed and the people to be exiled. As if to underscore the point about the willfulness of the people, the story is told of how, after God had already devastated the city and sent the elite of the country into exile, "all the people, from the young to the old," fled to Egypt because of their misplaced fear (25:26). The story thus justifies God's judgment in the face of recalcitrant human will.

That is by no means the last word in Kings, however. Rather, alongside the story of God's inevitable judgment because of human will to disobey, is a hint that the last word has not yet been spoken. Despite the willful reversal of the exodus that "all the people" of Judah effected (25:26), the final word is an unexpected account of liberation, however tentative; after thirty-seven years in exile, there is the inexplicable good news of freedom for Jehoiachin. Despite the capture and humiliation of Zedekiah, the last king in Jerusalem, the final episode of Kings reports the exaltation of Jehoiachin above other kings in Babylonian captivity. It was the Lord who had sent the Babylonians to punish Judah, the narrator has asserted (23:26; 24:2-3). Though God is not mentioned in the closing words of Kings, one is invited to ponder if the reality of liberation and favor amid exile is not, finally, also a sign of divine grace. The tentative ending suggests an incomplete story that will be continued another time.

Davidic kingship, as one knows it from the book of Kings, has ended. The house of David, however, lives on. In the post-exilic period, Zerubbabel, a scion of Jehoiachin, would be called upon to join with the high priest to rebuild the Temple of Jerusalem (Hag 1:1; 2:2). Zerubbabel, though, would never become king in Jerusalem. Yet, in time, a descendant of Jehoiachin and Zerubbabel would be born (Matt 1:12-16; 2:2, 6), who would go on to play the role of king (cf. Matt 21:6-9; 27:11, 29, 37, 42), although his kingship would not be "of this world" (John 18:36 NIV). In him, God's expectations of a righteous king would finally be met (see Heb 7:1-2). Instead of leading people to sin and finally to destruction, that King would save people from darkness and bring about the forgiveness of sins (Col 1:13-14).

THE FIRST AND SECOND BOOKS
OF CHRONICLES

INTRODUCTION, COMMENTARY, AND REFLECTIONS
BY
LESLIE C. ALLEN

THE FIRST AND SECOND BOOKS OF
CHRONICLES

INTRODUCTION

T he books of Chronicles are the Bible's best-kept secret. Pastors who base their preaching on *The Revised Common Lectionary*[1] will find Chronicles absent from its readings. In Christian tradition these books have suffered by being placed behind 1 and 2 Samuel and 1 and 2 Kings, as if they were some pale shadow instead of an epic work in their own right. In the Hebrew Bible they stand impressively at the end, at the close of the Writings, or else before Psalms and after Malachi. That canonical distance from Samuel–Kings is necessary to symbolize a later time frame and different perspective. Still, the first nine chapters of genealogies are like lions guarding the gates, driving away the fainthearted from the treasures inside. S. De Vries has testified: "I regard Chronicles as one of the richest mines of spirituality in all Scripture."[2] The assessment of an earlier commentator may be added: "Chronicles is one of the most stimulating books in the Bible, courageous and practical—a splendid achievement."[3]

THE DATING OF CHRONICLES

There is a growing tendency to regard Chronicles as distinct from Ezra–Nehemiah, over against the traditional view of the two texts as a composite document. Although more work needs to be done to establish their precise relationship, enough evidence of their basic independence has emerged.[4] This discovery has released the books of Chronicles from the burden of interpretation dictated by Ezra–Nehemiah, which as a post-exilic document dealing with post-exilic events has a plainer agenda than Chronicles.

Chronicles appears to have been written after the bulk of Ezra–Nehemiah. It cites the latter, just as it does other written texts. Ezra 1:1-3 is quoted in 2 Chr 36:22-23, and Neh 11:3-19 in

---

1. *The Revised Common Lectionary* (Nashville: Abingdon, 1992).
2. S. J. De Vries, *1 and 2 Chronicles*, FOTL 11 (Grand Rapids: Eerdmans, 1989) xiv.
3. W. A. Elmslie, *The First and Second Books of Chronicles*, IB, 12 vols. (New York: Abingdon, 1954) 3:341.
4. See T. C. Eskenazi, *In an Age of Prose: A Literary Approach to Ezra–Nehemiah*, SBLMS 36 (Atlanta: Scholars Press, 1988) 14-36; S. Japhet, *I & II Chronicles*, OTL (Louisville: Westminster/John Knox, 1993) 3-5.

---

1 Chr 9:2-17, while Ezra 9–10 is reflected in 2 Chr 24:26. Chronicles also depends on Zechariah 1–8, as it does on pre-exilic prophetic texts. Zechariah 1:2-4 is presupposed in 2 Chr 30:6-7, Zech 4:10 in 2 Chr 16:9, and Zech 8:10 in 2 Chr 15:5-6. Since Zechariah 1–8 was written in the early post-exilic period, Chronicles must have been written sometime later. Moreover, it is significant that Chronicles used the Pentateuch in its final form.[5]

Archaeologists have found that the Persian period of Judean history falls into two parts. The second part, from about 450 to 332 BCE, is marked by an increase in prosperity.[6] David's appeal for contributions to the Temple and prayer of praise for a generous response in 1 Chronicles 29 and the narrative of the people's provision of ample support for the temple personnel in 2 Chronicles 31 are significant in this respect. Both chapters are transparently addressed to the constituency for whom the book was intended. The difficulty to be surmounted was evidently not an inability to give but an unwillingness to do so. The motif of willingness pervades the account in 1 Chronicles 29, and it is accompanied by references to the wealthy patriarchs as models. Such references fit the relative affluence of the second part of the Persian period.

A late Persian period dating is also supported by the levitical claims made in the course of Chronicles. There seems to have been considerable development in the standing of subordinate personnel of the post-exilic Temple. At an early stage the singing musicians were not regarded as Levites (Ezra 2:41 = Neh 7:44). By Nehemiah's time they were considered as such and were composed of two groups, the descendants of Asaph and the descendants of Jeduthun (Neh 11:3-19). At a later period the choir of Heman was added; eventually it became more prominent than that of Asaph, while the choir of Jeduthun was displaced by that of Ethan.[7] The evidence of Chronicles spans both stages of the third period, the former in 1 Chr 16:37-42; 2 Chr 5:12; 29:13-14; 35:15, and the latter in 1 Chr 6:31-48; 15:16-21, while the citation of Neh 11:3-19 in 1 Chronicles 9 naturally echoes the second period. Similarly, the gatekeepers were not yet Levites at the time of Ezra 2:42 (= Neh 7:45), nor had they yet graduated to this position by Neh 11:19, cited at 1 Chr 9:17. However, a later source employed in 1 Chr 9:18 firmly identifies them as such.

The same impression of a dating late in the Persian period is given by the post-exilic continuation of the Davidic genealogy in 1 Chronicles 3. The exact number of generations involved cannot be ascertained, but the genealogy extends into the fourth century BCE and was presumably meant to reflect the time of Chronicles. In the light of this and the earlier evidence, the first half of the fourth century BCE seems to be the period when it was written. No Hellenistic features are present to warrant a later date.

THE SETTING AND PURPOSE OF CHRONICLES

A dominant feature of Chronicles is an emphasis on exile and restoration, both as a historical fact and as a metaphor that providentially relates the overall success or failure of the community to its spiritual relationship to the Lord. The chronicler—the homogeneity of most of the work suggests that an individual rather than a group was responsible, and one may presume that the author was male—envisioned in 2 Chronicles 28–36 not one exile but a series of exiles toward the end of the pre-exilic period. He conceived of not only one literal and national restoration but also a royal one in the case of Manasseh and a metaphorical one under Hezekiah, which repeated the restoration represented by David's reign after the "exilic" fate of Saul and Israel.[8]

The novelty of the chronicler lies in his application of the theme and not in his creation of it. A later author (Daniel 9) would claim that the exile was to last 490 years, not seventy, and

5. See W. M. Schniedewind, *The Word of God in Transition: From Prophet to Exegete in the Second Temple Period,* JSOTSup 197 (Sheffield: Sheffield Academic, 1995) 133n. 11, 194n. 16.

6. See C. L. Myers and E. M. Myers, *Zechariah 9–14,* AB 25C (Garden City, N.Y.: Doubleday, 1993) 22-26.

7. See H. Gese, "Zur Geschichte der Kultsänger am zweiten Tempel," *Abraham unser Vater: Juden und Christen im Gespräch über die Bibel,* ed. O. Betz et al. (Leiden: Brill, 1963) 222-34 (= *Vom Sinai zum Zion. Alttestamentliche Beiträge zur biblischen Theologie,* BEvT 64 [Munich: Chr Kaiser, 1974] 147-58); H. G. M. Williamson, "The Origins of the Twenty-Four Priestly Courses: A Study of 1 Chronicles xxiii-xxvii," in *Studies in the Historical Books of the Old Testament,* ed. J. A. Emerton, VTSup 30 (Leiden: Brill, 1979) 251-68, esp. 263.

8. See R. Mosis, *Untersuchungen zur Theologie des chronisten Geschichtswerks,* Freiburger theologische Studien 92 (Freiburg: Herder, 1973) 31-43; P. R. Ackroyd, "The Chronicler as Exegete," *JSOT* 2 (1977) 2-32, esp. 3-9 (= *The Chronicler in His Age,* JSOTSup 101 [Sheffield: JSOT, 1991] 314-18).

was a negative condition still experienced by the so-called post-exilic community.[9] This notion of exile as a metaphor for a continuing experience is also found in earlier post-exilic literature. Psalm 126 celebrates the Lord's restoration of Zion's fortunes in the return from exile. Yet all was not well. The worshiping community prayed afresh, "Restore our fortunes." They were still suffering a virtual exile, though they lived in the land again. The same point is made in the first half of Psalm 85:1, where the Lord's past restoration of Jacob's fortunes is the basis for hope of a renewed restoration (Ps 85:1, 4). The cessation of divine anger indicated by the return from literal exile needed to be repeated, since the community was still suffering from that anger (Ps 85:3, 4-5). This superimposing of an exilic condition as a way to understand the post-exilic situation also occurs in Zech 1:2-6, which as has been observed is reflected in 2 Chr 30:6-7. The Lord's anger with the pre-exilic people, which resulted in their exile, is used as a symbol of warning for the post-exilic community.

The prayers in Ezra 9 and Nehemiah 9 demonstrate the ways in which exile as a metaphor can be traced to the present. In the former case it is lamented that "from the days of our ancestors to this day we have been deep in guilt, and for our iniquities we, our kings, and our priests have been handed over to the kings of the lands, to the sword, to captivity, to plundering, and to utter shame, as is now the case" (Ezra 9:7 NRSV). Divine alleviation of this condition is described in grudging terms (Ezra 9:8-9). Similarly, Nehemiah 9 speaks of the hardships endured by the community "since the time of the kings of Assyria until today" and of the "great distress" caused by foreign domination (Neh 9:32, 37). Despite domicile in the land, the people understood themselves to be "in exile."

In this connection the reader should consider the partial spiritualization of terms relating to the land in the psalms. Although the process began in the pre-exilic period, its continuing use in the post-exilic age is significant. The psalms use the levitical phrase "the LORD is my portion"—the Levites had received no portion of tribal land—to express the faith of the laity (Pss 16:5; 73:26; 142:6; cf. Lam 3:24). They also freely employ terms of inheriting the land as metaphors of blessing in store for the faithful (Pss 16:6; 25:13; 37 [5 times]; 44:4; 69:36-37).[10] The concept of a spiritual restoration to the land is reinforced by this use of language.

Chronicles acknowledges the problematic condition of metaphorical exile. The chronicler utilized this well-established imagery of exile and restoration, and he deliberately echoed it thoughout his work. He used three religious texts that deal with the literal exile and pointed forward to restoration, reapplying them to people in other conditions. These texts became guidelines for his constituency to follow, commending to them the cures advocated in the texts.

The first text is Lev 26:34-45, which reviews Israel's sin, exile, and return to the land. Leviticus 26:34 is given a structurally significant place in 2 Chr 36:21 to define the duration of the literal exile as limited to a set period of sabbath rest. According to Jeremiah 29:1, this exile was to last seventy years. There never was a fatalistic decree that exile should continue for centuries. The metaphorical exile was the people's fault, not the Lord's. To describe the spiritual conditions for such exile the chronicler drew upon the expression מעל מעל (*māʿal maʿal*), "practice unfaithfulness" (Lev 26:40; "committed treachery," NRSV). He used either the phrase or its separate elements of verb and noun as a key term. In the light of Lev 26:15, 43, this vocabulary is used in the general sense of breaking the covenant, though in a few contexts it gains a cultic nuance. He employed the term to define the cause of literal exile in 1 Chr 5:25 ("were unfaithful," NIV); 9:1; and 2 Chr 36:14. This same vocabulary appears elsewhere in his regular diagnosis for metaphorical exile, notably in the evaluation of the reigns of Saul and Ahaz (1 Chr 10:13; 2 Chr 29:6). The Leviticus passage also supplies one of the characteristic terms used by the chronicler when he refers to restoration, "to be humbled" (נכנע *niknaʿ*, in the niphal; Lev 26:41), e.g., in 2 Chr 7:14, a text that puts in a nutshell the chronicler's remedy for spiritual exile.

The second text imbued with religious authority to which the chronicler made frequent reference is Jer 29:10-19. It, too, discusses literal exile and restoration, and so might be used as a basis for comparison for their metaphorical counterparts. The description of the desolation

9. See M. A. Knibb, "The Exile in the Literature of the Intertestamental Period," *HeyJ* 17 (1976) 253-72.
10. See H. D. Preuss, *Old Testament Theology I*, trans. L. G. Perdue (Louisville: Westminster/John Knox, 1995) 123.

of the land in Jer 29:18 is applied to the outworking of divine wrath inherited by Hezekiah in 2 Chr 29:8. The prophecy of seventy years of exile is used positively as a limit of the Lord's judgment of exile in 2 Chr 36:21-22. However, the passage was primarily used to define how God's people might be spiritually restored: "when you call upon me and come and pray to me, I will hear you . . . If you seek me with all your heart, I will let you find me, says the Lord, and I will restore your fortunes" (Jer 29:12-14 NRSV). The divine promise became the substance of the chronicler's own message. It is the basis of the epigrammatic 2 Chr 7:14 and of the spiritual principle, "If you seek [the Lord], he will be found by you" in 1 Chr 28:9 and 2 Chr 15:2. Most notably the Jeremian text supplies the chronicler's devotional key word דרש (dāraš, "seek"), which is extensively used to characterize repentant return to the Lord and normative worship and way of life. The chronicler uses the parallel verb בקש (biqqēš, "seek"), which occurs in Jer 29:13, less often.

The third text about exile and return from which the chronicler drew heavily is Ezekiel 18, which grounds an appeal to the exiles for repentance in a sequence of good and bad generations, and also generations who changed in midcourse from bad to good and from good to bad.[11] The text provides structural models for the royal narratives of both the divided kingdom in 2 Chronicles 10–28 and the reunited kingdom in chaps. 29–36. Moreover, it uses the idiom mā'al ma'al, "practice unfaithfulness" [Lev 26:40; Ezek 18:24]), in the general sense of breaking the Torah. The chronicler's teaching of immediate retribution is generally worked out at the level of individual kings, but who symbolize separate generations. We have learned to exegete Ezekiel 18 in terms of generations, and we must also do so in the case of Chronicles. The chronicler regarded members of each generation as controlling their own destiny, free to start again with or against the Lord.

A clue to the importance of each generation in Chronicles is the recurring phrase "the God of their/your/our fathers" (NIV). The NRSV, true to its inclusive concern, renders "the God of . . . ancestors," but this is rarely the meaning. The singular counterpart "the God of your/his father" in 1 Chr 28:9; 2 Chr 17:4 is significant. Each generation had the responsibility of appropriating the faith handed down by its immediate predecessors. The chronicler was calling on his own generation to pursue the path that led to spiritual restoration. It was this policy that, by God's grace, made possible a break with the oppressive past that otherwise haunted each post-exilic generation.

THE DAVIDIC ERA

The literary backbone of Chronicles is the account of the joint reigns of David and Solomon, to which nearly half the work is devoted. Correspondingly their reigns constitute the theological mainstay of the book. The chronicler used the verb "choose" (בחר bāḥar) to indicate special agents or agencies in the Lord's long-term purposes. Of the seven entities so described, five are closely associated with these two reigns: David (2 Chr 6:6), Solomon (1 Chr 28:10), the Temple (2 Chr 7:12, 16; 33:7), Jerusalem (2 Chr 6:6, 34, 38; 12:13), and the tribe of Judah in its royal role (1 Chr 28:4). The two other entities, Israel (1 Chr 16:13) and the Levites (1 Chr 15:2; 2 Chr 29:11), are swept into this new work.

Another term for theological destiny used by the chronicler is "forever" (עד עולם 'ad 'ôlām) or variations involving this word. Apart from two references to God, it is employed twenty-seven times in Chronicles, of which sixteen occurrences relate either to the Davidic dynasty (7 times) or to the Temple (9 times). Again the joint reigns supply the arena for the majority of cases. As for the other instances, three entities were radically affected by the two reigns, the land (3 times), Israel (twice), and the covenant love (חסד ḥesed, "[steadfast] love") extended by the Lord to Israel (6 times).

The way these weighty terms are used discloses the chronicler's perception of a Davidic era launched under David and Solomon and continuing until the chronicler's own time. It

11. See R. B. Dillard, "Reward and Punishment in Chronicles: The Theology of Immediate Retribution," *WTJ* 46 (1984) 164-72, esp. 171.

superseded the Mosaic dispensation and covenant, to which Israel failed to adhere. Hence Chronicles plays down, though without denying, the exodus traditions. They are given a swan song in 1 Chr 17:21-22, to be replaced, in effect, by new traditions. The concept of a new dispensation was probably suggested to the chronicler by Psalm 78, especially vv. 67-72; the chronicler alludes to Ps 78:68, 70 in 1 Chr 28:4. There was continuity with the old dispensation; the religious and general duties of the Mosaic Torah were still obligatory for Israel. Yet the Jerusalem Temple now replaced the tabernacle of the Torah, and the Levites received a new role. The chronicler indulged in a host of typological parallels to demonstrate the divine authority of the new sanctuary, over against the representations of the written Torah. And for those who broke the Torah and repented, there was a way back to the Lord.

There is also a concern to establish the permanent nature of the Davidic dynasty. It was guaranteed, the chronicler claimed, by Solomon's construction of the Temple and general obedience to the Torah (1 Chr 28:6-7). Thereby Israel's relationship to the Lord was made permanent, as especially 2 Chr 9:8 affirms. The hymnic snatch "for [the Lord's] [steadfast] love endures forever" ties Israel's covenant to the Davidic covenant (1 Chr 16:34, 41; 2 Chr 5:13; 7:3, 6; 20:21). The permanent gift of the land to the patriarchs was reinforced by the Davidic covenant (1 Chr 16:17; 2 Chr 20:7).

There is a delicate balance between the once-for-all theological privilege established under David and Solomon and the onus of covenant obedience laid on kings and commoners thereafter. These twin phenomena find common ground in 1 Chronicles 28: In v. 8 the latter responsibility is added to a declaration of the God-given privilege. Israel's future oscillates in Chronicles between objective certainty in principle (2 Chr 9:8) and subjective uncertainty in particular (2 Chr 7:19-20).

In the interests of a moral and spiritual challenge the royal narratives after David's and Solomon's reigns focus on tracing the obedience or disobedience of each king to the guidelines laid down in those reigns. Yet there are also reminders of the permanent nature of Davidic kingship (2 Chr 13:5; 21:7), reaffirming the earlier narratives. Similarly, in 1 Chronicles 2–9 the extension of the Davidic genealogy into the post-exilic period at 1 Chronicles 3 strikes a unique note of permanence. The Davidic covenant's divinely pledged permanence—and hence certainty of restoration—was also the sign of Israel's permanence. Pastoral needs loom large in the emphasis on Israel's responsibility after 2 Chronicles 9. The lack of any royal reaffirmation near or at the end of the book also reflects the historical fact of the Davidic dynasty's eclipse, an eclipse that stretched far into the post-exilic period. One suspects that the dynasty's restoration was a distant item on the chronicler's eschatological calendar, doubtless as a negative response to political and perhaps proto-apocalyptic pressures.[12] It would be restored in God's good time. Moreover, that restoration was separate from the blessings each post-exilic generation had the potential to inherit, even within the context of Persian hegemony (see 2 Chr 12:7-8).

The Temple provided a pivot between theological stability and spiritual alternatives in the chronicler's thought. Its choirs brought a constant reminder that the Lord's "[steadfast] love endures forever." The Temple was the divinely instituted setting for the normative obligations of worship and maintenance of its fabric and personnel. In the course of the royal narratives, the chronicler covered each of the Torah-based festivals in turn, the Feast of Tabernacles in 2 Chronicles 7, the Feast of Weeks in 2 Chronicles 15, and the double feast of Passover and Unleavened Bread in 2 Chronicles 30 and 35.[13] Both in these chapters and in 1 Chronicles 15–16, he affirmed the joy of celebrating regular worship. Yet the Temple was also the center of an emergency system that offered restoration to the repentant. Redemptive grace could prevail over the breaking of the Torah (see esp. 2 Chr 7:3-16; 30:18-20; 32:25-26).

---

12. See H. H. Rowley's refusal to see eschatological significance in World War II in *The Relevance of Apocalyptic* (London: Lutterworth, 1944) 7-8. Very little is known of Judah's history in this period. For the unsettled political history of the later Persian period in the West, see E. Stern, *The Cambridge History of Judaism*, ed. W. D. Davies and L. Finkelstein (Cambridge: Cambridge University Press, 1984) 1:73-77.

13. See H. Cancik, "Des jüdische Fest," *TQ* 105 (1970) 335-48, esp. 338-39.

AN INCLUSIVE ISRAEL

A constant issue in the teaching of Chronicles is the inclusiveness of the people of God. In this respect the work stands at a remarkable distance from Ezra and Nehemiah, who at an earlier period advocated a separatist community made up of Judeans who had returned from exile. Doubtless the chronicler judged that the time was ripe for a less rigorous policy, now that the community was more established. His insistence on the spiritual potential of a wider religious community made up of "all Israel" is integrated with his presentation of the united kingdom of David and Solomon, and that insistence is reaffirmed under the reunited kingdom of Hezekiah. In the genealogical prologue, it is undergirded by appeals to the traditions of the twelve tribes in the wilderness period, attested by the Torah, and affirmed in the settlement of the promised land.

In this respect the chronicler steered a middle course between separatist and assimilationist parties in Jerusalem.[14] He rigorously maintained the unique role of the Jerusalem Temple in Israel's worship. The well-established traditions of a united Israel laid on Judah the obligation to attempt to win back Israelites still in the north to allegiance to the God of the Temple. Hezekiah is presented as a model for this obligation (2 Chronicles 30).

THE LEVITES

The chronicler's attitude toward the Levites breaks the pattern of his overall teaching. Certainly it is stitched neatly into the Davidic organization of the Temple, and their work is thus invested with the highest religious authority. Yet his teaching would have been coherent, theologically and spiritually, without his pervasive attention to the Levites. The chronicler acted as advocate for the Levites, regarding them as a disadvantaged group. His enthusiasm, which extends to a call for affirmative action, opens for us an otherwise closed window to the music and song provided by the singing Levites and the security system operated by the gatekeeping Levites. The chronicler urges that they be given a greater role in sacrificial worship and attaches names and pedigrees to the faceless members of these lower ranks of the temple staff.

The chronicler's advocacy of the Levites led to the redactional introduction of material emphasizing the role of the priesthood. A pro-priestly reviser was active mainly in 1 Chronicles 23–27, but also in a few passages elsewhere; he may have lived a generation later than the chronicler.[15] The redactor's aim was not to silence his predecessor's advocacy but to supplement it and so redress the balance somewhat, making Chronicles more comprehensive in its outlook.

THE FORM OF CHRONICLES

The Outline below will show that the work falls into four literary blocks. The longest and most important block deals with the reigns of David and Solomon, which established under God the institutions of the dynasty and the Temple. It is followed by accounts of the divided kingdom of Judah and of the reunited kingdom. These latter two blocks reaffirm the spiritual guidelines laid down in the main one, sometimes positively but more often negatively. The introduction to Chronicles provides a block of genealogies, which presents the themes of Israel's election, its inclusive nature as traditionally made up of twelve tribes, and its territorial heritage. These themes are set against a gradually emerging background of the people's unfaithfulness, exile, and restoration, which the royal narratives will repeat.

The chronicler had only a few tunes in his literary repertoire. He played them over and over again in the interests of spiritual challenge and encouragement, mainly with the present and immediate future in mind, but also on a long-term scale. It has been observed that Chronicles could "have been utilised section by section as a series of connected homilies."[16] I have traced

---

14. H. G. M. Williamson, *Israel in the Books of Chronicles* (Cambridge: Cambridge University Press, 1977) 139.

15. See Williamson, "The Origins of the Twenty-Four Priestly Courses," 251-68, esp. 266; cf. in principle A. C. Welch, *The Work of the Chronicler: Its Purpose and Date* (London: British Academy, 1939) 71-73, 85-96.

16. P. R. Ackroyd, *The Age of the Chronicler* (Aukland: Colloquium, 1970) 45 (= *The Chronicler in His Age*, 64).

in an article, and reproduced in this commentary, the quasi-homiletic stylization of the subdivisions in the four literary blocks of Chronicles.[17] The chronicler used standard rhetorical devices to present his material in assimilable portions in order to stimulate spiritual commitment to theological principles.

The question of the relation of Chronicles to "real" history is often raised. A thorough answer would be complex. Sometimes the chronicler evidently reproduced ancient, authentic documents, for instance in 1 Chr 27:25-31; sometimes he wrote up a grand tale out of a little incident, for example in 2 Chr 20:1-30; and once he stood an earlier narrative on its head to adapt it to his own perspective, in 2 Chr 20:35-37. In general modern readers need to be warned against false expectations. The chronicler was writing to help his own generation. Hence readers must focus on his situation and message—and not only on earlier history—if they are to do him justice. His royal narratives in 2 Chronicles 10–36 are a series of spiritual parables, and the speeches put into the mouths of his characters are vehicles by means of which he interprets these stories. The earlier narratives of Samuel–Kings, which were his sources, are put through a hermeneutical filter to convey the truths his constituency needed to learn. The particular genre of historiography exhibited in Chronicles must be considered in the light of its homiletic function.

THE TEXT OF CHRONICLES

Discussion of the Masoretic Text (MT) has been limited to explaining cases of divergence from it by the NRSV and the NIV, which are both alert to textual problems, and between these versions and also to other instances judged to be of exegetical importance. For further discussion, readers will often be directed to my earlier work, *The Greek Chronicles: The Relation of the Septuagint of 1 and 2 Chronicles to the Massoretic Text.*[18] It may be mentioned here that for convenience the English versification is followed throughout.

An important issue is what type of text of Samuel–Kings was available to the chronicler. For Kings, he had the type preserved in the MT.[19] In the case of Samuel, his text was close to that of the first-century BCE Qumran manuscript 4QSam[a].[20] It is crucial to trace this textual relationship because a number of idiosyncratic features previously credited to the chronicler are now seen to be already part of the textual tradition of Samuel that he used.

EXEGETING AND APPLYING CHRONICLES

Chronicles is inspirational literature, and so an exegetical and hermeneutical commentary has the duty to convey with warmth the inspirational message. The chronicler had a pastor's heart and a teacher's mind, and his concern for his constituency surfaces throughout. Application depends on the particular circumstances of the modern pastor. In the Reflections, the aim will be to make general applications, especially by building a bridge to the NT and showing how the spiritual concerns of the chronicler reappear in its Christian contexts. There will also be an endeavor to note and discuss as necessary our own distance, real or perceived, from the chronicler.

In the Commentary sections the goal will be to enter into the chronicler's world by discerning his particular agenda in each passage, and to appreciate his passion. The focus will be on Chronicles itself, rather than on looking through it or behind it to historical details. The chronicler does invite us to take an interest in his literary sources (see, e.g., 2 Chr 13:22), and so some attention will be paid to this aspect. But the main endeavor will be to examine Chronicles as a work in its own right and to listen to the spiritual message it wants to bring. As we readers first overhear it

17. L. C. Allen, "Kerygmatic Units in 1 and 2 Chronicles," *JSOT* 41 (1988) 21-36.
18. L. C. Allen, *The Greek Chronicles: The Relation of the Septuagint of 1 and 2 Chronicles to the Massoretic Text,* Part 1: *The Translator's Craft;* Part 2: *Textual Criticism,* VTSup 25, 27 (Leiden: Brill, 1974).
19. See S. L. McKenzie, *The Chronicler's Use of the Deuteronomistic History,* HSM 33 (Atlanta: Scholars Press, 1985) 83-84, 33-81.
20. See McKenzie, *The Chronicler's Use of the Deuteronomistic History,* 83-84, 119-58.

and then make an effort to hear it in the context of our particular situations, we shall find that message to be both biblical and contemporary, both inspired and inspiring.[21]

21. Portions of the treatment of the books of Chronicles in the following commentary are similar to the author's comments in Leslie C. Allen, *1, 2 Chronicles*, Communicator's Commentary 10 (Waco, Tex.: Word, 1987). Thanks are due to my colleague Francis I. Andersen for giving me a copy of the unpublished "A Key-Word-in-Context Concordance to Chronicles," edited by himself and A. D. Forbes, which proved of inestimable help; to the staff of the word processing office of Fuller Seminary for their labors on my behalf; and to my research assistant Curtis McNeil for his careful editing of the manuscript.

BIBLIOGRAPHY

Ackroyd, P. R. *1 & 2 Chronicles, Ezra, Nehemiah.* Torch Bible. London: SCM, 1973. A short, judicious commentary for general readers.

Braun, R. L. *1 Chronicles.* WBC 14. Waco, Tex.: Word, 1986. A technical and exegetical commentary reflecting informed scholarship.

De Vries, S. J. *1 and 2 Chronicles.* FOTL 11. Grand Rapids: Eerdmans, 1989. A form-critical analysis; an excellent contribution to this series, which lays an invaluable foundation for exegesis.

Dillard, R. B. *2 Chronicles.* WBC 15. Waco, Tex.: Word, 1987. A companion volume to Braun's book; equally helpful.

Japhet, S. *I & II Chronicles.* OTL. Louisville: Westminster/John Knox, 1993. The definitive commentary on Chronicles; embodies the author's comprehensive study, *The Ideology of the Book of Chronicles and Its Place in Biblical Thought.* Translated by A. Barber. BEATAJ 9. Frankfurt am Main: Peter Lang, 1989.

McConville, J. G. *1 & 2 Chronicles.* Daily Study Bible. Philadelphia: Westminster, 1984. A good devotional commentary for the general reader.

Selman, M. J. *1 Chronicles; 2 Chronicles.* TOTC. Downers Grove: Inter-Varsity, 1994. A thorough commentary written from a conservative perspective and concerned to relate Chronicles to history.

Williamson, H. G. M. *1 and 2 Chronicles.* NCB. Grand Rapids: Eerdmans, 1982. A masterly, detailed commentary that incorporates his insightful *Israel in the Books of Chronicles.* Cambridge: Cambridge University Press, 1977.

OUTLINE OF FIRST AND SECOND CHRONICLES

1 CHRONICLES 1:1–9:34

ISRAEL: ELECT AND INCLUSIVE, UNFAITHFUL BUT RESTORED

OVERVIEW

This unit supplies a genealogical prologue for the chronicler's history. The latter will consist of royal narratives, the stories of the Davidic dynasty. The prologue has a wider national and chronological focus. It considers the people of Israel, first in relation to the world at large, as the elect people of God, then in terms of pre-exilic tribal records that provocatively reproduce both southern and northern traditions, and finally in the light of a provisional post-exilic restoration that hopefully would lead to bigger and better things.

Lists of names do not make for easy reading. Students of the genealogies will benefit from J. M. Myers's presentation of them in the form of charts.[22] But there is more than names here. The genealogies are used for the chronicler's literary and theological ends, both negative and positive. They exhibit close thematic links with the royal narratives, which the sectional commentaries will trace.[23] The plainer teaching of the narratives helps the reader of the genealogies to decode them.

Israel stood in a special relationship with the Lord. Yet what was the identity of Israel? The title could not be monopolized by the members of the post-exilic province of Yehud whose predecessors returned from Babylonian exile. They were only a nucleus of a larger entity, attested traditionally in the wilderness period, in the settlement and division of the promised land, and in the united kingdom of David and Solomon. It was with that larger Israel, for whom the sanctuary was so important, that the post-exilic community should identify and find its continuity. They must also reckon with failure, the common failure that led north and south to the divine punishment of exile (5:25-26; 6:15; 9:1). Yet beyond failure lay restoring grace, already realized in part (9:2). The path to complete restoration lay via heartfelt need and earnest prayer (4:9-10; 5:20).

The sequence of generations held a fascination for the chronicler, for whom each generation had the privilege and responsibility of commitment to the God of its predecessors. There are two examples of consecutive generations' taking opposite decisions and reaping what they severally sowed, in 5:19-22, 25-26 and 7:21-24. Which generation, the chronicler was implicitly asking, did his readers wish to take for their model?

22. J. M. Myers, *2 Chronicles*, AB 13 (Garden City, N.Y.: Doubleday, 1965) 233-50.
23. See M. D. Johnson, *The Purpose of the Biblical Genealogies*, SNTSMS 8 (Cambridge: Cambridge University Press, 1969) 47-55; W. L. Osborne, "The Genealogies of 1 Chronicles 1–9" (Ph.d. diss., Dropsie University, 1979) 21-74.

1 CHRONICLES 1:1–2:2, ISRAEL'S ELECTION

COMMENTARY

This section is a genealogical list that traces a narrowing process from the world of humanity to the founder of the twelve tribes of Israel. The chronicler's intention may be deduced from a speech in which he used a similar process. David told Israel's leaders in

28:4-5: "The LORD . . . chose Judah as leader, and from the house of Judah he chose my family, and from my father's sons he was pleased to make me king over all Israel. Of all my sons . . . he has chosen my son Solomon" (NIV). These specific references to divine selection explain the implicit purpose here. Support for this interpretation comes from 16:13, where the chronicler borrowed from Ps 105:6 the description of the "sons of Jacob" (NIV) as the Lord's "chosen ones."

Structurally the section falls into two halves. Name lists devoid of any kinship terms occur in 1:1-4 and 24-27. Each list is followed by a series of genealogies, though in the second case it is amplified by lists of kings and chiefs in 1:43-54. The genealogies fall into groups of three. In the first half of the section the descendants of the three sons of Noah are listed. In the second half, this phenomenon occurs twice, relating first to the sons of Abraham—namely Ishmael, those born to Keturah, and Isaac—and then to the family of Isaac—namely Esau, Seir, and Israel. In accord with the theme of election, the chosen line is put last, after the two other lines are disposed of. In the first case the chronicler was following the order of his Genesis source, but he reversed it in putting Israel's sons after those of Esau and Seir. His reordering suggests his intention: to conclude with the elect line.

So, apart from 1:43-54, the whole genealogical list has an ABCD/ABCDB'C'D' pattern. There is first a dash from creation to the flood, then a lingering over the triple, postdiluvian descendants of Noah. This is followed by a further dash from the flood to the first patriarch, Abraham, and a lingering over the triple descendants of both Abraham and Isaac. The tripling enhances the principle of election. The genealogical list culminates in the sons of Jacob, or "Israel." The latter name, divinely conferred in Gen 35:10, is the chronicler's preferred name for Jacob, which occurs only in the quoted material of 1 Chr 16:13, 17. He used it to highlight the relationship between the chosen nation and its ancestor. That relationship is facilitated by the linguistic fact that the standard Hebrew phrase for Israelites is בני ישראל (běnê yiśrā'ēl), literally "sons of Israel." The phrase occurs in 1:43, so that in 2:2 the reader is made aware of

an intentional ambiguity between persons and tribes. In the NT, Paul focuses on a son of Abraham as a prime figure of theological history: "You . . . like Isaac, are children of the promise" (Gal 4:28 NRSV). The chronicler's perspective moved two generations down the line, but made the same point, as if saying to his Judean contemporaries, "You, like Israel's sons, are children of the promise."

The chronicler derived his genealogical material from the book of Genesis. His principle was not to use all its genealogies, but to select only those that have the heading "These are the generations of . . ." (KJV, Gen 6:9; 10:1; 11:10, 27; 25:12, 19; 36:1, 9; also Gen 5:1, which has a longer heading). The headings in 25:12, 19 are actually cited in 1:29, in the form "These are their generations" (KJV). In the case of Jacob's sons he presumably took his cue from the heading "These are the genealogies of Jacob" in Gen 37:2 (KJV), which introduces not a genealogy but a narrative, and defined it in terms of the genealogy in Gen 35:22b-26. The genealogy of Keturah's sons (Gen 25:1-4) lacks such a heading, but the chronicler used it anyway, inserting it in 1:32-33 between the descendants of Ishmael and those of Isaac, in keeping with the triple structure. There are a few textual discrepancies between the Genesis lists and the readings of the MT in Chronicles, and between the MT and the LXX of Chronicles. The NIV tends to emend in line with Genesis, while the NRSV has retained the MT (apart from a small change in 1:42 and a conjectural transposition in 1:12), presumably judging that the differences were already in the text of Genesis used by the chronicler.

1:1-42. The name list from Adam to Noah has been distilled from the names given in the course of Genesis 5, minus the narrative of ages. Knowledge of the source is presupposed, so that it now functions as a linear genealogy. The last three names in v. 4 introduce what follows and were taken from a fusion of Gen 6:9 and 10:1. There is parallelism between the ten names in vv. 1-4 (as far as Noah) and the ten in vv. 24-27. The linear character of both passages contrasts with the following segmented genealogies, which branch out in the form of a family tree. Verses 5-23 continue using Genesis 10, with deletion of its historical and geographical material. Verses 24-27 are derived from Gen 11:10-27; its names overlap with those of the previous genealogy. Details of age are again omitted. The explanation of Abram as Abraham paves the way for v. 28. Verses 28-31, 34a are extracted from Gen 25:12-16, 19 and vv. 32-33 from Gen 25:1-4, while v. 34b has been distilled from Gen 25:20-26. Verses 35-42 have been compressed from Gen 36:1-4, 9-28 (bypassing vv. 15-19). Seir is nowhere given a genealogical relationship to Esau; Gen 36:20-21 states, and the chronicler assumed, that he lived in Edom. Timna in v. 36 was actually not a son of Eliphaz but his concubine (Gen 36:12). The chronicler, in compressing his material, assumed that readers would know Genesis and not be confused.

1:43-54. The structurally anomalous lists of kings and chiefs are taken practically verbatim from Gen 36:31-43, apart from the insertion of v. 51a. The list of chiefs is related to Edom in v. 51, as in the closing v. 54 (= Gen 36:43); in Gen 36:40, chiefs of Esau are specified. So there are standardizing references to Edom in vv. 43, 51, and 54. The NRSV renders the Hebrew term אלופים (ʾallûpîm) as "clans" both here and in Genesis 36; the NIV prefers "chiefs," which seems to reflect the chronicler's intention.

Why was this Edomite material included, with the preservation of its narrative, in the first case? It can hardly have been for the sake of completeness, since Gen 36:15-19 finds no place here. There must have been good reason for the chronicler to interrupt his structural pattern. The material traces the fortunes of the Edomite monarchy. The focus of the chronicler's history will be the Davidic monarchy, and David's genealogy will begin a few verses later in 2:9. Was the chronicler influenced by the promise of Gen 35:11, that (proper) kings would spring from Jacob? In comparison to the Davidic monarchy, the Edomite one was a travesty. David's dynasty lasted in Jerusalem from generation to generation by the Lord's appointment, while Edom had a chaotic assortment of unrelated kings

and different capitals. By adding a reference to the death of Hadad in 1:51a, the chronicler interpreted 1:51b-54 as a sequel to the monarchy, a series of chieftains after the monarchy collapsed. In the post-exilic period, Judah had a strong sense of grievance against Edom for various reasons, a grievance that emerges at 1 Chr 18:12-13 and 2 Chr 25:11-12. A scoring over Edom fits this historical mood. The implicit contrast assumes a future for the house of David. Although historically it was swept away at the exile and not restored, it lived on in the chronicler's heart. Its eventual restoration was guaranteed by a divine "forever" (2 Chr 13:5).

2:1-2. It has already been noted that the genealogy of Israel's sons comes from Gen 35:22b-26. The arrangement by maternal rank has been kept, but pruned to a list of paternal brothers. The upgrading of Dan, born to Rachel's maid Bilhah, to a position before Rachel's sons, Joseph and Benjamin, presupposes Rachel's adoption of Dan in Gen 30:6, before her natural children were born.

The chronicler has presented the book of Genesis in potted form. Its divine plan, moving from primeval history to patriarchal history, from creation to covenant, from the universal to the national, has been echoed via its genealogical lists. The principle of this section is that of Samuel's review of Jesse's sons one by one in 1 Sam 16:1-13: "The LORD has not chosen any of these. . . . This is the one" (NRSV). Israel was the elect people of God. Much important truth in Genesis has been passed over in the process, such as the divine command to multiply and be fruitful, which the table of nations in Genesis 10 illustrates, and the checkered pattern of blessing, judgment, and grace that runs through Genesis 1–11. The chronicler's constituency needed to hear their election reaffirmed. Assurance was the basic need for these subjects of the Persian Empire, to hear that "the LORD . . . chose Abram" (Neh 9:7). In due course the chronicler would have much to say by way of challenge and warning.

REFLECTIONS

Genesis is a book of beginnings and basics, with which post-exilic Judah identified. The Christian church, in prizing the Gospels and Acts, takes a similar stand. Here is decisive divine/human interaction that refuses to stay in its own historical place but chases humanity down the corridors of time, demanding recognition and response and identifying the church thereafter as "children of the promise" through Christ. We have inherited the doxology generated by divine election, "Blessed be the God and Father of our Lord Jesus Christ" for choosing us in him (Eph 1:3-4).

As we have seen, the figure of David, who will dominate Chronicles, haunts even this section, in providing a normative perspective for critiquing the Edomite monarchy and its supposed aftermath in 1:43-54. The Lord's Davidic goal in history and in hope colored the chronicler's interpretation of Genesis, just as a christological hermeneutic controls some Christians' reading of the OT.

A note of challenge creeps into the climax of the section, though its implications await spelling out in the tribal material of the following chapters. Was the little post-exilic community of Judah the true Israel? Only as a nucleus for a larger entity. The twelve sons of Israel had a relevance for the chronicler's own time. Every descendant of Jacob or Israel could claim a stake in Judah's heritage. It is the first occurrence of an "ecumenical" note that will pervade the chronicler's work, dispelling complacency. In turn, to be members of the "chosen race . . . holy nation, God's own people" (1 Pet 2:9) means grappling with different traditions and unappropriated insights. "I have other sheep," Jesus has warned us, "that do not belong to this fold" (John 10:16 NRSV).

1 CHRONICLES 2:3–9:1, A PANORAMA OF PRE-EXILIC ISRAEL

OVERVIEW

The framework of this unit is provided by the placing of the three southern tribes of Judah, Levi, and Benjamin at beginning, middle, and end. The circumference and center are used as a setting for the northern tribes, as joint members of "all Israel" (9:1): "The other tribes are not excluded, but rather enclosed by this framework."[24] The ordering of the tribes represents a chiastic pattern:

A 2:3–4:43, Judah and its ancillary tribe, Simeon
  B 5:1-26, the Transjordanian tribes
    C 6:1-81, the religious tribe of Levi
  B´ 7:1-40, the remaining northern tribes
A´ 8:1-40, the other Judean tribe, Benjamin

At the conclusion mention of "all Israel" harks back to the listing of the sons of Israel, after whom the tribes were named (2:1-2), though a schematic total of twelve tribes prevents exact correspondence.

Just as 9:2-34 will provide a post-exilic list of Israelites in Jerusalem, so also the purpose here is to present a pre-exilic survey of the tribes.[25] A striking exception is the genealogy of David's descendants in chap. 3, which pushes deep into the post-exilic period, in line with the chronicler's royalist hopes, expressed in his narratives. The blend of genealogical historical and geographical concerns exhibited in this unit corresponds to a pattern found in the Safaitic inscriptions of the first centuries BCE and CE.[26] The chronicler was able to copy comparable mixed sources for his own ends. He also drew on biblical material, especially Genesis 46, Numbers 26, and parts of Joshua 15–21, and on a military census list for the Transjordanian tribes and for Issachar, Benjamin, and Asher. The listing of tribal territories outside the post-exilic province of Yehud and the tales of vigorous expansion to adjacent areas present a paradigm of territorial hope.

24. H. W. M. Williamson, *1 and 2 Chronicles*, NCB (Grand Rapids: Eerdmans, 1982) 47.

25. See J. P. Weinberg, "Die Wesen und die funktionelle Bestimmung der Listen in 1 Chr 1–9," *ZAW* 93 (1981) 91-114.

26. See Johnson, *The Purpose of the Biblical Genealogies*, 60-62; Williamson, *Israel in the Books of Chronicles*, 76-80.

1 Chronicles 2:3–4:23, The Royal Tribe of Judah

COMMENTARY

This section supplies a genealogical list for Judah. The key to understanding this composite text is its present structuring as a chiasm.[27] It has a large center of three concentric rings forming an ABCC'B'A' pattern. In 2:9 we are introduced to the three sons of Hezron, Judah's grandson and Perez's son—namely Jerahmeel, Ram, and Chelubai (or Caleb). Their lineage is explored in 2:10-33. Ram's descendants are listed as far as David in 2:10-17, Caleb's descendants are presented in 2:18-24, and Jerahmeel's in 2:25-33. Then supplementary material relating to these three lineages is given in 2:34–3:24, in reverse order, Jerahmeel's in 2:34-41, Caleb's in 2:42-55, and finally Ram's in 3:1-24 in the form of David's descendants. This chiasm is provided with two outer rings concerning the lineages of Judah's sons, that of Shelah in 2:3 and 4:21-23, and a further one of Perez, Hezron's father, in 2:4-8 (including that of a third son, Zerah) and 4:1-20.

The overall effect of this intricate chiasm is to let David's clan dominate the center of the composition, so that it begins with his ancestors and ends with his descendants. The split conveys a sense of the overarching theological importance of David's kingship, not only as a historical phenomenon but also in terms of an expectation for its restoration.

The intention of presenting the double genealogy of Jerahmeel is to take it down to the end of the pre-exilic period. The Caleb genealogies are concerned at their close to give the traditional localities of various clans (2:50b-55). The reference to the royal service of the guild of potters mentioned at the end of the genealogy of Shelah (4:23) strikes an explicitly pre-exilic note. In general the chronicler understood the genealogies as pre-exilic. It is remarkable, therefore, that the second genealogy of Ram does not stop at the exile but overshoots it at 3:17 ("the captive") and takes the Davidic family down

into the fourth century BCE. They were waiting in the wings, ready to take center stage again at the time of the Lord's choosing. The permanent nature of the Davidic dynasty is a theme emphasized in Chronicles ("forever," 1 Chr 17:12, 14, 23, 27; 28:4; 2 Chr 13:5). The chronicler used the genre of genealogy to reaffirm this conviction.

In 28:4-5 this genre is echoed in narrative form to express David's testimony that "the LORD God of Israel chose me from all my ancestral house to be king over Israel forever; for he chose Judah as leader, and in the house of Judah my father's house. . . . And of all my sons . . . he has chosen my son Solomon" (NRSV). Such sentiments are here expressed in a genealogical form. The leadership of Judah among the tribes and its royal associations will also be attested in 5:2: "Judah became prominent among his brothers and a ruler came from him" (NRSV). Accordingly Judah is here put first and presented as the matrix of the monarchy. In Jacob's blessing, his sons Reuben, Simeon, and Levi were virtually passed over (Gen 49:2-7), so that Judah, next in line among the sons of Judah's first wife, Leah, assumed the headship (Gen 35:23; 49:8-12).[28]

In 2:3-8, 10-17, 20; 3:1-6, the backbone of the Judah genealogy has been copied substantially from earlier biblical texts, with minor variations. This material has been interwoven with extra-biblical genealogies, three of which have been incorporated with their parallel opening and closing formulas: 2:25-33, relating to Jerahmeel; 2:42-50a, relating to Caleb; and 2:50b-55 + 4:2-4, relating to Hur (cf. the introductory 2:18-19).

2:3-4. Judah's lineage came down only through Shelah, Perez, and Zerah; his other sons, Er and Onan, died without heirs (Gen 46:12). The story of the latter, told in Gen 38:8-10, is presupposed, while in v. 3b the chronicler has copied out Gen 38:7 concerning Er. It corresponds to his general teaching that for each generation the wages of sin can

27. Curtis and Madsen, *The Books of Chronicles*, 82-84; H. G. M. Williamson, "Sources and Redaction in the Chronicler's Genealogy of Judah," *JBL* 98 (1979) 351-59; *1 and 2 Chronicles*, 48-50; cf. the comments of R. L. Braun, *1 Chronicles*, WBC 14 (Waco, Tex.: Word, 1986) 25-28.

28. See T. J. Prewitt, "Kinship and the Genesis Genealogies," *JNES* 40 (1981) 87-98, esp. 97-98.

be death. Genesis 38:11-26, a tangled tale of grievance and disappointment and of a willful attempt to get one's rights, is presupposed. It ended in the shocking fact of v. 4: "Tamar, his daughter-in-law, bore him Perez and Zerah." This relationship was incestuous according to the Torah (Lev 18:15), and both parties should have died (Lev 20:12). The chronicler has juxtaposed the striking disparity of vv. 3*b* and 4: The wicked son lost his life, while the wicked father and wife found places in the line leading to David. Elsewhere the chronicler ties such grace to prior repentance. Presumably he deduced it from Judah's declaration in Gen 38:26, on the lines of the confession attributed to him in the *Testaments of the Twelve Patriarchs*: "Before the eyes of all I turned aside to Tamar and committed a great sin."[29]

Mention of Judah's Canaanite wife initiates a recurring phenomenon in the Judah genealogy. Marrying a Canaanite defied not only Gen 24:3; 28:1, but also Ezra 9:1. In 2:17 an Ishmaelite father appears, and in 2:34 an Egyptian slave. At 3:2 one of David's wives is a princess from the Aramean state of Geshur, and in 4:18 an Egyptian princess is mentioned. The chronicler allowed these references to stand. Throughout his history he took a softer line on intermarriage than did Ezra and Nehemiah. Writing later, he evidently regarded their rigorous stand as no longer so necessary. He did not censor out from 1 Kings a portion of Solomon's prayer in 2 Chr 6:32-33, to the effect that foreigners were welcome to worship the Lord at the Temple.

2:5-8. After reflecting Gen 46:12a, the text cites Gen 46:12b at v. 5. Zerah's sons in v. 6 include Zimri, the equivalent of Zabdi in Josh 7:1, the two forms being similar in the old Hebrew script. So in v. 7 the line leads via Carmi to Achan. Mention of Ethan, Heman, Calcol, and Dara in v. 6 comes from 1 Kgs 4:31, where the fourth name is Darda. It depends on equating "[Ethan] the Ezrahite" and Zerah's clan, the Zerahites. In the headings to Psalms 88 and 89, Heman and Ethan are called Ezrahites. Temple music guilds, elsewhere levitical in Chronicles, are here adopted into the tribe of Judah. There is considerable telescoping involved in v. 6: These figures are associated with the age of Solomon, while v. 7 moves back to the period of conquest.[30] The music of the Temple is a key concern of the chronicler, and here genealogical tribute is paid to it.

Verse 7 presupposes knowledge of the story of Achan in Joshua 7. He is called "Achar" by wordplay with the Valley of Achar ("trouble") in Josh 7:26. Similarly he is branded "troubler (עוכר *'ôkēr*) of Israel," the contemptuous term Elijah threw back at Ahab in 1 Kgs 18:17-18. Here it alludes to his contaminating Israel by disobeying a holy war ruling: "Israel has sinned" and he "troubled us" (Josh 7:11, 25). His "being unfaithful" (NJB) reflects the text of Josh 7:1. The Hebrew expression used there (מעל מעל *mā'al ma'al*, "practice unfaithfulness") is only the first in a series within 1 Chronicles 2–9. In 5:25 and 9:1 the verb מעל (*mā'al*) and the noun מעל (*ma'al*) refer to the sin that leads to exile, a characteristic use in Chronicles derived from Lev 26:40. In 9:1, Judah's own sin is here prefigured in Achan's.

2:9-17. Verse 9 provides the framework for the central part of Judah's genealogy. "Chelubai" (NRSV) refers to Caleb later (vv. 18, 42, etc). The chronicler distinguished between this archetypal figure and "Caleb son of Yephunneh," who is mentioned in another connection in 4:15. David's genealogy recalls Num 2:3; Ruth 4:19-22; 1 Sam 16:6-9; and narratives of 1–2 Samuel. It has been telescoped into ten members. Jesse had eight sons, according to 1 Sam 16:10-11; 17:12, and 1 Chr 27:18 suggests that the name of the eighth was Elihu. The names in vv. 16-17 are included because of the role these persons played in David's rise to power.

2:18-24. The Caleb clan, who lived in the southern part of the mountains of Judah, was originally distinct from the tribe of Judah (1 Sam 25:3; 30:14), but was later incorporated into it, as this next genealogy implies. The Caleb genealogy, which basically lists children according to Caleb's two wives, reflects the amalgamation of different types of material. The Bezalel lineage in v. 20 has been inserted from Exod 31:2, though it remains unharmonized with the Hur genealogy given in 2:50b-55; 4:2-4. It will be cited again at 2 Chr 1:5. It pays tribute to the craftsman of

29. *T. Jud.* 14:5.

30. Osborne, "The Genealogies of 1 Chronicles 1–9," 213.

the Mosaic tabernacle, the precursor of the Solomonic Temple. The chronicler will represent Solomon as his antitype, so room is made for him here. Separate information about a fourth son of Hezron in vv. 21-23 interrupts the story of the progeny of Caleb's marriages. It was presumably placed here before the mention of Hezron's death in v. 24; it records links with the Transjordanian tribe of Manasseh (see Num 27:1; 32:39-42). The loss of cities to the Arameans is not related to sin, but it paves the way for the theological association in 5:23-26. In v. 24, which continues v. 19, a preferable textual tradition yields the translation "Caleb went in to Ephrath" (cf. the RSV and REB, and see *BHS*; for intercourse with one's wife after bereavement, see 2 Sam 12:24).[31] The isolated Hebrew sentence "and Abijah [was] the wife of Hezron" may originally have been attached to v. 21, itself part of the insertion of vv. 21-23.[32] The Ashhur genealogy will be continued in 4:5-8. Ashhur was the "founder" (REB) of Tekoa, an idiomatic use of "father" that occurs several times in chaps. 2 and 4.

2:25-33. The first Jerahmeel genealogy rounds off the first half of the chiasm. Like the clan of Caleb, this group was originally distinct from Judah (see 1 Sam 27:10; 30:29) and was incorporated subsequently. Ancient genealogies reflected social relationships as well as physical descent. The Jerahmeelites lived in the Negeb, either in the northeast or in the southeast.[33]

2:34-41. Whereas in the previous segmented genealogy Sheshan has a son named Ahlai, Sheshan's own linear genealogy reflects a different tradition. Such fluidity was common in ancient genealogies.[34] The chronicler assumed that this genealogy extended to the close of the pre-exilic period. If one compares Sheshan's position as the tenth generation from Judah and the subsequent fifteen generations with David's genealogy in 2:9-17; 3:1-24, then Sheshan corresponds with Jesse, and

Elishama (v. 41) with Josiah, near the end of the monarchical period.[35]

2:42-55. The second Caleb genealogy relates to an unnamed wife and two concubines, Ephah (v. 46) and Maachah (v. 48). The seemingly unconnected v. 42*a* and v. 42*b* (reflected in the NRSV, except that "and" should precede the second phrase) define the descendants of Caleb as both Mesha and the unidentified descendants of Mareshah.[36] The connection between v. 47 and what precedes is not indicated by a kinship term. In v. 49 Achsah was actually the daughter of Caleb son of Yephunneh, according to Josh 15:16-17 and Judg 1:12-13. The clause may have originated as a note on v. 50*a*, which equated the two Calebs, something the chronicler himself did not do.

Hur's genealogy in vv. 50*b*-55 continues vv. 18-19, giving the descendants of Caleb and his wife, Ephrath(ah), via Hur and then via his sons Shobal and Salma. The descendants of the latter two are mainly described in terms of clans. "Haroeh" in v. 52 is called Reaiah in 4:2 and has probably been corrupted from that form (REB; see *BHS*). For "the Menuhoth" (NRSV), one should doubtless read "the Manahathites" (NIV; cf. the REB; see also *BHS*), in line with v. 54. Verse 55 probably refers to "Sophrites" (REB) rather than to "scribes" (NRSV, NIV; there is no article in the Hebrew), with reference to Kiriath-sepher southwest of Hebron. The Kenites were an independent tribe in the eastern Negeb (see 1 Sam 27:10), here affiliated with the (Judaized) Calebites.

3:1-9. David's descendants in chap. 3 provide the outer rim of the main chiastic structure. The list in vv. 1-8 is related primarily to 2 Sam 3:2-5 and 5:5, 13-16; vv. 5-8 will recur in 14:4-7 to illustrate divine blessing. The attribution of four sons to Bathshua (= Bathsheba) occurs only here, and the position of Solomon is surprising. For Elishama (NRSV) in v. 6 one expects "Elishua," as in 14:5 and 2 Sam 5:15 (the NIV has duly emended the text, assuming assimilation to the name in v. 8).

31. See Allen, *The Greek Chronicles,* 2:87, 106; D. Barthélemy et al., *Critique textuelle de l'Ancien Testament,* OBO 50/1 (Fribourg: Editions Universitaires; and Göttingen: Vandenhoeck & Ruprecht, 1982) 1:431.

32. H. G. M. Williamson, *1 and 2 Chronicles,* NCB (Grand Rapids: Eerdmans, 1982) 53-54.

33. See Y. Aharoni, "The Negeb of Judah," *IEJ* 8 (1958) 26-38, esp. 30.

34. For fluidity whereby a change of genealogical function caused a change in form, see R. R. Wilson, *Genealogy and History in the Biblical World,* (New Haven: Yale University Press, 1977) 27-36.

35. S. Japhet, "The Israelite Legal and Social Reality as Reflected in Chronicles: A Case Study," in *"Shaarei Talmon": Studies in the Bible, Qumran and the Ancient Near East Presented to Shemaryahu Talmon,* ed. M. Fishbane et al. (Winona Lake: Eisenbrauns, 1992) 79-91, esp. 82-83.

36. M. Kartveit, *Motive und Schichten der Landtheologie in 1 Chronik 1–9,* ConBOT 28 (Stockholm: Almqvist & Wiksell, 1989) 46.

3:10-24. The linear list of Solomon's descendants up to v. 14 simply follows the order of Davidic monarchs in the books of Kings. It changes style in v. 15 by enumerating the four sons of Josiah not by succession but by age, including an otherwise unknown Johanan. From now on a segmented list is used from another source. Shallum, as in Jer 22:11, is elsewhere known as Jehoahaz. In v. 16 Jehoiachin is called Jeconiah, as in Jer 24:1; 29:2. The repeated "his son" in this verse does not refer to separate generations as in vv. 10-14, since Jeconiah's sons are listed in vv. 17-18; thus sons of Jehoiakim are meant. The Zedekiah of v. 16 will be equated with the king in 2 Chr 36:10, whereas 2 Kgs 24:17 relates him to his namesake uncle in v. 15. Zerubbabel is listed as a son of Pedaiah in v. 18; he is Shealtiel's son in Ezra 3:28; 5:2; Neh 12:1. Perhaps Pedaiah engaged in a levirate marriage with Shealtiel's widow after he died without a son. In v. 20 there is no kinship term, and so the relation of these five persons is not clarified; the reference to Hananiah in v. 21 may suggest that they were sons of Meshullam. In v. 21 the NIV reflects the MT, which may be retained. After Hananiah's two sons, four generations are represented in the form of an empty horizontal framework, introductions to name lists for which no names were available.[37] The errant arithmetic in v. 22 may be resolved by regarding "and the sons of Shemaiah" (NRSV) as an erroneous repetition of part of what precedes, so that Shemaiah is the first of the six sons of Shecaniah (REB; see *BHS*).[38] Whether Hattush is the Davidide of Ezra 8:2-3 is a moot issue. Although the number of generations involved in this genealogy is uncertain, it seems to extend well into the fourth century, down to the chronicler's period. Fecundity marks out this family as the object of divine blessing.

4:1-4. The first of the outer rings of the chiasm, 4:1-20, begins here. It corresponds to 2:4-8 and is intended as a genealogy of Perez according to the recapitulating heading in v. 1. It uses to this end supplements to various genealogies that appeared in chap. 2. In place of Carmi in v. 1 one expects a reference to Caleb; confusion with Reuben's sons Hezron and Carmi (5:3; Gen 46:9) seems to have occurred at some stage. Verse 2 restates 2:52-53 in different terms, giving more background information about the Zorathite clan. In v. 3, the NIV and the NRSV have replaced the MT's "father" (in the sense of founder) with a minority reading "sons," but some words may have dropped out earlier,[39] perhaps referring to Hur's third son, Hareph (2:51), whose genealogy is not otherwise supplied.

4:5-8. The genealogy of Caleb's son Ashhur is continued from 2:24. In v. 6 "Haahashtari" seems to refer to a clan, "the Ahashtarites" (NJB). The name is evidently Persian in origin, so that this reference is post-exilic. Verse 8 is unrelated in the MT to what precedes; the NIV, together with the REB, has supplied "and Koz" at the end of v. 7, attested only in the Targum, a procedure that all three versions adopt in v. 13.

4:9-10. Mention of Jabez in v. 9 may be linked with the place-name in 2:55, here treated as a person associated with "territory" (v. 10 NIV). Verse 9 presents a paradox, and v. 10 resolves it. Jabez enjoyed a higher status in the community than did his brothers—surprisingly so, since he was dogged by an ill-omened name. The story engages in wordplay between עֹצֶב (*ʿōṣeb*, "pain") and the (metathesized—the name of the Hebrew consonants *b* and *ṣ* is switched) name יַעְבֵּץ (*yaʿbēṣ*), assuming that the name means "he [God] inflicts pain" and commemorates his mother's painful delivery. In popular thinking such a name made Jabez a born loser. His name should have been changed for his own good, as in Gen 35:18. Yet his life turned into a success story. The secret was God's answering his prayer. What his mother "called" him (REB) was countered by his calling on God. He prayed that God bless him with territorial growth and protection from the "pain" (NIV) that would otherwise have been his lot. This little narrative must have appealed to the chronicler, since it accords with his own emphasis on prayer as the remedy for crisis. Like Asa in 2 Chr 15:2 and like Jehoshaphat in 20:17, Jabez enjoyed the protective presence of God in response to trusting prayer. Jabez's experience in desiring and obtaining an enlarged border constituted a vignette of

---

37. De Vries, *1 and 2 Chronicles*, 42.
38. See Barthélemy, *Critique textuelle de l'Ancien Testament*, 1:434-35.

39. See *BHS*.

hope for post-exilic Israel. References to the southern part of the Judean mountain country and to the Negeb, areas lost by post-exilic times to the Edomites, suggest that the chronicler intended his constituency to identify with the prayer in v. 10.

4:11-20. The genealogy of the Recah clan in vv. 11-12 is not related to anything in the preceding context. The LXX refers instead to Rechab, linking with the Rechabites of 2:55; but that may reflect ingenuity rather than a sound tradition. In vv. 13-15 the Kenizzite genealogy refers more certainly to 2:55; it is presupposed that Othniel and Caleb son of Yephunneh were brothers associated with the conquest of Kiriath-sepher, home of the Sophrites (REB; cf. Josh 15:15-19; Judg 1:11-15). The Kenizzites were another southern group who were incorporated into the tribe of Judah. They lived in the southern mountain country of Judah in the area of Debir.

Verses 16-20 present a series of fragmentary genealogies. In vv. 17-18 the NRSV, along with the REB, has transposed the order and secured better sense, while the NIV bravely struggles with the MT.

4:21-23. The Shelah genealogy rounds off the whole chiasm, harking back to Judah's oldest son in 2:3. It preserves traditions of weaving and pottery guilds, continuing a theme broached in v. 14. Since the potters worked for Judean kings, the records in which these details were preserved may have been royal ones. Reference to those "who ruled in Moab" reflects the period of the united monarchy when Moab was under Israelite control (see Ezra 2:6). If the slight emendation reflected in the NRSV's "but returned to Lehem" is correct, Lehem is short for Bethlehem.[40]

---

40. Y. Aharoni, *The Land of the Bible: A Historical Geography*, 2nd rev. ed., trans. A. F. Rainey (Philadelphia: Westminster, 1979) 108.

REFLECTIONS

1 The length and artistic structure of the genealogy of the tribe of Judah emphasizes its importance for the chronicler. The tribe was the bastion of Israel, shaping its religious and national traditions down through the centuries. Its value lay particularly in its role as tribal matrix of the Davidic monarchy. As in 28:4, we can observe divine election flowing from Judah to David. Two of the evangelists took a leaf out of the chronicler's book. Both Matthew and Luke prefaced their accounts of the ministry of Jesus with linear genealogies that traced Jesus' ancestry from Abraham, in the former case, and back to Adam, in the latter (Matt 1:11-17; Luke 3:23-28).

Matthew's periodization in terms of Abraham, David, the Babylonian exile, and the coming of Jesus as the Messiah is similar to the standpoint of the chronicler, for whom Jacob or Israel replaced Abraham. The interruption of exile (3:17) meant not the collapse of Davidic hopes, but an open-ended continuation of the register of the royal family, evidently down to the chronicler's own time. What the chronicler awaited, Matthew proclaimed as fulfilled in the person of Jesus. In briefer, Pauline terms, Jesus was "descended from David according to the flesh" (Rom 1:3 NRSV).

2. The genealogical open-endedness of the chronicler is matched by an ethnic open-heartedness. Foreigners found an undisputed place in Judah's heritage. Clans were adopted into the family; individuals joined it by marriage. This perspective recalls the post-exilic oracle in Isa 56:2-8, which extended a welcome to foreigners who joined themselves to the Lord and aspired to worshiping in the Jerusalem Temple. Matthew's Gospel strikes a similar note by incorporating the motherhood of the Moabite Ruth into the royal genealogy of Jesus (Matt 1:5). In the framework of the Gospel, that element and the visit of the magi are matched by the commission of the risen Jesus to go and "make disciples of all nations" (Matt 28:19). This openness should not be regarded as a missiological truism, but must challenge us to its domestic implications, such as integration within local churches and fellowship between homogeneous churches of different sorts. Such applications will be true to the antidiscriminatory religious intention the chronicler himself had.

3. In 2:3-4 the chronicler knew more than he wrote, expecting his readers to reflect on the underlying Genesis narrative. Matthew picked up the implicit message of Tamar from the Chronicles genealogy and passed it on in his own (Matt 1:3). Judah and Tamar were links in the chain that led ultimately to Jesus. Grace was at work here, as the chronicler underlined by his dramatic contrast. Human failure was transcended in the ongoing purposes of a merciful God. In the Midrash Rabbah the pregnant Tamar exclaims, "I am big with kings and redeemers."[41] Matthew the Evangelist was one reader who picked up this implicit message from the Chronicles genealogy and passed it on in his own (Matt 1:3). Judah and Tamar, though they deserved to die like Er, were links in the chain that led ultimately to Jesus.

4. Achar, Mr. Trouble, is another character over whom we are invited to pause. He disobeyed a divine mandate by keeping loot for himself. The selfish act had wider consequences, as selfish acts do. It contaminated the entire community and laid it under a divine curse. Their existence was threatened almost as soon as they set foot in the promised land. Achar would have brought total disaster on them, if the Lord had not arranged a way to decontaminate Israel. It was a sad beginning, curiously like the story of greedy Ananias and Sapphira in Acts 5. Human nature soon raises its ugly head, spoiling the work of God, and it requires a quick response. If 2:3-4 points to divine forgiveness, 2:7 poses a serious warning.

5. Food for thought is provided in the reference to "Bathshua," or Bathsheba, among David's wives, through whom the blessing of a large family came from God (3:5; cf. 26:4-5). As if incest and greed were not bad enough, now the crimson threads of adultery and murder are woven into the tapestry of divine providence (see 2 Samuel 11–12). The chronicler did not have occasion to incorporate the sordid narrative into his presentation of David. He was constrained by the religious nature of that presentation to illustrate David's sin as the pride that led to the military census, which led eventually to the gracious revelation of the temple site (1 Chronicles 21). He did, however, echo a striking sentence from the Bathsheba narrative at 21:7. The incident carries a message of sin and repentance, of judgment and grace. Once more Matthew—in his own genealogy—wondered at God's graciousness, pointedly referring to Bathsheba as simply "the wife of Uriah" (Matt 1:6). Where sin abounded, divine grace superabounded.

6. One can sense the chronicler's relishing of the story of Jabez in 4:9-10. Prayer changes things, he testifies throughout his work, because the Lord answers prayer. Jabez could participate in the dynamics of change. He knew of available resources in the communal faith: He "called on the God of Israel." As in the Aaronic benediction (Num 6:24-26), blessing and keeping trouble at bay are positive and negative factors that belong together. Jabez's name created an emotional hang-up that society endorsed. It stopped him from leading a satisfying life: Only God could deal with that negative image and flood his life with blessing. He was enabled to get release from its grip and enjoy a social role beyond all expectations.

41. *Gen. Rab.* 85. 11.

1 Chronicles 4:24–5:26, Simeon and the Transjordanian Tribes

COMMENTARY

The little tribe of Simeon is tucked behind Judah, into whose tribal territory it became incorporated at a very early date. However, the southern tribe and the northern tribes across the Jordan have also been blatantly juxtaposed to form a contrasting pair. The passages 4:24-43 and 5:1-26 have parallel conclusions: "to this day." Both are also matched in their formal content, exhibiting a mixture of genealogy, geography, and history. This parallelism takes an ironic turn at the end: One group survived in the land "to this day," while the other was exiled from it "to this day." The polarization throws into relief a homiletic contrast between the deportation suffered by the bad group of tribes and the territorial permanence enjoyed by the evidently good tribe, Simeon. An option confronts the people of God, exemplified by the fate and fortune of these groups. They may either stay loyal to the Lord and keep the land or stray from their allegiance and lose it. The motif of exile often functions in Chronicles as a symbol of spiritual loss that any generation was liable to suffer, should they rebel against the divine will.

Simeon's genealogy falls into three parts, a descending genealogy in 4:24-27, a list of towns and villages to define the tribal area in 4:28-33, and two reports of territorial expansion in 4:34-43, introduced by a list of clan leaders in 4:34-38, to which 4:41 refers. Historically the passage specifies a pre-David period (4:31) and dates one of the expansions in Hezekiah's reign (4:41). So what the chronicler intends is to give a pre-exilic account of the tribe.

4:24-33. The genealogy begins with a linear list that has extracted names from the catalog of Simeonite clans in Num 26:12-24, except that Jarib replaces Jachin, which may have died out. Verses 25-27a add a total of five more generations from an unknown source. An example of fertility is given, as also in v. 38, to pay maximum respect to a tribe so overshadowed by Judah. Historically this

genealogy must have survived because of the importance of this particular clan. The geographical area they occupied was mostly in the Negeb of Judah, though it extended into the southern Shephelah and other areas of the Negeb.[42] The list of places has been taken from Josh 19:2-9, which it reflects pretty closely. A historical note has been inserted into v. 31. The towns were absorbed into Judah for administrative purposes, though local consciousness of their association with Simeonite clans survived. The last sentence in v. 33 means, "And they were placed on the muster roll," referring to a military census.[43] It is the chronicler's interpretation of "according to its families" in Josh 19:8 (NRSV).[44]

4:34-43. An example of such a census is supplied in vv. 34-38, in a partially genealogical listing of clan leaders who were officers in the tribal or regional militia. According to v. 41, this listing relates to the eighth century BCE. A campaign was mounted to secure grazing grounds for flocks, as the literary frame in vv. 39 and 41 informs us. It is not possible to locate "Gedor," read by the MT; "Gerar," attested by the LXX (cf. the NJB), would make good sense. It was a city between Beersheba and Gaza, on the edge of the Philistine coastal plain, and will be important in 2 Chr 14:13. The valley named after it, to be identified with Wadi esh-Sharieh, extends to the east.[45] The campaign may have been part of Hezekiah's expansion into Philistia (see 2 Kgs 18:8).[46] The "Meunim" or "Meunites" hardly fit such a location; Maon was in southeastern Judah. Originally there may have been a reference to "the dwellings [which]" (NJB; cf. *BHS*). Another campaign marked an expansion to the southeast, to the south of the Dead Sea. Again militia officers are named; evidently a group of Amalekites had taken refuge in the area.

---

42. See Aharoni, *The Land of the Bible*, 260-62.
43. De Vries, *1 and 2 Chronicles*, 49.
44. Curtis and Madsen, *The Books of Chronicles*, 116.
45. See Y. Aharoni, "The Land of Gerar," *IEJ* 6 (1956) 26-32.
46. See B. Oded, *Israelite and Judean History*, ed. J. H. Hayes and J. M. Miller (Philadelphia: Westminster, 1977) 444-46.

Both of the battle reports are set in the context of a schema of territorial claims, which not only states how a group came into possession of an area but also affirms continuous and still-existing occupation.[47] The formula "to this day," used in vv. 41 and 43, clearly belongs to the source, as it does in 2 Chr 5:9 in dependence on 1 Kgs 8:8. In 5:26 the phrase will involve reference to the post-exilic era. Did the chronicler regard the two districts, respectively in the province of Ashdod and in Idumea by his time, as still occupied by Simeonite families? He might have assumed the contemporary validity of the source. If so, he was maintaining membership in the people of God not only of returned exiles, but also of those who were not deported. His inclusivity in other respects would accord with such a conclusion. At least the story holds out this ideal. In retrospect, after reading the drab sequence of sin and exile in 5:25-26, successful Simeon seems to exemplify an obedient people who possess the land forever (28:8). He stands for the hope that old national boundaries would one day be reestablished. The Abrahamic covenant concerning the land would find renewed and lasting fulfillment (16:15-18; cf. 2 Chr 6:25; 20:7, 11; 33:8).

The genealogical account of the two and a half eastern tribes in chap. 5 is intended as a single passage, as the comprehensive references in vv. 18-22 and 26 indicate. There is the same mixture of concerns in the individual paragraphs that we saw in the case of Simeon, though now the genealogical concern is oriented toward military registration. The function of the text is to give pre-exilic sketches of the tribes, anchored by references to domestic and foreign kings in vv. 6, 10, 17, and 26 and conscious of looming exile in vv. 6, 22, and 26.

5:1-10. The Reuben genealogy opens with a list of sons in vv. 1a and 3, extracted from Num 26:5-6, just as Num 26:12-14 was used in 4:24. It is broken off by an observation of the chronicler in vv. 1b-2 and then resumed. If Reuben was the firstborn (Num 26:5), the chronicler asks, then why did I begin my genealogy of the twelve individual tribes with Judah, rather than Reuben, whom I placed first in the list of 2:1-2? He gives the answer

47. De Vries, *1 and 2 Chronicles*, 51, 426.

in v. 2a: "For" (KJV) Judah eclipsed Reuben. The explanation is not merely historical but scriptural. It is based on Jacob's blessing of Judah in Gen 49:8-10, which specifies his brothers' subordination to him and his royal progeny. The chronicler also interprets incestuous Reuben's loss of excellence (Gen 49:4) in terms of his loss of the birthright. He maintains that such privilege passed to Joseph, presumably deducing from Jacob's adoption of his grandsons Ephraim and Manasseh that Joseph received the double portion reserved for the firstborn (Deut 21:17). The repetition of Joseph's privilege in vv. 1-2 indicates its importance for the chronicler and reflects his tribal inclusivity. These major northern tribes were key members of the ideal community of Israel. He sometimes used "Ephraim and Manasseh" as a shorthand reference to the northern tribes in general (9:3; 2 Chr 30:10; 31:1).

The genealogy of Reuben is supplied from both ends, first moving down five generations and then providing a lineage for the exiled tribal leader Beerah for eight generations in vv. 4-6, though the two linear genealogies do not meet in the middle. "Tiglath-pilneser" is the chronicler's version of Tiglath-pileser (v. 26; 2 Chr 28:20). Other military leaders, presumably contemporary with Beerah, are listed in vv. 7-8a. We do not know whether the Joel of v. 8a is intended to be that of v. 4; if so, this genealogy is telescoped. In vv. 8b-9 the territory of the Reubenites is defined: In the Hebrew the singular verb agrees with the Hebrew collective term "the Reubenite" at v. 6, as the NIV (and the REB) recognizes. From south to north they occupied the area to the east of the Dead Sea. They also expanded eastward into the desert "that extends to the Euphrates River" (NIV) to gain grazing land for their cattle. A historical example of such expansion is supplied in v. 10, the taking of land from a bedouin tribe.

5:11-17. The genealogy of Gad actually gives a list of tribal chiefs (v. 12), then a list of military leaders of interrelated clans, which are traced back through Abihail nine generations to Buz (vv. 13-14), and finally the name of a further leader whose genealogy is traced to a depth of three generations (v. 15). The first list is interrupted after "the sons of Gad" by a brief description of the tribal territory, which abbreviates v. 16. Elsewhere in the OT, Gad's region is Gilead, the area to the east of the river Jordan; here it includes Bashan, the region east of the Sea of Chinnereth. The description of Bashani territory in v. 11 may be a rationalization from the description of Reubenite territory as Gilead (originally intended in a wider sense?) in v. 9. The military census material of vv. 12-15 is given a dating by the synchronism of v. 17 at about 750 BCE.

5:18-22. One gets the impression that the Gadite census details were meant to prepare for this intertribal campaign, especially as it begins with an analysis of the conscript army in terms of expertise and size. The enemies were a bedouin confederation (cf. 1:31). The style of the battle report is so typical of the chronicler that he has probably edited his source at this point. The divine initiative (v. 22), which serves to explain the great victory (vv. 21-22a [NIV]), finds Hebrew parallels at 2 Chr 22:7; 25:20 (cf. 10:15). Here it is grounded in the trust that motivates an appeal for divine help, very much like Asa's in 2 Chr 14:11 and Jehoshaphat's in 18:31 (cf. 26:17; 32:8, 20-22). The observation that the Transjordanian tribes occupied their foes' territory until the exile introduces a somber note. Blessing is not cast in concrete. Each generation determines its own fate or fortune under God.

5:23-24. The chronicler will present that agenda in vv. 25-26. Meanwhile, it is necessary to round off the genealogical input by referring to the half tribe of Manasseh. Instead of a genealogy proper, territorial information is initially provided (which reads better in the NIV, although it deviates from the MT's accentuation), and then a military list of clan leaders, which supplements the information of vv. 17-22, is given. The former datum locates them in Bashan, with a northward expansion. Elsewhere they are also located in the northern part of Gilead. There seems to be a trend in this chapter to push the two northern tribes farther north, so that Reuben has more space.

5:25-26. Another summary from the chronicler appears here. The unfaithfulness (NIV) that leads to exile is characteristic of the chronicler, as was observed at 2:7. So is the challenge that faces a new generation, implied in the phrase "the God of their fathers" (NIV). Such language will be combined again in 2 Chr 36:14-16 as the tragic cause of Judah's exile. In presenting the exile of the eastern tribes in 733 BCE, the chronicler blends their fate with that of the rest of the northern kingdom in 721. He draws upon 2 Kgs 15:19, 29; 17:6; 18:11 and includes a short summary of 17:7-23. Was all lost? Not necessarily. In 2 Chr 30:9 he will hold out hope that the northern exiles would return, as a consequence of the repentance of their kinsfolk still in the land. The eastern tribes, no less than the rest, belonged to the chronicler's ideal Israel. Their pre-exilic gains and losses were presented as respective incentive and challenge to his post-exilic contemporaries in Judah, both to motivate their own response to the Lord and to reinforce a larger hope.

REFLECTIONS

The basic theology of the OT is a triangle with three points: God, Israel, and the land. The theme of the land—promised, given, taken away, and given back—is a thread that weaves in and out of the OT story. The land is a barometer that registers Israel's level of obedience or disobedience to the Lord. This land-based spirituality dominates the present section. The post-exilic community, relishing the land because in their history they knew what it meant to lose it (9:1-2) and had only partially regained it, is confronted with contrasting stories of winning and losing the land as corollaries of obedience and backsliding. Such morally based contrasts are typical of the chronicler. Here the land features as prize or penalty. Israel's right to the land was conditional, according to 1 Chr 28:8. Yet, once forfeited, it could be won back by repentance, according to 2 Chr 6:24-25; 30:9.

The chronicler drew a contrast not only between Simeon's survival and the Transjordanians' loss of the land, but also between the differing attitude to the Lord in the experience of the latter group. One generation trusted in the Lord; the next was disloyal to the God of that generation (5:20, 25). God has no grandchildren. The call to allegiance comes afresh to each generation in turn. This was a conviction the chronicler habitually reaffirmed. Christians, too, are called to take the baton from their predecessors and carry it faithfully for their lap of the relay race.

> Remember your [deceased] leaders, who spoke the word of God to you. Consider the outcome of their way of life and imitate their faith. Jesus Christ is the same yesterday and today and forever. (Heb 13:7-8 NIV)

> So do not throw away your confidence; it will be richly rewarded. You need to persevere so that when you have done the will of God, you will receive what he has promised. (Heb 10:35-36 NIV)

The writer to the Hebrews strikingly echoes the chronicler's call to commitment, constancy, and hope.

1 Chronicles 6:1-81, The Religious Tribe of Levi

COMMENTARY

In the tribal genealogies, a central place is allotted to the tribe of Levi. Moreover, a great deal of coverage is given to it, amounting to eighty-one verses, not much less than the hundred devoted to Judah. The emphasis on Levi carries both a religious and a theological message. The Temple was of crucial importance for the postexilic community of Judah, and the tribe of Levi, made up of priests and Levites, had been commissioned to minister to the special presence of God that it represented. From a human perspective, the size of the genealogy reflects the extensiveness of the available records. In order to officiate at the Temple, hereditary legitimacy had to be proved (see Ezra 2:62-63).

The chronicler wrote his history to promote the interests of the Temple. He leaves readers in no doubt about his convictions that the Temple merited the community's unstinting support and that worship should be conducted in a traditional and proper manner. Putting Levi at the middle of the tribal genealogies reflects the chronicler's belief that the Temple stood at the heart of the community of faith. He also uses this section as an opportunity to maintain for the first time the validity of the Temple as a religious institution. The Torah regarded the Mosaic tabernacle as the focus of the Lord's holy presence,

and, true to its historical context, had nothing to say about the Temple, apart from the annotation in Gen 22:14, which the chronicler will exploit in 2 Chr 3:1, and of course Deut 12:10-11, which he so interprets in 1 Chr 22:9-10, 18-19. A new Temple-related dispensation was launched under David and Solomon (vv. 10, 31-32, 48). It continued the sacrificial system of the Mosaic era (v. 49), but gave new and permanent duties of music and song to the Levites. As the chronicler's community worshiped at the post-exilic Temple, they could be confident that it perpetuated pre-exilic ideals and reflected the will of the Lord.

The chronicler is concerned with giving a sketch of temple personnel in pre-exilic times, as v. 15 indicates with its reference to the exile. He focused on Aaron, Moses, David, and Solomon as founders of Israel's religion under God. The same concerns of genealogy, history, and geography reappear in this section, with the religious character of the tribe providing a unique slant. After a basic tribal lineage in vv. 1-3, a genealogy of the high priesthood appears in vv. 4-15, then one of the clans of Levites in vv. 16-30, and another of the levitical guilds of music in vv. 31-47, with a brief indication of the roles of the other Levites and of the priests in vv. 48-49 and a short list of high priests up to David's time in vv. 50-53. The rest of the chapter is devoted to the territorial holdings of the tribe of Levi among the other tribes (vv. 54-81). One should notice that much more space is devoted to the Levites than to priests. This inequity reflects the chronicler's perennial concern to promote the cause of the former.

6:1-15. The genealogy begins by listing the eponymous ancestors of the three tribal clans: Gershon (NIV), Kohath, and Merari. Gershom is the chronicler's preferred form; the variant Gershon used in the priestly texts of the Pentateuch appears here as a reflection of his source, reverting in v. 16 to Gershom (NRSV; the NRSV and the NIV have standardized differently in this chapter). Priests traced their descent from a branch of the tribe, through Kohath, Amram, and Aaron, and the high priests belonged to this line. The chronicler does not mention here that other priests were also descended from Ithamar (cf. 24:1-4). The genealogy takes a segmented form in vv. 1-3; its names have been extracted from the record in Exod 6:16-23, with the difference that Miriam is now included alongside Amram's sons (see Num 26:59). Her role in the pentateuchal narratives merited a place in the genealogy.

The continuation of the genealogy in vv. 4-15 takes a linear form. Although given a genealogical shaping, it is taken from an official list of high priests with a variety of family ties or even none. The list is related to that in Ezra 7:1-5. It probably belonged to a slightly longer list ending in Joshua, the first high priest after the exile (see Hag 1:1); it contained interesting symbolic features, but they were not the chronicler's concern.[48] He cut it off at the point of exile, true to his time frame in the genealogical chapters, and added two historical notes. The one in v. 15 ends with exile; the other in v. 10 draws attention to the first high priest of the Solomonic Temple, though it is misplaced and historically belongs next to the Azariah of v. 9 (see 1 Kgs 4:2).

6:16-30. The Levites are given a corresponding genealogy. The Davidic emphasis of the next paragraph, announced in v. 31, suggests that the chronicler regarded his genealogy as tracing the levitical line down to that period. The closing of the Kohathite lineage a generation after Samuel in v. 28 also suggests this point. In v. 30 Asaiah nicely aligns with 15:6, where Asaiah leads the Merarites in the levitical guard of honor for the ark. But comparison with vv. 39-41 implies that the final representative of the Gershom lineage in v. 21, Jeatherai, marks a somewhat earlier stage. As in the former listing, the initial generations are segmented with reference to the three tribal clans, and the rest is supplied in a linear form. The material in vv. 16-19 has been abbreviated from Num 3:17-20, with the closing statement in v. 19b now serving as a heading to another, non-biblical list of clan genealogies in vv. 20-30. Gershom (NRSV) in v. 16 is doubtless an adaptation of Gershon, to accord with Gershom in the new list at v. 20.

The clan genealogies are developed from the first sons of the three eponymous clan founders, at least in the case of Gershom (Libni, vv. 17, 20) and Merari (Mahli, vv. 19, 29). In the case of Kohath, the line of the firstborn Amram has been preempted as a priestly pedigree. Izhar is expected here, as the father of Korah (cf. vv. 37-38). Instead the name of Amminadab appears. We do not know whether this is intended to refer to Aaron's father-in-law (Exod 6:23), of the same generation as Amram, and if some link was being claimed between David and the tribe of Levi via Ruth (see Ruth 4:18-22).[49] Kohath's genealogy is longer than the other two. It includes a collateral branch descended from Elkanah (v. 23) in vv. 25-28. It attests the adoption of Samuel into the levitical chain, legitimating the religious activity of this Ephraimite, to which his mother especially dedicated him (1 Sam 1:1, 11, 28). The chronicler will exploit this levitical link at 2 Chr 35:18 as part of his crusade to promote the Levites' cause. The attribution of different sons to Elkanah in vv. 23 and 25 is a clue to the fact that the vertical listing in vv. 22-23 has replaced an earlier horizontal grouping of three brothers, Assir, Elkanah and Ebiasaph, with Tahath functioning as Assir's son (see Exod 6:24).[50] Verse 28 has come down to us in a damaged form; our

---

48. For its schematic and partial character see Williamson, *1 and 2 Chronicles*, 70-71.

49. Osborne, "The Genealogies of 1 Chronicles 1–9," 272.

50. See Johnson, *The Purpose of the Biblical Genealogies*, 71-73, summarizing the contribution of A. Lefèvre.

versions represent an attempt to repair it (see the NRSV note; cf. *BHS*). Verse 48 implies that this genealogy was meant to represent the large group of Levites responsible for assisting the priests by carrying out a range of general duties (cf. 23:4, 24, 28-29).

6:31-49. The next series of ascending genealogies in vv. 33-47 involves a specialist group of Levites, the singing musicians organized into a threefold ancestral guild. The chronicler has set it in an explanatory narrative frame, vv. 31-32 and 48-49. At the beginning of the post-exilic period, these choirs were not yet regarded as Levites, but gradually they were integrated into the levitical order and equipped with legitimating genealogies. The present arrangement of Heman, Asaph, and Ethan attests the latest historical development found in Chronicles (see 15:16-21; see also the Introduction). The three choirs are represented as they performed in the temple court, with Heman's at the center and Asaph's and Ethan's on each side. This genealogy differs from the preceding one by claiming to trace the guild from the second sons of Gershom, Kohath and Merari (vv. 16-19), at least in the cases of Izhar and Mushi. The inclusion of Shimei, now in v. 42 near the end of the Gershom list, may have the same intent. Perhaps it originally stood in v. 43, leaving Zimmah and Jahath as father and son as in v. 20. This overlap with the earlier genealogy based on first sons also occurs in the line of Kohath, which has coordinated the independent Elkanah genealogy into a vertical, and so longer, list.

Verses 31-32 possess chiastic structure.[51] The chronicler puts in the middle the overlap of dispensations, when the new choirs officiated at the old tabernacle in Gibeon (see 16:39-42). He contrasts it with the new sanctuary built by Solomon, where the choirs found their proper place, in fulfillment of preparations David had made for their role in the Temple (see 23:5; 25:1-6). He has in mind the installation of the ark in the Temple (2 Chr 5:12-13; 6:41; 7:6). They symbolized the beginning of a new era to which the chronicler's community of faith still belonged. The ending of the Levites' duties to carry the

ark, reflected in the name of Asaiah at v. 31 (cf. 15:6), provided opportunities for their temple ministry, especially that of music and song (cf. 23:26, 30; 2 Chr 35:3). The Temple had the same value for Israel as had the old tabernacle, as the juxtaposition of terms in v. 48 signifies; according to 2 Chr 5:5 the tabernacle was placed inside the Temple.

Apart from the replacement of the tabernacle, featured in the Torah, with the Temple and the extension of levitical duties, the old Mosaic dispensation continued, with the perpetuation of the Levites' other responsibilities (see Num 18:1-6). The priests kept their regular duties. The latter are summarized in v. 49, first in terms of sacrificing burnt offerings and burning incense, both done twice a day (Exod 30:7; Num 28:1-8; 29:38-42; 2 Chr 2:4). Their responsibility for "the most holy things" (NJB; cf. the REB) relates to other offerings: the grain offering, the sin offering, and the guilt offering, which were regarded as especially holy (Num 18:9). Their work of atonement, associated with all animal sacrifices, refers to the blood rite of Lev 4:16-20; 17:11. This aspect of their work will come to the fore in 2 Chr 29:22-24.

6:50-53. The linear list of high priests up to David's reign is a partial repetition of the one at the head of the chapter. It appears to be a redactional addition: "Aaron's sons," an expression used for priests in general (v. 49), are here restricted to high priests.[52] The list was added to match the genealogy of levitical singers as far as David's time in vv. 33-47, but it does not involve a new role. Its intent was to illustrate from a priestly perspective the shift from tabernacle to Temple.

6:54-81. The geographical component of the Levi genealogy relates to the towns and pasturelands set aside for the tribe throughout Israel's territory according to Joshua 21, from which this passage has adapted vv. 4-39.[53] The chronicler has supplied an introduction in v. 54*a*. The earlier list summarized the towns assigned to priests and the three levitical clans in terms of tribal areas and numbers, and then itemized the particular

52. See Williamson, *1 and 2 Chronicles*, 74; De Vries, *1 and 2 Chronicles*, 64.

53. See Braun, *1 Chronicles*, 98-100; M. Kartveit, *Motive und Schichten der Landtheologie in 1 Chronik 1–9*, ConBOT 28 (Stockholm: Almqvist & Wiksell, 1989) 69-77; E. Ben Zvi, "The List of the Levitical Cities," *JSOT* 54 (1992) 77-106, esp. 77n. 1.

51. John W. Kleinig, *The Lord's Song: The Basis, Function and Significance of Choral Music in Chronicles*, JSOTSup 156 (Sheffield: JSOT, 1993) 43.

towns in each of the four cases. Here the priestly towns in the south are itemized first in vv. 55-60 (= Josh 21:10-19). Doubtless the intent was to bunch together the priestly details with those of v. 49 (plus vv. 50-53). Then the summaries relating to the levitical clans in the north follow in vv. 61-63 and their detailed listings in vv. 66-81. Verses 64-65 provide a comprehensive summary of the towns located among the northern and the southern tribes, respectively. Verse 65 has been adapted from the heading to the specific list of priestly towns in Josh 21:9. This adaptation with an unspecified subject means that in v. 64 "Levites" now refers generally to members of the tribe of Levi rather than only to its non-priestly members.

The chronicler seems to assign the dating of the initial occupation of these areas to the end of the period of conquest, in line with a plain reading of Joshua 21. According to 1 Chr 13:2, the priests and the Levites were already settled there immediately after David's coronation. According to 2 Chr 11:14, in Rehoboam's reign the Levites abandoned their "pasturelands" (NIV) in the newly formed northern kingdom and moved to the south, evidently to all the towns in Judah (23:2). In 31:15, 19 the priestly towns and "pasture lands" (NJB) in the southern kingdom find mention in the account of Hezekiah's reign. A number of scholars regard this system as a historical fact and date it to the period of the united kingdom.[54] The chronicler took it seriously as a normative means of supporting the temple clergy.

The tribe of Levi had no land holdings comparable with those of its fellow tribes. The tribe was maintained partly by the tithes and offerings given to the Lord, as 2 Chr 31:4-19 will recount and commend, and partly by the allocation of land from the territory of the other tribes in recognition of its religious service. The Lord, not land, was Levi's inheritance (Deut 10:9). The devotional saying "The LORD is my portion" (Pss 16:5; 73:26; 119:57; 142:5; Lam 3:24) seems to have originated among the tribe of Levi in acknowledgment of this fact. In the Psalms it gained a wider, spiritualized sense as a

beautiful expression of faith in the Lord as the mainstay of the believer's life. The present listing had become a dead letter by the chronicler's time. The province of Yehud did not even match the traditional area of the state of Judah, let alone other tribal areas. It conveyed a double message to his constituency: the hope of eventual territorial restoration and a contemporary challenge to make room for priests and Levites in the priestly towns and elsewhere within their borders (cf. 2 Chr 23:2; 31:11-19, esp. vv. 15, 19; Neh 12:27). Traditionally each of the tribes gave up part of its territory to the Lord's ministers. It was like rent, surrendering part in acknowledgment of God's claim on the whole. The community of faith was still obligated to make space for the temple personnel. According to 2 Chronicles 31, they were to support them by sacrificial offerings and gifts in kind to the Temple. A firm part of Israel's understanding of the land was that it belonged to the Lord: "The land is mine" (Lev 25:23). Each tribe gave over towns for them to reside in and grazing land for their cattle (Josh 21:2).

A total of forty-eight towns was assigned for this purpose. Verse 60b, with its closing number of priestly towns, nicely prefaces the summaries in vv. 61-63, each of which has a numerical component for the levitical towns. Sometimes the totals do not align with the listings in the MT. Accordingly in the NIV, Juttah and Gibeon have been supplied from Joshua 21 in vv. 59-60, and Jokneam and Kartah in v. 77. It is noticeable that the tribe of Dan, included in Josh 21:23-25, is not cited in vv. 61 and 69, though two of its four towns survive in the latter verse. The omission of Dan is consistent with its absence from the tribal listings in chap. 7. Here, however, the lack of apparently vital information—the absence of Ephraim in v. 61 (contrast vv. 66-67) and of two towns in v. 69—suggests that the material has been clumsily wrenched out of the text of Chronicles, perhaps because the Danites built an idolatrous sanctuary (cf. Judges 18; see *BHS* here). Joshua 21 leans on the account of the institution of six cities of refuge in Joshua 20, by noting their inclusion in the list of towns, notably Hebron and Shechem in Josh 21:13, 21. These two references are reproduced in 1 Chr 6:57, 67, but in a plural form as if the towns were all cities of refuge. Although no variant reading occurs

54. See C. Hauer, Jr., "David and the Levites," *JSOT* 23 (1982) 33-54; Z. Kallai, *Historical Geography of the Bible: The Tribal Territories of Israel* (Jerusalem: Magnes, 1986) 447-58.

in the textual tradition of Chronicles, the NIV along with the REB has adopted the singulars of Joshua 21.[55] In view of the chronicler's extensive knowledge of OT sources, it is difficult to envision his sanctioning so serious a change.

55. See *BHS.*

REFLECTIONS

The centrality of Levi among the tribes implies the centrality of the Temple in Israel's culture and the centrality of the Lord in their lives. Lyonel Feininger's painting *The Church*, executed in the cubist tradition, translates this concept into a Christian idiom. In his picture of houses surrounding a church, all the lines bring the eye toward the central feature. Then the eye is taken up by the spire into the sky. It expresses the ideal of the church as the living heart of society, drawing the community to itself and then directing it to God.

One may conceive of many ways in which Christians can appropriate the chronicler's focus on the Temple, in view of the NT's multifaceted interpretation. Yet we would not represent his mind adequately if we simply spoke of putting God at the center of the individual's life. A truth faithful to his intent is the importance of institutional religion for the people of God. No church building has the theological value assigned to the Temple in the OT; yet, the Christian faith necessarily has its institutional forms. Those who seek to worship only in front of a television set or in private devotions lack a key dimension of Christian experience. Over against such a solitary form of faith we may set the testimony of Psalm 42. Enforced deprivation of corporate worship was a source of anguish for the psalmist. Times were nostalgically recalled when "I went with the throng,/ and led them in procession to the house of God,/ with glad shouts and songs of thanksgiving,/ a multitude keeping festival" (Ps 42:4 NRSV).

There is a healthy ring to the declaration of Ps 122:1:

I was glad when they said to me,
  "Let us go to the house of the LORD!"
Our feet are standing
  within your gates, O Jerusalem. (NRSV)

This communal enthusiasm defies the individualism rampant in modern Western societies. The chronicler will amply illustrate in ensuing narratives about the Temple the communal aspect of putting God at the center of life. Seeking the Lord very often has for him an institutional meaning. Personal faith must find communal expression if it is to be true to the Bible. "Christianity is essentially a social religion; and . . . to turn it into a solitary religion is indeed to destroy it," affirmed John Wesley.[56] The same is true of the faith of the Old Testament. The exhortation "Let us not give up meeting together, as some are in the habit of doing" (Heb 10:25 NIV) echoes the OT's own emphasis on temple worship.

One of the chronicler's aims in his work was to establish the validity of post-exilic worship. For us, he tells his readers, the Temple corresponds to the tabernacle, which the Torah associates with the Lord's special presence. He envisioned an old order, still largely valid, and a new order that added to God's earlier revelation as to how to worship. In juggling things old and new, the chronicler offers a model for us in treating the Old Testament and the New Testament, with their respective eras of revelation and response. He knew such tension as Christian preachers feel in handling the OT, the Bible

56. John Wesley, *The Works of John Wesley*, ed. A. C. Outler (Nashville: Abingdon, 1984) 1:533.

of the early church but much less so for the modern church. Fortunately for him, he could not indulge in our temptation to replace a Hebrew Bible with a Christian New Testament. He had to wrestle with the tension of development and adaptation evident in the Law and the Prophets and in the ongoing history of the community of faith. We read "Jesus" in place of David and Solomon as founders of a new spiritual era under God. Just as David's work did not cancel out the former revelation but vitally supplemented it, so also it has been the traditional conviction of the church that the New Testament is set alongside the Old Testament to form a completed revelation.

The Temple did not run itself. No magic broomstick kept its courts clean. The daily duties of sacrificing to the accompaniment of music and song and the less spectacular routines of preparation and maintenance were the responsibility of priests and Levites. The system came with a necessary price tag for Israel, including the setting aside of some of their territory directly for the Lord to be used by temple personnel. This principle correlates with the divine claim on the lives of Christians. It is not enough to speak of surrendering oneself to God or to sing "All for Jesus." Such sincere sentiments require translation into the allocation of one's resources to God and so to God's human agencies. Surrender means stewardship, part of which is to devote a portion of what one has directly to God's work and workers.

1 Chronicles 7:1-40, The Other Northern Tribes

COMMENTARY

In the tribal genealogies the Transjordanian tribes were dovetailed between Judah and Simeon on one side and Levi on the other. Now the remaining northern tribes are placed as a bloc between Levi and Benjamin. The framework of southern tribes embraces within it the clusters of northern ones. The symbolism is clear. The southern tribes, marked by allegiance to the Jerusalem Temple and dynasty and so to the Lord, were incomplete apart from the other tribes. In the case of Issachar, mention of David (v. 2) recalls a long-lost period of unity. The northern tribes still had a place reserved for them in the ideal Israel, which they should claim by faith. Southerners must encourage them to do so, rather than stand in their way.

The tribes in this section are not listed in any special order, in relation to listings elsewhere or to geographical position. The military slant of the Issachar, Benjamin, and Asher genealogies indicates that the chronicler found them in the census source he used for the Transjordanian tribes (cf. 5:18), deliberately breaking into it by his insertion of the tribe of Levi in chap. 6. The placing of Asher after west Manasseh and Ephraim reflects the southern setting of this particular list, as we shall see.

Unlike the listing in 2:1-2, Zebulun and Dan find no place here, presumably under the constraint of the conventional schematic representation of Israel's tribes as twelve in number. The splitting of Joseph into Manasseh and Ephraim and the further division of Manasseh into its eastern and western areas meant that two others had to be dropped. In 12:24-37 the problem will be resolved by treating the eastern tribes as one group, and in 27:16-22 by omitting Asher and Gad. Here the omission was not motivated by lack of material. Some earlier genealogical material was available to the chronicler in Gen 46:14-23 and Num 26:26, 42, and geographical information, in Josh 19:10-16, 40-48. All three sources are used in his other tribal genealogies. Lack of later material was not a factor; in the case of Naphtali (v. 13) he coped without it.

7:1-5. The Issachar genealogy falls into three parts. The first in v. 1 has been extracted from the clan information in Num 26:23-24. The other two parts, in vv. 2 and 3-5, give details of a military census. In v. 5, "enrolled by genealogy" (NRSV) signifies rather "enrolled for war."[57] In vv. 2 and 4 and also in v. 9, "of/by/according to their generations" (NRSV) means "according to their genealogical divisions." In v. 2, a census list credited to the time of David names six officers in the clan descended from Tola, who commanded conscripts from their extended families. One thinks, as presumably the chronicler did, of David's census in chap. 21. The item also invites comparison with the list of tribal heads in 27:16-22, related to that census, and with the enumeration of tribal contingents in 12:24-37, where Issachar is uniquely represented not by a number but by "200 chiefs, with all their relatives" (NIV). In the next census extract, five officers, Izrahiah and his four sons, all related to the subclan of Uzzi, are listed with the number of their conscripts. The total in v. 5 seems to include troops from the other three clans of v. 1, though the Hebrew is unclear.

7:6-12. The Benjaminite listing is unexpected in view of the long entry in chap. 8, where its presence accords with the overall design of the literary unit. The listing was evidently included in the longer source used by the chronicler, and he may have appreciated its military data as providing a sense of community and chose to use it here rather than incorporating it into chap. 8. The listing may also reflect a tradition that part of Benjamin belonged to the northern kingdom, as the double listing of tribal towns in Josh 18:21-28 seems to attest.[58] Verses 6-11 are taken from a military census document; in vv. 7 and 9 enrollment for military service is again in view. Three clans are listed, first according to their eponymous founders and then in terms of the numbers and names of their commanders and the numbers of their conscripts. In v. 6, neither Num 26:38-40 nor Gen 46:21 is followed precisely. No date is supplied for the census, though the chronicler probably assumed it was Davidic. The comparatively late name Elioenai may point to the period of Hezekiah, as in 4:36. Verse 12 gives a fragment of a genealogy of Benjamin, related to Num 26:39. It betrays an awareness that Benjamin had more than three clans and supplies

two more in v. 12a; Ir may be meant to refer to Iri in v. 7. In v. 12b the name of a third clan or subclan founder, Hushim, seems to be Benjaminite; it is used of a woman in 8:8, 11. Aher appears to be a variant of either Aharah in 8:1 or Ahiram in Num 26:38. There is little merit in the conjecture that a lost genealogy of Dan underlies v. 12b (see the REB; see also Gen 46:23).

7:13. The terse genealogy of Naphtali is derived from Gen 46:24-25a. It gives the founders of its four clans and calls them "descendants" of the tribal mother Bilhah. In the parent text, the reference was to Dan and Naphtali as sons of Bilhah, but the chronicler has reused it to augment his scanty source material; Num 26:48-49 could supply him with nothing more.

7:14-19. The genealogy of Manasseh is closely related to that of Ephraim in vv. 20-27, as the joint geographical description in vv. 28-29 shows. That description also makes clear that west Manasseh is in view, notwithstanding the eastern flavor of the names "Machir" and "Gilead" (cf. Josh 17:3).[59] The eastern half of the tribe has already been featured in chap. 4. This genealogy has no solid basis in biblical precedents, though a number of names overlap with Numbers 26 and Joshua 17. It makes lavish use of birth reports. In its present form it reads like a series of disjointed statements. Its lack of coherence may be overcome by assuming that (1) "Asriel" in v. 14 originated as an early annotation specifying a further clan (see Num 26:31; Josh 17:2); (2) in v. 15 Machir's wife was taken (in relation to and so) "from" (NIV) the Benjaminite family of Huppim and Shuppim in v. 12; and (3) originally it was "their" sister, Maacah, who became his wife (see v. 16; cf. *BHS*). Mention of Zelophehad as "the second" (son) presupposes the role of Machir as the firstborn (Josh 17:1), though in Josh 17:3 Zelophehad is placed later in the genealogical chain.

This genealogy identifies first Manasseh's two sons Machir and Zelophehad by an Aramean concubine (vv. 14-15) and then specifies the lineage of Machir and his wife, Maacah, to a depth of four generations (vv. 16-17a). The derivation from Gilead in v. 17b

57. De Vries, *1 and 2 Chronicles*, 74.
58. See Aharoni, *Land of the Bible*, 315; cf. Osborne, "The Genealogies of 1 Chronicles 1–9," 28-87; M. Oeming, *Das wahre Israel: die "genealogische Vorhalle" 1 Chronik 1-9*, BWANT 128 (Stuttgart: Kohlhammer, 1990) 161-63.

59. See D. Edelman, "The Manasseh Genealogy in 1 Chronicles 7:14-19: Form and Source," *CBQ* 53 (1991) 179-201, esp. 192-93.

offers an instance of genealogical fluidity; it accords with the tradition of Josh 17:3. It is uncertain whether Machir's sister or Gilead's is in view in v. 18. The lineage in v. 19 is not coordinated with what precedes it, but Shemida is known as a clan ancestor (Num 26:32; Josh 17:2). Mention of Zelophehad's daughters in v. 15 reminds readers of their role as heirs in Josh 17:3-6 by a special dispensation that extended a male privilege to them.

7:20-27. The genealogy of Ephraim, like the former one, does not depend directly on OT sources. It provides two separate linear genealogies that are interrupted by a narrative. The first is the line from Ephraim to an unknown Zabad, traced to a depth of seven generations. The second, beginning in v. 25, is that of Joshua; it has a depth of ten generations. At the start of the first genealogy, the vertical listing is an adaptation of an earlier horizontal one, in the light of the clan founders named in Num 26:36. The second overlaps with the first to some extent, with variations in spelling. In the course of v. 21 the phrase "Shuthelah his son" resumes the reference to Ephraim's son in v. 20 as an introduction to the story of the killing of two other sons and its sequel (cf. 2:3-4). The sense is: "Now Shuthelah was Ephraim's son, and so were Ezer and Elead."[60]

Ephraim's involvement in this Palestinian narrative stands in tension with his birth in Egypt (Gen 41:50-52). Whether the narrative is set in the patriarchal period or in the period of conquest cannot be ascertained. Gath is probably Gittaim, a dozen miles west of the Beth-horons.[61] This city-state was still a Canaanite enclave early in the monarchical period (2 Sam 4:3). The death of the cattle rustlers caused grief that their father found impossible to shake off, though his "relatives" (NIV) or "kinsmen" (REB)—he had only one brother—rallied around him in sympathy. His next son was given the name Beriah to commemorate the loss: It is explained as "in disaster" or "in misfortune" (ברעה *bĕrāʿâ*). What was the moral of the story for the chronicler? Two contrasted generations are often juxtaposed in his narratives, and so the little success story of Ephraim's daughter Sheerah in v. 24 is significant. Building is a sign of divine blessing in Chronicles (e.g., 2 Chr 26:5-6). The message is that disaster in one generation need not hold the next generation hostage. A Saul may give way to a David, an Ahaz to a Hezekiah.

7:28-29. The territory occupied by west Manasseh and Ephraim is defined together. Ephraim's boundaries are described in v. 28 and the boundaries of the northern area of west Manasseh in v. 29. Shechem was variously aligned in different historical periods; v. 19 suggests its attachment to Manasseh.

7:30-40. In the Asher genealogy, there is a return to the military census list used for a number of the earlier genealogies, most recently Benjamin's. Its introduction in vv. 30-31a is taken from Gen 46:17. Verses 30-32 take the form of a segmented genealogy to a depth of four generations. The attached list of clan commanders now functions as its continuation, though the partial alignment of names betrays its independent origin; the clan in v. 39 has no counterpart in the genealogy. The phrase "enrolled by genealogies" (v. 40) refers rather to military registration. The listing refers not to the tribe in its northern setting, but to an Asherite enclave in the southern part of the hill country of Ephraim, as some of the names show.[62]

---

60. See W. Rudolph, *Chronikbücher*, HAT 1:21 (Tübingen: Mohr [Siebeck], 1955) 71-72.

61. See B. Mazar, "Gath and Gittaim," *IEJ* 4 (1954) 227-35.

62. See D. Edelman, "The Asherite Genealogy in 1 Chronicles 7:30-40," *BR* 33 (1988) 13-23; N. Na'aman, "Sources and Redaction in the Chronicler's Genealogies of Asher and Ephraim," *JSOT* 49 (1991) 99-111, esp. 100-105; Aharoni, *The Land of the Bible*, 244.

REFLECTIONS

1. Who belongs to the people of God? The chronicler gives a provocative answer. The earlier leaders Ezra and Nehemiah had given a minimal answer, understandable in a hard-pressed, relatively new community. The chronicler judged that a broader answer grounded in ancient tradition could be given. He endeavored to prevent a particular religious emphasis driven by temporary need from hardening into a permanent attitude. He conceived of an ideal Israel to which the northern tribes belonged in principle just as much as did the southern tribes. Such completeness would replicate the united kingdom and the allocation of the land of Israel to each of the twelve tribes. No wonder David finds mention early in the section (7:2). No wonder an honored place is given to the genealogy of Joshua, under whose leadership the land was won and allocated (7:25-27).

Each new work of God throws into focus a particular truth and creates champions for it. A new denomination builds a shrine to its truth and makes it a permanent tradition and the reason for its continued existence. Anthony Norris Groves, a nineteenth-century Christian leader, after receiving adult baptism, was informed by a Baptist pastor, "Of course, you must be a Baptist now." "No," Groves replied, "I desire to follow all in those things in which they follow Christ, but I would not by joining one party cut myself off from others."[63] There is an idealism in this response that is difficult to attain in practice. Each local church has its own emphases and affiliation with like-minded believers. The chronicler was protesting at the iron curtain that was erected between members of the Lord's people. Have we in turn built walls of partition to cut ourselves off from fellow Christians?

2. There is a Wild West flavor about the first of the two scenarios sketched in 7:21-24. It easily translates into a celluloid world of cattle rustling and lynching at the hands of a posse who galloped after the rustlers. The genre is less evident in the sequel of family mourning. The father could not get over the overwhelming loss of two grown sons, and he perpetuated his grief in the name of his infant son. The baby was made to bear the brunt of an unending grief. We have already learned from 4:9-10 the cultural consequences of such unlucky naming, which only prayer to a powerful God could avert. Here the vignette is set against a scene of blessing. Sheerah is the only woman in the Old Testament to found cities. Like Dido, traditionally the founder of Carthage, she enjoyed a rare privilege. The chronicler contrasted bane and blessing, in line with his regular teaching that each generation could beat its past and win blessing from the Lord. Elsewhere he included moral and religious factors. Here the constraint of his source produced a contrast of blessedly achieving and fatalistically putting life on hold.

To those in the chronicler's constituency with ears to hear, the question posed was, Should we cast ourselves as victims of past tragedy? Zechariah had the right answer, when asked whether fast days commemorating the onset of conquest and exile should be perpetuated. No, turn them into happy holidays, he replied, and build a community where truth and peace are cherished (Zech 7:1-7; 8:18). Sowing in tears is meant to result in reaping with shouts of joy (Ps 126:5-6). The people themselves had a part to play in shaking off the past and beginning again with the Lord. The passage served the chronicler as an illustration of one of his model texts, Ezekiel 18. Pessimism could give way to optimism. The chains of a demoralizing past could be broken. A door of hope stands open, and readers are challenged to walk through and achieve great things with God. This is a message many believers still need to hear.

63. G. H. Lang, *Anthony Norris Groves* (London: Paternoster, 1949) 279.

1 Chronicles 8:1–9:1, The Tribe of Benjamin

COMMENTARY

The massive textual unit that began in 2:2 is now brought to a conclusion. Benjamin, in whose territory Jerusalem lay (according to a prominent OT claim), was one of the triumvirate of tribes that for centuries preserved Israel's religious and dynastic traditions. So in the chronicler's genealogies Judah and Benjamin stand at either end of a literary rainbow, red and violet, with Levi as the central green. The rainbow represents the whole people of God, who were given stakes in the land and a religious center in acknowledgment of God's divine patronage and presence. The spectrum comprised many more than three colors, or four including the vestigial tribe of Simeon. The southern tribes needed the rest to complete the rainbow.

The Benjaminite genealogy reflects a compilation available to the chronicler that evidently contained a range of earlier listings. They were largely made up of local community records of a military nature. The combination of genealogical, geographical, and historical data that featured in many of the earlier genealogies reappears in this one. The Benjaminite clans who traditionally lived at Geba are represented in vv. 1-7; those associated with Moab and with Ono and Lod, in vv. 8-12; residents of Aijalon, Gath, and Jerusalem, in vv. 13-28; and others who lived in Gibeon and Jerusalem, in vv. 29-32. With this last listing is linked a genealogy of Saul in vv 33-40a, while the whole section is concluded in v. 40b. The unit of twelve tribal genealogies is brought to a close in 9:1. The emphasis on Jerusalem in this chapter nicely anticipates a post-exilic concern in 9:3, 34 and its dynastic and religious roles inaugurated by David in 11:4-8 and chaps. 15–16.

8:1-7. The first record is associated with the town of Geba. It is prefaced in vv. 1-2 by Benjamin's sons, five eponymous founders of clans. This listing is close to that in Num 26:38-40, though the last two names are different. The genealogy is then traced from a son, Bela, to representatives of nine subclans. Some of these recur in v. 7, with Ahijah replacing Ahoah. Verse 6 indicates that these are the names of militia commanders at some point in history (cf. 7:40). There is a partial generational update at the end of v. 7. Rather awkwardly, they are also called the "descendants" of Ehud in v. 6. It is tempting to identify him with Ehud ben-Gera, the left-handed Benjaminite judge who delivered Israel from Moab (Judg 3:12-30), but the Hebrew form of the name is slightly different (אחוד [ʾēḥûd], not אהוד [ʾēhûd]). These commanders are located at Geba and, after

migration, at Manahat, whether the Edomite one of 1:40 or the Judean one of 2:52, 54. The interpretation of the NIV and the REB in v. 7 is probably correct: Gera did lead the transplanted group.

8:8-12. The next listing is also credited with settlement outside tribal territory, in this case wholly so. A subclan descended from Shaharaim is located in Moab and is supplied with contemporary representatives. This settlement must have taken place before Moab gained independence in the middle of the ninth century BCE. "Mesha" (v. 9) is a Moabite name, shared by the king who successfully rebelled against Israel. A collateral branch, traced through an earlier wife and a second son of the union, Elpaal, is linked with the western enterprise of Shemed, rebuilding or fortifying Ono and Lod on the eastern edge of the coastal plain.

8:13-28. Verse 13 begins a new sentence (as in the NJB). Five militia leaders of Aijalon are named, the first two of whom are associated with expansion to Gath-Gittaim to the south of Lod (cf. 7:21). Their family counterparts in a later generation are named in vv. 15-21. In the latter listing, Shimei stands for Shema, and there is mention of another group under Elpaal, presumably a different person from the one in listed v. 12. Over against the Aijalon-based groups are two other groups of commanders descended from Shashak and Jeremoth (v. 14), who settled in Jerusalem (vv. 22-28). In the later list, "Jeroham" appears as the equivalent of "Jeremoth." It is clear that the later information in vv. 15-28 was originally independent of that in vv. 13-14. The two records were combined with their deviations intact, including the dropping of Ahio in v. 14, unless it really means "his brother" (NJB, following the LXX).

8:29-32. In this last localized listing, a family group moved to Jerusalem and, not surprisingly, took up residence near their fellow Benjaminites whose leaders were named in vv. 22-27. This group originally came from Gibeon; it is traced back to the Israelite "founder" (REB) of this older, Canaanite town, otherwise known in Chronicles as the honorable site of the tabernacle until Solomon's reign (16:39-40; 2 Chr 1:3). His name is not supplied, but in the parallel text at 9:35 it is given as "Jeiel," which the NIV and the NRSV have repeated here. Presumably most of the ensuing family listed in vv. 30-32a remained in Gibeon. Perhaps those who relocated were the families mentioned in v. 32 (cf. the REB). The name "Baal" in v. 30 implies an early dating for the list.

8:33-40a. The Gibeon-Jerusalem listing continues with a genealogy of King Saul, Benjamin's best-known scion (except for a later Saul of NT fame) and so ancestor of a prominent family. He evidently came from Gibeon.[64] This lineage connects with the preceding listing at the point of "Ner" (v. 30; cf. 1 Sam 14:50-51). The name appears at 9:36 before "Nadab" (the first part of this name, "Nadab" [נדב *nādāb*], looks very similar in the Hebrew script to "Ner" [נר *nēr*]; evidently it fell out of the text). His "brother" Kish fluidly reappears as a son. In fact, a strictly genealogical relationship is now given, over against the horizontal grouping of subclans in vv. 30-31. The genealogy basically represents the lineage of Azal (v. 37); it is mainly linear, with segmented details at three points. It has been updated by one generation and by a collateral branch of conscripts specializing in archery (vv. 38-40a). This genealogy was probably composed toward the end of the monarchical period.[65]

8:40b–9:1. After the sectional summary in 8:40b, the chronicler looked back over the whole unit with its twelve tribal genealogies. Since the sons of Israel or Jacob (2:1-2) had been treated in principle, "all Israel" had been presented in genealogical form. This entity of twelve tribes comprised the people of God, and no lesser, sectarian definition could satisfy. The source, unlike in 2 Chr 20:34, appears to be a royal document, from which the tribal census information given for a number of the tribes, and perhaps also the guild records of 4:21-23, had been taken.

A final statement was necessary—namely, a historical and theological comment on the southern tribes. In 5:25-26 the chronicler had recorded the unfaithfulness and exile of the northern tribes. Now a precise parallel needed to be drawn; that of 6:15 was not enough. The southern tribes, who comprised the state of Judah, were no less partners in such sin and punishment. They, too, were covenant breakers (cf. Lev 26:40, where "treachery" translates מעל [*ma'al*, here rendered "unfaithfulness"). So they in turn had to lose the land. Eventually the royal narrative will return to this point at 2 Chr 36:14, 20a.

64. See J. Blenkinsopp, *Gibeon and Israel: The Role of Gibeon and the Gibeonites in the Political and Religious History of Early Israel*, SOTSMS 2 (Cambridge: Cambridge University Press, 1972) 58-59.

65. See A. Demsky, "The Genealogy of Gibeon (1 Chronicles 9:35-44): Biblical and Epigraphic Considerations," *BASOR* 202 (April 1971) 16-23.

REFLECTIONS

If the chronicler were alive and active in the Jewish community today, he would surely be a member of Habad, encouraging assimilated Jews to appreciate their heritage and to be true to its glorious traditions. Benjamin and Judah stood for him as pre-exilic models for his own constituency, insofar as they were guardians of covenant truths centered in Jerusalem's Temple and dynasty. As guardians they had a responsibility to the other tribes, who had long ago lost their allegiance to these truths. They were not to be an inner circle, hugging to themselves their relationship with the Lord. Rather, as the structure of chaps. 2–8 indicates, they were to be an outer circle, inviting the others back into their midst and acknowledging their equality as fellow children of Israel. Although Judah was historically preeminent, the birthright still belonged to Ephraim and Manasseh (5:1-2).

How may we apply this principle, which was so important for the chronicler's time? There tends to be a denominational hierarchy in Christian circles. Traditional denominations are valued by their members for their links with the religious past. Younger denominations are dismissed to the end of the pecking order. It also works the other way. The newer groups see themselves as more open to the Holy Spirit and in touch with modernity. They look on older denominations as worn-out wineskins that held the spiritual wine of yesteryear. Either way, our denominational selves align easily with Judah and Benjamin. The chronicler would grant us our elitism, for whatever reason, yet urge that we are thereby responsible for initiating moves to express our unity with the "lesser" groups. We are the ones, he would tell us, who must work at producing a cross-fertilizing commonwealth of churches, devoted alike to worship, service, and outreach. "From everyone to whom much has been given, much will be required; and from the one to whom much has been entrusted, even more will be demanded" (Luke 12:48 NRSV).

There is a sting in the tail at 9:1. The state of Judah fell into the same fate of exile as had the northern state earlier, victim of the same failure. Each of the two groups could come before God only as repentant sinners, saved by repeated grace in spite of the skeletons in their closets. Unity is best achieved by crowding together at the mercy seat in a common humility, aware that "God has imprisoned all in disobedience so that he may be merciful to all" (Rom 11:32 NRSV).

1 CHRONICLES 9:2-34, ISRAEL'S RESTORATION IN PRINCIPLE

COMMENTARY

Exile was not the end of the story. Restoration to the land and so, in the light of v. 1, to the Lord's favor eventually occurred. Only here does the chronicler deal with resettlement as a fact. (In 2 Chr 36:20b-23 he will tantalizingly look forward to it, like Moses viewing the land from Mt. Nebo.) This section has a partial, preliminary tone, for all its solid data. Only mention of the resettlement of Judah is made in the brief note of v. 2, despite the fact that the northern tribes had "possessions" in the land (7:28 NRSV; cf. 2 Chr 31:1). The next focus is narrower still: the reoccupation of Jerusalem, stated at the beginning and the end (vv. 3, 34), though a bit more information is included in vv. 16 and 22. The singling out of Jerusalem has symbolic value—as an earnest of the eventual reoccupation of the whole land, a promise the Lord could fulfill only if the people played their part (28:8). Moreover, it surely echoes earlier prophetic hopes, from First Isaiah (Isa 1:26), via a package of promises in Second Isaiah (esp. Isa 49:14-21; 52:12; 54:1-3), and via Ezekiel (Ezek 16:53-63; 48:30-35), to Zechariah (Zech 8:1-10). The word of the Lord had begun to come true.

The chronicler affirms the continuity of the post-exilic community with the pre-exilic one, whose story is told in the ensuing narratives. The tribal groupings of chaps. 2–8 were represented in the resettlement of Jerusalem not only by the secular tribes but also by the tribe of Levi, divided into priests and Levites. Jerusalem had been chosen by the Lord to be the home of the Temple (2 Chr 6:6). The emphasis on its sacred personnel in vv. 10-34 reflects continuity of worship at the Temple, which was duly rebuilt, as 2 Chr 36:23 was to announce.

The issue of continuity, lay and religious, comes to the fore in the different form the genealogies now take. In chaps. 1–8 they had mainly been descending, apart from the levitical links between the ages of David and Moses, forged for dispensational purposes in 6:33-48 (also 5:8, 14-15). Now they are ascending, tracing the perpetuation of older lines in the post-exilic community. Provisionally at least, Israel is alive and well, and through its religious representatives is faithful to its duty to maintain the worship of the Lord. Ideals are presented here with an implicit challenge that they should be cherished.

Verses 2-17 appear to depend on Neh 11:3-11, despite substantial differences. The echoing of the editorial introduction of Neh 11:3 is a strong argument for literary dependence. Apart from textual variants and subsequent omissions in Nehemiah 11, most differences may be understood in terms of updating to a later generation, both by replacing older with more contemporary names and by increasing the numbers of figures. The Nehemiah list records those who were drafted to Jerusalem as a defensive measure after its walls were rebuilt.

9:2-9. Verse 2, adapted from Neh 11:3, views the population of Judah returning to their ancestral properties. "Again" (NRSV; "resettle," NIV) is not in the Hebrew, but is implied after v. 1 and agrees with the post-exilic nature of the source. "Israelites" refers to lay members. A tolerable tension is created by the chronicler's including in v. 3 "Ephraim and Manasseh," which is lacking in Neh 11:4. He not only relegated "Israelites" in Neh 11:3 (NIV) to lay status but also invested the term with intertribal significance, in line with "all Israel" in v. 1. The pair of tribes is a shorthand reference to all the northern tribes (as in 2 Chr 30:1; 31:4; 34:9), though no tribal representatives have been inserted into the list that follows. The spiritual reunion of Judah and members of the old northern kingdom is portrayed in 2 Chr 28:8-15; 30:11, 18; 34:9 is presupposed here. The chronicler's addition is motivated by his idealism. He may have been influenced by Ezekiel's description of the new Jerusalem as being entered by gates named after the tribes of Israel (Ezek 48:30-35).

In accord with its heading, the list details the lay population in vv. 4-9 and priests and Levites in vv. 10-34. The "temple servants" (cf. Neh 11:21), though retained in the heading, are not elaborated upon, because they never feature among the chronicler's temple personnel. As for Judah, three family heads represent the three clans of Perez, Shelah, and Zerah (see 2:3-4; in v. 5 "Shelanites" [REB] is to be read with the LXX by repointing the Hebrew). The representative of the Perez clan has been replaced. A reference to Zerah probably followed in Nehemiah 11 at an earlier stage; the low number in Neh 11:6 relates only to the Perez clan. Consistent with the source, there is no listing for the family of David (cf. Ezra 8:2). The chronicler has already supplied its post-exilic genealogy in 3:18-24.

The four Benjaminite family heads represent a considerable amplification of the parallel in Nehemiah 11, but the two officials of Neh 11:9 are not reproduced. The family heads are not distinguished by clan, though "according to their generations" (v. 9, also v. 34), which means "according to their genealogical divisions," implies clan ancestry.

9:10-13. The priestly list traces the lineage of two out of six priestly heads of families, one by telescoping to the ancient high priest Ahitub (see 6:11-12), and the other by tracing to Immer, presumably the ancestor mentioned in Ezra 2:37; Neh 7:40; 10:20. The number of priests reflects a total of the individual numbers in Neh 11:12-14 with an updating from 1,192 to 1,760.

9:14-16. The listing of Levites does not give a straightforward derivation from the three clans of Merari, Gershom, and Kohath, apart from Merari in v. 14. Two singing groups are represented in the course of vv. 15-16. That of Asaph was descended from Gershom, according to 6:39-43; that of Jeduthun is nowhere traced to a clan. The Kohath clan will feature in v. 32 and by implication in vv. 19 and 31 via its Korahite subclan. The list here has added a reference to Berechiah and his home at Netophah, where singers lived, according to Neh 12:28. Presumably his family rose to prominence later. His presence does not fit comfortably in a list of Jerusalem residents; doubtless his part-time residence when on duty is in view (see vv. 25, 33).

9:17-27. The source already regarded temple singers as Levites, unlike that of Ezra 2:41 (= Neh 7:44). Gatekeepers were not yet included, just as they were not in Ezra 2:42 (= Neh 7:45). The chronicler turns to use another source, beginning in v. 17. It overlapped with Neh 11:19, but mentioned four rather than two family heads of the gatekeepers.[66] In this later source, gatekeepers are firmly identified as Levites (v. 18; cf. v. 26), as the chronicler himself identified them in 23:5 and in the primary layer of chap. 26. In the rest of the section the focus shifts from names to duties. The shortest listing, that of the Levites in vv. 14-17, receives an extensive analysis of duties in vv. 18-33, in terms of security (vv. 18-27), supplies and equipment (vv. 28-32), and singing (v. 33). This range of duties accords with three of the four categories of Levites in 23:4-5 and is amplified in subsequent chapters—namely, maintenance

66. Williamson, *1 and 2 Chronicles,* 90.

staff, gatekeepers, and singers. The chronicler consistently regarded Levites as the solid bedrock of temple service. He regularly championed them and encouraged appreciation of their work, which lacked the attention and honor attached to the priesthood.

The issue of continuity is treated in a distinctive way (vv. 18-33). Shallum was currently head of the security force and formerly in the prestigious position of controlling the east gate, still called the royal gate, before he was replaced by Zechariah (v. 21). Shallum is credited with a magnificent pedigree stretching back to the wilderness period of the tabernacle, to which there is a flashback in vv. 19b-20 (cf. Num 1:53). Then the gatekeepers came under the supervision of the chief priest Eleazar in Num 3:32 and so later of his illustrious son Phineas, who was a blessed model of temple service (Num 25:7-13; cf. 1 Chr 6:4; Ps 106:30-31). In the temple dispensation, the gatekeepers' office was renewed by no less than David and the prophet Samuel. The reference to David accords with 23:2-6. Samuel's patronage is of a vaguer nature. Although he predicted David's reign (11.3), he did not live to see it or his organization of the Temple (see 1 Sam 25:1; 28:3). Presumably young Samuel's service in the Shiloh temple (1 Sam 3:2-18) was a levitical precedent; his adoption into the family tree of the Levites in 6:28, 33 is noteworthy.

Direct reference to the ancient tabernacle in v. 19b is accompanied by typological allusions to it in vv. 18b, 19a, 21, and 23; in the first case, "the camp of the LORD" refers to the temple precincts, as in 2 Chr 31:2. The Temple was the dispensational counterpart of the tabernacle, featured in the Torah. So the post-exilic gatekeepers, bridging the two dispensations in their ancient and current work, had a double validity. As in v. 16, their commuting "for seven-day periods" in vv. 22 and 25 (cf. Neh 12:28-29) does not fit the impression of permanent residence in the context. As if aware of this, v. 26a states that "the four head gatekeepers were on permanent duty" (NJB) and thus were residents.

There seems to be a shift in the course of v. 26 to another source or to another part of the same source (see the new paragraph in the NJB). The Hebrew clause "they were Levites" may be intended to indicate that a range of levitical categories is in view hereafter, and not just gatekeepers. First, security work continues to be in mind. The reference in v. 28b is not to the administrative posts of 26:20-28 but to sentry duty, like that at "the storehouse" in 26:15, 17. Their crucial responsibilities are highlighted in v. 27.

9:28-32. Another group of Levites comes into view: the maintenance workers of 23:4, 6-24 (cf. 23:28-29). They worked faithfully behind the scenes, caring as conscientiously for mundane utensils as for the sacred vessels used in temple services. The aside in v. 30 may be attributed to the pro-priestly reviser who embellished Chronicles at various points to redress the balance.[67] The "flat cakes" (v. 31) were for the daily grain offerings (see Lev 6:19-23).

9:33-34. Another source break occurs at v. 33, which must have been the heading or conclusion for a list of family heads of levitical singers. The chronicler used this extract for the light it shed on their duties, especially their dedication in serving by night as well as by day (cf. Ps 134:1). Before the chronicler turns to repeat in vv. 35-44 the genealogy of Saul from 8:29-38, he puts 8:28 to new use by slipping in a reference to Levites. It becomes a conclusion both to vv. 14-33 and to the whole section, corresponding to v. 3.

67. Williamson, *1 and 2 Chronicles*, 91.

REFLECTIONS

Exile gave way to return. Although the wording stays at the human level, there were divine overtones for the chronicler in the light of Solomon's prayers that the sinning and repentant people might be restored to their God-given land (2 Chr 6:24-25, 36-39) and the reference to Jeremiah's prediction of restoration at 2 Chr 36:21-22. The story is symbol as well as event, since it is related to the chronicler's use of return from exile as a metaphor for the spiritual and complete restoration available to the post-exilic people of God. The historical return has a provisional character, limited as it was to Judah and Jerusalem. The tribal boundaries and towns covered in chapters 2–8 are woefully contracted. Yet that return was consistent with earlier prophetic words, and the concentration on Jerusalem seems to underline the implicit theme of prophecy's coming true.

These are themes the New Testament also celebrates. The gospel of Christ is no novelty but was promised by God through the prophets in the Holy Scriptures (Rom 1:2). The Christian church enjoys both present grace and the prospect of final salvation foretold by the prophets (1 Pet 1:3-12). We, too, have a "pledge of our inheritance as God's own people" (Eph 1:14 NRSV) and are challenged to make every effort to enter it (Heb 4:1, 10; 12:1-2).

The chronicler insists that Israel was present in the post-exilic capital, in its wider, grander sense. North and south, sinners both (5:26-27; 9:1-2), found in Jerusalem a big enough umbrella of divine grace to cover them all in token of their common heritage and future enjoyment of it on a larger scale. Paul expressed a remarkably similar conviction in his defense before Agrippa, when he testified of his "hope in the promise made by God to our ancestors, a promise that our twelve tribes hope to attain" (Acts 26:6-7 NRSV). The theme is repeated in a typological sense at Rev 21:12-14 in borrowing from Ezekiel 48 the vision of the new Jerusalem's twelve gates inscribed with the names of the twelve tribes (see Rev 7:4-8). All of God's people were to be represented there. Accordingly here and now we are to extend the right hand of fellowship that transcends different spheres of the faith as James, Cephas, and John did to Paul and Barnabas (Gal 2:9).

For the chronicler, the restored Jerusalem was home to the Temple. He used the opportunity to extol the work of the Levites. His exuberant description is reminiscent of C. S. Lewis's depiction of Sarah Smith, who used to live in Golders Green, now radiantly transformed into a veritable Queen of Heaven.[68] The message there is to respect and honor people like Mrs. Smith, whose labors for good and for God will redound to surprising fame in heaven. So here a glorious picture of heritage and devotion is painted in honor of these lesser members of the temple staff. We may apply this call for appreciation to our particular ecclesiastical settings and elsewhere.

The chronicler is also concerned to validate post-exilic worship, for which the work of the Levites is used as a test case. Their heritage stretched back to the wilderness period of Israel's history, when their predecessors worked for the tabernacle. Their work was validated afresh by Samuel and by David. Along the chain of generations, God's work went on. We do not readily warm to this saga of hereditary succession. It clashes with a cultural commitment to modernity and a strange disdain for the past. Yet it is a necessary message for Christians, if we are to stand on solid spiritual foundations, true to a historically given revelation. The call comes in turn to us to maintain the traditions of the ancient faith handed on to us, proudly and appropriately (see 1 Cor 11:2; 15:1-2).

68. C. S. Lewis, *The Great Divorce* (New York: Macmillan, 1946) 108-23.

1 CHRONICLES 9:35–
2 CHRONICLES 9:31

THE REIGNS OF DAVID AND SOLOMON

OVERVIEW

The chronicler highlighted the reigns of David and Solomon as a key period of theological history. During that time, there was a special manifestation of the covenant goodness of the Lord and a revelation of guidelines for Israel thereafter. The chronicler set the period inside its own literary frame, which serves to isolate it from the comparative mundaneness of history before and after. The frame occurs in 10:14, "the Lord turned the kingdom over to David," and in 2 Chr 10:15, the "turn" in events predicted for Rehoboam. These two turning points in sacred history, at the end of Saul's reign and at the beginning of Rehoboam's, draw attention to the intervening reigns of David and Solomon as a period when God's will for Israel then and thereafter was supremely realized. First Chronicles 11–2 Chronicles 9, prefaced by 1 Chr 9:35–10:14, is a single overarching unit and nearly half the chronicler's work. We must listen carefully to his presentation of the double reign, if we want to catch his message.

1 CHRONICLES 9:35–29:30, THE REIGN OF DAVID

OVERVIEW

The account of David's reign is dominated by two religious enterprises: his moving the ark to Jerusalem (chaps. 13–16) and his preparations for the building of the Temple, where the ark was to be housed (chaps. 23–29). The accomplishment of each task is marked by public praise of God (16:7-36; 29:10-19). Chapters 17–22 are introduced by a prophetic oracle in chap. 17. It sets out the divine program for the reigns of David and Solomon—David's preparatory role as a warrior king and Solomon's as temple builder—and announces a Davidic dynasty. David's role is discharged in chaps. 18–20. Chapters 21–22 are concerned with the temple site, which is essentially linked with divine grace, and with Solomon's double mandate as temple builder and guarantor of the dynasty. These latter themes are revisited in chap. 28. The initial section, chaps. 9–12, by recounting the disastrous end of Saul's reign and the beginning of David's blessed one, contrasts the motifs of spiritual exile and the restoration begun by David's coronation and his occupation of Jerusalem.

1 Chronicles 9:35–12:40, A Decisive Change of King

OVERVIEW

Saul and David are like night and day. They function as models of right and wrong, of defeat and victory. The chronicler has given a pointer to their typological meaning by speaking plainly of Judah as first unfaithful to God and so exiled, and then returning to live again in their cities, especially in Jerusalem (9:1-3). Now Saul is unfaithful and dies; his subjects are scattered from their homes. But David is raised up as the new king of a united people and comes to live in Jerusalem. So David becomes a pledge that exile will finally be put behind the people of God and that full restoration will eventually come, if only they will follow in David's footsteps and not Saul's.

1 Chronicles 9:35–10:14, Saul's Infidelity and Death

COMMENTARY

For the chronicler, the monarchy was important because it provided models for the contemporary people of God, against which they could evaluate their own spiritual lives. Saul functions as a negative model, as 10:13-14 will show.

9:35-44. The genealogy is a reprise of 8:29-38, part of the listing relating to the tribe of Benjamin. This genealogy is presented in a slightly better form than was the earlier one. A few names are spelled a little differently; the NRSV and the NIV rightly restore "and Ahaz" at the end of v. 41, as in 8:35, to prepare for Ahaz's own genealogy in v. 42. The genealogy is intended to pave the way for the narrative of chap. 10. It traces Saul's ancestry back four generations and his posterity to a depth of twelve generations, down to late pre-exilic times. The genealogy intersects in v. 39 with 10:2, with the cluster of names of Saul and his sons. At first sight mention of Saul's posterity awkwardly conflicts with the statement in 10:6 that "all" of Saul's "house" perished in battle. The reference is to Saul's royal house or dynasty, in the light of v. 14b. The short-lived reign of Eshbaal (2 Samuel 2–4) did not count for the chronicler; he mentions Saul's daughter Michal as living at a later time (15:29). What did the genealogy signify for the chronicler, for whom Saul was a villain of the deepest dye? It illustrated his characteristic view of separate generations. Each generation enjoyed a fresh start before God and was not doomed by the wickedness of its predecessors. While royal status passed to David's house, Saul's descendant Azel received rich blessing in the gift of six sons (see Ps 127:3).

10:1-14. The narrative in these verses concentrates on Saul's death and its implications. It falls into two roughly parallel halves, vv. 1-7 and vv. 8-14. Each half has three parts in an ABCA'C'B' order. A series of Philistine-related actions concerning Saul is presented in vv. 1-5 and 8-10. They trigger reactions in Israel (v. 7, "saw"; vv. 11-12, "heard") and are given an evaluative summary in both v. 6 and vv. 13-14.

The chronicler does not linger over Saul's reign in its own right, but abruptly passes to its lamentable outcome. He will interpret it (vv. 13-14) as the grim harvest of wrong choices previously made. He repeats the narrative of 1 Samuel 31, which describes Israel's luckless stand against the Philistines on Mt. Gilboa. The source used by the chronicler appears to have been a shorter version than we read in the MT of Samuel.[69] The chronicler has amplified his source into a new structure by expanding "together" in 1 Sam 31:6 with an evaluative element, "and all his house," in v. 6 and by matching this evaluative summary with his own longer interpretive conclusion in vv. 13-14.

---

69. See the comparative textual analyses of P. K. McCarter, *1 Samuel,* AB 8 (Garden City, N.Y.: Doubleday, 1980) 440-42, and McKenzie, *The Chronicler's Use of the Deuteronomistic History,* 58-60.

10:1-7. The first half of the chapter may be viewed not only as a succession of statements moving toward a conclusion, but also as a series of concentric circles. The center of the account is Saul's face-saving death by his own hand in vv. 4-6*a*. From this center the story spreads out to the fate of others bound up with the king's own death in vv. 2*a* and 6*b*. The boundaries of the story are marked in vv. 1 and 7 by the flight of such Israelites as survived, both soldiers from the battlefield and local citizens from their homes. Saul dragged down with him both his sons and his subjects.

Verse 6 provides a crucial statement. The chronicler has not merely added to his source a negative reference to a possible dynasty, but has highlighted the verse by creating a chiasm.[70] This he has done by adding "they died" at the end of the verse, which matches the initial "and he died" in the Hebrew.

10:8-10. The chronicler underscores the deaths of Saul and his sons, to which v. 6 has drawn particular attention. The burial of their bodies reinforces the fact of their deaths. These verses have their own agenda: The humiliation Saul evaded in life (v. 4) over took him in death. So when the chronicler refers again to Saul's death (vv. 13-14), the reference now carries with it an allusion to this humiliation. Whereas he has generalized the original reference to Ashtaroth (1 Sam 31:10), in whose temple Saul's armor was placed, replacing it with "their gods," the chronicler has evidently imported mention of the temple of Dagon as the repository of Saul's severed head. Once the ark was taken as a prize of war to this very temple—and the idol of Dagon fell flat on its face in virtual homage (1 Sam 5:1-4)! And when David slew Goliath, the Philistines fled and Goliath's head was taken to Jerusalem (1 Sam 17:50-54). Now the boot was very much on the other foot. The allusions highlight by contrast the grimness of the present situation as one of utter defeat.[71]

10:11-12. The only glimmer of hope was the loyal bravery of the citizens of Jabesh-gilead, who had good reason to be grateful to Saul (see 1 Sam 11:1-11). But even this incident differentiates disparagingly between Saul's early promise and his tragic end. How the mighty are fallen!

10:13-14. The chronicler writes his own obituary for Saul. He develops the dynastic reference of his previous summary (v. 6), which becomes an appropriate transition to David's dynasty. So tragic and humiliating a death narrated in vv. 1-12 could only be due to cardinal sins committed in Saul's lifetime. These sins are first summarized as "unfaithfulness." This key term (מעל *ma'al*), here used with the cognate verb, has occurred earlier at significant points. In 5:25 the verb (NIV, "were unfaithful"; NRSV, "transgressed") described the sins of the northern tribes, which led to exile. In 9:1 the noun defined the sins of the southern kingdom of Judah, which likewise caused their exile (see 2 Chr 36:14). These previous cases suggest that here the chronicler found in his narrative about Saul a picture of Israel's fate of military defeat and exile (see vv. 7, 10), a paradigm for the sorry state of the contemporary people of God.

The reader's knowledge of Samuel–Kings is assumed, as is often the case in Chronicles. Two damning reasons from earlier places in the Samuel narrative are discovered, to unpack the charge of unfaithfulness.[72] (A third sin, neglecting the ark, will be added in 13:3; cf. 15:29.) The first sin is rejection of the prophetic word narrated in 1 Samuel 13:1 and 15. In 1 Sam 13:13-14, the verb "keep" is negatively associated with Saul's loss of kingship, as here, in a framework of accusation and punishment. The "word" (NIV; NRSV, "command") that Saul disobeyed is the prophet's message in 1 Sam 10:8. In 1 Sam 15:23, 26 the divine "word" that is flouted is that given through Samuel in 1 Sam 15:1-3. The chronicler is echoing Samuel's judgment oracles in 1 Samuel 13 and 15 and finds their fulfillment here. The second sin occurs in the incident narrated by 1 Sam 28:6-14: consulting the witch of Endor, which is interpreted as a religious sin, as 1 Sam 28:3 implies (cf. 2 Chr 33:6, in the light of Lev 19:31; Deut 18:11). It was no less than disobedience of

---

70. Williamson, *1 and 2 Chronicles*, 93.

71. Williamson, *1 and 2 Chronicles*, 92-95, with reference to Mosis, *Untersuchungen zur Theologie des chronisten Geschichtswerks*, 17-43, though he recognizes that not all of his argumentation is valid; Ackroyd, "The Chronicler As Exegete," 2-32, esp. 3-9 (= *The Chronicler in His Age*, 313-23). All these authors see a paradigmatic reference to exile, which will be considered below.

72. לשאול (*liš'ôl*) continues the previous על ('*al*), "because of [the word] . . . and because he consulted." See Rudolph, *Chronikbücher*, 94.

the Torah. Those conversant with the Samuel narrative will recall that Saul tried to consult the Lord and turned to a medium only when he received no answer (1 Sam 28:6). The chronicler found no room for this gray detail in his black and white presentation.

The verb דרש (*dāraš*), rendered "seek guidance" (NRSV; NIV, "guidance," "inquire") is another key term in the chronicler's religious vocabulary. It stands for a spiritual commitment that takes God's revealed will as normative for life (see 2 Chr 14:4). By consulting the witch of Endor, Saul showed himself essentially unspiritual, hostile to the Torah as well as to the Prophets.

The chronicler states baldly that "the LORD put him to death," recalling Samuel's forecast in 1 Sam 28:19 of the divinely instigated defeat of Israel's army and the death of the royal family. Behind the hand of Saul in taking his own life and behind the Philistine victory that occasioned it stood the figure of the divine judge as agent of warranted punishment. The loss of Saul's kingship necessitated a new king, David, the man after the Lord's own heart (1 Sam 13:14). For the transfer from one royal house to another, the chronicler uses a verb (סבב *sābab*) derived from 1 Kgs 12:15 (= 2 Chr 10:15). His intention is to demarcate structurally the special reigns of David and Solomon from preceding and subsequent history. The last clause of v. 14 is a theological interpretation of the human events of 11:1-3, as the final wording of 11:3, repeated in 12:23, shows. It may be taken as a heading for the next section, 11:1–12:40.

REFLECTIONS

If we compare this section with the long and complex account of Saul's reign in 1 Samuel 9–31, we see the starkness of the Chronicles version standing out. There is no room in it for his victories mentioned in 1 Chr 26:28, only for a story of shocking death and national defeat and a sketch of the personal defeats that led to them. Here is an illustration of the chronicler's use of narrative as a sermon to his contemporaries. Historiography has become a source of spiritual reflection. Particulars of one human life have been used as a window onto general issues that confront any reader who belongs to the community of faith in a later age. The New Testament uses this same approach. In 1 Cor 10:1-11, Paul interpreted the destruction of the Israelites in the wilderness as warnings not to sin against God: "These things happened to them as examples and were written down as warnings for us" (1 Cor 10:11 NIV).

At first sight, one might think of adducing as a New Testament parallel to this passage the text "the wages of sin is death, but the gift of God is eternal life" (Rom 6:23 NIV). Yet the widespread use of that text in an evangelistic context may lead us away from an understanding of what the chronicler intended. He was a spiritual director to the community of faith. So a better parallel would be Rom 8:13, clearly addressed to believers: "If you live according to the flesh, you will die; but if . . . you put to death the deeds of the body, you will live" (NRSV). We are meant to read the text as a challenge, to measure our own lives against the parable of Saul's experience and so to keep away from the broad road that leads to destruction (Matt 7:13).

While the narrative gives a good deal of space to Saul's death as a deterrent, the climax of the narrative looks back briefly to the seeds that yielded such a terrible harvest. The chronicler could appeal to his contemporaries' knowledge of the Saul narratives in 1 Samuel as background to his summary, while we modern readers are at a disadvantage unless we turn back to read them. The chronicler did not merely presuppose them, but imposed his own generalizing vocabulary of spirituality upon them. The key to the divine will was found in the revelation of the Law and the Prophets. Correspondingly, the teaching of our own canon of Scripture provides standards for our own spirituality. By such means we shall avoid, in Paul's terms, sowing to our own flesh and reaping corruption. Instead we will sow to the Spirit by doing what is right and contributing to the good of others (Gal 6:7-10).

1 Chronicles 11:1–12:40, David Crowned by All Israel

COMMENTARY

These next two chapters make up a literary unit. Its theme is the transfer of royal power to David, as the end of chap. 10 has announced. There David's kingship was represented as the Lord's work. Here the narrative emphasizes its human outworking; yet, at crucial points there are indications that God's will was being done.

At first sight the narrative hops disconcertingly from period to period, from place to place. David is anointed king at Hebron (11:1-3) and at once marches off to capture Jerusalem (11:4-9). A list of the high-ranking soldiers who participated in the coronation at Hebron (11:10-47) follows. Then there are flashbacks to tribal groups who threw in their lot with David at two earlier periods in his life (12:1-22). David's coronation at Hebron is again the topic of 12:23-40, with lists of the tribal contingents who attended (12:23-37), followed by an account of the celebrations (12:38-40).

There is method in this seeming randomness. A chiastic structuring dominates the section and gives it coherence, in an ABCDD'C'B'A' pattern.[73] The coronation and the celebratory meal that seals it make up the Hebron-based outer framework (A, 11:1-3; A', 12:38-40). Next to it are placed lists of the officers and conscript soldiers who attended (B, 11:10-47; B', 12:23-37). Military support for David at an earlier period, when he was based at Ziklag, is presented in an inner ring (C, 12:1-7; C', 12:19-22). At the double center stand reports of backing for David at an even earlier stage, while he was an outlaw in the wilderness, at "the stronghold" (D, 12:8-15; D', 12:16-18). The chiasm is used to present growing support for David and his transformation from a nervous victim of harassment (12:1, 17) to the secure bearer of power at the time of his coronation (11:9; 12:22).

Alongside this structural concern is another, in part independent, scheme: a roll call of David's army, from its commander Joab (11:6) and the Three and the Thirty and other leaders (11:10-47), to veterans who were "mighty warriors" (12:1-21), and finally down to the rank and file of this "great army" (12:22-37).[74]

The end of chap. 10 left the people of God defenseless, at the mercy of their enemies, and, in principle, bereft of land and liberty. Now they are portrayed as militarily strong. Over against the flight narrated in chap. 10, occasioned by Saul, strength and unity surround the figure of David. By the end of 1 Chronicles 12, king and people stand together, ready to win freedom under God. The Israel of David's days was intended to be an inspirational example. The unity of God's people was an ideal for which contemporary Judah must begin training! In 11:1-9 and 12:23-40 unity was finally achieved, but only gradually as one group after another pledged its allegiance to the new king, who had a divine claim on their support.

In 11:1-3 the chronicler rushes from Saul's death to the anointing of his successor as king of Israel in order to point out the contrast. In his biblical source four traumatic chapters elapsed between 1 Samuel 31 and 2 Samuel 5, on which latter chapter he relies in 11:1-9. He leaps to its eventual outcome. Afterward, however, he goes back to portray the hard climb to the top and the outstretching of hands that enabled David to get there. So this material is not so triumphalist as it first appears. An impressionistic contrast is drawn between the defeated, leaderless nation and a united, virile people under a God-given leader. It accentuates the slow but sure triumph of divine grace and also functions as a vision for the chronicler's constituency.

11:1-3. This paragraph is taken from 2 Sam 5:1-3, in which Israel confirms David's divine right to the throne (v. 2). At the end of v. 3, the chronicler adds his own theological commentary, as he often does. What has been narrated was a fulfillment of "the word of the

73. H. G. M. Williamson, " 'We Are Yours, O David': The Setting and Purpose of 1 Chronicles xii 1-23," *OTS* 21 (1981) 168-70; *1 and 2 Chronicles*, 105.

74. T. Willi, *Die Chronik als Auslegung* (Göttingen: Vandenhoeck & Ruprecht, 1972) 224n. 30.

LORD by Samuel" (NRSV). He has in mind the prophet's message of judgment to Saul in 1 Sam 15:28 and his mission to anoint David in advance in 1 Sam 16:1-13. He presupposes knowledge of this material. This accent on the divine "word" will reappear later, in his comments at 11:10 and 12:23 (NRSV).

The chronicler emphasizes the involvement of "all Israel" in this event (v. 1; cf. v. 3). In 2 Samuel 5 the context shows that the original phrase "all the tribes of Israel" (2 Sam 5:1) refers only to the northern tribes, and "all the elders of Israel" (2 Sam 5:3) to a northern delegation. The chronicler adapts the passage to reflect one of his favorite motifs. He will unpack the phrase "all Israel" as essentially composed of members of all the traditional tribes of Israel, northern and southern, in 12:38.

The chronicler also glosses over the fact that David had earlier been made king over Judah, before the northerners recognized him. In fact, the distinction drawn in 2 Sam 5:4-5 between Hebron as David's capital while king of Judah, and Jerusalem as his capital while he reigned over all Israel may not have been present in the text of Samuel used by the chronicler. It was evidently lacking in the Hebrew scroll 4QSamª, as it is in the Old Latin.[75] Mention of "the king" in 11:3 is a clue that the chronicler was aware of the two stages of kingship, but preferred not to draw further attention to it, as a distraction from his main theme.

11:4-9. The report of the capture of Jerusalem derives from 2 Sam 5:6-10. The material was significant for the chronicler in several ways.[76] For later readers, Jerusalem would automatically have been associated with David as his capital, and so crown and capital are naturally paired. It was also an opportunity to introduce Israel's army commander, as we have seen, initiating a review of David's army. Most significantly, it fits neatly into a larger scheme broached in chap. 9. After the unfaithfulness that caused Judah's exile, representatives of Judah returned and dwelt in their cities again and sacramentally, as it were, in Jerusalem, the traditional capital

(9:1-3). For the chronicler, Saul and David were archetypes of exile and restoration. After Saul's unfaithfulness (10:13), David comes to dwell in Jerusalem (11:7; unlike the NRSV and the NIV, the RSV uses "dwell" in both chap. 9 and chap. 11 for ישב [yāšăb]). This passage allows the chronicler to express the paradigmatic parallel. The union of Israel centered around David in Jerusalem was an ideal the chronicler hoped would again be realized eventually.

He once more introduces the concept of a united Israel into his text at v. 4. The 2 Samuel text has "his men," referring to David's mercenary troops. From the chronicler's ideal perspective it is "all Israel," who had just sworn allegiance to David and marched off with him to capture Jerusalem as a national undertaking in token of their allegiance. The city is graced with an antiquarian note, "that is Jebus," a literary borrowing from Judg 19:10-11.

In v. 5, the chronicler leaves out the rather obscure taunting from the Jebusites in 2 Sam 5:6. We do not know whether or how the novel reference to Joab related to the 2 Samuel text; 2 Sam 5:8 contains quite different material. Did it originate in a textual variant? Was it derived from an amplified text? It fits well into the overall text of 1 Chronicles, which otherwise mentions only the names of Joab's brothers, identifying them as such (11:20, 26). The reference may depend on a historical tradition. Joab was already commander in 2 Sam 2:13, but perhaps permanently so only from this time on.

In v. 7 the chronicler introduces the conjunction "therefore," so that not conquest but residence—important for him—explained the title "city of David." In v. 8, "the city" reflects a reading different from the Samuel text, shared by 4QSamª and the Greek Codex Vaticanus in place of the MT's "David." The relation of v. 8b to the text the chronicler used is uncertain, and so is the meaning of the verb rendered "restored" or "repaired" (יחיה yĕhayyeh). A building reference links well with the earlier part of the verse. It would also reflect a regular motif in the books of Chronicles, where building is often a mark of blessing that comes to faithful kings. So it is a fitting illustration of the divine presence bestowing favor on David (v. 9).

75. See P. K. McCarter, *2 Samuel*, AB 9 (Garden City, N.Y.: Doubleday, 1984) 130-31; McKenzie, *The Chronicler's Use of the Deuteronomistic History*, 42-43.
76. See D. A. Glatt, *Chronological Displacement in Biblical and Related Literatures* (Atlanta: Scholars Press, 1993) 174-78.

11:10-47. For vv. 10-41 the chronicler depends on the appendix in 2 Sam 23:8-39. The passage was meant to illustrate the exploits of David's military heroes, but he reinterprets it as a list of supporters present at the coronation, as v. 10 makes clear. So the list of names now gives examples of "all Israel," who recognized the divinely willed kingship of David. At the end of v. 10, the NIV and the NRSV reflect different renditions: either to follow the accentuation in the MT and render "concerning Israel" (NRSV), which accords with 15:2, or to relate the phrase to the verb, "[make king] over Israel," paraphrased in the NIV as "over the whole land," an option that agrees with 12:38.

There seems to be some textual confusion between the Three and the Thirty, two high-ranking groups, in v. 11 and again in vv. 20-21. It is difficult to be sure, but it seems logical at least to find reference to the Thirty (NRSV) in v. 21 in the light of the seemingly parallel v. 25 (cf. 27:6) and then so to read in v. 20a, as again the NRSV does. Similarly a reference to the Three is contextually fitting in v. 11 and has some support from 2 Sam 23:8, over against the MT, which the NIV reflects with "the officers."

11:10-14. Exploits of two of the Three are related. Comparison with 2 Samuel 23:1 shows that a chunk of text has fallen out. Two separate feats of the second and third of the Three have been telescoped. It is often suggested that this omission occurred only within the Chronicles tradition, but it may already have befallen the text of Samuel used by the chronicler. Certainly there is a coherent structural pattern in the present text of vv. 11-25. The exploits of two heroes, each introduced with an emphatic "he" (הוא *hû*), form an outer framework in vv. 11-14 and 20-25.[77] The reference to God-given victory at the end of v. 14 is in tune with the chronicler's own thinking, as is the similar refrain in 18:6, 13. Military victory was for him evidence of divine blessing on obedient kings.

11:15-19. This episode encapsulates both the devotion of David's supporters and his own devotion to God. It is taken from 2 Sam 23:13-17. David, with a soldier's nostalgia for home, longs for a drink from the well of enemy-occupied Bethlehem. For three anonymous members of the Thirty, his wish is their command, and they break through enemy lines to get the water for him. David cannot bring himself to drink it. He pours it on the ground as a sort of libation to God, regarding it as significant as the blood of those who had risked their lives for him. By this dramatic gesture, David both acknowledges his appreciation of their self-sacrificial loyalty and gives God the glory.

11:20-25. The "sons of Ariel" in v. 22 are better translated "champions" (REB). In v. 23 the chronicler evidently had a fuller text than the MT of 2 Sam 23:21, which is also reflected in some Greek traditions of 2 Samuel. The expansion recalls Goliath's height and his having a spear "like a weaver's beam" (1 Sam 17:4, 7; the ancient texts differ concerning the giant's stature).

11:26-47. At v. 26 the chronicler makes a break in the 2 Samuel 23 list by supplying a short heading before Asahel's name. Although "among the Thirty" in 2 Sam 23:24 is omitted here, he probably took the following names up to v. 41a as an enumeration of the Thirty, so warranting a separate heading. They are ranked with those from the Bethlehem area placed first, and include officers of mercenary contingents, notably "Uriah the Hittite" (v. 41). Verses 41b-47 comprise an independent list evidently available to the chronicler from another source. It is stylistically different from the preceding list and appears to enumerate a group of soldiers from the Transjordan.

12:1-7. There is a glance back to David's stay at Ziklag, a Philistine city in which the king of Gath established David in return for his military support (1 Sam 27:6). There is no parallel text in 1 or 2 Samuel. The chronicler depended to a greater or lesser extent on independent material for vv. 1-21, using it to promote his "all Israel" theme.[78] Irony is present in that, while Saul restricted David's movements, members of Saul's own tribe of Benjamin joined David's militia. A motif of help proffered to David at a time of weakness by various tribal groups comes to the fore in each of the next three paragraphs (vv. 1-22). The verbal forms in vv. 1, 17-19, 21-22 relating to "help" (עזר *'āzar*) are supplemented by some names in the lists: Ahiezer (v. 3), Joezer

77. De Vries, *1 and 2 Chronicles*, 128.

78. See Japhet, *1 & 2 Chronicles*, 257-58.

(v. 6), and Ezer (v. 9), the first and third receiving emphasis from the accompanying epithet "the chief."[79] We can now see that preparation for the wordplay was made in the list of names in chap. 11; i.e., Eleazar (v. 12) and Abiezer (v. 28).

12:8-15. David had received such support before. During his preceding period as an outlaw, when he had established a base in the wilds of Judah, a contingent of commandos from the tribe of Gad in the Transjordan "defected" (NIV) and threw in their lot with him. A number of such bases are mentioned in 1–2 Samuel: Adullam (1 Sam 22:14; 2 Sam 23:13-14), Ziph (1 Sam 23:14), Maon (1 Sam 23:24), and En-gedi (1 Sam 23:29). Perhaps the last one is in view here, since it is closest to the Transjordan.

12:16-18. These early days are now featured again. Two groups from Benjamin and Judah arrived at one of the bases. David's weakness, evidenced in his political circumstances in v. 1, is now expressed in terms of lack of morale. Friend or foe? All he can do is to appeal to God to expose them and bring about their downfall, if they are spies. The appeal, spoken out of human helplessness, receives a gracious answer from God. On the spot, Amasai, no regular prophet, is endowed with the spirit of prophecy to give a reassuring pledge of support from the new arrivals and from God.[80] The triple greeting of "peace" (NRSV), woven into his answer, is meant to give encouragement to David. It picks up a term used by David himself in v. 17: "peace" (NIV). He is surrounded by helpers and is even aided by God as patron of his cause, and so victory is assured. In fact, the complex term שָׁלוֹם (šālôm) here takes on the flavor of "success" (NIV). In the overall context this oracle of salvation reinforces Samuel's prophecy of kingship for David, mentioned in 11:3, 10.

12:19-22. The narrative revisits Ziklag to show how fresh followers were added, this time from the northern tribe of Manasseh, doubtless along with their contingents. David would have approached or even entered Manassite territory while accompanying the Philistine army, marching to its decisive encounter with Saul at Mt. Gilboa (cf.

1 Sam 29:1, 11), before he was dismissed and spared fighting against his own nation. They were able to aid him as he rescued prisoners from Amalekite raiders, who had sacked Ziklag in David's absence (1 Sam 30:1-20).

Verse 22 provides a transition to a new section, which reverts to the coronation at Hebron. The trickle of support in the early days turned into a stream and then a river, until each of Israel's tribes was amply represented in the army present at Hebron. He enthusiastically compares it to "an army of God," an army even by God's definition, "a camp of prodigious size" (NJB).

12:23-37. The tribal list is presented idealistically as the report of a muster of David's troops at Hebron.[81] Again the fulfillment of the Lord's prophetic word is brought to the fore, and the divinely formulated language of 10:14*b* is echoed in human terms. The list suits well the chronicler's intention, being a catalog of all the tribes with enormous numbers attached. Mention of "help" in v. 33 (here עֵדֶר *ʿādar*, an Aramaism) reiterates the earlier emphasis. He evidently made use of an existing list based on a military census. The grand total of 340,822 may be contrasted with the national conscript army of 30,000 in 2 Sam 6:1. It is possible to rationalize the numbers by regarding a "thousand" as a nominal term for what was a much smaller contingent.[82] However, the chronicler himself wanted to take the numbers at their maximum value, as an exuberant expression of an "army of God" (v. 22).

The list enumerates first the tribes associated with the kingdom and province of Judah (Judah, Simeon, Levi, Benjamin), and then the tribes to the north and in the Transjordan. The traditional number of twelve tribal groups is here achieved by amalgamating the two and a half Transjordanian tribes in v. 37. The numbers assigned to Judah and Benjamin are comparatively small, and an apology is felt to be necessary in the latter case.[83] The overall impression is to play up the contribution of the remaining tribes.

In v. 26 the Levites would naturally refer to the tribe of Levi, if vv. 27-28 did not add

---

79. Willi, *Die Chronik als Auslegung*, 224n. 30.
80. See Schniedewind, *The Word of God in Transition*, 70-74.

81. De Vries, *1 and 2 Chronicles*, 131.
82. For details see G. E. Mendenhall, "The Census Lists of Numbers 1 and 26," *JBL* 77 (1958) 61-63.
83. See Braun's suggestion that two separate lists have been joined. Braun, *1 Chronicles*, 169.

priestly contingents, so that now the Levites relate to the non-priestly part of the tribe. It is probable that the latter verses represent a supplement from the pro-priestly reviser to make room for the participation of priests on this great occasion. The twenty-two commanders of Zadok's house may be a link with the twenty-two priestly families in the late list of Neh 12:1-7.

12:38-40. The chronicler rounds off the unit with his own fervent description of the climactic coronation event. The phrase "arrayed in battle order" (NRSV) is better rendered "helping [עדרי *'ōdĕrê*] in battle" (cf. v. 11), echoing the prominent motif used earlier.[84] The narrative continues where 11:1-3

84. Williamson, *1 and 2 Chronicles*, 111.

left off, repeating the understanding of the previous list (v. 23) as Israel's conscript army, which represented "all Israel" (11:1-2) at the coronation. The chronicler typically refers to the feasting and joy that befitted this national occasion. The resolution and unanimity of David's support are emphasized. The covenant between king and people (11:3) is capped with a covenant meal by way of commitment and celebration (cf. Gen 26:30; Josh 9:11-15). It is an expression of solidarity and fellowship. The chronicler cannot resist a reference to three far-flung northern tribes among those who brought supplies for the potluck meal. They, too, belonged to Israel, he insists, and thus had a vital contribution to make.

REFLECTIONS

The chronicler highlights the reigns of David and Solomon as a special manifestation of divine blessing and as a revelation of guidelines for God's people thereafter. Saul's death was a graphic illustration of the road to exile, leading away from God. Yet it did not spell the demise of the divine purpose. From the ashes of failure and judgment arose a new flame of achievement. The Lord raised up a new king for Israel. God's redemptive grace stooped to the lowest point of human failure, lifting its victims to new life.

1. Both 11:1-3 and 11:4-9 start with one of the chronicler's beloved phrases, "all Israel"; and much of this literary unit amplifies its meaning. Just as the genealogies of chapters 1–9 were intended to teach, and as the renewed listing of tribal units in 12:23-37 will reinforce, so also the chronicler refused to identify the spiritual heirs of God's pre-exilic people as merely the tribes of Judah, Benjamin, Levi, and Simeon. Although many in post-exilic Judah so defined the latter-day Israel (see Ezra 4:1-3), the chronicler represents a broader view.

Many Christians belong to a particular group with which they strongly identify. They look over its walls with suspicion and distrust at other, unfamiliar manifestations of the Christian faith. And many more of us have such a background from which we have reached a wider standpoint. If the chronicler could have read John's Gospel, one of his favorite texts may have been from the prayer of Jesus: "that they may all be one . . . so that the world may believe that you sent me" (John 17:21). The way forward is not via the holy huddle that nervously finds security in its own rarefied traditions of the faith and pays lip service to some hidden, mystical unity that only God can see. Needed in each denomination are intrepid visionaries who are open to the potential of rich fellowship with others of God's flock outside their particular fold. If the Gospel of John was originally composed for the church to whom the First Letter of John was written—a dispirited group who had been victims of dissension and schism (see 1 John 2:18-19)—then one of the Evangelist's aims was to encourage them not to be so embittered by the experience as to withdraw into their shells, but to maintain a broad perspective.

The chronicler used David's coronation as an opportunity to encourage his fellow Judeans to think big about the dimensions of the community of faith. However, he had no vague, amorphous view of the spiritual traditions he espoused. God's revelation for him stood firmly within the tradition of the Davidic dynasty and of Jerusalem as its capital, which was to be the home of the Temple. "All Israel" travels to Jerusalem in David's company (11:4), and in spirit God's people had to continue making that journey. The chronicler had convictions that many "separated brethren" of his own day would have opposed (see 2 Chr 30:10-11). With evangelical fervor he was urging narrower believers in his constituency to invite them back to the purity of the traditional faith (12:17) and to regard themselves as incomplete until that task was achieved.

2. The chronicler acknowledged that his vision outstrips present realities—frustratingly so. The leap from chapter 10 to 11:1-9 did not occur overnight. In the middle of the unit readers are taken back to David at his wilderness base. Superficially it had a Robin Hood glamour (see 1 Sam 22:1-2), but the reality was far different. David was emotionally low, forced to flee from court and hounded by a psychotic king, his former patron turned foe. He did not know whom to trust or which of his companions might turn traitor. Politically there was a rival cause: the house of Saul, which enjoyed the support especially of his own tribe for a long time (12:29). It was an act of religious and political courage to throw in one's lot with David, daring to believe in God's prophetic word. Until that cause triumphed, it meant swimming against the tide and anticipating the "trouble" in this world that Jesus promised his own followers, with the encouragement that in principle he had already "overcome the world" (John 16:33 NIV).

The chronicler meant to echo the comparative weakness and discouragement of post-exilic Judah. Even as he did so, he laid before his readers the vision of David's ascent from weakness to strength. He skillfully wove it into his larger plan for a united Israel, challenging them to make it their own and advising them that the task would be arduous but worthwhile.

3. The divine thread that holds these two chapters together is the prophetic word of promise (11:3, 10; 12:23; cf. 12:18). Saul fatally ignored the word of the Lord (10:13) when it came in the form of a command. Now "all Israel" took as their command the divine promise of David's kingship (11:2). The chronicler placed a high value on the words of the prophets as divine revelation. To believe in the Lord involved believing the prophets (2 Chr 20:20). The prophetic word will often be quoted and applied in the so-called sermons scattered throughout Chronicles, but its fundamental role here is to affirm the new era of David and Solomon as a dispensation that stretched down to the chronicler's day and beyond. In New Testament terms, his perspective finds a parallel in the gospel about the Son of God descended from David, promised beforehand through God's prophets in the Holy Scriptures (Rom 1:2-3). In both cases the prophetic word functions as a warranty that a new era of divine grace has dawned, destined to reverberate through human history and challenge it to its core.

Working within the parameters of Old Testament history and theology, the chronicler promised that if God's people threw in their lot with David and the divine revelation associated with him, they would experience fully the restoration that lay beyond their "exile" of failure and frustration. Jerusalem, David's new home, was part and pledge of the whole land. United under a restored Davidic monarchy ruling from Jerusalem, Israel would win back the land in part of which they now lived by the grace of the Persian emperor. The patriarchs, too, were prophets, through whom the land of Israel was promised to Israel (16:15-18, 22). And salvation oracles in prophetic texts provided promises that the judgment of exile would one day be fully over and that the day of salvation, anticipated and inaugurated in the era of David and Solomon, would dawn for Israel. The chronicler, like the Christian, saw himself as standing in the middle of time, looking back in faith to the beginning of God's great work and looking forward in hope to its blessed fulfillment.

Meanwhile the believing, hoping community was not to sit idly, but to prepare for that day by embracing the unity that was theirs in principle and living in the light of their faith and hope. In New Testament terms, the chronicler brought a challenge to encompass in their vision the panorama of "all the saints" (Eph 3:18) and to make every effort "to maintain the unity of the Spirit in the bond of peace" as "one body" (Eph 4:3-4 NRSV). This single body could only progress as each part was working properly (Eph 4:16). Accordingly, the chronicler not only surveys the army of Israel en masse and enumerates its tribal dimensions, but also gives examples of individual commitment to the cause of David and his kingdom.

4. This emphasis is also served by the motif of help, which runs throughout these two chapters and elsewhere in the books of Chronicles. It is a comprehensive motif, covering not only help from other members of God's people, but also help from God and an obligation not to help the ungodly.[85] The element of divine help appears plainly in 12:18. The God who made promises did not stand aside, but provided gracious help, ensuring that the promises came true. David's role was not only to obey the revelation but also to accept divine help to that end. And such is always the case, as Paul attested in Acts 26:22. The element of divine help is accentuated by some of the names of David's supporters: Eleazar ("God helps," 11:12), Abiezer ("the [divine] father helps," 11:28), Ahiezer ("the [divine] brother helps," 12:3), and Joezer ("the Lord helps," 12:6).

The factor of not helping the enemy emerges in 12:19 in principle and will reappear in 2 Chr 19:2 (cf. 28:16, 23). There are boundaries that separate God's people from the world. The wise will discern occasions when they apply, lest they be "mismatched with unbelievers" (2 Cor 6:14 NRSV). Mostly, however, the motif of help is associated with cooperation, as we have seen. Behind David stood an army of active supporters. They rallied around their leader and so promoted God's work. The Letter to the Romans joins Chronicles in featuring at least two of these aspects of help. Paul celebrated the Spirit of God who "helps us in our weakness" (Rom 8:26) and also honored Phoebe as "a great help to many people, including me" (Rom 16:2 NIV).

5. Chapters 10–12 laid before post-exilic Judah two possibilities. For the chronicler, the current generation stood at a crossroads, to decide either for or against God. Saul still lurked in contemporary hearts, seeking to drag them down the path that led to continued exile from God and God's blessing. Yet David beckoned, challenging them to a breadth of spirit, exemplifying commitment to God and to Israel, and summoning them to a hope that the Lord would again work in such a fashion. It is helpful for us later readers to formulate this positive appeal in terms of Heb 12:1-2. The chronicler, taking David as pioneer, urged all of his readers, including us, to run with perseverance this arduous but rewarding race. Only of those who do so can it be truly said that they have "understanding of the times, to know what Israel ought to do" (12:32 NRSV).

85. Williamson, "We Are Yours, O David," 166-67; *1 and 2 Chronicles*, 105.

1 Chronicles 13:1–16:43, Giving God Pride of Place

OVERVIEW

David's two attempts to install the ark in Jerusalem, the first unsuccessful and the second successful, are the narrative framework that binds these chapters together. The section is united structurally by two series of repeated Hebrew terms. The English reader is made aware of two instances in the first series by the transliterated place-names "Perez

Uzzah," or "outburst against Uzzah" (13:11), and "Baal Perazim," or "Lord of break-throughs" (14:11). Both place-names are explained with the verbal form פָרַץ (*pāraṣ*), rendered "burst/broken out." These two cases are taken over from the source material in 2 Samuel 5:1–6, but are presented in reverse order. The chronicler uses the verb in two other ways. The first is in 13:2, rendered together with a second verb as "Let us send abroad" (NRSV) or "let us send word far and wide" (NIV). The other is in 15:13, which picks up 13:11. This fourfold wordplay will be investigated as it is encountered.

The other series of repetitions is more straightforward, except that both of the English versions lack consistency. One of the chronicler's key verbs, דרש (*dāraš*, "seek"), which was used twice in 10:13-14, surfaces again three times in this section. In 16:11 there is a call to "seek the LORD" (NRSV). It echoes two references to seeking the ark in 13:3 ("inquire of," NIV; "turn to," NRSV) and 15:13 ("inquire of [him]," NIV; "give proper care," NRSV). Here is a clue that seeking God and doing so by proper means constitute the message of this section.

1 Chronicles 13:1-14, David Tries to Move the Ark

COMMENTARY

God has been present behind the scenes in chaps. 10–12. The Lord was responsible for both Saul's death (10:14) and for David's growth to greatness (11:9). Now there is a national resolve to give God a central place in the community. This was to be achieved by paying tribute to the ark, the religious symbol of God's presence.

The chronicler draws a pointed contrast (v. 3) between the negative attitude toward the ark during Saul's reign and the positive one now displayed at the beginning of David's.[86] By using his spiritual key word דרש (*dāraš*), the chronicler recalls to his readers Saul's failure to "seek" the Lord (10:14) and offers another example of such behavior. To neglect the ark by leaving it in Kiriath-jearim (cf. 1 Sam 7:2) was symptomatic of Saul's neglect of God. The chronicler assumes that his readers know the history of the ark from 1 Samuel 4–7. For a generation the ark had languished at Kiriath-jearim, some eight miles west of Jerusalem. Now that a new era had dawned with David, this aberration could be tolerated no longer. It was necessary to restore the ark as a way of putting God at the heart of the community's life.

13:1. Verses 6-14 correspond to 2 Sam 6:2-11. The chronicler has supplied his own introduction in vv. 1-5. David consults first with the leaders of tribal contingents and then with the rank and file as an assembly that represents the nation. Both groups were present at Hebron for the coronation (12:23, 38), so that the narrative runs on without a break. David proposes to bring the ark to Jerusalem (cf. v. 13). The conquest of Jerusalem lies in the past (11:4). The chronicler loosely implies that the national army, gathered at Hebron, marched to Jerusalem to conquer it and then returned to continue the coronation celebrations. David's residence in Jerusalem (11:7; 13:13) does not square with this overall impression.

In 2 Samuel, the moving of the ark follows the two victories over the Philistines, but here it precedes them. One reason for this reordering is to make David's first act after the coronation a religious one, the transportation of the ark. The chronicler claims that the city of David (11:7; 13:13) soon becomes the city of God. The residence of the human king becomes that of the divine king (cf. v. 6).

13:2-4. In v. 2 a change in the MT's accentuation would supply an impersonal verb in the second condition, with the force "and if there is a breakthrough brought about by the LORD our God." The LXX understood it similarly: "and if success is brought about by the LORD our God."[87] So does the REB: "and if the LORD our God opens a way." This is the first instance of one of the key words

86. For 1 Sam 14:18, see McCarter, *I Samuel*, 237, 240.

87. See Allen, *The Greek Chronicles*, 1:128.

in the section, פרץ (*pāraṣ*). The chronicler appears to be anticipating the third, positive instance in 14:11, God's breaking through the Philistines and giving David victory. This evidence of blessing will encourage the king to continue his quest to bring the ark to Jerusalem. In the chronicler's narrative it acquires the value of a divine affirmation that David may go ahead. This wordplay supplies a further reason why the chronicler places David's victories over the Philistines after his initial attempt to transport the ark.

First, however, there has to be a full assembling of the people. "The whole assembly" (v. 2) and "all the people" (v. 4) were in fact the representative body of tribal contingents. The new enterprise merits even greater representation than David's coronation, as God is greater than the human king. So the rest of Israel, absent in 12:38, is now summoned. Along with the laity, the presence of the priests and the Levites is sought for this religious occasion (the NIV's "and also" is better than the NRSV's "including"). They will feature prominently in the chronicler's narrative in chap. 15, but allusion will also be made to them at 13:8. Reference to the cities and pasturelands of the priests and Levites directs the reader back to the list in 6:50-81.

13:5-6. The chronicler's inclusive term "all Israel" in v. 5 is pointedly repeated in v. 6 and also in v. 8. This threefold occurrence shows its importance for the passage. In v. 6, as the chronicler joins the 2 Samuel text, he makes this point by replacing with the idealized "all Israel" the limited reference to a representative group of 30,000 conscripts. This theme of "all Israel" is underscored by making the northern and southern frontiers of Israel as wide as possible. They are evidently defined in terms of the Davidic Empire and accord with the frontiers of Solomon's kingdom in 2 Chr 7:8.[88] Accordingly, "Shihor," the easternmost branch of the Nile, is used loosely for Wadi el-Arish, corresponding to "the Wadi of Egypt" at 2 Chr 7:8. It is significant that such boundaries are drawn for the ideal Israel in Num 34:2-12 (cf. Ezek 47:15-19), while in Josh 13:1-7 the promised land is similarly defined, with precise mention of Shihor, which clearly inspired the present

reference.[89] The Davidic Empire and the promised land are fused in the chronicler's mind as the ideal shape of Israel's territory. The land that belonged to Israel by divine gift would one day be restored to the people of God, who now occupied far less (see 16:15-20, 35).

13:7-10. In v. 7 the chronicler has omitted the second verbal form in 2 Sam 6:3, "and they brought it." This verb, נשא (*nāśāʾ*), bears religious connotation, as its use with reference to the Levites in 15:2, 15 (rendered "carry") will make clear.[90] To keep the word here would have brought confusion into the story. Another significant change occurs in v. 8, with the addition of "trumpets" to the list of musical instruments (2 Sam 6:5) that were used to celebrate the transportation of the ark. The lyres, harps, and cymbals have now implicitly become the instruments played by the Levites of v. 2, while the trumpets are blown by the priests, as the description of the second ceremony will explicitly mention (15:16, 24; cf. 15:28). In the chronicler's own day, music had an official religious setting, and he sees the ancient ceremony through contemporary lenses.

On the other hand, it is unlikely that the difference in v. 9 between the infinitive "to hold" or "to steady" and the past tense in the text of 2 Sam 6:6 is an intensification on the chronicler's part. The infinitive was probably already in the text he used.[91] Nor is the immediacy of the phrase "before God" in v. 10 a heightening of the chronicler's narrative. His text of 2 Samuel seems to have had the same reading, rather than "beside the ark of God," which appears in the MT of 2 Samuel.[92]

13:11-14. To a large extent the story follows the contours it has in 2 Samuel. The introduction (vv. 1-4) increases the sense of shock and anticlimax at the failure of the venture. The chronicler will explain it in chap. 15, but one must respect the narrative sequence and wait until then. The mission is disastrously short-circuited. The numinous

88. Williamson, *Israel in the Books of Chronicles*, 123-24; *1 and 2 Chronicles*, 115.

89. See S. Japhet, "Conquest and Settlement," 209-10; *1 & 2 Chronicles*, 277-78.

90. M. Fishbane, *Biblical Interpretation in Ancient Israel* (Oxford: Clarendon, 1985) 393.

91. See McKenzie, *The Chronicler's Use of the Deuteronomistic History*, 49. For the name variants "Chidon" in Chronicles and "Nacon" in the MT of 2 Samuel, see McCarter, *2 Samuel*, who regards both as secondary to "Nodan" in 4QSamª.

92. McCarter, *2 Samuel*, 165; McKenzie, *The Chronicler's Use of the Deuteronomistic History*, 49-50. Cf. v. 8 and the parallel 2 Sam 6:5.

holiness of which the ark partook has here a dangerous physical quality like an electrical charge (cf. Num 4:18-20; 1 Sam 6:19-20). As with the parallel in 2 Samuel, the episode is an installment of a larger story, but the chronicler's insertion of chap. 14 increases the tension. He tantalizingly leaves loose ends dangling until, like a mystery writer, he finally explains its twists and turns. The narrative does end with a glimmer of hope, blessing enjoyed by the family of Obed-edom, which will be explained in terms of a large family in 26:4-5. The ark is left with him for three months.

REFLECTIONS

1. The chronicler's introduction brings David's good intentions to the fore—not the good intentions the proverb tells us the road to hell is paved with, mental aspirations that die before seeing the light of day. David's intentions are matched with an energetic endeavor to realize them and are backed with sincere integrity. This dedication makes the subsequent failure hard to handle. Who has not known the consternation of a serious setback, when all seemed to be going well in a life committed, one thought, to God's will? It is at this realistic midpoint that the chapter ends.

2. Another favorite theme of the chronicler appears here: seeking God. Verse 3 mentions seeking the Lord via the ark. To neglect the ark was to neglect God, a symptom of the way to exile chosen by Saul. The road to restoration calls for an active concern for God and so for the discharge of religious duties that serve to express it. Whatever denomination we belong to, we all have religious rites and forms that are part of that denominational tradition, whether high or low, traditional or contemporary. Of course, any means of grace can degenerate into "a human commandment learned by rote," if "the hearts" of those who perform it are "far from" the Lord (Isa 29:13 NRSV). There is an opposite danger when religious habits are disregarded. As the Jewish scholar Israel Abrahams shrewdly observed, "What can be done at any time and in any manner is liable to be done at no time and in no manner."[93]

The chronicler's ordering of his material gives top priority to the things of God. Here David seeks first the kingdom of God (cf. Matt 6:33) in seeking the ark that celebrated God's kingship ("enthroned on/between the cherubim," 13:6). For the chronicler and his first readers, just as for us, the story needed mental reinterpretation. The ark no longer rested as a nucleus of worship in the holy of holies of the Second Temple. Although the ark was gone, what it stood for remained. There was still a conviction of the vital presence of God with the worshiping community, and still a need to acknowledge the Lord as King of kings.

3. As the story proceeds, these ideals shatter into (as yet) inexplicable fragments. David reacts in two ways to this crisis. First, he is angry. It is the anger of frustration hammering impotently at a slammed door. Such anger underlies the laments in the psalms, expressing the disappointment and resentment with which we typically respond to crisis. Second, David is afraid (cf. Acts 5:11), realizing that he is in the presence of a mysterious power he can neither control nor comprehend. He has lost the rapport with God he seemed to enjoy up to 13:8. One might regard this fear as a more appropriate response than anger, but the human frame is too weak to attain to spirituality at a single leap. One must work steadily through emotions triggered by crisis. David and reader alike can only wait, clinging to such redeeming features as bolster faith and hope.

93. I. Abrahams, *Studies in Pharisaism and the Gospels*, 2nd ser. (Cambridge: Cambridge University Press, 1924) 84.

1 Chronicles 14:1-17, God Honors David's Intentions

COMMENTARY

Chapter 14 fills the three-month gap—a literary device that conveys a sense of waiting—between the two attempts to bring the ark to Jerusalem. Material from 2 Sam 5:11-23, placed there before the first attempt, is used here to fill the intervening period, though historically the reports of both David's involvement with Hiram and the birth of thirteen children in Jerusalem belong much later in his reign.

Three incidents are borrowed from 2 Samuel 5: Hiram's gifts to David, his growing family, and his double victory over the Philistines. They represent a flood of divine blessings filling David's life. For the chronicler such blessings result from David's seeking God via the ark (see 13:3). Later in Chronicles he will present King Asa as seeking God and victorious (2 Chr 14:4, 7, 9-15) and King Jehoshaphat as receiving tribute and riches after seeking the Lord (2 Chr 17:4-5). David's reversal of Saul's bad example meant that he could receive divine approval.[94]

14:1-2. God's blessing is first traced in the area of foreign tribute. The chronicler appears to have understood the gifts of the king of Tyre as tribute from a vassal. In 2 Chr 2:14, in a letter from Hiram to Solomon, David is referred to as "my lord." In v. 2 he gladly takes over the interpretation of this event given in 2 Samuel. Behind the human honor was the Lord's providential purpose to confirm David's royal power, as will also be the case for Jehoshaphat (2 Chr 17:5). Whereas Saul lost his kingship (10:14), David's was put on a firm footing. It was "exalted," as Hezekiah's will be, another good king (2 Chr 32:23). The chronicler adds a characteristic word, למעלה (lĕma'lâ, "highly"), to recognize David's imperial greatness. Such recognition is balanced with an acknowledgment of the Lord as the power behind the throne and the source of David's success, and also with an awareness of his role as servant to his subjects. The king's function was to serve the

interests of the God who supported him and the people he ruled (cf. 13:6; 17:14).

The chronicler doubtless saw a deeper significance in v. 2b than social justice or economic prosperity enjoyed by David's subjects. His monarchy was the means by which God's will was being realized for the people of Israel. The hint of a continuing dynasty broached in vv. 3-7 fits this broader horizon. The chronicler could not conceive of Israel's ultimate future without a descendant of David (cf. 3:1-24).

14:3-7. Sons and daughters born to David are understood as a further indication of divine blessing. The chronicler has retained "more" from his text of 2 Samuel in v. 3, indicating that he was aware of the earlier list of children born at Hebron (2 Sam 3:2-5), which in fact he cited in 3:1-4. Mention of concubines in the master text, alongside wives, is omitted, presumably to safeguard the legitimacy of the children.[95] There is an implicit contrast with Saul's loss of his sons in 10:6. David's family raises dynastic hopes. Solomon will turn out to be the chosen successor (22:9-10; 28:6).

14:8-12. The rest of the chapter is devoted to David's victories over the Philistines. Again Saul's negative experience lies in the background, as one defeated by them. Whereas the king who did not seek God became a loser, this king who put the Lord first is a winner. In the chronicler's hands the Samuel text takes on new significance.

There is a slight harmonization with chaps. 11–12. "Israel" in the text of 2 Samuel becomes "all Israel," in line with the chronicler's earlier emphasis. "Baal-perazim" in v. 11 and David's accompanying interpretation also reflect a previous concern of Chronicles. Perez-Uzzah, God's outbreak against Uzzah (13:11), is compensated for by a breakthrough against David's enemies. Divine curse gives way to blessing. This use of the key word פרץ (pāraṣ) recalls the first use in 13:2. The Lord has now broken through in

94. Williamson, *1 and 2 Chronicles*, 116-19, judiciously following Mosis, *Untersuchungen zur Theologie des chronisten Geschichtswerks*, 55-79.

95. McCarter, *2 Samuel*, 147.

a clear demonstration of favor. The initial condition is satisfied. Now David can resume his honorable attempt to move the ark to Jerusalem.

This seeker after God lived up to his reputation. He "inquired of God" before both campaigns (vv. 10, 14). It is no accident that this verb (שאל *šā'al*) occurred with reference to Saul in 10:13 ("consulted," NRSV, NIV), where he inquired of a medium instead of the Lord. The burning of the captured images of the Philistines' gods (v. 12) conspicuously differs from their being taken back as trophies of war in the MT of 2 Sam 5:21. There is disagreement as to whether the chronicler's text of 2 Samuel already had this different reading.[96] Anyway, it was probably significant for the chronicler that David follows in such matters the dictate of the Torah, as laid down in Deut 7:5, 25.

14:13-16. In the second campaign an attack from the rear evidently made it impossible for the Philistines to withdraw at the western end of the valley of Rephaim, to the southwest of Jerusalem. They are forced to retreat by a northern route. In Chronicles the retreat is made by way of Gibeon, rather than Geba (so 2 Sam 5:25 MT). The LXX of 2 Samuel reflects the same reading as does Chronicles, and so it may already have been present in the chronicler's text of 2 Samuel, unless the LXX reading is simply the result of textual assimilation. The variant is often explained as an allusion to Isa 28:21.[97] That text celebrates great victories wrought by the Lord on Israel's behalf at Mt. Perazim and in the valley of Gibeon, with the latter probably referring to Joshua 10. The chronicler, no stranger to prophetic literature, may have had Isa 28:21 in mind and hence intended to glorify David's victories.

14:17. This observation is found only in 1 Chronicles. The historian is meditating on David's foreign relations, most particularly those with Tyre and the Philistines. He regards them as striking examples of general international renown, doubtless thinking of chaps. 18–20 (esp. 18:11). He interprets this phenomenon in line with the reflection he took over from 2 Samuel in v. 2. These international dealings reflect the Lord at work, providentially bestowing blessing, and will find echoes in the reigns of David's faithful heirs Jehoshaphat and Hezekiah (2 Chr 17:10-11; 20:29; 32:22-23). Such weal in the foreign affairs of the Davidic dynasty created an expectation that an illustrious king would be restored in God's good time.

96. See W. E. Lemke, "The Synoptic Problem in the Chronicler's History," *HTR* 58 (1965) 352; McKenzie, *The Chronicler's Use of the Deuteronomistic History*, 62; but note Williamson's reply, *1 and 2 Chronicles*, 118-19.

97. Notably by Mosis, *Untersuchungen zur Theologie des chronisten Geschichtswerks*, 65. See also Williamson, *1 and 2 Chronicles, 119.*

REFLECTIONS

1. The chronicler's new placement of this material has made it serve his own concerns, functioning as a literary interlude. Its present message is that God has honored David's good intentions, though not Uzzah's, unfortunately. Did the ancient writer, too, experience a sense of unfairness that well-intentioned Uzzah should die? Life, like war, is often so unfair. One person, too close to the catastrophe, is engulfed by it. Another survives, shell-shocked and wondering at the randomness of providence. At last there comes the signal of God's will, expressed in terms of the wordplay of the section (13:2; 14:11). David's efforts at seeking God brought an appreciative response, for the Lord stood behind these human experiences, we are told in 14:2 and 17. God measures spiritual progress by endeavors, not by results.

2. The chronicler wanted his readers to find in these happy consequences an incentive for their own spiritual lives. Jesus also proclaimed such an incentive in his exhortation, "Seek first [God's] kingdom and his righteousness, and all these things will be given to you as well" (Matt 6:33 NIV; cf. Heb. 6:10). David's heart was in the right place. There is a close parallel in 2 Chr 30:19, where again the chronicler traces the blessed outcome of seeking God. Hezekiah prayed that Israelites who had unavoidably failed to undergo proper purification rites might participate with impunity in the Passover celebrations. The ground of his prayer is that they had "set their hearts to seek God . . . even though not in accordance with the sanctuary's rules of cleanness" (NRSV). David, too, it will be revealed in chapter 15, had made a ritual mistake, but he had certainly set his heart to seek God. In his case he had to go through the whole ceremony again, but his efforts did not go unrewarded. The chronicler's emphasis on motivation shows how far from legalism his concept of spirituality was.

3. David has taken the high road, while Saul took the low road to failure. Chapter 10 must reverberate in readers' ears as they study chapter 14. Where foreigners were concerned, David was the head, and Saul was the tail (Deut 28:13, 44). The chronicler is posing a warning: Along which road are you traveling, my readers—a road of backsliding and virtual exile or a road of restoration and blessing? As we identify with the things of God and live accordingly, the chronicler's purpose will be honored.

4. The reflection borrowed in 14:2 sets before us ideals of human leaders, who are to be subject to God and sensitive to the needs of subordinates. David is empowered not for his own sake, but to do the will of God and to promote the interests of the nation. Power tends to corrupt, but as David's star reaches its zenith, his resolve is that God should be glorified and the people should profit. His consultation with national representatives and concern for the divine will in 13:1-2 already illustrated such ideals.

5. The reflections in 14:2 and 17 also point toward the future by tracing the inauguration of eschatological ideals. The establishment of the dynasty, at which 14:3-7 hints, gave birth to a hope still dear to the chronicler's heart centuries later and shaped his understanding of Israel's future under God. The David of 14:2 and 17 finds a parallel in the Christ of Eph 1:21-22. God has made him "the head over all things for the church" and already placed him "above every name that is named, not only in this age but also in the age to come" (NRSV). Here "all lands" and "all nations" (NRSV) in 14:17 hint at the universal submission promised to David's line from "the nations" and "the ends of the earth" in Ps 2:8-9, a psalm that has an eschatological function in the psalter and to which the christology of the NT is no stranger. A divine arc is drawn for both the chronicler and the Christian between past revelation and future hope. Both stand in the gap between those two points, looking forward to a hope stamped by that past.

1 Chronicles 15:1–16:3, David Moves the Ark Properly

COMMENTARY

Chapter 14 left unresolved the issue of bringing the ark to Jerusalem, though it did establish favorable conditions for doing so. Now the narrative reaches a climax, explaining what went wrong the first time and how it was to be done. The ark is duly moved, and worship is offered in Jerusalem—worship that constitutes a spiritual landmark. The passage is based on the account of the second, successful attempt to convey the ark in 2 Sam 6:12a-19a. The chronicler expands these eight verses fourfold, making the

episode especially important. He turns it into an injunction to honor the Torah, specifically its guidelines for worship.

15:1-24. Reproduction of the 2 Samuel narrative is left until the end of the passage (15:25–16:3). What precedes is concerned with preparations for and clarification of the ark narrative, which will itself be correspondingly amplified as it is quoted. First, 2 Sam 6:17 (= 1 Chr 16:1) mentions a tent David had set up for the ark in Jerusalem. Room needed to be made, so in v. 1 the king carefully prepares a site for the ark and erects the tent, in addition to engaging in his own building projects (14:1). This preparation is underlined in vv. 3 and 12. It is a key motif of the passage, revealing David's active concern for the ark, which is the opposite of the neglect shown by Saul (13:3). Did the chronicler have in mind Ps 132:3-5, which mentions David's vow not to enter his own home or rest until he had found "a place for the LORD," by bringing the ark to Jerusalem? Although David builds houses for himself (v. 1), it is not stated until 17:1, after the installation of the ark in the place prepared for it, that David took up residence in his house. Here is diligence, indeed, for the things of God and a spiritual lesson for others to emulate.

Second, the story in 2 Samuel speaks first of David's bringing up the ark and then of "David and all the house of Israel" (the latter group is also mentioned at the end of the account, 2 Sam 6:12, 15, 19). This information calls for an explanation about another assembling of "all Israel" after the three months time lag. This explanation duly appears in v. 3. The chronicler is alluding to 13:5, the total participation of the believing community envisioned there. When, however, he quotes 2 Sam 5:12b in v. 25, David is joined by "the elders of Israel and the commanders of thousands" as his fellow participants, echoing the partial representation in 11:3 and 13:1. Did the chronicler have in view a representational procession over to Obed-edom's house and a comprehensive one back to the temple site? Perhaps, but the main point is a literary one, that earlier threads of the coronation celebration and of deliberations to move the ark are being drawn together in order to convey its climactic importance.

The chronicler's third and crucial clarification concerns the preparing of personnel for the procession and its aftermath. The ark narrative in 2 Samuel no longer spoke of "transporting" (הרכיב *hirkîb*) the ark on a new cart. Instead, it mentioned those who were "carrying" (נשא *nāśā*) the ark in 2 Sam 6:13, with which 1 Chr 15:26 is parallel.[98] This information provides the chronicler with a clue that David had to pursue his seeking

of God at a deeper level. In v. 13 there is an admission from David that, literally, "we did not seek (דרש *dāraš*) it in the proper way." So they had to search the Torah to discover the appropriate manner to transport the ark. The chronicler found it in Deut 10:8, which stipulated that the tribe of Levi is to "carry [*nāśā*] the ark of the covenant of the LORD." In the priestly writings of the Pentateuch, this work was allocated to the associate clergy, the Levites, and so it is in Chronicles (v. 2). The exact procedure is spelled out in v. 15. The Levites were to carry on their shoulders poles that supported the suspended ark. In this case explicit reference to the Torah is made, presumably to Exod 25:13-15 (cf. Num 7:9; בדים [*baddîm*] is used for poles in Exodus 25:1, but here a different word, מטות [*mōṭōt*]; cf. the use of מוט [*môṭ*] as a flat carrying frame for vessels in Num 4:10, 12). These priestly texts already have the Levites in view, specifically the Kohathite clan. The poles kept the carriers at a safe distance from the ark, respecting its holiness: "They must not touch the holy things, or they will die" (Num 4:15 NIV). Repetition of poor Uzzah's fate is avoided by maintaining an insulating space around the holy ark.

The "word of the LORD" (v. 15) was of paramount importance for the chronicler. In chaps. 10–12 it had been a prophetic word. Now it stands for the Torah, "as Moses had commanded." The Lord was honored by obeying Scripture. The chronicler highlights this solution by recalling the negative use of the section's key word: פרץ (*pāraṣ*, "burst/broken out") in 13:11 and explaining in David's speech that the judgment on Uzzah had been evidence of the Lord's displeasure for disobeying the Torah's prescription.

The chronicler understood this event to have affected later levitical responsibilities. In v. 2 he fused Deut 10:8 with the overlapping Deut 18:5, where the tribe of Levi, including the Levites, is given a divine commission to "minister in the LORD's name always" (NIV). The chronicler found in the ark narratives a definition of part of the Levites' ministry. He will argue in 16:4, 37 that this ministry entailed choral music. He associated the first attempt to move the ark with their musical participation, as the list of musical instruments in 13:8 is meant to convey (cf. 13:2).

---

98. This verb also occurred in a general sense ("brought") at 2 Sam 6:3 and was omitted in 1 Chr 13:7.

Now they come into their own, again implicitly playing

the cymbals, harps, and lyres in v. 28 as well as conveying the ark. In vv. 16-24 the chronicler will take the opportunity to trace back to David's initiative the organization of the levitical singing musicians, which developed in post-exilic times. It is uncertain whether these verses represent the stage of development in the chronicler's day or a little later. They represent the latest post-exilic stage, with Heman in first place, before Asaph, and the third group associated not with Jeduthun but with Ethan, as in 6:31-48. In 16:37-41, however, a slightly earlier stage, probably a generation earlier, is reflected, with Asaph in first place, Heman in second, and Jeduthun in third (see the Introduction).[99]

In vv. 5-10 a list of Levites available to the chronicler is applied to the present situation by means of the heading in v. 4 and the summary in v. 11. It cites representatives of the three clans of Levites, the clans of Kohath, Merari, and Gershom, together with their family heads at the particular time when the list was composed. In addition, three Kohathite subclans, those of Elizaphan, Hebron, and Uzziel (cf. 6:18; Num 3:30) are here elevated to independent status, as in the case of Elizaphan in 2 Chr 29:13. Mention is also made of priests who participated in vv. 4, 11, 14, and 24, in the last case as trumpeters. This last reference presupposes Num 10:10. Otherwise, their presence may stem from an awareness of Num 4:5, where they are to be responsible for covering the ark. Their normative role in sacrifices (15:26; 16:1) and their responsibility to place the ark in the tent (16:1) may also be in view.[100]

So vv. 1-24 are concerned with preparations for the ceremony of 15:25–16:3. The passage is structurally governed by the two commands of David in vv. 2 and 16 for Levites to carry the ark and to be responsible for the choral music. There are two subdivisions, vv. 2-15 and vv. 16-24. Verse 15 has an anticipatory role, as a comment on v. 26. This text presents arrangements that would guide the procession of the ark.

Verse 16 announces the second great preparation, with a double list of participants and the instruments they were to play provided in vv. 17-21.[101] The religious musicians of the post-exilic period were only gradually given levitical status, which they lacked at the early stage represented by the list preserved in Ezra 2:41; Neh 7:44. The chronicler typically projects later customs back to an earlier period. Obed-edom, presumably the naturalized Gittite who took care of the ark in 13:14, is adopted into the musicians' ranks in vv. 18, 21 (and in 16:5). Footnotes incorporated into the text at v. 18 ("gatekeepers") and v. 24 ("Obed-edom . . . ark") about his status as a gatekeeper seem to reflect different claims about the post-exilic role of Obed-edom's descendants. Two brief items concerning the musical director and the "gatekeepers" are supplied in vv. 22-23. Presumably the latter were responsible for security during the ceremony.

15:25-28. The chronicler now joins the text of 2 Samuel. In v. 26 the same number of sacrificial animals appears in 4QSam[a] (cf. 2 Sam 6:13 MT). In v. 27 the aberrant first clause represents probably the chronicler's attempt to deal with an indistinct text, reading the verb מכרכר (*mĕkarkēr*, "was dancing") in 2 Sam 6:14a as מכרבל (*mĕkurbāl*, "was clothed"), an interpretation influenced by v. 14*b*. Certain additions are made to harmonize the text with his own earlier perceptions. The Levites are duly given a prominent part in vv. 26-27. The success of the new mode of moving the ark is credited to divine help, an echo of 12:18. This time God did not hinder, but blessed human compliance with the divine will. In a major change from the 2 Samuel text, the ark is now repeatedly called "the ark of the covenant of the LORD/God" (vv. 25-26, 28-29; also 16:6, 37). This designation has been formally triggered by Deut 10:8, cited earlier. The ark was a symbol of the covenant relationship between God and

99. Williamson, *1 and 2 Chronicles*, 120-25, attributes the list in 15:16-24 to the chronicler, rather than to a redactor.

100. See Kleinig, *The Lord's Song*, 50n. 3. Kleinig's understanding of 15:16-24 in terms of a processional order at the ark ceremony can hardly stand without consideration of diachronic factors. Williamson, *1 and 2 Chronicles*, 123, among others, has taken the references to priests as the work of the pro-priestly reviser. Some mention of priestly participation by the chronicler is not unexpected; see 13:2 and the pointed reference to trumpets in 13:8. In v. 4, however, the sole designation of the priests as "the descendants of Aaron" is characteristic of secondary passages, and the context refers only to the Levites' duties. 15:24*a* is set in a secondary context and may be an addition developed from 16:6, designed to restore a priestly balance.

101. The terms "Alamoth" and "Sheminith" in vv. 20-21 are transliterated because they are no longer understood. They refer to musical modes or melodies.

Israel. When the chronicler thought of the ark, he was reminded that Israel was God's people, the object of divine care and claim. These instances cluster around the three references to the covenant (16:15-17). Overall, the chronicler seems to have taken the Lord's covenant with David as a new, once-for-all arrangement that subsumed within it all that was best in God's earlier relations with Israel (cf. 2 Chr 13:5; 21:7). We shall observe the development of this thought in chap. 16.

15:29. The incident of Michal's scorn takes on new meaning in this context. It becomes a reminder of Saul's neglect of the ark. This "daughter of Saul" was the odd person out that day. She was the would-be killjoy in this atmosphere of communal joy. As David and "all Israel" honored the ark and worshiped God, she failed to perceive the significance of the event. It was a case of "like father, like daughter." Michal chose to follow Saul's path away from God and God's people.

REFLECTIONS

1. The chronicler's resolution of the failure of the first attempt to move the ark to Jerusalem is achieved by recourse to the Torah. The new, unprofaned cart and the willing helpers in chapter 13 were not good enough. Seeking God was not to be an arbitrary human endeavor (cf. 1 Sam 6:7), but was to follow a sacred pattern already revealed in the Torah. Christians have not been furnished in the New Testament such detailed information about institutional aspects of their faith. "If every church must be built on the exact model of the Church at Corinth, at Ephesus or at Antioch, we are in hopeless difficulties. The plans have been lost, and the specifications destroyed."[102] The New Testament does not echo the Old Testament's prescriptions of institutional order. The sacraments of baptism and communion and such general principles as unity, faith, love, and the need that "all things be done decently and in order" (see 1 Corinthians 10:1–14) are what the church has received as its heritage. Denominational traditions have variously clothed with culturally appropriate flesh and blood the skeletons of these practices and principles.

From a broader perspective, however, the chronicler and the Christian think alike. The new order, originated under David and commended by the chronicler as still relevant to believers in his own day, continued to take its cue from the Torah. Each new revelation of God in the Bible takes a step forward in one or a few great respects, and otherwise preserves the older faith. In chapters 10–12, the "word of the LORD" was prophetic. Now, in 15:15, it is from the Torah. The chronicler regarded the Law and the Prophets as the divine word for contemporary Israel. In them was to be sought expression of God's will for each generation. This emphasis on the Scriptures is an essential trait of the books of Chronicles. Invested with divine authority, Scripture was to be the basis of Judah's self-understanding and life-style. Similarly the New Testament church was later to echo this value attached to the Old Testament scriptures, now composed of a greater canonical whole, and to find in them positive and negative guidelines as to what to believe and how to behave (2 Tim 3:16).

2. If the chronicler turned back to the Torah to hear a recording of the divine voice, here about religious practice, then he also had a dynamic conception of the living presence of God at work in the community of faith. "God [had] helped the Levites" who were carrying the ark (15:26). The Lord is envisioned not as the inspirer of the Torah who then left Israel to obey ancient commands as best they could, but as providentially present with them and promoting their participation in the divine will. The same sentiments will reappear in David's prayer in 28:18-19—namely, that God would turn Israel's hearts toward the light and help Solomon keep the Torah. Similarly, according

102. R. W. Dale, *Essays and Addresses* (London: Hodder and Stoughton, 1909) 31.

to Psalm 119, where God's "law" or Torah is more than the Pentateuch and included at least Isaiah, Jeremiah, and Proverbs, Israel is to depend not only on written revelation but also on the living God, whose constant help is sought in prayer.

3. The new era associated with David and Solomon meant a step forward, supremely in the building of the Temple, for which a vital beginning is made here. The Second Temple had the same value as the First for the chronicler. These pre-temple chapters implicitly present a message about temple worship for God's people in the chronicler's time to heed. Solomon duly incorporated the Davidic innovations into temple practice, especially "the Levites for their offices of praise . . . for so David the man of God had commanded" (2 Chr 8:14 NRSV). Chapter 15 is one key place where we read of this new practice. As the chronicler and his generation enjoyed listening to the Levites singing to their own music at temple services, he encouraged them to prize the tradition as ultimately grounded in the glorious work of David, "the man of God" and so agent of divine revelation. This spanning of the centuries corresponds to the way Christians look back to the dawn of a new era in Christ and celebrate it as the revelation of God (Heb 1:1-2).

4. The note of joy struck at the end of the previous section (12:40) also comes to the fore in 15:16, 25. Comparison of these two verses shows that the chronicler regarded the Levites' music and song as inspiring the people's joy. Such joy was not a spontaneous phenomenon but was promoted by this new institutional practice. Likewise, every church has the task of translating the spirit of worship into appropriate religious forms. Forms there must be, and their character should be a constant challenge. Forms can turn into formality, and so new Christian groups appear with fresh and "informal" forms, for the eventual edification of the church at large. Tradition and adaptability are the two poles within which the church legitimately moves. Worship is to be alive and joyful, ascending to God from hearts and minds in culturally appropriate language and modes.

5. The Saul/David antithesis returns to haunt this passage. Saul is typical of those who do not seek the things of God and are blind to such endeavors. The challenge came, as ever, to the next generation. Michal took the wrong direction by siding with her father. In the chronicler's thinking, every generation in turn is confronted with the need to make a fresh decision for God. He here poses an implicit warning as to which direction his own generation wants to take at its own crossroads: the low road away from God or the high road of spiritual commitment. Michal had the same chance we all have, but she made the wrong choice.

1 Chronicles 16:4-43, Praise and Worship Inaugurated

COMMENTARY

The chronicler brings to a close his convoluted account of the installation of the ark in Jerusalem, the first step toward the goal of building a temple. The only point of contact with his 2 Samuel text is the quotation of 2 Sam 6:19b-20 in 16:43. He uses it as his conclusion, having no use on this celebratory occasion for Michal's bitter confrontation with David (2 Sam 6:20b-23). Verse 43b has

an important anticipatory role in the Chronicles narrative, paving the way for chap. 17. David returns home to pray for divine blessing on his "household" or "family." His prayer will be answered in the prophetic announcement of a Davidic dynasty.

16:4-7, 37-42. Apart from this borrowed conclusion, the prose narrative falls into two parts: David's appointment of personnel to be responsible for choral music at the site of the ark (vv. 4-6) and the implementation of these arrangements (vv. 37-42). The chronicler was concerned to trace the ministry of levitical musicians back to the establishment of the ark in Jerusalem, before the Temple was built. He had expressed this concern in 6:31-32. However, he had to address another issue: Solomon's sacrificing at Gibeon in 2 Chr 1:2-6. To be sure, the ark was safely installed at Jerusalem. However, the chronicler also affirmed that at one time the tabernacle was located at Gibeon, along with the altar of burnt offering on which sacrifices were regularly offered. We do not know whether he reasoned to this end or had recourse to an older tradition that attested the later history of the tabernacle after its stay in Shiloh (Josh 18:1; cf. 19:51). The chronicler describes the sacrificial calendar of the Pentateuch for the tabernacle as in full operation at Gibeon (see Exod 29:38-42; Num 28:2-8). In v. 40, he emphasizes that all ritual activity is based on what was written in the Torah, as was the case in 15:15 with respect to the carrying of the ark. At Gibeon the newly appointed levitical musicians were to play a supporting role, as later they would in the Temple.

The description of sacrifice in Gibeon (v. 39) helps to explain vv. 4-6. A key word in the prose narrative is "regularly" (תמיד *tāmîd*, vv. 6, 37, 40). Its most natural usage occurs in v. 37, where it is used to describe the regular morning and evening sacrifices. In v. 37 the chronicler transfers this term to the Levites' music and song in the vicinity of the ark, and in v. 6 to the priests' trumpet blasts there. Evidently the simultaneous accompaniment of the sacrificial procedure with musical songs in the Temple, envisioned in 23:30-31, was to happen even now. The singing element was to take place together, at the same time, with the sacrificial element in Gibeon, but by itself in Jerusalem.[103] Proper worship could occur in two places: Gibeon and Jerusalem.

The comprehensive choral arrangements recorded as having been set up in the list of personnel and instruments in 15:16-21 are now implemented. There is a slight inconsistency, noted earlier, in that the scheme reflected in vv. 5, 37, 41-42 does not quite accord with the previous arrangements. It attests an earlier stage of post-exilic development. The two stages are loosely treated as the same. In v. 41, five of the fourteen names in 15:20-21 are presupposed ("the rest of those . . . expressly named," NRSV), after the citation of the other nine in v. 5. The same dispute in 15:18, 24—over whether Obed-edom was a musician or a gatekeeper—reappears in v. 38.

The task of the singing musicians was to praise God, as v. 4 indicates with an enthusiastic amassing of synonymous verbs. The first verb, rendered "invoke" (להזכיר *lĕhazkîr*) in the NRSV, is a general term for making mention of the Lord's name either in praise or in prayer. The NIV opts for the latter sense ("make petition"), but here the former is preferable. The second verb (להודות *lĕhôdôt*), involves primarily the thanksgiving song of an individual delivered from a crisis. By post-exilic times, however, it had also become part of the vocabulary for hymnic praise, as in v. 7, where *lĕhôdôt* reappears ("psalm of thanks," NIV). So the chronicler is concerned about the singing of hymns, as vv. 8-36 will illustrate. The chronicler introduces this sacred poetry in v. 7; afterward he resumes his narrative in v. 37.[104]

16:8-43. The poem is an anthology of elements drawn from three post-exilic psalms: Ps 105:1-15 in vv. 8-22, Ps 96:1b-13a in vv. 23-33, and Ps 106:1, 47-48 in vv. 4-36. Psalm 105:1 is a hymn that reviews the Lord's saving work on Israel's behalf. Psalm 96 is an eschatological hymn celebrating divine kingship, already grounded in creation and one day to be consummated worldwide. Psalm 106 is best understood as a communal lament; it praises God for past acts of grace because they provide hope of renewed help for Israel. The chronicler uses his anthology as an example of what the guild of singers contributed to public worship. Still the content of the psalm extracts was also important for him. The overlap of vocabulary with the narrative context shows that he anchored the medley to his story of David. The process is akin to that which underlies historicizing headings in the book of Psalms, which apply

---

103. Kleinig, *The Lord's Song*, 53.

104. See T. C. Butler, "A Forgotten Passage from a Forgotten Era (1 Chr xvi 8-36)," *VT* 28 (1978) 146; J. W. Watts, *Inset Hymns in Hebrew Narrative*, JSOTSup 139 (Sheffield: JSOT, 1992) 163 and nn. 4-5.

a psalm to a particular incident in David's life.[105] The anthology constitutes a complex hymn that at the end weaves petition into its praise. It is used as a song of adoration for what God had done thus far in David's career and as an appeal that the Lord will bring it to a successful conclusion.

The Temple is presupposed in the source behind vv. 27 and 29 (Ps 96:6, "in his sanctuary"; Ps 96:8, "to his courts"). The chronicler adapts these historically unsuitable phrases to "in his place" and "before him" respectively. In doing so, he achieves references to "the place" David had prepared for the ark (15:1, 3, 12) and to God's presence through the ark (13:8, 10; 16:1). The regular system of music and song just set up before the ark (vv. 6, 37) to synchronize with the sacrifices and songs offered at Gibeon (v. 40) is echoed in v. 11 ("continually" [tāmîd]). It occurs in a summons to resort to the Lord's "presence" (NRSV), now via the ark. The call in v. 11a to "seek" (דרש dāraš) the Lord reinforces the motivation of David and the believing community in bringing the ark to Jerusalem (cf. 13:3; 15:13). The thrice-mentioned patriarchal "covenant" comprising the promise of the land of Canaan (vv. 15-17) relates to the frequent designation of the ark as the ark of the covenant in recent narrative (vv. 6, 37; see also 15:25-26, 28-29). The chronicler is aware of the close links between the patriarchal and the Davidic covenants. Reference to the land echoes the imperial frontiers of 13:5, while the everlastingness of the covenant (vv. 15, 17) alludes to the permanency of the Davidic dynasty in 17:13-14. The covenant with the patriarchs was taken up into the Davidic one and through David became Israel's heritage. Similarly, the Lord's "[steadfast] love," which "endures for ever" (v. 34, echoed in v. 41), presupposes the divine blessing promised to the Davidic line through Solomon in 17:13.

The accent on rejoicing in v. 10 reflects the festive joy of 15:16, 25; the hearers are urged to share it in v. 31 ("rejoice," NRSV). Hebrew synonyms for "rejoice" appear in vv. 27, 31-33 in an outflowing of joy that spreads throughout the world. Likewise, the

"strength" of v. 27 harks back to Israel's celebrating "with all their might" in 13:8 (עז 'oz in both cases). Here are Asaph and his fellow choristers doing their work, singing and encouraging song (vv. 9, 23). Called to "thank" (v. 4), they promote thanksgiving in vv. 8, 34-35. Summoned to "praise," they stimulate it in vv. 10 (rendered "glory"), 25, 35-36.

If the new psalm majors in David's present, it also looks back to his past. The small number of David's followers in his wilderness and mercenary periods, when God protected them (see 12:18), is paralleled in vv. 19-22. God's "wonders" (v. 12 NIV; v. 24, "marvelous works/deeds") are now the exploits wrought by the Lord through David and his troops in chaps. 11–12 and 14. The divine causation of these exploits will be emphasized in 17:8a. The kingship of the Lord (v. 31) had recently been shown to be reflected in the ark (13:6), while David's kingdom will turn out to be God's own kingdom (17:14). This psalm medley also has in view the future of David. Appeal is made to the God who had already proved to be "our savior" (v. 35 NIV; cf. the related noun for "victory" in 11:14), for further feats of salvation. They will duly be accomplished in 18:6, 13.

The historicizing Davidic titles in the psalms were designed to present David as a model for post-exilic Judah.[106] The chronicler also had his contemporaries in mind in the new entity he created. Hermeneutical application pervades its stanzas. It falls into four stanzas: a call to Israel to praise God (vv. 8-22), a call for praise throughout the earth (vv. 23-30), a call for cosmic praise (vv. 31-33), and a call for Israel not only to praise but also to pray that fresh potential for praise may be theirs (vv. 34-36).[107] The clarion call to seek the Lord (v. 11) rings through the ages from Asaph to post-exilic readers. Contemporary Judah is meant to heed the double call to remember God's intervention in history to launch the new Davidic era (v. 12) and the

105. For the intricate intertextuality involved in this procedure, see E. Slomovic, "Toward an Understanding of the Formation of Historical Titles in the Book of Psalms," ZAW 91 (1979) 350-80.

106. See B. S. Childs, "Psalm Titles and Midrashic Exegesis," JSS 16 (1971) 137-50; Introduction to the OT as Scripture (Philadelphia: Fortress, 1979) 520-22. David is presented in the psalter both as a model of ethical spirituality and as a source of eschatological hope.

107. Kleinig, The Lord's Song, 65n. 1, has cited C. Becker's observation that pushing Ps 96:11a into a leading place in 16:31a was intended to highlight the cosmic reference. He also draws attention to the use of "all the earth" as a framework in vv. 23, 30 (p. 142). Verse 36 (= Ps 106:48), originally a redactional doxology to the fourth book of the psalter, is here partly woven into the poem and partly made a narrative response.

everlasting patriarchal covenant received anew by David and passed on to Israel (vv. 15-18; the NRSV's imperative "Remember" in v. 15 suits the chronicler's exhortatory intent, while the NIV's "He remembers" has harmonized with the parent text, Ps 105:8). These old truths assure post-exilic Judah that it is only part of a wider Israel and that the whole land would one day be theirs. In v. 13 the chronicler has changed "Abraham" in Ps 105:6 to "Israel," thereby achieving the same parallelism as in v. 17. He sought to draw attention to the ancestor of the twelve tribes, whom he calls Israel rather than Jacob. As to the promise of the land, the patriarchs were God's veritable "prophets" (v. 22). Verses 19-22 had relevance for post-exilic Judah, territorially cramped yet assured of God's protection. In v. 19 the MT has "you" rather than "they." One wonders whether the "you" is directed to the chronicler's audience or if it implies reference to a continuation of direct speech from v. 18, as the NJB takes it.

Psalm 96, which underlies vv. 23-33, is an eschatological hymn, urging confident praise for what the Lord is yet to do. The chronicler still wanted the psalm to be understood this way. Judah's witness to the nations about the Lord's purposes (v. 18) would one day trigger an echoing response (v. 23). The world belongs to the Lord by virtue of creation,

and so the fear inspired by God in all nations (14:17) would eventually issue into universal submission. The final clause in v. 29 is probably to be rendered "Worship the LORD for his holy splendor."[108] One day the universe would dance in honor of the ultimate outworking of Davidic kingship, when the whole earth welcomed the Lord coming to reign and to establish justice.

But not yet. The nations still jostled the people of God, who were "strangers" in their own "land" (v. 19). God's everlasting "[steadfast] love" (v. 34), like the covenant promises (vv. 15-18), was assurance enough that the full salvation celebrated in anticipation in v. 23 would eventually be theirs. Even now Israel should begin to give God everlasting praise to match that everlasting love. In v. 35 the vocative "O God, our savior" is provided by the chronicler, and so is the imperative "and deliver us" (the two verbal forms for "and gather us" [not reflected in the LXX] and "and deliver us" probably reflect a conflated text in the MT). He probably took both elements from Ps 79:9, attracted by the potential of a new generation in Ps 79:8.[109] The focus changes from a concern of the diaspora to the needs of the returned exiles.

108. See Kleinig, *The Lord's Song*, 176n. 2.
109. See Allen, *The Greek Chronicles*, 1:217.

REFLECTIONS

1. The chronicler has used his psalm extracts as hermeneutical stepping-stones from a unique but incomplete past to an inadequate, still incomplete present. David's growth from weakness to power has turned into an omen that post-exilic Judah's own prayers would be answered. Israel's glorious past is held up as a mirror to Israel's future. Partial restoration would give way to full rehabilitation. God's kingdom was to come on earth. The secret is the spiritual lesson the chronicler has been teaching since chapter 10: to seek the Lord. This means giving God the rightful place of honor in the religious life of the community, as the journey of the ark had symbolized. It also means expressing appreciative praise for what God had already done and would yet do.

"Let the hearts of those who seek the LORD" (16:10) rejoice over the purposes God had for them. The believing community in the chronicler's time, as in David's, was God's "chosen ones" (v. 13), as recipients of the divine promise, good for a thousand generations (v. 16). We are the chosen people, affirms the chronicler in healthy pride, in order to convey to his contemporaries a necessary continuity and destiny. When pride is the opposite of humility, it is bad; when it is the opposite of shame, it is good. At a time when so much in Judah's environment shouted no at their claims, the chronicler's faith dared to shout yes. They were tantalizingly close to and yet so far from the promise, like the patriarchs and like outlawed David. Yet they stood under the same protection of God (16:21-22). Promise, privation, protection—such was the dappled pattern of light and shade that covered the Judean community. We Christians recognize this clash of perspectives. Our hope is veiled: "We walk by faith, not by sight" (2 Cor 5:7 NRSV).

2. Accordingly, 16:23-33 presents a vision of victorious hope. Verse 23*b* has a remarkably Christian ring: It may be rendered "Proclaim . . . the good news that [the LORD] has saved us" (GNB). It was a mark of the new age God had established through David. It replaced the defeatism of the way of exile, which encouraged the impression that the Lord had lost and other powers had won. The same verb occurs in 10:9, where messengers were sent all through Philistine territory "to convey the good news" of Israel's defeat "to their idols and to the people." Underlying David's great power in 11:9 and 12:2 was the Lord's own greatness (16:25). Divine kingship in the psalms is often associated with the Lord's work as creator and maintainer of the world (16:26, 30). The Judeans, like us, could entrust themselves to a faithful creator (1 Pet 4:19). Psalm 96, used here, reflects the faith of post-exilic Judah in a universal God of creation and its hope that this universal role would be matched by a future intervention, when the Lord was to lay redemptive claim to the world and set it right (see Acts 17:31; 2 Pet 3:13). For the chronicler, there had already been a significant revelation of this God in the period of David, which confirmed the earlier disclosure to the patriarchs. The first chapter of 1 Chronicles had begun with the world, and so this message about its destiny is appropriate. To the post-exilic community living in "a day of small things" (Zech 4:10) are offered the narratives of a great David as encouraging signs of a great hope. "Sit at my right hand, until I make your enemies your footstool" (Ps 110:1) was the Lord's similar word to David elsewhere, and it came to pervade the New Testament, now addressed to Jesus enthroned in token of a greater throne hereafter.

3. The ambivalence of 16:8-22 returns in 16:34-36. On the one hand, the believing community is the recipient of God's goodness and love forever. On the other hand, they pray to the Lord for deliverance. Full restoration is conspicuous by its absence. The chronicler opens his contemporaries' eyes to their great traditions and urges this small community to appropriate these traditions, to live in the good of them and to make them the basis of a sure hope in the God who is preserving them for a purpose.

Here is theology set to music. As the hearts of God's people open in praise, divine truths take root. This theology functions as encouragement, giving renewed strength to the weary: "The LORD is great" and "the LORD is coming" (16:25, 33). The chronicler's old, yet new, psalm is matched in the New Testament by Rom 5:1-11 and 8:18-39. The church is represented as subject to limitations. Yet its members raise joyful voices because they look beyond brute facts to see God at work, preparing future glory. They feel the rain, but see a rainbow. God's electing love embraces them in its strong grip. That love brings assurance of victory, even now enjoyed in spirit. The work of God in Christ is the guarantee of their own destiny.

Doxology is here used as an antidote to despair. On other occasions both Paul and the chronicler challenged their constituencies. However, the need of this hour was to ensure that they were strengthened in faith and hope, with a power that came from God: "Seek the LORD and his strength" (16:11 NRSV).

1 Chronicles 17:1–20:8, Thy Kingdom Come!

OVERVIEW

This section presents the divine program for the reigns of David and Solomon. First, it is revealed in chap. 17 that David is to play the part of a warrior king. He will bring about stability and thus provide the people of Israel with a place of freedom and security. Second, Solomon (as yet unnamed) may then do his own work, building the Temple in Jerusalem. Solomon's accomplishment of this task will win lasting blessing from the Lord, the foundation of a permanent dynasty, which will be an inaugural manifestation of the kingdom of God. In chaps. 18–20, David duly fulfills the role assigned to him, in accord with the promise that God "will subdue all his enemies" (17:10). The verb "subdue" (הכניע *hiknîʿa*, in the hiphil) becomes a key word of the unit. It is echoed at the beginning of the first and third subunits in chaps. 18–20. At 18:1 David "subdued" the Philistines, and at 20:4 they "were subdued" (NRSV) again.

1 Chronicles 17:1-27, God's Program for David and Solomon

COMMENTARY

This chapter falls into three parts: David's plan to build a temple to house the ark (vv. 1-2), the Lord's negative and positive answers (vv. 3-15), and David's prayer of thanksgiving and petition (vv. 16-27). What binds the chapter together is a series of wordplays on the term "house" (בית *bayit*). David, now residing in his house or palace (v. 1), wants to build a comparable house for the Lord, a temple (v. 6). God has other plans: to build a house or dynasty for David (vv. 11, 17-27) and for one of David's sons to build a house or temple for the Lord (vv. 12, 14).

The chapter follows 2 Samuel 7 fairly closely; differences will be pointed out as they are encountered. The major convictions associated with the deuteronomistic form of the oracle in 2 Sam 7:5-16 (= 1 Chr 17:4-14) are that David's reign is a period of promise and preparation, looking forward to the establishment of the royal dynasty and to the building of the Temple in Solomon's reign. David was to prepare for this period of fulfillment by pacifying the land, as 2 Samuel 8 records.[110] All this was grist for the chronicler's mill, and he took it over with a few refinements.

The reader of 1 Chronicles will recognize here another version of chaps. 13–15. A spiritual proposal is followed first by a divine setback and then by divine blessing as a reward for the previous spiritual intention. This was how the chronicler perceived the episode, in the light of 2 Chr 6:8 (= 1 Kgs 8:18). In these circumstances even a divine no can be worth having. God prizes spiritual initiatives, even if they eventually prove impracticable for reasons beyond the initiator's knowledge. David is still seeking the Lord with all his heart, and he is presented as an implicit model for later believers.

17:1-2. The king is concerned by the imbalance between his own palace and a mere tent for the ark. Why should he be better housed (cf. Hag 1:4)? The chronicler has been building up to this point in his narrative by mentioning David's palace at structurally significant points (v. 1; 14:1; 15:1). In v. 2, he makes a pregnant statement in calling "the ark of God" (2 Sam 7:2) "the ark of the covenant of the LORD." The issue of housing the ark will involve a divine covenant as the chapter progresses, the all-important covenant with David (cf. 2 Sam 23:5; Ps 89:3, 28, 34). As in chaps. 15–16, the value of the ark

110. McCarter, *2 Samuel*, 217-20, 241.

as a symbol of the Davidic covenant comes to the fore.

17:3-6. Nathan's general promise of divine support for building the Temple is countermanded by a detailed and complex oracle, which includes the ruling that on God's calendar the time for such a venture has not yet arrived. The oracle's initial sentence forms the first side of a triangle of statements. "You are not the one to build me a house to dwell in" (v. 4), says God. Instead, "the LORD will build you a house" (v. 10). And of one of David's sons, it is said, "He is the one who will build a house for me" (v. 12). In 2 Sam 7:5, the first statement appears in the form of a question. Here it is rephrased as a statement, as in 1 Kgs 8:19, and it looks forward to the two other contrasting ones. Verses 5-6 begin to explain the refusal in terms of the divine program for the reigns of David and Solomon. The long-standing precedent of housing the ark in a tent was to continue for a little longer. The ark had gone "from tent to tent and from tabernacle" (MT, which the NRSV has emended according to the parallel 2 Sam 7:6, following the harmonistic LXX, while the NIV has implicitly indulged in a popular conjectural addition, for which some have claimed support from the Targum). Once located in the tabernacle of the tent of meeting according to Exod 39:32 (cf. 1 Chr 6:32), it had now been moved to another tent, David's tent.[111] This distinction between the tabernacle and the tent provided by David follows naturally that made by the chronicler in 15:1; 16:1, 39.

17:7-10a. The initial "And now" ("Now then," NIV; "Now therefore," NRSV) in v. 7 typically signals that the main point is to be announced after introductory material. The renewed messenger formula "thus says the LORD of Hosts" lends further emphasis. In God's program, David's role was to be a warrior king. David's reign was to be the Lord's means of providing a secure land for Israel. To accomplish this goal, David is guaranteed complete victory. Whereas 2 Sam 7:11 promises David rest from all his enemies, here in v. 10 a verb of subjection is substituted. The chronicler associated Solomon with rest and

David with warfare, and so found this reference to rest inappropriate (see Commentary on 22:9).[112] Both the deuteronomist and the chronicler presumed the condition laid down in Deut 12:10-11 that only after God had given Israel rest from all their enemies could they offer worship, at the place of the Lord's choosing. They differed as to when that rest occurred. The chronicler associated David with necessary warfare as his role in a pre-Temple program. Accordingly, he replaced the verb of rest, borrowing his new verb of subjection from 2 Sam 8:1 (= 1 Chr 18:1). By so doing, he created a structural marker for the section, using it yet again in 20:4.

17:10b-15. The second half of the program is presented in these verses. It supplies the other two sides of the triangle of statements in quick succession. Dynasty building and temple building are intertwined. The chronicler and his first readers knew what it was not yet time to say, that Solomon was in view as temple builder.[113] A temple was indeed to be built, but not yet, and by Solomon, not by David. His building of the Temple was to constitute a guarantee of the Davidic dynasty and its perpetuity. For the chronicler, the two halves of v. 12 constitute cause and effect. Another condition Solomon must keep will be presented in 28:7 (cf. 2 Chr 7:17-18). The divine side of the agreement was that the "[steadfast] love" forfeited by Saul would be permanently bestowed on Solomon. The post-exilic community often sang of the Lord's "[steadfast] love" in their hymns (see 16:34, 41). The chronicler traced it back to God's covenant with David and Solomon, which he regarded as the foundation of a permanent relationship with Israel. The reference to divine punishment in 2 Sam 7:14b is omitted as irrelevant after 1 Chr 17:13a. At this point the chronicler focuses solely on Solomon, whom he regarded as fulfilling the condition of obedience, the other factor that was to seal the dynastic promise. So Solomon was not liable to punishment at the hands of the divine patron of the monarchy.[114]

111. R. E. Friedman, *The Exile and Biblical Narrative*, HSM 22 (Chico, Calif.: Scholars Press, 1981) 54. In the priestly literature the inner curtains of the tabernacle structure are referred to as the tabernacle, and the outer curtains as the tent. See Exod 26:1-13.

112. R. L. Braun, "Solomon, the Chosen Temple Builder: The Significance of 1 Chronicles 22, 28, and 29 for the Theology of the Chronicler," *JBL* 95 (1976) 582-86; and *1 Chronicles*, 198-99.

113. For the slight change in 17:11, "one of your own sons" in place of "[one] who will come from your own body" (2 Sam 7:12 NIV), see H. G. M. Williamson, "The Dynastic Oracle in the Books of Chronicles," *I. L. Seeligmann Volume*, ed. A. Rof' and Y. Zakovitch (Jerusalem: Rubinstein, 1983) 305-9.

114. See Williamson, *1 and 2 Chronicles*, 135-36.

Solomon's dual role is summed up in v. 14. God would "set him over" the Temple and the theocracy, giving him a once-for-all supervisory role in these two areas. Second Samuel 7:16a reads "your house and your kingdom," but the chronicler prefers a concluding summary that repeats the substance of vv. 11b-12a. The new reference to God's kingdom introduces a motif characteristic of the books of Chronicles (28:5; 29:23; 2 Chr 9:8; 13:8). The Lord was to reign not only via the religious symbolism of the ark (13:6), but also from the palace itself. The human king would be regent, responsible to the heavenly king. It is difficult not to recognize an eschatological reference, especially after 16:31, in the sense of an inaugurated rather than a realized eschatology. The character of v. 14 as a recapitulating conclusion extends to the last clause. Instead of David's throne being established forever (2 Sam 7:16), Solomon's would be, in repetition of v. 12.

The portrayal of a new era founded on the Jerusalem Temple and dynasty finds a parallel in Psalm 78. Its review of the twists and turns of Israelite history culminates in the opening of a new age. This age is marked by God's building on Mt. Zion "his sanctuary," as secure as heaven and earth, and by choosing "his servant David" as Israel's shepherd (Ps 78:69-71; cf. 1 Chr 28:4 and Commentary on 28:4-7). Israel's history was to witness many more twists and turns after the basic 2 Samuel 7 and Psalm 78 were composed. The Temple would be destroyed, as Psalm 79 attests, and David's house with it, as Psalm 89 laments. Yet from those ruins, the Temple had now been rebuilt, and the chronicler rejoiced in the Davidic era of God's grace, which still continued. One element was missing: a restored house of David. Spiritual logic required that it would be only a matter of time before that, too, occurred. The perpetuity of vv. 12 and 14 was God's pledge.

17:16-19. David's response of prayer closely reflects the source, 2 Sam 7:18-29. The chronicler's version falls into two parts, vv. 16-22 and 23-27. The second part is introduced by "And now," which indicates a transition to the main part of the prayer, just as in the prophetic oracle at v. 7. The first part is devoted to thanksgiving. There is a convention in the OT that a person endowed with

a divine revelation and mission responds in tones disparaging to oneself and one's family. Moses did so in Exod 3:11 ("Who am I . . . ?"), and so did Gideon in Judg 6:11. David continues this healthy tradition (see 1 Sam 8:18). Here the prayer strikes a note of surprise at God's gracious initiative, both in advancing David's career thus far, as the oracle had mentioned in vv. 7-8a, and in making the dynastic promise of vv. 10b-14. David's heart is too full for words, but God could read his gratitude there (v. 18). The "great thing" the Lord had done (v. 19), as the continuation explains, is the revelation of God's great promise of a dynasty.

17:20-22. The thanksgiving moves into general praise, rehearsing the past work of God on Israel's behalf, which religious tradition had handed down, and deducing from it a conviction of the Lord's uniqueness. Redemption from Egypt (cf. v. 5) and divinely aided entry into the promised land were evidence of God's praiseworthiness. Associated with such crucial demonstrations of grace was the covenant bonding of God and people. The *foreverness* of the Mosaic covenant strikes a late, deuteronomistic note (cf. Deut 4:30-31; 30:4-6), which for the chronicler was taken up and confirmed in the Davidic covenant.

17:23-24. The second half of the prayer moves from thanksgiving to petition. Nathan has initially encouraged the king to do what he had in mind (v. 2), and David would have been glad to do so. Now he bows to God's better will: "Do as you [have] promised." David adds his amen to the Lord's revelation. Behind the verb "be established," used three times, is the verb יֵאָמֵן (*yēʾāmēn*). He prays that God will keep the promises about himself (vv. 8-10a) and the ensuing dynasty (vv. 10b-14). For the promises to come true, the Lord's help was necessary. And such help would redound to continuing and greater praise.

17:25-27. The dynastic promise becomes the closing focus. David would never have dared invent such a pretentious-sounding petition. Two present factors (v. 26, "now," NRSV; v. 27, "Now," NIV) encourage David to envision its fulfillment. The first is the oracular promise made by God through Nathan. The second factor is the blessing already experienced by the royal house (cf.

chap. 14), a guarantee that it would, indeed, enjoy God's perennial favor.[115] The Lord had already blessed it, and so "it will be blessed forever" (NIV, similarly REB; see NRSV note). The chronicler alters slightly the ending in the prayer in 2 Samuel 7 so that cognizance may be taken of the previous establishment of David's kingship (1 Chr 14:2). God had laid a good foundation, as the oracle itself observed in vv. 7-8a. The chronicler draws a little tighter the threads between the prayer, the oracle, and the preceding narrative.

Oracle and prayer fit the chronicler's purposes well. The oracle announces the divine program for David and Solomon and establishes the once-for-all character of their reigns for the future of God's people. For the deuteronomist, the theology of grace fits imperfectly a historical context of failure and exile. From the chronicler's post-exilic perspective it could be embraced afresh as grounds of hope for a partially restored people.

Accordingly, mention of the exodus and entry into the land of promise in David's prayer (v. 21) becomes a swan song for the old Mosaic era. Divine revelation had taken a dynamic step forward. Just as David looked back to the exodus and the Mosaic covenant, so also thereafter Israel should look back to

the Davidic covenant and its establishment by Solomon. It subsumed the best of what had gone before, but marked a real and irreversible advance. The prayer of 2 Sam 7:24, paralleled here in v. 22, speaks of the Mosaic covenant as revealing the triumph of divine grace and so is everlasting like the patriarchal covenant. The chronicler took over this concept, but would have explained it differently, in the light of chap. 16. He saw in God's relationship with Israel a reflection of the promise of perpetuity associated with the Davidic dynasty. This promise, celebrated in vv. 12, 14, 23, and 27 (cf. v. 13), resumed God's everlasting "[steadfast] love" in 16:24, 41, which itself echoed the "everlasting covenant" with the patriarchs in 16:17.

One might be surprised that there is no mention of the Temple in David's response. While it is possible to explain this lack in 2 Samuel 7:1 as a pre-redactional phenomenon, it is significant that the chronicler did not add such a reference, though he had augmented the allusion to the Temple in the oracle. Many scholars view David's and Solomon's kingship as a means to an end in the chronicler's thought, a step toward the establishment of the Temple as the divinely authorized place of worship. Here, however, the Davidic dynasty stands in its own right. The chronicler intended his readers to add their own amen to David's, that in God's good time the Davidic house would be reestablished.

115. הואלת (*hôaltā*) is rendered "you have been pleased" in the NIV and as a precative perfect, "may it please you" in the NRSV. The context suggests a different sense, "you have begun." See Braun, *1 Chronicles*, 196, 199; *BDB* 384a.

REFLECTIONS

1. The chronicler took over without a qualm the discrepancy between the prophet's initial *yes* and later *no*, or rather *not yet*. It is reassuring to us less inspired humans that even a prophet apprehended God's will in stages. Nathan's general awareness that a temple should be built was correct, but he did not initially know when and by whom. God's servants in every age have experienced this slow progress in the right direction. Paul had a similar experience in seeking where to go on his first missionary journey (Acts 16:6-10). He wanted to go west to the Roman province of Asia, but found his way blocked by the Holy Spirit. He turned north to Bithynia, with the same result. He traveled west to the port of Troas and at last received clear guidance to catch a boat to Macedonia. In 1 Chronicles 17 and in Acts 16, guidance comes through a sincere desire to be led by God. In spite of our best intentions, we may sometimes be mistaken initially in perceiving what the Lord wants of us. We are to act boldly in accordance with what we believe to be God's purpose, putting that belief to the test even as we wait for clarification.

David was not to build the Temple, after all. A need was there, but it did not constitute a call, eager volunteer though he was. He might have been resentful that another was to do what he wanted to do. Unlike in 13:11, there is no outburst of anger at the overruling of his well-intentioned wishes. David's prayer shows that he accepted his different preparatory role. Here is the generous spirit of 1 Cor 3:6, "I planted the seed, Apollos watered it, but God made it grow" (NIV).

2. We encounter here for the first time the chronicler's emphasis that the earthly kingdom was a manifestation of the *kingdom of God.* Henceforth the truth that "the LORD reigns" (16:31) was to take on new meaning. God would rule in Israel through the Davidic throne. The chronicler seems to have regarded the eschatological kingdom of God (see Dan 7:14, 27; Obad 21:1; Mic 4:7; Zech 14:9) as having been inaugurated in Israel's past history. The end time had been anticipated in principle, in a historical manifestation that fostered hope that its consummation was no less certain. Readers of the New Testament are no strangers to the idea of a once-for-all revelation. It is not difficult to draw parallels between the new era of David and Solomon and the new age manifested in Christ. The manifestation of the eschatological kingdom of God was proclaimed in the ministry of Jesus (Luke 11:20; see also Luke 7:22; 17:21). In Christ we meet a new Son of God, heir of the royal promise and more besides. He has provided a spiritual temple, giving us access to God so that we may approach the throne of grace with confidence and through him offer sacrifices of praise (Heb 4:16; 13:15). He has established the kingdom of God in fact and in hope. We are in the process of receiving "a kingdom that cannot be shaken" (Heb 12:28).

3. A notable feature of David's prayer is the reflection of elements of the prophetic oracle. The term "servant" occurs twice in the oracle, in the messenger formula of 17:4 and 17:7. The term occurs no less than ten times in the prayer. David affirms his subordinate role in the divine program. A response of humility is made to the honor of stabilizing the land and to the privilege of founding a dynasty, firmly keeping down the peacock's feathers that the human heart loves to display. "All who exalt themselves will be humbled, and all who humble themselves will be exalted" (Matt 23:12 NRSV).

The plea for God to keep the promises relating to David and his dynasty (17:23) is grounded in human need. The divine commission could be carried out only with the Lord's help. Beyond necessary human endeavors there must be dependence on God to fulfill the promises. Prayer is a means by which believers may acknowledge their sense of weakness and ask for divine strength to accomplish the tasks they have been given.[116]

116. R. E. Clements, *In Spirit and in Truth: Insights from Biblical Prayers* (Atlanta: John Knox, 1985) 76-77, 79.

1 Chronicles 18:1–20:8, A Place for God's People

COMMENTARY

This long passage develops the Davidic part of the divine program, laid down in 17:8*b*-10*a*, the promise that the Lord "will subdue all" David's "enemies" (17:10). This verb becomes a key word in the section. It is repeated in 18:1 from 2 Sam 8:1: David "subdued" (יכניעם *yaknî'ēm*) The Philistines. The chronicler also worked it into the final narrative at 20:4: The Philistines "were

subdued" (NRSV). Another structural marker is present at both the beginning and the end of the present passage. We have to turn to the KJV, however, to find it. In 18:1, David takes the Philistine city of Gath and its villages "out of *the hand* of the Philistines." In 20:8, the Philistine giants "fell by *the hand* of David and by *the hand* of his servants." This rhetorical framework expresses well the loss of Philistine control and its passing to David. Both the first paragraph (18:1) and the final, longer one (20:4-8) relate to the Philistines as archetypal enemies of Israel. They were the ones who defeated Saul and the Israelite army. Now the tide turns. Where there was once divinely instigated failure, there is now God-given victory. The Philistines, who had sought to conquer the Israelite interior (chap. 14) and were defeated, lose control of some of their own territory. God, through David, is providing a place for the covenant people and putting an end to external oppression (17:9).

The sequence of subunits within chaps. 18–20 is indicated structurally by a common opening formula. The NIV reproduces the repeated Hebrew phrase as "In the course of time" in 18:1; 19:1; and 20:4. These three initial markers indicate separate blocks of material taken over from 2 Samuel. First Chronicles 18:1-17 comes from 2 Sam 8:1-18; 1 Chr 19:1–20:3 from 2 Sam 10:1–11:1; 1 Chr 12:26, 30-31; and 20:4-8 from 2 Sam 21:18-22. The chronicler has selected three blocks from 2 Samuel dealing with military victories, which provided him with a set of initial markers. The combination of material from 2 Samuel 8 and 21 also furnished him with the framework for the transfer of power from the Philistines to David. As for 1 Chr 20:4-8, one might ask why the chronicler did not include 2 Sam 21:15-17. The chronicler's eye lighted on the introductory phrase in 2 Sam 21:18. His desire for structural symmetry committed him to beginning the last of his three subunits at that point, which became 2 Chr 20:4.

Mention may also be made of a pervasive and appropriate key word in the passage, the verb הכה (hikkâ, in the hiphil), which occurs seven times in chap. 18 (vv. 1, 2, 3, 5, 9, 10, 12), once in 19:1–20:3 (20:1), and three times in 20:4-8 (vv. 4, 5, 7). It has a wide range of meanings, such as "attack," "defeat," and "kill." The useful archaic verb "smite" allowed the KJV closer reproduction of this drumbeat of doom for Israel's enemies. Apart from 18:10, the Hebrew verb supplies a marker for the separate military episodes.

The chronicler vigorously ransacked 2 Samuel for material relating to David's military victories and, as a result of this single-mindedness, refrained from using a lot of other material in 2 Samuel. In particular he pruned 2 Samuel 10–12 of David's affair with Bathsheba and murder of her husband. One can hardly accuse the chronicler of tendentiously cutting out conduct unbefitting the gentleman he wanted David to be; he fully acknowledges David's sin over the census in chap. 21. The difference is that it fits the chronicler's emphasis on the Temple.

The series of victories (18:1-12) already had in 2 Samuel 8 an all-encompassing character. The victories fan out in all directions. The Philistines were subdued to the west, Moab to the east, Hadadezer of Zobah to the north (and in the far north Tou of Hamath became an ally), and in the south Edom was defeated. Second Samuel 8 presents a spectrum of victory throughout the land, and it fit the chronicler's own purposes to take it over. In fulfilling the pre-temple program, David was pushing out to the ideal limits of the land expressed in 13:5.

18:1-6. A number of battle reports are presented. In the defeat of the Philistines (v. 1) the capture of "Gath and its villages" is pinpointed. The corresponding phrase in 2 Sam 8:1, "Metheg-ammah," is obscure. In order to make sense out of this dubious text, the chronicler was probably influenced by the occurrence of Gath in 2 Sam 21:20, 22 (= 1 Chr 20:6, 8). Transposition of the last two Hebrew consonants of "Metheg" (מתג mtg) produced "Gath" (גת gt). In turn, אמה ('ammâ) suggested to him a mother city, and so "daughter settlements," as the Hebrew term for "villages" may be more literally rendered.

The executions meted out to the Moabite army (2 Sam 8:2) are not reproduced here, perhaps simply for the sake of brevity.[117] The Moabite campaign is the first of a series of victorious battles waged in the Transjordan, which the chronicler narrates according to the sequence in 2 Samuel, before he comes full circle to fresh Philistine episodes in 20:4-8.

Zobah was the strongest of the Aramean states in David's period, and David was a threat to their sphere of power in the north Transjordan, just as he was to the Philistines

---

117. McKenzie, *The Chronicler's Use of the Deuteronomistic History*, 64, suggests simply a textual oversight. He is probably correct in considering idealization of David an unlikely cause for the omission.

in the west. The chronicler was not responsible for the increase of military numbers of v. 4. The LXX of 2 Sam 8:4 and, probably, 4QSam^a have the same reading.

The series of battle reports is brought to a close in v. 6*b* with a statement attributing such victories to the Lord. This generalizing conclusion will recur at the end of the next series, in v. 13*b*. These refrains were gladly reproduced by our historian, since they fit his reports about God subduing David's enemies and then David doing so himself (v. 1; 17:10; see also 20:4). The divine program relating to David's battles was being realized, as God crowned all his campaigns with blessing.

18:7-11. The spoils of war and related tribute are now the topic. The city of "Berothai" in 2 Sam 8:8 is replaced in v. 8*a* with "Cun," perhaps a place better known to post-exilic readers. Verse 8*b* represents an addition to the MT of 2 Samuel. The text 4QSam^a is not extant at this point, but the addition is present in the LXX of 2 Samuel, possibly by assimilation to the text of Chronicles. Whether the chronicler found it or added it, it suits his overall theme from chap. 17, in pointing to the Solomonic Temple on the horizon of his thought (see 2 Chr 4:12, 15-16). The gifts of metals from Tou of Hamath and similar spoils from the campaigns are "dedicated to the LORD," as an acknowledgment that the glory should go to David's patron. The dedication corresponds in placing and purport to the refrain of God's help in vv. 6 and 12. Within 1 Chronicles the dedication is picked up in 26:26 and then in 2 Chr 5:1 (= 1 Kgs 7:51). Verses 8*b* and 11 anticipate the theme of David's preparations for the Temple, to be announced in 22:5.

18:12-13. A second, shorter battle report is supplied, followed by a refrain that gives the Lord credit for the victories. There is a lack of concord between v. 12 and v. 13*a*. In the latter verse, David is the subject, and one expects him to be so in v. 12, as in the parallel 2 Sam 8:13. But Abishai appears in v. 12. Perhaps Abishai's victory was regarded the same as David's, like the killing of the giants in 1 Chr 20:4-8. The heading to Psalm 60:1 attributes the slaughter to Joab, another son of Zeruiah. So both the MT of 2 Samuel and the text of 1 Chronicles may have preserved different parts of a longer narrative.[118] The

initial clause in 2 Sam 8:13, concerning David's making a name for himself, is not included. It would have accorded with 17:8. The fact that David is the subject here, while the Lord is the subject there, may have encouraged its omission.

18:14-17. The chronicler continues to use the 2 Samuel text, describing the stability enjoyed by "all Israel" as a result of David's military successes. The secure place God was to create through David is now realized. The terms "Israel" and "people" in v. 14 are links with 17:9. The list of members of the royal administration in vv. 15-17*a* exhibits a chiastic order of military/civilian/religious/civilian/military leadership.[119] The bureau provides yet another indication that David's kingdom has been set on a firm footing. His imperial reign, marked by "justice," constitutes the inauguration of the kingdom in which the Lord will come to judge the earth (16:31-33).

In v. 16, the NRSV and the NIV, in place of the MT's "Abimelech," have followed a minority reading, "Ahimelech," as the name of the second priest, which accords with 2 Sam 8:17. The reconstructed reading underlying both texts may have been "Abiathar son of Ahimelech" (Ahitub may have been the grandfather of Abiathar).[120] But the chronicler knows nothing of this (see 6:12; the REB's "Zadok and Abiathar son of Ahimelech, son of Ahitub" represents a hypercorrection in which historical reconstruction has triumphed over respect for the text of Chronicles). David's sons are called "priests" in 2 Sam 8:19, and the change is generally credited to the chronicler's reluctance, in a post-exilic context, to envision any priesthood other than the Aaronic one.[121] Verses 15-17 have a new, prospective role. They reintroduce readers to Joab, who is to play a prominent role in the next three chapters. In referring to the priests Zadok and Ahimelech, the verses anticipate David's organization of temple personnel with their help (24:3, 6, 31).

---

118. McCarter, *2 Samuel*, 246.

119. De Vries, *1 and 2 Chronicles*, 162.

120. See the discussion in McCarter, *2 Samuel*, 253-54.

121. Armerding has observed that Israel knew of several orders of priesthood, citing 2 Sam 20:26; 1 Kgs 4:5. See C. E. Armerding, "Were David's Sons Really Priests?" in *Current Issues in Biblical and Patristic Interpretation*, ed. G. F. Hawthorne (Grand Rapids: Eerdmans, 1975) 75-86. Alternatively, Wenham has suggested that the chronicler has paraphrased a term for administrators of royal estates, סכנים (*sknym*), found in his text of 2 Samuel, which was subsequently corrupted to כהנים (*khnym*), "priests." See G. J. Wenham, "Were David's Sons Priests?" *ZAW* 87 (1975) 79-82.

19:1–20:3. The narrative, like that in 2 Samuel but to a much lesser extent, functions as an extended note, explaining the defeat of Ammon, briefly mentioned in 18:11. It also supplies further information on the defeat of Hadadezer, covered in 18:3-4. The narrative has been pruned of the complication of David's adultery and murder in 2 Samuel; otherwise, it follows that text by and large. It tells of the new Ammonite king's provocation of David (19:1-5) and both sides' preparations for battle (19:6-13), reports the defeat of the Aramean mercenary troops and withdrawal of the Ammonite army to the capital (19:14-19), and reports the next season's victorious campaign (20:1-3). The chronicler must have appreciated the way 19:11 mentions "all Israel" as being conscripted to fight under David, an echo for him of the concerted campaign against Jerusalem in 11:4-6. He would also have liked the fresh affirmation in 19:13 that, when victory comes, God is the giver. Both Israelite companies were to do their best and leave the rest to the Lord, who "will do [rather than "may the Lord do," NRSV] what is good in his sight" (NIV). A greater role is given to David in a few places. He takes the initiative in 19:17b, over against 2 Sam 10:17b, and in 19:19 peace is made with him, not with Israel, as in 2 Sam 10:19. On the other hand, in 20:1 the 2 Samuel text has been roughly condensed, and Joab's concern to give David the glory by capturing Rabbah in 2 Sam 12:27-30 has been dropped.

In 19:6-7 there are a few differences from the MT of 2 Samuel. The chronicler's reference to "Mesopotamia" in place of "Beth-Rehob" in 2 Sam 10:6 probably reflects a later readership's unfamiliarity with that Aramean state, and so does the dropping of "the men of Tob." The sum of 1,000 talents of silver in 19:6 is not an embellishment by the chronicler. It also occurs in 4QSam^a and so was shared by the chronicler's 2 Samuel text. Apparently 4QSam^a also read "thirty-two thousand chariots," which explains its presence in 19:7, over against 2 Sam 10:6. The final sentence in 19:7, absent from the MT of 2 Sam 10:7, also occurs in 4QSam^a, though in a slightly different form. The penultimate Hebrew sentence in 19:7 ("who . . . Medeba"), which does not occur in 4QSam^a, presents a logistical problem. Moabite Medeba

is too far to the south to permit the reciprocal emergency arrangements envisioned in 19:12 for the two obviously adjacent Israelite companies. An underlying מי רבה (*my rbh*), "waters of Rabbah," has been conjectured for מידבא (*mydb'*) with reference to 2 Sam 12:27.[122]

In 19:19 the "servants" (NRSV) of Hadadezer are his "vassals" (NIV), the junior Aramean kings who had committed their armies to the enterprise (cf. 2 Sam 10:19). With their capitulation only the Ammonite sector had still to be overcome, which duly takes place in 20:1. The English versions attest the ambiguity of the consonantal Hebrew text in 20:2. Was it the crown of "their king" (מלכם *malkām*, NIV) or of "Milcom" (מלכם *milkōm*, NRSV), the Ammonite god in iconic form? In 20:3 both versions emend the verb of sawing to one of setting or consigning to work, in line with 2 Sam 12:31. However, the MT may refer, not to a gruesome act of cruelty, but to dismantling fortifications.[123]

20:4-8. The narrative returns to the Philistines. They are the A and Z of opposition to God's people, who typically needed to be "subdued," as representatives of all of David's enemies (17:10). These agents of defeat in chap. 10 now meet their match. Whereas Saul lost, David won and won again. Power passed from Israel's enemies to David and his troops (18:1; 20:8).

Three Israelite exploits against aboriginal "giants" (NRSV) or "Rephaim" (REB) who were allied with the Philistines are recounted. The perpetrators of these exploits are assumed in v. 8b (as in the parallel 2 Sam 21:22) to be soldiers in David's service, though he was not personally involved. "Gezer" in v. 4 corresponds to "Gob" in 2 Sam 21:18. Whatever the reason for the variant, in the overall narrative of Chronicles it nicely picks up where the campaign against the Philistines in 14:16 left off.[124] Verse 5 appears to be the result of an exegetical crux that confronted the chronicler, a crux that presupposes knowledge of 1 Samuel 17:1 (cf. 11:23). Who killed Goliath: Elhanan (2 Sam 21:19) or David (1 Samuel 17:1)? The chronicler may have

---

122. Rudolph, *Chronikbücher*, 137, following Rothstein and *BHS*.

123. McCarter, *2 Samuel*, 313.

124. McCarter considers the 1 Chronicles reading superior and the MT of 2 Samuel the product of assimilation to the city in 2 Sam 21:19. See K. McCarter, *2 Samuel*, 448.

been making the best of a corrupt text (בֵית-הלחמי [bêt-hallaḥmî, "the Bethle-hemite"] is represented as את-לחמי [ʾet-laḥmî], now the slain giant's name, and the sign of the direct object את [ʾēt] has become אחי [ʾăḥî, "brother of"]). However, the rec-onciliation of rival traditions seems to have played a part in the history of this text.

These territorial victories gave Israel room to dwell in all directions. There were also respectful overtures from Tou, king of Hamath, who is Huram of Tyre all over again (14:1). David's fame was, indeed, going out into all lands (14:17). The chronicler finds here evidence of God's immediate purpose: to give Israel a secure place, free of the oppres-sion that has dogged them since the days of the Judges (17:9-10a). It was part of the Lord's overall plan, which required a peaceful setting for the building of the Temple, which in turn would guarantee the continuance of the Davidic dynasty (17:10b-14). The goal of the Temple has received some minor atten-tion in 18:8 and, implicitly, in 18:11.

The forward-looking prayer in 16:35, "Save us from the nations," which fuses his-torical and contemporary concerns, raises the issue of an implicit eschatological agenda in these chapters, according to which David won victories over "all the nations" (18:11 NRSV). Judah's territorial weakness in the post-exilic period must have filled the chroni-cler's first readers with nostalgia. The relish with which he narrates royal victories sug-gests that this victorious past was intended to point toward Israel's own future.

REFLECTIONS

1. A triangle dominates Old Testament theology: the Lord, Israel, and the land. In the New Testament, the issue of the land falls away. The Old Testament promise of the land as Abraham's inheritance is transformed into the world in Rom 4:13 and into a heavenly country in Heb 11:16. Moreover, prophetic and apocalyptic talk of warfare largely gives way to a sublimated and spiritualized form of cosmic struggle, which occa-sions impressive imagery for the development of Christian virtues, as Eph 6:10-17 illus-trates. Perhaps we modern readers need a stronger sense of the supernatural conflict of which the later chapters of Daniel and such New Testament writings as Ephesians are so conscious in order to draw a fair typological parallel with the chronicler's concerns.

His portrayal of the warrior king fighting at God's behest and with God's help was associated with the inauguration of a new age. There is a close spiritual rapport at this point between 1 Chronicles and the Letter to the Colossians. God has rescued us believers (1 Chr 16:35 NRSV) from the power of darkness and transferred us into the kingdom of Christ (Col 1:13; cf. 1 Chr 10:14). Peace has been won through the cross (Col 1:19). Christ has triumphed, disarming hostile powers (Col 2:15).

The chronicler lived in an age much less glorious than David's. While desiring eschatological fulfillment, the chronicler seems to have perceived that it would not be manifested soon. Yet, he wished his readers to sense that they were on God's side and identified with a cause that would ultimately enjoy victory. Likewise, the Christian affirmation that "we are more than conquerors" was spoken in defiance of present tribulation (Rom 8:35, 37).

The New Testament speaks of the Christian life in tones agreeable to the paci-fism, implicit or radical, of modern Christians. It must not be forgotten, however, that Christianity also directly inherits the theme of eschatological warfare from the Old Testament and intertestamental writings. The theological sublimation of an inaugu-rated eschatology, expressed in the once-for-all achievement of Christ and the ongoing struggle of Christians in an alien universe, does not exclude a coming showdown. The old language of military violence is dramatically revived for this event (see 2 Thess 1:7-9; 2:8; Rev 19:1; 20:7-9).

2. The section glides easily from God's subduing of David's enemies to David's doing it himself, and back again (17:10; 18:1; 20:4). The chronicler borrows from the description of the king's victories in 2 Samuel 8 the conviction that they were the gifts of the Lord (18:6, 13). He both borrows and enhances David's own desire to give God the credit (18:8, 11). In the same vein, Paul, returning from his third missionary trip, reported to the church leaders in Jerusalem "what God had done . . . through his ministry," and the hearers "praised God" (Acts 21:19-20). Both David and Paul were God's responsible agents in their different spheres. There is an exaggerated type of spirituality that makes God big by making humans small, urging them to be nothing so that God may be everything. David and Paul were individuals with their own identities, which they used for God even as God was using them.

3. Just as the verb of subduing has both divine and human subjects, so also human and divine factors are coordinated in Joab's battle speech (19:12-13). Each has its place, as in the not insincere summons to "put your trust in God and keep your powder dry." One human factor through which the Lord worked was mutual help. The motif of human help is reminiscent of chaps. 11–12, where it is associated with God's own help. Here it makes use of proven ability, in the sphere of shrewd military tactics. The second factor is sheer courage, the grit that is necessary to pursue doggedly an endeavor to its close. The third is loyal commitment to those for whom one is laboring and to God ("our people," "our God"). The expression of the divine factor conveys a calm sense of the Lord's sovereignty. Entrusting the venture to God releases us from crippling anxiety and enables us to do our best in God's service.

1 Chronicles 21:1–22:19, Temple Site and Builder Announced

OVERVIEW

Chapters 17–29 all relate to the Temple. The purpose of chap. 21 is to designate the site of the Temple, and of chap. 22 to specify Solomon as the son of David who will build it (cf. 17:11-12, 14). Solomon's name is mentioned in this connection for the first time. Both chapters use at their close the chronicler's key term for spirituality: "seek" (דרש *dāraš*; 21:30; 22:19). In this new era, the Lord is to be sought in the Temple, which is about to be built in Jerusalem. Both chapters focus on human failure or weakness as a means of bringing glory to God and highlighting God's own role.

1 Chronicles 21:1–22:1, Discovery of the Site by Grace

COMMENTARY

The climax of this episode comes in 22:1: the announcement of the site chosen by God for the future Temple, where Israel was to worship the Lord. For the chronicler and his post-exilic readers, it was a story full of spiritual relevance. It laid the foundation for their own worship of God in the Second Temple on the same site. Incongruously, it seems at first, the discovery was the result of a shameful act of presumption, narrated in chap. 21. Yet the very association of human sin with the Temple will turn out to be crucial for the chronicler's concept of spirituality.

The chronicler is sometimes accused of triumphalism and idealism in his depiction of David. He passed over the Bathsheba affair and the Uriah cover-up, narrated in 2 Samuel 11–12, which in 1 Chronicles is telescoped into a single, blame-free verse (20:1). That criticism is hardly fair. Those chapters in 2 Samuel belong to narrative about the royal succession and were designed to show that the Davidic dynasty was rooted in divine grace that overcame human sinfulness. As for the succession, the chronicler's interests in the dynasty were better served, he judged, by concentrating on the outcome, the passing of the crown to Solomon. The temple-building project was a major concern for the chronicler, and he wanted to establish from the outset its grounding in divine grace, the "mercy" of God, which is "very great" (21:13). At one point in the narrative, he departs from the basic text of 2 Samuel 24 and inserts a clause borrowed from the Bathsheba episode, "But God was displeased with this thing" (21:7 NRSV), in the Hebrew a virtual copy of 2 Sam 11:27b. The chronicler's awareness of Bathsheba is shown by 3:5, where she is called Bathshua. The echo in 21:7 is tantamount to saying that in his estimation this was an equivalent story. His David, too, had feet of clay. The chronicler wanted to affirm, in principle, that the Temple afforded the opportunity for the forgiveness of sins not only in David's case, but also for all the people of God during the centuries-long dispensation launched under David and Solomon (cf. 2 Chr 7:14-16).

The original story in 2 Samuel 24 reflected the conviction that the altar built at the threshing floor was the altar of burnt offering at the Temple. The story implicitly looked beyond David's reign to Solomon's building of the Temple.[125] The chronicler makes this conviction his own in the interpretive conclusion he adds at 22:1. His version of the story depends heavily on literary flashbacks. David's transgression in having taken a military census is narrated straightforwardly in 21:1-6; 21:7 is a summary statement of consequent divine punishment, which is explained in 21:8-14, with 21:14 eventually catching up with 21:7b. Another summary is found in 21:15a, now about God's relenting, which is told in 21:15b-27, with 21:27 giving actual expression

to the divine change of heart. Finally, 21:28–22:1 represents the chronicler's own ending to the story. It explains the divine legitimacy of the altar David had built.

The narrative of 1 Chronicles deviates from that in the MT of 2 Samuel 24 at a number of places. The discovery of 4QSamᵃ, fragmentary though it is, shows that many of these variants were inherited by the chronicler from the text he used, an important factor in assessing his own contribution. However, 4QSamᵃ is extant only for 21:15-21 (= 2 Sam 24:16-20).

21:1-2. A fascinating change occurs in v. 1, with mention of Satan as the initiating factor behind David's sin. Whether the chronicler made the change or it had already occurred in his text, it clearly represents theological rewriting. The Lord's anger is referred to in 2 Sam 24:1 as the reason for inciting David to sin. Sometimes in the psalms divine anger is not a reaction to human sinning, but an amoral violent force beyond human control (e.g., Pss 6:1; 74:1; 88:16; 102:10-11). It corresponds in some respects to the modern term used by insurance companies, "act of God." Old Testament theology often traces human experience directly back to God. Here the directness illustrates a logical difficulty occasioned by a monotheistic faith. Polytheism can simply assign misfortune to one or another god or goddess. Both Jews and Christians can appreciate that a later generation of believers required a more indirect explanation of both the divine anger and the entrapment policy, here associated with it. Divine enticement finds parallels in 1 Sam 26:19 and 1 Kgs 22:21-22, paralleled as well in 2 Chr 18:19-21, although a different verb is used. The latter reference was not changed, presumably because Ahab was regarded as already wicked (2 Chr 19:2) and so ripe for punishment.

Here, by way of explanation, help is obtained from Job 1–2 and Zech 3:1-5, where the שָׂטָן (śāṭān), "accuser," a supernatural member of the heavenly council, is represented as the malicious prosecutor in the celestial law court, gloating over human weakness and exploiting it. He has a mysterious role in God's purposes, but the harm he is permitted to do is limited by the Lord's control. The use of the verb "incite" with him as

125. McCarter, *II Samuel*, 517.

subject in Job 2:3 underlies the usage here. In Zech 3:1, he stood to accuse the high priest, and this expression, too, is borrowed as a posture of hostility. Both of these texts have been used to shed light on 2 Sam 24:1. In addition to borrowing, there is also development, in that here for the first time "Satan" appears as a name instead of a descriptive noun.[126]

The test relates to the taking of a military "census." Its military intent is indicated by the report of the results (v. 5) and by its being organized by army officers (v. 2). Here it is regarded as a sinful act to ascertain the precise number of the Israelite conscripts. In the context of 1 Chronicles it indicates a lack of trust in God as the giver of victory (cf. 18:6, 13). The Lord is able to achieve victory with an insignificant force (2 Chr 14:10-15). Chapters 18–20 described David's military successes as part of the overall divine plan for building the Temple. David gave God the glory and acknowledged that his success reflected God's blessing (17:8, 24; 18:1). Now his decision to take a census betrays a trust in human resources, rather than in God as their giver and user.

21:3. Joab objects that David is trespassing on God's prerogatives. Divine blessing is what counts. The 1 Chronicles text adduces another factor: that David has the whole people behind him (cf. 12:38), a boon with which the king should be content. It also intensifies Joab's objection by adding the warning that Israel would be imperiled by the guilt triggered by the census. The warning points the reader to v. 1, Satan's aim to attack Israel, and then forward to v. 7, the divine punishment of Israel, another adaptation in the text of 1 Chronicles. For the negative cultural presuppositions of census taking, one may compare Exod 30:12.

21:4-5. The detailed itinerary in 2 Sam 24:5-8 is omitted, and the chronicler moves quickly to the total obtained. He engages in two mathematical sums to revise the numbers given in 2 Sam 24:9. Instead of listing separately the totals for the northern

tribes ("Israel") and the later southern state ("Judah"), he gives a grand total for "all Israel," over which David reigns, according to chaps. 11–12. He also provides a separate, partial sum ("including," NIV) for the tribe of Judah. The grand total of 1,100,000 represents the addition of 800,000 and 500,000, the numbers in 2 Samuel, minus the two omitted tribes of v. 6, assuming 100,000 per tribe. The numbers in 2 Samuel may reflect a use of אלף (*'elep*), not numerically as 1,000, but as a smaller contingent.[127] The chronicler, however, would have appreciated enormous numbers as reflecting the glory of David's reign. The total of 470,000 for the tribe of Judah inconsistently presupposes the subtraction of only 30,000 for the tribe of Benjamin, which belonged to the state of Judah.

21:6. In this supplement to the text of 2 Samuel, Joab refuses to include all the tribes. The exclusion of Levi reflects the pentateuchal precedent in Num 1:49; 2:33, with which בתוכם (*bĕtôkām*; lit., "among them") provides an intertextual link.[128] The reason for the exclusion of Benjamin is less obvious. It is probably because of the presence of the tabernacle in Gibeon within its tribal territory (cf. Josh 18:25). The 1 Chronicles text assigns to Joab, in his abhorrence and greater vehemence, the role of spokesperson for the Lord's displeasure.

21:7. The text turns to the divine reaction. A direct reference to God is necessary after the adaptation of v. 1. "This thing" or "command" refers to the taking of the census, in the light of vv. 8 and 17. The clause is borrowed from 2 Sam 11:27, the Lord's reaction to David's murder of Uriah after having committed adultery with his wife. There is only a loose connection between 2 Sam 24:10 and v. 7, the verb of striking. Israel, the object of David's selfish pride, is punished, and Satan's initial aim of attacking Israel (v. 1) is achieved. By using the verb "to strike" (הכה *hikkâ*, in the hiphil) in this new way, the text has anticipated v. 14. Hence, vv. 8-14 function as a detailed flashback. Moreover, David's prayer (v. 8) lacks the introduction of repentance it has in the parent text.

126. Day, observing that the name does not occur until c. 168 BCE, takes the noun as "a *satan*," an unspecified celestial accuser. See P. Day, *An Adversary in Heaven: Satan in the Hebrew Bible*, HSM 43 (Atlanta: Scholars Press, 1988) 128-29, 142-44. Japhet interprets it as a human figure. See Japhet, *I & II Chronicles*, 374-75. And Wright takes it as a national enemy. See J. W. Wright, "The Innocence of David in 1 Chronicles 21," *JSOT* 60 (1993) 93. However, the intertextual links with Job and Zechariah suggest hermeneutical dependence on both passages.

127. See McCarter, *2 Samuel*, 510.

128. Mosis, *Untersuchungen zur Theologie des chronisten Geschichtswerks*, 108.

21:8-14. The king prays for the alleviation of the burden of guilt that his sin has brought upon Israel (v. 3). The flow of the narrative and a comparison with Num 14:19-23 suggest that what David sought was mitigation of punishment, escape from the crushing weight of merited annihilation (cf. 2 Sam 12:13-14). The court prophet Gad gives David a choice—not as to whether Israel is to suffer, but as to how they should suffer: by famine, foreign invasion, or pestilence. The Lord is represented as being capable of using nature and humanity as instruments of moral providence (cf. Amos 4:6-11). David opts for the shorter form of direct punishment from God as a judge who has the quality of mercy, rather than for punishment mediated through human agents, who might cruelly overstep the divine mandate (see Isa 10:5-12; 37:26-29). The 1 Chronicles text has been amplified in v. 12 by polarizing two new elements, "the sword of your enemies" and "the sword of the Lord," which paves the way for the contrast drawn in v. 13. The second phrase also prepares for the angelic sword in vv. 16 and 27. This is the role of a further amplification: the reference to the angel of the Lord destroying the land, which also anticipates v. 15. The great sin (v. 8) was to be mitigated through God's very great mercy. The chronicler draws an arc between these two points by adding "very" (מאד *mĕʾōd*) in v. 13, the term rendered "greatly" in v. 8. Verse 14 reports the pestilence as the method by which the Lord duly "struck" or "punished" Israel (v. 7), thus reducing sizably the large forces in which David trusted.

21:15-17. Once again an initial statement summarizes the whole and traces a process that is eventually reached in v. 27. The chronicler's own conclusion to the episode is in 21:26b–22:1. The addition of v. 27 achieves the eventual resolution of the threat posed in v. 15a. In the 2 Samuel text the parallel v. 16a does not have an anticipatory role. However, the drawn sword of 1 Chr 21:16 is found in 4QSamᵃ. Here, in vv. 16 and 27, the angel's sword begins and ends the episode as a symbol of destruction. It is brandished in threat until finally it is sheathed in implicit response to the Lord's command (v. 15a). The 1 Chronicles text adds a reference to the Lord's seeing (NIV) or taking

note (NRSV). It anticipates David's response, physical and verbal, of repentance and intercession (vv. 16b-17). The verb is used as in Ps 106:44, where God "regarded their distress [with compassion] when he heard their cry" (NRSV). The contingent nature of the divine word of judgment is expounded well in Jer 18:1-11 and illustrated even better in Jonah 3–4:2. The prophetic word of judgment assumes that the sinners threatened at the outset remain identified with their sin. If they distance themselves from it, the situation changes and the message of judgment does not apply. This prophetic contingency stands in tension with the emphasis on the absoluteness of the divine word in other parts of the OT (e.g., Isa 55:11). The chronicler does not employ the motif of divine relenting apart from this citation of 2 Sam 24:16, but the motif is similar to his regular message of divine forgiveness for the repentant, which appears in a classic formulation at 2 Chr 7:14.

The threshing floor, which will be the site for the Temple, is mentioned for the first time in v. 15b. It plays an increasingly prominent role throughout the paragraph, here simply as the angel's location, in v. 18 as the place where David is told to build an altar, in vv. 21-22 as the scene of David's negotiations to purchase it, and finally as the site of the duly built altar ("there," v. 26).

Verse 16 is much longer than the parallel text in 2 Sam 24:17. It was already in the chronicler's parent text, for it appears in almost identical form in 4QSamᵃ and may well have been largely lost in the MT.[129] The angel of destruction, hovering in midair, threatened Jerusalem with his drawn sword, ready to strike it. The drawn sword provides a counterpoint to the soldiers of the sinister census, "who drew the sword" (v. 5 NRSV). The punishment fits the crime.

David, together with the nation's representatives (cf. 11:3; 15:25), responds to the threat with renewed submission and repentant prayer. He now urges that he, as the instigator of the census, should bear the punishment—and not only he, but his family as well, despite the high expectations that were forecast for it in chap. 17 (note "my God," as in 17:25). The Lord's people, sheep in God's

129. See McKenzie, *The Chronicler's Use of the Deuteronomistic History,* 55-56.

covenant flock who are innocently led to the slaughter (cf. Jer 11:19), should not suffer. Such seems to be the force of the metaphor in the present text. The LXX of Samuel and 4QSam[a] develop the metaphor with reference to David as a shepherd, responsible for the sheep. This was surely the original text there.[130] The REB, indulging in hypercorrection, imports this longer text into 1 Chr 21:17, "It is I who have sinned, I, the shepherd who have committed wrong."

21:18-19. The chronicler introduces the angel of the Lord as the originator of the command to build an altar. He had in mind the story of Balaam, where the angel of the Lord first confronts Balaam with a drawn sword, causing him to fall to the ground in submission, and then reveals a message to him (Num 22:31, 35). Arrangements for a means of reconciliation now begin. In terms of the summary in v. 15a, they happen between the Lord's relenting and the restraint of the angel (v. 27). God listens, not to the logic, but to the spirit of David's prayer. A new prophetic word has come to David through God, as v. 19 underlines—a word as momentous as that which came through Samuel for him to become king (11:3, 10; 12:23). This word constitutes a significant step toward the implementation of the building of the Temple, as 22:1 will affirm. The erection of an altar is the task assigned to David as an act of penance and the means of his reconciliation to God, which would lead to the cessation of the pestilence (cf. v. 22).

21:20-21. Verses 20-21a reflect a conflated text (cf. 2 Sam 24:20). The first part may reflect a rewriting of an illegible text, as in 15:27, which has subsequently had a correction added. But the detail of Ornan's threshing wheat, absent from the MT of 2 Samuel, is confirmed by 4QSam[a].[131] The hiding of Ornan's sons reflects a fear that looking at the angel of the Lord would be fatal (cf. Judg 6:22-23).

21:22-25. The negotiations have been flavored with several details drawn from Abraham's bargaining for a burial place for Sarah in Genesis 23:1. In v. 22, David's taking the initiative echoes Gen 23:3-4, and the two instances of the verb "give" (נתן nātan)

reflect Gen 23:4, 9. The insistence on paying "the full price" in vv. 22, 24a corresponds to Gen 23:9. Abraham's purchase was a landmark in Israel's history, since it was the first piece of real estate owned in the promised land. The purchase of the threshing floor was a comparable landmark for the chronicler. Ornan's throwing in the wheat he had been threshing as part of the deal (v. 23), to be used as a grain offering, is a new touch. The citing of a grain offering alongside burnt offerings meant that David's foundational sacrifices in v. 26 included the statutory pair of offerings laid down in the Torah (see Exod 29:38-41; Num 15:2-10; 2 Chr 7:7). The fine or choice flour of the grain offering was ground from wheat (Exod 29:2).

David's insistence that he will not offer free burnt offerings is reinforced in 1 Chronicles with the prefatory statement that he will not use for the Lord another person's property (v. 24). Since David is sacrificing on Israel's behalf, he must bear the cost. In v. 25 the price of 600 gold shekels contrasts with that of 50 silver shekels in 2 Sam 24:24. There it is the cost of the threshing floor and oxen, here it is the price for "the site" (vv. 22, 25), which covers a larger area, sufficient for the Temple (cf. 2 Chr 3:1). The change from silver to gold may reflect the lavish use of gold for the Temple. The medieval commentator Rashi suggested that the number 600 had symbolic value as a multiple of twelve: Whereas the 50 shekels of 2 Samuel were paid by David as a member of the tribe of Judah, 600 were sufficient for the twelve tribes.

21:26-27. Verse 26a marks the completion of the commission to erect an altar in v. 18. It is sealed by the inaugural sacrificing of the two standard types of offerings, as in 16:1. We were not told on what altar the offerings in 16:1 were sacrificed (cf. 29:21). The chronicler simply took over the rite from his 2 Samuel text. What the chronicler adds begins in v. 26b and extends to 22:1. First, the narrative is brought to a close in vv. 26b-27. David presumably asked that this inaugural rite of worship be accepted as a sign of forgiveness. The prayer appears to be modeled on Elijah's prayer in 1 Kgs 18:36-37. That earlier prayer appealed for an answer, which came in the form of fire devouring the sacrifice on the altar Elijah had built.

---

130. McKenzie, *The Chronicler's Use of the Deuteronomistic History,* 56.
131. See McKenzie, *The Chronicler's Use of the Deuteronomistic History,* 57.

Here God "answered" similarly. Acceptance by divine fire will reappear in 2 Chr 7:1, in another addition made by the chronicler, after the inaugural sacrificial rite in Solomon's Temple. Both instances depend on Lev 9:24, which associates the fire of acceptance with the inauguration of Aaron's priesthood. The fire puts David's altar on a par with the altar of the old tabernacle, featured in the Torah. It also marks the reconciliation and reinstatement of David and Israel before God. Verse 27 returns to this more immediate concern. The crisis is over.

21:28–22:1. The chronicler regularly appends an interpretive conclusion to a narrative. The Hebrew syntax of this passage is complex, and the English versions simplify it into a series of separate sentences. The main clause consists of David's pronouncement in 22:1. Verse 28 is best understood as a two-part temporal clause. It recapitulates the two significant facts of v. 26 in reverse order, mentioning first David's appreciation of the divine answer of v. 26b and then continuing "and he had [earlier] sacrificed there," with reference to v. 26a.[132] Verses 29-30 are in parenthesis between the temporal clause and the main clause. But first v. 28, recapitulating v. 26, underscores the divine endorsement of David's sacrifice by means of supernatural fire. His sacrifice was a trial offer, one might say. God's acceptance proved that the altar bore a greater significance: It was good enough for both God and the king, so it would be good enough for Israel. The national dimensions of the event have been hinted at in v. 22: Relief of Israel's present suffering was at stake. Now sacrifices and altar are hailed as possessing "a once-for-all" value. Israel had a new altar of burnt offering; it had been prophetically commissioned (21:18). It was the nucleus of a new sanctuary, which in terms of chap. 17 may be called God's "house," the temple that David's successor was to build (cf. 2 Chr 3:1).

The parenthesis in vv. 29-30 raises the question of the old altar and the old sanctuary at Gibeon (cf. 16:39-40) and implies that its days were numbered. For all its traditional authenticity, traced back to Moses (cf. Exodus 26:1), it could not for long remain Israel's religious center. The Torah had been superseded in this respect. The chronicler could have appealed to the prophetic warrant of 21:18. In fact, he appeals to a higher authority; the revelation of the angel of the Lord, whose intervention the chronicler had claimed, lay behind the prophetic oracle in 21:18. This remarkable figure appears with his full title in the MT of 2 Sam 24:16b, and also as "the angel" in 2 Sam 24:16a, 17. In 1 Chronicles, however, he is called "the angel of the LORD" five times (21:12, 15b, 16 [= 4QSam[a]], 18, and 30) and four times "the [or an] angel" (21:15[twice], 20, and 27). The chronicler, encouraged by 2 Sam 24:16, echoes older traditions in crediting the figure with divine authority.[133] He stands at a distance from them; they have lost their original complex significance. He has little interest in angelology elsewhere. Here a greater significance is assigned to this figure, and the punch line in v. 30 explains why. It refers back to 21:16, now interpreted as a supernatural, deliberate barring of the way. The chronicler again had in mind Num 22:21, where the angel of the Lord is described in similar language and has this role. David's temporary inability to "seek" (דרש dāraš; NRSV and NIV, "inquire [of]") God, here not only in a formal religious sense, but also tinged with a sense of repentance and finding God anew, is invested with a once-for-all significance. This event points forward to the Temple to be built in Jerusalem as the divinely intended place at which Israel would seek the Lord. The Temple was to be dedicated especially to bringing repentant sinners, like David, back to God. The divinely nominated place is associated with a theology of grace, as 2 Chr 7:14 will explain.[134] David serves as a model for every backslider.

---

132. For inverse order in recapitulation as a Hebrew literary technique, see S. Talmon, "The Textual Study of the Bible—A New Outlook," in *Qumran and the History of the Biblical Text*, ed. F. M. Cross and S. Talmon (Cambridge, Mass.: Harvard University Press, 1975) 359-62.

133. For these traditions see T. Fretheim, *The Suffering of God*, OBT 14 (Philadelphia: Fortress, 1989) 93-95.

134. T.-S. Im, *Das Davidbild in den Chronikbüchern*, Europäische Hochschulschriften 23:263 (Frankfurt am Main: Peter Lang, 1985) 152.

REFLECTIONS

The altar David is commanded to build is, for the chronicler, a monument to God's forgiving grace. Hitherto the narrative had witnessed to a David dedicated to the will of God whose only fault was an unwitting ritual ignorance that he gladly resolved. But sooner or later forgiving grace cannot stay out of any divine/human relationship. There is a need for a "God who is rich in mercy," who redirects misused energies into new and wholesome channels (see Eph 2:1-10).

1. The reference to Satan in 21:1 is a milestone in the development of the theological explanation of human wrongdoing in the Bible. The echoing of phraseology from passages in Job and Zechariah reflects a constructive use of Scripture to grapple with issues of theodicy. Second Samuel 24:1 had referred simply to the mysterious will of the sovereign Lord, using the category of divine wrath, to which a number of the psalms attribute human suffering. However, in this context it involves David's being tempted to do wrong. So a means was sought to avoid associating God directly with such temptation. James 1:13-15 bears witness to a similar endeavor, but grounds temptation in the human self. The text of 1 Chronicles retains a supernatural reference. As in the book of Job, Satan is an angelic member of the divine administration who is permitted to initiate moral challenges and to appeal to what is base in human nature. He is permitted to inflict suffering and to provoke his victim to sin against God. The text has not reached the stage of an open rival to God's sovereignty that appears in the New Testament, for instance in Eph 2:2, where "the ruler of the power/kingdom of the air" is considered to be the agent of evil.

At no stage in the biblical development is there any denial of human responsibility for human actions. There is never a suggestion that the buck may be passed back with the excuse, "The devil made me do it." Moreover, the text of 1 Chronicles, like the underlying texts in Job and Zechariah, firmly encloses evil in a larger framework of divine providence. As in Zechariah 3, it is ultimately eclipsed by forgiving grace. In turn, the New Testament regards the celestial powers of evil as already being defeated in principle at the crucifixion and doomed finally to submit to God's benevolent sovereignty (see Rom 16:20; Col 2:15; Rev 20:10).

2. According to the chronicler, David's demand for a military census betrayed a lack of faith, an ungodly determination to walk by sight, not by faith, to adapt the language of 2 Cor 5:7. Joab's protest implies that David's sin was an act of presumption against the Lord as giver of national blessing. If we consider the chronicler's standpoint out of place in the real world, we may compare it to the warning of Jesus not to worry over such mundane matters as food and clothing, but to "seek first" God's "kingship over you" (Matt 6:33 NAB).

3. The social consequences of a person's sinning come to the fore in 21:1–22:1. Israel features as the object of Satan's challenge and the victim of God's displeasure. David did not function simply as an individual. He was Israel's representative before God and the agent of the whole people's destiny. He will magnanimously plead to bear the punishment alone (21:17)—a noble offer and an appropriate sign of remorse, but unrealistic nevertheless. Self-centered willfulness begins with oneself, but ends by dragging others down. This truth applies to commoners as well as to kings. Apparently private acts, such as personal infidelity or substance abuse, have social consequences. It was too late for David to say he did not want others to be involved as victims of his folly.

4. The king pleaded to be forgiven (21:8), but the forgiveness is not straightforward. In 21:10-15, as often in the Old Testament, God's grace is displayed after an experience of judgment. In the New Testament, the peace that spells reconciliation with God could only be made through the blood of the cross (Col 1:20). On the human plane this principle is also true to life. Sinning tends to unleash unchecked suffering. Repentance cannot undo the results of drunk driving. Confession of sin and recognition of accountability before God do not turn the clock back.

5. Divine grace is celebrated in 21:1–22:1. David opts to "fall into the hand[s] of the LORD, for his mercy is very great." The reader of the New Testament is superficially reminded of the grim words and grimmer context of Heb 10:31 that it is "a terrifying thing to fall into the hands of the living God" (REB). The contrast warns against the all-too-common generalization that the Old Testament is full of God's wrath, but the New Testament of God's love. Here the chronicler takes over from 2 Samuel a message that stands at the heart of his own overall presentation: Forgiving grace predominates in the Lord's attitude to the covenant people. The combination of divine mercy and relenting accords with a version of part of the great theological proposition in Exod 34:6-7, which appears in Joel 2:13 and Jonah 4:2, "The LORD is merciful . . . and relents from punishing" (NRSV). It is the theme of Psalm 103:1, a hymn celebrating God's forgiving grace: "The LORD is merciful. . . . He does not deal with us according to our sins" (Ps 103:8, 10 NRSV).

6. Personal cost is an essential factor in biblical spirituality. David's protest that he must pay for the threshing floor and its accoutrements (21:24) is prefaced in the text by the extra clause, "I will not take for the LORD what is yours." The offering of sacrifices had to reflect personal spirituality. Malachi complained that some of the sacrificial animals that worshipers were bringing to the Temple had been misappropriated, while others were blind or lame (Mal 1:8, 13). For integrity's sake, an offering had to be of true value. This is a principle worth pondering by the Christian in offering to God the spiritual sacrifices of praise and shared resources (Heb 13:15-16). The ostensible price tags do not necessarily represent the value, as Jesus shrewdly taught in contrasting the respective donations of the widow and the wealthy (Luke 21:1-4).

1 Chronicles 22:2-19, Solomon's Mandate to Build

COMMENTARY

According to 17:11-12, one of David's sons would build the Temple. Now that son is identified as Solomon, who duly receives a commission from David to undertake his divinely assigned task. The identification of the site for the Temple (v. 1) made it possible to proceed with plans for its construction. The passage is structurally bound together as a threefold series of instructions toward this end, vv. 2-5, 6-16, and 17-19.

22:2-5. David's provision of materials for the future Temple was an ongoing task that he pursued for many years (v. 5b). The Hebrew verb "to provide" (הכין hēkîn, in the hiphil) is the key word, occurring three times (v. 3, "provided"; v. 5a, "make provision," REB; "make preparation[s]," NRSV, NIV; v.

5b, "provided," NRSV). These verses function as narrative background for David's mention of his provision (v. 14). The stone had to be hewn, and so stonecutters were procured from among the resident aliens, who were used for forced labor. The chronicler has transferred back to David's reign material he has also used for Solomon's (cf. 1 Kgs 5:15; 9:20-21; 2 Chr 2:17-18; 8:7-8). Bronze, which was used extensively in Solomon's Temple, had been obtained in David's wars and would be used for the molten sea, the pillars in front of the Temple, and temple vessels (18:8; cf. 1 Kgs 7:15-47; 2 Chr 4:11-18). The Phoenicians' supply of cedar anticipates Solomon's own request for cedar from King Huram of Tyre (2 Chr 2:8 = 1 Kgs 5:6). The chronicler does not specify its use, but the 1 Kings account mentions the cedar paneling of the main walls and roof of the Temple and the inner wall of the holy of holies (1 Kgs 6:9, 15-16). The note of hyperbole sounded in vv. 3-4 concerning the amounts of bronze and cedar used, which v. 14 repeats to a greater degree, is explained in v. 5.

David's reflection in v. 5a provides the reader with two inter-related reasons for his policy of preparation: Solomon's youthfulness and inexperience. The gist of it will recur in 29:1. Mention of Solomon's youth is a wisdom motif (cf. 1 Kgs 3:7, where the motif refers to his ruling), applied here to his role as temple builder. David's building experience (cf. 14:1; 15:1) could be put to good use, not for building the Temple, from which he had been debarred (17:4), but for amassing appropriate materials and for other preparations listed in 28:11-19. The chronicler gives the Temple greater legitimacy by closely associating it with David, already a theological hero and a role model for Israel.

The end product had to be worthy of God. It would be a showpiece commanding universal admiration and reflect its divine patron. One of the Songs of Zion, with the Temple in mind, celebrates Mount Zion as "beautiful in elevation . . . the joy of all the earth" (Ps 48:2 NRSV); another psalm calls Zion "the perfection of beauty" (Ps 50:2), and Lam 2:15 echoes both these acolades. The chronicler's actual vocabulary, "fame" (שֵׁם šēm) and "glory" (תפארת tif'eret), is borrowed from the description of Israel's eschatological supremacy (šēm, tif'eret [Deut 26:19; Jer 13:11]; šēm [Zeph 3:19-20]). In Jer 33:9 tif'eret is applied to Jerusalem, which probably encouraged the chronicler's reapplication of it to the Temple. Indeed, in 29:11 similar language appears in an effusive description of God. The Temple was to be as adequately as possible a reflection of divine glory. This idealistic representation explains the language of limitlessness in vv. 3-4 and in v. 14 below. Verse 5 reaffirms the complementary nature of the respective work of David and Solomon. Their reigns represented a joint venture in completing the institution that thereafter in Israel's experience would be the channel of divine grace and human worship.

22:6-10. Chapter 28 will contain the public charge to Solomon to build the Temple. This charge is a preliminary, private commissioning. In David's speech the previous divine warrant for Solomon to be temple builder (17:4-14) is repeated in vv. 7-10, and Solomon is encouraged to assume this role in vv. 11-16. Each half of the speech is introduced by the vocative "my son" (vv. 7, 11). Verses 7-10 obviously depend on Nathan's oracle in 17:4-14. However, the chronicler takes the opportunity to import some fresh nuances. He leans on Solomon's retelling of the event in his letter to Hiram at 1 Kgs 5:3-4 and in his prayer at 1 Kgs 8:17. First, Solomon's words in 1 Kgs 8:17, which the chronicler uses directly in 2 Chr 6:7, are put back into David's mouth in v. 7, to give expression to his own frustrated ambition to build the Temple. Then in vv. 8-9a David's leadership in war is presented as that which disqualifies him from building the Temple (cf. 1 Kgs 5:3), while the absence of warfare qualifies Solomon as the temple builder (cf. 1 Kgs 5:4). In Samuel–Kings, both David and Solomon are created with enjoying rest from war (2 Sam 7:11; 1 Kgs 5:4), which was a precondition for building the Temple (Deut 12:10-11; cf. 2 Chr 7:12). The chronicler tended to view David as a warrior, and to that end edited the reference to rest (2 Sam 7:11) out of 17:10, as we saw. Here the NRSV and NIV conceal the connection with 1 Kgs 5:4 by rendering שלום (šālôm) as "peace" instead of as "rest" twice in v. 9a. The chronicler clinches his attribution of rest to Solomon by a wordplay between his name (שלמה šĕlōmōh) and šālôm in v. 9b.

The description of David as a warrior king in v. 8a has a different nuance from that in 17:8b-10a. There it has a positive ring, as the result of divine initiative and blessing. This interpretation of David's warfare is actually echoed in v. 18 below. Here David's actions are his own, while God is a comparative bystander. The basis for the change may be Shimei's accusation that David was "a man of blood" (2 Sam 16:7 NIV), though it has been completely reapplied, if so. The repeated mention of shedding much blood suggests that it had a polluting effect (cf. Num 35:33; Ps 106:38-39). This dual interpretation of David's fighting finds a parallel in Numbers

31:1.[135] There, on the one hand, Israelite troops engaged in a divinely initiated campaign to execute the Lord's vengeance on Midian (Num 31:3); yet, on the other hand, any who killed became unclean and had to purify themselves (Num 31:20, 24). In Israelite culture uncleanness was differentiated from moral culpability.[136] The unclean were debarred from approaching the temple (2 Chr 23:19). It was an easy step for the chronicler to extend the ban to David's building the Temple, after repeated bouts of uncleanness. Such a firm ban enhanced Solomon's legitimacy as temple builder.

Verse 10 is paralleled in 17:12-13a, but is closer to 2 Sam 7:13-14a. The last three clauses are inverted so that greater emphasis falls on Solomon's divinely backed kingship. David's son (v. 9) would also be the Lord's son, adopted into divine patronage (cf. Ps 2:7). Modern versions are much more staccato than the Hebrew; the KJV's "*and* he shall be my son" expresses the consequence. The building of the Temple would clinch Solomon's special relation to the Lord, which in turn would lead to a further consequence: the perpetuity of the dynasty descended from him.

22:11-16. Verse 11 moves to the imminent task of temple building. The commissioning proper begins at this point. It typically consists of three elements.[137] One is the assurance that the Lord's presence will bring success to the task. Expressed as a wish, it is placed at the beginning and repeated at the end, functioning as a framework in the commissioning (vv. 11, 16). The second element is the description of the task (v. 11). The third element is one of encouragement, to be strong and free of needless fears (v. 13). In v. 12, God's supporting presence is reformulated as a divine gift of wisdom, which David covets for Solomon (cf. 1 Kgs 3:12). Here Solomon's general task of ruling appears to be in view. Solomon had a double duty: to be Israel's king and to build the Temple (vv. 10-12; these general and specific duties are also combined in 29:19). Wisdom here refers to the Torah, which Solomon must use to rule well.

The NRSV differentiates between "succeed" in the temple project (v. 11) and "prosper" generally (v. 13). Although the same Hebrew verb (צלח *ṣālēaḥ*) is used, the context indicates different references. This advice to obey the Torah echoes David's charge to Solomon just before his death in 1 Kgs 2:2-3. The exhortation to be strong in v. 13b reverts to the building of the Temple. The new link forged by the chronicler between the wise rule of 1 Kings 3 and obedience to the Torah in 1 Kings 2 reflects a late development in wisdom thinking, which defined wisdom in terms of the Torah (see Psalms 19; 119).

David grounds the encouragement in a further factor: his own provision of resources for the task. Solomon would not have to start from scratch, but could use materials and workers that have already been supplied. The NIV and the NRSV rightly take v. 16a closely with v. 15, so that "without number" refers to the workers. The chiastic order confirms this connection: metals, timber, stone, stone-workers, timberworkers, metalworkers.[138]

A striking feature of David's description of his provision is the incredibly large amounts mentioned in v. 14. The qualifications "beyond weighing" and "without number" in vv. 14-15 echo those of vv. 3-4, where the divine associations of the Temple encouraged hyperbole. Here the same motivation is implicitly at work. According to 1 Kgs 10:14, Solomon's annual income was 666 gold talents, which was intended to be a breathtaking amount. This comparison enables the reader to judge the colossal nature of the present figures and calls into question a literal interpretation. Earlier figures in 1 Chronicles all seemed to have had some rational basis in relation to the literary source or context. Here, as elsewhere, the chronicler resorts to his own branch of mathematics, rhetorical mathematics, which must be respected for its intention. English idioms can use mathematical language to express hyperbole, as when we say, "Thanks a million" or "A thousand pardons." Here the exaggeration is akin to the extravagant language of praise in the hymns and thanksgiving songs of the psalms. Just as they attempt to convey in words God's incomparability, so also these incredible

135. See Im, *Das Davidbild in den Chronikbüchern*, 139.

136. See T. Frymer-Kensky, "Pollution, Purification, and Purgation in Biblical Israel," in *The Word of the Lord Shall Go Forth*, ed. C. L. Myers et al. (Winona Lake: Eisenbrauns, 1983) 399-404.

137. See D. McCarthy, "An Installation Genre?" *JBL* 90 (1971) 31-41.

138. Curtis and Madsen, *The Books of Chronicles*, 258.

numbers express in material terms the magnificence of this God of the Temple.

A further agenda is found in this commissioning speech: The double charge to Solomon, private and public, in chaps. 22 and 28 recalls the commissioning of Joshua in Deut 31:7-8, where Moses addresses him, and in Josh 1:2-9, where the Lord communicates to him directly (cf. Deut 31:23). All three of the formal elements are found in both passages: (1) the call for courage and the banishing of fear (Deut 31:7-8; Josh 1:6-7, 9); (2) the description of the new task (Deut 31:7; Josh 1:2, 6); and (3) the assurance of divine aid (Deut 31:8; Josh 1:5, 9). The duty of obeying the Torah reappears in Josh 1:7-8, with mention of general prosperity (*ṣālēaḥ*), the same verb used in 1 Chr 22:13. A deliberate parallel is being drawn between Joshua as successor to Moses and Solomon as successor to David.[139] Just as Joshua, rather than Moses, crossed the Jordan as the divinely appointed leader to win the land (Deut 31:2-3), so also Solomon, rather than David, is commissioned to build the Temple. The chronicler affirms a dispensational relationship of type and antitype between the old pair of God's servants and this new pair. This typologizing functioned as an argument that a temple age had succeeded the tabernacle era of Moses and

139. Braun, "Solomon, the Chosen Temple Builder," 586-88; *1 Chronicles*, 221-23; H. G. M. Williamson, "The Accession of Solomon in the Books of Chronicles," *VT* 26 (1976) 351-61.

Joshua. The Lord was doing a comparable new work and resetting the stopwatch of theological history.

22:17-19. David now urges Israel's leaders to support Solomon in the project. This charge was meant as a private lobbying meeting before the public one in 28:1-8. The speech in vv. 18-19 falls into the same double pattern found in vv. 7-16. In v. 18, David concentrates on God's work (rather than God's Word, vv. 7-10), and in v. 19 on building the Temple (as in vv. 11-16). The leaders, too, receive a charge, with two of the standard three elements represented: the Lord's presence and the task. The Lord's presence had been manifested in the momentous achievements of David's reign, which had by its close brought about "rest" from warfare. So, implicitly, it was time to build the Temple, according to the divine calendar of Deut 12:10-11. Their task is first defined in general terms in a call to "devote your heart and soul" to seeking the Lord. As "your God" (vv. 18-19), the Lord had a claim on their lives. Again the chronicler's key term for spirituality is used ("seek," דרש *dāraš*; cf. 10:13-14; 13:3; 15:13; 21:30). Spirituality is worked out in various ways in 1 Chronicles; here it takes the specific form of assisting in building the Temple, so that the ark and the holy vessels (2 Chr 5:5) might receive due honor. To respect the things of God in this way was to honor God.

REFLECTIONS

1. David and Solomon have complementary roles in their great work for God, David as a warrior king and a provider and Solomon as a king in peacetime and a builder. Each brought to his particular tasks his personal qualities, resources, and opportunities. Paul, in turn, testified to this principle of complementarity in Christian service: "I planted the seed, Apollos watered it, but God made it grow . . . and each will be rewarded according to his own labor" (1 Cor 3:6, 8 NIV). While Paul "laid a foundation," others had opportunities to build on it with such resources as they were able to contribute, "gold, silver, costly stones" (1 Cor 3:10-12).

According to the chronicler, the overall criterion in building the Temple was that the end product should be worthy of the Lord and reflect divine glory. Likewise, the high appreciation of God we voice in our hymns and prayers should emerge from our commitment to God as we work and live for God.

2. A new era of divine revelation dawned with David's and Solomon's reigns. David had the role of being the forerunner, and Solomon was the fulfiller in a glorious outworking of God's Word in Deut 12:10-11. This day of grace, though old in time, was still operating for the chronicler, since God had promised David that Solomon's throne would be forever (22:10). In the New Testament, there is a comparable ring about the advent of Christ: "When the fullness of time had come, God sent his son" (Gal 4:4 NRSV). Like Solomon for Israel, Christ is "our peace," a claim that echoes the royal prophecy of Mic 5:5, "and he shall be the one of peace" (NRSV).

The typological comparison between Joshua and Solomon as fellow fulfillers of a task begun by others also affirms that a new epoch of revelation had arrived, authentically like the old, but superseding it. Second Isaiah engaged in this theological argumentation, for instance with the language of a new exodus in Isa 43:16-21; 52:12, over against Deut 16:3.[140] The Christian is reminded of the way temple language is reapplied to Jesus and the church in the New Testament, with similar claims that the God of former revelation has now moved on further (see John 2:19-22; 1 Cor 3:16; 6:19; Eph 2:21). The Bible urges us to appreciate the continuity and development of God's purposes. Old and new elements are intermingled in the New Testament. Their significance cannot be understood, however, until the Old Testament is taken seriously, rather than slighted as an antiquarian millstone around the neck of the modern church.

3. Verses 11-13 have an obvious value for the commissioning of any servant of God to a new work. Fears are admitted and faced, and God's enabling presence is offered as an antidote. Especially important is the truth that a special task does not exempt any believer from the general standards of God's will. The lesson was taken over from the deuteronomist in Josh 1:7-8. In this respect, also, Solomon was meant to be a latter-day Joshua. None of God's servants is ever placed in a privileged position above the moral law. That is a much-needed lesson, because in the shadow of prestige and power lurks the temptation to consider oneself untrammeled by ordinary conventions. However special the task, it grants no immunity from standards laid on all the people of God.

The new temple-oriented age was not exempt from the moral claims of the Torah in the old one. The Christian, in turn, rejoicing over God's grace in Christ, dares not dispense with the New Testament's affirmation that to love God still involves keeping God's commandments (1 John 5:3), as truly as in Exod 20:6. To live in the Spirit means to meet fully "the righteous requirements of the law" (Rom 8:4 NIV).

The "help" sought from Israel's leaders for Solomon in his task of building the Temple echoes the help David himself received in chaps. 11–12. God's servant does not stand alone or even receive help only from God directly, but is encouraged to look around for support from others. These leaders, however, especially needed the assurance of the Lord's presence with them. Their eyes are directed back to what their God had done. This recollection is to be equated, not with a proud self-congratulation for one's own efforts, which one may easily duplicate in the future, but with a sober assessment of what God has accomplished through one's ministry (see Acts 21:19). It functions as encouragement to the anxious that the same God will also be with them at the next stage.

140. See B. W. Anderson, "Exodus Typology in Second Isaiah," in *Israel's Prophetic Heritage*, ed. B. W. Anderson and W. Harrelson (New York: Harper, 1962) 177-95.

1 Chronicles 23:1–29:30, Preparing Personnel for the Temple

OVERVIEW

The structural bookends holding these chapters together are the partly parallel sentences of 23:1 and 29:28. First, David, "full of days," makes Solomon king, and finally David dies, "full of days," and Solomon becomes king. Co-regency was followed by sole rule. In chap. 28, David publicly commissions Solomon as temple builder, after the private ceremony in chap. 22. The bulk of chap. 29 is taken up with David's prayer of praise. This prayer is formally parallel to the psalm of praise and petition in chap. 16. The two great religious events of David's life, the installation of the ark in Jerusalem and preparation for the Temple, are both concluded with appropriate praise of God (16:8-36; 29:10-22).

The account of the private commissioning of Solomon as temple builder in chap. 22 was closely associated with David's material preparations for the Temple. This motif reappears in 29:2-5. Similarly, a little earlier David presents Solomon with a set of plans for the Temple and its furnishings (28:11-19),

and also for the personnel (28:13; cf. 28:21). The preceding chapters in this unit pave the way for this last statement by tracing back to David the complex organization of Levites at the Temple in the period of the chronicler. As De Vries comments on 28:13, "Now we know why [the chronicler] has insisted on inserting his regulations for the clergy into his narrative of the investiture."[141] Readers have been prepared for such a comprehensive ordering by the account of David's appointment of levitical and priestly musicians and security officers for the ark procession, for the ark installed in Jerusalem, and for the tabernacle in Gibeon (15:16-24; 16:4-6, 37-42).

141. De Vries, *1 and 2 Chronicles*, 219.

1 Chronicles 23:1-32, Organization and Duties of the Levites

COMMENTARY

23:1-6a. Verse 1 briefly alludes to the narrative of 1 Kings 1–2, characteristically omitting the struggle for succession to the throne described there, and presents the destined conclusion. Verse 2 refers to a preliminary meeting in which David gives assignments and instructions in preparation for Solomon's succession and commission as temple builder. The verse has often been regarded as a duplicate of 28:1, but the two meetings, for which different Hebrew verbs are used, are distinct. This meeting is an informal briefing, while the meeting in 28:1 is a formal convocation.[142] In vv. 3-6a, the chronicler has used a list older than his own time, related to a census of the Levites and to their proportionate division of duties. It appears to be post-exilic, since it regards gatekeepers and singers as Levites, a phenomenon that developed after the return from exile. It is attributed to the reign of David and had the function of legitimating the roles the Levites had in the Temple just before the time of the chronicler. Unlike the ill-fated military census of chap. 21, no exception is taken to this census, which has a different purpose. A similar census of Levites that assigns duties is found in Num 3:14-39;

142. See J. W. Wright, "The Legacy of David in Chronicles: The Narrative Function of 1 Chronicles 23-27," *JBL* 110 (1991) 229-42, esp. 229-31.

4:1-49. The total of 38,000 Levites is generally regarded as exaggerated. The value of the list for the chronicler is the fourfold division of duties, which he uses as a framework for the presentation of Levites in the following chapters. Here the groups are listed in descending numerical order, but in the expanded analysis their contribution to temple worship determines their order. Those responsible for maintenance of the Temple are featured in 23:6b-24. The Levites involved in administration and those assigned to secular work, here loosely called "officials and judges," are dealt with in 26:20-32. The gatekeepers appear in 26:1-19, and the musicians in 25:1-31. The tradition that David made the instruments used for sacred music also occurs in 2 Chr 7:6; 29:26; Neh 12:36. That it is an old tradition is indicated by its presence in Amos 6:5.

23:6b-24. The chronicler now uses another list, structured not according to total numbers of individuals involved but by family heads. The NIV uses a reader-friendly layout. One might judge it to be a general list of Levites, but it relates to the first category, as v. 24 shows by its echo of temple work. This group was probably the oldest of the levitical groups, which gradually adopted others into its ranks. The list begins in v. 6b, "The sons of Levi: Gershon, Kohath and Merari"

(TNK). It is not a proper genealogy, but a representative list of family heads current when it was composed, with narrative explanations where the list was incomplete. It runs from clan founder to a second or third generation and then jumps to contemporary heads of families. So "sons" with reference to these heads is used in the loose sense of descendants, as the NIV renders sketchily in vv. 16-17 and 24. Twenty-two family heads are listed.[143] Verses 10-11 regard Shimei's four sons as constituting only three families; v. 22 incorporates Eleazar's family into that of Kish. It is uncertain whether the law of inheritance in Numbers 27:1 would have been applied to exclusively male families of serving Levites. Japhet admits that in 24:28 Eleazar has no father's house.[144]

In vv. 7-8 (and 26:21), "Ladan" appears in place of "Libni" elsewhere (6:16-17; Exod 6:17; Num 3:18). Mention of "Shimei" in v. 9 seems to anticipate v. 10. The general structure of the list, in which the eldest son's children begin the listing of the next generation, leads one to expect the name "Jehiel" at this point.[145] Moses (v. 15) is a necessary exception to this pattern. In vv. 10-11, "Zina" and "Ziza(h)" must be the same person; the NIV and the REB emend the first name. The chronicler adds his own conclusion to the list in v. 24, relating this list of family heads to the previous total of individuals in v. 4a. The final phrase in the Hebrew, "from twenty years old and upwards," seems to be an annotation correcting the thirty-year lower limit of v. 3 (cf. Num 4:3). The lower limit evidently fluctuated according to supply and demand, and another limit was cited, which accords with 2 Chr 31:17; Ezra 3:8. A further annotation entered the text at v. 27, crediting the change of the minimum age of service to a later ruling by David.

Two aberrant factors of this levitical list are the aside in v. 13b and the complementary information of v. 14, concerning Aaron's status as a priest distinct from Moses and other Levites. This report apparently emanated from a pro-priestly redactor who wanted to present a more balanced view of the temple

personnel than the rather one-sided approach of the chronicler.[146] Since this summary of the priests' work is best understood as sketching their duties, the word לשׁרתו (lĕšortô) ought to be translated as "in serving him."[147] The first duty involved "the most holy things"— that is, things to be sacrificed. They were consecrated or kept holy through the following of proper sacrificial rituals. The second duty was that of communicating the Lord's blessing to the people (cf. Num 6:22-27). The benediction formed a bridge between temple worship and the worshipers' lives, promising fulfillment and satisfaction to those who had met with God at the Temple.

23:25-32. These verses, apart from the annotation in v. 27, should also be attributed to a pro-priestly redactor. They complement v. 13b by giving a review of the work of the Levites. The redactor stresses the Levites' subordination in rank to the priesthood. Their essential duty to "assist" and to "attend" the priests in a number of respects is stated emphatically at the beginning (v. 28) and the end (v. 32). In the temple age, they were no longer porters, as they had been in the earlier period of the portable tabernacle. In 15:2, the chronicler traced the Levites' old task back to Deut 10:8; 18:5, whereas here it is related to Num 3:6-9; 4:15, 27, 33 and is replaced by tasks that demonstrate their continued subordination to the priests.[148] Now some had become temple janitors, responsible for keeping everything clean. Others were bakers, scrupulously preparing various items for the standard offerings made by the priests. Yet others were musicians, accompanying the priests' regular sacrifices of burnt offerings with their music and songs of worship.

One can appreciate the redactor's desire to present a more balanced view of the Levites' work. What brands these verses as supplementary is the misunderstanding of the role of vv. 6b-24. Verse 24 harks back to v. 4a and indicates that only the first category of Levites is in view in the preceding list. Verses 25-32 assume that the list referred to all the categories in vv. 4-5 and so may include the musicians in vv. 30-31. The phrase "for

---

143. Japhet finds 24, including 10 from Gershon and 5 from Merari. Her total, however, disregards conclusions the text itself draws. See Japhet, *I & II Chronicles*, 413-17.

144. Japhet, *I & II Chronicles*, 433-34.

145. K. Hognesius, "A Note on 1 Chr 23," *SJOT* 1 (1987) 123-27.

146. See Williamson, "The Origins of the Twenty-Four Priestly Courses," 257n18; *1 and 2 Chronicles*, 161.

147. Kleinig, *The Lord's Song*, 105-6.

148. Rudolph, *Chronikbücher*, 157.

the service of the house of the LORD" is deliberately repeated three times (vv. 24, 28, 32), but inclusion of the musicians shows that the phrase is related to the Levites generally. Verses 25-32 function as an explanation of this "service." The accent on God's gift of rest to Israel in v. 25 recalls 22:18. There is a hint that the Lord also shared the rest, which anticipates the chronicler's perspective in 28:2; 2 Chr 6:41. The "forever" in v. 25 assumes continuity of worship despite the hiatus of the exile. It matches the double "forever" associated with the priests' duties in v. 13. Verse 32 gives the gist of Num 18:3-5, with the phrase "service of the tent" updated as "service of the house of the LORD" to fit the new context. This change suggests that in v. 32 the expression "tent of meeting," another term that could refer to the tabernacle, is used metaphorically for the Temple, which is the new counterpart of and replacement for the tabernacle.

REFLECTIONS

1. Chapter 23 begins a series of lists concerning temple administration. They are perhaps the most difficult part of Chronicles for Christian readers to apply. When the ark was brought to Jerusalem, lists of religious personnel and their roles were presented in chaps. 15–16. Now sacred history had moved on, and a more extensive organization was necessary. David is credited with having set up a complex system involving classes of Levites in the areas of maintenance, security, music, and secular duties. There is an outworking of a principle affirmed in the New Testament: "All things should be done decently and in order" (1 Cor 14:40 NRSV).

2. Essentially, the chronicler is investing the temple organization of his own day with the glory of past tradition. The chronicler belonged to a community of relatively little political importance. Thus he endeavored to give it a spiritual identity by postulating the Temple as the center of the community's life. To this end he used David and Solomon as religious models. This ideology brought meaning into life and crowned contemporary worship with the past glory. The thread of Davidic organization that runs through this chapter and succeeding ones helped the community to understand that the expression of post-exilic faith in worship rested on ancient, divinely sponsored foundations.

Modern Christians have to juggle cultural pressures and biblical roots and, as citizens of one world and heirs of another, try to find what to stand for. Aversion to modern-day bureaucracy has made us weary of organization and highly developed structures. Many Christians want to start again with smaller groups that can relate heart to heart and to shrug off the burden of large religious institutions with top-heavy appendages. Nevertheless, each religious group develops its own traditions, if only to differentiate itself from other groups, and needs organization in order to function effectively in worship, teaching, and faith development. The Christian who visits a church on vacation and enjoys a Sunday service knows nothing about the labors of love that lie behind it. In thanking the pastor, one should add thanks for others who have contributed behind the scenes. Commitment to the Lord necessarily means commitment to many details. They become windows through which others may glimpse the Lord. This is the chronicler's attitude as he takes us into a hive of religious industry.

3. The second half of the chapter (23:25-32, and also the earlier vv. 13b-14) reflects a need to redress the emphasis placed on the Levites. Nothing the chronicler has said is denied, but an editor considered a different perspective necessary. The chronicler wrote as an enthusiast, with the lopsidedness that often goes with zeal for a beloved cause. He crusaded for recognition and appreciation of the Levites. The editor also wanted the contribution made by priests to be prized. He wanted Chronicles to be more widely representative of temple traditions. We need the enthusiast, especially the champion of unappreciated worth. We also need the generalist who restores the balance. May God give us wisdom to know which to be and when.

4. The brief job description of the priests (23:13*b*) focuses on their roles in bringing the people's sacrifices to God and in bringing God's blessing to the people. Like the priest, the pastor stands in the middle, representative of earth to heaven and of heaven to earth.

1 Chronicles 24:1-31, The Divisions of Priests and Levites

COMMENTARY

The priests were organized into divisions in order to establish a rotational system of temple service, "their appointed order of ministering" (v. 3). These divisions correspond to the organization of Levites into four divisions (credited to David in 23:6*a*). Those levitical divisions related to different functions, but these twenty-four priestly divisions refer to different periods of temple duty. In Jewish practice, each division served for a week twice in a year of forty-eight weeks, based on a lunar calendar. Since 24:1 closely follows the mention of "the descendants of Aaron" in 23:32, the passage appears to be part of the same redactional complex. Like 23:25-32, 24:1-19 interrupts the exposition of the four divisions of Levites, announced in 23:4-6*a*.

This system of twenty-four divisions based on priestly families continued throughout the rest of the period of the Second Temple, and so it constitutes an important development. It reflects an overabundance of priests, who had to take their turn to exercise their right to serve in the Temple. Here this arrangement is attributed to David's supervision, but it appears to have occurred within the post-exilic period. At the beginning of that period, a time reflected in Ezra 2:36-39, there were only four priestly families. In Neh 12:12-31, an original fifteen or sixteen families at the time of the high priest Joiakim (Neh 12:12-18) had been editorially augmented with an extra six, which corresponded to a later situation (Neh 12:19-21).[149] By then the present twenty-four divisions had nearly been attained; ten names appearing here overlap with those in Neh 12:12-21, sometimes in

slightly different forms.[150] This final stage of development probably took place near the end of the Persian period, a little later than the chronicler's own time.

24:1-19. The numbered list (vv. 7-18) reflects this later development. It was inserted to amplify the description of priestly divisions in 28:13, 21, together with the divisions of Levites (cf. 2 Chr 8:14; 23:18; 31:2). Presumably these references were related to different priestly functions, although the original block of material contained within chaps. 23–27 does not contain such information. David was regarded as simply endorsing the functions of priests in the Torah and ordering that they be put into operation in the Temple.

The method for selecting the priests is reported in vv. 1*b*-6. They are described as descendants of only two of the four sons of Aaron: Eleazar and Ithamar. The scandal of the sacrilege committed by Nadab and Abihu, which led to their deaths (Num 3:4), is treated with reserve (v. 2), out of respect for the priesthood. In the Torah, Eleazar and Ithamar are mentioned as sharing certain responsibilities for transporting the tabernacle (Num 4:16, 28, 33). The presence of the names of the two leading priests in David's reign, Zadok and Ahimelech, reflects literary dependence on 18:16; these two priests are credited to the two surviving lines of priestly descent. Zadok's descent from Eleazar was derived from 6:8, 53, where his adoption into that priestly group is evidently in view. One may infer that Ahimelech was associated with the remaining line of Ithamar. The numerical

149. See H. G. M. Williamson, *Ezra, Nehemiah*, WBC 16 (Waco, Tex.: Word, 1985) 358-62.

150. See Japhet, *I & II Chronicles*, 429.

dominance of Eleazar's line presumably corresponds to the situation in the period of the redactor. The necessary adjustments to create twenty-four divisions are legitimated by tracing them back to David. Both groups win approval by having among them "sacred officers" (REB) and "officers of God" (NRSV). These titles do not refer to particular offices but are general descriptions of qualification for the priesthood.

The order of shifts is achieved by casting lots.[151] Apparently, one each of the families belonging to Eleazar's line and those of Ithamar's were chosen in turn, until the latter's families were exhausted. Then, the last eight families were confined to the line of Eleazar. A parallel for this pattern occurs in chap. 25. Accordingly, Ithamar's line is made up of numbers 2, 4, 6, 8, 10, 12, 14, and 16. The resulting roster by families is presented in vv. 7-18. Verse 19 carefully observes that the functions of the priests had been laid down in the Torah, presented by the Lord via Aaron, the priests' ancestor (see, e.g., Lev 10:8-11; 17:1-7). Only the number and order of the shifts were established by the present system.

24:20-31. A corresponding roster of Levites is given. The heading in v. 20a differentiates between the priestly line of Aaron, dealt with in vv. 1-19, and the rest of the "descendants" of Levi, the Levites. The list that follows in vv. 20b-30 bears a close relationship to that of the maintenance staff, grouped by family heads in 23:12-23. Once again, however, as in the redactional addition (23:25-32), it is assumed that the list represents Levites generally, and not just one group of them. The system of levitical divisions parallel to that of the priests presupposes the role of the Levites as assistants to the priests (23:28-32), which is here developed into a corresponding roster.

This list makes no mention of the Gershonites, who were featured in 23:7-11. It begins with the clan of Kohath, who is not actually mentioned in vv. 20b-25, and continues with the clan of Merari in vv. 26-30. It represents a slightly later stage of the previous list of family heads. In most cases, it is advanced one

generation. Thus Shubael (= Shebuel, 23:16 NRSV) is replaced by Jehdeiah (v. 20b). Other replacements are Isshiah (v. 21), Jahath (v. 22), Shamir (v. 24), Zechariah (v. 25), and Jerahmeel (v. 29). The descendants of Merari stay the same in v. 27 as in 23:21. Another recapitulation occurs in v. 23 concerning the family heads descended from Hebron, reference to which needs to be restored in line with 23:19, as the NRSV and the NIV recognize. The mixture of recapitulation and replacement indicates that the updated list reflects a period shortly after that of the preceding one. This phenomenon suggests that the pro-priestly reviser was at work one generation later than the chronicler.[152]

In vv. 26-27, "Beno" is simply a transliteration of the Hebrew term בנו (běnô, "his son"). The consequent rendering in v. 26, "the sons of Jaaziah, his son," refers to a newly recognized descendant of Merari, now included by adoption into the clan. In v. 27a, an explanatory annotation has probably been incorporated, with the sense "the descendants of Merari via Jaaziah were" (cf. the NJB).

After a closing summary in v. 30b, the procedure of casting lots is narrated in v. 31, with material from vv. 1, 3, and 5-6 included. The comparisons with the priests chosen by lot implies twenty-four divisions. We are not told how this number was attained. Presumably, in addition to the nine family heads credited to the clan of Kohath and the seven allocated to the clan of Merari, eight of the nine family heads associated with the clan of Gershon in 23:7-11 must be included.[153] The recapitulation of the earlier list in vv. 23 and 30 supports this explanation, and a reason is supplied for the omission of the Gershon clan members, who are assumed to stay the same. The principle of equality, which in the case of the priests related to the two priestly houses, is here applied to a lack of preferential treatment of closely related family heads. A "chief" (cf. vv. 21, 23; 23:8, 11) received no different treatment from his juniors. All "were treated the same."

---

151. In v. 6b a slight emendation is followed implicitly by both the NIV and the NRSV. See the notes in the REB and *BHS*.

152. Williamson, "The Origins of the Twenty-Four Priestly Courses," 266.

153. Japhet, *I & II Chronicles*, 433.

REFLECTIONS

1. Mention of Abijah in 24:10 spans the testaments. Zechariah, the father of John the Baptist, belonged to the eighth division (according to Luke 1:5). He was on duty in the Temple, burning incense, when he received an angelic vision and message about the birth of John and his mission. Struck dumb, Zechariah was unable to deliver the priestly benediction in the temple court. Thus 1 Chr 23:13 and 24:10 may be understood as background material for that New Testament passage.

2. This system of twenty-four divisions became an established custom until the Temple fell in 70 CE. The system gradually evolved after the exile; 24:1-19 is the first evidence that it reached its final form. The attribution to the period of David reflects a sincere and evidently successful attempt to have its value recognized and its permanence guaranteed. Christian denominations and movements that honestly claim New Testament support for their distinctive teachings work in a similar fashion.

The passage gives the impression that "all things should be done decently and in order" (1 Cor 14:40 NRSV). To worship in spirit and in truth is not incompatible with the implementation of a mass of necessary details.

The principle of equality achieved by casting lots (24:5) was, presumably, to prevent more powerful priestly families from controlling the system. While the most desirable case is for the best people do the work, a principle of fair sharing is also required in order that no one becomes too heavily burdened and that the gifts of other persons may be developed.

3. The parallel levitical roster (24:20-31) presupposes the role of the Levites as assistants to the priests, outlined in 23:28-32. The priest depended on the partnership of the lesser staff member, if the job was to be done. The significant difference between the new list and the old one in 23:7-21 is that time had moved on. While some of the heads of families were still in office, others had been succeeded by the next generation. The principle of a new generation taking over from the preceding one has a major part to play in 1 Chronicles. The work can only go on insofar as younger persons take over ministry in God's service.

Again the principle of equality is featured. We tend to assume that the biblical tradition ascribes honor to age. Here, however, age plays no part. The chronicler envisions that these family heads stood on a level playing field and gained no advantage from their degree of maturity. Seniority is a prized ingredient of many aspects of our culture. The notion of equality that has been running through recent passages represents a challenge. We need to ask ourselves when this factor should reasonably prevail and when it should be discarded in the name of God.

1 Chronicles 25:1-31, Temple Musicians

COMMENTARY

Exposition of the four divisions of Levites, announced in 23:4-5 and begun with the maintenance staff in 23:6b-24, now continues with attention devoted to the singing musicians.[154] According to 15:16-24, these musicians attended David's second and

154. Williamson, "The Origins of the Twenty-Four Priestly Courses," 255-57.

successful attempt to install the ark in Jerusalem. They were appointed by the chiefs of the Levites at David's command. Then, according to 16:4-6, 41-42, the king also appointed two groups: one led by Asaph to sing and play at the tent of the ark and another led by Heman and Jeduthun to serve at the tabernacle in Gibeon. The chronicler emphasizes David's initiation of the levitical system of sacred music and song. The same claim is made in the course of the genealogy of Levi at 6:31-48.

25:1a. The singers were set apart from other levitical duties. The army officers were presumably present to add formality to the occasion, occasion, as "all the leaders of Israel" were in 23:2. It is possible, however, that the term צבא (ṣābā´) refers to the "host" of Levites, as both the noun and its cognate verb are used in Numbers 4 and 8, rather than "army."[155] Then these officers are the equivalent of "the chiefs of the Levites" in 15:16 (NRSV). The listing of the choir heads as Asaph, Heman, and Jeduthun permits us to place this account within the post-exilic developments of the singers' role. This list reflects the penultimate stage, but is already leaning toward the final stage listing Heman, Asaph, and Ethan, in that Heman is pushed to the fore (v. 5; see the Introduction).

Their ministry is strikingly defined as prophesying. It refers to the oral aspect of their combined music and song. The description is repeated for each of the guild leaders in the list of vv. 1b-6. Asaph "prophesied" (v. 2), and so did Jeduthun as he praised with the lyre (v. 3), while Heman is called "the king's seer" (v. 5). In v. 1a, however, it is the rank and file who are said to prophesy. Much discussion has been devoted to the nature of this prophesying.[156] It is best taken as being related to the nature of their songs, the texts of the psalms regarded as the words of God given by inspiration.[157] The guild leaders are reckoned as inspired authors of certain psalms. Indeed, in 2 Chr 29:30 Hezekiah ordered the Levites to worship "with the words of David and of the seer Asaph" (NRSV). This phrase refers to the collections of psalms ascribed to David and to Asaph in the psalter. Heman features in the heading to Psalm 88:1, and Jeduthun in those to Psalms 39, 62, and 77. In the NT, one may add, David is considered a prophet in Mark 12:36 and Acts 2:25-35; 4:25, and Asaph in Matt 13:35.

25:1b-6. The chronicler supplies a list of the three-part guild and its members. The founders are regarded as contemporary with David, whom vv. 2 and 6 identify as their patron, which is consistent with his setting aside their families in v. 1a. The list in vv. 9-31 and the need for an extra name to make up the stated total of six (v. 3) indicate that the name "Shimel," preserved in the LXX, has accidentally fallen out of v. 3 in the MT. Heman is singled out because of the exceptional size of his family, which is viewed as the object of divine blessing. There is a deliberate intent to promote him as the leading figure among the guild founders. The repeated "All these" at the beginning of vv. 5 and 6 accentuates this singular emphasis. There is some question about the translation of v. 5a. The TNK takes the words following "seer" as descriptive of Heman's prophetic role: "who uttered the prophecies of God for His greater glory." The latter part of this rendering is doubtful, since elsewhere the Hebrew phrase "raise the horn" is used with a human object. Rather, the phrase seems to qualify Heman's sons, whose numbers give him prominence. It is attractive to take the earlier part of the phrase as qualifying "seer," with the sense "the king's seer with [= using] the words of God." Reference is then made to the psalms he was regarded as having composed for future use in the Temple.[158]

The names after Jerimoth in v. 4 have a strange, exotic ring. They do not look like Hebrew names at all, but ordinary words. It is possible to regard them as slightly adapted in form from a snatch of psalm poetry, specifically an individual lament or, since the sequence of clauses becomes rather ragged as it continues, a series of beginning phrases (incipits) used as psalm titles.[159] One feasible rendering of v. 4b is "Have mercy on me, O LORD, have mercy. You are my God. I magnify and exalt [your] help. As one living in adversity, I speak. Give an abundance of visions." An attempt has been made to find a Sumerian parallel for using quotations from religious songs as names, but it is unconvincing.[160] The latter part of the list of Heman's fourteen sons seems to be a literary formulation rather than a historical report.

155. Curtis and Madsen, *The Books of Chronicles*, 279.

156. See esp. D. L. Petersen, *Late Israelite Prophecy*, SBLMS 23 (Missoula, Mont.: Scholars Press, 1977) 62-87; Kleinig, *The Lord's Song*, 154-57; Schniedewind, *The Word of God in Transition*,170-88.

157. S. Zalewski, cited in Kleinig, *The Lord's Song*, 155. See also A. H. J. Gunneweg, *Leviten und Priester*, FRLANT 89 (Göttingen: Vandenhoeck & Ruprecht, 1965) 215; Japhet, *I & II Chronicles*, 440.

158. See Petersen, *Late Israelite Prophecy*, 64 and n. 43.

159. J. M. Myers, *1 Chronicles*, AB 12 (Garden City, N.Y.: Doubleday, 1965) 173.

160. See Petersen, *Late Israelite Prophecy*, 65-66.

The list of names "Asaph, Jeduthun, and Heman" is abrupt in the Hebrew of v. 6b. It is often taken as an annotation indicating that v. 6 refers to the descendants of all three founders, so that "their father" functions as a distributive singular. If so, the reference to the king in v. 6b relates to the royal patronage of the Heman group; likewise, the reference to the king in v. 2 relates to the royal patronage of the Asaph group. "All these" at the start of v. 6 (NIV) brackets the verse with v. 5, which begins identically. Moreover, one does expect a general statement relating to the Heman group, parallel with those in vv. 2 and 3b, which refer to the other Asaph and Jeduthun groups. The only reason for considering v. 6 a summary of vv. 1b-5 is the repetition of the instruments of v. 1a, but the repetition only rounds off the paragraph with a rhetorical inversion.

25:7-31. This roster is based on the preceding list of names. Although the term "division" is not used, the roster is modeled on the twenty-four priestly divisions of 24:1-19. This rotation of shifts was motivated by the reviser's description of the levitical singers who accompanied with music and song the priests' sacrificing of the regular burnt offerings (23:30-31). The priestly divisions are given a matching roster of twenty-four choirs, each led by one of the named persons. This arrangement depends on the work of the pro-priestly reviser and, since it ministers to priestly ends, was probably added by him. It is possible that the names of the extra sons of Heman were added along with the roster, which depends on their presence to make up the required number.

An introduction to the roster is given in vv. 7-8. It uses as a catchword מספר (mispār), with which the former list opened (v. 16),

therein the sense of "list" and now meaning "number." Emphasis is laid on the professional standards of the singers, which included a training program. The total number of 288 is made up of twenty-four choirs of twelve members each. According to the Mishnah, in later times such a musical choir would comprise nine lyre players, two harp players, and one cymbal player.[161] The casting of lots accords with redactional elements (24:5, 31). Based on vv. 9-31, one expects selection of the order of choirs to be the object of the lot, but v. 8 has individuals in view, from whom the choirs were formed. So not one but two separate lot castings are envisioned. The principle of equality characteristic of the other selections by lot is at work here, so that experience ("young and old," NIV) and expertise are not of particular value at this stage.

The form of the roster is remarkably full and repetitive. Some of the names vary slightly from those in vv. 2-4. In v. 9 one expects a reference to the choir, which the LXX attests in an abbreviated and misplaced note.[162] Both the analogy of the following verses and the total of 288 in v. 7 suggest its original presence (the NIV has restored it). At each round of lots a choice was made between two previously selected candidates for two positions.[163]

The chronicler has given three extended treatments of the levitical singing musicians: 6:31-48 in a genealogy, chaps. 15–16 in the narrative of the installation of the ark, and here. Other parts of his narrative will feature them further. This aspect of levitical duties was especially dear to the chronicler's heart as a mark of the new dispensation associated with David and still valid in his own day.

161. b. 'Arak. 13b.
162. See Allen, The Greek Chronicles, 2:140.
163. See the table in Kleinig, The Lord's Song, 59.

REFLECTIONS

1. A striking characteristic of the chronicler's description of the choirs' ministry is the use of the concept of prophecy. The temple choirs were so credited because they sang items from the authoritative psalms and also because the composition of inspired psalms was attributed to the choirs' founders. The medley of psalm extracts in chapter 16 is an example of the Levites' contribution to temple worship. With divinely inspired words, they lifted up to God the hearts and minds of the congregation and stimulated them to a loftier spirituality. They led the worship and voiced the praises and prayers to which the congregation added their amens and hallelujahs (16:36). No choir could be paid a greater tribute. Ideals are presented that church choirs today may want to take seriously.

2. In 25:7-8 the high standards expected of the choirs' ministry are mentioned. Evidently a general training scheme tested and improved professional competence, and rehearsals were designed to teach accomplished renderings of the psalms. According to the Talmud,[164] in later times temple choristers underwent five years of training. These references, tantalizingly brief though they are, suggest that Christian churches should have high standards of music and song.

3. The book of Revelation describes the hymns sung to the music of the harp (Rev 5:8; 15:2), mentioning "harps of God" (Rev 15:2 NRSV), presumably harps used in the worship of God. Music appeals to the emotions, with the accompanying words appealing more to the intellect. Thereby the whole person is brought nearer to God. Martin Luther testified to the power of music: "With all my heart I would extol the precious gift of God in the noble art of music. . . . Music is to be praised as second only to the Word of God, because by her are all the emotions swayed. Nothing on earth is more mighty . . . to hearten the downcast, mellow the overweening, temper the exuberant, or mollify the vengeful. . . . When natural music is sharpened and polished by art, then one begins to see with amazement the great and perfect wisdom of God."[165]

164. *b. Ḥul.* 24a.
165. Martin Luther, cited in R. H. Bainton, *Here I Stand: A Life of Martin Luther* (Nashville: Abingdon, 1950) 343.

1 Chronicles 26:1-32, Temple Security and Secular Assignments

COMMENTARY

This chapter completes the exposition of the various groups of Levites appointed by David, which had been announced in 23:4-5. In vv. 1-19 the chronicler deals with the gatekeepers and in vv. 20-32 with the miscellaneous group called "officials and judges" (23:4 NIV). Verse 1*a* provides a heading for vv. 1*b*-19, and v. 19 a summary of the two levitical clans involved. The term "division" refers here to the assignment of personnel to particular tasks of gatekeeping. Somewhat surprisingly, David is not mentioned in this passage, whereas in 9:22 the organization of the temple gatekeepers is credited to David and Samuel. The earliest layer in this material is probably vv. 1-3, 9-11, and 19.[166] In the early post-exilic period, gatekeepers were not regarded as Levites. Indeed, they are not so viewed in the source from Neh 11:19, which is used in 9:17. By the chronicler's time they were classed as Levites and their descent was traced from Levi.

166. See Williamson, "The Origins of the Twenty-Four Priestly Courses," 253-54.

26:1-3, 9-11. Here the Levites are traced back to Merari, a son of Levi, and to Korah, who in Num 16:1 is descended from Kohath, another son of Levi. Meshelemiah, called Shelemiah in v. 14, is possibly the Shallum of 9:17 and Ezra 2:42 (= Neh 7:45). The appearance of Asaph, head of one of the branches of the singing guild, is unexpected here. He belongs to a different part of the family tree of Levi, one who descended from Gershom, another son of Levi (6:39-43). By comparison with 9:19, we expect "Ebiasaph" at this point, which is found in the LXX in a corrupted form and is restored in the REB.

26:4-8. The information about Obed-edom cuts across the data about Meshelemiah in vv. 1*b*-3 and 9. In the primary tradition present in chaps. 15–16, Obed-edom was regarded as a singer; references to his status as a gatekeeper in 15:18, 24; 16:38*b* are secondary. His reappearance here represents a redactional addition, since a genealogical link is lacking. He has been adopted into the Kohathite clan and is identified with the Gittite who was temporary keeper of the ark (13:14). The Lord's blessing mentioned there is here defined in terms of an abundance of children. The emphasis on the ability of his family (v. 6) reflects an attempt to have them accepted as members of the guild of gatekeepers. Another motivation for the insertion at this point is the goal of attaining a total of twenty-four divisions, on the model of the priests in chap. 24. The total of twenty-four family heads is achieved by adding the seven sons of Meshelemiah, the four of Hosah, seven of the sons of Obed-edom, and the six sons of his firstborn son, Shemaiah. Hosah features outside this passage only in 16:38. His role with Obed-edom there suggests that verse depends on the expanded 1 Chronicles 26:1.

26:12-19. The duties of the gatekeepers rely on the expanded text of vv. 1-11. The term מחלקות (*maḥlĕqôt*, "divisions," v. 1) is related to "shifts" in v. 12. The use of lots has been a redactional feature in the accounts of the priestly and derivative divisions. The lots are cast according to ancestral houses. Presumably the twenty-four family heads of the previous expanded paragraph are in view. The principle of equality achieved by taking the lot is here applied to the family groups, whether "small or great." In this case, the casting of lots is related, not to the order of divisions on duty, as elsewhere, but to the particular gates to which the three major groups were assigned. Since there were four gates, one group had to take charge of two gates. One might have expected Obed-edom's family to qualify, but, upstart that he was, this was not to be the case. The east gate, which was the most important, honored by the title "the king's gate" (9:18), was manned by the greatest number of guards (v. 17). The "storehouse" refers to a temple treasury (cf. 2 Chr 25:24). In v. 16, the name of a newcomer to the passage, "Shuppim," should be deleted (so REB); a marginal variant reading for ולאספים (*wĕlāʾăsuppîm*, "and for the storehouses") in v. 17 was wrongly related to the noun האספים (*hāʾăsuppîm*) in v. 15 and was incorporated into the text. The west gate was approached from the Tyropocon Valley; its name, "Shallecheth," does not occur elsewhere.

Verse 16*b* functions as a heading for the distribution of guards in vv. 17-18, as the paragraphing in the NIV indicates. The total of twenty-four guards on duty at any one time is a permutation of the dominant priestly number, to which v. 12 refers in its echo of 24:31 ("just as their kindred did," NRSV). Extensive topographical knowledge of the temple area is displayed here, knowledge to which, unfortunately, we do not have access. In v. 17, "each day" needs to be restored to the MT, as the NIV does implicitly and the NRSV explicitly.[167] The rare term פרבר (*parbār*) in v. 18, long unexplained, has been clarified by its use in the *Temple Scroll*, found at Qumran. In the form פרור (*prwr*) it is there used of a porch with columns at the west side of the Temple, in connection with priests' sin offerings and guilt offerings.[168] This context suggests the rendering "colonnade" (NRSV, REB; the first instance of "colonnade" in v. 18 should be deleted with *BHS* as an erroneous anticipation of the second).

The temple gatekeepers were security police, as their placement at the storehouse indicates.[169] Much of the security for which they were responsible had a religious motivation. According to 2 Chr 23:19, they ensured that anyone unclean would not enter the temple grounds. The temple gates were evidently ritual checkpoints. Psalm 15 seems to be based on an interchange between a pilgrim and a gatekeeper about God's moral standards for the would-be worshiper (see also Pss 24:3-6; 118:19-20; Isa 33:14-16). The condemnation of temple worshipers in Isa 1:10-17 implies that in Isaiah's day this check was a perfunctory one, if done at all. Isaiah, speaking as a substitute gatekeeper, challenges pilgrims to "cease to do evil, learn to do good" (Isa 1:16-17 NRSV). Zechariah's qualification as "a prudent counselor" (v. 14 NRSV) apparently legitimated him in his role at the gate.

26:20-32. The last levitical category of "officials and judges" (NIV) in 23:4 is defined in terms of personnel and duties in these verses. At first sight, one might think that this section deals with two distinct groups,

---

167. The *BHS* apparatus is a better guide than the note in the NRSV.
168. 11QTemple 35:10-15.
169. For the paramilitary role of gatekeepers, see J. W. Wright, "Guarding the Gates: 1 Chronicles 26.1-19 and the Roles of Gatekeepers in Chronicles," *JSOT* 48 (1990) 69-81, esp. 69-74.

temple treasurers (vv. 20-28) and secular officials (vv. 29-32). But it has a common genealogical framework, at least from v. 23 on. The diverse Levites mentioned in vv. 24-32 were all Kohathites, attributed to the subclans of Amram, Izhar, Hebron, and Uzziel (cf. 23:16). The Uzzielites do not feature in the detailed presentation extracted by the chronicler from a longer list.

Apart from the genealogical framework that binds this passage together, in terms of temple duties it falls into two distinct parts, vv. 20-28 and vv. 29-32. The first part is supplied with an introduction in v. 20, referring to two types of treasuries. Then vv. 21-22 deal with those in charge of the temple treasuries, and vv. 25-28 with the staffing of the treasuries of dedicated gifts. Verse 23 is a genealogical heading for vv. 24-32 (see the NIV). Verse 24 specifies Shebuel as the overall supervisor of both kinds of treasuries. So there is no room for "Ahijah" (NRSV = MT) in this role (v. 20). This name has arisen from misunderstanding of an abbreviated form of "their brothers" or "their fellow [Levites]" (NIV).[170]

The first type of treasury stored sacred vessels and sacrificial materials, such as fine flour, wine, and oil (9:29).[171] Verses 21-22 should be read together, as in the NIV. These storerooms were staffed not by Kohathites but by Gershonites, who are traced through Ladan, as in 23:7-9. "Jehieli" is probably the same person as "Jehiel" there.

170. See Allen, *The Greek Chronicles*, 2:89.
171. In Ezra 8:33-34, we get a glimpse of activity there on a special day, when Ezra arrived from Babylonia with a consignment of money and vessels.

The other type of treasury was a combined bank and museum. Ancient temples regularly contained valuable objects that had been accumulated over centuries. These treasuries contained spoils of war and could be used as necessary for the "maintenance" (NRSV) or upkeep of the Temple. According to 18:11, David contributed to such a treasury. Objects associated with various military campaigns were placed in this treasury, presented as trophies to God's grace.

In vv. 29-32, the genealogical framework introduced in v. 23 is developed in terms of another group of Levites, who had been relieved of temple duties to play a role in the community at large. The Izharites (v. 29) had a judicial role as judges and "officials" or "officers"; their responsibilities fell somewhere between those of clerks and the police (see Deut 17:8-13; 2 Chr 29:11). Levitical experience in interpreting the Torah (see 2 Chr 17:7-9) and in security work was used for a broader purpose. According to vv. 30-32, the Hebronites had a national role, on both sides of the Jordan. This tradition evidently goes back to the period of the united monarchy. Their duties, on behalf of palace and Temple, probably involved the collection of taxes, in which case these Levites were appropriately listed alongside the temple treasurers. In v. 31, the chronicler assigns to David's last year a search for Hebronites at the levitical city of Jazer (cf. 6:81), who were given the same role among the Transjordanian tribes as their western counterparts had in v. 30.

REFLECTIONS

1. The lists of traditional groups responsible for gates, goods, and gifts and for trials and taxes described in chapter 26 illustrate the extensive organization of the Levites. They are concerned with security in many forms. The sacred grounds of the Temple had to be protected from ritually unclean people. In Rev 21:27, this concept is developed with reference to the heavenly Jerusalem. That holy city *par excellence* can have nothing unclean entering it, and a strict demarcation is drawn between faith and immorality. The temple gatekeepers were evidently responsible for setting worship standards. In the Sermon on the Mount (Matt 5:23-24), Jesus echoed the entrance liturgy of Psalm 15. He counseled that his disciples be their own gatekeepers in monitoring their approach to the altar of the Temple. Anyone who brought offerings in worship was to examine the self about his or her treatment of others. If a problem existed for which one bore responsibility, the offering was not to be completed until the matter had been put right. Consistency between worship and way of life is as necessary for the Christian as it was for the people of God in the Old Testament.

2. De Vries thinks it is significant that two brothers were in charge of the temple stores (26:22): "We take note of Zetham's and Joel's joint tenure, as though the one was needed to keep check on the other."[172] God's property must receive good care, not least so as to keep faith with the donors. Occasionally we hear of church treasurers embezzling funds or otherwise using them improperly. We, too, require a foolproof system of precautions to protect church funds from misappropriation and their stewards from temptation.

3. The wider ministry described in 26:29-32 will not be found in countries that strictly separate church and state. In the British House of Lords, the Anglican archbishops and bishops sit as "lords spiritual." This civil appointment is a traditional part of their overall duties as servants of God. On a less grandiose scale, many ordained pastors sit on social committees concerned with welfare work or education. Although nation and people of God are not coterminous as they were for ancient Israel, Christian love and concern cannot stay in the church, but must overflow into a needy world and seek to give direction in societies where so many people lack moral and spiritual bearings. Only thus will Christians fulfill their mandate to be salt of the earth and light of the world.

172. De Vries, *1 and 2 Chronicles*, 210.

1 Chronicles 27:1-34, Lay Leaders

COMMENTARY

This chapter consists of four secular lists, two relating to Israel's tribes and two to Israel's king, though David is also associated with the first two (vv. 1, 23). The lists tend to supplement the religious, temple-related lists of the previous four chapters. Levitical involvement in secular work (chap. 26) has eased the transition. These four lists are inserted with a consciousness that with David's reign drawing to a close this was the only place to insert such information. This feeling surfaces especially in the last pair of lists, the stewards of royal property (vv. 25-31) and the members of the privy council (vv. 32-34).

However, the first two lists, the tribal divisions (vv. 1-15) and the tribal leaders (vv. 16-24), are motivated by priestly interests. The basic structure of chaps. 23–27 was dictated by the skeleton list of Levites in 23:4-5, and a pro-priestly editor took the opportunity to add material. By this token not only does chap. 27 have no place in the original levitical structuring of chaps. 24–27, but also one expects priestly interests to surface in it, as they do in the first two lists.

27:1-15. Verse 1 functions as a heading for the first list. "The people of Israel [בני ישראל *běnê yiśrā'ēl*]" here refers to the laity, as distinct from the religious personnel of previous chapters. The list consists of twelve heads of monthly divisions. The introduction provides information about levels of leadership in these divisions and their monthly royal service. The list postulates twelve divisions of conscripts, each consisting of 24,000 men, amounting to 288,000 in all. This idealistic presentation was probably inspired by the list of twelve district leaders who supplied Solomon's court with food each month of the year (1 Kgs 4:7-19, 27). It not only adopts a military format, but also reflects the influence of the twenty-four divisions of priests in 24:1-19. Israel is made to march to a priestly tune, like the levitical groups in earlier chapters. This microcosm of divine order provides a pattern for society.

The names of the divisional leaders are closely related to the list of David's prominent warriors in 11:11-31, particularly to names appearing in 11:11-12, 26-31. These individual warriors receive an administrative role in the present list. In fact, Asahel (v. 7) was already dead before David became king of all Israel (2 Sam 2:18-32); mention of his son's succession shows a recognition, though hardly a resolution, of the difficulty. The assigning of Benaiah to the priesthood (v. 5) reflects 12:27, itself an addition of the propriestly reviser. Other features of the list seem to supply older information independent of the list of warriors in chap. 11. Benaiah is credited with leadership of the Thirty, a role only Abishai has in 11:21. This list knows the names of Benaiah's and Asahel's sons (vv. 6-7), and in general more family information is given.[173]

27:16-24. The list of tribal leaders in vv. 16-22 has been taken from older material associated with David's census, as the closing material in the list shows. The narrative is more closely linked with the list than either the NIV or the NRSV indicates. The Hebrew for "their number" (KJV; חספרם *mispārām*, v. 23) refers to the number of the tribes of Israel mentioned in v. 22. This account of the census has a different tone from the story in chap. 21. The account shows that David did no wrong in ordering the census. It makes the implicit claim that David followed the procedure of the Torah by not including those under twenty years old (Num 1:3), thus respecting the Lord's sovereignty. The full number of Israelites would be known only to God and would be allowed to grow as indefinitely large as divine promises to the patriarchs had foretold (see Gen 15:5; 22:17; 26:4). As in chap. 21, Joab was evidently assigned the task of taking the census, but according to this account he was interrupted by divine wrath (v. 24). According to chap. 21, he reluctantly obeyed David's orders and completed the census, but registered a protest by omitting two tribes, Levi and Benjamin, though here their leaders are included (vv. 17, 21). The narrative is terse, but the reviser evidently wants to exonerate David of

173. The clause relating to Mikloth in v. 4, omitted in the RSV, probably originated as an explanatory gloss. See Rudolph, *Chronikbücher*, 178; Allen, *The Greek Chronicles*, 2:144-45.

any blame and implicitly to cast some blame on Joab. Joab ceases to be the good guy, and his respect for God (21:3) is transferred to David. This account represents an idealized view of David that the chronicler did not share. Since the census was broken off, only the tribal leaders were inserted in the Davidic record, not the full numbers. In taking over the narrative appended to the list, the editor may have wanted to highlight the list as authentically Davidic.

The touch of the priestly editor appears in the reference to Zadok as head of (the house of) Aaron (v. 17). The point of the insertion was the same as in 12:27-28: to make room for explicit participation, on the assumption that "Levi" represented not the tribe but merely the non-priestly members.

Apart from this insertion, the nominal number of twelve tribes for Israel is here achieved by taking the two halves of Manasseh separately and then omitting Gad and Asher. The list of Jacob's sons in Gen 35:23-26 provides the basis for the ordering of the tribes. The first six tribes (vv. 16-19*a*) correspond to the order of the sons born to Jacob by Leah. Those in vv. 20-21 represent his sons by Rachel. Dan and Naphtali, here strangely separated in vv. 22*a* and 19*b* respectively, were sons of Bilhah, Rachel's maid, while those by Leah's maid Zilpah, Gad and Asher, are omitted as being outside the traditional number of twelve. Judah's representative "Elihu" (v. 18) is not otherwise known as a brother of David. He may have been the unnamed eighth brother in 1 Sam 16:10 (in addition to the seven names in 1 Chr 2:13-15). The emphasis on the twelve tribes of Israel accords with the chronicler's own concern for the traditional unity of north and south, a concern for all Israel. The redactor, by including this list, was adding his own "amen" to this element of the chronicler's agenda.

27:25-31. The list of David's administrators of crown property is generally recognized as historically reliable. It is arranged in three groups, according to storage places in the capital (implicitly) and in the country (v. 25), agriculture and agricultural products (vv. 26-28), and livestock (vv. 29-31*a*). A descriptive summary in v. 31*b* concludes the list. The royal property was spread throughout the united kingdom, as vv. 28-29 attest. The list illustrates David's riches (29:28), painting a beautiful picture of God's blessing on the land and a nostalgic ideal that implicitly included economic and political hopes for full restoration.

27:32-34. The final list, which is also viewed as historically authentic, presents David's inner circle of confidants. It complements the list of members of his administration (18:15-17). The inclusion of Joab, defined by his administrative role and not by a counseling function, has been regarded as secondary. He was certainly a member of the old guard; in 2 Sam 19:5-8, he speaks candidly as an intimate adviser. The tutor of the royal princes is given a place in the list. Replacements for Ahithophel were necessary in view of his suicide after supporting Absalom's rebellion (2 Sam 17:23). Hushai's epithet, "the king's friend," was an official title, which 2 Sam 15:37 uses of him and to which 2 Sam 16:17 ironically alludes.

REFLECTIONS

The first list in chap. 27 is dedicated to order, which, as closely as it can, takes its cue from the organization of the priesthood into divisions. Each family took its turn serving at the Temple. This modeling of a secular list on a religious background means that the Temple is regarded as a pattern for society. It resembles attempts to set up a civil community based on Christian principles, such as Calvin's Geneva and the colonies established by the Puritans in New England.

The second list, here garnished with an extra, priestly flavor, reinforces the chronicler's own ecumenical concern. It challenges readers to endorse the larger dimensions of the people of God and to recognize as separatist any smaller grouping that claims to be the whole. A second point of interest in the list is a redeeming feature claimed for the ill-fated census in 27:23. Israelites under the age of twenty were not included in the census, in order that the full number of God's people should not be known. In this way a balance was struck between human practicality and divine promise.

The third list may be read in the light of the Old Testament theology of the land. It finds an echo in Uzziah's love of the soil and devotion to agricultural enterprises (2 Chr 26:10). Such a concern has a theological basis in Deut 8:7-10, which describes the gift of a good land that provides food for God's people. From Paul's perspective, "the earth and its fullness are the Lord's," and so they are to be enjoyed, affirms 1 Cor 10:26 (NRSV) in an application of Ps. 24:1.

The fourth list in the chapter sets out the members of David's privy council. In terms of the themes to be found elsewhere in the books of Chronicles, it recalls the help given by the people of God, which came to the fore in 1 Chronicles 11:1–12. David, in his rise to power, did not stand alone. Here, in his heyday, he still leaned on others to help him rule. The help is defined in terms of counseling (27:32-33a, 34a). Joab's unpalatable advice in 2 Sam 19:5-8 encouraged David to act like a king when he was tempted to withdraw into private grief, just as Queen Victoria did at the death of her husband, Prince Albert. Counseling is especially prized in the wisdom traditions of the Old Testament: "Without counsel plans go wrong, but with many advisers they succeed" (Prov 15:22 NRSV; cf. Prov 11:14; 13:10; 24:6; Eccl 4:13). Second Chronicles 10 and 22 will develop this motif in terms of both good and bad advice.

1 Chronicles 28:1-21, Solomon's Renewed Mandate to Build the Temple

COMMENTARY

In chap. 22 David gave Solomon a private charge to build the Temple as the chief task of his reign. Now David assembles representatives of the people and delivers a public charge, rehearsing Solomon's divinely authored qualifications (vv. 1-10). Then David ceremoniously hands over a set of plans for the Temple (vv. 11-19) and adds words of encouragement, as he commissions Solomon to undertake the task and carry it through (vv. 20-21). David's speech primarily recapitulates themes announced earlier (chaps. 17 and 22). The speech falls into the regular pattern of explanatory introduction (vv. 2*b*-7) and a main exhortatory part headed by "So now" (vv. 8-10).

28:1. This meeting is different from that in 23:2, which was of a preparatory, private nature. Here David summons the leaders of the nation and of the court and members of the army, as representatives of "all Israel" (v. 8), to present Solomon to them as his successor. An editor has introduced five titles for leaders of the groups mentioned in 27:1-31, in order to integrate that later material into the Chronicles history. The fifth group, the royal stewards, strictly belongs with the palace officials. The complex organization associated with David's successful reign is impressive.

28:2-3. David's addressing the assembly as both his brothers (cf. 13:2) and his people paves the way for the statement in v. 4 that God had promoted him up from the ranks (cf. Deut 17:20). God's declaration to David (v. 3; see also v. 6) is the primary theme. The contrast between the veto of the father's building of the Temple and the mandate to the son to do so instead is based on 17:4, 12, while the disqualification summarizes 22:8 and the specification of Solomon repeats 22:9-10.

Reference to David's original plan in v. 2 builds on 17:1 and 22:7, putting the motif of rest to new use. There it was rest for Israel achieved by David's victories (22:9, 18). Now it has a religious sense with the ark

as subject. The chronicler reflects Ps 132:8 (cf. Ps 132:14): the description of the ark as God's "footstool" occurs elsewhere only in Ps 132:7. In Ps 132:8 the permanent installation of the ark in Jerusalem is dramatically represented as an invitation to the Lord to go to "your resting place," the Temple. David's "preparations" sound like those made by the king in 22:2-5; yet, the text reads as if they occurred before the prophetic oracle of chap. 17. The clause "and I made preparations for building" (v. 2) probably breaks the continuity and has the sense "and [subsequently] I have in fact . . ." (see the GNB).

28:4-7. David's roles as founder of the dynasty and father of the builder of the Temple are drawn from 17:7-14. This repetition emphasizes the divine purpose, which would affect Israel thereafter. God's choosing of David from within his family recalls the narrative of his being anointed in 1 Samuel 16 (cf. 2 Sam 6:21). A narrowing process has transpired. First, Judah was chosen as "ruling tribe" (REB), then David's family was chosen (1 Samuel 16). The choice of Judah echoes Ps 78:68-69, where it is associated with God's choice of "his servant David" (Ps 78:70).[174] God's word through Nathan pointed to Solomon's election from among David's many sons, repeating the process of a generation earlier. As in chap. 22, with hindsight the chronicler cuts through the complex succession narrative in 2 Samuel 9–1 Kings 2. Here a new factor, the divine election of Solomon, is introduced, indicated by the term "chosen" (בחר *bāḥar*) in vv. 5-6 and 10.[175] Solomon stood alongside David as elected by God. They are twin agents of the divine purpose, joint founders of a new era under God, an era that was to last "forever" (vv. 4, 7).

174. See R. J. Clifford, "In Zion and David a New Beginning: An Interpretation of Psalm 78," in *Traditions in Transformation*, ed. F. M. Cross (Winona Lake: Eisenbrauns, 1981) 121-41, esp. 137-41.

175. The application of the concept of election to Solomon (28:5-6) is unparalleled in the OT. See Braun, "Solomon, the Chosen Temple Builder," 588-90.

As in 17:14 and later in 29:23, Solomon was to represent the Lord's own kingship (v. 5). We may compare Solomon's throne to the description of the ark as the "footstool" of God (v. 2). A parallel is drawn between the Temple and the palace as two disclosures of God's kingship (cf. 16:31). The "ark of the covenant of the LORD" is mentioned twice in this chapter (vv. 2, 18). In chaps. 16 and 17, the ark was associated with the Davidic covenant, as it is in this chapter. God's earlier covenant with Israel was now subsumed under the present one and thus guaranteed "forever" for the community of faith.

Solomon is assigned the double role of temple builder and guarantor of the dynasty. Although the Temple is the focus of David's speech (vv. 2b-3, 6a, 10), much space is devoted to the dynasty, which was important for Israel's future. Verse 7 lays down a condition for the permanence of the dynasty: Solomon's overall obedience to the Torah.[176] The issue had been introduced in a lower key at 22:12-13a. Now it is elevated to a condition, supplementing the earlier condition of building the Temple (17:12; 22:10). Obedience is envisioned as humanly possible, as in Deut 30:11-14. The chronicler's account of Solomon's reign never contradicts this statement. That reign ends on the laudatory notes of wisdom and wealth as implicit signs of God's blessing and approval (2 Chronicles 9). The chronicler thus insists that Solomon's adherence to God's general requirements was still sufficient to guarantee the dynasty (see 2 Chr 13:5; 21:7; 23:3). He is implicitly challenging the deuteronomist's perspective in 1 Kings 11 (see esp. 1 Kgs 11:31-34, 38) and also the strict line taken against intermarriage in Ezra–Nehemiah, which was partially grounded in 1 Kings 11 (see Neh 13:26). The chronicler undoubtedly found a basis for the condition in 1 Kgs 6:11-13; 9:4-5 (see also 1 Kgs 3:14), which he interpreted in terms of a general dynastic promise that would hold good after Solomon had successfully undergone a probationary period.

28:8-10. Solomon received two mandates, one of general obedience and the specific one of building the Temple. This part of the speech focuses on exhortations to carry out these mandates. The reader expects Solomon

176. See Williamson, "The Dynastic Oracle in the Books of Chronicles," 313-18.

to be addressed throughout, and v. 8a encourages this expectation. But v. 8b, with its plural verbs and pronouns in the Hebrew, goes off on a tangent. David turns for a moment to address the representative assembly, applying Solomon's role homiletically to the people. In obeying the Torah, he would not only secure the dynasty but also become a role model for the people. The appeal borrows from Deuteronomy the association of obedience to the Torah and enjoyment of "the good land" (seeDeut 4:22-23; 6:17-18), but the chronicler slips in his own spiritual key word, דרש (dāraš), "seek" ("search out," NRSV; "follow," NIV). Seeking God meant the people must obey the Torah. God's covenant with Israel through David included the land as a vital component, but Israel's prayers to this end (16:35) had to be backed by lives dedicated to the Lord's requirement. Verse 8b is intended to transcend its historical context. Every reader's mind rushes to the disappointing fact that the people failed in this obligation and lost the land. Yet the chronicler and his first readers rejoiced in the partial renewal of the gift. He was challenging them to qualify for full restoration.

In the charge to Solomon (vv. 9-10), the condition of v. 7 is reiterated in a fervent call to spiritual commitment. The reference to a devoted heart and mind again borrows from Deuteronomy (Deut 4:29; 10:12). The chronicler includes his own emphasis: the obligation of each generation to appropriate the faith of the preceding one. The call is undergirded by a reference to divine omniscience, a motif that will recur in 29:17.

The pair of conditional statements that follows is based on Jer 29:13-14, as is indicated by the passive form "be found" (or "let himself be found"; cf. the active verb in Deut 4:29), so that in this respect, too, Solomon turns out to be a model for later generations. In this context, however, the idea of "being found" gives expression to the unique responsibility that rests on Solomon to "make" his "election sure," to use a NT phrase (2 Pet 1:10 NIV). The exhortations and dire warning stress the human side of the matter. In 29:19, as already in 22:12, they are balanced by David's request that God empower Solomon. At its end, the speech returns to Solomon's other mandate. The chosen king was also the chosen temple builder. He is encouraged in this future task, in anticipation of the charge in vv. 20-21.

28:11-19. The chronicler narrates a ceremonial handing over of a set of plans for the Temple, drawn up by David as a further part of his preparations. Although he could not build the Temple, David did everything he could to help Solomon achieve that goal. According to the chronicler, David was not only the supplier of materials but also the designer of the Temple and its furnishings. The Temple's legitimacy was thus enhanced by such close association with this traditional hero of the faith.

Verse 12 probably refers to David's own planning, as an amplification of v. 2 (NRSV; cf. the NIV). Verse 19 will trace these plans, evidently in the form of a written description, to divine inspiration. The Lord's "hand . . . upon me" is a prophetic expression (cf. Ezek 1:3; 3:14). The chronicler intends to prove that the Temple is the product of divine revelation. Even "the details" were divinely inspired.

The description moves from architectural layout and ritual procedure to particular vessels and furnishings and the amounts of gold and silver required in each case. In v. 18, the ark is singled out for special mention. The golden cherubim on each side are related to a chariot, which alludes to Ezekiel's visions (Ezekiel 1; 10–11; 43); both v. 18 and v. 19 depend on the book of Ezekiel. The cherubim are part of what Ezekiel experienced of the divine presence, which rested in the earthly temple (cf. Ezek 10:4, 18-19).

The chronicler's enthusiasm shines through. Although he lived many centuries later and knew only the Second Temple, he rejoiced in the wonder of it all. The ark and the gold-plated cherubim were no more, nor was Solomon's Temple standing in all its glory (cf. Ezra 3:10-13; Hag 2:3). Still, the Second Temple was its successor in spiritual, if not material, terms. The temple "vessels" (vv. 13-14) provided continuity between the old and the new buildings.[177] Some were recovered, others took on the aura of the old (Ezra 1:6-11).

The legitimacy of the old temple, inherited by the new one, was confirmed by the plans (תבנית *tabnît*) of vv. 11, 18-19. The same Hebrew word is used of the revealed

"pattern" of the tabernacle and its furnishings in Exod 25:1-40, which contains a list very similar to the one supplied here. David is represented as a second Moses, doing for the Temple what Moses had done for the tabernacle. Another allusion to the tabernacle will appear in v. 21, where the skilled volunteers who work on the Temple reflect Exod 35:10. The Temple corresponded to the tabernacle and would function as a divine replacement for it. There was a new era of worship, which authentically corresponded to the old one prescribed in the Torah, but represented a fresh, prophetic revelation. David was a prophet for the new age, in which the chronicler and his contemporaries still lived.

28:20-21. The formal public commissioning of Solomon to build the Temple, like the private one in 22:11-16, includes three standard elements: exhortations of encouragement, including the facing and overcoming of natural fears, an assurance of the Lord's enabling presence, and a description of the job to be done. The Lord is David's own God (v. 20). David is testifying that God had seen him through every problem (see 2 Sam 4:9; 1 Kgs 1:29) and would be there to help Solomon to the end. Such a privilege accompanied the responsibility to appropriate a parent's faith (v. 9). This incentive was accompanied by another: the cooperation of qualified personnel. Yet another was the good will of "all the people," for whom Solomon's word was to be their command. The motif of help, from human beings and from God, proclaimed earlier in chaps. 11–12, reappears here.

Another agenda, repeated from chap. 22, is pursued in this commissioning speech. No one who has read Deut 31:7-8 and Josh 1:2-9 can be blind to the intertextual themes in vv. 20-21, including the assurance that the Lord would not fail or forsake this new servant (cf. Deut 31:8; Josh 1:5). The transition of leadership from Moses to Joshua is used as a model. On the human plane, David and Solomon belong together, with the second taking over from the first and completing the unfinished business he left. Theologically, activity in the Second Temple period was a comparable work of God. The new age that continued until the chronicler's time was as divinely authentic as the age launched by the exodus and entry into the promised land.

177. See P. R. Ackroyd, "The Temple Vessels: A Continuity Theme," in *Studies in the Religion of Ancient Israel*, ed. G. W. Anderson et al., VTSup 23 (Leiden: Brill, 1972) 166-81 (= *Studies in the Religious Tradition of Ancient Israel* [London: SCM, 1987] 46-60).

REFLECTIONS

1. The chronicler devoted three speeches to the Davidic covenant, the prophetic oracle in chap. 17, and the royal speeches in chapters 22 and 28. A new element found here is the motif of election applied not only to David but also to Solomon. The motif reinforces the theological principles of the earlier speeches. The Lord worked through both David and Solomon on behalf of the people's future. Matthew and Luke identified Jesus as God's chosen servant of Isa 42:1 (cf. Matt 12:18; Luke 9:35). In Eph 1:4, 6, God's election of the church is grounded in that of Christ, the beloved. Karl Barth well observed that "as elected man, He is the Lord and Head of all the elect, the revelation and reflection of their election, and the organ and instrument of all divine electing."[178] In the Christian era, the spotlight of revelation has singled out Christ as the embodiment of the divine purposes.

2. The aside in 28:8*b* makes Solomon a model for God's people. They also are called to obey, if they are to enjoy the Lord's continued blessing. The royal "if" (28:7 and 9) is implicitly transferred to the king's subjects as beneficiaries of the royal covenant. The chronicler's readers were meant to overhear the challenge, generation by generation. Likewise, we need to hear the somber conditions of Rom 11:22 and Col 1:23.

3. Commitment comes to the fore in 28:9 as David addresses Solomon. It would be difficult to find in Scripture a more fervent call to spiritual commitment. The chronicler's echoing of Deuteronomy and his use of similar language elsewhere indicates that here, too, Solomon is meant to be a model for all believers, especially as they receive the torch of faith from the preceding generation. The call to consciously live a life that is an open book to God is repeated in Heb 4:13: "Before him no creature is hidden" (NRSV). The ill-fated attempt of Ananias and Sapphira to deceive the church (Acts 5:1-11) is a dire example of the need to hear as a challenge the message of God's insight.

4. A love for the Temple and a pride even in its bygone glory shine through the descriptive list in 28:11-18. It is true that today's means of grace may become tomorrow's superstition (see 2 Kgs 18:4). Yet a spiritual beauty emanates from sacred use. In the most austere of churches a communion table, given pride of place at the front, has a sacred role attached to it. We could empathize with the chronicler as he listed the objects that spoke to him of God and mostly still functioned for him as a means of grace.

5. The typological move from tabernacle to Temple is reminiscent of the careful arguments in the Letter to the Hebrews. The tabernacle described in the Torah was a foreshadowing of the heavenly sanctuary into which the ascended Christ had entered (Hebrews 5–10). Writing for Hellenistic Jews who were more oriented to the Torah than to the Temple, the author of Hebrews needed to start with the Torah. For us modern Christians, the New Testament and its revelation have gained a venerable authenticity of their own, but originally it was necessary to trace the consistency and consecutiveness of the work of God by balancing things old and new. The Old Testament and the New Testament together represent the total Word of God, and their mutual relationship deserves careful evaluation. The chronicler had a similar task in his own day. He valued the law, but was aware that it had been supplemented by the prophets, here by a prophetic type of revelation for his own age. Diligent study and careful discrimination were necessary to show their complexity and the contemporary value of each part of God's revelation. Let us, as heirs of both testaments, listen to the chronicler.

---

178. Karl Barth, *Church Dogmatics*, ed. G. W. Bromiley and T. F. Torrance (Edinburgh: T. & T. Clark, 1957) 2:2.117.

A similar message is carried by the comparison of David and Solomon with Moses and Joshua. The old was a model for the new, and the new was an updated, revised version of the old. Typology, properly understood, traces correspondences with former phases of divine revelation in order to recognize the subsequent work of God. The New Testament follows in the wake of the books of Chronicles by making much use of typology. The New Testament knows of a last Adam, a heavenly Jerusalem, and a new sacrifice for sins.

1 Chronicles 29:1-30, David's Public Appeal and Prayer of Praise

COMMENTARY

In his last speech, David appeals for contributions so that the community of faith may share in the cost of building the Temple (vv. 1-5). They respond positively to his appeal (vv. 6-9). Then the king gives thanks to the Lord (vv. 10-19), and the whole community responds by celebrating in worship (vv. 20-22a). Both passages of public response end on notes of joy (vv. 9, 22a). Solomon is duly made king and is eulogized by the chronicler (vv. 22b-25). David's reign is concluded with a formal epilogue (vv. 26-30).

The key word that begins the first of David's speeches and closes the second is the verb הכינותי (hăkînôtî), denoting the preparation that pervaded 22:2-5 and is here rendered "provided" or "made provision" (vv. 2-3, 16, 19). It primarily refers to David, appropriately summing up his role as the human author of the temple project, while Solomon would finish it. Under God both kings established the religious institution that would be the channel of Israel's faith and worship down to the chronicler's day and beyond. The chronicler uses another term for the Temple in vv. 1 and 19, בירה (bîrâ), "fortress," rendered "palatial structure" in the NIV. It evokes the Temple's imposing grandeur.

29:1-5. David makes an appeal to the representative assembly convened in 28:1 (cf. 28:8). The purpose of the speech is disclosed at the end. The flow of the passage from 28:21 to 29:5 suggests that there was a practical way in which the people could help Solomon fulfill the mandate for which he had been chosen (v. 1; cf. 28:10). Just as the formidable nature of this task encouraged David to make advance preparations (22:5),

so also here it motivates contributions from the people as well as from David. David led with his pocket, giving not public money but his own (v. 3), thus setting an example of generosity. His provision for the Temple in 22:14 was expressed in a colossal number of talents. The same rhetorical use of numbers occurs here in v. 4, though the figures are smaller than before. Still, the motivation is the same; his provisions reflect the worth of the God for whom the Temple was to be built (v. 1).

The king's appeal for voluntary contributions (v. 5) contains a striking phrase. It is employed in Exod 28:41 (also in 2 Chr 13:9) when a newly ordained priest offered his first sacrifice. The exact sense of the phrase "fill one's hand" (מלא יד millē' yād) is unclear, but it seems to invest the sacrifice with symbolic value, ratifying the offerer's admission to the priesthood. Here it is used as a spiritual metaphor. It is not simply the gift that is consecrated to God but also the giver to God's service. The financial sponsors declared themselves committed to the Lord's work and its success.

29:6-9. The representatives of the people, inspired by David's example and moved by his appeal, gave unstintingly. The storage of precious stones (v. 8) reflects personnel created by 26:21-22. In v. 7, fabulous sums are also mentioned. The reference to "ten thousand darics" (a Persian unit of currency) breaks the pattern in v. 7. It amounts to about 185 pounds, whereas one talent weighed about 75 pounds. The conversion is an admission that the chronicler's constituency was unable to give such vast sums, but was affluent enough to give substantially. The chronicler was appealing to his contemporaries to give according to their means (cf. Deut 16:17). An impression of overwhelming generosity is conveyed by their "single mind" (NRSV) or "wholeheartedness" (NIV; בלב שלם *bĕlēb šālēm*). This virtue marked spiritual service of God in 28:9, and here it represents an outworking of that service.

In Exod 35:4-9, Moses appealed for similar contributions to the construction of the tabernacle and its contents, and the people willingly responded (Exod 35:20-29; see also Exod 25:1-7). The chronicler has written vv. 1-9 with one eye on these Exodus passages. Again the Temple is being put on a par with the tabernacle. The chronicler is announcing a new era launched by the same God of Israel.

29:10-19. The chronicler's account of David's reign consists of two phases: bringing the ark to Jerusalem and preparing for the Temple. Each phase ends in praise, in chap. 16 and here. This magnificent prayer reflects the joy of David and the people over the leaders' generous giving (v. 9) and turns it Godward. Not surprisingly, the prayer has an exuberant tone, reflected in its expressions of totality. "All" (כל *kōl*) occurs no less than ten times. The prayer falls into three parts, each introduced by a fresh address of God: praise in vv. 10*b*-12, thanksgiving in vv. 13-17, and petition in vv. 18-19. Thanksgiving is the main element. It is prefaced by hymnic praise, which seems to reflect liturgical language of the chronicler's period.

29:10-12. David functions as spokesperson for the worshiping community. God deserves their never-ending praise. The reference to the patriarch Jacob, pointedly called Israel in Chronicles, reflects the fact that he, too, was blessed with wealth for which he gave God the credit (Gen 30:43; 31:7; 33:11). The doxology (v. 11*a*) effusively piles up terms for God's sovereign power. Four reasons for praise are given in vv. 11*b*-12: (1) the Lord, as creator, owns the world; (2) as its king, the Lord is supreme over the world; (3) the Lord is the source of all human wealth; and (4) the Lord is the providential supplier of human power.

29:13-15. "And now" (ועתה *wĕʿattâ*) typically marks a transition to the main point, here to thanksgiving directed to the God who acts not only on a universal plane but also

as "our God," dispensing wealth to Israel. King and people could claim no credit for their own generous giving. They were channels of resources first given by God, "what comes from your hand" (v. 14). Everything depended on God's prevenient grace. The people of Israel, like the patriarchs, lived as aliens in the promised land (cf. 16:19-20). The land—and all the resources in it—"is mine," declared the Lord; "with me you are but aliens and tenants" (Lev 25:23 NRSV) or "aliens and transients," as the NRSV renders the same Hebrew nouns. Whereas in 16:19-20, the term "alien" had a political sense and in Lev 25:23 a socioeconomic connotation, here גרים (*gērîm*) involves a spiritual meaning.[179] Although David and Israel were firmly in possession of the land, nothing belonged to them by right. They were stewards of God's property, spiritual counterparts of the royal stewards in 27:25-31. This generation must seize the opportunity while it can (see Job 8:9; 14:2).

29:16-17. Wealth, God-given to the last penny, had been returned to God for work on the Temple. In the end, the offering was more than a material one, for its substance already belonged to the Lord. The real offerings were spiritual, matters of "the heart": a sincere motivation to honor God and a readiness to give.

29:18-19. The passage ends with petitions, asking that God's help continue into the future. As at the start, there is a reference to the patriarchs. Not only Jacob but also Abraham and Isaac depended on the Lord for the resources they enjoyed (Gen 13:2; 24:1; 26:12-14). They are no longer models of weakness and hope, as in chap. 16, but of stewardship. The Lord both gives resources and inspires the heart to part with them. So David prays for God to keep fresh and sweet the people's devotion in this area. It was a prayer the chronicler meant his own generation to hear.

The final petitions transcend the immediate context. They revert to a concern of chap. 28: the two mandates, general and particular, that pressed heavily on Solomon's shoulders. The survival of the dynasty depended on his obedience to God in the areas of Torah and

---

179. D. J. Estes, "Metaphorical Sojourning in 1 Chronicles 29:15," *CBQ* 53 (1991) 45-49.

Temple (17:12; 22:12; 28:7). How could he maintain the required compliance? The Lord, who gave these duties, also is asked to give Solomon "wholehearted devotion" so that he might live for God and "do everything" necessary for the building of the Temple. Only the Lord's help could make this possible (cf. 1 Kgs 8:58; Ps 119:33-36, 133). The chronicler acknowledged that "there is no one who does not sin" (2 Chr 6:36 = 1 Kgs 8:46). Here, David asks God to give special grace to Solomon.

29:20-22a. Then David urges the assembly to praise God. They worship in word and gesture and also offer homage to the king as a mark of respect and of appreciation for his long reign. They also worship with sacrifices. With meat from the sacrifices other than burnt offerings, they engage in a sacred meal to celebrate their spiritual "joy." The united worship of "all Israel" was an ideal the chronicler coveted for his own generation.

29:22b-25. The coronation of Solomon as co-regent is an idealistic version of the material in 1 Kings. The intertwining of David's and Solomon's reigns is a hook-and-eye bonding into a single whole. Royal appointment functions as an outer framework for David's reign, which started with Israel's anointing David king in chaps. 11–12 and then with their anointing of Solomon as king here. The "second" coronation may reflect the chronicler's view that the ceremony in 1 Kgs 1:38-40 was a hasty, improvised affair, followed by this more formal event. The anointing of Zadok, presumably as (sole) high priest (15:11; 16:39) seems to reflect Solomon's act early in his reign (1 Kgs 2:35). His sitting on God's throne is a typical rewriting of 1 Kgs 1:46; 2:12 (cf. 1 Chr 17:14; 28:5). Solomon's

prosperity represents a fulfillment of 22:13, and so the implicit guarantee of the Davidic dynasty. The obedience of "all Israel" characterized the reigns of both David and Solomon. Solomon won the support of all the other sons of David; thereby hangs a long tale, told in the succession narrative of 2 Samuel 9:1–20 and 1 Kings 1–2. As in the case of David's accession, the chronicler was not concerned with this tangled process but instead passed to the outcome. Solomon is even presented as greater than David (v. 25; cf. 1 Kgs 1:47).

The reader will be reminded of Joshua in the chronicler's depiction of Solomon. Joshua was the object of Israel's obedience (Deut 34:9; Josh 1:17), and the Lord exalted him in the sight of all Israel (Josh 3:7; 4:14). Solomon was a second Joshua, as David was another Moses. God's new age had the authenticating hallmarks of the previous one.

29:26-30. The chronicler recapitulates David's reign in the course of a royal epilogue, an expanded version of the one in 1 Kgs 2:10-12. Tribute is paid to the blessings he enjoyed from God's hand: a long life, riches, and honor (cf. v. 12; 23:1). The chronicler copies other royal epilogues in 1–2 Kings by closing with a reference to the literary sources (v. 29) he used for his digest in chaps. 10–29. He casts 1 and 2 Samuel as a series of prophetic narratives (cf. 2 Chr 29:25). In Samuel's case, he had particularly in mind 1 Samuel 16 (cf. 1 Chr 28:4); for Nathan, 2 Samuel 7 (= 1 Chronicles 17); and for Gad, 2 Samuel 24 (= 1 Chronicles 21). In the Jewish canon, 1–2 Samuel are included in the Former Prophets and carry prophetic authority. Even in the chronicler's day they appear to have been invested with a prophetic role.

REFLECTIONS

1. David's appeal for contributions to the building of the Temple reminds the Christian reader of the emergency fund Paul set up on behalf of the needy church in Jerusalem, for which he appealed in 2 Corinthians 8–9. For both Paul and the chronicler, cheerful giving was a measure of spirituality. While in 1 Chronicles David is the model, in 2 Cor 8:9 the "generous act" (NRSV) of Christ in choosing human poverty is the example. If the people and the king rejoiced at the willingness of the giving, God, too, "loves a cheerful giver" (2 Cor 9:7), as 1 Chr 29:17 hints. Consumers experience self-gratification in their spending, and so do misers in their saving; but givers know a deeper joy and a greater gain.

2. The thanksgiving prayer (29:14-17) wrestles reverently with the paradox that one cannot give to God, who is the prior giver of everything. C. S. Lewis expressed this problem well:

> It is like a small child going to its father and saying, "Daddy, give me sixpence to buy you a birthday present." Of course, the father does and is pleased with the present. It is all very nice and proper, but only an idiot would think that the father is sixpence to the good in the transaction.[180]

Israel was like a child without sixpence to call its own. It could be asked of them, "What do you have that you did not receive?" (1 Cor 4:7 NRSV). There could be no self-congratulation on the part of the donors. The thanksgiving emphasizes this point as it traces all giving back to the Lord. As well, God's prior giving constrains Christian giving. As one version of a popular hymn declares, "The gifts we have to offer are what thy love imparts, but chiefly thou desirest our humble, thankful hearts."[181]

Dependence on God is given a twist in the petitions of 29:18-19. If the means of giving is given first by God, we humans depend on God also for a continuing sense of motivation. We need the prodding of the Holy Spirit to stimulate our self-centered hearts Godward.

3. The second petition is conscious of the burdens resting on young Solomon. God never gives burdens for us to bear alone, but wants to share them. In fact, "we do not have to do any carrying without remembering that we *are* carried."[182] There is a beautiful prayer in the *bar mitzvah* service used in Great Britain, when a thirteen-year-old Jewish boy assumes the yoke of the Torah. It speaks, rightly, of duty and resolve, but it manifests throughout a sense of utter dependence on God's help, as in this extract: "I pray humbly and hopefully before thee, to grant me thy gracious help, so that I have the will and the understanding to walk firmly in thy ways all the days of my life. Implant [literally "create"] in me a spirit of sincere devotion to thy service."[183] Christians, too, are called to trust and obey—to trust in God's enabling even as they obey. "It is God who is at work in you, enabling you both to will and to work for his good pleasure" (Phil 2:13 NRSV).

4. David's thanksgiving and praise in vv. 10-19 provide a counterpart to the praise and petitioning taken from the psalms in 1 Chr 16:7-36. Both have similar themes: The Lord is the sovereign King. The people, insignificant in and of themselves, are caught up in God's great purposes. There are also differences. According to 1 Chr 16:7-36, the patriarchs are models for a needy Israel as they wander through the land and receive the divine promise of a future inheritance. Here the patriarchs and Israel are recipients of God-given assets, which are humbly owned as such. Whereas in 1 Chr 16:7-36 Israel's appeal is brought to God, in David's prayer the chronicler implicitly brings the Lord's appeal to contemporary Israel and stakes God's claim on their lives and especially their monetary resources. Challenge rather than assurance is the dominant note. In these prayers of praise, different facets of theology are presented, and both end in petitions. In the psalm it was an eschatological petition, while here it is an existential plea for God's help in life's divinely assigned duties. We need both types of prayer, for life is both performance and preparation.

180. C. S. Lewis, *Mere Christianity* (New York: Macmillan, 1952) 110-11.

181. From "We Plow the Fields and Scatter" by M. Claudius, trans. J. M. Campbell, an altered version in *The Hymnal 1982* (New York: Church Hymnal Corporation) 291.

182. Karl Barth, *Ethics*, trans. G. W. Bromiley (New York; Seabury, 1981) 516.

183. *The Authorised Daily Prayer Book of the United Hebrew Congregations of the British Commonwealth of Nations*, 2nd ed., trans. S. Singer (London: Eyre and Spottiswoode, 1962) 407.

2 CHRONICLES 1:1–9:31, THE REIGN OF SOLOMON

OVERVIEW

The account of Solomon's reign has been analyzed as if it were a complex chiasm.[184] More probably it falls into two parallel halves, 1:1–5:1 and 5:2–9:31. Each half is initiated by the king's organizing a national assembly to worship at a sanctuary and receiving a nocturnal theophany in which a prayer of Solomon is answered (1:1-13; 5:2–7:22). The fact that the first sanctuary visited is the old one at Gibeon and the second is the new Temple in

Jerusalem shows the crucial development that the reign of Solomon brought. While much of the material is devoted to temple matters, the focus on Solomon's prosperous reign in chaps. 1 and 9 provides a different framework for the unit. Chapter 2 is concerned with his preparations for building the Temple and 3:1–5:1 with the actual building. Chapter 8 looks backward and forward: 8:1-11 anticipates the royal initiatives of 8:17–9:31, while 8:12-16 rounds off a description of temple ritual.

184. R. B. Dillard, *2 Chronicles*, WBC 15 (Waco, Tex.: Word, 1987) 5-7. See also Kleinig, *The Lord's Song*, 159-60.

2 Chronicles 1:1-17, Seeking God and Receiving Blessing

COMMENTARY

This chapter has two agendas. The first involves its relationship with chap. 9, as one of two literary bookends for this unit. Although the theme of the Temple dominates most of the account of Solomon's reign, his kingship is pushed to the fore at the beginning and the end. The root מלך (*mlk*), which denotes aspects of kingship, occurs no fewer than six times in vv. 1-13 and twice more in vv. 14-17. And this repetition is not surprising: Solomon's role in establishing the Davidic dynasty has been emphasized in 1 Chronicles 17; 22; and 28. Both his building of the Temple and his overall obedience to God were the conditions that had to be fulfilled if the dynasty were to last. Prosperity, it had been hinted, would be the signal that he had been obedient (1 Chr 22:13; cf. 1 Chr 29:23). So his reign is pointedly described as a success story at both its beginning and its ending. At the outset, his reign is grounded in his spirituality—namely, seeking the Lord. This fits the prescription for finding God that David gave him: "If you seek him, he will be found by you" (1 Chr 28:9). The second agenda of the

chapter involves a description of the old pre-Temple religious order, in preparation for the claim in later chapters that it had been superseded by the new Temple.

1:1. Solomon's accession to the throne carries with it a suggestion of opposition. The negative undercurrents are probed in 1 Kings 2, while 2 Chronicles sums up their resolution in a sentence. Solomon succeeded, as 1 Kgs 2:46b records, but only because he had divine backing. It is 1 Chr 11:9 all over again: "David became greater and greater, for the Lord of hosts was with him" (NRSV). The boon of the Lord's presence with Solomon begins to fulfill David's encouraging wish and affirmation in 1 Chr 22:11; 28:20. There the temple project was in view, but here it is the wider matter of Solomon's reign, as was the case with David (1 Chr 11:9). The statement that the Lord "made him exceedingly great" is a recapitulation of the same Hebrew wording in 1 Chr 29:25a (cf. KJV; TNK).

1:2-6. The chronicler makes clear that Solomon's first act as king was to seek the Lord. The writer of 1 Kgs 3:2-3 is apologetic about

Solomon's visit to the high place at Gibeon, excusing him grudgingly.[185] The chronicler had no such misgivings. Elsewhere he distinguishes between sincere worship of the Lord and idolatrous religion at high places (33:17). What made Solomon's visit to Gibeon unimpeachably legitimate was the claim, already encountered in 1 Chr 16:39-40; 21:29, that Gibeon was the national sanctuary for sacrifice, complete with the accoutrements of Mosaic religion. In 1 Kings 3, the sanctuary is of importance only as the place of ensuing theophany. In 2 Chronicles, Solomon's private visit is developed into a national pilgrimage. "All Israel" and "the whole assembly" are descriptions of a representative group of leaders, as v. 2 suggests.

According to 1 Chronicles, the first thing David had done after becoming king was to seek out the ark (1 Chr 13:3; cf. 1 Chr 15:13) with a national pilgrimage to its location (1 Chr 13:6). It was a case of like father, like son. Solomon and Israel "sought" (דרש *dāraš*; NRSV, "Inquired at it," a more likely interpretation than the NIV's "inquired of him," in view of the intended reminiscence of 1 Chr 13:3 and the fact that in the Hebrew single compound sentence of v. 5 the object of the verb is naturally the subject of the first clause, "the altar") the bronze altar for burnt offerings.[186] Verses 3 and 5 paint a beautiful picture of a united people worshiping together under God's chosen king. This expression of Solomon's spiritual faithfulness to God boded well for the perpetuity of the dynasty. It also sent reverberations of challenge and hope down through the centuries.

The legitimacy of the enterprise is painstakingly spelled out. The Mosaic "tent of meeting" (v. 3) or "tabernacle" (v. 5) had been preserved at Gibeon. The presence of the ancient altar at Gibeon (v. 5) made sacrificial worship there legitimate. Yet, there are hints of changes to come, heralded already by the installation of the ark in David's new tent in Jerusalem. The reference to Bezalel (cf. Exod 31:2; 1 Chr 2:20) prepares readers for a typological application in chap. 2, which will authorize a new order of worship. In 1 Kgs 3:4, the "thousand burnt offerings" on the

altar (v. 6) refer to Solomon's general custom. Here they are applied to this event and constitute a grand farewell to the tabernacle in its old setting. This moment marked the phasing out of Torah-based tabernacle worship, before the launching of the temple age.

1:7-9. In a private theophany, the Lord's invitation, "Ask what I should give you," has a royal flavor. In Ps 2:8, God offers to the king universal rule and in Ps 21:4 long life. Verse 8 is an abbreviation of 1 Kgs 3:6-7. One missing element, Solomon's inexperience, has been transferred to 1 Chr 22:5; 29:1. Two elements have been added. The first, an appeal for the Lord to keep the promise made to David, has been borrowed from 1 Kgs 8:26, which reappears in 2 Chr 6:17. We hear an echo of David's own prayer (1 Chr 17:23-24). These other contexts show that Solomon is requesting realization of that dynasty. This dynastic reference suggests that here Solomon's obedience is in view as a condition for the dynastic continuity. In fact, the motif of royal obedience accompanies the references to the divine promises in 1 Kgs 8:26 and the parallel 2 Chr 6:17. The second addition is the interpretation of the vast number of the people in terms of dust, recalling the promise made to Jacob in Gen 28:14.[187] So this interpretation represents an idealization of Solomon's reign as the keeping of a much older divine promise.

1:10-12. The king's request for wisdom in governing God's people, a purpose underlined by the chronicler in v. 12, is granted with the bonus of great riches and status. Whereas 1 Kgs 3:12 focuses on Solomon's imcomparable wisdom, here his wealth is brought to the fore, as vv. 14-17 will illustrate.

1:13. Solomon returns to Jerusalem "from the high place" (rightly emended in the NRSV with a note and implicitly in the NIV).[188] His celebratory sacrificing in Jerusalem (1 Kgs 3:15) is not mentioned here. Did the chronicler consider Gibeon the only rightful place of sacrifice at the time (cf. 1 Chr 16:39-40)? No, the presence of an altar in Jerusalem (1 Chr 21:26–22:1; cf. 1 Kgs 2:28) would have satisfied him, and he even took over the earlier reference to sacrificing there in 1 Chr 15:26. But the omission did underline the legitimacy of Gibeon.[189]

185. See the comparative analysis of D. M. Carr, *From D to Q: A Study of Early Jewish Interpretations of Solomon's Dream at Gibeon,* SBLMS 44 (Atlanta: Scholars Press, 1991) 90-114.

186. Japhet, *I & II Chronicles,* 529.

187. See Williamson, *Israel in the Books of Chronicles,* 64.

188. See Allen, *The Greek Chronicles,* 2:131.

189. Williamson, *1 and 2 Chronicles,* 196.

1:14-17. The cluster of items about horses has been taken from 1 Kgs 10:26-29. One expects to find it in the parallel 2 Chr 9:25-28. What does appear there has been influenced by the similar report in 1 Kgs 4:26. The chronicler regarded the 1 Kings texts as two separate summaries of Solomon's chariotry at the beginning and end of his reign. He put the smaller number first, encouraged by the verb "gathered together."[190] The paragraph

190. Curtis and Madsen, *The Books of Chronicles*, 318.

was put here to illustrate the fulfillment of the promise of riches in v. 12; it represents divine blessing for Solomon's seeking the things of God. Mention of "silver and gold" in v. 15, over against "silver" in 1 Kgs 10:27 and 2 Chr 9:27, paves the way for 2:7, as "cedar" does for 2:8, though here temple building is not yet in view. Readers may consult the 1 Kings commentary for the details of vv. 16-17. For the chronicler, the broad picture was sufficient.

REFLECTIONS

Like the account of David's reign, the chapters devoted to Solomon are vibrant with the excitement of change. These were times of transition from an old order to a new one. A royal dynasty was in the process of being founded, which was to reverberate through later history and become the basis of eschatological hope. A temple was to be built as the focus of offering worship and finding God's love thereafter for Israel. As Christian readers enter into the chronicler's excitement, they will appreciate in turn Jesus' claim that "something [even] greater than Solomon is here" (Matt 12:42 NRSV).

Solomon is represented as a model of spirituality. His first royal act was to urge "all Israel" to "seek" the Lord with him at a national sanctuary, replete with religious objects endorsed by the Torah. "Seek first . . ." is the chronicler's message, like that of Jesus (Matt 6:33 NIV). As a consequence, the king was rewarded with divine blessing. Solomon gained wealth (and also wisdom, but the chapter concentrates on the wealth) as a prize for seeking the Lord.

"Wealth . . . and honor" (1:12 NIV) come from God, according to 1 Chr 29:12. In the books of Chronicles these are the blessings poured out on good kings: David (1 Chr 29:28), Jehoshaphat (2 Chr 17:5; 18:1), Hezekiah (32:27), and here Solomon (also 9:22). In Jehoshaphat's case, it is also the result of seeking God (2 Chr 17:4). In Proverbs, wealth and honor are held out as incentives for seeking wisdom (Prov 8:17-18; see also Prov 22:4). Other parts of the Old Testament are not so sanguine in their attitude to wealth. While it fits snugly into the Old Testament's land-oriented theology, there are warnings about confusing material blessings and materialism (Deut 8:12-14, 17-18; Jer 9:23). The prophets complain of the wealth of the wicked (Jer 5:27; Hos 12:7-8; Mic 6:12; Zech 11:5), while Ecclesiastes is dubious about a providential explanation of wealth (Eccl 9:11). We are uneasily aware of such caveats. Yet, the chronicler was careful to take over the emphasis in 1 Kings that no self-seeking was involved and that it was in the context of discharging difficult responsibilities and seeking help in so doing that blessing came.

The one who seeks is invited to ask (1:7). Verses 5 and 7 of this chapter are reminiscent of the promise-laden invitations in the Sermon on the Mount: "Ask and it will be given to you; seek and you will find. . . . For everyone who asks receives; he who seeks finds" (Matt 7:7-8 NIV). Indeed, seeking God's kingdom results in the meeting of material needs (Matt 6:33) and the receipt of benefits ironically comparable with those enjoyed by "Solomon in all his glory" (Matt 6:29 NRSV). Again, we modern readers find it easier to separate spirituality from material things and to psychologize by focusing on the peace of mind we forfeit by not seeking God. Nevertheless, there is a refreshing simplicity about the link between body and spirit that often underlies biblical thinking and that we still honor when we pray at mealtime.

If, during Solomon's reign, gold was as common as stone in Jerusalem, in the new Jerusalem the very streets are to be paved with gold (Rev 21:21). One can hardly exclude an eschatological dimension from the text of 2 Chronicles (cf. Isa 60:5, 11; 61:6; 66:12). Here was the inauguration of future hope; here was a fitting earthly manifestation of God's kingdom (cf. 1 Chr 29:11-12). Jesus, too, received gold as an implicit pledge of his royal glory (Matt 2:11; 25:31).

2 Chronicles 2:1-18, Preparing for the Temple

COMMENTARY

2:1. Now the king can make the necessary arrangements for carrying out his God-appointed task of building the Temple. This verse is a headline for the chapter. It brings the Temple project to the fore and only glances at matters of royalty. Such side glances also occur in 2:12; 7:11; 8:1; 9:11, and presuppose knowledge of the account of building the palace in 1 Kgs 7:1-12. The chronicler turns into a narrative introduction Solomon's statement in his message to Hiram (Huram in Chronicles) at 1 Kgs 5:5 about the intention to build the Temple.

2:2. Two factors were necessary for building the Temple. The first is treated in this verse: personnel. The need for personnel provides a literary framework for the chapter. It is mentioned here and given fuller treatment in vv. 17-18. The need for a particular artisan appears in vv. 7 and 13-14. In ancient times, building projects were labor-intensive. An adequate labor force had to be prepared. This recruitment parallels the work of Solomon to that of David in 1 Chr 22:2.

2:3-16. Materials were also needed to build the Temple. Although David had provided much, 1 Chr 22:14 indicated the need for more. Verse 9 suggests that the splendor of Solomon's project made more materials required, harking back to 1 Chr 22:5. His negotiations with the Phoenician king Huram take up most of the chapter (vv. 3-16). They open with a message that falls into two parts: an introduction in vv. 3b-6 and its substance in vv. 7-10. Verses 3b-9 are bound together as a single meandering sentence in the Hebrew, with the core meaning "As you sent David cedar . . . send me also cedar" (vv. 3, 8).

2:3-6. Solomon's message to Huram is based on 1 Kgs 5:2-6, but here the Israelite king takes the initiative, and Hiram's prior

congratulations in 1 Kgs 5:1 are relegated to his reply at v. 11. The text of 1 Kgs 5:3-5 consists of Solomon's preliminary statements before his request in 1 Kgs 5:6. The chronicler had already used the motif of David's disqualifying warfare in 1 Chr 22:8-9, and has moved Solomon's intention to build the Temple back to 2 Chr 2:1.

That intention is repeated in v. 4a, but the rest of the introductory passage in vv. 3b-6 is given over to the chronicler's own concerns. First, a parallel is drawn between David and Solomon to call attention to their joint status. The chronicler deems Solomon to be as great a king as his father, since Solomon asked Huram for tribute (see vv. 14-15; cf. 1 Chr 14:1-2). Verse 7 will discriminate between the respective roles of David and Solomon vis-à-vis the Temple by presenting David as provider (cf. 1 Chr 22:15) and Solomon as executor.

Second, before the building narrative begins, the chronicler takes the opportunity to define the function of the Temple as a place of sacrificial worship (vv. 4b, 6; cf. 7:12). Although the Temple was a religious innovation, it was to operate on traditional lines laid down in the Lord's earlier revelation. The new era was to be marked by religious conformity to the old tabernacle era, as the priestly material in the Torah presented it. The offerings of incense (Exod 30:7-8), the bread of the presence (Exod 25:30; Lev 24:5-8), and the regular burnt offerings (Numbers 28:1–29) were to be maintained as permanent obligations for God's people to honor. These regular rites became a feature of the macrostructure of the chronicler's narrative as a yardstick by which to measure the spiritual loyalty of future kings.[191] In the divided

191. Williamson, *1 and 2 Chronicles*, 198.

kingdom, temple duties are reaffirmed at the outset as at least still being honored in Judah (13:10-11). At the end they are recorded as being tragically neglected even in Judah (29:7). In the reunited kingdom, Hezekiah reestablished these rites (29:18; 31:2-3), restoring the Temple to the religious standards of the Torah (31:3).

Third, in vv. 5-6 the theology of the Temple's structure and decor is discussed, in a development of David's statements at 1 Chr 22:5; 29:1. If Israel's "God is greater than all other gods" (1 Chr 16:25 NIV), then an edifice to honor such a God must itself be correspondingly great. It must be a visible witness to the wonderful glory of the Lord (v. 9). Yet too much should not be claimed for the Temple. It was only in a limited sense God's house (cf. Exod 25:8), though it did enjoy the partial presence of the Lord ("before him," vv. 4, 6). The chronicler borrows material from Solomon's prayer in 1 Kgs 8:27 that he will use again in its proper place at 6:18. It is an assertion of divine omnipresence by which the Lord is shown to be beyond all manipulation (cf. Ps 139:7-12).

2:7-10. Solomon asks for a master craftsman (v. 7) and for lumber (vv. 8-10). In a letter Huram will consent to both requests (vv. 13-16). The chronicler's source is 1 Kgs 7:13-14, a separate narrative whose gist he weaves into Solomon's message. There the craftsman was called simply Hiram and is a bronzesmith, while ethnically he was a Phoenician with an Israelite mother from the tribe of Naphtali. Here he is called Huram-abi and is an artisan skilled in many crafts, and his mother's tribe is Dan.

As elsewhere, the chronicler writes with one eye on the historical source and the other on the tabernacle account, specifically the description of its construction in Exodus 35. Its chief craftsman was Bezalel, from the tribe of Judah. He was mentioned in 2 Chr 1:5 in anticipation of this passage (cf. 1 Chr 2:20). Bezalel had an assistant named Aholiab (Exod 35:34), from the tribe of Dan, and between them they had the manifold skills of vv. 7 and 14. Solomon is regarded typologically as a second Bezalel from Judah, and Huram-abi as a second Aholiab from Dan. In the latter case, the longer name "Huram-abi" is a clue to the typologizing. We shall read repeatedly

in chaps. 3–4 the statement "and he made" (ויעש *wayya'aś*) about Solomon's work for the Temple. It is used much more often than in the 1 Kings source and echoes the same frequent refrain concerning Bezalel in Exodus 36–39. With these echoes, the chronicler affirms theologically that the Temple is a second tabernacle. In 1 Kgs 7:14, Hiram had been modeled in part on Bezalel (cf. Exod 35:3-35),[192] while the temple furnishings in 1 Kgs 7:40, 48-50 reflected those of the tabernacle.[193] The chronicler takes these hints seriously and develops them in his own way. Typological comparison serves to describe the new era as comparable to and succeeding the old one.

2:11-16. Huram's reply is cast in the form of a letter. It corresponds closely to Solomon's message, both in content and in structure, which consists of introduction and main part (vv. 13-16). The introduction, like Solomon's, is theologically oriented. The description of Solomon as the Lord's love gift to Israel is borrowed from another foreign testimony (1 Kgs 10:9), which will be used again in 2 Chr 9:8. It fits Solomon's role as the chosen agent of a new era for Israel (cf. 1 Chr 28:5-7). It is adapted from Hiram's love for David, mentioned in the narrative of 1 Kgs 5:1 (KJV). The shift was encouraged by the pair of blessing formulas in 1 Kgs 5:7 and 10:9.

Huram's praise in v. 12 changes 1 Kgs 5:7b in two ways. First, it adds a reference to the Lord as creator (cf. Ps 78:69), which is consistent with Solomon's witness to God (vv. 5-6). Second, and in accord with the literary context, it envisions Solomon's wisdom as being manifested in his building of the Temple rather than in his reign. The theological program of 1 Chr 16:25-30 finds partial realization here. The Phoenician king represents Gentile peoples who were urged to "ascribe to the LORD the glory due to his name," as the God who "made the heavens." The new era inaugurated by David and Solomon awaited the consummation, the Gentiles' acknowledgment of the praiseworthiness of Israel's God (cf. Ps 22:27-28; 102:21-22; Isa 45:14; 66:18-23). King Huram is also represented as vassal of David and Solomon ("my lord,"

192. See McKenzie, *The Chronicler's Use of the Deuteronomistic History,* 107.
193. R. D. Nelson, *First and Second Kings,* Interpretation (Louisville: John Knox, 1987) 47.

vv. 14-15). Solomon receives foreign homage on the Lord's behalf, sitting as he does on God's throne (1 Chr 29:23). This is an aspect of Solomon's reign that chap. 9 will develop.

The NRSV and the NIV omit the transitional "And now" (v. 13 KJV), which is repeated in v. 15. Huram assents to Solomon's two requests and agrees with the wages to be paid Huram's woodcutters, offered in v. 10. In 1 Kgs 5:6, Solomon left it to the king of Tyre to fix the wages, but here Solomon again takes the initiative. The quantities involved are loosely based on the annual contribution specified in 1 Kgs 5:11, but here a single fee is envisioned.

2:17-18. The issue of local workers, broached in v. 2, is elaborated in a resumptive conclusion. The chronicler is now following the order of his parent text, 1 Kgs 5:13-18. The numbers and job descriptions of 1 Kgs 5:15-16 are closely followed and supplied with a total (v. 17). There is one other passage about forced labor in 1 Kgs 9:20-22, which states categorically that Solomon used no Israelites for the labor gangs, but only indigenous groups. The chronicler, who will make explicit use of 1 Kgs 9:20-22 in 2 Chr 8:7-9, follows that tradition, encouraged by his view of Solomon as one who follows the Torah. He is mindful of Lev 25:39-45 and Deut 20:11, which prohibit harsh rule over Israelites and permit the use of indigenous subjects as forced labor.[194] Accordingly, both here and in 1 Chr 22:2, to which he refers (אחרי [*'aḥărê*] is better rendered "similar to," with the REB, than "after"), he interpreted "out of all Israel" in 1 Kgs 5:13 not nationally but territorially, as "the aliens who were residing in the land of Israel" (NRSV). The chronicler's interpretation seems forced. It does not accord with Jeroboam's position as overseer of the forced labor of the house of Joseph (1 Kgs 11:28). Moreover, the antipathy of the northern tribes to Rehoboam and their stoning of the administrator of the forced labor program (1 Kgs 12:3-4, 18), both of which are taken over in 2 Chr 10:3-4, 18, are left unexplained.[195]

194. See Williamson, *1 and 2 Chronicles*, 202.
195. For further study see R. H. Lowery, *The Reforming Kings: Cults and Society in First Temple Judah*, JSOTSup 120 (Sheffield: JSOT, 1991) 80-88.

REFLECTIONS

The chronicler has used Solomon's preparations for building the Temple as an opportunity to express a number of theological themes relating to the Temple and to Solomon himself. The Torah is honored both as a continuing model for temple worship (2:4) and implicitly as a guide for Solomon's use of labor gangs for construction (2:17). The chronicler was sensitive to the blend of old and new. The new era, even as it forged ahead in certain areas, respected older norms and took them seriously. One covets for the Christian similar conscientiousness in honoring the Old Testament as God's Word and carefully tracing the New Testament's relation to it.

1. The greatness of God is reflected in two ways. First, it is reflected through Solomon, who receives the homage of the Phoenician king and takes the initiative to procure lumber and an artisan from him. Moreover, the aliens in Israel also served him (2:17). The Lord gives Solomon greatness (1:1) in a Gentile setting, such as David before him had enjoyed (1 Chr 14:17). Solomon, builder of a palace and a temple (v. 1), was God's viceroy. His reign represented the inauguration of an era that was to be consummated in the future, when the Lord was revealed fully as king over the nations (1 Chr 16:31). Would not God's future king of David's line be "great to the ends of the earth" (Mic 5:4 NRSV)? History and hope are intertwined in the theology of the new era. Likewise, according to the New Testament, God has already highly exalted the risen Jesus, with the eventual purpose that "every knee should bow" at the supreme name given to him (Phil 2:9-10). In Christian worship, we find God's work in past and future time having an impact on our present lives.

Second, the Lord's greatness would be reflected in the Temple. It, too, would be "great" (2:5, 9). Solomon's principle of a great building for a great God was taken over by the medieval church, which channeled immense economic resources into magnificent cathedrals that were showpieces of artistic beauty. The modern church, poorer and also alert to human need, can hardly emulate such architectural masterpieces. Yet, church buildings are silent witnesses to the faith of those who worship inside them. Outsiders receive from these buildings a visual impression of the God who is worshiped there. The role of the church building committee, therefore, is to communicate theology.

2. The magnificence of the Temple was to be only a relative reflection of God's greatness. The Lord was near, yet also enthroned beyond the stars. The God of the covenant was also the God of creation (2:11-12). There are Christians whose conceptions of God are too limited, yet who are confident about their version of the Christian faith and God's predictability. Here, by contrast, is a conception of God that testifies to the mystery of God's being. God is never so accessible as to be caged. The Lord could only be worshiped with a regularity that created its own calendar. Only by that *forever-ness* (see 2:4) could Israel hope to reflect the truth that God is great and greatly to be praised (1 Chr 16:25).

3. Typological comparisons, like the one manifested in the description of the craftsman Huram-abi, appear in the New Testament. The phenomenon of a new revelation, echoing language relevant to an older one, even as it supersedes it, is found in the description of Christ as "the last Adam" (1 Cor 15:45), head of a new humanity. There is the same painstaking concern as here in 2 Chronicles to trace continuity between revelations both old and new. Theological history is a series of divine interventions, with each new one bearing the familiar signature of the earlier intervention in token of its authenticity.

2 Chronicles 3:1–5:1, Building the Temple

COMMENTARY

These two chapters follow a clearly marked route defined by Solomon's beginning and finishing the construction of the Temple (3:1-2; 5:1) and by a series of literary milestones along the way, the repeated "and he made" (ויעש *wayyaʿaś*) from 3:8 onward. The chronicler has considerably shortened his source, 1 Kings 6–7, to about half its length. He does not attach precise significance to each detail. The details were evidently regarded as a means to a more important end, the worship of God. The theology of the Temple had been broached in chap. 2 and will be treated further in chaps. 5–7; it finds little expression here.

Second Chronicles 3:1–4:9 represents an integral block of material. The location of the Temple and the date for starting its construction are the concerns of 3:1-2; 3:3-14

presents the dimensions and ornamentation of the temple building, as a whole and in its parts. Details of the items with which the Temple was furnished are provided in 3:15–4:8, while 4:9 takes in the courts around the Temple.

3:1-2. The chronicler omits the exodus dating found in 1 Kgs 6:1, since a new religious era had dawned for Israel with the Davidic monarchy. He inserts fresh evidence of its divine authenticity, reminding readers of the choice of the Temple site in 1 Chronicles 21:1. David's encounter with the angel of the Lord and the supernatural fire are described as divine revelation. The translation "the LORD has appeared" stands for a Hebrew verb lacking a subject (נראה *nirʾâ*). It may more properly be regarded as an impersonal passive, "revelation was made." The chronicler alludes to Gen 22:14, which associates the place where Abraham almost sacrificed Isaac with a future revelation. There is wordplay in Gen 22:14—between God's provision of an alternative sacrifice and a future theophany. The Hebrew verb rendered "see" also means "see to," "provide." So the promise that "on the mount of the LORD it shall be provided" (Gen 22:14 NRSV) could also mean "revelation shall be made." The phrase "the mountain of the LORD" is used of the Jerusalem Temple in Ps 24:3; Isa 2:3. The chronicler took over a tradition in the book of Genesis and claimed that this omen associated with a patriarchal experience had now come true. Here was "Mount Moriah" (cf. Gen 22:2), understood by popular etymology as "the mountain of the revelation of the LORD." It was David who received the promised revelation. So there was further good reason for David to pass over the Gibeon sanctuary in 1 Chr 21:28–22:1, even though it contained the tabernacle. In the Torah there was a warrant for worship that was more ancient than the tabernacle and pointed beyond the tabernacle to the Temple.

3:3-14. This passage is concerned with the overall size and appearance of the Temple. It was an opulent and artistically ornamented structure. Here was splendor and beauty as worthy of God as any funded and fashioned by human hands (cf. 1 Chr 29:1-9; 2 Chr 2:5-9). Verse 3 presents a ground plan (the NIV's "foundation" [הוסד *hûsad*; cf. the REB] need not be emended with the NRSV; the plural "these" [אלה *'elleh*] is attracted to the dimensions). The chronicler observes that the size of the cubit was obsolete by his time; it was seven handbreadths rather than six (cf. Ezek 43:13). The height of the vestibule or portico in the MT, and preserved in the NRSV, is surprising. Some 180 feet high, it was an enormous tower. The height of the vestibule of the Herodian Temple was 100 cubits high. The writers of 1 Kgs 6:3 are silent about the height; the rest of the Temple was thirty cubits high according to 1 Kgs 6:2. The textual evidence for "twenty cubits," to which the NIV and the REB appeal, is not impressive.[196]

The rest of the Temple was divided into the nave, or main hall, and the "most holy place," or holy of holies, with its gold-plated cherubim (see 1 Kgs 6:15-30). The rear room in which the ark was to be placed is described as the "most holy place," the ultimate in gradations of holiness. It symbolizes the sovereign mystery of the Lord, whose gracious fellowship with Israel was never to be interpreted as familiarity. The chronicler highlights the presence of the images of cherubim in the Temple, which the Second Temple no longer contained. They were featured not only as statues in the most holy place, but also as engravings on the wood lining the Temple's walls (v. 7; cf. 1 Kgs 6:29); figures of cherubim were also embroidered on the curtain covering the "most holy place" (v. 14; cf. Ezek 36:25). They functioned as symbols of the divine presence. As in 1 Chr 28:18, these cherubim reflect the chronicler's fascination with the visions of Ezekiel 1; 8–10; and 43. Mention of the cherubim also drew implicit attention to "the ark of God the Lord who is enthroned between the cherubim" (1 Chr 13:6) and served as a reminder that the Temple was to house the ark (5:7).

The repeated "And he made" (*wayya'as*), which occurs thirteen times between 3:8 and 4:9, systematically demarcates the progression of the narrative. The chronicler develops the four instances of *wayya'as* in 1 Kgs 6:23; 7:23, 38, 48, in line with the description of the tabernacle and its furnishings (Exodus 36:1–39). The chronicler is teaching his Torah-versed readers that what Solomon made corresponds to what Bezalel had made. There are further features borrowed from the tabernacle in this account. The small weight of gold for the nails in the most holy place (v. 9) indicates the use of gold plating. These golden nails correspond to the gold hooks used for the screen of the tabernacle in Exod 26:32, 37; 36:36. The curtain between the rear room and the nave (v. 14) was a feature of the Herodian Temple, but is not mentioned in the 1 Kings narrative, which has doors instead (1 Kgs 7:50; cf. 2 Chr 4:22), though 1 Kgs 8:8 may presuppose it.[197] The chronicler again has the tabernacle screen in mind, as the verbal parallelism with Exod 36:35 (and 26:31) indicates.

196. See Williamson, *1 and 2 Chronicles*, 206-7; Barthélemy, *Critique textuelle de l'Ancien Testament,* 1:477-78.

197. See J. A. Montgomery and H. S. Gehman, *The Books of Kings*, ICC (Edinburgh: T. & T. Clark, 1951) 189.

3:15-17. The chronicler draws attention to the two ornate pillars at the entrance to the vestibule, abbreviating 1 Kgs 7:15-22, to which he jumps in his source from 1 Kgs 6:29. Did their names, "Jachin" and "Boaz," have any special meaning for the chronicler? "Jachin" means "he establishes," or "he prepares." The related verb הכין (hēkîn, in the hiphil) has been used of God's permanent establishment of the Davidic dynasty once the condition of erecting the Temple had been met (1 Chr 17:11-12; 22:10; cf. 1 Chr 28:7). On the human plane the verb was used when the chronicler described David's preparations for the Temple. Boaz, if the vocalization suggests "in him is strength," attests the Lord's power, mentioned in 1 Chr 16:11, 27-28; 2 Chr 6:41, which is associated with the sanctuary in 1 Chr 16:27. Both names resonate with literary connotations.

In v. 16, in place of the MT's בדביר (baddĕbîr, "in the rear room") the NRSV and the NIV rightly adopt the conjectural emendation כרביד (kĕrābîd, "encircling," "interwoven," or "like a necklace" [REB]; see the REB; the MT probably arose from a displacing gloss that loosely compared it to 1 Kgs 6:21).[198] The pillars are said to be thirty five cubits "high" (NRSV), literally "long" (NIV). This dimension clashes with the eighteen cubits of 1 Kgs 7:15; 2 Kgs 25:17; Jer 52:21. The change recalls the increased height of the vestibule in v. 4; in this case it may have arisen from the chronicler's confused understanding of the numbers in 1 Kgs 7:15.[199]

4:1-8. The chronicler continues describing the items installed in the Temple and its court. The bronze altar is not mentioned in the MT of 1 Kings 6–7, but 1 Kgs 9:25 (= 2 Chr 8:12) states that Solomon built it, and 1 Kgs 8:22, 64; 2 Kgs 16:14 presuppose it. It was probably in the chronicler's text of 1 Kings between 1 Kgs 7:22 and 23, and was lost from the MT.[200] Its presence here is consonant with the emphasis on the sacrificial function of the Temple in 2:4, 6. Whereas religious items were brought from Gibeon (5:5), the altar of 2 Chr 1:5-6 (cf. 1 Chr 21:29) is not mentioned there. Solomon, a second Bezalel (Exod 38:1-7), made a fresh altar for the new era of temple worship. David's altar in 1 Chr 21:26 was presumably regarded as provisional, so that the altar announced in 1 Chr 22:1 anticipates this one, made by Solomon.

The description of the vast bronze "sea" or "tank" (GNB) in vv. 2-5 is taken closely from 1 Kgs 7:23-26. In v. 6b, its function is defined in terms of the bronze laver of the tabernacle in Exod 30:19-21, linking it with sacrificial ritual. Mathematicians will notice that in v. 2 π is given the numerical value of 3, rather than 3.14. The circumference is given as a round figure; possibly it was measured with a line more easily placed beneath the flared rim.[201] The "gourds" (NIV) of 1 Kgs 7:24, embossed under the rim, have here become "figures of bulls." The chronicler probably misread or misunderstood his source. The capacity of 3,000 baths contrasts with the 2,000 in 1 Kgs 7:26, either because of a textual error or because of the conversion to a smaller, post-exilic unit of capacity.[202]

The material about lampstands is taken from 1 Kgs 7:49a, to which the chronicler leaps. The appeal to earlier prescription hardly refers to the Torah, as it usually does in Chronicles, since only one lampstand stood in the tabernacle, as in the Second Temple (cf. Exod 25:31-40; 37:17-24). But the use of the lampstands does allude to the plans for the Temple and its furnishings that were drawn up by David and presented to Solomon (see 1 Chr 28:15).[203] The burning of the Temple lamps, an element of special importance to the chronicler, was the fourth traditional medium of worship that belonged with the other three listed in 2:4. All four are enumerated in 13:11; 29:7.

What were the ten tables used for? The reference in 1 Chr 28:16 to a number of tables used for the bread of the presence (cf. v. 19) suggests that this was their purpose, though only one table is mentioned in 2 Chr 13:11; 29:18, as in 1 Kgs 7:48. One hundred gold "sprinkling bowls" (NIV) were used to dash sacrificial blood against the altar (see 1 Kgs 7:50, where the number of bowls is unspecified).

198. See Williamson, *1 and 2 Chronicles*, 210.
199. See Japhet, *I & II Chronicles*, 557.
200. See Rudolph, *Chronikbücher*, 207; McKenzie, *The Chronicler's Use of the Deuteronomistic History*, 88.

201. A. Zuidhof, "King Solomon's Molten Sea and (π)," *BA* 45 (1982) 179-84, esp. 181.
202. Zuidhof, "King Solomon's Molten Sea and (π)," 181.
203. S. J. De Vries, "Moses and David as Cult Founders in Chronicles," *JBL* 107 (1988) 619-39, esp. 630.

4:9. The closing reference to the two courts has been loosely derived from 1 Kgs 6:36; 7:12. There the temple court, or "inner court," was distinguished from the "great court" that surrounded the complex of palace buildings and the temple area. The chronicler, however, in accord with Second Temple practice and with Ezekiel 40–48, conceives of two temple courts, an inner one restricted to priests and Levites and an outer one for laity. The bronze doors are not mentioned in 1 Kings.

4:10-22. This passage is a close copy of 1 Kgs 7:39b-50. It does not match the earlier material in 3:1–4:9, which was marked by selectivity, summarizing, and precise copying of short passages. The lampstands of 1 Kgs 7:49a (2 Chr 4:20) have already been dealt with in 4:7, and the "sprinkling bowls" of 1 Kgs 7:50 (= 2 Chr 4:22) have been mentioned in v. 8*b*. One does not expect a return to the pillars of 3:15-17 in such detail as is found in vv. 12-13. Renewed mention of the basins and the sea (vv. 14-15) is also surprising, as is mention of the stands for the basins, since the chronicler appeared to have chosen to omit reference to them in v. 6. The overall impression is that the passage has been subsequently inserted to fill a gap between citation of 1 Kgs 7:39a in v. 7 and of 1 Kgs 7:51 in 5:1.[204] One may explain the abrupt resumption of the topic of the sea in 4:10 (= 1 Kgs 7:39b) in this fashion.

This new material improves the earlier text of Chronicles by incorporating the work of Huram-abi, which 2:13-14 led the reader to expect. The unweighed amounts of bronze in v. 18 recall the same factor in David's preparations at 1 Chr 22:3, 14 and so reintroduce the pervasive theme of the Temple's grandeur. The golden altar (v. 19) refers to the incense

204. See Willi, *Die Chronik als Auslegung*, 94n. 78; Williamson, *1 and 2 Chronicles*, 211-12; Dillard, *2 Chronicles*, 34. See also Japhet, *I & II Chronicles*, 560-64.

altar in the nave. Its presence builds a literary bridge between David's prescription in 1 Chr 28:18 and the narrative about Uzziah's misuse of it in 2 Chr 26:16-20. There are a few departures from 1 Kings 7. In v. 19 the table for the bread of the presence is made plural, in line with v. 8. In v. 22 "entrance" or "door" (פתח *petaḥ*) represents a different reading; 1 Kgs 7:50 has "sockets" (פתות *pōtôt*). In v. 20, the prescriptive formula of v. 7 has been added and supplied with a new basis, the use of the lampstands rather than their form, corresponding more precisely to 13:11; 29:7.

5:1. The chronicler uses 1 Kgs 7:51 to round off his narrative of the Temple's construction. In 1 Chr 22:9 we observed a Hebrew wordplay on Solomon's name (שלמה *šělōmōh*) and "peace" (שלום *šālôm*). Another wordplay seems to occur here, with reference to Solomon's work having been finished (ותשלם *wattišlam*). Both wordplays underline the divine program for Solomon's reign, in this case as temple builder. However, in another sense, there was more to be done. The empty Temple had yet to be filled with the personnel and rites of regular worship; this dynamic aspect will be covered in 8:12-16. Here a finishing touch is supplied by the installation of David's victory trophies (cf. 1 Chr 18:10-11), in tribute to the labors of the warrior king who had earlier played his part in the Lord's program. David's and Solomon's joint work is affirmed here, as at the beginning of the passage (3:1). Mention of the "treasuries" also helps the reader to recall David's work in 1 Chr 26:20-28. The treasuries have not been mentioned in the account of building the Temple. Presumably they were on the first floor of the structure surrounding three sides of the Temple, described in 1 Kgs 6:5-10, while the "upper rooms" of 1 Chr 28:11 and 2 Chr 3:9 were its second and third stories.

REFLECTIONS

1. The completion of the Temple (5:1) was a decisive step forward, laying a divine foundation for the future. At the outset of construction, the reader is reminded that the human activity is based on the purposes of God. According to 3:1, David's preparatory work in designating the Temple site had been grounded in a divine revelation, which the Torah itself had forecast. Thus the divine authenticity of the Temple was doubly established as successor to the Mosaic tabernacle, first in the Torah and then in a new revelation to David. In appealing to the Torah the chronicler is giving a solid theological argument for the importance of the contemporary Temple.

The argument is similar to that used in Hebrews 7. How may Jesus, a member of the non-priestly tribe of Judah, be high priest of the heavenly tabernacle? The answer lies in Gen 14:18-20 and Ps 110:4: Jesus, in inheriting this royal role, also became an heir of the priest-king Melchizedek. Another example is Paul's grounding of justification by faith in Gen 15:6 at Romans 4 and Galatians 3. The authors of the New Testament used the Old Testament as a theological dictionary, turning to it for clarification and finding special authority in the Torah. Sometimes we modern Christians hide behind an appeal to blind faith and ignore such unashamedly intellectual concerns to gain a hearing for what was held to be the truth by culturally relevant arguments. The Bible constantly appeals to the mind, with careful argumentation to support its claims. Faith has to find corroboration if it is to satisfy and survive. Such corroboration is worth seeking, both in the theological reasoning of the Bible and in contemporary theological and ethical reflection.

2. The accent on gold and precious stones, which the redactional supplement enhances in 4:19-22, envisions a past glory that the chronicler's contemporaries could not copy. Even for David the qualification "so far as I was able" (1 Chr 29:2 NRSV) posed a limit as well as a target. Only the best—always a relative best—that particular human hands can give and do is good enough for God. Neither more nor less is sought. It was that human best that was to be graciously filled with divine glory (5:14).

3. The ever-burning lampstands, singled out in 4:7 and editorially underlined in 4:20, were a vital element of worship for the chronicler, according to 13:11. In 29:7, he will deplore their temporary absence. Worship is grounded in certain traditional sacred acts that transcend the present and the personal concerns of worshipers. They remind us that we are part of a sacred entity much greater than ourselves.

4. The completion of Solomon's task (5:1) recalls David's work as pioneer, as the rest of the verse suggests. We are reminded of another who became both "pioneer and perfecter" (Heb 12:2 NRSV) and who was to cry, "It is finished" (John 19:30 NIV). In both eras, a solid foundation was being laid for future believers to stand on before God.

5. Paul, reading 2 Chronicles 3–4, may have reflected on its relevance for his own ministry and incorporated his reflections into a letter to the church he had recently planted in Corinth (1 Cor 3:10-17). He would have been reading the 2 Chronicles account rather than the one in 1 Kings, since the chronicler's account refers to laying a foundation and to precious stones. Paul was probably reading the Hebrew text because the LXX does not mention laying a foundation. The apostle represented himself as another Solomon for the Christians in Corinth, a temple builder who had laid a foundation in evangelism and basic teaching. Now each member was responsible for continuing the work, making his or her contribution to the fellowship, like Huramabi and like the craftsmen of 2 Chr 2:13. The latter contributed a golden bowl and a silver dish or jeweled ornamentation, each item skillfully and lovingly made—no hay or stubble, ludicrous examples of the ephemeral, but contributions of solid and lasting worth. The apostle was typologizing, using elements of the old era to teach principles of the new era. If 2 Chronicles 3–4 strikes us as unpromising preaching material, Paul's hermeneutical creativity is worth studying.

2 Chronicles 5:2–7:22, The Temple: Place of Worship and Means of Grace

COMMENTARY

The reign of Solomon is divided into two halves in 2 Chronicles (1:1–5:1; 5:2–9:31). Each half begins with the king's organizing a national assembly to worship at a sanctuary and his receiving a theophany in which one of his prayers is answered at night. The second half of Solomon's reign is addressed in this section. The main agenda of the first half was the construction and equipping of the Temple. Now the chronicler fills the building with the Lord's presence and with Israel's worship and prayers. The Temple comes to life and becomes a dynamic element in maintaining the relationship between Israel and their God.

5:2-10. This spiritual landmark in Israel's history is appropriately initiated by a representative assembly at the Temple. The installation of the ark in the Temple fittingly launches the new section, because the ark symbolized the divine presence. Housed in the Temple, it became the implicit focus of Israel's prayers ("in your presence," 6:19) and sacrificial worship ("before the LORD," 7:4). The chronicler used 1 Kgs 8:1-9 as his source for the account of the ark's installation, only supplementing it with the role of the Levites in carrying the ark, evidently for the last time. There is a grand procession from "the city of David," where the ark had stood in David's tent (1 Chr 13:13; 16:1), to the Temple, a few hundred yards to the north. The occasion was the Feast of Tabernacles (v. 3; cf. Lev 23:34). The account in 1 Kings 8:1 uses the generic term "priests" (כהנים *kōhănîm*) for those who carried the ark (1 Kgs 8:3), as in Joshua 3, and then adds the note that both priests and Levites were involved (1 Kgs 8:4). The chronicler scrupulously changes "priests" (*kōhănîm*) to "Levites" (לוים *lĕwiyyim*) in v. 4, to conform with the emphasis on the Levites in 1 Chronicles 15. The text in v. 5 is not certain; both "the Levitical priests" and "the priests and the Levites" appear in ancient manuscripts.

The installation of the ark and its "vessels" (NRSV) marks a fulfillment of David's directions (1 Chr 22:19). The presence of the "tent of meeting," or tabernacle, presumably brought earlier from Gibeon, builds on the dual system of worship set up by David (1 Chronicles 16:1). In v. 7, the priests install the ark in the Temple (see Num 4:5-15, 20). In v. 9 "the ark" (הארון *hāʾārôn*) accords with the Masoretic Text. More probably "the ark" represents a gloss that has displaced the NRSV's "the holy place" (הקדש *haqqōdeš*), which appears in the parallel text, 1 Kgs 8:8.[205] The phrase "to this day" is retained in 2 Chronicles as an antiquarian reference. The Second Temple had no ark, but it did possess the ritual vessels (v. 5), which provided essential continuity with the First Temple and affirmed its legitimacy. The contents of the ark, the tablets inscribed with the Ten Commandments, represented the Torah, a continuing mandate for king and people (6:16; 7:17, 19). The new, temple-oriented revelation did not eclipse the obligations of the old, though it did demonstrate a remarkably qualified perspective toward them (6:24-39; 7:14).

5:11-14. The chronicler interrupts the account of the priests' leaving the Temple and the supernatural cloud that fills it (1 Kgs 8:10) with his own snapshot of the scene. He enthusiastically portrays the massed presence of the priests exiting the Temple and the levitical singing musicians in white robes in front of the altar in the temple court, accompanied by the priestly trumpeters. The choirs, formerly separated at different sanctuaries (1 Chr 16:37-42), were now united at the new Temple. The chronicler envisions a service of music and song to complement the sacrificial worship (v. 6).

The hymn fragment, sung earlier in 1 Chr 16:41, offers praise for the permanent "[steadfast] love" (חסד *ḥesed*) which is the Lord's attribute as God of the covenant. It fits the inauguration of the new age, founded on the Davidic covenant and centered in Temple and dynasty. Although the Torah was associated first with the Mosaic covenant (v. 10; 6:11), that covenant was now taken up into the new

205. See Allen, *The Greek Chronicles*, 2:145.

Davidic covenant (cf. 6:14, 42; 7:18), and so was secured with a fresh guarantee: God's "[steadfast] love endures forever." For the chronicler, this song results in the appearance of the cloud of glory in the Temple, which marks an intensified mode of the divine presence.[206] It constitutes an implicit parallel with the cloud in Exod 40:34-35, as God's seal of approval on the Temple.

6:1-2. In two speeches (vv. 1-11), Solomon takes stock of the situation and comments on its theological significance, consistent with 1 Kgs 8:12-21. Facing the Temple, the king formally presents it to the Lord. The theophanic cloud, which concealed even as it revealed, is implicitly compared with the dark holy of holies in which the ark had been placed. The holy of holies marked the permanent presence of the transcendent and mysterious God.

6:3-11. The second speech is made to the assembled Israel, whom Solomon turns to face. It opens with a formula of praise ("Blessed be . . ." NRSV); the verb "blessed" (ויברך *wayyĕbārek*) in v. 3 refers to the use of this formula in the address. Solomon explains why he built the Temple and installed the ark in it. The speech is constructed around two divine promises to David (vv. 5-6 and vv. 8b-9). David was to be king, but the privilege of being temple builder was reserved for one of his sons, who would succeed him and would build the sanctuary. The Lord's promise had been kept, and for that Solomon gave praise (v. 4). The speech here does not have the force it has in 1 Kings 8, since, according to 1 Chr 22:9, David had already disclosed Solomon's identity as the divinely revealed successor and temple builder, while 1 Kings 8 knows of no such disclosure. Here the speech endorses the earlier revelation. The emphasis on the Lord's name being in the Temple (vv. 5-6, preserving a longer text than the MT of 1 Kgs 8:16) identified the Temple as the legitimate sanctuary—*the* place at which invoking the divine name was authorized (cf. Exod 20:24 REB: "wherever I cause my name to be invoked"; see also 2 Chr 6:24, 26).[207]

Verse 11 recalls 5:10. The ark is again identified as the container for the tablets summarizing the Torah, here briefly called "the covenant." It conveyed for the chronicler the importance of the Torah as a basis for the covenant relationship (see vv. 16, 27). In the books of Chronicles, "the ark of the covenant" appears prominently in passages that celebrate the Davidic covenant. The chronicler regarded the Mosaic covenant as substantially taken up into the Davidic one (see also 1 Chr 16:15-22).

6:12-42. The prayer in vv. 12-42 primarily introduces a fresh topic: the ongoing function of the Temple in Israel's relationship with the Lord. The text of 1 Kgs 8:22-53 is followed closely in vv. 12-42, except for the addition of minimal material in the initial narrative and a change in the ending of the prayer. There is also unfinished business concerning the dynasty, left over from Solomon's second speech. The opening part of the prayer is devoted to this matter.

6:12-13. Solomon's position is clarified (v. 13) by an addition to 1 Kgs 8:22, which may antedate the chronicler.[208] First, the king does not stand in the inner court, "the court of the priests," but in "the great court" of 4:9, and so "the outer court." Holy space was thus safeguarded even from this distinguished layperson. Second, Solomon stands on a platform so that he can be seen and heard by the large company, "the whole assembly of Israel." Third, the chronicler carefully notes that Solomon knelt to pray, which his source states later (1 Kgs 8:54). After the addition, 1 Kgs 8:22b is recapitulated.

6:14-17. The unfinished business is an issue high on the chronicler's agenda: the guarantee of a permanent dynasty, secured by Solomon's building the Temple and his keeping the Torah (cf. 1:9; 1 Chr 17:12-14; 22:10; 28:5-7). The introductory praise (vv. 14-15) echoes the king's testimony of praise (vv. 4-10). The Lord is faithful to those who are faithful to the Lord. This theological proposition is taken from Exod 20:4; Deut 7:9 (cf. 1 Sam 2:30b ; see also Matt 10:32-33). It leads on to a particular example: The completed Temple testifies to God's faithfulness to David as a keeper of promises. (The praise is a preamble to the petition of vv. 16-17:

206. Fretheim, *The Suffering of God*, 64.

207. See A. S. van der Woude, "שׁם *šēm*, Name," *Theologische Handwörterbuch zum Alten Testament*, ed. E. Jenni and C. Westermann (Munchen: Kaiser, 1976) 2:935-63, esp. 951-55; E. Talstra, *Solomon's Prayer*, Contributions to Biblical Exegesis and Theology 3, trans. G. Runia-Deenick (Kampen: Pharos, 1993) 139-40.

208. See Japhet, *I & II Chronicles*, 586.

"Now . . . And now" [NIV].) And there was a further promise. For the chronicler, who has Solomon in mind, it was the promise of a permanent Davidic dynasty, hedged by the condition of human faithfulness. David's own petition to this end (1 Chr 17:23) is echoed in v. 17. The chronicler relates the reference to David's "sons" in 1 Kgs 8:25 explicitly to Solomon (see 1 Chr 28:7-10; 2 Chr 7:17-18). The outworking of the theological proposition of v. 14, relating to God's faithfulness, implied that the survival, and so restoration, of the Davidic dynasty was grounded in the character of God.

Instead of simply repeating the phrase "walking before God" (vv. 14, 16; cf. 1 Kgs 8:23, 25), the chronicler offers a stylistic variation, "walk in my law." To walk before the Lord is to adopt a way of life that complies with God's will. This spelled Torah for the chronicler. Indeed, the very word תורה (tôrâ) suggests a metaphor that pictures life as a journey. The related verb הורה (hôrâ, in the hiphil), which occurs in v. 27, can mean to give directions to a place (Gen 46:28 NIV). So the Torah constitutes God's guiding principles for the journey of life. The chronicler may have been influenced by v. 27, which can be translated "when you give directions to the good way in which they should walk," to make the change here.

6:18-21. The rest of Solomon's prayer is about prayer. It envisions seven scenarios of prayer (vv. 22-39). By way of introduction, these verses explore the relationship between the Temple and prayer in an all-embracing petition that is resumed in v. 40 after the intervening examples. As in v. 14, a theological proposition is the starting point and qualifies the concept of the Temple as God's residence, expressed in v. 2. Those who came to the Temple area to pray did indeed find the Lord there. Solomon was praying "in your presence" (v. 19; cf. 7:4). Certainly God's "heart" was there (7:16), but the chronicler reaffirms the principle, already expressed in 2:6, that divine immanence had to be held in tension with divine transcendence. Here the text reflects the traditional OT dialectic that the Lord is present both in heaven and in an earthly counterpart, the Temple in Jerusalem (see Pss 14:2, 7; 20:2, 6; 76:2, 8; Isa 31:4, 9).

The outer court of the Temple was the place where the laity prayed facing the Temple. The only exception was when those who prayed were detained outside the country (vv. 34, 38). Daniel fits this category; he compensated for being outside Jerusalem by praying in his upper room with the window shutters open toward Jerusalem (Dan 6:10). As the location of God's earthly presence, the Temple was a means of access to the heavenly God.

6:22-23. The framework of Solomon's prayer makes forgiveness the keynote of the divine response. The following seven petitions are grounded in basic conditions of human sin and so function as penitential prayers. Four of the seven fall into this category. The first, fifth, and sixth do not. The first petition is for social justice. It has in view a self-cursing oath sworn at the sanctuary (cf. Num 5:11-31; Ps 7:3-5). Solomon's request that the sinner be exposed and the one sinned against be vindicated by the curse parallels the standard covenant relationship between the Lord and Israel (v. 14). Most of the other petitions postulate emergency situations in which the usual order has irretrievably broken down so that people no longer call for justice but for grace instead. In human failure, which turns out to be the rule rather than the exception, the Temple is the place to go to find forgiveness and a new start in life.

6:24-27. The second to seventh petitions fall, basically, into three pairs.[209] The first pair occurs in vv. 24-25 and vv. 26-27. Verses 24-25 reflect a covenant curse of a military defeat coming true (cf. Lev 26:17; Deut 28:25). The nation finds itself collectively in the role of the sinner (v. 22), whose self-curse has become effective. Is there a way back to the Lord? The king asks God to make it possible. Part of the population is regarded as being in exile; the rest are still in the land and able to come to the Temple. The gift of the land is understood in v. 25 as made not only to Israel's "ancestors," as in 1 Kgs 8:34, but also to the generation featured in this scenario. It was not automatically inherited; each generation had to prove itself worthy of it.[210] Solomon dares to pray for resolution

209. See Talstra, *Solomon's Prayer*, 112-26.
210. Japhet, *I & II Chronicles*, 595.

of this hopeless sitation and for restoration of the land. The scenario of vv. 26-27 envisions the covenant curse of Deut 28:24. The king prays that the God who justly punishes sinners may be further revealed as the one who saves from crisis and restores the relationship, pointing the people back to "the right way to live" (v. 27).

6:28-33. The second pair of scenarios has substantial differences; both stress, however, the importance of fearing God. The first continues the theme of Israel's experience of covenant curses (v. 28*a* ; cf. Deut 28:21-22, 38, 48, 52). The situations reflect a variety of dire possibilities. Humans can respond in both communal and individual laments. These particular laments affirm an awareness of human guilt (cf. Pss 25:7; 38:3-4; 39:8-11; 51:1-4, 9; 106:6; Jer 14:7). Forgiveness after sincere repentance is meant to lead to respectful obedience (cf. Jer 32:39). "The foreigner too" (REB) is given a place in these scenarios. Here divine forgiveness extends to one who cannot claim the help offered to God's covenant people. The prospect of international respect for the Lord is reminiscent of 1 Chr 14:17 and 2 Chr 20:29, except that here it is a response to answered prayer.

6:34-39. The sixth petition recalls the first in the way it prepares for and contrasts with the following one. It presents the situation of a holy war obediently undertaken at God's command and so warranting divine help (cf. 1 Sam 15:20). Such respectability is replaced by culpable crisis in the contrasting seventh scenario. Now defeat and deportation function as instruments of divine punishment. It is the second scenario blown up to horrendous proportions. Solomon dares to hope that the Lord will acknowledge Israel as covenant partner again, if the people will repent of their apostasy. Sinning is no longer an option, but has become inevitable and fateful. So there is an emphasis on a complete "change of heart" (v. 37). A communal lament is put on the people's lips, addressed to the God of the Temple, who has driven them from the land.

A glance ahead at the divine response in 7:12-16 (cf. 1 Kgs 9:2-3) shows that Solomon's prayer is meant to contribute to a theological manifesto for the Temple. The chronicler uses the prayer and its answer to develop the thesis he propounded in 1 Chronicles 21

that the Temple was based on divine grace. He copied out this long prayer from 1 Kings 8 because it illustrates so well that the Temple provided a means of grace for the people of God. When the Torah had been broken, the Lord honored the prayers of individuals or the community. But sinning was not condoned. Repentance features not only in vv. 37-38 but also in the "turning back" of v. 24 and the turning from sin in v. 26. In v. 37, the "change of heart" (NIV) or "coming to one's senses" (NRSV) means recalling what one did when carried away by self-will and reconsidering it in the cold light of day. An ethical life-style is anticipated as the sequel to repentance in vv. 27 and 31.

6:40-42. After reverting to the framework of the prayer in v. 40, the chronicler's version ends on a different note. Both the exodus as the basis of Israel's covenant relationship and the Lord's assurance given "through Moses your servant" were recalled in 1 Kgs 8:51-53. For the chronicler, this recollection turned the clock back to an earlier era of revelation. The time had come to concentrate on "David your servant" (v. 42), in line with the emphasis at the start of the prayer (vv 15-17). What follows in vv. 41-42 is largely drawn from Ps 132:8-10. Psalm 132 associates the transportation of the ark with the establishment of the Davidic dynasty, which the chronicler found congenial to his own interests. He may initially have been attracted to it by its motif of rest. He omitted the speech to Israel (1 Kgs 8:56-61), probably because it began by again harking back to the Lord's "servant Moses." But its reference to divine rest for Israel may have reminded him of the rest the Lord achieved with the installation of the ark (cf. 1 Chr 28:2).

The quotation of Ps 132:8-10 associates God with the ark as a symbol of the divine presence. The invitation to the Lord to take up residence in the Temple by means of the ark could more appropriately have accompanied 5:2-11, but the remainder of the block of quoted material made it a suitable conclusion to Solomon's prayer. The three added vocatives, "O LORD God," though turning the poetry into prose, now recall the opening of the prayer, with its triple "O LORD, God of Israel" (6:14-17 NRSV), and so welds the quotation to its new context.

God's presence in the Temple inaugurated a new era in which its priests would be mediators of divine "salvation" (תשועה *těšuʿâ*), a term borrowed from Ps 132:16. The term is used here, as it is in the psalter (in psalms of lament and thanksgiving), to signify the Lord's rescuing humans from situations of crisis (cf. 20:9). It alludes to the granting of the petitions in the body of Solomon's prayer. Priests, it is hoped, would pass on God's favorable answers and promises of restoration (see Pss 28:6; 85:8-9). The final clause, "and let your faithful rejoice in your goodness," paraphrases "and let the faithful exult" (Ps 132:9), intended to provide intertextual links with 7:10. The reference to God's "faithful ones" (חסידים *ḥăsîdîm*) may refer to the Levites whose role required them to sing of the Lord's goodness and (steadfast) love (5:13). However, the term *ḥăsîdîm*, which connotes those who are faithful or who evince steadfast love, probably refers to the people. In v. 14, the related word חסד (*ḥesed*) was used to describe the covenant relationship between the Lord and Israel. Not only the combination of the people's joy and God's goodness in 7:10, but also the people's singing of the levitical chorus in 7:3 will indicate the fulfillment of the prayerful wish of 6:41.

The final verse of the prayer blends part of Ps 132:10 with a phrase taken from Isa 55:3. The chronicler may have been attracted to the prophetic oracle because Isa 55:6-7 issues an invitation to "seek the LORD . . . call upon him. . . . Let the wicked forsake his way. . . . Let him turn to the LORD . . . for he will freely pardon" (NIV). Such motifs have been the burden of Solomon's prayer earlier in the chapter, while "seeking the LORD" is the chronicler's key term for spirituality. The citation of Isa 55:3 becomes Solomon's appeal to God to fulfill the dynastic promise made to David, as the paraphrase in the NIV suggests.[211] The temple prayer ends as it began in 6:16-17. Solomon's building of the Temple for the Lord and the establishment of a permanent dynasty were intertwined in the purposes of God.

According to Isa 55:3, the Davidic covenant is made with Israel. In the light of

Second Isaiah's overall message, this represents a democratization of the royal covenant. Royal benefits were to be transferred to the people as a whole. The chronicler understood the text differently. From his perspective, the Davidic covenant enlarged the divine relationship with Israel, undergirding with divine permanence what is often in the Torah represented as perishable. The everlasting nature of the covenant was bound up with the permanence of the dynasty (cf. 13:5; 21:7; 23:3).

7:1-3. Solomon's prayer, apart from its dynastic framing, has been concerned with the religious functioning of the Temple, now that the ark had been installed in it and it had been graced with a special manifestation of God's presence (5:2-14). The Temple has two functions in the books of Chronicles: to be a place of prayer and "a house of sacrifice" (v. 12). The latter element is missing from the account in 1 Kings 8; sacrifices are offered there without explicit divine warrant (1 Kgs 8:62-64). So the chronicler has supplied it in these verses.

"Fire came down from heaven," which symbolizes acceptance of the sacrifices (5:6) that were made in conjunction with the ark's installation. The miracle echoes 1 Chr 21:26, where the temple site was divinely sanctioned for worship in this way. The Temple, approved then in principle, is now formally designated as the legitimate place of worship. This fire adds to the endorsement of 5:13-14. The circumstantial clause in v. 1*b* is better translated "and the glory of the LORD was [still] filling the temple."[212] However, a new note is introduced in v. 3. Whereas the revelation in 5:13-14 affected only the priests, as 7:2 reminds us, now God's people were witnesses. Seeing the fire on the altar of burnt offering and now also an aura of glory "on" the Temple, they received assurance of the Lord's commitment to the Temple. The chronicler has in mind Lev 9:23-24, where the tabernacle sacrifices were authenticated by supernatural fire before all the people. This repetition teaches that the Temple had taken over the role of the tabernacle.

The people responded to the divine revelation with vocal worship. If in chap. 5 revelation was a gracious response to the singing

211. See H. G. M. Williamson, " 'The Sure Mercies of David': Subjective or Objective Genitive?" *JSS* 23 (1978) 31-49. Cf. Japhet, *I & II Chronicles*, 604-5.

212. Williamson, *1 and 2 Chronicles*, 222.

of praise, here it inspires praise in a service of dedication (cf. 7:5b). Israel takes over the Levites' chorus (5:13), duly enabled to rejoice in the Lord's goodness, as Solomon had asked in 6:41. They celebrate God's "[steadfast] love" (ḥesed) as a feature not merely of the Mosaic covenant (6:14) but of the Davidic covenant, which inaugurated a new era of grace for Israel (6:42; 7:10).

7:4-11. In vv. 4-5 the text of 1 Kgs 8:62-63 is rejoined, while vv. 7-10 are based on 1 Kgs 8:64-66. In v. 6 the chronicler introduces the component of worship, which for him necessarily supplemented sacrifice, the blasts of the priestly trumpeters, and the music and song of the Levites. Appeal is made to David's traditional association with musical instruments, which enhances the prestige of temple music (cf. 1 Chr 23:5). For the first time, sacrifice and song were offered together in Jerusalem, as formerly had been done in Gibeon (1 Chr 16:37-42). The service of dedicating the "house" (v. 5) or the "altar" (v. 9) was so lavishly supplied with sacrificial animals that the altar proved too small to accommodate the burnable parts, and the celebrations lasted a week. Then the Feast of Tabernacles provided a further week of worship, which reached a finale on the eighth day. The narrative in 1 Kgs 8:65-66 (in the emended form of the NRSV) follows the seven-day festival of Deut 16:13-15. The chronicler carefully realigns it with the Torah's detailed requirements for an eight-day festival in Lev 23:34-36, 39-43 (cf. Num 29:15-38). The "eighth day" of dismissal in 1 Kgs 8:66 now becomes the ninth day as the twenty-third day of the month, after the dedication of the altar from the eighth to the fourteenth day and the Feast of Tabernacles from the fifteenth to the twenty-second.[213] The Torah's festivals, in their priestly form, as practiced in the post-exilic period, continued into the new era, with a new rendezvous. The chronicler made the dedicatory celebrations separate from the Feast of Tabernacles. Accordingly, pilgrims were summoned a week before the feast (5:3 is now implicitly revised).

The reference in 1 Kgs 8:65 to Israel's north and south frontiers as Lebo-hamath and the Wadi of Egypt serves as a parallel to

213. See J. R. Shaver, *Torah and the Chronicler's History Work*, BJS 196 (Atlanta: Scholars Press, 1989) 99-100.

David's assembly for the original transportation of the ark (1 Chr 13:5) and underlines the significance of "all Israel." It also alludes to the joint nature of David's and Solomon's reigns. The reference to Solomon, added by the chronicler (v. 10), reminds the reader that their reigns were two halves of a single episode of divine revelation (cf. 11:17; 35:4). Verse 11 is also added as a development of 1 Kgs 9:1. Here was a further stage in the completion of the Temple, now that its sacrificial system had been representatively inaugurated. The success for which David had prayed concerning the building of the Temple (1 Chr 22:11) was duly attained. "Mission accomplished," reports the chronicler.

7:12. The account of the personal theophany in 7:12-22 amplifies 1 Kgs 9:2-9. Verse 12b embraces Solomon's prayer in 6:14-42 and the ensuing narrative in 7:1. The Lord had heard the prayer and chose the Temple as "a house of sacrifice." What was expressed in symbol (v. 1) is now put into words. Sacrifice was of prime importance at the Temple, so much so that its dedication (v. 5) could be called a dedication of the altar (v. 9); Solomon had summed up the Temple's function thus in 2:4, 6. By means of the distinctive verb "chosen" (בחר bāḥar; cf. 6:6), the Temple was now accredited as the place to sacrificially worship the Lord. Now, at last, the promise of the Lord's choosing such a place in Deut 12:4-6, 11 had come true.

7:13-14. This section returns to the other great role of the Temple: It was a place of prayer, the topic of most of Solomon's prayer. A digest of that prayer is provided in vv. 13-14, especially in terms of the third and fourth scenarios (6:26, 28). They dealt with crisis suffered by the land in reprisal for the people's sinning and so were relevant to the chronicler's post-exilic constituency. The other key scenarios that depict exile (the second and especially the seventh), now function as metaphors for their spiritual state: They are still alienated from the Lord and so deprived of blessing. In response, the Lord first acknowledges the truth of the phrase "your people" in the king's prayer, reaffirming it with an idiom of ownership, "called by my name" (נקרא-שמי niqrā'-šĕmî). Israel was still the object of God's care and claim. Prayer—humble prayer (cf. Lev 26:41) that abandoned the brazenness of disobedience—is endorsed as the means of triggering divine love. This prayer was to be an expression of seeking God's face. Instead of the standard term for "spirituality" (דרש *dāraš*, lit., "seek"), a synonym (בקש *biqqēš*) appears, which had occurred alongside it in one of the chronicler's basic texts, Jer 29:13-14. The word *biqqēš* is appropriate in 2 Chr 7:14 because to seek God's face was a religious idiom for worship at the Temple (see also Pss 24:6; 27:8; 105:4). The chronicler used Ps 105:4 in 1 Chr 16:11. Here it relates not to standard worship, but to prodigal sons and daughters returning to the Lord.

The Lord promised to honor such prayer and to wipe the slate clean in forgiveness, as Solomon had asked. Curses resting on the land would be removed. Rain would fall again on the drought-stricken land (6:26-27). The locusts of 6:28 would be banished, as in the book of Joel. Where there had been failure and loss, healing would be given. In Solomon's prayer, the land of Israel had featured as an area of both deprivation and blessing (6:25, 27-28, 31). As generally in the OT, the land functioned as a spiritual barometer, registering the people's loyalty to the Lord. The chronicler's exposition of the Lord's response to the king's prayer sums up a crucial aspect of his message: Through worship at the Temple, God had provided a way of ending guilt and the spiritual and material crises it caused. Beyond a broken covenant lay divine resources of healing and restoration. The chronicler will weave this divine promise into the narratives that follow in order to reinforce a message of human guilt and divine love for the people of God.[214]

7:15-16. These verses substantially return to 1 Kgs 9:3b, making God's response apply to the royal request in 6:40 and ·adding the motif of divine choice, repeated from 6:6; 7:12. The new parallelism with v. 12 brackets the two roles of the Temple, a· normative one of worship and praise and a special· one of finding a welcome after falling away. God waits, ever ready to hear Temple-centered prayers of repentance.

7:17-18. God responds to the initial and final requests of Solomon's prayer, concerning the dynastic succession of Davidic kings.

The chronicler follows 1 Kgs 9:4-5 but with his own emphases. The dynastic condition of building the Temple, laid down in 1 Chr 17:12, has been met. The other proviso, Solomon's general obedience, reported by David as having been met thus far in 1 Chr 28:7, was still ahead. It was the chronicler's conviction that Solomon did meet the latter condition, and the next section will address this issue. The account of Solomon's reign will end with glorious tributes to him and to his God. The omission of "over Israel forever" (1 Kgs 9:5) from v. 18 may indicate an expansion in the MT of 1 Kings.[215] At the end of the verse, the chronicler makes a significant change, upgrading the verb "promised" (דבר *dibber*, in the piel) in the 1 Kings text to "covenanted" (כרת *kārat*) here. The change recalls the divine faithfulness to David in 6:14 and advances the Mosaic reference in 5:10. The Mosaic covenant had been amplified by the Davidic covenant, which strengthened Israel's relationship with the Lord. The new verb, "covenanted" (כרתי *kāratî*), is also a pun on God's assurance that the people would never "lack" (יכרת *yikkārēt*) a Davidic successor. The pun reinforces the promise. The promise to David, as found in the MT of 1 Kings, "on the throne of Israel," is replaced by (literally) "ruling in Israel." The reading is shared by the LXX of 1 Kings, and the MT may reflect assimilation to 1 Kgs 2:4; 8:25.[216]

7:19-22. The text takes over the dire warning of 1 Kgs 9:6-9, which not only amplifies 1 Kgs 8:46 (= 2 Chr 6:36), but also spells out the possibility of withdrawing the Temple-centered relationship between Israel and the Lord. In v. 19, both the king and the people are addressed together with plural verbs, while in vv. 20-22 the people are in view. Solomon could have been punished (cf. 1 Chr 28:9b), but he eluded it, at least according to the chronicler. For the people such punishment was a recurring threat. According to 1 Chr 28:8, continued possession of the land was tied to obedience. Here its loss is envisioned as a result of disobedience. The exodus, if forgotten, could give way to exile. The rhetorical device of question and answer in vv. 21-22 conveys in a dramatic way the folly

---

214. See Williamson, *1 and 2 Chronicles*, 226.

215. See McKenzie, *The Chronicler's Use of the Deuteronomistic History*, 97.

216. S. J. De Vries, *1 Kings*, WBC 12 (Waco, Tex.: Word, 1985) 119.

of turning one's back on the Lord. The stark warning alludes to Judah's fate in 587 BCE.

There are two redeeming features, however, in the 2 Chronicles presentation. First, there is no suggestion that the dynastic promise would die. Once Solomon's reign was over, it became a guarantee for the long-term future of God's people. Second, the post-exilic Temple had arisen from the ashes of the first, and so the Temple-related promise of forgiveness and a fresh start still stood. Yet, each generation had the threat of spiritual exile hanging over it (cf. 1 Chr 10:7, 13; 16:19-20), if

they turned their backs on "the God of their fathers" (v. 22). On the other hand, obedience or doom-laden disobedience were not the only options open to Israel. Repentance leading to restoration and blessing was a third alternative that still was made available, as ensuing narratives in 2 Chronicles will amply testify. The chronicler chose not to end on this note. He knew that the repentance of heart and soul sought by the Lord (6:38) did not come about easily. A hefty stick was needed to break down human willfulness and induce a healthy fear of God (6:31).

REFLECTIONS

Much of the chronicler's theology is showcased in these chapters. The concentration on the Temple and its dynamic roles in the life of God's people is at first alien to the Christian reader. However, the chronicler offers a clue about why the Temple features so prominently in spiritual metaphors in the New Testament. The chronicler was proud to live in a temple age. The narrative of Solomon's work under God resonates with new beginnings. The chronicler looked back over the centuries to a significant, sacred moment in history. In the same vein, we read of "the beginning of the gospel" in Mark 1:1 and join the Evangelist in investing particular incidents with profound meaning.

1. The older covenant between the Lord and Israel attested mutual commitment (cf. 6:14), to which the ark's contents testified. The Lord's redeeming love in the exodus established an obligation for Israel to adopt a particular life-style, reflected in the Ten Commandments. The Torah, to which 6:11 alludes, surfaces again as a continuing mandate for king and people in 7:17-22. The new revelation did not suspend the broader obligations of the old. In eighteenth-century Jewish history, the charismatic Hasidim emerged in Poland, emphasizing joy and God's presence in one's heart and mind every waking moment. This movement within Judaism was a dynamic reaction against religious scholarship, which had not gloried in the joy of Torah study. It was left to the second generation of Hasidim to restore the balance and learn again that the Torah comprised God-given guidelines for living.

In the early Christian church, there were those who identified the new wine of Christianity with antinomianism and made divine grace an argument for human licentiousness (see Jude 4). Paul himself was so accused (Rom 3:8; 6:1-2). Firmly rebutting the charge, he insisted on obedience "from the heart to the standard of teaching" to which Christians had been "committed" (Rom 6:17 RSV) and even on the fulfilling of "the righteous requirements of the law" in the power of the Spirit (Rom 8:4 NIV). The metaphor of the Torah as the basis for "the good way" of life (2 Chr 6:27) finds a parallel in the New Testament at Eph 2:10. God has prepared in advance "good works" for Christians to "walk in" (KJV) or "to be our way of life" (NRSV).

2. Temple and covenant were linked by more than the Torah inside the ark. Temple worship testified to the covenant love of the Lord, present in the songs of the levitical choirs and repeated by the congregation (5:13; 7:3, 6). Such worship had been revealed in a richer way in the promises to David, which trickled down to Israel (6:41-42; 7:10). A new, "forever" age was dawning for God's people with a fresh manifestation of covenant grace as its keynote, a "[steadfast] love" so deep and wide that it met their repentance with forgiveness and renewed blessing (7:14). Christian readers can draw parallels of their own. In Rom 5:1-11, the beginning of a new era is celebrated ("at the right time," Rom 5:6 NRSV). God's love had been demonstrated toward sinners in Christ's death, so that they are friends of God and are blessed with everlasting salvation. No wonder joy is the response that frames this passage! Christians have fresh grounds to join in Israel's worship in 7:3.

3. The typological parallel drawn between tabernacle and Temple in the descent of the cloud of glory upon the sanctuary is repeated in John 1:14: "The Word became flesh and made his dwelling among us. We have seen his glory . . . full of grace and truth" (NIV). In Jesus there was a new manifestation of divine presence. The Fourth Gospel develops that imagery by assigning to the risen Jesus the role of a miraculously rebuilt temple, like Ezekiel's new temple (John 2:19-22).

Solomon's first speech (6:1-2) compares the cloud to the home of the unseen ark. Although the New Testament rejoices in the rending of the veil and in fuller access to God, there will always be a sense of divine mystery. It is a feature of traditional Jewish theology to maintain from an intellectual standpoint, though not from a spiritual one, that God is unknowable. Paul also affirmed such human inadequacy of knowledge of God in stating that "we know only in part" (1 Cor 13:9 NRSV).

This section of 2 Chronicles is full of theological tension, between the concealing and revealing of the deity in the cloud of glory, between the Lord's dwelling in earthly and heavenly temples, and between the latter and a divine presence that spills everywhere. Such divine paradoxes defy our tidy systems.

4. Solomon's sanctuary was meant to be a great temple for a great God (2:5); yet, it could not contain the Lord (6:18). Likewise, God is too magnificent to fit snugly into our church, our denomination, our present conception of deity. God is a veritable Gulliver in our Lilliputian world.

5. The petitions in Solomon's prayer move primarily from a situation of existential crisis caused by human sinning to Temple-centered prayer. They look forward to divine hearing, forgiveness, and reversal of the crisis. Solomon is concerned that the spiritual relationship between the Lord and the believing community (or individual, 7:29) be restored and reflected sacramentally in land-related blessing. The repeated emphasis on human sinning, which necessitates divine forgiveness (7:21 onward), stands in conflict with the calm, orderly situation of 6:14. An adequate theology must recognize and deal with the abnormal, because "there is no one who does not sin" (7:36), and sooner or later everybody falls into a self-inflicted predicament. In order to address such situations realistically, the chronicler took over the deuteronomistic emphasis on temple prayer as a means of forgiveness. It conformed to his Davidic prototype of a sinner's plea that found a divine response (1 Chr 21:26). Sin was not thereby condoned, but it was confronted and held at a distance (6:24, 26, 29, 37-38). We modern worshipers find such an opportunity in our own corporate prayer, especially in the confession of sins and the laying hold of forgiveness in Christ.

6. The fifth scenario (7:32-33) makes those of us who are Gentiles feel at home. The chronicler, no xenophobe and no hoarder of divine grace, took over this scenario gladly. A foreigner, Naaman-like, is drawn to the Temple because of God's exploits on Israel's behalf. Isaiah 56:7 likewise speaks of the Temple as "a house of prayer for all nations." According to Mark 11:17, Jesus cited that text when he condemned blatant commercialization in the Court of the Gentiles. Such behavior presented a poor testimony to Gentiles who frequented that part of the Temple that was open to them. We inherit Scripture that invites all to come, and so we must ensure that all groups in our community find a welcome in our church.

7. When normal life collapsed, the Temple had a role other than that of a "house of sacrifice," as the channel of penitential prayer and restorative love. This latter role is developed in 2 Chr 7:13-14. Solomon's prayer laid the foundation by identifying the need. Now the forgiveness he sought is duly pledged. The pall of judgment, guilt, and frustration that hung over the post-exilic community (cf. Neh 9:32-37; Dan 9:4-14) could be dispelled. When the Torah had been broken and covenant curses rested on people and land, there was a way forward. The low road from sin to disaster could be left by a new track winding back to the high road from obedience to blessing, according to 7:14. God's people find two divine claims on their lives. The first is for obedience to the divine will. However, if they go down a path of their own choosing, they find the Lord standing in the way, ready to make a second claim and offer another chance.

The chronicler articulates an evangelical theology, meeting sin with forgiveness, while safeguarding morality by means of repentance and renewed commitment. Some Christians want to see a theology of grace in the New Testament and deny its presence in the Old, but the chronicler attests otherwise. The God of the Torah coped with failure, picking up the broken pieces as soon as the covenant was broken (Exodus 32–34; note Exod 34:6). The chronicler, too, found in the Temple a means to reaffirm God's compassion.

Those who would not accept the carrot of 7:14, the chronicler consigned to the stick of 7:19-22. The divine presentations stand as alternatives. The broken covenant, apart from the Lord's provision, must lead to an intensification of the curses in the Torah. There is a tension in this section that the New Testament expresses and every pastor knows. On the one hand, the Lord issues a solemn call for compliance and integrity, backed by due warnings. On the other hand, there is fervent assurance of forgiveness and a fresh chance. Untidy as this double message is, it is realistic. The logic of the double message is supplied in 1 John 2:1, "I write this to you so that you will not sin. But if anybody does sin . . ." (NIV). The literary movement from grace to judgment at the end of 2 Chronicles 7 finds a parallel in the Letter to the Galatians. From justification by grace through faith (Gal 2:20–3:25), the apostle moved to a threatening message of judgment: "God is not mocked, for you reap whatever you sow" (Gal 6:7 NRSV).

For the chronicler, as for the deuteronomist, the moral issue was resolved by an emphasis on repentance. As a second best, God is prepared to take the thought for the deed and to accept conscience in place of constancy, if commitment to the good ensued (6:27). It is not only talking the talk of penitential prayer that is envisioned, but also walking a corresponding walk thereafter. The grim either/or of 7:17-22 is not God's last word. The post-exilic community had seen that beyond "just deserts" lay God's helping hand. Sometimes, like the chronicler's constituency, even we need to hear strident threats, in the hope that we may be saved from willful apathy.

2 Chronicles 8:1-16, Finding Blessing and Finishing the Temple

COMMENTARY

This section takes its cue from 1 Kgs 9:10-25. The chronicler follows the order of its twists and turns tenaciously and at times puts his own spin on the material. The key word is the verb "build" (בנה *bānâ*), which occurs seven times here and only five times in the

source. The building of the Temple and the altar (vv. 1, 12) is the pervasive theme for Solomon's reign up to this point. The rest of the references to building reflect another agenda. The chronicler will regularly use building in later narratives as a symbol of divine blessing for a king's obedience (cf. 1 Chr 11:8). For example, Asa's building program is a sign of prosperity after seeking the Lord and keeping the Torah (14:1*b*-7). The terms "fortified cities," "walls," and "gates and bars" in v. 5 occur again in 2 Chronicles only in 14:6-7. The motif of rest also links the reigns of Solomon and Asa. The Lord gave Asa rest because he had sought God (14:6-7 NIV). Rest is especially associated in the books of Chronicles with Solomon's reign (1 Chr 22:9).

Building also belongs to a network of other motifs: seeking the Lord, keeping the Torah, and so enjoying divine blessing. These motifs appear in the account of Asa's reign and are implicit here. The chronicler is answering the question set against Solomon's reign in 7:17-18: Would Solomon keep the Torah and so fulfill the dynastic condition of 1 Chr 28:7? The answer is yes, because the prosperity enjoyed by Asa and linked with building (14:7*b*) was also enjoyed by Solomon, which would fulfill the promise of 1 Chr 22:13. The prosperity credited to Solomon in 1 Chr 29:23 finds illustration here.

8:1-6. The account of Huram's cities in v. 2 reads differently from the longer one in 1 Kgs 9:10-14. It is unlikely that the chronicler contradicted the 1 Kings account, though he would have wanted to put his own construction on the text.[217] His copy may have had a corrupted text, so that in 1 Kgs 9:12 he read "the cities which he had given Solomon" and took that as the basis for his own account, omitting the rest as irrelevant to his agenda.[218] Some scholars have objected that the chronicler must have been well aware of the Samuel–Kings narratives, since he often presupposes them.[219] However, one may question whether he would have known such precise details as to be able to override a divergent text.

The motif of (re)building is imported from the context. The addition about settling Israelites in the Galilean cities introduces the motif of restoration from exile (see Isa 54:3; Jer 32:37; Ezek 36:33; cf. 1 Chr 10:7). Perhaps the insertion of both topics was inspired by the information about Gezer in 1 Kgs 9:16-17*a*. It was a little step forward in the

enjoyment of the land promised in 1 Chr 16:18, an earnest of future hope. Both here and in 2 Chr 8:9 Israel's interests are represented as a goal of Solomon's rule.

In v. 4, the reference to Tadmor follows a variant tradition reflected in the oral text (the Qere) of 1 Kgs 9:17 and in the LXX at 3 Kgdms 2:46*d*, though both may depend on Chronicles. The context shows that Tamar in the Negeb was original in the 1 Kings text. However, the chronicler alludes to the northern Tadmor or Palmyra in the Syrian desert, and so it is separated from the building projects in Israel. The reference to its storage towns as well as to Baalath's in v. 6 represents a double use of 1 Kgs 9:19a. The reading "Tadmor" encouraged another textual variant, the earlier reference to Hamath-Zobah. Again a damaged parent text appears responsible, with the "wall" in 1 Kgs 9:15 (חומת [*ḥômat*], read defectively as חמת [*ḥmt*]), being understood as Hamath.[220] Zobah was also added, which reflected the later administrative system of provinces set up by the Assyrians and retained under the Persians.

8:7-11. The chronicler follows in a straightforward fashion the narrative concerning forced labor in 1 Kgs 9:20-23. As was observed at 2:17, the chronicler preferred this aspect of the double tradition preserved in 1 Kings. He presupposes knowledge of Solomon's wife, provided in 1 Kgs 3:1; 7:8; 9:16. The information that she was moved up from the city of David reminds the chronicler that the ark had also been brought up from there (5:2). He thinks in terms of a residual holiness at its former site, with which a woman's regular states of impurity would clash (see Lev 12:1-4; 15:19-31*a*).[221] Unlike the deuteronomist, the chronicler finds her gender greater cause for concern than her foreignness. His Torah-based reasoning accords with a presupposition of the preceding narrative, Solomon's spiritual qualification for divine blessing.

8:12-16. This passage expands 1 Kgs 9:25. For the chronicler, preoccupied with the Torah, it represents the last of the various stages of the completion of the Temple project (cf. 5:1; 7:11). Whereas the ritual festivities of chap. 7 mark the inauguration of the religious calendar, the lapse of time permits

217. McKenzie, *The Chronicler's Use of the Deuteronomistic History*, 108.
218. Willi, *Die Chronik als Auslegung*, 77.
219. Dillard, *2 Chronicles*, 63.

220. De Vries, *1 and 2 Chronicles*, 238.
221. Rudolph, *Chronikbücher*, 220.

the institution of the whole calendar, in line with Solomon's intention in 2:4. The priestly calendar of Numbers 28–29 is in view, but whereas it stipulates five annual festivals, the chronicler is limited by the reference to three in the parent text and so reflects the deutero-nomic system of three feasts (Deut 16:1-16; cf. Exod 23:14-17; 34:18-24).[222] The Torah's program of sacrificial worship is transferred from the tabernacle to the Temple.

The revelation given to Moses had been supplemented by that granted to David. The new temple order had been enriched by specifications for its administrative staffing (see 1 Chr 24:1-26; 28:13, 21). Moses was not the only "man of God" (1 Chr 23:14; 2 Chr 30:16). David, too, possessed such inspiration, as he had claimed in 1 Chr 28:19 (cf. 2 Sam 23:1-2). A prophetic type of rev-elation had been added to that of the Torah. The chronicler found in both of them bind-ing models for contemporary temple worship.

Now Solomon's command puts into operation for the first time David's commands, while perpetuating those of Moses. The NRSV and the NIV are correct in reading "from the day" in place of "to the day" at v. 16. The ungram-matical MT has in initial view the period of preparation in chap. 2 before the actual build-ing began in 3:1-3.[223] Verse 16 marks the ful-fillment of David's blessing in 1 Chr 28:20b. The Lord had, indeed, brought Solomon through to the end.

The information that Solomon had fin-ished his God-given work was no matter-of-fact statement for the chronicler. It involved the start of a new era of temple worship. Sol-omon had started religious worship, which would operate into post-exilic times, tran-scending the brief silence of the exile. Day after day, year after year it would continue to glorify God, in a tradition of worship that gave the Lord pride of place in the community.

222. Shaver, *Torah and the Chronicler's History Work*, 94-96.

223. See Barthélemy et al., *Critique textuelle de l'Ancien Testament*, 1:486-87; Allen, *The Greek Chronicles*, 2:97.

REFLECTIONS

1. Israel's religious faith stood firmly on a double foundation: the revelations to Moses and David. Likewise, the church must never forget that its faith is based on God's double revelation in the Old Testament and the New Testament. Christians are offered assurance of God's revelation when they attend services that include readings from both testaments and so are taken back to the roots of their faith.

Those roots are as person-centered today as they were in the chronicler's teach-ing. A firm foundation was laid by Christ's "finishing the work" that God "gave" him "to do" (John 17:4). In the Chronicles program, Solomon's obedience to God, which underlies the prosperity of his building projects, sealed the dynasty and so undergirded the covenant relationship between Israel and the Lord. In Christ's prayer of John 17, too, there is a strong sense that the community would last, committed to God's safe-keeping. The theological history the chronicler recognized as being made in Solomon, John the Evangelist saw reproduced in Jesus Christ for the church.

2. The explanation the chronicler gives for Solomon's removal of his Egyptian wife from Jerusalem is unwelcome to modern ears. It perpetuates the Torah's reference to ritual (rather than moral) uncleanness, here associated with the female gender. For the chronicler, however, Solomon's action meant that he was honoring the Torah. His first readers might have disliked his refusal to attack racially mixed marriages (see Neh 13:23-27). In such a debate, the chronicler would have taken the side of the writer of the book of Ruth. We should applaud the chronicler for denying the need to end ethni-cally mixed marriages. Not even much of what is in the New Testament lives up to the great affirmation of Gal 3:28, which calls for men and women to be treated as equally by others as they are regarded in God's sight.

2 Chronicles 8:17–9:31, Solomon's Significant Prosperity

COMMENTARY

The account of Solomon's reign draws to a close with an emphasis on his wealth, wisdom, and international fame. As far as 9:28, the narrative has been largely a straightforward transcription of 1 Kgs 9:26–10:29. What was the point of copying out so much material? The only other king for whom such details of wealth are given is Hezekiah (32:27-29). His international fame also aligns him with Solomon (32:23). In Hezekiah's case, wealth and fame illustrate God-given success or prosperity that accrued to him after having sought the Lord by observing the Torah (31:21; 32:30). Prosperity that follows obedience implicitly ties the present section into the overall presentation of Solomon's reign in 2 Chronicles. The same verb used in the Hezekiah account (הצליח *hisliah*, in the hiphil) occurs in the programmatic 1 Chr 22:13: Solomon would "prosper" or "succeed" if he observed the Torah. This condition was elevated into a stipulation for guaranteeing the dynasty in 1 Chr 28:7. This section, as does the preceding one, answers with a resounding yes the vital question of whether the king obeyed the Torah (cf. 11:17; 12:1). Not only did he carry out the other, specific stipulation of building the Temple (1 Chr 22:11; 2 Chr 7:11), but also in this general area he set the dynasty on a permanent foundation, as was also affirmed in 2 Chr 1:1-13. The chronicler has framed his account of Solomon's reign with this good news, in elaboration of his preliminary claim in 1 Chr 29:23.

Solomon's maritime ventures appear at the circumference and center of 8:17–9:21 (8:17-18; 9:10, 21). They present an exotic backdrop to the narrative, especially for Judean landlubbers who, throughout most of their history, had no direct territorial access to the sea. The sea and ships are balanced by the mention of land (9:5, 11-12, 14) and overland caravans, and this theme is generalized in 9:22-28 ("earth," vv. 22-23; "land," v. 26; "lands," v. 28). A term that cascades through 8:17–9:21 is "gold": how much gold Solomon received and from whom, to what uses he put it in the Temple. The chronicler

emphasizes unique elements that distinguish Solomon's reign (cf. 1:12; 1 Chr 29:25). Exuberant denials minister to this theme. There was nothing Solomon could not explain to the queen of Sheba (9:2). No breath was left in her, so breathtaking were Solomon's wisdom and flair (9:4). Statements of the same type appear in 9:9, 11, 19-20.

Use of the word "all" also underlines the magnificence of Solomon's reign. The beginning and end of the narrative concerning the queen of Sheba is especially so marked. Wise Solomon listened to all her questions and could answer them all (9:1*b*-2). He gave her everything she wanted (9:12). The word "all" also forms a frame for the next passage, 9:13-21, in 9:14, and 20. The final passage, 9:22-28, even more stresses this element, at the beginning, the middle, and the end: 9:22-23, "all the kings of the earth"; 9:26, "all the kings"; and 9:28, "all lands."

Both wealth and wisdom are featured, as 9:22 summarizes. The definition of wisdom as God's gift in 9:23 echoes the endowment in the theophany in 1:11-12. Whereas in 2:12 it was diverted to the service of the Temple, here such wisdom returns to its initial regal setting. The emphasis placed on wisdom in the story of the queen of Sheba (9:22-23) illustrates the Lord's spectacular blessing on Solomon's reign.

8:17–9:12. In its context, "house" (9:3 NRSV) refers to the "palace" (NIV), rather than the Temple. The context also makes it a little more likely that the "burnt offerings" in the Temple, which the English versions envision in 9:4, (adopting the reading of the ancient versions and of the parallel 1 Kgs 10:5), should be rejected in favor of the MT's reference to "the procession with which he went up" to the Temple (TNK; cf. NIV). A characteristic change is made at 9:8. Israel's throne (1 Kgs 10:9) becomes the throne of God (cf. 13:8; 1 Chr 17:14; 28:5; 29:23). Solomon in all his glory had no independent role but was the Lord's viceroy, pointing beyond himself to the divine rule for whose final establishment on earth the chronicler yearned (1 Chr 16:31). The queen's reference to Solomon's reign as evidence of God's love for Israel matches Huram's testimony in 2:11. Whether the phrase "to uphold them" is a part of the original text or is a later addition is debatable, but the phrase does represent a thought high on the agenda of 2 Chronicles: The permanent dynastic covenant brought a payoff for the people of God. In its permanence, they enjoyed their own and found a warranty of the Lord's continuing purposes for Israel and so of their eventual vindication.

The translations of 9:12 in both the NRSV and the NIV are doubtful. The text seems to refer to Solomon's gifts of exotic articles, far different from the type of gifts brought by the queen. It represents a misunderstanding of "besides what he gave her according to king Solomon's [generous] hand" in 1 Kgs 10:13 as "besides what she gave into the hand of king Solomon (נתנה ביד *nātĕnâ bĕyad* in place of נתן-לה כיד *nātan-lāh kĕyad*)."[224]

9:13-21. The text of v. 14 probably reflects the already corrupted MT of 1 Kgs 10:15 (the NIV ["revenues"] implicitly and the REB ["tolls"] explicitly have emended the awkward אנשי [*'anšê*, "men"] to ענשי [*'onšê*]).[225] The amount of gold used for each type of ceremonial shield in vv. 15-16 is represented in 1 Kgs 10:16-17 as 600 shekels for each large, body-length shield and three minas for each small round shield. The unit of weight is not expressed in the first case, but common use requires shekels. Here the weights are given as 600 and 300 shekels respectively (NRSV). The NIV of 1 Kgs 10:16 and 2 Chr 9:15-16 has assumed that the unexpressed unit of weight is the beka, or half shekel. This produces a solution for the discrepancy, since a mina is fifty shekels, and so three minas are 150 shekels, or 300 bekas. Dillard has rightly judged the harmonization ingenious, but not conforming to standard use; he prefers to think in terms of a heavy mina of 100 shekels.[226]

Solomon's throne, "inlaid with ivory" (v. 17) and overlaid with gold, had "the top . . . rounded in the back" according to 1 Kgs 10:19 (NRSV), but in v. 18 a "footstool" is "attached" to it. Of the two textual

differences involved, the second probably reflects an indistinct text in the chronicler's source, but there is no convincing reason for the first.[227] In v. 21, the royal fleet is presumably that based in the Red Sea port of Eziongeber (8:17). Mention of Tarshish as a destination is embarrassing; it is mentioned as a Mediterranean port elsewhere in the OT. The writer of 1 Kgs 10:22 speaks simply of "ships of Tarshish," in the sense of large oceangoing vessels. The chronicler's change, reflected in the NRSV, suggests that the chronicler knew less than we do about the location of Tarshish. The NIV's rendering is a harmonization with the parallel text.

9:22-28. The mention of "weaponry" or "weapons" in v. 24 is more likely a reference to "perfumes" (REB), as the LXX rendered it. The association with spices favors this explanation. Verse 25*a* reflects an abandoning of the parallel 1 Kgs 10:26a in favor of 1 Kgs 4:26, except that the 40,000 horse stalls are 4,000 here. The change is bound up with the chronicler's choice to make use of 1 Kgs 10:26a in 2 Chr 1:14. A numerical progression is assumed, so that Solomon had more stalls/chariots at the end of his reign than at the beginning. Another deviation from the parent text occurs in v. 26, which reflects an insertion from 1 Kgs 4:21a. The chronicler sometimes uses Solomonic material at different points. Here the added material provides an impressive generalization for the close of Solomon's reign. Moreover, it ministers to the element of comprehensiveness that pervades this paragraph. Verses 26b-28 (parallel to 1 Kgs 10:27-29) have already been used in 1:14*b*-17. The repetition seems to be more a matter of rhetoric than of redaction, providing a roughly parallel framework for Solomon's reign.[228] So v. 28 does not repeat the details of the source but gives the gist, adapting it stylistically to the context by mentioning "all lands."

9:29-31. The epilogue makes use of the end of 1 Kings 11. There is a blatant jump from 1 Kgs 10:29. Every commentator, given the chance to put one question to the chronicler, would choose to interrogate him on his omission of the deuteronomist's negative

---

224. Barthélemy, *Critique textuelle de l'Ancien Testament*, 1:488.

225. So *BHS*. See Barthélemy, *Critique textuelle de l'Ancien Testament*, 1:358-59.

226. Dillard, *2 Chronicles*, 73.

227. See McKenzie, *The Chronicler's Use of the Deuteronomistic History*, 98.

228. De Vries, *I and II Chronicles*, 238.

material concerning Solomon in 1 Kgs 11:1-40. In both 9:29 and 10:15, the chronicler reflects the prophet Ahijah's oracle of judgment in 1 Kgs 11:29-40, though the chronicler blames Rehoboam for the division of the kingdom. The omission contrasts with the condemnation of Solomon's sin in marrying foreign women in Neh 13:26 as a supporting argument against a post-exilic practice. The chronicler evidently sided with the leading figures in Judah who had engaged in mixed marriages (see Ezra 9:2), or at least regarded intermarriage as permissible in his own later time. He refers to the practice without qualm in the course of his history (1 Chr 2:3, 17, 34-35; 3:1; 4:17; 7:14; 8:8; 2 Chr 2:14; 8:11; 12:13; 24:26). While he was bitterly opposed to foreign alliances, he does not seem to have felt so strongly about foreign marriages. Only such acts by northern royalty provoked his anger (18:1; 21:6; 22:2-3, 10) as a threat to the Davidic dynasty.

The chronicler appears to have been motivated by two factors: his opposition to the rigorism advocated by Ezra and Nehemiah as a policy for his own period, and his theological contention that Solomon was not guilty of alleged apostasy but had met the requirements laid down for the perpetuation of the dynasty. In his story, Solomon did nothing to threaten this consequence. Special grace was given him by the Lord (see the Commentary on 1 Chr 29:19). The king rode into a golden sunset, his double mission accomplished in the building of the Temple and the securing of the dynasty (13:5-8; 21:7). The chronicler leaned heavily on 2 Samuel 7 (= 1 Chronicles 17) and 1 Kings 1–10, which consistently share his conviction that Solomon discharged his obligations and guaranteed the dynasty.[229] So he considered himself justified in silencing the discordant voice of 1 Kings 11, just as he dropped one of the two traditions concerning forced labor.

The epilogue to Solomon's reign is adapted from 1 Kgs 11:41-43. Here the chronicler refers to 1 Kings in terms of prophetic announcement, with the initial involvement of Nathan (1 Kings 1) and the final prophecy of Ahijah (1 Kgs 11:29-39). According to Josephus, "Iddo," who prophesied about Rehoboam's rival Jeroboam, was the name of the anonymous prophet of 1 Kgs 13:1-10.[230] The last reference was important to the chronicler, since it affirmed the continuation of the Davidic dynasty and the importance of the Temple in Jerusalem as Israel's religious center (1 Kgs 13:2; cf. 1 Kgs 13:32). Like Ahijah's oracle, it dealt primarily with Jeroboam, but also provided a comment on his picture of Solomon. The chronicler understood the reign of Solomon from a prophetic perspective, as he did that of David (1 Chr 29:29). The later view of Joshua–Kings as the Former Prophets is anticipated here. The chronicler stood foursquare on the foundation of the Law and the Prophets, faithful to the revelation associated with Moses, on the one hand, and with David and Solomon, on the other.

229. Baruch Halpern, *The Constitution of the Monarchy in Israel*, HSM 25 (Chico, Calif.: Scholar's Press, 1981) 40.
230. Josephus *Antiquities of the Jews* VIII.8.5 231.

REFLECTIONS

1. The picture of Solomon in all his glory, master of land and sea, ruling over an independent, enlarged Israel and receiving tribute and respect from the kings of the earth must have aroused nostalgia in the chronicler's post-exilic constituency. The chronicler mainly used Solomon's glory as a window through which to view a theological truth. It was proof of the Lord's love for Israel (9:8b), an affirmation that the anticipatory declaration in 2:11 shows to be crucial for the chronicler. It laid a foundation for Israel's security and brought guarantees to the dynasty and so to the Lord's covenant with Israel, since Israel was heir to the permanent royal covenant.

In turn the faith of Christian believers is continually strengthened as they remind themselves of the guarantees God has given in Christ. God's love, revealed through Jesus, has embraced generations of Christians (John 17:20, 23). The love of God in Christ is so strong that nothing can separate us from it (Rom 8:35-39). The work of

Christ mediates God's love and guarantees for the church the success already told in the resurrection and ascension of Christ (Eph 2:4-7). The Lord's purpose of establishing Israel forever was a concept Paul took seriously, wrestling with it in Romans 9–11 and finally affirming it.

2. Also evident in this narrative of Solomon's royal glory is an eschatological dimension. Here the kingdom of God (9:8*a*) was glimpsed, and so the veil of the future was drawn back when, as the prophets encouraged the chronicler to believe, God's king would "be great to the ends of the earth" (Mic 5:4 NRSV; cf. 2 Chr 20:20). Solomon's establishment of justice and righteousness within Israel's frontiers (9:8*b*) prefigured the just society to be set up by the coming Davidic king (see 1 Chr 16:3; 18:14; Isa 9:7; 11:1-5). Indeed, royal tribute from Sheba was promised in one of the royal psalms (Ps 72:10, 15), which already in the post-exilic psalter was imbued with hope: "Let all kings pay him homage" was the hope set in the Davidic dynasty (Ps 72:11 REB).

The reader of the first Gospel is familiar with prodigious history of this type. The magi from the east brought gifts of gold, frankincense, and myrrh to the infant Jesus in homage to him in his role as King of the Jews (Matt 2:1-11). Implicit in Matthew's account is a fulfillment of Psalm 72 and the related Isa 60:5-6. It was an anticipatory fulfillment, just as the triumphal entry of Jesus proclaimed his kingship in principle (Matt 21:1-11). Something even greater than Solomon was manifested in Christ, which so many of Jesus' generation could not see, though the queen of Sheba had recognized Solomon's worth (Matt 12:42 NRSV). For both the chronicler and Christians, eschatology puts the present into perspective and challenges its limitations with ideals to work for.

3. The chronicler's discriminating dependence on the Law and the Prophets is attested in this section. The ancient texts spoke to him with religious authority. The church is called to study a larger canon of Scripture and to make it their own in a modern age that has experienced a crisis of authority in so many ways. The chronicler invites us to follow in his tracks, assuring us from his productive example that the human mind is not thereby locked passively into thinking about the past but may find stimulation for creative theological reflection.

4. Solomon's wisdom plays a prime role as the object of the queen's adulation. The resumption of this motif on a wider scale in 9:22-23 gives the chronicler the opportunity to affirm a truth associated with 1:1-12: The wisdom of Solomon was a divine gift, and so credit for it must go to the Lord. Since Solomon is the "patron saint" of wisdom in the Old Testament, it is not surprising that this divine origination is also found in the wisdom literature, notably at Prov 2:6, "The LORD gives wisdom;/ from his mouth come knowledge and understanding" (NRSV). The virtues so prized in wisdom teaching, one's own experience and learning from the experience of others, were the very means by which the Lord communicated truth and provided answers to perplexing questions that life poses. In the New Testament, Solomon's gift is offered in principle to all believers: "If any of you is lacking in wisdom, ask God . . . and it will be given you" (Jas 1:5 NRSV).

2 CHRONICLES 10:1–28:27

THE DIVIDED KINGDOM

OVERVIEW

These chapters make up the third block of the chronicler's history: the period of the divided kingdom. A new age marked by a permanent dynasty and temple worship had been inaugurated in the reigns of David and Solomon (7:10). The continued enjoyment of these privileges by the southern kingdom and their forfeiture by the northern kingdom are affirmed in a royal speech in 13:5-12. The dynastic privilege is reaffirmed at a significant moment of threat in 21:7, whose passing is celebrated at 23:3. Davidic kingship was restored against all odds, and its survival then spelled hope thereafter.

David and Solomon function as role models (11:17). The reigns of the kings of Judah are used in this literary block to illustrate the spiritual principle propounded to Solomon by David, the principle of seeking rather than forsaking the Lord (1 Chr 28:9), which finds full expression in 15:2. Such normative spirituality is worked out with reference to both the Temple and the Torah, maintaining the worship and fabric of the Temple and complying with the guidelines of the Torah. These obligations, previously the two conditions for the establishment of the dynasty, now operate as criteria for blessing or bane for successive Judean kings. Blessing shows itself in the gift of children, building operations, and victory over invaders, while military defeat, illness, and premature death are reaped by sinners.

The Temple was built not only for worship but also for prayer in time of trouble. Judah's kings, like any believer, needed the sort of help outlined in 7:14. God's help comes into operation in chaps. 12; 15 (momentarily); and 20 and, surprisingly, in the northern kingdom in chap. 28. However, appropriate human humility is tragically missing in the pride exhibited in chaps. 25–26.

The varying levels of virtue and vice registered in the kings' lives seem to function as royal versions of the successive scenarios listed in Ezekiel 18: a good king, a bad king, a good king who degenerates, and a sinning king who reforms. The principle of each generation's standing or falling on its own showing, which Ezekiel attested, also finds explicit illustration in these chapters, signaled by the chronicler's phrase "the God of one's fathers" or predecessors.

The ecumenical ideal cherished by the chronicler is particularly evident at both the beginning and the end of this literary block. The status of the two kingdoms as "brothers" before the Lord is affirmed in chaps. 11 and 28. Yet their roles become skewed. The people of the north, the straying sheep of the family of God in chap. 13, become models of restoration and reconciliation in chap. 28. Conversely, the people of the south, pillars of orthodoxy in chap. 13, degenerate into religious apostasy in chap. 28. This leveling was the chronicler's challenge to the separatism of post-exilic Judah.

The text falls into six units: (1) lessons from Rehoboam's reign, 10:1–12:26; (2) three examples of trust, 13:1–16:14; (3) lessons of fellowship with the Lord from Jehoshaphat's reign, 17:1–21:1*a* ; (4) the averting of a threat to the Davidic dynasty, 21:1*b*–23:21; (5) three examples of good kings who became apostate, 24:1–26:23; and (6) examples of a good king and a bad king, 27:1–28:27.

2 CHRONICLES 10:1–12:16, REHOBOAM'S CHECKERED REIGN

OVERVIEW

Rehoboam's reign is presented as a spiritual roller coaster. First, he plunges deep into failure. His immature folly is responsible for the loss of most of his kingdom. The only good that emerges from the disaster is that the Lord is glorified by vindication of an earlier prophetic word. The king's paying heed to another prophetic revelation is made the basis of a high period of blessing. Then he falls into apostasy and experiences further loss. A third prophetic intervention brings a challenge that is heeded, and utter disaster is averted. Prophecy is assigned a role in each of the three sections of the chronicler's narrative of the reign of Rehoboam. This prophetic message was addressed to his contemporaries, that they heed God's written prophetic revelation and, for their own good, apply to their own lives its challenge and warning as an alternative to experiencing its judgment.

2 Chronicles 10:1-19, The King Who Would Not Listen

COMMENTARY

The chronicler used from the 1 Kings account a contrast between Rehoboam's refusal to listen to the people, mentioned twice in 10:15-16, and his and Judah's willingness to listen to the Lord in 11:4 ("They listened to the word of the Lord," REB). In each case the verb שׁמע (šāmaʿ) is used. The prophet's name, Shemaiah, in 11:2 must have suggested to the chronicler the sense of "listening to the LORD," and so it accentuates the contrast.

The chronicler follows the MT of 1 Kgs 12:1-19 closely. Scholars disagree over the role of Jeroboam in the original form of the 1 Kings narrative and whether its present text is the result of assimilation to the Chronicles form of the story. Whether the chronicler was the first to push Jeroboam to the fore or not, his interest in the rival king was not his culpability, at this stage at least, but as a historical sequel to Ahijah's prophecy concerning Jeroboam in 9:29, which finds a subsequent echo at 10:15. Jeroboam's seizure of power on justifiable grounds had been predicted by the Lord. The chronicler omitted 1 Kgs 12:20 because of the redundancy of its first half and because political information about the northern kingdom is filtered out as much as possible in this book.

The section begins with Rehoboam's expectation of becoming king over "all Israel" (v. 1), which in 1 Kgs 12:1 meant the northern tribes, but here signifies all twelve. His reign concludes with a report about his reign over Judah (v. 17). So ended an eighty-year-old bond between king and unified nation (cf. 9:30; 1 Chr 29:26-27). The chronicler does not let the shattering of this ideal pass without comment, but makes small adaptations later in the narrative to express his viewpoint.

10:1-14. The coronation at Shechem never took place. The people, weary of conscription and subscription to Solomon's projects, laid down conditions, which delayed the ceremony. Wisely, Rehoboam consulted Solomon's counselors. Foolishly, he rejected their counsel of conciliation, preferring the tough policy urged by his contemporaries. The royal wisdom of chap. 9 is conspicuous by its absence. The divine purpose that the monarchy should minister to the people's interests, advocated in 9:8 and in 1 Chr 14:2, finds no place now. The chronicler cannot stomach the two references to the king's serving the people in 1 Kgs 12:7, replacing them in v. 7 with a reference to treating them kindly and pleasing them. In fact, the omission of "today" (1 Kgs 12:7) advocates a policy, not of temporary blandishment, but of permanent benevolence.

10:15. The word of the Lord had dominated David's coronation in 1 Chr 11:1-3, 10; 12:23 in a positive way. Here the Lord's word controls the absence of a coronation for Rehoboam, providing a framework for the coronation narrative (vv. 1-15*a*) at 9:29 and 10:15*b*. The chronicler retains without explanation the theological comment that the Lord's prophetic revelation was realized. The narrative in 1 Kgs 11:29-39 is more lucid, but one can read into the present reference only Ahijah's prediction that Jeroboam would reign over ten of Israel's tribes. In 1 Kings that prediction constitutes a reprisal for Solomon's wrongdoing, whereas the chronicler's concern in his presentation of Solomon's reign was to avoid such negative factors, so that the accusation in v. 4, with which he could hardly dispense, now stands in tension with his earlier account. God's prediction is here a reprisal for Rehoboam's willful folly. The chronicler's propensity for giving a clean slate to each generation, and so control over its own destiny, favors this explanation, though some adaptation of the language of 1 Kgs 12:15 might have made it clearer. Ironically, Rehoboam had more power in his "little finger" (v. 10) than even he realized. The resumption of v. 15*a* in v. 16*a* shows how the divine purpose was realized in human experience.

This expression of the divine will has an overarching function in the narrative. At 1 Chr 10:14, mention was made of the Lord's turning Saul's kingdom over to David. Similar language was used in 1 Chr 12:23, with a reference to the Lord's predictive word. A noun relating to the verb used there occurs here: "It was a turn of affairs brought about by God" (NRSV). These parallel statements isolate the reigns of David and Solomon from earlier and later history. Prophets bore witness that they constituted a special period. With David's accession, the outgoing tide turned and brought special revelation on its crest. With Solomon's death, the tide turned again. It left on Israel's shores three witnesses to God's dynamic will: the Temple, the Davidic dynasty, and, in memory at least, the union of God's people. The Temple that stood in the chronicler's day had been rebuilt on the same site as the First Temple and had the same validity as its predecessor. Restoration of the dynasty and a united people belonged to his vision of a divinely ordered future.

10:16-19. To this last ideal the chronicler testifies in v. 17 (cf. 11:3) in referring to "the people of Israel who were living in the cities of Judah." They matched "the people of Israel" in the north (v. 18).[231] He never forgot that twelve tribes, not two, were the Lord's ideal. He was implicitly calling for a halt to the separatism of Ezra and Nehemiah.

Rehoboam underestimated the power of his constituents. Their anti-Davidic slogan (v. 16) functions as a reversal of the affirmation of loyalty in 1 Chr 12:18. With one stroke he had undone the achievement of David and decimated his subjects. Still expecting business as usual, he dispatched the administrator of national conscription. His lynching forced him, so rigidly standing on his dignity hitherto, to retreat to the safety of Jerusalem.[232] He "managed to get into his chariot and escape" (NIV). The northern kingdom's rebellion against the Davidic dynasty remained an unresolved issue. Sadly, the chronicler had no reason to correct the time limit of 1 Kgs 12:19, "to this day." The renunciation of David's house reverberated through the centuries—but would not be forever, the chronicler hoped and prayed.

---

231. See Williamson, *Israel in the Books of Chronicles*, 108-10.
232. See L. Koehler and W. Baumgartner, *The Hebrew and Aramaic Lexicon of the Old Testament* (Leiden: Brill, 1994) 1:65.

REFLECTIONS

The text sides with the rejected counsel of Solomon's old advisers and so with the people's demand for their national burdens to be lightened. We can understand the chronicler's reluctance to reflect on the significance of this demand to Solomon's reign. Not even the deuteronomist gave a clear lead in this respect. For both historians, it carried a message about the new reign, the folly of inexperience that refuses conciliation and blunders into alienation. Power went to Rehoboam's head, and he listened to advice to put his foot down from the start, as if he were a novice schoolteacher. He lacked respect for those over whom he had been given authority. His threats were an overreaction born of insecurity. He heard the weary people's conditions as threats to his power and reacted with counterthreats. Power was misconstrued as force to be exercised "harshly" (10:13) without regard for human feelings or any real understanding of the situation. The chapter should be required reading for persons embarking on new tasks involving authority over others.

Rehoboam's brash threat to increase his subjects' yoke contrasts with the offer Jesus made to the weary and burdened: "Take my yoke upon you and learn from me . . . for I am gentle and humble in heart, and you will find rest for your souls. For my yoke is easy, and my burden is light" (Matt 11:29-30). The tension between challenge and assurance is a delicate one for pastors and church authorities to hold in balance. The Scylla of a lax attitude with regard to the spiritual and moral lives of members is as reprehensible as the Charybdis of tyranny that some groups exercise over their adherents. This passage is concerned with the Charybdis, just as in religious terms the yoke of the Torah is deplored in Acts 15:10. More generally, and with a different metaphor, lording it over the flock is deprecated in 1 Pet 5:3, an echo of Ezek 34:4. Yet there must be a yoke. The invitation of Jesus spoke not only of rest but also of discipline, learning to change the way we would otherwise live.

2 Chronicles 11:1-23, Strength from Listening

COMMENTARY

Rehoboam had closed his ears to his northern constituents' demands for a lighter load. He responded to their cries of good riddance with an arrogant and vain dispatch of Hadoram. The lesson was not learned until 11:4, when king and southerners listened to a prophetic word and desisted from any attempt to take back the kingdom by force. In vv. 1-4 the text of 1 Kgs 12:21-24 is followed, but the chronicler makes it a preliminary to a receipt of blessing. By means of his extra narrative in vv. 5-23, he preaches a message to his contemporaries advocating obedience to the Lord's written prophetic word and offering incentives for so doing.

11:1-4. The intervention of Shemaiah is typical of prophetic behavior before a battle—inquiry about the military campaign's success (cf. 18:4-27; 25:7-8; 1 Chr 14:10, 14). Whereas Ahijah had pronounced judgment in advance on Rehoboam's high-handedness (10:15), here a new prophecy intrudes, banning Rehoboam's military reprisal. Just as that "turn of events was from God" (10:15 NIV), so also "this thing is from me," declares the Lord (v. 4). The division of the kingdom, and so Jeroboam's reign over the ten tribes, was

God's will for the moment at least. Civil war was not the answer. "Brothers" in the family of God were not to be treated as enemies. For the chronicler, this appeal to brotherhood had a special attraction. It belonged to his agenda for a complete Israel, to which he draws attention in v. 3 by importing a reference to Israel into 1 Kgs 10:23: "all Israel in Judah and Benjamin" (NRSV). The new southern kingdom was only a partial representation of the true Israel.

The king who would not hear what his constituents were saying now listens to the Lord. "The courage, flexibility and humility which were so urgently needed in the preceding episode suddenly appear here in full bloom."[233] Rehoboam's compliance with the divine will motivates three responses of divine blessing: vv. 5-12a, vv. 12b-17, and vv. 18-23. The first two responses have strength as their keynote, the strength of the fortified cities in vv. 11-12 and the strengthening of the kingdom by an influx of believers from the north in v. 17. In the third paragraph, the king's vigor in producing a huge

233. Japhet, *I & II Chronicles*, 660.

family strikes a similar chord. In a retrospective summary he is described as strong. The chronicler's perspective at 12:1 is the same as that expressed in 16:9: The Lord's policy was to "strengthen those whose hearts are fully committed to him" (NIV). Rehoboam and the later Uzziah are a parallel pair of kings, obedient and strong in the early parts of their reigns (see 26:8, 15-16; cf. 27:6). Moreover, the three paragraphs are deliberately modeled on 1 Kgs 12:25–13:10; 14:1-18.[234] If Jeroboam resided in his own capital and built a frontier fortress, Rehoboam did likewise. If Jeroboam engaged in religious reforms and encountered adverse reactions to them, such reactions involved Judah too. If Jeroboam's royal house was cursed, Rehoboam's family was blessed, and an ordered succession was secured.

11:5-12a. It is generally acknowledged that in vv. 6-10a the chronicler had available a source other than 1 Kings: a list of Judah's military defenses. If it did originally relate to Rehoboam's reign, at least in part the list seems to reflect a period after Shishak's invasion in chap. 12. The lines of fortification were set up in the east, south, and west along important roads.[235] The northern side was left unprotected, either because the king anticipated no invasion from that quarter or because he expected to recover the lost territory to the north.

In the books of Chronicles, building operations symbolize God's blessing as a response to obedient behavior (see 8:2-6). The Lord was building and guarding through Rehoboam, on the principle of Ps 127:1: "Unless the LORD builds the house, those who build it labor in vain" (NRSV). The security of having a good defense system was not regarded as inconsistent with trust in God, a perspective that suits in principle the land-based theology of the OT. Elsewhere in the OT, prophets criticize the presence of military power in the OT as a sinister shift whereby it became a substitute object of faith (see Isa 31:1). Occasionally biblical perspectives clash. Hezekiah's defense measures against Assyria were, for Isaiah, evidence of a lack of faith, but they were proof

of faith for the chronicler (Isa 22:8b-11; 2 Chr 32:1-8).

11:12b-17. Verse 12b introduces the next paragraph.[236] Extra support was forthcoming from the north, initially in the form of religious personnel, who "sided with" Rehoboam. The chronicler deduces from Jeroboam's appointing of his own priesthood that the former ones who officiated at the Jerusalem Temple and lived in the northern kingdom had been expelled (cf. 13:9). The account of the division of the kingdom in chap. 10 had laid little, if any, blame on Jeroboam. Rehoboam had been the foolish villain and Jeroboam the divinely specified agent in an oracle of judgment (9:29; 10:15). Now the roles of saint and sinner are reversed. The role of sinner is even extended to all succeeding kings of the north, as "sons" in v. 14 appears to signify. Not only is the idolatrous interpretation of Jeroboam's calves taken over from the deuteronomist and Hosea (Hos 8:4-6; 10:5; 13:2), but also his pernicious innovations are intensified by a new mention of "goat-demons," an infringement of the Torah's prohibition at Lev 17:7. Priests and Levites defected to the south, prepared to lose their land holdings for the sake of maintaining their religious integrity (cf. 1 Chr 6:54-81; 13:2).

Whether the northern laity who came to Jerusalem to worship are meant as pilgrims or as immigrants is uncertain; the parallel of 15:9 suggests the latter. Verse 16 is redolent with the chronicler's language of religious faith. The Temple is recognized as the only "house of sacrifice" (7:12) authorized for worship of the Lord. People came to "seek" (בקש *biqqēš*) the Lord, a term associated especially with going to the Temple. They "set their hearts" or "were resolved" (REB) to do so, a phrase used earlier at 1 Chr 22:19; 29:19 and part of the chronicler's vocabulary of spiritual zeal. Their devotion to "the God of their fathers" indicates the stand taken by this particular generation in converting their parents' faith into their own. The chronicler has in mind an ideal for his own day: the status of the Temple as a place of worship for all the tribes of Israel. He lavishes the riches of his spiritual vocabulary on northerners, hoping for an influx of northern pilgrims who

234. Japhet, *1 & II Chronicles*, 663.
235. See Aharoni, *The Land of the Bible*, 330. For the dating and the strange order of place-names see Williamson, *1 and 2 Chronicles*, 240-42.

236. P. R. Ackroyd, *1 & 2 Chronicles, Ezra, Nehemiah*, Torch Bible (London: SCM, 1973) 128.

recognize the Temple as God's appointed sanctuary. In doing so, he appeals to his fellow Judeans to open their hearts to their neighbors.

The southern kingdom, bolstered by such northern saints, basked in the Lord's blessing. The early period of Rehoboam's reign is presented as a spiritual heyday. The three-year duration of security for the land (v. 17) appears to have been calculated by counting back from the fifth year of his reign (12:2) and by allowing one year for backsliding. The period allows room for the blessings of military defense and a family for Rehoboam. David and Solomon are portrayed as ideals of obedience. The chronicler conceives of a joint era of blessing, finding no room for the deuteronomist's toppling of Solomon from his pedestal of faith in 1 Kgs 11:4-6.

11:18-23. The third paragraph presents Rehoboam's enormous family as an implicit sign of divine blessing, in line with 1 Chr 25:5; 26:4-5; it accords with the reference to David's family in 1 Chr 14:3-7. Solomon's harem was passed over because of the sinister interpretation the deuteronomist had put on it. We have no parallel for the description of Rehoboam's family in 1 Kings, gleaning only the name of Abijah's mother, Maacah daughter of Absalom (1 Kgs 15:2), who now turns out to be the king's second wife. The list presumably came from a source at the chronicler's disposal.[237] This special material explains why the firstborn son did not become king, though Deut 21:15-17 was thereby contravened. The list obviously relates to Rehoboam's whole reign and has been placed here to fit the chronicler's agenda of obedience and blessing. The first wife was the king's second cousin, another grandchild of David. It is unlikely that the Absalom mentioned here as the father of Rehoboam's second wife was David's son; the link would have been expressed, as in v. 18. Another tradition about Abijah's mother is followed in 13:2 (see also 1 Kgs 15:10).[238] In ancient royal circles, sons of the harem were trained as civil and military leaders (v. 23). Family bonds ensured the loyalty of persons in high places, and so the king acted "wisely." At the end of the verse both the NIV and the NRSV have implicitly followed a common conjectural emendation made by textual critics.

237. McKenzie, *The Chronicler's Use of the Deuteronomistic History*, 89-90.
238. See Japhet, *I & II Chronicles*, 670-71.

REFLECTIONS

1. At the close of the account of the divided kingdom the chronicler shows that calling the people of the north "brothers" was a very important concern (28:8-15 NIV). His heart ached over a truncated people of God, as Paul's had over his unconverted Jewish brothers and sisters in Rom 9:1. Like Paul in Romans 9–11, the chronicler dreamed that one day God would be glorified by a reunited covenant people. The separated "brothers" of the north were "brothers" still and even potential saints, as the chronicler suggests with some irony in 11:16.

The New Testament bids us take the family relationship seriously in our treatment of fellow Christians (Matt 5:22; Rom 14:10, 21; 1 Thess 4:6-10; 1 John 3:17; 4:20-21; see also Acts 7:26). The chronicler's concern, however, translates less readily into fellowship within the local church, as most of these texts envision, but more into a wider fellowship of God's people that transcends denominational barriers. Recent overtures between evangelicals and Roman Catholics in the United States are a beautiful example of the melting of traditional antagonism.

2. This story of polygamy and concubinage, including Rehoboam's intent to make a son of his favorite wife his heir, strikes a discordant note for the modern reader. One must try to rise above cultural prejudices, even when they may seem well founded, and appreciate the concerns of the text. In the Old Testament, polygamy was an accepted form of marriage, and concubines did not lack legal rights. Indeed, Judaism has sometimes permitted polygamy for Jews residing in Muslim countries. In practice, economic factors probably made monogamy more expedient. However, the cultural ethos of polygamy is so ingrained in the Old Testament that the Lord is symbolically represented as having two wives in the allegory of Ezekiel 23 (see also Jer 3:6-10). Similarly, in the New Testament the cultural phenomenon of slavery can be used as a model for Christian service (Rom 6:16-22; Gal 5:13).

3. This particular text refers to God's gift of children. In the Old Testament fertility is traced directly back to God's providential blessing (see Job 10:8-12; Ps 139:13-15), while infertility is regarded as an unnatural and divinely wrought situation, as 1 Sam 1:6, 11 illustrates. Many people in the ancient world equated nature and deity, while Israel viewed nature as the arena by which the Lord's will was worked out. Too close and too remote a correlation between God and the natural world is dangerous, but that there is some relation is a necessary Christian belief, in tune with the biblical concept of God as creator and sustainer of the natural world. Parents rejoicing over a new baby respond to a wise spiritual instinct when they praise God for the gift.

2 Chronicles 12:1-16, Failure and a Fresh Start

COMMENTARY

The chronicler uses the passages in 1 Kgs 14:22-28 about Judah's religious sins and Shishak's invasion and exaction of tribute from palace and Temple as the basis for his narrative in vv. 1-12. Whereas the 1 Kings story places apostasy and foreign invasion side by side without comment, it implicitly invites its readers to draw a moral. The chronicler is one reader who does moralize. He summarizes the detailed circumstances of 1 Kgs 14:22-24 in his own way in vv. 1-2 and 5 as forsaking the Torah and being unfaithful to the Lord. The first verb, here rendered "abandon" (עזב *'āzab*) in order to capture the wordplay in v. 5, was used earlier (1 Chr 28:9) in a polarized proposition of spirituality versus apostasy: "If you seek [the LORD], he will be found by you, but if you forsake him, he will reject you forever" [NIV]). The other verb (מעל *mā'al*, "to be unfaithful") or a related noun was used of the dire cause of the exile in 1 Chr 5:25; 9:1 and was applied to Saul's apostasy in 1 Chr 10:13. Like Saul, Rehoboam, scion of David though he was, found that unfaithfulness exposed him to military defeat.

12:1. Whereas the MT of 1 Kgs 14:22-24 puts the blame on the people of Judah, our text includes the king in that blame. In the LXX of 1 Kgs 14:22 Rehoboam is made the subject of v. 22a, as indeed in v. 14 of the Chronicles text, and the plural verb "they provoked him to jealousy" in v. 22b is correspondingly singular. The chronicler may have read a complex text, with a singular verb in v. 22a, like the LXX, and a plural verb at the start of v. 22b, like the MT. The reference to "all Israel with him" refers to the representatives of the total Israel to be found in the southern kingdom.

What did he mean by saying that the Torah had been abandoned by Rehoboam? In view of the details in 1 Kgs 14:23, the chronicler probably had in view Deut 12:1-14. Such pagan worship contrasts with worship of the true God in the chosen sanctuary. For the chronicler, as for the deuteronomist, this was the Jerusalem Temple (2 Chr 7:12). To seek the Lord meant to worship at the Temple (11:16). Conversely, to forsake the Lord was to forsake the Torah (cf. 7:19, 22).

Verse 1 draws an arc between becoming "strong," the key word of 11:5-23, and forsaking the Torah. As in the later case of Uzziah (26:16), Rehoboam fell into a trap of self-sufficiency, believing that "my power and the might of my own hand have gotten me this wealth" or strength (Deut 8:17 NRSV). Behind the blatant sins of religious perversity, the chronicler glimpsed an intellectual sin of failing to interpret success as the Lord's blessing.

12:2-4. Punishment for apostasy comes in the form of military attack and defeat.

Shishak's own description of the campaign is extant today; it lists cities in southern Judah throughout the northern kingdom. Only the mention of Aijalon overlaps with the list of Rehoboam's fortress cities in 11:6-10. Demand for a heavy tribute from Jerusalem must have been issued from Gibeon, which is also mentioned in Shishak's account. The chronicler magnifies the effect on the southern kingdom to make his point. The mention of 60,000 cavalry (v. 3) seems to be a further example of his rhetorical use of mathematics, as his use of "innumerable" or "countless" suggests. The chronicler paints a sensational picture as a deterrent to such behavior. It gives him the opportunity to revisit the fortified cities of chap. 11. They had been tokens of divine blessing and expressions of the king's trust in the Lord to protect Judah. Only as strong as their builder's faith, they became houses built on sand. Rehoboam could no longer expect God's positive presence.

12:5. To make the religious point, Shemaiah, the prophet active in 11:2-4, steps onstage again. His one-sentence message, expressed in a powerful chiastic style, is delivered to the king and the government officials huddled in Jerusalem. After vv. 2-4 the Lord had providentially treated Judah as they had treated the Lord (see the NRSV; the rendering in the NIV and the REB, "I now abandon you," takes the perfect as performative).

A typical role for a prophet in 2 Chronicles is that of a sentry posted to warn of trouble ahead. Thus in 24:19 prophets are sent to bring the people back to the Lord, while in 36:15 they are dispatched out of the Lord's compassion to prevent the destruction of people and sanctuary. Prophets feature as well as agents of the redemptive policy disclosed in 7:14.

12:6. Rehoboam had let himself be sucked into the fatal vortex of 1 Chr 10:13 and 28:9. Death and utter dereliction loomed ominously near. Help came in the form of the gracious option announced in 2 Chr 7:14, set against the scenario of 6:24-25. Rehoboam and the officials escaped judgment by humbling themselves and confessing the Lord's name (6:24; 7:14); the officials acted as representatives of the people of God ("Israel," v. 6). God had offered a way back to spiritual security and a new lease on life. Four times

the chronicler mentions people humbling themselves (vv. 6-7, 12). It is his call to those with ears to hear that the good news of 7:14 can work for anybody. The liturgical formula "The LORD is righteous" works as a confession of sin, implying that the Lord is in the right and correspondingly the people are in the wrong and thus are receiving their just deserts (cf. Exod 9:27; Dan 9:14).

12:7-8. The people's admission that the Lord was in the right made possible a reprieve, announced in Shemaiah's further message. Yet it came with a condition. Just as Jacob was left with a limp as a poignant reminder of having fought with God (Gen 32:25, 31), so also Rehoboam became Shishak's vassal, which left Rehoboam the capital and the throne. King and country were to be taught a lesson by this partial deliverance ("some," NRSV, fits the context better than "soon," NIV). They would find that the Lord's yoke was light in comparison with being in the service of a foreign power. Experience of both alternatives would enable them to appreciate the former. These verses are transparent. Rehoboam under Shishak is a mirror for post-exilic Judah, restored to the land but still subject to Persia (Ezra 9:8-9; Neh 9:36-37; see also 2 Chr 36:20). The healing envisioned in 7:14 does not materialize fully in this presentation. The chronicler hints that spiritual return to the Lord would not necessarily spell immediate liberation. This cautious scenario indicates that the glorious descriptions elsewhere in 2 Chronicles were meant to serve as incentives to appropriate behavior.

12:9-12. Verses 9-11 are a copy of 1 Kgs 14:25-28. The ceremonial gold shields of 9:15 had to be replaced with bronze copies for the palace escort. Did the chronicler think ironically of the prophetic promise, "Instead of bronze I will bring gold" (Isa 60:17)? Verse 12 sums up the situation positively. Rehoboam's self-humbling was the factor that "under God" saved the day. The king had climbed down from the daredevil stance of v. 1 and so averted utter destruction from the Lord's indignation. The last clause has a religious reference, as the parallel in 19:3 suggests. Once again "conditions were good in Judah." That comment paves the way for the favorable portrayal of Judean religion in 13:10-11. The cultic aberrations of 1 Kgs

14:23-24 had been eliminated. The chronicler's introduction of Rehoboam's repentance was intended both to teach its own spiritual lesson and to build a literary bridge back to the religious orthodoxy to be portrayed in chap. 13.

12:13-14. In vv. 13*b*-14 the chronicler cites part of the royal prologue to Rehoboam's reign in 1 Kgs 14:21*b*-22*a*, using it for his own ends. He prefaces it with the statement that Rehoboam "grew strong" (TNK) and "continued as king" (NIV). He introduces the actual citation with "because" (כִּי *kî*, "for," KJV), left untranslated in modern English versions. The king must have regained the sorts of strength described in 11:5-23, which indicated divine blessing, because according to 1 Kings he went on to enjoy twelve more years on the throne. Mention of his ruling in Jerusalem takes on special significance; it confirms the Lord's promise to spare the capital in v. 7.[239] Verse 14, which he relates

to the king, is a reflective flashback to v. 1*b*, itself a paraphrase of 1 Kgs 14:22-23. Why did Rehoboam commit such evil deeds? Because he did not persevere in the seeking of the Lord to which 11:16-17 had referred. He "did not make a practice of" seeking God (REB; for the sense of perseverance, see 19:3; Ps 78:8). Rehoboam did eventually get back on track, but how much better it would have been had he followed the high road of chap. 11 without the detour of 12:1-12!

12:15-16. The epilogue is modeled on 1 Kgs 14:29-31, which the chronicler has adapted to his prophetic format. The Shemaiah story of 1 Kgs 12:21-24 (= 2 Chr 11:1-4) is singled out, and (as in 9:29) the oracle of the prophet in 1 Kgs 13:1-3 is mentioned as significant. The reference to a genealogy, or muster, is awkward in the Hebrew and may be a gloss.[240] It relates either to a genealogical source for the royal family in 11:18-22 (cf. 1 Chr 9:1) or to a military source for 11:5-12 and possibly 12:3-4.

239. Myers, *2 Chronicles*, 75.

240. Cf. the REB and *BHS*.

REFLECTIONS

1. The spiritual mountaintop of 11:5-23 brings its own temptations. The chronicler sees in Rehoboam the pride that would ruin the later kings Amaziah and Uzziah and that marred for a time Hezekiah's spiritual journey (25:19; 26:16; 32:25). As in 32:26, spiritual humbling is a reversal of such pride that demoted the Lord from rightful sovereignty. There was a flouting of the Torah, the expression of the divine will, "that pattern of teaching" to which God's people had been "made subject" (Rom 6:17 REB). There was no longer a resolve to "obey [God's] commandments and do what pleases him" (1 John 3:22).

The chronicler affirms that there was still hope beyond such disobedience, according to the provision of 7:14. Yet he has a pastoral concern not to minimize the seriousness of Rehoboam's departure from the divine norm. In 12:14 he deplores this abandoning of the Torah. There is a risk that leaving an opportunity for repentance may lull believers into carelessness. John was sensitive to this danger in emphasizing that his prime purpose was to encourage Christians not to sin and that God's emergency system should not be trivialized (1 John 2:1-2). This is why the chronicler deplores the king's lack of spiritual stamina. Similarly, Christian believers are urged to "remain faithful to the Lord with steadfast devotion" (Acts 11:23 NRSV) and to "continue securely established and steadfast in the faith" (Col 1:23 NRSV). Redeeming grace can put Humpty Dumpty together again, but it is better for him not to fall.

2. In Shemaiah's first oracle there is a dire pronouncement, a quid pro quo that deals in direct retribution. Repentance is the intention, and so a second chance for king and country. Human intransigence ties even God's hands, but a humble heart permits the Lord to work miracles.

3. The divinely sanctioned vassalage of 12:8 serves as a reminder that frustrating hindrances may teach spiritual lessons, if only by directing us toward God in prayer and a renewed sense of dependence. Paul came to regard his "thorn in the flesh" as not merely necessary but a fresh opportunity to appreciate God's power and grace (2 Cor 12:7-10).

2 CHRONICLES 13:1–16:14, TRUSTING THE TRUE GOD IN TIMES OF CRISIS

OVERVIEW

The accounts of Abijah's and Asa's reigns are dominated by the theme of reliance on God. Forms of the key term "rely" (נשען *niš'an*, in the niphal) occur here five times and nowhere else in Chronicles, though the general motif of turning to God in emergencies and to God alone is common elsewhere. The repetition creates a literary unit with three sections. The first occurrence of the word (13:18) helps us to identify the first section, 13:1–14:1a, in which Abijah's and Judah's trust in the Lord is vindicated over against the infidelity of Jeroboam and the people of the northern kingdom. The second case (14:11) is set within the section 14:1b–15:19, in which Asa's initial trust is vindicated. The remaining three instances (16:7-8) occur in the third section, 16:1-14, where Asa's counterfeit trust is punished.

The chronicler uses the two reigns to preach a series of sermons that are variations on a single theme: trust in the Lord. Moreover, if trust in the Lord is the main thread that runs through these chapters, it is interwoven with two other threads taken from the general religious vocabulary of Chronicles: forsaking the Lord (13:10-11) and its polar opposite, seeking the Lord (14:4, 7; 15:2, 4, 12, 15; 16:12) Also, in each of the first two sections the chronicler refers to the Lord twice as "God of your/their fathers" (NIV, 13:12, 18; 14:4; 15:3).

2 Chronicles 13:1–14:1a, Abijah's Loyal Trust Vindicated

COMMENTARY

Abijah is called Abijam in 1 Kgs 15:1-8. We do not know why the names are different; they may represent a throne name and a personal name. According to 1 Kings 15, this king is a worthless nonentity who does so little to enhance the Davidic line that its survival is credited to the Lord's gracious covenant with David. One of the few significant contacts between the 1 Kings account and the text in 2 Chronicles is the mention of warfare between Abijah and Jeroboam, of which the chronicler indulges in an example in vv. 3-19. There is controversy over whether he invented it or wrote it up from a historical source that specified the territorial

gains of v. 19. It has been argued that the place-names have been borrowed from a longer text of Josh 18:21-24 that is preserved in the LXX.[241] Others find it difficult to believe that the chronicler reversed the verdict of 1 Kings 15 on Abijah's reign without a written tradition of even a fleeting victory over the north.[242] The evidence of 1 Kgs 15:19 (= 2 Chr 16:3) concerning an alliance between Abijah and Aram to secure dominance over

241. R. W. Klein, "Abijah's Campaign Against the North (2 Chr 13)—What Were the Chronicler's Sources?" *ZAW* 95 (1983) 210-17. See the critique of D. G. Deboys, "History and Theology in the Chronicler's Portrayal of Abijah," *Bib* 71 (1990) 48-62, esp. 60-61.

242. Rudolph, *Chronikbücher*, 235-36, with reference to M. Noth.

their common neighbor Jeroboam, lends support to this judgment. The chronicler appears to have written up such a tradition into a holy war type of narrative akin to that in chap. 20. Victory in warfare is a standard motif in the books of Chronicles to show divine favor for obedience. The chronicler found support for this positive assessment in another available tradition concerning Abijah's large family (v. 21).

These traditions gave him grounds for his description of the healthy state of the southern kingdom at this time. He assumed the continuing orthodoxy of temple worship, which he had affirmed in 11:16, and wove both this factor and the issue of the Davidic dynasty (specified in 1 Kgs 15:4) into a pre-battle type of speech in vv. 4-12. They became the basis for miraculous victory and remarkable blessing that come later in the chapter. Tension was thereby created with Asa's reforming zeal in 2 Chr 14:3-5*a* (what was there to reform?), but the chronicler was not concerned to iron out such inconsistencies, as his retention of the negotiations between the northerners and Rehoboam in chap. 10 illustrated.

13:1. Only here is a synchronism with a northern king repeated from 1–2 Kings. Its presence reflects the fact that the whole chapter hangs on the respective relations of the two kingdoms to the Lord. The people of God had radically split in two. The initial split was ratified by prophetic prediction, while on the human plane Rehoboam's folly was warrant enough for the bulk of his subjects to reject his rule. The chronicler knew from 1 Kgs 11:37-38 that the perpetuation of the northern line of kings depended on Jeroboam's fidelity to the Lord. He had failed in this respect, as his religious innovations proved (2 Chr 11:14-15). Accordingly, the death of foolish Rehoboam and the accession of a new Judean king afforded an opportunity for the northerners to reject Jeroboam and revert to allegiance to the true Davidic king and temple worship.[243]

13:2. Abijah's mother was Maacah (LXX and NIV), as mentioned in 11:20-22 and the parallel 1 Kgs 15:2, rather than Micaiah (MT and NRSV).[244] The different patronymic represents another tradition.

13:3. The numbers are a further example of the rhetorical mathematics in which the chronicler sometimes indulged for dramatic effect. The size of the northern army may symbolize the total commitment of available forces, corresponding to the northern census number in 2 Sam 24:9. Then Judah's forces were a mere half, a feature that enhances their eventual victory. It is possible to rationalize the figures by interpreting them as 400 and 800 units, but such an approach destroys the intended grandiose effect.

13:4-12. The unidentified Mount Zemaraim was evidently in the region of Bethel (see Josh 18:22). The royal speech, like other speeches that have no parallel in 1–2 Kings, is a vehicle of the chronicler's theological interpretation.[245] The punch line at the end of v. 12 gives the main point of the king's speech: The northerners should recognize that the Lord is on the other side, so to fight Judah is to fight Judah's divine patron. What precedes is a two-pronged argument for this conclusion (vv. 5-8*a* and vv. 8*b*-12*a*). The first prong is the legitimacy of the Davidic dynasty, which earlier chapters have already established for the reader, and the second is the authenticity of the worship offered only at the Jerusalem Temple.

The expression "covenant of salt" is borrowed from Num 18:19 (cf. Lev 2:13) and has been reapplied to the Davidic covenant. Whatever its original meaning, the phrase clearly reinforces the notion of a perpetual covenant. In the light of the chronicler's overall presentation, his description of Jeroboam's rebellion (v. 6) probably has in view not the narrative of 1 Kgs 11:26-27, 40, which is set in Solomon's reign, but that of 2 Chronicles 10:1, in Rehoboam's reign (see esp. 10:19), so that "his master" is in fact Rehoboam. Then v. 7 reflects mitigating circumstances: the bad influence of younger counselors on Rehoboam, who persuaded him to adopt a high-handed attitude and so prevailed over him (התאמץ *hit'ammēṣ*; cf. the Qal in v. 18, rather than the NRSV's "defied" or the NIV's "opposed").[246] Josephus interpreted the text

243. See Williamson, *Israel in the Books of Chronicles*, 110-14.
244. See Allen, *The Greek Chronicles*, 2:99.

245. See Deboys, "History and Theology in the Chronicler's Portrayal of Abijah," 55-59.
246. Williamson, *Israel in the Books of Chronicles*, 112-13; *1 and 2 Chronicles*, 252-53; De Vries, *1 and 2 Chronicles*, 292. See also G. N. Knoppers, "Rehoboam in Chronicles: Villain or Victim?" *JBL* 109 (1990) 423-44, esp. 437-39.

in this way,[247] and a small group seems more apposite than "Jeroboam and all Israel" (10:3). According to 10:15, the chronicler respected the necessity of Jeroboam's rebellious role in the light of Rehoboam's conduct. His successor apologizes for Rehoboam's immature mistake and its tragic consequences. There was now no reason to persist in secession. The rule of David's sons had been approved by God (cf. 1 Chr 17:14; 29:23). As the speech progresses, Abijah increasingly bypasses Jeroboam. He is jointly addressed in v. 4, but is mentioned obliquely in vv. 6, 8; by the end of the speech, only the people are addressed (v. 12). Jeroboam was no longer in the picture, just as Rehoboam had ceased to be a material factor in the contemporary situation. The reason for Jeroboam's exclusion is given in v. 8*b* : He had appointed his own priests and had encouraged idol worship (11:15).

In formal structure, the speech consists of a historical introduction (vv. 5-7) and contemporary consequences (vv. 8-12), with a recapitulation of the argument of vv. 5-7 in v. 8*a*. Verses 10-12*a* form a smaller section counterpointing at beginning and end Judah's not having forsaken the Lord and Israel's having done so.

The new era established by David and Solomon determined criteria of worship for the people of God. The reader of the books of Chronicles is no stranger to these criteria: proper personnel and four archetypical features of worship. Their presence or absence defined the seeking or forsaking of the Lord. Implicit conformity of temple worship with the Torah determined which elements should be mentioned here, as a citation of Lev 24:6 in v. 11 ("table of pure gold") and an appeal to Num 10:8-9 (cf. Num 31:6) for the priestly trumpets in v. 12 indicate. So the role of levitical singers went unnoticed, and the single lampstand of the tabernacle surreptitiously replaced the ten that were actually present in the Temple, according to 4:7 (cf. Exod 25:31-39; 37:17-24).

Abijah's challenge to the northerners not to fight the southerners is a counterpart to the call to Rehoboam and his army not to attack the northerners in 11:4. Now the shoe was on the other foot. Any justification for the secession of the northern kingdom had

disappeared. Abijah appeals for reunification under the banner of "the God of your fathers." The parents of these northerners had worshiped the Lord as citizens of a united kingdom. Now it was the new generation's turn to make such a decision and break with recent religious aberrations. Accordingly, the term "Israelites" or "sons of Israel" carries theological overtones. Prodigal children are invited back into God's family. If they had forsaken the Lord, so had Rehoboam earlier, and a door of repentance had stood open for him (12:5-6).

13:13-18. No such hopes prevailed. The huge northern army, surrounding the Judean troops with a pincer movement, expected victory. But neither strategy nor statistics won the day against the Lord. The claim and challenge of v. 12 are translated into narrative in vv. 14 and 18. The priestly trumpets sounded an alarm to summon divine aid (cf. Num 10:9), and it was the new generation in the south that prevailed. Unlike those in the north, the southern army had laid hold of their parents' faith (vv. 12, 18). The battle is described in an archaic fashion, in the style of holy war used in the military narratives of Joshua and Judges. The secret of the southern army's success is revealed in the verb "relied" (נשׁען *niš'an*, in the niphal) in v. 18, the first appearance of this key word in this literary unit. Its use harks back to the shout of allegiance in v. 15 (cf. Judg 7:18), which the Lord honored. "To rely" is literally "to lean." A related noun (משׁען *miš'ān*) occurs in Ps 18:18, where the victorious king testifies that "the LORD was my support." The contexts of both v. 18 and Ps 18:18 are situations of desperate crisis, and in each case there is a divine acknowledgment of human fidelity (cf. Ps 18:19-27). The victory confirmed Abijah's arguments that the southern kingdom had remained loyal.

13:19-21. The frontier between the kingdoms was redrawn to the north of Bethel. As in 2 Kgs 19:37, the battle report concludes by looking ahead to the premature death of the enemy king, which stands in contrast to Abijah's fruitful reign. The point is a religious rather than a chronological one; Abijah died before Jeroboam, according to 1 Kgs 14:20; 15:9, though the chronicler may have overlooked these texts. The path of fidelity is

247. Josephus *Antiquities of the Jews* 8.11.2 277.

paved with blessing, while infidelity leads to destruction (cf. Deut 30:15-20).

13:22–14:1a. The royal epilogue is based on 1 Kgs 15:7a, 8. By referring to Iddo, the chronicler appeals to 1 Kgs 13:1-10 to bolster his case. That oracle denounced Jeroboam's religious innovations and affirmed the Davidic dynasty. Such an allusion adds an authoritative "amen" to Abijah's speech.

REFLECTIONS

Abijah's appeal to the northerners has at first sight the ring of civil war propaganda. For the chronicler, it was not simply a reconstruction of ancient history. The controversy between south and north opened a window on contemporary issues. It concerned the warrant of post-exilic Judah to regard itself as the preserver of true faith and worship. Abijah's speech lays down basic theological convictions about Judah's status before the Lord.

1. The Torah-based worship practiced in the Jerusalem Temple is one of the standards by which the fidelity of the southern kingdom is measured. Faith was no vague belief, but was clothed in specific religious forms. A striking feature typical of the culture of which the chronicler spoke and to which he still belonged is that for both the north and the south religious forms stood at the center of controversy. Religious worship loomed large, as it does in most ages—but less so our own. Very many who sincerely regard themselves as Christians consider their faith a matter of the mind and heart rather than essentially expressed in religious habits, private or communal. We need to listen with respect to the chronicler's affirmation that those who rely on God are also those who prize institutional forms of faith.

2. Abijah's challenge at the end of 13:12 is virtually an appeal for reunification of the divided kingdom under one God and king. Prodigal children are invited back into the family. Through Abijah, the chronicler's voice rang out for the Judeans to accept their role as hosts and welcome the prodigals back. In an age of religious resentment, not untinged with political factors, he refused to budge from this inclusive ideal, undergirding it with even more powerful arguments in chapter 28. Within his ecumenicity, he had non-negotiable standards of traditional religion and theology; but his arms were wide open to religious union.

But subsequent generations paid no heed to history. They followed a downward path to the point where some Jews did "not associate with Samaritans" (John 4:9 NIV). In principle, Jesus was affirming the chronicler's stand when he built bridges between himself and the Samaritan community of Sychar (John 4:39-41). He insisted on the historical priority of Jerusalem, just as the chronicler had done: "salvation is from the Jews" (John 4:21). Jesus went on to announce a new era of worship, based on criteria of "spirit and truth" (John 4:22-26). These criteria, while denying a single religious center, by no means promote an amorphous religion. The phrase "spirit and truth" does not replace the solid verb "worship," but rather qualifies it.

3. The warning against fighting God in 13:12 has a striking parallel in Gamaliel's caution to the Sanhedrin, who wanted to kill the apostles: "If it is from God, you will not be able to stop these men; you will only find yourselves fighting against God" (Acts 5:39 NIV). Just as the apostles were bravely determined to "obey God rather than any human authority" (Acts 5:29 NRSV), so also Abijah, at the head of an outnumbered army, stood staunchly by his principles. The spirit of Martin Luther sums up both scenarios: "Here I stand, I can do not other."[248]

248. See Bainton, *Here I Stand*, 185.

4. The winners relied on "the God of their fathers" (13:18 NIV). The chronicler saw himself as an upholder of tradition. He defined tradition not as a dead thing to be mechanically perpetuated for its own sake, but in terms of a reincarnation of the living faith of previous generations. To each generation the call of God comes afresh to take a positive stand as champions of the faith their parents held.

5. The chronicler conjures up a scenario of faith vindicated in time of crisis. In the case of Abijah and Judah, it was no foxhole religion. Their cry of trust drew credit from a spiritual bank account that had already been set up and was regularly used. Crisis can befall sincere believers as well as backsliders. For the former, the chronicler envisioned the certainty of divine help. Times of crisis, which may seem beyond human ability to resolve, can be a challenge to faith and an opportunity to rely on God.

2 Chronicles 14:1*b*–15:19, Asa's Valid Trust Vindicated

COMMENTARY

In 1 Kgs 15:10-11, 15, Asa is judged to be a consistently good king who reigned for forty-one years. The picture presented in 2 Chronicles 14–16 is different. Two contrasting vignettes of a long good period and a short bad one are sketched in a schematic fashion. The first period did justice to his long reign, interpreted as a recompense for goodness. But there were negative features in 1 Kings 15 to be explained: his alliance with Aram and illness in old age. Interpreting these features providentially, the chronicler reasoned back to a radical change in Asa's spiritual stance, as 16:7-8 explains.

There are chronological difficulties in the different presentations of Asa's reign. According to 1 Kgs 16:6, 8, the northern king Baasha died in Asa's twenty-sixth year, yet 2 Chr 16:1 presents him as still active in Asa's thirty-sixth year. The best way to explain this chronological anomaly is to assume that the chronicler reshuffled the events and timing in 1 Kings 15 in order to create a clear-cut division into a very long period of blessing for fidelity and a short period of infidelity. His account of Asa's reign reads as a powerful two-part lesson of spiritual greatness and a tragic fall, bringing messages of both assurance and challenge.

14:1b-8. The phrase "at peace" (vv. 1*b*, 5) provides a framework for vv. 1-5. In vv. 6-7, which describe the building of fortified cities, it is repeated in v. 6*a* and is modified by the Lord's gift of "rest" in vv. 6*b*-7. Rest from enemies was an ancient promise (Deut 12:10), associated with the land, which is mentioned three times (vv. 1*b*, 6, 7). The designation of certain periods as times of peace for the land recalls Judg 3:11, 30; 5:31; 8:28, all of which use the same Hebrew verb (שָׁקַט *šāqaṭ*, "to be quiet") and punctuate periods of backsliding and providential punishment by invasion.[249] The chronicler imposed on Asa's reign the periodization of Judges. His allusion to the judges era in 15:3-6 develops this parallel.

For the chronicler, rest had been realized in Solomon's reign, marking the onset of a new era of grace (1 Chr 22:9). It was a heritage that each succeeding king had the potential to enjoy, but its enjoyment depended on meeting two God-given responsibilities relating to the Temple and to the Torah, both of which Solomon had successfully discharged (1 Chr 28:7-10). Asa is portrayed in vv. 1*b*-7 as another Solomon. The material in vv. 1*b*-5 does not appear in the 1 Kings account, apart from the accolade of v. 2, which reproduces 1 Kgs 15:11a, though the reform measures of vv. 3 and 5*a* are thematically related to those in 1 Kgs 15:12. The chronicler has developed the motif of peace by arguing back from his dating of warfare between the two kingdoms in the latter part of Asa's reign in 15:19. He has shortened the period of warfare of 1 Kgs 15:16. Aware of open conflict only in the Ramah incident of 1 Kgs 15:17-22 (= 2 Chr 16:1-6), he assumed a state of cold war in the preceding period.[250]

249. Williamson, *1 and 2 Chronicles*, 259.
250. Williamson, *1 and 2 Chronicles*, 272.

Divinely given rest and peace provide a frame for Asa's loyal discharge of the obligations relating to Temple and Torah. The accolade of v. 2, taken over from 1 Kings, is unpacked in vv. 3-5*a*. Asa's concern for the Temple is illustrated in vv. 3 and 5*a*. Only Solomon could build the Temple; his successors were to maintain it as the sole focus of worship. This concern dictated the rewriting of the religious reform in 1 Kgs 15:12. The vocabulary of cultic perversions is implicitly antithetical to pure temple worship. The chronicler echoes the language of Lev 26:30 and Deut 12:2-3 and anticipates the pro-temple reforms of Hezekiah and Josiah in 2 Chr 21:1 (cf. 2 Kgs 18:4a) and 34:3-7. Mention of the idols in 1 Kgs 15:2 is held over until Asa's second reform in 15:8. "Incense altars" (חמנים *ḥammānîm*), not to be confused with the altar in the Temple, bore pagan associations, as Isa 17:7-8 illustrates. The removal of high places conflicts with the explicit statement of 1 Kgs 15:14. The chronicler will deal with this inconsistency later in his own way. He leaves unsettled the matter of when such deviations occurred; in his view, Asa's predecessor was a saint, and not the sinner of 1 Kgs 15:3.

If the Temple was important, so was the Torah (v. 4). The spiritual catchword of Chronicles, "seeking [שׁרד *dāraš*] the LORD," reappears here. Traditional faith and personal commitment are correlated in the phrase "seek the LORD, the God of their fathers" or predecessors. Here is the chronicler's ideal, for a new generation to appropriate their spiritual heritage, so that the community would be renewed from age to age. Such spiritual renewal is here measured by an adherence to the Torah.

The references to building fortified cities in vv. 6-7 and later to the army in v. 8 represent in the idiom of Chronicles God's blessings in response to the king's faithfulness. The building of the cities is derived from 1 Kgs 15:23 (cf. Jer 41:9), while the details of Asa's conscript army seem to depend on a military census list available to the chronicler.[251] When did these military developments take place? The chronology of chaps. 14–15 is left hazy. Verses 1*b*-8 read as if they relate to a ten-year period. Yet the battle of vv. 9-15 took place in Asa's fifteenth year, according to 15:10-11.

De Vries seems to be right in assigning vv. 6-7 to a period of five years of special blessing after the initial ten years of reform and rest.[252] He has drawn attention to the stylistic differentiation of vv. 1*b*-5 and 6-7 as separate passages. In v. 6, "while" in the NRSV is confusing; the NIV's "since" is preferable. Verse 7 distinguishes a phase of seeking the Lord and finding rest from a phase of building (in v. 7*b* the MT may be retained, instead of emending with the REB and NJB).[253] The royal speech reinforces the narrative, implicitly conveying to the chronicler's contemporaries an incentive for their own seeking of God in Temple and Torah. The prophetic speech in chap. 15 will develop this message.

14:9-15. Verse 8 marks a transition, capping the blessings of vv. 6-7, yet ironically preparing for the anticlimax of v. 9, which rudely shatters the peace of the earlier passage. The story of vv. 9-15 appears to be an extravagant rewriting of an extant historical tradition about the defeat of a semi-nomadic group based in the region of Gerar but originally from Cush to the south of the Dead Sea (cf. 21:16).[254] A raid on Mareshah was repulsed, and the raiders were chased back to Gerar. The Judeans "killed the herdsmen" (v. 15 REB; cf. *BHS*) and captured livestock, which will reappear in 15:11. The chronicler transformed history to story, enlarging the raiders into a huge exotic force from Cush in Africa ("Ethiopians," NRSV), as the reference to "Libyans" in 16:8 makes clear. The chronicler had in mind an invasion like that in 12:3. In his hands, the account became a spiritual call to faith and a portrayal of the Lord as able to meet any need, however great the human odds. The odds are grandiloquently presented as "a thousand thousand men" ("million," NRSV). The NIV's less colorful rendering, "vast," recognizes the rhetoric of this figure.

Had not the Lord already provided the answer to Asa's problem in vv. 7-8? The capture of Abijah's fortified cities in 12:4 has prepared for a negative answer here. There had to be a fresh turning of the heart to the Lord, rather than trusting in earlier provision. In fact, God proved to be a very present help in trouble. That help is triggered by

251. See Williamson, *1 and 2 Chronicles*, 261-63.

252. De Vries, *1 and 2 Chronicles*, 297-98.
253. See Dillard, *2 Chronicles*, 114.
254. See Aharoni, *The Land of the Bible*, 146.

prayer, which admits to human helplessness and claims the Lord's patronage ("our God" twice) and unique power. Asa's prayer opens with praise of the Lord's incomparable protective power: "There is no one like you to help the powerless against the mighty" (NIV, rightly interpreting the literal "help [in a conflict] between the mighty and the powerless"). Appeals for that help surround avowals of trust.

The account of God-given victory, laden with holy war motifs, reinforces the message of its twin in chap. 13. The key word of the literary unit, "rely" (נשען *niš'an*, niphal), is used in the royal prayer, alongside a claim that the people are the Lord's representatives ("in your name"; cf. 1 Sam 17:45). The trust of the faithful is vindicated.

15:1-7. Azariah's prophetic message builds an interpretative bridge between the preceding and the following accounts of Asa's reign. In the ungrammatical MT of v. 8, the prophet seems disconcertingly to turn into his father ("the prophecy, Oded the prophet"). The text is in disorder; the NIV and the NRSV have taken over an attested, but secondary, reading in an attempt to correct it. "Oded the prophet" seems to be a misplaced marginal annotation to v. 1, intending to add "the prophet," qualifying Azariah, to the phrase ending in "Oded" there. Azariah is mentioned only here. Whether the chronicler knew of him from a historical tradition or invented him along with his religious message, the name, which means "Yahweh has helped," fits the situation of 14:9-15. The Lord answers the petition for help in 14:11. Such help had been shown in the Lord's protective presence "with" them (cf. 20:17; "you" and "your" are plural throughout the address). God's continued presence in blessing was possible only if the people remained committed to the Lord.

Two alternative prospects are presented, underlined by prophetic authority. The chronicler has already introduced them to his readers in David's challenge to Solomon in 1 Chr 28:9: "If you seek him, he will be found by you; but if you forsake him, he will reject you forever" (NIV). The first alternative is taken from one of the chronicler's favorite texts, Jer 29:13-14, while the second is his own formulation, a negative foil to reinforce the

first. This pair of alternatives expresses what has been called mirror-image theology.[255] It sums up the Lord's normal dealings with Israel according to the Torah, though God also has an emergency system of restoration, proclaimed in 7:14. Here it serves to point forward to Asa's remaining years, which split into two contrasting periods. The clause "The LORD is with you while you are with him" will work itself out in vv. 8-19. While Asa and the people engaged in God's work, "the LORD . . . was with him" (v. 9). The opposite scenario, being forsaken by the forsaken God, will appear in chap. 16. A contrast between the two narratives is afforded by the double reference to commitment of heart in 15:17 and 16:19. Asa's commitment proved temporary.

Azariah gives a historical illustration in vv. 3-6. The alternatives of seeking and finding or leaving and losing the Lord were not foreign to Israel's pre-monarchical history. The book of Judges presents that period as a revolving wheel of fortune, a wheel segmented into declension, invasion, cry for help, divine deliverance, and peace (Judg 2:11-16; 3:7-11; 10:6-16). These segments are used to illustrate the alternatives facing Asa. In declension, Israel forsook the Lord, the legitimate priestly order, and the Torah for pagan religion (see Judg 2:12; 17:5-6). Yet, they were able to bypass the divine law of cause and effect by crying to God for help.

In Judges, the wheel turned on, and punitive crisis soon loomed again, with danger lurking on every journey, so prevalent was the enemy (cf. Judg 5:6; 6:2). In the absence of a true return, things went from bad to worse under God's chastising hand. If 2 Chr 15:3-4 illustrates the first alternative of v. 2, the vehemently negative vv. 5-6 function as a warning to Asa not to become embroiled in the second alternative. This rhetorical stick is replaced by a carrot in the concluding direct appeal to king and people. They are encouraged to keep up the good "work" and are urged not to rest on their laurels.

The chronicler wove into vv. 5-6 material from Zech 8:10. It is his way of challenging his post-exilic readers. Was not the return from exile marked by national distress? Was not this a case of forsaking God and incurring

255. J. G. McConville, *I & II Chronicles*, Daily Study Bible (Philadelphia: Westminster, 1984) 168-69.

punishment? Such a history teaches one to seek the Lord and find in God the answer to one's needs. Just as Azariah was exhorting pre-exilic Judah by referring to past history, so also the chronicler was challenging post-exilic Judah and using Azariah's address as his own.

15:8-15. The rest of the chapter presents the development of the first of the two scenarios of v. 2. These verses are marked by positive answers to the prophetic word. In v. 8, "took courage" echoes the imperative in v. 7, an echo captured in the NRSV. The seeking and finding of vv. 12 and 15 pick up the principle laid down in v. 2 and illustrated in v. 4. King and people constitute a model congregation, taking the message to heart and living it out. Their behavior triggers a revival, a deepening of the nation's spiritual life. Further temple-related reform took place, and maintenance work was carried out on the altar. The Feast of Weeks evidently provided an opportunity for a special service of recommitment to the Lord (cf. Lev 23:15-21; there seems to be a wordplay between the root שבע [*šāba'*, "swore," "oath"] and שבועות [*šābu'ôt*, "weeks"]). Verses 9-15 are awash with expressions of totality and enthusiasm. Verse 9 mentions the representative wholeness of God's people, continuing the trend of 11:13-17. The sacrificial worship of v. 11 indicates their indebtedness to the Lord in the earlier battle.

This feast provided an incentive for the community to dedicate themselves to the Lord afresh. The royal command of 14:4 is now enthusiastically endorsed. Whereas the king was the subject there, now the people are actively involved. The total commitment of v. 12 echoes Jer 29:13 (cf. Deut 4:29). The obligation of each generation to decide anew for the God of earlier generations was honored in this communal pledge ("covenant"). It was an experience the chronicler yearned for his contemporaries to share. The somber note of v. 13 only adds to the impression of solidarity. It borrows from Deut 13:1-10; 17:2-7 a negative consequence of group solidarity (see Ezra 7:16; see also 1 Cor 5:5). The community's oath of allegiance, sealing the pledge of v. 12, is made to the accompaniment of hallelujahs and musical blasts, which expresses the fervor of human hearts. The chronicler was presenting a model of temple worship, a joyful celebration of spiritual commitment in which religious forms reflected the adoration of the heart. The paragraph ends on the satisfying note that the people had found the Lord and had, consequently, been given rest in the land.

15:16-19. These verses provide a fitting sequel, with their motifs of reform, thankfulness to the Lord, and peace. Apart from v. 19 they are cited en bloc from 1 Kgs 15:13-15, to capture the theme of Asa's reforming zeal. The presence of the high places, which in 1 Kings clashes with the chronicler's claim in 14:3, is harmonized by locating them in the northern kingdom (in cities captured, according to v. 8). The chronicler may have had in view the extension of the frontier as far north as Mizpah, recorded in 16:6 (cf. 17:2), despite the chronological anomaly. In the light of Asa's backsliding (chap. 16) the chronicler must have understood Asa's lifelong commitment as a reference to his life up to this point. The continual warfare of 1 Kgs 15:16 is deliberately adapted to accord with his periodization of Asa's reign.

REFLECTIONS

1. The chronicler presents his religious ideals in this section. The seeking of the Lord is its basic theme, mentioned no less than eight times. Seeking the Lord, in our idiom, refers to uncommitted persons' feeling their way toward faith. Here it stands for commitment that is worked out in positive ways. One prime way related to the Temple: worshiping there and not elsewhere, worshiping in the traditional monotheistic way and according to standard rites, and maintaining the fabric of the Temple. Such fidelity to the Temple in 14:3, 5*a* and 15:8 was a measure of fidelity to the Lord. Christian readers may be tempted to dismiss this focus as a typical Old Testament stress on the material, which in the New Testament gives way to spiritual concerns. This conclusion would ignore the coexistence of the material and the spiritual. Although John

4:21-26 announces a new era in which the Temple is superseded, the spirit of worship can be demonstrated only in material ways, and the inner attitude of the heart only in external forms. Belonging to the spiritual temple of the church carries with it the obligations of communal worship and commitment to a local congregation of believers (Heb 13:15; 1 Pet 2:5).

2. Each generation in turn was called to be a steward of temple worship. In seeking the Lord, they were also called to commitment to the Torah, to its revealed guidelines for life. John's appeal, in his first letter, to Christians to keep God's commandments in token of their love for God (1 John 5:2-3; see also 2:3-5), may be regarded as a renewed application of the message of 2 Chronicles. In the church to which John wrote, there were people claiming to love God, whose bluff he called by demanding that spiritual claims be grounded in keeping God's commandments.

3. The violent turn the narrative takes at 14:9 shows the chronicler's awareness that crisis is a fact of life that does not always discriminate between the worthy and the unworthy in its choice of victims. If it could not be explained in terms of moral providence, the pragmatic answer was that the Lord had provided resources so that one could deal with the situation. In the laments and thanksgiving songs in the book of Psalms, there is a turning to the Lord, even in the voicing of doubt and anger. In turn, we Christians are urged to "approach the throne of grace with confidence" and to find through prayer "grace to help us in our time of need" (Heb 4:16 NIV).

4. Asa's prayer in 14:11 is well known to Christian congregations in the form of the beautiful hymn written by Edith G. Cherry, "We rest on thee, our shield and our defender," happily set to Sibelius's *Finlandia*. As in 13:18, this kind of faith is not the everyday variety. It is trust exercised in crisis. Again in the laments of the psalms such faith is heard in ardent prayer, when life had inflicted bleeding wounds.

5. The mirror-image formula of spirituality in 15:2 reappears in principle in the teaching of Jesus, as an incentive to fulfill God-given obligations. It always has an unexpected ring, jolting readers out of complacency. In the Lord's prayer, God is asked with some irony to "forgive us our debts, as we also have forgiven our debtors" (Matt 6:12). Yes, God does take the initiative in forgiveness, but God sets up an obligation for us to forgive in turn, which if not heeded can damage our relationship with God and impede further forgiveness. So Jesus taught in his parable of forgiveness in Matt 18:21-35, which explains the petition in the prayer he gave the church. Mirror-image spirituality is the norm in God's dealings with believers (see Ps 18:25-26). The New Testament equivalent of 2 Chr 15:2 is the solemn either/or message of Gal 6:7-9 about sowing and reaping. Paul could use it along with the doctrine of justification by faith earlier in the letter, ill matched though the association may look in terms of human logic.

6. The use of Judges in Azariah's address (15:3-6) offers an instance of the use of past history in Scripture as a spur to the life of faith. It is a microcosm of what the books of Chronicles as a whole were meant to convey. The practice occurs elsewhere in the Bible as a means of conveying moral and spiritual lessons. Psalm 95 harks back to the wilderness period and is reused in Heb 3:7–4:13. Paul also employed that period for "examples" and "warnings" to believers (1 Cor 10:1-11 NIV). As we read scriptural narratives, we will find their relevance to our lives.

2 Chronicles 16:1-14, Asa's False Trust Punished

COMMENTARY

In the macrostructure of the unit (13:1–16:14), Asa's new trust in human allies stands as a negative counterpart to the trust in the Lord, expressed in the two earlier sections. From a narrower perspective, this section describes the outworking of the second of the two scenarios offered by Azariah in 15:2-7, to abandon the Lord and suffer the bitter consequences. So, as the illustration in 15:6 warned, Asa will find himself troubled by God with every kind of distress. The section is a hellish reversal of the previous two. Victory is now won by unworthy means, the Lord's word is rejected, and, in contrast to earlier fidelity, infidelity is compounded. Asa becomes for the chronicler's readers a dramatic warning against backsliding (cf. Ezek 18:24).

16:1-6. The chronicler substantially repeats 1 Kgs 15:17-22 in vv. 1*b*-6. "Abel-maim" (v. 4) was probably the post-exilic name for "Abel-beth-maacah" (1 Kgs 15:20). The reference in v. 5 to Asa's having abandoned his work is probably the chronicler's attempt to make sense of a partially illegible text in 1 Kgs 15:21. He lets the 1 Kings passage speak for itself, reserving comment until the speech of Hanani in vv. 7-10. However, his underlying sense of outrage is easily appreciated. Where now is the faith expressed in 14:11? How can treasures consecrated to the Lord, including Asa's own votive gifts put in the Temple in the halcyon days of 15:18, be seized and used as payment for foreign aid?

The chronological notice added in v. 1*a* corresponds to the previous one in 15:19. The chronicler appears to have envisioned Asa's forty-one-year reign as being divided into two long periods of spirituality and blessing (15 + 20 years) and two short periods of unspirituality and misfortune (3 + 3 years). Some scholars have attempted to relate the thirty-fifth and thirty-sixth years to the length of time since the division of the monarchy, equating them with the fifteenth and sixteenth years of Asa's reign.[256] However, Asa's

death in the forty-first year of his reign is a given, taken over from 1 Kgs 15:10, and the earlier numbers are more likely the product of the chronicler's schematization. He probably overlooked the chronological discrepancy with 1 Kgs 15:33; 16:8.

The chronicler did not view Baasha's aggressive move into Judean territory as providential retaliation for disobedience (cf. 12:1-2). Rather, he saw it as a counterpart to Zerah's invasion earlier in the reign (14:19) and as an opportunity to put renewed trust in the Lord, whereupon Baasha would have been repulsed by supernatural means.

16:7-9. Whereas in 1 Kings Asa is not blamed for his alliance with Aram, the chronicler uses the prophetic speech of Hanani to condemn it as a breach of faith in the Lord. He derives the name from the reference to the prophet "Jehu the son of Hanani" in 1 Kgs 16:1, 7, an opponent of Baasha, and he will make use of the son's name in 19:2; 20:34 in his account of Jehoshaphat's reign. Hanani's address is made up of essentially an initial accusation followed by an announcement of punishment, with the accusation enhanced by an elaboration of Asa's folly. In prophetic oracles, the accusation is at times made to appear more shocking by setting it against a background of divine grace (e.g., Isa 5:4; Amos 2:9-11; Mic 6:3-5). Asa's folly was to disregard the gracious aid he had enjoyed previously and that would still have been available to him. If the king was congratulating himself on the success of his stratagem, he needed to hear how shortsighted he had been. Not only would he have secured the retreat of Baasha, but also the Aramean army would have fallen into his lap![257]

The reference to Asa's earlier victory is described in terms of reliance on the Lord, and by contrast the alliance with Aram is regarded as a switch of allegiance. The key word of the literary unit, "rely," bombards Asa's ears and the reader's eyes, recalling 14:11. Again crisis gave an opportunity to

256. E.g., Williamson, *1 and 2 Chronicles*, 256-58; De Vries, *1 and 2 Chronicles*, 296.

257. Curtis and Madsen, *The Books of Chronicles*, 389.

prove the Lord, but this time trust was put in human aid. The chronicler seems to have had Isa 10:20 in mind, which mentions relying (NIV; NRSV, "lean") on the Lord instead of on Assyria. Isaiah had considered reliance on foreign aid a besetting sin of the Judean monarchy (Isa 30:1-2; 31:1), while earlier Hosea had berated the northern kingdom for such improper action (Hos 7:8-12; 14:3). Such is the prophetic standpoint that the chronicler puts in the mouth of the prophet Hanani.

Verse 9 cites Zech 4:10, affirming the universality of the Lord's protection. God could cope with crisis from any quarter, ever ready to respond to faith with a demonstration of divine power. In fact, narratives of divine deliverance throughout chaps. 13–25 illustrate victory over the north in chap. 13, the west in chap. 14, the east in chap. 20, and the south in chap. 25. In this case, however, faith had been replaced by folly. In reprisal, Asa's lot would be warfare, not peace as before. The chronicler found a providential role for the warfare of 1 Kgs 15:16, which for him lasted the remaining five or six years of Asa's reign. This final period was no longer a test of faith but retribution for lack of faith.

16:10. Asa had responded in model fashion to a sermon in chap. 15. Now he compounds his errant spiritual attitude by rejecting the divine message. He takes out on God's messenger his resentment against God, putting the messenger in the prison "stocks," a fate for a prophet that the chronicler derived from the book of Jeremiah (Jer 20:3; 29:26). Some of the people were tortured. The ideal of a king's proper rule (2:1; 9:8; see also 1 Chr 14:2) has been left far behind. Presumably the chronicler adduced this persecution of prophet and people as the reason for Asa's illness in v. 12, which we are not given enough information to identify.

16:11-14. The royal epilogue in 1 Kgs 15:23-24 is used, with extra focus on the king's illness and burial and specifying the length of his reign from 1 Kgs 15:10. The chronicler identifies his main source as a document identified with the canonical books of 1–2 Kings, blocks of which have been used in his account, though he seems to have had access to other written traditions. If Asa failed to rely on the Lord in his military crisis, he also failed to "seek the Lord" in a personal crisis generated by his own wrongdoing, and instead turned to physicians. Asa did not take the opportunity to resort to God in prayer in his sickness (6:28), humbling himself and turning from his wicked ways (7:14). We are meant to understand that Asa's lack of repentance led to his death.

The report of an elaborate funeral, with lavish burning of spices (cf. 21:19; Jer 34:5), is a device the chronicler often used to give an overall evaluation of a reign. In fairness he wanted readers to remember that even if Asa fell from grace in his final six years, for thirty-five years he had been a good king. The chronicler so characterized him in 20:32 and 21:12 (cf. 17:3-4). Yesterday's scandals were not allowed to obliterate the integrity of yesteryear. The chronicler could not bring himself to apply the rigorous standard offered as a deterrent in Ezek 18:24, that "none of the righteous deeds . . . shall be remembered" (NRSV).

REFLECTIONS

1. Asa exemplifies a good person who turns bad. His story warns against spiritual complacency. In the terms of 1 Tim 1:19, Asa suffered a shipwreck in the faith. What counts is for the believer to have a steady walk with God in ordinary days, finding resources from God to cope with emergencies, and, if sin intrudes, repairing the damage by humbly seeking divine forgiveness. Asa failed the third test, fool that he was (16:9).

2. The heart of the chapter is Hanani's interpretive message. He is another Isaiah, contrasting recourse to foreign military aid with reliance on God. In a crisis, Asa looked around rather than up, forgetting the proven help the Lord gives to committed believers. Lessons of trust, once we have learned them, are to be reapplied when crisis strikes again. According to Paul: God, "who rescued us from so deadly a peril will continue to rescue us; on him we have set our hope that he will rescue us again" (2 Cor 1:10 NRSV).

3. Hanani, like Jeremiah, suffered persecution for his faithful witness for the Lord. The chronicler will return to the motif of persecution in 18:26 and 24:20-22; it stands out starkly against the mellow background of his standard teaching that loyalty to God spells blessing. Jesus echoes the motif in one of his ironical beatutitudes: "Blessed are you when people . . . persecute you. In the same way they persecuted the prophets" (Matt 5:11-12). It takes courage to witness for God in a hostile or potentially hostile environment. The writer of the Letter to the Hebrews, addressing a group who had previously suffered persecution and were likely to do so again, challenged them to recall the persecution that God's people in the Old Testament had endured (Heb 10:32-35; 11:35-37). He pointed them to the supreme example of Jesus (Heb 12:3).

4. Healing is a perennial topic on which Christians seek spiritual enlightenment. This passage gives only part of the biblical answer. The chronicler brackets recourse to physicians together with an alliance with a foreign king as a further example of resorting to human aid, rather than divine. Morally lapsed as Asa was, his disease should have been a warning of the Lord's displeasure. This malady went too deep for doctors to cure, irrespective of the limitations of ancient medical lore. Asa's reaction represented an evasive tactic, dealing with a symptom instead of going to the root of the problem and seeking God in the spirit of 7:14. It was like treating a decayed tooth with a pain reliever. In the New Testament, too, are envisioned cases of sickness linked with unfaithfulness to God (1 Cor 11:30). According to Paul's diagnosis, the sick Christians at Corinth would have been remiss to seek medical help rather than putting their spiritual malady aright. This text is not the only biblical tradition concerning medical help; Paul's reference to Luke as "the beloved physician" (Col 4:14 NRSV) reflects positive appreciation, while the intertestamental Ben Sira taught God's healing through the agency of doctors (Sir 38:1-15).

2 CHRONICLES 17:1–21:1*a*, JEHOSHAPHAT CHOOSES AND LOSES THE LORD'S PRESENCE

OVERVIEW

The four chapters devoted to Jehoshaphat indicate his importance in the chronicler's eyes. He has used the motif of divine presence, expressed by means of the preposition "with" (עם *'im*), to describe the reigns of David (1 Chr 11:9; 17:2, 8) and Solomon (1 Chr 22:11, 16; 28:20; 2 Chr 1:1). It has previously surfaced in important passages (13:12; 15:2, 9; cf. 13:8). Now it takes on a structural role in this literary unit, concerned with Jehoshaphat's reign. He and his subjects had opportunities to enjoy the Lord's presence in blessing that followed obedience (17:3), in the maintenance of social justice (19:6, 11) and in help against an external threat (20:17). This positive motif is interspersed with a negative one, alliance with sinners, represented by the northern kings Ahab and Ahaziah (18:3; 20:35-37). So the chronicler's account of the reign of Jehoshaphat provides a challenging sermon on the alternatives of association with God or with human allies, somewhat on the lines of a NT text: "As God has said, 'I will live with them. . . . Therefore come out from them and be separate, says the Lord' " (2 Cor 6:16-17 NIV).

At one point the chronicler slightly alters his source in order to highlight the motif. The word אתי ('*ittî*, "with me") in 1 Kgs 22:4 is standardized to עמי ('*immî*) in 2 Chr 18:3, and "we will be with you in the war" (NRSV)

is added. The use of the key word establishes five sections in an ABAAB pattern. These sections accord with the five narratives that make up the unit: 17:1-19; 18:1–19:3; 19:4-11; 20:1-30; and 20:31–21:1*a*. Three of the sections are also graced with the chronicler's prime term for spirituality, "seek" (דרש *dāraš*), in 17:3-4; 18:4 (NIV; NRSV, "inquire"); 19:3; and 20:3 (cf. the use of בקש [*biqqēš*, "seek"] in v. 4). In the fourth section, verbal phrases with the same role appear (20:32-33).

2 Chronicles 17:1-19, Finding God in Obedience and Blessing

COMMENTARY

The presentation of Jehoshaphat's reign in 1–2 Kings often involves relations with the northern kingdom (1 Kgs 15:24b; 22:1-50; 2 Kgs 3:4-27). Here he is considered in his own right as a Judahite king. This chapter functions as an introduction describing his rule. The following chapters either endorse the high assessment of Jehoshaphat or provide exceptions to the general tenor of his reign. Only at 17:1, 3 is there use of the 1 Kings narrative (1 Kgs 15:24; 22:43).

17:1-5. The gist of the section is provided here in summary form. It is structured with a spiritual center (vv. 3*b*-4) and a framework of divinely authored success (vv. 1-3*a*, 5). Jehoshaphat's life was characterized by loyalty to God. The accolade of spirituality is bestowed on him: He "sought" the Lord. An even more glowing testimony will be given in 22:9: "He sought the LORD with all his heart."

The observation is clarified by a comparison and a contrast. Jehoshaphat lived up to the chronicler's ideal of appropriating his father's faith, keeping the spiritual flag flying in the next generation. The chronicler follows 1 Kgs 22:43 in comparing him with Asa. But his own representation of Asa required him to distinguish between Asa's "earlier" period of faith, described in chaps. 14–15, and his later period of decline in chap. 16 (NRSV, following the shorter reading of the LXX [cf. v. 4*a*]; the NIV retains the MT's "David" and then gives the unlikely rendering "in his [= Jehoshaphat's] early years"). Jehoshaphat is

compared to his sinful northern contemporary Ahab in oblique terms. The chronicler presupposes knowledge of the final chapters of 1 Kings, where Ahab's devotion to Canaanite religion is narrated. By contrast, Jehoshaphat exemplifies devotion to the Torah. Such spirituality invited the Lord's presence in blessing, which is described in terms of military defense in vv. 1*b*-2. As in 11:5-12, the royal defense system was a mark of divine help, making Judah a strong nation. Blessing is further elaborated in v. 5, in terms of consolidation of his rule and riches and honor.

17:6-9. Verses 1-5 offer a digest of the rest of the chapter, where its themes are amplified. Jehoshaphat's adherence to the religious purity of the Torah, and so to that of the Temple, is illustrated in v. 6*b* with loose reference to Deut 7:5; 12:2-3. As in 14:3, the chronicler is writing idealistically and so does not use 1 Kgs 22:43, which he will cite later in 20:33. The compliment in v. 6*a* refers literally to a high heart. Elsewhere it connotes pride ("He took pride in the service of the Lord" [REB]). It here refers to high ideals and serves as a headline for both v. 6*b* and vv. 7-9. The king's wider commitment to the Torah finds illustration in vv. 7-9. The dating in Jehoshaphat's third year may be simply a literary device for the close of a short period of time.[258] An itinerant

---

258. M. Cogan, "The Chronicler's Use of Chronology as Illuminated by Neo-Assyrian Royal Inscription," in *Empirical Models for Biblical Criticism*, ed. J. H. Tigay (Philadelphia: University of Pennsylvania Press, 1980) 197-209, esp. 207-8.

team of teachers is envisioned as having been commissioned by the king. Here and in the related 19:4-11 the chronicler appears to have drawn from a source describing Jehoshaphat's judicial reforms. In this case, the promulgation of the royal law code was doubtless in view, and the chronicler adapted it anachronistically into a concern for the Torah, or Pentateuch.[259] In the light of 15:3, teaching and Torah went together—naturally so, since Torah relates to directions for life's journey, as was noted at 6:16, 27. A team of Levites and priests, backed by royal officials to lend authority to the enterprise, was dispatched throughout Judah on a teaching mission. There are post-exilic similarities with Ezra's commission from the Persian king in Ezra 7:6, 11-26 and with the expository task of the Levites in Neh 8:7-8. Here was a further example of Jehoshaphat's high ideals, instructing the people in divine revelation so that it might govern their lives. Such activity corresponds to Asa's concerns expressed in 14:4.

17:10-12a. The blessing mentioned in v. 5*b* is amplified in vv. 10-11. The gift of Solomonic peace, enjoyed by Asa in 14:1, 6-7, is combined with fear typical of a holy war, such as foreigners had of Asa (14:14). Another of Solomon's blessings, tribute from other nations (9:14, 23-24), appears in v. 11, while the increasing prominence of the king echoes that of David in 1 Chr 11:9, where it is accompanied by the formula of divine presence. Here was a noble scion of the Davidic dynasty.

17:12b-19. The theme of troops and fortified cities, broached in v. 2, is now expanded. Fortresses and military "supplies" were part of the defense system, which was manned by a standing army (vv. 13, 19*b*). As backup there was a large conscript army, whose commanding officers are listed in vv. 14-18. Along with the notice in 14:8, vv. 14-18 probably derive from a royal military census list that was available to the chronicler.[260] Doubtless the word אֶלֶף (*'elep*), here rendered in terms of thousands, referred there to much smaller units, though the chronicler has maximized them. In v. 14, the conscript army available in wartime seems to be equated with the standing army stationed in Jerusalem. The list was not adequately coordinated with its new context.

259. See Williamson, *1 and 2 Chronicles*, 282-83.

260. See Williamson, *1 and 2 Chronicles*, 261-63.

REFLECTIONS

1. The blessings of the divine presence enjoyed by a spiritually minded king are the topic of this chapter. In principle this theme corresponds to Paul's promise that the presence of the God of love and peace would attend in blessing those who pursued such virtues among their fellow Christians (2 Cor 13:11). A similar promise appears in Phil 4:9, that continuance in apostolic teaching and practice would secure the presence of the God of peace. We who want God to be with us in our lives are here given clues as to how to achieve such a blessing.

2. The theme of 17:1-5 is seeking and finding. The narrative develops the spiritual principle enunciated by Azariah in 15:2, "The LORD is with you, while you are with him. If you seek him, he will be found by you" (NRSV). The chronicler encourages his own constituency to commit themselves to God. The king's success is traced back to his dedication to the Lord. Seeking God, he found evidence of God's goodness flooding his life. For the chronicler, a living faith and well-being went together, and exceptions only proved the rule. Jehoshaphat stands as a spiritual role model for the chronicler.

3. The developments described in 17:6-19 are prefaced by a reference to Jehoshaphat's high ideals or spiritual ambitions. A strikingly similar reference occurs in the New Testament in the exhortation of Col 3:2, which literally may be rendered, "Think high things." Ambition is a virtue when practiced within the guidelines of "the ways of the LORD." The king's high aims were achieved in the twin areas of love of God and love of neighbor (17:6*b*, 7-9). The community was encouraged to take seriously the standards of the Torah for their lives. The chronicler's own communal ideal is transparent here.

4. The muster list at the close of the chapter describes one of the officers as "a volunteer for the service of the LORD" (17:16 NRSV). He evidently volunteered and rose to a responsible rank, but interestingly his work is described in religious terms. A word with the same root occurs in a royal psalm at Ps 110:3, which speaks of the king's subjects as volunteers to serve him in his divinely authorized campaigns. Similarly, the New Testament urges Christian slaves as they serve their masters to "work willingly for the sake of the Lord" (Eph 6:7 NJB; cf. Col 3:23). Happy is the person whose job is his or her hobby, to paraphrase George Bernard Shaw. Even happier is the person whose daily work is dedicated to God and done to please the Lord.

2 Chronicles 18:1–19:3, Collusion with a Northern King

COMMENTARY

The moral of this story is spelled out in the prophet Jehu's interpretation in 19:2: Jehoshaphat ended up in the wrong camp, helping the Lord's enemies. The king entered into an alliance with the northern king Ahab. The story is taken from 1 Kgs 22:2, 4-35, which is closely followed in 18:2*a*, 3-34. The focus of the narrative in 1 Kings 22 lies in the fate of the wicked king Ahab, unable to evade God's punishment. Here Jehoshaphat is the center of the story, as new material at the beginning, partway through, and at the end indicates (18:1, 2*b*, 31*b*; 19:1-3). If improper association with the Lord's enemies is the point of the story in the larger literary context (17:1–20:37), then such behavior also carries its own message, as is indicated by the chronicler's addition of the verb הסית (*hēsît*, in the hiphil, "entice") with a human subject at 18:2 (NRSV, "induced"; NIV, "urged") and with God as subject at 18:31 ("drew away"). This new verb acts as a counterfoil to the synonymous divine enticing of 18:19-21 (= 1 Kgs 22:20-22: יפתה [*yĕpatteh*]). The story becomes a study in manipulation, both human and divine. The three appearances of the verb, taken over from 1 Kings, are set in a new framework of enticement. The celestial scheme of enticing Ahab to his death is presented as a reprisal for Ahab's own scheming in 18:2. Ahab is outmaneuvered, and the punishment is shown to fit his recent crime. As for 18:31, Ahab's further plotting against Jehoshaphat is foiled. The Lord manipulated the tactics of the enemy charioteers to save

Jehoshaphat. So justice was done by punishing the bad king and protecting the good but gullible king.

18:1-3. Verse 1*a* repeats 17:5*b* as a critical comment on Jehoshaphat's marriage alliance in v. 1*b*, which anticipates 21:6 (= 2 Kgs 8:18). Although the Lord had lavished "great riches and honor" on him, he ventured into the marriage treaty, which was contracted among royalty for political and economic advantage. Ahab's name is introduced into the narrative from the start, whereas in the parent text it is delayed until 1 Kgs 22:20. The name spoke volumes to anyone who knew the account of his reign in 1 Kings, which the chronicler presupposes. His own comments in 21:6; 22:2-3 indicate his low estimate of Ahab. Earlier Jehoshaphat had resolutely followed a path of spiritual purity. Now he entangled himself with the apostate Ahab. The text drops a hint of the theme of the next unit, chaps. 21–23: the danger posed to the Davidic dynasty by this marriage alliance. The marriage of the crown prince Jehoram and Athaliah, daughter of Ahab and Jezebel, introduced a viper into the Judean nest.

This negative account of the association with Ahab is also colored by the theological judgment of chap. 13, where the chronicler distinguished between the people of the northern kingdom and the kings who led them astray from the Lord's chosen dynasty and sanctuary. Ahab had aggravated the sins of his royal predecessors by sanctioning an alien religion (17:3-4). So the northern troops and Jehoshaphat, both misled, were eventually to return home in peace, but Ahab had to die on the battlefield (18:16, 27, 34; 19:1).

Verse 1*a* also serves as an interpretative foil for v. 2 and judges Jehosaphat's agreement with Ahab to fight against the Arameans to be an act of folly. Jehoshaphat was dazzled by the extravagance of his state visit to Samaria, falling a naive victim to Ahab's wishes. As noted above, the verb of enticement (*hēsît*) becomes a key word in the chronicler's version of the story. It is used in Deut 13:6 of enticement to apostasy and so connotes leading someone spiritually astray. Such manipulation would not go unchecked.

The key word of the unit occurs in this section (v. 3). The chronicler stated in 15:2 that "the LORD is with you, while you are with him" (NRSV). Now Jehoshaphat promised to be with Ahab, the Lord's enemy. The chronicler adds the last clause of v. 3: *with him*. At least Jehoshaphat insisted on a prophetic seeking (דרש *dāraš*) of the Lord's will, with a spark of his old spiritual fire. Yet, when his request was honored and defeat was foretold, he persisted in the military enterprise, a campaign to capture Ramoth-gilead, a border town in the north Transjordan.

18:4-8. The scene of prophetic inquiry concerning the success or otherwise of the campaign is a variant of a conventional type scene illustrated in Judg 4:12-16 and 1 Kgs 20:26-30. The campaign is presented as a fiasco from beginning to end. It is a game Ahab wrongly thought he had won, ignoring the checkmate moves of his prophetic opponent. Jehoshaphat, again displaying a modicum of spiritual insight, was not satisfied with the glib replies of Ahab's seeming yes-men and asked for a second opinion. Ahab, with a cynical comment, had Micaiah brought to Jehoshaphat.

18:9-17. Zedekiah's symbolic action of vv. 9-11 affirms the sincerity of Ahab's prophets—a disconcerting affirmation, on reflection—and fills the time it takes for Micaiah to arrive. Zedekiah at first refuses to speak other than God's truth, then confirms the previous promises of victory—another disconcerting element. Ahab draws attention to it in v. 15, finding it out of character (cf. v. 7). How can these tensions in the story find resolution? The reader is disappointed by Micaiah's

parroting of the court prophets' assurances of victory. Yet Micaiah had to do this: He was affirming that it was a divinely given word. The sequel will show that it was deliberately deceptive, a genuine but wrong prophecy.[261] His provocative reply in v. 14 is justified by two reports of prophetic visions. The first, described and given a divine interpretation in v. 16, envisions a leaderless rout. The troops' trudging home unscathed implicitly contrasts with Ahab's fate.

18:18-22. The second vision is narrated and given a prophetic interpretation, resolving the paradox of Micaiah's two answers in vv. 14 and 16. It features the heavenly council, whose traditional role in war was to muster a celestial army to fight for Israel. Here its role is reversed, and it plans Ahab's providential defeat and death.[262] The heavenly court is the counterpart of the human court depicted in v. 9. The heavenly court has higher authority and greater power[263] and controls not only the outcome of the battle but also the means by which the prophets of the earthly court enticed Ahab to his fate. In the context of 1 Kings 22, the entrapment is regarded as morally justified, as the punishment of a wicked king. In 2 Chronicles the justification of this entrapment is reinforced by Ahab's reaping the harvest of enticement he had sown. The Machiavellian manipulator of v. 2 was lured by a countermanipulation to the doom he deserved. Ahab was told the truth (vv. 15-16), but the narrator can safely gamble that he would consider himself master of his own fate. In effect, the Lord gave him up to his own perversity (cf. Rom 1:24, 26, 28).

18:23-27. Zedekiah killed the moment of truth by refusing to believe Micaiah's sophisticated explanation. He rejected that complex kind of inspiration, genuine as to source but deceptive in content. In the wake of this convenient attack, Ahab ordered the prophet's incarceration, somewhat like that of Asa in 16:10, until Ahab returned "in peace," thus defying the prophetic vision in v. 16 and the oracle of judgment in v. 22. Micaiah's confident answer to both Zedekiah and Ahab was,

---

261. Nelson, *First and Second Kings*, 146, 148.

262. Dillard, *2 Chronicles*, 142.

263. S. J. De Vries, *Prophet Against Prophet: The Role of the Micaiah Narrative (1 Kings 22) in the Development of Early Prophetic Tradition* (Grand Rapids: Eerdmans, 1978) 42.

"Wait and see," a deuteronomic test of prophecy (Deut 18:22). His final word of appeal to the nations (NRSV, "peoples") is a gloss citing Mic 1:2 in the text of 1 Kgs 22:28, which the chronicler found and took over; its omission in the REB is a textual hypercorrection. It becomes an appeal for the chronicler's readers to listen open-mindedly, after Ahab had refused to listen in v. 18, and to be witness to Micaiah's vision of judgment and eventual vindication.

18:28-34. The text now takes the form of a battle report. Ahab still had a card to play, donning a disguise so that Jehoshaphat would be the only royal figure in sight. The two kings are deceitful and naive to the last. The rest of the battle story is devoted to the undoing of Ahab's ruse to endanger Jehoshaphat and save his own skin. Jehoshaphat was duly mistaken for Ahab, but had only a close shave with death. His cry, left undefined in 1 Kgs 22:32, is here interpreted as a prayer (cf. 13:14; 14:10). The prayer of this believer, though the trouble was of his own making, was charitably answered with divine help. The chronicler understands the efficacy of prayer to trigger the gracious help of the Lord. He also draws attention to the divine manipulation of events. Ahab had wanted to make Jehoshaphat the fall guy. God foiled him by showing the Aramean charioteers that this royal figure was not their intended quarry, enticing them away from him. The human manipulator of v. 2 met his match in the Lord. Ahab, still safe from overt Aramean attack, had the bad luck to be hit by a stray arrow, which found its way between the plates of his armor. Readers are invited to recognize divine intervention at work here.[264]

19:1-3. The chronicler skips details crucial for the Ahab-centered account of 1 Kgs

22:36-38, leaping to his own account of Jehoshaphat's safe return. The motif of peaceful return in 2 Chr 18:16, 26-27 parallels the account in 1 Kgs 22:17, 27-28; now it is extended and applied to the Judean king "in peace" (בשלום *bĕšālôm*; NRSV, "in safety"; NIV, "safely"). In accordance with the divine word, only Ahab died. The chronicler puts an interpretive message in Jehu's mouth, retrieving him from a northern context in 1 Kgs 16:1, 7. The prophetic postmortem begins with an accusatory question (as later in 24:20; 25:15). Jehoshaphat is taken to task for his association with Ahab. Divine mercy does not condone wrongdoing. "Love" (אהב *'āhēb*) is used in the Hebrew idiomatic sense of alliance, but the contrasted hating of the Lord gives it a nuance of unspirituality. The reference to divine "wrath" lacks a verb, so its tense may be past (NRSV), present (NIV), or future (REB, "will strike you"). The NRSV is probably right; it relates to Jehoshaphat's humiliating defeat (18:16; cf. 20:37).[265] Many commentators find a forward-looking reference, to a kind of sword of Damocles poised over the king's head and kept aloft by his repentant deeds in 19:14–20:30, but eventually falling on him in 20:1 or 20:35-37. In the latter passage, however, the judgment has its own adequate reasons, while Jehoshaphat's prayer in 20:6-12 lacks a corresponding confession of sin.

The divine deliverance (18:31) had taken into account the king's "good" qualities, his reform (17:6), and his spiritual commitment (17:3-4). He had "made a practice" (REB) of seeking the Lord. So God's rescue falls into the category of normative help, rather than redemptive help of the variety described in 7:14. Jehoshaphat had been more simpleton than sinner.

---

264. This reference to divine help is an addition of the chronicler. The Lucianic recension of the LXX of 1 Kings has it, but by assimilation to the LXX of 2 Chronicles, since the distinctive Greek rendering is the same and the motif of divine help is so typical of the chronicler.

265. See Schniedewind, *The Word of God in Transition,* 94, 96.

REFLECTIONS

1. Should one lie if lying leads to a good end? This question makes us uneasy. Doubtless we would become even more uneasy at the suggestion that God might give false messages to prophets, to lure the recipient to his or her death. Yet, that is what we find in these chapters. The chronicler himself was a little uneasy at taking over the story from 1 Kings 22 and so made a few changes. Does the New Testament contain any parallels to the chronicler's presentation of God's punitive providence in 2 Chronicles 18–19? A close parallel may be presented in 2 Thess 2:11: A fate reserved for those who refuse to love the truth and be saved is that "God sends them a powerful delusion, leading them to believe what is false" (NRSV; similarly NIV). If chapters 18–19 pose a problem, it is a biblical problem. "Can one trust God? Maybe, but only at the price of obedience and a genuine love for the truth, no matter how unpleasant that truth may be. Without these ingredients in one's response to God, the divine lie remains a distinct and terrifying possibility."[266]

We must examine how far our difficulties are due to an idealized, static conception of God, which may make us uneasy with the portrayal of a dynamic player in the ever-changing game of life, who responds to each new move with an appropriate counter-move. Certainly the chronicler's view of moral contingency accords with the last of the theological propositions expressed in Ps 18:26, "with the crooked you show yourself perverse" (NRSV; unconscionably toned down in the NIV). If the thesis of a just war is granted, one may compare this divine deception to the cracking of encoded messages sent by the enemy and the consequent feeding of misinformation to them to bring about their necessary defeat. In 2 Sam 17:14, there is a similar incident: Hushai misrepresents the truth at Absalom's court in order that the rightful king might be restored to his throne; Hushai's deception is then credited to the Lord's providential overruling. Ahab's death by entrapment is similar, as a case of his reaping what he had sown.

A theological protest against such a presentation of God arose within the Old Testament itself. Habakkuk complained that the Lord, in using the Chaldeans to punish Judean immorality, was using a thief to catch a thief (Hab 1:13). Yet the answer offered in Hab 2:1-13 appears to be that this was a necessary part of a long process of gradually establishing justice in the world. The mills of God grind slowly; yet, they grind exceedingly small.

2. Did the chronicler have in mind a post-exilic situation comparable to Jehoshaphat's ill-advised venture? He would not have taken the narrow stance of Ezra and Nehemiah with regard to mixed marriages, especially since he differentiated between members of the northern kingdom and their leaders. Perhaps political involvement with Samaria was an equivalent temptation (see 19:2). He leaves his readers with a black-and-white picture to apply for themselves. This principle comes to us through 2 Cor 6:14, "Do not be mismatched with unbelievers. . . . What fellowship is there between light and darkness?" (NRSV). May the Spirit help us to apply this principle aright, remembering that in this impure world the Christian cause is not necessarily advanced by insulation from sinners (see 1 Cor 5:9-13).

266. J. J. M. Roberts, "Does God Lie? Divine Deceit as a Theological Problem in Israelite Prophetic Literature," *Congress Volume Jerusalem 1986*, ed. J. A. Emerton, VTSup 40 (Leiden: Brill, 1988) 211-20, esp. 220.

2 Chronicles 19:4-11, Finding God in Social Reform

COMMENTARY

The keynote of the unit, the Lord's presence, appears in two places: as a cautionary assurance at the beginning of the king's first speech (v. 6) and as a prayerful wish at the end of his second speech (v. 11). We are led out of the shadows of chap. 18 and back into the sunshine of chap. 17. The chronicler split Jehoshaphat's reign into two periods of social reform, as he did with Asa's reign and his religious reforms (14:3-5; 15:8-15). He seems to have followed a source other than 1 Kings in his description of a judicial reform instigated by Jehoshaphat.[267] Underlying the reform was a shift from the old tribal system of justice to a centralized royal administration.[268] This shift is reproduced in vv. 5, 8, and 11 a, which frame the section. The chronicler supplied the two speeches, drawing on Deuteronomy for the content, and furnished the section with a headline in v. 4. He was doubtless conscious of the wordplay of Jehoshaphat's name, which means "the LORD judges," and it probably influenced v. 6. This unit is an amalgamation of a historical tradition, material from Deuteronomy, and post-exilic judicial practice, all wrapped up in the chronicler's distinctive vocabulary.[269]

19:4-7. Jehoshaphat learned his lesson, at least initially. He did not return to the northern kingdom, but devoted himself to Judean affairs. He set up a nationwide system of social reform from the southern to the northern frontier (17:7-9; cf. 15:8). This reform was enacted through judicial administration. To effect justice for the people was a king's divinely sanctioned duty; it had Davidic and Solomonic precedents (1 Chr 18:14; 2 Chr 9:8). It was a way in which the king could show concern for the people's welfare, as in 17:9. Earlier, Jehoshaphat had taken seriously the responsibility to affirm his faith as a member of a new generation (17:4). Now he encourages the people to respond to the challenge in the area of social ethics.

The national system of law courts is described in v. 5, and the king's commissioning of the judges is presented in vv. 6-7. The system included fortified cities as locations for courts. We are meant to think of Rehoboam's defense network in 11:5-10, situated along major roads, thus accessible to the surrounding areas. The commissioning speech is concerned with maintaining high standards in these local courts. Its form falls into the chronicler's pattern for speeches: an introduction

(v. 6) and a main part prefaced with "And now" (v. 7 [ועתה wĕʿattâ]). In content both parts run on parallel lines, arguing that divine considerations should affect human practice. Deuteronomy 1:17 influences v. 6. The local judges were to regard themselves as the Lord's representatives in their communities. Answerable to God, they were to be conscientiously aware of the divine presence with them, guiding their decisions. In v. 7, the influence of Deut 16:19 is evident in the warning against unjust decisions, especially when made under the influence of partiality or bribery. Such scrupulous standards are grounded in the Lord's character, portrayed as it is in Deut 10:17.

19:8-11. A higher court is set up in Jerusalem, and it, too, is launched with a commissioning speech. The MT at the end of v. 8 has "and they returned [וישבו wayyāšubû] to Jerusalem," which can hardly be right. If it refers to returning from the mission of v. 4, which is not consistent with the plural verb, this expression should have come at the beginning of v. 8. The reading of the phrase in the LXX, which the NEB adopted, is more reasonable: "[and the disputed cases of] the citizens of Jerusalem." This reading of ישבי (yōšĕbê) as "citizens" envisions the Jerusalem court not only as having an appellate function but also as serving as a lower court for the area of the capital. However, in v. 10 the reference to "every case" seems to resume the concern "to settle cases" at the end of v. 8. This resumption suggests that, as in v. 10, provincial cases are in view, rather than local cases from the Jerusalem area. Accordingly another option is to be followed, revocalizing the verb as the NRSV and the NIV have done (וישבו wayyēšĕbû; NIV, "lived"; NRSV, "had their seat at").

This higher court was made up of three groups: Levites, priests, and laypersons ("Israel") who were clan chiefs. In specifying Levites, the chronicler had in mind the Davidic appointment of levitical "officials and judges" (1 Chr 23:4; 26:29). The spiritual aspect of their role is spelled out: "to give judgment for the LORD," like the judges of the lower courts (v. 6).

In form the commissioning speech is like the one David addressed to Solomon in 1 Chr 28:20-21. It has a formula of encouragement

267. See K. W. Whitelam, *The Just King: Monarchical Judicial Authority in Ancient Israel*, JSOTSup 12 (Sheffield: JSOT, 1979) 185-206. See also Knoppers, "Jehoshaphat's Judiciary and 'the Scroll of YHWH's Torah,' " *JBL* 113 (1994) 59-80.

268. See Williamson, *1 and 2 Chronicles*, 287-89; Japhet, *I & II Chronicles*, 770-74.

269. See R. R. Wilson, "Israel's Judicial System in the Pre-exilic Period," *JQR* 74 (1983) 229-48, esp. 245-48.

(v. 11*b*). It gives a job description, which in this case is lengthy and given pride of place (vv. 9-10). It also mentions the provision of personnel, here chairpersons and supporting staff, beginning (as in 1 Chr 28:21) with והנה (*wěhinnēh*, "And behold" [KJV]). Verses 9-10 are framed in the Hebrew with the same clause, "thus you shall act." The speech includes norms to be followed as well as judicial procedures. The motive, "the fear of the LORD," is repeated from v. 7 and is coupled with virtues found elsewhere in 2 Chronicles: devotion to their work (cf. 31:12, 15; 34:12) and integrity (e.g., 15:17; 16:9). The procedures in v. 10 depend on Deut 17:8-13. The superior court was to review difficult cases referred by the judges of the lower courts, with the tasks of specifying types of homicide and establishing which laws were applicable.

The issue of motivation recurs in the latter part of v. 10. For both the superior judges and their provincial colleagues, handing down ("instruct," NRSV; cf. Exod 18:20 for הזכיר [*hizkîr*, in the hiphil] in a forensic sense) and receiving verdicts was a serious matter. The Lord would hold both groups responsible for doing justice, repaying unjust verdicts with reprisals. The superior court was to have two departments, religious and secular, the former headed by the chief priest (presumably the Amariah of 1 Chr 6:11) and the latter by the senior elder of the tribe of Judah. Levites were to function as court officers, with clerical and policing duties. At the end, the judges are encouraged to work well and are blessed with the incentive of enjoying the beneficent presence of the Lord.

REFLECTIONS

Uncontrolled power is frightening, and sanctions are necessary if it is not to be abused. The lower courts established by Jehoshaphat are presented as being free to make their own decisions, though if they referred cases to the higher court its verdicts were binding. Both types of courts were still subject to a higher mandate: the divine will. Since the Lord was the supreme judge, God's moral character was to be shared by the human judges. They were on trial even as they tried others.

Such spiritual ethics are worthy of Christian judges and of any believer who makes authoritative evaluations. In the New Testament, such considerations are applied to Christian slave owners. In Eph 6:9, both masters and slaves are told that they have "the same Master in heaven, and with him there is no partiality" (NRSV). Another perspective relating to Christian respect for secular authority may be found in Rom 13:1-7. In principle, officers of the state are God's ministers in enforcing law and order. God is the Lord of social order in the secular world. So Christians, for example, who cheat on their taxes are obstructing God's purposes for society. A commitment to social justice must be a prime concern of the church, even in the midst of a secular society.

2 Chronicles 20:1-30, Finding God in Trust and Deliverance

COMMENTARY

The unit's motif of divine presence surfaces as the climax of a prophet's speech of assurance, "and the LORD will be with you" (v. 17). The prophet refers to rescue from crisis, which God provides for faithful believers. That issue is closely tied to the secondary theme of the unit, "seeking the LORD" (v.

3, דרש *dāraš*, v. 4, בקש *biqqēš*, twice), here turning to God in religious rites as a response to an overwhelming attack. Once again the spiritual presupposition of 15:2 finds illustration: "The LORD is with you, while you are with him. If you seek him, he will be found by you" (NRSV).

The chronicler uses again the type scene of Asa and Zerah (14:9-15), but the narrative here is more complex. The chronicler breaks away from 1 Kings, evidently following a tradition of a successful military engagement—perhaps a minor conflict—at the northwest of the Dead Sea. The use of local names and locations in vv. 16, 20, and 24, the modernizing reinterpretation of Hazazon-tamar as En-gedi in v. 2, and the etymologizing of the Valley of Berachah in v. 26 appear to reflect a written tradition.[270] The present narrative reflects a rewriting in the grand style of holy war. According to De Vries, "Chapter 20 represents the ultimate in idealization" and brings "together a wide variety of formulae and motifs from the Holy War tradition, being surpassed in rigid stylization only by 1QM."[271]

20:1-5. Judah's enemies are described (vv. 10, 22-23) as a coalition of Moab, Ammon, and Mount Seir or Edom. This tripartite grouping suggests that in place of the impossible repetition of the Ammonites in v. 1, the MT should be emended to "Meunites" in line with the LXX, as is commonly done (cf. 26:7). This name survives in the later place-name Maʿan, twelve miles southeast of Petra. The chronicler understood it in this way, though in the original story Maʿan in the southeast of Judah, ten miles south of Hebron, may have been in view (see 1 Sam 23:24-26; 25:2). Moreover, the inappropriate "Aram" in the MT of v. 2 is generally emended to "Edom."[272]

Jehoshaphat's initial reaction of fear (v. 3) leads to a chain of religious events that culminate in his receiving the divine message "Do not fear" in vv. 15, 17. The cause of this fear, the "great multitude" of v. 2, is given an important role in the lament at v. 12, in the positive answer at v. 15, and in the battle report at v. 24, where, however, "the multitude" is no longer great (despite the NIV) but is diminished in death. The secret of the reversal is disclosed in v. 3: Jehoshaphat seeks the Lord in a series of religious measures that bring the whole community to the Temple to implore God's help, complete with wives and children (v. 13; cf. Joel 2:16). King and people adopt a united front in an all-out

mobilization, not for war, but for worship. As in the story of Asa in chap. 14, Jehoshaphat's vast army (17:14-18) was not to be used as a surrogate for faith in the Lord. The enormity of the crisis required all the people's involvement, by fasting to show the earnestness of the ensuing prayer and by offering communal prayer in front of the Temple. Jehoshaphat's location as he leads the prayer, "before the new court," reflects the post-exilic Temple. This court replaced the pre-exilic royal court outside the temple area. When the Second Temple was built, it was recognized as new and the name stuck.[273]

20:6-12. The prayer is a beautiful expression of human despair and dependence on the Lord. It follows the general structure of the communal laments in the psalter, such as Psalms 44 and 83.[274] Jehoshaphat recounts the Lord's past favors, which exemplify divine praiseworthiness (vv. 6-7), affirms the people's grounds for confidence in God (vv. 8-9), narrates the human predicament (vv. 10-11), and closes with a petition for divine intervention and an affirmation of total trust (v. 12). The barrage of rhetorical questions in which the initial praise of v. 6 is cast is unusual. It expresses well the customary role of praise in laments—namely, to challenge the Lord to live up to earlier saving help.

Two issues were at stake: the promised land as the gift of God (vv. 7, 11; cf. Ps 44:1-3) and the Temple as the place where God answers prayer. The Lord's people were heirs to two dispensations, inheriting two blessings to which they could lay claim. The promise of the land to God's "friend" Abraham (cf. Isa 41:8), realized in the initial occupation, still played a part in the Lord's ongoing will for Israel, as 1 Chr 16:14-22 had reaffirmed. The temple promise of 2 Chr 7:14, in response to the prayers of 6:28, 34, was valid as long as the Temple stood. In this context the somber background of human sin requiring divine forgiveness (6:30) is less relevant than the optimistic scenario of compliance with the Lord's will in 6:34-35. So in v. 9 the translation "the sword, judgment" (NRSV) is preferable to "the sword of judgment" (NIV).

The prayer takes a new turn with the "But now" of v. 10. What preceded was theological

270. See Williamson, *1 and 2 Chronicles*, 291-93.
271. S. J. De Vries, "Temporal Terms as Structural Elements in the Holy War Tradition," *VT* 25 (1975) 80-105, esp. 103.
272. See *BHS*.

273. Curtis and Madsen, *The Books of Chronicles*, 406.
274. See Petersen, *Late Israelite Prophecy*, 72.

preamble; here the main point is a crisis that required the Lord's presence. (A continuing element is the persuasive argumentation that persists into vv. 10-12a.) The invasion not only violated the Lord's will, but also constituted an act of ingratitude after Israel had spared their territory at God's bidding (cf. Deut 2:1-19; Judg 11:15-18). So there was a host of reasons for the Lord to intervene in the role of "our God" (vv. 7, 12), whose care extended to the present generation of Israel. Their powerlessness stands in contrast to God's "power" in v. 6. The final affirmation of trust, looking to the Lord for help, is a lovely expression of hope and faith, reminiscent of Ps 123:2.

20:13-17. In the temple system, prayer was sometimes answered by a prophetic message (as Joel 2:18-27 illustrates). This religious tradition appears here as a response to the expectantly waiting people. This message introduces the literary tradition of holy war that pervades vv. 14-29. The inspired oracle of the Levite stands in contrast to the travesty and confusion of 18:4-27. The pedigree of the temple singer Jahaziel is traced back four generations, presumably to David's time as a reminder of that new era of temple worship, which also anticipates vv. 19 and 21. The use of the possession formula "the spirit of the LORD came upon" indicates that Jahaziel was not a regular prophet.[275]

Jehaziel's message is a summons to holy war.[276] It has the three basic elements of assignments to a task: a call to fearless courage, a detailed description of the task, and an assurance of the Lord's enabling presence, like Solomon's commissioning in 1 Chr 28:20-21. The message also fulfills more specific functions appropriate to the context. The call not to fear is typical of the oracle of salvation that responds to a prayer of lament (e.g., Lam 3:57). The call is backed with a promise of divine help, which also characterizes this form (see Isa 41:8-14). The call not to fear is also a holy war motif (see Exod 14:13-14; Josh 11:6). So a variety of literary traditions is blended into this prophetic answer. The description of the task (v. 16) was presumably

derived from details of the underlying historical tradition. Verse 17 has a resumptive role; it is reinforced with an appeal to Exod 14:13. The God who could defeat Pharaoh was still Israel's God.

20:18-19. The reassuring message is followed by worship and praise. In usual worship practice, a prayer of lament was later followed by a song of thanksgiving, when the crisis was over. Praise after the prayer might anticipate this song, if the prayer received an affirmative response (cf. Ps 28:6-7). Such praise took the divine answer on trust, unresolved though the crisis was. This type of praise, which dared to take the Lord's promise seriously, is featured here. The group of levitical singers is presented: "Kohathites and [specifically] Korahites." In terms of the customary choral designations in the books of Chronicles, this group appears to be related to the later clan of Heman (cf. 1 Chr 6:33-38). In the post-exilic development of temple music, the appellation "Korahites" reflects a stage just before the singling out of the Heman group, which subsequently took a dominant role in the choral guild.[277] The chronicler here made use of a tradition older than his own time, which is also reflected in the Korahite collection of psalms (Psalms 42–49; 84–85; 87–88; in Psalm 88, Heman also appears in the heading). This use of an older tradition may indicate that, in chap. 20, the chronicler employed a source that had been written a little before his own period.

20:20-25. The narrative moves to an account of the battle. The "morrow" of vv. 16-17 had dawned. The royal speech of encouragement places a premium on faith. It echoes Isaiah's message from God in a similar context of military threat, a message sharpened by Hebrew wordplay: "If you will not take your stand on me, you will not stand firm" (Isa 7:9 NJB). There the oracle was presented negatively as a challenge; here it is recast into a word of assurance. Historically Isaiah belonged to the century after Jehoshaphat. The speech, as elsewhere, is the work of the chronicler, communicating spiritual issues to his own constituency. This function becomes transparent in the following exhortation, "Have faith in his prophets, and you will be successful" (NIV; the last clause

275. Schniedewind, *The Word of God in Transition*, 70-74, 116-17.
276. R. A. Mason, *Preaching the Tradition: Homily and Hermeneutics After the Exile* (Cambridge: Cambridge University Press, 1990) 64.

277. See Petersen, *Late Israelite Prophecy*, 75-76.

is unaccountably omitted in the NRSV). The message was to be found not only in Isaiah's prophecy but also in a larger collection of prophetic works that looked beyond judgment to salvation.

In an outworking of such faith, Jehoshaphat ordered anticipatory praise to be sung again, as on the previous day in the temple court. No particular choir is specified. Positioned as the army's vanguard, they were to praise the Lord for "the splendor of his holiness" (NIV, REB; cf. 1 Chr 16:29)—that is, for the radiant power they hoped would be demonstrated. From another perspective, the Lord's "[steadfast] love" in deliverance was anticipated. Promised "forever," it was claimed for that day. The praise here replaces the shout in holy war contexts (13:14-15; Judg 7:20; cf. Isa 30:29-32) or the trumpet blast of Num 10:9 (cf. 2 Chr 13:12, 14). The focus on the Lord accentuates the conviction that the battle was not theirs but God's (v. 15). The people were not to fight but were to watch the Lord defeating the enemy, as v. 17 had promised. Divine intervention duly came in v. 22, which is interpreted in v. 23 in terms of an act of self-destruction on the part of Judah's enemies. It is a conventional holy war motif, illustrated in Judg 7:22; 1 Sam 14:20; Ezek 38:21; and Hag 2:22. The enormous amount of booty reflects both the magnitude of the Lord's victory and the blessing enjoyed by the believing people. "Livestock" and "clothing" represent neccessary emendations.[278]

20:26-30. While anticipatory praise was featured in vv. 19 and 21, this passage represents standard praise celebrating what the Lord had done. The army, assembled to march back to Jerusalem, first engaged in a service of thanksgiving. The site, Berachah, which can mean "praise," is associated with a testimony to the God-given victory. Further celebration followed their return to the capital, in a processional service in which levitical

music and song and priestly trumpets stimulated praise. As in 1 Chr 15:25, 28, the jubilation took a religious form. The passage closes by mentioning a further consequence of the Lord's intervention in the battle (v. 29), while the whole section concludes with a notice of the cessation of warfare (v. 30).[279] The king who had trusted the Lord now receives the blessing of rest and quiet, like Asa before him.

In the chronicler's accounts of David's victories and of Solomon's power and prestige, it could be inferred that another agenda was being pursued: presenting a model of Israel's future hope. That agenda now reappears. Here was an earnest of prophetic salvation (v. 20). The hymn in 1 Chronicles 16 had offered the hope of enjoying to the full the Lord's gift of the land and the realization of God's kingship over the earth. Fulfillment of this double hope was inaugurated in the reigns of David and Solomon. According to Jehoshaphat's prayer, Israel's divine right to the land was at stake and so was the Lord's "rule over all of the kingdoms of the nations" (v. 6), while the aftermath attested to the fear of God falling on "all the kingdoms of the countries" (v. 29). The victory was intended as an anticipatory pledge of an eschatological kingdom.

The post-exilic community prized the message of salvation they found in the prophetic books. Correspondingly, the chronicler's message to his own generation is unmistakable in the exhortation, "Believe [the LORD's] prophets." The divine hope revealed there gave shape to Israel's future. Yet, even as the holy war narrative was a parable of eschatological hope, it issued a call for quietism, to wait in faith for divine intervention. Herein lies the relevance of the holy war theme, which leaves everything to God. The Lord's good time would surely come. Meanwhile, Judah was not to plunge into apocalyptic battles of its own devising.[280]

278. See *BHS*. See also Allen, *Greek Chronicles*, 2:89, 98.

279. De Vries, *1 and 2 Chronicles*, 326.
280. See Ackroyd, *1 & 2 Chronicles, Ezra, Nehemiah*, 151-52.

REFLECTIONS

1. This is a classic story of faith, gripping in its portrayal of commitment to God as ally when life wages war against us and "we do not know what to do" (20:2). It carries an existential message as well as an eschatological one. It is a beautiful paradigm of taking seriously grounds for fear and yet transcending them by a conviction of the divine presence that could cope with the monster and bring God's people safely through the crisis. Believers are not exempt from fear, but they have a God to whom to take their fears. Fear is like a smoke detector, warning that appropriate action should be taken against a fiery disaster. Recourse to God must be one such action; here it was the only option. Fear banishes our self-sufficiency, driving us to "seek" God by resorting to religious measures. At times of crisis, we need religious forms as vehicles of divine comfort. The temple laments in the book of Psalms were the Lord's provision for believers in need (2 Chr 20:9).

2. Using praise to challenge God is no part of ordinary prayer, but when crisis strikes it can express human frustration. It is a cry for God to become real in our situation, to live up to the creeds and hymns we tend to take for granted in calmer times. The chronicler had spiritual insight in linking faith with periods of crisis.

3. Apocalyptic fervor brought a temptation to take matters into one's own hands. Centuries later in Jewish history, orthodox Jews opposed the rise of Zionism as usurping the Messiah's role in taking the people of Israel back to their land. The chronicler used the model of the holy war, which left everything to the Lord as a warning not to try to help God by abortive rebellion against the secular powers. Meanwhile, there was plenty to be done for the Lord by inculcating the standards of the Torah in Judah's social life (17:9) and by promoting law and order as the divine will for the community the Lord had set in their own land (19:5-11; 20:7).

In a similar vein, the New Testament has distinguished between the work God has done and will do in Christ and the work to be done by the church. It looks forward to the second advent as a dynamic breaking into human history, like a thief in the night. In Rev 19:11-21, it is the King of kings and a celestial army who fight against human and superhuman forces of evil. There is a distinction in the books of Chronicles between the type of war a king fought with the Lord's help (e.g., 1 Chr 18:1-6, 9-14; 2 Chr 6:34-35) and the form presented in chapter 20, in which God fought without their participation. The New Testament speaks of the once-for-all campaign Christ fought against evil principalities and powers (Col 2:15). It also proclaims the ongoing fight of Christians in the Lord's strength against those very forces (Eph 6:10-17). The church trusts in a work only its Lord can do and that God will consummate. Within these parameters, Christians strenuously "fight the good fight of the faith" (1 Tim 6:12).

2 Chronicles 20:31–21:1a, Collusion with Another Northern King

COMMENTARY

The religious message of 20:1-30 was an application of the positive side of the proposition in 15:2. Now the alternative implicitly comes to the fore, "But if you forsake him, he will forsake you" (NIV). Jehoshaphat, no longer "with" the Lord, was "with" the northern king Ahaziah instead. The preposition occurs three times in the MT in the course of vv. 35-37, as the NIV attests. The dynamics of chap. 18 appear again.

20:31-34. The section depends on 1 Kgs 22:41-51 and takes it over as a block, though with a few small omissions and adaptations. The review of Jehoshaphat's reign in vv. 31-33 stands in some tension with the representation in earlier chapters. Presumably the chronicler regarded the positive assessment of v. 32 as a generalization, as in the more blatant case of Asa (14:2), which was also taken over from 1 Kings. The chronicler's view of Jehoshaphat's relation to Asa was more adequately expressed in 17:3. The king's life was good despite some temporary lapses. More seriously, v. 33a contradicts the statement in 17:6 as well as the tone of 19:3. The rewriting of the last part of 1 Kgs 22:43 in v. 33b shows that pagan high places are in view as they were in 17:6. The chronicler differentiated between the king and the people; the spiritual language of v. 33b was used positively of the king in 19:3. The chronicler may have meant that the people resisted the king's efforts at reform. Certainly the reference to traditional faith directs the reader to Jehoshaphat's endeavors in 19:4. The mention of Jehu in the source formula of v. 34 picks up his prophetic speech in 19:2-3, where he condemned Jehoshaphat's participation with Ahab. The reference leads nicely to a similar misadventure in vv. 35-37. The chronicler put the source formula to a new use in order to remind readers of 1 Kgs 16:1-4, 7, 12, an instance in which Jehu condemned the northern king Baasha for having led his people astray religiously. The text has nothing to do with Jehoshaphat, but in this way the chronicler justified his use of Jehu's name to condemn the alliance with a northern king.

20:35–21:1a. The disastrous enterprise is not military this time but commercial.

The 1 Kings account has been stood on its head. The chronicler evidently took Ahaziah's offer to Jehoshaphat in 1 Kgs 22:49 as having taken place prior to the shipwreck by interpreting the verb "said" as a pluperfect.[281] He construed it in terms of seeking a human ally instead of the Lord and assumed that Jehoshaphat's unwillingness to agree to Ahaziah's offer in 1 Kgs 22:49 was overridden in the light of the expedition in 1 Kgs 22:48. Then he gave his interpretation of the narrative by adding an oracle of judgment. The prophet Eliezer is not otherwise known, but his very name, which means "God is help," reinforces the rebuke and ties in with Jehu's complaint that Jehoshaphat had helped wicked Ahab (19:2). The reference to acting wickedly, added by the chronicler in v. 35, is ambiguous. Is the subject Jehoshaphat, as the REB, the NJB, and the TNK take it to be? The answer may seem more obvious, but the labeling of Ahab as wicked in 19:2 suggests that the NRSV and the NIV are correct in referring to Ahaziah. As in 9:21, the chronicler seems not to have known where in the world Tarshish was; the NIV again tones down the tenor of the Hebrew.

281. Willi, *Die Chronik als Auslegung*, 219; Williamson, *1 and 2 Chronicles, 303.*

REFLECTIONS

The chronicler allowed Solomon to go through life unscathed by failure, although he took seriously Solomon's own testimony that "there is no one who does not sin" (1 Kgs 8:46 = 2 Chr 6:36). Jehoshaphat was basically good (20:32), but he had a blind spot, a besetting sin to which he surrenders again in 20:35-37. Yet, despite temporary lapses, the tenor of his life was positive. God was "not unjust" so as "to overlook" his "work" (Heb 6:10 NRSV). The reassurance brings comfort to us all.

The people's unspiritual behavior contrasts with the king's own spirituality and efforts to encourage the people in this direction in 19:3-4. Jehoshaphat had shown the people the right way; it was their fault and not his that they failed to follow. This situation is in line with the principle of Ezek 33:7-9 that the wicked must be warned to repent even if they decide not to repent. Parents can find reassurance in this passage, when they are tempted to blame themselves for the actions of adult children who stray from the good ways they were taught.

2 CHRONICLES 21:1b–23:21, THE THREAT TO THE DYNASTY AVERTED

OVERVIEW

The accounts of the reigns of Jehoram, Ahaziah, and Athaliah make up a single unit. It traces in two sections the annulling of threats that the Davidic dynasty would be extinguished in spirit and in fact. The reigns of Jehoram and Ahaziah are presented as a pair, correlated in 21:2 and 22:3 with the linking "also" or "too." So the first section is 21:1b–22:9. Its first half, 21:1b-20, introduces the pernicious influence of "the house of Ahab" through "the daughter of Ahab" (21:6 = 2 Kgs 8:18). A fresh reference to it is created at 21:13.[282] That "house" stands in contrast with "the house of David" (21:7), which replaces "Judah" in 2 Kgs 8:19, a variation that strengthens the theological assertion of the permanence of the Davidic dynasty. The contrasting fates of their houses was suggested by "David" (2 Kgs 8:19), which is retained in 2 Chr 21:7. A new reference to "David" appears in 21:12, a challenge to the current Davidic king to live up to his royal heritage. That reference is matched by another comment about "the house of Ahab" in 21:13. The alternating references to rival dynasties sum up the passage's agenda.

The second half of the first section (22:1-9) contains two references to "the house of Ahab" (22:3-4), which are derived from 2 Kgs 8:27. They are echoed in 22:7-8 by two final references unparalleled in 2 Kings. Two

intervening references to J(eh)oram son of Ahab in 22:5-6 (= 2 Kgs 8:28-29) reinforce the ominous phrase. But the allusions to David in chap. 21 are absent. This stylistic monopoly prepares the reader for the despairing final sentence, "And the house of Ahaziah had no one able to rule the kingdom" (NRSV).

The second section, 22:10–23:21, records the reversal of this sinister situation. The house of Ahab receives no comment now. Restoration of Davidic rule is celebrated by two references introduced by the chronicler: an affirmation of the Lord's promise about the dynasty (23:3) and an account of the reintroduction of cultic worship inaugurated by David (23:18). The triumph of the Judean dynasty gave the chronicler an opportunity to draw attention to the permanence of the Davidic covenant and to the temple worship associated closely with it.

Jehoshaphat's reign marked a zenith in the fortunes of the Judean monarchy during the period of the divided kingdom. The next two reigns registered an all-time low. The chronicler polarizes the two periods in 21:12 and 22:9. Northern kingship, camel-like, poked its nose into the Davidic tent in Jehoshaphat's reign. Now it made its presence felt so blatantly that the Judean dynasty was almost wiped out by a combination of divine judgment (21:14, 16, 18; 22:7) and human sin. Almost, for the Lord's promise guaranteed its survival.

282. For the epigrammatic nature of this phrase in the OT, see T. Ishida, "The House of Ahab," *IEJ* 25 (1975) 135-37.

2 Chronicles 21:1b–22:9, The Apostasy of Jehoram and Ahaziah

COMMENTARY

21:1-7. Jehoram's reign is the first to be judged in totally negative terms. His successor's reign will be the next. These reigns form a dark backdrop to the Lord's redeeming

purpose, described in v. 7. The citing of 1 Kgs 22:50 in v. 1 is followed in vv. 2-4 by a grim tale of fratricide, which is generally attributed to the chronicler's use of another source. A flashback (see the NIV of v. 3) establishes Jehoshaphat's generosity to his other sons. Not content with the throne, the new king had all of his brothers murdered for their possessions. So the chronicler implies that Jehoram's punishment would affect his own possessions (vv. 14, 17; the Hebrew word for "possessions" is different in vv. 14, 17). This fratricide introduces the theme that runs throughout the unit: a threat to the royal family that puts at risk the very purposes of God. Here it is a threat from within, a multiplication of Cain's primeval sin.

Jehoram chalked up further crimes on his slate. The chronicler cites 2 Kgs 8:17-22 in vv. 5-10*a*, significantly varied by importing "the house of David" into v. 7. Mention of Jehoshaphat's marriage alliance in 18:1 warned readers of the grim legacy of the influence of the ill-famed house of Ahab. The house of David, chameleon-like, assumed the morally and religiously evil character of the house of Ahab so that it deserved the same fate (see 1 Kgs 21:22, 29; 2 Kgs 9:7-9). Divine grace, in the form of the covenant promise made to David, intervened, replacing the wages of sin with everlasting life for the dynasty (see 1 Chr 17:12; 28:7). It was a lamp that would keep burning, however dark and long the night (cf. Ps 132:17). It might even be extinguished for a time, like the temple lamps (cf. 2 Chr 29:7), but it would eventually be relit. This assurance looks beyond the coup of chap. 23 to a hope that the Davidic monarchy would one day be restored.

21:8-10. Verse 9*b* takes over the uncertain text of 2 Kgs 8:20, which speaks first in terms of victory and then of defeat. Here it presumably means that the king escaped by the skin of his teeth. The NIV paraphrases to this effect, while the NRSV gives a literal rendering. The narrative of the loss of Edom and of Libnah on the Philistine border spelled for the chronicler the providential punishment of Jehoram. The chronicler added his own theological interpretation of these territorial losses in v. 10*b*, using his term "forsake" and so reminding readers of the proposition in 15:2. In 2 Chronicles, the Lord keeps short accounts in claiming moral debts, if a new generation disdains the spiritual baton passed down from its predecessors.

21:11-20. Except for parts of v. 20, vv. 11-20 are unique to 2 Chronicles.

21:11. The chronicler drives another nail into Jehoram's coffin by accusing him of disparaging the Temple by constructing high places as alternative sanctuaries. This new sin is an example of assimilation to the northern kingdom (v. 6), specifically in its adoption of Canaanite religion. The mention of religious prostitution echoes 1 Chr 5:25, where the same verb is used of the northern tribes. Likewise, the Lord's stirring up the "spirit" (TNK) of foreign groups (v. 16) repeats the phrase used in 1 Chr 5:26 with reference to Assyria's deportation of the northerners. Judah under Jehoram sank as low morally as had its northern neighbor. This theme will be developed in chap. 28.

21:12-15. A letter from Elijah, the great prophet to the northern kingdom (1 Kings 17–19; 21; 2 Kings 1–2), is cited. The letter's historicity is questionable. It is implied in 2 Kgs 3:11 that Elijah was dead by the time Jehoram came to the throne, while 2 Kgs 1:17 suggests that he died early in his reign. The chronicler's recourse to a northern prophet reinforces his equation of the two kingdoms. He honored the tradition represented by the prophet, a tradition of opposition in the Lord's name to Ahab's immorality and Jezebel's patronage of pagan worship. Who better than Elijah to be the vehicle of this theology of providential retribution? The notes of accusation and punishment that run through the surrounding narratives are given a distinctively theological orientation in the letter, which takes the classic two-part form of a prophetic oracle of judgment. A general accusation of choosing a wrong role model, the house of Ahab, is followed by the specific one of murdering innocent brothers. "Better" is used in a judicial sense.[283] A double punishment is announced, a "heavy blow" to befall the people and the royal household and a serious illness for the king.

21:16-17. The narrative traces the detailed fulfillment of both reprisals. The chronicler evidently drew on historical traditions, which he also incorporated into the letter. The first concerned a local border raid, typically magnified by the chronicler.[284] The rendering "Cushites" (NIV) represents the standpoint of the tradition and "Ethiopians"

283. De Vries, *I and 2 Chronicles*, 334.
284. See Japhet, *I & II Chronicles*, 814-15.

(NRSV) that of the chronicler (see the Commentary on 14:9-15). A conquest of Jerusalem is not envisioned even by the chronicler, as 22:1 confirms. In v. 17, "the goods found in the king's palace" (NIV) are not in view, but those "that belonged to the king's house" (NRSV), meaning crown property. Ahaziah is called "Jehoahaz" with a reversal of the two elements of his name; perhaps this was his personal name, which was replaced by a throne name. Justice had been done. The killing of Jehoram's brothers was repaid by the killing of all but one of his sons (cf. 22:1). When he gained his brothers' possessions, he forfeited his own. The survival of a single son to ensure Davidic succession is consistent with the principle that the house of David would survive (v. 7). The motif of the dynasty's hanging by a single thread will be repeated in 22:10-11. In 2 Chronicles, as is also probably the case in 2 Kings 11:1, collateral lines may not provide an heir.[285]

21:18-20. The outworking of the second prophetic curse follows in vv. 18-19*a*. As in 16:12 (and in 1 Cor 11:30) fatal sickness is the mode of punishment, a premature and painful death that satisfies the chronicler's sense of outrage over Jehoram's evil reign. The repetition of v. 5 (= 2 Kgs 8:17) in v. 20*a* draws attention to the providential brevity of his reign. The quotation continues in the following verb, which repeats "He walked" (v. 6 = 2 Kgs 8:18), but now in a new, fatal sense, "He departed" or "passed away." It is as if the chronicler were saying, "There is a way that seems right to a person, but its end is the way to death" (Prov 14:12 NRSV). As he often does, the chronicler uses as an obituary the final circumstances, here the lack of a fire in his honor (cf. 16:14) and of burial in the royal cemetery. It may be significant that there is no reference to a literary source corresponding to 2 Kgs 8:23. Jehoram was best forgotten.

22:1-9. The attack of 21:16-17 is rounded off in the course of 22:1*a*. The chronicler follows 2 Kgs 8:26-29 fairly closely in vv. 1*b*-6. Ahaziah's age is given as twenty-two in 2 Kgs 8:26 (thus the NIV and the REB are preferred here, following the Lucanic recension of the LXX and the Syriac, whose reading is probably due to synoptic assimilation). The king

could hardly have been forty-two (NRSV with the MT), which would make him older than his father, according to 21:5, 20. The LXX has "twenty"; the MT may have arisen from conflation of twenty and twenty-two.[286] Ahaziah is another Jehoram in treading "the ways of the house of Ahab." The chronicler introduces three references to evil counsel in vv. 3-5. The NRSV has preserved the first two ("counselor," "counselors"), and the NIV the third ("counsel"). Ahaziah took the wrong advice, which led first to moral wrongdoing and then to the king's ruin. This reference to unethical behavior is here interwoven with the overarching theme, the influence of the house of Ahab. The queen mother, who *ex officio h*ad an influential role in the Judean monarchy (see 1 Kgs 2:19), was Athaliah, a member of the northern royal family.

The writing was on the wall for the northern dynasty, and Ahaziah was caught up in its destruction. His joining in a campaign at Ramoth-gilead resembles the story about Jehoshaphat's campaign at Ramoth-gilead in chap. 18, and it carries the same negative overtones as that account. In vv. 7*b*-9*a* the chronicler assumes knowledge of 2 Kgs 9:1-28; 10:12-14, abbreviating his source and concentrating on the southern royal family. In v. 8, reference to "the sons of Ahaziah's brothers" involves a harmonistic addition. Either the chronicler or a later copyist took "brothers" literally and adjusted the text to their having died earlier. At 2 Kgs 10:13-14, Ahaziah's "relatives" are the ones killed.

The chronicler supplies an interpretive framework in vv. 7*a* and 9*b*. The former verse brings to the fore the providential work of God, effecting the destruction that must lie at the end of Ahaziah's self-chosen path. Mention of Jehoshaphat's spirituality, which allows the corpse decent burial, widens the gap between grandfather and grandson (like 21:12). The reforming zeal of Jehu, commissioned by Elisha to crusade in the Lord's name against the house of Ahab, extended not only to the southern ally Ahaziah but also to other princes. It meant the radical depletion of the house of David. There was nobody of sufficient maturity and influence to take over. Was all lost?

---

285. De Vries, *1 and 2 Chronicles*, 333.

286. Myers, *2 Chronicles*, 125. See also Barthélemy, *Critique textuelle de l'Ancien Testament*, 1:499-500.

REFLECTIONS

1. Divine grace and justice clash in this section. On one side stood the "lamp" (21:7), which in 13:5, 8 the chronicler had interpreted as the sons of David perpetually ruling over the kingdom of the Lord (see also 1 Kgs 15:4). Confronting this promise of irrevocable grace was Jehoram's and Ahaziah's defiance of basic religious and ethical standards. The Lord had promised to wipe out the house of Ahab. Logically one expects the same fate for David's house, now that it had sunk as low as its northern counterpart. In the way, however, stood the promise of 21:7. Yet divine judgment brought the chosen royal family to the verge of extinction by the end of the section (22:1, 8-9). The story was a parable for the chronicler. The days of the post-exilic period without a king were an interim phase. The Lord's royal promises, affirmed in the prophetic books, could not be gainsaid. No less sure is the hope of the church, which has its own "lamp shining in a dark place, until . . . the morning star rises in your hearts" (2 Pet 1:19 NRSV). This hope is centered in "the root and the descendant of David, the bright morning star" (Rev 22:16 NRSV).

2. The spiritual correlation between north and south implied in the language of 21:11 represents a call for humility at this point. He was preaching against the Judah of his day, a proud elder brother who despised the northern prodigal. He reminded them that in their own past they, too, had been prodigal sons and daughters, needing the same grace from a forgiving Parent. Paul had a similar word of rebuke for Jew-despising Gentile Christians in Rom 11:17-22.

3. The motif of bad counsel, added in 22:3-5, builds on the precedent of Rehoboam in chapter 10. Ahaziah might have pleaded that he was not to blame, as the pawn of stronger personalities. But his plea would have been to no avail· The buck stopped here, in the decisions of the leader. The dice of heredity and environment were loaded against Ahaziah, but it was his own succumbing that plunged the dynasty into danger. The chronicler teaches personal responsibility here. Ahaziah forfeited the beatitude of those who do "not walk in the counsel of the wicked" (Ps 1:1 NIV). He was no Job, who testified, "I stand aloof from the counsel of the wicked" (Job 21:16 NIV).

2 Chronicles 22:10–23:21, The Coup in Support of Joash

COMMENTARY

This thrilling section depends on 2 Kgs 11:1-20, though the chronicler has left his fingerprints all over 23:1-21.

22:10-12. This episode stays rather close to the 2 Kings narrative. Athaliah usurped the throne, a double shock because she did·not belong to the Davidic line and was Ahab's daughter (21:6), with a history of leading the former kings astray (v. 3; 21:6). In four centuries of southern rule, this was the only break in the Davidic succession, brief though it was. The divine principle of the permanence of the house of David, enunciated in 21:7, invites readers to see the Lord's hand in events. At first, the situation became more hopeless.

The queen tried to kill off the remaining male heirs, in reprisal for her family members' deaths. The theme of the royal family's being whittled down reaches a climax.

This first passage is a tale of two women. Athaliah was in control, indulging to the full her opposition to the true God (cf. 24:7) and thinking she has dealt the same death blow to the house of David that Jehu had to the house of Ahab. She met her match in Jehoshabeath (a feminine form of "Jehosheba" in 2 Kgs 11:2), a Davidic princess born to Jehoram by another wife, according to Josephus.[287] The

287. Josephus *Antiquities of the Jews* IX.7.1-141.

chronicler adds that she was the wife of the chief priest, which would explain her hiding Joash in the married priest's quarters in the temple compound. It is not known whether this statement was the chronicler's inference or was based on a historical tradition. The princess kidnapped the baby Joash with his wet nurse, taking on herself the hazardous mission of preserving the Davidic line. The mission will pass to her husband in chap. 23, but she spent six long years guarding her secret.

23:1-21. Another contrast is posed, between the usurper and the baby king. Even before the boy Joash was crowned, the chronicler honored him with the title of king (v. 3), regarding him as the legitimate Davidic king during the queen mother's interregnum. In his version of the coup to restore the Davidic monarch, the chronicler closely followed 2 Kings 11, apart from working into its narrative three particular interests. The first is a concern to replace the foreign palace guards by Levites; by his time temple security was the responsibility of Levites.[288] The change was given theological warrant in Ezek 44:6-14: The intrusion of "foreigners uncircumcised in heart and flesh" profaned holy space. So the palace guards have been edited out of the text, and an idealized account has been put in its place in the interest of religious propriety. The plot fomented by Jehoiada with the officers of the palace guard now involved officers of the levitical security force. They mobilized Levites to carry out the plot, which was evidently planned to take place on a particular sabbath.

The proposed deployment of different groups of guards in various areas of the palace and temple complex described in 2 Kgs 11:5-8 is given a religious coloring in vv. 4-7. The orders are complicated in the 2 Kings account because of the addition of v. 6a to 2 Kings, which the chronicler appropriated. The 2 Kings account includes one set of instructions for those coming off duty who were to guard the palace in three groups, and another set for those coming on duty, consisting of two platoons, who were to guard the Temple and the boy king. "The probability is that the chronicler neither understood nor cared about the details of the arrangements."[289] He identified the first group with priests and Levites and made the orders include a specific ban on anybody else entering the Temple (vv. 4, 6). The second watch is identified with Levites (v. 7).

The chronicler took the reference to "whoever approaches the ranks [of the palace guards] is to be killed" in 2 Kgs 11:8 (NRSV) to refer to the temple precincts, and he chose to elaborate this order to kill in the anticipatory ban of v. 6. The same term (שְׂדֵרוֹת *šĕdērôt*) occurs in 2 Kgs 11:15 and the parallel 2 Chr 23:14. Was Athaliah to be brought out "between the ranks" or "out from the precincts" (NIV note; cf. the REB)? The chronicler's interpretation (v. 7) suggests that he interpreted this phrase in the latter sense. Jehoiada's command not to profane temple area with homicide in v. 14b is closely related to his instructions about where to take her in v. 14a. In both v. 6 and v. 14, a concern to protect holy space comes to the fore.

The second feature the chronicler worked into the narrative is the pervasive inclusion of the people in the plot. He took the mention of "the people" or "the people of the land," who suddenly appear in 2 Kgs 11:13-14, 17-20 (= 2 Chr 23:12-13, 16-17, 20-21), as his cue to project them back into the earlier narrative for both logical and theological reasons. Whatever political flavor "the people of the land" may have had in 2 Kings, in 2 Chronicles the phrase simply refers to the covenant nation, as the use of "the people" in v. 17 indicates. The first new reference to the people occurs in v. 2, where "the heads of families of Israel" are gathered from Judah. They form the representative members of "the whole assembly" (v. 3). The compact with the officers of the guard (according to 2 Kgs 11:4) is doubled, thus also becoming a pact with the representative assembly of God's people. The chronicler found warrant for this pact in 2 Kgs 11:17b, which he transposed here.[290] This compact with the people repeats on a smaller scale the pact that the newly crowned Solomon made with the nation gathered in 2 Chr 1:2-3. Moreover, the unity of king and people under God, which had characterized David's coronation in 1 Chronicles 11–12,

---

288. For the paramilitary role of the Levites, see Wright, "Guarding the Gates," 69-74.

289. Curtis and Madsen, *The Books of Chronicles*, 427.
290. Japhet, *I & II Chronicles*, 835.

finds its first echo in this chapter. Just as David depended on the help of his supporters who pledged themselves to him and to the Lord, so also the boy king Joash was backed by a loyal populace, or at least a representative group. The pact marks the triumph of the Lord's word concerning "the sons of David," the promise of a perpetual dynasty made to David "and to his sons" (21:7 NJB).

The presentation to the people assumed in the NRSV, "Here is the king's son," presupposes and puts into direct speech the narrative detail in 2 Kgs 11:4 that Jehoiada showed them the king's son. This translation is preferable to the more low-key rendering of the NIV, which reflects the punctuation in the MT and leaves the presentation to the people until v. 11. The former interpretation fits the popular sequence of the plot, injected into the text by the chronicler. The people are next introduced at v. 5, posing as ordinary worshipers. According to v. 10, "all the people" were to share in guarding the king, positioned in the temple court, while in v. 6 "all the people" (REB) were to observe religious protocol by staying out of the temple building. A careful distinction is drawn between the people's theological inclusion and religious exclusion, though in this emergency they are allowed access to the temple court.

The chronicler appears to have had a hermeneutical basis for introducing the people in vv. 2, 5-6. In the 2 Kings story "the guards" or "the runners" (2 Kgs 11:13) is a term that, in the Hebrew, stands in apposition to "the people." The chronicler understood the two terms as a single entity, "the people running," and also as objective warrant for changing "the guards" in 2 Kgs 11:4, 6 (in the standard Hebrew form הרצים [hārāṣîm]) into "the people," as the group who were running when the plot was put into action (cf. v. 20a, where this expedient was impossible and he converted them into "governors/rulers of the people"; in v. 20b, "the gate of the guards" [2 Kgs 11:19] became simply "the upper gate"). The renderings "all the other men" and "all the men" in the NIV at vv. 5-6, 10 and also "all the other people" in the NRSV at v. 6 miss the point. The unambiguous mention of "all [the men of] Judah" in v. 8 shows how the chronicler's mind was working.

The third concern in the chronicler's version is to parade the religious music and song he prized and associated with the temple era founded by David. The reference to trumpeters in 2 Kgs 11:14 suggested to him the priestly trumpeters. While he allowed the next mention of the people trumpeting to stand, he quickly followed it up with a reference to levitical singers, who were leading the cheers with religious songs (v. 13; cf. 1 Chr 15:16, 27-28). The destruction of the temple of Baal, along with its altars, images, and priest invited the promotion of the interests of the true Temple. The setting of "guards" at the Temple (2 Kgs 11:18) gave him an opportunity. The chronicler first applied פקדות (pĕquddôt) to the levitical gatekeepers, ascribing to them the role of protecting holy space, which is a strong theme of the section (v. 19). He also understood pĕquddôt as "oversight" and explained it in terms of the double system planned by David, who retained the Mosaic order of priestly sacrifice and supplemented it with his own order of levitical music and song (v. 18). It was a reestablishment of Solomon's institution in 8:12-15. The restoration of Davidic rule and of David's worship in the Temple meant the fulfillment of ideals cherished by the chronicler.

The preliminary "covenant" made with the people to carry out the enthronement of the Davidic claimant (v. 3) is fittingly followed by renewed commitment to the covenant with the Lord (v. 16). For the chronicler, it was a repetition of the people's covenant pledge in Asa's reign (15:12) and a model of spiritual devotion to God, which he commended to his own generation. The language of 2 Kgs 11:17, involving both people and king, and with the priest now acting as the Lord's representative, suited the chronicler's conception of covenant. The Lord's covenant with David (21:7) and the covenant with Israel overlapped, with the former providing a guarantee of the continuance of the covenant. The quiet of the city after the coup carried political overtones in 2 Kgs 11:21; in 2 Chr 23:21 it connotes divine blessing on the faithful (as in 15:15).

REFLECTIONS

1. The dramatic contrast in 22:10-12 is a link in a biblical chain. It begins with the hiding of baby Moses in the bulrushes and culminates in the spiriting away of the infant Jesus from the wrath of King Herod. Whether it was a pharaoh, an Athaliah, or a Herod, the wicked ruler met his or her match in the providential working of God. They did their worst and thought they had triumphed, unaware of the loophole that spelled their failure. In this episode, a seminal victory is won, which, like the moral victory of Dunkirk in World War II, allows a decisive encounter to be mounted at a later stage. It crystallizes the theme that runs throughout the Bible and throughout the history of the church and the synagogue: the triumph of the remnant. It speaks to the people of God whenever they find themselves a beleaguered minority.

2. The *leitmotif* of the two royal houses runs through this unit, with that of the house of Ahab rising to a savage crescendo until it is silenced and followed by a resurgence of the sweeter melody. This saga of an overwhelming threat to the Davidic dynasty and its eventual removal is reminiscent of Rimsky-Korsakov's arrangement of Mussorgsky's *A Night on Bald Mountain*. The increasingly strident music represented in the dance of the witches of the power of evil is stilled by the dawning of a new day and the tolling of a church bell. Corresponding to that finale is the closing paragraph, 23:16-21, which speaks of the triumph of good and the enjoyment of rest. God is the ultimate winner in this terrible struggle. The Davidic line, the Temple, and the community of faith are all beneficiaries of the divine victory. The story became for the chronicler a parable of hope. All who live in dark days and labor for a good cause can read it as such for themselves as well.

3. The tale of the two women presents contrasted cameos of self-seeking evil and unselfish heroism in the Lord's service. Athaliah stands for a regime of cruel oppression. Jehoshabeath is the heroine of a resistance movement, risking her life in order that good may eventually triumph. She is a role model for all who take a stand with God when evil is rampant (cf. Heb 11:33).

4. The rivalry of royal houses comes to a poignant interim climax in the course of this section. The house of David lives on in a baby. Is this the King? Yes, the chronicler claims, as surely as Matthew does in his birth narrative. In Matt 2:1-18, King Herod pits his power against one who is born King of the Jews. In both narratives, weakness and power are polarized. As in a later age, here "God chose what is weak in the world to shame the strong" (1 Cor 1:27 NRSV). Christians still know of hiddenness, awaiting the revelation of the Son of David as the key to truth and right (Col 3:1-10).

5. Restoration of royalty and of right religion is intertwined in chapter 23. Its most obvious feature is the protection of holy space devoted to the Lord. So gatekeepers are stationed to keep out those of the people who are unclean (23:19). The chronicler acts as a literary gatekeeper throughout the story, taking Ezekiel 44 to heart and idealistically expelling the foreign palace guard from the original narrative. In fact, the old guard is replaced not only by the Torah-accredited priests and Levites (cf. Numbers 18), but also by the covenant people, who had an essential stake in the vindication of King and Temple. The New Testament, especially in the Letter to the Hebrews, fuses the themes of holiness and the people still further. Now "we have confidence to enter the Most Holy Place . . . by a new and living way" (Heb 10:19-20 NIV). Yet, just as the chronicler's story is a paradigm of promise and hope to work toward, so, too, this new spiritual access has been inaugurated but not yet consummated: "Let us hold unswervingly to the hope we profess, for he who promised is faithful" (Heb 10:23 NIV).

6. Many themes cherished by the chronicler crowd into this section. It is a glorious moment of revelation and attained potential. It portrays ideals concerning what ought to be and what was yet to be. No wonder the section closes with notes of joy and peace, inspired by the recognition of the true King. In like spirit, Luke's Gospel lets us hear the angels' song of peace and joy at the birth of the Davidic Messiah, in fulfillment of God's ancient word of covenant promise (Luke 1:69-75; 2:4-14).

2 CHRONICLES 24:1–26:23, HOW TO LOSE THE RACE, IN THREE LESSONS

OVERVIEW

These chapters present three Jekyll and Hyde scenarios of initial obedience to God and subsequent apostasy. They preach in narrative form a triple warning against abandoning the true faith. In each case, the first half opens with a commendatory "did what was right in the sight of the LORD" (NRSV), followed by a negative qualifying clause about the king's short-lived virtue (24:2, from 2 Kgs 12:3; 25:2; 26:4-5). In the first and third of the three reigns described, virtue is credited to heeding a wise old counselor (24.17; 26:5), and in the first and second wise counsel is rejected (24:21-22; 25:16, 20). In the second and third reigns, the second phase features pride (25:19, from 2 Kgs 14:10; 26:16).

Each of the three kings was "running well" for a time, to use the metaphor of Gal 5:7 (NRSV), but each failed to finish the race. The chronicler seems to be using them to illustrate the case in Ezek 18:24, 26 (cf. 33:12-13), where "the righteous turn away from their righteousness and commit iniquity" (NRSV) and are punished with premature death. He wrote from a pastor's heart, providing spiritual case studies for his own generation to heed.

2 Chronicles 24:1-27, Joash Listens to the Wrong Advice

COMMENTARY

For the most part, the chronicler followed the account of Joash's reign in 2 Kings 12, but he interpreted it differently. He understood in a restrictive sense the statement in 2 Kgs 12:3 about lifelong loyalty to the Lord because of Jehoiada's influence, taking it like the NIV's (harmonistic) rendering, "All the years Jehoiada the priest instructed him." The chronicler's report of regular sacrificing while Jehoiada was alive (v. 14) provides a summary for vv. 2-13 and reinforces his understanding of v. 2. This latter end is also served by Jehoiada's involvement in organizing the temple repairs (vv. 12, 14). Why did the chronicler split Joash's reign into good and bad periods? He was encouraged to do so by the misfortunes at the end of his reign,

foreign invasion, and an internal conspiracy that led to his assassination. He conceived of two providentially coherent phases, before and after Jehoiada's demise, the first marked by obedience and blessing and the second by disobedience and unmitigated disaster.[291] This structuring made it expedient to omit, or at least postpone, 2 Kgs 12:3 with its negative mention of worship at the high places.

Chapter 23 has left readers with a sense of relief that now all was well in the palace and the Temple and throughout the land. And so it was at first under Jehoiada's tutelage. In 24:3, the chronicler adds a vignette of divine

291. See the parallel reversal found in the two phrases by M. P. Graham, "The Composition of 2 Chronicles 24," in *Christian Teaching: Studies in Honor of LeMoine G. Lewis*, ed. E. Ferguson (Abilene: Abilene Christian University, 1981) 138-55, esp. 140.

blessing to cap the obedience of 24:2. After the decimation of the royal family in the previous unit, their increase is a welcome sign that the threat to the dynasty was now over.

24:1-14. The account of the temple repairs in 2 Kgs 12:14-16 has been used loosely to illustrate Joash's obedience, which relates both to the Torah and to the Temple. The theme of repairing the Temple, which runs throughout the 2 Kings account in speech and narrative (2 Kgs 12:5-7, 12, 14), is precisely paralleled only at vv. 5 and 12 (= 2 Kgs 12:5, 12), but the chronicler begins his account by announcing Joash's plans for restoration in v. 4 and ends it by adding a long sentence about its having been accomplished in v. 13. This generalized packaging suggests that he intended to inspire his contemporaries to maintain the Temple—joyfully (v. 10). This idealistic perspective explains in part the reversal of 2 Kgs 12:13 in v. 14; so liberal was the funding that vessels could be provided for the Temple (cf. Ezra 8:25). The chronicler also wanted to supply a positive counterpart to the note he had added in v. 7 about the misappropriation of consecrated articles in Athaliah's reign. Moreover, the chronicler has in mind the tabernacle tax, part of which was used to furnish the sanctuary (Exod 38:24-31). The tabernacle had been replaced by the Temple as the sanctuary Israel was obliged to maintain and keep equipped.

The chronicler was concerned to honor the Torah stipulations that related to the sanctuary. In Israel's wilderness period, the tabernacle had been maintained by an annual tax of half a shekel (see Exod 30:11-16). Scholars differ as to whether 2 Kgs 12:4 refers to this tax, but the chronicler explicitly cites it. He characteristically emphasized the Torah by twice naming "Moses the servant of the LORD/God" (vv. 6, 9) as the venerable author of the tax. In mentioning the initial hesitation of the temple personnel (a simplification of the religious politics in 2 Kgs 12:5-8) and the eventual glad giving of leaders and people, strong hints were dropped to his own generation.[292] In the post-exilic period, there seems to have been a reluctance to pay the temple tax, perhaps due to economic difficulties

in the early part of the period. A pledge to pay the tax is written into the covenant of rededication to the Lord in Neh 10:32-33. The chronicler used both 1 Chronicles 29 and the present narrative, notably v. 10, to provide models for his readers of joyful giving to God's work. Whereas in the former passage it was presented as a Davidic ideal, here it has the backing of the Torah.

Two aspects of proper religious practice are introduced. First, in v. 8 the location of the chest is specified as being outside the temple gate—that is, outside the inner or temple court. In deference to the Temple's sanctity, the laity was restricted to the outer court, though in the emergency of 23:5 the chronicler had relaxed this ruling. Second, in v. 14b the regular sacrifices of burnt offering align with both the Torah and Solomon's institution of them at the Temple (2:4; 8:12-13).

24:15-16. The chronicler pauses to note the honorable burial of Joash's mentor, after a patricharchal-like longevity that reflected God's blessing on his good work on behalf of the Temple and the dynasty. This latter work is defined in terms of "Israel," so close were the respective covenants in the chronicler's thinking. Jehoiada's burial in the royal cemetery, unlike that of his royal protégé (v. 25), communicates his high regard for the priest's achievements.

24:17-19. The rest of Joash's reign takes a shockingly different turn. As with Asa in chap. 16, the chronicler reasoned back from the military and political crises of 2 Kgs 13:17-18, 20-21 and thought that Asa had forsaken the Lord. The king's life-style degenerated into a vicious cycle of wrongdoing. Joash lent his ear to less worthy counselors who hankered after precedents set by Athaliah. Verse 18a is the chronicler's elaboration of the worship at high places in 2 Kgs 12:3, moved here for schematic reasons. Asa had rejected the religious orthodoxy of vv. 4-14, abandoning the Temple. This time also spells a generational shift from "the God of their fathers." Jehoiada's piety was forgotten. Divine "wrath" was incurred, to which Zechariah would give vent. Yet, the Lord gave a second chance by sending prophets to urge repentance. In the Hebrew the phrase "bring them back" (להשׁיבם *lahăšîbām*) is the causative form of the verb "turn" (שׁוב *šûb*) in

---

292. For the non-secondary nature of 24:5*b*-6, see Dillard, *2 Chronicles*, 189-90.

7:14. It was a cue for the people to claim that divine provision for backsliders. Their refusal augments the wrong listening of v. 17.

24:20-22. When these warnings went unheeded, the Lord gave a third chance through Zechariah, the son of the venerable Jehoiada, not willing that any should perish (Ezek 33:11; see also 2 Pet 3:9). The chronicler may have known a prophetic tradition referring to Zechariah; here Zechariah's words reflect the perspective of the chronicler. The message of judgment was not final but was intended to bring repentance (cf. 12:5-6). The accusation is framed in a rhetorical question, as in 19:3 and 25:15. It draws on Num 14:41, citing the Torah even as it charges its breach as worshiping at the pagan high places (cf. Deut 12:2-6). The grim mirror-image principle of 1 Chr 28:9; 2 Chr 12:5; 15:2 is repeated, but to no avail. Zechariah's patronym did not protect him from lynching, at the king's urging. This inspired priest, standing on a platform inside the temple court, was an easy target for rocks hurled by a mob undeterred by the sanctity of the location. The chronicler lays the responsibility on the king's shoulders, finding it a shocking response to Jehoiada's loyal service. His failure to remember provides a play on the victim's name, which means "The LORD remembers." The Lord did indeed remember, by answering Zechariah's prayer. The dying priest had the last word, indicating that the fate of king and priest was now sealed. Judgment incurred after prophetic warnings had been rejected is a repeated theme until it culminates in exile (16:7-10; 25:15-16; 33:10-11; 36:15-16).

24:23-27. Now the moral stage has been set for the calamities described in 2 Kgs 12:17-18, 20-21. The divine wrath (v. 18) is realized through foreign invasion and a palace coup. Precise correspondence between fault and fate is traced. The national leaders, Joash's misleaders, are targeted for death (vv. 17, 23). Conspiracy against Zechariah, in which the king was involved, is requited by a court conspiracy against him (vv. 21, 25-26). The king who killed God's messenger is himself killed; the chronicler interprets the conspiracy as divine judgment for the murder of Zechariah (see vv. 22, 25, where "sons" in the MT is rightly emended to "son"). Forsaking the Lord is duly repaid (vv. 20, 24). So the

tables are turned. Ironically, a small Aramean force defeated "a very great army" (v. 24). The Lord sided with the outnumbered, as in 13:3-18 and 14:8-15, this time backing Judah's foes. Mention of the king's dishonorable burial place is a last word of evaluation, though it formally disagrees with 2 Kgs 12:21. The common grave contrasts with the honor paid to the non-royal Jehoiada in v. 16. In v. 26, the extra information that the conspirators were sons of Ammonite and Moabite women may be due to the chronicler's having associated their names with their presence in a list relating to interracial marriages in Ezra 10:22-23, 27, 33, 43.[293]

At the close, the chronicler tries to find a good word to say about Joash concerning the repair of the Temple, but it enhances the heinousness of his idolatry and his execution of Zechariah in vv. 18 and 21. The reference to a literary source in v. 27 is probably a device to sum up key aspects of Joash's reign.[294]

The figure of Jehoiada not only dominates the first half of the chapter, but also haunts the second half (vv. 17, 20, 22, 25) as a symbolic measure of the king's degeneration. A term that pervades the second half is the verb "forsake" or "abandon" (עָזַב *'āzab*), in a literary pattern of wrongdoing and retribution. Each of the four parts into which it falls, vv. 17-19, vv. 20-22, vv. 23-24, and vv. 25-26, uses this verb. In v. 18, the forsaking of the Temple marks the abandoning of true, traditional faith. In v. 20, it is interpreted as forsaking the Lord, which incurs the curse of being forsaken in turn. Verse 24 reiterates the sin of vv. 18 and 20, now as the reason for Judah's punishment, with repetition of the generational implications of v. 18. The last case, in v. 25, is concealed by the English translations. Half dead, Joash was abandoned by his enemies, left to die. The verb traces the final outworking of the king's God-forsakenness. It is the polar opposite of the fellowship with the Lord, highlighted in the Jehoshaphat unit.

293. M. P. Graham, "A Connection Proposed Between 2 Chr 24, 26, and Ezra 9–10," *ZAW* 97 (1985) 256-58.

294. See Williamson, *1 and 2 Chronicles*, 326. See also McKenzie, *The Chronicler's Use of the Deuteronomistic History*, 111-12.

REFLECTIONS

1. Joash's spirituality is illustrated in his efforts to repair the Temple. His is a down-to-earth piety, concerned with renovation of fabric and woodwork. The instruments of human faith have a built-in obsolescence. Maintaining a practical faith is like going up a down escalator. One has to move to stay in the same place on the escalator, in order to offset a downward pull. A church, understood in terms of place or people, needs effort to counteract natural wear and tear.

In the case of the Temple, a special factor made repairs necessary: damage and defilement caused in the interregnum of the "wicked" queen (24:7). The repair work was an implementation of the king's and the people's rededication to the Lord (23:16). It was a positive counterpart to the negative work of 23:17: the tearing down of Baal's images and altars. The undoing of wrong had to be succeeded by doing "what was right in the sight of the LORD" (24:2). Only thus is true spirituality attained.

2. Joash was also alert to the relevance of the Torah. The chronicler emphasizes the Torah's stipulation of the tabernacle tax and reapplies it to the Temple. Similarly, Paul appears to have translated the temple tax into a corresponding obligation laid on the churches he planted to support the poor church in Jerusalem (Rom 15:25-28; 2 Corinthians 8–9).[295] Both the chronicler and Paul were using a typological principle. Each transferred a responsibility in the old dispensation to another in the new. This typologizing insists that dipping regularly into pocket and purse remains a measure of the believer's spirituality.

3. The spiritual shift after Jehoiada's death provides the chronicler with an opportunity to dwell on the generational aspect of his doctrine. "The LORD, God of their fathers" (24:18, 24 NIV) had been abandoned. Jehoiada's faith was not taken over by the next generation. So in the person of the king they reaped what they had sown, as the precise parallels drawn between offense and punishment show. A positive counterpart to this lesson occurs in Heb 13:7-9: "Remember your leaders, those who spoke the word of God to you; consider the outcome of their way of life, and imitate their faith. Jesus Christ is the same yesterday and today and forever. Do not be carried away by all kinds of strange teachings" (NRSV).

4. Justice and grace tussled in the divine heart. The opportunity of 7:14 stayed open longer than one might have expected. Eventually Zechariah had to utter a grim prayer of requital. Christian readers may be tempted to contrast the gracious prayer of Jesus on the cross, "Father, forgive them, for they do not know what they are doing" (Luke 23:34), or the cry of Stephen, the first Christian martyr, "Lord, do not hold this sin against them" (Acts 7:60). But one may not contrast New Testament grace with Old Testament wrath; Luke 11:47-51 and Rev 6:10; 19:2 are worth comparing with Zechariah's stern prayer (2 Chr 24:22). The inspired priest was not praying a personal prayer of vengeance. Divine overtures had been spurned time after time, and this last refusal sealed the people's fate. They had lost their last chance. It could hardly be said that they did not know what they were doing. The Lord's hands were tied, as if to say, "What else can I do?" (see Jer 9:7).[296] The redeeming feature in the chronicler's program is that God gives each generation a fresh opportunity to respond. God offers chance after chance, but these moments leave us in God's debt, accountable if we fail to respond.

The assassination of Zechariah finds a place in a woe uttered by Jesus that discerns a crimson thread "from the blood of Abel to the blood of Zechariah, who perished between the altar and the sanctuary" (Luke 11:51 NRSV: cf. Matt 23:35). This incident in Chronicles is regarded as the culmination of the Old Testament record of human rejection of God.

295. See K. F. Nickle, *The Collection: A Study in Paul's Strategy*, SBT 48 (Naperville, Ill.: Allenson, 1966) 87-93.
296. Cf. Fretheim, *The Suffering of God*, 122-26.

2 Chronicles 25:1-28, Amaziah Finds a New Faith

COMMENTARY

Once again the reign is split down the middle with an initial period of favor and then a fall from grace. The chronicler's added reference to Amaziah's lack of wholehearted-ness (v. 2) relates to this spiritual inconsistency. This verse anticipates the judgment in vv. 14-16, but also alludes to the lesser flaw (v. 6), which at least the king was prepared to put right.

The chronicler found in the account of Amaziah's reign in 2 Kgs 14:1-20 four pieces of an incomplete jigsaw, two relating to positive events and two to negative ones. They dictated his schematic division of the reign, but failed to give a complete theological picture. The chronicler supplied vv. 14-16 as the missing piece, which explained the following two negative incidents. He harked back to it in the material he added at vv. 20b and 27a.[297]

25:1-4. The first episode (vv. 3-4) is taken over, along with vv. 1-2a, from 2 Kgs 14:1-3, 5-6. The reference to compliance with the Torah (v. 4) obviously coincides with one of the chronicler's interests. Honoring the Torah illustrates the king's having done right in the Lord's sight. Although Joash's murderers had been agents of divine providence (according to 24:25), their recourse to illegality could not be condoned. The Torah citation about limiting reprisals is taken from Deut 24:16, which states that parents and children will not be punished for each other's offenses. Appeal is also made to the law in Ezek 18:20 that only the offender will receive punishment. The judicial principle provided the prophet's theological tenet that the Lord operated providentially within a single generation, a tenet that finds ample illustration in the chronicler's narratives about kings.

25:5-13. The second episode concerns a successful campaign against Edom. It is an expansion of a single verse, 2 Kgs 14:7, which is reflected at v. 11. In vv. 5-6, the chronicler

was probably able to amplify it with a detail from military census lists arranged according to the reigns of kings (see 14:8; 17:14-17). The damage that the Emphraimite merce-naries inflicted on Judah probably also had an objective basis; its inconsistency with the promise of v. 9 is an argument against free composition at this point. Amaziah's having supplemented the national army with north-erners draws a rebuke from an unnamed prophet. The type of alliance that Jehoshapat made with Ahab in chap. 18 is repeated here. Defeat is forecast as the price to pay for such reliance on the northern kingdom. As long as that nation persisted in rejecting the Lord, it was out of fellowship with God, as the chron-icler explained in 13:4-12 (see also 15:2).

The first half of v. 8 is a textual crux. A feasible reconstruction is, "For if with these you act strongly in war, God . . .," which under-lies the REB's paraphrase, "For, if you make these people your allies in war   " (cf. the LXX).[298] The issue was not numerical superi-ority but the will of God, who could grant vic-tory or defeat irrespective of numbers. It is a trust-oriented argument we have heard from the chronicler before (14:11 and esp. chap. 20). The rueful inquiry for an oracle in v. 9a leads to a repetition of the motif of divine power, now to compensate for loss incurred out of loyalty to the Lord. We have not heard the last of the mercenaries. Deprived of the customary spoils of war, they returned home bent on reprisal and launched their own attack on Judean territory (vv. 10, 13). Verse 13 is not clearly expressed, since Samaria was in no way a Judean town.[299]

The account of the successful Edomite campaign (vv. 11-12) has a bloodthirsty ring. While v. 11 is based on 2 Kgs 14:7, v. 12 may have arisen as a variant interpretation of it. One must take into account the long-standing hostility between Judah and Edom, which in post-exilic times was exacerbated by the fail-ure of Edom to support its ally Judah in the disaster of 587 BCE and by their infiltration

---

297. See M. P. Graham, "Aspects of the Structure and Rhetoric of 2 Chronicles 25," in *History and Interpretation: Essays in Honour of John H. Hayes*, ed. M. P. Graham et al., JSOTSup 123 (Sheffield: JSOT, 1993) 78-89, who finds in 25:14-16 a pivot for the concentric structure of this chapter.

298. See Allen, *The Greek Chronicles*, 2:85-86.
299. See *BHS*.

of Judah's southern territory during the exile. The prophecy of Obadiah reflects this animosity, and so does the passionate Psalm 137. Consequently, the subjugation of Edom played a key role in the conception of the coming kingdom of God, as Amos 9:12 and Obad 21:1 indicate. Edom became a symbol for human opposition to God's people and so to God, which required that justice be done. This prophetic, eschatologically tinged way of thinking is the animating force behind the hostility of the text.

25:14-19. After 20:20-28, the sequel to the campaign is a shocking disappointment to the reader; worship from grateful hearts is given to the wrong deities. The worship of other people's gods becomes a new negative pivot for the rest of the chapter and explains the reversals copied from 2 Kings 14. The unusual character of the incident, to which v. 15 b will refer, has an ideological basis in the ancient Near Eastern notion that gods abandoned a conquered nation and joined the conquerors' side, to whose country their images were duly transferred.[300] So it may have had some historical basis.

The chronicler uses the intervention of another unnamed prophet to express an adverse theological perspective. The divine anger, expressed in the prophet's accusation, functions as a warning to Amaziah to turn from his folly and reverts implicitly to the motif of divine power, used by the earlier prophet in v. 8. The dire charge of "seeking" (דרש *dāraš*; NIV, "consult"; NRSV, "resorted to") gods other than the Lord is a denial of true spirituality, which will be echoed in v. 20 ("sought"). Now the royal response is not assent but protest and threat. For the chronicler, the greater sin was the spurning of a second chance. The king's fate was sealed by his refusal to heed the prophet's counsel.

Verses 16-17 a contain a fourfold Hebrew play on the word "counsel" (יעץ *yāʿaṣ*). Amaziah rejected the prophet's right to take part in royal deliberations and threatened death. In reply, the prophet blamed the king for refusing to listen to his sound deliberation and retorted that in reprisal God had deliberated Amaziah's destruction. Finally, the king

proceeded to deliberate a foolish military confrontation with the northern kingdom, which is the chronicler's preface to his citation of 2 Kgs 14:8-14. This episode was intended as an ironic echo of the divine decision and marks a significant stage in its providential outworking. Divine and human wisdom are contrasted, with the latter shown to be arrogant folly in this political fable of the northern king—"God has made the wisdom of this world look foolish!" (1 Cor 1:20 NRSV). It is a tragic antithesis of the humble repentance that the prophet's accusation was meant to elicit (cf. 7:14; 24:19).

25:20-24. Capital, palace, and Temple all suffered, their destruction foreshadowing the later conquests of 597 and 587 BCE that led to exile. Twice in quick succession, in 24:23 and here, the chronicler has mentioned Jerusalem's exposure to enemy attack, both deliberately repeated from 2 Kings. The taking of hostages sounds an exilic note. The chronicler regarded such exile-related disaster as a recurring phenomenon, rather than a unique climax. It functions as a theological image of divine punishment confronting any generation who turns away from the Lord. The insertion of v. 20 b into the 2 Kings narrative interprets the disaster as providential punishment for apostasy. Another addition, this time redactional, appears in v. 24, referring to Obed-edom's liability for religious artifacts that had been looted (NIV: cf. 1 Chr 26:15). It is a breach of temple security, while the looting marks a reversal of 2 Chr 24:14a.

25:25-28. A further block of material from 2 Kgs 14:17-22 is quoted in 25:25–26:2, spilling over into Uzziah's reign. Amaziah lived on, only to fall victim to a conspiracy, as had his predecessor. His flight from fatality just postponed it, for the wages of sin is death. The chronicler adds a theological comment in v. 27 a. He regards Amaziah's steps as being dogged thereafter by a resistance movement that issued into conspiracy. Apostasy was a slippery slope toward destruction; his remaining fifteen years were not blessed but blighted. Such is the fate of those who turn away from the Lord. There are extra-biblical parallels for calling Jerusalem "the City of Judah," a variant of "the city of David" in the 2 Kings text.[301]

300. See M. Cogan, *Imperialism and Religion: Assyria, Judah and Israel in the Eighth and Seventh Centuries BCE*, SBLMS 19 (Missoula, Mont.: Scholars Press, 1974) 9-21; Dillard, *2 Chronicles*, 201.

301. See Selman, *2 Chronicles*, 464 and n. 1.

REFLECTIONS

1. The chronicler relished the citation of Deut 24:16 in 2 Chr 25:4 (taken over from 2 Kings), because it favored his concept of the independence of each generation before God. He was not always consistent; in 22:9, Ahaziah was permitted a decent burial for his grandfather's sake. But that incident leans positively on the side of graciousness, recalling good qualities and forgetting bad ones. The chronicler was not such a stickler for logical consistency as was Ezekiel, who held that God remembered neither the good of those who turned away from righteousness nor the bad of those who turned back to righteousness (Ezek 18:22, 24). Human memories tend to be less charitable, holding on to grudges more readily than to good opinions.

Amaziah's moderation speaks to all persons in positions of authority. Parents know the temptation to crack the nut of a child's offense with a sledgehammer of fury. Police, eyeing a surging crowd of demonstrators, need to decide whether or when to resort to a crack down. Who does not sympathize with James and John, who wanted to call down fire from heaven when the Samaritan villager rejected Jesus? And who does not agree on reflection with Jesus' branding their impulse as an overreaction (Luke 9:25-56; cf. 2 Sam 16:5-13)?

2. The king's complaint in 25:8 also hits home. Virtue and an appropriate grace do not always go together. We can all look back and regret the expenditure of resources to no good purpose. Hopefully, we are wiser as a result, though sadder. The prophet's reply that God can compensate for losses is not neatly worked out in the ensuing narrative. A lesson learned has value in itself. In fact, Amaziah incurred further losses. Even when amends have been made, mistakes sometimes cast long shadows and dim future potential.

3. The vehemence underlying 25:12 is something we all find abhorrent but need to try to understand. In the same vein it is too easy to read only Ps 137:1-6 and to silence its last three verses. Implicit in both post-exilic passages are a deep sense that injustice has been done and a passionate craving for justice to prevail (cf. 1 Chr 16:33). The same aggrieved vehemence reappears in 2 Thess 1:5-10 and the book of Revelation.

4. Is the emphasis in the second half of the chapter on a working out of providential punishment the shadow side of Rom 8:28? If eventual good is the prospect of those who love God, what awaits those who go on to repudiate that love? The chronicler intended his moral narrative to be a warning. He was pleading with his readers not to "abandon" their "confidence." His message resonates with the New Testament affirmation that "we are not among those who shrink back and so are lost, but among those who have faith and so are saved" (Heb 10:35, 39 NRSV).

2 Chronicles 26:1-23, Uzziah Oversteps God's Limits

COMMENTARY

Amaziah, his father before him, and his son after him were all tarred with the same brush, first faithful to the Lord and then faithless. The royal trilogy is meant to function as a powerful sermon to believers to "hold" their "first confidence firm to the end" (Heb 3:14 NRSV).

The royal name "Uzziah" appears to be an alternative form of "Azariah," which this king bears in the Davidic genealogy of 1 Chr 3:12 and, most of the time, in 2 Kings 14–15. The chronicler may have preferred "Uzziah" to avoid confusion with the high priest Azariah (vv. 17, 20). He was aware of both names and provides wordplays on their meanings, "Yahweh helps" (Azariah) and "Yahweh is my strength" (Uzziah) in vv. 7-8, 13, 15. Only about seven verses of the section have been copied from 2 Kings, at the beginning and at the end of the chapter. Verses 1-2 were taken over from 2 Kgs 14:21-22, and vv. 3-4 from 2 Kgs 15:2-3. Verses 20b-22 were supplied from 2 Kgs 15:5-6, apart from the temple reference, and v. 23 from 2 Kgs 15:7, except for mention of the royal burial field.

26:1-5. Uzziah's military success, long reign, and approbation, echoed in vv. 2-4, and the Lord's afflicting him with leprosy in his final years provided scaffolding for a further sequence of blessing and backsliding. The comparison with Amaziah in v. 4 gave the chronicler, though not the deuteronomist, support for this structuring. The high and low points of the section are featured by two contrasting statements, "God gave him success" (v. 5) and "the LORD had afflicted him" (v. 20).

26:6-15. The good period of the reign is elaborated with three examples of divine blessing: military success, vv. 6-8; building projects, vv. 9-10; and an army and armaments, vv. 11-15. At beginning and end, God's help is celebrated (vv. 7, 15). In the latter case, the passive verb and the adverb point to the Lord as the source of the help. Historians regard Uzziah's long reign as a prosperous one, though the deuteronomist took little interest in it. Control of the port of Eloth or Elath (v. 2) gave access to Arabia, Africa, and India via maritime trade. The accounts of Uzziah's enterprise in vv. 6-15 are all feasible in principle and appear to depend on solid tradition, the last item doubtless relying on a royal military source. The chronicler also seems to have known from elsewhere a mentor called Zechariah (v. 5) and the king's officiating in the Temple (v. 16).

The chronicler introduces Uzziah's period of blessing in v. 5. It spells out the spiritual accolade of v. 4 and adds its corollary of prosperity, limited though it was. This period reiterates the situation of the pious Jehoiada's mentoring of Joash (24:2-16).[302] Uzziah was like Joash, too, in that his prosperity lasted only as long as did a positive attitude toward God (24:20). This attitude is typically defined as seeking (דרש *dāraš*) the Lord and is closely linked with a successful life. The link, loosely made in 14:7, will be repeated in Hezekiah's case (31:21). The pattern of obedience and prosperity finds a parallel in 1 Chr 22:13 and is a more tangible version of the basic proposition that to seek the Lord leads to a manifestation of the divine presence (15:2; 1 Chr 28:9). The list of military victories draws an impressive semicircle, west, southwest, south, and east. The lack of such activity to the north reflects détente with the northern kingdom. The campaign against the Philistines was followed by the building of Judean settlements in the area. The reference to Gur-baal is textually and exegetically uncertain and may conceal mention of Gerar;[303] in that case the Arabs are the Cushites (cf. 14:13-14). The Meunites are to be located in Edom (see 20:1). The mention of Ammonites is uncertain; the LXX refers instead to the Meunites, which suits better the directional reference to the border of Egypt. Uzziah's power and prestige are traced to the backing of his divine patron, directly in v. 7 and indirectly in v. 8, where his strength alludes to the meaning of his name, "Yahweh is my strength."

The triple themes of vv. 6-15 fall into two paragraphs, vv. 6-8 and vv. 9-15, each ending in the same refrain of fame and divinely given strength. The first paragraph highlights external success, and the other internal. Building work is always an indication of blessing in the books of Chronicles; here it embraces both urban and rural enterprises. The latter relate to livestock and crops in the development of the royal estates (cf. 1 Chr 27:25-31), for which there is considerable archaeological support.[304] The description of Uzziah as a lover of the soil reflects the chronicler's own regard for the good land of Israel (cf. Deut 8:7-10). The details of the conscript army include a list of weapons provided by the king, which have an impression of increasing sophistication and include a description of a new invention for defense against a siege. This innovation consisted of attaching to towers and battlements wooden frames into which round shields were inserted to form a protective barrier behind which archers and stone throwers could safely stand instead of

302. For the "fear" of God see *BHS* and Japhet, *I & II Chronicles*, 878.

303. See *BHS*.
304. See Williamson, *1 and 2 Chronicles*, 336-37.

crouching awkwardly. These devices were used at Lachish at the end of the eighth century, according to the scenes of the siege depicted on Sennacherib's reliefs.[305]

All this military power illustrated for the chronicler not simply Judah's defensive capability (v. 13) but also further signs of divine blessing. Old Testament theology often involves a triangle made up of God, the land, and Israel. So land-related work and territorial security were necessarily drawn into the sphere of the divine/human relationship. In v. 15, the developments in military technology are linked to miraculous assistance ("marvelously helped"), which is an aspect of the protective power of God (cf. Ps 127:1).

26:16-21. Uzziah's sudden fall from grace, anticipated in the qualification of v. 5, serves to explain his leprosy late in life. The chronicler has in view the apostasy of the good person in Ezek 18:24, borrowing from there the term for "unfaithfulness" (מעל *māʿal*), which is twice used for the royal sin (vv. 16, 18). It fits well here because it can have a religious nuance as well as referring to breaking of the covenant (cf. Lev 5:15; 26:40). The chronicler may have known a tradition of Uzziah's officiating in the Temple and then imaginatively wrote it up from the post-exilic perspective that only Aaronic priests might "burn incense" (v. 18), which is reflected in the Torah at Exod 30:7 and Num 16:39-40. In 1 Kgs 9:25, there is a reference to Solomon's burning incense, which the chronicler left out of his account. The Davidic king evidently engaged in certain religious rituals apart from those restricted to the regular priesthood (see Ps 110:4). The incense altar stood in the nave of the Temple near the holy of holies (see 1 Kgs 6:22). So, for the chronicler, there was a violation of sacred space and sacred ritual, a double trespass. Biblical evidence is insufficient to reconstruct the precise ceremony, in this case involving both the incense altar and use of a censer.[306]

In the story of Rehoboam, royal strength led to an abandoning of the Torah, which was followed by a prophetic challenge and subsequent repentence (12:1, 6-7; cf. 7:14). A less happy permutation of such motifs appears here. Strength leads to pride, which is unrelieved by repentance, even when the king is challenged by the high priest. Uzziah displayed his father's sin of pride (25:19), now demonstrated against the Lord. Yet v. 19 emphasizes that judgment struck only after Azariah's warning had been rejected. In each of the cases of the three apostate kings, the chronicler was concerned to highlight the Lord's patience in giving an opportunity for a change of heart. Punishment came as a last resort, after a challenge had fallen on deaf ears (24:19-21; 25:15-16; 26:18-19).

The first part of v. 20 is colored by Aaron's reaction to Miriam's leprosy (Num 12:10). The term for "leprosy" (מצרע *měṣōrāʿ*) carried emotive overtones, reflected in its fivefold occurrence in vv. 19-21 and in the chronicler's addition at v. 23. The annotations in the NRSV and the NIV remind us that in the Bible leprosy is not the same malady we think of as leprosy today. It was a severe skin disease, dire in that it rendered its victim ritually unclean (cf. Lev 13:44-46). So, commented the chronicler with Lev 13:46 in mind, Uzziah was excluded from worship in the temple area and so was stripped of the religious privilege of every believer. He also lost his right to rule, surrendering it to his son as regent.

26:22-23. The chronicler writes Uzziah's obituary in consigning him in death, not to the royal cemetery, but to adjoining crown property. In referring to the underlying 2 Kings narrative, the chronicler assumes that Isaiah was the author, since the prophet lived during part of Uzziah's reign (Isa 6:1) and because the same material concerning Hezekiah appears in both his book and 2 Kings. Once more the basic narrative is invested with prophetic authority.

305. See Y. Yadin, *The Art of Warfare in Biblical Lands* (New York: McGraw-Hill, 1963) 2:324-26, 431, 434.

306. See Petersen, *Late Israelite Prophecy*, 80-81; K. Nielsen, *Incense in Ancient Israel*, VTSup 38 (Leiden: Brill, 1986) 57, 79.

REFLECTIONS

1. The chronicler tended to work with a theology of prosperity—that is, a conviction that God would materially reward the virtuous in their lifetime. True, the chronicler allowed for crisis to break into the life of obedient believers, as precursor to a new experience of trust in the Lord, who saves and blesses them (see 20:1-30). His prosperity theology had a pastoral intent, using the prospect of well-being as an incentive for his fellow believers to adopt a spirituality that honored the Torah and the Temple. We human beings all seem to require incentives. The New Testament writers sometimes retain such a material, this-worldly perspective. When they enlarge the scale of life to encompass a heavenly reward, they are still within the scope of giving an incentive. Disciples are urged to lay up for themselves treasures in heaven (Matt 6:20). An ideal of virtue for virtue's sake is intellectually appealing, but inadequate for most of us. A practicable system of ethics needs to argue long-term expediency—for example, warning couples who enjoy the stolen waters of premarital sex not to be surprised if they find marital sex disappointing.

2. Chapters 24–26 depict a shift from spirituality to willful disobedience. The chronicler's positive aim was that of the writer of the Letter to the Hebrews in its passages of grim warning. The kindly intent of both authors was the same: The writer of Hebrews cautioned: "Take care, brothers and sisters, that none of you may have an evil, unbelieving heart that turns away from the living God" (Heb 3:12 NRSV). The chronicler, too, wrote sadly of such turning away (25:27).

One has to ask whether the well-intentioned assurance current in some circles that the Christian is "once saved always saved" does not show a false kindness, evading the tension of the challenges that balance the assurances of Scripture. The somber proviso "if only we hold our first confidence firm to the end" (Heb 3:14 NRSV) is part of a chorus of New Testament conditions. It is heard not only in the "if" of Heb 3:6 but also in the Pauline caution of Rom 11:22 ("provided you continue in [God's] kindness"), of 1 Cor 15:2 ("if you hold firmly to the word I preached to you" [NIV]), and of Col 1:23 ("if you continue in your faith, established and firm" [NIV]). In such texts, Paul added his "amen" to the message of 2 Chronicles.

2 CHRONICLES 27:1–28:27, ROYAL MODELS OF RIGHT AND WRONG

OVERVIEW

Two reigns are set back-to-back as polar opposites of right and wrong. Jotham the good is presented alongside Ahaz the bad. The assessments of their reigns function as rhetorical markers: Jotham "did what was right in the sight of the LORD," while Ahaz "did not do what was right in the sight of the LORD" (27:2 [= 2 Kgs 15:34]; 28:1 [= 2 Kgs 16:2]).

The chronicler seems to have had in mind the case histories of Ezek 18:5-13, in which a good father is succeeded by a wretch of a son. Chapter 28 also has its own agenda. It marks the end of the narrative of the divided kingdom in chaps. 10–28, which accounts for its greater length and special features.

2 Chronicles 27:1-9, Jotham the Good

COMMENTARY

The first story with a moral is short and sweet, if unexciting. Jotham's reign is presented as a compact vignette of obedience and blessing. The chapter is structured in a symmetrical fashion. At its center lie two pieces of evidence of the Lord's favor (vv. 3-5). This pair of elements is surrounded by statements revealing the secret of Jotham's success (vv. 2, 6). They are encircled by the royal prologue and epilogue to his reign (vv. 1, 7-9), the latter echoing the former by repeating v. 1a in v. 8. This presentation is as neat as a piece of embroidery, each stitch carefully sewn. On a smaller scale, the neatness is reflected in the Hebrew by chiastic sentences at vv. 3-4 and in parallel beginnings at vv. 3 and 5 (הוא . . . והוא *hû' . . . wěhû'*, "he . . . and he"). The chronicler has stressed, using such literary technique, his admiration for Jotham.

27:1-5. The chronicler cites the short account of Jotham's reign, found in 2 Kgs 15:32-38. He amplified that account with details of further building operations (vv. 3b-4) and with a reference to an Ammonite victory (v. 5). The lavish presence of literary features often used by the chronicler means that if he was depending on sources, he edited heavily, though the report remains reasonable.[307] An Ammonite victory would imply the weakening of the northern kingdom's control over the Transjordan. The chronicler held over the reference to the Syro-Ephraimite war in 2 Kgs 15:37 until Ahaz's reign (26:5), which was more appropriate to his polarized conception. The accounts of tribute are presented in an inflated form.

---

307. See Williamson, *1 and 2 Chronicles*, 342; Japhet, *I & II Chronicles*, 892.

At the heart of the chapter lie two forms of evidence of the security given by the Lord. Building operations and military victory belong to the chronicler's code for divine blessing. If the Lord is the unnamed benefactor in vv. 3-5, such blessing is grounded explicitly in the king's honoring of God (v. 2). The blanket affirmation of 2 Kgs 15:34 had to be adjusted by reference to Uzziah's lack of respect for holy space in 26:16. The verbal echo of that verse in Hebrew (בא *bā'*) favors "enter" (NIV) rather than the vehement "invade" (NRSV). The paraphrase of 2 Kgs 15:35a in v. 2b seems to reflect a continuing agenda to discredit the people of Judah. It began in 20:33, will come to a head in 28:6, and will be reversed in 30:12 and 31:1, only to rise to a fatal climax in 36:14-17. Neither Jehoshaphat nor Jotham could force them into paths of righteousness. Jotham's goodness shines all the brighter against the background of the people's unspirituality.

27:6-9. The elements given in vv. 2a and 3-5 are combined in v. 6. Jotham's strength echoes that of Uzziah (26:6-15) and also of Rehoboam (12:2). The key was Jotham's consistency, which both Rehoboam and Uzziah lacked: "He maintained a steady course of obedience" (REB; cf. the NIV; see 12:14). The reference in v. 7 to "all his wars and all his ways" may simply be an impressionistic way of alluding to a supposed wealth of military and spiritual exploits. Amid the details of v. 8, the chronicler focuses on the length of Jotham's reign. He cited a similar block of material at the close of the reigns of Rehoboam and Jehoshaphat to focus on their length (12:13; 20:31). Here the material is repeated from v. 1a, as in the case of Jehoram (21:5, 20).

REFLECTIONS

Chapters 24–26 warned three times over that human fortunes can plummet when spirituality ceases to be a priority. In chaps. 27–28, the chronicler uses a different format to preach the same message, setting two reigns side by side. We shall see that chap. 28, similar in form to chap. 27 but diverse in content, functions as its negative counterpart. Yet chap. 27 poses its own contrast with chaps. 24–26. Verse 6 puts the chapter in a nutshell: The Lord honors consistent commitment to moral and spiritual excellence. So the chronicler's challenge to his constituency to continue all their days in a living faith, presented negatively in the preceding unit, is now repeated in a positive package. In New Testament terms, it corresponds to Paul's missionary concern that newly planted churches should remain faithful to the Lord (Acts 11:23; 13:43; 14:22). In the ups and downs of human experience, we are called to stay on an even keel in living out our faith.

2 Chronicles 28:1-27, Ahaz the Bad

COMMENTARY

Alongside Jotham's good reign is set Ahaz's shockingly bad one. The chronicler wants his readers to view them together as alternative role members, as if saying, "See, I . . . set before you . . . life and prosperity, death and adversity" (Deut 30:15 NRSV). Jotham's sixteen worthy years are succeeded by Ahaz's sixteen wasted years (27:1, 8; 28:1). Jotham's strength through spirituality is contrasted with Ahaz's lack of strength after turning to a secular power for help (27:6; 28:20 in the NRSV). The structure of concentric rings in chap. 27 is matched in chap. 28. The opening and closing formulas appear in vv. 1a and 26-27. The next ring (vv. 1b-4, 22-25) involves religious apostasy; each features sacrificing and making offerings and specifies high places. Further into the chapter appear two pairs of divinely instigated military defeats suffered by Judah at the hands of Aram and Israel (vv. 5-7) and of Edom and Philistia (vv. 17-19). The latter pair of disasters is set in its own framework, Ahaz's turning to Assyria for help (vv. 16, 20-21). At the heart of the chapter (vv. 8-15), stands a prophetic appeal to the northern troops to repatriate their Judean prisoners of war. Their affirmative response shows up, in an even worse light, in the unspirituality of Ahaz and Judah.

The chronicler has based his version of Ahaz's reign on the unsavory account in 2 Kings 16. He follows it primarily at the beginning and the end (vv. 1-4, 26-27) and loosely echoes it (vv. 5, 16a, 21a, 24a). The general outline of 2 Kings 16:1 is maintained: religious apostasy, the invasion of Aram and Israel, and cultic innovations. The details of v. 7 point to a tradition other than 2 Kings, and so does the second pair of invasions (vv.

17-19). The specification of personal names in v. 2 and the evident suppression of names (cf. "men nominated for this duty," NEB) and the place-name "Jericho" in v. 15 also appear to reflect a separate source. The chronicler has woven various items into a powerful piece of writing that makes liberal use of his own interpretive language.

The war waged by Israel and Aram Judah provides the historical background. It sprang from an attempt to form a multinational alliance against attack from the eastern power Assyria. Judah, nestling in its out-of-the-way hills, refused to cooperate, judging discretion to be the better part of valor and unwilling to antagonize Assyria, should an attack materialize. This policy provoked its northern neighbors to increasing pressure, culminating in an attack on Jerusalem. There are various divergent accounts of this complex conflict in the OT (see 2 Kgs 15:37; 16:5; Isaiah 7:1; Hos 5:8–6:6). Each account is written from a specific perspective; the 2 Chronicles account complements the others with its own theological emphasis.[308] The conflict led to Judah's loss of independence and vassalage under Assyria, to which vv. 20-21 allude. It also brought about the end of the northern kingdom and the exile of many of its citizens at Assyria's hands. This catastrophe is not mentioned here (cf. 30:6; 1 Chr 5:6, 26), but the chronicler presupposes that it occurred in Ahaz's reign, leaving Judah as the only kingdom in which the Lord is worshiped. The chronicler calls Ahaz king of Israel and speaks of his subjects as all Israel (vv. 19, 23).

308. See M. E. W. Thompson, *Situation and Theology: OT Interpretations of the Syro-Ephraimite War* (Sheffield: Almond, 1982) 91-124.

28:1-4. The contrast between David and the kings of Israel in vv. 1-2 (= 2 Kgs 16:2-3) recalls Abijah's speech in 13:4-12, in which the ideals of Davidic worship were set against Jeroboam's innovations. This similarity signals the close relationship between the present chapter and chap. 13. The chronicler has added in v. 2*b* the sentence about casting images for the Baals. That addition evokes Jeroboam's sin of making images in 1 Kgs 14:9 and, even more closely, the indictment of the northern kingdom in 2 Kgs 17:16 that they cast images of two calves and served Baal, sins that merited exile. Ahaz is painted in northern hues. In the addition of v. 3*a*, local coloring is provided by specifying the Valley of Hinnom as the site of a cult of child sacrifice (cf. 2 Kgs 23:10). The change from "his son" (2 Kgs 16:3) to "his sons" probably marks an intentional rhetorical intensification—i.e., a general practice rather than a single occurrence. The reference to "the kings of Assyria" in the MT of v. 16, rather than the singular at 2 Kgs 16:7, reflects similar intensification.

28:5-7. The chronicler links religious apostasy and military defeat as cause and effect. He portrays separately the attacks of the allies (vv. 5*a*, 5*b*-7) to prepare for his focus on Israel's Judean prisoners (vv. 8-15). Israel's sword, ranging wide and high, is described as the Lord's reprisal for Judah's apostasy. They had failed the test confronting each new generation and had to face the consequences. Similarly, the disaster is credited to the Lord's anger against the southern kingdom (v. 9). The number of the casualties, whether or not they can be rationally reduced to 120 units, reflects the rhetorical mathematics we have noticed the chronicler using elsewhere. Together with the phrase "in one day," it contributes to a dramatic effect intended as a deterrent. A NT parallel occurs in 1 Cor 10:6-10.

28:8-15. A defeat leads into this narrative and prophetic speech. Its key word is "brothers," at beginning, middle, and end (vv. 8, 11, 15 NJB). An otherwise unknown prophet, Oded urges the release of the families of Judean conscripts, rather than enslavement. His main argument seems to be based on the mandate in Lev 25:39-43, 46 that "brother-Israelites" (NJB) should not be enslaved. He also offers a supporting argument: Although the victory was theologically justified, the slaughter had exceeded what the Lord had intended (cf. Isa 10:5-19). There is also a hint at a backlog of guilt: "Aren't you also [as well as Judah] guilty?" (NIV).

The message hits home to four leading Ephraimites, who add their own warning to Oded's, grounded in a confession of the sins of which he had accused them. It works. The prisoners and the spoils are given up—not only that, but a task force is also designated to meet the immediate needs of the naked, hungry, wounded prisoners and to escort them compassionately back to the border town of Jericho for repatriation. In a structurally central place, this message of sensitivity to the Lord's will forms a sharp contrast to Ahaz's growing intransigence.

28:16-21. The rest of the chapter returns to that latter theme. Attacks by Edomites (cf. 2 Kgs 16:6) and Philistines are framed with an appeal to Assyria, help that was not forthcoming (vv. 16, 21). By putting the appeal in the context of the defeats at the hands of Aram and Israel ("At that time," v. 16), the chronicler implies that their attacks, as well as these new ones from the south and west, motivated the appeal. The Philistine incursions are illustrated by a list of towns in the northern Shephelah that were captured and occupied.

The chronicler supplies a theological interpretation of these attacks (v. 19) in terms of providential punishment. Ahaz's loss of "restraint" in Judah looks back to v. 4. "Faithlessness" or "unfaithfulness" (מעל *mā'al*) is the chronicler's key term for describing sin that leads straight to exile (1 Chr 5:25 NIV; *ma'al* in 9:1), which had found illustration in Saul's experience (1 Chr 10:10-14, esp. v. 13). Indeed, the Philistines' attack and their occupation of Judean towns reads like a rerun of 1 Chr 10:1-2, 7. The note of exile is sounded elsewhere in the chapter in the deportation of Judean prisoners of war to Aram, Israel, and Edom (vv. 5, 8, 17). Post-exilic Judah looked back to the Babylonian exile as the ultimate of woe, in tune with the representation of national defeat in 2 Kings and pre-exilic prophecy of divine judgment in terms of exile. The chronicler also regarded exile as the worst of calamities, but he refused to see it as a chasm separating pre-exilic and post-exilic Judah. He found that exile was repeated in Judean history, and each time the Lord created a new beginning as its positive aftermath. Each generation contained within itself seeds of exile, which it could cultivate into fast-growing weeds or firmly suppress with God's help.

Judah so disdained the Lord's help that they put the Assyrian monarchy in God's place. It was no help, the chronicler concludes with grim satisfaction. In the short term, the ploy did get Aram and Israel off Judah's back. However, the chronicler has in mind the long-term consequences of becoming entangled with an oppressive empire (so Isa 7:17; 8:7-8). How could robbing the Temple (v. 21) turn out otherwise?

28:22-27. The faithlessness of vv. 2-4 (and referred to in v. 19), is now surpassed. There is also development of the motif of inappropriate help, broached in vv. 16 and 21. Now help was being sought from other gods (v. 23). Ahaz turned everywhere for help except to the Lord. The chronicler interprets Ahaz's having a copy made of an altar seen in Damascus and installing it in the temple court (2 Kgs 16:10-16) as worship of the gods of Damascus (cf. v. 5 and the different theological explanation there). The 2 Kings narrative is written in such neutral terms that its interpretation is uncertain, though it implies that the altar was used for sacrifice to the Lord (2 Kgs 16:13, 15). The chronicler found the narrative sinister, not only because of Ahaz's bad reputation even in 2 Kings, but also because for him Solomon's temple arrangements were cast in concrete (cf. 4:1; 7:9; 8:12-13), and not to be changed. With 2 Kings 16:17a in mind, the chronicler thought of desecration as he wrote of cutting holy implements into pieces. He extrapolated the complete closing of the temple doors from Ahaz's closing of the royal entrance to the Temple (2 Kgs 16:18) and from Hezekiah's later plating of its doorposts (2 Kgs 18:16).[309]

The theme of worshiping other gods is resumed (vv. 24b-25), a practice that summoned storm clouds of further divine anger. The way the narrative breaks off implies that this dire situation was inherited by Hezekiah. He had to reverse the religious trend in order to remove the threat. This situation explains

the careful tracking of its reversal, drawn in chap. 29. The chronicler writes the obituary of Ahaz in his notice of the burial, by denying Ahaz a place in the royal cemetery. This contradicts 2 Kgs 16:20 (at least in the MT; the text used by the chronicler may have lacked the second reference to his ancestors, as did the LXX of 2 Kings).

Chapter 28 brings to a close coverage of the divided kingdom, which began in chap. 10. It was the chronicler's concern to draw contrasts between the end of this phase and its beginning.[310] At first sight, Rehoboam was as bad as Ahaz in forsaking and being unfaithful to the Lord and robbing the Temple to pay tribute (12:2, 5, 9). But whereas in Rehoboam's case divine wrath was averted by self-humbling (12:6, 7, 12), for Ahaz God's anger brought about defeat (28:9) and was a legacy he left to Hezekiah (28:25).

In 11:4 and 28:11, a prophet takes an army to task for improper treatment of their "brothers," first a southern army preparing to fight the north, then a northern army that had captured southerners. Now the northern kingdom is given an opportunity to celebrate the wholeness of the covenant people, and takes it. The stereotype of the southerners as good guys and the northerners as bad guys, which the chronicler has tended to accept, is discarded and even reversed in some respects. In v. 5 the "great slaughter" (NRSV) experienced by Judah was the fate of Israel at Abijah's hands in 13:17. In 12:5-6, Judah listened to a prophet and repented in self-humbling (on the lines of 7:1), while Israel rejected Abijah's implicit appeal to stop turning away from the God they used to worship (13:8). Now it was Israel's turn to hear a prophet who spoke of their traditional God (v. 9). They took a step in the right direction by confessing the backlog of sins they had inherited and retained, the dynastic and religious sins of 13:8-9, and by complying with the prophet's advice to return the prisoners (v. 11). The verb "send back" (השׁיבו *hăšîbû*) echoes the injunction of 7:14 to "turn" (ישׁבו *yāšubû*) from wicked ways. In 13:16, God gave Israel into Judah's hands, but in 28:9 the opposite occurred. Different renderings of the same verb (כנע *kāna‘*) conceal the fact that in v. 19 the Lord "brought Judah low," while

309. See Japhet, *I & II Chronicles*, 918.

310. See Williamson, *Israel in the Books of Chronicles*, 114-18.

in 13:18 Israel was "brought low." Judah had lost its position of privilege, grounded in the Temple as the center of orthodox worship (13:10-11). Now its doors were closed (28:24; 29:7).

The note of exile is sounded for Judah in this chapter, a note that will be developed in later chapters. Israel was now exiled, and a mere remnant was left; but in principle Judah had undergone a similar experience (29:9; 30:6). Judah was leveled to the same low state of unworthiness before the Lord that Israel had reached. The chronicler was bidding post-exilic Judah to remember the skeletons in its closet when it thought of disowning brothers and sisters in the north. He was also urging them to take seriously a provocative potential for confession and conciliation, taught here by northern role models.

REFLECTIONS

1. The chronicler regards Ahaz as a despicable traitor, although the deuteronomist reserved that role for Manasseh. No other Davidic king is portrayed in such disparaging tones; he is as bad as Saul or Athaliah, neither of whom was part of David's house. Through Ahaz, the chronicler warns of the terrible fate that overwhelms apostates. This account is a lesson "written down to instruct later readers" (1 Cor 10:11 NRSV).

2. In comparison to chapters 11–13, Judah's role vis-à-vis Israel has been stood on its head. The message is like that of the parable of the prodigal son in Luke 15:11-32, where the older brother stands for the Judean establishment as he objects to the welcome extended to the prodigal, who represents repentant tax collectors and sinners (Luke 15:1-2). The former, faithful to God in their own eyes, are portrayed in a bad light for criticizing the claims of Jesus that his work of love was a God-given mission. The chronicler was playing a similar tune. Judah should be prepared to make warm advances to their northern kinsfolk. They stood in the same needy position before the Lord as did their neighbors.

Paul had occasion to condemn such a spirit of arrogant distancing (Rom 11:13-22). Gentile Christians were proud of their own response to the gospel and of their role as members of the people of God. They snobbishly looked down on Jews as spiritual has-beens—they had become God's favorites. For the apostle, it was a dangerous perspective. Privilege never warrants pride, let alone prejudice. Do not boast, Paul warned, or else you will find yourself outside the circle of God's active favor. Every group of believers is prone to arrogance, letting new wine go to their heads. Jesus had to correct John, when he and the other disciples forbade a man they saw casting out demons in his name, "because he is not one of us" (Luke 9:49-50 NIV).

3. Christians, when reading 28:15, may recall the parable of the good Samaritan (Luke 10:25-37). In fact, this passage may have been the literary inspiration for the parable.[311] Jesus told it at a time when religious relations between Jerusalem and Samaria had degenerated much further. Yet, in the parable the good Samaritan, as we ironically call him, shows up the Judean priest and the Levite, who each passed by on the other side of the injured man. There is the same reversal of expected roles as in the chronicler's narrative. The northerners' actions were "deeds consistent with repentance" (Acts 26:20 NRSV) or "fruit in keeping with repentance" (Matt 3:8 NIV).

4. Another part of the ministry of Jesus may have been influenced by this passage: his teaching on the last judgment in Matt 25:31-46. Those who gave food and drink or clothing to others were themselves honored and credited with having also done it to Jesus. It is a measure of the premium the Bible places on loving actions.

---

311. See F. S. Spencer, "2 Chronicles 28:5-15 and the Parable of the Good Samaritan," *WTJ* 46 (1984) 317-49, though some of his treatment is a little forced.

2 CHRONICLES 29:1–36:23

THE REUNITED KINGDOM

OVERVIEW

This is the last and shortest of the four literary blocks that make up the chronicler's selective retelling of Israel's history. It mirrors on a smaller scale the two preceding blocks. Hezekiah is portrayed as a second David and Solomon, reenacting their devotion to the ideals of Temple and Torah, and so reversing the degenerate state of Judah in chap. 28. He also availed himself of the Solomonic revelation (7:14) in his appeal for self-humbling, in his own recourse to it (30:11; 32:26), and in his prayer on behalf of unclean worshipers (30:18-20). In the second case, he became another Rehoboam, averting divine wrath by humbling himself (12:6-7; 32:25-26). Like Abijah, he laid the claims of the Jerusalem sanctuary before the people of the north (13:8-12; 30:5-9).

The kaleidoscope of good and bad royal models in the previous block continues to flash before our eyes, as we are shown a good reign, a bad one that turns good, an utterly bad one, a good one that turns bad at the end, and then a series of utterly bad reigns. The variety of options offered in Ezekiel 18 is illustrated once more in the interests of spiritual challenge and encouragement.

In the previous block, we noticed a sharp contrast between Judah's spiritual well-being near the beginning and its sorry state by the end, as bad as and, in fact, worse than that of the northern kingdom. The same impression is given here. Zedekiah's people scorned the prophetic messengers the Lord sent to warn and coax them, as had the northern tribes earlier in reaction to Hezekiah's courier (30:10; 36:16). Some of the latter did humble themselves (7:14), but not Zedekiah (30:11; 36:12). In this respect, he was no Hezekiah, whose example had been followed by Manasseh and Josiah; Zedekiah took after Amon (32:26; 33:12, 19, 23; 34:27). Both the northerners and Zedekiah are called stiff-necked (30:8; 36:13), and both they and his subjects are confronted with the divinely consecrated role of the Temple (30:8; 36:14).

The fall of the northern kingdom at the end of the preceding block removed a stumbling block of wicked alliance from Judah's kings, leaving the Davidic dynasty unchallenged and giving the opportunity for good kings of Judah to make spiritual overtures to the members of the tribes of Israel left in the north. Hezekiah, in line with his Davidic and Solomonic orientation, went to great lengths to hold a festival for all Israelites, whereupon religious reform ensued in north and south (30:1–31:1). Josiah, a paler reflection of Hezekiah, is credited with similar, if less vigorously stated, roles (34:33; 35:17-18).

This final block resembles the first in moving at its close from exile to restoration (1 Chr 9:1-34; 2 Chr 36:20-23). Punishment was not the Lord's last word. A day of opportunity dawned for a new generation. Solomon's petition that a repentant people might return to the land found a gracious hearing (2 Chr 6:24-25; cf. Zech 1:4-6). For the chronicler, such restoration created a precedent still available to any generation aware of their spiritual exile from the Lord. "Return to me . . . and I will return to you" (Zech 1:3 NIV) was the divine word to an earlier post-exilic generation, and it was still the Lord's gracious invitation, this last block affirms (30:8-9).

The block is made up of three units: (1) 29:1–32:33 presents Hezekiah's model reign; (2) 33:1–35:27 portrays two dramatic shifts from apostasy to spirituality, though flawed at the close in the latter case; and (3) 36:1-23 contrasts the finale of decline and destruction with the divinely endorsed hope of a fresh beginning.

2 CHRONICLES 29:1–32:33, HEZEKIAH ATTAINS ROYAL POTENTIAL

OVERVIEW

This unit divides Hezekiah's reign into two unequal halves, 29:1–31:21 and 32:1-33. In the first, the king is held up as a model of loyalty to the Lord. This section is introduced by the statement that he did right in the Lord's sight (29:2), which reuses a standard element of the deuteronomistic prologue to a monarch's reign (2 Kgs 18:3). Hezekiah's behavior is described at length and then recapitulated in a longer sentence, including "he did what was . . . right . . . before the LORD" (31:20 NRSV). The second half also uses a framing device. Now Hezekiah is presented as a paradigm for the prosperity that follows faithfulness to the Lord. The chronicler announces his theme in 31:21, "In everything that he undertook . . . he prospered" (NIV). He reinforces it with a final summary in 32:30, "He succeeded in everything he undertook" (NIV).

Throughout the account, Hezekiah is represented as reestablishing royal ideals associated with the reigns of David and Solomon.[312] The founders of a new era of revelation found a worthy heir in Hezekiah, in his honoring of the Lord's chosen shrine and in his efforts to unite the people of God in worship. When the accounts of his reign in 2 Kings and 2 Chronicles are compared, a shift of emphasis becomes apparent. For the writer of the books of Kings, deliverance from crisis was the primary theme, in a context of political threat and military invasion. The chronicler found room for this theme as well, but inserted it in a panorama of spiritual restoration, united worship, religious reformation, and divine blessing. In reliving such Davidic and Solomonic ideals, Hezekiah became a role model for the post-exilic community.

312. See M. A. Throntveit, *When Kings Speak: Royal Speech and Royal Prayer in Chronicles*, SBLDS 93 (Atlanta: Scholars Press, 1987) 121-24.

2 Chronicles 29:1-36, Temple Cleansing, Atonement, and Worship

COMMENTARY

29:1-2. This passage is taken from 2 Kgs 18:1-3. Verse 2 now functions as a basic statement about Hezekiah's reign. The comparison with David reminds us of his religious devotion, both to the ark of the covenant and to preparations for the building of the Temple. The chronicler saw this spirit reborn in Hezekiah. Taking his cue from the single verse concerning religious reform, 2 Kgs 18:4, he divided his definition of the king's spirituality into three parts, all relating to the Temple. The first (vv. 3-35) is concerned with the cleansing of the Temple, desecrated and discounted by Ahaz (chap. 28). This narrative matches the schematic interpretation of Ahaz's religious measures in 28:24 and serves as a positive counterpart.

29:3-11. The divine wrath that threatened Judah (28:25) demanded an immediate response (vv. 8, 10). So top priority was given to opening up the Temple, which Ahaz had closed down. This task had to fall on its official personnel, and the first opportunity is taken to summon them to a meeting. Comparison with 30:2-3 suggests that the first calendar month of Hezekiah's first official year as king is in view (v. 3), rather than the first month he came to the throne. The date was chosen to accord with priestly tradition, in the light of the sin offering on that date (see

Ezek 45:18-19).[313] Verse 3 functions as an initial summary; v. 17 suggests that the doors were opened on the eighth day of the project.

The speech ascribed to Hezekiah gives the chronicler a chance to provide a theological interpretation. He understood the "square" from a post-exilic perspective, situating Hezekiah, as he gave his speech, outside the uncleansed temple area, between that and the eastern wall of the city. The Levites are addressed in v. 5, which accords with their response in vv. 12-15. Yet priests, too, were summoned (v. 4) to hear the speech. The double reference to ministering (v. 11) embraces both groups, while mention of making offerings or burning incense relates to priests. So both are in view throughout. The singling out of the Levites accords with the chronicler's special interest in them and may also stem from the fact that they would do most of the work. There is a parallel in 1 Chr 15:11-14, where again a mainly levitical task is in view.

The speech uses calls for action (vv. 5, 11) as a frame for interpreting Ahaz's reign in terms of communal sin and punishment (vv. 6-9) and announcing Hezekiah's positive intent, for which the action will prepare (v. 10). The new generation had the responsibility of relating spiritually to the God of the previous generation ("fathers," NIV; the NRSV's "ancestors" is patently wrong in vv. 5-6; see v. 19 and its rendering of "fathers" in v. 9). Now their turn had come, and the Lord had become "our God" (v. 6). That meant correcting the abuses of their predecessors and making a total change, like the good son of the wicked father in Ezek 18:14-18. Their parents' sins are described in terms of general spirituality (v. 6) and more specifically (v. 7). Their unfaithfulness (מעל māʿal) echoes that of 28:19, 22, with reference to the Temple-related offenses of 28:2-4, 23-25. Their having forsaken the Lord picks up the reference in 28:6. Their rejection of the Lord's earthly home had been a token of their rejection of God. The specific sins begin with the datum in 28:24. They continue with the cessation of the Temple's archetypal functions, initiated by Solomon and affirmed by Abijah (2:4; 4:7; 13:11). Judah could no longer claim that, in Adijah's words, "we are observing the requirements of the Lord our God" (NIV).

313. Japhet, *I & II Chronicles*, 922-23.

The consequent wrath of the Lord recalls the divine anger depicted in 24:18, which was a response to temple-related sins. The chronicler here describes the divine motivation for surrendering Judah to Aram and Israel (28:5, 9). Verse 8*b* cites part of Jer 29:18b, essentially a description of the Judean exile of 587 BCE. The program of restoration in Jer 29:12-14 was dear to the chronicler, and he related it metaphorically to post-exilic Judah. Here he does the same with a verse in the context, reapplying it to the exile-like conditions of Hezekiah's reign, after many of the people had been killed or deported by their enemies. Verse 9 describes this very situation, echoing 28:5-8, 17-18. Although most Judeans still occupied the land, they had undergone a virtual exile. It was the situation of Saul's time all over again (1 Chr 10:1, 7). From this perspective, the reference to unfaithfulness in v. 6 takes on new significance. In 1 Chr 10:13, the chronicler made it the trigger for metaphorical exile, echoing Lev 26:40, where it describes the sin of covenant breaking, which leads to exile. Hezekiah was another David whose reign brought spiritual restoration. His task was to re-call the people from their exile.

Hezekiah's eventual aim of making a covenant pledge to the Lord is reminiscent of the pledges in Asa's (15:12) and Jehoiada's (23:16) reigns, and it anticipates Josiah's (34:31; cf. Ezra 10:3). It suggests a service at which this sinful state would be renounced, which is presumably reflected in vv. 20-31 (see also v. 31). This goal required preparation: the cleansing of the neglected and defiled Temple, including the removal of pagan objects (implied in v. 16). The task fell to the priests and Levites. The former alone had access to the temple building (cf. 5:7), while the latter had access to the temple court and were responsible for maintenance work. Challenged to do their God-given duty and coaxed by the epithet "my sons," they are encouraged to get on with the work.

In this address, the chronicler uses Hezekiah's situation as a means of preaching to his contemporaries. They were heirs of the message of the Torah (Lev 26:40) and of the prophetic message in Jer 29:18, to the effect that sin had caused the Babylonian exile, which still haunted the descendants of the returnees (see Neh 9:32-37). The chronicler offers the success story of Hezekiah's reign as a model for escape from such frustration. The Temple was the key to appropriate religion, and the priests and especially the Levites—the workhorses of the Temple—had a vital role in its worship. Only thus could worship be given pride of place in the community's life. "Do not be negligent" is his appeal to the temple personnel of his day.

29:12-17. The historical response was positive. All the main groups of the Levites were represented, even the choral families (cf. 1 Chr 15:5-8; 28:1). The priests were not unresponsive; they worked in areas inaccessible to the Levites. They all worked with devotion, heeding not only the king's appeal but also the inspired messages implicitly brought to their notice (cf. 30:12). They spent a week in the temple court and another in the sanctuary, where the priests first became involved, and by day sixteen the task was done. The references to beginning and ending are a faint but proud echo of Solomon's basic work in 3:1-2; 5:1. As in Asa's reign (15:16), pagan religious objects were burned in the Kidron Valley. The cleansing rites had to be repeated on successive days (cf. Exod 29:37; Ezek 43:18-27) and carried out on different items. Evidently the priests who performed this task were insufficiently represented (cf. 30:3). Consequently, the date of the passover, the fourteenth of Nisan, was overshot and had to be reset (30:5).

29:18-19. In this conclusion of Hezekiah's appeal, the chronicler focuses first on the altar of burnt offering in the temple court and the table for the bread of the presence in the Temple, and then on the replacement of utensils that had been "removed" or discarded by faithless Ahaz (see 28:22, 24). The first case presupposes knowledge of Ahaz's having displaced the altar in 2 Kgs 16:14-15 (see "the altar of the LORD," instead of "the pagan one," in vv. 19, 21). Mention of the table together with the altar recalls their archetypal role in 2:4; 13:11. The "utensils" (NRSV) or "vessels" (REB) in vv. 18-19 were important for the chronicler. In the post-exilic Temple, the vessels were especially prized as providing continuity with the pre-exilic sanctuary; extra ones came to share their pristine sanctity (cf. Ezra 1:6-11; 6:5; 8:30, 33).

29:20-35a. With the preliminary work of cleansing completed, it was now time for the pledge of loyalty to the Lord to deflect the divine anger of 28:25, in accordance with the program of v. 10. The pledge takes the form of a service involving complex ritual, narrated in vv. 20-35a. It gave the chronicler an opportunity to portray a post-exilic service of ritual reconsecration for the spiritual enlightenment of his constituency. The course of the service is demarcated by four stages, beginning with Hezekiah's command in vv. 21, 27, 30-31. The service, conducted by priests and Levites, was organized by the king and the city officials (vv. 20, 30; 30:12; see also 18:25; 34:8). As the service proceeds, there is also mention of "the assembly" (vv. 23, 28, 31-32) and "all the people" (v. 36). Moreover, in v. 29 "all who were present" refers to the congregation, as in 30:21; 31:1; 34:32-33; 35:7, 17-18.[314] In the light of 30:2, these terms refer to a body of Jerusalem residents who represented the people of Judah (cf. v. 21). The leaders provided the sacrificial animals (see 30:24), as did the prince in Ezekiel 45–46. The details given in vv. 22-24 show that the first three sets of seven animals were to be burnt offerings, and only the goats were to be used as sin offerings. The groups on whose behalf they were to be sacrificed were "the royal house" (NJB), the temple personnel, and Judah.

The first royal command initiates the general sacrificial procedure (v. 21b). Thereafter the ritual is divided into two separate stages: the blood rite (vv. 22-24) and the actual sacrificing of the public burnt offerings (vv. 25-30).[315] Then a third stage of voluntary private offerings is given by individual members of the congregation (v. 31). The whole ritual sequence follows a standard pattern of atonement and then worship.[316] The various parts of the burnt offering ritual for animals from the herd and flock are laid down in the priestly source at Lev 1:3-9, 10-13. The present account, though shorter, seems to presuppose that procedure. In vv. 22-24, the chronicler focuses on the treatment of the blood (cf. Lev 1:5, 11). After the offerers

314. Kleinig, *The Lord's Song,* 121 n. 1.
315. Petersen, *Late Israelite Prophecy,* 83.
316. See A. F. Rainey, "The Order of Sacrifices in OT Ritual Texts," *Bib* 51 (1970) 485-98; note the modification of Kleinig, *The Lord's Song,* 101 n. 2.

had slaughtered the animals, the blood was drained out of the carcasses and collected in a basin. The blood was then splashed against the sides of the altar in the temple court. Blood had an atoning role in the sacrificial ritual. The subject of the verbs of slaughtering (v. 22) are the king and officials depicted in vv. 20-21a. Such a picture differentiates the priests' dealing with the blood in the first two cases, which is consistent with Lev 1:5, 11. The NRSV, unlike the NIV, allows for this interpretation.

Next came the sin offerings. The Hebrew term חטאת (ḥaṭṭā't) is literally a de-sinning offering or "purification-offering" (REB). The full ritual is described in Lev 4:1–5:13, though there it is prescribed for inadvertent sins and sins of omission. Here it involves much more, as it does in the Day of Atonement ceremony of Leviticus 16. The theory behind the sin offering in Leviticus is related, in part at least, to the sanctuary. Human sins had a polluting effect on it, "defiling [God's] tabernacle that is in their midst" (Lev 15:31 NRSV). The effect of the sin offering was "to cleanse it and consecrate it from the uncleanness of the Israelites" (Lev 16:19 NIV). Leviticus knows two types of sin offering: One type had the specific role of cleansing the altar (Lev 4:30), which is the one envisioned here.[317] Again, the treatment of the blood was the important element for the chronicler, but there was a different procedure in the case of the sin offering. After the blood was drained, most of it was poured out at the bottom of the altar and a little was put in a basin and smeared on the altar. As in vv. 18-19, 21, continuing emphasis is placed on the altar of burnt offering, which had suffered at Ahaz's hands.

Mention is made of the rite of the laying on of hands in v. 23. This is specified at Lev 4:24 in the case of the sin offering, in which each worshiper pressed one hand on the goat's head. This action represented the self-identification of the offerer with the victim[318] and was a personal affirmation of a sinful status before the Lord and of the sincere desire to mend the broken relationship. In this case, the king and the congregation represented not only themselves but the rest of the people

as well, "to make atonement for all Israel." In the light of the clarification in v. 24b, his reference to "all Israel" functions as a correction made by the king, so that not only Judah was covered, as v. 21 envisions, but all the tribes as well.[319] Hezekiah's sense of responsibility for the northern tribes, evidenced in the next chapter, is already in view here. He would not rest until separated members of the covenant family were visibly reunited in worship of their one God.

Much scholarly ink has been spilled to determine the meaning of the verb כפר (kipper), rendered "atone" or "make atonement." An explanation that is widely preferred is a denominative sense, "pay a ransom." Sacrificial animals were a ransom, the alternative to the sinful offerers' losing their own lives. In the overall context, a propitiatory value for these atoning sacrifices can hardly be avoided. They function as God's answer to the question of what will appease the divine wrath (v. 10). A novel feature of v. 24, in comparison with earlier verses, is that the priests carry out the slaughtering. The solemnity of the occasion may have led the chronicler to base this stage on the Day of Atonement ritual, in which the high priest killed the goat for the people's sin offering (Lev 16:15).[320]

Verses 25-30 are concerned with the placing of burnt offerings on the altar (cf. Lev 1:6-9, 12-13). This stage is inaugurated by royal command in v. 27a. Its being accompanied by sacred music and song is narrated in v. 27b, as in 1 Chr 23:30-31. Verses 25-26 describe a preliminary procedure for v. 27b, placing the levitical singing musicians and the priestly trumpeters in position. It gives the chronicler another chance to reaffirm the ancient authority vested in the post-exilic musical guilds of Levites. In vv. 26-27, David's traditional association with musical instruments is applied to those played by the Levites, as earlier in 1 Chr 23:5; 2 Chr 7:6. This link enhanced the venerability with which the chronicler invested levitical music. Moreover, in v. 25 the use of music is traced back to David's organization of the Temple. Readers are meant to read this text from the perspective of 1 Chr 15:16-21; 25:1-6. However, in

317. See J. Milgrom, "Two Kings of Ḥaṭṭā't," VT 26 (1976) 333-37.
318. See D. P. Wright, "Hands, Laying on of. Old Testament," ABD, 3:47-48.
319. See Williamson, Israel in the Books of Chronicles, 126-27.
320. Williamson, 1 and 2 Chronicles, 357.

v. 25 David's authority as founder of this aspect of the temple era is backed by the prophetic sanction of Gad and Nathan and through them by divine warrant.[321] A prophetic role also appears in 1 Chronicles 25, but there it is associated with the musical choirs and especially their leaders. Here the wider God-given mission of Nathan and Gad as prophets involved in the location and building of the Temple (1 Chr 17:3-15; 21:18-19) is invoked. Hezekiah honored the Davidic command, as did Solomon in 8:14.

The accompaniment of burnt offerings with song and trumpet blasts accords with and clarifies the representations of 1 Chr 23:30-31; 2 Chr 8:12-14; 23:18. Worship ascended to the Lord in both ritual and music. It was echoed by the prostration of the congregation at beginning and end and also of the singers at the end after having laid down their instruments.[322] The royal command to the Levites (v. 30) is not chronologically placed, but serves as a footnote qualifying v. 27b and as a parallel to the ritual command of v. 27a. The command provides a fitting climax, with its further affirmation of the Levites' venerable role, which dominates the paragraph. Here the chronicler focuses on the content of the singing—namely, the psalms attributed to David and Asaph in the psalter. This reference to inspired songs is closest to 1 Chr 25:1-6, where Asaph is also mentioned in prophetic terms (1 Chr 25:2). The chronicler's message is that the Lord had authorized practices and texts that were to be perpetuated in temple worship. For post-exilic Judeans, remote from the origins of their faith, this was to be an anchor securing them to divine revelation and, hence, keeping them true to the Lord. The chronicler was particularly concerned to endorse the Levites' ministry as an indispensable part of temple worship.

The last stage of this model service of temple cleansing and spiritual restoration occurs in vv. 31-35a. The accent thus far has been on bridging the gap between the community and the Lord. The praise of v. 30 is a welcome indication that the gap had been closed. The previous public sacrifices of worship represented self-dedication on the part of the worshiping congregation. The Hebrew verbal

321. See Schniedewind, *The Word of God in Transition*, 197-98.
322. See Kleinig, *The Lord's Song*, 122.

phrase usually refers to the consecration of a new priest by offering his first sacrifice. In 1 Chr 29:5, it was used metaphorically of commitment to the Lord's work by giving money. Here מלא יד (*mālē' yād*) relates to reconsecration to God's service after the burden of guilt had been lifted. While the "covenant," or pledge, of v. 10 looked forward to the service of atonement, this phrase looks back to it.

The "sacrifices and thank offerings" (v. 31) are better taken as idiomatic for "thanksgiving sacrifices" (NJB). Such sacrifices celebrated the end of a crisis for an individual. Here these private offerings reflect individuals' gratitude for deliverance from the divine wrath that had loomed over the community. These offerings took the form of שלמים (*šělāmîm*, "offerings of well-being" or "fellowship offerings," v. 35), of which only the fat and a few other parts of the animal were sacrificed (Lev 3:3-4, 16b). Yet other parts were donated to the priests, and the rest was returned to the worshiper for a sacred meal with his family (Lev 7:15-17, 29-36). In v. 33, these are called "consecrated offerings" because they could be eaten only at the sanctuary (cf. Lev 19:8). People could elect to present a burnt offering instead, which was completely given over to the Lord with nothing returned to the individual. It expressed a generosity of devotion beyond that of the other offering (see Ps 66:15). Of course, all the private offerings were given out of "a willing heart," but the chronicler was issuing a challenge to his own constituency to go the extra mile in their worship. The data in vv. 32-33 suggest that about a tenth of the heads of households present elected to do so.

Staffing the temple became a problem. The responsibility of priests to skin burnt offerings may reflect the custom in the chronicler's day; in Lev 1:6 it is the duty of the lay offerer. The co-opting of Levites for this task is used as an opportunity not only to highlight their spiritual alacrity but also to advocate a policy change. In the narrative of sacrificial procedures during Josiah's reign, the Levites are reported in a more matter-of-fact way to have engaged in skinning sacrificial animals (35:11). The emergency measures described in this story become virtually the norm in the next. By such means, the chronicler was urging that Levites be given a greater role in sacrificial ritual. Further reasons why the priests were hard-pressed are supplied in v. 35a. They had to burn the fat of the offerings of well-being with the burnt offerings and to make the drink offerings that accompanied the burnt offerings (see Exod 29:40; 1 Chr 9:29; Ezra 7:17).

29:35b-36. This catalog of priestly duties serves as a glad reminder that normal services at the Temple had resumed. A restored Temple and a restored people worshiping their God constituted spiritual normality. This switch from apostasy to piety had occurred "so quickly," in less than three weeks. King and congregation took none of the credit. God must have been at work among them, they concluded. They gave thanks for this miracle of grace.

REFLECTIONS

1. The Temple had a sacramental value in the life of God's people, for it mediated the blessing of God. It was the touchstone of their reverence, the place where God's honor was most obviously acknowledged. A right regard for the Lord was grounded in pure and regular worship at the sanctuary. Hezekiah found the Temple to be in a shocking state of neglect and disuse. It mirrored the people's condition before God. Restoration from the spiritual exile of Ahaz's reign required cleansing rites and reestablishment of Torah-based patterns of worship. These patterns were to be supplemented with levitical music and song attributed to David's inspired institution. The reorganization of the Temple is presented as normative for later generations, a model for the chronicler's constituency. "Go and do likewise" is his message, one that we in turn must try to hear as we search for principles to govern our own worship.

A locked Temple was unthinkable for God's people; the Temple provided regular access to the Lord. The New Testament uses this function of the Temple as a spiritual metaphor. In Eph 2:18-22, access to God and status within the new Temple-church are mentioned side by side. Hebrews 10:19-22 celebrates the privilege of entering the heavenly sanctuary won by Jesus for his followers.

Only priests could enter the temple building, but they did so on the people's behalf. Israel's supreme task was to worship the Lord both indirectly through the regular rites of the Temple and directly by their participating presence in the temple area. This priority of worship comes over into the Christian era. In 1 Pet 2:5, 9, the role of believers in a local church is described as "offering spiritual sacrifices acceptable to God through Jesus Christ" and declaring "the praises" of a gracious God (NIV). The "prayers of the saints" are represented as incense in a vision at Rev 5:8 (cf. 2 Chr 29:7). Christians are to offer their whole selves as "living sacrifices, holy and pleasing to God—this is your spiritual act of worship" (Rom 12:1 NIV). Here religious worship spills over into the rest of life. First, however, those of us who culturally tend to shy away from the institutional and the congregational must hear the more literal side of the message. Psalm 133:1, 3 suggests that the communal experience of temple worship was a prime source of blessing and vitality for ancient Israelites. In turn, the writer to the Hebrews could not conceive of exercising the privilege of access to God apart from the responsibility of loyal attendance at Christian meetings for mutual encouragement (Heb 10:19, 25).

2. In Hezekiah's appeal to the temple clergy to play their preliminary role in restoring the sanctuary, we hear the chronicler addressing the temple personnel of his own day. His message may be updated as a call to pastors of the church for continued consecration. Thus their example of spiritual living and reverent service can work to prompt lay Christians to turn their own hearts toward God.

3. The post-exilic community prized the vessels of the Temple, highlighted in 29:18-19. They were heirlooms that could be traced back to the temple builder, Solomon, and even to David (1 Chr 28:13-17; 2 Chronicles 4:1). In a spiritual sense, we Christians receive the communion cup ultimately from our Lord, who first passed it to his disciples' hands. In validation of our faith we take the morsel of bread broken first by Jesus and by faith hear his voice across the centuries, "Do this in remembrance of me."

4. At first sight, 29:21-24 gives an account of antiquated rites irrelevant to Christians today. On the contrary, however, they provide a necessary background to the thinking of the New Testament. The New Testament depends heavily on the concept of sacrifice in the Old Testament, especially as a way of expressing the meaning of the crucifixion. The problem of sin had not gone away by the first century CE, nor has it vanished in our own day. The early church lived and thought in a period when religious sacrifice was still common, not least in a Jewish context, as a means of dealing with sinfulness. Although such rituals are absent from modern culture, the church's theology—if it is to be a biblical one—cannot dispense with this dynamic concept, whose roots delve deep into the Old Testament. The New Testament's description of the death of Jesus in terms of "blood" takes its readers back to the blood rite described here. The atoning value of the burnt offering is echoed in important New Testament passages, even though the precise term is not used. In Mark 10:45, it partly underlies the explanation that Jesus came "to give his life [as] a ransom for many." The definition of the devoted love of Christ in Eph 5:2 refers to it: He "gave himself up for us [as] a fragrant offering and sacrifice to God" (cf. Lev 1:9). In 1 Pet 1:18-19, Christians are similarly described as "ransomed . . . with the precious blood of Christ, like that of a lamb without defect or blemish" (NRSV; cf. Lev 1:10).

The sense of propitiation implied in 2 Chronicles 29 is matched in the Letter to the Romans. Just as atoning sacrifices were the God-given answer to the divine wrath that loomed over the people, so also "God put forward" Jesus "as a sacrifice of atonement by his blood," as God's own solution to the wrath that threatened humanity (Rom 3:25 NRSV: cf. Rom 1:18; 2:5; 3:5-6; 4:15). Divine wrath coexists with divine love (Rom 5:8-9), just as in 2 Chronicles escaping it was possible because of the Lord's gracious provision of a means of atonement.

As for the purification offering, the writer to the Hebrews was aware of its importance in the Old Testament economy (Heb 9:22). He used its function on the Day of Atonement in Hebrews 9–10 to explain the work of Christ in dying and ascending alive to heaven. Just as the sanctuary was sprinkled with the blood of the purification offering, so also in the earthly counterpart of the heavenly sanctuary, elements have been purified through the sacrificial death of Christ—namely, the bad consciences and sinful hearts of those who have availed themselves of God's provision (Heb 9:14, 23; 10:22; cf. 1 John 1:7, 9).

In 1 Chr 29:23, this appropriation is symbolized by the laying of the offerer's right hand on the sacrificial victim. Such acts of self-identification touch the heart of the Christian gospel as the personal means of turning the bad news of human sinfulness into the good news of divine forgiveness. In 1 John 1:9, the verbal aspect of such appropriation is made explicit: "If we confess our sins, he who is faithful and just will forgive us our sins and cleanse us from all unrighteousness" (NRSV). Significantly, this New Testament promise is related not to the beginning of the Christian life, but to its continuation, as a means of maintaining pre-existing fellowship with God. In this respect, it aligns itself with the perspective of 2 Chronicles.

5. In 29:25-30 the chronicler values greatly following a Davidic blueprint for the use of music and song in worship. No such biblical blueprint is available to the local church. The New Testament principles of proclaiming Christ and worshiping both in spirit and truth, "and decently and in order" (1 Cor 14:40) apply to every Christian gathering, though the more liturgical churches have filled the gap with ancient traditions. The singing of psalms, or at least hymnic paraphrases, has been a healthy tradition, presumably based partly on the authority of Eph 5:19, which could be described as a New Testament counterpart to 2 Chr 29:25-30.

6. Worship in this chapter accents the public burnt offerings. This communal function underlies the reference to the burnt offering as a metaphor for Christian living in Rom 12:1. Worship was also offered by means of the private offerings of 29:30-35. These offerings comprise a large category of voluntary sacrifices, brought not because they were mandatory but to express personal devotion. Some churches use the phrase "tithes and offerings" for the collection; those offerings correspond to this type of sacrifice. Christians who categorize Old Testament religion as being marked by joyless formality and compulsion must reckon with the offerings and with the enthusiasm of 29:30, 36. Such offerings were the expression of willing hearts, and the chronicler placed a premium on voluntary contributions. The offerings of well-being are invested with a metaphorical interpretation in Heb 13:15-16, as vocal praise, doing good, and sharing one's resources with others: "Such sacrifices are pleasing to God" (NRSV).

2 Chronicles 30:1–31:1, United Passover Worship

COMMENTARY

This section provides the second example of Hezekiah's having acted properly in the Lord's sight (29:2). He was intended as a model for the post-exilic community to follow. Already in 29:24 we noticed the chronicler's interest in showing the king's concern for "all Israel." The joint celebration of passover and the Feast of Unleavened Bread provided an opportunity to invite all members of the covenant people to Jerusalem to worship at the Temple. The repentance of the northerners in 28:13 and their overtures to Judah in 28:14-15 had paved the way for such a united venture. The phrase "all Israel" in this comprehensive sense occurs at significant points in the narrative (30:5; 31:1). Unity meant for the chronicler a religious unity, worshiping "the God of Israel" (30:1, 5). He affirmed it over against the exclusivism associated with Ezra and Nehemiah.

This section lays stress not only on a common faith but on a continuity of faith from generation to generation as well. The present generation was to become a living link in the chain of faith. The Lord was the God of their common ancestors, Abraham, Isaac, and Israel (v. 6), and the God of their immediate predecessors (NIV, "fathers," vv. 7, 19, 22; cf. 28:9, 22; 29:6) and now "your God" (v. 9). The challenge went out to northerners and southerners alike in Hezekiah's day to live up to God's claims and to honor the

common roots of their faith by worshiping together. Hezekiah is the chronicler's hero in his refusal to write off the people of the north as apostates, but recognizing them instead as brothers and sisters in the faith who were to be welcomed in God's name.

The chronicler has left 2 Kings far behind, citing it last in 29:1-2 and about to echo it briefly in 31:1, 21. We do not know what sources he had available for these three chapters or to what extent they are simply his own reconstruction. An appeal to the north is historically fitting. The northern kingdom, earlier diminished territorially by the Assyrians, was brought to an end in 721 BCE; its land was incorporated into their provincial system. Hezekiah's naming of his son Manasseh, after the northern tribe, indicates his interest in the citizens of the old northern state halfway through his reign. Moreover, scholars now recognize that the deuteronomists had their own agenda. Religious information about Hezekiah may have been suppressed in order to promote the stock of Josiah, their own hero of the faith. Certainly the chronicler did not take over his account of a combined passover and Festival of Unleavened Bread from Josiah's celebration in 2 Kings 23. The irregularities of its timing and the admission of unclean participants look authentic. Yet the section is so full of expressions and concerns typical of the chronicler that it is difficult to disentangle his own contribution from older elements.[323]

The Pentateuch contains a number of different traditions concerning the passover and whether and in what respects it was linked with the Festival of Unleavened Bread.[324] Although the present account alludes freely to a variety of these traditions, it seems to come closest to the representation in the holiness code of Lev 23:5-8 and the later Num 28:16-25, in which the two are closely associated as sanctuary-based celebrations; the passover is held on the evening of Nisan 14, and the seven-day Festival of Unleavened Bread is held from Nisan 15.

30:1-5. Verse 1 provides a summary of a verbal proclamation accompanied by a letter, while the details are unpacked in vv. 2-9. "Ephraim and Mannasseh" refer to the northern tribes, as in 1 Chr 9:3. The failure to keep the passover in the first month could have been explained simply: It was now too late (cf. 29:17). The chronicler was concerned to relate the issue to the permission granted in Num 9:6-12 for an individual to hold it in the second month on grounds of uncleanness or absence. Numbers 9:6 is quoted in v. 3: "They could not keep the passover on that day" (cf. the REB; the renderings of the NRSV and the NIV are paraphrases that obscure the allusion).[325] Justification is found in the Torah in a provision for an individual, which is here applied more broadly. The grounds of ritual impurity and absence are hermeneutically applied to the priests' failure to purify themselves in adequate numbers, a circumstance borrowed from 29:34, and to the absence of "the people," which here refers not to the representative assembly of 29:36 but to the larger, ideal assembly. Its territorial extent from Beer-sheba to Dan, as in the Davidic narrative at 1 Chr 21:2, reflects the ideal boundaries of the united kingdom, now existing, in principle, under the reign of a Davidic king. The chronicler makes another reference to the Torah (v. 5), now to Deut 16:1-8, where a pilgrimage festival of sacrifice at the central sanctuary is envisioned, rather than the home-based celebration of Exodus 12:1. Temple worship had to be grounded in the Torah. The nature of the celebration as pilgrimage will be affirmed in v. 13.

30:6-9. The message is presented at the center, an invitation to come to the divinely accredited Temple, echoing the narrative of vv. 1 and 5. The rest of the proclamation alludes to restoration after exile. Accordingly, the chronicler borrows from Zech 1:2-4, an appeal to an early post-exilic constituency to live up to the spiritual ideals of returning to the land by returning to the Lord. Then the Lord would return to them in the fullness of a restoration blessing. The message transcends its explicit audience in the narrative and speaks also to the chronicler's contemporaries, setting out conditions for their enjoying the fulfillment of divine promises. There was a way to escape from a perpetuation of exile, a way outlined in the prophetic text. Not only the Law but also the Prophets provide biblical models for the chronicler to commend to his constituency. The appeals to "return to the LORD . . . that he may return to you" and "Do not be like your fathers" (NIV) are cited from Zech 1:2-4. They are given backing from the Torah by the warning "Do not be stiffnecked," taken from Deut 10:16, which is set in a context of the Lord's renewed grace to Israel after their disobedience.

The proclamation involves a series of appeals backed by incentives and reasons. Although it is addressed to both Judah and the northern tribes, it is angled toward the latter, as the references to Assyrian destruction at the hands of Tiglath-pileser III and Shalmaneser V (see 2 Kgs 15:29; 17:3; 18:9) and exile make clear. Judah, too, is in view: It was described in similar terms in Hezekiah's speech at 29:6, 8-10. The leveling down to the fate of the northern kingdom, implied in chaps. 28–29, now becomes explicit. South and north stood before their God as sinners and as victims of the Lord's fair judgment. They all stood in an exilic situation after unfaithfulness to God. The spirit of 7:14 permeates the speech. The people are virtually called to humble themselves, seek the Lord's face, and turn from their wicked ways, so that God may accept them back. In fact, the chronicler has reserved until now Solomon's petition that the Lord may arrange

323. See J. Rosenbaum, "Hezekiah's Reform and the Deuteronomistic Tradition," *HTR* 72 (1979) 23-43; McKenzie, *The Chronicler's Use of the Deuteronomistic History*, 170-72; Lowery, *The Reforming Kings*, 162-67.

324. See the survey in Shaver, *Torah and the Chronicler's History Work*, 105-9.

325. See Fishbane, *Biblical Interpretation in Ancient Israel*, 154-57.

compassionate treatment for the exiles (1 Kgs 8:50). In the light of 2 Chr 7:14, petition becomes promise, a promise of response to Israel's repentance. Although explicit vocabulary links with 7:14 are scanty, the repeated motif of turning or returning is important. In the narrative of response, however, the reference to self-humbling in v. 11 provides an intratextual echo. The definition of God as "gracious and merciful" is inspired by Exod 34:6, a text from the same narrative setting as Deut 10:16, cited earlier. The definition commemorates forgiveness that was originally extended to those who had broken a brand-new covenant by worshiping the golden calf. Just as the old dispensation of the Torah offered a second chance, so, too, did the new, temple-based dispensation. History repeated itself, bringing new hope to victims of exile in Hezekiah's time and also to their counterparts in the chronicler's age.

30:10-12. The response to Hezekiah's proclamation was mixed. In v. 11, "some men" (NIV) is a superior rendering to "only a few" (NRSV) in describing the northern pilgrims. The religious unity rejected by the north in chap. 13 was again rejected by most, but at least the offer had been made in good faith. The tribal list is only representative, in the light of v. 18. Mention of Zebulun as the tribe farthest north contrasts with Dan (v. 5). The discrepancy may point to use of a historical detail here, though consistency is not the chronicler's strong suit. Judah's unanimous response is sensitively presented, not as a feather in its cap, but as the result of the Lord's gracious nudging. The chronicler, himself a Judean, will not allow his fellow Judeans to take the credit, as if they were doing God a favor. The unanimity is a partial echo of a Davidic phenomenon in 1 Chr 12:38. The "word of the LORD" refers to Zech 1:2-4, which was used in the king's message (cf. 2 Chr 29:15).

30:13-14. The spiritual commitment of the pilgrims to the God of the Temple led to reform in Jerusalem and the destruction of altars built at Ahaz's behest (28:24). Just as the Levites and priests had cleansed the Temple, so also the people purified the city of pagan worship paraphernalia, each group acting in its own sphere.

30:15-20. The chronicler describes the combined festivals of passover and Unleavened Bread. The laity's slaughtering of the passover lambs (v. 15a) is followed by a statement that the Levites took over this task (v. 17b). What precedes in vv. 15b-17a parenthetically explains v. 17b and should be translated with pluperfect verbs (as in the NJB). Criticism of the religious professionals, confined in 29:34; 30:3 to priests, is now extended ·to the Levites (cf. 24:5-6). Stung by the laity's enthusiasm, they now prepared for their ritual roles. Opposition to the united festival, and perhaps to Hezekiah's reform, was found not only among the northerners but also at home among the temple staff. Some priests and even Levites stood aloof until their hardness of heart was melted by the devotion of the pilgrims. They duly joined in, after offering their purificatory burnt offerings (cf. 29:21). The reference to the Torah is a general one, as a reference to the prominence of priests in the ritual.[326] The description also demarcates the non-traditional role to be adopted by the Levites in v. 17b. Just as penitential pilgrimage gave honor to the prophetic word (v. 12), so also the ritual paid tribute to the Torah. The passover lambs slain in a temple setting were naturally subject to the blood rite. The innovation to which the chronicler draws attention is the Levites' taking over from the laity the rite of slaughtering the sacrificial animals. It is explained in v. 18 as an emergency procedure, like the skinning in 29:34. In chap. 35, such levitical participation will be presented as normative. A subplot runs through these chapters, to give Levites new roles in the sacrificial procedure.

The explanation concerns especially the northern pilgrims as lacking ritual purity and so unable to slaughter their own passover lambs. The Levites stood in for the pilgrims, while the priests cooperated in the arrangements. Yet it was not enough, for the essence of the passover was eating the lamb. In 30:18-19, Hezekiah availed himself of the provision of 7:14, conscious that the provisions about the passover in Numbers 9 had been exhausted. The Torah was not God's last word, though it was the norm, as v. 16 makes clear and the rest of 2 Chronicles overwhelmingly testifies. In the temple dispensation,

326. Williamson, *1 and 2 Chronicles*, 369-70.

there was a higher principle of grace, a Solomonic ideal whereby the sanctuary was a house of prayer as well as a place of sacrifice. Moreover, the Lord had shown that spiritual intentions are honored in the blessing that followed David's first attempt to bring the ark to Jerusalem (1 Chronicles 13–14). So Hezekiah prayed, treading in the noble tradition of Solomon, who prayed on the people's behalf in chap. 6. In Hezekiah's prayer that the Lord may "provide atonement" (v. 18 TNK) there is minimal verbal contact with 7:14, but again the ensuing narrative expresses the link, the divine hearing and healing. The golden text was gloriously fulfilled. The verb of healing had to be stretched. The chronicler used it to refer to some objective evidence of the Lord's affirmative answer. Doubtless he extrapolated from Num 9:13 (cf. Lev 15:31) a punishment of being cut off from the people for improper eating (cf. Ezek 14:8-9; Acts 5:5, 10; 1 Cor 11:29-30). He envisioned for them a fate like Uzzah's in 1 Chr 13:10. Instead, the Lord left them unharmed, like the household of Obed-edom in 1 Chr 13:14.[327] It was a divine tribute to the spirituality of the northern pilgrims. The language used to describe an earlier generation of such pilgrims, setting hearts to seek the Lord (2 Chr 11:16), has been reused here.

30:21-22. This is a short description of the weeklong Festival of Unleavened Bread, which concentrates on the private offerings brought by the people rather than on the official sacrifices of Lev 23:8 and Num 28:19-24. The chiastic structure of these verses highlights the link between the people's daily praise and the contribution of levitical music and song and priestly trumpet blasts, which stimulated their praise.[328] Hezekiah congratulated the Levites; their standard of choral and musical excellence was not something to be taken for granted. "Hear, hear!" is the chronicler's implicit comment. The "offerings of well-being" (NRSV) were brought by individuals, as in 29:31, 35. They were tokens of willing worship and expressions of personal thanksgiving.

30:23–31:1. The festivities spilled into a second week. In this paragraph, the theme of the united people of God is prominent once more. The chronicler bids his readers to think of Solomon, who also engaged in two weeks of enthusiastic celebration (v. 26; 7:8-10). So generous were the king and the officials and so ample now the supply of priests identifying themselves with Hezekiah's vision that sacrifices abounded and sacred meals of veal and lamb lasted through the second week. The inclusion of resident aliens or non-Israelite proselytes from north and south echoes their presence at the passover laid down in Num 9:14 (also Exod 12:19, 48-49). In this section, the chronicler has used Numbers 9 both to exemplify obedience to the Torah and to expose its limitations, which further divine revelation had made good. The aliens from the north presumably included the foreigners brought into Israel (the chronicler presupposes and counters 2 Kgs 17:24-41).[329]

The united gathering was dismissed by the "levitical priests" (NJB with the MT, similarly the TNK; the NIV and the NRSV insert "and" with some ancient MSS, but only priests gave the blessing). They offered the priestly benediction of Num 6:24-26 (cf. Lev 9:22; 1 Chr 23:13). It was no magic formula but a prayer, which God duly heard and answered in the agricultural blessing of 31:10 and also in the protection and prosperity of chap. 32. The use of the deuteronomic term "levitical priests" and the linguistic echoes of the divine blessing of Israel in the tithe-related Deut 26:15 at v. 27b suggest that the chronicler's mind was already moving on to the deuteronomic topic of the tithe in the next section. The removal of Judean pagan shrines (v. 1) reflects 2 Kgs 18:4 (cf. 2 Kgs 18:22), but enthusiastically extends the reform to northern territory in keeping with the dominant theme of the section. It spelled the last undoing of Ahaz's pernicious work (28:25). The Temple now stood in solitary splendor, unchallenged in its testimony to the Lord as God of a bigger Israel.

---

327. See Japhet, *I & II Chronicles*, 953.
328. Kleinig, *The Lord's Song*, 76, 88.

See M. Cogan, "For We, Like You, Worship Your God: Three Biblical Portrayals of Samaritan Origins," *VT* 38 (1988) 286-92, esp. 290-91.

REFLECTIONS

This section provides food for thought for translating the truth of a universal church into a practical demonstration of unity among various Christian traditions. Hezekiah used the common origins of now diverse groups (30:6) as the basis for his call to joint celebration of worship and fellowship.

1. The chronicler's account of Ahaz's reign revealed the privations suffered by Judah. So Hezekiah's message in 30:6-10 could appeal to needs shared by north and south, and so to a common yearning for renewal and grace. All the people must humble themselves before the Lord. A call for renewed commitment is likely to be heard by people when it is addressed to a sense of spiritual dissatisfaction. Dietrich Bonhoeffer wrote eloquently about a formal brand of Christianity into which we can all fall. Cheap grace, as he called it, is "the preaching of forgiveness without requiring repentance, baptism without church discipline, Communion without confession. . . . Cheap grace is grace without discipleship, grace without the cross, grace without Jesus Christ living and incarnate."[330]

2. What if the enthusiasm of one group is largely snubbed by another group (30:10)? Pessimists would have forecast such a rejection and deplored the enterprise as a waste of time. But that is no reason not to make the effort, urged the chronicler. The powerful presence of separatist traditions and conventions must not be minimized. Hezekiah reaffirmed as non-negotiable Abijah's claim that the Jerusalem Temple was the true focus of the ancestral faith (13:10-11), claiming that the decisive sign of fellowship with the Lord was to share in worship there. For the north, it meant going against a religious current that had been flowing the other way for centuries. It meant abandoning an entrenched position. Concessions had to be made on Judah's side by lowering temporarily the standards of the Temple and the Torah (30:18-19). The need to build bridges across Christian divisions may press us to surrender what is emotionally dear and challenge us to reexamine cherished convictions.

What if one group's feelings of superiority are well founded? The chronicler refuses to give credit to Judah, but says, "Thanks to God," to divine enabling, which alone brings us where we are in our best moments. The whole section concerning divisions in the local church in 1 Corinthians 3–5 is applicable on a larger scale. It is a sad irony that the mocking of the northern tribes will become Judah's response in 36:16.

3. United worship is excellent, but it cannot stand alone. Changes follow, in areas for which different groups realize themselves to be responsible (30:14; 31:1). Circles of reform gradually widened. Lives that know God's blessing must banish that which is alien to the true God. Further steps of faith grant new insights for bringing our lives more into line with God's will.

4. Irony appears in the reluctance of religious professionals to commit themselves to Hezekiah's efforts at religious integration. Put to shame by lay enthusiasm, they eventually joined in the revival movement. For Christian ecumenism to flourish, it must light its fire in the hearts of all believers and in local churches that go out of their way to bear a common witness to their Lord.

5. When people work together, concessions have to be made to ensure amicable relations. The chronicler shows the lengths he was prepared to go to in the cause of religious reunification, presenting a scene in which the temple rules of purity were waived for northern worshipers. There were times when the Torah had to stay broken in the interests of a higher ideal and God's greater glory. We may welcome this

---

330. Dietrich Bonhoeffer, *The Cost of Discipleship*, 2nd ed., trans. R. H. Fuller (New York: Macmillan, 1959) 36.

distinction between law and spirit. Or it may leave us murmuring uneasily about compromise, relativism, and situational ethics. May God give us insight as to how and when to apply this risky principle.

The chronicler's teaching on this point is part of a wider paradigm of a divine double standard. On the one hand, believers had a normative relationship with the Lord, governed by responsibilities and expectations determined by the Torah. On the other hand, there were emergency situations when the Torah hindered rather than helped. In such cases, there had to be a redemptive breakthrough if the momentum of spiritual life was to be restored. Here the Lord looked at people's motives and took the spiritual thought for the deed and the repentant spirit for obedience (30:11, 19). This shift cannot be equated with the move from the law to the gospel. The parallel for Christian believers appears in the First Letter of John, in the tension between obeying God's commandments and finding a fresh start in divine forgiveness and renewal (1 John 2:1; 5:2-3) after moral breakdown.

2 Chronicles 31:2-21, Temple Reorganization

COMMENTARY

This section is the third and last result of Hezekiah's spiritual activity, introduced in 29:2 and enthusiastically recapitulated in 31:20b-21. The theme of this section reverts to Ahaz's closing down of the Temple (28:4), which is envisioned as having been reopened (chap. 29). Still, more remained to be done. Presumably the system of staffing the Temple had collapsed. Hezekiah had to reorganize it, just as Jehoiada had done (23:18-19).

31:2. Hezekiah implemented the system of coordinating personnel and duties, set up by David and administered by Solomon, after the Temple was built (1 Chr 28:21; 2 Chr 8:14; cf. 1 Chr 16:37-42; 23:5). This moment gave the chronicler an opportunity to instruct his own generation, urging them to make the Temple services run like clockwork. This was part of what it meant to "seek" God (v. 21). David's and Solomon's system of sacrifice, security, and singing was the Lord's way for them to follow. Moreover, there is an allusion to an even older heritage. Temple procedure stood in line with gatekeeping duties for the tabernacle. This role had passed to the Temple, so that its precincts in turn became the Lord's "camp" (v. 2 NRSV, which implicitly adopts the order of words in the LXX; cf. 1 Chr 9:18).[331] Moreover, the sacrificial calendar followed the one laid down in the Torah (v. 3; see Numbers 28–29), duly transferred

to the Temple by Solomon (8:13). Sanctions regarding the tabernacle constituted a religious mandate "ordained forever for Israel" (2:4). Each generation of the Lord's people was responsible for maintaining these commands. The chronicler is here expanding in a religious direction the information that Hezekiah "kept the commandments that the Lord commanded Moses" (2 Kgs 18:6 NRSV; cf. 2 Chr 31:21).[332]

31:3. The king undertook to provide the regular burnt offerings that made up regular worship practice. It was a costly responsibility, such as Josiah was to assume in the case of passover lambs (35:7). Such support echoes the gifts of sacrificial victims made by Hezekiah and the officials (30:24). There was a precedent in Solomon's special gift of offerings in 7:5, while 8:12-13 implies his responsibility for the regular sacrifices. Presumably the chronicler, writing when the monarchy no longer existed, was arguing that such burdens should be borne by the private resources of the governor and leading officials or by state funds (see Ezra 6:9-10), not, at any rate, by the people (cf. Neh 10:32-33).

31:4-10. The people had their own responsibility: to provide consistent financial support for the temple staff (see Neh 10:35-39). Administrative ramifications will occupy

331. Allen, The Greek Chronicles, 2:108.

332. Shaver, Torah and the Chronicler's History Work, 91.

the text up to to v. 19. The amount of space the chronicler devoted to this concern reflects the difficulty of maintaining full staffing in the Temple of the post-exilic period (see Neh 13:10-13; Mal 3:8-10). In the early days, economic stringency was a significant factor (cf. Hag 1:2-11). By the more settled time of the chronicler, it was a question of unwillingness rather than want, as he implied in 1 Chronicles 29. The message of these verses is threefold: that such support was (1) a divine mandate, (2) a human obligation to be discharged with good grace, and (3) a source of divine blessing. The chronicler leaned heavily on the Torah for his terminology, expecting his Torah-versed readers to catch the allusions and hear the solemn call of duty. His prime source was Num 18:8-32, whose phrases, including the verb "bring [in]," are echoed in vv. 5-6, 12.[333] The "portion due to the priests and the Levites" bought them time for Torah-mandated duties by releasing them from the need to work to support themselves and their families (v. 4; cf. Neh 13:10).

The royal command came first to the citizens of Jerusalem. As soon as it went out, there was a generous response from these Israelites, or members of God's people. Then others responded, those of the community of faith living in Judean towns.[334] The responses took the form of offerings of firstfruits and tithes. According to Numbers 18:1, the former went to priests and the latter to Levites. A tithe of honey is mentioned in Lev 2:11-12, and a tithe of livestock in Lev 27:32. The "holy things" (NIV; NRSV, "dedicated things") refer generally to these donations in v. 6 and in v. 12 (see Num 18:8, "holy gifts/offerings"), while they are called "contributions" in vv. 10, 12-13 (see Num 18:8, 11 REB). These holy things were tithes and were not themselves tithed, as v. 6 seems to imply. The phrase there must mean "and [the rest of] the tithes consisting of holy things." The third and seventh months were key agricultural periods, marking respectively the grain harvest and the grape and other fruit harvest.

The lavishness of the people's response, strategically mentioned in vv. 5 and 10, carries a message of challenge to readers. The

copious contributions evoke exclamations of blessing upon God and the people. They refer to two formulas of blessing, "Blessed be the LORD who . . ." (see Ruth 4:14) and "May you be blessed by the LORD for . . ." (see Ruth 2:20). In fact, the Lord had already provided a bumper harvest, so that the people lost nothing by their gifts. The windows of heaven had been opened for them (Mal 3:10)!

31:11-19. Arrangements had to be made for storing the contributions (vv. 11-13) and then for allocating them (vv. 14-19). Two Levites with ten assistants were given charge of the stored items, for which the chronicler in v. 12 loosely piles up three earlier terms. A high-ranking security officer (see Commentary on 1 Chr 26:14, 17) was given the responsibility of distributing the mandated items, "the contributions made to the LORD" (v. 14). These were supplemented, we are now told, with voluntary gifts. The chronicler took the opportunity to mention further priestly dues, "the most holy offerings." He had in view their definition in Num 18:9-10 as food derived from the grain offering, the sin offering, and the guilt offering, which had to be eaten in the sacred precincts. The distribution officer had six assistants, posted in the tribal areas where the priests and Levites lived when not on duty (cf. 1 Chr 6:54-81).

Verses 16-18 define more exactly the regulations for distribution to serving personnel, specifying who was eligible, though the definition is not crystal clear. Registration for receiving food differed for priests and Levites (v. 17 NRSV, REB, NJB; the NIV interprets otherwise, following the punctuation of the MT, which does not fit the context so well). Priests were registered according to their ancestral families. For v. 18, the NRSV appears to be correct in taking priests as the implicit subject. The family members of priests were also eligible to receive food; evidently priests brought their immediate families to Jerusalem. Verse 18b may mean that the priests had greater holiness (cf. Lev 21:1-15; Ezek 44:15-31), which isolated them from the rest of society so that they needed their families there for companionship. In the case of Levites, who apparently did not bring their families, only (male) serving staff were registered, according to their particular duties (see 1 Chr 23:4-5).

---

333. Fishbane, *Biblical Interpretation*, 214-15.
334. The inclusion of "and Judah" in 32:6 is difficult to construe and may be an addition. See *BHS.*

The limitation at the beginning of v. 16 is best attached to the end of v. 15 as an elaboration of "old and young alike." Verse 16*a* implies that, in the case of off-duty staff, registration was not necessary for the young (see the REB's "irrespective of their registration"). The reason was that all males ages three and over (children were breast-fed up to that age) were automatically eligible for food from the sanctuary. After that a new topic begins, the procedures for serving priests and Levites. The arrangements for off-duty staff resume in v. 19. The assistants mentioned in v. 15 allocated food to every male of the priestly line and to every registered Levite. We may deduce that the beginning of v. 16 applies only to priestly males, as in fact the phrase "the cities/towns of the priests" in v. 15 suggests (cf. 1 Chr 6:54-60). Evidently females within priests' families could not obtain food when the priests were not on duty, while the families of registered Levites were never recipients. In both cases, there was opportunity to provide food by other means.

Overall, vv. 14-19 give the impression of being angled toward priests, with levitical regulations inserted somewhat awkwardly as necessary. This suggests that the chronicler adapted a post-exilic priestly document. All these details, whatever their precise meaning, indicate scrupulous thoroughness and conscientious stewardship. Contributions given in good faith (v. 12) had to be allocated in good faith (v. 15). So rules had to be followed for responsible allocation.

31:20-21. The chronicler loosely followed 2 Kgs 18:6-7*a* in these verses to create a summary of chaps. 29–31. Verse 20*a* summarizes vv. 4-19, and vv. 20b-21 enthusiastically develop 29:2 as a sweeping résumé of the intervening material. Hezekiah's devotion to God in matters pertaining to Temple and Torah was exemplary. His ambition was to apply himself to the revealed will of God and to the right worship of God. In seeking the Lord with all his heart, Hezekiah was a king like Jehoshaphat (22:9). The king's ensuing prosperity opens a window to the next section.

REFLECTIONS

The theme of chapter 31 is the maintenance of temple worship. Sacrifices did not appear on the altar by themselves, nor could the staff live on air. Human resources and organization were necessary to keep the system going to the glory of God. There is a type of piety that regards efficient methods as carnal. The chronicler adduced Hezekiah's organizational acumen as one fine way in which he was able to seek the Lord, thereby endowing the most mundane of religious tasks with an aura of devotion. The chronicler was encouraged to think this way because he inherited the details of the priestly strata of the Torah. Every church requires efficient administration and coordination, of which the visitor is hardly aware unless they are lacking.

Most of the section 31:2-21 is concerned with funding. The chronicler's portrayal of the king as the donor-patron of the Temple uses a pre-exilic ideal to take some of the burden off the worshiping people. We may compare tax concessions, such as the exemption of church buildings from property taxes and the parsonage allowance for pastors, that apply to churches in the United States (cf. Ezra 7:24).

Yet much of the burden had to fall on the people. Every church or parachurch organization knows the time and energy that must be devoted to fund-raising. A few Christian organizations operate on the lofty principle that "the Lord will provide." Yet the chronicler's axiom is reasonable. Paul expressed it thus: "Those who work in the temple get their food from the temple, and those who serve at the altar share in what is offered on the altar" (1 Cor 9:13 NIV). The apostle deduced from this axiom a corresponding Christian tenet that "those who preach the gospel should receive their living from the gospel" (1 Cor 9:14 NIV; cf. Luke 10:7; 1 Tim 5:18). There need be no embarrassment in soliciting funds for Christian work from the Christian public, nor should it be resented as unspiritual, provided that fitting approaches are used. And, the chronicler would add, there must be scrupulous integrity in the allocation of funds. The gospel has not been advanced by tales of the lavish spending of countless widows' mites.

The chronicler, never slow to provide incentives for his challenges, gives an agricultural blessing (31:10). Paul used a similar argument when he wrote that God is generous to those who were generous to support the poor church in Jerusalem: "God is able to provide you with every blessing in abundance, so that by always having enough of everything you may share abundantly in every good work" (2 Cor 9:8 NRSV; cf. Phil 4:19). Obviously his words are intended not to provide a selfish motivation for giving, but as an assurance that God is nobody's debtor and blesses even the disinterested giver (cf. Luke 6:32-38). Another incentive appears at the end of the chapter: The one who seeks the Lord finds success also (31:21). We may think once more of the spiritual arithmetic of Matt 6:33, "Seek first [the Father's] kingdom . . . and all these things will be given to you as well" (NIV).

2 Chronicles 32:1-33, Deliverance and Blessing

COMMENTARY

We have seen that, when compared with the writer of 2 Kings, the chronicler gave much more space to temple matters in his account of Hezekiah's reign. Correspondingly, he reduced the amount of material devoted in 2 Kgs 18:13–19:37 to the Assyrian crisis of 701 BCE. Besides 2 Kings, he seems also to have had at his disposal another source concerning his measures taken to defend Jerusalem (vv. 2-6) and his projects (vv. 27-30). The narrative is set within a framework that interprets Hezekiah's success as a direct result of his spirituality. The summary of the latter in 31:21, repeated at the start of chap. 32, introduces the theme of the king's success. Hezekiah is commended as a spiritual model. His spirituality, already demonstrated in his zeal for the Temple, now takes on new dimensions: trust when attacked and repentance. The chronicler's hero is realistically unexempt from threats and scars.

The section covers the king's deliverance (vv. 1-26) and his general success (vv. 27-33), though the latter also breaks into vv. 5-6 and 22b-23. Three examples of deliverance at God's hands are given: from Assyrian invasion (vv. 1-22), from deadly sickness (v. 24), and from divine wrath (vv. 25-26; cf. v. 31). Most attention is paid to the first. The 2 Kings account celebrates Hezekiah's reign by highlighting Sennacherib's failure to capture Jerusalem, interpreting it as a tribute to the power of the Lord. The chronicler echoed this interpretation, but wove it into his own literary tapestry of holy war, in which supernatural deliverance comes when committed believers demonstrate fresh trust in God. Again, war comes as a providential surprise, unprovoked by previous sin on the king's part. The Lord's protective presence is itself a blessing bestowed on the good king. The catchword that marked Jehoshaphat's and Asa's God-given victories, the Lord's being "with" each king at a time of unprovoked attack, recurs in v. 8, echoing 15:2 and 20:17 (see also 13:12).

32:1-6a. The chronicler begins with Sennacherib's invasion of Judah in 2 Kgs 18:13, but, in line with his overall perspective, regards the capture of fortified cities as a threat rather than a fact, presumably by interpreting the verbal form differently from the MT (as "in order that he might capture them"). Verses 2-6 have no counterpart in 2 Kings. The topics of v. 5 also appear in Isa 22:8-11, but the blatantly different treatment and lack of intertextual correspondence suggest that the chronicler knew them from another written tradition. Hezekiah's practical measures concerning Jerusalem's water supply (vv. 3-4, 30) give the same impression, while the organization of a conscript army, mentioned obliquely in v. 6, aligns with more specific information supplied for earlier reigns.

The king took defensive measures against a siege. Isaiah condemned such precautions as indications of lack of faith (Isa 22:8-11). The chronicler regularly gave defensive building and conscription a positive significance. Such actions were associated with divine blessing in the cases of Asa and Jehoshaphat (14:6-8; 17:12-19). In each instance, such measures were not used in the ensuing war. The divine and human help (vv. 3 and 8) echoes a Davidic pattern in 1 Chronicles 11–12. The first measure was control of the water supply. It was a separate procedure from the construction of the Siloam tunnel (v. 30), an extensive enterprise that must have occurred earlier. The water supply from the Gihon Spring had been channeled into outlets to irrigate the cultivated terraces on the western slope of the Kidron Valley, which then produced a runoff stream at the bottom of the valley. These outlets were now blocked off to prevent Assyrian access to the water.[335] A second measure was the improvement of Jerusalem's fortifications ("and raised towers on it," NRSV, similarly NIV; this rendering involves a slight change; see *BHS*). The other wall built by Hezekiah is probably that of which a portion was found in 1969–71. It enclosed part of the western hill of Jerusalem, which had become populated.[336] The third measure was the organization and arming of a defensive force.

32:6b-8. It was the chronicler's practice to preface a battle report with a speech or prayer or both in which trust in the Lord was affirmed in reaction to the military crisis. The speech in vv. 7-8, perhaps set in the square (mentioned in 29:4), takes the form of an encouragement for a task, here adapted to a pre-battle speech.[337] It has the standard elements of a call for courage and an assurance of the divine presence, but it does so as a vehicle for expressing trust in the Lord's power to save. Such trust could put natural fears to flight and impart strength to face opposition unflinchingly. The motif of the divine presence in a military context was borrowed from 2 Kgs 18:7a, already echoed more generally

in 31:21. The belittling phrase "arm of flesh" reflects biblical language (e.g., Isa 31:3; Jer 17:5), while v. 7b recalls such texts as 2 Kgs 6:16 and Isa 7:14.

32:9-15. The shift from v. 8 to v. 9 brings to the fore a contrast that runs throughout vv. 1-22, that between the God-honoring believer and the blasphemous infidel. The counterpointing is accentuated by the parallel titles "King Hezekiah of Judah" and "King Sennacherib of Assyria." To be for or against the Lord is the basic issue for the chronicler. The shocking nature of Sennacherib's blasphemies, underlined in v. 19, is an implicit call to faith, intended to put Judean readers on their mettle and to transform nominal faith into keenness. The core of Israel's faith was under attack.

As v. 16 hints, the chronicler selectively condensed the composite account of 2 Kgs 18:13–19:37 into a single narrative to express a barrage of threats via an oral message (vv. 9-16), a letter (v. 17), and intimidating shouts (v. 18). He omitted and adapted material that did not fit his holy war perspective. Already the calm, resolute believer of vv. 7-8 looks different from the desperate figure of 2 Kgs 19:1-4. Jehoshaphat was allowed his fear in 2 Chr 20:3, 12, but Hezekiah was not, though he will be presented as more human in vv. 25-26. The very form of the speech made the transformation inevitable.

Hezekiah's speech deactivates the verbal warheads launched by Sennacherib, reducing them to fireworks. The Assyrian king was only accumulating providential grounds for his eventual disgrace and premature death (v. 21). Although the chronicler imagines the worst, going beyond 2 Kings in representing Jerusalem as already under siege (v. 10), Sennacherib turned out to be a paper tiger. His speech follows the Chronicles pattern of introductory arguments (vv. 10-14) and a main challenge prefaced by "And now" (v. 15). The arguments consist of a series of sneering questions. As in the 2 Kings presentation, there is a shift in Sennacherib's denials from the divine will to save to the power to do so. The speech amalgamates Rabshakeh's first speech in 2 Kgs 18:19-25 (vv. 10, 12) with his second speech in 2 Kgs 18:28-35 (vv. 11, 13-14) and anticipates Sennacherib's letter in 2 Kgs 19:10-13 (v. 13; "predecessors"

---

335. J. Simons, *Jerusalem in the OT* (Leiden; Brill, 1952) 177.
336. See N. Avigad, "Excavations in the Jewish Quarter of the Old City 1968-1974," in *Jerusalem Revealed: Archaeology in the Holy City 1968-1974*," ed. Y. Yadin (Jerusalem: Israel Exploration Society, 1975) 41-51, esp. 43-44.
337. R. A. Mason, *Preaching the Tradition: Homily and Hermeneutics After the Exile* (Cambridge: Cambridge University Press, 1990) 110.

would be a better rendering than the NRSV's "ancestors" in vv. 13-15). References to Judah's alliance with Egypt in 2 Kgs 18:21, 24*b* are understandably filtered out. So, too, are the now unnecessary warnings to Hezekiah about trusting in his own strength in 2 Kgs 18:20, 23, 24*a*.

32:16-19. If Sennacherib was counterpointed with Hezekiah in vv. 8-9, he is the arrogant rival of the Lord in v. 16, where his "servants" match God's "servant Hezekiah." The chronicler expresses the same royal ideology as that found in Psalm 2, where the kings of the earth "set themselves . . . against the LORD and his anointed" (Ps 2:2 NRSV). Here, too, the Lord is the unseen power behind the Judean throne, guaranteeing the eventual triumph of king and people and the downfall of their blasphemous foes. The mention of "the gods of the nations" (v. 17) focuses on 2 Kgs 19:12 and develops it into a plain statement of denial. Its "insulting" nature is derived from Hezekiah's reaction in 2 Kgs 19:16 (חרף *ḥērēp*, in the piel; NRSV, "mock"; NIV, "insult"; cf. 2 Kgs 19:4, 22-23). The intimidating shouts of v. 18 come from 2 Kgs 18:26, 28, transposed in order to form a climactic conclusion. The chronicler has the last word in v. 19, derived from Hezekiah's prayer in 2 Kgs 19:18. If in v. 16 he echoed a royal tradition, in referring to "the God of Jerusalem" he draws on Zion ideology, in which it is celebrated as God's own city (see Psalms 46; 48; 87). Such thinking would be dealt a cruel blow in 36:19 (cf. Lam 4:12), but it could spring to new life in post-exilic times. Jerusalem was an essential ingredient in the chronicler's restoration hope (cf. 6:6; 12:13; 1 Chr 9:3, 34; 11:4-9).

32:20-23. The prayers of trust (v. 20) echo 2 Kgs 19:4, 15, 30. They are the human factor that tipped the scales from defeat to deliverance. Jehoshaphat had said about prayer to a powerful God at a time of crisis: "You will hear and save" (20:9; cf. 13:15; 14:11; 18:31). The Lord did save (v. 22). The verb הציל (*hiṣṣîl*, in the hiphil, "rescue"), variously rendered in the NRSV and the NIV, has run negatively through vv. 11-17, but now a synonym celebrates its positive truth. Deliverance takes two appropriate forms, abbreviated from 2 Kgs 19:35-37: the supernatural defeat of Sennacherib's forces and the ironic

failure of a pagan god to protect his devotee from providential punishment. The menacing "hand" so blatantly brandished in Sennacherib's speech was rendered powerless.

The chronicler used the event as an example of numerous victories (cf. 2 Kgs 18:7-8). He deduced that, like Jehoshaphat in 20:30, Hezekiah entered into the Solomonic heritage of divinely given "rest" (NRSV, following the LXX, the Old Latin, and the Vulgate; the MT's "guided" in the sense of "took care" [so NIV; cf. Gen 47:17] is contextually less likely).[338] Another of his blessings, he infers, was the international prestige like that which Solomon (9:23-24) and Jehoshaphat (17:10-11) had enjoyed. The indemnity Hezekiah paid to Assyria in 2 Kgs 18:14-16 finds no place in the chronicler's idealistic narrative. He had a bigger agenda to promote, one with eschatological implications. Solomon's golden age had represented for him one end of a rainbow, while its other end rested out of sight in a coming age. In the same way, Hezekiah's glory was a sign pointing to eschatological splendor. Sacred traditions pertaining to the dynasty and to Zion found anticipatory fulfillment in his reign (see Pss 72:10; 76:11).

32:24-26. If deliverance from Sennacherib was the chronicler's main example of deliverance, he now offers instances in other areas. Hezekiah is now brought down to earth as a fallible mortal. The chronicler assumes that his readers know the account of the king's sickness and the visit of envoys from Babylon (2 Kgs 20:1-9). At death's door, Hezekiah once more offers a trusting prayer, which the Lord not only answers but confirms with a miraculous sign. In spite of this favor, the king ostentatiously displays all his wealth to the envoys. In the 2 Kings narrative, Isaiah had judged this a reprehensible act. It is characterized here as an exhibition of pride that left God out of account. The sin of Amaziah and Uzziah all over again (25:19; 26:16), it could have led to terrible punishment such as those kings had incurred. Instead, Hezekiah resorted to the Solomonic principle of 7:14, not for others (as in 30:18-20) but for himself. The chronicler regarded the royal submission of 2 Kgs 20:19a as an example of the self-humbling required by the gracious provision

---

338. See Barthélemy, *Critique textuelle de l'Ancien Testament,* 1:511.

of 7:14. So the king avoided the divine wrath expressed in Isaiah's oracles of judgment in 2 Kgs 20:16-18, which would have overwhelmed the palace and implicitly the capital and the country.

God's grace opened a new chapter of life for Hezekiah and his people. The threat of exile was averted. The chronicler used the story to hold out to his contemporaries the divinely authored way out of the metaphorical exile that loomed over them as a manifestation of God's wrath. He gave it a communal slant in vv. 25*b*-26. Each generation had to decide for or against the Lord, and its fate was decided accordingly. A later generation would sin and face exile as an expression of wrath (36:16, 20), but this one was spared, according to 2 Kgs 20:19b.

32:27-31. The chronicler recounts Hezekiah's blessings. Verse 27 elaborates 2 Kgs 20:13. His possessions are recognized as God's gifts (v. 29*b*), unlike his own denial of stewardship (v. 25). Verses 28-29*a* and 30a probably depend on an independent source. Evidence of his storage cities has survived, directly or indirectly, in the royal seal impressions on jars dating from his reign.[339] The description of the Siloam tunnel is too detailed to depend on 2 Kgs 20:20. The chronicler concluded by recapitulating the theme of the

section, which is that Hezekiah experienced the success that follows spirituality. The chronicler could not resist adding "even in the affair of the envoys" (REB), assuming that the Babylonians came as astronomical experts to investigate the sun-related sign of v. 24. It was a different kind of success, however—a victory over himself. The king's relations with the Lord reached a critical point. God had to confront him with wrath and forsake him (cf. 15:2). In the end, his "heart" was loyal, as was demonstrated by his return to the Lord's way of thinking. He had passed the test. The notion of testing recalls Deut 8:2, but there it was to determine whether Israel would obey the Torah, whereas here it relates to response to the divine provision of 7:14. The chronicler drew renewed attention to this incident, inviting his readers to ponder it.

32:32-33. The standard conclusion to the reign was inspired by 2 Kgs 20:20-21. There is a focus on the king's "acts of devotion," doubtless with 2 Kgs 18:3-6 in mind. Isaiah's vision refers to 2 Kings 19–20, in which the prophet played a key role and issued oracles. The chronicler treats the funeral report as an obituary by adding references to a special burial place and the honor his people paid him (cf. 16:14; 21:19-20). He commended Hezekiah as a positive role model so that his readers would honor this king in turn by emulating his acts of devotion.

339. See Aharoni, *The Land of the Bible,* 394-400.

REFLECTIONS

1. The chronicler was a good student of human nature in refusing to let virtue be its own reward but ever dangling incentives before his readers. He also recognized the mystery of life and admitted that disaster strikes even the virtuous, here in the forms of invasion and sickness (cf. 2 Kgs 20:3). He devoted more space to the blessing of deliverance from such random ills than to the blessing of material prosperity. The virtuous could overcome such disasters. The secret was trust in the Lord. The Assyrian invasion was another opportunity to preach this message, highlighted in the affirmation of faith in 32:7-8. If it left no room for the human fear found in the basic narrative, at least Hezekiah comes over as an encourager in 32:6*b*, 8*b*. Leaders had to rise above the crisis and direct God's people to God's "grace to help in time of need" (Heb 4:16 NRSV).

The chronicler may irritate us by reducing complex issues to simplistic and seemingly unrealistic terms. Isaiah has the same effect on us. In fact, so do any number of biblical writers. They want us to take the simple message more seriously. We are invited to look beyond the crisis and its array of factors that fill us with justifiable fear. The testimony that God saves believers from existential crisis is reiterated in the New Testament at 2 Cor 1:8-10; 2 Tim 4:17-18; and 2 Pet 2:7-9.

2. Hezekiah's deliverance from a potentially fatal illness is the next blessing. James would have approved: "The prayer of faith will save the sick. . . . The prayer of the righteous is powerful and effective" (Jas 5:15-16 NRSV). Such miraculous healing does not always happen—or saints would never die—but at least we are encouraged to pray and leave the result to God in faith (see 2 Cor 12:7-10). It is ironic, then, that this seeming supersaint responded to his deliverance from fatal illness by falling into pride. The king received a warning about this fall from favor. The fuller narrative in 2 Kings shows that the chronicler had in mind the gracious role of the prophet as the bearer of divine wrath, which had the goal of turning the backslider from erring ways (cf. 36:15-16).

3. One could forsake—and so be forsaken by—God not only by breaking the Torah or adopting another religion but also by simply putting oneself in God's place as the provider of all one's assets. It is the sin of Deut 8:17: "My power and the might of my own hand have gotten me this wealth" (NRSV). The chronicler noticed the five third-person and two first-person pronouns relating to Hezekiah's pride of ownership in 2 Kgs 20:13, 15 and exegeted accordingly. He interpreted the aftermath in terms of a key element in his own message, the divine provision in 7:14, and was sufficiently impressed by the incident to remind his readers about it in 32:31. True believers are not those who never sin, "for there is no one who does not sin" (6:36), in the sense of falling into grave sin that upsets the even tenor of spiritual life. No, the true believer is the person who repents sincerely. Drawing on divine grace, one may continue along the spiritual path, chastened but not devastated by the experience. To "walk in the light" includes bringing into God's light willful mistakes one makes and finding forgiveness and new confidence to carry on (1 John 1:7–2:2). Such is God's provision—and from another perspective God's test as to whether we appropriate it. "With the testing he will also provide the way out" (1 Cor 10:13 NRSV)—whether we take the way out is up to us.

2 CHRONICLES 33:1–35:27, DROSS INTO GOLD

OVERVIEW

Like chaps. 21–23 and 24–26, this unit features three kings. In 33:1-20, Manasseh is portrayed as a renegade who makes good. The chronicler then parallels his apostasy and reformation with the next two reigns. In 33:21-25, Amon is a carbon copy of Manasseh in his pre-reformation period, while Josiah's reign in chaps. 34–35 reflects the later, better part of his grandfather's life. The two phases of Manasseh's reign, degenerate and regenerate, are paired with Amon's negative reign and Josiah's positive one.

The negative parallels are threefold, the first two of which were taken from 2 Kings 21. Manasseh did evil in the Lord's sight, and Amon copied him (33:2 = 2 Kgs 21:2;

33:22 = 2 Kgs 21:20). Manasseh "worshiped all the host of heaven and served them," and Amon "served" his father's gods (33:3 = 2 Kgs 21:3; 33:23 = 2 Kgs 21:21). The chronicler reinforced this parallelism with his own third case: Manasseh set up "images," and in turn Amon "sacrificed to all the images that his father Manasseh had made" (33:19, 22 NRSV). The positive parallels the chronicler drew between the redeemed Manasseh and Josiah are also threefold. First, he found a precedent for Josiah's self-humbling at 34:27, based on 2 Kgs 22:19, in Manasseh's own submission in 33:12, 19, 23; in the last case, he differentiated it from Amon's negative attitude. Second, he provided a parallel for the Lord's hearing Josiah's repentant prayer at 34:27 (= 2 Kgs 22:19) in Manasseh's experience at 33:13. In both cases, features of Josiah's reign were transferred to Manasseh's by way of anticipation. Third, he credited both Manasseh and Josiah with having established true worship and for commending it to the people (33:16; 34:33; 35:16). Josiah's reign reinforces the lessons of Manasseh's regenerate phase.

The chronicler found in these three kings two paradigms of the way back to the Lord from apostasy via repentance. Once more

he seems to have had in view the range of vignettes in Ezekiel 18. Manasseh lived out the instructions in Ezek 18:21-23, a trophy to the grace of a God who forgives repentant sinners, forgets their past, and inspires a new integrity. Amon is the sinner who never detached himself from his sins, like the person in Ezek 18:10-13. Josiah's reversal of Amon's evil reign captures in story form Ezek 18:14-18, the case of the son who rises above an evil family background. His unexpected relapse brings him closer to the character of Ezek 18:24.

2 Chronicles 33:1-20, Manasseh, a Model of Repentance

COMMENTARY

In 2 Kings 21, Manasseh is an unmitigated villain, the king at whose doorstep liability for Judah's exile is laid (cf. Jer 15:4). The chronicler put Zedekiah in the dastardly role of Judas-like betrayer, true to his tenet that each generation was master of its own fate. Instead, Manasseh became a counterpart to Simon Peter, restored through repentance. It is reasonable to assume that the king's long reign influenced the chronicler, who took it as divine blessing for obedience. It is difficult to imagine, however, that this was the sole justification for the crucial episode in vv. 11 and 13, though we may only surmise how the otherwise unknown incident might fit into Assyrian history, in which Manasseh had the role of a vassal king.[340] There was political unrest in much of the western sector of the empire at a certain point, and the otherwise loyal Manasseh could have been caught up in it. If that was the case, Ashurbanipal's attested leniency toward defiant vassals makes Manasseh's restoration to his throne credible. However, we do not know whether or to what extent the chronicler was extrapolating from Isaiah's forecast in 2 Kgs 20:18 that Hezekiah's sons would end up in Babylon. He did sometimes hold material over, for instance reserving 1 Kgs 8:50 until 2 Chr 30:9. But the 2 Kings reference does not account for the king's return or for his having built the city walls, specifically

described in vv. 13-14. Whatever the political background, the spiritual significance of Manasseh's adventure was what mattered for the chronicler. He saw in the incident a pattern of exile and return and in Manasseh's reign generally an outworking of the temple theology broached in chap. 7.

The section is artistically structured with a chiastic framework. Between the royal prologue and epilogue in vv. 1 and 18-20 are set narratives of apostasy and reformation in vv. 2-9 and 14-17, which have as their pivot Manasseh's change of heart in vv. 10-13.[341]

33:1-9. This passage is taken over practically verbatim from 2 Kgs 21:1-9, an impassioned piece of writing that was well worth repeating. The double declaration of the flouting of the Lord's express will (vv. 4, 7-8) is enveloped in a refrain of Manasseh's wrongdoing, escalating from "evil" to "much evil" to "more evil" than what the destroyed Canaanites perpetrated (vv. 2, 6, 9). Whereas the formula of v. 2a refers in the parent text to the whole reign, here it is limited in duration. The chronicler seems to have divided the paragraph into vv. 2-3, vv. 4-6, and vv. 7-9, applying the evil of v. 2a to pagan worship at the high places in vv. 2b-3 and summarizing the offenses in the environs of the temple building in vv. 4-6a as "much evil" in v. 6b, and the temple sin of v. 7a as egregiously evil

340. See Williamson, *1 and 2 Chronicles*, 391-93; Japhet, *I & II Chronicles*, 1002-4, 1009.

341. See K. A. D. Smelik's more complex structuring in *Converting the Past*, OTS 28 (Leiden: Brill, 1992) 169-74.

in v. 9. In the light of v. 19, v. 3 refers wholly to the high places, which explains the plural versions of the singular "Baal" and "sacred pole" at 2 Kgs 21:3 (NRSV).[342] Manasseh's child sacrifice in v. 6 is brought into line with that of Ahaz in 28:3 by specification of the place and by the plural "sons" (NIV; the NRSV unaccountably has a singular).

Mention of the Lord's will concerning the Temple (vv. 4, 7-8) reminds the chronicler of God's revelation to Solomon in chap. 7, which represented for him the theological basis of the era in which he and his contemporaries lived. The deuteronomist's "In Jerusalem I will put my name" (2 Kgs 21:4) becomes the chronicler's "In Jerusalem shall my name be forever" (v. 4) to align with the divine statement of 7:16. "Forever" recurs in v. 7, affirming the permanence of the temple age. Chapter 7 went on to speak of human behavior that could interfere with the promise—namely, abandoning the Torah and exclusive worship of the Lord. Manasseh became guilty of those very sins. Verse 6a evokes a directive in Deut 18:10-11 in the reference to "sorcery" or "witchcraft." Moreover, the reference to the Torah in v. 8 has been expanded. The NIV captures the flagrancy of Manasseh's apostasy (v. 7), taken from the basic text: Manasseh "put" the image of the idol in the very sanctuary where the Lord had "put" the divine name, as if to assert, "Not thy will but mine be done."

The king had fallen into the traps of 7:19 and shown himself at odds with the Lord's Temple-centered revelation. The fate prescribed in 7:20 was exile from the land, to which v. 8 also refers. Verse 2 had already let us hear the rumbling of this volcano in its flashback to the dispossessed nations, warning that the king was even then walking a road that led to exile. By v. 9, he has qualified for a further flashback to the destruction of those nations. Now his subjects had fallen under his pernicious spell: Loss of life would be fitting reprisal for the way the king and the people had spurned their religious heritage.

33:10-13. This core part of the section relates Manasseh's roundabout return to the Lord. At first matters got worse, with the Lord setting punishment in motion after divine warnings went unheeded. Verse 10a

encapsulates the prophetic revelation of 2 Kgs 21:10-15, while v. 10b relocates 2 Kgs 21:9a, "But they did not listen" (NRSV), retaining the plural reference of v. 9. The chronicler now leaves the 2 Kings account until vv. 18 and 20, staying under the influence of 2 Chronicles 7. The oracle of 2 Kgs 21:10-15 sealed the nation's fate by predicting national calamity. The chronicler has a different perspective, inspired by his understanding of prophecy as meant to bring the people back to the Lord (see 24:19; 36:15) and so as a warning to the people to turn from their wicked ways, which is consistent with 7:14. Here, as in 24:19, this second chance was rejected. The Assyrian invaders whom the Lord "brought upon them" (KJV) were marching in step with the negative part of chap. 7: "He has brought all this calamity upon them" (7:22 NRSV). The punishment actually fell on Manasseh, presumably to comply with the source followed by the chronicler. The king functions theologically as the representative victim of providential punishment. The specification of Babylon, at a time when Nineveh was the Assyrian capital, may reflect a summons in 648 BCE, after the emperor suppressed in Babylon the rebellion of his brother, who had also fomented unrest in the western provinces.

For the chronicler, the "exile" of Manasseh was an anticipation of Judah's own exile in Babylon. Return from exile was envisioned in Solomon's prayer in the scenario of 6:24-25, after prayer offered by penitents still in the land, and implicitly in 6:36-39, where the exiles themselves repent. Those scenarios were affirmed by the divine promise of 7:14. The promise finds verbal echoes in Manasseh's humbling himself and praying to the Lord for help. The king is represented as a textbook case of fulfillment of the golden promise. In 6:24, the chronicler refers to the confession of the divine name before return to the land. Here the perception that the Lord was the true God is a testimony inspired by Manasseh's return. Human intermediaries had fallen away; it was God who restored him, rather than the Assyrians. An experience interpreted by faith as divine deliverance created the Lord's exclusive claims on his life. Even before that experience he put his trust in the Lord as "his God" (v. 12).

342. Curtis and Madsen, *The Books of Chronicles*, 495.

Manasseh now became a living link in the chain of believers by owning "the God of his fathers." The chronicler was speaking to his post-exilic contemporaries here. Exile did not constitute a great gulf whereby pre-exilic Judah had to give way to a second-rate community that perpetuated exile in failing to realize full restoration. The Lord's redemptive power was just one earnest prayer away for each generation of God's people. Even a religious renegade like Manasseh could be restored to blessing. Exile is used as a parable of alienation from God and a temporary precursor of restoration, in line with the gracious promise the Lord gave Solomon in launching the temple era.[343]

33:14-17. The repentant sinner lives a saintly life. He steps into the shoes of Rehoboam, who after obedience found blessing in the form of building operations (11:5-12). To repent was to obey, and to obey was to be eligible for blessing. Manasseh's repentance bore religious fruit: The Lord's exclusive role in the Temple and in the city was now honored. The idolatry of vv. 4-5, 7 was reversed because of the truth he had learned (v. 13b). A directive to the people "to serve the LORD God of Israel" now countermanded the commending of his own service of other gods (v. 9). Outside the capital, the high places of v. 3, though not removed, were restricted to worship of the Lord. Step by step, religious aberrations were replaced by reforms.

The chronicler appears to be writing idealistically in penning such reforms. He will preserve evidence from 2 Kings that Amon perpetuated his father's religious deviations and that only Josiah removed them, even as he transfers back to Manasseh's reign Josiah's own reforms (2 Kgs 23:12, echoed in 2 Chr 33:15). The symmetrical grid into which he divided the three reigns encouraged him to preserve this impression. Narrative consistency was sacrificed in presenting religious models that created their own logic.

33:18-20. The customary source citation formula of 2 Kgs 21:17 has been reconstructed to describe Manasseh's checkered life. The chronicler's elaboration made it expedient to split his usual citation of the deuteronomistic narrative in prophetic terms into two parallel parts.[344] The basic text spoke only of the king's sin, in line with its uniformly negative presentation. The chronicler granted its presence and reinforced it with the qualifying "all" and with his key term for unspirituality: "being unfaithful" or "being faithless" (מעל *ma'al*). He also recapitulates the religious deviations of vv. 3 and 7. Yet, he wanted to make clear that divine grace triumphed over godlessness. The Lord would not let Manasseh alone, but tried to coax him back through "seers" (see v. 10; see also 2 Kgs 21:10-15). Eventually Manasseh succumbed to this persistent tough love and found in 7:14 a prescription for returning to the Lord. Prayer is mentioned twice as a spiritual key to securing a favorable response from God. The elaboration of his sin serves as a pastoral reminder that no one is too bad to be welcomed back to divine favor.

343. Mosis, *Untersuchungen zur Theologie des chronisten Geschichtswerks*, 389-90.

344. See *BHS* for the end of 33:19, where the conjectured "his seers" is an abbreviated reference to "the seers who spoke to him" in 33:18.

REFLECTIONS

The chronicler's account of Hezekiah's reign had given him the opportunity to present the best possible spiritual life for his own constituency to emulate. Best possible, because to err is human. Now he presented another potential: The worst apostates may turn their lives around and find blessing. It starts as a worst-case scenario, in which sinning against God is turned into a major element. It is said that the Christian journalist Hugh Redwood used to say that God is able to save "from the guttermost to the uttermost." Manasseh was an ideal candidate for this presentation.

There is a beautiful inconsistency in the temple theology of chapter 7. It sets up high standards of obedience, but provides a loophole for those who fail to meet them (cf. 1 John 1:5–2:2). This illogicality is a concession to human infirmity made by a gracious

God. It is celebrated in the thanksgiving hymn, Psalm 103: "[The LORD] does not treat us as our sins deserve . . . for he knows how we are formed, he remembers that we are dust" (Ps 103:10, 14 NIV).

When Manasseh rejected his second chance, the Lord reluctantly had to activate providential judgment. He had failure written all over him (33:11), but God had not given him up, using "distress" as a megaphone to appeal to the unhearing king. Manasseh's positive reaction contrasts with that of Ahaz, who plunged into deeper sin (28:22). These alternative responses to suffering are true to life. Manasseh availed himself of the promise of 7:14, as any backslider may. Jesus taught this perspective in the parable of the fig tree (Luke 13:6-9). For three years, the owner looked for figs in vain. Even then he was prevailed upon not to cut the tree down but to give it another chance—after which it did produce fruit. This divine opportunity may not be restricted to an evangelistic setting; it also belongs to Christian counseling. It is significant that Jewish theology uses the metaphor of being born again for any occasion of repentance.

Restoration to divine favor also requires becoming sensitive to divine claims on one's life. Manasseh rectified those areas where he had erred. After failure, there is first a call to rest in God's acceptance and then to rise to God's expectations, and thereby find blessing.

2 Chronicles 33:21–35:27, Amon's Wrongdoing; Josiah's Repentance, Reform, and Relapse

COMMENTARY

This section reiterates the truth that a situation of spiritual failure can be redeemed. The transition from Amon to Josiah repeats the good news, but now it spreads the process over two generations.

33:21-25. The chronicler based his account of Amon's reign on 2 Kgs 21:19-24. The epilogue in 2 Kgs 21:25-26 is not represented. Either his eye slipped over it because of the similar endings in vv. 24 and 26 or this omission had already occurred in his text. His concern was to present the reign as a parallel rerun of Manasseh's first, evil period. So he adapted the vocabulary of apostasy in 2 Kgs 21:21-22 by echoing the "images" and self-humbling of v. 19. In hindsight, that verse has another agenda, to recapitulate negative elements that would resurface in Amon's reign in order to facilitate the comparison. Now self-humbling before the Lord, the back door to blessing, was conspicuous by its absence (v. 23).

The convoluted political maneuverings of vv. 24-25 are intended as providential retribution and reordering, like the regicidal conspiracies of 24:25; 25:27. The "people of the land," duly copied from 2 Kings, here has

no special meaning; it picks up the reference to the people in v. 17. Under Manasseh they had been the willing dupes of his evil genius. By v. 17, they lagged somewhat behind the momentum of his new spirituality. Now they have gotten the message and instigated a turn for the better.

Spirituality is restored in 34:1–35:19. The people retained and developed their new commitment, as 34:33 b attests. In this exemplary pilgrimage, they now had the encouragement and role modeling of Josiah (v. 33a), whose reign is now described. It was a more elaborate parallel of Manasseh's new lease on life. While Manasseh's first period was marked by failure to keep the Torah (33:8), Josiah's reign is characterized not only by an admission of such failure but also by a resolve to give the Torah priority and to subordinate communal life to the Lord's revealed will (34:14, 21, 31; cf. 35:26). There was a devout spirit of self-humbling before God and a desire to honor the Temple as the center of proper worship.

34:1-13. Amon had negatively modeled exile from the Lord and from the divine will for Israel's worship. Now Josiah became an example of restoration and religious renewal.

The chronicler took over the introduction to the reign he found in 2 Kgs 22:1-2 and used v. 2 as a headline for 34:3–35:19, which provides four examples of its outworking. The Davidic idealism of v. 2 is reinforced in v. 3 with the help of the term for spirituality, "seek" (דרש *dāraš*).

In 2 Kings the record of Josiah's reforms clusters around the eighteenth year of his reign, 622 BCE, and his discovery of the Torah book, so that reform took its motivation and direction from it. Here, however, the reform is staggered over two stages and the book has a lesser role. Did the chronicler know more than we do from reading 2 Kings? It is significant that the data of vv. 3*b*-7, applied to Josiah's twelfth year (628 BCE), are borrowed from the phase of reform after the discovery of the book, described in 2 Kgs 23:4-20, as is shown by the quotation of "Then he went back/returned to Jerusalem" (v. 7 = 2 Kgs 23:20).

There is no objective indication in the chronicler's material that he was using a different source at this point. Suggestions to the contrary stem from uneasiness felt by readers of the account of the reform in 2 Kings 22–23. There reforms are all squeezed into a single year, and the Torah book is given enormous weight in providing impetus for the religious reform. The deuteronomists had a vested interest in the discovery and impact of the book, evidently a form of Deuteronomy, and so the emphasis placed on it is not necessarily to be taken at face value. For the chronicler, the book was largely important because its discovery led to Huldah's prophetic oracle and then to a communal pledge of renewal. He represents the reform as a long process, begun in the twelfth year (v. 3*b*), continued in the eighteenth (v. 8; better translated "in the course of purifying the land and the temple"), and resumed after the book turned up (v. 33). This spacing looks more feasible than the one presented in 2 Kings, but it must be weighed against the fact that the chronicler retained Huldah's accusation of contemporary backsliding in 34:24-25 (= 2 Kgs 22:16-17) and praise of Josiah for his repentance in response to the book. In 2 Chronicles, the prophet is still allowed to speak as if no reform had occurred in Jerusalem. Moreover, Josiah's panic over the dire message of the book has been robbed of justification by the earlier account of reforms. As elsewhere, and indeed in this very unit, the chronicler has evidently sacrificed the consistency he found in 2 Kings to a more atomistic presentation of spiritual themes.

A further factor is a historical one: whether Assyria's growing loss of control over the west had reached by 628 BCE a point of allowing the northern religious measures described in vv. 6-7. It is questionable whether there was a political vacuum sufficient for Josiah to exercise such control until after Ashurbanipal's death in 627. Two factors emerge from the chronicler's presentation. First, he has left no objective evidence that he was following an independent historical tradition. Second, there are a number of signs that he took his cue from 2 Kings, adapting it to accord with his own concerns.[345]

David, with whom Josiah is compared in v. 2, had put religious matters first, capturing Jerusalem and planning the installation of the ark there in the very context of his coronation (1 Chr 11:4-8; 13:1-4). Josiah showed a similar alacrity, also like Jehoshaphat, who was spiritually active in the third year of his reign, and like Hezekiah, who set to work in the first month of his (official) first year (17:7; 29:3).[346] When still a minor, Josiah determined to walk spiritually in David's footsteps and make David's religious devotion his own. At the first opportunity, presumably as soon as a regent no longer ruled on his behalf, he used his new royal power to this end. The twelfth year of his reign, when he became twenty years old, appears to function as the age of majority, as in the case of the Levites at 31:17.

A start was made to undo Amon's religious apostasy. "Carved images" or "idols" (פסלים *pĕsilîm*, vv. 3-4) had been a mark of Amon's backsliding, renewed from Manasseh's early period and set up at high places (33:19, 22). So the pagan high places had to go, along with their other furnishings, including incense altars (vv. 4, 7; cf. 14:5), whether in Jerusalem (cf. 2 Kgs 23:8b, 13) or in Judah (cf. 2 Kgs 23:5, 8*a*). In this period of the reunited

345. See Williamson, *1 and 2 Chronicles*, 397-98; Japhet, *I & II Chronicles*, 1018-20.

346. See Cogan, "The Chronicler's Use of Chronology as Illuminated by Neo-Assyrian Royal Inscription," 203-5; Glatt, *Chronological Displacement in Biblical and Related Literatures*, 68-72.

kingdom, beginning with Hezekiah, Josiah also removed high places from the former northern kingdom (cf. 2 Kgs 23:15-20; in v. 6, בער בתיהם [bi'er bātêhem, "he destroyed their sanctuaries"] is the best emendation of the corrupt MT, here rendered "in the/their ruins"; cf. the REB).[347] The general reference to purging the Temple (v. 8) presupposes and sums up Josiah's measures, narrated in 2 Kgs 23:4, 6-7, 11-12, though the chronicler had already borrowed 2 Kgs 23:6, 12 for Manasseh's reforms at 33:15.

The 2 Kings account focuses on the discovery of the Torah book, and the issue of temple repairs is relegated to a preliminary royal speech. Here the repairs are given their own narrative as further evidence of Josiah's religious enthusiasm. The commands of 2 Kgs 23:3-7 become the basis of the account in 2 Chr 34:8-13. The topic is woven into this unit by citing impairment in the reigns of "the kings of Judah," meaning Manasseh and Amon (v. 11). In v. 8, the details about the royal delegation are striking; they may preserve information that has fallen out of 2 Kgs 22:3 as we know it.

The chronicler takes the opportunity to repeat and develop lessons he has taught in chaps. 24 and 31 about the responsibility of God's people to contribute to the upkeep of the sanctuary. The new emphasis here is that they all participated, including members of northern tribes. Whether "the remnant of Israel" refers to non-exiled members of the northern kingdom or includes southerners (in the light of chap. 28), as the longer definition in v. 21 certainly does, the chronicler was expressing a viewpoint at variance with that of Ezra 4:1-3. Both groups had a stake in the Temple, he insisted, and there was no room for a separatist claim that only survivors of the Judean exile could comprise the Lord's people. In his account of Hezekiah's reign, he had asserted that all of them have a right and duty to worship at the Jerusalem Temple (30:1-12), though evidently Judeans were assigned the responsibility of supporting its workers (31:4-6; cf. 24:9). Here the overall theme of the reunited kingdom is taken a step further. If the instigation of repairs was the king's responsibility, its financing rested on the whole people of God. In the chronicler's day, Judah's religious policy meant a higher financial burden than was necessary!

In the 2 Chronicles version, another opportunity is taken to give maximum visibility to the contribution of the Levites. The "keepers of the threshold" (2 Kgs 22:24), who are priests in 2 Kgs 12:9, are identified here as Levites (cf. 24:6, 11; 1 Chr 9:19). They are also given a supervisory role in the repairs. The clans of Merari and Kohath are specified in v. 12, though not that of Gershom, unlike in 29:12. The levitical arrangements of chronicler's day are projected back. The temple musicians evidently provided timing and rhythm for the workers' tasks, as regularly happened in ancient times, while other levitical skills were harnessed to this work (cf. 1 Chr 23:4-5).

34:14-33. Communal commitment to the Lord is the overall theme of these verses. The chronicler has repeatedly mentioned the habit of good kings to hold a special service in which they and the people pledged their lives to the Lord. It occurred in Asa's reign and during Jehoiada's regency; most recently Hezekiah had instigated it (15:9-12; 23:16; 29:10). Josiah took his place in this noble succession. In 2 Chronicles such a pledge is always part of a larger reform program and is preceded or followed by corrective measures. Verses 15-32a have been largely copied from 2 Kgs 22:8–23:3, with the chronicler supplying his own introduction and conclusion at vv. 14 and 32b-33. Verse 14 serves as a recapitulation after the expanded narrative of vv. 10-13, synchronizing the mission of vv. 8-9 and 15. The chronicler used this long extract because it fit his pattern of making pledges of covenant renewal, which he considered a spiritual ideal relevant to his own time.

The striking prelude to the ceremony must also have intrigued him because it coincided with his own spiritual program in three other respects. First, it showed a healthy respect for the Torah and its demand for exclusive worship of the Lord (v. 25). Second, the prelude featured an inquiry for God's will through a prophet. This inquiry or seeking (vv. 21, 23) echoes and develops in a specific direction the seeking that characterized the king's early commitment (v. 3). Third, the divine revelation of Torah and the prophetic oracle are

347. See Williamson, *1 and 2 Chronicles,* 399; Dillard, *2 Chronicles,* 275.

associated with a response of self-humbling, which accords with a goal of prophecy elsewhere (12:5-7; 36:12; cf. 32:24-26). The single reference to self-humbling in 2 Kgs 22:19 is doubled in v. 27, perhaps to highlight Josiah's parallel role to that of Manasseh (33:12, 19). Self-humbling in 33:12, 19 was a pointer to the divine provision of 7:14, and it functions here in the same way.

The negative side of the revelation in chap. 7 emerges in the forsaking of the Lord and the espousal of other gods (v. 25; cf. 7:19, 22), which result in "all the disaster" of v. 28 (cf. v. 24 and 7:22 NIV). However, the positive side surfaces not only in self-humbling but also in the Lord's hearing the king's penitent plea (v. 27; cf. 7:14). As a result, king and people resolved to keep the Lord's "commandments" and "statutes" (v. 31), in line with 7:19, acutely aware that they had been disobedient. Once more grace provided a way back to God.

The book of the Torah, found in the Temple before the repairs had started, is generally identified with some form of Deuteronomy. The account of its discovery in 2 Kings furnishes evidence to support this identification. The chronicler replaces "all the words of the book" (2 Kgs 22:16) with "all the curses [that are] written in the book" (v. 24). This formulation forges an intertextual link with Deut 29:21, "all the curses . . . written in this book of the law," with reference to the lists of curses in Deut 28:15-68; 29:19-28. It is likely, however, that the chronicler had the entire Pentateuch in mind. It has been claimed that the issue turns on v. 18, where Josiah's reading "of the book" (2 Kgs 22:10) is replaced in the Hebrew by his reading "in the book." Does this imply a complete Torah, read partially in v. 18? The NIV's "read from it" might so indicate, over against the NRSV's "read it." The Hebrew diction of the chronicler is also found in Jer 36:6, 8, 10, 13, where the reading of a whole document is meant.[348] It is significant, however, that in 2 Chr 34:19 the book is referred to as "the law," rather than "the book of the law" (cf. 2 Kgs 22:11). Moreover, in 35:6, 12 "the word of the LORD by Moses" (NRSV) and "the book of Moses," to which appeal is made in an echo of the reference in 2 Kgs 23:21 to "this book of the

covenant," seems to have contained both deuteronomic and priestly material.

An interesting change occurs in the comprehensive description of the participants in the ceremony of rededication (v. 30). Whereas 2 Kgs 23:2 mentions "priests and prophets," the chronicler has "priests and Levites." In view of the chronicler's special interest in Levites, it is hardly likely that we are to conclude from the presence of this reading in a few MT manuscripts of 2 Kings that he found it in his source.[349] The change can be explained as his furnishing a description in terms of the post-exilic scene he knew, rather than a conscious identification of Levites with earlier prophets.[350]

Verses 32b-33 are the chronicler's own finale to this passage. It shows how king and people alike lived up to the pledge of obedience. As for the king, there is further use of 2 Kgs 23:4-20 to illustrate his reforms throughout the area of the old northern kingdom. The chronicler achieved maximum mileage out of the passage, having used it also for describing Manasseh's reforms and for Josiah's early endeavors. He singled out "the inhabitants of Jerusalem" as participants, as he will do later in the course of the passover (35:18). After all, they had been the target of Huldah's oracle of judgment (vv. 24-25, 27-28). He demoted her pronouncement of inexorable wrath to a warning to draw back from the brink of destruction. They heeded the threat and were spared. The same impression is given in v. 33, where the people are responsive to Josiah's efforts. The "God of their fathers" became "their God." The chronicler was countering the intergenerational pronouncement copied from 2 Kings in 2 Chr 34:21 (cf. v. 25). There was a sure way to escape divine wrath that was open to every generation: a new and continuing allegiance to the Lord "all [Josiah's] days." Divine wrath was intended to be a provocative precursor to grace and a new spiritual start, and so it proved in this chapter not only for Josiah but also for the people.

35:1-19. The chronicler found three pieces of evidence that Josiah had acted properly in the Lord's sight (34:2): his religious reforms

348. Ackroyd, *1 & 2 Chronicles, Ezra, Nehemiah*, 202.

349. Contra McKenzie, *The Chronicler's Use of the Deuteronomistic History*, 166.

350. See Schniedewind, *The Word of God in Transition*, 184-86.

throughout the land, his arrangements to repair the Temple with public money, and his service of spiritual renewal (34:3-7, 8-13, 14-33). Now the chronicler adds a fourth, Josiah's celebration of the passover as a token of his respect for traditional temple procedure (35:1-19). This fourth element also illustrates the spirituality of the reunited people in general and of the inhabitants of Jerusalem in particular (vv. 17-18; 34:32-33). The 2 Kings account had devoted three verses to the celebration (2 Kgs 23:21-23). The chronicler expanded it to nineteen verses, incorporating its material into the beginning and the end (vv. 1a, 18a, 19). He altered the royal directive of 2 Kgs 23:21 into narrative in v. 1a, but referred to it as such in v. 16. "This book of the covenant" has been transmuted into "the word of the LORD by Moses" and "the book of Moses" as the basis for the festival (vv. 6, 12). Its content begins to be unfolded in v. 1.

This passover was held at the sanctuary, which is consistent with Deut 16:5 6, while its precise dating accords with later priestly texts (Exod 12:6; Lev 23:5; Num 9:3) and conforms with the cultic calendar, over against Hezekiah's emergency, dating in 30:2, 13.[351] The accent on slaughtering the passover lamb, which echoes the terminology of Exodus 12, anticipates an issue that will loom large in the chronicler's account (esp. vv. 6, 11) and as an implicit element in the preparations of vv. 14-15.

This is the final description of a festival given in the royal narratives. In Hezekiah's reign, the Festival of Unleavened Bread received greater emphasis than it does here; in this case, the passover is brought to the fore and the festival that followed is mentioned in passing (v. 17). The passage falls into four paragraphs: preparation of the Temple staff (vv. 2-6), donations of sacrificial victims (vv. 7-9), details of the ritual (vv. 10-15), and closing observations (vv. 16-19). The third paragraph has its own summarizing frame, "So the service was arranged" and "so the whole service of Yahweh was arranged that day" (vv. 10, 16 NJB). There are two agendas in the account. First, the grounding of worship in the Lord's past revelation is emphasized. The ceremony took over the rulings for sacrificial worship laid down in the Torah (vv. 6b,

12-13) and also the organizational prescriptions established by David and Solomon with prophetic authorization (vv. 4, 15, reading "the king's seers" [REB], whether by emendation [see *BHS*] or by giving a plural sense to the Hebrew singular form).[352] This celebration honored a blend of truths imparted in the old and new eras of revelation and paid tribute to both the Law and the Prophets.

This passover celebration reflects a number of different traditions preserved in the Torah.[353] As in the case of Hezekiah's festival, described in chap. 30, in principle Deuteronomy 16 is followed, with its prescription of a centralized service of sacrifice, rather than the home celebration of Exodus 12:1. Taking the passover animals from the flock and the herd accords with Deut 16:2, whereas Exod 12:5 ruled that only a lamb or a kid should be used. In v. 13, the cooking of the passover offerings over fire reflects a harmonization of the two traditions. The verb בשל (*biššēl*) means primarily "boil" and more generally "cook." It is used in the latter sense in Deut 16:7. However, Exod 12:9 creates tension: The passover lamb was not to be "boiled" (בשל מבשל *bāšēl mĕbuššāl*) in water, but "roasted" (צלי *sĕlî*) over fire. The chronicler harmonized the double mandate by using the verb of one tradition with the qualifying phrase of the other. The "holy offerings" that were boiled rather than roasted are not explained. They seem to refer to the bulls, which for some reason were treated differently from the other passover animals. The tradition of boiling sacrificial animals is attested outside the Pentateuch in 1 Sam 2:13-14 and 1 Kgs 19:21 (cf. Ezek 46:20, 24; Zech 14:21), but in the priestly material of the Pentateuch only in connection with certain other rituals (Exod 29:31; Lev 6:28; 8:31; Num 6:19). Temple custom in the chronicler's day may be reflected here, but it may also express his desire to honor Deut 16:7 in another way, by retaining the primary sense of its Hebrew verb "boil."

Observing the passover in the sanctuary necessitated a degree of institutionalization not previously encountered in the Torah. In 30:16, the blood rite associated with all animal offerings was applied to the passover animals, and so it is in v. 11. In terms of temple

---

351. Shaver, *Torah and the Chronicler's History Work*, 115.

352. Barthélemy, *Critique textuelle de l'Ancien Testament*, 1:618-19.
353. Fishbane, *Biblical Interpretation in Ancient Israel*, 136-38.

sacrifices, the passover offering was justifiably put in the category of the שלמים (*šĕlāmîm*), the "offerings of well-being" or "fellowship offerings," which were partly eaten by the worshiper and partly burned on the altar. The latter parts are called "burnt offerings" in vv. 12 and 14 and are given a prominent place in the summary at v. 16. This label is defined as "the fat parts" of the victims (v. 14; "and" is explicative, meaning "namely," as in 29:31). This phrase also referred to the kidneys and the heart of sheep and goats (Lev 3:9-11, 14-15) and cattle (Lev 3:3-4). The rules of Leviticus 3 seem to be reflected in the formula "as it is written in the book of Moses."[354] The process relating to the lambs or kids (vv. 11-12*a*) was repeated for the bulls (v. 12*b*).

The chronicler had another message, a more sensitive one, to deliver in his passover story. The Levites are assigned a strikingly prominent role, which was his way of proposing innovations in the range of their ministry. Josiah's speech (vv. 3-5) sets the scene. The introduction to the speech boosts the Levites' image, after the priests have been organized and given their own word of encouragement (cf. 1 Chr 28:20).[355] The Levites are honored as teachers, as they were represented in 17:8-9 (cf. Neh 8:7, 9-12), and are given the epithet "holy" by virtue of their right of access to the temple court, which they were to exercise in the ensuing ceremony (v. 5).[356] The opening command is puzzling, since there has been no prior notice of the removal of the ark from the Temple. The MT may have been corrupted from a past tense,[357] with reference to the ark's installation at Solomon's dedication of the Temple, when the Levites carried it and the priests actually installed it in the inner room (5:4-7). Their Mosaic task of carrying the "holy" ark was over. What was their new ritual role to be?

Already in the temple era, the Levites had been assigned the roles of musicians and gatekeepers; in vv. 4 and 10 the reference to their divisions relates to their assignments in 1 Chr

23:4-5, two of which are mentioned in v. 15. The "written directions" of David and Solomon (v. 4) pose a problem in the latter case. The chronicler seems to refer to the David narrative and the Solomon narrative in his own writings, in the first case to 1 Chronicles 16 and to the primary layer of 1 Chronicles 23–27 and in the second to 2 Chr 8:14.[358] As for the Levites, v. 5 proposes a new role for the third group of Levites, the temple workers—namely, to take over the tasks of slaughtering and skinning the passover animals. The latter task is stated in v. 11 and alluded to in v. 6, while in vv. 14-15 the preparations also include slaughtering and cooking. Ordinarily the first two tasks were carried out by the lay worshiper, according to Lev 1:5-6 and to 2 Chr 29:22 in the case of slaughtering. Verse 6 implies as much: The Levites were to "prepare for" their "brothers to fulfill the word of the Lord given through Moses" (REB)—that is, it was their duty to help laypeople carry out their religious responsibilities by doing them on their behalf. In v. 11, it can only be the Levites who did the slaughtering, in view of v. 6.[359] In 29:34 and 30:16-17, the skinning and slaughtering respectively were assigned to Levites as emergency measures. Now the chronicler was urging that such preparatory work should be their regular prerogative in recognition of their holy status.

To this end Levites were assigned to lay family groups as their representatives in v. 5, and also in vv. 12-13, where their duties include delivering the meat for the passover meal. Respect was thereby paid to the family setting of Exod 12:3-4. The Levites' haste may be a reenactment of the haste of Exod 12:11; Deut 10:3. These new arrangements presuppose that in post-exilic times laypeople were not usually admitted into the temple court. The chronicler's proposal rationalized this situation, though it did not become normative for later Judaism. Ezra 6:20 is the only other place where the Levites slaughter the passover animals. The role of the Levites as the people's representatives is also prominent in Ezek 44:11; 46:24, though in other respects the chronicler goes further. Verses 11-15 portray the Levites as duly discharging

---

354. H. G. M. Williamson, "History," in *It Is Written: Scripture Citing Scripture: Essays in Honour of Barnabas Lindars SSR*, ed. D. A. Carson and H. G. M. Williamson (Cambridge: Cambridge University Press, 1988) 25-38, esp. 29.

355. See *BHS*. See also Mason, *Preaching the Tradition in Ancient Israel*, 115.

356. See Kleinig, *The Lord's Song*, 94.

357. See *BHS*.

358. De Vries, *1 and 2 Chronicles*, 415.

359. For the text of 35:11, see Barthélemy, *Critique textuelle de l'Ancien Testament*, 1:518.

these preliminary activities and so playing a key role in the passover ritual. It was a facilitating role, allowing other personnel—priests and gatekeepers—to carry out their duties uninterrupted. This observation functions as a further argument adduced by the chronicler.

The other levitical groups—musicians and gatekeepers—also played their part. The former group is described in terms of the same developmental stage as in 1 Chr 16:37-42 and 2 Chr 5:12; 29:13-14, which prevailed in the chronicler's period or just before. The musicians are assigned to the Asaph group, perhaps here only a shorthand reference to all three groups.[360] Their music accompanied the burning of the fat, which accords with their having played at the regular burnt offerings in 1 Chr 23:30-31; 2 Chr 29:27, and they performed at the place specified in 2 Chr 5:12.

The donations of the king and the members of the civil and religious administration (vv. 7-9) recall 30:24 and the regular royal contributions of 31:3. The leaders' having given "willingly" (v. 8) and the rhetorical number of the king's gift function as an exhortation to leaders in the chronicler's day.

The closing observations in vv. 16-19 mention the unified nature of the celebration, but do not belabor the point, which was adequately covered in the account of Hezekiah's passover in chap. 30. The same brevity extends to mention of the accompanying Festival of Unleavened Bread. The notice in 2 Kgs 23:22 that an ancient precedent from "the days of the judges" was revived is changed to "since the days of the prophet Samuel." At first glance, the alteration says little: Samuel was the last of the judges. However, in 1 Chr 6:26-28, 33-38 Samuel was represented as an adoptee of the levitical clan. A Levite once led Israel's worship! Here was precedent for Levites to take a more prominent role in sacrificial worship. The chronicler used this narrative to argue a cause dear to his heart—the Levites' leadership—and to advocate their importance in his own day.

35:20-27. Josiah's observance of the festival is interpreted in v. 20 as his reorganization of the temple worship and functioned as an example of his reinstating of services, as Manasseh had done (33:16). The resumption of the religious calendar was evidence

of a response to the Lord on the part of king and people (34:2, 33). However, the chronicler now has a less happy incident to record, jumping thirteen years to the time of Josiah's death. The disappointment of "after all this" recalls 20:35. The brief account of his tragic death in 2 Kgs 23:29-30, tucked into an appendix there, appears here in a longer version, integrated into the ongoing narrative, which thus culminates in his death and burial. The chronicler writes independently of the 2 Kings account, avoiding its erroneous statement that Pharaoh Neco was campaigning "against the king of Assyria" (TNK), specifying Carchemish as the place of battle and adding such objective details as Josiah's being moved to another chariot and dying in Jerusalem. These and perhaps other points appear to have been taken from another account, though the reference to Carchemish may have come from Jer 46:2 and the details of Josiah's death may have been influenced in part by Ahaziah's in 2 Kgs 9:27-28. The chronicler wove it into a theological explanation of Josiah's unexpected end, employing as usual a speech for this purpose.

Josiah had been caught up in the death throes of a superpower, Assyria, and collided with the efforts of Egypt, the other superpower, to preserve its ally Assyria from the vigorous attacks of the Babylonians for as long as possible.[361] The chronicler had an ideological framework into which the incident could be slotted. Surprise attacks on good kings did happen, as opportunities for them to put their faith in the Lord and thus be victorious. Such a category does not fit here. Josiah initiated the conflict, and his death meant that he was culpable. He was like Rehoboam, who was ready to fight and encountered a prophet who warned him that it was not the Lord's will. Unlike Josiah, Rehoboam was dissuaded and won divine blessing as a consequence (11:1-12). Josiah was close to Jeroboam I of Israel, whom Abijah urged not to fight against the Judean army because the Lord was with Judah and whose refusal led to military defeat and an early death (13:3-20). Here, too, the opposing king claims the advantage of the divine presence as a foreigner speaking more

360. Japhet, *I & II Chronicles*, 1053.

361. See A. Malamat, "Josiah's Bid for Armageddon," *JANESCU* 5 (1973) 267-79.

appropriately of "God." The story may also have been influenced by the divine revelation to Abimelech, king of Gerar, in Gen 20:3-7. We are meant to take the claim of revelation at face value and not stray outside the boundaries of the story by asking how it could have been recognized as such (cf. 2 Kgs 18:25).

Reformers do not stay the course in 2 Chronicles. Josiah went the way of Joash and Hezekiah, more like the former in not listening to the warning sent by God (24:19; cf. 32:26). The chronicler went so far as to present Josiah as a second Ahab, who disguised himself in an attempt to prevent the wound from the predicted arrow that necessitated his removal from the fray (18:19, 29, 33). The king's having died in Jerusalem instead of Megiddo seems to reflect Huldah's oracle (34:28) and may have already featured in the chronicler's independent source. This issue would not have caused him concern: If repentance could cancel out oracles of judgment, presumably, then, defiance could annul an oracle of salvation (so Jer 18:9-10).

From the chronicler's perspective, the incident constituted a warning that to disregard God's revealed will was dire folly and that, if one of the most spiritual of kings was not immune from backsliding, constant vigilance was required by all believers.

Yet he did not want the aberration of Josiah's premature and humiliating end to overshadow this king's extremely positive contribution to the life of God's people. The threefold reference to mourning takes the place of the funeral fires (16:14; 21:19) as a tribute. Jeremiah's laments (v. 25) have not been preserved, but they are consistent with his high regard for Josiah (see Jer 22:11, 15-16). The chronicler used v. 26 as an obituary notice to express his conviction that Josiah was a spiritually good king whose reign was characterized by honoring the Torah. The chronicler ranged over the narrative and alluded to such passages as 34:19, 27, 31; 35:6, 12. On the scales of history, Josiah's obedience to the divine Word far outweighed his final, fatal disobedience.

REFLECTIONS

1. The homiletic melodies the chronicler played in this part of his composition are by now familiar. By dint of repetition, he wanted his hearers to go away humming them and taking them to heart, especially the second half of the two-part unit, which compares Amon and Josiah to Manasseh's "before and after" life. If a single generation could experience transformation from apostasy to spirituality, then equally so a wicked generation, doomed to failure, could be succeeded by a reforming, virtuous one. The chains of the past could be unshackled; lives dedicated to the Lord could find freedom. It is the quintessential message of Ezekiel 18, a denial that when parents ate sour grapes the children's teeth were inevitably set on edge (Ezek 18:2). The wrath of God was no fatalistic process engulfing generation after generation. The Lord had provided an opportunity for people to live new, unfettered lives. Yet, a note of challenge is mixed with this encouragement. If the story of Manasseh taught, over against 2 Kings, that failure need not be final, then Josiah's tale reinforces the truth that failure dogs the steps of any believer (cf. 1 Cor 10:12).

2. "First things first" is a principle the chronicler has preached before. Josiah's reign teaches a lesson of spiritual priorities. His religious aspirations appear in his eighth year, when he was sixteen. Many Christians look back to their teenage years or even earlier as the period when faith in God first found a place in their hearts and decisions were made that set a course for the rest of their lives. Church work among young people has a tremendous potential in urging them to "begin to seek" the God of their parents' generation and gain a living faith for themselves, a faith that fits their new circumstances.

3. Josiah's resolve to repair the Temple reinforces the message of chapter 24 that the people were responsible for providing funds, with no group being exempt (34:9). The chronicler's spirituality included such a down-to-earth element, which he hoped would not fall on unlistening ears in his own day. Routine maintenance of church premises is not the most glamorous of calls on the Christian's resources, but it belongs to the needs of real life, which we disregard at our peril.

4. The chronicler also found room for the extraordinary—here a special service of rededication to the Lord—confronting human lives with divine revelation and calling for deep commitment to God's Word and an enthusiastic embrace of the obligations it brought (34:29-32). It caused changes in the religious life of the nation (35:33a) and reflected on a larger scale Josiah's having come to terms with his sense of failure and remorse (35:27). Once again, the message is that grace can triumph over human failure and that disappointing lives can be rechanneled into satisfying paths of allegiance to God. Josiah influenced the nation for good, bringing others to the point he had reached earlier: appropriation of a traditional faith.

5. Traditions of worship are brought to the fore in the description of Josiah's passover celebration. Revelation mediated both through Moses and through David and Solomon (35:6, 12, 19) is emphasized. Guidelines had been provided in the old and the new eras of revelation, in the Law and in the (Former) Prophets. To worship God meant to stay respectfully within the parameters of revelation and to grapple conscientiously with different traditions reflected in it. These traditions had been developed over the centuries and reflect the stage they had reached by the chronicler's time. He belongs to those who raise their voices today in favor of traditional forms of worship.

6. Inconsistently, but at the same time healthily, the chronicler also fought for innovation and used his narrative as a platform for religious development. The role of the Levites, he believed, should be extended because its expansion would be advantageous, both for other temple personnel and for worshipers. Levites were held back from the ministry of which they were capable, which in fact the editorial material in 1 Chr 23:25-32 served to reinforce. One cannot help comparing the movement at work in Christian denominations, with varying success, to promote the ministry of women.

7. Unlike the deuteronomist, the chronicler could take in stride Josiah's tragic end, though it spoiled somewhat the structural agenda of the literary unit. It took little adaptation, helped doubtless by another version of the story available to him, to weave it into a pattern of spiritual experience. Josiah had to be a lesser king than Hezekiah in 2 Chronicles because Josiah fatally succumbed to his flaw, whereas Hezekiah came successfully through his. As for an inspired pharaoh, the lesson is that God's message, however unlikely the medium, must be sensitively recognized as such by the believer and taken seriously after testing whether such a spirit is from God (see 1 John 4:1). This section challenges us in a number of respects to decide when to change course and when to stand our ground. The principle at stake is that changing is not expediency but rather reasonable openness to adaptability.

2 CHRONICLES 36:1-23, RECURRING EXILE AND THE PROSPECT OF RESTORATION

COMMENTARY

The chronicler insisted that the Judean exile of 587 BCE was not a unique or final event; it had counterparts in earlier generations. The motifs of death, deportation, and deprivation of temple worship had materialized at the end of the divided kingdom, in the reign of Ahaz (28:5-6, 8, 17; 29:8-9), and had been succeeded by a spiritual restoration under Hezekiah. In turn, Manasseh was exiled to Babylon and after his repentance was restored to the throne (33:11-13). The last four reigns, summarized in this last section of the book, are also sketched in terms of as many exiles. The first three of the four kings were deported, and in the reign of the last the people suffered exile. The cessation of temple worship at the conclusion is anticipated by the removal of temple vessels by foreigners in two of the three preceding reigns. None of the earlier royal exiles is reversed, but the continuity of people and monarchy in the land does not give a repeated impression of finality. At the end, this impression bursts into an explicit announcement of restoration, with the dawn of the Persian Empire. So the last nine chapters of the book major in presenting exile as a judgment borne by generation after generation, yet one that can be followed by renewal.

The vignettes of successive reigns function as parables of a potential for good or evil confronting each generation. The chronicler took up the metaphor of a prolonged exile that dominated Judean thinking after the Babylonian exile had ended, both accepting it and pointing beyond it. His royal parables of exile and restoration all presuppose and reinforce his master plot of exile under Saul and restoration under David and Solomon. Davidic kings though these last monarchs were, they were spiritual Sauls. Each generation could take Saul's low road of unfaithfulness to the Lord, which led to failure. With such warnings came an implicit challenge to lay hold of restoring grace and to embrace in heart and life the positive purposes God had for the people. At the end of the chapter, the chronicler had Jer 29:10 in view. He would have agreed with the representation of the divine purpose in Jer 29:11: "I know the plans I have for you, says the LORD, plans for your welfare and not for harm, to give you a future with hope" (NRSV).

36:1-10. The pace of the narrative quickens. Kings tumble into exile like lemmings into the sea. The pace of the source (2 Kgs 23:30b–24:17) is rapid, but the chronicler's account is still much more accelerated than that in 2 Kings, cut to less than half. The chronicler's account emphasizes the fate of exile suffered by each king. It is like a series of clips of automobile crashes shown in a public service announcement.

The message of the reigns of Jehoiakim and Jehoiachin in vv. 5-10 is that the wages of sin is exile. In Jehoahaz's case, the expected formula of wrongdoing, which appears in 2 Kgs 23:32, is missing—not because of his short reign; Jehoiachin's was little longer. Did the chronicler think of him as being caught up in Josiah's catastrophe, which politically was in fact the case? He does not usually work with the deuteronomistic concept of transgenerational punishment. The wham-bam style he adopted here may have run away with him, making him prune his source overmuch. The account of the first two reigns reflects Egypt's brief period of control over Syria and Palestine, until Babylonia took over Assyria's western provinces and vassal states. Judah's payment of tribute and enforced change of king were a far cry from the glorious reigns of David and Solomon, when tribute flowed into Jerusalem. Neco's heavy fine reminds the reader of another pharaoh who rode roughshod over Judah as an agent of divine punishment (12:1-12). With Jehoahaz being held hostage in Egypt to ensure his people's loyalty, Judah's new puppet king was devoid of power. He had trappings of traditional royalty, his new throne name "Jehoiakim" emptily honoring Yahweh. Ironically, though, the Lord was in control through Neco.

The account of Jehoiakim's reign (vv. 5-8) is a truncated version of 2 Kgs 23:36–24:7, with a new item inserted about his exile to Babylon and the closing source formula expanded. He noticeably stands and falls as an individual, unshackled by the inherited ball and chain so prominent in the 2 Kings account. It is possible that the 2 Chronicles version depends on the chronicler's understanding of that source. He found in it a record of Jehoiakim's "abominations" and "what happened to him in consequence" (NJB). The latter clause refers to the divinely instigated military attacks of 2 Kgs 24:2. The "sins of Manasseh," related in 2 Kgs 24:3-4, became Jehoiakim's own abominations that providentially triggered the attacks. The chronicler apparently took the king, rather than Judah, as the object of the Lord's command "to remove from his face because of the sins of Manasseh" and interpreted the last phrase as sins such as Manasseh had committed. Then he understood the sequel as "according to all that he [the Lord] did [to Manasseh]." What the Lord did was to arrange that the Assyrian king "bound him with fetters" (33:11). So the same fate, including subsequent removal to Babylon, could be predicated of Jehoiakim. The infinitive form, "to take him" (להליכו *lĕhōlîkô*), does not imply unfulfilled purpose; it may echo the infinitive defining the Lord's command in 2 Kings, "to remove [him] from his face." The plausibility of this interpretation is shown by the partial parallel in the LXX, which here uses a longer Hebrew text assimilated to that of 2 Kings. It specifies Jehoiakim as the object of "to remove from his face" (2 Kgs 24:3) and also as the subject of "filled Jerusalem with innocent blood" (2 Kgs 24:4).

What is left unexplained by this hypothesis is Nebuchadnezzar's having taken temple vessels and putting them in his palace (v. 7; or "temple," KJV; cf. Dan 1:2). It is possible that the incidents of vv. 6-7 are associated with the king's appropriation of these vessels, which the chronicler magnified into a long-term exile.[362] If so, the chronicler found extra support for deportation and its spiritual cause in his treatment of 2 Kings. Mention of the loss of temple vessels symbolizes the Lord's abandonment of the sanctuary. It is a theme of this chapter, rising to a crescendo in the destruction of the Temple. In each case (vv. 7, 10, 18), the chronicler added the plundering of its vessels, which prevented true worship.[363] It is a divinely authored action that works out the threat against the Temple, "I will cast [it] out of my sight" (7:20 = 1 Kgs 9:7).

The account of Jehoiachin's short reign is abbreviated from 2 Kgs 24:8-17 to correspond to the triple pattern of the section: evil, exile, and looting of the Temple. The chronicler leaves out the partial deportation of the people (2 Kgs 24:14-16), preferring for literary effect to continue the motif of royal exile and to reserve national exile as a terrible climax. In 2 Kgs 24:17, Zedekiah is identified with Jehoiachin's uncle, but here he is equated with his "brother" (NRSV; the NIV harmonistically has "relative" and so "uncle").[364] Both persons with the same name are featured in a royal genealogy (1 Chr 3:15-16).

36:11-20a. The chronicler's account of Zedekiah's rule in vv. 11-12a, 13a, 19-20a is based on 2 Kgs 24:18–25:11. The account falls into two parts: (1) the willful sins of Zedekiah and other leaders, including their rejection of opportunities to repent (vv. 12-16), and, as a consequence, (2) inexorable punishment (vv. 17-20a). This climactic passage is written in an emotional vein, indicated in Hebrew narrative by a poetic piling up of terms and clauses in parallel arrangements. Thus the totality of the catastrophe in vv. 17-18 is described in two parallel, three-beat clauses at the end of adjacent sentences: "all he gave into his hand" (such is the Hebrew order) and "all he brought to Babylon."

Mention of the prophet Jeremiah provides a frame in vv. 12 and 21. The first case met with rejection, as the middle part (vv. 15-16) elaborates. In Jeremiah 37:1–38, Zedekiah is portrayed as two-faced, but his dominant attitude is summed up at the outset of that narrative:

Neither he nor his attendants nor the people of the land paid any attention to the words the Lord had spoken through Jeremiah the prophet. (Jer 37:2 NIV)

The chronicler echoes that sentiment in the double indictment of vv. 12-16, blaming the king in vv. 12-13 and the religious and civil leaders in v. 14.

The chronicler brings together a number of his spiritual principles in this passage. The first is the offer of a fresh start, enshrined in 7:14. Zedekiah's attitude is defined in terms of its vocabulary in vv. 12-13. He "did not humble himself" before the Lord's agent and in that respect took after Amon rather than Manasseh or Josiah (33:12, 19, 23; 34:27). He also resisted "turning" from his wicked ways. Zedekiah's twofold rejection of the Lord's overtures was reproduced in the community. "His people" (vv. 15-16) poignantly echoes "my people" in the promise of 7:14. Their blatant refusal blocked the promise; there could be "no remedy," or more literally, "healing" (מרפא *marpē*). Reluctantly, divine wrath had to prevail over grace.

Chapter 7 also has a shadow side: the sinister consequences of opposing the Lord (7:19-22). It would mean the divine uprooting of

---

362. See Williamson, *1 and 2 Chronicles,* 413-14.
363. Ackroyd, "The Temple Vessels," 56-57.
364. See Barthélemy et al., *Critique textuelle de l'Ancien Testament,* 1:520-21.

the people and rejection of the Temple, "consecrated" to God though it was. Verse 14, where Judah defiled what the Lord had consecrated, opens the floodgates to those disasters. The Temple was indeed reduced to a shocking condition (7:21-22), first despoiled and then burned, while exile awaited the people left alive.

Exile is the result of unfaithfulness, in the general sense of breaking the covenant, as the chronicler had learned from Lev 26:40. It was a historical lesson he often taught (1 Chr 5:25-26; 9:1; 2 Chr 33:19) and also applied metaphorically (1 Chr 10:13; 2 Chr 28:19, 22; 29:6-9, 19). The ominous term occurs in v. 14. In the absence of a response to God's overtures, unfaithfulness led inexorably to exile (v. 20). It was the chronicler's custom to link those overtures with prophetic warnings (as in 24:19; 33:18) and to regard prophets as those who announced the promise of 7:14. He makes such a link in vv. 12, 15-16 for the last time.

He evidently had in mind particular oracles that forecast the calamity of 587 BCE. As was noted above, Jer 37:2 seems to be in view in v. 12. The phrase "stiffen one's neck" (v. 13) and the term "persistently" or "again and again" (v. 15) are characteristic of Jeremiah. Since they occur together in Jer 7:25-26, it is likely that the chronicler was principally thinking of that oracle, forecasting the destruction of the Temple. Moreover, "defiling the temple" (v. 14) and "abominations" (v. 14) are mentioned in Jer 7:30. The chronicler also made use of the book of Ezekiel. In v. 13 he referred to the charge of Ezek 17:18-19 that Zedekiah's political rebellion involved breaking an oath made in the name of the Lord. It is likely, too, that the abominations of v. 14 echo not only Jer 7:30 but also the abominations that are repeated in Ezek 8:6, 13, 15. The chronicler was drawing on Ezekiel's vision of the destruction of the Temple. Certainly the carnage in the Temple (v. 17) depends on the visionary slaughter carried out by angelic executioners (Ezek 9:5-6), who were to show no compassion, and the killing was to begin at the sanctuary and to embrace old men, young men, and young women.[365]

365. C. Begg, "Babylon and Judah in Chronicles," *ETL* 64 (1988) 142-52, esp. 149-50.

The destroying angels turned into flesh and blood, wearing Babylonian uniforms. The chronicler has used prophetic texts involving the Temple to illustrate his account of the fall of Judah.

The slaughter spelled the withdrawal of the earlier divine compassion (v. 15). Invasion similar to that of Shishak was occurring all over again, when palace and royal treasuries were completely emptied and Judah became his servant (12:8-9). Now the city felt the full force of that wrath against the covenant people (vv. 16, 19). The curses of an empty land and a ruined Temple made in 7:20-22 now had come true.

36:20b-21. The narrative glides into a positive aftermath. The Lord never intended that the exile would go on interminably, but set limits for its duration. The divine purpose and human history, in the form of Persian seizure of power, coalesced in the interests of God's people. The "until" of history in v. 20 finds a parallel in the "until" set by the Torah at v. 21, while the human "until" fulfills the prophetic "word of the LORD." This word might be that of Jer 25:11-12, which continues the western nations' service of Babylon with a seventy-year limit to Babylonian control. More likely, Jer 29:10 is in view, which is addressed specifically to Judean exiles. The chronicler regularly employed Jer 29:12-14 as a spiritual formula for conditional release from a metaphorical exile. Here his use of an adjacent verse involves the same theme. The divine judgment of Babylonian exile had ended long ago. There was no barrier to blessing on God's side; the onus rested on the covenant people. So the seventy years—how one reckoned them was not the chronicler's concern—were not simply a historical datum but a divine closure.

With the prophetic word, the chronicler intertwined the covenant curse of the Torah at Lev 26:34, a reprisal for sabbath breaking (cf. Lev 26:2). He cited it word for word, simply changing the tenses from future to past to indicate fulfillment. The Torah, too, set a time limit to the exile. It spoke of a sabbath year, a seventh year of letting the land lie fallow after six years of cultivation. As many years as were missed before the exile were to be "made up" (NRSV) or else "enjoyed" (NIV) by the land, in the latter case by way of recuperation for the new life of the post-exilic period.[366] The chronicler read the Torah text in the light of Jer 29:10 and envisioned a period of disobedience lasting 490 years, though he does not develop this point. Exile was the punishment for unfaithfulness (Lev 26:40, 43; cf. 2 Chr 36:14). Yet, like Jer 29:10, the word of judgment was given in a context of conditional restoration: "If . . . their . . . heart . . . is humbled . . . then will I remember my covenant" (Lev 26:41-42 NRSV).

36:22-23. A quotation from Ezra 1:1-3, broken off at the end, expresses in plain terms the promise of v. 21. Scholars dispute whether it is a redactional addition.[367] It is probably the chronicler's own quotation from the earlier book of Ezra–Nehemiah, just as he quoted Nehemiah 11 in 1 Chronicles 9. He had intruded into the later period in 1 Chr 9:2-34, so as to bring out the continuity of God's purposes. The concentration on Temple and people in the quotation develops the negative emphasis in vv. 15-20a in a positive direction, while vv. 20b-21 are a typical theological summary introducing a quotation. The royal speech of v. 23 coincides with the chronicler's own pattern of speechmaking as an encouragement to a task.[368]

As in the case of many of his citations of earlier material, there is a measure of reinterpretation in these verses. The prophetic oracle, originally related to Jer 51:1, 11, was understood in terms of the promises of Second Isaiah.[369] Here it refers to Jer 29:10, echoing v. 21. The seventy years were over, and Cyrus functioned as agent of divine grace. In Ezra 1:3, the Judeans' return to Jerusalem was in view. Here restoration of "all" the Lord's "people" residing throughout "all" Cyrus's "kingdom" reads like a comprehensive reference to displaced northern as well as southern tribes and as an implicit call for them to return to the land (cf. 1 Chr 5:26; 17:5; 2 Chr 30:9; 34:9, 21).

Cyrus's recognition of the Lord meant that God's kingship was acknowledged among the nations and that God's people were in principle rescued from among the nations, as 1 Chr 16:31, 35 had hoped (cf. 2 Chr 20:6). It was an earnest of greater blessing yet to come. As in 35:21, a non-Israelite king was steward of divine power. Ultimately a Davidic king was to wield such universal influence (cf. 1 Chr 14:17; 2 Chr 9:23-24, 26; 17:10; 20:29; 32:17). History had witnessed a lesser restoration, akin to that of Rehoboam, though with only fleeting Davidic control under Zerubbabel (cf. 1 Chr 3:19). Yet, the returning exiles were to enjoy the presence of the Lord. The prayerful wish of Cyrus is turned into a ringing affirmation, "The LORD will be with him."[370] The promise functions as an echo of the great model of restoration under Solomon: "and the LORD his God was with him" (1:1; cf. 1 Chr 28:20). David had known such a blessing, and other good kings, such as Abijah, Asa, Jehoshaphat, and Hezekiah, were no stranger to it (2 Chr 13:12; 15:2; 17:3; 20:17; 32:8).

As in 13:10-12, the Lord's supportive presence with the covenant people would be mediated through temple worship. The Temple, destroyed under Nebuchadnezzar, was to be rebuilt under Cyrus by divine behest. The temple age would continue, and so the grace associated with the Temple would still be available. Solomon's temple prayer—that the Lord bring Israel back to the land (6:25)— was now to be answered. All that remained was for each Israelite generation to respond to divine grace and to honor divine revelation in their worship and way of life. Each had to "go up," embracing the proferred inheritance. The prerequisite was repentance, specified at the beginning of this literary unit (30:8-9; cf. Zech 1:3).

---

366. See P. R. Ackroyd, *Exile and Restoration* (London: SCM, 1968) 241-42.

367. For opposing viewpoints, see Williamson, *Israel in the Books of Chronicles*, 7-10; W. Riley, *King and Cultus in Chronicles: Worship and the Reinterpretation of History*, JSOTSup 160 (Sheffield: JSOT, 1993) 149-55.

368. See Mason, *Preaching the Tradition in Ancient Israel*, 118.

369. Williamson, *Ezra and Nehemiah*, 9-10.

370. Cf. 1 Chr 28:20; 2 Chr 20:17 for the Hebrew ellipsis. The NRSV and the NIV presuppose a jussive sense, but the change from יהי (*yĕhî*, "may he be") to the divine name יהוה (*yhwh*) seems to have been intended to change the meaning. See also the LXX, which reflects יהיה (*yihyeh*, "will be") in place of *yhwh*.

REFLECTIONS

1. John Bunyan ended the first part of *Pilgrim's Progress* with Ignorance being turned away from the gate of the celestial city. The shining ones were commanded "to bind him hand and foot and have him away." "Then I saw," added Christian, "that there was a way to hell even from the gates of heaven, as well as from the city of destruction."[371] The Sermon on the Mount, addressed to disciples, concludes with the same warning: "and it fell—and great was its fall" (Matt 7:27 NRSV). The chronicler ends his work on the same warning note, speaking of expulsion from Jerusalem in language close to Bunyan's. The last two decades of the monarchy provided the chronicler with a series of spiritual parables of the consequences of being out of fellowship with the Lord. To do evil meant to lose God's favor and land-centered blessings. The New Testament speaks just as bluntly: "Do you not know that wrongdoers will not inherit the kingdom of God? Do not be deceived!" (1 Cor 6:9; cf. Gal 6:7-8*a*). In Romans 8, the message of liberation, life, and divine love realistically includes a warning: "If you live according to the flesh, you will die" (Rom 8:13 NRSV).

2. Zedekiah and his generation function as the ultimate of negative role models. The chronicler typically works with a double definition of *sin*, a basic sin of rejecting the Lord's revealed will and compounding that sin by rejecting the Lord's call to repent. This doubling is emphasized in this chapter, receiving three parallel statements in 36:12-16, twice with reference to the king and once with reference to his people. After the normative standard of obedience had been abandoned, all was not lost, however. Sinners could qualify for God's grace. The emergency system enunciated in 7:14 could rescue them from merited destruction. Unfortunately, prophetic overtures intended to foster that promise found no welcome, and so the promise could not work. The parable of the fig tree in Luke 13:6-9 acknowledges such a point of no return.

3. The chronicler was not tied to a legalistic mode of thought. The doom of exile came about not primarily because of broken laws but because of the rejection of the Lord's prophetic warnings and offers of forgiveness and a further chance. Spurning this initiative is the sin of sins in the chronicler's book, just as in John 16:9 sin is defined as not believing in Christ. Lesser sins do not drive anyone beyond the pale—only the sinner's refusal to repent and start over again with God. In case Christian readers complacently agree, contrasting their security with the fate of unbelievers, it is wise to recall that the chronicler had in mind a falling away from within the believing community.

4. The worst of fates befell Zedekiah's generation. Yet by setting *the* exile against a background of earlier exiles, it became just *an* exile. That generation had to be written off, but the Lord's purposes for the covenant people continued. In no way did the exile of 587 BCE represent a divine intention to "destroy them and blot out their name from under heaven" (Deut 9:14). Nor by an extension of deuteronomistic doctrine did it leave in the Lord's heart a lingering grudge such as parents sometimes inflict on their children long after an offense has been dealt with. As in Ezekiel 18, each generation is given a nontransferable ticket. Human responsibility is real; humanity has a free choice for good, which the Lord encourages. A balanced theological presentation would tinker with this partial truth, but it was the message that the chronicler's generation, like Ezekiel's, badly needed to hear.

5. A picture of restoration is displayed in 36:20*b*-23. The chronicler appealed to the Law and the Prophets to substantiate his affirmation that from the Lord's perspective the historical exile was long over. His encouraging message is akin to that of Second Isaiah, for whom ruined Jerusalem, a cipher for the exiled people, "has served her

371. John Bunyan *Pilgrim's Progress* in *The Complete Works of John Bunyan* (Philadelphia: Bradley, Garretson, 1873) 170.

term . . . her penalty is paid" (Isa 40:2 NRSV). The Lord was ready to "renew [Zion] in his love" (Zeph 3:17 NRSV). The wrath of 36:16 was spent, and healing was once again a live option. A hallmark of restoration for the chronicler was God's enabling presence with the recommitted people. It has passed as a rich blessing into the Christian era. An Immanuel, "God with us," is enthroned at the heart of the Christian faith. The Gospel of Matthew exults in this powerful truth at its beginning, middle, and end (Matt 1:23; 18:20; 28:20). An assurance of the divine presence was the old message given Israel on the verge of entering the promised land: "It is the LORD your God who goes with you; he will not fail you or forsake you" (Deut 31:6 NRSV). It became the chronicler's new message for each generation of God's people, as he urged them to commit themselves to pilgrimage with the Lord. In turn, this challenge and assurance pass to us and then to those who will take our place.

ABBREVIATIONS

BCE	before the Common Era
ca.	circa
CE	Common Era
cent.	century
cf.	compare
chap(s).	chapter(s)
d.	died
Dtr	Deuteronomistic historian
esp.	especially
fem.	feminine
HB	Hebrew Bible
l(l).	line(s)
lit.	literally
LXX	Septuagint
masc.	masculine
MS(S)	manuscript(s)
MT	Masoretic Text
n(n).	note(s)
neut.	neuter
NT	New Testament
OG	Old Greek
OL	Old Latin
OT	Old Testament
par(r).	parallel(s)
pl(s).	plate(s)
SP	Samaritan Pentateuch
v(v).	verse(s)
Vg	Vulgate
\\	between Scripture references indicates parallelism

Names of Pseudepigraphical and Early Patristic Books

Apoc. Abr.	*Apocalypse of Abraham*
2–3 Apoc. Bar.	Syriac, Greek *Apocalypse of Baruch*
Apoc. Mos.	*Apocalypse of Moses*

Ascen. Isa.	*Ascension of Isaiah*
As. Mos.	*Assumption of Moses*
Barn.	*Barnabas*
Bib. Ant.	Pseudo-Philo, *Biblical Antiquities*
1–2 Clem.	*1–2 Clement*
Did.	*Didache*
1–2–3 Enoch	Ethiopic, Slavonic, Hebrew *Enoch*
Ep. Arist.	*Epistle of Aristeas*
Gos. Pet.	*Gospel of Peter*
Herm. Sim.	Hermas, *Similitude(s)*
Ign. Eph.	Ignatius, *Letter to the Ephesians*
Ign. Magn.	Ignatius, *Letter to the Magnesians*
Ign. Phld.	Ignatius, *Letter to the Philadelphians*
Ign. Pol.	Ignatius, *Letter to Polycarp*
Ign. Rom.	Ignatius, *Letter to the Romans*
Ign. Smyrn.	Ignatius, *Letter to the Smyrnaeans*
Ign. Trall.	Ignatius, *Letter to the Trallians*
Jub.	*Jubilees*
POxy	B. P. Grenfell and A. S. Hunt (eds.), *Oxyrhynchus Papyri*
Pss. Sol.	*Psalms of Solomon*
Sib. Or.	*Sibylline Oracles*
T. Benj.	*Testament of Benjamin*
T. Dan	*Testament of Dan*
T. Iss.	*Testament of Issachar*
T. Job	*Testament of Job*
T. Jud.	*Testament of Judah*
T. Levi	*Testament of Levi*
T. Naph.	*Testament of Naphtali*
T. Reub.	*Testament of Reuben*
T. Sim.	*Testament of Simeon*

Names of Dead Sea Scrolls and Related Texts

CD	Cairo (Genizah text of the) Damascus Document
DSS	Dead Sea Scrolls
8HevXII gr	Greek scroll of the Minor Prophets from Naḥal Ḥever
Q	Qumran
1Q, 2Q, etc.	numbered caves of Qumran, yielding written material; followed by abbreviation of biblical or apocryphal book
1Q28b	Rule of the Blessings (Appendix b to 1QS)
1QH	Thanksgiving Hymns (Qumran Cave 1)
1QM	War Scroll (Qumran Cave 1)
1QpHab	Pesher on Habakkuk (Qumran Cave 1)
1QpPs	Pesher on Psalms (Qumran Cave 1)
1QS	Rule of the Community (Qumran Cave 1)
1QSa	Rule of the Congregation (Appendix a to 1QS)
1QSb	Rule of the Blessings (Appendix b to 1QS)
4Q175	Testimonia text (Qumran Cave 4)
4Q246	Apocryphon of Daniel (Qumran Cave 4)
4Q298	Words of the Sage to the Sons of Dawn (Qumran Cave 4)
4Q385b	fragmentary remains of Pseudo-Jeremiah that implies that Jeremiah went into Babylonian exile. Also known as ApocJer^C or 4Q385 16. (Qumran Cave 4)

4Q389a	several scroll fragments now thought to contain portions of three pseudepigraphical works including Pseudo-Jeremiah. Also known as 4QApocJer[e]. (Qumran Cave 4)
4Q390	contains a schematized history of Israel's sin and divine punishment. Also known as psMos[e]. (Qumran Cave 4)
4Q394–399	Halakhic Letter (Qumran Cave 4)
4Q416	Instruction[b] (Qumran Cave 4)
4Q521	Messianic Apocalypse (Qumran Cave 4)
4Q550	Proto-Esther[a-f] (Qumran Cave 4)
4QFlor	Florilegium (or Eschatological Midrashim) (Qumran Cave 4)
4QMMT	Halakhic Letter (Qumran Cave 4)
4QpaleoDeutr	copy of Deuteronomy in paleo-Hebrew script (Qumran Cave 4)
4QpaleoExod	copy of Exodus in paleo-Hebrew script (Qumran Cave 4)
4QpNah	Pesher on Nahum (Qumran Cave 4)
4QpPs	Psalm Pesher A (Qumran Cave 4)
4QPrNab	Prayer of Nabonidus (Qumran Cave 4)
4QPs37	Psalm Scroll (Qumran Cave 4)
4QpsDan	Pseudo-Daniel (Qumran Cave 4)
4QSam	First copy of Samuel (Qumran Cave 4)
4QTestim	Testimonia text (Qumran Cave 4)
4QTob	Copy of Tobit (Qumran Cave 4)
11QMelch	Melchizedek text (Qumran Cave 11)
11QPs[a]	Psalms Scroll (Qumran Cave 11)
11QT	Temple Scroll (Qumran Cave 11)
11QtgJob	Targum of Job (Qumran Cave 11)

Targumic Material

Tg. Esth. I, II	First or Second Targum of Esther
Tg. Neb.	Targum of the Prophets
Tg. Neof.	Targum Neofiti

Orders and Tractates in Mishnaic and Related Literature

To distinguish the same-named tractates in the Mishnah, Tosefta, Babylonian Talmud, and Jerusalem Talmud, *m., t., b.,* or *y.* precedes the title of the tractate.

ʾAbot	ʾAbot
ʿArak.	ʿArakin
B. Bat.	Baba Batra
B. Meṣ.	Baba Meṣiʿa
B. Qam.	Baba Qamma
Ber.	Berakot
Dem.	Demai
Giṭ.	Giṭṭin
Ḥag.	Ḥagigah
Hor.	Horayot
Ḥul.	Ḥullin
Ket.	Ketubbot
Maʿaś.	Maʿaśerot
Meg.	Megilla
Menaḥ.	Menaḥot

Mid.	Middot
Mo'ed Qaṭ.	Mo'ed Qaṭan
Nazir	Nazir
Ned.	Nedarim
p. Šeqal.	pesachim Šeqalim
Pesaḥ.	Pesaḥim
Qidd.	Quddušin
Šabb.	Šabbat
Sanh.	Sanhedrin
Soṭah	Soṭah
Sukk.	Sukkah
Ta'an.	Ta'anit
Tamid	Tamid
Yad.	Yadayim
Yoma	Yoma (=Kippurim)

Other Rabbinic Works

'Abot R. Nat.	'Abot de Rabbi Nathan
Pesiq. R.	Pesiqta Rabbati
Rab.	Rabbah (following abbreviation of biblical book—e.g., Gen. Rab. = Genesis Rabbah)
Sipra	Sipra

Greek Manuscripts and Ancient Versions

Papyrus Manuscripts

$\mathfrak{P}^1$	third-century Greek papyrus manuscript of the Gospels
$\mathfrak{P}^{29}$	third- or fourth-century Greek papyrus manuscript
$\mathfrak{P}^{33}$	sixth-century Greek papyrus manuscript of Acts
$\mathfrak{P}^{37}$	third- or fourth-century Greek papyrus manuscript of the Gospels
$\mathfrak{P}^{38}$	fourth-century Greek papyrus manuscript of Acts
$\mathfrak{P}^{45}$	third-century Greek papyrus manuscript of the Gospels
$\mathfrak{P}^{46}$	third-century Greek papyrus manuscript of the letters
$\mathfrak{P}^{47}$	third-century Greek papyrus manuscript of Revelation
$\mathfrak{P}^{48}$	third-century Greek papyrus manuscript of Acts
$\mathfrak{P}^{52}$	second-century Greek papyrus manuscript of John 18:31-33, 37-38
$\mathfrak{P}^{58}$	sixth-century Greek papyrus manuscript of Acts
$\mathfrak{P}^{64}$	third-century Greek papyrus fragment of Matthew
$\mathfrak{P}^{66}$	second- or third-century Greek papyrus manuscript of John (incomplete)
$\mathfrak{P}^{67}$	third-century Greek papyrus fragment of Matthew
$\mathfrak{P}^{69}$	third-century Greek papyrus manuscript of the Gospel of Luke
$\mathfrak{P}^{75}$	third-century Greek papyrus manuscript of the Gospels

Lettered Uncials

ℵ	Codex Sinaiticus, fourth-century manuscript of LXX, NT, Epistle of Barnabas, and Shepherd of Hermas
A	Codex Alexandrinus, fifth-century manuscript of LXX, NT, 1 and 2 Clement, and Psalms of Solomon
B	Codex Vaticanus, fourth-century manuscript of LXX and parts of the NT

C	Codex Ephraemi, fifth-century manuscript of parts of LXX and NT
D	Codex Bezae, fifth-century bilingual (Greek and Latin) manuscript of the Gospels and Acts
G	ninth-century manuscript of the Gospels
K	ninth-century manuscript of the Gospels
L	eighth-century manuscript of the Gospels
W	Washington Codex, fifth-century manuscript of the Gospels
X	Codex Monacensis, ninth- or tenth-century manuscript of the Gospels
Z	sixth-century manuscript of Matthew
Θ	Koridethi Codex, ninth-century manuscript of the Gospels
Ψ	Athous Laurae Codex, eighth- or ninth-century manuscript of the Gospels (incomplete), Acts, the Catholic and Pauline Epistles, and Hebrews

Numbered Uncials

058	fourth-century fragment of Matthew 18
074	sixth-century fragment of Matthew
078	sixth-century fragment of Matthew, Luke, and John
0170	fifth- or sixth-century manuscript of Matthew
0181	fourth- or fifth-century partial manuscript of Luke 9:59–10:14

Numbered Minuscules

33	tenth-century manuscript of the Gospels
75	eleventh-century manuscript of the Gospels
565	ninth-century manuscript of the Gospels
700	eleventh-century manuscript of the Gospels
892	ninth-century manuscript of the Gospels

Names of Nag Hammadi Tractates

Ap. John	Apocryphon of John (also called the Secret Book of John)
Apoc. Adam	Apocalypse of Adam (also called the Revelation of Adam)
Ep. Pet.	Letter of Peter to Philip
Exeg. Soul	Exegesis on the Soul
Gos. Phil.	Gospel of Philip
Gos. Truth	Gospel of Truth

Ancient Versions

bo	the Bohairic (Memphitic) Coptic version
bo[mss]	some manuscripts in the Bohairic tradition
d	the Latin text of Codex Bezae
e	Codex Palatinus, fifth-century Latin manuscript of the Gospels
$f\!f^2$	Old Latin manuscript, fifth-century translation of the Gospels
Ir[lat]	the Latin translation of Irenaeus
latt	the whole Latin tradition (including the Vulgate)
mae	Middle Egyptian
sa	the Sahidic (Thebaic) Coptic version
sy	the Syriac version
sy[s]	the Sinaitic Syriac version

<u>Other Abbreviations</u>

700*	the original reading of manuscript 700
ℵ*	the original reading of Codex Sinaiticus
ℵ¹	the first corrector of Codex Sinaiticus
ℵ²	the second corrector of Codex Sinaiticus
𝔐	the Majority text (the mass of later manuscripts)
C²	the corrected text of Codex Ephraemi
D*	the original reading of Codex Bezae
D²	the second corrector (c. fifth century) of Codex Bezae
f^1	Family 1: minuscule manuscripts belonging to the Lake Group (1, 118, 131, 209, 1582)
f^{13}	Family 13: minuscule manuscripts belonging to the Ferrar Group (13, 69, 124, 174, 230, 346, 543, 788, 826, 828, 983, 1689, 1709)
pc	a few other manuscripts

Commonly Used Periodicals, Reference Works, and Serials

AAR	American Academy of Religion
AASOR	Annual of the American Schools of Oriental Research
AB	Anchor Bible
ABD	*Anchor Bible Dictionary*
ABR	*Australian Biblical Review*
ABRL	Anchor Bible Reference Library
ACNT	Augsburg Commentaries on the New Testament
AcOr	*Acta Orientalia*
AfO	*Archiv für Orientforschung*
AfOB	Archiv für Orientforschung: Beiheft
AGJU	Arbeiten zur Geschichte des antiken Judentums und des Urchristentums
AJP	*American Journal of Philology*
AJSL	*American Journal of Semitic Languages and Literature*
AJT	*American Journal of Theology*
AnBib	Analecta Biblica
ANEP	J. B. Pritchard (ed.), *The Ancient Near East in Pictures Relating to the Old Testament*
ANET	J. B. Pritchard (ed.), *Ancient Near Eastern Texts Relating to the Old Testament*
ANF	*Ante-Nicene Fathers*
ANRW	*Aufstieg und Niedergang der römischen Welt*
ANTC	Abingdon New Testament Commentaries
ANTJ	Arbeiten zum Neuen Testament und Judentum
APOT	R. H. Charles (ed.), *The Apocrypha and Pseudepigrapha of the Old Testament*
ASNU	Acta Seminarii Neotestamentici Upsaliensis
ATANT	Abhandlungen zur Theologie des Alten und Neuen Testaments
ATD	Das Alte Testament Deutsch
ATDan	Acta Theologica Danica
Aug	*Augustinianum*
AusBR	*Australian Biblical Review*
BA	*Biblical Archaeologist*

BAGD	W. Bauer, W. F. Arndt, F. W. Gingrich, and F. W. Danker, *Greek-English Lexicon of the New Testament and Other Early Christian Literature*, 2nd ed. (Bauer-Arndt-Gingrich-Danker)
BAR	*Biblical Archaeology Review*
BASOR	*Bulletin of the American Schools of Oriental Research*
BBB	Bonner biblische Beiträge
BBET	Beiträge zur biblischen Exegese und Theologie
BBR	*Bulletin for Biblical Research*
BDAG	W. Bauer, W. F. Arndt, F. W. Gingrich, and F. W. Danker, *Greek-English Lexicon of the New Testament and Other Early Christian Literature*, 3rd ed. (Bauer-Danker-Arndt-Gingrich)
BDB	F. Brown, S. R. Driver, and C. A. Briggs, *A Hebrew and English Lexicon of the Old Testament*
BDF	F. Blass, A. Debrunner, and R. W. Funk, *A Greek Grammar of the New Testament and Other Early Christian Literature*
BEATAJ	Beiträge zur Erforschung des Alten Testaments und des antiken Judentum
BETL	Bibliotheca Ephemeridum Theologicarum Lovaniensium
BEvT	Beiträge zur evangelischen Theologie
BHS	*Biblia Hebraica Stuttgartensia*
BHT	Beiträge zur historischen Theologie
Bib	*Biblica*
BibInt	*Biblical Interpretation*
BibOr	Biblica et Orientalia
BJRL	*Bulletin of the John Rylands University Library of Manchester*
BJS	Brown Judaic Studies
BK	*Bibel und Kirche*
BKAT	Biblischer Kommentar, Altes Testament
BLS	Bible and Literature Series
BN	*Biblische Notizen*
BNTC	Black's New Testament Commentaries
BR	*Biblical Research*
BSac	*Bibliotheca Sacra*
BSOAS	*Bulletin of the School of Oriental and African Studies*
BT	*The Bible Translator*
BTB	*Biblical Theology Bulletin*
BVC	*Bible et vie chrétienne*
BWA(N)T	Beiträge zur Wissenschaft vom Alten (und Neuen) Testament
BZ	*Biblische Zeitschrift*
BZAW	Beihefte zur Zeitschrift für die alttestamentliche Wissenschaft
BZNW	Beihefte zur Zeitschrift für die neutestamentliche Wissenschaft
CAD	*The Assyrian Dictionary of the Oriental Institute of the University of Chicago*
CB	*Cultura Bíblica*
CBC	Cambridge Bible Commentary
CBOTS	Coniectanea Biblica: Old Testament Series
CBQ	*Catholic Biblical Quarterly*
CBQMS	Catholic Biblical Quarterly Monograph Series
ConBNT	Coniectanea Neotestamentica or Coniectanea Biblica: New Testament Series
ConBOT	Coniectanea Biblica: Old Testament Series
CP	*Classical Philology*
CRAI	Comptes rendus de l'Académie des inscriptions et belles-lettres

CRINT	Compendia Rerum Iudaicarum ad Novum Testamentum
CTM	*Concordia Theological Monthly*
DJD	Discoveries in the Judaean Desert
EB	Echter Bibel
EI	*Encyclopaedia of Islam*
EKKNT	Evangelisch-katholischer Kommentar zum Neuen Testament
Enc	*Encounter*
EncJud	C. Roth and G. Wigoder (eds.), *Encyclopedia Judaica*
EPRO	Etudes préliminaires aux religions orientales dans l'empire romain
ErIsr	*Eretz-Israel*
EstBib	*Estudios bíblicos*
ETL	*Ephemerides Theologicae Lovanienses*
ETS	Erfurter theologische Studien
EvQ	*Evangelical Quarterly*
EvT	*Evangelische Theologie*
ExAud	*Ex Auditu*
ExpTim	*Expository Times*
FAT	Forschungen zum Alten Testament
FB	Forschung zur Bibel
FBBS	Facet Books, Biblical Series
FFNT	Foundations and Facets: New Testament
FOTL	Forms of the Old Testament Literature
FRLANT	Forschungen zur Religion und Literatur des Alten und Neuen Testaments
FTS	Frankfurter Theologische Studien
GBS.OTS	Guides to Biblical Scholarship. Old Testament Series
GCS	Die griechischen christlichen Schriftsteller der ersten [drei] Jahrhunderte
GKC	Emil Kautzsch (ed.), *Gesenius' Hebrew Grammar*, trans. A. E. Cowley, 2nd ed.
GNS	*Good News Studies*
GTA	Göttinger theologischer Arbeiten
HALAT	*Hebräisches und aramäisches Lexikon zum Alten Testament*
HAR	*Hebrew Annual Review*
HAT	Handbuch zum Alten Testament
HBC	*Harper's Bible Commentary*
HBT	*Horizons in Biblical Theology*
HDB	*Hastings' Dictionary of the Bible*
HDR	Harvard Dissertations in Religion
HeyJ	Heythrop Journal
HNT	Handbuch zum Neuen Testament
HNTC	Harper's New Testament Commentaries
HR	*History of Religions*
HSM	Harvard Semitic Monographs
HSS	Harvard Semitic Studies
HTKNT	Herders Theologischer Kommentar zum Neuen Testament
HTR	*Harvard Theological Review*
HTS	Harvard Theological Studies
HUCA	*Hebrew Union College Annual*
IB	*Interpreter's Bible*
IBC	Interpretation: A Bible Commentary for Teaching and Preaching
IBS	*Irish Biblical Studies*
ICC	International Critical Commentary

IDB	*The Interpreter's Dictionary of the Bible*
IDBSup	supplementary volume to *The Interpreter's Dictionary of the Bible*
IEJ	*Israel Exploration Journal*
Int	*Interpretation*
IRT	Issues in Religion and Theology
ITC	International Theological Commentary
JAAR	*Journal of the American Academy of Religion*
JAL	Jewish Apocryphal Literature Series
JANESCU	*Journal of the Ancient Near Eastern Society of Columbia University*
JAOS	*Journal of the American Oriental Society*
JBL	*Journal of Biblical Literature*
JETS	*Journal of the Evangelical Theological Society*
JJS	*Journal of Jewish Studies*
JNES	*Journal of Near Eastern Studies*
JNSL	*Journal of Northwest Semitic Languages*
JPS	Jewish Publication Society
JQR	*Jewish Quarterly Review*
JR	*Journal of Religion*
JRH	*Journal of Religious History*
JSJ	*Journal for the Study of Judaism in the Persian, Hellenistic, and Roman Periods*
JSNT	*Journal for the Study of the New Testament*
JSNTSup	Journal for the Study of the New Testament Supplement Series
JSOT	*Journal for the Study of the Old Testament*
JSOTSup	Journal for the Study of the Old Testament Supplement Series
JSP	*Journal for the Study of the Pseudepigrapha*
JSS	*Journal of Semitic Studies*
JTC	*Journal for Theology and the Church*
JTS	*Journal of Theological Studies*
KAT	Kommentar zum Alten Testament
KB	L. Koehler and W. Baumgartner, *Lexicon in Veteris Testamenti libros*
KEK	Kritisch-exegetischer Kommentar über das Neue Testament (Meyer-Kommentar)
KPG	Knox Preaching Guides
LCL	Loeb Classical Library
LTQ	Lexington Theological Quarterly
MNTC	*Moffatt New Testament Commentary*
NCBC	New Century Bible Commentary
NHS	*Nag Hammadi Studies*
NIB	*The New Interpreter's Bible*
NIBC	*The New Interpreter's Bible Commentary*
NICNT	New International Commentary on the New Testament
NICOT	New International Commentary on the Old Testament
NIGTC	The New International Greek Testament Commentary
NJBC	*The New Jerome Biblical Commentary*
NovT	*Novum Testamentum*
NovTSup	Supplements to Novum Testamentum
NPNF	*Nicene and Post-Nicene Fathers*
NTC	New Testament in Context
NTG	New Testament Guides
NTS	*New Testament Studies*
NTT	*Norsk Teologisk Tidsskrift*

OBC	*The Oxford Bible Commentary*
OBO	Orbis Biblicus et Orientalis
OBT	Overtures to Biblical Theology
OIP	Oriental Institute Publications
Or	*Orientalia* (NS)
OTG	Old Testament Guides
OTL	Old Testament Library
OTM	Old Testament Message
OTP	*Old Testament Pseudepigrapha*
OTS	*Oudtestamentische Studiën*
PAAJR	*Proceedings of the American Academy of Jewish Research*
PEFQS	Palestine Exploration Fund Quarterly Statement
PEQ	*Palestine Exploration Quarterly*
PGM	K. Preisendanz (ed.), *Papyri Graecae Magicae*
PTMS	Pittsburgh Theological Monograph Series
QD	Quaestiones Disputatae
RANE	Records of the Ancient Near East
RB	*Revue biblique*
ResQ	*Restoration Quarterly*
RevExp	*Review and Expositor*
RevQ	*Revue de Qumran*
RSRel	*Recherches de science religieuse*
RTL	*Revue théologique de Louvain*
SAA	State Archives of Assyria
SB	H. L. Strack and P. Billerbeck, *Kommentar zum Neuen Testament aus Talmud und Midrasch,* 6 vols. 1922–61
SBAB	Stuttgarter biblische Aufsatzbände
SBB	Stuttgarter biblische Beiträge
SBL	Society of Biblical Literature
SBLDS	SBL Dissertation Series
SBLMS	SBL Monograph Series
SBLRBS	SBL Resources for Biblical Study
SBLSCS	SBL Septuagint and Cognate Studies
SBLSP	SBL Seminar Papers
SBLSS	SBL *Semeia* Studies
SBLSymS	SBL Symposium Series
SBLWAW	SBL Writings from the Ancient World
SBM	Stuttgarter biblische Monographien
SBS	Stuttgarter Bibelstudien
SBT	Studies in Biblical Theology
SEÅ	*Svensk exegetisk årsbok*
SJLA	Studies in Judaism in Late Antiquity
SJOT	*Scandinavian Journal of the Old Testament*
SJT	*Scottish Journal of Theology*
SKK	Stuttgarter kleiner Kommentar
SNTSMS	Society for New Testament Studies Monograph Series
SOTSMS	Society for Old Testament Studies Monograph Series
SP	Sacra Pagina
SR	*Studies in Religion/Sciences religieuses*
SSN	Studia Semitica Neerlandica
ST	*Studia Theologica*
SUNT	Studien zur Umwelt des Neuen Testaments
SVT	Supplements to Vetus Testamentum

SVTP	Studia in Veteris Testamenti Pseudepigraphica
SWBA	Social World of Biblical Antiquity
TB	Theologische Bücherei: Neudrucke und Berichte aus dem 20. Jahrhundert
TD	*Theology Digest*
TDNT	*Theological Dictionary of the New Testament*
TDOT	*Theological Dictionary of the Old Testament*
TextS	Texts and Studies
THKNT	Theologischer Handkommentar zum Neuen Testament
TLZ	*Theologische Literaturzeitung*
TOTC	Tyndale Old Testament Commentaries
TQ	*Theologische Quartalschrift*
TSK	*Theologische Studien und Kritiken*
TSSI	*Textbook of Syrian Semitic Inscriptions*
TToday	*Theology Today*
TynBul	*Tyndale Bulletin*
TZ	*Theologische Zeitschrift*
UBS	United Bible Societies
UBSGNT	*United Bible Societies Greek New Testament*
UF	*Ugarit-Forschungen*
USQR	*Union Seminary Quarterly Review*
UUÅ	Uppsala Universitetsårsskrift
VC	*Vigiliae Christianae*
VT	*Vetus Testamentum*
VTSup	Supplements to Vetus Testamentum
WA	M. Luther, *Kritische Gesamtausgabe* (= "Weimar" edition)
WDC	Word Biblical Commentary
WBT	Word Biblical Themes
WMANT	Wissenschaftliche Monographien zum Alten und Neuen Testament
WTJ	*Westminster Theological Journal*
WUNT	Wissenschaftliche Untersuchungen zum Neuen Testament
ZAH	*Zeitschrift für Althebräistik*
ZAW	*Zeitschrift für die alttestamentliche Wissenschaft*
ZNW	*Zeitschrift für die neutestamentliche Wissenschaft und die Kunde der älteren Kirche*
ZTK	*Zeitschrift für Theologie und Kirche*